ANNUAL BIBLIOGRAPHY OF ENGLISH LANGUAGE AND LITERATURE FOR 2005

GENERAL EDITOR
GERARD LOWE

ANNUAL

BIBLIOGRAPHY

OF

ENGLISH LANGUAGE
AND LITERATURE
FOR 2005

VOLUME 80

ACADEMIC EDITOR
JENNIFER FELLOWS

AMERICAN EDITORS
BRUCE T. SAJDAK
and
JAMES R. KELLY

Published by
Maney Publishing
for the
Modern Humanities Research Association
2006

The *Annual Bibliography*
of English Language and Literature
may be ordered from Maney Publishing,
Hudson Road, Leeds LS9 7DL

Unsolicited offprints, photocopies or other material for reporting, and correspondence about such matters, ought to be sent direct to the Academic Editor, *Annual Bibliography of English Language and Literature,* University Library, West Road, Cambridge CB3 9DR, England

(E-mail: abell@bibl.org)

(http://www.mhra.org.uk/Publications/Journals/abell.html)

© MODERN HUMANITIES RESEARCH ASSOCIATION 2006

ISBN 1-904350-89-5 / 978-1-904350-89-7
ISSN 0066-3786

Printed in Great Britain by
MANEY PUBLISHING
HUDSON ROAD LEEDS LS9 7DL

PREFACE

As always at this time of year, it is my pleasant duty to express my gratitude to all involved in the production of the *Annual Bibliography*: our American Editors, James Kelly and Bruce Sajdak; our contributors worldwide; the General Editor, Gerard Lowe, especially for his technological support; and, last but by no means least, the Assistant Editor, Dr Lucy Lewis, who has unflinchingly shouldered many additional responsibilities since the departure of Jon Coe and has discharged them admirably.

We say farewell this year to two US contributors, Madeline Copp and Jane Segal, thanking them for their bibliographical contributions and wishing them well for the future; at the same time, we welcome Jen Stevens as a new member of our North American team.

Finally, we are always glad to hear from potential contributors and to be alerted to any errors or omissions.

24 July 2006   JENNIFER FELLOWS

CANDACE R. BENEFIEL, Stirling C. Evans Library, Texas A&M University, College Station

KAREN W. BROWN, Thomas Cooper Library, University of South Carolina, Columbia

GERALD T. BURKE, University Library, Albany, NY

DAN COFFEY, Parks Library, Iowa State University, Ames

ANGELA COURTNEY, Main Library, Indiana University, Bloomington

CHARLOTTE CUBBAGE, Northwestern University Library, Evanston, IL

CHRISTINE DEZELAR-TIEDMAN, University of Minnesota Libraries, Minneapolis

*G. RONALD DOBLER, Morehead State University, Morehead, KY

MARIE GARRETT, University of Tennessee Libraries, Knoxville

* MARC GLASSER, Salem State University, Salem, MA

*LILA M. HARPER, Central Washington State University, Ellensburg

*STYRON HARRIS, East Tennessee State University, Johnson City

SUSAN HOPWOOD , Marquette University Libraries, Milwaukee, WI

EMILY J. HORNING, Sterling Memorial Library, Yale University, New Haven, CT

*CECILE M. JAGODZINSKI, Main Library, Indiana University, Bloomington

NAOMI LEDERER, Morgan Library, Colorado State University, Fort Collins

LESLIE MADDEN, Georgia State University Library, Atlanta

DIANE MAHER, Copley Library, University of San Diego, CA

FRED MURATORI, Olin Library, Cornell University, Ithaca, NY

KRISTIN NIELSEN, University of Georgia Libraries, Athens

DARBY ORCUTT, North Carolina State University Library, Raleigh

MICHAEL RODRIGUEZ, Michigan State University Library, East Lansing

YVONNE SCHOFER, Memorial Library, University of Wisconsin, Madison

JANE SEGAL, Fondren Library, Rice University, Houston, TX

JEN STEVENS, George Mason University Library, Fairfax, VA

*GLENN ELLEN STARR STILLING, Belk Library, Appalachian State University, Boone, NC

LAURA TADDEO, University at Buffalo Libraries, Buffalo, NY

*STEPHEN L. THOMPSON, Rockefeller Library, Brown University, Providence, RI

*MARKEL D. TUMLIN, University Library, San Diego State University, San Diego, CA

SHARON VERBA, Thomas Cooper Library, University of South Carolina, Columbia

TAMMY J. ESCHEDOR VOELKER, Main Library, Kent State University, Kent, OH

* Senior contributor

CONTENTS

SOURCES AND ABBREVIATIONS
2005

What follows is a list of the periodicals consulted in the compilation of the Bibliography; an asterisk indicates that relevant items have been found and are indexed in this volume. The editors are always glad to hear of journals requiring coverage.

*1650–1850	1650–1850: ideas, aesthetics, and inquiries in the early modern era (New York)
4thG	Fourth Genre: explorations in nonfiction (East Lansing, MI)
*AAR	African American Review (Indiana State Univ., Terre Haute)
*A/B	A/B: Auto/Biography Studies (Univ. of North Carolina, Chapel Hill)
*ABPR	American Book Publishing Record (New Providence, NJ)
ABR	American Benedictine Review (Assumption Abbey, Richardton, ND)
*Acme	Acme: annali della Facoltà di Lettere e Filosofia dell'Università degli Studi di Milano (Milan)
*Àcoma	Àcoma: rivista internazionale di studi nordamericani (Milan)
ACPQ	American Catholic Philosophical Quarterly (American Catholic Philosophical Assn, Washington, DC)
*ADS	Australasian Drama Studies (Univ. of Queensland, St Lucia)
*Aethlon	Aethlon: the journal of sport literature (East Tennessee State Univ., Johnson City)
*AF	Australian Folklore: a yearly journal of folklore studies (Australian Folklore Assn) (Armidale, N.S.W.)
AFSN	American Folklore Society News (American Folklore Soc., Ohio State Univ., Columbus)
*AfSR	African Studies Review (Dept of Anthropology, Univ. of Massachusetts, Amherst)
*Agenda	Agenda (London)
*Agni	Agni (Boston Univ., Boston, MA)
*AH	American Heritage (Soc. of American Historians, New York)
*AI	American Imago (Assn for Applied Psychoanalysis) (Baltimore, MD)
*AICRJ	American Indian Culture and Research Journal (American Indian Studies Center, Univ. of California, Los Angeles)
*AIQ	American Indian Quarterly (Southwestern American Indian Soc.; Soc. for American Indian Studies & Research, Lincoln, NE)
*AJH	American Jewish History: an American Jewish History Society quarterly publication (Baltimore, MD)
*AL	American Literature: a journal of literary history, criticism, and bibliography (Durham, NC)
AlaLR	Alabama Literary Review (Troy State Univ., Troy, AL)
*Albion	Albion: a quarterly journal concerned with British studies (Dept of History, Appalachian State Univ., Boone, NC; North American Conference on British Studies)
*ALR	American Literary Realism (Champaign, IL)
*ALS	Australian Literary Studies (Univ. of Queensland, St Lucia)
*ALSCN	ALSC Newsletter (Assn of Literary Scholars and Critics, Mount Pleasant, MI)
*Aluze	Aluze: revue pro literaturu, filozofia jiné (Olomouc)
*ALyr	Ars Lyrica: journal of LYRICA Society for Word–Music Relations (Georgia Inst. of Technology, Atlanta)
*AMacJ	Archibald MacLeish Journal (Friends of the Archibald MacLeish Collection, Greenfield Community College, Greenfield, MA)
*AmBR	American Book Review (Illinois State Univ., Normal)
*AmDr	American Drama (Dept of English, Helen Weinberger Center, McMicken College of Arts and Sciences, Univ. of Cincinnati, OH)
*AmerJ	Amerasia Journal (Univ. of California, Los Angeles)
*AmJ	American Journalism: a journal of media history (Sacramento, CA)

*AmJP	American Journal of Psychoanalysis (New York)
*AmLH	American Literary History (Cary, NC; Oxford)
*AmP	American Periodicals: a journal of history, criticism and bibliography (Research Soc. for American Periodicals) (Columbus, OH)
*Amphora	Amphora (Alcuin Society, Vancouver, BC)
*AmQ	American Quarterly (American Studies Assn) (Baltimore, MD)
*AmS	American Studies: a tri-annual interdisciplinary journal (Mid-America American Studies Assn; Univ. of Kansas, Lawrence)
*Amst	Amerikastudien / American Studies (Heidelberg)
*ANCW	America: the national Catholic weekly (New York)
*Anglophonia	Anglophonia: French journal of English studies (Univ. of Toulouse–Le Mirail)
*AngP	Anglistica Pisana (Pisa)
*ANQ	ANQ: a quarterly journal of short articles, notes, and reviews (Univ. of Kentucky, Lexington)
AnthQ	Anthropological Quarterly (Washington, DC)
Anthrop	Anthropologica (Wilfrid Laurier Univ., Waterloo, Ont.)
*Anthropoetics	Anthropoetics: the electronic journal of generative anthropology (Univ. of California, Los Angeles) (http://www.humnet.ucla.edu/humnet/anthropoetics/home.html)
*Antipodes	Antipodes: a North American journal of Australian literature (American Assn of Australian Literary Studies, Brooklyn, NY)
*AppalJ	Appalachian Journal: a regional studies review (Boone, NC)
*AppH	Appalachian Heritage (Appalachian Center, Berea College, Berea, KY)
*AppL	Applied Linguistics (Oxford)
*APQ	American Philosophical Quarterly (Bowling Green State Univ., Bowling Green, OH)
*APR	American Poetry Review (Philadelphia, PA)
*AQ	Arizona Quarterly: a journal of American literature, culture and theory (Univ. of Arizona, Tucson)
AQR	Alaska Quarterly Review (Univ. of Alaska, Anchorage)
*AR	Antioch Review (Yellow Springs, OH)
ARAL	Annual Review of Applied Linguistics (Cambridge; New York)
*Archives	Archives: the journal of the British Records Association (Exeter)
*ArkR	Arkansas Review: a journal of Delta studies (Arkansas State Univ., Springdale)
*ARSCJ	Association for Recorded Sound Collection Journal (Toronto)
ArtD	Artful Dodge (Wooster, OH)
*Arthuriana	Arthuriana (International Arthurian Soc. – North American Branch) (Southern Methodist Univ., Dallas, TX)
*AS	American Speech: a quarterly of linguistic usage (American Dialect Soc.) (Durham, NC)
*ASch	American Scholar (Washington, DC)
*ASE	Anglo-Saxon England (Cambridge)
ASSA	Applied Semiotics / Semiotique appliquée: a learned journal of literary research on the World Wide Web (Univ. of Toronto) (http://www.chass.utoronto.ca/french/as-sa/)
*ATJ	Asian Theatre Journal (Assn for Asian Performance, Honolulu, HI)
*Atl	Atlantis: journal of the Spanish Association for Anglo-American studies (Univ. de La Laguna, Tenerife)
Atlantis	Atlantis: a women's studies journal (Mount Saint Vincent Univ., Halifax, N.S.)
*AtlR	Atlanta Review (Atlanta, GA)

*ATQ	American Transcendental Quarterly: 19th century American literature and culture (Univ. of Rhode Island, Kingston)
AU	Art & Understanding (Albany, NY)
*AUMLA	AUMLA: journal of the Australasian Universities Language and Literature Association: a journal of literary criticism and linguistics (Christchurch, New Zealand)
AUPO	Acta Universitatis Palackianae Olomucensis: Philologica (Olomouc)
*AUR	Aberdeen University Review (Alumnus Assn, Univ. of Aberdeen)
*Auto/Biography	Auto/Biography: an international and interdisciplinary journal (London)
*Aztlan	Aztlan: a journal of Chicano studies (Los Angeles, CA)
*B2	Boundary 2: an international journal of literature and culture (Durham, NC)
*BBIAS	Bibliographical Bulletin of the International Arthurian Society (Univ. of Oklahoma, Norman)
*BC	Book Collector (London)
BCS	B.C. Studies (Vancouver)
*BecC	Beckett Circle: newsletter of the Samuel Beckett Society (Dept of English, Univ. of Wisconsin, Madison)
*Bel	Belfagor: rassegna di varia umanità fondata da Luigi Russo (Florence)
*BELL	BELL: Belgian essays on language and literature (Belgian Assn of Anglicists in Higher Education, Liège)
*BH	Book History (University Park, PA)
*BHM	Bulletin of the History of Medicine (Baltimore, MD)
*Bibliofilia	Bibliofilia (Florence)
*Bibliotheck	Bibliotheck: a journal of Scottish bibliography and book history (Scottish Centre for the Book, Napier Univ., Edinburgh)
*Biography	Biography: an interdisciplinary quarterly (Center for Biographical Research, Univ. of Hawaii, Honolulu)
*BJ	Byron Journal (Byron Soc., London)
*BJA	British Journal of Aesthetics (Oxford)
*BJCS	British Journal of Canadian Studies (British Assn for Canadian Studies, Univ. of Edinburgh)
*BJECS	British Journal for Eighteenth-Century Studies (Voltaire Foundation, Oxford)
*BJJ	Ben Jonson Journal: literary contexts in the age of Elizabeth, James, and Charles (Las Vegas, NV)
*BkW	Book World (Washington, DC)
*Blake	Blake: an illustrated quarterly (Rochester Univ., Rochester, NY)
*BLFSEB	Bulletin de liaison de la Société Française des Études Byroniennes (Paris)
*BLR	Bodleian Library Record (Oxford)
Blueline	Blueline (State Univ. of New York, Potsdam)
*BMGS	Byzantine and Modern Greek Studies (Centre for Byzantine, Ottoman and Modern Greek Studies, Univ. of Birmingham) (Leeds)
*Book	Book: newsletter of the Program in the History of the Book in American Culture (Worcester, MA)
*BosR	Boston Review: a political and literary forum (Cambridge, MA)
BPJ	Beloit Poetry Journal (Beloit, WI)
*BR	Bilingual Review / La revista bilingue (Arizona State Univ., Tempe)
BrC	Brilliant Corners: a journal of jazz and literature (Lycoming College, Williamsport, PA)
*BRev	Bloomsbury Review: a book magazine (Denver, CO)
*Brick	Brick (Toronto)

*BrSt	Brontë Studies: the journal of the Brontë Society (Brontë Soc., Haworth) (Leeds)
*BSANZB	Bibliographical Society of Australia and New Zealand Bulletin (Victoria Univ. of Wellington, Wellington, New Zealand)
*BSch	Black Scholar: journal of Black studies and research (Black World Foundation, Oakland, CA)
*BSJ	Baker Street Journal: an irregular quarterly of Sherlockiana (Indianapolis, IN)
*BuR	Bucknell Review (Bucknell Univ., Lewisburg, PA)
BWR	Black Warrior Review (Univ. of Alabama, Tuscaloosa)
BYUS	Brigham Young University Studies: a multidisciplinary Latter-Day Saint journal (Provo, UT)
*Callaloo	Callaloo: a journal of African American and African arts and letters (Univ. of Virginia, Charlottesville) (Baltimore, MD)
Calyx	Calyx: a journal of art and literature by women (Corvallis, OR)
*CamOb	Camera Obscura: feminism, culture, and media studies (Dept of Film Studies, Univ. of California, Santa Barbara)
*CamQ	Cambridge Quarterly (Cambridge Quarterly Assn, Clare College, Cambridge) (Oxford)
*CanJAS	Canadian Journal of African Studies (Toronto)
*CanJP	Canadian Journal of Philosophy (Calgary, Alta)
*CanL	Canadian Literature / Littérature canadienne: a quarterly of criticism and review (Univ. of British Columbia, Vancouver)
*CanP	Canadian Poetry (Univ. of Western Ontario, London)
*CanRCL	Canadian Review of Comparative Literature / Revue canadienne de littérature comparée (Dept of Comparative Literature, Univ. of Alberta, Edmonton)
*CanTR	Canadian Theatre Review (School of Literatures and Performing Studies in English, Univ. of Guelph, Ont.)
CaribS	Caribbean Studies (Puerto Rico Univ., San Juan)
*CaroQ	Carolina Quarterly (Univ. of North Carolina, Chapel Hill)
CarQ	Caribbean Quarterly (Univ. of the West Indies, Kingston, Jamaica)
*Carrollian	Carrollian (Lewis Carroll Soc., Clifford, Herefordshire)
*CathHR	Catholic Historical Review (Catholic Univ. of America, Washington, DC)
*CC	Cross Currents (Assn for Religion and Intellectual Life, College of New Rochelle, NY)
*CE	College English (Urbana, IL)
*CEACrit	CEA Critic (Dept of English, Widener Univ., Chester, PA)
*CEAF	CEA Forum (Youngstown State Univ., Youngstown, OH)
*CEl	Cahiers élisabéthains: late medieval and Renaissance English studies (Centre d'Études et de Recherches Élisabéthaines de l'Univ. Paul-Valéry, Montpellier)
*CFMB	Canadian Folk Music Bulletin (Calgary, Alta)
Chain	Chain (Buffalo, NY)
*ChattR	Chattahoochee Review (DeKalb Community College, Dunwoody, GA)
*ChauR	Chaucer Review: a journal of medieval studies and literary criticism (University Park, PA)
*ChE	Changing English: studies in reading and culture (Univ. of London Inst. of Education)
Chelsea	Chelsea (New York)
*ChildLit	Children's Literature: annual of the Modern Language Association Division on Children's Literature and the Children's Literature Association (New Haven, CT)

*ChiR	Chicago Review (Division of the Humanities, Univ. of Chicago, Chicago, IL)
*CHist	Church History (American Soc. of Church History, Chicago, IL)
*ChrisL	Christianity and Literature (Conference on Christianity and Literature, State Univ. of West Georgia, Carrollton)
*Chronicles	Chronicles: a magazine of American culture (Rockford, IL)
*ChronOkla	Chronicles of Oklahoma (Oklahoma Historical Soc., Oklahoma City)
*CI	Critical Inquiry (Chicago, IL)
*Cineaste	Cineaste (Union City, NJ)
*CinJ	Cinema Journal (Soc. for Cinema Studies, Univ. of Texas, Austin)
*Cithara	Cithara: essays in the Judaeo-Christian tradition (St Bonaventure Univ., St Bonaventure, NY)
CJa	Cizí jazyky ve škole (Prague)
*CJIS	Canadian Journal of Irish Studies (Canadian Assn for Irish Studies, St John's, Nfld)
*CL	Comparative Literature (Univ. of Oregon, Eugene)
*CLAJ	CLA Journal (College Language Assn, Morehouse College, Atlanta, GA)
*CLAQ	Children's Literature Association Quarterly (Battle Creek, MI)
*CLB	Charles Lamb Bulletin: journal of the Charles Lamb Society (London)
*CLCWeb	CLCWeb: computers, literature, and culture, a WWWeb journal (Purdue Univ., West Lafayette, IN) (http://clcwebjournal.lib.purdue.edu/)
*CLIN	Cuadernos de literatura inglesa y norteamericana (Facultad de Filosofía y Letras, Pontificia Univ. Católica Argentina (Buenos Aires)
*CLIO	CLIO: a journal of literature, history, and the philosophy of history (Indiana Univ.–Purdue Univ., Fort Wayne)
*CLS	Comparative Literature Studies (Pennsylvania State Univ., University Park)
*Clues	Clues: a journal of detection (Bowling Green State Univ., OH)
*ČMF	Časopis pro moderní filologii (Czech Academy of Sciences) (Amsterdam; Philadelphia, PA)
*CML	Classical and Modern Literature: a quarterly (Terre Haute, IN)
*CogL	Cognitive Linguistics: an interdisciplinary journal of cognitive science (Berlin; New York)
*ColB	Coleridge Bulletin: the journal of the Friends of Coleridge (Nether Stowey, Som.)
*ColJR	Columbia Journalism Review (Columbia Univ., New York)
*ColLit	College Literature (West Chester Univ., PA)
ColoH	Colorado Heritage (Colorado Historical Soc., Denver)
*ColoR	Colorado Review: a journal of contemporary literature (Colorado State Univ., Fort Collins)
ColUL	College and Undergraduate Libraries (Binghamton, NY)
ComCog	Communication and Cognition (Ghent, Belgium)
*Comitatus	Comitatus: a journal of medieval and Renaissance studies (Center for Medieval and Renaissance Studies, Univ. of California, Los Angeles)
CommEd	Communication Education (National Communication Assn, Annandale, VA)
ComMon	Communication Monographs (Falls Creek, VA)
*CommRev	Common Review: the magazine of the Great Books Foundation (Chicago, IL)
*Comparatist	Comparatist: journal of the Southern Comparative Literature Association (Fairfax, VA)
*CompDr	Comparative Drama (Western Michigan Univ., Kalamazoo)

*CompLing	Computational Linguistics (Assn for Computational Linguistics, Cambridge, MA)
*ComQ	Communication Quarterly (Eastern Communication Assn, Salisbury State Univ., Salisbury, MD)
*Configurations	Configurations: a journal of literature, science, and technology (Soc. for Literature and Science; Georgia Inst. of Technology) (Baltimore, MD)
Confrontation	Confrontation (English Dept, C. W. Post College of Long Island Univ., Brookville, NY)
*ConLit	Contemporary Literature (Univ. of Wisconsin, Madison)
*Connotations	Connotations: a journal for critical debate (Münster; New York)
*ConnR	Connecticut Review (Southern Connecticut State Univ., New Haven)
*Conradian	Conradian: journal of the Joseph Conrad Society (UK) (Amsterdam; Atlanta, GA)
*Conradiana	Conradiana: a journal of Joseph Conrad studies (Texas Tech Univ., Lubbock)
*ConS	Concord Saunterer (Thoreau Lyceum, Concord, MA)
*ContRev	Contemporary Review (London)
*CRAS	Canadian Review of American Studies (Carleton Univ., Ottawa)
*Cresset	Cresset: a review of literature, arts and public affairs (Valparaiso Univ., Valparaiso, IN)
*Criticism	Criticism: a quarterly for literature and the arts (Wayne State Univ., Detroit, MI)
*CritQ	Critical Quarterly (Oxford)
*CritR	Critical Review: an interdisciplinary journal of politics and society (Newton, CT)
*CritS	Critical Survey (New York; Oxford)
*CritW	Critique: studies in contemporary fiction (Washington, DC)
*CrN	Creative Nonfiction (Pittsburgh, PA)
*CRNew	CR: the new centennial review (Michigan State Univ., East Lansing)
*CSL	CSL: bulletin of the New York C. S. Lewis Society (Glendale, NY)
*CSR	Christian Scholar's Review (Holland, MI)
*CTHEORY	CTHEORY: theory, technology, culture (Concordia Univ., Montreal) (http://www.ctheory.com/)
*CulL	Cultural Logic: an electronic journal of Marxist theory and practice (Wichita, KS) (http://eserver.org/clogic/default.html)
*CultC	Cultural Critique (Cary, NC)
*Culture	Culture: annali dell'Istituto di Lingue della Facoltà di Scienze Politiche dell'Univ. degli Studi di Milano (Milan)
CurA	Current Anthropology: a world journal of the human sciences (St Louis, MO)
*CVE	Cahiers victoriens et édouardiens (Univ. Paul-Valéry, Montpellier)
*Cweal	Commonweal (Commonweal Foundation, New York)
*CWH	Civil War History: a journal of the Middle Period (Dept of History, Kent State Univ., Kent, OH)
*Cycnos	Cycnos (Centre de Recherche sur les Écritures de Langue Anglaise, Univ. of Nice)
*DalR	Dalhousie Review (Dalhousie Univ., Halifax, N.S.)
Descant	Descant (Toronto)
*Diacritics	Diacritics: a review of contemporary criticism (Dept of Romance Studies, Cornell Univ., Ithaca, NY) (Baltimore, MD)
*Dialogue	Dialogue: Canadian philosophical review (Univ. du Québec à Trois-Rivières)
*Dic	Dictionaries: journal of the Dictionary Society of North America (Madison, WI)

*Dickensian	Dickensian (Dickens Fellowship, Eliot College, Univ. of Kent, Canterbury)
*DickQ	Dickens Quarterly: a scholarly journal devoted to the study of the life, times, & works of Charles Dickens (Univ. of Massachusetts, Amherst)
*Discourse	Discourse: journal for theoretical studies in media and culture (Wayne State Univ., Detroit, MI)
*DNR	Dime Novel Roundup: a magazine devoted to the collecting, conservation and study of old-time dime and nickel novels, popular story papers, series books, and pulp magazines (Dundas, MN)
*DP	Discourse Processes: a multidisciplinary journal (Univ. of Memphis, TN)
*DQ	Denver Quarterly (Dept of English, Univ. of Denver, CO)
*Dramatist	Dramatist (New York)
*DreiS	Dreiser Studies (Dept of English, Univ. of North Carolina, Wilmington)
*DRM	Drood Review of Mystery (Kalamazoo, MI)
*DSA	Dickens Studies Annual: essays on Victorian fiction (Graduate Center, City Univ. of New York)
DSNA	DSNA: Dictionary Society of North America newsletter (Madison, WI)
*EA	Études anglaises: Grande-Bretagne, États-Unis (Paris)
*EAL	Early American Literature (Chapel Hill, NC)
*EAPR	Edgar Allan Poe Review (Poe Studies Assn, Ohio Univ., Athens)
*EAS	Essays and Studies (English Assn) (Cambridge)
*EC	Essays in Criticism: a quarterly journal founded by F. W. Bateson (Oxford)
*ECF	Eighteenth-Century Fiction (McMaster Univ., Hamilton, Ont.)
*ECInt	Eighteenth-Century Intelligencer (East-Central/American Soc. for Eighteenth-Century Studies, DuBois, PA)
*ECL	Eighteenth-Century Life (College of William and Mary, Williamsburg, VA)
*ECN	Eighteenth-Century Novel (New York)
*ECS	Eighteenth-Century Studies (American Soc. for Eighteenth Century Studies, Wake Forest Univ., Winston-Salem, NC)
*EDISB	Emily Dickinson International Society Bulletin (Lexington, KY)
*EDJ	Emily Dickinson Journal (Emily Dickinson International Soc.) (Baltimore, MD)
*EDS	English Dance and Song (English Folk Dance and Song Soc., London)
*EGN	Ellen Glasgow Newsletter (Austin, TX)
*EI	Éire-Ireland: a journal of Irish studies (Irish American Cultural Inst., St Paul, MN)
*EIUC	Estudios ingleses de la Universidad Complutense (Madrid)
*EJES	European Journal of English Studies (Lisse)
*ELH	ELH: journal of English literary history (Baltimore, MD)
*ELN	English Language Notes (Univ. of Colorado, Boulder)
*ELR	English Literary Renaissance (Univ. of Massachusetts, Amherst)
*ELT	English Literature in Transition (1880–1920) (Univ. of North Carolina, Greensboro)
*EMS	Essays in Medieval Studies: proceedings of the Illinois Medieval Association (West Virginia Univ., Morgantown)
*Encomia	Encomia: bibliographical bulletin of the International Courtly Literature Society (Univ. of Nebraska, Omaha)
*Eng	English (English Assn, Leicester)
*EngMS	English Manuscript Studies, 1100–1700 (British Library, London)
*EngS	English Studies: a journal of English language and literature (Lisse, The Netherlands)

*Envoi	Envoi: a review journal of medieval literature (New York)
*EOR	Eugene O'Neill Review (Suffolk Univ., Boston, MA)
Epoch	Epoch (Cornell Univ., Ithaca, NY)
*EREA	EREA: revue d'études anglophones (Univ. de Provence (Aix-Marseille 1), Aix-en-Provence) (www.e-rea.org)
ERec	English Record (New York State English Council, Schenectady)
*ERR	European Romantic Review (North American Soc. for the Study of Romanticism, San Francisco, CA)
*ESA	English Studies in Africa: a journal of the humanities (Univ. of the Witwatersrand, South Africa)
*ESpP	English for Specific Purposes (Oxford)
*ESQ	ESQ: a journal of the American renaissance (Washington State Univ., Pullman)
*Esquire	Esquire (New York)
*EtBr	Études britanniques contemporaines (Univ. Paul-Valéry, Montpellier)
*ETh	Early Theatre: a journal associated with the Records of Early English Drama (Hamilton, Ont.)
Ethnology	Ethnology: an international journal of cultural and social anthropology (Pittsburgh Univ., Pittsburgh, PA)
Ethnomusicology	Ethnomusicology: journal of the Society for Ethnomusicology (Univ. of Illinois, Urbana)
*EtIr	Études irlandaises: revue française d'histoire, civilisation et littérature de l'Irlande (Sainghin-en-Melantois)
EtLitt	Études littéraires (Univ. Laval, Que.)
*EurJAC	European Journal of American Culture (Exeter)
*EWeltyN	Eudora Welty Newsletter (Atlanta, GA)
*EWR	Edith Wharton Review (Kean Univ., Union, NJ)
*EWW	English World-Wide: a journal of varieties of English (Amsterdam; Philadelphia, PA)
*Exemplaria	Exemplaria: a journal of theory in medieval and Renaissance studies (Asheville, NC)
*Exp	Explicator (Helen Dwight Reid Educational Foundation, Washington, DC)
*ExRC	Explorations in Renaissance Culture (Dept of English, Southwest Missouri State Univ., Springfield)
*Extrapolation	Extrapolation (Kent State Univ., Kent, OH)
*FCS	Fifteenth-Century Studies (Univ. of Virginia, Charlottesville) (Columbia, SC)
FemSt	Feminist Studies (Univ. of Maryland, College Park)
*FF	Folklore Forum (Bloomington, IN)
*FHist	Folklore Historian (Dept of English, Indiana State Univ., Terre Haute)
*Fiddlehead	Fiddlehead: Atlantic Canada's international literary journal (Univ. of New Brunswick, Fredericton)
*FilCr	Film Criticism (Allegheny College, Meadville, PA)
*FilmH	Film and History: an interdisciplinary journal of film and television studies (Popular Culture Center, Cleveland, OK)
*FilmQ	Film Quarterly (Univ. of California, Berkeley)
*FiveP	Five Points: a journal of literature and art (Atlanta, GA)
*FJ	Faulkner Journal (Dept. of English, Univ. of Akron, OH)
FlR	Florida Review (Univ. of Central Florida, Orlando)
*FLS	Foreign Literature Studies (Wuhan, China)
*FMJ	Folk Music Journal: the journal of traditional music and dance (London)
*FMLS	Forum for Modern Language Studies (Univ. of St Andrews) (Oxford)

*FOAFN	FOAFtale News (International Soc. for Contemporary Legend Research, Memorial Univ. of Newfoundland, St John's)
*FolkL	Folk Life: journal of ethnological studies (Soc. for Folk Life Studies, Leeds)
*Folklore	Folklore (Folklore Soc., University College, London)
*FOR	Flannery O'Connor Review (Dept of English and Speech, Georgia College & State Univ., Milledgeville)
*FortT	Fortean Times (London)
*Foundation	Foundation: the review of science fiction (Science Fiction Foundation, Liverpool)
FoxM	Foxfire Magazine (Mountain City, GA)
*Frontiers	Frontiers: a journal of women studies (Washington State Univ., Pullman)
*GaR	Georgia Review (Univ. of Georgia, Athens)
*Gastronomica	Gastronomica: the journal of food and culture (Berkeley, CA)
Gateway	Gateway: the quarterly magazine of the Missouri Historical Society (St Louis, MO)
*GBB	George Borrow Bulletin (George Borrow Soc., Wallingford, Oxon.)
*GC	Gulf Coast (Univ. of Houston, Texas)
*GEGHLS	George Eliot – George Henry Lewes Studies (Northern Illinois Univ., DeKalb)
*Genre	Genre: forms of discourse and culture (Dept of English, Univ. of Oklahoma, Norman)
*GER	George Eliot Review (George Eliot Fellowship, Coventry)
*GetR	Gettysburg Review (Gettysburg College, Gettysburg, PA)
*GHJ	George Herbert Journal (Sacred Heart Univ., Fairfield, CT)
*GissJ	Gissing Journal (Bradford)
*GLQ	GLQ: a journal of lesbian and gay studies (Durham, NC)
*GLRW	Gay and Lesbian Review Worldwide (Boston, MA)
*GothS	Gothic Studies (Manchester)
*GPQ	Great Plains Quarterly (Center for Great Plains Studies, Univ. of Nebraska, Lincoln)
*Gramma	Gramma: periodiko theorias & kritikes (Dept of English, Aristotle Univ., Thessaloniki)
*GreRR	Great River Review (Winona, MN)
*GWR	G.W. Review (Marvin Center, George Washington Univ., Washington, DC)
*HAge	Heroic Age: journal of early medieval Northwestern Europe (Belleville, IL) (http://members.aol.com/heroicage1/homepage.html)
*HaR	Hardy Review (New Haven, CT)
*HarSJ	Hardy Society Journal (Thomas Hardy Soc., Dorchester)
*HC	Hollins Critic (Hollins Univ., Hollins, VA)
*HemR	Hemingway Review (Hemingway Soc., Nantucket, MA)
*HGP	Heritage of the Great Plains (Emporia State Univ., Emporia, KS)
*Historian	Historian (Univ. of South Florida, Tampa)
*HJR	Henry James Review (Henry James Soc., Univ. of Louisville, KY) (Baltimore, MD)
*HJS	Hypermedia Joyce Studies (http://www.geocities.com/hypermedia_joyce/archive.html)
*HLQ	Huntington Library Quarterly: studies in English and American history and literature (Henry E. Huntington Library and Art Gallery, San Marino, CA)
*HN	History Now: te pae tawito o te wa (History Dept, Univ. of Canterbury, Christchurch, New Zealand)

*HopQ	Hopkins Quarterly (St Joseph's Univ., Philadelphia, PA)
HotelA	Hotel Amerika (Dept of English, Ohio Univ., Athens)
*HR	Hudson Review: a magazine of literature and the arts (New York)
*HSJ	Housman Society Journal (Bromsgrove, Worcs.)
HTR	Harvard Theological Review (Cambridge, MA)
Humanist	Humanist: a magazine of critical inquiry and social concern (American Humanist Assn, Amherst, NY)
*Humor	Humor: international journal of humor research (The Hague)
*HWSJ	Henry Williamson Society Journal (Chichester)
*Hypatia	Hypatia: a journal of feminist philosophy (Univ. of Oregon, Eugene)
*IE	Indiana English (Indiana State Univ., Terre Haute)
*IGSJ	Ivor Gurney Society Journal (Ivor Gurney Soc., School of English, Univ. of Birmingham)
IHI	Iowa Heritage Illustrated (State Historical Soc. of Iowa, Iowa City)
*IJES	International Journal of English Studies (Univ. de Murcia)
*IJPP	Interpretation: a journal of political philosophy (Queen's College, City Univ. of New York, Flushing)
*Illusions	Illusions: a New Zealand magazine of film, television and theatre criticism (Wellington, New Zealand)
*ILS	Irish Literary Supplement (Wading River, NY)
*ImN	Image & Narrative: online magazine of the visual narrative (Louvain)
*IMR	Iron Mountain Review (Emory, VA)
*Indice	Indice (Turin)
*IndS	Independent Shavian (Bernard Shaw Soc., New York)
*InR	Indiana Review (Bloomington, IN)
Interpretation	Interpretation: a journal of Bible and theology (Union Theological Seminar in Virginia, Richmond)
*Intertexts	Intertexts (Texas Tech Univ., Lubbock)
*IowaR	Iowa Review (Univ. of Iowa, Iowa City)
*Iris	Iris: a journal about women (Univ. of Virginia, Charlottesville)
*Isis	Isis: an international review devoted to the history of science and its cultural influences (History of Science Soc.) (Chicago, IL)
*ISLE	ISLE: interdisciplinary studies in literature and environment (Assn for the Study of Literature and Environment, Univ. of Nevada, Reno)
*ItalA	Italian Americana (State Univ. of New York, Buffalo)
*Italica	Italica (Columbia Univ., New York)
*IW	Issues in Writing (Univ. of Wisconsin, Stevens Point)
*JAAH	Journal of African American History (Assn for the Study of African American Life and History, Silver Spring, MD)
*JAAL	Journal of Adolescent and Adult Literacy (International Reading Assn, Newark, DE)
*JAAR	Journal of the American Academy of Religion (Whittier College, Whittier, CA)
*JAAS	Journal of Asian American Studies (Assn for Asian American Studies) (Baltimore, MD)
*JAC	Journal of American Culture: studies of a civilization (American Culture Assn, Bowling Green State Univ., Bowling Green, OH)
*JACJ	JAC: a journal of composition theory (Dept of English, Iowa State Univ., Ames)
*JADT	Journal of American Drama and Theatre (Graduate School, City Univ. of New York)
*JAE	Journal of Aesthetic Education (Univ. of Illinois, Champaign)

*JAF	Journal of American Folklore: journal of the American Folklore Society (Arlington, VA)
*JAH	Journal of American History (Indiana Univ., Bloomington)
JAMLS	Journal of Arts Management, Law, and Society (Washington, DC)
*JAMS	Journal of the American Musicological Society (Stanford Univ., Stanford, CA)
JAR	Journal of Anthropological Research (Univ. of New Mexico, Albuquerque)
*JArizH	Journal of Arizona History (Arizona Historical Soc., Tucson)
*JAStud	Journal of American Studies (Cambridge)
*JATS	Journal of the Angela Thirkell Society (Leeds)
*JazA	Jazykovědné aktuality (Prague)
*JBecS	Journal of Beckett Studies (Florida State Univ., Tallahassee)
*JBJ	John Buchan Journal (John Buchan Soc., Bridge of Weir, Renfrewshire)
*JBlaS	Journal of Black Studies (Thousand Oaks, CA)
*JBS	Journal of British Studies (Chicago, IL)
*JCanStud	Journal of Canadian Studies / Revue d'études canadiennes (Trent Univ., Peterborough, Ont.)
*JCarL	Journal of Caribbean Literatures (Dept of English, Univ. of Northern Iowa, Cedar Falls)
*JCG	Journal of Cultural Geography (Bowling Green State Univ., Bowling Green, OH)
*JCI	Journal of Communication Inquiry (Univ. of Iowa, Iowa City)
*JCL	Journal of Commonwealth Literature (East Grinstead, W. Sussex)
*JCM	Journal of Country Music (Nashville, TN)
JCP	Journal of Canadian Poetry: the poetry review (Nepean, Ont.)
*JCPS	Journal of Commonwealth and Postcolonial Studies (Georgia Southern Univ., Statesboro)
*JCSJ	John Clare Society Journal (Helpston, Peterborough)
*JDN	James Dickey Newsletter (DeKalb Community College, Dunwoody, GA)
*JDTC	Journal of Dramatic Theory and Criticism (Univ. of Kansas, Lawrence)
*JEBS	Journal of the Early Book Society for the Study of Manuscripts and Printing History (New York)
JECS	Journal of Early Christian Studies (North American Patristics Soc.) (Baltimore, MD)
*JEGP	Journal of English and Germanic Philology: a quarterly devoted to the English, German, and Scandinavian languages and literatures (Champaign, IL)
*JEL	Journal of English Linguistics (Thousand Oaks, CA)
*JEPNS	Journal of the English Place-Name Society (Univ. of Nottingham)
*JFA	Journal of the Fantastic in the Arts (International Assn for the Fantastic in the Arts) (Boca Raton, FL)
*JFR	Journal of Folklore Research (Indiana Univ. Folklore Inst., Bloomington)
*JFV	Journal of Film and Video (University Film and Video Assn, California State Univ., Los Angeles)
JGE	Journal of General Education (Pennsylvania State Univ., University Park)
*JHI	Journal of the History of Ideas (Rutgers Univ., New Brunswick, NJ)
*JHM	Journal of the History of Medicine and Allied Sciences (New Haven, CT)
*JHo	Journal of Homosexuality (Binghamton, NY)
JHP	Journal of the History of Philosophy (Emory Univ., Atlanta, GA)
*JHS	Journal of the History of Sexuality (Bard College, Annandale-on-Hudson, NY)
*JJLS	James Joyce Literary Supplement (Miami Univ., Coral Gables, FL)

*JJQ	James Joyce Quarterly (Univ. of Tulsa, OK)
*JLSP	Journal of Language and Social Psychology (Univ. of California, Santa Barbara)
*JMCQ	Journalism and Mass Communication Quarterly (Assn for Education in Journalism and Mass Communication, Columbia, SC)
*JMEMS	Journal of Medieval and Early Modern Studies (Durham, NC)
*JMH	Journal of Modern History (Chicago, IL)
*JML	Journal of Modern Literature (Foundation for Modern Literature, Bloomington, IN)
*JMMLA	Journal of the Midwest Modern Language Association (Univ. of Iowa, Iowa City)
*JNT	Journal of Narrative Theory (Soc. for the Study of Narrative Literature, Eastern Michigan Univ., Ypsilanti)
*JNZL	Journal of New Zealand Literature (Dept of English, Univ. of Otago, Dunedin)
*JoH	Journalism History (Univ. of Nevada, Las Vegas)
*Journeys	Journeys: the international journal of travel and travel writing (London)
*JPC	Journal of Popular Culture (Popular Culture Center, Bowling Green State Univ., OH)
*JPCL	Journal of Pidgin and Creole Languages (Amsterdam)
*JPFT	Journal of Popular Film and Television (Helen Dwight Reid Educational Foundation) (Washington, DC)
JPH	Journal of Presbyterian History (Presbyterian Historical Soc., Philadelphia, PA)
*JPHS	Journal of the Printing Historical Society (London)
*JPrag	Journal of Pragmatics: an interdisciplinary monthly of language studies (Amsterdam)
*JPRS	Journal of Pre-Raphaelite Studies (Strong College, York Univ., Toronto)
*JPW	Journal of Postcolonial Writing (Abingdon, Oxon.)
*JR	Journal of Religion (Chicago, IL)
JRS	Journal of Ritual Studies (Pittsburgh Univ., Pittsburgh, PA)
*JSBC	Journal for the Study of British Cultures (British Council, Tübingen)
*JSchP	Journal of Scholarly Publishing (North York, Ont.)
*JSH	Journal of Southern History (Rice Univ., Houston, TX)
*JSoc	Journal of Sociolinguistics (Oxford)
*JSSE	Journal of the Short Story in English / Les Cahiers de la nouvelle (Univ. d'Angers)
*JSwest	Journal of the Southwest (Univ. of Arizona, Tucson)
*JTLBS	Journal of the Thomas Lovell Beddoes Society (Belper, Derbyshire)
*Jubilat	Jubilat (Dept of English, Univ. of Massachusetts, Amherst)
*JuC	Jump Cut: a review of contemporary media (Berkeley, CA) (http://www.ejumpcut.org/)
*JudQ	Judaism: a quarterly journal of Jewish life and thought (Univ. of California, Santa Cruz)
*JVC	Journal of Victorian Culture (Edinburgh)
*JWest	Journal of the West: an illustrated quarterly of Western American history and culture (Manhattan, KS)
*JWMS	Journal of the William Morris Society (Hammersmith)
*Kalliope	Kalliope: a journal of women's literature & art (Florida Community College, Jacksonville)
*KenEB	Kentucky English Bulletin (Bowling Green, KY)
*KenPR	Kentucky Philological Review (Highland Heights, KY)
*KJ	Kipling Journal (Kipling Soc., Brighton)

*KnLet	Knight Letter (Lewis Carroll Soc. of North America, Nappa, CA)
*KR	Kenyon Review (Kenyon College, Gambier, OH)
*KSR	Keats–Shelley Review (Keats–Shelley Memorial Assn, Windsor)
*LAm	Letterature d'America: rivista trimestrale (Rome)
*Landfall	Landfall: New Zealand arts and letters (Dunedin)
*Lang	Language: journal of the Linguistic Society of America (Baltimore, MD)
LauR	Laurel Review (Northwest Missouri State Univ., Maryville)
LB	Living Blues: a journal of the African American Blues tradition (University, MS)
*Legacy	Legacy: a journal of American women writers (Pennsylvania State Univ., University Park)
*Lembas-extra	Lembas-extra (Tolkien Genootschap 'Unquendor') (Leiden)
*Leviathan	Leviathan: a journal of Melville studies (Melville Soc.; Hofstra Univ., Hempstead, NY)
*LFil	Linguistica e Filologia (Bergamo)
LH	Lincoln Herald (Harrogate, TN)
*LHR	Langston Hughes Review: official publication of the Langston Hughes Society (Athens, GA)
*LibC	Libraries & Culture: a journal of library history (Austin, TX)
*LibH	Library History: journal of the Library History Group of the Library Association (London)
*Library	Library: the transactions of the Bibliographical Society (Oxford)
*LingPr	Linguistica Pragensia (Czech Academy of Sciences) (Amsterdam; Philadelphia, PA)
*Lit	Lit: literature, interpretation, theory (Reading)
*LitB	Literature and Belief (Provo, UT)
*LitFQ	Literature/Film Quarterly (Salisbury State Univ., Salisbury, MD)
*LitH	Literature and History (Univ. of Manchester)
*LitIm	Literary Imagination: the review of the Association of Literary Scholars and Critics (Athens, GA)
*LitMed	Literature and Medicine (Baltimore, MD)
*LitR	Literary Review: an international journal of contemporary writing (Fairleigh Dickinson Univ., Madison, NJ)
*LitTheol	Literature & Theology: an interdisciplinary journal of theory and criticism (Oxford)
*LittPr	Litteraria Pragensia: studies in literature and culture (Czech Academy of Sciences) (Amsterdam; Philadelphia, PA)
*LJH	Lamar Journal of the Humanities (College of Arts and Sciences, Lamar Univ., Beaumont, TX)
*LLit	Language and Literature: journal of the Poetics and Linguistics Association (Harlow)
*LovS	Lovecraft Studies (West Warwick, RI)
*LProv	Lettore di provincia (Ravenna)
*LPub	Learned Publishing: the journal of the Association of Learned and Professional Society Publishers (London)
*LQ	Library Quarterly: a journal of investigation in library and information sciences (Chicago, UL)
*LRB	London Review of Books (London)
*LRC	Literary Review of Canada: a review of Canadian books on culture, politics and society (Toronto)
*LSE	Leeds Studies in English (Univ. of Leeds)
*LT	Linea Tempo (Milan)

*LU	Lion and the Unicorn: a critical journal of children's literature (Baltimore, MD)
MacGuffin	MacGuffin (Dept of English, Schoolcraft College, Livonia, Ml)
*MÆ	Medium Ævum (Soc. for the Study of Medieval Languages and Literature, Oxford)
*MaHR	Massachusetts Historical Review (Massachusetts Historical Soc., Boston)
*MalaR	Malahat Review (Univ. of Victoria, B.C.)
Manoa	Manoa: Pacific journal of international writing (Honolulu, HI)
*ManQ	Mankind Quarterly (Washington, DC)
*MarvT	Marvels & Tales: journal of fairy-tale studies (Wayne State Univ., Detroit, MI)
*MassR	Massachusetts Review: a quarterly of literature, the arts, and public affairs (Univ. of Massachusetts, Amherst)
*McNR	McNeese Review (McNeese State Univ., Lake Charles, LA)
*Meanjin	Meanjin (Univ. of Melbourne, Parkville, Vic.)
*MedH	Media History (Oxford)
*MedRen	Medieval and Renaissance Drama in England (Madison, NJ)
*MelSE	Melville Society Extracts (Hempstead, NY)
*MELUS	MELUS (Univ. of Southern California, Los Angeles)
*Menckeniana	Menckeniana: a quarterly review (Enoch Pratt Free Library, Baltimore, MD)
*MerA	Merton Annual: studies in culture, spirituality, and social concerns (Decatur, GA)
*Meridians	Meridians: feminism, race, transnationalism (Wesleyan Univ., Middletown, CT)
Metamorphoses	Metamorphoses (Amherst, MA)
*Metro	Metro (Auckland)
*MetS	Metaphor and Symbol (Mahwah, NJ)
*MFS	Modern Fiction Studies (Dept of English, Purdue Univ., West Lafayette, IN) (Baltimore, MD)
MichH	Michigan History Magazine (Dept of State, Michigan Historical Center, Lansing)
*MichQR	Michigan Quarterly Review (Univ. of Michigan, Ann Arbor)
*MidAmerica	MidAmerica: the yearbook of the Society for the Study of Midwestern Literature (East Lansing, MI)
*MidF	Midwestern Folklore: journal of the Hoosier Folklore Society (Terre Haute, IN)
*MidQ	Midwest Quarterly: a journal of contemporary thought (Pittsburg State Univ., Pittsburg, KS)
*MiE	Mind's Eye: a liberal arts journal (North Adams, MA)
*MinnR	Minnesota Review (Univ. of Missouri, Columbia)
*Misc	Miscelánea: a journal of English and American studies (Zaragoza Univ.)
MisR	Mississippi Review (Center for Writers, Univ. of Southern Mississippi, Hattiesburg)
*MLN	MLN (Baltimore, MD)
*MLQ	Modern Language Quarterly: a journal of literary history (Duke Univ., Durham, NC)
*MLR	Modern Language Review (Modern Humanities Research Assn) (Leeds)
*MLS	Modern Language Studies (Northeast Modern Language Assn, Univ. of Rhode Island, Kingston)
*M/M	Mentalities/Mentalités (Hamilton, New Zealand)
*ModAge	Modern Age: a quarterly review (Intercollegiate Studies Inst., Univ. of Maryland, College Park)

*ModDr	Modern Drama (Graduate Centre for Study of Drama, Univ. of Toronto) (Downsview, Ont.)
*Mod/Mod	Modernism/Modernity (Baltimore, MD)
ModSch	Modern Schoolman (St Louis Univ., St Louis, MO)
*Monist	Monist: an international quarterly journal of general philosophical inquiry (Chicago / La Salle, IL)
*Montana	Montana: the magazine of Western history (Montana Historical Soc., Helena)
*Moreana	Moreana (Angers)
*Mosaic	Mosaic: a journal for the interdisciplinary study of literature (Univ. of Manitoba, Winnipeg)
*MovIm	Moving Image: the journal of the Association of Moving Image Archivists (Minneapolis, MN)
*MP	Modern Philology: a journal devoted to research in medieval and modern literature (Chicago, IL)
*MQ	Milton Quarterly (Baltimore, MD)
*MR	Missouri Review (Univ. of Missouri, Columbia)
*MSAN	MSAN: Marlowe Society of America newsletter (South Dakota State Univ., Brookings)
MsM	Ms Magazine (New York)
*MSS	Manuscripts (Manuscript Soc., Burbank, CA)
*MTJ	Mark Twain Journal (English Dept, The Citadel, Charleston, SC)
*MusL	Music & Letters (Oxford)
*Mythprint	Mythprint: the monthly bulletin of the Mythopoeic Society (San Francisco, CA)
*Nabokovian	Nabokovian (Vladimir Nabokov Soc., Univ. of Kansas, Lawrence)
*NabSt	Nabokov Studies (Los Angeles, CA)
NADS	Newsletter of the American Dialect Society (MacMurray College, Jacksonville, IL)
*Narrative	Narrative (Soc. for the Study of Narrative Literature, Columbus, OH)
*NCarF	North Carolina Folklore Journal (Greenville, NC)
*NCC	Nineteenth-Century Contexts: an interdisciplinary journal (Dept of English, Univ. of Notre Dame, IN; Dept of English, Univ. of Lancaster) (Amsterdam)
*NCFrS	Nineteenth-Century French Studies (Fredonia, NY)
*NCHR	North Carolina Historical Review (Raleigh, NC)
*NCL	Notes on Contemporary Literature (Carrollton, GA)
*NCLR	North Carolina Literary Review (North Carolina Literary and Historical Assn, Dept of English, East Carolina Univ., Greenville)
*NCorr	Nuova Corrente (Genoa)
*NCP	Nineteenth Century Prose (Dept of Literature and Language, Mesa State College, Grand Junction, CO)
*NCS	Nineteenth Century Studies (Lancaster, PA)
*NCT	Nineteenth Century Theatre and Film (Manchester)
NebH	Nebraska History (Nebraska State Historical Soc., Lincoln)
*Neophilologus	Neophilologus: an international journal of modern and mediaeval language and literature (Dordrecht; Boston, MA; London)
*NER	New England Review (Middlebury College, Middlebury, VT)
*NewHR	New Hibernia Review / Irís Éireannach Nua: a quarterly record of Irish studies (Center for Irish Studies / Lárionad an Léinn Éireannaigh, Univ. of St Thomas, St Paul, MN)
*NewL	New Leader (American Labor Conference on International Affairs, New York)

*NewLet	New Letters (Univ. of Missouri, Kansas City)
*NewR	New Renaissance: an international magazine of ideas and opinions emphasizing literature and the arts (Arlington, MA)
NF	Northeast Folklore (Univ. of Maine, Orono)
*NHR	Nathaniel Hawthorne Review (Dept of English, Duquesne Univ., Pittsburgh, PA)
NiemR	Nieman Reports (Cambridge, MA)
*Nimrod	Nimrod: international journal of prose and poetry (Tulsa, OK)
*NineL	Nineteenth-Century Literature (Berkeley; Los Angeles, CA)
*NLH	New Literary History: a journal of theory and interpretation (Univ. of Virginia, Charlottesville) (Baltimore, MD)
NLStud	Newfoundland and Labrador Studies (Memorial Univ., St John's, Nfld)
*NM	Neuphilologische Mitteilungen: bulletin de la Société Néophilologique / bulletin of the Modern Language Society (Helsinki)
*NMAS	Newsletter of the Margaret Atwood Society (Oxford, OH)
*NML	New Medieval Literatures (Oxford)
NOR	New Orleans Review (Loyola Univ., New Orleans, LA)
*NorS	North and South (Auckland)
*Novel	Novel: a forum on fiction (Brown Univ., Providence, RI)
*Now	Now and Then (East Tennessee State Univ., Johnson City)
*NQ	Notes and Queries: for readers and writers, collectors and librarians (Oxford)
*NRCLL	New Review of Children's Literature and Librarianship (London)
*NwOH	Northwest Ohio History (Lucas / Maumee Valley Historical Soc., Toledo-Lucas Public Library, Dept of History, Bowling Green State Univ., Bowling Green, OH)
*NwR	Northwest Review (Univ. of Oregon, Eugene)
*NWSAJ	NWSA Journal: a publication of the National Women's Studies Association (Indiana Univ., Bloomington)
*NYH	New York History (New York State Historical Assn, Cooperstown)
*NYRSF	New York Review of Science Fiction (Pleasantville, NY)
*NYTM	New York Times Magazine (New York)
*NZBooks	New Zealand Books (Wellington, New Zealand)
*NZEJ	New Zealand English Journal (Univ. of Canterbury, Christchurch)
NZHP	New Zealand Historic Places (Wellington, New Zealand)
*NZW	NZ Words (New Zealand Dictionary Centre, Victoria Univ. of Wellington) (Auckland; Oxford)
*OEN	Old English Newsletter (Medieval Inst., Western Michigan Univ., Kalamazoo)
*OENS	Old English Newsletter: Subsidia (Medieval Inst., Western Michigan Univ., Kalamazoo)
*OHR	Oral History Review: journal of the Oral History Association (Univ. of Connecticut, Storrs)
*OnCan	Onomastica Canadiana: journal of the Canadian Society for the Study of Names / revue de la Société Canadienne d'Onomastique (Ottawa)
*Onthebus	Onthebus (Los Angeles, CA)
OntR	Ontario Review (Princeton, NJ)
OpC	Open City Magazine (New York)
OpL	Open Letter (London, Ont.)
OreHQ	Oregon Historical Quarterly (Oregon Historical Soc., Portland)
*OT	Oral Tradition (Univ. of Missouri, Columbia)
*OurS	Our State: down home in North Carolina (Greensboro, NC)

*OV	Other Voices (Dept of English, Univ. of Pennsylvania, Philadelphia)
OVH	Ohio Valley History: the journal of the Cincinnati Historical Society (Cincinnati, OH)
*OvR	Overland Review (Kansas Folklore Soc., Paola)
*OxAm	Oxford American: a magazine from the South (Univ. of Central Arkansas, Conway)
*PAAS	Proceedings of the American Antiquarian Society: a journal of American history and culture through 1876 (Worcester, MA)
*PacHR	Pacific Historical Review (Univ. of California, Los Angeles)
*PacNQ	Pacific Northwest Quarterly: a scholarly journal of Northwest history (Univ. of Washington, Seattle)
*Paideuma	Paideuma: a journal devoted to Ezra Pound scholarship (Univ. of Maine, Orono)
*PAJ	Performing Arts Journal: a journal of performance and art (Baltimore, MD)
*Palacio	Palacio: magazine of the Museum of New Mexico (Santa Fe, NM)
*PAPS	Proceedings of the American Philosophical Society (Philadelphia, PA)
Para	Paragraph (Oxford)
*Parabola	Parabola: the magazine of myth and tradition
*Parergon	Parergon: journal of the Australian and New Zealand Association for Medieval and Early Modern Studies (Nedlands, W. Australia)
*Parnassus	Parnassus: poetry in review (New York)
*PartA	Partial Answers: journal of literature and the history of ideas (School of Literatures, Hebrew Univ. of Jerusalem)
PassS	Passing Show (Shubert Foundation, New York)
*PBSA	Papers of the Bibliographical Society of America (New York)
*PCP	Pacific Coast Philology (Pacific Ancient and Modern Language Assn, California State Univ., Northridge)
*PCR	Popular Culture Review: journal of the Far West Popular and American Culture Association (Dept of English, Univ. of Nevada, Las Vegas)
*PeakeS	Peake Studies (Orzens, Vaud, Switzerland)
*PemM	Pembroke Magazine (Univ. of North Carolina, Pembroke)
*Persuasions	Persuasions (Jane Austen Soc. of North America, New York)
PEW	Philosophy East and West: a quarterly of Asian and comparative thought (Univ. of Hawaii, Honolulu)
*PhilL	Philosophy and Literature (Baltimore, MD)
Philosophy	Philosophy: the journal of the Royal Institute of Philosophy (London)
*PhilR	Philosophy and Rhetoric (University Park, PA)
*PhRSN	Philip Roth Society Newsletter (Dept of Languages and Communications, Prairie View A&M Univ., Prairie View, TX)
*PinR	Pinter Review (Tampa Univ., Florida) (http://www.haroldpinter.org/pinterreview/index.shmtl)
*PInt	Poetry International (Dept of English and Comparative Literature, San Diego State Univ., San Diego, CA)
PJCAC	Phoenix: the journal of the Classics Association of Canada (Trinity College, Toronto)
*PJCL	Prairie Journal of Canadian Literature (Calgary, Alta)
*PLL	Papers on Language & Literature: a quarterly journal for scholars and critics of language and literature (Southern Illinois Univ., Edwardsville)
*Ploughshares	Ploughshares: a journal of new writing (Emerson College, Boston, MA)
*PMC	Postmodern Culture: an electronic journal of interdisciplinary criticism (Raleigh, NC) (http://jefferson.village.virginia.edu/pmc/)
*PNZ	Poetry New Zealand (Auckland)

*PoeS	Poe Studies / Dark Romanticism: history, theory, interpretation (Washington State Univ., Pullman)
*PoesiaM	Poesia (Milan)
*Poetics	Poetics: journal of empirical research on culture, the media and the arts (Amsterdam)
*Poetry	Poetry (New York; Chicago, IL)
*PowJ	Powys Journal (Powys Soc., Wexham, Bucks.)
PPR	Philosophy and Phenomenological Research (State Univ. of New York, Buffalo)
*PQ	Philological Quarterly (Univ. of Iowa, Iowa City)
*PRes	Performance Research: a journal of performing arts (London)
*PrF	Prairie Fire: a Manitoba literary review (Winnipeg, Man.)
*PrH	Printing History: journal of the American Printing History Association (New York)
*Prism(s)	Prism(s): essays in Romanticism (American Conference on Romanticism, Brigham Young Univ., Provo, UT)
*Profession	Profession (Modern Language Assn of America, New York)
*Proteus	Proteus: a journal of ideas (Shippensburg, PA)
*Proverbium	Proverbium (Ohio State Univ., Columbus)
*PrQ	Print Quarterly (London)
*PrS	Prairie Schooner (Univ. of Nebraska, Lincoln)
*PrSt	Prose Studies: history, theory, criticism (London)
PRv	Philosophical Review (Cornell Univ., Ithaca, NY)
*PS	Post Script: essays in film and the humanities (Commerce, TX)
*PsCS	Psychoanalysis, Culture & Society (Basingstoke)
*PsyArt	PsyArt: a hyperlink journal for the psychological study of the arts (Dept of English, Univ. of Florida, Gainesville) (http://web.clas.ufl.edu/ipsa/journal/)
*PubRQ	Publishing Research Quarterly (New Brunswick, NJ)
QH	Quaker History: the bulletin of Friends Historical Association (Haverford College, Haverford, PA)
*QRFV	Quarterly Review of Film and Video (London)
*QStud	Québec Studies (Univ. of Vermont, Burlington)
QW	Quarterly West (Univ. of Utah, Salt Lake City)
*RAC	Religion and American Culture: a journal of interpretation (Center for the Study of Religion and American Culture) (Berkeley, CA)
*RAEI	Revista alicantina de estudios ingleses (Univ. de Alicante, Alicante)
*RAL	Research in African Literatures (Bloomington, IN)
*Rampike	Rampike (Sault St Marie, Ont.)
*RANAM	Recherches anglaises et nord-américaines (Univ. des Sciences Humaines de Strasbourg)
*Raritan	Raritan: a quarterly review (Rutgers Univ., New Brunswick, NJ)
*RCF	Review of Contemporary Fiction (Illinois State Univ., Normal)
*Reader	Reader: essays in reader-oriented theory, criticism, and pedagogy (Houghton, MI)
*RECTR	Restoration and 18th Century Theatre Research (Loyola Univ., Chicago, IL)
*RelArts	Religion and the Arts: a journal from Boston College (Chestnut Hill, MA)
*ReLit	Religion and Literature (Univ. of Notre Dame, Notre Dame, IN)
*Ren	Renascence: essays on values in literature (Marquette Univ., Milwaukee, WI)
*RenD	Renaissance Drama (Evanston, IL)

*RenP	Renaissance Papers (Southeastern Renaissance Conference) (Columbia, SC)
*RenSt	Renaissance Studies: journal of the Society for Renaissance Studies (Oxford)
*Representations	Representations (Univ. of California, Berkeley)
*RES	Review of English Studies: the quarterly journal of English literature and the English language (Oxford)
*Restoration	Restoration: studies in English literary culture, 1660–1700 (Tennessee Technological Univ., Cookeville)
RevR	Revolver Review (Prague)
*RFR	Robert Frost Review (Rock Hill, SC)
*Rhetorica	Rhetorica: a journal for the history of rhetoric (Berkeley, CA)
*RhR	Rhetoric Review (Dept of English, Univ. of Arizona, Tucson)
*RLC	Revue de littérature comparée (Paris)
*RMER	Rocky Mountain E-Review (Rocky Mountain Modern Language Assn, Pullman, WA) (http://rmmla.wsu.edu/)
*Romanticism	Romanticism (Edinburgh)
*RomNet	Romanticism on the Net (Univ. of Montreal) (http://www.ron.umontreal.ca/)
*RORD	Research Opportunities in Renaissance Drama (Univ. of New Orleans, LA)
*RQ	Renaissance Quarterly (Renaissance Soc. of America, New York)
RR	Romanic Review (Dept of French and Romance Philology, Columbia Univ., New York)
*R/R/R	Ricerca/Research/Recherche (Lecce)
*RSA	RSA Journal: rivista di studi nord americani (Associazione Italiana di Studi Nord-Americani, Venice)
*RSQ	Rhetoric Society Quarterly (Rhetoric Soc. of America, Dept of English, Pennsylvania State Univ., University Park)
*RT	Radical Teacher: a Socialist and feminist journal on the theory and practice of teaching (Cambridge, MA)
*RWP	RWP: an annual of Robert Penn Warren studies (Center for Robert Penn Warren Studies) (Western Kentucky Univ., Bowling Green)
*SAC	Studies in the Age of Chaucer (New Chaucer Soc., Ohio State Univ., Columbus)
*SAH	Studies in American Humor: the journal of the American Humor Studies Association (Univ. of North Carolina, Greensboro)
*SAIL	Studies in American Indian Literatures (Western Washington Univ., Bellingham)
*SAP	Studia Anglica Posnaniensia: an international review of English studies (Adam Mickiewicz Univ., Poznań, Poland)
*SAQ	South Atlantic Quarterly (Duke Univ., Durham, NC)
*SaS	Slovo a slovesnost / Word and Writing: časopis pro otazky teorie a kultury jazyka (Prague)
*SAtlR	South Atlantic Review: the journal of the South Atlantic Modern Language Association (Georgia State Univ., Atlanta)
*SBJ	Saul Bellow Journal (West Bloomfield, MI)
*Scandinavica	Scandinavica (London)
*Scintilla	Scintilla (Usk Valley Vaughan Assn, Llantrisant, Usk, Gwent)
*SCJ	Southern Communication Journal (Southern States Communication Assn, Univ. of Memphis, TN)
*ScLang	Scottish Language (Assn for Scottish Literary Studies, Univ. of Aberdeen)
*SCN	Seventeenth-Century News (Texas A&M Univ., College Station)

*SCR	South Central Review: the journal of the South Central Modern Language Association (Texas A&M Univ., College Station)
*Scriblerian	Scriblerian and the Kit-Cats (Temple Univ., Philadelphia, PA)
*SCrit	Strumenti critici (Turin)
*ScSR	Scottish Studies Review (Assn for Scottish Literary Studies, Glasgow)
*SDR	South Dakota Review (Dept of English, Univ. of South Dakota, Vermillion)
*SEDERI	SEDERI: yearbook of the Spanish and Portuguese Society for English Renaissance Studies (Univ. of Valladolid)
*SEEJ	Slavic and East European Journal (Univ. of Arizona, Tucson)
*SELIM	SELIM: revista de la Sociedad Española de Lengua y Literatura Inglesa Medieval (Univ. of Oviedo)
*SELit	Studies in English Literature 1500–1900 (Rice Univ., Houston, TX)
*SevC	Seventeenth Century (Centre for Seventeenth-Century Studies, Univ. of Durham)
*SEVEN	SEVEN: an Anglo-American literary review (Wheaton College, IL)
*SewR	Sewanee Review (Univ. of the South, Sewanee, TN)
*SHARP	SHARP News (Macon, GA)
*Shaw	Shaw: the annual of Bernard Shaw studies (University Park, PA)
*ShB	Shakespeare Bulletin: a journal of performance criticism and scholarship (Baltimore, MD)
*Shen	Shenandoah: the Washington and Lee University review (Lexington, VA)
*SHogg	Studies in Hogg and His World (James Hogg Soc., Univ. of Stirling)
*ShQ	Shakespeare Quarterly (Folger Shakespeare Library, Washington, DC)
*ShS	Shakespeare Survey: an annual survey of Shakespearean studies and production (Cambridge)
*ShSt	Short Story (Columbia, SC)
*ShY	Shakespeare Yearbook (Lewiston, NY)
*SidJ	Sidney Journal (Univ. of Guelph, Ont.)
*Sionnach	An Sionnach: a journal of literature, arts, and culture (Omaha, NB)
*SixCJ	Sixteenth-Century Journal: the journal of early modern studies (Truman State Univ., Kirksville, MO)
*SJ	Shakespeare Jahrbuch (Deutsche Shakespeare-Gesellschaft, Bochum)
*SlavR	Slavic Review: American quarterly of Soviet and East European studies (Stanford, CA)
*SLI	Studies in the Literary Imagination (Georgia State Univ., Atlanta)
*SlStE	Slovak Studies in English (Univ. Komenského, Bratislava)
*SmAx	Small Axe (Indiana Univ., Bloomington)
*SNL	Shakespeare Newsletter (Dept of English, Iona College, New Rochelle, NY)
*SoCR	South Carolina Review (Clemson Univ., Clemson, SC)
*SoCult	Southern Cultures (Center for the Study of the South, Univ. of North Carolina, Chapel Hill)
*SoHR	Southern Humanities Review (Southern Humanities Council, Auburn Univ., Auburn, AL)
*SoLJ	Southern Literary Journal (Dept of English, Univ. of North Carolina, Chapel Hill)
*SondR	Sondheim Review (Milwaukee, WI)
*SoQ	Southern Quarterly (Univ. of Southern Mississippi, Hattiesburg)
*SoR	Southern Review (State Univ. of Louisiana, Baton Rouge)
*Southerly	Southerly (English Assn, Sydney)
*SP	Studies in Philology (Chapel Hill, NC)

*SPACVW	Selected Papers from the Annual Conference on Virginia Woolf (Center for Virginia Woolf Studies, Univ. of California, Berkeley)
*SPAS	Studies in Puritan American Spirituality (Univ. of Alaska, Fairbanks)
*SPC	Studies in Popular Culture (Dept of English, Middle Tennessee State Univ., Murfreesboro)
*Spec	Speculum: a journal of medieval studies (Medieval Academy of America, Cambridge, MA)
*SPELL	Swiss Papers in English Language and Literature (Tübingen)
*SpenR	Spenser Review (Macalester College, St Paul, MN)
*SPFFOU	Sborník prací filozofické fakulty Ostravské univerzity (Ostrava)
*SR	Studies in Romanticism (Boston Univ., Boston, MA)
*SRASP	Shakespeare and Renaissance Association of West Virginia: selected papers (Marshall Univ., Huntington, VA)
*SRev	Southwest Review (Southern Methodist Univ., Dallas, TX)
*SS	Scandinavian Studies (Lawrence, KS)
*SSE	Sydney Studies in English (Univ. of Sydney)
SShaK	SShA, Kanada: ekonomika, politika, kul'tura = USA, Canada: economics, politics, culture (Moscow, Russia)
*SStud	Shakespeare Studies (Madison, NJ)
*SStudT	Shakespeare Studies (Shakespeare Soc. of Japan, Tokyo)
*StAL	Studies in American Literature / Amerika bungaku kenkyu (Kobe, Japan)
*StCS	Stephen Crane Studies (Dept of English / Stephen Crane Soc., Virginia Polytechnic Inst. and State Univ., Blacksburg)
*StIll	Studies in Illustration (Imaginative Book Illustration Soc., London)
*Storytelling	Storytelling: a critical journal of popular narrative (Washington, DC)
*StStud	Steinbeck Studies (Martha Heasley Cox Center for Steinbeck Studies, San Jose State Univ., San Jose, CA)
*StudAJL	Studies in American Jewish Literature (Dept of English, Pennsylvania State Univ., University Park)
*StudCanL	Studies in Canadian Literature / Études en littérature canadienne (Univ. of New Brunswick, Fredericton)
*StudECC	Studies in Eighteenth-Century Culture (American Soc. for Eighteenth-Century Studies) (Baltimore, MD)
*StudMed	Studies in Medievalism (Cambridge)
*StudN	Studies in the Novel (Univ. of North Texas, Denton)
*Style	Style (Northern Illinois Univ., DeKalb)
*SubStance	SubStance: a review of theory and literary criticism (Univ. of Wisconsin, Madison)
*SvL	Svět literatury (Kruh moderních filologů, Prague) (Amsterdam; Philadelphia, PA)
*SwSt	Swift Studies: annual of the Ehrenpreis Centre for Swift Studies (Münster)
*Symbiosis	Symbiosis: a journal of Anglo-American literary relations (College of St Mark and St John, Plymouth)
*Symplokē	Symplokē: a journal for the intermingling of literary, cultural and theoretical scholarship (Univ. of Illinois, Chicago)
*Symposium	Symposium: a quarterly journal in modern literatures (Washington, DC)
*Syncrise	Syncrise (Annual of the Hellenic Comparative Literature Assn, Athens)
Talisman	Talisman: a journal of contemporary poetry and poetics (Jersey City, NJ)
*TBR	Texas Books in Review (Stephenville, TX)
*TCL	Twentieth Century Literature: a scholarly and critical journal (Hofstra Univ., Hempstead, NY)

*TDR	TDR / The Drama Review: the journal of performance studies (Cambridge, MA)
*TEJ	Tennessee English Journal (Tennessee Tech Univ., Cookeville)
*Te Reo	Te Reo: journal of the Linguistic Society of New Zealand (Auckland)
*TexP	Textual Practice (London)
*TextB	Text: an interdisciplinary journal for the study of discourse (Berlin)
*TextT	TEXT Technology (McMaster Univ., Hamilton, Ont.)
*Textus	Textus: English studies in Italy (Genoa)
*TFr	Testo a fronte (Milan)
*TFSB	Tennessee Folklore Society Bulletin (Middle Tennessee State Univ., Murfreesboro)
*Theater	Theater (Yale School of Drama / Yale Repertory Theater, New Haven, CT)
*TheatreA	Theatre Annual: a journal of performance studies (College of William and Mary, Williamsburg, VA)
*TheatreForum	TheatreForum (Univ. of California at San Diego, La Jolla)
*TheatreS	Theatre Survey: the journal of the American Society for Theatre Research (Dept of Drama, Catholic Univ. of America, Washington, DC)
*THJ	Thomas Hardy Journal (Thomas Hardy Soc., Dorchester)
*THQ	Tennessee Historical Quarterly (Tennessee Historical Soc., Nashville)
*THS	Theatre History Studies (Mid-America Theatre Assn, Central College, Pella, IA)
*THSC	Transactions of the Honourable Society of Cymmrodorion / Trafodion Anrhydeddus Gymdeithas y Cymmrodorion (London)
*ThSym	Theatre Symposium: a journal of the Southeastern Theatre Conference (Tuscaloosa, AL)
*TJ	Theatre Journal (Assn for Theatre in Higher Education) (Baltimore, MD)
*TLS	Times Literary Supplement (London)
*TMR	The Medieval Review (Univ. of Michigan, Ann Arbor) (http://www.hti.umich.edu/b/bmr/tmr.html)
*TN	Theatre Notebook (Soc. for Theatre Research, London)
*TolStud	Tolkien Studies: an annual scholarly review (Morgantown, VA)
*TPB	Tennessee Philological Bulletin (Univ. of Tennessee, Chattanooga)
*TPQ	Text and Performance Quarterly (Speech Communication Assn, Annandale, VA)
*Traditio	Traditio: studies in ancient and medieval history, thought, and religion (Fordham Univ., New York)
*Transition	Transition (Cambridge, MA)
*TransR	Translation Review (Dallas, TX)
*TRB	Tennyson Research Bulletin (Tennyson Soc., Lincoln)
*TRC	Theatre Research in Canada (Univ. of Toronto)
*TRI	Theatre Research International (Oxford)
*TriQ	TriQuarterly: an international journal of arts, letters, and opinions (Northwestern Univ., Evanston, IL)
*Tristania	Tristania: a journal devoted to Tristan studies (Lewiston, NY)
*TSB	Thoreau Society Bulletin (Lincoln, MA)
*TSLL	Texas Studies in Literature and Language (Austin, TX)
*TSWL	Tulsa Studies in Women's Literature (Univ. of Tulsa, OK)
*TT	Theatre Topics (Baltimore, MD)
*Twainian	Twainian (Mark Twain Research Foundation, Culver Stockton College, Canton, MO)
*TWAR	Tennessee Williams Annual Review (Middle Tennessee State Univ., Murfreesboro) (http://www.tennesseewilliamsstudies.org/)

*UC	Upstart Crow: a Shakespeare journal (Dept of English, Clemson Univ., Clemson, SC)
*VH	Vermont History (Vermont Historical Soc., Montpelier)
*VIA	VIA: voices in Italian America (Chicago, IL)
*VicR	Victorian Review (Victorian Studies Assn of Western Canada, Univ. of Lethbridge, Alta)
*VIJ	Victorians Institute Journal: Victorian literature, art, and culture (Victorians Inst., Depts of English, Virginia Commonwealth Univ., Richmond, and Univ. of Richmond)
*VLC	Victorian Literature and Culture (New York)
*VLT	Velvet Light Trap (Austin, TX)
*VN	Victorian Newsletter (Western Kentucky Univ., Bowling Green)
*VocR	Vocabula Review (http://www.vocabula.com/)
*VoicesNY	Voices: journal of the New York Folklore Society (Schenectady, NY)
*VP	Victorian Poetry (Univ. of West Virginia, Morgantown)
*VPR	Victorian Periodicals Review (Niwot, CO)
*VQR	Virginia Quarterly Review: a national journal of literature and discussion (Univ. of Virginia, Charlottesville)
*VS	Victorian Studies: an interdisciplinary journal of social, political, and cultural studies (Univ. of Indiana, Bloomington)
*VWB	Virginia Woolf Bulletin (Virginia Woolf Soc. of Great Britain, London)
*VWM	Virginia Woolf Miscellany (Southern Connecticut State Univ., New Haven)
*WAL	Western American Literature: quarterly journal of the Western Literature Association (Utah State Univ., Logan)
*WAR	Wisconsin Academy Review (Madison, WI)
*WasRCPSF	Wascana Review of Contemporary Poetry and Short Fiction (Dept of English and Canadian Plains' Research Center, Univ. of Regina, Sask.)
*WB	Weimarer Beiträge: Zeitschrift für Literaturwissenschaft, Ästhetik und Kulturwissenschaften (Berlin)
*WCL	West Coast Line: writing, images, criticism (Burnaby, B.C.)
*WCPMN	Willa Cather Pioneer Memorial and Educational Foundation Newsletter and Review (Omaha, NB)
*WCWR	William Carlos Williams Review (Univ. of Texas, Austin)
WD	Writer's Digest (Cincinnati, OH)
*WeBr	West Branch (Bucknell Univ., Lewisburg, PA)
*WebS	Weber Studies: voices and viewpoints of the contemporary West (Ogden, UT)
*Wellsian	Wellsian: the journal of the H. G. Wells Society (Reading)
*WF	Western Folklore (California Folklore Soc., Long Beach)
*WHR	Western Humanities Review (Univ. of Utah, Salt Lake City)
*WI	Word & Image: a journal of verbal/visual enquiry (London)
*Wildean	Wildean: the journal of the Oscar Wilde Society (Kingston upon Thames)
*WinP	Winterthur Portfolio: a journal of American material culture (Chicago, IL)
*WJBS	Western Journal of Black Studies (Washington State Univ., Pullman)
*WL	Women and Language (Fairfax, VA)
*WLA	War, Literature, and the Arts (US Air Force Academy, Colorado Springs, CO)
*WLT	World Literature Today: a literary quarterly of the University of Oklahoma (Norman, OK)
*WLWE	World Literature Written in English (Univ. of Texas, Arlington)
*WordsC	Wordsworth Circle (Temple Univ., Philadelphia, PA)

*WorldE	World Englishes: journal of English as an international and intranational language (Oxford)
*WP	Women and Performance: a journal of feminist theory (New York)
*WRB	Women's Review of Books (Center for Research on Women, Wellesley, MA)
*Writing	Writing (Stamford, CT)
*WrLL	Written Language and Literacy (Boulder, CO)
*WS	Women's Studies: an interdisciplinary journal (New York)
*WSA	Woolf Studies Annual (Pace Univ., New York)
WSC	Women's Studies in Communication (California State Univ., Long Beach)
*WSJ	Wallace Stevens Journal (Wallace Stevens Soc., Clarkson Univ., Potsdam, NY)
*WWQR	Walt Whitman Quarterly Review (Dept of English, Univ. of Iowa, Iowa City)
*WWr	Women's Writing: the Elizabethan to Victorian period (Wallingford, Oxon.)
*WWrE	Welsh Writing in English: a yearbook of critical essays (Bangor, Gwynedd)
*XavR	Xavier Review: a journal of literature and culture (Xavier Univ., New Orleans, LA)
*YA	Yeats Annual (Basingstoke)
*YER	Yeats Eliot Review: an independent journal of scholarship, criticism, and opinion (Little Rock, AR)
*YES	Yearbook of English Studies (Modern Humanities Research Assn) (Leeds)
*YJC	Yale Journal of Criticism: interpretation in the humanities (Whitney Humanities Center, Yale Univ., New Haven, CT) (Baltimore, MD)
YJLF	Yale Journal of Law and Feminism (New Haven, CT)
*YLG	Yale University Library Gazette (New Haven, CT)
YLM	Yale Literary Magazine (New Haven, CT)
*YLS	Yearbook of Langland Studies (Asheville, NC)
*YREAL	REAL: yearbook of research in English and American literature (Tübingen)
*YWCCT	Year's Work in Critical and Cultural Theory (English Assn) (Oxford)
*ZNHF	Zora Neale Hurston Forum: official publication of the Zora Neale Hurston Society (Morgan State Univ., Baltimore, MD)
ZYZZYVA	ZYZZYVA (San Francisco, CA)

ANNUAL BIBLIOGRAPHY OF ENGLISH LANGUAGE AND LITERATURE

2005

BIBLIOGRAPHY

GENERAL STUDIES

1. ALMOND, PHILIP C. The Witches of Warboys: a bibliographical note. *See* **5328**.

2. BARKER, NICOLAS. Form and meaning in the history of the book: selected essays. (Bibl. 2004, 3.) Rev. by Derek Pearsall in JEBS (8) 2005, 269–71; by Alexandra Gillespie in SHARP (14:3) 2005, 5–6.

3. BARNARD, JOHN; MCKENZIE, D. F. (eds); BELL, MAUREEN (asst ed.). The Cambridge history of the book in Britain: vol. 4, 1557–1695. (Bibl. 2004, 4.) Rev. by David L. Gants in HLQ (67:3) 2004, 473–9; by Andrew Pettegree in JMH (77:2) 2005, 418–20.

4. BASBANES, NICHOLAS A. A splendor of letters: the permanence of books in an impermanent world. (Bibl. 2004, 5.) Rev. by Phyllis Reeve in Amphora (138) 2005, 28–9.

5. CHARTIER, ROGER. Crossing borders in early modern Europe: sociology of texts and literature. Trans. by Maurice Elton. *See* **6525**.

6. DANE, JOSEPH A. In search of Stow's Chaucer. *In* (pp. 145–55) **5746**.

7. —— The myth of print culture: essays on evidence, textuality and bibliographical method. (Bibl. 2004, 9.) Rev. by Seth Lerer in MLR (100:2) 2005, 475–7; by James McLaverty in RES (56:224) 2005, 313–15; by Ashby Kinch in JEGP (104:3) 2005, 412–16.

8. DEVRIES, DUANE. Bibliographies, catalogues, collections, and bibliographical and textual studies of Dickens's works. *See* **10671**.

9. FINKELSTEIN, DAVID; MCCLEERY, ALISTAIR. An introduction to book history. London; New York: Routledge, 2005. pp. 160.

10. FISHER, NICHOLAS. Jacob Tonson and the Earl of Rochester. *See* **7827**.

11. FLIEGELMAN, JAY. The thing itself. PCP (40:2) 2005, 21–6.

12. GANTS, DAVID L. Bibliographical scholarship and the history of the book. HLQ (67:3) 2004, 473–9 (review-article).

13. GILLESPIE, ALEXANDRA. Introduction: bibliography and early Tudor texts. HLQ (67:2) 2004, 157–71.

14. GURA, PHILIP. *Magnalia historiae libri Americana*; or, How AAS brought the history of the book into the new millennium. PAAS (114:2) 2004, 249–80.

15. HAMMOND, MARY. The Reading Experience Database 1450–1945 (RED). *In* (pp. 175–87) **19**.

16. HARRIS, IAN C.   *The Case of the Suffering Clergy of France*: a short study in bibliography, history, and textual criticism. *See* **8431**.

17. HOOGVLIET, MARGRIET (ed.).   Multi-media compositions from the Middle Ages to the early modern period. Louvain; Dudley, MA: Peeters, 2004. pp. xiii, 195. (Groningen studies in cultural change, 9.)

18. HOWARD, NICOLE.   The book: the life story of a technology. Westport, CT; London: Greenwood Press, 2005. pp. xvi, 171. (Greenwood technographies.)

19. MYERS, ROBIN; HARRIS, MICHAEL; MANDELBROTE, GILES (eds).   Owners, annotators and the signs of reading. New Castle, DE: Oak Knoll Press; London: British Library, 2005. pp. xv, 231. (Publishing pathways.)

20. RUBIN, JOAN SHELLEY.   What is the history of history of books? JAH (90:2) 2003, 555–75.

21. SNYDER, HENRY L.; SMITH, MICHAEL S. (eds).   The *English Short-Title Catalogue*: past, present, future. (Bibl. 2003, 25.) Rev. by James E. May in Scriblerian (37:2 / 38:1) 2005, 108–9.

22. STALLYBRASS, PETER, *et al*.   Hamlet's tables and the technologies of writing in Renaissance England. *See* **6372**.

23. TANSELLE, G. THOMAS.   Fifty years on: bibliography then and now. BC (52:4) 2003, 459–70.

24. THORBURN, DAVID; JENKINS, HENRY (eds); SEAWELL, BRAD (assoc. ed.). Rethinking media change: the aesthetics of transition. Cambridge, MA; London: MIT Press, 2003. pp. x, 404. (Media in transition.) Rev. by Heather Hendershot in FilmQ (59:1) 2005, 67–9.

BINDING

25. BENNETT, STUART.   Trade bookbinding in the British Isles 1660–1800. (Bibl. 2004, 32.) Rev. by David Pearson in TLS, 28 Jan. 2005, 34; by Randy Silverman in SHARP (14:1/2) 2005, 11; by Melvyn New in Scriblerian (37:2/38:1) 2005, 171–2; by Mirjam M. Foot in BC (54:4) 2005, 612–14.

26. DE HAMEL, CHRISTOPHER.   Book thefts in the Middle Ages. *In* (pp. 1–14) **937**.

27. FOOT, MIRJAM M.   Bookbinding research: pitfalls, possibilities and needs. *In* (pp. 13–29) **30**.

28. —— The decorated bindings in Marsh's Library, Dublin. (Bibl. 2004, 34.) Rev. by David Pearson in Library (6:1) 2005, 90–1.

29. —— 'A magnificent and bewildering variety': Irish bookbinding in the eighteenth century. *In* (pp. 206–36) **30**.

30. —— (ed.).   Eloquent witnesses: bookbindings and their history. A volume of essays dedicated to the memory of Dr Phiroze Randeria. New Castle, DE: Oak Knoll Press; London: British Library for the Bibliographical Soc. of London, 2004. pp. 328. Rev. by Consuela Metzger in SHARP (14:1/2) 2005, 13–14; by Anthony Hobson in TLS, 7 Jan. 2005, 29.

31. FORD, LYLE.   The Art Nouveau book designs of Talwin Morris. Amphora (135) 2004, 4–8.

32. Hobson, Anthony; Woodcock, Thomas. The owners of the 'Carpe Diem' armorial binding stamp. BC (54:4) 2005, 539–43.

33. Jones, Gregory V.; Brown, Jane E. Victorian binding designer WR: William Ralston (1841–1911), not William Harry Rogers. BC (52:2) 2003, 171–98.

34. Lock, Margaret. Bookbinding materials and techniques, 1700–1920. (Bibl. 2004, 41.) Rev. by Keith Valentine in Amphora (136) 2004, 31–2.

35. Pearson, David. English bookbinding styles, 1450–1800: a handbook. New Castle, DE: Oak Knoll Press; London: British Library, 2005. pp. xii, 221, (plates) 16. Rev. by David McKitterick in TLS, 23 & 30 Dec. 2005, 40–1; by Anthony Hobson in BC (54:4) 2005, 614–16.

36. —— English centre-piece bookbindings 1560–1640. In (pp. 106–26) 30.

37. Pickwoad, Nicholas. The history of the false raised band. In (pp. 103–31) 937.

38. Potter, Esther. Benjamin West 1805–1883. In (pp. 237–63) 30.

39. Ratcliffe, Stephen. Jewelled bindings: missing masterpieces. BC (54:4) 2005, 545–51.

40. Rodriguez, Catherine M. The use of web seam evidence to determine format. See 176.

41. Tidcombe, Marianne. Women bookbinders in Britain before the First World War. In (pp. 282–303) 30.

BOOK ILLUSTRATION

42. Anon. Illustrations. In (pp. 15–22) 10222.

43. Alderson, Brian. Edward Ardizzone: a bibliographic commentary. New Castle, DE: Oak Knoll Press; London: British Library for the Private Libraries Assn, 2003. pp. 309, (plates) 4. Rev. by Robin Greer in PBSA (99:1) 2005, 153–4; by Andrea Immel in Library (6:2) 2005, 210–12.

44. Ali, Barish. The violence of criticism: the mutilation and exhibition of history in From Hell. JPC (38:4) 2005, 605–31.

45. Baltes, Sabine. Father Time: the emblematic and iconographic context of 'The Epistle Dedicatory to His Royal Highness Prince Posterity' in Swift's Tale. See 9045.

46. Bayne, John. Barry Moser, the robber, and Eudora Welty. See 20072.

47. Benes, Rebecca C. Native American picture books of change: the art of historic children's editions. See 14325.

48. Billings, Timothy. Squashing the 'shard-borne beetle' crux: a hard case with a few pat readings. See 6532.

49. Bristow, Joseph. Biographies: Oscar Wilde – the man, the life, the legend. In (pp. 6–35) 12414.

50. Clarke, Stuart N. Now you see them, now you don't: Woolf's illustrated books. See 20328.

51. Connelly, William. The illustrators of The Merry-Go-Round. See 1180.

52. Cooke, Simon. 'A man of sound judgement and sure taste': Samuel Lucas, Once a Week and sixties illustration. StIll (23) 2003, 12–20.

53. CORDERY, GARETH. Harry Furniss and the 'Boom in Boz' (part one). *See* **10663**.

54. —— Harry Furniss and the 'Boom in Boz' (part two). *See* **10664**.

55. —— A special relationship: Stiggins in England and America (part one). *See* **10665**.

56. —— A special relationship: Stiggins in England and America (part two). *See* **10666**.

57. DALY, NICHOLAS. The woman in white: Whistler, Hiffernan, Courbet, du Maurier. *See* **10876**.

58. DANE, JOSEPH A. 'Wanting the first blank': frontispiece to the Huntington copy of Caxton's *Recuyell of the Historyes of Troye*. *See* **4778**.

59. —— DJANANOVA, SVETLANA. The typographical gothic: a cautionary note on the title page to Percy's *Reliques of Ancient English Poetry*. *See* **8857**.

60. DAWSON, MUIR. Two children's books illustrated by Bewick, with notes on printing from the original blocks. *See* **8168**.

61. DOCHERTY, JOHN. A Christmas Carroll. *See* **10398**.

62. DRIVER, MARTHA W. The image in print: book illustration in late medieval England and its sources. London: British Library, 2004. pp. xi, 302. Rev. by Jessica Brantley in TMR, Aug. 2005; by M. M. Smith in SHARP (14:1/2) 2005, 12–13; by Lawrence B. Hobson in Comitatus (36) 2005, 216–19.

63. EELLS, EMILY. From word to image: illustrating *Great Expectations*. *See* **10678**.

64. FLANERY, PATRICK DENMAN. (Re-)marking Coetzee & Costello: The (textual) *Lives of Animals*. *See* **15828**.

65. FORD-SMITH, ALICE. Confessions: the Midlands execution broadside trade. *In* (pp. 153–67) **880**.

66. FURMAN-ADAMS, WENDY; TUFTE, VIRGINIA JAMES. Saying it with flowers: Jane Giraud's ecofeminist *Paradise Lost* (1846). *In* (pp. 223–53) **7717**.

67. GANIM, JOHN M. Chaucer and free love. *In* (pp. 344–63) **4485**.

68. GENOVA, JOHN. Sydney Paget's successor: the life of Arthur Twidle. BSJ (55:3) 2005, 12–19.

69. GERARD, W. B. 'All that the heart wishes': changing views toward sentimentality reflected in visualizations of Sterne's Maria, 1773–1888. *See* **9032**.

70. GILL, KULDIP. Barbarian Press. *See* **1040**.

71. GILLMAN, SUSAN. In Twain's times. *See* **12241**.

72. GILSON, DAVID. Later publishing history, with illustrations. *In* (pp. 121–59) **10060**.

73. GOESER, CAROLINE. The case of *Ebony and Topaz*: racial and sexual hybridity in Harlem renaissance illustrations. *See* **1208**.

74. GOLDEN, CATHERINE. *The Yellow Wall-Paper* and Joseph Henry Hatfield's original magazine illustrations. *See* **16685**.

75. GOLDMAN, PAUL. Beyond decoration: the illustrations of John Everett Millais. New Castle, DE: Oak Knoll Press, 2005. pp. 337.

76. GOLLAPUDI, APARNA. Unraveling the invisible seam: text and image in Maurice Sendak's *Higglety Pigglety Pop! See* **19356.**

77. GOULART, RON. Comic book encyclopedia: the ultimate guide to characters, graphic novels, writers, and artists in the comic book universe. New York: HarperEntertainment, 2004. pp. v, 378.

78. GREER, ROBIN. Variants and addenda to Richard Riall's *A New Bbliography of Arthur Rackham*, 1995. StIll (23) 2003, 39–57.

79. GRESH, LOIS H.; WEINBERG, ROBERT E. The science of supervillains. Chichester; Hoboken, NJ: Wiley, 2005. pp. xi, 212.

80. HAMILTON, DONNA B. Richard Verstegan and Catholic resistance: the encoding of antiquarianism and love. *In* (pp. 87–104) **5915.**

81. HAMMERSCHMIDT-HUMMEL, HILDEGARD (ed.). Die Shakespeare-Illustration (1594–2000): bildkünstlerische Darstellungen zu den Dramen William Shakespeares: Katalog, Geschichte, Funktion und Deutung; mit Künstlerlexikon, klassifizierter Bibliographie und Registern. *See* **5957.**

82. HANSON, DAVID A. John Carbutt and the woodburytype in America. PrH (24:2) 2005, 41–54.

83. HARDY, ANNE. Tennyson, Millais, and the depiction of mood in *Mariana* and *St Agnes Eve. See* **12145.**

84. HARROD, TANYA. A missing bird. *See* **872.**

85. HATFIELD, CHARLES. Alternative comics: an emerging literature. Jackson; London: Mississippi UP, 2005. pp. xv, 182.

86. HAUT, ASIA. Reading Flora: Erasmus Darwin's *The Botanic Garden*, Henry Fuseli's illustrations, and various literary responses. *See* **8497.**

87. HEER, JEET; WORCESTER, KENT (eds). Arguing comics: literary masters on a popular medium. Jackson; London: Mississippi UP, 2004. pp. xxiii, 176.

88. HOLLANDS, HOWARD. Drawing a blank: picturing nothing on the page. *See* **14336.**

89. HOLLIS, CATHERINE W. Virginia Woolf's double signature. *See* **20366.**

90. IRWIN, ROBERT. Omar's metamorphosis. *See* **11017.**

91. JONES, GERARD. Men of tomorrow: geeks, gangsters, and the birth of the comic book. (Bibl. 2004, 79.) Rev. by Jared Gardner in AmP (15:1) 2005, 116–18.

92. KELLER, YVONNE. 'Was it right to love her brother's wife so passionately?': lesbian pulp novels and US lesbian identity, 1950–1965. *See* **14186.**

93. KIRK, CONNIE ANN. Companion to American children's picture books. *See* **4088.**

94. KNAPP, JAMES A. Illustrating the past in early modern England: the representation of history in printed books. (Bibl. 2004, 81.) Rev. by Christopher Highley in CLIO (34:4) 2005, 475–80; by Janine Barchas in SHARP (14:3) 2005, 7.

95. KOOISTRA, LORRAINE JANZEN. The illustrated *Enoch Arden* and Victorian visual culture. *See* **12148.**

96. LENDRUM, ROB. The super Black Macho, one baaad mutha: Black superhero masculinity in 1970s mainstream comic books. Extrapolation (46:3) 2005, 360–72.

97. LESTER, VALERIE BROWNE. Phiz: the man who drew Dickens. (Bibl. 2004, 86.) Rev. by Gareth Cordery in DickQ (22:4) 2005, 255–8.

98. LOCKE, GEORGE. The Sketch: an annotated checklist of certain illustrators, based on a partial run. See 1257.

99. LOCKWOOD, DAVID. Pictorial puzzles from Alice. See 10405.

100. MCMASTER, JULIET. Illustrating Jane's juvenilia. See 10017.

101. MCNEIL, DAVID. Collage and social theories: an examination of Bowles's 'Medley' prints of the 1720 South Sea Bubble. See 8194.

102. MILLER, P. ANDREW. Mutants, metaphor, and marginalism: what x-actly do the X-Men stand for? See 14227.

103. MORRIS, FRANKIE. Artist of Wonderland: the life, political cartoons, and illustrations of Tenniel. Charlottesville; London: Virginia UP, 2005. pp. xv, 405. (Victorian literature and culture.)

104. —— Researching Artist of Wonderland. KnLet (75) 2005, 15–19.

105. MORRIS, TOM; MORRIS, MATT (eds). Superheroes and philosophy: truth, justice, and the Socratic way. Chicago, IL: Open Court, 2005. pp. xiii, 281. (Popular culture and philosophy, 13.)

106. MOSER, BARRY. From where it is to where it ain't: illustration as an act of vision. See 18571.

107. MÜLLER, ANJA. Picturing Æsops: re-visions of Æsop's Fables from L'Estrange to Richardson. 1650–1850 (10) 2004, 33–62.

108. NICHOLSON, EIRWEN. Soggy prose and verbiage: English graphic political satire as a visual/verbal construct. See 1288.

109. NICULESCU, EMIL. The link between Ronald (sic) Pym and 'La Petite Dormeuse' in Lolita. See 18465.

110. OP DE BEECK, NATHALIE. 'The first picture book for modern children': Mary Liddell's Little Machinery and the fairy tale of modernity. See 17820.

111. PADGETT, RON. Joe: a memoir of Joe Brainard. Minneapolis, MN: Coffee House Press, 2004. pp. xiv, 357, (plates) 8. Rev. by Stephen Paul Miller in AmBR (26:2) 2005, 13–15.

112. PARR, ANTHONY. Time and the satyr. HLQ (68:3) 2005, 429–65.

113. PLATE, LIEDEKE. Intermedial Woolf: text, image, and in-between. See 20399.

114. PRICHARD, MAUREEN. Christine Macgregor's illustrated private press books. See 968.

115. QUEYSSI, LAURENT. La révolution des super-héros: Watchmen d'Alan Moore et Dave Gibbons. Cycnos (22:2) 2005, 55–65.

116. RICHMOND, VELMA BOURGEOIS. Edward Burne-Jones's Chaucer portraits in the Kelmscott Chaucer. See 4964.

117. ROBINSON, LILLIAN S. Wonder women: feminisms and superheroes. (Bibl. 2004, 113.) Rev. by Ximena Gallardo in JPC (38:6) 2005, 1109–11; by Shelley Armitage in TSWL (24:1) 2005, 155–7; by Devoney Looser in MinnR (63/64) 2005, 239–43.

118. ROCKMAN, CONNIE C. (ed.). The ninth book of junior authors and illustrators. See 4097.

119. ROMANSKA, MAGDA. Ontology and eroticism: two bodies of Ophelia. *See* **6362**.

120. SALOMON, DAVID A. *Corpus mysticum*: text as body / body as text. *In* (pp. 141–55) **4411**.

121. SARACENI, MARIO. The language of comics. (Bibl. 2004, 116.) Rev. by Francisco Yus in Lang (81:1) 2005, 289.

122. SHERMAN, FRASER A. *The Wizard of Oz* catalog: L. Frank Baum's novel, its sequels, their adaptations for stage, television, movies, radio, music videos, comic books, commercials, and more. *See* **15363**.

123. SIKORSKA, MAGDALENA. The stories illustrations tell: the creative illustrating strategy in the pictures by Beatrix Potter and Janosch. *See* **18852**.

124. SILLARS, STUART. Seeing, studying, performing: *Bell's Edition of Shakespeare* and performative reading. *See* **5830**.

125. STANTON, JOSEPH. The important books: children's picture books as art and literature. *See* **4098**.

126. STOTT, JON C. Gerald McDermott and you. Foreword by Gerald McDermott. Westport, CT: Libraries Unlimited, 2004. pp. xiv, 109. (Author and you.)

127. THOMAS, JULIA. Pictorial Victorians: the inscription of values in word and image. Athens: Ohio UP, 2004. pp. ix, 203, (plates) 8. Rev. by Richard D. Altick in JPRS (14:1) 2005, 98–100; by Alison Byerly in VS (48:1) 2005, 173–5.

128. THORNTON, EDITH. 'Innocence' consumed: packaging Edith Wharton with Kathleen Norris in *Pictorial Review* magazine, 1920–21. *See* **20136**.

129. TILLEY, ELIZABETH. Science, industry, and nationalism in the *Dublin Penny Journal*. *In* (pp. 139–49) **1226**.

130. TOPLISS, IAIN. The comic worlds of Peter Arno, William Steig, Charles Addams, and Saul Steinberg. *See* **1349**.

131. WEBBY, ELIZABETH. Books and covers: reflections on some recent Australian novels. SSE (29) 2003, 79–86.

132. WEIMERSKIRCH, PHILIP J. The beginning of color printing in America. PrH (24:2) 2005, 25–40.

133. WEINSTEIN, AMY. Once upon a time: illustrations from fairytales, fables, primers, pop-ups, and other children's books. New York: Princeton Architectural Press, 2005. pp. xi, 179.

134. WENDLAND, ALBERT. Touching the night sky: 'progressing' the 50s in *Strange Adventures* and *Mystery in Space*. JFA (13:4) 2003, 389–402.

135. WESTERWEEL, BART. Some reflections on William Blake and the emblem. *In* (pp. 11–25) **9237**.

136. WILHELM, RANDALL S. Faulkner's big picture book: word and image in *The Marionettes*. *See* **16457**.

137. YAMPBELL, CAT. Judging a book by its cover: publishing trends in young adult literature. *See* **1028**.

138. ZACHARIAS, GREG. Henry James cartoons. *See* **11466**.

BOOK PRODUCTION, PRINTING, TYPOGRAPHY

139. ANON. The title-page. BC (52:4) 2003, 447–58 (review-article).

140. ALLSOPP, RIC. Itinerant pages: the page as performance space. PRes (9:2) 2004, 2–6.

141. BAINES, PHIL. Penguin by design: a cover story, 1935–2005. London: Allen Lane, 2005. pp. 256. Rev. by Tanya Harrod in TLS, 2 Sept. 2005, 8.

142. BALE, ANTHONY. Stow's medievalism and antique Judaism in early modern London. *In* (pp. 69–80) **5746**.

143. BEETHAM, MARGARET. Of recipe books and reading in the nineteenth century: Mrs Beeton and her cultural consequences. *In* (pp. 15–30) **9257**.

144. BRACK, O. M., JR; CARLILE, SUSAN. Samuel Johnson's contributions to Charlotte Lennox's *The Female Quixote*. *See* **8788**.

145. BRIGGS, JULIA. 'Printing hope': Virginia Woolf, Hope Mirrlees, and the iconic imagery of *Paris*. *See* **20316**.

146. BRIGHT, BETTY. No longer innocent: book art in America: 1960–1980. New York: New York Public Library/Granary, 2005. pp. xix, 301, (plates) 8.

147. BRODY, JENNIFER DEVERE. The blackness of Blackness …: reading the typography of *Invisible Man*. *See* **16327**.

148. CARMINATI, MARIA NELLA, *et al.* The visual impact of *ottava rima*. *See* **10294**.

149. CLEMIT, PAMELA. William Godwin and James Watt's copying machine: wet transfer copies in the Abinger papers. *See* **8670**.

150. COOK, HARDY M. Unnoticed variant reading in Q1 *Lucrece*, 1594. *See* **6680**.

151. DANE, JOSEPH A.; DJANANOVA, SVETLANA. The typographical gothic: a cautionary note on the title page to Percy's *Reliques of Ancient English Poetry*. *See* **8857**.

152. DAVIDSON, IAN. Visual poetry as performance. *See* **15814**.

153. DE HAMEL, CHRISTOPHER; SILVER, JOEL. Disbound and dispersed: the leaf book considered. *See* **375**.

154. DONOVAN, STEPHEN. 'Short but to the point': newspaper typography in 'Aeolus'. *See* **17269**.

155. DWORKIN, CRAIG. Textual prostheses. CL (57:1) 2005, 1–24.

156. FRANKEL, NICHOLAS. 'A wreath for the brows of time': the books of the Rhymers' Club as material texts. *In* (pp. 131–57) **9675**.

157. GILL, KULDIP. Barbarian Press. *See* **1040**.

158. —— Frog Hollow Press, Victoria, B.C. *See* **1041**.

159. —— Greenboathouse Books. *See* **1042**.

160. HANSON, DAVID A. John Carbutt and the woodburytype in America. *See* **82**.

161. HENRY, BARBARA. Why I like to set type by hand. LU (29:1) 2005, 12–15.

162. HOLLANDS, HOWARD. Drawing a blank: picturing nothing on the page. *See* **14336**.

163. HOLZENBERG, ERIC; PENA, J. FERNANDO. Lasting impressions: the Grolier Club Library. New York: Grolier Club, 2004. pp. 205.

164. HOPKINS, RICHARD. Poppy Press. *See* **887**.

165. HUTNER, MARTIN; KELLY, JERRY. A century for the century: fine printed books from 1900 to 1999. Danbury, CT: Grolier Club; Jaffrey, NH: Godine, 2004. pp. lxii, 110. (Second. ed.: first ed. 1999.)

166. JOSEPH, MICHAEL. The rise and maiden flight of *Hannah Goose Nursery Rhymes*. *See* **3680**.

167. LEE, MARSHALL. Bookmaking: editing/design/production. (Bibl. 1982, 429.) New York; London: Norton, 2004. pp. 494. (Third ed.: first ed. 1965.) Rev. by Noel Waite in SHARP (14:3) 2005, 7–8.

168. LEWIS, LUCY. The Tavistock Boethius: one of the earliest examples of provincial printing. *In* (pp. 1–14) **880**.

169. MCCORKLE, BEN. Harbingers of the printed page: nineteenth-century theories of delivery as remediation. *See* **2389**.

170. MOUNT, KEVIN. Woman in white meets man in black. *See* **15711**.

171. PHILLIPS, MICHAEL. The printing of Blake's *Illustrations of the Book of Job*. *See* **8381**.

172. PURDON, JOHN JAMES. John Aubrey's 'discourse in paper'. *See* **7199**.

173. RAVEN, JAMES. Book production. *In* (pp. 194–203) **10060**.

174. REEVE, PHYLLIS. *Plantation Printer's Pie*: grandmother and the Multigraph. Amphora (138) 2005, 9–12.

175. ROBINSON, FRED C. *Mise en page* in Old English manuscripts and printed texts. *In* (pp. 363–75) **4221**.

176. RODRIGUEZ, CATHERINE M. The use of web seam evidence to determine format. BSANZB (28:3) 2004, 122–4.

177. SHERMAN, WILLIAM H. Toward a history of the manicule. *In* (pp. 19–48) **19**.

178. SHRANK, CATHY. 'These fewe scribbled rules': representing scribal intimacy in early modern print. *See* **5349**.

179. SOUTHALL, RICHARD. Printer's type in the twentieth century: manufacturing and design methods. New Castle, DE: Oak Knoll Press; London: British Library, 2005. pp. xv, 238. Rev. by Kay Amert in SHARP (14:4) 2005, 17.

180. SPEDDING, PATRICK. A note on the ornament usage of Henry Woodfall. BSANZB (27:1/2) 2003, 109–16.

181. STAUFFER, ANDREW M. Byron, the pyramids, and 'uncertain paper'. *See* **10336**.

182. STEEVES, ANDREW. Why design required a good chair: reflections on learning a trade. Amphora (138) 2005, 4–8.

183. STOICHEFF, PETER; TAYLOR, ANDREW (eds). The future of the page. (Bibl. 2004, 177.) Rev. by Kate Eichhorn in JSchP (37:1) 2005, 58–67.

184. STOKER, DAVID. Francis Burges's *Observations on Printing*, 1701: a reconstruction of the text. Library (6:2) 2005, 161–77.

185. TAYLOR, ANDREA. Cotton Socks Press. *See* **1062**.

186. TOKUNAGA, SATOKO. Early English printing and the hands of compositors. *See* **5036**.

187. Wakely, Maria; Rees, Graham. Folios fit for a king: James I, John Bill, and the King's Printers, 1616–1620. See **1013**.

188. Wallis, Lawrence. George W. Jones, printer laureate. Kidlington, Oxon.: Plough, 2004. pp. 128, (plates) 8. Rev. by Sebastian Carter in TLS, 8 July 2005, 27.

189. Weimerskirch, Philip J. The beginning of color printing in America. See **132**.

190. Whitesell, David R. Thomas Jefferson and the book arts. See **8744**.

MANUSCRIPTS

191. Anon. The medieval libraries of Britain. BC (52:2) 2003, 151–70 (review-article).

192. —— Script and its names. See **1509**.

193. Adams, Gillian. In the hands of children. LU (29:1) 2005, 38–51.

194. Aldrich-Watson, Deborah. Notes on editing *The Verse Miscellany of Constance Aston Fowler: a Diplomatic Edition. In* (pp. 157–65) **587**.

195. Alexander, Jonathan J. G., *et al.* The splendor of the word: medieval and Renaissance illuminated manuscripts at the New York Public Library. New York: New York Public Library / Miller, 2005. pp. 480. (Exhibition catalogue.)

196. Alonso Almeida, Francisco. All gathered together: on the construction of scientific and technical books in 15th-century England. See **4698**.

197. Archibald, Elizabeth. Given the old razzle-dazzle. TLS, 30 Sept. 2005, 18–19 (review-article). (Cambridge Illuminations exhibition.)

198. Babcock, Robert G.; Davis, Lisa Fagin; Rusche, Philip G. Catalogue of medieval and Renaissance manuscripts in the Beinecke Rare Book and Manuscript Library, Yale University: vol. 4, MSS 481–485. Turnhout: Brepols; Tempe, AZ: Center for Medieval and Renaissance Studies, 2004. pp. xxvi, 459, (plates) 152. (Arizona studies in the Middle Ages and the Renaissance, 11.) (Medieval & Renaissance texts & studies, 176.) Rev. by Craig Kallendorf in SCN (63:1/2) 2005, 130–1.

199. Babcock, Robert Gary, *et al.* A book of her own: an exhibition of manuscripts and printed books in the Yale University Library that were owned by women before 1700. See **353**.

200. Bawcutt, Priscilla. Scottish manuscript miscellanies from the fifteenth to the seventeenth century. EngMS (12) 2005, 46–73.

201. Beckett, Katharine Scarfe. Worcester sauce: Malchus in Anglo-Saxon England. *In* (pp. 212–31) **4221**.

202. Binski, Paul; Panayotova, Stella (eds). The Cambridge illuminations: ten centuries of book production in the medieval West. London: Miller, 2005. pp. 415. (Exhibition catalogue.) Rev. by Elizabeth Archibald in TLS, 30 Sept. 2005, 18–19.

203. Bowers, John M. Two professional readers of Chaucer and Langland: Scribe D and the HM 114 scribe. SAC (26) 2004, 113–46.

204. BRAYMAN HACKEL, HEIDI; MANCALL, PETER C. Richard Hakluyt the Younger's notes for the East India Company in 1601: a transcription of Huntington Library Manuscript EL 2360. *See* **5467.**

205. BREGMAN, ALVAN. A Gabriel Harvey manuscript brought to light. *See* **5476.**

206. BROCKMAN, WILLIAM S. Collecting Joyce. *In* (pp. 273–84) **17274.**

207. BROWN, MICHELLE P. The Lindisfarne Gospels: society, spirituality and the scribe. (Bibl. 2004, 201.) Rev. by Bernard J. Muir in Spec (80:4) 2005, 1242–4.

208. BURKE, VICTORIA E.; CLARKE, ELIZABETH. Julia Palmer's *Centuries*: the politics of editing and anthologizing early modern women's manuscript compilations. *In* (pp. 47–64) **587.**

209. —— GIBSON, JONATHAN (eds). Early modern women's manuscript writing: selected papers from the Trinity/Trent Colloquium. (Bibl. 2004, 204.) Rev. by Warren Chernaik in Library (6:3) 2005, 348–50; by Carlo M. Bajetta in NQ (52:3) 2005, 398–400; by Mihoko Suzuki in RQ (58:3) 2005, 1025–8.

210. BURLINSON, CHRISTOPHER; ZURCHER, ANDREW. 'Secretary to the Lord Grey Lord Deputie here': Edmund Spenser's Irish papers. *See* **5683.**

211. CAIE, GRAHAM D. 'I do not wish to be called auctour, but the pore compilatour': the plight of the medieval vernacular poet. *See* **4601.**

212. CALKIN, SIOBHAIN BLY. Saracens and the making of English identity: the Auchinleck Manuscript. *See* **4577.**

213. CARRILLO LINARES, Mᴬ JOSÉ. Middle English *Antidotarium Nicholai*: evidence for linguistic distribution and dissemination in the vernacular. *See* **4699.**

214. CERASANO, S. P. The geography of Henslowe's diary. *See* **5484.**

215. —— Henslowe's 'curious' diary. *See* **5485.**

216. CLAYTON, MARY. Ælfric's *De auguriis* and Cambridge, Corpus Christi College 178. *In* (pp. 376–94) **4221.**

217. COATALEN, GUILLAUME. 'Lô a timorous correction': unrecorded extracts from Spenser and Harington and negative criticism of *The Faerie Queene* in a folio from the Bodleian Library. *See* **5687.**

218. COLCLOUGH, DAVID. Freedom of speech, libel and the law in early Stuart England. *In* (pp. 170–88) **5196.**

219. COLCLOUGH, STEPHEN. 'A grey goose quill and an album': the manuscript book and text transmission, 1800–1850. *In* (pp. 153–73) **19.**

220. COOPER, HELEN. Lancelot, Roger Mortimer and the date of the Auchinleck Manuscript. *In* (pp. 91–9) **4419.**

221. CRICK, JULIA; WALSHAM, ALEXANDRA (eds). The uses of script and print, 1300–1700. (Bibl. 2004, 210.) Rev. by Mary Erler in TMR, Jan. 2005; by Julia Boffey in Library (6:1) 2005, 88–90; by William E. Engel in SCN (63:1/2) 2005, 50–3; by Holly A. Crocker in SStud (33) 2005, 217–20; by Elisabeth Dutton in NQ (52:4) 2005, 531–2; by William H. Sherman in RQ (58:1) 2005, 317–19.

222. D'ARCY, ANNE MARIE; FLETCHER, ALAN J. (eds). Studies in late medieval and early Renaissance texts in honour of John Scattergood: 'the key of all good remembrance'. *See* **4419.**

223. D'ARONCO, MARIA AMALIA. Anglo-Saxon plant pharmacy and the Latin medical tradition. *In* (pp. 133–51) **1773**.

224. DE HAMEL, CHRISTOPHER. Book thefts in the Middle Ages. *In* (pp. 1–14) **937**.

225. DENBO, MICHAEL ROY. Editing a Renaissance commonplace book: the Holgate Miscellany. *In* (pp. 65–73) **587**.

226. DOCKRAY-MILLER, MARY. The *eadgiþ* erasure: a gloss on the Old English *Andreas*. *See* **4281**.

227. DUMVILLE, DAVID; KEYNES, SIMON (gen. eds). The *Anglo-Saxon Chronicle*: a collaborative edition: vol. 7, MS E: a semi-diplomatic edition with introduction and indices. Ed. by Susan Irvine. *See* **4282**.

228. DUMVILLE, DAVID N. English script in the second half of the ninth century. *In* (pp. 305–25) **4220**.

229. EDWARDS, A. S. G. Duke Humfrey's Middle English Palladius manuscript. *In* (pp. 68–77) **4488**.

230. —— John Stow and Middle English literature. *In* (pp. 109–18) **5746**.

231. —— Manuscripts at auction: January 2002 to December 2003. EngMS (12) 2005, 254–9.

232. —— Manuscripts of the verse of Henry Howard, Earl of Surrey. *See* **5758**.

233. —— A new text of the *Canterbury Tales*? *In* (pp. 121–8) **4419**.

234. —— Surrey's Martial epigram: scribes and transmission. *See* **5759**.

235. EZELL, MARGARET J. M. Eclectic circulation: the functional dynamics of manuscript and electronic literary cultures. *In* (pp. 27–35) **587**.

236. FISHER, CELIA. Flowers in medieval manuscripts. Toronto; Buffalo, NY; London: Toronto UP, 2004. pp. 64.

237. FOREY, MARGARET. Manuscript evidence and the author of *Aske Me No More*: William Strode, not Thomas Carew. *See* **7853**.

238. FULK, R. D. Some contested readings in the *Beowulf* manuscript. *See* **4296**.

239. FULTON, JOE B. The lost manuscript conclusion to Mark Twain's *Corn-Pone Opinions*: an editorial history and an edition of the restored text. *See* **12240**.

240. GARRIDO ANES, EDURNE. Geographical and dialectal distribution of Platearius' *Liber de simplici medicina* in England. *See* **4700**.

241. GILLESPIE, ALEXANDRA. Poets, printers, and early English *Sammelbände*. *See* **852**.

242. —— Stow's 'owlde' manuscripts of London chronicles. *In* (pp. 57–67) **5746**.

243. GNEUSS, HELMUT. The homiliary of the Taunton fragments. *See* **4345**.

244. GODDEN, MALCOLM. Alfred, Asser, and Boethius. *In* (pp. 326–48) **4220**.

245. GRAHAM, TIMOTHY. The opening of King Alfred's preface to the Old English *Pastoral Care*: Oxford, Bodleian Library, MS Hatton 20. *See* **4272**.

246. GREEN, RICHARD FIRTH. *The Hunting of the Hare*: an edition. *In* (pp. 129–47) **4419**.

247. GRIFFITHS, JANE. What's in a name? The transmission of 'John Skelton, Laureate' in manuscript and print. *See* **5668**.

248. GUY, JOSEPHINE M. Oscar Wilde's 'self-plagiarism': some new manuscript evidence. *See* **12395**.

249. HANNA, RALPH. English biblical texts before Lollardy and their fate. *In* (pp. 141–53) **4482**.

250. —— Middle English books and Middle English literary history. *See* **4585**.

251. —— Notes on some Trinity College Dublin manuscripts. *In* (pp. 171–80) **4419**.

252. HARLEY, JOHN. 'My Ladye Nevell' revealed. *See* **5396**.

253. HARRIS, OLIVER. 'Motheaten, mouldye, and rotten': the early custodial history and dissemination of John Leland's manuscript remains. *See* **5508**.

254. HAVENS, EARLE. English manuscript culture and the ambiguous triumph of print: seventy years of the Osborn Collection, 1934–2004. *See* **400**.

255. HILL, BETTY. The writing of the septenary couplet. *See* **4645**.

256. HILL, JOYCE. Ælfric's *Colloquy*: the Antwerp/London version. *In* (pp. 331–48) **4221**.

257. HILL, W. SPEED (ed.). New ways of looking at old texts III: papers of the Renaissance English Text Society, 1997–2001. *See* **587**.

258. HILMO, MAIDIE. Medieval images, icons, and illustrated English literary texts: from the Ruthwell Cross to the Ellesmere Chaucer. (Bibl. 2004, 240.) Rev. by Susan Yager in TMR, Feb. 2005; by Charlotte C. Morse in JEBS (8) 2005, 288–9; by Catherine E. Karkov in NQ (52:1) 2005, 111; by Kathleen Kamerick in SHARP (14:1/2) 2005, 15.

259. HOLBERTON, EDWARD. The textual transmission of Marvell's *A Letter to Doctor Ingelo*: the Longleat manuscript. *See* **7627**.

260. HOROBIN, SIMON. The angle of oblivioun: a lost medieval manuscript discovered in Walter Scott's collection. TLS, 11 Nov. 2005, 12–13.

261. —— 'In London and opelond': the dialect and circulation of the C version of *Piers Plowman*. *See* **4850**.

262. —— MOONEY, LINNE R. A *Piers Plowman* manuscript by the Hengwrt/Ellesmere scribe and its implications for London Standard English. *See* **4851**.

263. —— MOSSER, DANIEL W. Scribe D's SW Midlands roots: a reconsideration. *See* **2939**.

264. HOURIHANE, COLUM (ed.). Between the picture and the word: manuscript studies from the Index of Christian Art. Princeton, NJ: Index of Christian Art, Dept of Art and Archaeology, Princeton Univ., 2005. pp. xxvii, 216, (plates) 142. (Index of Christian Art occasional papers, 8.)

265. IRVINE, SUSAN. Fragments of Boethius: the reconstruction of the Cotton manuscript of the Alfredian text. *See* **4273**.

266. JEFFERSON, JUDITH A.; PUTTER, AD. Alliterative patterning in the *Morte Arthure*. *See* **4579**.

267. JUSTICE, GEORGE L.; TINKER, NATHAN (eds). Women's writing and the circulation of ideas: manuscript publication in England, 1550–1800. (Bibl. 2004, 246.) Rev. by Shawndra Holderby in SixCJ (34:3) 2003, 835–6.

268. KATO, TAKAKO. Towards the digital Winchester: editing the Winchester manuscript of Malory's *Morte Darthur. See* 4889.

269. KAUFFMANN, MICHAEL. Biblical imagery in medieval England, 700–1550. (Bibl. 2004, 4417.) Rev. by Anne Rudloff Stanton in Spec (80:3) 2005, 909–11.

270. KEISER, GEORGE R. A Middle English rosemary treatise in verse and prose. ANQ (18:3) 2005, 7–17.

271. KENNEDY, RUTH. The Evangelist in Robert Thornton's devotional book: organizing principles at the level of the quire. *See* 4443.

272. KEYNES, SIMON. Between Bede and the *Chronicle*: London, BL, Cotton Vespasian B.vi, fols 104–9. *In* (pp. 47–67) 4220.

273. KLENE, JEAN. Working with a complex document: the Southwell–Sibthorpe Commonplace Book. *In* (pp. 170–5) 587.

274. LABRIOLA, ALBERT C. The begetting and exaltation of the Son: the Junius Manuscript and Milton's *Paradise Lost. In* (pp. 22–32) 7738.

275. LAWRENCE-MATHERS, ANNE. Manuscripts in Northumbria in the eleventh and twelfth centuries. (Bibl. 2003, 242.) Rev. by Elaine Treharne in Spec (80:1) 2005, 255–7.

276. LINENTHAL, RICHARD A. Medieval and Renaissance manuscripts: a handlist of the collection of B. S. Cron. BC (54:4) 2005, 553–63.

277. LIVINGSTON, MICHAEL. A sixth hand in Cambridge, Trinity College, MS R.3.19. *See* 1529.

278. LOFARO, MICHAEL A.; DAVIS, HUGH (eds). James Agee rediscovered: the journals of *Let Us Now Praise Famous Men* and other new manuscripts. *See* 15087.

279. LONG, WILLIAM B. Dulwich MS XX, *The Telltale*: clues to provenance. *See* 7022.

280. MCKITTERICK, ROSAMOND; BINSKI, PAUL. History and literature: sacred and secular. *In* (pp. 235–95) 202.

281. MCLEOD, RANDALL. Obliterature: reading a censored text of Donne's *To His Mistress Going to Bed. See* 7382.

282. MALCOLM, NOEL. Hobbes, the Latin optical manuscript, and the Parisian scribe. EngMS (12) 2005, 210–32.

283. MARSDEN, RICHARD. Latin in the ascendant: the interlinear gloss of Oxford, Bodleian Library, Laud Misc. 509. *In* (pp. 132–52) 4221.

284. MATHESON, LISTER M. *Médecin sans frontières?* The European dissemination of John of Burgundy's plague treatise. *See* 4704.

285. MATSUDA, TAKAMI (ed.). *Codices Keionenses*: essays on Western manuscripts and early printed books in Keio University Library. *See* 430.

286. —— LINENTHAL, RICHARD A.; SCAHILL, JOHN (eds). The medieval book and a modern collector: essays in honour of Toshiyuki Takamiya. (Bibl. 2004, 260.) Rev. by Justin Croft in BC (54:3) 2005, 464–72.

287. MAYS, J. C. C. (ed.). *Diarmuid and Grania*: manuscript materials. *See* **20515**.

288. MEYERS, TERRY L.   A manuscript of Swinburne's *The Garden of Proserpine*. *See* **12124**.

289. MITCHELL, DOMHNALL.   Measures of possibility: Emily Dickinson's manuscripts. *See* **10797**.

290. MORGAN, NIGEL.   An SS collar in the devotional context of the shield of the Five Wounds. *In* (pp. 147–62) **4488**.

291. MOSSER, DANIEL W.   The scribe(s) of British Library MSS Egerton 2864 and Additional 5140: to 'lump' or 'split'? JEBS (8) 2005, 215–28.

292. NEWLYN, EVELYN S.   A methodology for reading against the culture: anonymous, women poets, and the Maitland Quarto manuscript (*c*.1586). *In* (pp. 89–103) **3754**.

293. NICHOLLS, MARK.   The authorship of *Thomas Bastard's Oxford Libel*. *See* **5386**.

294. O'KEEFFE, KATHERINE O'BRIEN; ORCHARD, ANDY (eds).   Latin literature and English lore: studies in Anglo-Saxon literature for Michael Lapidge: vol. I. *See* **4220**.

295. —— ——   Latin literature and English lore: studies in Anglo-Saxon literature for Michael Lapidge: vol. II. *See* **4221**.

296. O'ROURKE, JASON; TAKAMIYA, TOSHIYUKI.   Two hitherto unrecorded fragments of the *Brut*. *See* **4719**.

297. PAGE, SOPHIE.   Magic in medieval manuscripts. London: British Library in assn with Toronto UP, 2004. pp. 64. Rev. by Michael D. Bailey in TMR, Aug. 2005.

298. PANAYOTOVA, STELLA.   Art and politics in a royal prayerbook. BLR (18:5) 2005, 440–59.

299. —— A Ruskinian project with a Cockerellian flavour. *See* **11895**.

300. PICKERING, OLIVER.   Stanzaic verse in the Auchinleck Manuscript: *The Alphabetical Praise of Women*. *In* (pp. 287–304) **4419**.

301. POPE, NANCY P.   A Middle English satirical letter in Brogyntyn MS II.1. ANQ (18:3) 2005, 35–9.

302. POWELL, JASON.   Thomas Wyatt's poetry in embassy: Egerton 2711 and the production of literary manuscripts abroad. *See* **5782**.

303. RANKIN, SUSAN.   An early eleventh-century missal fragment copied by Eadwig Basan: Bodleian Library, MS Lat. Liturg. d.3, fols 4–5. BLR (18:3) 2004, 220–52.

304. RAY, MARTIN.   The Bodleian manuscript of *Poems of the Past and the Present*. *See* **11154**.

305. RAYLOR, TIMOTHY.   The date and script of Hobbes's Latin optical manuscript. EngMS (12) 2005, 201–9.

306. REVARD, CARTER.   Four fabliaux from London, British Library MS Harley 2253, translated into English verse. ChauR (40:2) 2005, 111–40.

307. ROBINSON, FRED C.   *Mise en page* in Old English manuscripts and printed texts. *In* (pp. 363–75) **4221**.

308. ROBINSON, P. R. Catalogue of dated and datable manuscripts *c*.888–1600 in London libraries. (Bibl. 2004, 281.) Rev. in BC (54:2) 2005, 171–94; by Jeanne Krochalis in JEBS (8) 2005, 293–7; by Ralph Hanna in MÆ (74:1) 2005, 122–3; by Richard Gameson in NQ (52:2) 2005, 234–6.

309. ROWLEY, SHARON M. 'A *wese\n/dan nacodnisse and þa ecan þistru*': language and mortality in the homily for Doomsday in Cambridge, Corpus Christi College MS 41. See **4349**.

310. RUNDLE, DAVID. The scribe Thomas Candour and the making of Poggio Bracciolini's English reputation. EngMS (12) 2005, 1–25.

311. RUSHFORTH, REBECCA; ORCHARD, NICHOLAS. A lost eleventh-century missal from Bury St Edmunds Abbey. BLR (18:5) 2005, 565–76.

312. SÁNCHEZ MARTÍ, JORDI. Longleat House MS 257: a description. Atl (27:1) 2005, 79–89.

313. —— *The Sowdoun of Babyloyne*: a description of the manuscript. See **4595**.

314. SANDLER, LUCY. The Lichtenthal Psalter and the manuscript patronage of the Bohun family. (Bibl. 2004, 287.) Rev. in BC (54:2) 2005, 171–94; by Stella Panayotova in TLS, 18 Mar. 2005, 27.

315. SANDLER, LUCY FREEMAN. Lancastrian heraldry in the Bohun manuscripts. *In* (pp. 221–32) **4488**.

316. SAUER, MICHELLE M. The legend of St Juliana from Lambeth MS 72. See **4688**.

317. SCASE, WENDY. *Satire on the Retinues of the Great* (MS Harley 2253): unpaid bills and the politics of purveyance. *In* (pp. 305–20) **4419**.

318. SCHAPIRO, MEYER. The language of forms: lectures on Insular manuscript art. Foreword by Charles E. Pierce, Jr. Introd. by Jane E. Rosenthal. New York: Pierpont Morgan Library, 2005. pp. vii, 199.

319. SCHMITT, NATALIE CROHN. Continuous narration in the Holkham Bible Picture Book and Queen Mary's Psalter. WI (20:2) 2004, 123–37.

320. SCHWAMB, SARA. Introduction to Lambeth MS 546, fols 1r–7r: *The Fifteen Places Mary Visited after Christ's Ascension*. See **4687**.

321. SCRAGG, DONALD. A late Old English Harrowing of Hell homily from Worcester and Blickling Homily VII. *In* (pp. 197–211) **4221**.

322. SEALS, MARC. Trauma theory and Hemingway's lost Paris manuscripts. See **16992**.

323. SHARMA, MANISH. Nebuchadnezzar and the defiance of measure in the Old English *Daniel*. See **4329**.

324. SHERMAN, WILLIAM H. Toward a history of the manicule. *In* (pp. 19–48) **19**.

325. SINISI, LUCIA. Urbanization and pollution in an Irish (?) town in the 14th century. See **4612**.

326. SMITH, KATHRYN ANN. Art, identity, and devotion in fourteenth-century England: three women and their Books of Hours. (Bibl. 2004, 294.) Rev. by Linda E. Mitchell in TMR, Nov. 2005.

327. STOCK, RANDALL. The trail of the semi-solitary manuscript. See **10870**.

328. STRATFORD, JENNY (ed.). The Lancastrian court: proceedings of the 2001 Harlaxton Symposium. *See* **4488**.

329. SZARMACH, PAUL E. Alfred's *Soliloquies* in London, BL, Cotton Tiberius A.iii (art. 9g, fols 50v–51v). *In* (pp. 153–79) **4221**.

330. TAVORMINA, M. TERESA. The twenty-jordan series: an illustrated Middle English uroscopy text. *See* **4708**.

331. VALDÉS MIYARES, RUBÉN. Sturdy stories: medieval narrative into popular ballad. *See* **4490**.

332. VOIGTS, LINDA EHRSAM. The Master of the King's Stillatories. *In* (pp. 233–52) **4488**.

333. WAKELIN, DANIEL. Scholarly scribes and the creation of *Knyghthode and Bataile*. *See* **4629**.

334. WALLS, KATHRYN. 'A prophetique dreame of the churche': William Baspoole's Laudian reception of the medieval *Pilgrimage of the Lyfe of the Manhode*. *In* (pp. 245–76) **6872**.

335. WALTER, JOHN PAUL. The Arthurian material in Holkham Hall MS 669. *See* **4681**.

336. WATSON, ROWAN. Illuminated manuscripts and their makers: an account based on the collection of the Victoria and Albert Museum. London: V&A, 2003. pp. 144. Rev. in BC (54:2) 2005, 171–94.

337. WITHERS, BENJAMIN C.; WILCOX, JONATHAN (eds). Naked before God: uncovering the body in Anglo-Saxon England. *See* **4234**.

338. WRIGHT, CHARLES D. The persecuted Church and the *mysterium lunae*: Cynewulf's *Ascension*, lines 252b–272 (*Christ II*, lines 691b–711). *In* (pp. 293–314) **4221**.

339. ZACHARIAS, GREG. Henry James cartoons. *See* **11466**.

340. ZACHER, SAMANTHA. The rewards of poetry: 'homiletic' verse in Cambridge, Corpus Christi College 201. *See* **4235**.

341. ZIEGLER, GEORGIANNA (comp.). Elizabeth I: then and now. *See* **489**.

COLLECTING AND THE LIBRARY

342. ANON. Gissing returns to Manchester. *See* **11065**.

343. —— The medieval libraries of Britain. *See* **191**.

344. —— Selected recent acquisitions briefly noted. YLG (77:3/4) 2003, 192–222. (Beinecke Rare Book and Manuscript Library.)

345. —— Selected recent acquisitions briefly noted. YLG (79:1/2) 2004, 78–96. (Beinecke Rare Book and Manuscript Library.)

346. —— Selected recent acquisitions briefly noted. YLG (79:3/4) 2005, 180–92. (Beinecke Rare Book and Manuscript Library.)

347. —— Selected recent acquisitions briefly noted. YLG (80:1/2) 2005, 77–81. (Beinecke Rare Book and Manuscript Library.)

348. ALEXANDER, JONATHAN J. G., *et al.* The splendor of the word: medieval and Renaissance illuminated manuscripts at the New York Public Library. *See* **195**.

349. ALLISON, JONATHAN.   *Friendship's Garland* and the manuscripts of Seamus Heaney's *Fosterage*. See **16932**.

350. ARCHIBALD, ELIZABETH.   Given the old razzle-dazzle. See **197**.

351. ATTAR, K. E.   George Thackeray of King's College, Cambridge. BC (54:3) 2005, 389–407. (Portrait of a bibliophile, 38.)

352. BABCOCK, ROBERT G.; DAVIS, LISA FAGIN; RUSCHE, PHILIP G.   Catalogue of medieval and Renaissance manuscripts in the Beinecke Rare Book and Manuscript Library, Yale University: vol. 4, MSS 481–485. See **198**.

353. BABCOCK, ROBERT GARY, *et al.*   A book of her own: an exhibition of manuscripts and printed books in the Yale University Library that were owned by women before 1700. New Haven, CT: Beinecke Rare Book & Manuscript Library, Yale Univ., 2005. pp. 78.

354. BARKER, NICOLAS.   Arthur Edward Wrigley (1865–1952), author of *A Book-Hunter's Yesterdays*. BC (52:4) 2003, 528–36. (Portrait of a bibliophile, 37.)

355. —— Notes on the origins of the second-hand book trade. See **760**.

356. BARLOW, GILLIAN F.   Of spats and moccasins: reflections on archiving and curating the John Buchan papers in Canada. See **15600**.

357. BATCHELOR, RHONDA.   *Ex libris*: too many books. Amphora (131) 2003, 13–18.

358. BERNER, SETH.   Collecting Faulkner. *In* (pp. 153–67) **16453**.

359. BINSKI, PAUL; PANAYOTOVA, STELLA (eds).   The Cambridge illuminations: ten centuries of book production in the medieval West. See **202**.

360. BLAND, MARK.   The James A. Riddell collection of Jonson's 1616 and 1640 *Workes*. See **7537**.

361. BORO, JOYCE.   Lord Berners and his books: a new survey. See **5388**.

362. BOWDEN, CAROLINE.   The library of Mildred Cooke Cecil, Lady Burghley. Library (6:1) 2005, 3–29.

363. BROCKMAN, WILLIAM S.   Collecting Joyce. *In* (pp. 273–84) **17274**.

364. BUCKER, PARK (comp.).   The Matthew J. and Arlyn Bruccoli Collection of F. Scott Fitzgerald at the University of South Carolina: an illustrated catalogue. See **16487**.

365. BUSH, ERWIN H.   The future of used bookselling: an observation. See **1033**.

366. CARLEY, JAMES P.   The books of King Henry VIII and his wives. Preface by David Starkey. (Bibl. 2004, 338.) Rev. by J. B. Trapp in TLS, 8 Apr. 2005, 31.

367. CARROLL-HORROCKS, BETH.   A working relationship: the Dorothy Nevile Lees papers relating to Edward Gordon Craig and *The Mask*, at the Harvard Theatre Collection. See **1171**.

368. CAVE, MARK.   Fred W. Todd and the Tennessee Williams holdings at the Historic New Orleans Collection. See **20182**.

369. CERASANO, S. P.   Henslowe's 'curious' diary. See **5485**.

370. CLEMIT, PAMELA.   William Godwin's papers in the Abinger deposit: an unmapped country. See **8671**.

371. COATES, ALAN, *et al.*   Catalogue of books printed in the fifteenth century now in the Bodleian Library. Oxford; New York: OUP, 2005. 6 vols. pp. lxxxvii, 2956. Rev. by David McKitterick in TLS, 9 Dec. 2005, 5–7.

372. CROFT, CLARY.   The Helen Creighton Fonds at the Public Archives of Nova Scotia. See **3540**.

373. CROFT, PAULINE.   Mildred, Lady Burghley: the matriarch. *In* (pp. 283–300) **5121**.

374. DAWSON, MUIR.   Two children's books illustrated by Bewick, with notes on printing from the original blocks. See **8168**.

375. DE HAMEL, CHRISTOPHER; SILVER, JOEL.   Disbound and dispersed: the leaf book considered. Chicago, IL: Caxton Club, 2005. pp. 152. (Exhibition catalogue.) Rev. by A. S. G. Edwards in BC (54:4) 2005, 608–9.

376. DICKINSON, DONALD C.   John Carter: the taste & technique of a bookman. Preface by Sebastian Carter. (Bibl. 2004, 347.) Rev. by Anthony Hobson in TLS, 13 May 2005, 32; by David McKitterick in Library (6:2) 2005, 213–16; by Michael Levine-Clark in LibC (40:2) 2005, 198–9.

377. DICKSON, DONALD R.   Henry Vaughan's medical library. See **7880**.

378. DIJKGRAAF, HENDRIK.   The library of a Jesuit community at Holbeck, Nottinghamshire (1679). (Bibl. 2004, 348.) Rev. by Mark Purcell in LibH (21:1) 2005, 66–8.

379. DIZER, JOHN T.   How I started collecting books. DNR (74:1) 2005, 18–24.

380. DRIVER, MARTHA W.   Stow's books bequeathed: some notes on William Browne (1591–*c*.1643) and Peter Le Neve (1661–1729). *In* (pp. 135–43) **5746**.

381. EDWARDS, A. S. G.   Manuscripts at auction: January 2002 to December 2003. See **231**.

382. —— (foreword).   The pleasures of bibliophily: fifty years of *The Book Collector*: an anthology. (Bibl. 2004, 352.) Rev. by David Pearson in SHARP (14:1/2) 2005, 10; by Robert L. Dawson in LibC (40:2) 2005, 194–7.

383. EDWARDS, BRENDAN FREDERICK R.   Paper talk: a history of libraries, print culture, and aboriginal peoples in Canada before 1960. Lanham, MD; London: Scarecrow Press, 2005. pp. xx, 221. Rev. by Joanie Crandall in SHARP (14:4) 2005, 12–13.

384. EDWARDS, CHRISTOPHER.   From Pope to Swift: a book from Swift's library. See **9058**.

385. ELDRIDGE, BOB.   Mark David Chapman, science fiction fan. See **4018**.

386. EMMERSON, J. McL.   Dan Fleming and John Evelyn: two seventeenth-century book collectors. BSANZB (27:1/2) 2003, 48–61.

387. FOOT, MIRJAM M.   'A magnificent and bewildering variety': Irish bookbinding in the eighteenth century. *In* (pp. 206–36) **30**.

388. FORKER, CHARLES R.   How did Shakespeare come by his books? See **5935**.

389. FOSS, PETER J.   An inventory of the Llewelyn Powys holdings: manuscripts of works (part two). See **18924**.

390. GIBSON, WILLIAM.   Benjamin Hoadly: myth and archives. See **8718**.

391. GILLESPIE, ALEXANDRA.   Poets, printers, and early English *Sammelbände*. See 852.

392. —— Stow's 'owlde' manuscripts of London chronicles. *In* (pp. 57–67) 5746.

393. GILLESPIE, VINCENT.   Syon and the English market for Continental printed books: the incunable phase. ReLit (37:2) 2005, 27–49.

394. GRAHAM, TIM (comp.).   Penguin in print: a bibliography. *See* 858.

395. GUIGENO, VINCENT.   Engineering the words: Robert Louis Stevenson and the Bell Rock lighthouse. *See* 12068.

396. HABEGGER, ALFRED.   Some notes on the Emily Dickinson Collection at Sophia University in Tokyo. *See* 10783.

397. HANNA, RALPH.   Notes on some Trinity College Dublin manuscripts. *In* (pp. 171–80) 4419.

398. HARRIS, OLIVER.   'Motheaten, mouldye, and rotten': the early custodial history and dissemination of John Leland's manuscript remains. *See* 5508.

399. HARTMAN, STEVEN.   'Invading *Walden*': part 1, An exchange between Walter Harding and Wallace Stegner. *See* 12193.

400. HAVENS, EARLE.   English manuscript culture and the ambiguous triumph of print: seventy years of the Osborn Collection, 1934–2004. YLG (79:1/2) 2004, 5–52.

401. HESTER, M. THOMAS; SORLIEN, ROBERT PARKER; FLYNN, DENNIS (eds).   John Donne's marriage letters in the Folger Shakespeare Library. *See* 7378.

402. HEYWOOD, CHRISTOPHER.   The mark 'Bronte' on Frederic Montagu's *Gleanings in Craven*. *See* 11731.

403. HOBSON, ANTHONY; WOODCOCK, THOMAS.   The owners of the '*Carpe Diem*' armorial binding stamp. *See* 32.

404. HOPKINS, RICHARD.   Book signing: the view from both sides of the table. Amphora (136) 2004, 6–10.

405. HOROBIN, SIMON.   The angle of oblivioun: a lost medieval manuscript discovered in Walter Scott's collection. *See* 260.

406. HUGHES, AMY (ed.).   Theatre research resources in New York City. *See* 3979.

407. HUNTER-RUTTER, KATHLEEN.   Another distinguished Borrovian: Theodore Roosevelt. *See* 10112.

408. JACKSON, H. J.   'Marginal frivolities': readers' notes as evidence for the history of reading. *In* (pp. 137–51) 19.

409. JONES, JACQUELINE C.   The unknown patron: Harold Jackman and the Harlem renaissance archives. *See* 19907.

410. KEENAN, THOMAS.   The Theatre Guild archive at the Beinecke. YLG (80:1/2) 2005, 65–70.

411. KIESSLING, NICOLAS K.   The library of Anthony Wood. (Bibl. 2004, 384.) Rev. by David Stoker in LibH (21:1) 2005, 70–1.

412. KING, JULIA; MILETIC-VEJZOVIC, LAILA (eds).   The library of Leonard and Virginia Woolf: a short-title catalog. Introd. by Diane F. Gillespie. (Bibl. 2004,

385.) Rev. by Ruth Hoberman in PacNQ (96:1) 2004/05, 52–3; by Stuart N. Clarke in WSA (11) 2005, 224–7; by Paul W. Nash in Library (6:1) 2005, 103–4.

413. KIRSOP, WALLACE. Boulard's syndrome. BSANZB (27:1/2) 2003, 3–13. (Private libraries.)

414. —— Writing a history of nineteenth-century commercial circulating libraries: problems and possibilities. BSANZB (27:3/4) 2003, 71–82.

415. LE FAYE, DEIRDRE. Memoirs and biographies. In (pp. 51–8) **10060**.

416. LEWIS, LUCY. The Tavistock Boethius: one of the earliest examples of provincial printing. In (pp. 1–14) **880**.

417. LIGHTBOURNE, RUTH. Bookplates, book labels, and handwritten inscriptions in a New Zealand colonial library. BSANZB (28:3) 2004, 62–77.

418. LINENTHAL, RICHARD A. Medieval and Renaissance manuscripts: a hand-list of the collection of B. S. Cron. See **276**.

419. LOCKWOOD, TOM. Edmond Malone and early modern textual culture. See **8820**.

420. LONG, WILLIAM B. Dulwich MS XX, *The Telltale*: clues to provenance. See **7022**.

421. LOPEZ, KEN. Collecting authors' first books. Amphora (134) 2004, 10–15.

422. —— Signed *vs* inscribed. Amphora (131) 2003, 19–23.

423. LOVETT, CHARLIE. Lewis Carroll among his books: a descriptive catalogue of the private library of Charles L. Dodgson. See **10406**.

424. MCKITTERICK, DAVID. Out of the cradle. TLS, 9 Dec. 2005, 5–7 (review-article). (Incunabula in the Bodleian.)

425. MCKITTERICK, ROSAMOND; BINSKI, PAUL. History and literature: sacred and secular. In (pp. 235–95) **202**.

426. MANDELBROTE, GILES; LEWIS, YVONNE. Learning to collect: the library of Sir Richard Ellys (1682–1742) at Blickling Hall. London: National Trust, 2004. pp. 27. (Exhibition catalogue.) Rev. by David Stoker in LibH (21:1) 2005, 74–5.

427. MANLEY, K. A. Lounging places and frivolous literature: subscription and circulating libraries in the West Country to 1825. In (pp. 107–20) **880**.

428. MARTIN, PATRICK; FINNIS, JOHN. A gunpowder priest? *Benedicam dominum* – Ben Jonson's strange 1605 inscription. See **7567**.

429. MASON, EMMA. 'Some kind friends': Scott's *Harold the Dauntless* (HM 1937) and Frederick Locker-Lampson. See **11936**.

430. MATSUDA, TAKAMI (ed.). *Codices Keionenses*: essays on Western manuscripts and early printed books in Keio University Library. Tokyo: Keio UP, 2005. pp. 211. Rev. by John McQuillen in Arthuriana (15:4) 2005, 72–3.

431. MATTESON, ROBERT S.; BARTON, GAYLE. A large private park: the collection of Archbishop William King 1650–1729. (Bibl. 2004, 406.) Rev. by Charles Benson in LibH (21:1) 2005, 68–70; by Mark Purcell in Library (6:2) 2005, 198–200.

432. MATTHEWS, JACK. Rare books as instruments of the past. AR (63:2) 2005, 278–88.

433. MAY, JAMES E. Scribleriana transferred: manuscripts and books at auction and in dealer's catalogues, 2002–2003. See **8031**.

434. —— Swift and Swiftiana offered, sold, and acquired, 2002–2005. See **9076**.

435. MEYERS, TERRY L. A manuscript of Swinburne's *The Garden of Proserpine*. See **12124**.

436. MORTIMER, IAN. The Henry Williamson archive at Exeter University Library. See **20230**.

437. NAIDITCH, P. G. The extant portion of the library of A. E. Housman: part IV, Non-Classical materials. See **17064**.

438. NELSON, ALAN H. Shakespeare and the bibliophiles: from the earliest years to 1616. *In* (pp. 49–73) **19**.

439. NOLAN, MARIE E.; REID, PETER H. Pride and glory: Aberdeen Public Library during the Second World War. LibH (21:1) 2005, 9–27.

440. PANAYOTOVA, STELLA. A Ruskinian project with a Cockerellian flavour. See **11895**.

441. PANOFSKY, RUTH; MOIR, MICHAEL. Halted by the archive: the impact of excessive archival restrictions on scholars. See **1086**.

442. PARKS, STEPHEN (ed.). The Beinecke Library of Yale University. (Bibl. 2004, 415.) Rev. by Bruce Whiteman in PBSA (99:1) 2005, 164–5.

443. PHILLIPS, MICHAEL. Blake's annotations in context. See **8380**.

444. PITCHER, JOHN. Samuel Daniel's gifts of books to Lord Chancellor Egerton. See **7341**.

445. PITTOCK, MURRAY G. H. Sources and dates for the Jacobite song: II. See **3577**.

446. POOLE, WILLIAM; THORP, JENNIFER. Women among the prisoners: New College fragments of a new Jacobean play. See **7036**.

447. PRESCOTT, ANNE LAKE. Getting a record: Stubbs, Singleton, and a 1579 almanac. See **5757**.

448. PURCELL, JANE. Not of an age, but for all time: Shakespeare at the Huntington. See **6058**.

449. PURCELL, MARK. The library at Lanhydrock. BC (54:2) 2005, 195–230. (National Trust libraries, 1.)

450. —— SHENTON, CAROLINE. National Trust libraries: introduction and select bibliography. BC (54:1) 2005, 53–9.

451. RANSOME, JOYCE. Monotessaron: the harmonies of Little Gidding. See **7444**.

452. REED, JOSEPH W. The Pottles at Glen Cove: education of a country mouse. See **8411**.

453. RIBBLE, FREDERICK G. New light on Henry Fielding from the Malmesbury Papers. See **8617**.

454. ROBERTSON, GUY. Library gold in the garbage. Amphora (136) 2004, 12–15.

455. ROBERTSON, RANDY. Swift's *Leviathan* and the end of licensing. See **9086**.

456. ROSE, MARILYN. The literary archive and the telling of Modernist lives: retrieving Anne Marriott. *In* (pp. 231–49) **12739**.

457. ROSSINGTON, MICHAEL.   Commemorating the relic: the beginnings of the Bodleian Shelley collections. *See* **12028.**

458. RUNDLE, DAVID.   The scribe Thomas Candour and the making of Poggio Bracciolini's English reputation. *See* **310.**

459. SCHUCHARD, RONALD.   The Robert Penn Warren collection at Emory University: a personal account. *See* **19996.**

460. SHERBO, ARTHUR.   From the sale catalogue of the library of Samuel Rogers. *See* **11852.**

461. SHERMAN, WILLIAM H.   'Rather soiled by use': attitudes towards readers' marks. BC (52:4) 2003, 471–90.

462. —— Toward a history of the manicule. *In* (pp. 19–48) **19.**

463. SHUFFELTON, GEORGE.   *Piers Plowman* and the case of the missing book. *See* **4861.**

464. SIM, GARY.   Thoughts on antiquarian booksellers. *See* **1058.**

465. SMITH, NICHOLAS D.   An annotated copy of the third Hawkins edition of Izaak Walton's *The Complete Angler. See* **7892.**

466. SNART, JASON.   Blake's Milton: did Blake own and annotate the 1732 Bentley edition of Milton's *Paradise Lost? See* **8390.**

467. STALKER, LAURA.   Intramuralia acquisitions of rare materials, 2002. HLQ (67:4) 2004, 669–89. (Henry E. Huntington Library.)

468. —— Intramuralia acquisitions of rare materials, 2003. HLQ (68:3) 2005, 567–82. (Henry E. Huntington Library.)

469. STILLMAN, TERRY A.   What a difference fifty years makes: used book prices skyrocket since 1953. *See* **998.**

470. THOMPSON, GEORGE H.   The art of collecting H. L. Mencken. *See* **18186.**

471. THORMÄHLEN, MARIANNE.   Anne Brontë's *Sacred Harmony*: a discovery. *See* **10147.**

472. TITE, COLIN G. C.   The early records of Sir Robert Cotton's Library: formation, cataloguing, use. (Bibl. 2004, 445.) Rev. by Ian Mortimer in SixCJ (36:1) 2005, 188–90; by Simon Keynes in BC (54:3) 2005, 461–4.

473. TRILL, SUZANNE.   Early modern women's writing in the Edinburgh Archives, c.1550–1740: a preliminary checklist. *In* (pp. 201–25) **3754.**

474. WAKELIN, DANIEL.   William Worcester writes a history of his reading. *See* **4930.**

475. WALKER, GREGORY; CLAPINSON, MARY; FORBES, LESLEY (eds).   The Bodleian Library: a subject guide to the collections. Oxford: Bodleian Library, 2004. pp. 240, (plates) 49.

476. WATSON, JAMES G.   Man writing: the Watson trilogy: Peter Matthiessen in archive. *See* **18146.**

477. WATSON, ROWAN.   Illuminated manuscripts and their makers: an account based on the collection of the Victoria and Albert Museum. *See* **336.**

478. WHITEHEAD, STEPHEN.   Henry Bonnell: guardian of the relics of passion. *See* **10228.**

479. WHITLOCK, KEITH.   The Robert Ashley founding bequest to the Middle Temple Library and John Donne's library. *See* **7401.**

480. WIEGAND, WAYNE. Collecting contested titles: the experience of five small public libraries in the rural Midwest, 1893–1956. LibC (40:3) 2005, 368–84.
481. WILSON, LESLIE PERRIN. 'No worthless books': Elizabeth Peabody's Foreign Library, 1840–52. *See* **9449**.
482. WOLZ, LYN A. Resources in the Vaughan Williams Memorial Library: the Anne Geddes Gilchrist manuscript collection. *See* **3598**.
483. WOUDHUYSEN, H. R. A good morning's work. *See* **12970**.
484. —— Not lonely, but alone. *See* **17642**.
485. WRYNN, SUSAN. News from the Hemingway Collection. *See* **16998**.
486. —— News from the Hemingway Collection. *See* **16999**.
487. —— News from the Hemingway Collection. *See* **17000**.
488. YOUNG, TIMOTHY. The Robert Graves collection of William S. Reese. *See* **16806**.
489. ZIEGLER, GEORGIANNA (comp.). Elizabeth I: then and now. Washington, DC: Folger Shakespeare Library, 2003. pp. 190. (Exhibition catalogue.) Rev. by Sarah Jett in LibC (40:1) 2005, 92–3.
490. ZUKOFSKY, PAUL. Louis Zukofsky's marginalia. *See* **20541**.

TEXTUAL STUDIES

491. ANON. An addendum to *Buddhist Duality in William Gaddis's 'Carpenter's Gothic'*. *See* **16624**.
492. ABATE, MICHELLE ANN. Oversight as insight: reading *The Second Shepherds' Play* as *The Second Shepherd's Play*. *See* **4529**.
493. ALDRICH-WATSON, DEBORAH. Notes on editing *The Verse Miscellany of Constance Aston Fowler: a Diplomatic Edition*. *In* (pp. 157–65) **587**.
494. ALEXANDER, CHRISTINE. Defining and representing literary juvenilia. *In* (pp. 70–97) **9164**.
495. ALLISON, JONATHAN. *Friendship's Garland* and the manuscripts of Seamus Heaney's *Fosterage*. *See* **16932**.
496. ANSELMENT, RAYMOND A. Seventeenth-century manuscript sources of Alice Thornton's life. *See* **7866**.
497. APPLEFORD, ROB. The Indian act(ing): proximate perversions in Genet's *The Blacks* and Floyd Favel Starr's *Lady of Silences* (1993, 2003). *See* **19567**.
498. ARDOLINO, FRANK R. 'Sweete mistresse where as I loue you nothing at all': indeterminacy and ambiguity in *Roister Doister*. *See* **5770**.
499. ARNER, ROBERT D. Textual transmission and the transformation of texts: on the dialogic margins of Dorothy Parker's *The Waltz*. *In* (pp. 86–113) **18738**.
500. BACIGALUPO, MASSIMO. America in Ezra Pound's posthumous cantos. *See* **18855**.
501. BAJETTA, CARLO M. Sir Walter Ralegh ed Elisabetta I: poesie per tre occasioni. *See* **5617**.
502. BAMMESBERGER, ALFRED. The coastguard's maxim reconsidered (*Beowulf*, lines 287b–289). *See* **4288**.
503. BLAND, MARK. Ben Jonson and the legacies of the past. *See* **7535**.

504. —— Francis Beaumont's verse letters to Ben Jonson and 'the Mermaid Club'. *See* **7224.**

505. —— The James A. Riddell collection of Jonson's 1616 and 1640 *Workes. See* **7537.**

506. BLOOM, JONATHAN.   Revision as transformation: the making and re-making of V. S. Pritchett's *You Make Your Own Life. See* **18935.**

507. BORDALEJO, BÁRBARA.   The text of Caxton's second edition of the *Canterbury Tales. See* **4984.**

508. BRAY, ROBERT.   Foreword to *His Father's House. See* **20179.**

509. —— *et al.*   The early plays of Tennessee Williams. *See* **20180.**

510. BREEN, JENNIFER.   And asunder to remain. *See* **17058.**

511. BRICE, XAVIER.   Ford Madox Ford and the composition of *Nostromo. See* **15859.**

512. BRIGGS, JULIA.   The conversation behind the conversation: speaking the unspeakable in Virginia Woolf. *See* **20315.**

513. BURKE, VICTORIA E.; CLARKE, ELIZABETH.   Julia Palmer's *Centuries*: the politics of editing and anthologizing early modern women's manuscript compilations. *In* (pp. 47–64) **587.**

514. BURT, JOHN.   A note on *Uncertain Season in High Country. See* **19982.**

515. BUSH, RONALD.   Remaking Canto 74. *See* **18865.**

516. BUSHELL, SALLY.   Meaning in Dickinson's manuscripts: intending the unintentional. *See* **10771.**

517. —— Wordsworthian composition: the micro-*Prelude. See* **12464.**

518. CALLE MARTÍN, JAVIER; MIRANDA GARCÍA, ANTONIO.   Editing Middle English punctuation: the case of MS Egerton 2622 (ff. 136–152). *See* **4684.**

519. CAMAIORA CONTI, LUISA.   Keats's *La Belle Dame sans Merci*: the story of two versions. *See* **11507.**

520. CARPENTER, ANDREW.   *A Tale of a Tub* as an Irish text. *See* **9052.**

521. CHAPMAN, WAYNE K.   Yeats's dislocated Rebellion poems and the Great War: the case of *The Wild Swans at Coole* and *Michael Robartes and the Dancer. See* **20485.**

522. CLARKE, COLIN A.   'Only man is miserable': the evolving view of imprisonment in Robert Lowell's poetry. *In* (pp. 131–46) **12821.**

523. COELSCH-FOISNER, SABINE; GÖRTSCHACHER, WOLFGANG (eds).   The author as reader: textual visions and revisions. New York; Frankfurt: Lang, 2005. pp. xi, 259. (Salzburg studies in English literature and culture, 2.)

524. COHEN, DANIEL A.   Martha Buck's copybook: New England tragedy verse and the scribal lineage of the American ballad tradition. *See* **3536.**

525. COLCLOUGH, STEPHEN.   'Designated in print as "Mr John Clare"': the annuals and the field of reading, 1827–1835. *See* **10434.**

526. —— 'A grey goose quill and an album': the manuscript book and text transmission, 1800–1850. *In* (pp. 153–73) **19.**

527. COOK, ELIZABETH.   From Pandemonium. *See* **19122.**

528. COX, CHARLES.   *A Tale of Tucuman*: a Tennyson reference of 1831. *See* **12139.**

529. CRESWELL, ROBYN. Reimagining Robert Lowell. *See* **17870.**

530. D'ARCY, ANNE MARIE; FLETCHER, ALAN J. (eds). Studies in late medieval and early Renaissance texts in honour of John Scattergood: 'the key of all good remembrance'. *See* **4419.**

531. D'ARONCO, MARIA AMALIA. Anglo-Saxon plant pharmacy and the Latin medical tradition. *In* (pp. 133–51) **1773.**

532. DAVIDSON, JULIE E. William Roberts's dating of Hannah More's memoirs. *See* **8842.**

533. DAWSON, P. M. S. The making of Clare's *Poems Descriptive of Rural Life and Scenery* (1820). *See* **10435.**

534. DE LA CRUZ, ISABEL; VÁZQUEZ, NILA. New approaches in textual editing: a selection of electronic editions under analysis. IJES (5:2) 2005, 193–208.

535. DE LA CRUZ CABANILLAS, ISABEL. The language of the extant versions of Rolle's *Ego Dormio. See* **4915.**

536. DENBO, MICHAEL ROY. Editing a Renaissance commonplace book: the Holgate Miscellany. *In* (pp. 65–73) **587.**

537. DEVER, MARYANNE. 'A friendship that is grown on paper': reflections on editing Marjorie Barnard's letters to Nettie Palmer. *See* **16235.**

538. DIRST, SHELLEY SHARP. From *The Hour-Glass* to *At the Hawk's Well*: revisions toward an idealized theater. *See* **20488.**

539. DRABECK, BERNARD A. Scratch revisited. *See* **18012.**

540. DRIVER, MARTHA W. Stow's books bequeathed: some notes on William Browne (1591–c.1643) and Peter Le Neve (1661–1729). *In* (pp. 135–43) **5746.**

541. DUTTON, ELISABETH. Augustine Baker and two manuscripts of Julian of Norwich's *Revelation of Love. See* **4823.**

542. ECONOMOU, GEORGE D. Chaucer and Langland: a fellowship of makers. *In* (pp. 290–301) **4485.**

543. EDWARDS, A. S. G. Manuscripts of the verse of Henry Howard, Earl of Surrey. *See* **5758.**

544. —— A new text of the *Canterbury Tales*? *In* (pp. 121–8) **4419.**

545. —— Surrey's Martial epigram: scribes and transmission. *See* **5759.**

546. ENGEL, MARK. Collating Carlyle: patterns of revision in *Heroes, Sartor Resartus*, and *The French Revolution. In* (pp. 240–7) **10393.**

547. ERNE, LUKAS. Words in space: the reproduction of texts and the semiotics of the page. *See* **4991.**

548. ESDALE, LOGAN. Dickinson's epistolary 'naturalness'. *See* **10777.**

549. EZELL, MARGARET J. M. Eclectic circulation: the functional dynamics of manuscript and electronic literary cultures. *In* (pp. 27–35) **587.**

550. FERRY, ANNE. Frost's design. *See* **16602.**

551. FLANERY, PATRICK DENMAN. (Re-)marking Coetzee & Costello: The (textual) *Lives of Animals. See* **15828.**

552. FOREY, MARGARET. Manuscript evidence and the author of *Aske Me No More*: William Strode, not Thomas Carew. *See* **7853.**

553. FORNERO, CATERINA. Chess is the game wherein I'll catch the conscience of the king: the metaphor of the game of chess in T. S. Eliot's *The Waste Land*. See **16267**.

554. FOSS, PETER J. An inventory of the Llewelyn Powys holdings: manuscripts of works (part two). See **18924**.

555. FRANKEL, NICHOLAS. On the dates of composition and completion for Wilde's *Salome* and *Lady Windermere's Fan*. See **12390**.

556. FREIDRICH, MARIANNE M. 'Something to remember me by': from early fragments to finished story. See **15443**.

557. FRÓES, JOÃO. 'A part omitted' from Swift's *Sentiments of a Church-of-England Man*. See **9065**.

558. FULK, R. D. Six cruces in *Beowulf* (lines 31, 83, 404, 445, 1198, and 3074–5). In (pp. 349–67) **4220**.

559. —— Six cruces in the Finnsburg fragment and episode. See **4338**.

560. —— Some contested readings in the *Beowulf* manuscript. See **4296**.

561. FULTON, JOE B. The lost manuscript conclusion to Mark Twain's *Corn-Pone Opinions*: an editorial history and an edition of the restored text. See **12240**.

562. GANTOS, JACK. Evidence of books not yet written. See **16639**.

563. GARRIDO ANES, EDURNE. Geographical and dialectal distribution of Platearius' *Liber de simplici medicina* in England. See **4700**.

564. GERSHENOWITZ, DEBORAH A. Negotiating voices: biography and the curious triangle between subject, author and editor. See **14594**.

565. GILLES, SEALY; TOMASCH, SYLVIA. Professionalizing Chaucer: John Matthews Manly, Edith Rickert, and the *Canterbury Tales* as cultural capital. In (pp. 364–83) **4485**.

566. GILLESPIE, ALEXANDRA. Introduction. In (pp. 1–11) **5746**.

567. GLADDEN, SAMUEL LYNDON. Mary Shelley's editions of *The Collected Poems of Percy Bysshe Shelley*: the editor as subject. See **11971**.

568. GNEUSS, HELMUT. The homiliary of the Taunton fragments. See **4345**.

569. GOSSETT, SUZANNE. The ethics of post-mortem editing. In (pp. 147–55) **587**.

570. GOULD, WARWICK. Writing the life of the text: the case of W. B. Yeats. See **20494**.

571. GOUWS, JOHN. Book and text studies in Grahamstown. See **857**.

572. GREEN, RICHARD FIRTH. *The Hunting of the Hare*: an edition. In (pp. 129–47) **4419**.

573. GRIFFIN, ROBERT J. The text in motion: eighteenth-century *Roxana*s. See **8517**.

574. GRIFFITHS, JANE. Text and authority: John Stow's 1568 edition of Skelton's *Workes*. In (pp. 127–34) **5746**.

575. —— What's in a name? The transmission of 'John Skelton, Laureate' in manuscript and print. See **5668**.

576. GUIGENO, VINCENT. Engineering the words: Robert Louis Stevenson and the Bell Rock lighthouse. See **12068**.

577. GUMBRECHT, HANS ULRICH.   The powers of philology: dynamics of textual scholarship. Urbana: Illinois UP, 2003. pp. 93. Rev. by Jan M. Ziolkowski in JEGP (104:2) 2005, 239–72.

578. GUY, JOSEPHINE M.   Oscar Wilde's 'self-plagiarism': some new manuscript evidence. See 12395.

579. HAGEMAN, ELIZABETH H.   Treacherous accidents and the abominable printing of Katherine Philips's 1664 Poems. In (pp. 85–95) 587.

580. HALE, ALLEAN.   Tennessee Williams' Three Plays for the Lyric Theatre. See 20188.

581. HANNA, RALPH.   English biblical texts before Lollardy and their fate. In (pp. 141–53) 4482.

582. —— Middle English books and Middle English literary history. See 4585.

583. HARSH, CONSTANCE.   The text of Eve's Ransom: insights from the Illustrated London News serialization. See 11073.

584. HENIGE, DAVID.   Commas, Christians, and editors. JSchP (36:2) 2005, 58–74.

585. HENNESSEY, OLIVER.   'I shall find the dark grow luminous when I understand I have nothing': Yeats's failing Vision. See 20501.

586. HILL, JOYCE.   Ælfric's Colloquy: the Antwerp/London version. In (pp. 331–48) 4221.

587. HILL, W. SPEED (ed.).   New ways of looking at old texts III: papers of the Renaissance English Text Society, 1997–2001. Tempe: Arizona Center for Medieval and Renaissance Studies for the Renaissance English Text Soc., 2004. pp. vii, 210. (Medieval & Renaissance texts & studies, 270.)

588. HOLBROOK, PETER.   An earthy muse. See 7504.

589. HOLLAND, PETER; ORGEL, STEPHEN (eds).   From script to stage in early modern England. See 5260.

590. HOROBIN, S. C. P.   Pennies, pence and pans: some Chaucerian misreadings. See 5005.

591. HOROBIN, SIMON.   'In London and opelond': the dialect and circulation of the C version of Piers Plowman. See 4850.

592. HOSPITAL, JANETTE TURNER.   West's Survivors in Mexico. See 20107.

593. HUBBARD, MELANIE.   'Turn it, a little': the influence of the daguerreotype and the stereograph on Emily Dickinson's use of manuscript variants. See 10788.

594. HUME, ROBERT D.   The aims and uses of 'textual studies'. PBSA (99:2) 2005, 197–230.

595. IRVINE, SUSAN.   Fragments of Boethius: the reconstruction of the Cotton manuscript of the Alfredian text. See 4273.

596. JACKSON, JEFFREY E.   Elizabeth Gaskell and the dangerous edge of things: epigraphs in North and South and Victorian publishing practices. See 11044.

597. JACKSON, VIRGINIA.   Dickinson undone. See 10789.

598. JAECKLE, JEFF.   'These minutiae mean more': five editions of Wallace Stevens' Esthétique du Mal. See 19667.

599. JEFFERSON, JUDITH A.; PUTTER, AD. Alliterative patterning in the *Morte Arthure*. See **4579**.

600. —— —— The distribution of infinitives in -*e* and -*en* in some Middle English alliterative poems. See **1563**.

601. JOLLY, MARGARETTA. Myths of unity: remembering the Second World War through letters and their editing. In (pp. 144–70) **14645**.

602. JONES, CHRIS. Knight or wight in Keats's *La Belle Dame*? An ancient ditty reconsidered. See **11516**.

603. JONES, PETER MURRAY. Surgical narrative in Middle English. See **4701**.

604. JUNG, SANDRO. John Gilbert Cooper's revisions of *The Tomb of Shakespear: a Vision*. See **8483**.

605. —— John Gilbert Cooper's *The Tomb of Shakespear*: an edition. See **8484**.

606. KATO, TAKAKO. Towards the digital Winchester: editing the Winchester manuscript of Malory's *Morte Darthur*. See **4889**.

607. KEISER, GEORGE R. Verse introductions to Middle English medical treatises. See **4703**.

608. KELLY, STUART. The book of lost books. See **3824**.

609. KENNEDY, RUTH. The Evangelist in Robert Thornton's devotional book: organizing principles at the level of the quire. See **4443**.

610. KETTERER, DAVID. John Wyndham and the sins of his father: damaging disclosures in court. See **20474**.

611. KING, JOHN N. Guides to reading Foxe's *Book of Martyrs*. See **5438**.

612. KLENE, JEAN. Working with a complex document: the Southwell–Sibthorpe Commonplace Book. In (pp. 170–5) **587**.

613. KNOWLES, OWEN; STAPE, J. H. The rationale of punctuation in Conrad's *Blackwood's* fictions. See **15886**.

614. KOBAYASHI, JUNJI. *Gorboduc* and the Inner Temple revels of Christmas. See **5630**.

615. KRIES, SUSANNE. English–Danish rivalry and the mutilation of Alfred in the eleventh-century *Chronicle* poem *The Death of Alfred*. See **4283**.

616. LEE, MARSHALL. Bookmaking: editing/design/production. See **167**.

617. LINDSTRÖM, BENGT. A note on anagrammatic corruption in *Havelok*. See **4567**.

618. LOCKWOOD, TOM. Edmond Malone and early modern textual culture. See **8820**.

619. LOFARO, MICHAEL A.; DAVIS, HUGH (eds). James Agee rediscovered: the journals of *Let Us Now Praise Famous Men* and other new manuscripts. See **15087**.

620. LUPTON, CHRISTINA. Two texts told twice: poor Richard, Pastor Yorick, and the case of the word's return. See **9037**.

621. MACK, DOUGLAS; MACK, WILMA (eds). *Tales of Fathers and Daughters* no. 2. See **11284**.

622. McKENNA, BERNARD. George Shiels' *The Passing Day* – the author's text with deletions and emendations. See **19439**.

623. McLeod, Randall.   Obliterature: reading a censored text of Donne's *To His Mistress Going to Bed. See* **7382.**

624. McNamee, Brendan.   'What then?': poststructuralism, authorial intention and W. B. Yeats. *See* **20513.**

625. Magee, Rosemary M.; Wright, Emily.   A good guide: a final conversation with Sally Fitzgerald. *See* **18570.**

626. Mamigonian, Marc A.; Turner, John Noel.   Annotations for *Stephen Hero. See* **17311.**

627. Marotti, Arthur F.   A response to Michael Rudick. *In* (pp. 143–6) **587.**

628. Marshik, Celia.   The case of *Jenny*: Dante Gabriel Rossetti and the censorship dialectic. *See* **11872.**

629. Martin, Susan M.   Robert Gould's attacks on the London stage, 1689 and 1709: the two versions of *The Playhouse: a Satyr. See* **7457.**

630. Mason, Emma.   'Some kind friends': Scott's *Harold the Dauntless* (HM 1937) and Frederick Locker-Lampson. *See* **11936.**

631. May, Steven W.   Queen Elizabeth's *Future Foes*: editing manuscripts with the first-line index of Elizabethan verse (a future friend). *In* (pp. 1–12) **587.**

632. May, William.   *The Choosers*: posthumous collections of Stevie Smith's poetry. *See* **19492.**

633. Mayhew, Robert.   Anthem: '38 & '46. *In* (pp. 28–54) **19013.**

634. Mayo, Christopher.   Manners and manuscripts: the editorial manufacture of Lord Chesterfield in *Letters to His Son. See* **8471.**

635. Mays, J. C. C. (ed.).   *Diarmuid and Grania*: manuscript materials. *See* **20515.**

636. Melnikoff, Kirk.   Jones's pen and Marlowe's socks: Richard Jones, print culture, and the beginnings of English dramatic literature. *See* **5545.**

637. Meskill, Lynn Sermin.   Exorcising the Gorgon of terror: Jonson's *Masque of Queenes. See* **7571.**

638. Meyer, Susan.   Antisemitism and social critique in Dickens's *Oliver Twist. See* **10716.**

639. Meyers, Terry L.   A manuscript of Swinburne's *The Garden of Proserpine. See* **12124.**

640. Milgram, Shoshana.   *Anthem* in manuscript: finding the words. *In* (pp. 3–23) **19013.**

641. Miller, Anthony.   Corrections to the Womersley text of Gibbon's *Decline and Fall. See* **8656.**

642. Mitchell, Domhnall.   Measures of possibility: Emily Dickinson's manuscripts. *See* **10797.**

643. Mitchell, Paul.   Reading (and) the late poems of Sylvia Plath. *See* **18826.**

644. Monteiro, George.   An Emerson letter re-edited. *See* **10987.**

645. Mooney, Rodney.   Journey through *A Wrinkle in Time* and explore the world of 'sacred idleness'. *See* **17685.**

646. Moore, Helen.   Succeeding Stow: Anthony Munday and the 1618 *Survey of London. In* (pp. 99–108) **5746.**

647. MORGAN, ROSEMARIE.　Editing Hardy. *In* (pp. 90–110) **11140**.

648. MORTIMER, IAN.　The Henry Williamson archive at Exeter University Library. *See* **20230**.

649. NESVET, REBECCA.　'Have you thought of a story?': Galland's Scheherazade and Mary Shelley's 1831 *Frankenstein*. *See* **11981**.

650. NORBROOK, DAVID.　'But a copy': textual authority and gender in editions of *The Life of John Hutchinson*. *In* (pp. 109–30) **587**.

651. NORRIS, MARGOT.　*Finnegans Wake*. *In* (pp. 149–71) **17244**.

652. NOVAK, MAXIMILLIAN; FISHER, CARL.　Publishing history and modern editions. *In* (pp. 3–5) **8537**.

653. NOWLIN, STEELE.　Narratives of incest and incestuous narrative: memory, process, and the *Confessio Amantis*'s 'middel weie'. *See* **4800**.

654. OBENZINGER, HILTON.　Better dreams: political satire and Twain's final 'exploding' novel. *See* **12261**.

655. OBER, K. PATRICK.　The body in the cave: Dr Joseph McDowell's influence on Mark Twain. *See* **12262**.

656. O'DONNELL, DANIEL PAU.　O captain! My captain! Using technology to guide readers through an electronic edition. *See* **1124**.

657. O'KEEFFE, KATHERINE O'BRIEN; ORCHARD, ANDY (eds).　Latin literature and English lore: studies in Anglo-Saxon literature for Michael Lapidge: vol. I. *See* **4220**.

658. —— ——　Latin literature and English lore: studies in Anglo-Saxon literature for Michael Lapidge: vol. II. *See* **4221**.

659. O'ROURKE, JASON; TAKAMIYA, TOSHIYUKI.　Two hitherto unrecorded fragments of the *Brut*. *See* **4719**.

660. ORTIZ, RICARDO.　Fables of (Cuban) exile: special periods and queer moments in Eduardo Machado's Floating Island plays. *See* **17993**.

661. OTT, MARK P.　Nick Adams at a windy cross roads: echoes of past and future fictions in Ernest Hemingway's *Che ti dice la patria*? *See* **16986**.

662. PAPAHAGI, ADRIAN.　*(Ge)wyrd*: emendations to three anonymous Old English homilies and saints' lives. *See* **4348**.

663. PARFECT, RALPH.　Robert Louis Stevenson's *The Clockmaker* and *The Scientific Ape*: two unpublished fables. *See* **12076**.

664. PARR, BRUCE.　The misfit male body in Adelaide theatre, 1959. *See* **13091**.

665. PEARSALL, DEREK.　John Stow and Thomas Speght as editors of Chaucer: a question of class. *In* (pp. 119–25) **5746**.

666. PERRET, XAVIER.　An annotated text of *The Hunting of the Cheviot*, with a French rendition. *See* **3575**.

667. PERRY, SEAMUS.　The little horror show. *See* **12510**.

668. PITTOCK, MURRAY G. H.　Sources and dates for the Jacobite song: II. *See* **3577**.

669. PLOWDEN, GEOFFREY.　Housman's blottings. *See* **17066**.

670. POLLNITZ, CHRISTOPHER.　The censorship and transmission of D. H. Lawrence's *Pansies*: the Home Office and the 'foul-mouthed fellow'. *See* **17623**.

671. —— Editing D. H. Lawrence's *Collected Poems*: the composite typescript and base-text. *See* **17624**.

672. POPE, JON C. The printing of 'this written book': G.T. and H.W.'s editorial disputes in *The Adventures of Master F.J. See* **5449**.

673. PRESTWICH, NATALIE K. Ghostly metaphysicality: a manuscript variant of Robert Herrick's *The Apparition. See* **7496**.

674. PURDON, JOHN JAMES. John Aubrey's 'discourse in paper'. *See* **7199**.

675. RAINEY, LAWRENCE. Eliot among the typists: writing *The Waste Land. See* **16296**.

676. RAVENSCROFT, ALISON. Recasting indigenous lives along the lines of Western desire: editing, autobiography, and the colonizing project. *See* **14631**.

677. RAY, MARTIN. The Bodleian manuscript of *Poems of the Past and the Present. See* **11154**.

678. REX, RICHARD. Thorpe's *Testament*: a conjectural emendation. *See* **4924**.

679. RICKS, CHRISTOPHER. Decisions and revisions in T. S. Eliot. *See* **16300**.

680. RIDDY, FELICITY. Text and self in *The Book of Margery Kempe. In* (pp. 435–57) **4460**.

681. ROBERTSON, ELIZABETH; SHEPHERD, STEPHEN H. A. (eds). *Piers Plowman*: the Donaldson translation, select authoritative Middle English text, sources and backgrounds, criticism. *See* **4857**.

682. ROBERTSON, IAN. Wry aspersions in the *Rye. See* **10124**.

683. ROBINSON, FRED C. *Mise en page* in Old English manuscripts and printed texts. *In* (pp. 363–75) **4221**.

684. ROBINSON, PETER. The identification and use of authorial variants in the Miller's Tale. *See* **5026**.

685. ROCHER, ROSANE. Sir William Jones as a satirist: an ethic epistle to the Second Earl Spencer. *See* **8782**.

686. ROWLEY, SHARON M. 'A *wese\n/dan nacodnisse and þa ecan þistru*': language and mortality in the homily for Doomsday in Cambridge, Corpus Christi College MS 41. *See* **4349**.

687. RUDICK, MICHAEL. Editing Ralegh's poems historically. *In* (pp. 133–42) **587**.

688. RUDMAN, JOSEPH. Unediting, de-editing, and editing in non-traditional authorship attribution studies: with an emphasis on the canon of Daniel Defoe. *See* **8542**.

689. RUMBOLD, VALERIE; MCGEARY, THOMAS. *Folly*, session poems, and the preparations for Pope's *Dunciads. See* **8626**.

690. RUTKOWSKA, HANNA. Selected orthographic features in English editions of the *Book of Good Maners* (1487–1507). *See* **4673**.

691. SAJÉ, NATASHA. Dynamic design: the structure of books of poems. *See* **20938**.

692. SAKAMOTO, TADANOBU. A new relation between the narrator and the reader in *Jacob's Room. See* **20413**.

693. SÁNCHEZ MARTÍ, JORDI.   Wynkyn de Worde's editions of *Ipomydon*: a reassessment of the evidence. *See* **4573.**

694. SAUER, MICHELLE M.   The legend of St Juliana from Lambeth MS 72. *See* **4688.**

695. SCHAEFER, MICHAEL.   Stephen Crane in the time of shock and awe: teaching *The Red Badge of Courage* during the Iraq War. *See* **10584.**

696. SCHARNHORST, GARY.   Nabokov and Bret Harte: an overlooked allusion in *Lolita*. *See* **18467.**

697. SCHLICKE, PAUL.   Revisions to *Sketches by Boz*. *See* **10738.**

698. SCHMIDT, A. V. C.   *Ars* or *scientia*? Reflections on editing *Piers Plowman*. *See* **4859.**

699. SCHNEIDER, ERIK.   Towards *Ulysses*: some unpublished Joyce documents from Trieste. *See* **17336.**

700. SCHWAMB, SARA.   Introduction to Lambeth MS 546, fols 1r–7r: *The Fifteen Places Mary Visited after Christ's Ascension*. *See* **4687.**

701. SCRAGG, DONALD.   A late Old English Harrowing of Hell homily from Worcester and Blickling Homily VII. *In* (pp. 197–211) **4221.**

702. SEYMOUR, M. C.   Chaucer's *Book of the Duchess*: a proposal. *See* **4976.**

703. SHAW, JOHN.   *Luriana, Lurilee* revisited: I, *A Garden Song*: Leonard Woolf's manuscript copy: the 'right version' of the poem. *See* **10962.**

704. SHIH, ELIZABETH A.; KENNEY, SUSAN M.   Editing the palimpsestic text: the case of Virginia Woolf's *A Sketch of the Past*. *See* **20421.**

705. SHIPPEY, TOM.   The Merov(ich)ingian again: *dramatio memoriae* and the *usus scholarum*. *In* (pp. 389–406) **4220.**

706. SHOWALTER, ELAINE; SHOWALTER, ENGLISH.   Every single one matters. *See* **10577.**

707. SIEMENS, R. G.   'What two crownes shall they be?': 'lower' criticism, 'higher' criticism, and the impact of the electronic scholarly edition. *In* (pp. 37–46) **587.**

708. SMITH, NICHOLAS D.   An annotated copy of the third Hawkins edition of Izaak Walton's *The Complete Angler*. *See* **7892.**

709. STAUFFER, ANDREW M.   Dante Gabriel Rossetti and the burdens of Nineveh. *See* **11878.**

710. STEGGLE, MATTHEW, *et al.*   Jonson and his era: overviews of modern research. *See* **7586.**

711. STEINBERG, ERWIN R.; HALLSTEIN, CHRISTIAN W.   Probing silences in Joyce's *Ulysses* and the question of authorial intention. *See* **17341.**

712. STEINER, EMILY.   Lollardy and the legal document. *In* (pp. 155–74) **4482.**

713. STEVENSON, KAY GILLILAND.   Beyond 'no end': the shape of *Paradise Lost*, x. *See* **7763.**

714. STEVENSON, LUCY.   Two drafts of an unpublished story by Dorothy Edwards. *See* **16231.**

715. STOCK, RANDALL.   The trail of the semi-solitary manuscript. *See* **10870.**

716. STRINGER, GARY A.   Words, artifacts, and the editing of Donne's *Elegies*. *In* (pp. 13–26) **587.**

717. SUAREZ, MICHAEL F. A crisis in English public life: the Popish Plot, *Naboth's Vineyard* (1679), and mock-biblical satire's exemplary redress. *See* **7308**.

718. SUTHERLAND, KATHRYN. Chronology of composition and publication. *In* (pp. 12–22) **10060**.

719. —— Jane Austen's textual lives: from Aeschylus to Bollywood. *See* **10057**.

720. SWAN, JESSE G. Towards a textual history of the 1680 folio *The History of the Life, Reign and Death of Edward II* (attributed to Elizabeth Cary, Lady Falkland): understanding the collateral 1680 octavo *The History of the Most Unfortunate Prince*. *In* (pp. 177–90) **587**.

721. SZARMACH, PAUL E. Alfred's *Soliloquies* in London, BL, Cotton Tiberius A.iii (art. 9g, fols 50v–51v). *In* (pp. 153–79) **4221**.

722. TANSELLE, G. THOMAS. The prospect for textual criticism. Raritan (25:1) 2005, 137–46.

723. —— Textual criticism since Greg: a chronicle, 1950–2000. Charlottesville: Bibliographical Soc. of the Univ. of Virginia, 2005. pp. xiii, 373.

724. TEBBETTS, TERRELL. *Sanctuary*, marriage, and the status of women in 1920s America. *See* **16449**.

725. THOMPSON, CHRIS. Voicing Joyce: crossmess parzels from Cage to Beuys. *See* **17345**.

726. THOMPSON, JOHN J. Patch and repair and making do in manuscripts and texts associated with John Stow. *In* (pp. 353–61) **4419**.

727. TINKLER-VILLANI, VALERIA. Victorian Shelley: perspectives on a Romantic poet. *In* (pp. 89–104) **9237**.

728. TOKUNAGA, SATOKO. Early English printing and the hands of compositors. *See* **5036**.

729. TULLOCH, GRAHAM. Writing 'by advice': *Ivanhoe* and *The Three Perils of Man*. *See* **11946**.

730. UPTON, LEE. 'I / Have a self to recover': the restored *Ariel*. *See* **18838**.

731. UTARD, JULIETTE. Collecting oneself: the late poetry of Wallace Stevens. *See* **19688**.

732. VAN HULLE, DIRK. Textual awareness: a genetic study of late manuscripts by Joyce, Proust, and Mann. *See* **17350**.

733. VAN REENEN, PIETER; DEN HOLLANDER, AUGUST A.; VAN MULKEN, MARGOT (eds). Studies in stemmatology II. Amsterdam; Philadelphia, PA: Benjamins, 2004. pp. xii, 312.

734. VANWINKLE, MATTHEW. Fluttering on the grate: revision in *Frost at Midnight*. *See* **10530**.

735. VÁZQUEZ, NILA. The need for 're-editing' *Gamelyn*. *See* **4563**.

736. WAKELIN, DANIEL. Scholarly scribes and the creation of *Knyghthode and Bataile*. *See* **4629**.

737. WALKER, GREG. The textual archaeology of *The Plowman's Tale*. *In* (pp. 375–401) **4419**.

738. WARNER, LAWRENCE. John But and the other works that Will wrought (*Piers Plowman* A XII 101–2). *See* **4864**.

739. WATSON, JAMES G. Man writing: the Watson trilogy: Peter Matthiessen in archive. *See* **18146**.

740. WATSON, NICHOLAS. The making of *The Book of Margery Kempe*. *In* (pp. 395–434, 453–7) **4460**.

741. WILLIAMS, GEORGE WALTON. Addendum. *See* **7336**.

742. WILTSHIRE, IRENE. Speech in *Wuthering Heights*: Joseph's dialect and Charlotte's emendations. *See* **10209**.

743. WINNINGTON, G. PETER (introd.). Mervyn Peake's two radio plays for Christmas. *See* **18755**.

744. WOLFE, HEATHER. A family affair: the life and letters of Elizabeth Cary, Lady Falkland. *In* (pp. 97–108) **587**.

745. WORTHEN, JOHN. 'Wild turkeys': some versions of America by D. H. Lawrence. *See* **17637**.

746. ZIOLKOWSKI, JAN M. Metaphilology. *See* **15064**.

HISTORY OF PUBLISHING AND BOOKSELLING

747. ANON. For as long as we read: essays in honor of Ivan Dee. Chicago, IL: Dee, 2005. pp. xiv, 403.

748. —— The persistence of folly: 40 years of Gnomon Press: an interview with Jonathan Greene. AppalJ (32:4) 2005, 442–57.

749. —— The Stationers' Company. BC (52:3) 2003, 295–316 (review-article).

750. —— The title-page. *See* **139**.

751. ABEL, JONATHAN E. Canon and censor: how war wounds bodies of writing. *See* **19876**.

752. ADKINS, KEITH. Orger and Meryon: booksellers to the colony. BSANZB (28:1/2) 2004, 9–16.

753. AITKEN, KELLEY; GOYETTE, SUE; SCOTT, BARBARA (eds). First writes. Banff, Alta: Banff Centre Press, 2005. pp. viii, 149.

754. AMORY, HUGH. Bibliography and the book trades: studies in the print culture of early New England. Ed. by David D. Hall. Philadelphia: Pennsylvania UP, 2004. pp. ix, 174. (Material texts.) Rev. by William J. Scheick in SCN (63:3/4) 2005, 169–71; by Lisa M. Gordis in Book (65) 2005, 2–3.

755. ANDERSON, KATHARINE. Almanacs and the profits of natural knowledge. *In* (pp. 97–111) **1226**.

756. ARMSTRONG, CATHERINE. The bookseller and the pedlar: the spread of knowledge of the New World in early modern England, 1580–1640. *In* (pp. 15–29) **880**.

757. ARNER, ROBERT D. Textual transmission and the transformation of texts: on the dialogic margins of Dorothy Parker's *The Waltz*. *In* (pp. 86–113) **18738**.

758. ASTINGTON, JOHN H. John Rhodes: draper, bookseller and man of the theatre. *See* **6968**.

759. BAINES, PHIL. Penguin by design: a cover story, 1935–2005. *See* **141**.

760. BARKER, NICOLAS.   Notes on the origins of the second-hand book trade. BC (52:3) 2003, 356–70.

761. BARNHISEL, GREGORY.   James Laughlin, New Directions, and the remaking of Ezra Pound. See 17589.

762. BARRETT, SUSAN.   'What I say will not be understood': intertextuality as a subversive force in Nadine Gordimer's Burger's Daughter. See 16750.

763. BASSETT, TROY J.   Circulating morals: George Moore's attack on late Victorian literary censorship. See 18300.

764. BAUMAN, SUSAN R.   In the market for fame: the Victorian publication history of the Brontë poems. See 10214.

765. BEAVAN, IAIN.   John Murray, Richard Griffin and Oliver & Boyd: some supplementary observations. In (pp. 147–51) 880.

766. BEETHAM, MARGARET.   Of recipe books and reading in the nineteenth century: Mrs Beeton and her cultural consequences. In (pp. 15–30) 9257.

767. BELL, MAUREEN.   Offensive behaviour in the English book trade, 1641–1700. In (pp. 61–79) 937.

768. BENEDICT, BARBARA M.   Readers, writers, reviewers, and the professionalization of literature. In (pp. 3–23) 8014.

769. BERRY, HELEN.   Crimes of conscience: the last will and testament of John Dunton. In (pp. 81–101) 937.

770. BLAYNEY, PETER W. M.   The alleged popularity of playbooks. ShQ (56:1) 2005, 33–50.

771. BLOOM, LYNN Z.   Once more to the essay canon. In (pp. 90–111) 3749.

772. BOFFEY, JULIA.   Chaucer's Fortune in the 1530s: some sixteenth-century recycling. In (pp. 53–64) 4419.

773. ——   John Mychell and the printing of Lydgate in the 1530s. See 4869.

774. BOHAN, EDMUND.   The house of Reed 1907–1983: great days in New Zealand publishing. Christchurch, New Zealand: Canterbury UP, 2005. pp. 311, (plates) 8.

775. BORO, JOYCE.   Lord Berners and his books: a new survey. See 5388.

776. BOTTIGHEIMER, RUTH B.   The book on the bookseller's shelf and the book in the English child's hand. In (pp. 3–28) 8171.

777. BOYER, PAUL S.   Purity in print: book censorship in America from the Gilded Age to the computer age. (Bibl. 2004, 757.) Rev. by Rebecca Knuth in LQ (74:4) 2004, 475–7.

778. BRACK, O. M., JR; CARLILE, SUSAN.   Samuel Johnson's contributions to Charlotte Lennox's The Female Quixote. See 8788.

779. BRAITHWAITE, HELEN.   Romanticism, publishing, and Dissent: Joseph Johnson and the cause of liberty. (Bibl. 2004, 758.) Rev. by Robert Morrison in ERR (16:1) 2005, 111–15.

780. BRAYMAN HACKEL, HEIDI.   Reading material in early modern England: print, gender, and literacy. Cambridge; New York: CUP, 2005. pp. xii, 322. Rev. by Maureen Bell in TLS, 18 Nov. 2005, 32; by Cathy Conder in WS (34:7) 2005, 611–15.

781. BRENNAN, GILLIAN E.   Patriotism, power and print: national consciousness in Tudor England. (Bibl. 2004, 759.) Rev. by Rudolph P. Almasy in SRASP (28) 2005, 110–11.

782. BROUILLETTE, SARAH.   Authorship as crisis in Salman Rushdie's *Fury*. See **19264**.

783. BROWN, CANDY GUNTHER.   The Word in the world: evangelical writing, publishing, and reading in America, 1789–1880. (Bibl. 2004, 762.) Rev. by Michael Van Dyke in CSR (34:3) 2005, 401–2; by Richard D. Brown in JAH (91:4) 2005, 1456; by Susanna Ashton in SHARP (14:1/2) 2005, 11–12; by Cathy Conder in WS (34:7) 2005, 611–15; by Beth Barton Schweiger in JSH (71:2) 2005, 432–3.

784. BROWN, STEPHEN.   James Tytler's misadventures in the late eighteenth-century Edinburgh book trade. *In* (pp. 47–63) **880**.

785. BURNS, WILLIAM E.   Astrology and politics in seventeenth-century England: King James II and the almanac men. SevC (20:2) 2005, 242–53.

786. CAPONI, PAOLO.   La commercializzazione di *Lolita*: sulla circolazione dei testi nell'era del mercato globale. See **18450**.

787. CARPENTER, ANDREW.   A *Tale of a Tub* as an Irish text. See **9052**.

788. CARPENTER, MARY WILSON.   Imperial Bibles, domestic bodies: women, sexuality, and religion in the Victorian market. See **9211**.

789. CESERANI, GIOVANNA.   Narrative, interpretation, and plagiarism in Mr Robertson's 1778 *History of Ancient Greece*. See **8222**.

790. CHAPMAN, WAYNE K.   Yeats's dislocated Rebellion poems and the Great War: the case of *The Wild Swans at Coole* and *Michael Robartes and the Dancer*. See **20485**.

791. CIRILLO, NANCY.   Anthologizing the Caribbean; or, Squaring beaches, bananas, and Nobel laureates. *In* (pp. 222–46) **3749**.

792. CLARKE, ELIZABETH.   George Herbert and Cambridge scholars. See **7467**.

793. CLARKE, STUART N.   Now you see them, now you don't: Woolf's illustrated books. See **20328**.

794. CLEGG, CYNDIA SUSAN.   'The aucthor of this book': attributing authorship, 1580–1640. See **5113**.

795. COATES, ALAN, *et al*.   Catalogue of books printed in the fifteenth century now in the Bodleian Library. See **371**.

796. COLCLOUGH, STEPHEN.   'Designated in print as "Mr John Clare"': the annuals and the field of reading, 1827–1835. See **10434**.

797. —— Station to station: the LNWR and the emergence of the railway bookstall, 1840–1875. *In* (pp. 169–84) **880**.

798. COLLIGAN, COLETTE.   The unruly copies of Byron's *Don Juan*: harems, underground print culture, and the age of mechanical reproduction. See **10300**.

799. CONAWAY, CHARLES.   Shakespeare, molly house culture, and the eighteenth-century stage. See **6732**.

800. CONLEY, TIM.   *Samizdat* odyssey: *Ulysses* above the 42nd parallel. *In* (pp. 139–51) **12739**.

801. Cox, J. Randolph.   Premiums in dime novels. *See* **9533.**

802. Cramer, Janet M.   Cross purposes: publishing practices and social priorities of nineteenth-century US missionary women. *See* **9745.**

803. Cressy, David.   Book burning in Tudor and Stuart England. SixCJ (36:2) 2005, 359–74.

804. Damrosch, David.   From the Old World to the whole world. *In* (pp. 31–46) **3749.**

805. Davis, Caroline.   The politics of postcolonial publishing: Oxford University Press's Three Crowns series 1962–1976. BH (8) 2005, 227–44.

806. Dawson, P. M. S.   The making of Clare's *Poems Descriptive of Rural Life and Scenery* (1820). *See* **10435.**

807. Dean, Ann C.   Authorship, print, and public in Chesterfield's *Letters to His Son. See* **8470.**

808. Deazley, Ronan.   On the origin of the right to copy: charting the movement of copyright law in eighteenth-century Britain (1695–1775). Oxford: Hart, 2004. pp. xxvi, 261. Rev. by Adam Budd in TLS, 15 July 2005, 24.

809. de Bellaigue, Eric.   British book publishing as a business since the 1960s: selected essays. (Bibl. 2004, 783.) Rev. by Robin Baird-Smith in TLS, 26 Nov. 2004, 30; by Robert Denniston in Library (5:3) 2004, 333–4; by John Sutherland in LRB (27:9) 2005, 28–9.

810. Di Leo, Jeffrey R. (ed.).   On anthologies: politics and pedagogy. *See* **3749.**

811. Dougherty, Ian.   Books and boots: the story of New Zealand publisher, writer and long-distance walker Alfred Hamish Reed. Dunedin: Otago UP, 2005. pp. 252.

812. Driver, Martha W.   The image in print: book illustration in late medieval England and its sources. *See* **62.**

813. —— Stow's books bequeathed: some notes on William Browne (1591–*c.*1643) and Peter Le Neve (1661–1729). *In* (pp. 135–43) **5746.**

814. Duffy, Dennis.   The robber baron of Canadian literature. LRC (12:3) 2004, 20–2. (Louis Coues Page, US publisher.)

815. Edwards, A. S. G.   Manuscripts of the verse of Henry Howard, Earl of Surrey. *See* **5758.**

816. Edwards, Brendan Frederick R.   Paper talk: a history of libraries, print culture, and aboriginal peoples in Canada before 1960. *See* **383.**

817. Eells, Emily.   The mystery of *Kitty Bell*: a possible solution? *See* **10158.**

818. Emblidge, David M.   City Lights Bookstore: 'a finger in the dike'. PubRQ (21:4) 2005, 30–9.

819. English, James F.   The economy of prestige: prizes, awards, and the circulation of cultural value. Cambridge, MA; London: Harvard UP, 2005. pp. xii, 409.

820. Epp, Michael.   Full contact: Robert McAlmon, Gertrude Stein, and Modernist book making. *See* **19585.**

821. ERDAL, JENNIE. Ghosting. Edinburgh: Canongate, 2004. pp. xiii, 273. Rev. by Sarah Curtis in TLS, 5 Nov. 2004, 40; by Jenny Diski in LRB (26:21) 2004, 33–4.

822. EVERTON, MICHAEL. 'The would-be author and the real bookseller': Thomas Paine and eighteenth-century printing ethics. *See* **8853**.

823. FAFLIK, DAVID. The case for *Charles Anderson Chester*. *See* **11607**.

824. FARMER, ALAN B.; LESSER, ZACHARY. The popularity of playbooks revisited. ShQ (56:1) 2005, 1–32.

825. —— —— Structures of popularity in the early modern book trade. ShQ (56:2) 2005, 206–13.

826. FARR, CECILIA KONCHAR. Reading Oprah: how Oprah's Book Club changed the way America reads. *See* **14132**.

827. FERGUS, JAN. Biography. *In* (pp. 3–11) **10060**.

828. FISCHER, HEINZ-D.; FISCHER, ERIKA J. Complete bibliographical manual of books about the Pulitzer Prizes, 1935–2003: monographs and anthologies on the coveted awards. *See* **12675**.

829. FITZGERALD, LAUREN. The gothic villain and the vilification of the plagiarist: the case of *The Castle Spectre*. *See* **8794**.

830. FLANERY, PATRICK DENMAN. (Re-)marking Coetzee & Costello: *The* (textual) *Lives of Animals*. *See* **15828**.

831. FLEMING, PATRICIA LOCKHART; LAMONDE, YVAN (gen. eds). History of the book in Canada: vol. 1, Beginnings to 1840. Ed. by Patricia Lockhart Fleming, Giles Gallichan and Yvan Lamonde. Toronto; Buffalo, NY; London: Toronto UP, 2004. pp. xxx, 540. Rev. by Dean Irvine in DalR (85:3) 2005, 483–5.

832. —— —— History of the book in Canada: vol. 2, 1841–1918. Ed. by Yvan Lamonde, Patricia Lockhart Fleming, and Fiona A. Black. Toronto; Buffalo, NY; London: Toronto UP, 2004. pp. xxxiii, 659.

833. FOOT, MIRJAM M. 'A magnificent and bewildering variety': Irish bookbinding in the eighteenth century. *In* (pp. 206–36) **30**.

834. FORD-SMITH, ALICE. Confessions: the Midlands execution broadside trade. *In* (pp. 153–67) **880**.

835. FORKER, CHARLES R. How did Shakespeare come by his books? *See* **5935**.

836. FREEMAN, JAN. The Paris Press publication of *On Being Ill*. *See* **20351**.

837. FREEMAN, JANET ING. 'Lyes' and 'hyghe treason' in 1570: John Stow annotates Grafton's *Abridgement of the Chronicles*. *See* **5744**.

838. FYFE, AILEEN. Commerce and philanthropy: the Religious Tract Society and the business of publishing. JVC (9:2) 2004, 164–88.

839. —— Periodicals and book series: complementary aspects of a publisher's mission. *In* (pp. 71–82) **1226**.

840. —— Science and salvation: evangelical popular science publishing in Victorian Britain. Chicago, IL; London: Chicago UP, 2004. pp. xiv, 325. Rev. by David Knight in SHARP (14:4) 2005, 14.

841. GADD, IAN; FERGUSON, MERAUD GRANT. 'For his paynes': John Stow and the Stationers. *In* (pp. 37–44) **5746**.

842. GALLOWAY, FRANCIS.   Notes on the usefulness of publishing statistics for a broader South African book history. ESA (47:1) 2004, 109–18.

843. GAMER, MICHAEL.   'Bell's poetics': *The Baviad*, the Della Cruscans, and the book of *The World*. *In* (pp. 31–53) **9305**.

844. GAMMON, SUSAN R.   Heroism reconsidered: negotiating autonomy in *St Nicholas* magazine (1873–1914). *In* (pp. 179–98) **8171**.

845. GARSIDE, PETER.   Hogg and the Blackwoodian novel. *See* **11271**.

846. GASSMAN, RICHARD.   The first American tourist guidebooks: authorship and the print culture of the 1820s. BH (8) 2005, 51–74.

847. GATES, SONDRA SMITH.   The edge of possibility: Susan Warner and the world of Sunday school fiction. *See* **12285**.

848. GEMMELL, NIKKI.   The identity trap. *See* **16658**.

849. GENZ, MARCELLA D.   A history of the Eragny Press, 1894–1914. (Bibl. 2004, 810.) Rev. by Paul W. Nash in PBSA (99:2) 2005, 327–8; by Jacquelynn Baas in Library (6:3) 2005, 354–6; by Colin Franklin in BC (54:2) 2005, 310–12.

850. GILLESPIE, ALEXANDRA.   Introduction. *In* (pp. 1–11) **5746**.

851. ——— Introduction: bibliography and early Tudor texts. *See* **13**.

852. ——— Poets, printers, and early English *Sammelbände*. HLQ (67:2) 2004, 189–214.

853. GILLESPIE, RAYMOND.   Reading Ireland: print, reading and social change in early modern Ireland. Manchester; New York: Manchester UP, 2005. pp. 222. (Politics, culture and society in early modern Britain.) Rev. by Sebastian Carter in TLS, 16 Sept. 2005, 28.

854. GILMOUR, IAN.   Out of bounds. LRB (27:2) 2005, 26–8 (review-article). (Romantic-period publishing and reading.)

855. GILSON, DAVID.   Later publishing history, with illustrations. *In* (pp. 121–59) **10060**.

856. GLADFELDER, HAL.   Obscenity, censorship, and the eighteenth-century novel: the case of John Cleland. *See* **8477**.

857. GOUWS, JOHN.   Book and text studies in Grahamstown. ESA (47:1) 2004, 119–24.

858. GRAHAM, TIM (comp.).   Penguin in print: a bibliography. Edinburgh: Penguin Collectors' Soc., 2003. pp. 112. Rev. by Richard W. Eiger in PubRQ (21:3) 2005, 93–4.

859. GRECO, ALBERT N.   A bibliography of books and journal articles on scholarly publishing. JSchP (37:1) 2005, 48–54.

860. ——— WHARTON, ROBERT M.; ESTELAMI, HOOMAN.   The changing market for university press books in the United States: 1997–2002. JSchP (36:4) 2005, 187–220.

861. GREENBERG, STEPHEN.   Plague, the printing press, and public health in seventeenth-century London. HLQ (67:4) 2004, 509–27.

862. GREENE, JODY.   The trouble with ownership: literary property and authorial liability in England, 1660–1730. *See* **6881**.

863. GRIFFIN, ROBERT J.   The text in motion: eighteenth-century *Roxanas*. *See* **8517**.

864. GRIFFITHS, JANE. Text and authority: John Stow's 1568 edition of Skelton's *Workes*. *In* (pp. 127–34) **5746**.

865. —— What's in a name? The transmission of 'John Skelton, Laureate' in manuscript and print. *See* **5668**.

866. GRIMES, KYLE. Verbal jujitsu: William Hone and the tactics of satirical conflict. *In* (pp. 173–84) **9305**.

867. GROSS, ROBERT A. Courtesies of the trade: an overview of American book history. Book (66/67) 2005, 6–10.

868. GROVIER, KELLY. The dumpling one. *See* **11290**.

869. GUPTA, SUMAN. In search of genius: T. S. Eliot as publisher. *See* **16272**.

870. HAGEMAN, ELIZABETH H. Treacherous accidents and the abominable printing of Katherine Philips's *1664 Poems*. *In* (pp. 85–95) **587**.

871. HAGLUND, DAVID. 'Puke or prude': Frost and Stevens in the literary market place of 1922. *See* **16604**.

872. HARROD, TANYA. A missing bird. TLS, 2 Sept. 2005, 8 (review-article). (Penguin Books.)

873. HARSH, CONSTANCE. The text of *Eve's Ransom*: insights from the *Illustrated London News* serialization. *See* **11073**.

874. HAWKINS, ANN R. Marketing gender and nationalism: Blessington's *Gems of Beauty*/*L'Écrin* and the mid-century book trade. *See* **10100**.

875. HAYNES, CHRISTINE. Reassessing 'genius' in studies of authorship: the state of the discipline. BH (8) 2005, 287–320.

876. HENEGHAN, THOMAS. Secrets behind the forbidden books. ANCW (192:4) 2005, 22–7.

877. HEYES, BOB. Selling John Clare: the poet in the marketplace. *See* **10439**.

878. HIATT, ALFRED. Stow, Grafton, and fifteenth-century historiography. *In* (pp. 45–55) **5746**.

879. HIGGINS, IAN. Remarks on *Cato's Letters*. *In* (pp. 127–46) **8091**.

880. HINKS, JOHN; ARMSTRONG, CATHERINE (eds). Printing places: locations of book production & distribution since 1500. New Castle, DE: Oak Knoll Press; London: British Library, 2005. pp. xiii, 208. (Print networks.)

881. HOAGWOOD, TERENCE ALLAN; LEDBETTER, KATHRYN. 'Colour'd shadows': contexts in publishing, printing, and reading nineteenth-century British women writers. *See* **9292**.

882. HOFMEYER, ISABEL. 'Spread far and wide over the surface of the earth': evangelical reading formations and the rise of a transnational public sphere – the case of the Cape Town Ladies' Bible Association. ESA (47:1) 2004, 17–29.

883. HOLLIS, CATHERINE W. Virginia Woolf's double signature. *See* **20366**.

884. HOLMAN, VALERIE. Carefully concealed connections: the Ministry of Information and British publishing, 1939–1946. BH (8) 2005, 197–226.

885. HOLT, PATRICIA. 'It's enough to drive a bloke mad': Norman Lindsay's art and literature. *See* **17834**.

886. HOMESTEAD, MELISSA J. American women authors and literary property, 1822–1869. *See* **9295**.

887. HOPKINS, RICHARD. Poppy Press. Amphora (130) 2003, 22–5.

888. HOUNSLOW, DAVID. 'Self-interested and evil-minded persons': the book-trade activities of Thomas Wilson, Robert Spence and Joseph Mawman of York and the Mozleys of Gainsborough. *In* (pp. 89–106) **880**.

889. HUGHES, LINDA K. Constructing fictions of authorship in George Eliot's *Middlemarch*, 1871–1872. *See* **10931**.

890. HUNTLEY-SMITH, JEN A. 'Such is change in California': James Mason Hutchings and the print metropolis, 1854–1862. PAAS (114:1) 2004, 35–85.

891. HUTNER, MARTIN; KELLY, JERRY. A century for the century: fine printed books from 1900 to 1999. *See* **165**.

892. HUTTON, CLARE (ed.). The Irish book in the twentieth century. Dublin; Portland, OR: Irish Academic Press, 2004. pp. ix, 211. Rev. by Sebastian Carter in TLS, 16 Sept. 2005, 28.

893. ISAAC, PETER. John Murray II and Oliver & Boyd, his Edinburgh agents, 1819–1835. *In* (pp. 131–46) **880**.

894. JACKSON, H. J. Romantic readers: the evidence of marginalia. *See* **9301**.

895. JACKSON, JEFFREY E. Elizabeth Gaskell and the dangerous edge of things: epigraphs in *North and South* and Victorian publishing practices. *See* **11044**.

896. JENKINSON, MATTHEW T. A new author for the 'observations' in *Rebels No Saints* (1661)? *See* **7124**.

897. JENSEN, KRISTIAN (ed.). Incunabula and their readers: printing, selling and using books in the fifteenth century. (Bibl. 2004, 844.) Rev. by Alexandra Barratt in RenSt (18:2) 2004, 331–4; by Paul Needham in PBSA (99:2) 2005, 329–33; by Margaret Lane Ford in BC (54:1) 2005, 139–41.

898. JUNG, SANDRO. David Mallet and Lord Bolingbroke. *See* **8819**.

899. KARELL, LINDA. The postmodern author on stage: *Fair Use* and Wallace Stegner. *See* **19576**.

900. KEISER, GEORGE R. Verse introductions to Middle English medical treatises. *See* **4703**.

901. KELLER, YVONNE. 'Was it right to love her brother's wife so passionately?': lesbian pulp novels and US lesbian identity, 1950–1965. *See* **14186**.

902. KELMAN, SUANNE. The glittering prizes: the struggle between merit and Mammon continues, ten years after the birth of the Giller. *See* **14188**.

903. KEYMER, THOMAS. Parliamentary printing, paper credit, and corporate fraud: a new episode in Richardson's early career. *See* **8943**.

904. —— SABOR, PETER. *Pamela* in the marketplace: literary controversy and print culture in eighteenth-century Britain and Ireland. *See* **8944**.

905. KILCUP, KAREN L. The poetry and prose of recovery work. *In* (pp. 112–38) **3749**.

906. KRUMMEL, DONALD W. Early American imprint bibliography and its stories: an introductory course in bibliographical civics. LibC (40:3) 2005, 239–50.

907. LANDAU, LEYA. Street sisters. *See* **7521**.

908. LAROCQUE-POIRIER, JOANNE. John Buchan's legacy: the Governor-General's Literary Awards. *See* **15609**.

909. LECKIE, BARBARA. The simple case of adultery. *See* **17299**.

910. LESSER, ZACHARY.   Renaissance drama and the politics of publication: readings in the English book trade. *See* **5271**.

911. LEWIS, JEREMY.   Penguin special: the life and times of Allen Lane. London: Penguin; New York: Viking, 2005. pp. xii, 484, (plates) 16. Rev. by John Sutherland in LRB (27:9) 2005, 28–9; by Tanya Harrod in TLS, 2 Sept. 2005, 8; by Michael Karwowski in ContRev (287:1677) 2005, 243–4.

912. LIVINGSTON, MEG POWERS.   *The Tragedy of Sir John Van Olden Barnavelt*: a re-examination of Fletcher and Massinger's sources. *See* **7447**.

913. MCCLEERY, ALISTAIR; FINKELSTEIN, DAVID.   Archie Turnbull and Edinburgh University Press. JSchP (37:1) 2005, 33–47.

914. MCCLUSKEY, PETER M.   Sir Edmond (*sic*) Tilney, *Sir Thomas More*, and the Netherlandic immigrant community. *See* **6709**.

915. MCDONALD, PETER D.   The politics of obscenity: *Lady Chatterley's Lover* and the apartheid State. *See* **17617**.

916. MCKAY, BARRY; HINKS, JOHN; BELL, MAUREEN (eds).   Light on the book trade: essays in honour of Peter Isaac. (Bibl. 2004, 884.) Rev. by Julian Roberts in Library (6:2) 2005, 202–4; by John R. Turner in SHARP (14:1/2) 2005, 17.

917. MCKITTERICK, DAVID.   A history of Cambridge University Press: vol. 3, New worlds for learning, 1873–1972. Cambridge; New York: CUP, 2004. pp. xxii, 513. Rev. by Willis G. Regier in JSchP (36:2) 2005, 123–5.

918. ——   'Not in *STC*': opportunities and challenges in the *ESTC*. Library (6:2) 2005, 178–94.

919. ——   Out of the cradle. *See* **424**.

920. ——   Print, manuscript, and the search for order, 1450–1830. (Bibl. 2004, 885.) Rev. by Freya Johnston in EC (54:4) 2004, 398–405; by Harold Love in MLQ (66:3) 2005, 396–9; by Dosia Reichardt in Parergon (22:2) 2005, 235–6.

921. MCLEOD, RANDALL.   Obliterature: reading a censored text of Donne's *To His Mistress Going to Bed. See* **7382**.

922. MACSKIMMING, ROY.   The perilous trade: publishing Canada's writers. Toronto: McClelland & Stewart, 2003. pp. viii, 464. Rev. by Peter Mitham in Amphora (136) 2004, 33–4; by Sandra Martin in LRC (12:5) 2004, 16–17.

923. MAGNUSON, PAUL.   The Lake School: Wordsworth and Coleridge. *In* (pp. 227–43) **8014**.

924. MALONE, RICHARD.   Etiquette in Pandemonium: Grant Richards and the early American editions of A. E. Housman's *A Shropshire Lad. See* **17062**.

925. MANN, ALASTAIR J.   'Some property is theft': copyright law and illegal activity in early modern Scotland. *In* (pp. 31–60) **937**.

926. ——   A spirit of literature – Melville, Baillie, Wodrow, and a cast of thousands: the clergy in Scotland's long Renaissance. RenSt (18:1) 2004, 90–108.

927. MASON, NICHOLAS.   'The quack has become God': puffery, print, and the 'death' of literature in Romantic-era Britain. *See* **1271**.

928. MAY, WILLIAM.   *The Choosers*: posthumous collections of Stevie Smith's poetry. *See* **19492**.

929. MAYHEW, ROBERT.   *Anthem*: '38 & '46. *In* (pp. 28–54) **19013**.

930. MELNIKOFF, KIRK. Jones's pen and Marlowe's socks: Richard Jones, print culture, and the beginnings of English dramatic literature. *See* **5545**.

931. MENNELL, BARBARA. The durable past. ILS (25:1) 2005, 12–13.

932. MITCHELL, SALLY. Victorian 'companions': forward to the past? *See* **21091**.

933. MORGAN, SPEER; SOWIENSKI, RICHARD; SOMERVILLE, KRISTINE (introds). Ray Bradbury's letters to Rupert Hart-Davis. *See* **15556**.

934. MOUNT, NICK. The expatriate origins of Canadian literature. *In* (pp. 237–55) **9191**.

935. —— When Canadian literature moved to New York. *See* **9359**.

936. MURPHY, ANDREW. Shakespeare goes to Scotland: a brief history of Scottish editions. *In* (pp. 157–71) **6561**.

937. MYERS, ROBIN; HARRIS, MICHAEL; MANDELBROTE, GILES (eds). Against the law: crime, sharp practice, and the control of print. New Castle, DE: Oak Knoll Press; London: British Library, 2004. pp. xv, 184. (Publishing pathways.) Rev. by Barbara Ryan in SHARP (14:3) 2005, 8.

938. —— —— —— The London book trade: topographies of print in the metropolis from the sixteenth century. (Bibl. 2004, 911.) Rev. by Laurence Worms in BC (54:1) 2005, 147–9.

939. NASH, ANDREW. *At the Gates*: new commentaries on a lost text by D. H. Lawrence. *See* **17619**.

940. —— The publication of Catherine Carswell's novels. *See* **15703**.

941. —— Walter Besant's *All Sorts and Conditions of Men* and Robert Louis Stevenson's *The Strange Case of Dr Jekyll and Mr Hyde*. *See* **10093**.

942. —— (ed.). The culture of collected editions. (Bibl. 2004, 913.) Rev. by Seth Lerer in MLR (100:2) 2005, 475–7.

943. NELSON, CARY. The economic challenges to anthologies. *In* (pp. 170–85) **3749**.

944. NELSON, JAMES G. 'A delightful companion': Leonard Smithers and the Decadents. *See* **12404**.

945. NICHOLAS, DAVID, *et al.* The Big Deal – ten years on. *See* **1123**.

946. NORD, DAVID PAUL. Faith in reading: religious publishing and the birth of mass media in America. (Bibl. 2004, 918.) Rev. by Meredith L. McGill in JAH (92:2) 2005, 608–9; by Jennifer Harris in SHARP (14:4) 2005, 15–16; by Candy Gunther Brown in JR (85:4) 2005, 707–8; by John P. Ferré in JoH (30:4) 2005, 220.

947. NOVAK, MAXIMILLIAN; FISHER, CARL. Publishing history and modern editions. *In* (pp. 3–5) **8537**.

948. O'CALLAGHAN, MICHELLE. Taking liberties: George Wither's *A Satyre*, libel and the law. *In* (pp. 146–69) **5196**.

949. Ó DRISCEOIL, DONAL. 'The best banned in the land': censorship and Irish writing since 1950. *See* **12842**.

950. O'NEILL, ANGELINE. Distinguishing the map from the territory. *In* (pp. 247–63) **3749**.

951. PANOFSKY, RUTH.   Barometers of change: Presidents Hugh Eayrs and John Gray of the Macmillan Company of Canada. JCanStud (37:4) 2002/03, 92–111.

952. PARFECT, RALPH.   Robert Louis Stevenson's *The Clockmaker* and *The Scientific Ape*: two unpublished fables. See **12076**.

953. PARKER, ALLENE M.   Of death, life, and virtue in Steinbeck's *Of Mice and Men* and *The Grapes of Wrath*. *In* (pp. 73–85) **19612**.

954. PARKER, EMMA.   Introduction: 'the proper stuff of fiction': defending the domestic, reappraising the parochial. See **14245**.

955. PASSET, JOANNE E.   Reading *Hilda's Home*: gender, print culture, and the dissemination of utopian thought in late nineteenth-century America. See **11095**.

956. PATTERSON, PAUL J.   Reforming Chaucer: margins and religion in an apocryphal *Canterbury Tale*. See **4643**.

957. PAYNE, DAVID.   The reenchantment of nineteenth-century fiction: Dickens, Thackeray, George Eliot, and serialization. See **10730**.

958. PEARSALL, DEREK.   John Stow and Thomas Speght as editors of Chaucer: a question of class. *In* (pp. 119–25) **5746**.

959. PENNY, SARAH.   A literary *vox pop*. See **14251**.

960. PETERS, KATE.   Print culture and the early Quakers. See **7142**.

961. PHARAND, MICHEL W.   Billions of letters. See **19412**.

962. PIPES, DANIEL.   The Rushdie affair: the novel, the Ayatollah, and the West. Postscript by Konraad Elst. See **19274**.

963. POLLNITZ, CHRISTOPHER.   The censorship and transmission of D. H. Lawrence's *Pansies*: the Home Office and the 'foul-mouthed fellow'. See **17623**.

964. POPE, JON C.   The printing of 'this written book': G.T. and H.W.'s editorial disputes in *The Adventures of Master F.J.* See **5449**.

965. POTTER, FRANZ J.   The history of gothic publishing, 1800–1835: exhuming the trade. Basingstoke; New York: Palgrave Macmillan, 2005. pp. xii, 213.

966. POTTER, RACHEL.   'Can my daughter of 18 read this book?': *Ulysses* and obscenity. See **17328**.

967. PRICE, DAVID.   George on the Net. See **10119**.

968. PRICHARD, MAUREEN.   Christine Macgregor's illustrated private press books. BSANZB (27:1/2) 2003, 34–47.

969. QUIGLEY, THOMAS.   Of frigates, wings, and maple leaves: a centre for the book in Canada. Amphora (134) 2004, 22–5.

970. RALSTON, RICHARD E.   Publishing *Anthem*. *In* (pp. 24–7) **19013**.

971. RANSOME, JOYCE.   Monotessaron: the harmonies of Little Gidding. See **7444**.

972. RAVEN, JAMES.   Book production. *In* (pp. 194–203) **10060**.

973. RAYMOND, JOAD.   'The language of the public': print, politics, and the book trade in 1614. *In* (pp. 95–112) **6860**.

974. READ, DAPHNE.   From Clinton to Bush, literacy to war: the political contexts of Oprah's Book Club. PubRQ (21:4) 2005, 40–9.

975. REDSHAW, THOMAS DILLON.   By James Liddy: a descriptive checklist, 1962–2004. See **17826**.

976. REID, CHAD. 'Widely read by American patriots': the *New-York Weekly Journal* and the influence of *Cato's Letters* on Colonial America. *In* (pp. 109–42) **1244**.

977. RIDLER, ANN. Censorship and *The Sleeping Bard*. *See* **10120**.

978. RIPP, JOSEPH. Middle America meets Middle-earth: American discussion and readership of J. R. R. Tolkien's *The Lord of the Rings*, 1965–1969. *See* **19842**.

979. ROBERTSON, RANDY. Censors of the mind: Samuel Pepys and the Restoration licensers. *See* **7814**.

980. —— Swift's *Leviathan* and the end of licensing. *See* **9086**.

981. ROLDÁN VERA, EUGENIA. The British book trade and Spanish American independence: education and knowledge transmission in transcontinental perspective. (Bibl. 2004, 949.) Rev. by Joseph Gwara in PBSA (99:2) 2005, 342–4.

982. RUSSELL, GILLIAN. Theatrical culture. *In* (pp. 100–18) **8014**.

983. RUTKOWSKA, HANNA. Selected orthographic features in English editions of the *Book of Good Maners* (1487–1507). *See* **4673**.

984. RUWE, DONELLE R. Satirical birds and natural bugs: J. Harris' chapbooks and the aesthetic of children's literature. *In* (pp. 115–37) **9305**.

985. SABOR, PETER. Richardson, Henry Fielding, and Sarah Fielding. *In* (pp. 139–56) **8014**.

986. SAINT-AMOUR, PAUL K. The copywrights: intellectual property and the literary imagination. (Bibl. 2004, 955.) Rev. by Robert Spoo in JJLS (19:1) 2005, 10–11.

987. —— Ride 'em cowpoyride: literary property metadiscourse in *Ulysses*. *In* (pp. 229–54) **17274**.

988. SÁNCHEZ MARTÍ, JORDI. Wynkyn de Worde's editions of *Ipomydon*: a reassessment of the evidence. *See* **4573**.

989. SCHMIDT, ARNOLD A. Bligh, Christian, Murray, and Napoleon: Byronic mutiny from London to the South Seas. *See* **10333**.

990. SEYMOUR, M. C. Chaucer's *Book of the Duchess*: a proposal. *See* **4976**.

991. SHRANK, CATHY. 'These fewe scribbled rules': representing scribal intimacy in early modern print. *See* **5349**.

992. SONODA, AKIKO. Coleridge's later poetry and the rise of literary annuals. *See* **10523**.

993. SPEDDING, PATRICK. A note on the ornament usage of Henry Woodfall. *See* **180**.

994. SPIERS, JOHN. For flag and fortune? The colonial edition, 1843–1972: a Gissing perspective. *See* **11084**.

995. STAVES, SUSAN. Gendering texts: 'the abuse of title pages': men writing as women. *In* (pp. 162–82) **6958**.

996. STEGGLE, MATTHEW. Richard Head's *The Floating Island* (1673) plagiarizes Thomas Powell. *See* **7462**.

997. —— et al. Jonson and his era: overviews of modern research. *See* **7586**.

998. STILLMAN, TERRY A.   What a difference fifty years makes: used book prices skyrocket since 1953. Amphora (133) 2003, 20–4.

999. STOKER, DAVID.   Norwich 'publishing' in the seventeenth century. *In* (pp. 31–46) **880.**

1000. SUTHERLAND, JOHN.   Wolfish. LRB (27:9) 2005, 28–9 (review-article). (British publishing.)

1001. SUTHERLAND, KATHRYN.   Chronology of composition and publication. *In* (pp. 12–22) **10060.**

1002. SWAN, JESSE G.   Towards a textual history of the 1680 folio *The History of the Life, Reign and Death of Edward II* (attributed to Elizabeth Cary, Lady Falkland): understanding the collateral 1680 octavo *The History of the Most Unfortunate Prince. In* (pp. 177–90) **587.**

1003. TAYLOR, HENRY.   The publishing legacy of Leslie E. Phillabaum. HC (42:2) 2005, 1–13. (Louisiana State Univ. Press.)

1004. THOMAS, SUE.   *Pringle v. Cadell* and *Wood v. Pringle*: the libel cases over *The History of Mary Prince. See* **9831.**

1005. THOMPSON, JOHN J.   Patch and repair and making do in manuscripts and texts associated with John Stow. *In* (pp. 353–61) **4419.**

1006. TIGHE, CARL.   Writing and responsibility. *See* **12947.**

1007. TOPHAM, JONATHAN R.   John Limbird, Thomas Byerley, and the production of cheap periodicals in the 1820s. BH (8) 2005, 75–106.

1008. TOTTEN, GARY.   Dreiser and the writing market: new letters on the publication history of *Jennie Gerhardt. See* **16150.**

1009. TOWERS, S. MUTCHOW.   Control of religious printing in early Stuart England. (Bibl. 2004, 992.) Rev. by David Woolf in SixCJ (36:1) 2005, 176–8.

1010. TOWHEED, SHAFQUAT.   Rudyard Kipling's literary property, international copyright law and *The Naulahka. See* **17491.**

1011. TURNER, JAMES GRANTHAM.   Libertine literature forty years on: part 1, From Aretino to *The School of Venus. See* **6952.**

1012. VICKERS, DAVID.   Gwas Gregynog Press. Amphora (136) 2004, 4–5.

1013. WAKELY, MARIA; REES, GRAHAM.   Folios fit for a king: James I, John Bill, and the King's Printers, 1616–1620. HLQ (68:3) 2005, 467–95.

1014. WALKER, GREG.   The textual archaeology of *The Plowman's Tale. In* (pp. 375–401) **4419.**

1015. WATERS, LINDSAY.   Enemies of promise: publishing, perishing, and the eclipse of scholarship. Chicago, IL: Prickly Paradigm Press, 2004. pp. 89. (Paradigm, 15.) Rev. by William W. Savage, Jr, in JSchP (36:2) 2005, 120–2.

1016. WATRY, MAUREEN (ed.).   The Vale Press: Charles Ricketts, a publisher in earnest. (Bibl. 2004, 1001.) Rev. by Sebastian Carter in TLS, 18 Feb. 2005, 33.

1017. WEEDON, ALEXIS.   Victorian publishing: the economics of book production for a mass market, 1836–1916. (Bibl. 2004, 1002.) Rev. by David Finkelstein in LibH (21:1) 2005, 71–2; by Solveig C. Robinson in VPR (38:3) 2005, 332–3; by Michael Winship in NQ (52:4) 2005, 548–9.

1018. WEIDENFELD, GEORGE.   The imperishable matrix: past, present, and future of books. PubRQ (20:4) 2005, 47–51.

1019. WEINTRAUB, STANLEY.   Reggie Turner, forgotten Edwardian novelist. *See* **19881.**

1020. WHITEHEAD, ANGUS.   A reference to William Blake and James Parker, printsellers, in *Bailey's British Directory* (1785). *See* **8397.**

1021. WIEGAND, WAYNE.   Collecting contested titles: the experience of five small public libraries in the rural Midwest, 1893–1956. *See* **480.**

1022. WILKINSON, CRYSTAL E.   Harvesting *Blackberries, Blackberries*: a Black woman's publishing tale. *In* (pp. 189–93) **14204.**

1023. WILSON, BEN.   The laughter of triumph: William Hone and the fight for the free press. *See* **11291.**

1024. WIRTÉN, EVA HEMMUNGS.   No trespassing: authorship, intellectual property rights, and the boundaries of globalization. Toronto; Buffalo, NY; London: Toronto UP, 2004. pp. xii, 224. (Studies in book and print culture.) Rev. by Lindsay Gledhill in SHARP (14:1/2) 2005, 20–1.

1025. WOODWARD, FRED M.   *Ad astra per aspera*: University Press of Kansas, 1946–2005. JSchP (36:2) 2005, 75–88.

1026. WU, DUNCAN.   Hazlitt's *Essay on the Principles of Human Action*: a bibliographical note. *In* (pp. xv–xviii) **11245.**

1027. WYNNE-TYSON, JON.   Finding the words: a publishing life. Norwich: Russell, 2004. pp. 318, (plates) 16. Rev. by David McKitterick in TLS, 27 May 2005, 27.

1028. YAMPBELL, CAT.   Judging a book by its cover: publishing trends in young adult literature. LU (29:3) 2005, 348–72.

1029. YU, PAULINE.   On synthetic technologies: the book, the university, the Internet. *See* **1142.**

1030. ZIEGLER, GEORGIANNA (comp.).   Elizabeth I: then and now. *See* **489.**

1031. ZIMBLER, JARAD.   Under local eyes: the South African publishing context of J. M. Coetzee's *Foe*. *See* **15843.**

CONTEMPORARY PUBLISHING AND BOOKSELLING

1032. BROWER, BRYAN.   Articles of chap. *See* **20910.**

1033. BUSH, ERWIN H.   The future of used bookselling: an observation. Amphora (134) 2004, 4–9.

1034. BUTLER, RICHARD J.; COWAN, BENJAMIN W.; NILSSON, SEBASTIAN.   From obscurity to bestseller: examining the impact of Oprah's Book Club selections. PubRQ (20:4) 2005, 23–34.

1035. COUSINS, JILL; NEYLON, EAMONN.   Information objects are hot, documents are not: the use of identifiers in online publishing. *See* **1105.**

1036. DARKO-AMPEM, KWASI.   A university press publishing consortium for Africa: lessons from academic libraries. JSchP (36:2) 2005, 89–114.

1037. FITZPATRICK, KATHLEEN.   From the crisis to the commons. CinJ (44:3) 2005, 92–5. (Crisis in academic publishing, especially Film Studies.)

1038. GANGI, JANE M.   Inclusive aesthetics and social justice: the vanguard of small, multicultural presses. CLAQ (30:3) 2005, 243–64.

1039. GILES, PAUL; ELLIS, R. J.   *E pluribus multitudinum*: the new world of journal publishing in American Studies. AmQ (57:4) 2005, 1033–78.

1040. GILL, KULDIP.   Barbarian Press. Amphora (137) 2004, 5–21.

1041. —— Frog Hollow Press, Victoria, B.C. Amphora (133) 2003, 13–18.

1042. —— Greenboathouse Books. Amphora (135) 2004, 9–16.

1043. GRAFF, GERALD; DI LEO, JEFFREY R.   Anthologies, literary theory, and the teaching of literature. *In* (pp. 279–97) **3749.**

1044. HOPKINS, RICHARD.   Book signing: the view from both sides of the table. *See* **404.**

1045. KINDSETH, TIM.   The wide, wide world of chapbooks. *See* **14430.**

1046. LOOTENS, TRICIA.   Between treasuries and the Web: compendious Victorian poetry anthologies in transition. *See* **9702.**

1047. MCLAUGHLIN, ROBERT L.   Anthologizing contemporary literature. *In* (pp. 141–54) **3749.**

1048. MAZZA, CRIS.   Finding the chic in lit. *In* (pp. 155–69) **3749.**

1049. MILLER, WAYNE.   Chapbooks: democratic ephemera. *See* **14457.**

1050. MITCHNER, LESLIE.   'Oy vey! Is it a crisis or is it just me?' *See* **13315.**

1051. NICHOLAS, DAVID, *et al.*   In their very own words: authors and scholarly journal publishing. *See* **1287.**

1052. PETRO, PATRICE.   Whose crisis is it? *See* **13333.**

1053. POLETTI, ANNA.   Self-publishing in the global and local: situating life writing in zines. *See* **14625.**

1054. POSTER, JAMIE.   Code orange: career fear and publishing. *See* **13343.**

1055. PRESSMAN, RICHARD S.   Is there a future for the *Heath Anthology* in the neoliberal State? *In* (pp. 264–76) **3749.**

1056. SCHOLES, ROBERT.   What is happening in literary studies? *See* **21122.**

1057. SCHRIFT, ALAN D.   Confessions of an anthology editor. *In* (pp. 186–204) **3749.**

1058. SIM, GARY.   Thoughts on antiquarian booksellers. Amphora (135) 2004, 20–6.

1059. SINGLETON, ALAN.   Open access and learned societies. *See* **1137.**

1060. SMOODIN, ERIC.   How I learned to stop worrying and love the crisis in publishing. *See* **13393.**

1061. SZIRTES, GEORGE.   An update on British poetry. *See* **20945.**

1062. TAYLOR, ANDREA.   Cotton Socks Press. Amphora (134) 2004, 26–9.

1063. WARE, MARK.   E-only journals: is it time to drop print? *See* **1357.**

1064. —— Online submission and peer-review systems. *See* **1358.**

1065. WILLIAMS, JEFFREY J.   Anthology disdain. *In* (pp. 207–21) **3749.**

1066. —— Visualizing books: an interview with Ken Wissoker. MinnR (63/64) 2005, 141–57. (Duke University Press.)

1067. WRIGHT, ZACHARY C.; RABKIN, ERIC S.; SIMON, CARL P.   The exaggerated reports of the death of science fiction. *See* **20895.**

SCHOLARLY METHOD

1068. ANON. The American Heritage guide to contemporary usage and style. Boston, MA: Houghton Mifflin, 2005. pp. xv, 512.

1069. BAILEY, GUY; TILLERY, JAN; ANDRES, CLAIRE. Some effects of transcribers on data in dialectology. *See* **2977.**

1070. BAXTER, JUDITH. Positioning gender in discourse: a feminist methodology. *See* **3148.**

1071. BELL, HAZEL K. Indexing biographies and other stories of human lives. Sheffield: Soc. of Indexers, 2004. pp. vi, 106. (Third ed.: first ed. 1992.) Rev. by Carrie Pedersen in JSchP (36:3) 2005, 173–6.

1072. BOBERG, CHARLES. The North American Regional Vocabulary Survey: new variables and methods in the study of North American English. *See* **2985.**

1073. CARPENTER, CHARLES A. Tracking down Shaw studies: the effective use of printed and online bibliographical sources. *See* **19384.**

1074. DOSSENA, MARINA; LASS, ROGER (eds). Methods and data in English historical dialectology. *See* **2909.**

1075. FAIRCLOUGH, NORMAN. Analysing discourse: textual analysis for social research. *See* **1372.**

1076. FLOWERDEW, LYNNE. An integration of corpus-based and genre-based approaches to text analysis in EAP/ESP: countering criticisms against corpus-based methodologies. ESpP (24:3) 2005, 321–32.

1077. FOOT, MIRJAM M. Bookbinding research: pitfalls, possibilities and needs. *In* (pp. 13–29) **30.**

1078. GERMANO, WILLIAM. Final thoughts. Profession (2005) 176–9.

1079. —— From dissertation to book. Chicago, IL; London: Chicago UP, 2005. pp. x, 141. (Chicago guides to writing, editing, and publishing.)

1080. HARTLEY, JAMES. Down with 'op. cit.'. LPub (18:1) 2005, 75–7. (Personal view.)

1081. HENIGE, DAVID. Commas, Christians, and editors. *See* **584.**

1082. LANCASTER, F. W. Indexing and abstracting in theory and practice. (Bibl. 1998, 1169.) London: Facet, 2003. pp. xxi, 451. (Third ed.: first ed. 1991.) Rev. by Janet Halsall in LPub (17:2) 2004, 172.

1083. MCKITTERICK, DAVID. 'Not in STC': opportunities and challenges in the *ESTC*. *See* **918.**

1084. MILROY, LESLEY; GORDON, MATTHEW. Sociolinguistics: method and interpretation. *See* **3190.**

1085. PALMQUIST, MIKE. The Bedford researcher: an integrated text, CD-ROM, and Web site. Basingstoke: Macmillan; Boston, MA: Bedford Books of St Martin's Press, 2003. pp. xxxv, 438 + 1 CD-ROM.

1086. PANOFSKY, RUTH; MOIR, MICHAEL. Halted by the archive: the impact of excessive archival restrictions on scholars. JSchP (37:1) 2005, 19–32.

1087. PINNEY, THOMAS. Some reflections on Kipling's letters. *See* **17483.**

1088. POSNER, DAVID M. Rhetoric, redemption, and fraud: what we do when we end books. Profession (2005) 179–82.

1089. ROBERTS, ROSEMARY, et al. (eds). New Hart's rules. (Bibl. 2002, 820.) Oxford; New York: OUP, 2005. pp. viii, 417. (New ed.: first ed. 1893.)

1090. ROGERS, REBECCA. A critical discourse analysis of family literacy practices: power in and out of print. See **3199**.

1091. SCHOENFELDT, MICHAEL. First impressions and last thoughts: the importance of scholarly introductions. Profession (2005) 169–71.

1092. STEVENSON, ANGUS; BROWN, LESLEY (eds). New Oxford dictionary for writers and editors. (Bibl. 2001, 887.) Oxford; New York: OUP, 2005. pp. xiv, 434. (Third ed.: first ed. 1981.)

1093. TARTAR, HELEN. Introductions: an editor's view. Profession (2005) 172–5.

1094. TEICH, ELKE. Cross-linguistic variation in system and text: a methodology for the investigation of translations and comparable texts. See **3387**.

1095. TRIMMER, JOSEPH F. A guide to MLA documentation: with an appendix on APA style. (Bibl. 1999, 988.) Boston, MA: Houghton Mifflin, 2004. pp. iii, 46. (Sixth ed.: first ed. 1984.)

1096. WILLIAMS, JOSEPH M. Style: ten lessons in clarity and grace. See **2902**.

LANGUAGE, LITERATURE AND THE COMPUTER

1097. BEST, MICHAEL. 'Is this a vision? Is this a dream?': finding new dimensions in Shakespeare's texts. *See* **5789**.

1098. BOND, FRANCIS. Translating the untranslatable: a solution to the problem of generating English determiners. *See* **3227**.

1099. BREWER, CHARLOTTE. The electronification of the *Oxford English Dictionary. See* **1920**.

1100. BROGAN, MARTHA L. A kaleidoscope of digital American literature. *See* **3715**.

1101. BURROWS, JOHN. Andrew Marvell and the 'painter satires': a computational approach to their authorship. *See* **7620**.

1102. CARPENTER, CHARLES A. Tracking down Shaw studies: the effective use of printed and online bibliographical sources. *See* **19384**.

1103. CARSON, CHRISTIE. Digitizing performance history: where do we go from here? PRes (10:3) 2005, 4–17.

1104. CHARTERIS-BLACK, JONATHAN. Corpus approaches to critical metaphor analysis. *See* **2251**.

1105. COUSINS, JILL; NEYLON, EAMONN. Information objects are hot, documents are not: the use of identifiers in online publishing. LPub (18:1) 2005, 5–12.

1106. DE LA CRUZ, ISABEL; VÁZQUEZ, NILA. New approaches in textual editing: a selection of electronic editions under analysis. *See* **534**.

1107. DUEÑAS VINUESA, MARÍA. Border Studies: an annotated list of cultural and academic Web sources. *See* **12643**.

1108. EVERETT, GLENN. Electronic resources for Victorian researchers – 2005 and beyond. VLC (33:2) 2005, 601–14.

1109. EZELL, MARGARET J. M. Eclectic circulation: the functional dynamics of manuscript and electronic literary cultures. *In* (pp. 27–35) **587**.

1110. FOYS, MARTIN K. *Circolwyrde* 2004: new electronic resources for Anglo-Saxon studies. *See* **4207**.

1111. FREDERKING, ROBERT E.; TAYLOR, KATHRYN B. (eds). Machine translation: from real users to research: 6th Conference of the Association for Machine Translation in the Americas, AMTA 2004. *See* **3275**.

1112. HAMMOND, MARY. The Reading Experience Database 1450–1945 (RED). *In* (pp. 175–87) **19**.

1113. HARDY, DONALD E. Collocational analysis as a stylistic discovery procedure: the case of Flannery O'Connor's *eyes. See* **18560**.

1114. HARGRAVES, ORIN. Long-distance lexicography: a view from the field. *See* **1927**.

1115. HILL, W. SPEED (ed.). New ways of looking at old texts III: papers of the Renaissance English Text Society, 1997–2001. *See* **587**.

1116. JACKSON, VIRGINIA. Dickinson undone. *See* **10789**.

1117. KATO, TAKAKO. Towards the digital Winchester: editing the Winchester manuscript of Malory's *Morte Darthur. See* **4889**.

1118. LEARY, PATRICK. Googling the Victorians. JVC (10:1) 2005, 72–86. (Perspectives, 1.)

1119. LOOTENS, TRICIA. Between treasuries and the Web: compendious Victorian poetry anthologies in transition. *See* **9702**.

1120. MAY, STEVEN W. Queen Elizabeth's *Future Foes*: editing manuscripts with the first-line index of Elizabethan verse (a future friend). *In* (pp. 1–12) **587**.

1121. MERRIAM, THOMAS. Anomalous verse in *Henry IV* and *Henry V. See* **6409**.

1122. MUELLER, MARTIN. *The Nameless Shakespeare. See* **5818**.

1123. NICHOLAS, DAVID, *et al.* The Big Deal – ten years on. LPub (18:4) 2005, 251–7. (Online journal usage.)

1124. O'DONNELL, DANIEL PAU. O captain! My captain! Using technology to guide readers through an electronic edition. HAge (8) 2005.

1125. PARTRIDGE, JEFFREY F. L. Hypertext past and present: a conversation with George P. Landow. ConnR (27:2) 2005, 159–73.

1126. PETTER, CHRIS; ROBERTS, LINDA; ROSE, SPENCER. The Robert Graves diary (1935–39). *See* **16803**.

1127. PINNEY, THOMAS. Some reflections on Kipling's letters. *See* **17483**.

1128. POSTER, JAMIE. Code orange: career fear and publishing. *See* **13343**.

1129. POWELL, KATHRYN. The MANCASS C11 database: a tool for studying script and spelling in the eleventh century. *See* **1410**.

1130. PRICE, DAVID. George on the Net. *See* **10119**.

1131. RENOUF, ANTOINETTE. Phrasal creativity viewed from an IT perspective. *See* **1762**.

1132. RITTERSBACHER, CHRISTA; MÖSCH, MATTHIAS. A haystack full of precious needles: the Internet and its utility for paremiologists. *See* **3456**.

1133. ROBINSON, PETER. The identification and use of authorial variants in the Miller's Tale. *See* **5026**.

1134. ROFF, SANDRA SHOIOCK. The return of the armchair scholar. JSchP (36:2) 2005, 49–57.

1135. RUDMAN, JOSEPH. Unediting, de-editing, and editing in non-traditional authorship attribution studies: with an emphasis on the canon of Daniel Defoe. *See* **8542**.

1136. SIEMENS, R. G. 'What two crownes shall they be?': 'lower' criticism, 'higher' criticism, and the impact of the electronic scholarly edition. *In* (pp. 37–46) **587**.

1137. SINGLETON, ALAN. Open access and learned societies. LPub (18:3) 2005, 223–8. (Personal view.)

1138. STUBBS, MICHAEL. Conrad in the computer: examples of quantitative stylistic methods. *See* **15926**.

1139. THORBURN, DAVID; JENKINS, HENRY (eds); SEAWELL, BRAD (assoc. ed.). Rethinking media change: the aesthetics of transition. *See* **24**.

1140. WARE, MARK. E-only journals: is it time to drop print? *See* **1357**.

1141. —— Online submission and peer-review systems. *See* **1358**.

1142. Yu, Pauline.   On synthetic technologies: the book, the university, the Internet. LPub (18:1) 2005, 41–50.

NEWSPAPERS AND OTHER PERIODICALS

1143. ANON. Mencken's many identities. *See* **18166**.

1144. BEN-AARON, DIANA. Given and news: evaluation in newspaper stories about national anniversaries. *See* **2802**.

1145. ACKLAND, MICHAEL. Polemics anonymous: James McAuley's *nom de plume* contributions from *Hermes* to *Quadrant*. *See* **17922**.

1146. ADAMS, JAMES ELI. The function of journals at the present time. *See* **20988**.

1147. ALEXANDER, CHRISTINE. Play and apprenticeship: the culture of family magazines. *In* (pp. 31–50) **9164**.

1148. AMIGONI, DAVID. Carving coconuts, the philosophy of drawing rooms, and the politics of dates: Grant Allen, popular scientific journalism, evolution, and culture in the *Cornhill Magazine*. *In* (pp. 251–61) **1226**.

1149. ANDERSON, KATHARINE. Almanacs and the profits of natural knowledge. *In* (pp. 97–111) **1226**.

1150. ARNER, ROBERT D. Textual transmission and the transformation of texts: on the dialogic margins of Dorothy Parker's *The Waltz*. *In* (pp. 86–113) **18738**.

1151. ASHLEY, MIKE. Transformations: the story of the science-fiction magazines from 1950 to 1970. *See* **14079**.

1152. BAGGS, CHRIS. 'In the separate reading room for ladies are provided those publications specially interesting to them': ladies' reading rooms and British public libraries 1850–1914. VPR (38:3) 2005, 280–306.

1153. BANNET, EVE TAVOR. 'Epistolary commerce' in *The Spectator*. *In* (pp. 220–47) **1285**.

1154. BECKER, JEFF. Twenty-five *Blue Canary* years. *See* **17822**.

1155. BERRY, HELEN. Gender, society and print culture in late Stuart England: the cultural world of the *Athenian Mercury*. (Bibl. 2004, 1187.) Rev. by Marja Smolenaars in JPHS (ns 7) 2004, 74–5; by Maureen Bell in Library (5:1) 2004, 87–9; by Anna Marie Roos in Albion (36:3) 2004, 523–4; by Erin Mackie in CLIO (34:3) 2005, 376–81; by Amara Graf in LibC (40:1) 2005, 93–4.

1156. BIRNS, NICHOLAS. 'Thy world, Columbus!': Barbauld and global space, 1803, *1811*, 1812, 2003. *See* **8341**.

1157. BOWERS, TERENCE. Universalizing sociability: *The Spectator*, civic enfranchisement, and the rule(s) of the public sphere. *In* (pp. 150–74) **1285**.

1158. BOYD, KELLY. Manliness and the boys' story paper in Britain: a cultural history, 1855–1940. (Bibl. 2004, 1194.) Rev. by Michael Rupert Taylor in VicR (29:2) 2004, 107–10; by Asa Briggs in LitH (14:1) 2005, 99–100.

1159. BRADLEY, JENNIFER L. To entertain, to educate, to elevate: Cather and the commodification of manners at the *Home Monthly*. *In* (pp. 37–65) **15749**.

1160. BRAKE, LAUREL; CODELL, JULIE F. (eds). Encounters in the Victorian press: editors, authors, readers. Basingstoke; New York: Palgrave Macmillan,

2005. pp. xiv, 268. (Palgrave studies in nineteenth-century writing and culture.)

1161. BROWN, GILLIAN. Thinking in the future perfect: consent, childhood, and minority rights. YREAL (19) 2003, 113–28.

1162. BROWN, STEPHEN. James Tytler's misadventures in the late eighteenth-century Edinburgh book trade. *In* (pp. 47–63) **880.**

1163. BUCKER, PARK. 'That kitchen with the shining windows': Willa Cather's *Neighbour Rosicky* and the *Woman's Home Companion. In* (pp. 66–112) **15749.**

1164. BURLEY, STEPHEN. Hazlitt and John Stoddart: brothers-in-law or brothers at war? *See* **11231.**

1165. BURNS, WALKER. Golden days. *See* **20223.**

1166. BURT, STEPHEN. R. P. Blackmur and Randall Jarrell on literary magazines: an exchange. RWP (5) 2005, 139–45.

1167. BUTTERSS, PHILIP. Gadding about: C. J. Dennis and the *Gadfly. See* **16054.**

1168. CALHOUN, RICHARD J. The unremembered heritage: Charleston's antebellum literary magazines. SoCR (38:1) 2005, 34–40.

1169. CANTOR, GEOFFREY. Friends of science? The role of science in Quaker periodicals. *In* (pp. 83–93) **1226.**

1170. CAREY, BRYCCHAN. 'Accounts of savage nations': *The Spectator* and the Americas. *In* (pp. 129–49) **1285.**

1171. CARROLL-HORROCKS, BETH. A working relationship: the Dorothy Nevile Lees papers relating to Edward Gordon Craig and *The Mask*, at the Harvard Theatre Collection. TheatreS (46:1) 2005, 103–13. (*Re:* sources.)

1172. CHANDLER, ANNE. The 'seeds of order and taste': Wollstonecraft, the *Analytical Review*, and critical idiom. *See* **9132.**

1173. CHANDLER, DAVID. The early development of the 'Lake School' idea. *See* **12466.**

1174. CLARKE, BOB. From Grub Street to Fleet Street: an illustrated history of English newspapers to 1899. Aldershot; Burlington, VT: Ashgate, 2004. pp. viii, 283. Rev. by Gregory Dart in TLS, 7 Jan. 2005, 22; by Ian Jackson in SHARP (14:1/2) 2005, 12.

1175. CLEMM, SABINE. 'Amidst the heterogeneous masses': Charles Dickens's *Household Words* and the Great Exhibition of 1851. *See* **10660.**

1176. CLYDE, TOM. Irish literary magazines: an outline history and descriptive bibliography. (Bibl. 2004, 1203.) Rev. by Elizabeth Tilley in VPR (38:1) 2005, 115–17.

1177. CODELL, JULIE F. (ed.). Imperial co-histories: national identities and the British and colonial press. (Bibl. 2004, 1204.) Rev. by Thomas C. Howard in Albion (36:3) 2004, 576–8; by Margaret Beetham in VPR (38:1) 2005, 104–6; by Matthew Dimmock in YES (35) 2005, 348–9; by Lynn Zastoupil in VS (48:1) 2005, 153–5.

1178. COLBERT, BENJAMIN. Petrio-pindarics: John Wolcot and the Romantics. *See* **9128.**

1179. COLEY, WILLIAM B. (ed.). Contributions to *The Champion* and related writings. *See* **8605**.

1180. CONNELLY, WILLIAM. The illustrators of *The Merry-Go-Round*. StIll (23) 2003, 36–8.

1181. COOK, MALCOLM. The *Modern Language Review*: the first hundred years. MLR (100:4:supp.) 2005, 1–4.

1182. COOKE, SIMON. 'A man of sound judgement and sure taste': Samuel Lucas, *Once a Week* and sixties illustration. *See* **52**.

1183. DANIEL, ANNE MARGARET. Arthur Symons and *The Savoy*. *See* **12127**.

1184. DAVIS, JAMES P. *Maxim* magazine and the management of contempt. JPC (38:6) 2005, 1011–21.

1185. DAWSON, GOWAN. Walter Pater's *Marius the Epicurean* and the discourse of science in *Macmillan's Magazine*: 'a creature of the nineteenth century'. *See* **11779**.

1186. DE MICHELIS, LIDIA. Daniel Defoe and the aesthetics of discovery. *See* **8512**.

1187. DE MONTLUZIN, EMILY LORRAINE. The *Anti-Jacobin Review* after Gifford: contributions by identified authors, 1807–21. Library (6:3) 2005, 274–320.

1188. —— Attributions of authorship in the *Gentleman's Magazine*, 1745–1754: a supplement to the *Union List*. NQ (52:3) 2005, 360–9.

1189. —— Attributions of authorship in the *Gentleman's Magazine*, 1755–64: a supplement to the *Union List*. ANQ (18:1) 2005, 32–42.

1190. DENHAM, ROBERT D. Thou art that: Woolylamb Hormone, Northcote Fricassee, and chap named Denim. *See* **16894**.

1191. DE TOLEDANO, RALPH. Erato in the throes. *See* **14388**.

1192. DUMAS, FRÉDÉRIC. Éros est mort à Chicago: Nelson Algren accuse *Playboy*. *See* **15115**.

1193. DUNCAN, IAN. Edinburgh, capital of the nineteenth century. *In* (pp. 45–64) **9217**.

1194. EASLEY, ALEXIS. *Tait's Edinburgh Magazine* in the 1830s: dialogues on gender, class, and reform. VPR (38:3) 2005, 263–79.

1195. EDWARDS, OWEN DUDLEY. 'True Thomas': Carlyle, Young Ireland, and the legacy of millenialism. *In* (pp. 60–76) **10393**.

1196. FEE, FRANK E., JR. Intelligent union of Black with White: Frederick Douglass and the Rochester press, 1847–48. *See* **10826**.

1197. FEHLBAUM, VALERIE. As she knew him: as Ella Hepworth Dixon knew Oscar Wilde. *See* **12385**.

1198. FORSTER, LAUREL. Liberating the recipe: a study of the relationship between food and feminism in the early 1970s. *In* (pp. 147–68) **9257**.

1199. FOSDICK, SCOTT. From discussion leader to consumer guide: a century of theater criticism in Chicago newspapers. *See* **13022**.

1200. FRASER, HILARY; JOHNSTON, JUDITH; GREEN, STEPHANIE. Gender and the Victorian periodical. (Bibl. 2004, 1236.) Rev. by Janice Schroeder in VicR (30:2) 2004, 103–5; by George Mariz in VPR (38:1) 2005, 112–13; by Josephine

McDonagh in RES (56:225) 2005, 465–6; by Linda K. Hughes in NineL (60:2) 2005, 254–8.

1201. FRAWLEY, MARIA.   Behind the scenes of history: Harriet Martineau and *The Lowell Offering*. See **11652**.

1202. FRIGERIO, FRANCESCA.   'A filmless London': *flânerie* and urban culture in Dorothy Richardson's articles for *Close Up*. *In* (pp. 19–31) **14254**.

1203. FYFE, AILEEN.   Periodicals and book series: complementary aspects of a publisher's mission. *In* (pp. 71–82) **1226**.

1204. GAMER, MICHAEL.   'Bell's poetics': *The Baviad*, the Della Cruscans, and the book of *The World*. *In* (pp. 31–53) **9305**.

1205. GANNON, SUSAN R.; RAHN, SUZANNE; THOMPSON, RUTH ANNE (eds). *St Nicholas* and Mary Mapes Dodge: the legacy of a children's magazine editor, 1873–1905. (Bibl. 2004, 1240.) Rev. by Lorinda B. Cohoon in CLAQ (30:1) 2005, 128–32.

1206. GARDINER, DAVID.   'The last summer': James Liddy's *Arena*. See **17823**.

1207. GILES, PAUL; ELLIS, R. J.   E *pluribus multitudinum*: the new world of journal publishing in American Studies. See **1039**.

1208. GOESER, CAROLINE.   The case of *Ebony and Topaz*: racial and sexual hybridity in Harlem renaissance illustrations. AmP (15:1) 2005, 86–111.

1209. GOLDEN, CATHERINE.   *The Yellow Wall-Paper* and Joseph Henry Hatfield's original magazine illustrations. See **16685**.

1210. GOLDING, ALAN C.   *The Dial, The Little Review*, and the dialogics of Modernism. AmP (15:1) 2005, 42–55.

1211. GOODAY, GRAEME J. N.   'I never will have the electric light in my house': Alice Gordon and the gendered periodical representation of a contentious new technology. *In* (pp. 173–85) **1226**.

1212. GOULD, MARTY.   Flirting with disaster: sexual play in the Victorian periodical. VPR (37:3) 2004, 273–88.

1213. GOULD, PHILIP.   The African slave trade and Abolitionism: rereading antislavery literature, 1776–1800. *In* (pp. 201–19) **1244**.

1214. GREGORY, JOHN.   Journalism: the public face of the Norfolk farm. See **20225**.

1215. GRENBY, M. O.   'A conservative woman doing radical things': Sarah Trimmer and *The Guardian of Education*. *In* (pp. 137–61) **8171**.

1216. GUNDY, JEFF.   Taste and the open door. See **14402**.

1217. GUPTA, SUMAN.   In search of genius: T. S. Eliot as publisher. See **16272**.

1218. HAMILTON, DAVID.   The common writer. See **14407**.

1219. HAMPTON, MARK.   Rethinking the 'New Journalism', 1850s–1930s. JBS (43:2) 2004, 278–90 (review-article).

1220. HARRIS, SHARON M.   The *New-York Magazine*: cultural repository. *In* (pp. 339–64) **1244**.

1221. —— GARVEY, ELLEN GRUBER (eds).   Blue pencils & hidden hands: women editing periodicals, 1830–1910. (Bibl. 2004, 1253.) Rev. by Melissa J. Homestead in Legacy (22:1) 2005, 84–6.

1222. HARSH, CONSTANCE. The text of *Eve's Ransom*: insights from the *Illustrated London News* serialization. *See* **11073**.

1223. HARVEY, ROSS. Sources of 'literary' copy for New Zealand newspapers. BSANZB (27:3/4) 2003, 83–93.

1224. HATFIELD, CHARLES. Alternative comics: an emerging literature. *See* **85**.

1225. HENSON, LOUISE. 'In the natural course of physical things': ghosts and science in Charles Dickens's *All the Year Round*. *In* (pp. 113–23) **1226**.

1226. —— *et al.* (eds). Culture and science in the nineteenth-century media. Aldershot; Burlington, VT: Ashgate, 2004. pp. xxv, 296. (Nineteenth century.) Rev. by Lisa Gitelman in SHARP (13:3) 2004, 6–7.

1227. HETHERINGTON, NAOMI. New Woman, 'new boots': Amy Levy as child journalist. *In* (pp. 254–68) **9164**.

1228. HIGGINS, DAVID MINDEN. Romantic genius and the literary magazine: biography, celebrity, and politics. *See* **11227**.

1229. HOBERMAN, RUTH. Constructing the turn-of-the-century shopper: narratives about purchased objects in the *Strand* magazine, 1891–1910. *See* **9563**.

1230. HOLMAN, VALERIE. Carefully concealed connections: the Ministry of Information and British publishing, 1939–1946. *See* **884**.

1231. HOWE, NICHOLAS. *Beowulf* in the house of Dickens. *In* (pp. 421–39) **4220**.

1232. HUETT, LORNA. Among the unknown public: *Household Words*, *All the Year Round* and the mass-market weekly periodical in the mid-nineteenth century. VPR (38:1) 2005, 61–82.

1233. HUGHES, GILLIAN. Hogg and the *Monthly Musical and Literary Magazine*. *See* **11274**.

1234. —— James Hogg and *The Metropolitan*. *See* **11277**.

1235. HUGHES, LINDA K. Constructing fictions of authorship in George Eliot's *Middlemarch*, 1871–1872. *See* **10931**.

1236. —— Women poets and contested spaces in *The Yellow Book*. SELit (44:4) 2004, 849–72.

1237. HUNT, PAUL. Serial fiction in the *Otago Witness*, 1851–1906. *See* **9565**.

1238. ITALIA, IONA. The rise of literary journalism in the eighteenth century: anxious employment. *See* **8232**.

1239. IVES, MAURA. Further evidence for Eliza Straffen's authorship of *Some Recollections of Jean Ingelow and Her Early Friends*. *See* **11364**.

1240. JONES, JULIA. 'A fine, sturdy piece of work [...]': Margery Allingham's book reviews for *Time & Tide* 1938–1944. *See* **15121**.

1241. JOUKOVSKY, NICHOLAS A. Keats, Shelley, and *The Troubadour*. KSR (19) 2005, 132–41.

1242. JUSTICE, GEORGE. *The Spectator* and distance education. *In* (pp. 265–99) **1285**.

1243. KAMRATH, MARK L. American Indian oration and discourses of the Republic in eighteenth-century American periodicals. *In* (pp. 143–78) **1244**.

1244. —— HARRIS, SHARON M. (eds). Periodical literature in eighteenth-century America. Knoxville: Tennessee UP, 2005. pp. xxvii, 394.

1245. KIJINSKI, JOHN L. Respectable reading in the late nineties: H. D. Traill's *Literature*. NCC (25:4) 2003, 357–72.

1246. KING, ANDREW. The *London Journal* 1845–83: periodicals, production, and gender. (Bibl. 2004, 1277.) Rev. by Alexis Easley in Library (6:1) 2005, 99–101; by Gowan Dawson in SHARP (14:1/2) 2005, 15–16.

1247. KITCH, CAROLYN. Pages from the past: history and memory in American magazines. Chapel Hill; London: North Carolina UP, 2005. pp. 256. Rev. by Berkley Hudson in AmJ (22:4) 2005, 105–6.

1248. KLEIN, LAWRENCE E. Joseph Addison's Whiggism. *In* (pp. 108–26) **8091**.

1249. KNOWLES, OWEN; STAPE, J. H. The rationale of punctuation in Conrad's *Blackwood's* fictions. *See* **15886**.

1250. KRAFT, ELIZABETH. Wit and *The Spectator's* ethics of desire. SELit (45:3) 2005, 625–46.

1251. LAW, GRAHAM. Imagined local communities: three Victorian newspaper novelists. *In* (pp. 185–203) **880**.

1252. —— Savouring of the Australian soil? On the sources and affiliations of colonial newspaper fiction. VPR (37:4) 2003, 75–97.

1253. LEDBETTER, KATHRYN. Bonnets and rebellions: imperialism in *The Lady's Newspaper*. VPR (37:3) 2004, 252–72.

1254. —— Protesting success: Tennyson's 'indecent exposure' in the periodicals. *See* **12149**.

1255. LILLY, THOMAS. The national archive: *Harper's New Monthly Magazine* and the civic responsibilities of a commercial literary periodical, 1850–1853. AmP (15:2) 2005, 142–62.

1256. LITVACK, LEON. *The Dickensian*: editors, contributors and readers, 1905–2005. *See* **10711**.

1257. LOCKE, GEORGE. *The Sketch*: an annotated checklist of certain illustrators, based on a partial run. StIll (23) 2003, 21–33.

1258. LOCKWOOD, DAVID. Pictorial puzzles from *Alice*. *See* **10405**.

1259. LOFTS, W. O. G.; ADLEY, DEREK. *Scoops*: the first British science-fiction boys' paper. DNR (74:3) 2005, 79–89.

1260. LOGAN, LISA M. 'Dear matron —': constructions of women in eighteenth-century American periodical columns. SAH (11) 2004, 57–61.

1261. —— 'The ladies in particular': constructions of femininity in the *Gentlemen and Ladies Town and Country Magazine* and the *Lady's Magazine; and Repository of Entertaining Knowledge*. *In* (pp. 277–306) **1244**.

1262. LOW, DENNIS. Gold and silver fishes in a vase: a portrait of Wordsworth and Maria Jane Jewsbury. *See* **12497**.

1263. LUCKHURST, ROGER. W. T. Stead's occult economies. *In* (pp. 125–35) **1226**.

1264. MCCREA, BRIAN. The virtue of repetition: Mr Spectator trains Benjamin Franklin. *In* (pp. 248–64) **1285**.

1265. McGrane, Laura.   Fielding's fallen oracles: print culture and the elusiveness of common sense. *See* **8614**.

1266. McKenry, Keith.   *Australian Folklore*: an appraisal. *See* **3420**.

1267. McKible, Adam.   'Life is real and life is earnest': Mike Gold, Claude McKay, and the Baroness Elsa von Freytag-Loringhoven. *See* **16732**.

1268. Mackie, Erin Skye.   Being too positive about the public sphere. *In* (pp. 81–104) **1285**.

1269. McNees, Eleanor.   *Punch* and the Pope: three decades of anti-Catholic caricature. VPR (37:1) 2004, 18–45.

1270. McNeill, Laurie.   Writing lives in death: Canadian death notices as auto/biography. *In* (pp. 187–205) **14629**.

1271. Mason, Nicholas.   'The quack has become God': puffery, print, and the 'death' of literature in Romantic-era Britain. NineL (60:1) 2005, 1–31.

1272. Masteller, Jean Carwile.   Serial romance: Laura Jean Libbey and nineteenth-century story papers. *See* **11602**.

1273. Mémet, Monique.   Letters to the editor: a multi-faceted genre. *See* **2868**.

1274. Merritt, Juliette.   Originals, copies, and the iconography of femininity in *The Spectator*. *In* (pp. 41–58) **1285**.

1275. Miller, Char.   Proving ground: Richard Harding Davis in the American West. *See* **10595**.

1276. Montgomery, Paul.   Hemingway and Guy Hickock in Italy: the *Brooklyn Eagle* articles. *See* **16985**.

1277. Morrison, Ian; Perkins, Maureen; Caulfield, Tracey (comps).   Australian almanacs 1806–1930: a bibliography. Auburn, Vic.: Quiddlers Press, 2003. pp. xiii, 166. Rev. by Elizabeth Morrison in SHARP (13:2) 2004, 7–8.

1278. Morrison, Robert.   *De Quincey's Revenge*: David Macbeth Moir and *Confessions of an English Opium-Eater*. *See* **11729**.

1279. Morrison, Sarah R.   Truth or consequences: Johnson's *Life of Milton* and the moral biographer's dilemma. *In* (pp. 220–33) **7738**.

1280. Mouton, Michelle.   Margaret Oliphant and John Stuart Mill: disinterested politicians and the 1865 General Election. *See* **11767**.

1281. Mulford, Carla.   Pox and 'hell-fire': Boston's smallpox controversy, the New Science, and early modern liberalism. *In* (pp. 7–27) **1244**.

1282. Müller, Anja.   Putting the child into discourse: framing children in *The Spectator*. *In* (pp. 59–80) **1285**.

1283. Mutch, Deborah.   The *Merrie England* triptych: Robert Blatchford, Edward Fay and the didactic use of *Clarion* fiction. VPR (38:1) 2005, 83–103.

1284. Newcomb, John Timberman.   *Poetry*'s opening door: Harriet Monroe and American Modernism. AmP (15:1) 2005, 6–22.

1285. Newman, Donald J. (ed.).   *The Spectator*: emerging discourses. Newark: Delaware UP, 2005. pp. 313.

1286. Nicholas, David, *et al.*   The Big Deal – ten years on. *See* **1123**.

1287. ——   In their very own words: authors and scholarly journal publishing. LPub (18:3) 2005, 212–20.

1288. NICHOLSON, EIRWEN.   Soggy prose and verbiage: English graphic political satire as a visual/verbal construct. WI (20:1) 2004, 28–40.

1289. NICOLAY, CLAIRE.   The anxiety of 'Mosaic' influence: Thackeray, Disraeli, and Anglo-Jewish assimilation in the 1840s. *See* **12168.**

1290. NIXON, JUDE V.   'Lost in the vast worlds of wonder': Dickens and science. *See* **10724.**

1291. NOAKES, RICHARD.   Representing 'a century of inventions': nineteenth-century technology and Victorian *Punch. In* (pp. 151–63) **1226.**

1292. OLIVER, SUSAN.   Transatlantic influences in periodical editing: from Francis Jeffrey's *Edinburgh Review* to Horace Greeley's *New-York Tribune.* Symbiosis (9:1) 2005, 45–62.

1293. OSELL, TEDRA.   Tatling women in the public sphere: rhetorical femininity and the English essay periodical. ECS (38:2) 2004, 283–300.

1294. PALMERI, FRANK.   Cruikshank, Thackeray, and the Victorian eclipse of satire. *See* **12169.**

1295. PARISI, JOSEPH.   Poetry and the embarrassment of riches. *See* **14469.**

1296. PARRIS, BRANDY.   Difficult sympathy in the Reconstruction-era animal stories of *Our Young Folks. See* **9652.**

1297. PASSET, JOANNE E.   Freethought children's literature and the construction of religious identity in late nineteenth-century America. *See* **9653.**

1298. PATTEE, AMY S.   Mass-market mortification: the developmental appropriateness of teen magazines and the embarrassing story standard. LQ (74:1) 2004, 1–20.

1299. PAYNE, DAVID.   The reenchantment of nineteenth-century fiction: Dickens, Thackeray, George Eliot, and serialization. *See* **10730.**

1300. PEACEY, JASON.   The struggle for *Mercurius Britanicus*: factional politics and the Parliamentarian press, 1643–1646. HLQ (68:3) 2005, 517–43.

1301. PELIZZON, V. PENELOPE; WEST, NANCY M.   Multiple indemnity: *film noir*, James M. Cain, and adaptations of a tabloid case. *See* **13332.**

1302. PHEGLEY, JENNIFER.   Domesticating the sensation novelist: Ellen Price Wood as author and editor of the *Argosy Magazine.* VPR (38:2) 2005, 180–98.

1303. —— Educating the proper woman reader: Victorian family literary magazines and the cultural health of the nation. Columbus: Ohio State UP, 2004. pp. x, 233. Rev. by Margaret Beetham in VS (47:4) 2005, 615–17.

1304. —— 'I should no more think of dictating ... what kinds of books she should read': images of women readers in Victorian family literary magazines. *In* (pp. 105–28) **12549.**

1305. PHILLIPS, MARK SALBER.   Criticism: literary history and literary historicism. *In* (pp. 247–65) **6958.**

1306. PITCHER, EDWARD W. R. (comp.)   *The Literary Miscellany* (Philadelphia 1795), *Lady and Gentleman's Pocket Magazine* (New York 1796), and *Literary Museum; or, Monthly Magazine* (Westchester 1797): three annotated catalogues for American literary magazines. Lewiston, NY; Lampeter: Mellen Press, 2004. pp. 207. (Studies in British and American magazines, 31.)

1307. —— The *New American Magazine* (Woodbridge, New Jersey, January 1758 – March 1760): an annotated catalogue of the literary contents with an appendix on *The Instructor* (New York, March 6 – May 10, 1755). Lewiston, NY; Lampeter: Mellen Press, 2004. pp. 255. (Studies in British and American magazines, 29.)

1308. PLATE, LIEDEKE. Intermedial Woolf: text, image, and in-between. *See* **20399**.

1309. POLETTI, ANNA. Self-publishing in the global and local: situating life writing in zines. *See* **14625**.

1310. POLLY, GREG. Leviathan of letters. *In* (pp. 105–28) **1285**.

1311. QUINN, WILLIAM A. Harriet Monroe as queen-critic of Chaucer and Langland (*viz.* Ezra Pound). *See* **4962**.

1312. REDSHAW, THOMAS DILLON. 'We done our best when we were let': James Liddy's *Arena*, 1963–1965. *See* **17827**.

1313. REED, BEVERLY J. Exhibiting the fair sex: the *Massachusetts Magazine* and the bodily order of the American woman. *In* (pp. 227–54) **1244**.

1314. REID, CHAD. 'Widely read by American patriots': the *New-York Weekly Journal* and the influence of *Cato's Letters* on Colonial America. *In* (pp. 109–42) **1244**.

1315. REID, CHRISTOPHER. Speaking candidly: rhetoric, politics, and the meaning of candour in the later eighteenth century. *See* **8052**.

1316. REID, JULIA. The *Academy* and *Cosmopolis*: evolution and culture in Robert Louis Stevenson's periodical encounters. *In* (pp. 263–73) **1226**.

1317. REYNOLDS, TOM. Selling college literacy: the mass-market magazine as early 20th-century literacy sponsor. AmP (15:2) 2005, 163–77.

1318. RICHARDS, ALAN. Between tradition and counter-tradition: the poems of A. J. M. Smith and F. R. Scott in *The Canadian Mercury* (1928–1929). *See* **19480**.

1319. RICHARDSON, ANGELIQUE. Eugenics and freedom at the *fin de siècle*. *In* (pp. 275–86) **1226**.

1320. RITVO, HARRIET. The view from the hills: environment and technology in Victorian periodicals. *In* (pp. 165–72) **1226**.

1321. ROBINSON, SOLVEIG C. Expanding a 'limited orbit': Margaret Oliphant, *Blackwood's Edinburgh Magazine*, and the development of a critical voice. *See* **11768**.

1322. —— RSVP bibliography: 2001–2003. VPR (38:1) 2005, 5–60. (Research Soc. for Victorian Periodicals.)

1323. ROOKS, NOLIWE M. Ladies' pages: African American women's magazines and the culture that made them. (Bibl. 2004, 1343.) Rev. by Frances Foster Smith in AmP (15:2) 2005, 223–4.

1324. ROWLINSON, MATTHEW. Theory of Victorian Studies: anachronism and self-reflexivity. *See* **21115**.

1325. RUDNICK, LOIS. Modernism in the high desert: the multivocal ecology of Alice Corbin Henderson's *Red Earth*. *See* **17003**.

1326. RYLANCE, RICK. 'The disturbing anarchy of investigation': psychological debate and the Victorian periodical. *In* (pp. 239–50) **1226.**

1327. SHEFFIELD, SUZANNE LE-MAY. The 'empty-headed beauty' and the 'sweet girl graduate': women's science education in *Punch*, 1860–90. *In* (pp. 16–28) **1226.**

1328. SHERBO, ARTHUR. More Johnsoniana from the *Gentleman's Magazine*. *See* **8777.**

1329. SHOVLIN, FRANK. The Irish literary periodical, 1923–1958. (Bibl. 2004, 1359.) Rev. by Bruce Stewart in NQ (52:1) 2005, 146–8.

1330. SHTEIR, ANN B. Green-stocking or blue? Science in three women's magazines, 1800–50. *In* (pp. 3–13) **1226.**

1331. SHUFFELTON, FRANK. Thomas Jefferson, Francis Hopkinson, and the representation of the *Notes on the State of Virginia*. *In* (pp. 255–76) **1244.**

1332. SIVASUNDARAM, SUJIT. The periodical as barometer: spiritual measurement and the *Evangelical Magazine*. *In* (pp. 43–55) **1226.**

1333. SLAWINSKI, SCOTT. Validating bachelorhood: audience, patriarchy, and Charles Brockden Brown's editorship of the *Monthly Magazine* and *American Review*. *See* **10241.**

1334. SMITH, MICHELLE DENISE. Guns, lies, and ice: the Canadian pulp magazine industry and the crime fiction of Raymond Chandler and Niel Perrin. *See* **15760.**

1335. SMYTHE, TED CURTIS. The Gilded Age press 1865–1900. Westport, CT; London: Praeger, 2003. pp. x, 240. (History of American journalism, 4.) Rev. by W. Joseph Campbell in JAH (91:2) 2004, 644–5.

1336. SOLIE, RUTH. Music in other words: Victorian conversations. *See* **10955.**

1337. SONODA, AKIKO. Coleridge's later poetry and the rise of literary annuals. *See* **10523.**

1338. STREETS, HEATHER. Military influence in late Victorian and Edwardian popular media: the case of Frederick Roberts. *See* **9830.**

1339. SUMPTER, CAROLINE. Making Socialists or murdering to dissect? Natural history and child socialization in the *Labour Prophet* and *Labour Leader*. *In* (pp. 29–40) **1226.**

1340. SUSSEX, LUCY. 'Bobbing around': James Skipp Borlase, Adam Lindsay Gordon, and surviving in the literary market of Australia, 1860s. *See* **10106.**

1341. SWAIM, BARTON. Murray, Lockhart, Croker, and the *Quarterly*. *See* **11609.**

1342. TANSELLE, G. THOMAS. Fifty years on: bibliography then and now. *See* **23.**

1343. THERNSTROM, MELANIE. A woman of verse. NYTM, 25 Dec. 2005, 36–8. (Elizabeth McFarland, poetry editor of *The Ladies' Home Journal*.)

1344. THOMAS, KEITH. How it strikes a contemporary. *See* **14642.**

1345. THORNTON, EDITH. 'Innocence' consumed: packaging Edith Wharton with Kathleen Norris in *Pictorial Review* magazine, 1920–21. *See* **20136.**

1346. TILLEY, ELIZABETH. Science, industry, and nationalism in the *Dublin Penny Journal*. *In* (pp. 139–49) **1226**.

1347. TOPHAM, JONATHAN R. John Limbird, Thomas Byerley, and the production of cheap periodicals in the 1820s. *See* **1007**.

1348. —— Periodicals and the making of reading audiences for science in early nineteenth-century Britain: the *Youth's Magazine*, 1828–37. *In* (pp. 57–69) **1226**.

1349. TOPLISS, IAIN. The comic worlds of Peter Arno, William Steig, Charles Addams, and Saul Steinberg. Baltimore, MD; London: Johns Hopkins UP, 2005. pp. xiii, 325. Rev. by Brian Thornton in AmJ (22:4) 2005, 119–20.

1350. TROLANDER, PAUL; TENGER, ZAYNEP. Addison and the personality of the critic. *In* (pp. 175–99) **1285**.

1351. TURLEY, RICHARD MARGGRAF. 'Amorous cavaliers': Keats, Barry Cornwall, and Francis Jeffrey. *See* **11537**.

1352. UCHIDA, MASAKO. The activities of the Chancery Reform Association and Dickens's writing of *A December Vision*: part II. *See* **10755**.

1353. VAN BRONSWIJK, R. Driving the darkness: W. E. Henley's *The Song of the Sword* as uneasy battle cry. *See* **11266**.

1354. VITA, PAUL. Returning the look: Victorian writers and the Paris morgue. *See* **10759**.

1355. WALL, EAMONN. James Liddy: editor and poet. *See* **17829**.

1356. WALMSLEY, PETER. Death and the nation in *The Spectator*. *In* (pp. 200–19) **1285**.

1357. WARE, MARK. E-only journals: is it time to drop print? LPub (18:3) 2005, 193–9.

1358. —— Online submission and peer-review systems. LPub (18:4) 2005, 245–50.

1359. WEAVER, RACHAEL. Reflecting the detectives: crime fiction and the New Journalism in late nineteenth-century Australia. *See* **9885**.

1360. WEBBY, ELIZABETH. Images of Europe in two nineteenth-century Australian illustrated magazines. VPR (37:4) 2003, 10–24.

1361. WELLS, DANIEL A.; WELLS, JONATHAN DANIEL. The literary and historical index to American magazines, 1800–1850. Westport, CT; London: Praeger, 2004. pp. xxi, 506. (Bibliographies and indexes in American literature, 32.)

1362. WINKIEL, LAURA. Cabaret Modernism: Vorticism and racial spectacle. *In* (pp. 206–24) **12640**.

1363. WONHAM, HENRY B. Amerigo's miraculous metamorphosis; or, The logic of ethnic caricature in *The Golden Bowl*. *See* **11464**.

1364. WOODSWORTH, GLENN. *The Adder's* tale: memories of a little magazine of the 1960s. Amphora (138) 2005, 21–4.

1365. WORTH, GEORGE J. *Macmillan's Magazine*, 1859–1907: no flippancy or abuse allowed. (Bibl. 2004, 1387.) Rev. by David McKitterick in BC (54:1) 2005, 136–8.

1366. YOUNG, PAUL. Economy, empire, extermination: the Christmas Pudding, the Crystal Palace and the narrative of capitalist progress. *See* **9638**.

1367. YOUNGKIN, MOLLY. 'Independent in thought and expression, kindly and tolerant in tone': Henrietta Stannard, *Golden Gates*, and gender controversies in *fin-de-siècle* periodicals. VPR (38:3) 2005, 307–29.

THE ENGLISH LANGUAGE

GENERAL STUDIES

1368. ANON. (ed.). Insights into the dynamics of the English language and culture: conference proceedings. Prešov: Prešov UP, 2005. pp. 565.

1369. ČERMÁK, JAN, *et al.* (eds). Patterns: a Festschrift for Libuše Dušková. Prague: Charles Univ., 2005. pp. 305.

1370. CHOVANEC, JAN (ed.). Theory and practice in English Studies: proceedings from the eighth conference of English, American and Canadian studies: vol. 3. Brno: Masarykova Univ., 2005. pp. 256.

1371. CRYSTAL, DAVID. The Cambridge encyclopedia of the English language. (Bibl. 2004, 1391.) Rev. by Agnieszka Mrowiec in JPrag (36:11) 2004, 2085–7; by Roderick A. Jacobs in JEL (33:1) 2005, 83–7.

1372. FAIRCLOUGH, NORMAN. Analysing discourse: textual analysis for social research. London; New York: Routledge, 2003. pp. 270. Rev. by David Banks in LLit (14:2) 2005, 199–202.

1373. GRMELOVÁ, ANNA; DUŠKOVÁ, LIBUŠE; FARRELL, MARK (eds). 2nd Prague Conference on Linguistic and Literary Studies: proceedings. Prague: Charles Univ., 2005. pp. 198.

1374. HAMM, ALBERT. Language chunks and the levels of linguistic analysis. RANAM (38) 2005, 9–24.

1375. KITIS, ELIZA (ed.). Working papers in linguistics. Thessaloniki: School of English, Aristotle Univ., 2004. pp. 181.

1376. MARMARIDOU, SOPHIA, *et al.* (eds). Reviewing linguistic thought: converging trends for the 21st century. Berlin; New York: Mouton de Gruyter, 2005. pp. xii, 436. (Trends in linguistics: Studies and monographs, 161.)

1377. MATTHEOUDAKIS, MARINA; PSALTOU-JOYCEY, ANGELIKI (eds). Selected papers on theoretical and applied linguistics from the 16th international symposium. Thessaloniki: Aristotle Univ., 2005. pp. 575.

1378. PETERS, PAM. The Cambridge guide to English usage. (Bibl. 2004, 1406.) Rev. by Edgar W. Schneider in EWW (26:1) 2005, 116–18.

1379. WILSON, DAVID. Mugging de Queen's English? Mapping mental spaces of English. SPELL (17) 2005, 265–85.

HISTORY AND DEVELOPMENT OF ENGLISH

1380. ALTVATER, FRANCES, *et al.* (comps). The year's work in Old English studies 2002. *See* **4195**.

1381. BAKER, PETER S. Introduction to Old English. (Bibl. 2003, 1319.) Rev. by Robert D. Stevick in Envoi (10:2) 2003 for 2001, 100–3; by Richard Dance in NQ (52:1) 2005, 110.

1382. BASWELL, CHRISTOPHER. Troy, Arthur, and the languages of 'Brutis Albyoun'. *In* (pp. 170–97) **4485**.

1383. BERTACCA, ANTONIO (ed.). Historical linguistic studies of spoken English: papers read at the 11th Italian Conference on the History of the English Language, Pisa, 5–7 June 2003. *See* **2537.**

1384. BRAGG, MELVYN. The adventure of English: the biography of a language. New York: Arcade, 2004. pp. xii, 322. Rev. by James Jamieson in ManQ (45:2) 2004, 252–4.

1385. CANNON, CHRISTOPHER. Between the Old and the Middle of English. NML (7) 2005, 203–21.

1386. CARRILLO LINARES, Mᴬ JOSÉ. Middle English *Antidotarium Nicholai*: evidence for linguistic distribution and dissemination in the vernacular. *See* **4699.**

1387. CORÈDON, CHRISTOPHER; WILLIAMS, ANN. A dictionary of medieval terms and phrases. *See* **1955.**

1388. CRYSTAL, DAVID. The stories of English. (Bibl. 2004, 1427.) Rev. by Daniel Schreier in EWW (26:2) 2005, 243–5.

1389. CULPEPER, JONATHAN. History of English. (Bibl. 2000, 1703.) London; New York: Routledge, 2005. pp. x, 134. (Second ed.: first ed. 1997.)

1390. DOSSENA, MARINA; LASS, ROGER (eds). Methods and data in English historical dialectology. *See* **2909.**

1391. GARRIDO ANES, EDURNE. Geographical and dialectal distribution of Platearius' *Liber de simplici medicina* in England. *See* **4700.**

1392. GOYENS, MICHELE; VERBEKE, WERNER (eds). The dawn of the written vernacular in Western Europe. Louvain: Louvain UP, 2003. pp. xiv, 484. (Mediaevalia Lovaniensia, 1:33.) Rev. by Charles F. Briggs in TMR, Nov. 2005.

1393. GUZMÁN-GONZÁLEZ, TRINIDAD. Out of the past: a walk with labels and concepts, raiders of the lost evidence, and a vindication of the role of writing. *See* **3173.**

1394. HERNÁNDEZ-CAMPOY, JUAN MANUEL; CONDE-SILVESTRE, JUAN CAMILO. Sociolinguistic and geolinguistic approaches to the historical diffusion of linguistic innovations: incipient standardisation in Late Middle English. *See* **3177.**

1395. HICKEY, RAYMOND. Dublin English: evolution and change. *See* **2932.**

1396. HILTUNEN, RISTO; SKAFFARI, JANNE (eds). Discourse perspectives on English: medieval to modern. (Bibl. 2004, 1440.) Rev. by Peter Grund in JEL (33:1) 2005, 87–91.

1397. HOLM, JOHN. Languages in contact: the partial restructuring of vernaculars. Cambridge; New York: CUP, 2004. pp. xx, 175. Rev. by Edgar W. Schneider in EWW (26:1) 2005, 125–6.

1398. HOROBIN, SIMON. 'In London and opelond': the dialect and circulation of the C version of *Piers Plowman*. *See* **4850.**

1399. HOWE, JOHN R. Language and political meaning in Revolutionary America. *See* **8230.**

1400. KRIES, SUSANNE. Skandinavisch–schottische Sprachbeziehungen im Mittelalter: der altnordische Lehneinfluss. *See* **2941.**

1401. KRYGIER, MARCIN; SIKORSKA, LILIANA (eds). For the loue of Inglis lede. *See* **4445.**

2005]   HISTORY OF LINGUISTICS   71

1402. KYTÖ, MERJA; WALKER, TERRY. The linguistic study of Early Modern English speech-related texts: how 'bad' can 'bad' data be? *See* **2565**.

1403. LONGMORE, PAUL K. 'They ... speak better English than the English do': colonialism and the origins of national linguistic standardization in America. *See* **3011**.

1404. MACHAN, TIM WILLIAM. English in the Middle Ages. (Bibl. 2004, 1448.) Rev. by Jeremy J. Smith in MLR (100:4) 2005, 1079–80; by Christopher Cannon in Spec (80:2) 2005, 629–31.

1405. MARSDEN, RICHARD. The Cambridge Old English reader. (Bibl. 2004, 1450.) Rev. by Robert D. Fulk in NQ (52:2) 2005, 236–7.

1406. MARSHALL, JONATHAN. Language change and sociolinguistics: rethinking social networks. *See* **3187**.

1407. MICHIE, ALLEN; BUCKLEY, ERIC (eds). Style: essays on Renaissance and Restoration language and culture in memory of Harriett Hawkins. *See* **5167**.

1408. NEVALA, MINNA. Accessing politeness axes: forms of address and terms of reference in early English correspondence. *See* **5343**.

1409. NEVALAINEN, TERTTU; RAUMOLIN-BRUNBERG, HELENA. Sociolinguistics and the history of English: a survey. *See* **3195**.

1410. POWELL, KATHRYN. The MANCASS C11 database: a tool for studying script and spelling in the eleventh century. OEN (38:1) 2004, 29–42.

1411. RAUMOLIN-BRUNBERG, HELENA, *et al.* (eds). Variation past and present: VARIENG studies on English for Terttu Nevalainen. (Bibl. 2003, 1356.) Rev. by Roberta Facchinetti in JEL (31:4) 2003, 363–9; by Matthew J. Gordon in AS (80:1) 2005, 87–91.

1412. RITT, NIKOLAUS; SCHENDL, HERBERT (eds). Rethinking Middle English: linguistic and literary approaches. New York; Frankfurt: Lang, 2005. pp. xi, 339. (Studies in English medieval language and literature, 10.)

1413. SHERBO, ARTHUR. The appendix to Edmond Malone's 1790 *Shakespeare*, the 1821 Boswell–Malone *Shakespeare*, and Elizabethan language. *See* **5828**.

1414. SIEGEL, JEFF. Creolization outside creolistics. *See* **3137**.

1415. TAAVITSAINEN, IRMA. Genres of secular instruction: a linguistic history of useful entertainment. Misc (29) 2004, 75–94.

1416. TINTI, FRANCESCA (ed.). Pastoral care in late Anglo-Saxon England. *See* **4259**.

1417. TRYON, DARRELL T.; CHARPENTIER, JEAN-MICHEL. Pacific pidgins and creoles: origins, growth and development. *See* **3139**.

1418. WATTS, RICHARD; TRUDGILL, PETER (eds). Alternative histories of English. (Bibl. 2004, 1464.) Rev. by Kingsley Bolton in EJES (9:1) 2004, 96–8.

HISTORY OF LINGUISTICS

1419. BOISSON, CLAUDE. La terre, la barre de fer et le Préfet de l'Isère: faits, lois et modèles, théories. Anglophonia (18) 2005, 7–27.

1420. CAMBONI, MARINA. Walt Whitman e la lingua del Mondo Nuovo: con tre testi di Walt Whitman. *See* **12300**.

1421. CANNON, GARLAND; FRANKLIN, MICHAEL J. A Cymmrodor claims kin in Calcutta: an assessment of Sir William Jones as philologer, polymath, and pluralist. *See* **8780.**

1422. CHAPMAN, DON. Composing and joining: how the Anglo-Saxons talked about compounding. *In* (pp. 39–54) **1786.**

1423. CHRISTIDIS, ANASTASIOS FIVOS. The nature of language: twentieth-century approaches. *In* (pp. 291–312) **1376.**

1424. GILLIES, MALCOLM. Percy Grainger's word games. Meanjin (64:3) 2005, 145–51. ('Nordic English'.)

1425. GOLD, DAVID L. An aspect of lexicography still not fully professionalized: the search for antedatings and postdatings (with examples mostly from English and some from other languages). *See* **1925.**

1426. JOSEPH, BRIAN D.; JANDA, RICHARD D. (eds). The handbook of historical linguistics. Oxford; Malden, MA: Blackwell, 2003. pp. xviii, 881. (Blackwell handbooks in linguistics.) Rev. by François Chevillet in EA (58:1) 2005, 102–4.

1427. MARMARIDOU, SOPHIA; NIKIFORIDOU, KIKI; ANTONOPOULOU, ELENI. Introduction: converging trends for 21st-century linguistics: a theoretical background. *In* (pp. 1–11) **1376.**

1428. OSSELTON, N. E. Bishop Lowth converted: an English grammar for Catholics in the late eighteenth century. EngS (84:5) 2003, 448–52.

1429. SHORROCKS, GRAHAM. The Rev. William Hutton's *A Bran New Wark*: the Westmorland dialect in the late early modern period. *See* **2961.**

1430. STEEN, GERARD. Metonymy goes cognitive-linguistic. *See* **2488.**

1431. TEN HACKEN, PIUS. The disappearance of the geographical dimension of language in American linguistics. SPELL (17) 2005, 249–64.

1432. TIEKEN-BOON VAN OSTADE, INGRID. Of social networks and linguistic influence: the language of Robert Lowth and his correspondents. *See* **3206.**

1433. WOLF, GÖRAN. Grammarians assess the English language. *In* (pp. 173–9) **1370.**

PHONETICS AND PHONOLOGY

HISTORICAL PHONETICS AND PHONOLOGY OF ENGLISH

1434. BRITAIN, DAVID. Where did New Zealand English come from? *In* (pp. 156–93) **3044.**

1435. —— TRUDGILL, PETER. New dialect formation and contact-induced reallocation: three case studies from the English Fens. *See* **2916.**

1436. CARPENTER, JEANNINE. The invisible community of the lost colony: African American English on Roanoke Island. *See* **2988.**

1437. CRYSTAL, DAVID. Pronouncing Shakespeare: the Globe experiment. *See* **6152.**

1438. GREEN, MARTIN. The pronunciation of *Wriothesley*. *See* **2061.**

1439. HÄCKER, MARTINA. Linking [ɹ] and the variation between linking /r/ and glottal onsets in South African English. *See* **3057.**

1440. HOUGH, CAROLE.   Old English *gefnesan*, present-day English *sneeze*, and the place-names Snogsash and Sneachill. See **1842.**

1441. IVERSON, GREGORY K.; SALMONS, JOSEPH C.   Filling the gap: English tense vowel plus final /š/. JEL (33:3) 2005, 207–21.

1442. MILROY, JAMES.   Variability, language change, and the history of English. IJES (5:1) 2005, 1–11.

1443. MINKOVA, DONKA.   Alliteration and sound change in early English. (Bibl. 2004, 1492.) Rev. by Christopher M. Cain in JEGP (104:3) 2005, 394–6; by Marc Pierce in Spec (80:4) 2005, 1331–3.

1444. MUGGLESTONE, LYNDA.   'Talking proper': the rise of accent as social symbol. (Bibl. 1999, 1378.) Oxford; New York: OUP, 2003. pp. viii, 354. (Second ed.: first ed. 1995.) Rev. by Richard W. Bailey in Lang (81:1) 2005, 269–71; by François Chevillet in EA (58:2) 2005, 193–4.

1445. ROBINSON, CHRISTINE.   Changes in the dialect of Livingston. See **2955.**

1446. SCHREIER, DANIEL.   CCV-> #CV-: corpus-based evidence of historical change in English phonotactics. IJES (5:1) 2005, 77–99.

1447. —— Consonant change in English worldwide: synchrony meets diachrony. Basingstoke; New York: Palgrave Macmillan, 2005. pp. xvi, 248. (Palgrave studies in language history and language change.)

1448. TROUSDALE, GRAEME.   The social context of Kentish Raising: issues in Old English sociolinguistics. See **2962.**

1449. WRIGHT, LAURA.   The space of English: geographic space, temporal space and social space. See **2914.**

PHONETICS AND PHONOLOGY OF CONTEMPORARY ENGLISH

1450. ADJAYE, SOPHIA A.   Ghanaian English pronunciation. See **3035.**

1451. BAILEY, GUY; TILLERY, JAN; ANDRES, CLAIRE.   Some effects of transcribers on data in dialectology. See **2977.**

1452. BAYARD, DONN; GREEN, JAMES A.   Evaluating English accents worldwide. Te Reo (48) 2005, 21–8.

1453. —— SULLIVAN, KIRK P. H.   A taste of Kiwi: does the Swedish palate differ in sensitivity and preference from the New Zealanders'? Te Reo (48) 2005, 29–40.

1454. BECK, JANET MACKENZIE.   Perceptual analysis of voice quality: the place of vocal profile analysis. *In* (pp. 285–322) **1472.**

1455. BECKETT, DAN.   Sociolinguistic individuality in a remnant dialect community. See **2981.**

1456. BELL, ALLAN; HARLOW, RAY; STARKS, DONNA (eds).   Languages of New Zealand. See **3044.**

1457. CONOLLY, L. W.   Shaw and BBC English. See **19387.**

1458. COWPER, ELIZABETH.   The geometry of interpretable features: INFL in Spanish and English. See **1588.**

1459. CURL, TRACI S.   Practices in other-initiated repair resolution: the phonetic differentiation of 'repetitions'. DP (39:1) 2005, 1–43.

1460. CUTLER, ANNE; BROERSMA, MIRJAM.   Phonetic precision in listening. *In* (pp. 63–91) **1472.**

1461. DETERDING, DAVID.   Emergent patterns in the vowels of Singapore English. *See* **3052.**

1462. DOCHERTY, G. J.; FOULKES, P.   Glottal variants of *t* in the Tyneside variety of English. *In* (pp. 173–97) **1472.**

1463. DODSWORTH, ROBIN.   Attribute networking: a technique for modeling social perceptions. *See* **3162.**

1464. DRAGER, KATIE.   From *bad* to *bed*: the relationship between perceived age and vowel perception in New Zealand English. Te Reo (48) 2005, 55–68.

1465. FRASER, HELEN.   Constraining abstractness: phonological representation in the light of color terms. *See* **1732.**

1466. —— Representing speech in practice and theory. *In* (pp. 93–128) **1472.**

1467. FRIDLAND, VALERIE; BARTLETT, KATHRYN; KREUZ, ROGER.   Making sense of variation: pleasantness and education ratings of Southern vowel variants. *See* **2996.**

1468. GEORGIAFENTIS, MICHALIS.   Focus: the interplay of phonology, syntax, semantics, and pragmatics. *In* (pp. 163–78) **1376.**

1469. GIBSON, ANDREW M.   Non-prevocalic /r/ in New Zealand Hip Hop. NZEJ (19) 2005, 5–12.

1470. GOODEN, SHELOME.   Prosodic contrast in Jamaican Creole reduplication. *In* (pp. 193–208) **3133.**

1471. GUT, ULRIKE.   Nigerian English prosody. *See* **3056.**

1472. HARDCASTLE, WILLIAM J.; BECK, J. MACKENZIE (eds).   A figure of speech: a Festschrift for John Laver. Mahwah, NJ; London: Erlbaum, 2005. pp. xxxix, 428.

1473. HARRINGTON, JOHN; PALETHORPE, SALLYANNE; WATSON, CATHERINE.   Deepening or lessening the divide between diphthongs: an analysis of the Queen's annual Christmas broadcasts. *In* (pp. 227–61) **1472.**

1474. HARRISON, CAREY.   Hey-days. VocR (7:7) 2005. (Received Pronunciation.)

1475. HAZEN, KIRK.   Mergers in the mountains: West Virginia division and unification. *See* **3003.**

1476. JAMES, WINFORD.   The role of tone and rhyme structure in the organisation of grammatical morphemes in Tobagonian. *In* (pp. 165–92) **3133.**

1477. KIESLING, SCOTT F.   Variation, stance and style: word-final -*er*, high rising tone, and ethnicity in Australian English. *See* **3060.**

1478. KILGORE, JOHN.   The uses of euphony. *See* **2563.**

1479. LADEFOGED, PETER.   Speculations on the control of speech. *In* (pp. 3–21) **1472.**

1480. LAPPE, SABINE; PLAG, INGO.   Rules *vs* analogy: modeling variation in word-final epenthesis in Sranan. *In* (pp. 71–90) **3133.**

1481. LOCAL, JOHN.   On the interactional and phonetic design of collaborative completions. *In* (pp. 263–82) **1472.**

1482. —— WALKER, GARETH.   Abrupt-joins as a resource for the production of multi-unit, multi-action turns. *See* **2569.**

1483. McKenzie, Jayne. 'But he's not supposed to see me in my weeding dress!': the relationship between *dress* and *fleece* in Modern New Zealand English. NZEJ (19) 2005, 13–25.

1484. Majors, Tivoli. Low back vowel merger in Missouri speech: acoustic description and explanation. *See* **3014**.

1485. Mompeán-González, José A. Category overlap and neutralization: the importance of speakers' classifications in phonology. CogL (15:4) 2004, 429–69.

1486. Ní Chasaide, Ailbhe; Gobl, Christer. On the relation between phonatory quality and affect. *In* (pp. 323–46) **1472**.

1487. Nielsen, Daniel; Hay, Jennifer. Perceptions of regional dialects in New Zealand. Te Reo (48) 2005, 95–110.

1488. Ohala, John J. Phonetic explanations for sound patterns: implications for grammars of competence. *In* (pp. 23–38) **1472**.

1489. Plag, Ingo (ed.). Phonology and morphology of creole languages. *See* **3133**.

1490. Purnell, Thomas; Tepeli, Dilara; Salmons, Joseph. German substrate effects in Wisconsin English: evidence for final fortition. *See* **3020**.

1491. Rodriguez, José I.; Cargile, Aaron Castelan; Rich, Marc D. Reactions to African American Vernacular English: do more phonological features matter? *See* **3024**.

1492. Rubinstein, George. Linguistic bioacoustics: frames of Russian and English. *See* **3369**.

1493. Sharma, Devyani. Dialect stabilization and speaker awareness in non-native varieties of English. *See* **2911**.

1494. Shockey, Linda. Sound patterns of spoken English. (Bibl. 2003, 1424.) Rev. by Wolfgang U. Dressler and Katarzyna Dziubalska-Kołaczyk in Lang (81:1) 2005, 274–6.

1495. Shurbanov, Alexander. The Shakespearean sound in translation. *In* (pp. 239–57) **6000**.

1496. Silverman, Daniel. On the phonetic and cognitive nature of alveolar stop allophony in American English. CogL (15:1) 2004, 69–93.

1497. Skarnitzl, Radek. English word stress in the perception of Czech listeners. *In* (pp. 183–94) **1369**.

1498. Smith, Norval. New evidence from the past: to epenthesize or not to epenthesize? That is the question. *In* (pp. 91–107) **3133**.

1499. Starks, Donna; Allan, Scott. What comes before *t*? Nonalveolar *s* in Auckland. *See* **3074**.

1500. —— Reffell, Hayley. Pronouncing your /r/s in New Zealand English? A study of Pasifika and Maori students. NZEJ (19) 2005, 36–48.

1501. Sutcliffe, David. African American English suprasegmentals: a study of pitch patterns in the Black English of the United States. *In* (pp. 147–62) **3133**.

1502. Thomas, Brynmor; Hay, Jennifer. A pleasant malady: the *Ellen/Allan* merger in New Zealand English. Te Reo (48) 2005, 69–93.

1503. TRUDGILL, PETER; MACLAGAN, MARGARET; LEWIS, GILLIAN.   Linguistic archaeology: the Scottish input to New Zealand English phonology. *See* **3078.**

1504. VAN LEYDEN, KLASKE.   Prosodic characteristics of Orkney and Shetland dialects: an experimental approach. *See* **2964.**

1505. VOLÍN, JAN.   Rhythmical properties of polysyllabic words in British and Czech English. *In* (pp. 279–92) **1369.**

1506. WARREN, PAUL; DALY, NICOLA.   Characterising New Zealand English intonation: broad and narrow analysis. *In* (pp. 217–37) **3044.**

1507. WICHMANN, ANNE.   The intonation of *please*-requests: a corpus-based study. *See* **1701.**

1508. YAVAS, MEHMET.   Applied English phonology. Oxford; Malden, MA: Blackwell, 2005. pp. viii, 245.

SPELLING, PUNCTUATION, HANDWRITING

1509. ANON.   Script and its names. BC (54:2) 2005, 171–94 (review-article).

1510. AFROS, ELENA.   Syntactic variaton in Riddles 30A and 30B. *See* **4370.**

1511. BURLINSON, CHRISTOPHER; ZURCHER, ANDREW.   'Secretary to the Lord Grey Lord Deputie here': Edmund Spenser's Irish papers. *See* **5683.**

1512. CALLE MARTÍN, JAVIER.   Punctuation practice in a 15th-century arithmetical treatise (MS Bodley 790). NM (105:4) 2004, 407–22.

1513. —— MIRANDA GARCÍA, ANTONIO.   Editing Middle English punctuation: the case of MS Egerton 2622 (ff. 136–152). *See* **4684.**

1514. COOK, VIVIAN.   The English writing system. Oxford; New York: OUP, 2004. pp. vi, 229. (English language.)

1515. COOPER, LISA H.   Urban utterances: merchants, artisans, and the alphabet in Caxton's *Dialogues in French and English*. *See* **4777.**

1516. COOPERMAN, MATTHEW.   Between the brackets: an interview with D. A. Powell. *See* **18912.**

1517. DEROLEZ, ALBERT.   The palaeography of gothic manuscript books: from the twelfth to the early sixteenth century. (Bibl. 2004, 213.) Rev. in BC (54:2) 2005, 171–94; by A. I. Doyle in MÆ (74:1) 2005, 119–20.

1518. DiNAPOLI, ROBERT.   Odd characters: runes in Old English poetry. *In* (pp. 145–61) **1786.**

1519. DUMVILLE, DAVID N.   English script in the second half of the ninth century. *In* (pp. 305–25) **4220.**

1520. ESTEBAN SEGURA, MARIA LAURA.   The punctuation system of the West Saxon version of the Gospel according to Saint John. *See* **4344.**

1521. FRASER, HELEN.   Representing speech in practice and theory. *In* (pp. 93–128) **1472.**

1522. HARRISON, CASEY.   Outré-days. VocR (7:12) 2005. (Whether commas etc. go inside or outside inverted commas.)

1523. HEYMAN, MICHAEL.   The performative letter, from medieval to modern. CLAQ (30:1) 2005, 100–7.

1524. HILL, BETTY.   The writing of the septenary couplet. *See* **4645.**

1525. HOLLIS, CATHERINE W.   Virginia Woolf's double signature. *See* **20366.**

2005]   SPELLING, PUNCTUATION, HANDWRITING   77

1526. KNOWLES, OWEN; STAPE, J. H.   The rationale of punctuation in Conrad's *Blackwood's* fictions. *See* **15886.**

1527. LEDERER, RICHARD.   A little bit of comma sense. VocR (7:7) 2005.

1528. LINDSTRÖM, BENGT.   A note on anagrammatic corruption in *Havelok*. *See* **4567.**

1529. LIVINGSTON, MICHAEL.   A sixth hand in Cambridge, Trinity College, MS R.3.19. JEBS (8) 2005, 229–37.

1530. LÓPEZ RÚA, PAULA.   Shortening devices in text messaging: a multilingual approach. NM (106:2) 2005, 139–55.

1531. MEDOVARSKI, ANDREA.   Unstable post(-)colonialities: speculations through punctuation. *See* **14910.**

1532. POWELL, KATHRYN.   The MANCASS C11 database: a tool for studying script and spelling in the eleventh century. *See* **1410.**

1533. PURDON, JOHN JAMES.   John Aubrey's 'discourse in paper'. *See* **7199.**

1534. PUTTER, AD.   Weak *e* and the metre of Richard Spalding's *Alliterative Katherine Hymn*. *See* **4921.**

1535. RAYLOR, TIMOTHY.   The date and script of Hobbes's Latin optical manuscript. *See* **305.**

1536. ROLLINGS, ANDREW G.   The spelling patterns of English. Munich: LINCOM Europa, 2004. pp. ix, 239. (LINCOM studies in English linguistics, 4.)

1537. ROMAINE, SUZANNE.   Orthographic practices in the standardization of pidgins and creoles: pidgin in Hawai'i as anti-language and anti-standard. *See* **3134.**

1538. RUTKOWSKA, HANNA.   Selected orthographic features in English editions of the *Book of Good Maners* (1487–1507). *See* **4673.**

1539. SALE, CAROLYN.   The 'Roman hand': women, writing and the law in the *Att.-Gen. v. Chatterton* and the letters of the Lady Arbella Stuart. *See* **7149.**

1540. SEELY, JOHN.   Oxford A–Z of grammar and punctuation. *See* **1640.**

1541. SHRANK, CATHY.   'These fewe scribbled rules': representing scribal intimacy in early modern print. *See* **5349.**

1542. SOANES, CATHERINE; FERGUSON, SHEILA.   Oxford A–Z of spelling. *See* **1969.**

1543. TRUSS, LYNNE.   Eats, shoots & leaves: the zero tolerance approach to punctuation. (Bibl. 2004, 1558.) Rev. by Myles Weber in SewR (113:1) 2005, xx–xxii.

1544. WAITE, MAURICE (ed.).   New Oxford spelling dictionary. *See* **1976.**

1545. WEINGARTEN, RUEDIGER.   Subsyllabic units in written word production. *See* **1561.**

1546. WINNICK, R. H.   Anagrammatic patterns in Shakespeare's Sonnet 69. *See* **6727.**

GRAMMAR

MORPHOLOGY OF CONTEMPORARY ENGLISH

1547. ADAMS, MICHAEL. Meaningful interposing: a countervalent form. AS (80:4) 2005, 437–41. (Slayer slang.)

1548. BAPTISTA, MARLYSE. Inflectional plural marking in pidgins and creoles: a comparative study. *In* (pp. 315–32) **3133.**

1549. COWPER, ELIZABETH. The geometry of interpretable features: INFL in Spanish and English. *See* **1588.**

1550. DUBOIS, SYLVIE; HORVATH, BARBARA M. Verbal morphology in Cajun Vernacular English: a comparison with other varieties of Southern English. *See* **2995.**

1551. FRATH, PIERRE. Why is there no ham in a hamburger? A study of lexical blends and reanalysed morphemisation. *See* **1733.**

1552. JAMES, WINFORD. The role of tone and rhyme structure in the organisation of grammatical morphemes in Tobagonian. *In* (pp. 165–92) **3133.**

1553. KAVKA, STANISLAV. Inflectional and/*versus* derivational morphology: clear-cut types or continua? SAP (39) 2003, 177–90.

1554. KOUWENBERG, SILVIA (ed.). Twice as meaningful: reduplication in pidgins, creoles and other contact languages. *See* **3126.**

1555. LÓPEZ RÚA, PAULA. The manipulative power of word-formation devices in Margaret Atwood's *Oryx and Crake. See* **15218.**

1556. MELA-ATHANASOPOULOU, ELIZABETH. The derivational suffix in English: its categorial and semantic effect. *In* (pp. 85–102) **1375.**

1557. —— Morphologization of synthetic prepositions in English and Modern Greek. *In* (pp. 118–32) **1377.**

1558. MICHAELIS, LAURA A. Type shifting in construction grammar: an integrated approach to aspectual coercion. *See* **1623.**

1559. PLAG, INGO (ed.). Phonology and morphology of creole languages. *See* **3133.**

1560. SMITH, NORVAL. New evidence from the past: to epenthesize or not to epenthesize? That is the question. *In* (pp. 91–107) **3133.**

1561. WEINGARTEN, RUEDIGER. Subsyllabic units in written word production. WrLL (8:1) 2005, 43–61.

HISTORICAL MORPHOLOGY OF ENGLISH

1562. CHAPMAN, DON. Composing and joining: how the Anglo-Saxons talked about compounding. *In* (pp. 39–54) **1786.**

1563. JEFFERSON, JUDITH A.; PUTTER, AD. The distribution of infinitives in -*e* and -*en* in some Middle English alliterative poems. MÆ (74:2) 2005, 221–47.

1564. LOUREIRO PORTO, LUCÍA. A corpus-based approach to eModE *have need. See* **1691.**

1565. NEVALAINEN, TERTTU. Sociolinguistic perspectives on Tudor English. *See* **3193.**

1566. SAUER, HANS. The morphology of the Old English plant-names. *In* (pp. 161–79) **1773.**

SINGLE MORPHEMES

1567. *-ing*] NÚÑEZ PERTEJO, PALOMA. Adjectival participles or present participles? On the classification of some dubious examples from the Helsinki Corpus. SEDERI (13) 2003, 141–53.

1568. *-ingas*] LAFLIN, SUSAN. Do *-ingas* place-names occur in pairs? JEPNS (35) 2002/03, 31–40.

1569. *-man*] VAN DEN BERG, MARGOT. Early 18th-century Sranan *-man*. *In* (pp. 231–51) **3133**.

1570. *-pela*] FARACLAS, NICHOLAS. The *-pela* suffix in Tok Pisin and the notion of 'simplicity' in pidgin and creole languages: what happens to morphology under contact? *In* (pp. 269–90) **3133**.

1571. *-tūn*] COATES, RICHARD. Two notes on names in *tūn* in relation to pre-English antiquities: Kirmington and Broughton, Lincolnshire. *See* **2038**.

1572. *-wican*] BRITTON, DEREK. Orm's *wikenn* and compounds with *-wican* in annal 1137 of the Peterborough Chronicle. *See* **4713**.

1573. *-wise*] YEZBICK, KA'ALA; TRAUGOTT, ELIZABETH CLOSS. Recent developments in viewpoints *-wise*. AS (80:1) 2005, 105–12.

SYNTAX OF CONTEMPORARY ENGLISH

1574. ANON. The American Heritage dictionary of phrasal verbs. *See* **1944**.

1575. ADAM, MARTIN. Functional *macrofield* perspective? *In* (pp. 27–34) **1370**.

1576. ARNAUD, PIERRE J. L.; MANIEZ, FRANÇOIS. Linguistique de corpus et nano-genre: temps et *be* + *ing* dans les légendes de photographies de trains. Anglophonia (18) 2005, 73–84.

1577. BAO, ZHIMING; LYE, HUI MIN. Systematic transfer, topic prominence, and the bare conditional in Singapore English. *See* **3038**.

1578. BAPTISTA, MARLYSE. Inflectional plural marking in pidgins and creoles: a comparative study. *In* (pp. 315–32) **3133**.

1579. BEHEYDT, GRIET. Bygone times …: the preterite and the present perfect in Dutch as compared to English. BELL (ns 3) 2005, 123–48.

1580. BERGE, SIGBJØRN L. The grammatical nature of the English modal auxiliaries: a hypothesis. *In* (pp. 35–41) **1370**.

1581. BERGEN, BENJAMIN K.; PLAUCHÉ, MADELAINE C. The convergent evolution of radial constructions: French and English deictics and existentials. CogL (16:1) 2005, 1–42.

1582. BOND, FRANCIS. Translating the untranslatable: a solution to the problem of generating English determiners. *See* **3227**.

1583. CASIELLES-SUAREZ, EUGENIA. The syntax–information structure interface: evidence from Spanish and English. London; New York: Routledge, 2004. pp. xv, 232. (Outstanding dissertations in linguistics.)

1584. CHAMONIKOLASOVÁ, JANA; ADAM, MARTIN. The presentation scale in the theory of functional sentence perspective. *In* (pp. 59–69) **1369**.

1585. CHOVANEC, JAN. The (un)conventional use of the simple past tense in news headlines. *In* (pp. 71–81) **1369**.

1586. CONSIGNY, ANTOINE. Chunks of meanings in English phrasal verbs. RANAM (38) 2005, 75–84.

1587. COOK, ANNE E.; MYERS, JEROME L.; O'BRIEN, EDWARD J. Processing an anaphor when there is no antecedent. DP (39:1) 2005, 101–20.

1588. COWPER, ELIZABETH. The geometry of interpretable features: INFL in Spanish and English. Lang (81:1) 2005, 10–46.

1589. DE KLERK, VIVIAN. Expressing levels of intensity in Xhosa English. *See* **3050.**

1590. DONTCHEVA-NAVRATILOVA, OLGA. Supplementive clauses in resolutions. *In* (pp. 43–52) **1370.**

1591. DUFFLEY, PATRICK J. The gerund and the *to*-infinitive as subject. JEL (31:4) 2003, 324–52.

1592. DUŠKOVÁ, LIBUŠE. From the heritage of Vilém Mathesius and Jan Firbas: syntax in the service of FSP. *In* (pp. 7–23) **1370.**

1593. —— Konstantnost syntaktické funkce mezi jazyky. (Syntactic constancy across languages.) SaS (66:4) 2005, 243–60.

1594. —— Syntactic constancy of the subject complement: part 2, A comparison between English and Czech. LingPr (15:1) 2005, 1–17.

1595. ESSEGBEY, JAMES. The basic locative construction in Gbe languages and Surinamese creoles. *See* **3120.**

1596. FANEGO, TERESA. Is cognitive grammar a usage-based model? Towards a realistic account of English sentential complements. Misc (29) 2004, 23–58.

1597. FARRELL, PATRICK. English verb–preposition constructions: constituency and order. Lang (81:1) 2005, 96–137.

1598. GEORGIAFENTIS, MICHALIS. Focus: the interplay of phonology, syntax, semantics, and pragmatics. *In* (pp. 163–78) **1376.**

1599. GIBSON, EDWARD, *et al.* Reading relative clauses in English. CogL (16:2) 2005, 313–53.

1600. GOODEN, SHELOME. Prosodic contrast in Jamaican Creole reduplication. *In* (pp. 193–208) **3133.**

1601. GORLACH, MARINA. Phrasal constructions and resultativeness in English: a sign-oriented analysis. Amsterdam; Philadelphia, PA: Benjamins, 2004. pp. vi, 150. (Studies in functional and structural linguistics, 52.)

1602. GRIES, STEFAN TH.; HAMPE, BEATE; SCHÖNEFELD, DORIS. Converging evidence: bringing together experimental and corpus data on the association of verbs and constructions. *See* **1680.**

1603. HANCOCK, CRAIG. Meaning-centered grammar: an introductory text. Oakville, CT: Equinox, 2004. pp. 260. (Equinox textbooks and surveys in linguistics.)

1604. HARRISON, CAREY. Away-days. VocR (7:8) 2005. (Verbal tenses.)

1605. HERBST, THOMAS, *et al.* (eds). A valency dictionary of English: a corpus-based analysis of the complementation patterns of English verbs, nouns, and adjectives. *See* **1959.**

1606. HEYVAERT, LIESBET; ROGIERS, HELLA; VERMEYLEN, NADINE. Pronominal determiners in gerundive nominalization: a 'case' study. EngS (86:1) 2005, 71–88.

1607. HOFFMANN, SEBASTIAN. Grammaticalization and English complex prepositions: a corpus-based study. London; New York: Routledge, 2005. pp. xiii, 214. (Routledge advances in corpus linguistics, 7.)

1608. HOFFMANN, THOMAS. Variable *vs* categorical effects: preposition pied piping and stranding in British English relative clauses. JEL (33:3) 2005, 257–97.

1609. JAMES, WINFORD. The role of tone and rhyme structure in the organisation of grammatical morphemes in Tobagonian. *In* (pp. 165–92) **3133**.

1610. KEIZER, EVELIEN. The discourse function of close appositions. Neophilologus (89:3) 2005, 447–67.

1611. KING, JEFFREY C. Context-dependent quantifiers and donkey anaphora. CanJP (supp.30) 2004, 97–127.

1612. KITIS, ELIZA. Conditional constructions as rhetorical structures. *In* (pp. 31–51) **1375**.

1613. KORTMANN, BERND (ed.). A comparative grammar of British English dialects: agreement, gender, relative clauses. *See* **2940**.

1614. KUDRNÁČOVÁ, NADĚŽDA. On one type of resultative minimal pair with agentive verbs of locomotion. *In* (pp. 107–14) **1369**.

1615. LANGLOTZ, ANDREAS. Are constructions the basic units of grammar? The phraseological turn in linguistic theory. RANAM (38) 2005, 45–63.

1616. LARROQUE, PATRICE. Variation et représentation linguistique. Anglophonia (18) 2005, 205–16.

1617. LEDERER, RICHARD. A tense time with verbs. VocR (7:9) 2005.

1618. LESTER, MARK; BEASON, LARRY. The McGraw-Hill handbook of English grammar and usage. Boston, MA: McGraw-Hill, 2005. pp. vii, 344.

1619. MALÁ, MARCELA. Syntactic and semantic differences between nominal relative clauses and dependent *wh*-interrogative clauses. *In* (pp. 85–9) **1370**.

1620. MALÁ, MARKÉTA. Semantic roles of adverbial participial clauses. *In* (pp. 91–7) **1370**.

1621. MALINIER, YVES-BERNARD. Du notionnel à l'énonciatif et retour: le cas de la construction *activo-passive* en anglais actuel. Anglophonia (18) 2005, 47–71.

1622. MERCHANT, JASON. Ellipsis and 'nonsentential speech'. *In* (pp. 175–89) **1377**.

1623. MICHAELIS, LAURA A. Type shifting in construction grammar: an integrated approach to aspectual coercion. CogL (15:1) 2004, 1–67.

1624. NARIYAMA, SHIGEKO. Subject ellipsis in English. JPrag (36:2) 2004, 237–64.

1625. OJEA, ANA. A syntactic approach to logical modality. Atl (27:1) 2005, 53–64.

1626. ONO, HARUHIKO. On the semantic difference between the *do*-form and the *doing*-form in perception verb complements: from the viewpoint of 'perception' and 'cognition'. JPrag (36:3) 2004, 407–39.

1627. PAP, DÁNIEL. A comparative approach to English, German and Hungarian verbal particles. *In* (pp. 113–19) **1370.**

1628. PÍPALOVÁ, RENATA. On central paragraphs with a stable P-theme. *In* (pp. 157–67) **1369.**

1629. —— On the structural aspect of textual hyperthemes. *In* (pp. 121–6) **1370.**

1630. POVOLNÁ, RENATA. On the role of some interactive D-items in different genres of spoken English. *In* (pp. 169–81) **1369.**

1631. QUINN, HEIDI. The distribution of pronoun case forms in English. Amsterdam; Philadelphia, PA: Benjamins, 2005. pp. x, 409. (Linguistik aktuell / Linguistics today, 82.)

1632. RAYMOND, JAMES C.; RUSSELL, I. WILLIS (eds). Essays in linguistics: dialectology, grammar, and lexicography in honor of James B. McMillan. *See* **3021.**

1633. RENOUF, ANTOINETTE. Phrasal creativity viewed from an IT perspective. *See* **1762.**

1634. RODRÍGUEZ JUÁREZ, CAROLINA. Priority hierarchies in subject assignment in English: cases of conflation. RAEI (18) 2005, 247–59.

1635. RÖMER, UTE. Progressives, patterns, pedagogy: a corpus-driven approach to English progressive forms, functions, contexts, and didactics. Amsterdam; Philadelphia, PA: Benjamins, 2005. pp. xi, 327. (Studies in corpus linguistics, 18.)

1636. ROUSSEL, EMMANUELLE. L'autonomie du passif anglais. Anglophonia (18) 2005, 185–203.

1637. SAKODA, KENT; SIEGEL, JEFF. Pidgin grammar: an introduction to the creole English of Hawai'i. *See* **3135.**

1638. ŠALDOVÁ, PAVLÍNA. The function of relative clauses (in comparison with postmodifying participles): foregrounding. *In* (pp. 38–46) **1373.**

1639. —— Presupposition in postmodifying participles: the assumptions made. *In* (pp. 231–45) **1369.**

1640. SEELY, JOHN. Oxford A–Z of grammar and punctuation. Oxford; New York: OUP, 2004. pp. xvii, 148.

1641. SHARMA, DEVYANI. Dialect stabilization and speaker awareness in non-native varieties of English. *See* **2911.**

1642. SIMON-VANDENBERGEN, A.-M.; TAVERNIERS, MIRIAM; RAVELLI, LOUISE (eds). Grammatical metaphor: views from systemic functional linguistics. (Bibl. 2004, 1693.) Rev. by Kay Wikberg in EJES (9:1) 2005, 91–4.

1643. SINCLAIR, JOHN M.; JONES, SUSAN; DALEY, ROBERT. English collocation studies: the OSTI report. Ed. by Ramesh Krishnamurthy. London; New York: Continuum, 2004. pp. xxix, 208. (Corpus and discourse.)

1644. SLUNEČKOVÁ, LENKA. Syntactic constancy of the object between Czech and English in fiction and technical writing: preliminary notes. *In* (pp. 197–207) **1369.**

1645. SMOLKA, VLADISLAV. Non-extraposed subject clauses. *In* (pp. 137–43) **1370**.

1646. SZMRECSANYI, BENEDIKT. Never change a winning chunk. *See* **2599**.

1647. TAGLIAMONTE, SALI; ROBERTS, CHRIS. So weird; so cool; so innovative: the use of intensifiers in the television series *Friends*. AS (80:3) 2005, 280–300.

1648. VALLÉE, RICHARD. Complex demonstratives, articulation, and overarticulation. *See* **2138**.

1649. VANDELANOTTE, LIEVEN. Deixis and grounding in speech and thought representation. JPrag (36:3) 2004, 489–520.

1650. VASKO, ANNA-LIISA. Up Cambridge: prepositional locative expressions in dialect speech: a corpus-based study of the Cambridgeshire dialect. *See* **2965**.

1651. WILAMOVÁ, SIRMA. Grammatical realizations of the avoidance strategy as a significant negative politeness strategy in English discourse. *In* (pp. 295–305) **1369**.

1652. WOLFE, MICHAEL B. W.; MAGLIANO, JOSEPH P.; LARSEN, BENJAMIN. Causal and semantic relatedness in discourse understanding and representation. *See* **2140**.

1653. YUASA, ETSUYO. Modularity in language: constructional and categorial mismatch in syntax and semantics. *See* **2143**.

HISTORICAL SYNTAX OF ENGLISH

1654. AFROS, ELENA. Syntactic variaton in Riddles 30A and 30B. *See* **4370**.

1655. BÆKKEN, BJØRG. Word order in 17th-century English: a study of the stabilisation of the XSV pattern. Oslo: Novus, 2003. pp. xiii, 220. Rev. by François Chevillet in EA (58:2) 2005, 198–9.

1656. BANKS, DAVID. On the historical origins of nominalized process in scientific text. *See* **2809**.

1657. CARPENTER, JEANNINE. The invisible community of the lost colony: African American English on Roanoke Island. *See* **2988**.

1658. CURZAN, ANNE. Gender shifts in the history of English. (Bibl. 2004, 1718.) Rev. by Mikko Laitinen in NM (106:1) 2005, 92–6.

1659. DORGELOH, HEIDRUN. Conjunction in sentence and discourse: sentence-initial *and* and discourse structure. *See* **1677**.

1660. GONZÁLEZ DÍAZ, VICTORINA. Adjective comparison in Renaissance English. SEDERI (13) 2003, 87–100.

1661. GONZÁLEZ ORTA, MARTA. The interrelation of semantic structure and syntactic variation in Old English verb classes: catalogue of syntactico-semantic constructions. RAEI (18) 2005, 111–28.

1662. —— The Old English verbs of *smell perception* and *emission*: analysis of the interface of their semantic and syntactic representation. *See* **1784**.

1663. HART, DAVID (ed.). English modality in context: diachronic perspectives. (Bibl. 2004, 1726.) Rev. by Lucía Loureiro Porto in SEDERI (15) 2005, 157–61.

1664. HEGARTY, MICHAEL. A feature-based syntax of functional categories: the structure, acquisition, and specific impairment of functional systems. Berlin; New York: Mouton de Gruyter, 2005. pp. xiii, 348. (Studies in generative grammar, 79.)

1665. LOUREIRO PORTO, LUCÍA. Force-dynamics: the key for an interpretation of modal necessity in Old English. NM (106:2) 2005, 211–27.

1666. MÉNDEZ-NAYA, BELÉN. On intensifiers and grammaticalization: the case of swīþe. See **1711.**

1667. NÚÑEZ PERTEJO, PALOMA. Adjectival participles or present participles? On the classification of some dubious examples from the Helsinki Corpus. See **1567.**

1668. OSSELTON, N. E. Bishop Lowth converted: an English grammar for Catholics in the late eighteenth century. See **1428.**

1669. RAUMOLIN-BRUNBERG, HELENA. Language change in adulthood: historical letters as evidence. See **2878.**

1670. RODRÍGUEZ-ÁLVAREZ, ALICIA; DOMÍNGUEZ-RODRÍGUEZ, Mᴬ VICTORIA. A Middle English text revised by a Renaissance reader: John Wotton's annotations to British Library MS Sloane 249 (ff. 180v–205v). See **4706.**

1671. ROHDENBURG, GÜNTER; MONDORF, BRITTA (eds). Determinants of grammatical variation in English. (Bibl. 2004, 1739.) Rev. by Alexander Bergs in Lang (81:1) 2005, 288–9.

1672. SCHLÜTER, JULIA. Rhythmic grammar: the influence of rhythm on grammatical variation and change in English. Berlin; New York: Mouton de Gruyter, 2005. pp. xi, 393. (Topics in English linguistics, 46.)

1673. TIEKEN-BOON VAN OSTADE, INGRID. Of social networks and linguistic influence: the language of Robert Lowth and his correspondents. See **3206.**

1674. TRETYAKOV, YURI P. The existential sentence: a diachronic model. NM (105:4) 2004, 437–43.

1675. WOODBRIDGE, LINDA. Shakespeare and magical grammar. In (pp. 84–98) **5167.**

SINGLE SYNTACTICAL ITEMS

1676. actually] DE KLERK, VIVIAN. The use of actually in spoken Xhosa English: a corpus study. WorldE (24:3) 2005, 275–88.

1677. and] DORGELOH, HEIDRUN. Conjunction in sentence and discourse: sentence-initial and and discourse structure. JPrag (36:10) 2004, 1761–79.

1678. and] PILLIÈRE, LINDA. And et les séries énumératives. Anglophonia (18) 2005, 135–56.

1679. as] BRŮHOVÁ, GABRIELA. Semantic roles of reason clauses introduced by the central conjunctions because, since, as and for. In (pp. 25–33) **1369.**

1680. as] GRIES, STEFAN TH.; HAMPE, BEATE; SCHÖNEFELD, DORIS. Converging evidence: bringing together experimental and corpus data on the association of verbs and constructions. CogL (16:4) 2005, 635–76.

1681. because] BRŮHOVÁ, GABRIELA. Semantic roles of reason clauses introduced by the central conjunctions because, since, as and for. In (pp. 25–33) **1369.**

1682. begin] CORRE, ERIC. Begin/start et leur complémentation: perspective diachronique et synchronique. Anglophonia (18) 2005, 157–72.

1683. *do*] MARGERIE, HÉLÈNE. La grammaticalisation de l'auxiliaire *do* revisitée: de Guillaume à Langacker. Anglophonia (18) 2005, 29–46.

1684. *do*] ZIEGELER, DEBRA. Reanalysis in the history of *do*: a view from construction grammar. CogL (15:4) 2004, 529–74.

1685. *for*] BRŮHOVÁ, GABRIELA. Semantic roles of reason clauses introduced by the central conjunctions *because, since, as* and *for*. In (pp. 25–33) **1369.**

1686. *forbid*] IYEIRI, YOKO. 'God forbid!': a historical study of the verb *forbid* in different versions of the English Bible. JEL (31:2) 2003, 149–62.

1687. *get*] GILQUIN, GAËTANELLE. Causative *get* and *have*: so close, so different. JEL (31:2) 2003, 125–48.

1688. *(be) going to*] SZMRECSANYI, BENEDIKT. Be going to versus *will/shall*: does syntax matter? JEL (31:4) 2003, 295–323.

1689. *have*] GAUDY-CAMPBELL, ISABELLE. *Have* en oral spontané: un comportement invariant au sein du travail de formulation? Anglophonia (18) 2005, 217–28.

1690. *have*] GILQUIN, GAËTANELLE. Causative *get* and *have*: so close, so different. See **1687.**

1691. *have need*] LOUREIRO PORTO, LUCÍA. A corpus-based approach to eModE *have need*. SEDERI (14) 2004, 217–26.

1692. *help (to)*] MCENERY, ANTHONY; XIAO, ZHONGHUA. HELP or HELP to: what do corpora have to say? EngS (86:2) 2005, 161–87.

1693. *I*] HARWOOD, NIGEL. 'I hoped to counteract the memory problem, but I made no impact whatsoever': discussing methods in computing science using *I*. See **2847.**

1694. *lie*] NEWMAN, JOHN; RICE, SALLY. Patterns of usage for English *sit, stand*, and *lie*: a cognitively inspired exploration in corpus linguistics. See **1706.**

1695. *like*] PAPADOPOULOU, IRIS. Discourse marker *like*: a unified account. In (pp. 190–202) **1377.**

1696. *like + to-infinitive*] DE SMET, HENDRIK; CUYCKENS, HUBERT. Pragmatic strengthening and the meaning of complement constructions: the case of *like* and *love* with the *to*-infinitive. JEL (33:1) 2005, 3–34.

1697. *love + to-infinitive*] —— —— Pragmatic strengthening and the meaning of complement constructions: the case of *like* and *love* with the *to*-infinitive. See **1696.**

1698. *may*] FURMANIAK, GRÉGORY. Le modal *may* dans les phrases optatives: étude syntaxique, sémantique et pragmatique. Anglophonia (18) 2005, 101–34.

1699. *me*] TEA, ALAN J. H.; LEE, BENNY P. H. Reference and blending in a computer role-playing game. JPrag (36:9) 2004, 1609–33.

1700. *ne*] BREMMER, ROLF H., JR; LAKER, STEPHEN. Earliest Middle English *ne*, 'than'. NQ (52:2) 2005, 163–4.

1701. *please*] WICHMANN, ANNE. The intonation of *please*-requests: a corpus-based study. JPrag (36:9) 2004, 1521–49.

1702. *provided (that)*] COUGIL ÁLVAREZ, ROSA MARÍA; GONZÁLEZ CRUZ, ANA I.   On the development of deverbal conjunctions: a case-study on the grammaticalisation of *provided (that)* in Early Modern English. SEDERI (13) 2003, 33–44.

1703. *sidle*] GOODBY, JOHN.   Whitman's influence on Dylan Thomas and the use of *sidle* as noun. *See* **19767**.

1704. *since*] BRŮHOVÁ, GABRIELA.   Semantic roles of reason clauses introduced by the central conjunctions *because, since, as* and *for. In* (pp. 25–33) **1369**.

1705. *since*] LATTES, TONY.   Sequitur et non-sequitur: *since* et alii. Anglophonia (18) 2005, 229–43.

1706. *sit*] NEWMAN, JOHN; RICE, SALLY.   Patterns of usage for English *sit, stand,* and *lie*: a cognitively inspired exploration in corpus linguistics. CogL (15:3) 2005, 351–96.

1707. *stand*] —— —— Patterns of usage for English *sit, stand,* and *lie*: a cognitively inspired exploration in corpus linguistics. *See* **1706**.

1708. *start*] CORRE, ERIC.   *Begin/start* et leur complémentation: perspective diachronique et synchronique. *See* **1682**.

1709. *sum*] BAMMESBERGER, ALFRED.   Old English *sum* in *Beowulf,* l. 271b. *See* **4290**.

1710. *(be) supposed to*] AGRAFOJO BLANCO, HÉCTOR.   The rise of modal meanings in Early Modern English: the case of the semiauxiliary verb BE *supposed to.* SEDERI (14) 2004, 189–97.

1711. *swīþe*] MÉNDEZ-NAYA, BELÉN.   On intensifiers and grammaticalization: the case of *swīþe.* EngS (84:4) 2003, 372–91.

1712. *that*] HYLAND, KEN; TSE, POLLY.   Hooking the reader: a corpus study of evaluative *that* in abstracts. ESpP (24:2) 2005, 123–39.

1713. *that*] SMOLKA, VLADISLAV.   Postposed subject *that* clauses. *In* (pp. 209–15) **1369**.

1714. *there + be*] CRAWFORD, WILLIAM J.   Verb agreement and disagreement: a corpus investigation of concord variation in existential *there + be* constructions. JEL (33:1) 2005, 35–61.

1715. *to*] LOS, BETTELOU.   The rise of the *to*-infinitive. Oxford; New York: OUP, 2005. pp. xv, 335.

1716. *will/shall*] SZMRECSANYI, BENEDIKT.   *Be going to* versus *will/shall*: does syntax matter? *See* **1688**.

1717. *with*] SANTIN-GUETTIER, ANNE-MARIE.   *With*: opérateur ambivalent? Anglophonia (18) 2005, 173–84.

1718. *with/without*] MALÁ, MARKÉTA.   *With* (and *without*) absolutes. *In* (pp. 117–27) **1369**.

1719. *you*] DE CLERCK, BERNARD.   Explicit *you*-subjects in English imperatives: a pragmatic corpus-based analysis. BELL (ns 3) 2005, 87–104.

1720. *you*] TEA, ALAN J. H.; LEE, BENNY P. H.   Reference and blending in a computer role-playing game. *See* **1699**.

VOCABULARY

VOCABULARY OF CONTEMPORARY ENGLISH

1721. ADAMS, MICHAEL. Meaningful interposing: a countervalent form. *See* **1547.**

1722. AZZARO, GABRIELE. Four-letter films: taboo language in movies. Rome: Aracne, 2005. pp. xi, 215. (Scienze dell'antichità filologico letteraria e storico artistiche, 152.)

1723. BATTISTELLA, EDWIN L. Bad language: are some words better than others? Oxford; New York: OUP, 2005. pp. vi, 230.

1724. BAUER, LAURIE; BAUER, WINIFRED. Regional dialects in New Zealand children's playground vocabulary. *In* (pp. 194–216) **3044.**

1725. BOBERG, CHARLES. The North American Regional Vocabulary Survey: new variables and methods in the study of North American English. *See* **2985.**

1726. BRADSTOCK, MIKE. Some Southern Sea lore. NZW (9) 2005, 1–3.

1727. BULTINCK, BERT. Numerous meanings: the meaning of English cardinals and the legacy of Paul Grice. *See* **2067.**

1728. COLLINS, VALERIE. Cutting and splicing. VocR (7:4) 2005. (Compound words.)

1729. DALY, NICOLA, *et al.* Expletives as solidarity signals in FTAs on the factory floor. *See* **2153.**

1730. DENT, SUSIE. Larpers and shroomers: the language report. Oxford; New York: OUP, 2004. pp. viii, 165.

1731. DONALD, RALPH. From 'knockout punch' to 'home run': masculinity's 'dirty dozen' sports metaphors in American combat films. *See* **13218.**

1732. FRASER, HELEN. Constraining abstractness: phonological representation in the light of color terms. CogL (15:3) 2004, 239–88.

1733. FRATH, PIERRE. Why is there no ham in a hamburger? A study of lexical blends and reanalysed morphemisation. RANAM (38) 2005, 99–112.

1734. —— GLEDHILL, CHRISTOPHER. Free-range clusters or frozen chunks? Reference as a defining criterion for linguistic units. RANAM (38) 2005, 25–43.

1735. GLOWKA, WAYNE, *et al.* Among the new words. AS (80:1) 2005, 78–86.

1736. —— Among the new words. AS (80:2) 2005, 207–15.

1737. —— Among the new words. AS (80:3) 2005, 301–20.

1738. —— Among the new words. AS (80:4) 2005, 406–24.

1739. IGNATOW, GABRIEL. 'Idea hamsters' on the 'bleeding edge': profane metaphors in high technology jargon. Poetics (31:1) 2003, 1–22.

1740. IWATA, SEIZI. Locative alternation and two levels of verb meaning. *See* **1853.**

1741. KACIRK, JEFFREY. Informal English: puncture ladies, egg harbors, Mississippi marbles, and other curious words and phrases of North America. *See* **3008.**

1742. KAVKA, STANISLAV J.   A book of idiomatology. Žilina, Czech Republic: Univ. of Žilina, 2003. pp. 150. Rev. by Miroslav Bázlik in LingPr (15:1) 2005, 49–51.

1743. LANGLOTZ, ANDREAS.   Are constructions the basic units of grammar? The phraseological turn in linguistic theory. See **1615**.

1744. LEDERER, RICHARD.   Euphemisms: the fig leaves of language. VocR (7:3) 2005.

1745. —— A guide to teenspeak. See **3185**.

1746. —— Serving up a tennis slogan: jest for the pun of it. VocR (7:8) 2005.

1747. —— The way we word. VocR (7:6) 2005.

1748. LEE, ALAN.   Colour and pictorial representation. See **11893**.

1749. LEE, PENNY.   'Feelings of the mind' in talk about thinking in English. See **2102**.

1750. LILLO, ANTONIO.   Celebrating slang and unconventional English, once again: an interview with Terry Victor. RAEI (18) 2005, 293–304.

1751. LORVIK, MARJORIE.   The distinctiveness of the Doric: home-grown or imported? See **2942**.

1752. MCHOUL, ALEX; RAPLEY, MARK.   Call me mad, but ... Meanjin (62:1) 2003, 214–24. (Vocabulary for referring to mental illness.)

1753. MALEKOVÁ, DANICA.   The status of term in the context of law writing. In (pp. 99–106) **1370**.

1754. MIMS, KEVIN.   The ultimate legal thriller. See **1935**.

1755. MURPHY, COLIN; O'DEA, DONAL.   The book of feckin' Irish slang that's great craic for cute hoors and bowsies. Dublin: O'Brien Press, 2004. pp. 63.

1756. NETTMANN-MULTANOWSKA, KINGA.   English loanwords in Polish and German after 1945: orthography and morphology. (Bibl. 2003, 1708.) Rev. by John Dingley in SEEJ (48:4) 2004, 711–12.

1757. OCASIO, WILLIAM; JOSEPH, JOHN.   Cultural adaptation and institutional change: the evolution of vocabularies of corporate governance, 1972–2003. Poetics (33:3/4) 2005, 163–78.

1758. ÖZÇALIŞKAN, ŞEYDA.   Metaphor meets typology: ways of moving metaphorically in English and Turkish. CogL (16:1) 2005, 207–46.

1759. PALUSZKIEWICZ-MISIACZEK, MAGDALENA.   Strategies and methods in dealing with culture-specific expressions on the basis of Polish–English translations of certain administrative and institutional terms. In (pp. 244–8) **1370**.

1760. PETERS, MARK.   The 'oohs' and 'ahs' and 'ooh-la-las': a look at interjections. VocR (7:6) 2005.

1761. QUIGLEY, KATHERINE.   Keeping company in the city: compounds in the lexicon of the New Zealand Treasury. NZEJ (19) 2005, 26–35.

1762. RENOUF, ANTOINETTE.   Phrasal creativity viewed from an IT perspective. RANAM (38) 2005, 113–22.

1763. RINGWALD, CHRISTOPHER D.   Bad writing kills. VocR (7:7) 2005.

1764. SKANDERA, PAUL.   Drawing a map of Africa: idiom in Kenyan English. See **3072**.

1765. TAYLOR, DOUGLAS. Prison slang and the poetics of imprisonment. *In* (pp. 233–45) **12821**.

1766. VOKÁČOVÁ, JANA. A comparative view of English, Czech, French and German idioms. *In* (pp. 163–71) **1370**.

1767. VOLÍN, JAN. Rhythmical properties of polysyllabic words in British and Czech English. *In* (pp. 279–92) **1369**.

1768. WAJNRYB, RUTH. Expletive deleted: a good look at bad language $&!@*. New York: Free Press, 2005. pp. vii, 290.

1769. WATSON, DON. Death sentences: how clichés, weasel and management-speak are strangling public language. New York: Gotham, 2005. pp. xxxii, 173.

1770. ZORN, JULIE ANNE. Making FUDGE: testing Metcalf's predictive method for new-word success. Dic (25) 2004, 122–36.

HISTORICAL VOCABULARY OF ENGLISH

1771. ANDERSON, EARL R. Folk-taxonomies in early English. (Bibl. 2003, 1719.) Rev. by Geoffrey Russom in Spec (80:3) 2005, 820–2.

1772. BIERBAUMER, PETER. Real and not-so-real plant-names in Old English glosses. *In* (pp. 153–60) **1773**.

1773. BIGGAM, C. P. (ed.). From earth to art: the many aspects of the plant-world in Anglo-Saxon England. Amsterdam; Atlanta, GA: Rodopi, 2003. pp. 342. (Costerus, ns 148.)

1774. ČERMÁK, JAN. Notes on obscured compounds in Old English. *In* (pp. 35–45) **1369**.

1775. CHAPMAN, DON. Composing and joining: how the Anglo-Saxons talked about compounding. *In* (pp. 39–54) **1786**.

1776. COOPER, MARTIN C. A mathematical model of historical semantics and the grouping of word meanings into concepts. *See* **2070**.

1777. CRISP, PETER. Leavings. NZW (9) 2005, 3–4. (Historical terms for 'leftovers'.)

1778. CRONAN, DENNIS. Poetic meanings in the Old English poetic vocabulary. *See* **4204**.

1779. DANCE, RICHARD. Words derived from Old Norse in Early Middle English: studies in the vocabulary of the South-West Midland texts. (Bibl. 2004, 1841.) Rev. by Heather O'Donoghue in RES (56:225) 2005, 447–8; by Anatoly Liberman in JEGP (104:4) 2005, 534–7.

1780. DÍAZ VERA, JAVIER. Onomasiological variation and change in the Older Scots vocabulary of marriage. *See* **2923**.

1781. DYER, GARY R. Reading as a criminal in early nineteenth-century fiction. *See* **11915**.

1782. ESPOSITO, ANTHONY. Medieval plant-names in the *Oxford English Dictionary*. *In* (pp. 231–48) **1773**.

1783. GODDEN, MALCOLM. Alfred, Asser, and Boethius. *In* (pp. 326–48) **4220**.

1784. GONZÁLEZ ORTA, MARTA. The Old English verbs of *smell perception* and *emission*: analysis of the interface of their semantic and syntactic representation. SELIM (12) 2003/04, 33–48.

1785. GRETSCH, MECHTHILD; GNEUSS, HELMUT. Anglo-Saxon glosses to a Theodorean poem? *In* (pp. 9–46) **4220**.

1786. HARBUS, ANTONINA; POOLE, RUSSELL (eds). Verbal encounters: Anglo-Saxon and Old Norse studies for Roberta Frank. Toronto; Buffalo, NY; London: Toronto UP, 2005. pp. x, 298. (Toronto Old English series, 13.) Rev. by Craig R. Davis in HAge (8) 2005; by Richard Dance in TMR, Sept. 2005.

1787. HOUGH, CAROLE. Place-name evidence for Anglo-Saxon plant-names. *In* (pp. 41–78) **1773**.

1788. HOUSTON, KERR. Phony histories: a vindication of false etymologies. VocR (7:7) 2005.

1789. JANICADISOVÁ, TEREZA. Latin words reflected in the Old English vocabulary. *In* (pp. 83–9) **1369**.

1790. LIBERMAN, ANATOLY. Word origins – and how we know them. Oxford; New York: OUP, 2005. pp. vii, 312.

1791. MARKUS, MANFRED. Terms for pregnancy in the history of English: an onomasiological approach based on the *OED*. NM (106:1) 2005, 7–21.

1792. MARSDEN, RICHARD. Latin in the ascendant: the interlinear gloss of Oxford, Bodleian Library, Laud Misc. 509. *In* (pp. 132–52) **4221**.

1793. O'KEEFFE, KATHERINE O'BRIEN; ORCHARD, ANDY (eds). Latin literature and English lore: studies in Anglo-Saxon literature for Michael Lapidge: vol. I. *See* **4220**.

1794. —— —— Latin literature and English lore: studies in Anglo-Saxon literature for Michael Lapidge: vol. II. *See* **4221**.

1795. PARKER, PATRICIA. Barbers and Barbary: early modern cultural semantics. *See* **6270**.

1796. QUINION, MICHAEL. Ballyhoo, buckaroo, and spuds: ingenious tales of words and their origins. Washington, DC: Smithsonian Institution Press; London: Penguin, 2004. pp. xvi, 282. (Pub. in UK as *Port Out, Starboard Home: and Other Language Myths*.)

1797. READ, ALLEN WALKER. Words crisscrossing the sea: how words have been borrowed between England and America. AS (80:2) 2005, 115–34.

1798. RIX, ROBERT (ed.). A political dictionary explaining the true meaning of words. *See* **8247**.

1799. RUSCHE, PHILIP G. Dioscorides' *De materia medica* and late Old English herbal glossaries. *In* (pp. 181–94) **1773**.

1800. —— Isidore's *Etymologiae* and the Canterbury Aldhelm *scholia*. *See* **4268**.

1801. RYDÉN, MATS. William Turner as botanist and plant-name scholar. *In* (pp. 249–62) **1773**.

1802. SAUER, HANS. The morphology of the Old English plant-names. *In* (pp. 161–79) **1773**.

1803. SHERK, BILL. 500 years of new words. Toronto: Dundurn, 2004. pp. 312.

1804. SIMPSON, JOHN. Will the *Oxford English Dictionary* be more 'European' after its first comprehensive revision since its first edition of 1884–1928? *See* **1941**.

1805. WILLIAMS, ALASTAIR (ed.). The vulgar tongue: buckish slang and pickpocket eloquence. By Francis Grose. *See* **1977**.

1806. WILTON, DAVID. Word myths: debunking linguistic urban legends. Oxford; New York: OUP, 2004. pp. x, 221.

SINGLE WORDS AND PHRASES

1807. *Adam-wits*] WALLS, KATHRYN. 'Adam-wits' in *Absalom and Achitophel*. *See* **7427**.

1808. *æspe*] BIGGAM, C. P. The *æspe* tree in Anglo-Saxon England. *In* (pp. 195–230) **1773**.

1809. *affection*] TISSARI, HELI. A corpus-based description of an emotion word and concept. *See* **1855**.

1810. *anymore*] GNANADESIKAN, AMALIA. The way we talk anymore. VocR (7:6) 2005.

1811. *autem*] GREEN, JONATHON. Hark, hark ... CritQ (46:3) 2004, 116–21.

1812. *autumn*] CASSELMAN, BILL. *Summer* and the words for seasons. *See* **1901**.

1813. *avalanche*] GOULDING, CHRISTOPHER. *Avalanche*: antedating the entry in the *Oxford English Dictionary*. NQ (52:1) 2005, 18–19.

1814. *broad*] MARTINKOVÁ, MICHAELA. Spatial concepts in *wide* and *broad*. *In* (pp. 107–12) **1370**.

1815. *bulwerk*] SAYERS, WILLIAM. Middle English and Scots *bulwerk* and some Continental reflexes. NQ (52:2) 2005, 164–70.

1816. *candour*] REID, CHRISTOPHER. Speaking candidly: rhetoric, politics, and the meaning of candour in the later eighteenth century. *See* **8052**.

1817. *cennan*] HEAD, PAULINE. *Cennan*, 'to cause to be born'/'to cause to know': Incarnation as revelation in Old English literature. *In* (pp. 55–75) **1786**.

1818. *chaos*] JONES, CHRISTOPHER A. Early medieval *chaos*. *In* (pp. 15–38) **1786**.

1819. *charity*] TISSARI, HELI. A corpus-based description of an emotion word and concept. *See* **1855**.

1820. *conscience*] EATON, R. D. From *inwit* to *conscience* in late Middle English literature. *See* **1850**.

1821. *conscience*] —— Sin and sensibility: the *conscience* of Chaucer's Prioress. JEGP (104:4) 2005, 495–513.

1822. *conservatism*] PANICHAS, GEORGE A. Restoring the meaning of Conservatism. ModAge (47:3) 2005, 195–200.

1823. *coon*] HAWTHORN, JEREMY. The use of *coon* in Conrad: British slang or racist slur? *See* **15880**.

1824. *corporate rule*] EUBANKS, PHILIP.   Globalization, 'corporate rule', and blended words: a conceptual–rhetorical analysis of metaphor, metonymy, and conceptual blending. *See* **2295**.

1825. *down*] HAMPE, BEATE.   When *down* is not bad, and *up* is not good enough: a usage-based assessment of the plus–minus parameter in image-schema theory. CogL (16:1) 2005, 81–112.

1826. *dunnoc(k)*] HOUGH, CAROLE.   Old English **dunnoc* 'hedge-sparrow': a ghost word? NQ (52:1) 2005, 11–13.

1827. *eggplant*] GNANADESIKAN, AMALIA.   Travels of an eggplant. VocR (7:5) 2005.

1828. *elf-shot*] HALL, ALARIC.   Calling the shots: the Old English remedy *Gif hors ofscoten sie* and Anglo-Saxon *elf-shot*. *See* **4357**.

1829. *even*] GIANNAKIDOU, ANASTASIA.   The three faces of *even*.   *In* (pp. 148–60) **1377**.

1830. *eyes*] HARDY, DONALD E.   Collocational analysis as a stylistic discovery procedure: the case of Flannery O'Connor's *eyes*. *See* **18560**.

1831. *fart*] BURNSIDE, JULIAN.   Naughty words. VocR (7:2) 2005.

1832. *feminist*] MANSBRIDGE, JANE; FLASTER, KATHERINE.   *Male chauvinist, feminist, sexist,* and *sexual harassment*: different trajectories in feminist linguistic innovation. *See* **1856**.

1833. *feorh*] SOLOMONIK-PANKRASOVA, TATYANA.   Semantics of Old English *feorh*: from pagan to Christian tradition. *In* (pp. 145–9) **1370**.

1834. *fiction*] BLESSINGTON, FRANCIS.   Finding the fictions. VocR (7:10) 2005.

1835. *filibuster*] RAWSON, HUGH.   Filibuster. AH (56:6) 2005, 14. (History now: why do we say that?)

1836. *fink*] SAYERS, WILLIAM.   The origin of *fink* 'informer, hired strikebreaker'. ANQ (18:1) 2005, 50–4.

1837. *free and clear*] PAINTER, MARK P.   Fallout from the Battle of Hastings. VocR (7:8) 2005.

1838. *freo*] BAMMESBERGER, ALFRED.   *Freo* 'woman' in *Genesis*, line 457a. NQ (52:3) 2005, 282–4.

1839. *galeie*] SOBECKI, SEBASTIAN I.   The 2000 Saracens of *King Horn*. *See* **4575**.

1840. *gameday*] SABINO, ROBIN.   Survey says … gameday. AS (80:1) 2005, 61–77.

1841. *(ge)wyrd*] PAPAHAGI, ADRIAN.   *(Ge)wyrd*: emendations to three anonymous Old English homilies and saints' lives. *See* **4348**.

1842. *gefnesan*] HOUGH, CAROLE.   Old English *gefnesan*, present-day English *sneeze*, and the place-names Snogsash and Sneachill. NM (106:3) 2005, 307–9.

1843. *gefreogum*] BAMMESBERGER, ALFRED.   Old English *gefreogum* in *The Phoenix*, line 29b. *See* **4364**.

1844. *gobbledygook*] RAWSON, HUGH.   Gobbledygook. AH (56:2) 2005, 20. (History now: why do we say that?)

1845. *green*] PEPRNÍK, JAROSLAV.   The colour *green* in English language and literature. *In* (pp. 143–55) **1369**.

1846. *gringo*] RAWSON, HUGH.   Gringo. AH (56:5) 2005, 14. (History now: why do we say that?)

1847. *happy*] PETERS, MARK.   Campers, mediums, and pigs: a look at the word *happy.* VocR (7:2) 2005.

1848. *hysteria*] CASSELMAN, BILL.   *Hysteria*: the just death of a medical word. VocR (7:9) 2005.

1849. *in fact*] AIJMER, KARIN; SIMON-VANDENBERGEN, ANNE-MARIE. A marker and a methodology for the study of pragmatic markers: the semantic field of expectation. JPrag (36:10) 2004, 1781–1805.

1850. *inwit*] EATON, R. D.   From *inwit* to *conscience* in late Middle English literature. NM (105:4) 2004, 423–35.

1851. *kitteback*] SMITH, J. B.   When is a shoe not a shoe? See **3458.**

1852. *loach*] BRATCHER, JAMES T.   *Loach* in the Peele jestbook. See **5606.**

1853. *load*] IWATA, SEIZI.   Locative alternation and two levels of verb meaning. CogL (16:2) 2005, 355–407.

1854. *lollare*] COLE, ANDREW.   William Langland and the invention of Lollardy. *In* (pp. 37–58) **4482.**

1855. *love*] TISSARI, HELI.   A corpus-based description of an emotion word and concept. NM (106:1) 2005, 89–91.

1856. *male chauvinist*] MANSBRIDGE, JANE; FLASTER, KATHERINE. *Male chauvinist, feminist, sexist,* and *sexual harassment*: different trajectories in feminist linguistic innovation. AS (80:3) 2005, 256–79.

1857. *mermaid*] FENKL, HEINZ INSU.   The mermaid. VocR (7:1) 2005.

1858. *mōd*] LOW, SOON-AI.   Pride, courage, and anger: the polysemousness of Old English *mōd*. *In* (pp. 77–88) **1786.**

1859. *mokes*] MEYERHOFF, MIRIAM.   Attitudes to gender and creoles: a case study on *mokes* and *titas. See* **3131.**

1860. *Ms*] ATKINS-SAYRE, WENDY.   Naming women: the emergence of 'Ms' as a liberatory title. WL (28:1) 2005, 8–16.

1861. *Ms*] FULLER, JANET M.   The uses and meanings of the female title *Ms.* AS (80:2) 2005, 180–206.

1862. *naughty*] BURNSIDE, JULIAN.   Naughty words. *See* **1831.**

1863. *nēadsibb*] PONS-SANZ, SARA M.   Friends and relatives in need of an explanation: Gr *anagkaîos*, L *necessarius*, and PGmc **nauð-. See* **1868.**

1864. *nēodfrēond*] —— Friends and relatives in need of an explanation: Gr *anagkaîos*, L *necessarius*, and PGmc **nauð-. See* **1868.**

1865. *neodian*] TAEYMANS, MARTINE.   On Old and Middle English *need* in positive and negative contexts. *See* **1905.**

1866. *netel*] COLE, ANN.   The use of *netel* in place-names. JEPNS (35) 2002/03, 49–58.

1867. *nugget*] ROBERTS, DANIEL SANJIV.   'A nugget of pure truth': Woolf's debt to De Quincey. *See* **20407.**

1868. *nȳdmǣg*] PONS-SANZ, SARA M.   Friends and relatives in need of an explanation: Gr *anagkaîos*, L *necessarius*, and PGmc **nauð-.* JEGP (104:1) 2005, 1–11.

1869. *of līfe forrǣdan*] —— An etymological note on OE *of līfe forrǣdan*. ANQ (18:2) 2005, 6–9.

1870. *off*] HAMPE, BEATE. When *down* is not bad, and *up* is not good enough: a usage-based assessment of the plus–minus parameter in image-schema theory. See **1825**.

1871. *on the other hand*] BELL, DAVID M. Correlative and non-correlative *on the other hand*. JPrag (36:12) 2004, 2179–84. (Squib.)

1872. *palmtwigede*] HILL, THOMAS D. The 'palmtwigede' Pater Noster: horticultural semantics and the Old English *Solomon and Saturn I*. See **4385**.

1873. *panne*] HOROBIN, S. C. P. Pennies, pence and pans: some Chaucerian misreadings. See **5005**.

1874. *paparazzo*] COUSTILLAS, PIERRE. Three companions in one: in turn Daniele Cristofaro takes the plunge and fully identifies Coriolano Paparazzo. See **11070**.

1875. *parlour boarder*] CRONIN, RICHARD; MCMILLAN, DOROTHY. *Emma*, Harriet Martin, and parlour boarders. See **9969**.

1876. *passion*] TISSARI, HELI. A corpus-based description of an emotion word and concept. See **1855**.

1877. *plain folk*] HYDE, SAMUEL C., JR. *Plain folk* reconsidered: historical ambiguity in search of a definition. JSH (71:4) 2005, 803–30.

1878. *plegscip*] HOUGH, CAROLE. Play-shields, play-ships and play-places in Old English. See **1879**.

1879. *plegscyld*] —— Play-shields, play-ships and play-places in Old English. NQ (52:2) 2005, 153–5. (*Responds to* bibl. 2004, 1916.)

1880. *plegstow*] —— Play-shields, play-ships and play-places in Old English. See **1879**.

1881. *poor*] PURDY, DWIGHT H. 'The one poor word' in *Middlemarch*. See **10950**.

1882. *poozle/poozling*] HURLEY, DESMOND. *Poozle* and *poozling*: a continuing story. NZW (9) 2005, 5.

1883. *ptarmigan*] CASSELMAN, BILL. The word *ptarmigan* looks pfunny. VocR (7:2) 2005.

1884. *puffin*] BREEZE, ANDREW. *Puffin*, a loanword from Cornish. NQ (52:2) 2005, 172–3.

1885. *Queen's chain*] BARDSLEY, DIANNE. Unravelling the Queen's chain. NZW (9) 2005, 10–11.

1886. *queer*] SAYERS, WILLIAM. The etymology of *queer*. ANQ (18:2) 2005, 15–18.

1887. *quere*] BURROW, COLIN. Henry Vaughan's *The Queer*: a note on queries. See **7877**.

1888. *robot*] GOULDING, CHRISTOPHER. *Robot*: antedating the entry in *The Oxford English Dictionary*. NQ (52:3) 2005, 380–1.

1889. *roddon*] COATES, RICHARD. The origin of *roddon*. NQ (52:2) 2005, 170–2.

1890. *rove*] JUNG, SANDRO. Collins's *Ode to Evening*. See **8480**.

1891. *sadness*] KLÉGR, ALEŠ. *Sadness/smutek*: a comparison of the verbal collocates. *In* (pp. 91–105) **1369.**

1892. *scone*] SAYERS, WILLIAM. Scones, *The Oxford English Dictionary*, and the Celtic element in English vocabulary. NQ (52:4) 2005, 447–50.

1893. *sexist*] MANSBRIDGE, JANE; FLASTER, KATHERINE. *Male chauvinist, feminist, sexist,* and *sexual harassment*: different trajectories in feminist linguistic innovation. *See* **1856.**

1894. *sexual harassment*] —— —— *Male chauvinist, feminist, sexist,* and *sexual harassment*: different trajectories in feminist linguistic innovation. *See* **1856.**

1895. *shall*] PHILPS, DENNIS. *Shall*, l'obligation, et le marqueur sub-lexical <sk>: une question de tailles? Anglophonia (18) 2005, 85–99.

1896. *small talk*] MALLINSON, ANNA JEAN. Small talk. VocR (7:2) 2005.

1897. *sneeze*] HOUGH, CAROLE. Old English *gefnesan*, present-day English *sneeze*, and the place-names Snogsash and Sneachill. *See* **1842.**

1898. *sockeye*] CASSELMAN, BILL. Sockeye salmon: a British Columbia word. VocR (7:10) 2005.

1899. *spray*] IWATA, SEIZI. Locative alternation and two levels of verb meaning. *See* **1853.**

1900. *spring*] CASSELMAN, BILL. Summer and the words for seasons. *See* **1901.**

1901. *summer*] —— Summer and the words for seasons. VocR (7:7) 2005.

1902. *sund*] FULK, R. D. Afloat in semantic space: Old English *sund* and the nature of Beowulf's exploit with Breca. *See* **4293.**

1903. *tæfl*] BAYLESS, MARTHA. *Alea, tæfl*, and related games: vocabulary and context. *In* (pp. 9–27) **4221.**

1904. *theory*] BENNETT-KASTOR, TINA. A battle of words: the land that evolution forgot. VocR (7:6) 2005.

1905. *þurfan/þurfen*] TAEYMANS, MARTINE. On Old and Middle English *need* in positive and negative contexts. BELL (ns 3) 2005, 105–21.

1906. *titas*] MEYERHOFF, MIRIAM. Attitudes to gender and creoles: a case study on *mokes* and *titas*. *See* **3131.**

1907. *up*] HAMPE, BEATE. When *down* is not bad, and *up* is not good enough: a usage-based assessment of the plus–minus parameter in image-schema theory. *See* **1825.**

1908. *urban legend*] BRUNVAND, JAN HAROLD. 'Urban legend' from 1925. *See* **3483.**

1909. *urban legend*] DOYLE, CHARLES CLAY; KNIGHT, LARA RENEE. On the term *urban legend*. FOAFN (63) 2005.

1910. *wabbit*] COBBY, A. E. An Old French source for Modern Scots *wabbit*? NM (106:2) 2005, 131–7.

1911. *war*] MONTGOMERY, MARTIN. The discourse of *war* after 9/11. LLit (14:2) 2005, 149–80.

1912. *war*] PINSKY, ROBERT. Myths of the workroom. *See* **18789.**

1913. *we*] RAY, ROBERT H. Uses of the royal plural in *King Lear*. *See* **6479.**

1914. *wide*] MARTINKOVÁ, MICHAELA.   Spatial concepts in *wide* and *broad*. *In* (pp. 107–12) **1370**.

1915. *wikenn*] BRITTON, DEREK.   Orm's *wikenn* and compounds with -*wican* in annal 1137 of the Peterborough Chronicle. *See* **4713**.

1916. *winter*] CASSELMAN, BILL.   *Summer* and the words for seasons. *See* **1901**.

1917. *wog*] —— 'Wog!': origin of a racist insult. VocR (7:8) 2005.

1918. *wop*] —— Origin of the racist slur *wop*. VocR (7:6) 2005.

LEXICOGRAPHY

GENERAL

1919. BRABCOVÁ, ALICE.   On six lexicographical myths: theory and practice of specialized lexicography contrasted. *In* (pp. 11–23) **1369**.

1920. BREWER, CHARLOTTE.   The electronification of the *Oxford English Dictionary*. Dic (25) 2004, 1–43.

1921. COLEMAN, JULIE.   A history of cant and slang dictionaries: vol. 1, 1567–1784. (Bibl. 2004, 1952.) Rev. by Carol Percy in NQ (52:2) 2005, 246–7.

1922. ESPOSITO, ANTHONY.   Medieval plant-names in the *Oxford English Dictionary*. *In* (pp. 231–48) **1773**.

1923. FUERTES OLIVERA, PEDRO A.   Specialized communication and English Studies: research proposals on specialized lexicography and English for specific purposes. Atl (27:2) 2005, 41–55.

1924. GILLIVER, PETER.   'That brownest of brown studies': the work of the editors and in-house staff of the *Oxford English Dictionary* in 1903. Dic (25) 2004, 44–64.

1925. GOLD, DAVID L.   An aspect of lexicography still not fully professionalized: the search for antedatings and postdatings (with examples mostly from English and some from other languages). RAEI (18) 2005, 25–69.

1926. GREEN, JONATHON.   Hark, hark ... *See* **1811**.

1927. HARGRAVES, ORIN.   Long-distance lexicography: a view from the field. Dic (25) 2004, 137–47.

1928. HITCHINGS, HENRY.   Dr Johnson's *Dictionary*: the extraordinary story of the book that defined the world. *See* **8758**.

1929. JACKSON, H. J.   Big and little matters: discrepancies in the genius of Samuel Johnson. *See* **8761**.

1930. KEYES, FRANK.   On some deficiencies in our American dictionaries (an editor writes to his son). VocR (7:6) 2005.

1931. KEYMER, THOMAS.   Meaning exuberant. *See* **8765**.

1932. KOLB, GWIN J.; DEMARIA, ROBERT, JR (eds).   Johnson on the English language. *See* **8766**.

1933. LEDERER, RICHARD.   No harmless drudge: a quatrimillenial celebration. VocR (7:4) 2005.

1934. LYNCH, JACK; MCDERMOTT, ANNE (eds). Anniversary essays on Johnson's dictionary. Cambridge; New York: CUP, 2005. pp. xi, 245. Rev. by H. J. Jackson in TLS, 11 Nov. 2005, 3–4.

1935. MIMS, KEVIN. The ultimate legal thriller. VocR (7:12) 2005. (*Black's Law Dictionary.*)

1936. MONTGOMERY, MICHAEL. Voices of my ancestors: a personal search for the language of the Scotch Irish. *See* **2947**.

1937. MUGGLESTONE, LYNDA. Lost for words: the hidden history of the *Oxford English Dictionary.* New Haven, CT; London: Yale UP, 2005. pp. xxi, 273. Rev. by Eric Korn in TLS, 16 Sept. 2005, 6–7; by Caroline Preston in ASch (74:3) 2005, 138–9.

1938. NAGY, ANDREA R. Life or lexicography: how popular culture imitates dictionaries. Dic (25) 2004, 107–21.

1939. RAYMOND, JAMES C.; RUSSELL, I. WILLIS (eds). Essays in linguistics: dialectology, grammar, and lexicography in honor of James B. McMillan. *See* **3021**.

1940. SAYERS, WILLIAM. Scones, *The Oxford English Dictionary*, and the Celtic element in English vocabulary. *See* **1892**.

1941. SIMPSON, JOHN. Will the *Oxford English Dictionary* be more 'European' after its first comprehensive revision since its first edition of 1884–1928? Misc (29) 2004, 59–74.

1942. WINCHESTER, SIMON. The meaning of everything: the story of the *Oxford English Dictionary.* (Bibl. 2004, 1976.) Rev. by Richard W. Bailey in Dic (25) 2004, 169–74.

DICTIONARIES OF ENGLISH

1943. ANON. The American Heritage desk dictionary and thesaurus. Boston, MA: Houghton Mifflin, 2005. pp. xii, 847.

1944. —— The American Heritage dictionary of phrasal verbs. Boston, MA: Houghton Mifflin, 2005. pp. xii, 466.

1945. —— The Merriam-Webster dictionary. Springfield, MA: Merriam-Webster, 2005. pp. xviii, 701.

1946. —— The new Webster's dictionary of the English language. New York: Lexicon International / Publishers Guild, 2004. 1 vol. (various pagings).

1947. —— Webster's new explorer dictionary of word origins. Springfield, MA: Federal Street Press, 2004. pp. xvii, 526.

1948. —— Word histories and mysteries: from abracadabra to Zeus. Boston, MA: Houghton Mifflin, 2004. pp. xvi, 348.

1949. ABRAMS, M. H. A glossary of literary terms. (Bibl. 1988, 290.) Belmont, CA: Wadsworth / Thomson Learning, 2005. pp. xi, 370. (Eighth ed.: first ed. 1957.)

1950. ADAMS, MICHAEL. Slayer slang: a *Buffy the Vampire Slayer* lexicon. (Bibl. 2004, 1981.) Rev. by Susan Tamasi in JEL (33:1) 2005, 91–4.

1951. AYTO, JOHN. The Oxford dictionary of slang. (Bibl. 1998, 2224.) Oxford; New York: OUP, 2003. pp. v, 474. (Second ed.: first ed. 1998.) Rev. by François Chevillet in EA (58:2) 2005, 194–6.

1952. BARDSLEY, DIANNE (comp.). The New Zealand mini thesaurus. Melbourne; Oxford: OUP, 2005. pp. 662.

1953. BENNETT, TONY; GROSSBERG, LAWRENCE; MORRIS, MEAGHAN (eds). New keywords: a revised vocabulary of culture and society. (Bibl. 1977, 44.) Oxford; Malden, MA: Blackwell, 2005. pp. xxvi, 427. (Revised ed.: first ed. 1976.)

1954. BLAKE, N. F. Shakespeare's non-Standard English: a dictionary of his informal language. (Bibl. 2004, 1984.) Rev. by Maurice Charney in SNL (54:4) 2004/05, 111–12; by Héloïse Sénéchal in TLS, 11 Feb. 2005, 13.

1955. CORÈDON, CHRISTOPHER; WILLIAMS, ANN. A dictionary of medieval terms and phrases. Woodbridge, Suffolk; Rochester, NY: Brewer, 2004. pp. ix, 308. Rev. by Elliot Kendall in TLS, 8 July 2005, 25.

1956. HALL, JOAN HOUSTON (ed.). Dictionary of American regional English: vol. 4, P–Sk. (Bibl. 2004, 1988.) Rev. by Richard W. Bailey in JEL (31:4) 2003, 358–62.

1957. HASSEL, RUDOLPH CHRIS, JR. Shakespeare's religious language: a dictionary. London: Thoemmes Press; New York: Continuum, 2005. pp. 432. (Athlone Shakespeare dictionaries.) Rev. by Alison Shell in TLS, 25 Nov. 2005, 25.

1958. HAWKER, SARA; COWLEY, CHRIS (eds). Oxford dictionary and thesaurus of current English. Oxford; New York: OUP, 2004. pp. x, 484.

1959. HERBST, THOMAS, et al. (eds). A valency dictionary of English: a corpus-based analysis of the complementation patterns of English verbs, nouns, and adjectives. Berlin; New York: Mouton de Gruyter, 2004. pp. xlii, 961. (Topics in English linguistics, 40.)

1960. ISAAC, PETER. The new gobbledygook: a New Zealand dictionary and guidebook. Wellington, New Zealand: Transpress, 2004. pp. 208.

1961. KIPFER, BARBARA ANN (comp.). Roget's descriptive word finder: a dictionary/thesaurus of adjectives. Cincinnati, OH: Writer's Digest, 2003. pp. 457.

1962. KURJIAN, DOUGLAS C. The dictionary of vital expressions: how to use expressions to persuade. Bethesda, MD: Academica Press, 2005. pp. 1415.

1963. MACALISTER, JOHN (ed.). A dictionary of Maori words in New Zealand English. Auckland; Oxford: OUP, 2005. pp. xxvi, 190.

1964. MIEDER, WOLFGANG; BRYAN, GEORGE B. A dictionary of Anglo-American proverbs and proverbial phrases found in literary sources of the nineteenth and twentieth centuries. See **3452**.

1965. RIDEOUT, PHILIP M. (ed.). Heinle's Newbury House dictionary of American English. Boston, MA: Thomson/Heinle, 2004. pp. xxiv, 1142; 1 CD-ROM. (Fourth ed.: first ed. 1996.)

1966. SEELY, JOHN. Oxford A–Z of grammar and punctuation. See **1640**.

1967. SIEFRING, JUDITH (ed.). The Oxford dictionary of idioms. (Bibl. 2003, 61221.) Oxford; New York: OUP, 2004. pp. 340. (Second ed.: first ed. 1999.)

1968. SMEAD, ROBERT N. Vocabulario vaquero/cowboy talk: a dictionary of Spanish terms from the American West. See **3029**.

1969. Soanes, Catherine; Ferguson, Sheila. Oxford A–Z of spelling. Oxford; New York: OUP, 2004. pp. xiv, 135.

1970. —— Stevenson, Angus (eds). Concise Oxford English dictionary. (Bibl. 1999, 1943.) Oxford; New York: OUP, 2004. pp. xx, 1708. (Eleventh ed.: first ed. 1914.)

1971. Speake, Jennifer (ed.). The Oxford dictionary of proverbs. *See* **3460**.

1972. Speares, Richard A. McGraw-Hill's dictionary of American idioms and phrasal verbs. Boston, MA: McGraw-Hill, 2005. pp. xvii, 1080.

1973. Stevenson, Angus; Brown, Lesley (eds). New Oxford dictionary for writers and editors. *See* **1092**.

1974. Trudgill, Peter. A glossary of sociolinguistics. Edinburgh: Edinburgh UP; Oxford; New York: OUP, 2003. pp. 148. Rev. by Łukasz Mokrzycki in NM (106:3) 2005, 373–5.

1975. Upton, Clive; Upton, Eben. Oxford rhyming dictionary. Oxford; New York: OUP, 2004. pp. viii, 659.

1976. Waite, Maurice (ed.). New Oxford spelling dictionary. (Bibl. 1986, 1726.) Oxford; New York: OUP, 2005. pp. xii, 596. (New ed.: first ed. 1986.)

1977. Williams, Alastair (ed.). The vulgar tongue: buckish slang and pickpocket eloquence. By Francis Grose. Chichester: Summersdale, 2004. pp. 316. Rev. by Michael Caines in TLS, 17 Sept. 2004, 24.

1978. Wilson, Christopher R.; Calore, Michela. Music in Shakespeare: a dictionary. London: Thoemmes Press; New York: Continuum, 2005. pp. xiv, 508. (Athlone Shakespeare dictionaries.)

1979. Wolfreys, Julian (ed.); Thomas, Harun Karim (asst ed.). Glossalalia: an alphabet of critical keywords. London; New York: Routledge, 2003. pp. vii, 400. Rev. by Clare Connors in Eng (54:208) 2005, 76–80.

NAMES

GENERAL

1980. Anon. Mencken's many identities. *See* **18166**.

1981. —— (comp.). Bibliography 2002. JEPNS (35) 2002/03, 61–6.

1982. —— Bibliography 2004. JEPNS (37) 2004/05, 61–5.

1983. Bates, Timothy. George Eliot's eclectic use of names in *Daniel Deronda*. *See* **10905**.

1984. Bredehoft, Thomas A. Secondary stress in compound Germanic names in Old English verse. *See* **4201**.

1985. Burnett, Paula. Walcott's intertextual method: non-Greek naming in *Omeros*. *See* **19936**.

1986. Cameron, Jean. Minor names of Norwell, Nottinghamshire. JEPNS (37) 2004/05, 53–8.

1987. Coates, Richard. A Tendring hundred miscellany. JEPNS (37) 2004/05, 37–47.

1988. Cole, Ann. The use of *netel* in place-names. *See* **1866**.

1989. CORNWELL, NEIL. 'A Dorset yokel's knuckles': Thomas Hardy and *Lolita*. *See* **18453**.

1990. DELABASTITA, DIRK. 'If I know the letters and the language': translation as a dramatic device in Shakespeare's plays. *In* (pp. 31–52) **5975**.

1991. DETRO, R. A.; WALKER, H. J. (comps). The wonderful world of geographic names: the writings of Meredith (Pete) F. Burrill (toponymist *extraordinaire*). Baton Rouge: Louisiana State UP, 2004. pp. xiii, 435. (Geoscience and man, 39.) Rev. by Alan Rayburn in OnCan (86:2) 2004, 109–12.

1992. EISIMINGER, SKIP. Dropping names. VocR (7:9) 2005.

1993. EVANS, MICHAEL R. Robin Hood in the landscape: place-name evidence and mythology. *In* (pp. 181–7) **3576**.

1994. GELLING, MARGARET. English place-name studies: some reflections. Being the first Cameron Lecture, delivered 11th December 2002, inaugurating the Institute for Name-Studies. JEPNS (35) 2002/03, 5–16.

1995. GOMES DA TORRE, M. The translation of proper names in *Measure for Measure*. *In* (pp. 203–15) **5874**.

1996. HOOKE, DELLA. Trees in the Anglo-Saxon landscape: the charter evidence. *In* (pp. 17–39) **1773**.

1997. HOUGH, CAROLE. Place-name evidence for Anglo-Saxon plant-names. *In* (pp. 41–78) **1773**.

1998. ISAACSON, DAVID. Getting nicked by nicknames. VocR (7:9) 2005.

1999. JOUSNI, STÉPHANE. Écrire Dublin après Joyce. *See* **17292**.

2000. KARLIN, DANIEL. Bob Dylan's names. *In* (pp. 27–49) **16207**.

2001. LAFLIN, SUSAN. Do *-ingas* place-names occur in pairs? *See* **1568**.

2002. LORE, TEREETEE; MCPHERSON, KAYE. Pickerdar: the black one. AF (20) 2005, 107–20.

2003. MCARTHUR, LEWIS A. Oregon geographic names. (Bibl. 2000, 25905.) Portland: Oregon Historical Soc. Press, 2003. pp. xiv, 1073; 1 CD-ROM. (Seventh ed.: first ed. 1928.) Rev. by Edward Callary in OnCan (86:1) 2004, 55–8.

2004. MACIÀ, JOSEP. Proper names: ideas and chains. CanJP (supp.30) 2004, 129–55.

2005. PRENTIS, MALCOLM D. M. Scottish place names in Australia. AF (19) 2004, 43–51.

2006. RAMSDEN, VALERIE. The use of names in the Barsetshire novels. *See* **19764**.

2007. ROMAINE, SUZANNE. Orthographic practices in the standardization of pidgins and creoles: pidgin in Hawai'i as anti-language and anti-standard. *See* **3134**.

2008. SHEVLIN, ELEANOR F. The titular claims of female surnames in eighteenth-century fiction. *In* (pp. 256–80) **6964**.

2009. SHURBANOV, ALEXANDER. The translatability of Shakespearean texts into an unrelated language/culture. *In* (pp. 51–64) **5874**.

2010. SIMMONS, JAMES R., JR. Did Willoughby join the Navy? Patrick O'Brian's thirty-year homage to Jane Austen. *See* **10045**.

2011. STEGGLE, MATTHEW. The names of Gabriel Harvey: cabbalistic, Russian, and fencing sources. *See* **5480.**

2012. TSE, GRACE Y. W. A corpus-based study of proper names in present-day English: aspects of gradience and article usage. New York; Frankfurt: Lang, 2005. pp. viii, 253. (English corpus linguistics, 2.)

2013. WARDROP, DANEEN. Collaboration in *Running a Thousand Miles for Freedom*: William's key and Ellen's renaming. *See* **9790.**

2014. WOODBRIDGE, LINDA. Shakespeare and magical grammar. *In* (pp. 84–98) **5167.**

SINGLE NAMES

2015. *Amy*] COONRADT, NICOLE M. To be loved: Amy Denver and human need – bridges to understanding in Toni Morrison's *Beloved*. *See* **18352.**

2016. *Arizonac*] GARATE, DONALD T. Arizonac: a twentieth-century myth. JArizH (46:2) 2005, 161–84.

2017. *Balack*] ROPER, ALAN. Doctor Balack and Bishop Boloch: nomenclature in Restoration parallel poems. *See* **7425.**

2018. *Belmarye*] KROCHALIS, JEANNE. 'And riden in Belmarye': Chaucer's General Prologue, line 57. *See* **5010.**

2019. *Boloch*] ROPER, ALAN. Doctor Balack and Bishop Boloch: nomenclature in Restoration parallel poems. *See* **7425.**

2020. *Broughton*] COATES, RICHARD. Two notes on names in *tūn* in relation to pre-English antiquities: Kirmington and Broughton, Lincolnshire. *See* **2038.**

2021. *Camel/Camelford*] BREEZE, ANDREW. The Battle of Camlan and Camelford, Cornwall. Arthuriana (15:3) 2005, 75–90.

2022. *Camlan*] —— The Battle of Camlan and Camelford, Cornwall. *See* **2021.**

2023. *Catte Streete*] BOWERS, RICK. Dick Whittington, Stow's *Survey*, and 'Catte Streete'. *See* **5738.**

2024. *Caulfield*] DUGAN, LAWRENCE. Holden and the Lunts. *See* **19294.**

2025. *Childrey Brook*] LOWE, KATHRYN A. *Mearcella* in S 703 and the etymology of Childrey Brook (Berkshire). JEPNS (37) 2004/05, 19–31.

2026. *Consett*] BREEZE, ANDREW. Middle Breton *Conek* and Consett near Durham. JEPNS (35) 2002/03, 41–3.

2027. *Eadgiþ*] DOCKRAY-MILLER, MARY. The *eadgiþ* erasure: a gloss on the Old English *Andreas*. *See* **4281.**

2028. *Edith Van Dyne*] PICKRELL, ALAN. L. Frank Baum's *Aunt Jane's Nieces*: pseudonyms can pay off. *See* **15362.**

2029. *Ellough*] PARSONS, DAVID N. Ellough: a Viking temple in Suffolk? JEPNS (35) 2002/03, 25–30.

2030. *Evangeline*] SHACKELFORD, LYNNE P. Stowe's *Uncle Tom's Cabin*. *See* **12113.**

2031. *Fagin*] ROWLAND, PETER. No sich a person? The hunt for Fagin. *See* **10736.**

2032. *Florida*] LOGAN, WILLIAM. The state with the prettiest name. *See* **4121.**

2033. *Gatsby*] CERVO, NATHAN A.   Fitzgerald's *The Great Gatsby. See* **16488.**

2034. *Hoon*] CRISP, BARRY, *et al.*   Hough and Hoon, Derbyshire. JEPNS (35) 2002/03, 45–8.

2035. *Hough*] —— Hough and Hoon, Derbyshire. *See* **2034.**

2036. *Jack Straw*] CAÑADAS, IVAN.   The naming of Jack Straw and Peter Ochello in Tennessee Williams's *Cat on a Hot Tin Roof. See* **20181.**

2037. *Jenny*] RIVERS, BRYAN.   Rossetti's *Jenny. See* **11874.**

2038. *Kirmington*] COATES, RICHARD.   Two notes on names in *tūn* in relation to pre-English antiquities: Kirmington and Broughton, Lincolnshire. JEPNS (37) 2004/05, 33–6.

2039. *Knightley*] COHEN, MICHÈLE.   'Manners' make the man: politeness, chivalry, and the construction of masculinity, 1750–1830. *See* **9965.**

2040. *Lollards*] SCASE, WENDY.   'Heu! *quanta desolatio Angliae praestatur'*: a Wycliffite libel and the naming of heretics, Oxford 1382. *In* (pp. 19–36) **4482.**

2041. *Lucy*] CHANDLER, DAVID.   Another Lucy poem about a glow-worm. *See* **12465.**

2042. *Mearcella*] LOWE, KATHRYN A.   *Mearcella* in S 703 and the etymology of Childrey Brook (Berkshire). *See* **2025.**

2043. *Moggerhanger*] COATES, RICHARD.   The antiquity of Moggerhanger, Bedfordshire. JEPNS (37) 2004/05, 48–51.

2044. *Mottram St Andrew*] LAUGHTON, JANE.   A note on the place-name Mottram St Andrew, Cheshire. JEPNS (37) 2004/05, 32.

2045. *Narnia*] FORTUNATI, GIUSEPPE.   Narnia e Narni: dalla storia al fantastico. Preface by Carlo M. Bajetta. *See* **17741.**

2046. *Nidder*] KENNEDY, SEÁN.   A note on Mr Nidder. *See* **15398.**

2047. *Parry*] HILL, JEN.   The Arctic genealogy of Clarissa Dalloway. *See* **20362.**

2048. *Peter Ochello*] CAÑADAS, IVAN.   The naming of Jack Straw and Peter Ochello in Tennessee Williams's *Cat on a Hot Tin Roof. See* **20181.**

2049. *Pity Me*] HOUGH, CAROLE.   Pity Me: a Borders place-name reconsidered. NQ (52:4) 2005, 445–7.

2050. *Rickleton*] JACKSON, RICHARD D.   Border line business: aspects of James Hogg's *The Three Perils of Woman. See* **11280.**

2051. *St Clare*] SHACKELFORD, LYNNE P.   Stowe's *Uncle Tom's Cabin. See* **12113.**

2052. *Sneachill*] HOUGH, CAROLE.   Old English *gefnesan*, present-day English *sneeze*, and the place-names Snogsash and Sneachill. *See* **1842.**

2053. *Snogsash*] —— Old English *gefnesan*, present-day English *sneeze*, and the place-names Snogsash and Sneachill. *See* **1842.**

2054. *Stevens*] EECKHOUT, BART.   How Dutch was Stevens? *See* **19655.**

2055. *Strensall*] HOUGH, CAROLE.   Strensall, *Steanaeshalch* and Stronsay. JEPNS (35) 2002/03, 17–24.

2056. *Stronsay*] —— Strensall, *Steanaeshalch* and Stronsay. *See* **2055.**

2057. *Talos*] WEATHERBY, HAROLD L.   Warren's Willie Talos: reflections on the name. *See* **20000.**

2058. *Ulalume*] KENYON, JOSEPH P.   Auber and Avernus: Poe's use of myth and ritual in *Ulalume*. See **11817**.

2059. *Uricon*] BREEZE, ANDREW.   Ashes under Uricon. See **17059**.

2060. *Wolf Rock*] —— Wolf Rock, off Land's End. JEPNS (37) 2004/05, 59–60.

2061. *Wriothesley*] GREEN, MARTIN.   The pronunciation of *Wriothesley*. EngS (86:2) 2005, 133–60.

MEANING

SEMANTICS

2062. AGRAFOJO BLANCO, HÉCTOR.   The rise of modal meanings in Early Modern English: the case of the semiauxiliary verb BE *supposed to*. See **1710**.

2063. AIJMER, KARIN; SIMON-VANDENBERGEN, ANNE-MARIE.   A marker and a methodology for the study of pragmatic markers: the semantic field of expectation. See **1849**.

2064. BENNETT-KASTOR, TINA.   A battle of words: the land that evolution forgot. See **1904**.

2065. BRANDT, LINE; BRANDT, PER AAGE.   Cognitive poetics and imagery. See **18227**.

2066. BRŮHOVÁ, GABRIELA.   Semantic roles of reason clauses introduced by the central conjunctions *because, since, as* and *for*. In (pp. 25–33) **1369**.

2067. BULTINCK, BERT.   Numerous meanings: the meaning of English cardinals and the legacy of Paul Grice. Amsterdam; New York: Elsevier, 2005. pp. xiii, 327. (Current research in the semantics/pragmatics interface, 15.)

2068. CIENKI, ALAN.   Metaphor in the 'strict father' and 'nurturant parent' cognitive models: theoretical issues in an empirical study. CogL (16:2) 2005, 279–311.

2069. CONSIGNY, ANTOINE.   Chunks of meanings in English phrasal verbs. See **1586**.

2070. COOPER, MARTIN C.   A mathematical model of historical semantics and the grouping of word meanings into concepts. CompLing (31:2) 2005, 217–48.

2071. CORRE, ERIC.   *Begin/start* et leur complémentation: perspective diachronique et synchronique. See **1682**.

2072. DE SMET, HENDRIK; CUYCKENS, HUBERT.   Pragmatic strengthening and the meaning of complement constructions: the case of *like* and *love* with the *to*-infinitive. See **1696**.

2073. DEVER, JOSHUA.   Binding into character. CanJP (supp.30) 2004, 29–80.

2074. FEYAERTS, KURT; BRÔNE, GEERT.   Expressivity and metonymic inferencing: stylistic variation in nonliterary language use. See **2547**.

2075. FRASER, HELEN.   Constraining abstractness: phonological representation in the light of color terms. See **1732**.

2076. FRATH, PIERRE; GLEDHILL, CHRISTOPHER.   Free-range clusters or frozen chunks? Reference as a defining criterion for linguistic units. See **1734**.

2077. FURMANIAK, GRÉGORY.   Le modal *may* dans les phrases optatives: étude syntaxique, sémantique et pragmatique. See **1698**.

2078. GEORGIAFENTIS, MICHALIS.   Focus: the interplay of phonology, syntax, semantics, and pragmatics. *In* (pp. 163–78) **1376.**

2079. GIANNAKIDOU, ANASTASIA.   The three faces of *even*. *In* (pp. 148–60) **1377.**

2080. GIBBS, RAYMOND W.; LIMA, PAULA LENZ COSTA; FRANCOZO, EDSON.   Metaphor is grounded in embodied experience. *See* **2315.**

2081. GIBSON, EDWARD, *et al.*   Reading relative clauses in English. *See* **1599.**

2082. GILQUIN, GAËTANELLE.   Causative *get* and *have*: so close, so different. *See* **1687.**

2083. GIORA, RACHEL, *et al.*   On negation as mitigation: the case of negative irony. DP (39:1) 2005, 81–100.

2084. GODDARD, CLIFF.   The ethnopragmatics and semantics of 'active metaphors'. *See* **2319.**

2085. GONZÁLEZ ORTA, MARTA.   The interrelation of semantic structure and syntactic variation in Old English verb classes: catalogue of syntactico-semantic constructions. *See* **1661.**

2086. —— The Old English verbs of *smell perception* and *emission*: analysis of the interface of their semantic and syntactic representation. *See* **1784.**

2087. GORLACH, MARINA.   Phrasal constructions and resultativeness in English: a sign-oriented analysis. *See* **1601.**

2088. HAJIČOVÁ, EVA.   On some aspects of translation. *In* (pp. 47–57) **1369.**

2089. HAMPE, BEATE.   When *down* is not bad, and *up* is not good enough: a usage-based assessment of the plus–minus parameter in image-schema theory. *See* **1825.**

2090. HANCOCK, CRAIG.   Meaning-centered grammar: an introductory text. *See* **1603.**

2091. HARDER, PETER.   Mental spaces: exactly when do we need them? CogL (14:1) 2003, 91–6.

2092. IWATA, SEIZI.   Locative alternation and two levels of verb meaning. *See* **1853.**

2093. JASZCZOLT, KATARZYNA.   Prolegomena to default semantics. *In* (pp. 107–42) **1376.**

2094. KANG, M. AGNES; LO, ADRIENNE.   Two ways of articulating heterogeneity in Korean American narratives of ethnic identity. *See* **2561.**

2095. KEIZER, EVELIEN.   The discourse function of close appositions. *See* **1610.**

2096. KILGORE, JOHN.   Crossing the Jordan: four meditations on usage: part 3. VocR (7:10) 2005.

2097. —— Crossing the Jordan: four meditations on usage: part 4. VocR (7:11) 2005.

2098. KINTSCH, WALTER.   An overview of top-down and bottom-up effects in comprehension: the CI perspective. DP (39:2/3) 2005, 125–8.

2099. KUDRNÁČOVÁ, NADĚŽDA.   On one type of resultative minimal pair with agentive verbs of locomotion. *In* (pp. 107–14) **1369.**

2100. —— On the semantics of English verbs of locomotion. *In* (pp. 79–84) **1370**.

2101. LANGLOTZ, ANDREAS. Are constructions the basic units of grammar? The phraseological turn in linguistic theory. *See* **1615**.

2102. LEE, PENNY. 'Feelings of the mind' in talk about thinking in English. CogL (14:2/3) 2003, 221–49.

2103. LIEBERSOHN, YOSEF Z.; NEUMAN, YAIR; BEKERMAN, ZVI. Oh baby, it's hard for me to say I'm sorry: public apologetic speech and cultural rhetorical resources. *See* **2177**.

2104. LOCAL, JOHN. On the interactional and phonetic design of collaborative completions. *In* (pp. 263–82) **1472**.

2105. LOUREIRO PORTO, LUCÍA. A corpus-based approach to eModE *have need*. *See* **1691**.

2106. LOW, SOON-AI. Pride, courage, and anger: the polysemousness of Old English *mōd. In* (pp. 77–88) **1786**.

2107. MCENERY, ANTHONY; XIAO, ZHONGHUA. *HELP* or *HELP to* : what do corpora have to say? *See* **1692**.

2108. MCGREEVY, MICHAEL WALLACE. Approaching experiential discourse iconicity from the field. *See* **8458**.

2109. MALÁ, MARCELA. Syntactic and semantic differences between nominal relative clauses and dependent *wh*-interrogative clauses. *In* (pp. 85–9) **1370**.

2110. MALÁ, MARKÉTA. Semantic roles of adverbial participial clauses. *In* (pp. 91–7) **1370**.

2111. MALINIER, YVES-BERNARD. Du notionnel à l'énonciatif et retour: le cas de la construction *activo-passive* en anglais actuel. *See* **1621**.

2112. MARMARIDOU, SOPHIA, *et al.* (eds). Reviewing linguistic thought: converging trends for the 21st century. *See* **1376**.

2113. MARTÍNEZ VÁZQUEZ, MONTSERRAT. What may words say, or what may words not say: a corpus-based approach to linguistic action. *See* **2403**.

2114. MARTINKOVÁ, MICHAELA. Spatial concepts in *wide* and *broad. In* (pp. 107–12) **1370**.

2115. MEDINA, JOSÉ. Anthropologism, naturalism, and the pragmatic study of language. *See* **2574**.

2116. MELA-ATHANASOPOULOU, ELIZABETH. The derivational suffix in English: its categorial and semantic effect. *In* (pp. 85–102) **1375**.

2117. MICHAELIS, LAURA A. Type shifting in construction grammar: an integrated approach to aspectual coercion. *See* **1623**.

2118. NARIYAMA, SHIGEKO. Subject ellipsis in English. *See* **1624**.

2119. NARROG, HEIKO. Modality, mood, and change of modal meanings: a new perspective. CogL (16:4) 2005, 677–731.

2120. NOLAN, JOHN; CLARK, ALAN J. (eds). Under the mind's watch: concerning issues of language, literature, life of contemporary bearing. *See* **19078**.

2121. OCASIO, WILLIAM; JOSEPH, JOHN. Cultural adaptation and institutional change: the evolution of vocabularies of corporate governance, 1972–2003. *See* **1757**.

2122. OLLER, JOHN W., JR, *et al.* Empirical predictions from a general theory of signs. DP (40:2) 2005, 115–44.

2123. ONO, HARUHIKO. On the semantic difference between the *do*-form and the *doing*-form in perception verb complements: from the viewpoint of 'perception' and 'cognition'. *See* **1626.**

2124. ÖZÇALIŞKAN, ŞEYDA. Metaphor meets typology: ways of moving metaphorically in English and Turkish. *See* **1758.**

2125. PEPRNÍK, JAROSLAV. The colour *green* in English language and literature. *In* (pp. 143–55) **1369.**

2126. RAKOVA, MARINA. The extent of the literal: metaphor, polyphony, and theories of concepts. Basingstoke; New York: Palgrave Macmillan, 2003. pp. x, 232. Rev. by Jürgen Van de Walle and Fieke Van der Gucht in CogL (16:4) 2005, 733–43.

2127. RIEMER, NICK. The semantics of polysemy: reading meaning in English and Warlpiri. Berlin; New York: Mouton de Gruyter, 2005. pp. xvi, 487. (Cognitive linguistics research, 30.)

2128. SANTIN-GUETTIER, ANNE-MARIE. *With*: opérateur ambivalent? *See* **1717.**

2129. SCHIAPPA, EDWARD. Defining reality: definitions and the politics of meaning. *See* **2463.**

2130. SHAPIRO, MICHAEL (ed.). From the critic's workbench: essays in literature and semiotics. By Marianne Shapiro. *See* **15197.**

2131. SOLOMONIK-PANKRASOVA, TATYANA. Semantics of Old English *feorh*: from pagan to Christian tradition. *In* (pp. 145–9) **1370.**

2132. SVOBODA, ALEŠ. Firbasian semantic scales and comparative studies. *In* (pp. 217–29) **1369.**

2133. SWEETSER, EVE. Putting the 'same' meaning together from different pieces. *In* (pp. 23–51) **1376.**

2134. TAEYMANS, MARTINE. On Old and Middle English *need* in positive and negative contexts. *See* **1905.**

2135. TISSARI, HELI. A corpus-based description of an emotion word and concept. *See* **1855.**

2136. —— *Love*scapes: changes in prototypical senses and cognitive metaphors since 1500. (Bibl. 2003, 2021.) Rev. by Lynda Mugglestone in NQ (52:2) 2005, 245–6.

2137. TRETYAKOV, YURI P. The existential sentence: a diachronic model. *See* **1674.**

2138. VALLÉE, RICHARD. Complex demonstratives, articulation, and overarticulation. Dialogue (44:1) 2005, 97–121.

2139. VANDELANOTTE, LIEVEN. Deixis and grounding in speech and thought representation. *See* **1649.**

2140. WOLFE, MICHAEL B. W.; MAGLIANO, JOSEPH P.; LARSEN, BENJAMIN. Causal and semantic relatedness in discourse understanding and representation. DP (39:2/3) 2005, 165–87.

2141. WONG, JOCK. The particles in Singapore English: a semantic and cultural interpretation. *See* **3082**.

2142. YU, NING. The eyes for sight and mind. JPrag (36:4) 2003, 663–86.

2143. YUASA, ETSUYO. Modularity in language: constructional and categorial mismatch in syntax and semantics. Berlin; New York: Mouton de Gruyter, 2005. pp. x, 209. (Trends in linguistics: Studies and monographs, 159.) (English and Japanese.)

PRAGMATICS

2144. AIJMER, KARIN; SIMON-VANDENBERGEN, ANNE-MARIE. A marker and a methodology for the study of pragmatic markers: the semantic field of expectation. *See* **1849**.

2145. AKHIMIEN, ERONMONSELE PIUS. The use of 'How are you?' in Nigerian society. *See* **3037**.

2146. ANDERSON, LAURIE. Information management in non-cooperative talk: a case study of two political discussion programmes. *See* **2531**.

2147. ARMINEN, ILKKA. Second stories: the salience of interpersonal communication for mutual help in Alcoholics Anonymous. JPrag (36:2) 2004, 319–47.

2148. BELL, DAVID M. Correlative and non-correlative *on the other hand*. *See* **1871**.

2149. BOSCO, FRANCESCA M.; BUCCIARELLI, MONICA; BARA, BRUNO G. The fundamental context categories in understanding communicative intention. JPrag (36:3) 2004, 467–88.

2150. BOWLES, HUGO; PALLOTTI, GABRIELE. Conversation analysis of opening sequences of telephone calls to bookstores in English and Italian. *See* **2539**.

2151. CLACHAR, ARLENE. Creole discourse effects on the speech conjunctive system in expository texts. *See* **3118**.

2152. CROOK, JOHN. On covert communication in advertising. JPrag (36:4) 2004, 715–38.

2153. DALY, NICOLA, *et al.* Expletives as solidarity signals in FTAs on the factory floor. JPrag (36:5) 2004, 945–64.

2154. DE CLERCK, BERNARD. Explicit *you*-subjects in English imperatives: a pragmatic corpus-based analysis. *See* **1719**.

2155. FERENČÍK, MILAN. Organization of repair in talk-in-interaction and politeness. *In* (pp. 69–78) **1370**.

2156. FILIPI, ANNA; WALES, ROGER. Perspective-taking and perspective-shifting as socially situated and collaborative actions. JPrag (36:10) 2004, 1851–84.

2157. FLEMING, BRUCE E. Art and argument: what words can't do and what they can. *See* **3167**.

2158. FLOWERDEW, JOHN. Identity politics and Hong Kong's return to Chinese sovereignty: analysing the discourse of Hong Kong's first Chief Executive. *See* **3054**.

2159. FUERTES OLIVERA, PEDRO A.   Specialized communication and English Studies: research proposals on specialized lexicography and English for specific purposes. *See* **1923**.

2160. FURMANIAK, GRÉGORY.   Le modal *may* dans les phrases optatives: étude syntaxique, sémantique et pragmatique. *See* **1698**.

2161. GARVER, EUGENE.   For the sake of argument: practical reasoning, character, and the ethics of belief. Chicago, IL; London: Chicago UP, 2004. pp. xi, 272. Rev. by James Kastely in RSQ (35:1) 2005, 115–18.

2162. GEORGIAFENTIS, MICHALIS.   Focus: the interplay of phonology, syntax, semantics, and pragmatics. *In* (pp. 163–78) **1376**.

2163. GREENBERG, GERALD S.   Poststructuralism and communication: an annotated bibliography. *See* **14811**.

2164. GUENDOUZI, JACKIE.   'She's very slim': talking about body-size in all-female interactions. *See* **2553**.

2165. HAGGAN, MADELINE.   Research paper titles in literature, linguistics and science: dimensions of attraction. JPrag (36:2) 2004, 293–317.

2166. HAJIČOVÁ, EVA.   On some aspects of translation. *In* (pp. 47–57) **1369**.

2167. HARWOOD, NIGEL.   'We do not seem to have a theory ... the theory I present here attempts to fill this gap': inclusive and exclusive pronouns in academic writing. *See* **2848**.

2168. HOLBERT, R. LANCE, *et al*.   *The West Wing* and depictions of the American Presidency: expanding the domains of framing in political communication. *See* **20817**.

2169. HYLAND, KEN; TSE, POLLY.   Hooking the reader: a corpus study of evaluative *that* in abstracts. *See* **1712**.

2170. JONES, DAVID K.; READ, STEPHEN J.   Expert–novice differences in the understanding and explanation of complex political conflicts. *See* **2560**.

2171. KALLIA, ALEXANDRA.   The social and psychological modalities of politeness. *In* (pp. 347–64) **1376**.

2172. KIHARA, YOSHIHIKO.   The mental space structure of verbal irony. CogL (16:3) 2005, 513–30.

2173. KITIS, ELIZA.   Conditional constructions as rhetorical structures. *In* (pp. 31–51) **1375**.

2174. KLINE, SUSAN L.   Interactive media systems: influence strategies in television home shopping. *See* **14010**.

2175. KOESTER, ALMUT JOSEPHA.   Relational sequences in workplace genres. *See* **2564**.

2176. KURJIAN, DOUGLAS C.   The dictionary of vital expressions: how to use expressions to persuade. *See* **1962**.

2177. LIEBERSOHN, YOSEF Z.; NEUMAN, YAIR; BEKERMAN, ZVI.   Oh baby, it's hard for me to say I'm sorry: public apologetic speech and cultural rhetorical resources. JPrag (36:5) 2004, 921–44.

2178. MARMARIDOU, SOPHIA, *et al*. (eds).   Reviewing linguistic thought: converging trends for the 21st century. *See* **1376**.

2179. Márquez Reiter, Rosina; Rainey, Isobel; Fulcher, Glenn. A comparative study of certainty and conventional indirectness: evidence from British English and Peninsular Spanish. AppL (26:1) 2005, 1–31.

2180. Mills, Sara. Gender and politeness. See 3189.

2181. Mooney, Annabelle. Co-operation, violations and making sense. JPrag (36:5) 2004, 899–920.

2182. Muilenberg, Gregg. The Cretan glance: toward a theory of metaphorical responsibility. See 2417.

2183. Murillo, Silvia. A relevance reassessment of reformulation markers. JPrag (36:11) 2004, 2059–68. (Discussion note.)

2184. Nariyama, Shigeko. Subject ellipsis in English. See 1624.

2185. Nevala, Minna. Address in early English correspondence: insights into historical socio-pragmatics. NM (106:1) 2005, 85–8.

2186. Ní Chasaide, Ailbhe; Gobl, Christer. On the relation between phonatory quality and affect. In (pp. 323–46) 1472.

2187. Ocasio, William; Joseph, John. Cultural adaptation and institutional change: the evolution of vocabularies of corporate governance, 1972–2003. See 1757.

2188. Padilla Cruz, Manuel. On the phatic interpretation of utterances: a complementary relevance-theoretic proposal. See 2582.

2189. Pagin, Peter. Is assertion social? JPrag (36:5) 2004, 833–59.

2190. Panther, Klaus-Uwe; Thornburg, Linda L. Motivation and convention in some speech act constructions: a cognitive linguistic approach. In (pp. 53–76) 1376.

2191. Pípalová, Renata. On the global textual theme and other textual hyperthemes. LingPr (15:2) 2005, 57–86.

2192. Povolná, Renata. Some discourse items as response elicitors in English face-to-face and telephone conversation. In (pp. 127–36) 1370.

2193. Recski, Leonardo. Interpersonal engagement in academic spoken discourse: a functional account of dissertation defenses. See 2589.

2194. Reid, Christopher. Speaking candidly: rhetoric, politics, and the meaning of candour in the later eighteenth century. See 8052.

2195. Roth, Wolff-Michael. Perceptual gestalts in workplace communication. JPrag (36:6) 2004, 1037–69.

2196. Tárnyiková, Jarmila; Válková, Silvie. Social deixis in addressing. In (pp. 247–59) 1369.

2197. Terkourafi, Marina. Pragmatic correlates of frequency of use: the case for a notion of 'minimal context'. In (pp. 209–33) 1376.

2198. Urbanová, Ludmila. On phatic function of language. In (pp. 271–7) 1369.

2199. van Eemeren, Frans H.; Houtlosser, Peter (eds). Argumentation in practice. Amsterdam; Philadelphia, PA: Benjamins, 2005. pp. vii, 368. (Controversies, 2.)

2200. Vuorela, Taina. How does a sales team reach goals in intercultural business negotiations? A case study. See 2604.

2201. WEE, LIONEL. 'Extreme illocutionary acts' and the boosting of illocutionary force. JPrag (36:12) 2004, 2161–78.

2202. WICHMANN, ANNE. The intonation of *please*-requests: a corpus-based study. See **1701**.

2203. WILAMOVÁ, SIRMA. Grammatical realizations of the avoidance strategy as a significant negative politeness strategy in English discourse. In (pp. 295–305) **1369**.

2204. —— On the function of pragmatic markers in negatively polite discourse. In (pp. 58–67) **1373**.

2205. —— On the nature, functions and linguistic realizations of 'thanking' and 'permission'. SPFFOU (220) 2005, 97–109. (Studia anglica.)

2206. WILSON, DEIRDRE. New directions for research on pragmatics and modularity. In (pp. 375–400) **1376**.

MEDIUM AND REGISTER

RHETORIC AND FIGURES OF SPEECH

2207. AKBARI, SUZANNE CONKLIN. Seeing through the veil: optical theory and medieval allegory. See **4395**.

2208. ALLEN, MICHAEL. Pax Hibernica/pax Americana: rhyme and reconciliation in Muldoon. In (pp. 62–95) **18404**.

2209. ALONSO ALMEIDA, FRANCISCO. All gathered together: on the construction of scientific and technical books in 15th-century England. See **4698**.

2210. ANDERSON, JUDITH H. Translating investments: metaphor and the dynamic of cultural change in Tudor–Stuart England. New York: Fordham UP, 2005. pp. xi, 324.

2211. BALTES, SABINE. Father Time: the emblematic and iconographic context of 'The Epistle Dedicatory to His Royal Highness Prince Posterity' in Swift's Tale. See **9045**.

2212. BARCELONA, ANTONIO (ed.). Metaphor and metonymy at the crossroads. (Bibl. 2002, 1815.) Berlin; New York: Mouton de Gruyter, 2003. pp. xii, 356. (Second ed.: first ed. 2000.) Rev. by Michael White in EIUC (11) 2003, 221–31.

2213. BEHRENDT, STEPHEN C. Mourning, myth, merchandising: the public death of Princess Charlotte. See **9667**.

2214. BELKNAP, ROBERT E. The list: the uses and pleasures of cataloguing. See **10965**.

2215. BENNETT, LYN. Boundaries and frontiers: metaphor and the rhetoric of interdisciplinarity in literary studies. See **14702**.

2216. BERRY, PHILIPPA. 'Salving the mail': perjury, grace and the disorder of things in Love's Labour's Lost. In (pp. 94–108) **5928**.

2217. BICK, ANGELA. 'Speak to one another with psalms': the unity of A. M. Klein's Psalter. See **17501**.

2218. BIDNEY, MARTIN. Peace and pathos in the sea epiphanies of Rupert Brooke: contours of narcissistic desire. See **15578**.

2219. BLACK, DANIEL P. Literary subterfuge: early African American writing and the trope of the mask. *See* **9190.**

2220. BOESKY, AMY. Samson and surrogacy. *In* (pp. 153–66) **7717.**

2221. BOOTH, SHERRY; FRISBIE, SUSAN. (Re)turning to Aristotle: metaphor and the rhetorical education of students. *In* (pp. 163–78) **2318.**

2222. BOOTH, WAYNE C. The rhetoric of rhetoric: the quest for effective communication. Oxford; Malden, MA: Blackwell, 2004. pp. xvi, 206. (Blackwell manifestos.) Rev. by Martin Jacobi in SoCR (37:2) 2005, 240–1.

2223. BOREN, MARK EDELMAN. A fiery furnace and a sugar train: metaphors that challenge the legacy of Phillis Wheatley's *On Being Brought from Africa to America*. *See* **9118.**

2224. BOUCHER, DAVID. Images and distorted facts: politics, poetry and protest in the songs of Bob Dylan. *In* (pp. 134–69) **16199.**

2225. BRADLEY, PATRICIA L. *The Birth of Tragedy* and *The Awakening*: influences and intertextualities. *See* **10426.**

2226. BRANDT, LINE; BRANDT, PER AAGE. Cognitive poetics and imagery. *See* **18227.**

2227. BRIDGEMAN, TERESA. Thinking ahead: a cognitive approach to prolepsis. *See* **19549.**

2228. BRIGANCE, LINDA CZUBA. Ballots and bullets: adapting women's rights arguments to the conditions of war. WL (28:1) 2005, 1–7.

2229. BRODY, JENNIFER DEVERE. The blackness of Blackness …: reading the typography of *Invisible Man*. *See* **16327.**

2230. BROMWICH, DAVID. Burke and the argument from human nature. *In* (pp. 37–58) **8425.**

2231. BROWN, STEPHEN. *Hugh Selwyn Mauberley* as Pound's *Sordello*. *In* (pp. 9–20) **3756.**

2232. BROWN, THEODORE L. Making the truth: metaphor in science. Urbana: Illinois UP, 2003. pp. xi, 215. Rev. by Richard D. Beset in SCJ (70:4) 2005, 349–50.

2233. BROWNE, STEPHEN HOWARD. Jefferson's call for nationhood: the first inaugural address. College Station: Texas A&M UP, 2003. pp. xvii, 155. (Library of Presidential rhetoric.) Rev. by S. Michael Halloran in RSQ (35:4) 2005, 115–22.

2234. BRUMMETT, BARRY. Rhetorical homologies: form, culture, experience. Tuscaloosa; London: Alabama UP, 2004. pp. 240. (Rhetoric, culture, and social critique.)

2235. BRYK, MARTA. Kaleidoscopic (dis)array of Graham Swift's *Waterland*. *In* (pp. 21–8) **3756.**

2236. BUCHANAN, LINDAL. Regendering delivery: the fifth canon and antebellum women rhetors. Carbondale: Southern Illinois UP, 2005. pp. xiv, 202. (Studies in rhetorics and feminisms.)

2237. BULLARD, PADDY. The meaning of the 'sublime and beautiful': Shaftesburian contexts and rhetorical issues in Edmund Burke's *Philosophical Enquiry*. *See* **8424.**

2238. BURGCHARDT, CARL R. (ed.).   Readings in rhetorical criticism. State College, PA: Strata, 2005. pp. xvii, 701. (Third ed.: first ed. 1995.)

2239. BURNHAM, DOUGLAS; GIACCHERINI, ENRICO (eds). The poetics of Transubstantiation: from theology to metaphor. *See* **3724**.

2240. BURNS, MARK K.   'A slave in form but not in fact': subversive humor and the rhetoric of irony in *Narrative of the Life of Frederick Douglass. See* **10825**.

2241. BURROW, J. A.   Lady Meed and the power of money. *See* **4844**.

2242. BUTTERWORTH, ROBERT D.   Hood's *Stanzas ('Farewell, Life ...'). See* **11292**.

2243. BYSTYDZIEŃSKA, GRAŻYNA.   The landscape in grey: the role of nature in the Ossianic epics. *In* (pp. 29–35) **3756**.

2244. CAMPBELL, KARLYN KOHRS.   Theory emerging from practice: the rhetorical theory of Frances Wright. *In* (pp. 125–41) **2410**.

2245. CANAKIS, COSTAS.   Metaphors of a body meant to die. Gramma (11) 2003, 13–29.

2246. CARSON, ANNE ELIZABETH.   The hunted stag and the beheaded king. *See* **7360**.

2247. CARTER, SUSAN.   Duessa: Spenser's Loathly Lady. *See* **5685**.

2248. CHANDRAN, K. NARAYANA.   T. S. Eliot and W. E. Henley: a source for the 'water-dripping song' in *The Waste Land. See* **16252**.

2249. CHANEY, CHRISTINE.   The rhetorical strategies of 'tumultuous emotions': Wollstonecraft's *Letters Written in Sweden. See* **9133**.

2250. CHARNEY, MAURICE.   Shakespeare's eloquence. *In* (pp. 99–112) **5167**.

2251. CHARTERIS-BLACK, JONATHAN.   Corpus approaches to critical metaphor analysis. Basingstoke; New York: Palgrave Macmillan, 2004. pp. xv, 263. Rev. by Kay Wikberg in EJES (9:1) 2005, 91–4; by Alice Deignan in MetS (20:4) 2005, 295–301.

2252. —— Politicians and rhetoric: the persuasive power of metaphor. Basingstoke; New York: Palgrave Macmillan, 2005. pp. xii, 239.

2253. CHEWNING, SUSANNAH MARY.   'Mi bodi henge/wið þi bodi': the paradox of sensuality in *Þe Wohunge of Ure Lauerd. In* (pp. 183–96) **4411**.

2254. CHIAPPE, DAN L.; KENNEDY, JOHN M.; CHIAPPE, PENNY.   Aptness is more important than comprehensibility in preference for metaphors and similes. Poetics (31:1) 2003, 51–68.

2255. CHODAT, ROBERT.   Real toads and imaginary gardens: Freud and Davidson on meaning and metaphor. *See* **16006**.

2256. CIENKI, ALAN.   Metaphor in the 'strict father' and 'nurturant parent' cognitive models: theoretical issues in an empirical study. *See* **2068**.

2257. CLARK, GREGORY.   Rhetorical landscapes in America: variations on a theme from Kenneth Burke. Columbia; London: South Carolina UP, 2004. pp. 181. (Studies in rhetoric/communication.) Rev. by Ann George in RSQ (35:3) 2005, 133–5.

2258. CLARKE, SUSAN A.   'Bright Heir t' th' Bird Imperial': Richard Lovelace's *The Falcon* in context. *See* **7607**.

2259. COHEN, ROBERT. 'The piano has been drinking': on the art of the rant. *See* 12614.

2260. COLCLOUGH, DAVID. 'Better becoming a senate of Venice'? The 'Addled Parliament' and Jacobean debates on freedom of speech. *In* (pp. 51–61) 6860.

2261. CORA ALONSO, JESÚS. 'This dream is all amiss interpreted': *Julius Caesar*, Shakespeare's alchemical tragedy. *See* 6380.

2262. CRISP, PETER. Allegory, blending, and possible situations. MetS (20:2) 2005, 115–31.

2263. CROSSAN, GREG. 'That wolf-howled, witch-prayed, owl-sung fool': Beddoes and the play of words. *See* 10088.

2264. CROWDER, ASHBY BLAND. Butler's *Subplot. See* 15634.

2265. CRUICKSHANK, FRANCES. Herbert's *Jordan (1). See* 7469.

2266. DAS, LIZA; BHUSHAN, BRAJ. From hard poetics to situated reading: a cognitive–empirical study of imagery and graded figurative language. *In* (pp. 219–36) 3888.

2267. DAU, DUC. The caress of God's breath in Gerard Manley Hopkins. *See* 11299.

2268. DAVIS, DIANE. Addressing alterity: rhetoric, hermeneutics, and nonappropriative relation. PhilR (38:3) 2005, 191–212.

2269. DAVIS, WHITNEY. Decadence and the organic metaphor. Representations (89) 2005, 131–49.

2270. DAVISON, PETER. Losing William Matthews. *See* 18128.

2271. DEAVER, KAREN. Updike's *No More Access to Her Underpants. See* 19889.

2272. DEIGNAN, ALICE. A corpus linguistic perspective on the relationship between metonymy and metaphor. Style (39:1) 2005, 72–91.

2273. —— Metaphor and corpus linguistics. Amsterdam; Philadelphia, PA: Benjamins, 2005. pp. viii, 235. (Converging evidence in language and communication research, 6.)

2274. —— POTTER, LIZ. A corpus study of metaphors and metonyms in English and Italian. JPrag (36:7) 2004, 1231–52.

2275. DE LA ZUNINO GARRIDO, MARÍA. Boscán and Garcilaso as rhetorical models in the English Renaissance: the case of Abraham Fraunce's *The Arcadian Rhetorike. See* 5445.

2276. DENMAN, WILLIAM N. Rhetoric, the 'citizen-orator', and the revitalization of civic discourse in American life. *In* (pp. 3–17) 2318.

2277. DEWAR-WATSON, SARAH. Dryden's *Aeneis* 2.718–41. *See* 7413.

2278. DICKERSON, VANESSA D. Performing Blackness: Carlyle and *The Nigger Question. In* (pp. 151–8) 10393.

2279. DIETRICH, JULIA. Women and authority in the rhetorical economy of the late Middle Ages. *In* (pp. 21–43) 2410.

2280. DOBRANSKI, STEPHEN B. Pondering Satan's shield in *Paradise Lost. See* 7669.

2281. DOLMAGE, JAY. Between the valley and the field: metaphor and disability. *See* 17984.

2282. DONALD, RALPH. From 'knockout punch' to 'home run': masculinity's 'dirty dozen' sports metaphors in American combat films. *See* **13218.**

2283. DORESKI, WILLIAM. Wallace Stevens at home in the wilderness. *See* **19654.**

2284. DOTY, MARK. Form, eros, and the unspeakable: Whitman's stanzas. *See* **12308.**

2285. DOW, WILLIAM. The perils of irony in Hemingway's *The Sun Also Rises*. *See* **16976.**

2286. DREHER, UTE. Sex, sermons and ornithology: Thomas Webbe, Edward Stokes and the Wiltshire Ranters. *See* **7109.**

2287. DUNCAN-JONES, KATHERINE. City limits: Nashe's *Choise of Valentines* and Jonson's *Famous Voyage*. *See* **5586.**

2288. DUTHEIL DE LA ROCHÈRE, MARTINE HENNARD. Body politics: Conrad's anatomy of empire in *Heart of Darkness*. *See* **15875.**

2289. DUTTON, RICHARD. *Volpone* and beast fable: early modern analogic reading. *See* **7548.**

2290. EARLEY, SAMANTHA MANCHESTER. Writing from the center or the margins? Olaudah Equiano's writing life reassessed. *See* **8592.**

2291. EDGECOMBE, RODNEY STENNING. Some literary uses of the manual. *See* **3757.**

2292. ELIA, ADRIANO. Sublime and word-painting in Ann Radcliffe's *The Mysteries of Udolpho*. *See* **8921.**

2293. EMSLEY, SARAH. Is Emily Dickinson a Metaphysical poet? *See* **10776.**

2294. ERICKSON, WAYNE. Amoret and Scudamour woo and wed: two courtly histories and a stalemate. *See* **5690.**

2295. EUBANKS, PHILIP. Globalization, 'corporate rule', and blended words: a conceptual–rhetorical analysis of metaphor, metonymy, and conceptual blending. MetS (20:3) 2005, 173–97.

2296. EZELL, MARGARET J. M. Looking glass histories. *See* **6875.**

2297. FELCH, SUSAN M. Doubt and the hermeneutics of delight. *See* **5692.**

2298. FENDT, GENE. Banquo: a false *faux ami*? *See* **6545.**

2299. FIAMENGO, JANICE. 'Baptized with tears and sighs': Sara Jeannette Duncan and the rhetoric of feminism. *In* (pp. 257–80) **9191.**

2300. FISHER, DEVON. In graceful service to the queen (bee): the politics of the hive in Tennyson's *The Princess*. *See* **12142.**

2301. FLANNERY, DENIS. The powers of apostrophe and the boundaries of mourning: Henry James, Alan Hollinghurst, and Toby Litt. *See* **11401.**

2302. FLECK, ANDREW. The limitations of narrative: Nashe's appropriation of Ovidian decorum in *The Unfortunate Traveller*. *See* **5587.**

2303. FLETCHER, CHRISTOPHER. Norman Nicholson's *The Blackberry* – a fruitful source for Sylvia Plath? *See* **18816.**

2304. FOWLER, ELIZABETH. *Macbeth* and the rhetoric of political forms. *In* (pp. 67–86) **6561.**

2305. FRANKS, JILL. Oxymorons and the pathetic fallacy in *The Narrow House*: a Lacanian reading. *See* **19342.**

2306. FREEMAN, LOUISE GILBERT.   Vision, metamorphosis, and the poetics of allegory in the *Mutabilitie Cantos*. *See* **5695**.

2307. FREEMAN, MARGARET H.   The poem as complex blend: conceptual mappings of metaphor in Sylvia Plath's *The Applicant*. *See* **18817**.

2308. FREINKEL, LISA.   The Shakespearean fetish. *In* (pp. 109–29) **5928**.

2309. GAGGERO, CHRISTOPHER.   Pleasure unreconciled to virtue: George Gascoigne and didactic drama. *In* (pp. 168–93) **5268**.

2310. GALLAGHER, LOWELL.   Waiting for Gobbo. *In* (pp. 73–93) **5928**.

2311. GATES, DANIEL.   Unpardonable sins: the hazards of performative language in the tragic cases of Francesco Spiera and *Doctor Faustus*. *See* **5524**.

2312. GERMANO, WILLIAM.   Final thoughts. *See* **1078**.

2313. GERTZ-ROBINSON, GENELLE.   Stepping into the pulpit? Women's preaching in *The Book of Margery Kempe* and *The Examination of Anne Askew*. With a response by David Wallace. *In* (pp. 459–91) **4460**.

2314. ——— Still martyred after all these years: generational suffering in Milton's *Areopagitica*. *See* **7677**.

2315. GIBBS, RAYMOND W.; LIMA, PAULA LENZ COSTA; FRANCOZO, EDSON. Metaphor is grounded in embodied experience. JPrag (36:7) 2004, 1189–1210.

2316. GIORA, RACHEL, *et al.*   On negation as mitigation: the case of negative irony. *See* **2083**.

2317. GLENN, CHERYL.   Unspoken: a rhetoric of silence. Carbondale: Southern Illinois UP, 2004. pp. xxii, 220. Rev. by Bradford Vivian in RSQ (35:4) 2005, 123–7.

2318. ——— LYDAY, MARGARET M.; SHARER, WENDY B. (eds).   Rhetorical education in America. Tuscaloosa; London: Alabama UP, 2004. pp. xvi, 245. Rev. by Jeffrey Walker in RSQ (35:3) 2005, 125–31; by Jane Donawerth in Rhetorica (23:4) 2005, 403–4.

2319. GODDARD, CLIFF.   The ethnopragmatics and semantics of 'active metaphors'. JPrag (36:7) 2004, 1211–30.

2320. GOLDFARB, LISA.   'Pure rhetoric of a language without words': Stevens's musical creation of belief in *Credences of Summer*. *See* **19658**.

2321. GORDON, DEXTER B.   Black identity: rhetoric, ideology, and nineteenth-century Black nationalism. (Bibl. 2003, 2247.) Rev. by Wilson J. Moses in JAH (91:1) 2004, 245–6.

2322. GORSKY, SUSAN RUBINOW.   The mask/masque of food: illness and art. *See* **20357**.

2323. GOULD, JOHN.   Making God: poetry as spiritual practice. *In* (pp. 13–37) **19115**.

2324. GRAFF, RICHARD; WALZER, ARTHUR E.; ATWILL, JANET M. (eds). The viability of the rhetorical tradition. Albany: New York State UP, 2005. pp. ix, 203.

2325. GRIBBEN, CRAWFORD.   Rhetoric, fiction and theology: James Ussher and the death of Jesus Christ. *See* **7875**.

2326. GUNN, JOSHUA.   Mourning speech: haunting and the spectral voices of nine-eleven. TPQ (24:2) 2004, 91–114.

2327. GURR, JENS MARTIN.   'Let me suppose thee for a ship a-while': nautical metaphors and contemporary politics in eighteenth-century translations of Horace's Ode I, xiv. *See* **9069.**

2328. HAINES, DOROTHY.   Courtroom drama and the homiletic monologues of the Vercelli Book. *In* (pp. 105–23) **1786.**

2329. HAMILTON, CRAIG A.   Toward a cognitive rhetoric of Imagism. *See* **14406.**

2330. HARBUS, ANTONINA.   Thinking in metaphors: figurative language and ideas on the mind. SSE (30) 2004, 3–20.

2331. HARDY, DONALD E.   Collocational analysis as a stylistic discovery procedure: the case of Flannery O'Connor's *eyes*. *See* **18560.**

2332. HARRAWOOD, MICHAEL.   Overreachers: hyperbole, the 'circle in the water', and force in *1 Henry 6*. *See* **6438.**

2333. HARRISON, CAREY.   Maydays. VocR (7:5) 2005. (Metathesis.)

2334. HARVEY, ANDREW.   Crossing wits: Donne, Herbert, and sacramental rhetoric. *See* **7377.**

2335. HATZITHEODOROU, ANNA-MARIA.   Repetition as a component of argumentation in written discourse. *In* (pp. 161–74) **1377.**

2336. HELGESON, KAREN.   Anding and ending: metaphor and closure in Stevens' *An Ordinary Evening in New Haven*. *See* **19664.**

2337. HIGGINS, ANDREW C.   Longfellow's *Snow-Flakes*. *See* **11615.**

2338. HIGGINS, LESLEY.   'To prove him with hard questions': degrees of answerability in Hopkins's writing. *See* **11306.**

2339. HILL, THOMAS D.   The failing torch: the Old English *Elene*, 1256–1259. *See* **4326.**

2340. HILL, W. SPEED.   Richard Hooker and the rhetoric of history. *In* (pp. 75–84) **587.**

2341. HOBSON, CHRISTOPHER Z.   Ralph Ellison, *Juneteenth*, and African American prophecy. *See* **16332.**

2342. HOLMES, DAVID G.   Say what? Rediscovering Hugh Blair and the racialization of language, culture, and pedagogy in eighteenth-century rhetoric. *In* (pp. 203–13) **2457.**

2343. HOLSINGER, BRUCE.   Lollard ekphrasis: situated aesthetics and literary history. *See* **4642.**

2344. HOOKER, DEBORAH ANNE.   Reanimating the trope of the talking book in Alice Walker's *Strong Horse Tea*. *See* **19961.**

2345. HOWE, SARAH.   'Pregnant images of life': visual art and representation in *Arcadia* and *The Faerie Queene*. *See* **5703.**

2346. HUDSON, NICHOLAS.   The alphabet of nature: writing as trope in early modern scientific and philosophical discourse. *See* **5340.**

2347. HUTSON, LORNA.   Rethinking the 'spectacle of the scaffold': juridical epistemologies and English revenge tragedy. *See* **6781.**

2348. HUTTON, CLARK.   Images of time and eternity in the religious poetry of Henry Vaughan. *See* **7882.**

2349. IGNATOW, GABRIEL. 'Idea hamsters' on the 'bleeding edge': profane metaphors in high technology jargon. *See* **1739.**

2350. INGRAM, CLAUDIA. 'Fission and fusion both liberate energy': James Merrill, Jorie Graham, and the metaphoric imagination. *See* **18189.**

2351. ITALIA, PAUL G. 'No joke!': the mediation of ironic humour in Conrad's *Lord Jim. See* **15884.**

2352. JACKSON, RICHARD. William Matthews' lovable weather. *See* **18130.**

2353. JAMES, STEPHEN. Seamus Heaney's sway. *See* **16944.**

2354. JANG, JEONG U. Thymotic misprision of self-evident truth. *See* **11604.**

2355. JOHNSON, CHRISTOPHER. Appropriating Troy: ekphrasis in Shakespeare's *The Rape of Lucrece. In* (pp. 193–212) **4479.**

2356. JOHNSON, NAN. Parlor rhetoric and the performance of gender in postbellum America. *In* (pp. 107–28) **2318.**

2357. JOHNSON, WILLIAM C. *In vino - et in amore - veritas*: transformational animation in Herrick's 'sack' poems. *See* **7495.**

2358. JOLLY, MARGARETTA. Corresponding in the sex and gender revolution: desire, education and feminist letters, 1970–2000. *In* (pp. 253–70) **8217.**

2359. JONES-DAVIES, MARGARET. Defacing the icon of the king: *Richard II* and the issues of iconoclasm. *In* (pp. 101–12) **6505.**

2360. JÖTTKANDT, SIGI. Effectively equivalent: Walter Pater, 'Sebastian van Storck', and the ethics of metaphor. *See* **11781.**

2361. JUNG, SANDRO. John Gilbert Cooper's revisions of *The Tomb of Shakespear: a Vision. See* **8483.**

2362. —— Unnoticed echoes of Collins's *Ode to Evening* in Mary Whateley's *Elegy on the Uses of Poetry. See* **8481.**

2363. KARDOKAS, LAIMA. The twilight zone of experience uncannily shared by Mark Strand and Edward Hopper. *See* **19714.**

2364. KASDORF, JULIA. Same, same! Pleasures and purposes of metaphor. Cresset (68:5) 2005, 9–15.

2365. KASKE, CAROL. Spenser's *Amoretti* and *Epithalamion*: a psalter of love. *In* (pp. 28–49) **6872.**

2366. KEARNS, JUDITH. Fashioning innocence: rhetorical construction of character in the *Memoirs* of Anne, Lady Halkett. *See* **7126.**

2367. KELLER, LYNN. Poems living with paintings: Cole Swensen's ekphrastic *Try. See* **21294.**

2368. KILGORE, JENNIFER. Tropes of memory in *The Orchards of Syon. See* **17026.**

2369. KILGORE, JOHN. Frisking the governor's daughter: on puns. VocR (7:1) 2005.

2370. KING, JANE. 'Images of flight ...': 'This time, Shabine, like you really gone!' *See* **19949.**

2371. KLINE, DANIEL T. Resisting the father in *Pearl. In* (pp. 1–29) **5069.**

2372. KOKERNOT, WALTER H. 'Where ignorant armies clash by night' and the Sikh rebellion: a contemporary source for Matthew Arnold's night-battle imagery. *See* **9935.**

2373. KOLÁŘ, STANISLAV. Animal imagery in Kosinski's *The Painted Bird* and Spiegelman's *Maus*. *In* (pp. 87–92) **3753**.

2374. KÖVECSES, ZOLTÁN. Metaphor: a practical introduction. (Bibl. 2004, 2422.) Rev. by Charles Forceville in JEL (31:2) 2003, 178–83.

2375. KRANIDAS, THOMAS. Milton and the rhetoric of zeal. *See* **7705**.

2376. KRŪMINIENĖ, JADVYGA. John Donne's sermons: paradox as a fundamental structural device. *In* (pp. 101–8) **3734**.

2377. KUCHAR, GARY. Divine subjection: the rhetoric of sacramental devotion in early modern England. *See* **5158**.

2378. LAWSON, JEREMY. Atomic and surface theories of matter in *Mrs Dalloway*: a comparative study of Clarissa and Septimus. *See* **20380**.

2379. LEAHY, MARK. Plantation and thicket: a double (sight) reading of Sir Thomas Browne's *Garden of Cyrus*. *See* **7274**.

2380. LEDERER, RICHARD. Serving up a tennis slogan: jest for the pun of it. *See* **1746**.

2381. —— A stylish inauguration speech. VocR (7:1) 2005. (John F. Kennedy.)

2382. LEIGH, DAVID. Firewatch in the belly of the whale: imagery of fire, water, and place in *The Sign of Jonas*. *See* **18200**.

2383. LOGAN, SHIRLEY WILSON. 'By the way, where did you learn to speak?': Black sites of rhetorical education. *In* (pp. 215–27) **2457**.

2384. LOMBARDY, ANTHONY. Allen Tate and the metaphysics of metaphor. *See* **19749**.

2385. LOW, GRAHAM. Explaining evolution: the use of animacy in an example of semi-formal science writing. *See* **2861**.

2386. MACARTHUR, FIONA. The competent horseman in a horseless world: observations on a conventional metaphor in Spanish and English. MetS (20:1) 2005, 71–94.

2387. MCCARTHY, MICHAEL; CARTER, RONALD. 'There's millions of them': hyperbole in everyday conversation. *See* **2570**.

2388. MCCLISH, GLEN. William G. Allen's 'Orators and Oratory': inventional amalgamation, pathos, and the characterization of violence in African American Abolitionist rhetoric. RSQ (35:1) 2005, 47–72.

2389. MCCORKLE, BEN. Harbingers of the printed page: nineteenth-century theories of delivery as remediation. RSQ (35:4) 2005, 25–49.

2390. MCCOY, RICHARD C. 'The grace of grace' and double-talk in *Macbeth*. *See* **6558**.

2391. MCCREA, BRIAN. The virtue of repetition: Mr Spectator trains Benjamin Franklin. *In* (pp. 248–64) **1285**.

2392. MCDONALD, PETER D. Stony ground. *See* **15835**.

2393. MCDOWELL, SEAN. Finding readers: Herbert's appeals to the passions. *See* **7478**.

2394. MCGOWAN, MARGARET M. Caesar's cloak: diversion as an art of persuasion in sixteenth-century writing. *See* **6381**.

2395. McIlvanney, Liam.　Hugh Blair, Robert Burns, and the invention of Scottish literature. *See* **8455.**

2396. McKenzie, Andrea.　Martyrs in low life? Dying 'game' in Augustan England. *See* **8236.**

2397. McKeown, Adam.　Looking at Britomart looking at pictures. *See* **5709.**

2398. McKim, A. Elizabeth.　Making poetry of pain: the headache poems of Jane Cave Winscom. *See* **9127.**

2399. Mallot, J. Edward.　Not drowning but waving: Stevie Smith and the language of the lake. *See* **19491.**

2400. Manolescu, Beth Innocenti.　Kames's legal career and writings as precedents for *Elements of Criticism. See* **8298.**

2401. Mansour, Wisam.　Gender ambivalence in Donne's *Valediction: Forbidding Mourning. See* **7383.**

2402. Mao, Douglas.　Privative synecdoches. *See* **19675.**

2403. Martínez Vázquez, Montserrat.　What may words say, or what may words not say: a corpus-based approach to linguistic action. RAEI (18) 2005, 189–214.

2404. May, Vivian M.; Ferri, Beth A.　Fixated on ability: questioning ableist metaphors in feminist theories of resistance. *See* **14908.**

2405. Mazur, Krystyna.　Poetry and repetition: Walt Whitman, Wallace Stevens, John Ashbery. *See* **12334.**

2406. Melas, Natalie.　Forgettable vacations and metaphor in ruins: Walcott's *Omeros. See* **19954.**

2407. Merrill, Yvonne.　The role of language in the construction of Mary Wortley Montagu's rhetorical identity. *In* (pp. 44–62) **2410.**

2408. Michie, Allen.　'New philosophy calls all in doubt': chaos theory and the fractal poetics of John Donne. *In* (pp. 150–77) **5167.**

2409. Miller, Anthony.　The proem to *The Faerie Queene*, Book ii: Spenser, Pliny, and undiscovered worlds. *See* **5711.**

2410. Miller, Hildy; Bridwell-Bowles, Lillian (eds).　Rhetorical women: roles and representations. Tuscaloosa; London: Alabama UP, 2005. pp. viii, 261.

2411. Monod, Sylvère.　Joseph Conrad's polyglot wordplay. *See* **15901.**

2412. Montgomery, Martin.　The discourse of *war* after 9/11. *See* **1911.**

2413. Moore, Candy.　Why feminists can't stop talking about voice. *In* (pp. 191–205) **2410.**

2414. Moretti, Franco.　Graphs, maps, trees: abstract models for a literary history. *See* **14926.**

2415. Mountford, Roxanne.　The gendered pulpit: preaching in American Protestant spaces. Carbondale: Southern Illinois UP, 2003. pp. xii, 194. (Studies in rhetorics and feminisms.) Rev. by Lindal Buchanan in Rhetorica (23:4) 2005, 401–3.

2416. Mousley, Andy.　Transubstantiating love: John Donne and cultural criticism. *In* (pp. 55–62) **3724.**

2417. MUILENBERG, GREGG. The Cretan glance: toward a theory of metaphorical responsibility. Cresset (68:5) 2005, 16–23.

2418. NEWMAN, BARBARA. The artifice of eternity: speaking of Heaven in three medieval poems. See 5076.

2419. NICHOLSON, MERVYN. 13 ways of looking at images: the logic of visualization in literature and society. See 3873.

2420. NIEDERHOFF, BURKHARD. Parody, paradox and play in *The Importance of Being Earnest*. See 12405.

2421. NOAKES, RICHARD. Representing 'a century of inventions': nineteenth-century technology and Victorian *Punch*. In (pp. 151–63) 1226.

2422. NORRICK, NEAL R. Hyperbole, extreme case formulation. JPrag (36:9) 2004, 1727–39.

2423. NUTTALL, A. D. Spenser and Elizabethan alienation. See 5714.

2424. OLSON, GRETA. Richard III's animalistic criminal body. See 6515.

2425. OSBORN, MARIJANE. 'Skep' (*Beinenkorb*, *beoleap) as a culture-specific solution to Exeter Book Riddle 17. See 4373.

2426. OSELL, TEDRA. Tatling women in the public sphere: rhetorical femininity and the English essay periodical. See 1293.

2427. OWLEY, STEVEN A. *Wynnere and Wastoure*. See 4658.

2428. ÖZÇALIŞKAN, ŞEYDA. Metaphor meets typology: ways of moving metaphorically in English and Turkish. See 1758.

2429. PANTHER, KLAUS-UWE; THORNBURG, LINDA L. Motivation and convention in some speech act constructions: a cognitive linguistic approach. In (pp. 53–76) 1376.

2430. PARKER, IAN C. Marvell and the 'Tygress fell'. See 7630.

2431. PARRY, JOSEPH. Petrarch's mourning, Spenser's Scudamour, and Britomart's gift of death. See 5716.

2432. PENDER, STEPHEN. The open use of living: prudence, decorum, and the 'square man'. Rhetorica (23:4) 2005, 363–400.

2433. PERRY, NANDRA. *Imitatio* and identity: Thomas Rogers, Philip Sidney, and the Protestant self. See 5628.

2434. PETERS, JASON. O'Connor's *Wise Blood*. See 18574.

2435. —— The source of Flannery O'Connor's 'flung' fish in *The Violent Bear It Away*. See 18575.

2436. PETERS, JULIE STONE. Theater and book in the history of memory: materializing Mnemosyne in the age of print. See 5548.

2437. PLOTKIN, CARY. Ametaphoricity and presence in Hopkins's poetics. See 11313.

2438. POLLY, GREG. Leviathan of letters. In (pp. 105–28) 1285.

2439. POSNER, DAVID M. Rhetoric, redemption, and fraud: what we do when we end books. See 1088.

2440. POTTER, URSULA. Performing arts in the Tudor classroom. In (pp. 143–65) 5268.

2441. POWELL, JASON. Puttenham's *Arte of English Poesie* and Thomas Wyatt's diplomacy. See 5614.

2442. POWELL, MALEA. Princess Sarah, the civilized Indian: the rhetoric of cultural literacies in Sarah Winnemucca Hopkins's *Life among the Piutes*. *In* (pp. 63–80) **2410**.

2443. RAINEY, LAWRENCE. Eliot among the typists: writing *The Waste Land*. *See* **16296**.

2444. RAKOVA, MARINA. The extent of the literal: metaphor, polyphony, and theories of concepts. *See* **2126**.

2445. RAMAZANI, JAHAN. Self-theorizing poetry: Yeats's *ars poetica* in '*The Green Helmet' and Other Poems*. *See* **20521**.

2446. REHDER, ROBERT. Stevens, Williams, Crane, and the motive for metaphor. *See* **19681**.

2447. REID, CHRISTOPHER. Character construction in the eighteenth-century House of Commons: evidence from the Cavendish diary (1768–74). Rhetorica (22:4) 2004, 375–99.

2448. REVAK, KELLY. 'As easy as collecting feathers in a hurricane': a re-definition of the genre of folk simile. *See* **3454**.

2449. RICHARDT, SUSANNE. Metaphor in languages for special purposes: the function of conceptual metaphor in written expert language and expert–lay communication in the domains of economics, medicine, and computing. New York; Frankfurt: Lang, 2005. pp. 290. (European univ. studies, XIV: Anglo-Saxon language and literature, 413.)

2450. RITVO, HARRIET. Narratives of nature: response. *See* **9780**.

2451. RIX, ROBERT W. Blake's *Auguries of Innocence, The French Revolution*, and *London*. *See* **8385**.

2452. RIZZO, BETTY. Male oratory and female prate: 'then hush and be an angel quite'. *See* **3197**.

2453. ROBERTS-MILLER, PATRICIA. Robert Montgomery Bird and the rhetoric of the improbable cause. *See* **10098**.

2454. ROEMER, KENNETH M. A 'touching man' brings Aacqu close. *See* **18666**.

2455. ROSS, MELANIE H. Conceiving jealousy: Othello's imitated pregnancy. *See* **6659**.

2456. ROUSSILLON, LAURENCE. '*All now is still'*: de la citation à l'œuvre dans *Ruggiero and Angelica* de Dante Gabriel Rossetti. *See* **11875**.

2457. ROYSTER, JACQUELINE JONES; SIMPKINS, ANN MARIE MANN (eds). Calling cards: theory and practice in studies of race, gender, and culture. Albany: New York State UP, 2005. pp. xiv, 303.

2458. RYKEN, LELAND. Milton's Sonnet 14 and Puritan funeral sermons for women. *In* (pp. 136–48) **7738**.

2459. SALE, CAROLYN. The 'Roman hand': women, writing and the law in the *Att.-Gen. v. Chatterton* and the letters of the Lady Arbella Stuart. *See* **7149**.

2460. SAVANT, JOHN. Follow that metaphor: what faith, jazz & poetry have in common. Cweal (132:20) 2005, 17–19.

2461. SCHÄFFNER, CHRISTINA. Metaphor and translation: some implications of a cognitive approach. JPrag (36:7) 2004, 1253–69.

2462. SCHEICK, WILLIAM J.   Taylor's *Meditation 1.7. See* **7862.**

2463. SCHIAPPA, EDWARD.   Defining reality: definitions and the politics of meaning. Carbondale: Southern Illinois UP, 2003. pp. xvi, 213. (Rhetorical philosophy and theory.) Rev. by John D. Schaeffer in Style (38:1) 2004, 134–8.

2464. SCHMITT-KILB, CHRISTIAN.   'Never was the Albion Nation without Poetrie': Poetik, Rhetorik und Nation im England der frühen Neuzeit. *See* **7343.**

2465. SCHÜRER, NORBERT.   Millay's *What Lips My Lips Have Kissed, and Where, and Why. See* **18228.**

2466. SCHWARTZ, BARRY.   The new Gettysburg Address: fusing history and memory. *See* **11605.**

2467. SCOLNICOV, HANNA.   Making ears serve for eyes: Stoppard's visual radio play. *See* **19700.**

2468. SEMINO, ELENA.   The metaphorical construction of complex domains: the case of speech activity in English. MetS (20:1) 2005, 35–70.

2469. —— Representing characters' speech and thought in narrative fiction: a study of *England, England* by Julian Barnes. *See* **15338.**

2470. —— HEYWOOD, JOHN; SHORT, MICK.   Methodological problems in the analysis of metaphors in a corpus of conversations about cancer. *See* **2593.**

2471. SHAMI, JEANNE.   Love and power: the rhetorical motives of John Donne's 1622 sermon to the Virginia Company. *See* **7394.**

2472. —— Squint-eyed, left-handed, half-deaf: *imperfect senses* and John Donne's interpretive middle way. *In* (pp. 173–92) **6872.**

2473. SHARMA, MANISH.   Metalepsis and monstrosity: the boundaries of narrative structure in *Beowulf. See* **4309.**

2474. SHARPE, PETER.   The ground of our beseeching: metaphor and the poetics of meditation. *See* **16305.**

2475. SHERIFF, STACEY.   Resituating Kenneth Burke's *My Approach to Communism*. Rhetorica (23:3) 2005, 281–96.

2476. SHURBANOV, ALEXANDER.   The translatability of Shakespearean texts into an unrelated language/culture. *In* (pp. 51–64) **5874.**

2477. SILBERSTEIN, SANDRA.   War of words: language, politics and 9/11. (Bibl. 2004, 2543.) Rev. by Nuria Lorenzo-Dus in LLit (12:3) 2004, 286–8; by Pepi Leistyna in JEL (32:2) 2004, 159–62.

2478. SIMPKINS, ANN MARIE MANN.   Rhetorical tradition(s) and the reform writing of Mary Ann Shadd Cary. *In* (pp. 229–41) **2457.**

2479. SIMPSON, KATHRYN.   Pearl-diving: inscriptions of desire and creativity in H.D. and Woolf. *See* **16114.**

2480. SIVASUNDARAM, SUJIT.   The periodical as barometer: spiritual measurement and the *Evangelical Magazine. In* (pp. 43–55) **1226.**

2481. SKLYARENKO, ALEXEY.   *Ada* as a Russian fairy tale spun by the Phoenix and sung by the Sirin. *See* **18472.**

2482. SMITH, TANIA SONA.   *The Lady's Rhetorick* (1707): the tip of the iceberg of women's rhetorical education in Enlightenment France and Britain. *See* **8251.**

2483. SNEDIKER, MICHAEL.   Hart Crane's smile. *See* **15959.**

2484. SOMERS-WILLETT, SUSAN B. A.   Slam poetry and the cultural politics of performing identity. *See* **14494**.

2485. SORENSEN, SUE.   A. S. Byatt and the life of the mind: a response to June Sturrock. *See* **15648**.

2486. SPURR, DAVID.   Architecture in Frost and Stevens. *See* **16617**.

2487. STEEN, GERARD.   Can discourse properties of metaphor affect metaphor recognition? JPrag (36:7) 2004, 1295–1313.

2488. —— Metonymy goes cognitive-linguistic. Style (39:1) 2005, 1–11.

2489. STEVENSON, WINIFRED.   Donne's nocturnal. *See* **7397**.

2490. STEWART, ALAN.   Instigating treason: the life and death of Henry Cuffe, secretary. *In* (pp. 50–70) **5196**.

2491. STOB, PAUL.   Kenneth Burke, John Dewey, and the pursuit of the public. PhilR (38:3) 2005, 226–47.

2492. STRACK, DANIEL C.   Who are the bridge-builders? Metaphor, metonymy, and the architecture of empire. *See* **17490**.

2493. SUAREZ, MICHAEL F.   A crisis in English public life: the Popish Plot, *Naboth's Vineyard* (1679), and mock-biblical satire's exemplary redress. *See* **7308**.

2494. SWENSON, RIVKA.   Representing modernity in Jane Barker's Galesia trilogy: Jacobite allegory and the patch-work aesthetic. *See* **7218**.

2495. SWIENCICKI, JILL.   Sew it seams: (a)mending civic rhetorics for our classrooms and for rhetorical history. *In* (pp. 55–73) **2318**.

2496. TACKACH, JAMES.   Abraham Lincoln's election jeremiad: the second inaugural address. *See* **11606**.

2497. TAYLOR, ANITA.   A treasure revisited: Rosalie Maggio's *New Beacon Book of Quotations by Women*. WL (28:2) 2005, 32–41.

2498. TAYLOR, CHERYL.   Paradox upon paradox: using and abusing language in *The Cloud of Unknowing* and related texts. *See* **4683**.

2499. THOMPSON, TERRY W.   Blackwood's *The Listener*. *See* **15506**.

2500. TILLEY, ELIZABETH.   Science, industry, and nationalism in the *Dublin Penny Journal*. *In* (pp. 139–49) **1226**.

2501. TILMOUTH, CHRISTOPHER.   Burton's 'turning picture': argument and anxiety in *The Anatomy of Melancholy*. *See* **7294**.

2502. TOMLINSON, BARBARA.   Authors on writing: metaphors and intellectual labor. Basingstoke; New York: Palgrave Macmillan, 2005. pp. vii, 233.

2503. TRUBEY, ELIZABETH FEKETE.   Emancipating the lettered slave: sentiment and slavery in Augusta Evans's *St Elmo*. *See* **11000**.

2504. TWU, KRISTA SUE-LO.   Chaucer's vision of the Tree of Life: crossing the road with the Rood in the Parson's Tale. *See* **5040**.

2505. URBANCZYK, AARON.   Analyzing the literary image. ModAge (47:4) 2005, 353–5 (review-article).

2506. VEEL, KRISTIN.   The irreducibility of space: labyrinths, cities, cyberspace. Diacritics (33:3/4) 2003, 151–72.

2507. VEIVO, HARRI; KNUUTTILA, TARJA.   Modelling, theorising and interpretation in cognitive literary studies. *In* (pp. 283–305) **3888**.

2508. Vivian, Bradford.   Being made strange: rhetoric beyond representation. (Bibl. 2004, 2578.) Rev. by Walter Jost in RSQ (35:1) 2005, 119–22.

2509. Vrbančić, Mario.   Burroughs's phantasmic maps. See 15630.

2510. Wai, Isabella.   Wilbur's *Walking to Sleep*. See 20172.

2511. Wallart, Kerry-Jane.   La métaphore chez Derek Walcott: à la recherche d'une 'arrière-langue'. See 19957.

2512. Watson, Elizabeth See.   George Puttenham as comedic artificer. See 5616.

2513. Watson, Jonathan.   Writing out 'Óðinn's Storm': the literary reception of an oral-derived template in the two versions of Laȝamon's *Brut*. In (pp. 209–236) 4197.

2514. Weseliński, Andrzej.   'Leopard' images in Graham Greene's fiction. In (pp. 275–82) 3756.

2515. West, Michael; Silberstein, Myron.   The controversial eloquence of Shakespeare's Coriolanus – an anti-Ciceronian orator? See 6287.

2516. White, Julianne.   Soto's *Oranges*. See 19541.

2517. Wicher, Andrzej.   The 'infantile' aspects of the 14th c. English mysticism: an introductory study. In (pp. 283–93) 3756.

2518. Williams, Lisa.   Momentous bodies: the poetry of Larissa Szporluk. See 19744.

2519. Wolfe, Jessica.   Spenser, Homer, and the mythography of strife. See 5729.

2520. Wolfreys, Julian.   'A self-referential density': *Glyph* and the 'theory' thing. See 21198.

2521. Wood, James.   The Jewish King James Version; or, Saul Bellow: not exactly English but biblically English. See 15459.

2522. Wright, Charles D.   The persecuted Church and the *mysterium lunae*: Cynewulf's *Ascension*, lines 252b–272 (*Christ II*, lines 691b–711). In (pp. 293–314) 4221.

2523. Xavier, Silvia.   Engaging George Campbell's 'sympathy' in the rhetoric of Charlotte Forten and Ann Plato, African American women of the antebellum North. RhR (24:4) 2005, 438–56.

2524. Yeager, R. F.   Death is a lady: *The Regement of Princes* as gendered political commentary. See 4816.

2525. Zappen, James P.   The rebirth of dialogue: Bakhtin, Socrates, and the rhetorical tradition. (Bibl. 2004, 2600.) Rev. by Kay Halasek in Rhetorica (23:3) 2005, 299–301.

2526. Zettel, Sarah.   Dust to dust: the destruction of fantasy trope and archetype in *His Dark Materials*. In (pp. 39–48) 18973.

2527. Zurcher, Amelia A.   Ethics and the politic agent of early seventeenth-century prose romance. See 7926.

2528. Zwicky, Jan.   Wisdom and metaphor. Kentville, N.S.: Gaspereau Press, 2003. pp. 118. Rev. by David R. Jarraway in MalaR (148) 2004, 101–3; by Brian Bartlett, Ross Leckie and Ann Simpson in Fiddlehead (222) 2004, 82–102.

SPOKEN DISCOURSE

2529. ALIM, H. SAMY. You know my steez: an ethnographic and sociolinguistic study of styleshifting in a Black American speech community. *See* **2975.**

2530. ALLISON, RAPHAEL C. David Antin's pragmatist technophobia. *See* **15174.**

2531. ANDERSON, LAURIE. Information management in non-cooperative talk: a case study of two political discussion programmes. Textus (17:1) 2004, 17–38.

2532. ARMINEN, ILKKA. Second stories: the salience of interpersonal communication for mutual help in Alcoholics Anonymous. *See* **2147.**

2533. BAKER, PAUL. Public discourses of gay men. *See* **3145.**

2534. BAYLEY, PAUL (ed.). Cross-cultural perspectives on parliamentary discourse. Amsterdam; Philadelphia, PA: Benjamins, 2004. pp. vi, 384. (Discourse approaches to politics, society, and culture, 10.) Rev. by Sandra Harris in AppL (26:3) 2005, 462–7.

2535. BECK, JANET MACKENZIE. Perceptual analysis of voice quality: the place of vocal profile analysis. *In* (pp. 285–322) **1472.**

2536. BELCHEM, JOHN. Radical language, meaning and identity in the age of the Chartists. *See* **2816.**

2537. BERTACCA, ANTONIO (ed.). Historical linguistic studies of spoken English: papers read at the 11th Italian Conference on the History of the English Language, Pisa, 5–7 June 2003. Pisa: PLUS, 2005. pp. 243. (Biblioteca: Atti di convegni.)

2538. BILMES, JACK. The call-on-hold as conversational resource. TextB (25:2) 2005, 149–70.

2539. BOWLES, HUGO; PALLOTTI, GABRIELE. Conversation analysis of opening sequences of telephone calls to bookstores in English and Italian. Textus (17:1) 2004, 63–88.

2540. BROWNE, STEPHEN HOWARD. Jefferson's call for nationhood: the first inaugural address. *See* **2233.**

2541. CRAWFORD, WILLIAM J. Verb agreement and disagreement: a corpus investigation of concord variation in existential *there + be* constructions. *See* **1714.**

2542. CURL, TRACI S. Practices in other-initiated repair resolution: the phonetic differentiation of 'repetitions'. *See* **1459.**

2543. DE CLERCK, BERNARD. Explicit *you*-subjects in English imperatives: a pragmatic corpus-based analysis. *See* **1719.**

2544. DE KLERK, VIVIAN. The use of *actually* in spoken Xhosa English: a corpus study. *See* **1676.**

2545. DENT, SUSIE. Larpers and shroomers: the language report. *See* **1730.**

2546. FERENČÍK, MILAN. Organization of repair in talk-in-interaction and politeness. *In* (pp. 69–78) **1370.**

2547. FEYAERTS, KURT; BRÔNE, GEERT. Expressivity and metonymic inferencing: stylistic variation in nonliterary language use. Style (39:1) 2005, 12–36.

2548. FILIPI, ANNA; WALES, ROGER. Perspective-taking and perspective-shifting as socially situated and collaborative actions. See **2156.**

2549. FRASER, HELEN. Representing speech in practice and theory. *In* (pp. 93–128) **1472.**

2550. GAUDY-CAMPBELL, ISABELLE. *Have* en oral spontané: un comportement invariant au sein du travail de formulation? See **1689.**

2551. GIBSON, ANDREW M. Non-prevocalic /r/ in New Zealand Hip Hop. See **1469.**

2552. GIORA, RACHEL, *et al.* On negation as mitigation: the case of negative irony. See **2083.**

2553. GUENDOUZI, JACKIE. 'She's very slim': talking about body-size in all-female interactions. JPrag (36:9) 2004, 1635–53.

2554. HARDCASTLE, WILLIAM J.; BECK, J. MACKENZIE (eds). A figure of speech: a Festschrift for John Laver. See **1472.**

2555. HARRINGTON, JOHN; PALETHORPE, SALLYANNE; WATSON, CATHERINE. Deepening or lessening the divide between diphthongs: an analysis of the Queen's annual Christmas broadcasts. *In* (pp. 227–61) **1472.**

2556. HILL, MARY LYNNE. The relationship between candidate sex and pronoun usage in a Louisiana governor's race. See **3178.**

2557. HORTON, WILLIAM S.; GERRIG, RICHARD J. Conversational common ground and memory processes in language production. DP (40:1) 2005, 1–35.

2558. HOUSE, JULIANE; KASPER, GABRIELE; ROSS, STEVEN (eds). Misunderstanding in social life: discourse approaches to problematic talk. (Bibl. 2004, 2632.) Rev. by Christina Kakava in JSoc (8:1) 2004, 150–4.

2559. JASZCZOLT, KATARZYNA. Prolegomena to default semantics. *In* (pp. 107–42) **1376.**

2560. JONES, DAVID K.; READ, STEPHEN J. Expert–novice differences in the understanding and explanation of complex political conflicts. DP (39:1) 2005, 45–80.

2561. KANG, M. AGNES; LO, ADRIENNE. Two ways of articulating heterogeneity in Korean American narratives of ethnic identity. JAAS (7:2) 2004, 93–116.

2562. KERBRAT-ORECCHIONI, CATHERINE. Introducing polylogue. JPrag (36:1) 2004, 1–24.

2563. KILGORE, JOHN. The uses of euphony. VocR (7:7) 2005.

2564. KOESTER, ALMUT JOSEPHA. Relational sequences in workplace genres. JPrag (36:8) 2004, 1405–28.

2565. KYTÖ, MERJA; WALKER, TERRY. The linguistic study of Early Modern English speech-related texts: how 'bad' can 'bad' data be? JEL (31:3) 2003, 221–48.

2566. LEDERER, RICHARD. A stylish inauguration speech. See **2381.**

2567. LEEDS-HURWITZ, WENDY. Making marriage visible: wedding anniversaries as the public component of private relationships. TextB (25:5) 2005, 595–631.

2568. LOCAL, JOHN. On the interactional and phonetic design of collaborative completions. *In* (pp. 263–82) **1472.**

2569. —— WALKER, GARETH.   Abrupt-joins as a resource for the production of multi-unit, multi-action turns. JPrag (36:8) 2004, 1375–1403.

2570. McCARTHY, MICHAEL; CARTER, RONALD.   'There's millions of them': hyperbole in everyday conversation. JPrag (36:2) 2004, 149–84.

2571. McKENZIE, JAYNE.   'But he's not supposed to see me in my weeding dress!': the relationship between *dress* and *fleece* in Modern New Zealand English. *See* **1483**.

2572. McWHORTER, JOHN.   Doing our own thing: the degradation of language and music and why we should, like, care. New York: Gotham, 2003. pp. xxiv, 279. Rev. by Jonathan Yardley in BkW, 19 Oct. 2003, 2; by Simon Stow in PhilL (28:1) 2004, 220–3; by Marlana Portolano in RSQ (34:4) 2004, 117–20; by Robert M. Martin in DalR (84:2) 2004, 336–8; by Eric J. Iannelli in TLS, 13 May 2005, 31.

2573. MAJORS, TIVOLI.   Low back vowel merger in Missouri speech: acoustic description and explanation. *See* **3014**.

2574. MEDINA, JOSÉ.   Anthropologism, naturalism, and the pragmatic study of language. JPrag (36:3) 2004, 549–73. (BBC interview with James Callaghan.)

2575. MERCHANT, JASON.   Ellipsis and 'nonsentential speech'. *In* (pp. 175–89) **1377**.

2576. MILLER, DONNA R.   '… to meet our common challenge': engagement strategies of alignment and alienation in current US international discourse. Textus (17:1) 2004, 39–62.

2577. MOMPEÁN-GONZÁLEZ, JOSÉ A.   Category overlap and neutralization: the importance of speakers' classifications in phonology. *See* **1485**.

2578. MOUNTFORD, ROXANNE.   The gendered pulpit: preaching in American Protestant spaces. *See* **2415**.

2579. MUGGLESTONE, LYNDA.   'Talking proper': the rise of accent as social symbol. *See* **1444**.

2580. NARIYAMA, SHIGEKO.   Subject ellipsis in English. *See* **1624**.

2581. O'CONNELL, DANIEL C.; KOWAL, SABINE; DILL, EDWARD J., III.   Dialogicality in TV news interviews. JPrag (36:2) 2004, 185–205.

2582. PADILLA CRUZ, MANUEL.   On the phatic interpretation of utterances: a complementary relevance-theoretic proposal. RAEI (18) 2005, 227–46.

2583. PAPADOPOULOU, IRIS.   Discourse marker *like*: a unified account. *In* (pp. 190–202) **1377**.

2584. PEARCE, MICHAEL.   Informalization in UK party election broadcasts, 1966–97. LLit (14:1) 2005, 65–90.

2585. PETERS, MARK.   The 'oohs' and 'ahs' and 'ooh-la-las': a look at interjections. *See* **1760**.

2586. POVOLNÁ, RENATA.   On the role of some interactive D-items in different genres of spoken English. *In* (pp. 169–81) **1369**.

2587. —— Some discourse items as response elicitors in English face-to-face and telephone conversation. *In* (pp. 127–36) **1370**.

2588. PURNELL, THOMAS; TEPELI, DILARA; SALMONS, JOSEPH.   German substrate effects in Wisconsin English: evidence for final fortition. *See* **3020**.

2589. RECSKI, LEONARDO. Interpersonal engagement in academic spoken discourse: a functional account of dissertation defenses. ESpP (24:1) 2005, 5–23.

2590. RUBINSTEIN, GEORGE. Linguistic bioacoustics: frames of Russian and English. *See* **3369**.

2591. SANTULLI, FRANCESCA. Dal politico al pubblico: forme e funzioni del discorso riportato. Culture (17) 2003, 191–210.

2592. SEMINO, ELENA. The metaphorical construction of complex domains: the case of speech activity in English. *See* **2468**.

2593. —— HEYWOOD, JOHN; SHORT, MICK. Methodological problems in the analysis of metaphors in a corpus of conversations about cancer. JPrag (36:7) 2004, 1271–94.

2594. SHACKLETON, ROBERT G., JR. English–American speech relationships: a quantitative approach. *See* **3027**.

2595. SHARMA, DEVYANI. Dialect stabilization and speaker awareness in non-native varieties of English. *See* **2911**.

2596. SHERZER, JOEL. Speech play and verbal art. (Bibl. 2004, 2672.) Rev. by Carolyn Temple Adger in JSoc (9:2) 2005, 273–6.

2597. STARKS, DONNA; ALLAN, SCOTT. What comes before *t*? Nonalveolar *s* in Auckland. *See* **3074**.

2598. —— REFFELL, HAYLEY. Pronouncing your /r/s in New Zealand English? A study of Pasifika and Maori students. *See* **1500**.

2599. SZMRECSANYI, BENEDIKT. Never change a winning chunk. RANAM (38) 2005, 85–98.

2600. TAYLOR, CHRISTOPHER JOHN. The language of film: corpora and statistics in the search for authenticity: *Notting Hill* (1998) – a case study. *See* **13692**.

2601. TERKOURAFI, MARINA. Pragmatic correlates of frequency of use: the case for a notion of 'minimal context'. *In* (pp. 209–33) **1376**.

2602. URBANOVÁ, LUDMILA. English conversation: authentic and fictional. *In* (pp. 155–62) **1370**.

2603. —— On expressing meaning in English conversation: semantic indeterminacy. (Bibl. 2003, 2584.) Rev. by Pavlína Šaldová and Aleš Klégr in LingPr (15:1) 2005, 46–9; by Renata Povolná in ČMF (87:2) 2005, 100–2.

2604. VUORELA, TAINA. How does a sales team reach goals in intercultural business negotiations? A case study. ESpP (24:1) 2005, 65–92.

2605. WEBBER, PAULINE. Interactive features in medical conference monologue. ESpP (24:2) 2005, 157–81.

2606. WILAMOVÁ, SIRMA. On the function of pragmatic markers in negatively polite discourse. *In* (pp. 58–67) **1373**.

2607. WILSON, JOHN; STAPLETON, KARYN. Voices of commemoration: the discourse of celebration and confrontation in Northern Ireland. TextB (25:5) 2005, 633–64.

2608. XIAO, ZHONGHUA; McENERY, ANTHONY. Two approaches to genre analysis: three genres in Modern American English. *See* **3034**.

STYLISTICS OF LITERARY TEXTS

2609. AFROS, ELENA. Linguistic ambiguities in some Exeter Book riddles. *See* **4369.**

2610. AHEARN, BARRY. Kenner, Eliot, and language. *See* **14684.**

2611. ALEXANDER, CATHERINE M. S. (ed.). Shakespeare and language. *See* **5841.**

2612. ANDREU, ALAIN. *Look at the Harlequins!* Dyslexia and aphasia, a vision through the looking glass. Trans. by Curt Robinson. *See* **18442.**

2613. ARCHER, JOHN MICHAEL. Citizen Shakespeare: freemen, city wives, and aliens in the language of the plays. *See* **5848.**

2614. BAMMESBERGER, ALFRED. The coastguard's maxim reconsidered (*Beowulf,* lines 287b–289). *See* **4288.**

2615. BANDERIER, GILLES. Enjeux linguistiques et idéologiques des traductions de Du Bartas (1579–1650). *See* **7856.**

2616. BASWELL, CHRISTOPHER. Troy, Arthur, and the languages of 'Brutis Albyoun'. *In* (pp. 170–97) **4485.**

2617. BAX, RANDY. Traces of Johnson in the language of Fanny Burney. *See* **8444.**

2618. BEASTON, LAWRENCE. The Wanderer's courage. *See* **4387.**

2619. BEDIENT, CALVIN. Toward a Jorie Graham lexicon. *In* (pp. 275–91) **16773.**

2620. BEPLATE, JUSTIN. Joyce, Bergson, and the memory of words. *See* **17248.**

2621. BILLINGS, TIMOTHY. Two new sources for Shakespeare's bawdy French in *Henry V. See* **6415.**

2622. BOLAM, ROBYN. *Richard II*: Shakespeare and the languages of the stage. *In* (pp. 141–57) **5964.**

2623. BOSE, MISHTOONI. Reginald Pecock's vernacular voice. *In* (pp. 217–36) **4482.**

2624. BRATCHER, JAMES T. The function of the jeweled bridle in Gower's 'Tale of Rosiphelee'. *See* **4795.**

2625. BREINER, LAURENCE A. Creole language in the poetry of Derek Walcott. *See* **19934.**

2626. BULLA, GUIDO. Il verso e la tragedia: forme del linguaggio in *Romeo and Juliet. See* **6687.**

2627. BURKE, MICHAEL. How cognition can augment stylistic analysis. *See* **17571.**

2628. BURROWS, JOHN. Andrew Marvell and the 'painter satires': a computational approach to their authorship. *See* **7620.**

2629. BUTLER, CHRISTOPHER. Joyce the Modernist. *In* (pp. 67–86) **17244.**

2630. CALVO, CLARA. Shakespeare and Cervantes in 1916: the politics of language. *In* (pp. 78–94) **6000.**

2631. CAMPBELL, JILL. Fielding's style. *See* **8604.**

2632. CAREY, JOHN. Henry Vaughan's poetry: pointful vagueness and the merging of contraries. *In* (pp. 69–83) **5167.**

2633. CARVALHO HOMEM, RUI. The feast and the scraps: translating *Love's Labour's Lost* into Portuguese. *In* (pp. 114–29) **5975.**

2634. CATHCART, CHARLES. Borrowings and the authorial domain: Gostanzo, Polonius, and Marston's Gonzago. *See* **7614.**

2635. CESARE, T. NIKKI. The fall of babble: an ontogenesic experiment on the fragmentation of language. *See* **15654.**

2636. CHARNEY, MAURICE. Parody – and self-parody in David Mamet. *See* **18072.**

2637. CHEN, PING. Language, reality, and desire: *The Bostonians* and the distorted reality. *See* **11387.**

2638. CHEUSE, ALAN. Reflections on dialogue: 'How d'yuh get t'Eighteent' Avenoo and Sixty-Sevent' Street?' *See* **14104.**

2639. CLAYTON, FREDERICK W.; TUDEAU-CLAYTON, MARGARET. Mercury, boy yet and the 'harsh' words of *Love's Labour's Lost. See* **6526.**

2640. COLLIER, MICHAEL. On Whitman's *To a Locomotive in Winter. See* **12303.**

2641. COONRADT, NICOLE M. To be loved: Amy Denver and human need – bridges to understanding in Toni Morrison's *Beloved. See* **18352.**

2642. CRONAN, DENNIS. Poetic meanings in the Old English poetic vocabulary. *See* **4204.**

2643. DANIEL, ANNE MARGARET. Wilde the writer. *In* (pp. 36–71) **12414.**

2644. DEANE, SEAMUS. Dumbness and eloquence: a note on English as we write it in Ireland. *In* (pp. 227–42) **2915.**

2645. DELABASTITA, DIRK. Cross-language comedy in Shakespeare. *See* **5894.**

2646. —— 'If I know the letters and the language': translation as a dramatic device in Shakespeare's plays. *In* (pp. 31–52) **5975.**

2647. DE LA CRUZ CABANILLAS, ISABEL. The language of the extant versions of Rolle's *Ego Dormio. See* **4915.**

2648. DÉPRATS, JEAN-MICHEL. Translation at the crossroads of the past and present. *In* (pp. 65–78) **5874.**

2649. DESKIS, SUSAN E. Exploring text and discourse in the Old English gnomic poems: the problem of narrative. *See* **4354.**

2650. DUPLESSIS, RACHEL BLAU. 'Lexicon's mixage': on multi-lingual strategies in my poetry. *In* (pp. 51–69) **14377.**

2651. DYER, GARY R. Reading as a criminal in early nineteenth-century fiction. *See* **11915.**

2652. EDGECOMBE, RODNEY STENNING. Dickens and the comedy of abbreviation. *See* **10676.**

2653. —— Dickens, Hunt and the waiter in *Somebody's Luggage. See* **10677.**

2654. —— 'The salt fish is an old coat' in *The Merry Wives of Windsor* 1.1. *See* **6616.**

2655. ERICKSEN, JANET SCHRUNK. Legalizing the Fall of Man. *See* **4342.**

2656. FALCONER, GAVIN. *Sched apon the rude?* Reflections on Scots and religion. *See* **2926.**

2657. FANEGO, TERESA.   'Fare thee well, dame': Shakespeare's forms of address and their socio-affective role. *See* **6260**.

2658. FARRELL, MICHAEL.   Counting and comparing personal etc. pronouns in and between Ryan's *Pure and Applied* and Ashbery's *Wakefulness. See* **19284**.

2659. FRANCIS, MATTHEW.   Syntax gram and the magic typewriter: W. S. Graham's automatic writing. *In* (pp. 86–105) **16793**.

2660. FRASER, KAYA.   Language to light on: Dionne Brand and the rebellious word. *See* **15560**.

2661. FULK, R. D.   Afloat in semantic space: Old English *sund* and the nature of Beowulf's exploit with Breca. *See* **4293**.

2662. GILBERT, GEOFF.   Words, flies, ~~Jews~~, Joyce, *Joint*: Wyndham Lewis and the unpublishing of obscenity. *See* **17815**.

2663. GOLDMAN, ERIC.   Bringing out the beast in Melville's *Billy Budd*: the dialogue of Darwinian and 'holy' lexicons on board the *Bellipotent. See* **11684**.

2664. GOLIGHTLY, VICTOR.   'Speak on a finger and thumb': Dylan Thomas, language and the deaf. *See* **19766**.

2665. GONZÁLEZ DÍAZ, VICTORINA.   Adjective comparison in Renaissance English. *See* **1660**.

2666. GOODERHAM, DAVID.   Fantasizing it as it is: religious language in Philip Pullman's trilogy *His Dark Materials. See* **18942**.

2667. GRAVES, ROY NEIL.   Blake's *London. See* **8363**.

2668. —— Raleigh's *Moral Advice. See* **5620**.

2669. GREENWOOD, EMILY.   'Still going on': temporal adverbs and the view of the past in Walcott's poetry. *See* **19944**.

2670. HAGEMANN, SUSANNE.   Postcolonial translation studies and James Kelman's *Translated Accounts. See* **17383**.

2671. HALLEN, CYNTHIA L.   The ways of possibility: Emily Dickinson and Dag Hammarskjöld. *See* **10784**.

2672. HAMILTON, PAUL.   Hazlitt and the 'kings of speech'. *In* (pp. 68–80) **11245**.

2673. HARBUS, ANTONINA.   Articulate contact in *Juliana. In* (pp. 183–200) **1786**.

2674. HARDY, DONALD E.   Collocational analysis as a stylistic discovery procedure: the case of Flannery O'Connor's *eyes. See* **18560**.

2675. HASSEL, RUDOLPH CHRIS, JR.   Shakespeare's religious language: a dictionary. *See* **1957**.

2676. HAYWARD, MALCOLM.   Are texts recognizably gendered? An experiment and analysis. Poetics (31:2) 2003, 87–101.

2677. HEITMAN, DANNY.   *Minority Report* reexamined. *See* **18174**.

2678. HELLER, MICHAEL.   Speaking the estranged: Oppen's poetics of the word. *See* **18656**.

2679. HERRINGTON, ELDRID.   Hopkins and Whitman. *See* **11305**.

2680. HIDALGO DOWNING, LAURA.   Reading R. Coover's *Quenby and Ola, Swede and Carl*: an empirical study on reference and story interpretation. *See* **15943**.

2681. Highley, Christopher. The place of Scots in the Scottish play: *Macbeth* and the politics of language. *In* (pp. 53–66) **6561.**

2682. Hillan, Sophia. Wintered into wisdom: Michael McLaverty, Seamus Heaney, and the Northern word-hoard. *See* **18011.**

2683. Holland, Norman N. 'The barge she sat in': psychoanalysis and diction. *See* **6262.**

2684. Holmes, David G. Revisiting racialized voice: African American ethos in language and literature. *See* **10418.**

2685. Hope, Jonathan. Shakespeare's grammar. *See* **5978.**

2686. Hori, Masahiro. Investigating Dickens' style: a collocational analysis. *See* **10697.**

2687. Horobin, Simon. The dialect and authorship of *Richard the Redeless* and *Mum and the Sothsegger*. *See* **4647.**

2688. —— The language of the Chaucer tradition. (Bibl. 2004, 5183.) Rev. by Jacob Thaisen in EngS (86:2) 2005, 188–9; by Derek Pearsall in Spec (80:3) 2005, 885–7.

2689. Hungerford, Amy. Postmodern supernaturalism: Ginsberg and the search for a supernatural language. *See* **16696.**

2690. Ilsemann, Hartmut. Some statistical observations on speech lengths in Shakespeare's plays. *See* **5983.**

2691. Janák, Petr. Fungování vícejazy čnosti v *Mechanickém pomeranč*. (The use of multilingualism in *A Clockwork Orange*.) *See* **15620.**

2692. Jansohn, Christa. The Shakespeare apocrypha: a reconsideration. *See* **6389.**

2693. Janssen, Anna; Murachver, Tamar. Readers' perceptions of author gender and literary genre. JLSP (24:2) 2005, 207–19.

2694. Jarrett, Gene. 'Entirely *black* verse from him would succeed': minstrel Realism and William Dean Howells. *See* **11342.**

2695. Jenkins, Lee M. The language of Caribbean poetry: boundaries of expression. *See* **14423.**

2696. Johnson, Mark. The dangerous poems of Dave Smith. *See* **19484.**

2697. Jones, George Fenwick. Of *inquit*s. *See* **14183.**

2698. Jones, Tom. Pope and Berkeley: the language of poetry and philosophy. *See* **8891.**

2699. Joseph, Clara A. B. Language in contact and literatures in conflict: text, context, and pedagogy. *See* **18264.**

2700. Joseph, Miriam. Shakespeare's use of the arts of language. *See* **5989.**

2701. Jost, Walter. Rhetorical investigations: studies in ordinary language criticism. Charlottesville; London: Virginia UP, 2004. pp. xiii, 346. Rev. by Robert Faggen in RFR (14) 2004, 121–5; by James Zeigler in RSQ (35:4) 2005, 133–7; by David Herman in PMC (16:1) 2005.

2702. Jousni, Stéphane; Goarzin, Anne (eds). Voix et langues dans la littérature irlandaise. *See* **12747.**

2703. Kaup, Monika. The neobaroque in Djuna Barnes. *See* **15326.**

2704. KNOTTENBELT, E. M. Romantic residues? Virgil's *Aeneid* 'in such a tongue as the people understandeth' or in a 'language really spoken by men'. *In* (pp. 235–57) **9237**.

2705. KUIPER, KONRAD. Shakespeare's Sonnet 116. *See* **6719**.

2706. LALLA, BARBARA. Creole and respec' in the development of Jamaican literary discourse. *See* **3127**.

2707. LANDON, RICHARD. Sport fiction and the untellable: cliché and language in Don DeLillo's *End Zone. See* **16035**.

2708. LAPAIRE, JEAN-RÉMI. Coordination et cognition. EA (58:4) 2005, 473–94.

2709. LECERCLE, JEAN-JACQUES. Jane Austen meets Dickens: a response to Thierry Labica. *See* **16864**.

2710. LEDENT, BÉNÉDICTE. A new wor(l)d order: language in the fiction of the new Caribbean diaspora. *See* **14203**.

2711. LEIGHTON, ANGELA. Pater's music. *See* **11784**.

2712. LIGGERA, J. Hawthorne coins a term in *The Scarlet Letter. See* **11207**.

2713. LIROLA, MARÍA. Reflections on some syntactical processes and their communicative implications in two short stories written by Julia Alvarez: *My English* and *A Genetics of Justice. See* **15145**.

2714. LOCK, CHARLES. Hardy and the critics. *In* (pp. 14–37) **11140**.

2715. LOGAN, WILLIAM. Prisoner, fancy-man, rowdy, lawyer, physician, priest: Whitman's brags. *See* **12330**.

2716. LOPEZ, JEREMY. Time and talk in *Richard III* I.iv. *See* **6511**.

2717. LÓPEZ RÚA, PAULA. The manipulative power of word-formation devices in Margaret Atwood's *Oryx and Crake. See* **15218**.

2718. MCCOURT, JOHN. An 'I' for an 'E', an Ireland for England: Trollope's Hiberno-English in *An Eye for an Eye. See* **12225**.

2719. MCGLYNN, MARY. Janice Galloway's alienated spaces. *See* **16636**.

2720. MAGNUSSON, LYNNE. Scoff power in *Love's Labour's Lost* and the Inns of Court: language in context. *See* **6528**.

2721. MANDAL, ANTHONY. Language. *In* (pp. 23–32) **10060**.

2722. MARINO, STEPHEN A. Language and metaphor in Arthur Miller's *After the Fall. See* **18248**.

2723. MATHESON, SUE. Psychic transformation and the regeneration of language in Peter S. Beagle's *The Last Unicorn. See* **15371**.

2724. MATHEWS, ALICE. Eve's 'sweet converse': conversational patterns in *Paradise Lost. See* **7718**.

2725. MATHOLÉ, PAUL. Milton's use of 'unking'd': an allusion to *Richard II. See* **7720**.

2726. MAYER, ARIC DAIN. Consciousness and being in equilibrium: good company for Beckett and Merleau-Ponty. *See* **15407**.

2727. MEJER, VALERIE. On awareness. *See* **17529**.

2728. MELNYCZUK, ASKOLD. Shadowboxing: style and time. Agni (61) 2005, 198–207.

2729. MERRIAM, THOMAS. Anomalous verse in *Henry IV* and *Henry V*. *See* **6409**.

2730. MICHAELS, CINDY SHEFFIELD. Welty's words for the birds ... and for children and scholars, too. *See* **20088**.

2731. MICHIE, ALLEN; BUCKLEY, ERIC (eds). Style: essays on Renaissance and Restoration language and culture in memory of Harriett Hawkins. *See* **5167**.

2732. MILESI, LAURENT (ed.). James Joyce and the difference of language. *See* **17315**.

2733. MILLER, J. HILLIS. Literature as conduct: speech acts in Henry James. *See* **11433**.

2734. MINIER, MARTA. Shakespeare translation and taboo: a case study in retranslation. *See* **6351**.

2735. MINOGUE, SALLY. Portrait of the artist: Ivor Gurney as modern maker. *See* **16847**.

2736. MITCHELL, BRUCE. The relation between Old English alliterative verse and Ælfric's alliterative prose. *In* (pp. 349–62) **4221**.

2737. MITCHELL, PAUL. Reading (and) the late poems of Sylvia Plath. *See* **18826**.

2738. MORISI, EVE CÉLIA. Poe's *To One in Paradise*. *See* **11818**.

2739. MUIRDEN, JAMES. Shakespeare well-versed: a rhyming guide to all his plays. *See* **6034**.

2740. NASH, JOHN. Reading Joyce in English. *In* (pp. 110–31) **17274**.

2741. NATARAJAN, UTTARA. Hazlitt, Lamb, and the philosophy of familiarity. *See* **11243**.

2742. NELSON, MARIE. *Beowulf*'s boast words. *See* **4306**.

2743. NERO, CLARENCE. A discursive trifecta: community, education, and language in *I Know Why the Caged Bird Sings*. *See* **15171**.

2744. NICHOLLS, PETER. George Oppen and 'that primitive, Hegel'. *See* **18657**.

2745. NURMI, ARJA. 'A jolly kind of letter': *The Documents in the Case* and Dorothy L. Sayers's correspondence on trial. *See* **19330**.

2746. O'CONNOR, LAURA. Neighborly hostility and literary creoles: the example of Hugh MacDiarmid. *See* **17943**.

2747. OHLGREN, THOMAS H. Merchant adventure in *Robin Hood and the Potter*. *In* (pp. 69–78) **3576**.

2748. ORCHARD, ANDY. Rhetoric and style in the Old English life of Mary of Egypt. *See* **4381**.

2749. PAKKALA-WECKSTRÖM, MARI. The dialogue of love, marriage and *maistrie* in Chaucer's *Canterbury Tales*. *See* **5020**.

2750. PECHEY, GRAHAM. 'Pharaoh's sjambok': Roy Campbell and the lexicon of emigration. *See* **15666**.

2751. PIKOULIS, JOHN. 'Some kind o' beginnin' ': Mike Jenkins and the voices of Cwmtaff. *See* **17198**.

2752. PURDY, DWIGHT H. 'The one poor word' in *Middlemarch*. *See* **10950**.

2753. RAY, ROBERT H. Uses of the royal plural in *King Lear*. *See* **6479**.

2754. REGNAULD, ARNAUD. L'érotisme dans *Virginie*; ou, Le décentrement du sens. *See* **16923**.

2755. RICKS, CHRISTOPHER. All praise to proper words: the new Oxford Professor of Poetry on equality for prose. *See* **3900**.

2756. ROBINSON, PETER. The identification and use of authorial variants in the Miller's Tale. *See* **5026**.

2757. ROBSON, MARK. Shakespeare's words of the future: promising *Richard III. See* **6516**.

2758. ROCHA, FLAVIA. Man talking to a mirror: on the attempt to translate Yusef Komunyakaa's vibrant verbal landscape into the mild undulations of Brazilian Portuguese. *See* **17533**.

2759. ROSEN, ALAN. Sounds of defiance: the Holocaust, multilingualism, and the problem of English. *See* **12887**.

2760. ROSS, STEPHEN. Authenticity betrayed: the 'idiotic folk' of *Love on the Dole. See* **16821**.

2761. RUBIK, MARGARETE. Provocative and unforgettable: Peter Carey's short fiction – a cognitive approach. *See* **15687**.

2762. RUDMAN, JOSEPH. Unediting, de-editing, and editing in non-traditional authorship attribution studies: with an emphasis on the canon of Daniel Defoe. *See* **8542**.

2763. SAINT-AMOUR, PAUL K. Ride 'em cowpoyride: literary property metadiscourse in *Ulysses. In* (pp. 229–54) **17274**.

2764. SCHÜRER, NORBERT. Millay's *What Lips My Lips Have Kissed, and Where, and Why. See* **18228**.

2765. SCRAGG, LEAH. John Lyly and the politics of language. *See* **5515**.

2766. SHERBO, ARTHUR. The appendix to Edmond Malone's 1790 *Shakespeare*, the 1821 Boswell–Malone *Shakespeare*, and Elizabethan language. *See* **5828**.

2767. SHERRY, VINCENT B. Liberal measures: language, Modernism, and the Great War. *In* (pp. 9–23) **12946**.

2768. SHRANK, CATHY. Civil tongues: language, law and Reformation. *In* (pp. 19–34) **5187**.

2769. SIMPSON, PAUL. On the discourse of satire: towards a stylistic model of satirical humor. *See* **3926**.

2770. SLUNEČKOVÁ, LENKA. Syntactic constancy of the object between Czech and English in fiction and technical writing: preliminary notes. *In* (pp. 197–207) **1369**.

2771. SMALL, HELEN. Tennyson and late style. *See* **12160**.

2772. SOTO VÁZQUEZ, ADOLFO LUIS. Charles Dickens makes fun of idiolects in *Martin Chuzzlewit. See* **10746**.

2773. STAPLETON, M. L. Making the woman of him: Shakespeare's Man Right Fair as sonnet lady. *See* **6726**.

2774. STEVENSON, WINIFRED. Donne's nocturnal. *See* **7397**.

2775. STOCKWELL, PETER. On cognitive poetics and stylistics. *In* (pp. 267–82) **3888**.

2776. —— Texture and identification. *See* **17489**.

2777. STROHM, PAUL. *Politique*: languages of statecraft between Chaucer and Shakespeare. *See* **4489**.

2778. STUBBS, MICHAEL. Conrad in the computer: examples of quantitative stylistic methods. *See* **15926**.

2779. TAAVITSAINEN, IRMA. Genres of secular instruction: a linguistic history of useful entertainment. *See* **1415**.

2780. TADIÉ, ALEXIS. 'An age of surfaces': le langage de la comédie dans *The Importance of Being Earnest* d'Oscar Wilde. *See* **12430**.

2781. TARLINSKAJA, MARINA. Who did NOT write *A Lover's Complaint*. *See* **6520**.

2782. TAYLOR, KARLA. Social aesthetics and the emergence of civic discourse from the Shipman's Tale to Melibee. *See* **5035**.

2783. TISCHLER, ALYSON. A rose is a pose: Steinian Modernism and mass culture. *See* **19597**.

2784. TOMÁŠKOVÁ, RENÁTA. On language and grafting in Jeanette Winterson's fiction. *In* (pp. 261–9) **1369**.

2785. TURNER, ALLAN. Translating Tolkien: philological elements in *The Lord of the Rings*. *See* **19851**.

2786. URBANOVÁ, LUDMILA. English conversation: authentic and fictional. *In* (pp. 155–62) **1370**.

2787. —— On phatic function of language. *In* (pp. 271–7) **1369**.

2788. WANG, SHANSHAN. On waiting in *Waiting for Godot*. *See* **15416**.

2789. WATKHAOLARM, PIMYUPA. Think in Thai, write in English: *Thainess* in Thai English literature. *See* **15085**.

2790. WAUGH, ROBERT H. 'Hey, yew, why don't ye say somethin'?': Lovecraft's dramatic monologues. *See* **17864**.

2791. WEBER, JEAN JACQUES. From 'bad' to 'worse': pragmatic scales and the (de)construction of cultural models. *See* **17429**.

2792. WILAMOVÁ, SIRMA. Grammatical realizations of the avoidance strategy as a significant negative politeness strategy in English discourse. *In* (pp. 295–305) **1369**.

2793. —— On expressing negative politeness in English fictional discourse. *See* **4072**.

2794. WILCOX, HELEN. Herbert's 'enchanting language': the poetry of a Cambridge orator. *See* **7488**.

2795. WILLIAMS, LEE. Telling as denouement in Charles Dickens's *Great Expectations* and Roberto Arlt's *El juguete rabioso* (*Mad Toy*). *See* **10762**.

2796. WILSON, PETER. The corpus of Jinglese: a syntactic profile of an idiolectal 'system of stenography'. *See* **10763**.

2797. WINDUO, STEVEN. Transition and transformation. *See* **20253**.

2798. WU, HUI. The paradigm of Margaret Cavendish: reading women's alternative rhetorics in a global context. *In* (pp. 171–85) **2457**.

2799. WU, QINGJUN. The defamiliarized language in *Ulysses*. *See* **17356**.

2800. ZARANDONA, JUAN MIGUEL.   The hybrid language and society (Afrikaans–English) of the South African postcolonial writing of Pauline Smith (1882–1959) in Spanish translation: *Anna's Marriage/La boda de Anna* (1925). See **19488**.

2801. ZINGG, GISELA.   Hiberno-English in Joyce's *Ulysses*. See **17357**.

STYLISTICS OF NON-LITERARY TEXTS

2802. BEN-AARON, DIANA.   Given and news: evaluation in newspaper stories about national anniversaries. TextB (25:5) 2005, 691–718.

2803. —— Given and news: media discourse and the construction of community on national days. Helsinki: Dept of English, Univ. of Helsinki, 2005. pp. 498. (Pragmatics, ideology and contacts monographs, 4.)

2804. AMIGONI, DAVID.   Carving coconuts, the philosophy of drawing rooms, and the politics of dates: Grant Allen, popular scientific journalism, evolution, and culture in the *Cornhill Magazine*. In (pp. 251–61) **1226**.

2805. ANDERSON, DAVID.   Down memory lane: nostalgia for the Old South in post-Civil War plantation reminiscences. See **9799**.

2806. ARGONDIZZO, CARMEN; PLASTINA, ANNA FRANCA.   Email text talk in institutional discourse. Textus (17:1) 2004, 89–110.

2807. ARNAUD, PIERRE J. L.; MANIEZ, FRANÇOIS.   Linguistique de corpus et nano-genre: temps et *be + ing* dans les légendes de photographies de trains. See **1576**.

2808. BANKS, DAVID.   The case of Perrin and Thomson: an example of the use of a mini-corpus. See **9736**.

2809. —— On the historical origins of nominalized process in scientific text. ESpP (24:3) 2005, 347–57.

2810. BANNET, EVE TAVOR.   'Epistolary commerce' in *The Spectator*. In (pp. 220–47) **1285**.

2811. —— 'Secret history'; or, Talebearing inside and outside the secretorie. See **7090**.

2812. BARTON, ELLEN; ARIAIL, JENNIE; SMITH, TOM.   The professional in the personal: the genre of personal statements in residency applications. IW (15:1) 2004, 76–124.

2813. BATTISTELLA, EDWIN.   The Pledge of Allegiance: a grammarian's view. VocR (7:7) 2005.

2814. BAUERLEIN, MARK.   Interpretation against the essay. See **20950**.

2815. BEKINS, LINN K.; HUCKIN, THOMAS N.; KIJAK, LAURA.   The personal statement in medical school applications: rhetorical structure in a diverse and unstable context. IW (15:1) 2004, 56–75.

2816. BELCHEM, JOHN.   Radical language, meaning and identity in the age of the Chartists. JVC (10:1) 2005, 1–14.

2817. BLOOM, LYNN Z.   Academic essays and the vertical pronoun. See **20951**.

2818. BRANT, CLARE.   'The tribunal of the public': eighteenth-century letters and the politics of vindication. In (pp. 15–28) **8217**.

2819. BROWN, THEODORE L. Making the truth: metaphor in science. *See* **2232**.

2820. BROWNLEY, MARTINE WATSON. Denzil Holles and the stylistic development of the early English memoir. *In* (pp. 135–49) **5167**.

2821. CALIENDO, GIUDITTA. EU language in cross-boundary communication. Textus (17:1) 2004, 159–178.

2822. CAMPAGNA, SANDRA. Investigating 'virtual' virtues: a comparative study of charity websites. Textus (17:1) 2004, 111–126.

2823. CARILLO, JOSE A. The deadly game of corporatese. VocR (7:3) 2005.

2824. CHILTON, PAUL. Analysing political discourse: theory and practice. (Bibl. 2004, 2913.) Rev. by Chad Nilep in JPrag (36:12) 2004, 2197–201; by Sandra Harris in AppL (26:3) 2005, 462–7.

2825. CHOVANEC, JAN. Czeching out pun and clichés in football reporting. *In* (pp. 61–7) **1370**.

2826. —— The (un)conventional use of the simple past tense in news headlines. *In* (pp. 71–81) **1369**.

2827. CLACHAR, ARLENE. Creole discourse effects on the speech conjunctive system in expository texts. *See* **3118**.

2828. COCKIN, KATHARINE. Slinging the ink about: Ellen Terry and women's suffrage agitation. *In* (pp. 201–11) **8217**.

2829. COOK, ANNE E.; MYERS, JEROME L.; O'BRIEN, EDWARD J. Processing an anaphor when there is no antecedent. *See* **1587**.

2830. CRAMER, JANET M. Cross purposes: publishing practices and social priorities of nineteenth-century US missionary women. *See* **9745**.

2831. CRANGLE, SARA. Epistolarity, audience, selfhood: the letters of Dorothy Osborne to William Temple. *See* **7802**.

2832. DAHL, TRINE. Textual discourse in research articles: a marker of national culture or of academic discipline? JPrag (36:10) 2005, 1807–25.

2833. DEAN, JANET. Nameless outrages: narrative authority, rape rhetoric, and the Dakota Conflict of 1862. *See* **9747**.

2834. DIEMERT, BRIAN. Uncontainable metaphor: George F. Kennan's 'X' article and Cold War discourse. CRAS (35:1) 2005, 21–55.

2835. DORGELOH, HEIDRUN. Conjunction in sentence and discourse: sentence-initial *and* and discourse structure. *See* **1677**.

2836. EPSTEIN, JAMES. In practice: studies in the language and culture of popular politics in modern Britain. (Bibl. 2004, 2928.) Rev. by Michael T. Saler in Albion (36:1) 2004, 174–6; by James Vernon in VS (46:4) 2004, 675–6; by Helen Rogers in JVC (10:2) 2005, 314–19.

2837. ESDALE, LOGAN. Dickinson's epistolary 'naturalness'. *See* **10777**.

2838. EUBANKS, PHILIP. Globalization, 'corporate rule', and blended words: a conceptual–rhetorical analysis of metaphor, metonymy, and conceptual blending. *See* **2295**.

2839. FEE, FRANK E., JR. Intelligent union of Black with White: Frederick Douglass and the Rochester press, 1847–48. *See* **10826**.

2840. FEYAERTS, KURT; BRÔNE, GEERT.   Expressivity and metonymic inferencing: stylistic variation in nonliterary language use. *See* 2547.

2841. FLOWERDEW, LYNNE.   An integration of corpus-based and genre-based approaches to text analysis in EAP/ESP: countering criticisms against corpus-based methodologies. *See* 1076.

2842. FLOYD, JANET.   Simple, honest food: Elizabeth David and the construction of nation in cookery writing. *In* (pp. 127–43) 9257.

2843. GELLES, EDITH B.   'Remember the ladies': politics in the letters of Abigail Adams. *In* (pp. 67–75) 8217.

2844. GIBSON, JOHN; HUEMER, WOLFGANG (eds).   The literary Wittgenstein. (Bibl. 2004, 14938.) Rev. by Ayal Donenfeld in PartA (3:2) 2005, 183–8.

2845. GOODAY, GRAEME J. N.   'I never will have the electric light in my house': Alice Gordon and the gendered periodical representation of a contentious new technology. *In* (pp. 173–85) 1226.

2846. HAGGAN, MADELINE.   Research paper titles in literature, linguistics and science: dimensions of attraction. *See* 2165.

2847. HARWOOD, NIGEL.   'I hoped to counteract the memory problem, but I made no impact whatsoever': discussing methods in computing science using *I*. ESpP (24:3) 2005, 243–67.

2848. —— 'We do not seem to have a theory ... the theory I present here attempts to fill this gap': inclusive and exclusive pronouns in academic writing. AppL (26:3) 2005, 343–75.

2849. HENSON, LOUISE, *et al.* (eds).   Culture and science in the nineteenth-century media. *See* 1226.

2850. HÖSLE, VITTORIO.   Philosophy and its languages: a philosopher's reflection on the rise of English as the universal academic language. *In* (pp. 245–62) 2915.

2851. HOWE, JOHN R.   Language and political meaning in Revolutionary America. *See* 8230.

2852. HYLAND, KEN; TSE, POLLY.   Hooking the reader: a corpus study of evaluative *that* in abstracts. *See* 1712.

2853. JONES, DAVID K.; READ, STEPHEN J.   Expert–novice differences in the understanding and explanation of complex political conflicts. *See* 2560.

2854. KAMRATH, MARK L.   American Indian oration and discourses of the Republic in eighteenth-century American periodicals. *In* (pp. 143–78) 1244.

2855. KANOKSILAPATHAM, BUDSABA.   Rhetorical structure of biochemistry research articles. ESpP (24:3) 2005, 269–92.

2856. KING, AMY M.   Re-orienting the scientific frontier: Victorian tide pools and literary realism. *See* 9765.

2857. KINTSCH, WALTER.   An overview of top-down and bottom-up effects in comprehension: the CI perspective. *See* 2098.

2858. KLINE, SUSAN L.   Interactive media systems: influence strategies in television home shopping. *See* 14010.

2859. LEVINE, GEORGE.   Darwin's romance. *See* 10591.

2860. LICONA, ADELA C. (B)orderlands' rhetorics and representations: the transformative potential of feminist third-space scholarship and zines. *See* **14881.**

2861. LOW, GRAHAM. Explaining evolution: the use of animacy in an example of semi-formal science writing. LLit (14:2) 2005, 129–48.

2862. LUPTON, JULIA REINHARD. Rights, commandments, and the literature of citizenship. *See* **7130.**

2863. MCNEILL, LAURIE. Writing lives in death: Canadian death notices as auto/biography. *In* (pp. 187–205) **14629.**

2864. MALEKOVÁ, DANICA. The status of term in the context of law writing. *In* (pp. 99–106) **1370.**

2865. MANKIN, ROBERT. Locke's education of the personality. *See* **7603.**

2866. MARTIN, GRETCHEN. A Louisiana swamp doctor's diagnosis: romantic fatality and the frontier roots of realism. *See* **11599.**

2867. MARTÍN-MARTÍN, PEDRO. The rhetoric of the abstract in English and Spanish scientific discourse: a cross-cultural genre-analytic approach. New York; Frankfurt: Lang, 2005. pp. x, 218. (European univ. studies, XXI: Linguistics, 279.)

2868. MÉMET, MONIQUE. Letters to the editor: a multi-faceted genre. EJES (9:1) 2005, 75–90.

2869. NEVALA, MINNA. Accessing politeness axes: forms of address and terms of reference in early English correspondence. *See* **5343.**

2870. NEWMAN, DONALD J. (ed.). *The Spectator*: emerging discourses. *See* **1285.**

2871. NEWMAN, STEVE. Tales of the professional imaginary: personal statements for medical school at Johns Hopkins, 1925 to the present. IW (15:1) 2004, 31–55.

2872. NICHOLSON, EIRWEN. Soggy prose and verbiage: English graphic political satire as a visual/verbal construct. *See* **1288.**

2873. NURMI, ARJA. 'A jolly kind of letter': *The Documents in the Case* and Dorothy L. Sayers's correspondence on trial. *See* **19330.**

2874. PETERLIN, AGNES PISANSKI. Text-organising metatext in research articles: an English–Slovene contrastive analysis. ESpP (24:3) 2005, 307–19.

2875. PHILLIPS, ALFRED. Lawyers' language: how and why legal language is different. (Bibl. 2004, 2987.) Rev. by Donald C. Freeman in LLit (13:4) 2004, 365–7.

2876. PÍPALOVÁ, RENATA. On central paragraphs with a stable P-theme. *In* (pp. 157–67) **1369.**

2877. RAMSEY, MICHELE. Selling social status: woman and automobile advertisements from 1910–1920. WL (28:1) 2005, 26–38.

2878. RAUMOLIN-BRUNBERG, HELENA. Language change in adulthood: historical letters as evidence. EJES (9:1) 2005, 37–51.

2879. RENDALL, JANE. 'Friends of liberty & virtue': women Radicals and transatlantic correspondence, 1789–1848. *In* (pp. 77–92) **8217.**

2880. RICHARDT, SUSANNE. Metaphor in languages for special purposes: the function of conceptual metaphor in written expert language and expert–lay communication in the domains of economics, medicine, and computing. *See* **2449**.

2881. RITVO, HARRIET. The view from the hills: environment and technology in Victorian periodicals. *In* (pp. 165–72) **1226**.

2882. RODRÍGUEZ-ÁLVAREZ, ALICIA; DOMÍNGUEZ-RODRÍGUEZ, Mᴬ VICTORIA. A Middle English text revised by a Renaissance reader: John Wotton's annotations to British Library MS Sloane 249 (ff. 180v–205v). *See* **4706**.

2883. ROWLEY-JOLIVET, ELIZABETH; CARTER-THOMAS, SHIRLEY. Genre awareness and rhetorical appropriacy: manipulation of information structure by NS and NNS scientists in the international conference setting. ESpP (24:1) 2005, 41–64.

2884. SAIRIO, ANNI. 'Sam of Streatham Park': a linguistic study of Dr Johnson's membership in the Thrale family. *See* **8775**.

2885. SALA, MICHELE. Equivalence and discrepancies between different versions of the EU Constitution. *See* **3105**.

2886. SAMRAJ, BETTY. An exploration of a genre set: research article abstracts and introductions in two disciplines. ESpP (24:2) 2005, 141–56.

2887. SCHAFFER, TALIA. The importance of being greedy: connoisseurship and domesticity in the writings of Elizabeth Robins Pennell. *In* (pp. 105–26) **9257**.

2888. SCHNEIDER, GARY. The culture of epistolarity: vernacular letters and letter writing in early modern England, 1500–1700. *See* **5348**.

2889. SCHOENFELDT, MICHAEL. First impressions and last thoughts: the importance of scholarly introductions. *See* **1091**.

2890. SCHULTE, RAINER. The dynamics of scholarly and essayistic writing. *See* **20960**.

2891. SHEFFIELD, SUZANNE LE-MAY. The 'empty-headed beauty' and the 'sweet girl graduate': women's science education in *Punch*, 1860–90. *In* (pp. 16–28) **1226**.

2892. SHTEIR, ANN B. Green-stocking or blue? Science in three women's magazines, 1800–50. *In* (pp. 3–13) **1226**.

2893. SLUNEČKOVÁ, LENKA. Syntactic constancy of the object between Czech and English in fiction and technical writing: preliminary notes. *In* (pp. 197–207) **1369**.

2894. SÖNMEZ, MARGARET J.-M. A study of request markers in English family letters from 1623 to 1660. *See* **7153**.

2895. STOTESBURY, HILKKA. Focus on business abstracts: considerations of rhetorical, lexico-grammatical and interpersonal perspectives. *In* (pp. 321–34) **3183**.

2896. SUMPTER, CAROLINE. Making Socialists or murdering to dissect? Natural history and child socialization in the *Labour Prophet* and *Labour Leader*. *In* (pp. 29–40) **1226**.

2897. TIEKEN-BOON VAN OSTADE, INGRID. Eighteenth-century English letters: in search of the vernacular. *See* **8252**.

2898. VAN MULKEN, MARGOT; VAN DER MEER, WOUTER. Are you being served? A genre analysis of American and Dutch company replies to customer inquiries. ESpP (24:1) 2005, 93–109.

2899. WARNES, CHRISTOPHER. The hermeneutics of vagueness: magical realism in current literary critical discourse. *See* **15047.**

2900. WILKINS, JOHN. Lost in translation: the bishops, the Vatican & the English liturgy. *See* **3398.**

2901. WILLIAMS, CHRISTOPHER. Pragmatic and cross-cultural considerations in translating verbal constructions in prescriptive legal texts in English and Italian. Textus (17:1) 2004, 217–245.

2902. WILLIAMS, JOSEPH M. Style: ten lessons in clarity and grace. London; New York: Pearson Longman, 2005. pp. xiii, 274. (Eighth ed.: first ed. 1981.)

2903. WOLFE, GARY K. Coming to terms. *In* (pp. 13–22) **4027.**

2904. XIAO, ZHONGHUA; MCENERY, ANTHONY. Two approaches to genre analysis: three genres in Modern American English. *See* **3034.**

2905. YOLTON, JOHN W. The two intellectual worlds of John Locke: man, person, and spirits in the *Essay. See* **7606.**

2906. ZIOLKOWSKI, THEODORE. The quest for cultural community. *See* **20963.**

DIALECTS

GENERAL

2907. BRITAIN, DAVID; CHESHIRE, JENNY (eds). Social dialectology: in honour of Peter Trudgill. Amsterdam; Philadelphia, PA: Benjamins, 2003. pp. viii, 343. (Impact: studies in language and society, 16.) Rev. by Edgar W. Schneider in EWW (26:1) 2005, 123–4; by Jennifer Smith in JSoc (9:1) 2005, 142–5.

2908. DAVIES, DIANE. Varieties of Modern English: an introduction. London; New York: Pearson Longman, 2005. pp. xi, 172. (Learning about language.)

2909. DOSSENA, MARINA; LASS, ROGER (eds). Methods and data in English historical dialectology. New York; Frankfurt: Lang, 2004. pp. 405. (Linguistic insights: studies in language and communication, 16.)

2910. SCHNEIDER, EDGAR WERNER, *et al.* (eds). A handbook of varieties of English: a multimedia reference tool. Berlin; New York: Mouton de Gruyter, 2004. 2 vols. pp. xxvi, 1168; xvii, 1226; 1 CD-ROM.

2911. SHARMA, DEVYANI. Dialect stabilization and speaker awareness in non-native varieties of English. JSoc (9:2) 2005, 194–224.

2912. TEN HACKEN, PIUS. The disappearance of the geographical dimension of language in American linguistics. *See* **1431.**

2913. TRUDGILL, PETER. New-dialect formation: the inevitability of colonial Englishes. (Bibl. 2004, 3226.) Rev. by Matthew J. Gordon in JSoc (9:1) 2005, 146–50.

2914. WRIGHT, LAURA. The space of English: geographic space, temporal space and social space. SPELL (17) 2005, 287–313.

DIALECTS OF THE BRITISH ISLES

2915. BLOOMER, W. MARTIN (ed.).   The contest of language: before and beyond nationalism. Notre Dame, IN: Notre Dame UP, 2005. pp. vi, 274.

2916. BRITAIN, DAVID; TRUDGILL, PETER.   New dialect formation and contact-induced reallocation: three case studies from the English Fens. IJES (5:1) 2005, 183–209.

2917. CARRILLO LINARES, Mᴬ JOSÉ.   Middle English *Antidotarium Nicholai*: evidence for linguistic distribution and dissemination in the vernacular. *See* **4699**.

2918. COBBY, A. E.   An Old French source for Modern Scots *wabbit*? *See* **1910**.

2919. CROWLEY, TONY.   Whose language is it anyway? The Irish and the English language. *In* (pp. 165–84) **2915**.

2920. DAVIES, CHRISTOPHER.   Divided by a common language: a guide to British and American English. (Bibl. 1999, 1923.) Boston, MA: Houghton Mifflin, 2005. pp. viii, 248. (New ed.: first ed. 1997.)

2921. DEANE, SEAMUS.   Dumbness and eloquence: a note on English as we write it in Ireland. *In* (pp. 227–42) **2915**.

2922. DE LA CRUZ CABANILLAS, ISABEL.   The language of the extant versions of Rolle's *Ego Dormio*. *See* **4915**.

2923. DÍAZ VERA, JAVIER.   Onomasiological variation and change in the Older Scots vocabulary of marriage. ScLang (24) 2005, 1–12.

2924. DOCHERTY, G. J.; FOULKES, P.   Glottal variants of *t* in the Tyneside variety of English. *In* (pp. 173–97) **1472**.

2925. ELMES, SIMON.   Talking for Britain: a journey through the nation's dialects. London; New York: Penguin, 2005. pp. xvii, 333.

2926. FALCONER, GAVIN.   *Sched apon the rude?* Reflections on Scots and religion. ScLang (24) 2005, 13–30.

2927. FINDLAY, BILL (ed.).   Frae ither tongues: essays on modern translations into Scots. Clevedon; Philadelphia, PA: Multilingual Matters, 2004. pp. viii, 272. (Topics in translation, 24.) Rev. by Tom Hubbard in ScLang (24) 2005, 75–7.

2928. GARRETT, PETER; COUPLAND, NIKOLAS; WILLIAMS, ANGIE.   Investigating language attitudes: social meanings of dialect, ethnicity and performance. Cardiff: UP of Wales, 2003. pp. x, 251. Rev. by Ronald Macaulay in JSoc (8:2) 2004, 290–5.

2929. GARRIDO ANES, EDURNE.   Geographical and dialectal distribution of Platearius' *Liber de simplici medicina* in England. *See* **4700**.

2930. HÄCKER, MARTINA.   Linking [fi] and the variation between linking /r/ and glottal onsets in South African English. *See* **3057**.

2931. HERNÁNDEZ-CAMPOY, JUAN MANUEL; CONDE-SILVESTRE, JUAN CAMILO.   Sociolinguistic and geolinguistic approaches to the historical diffusion of linguistic innovations: incipient standardisation in Late Middle English. *See* **3177**.

2932. HICKEY, RAYMOND.   Dublin English: evolution and change. Amsterdam; Philadelphia, PA: Benjamins, 2005. pp. x, 270. (Varieties of English around the world: General series, 35.)

2933. HIGHLEY, CHRISTOPHER.   The place of Scots in the Scottish play: *Macbeth* and the politics of language. *In* (pp. 53–66) **6561**.

2934. HIRAGA, YUKO.   British attitudes towards six varieties of English in the USA and Britain. WorldE (24:3) 2005, 289–308.

2935. HOROBIN, S. C. P.   Pennies, pence and pans: some Chaucerian misreadings. *See* **5005**.

2936. HOROBIN, SIMON.   The dialect and authorship of *Richard the Redeless* and *Mum and the Sothsegger. See* **4647**.

2937. —— 'In London and opelond': the dialect and circulation of the C version of *Piers Plowman. See* **4850**.

2938. —— MOONEY, LINNE R.   A *Piers Plowman* manuscript by the Hengwrt/ Ellesmere scribe and its implications for London Standard English. *See* **4851**.

2939. —— MOSSER, DANIEL W.   Scribe D's SW Midlands roots: a reconsideration. NM (106:3) 2005, 289–305. (Cambridge, Trinity College, MS R.3.2.)

2940. KORTMANN, BERND (ed.).   A comparative grammar of British English dialects: agreement, gender, relative clauses. Berlin; New York: Mouton de Gruyter, 2005. pp. x, 371. (Topics in English linguistics, 50:1.)

2941. KRIES, SUSANNE.   Skandinavisch–schottische Sprachbeziehungen im Mittelalter: der altnordische Lehneinfluss. Odense: UP of Southern Denmark, 2003. pp. xii, 500. (North-Western European language evolution, 20.) Rev. by Richard Dance in NQ (52:2) 2005, 244–5; by Anatoly Liberman in JEGP (104:4) 2005, 532–4.

2942. LORVIK, MARJORIE.   The distinctiveness of the Doric: home-grown or imported? ScLang (24) 2005, 31–63.

2943. MCCLURE, J. DERRICK.   Scots for Shakespeare. *In* (pp. 217–39) **5975**.

2944. MCCOURT, JOHN.   An 'I' for an 'E', an Ireland for England: Trollope's Hiberno-English in *An Eye for an Eye. See* **12225**.

2945. MCCULLOCH, MARGERY PALMER (introd.).   For the vernacular circle (*The Bulletin* January 1938): the re-emergence of a long-lost contribution to the *Scott and Scotland* controversy. *See* **18391**.

2946. MCMAHON, SEAN; O'DONOGHUE, JO.   Brewer's dictionary of Irish phrase and fable. Foreword by Maeve Binchy. (Bibl. 2004, 3064.) Rev. by Victor Price in TLS, 25 Feb. 2005, 27.

2947. MONTGOMERY, MICHAEL.   Voices of my ancestors: a personal search for the language of the Scotch Irish. AS (80:4) 2005, 341–65. (Presidential address.)

2948. MURPHY, COLIN; O'DEA, DONAL.   The book of feckin' Irish slang that's great craic for cute hoors and bowsies. *See* **1755**.

2949. NASH, JOHN.   Reading Joyce in English. *In* (pp. 110–31) **17274**.

2950. O'CONNELL, DANIEL C.; KOWAL, SABINE; DILL, EDWARD J., III. Dialogicality in TV news interviews. *See* **2581**.

2951. O'CONNOR, LAURA.   Neighborly hostility and literary creoles: the example of Hugh MacDiarmid. *See* 17943.

2952. O'ROURKE, JASON; TAKAMIYA, TOSHIYUKI.   Two hitherto unrecorded fragments of the *Brut. See* 4719.

2953. PIKOULIS, JOHN.   'Some kind o' beginnin'': Mike Jenkins and the voices of Cwmtaff. *See* 17198.

2954. READ, ALLEN WALKER.   Words crisscrossing the sea: how words have been borrowed between England and America. *See* 1797.

2955. ROBINSON, CHRISTINE.   Changes in the dialect of Livingston. LLit (14:2) 2005, 181–93.

2956. ROSS, STEPHEN.   Authenticity betrayed: the 'idiotic folk' of *Love on the Dole. See* 16821.

2957. RYDÉN, MATS.   William Turner as botanist and plant-name scholar. *In* (pp. 249–62) 1773.

2958. SAYERS, WILLIAM.   Middle English and Scots *bulwerk* and some Continental reflexes. *See* 1815.

2959. ——— Scones, *The Oxford English Dictionary*, and the Celtic element in English vocabulary. *See* 1892.

2960. SHACKLETON, ROBERT G., JR.   English–American speech relationships: a quantitative approach. *See* 3027.

2961. SHORROCKS, GRAHAM.   The Rev. William Hutton's *A Bran New Wark*: the Westmorland dialect in the late early modern period. SEDERI (14) 2004, 117–35.

2962. TROUSDALE, GRAEME.   The social context of Kentish Raising: issues in Old English sociolinguistics. IJES (5:1) 2005, 59–76.

2963. TRUDGILL, PETER; MACLAGAN, MARGARET; LEWIS, GILLIAN.   Linguistic archaeology: the Scottish input to New Zealand English phonology. *See* 3078.

2964. VAN LEYDEN, KLASKE.   Prosodic characteristics of Orkney and Shetland dialects: an experimental approach. Utrecht: LOT, 2004. pp. 133. (LOT: Landelijke Onderzoekschool Taalwetenschap, 92.) Rev. by Dominic Watt in ScLang (24) 2005, 78–81.

2965. VASKO, ANNA-LIISA.   Up Cambridge: prepositional locative expressions in dialect speech: a corpus-based study of the Cambridgeshire dialect. Helsinki: Soc. Néophilologique, 2005. pp. xvi, 340. (Mémoires de la Soc. Néophilologique de Helsinki, 65.)

2966. WILLIAMS, FIONNUALA CARSON.   Wellerisms in Ireland: towards a corpus from oral and literary sources. (Bibl. 2004, 3076.) Rev. by J. D. A. Widdowson in Folklore (116:1) 2005, 116–17.

2967. WILTSHIRE, IRENE.   Speech in *Wuthering Heights*: Joseph's dialect and Charlotte's emendations. *See* 10209.

2968. ZINGG, GISELA.   Hiberno-English in Joyce's *Ulysses. See* 17357.

DIALECTS OF NORTH AMERICA

2969. ANON. The American Heritage desk dictionary and thesaurus. *See* **1943**.

2970. —— The Merriam-Webster dictionary. *See* **1945**.

2971. —— The new Webster's dictionary of the English language. *See* **1946**.

2972. —— Webster's new explorer dictionary of word origins. *See* **1947**.

2973. ADAMS, MICHAEL. Meaningful interposing: a countervalent form. *See* **1547**.

2974. ALIM, H. SAMY. On some serious next millennium rap ishhh: Pharoahe Monch, Hip Hop poetics, and the internal rhymes of *Internal Affairs*. *See* **14362**.

2975. —— You know my steez: an ethnographic and sociolinguistic study of styleshifting in a Black American speech community. Durham, NC; London: Duke UP for the American Dialect Soc., 2004. pp. xxxii, 309. (Pubs of the American Dialect Soc., 89.)

2976. ANTONELLI, SARA; SCACCHI, ANNA; SCANNAVINI, ANNA. La babele americana: lingua e identità negli Stati Uniti d'oggi. Ed. by Anna Scacchi. *See* **3144**.

2977. BAILEY, GUY; TILLERY, JAN; ANDRES, CLAIRE. Some effects of transcribers on data in dialectology. AS (80:1) 2005, 3–21.

2978. BARBIERI, FEDERICA. Quotative use in American English: a corpus-based, cross-register comparison. JEL (33:3) 2005, 222–56.

2979. BATTISTELLA, EDWIN. The Pledge of Allegiance: a grammarian's view. *See* **2813**.

2980. BAYARD, DONN; GREEN, JAMES A. Evaluating English accents worldwide. *See* **1452**.

2981. BECKETT, DAN. Sociolinguistic individuality in a remnant dialect community. JEL (31:1) 2003, 3–33.

2982. BENDER, MARGARET (ed.). Linguistic diversity in the South: changing codes, practices, and ideology. (Bibl. 2004, 3088.) Rev. by Michael Montgomery in SoCult (11:2) 2005, 105–7.

2983. BICKFORD, DONNA M. A praxis of parataxis: epistemology and dissonance in Lucha Corpi's detective fiction. *See* **15947**.

2984. BILLINGS, ANDREW C. Beyond the Ebonics debate: attitudes about Black and Standard American English. JBlaS (36:1) 2005, 68–81.

2985. BOBERG, CHARLES. The North American Regional Vocabulary Survey: new variables and methods in the study of North American English. AS (80:1) 2005, 22–60.

2986. CAMBONI, MARINA. Walt Whitman e la lingua del Mondo Nuovo: con tre testi di Walt Whitman. *See* **12300**.

2987. CAMPBELL, KERMIT E. Gettin' our groove on: rhetoric, language, and literacy for the Hip Hop generation. Detroit, MI: Wayne State UP, 2005. pp. xii, 195. (African American life.)

2988. CARPENTER, JEANNINE. The invisible community of the lost colony: African American English on Roanoke Island. AS (80:3) 2005, 227–55.

2989. —— HILLIARD, SARAH.   Shifting parameters of individual and group variation: African American English on Roanoke Island. JEL (33:2) 2005, 161–83.

2990. CASSELMAN, BILL.   Sockeye salmon: a British Columbia word. *See* **1898**.

2991. CRAWFORD, WILLIAM J.   Verb agreement and disagreement: a corpus investigation of concord variation in existential *there + be* constructions. *See* **1714**.

2992. CURL, TRACI S.   Practices in other-initiated repair resolution: the phonetic differentiation of 'repetitions'. *See* **1459**.

2993. DAVIES, CHRISTOPHER.   Divided by a common language: a guide to British and American English. *See* **2920**.

2994. DODSWORTH, ROBIN.   Attribute networking: a technique for modeling social perceptions. *See* **3162**.

2995. DUBOIS, SYLVIE; HORVATH, BARBARA M.   Verbal morphology in Cajun Vernacular English: a comparison with other varieties of Southern English. JEL (31:1) 2003, 34–59.

2996. FRIDLAND, VALERIE; BARTLETT, KATHRYN; KREUZ, ROGER.   Making sense of variation: pleasantness and education ratings of Southern vowel variants. AS (80:4) 2005, 366–87.

2997. GIBBS, RAYMOND W.; LIMA, PAULA LENZ COSTA; FRANCOZO, EDSON.   Metaphor is grounded in embodied experience. *See* **2315**.

2998. GLOWKA, WAYNE, *et al.*   Among the new words. *See* **1735**.

2999. —— Among the new words. *See* **1736**.

3000. —— Among the new words. *See* **1737**.

3001. —— Among the new words. *See* **1738**.

3002. HARTLEY, LAURA C.   The consequences of conflicting stereotypes: Bostonian perceptions of US dialects. AS (80:4) 2005, 388–405.

3003. HAZEN, KIRK.   Mergers in the mountains: West Virginia division and unification. EWW (26:2) 2005, 199–221.

3004. HIRAGA, YUKO.   British attitudes towards six varieties of English in the USA and Britain. *See* **2934**.

3005. HOWE, JOHN R.   Language and political meaning in Revolutionary America. *See* **8230**.

3006. JARRETT, GENE.   'Entirely *black* verse from him would succeed': minstrel Realism and William Dean Howells. *See* **11342**.

3007. JONES, MALCOLM (ed.).   Essays in lore & language: presented to John Widdowson on the occasion of his retirement. *See* **3416**.

3008. KACIRK, JEFFREY.   Informal English: puncture ladies, egg harbors, Mississippi marbles, and other curious words and phrases of North America. New York: Simon & Schuster, 2005. pp. xiv, 239.

3009. KATES, SUSAN.   Politics, identity, and the language of Appalachia: James Watt Raine on 'mountain speech and song'. *In* (pp. 74–86) **2318**.

3010. KEYES, FRANK.   On some deficiencies in our American dictionaries (an editor writes to his son). *See* **1930**.

3011. Longmore, Paul K. 'They ... speak better English than the English do': colonialism and the origins of national linguistic standardization in America. EAL (40:2) 2005, 279–314.

3012. McNair, Elizabeth DuPree. Mill villagers and farmers: dialect and economics in a small Southern town. Durham, NC; London: Duke UP for the American Dialect Soc., 2005. pp. 160. (Pubs of the American Dialect Soc., 90.)

3013. McWhorter, John. Doing our own thing: the degradation of language and music and why we should, like, care. See **2572**.

3014. Majors, Tivoli. Low back vowel merger in Missouri speech: acoustic description and explanation. AS (80:2) 2005, 165–79.

3015. Mansbridge, Jane; Flaster, Katherine. *Male chauvinist, feminist, sexist*, and *sexual harassment*: different trajectories in feminist linguistic innovation. See **1856**.

3016. Miller, Donna R. '... to meet our common challenge': engagement strategies of alignment and alienation in current US international discourse. See **2576**.

3017. Montgomery, Michael. Voices of my ancestors: a personal search for the language of the Scotch Irish. See **2947**.

3018. Nagle, Stephen J.; Sanders, Sara L. (eds). English in the Southern United States. (Bibl. 2004, 3144.) Rev. by Mark J. Elson in Lang (81:1) 2005, 284.

3019. O'Connell, Daniel C.; Kowal, Sabine; Dill, Edward J., iii. Dialogicality in TV news interviews. See **2581**.

3020. Purnell, Thomas; Tepeli, Dilara; Salmons, Joseph. German substrate effects in Wisconsin English: evidence for final fortition. AS (80:2) 2005, 135–64.

3021. Raymond, James C.; Russell, I. Willis (eds). Essays in linguistics: dialectology, grammar, and lexicography in honor of James B. McMillan. Tuscaloosa; London: Alabama UP, 2004. pp. xvii, 184. (Second ed.: first ed. 1977.)

3022. Read, Allen Walker. Words crisscrossing the sea: how words have been borrowed between England and America. See **1797**.

3023. Rideout, Philip M. (ed.). Heinle's Newbury House dictionary of American English. See **1965**.

3024. Rodriguez, José I.; Cargile, Aaron Castelan; Rich, Marc D. Reactions to African American Vernacular English: do more phonological features matter? WJBS (28:3) 2004, 407–14.

3025. Sabino, Robin. Survey says ... gameday. See **1840**.

3026. Sayers, William. The origin of *fink* 'informer, hired strikebreaker'. See **1836**.

3027. Shackleton, Robert G., Jr. English–American speech relationships: a quantitative approach. JEL (33:2) 2005, 99–160.

3028. Silverman, Daniel. On the phonetic and cognitive nature of alveolar stop allophony in American English. See **1496**.

3029. SMEAD, ROBERT N. *Vocabulario vaquero* /cowboy talk: a dictionary of Spanish terms from the American West. Norman: Oklahoma UP, 2004. pp. xxxii, 197. Rev. by Angelo J. Disalvo in WorldE (24:2) 2005, 267–8.

3030. SOTO VÁZQUEZ, ADOLFO LUIS. Charles Dickens makes fun of idiolects in *Martin Chuzzlewit*. See **10746**.

3031. SPEARES, RICHARD A. McGraw-Hill's dictionary of American idioms and phrasal verbs. See **1972**.

3032. SUTCLIFFE, DAVID. African American English suprasegmentals: a study of pitch patterns in the Black English of the United States. *In* (pp. 147–62) **3133**.

3033. TAGLIAMONTE, SALI; ROBERTS, CHRIS. So weird; so cool; so innovative: the use of intensifiers in the television series *Friends*. See **1647**.

3034. XIAO, ZHONGHUA; MCENERY, ANTHONY. Two approaches to genre analysis: three genres in Modern American English. JEL (33:1) 2005, 62–82.

DIALECTS OF THE REST OF THE WORLD

3035. ADJAYE, SOPHIA A. Ghanaian English pronunciation. Lewiston, NY; Lampeter: Mellen Press, 2005. pp. xi, 322. (Studies in linguistics and semiotics, 22.)

3036. AGUILAR-SÁNCHEZ, JORGE. English in Costa Rica. WorldE (24:2) 2005, 160–72.

3037. AKHIMIEN, ERONMONSELE PIUS. The use of 'How are you?' in Nigerian society. JPrag (36:11) 2004, 2055–8. (Squib.)

3038. BAO, ZHIMING; LYE, HUI MIN. Systematic transfer, topic prominence, and the bare conditional in Singapore English. JPCL (20:2) 2005, 269–91.

3039. BARDSLEY, DIANNE. Unravelling the Queen's chain. See **1885**.

3040. —— (comp.). The New Zealand mini thesaurus. See **1952**.

3041. BAUER, LAURIE; BAUER, WINIFRED. Regional dialects in New Zealand children's playground vocabulary. *In* (pp. 194–216) **3044**.

3042. BAYARD, DONN; GREEN, JAMES A. Evaluating English accents worldwide. See **1452**.

3043. —— SULLIVAN, KIRK P. H. A taste of Kiwi: does the Swedish palate differ in sensitivity and preference from the New Zealanders'? See **1453**.

3044. BELL, ALLAN; HARLOW, RAY; STARKS, DONNA (eds). Languages of New Zealand. Wellington: Victoria UP, 2005. pp. 376.

3045. BOLTON, KINGSLEY. Chinese Englishes: a sociolinguistic history. Cambridge; New York: CUP, 2003. pp. xvii, 338. Rev. by Andrew Moody in EWW (26:2) 2005, 223–8; by Jerry Packard in WorldE (24:2) 2005, 271–3.

3046. BRADSTOCK, MIKE. Some Southern Sea lore. See **1726**.

3047. BRITAIN, DAVID. Where did New Zealand English come from? *In* (pp. 156–93) **3044**.

3048. COETZEE-VAN ROOY, SUSAN; VAN ROOY, BERTUS. South African English: labels, comprehensibility and status. WorldE (24:1) 2005, 1–19.

3049. CRISP, PETER. Leavings. See **1777**.

3050. DE KLERK, VIVIAN. Expressing levels of intensity in Xhosa English. EWW (26:1) 2005, 77–95.

3051. —— The use of *actually* in spoken Xhosa English: a corpus study. See **1676**.

3052. DETERDING, DAVID. Emergent patterns in the vowels of Singapore English. EWW (26:2) 2005, 179–97.

3053. DRAGER, KATIE. From *bad* to *bed*: the relationship between perceived age and vowel perception in New Zealand English. See **1464**.

3054. FLOWERDEW, JOHN. Identity politics and Hong Kong's return to Chinese sovereignty: analysing the discourse of Hong Kong's first Chief Executive. JPrag (36:9) 2004, 1551–78.

3055. GIBSON, ANDREW M. Non-prevocalic /r/ in New Zealand Hip Hop. See **1469**.

3056. GUT, ULRIKE. Nigerian English prosody. EWW (26:2) 2005, 153–77.

3057. HÄCKER, MARTINA. Linking [fi] and the variation between linking /r/ and glottal onsets in South African English. SPELL (17) 2005, 207–26.

3058. HURLEY, DESMOND. *Poozle* and *poozling*: a continuing story. See **1882**.

3059. ISAAC, PETER. The new gobbledygook: a New Zealand dictionary and guidebook. See **1960**.

3060. KIESLING, SCOTT F. Variation, stance and style: word-final *-er*, high rising tone, and ethnicity in Australian English. EWW (26:1) 2005, 1–42.

3061. LEITNER, GERHARD. Australia's many voices: Australian English – the national language. (Bibl. 2004, 3205.) Rev. by Pam Peters in JEL (33:2) 2005, 189–95.

3062. LIM, LISA (ed.). Singapore English: a grammatical description. (Bibl. 2004, 3206.) Rev. by Anthea Fraser Gupta in JEL (33:2) 2005, 185–9.

3063. MACALISTER, JOHN (ed.). A dictionary of Maori words in New Zealand English. See **1963**.

3064. McKENZIE, JAYNE. 'But he's not supposed to see me in my weeding dress!': the relationship between *dress* and *fleece* in Modern New Zealand English. See **1483**.

3065. MICHIEKA, MARTHA MORAA. English in Kenya: a sociolinguistic profile. WorldE (24:2) 2005, 173–86.

3066. MWANGI, SERAH. Prepositions in Kenyan English: a corpus-based study in lexico-grammatical variation. Aix-la-Chapelle: Shaker, 2003. pp. xi, 264. (Sprache & Kultur.) Rev. by Paul Skandera in EWW (26:2) 2005, 238–42.

3067. NICKELS, EDELMIRA L. English in Puerto Rico. WorldE (24:2) 2005, 226–37.

3068. NIELSEN, DANIEL; HAY, JENNIFER. Perceptions of regional dialects in New Zealand. See **1487**.

3069. PECHEY, GRAHAM. 'Pharaoh's sjambok': Roy Campbell and the lexicon of emigration. See **15666**.

3070. QUIGLEY, KATHERINE. Keeping company in the city: compounds in the lexicon of the New Zealand Treasury. See **1761**.

3071. SCHREIER, DANIEL. Insularity and linguistic endemicity. JEL (31:3) 2003, 249–72.

3072. SKANDERA, PAUL. Drawing a map of Africa: idiom in Kenyan English. Tübingen: Narr, 2003. pp. xv, 238. (Language in performance, 26.) Rev. by Frank Polzenhagen in EWW (26:1) 2005, 104–11.

3073. STANLAW, JAMES. Japanese English: language and culture contact. Hong Kong: Hong Kong UP, 2004. pp. xi, 375. Rev. by Paul Kei Matsuda in WorldE (24:1) 2005, 105–7.

3074. STARKS, DONNA; ALLAN, SCOTT. What comes before *t*? Nonalveolar *s* in Auckland. JEL (31:3) 2003, 273–80.

3075. —— REFFELL, HAYLEY. Pronouncing your /r/s in New Zealand English? A study of Pasifika and Maori students. See **1500**.

3076. THOMAS, BRYNMOR; HAY, JENNIFER. A pleasant malady: the *Ellen/Allan* merger in New Zealand English. See **1502**.

3077. THOMPSON, ROGER M. Filipino English and Taglish: language switching from multiple perspectives. (Bibl. 2004, 3225.) Rev. by Jamie Shinhee Lee in WorldE (24:1) 2005, 107–9.

3078. TRUDGILL, PETER; MACLAGAN, MARGARET; LEWIS, GILLIAN. Linguistic archaeology: the Scottish input to New Zealand English phonology. JEL (31:2) 2003, 103–24.

3079. WARREN, PAUL; DALY, NICOLA. Characterising New Zealand English intonation: broad and narrow analysis. In (pp. 217–37) **3044**.

3080. WATKHAOLARM, PIMYUPA. Think in Thai, write in English: *Thainess* in Thai English literature. See **15085**.

3081. WEE, LIONEL. Intra-language discrimination and linguistic human rights: the case of Singlish. AppL (26:1) 2005, 48–69.

3082. WONG, JOCK. The particles in Singapore English: a semantic and cultural interpretation. JPrag (36:4) 2004, 739–93.

ENGLISH AS A WORLD LANGUAGE

3083. BERNS, MARGIE. Expanding on the Expanding Circle: where do WE go from here? WorldE (24:1) 2005, 85–93.

3084. BLOMMAERT, JAN. Situating language rights: English and Swahili in Tanzania revisited. JSoc (9:3) 2005, 390–417.

3085. BLOOMER, W. MARTIN (ed.). The contest of language: before and beyond nationalism. See **2915**.

3086. BOLTON, KINGSLEY. Where WE stands: approaches, issues, and debate in world Englishes. WorldE (24:1) 2005, 69–83.

3087. CANAGARAJAH, A. SURESH. Dilemmas in planning English/vernacular relations in post-colonial communities. JSoc (9:3) 2005, 418–47.

3088. COHEN, ROGER. English in Mongolia. WorldE (24:2) 2005, 202–16.

3089. CRYSTAL, DAVID. English as a global language. (Bibl. 1999, 2753.) Cambridge; New York: CUP, 2003. pp. xv, 212. (Second ed.: first ed. 1997.) Rev. by Geoffrey Leech in JPrag (36:11) 2004, 2077–80.

3090. DIMOVA, SLOBODANKA. English in Macedonia. WorldE (24:2) 2005, 187–201.

3091. DOĞANÇAY-AKTUNA, SERAN; KIZILTEPE, ZEYNEP. English in Turkey. WorldE (24:2) 2005, 252–65.

3092. GONZÁLEZ FERNÁNDEZ, PAULA. Linguistic imperialism: a critical study. RAEI (18) 2005, 85–110.

3093. HÖSLE, VITTORIO. Philosophy and its languages: a philosopher's reflection on the rise of English as the universal academic language. In (pp. 245–62) **2915.**

3094. JENKINS, JENNIFER. World Englishes: a resource book for students. (Bibl. 2004, 3246.) Rev. by Kingsley Bolton in EJES (9:1) 2005, 96–8.

3095. JOSEPH, CLARA A. B. Language in contact and literatures in conflict: text, context, and pedagogy. See **18264.**

3096. KARMANI, SOHAIL. English, 'terror', and Islam. AppL (26:2) 2005, 262–7.

3097. KASANGA, LUANGA A. English(es) and the global context: the changing face of a *lingua franca* under siege. BELL (ns 3) 2005, 169–81.

3098. KOTHARI, RITA. Translating India: the cultural politics of English. Manchester; Northampton, MA: St Jerome, 2003. pp. 138.

3099. MANSOOR, SABIHA; MERAJ, SHAHEEN; TAHIR, ALIYA (eds). Language policy, planning, & practice: a South Asian perspective. Karachi; Oxford: OUP for Aga Khan Univ., 2004. pp. xx, 264. Rev. by Robert J. Baumgardner in WorldE (24:2) 2005, 268–70.

3100. MELCHERS, GUNNEL; SHAW, PHILIP. World Englishes. (Bibl. 2004, 3025.) Rev. by Edgar W. Schneider in EWW (26:1) 2005, 97–9.

3101. RAMANATHAN, VAIDEHI. The English–vernacular divide: postcolonial language politics and practice. Clevedon; Philadelphia, PA: Multilingual Matters, 2005. pp. xii, 143.

3102. REICHELT, MELINDA. English in Poland. WorldE (24:2) 2005, 217–25.

3103. RICENTO, THOMAS. Problems with the 'language-as-resource' discourse in the promotion of heritage languages in the USA. JSoc (9:3) 2005, 348–68.

3104. SAKAI, SANZO; D'ANGELO, JAMES F. A vision for world Englishes in the Expanding Circle. WorldE (24:3) 2005, 323–7.

3105. SALA, MICHELE. Equivalence and discrepancies between different versions of the EU Constitution. LFil (21) 2005, 147–83.

3106. SCHALLER-SCHWANER, IRIS; TSCHICHOLD, CORNELIA. Born to be wild: English in Swiss public space. SPELL (17) 2005, 227–47.

3107. SCHREIER, DANIEL. Consonant change in English worldwide: synchrony meets diachrony. See **1447.**

3108. SEARGEANT, PHILIP. Globalisation and reconfigured English in Japan. WorldE (24:3) 2005, 309–19.

3109. SONNTAG, SELMA K. The local politics of global English: case studies in linguistic globalization. (Bibl. 2004, 3261.) Rev. by Satoko Kobayashi in JSoc (9:2) 2005, 298–300; by Suzanne K. Hilgendorf in WorldE (24:3) 2005, 393–5.

3110. SPOLSKY, BERNARD.   Language policy. Cambridge; New York: CUP, 2004. pp. xi, 250. (Key topics in sociolinguistics.) Rev. by Giorgio Cadorini in SaS (66:4) 2005, 296–9.

3111. SWEETING, ANTHONY; VICKERS, EDWARD.   On colonizing 'colonialism': the discourses of the history of English in Hong Kong. WorldE (24:2) 2005, 113–30.

3112. USTINOVA, IRINA P.   English in Russia. WorldE (24:2) 2005, 239–51.

PIDGINS AND CREOLES

3113. ACETO, MICHAEL; WILLIAMS, JEFFREY P. (eds).   Contact Englishes of the Eastern Caribbean. (Bibl. 2003, 3118.) Rev. by Barbara Lalla in EWW (26:2) 2005, 228–34.

3114. ADONE, DANY (ed.).   Recent development in Creole Studies. Tübingen: Niemeyer, 2003. pp. 234. (Linguistische Arbeiten, 472.) Rev. by Teresa Griffith in JPCL (20:2) 2005, 369–74.

3115. BAPTISTA, MARLYSE.   Inflectional plural marking in pidgins and creoles: a comparative study. In (pp. 315–32) **3133**.

3116. BREINER, LAURENCE A.   Creole language in the poetry of Derek Walcott. See **19934**.

3117. CHRISTIE, PAULINE.   Language in Jamaica. Kingston, Jamaica: Arawak, 2003. pp. 73. (Caribbean language.) Rev. by Susanne Mühleisen in JPCL (20:2) 2005, 395–8.

3118. CLACHAR, ARLENE.   Creole discourse effects on the speech conjunctive system in expository texts. JPrag (36:10) 2004, 1827–50.

3119. COLLINS, MICHAEL.   What we mean when we say 'Creole': an interview with Salikoko S. Mufwene. Callaloo (28:2) 2005, 425–62.

3120. ESSEGBEY, JAMES.   The basic locative construction in Gbe languages and Surinamese creoles. JPCL (20:2) 2005, 229–67.

3121. FARACLAS, NICHOLAS.   The -pela suffix in Tok Pisin and the notion of 'simplicity' in pidgin and creole languages: what happens to morphology under contact? In (pp. 269–90) **3133**.

3122. GOODEN, SHELOME.   Prosodic contrast in Jamaican Creole reduplication. In (pp. 193–208) **3133**.

3123. GRAHAM, ROSS.   Partial creolization, restructuring and convergence in Bay Islands Englishes. EWW (26:1) 2005, 43–76.

3124. JAMES, WINFORD.   The role of tone and rhyme structure in the organisation of grammatical morphemes in Tobagonian. In (pp. 165–92) **3133**.

3125. KIHM, ALAIN.   Inflectional categories in creole languages. In (pp. 333–63) **3133**.

3126. KOUWENBERG, SILVIA (ed.).   Twice as meaningful: reduplication in pidgins, creoles and other contact languages. London: Battlebridge, 2003. pp. vi, 330. (Westminster creolistics, 8.) Rev. by George L. Huttar in JPCL (20:1) 2005, 194–8.

3127. LALLA, BARBARA.   Creole and respec' in the development of Jamaican literary discourse. JPCL (20:1) 2005, 53–84.

3128. LAPPE, SABINE; PLAG, INGO. Rules *vs* analogy: modeling variation in word-final epenthesis in Sranan. *In* (pp. 71–90) **3133**.

3129. LEDENT, BÉNÉDICTE. A new wor(l)d order: language in the fiction of the new Caribbean diaspora. *See* **14203**.

3130. LEFEBVRE, CLAIRE. Issues in the study of pidgin and creole languages. Amsterdam; Philadelphia, PA: Benjamins, 2004. pp. xiv, 358. (Studies in language companion series, 70.) Rev. by John McWhorter in JPCL (20:1) 2005, 211–18.

3131. MEYERHOFF, MIRIAM. Attitudes to gender and creoles: a case study on *mokes* and *titas*. Te Reo (47) 2004, 63–82.

3132. MIGGE, BETTINA. Creole formation as language contact: the case of the Suriname creoles. Amsterdam; Philadelphia, PA: Benjamins, 2003. pp. x, 149. (Creole language library, 25.) Rev. by Margot van den Berg in EWW (26:1) 2005, 100–4.

3133. PLAG, INGO (ed.). Phonology and morphology of creole languages. Tübingen: Niemeyer, 2003. pp. xi, 376. (Linguistische Arbeiten, 478.) Rev. by Stephanie Hackert in EWW (26:1) 2005, 120–3; by Malcolm Awadajin Finney in JPCL (20:1) 2005, 189–94.

3134. ROMAINE, SUZANNE. Orthographic practices in the standardization of pidgins and creoles: pidgin in Hawai'i as anti-language and anti-standard. JPCL (20:1) 2005, 101–40.

3135. SAKODA, KENT; SIEGEL, JEFF. Pidgin grammar: an introduction to the creole English of Hawai'i. Honolulu, HI: Bess Press, 2003. pp. viii, 120. Rev. by Suzanne Romaine in JPCL (20:2) 2005, 387–92.

3136. SIEGEL, JEFF. Applied creolistics revisited. JPCL (20:2) 2005, 293–323.

3137. —— Creolization outside creolistics. JPCL (20:1) 2005, 141–66.

3138. SMITH, NORVAL. New evidence from the past: to epenthesize or not to epenthesize? That is the question. *In* (pp. 91–107) **3133**.

3139. TRYON, DARRELL T.; CHARPENTIER, JEAN-MICHEL. Pacific pidgins and creoles: origins, growth and development. Berlin; New York: Mouton de Gruyter, 2004. pp. xix, 559. (Trends in linguistics: Studies and monographs, 132.) Rev. by Manfred Görlach in EWW (26:2) 2005, 234–8.

3140. VAN DEN BERG, MARGOT. Early 18th-century Sranan *-man*. *In* (pp. 231–51) **3133**.

3141. WINDUO, STEVEN. Transition and transformation. *See* **20253**.

SOCIOLINGUISTICS

3142. ALIM, H. SAMY. You know my steez: an ethnographic and sociolinguistic study of styleshifting in a Black American speech community. *See* **2975**.

3143. ANDROUTSOPOULOS, JANNIS K.; GEORGAKOPOULOU, ALEXANDRA (eds). Discourse constructions of youth identities. Amsterdam; Philadelphia, PA: Benjamins, 2003. pp. viii, 338. (Pragmatics & beyond, ns 110.) Rev. by Crispin Thurlow in JSoc (9:2) 2005, 276–9.

3144. ANTONELLI, SARA; SCACCHI, ANNA; SCANNAVINI, ANNA. La babele americana: lingua e identità negli Stati Uniti d'oggi. Ed. by Anna Scacchi. Rome: Donzelli, 2005. pp. iv, 280. (Virgole, 15.)

3145. BAKER, PAUL. Public discourses of gay men. London; New York: Routledge, 2005. pp. ix, 266. (Routledge advances in corpus linguistics, 8.)

3146. BARBIERI, FEDERICA. Quotative use in American English: a corpus-based, cross-register comparison. *See* **2978.**

3147. BAUER, LAURIE; BAUER, WINIFRED. Regional dialects in New Zealand children's playground vocabulary. *In* (pp. 194–216) **3044.**

3148. BAXTER, JUDITH. Positioning gender in discourse: a feminist methodology. Basingstoke; New York: Palgrave Macmillan, 2003. pp. v, 215. Rev. by Joan Swann in JSoc (9:1) 2005, 137–9.

3149. BECKETT, DAN. Sociolinguistic individuality in a remnant dialect community. *See* **2981.**

3150. BENNETT, TONY; GROSSBERG, LAWRENCE; MORRIS, MEAGHAN (eds). New keywords: a revised vocabulary of culture and society. *See* **1953.**

3151. BERNS, MARGIE. Expanding on the Expanding Circle: where do WE go from here? *See* **3083.**

3152. BOLONYAI, AGNES. 'Who was the best?': power, knowledge and rationality in bilingual girls' code choices. *See* **3226.**

3153. BOLTON, KINGSLEY. Chinese Englishes: a sociolinguistic history. *See* **3045.**

3154. BRITAIN, DAVID; CHESHIRE, JENNY (eds). Social dialectology: in honour of Peter Trudgill. *See* **2907.**

3155. —— TRUDGILL, PETER. New dialect formation and contact-induced reallocation: three case studies from the English Fens. *See* **2916.**

3156. CAMERON, DEBORAH; KULICK, DON. Language and sexuality. Cambridge; New York: CUP, 2003. pp. xvi, 176. Rev. by Susan Alice Fischer in ChE (11:1) 2004, 155–60; by Andrew Wong in JSoc (9:2) 2005, 254–66; by Jonathan Alexander in GLQ (11:1) 2005, 158–61.

3157. CARPENTER, JEANNINE; HILLIARD, SARAH. Shifting parameters of individual and group variation: African American English on Roanoke Island. *See* **2989.**

3158. COATES, JENNIFER. Men talk: stories in the making of masculinities. (Bibl. 2004, 3293.) Rev. by Beth Lee Simon in AS (80:4) 2005, 433–6.

3159. COLLINS, JAMES; BLOT, RICHARD. Literacy and literacies: texts, power, and identity. Cambridge; New York: CUP, 2003. pp. xx, 217. (Studies in the social and cultural foundations of language, 22.) Rev. by Weldu Weldeyesus in JSoc (9:1) 2005, 156–8.

3160. COOPER, LANA. Lore, language and rhyming in the Australian playground. *See* **3675.**

3161. DALY, NICOLA, *et al.* Expletives as solidarity signals in FTAs on the factory floor. *See* **2153.**

3162. DODSWORTH, ROBIN. Attribute networking: a technique for modeling social perceptions. JSoc (9:2) 2005, 225–53.

3163. DRAGER, KATIE. From *bad* to *bed*: the relationship between perceived age and vowel perception in New Zealand English. *See* **1464.**

3164. ECKERT, PENELOPE; MCCONNELL-GINET, SALLY. Language and gender. Cambridge; New York: CUP, 2003. pp. xii, 366. Rev. by Sara Mills in JSoc (9:1) 2005, 134–7.

3165. EICHER-CATT, DEBORAH. The myth of servant-leadership: a feminist perspective. WL (28:1) 2005, 17–25.

3166. FAIRCLOUGH, NORMAN. Analysing discourse: textual analysis for social research. *See* **1372**.

3167. FLEMING, BRUCE E. Art and argument: what words can't do and what they can. Dallas, TX: UP of America, 2003. pp. vi, 201. Rev. by Michael Weh in BJA (45:2) 2005, 202–4.

3168. FRIDLAND, VALERIE; BARTLETT, KATHRYN; KREUZ, ROGER. Making sense of variation: pleasantness and education ratings of Southern vowel variants. *See* **2996**.

3169. FULLER, JANET M. The uses and meanings of the female title *Ms*. *See* **1861**.

3170. GARRETT, PETER; COUPLAND, NIKOLAS; WILLIAMS, ANGIE. Investigating language attitudes: social meanings of dialect, ethnicity and performance. *See* **2928**.

3171. GREEN, ANN E. Guns, language, and beer: hunting for a working-class language in the academy. *In* (pp. 75–89) **2457**.

3172. GUENDOUZI, JACKIE. 'She's very slim': talking about body-size in all-female interactions. *See* **2553**.

3173. GUZMÁN-GONZÁLEZ, TRINIDAD. Out of the past: a walk with labels and concepts, raiders of the lost evidence, and a vindication of the role of writing. IJES (5:1) 2005, 13–31.

3174. HARTLEY, LAURA C. The consequences of conflicting stereotypes: Bostonian perceptions of US dialects. *See* **3002**.

3175. HAYWARD, MALCOLM. Are texts recognizably gendered? An experiment and analysis. *See* **2676**.

3176. HAZEN, KIRK. Mergers in the mountains: West Virginia division and unification. *See* **3003**.

3177. HERNÁNDEZ-CAMPOY, JUAN MANUEL; CONDE-SILVESTRE, JUAN CAMILO. Sociolinguistic and geolinguistic approaches to the historical diffusion of linguistic innovations: incipient standardisation in Late Middle English. IJES (5:1) 2005, 101–34.

3178. HILL, MARY LYNNE. The relationship between candidate sex and pronoun usage in a Louisiana governor's race. WL (28:2) 2005, 23–32.

3179. HIRAGA, YUKO. British attitudes towards six varieties of English in the USA and Britain. *See* **2934**.

3180. HOLMES, JANET; MEYERHOFF, MIRIAM (eds). The handbook of language and gender. Oxford; Malden, MA: Blackwell, 2003. pp. xvi, 759. (Blackwell handbooks in linguistics, 13.) Rev. by Elizabeth H. Stokoe in JSoc (9:1) 2005, 118–33; by E. Moore Quinn in JEL (33:3) 2005, 298–302.

3181. JOLLEY, PHILIP. The technological frontier: a view of some of its effects on the speech and play of today's children. AF (20) 2005, 74–9.

3182. KATES, SUSAN. Politics, identity, and the language of Appalachia: James Watt Raine on 'mountain speech and song'. *In* (pp. 74–86) **2318**.

3183. KUURE, LEENA; KÄRKKÄINEN, ELISE; SAARENKUNNAS, MAARIT (eds). Language and social action. Helsinki: Assn Finlandaise de Linguistique Appliquée, 2005. pp. 422. (Pubs de l'Assn Finlandaise de Linguistique Appliquée, 63.)

3184. LEAP, WILLIAM L.; BOELLSTORFF, TOM (eds). Speaking in queer tongues: globalization and gay language. Urbana: Illinois UP, 2003. pp. 288. Rev. by Andrew Wong in JSoc (9:2) 2005, 254–66.

3185. LEDERER, RICHARD. A guide to teenspeak. VocR (7:5) 2005.

3186. —— The way we word. *See* **1747**.

3187. MARSHALL, JONATHAN. Language change and sociolinguistics: rethinking social networks. Basingstoke; New York: Palgrave Macmillan, 2004. pp. xiii, 246. (Palgrave Macmillan studies in language variation.) Rev. by Robin Dodsworth and Elizabeth Hume in JSoc (9:2) 2004, 289–93.

3188. MICHIEKA, MARTHA MORAA. English in Kenya: a sociolinguistic profile. *See* **3065**.

3189. MILLS, SARA. Gender and politeness. Cambridge; New York: CUP, 2003. pp. viii, 270. (Studies in interactional sociolinguistics, 17.) Rev. by Janet Holmes in JSoc (9:1) 2005, 108–17.

3190. MILROY, LESLEY; GORDON, MATTHEW. Sociolinguistics: method and interpretation. Oxford; Malden, MA: Blackwell, 2003. pp. xv, 261. (Language in society, 12.) Rev. by Edgar W. Schneider in EWW (26:1) 2005, 118–20.

3191. MOUNTFORD, ROXANNE. The gendered pulpit: preaching in American Protestant spaces. *See* **2415**.

3192. MUGGLESTONE, LYNDA. 'Talking proper': the rise of accent as social symbol. *See* **1444**.

3193. NEVALAINEN, TERTTU. Sociolinguistic perspectives on Tudor English. SEDERI (13) 2003, 123–40.

3194. —— RAUMOLIN-BRUNBERG, HELENA. Historical sociolinguistics: language change in Tudor and Stuart England. (Bibl. 2004, 3333.) Rev. by Sara Ponce Serrano in RAEI (16) 2003, 361–2; by Sali A. Tagliamonte in JEL (33:2) 2005, 199–203; by Juan Camilo Conde-Silvestre in IJES (5:1) 2005, 211–22.

3195. —— —— Sociolinguistics and the history of English: a survey. IJES (5:1) 2005, 33–58.

3196. NICKELS, EDELMIRA L. English in Puerto Rico. *See* **3067**.

3197. RIZZO, BETTY. Male oratory and female prate: 'Then hush and be an angel quite.' ECL (29:1) 2005, 23–49.

3198. ROBINSON, CHRISTINE. Changes in the dialect of Livingston. *See* **2955**.

3199. ROGERS, REBECCA. A critical discourse analysis of family literacy practices: power in and out of print. Mahwah, NJ; London: Erlbaum, 2003. pp. xv, 225. Rev. by Kate Pahl in AppL (26:1) 2005, 131–4.

3200. SEALEY, ALISON; CARTER, BOB. Applied linguistics as social science. London; New York: Continuum, 2004. pp. xv, 239. (Advances in applied linguistics.) Rev. by Alan Davies in JSoc (9:2) 2005, 300–4.

3201. Siegel, Jeff.   Applied creolistics revisited. *See* **3136**.

3202. Spolsky, Bernard.   Language policy. *See* **3110**.

3203. Starks, Donna; Allan, Scott.   What comes before *t*? Nonalveolar *s* in Auckland. *See* **3074**.

3204. —— Reffell, Hayley.   Pronouncing your /r/s in New Zealand English? A study of Pasifika and Maori students. *See* **1500**.

3205. Stotesbury, Hilkka.   Focus on business abstracts: considerations of rhetorical, lexico-grammatical and interpersonal perspectives. *In* (pp. 321–34) **3183**.

3206. Tieken-Boon van Ostade, Ingrid.   Of social networks and linguistic influence: the language of Robert Lowth and his correspondents. IJES (5:1) 2005, 135–57.

3207. Trousdale, Graeme.   The social context of Kentish Raising: issues in Old English sociolinguistics. *See* **2962**.

3208. Trudgill, Peter.   A glossary of sociolinguistics. *See* **1974**.

3209. Wong, Andrew.   New directions in the study of language and sexuality. JSoc (9:2) 2005, 254–66 (review-article).

3210. Wright, Laura.   The space of English: geographic space, temporal space and social space. *See* **2914**.

TRANSLATION AND COMPARATIVE LINGUISTICS

3211. Aijmer, Karin; Simon-Vandenbergen, Anne-Marie.   A marker and a methodology for the study of pragmatic markers: the semantic field of expectation. *See* **1849**.

3212. Almeida Flor, João.   Shakespeare in the Bay of Portugal: a tribute to Luis Cardim (1879–1958). *In* (pp. 243–54) **5874**.

3213. Anderman, Gunilla; Rogers, Margaret (eds).   In and out of English: for better, for worse. Clevedon; Philadelphia, PA: Multilingual Matters, 2005. pp. xii, 303. (Translating Europe.)

3214. Andersen, Peter (ed.).   Pratiques de traduction au moyen âge: actes du colloque de l'Université de Copenhague 25 et 26 octobre 2002. (Bibl. 2004, 3363.) Rev. by Jeanette Beer in TMR, Mar. 2005.

3215. Azevedo, Milton M.   *Addio, adieu, adiós: A Farewell to Arms* in three Romance languages. *See* **16965**.

3216. Bammesberger, Alfred.   *Freo* 'woman' in *Genesis*, line 457a. *See* **1838**.

3217. Banks, David.   The case of Perrin and Thomson: an example of the use of a mini-corpus. *See* **9736**.

3218. ——   On the historical origins of nominalized process in scientific text. *See* **2809**.

3219. Bao, Zhiming; Lye, Hui Min.   Systematic transfer, topic prominence, and the bare conditional in Singapore English. *See* **3038**.

3220. Bartlett, Anne Clark.   Translation, self-representation, and statecraft: Lady Margaret Beaufort and Caxton's *Blanchardyn and Eglantine* (1489). *See* **4775**.

3221. BASWELL, CHRISTOPHER.   Troy, Arthur, and the languages of 'Brutis Albyoun'. *In* (pp. 170–97) 4485.

3222. BEHEYDT, GRIET.   Bygone times …: the preterite and the present perfect in Dutch as compared to English. *See* 1579.

3223. BERGEN, BENJAMIN K.; PLAUCHÉ, MADELAINE C.   The convergent evolution of radial constructions: French and English deictics and existentials. *See* 1581.

3224. BILLINGS, TIMOTHY.   Two new sources for Shakespeare's bawdy French in *Henry V*. *See* 6415.

3225. BOISSEAU, MARYVONNE.   Traduire/travestir: Derek Mahon détourne Molière. *See* 18036.

3226. BOLONYAI, AGNES.   'Who was the best?': power, knowledge and rationality in bilingual girls' code choices. JSoc (9:1) 2005, 3–27.

3227. BOND, FRANCIS.   Translating the untranslatable: a solution to the problem of generating English determiners. Stanford, CA: CSLI, 2005. pp. xv, 207. (CSLI studies in computational linguistics.)

3228. BOWLES, HUGO; PALLOTTI, GABRIELE.   Conversation analysis of opening sequences of telephone calls to bookstores in English and Italian. *See* 2539.

3229. BREEZE, ANDREW.   *Puffin*, a loanword from Cornish. *See* 1884.

3230. BRÖNNIMANN, WERNER.   Think-along edition: the bilingual *Studienausgabe* of Shakespeare. *In* (pp. 184–98) 5975.

3231. BRUNAZZI, ELIZABETH.   A conversation with Claire Malroux, contemporary French translator of Emily Dickinson. *See* 10770.

3232. CALIENDO, GIUDITTA.   EU language in cross-boundary communication. *See* 2821.

3233. CAMPAGNA, SANDRA.   Investigating 'virtual' virtues: a comparative study of charity websites. *See* 2822.

3234. CAMPILLO ARNÁIZ, LAURA.   Spanish translations of culture-bound elements in *The First Part of Henry IV*: a historical perspective. *See* 6394.

3235. CARVALHO HOMEM, RUI.   The feast and the scraps: translating *Love's Labour's Lost* into Portuguese. *In* (pp. 114–29) 5975.

3236. —— Gipsy queens: Portuguese Cleopatras and the fascination of opprobrium. *In* (pp. 225–41) 5874.

3237. —— Translating Shakespeare for the twenty-first century: introduction. *In* (pp. 1–24) 5874.

3238. —— HOENSELAARS, TON (eds).   Translating Shakespeare for the twenty-first century. *See* 5874.

3239. CASIELLES-SUAREZ, EUGENIA.   The syntax–information structure interface: evidence from Spanish and English. *See* 1583.

3240. CASTILLO, DEBRA A.   Redreaming America: toward a bilingual American culture. *See* 12593.

3241. CAWS, MARY ANN; JOSEPH, GERHARD.   Naming and not naming: Tennyson and Mallarmé. *See* 12135.

3242. ČERMÁK, JAN, *et al.* (eds).   Patterns: a Festschrift for Libuše Dušková. *See* 1369.

3243. CHAN, LEO TAK-HUNG. The poetics of recontextualization: intertextuality in a Chinese adaptive translation of *The Picture of Dorian Gray*. See **12372**.

3244. CHOVANEC, JAN. Czeching out pun and clichés in football reporting. *In* (pp. 61–7) **1370**.

3245. CIRINO, MARK. 'You don't know the Italian language well enough': the bilingual dialogue of *A Farewell to Arms*. See **16972**.

3246. CLAYTON, HUGH. Tom il Matto and Jar le Rétameur: aspects of T. F. Powys in Italian and French. See **18926**.

3247. COBBY, A. E. An Old French source for Modern Scots *wabbit*? See **1910**.

3248. COOPER, MARTIN C. A mathematical model of historical semantics and the grouping of word meanings into concepts. See **2070**.

3249. COWPER, ELIZABETH. The geometry of interpretable features: INFL in Spanish and English. See **1588**.

3250. CRISAFULLI, EDOARDO. The vision of Dante: Cary's translation of *The Divine Comedy*. See **10412**.

3251. DAHL, TRINE. Textual discourse in research articles: a marker of national culture or of academic discipline? See **2832**.

3252. DA ROCHA AFONSO, MARIA JOÃO. From words to action: translating Shakespeare for the Portuguese stage. *In* (pp. 163–80) **5874**.

3253. DEIGNAN, ALICE; POTTER, LIZ. A corpus study of metaphors and metonyms in English and Italian. See **2274**.

3254. DELABASTITA, DIRK. Cross-language comedy in Shakespeare. See **5894**.

3255. —— *Henry V* in the Low Countries: English, Dutch, and the other languages. See **6417**.

3256. —— 'If I know the letters and the language': translation as a dramatic device in Shakespeare's plays. *In* (pp. 31–52) **5975**.

3257. —— Notes on Shakespeare in Dutch translation: historical perspectives. *In* (pp. 99–116) **5874**.

3258. —— Shakespeare and translation: a guide to further reading. *In* (pp. 289–306) **5975**.

3259. DE LA ZUNINO GARRIDO, MARÍA. Boscán and Garcilaso as rhetorical models in the English Renaissance: the case of Abraham Fraunce's *The Arcadian Rhetorike*. See **5445**.

3260. DÉPRATS, JEAN-MICHEL. Translating Shakespeare's stagecraft. *In* (pp. 133–47) **5975**.

3261. —— Translation at the crossroads of the past and present. *In* (pp. 65–78) **5874**.

3262. DEWAR-WATSON, SARAH. Dryden's *Aeneis* 2.718–41. See **7413**.

3263. DI, JIN. Literary translation: quest for artistic integrity. Manchester; Northampton, MA: St Jerome, 2003. pp. 165. Rev. by Yu-chen Lin in JJLS (19:2) 2005, 12–13.

3264. DISCENZA, NICOLE. The King's English: strategies of translation in the Old English Boethius. See **4270**.

3265. DJORDJEVIĆ, IVANA.   Versification and translation in *Sir Beves of Hampton. See* **4588.**

3266. DUŠKOVÁ, LIBUŠE.   Konstantnost syntaktické funkce mezi jazyky. (Syntactic constancy across languages.) *See* **1593.**

3267. —— Syntactic constancy of the subject complement: part 2, A comparison between English and Czech. *See* **1594.**

3268. ESSEGBEY, JAMES.   The basic locative construction in Gbe languages and Surinamese creoles. *See* **3120.**

3269. EVERSON, JANE E.   Translating the Pope and the Apennines: Harington's version of the *Orlando furioso. See* **5471.**

3270. FARACLAS, NICHOLAS.   The *-pela* suffix in Tok Pisin and the notion of 'simplicity' in pidgin and creole languages: what happens to morphology under contact? *In* (pp. 269–90) **3133.**

3271. FEIJÓ, ANTÓNIO M.   Practically speaking: on translating *Hamlet. In* (pp. 193–202) **5874.**

3272. FINDLAY, BILL (ed.).   Frae ither tongues: essays on modern translations into Scots. *See* **2927.**

3273. FRANCE, PETER.   The rhetoric of translation. MLR (100:4:supp.) 2005, 255–68.

3274. FRANCINI, ANTONELLA.   Notes on translating Yusef Komunyakaa's poetry into Italian. *See* **17521.**

3275. FREDERKING, ROBERT E.; TAYLOR, KATHRYN B. (eds).   Machine translation: from real users to research: 6th Conference of the Association for Machine Translation in the Americas, AMTA 2004. Woodbury, NY: AIP Press; New York: Springer, 2004. pp. ix, 281. (Lecture notes in computer science, 3265: Lecture notes in artificial intelligence.)

3276. GIBBS, RAYMOND W.; LIMA, PAULA LENZ COSTA; FRANCOZO, EDSON. Metaphor is grounded in embodied experience. *See* **2315.**

3277. GOBETTI, NORMAN.   Pavese e Vittorini, traduttori di William Faulkner. *See* **16411.**

3278. GODDARD, CLIFF.   The ethnopragmatics and semantics of 'active metaphors'. *See* **2319.**

3279. GODDEN, MALCOLM.   Alfred, Asser, and Boethius. *In* (pp. 326–48) **4220.**

3280. GOMES DA TORRE, M.   The translation of proper names in *Measure for Measure. In* (pp. 203–15) **5874.**

3281. GOYENS, MICHELE; VERBEKE, WERNER (eds).   The dawn of the written vernacular in Western Europe. *See* **1392.**

3282. GRACE, DOMINICK.   Telling differences: Chaucer's *Tale of Melibee* and Renaud de Louens' *Livre de Mellibee et Prudence. See* **4998.**

3283. GRAHAM, KENNETH.   'Painting the eyes of the Circassians': Samuel Henley's mistranslations in *Vathek. See* **8714.**

3284. GRETSCH, MECHTHILD; GNEUSS, HELMUT.   Anglo-Saxon glosses to a Theodorean poem? *In* (pp. 9–46) **4220.**

3285. GURR, JENS MARTIN. 'Let me suppose thee for a ship a-while': nautical metaphors and contemporary politics in eighteenth-century translations of Horace's Ode I, xiv. See 9069.

3286. GUT, ULRIKE. Nigerian English prosody. See 3056.

3287. GUTSCH, JÜRGEN (ed.). '... lesen, wie kraß schön du bist konkret': William Shakespeare, Sonett 18, vermittelt durch deutsche Übersetzer in 154 + 1 Versionen. See 6717.

3288. GUY-BRAY, STEPHEN. Embracing Troy: Surrey's Aeneid. In (pp. 177–92) 4479.

3289. HÄCKER, MARTINA. Linking [fi] and the variation between linking /r/ and glottal onsets in South African English. See 3057.

3290. HAJIČOVÁ, EVA. On some aspects of translation. In (pp. 47–57) 1369.

3291. HAMBURGER, MAIK. 'If it be now': the knocking of Fate: reading Shakespeare for translation. In (pp. 117–28) 5874.

3292. —— Translating and copyright. In (pp. 148–66) 5975.

3293. HAMM, ALBERT. Language chunks and the levels of linguistic analysis. See 1374.

3294. HAYES, JULIE CANDLER. Tobias Smollett and the translators of the Quixote. See 9010.

3295. HEGARTY, MICHAEL. A feature-based syntax of functional categories: the structure, acquisition, and specific impairment of functional systems. See 1664.

3296. HEININGER, JOSEPH. Making a Dantean poetic: Seamus Heaney's Ugolino. See 16942.

3297. HOENSELAARS, TON. Introduction. In (pp. 1–27) 5975.

3298. —— 'There is tremendous poetry in killings': traditions of Shakespearean translation and adaptation in the Low Countries. In (pp. 79–98) 5874.

3299. —— (ed.). Shakespeare and the language of translation. See 5975.

3300. —— RIJSER, DAVID. From Homer to Shakespeare: an interview with H. J. de Roy van Zuydewijn. See 5976.

3301. HOLFORD-STREVENS, LEOFRANC. The first translation of Aulus Gellius. See 8833.

3302. HOLM, JOHN. Languages in contact: the partial restructuring of vernaculars. See 1397.

3303. HOOKER, MARK T. Schuchart vs Mensink-van Warmelo: round two. See 19820.

3304. IVERSON, GREGORY K.; SALMONS, JOSEPH C. Filling the gap: English tense vowel plus final /š/. See 1441.

3305. JAKUBIAK, KATARZYNA. Nienaturalny stan jednoro żca: translating Komunyakaa's Unicorn into Polish. See 17526.

3306. JANICADISOVÁ, TEREZA. Latin words reflected in the Old English vocabulary. In (pp. 83–9) 1369.

3307. KABELL, INGE. George Borrow and Finland (part 2). See 10114.

3308. KEOWN, DOMINIC. No time for the doves? Intrusion and redrafting in the English translation of La plaça del Diamant. MLR (100:3) 2005, 659–72.

3309. KIHM, ALAIN. Inflectional categories in creole languages. *In* (pp. 333–63) **3133.**

3310. KISHI, TETSUO. 'Our language of love': Shakespeare in Japanese translation. *In* (pp. 68–81) **5975.**

3311. —— BRADSHAW, GRAHAM. Shakespeare in Japan. *See* **5994.**

3312. KLÉGR, ALEŠ. *Sadness/smutek*: a comparison of the verbal collocates. *In* (pp. 91–105) **1369.**

3313. KLITGÅRD, EBBE. Chaucer reception and translation in Denmark. *See* **5007.**

3314. KNOTTENBELT, E. M. Romantic residues? Virgil's *Aeneid* 'in such a tongue as the people understandeth' or in a 'language really spoken by men'. *In* (pp. 235–57) **9237.**

3315. KOTHARI, RITA. Translating India: the cultural politics of English. *See* **3098.**

3316. KRIES, SUSANNE. Skandinavisch–schottische Sprachbeziehungen im Mittelalter: der altnordische Lehneinfluss. *See* **2941.**

3317. KRONTIRIS, TINA. Translation as appropriation: Vassilis Rotas, Shakespeare and Modern Greek. *See* **6554.**

3318. KURTES, SVETLANA. Contrastive linguistics: a 21st-century perspective. *In* (pp. 255–78) **1376.**

3319. LATTES, TONY. Sequitur et non-sequitur: *since* et alii. *See* **1705.**

3320. LEDERER, MARIANNE. Translation: the interpretive model. Trans. by Ninon Larché. Manchester; Northampton, MA: St Jerome, 2003. pp. 239.

3321. LIEBLEIN, LEANORE. 'Cette belle langue': the 'tradaptation' of Shakespeare in Quebec. *In* (pp. 255–69) **5975.**

3322. LIN, SHEN. A mirror up to 'human' nature: the case of the Chinese translator Liang Shi Qiu. *In* (pp. 98–113) **5975.**

3323. LONG, LYNNE (ed.). Translation and religion: holy untranslatable? Clevedon; Philadelphia, PA: Multilingual Matters, 2005. pp. vi, 209. (Topics in translation, 28.)

3324. LÓPEZ RÚA, PAULA. Shortening devices in text messaging: a multilingual approach. *See* **1530.**

3325. LORVIK, MARJORIE. The distinctiveness of the Doric: home-grown or imported? *See* **2942.**

3326. MACALISTER, JOHN (ed.). A dictionary of Maori words in New Zealand English. *See* **1963.**

3327. MACARTHUR, FIONA. The competent horseman in a horseless world: observations on a conventional metaphor in Spanish and English. *See* **2386.**

3328. McCLURE, J. DERRICK. Scots for Shakespeare. *In* (pp. 217–39) **5975.**

3329. McELROY, RUTH. 'For a mothertongue is a treasure but not a God': Gwyneth Lewis and the dynamics of language in contemporary Welsh poetry. *See* **17809.**

3330. McMURRAN, MARY HELEN. Aphra Behn from both sides: translation in the Atlantic world. *See* **7246.**

3331. MÅRD-MIETTINEN, KARITA; NIEMELÄ, NINA (eds). Erikoiskielet ja käännösteoria: VAKKI-symposiumi 25. (Languages for special purposes and translation theory: VAKKI symposium 25.) Vaasa: Univ. of Vaasa, 2005. pp. 357. (Vaasan yliopiston käänösteorian, ammattikielten ja monikielisyyden tutkijaryhmän jukaisut, 32 / Univ. of Vaasa Research Group for LSP, Translation and Multilingualism pubs, 32.)

3332. MÁRQUEZ REITER, ROSINA; RAINEY, ISOBEL; FULCHER, GLENN. A comparative study of certainty and conventional indirectness: evidence from British English and Peninsular Spanish. See 2179.

3333. MARSDEN, RICHARD. Latin in the ascendant: the interlinear gloss of Oxford, Bodleian Library, Laud Misc. 509. In (pp. 132–52) 4221.

3334. MARTÍN-MARTÍN, PEDRO. The rhetoric of the abstract in English and Spanish scientific discourse: a cross-cultural genre-analytic approach. See 2867.

3335. MEDDEMMEN, JOHN. L'estro comico della lingua inglese in italiano: a proposito di Alan Bennett. See 15465.

3336. MEJER, VALERIE. On awareness. See 17529.

3337. MELA-ATHANASOPOULOU, ELIZABETH. Morphologization of synthetic prepositions in English and Modern Greek. In (pp. 118–32) 1377.

3338. MICHAELIS, LAURA A. Type shifting in construction grammar: an integrated approach to aspectual coercion. See 1623.

3339. MINIER, MARTA. Shakespeare translation and taboo: a case study in retranslation. See 6351.

3340. MODENESSI, ALFREDO MICHEL. 'A double tongue within your mask': translating Shakespeare in/to Spanish-speaking Latin America. In (pp. 240–54) 5975.

3341. MONOD, SYLVÈRE. Joseph Conrad's polyglot wordplay. See 15901.

3342. —— Re-reading Il Conde. See 15902.

3343. MORINI, CARLA. The first English love romance without 'love'! The Old English Apollonius of Tyre. See 4284.

3344. NARROG, HEIKO. Modality, mood, and change of modal meanings: a new perspective. See 2119.

3345. NASI, FRANCO. Poetiche in transito: Sisifo e le fatiche del tradurre. (Bibl. 2004, 3488.) Rev. by Massimo Bacigalupo in Indice (2005:5) 17; by Emilio Mattioli in TFr (32:1) 2005, 226–31.

3346. NAUGHTON, JOHN (ed.). Shakespeare & the French poet: including an interview with Yves Bonnefoy. See 6038.

3347. O'CONNELL, DANIEL C.; KOWAL, SABINE; DILL, EDWARD J., III. Dialogicality in TV news interviews. See 2581.

3348. ORCHARD, ANDY. Reading Beowulf now and then. See 4308.

3349. ORKIN, MARTIN. 'I am the tusk of an elephant' – Macbeth, Titus and Caesar in Johannesburg. In (pp. 270–86) 5975.

3350. O'SHEA, JOSÉ ROBERTO. From printed text to performance text: Brazilian translations of Shakespearean drama. In (pp. 145–59) 5874.

3351. ÖZÇALIŞKAN, ŞEYDA.   Metaphor meets typology: ways of moving metaphorically in English and Turkish. *See* **1758**.

3352. PALUSZKIEWICZ-MISIACZEK, MAGDALENA.   Strategies and methods in dealing with culture-specific expressions on the basis of Polish–English translations of certain administrative and institutional terms. *In* (pp. 244–8) **1370**.

3353. PAP, DÁNIEL.   A comparative approach to English, German and Hungarian verbal particles. *In* (pp. 113–19) **1370**.

3354. PEETERS, JEAN (ed.).   On the relationships between translation theory and translation practice. New York; Frankfurt: Lang, 2005. pp. 258. (Studien zur romanischen Sprachwissenschaft und interkulturellen Kommunikation, 19.)

3355. PERRY, NANDRA.   *Imitatio* and identity: Thomas Rogers, Philip Sidney, and the Protestant self. *See* **5628**.

3356. PETERLIN, AGNES PISANSKI.   Text-organising metatext in research articles: an English–Slovene contrastive analysis. *See* **2874**.

3357. PETERSSON, IRMTRAUD; EICHHORN, THOMAS.   Translating *Fredy Neptune*: interview with Thomas Eichhorn. *See* **18435**.

3358. PIRES, MARIA JOÃO.   A palimpsest, or an image of a mutilated statue: the experience of translating Shakespeare. *In* (pp. 181–91) **5874**.

3359. PONS-SANZ, SARA M.   An etymological note on OE *of life forrǣdan*. *See* **1869**.

3360. ——   Friends and relatives in need of an explanation: Gr *anagkaîos*, L *necessarius*, and PGmc **nauð-*. *See* **1868**.

3361. PORTER, GERALD.   'No language, no land': bilingualism and the Irish rebel song. *In* (pp. 318–26) **3331**.

3362. PUJANTE, ÁNGEL LUIS; GREGOR, KEITH.   The four neoclassical Spanish *Hamlet*s: assimilation and revision. *See* **6356**.

3363. PURNELL, THOMAS; TEPELI, DILARA; SALMONS, JOSEPH.   German substrate effects in Wisconsin English: evidence for final fortition. *See* **3020**.

3364. RAMBOUSEK, JIŘÍ.   Unpublished translations of Poe's *The Raven* by František Nevrla. *In* (pp. 249–56) **1370**.

3365. RICHARDSON, DANIEL C.   Bridging the gulf: an analysis of a Brazilian translation of Faulkner's *The Wild Palms*. *See* **16440**.

3366. RIEMER, NICK.   The semantics of polysemy: reading meaning in English and Warlpiri. *See* **2127**.

3367. ROCHA, FLAVIA.   Man talking to a mirror: on the attempt to translate Yusef Komunyakaa's vibrant verbal landscape into the mild undulations of Brazilian Portuguese. *See* **17533**.

3368. RÖMER, UTE.   Progressives, patterns, pedagogy: a corpus-driven approach to English progressive forms, functions, contexts, and didactics. *See* **1635**.

3369. RUBINSTEIN, GEORGE.   Linguistic bioacoustics: frames of Russian and English. SEEJ (49:1) 2005, 95–120.

3370. SAYERS, WILLIAM.   The etymology of *queer*. *See* **1886**.

3371. ——   Middle English and Scots *bulwerk* and some Continental reflexes. *See* **1815**.

3372. SCHÄFFNER, CHRISTINA.   Metaphor and translation: some implications of a cognitive approach. *See* **2461**.

3373. SEARGEANT, PHILIP.   Globalisation and reconfigured English in Japan. *See* **3108**.

3374. SERPIERI, ALESSANDRO.   Translating Shakespeare: a brief survey of some problematic areas. *In* (pp. 27–49) **5874**.

3375. ——— Translation and performance. *In* (pp. 258–81) **6000**.

3376. ——— The translator as editor: the Quartos of *Hamlet*. *In* (pp. 167–83) **5975**.

3377. SHURBANOV, ALEXANDER.   The Shakespearean sound in translation. *In* (pp. 239–57) **6000**.

3378. ——— The translatability of Shakespearean texts into an unrelated language/culture. *In* (pp. 51–64) **5874**.

3379. ——— SOKOLOVA, BOIKA.   Translating Shakespeare under Communism: Bulgaria and beyond. *In* (pp. 82–97) **5975**.

3380. SIMPSON, JOHN.   Will the *Oxford English Dictionary* be more 'European' after its first comprehensive revision since its first edition of 1884–1928? *See* **1941**.

3381. SLUNEČKOVÁ, LENKA.   Syntactic constancy of the object between Czech and English in fiction and technical writing: preliminary notes. *In* (pp. 197–207) **1369**.

3382. SMEAD, ROBERT N.   *Vocabulario vaquero*/cowboy talk: a dictionary of Spanish terms from the American West. *See* **3029**.

3383. SULLIVAN, KEVIN M.   Chinese words in the 'verse. *In* (pp. 197–207) **20809**.

3384. SVOBODA, ALEŠ.   Firbasian semantic scales and comparative studies. *In* (pp. 217–29) **1369**.

3385. TABACZYNSKI, MICHAL.   Rhythm that survives, rhythm that saves. *See* **17535**.

3386. TAYLOR, JOHN.   Bonnefoy and Shakespeare. *See* **6092**.

3387. TEICH, ELKE.   Cross-linguistic variation in system and text: a methodology for the investigation of translations and comparable texts. Berlin; New York: Mouton de Gruyter, 2003. pp. x, 276.

3388. TURNER, ALLAN.   Translating Tolkien: philological elements in *The Lord of the Rings*. *See* **19851**.

3389. van DIJKHUIZEN, JAN FRANS.   An Arab in Venice: Hafid Bouazza translates *Othello* and the *Massacre at Paris*. *See* **6666**.

3390. van MULKEN, MARGOT; van der MEER, WOUTER.   Are you being served? A genre analysis of American and Dutch company replies to customer inquiries. *See* **2898**.

3391. VERDAGUER, ISABEL.   Shakespeare's 'poem unlimited' in eighteenth-century Spain. *In* (pp. 129–43) **5874**.

3392. VIEIRA, FÁTIMA.   The gender of spirits: Ariel and the Portuguese audience. *In* (pp. 217–23) **5874**.

3393. VOKÁČOVÁ, JANA.   A comparative view of English, Czech, French and German idioms. *In* (pp. 163–71) **1370.**

3394. VOLÍN, JAN.   Rhythmical properties of polysyllabic words in British and Czech English. *In* (pp. 279–92) **1369.**

3395. WATKHAOLARM, PIMYUPA.   Think in Thai, write in English: *Thainess* in Thai English literature. *See* **15085.**

3396. WEISSBORT, DANIEL.   From Russian with love: Joseph Brodsky in English: pages from a journal, 1996–97. *See* **15575.**

3397. WHITLA, WILLIAM.   William Morris's translation of Homer's *Iliad*, 1.1–214. *See* **11755.**

3398. WILKINS, JOHN.   Lost in translation: the bishops, the Vatican & the English liturgy. Cweal (132:21) 2005, 12–20.

3399. WILLIAMS, CHRISTOPHER.   Pragmatic and cross-cultural considerations in translating verbal constructions in prescriptive legal texts in English and Italian. *See* **2901.**

3400. WOOD, GILLEN D'ARCY.   Crying game: operatic strains in Wordsworth's lyrical ballads. *See* **12528.**

3401. WRAY, DAVID.   'cool rare air': Zukofsky's breathing with Catullus and Plautus. *See* **20540.**

3402. YU, NING.   The eyes for sight and mind. *See* **2142.**

3403. YUASA, ETSUYO.   Modularity in language: constructional and categorial mismatch in syntax and semantics. *See* **2143.**

3404. ZARANDONA, JUAN MIGUEL.   The hybrid language and society (Afrikaans–English) of the South African postcolonial writing of Pauline Smith (1882–1959) in Spanish translation: *Anna's Marriage / La boda de Anna* (1925). *See* **19488.**

3405. ZATLIN, PHYLLIS.   Theatrical translation and film adaptation: a practitioner's view. *See* **4006.**

TRADITIONAL CULTURE, FOLKLORE AND FOLKLIFE

GENERAL STUDIES

3406. ABRAHAMS, ROGER D. 'I must be doing something right': Don Américo among *los (g)rinches*. See **18730**.

3407. BELL, BERNARD W. The contemporary African American novel: its folk roots and modern literary branches. See **14082**.

3408. CASH, WILEY. 'Those folks downstairs believe in ghosts': the eradication of folklore in the literature of Charles W. Chesnutt. See **10417**.

3409. DE CARO, FRANK; JORDAN, ROSAN AUGUSTA. Re-situating folklore: folk contexts and twentieth-century literature and art. (Bibl. 2004, 3561.) Rev. by David A. Allred in JAF (118:470) 2005, 503–4; by John A. Burrison in SAtlR (70:2) 2005, 134–6.

3410. FREEMAN, MARK. Folklore collection and social investigation in late nineteenth- and early twentieth-century England. Folklore (116:1) 2005, 51–65.

3411. GORJI, MINA. Clare's 'Merry England'. See **10438**.

3412. HARKINS, ANTHONY. Hillbilly: a cultural history of an American icon. New York: OUP, 2004. pp. xii, 324. Rev. by Scott Saul in TLS, 28 May 2004, 9; by J. W. Williamson in AppalJ (31:2) 2004, 244–6; by Robert Sheardy in JAC (27:4) 2004, 446–7; by Rhonda Jenkins Armstrong in WF (63:4) 2004, 365–8; by Ronald D. Eller in JAH (91:4) 2005, 1513.

3413. HENDERSON, STUART. 'While there is still time …': J. Murray Gibbon and the spectacle of difference in three CPR folk festivals, 1928–1931. JCanStud (39:1) 2005, 139–74.

3414. HOFFMAN-JEEP, LYNDA. Creating ethnography: Zora Neale Hurston and Lydia Cabrera. See **17132**.

3415. JEMIE, ONWUCHEKWA (ed.). Yo' mama! New raps, toasts, dozens, jokes, and children's rhymes from urban Black America. Philadelphia, PA: Temple UP, 2003. pp. xxvii, 311. Rev. by Phil Samponaro in JPC (38:4) 2005, 785–7.

3416. JONES, MALCOLM (ed.). Essays in lore & language: presented to John Widdowson on the occasion of his retirement. Sheffield: National Centre for English Cultural Tradition, 2003. pp. 368, (plates) 16. Rev. by David Atkinson in Folklore (116:3) 2005, 356–8.

3417. JUPP, CATHERINE. Folklife: a definition. AF (20) 2005, 56–8.

3418. KERR, AUDREY ELISA. The paper bag principle: of the myth and the motion of colorism. JAF (118:469) 2005, 271–89.

3419. LEAL, LUIS. Américo Paredes and the culmination of Chicano folklore studies. See **18732**.

3420. MCKENRY, KEITH. *Australian Folklore*: an appraisal. AF (20) 2005, 197–207.

3421. MANN, JEFF. 'A beloved place and people': landscape and folk culture in the poetry of Maggie Anderson. See **15159**.

3422. MILLER, STEPHEN. 'A permanent and even European reputation': the lost work of the Reverend Walter Gregor. Folklore (116:2) 2005, 220–7.

3423. PRAHLAD, SW. ANAND. Africana folklore: history and challenges. JAF (118:469) 2005, 253–70.

3424. ROUNTREE, KATHRYN. Embracing the witch and the goddess: feminist ritual-makers in New Zealand. London; New York: Routledge, 2004. pp. xii, 223. Rev. by Marion Gibson in Folklore (116:3) 2005, 344–5.

3425. RYAN, J. S. Some account of the life and work of John White (1913–), Australia's most senior recorder of folk life, as well as a remarkable 'literary and music man'. AF (20) 2005, 1–10.

3426. SANDERS, LYNN MOSS. Howard W. Odum's folklore odyssey: transformation to tolerance through African American folk studies. Athens; London: Georgia UP, 2003. pp. xvii, 184, (plates) 6. Rev. by Wayne Mixon in JSH (71:1) 2005, 196–7.

3427. SHERMAN, SHARON R. Focusing in: film and the survival of Folklore Studies in the 21st century. WF (63:4) 2004, 291–318. (2004 Archer Taylor Memorial Lecture.)

3428. SPILLERS, HORTENSE J. A tale of three Zoras: Barbara Johnson and Black women writers. See 15023.

3429. STOREY, JOHN. Inventing popular culture: from folklore to globalization. Oxford; Malden, MA: Blackwell, 2003. pp. xii, 148. (Blackwell manifestos.) Rev. by Barry J. Faulk in Mod/Mod (12:2) 2005, 353–5.

AREA STUDIES AND COLLECTIONS

3430. BOCHEL, MARGARET M. Salt herring on Saturday: the fishertown of Nairn last century. East Linton, E. Lothian: Tuckwell Press, 2004. pp. vii, 95. (Flashbacks, 18.) Rev. by Fiona-Jane Brown in AUR (60:4) 2004, 338–9.

3431. EDELMAN, FOY ALLEN. Coming together at the North Carolina table: a sampling of Tar Heel recipes and stories. NCarF (52:2) 2005, 12–49.

3432. GARATE, DONALD T. Arizonac: a twentieth-century myth. See 2016.

3433. GREGORY, DAVID. The Elisabeth Greenleaf Collection at MUNFLA: an overview. CFMB (37:3) 2003, 10. (Memorial Univ. of Newfoundland Folklore Archives.)

3434. PALMER, ROY. The folklore of Shropshire. (Bibl. 2004, 3585.) Rev. by Emma Lile in FolkL (43) 2004/05, 129–30.

3435. —— The folklore of Warwickshire. (Bibl. 1979, 2242.) Rev. by Lewis Jones in EDS (67:2) 2005, 36.

3436. PHILLIPS, GRAHAM. Merlin and the discovery of Avalon in the New World. Rochester, VT: Bear, 2005. pp. vi, 231, (plates) 16.

3437. SATTERWHITE, EMILY. 'That's what they're all singing about': Appalachian heritage, Celtic pride, and American nationalism at the 2003 Smithsonian Folklife Festival. AppalJ (32:3) 2005, 302–38.

3438. SEMMENS, JASON. 'Whyler pystry': a breviate of the life and folklore-collecting practices of William Henry Paynter (1901–76) of Callington, Cornwall. Folklore (116:1) 2005, 75–94.

3439. SHELLER, MIMI.   Consuming the Caribbean: from Arawaks to zombies. (Bibl. 2004, 3590.) Rev. by Harvey Neptune in SmAx (8:2) 2004, 214–21.

3440. SIMPSON, JACQUELINE.   The folklore of the Welsh border. (Bibl. 1979, 2246.) Stroud; Charleston, SC: Tempus, 2003. pp. 224. (New ed.: first ed. 1976.) Rev. by Antone Minard in Folklore (116:1) 2005, 103–4.

3441. SMITH, JOHN B.   The devil of Croyden Hill: kinship, fiction, fact, tradition. Folklore (116:1) 2005, 66–74.

3442. WINKLER, WAYNE.   Walking toward the sunset: the Melungeons of Appalachia. Macon, GA: Mercer UP, 2004. pp. xx, 314. Rev. by Katherine C. Kurk in KenPR (19) 2004, 68–9.

PROVERBS, PROVERBIAL EXPRESSIONS, RIDDLES, RHYMES, DITES

3443. CASSELMAN, BILL.   Snow motto has ancient source. VocR (7:3) 2005.

3444. CROSSAN, GREG.   Proverbs and proverbial sayings in J. S. Le Fanu's *The Wyvern Mystery. See* **11585**.

3445. DESKIS, SUSAN E.; HILL, THOMAS D.   'The longe man ys seld wys': proverbial characterization and Langland's Long Will. *See* **4847**.

3446. GARNER, LORI ANN.   The role of proverbs in Middle English narrative. *In* (pp. 255–77) **4197**.

3447. MIEDER, WOLFGANG.   International bibliography of new and reprinted proverb collections. Proverbium (22) 2005, 477–84.

3448. ——   International proverb scholarship: an updated bibliography. Proverbium (22) 2005, 485–534.

3449. ——   'A proverb is worth a thousand words': folk wisdom in the modern mass media. Proverbium (22) 2005, 167–233.

3450. ——   Proverbs: a handbook. Westport, CT; London: Greenwood Press, 2004. pp. xvi, 304. (Greenwood folklore handbooks.)

3451. —— (ed.).   Proverbs and their lessons. Burlington: *Proverbium* in assn with the Dept of German and Russian, Univ. of Vermont, 2003. pp. ix, 179.

3452. —— BRYAN, GEORGE B.   A dictionary of Anglo-American proverbs and proverbial phrases found in literary sources of the nineteenth and twentieth centuries. New York; Frankfurt: Lang, 2005. pp. ix, 870.

3453. PETERS, JASON.   O'Connor's *Wise Blood. See* **18574**.

3454. REVAK, KELLY.   'As easy as collecting feathers in a hurricane': a redefinition of the genre of folk simile. Proverbium (22) 2005, 303–14.

3455. RICHARDSON, GAVIN.   Sex and secrecy in medieval antifeminist proverbs. Proverbium (22) 2005, 321–36.

3456. RITTERSBACHER, CHRISTA; MÖSCH, MATTHIAS.   A haystack full of precious needles: the Internet and its utility for paremiologists. Proverbium (22) 2005, 337–62.

3457. SCHIPPER, MINEKE.   Never marry a woman with big feet: women in proverbs from around the world. (Bibl. 2004, 3625.) Rev. by Kangi Alem Celfa in WLWE (40:1) 2002/03, 148–50; by Marina Warner in LRB (27:4) 2005, 19–20.

3458. SMITH, J. B.   When is a shoe not a shoe? FolkL (43) 2004/05, 121–4.

3459. SMITH, JOHN B. 'Riding knives to London'. Proverbium (22) 2005, 397–401.

3460. SPEAKE, JENNIFER (ed.). The Oxford dictionary of proverbs. (Bibl. 2001, 1710.) Oxford; New York: OUP, 2003. pp. xii, 375. (Fourth ed.: first ed. 1988.) (Orig. pub. as *The Concise Oxford Dictionary of Proverbs*.)

3461. WARNER, MARINA. Pick the small ones. LRB (27:4) 2005, 19–20 (review-article). (Women in proverbs.)

3462. WILTON, DAVID. Word myths: debunking linguistic urban legends. See **1806**.

WRITTEN AND PRINTED MATERIALS, INSCRIPTIONS, EPITAPHS, GRAFFITI

3463. CALDER, ANGUS. Disasters and heroes: on war, memory and representation. Cardiff: UP of Wales, 2004. pp. xiv, 281. Rev. by Robert Haworth in AF (19) 2004, 273–4.

3464. HALLORAN, S. MICHAEL. Writing history on the landscape: the tour road at the Saratoga Battlefield as text. In (pp. 129–44) **2318**.

3465. HEPWORTH, DAVID. Appendix: written epitaphs of Robin Hood. In (pp. 188–9) **3576**.

3466. —— A grave tale. In (pp. 91–112) **3576**.

3467. OLBRYS, STEPHEN GENCARELLA. Money talks: folklore in the public sphere. Folklore (116:3) 2005, 292–310. ('Currency chains', or messages written on bank notes.)

3468. PHILLIPS, HELEN (ed.). Robin Hood: medieval and post-medieval. See **3576**.

3469. SIMPSON, JACQUELINE. The Miller's Tomb: facts, gossip, and legend (1). Folklore (116:2) 2005, 189–200.

3470. WRIGHT, ELIZABETHADA A. Rhetorical spaces in memorial places: the cemetery as a rhetorical memory place/space. RSQ (35:4) 2005, 51–81.

NARRATIVE

3471. ANDERSON, MARK CRONLUND; BLAYER, IRENE MARIA F. (eds). Interdisciplinary and cross-cultural narratives in North America. See **9168**.

3472. ARDOLINO, FRANK. The Protestant context of George Peele's 'pleasant conceited' *Old Wives Tale*. See **5605**.

3473. BARBEITO, PATRICIA FELISA. 'He's making me feel things in my body that I don't feel': the body as a battleground in accounts of alien abduction. JAC (28:2) 2005, 201–15.

3474. BEHEREC, MARC A. The Devil, the terror, and the horror: the Whateley twins' further debts to folklore and fiction. See **17855**.

3475. BELSEY, CATHERINE. Remembering as re-inscription – with a difference. YREAL (21) 2005, 3–17.

3476. BENNETT, GILLIAN. Towards a revaluation of the legend of 'Saint' William of Norwich and its place in the blood libel legend. Folklore (116:2) 2005, 119–39.

3477. —— (comp.). The Superglue revenge. FOAFN (63) 2005.

3478. BOWERS, RICK. Dick Whittington, Stow's *Survey*, and 'Catte Streete'. See **5738**.

3479. BRAID, DONALD. Scottish traveller tales: lives shaped through stories. (Bibl. 2004, 3638.) Rev. by Ian Russell in WF (63:4) 2004, 362–5; by Licia Masoni in Folklore (116:1) 2005, 112–13.

3480. BRAMMER, REBEKAH. Bill Scott: a career overview. AF (20) 2005, 11–13.

3481. BROTTMAN, MIKITA. Funny peculiar: Gershon Legman and the psychopathology of humor. See **3717**.

3482. BRUNVAND, JAN H. Nostalgia ain't what it used to be: the case of 'Grandma's Washday'. OvR (32:1/2) 2005, 7–19.

3483. BRUNVAND, JAN HAROLD. 'Urban legend' from 1925. FOAFN (62) 2005.

3484. CAWSEY, KATHY. Tutivillus and the 'kyrkchaterars': strategies of control in the Middle Ages. See **4530**.

3485. COMPORA, DANIEL P. The legend of Dog Lady Island. FOAFN (61) 2005.

3486. DAVIDSON, HILDA ELLIS; CHAUDHRI, ANNA (eds). A companion to the fairy tale. (Bibl. 2004, 3645.) Rev. by Elizabeth Wanning Harries in MarvT (19:2) 2005, 319–22.

3487. DOYLE, CHARLES CLAY; KNIGHT, LARA RENEE. On the term *urban legend*. See **1909**.

3488. EBEL, JULIA TAYLOR (comp.). Orville Hicks: mountain stories, mountain roots. Boone, NC: Parkway, 2005. pp. x, 151.

3489. EVANS, MICHAEL R. Robin Hood in the landscape: place-name evidence and mythology. *In* (pp. 181–7) **3576**.

3490. GOLDSTEIN, DIANE E. Once upon a virus: AIDS legends and vernacular risk perception. Logan: Utah State UP, 2004. pp. xvi, 210. Rev. by Gillian Bennett in Folklore (116:3) 2005, 351–3; by the same in FOAFN (62) 2005; by Jennifer Orme in MarvT (19:2) 2005, 327–30.

3491. GRIFFIN, REBECCA. Courtship contests and the meaning of conflict in the folklore of slaves. JSH (71:4) 2005, 769–802.

3492. GRIFFITHS, TOM. Legend and lament. Southerly (64:2) 2004, 118–27.

3493. HATHAWAY, ROSEMARY V. 'Life in the TV': the visual nature of 9/11 lore and its impact on vernacular response. JFR (42:1) 2005, 33–56.

3494. HENKEN, ELISSA R. Gender shifts in contemporary legend. WF (63:3) 2004, 237–56.

3495. HEPWORTH, DAVID. A grave tale. *In* (pp. 91–112) **3576**.

3496. HILLARD, MOLLY CLARK. Dangerous exchange: fairy footsteps, goblin economies, and *The Old Curiosity Shop*. See **10695**.

3497. HOBBS, SANDY. The *Titanic* headline. FOAFN (61) 2005.

3498. HOLFORD, M. L. A local source for *Horn Child and Maiden Rimnild*. See **4570**.

3499. INNES, LYN. Resurrecting Ned Kelly. See **15685**.

3500. KILLICK, TIM. Hogg and the collection of short fiction in the 1820s. *See* **11281.**

3501. KNIGHT, STEPHEN. 'Meere English flocks': Ben Jonson's *The Sad Shepherd* and the Robin Hood tradition. *In* (pp. 129–44) **3576.**

3502. LADD, ROGER A. From 'sonne of marchaundy' to 'obscurely bred': the nine lives of Richard Whittington. *See* **4630.**

3503. LANGLOIS, JANET L. 'Celebrating Arabs': tracing legend and rumor labyrinths in post-9/11 Detroit. JAF (118:468) 2005, 219–36.

3504. LEARY, JAMES P. Storviken in the Old World and the New. JAF (118:468) 2005, 141–63.

3505. MAIN, DAVID; HOBBS, SANDY. Chinese restaurant legend still alive as a rumour. FOAFN (62) 2005.

3506. MATTHEWS, JOHN. King Arthur: Dark Age warrior and mythic hero. New York: Gramercy, 2004. pp. 128. Rev. by Ivana Mladenovic in Comitatus (36) 2005, 259–61.

3507. MORROW, JAMES. Once upon a time in the future: science fiction and the storytelling movement. *See* **14233.**

3508. NARVÁEZ, PETER. Of corpses: death and humor. Logan: Utah State UP, 2003. pp. 358. Rev. by J. S. Ryan in AF (19) 2004, 278–80.

3509. NEAL, MARK ANTHONY. Songs in the key of Black life: a rhythm and Blues nation. London; New York: Routledge, 2003. pp. xvii, 214. Rev. by Heather Duerre Humann in AAR (39:1/2) 2005, 255.

3510. NICOL, VALÉRIE DE COURVILLE. Personal ghost stories and the hyper-rationalization of fear. Storytelling (4:1) 2004, 23–43.

3511. NÜNNING, VERA. Fictions of collective memory. YREAL (21) 2005, 305–30.

3512. OAKLEY-BROWN, LIZ. Framing Robin Hood: temporality and textuality in Anthony Munday's Huntington plays. *In* (pp. 113–28) **3576.**

3513. PETERS, JILL. The role of Pocahontas and Sacagawea in the creation of new American mythology. *See* **7851.**

3514. PHILLIPS, HELEN. Introduction: studying Robin Hood. *In* (pp. 9–20) **3576.**

3515. —— Robin Hood, the prioress of Kirklees, and Charlotte Brontë. *In* (pp. 154–66) **3576.**

3516. —— (ed.). Robin Hood: medieval and post-medieval. *See* **3576.**

3517. POTTER, LOIS. Robin Hood and the fairies: Alfred Noyes' *Sherwood*. *In* (pp. 167–80) **3576.**

3518. QUINTELLI-NEARY, MARGUERITE. Establishing boundaries in the Irish American West. EtIr (29:2) 2004, 43–57.

3519. RODRIGUEZ, SUSANNAH. Universal harmony and the trickster in the works of Zora Neale Hurston and Lydia Cabrera. *See* **17138.**

3520. SAWIN, PATRICIA. Listening for a life: a dialogic ethnography of Bessie Eldreth through her songs and stories. *See* **3587.**

3521. SHARPE, JAMES. Dick Turpin: the myth of the English highway. (Bibl. 2004, 3677.) Rev. by David Wootton in LRB (27:3) 2005, 21–2.

3522. THOMAS, SEAN.   In search of Sawney Bean. FortT (195) 2005, 38–41.

3523. TROOST, LINDA.   The noble peasant. *In* (pp. 145–53) **3576.**

3524. WAGNER, BRYAN.   Disarmed and dangerous: the strange history of Bras-Coupé. *See* **10347.**

3525. WESTWOOD, JENNIFER; SIMPSON, JACQUELINE.   The lore of the land: a guide to England's legends, from Spring-Heeled Jack to the Witches of Warboys. London; New York: Penguin, 2005. pp. ix, 917.

3526. WOOTTON, DAVID.   The road is still open. LRB (27:3) 2005, 21–2 (review-article). (Dick Turpin.)

3527. YOLEN, JANE.   Sleeping Arthur. Parabola (30:1) 2005, 76–8.

SONG, MUSIC, BALLAD

3528. ATKIN, GAVIN.   Nelson's praise: the legacy of music associated with Admiral Nelson. EDS (67:3) 2005, 8–10.

3529. BARBER, DAVID.   What ever became of the ballad? Parnassus (28:1/2) 2005, 1–51.

3530. BAYLES, MARTHA.   The strange career of folk music. MichQR (44:2) 2005, 304–17.

3531. BRAMMER, REBEKAH.   Bill Scott: a career overview. *See* **3480.**

3532. BROCKEN, MICHAEL.   The British folk revival, 1944–2002. Aldershot; Burlington, VT: Ashgate, 2003. pp. xii, 236. (Ashgate popular and folk music.) Rev. by Norma Waterson and Martin Carthy in FMJ (8:5) 2005, 646–9.

3533. CARLIN, BOB.   String bands in the North Carolina Piedmont. Jefferson, NC; London: McFarland, 2004. pp. 275. Rev. by Amy Davis in NCarF (52:1) 2005, 64–7.

3534. CASS, EDDIE.   'He's a star on his breast.' EDS (67:3) 2005, 11.

3535. COCLANIS, ANGELO P.; COCLANIS, PETER A.   Jazz funeral: a living tradition. *See* **3625.**

3536. COHEN, DANIEL A.   Martha Buck's copybook: New England tragedy verse and the scribal lineage of the American ballad tradition. PAAS (114:1) 2004, 137–86.

3537. COHEN, NORM.   Folk music: a regional exploration. Westport, CT; London: Greenwood Press, 2005. pp. xliii, 335. (Greenwood guides to American roots music.)

3538. CONSTANTINE, MARY-ANN; PORTER, GERALD.   Fragments and meaning in traditional song: from the Blues to the Baltic. Foreword by Barre Toelken. Oxford; New York: OUP for the British Academy, 2003. pp. xiii, 261. (British Academy postdoctoral fellowship monographs.) Rev. by David Atkinson in Folklore (116:2) 2005, 236–8.

3539. COOPER, HELEN.   Thomas of Erceldoune: romance as prophecy. *In* (pp. 171–87) **4555.**

3540. CROFT, CLARY.   The Helen Creighton Fonds at the Public Archives of Nova Scotia. CFMB (38:2) 2004, 37–9.

3541. DAVIS, W. EUGENE.   Folk songs in the shearing-supper scene: John Schlesinger's movie version of *Far from the Madding Crowd*. *See* **11115.**

3542. DONLEAVY, KEVIN.   Strings of life: conversations with old-time musicians from Virginia and North Carolina. Blacksburg, VA: Pocahontas Press, 2004. pp. iv, 347. Rev. by Mark Freed in AppalJ (32:4) 2005, 495–7; by Ivan M. Tribe in JSH (71:4) 2005, 937–9.

3543. DOUGLAS, MALCOLM (reviser); CARTHY, MARTIN (foreword).   Classic English folk songs. Sel. and ed. by R. Vaughan Williams and A. L. Lloyd. With a new bibliography by David Atkinson. (Bibl. 2004, 3701.) Rev. by Roy Palmer in FMJ (8:5) 2005, 662–4.

3544. 'DUNGBEETLE'.   A veritable dungheap. EDS (67:2) 2005, 18. (*The Young Man's Lamentation.*)

3545. DUNNETT, BRIAN.   Railways: a popular theme in Australian country music. AF (19) 2004, 22–35.

3546. FANANY, REBECCA; FANANY, RUNA.   From Andersonville to the streets of New York: the evolution of a tune. See **3677**.

3547. FEFFER, STEVE.   Extending the breaks: *Fires in the Mirror* in the context of Hip Hop structure, style, and culture. See **19483**.

3548. GARABEDIAN, STEVEN.   Reds, Whites, and the Blues: Lawrence Gellert, *Negro Songs of Protest*, and the Left-wing folk-song revival. AmQ (57:1) 2005, 179–206.

3549. GOLDSMITH, THOMAS (ed.).   The bluegrass reader. Urbana: Illinois UP, 2004. pp. 376. Rev. by William S. Hamilton in AppalJ (32:3) 2005, 380.

3550. GRAY, DOUGLAS.   Everybody's Robin Hood. *In* (pp. 21–41) **3576**.

3551. GREEN, RICHARD FIRTH.   The hermit and the outlaw: new evidence for Robin Hood's death? *In* (pp. 51–9) **3576**.

3552. GREENHILL, PAULINE.   Radical? Feminist? Nationalist? The Canadian paradox of Edith Fowke. CFMB (37:3) 2003, 1–9.

3553. GREGORY, DAVID.   The Creighton–Senior collaboration, 1932–51. CFMB (38:2) 2004, 18–35.

3554. ——   Helen Creighton and the traditional songs of Nova Scotia. CFMB (38:2) 2004, 1–17.

3555. HALLI, ROBERT W., JR (ed.).   An Alabama songbook: ballads, folksongs, and spirituals. Collected by Byron Arnold. Tuscaloosa; London: Alabama UP, 2004. pp. xxv, 299. Rev. by Ray B. Browne in JAC (28:1) 2005, 132; by Ivan M. Tribe in JSH (71:4) 2005, 937–9.

3556. HAWORTH, ROBERT.   Chris Kempster, musician, 1933–2004: a true native voice. AF (19) 2004, 7–9.

3557. HEPPA, CHRISTOPHER.   Harry Cox and his friends: song transmission in an East Norfolk singing community c.1896–1960. FMJ (8:5) 2005, 569–93.

3558. HIRSH, JOHN C. (ed.).   Medieval lyric: Middle English lyrics, ballads, and carols. See **4618**.

3559. HOFFMAN, DEAN A.   'I wyll be thy true servaunte / And trewely serve thee': guildhall minstrelsy in the *Gest of Robyn Hode*. TDR (49:2) 2005, 119–34.

3560. HOWSON, KATIE (ed.).   Blyth voices: folk songs collected in Southwold by Ralph Vaughan Williams in 1910. Stowmarket: East Anglian Traditional

Music Trust, 2003. pp. 47. (Musical score.) Rev. by Jacqueline Patten in FMJ (8:5) 2005, 649–51.

3561. JONES, MICHAEL. Judas and the many 'betrayals' of Bob Dylan. *In* (pp. 55–78) **16199.**

3562. LEWIS, JACOB. The origins and evolution of *In the Jailhouse Now*. OvR (32:1/2) 2005, 37–44.

3563. LONG-WILGUS, ELEANOR R. Naomi Wise: creation, re-creation, and continuity in an American ballad tradition. (Bibl. 2004, 3728.) Rev. by Stephen D. Winick in WF (64:1/2) 2005, 149–51.

3564. MCKEAN, THOMAS A. (ed.). The flowering thorn: international ballad studies. (Bibl. 2004, 3733.) Rev. by Kirsten Kearney in ScSR (6:1) 2005, 133–4; by James Moreira in WF (64:1/2) 2005, 119–21.

3565. MILLS, JERRY LEATH (introd.). The spawning of *King Mackerel*. NCLR (14) 2005, 22–3.

3566. MOORE, SARAH J. Fostering local identity: great big sea, trad-pop and folkksong. CFMB (39:1) 2005, 6–13.

3567. MURPHY, ANTHONY G. Singing his America: narrative strategies of dissonance in the story songs of Steve Earle. *In* (pp. 137–49) **9168.**

3568. O'CONNOR, PATRICK. Minstrel and medicine shows: creating a market for the Blues. OvR (32:1/2) 2005, 57–68.

3569. OSTENDORF, ANN. Song catchers, ballad makers, and new social historians: the historiography of Appalachian music. THQ (63:3) 2004, 192–202.

3570. PALMER, ROY. Nelson's death. EDS (67:3) 2005, 6–7.

3571. PAPE, WALTER. Empathized with immediacy: improvisation, Romantic folk song and Goethe's concept of the 'born poet'. *See* **10328.**

3572. PAVLIĆ, ED. Open the unusual door: visions from the dark window in Yusef Komunyakaa's early poems. *See* **17531.**

3573. PEARCY, ROY. The literary Robin Hood: character and function in Fitts 1, 2, and 4 of the *Gest of Robyn Hode*. *In* (pp. 60–8) **3576.**

3574. PEARSALL, DEREK. Little John and the ballad of *Robin Hood and the Monk*. *In* (pp. 42–50) **3576.**

3575. PERRET, XAVIER. An annotated text of *The Hunting of the Cheviot*, with a French rendition. EngS (86:1) 2005, 1–39.

3576. PHILLIPS, HELEN (ed.). Robin Hood: medieval and post-medieval. Dublin; Portland, OR: Four Courts Press, 2005. pp. 197. Rev. by Jeffrey Richards in Arthuriana (15:4) 2005, 75–6.

3577. PITTOCK, MURRAY G. H. Sources and dates for the Jacobite song: II. Archives (31:112) 2005, 1–7.

3578. POLLARD, A. J. Imagining Robin Hood: the late medieval stories in historical context. *See* **4468.**

3579. PORTER, GERALD. 'The blood was frozen in their veins': survival at sea as a *topos* in Canadian song. *In* (pp. 130–47) **12912.**

3580. —— 'No language, no land': bilingualism and the Irish rebel song. *In* (pp. 318–26) **3331.**

3581. PORTER, JAMES. The traditional ballad: requickened text or performative genre? ScSR (4:1) 2003, 24–40.

3582. RADANO, RONALD. Lying up a nation: race and Black music. Chicago, IL; London: Chicago UP, 2003. pp. xix, 417. Rev. by William Kenney in AAR (39:1/2) 2005, 259–61.

3583. ROBSON, PETER. Thomas Hardy and *The Outlandish Knight*. See **11159**.

3584. ROUD, STEVE, *et al*. Still growing: English traditional songs and singers from the Cecil Sharp Collection. London: English Folk Dance and Song Soc. in assn with Folk South West, 2003. pp. 121. Rev. by Roy Palmer in FMJ (8:5) 2005, 662–4.

3585. ROUSE, ANDREW C. The remunerated vernacular singer: from medieval England to the post-war revival. New York; Frankfurt: Lang, 2005. pp. 212. (European univ. studies, XIV: Anglo-Saxon language and literature, 415.)

3586. RUTKOFF, PETER; SCOTT, WILL. Preaching the Blues: the Mississippi Delta of Muddy Waters. KR (27:2) 2005, 129–47.

3587. SAWIN, PATRICIA. Listening for a life: a dialogic ethnography of Bessie Eldreth through her songs and stories. Logan: Utah State UP, 2004. pp. xiv, 254. Rev. by Joyce Joines Newman in NCarF (52:1) 2005, 58–63; by Jill Stubington in AF (20) 2005, 238–44.

3588. SCHROEDER, PATRICIA R. Robert Johnson, mythmaking, and contemporary American culture. Urbana: Illinois UP, 2004. pp. x, 192. (Music in American life.) Rev. by Ben Harker in Mod/Mod (12:2) 2005, 348–9; by Mike Barry in CFMB (39:1) 2005, 30; by Robert Cochran in ArkR (36:3) 2005, 225–6.

3589. SMITH, BRUCE R. Female impersonation in early modern ballads. *In* (pp. 281–304) **5225**.

3590. SMITH, ROBERT JAMES. Swinging the swag: Warren Fahey A.M. today, fair dinkum. AF (20) 2005, 27–34.

3591. STUBINGTON, JILL. Phyl Lobl and the Australian folk revival. AF (19) 2004, 238–51.

3592. THOMAS, PHIL. *D'Ye Ken Sam Hughes?* and two other songs from the Great War, 1914–1918. CFMB (37:4) 2003, 10–15.

3593. THORN, JOHN. Murder and mayhem, tra-la! The Saugerties bard. VoicesNY (31:3/4) 2005, 38–43. (Henry Sherman Backus.)

3594. VALDÉS MIYARES, RUBÉN. Sturdy stories: medieval narrative into popular ballad. See **4490**.

3595. VIKÁR, LÁSZLÓ; PANAGAPKA, JEANETTE (eds). Songs of the north woods. Calgary, Alta: Calgary UP, 2004. pp. xviii, (music) 108. Rev. by David Gregory in CFMB (39:2) 2005, 18.

3596. WILENTZ, SEAN; MARCUS, GREIL. The rose & the briar: death, love, and liberty in the American ballad. New York; London: Norton, 2005. pp. viii, 406. Rev. by Paul Kingsbury in JCM (24:2) 2005, 50–4.

3597. WOLFE, CHARLES K.; AKENSON, JAMES E. (eds). Country music goes to war. Lexington: Kentucky UP, 2005. pp. viii, 250. Rev. by Paul Robertson in AppalJ (32:4) 2005, 492–5.

3598. WOLZ, LYN A.   Resources in the Vaughan Williams Memorial Library: the Anne Geddes Gilchrist manuscript collection. FMJ (8:5) 2005, 619–39.

DANCE AND DRAMA

3599. ATKIN, GAVIN.   Nelson's praise: the legacy of music associated with Admiral Nelson. *See* **3528**.

3600. BUNGERT, HEIKE.   'Feast of fools': German American carnival as a medium of identity formation, 1854–1914. Amst (48:3) 2003, 325–44.

3601. CASS, EDDIE.   The pace-egg plays of the Calder Valley. London: Folklore Soc., 2004. pp. 70. Rev. by Alan Gailey in FolkL (43) 2004/05, 128; by E. C. Cawte in FMJ (8:5) 2005, 664–6.

3602. FERRIS, LESLEY.   On the streets of Notting Hill: carnival as/is theatre. THS (25) 2005, 61–76.

3603. FORSE, JAMES H.   Secularizing the saint: the journey of St George's Day from feast day to horse race. PCR (16:2) 2005, 37–44.

3604. GREENFIELD, PETER.   Regional performance in Shakespeare's time. *In* (pp. 243–51) **5914**.

3605. PAYNE, IAN.   The almain in Britain, *c*.1549–*c*.1675. Aldershot; Burlington, VT: Ashgate, 2003. pp. xviii, 268, (plates) 3. Rev. by Anne Daye in FMJ (8:5) 2005, 666–8.

3606. SCHIEFFELIN, EDWARD L.   Moving performance to text: can performance be transcribed? OT (20:1) 2005, 80–92.

3607. SCHOFIELD, DEREK.   A black and white issue? EDS (67:2) 2005, 12–14.

3608. STOKES, JAMES.   Women and performance: evidences of universal cultural suffrage in medieval and early modern Lincolnshire. *In* (pp. 25–43) **5225**.

3609. TOMPSETT, ADELA RUTH.   'London is the place for me': performance and identity in Notting Hill Carnival. THS (25) 2005, 43–60.

3610. WATT, FRANCES.   Tapatak. EDS (67:2) 2005, 16–17.

3611. WEBB, ROWAN.   Notes from under the bed: Rowan's recollections of the Colonial Dancers. AF (19) 2004, 210–36.

3612. WHITE, PAUL WHITFIELD.   Holy Robin Hood! Carnival, parish guilds, and the outlaw tradition. *In* (pp. 67–89) **5268**.

3613. WILLIAMS, GWENO; FINDLAY, ALISON; HODGSON-WRIGHT, STEPHANIE.   Payments, permits and punishments: women performers and the politics of place. *In* (pp. 45–67) **5225**.

CUSTOM AND BELIEF

3614. ACKER, PAUL.   A Middle English prognostication by winds in Columbia University, Plimpton MS 260. *See* **4659**.

3615. ALMOND, PHILIP C. (comp.).   Demonic possession and exorcism in early modern England: contemporary texts and their cultural contexts. *See* **5329**.

3616. BAKER, RONALD L.   *Miracle Magazine* in the sixties: mass media narratives of healings and blessings. JAF (118:468) 2005, 204–18.

3617. BARKUN, MICHAEL.   A culture of conspiracy: apocalyptic visions in contemporary America. Berkeley; London: California UP, 2003. pp. xii, 243.

(Comparative studies in religion and society, 15.) Rev. by Reet Hiiemäe in WF (64:1/2) 2005, 121–3.

3618. BROWN, TOM. 'The Hunting of the Earl of Rone': the emergence of 'new' folklore motifs: individual creativity and group control. Folklore (116:2) 2005, 201–13.

3619. BURNS, WILLIAM E. Witch hunts in Europe and America: an encyclopedia. Westport, CT; London: Greenwood Press, 2003. pp. xli, 359. Rev. by Robert H. Landrum in SixCJ (36:1) 2005, 231–2.

3620. CAVENDER, ANTHONY. Folk medicine in southern Appalachia. (Bibl. 2004, 3783.) Rev. by Sandra Lee Barney in JAH (91:3) 2004, 1028–9; by J. K. Crellin in BHM (79:2) 2005, 351–2; by Kenneth DeShane in TFSB (61:1) 2005, 23–4.

3621. —— A midwife's commonplace book. AppalJ (32:2) 2005, 182–90.

3622. CHIREAU, YVONNE P. Black magic: religion and the African American conjuring tradition. Berkeley; London: California UP, 2003. pp. ix, 222. Rev. by Michael Pickering in Folklore (116:2) 2005, 231–2; by Eoghan C. Ballard in WF (64:1/2) 2005, 144–6.

3623. CLARK, LYNN SCHOFIELD. From angels to aliens: teenagers, the media, and the supernatural. Oxford; New York: OUP, 2003. pp. xii, 292. Rev. by Reet Hiiemäe in WF (64:1/2) 2005, 121–3.

3624. CLARKE, DAVID. The Angel of Mons: phantom soldiers and ghostly guardians. Chichester; Hoboken, NJ: Wiley, 2004. pp. x, 278, (plates) 8. Rev. by Jacqueline Simpson in Folklore (116:2) 2005, 232–3.

3625. COCLANIS, ANGELO P.; COCLANIS, PETER A. Jazz funeral: a living tradition. SoCult (11:2) 2005, 86–92.

3626. CRANE, SUSAN. The performance of self: ritual, clothing, and identity during the Hundred Years War. (Bibl. 2004, 3785.) Rev. by Claire Sponsler in SAC (26) 2004, 375–8; by Daisy Delogu in MP (103:1) 2005, 95–8.

3627. CRESSY, DAVID. Society and culture in early modern England. Aldershot: Ashgate Variorum, 2003. 1 vol. (various pagings). Rev. by Gary Jenkins in SixCJ (36:2) 2005, 475–6.

3628. DAYAN, COLIN. Legal terrors. See **7642.**

3629. DELONG, ANNE. 'What are these?': hunting for witches in Macbeth. See **6540.**

3630. EVANS, MICHAEL R. Robin Hood in the landscape: place-name evidence and mythology. In (pp. 181–7) **3576.**

3631. FAHS, ALICE; WAUGH, JOAN (eds). The memory of the Civil War in American culture. See **9644.**

3632. FISCHER-LICHTE, ERIKA. Theatre, sacrifice, ritual: exploring forms of political theatre. London; New York: Routledge, 2005. pp. viii, 290.

3633. GÓMEZ LARA, MANUEL. Discourses on health and leisure and modern constructions of holidays at the Restoration spas. In (pp. 202–27) **5167.**

3634. HALL, ALARIC. Calling the shots: the Old English remedy Gif hors ofscoten sie and Anglo-Saxon elf-shot. See **4357.**

3635. —— Getting shot of elves: healing, witchcraft and fairies in the Scottish witchcraft trials. Folklore (116:1) 2005, 19–36.

3636. JOHNSON, RICHARD FREEMAN. Saint Michael the Archangel in medieval English legend. *See* **4441.**

3637. JOYNER, GRAHAM. John Gale and the yahoo of the Brindabella Mountains. AF (19) 2004, 173–83.

3638. KACHUN, MITCH. Festivals of freedom: memory and meaning in African American emancipation celebrations, 1808–1915. (Bibl. 2004, 3809.) Rev. by Virginia Whatley Smith in AAR (38:3) 2004, 535–7; by Elizabeth Regosin in JAH (91:3) 2004, 1026–7; by Chiou-Ling Yeh in AmQ (57:1) 2005, 279–88.

3639. LIM, ENG-BENG. The Mardi Gras boys of Singapore's English-language theatre. *See* **20605.**

3640. LINDAHL, CARL. Ostensive healing: pilgrimage to the San Antonio ghost tracks. JAF (118:468) 2005, 164–85.

3641. MAGLIOCCO, SABINA. Witching culture: folklore and neo-paganism in America. Philadelphia: Pennsylvania UP, 2004. pp. 268. (Contemporary ethnography.) Rev. by Jacqueline Simpson in Folklore (116:2) 2005, 238–9.

3642. MAXWELL-STUART, P. G. Witch hunters: professional prickers, unwitchers & witch finders of the Renaissance. Stroud; Charleston, SC: Tempus, 2003. pp. 157, (plates) 8. Rev. by Charles W. Clark in RQ (58:3) 2005, 1007–8.

3643. MOFFITT, JOHN F. Picturing extraterrestrials: alien images in modern culture. Amherst, NY: Prometheus, 2003. pp. 595, (plates) 16. Rev. by Scott Lupo in JPC (38:3) 2005, 588–9.

3644. MORAVEC, MARK. Strange illuminations: 'Min Min Lights' – Australian 'ghost light' stories. AF (19) 2004, 184–209.

3645. NICOL, DAVID. Interrogating the Devil: social and demonic pressure in *The Witch of Edmonton. See* **7357.**

3646. NICOL, VALÉRIE DE COURVILLE. Personal ghost stories and the hyper-rationalization of fear. *See* **3510.**

3647. O'CONNOR, PATRICK. Minstrel and medicine shows: creating a market for the Blues. *See* **3568.**

3648. OLDBRIDGE, DARREN. Strange histories: the Trial of the Pig, the Walking Dead, and other matters of fact from the medieval and Renaissance worlds. London; New York: Routledge, 2005. pp. x, 198, (plates) 8. Rev. by Thomas V. Cohen in TMR, Sept. 2005.

3649. RADFORD, ANDREW. Hardy's Tess, Jane Harrison and the twilight of a goddess. *See* **11153.**

3650. RICHARDSON, JUDITH. Possessions: the history and uses of haunting in the Hudson Valley. Cambridge, MA; London: Harvard UP, 2003. pp. xi, 296. Rev. by John McWilliams in EAL (40:1) 2005, 206–9; by Russ Castronovo in JAH (91:4) 2005, 1477–8; by Karen Duffy in FHist (22) 2005, 59–60.

3651. ROGERS, NICHOLAS. Henry VI and the proposed canonisation of King Alfred. *In* (pp. 211–20) **4488.**

3652. ROGERS, PAT. The maypole in the Strand: Pope and the politics of revelry. *See* **8900.**

3653. ROUD, STEVE. The Penguin guide to the superstitions of Britain and Ireland. London; New York: Penguin, 2003. pp. xx, 546. Rev. by Gearóid Ó Crualaoich in FolkL (43) 2004/05, 127–8.

3654. ROWLANDS, ALISON. Contextualizing magic and witchcraft in the novels of Margery Allingham: the examples of *Sweet Danger* and *Look to the Lady*. See **15125**.

3655. RYAN, J. S. Folkloristic ways of looking at – and beyond – the recent phenomenon of roadside memorials, crosses and floral tributes. AF (19) 2004, 52–67.

3656. —— 'The great gaol by the sea' – the developing lore and associations of one such place of incarceration, Trial Bay Jail, New South Wales. See **17387**.

3657. RYTTING, ELIZABETH. Christmas as a reflexive commemoration. FF (36:1) 2005.

3658. SEAL, GRAHAM. Chook raffles, cracker nights and saints' days: the neglected study of Australian folk custom. AF (20) 2005, 209–26.

3659. SEMMENS, JASON. The witch of the west; or, The strange and wonderful history of Thomasine Blight; plainly setting forth her birth, life, death and prodigious burial. Plymouth: Jason Semmens, 2004. pp. 52. Rev. by Jacqueline Simpson in Folklore (116:3) 2005, 358–9.

3660. SMITH, J. B. Goats with cattle and hands from graves: towards a fresh look at our Insular superstitions. FolkL (43) 2004/05, 115–20.

3661. SMITH, ROBERT JAMES. The stockman and the legend. AF (19) 2004, 253–61 (review-article).

3662. STUBBS, CLARE; SUTTON, DAVID. A straunge and terrible wunder. FortT (195) 2005, 30–5. (Black Dog in British folklore.)

3663. TRUDEL, JEAN-LOUIS. Looking for little green men. See **14293**.

3664. TUCKER, ELIZABETH. Ghosts in mirrors: reflections of the self. JAF (118:468) 2005, 186–203.

3665. WOOD, SARAH. 'Serving the spirits': emergent identities in Nalo Hopkinson's *Brown Girl in the Ring*. See **17050**.

3666. WOODBRIDGE, LINDA. Shakespeare and magical grammar. In (pp. 84–98) **5167**.

3667. YOLEN, JANE. Sleeping Arthur. See **3527**.

MATERIAL CULTURE, TECHNIQUES AND OCCUPATIONS, FOLK ARTS AND CRAFTS

3668. BAYLESS, MARTHA. *Alea, tæfl*, and related games: vocabulary and context. In (pp. 9–27) **4221**.

3669. INCKLE, KAY. Who's hurting who? The ethics of engaging the marked body. See **20925**.

3670. LAMBKIN, BRIAN; MEEGAN, JENNIFER. The fabric of memory, identity and diaspora: an Irish needlework sampler in Australia with United States and Canadian connections. FolkL (43) 2004/05, 7–31.

3671. SCHEPER-HUGHES, NANCY. Anatomy of a quilt: the Gee's Bend Freedom Quilting Bee. SoCult (10:3) 2004, 88–98.

CHILDREN'S TRADITIONS

3672. BARTLETT, LESLEY.   It happened like this: the Dr Shoal stories of Shoal Creek Camp. OvR (32:1/2) 2005, 45–55.

3673. BENES, PETER (ed.); BENES, JANE MONTAGUE (assoc. ed.).   The worlds of children, 1620–1920. *See* **4078**.

3674. BRAMMER, REBEKAH.   Australian school playground games and rhyming from the 1950s. AF (20) 2005, 176–81.

3675. COOPER, LANA.   Lore, language and rhyming in the Australian playground. AF (20) 2005, 169–75.

3676. DARIEN-SMITH, KATE; FACTOR, JUNE (eds).   Child's play: Dorothy Howard and the folklore of Australian children. Carlton: Museum Victoria, 2005. pp. vii, 231. Rev. by J. S. Ryan in AF (20) 2005, 262–3.

3677. FANANY, REBECCA; FANANY, RUNA.   From Andersonville to the streets of New York: the evolution of a tune. AF (20) 2005, 227–37.

3678. JAMES, CYNTHIA.   From orature to literature in Jamaican and Trinidadian children's folk traditions. CLAQ (30:2) 2005, 164–78.

3679. JOLLEY, PHILIP.   The technological frontier: a view of some of its effects on the speech and play of today's children. *See* **3181**.

3680. JOSEPH, MICHAEL.   The rise and maiden flight of *Hannah Goose Nursery Rhymes.* LU (29:1) 2005, 16–37.

3681. THOMAS, JOSEPH T., JR.   Child poets and the poetry of the playground. ChildLit (32) 2004, 152–77.

ENGLISH LITERATURE

GENERAL LITERARY STUDIES

GENERAL

3682. Anon. Selected recent acquisitions briefly noted. *See* 344.

3683. —— Selected recent acquisitions briefly noted. *See* 345.

3684. —— Selected recent acquisitions briefly noted. *See* 346.

3685. —— Selected recent acquisitions briefly noted. *See* 347.

3686. —— (comp.). Bibliography. BBIAS (56) 2004, 11–391.

3687. —— (ed.). Insights into the dynamics of the English language and culture: conference proceedings. *See* 1368.

3688. Abbott, John L. (ed.). The selected essays of Donald Greene. Lewisburg, PA: Bucknell UP, 2004. pp. 355.

3689. Abelove, Henry. Deep gossip. Minneapolis; London: Minnesota UP, 2003. pp. xviii, 128. Rev. by Donald E. Hall in SAtlR (70:3) 2005, 124–7.

3690. Albertazzi, Silvia; Pelliconi, Claudia (eds). Cross-cultural encounters: literary perspectives. Rome: Officina, 2005. pp. 263. (Varietà di testi – varietà di lingue.)

3691. Altieri, Charles. The particulars of rapture: an aesthetics of the affects. Ithaca, NY; London: Cornell UP, 2004. pp. x, 299. Rev. by David Mikics in CL (57:2) 2005, 178–81; by Eric Rothstein in ConLit (46:1) 2005, 139–57; by Vincent Crapanzano in CLIO (35:1) 2005, 131–7.

3692. Antor, Heinz, *et al.* (eds). Refractions of Canada in European literature and culture. Berlin; New York: Mouton de Gruyter, 2005. pp. viii, 301.

3693. Applegate, Renae R. *Legacy* bookshelf. Legacy (22:1) 2005, 95–106.

3694. Aranda, José F., Jr. When we arrive: a new literary history of Mexican America. (Bibl. 2003, 3670.) Rev. by John M. Gonzalez in WAL (39:2) 2004, 244–5; by Ramon A. Gutierrez in PacHR (74:1) 2005, 140–1.

3695. Astell, Ann W. Joan of Arc and sacrificial authorship. (Bibl. 2004, 3842.) Rev. by Dominique Goy-Blanquet in MÆ (74:2) 2005, 337–8.

3696. Bak, Hans; Hoelbling, Walter (eds). 'Nature's nation' revisited: American concepts of nature from wonder to ecological crisis. Amsterdam: VU UP, 2003. pp. 478. (European contributions to American Studies, 49.)

3697. Balachandran, K. (ed.). Critical essays on American literature: a Festschrift to Dr L. Jeganatha Raja. New Delhi: Sarup, 2005. pp. xxiii, 307.

3698. —— Essays on Canadian literature. New Delhi: Sarup, 2003. pp. xvii, 162. Rev. by Kiriaki Massoura in BJCS (16:1) 2003, 205–6.

3699. Ballard, Sandra L.; Hudson, Patricia L. (eds). Listen here: women writing in Appalachia. (Bibl. 2004, 3847.) Rev. by Grace Toney Edwards in AppalJ (32:2) 2005, 269–71; by Carol Luther in TEJ (16) 2005, 57–8.

3700. Barash, David P.; Barash, Nanelle R. Madame Bovary's ovaries: a Darwinian look at literature. New York: Delacorte Press, 2005. pp. 262. Rev. by Denis Dutton in BkW, 7 Aug. 2005, 15.

3701. BARBER, RICHARD. The Holy Grail: imagination and belief. (Bibl. 2004, 3848.) Rev. by Julianne Smith in ChrisL (54:1) 2004, 133–5; by Laura D. Barefield in TMR, Sept. 2005; by Stefano Mula in JR (85:3) 2005, 494–5.

3702. BARTSCH, SHADI; BARTSCHERER, THOMAS (eds). Erotikon: essays on eros, ancient and modern. Chicago, IL; London: Chicago UP, 2005. pp. 338.

3703. BENNETT, ANDREW. The author. London; New York: Routledge, 2005. pp. vi, 151. (New critical idiom.)

3704. BERGER, HARRY, JR. Situated utterances: texts, bodies, and cultural representations. Introd. by Judith H. Anderson. New York: Fordham UP, 2005. pp. x, 585.

3705. BINHAMMER, KATHERINE; WOOD, JEANNE (eds). Women and literary history: 'for there she was'. (Bibl. 2003, 3687.) Rev. by Sasha Roberts in MLR (100:4) 2005, 1091–3; by Barbara K. Seeber in ECF (18:1) 2005, 147–9.

3706. BLACKBIRD, CHELSEA; NELSON, BARNEY (eds). Mary Austin's Southwest: an anthology of her literary criticism. See **15257**.

3707. BLACKFORD, HOLLY VIRGINIA. Out of this world: why literature matters to girls. Foreword by Carol Christ. (Bibl. 2004, 3855.) Rev. by Nathalie op de Beeck in CLAQ (30:1) 2005, 110–16.

3708. BLAUSTEIN, RICHARD. The thistle and the brier: historical links and cultural parallels between Scotland and Appalachia. Jefferson, NC; London: McFarland, 2003. pp. viii, 174. (Contributions to southern Appalachian studies, 7.) Rev. by Amy McNeese-Mechan in AppalJ (32:2) 2005, 214–32.

3709. BLODGETT, E. D. Five-part invention: a history of literary history in Canada. (Bibl. 2004, 3856.) Rev. by Robert Lecker in LRC (11:10) 2003, 22–3; by Faye Hammill in BJCS (17:1) 2004, 158–9.

3710. BOEHRER, BRUCE THOMAS. Parrot culture: our 2,500-year-long fascination with the world's most talkative bird. (Bibl. 2004, 3857.) Rev. by Robin Dix in MÆ (74:2) 2005, 339–40.

3711. BOGUE, RONALD. Deleuze on literature. London; New York: Routledge, 2003. pp. x, 213. (Deleuze and the arts.) Rev. by Jill Marsden in BJA (45:1) 2005, 97–101.

3712. BOOKER, CHRISTOPHER. The seven basic plots: why we tell stories. London; New York: Continuum, 2004. pp. viii, 278. Rev. by Carolyne Larrington in TLS, 21 Jan. 2005, 32; by Denis Dutton in BkW, 8 May 2005, 8; by David Parker in DickQ (22:3) 2005, 189–92.

3713. BRAY, ALAN. The friend. Chicago, IL; London: Chicago UP, 2003. pp. 380. Rev. by David Wallace in Spec (80:3) 2005, 845–8.

3714. BREEN, MARGARET SÖNSER. Understanding evil: an interdisciplinary approach. Amsterdam; Atlanta, GA: Rodopi, 2003. pp. xiii, 222. (At the interface/ Probing the boundaries.) Rev. by Claire Colebrook in EJES (9:1) 2005, 98–102.

3715. BROGAN, MARTHA L. A kaleidoscope of digital American literature. Washington, DC: Digital Library Federation, 2005. pp. x, 176. (Strategies and tools for the digital library.)

3716. BROOKS, JOANNA. American Lazarus: religion and the rise of African American and Native American literatures. (Bibl. 2004, 3860.) Rev. by Timothy

B. Powell in JAH (91:3) 2004, 998–9; by Lamont DeHaven King in JAAH (89:4) 2004, 362–3; by Laura Murray in EAL (40:2) 2005, 395–402; by Phillip H. Round in EAL (40:2) 2005, 375–85; by Karen A. Weyler in SAtlR (70:2) 2005, 186–91.

3717. BROTTMAN, MIKITA. Funny peculiar: Gershon Legman and the psychopathology of humor. Hillsdale, NJ: Analytic Press, 2004. pp. xxiii, 174. Rev. by Gretchen Martin in SAH (third series) (11) 2004, 99–101.

3718. BROWN, DEBORAH. What part of 'know' don't you understand? Monist (88:1) 2005, 11–35.

3719. BROWN, JAMES S.; YARBROUGH, SCOTT D. A practical introduction to literary study. Upper Saddle River, NJ: Prentice Hall, 2005. pp. ix, 342.

3720. BRUNEL, PIERRE. Mythopoétique des genres. (Bibl. 2004, 3862.) Rev. by Marc-Mathieu Munch in RLC (78:2) 2004, 245–6.

3721. BUBÍKOVÁ, ŠÁRKA. The formation and transformation of the American literary canon. In (pp. 25–8) 3753.

3722. BURGER, MARY (ed.). Biting the error: writers explore narrative. Toronto: Coach House, 2004. pp. 301.

3723. BURNETT, ARCHIE. Allusions and echoes in Kingsley Amis's letters. See 15147.

3724. BURNHAM, DOUGLAS; GIACCHERINI, ENRICO (eds). The poetics of Transubstantiation: from theology to metaphor. Aldershot; Burlington, VT: Ashgate, 2005. pp. xiv, 181. (Studies in European cultural transition, 27.)

3725. CAESAR, TERRY. Anthologies, literature, and theory in Japan. In (pp. 298–325) 3749.

3726. CAPLAN, BEN. Creatures of fiction, myth, and imagination. APQ (41:4) 2004, 331–9.

3727. CAREY, JOHN. What good are the arts? London; Boston, MA: Faber & Faber, 2005. pp. xii, 286. Rev. by Frank Kermode in LRB (27:12) 2005, 21–2.

3728. CARROLL, NOËL. Two comic plot structures. Monist (88:1) 2005, 154–83.

3729. CASANOVA, PASCALE. The world republic of letters. Trans. by M. B. DeBevoise. Cambridge, MA; London: Harvard UP, 2004. pp. xiii, 420. (Convergences.)

3730. CASTLE, TERRY (ed.). The literature of lesbianism: a historical anthology from Ariosto to Stonewall. (Bibl. 2004, 3874.) Rev. by Kate Chedgzoy in GLQ (11:3) 2005, 457–67.

3731. CHENEY, PATRICK; DE ARMAS, FREDERICK A. (eds). European literary careers: the author from Antiquity to the Renaissance. (Bibl. 2004, 5176.) Rev. by María Jesús Lorenzo Modia in MLR (100:1) 2005, 193–4.

3732. CHIALANT, MARIA TERESA (ed.). Il personaggio in letteratura. (Bibl. 2004, 3876.) Rev. by Chiara Lombardi in Indice (2005:7/8) 18.

3733. CHISHOLM, DIANNE. Queer constellations: subcultural space in the wake of the city. Minneapolis; London: Minnesota UP, 2005. pp. xix, 353.

3734. CHOVANEC, JAN (ed.). Theory and practice in English Studies: proceedings from the eighth conference of English, American and Canadian studies: vol. 4. Brno: Masaryk Univ., 2005. pp. 283.

3735. COELSCH-FOISNER, SABINE; GÖRTSCHACHER, WOLFGANG (eds). The author as reader: textual visions and revisions. *See* **523**.

3736. CONOLLY, OLIVER. Pleasure and pain in literature. PhilL (29:2) 2005, 305–20.

3737. COOK, JAMES L. Reproaching the military hero *sans peur*. WLA (17:1/2) 2005, 87–101.

3738. CROW, CHARLES L. (ed.). A companion to the regional literatures of America. (Bibl. 2004, 3883.) Rev. by Kathleen A. Boardman in GPQ (24:4) 2004, 298–9.

3739. CSICSILA, JOSEPH. Canons by consensus: critical trends and American literature anthologies. Foreword by Tom Quirk. Tuscaloosa; London: Alabama UP, 2004. pp. xx, 262. (Studies in American literary realism and naturalism.) Rev. by Christopher M. Kuipers in JMMLA (38:1) 2005, 140–3.

3740. CULLINAN, BERNICE E.; KUNZEL, BONNIE L.; WOOTEN, DEBORAH A. (eds). The Continuum encyclopedia of young adult literature. London; New York: Continuum, 2005. pp. 944.

3741. DAMROSCH, DAVID. From the Old World to the whole world. *In* (pp. 31–46) **3749**.

3742. —— What is world literature? (Bibl. 2004, 3886.) Rev. by Bruce Krajewski in ColLit (32:4) 2005, 234–6.

3743. DAVISON, CAROL MARGARET. Anti-Semitism and British gothic literature. Basingstoke; New York: Palgrave Macmillan, 2004. pp. ix, 227. Rev. by Max Fincher in TLS, 11 Nov. 2005, 27.

3744. DEATS, SARA MUNSON; LENKER, LAGRETTA TALLENT; PERRY, MERRY G. (eds). War and words: horror and heroism in the literature of warfare. Lanham, MD: Lexington, 2004. pp. x, 353.

3745. DE CHIARA, MARINA (ed.). Oltre la gabbia: ordine coloniale e arte di frontiera. Rome: Meltemi, 2005. pp. 167. (Meltemi.edu, 42.)

3746. DEGUZMÁN, MARÍA. Spain's long shadow: the Black Legend, off-Whiteness, and Anglo-American empire. Minneapolis; London: Minnesota UP, 2005. pp. xxxiii, 372.

3747. DE LA CRUZ, ISABEL; VÁZQUEZ, NILA. New approaches in textual editing: a selection of electronic editions under analysis. *See* **534**.

3748. DE PAULO, CRAIG J. N.; MESSINA, PATRICK; STIER, MARC (eds). Ambiguity in the Western mind. New York; Frankfurt: Lang, 2005. pp. xv, 248.

3749. DI LEO, JEFFREY R. (ed.). On anthologies: politics and pedagogy. Lincoln; London: Nebraska UP, 2004. pp. 431.

3750. DIRDA, MICHAEL. Bound to please: an extraordinary one-volume literary education: essays on great writers and their books. New York; London: Norton, 2005. pp. xxvii, 525. Rev. by George Garrett in HC (42:1) 2005, 22.

3751. DONIGER, WENDY. The woman who pretended to be who she was: myths of self-imitation. New Delhi; Oxford: OUP, 2005. pp. xii, 272. Rev. by Bharat Tandon in TLS, 19 & 26 Aug. 2005, 12–13; by Gillian Bennett in LRB (27:21) 2005, 29–30.

3752. DONOGHUE, DENIS. Speaking of beauty. (Bibl. 2004, 3896.) Rev. by David Mason in SewR (111:4) 2003, cxxvii–cxxix.

3753. DRÁBEK, PAVEL; CHOVANEC, JAN (eds). Theory and practice in English Studies: proceedings from the seventh conference of English, American and Canadian studies: vol. 2. Brno: Masarykova Univ., 2004. pp. 206.

3754. DUNNIGAN, SARAH M.; HARKER, C. MARIE; NEWLYN, EVELYN S. (eds). Women and the feminine in medieval and early modern Scottish writing. Basingstoke; New York: Palgrave Macmillan, 2004. pp. xxx, 238. Rev. by Joanna Martin in NQ (52:4) 2005, 529–31.

3755. ECO, UMBERTO. On literature. Trans. by Martin McLaughlin. Orlando, FL: Harcourt, 2004. pp. x, 334. Rev. by Paul Duguid in TLS, 10 June 2005, 26–7.

3756. EDELSON, MARIA (ed.). Studies in literature and culture in honour of Professor Irena Janicka-Świderska. Łódź: Łódź UP, 2002. pp. 308.

3757. EDGECOMBE, RODNEY STENNING. Some literary uses of the manual. Genre (37:3/4) 2004, 373–94.

3758. EDMOND, ROD; SMITH, VANESSA (eds). Islands in history and representation. (Bibl. 2004, 3900.) Rev. by Jürgen Kramer in JSBC (11:1) 2004, 98–9; by Susan Parman in Journeys (5:2) 2004, 100–2; by David James in TexP (19:2) 2005, 395–401.

3759. EDWARDS, PHILIP. Pilgrimage and literary tradition. Cambridge; New York: CUP, 2005. pp. ix, 218.

3760. EGAN, KEN, JR. Hope and dread in Montana literature. (Bibl. 2004, 3901.) Rev. by George Venn in PacHR (73:3) 2004, 499–500; by Daniel Lamberton in PacNQ (96:1) 2004/05, 39–40; by Sue Hart in GPQ (25:1) 2005, 48–9.

3761. EISENHAUER, ROBERT. Paradox and perspicacity: horizons of knowledge in the literary text. New York; Frankfurt: Lang, 2005. pp. xiii, 337. (Studies on themes and motifs in literature, 76.)

3762. ELIAS, CAMELIA. The fragment: towards a history and poetics of a performative genre. New York; Frankfurt: Lang, 2005. pp. ix, 397. (European univ. studies, XVIII: Comparative literature, 112.) Rev. by Franca Bellarsi in BELL (ns 3) 2005, 210–12.

3763. ELLIOTT, MICHAEL A.; STOKES, CLAUDIA (eds). American literary studies: a methodological reader. (Bibl. 2003, 3733.) Rev. by Winfried Fluck in CLIO (34:1/2) 2004, 229–35.

3764. ELLMANN, MAUD. Writing like a rat. See 16266.

3765. ENGELHARDT, ELIZABETH S. D. The tangled roots of feminism, environmentalism, and Appalachian literature. (Bibl. 2004, 3905.) Rev. by Judith Hatchett in KenPR (19) 2004, 64–5; by Amanda Hayes in AppH (33:2) 2005, 84–5; by Marjorie Pryse in Legacy (22:1) 2005, 83–4.

3766. ERMIDA, ISABEL. Humor, linguagem e narrativa: para una análise do discurso literário cómico. Minho, Portugal: Univ. do Minho, Centro de Estudos Humanísticos, 2003. pp. 352. (Poliedro, 14.) Rev. by Teresa Adão in Humor (18:1) 2005, 111–15.

3767. ESONWANNE, UZOMA. *Calibrations*: literary reference and the ethics of reading. *See* 21025.

3768. FADIMAN, ANNE (ed.). Rereadings. New York: Farrar, Straus, & Giroux, 2005. pp. xxi, 244.

3769. FALCONER, GAVIN. *Sched apon the rude?* Reflections on Scots and religion. *See* 2926.

3770. FETTERLEY, JUDITH; PRYSE, MARJORIE. Writing out of place: regionalism, women, and American literary culture. (Bibl. 2004, 3909.) Rev. by Carolyn Karcher in TSWL (24:1) 2005, 159–62.

3771. FINKE, LAURIE. The hidden curriculum. *In* (pp. 395–404) **3749**.

3772. FLANAGAN, THOMAS. There you are: writings on Irish and American literature and history. Ed. by Christopher Cahill. Preface by Seamus Heaney. New York: New York Review, 2004. pp. xx, 488. Rev. by Lawrence J. McCaffrey in ILS (25:1) 2005, 21–2.

3773. FOEHR-JANSSENS, YASMINA; MÉTRY, EMMANUELLE (eds). La Fortune: thèmes, représentations, discours. Geneva: Droz, 2003. pp. 220. (Recherches et rencontres, 19.) Rev. by Catherine Attwood in MÆ (73:1) 2004, 140–1.

3774. FOX, ROBIN. Male bonding in the epics and romances. *In* (pp. 126–44) **14807**.

3775. FREIBURG, RUDOLF; GRUSS, SUSANNE (eds). 'But vindicate the ways of God to man': literature and theodicy. Tübingen: Stauffenburg, 2004. pp. 571. (ZAA studies, 20.)

3776. FROHOCK, RICHARD. Heroes of empire: the British imperial protagonist in America, 1596–1764. *See* **7240**.

3777. FROST, BRIAN J. The essential guide to werewolf literature. (Bibl. 2004, 3916.) Rev. by J. Robert Craig in JFA (15:3) 2004, 254–6; by James P. Hammersmith in SoHR (39:2) 2005, 199–201.

3778. FUCHS, BARBARA. Romance. London; New York: Routledge, 2004. pp. viii, 146. (New critical idiom.)

3779. GARFITT, TOBY; MCMORRAN, EDITH; TAYLOR, JANE (eds). The anatomy of laughter. Leeds: Maney for the Modern Humanities Research Assn, 2005. pp. xi, 180. (Legenda.) (Studies in comparative religion, 8.)

3780. GATTA, JOHN. Making nature sacred: literature, religion, and environment in America from the Puritans to the present. Oxford; New York: OUP, 2004. pp. xii, 291.

3781. GAVINS, JOANNA; STEEN, GERARD (eds). Cognitive poetics in practice. London; New York: Routledge, 2003. pp. xii, 188. Rev. by Jean Jacques Weber in Style (38:4) 2004, 515–23.

3782. GEARY, JAMES. The world in a phrase: a brief history of the aphorism. London: Bloomsbury, 2005. pp. ix, 229.

3783. GENET, JACQUELINE; FIEROBE, CLAUDE. La littérature irlandaise. (Bibl. 1999, 3413.) Paris: L'Harmattan, 2004. pp. 364. (Second ed.: first ed. 1997.) Rev. by Jean Brihault in EtIr (30:1) 2005, 219.

3784. GIGANTE, DENISE. Taste: a literary history. New Haven, CT; London: Yale UP, 2005. pp. xii, 241. Rev. by Bharat Tandon in TLS, 28 Oct. 2005, 30.

3785. GIKANDI, SIMON (ed.). Encyclopedia of African literature. (Bibl. 2003, 3750.) Rev. by Eckhard Breitinger in AfSR (46:3) 2003, 154–7; by John Lemly in CanJAS (39:1) 2005, 160–2.

3786. GLANCY, DIANE. In-between places: essays. Tucson: Arizona UP, 2005. pp. 119.

3787. GRABES, HERBERT. The canon *pro* and *contra*: 'The canon is dead – long live pick and mix.' Misc (30) 2004, 35–49.

3788. GRAFF, GERALD; DI LEO, JEFFREY R. Anthologies, literary theory, and the teaching of literature. In (pp. 279–97) **3749**.

3789. GREEN, DIANE (comp.). Welsh writing in English: a bibliography of criticism 2004. WWrE (10) 2005, 190–8.

3790. GREENSPAN, EZRA; VASEY, LINDETH; WORTHEN, JOHN (eds). Studies in classic American literature. (Bibl. 2004, 3931.) Rev. by Neil Roberts in EREA (2:2) 2004.

3791. GREENWAY, BETTY (ed.). Twice-told children's tales: the influence of childhood reading on writers for adults. See **4086**.

3792. GRIFFIN, EDWARD M. Dancing around the maypole, ripping up the flag: the Merry Mount caper and issues in American history and art. See **17872**.

3793. GRMELOVÁ, ANNA; DUŠKOVÁ, LIBUŠE; FARRELL, MARK (eds). 2nd Prague Conference on Linguistic and Literary Studies: proceedings. See **1373**.

3794. GUNDY, JEFF. Walker in the fog: on Mennonite writing. Foreword by Hildi Froese Tiessen. Scottdale, PA: Herald Press, 2005. pp. 296. (C. Henry Smith series, 5.)

3795. HALLOWELL, CHRISTOPHER; LEVY, WALTER (eds). Listening to earth. London; New York: Pearson Longman, 2005. pp. xii, 241. (Longman topics reader.)

3796. HART, GEORGE; SLOVIC, SCOTT (eds). Literature and the environment. (Bibl. 2004, 3941.) Rev. by Ray B. Browne in JAC (28:1) 2005, 143.

3797. HAYNES, KENNETH. English literature and ancient languages. (Bibl. 2004, 3943.) Rev. by Robin Sowerby in MLR (100:3) 2005, 803–4; by Sylvia Adamson in EC (55:3) 2005, 255–62.

3798. HELLER, AGNES. Immortal comedy: the comic phenomenon in art, literature, and life. Lanham, MD: Lexington, 2005. pp. xiv, 225.

3799. HELMAN, KAREL. Cizinci v zaslíbené zemi: II, Nástin mapy americké přist ě hovalecké literatury. (Strangers in the Promised Land: II, A sketch map of American immigrant literature.) SvL (31) 2005, 15–30.

3800. HEMPFER, KLAUS W. Some problems concerning a theory of fiction(ality). See **14831**.

3801. HENTSCH, THIERRY. Truth or death: the quest for immortality in the Western narrative tradition. Trans. by Fred A. Reed. Vancouver: Talonbooks, 2004. pp. 412.

3802. HERMAN, LUC; VERVAECK, BART. Handbook of narrative analysis. See **21054**.

3803. HILLS, MATT. The pleasures of horror. London; New York: Continuum, 2005. pp. xiii, 250.

3804. HODGKINS, CHRISTOPHER. Reforming empire: Protestant colonialism and conscience in British literature. (Bibl. 2004, 3950.) Rev. by Colin Jager in JR (84:1) 2004, 164–5; by Paul Stevens in MP (103:1) 2005, 134–8.

3805. HODGSON, HEATHER (ed.). Saskatchewan writers: lives past and present. Regina, Sask.: Canadian Plains Research Center, 2004. pp. xiv, 247. (Sasketchewan lives past and present.)

3806. HOGAN, PATRICK COLM. The mind and its stories: narrative universals and human emotion. (Bibl. 2004, 3952.) Rev. by Stella Thompson in Style (38:4) 2004, 524–7.

3807. HOLMES, MARTHA STODDARD; CHAMBERS, TOD. Thinking through pain. LitMed (24:1) 2005, 127–41.

3808. HOPKINS, LISA. Screening the gothic. See **13263.**

3809. HORNER, AVRIL; ZLOSNIK, SUE. Gothic and the comic turn. Basingstoke; New York: Palgrave Macmillan, 2005. pp. ix, 205. Rev. by Jon Barnes in TLS, 2 Sept. 2005, 26.

3810. HOWARD, DAVID. Kingston: a cultural and literary history. Oxford: Signal, 2005. pp. xvi, 261. (Cities of the imagination, 10.) Rev. by Colin Channer in TLS, 20 May 2005, 29.

3811. HUANG, YUNXIA; HE, CHANGSHENG. 'Baroque' buried in oblivion: a survey of baroque literature studies. See **14839.**

3812. JACOBS, CAROL; SUSSMAN, HENRY (eds). Acts of narrative. (Bibl. 2004, 3958.) Rev. by Michael O'Sullivan in MFS (51:3) 2005, 724–7.

3813. JAHNER, ELAINE A. Spaces of the mind: narrative and community in the American West. Lincoln; London: Nebraska UP, 2004. pp. xviii, 191. (Frontiers of narrative.)

3814. JANSOHN, CHRISTA (ed.). Old age and ageing in British and American culture and literature. Münster: LIT, 2004. pp. vi, 265. (Studien zur englischen Literatur, 16.)

3815. JASPER, DAVID. The sacred desert: religion, literature, art, and culture. Oxford; Malden, MA: Blackwell, 2004. pp. xix, 208. Rev. by Kevin Hart in JR (85:4) 2005, 704–5.

3816. —— Wanderings in the desert: from the Exodus to *The English Patient.* LitTheol (18:2) 2004, 153–68.

3817. JAUSS, HANS ROBERT. Modernity and literary tradition. CI (31:2) 2005, 329–64.

3818. JOHNSON, BARBARA. Headnotes. In (pp. 384–94) **3749.**

3819. JORDAN, MICHAEL M. (ed.). On matters Southern: essays about literature and culture, 1964–2000. By Marion Montgomery. Foreword by Eugene D. Genovese. Jefferson, NC; London: McFarland, 2005. pp. vii, 205.

3820. JOSHI, S. T.; DZIEMIANOWICZ, STEFAN (eds). Supernatural literature of the world: an encyclopedia. Westport, CT; London: Greenwood Press, 2005. 3 vols. pp. xli, 1424.

3821. KALAGA, WOJCIECH H.; RACHWAŁ, TADEUSZ (eds). Feeding culture: the pleasures and perils of appetite. New York; Frankfurt: Lang, 2005. pp. 175. (Literary and cultural theory, 19.)

3822. KAMMEN, MICHAEL. A time to every purpose: the four seasons in American culture. (Bibl. 2004, 3967.) Rev. by David Bjelajac in JAH (92:1) 2005, 181–2; by Robert Sheardy, Jr, in JAC (28:4) 2005, 437.

3823. KEITH, W. J. Beyond novel, beyond romance: reading the complete *Porius*. See **18919**.

3824. KELLY, STUART. The book of lost books. London: Penguin; New York: Viking, 2005. pp. xxiii, 390.

3825. KESSLER, BRAD. One reader's digest: toward a gastronomic theory of literature. KR (27:2) 2005, 148–65.

3826. KIBERD, DECLAN. The Irish writer and the world. Cambridge; New York: CUP, 2005. pp. xi, 331. Rev. by Justin Beplate in TLS, 23 & 30 Dec. 2005, 13–14.

3827. KILCUP, KAREN L. The poetry and prose of recovery work. In (pp. 112–38) **3749**.

3828. KILLAM, DOUGLAS. Literature of Africa. Westport, CT; London: Greenwood Press, 2004. pp. xvii, 204. (Literature as windows to world cultures.) Rev. by M. Keith Booker in RAL (36:3) 2005, 157.

3829. KNAPP, JOHN V.; WOMACK, KENNETH (eds). Reading the family dance: family systems therapy and literary study. (Bibl. 2003, 3794.) Rev. by Jeffrey Adams in ColLit (32:3) 2005, 196–9; by Piotr Sadowski in Style (39:1) 2005, 97–100.

3830. KNIGHT, CHARLES A. The literature of satire. (Bibl. 2004, 3972.) Rev. by David Nokes in TLS, 11 Feb. 2005, 7; by Warren Chernaik in Scriblerian (37:2/ 38:1) 2005, 98–101.

3831. KNIGHT, STEPHEN. Robin Hood: a mythic biography. (Bibl. 2004, 3973.) Rev. by Edith L. Crowe in Mythprint (42:5) 2005, 4–5; by Pamela Allen Brown in SixCJ (36:1) 2005, 212–13; by Lois Potter in JEGP (104:3) 2005, 410–12.

3832. KNOWLES, ELIZABETH. Intelligent elasticity: the early years of the *Oxford Dictionary of Quotations*. Dic (25) 2004, 65–76.

3833. —— (ed.). The Oxford dictionary of quotations. (Bibl. 2004, 3974.) Rev. by E. S. Turner in TLS, 11 Feb. 2005, 10.

3834. KOŁEK, LESZEK; KĘDZIERSKA, ALEKSANDRA; KĘDRA-KARDELA, ANNA (eds). Perspectives on literature and culture. Lublin: Maria Curie-Skłodowska Univ., 2004. pp. 344.

3835. KRÖLLER, EVA-MARIE (ed.). The Cambridge companion to Canadian literature. (Bibl. 2004, 3977.) Rev. by Rocío G. Davis in CanL (183) 2004, 142–3; by Carolyne Van der Meer in LRC (12:7) 2004, 26–7; by Claire Omhovère in EA (58:2) 2005, 246–7.

3836. LACY, NORRIS J. (ed.). The fortunes of King Arthur. Woodbridge, Suffolk; Rochester, NY: Brewer, 2005. pp. xvi, 231, (plates) 29. (Arthurian studies, 64.)

3837. LAWALL, SARAH. Anthologizing 'world literature'. In (pp. 47–89) **3749**.

3838. LEE, JUDITH YAROSS. The year's work in American humor studies, 2003. SAH (11) 2004, 73–92.

3839. LEITCH, VINCENT B. Ideology of headnotes. In (pp. 373–83) **3749**.

3840. LENNON, JOSEPH.   Irish Orientalism: a literary and intellectual history. (Bibl. 2004, 3986.) Rev. by Nicholas Allen in NewHR (9:1) 2005, 157–9; by Mary Burke in ILS (25:1) 2005, 25–6; by Amy Bender in JJLS (19:1) 2005, 9.

3841. LENTRICCHIA, FRANK; DUBOIS, ANDREW (eds).   Close reading: the reader. (Bibl. 2004, 3987.) Rev. by Clare Connors in Eng (54:208) 2005, 76–80.

3842. LEVIN, CAROLE; CARNEY, JO ELDRIDGE; BARRETT-GRAVES, DEBRA (eds). 'High and mighty queens' of early modern England: realities and representations. (Bibl. 2003, 3802.) Rev. by Barbara Harris in Albion (36:3) 2004, 511–13; by D. A. J. Widmer in SixCJ (36:1) 2005, 273–5.

3843. LJUNGBERG, CHRISTINA.   Models of reading: diagrammatic aspects of literary texts. *In* (pp. 105–25) **3888.**

3844. LOVE, KAREN G.   Lies before our eyes: the denial of gender from the Bible to Shakespeare and beyond. New York; Frankfurt: Lang, 2005. pp. 259.

3845. LUPACK, ALAN.   The Oxford guide to Arthurian literature and legend. Oxford; New York: OUP, 2005. pp. xiv, 496. Rev. by Juliette Wood in Folklore (116:3) 2005, 343–4.

3846. LYALL, RODERICK J.   Writing towards the centre, reading around the periphery: the example of Scottish literature. BELL (ns 3) 2005, 5–21.

3847. LYNCH, JACK.   The age of Elizabeth in the age of Johnson. (Bibl. 2004, 3995.) Rev. by Barrett Kalter in MP (102:2) 2004, 279–82; by Bernice W. Kliman in MedRen (18) 2005, 220–2.

3848. LYNCH, WILLIAM F.   Christ & Apollo: the dimensions of the literary imagination. New introd. by Glenn C. Arbery. Wilmington, DE: ISI, 2003. pp. xl, 371. (Second ed.: first ed. 1960.) Rev. by Aaron Urbanczyk in ModAge (47:4) 2005, 353–5.

3849. MCCLATCHY, J. D.   American writers at home. New York: Library of America, 2004. pp. 224.

3850. MCCONKEY, JAMES.   The telescope in the parlor: essays on life and literature. Philadelphia, PA: Dry, 2004. pp. x, 196.

3851. MCCULLOCH, MARGERY PALMER (introd.).   For the vernacular circle (*The Bulletin* January 1938): the re-emergence of a long-lost contribution to the *Scott and Scotland* controversy. *See* **18391.**

3852. MCEWAN, IAN.   Literature, science, and human nature. *In* (pp. 5–19) **14807.**

3853. MCGOVERN, UNA (ed.).   Chambers dictionary of quotations. Edinburgh: Chambers Harrap, 2005. pp. vi, 1283. Rev. by Toby Lichtig in TLS, 16 Sept. 2005, 8.

3854. —— Dictionary of literary characters. (Bibl. 1998, 3678.) Edinburgh: Chambers Harrap, 2004. pp. xxix, 818. (Second ed.: first ed. 1994.) (Orig. pub. as *Larousse Dictionary of Literary Characters*.)

3855. MCILROY, BRIAN.   Irish horror: Neil Jordan and the Anglo-Irish gothic. *In* (pp. 128–40) **13374.**

3856. MALAK, AMIN.   Muslim narratives and the discourse of English. Albany: New York State UP, 2004. pp. ix, 181.

3857. MANCINI, BRUNA (ed.). Sguardi su Londra: immagini di una città mostruosa. Naples: Liguori, 2005. pp. 384.

3858. MANNING, ERIN. Ephemeral territories: representing nation, home, and identity in Canada. Minneapolis; London: Minnesota UP, 2003. pp. xxxi, 187. Rev. by Maria Truchan-Tataryn in CanL (183) 2004, 132–4.

3859. MARCUS, GREIL (introd.). American humor: a study of the national character. By Constance Rourke. New York: New York Review, 2004. pp. xxiv, 253. Rev. by Sean Zwagerman in JPC (38:3) 2005, 600–1.

3860. MATTHEW, H. C. G.; HARRISON, BRIAN (eds). Oxford dictionary of national biography: from the earliest times to the year 2000. (Bibl. 2004, 4005.) Rev. by Stefan Collini in LRB (27:2) 2005, 3–8; by Lawrence Goldman in TLS, 4 Feb. 2005, 12–13; by Joan Bellamy, et al., in BrSt (30:2) 2005, 171–7.

3861. MATTHEWS, JOHN. King Arthur: Dark Age warrior and mythic hero. See 3506.

3862. MEISTER, JAN CHRISTOPH (ed.); KINDT, TOM; SCHERNUS, WILHELM (asst eds). Narratology beyond literary criticism: mediality, disciplinarity. See 21087.

3863. MIKKELSEN, NINA. Powerful magic: learning from children's responses to fantasy literature. Foreword by Laurence Yep. New York: Teachers College Press, 2005. pp. x, 193. (Language and literacy.)

3864. MILLER, KEITH. Exquisite burning: tobacco or his toes: dilemmas for Sartre, Wilde and other literary smokers. TLS, 11 Feb. 2005, 3–4 (review-article).

3865. MITCHELL, MAREA; OSLAND, DIANNE. Representing women and female desire from Arcadia to Jane Eyre. Basingstoke; New York: Palgrave Macmillan, 2005. pp. viii, 247.

3866. MITSCHERLING, JEFF; DiTOMMASO, TANYA; NAYED, AREF. The author's intention. Lanham, MD: Lexington, 2004. pp. x, 143.

3867. MONTANDON, ALAIN (ed.). De soi à soi: l'écriture comme autohospitalité. Clermont-Ferrand: Presses Universitaires Blaise-Pascal, 2004. pp. 284. (Littératures.) Rev. by Claire Boyle in MLR (100:3) 2005, 747.

3868. MORRISON, KATHERINE L. Canadians & Americans: myths and literary traditions. New Brunswick, NJ: Transaction, 2005. pp. xix, 328.

3869. MORRISSEY, LEE (ed.). Debating the canon: a reader from Addison to Nafisi. Basingstoke; New York: Palgrave Macmillan, 2005. pp. v, 314.

3870. MYERS, JEFFREY. Converging stories: race, ecology, and environmental justice in American literature. Athens; London: Georgia UP, 2005. pp. ix, 188.

3871. NASTALI, DANIEL P.; BOARDMAN, PHILLIP C. The Arthurian annals: the tradition in English from 1250 to 2000. Oxford; New York: OUP, 2004. 2 vols. pp. 1120. Rev. by Kevin J. Harty in Arthuriana (15:2) 2005, 77–8; by Juliette Wood in Folklore (116:3) 2005, 343–4.

3872. NGAI, SIANNE. Ugly feelings. Cambridge, MA; London: Harvard UP, 2004. pp. 422.

3873. NICHOLSON, MERVYN. 13 ways of looking at images: the logic of visualization in literature and society. Beverly Hills, CA: Red Heifer Press, 2003. pp. 240. Rev. by Joseph Duemer in WSJ (29:1) 2005, 200–2.

3874. NÜNNING, ANSGAR. Where historiographic metafiction and narratology meet: towards an applied cultural narratology. Style (38:3) 2004, 352–75.

3875. O'DONNELL, KATHERINE; O'ROURKE, MICHAEL (eds). Love, sex, intimacy, and friendship between men, 1550–1800. (Bibl. 2004, 4022.) Rev. by Ian Frederick Moulton in HLQ (67:3) 2004, 481–7.

3876. O'DRISCOLL, DENNIS. The Library of Adventure. See **18591**.

3877. OGDEN, DARYL. The language of the eyes: science, sexuality, and female vision in English literature and culture, 1690–1927. Albany: New York State UP, 2005. pp. xiii, 272. (SUNY series in feminist criticism and theory.)

3878. OLSEN, STEIN HAUGOM; PETTERSSON, ANDERS (eds). From text to literature: new analytic and pragmatic approaches. Basingstoke; New York: Palgrave Macmillan, 2005. pp. x, 206.

3879. ONEGA, SUSANA; GUTLEBEN, CHRISTIAN (eds). Refracting the canon in contemporary British literature and film. Amsterdam; Atlanta, GA: Rodopi, 2004. pp. 261. (Postmodern studies, 35.) Rev. by Alain Blayac in EtBr (28) 2005, 151.

3880. PALMER, ALAN. Fictional minds. (Bibl. 2004, 4025.) Rev. by Craig Hamilton in TLS, 19 & 26 Aug. 2005, 35.

3881. PALTER, ROBERT. The Duchess of Malfi's apricots, and other literary fruits. (Bibl. 2004, 4026.) Rev. by David Karp in Gastronomica (5:2) 2005, 104–5.

3882. PEPRNÍK, JAROSLAV. The colour *green* in English language and literature. *In* (pp. 143–55) **1369**.

3883. PEPRNÍK, MICHAL. Topos lesa v americké literatuře. (The *topos* of the forest in American literature.) Brno: Host, 2005. pp. 250.

3884. PERCIVAL, MELISSA; TYTLER, GRAEME (eds). Physiognomy in profile: Lavater's impact on European culture. Newark: Delaware UP; London: Assoc. UPs, 2005. pp. 258.

3885. PETRILLI, SUSAN; PONZIO, AUGUSTO. Views in literary semiotics. Ottawa; New York: Legas, 2003. pp. 141. (Language, media & education studies, 30.)

3886. PHILLIPS, HELEN. Introduction: studying Robin Hood. *In* (pp. 9–20) **3576**.

3887. —— (ed.). Robin Hood: medieval and post-medieval. See **3576**.

3888. POLVINEN, MERJA (ed.). Cognition and literary interpretation in practice. Introd. by Harri Veivo. Afterword by Bo Pettersson. Helsinki: Helsinki UP, 2005. pp. 339.

3889. PORTER, LAURENCE M. Women's vision in Western literature: the empathic community. Westport, CT; London: Praeger, 2005. pp. 256. (Contributions in women's studies.)

3890. POTKAY, ADAM. The joy of *American Beauty*. See **13445**.

3891. POZZOBON, GIOVANNI MICHELE (ed.). Mosaici di orizzonti: società immaginari, comunicazione. Milan: Angeli, 2005. pp. 165.

3892. PRESSMAN, RICHARD S. Is there a future for the *Heath Anthology* in the neoliberal State? *In* (pp. 264–76) **3749**.

3893. PUNDAY, DANIEL. Narrative bodies: toward a corporeal narratology. Basingstoke; New York: Palgrave Macmillan, 2003. pp. x, 234. Rev. by Scott J. Juengel in Novel (37:3) 2004, 367–9; by Carolyn D. Williams in MLR (100:3) 2005, 748.

3894. QUINDLEN, ANNA. Imagined London: a tour of the world's greatest fictional city. Washington, DC: National Geographic Soc., 2004. pp. 162. (National Geographic directions.)

3895. RAI, SUDHA (comp.). Annual bibliography of Commonwealth literature 2004: India. JCL (40:4) 2005, 109–38.

3896. REICHARDT, MARY R. (ed.). The encyclopedia of Catholic literature. Westport, CT; London: Greenwood Press, 2004. 2 vols. pp. xxix, 842.

3897. REICHARDT, ULFRIED. The 'times' of the New World: future-orientation, American culture, and globalization. YREAL (19) 2003, 247–66.

3898. RIACH, ALAN. Representing Scotland in literature, popular culture and iconography: the masks of the modern nation. Basingstoke; New York: Palgrave Macmillan, 2005. pp. xxiv, 280. Rev. by Robert Crawford in TLS, 9 Sept. 2005, 8.

3899. RICE, ALAN. Radical narratives of the Black Atlantic. London; New York: Continuum, 2003. pp. ix, 244. (Black Atlantic.) Rev. by Rosie Wild in JAStud (38:1) 2004, 159–60; by Edward Margolies in AAR (39:1/2) 2005, 262–3; by Jonathan Elmer in AmLH (17:1) 2005, 160–70.

3900. RICKS, CHRISTOPHER. All praise to proper words: the new Oxford Professor of Poetry on equality for prose. TLS, 25 Feb. 2005, 13–15.

3901. ROBBINS, RUTH. Subjectivity. Basingstoke; New York: Palgrave Macmillan, 2005. pp. x, 216.

3902. ROBINSON, LORRAINE HALE. Dictionary of North Carolina writers, Mary Lynn Veach Sadler to Mark R. Sumner. NCLR (14) 2005, 191–216.

3903. ROCHE, MARK WILLIAM. Why literature matters in the 21st century. New Haven, CT; London: Yale UP, 2004. pp. xii, 308.

3904. RONALD, ANN. Reader of the purple sage: essays on Western writers and environmental literature. Foreword by Melody Graulich. (Bibl. 2004, 4045.) Rev. by Susan C. Rosen in WAL (39:1) 2004, 128–9.

3905. ROOD, TIM. The sea! The sea! The shout of the ten thousand in the modern imagination. London: Duckworth, 2005. pp. ix, 262, (plates) 12.

3906. ROTH, MARTY. Drunk the night before: an anatomy of intoxication. Minneapolis; London: Minnesota UP, 2005. pp. xxii, 228.

3907. ROUSH, JAN. Research in Western American literature, 2002 and 2003. WAL (39:1) 2004, 131–4.

3908. ROWE, M. W. Philosophy and literature: a book of essays. Aldershot; Burlington, VT: Ashgate, 2004. pp. xii, 238.

3909. ROYLE, NICHOLAS. The uncanny. (Bibl. 2004, 4047.) Rev. by Charles Benjamin in LitTheol (18:1) 2004, 109–11.

3910. SAMUELS, ROBERT; DA SOUSA CORREA, DELIA (eds). Phrase and subject: studies in music and literature. Oxford: Legenda; New York: Barnes & Noble, 2004. pp. 256.

3911. SANDERS, ANDREW. The short Oxford history of English literature. (Bibl. 2000, 3929.) Oxford; New York: OUP, 2004. pp. vii, 756. (Third ed.: first ed. 1994.)

3912. SANDHU, SUKHDEV. London calling: how Black and Asian writers imagined a city. (Bibl. 2004, 4049.) Rev. by Bruce King in WLWE (39:2) 2002/03, 135–40.

3913. SANDNER, DAVID (ed.). Fantastic literature: a critical reader. (Bibl. 2004, 4050.) Rev. by Christine Mains in JFA (15:2) 2004, 168–70.

3914. SAUNDERS, CORINNE; MACNAUGHTON, JANE (eds). Madness and creativity in literature and culture. Basingstoke; New York: Palgrave Macmillan, 2005. pp. xiv, 244.

3915. SAYRE, GORDON M. The Indian chief as tragic hero: native resistance and the literatures of America, from Moctezuma to Tecumseh. Chapel Hill; London: North Carolina UP, 2005. pp. x, 357.

3916. SCHECHET, NITA. Narrative fissures: reading and rhetoric. Madison, NJ: Fairleigh Dickinson UP, 2005. pp. 149.

3917. SCHECHTER, HAROLD. Savage pastimes: a cultural history of violent entertainment. New York: St Martin's Press, 2005. pp. 192. Rev. by Marshall W. Fishwick in JAC (28:3) 2005, 337.

3918. SCHRIFT, ALAN D. Confessions of an anthology editor. In (pp. 186–204) **3749.**

3919. SCOTT, MARIA M. Re-presenting 'Jane' Shore: harlot and heroine. Aldershot; Burlington, VT: Ashgate, 2005. pp. 141. Rev. by Emma Smith in RES (56:227) 2005, 787–8.

3920. SEAMON, ROGER. Why Poe? Why not Peirce? PhilL (29:2) 2005, 256–68.

3921. SELL, ROGER D. Literature, cultural memory, scholarship. See **15010.**

3922. SHARPE, JENNY. Ghosts of slavery: a literary archaeology of Black women's lives. (Bibl. 2004, 4054.) Rev. by Hilary McD. Beckles in JAH (91:2) 2004, 641–2; by Madhu Dubey in Novel (38:1) 2004, 107–10.

3923. SIEMERLING, WINFRIED. The new North American Studies: culture, writing and the politics of re/cognition. London; New York: Routledge, 2005. pp. x, 210.

3924. SIKORSKA, LILIANA (ed.). Ironies of art/tragedies of life: essays on Irish literature. New York; Frankfurt: Lang, 2005. pp. 300. (Polish studies in English language and literature, 13.)

3925. SIMO, MELANIE L. Literature of place: dwelling on the land before Earth Day 1970. Charlottesville; London: Virginia UP, 2005. pp. xv, 271.

3926. SIMPSON, PAUL. On the discourse of satire: towards a stylistic model of satirical humor. Amsterdam; Philadelphia, PA: Benjamins, 2003. pp. xiii, 242. (Linguistic approaches to literature, 2.) Rev. by John Morreall in Humor (18:3) 2005, 337–9.

3927. SINGER, ALAN. Aesthetic reason: artworks and the deliberative ethos. University Park: Pennsylvania State UP, 2003. pp. viii, 302. (Literature and philosophy.) Rev. by Daphna Erdinast-Vulcan in ELT (48:2) 2005, 206–9; by Eric Rothstein in ConLit (46:1) 2005, 139–57.

3928. SKOGAN, JOAN. Mary of Canada: the Virgin Mary in Canadian culture, spirituality, history and geography. Banff, Alta: Banff Centre Press, 2003. pp. xvii, 305. Rev. by Laurence Gillespie in PrF (25:4) 2004/05, 111–14.

3929. SLOVIC, SCOTT. There's something about your voice I cannot hear: environmental literature, public policy and ecocriticism. See 20199.

3930. SNODGRASS, MARY ELLEN. Facts on File encyclopedia of gothic literature. New York: Facts on File, 2005. pp. xvi, 480. (Facts on File library of world literature.)

3931. SOLWAY, DAVID. Director's cut. Erin, Ont.: Porcupine's Quill, 2003. pp. 209. (Canadian literature.) Rev. by Shane Neilson in LRC (12:6) 204, 25–6.

3932. SOMMER, DORIS. Bilingual aesthetics: a new sentimental education. Durham, NC; London: Duke UP, 2004. pp. xxv, 254. (Public planet.) Rev. by Marguerite Quintelli-Neary in SAH (third series) (11) 2004, 102–3.

3933. SPARGO, R. CLIFTON. The ethics of mourning: grief and responsibility in elegiac literature. Baltimore, MD; London: Johns Hopkins UP, 2004. pp. x, 314.

3934. SPURR, DAVID. The study of space in literature: some paradigms. SPELL (17) 2005, 15–34.

3935. STAM, ROBERT; RAENGO, ALESSANDRA (eds). Literature and film: a guide to the theory and practice of film adaptation. See 20681.

3936. STONEMAN, PATSY; SANCHEZ-ARCE, ANA MARIA; LEIGHTON, ANGELA (eds). European intertexts: women's writing in English in a European context. New York; Frankfurt: Lang, 2005. pp. 296. (European connections, 13.)

3937. STOTT, ANDREW. Comedy. London; New York: Routledge, 2005. pp. vi, 168. (New critical idiom.)

3938. SU, HUI. The comic sense: soul of comedy. FLS (115) 2005, 152–60. (In Chinese.)

3939. SWEENEY, MATTHEW; PEPRNÍK, MICHAL (eds). America: home of the brave. Olomouc: Palacky UP, 2005. pp. 219.

3940. TAAVITSAINEN, IRMA. Genres of secular instruction: a linguistic history of useful entertainment. See 1415.

3941. TINKLER-VILLANI, VALERIA (ed.). Babylon or New Jerusalem? Perceptions of the city in literature. Amsterdam; Atlanta, GA: Rodopi, 2005. pp. xii, 301. (DQR studies in literature, 32.) Rev. by Andrew Radford in EJES (9:3) 2005, 329–31.

3942. TOMLINSON, BARBARA. Authors on writing: metaphors and intellectual labor. See 2502.

3943. TREDINNICK, MARK (ed.). A place on earth: an anthology of nature writing from Australia & North America. Lincoln; London: Nebraska UP; Sydney: New South Wales UP, 2003. pp. 268. Rev. by Veronica Brady in Southerly (64:2) 2004, 176–82.

3944. TYMOCZKO, MARIA; IRELAND, COLIN (eds). Language and tradition in Ireland: continuities and displacements. (Bibl. 2004, 4071.) Rev. by Claude Fierobe in EtIr (30:1) 2005, 220–1.

3945. URBANOVÁ, LUDMILA. English conversation: authentic and fictional. *In* (pp. 155–62) **1370.**

3946. VAUGHT, JENNIFER C.; BRUCKNER, LYNNE DICKSON (eds). Grief and gender, 700–1700. (Bibl. 2004, 4074.) Rev. by Robin Norris in NQ (52:4) 2005, 514–15.

3947. VENDLER, HELEN. Can we conceive of Beatrice 'snapping' like a shrew? LRB (27:17) 2005, 9–10. (Dante's influence.)

3948. VERBOORD, MARC. Classification of authors by literary prestige. Poetics (31:3/4) 2003, 259–81.

3949. VERHAUL, JAAP (ed.). Dreams of paradise, visions of apocalypse: utopia and dystopia in American culture. Amsterdam: VU UP, 2004. pp. vii, 252. (European contributions to American Studies, 51.) Rev. by Charles J. Rooney, Jr, in JAH (92:1) 2005, 182–3.

3950. VIDA, VENDELA (ed.). The Believer book of writers talking to writers. San Francisco, CA: Believer, 2005. pp. 454.

3951. VOIGTS-VIRCHOW, ECKART (ed.). Janespotting and beyond: British heritage retrovisions since the mid-1990s. See **13415.**

3952. WARDI, ANISSA JANINE. Death and the arc of mourning in African American literature. (Bibl. 2004, 4083.) Rev. by James Coleman in SoLJ (38:1) 2005, 142–6.

3953. WARNER, MARINA. Angels and engines: apocalypse and its aftermath, from George W. Bush to Philip Pullman. See **18971.**

3954. —— Angels & engines: the culture of apocalypse. Raritan (25:2) 2005, 12–41.

3955. —— Fantastic metamorphoses, other worlds: ways of telling the self. (Bibl. 2004, 4084.) Rev. by Dolores Flores-Silva in SixCJ (35:4) 2004, 1206–7.

3956. WEINSTOCK, JEFFREY ANDREW (ed.). Spectral America: phantoms and the national imagination. (Bibl. 2004, 4087.) Rev. by Edward J. Ingebretsen in GothS (7:2) 2005, 207–10.

3957. WEST, M. GENEVIEVE. Zora Neale Hurston and American literary culture. See **17142.**

3958. WHITSON, KATHY J. Encyclopedia of feminist literature. Westport, CT; London: Greenwood Press, 2004. pp. xi, 300.

3959. WILLIAMS, JEFFREY J. Anthology disdain. *In* (pp. 207–21) **3749.**

3960. WILSON, DAVID SLOAN. Evolutionary social constructivism. *In* (pp. 20–37) **14807.**

3961. WINCHELL, MARK ROYDEN. Leslie Fiedler, ahead of the herd. See **15053.**

3962. WOLFE, CARY. Animal rites: American culture, the discourse of species, and posthumanist theory. Foreword by W. J. T. Mitchell. Chicago, IL; London: Chicago UP, 2003. pp. xv, 237. Rev. by T. J. Lustig in MLR (100:3) 2005, 755; by Bart H. Welling in ISLE (12:1) 2005, 280–2.

3963. WOOTTON, DAVID. The road is still open. *See* **3526.**

3964. WORTHEN, JOHN. 'Wild turkeys': some versions of America by D. H. Lawrence. *See* **17637.**

3965. YAO, JUNWEI. Xu Chi and his translation and introduction of American literature in China. FLS (114) 2005, 145–9. (In Chinese.)

3966. ZHANG, HAO; HOOSAIN, RUMJAHN. Activation of themes during narrative reading. DP (40:1) 2005, 57–82.

3967. ZIEGLER, GEORGIANNA (comp.). Elizabeth I: then and now. *See* **489.**

DRAMA AND THE THEATRE

3968. BANHAM, MARTIN (ed.). A history of theatre in Africa. (Bibl. 2004, 4097.) Rev. by Chimalum Nwankwo in AfSR (48:1) 2005, 196–9; by Loren Kruger in TJ (57:3) 2005, 548–50.

3969. BARKER, HOWARD. Death, the one and the art of theatre. *See* **15295.**

3970. BUSHNELL, REBECCA (ed.). A companion to tragedy. Oxford; Malden, MA: Blackwell, 2005. pp. xi, 556. (Blackwell companions to literature and culture, 32.)

3971. CAMERON, KENNETH M.; GILLESPIE, PATTI P. The enjoyment of theatre. Boston, MA: Allyn & Bacon, 2004. pp. xii, 452, (plates) 32.

3972. CHAMBERS, COLIN. Inside the Royal Shakespeare Company: creativity and the institution. (Bibl. 2004, 4106.) Rev. by Bridget Mary Aitchison in ADS (46) 2005, 143–5; by Dominic Shellard in TRI (30:1) 2005, 97–8.

3973. CHANG, WON-JAE. Irish influences on Korean theatre during the 1920s and 1930s. Gerrards Cross: Smythe; New York: OUP, 2003. pp. 262.

3974. CREMONA, VICKY ANN, *et al.* (eds). Theatrical events: borders, dynamics, frames. Amsterdam; Atlanta, GA: Rodopi, 2004. pp. 398.

3975. DAVIS, JESSICA MILNER. Farce. (Bibl. 2003, 3949.) Rev. by Mary Ann Rishel in Humor (18:4) 2005, 419–22.

3976. DAVIS, TRACY C.; POSTLEWAIT, THOMAS (eds). Theatricality. (Bibl. 2004, 4108.) Rev. by Janelle Reinelt in TheatreS (46:1) 2005, 123–7; by Dean Wilcox in TRI (30:1) 2005, 103–4.

3977. GOUNARIDOU, KIKI (ed.). Staging nationalism: essays on theatre and national identity. Jefferson, NC; London: McFarland, 2005. pp. viii, 235.

3978. HALL, EDITH; MACINTOSH, FIONA. Greek tragedy and the British theatre, 1660–1914. Oxford; New York: OUP, 2005. pp. xxxvi, 723.

3979. HUGHES, AMY (ed.). Theatre research resources in New York City. New York: Martin E. Segal Theatre Center, 2004. pp. 63. (Fifth ed.: first ed. 1992.)

3980. KAPLAN, ELLEN W.; RUDOLPH, SARAH J. (eds). Images of mental illness through text and performance. Lewiston, NY; Lampeter: Mellen Press, 2005. pp. iii, 166. (Studies in theatre arts, 33.)

3981. KAUFFMANN, STANLEY. The director reborn: an exploration. PAJ (73) 2003, 1–6.

3982. KENNEDY, DENNIS (ed.). The Oxford encyclopedia of theatre & performance. (Bibl. 2004, 4121.) Rev. by Mary Judith Dunbar in CompDr (38:2/3) 2004, 315–20.

3983. LOISELLE, ANDRÉ. Stage-bound: feature film adaptations of Canadian and Québécois drama. Montreal; Buffalo, NY; London: McGill-Queen's UP, 2003. pp. 260. Rev. by Stephen Johnson in CanTR (122) 2005, 92–4.

3984. LONDRÉ, FELICIA HARDISON. Words at play: creative writing and dramaturgy. Foreword by Barry Kyle. Carbondale: Southern Illinois UP, 2005. pp. xx, 249. (Theater in the Americas.)

3985. LUCKHURST, MARY; MOODY, JANE (eds). Theatre and celebrity in Britain, 1660–2000. Basingstoke; New York: Palgrave Macmillan, 2005. pp. xi, 248. Rev. by Michael Caines in TLS, 16 Dec. 2005, 31.

3986. McLAMORE, ALYSON. Musical theater: an appreciation. Upper Saddle River, NJ: Prentice Hall, 2004. pp. viii, 327.

3987. MANGAN, MICHAEL. Staging masculinities: history, gender, performance. (Bibl. 2004, 4125.) Rev. by Bob Vorlicky in TJ (57:2) 2005, 334–6; by Nicholas Radel in MedRen (18) 2005, 232–8.

3988. MENDICINO, KRISTINA; SELLAR, TOM. Classics under reconstruction. Theater (35:3) 2005, 62–73.

3989. NOVY, MARIANNE. Reading adoption: family and difference in fiction and drama. See **4048**.

3990. PATTERSON, MICHAEL. The Oxford dictionary of plays. Oxford; New York: OUP, 2005. pp. xxxv, 523.

3991. POOLE, ADRIAN. Tragedy: a very short introduction. (Bibl. 1993, 4116.) Oxford; New York: OUP, 2005. pp. 147. (Very short introductions.)

3992. PRITNER, CAL; WALTERS, SCOTT E. Introduction to play analysis. Boston, MA: McGraw-Hill, 2005. pp. xvi, 114, (plates) 16.

3993. PULLEN, KIRSTEN. Actresses and whores: on stage and in society. Cambridge; New York: CUP, 2005. pp. xii, 215. Rev. by Samantha Ellis in TLS, 3 June 2005, 27.

3994. REMSHARDT, RALF. Staging the savage God: the grotesque in performance. Carbondale: Southern Illinois UP, 2004. pp. xi, 304. Rev. by Nicholas Ridout in TJ (57:2) 2005, 344–5.

3995. SHEPHERD, SIMON; WALLIS, MICK. Drama/theatre/performance. London; New York: Routledge, 2004. pp. vii, 262. (New critical idiom.) Rev. by Peter M. Boenisch in TRI (30:3) 2005, 306–7.

3996. SOFER, ANDREW. The stage life of props. (Bibl. 2004, 4130.) Rev. by Frances Teague in CompDr (38:2/3) 2004, 336–8; by John Bell in TDR (49:2) 2005, 161–2.

3997. STŘÍBRNÝ, ZDENĚK. Proud času: stati o Shakespearovi. (The stream of time: essays on Shakespeare.) See **6088**.

3998. VAUGHAN, VIRGINIA MASON. Performing blackness on English stages, 1500–1800. Cambridge; New York: CUP, 2005. pp. xiv, 190. Rev. by Frédéric Delord in CEl (67) 2005, 87–91.

3999. WEBER, SAMUEL. Theatricality as medium. New York: Fordham UP, 2004. pp. xiv, 408.

4000. WEISEL, SANDRA RABEY (ed.). Great playwrights. San Diego, CA: Greenhaven Press, 2005. pp. 240. (Profiles in history.)

4001. WILES, DAVID. A short history of Western performance space. (Bibl. 2004, 4138.) Rev. by D. J. Hopkins in TJ (57:2) 2005, 319–20.

4002. WILLIAMS, GARY JAY. Athenian prologue to an American theatre. *In* (pp. 48–62) **3977.**

4003. WILMER, S. E. Theatre, society, and the nation: staging American identities. (Bibl. 2004, 4140.) Rev. by Bruce McConachie in NCT (31:2) 2004, 85–9.

4004. —— (ed.). Writing & rewriting national theatre histories. (Bibl. 2004, 4141.) Rev. by Patricia Ybarra in TJ (57:3) 2005, 550–1; by Roger Bechtel in THS (25) 2005, 207–9.

4005. WILSON, EDWIN. The theater experience. (Bibl. 1976, 2808.) Boston, MA: McGraw-Hill, 2004. 1 vol. (various pagings). (Ninth ed.: first ed. 1976.)

4006. ZATLIN, PHYLLIS. Theatrical translation and film adaptation: a practitioner's view. Clevedon; Philadelphia, PA: Multilingual Matters, 2005. pp. xii, 222. (Topics in translation, 29.)

FICTION

4007. ANDERSON, DOUGLAS A. Tales before Tolkien: the roots of modern fantasy. New York: Del Rey / Ballantine, 2003. pp. 436. Rev. by Charles E. Noad in TolStud (2) 2005, 261–2.

4008. BAETENS, JAN. Novelization, a contaminated genre? Trans. by Pieter Verrmeulen. CI (32:1) 2005, 43–60.

4009. BARRON, NEIL (ed.). Anatomy of wonder: a critical guide to science fiction. (Bibl. 1996, 4135.) Westport, CT: Libraries Unlimited, 2004. pp. xix, 995. (Fifth edition: first ed. 1976.) Rev. by Donald M. Hassler in Extrapolation (46:2) 2005, 268–70.

4010. BENSON, STEPHEN FRANK. Cycles of influence: fiction, folktale, theory. (Bibl. 2004, 4146.) Rev. by Thomas L. Cooksey in SAtlR (70:1) 2005, 154–6.

4011. BOYERS, ROBERT. The dictator's dictation: the politics of novels and novelists. New York: Columbia UP, 2005. pp. 218.

4012. BRODERICK, DAMIEN. x, y, z, t: dimensions of science fiction. Holicong, PA: Borgo Press / Wildside Press, 2004. pp. 268. Rev. by Russell Blackford in NYRSF (17:5) 2005, 19–20.

4013. BROWN, CHARLES N. Genre fiction; science fiction; the quest for utopia. FLS (116) 2005, 36–40.

4014. BROWN, KELLIE D. An annotated bibliography and reference list of musical fiction. Lewiston, NY; Lampeter: Mellen Press, 2005. pp. ii, 340. (Studies in the history and interpretation of music, 116.)

4015. BURNS, GRANT. The railroad in American fiction: an annotated bibliography. Jefferson, NC; London: McFarland, 2005. pp. ix, 281.

4016. BURROW, COLIN.   You and your bow and the gods. LRB (27:18) 2005, 23–4 (review-article). (Detective fiction.)

4017. DELANY, SAMUEL R.   Science fiction and 'literature'; or, The conscience of the king. *In* (pp. 95–117) **4027**.

4018. ELDRIDGE, BOB.   Mark David Chapman, science fiction fan. NYRSF (18:1) 2005, 1, 4–5.

4019. ELLIOTT, EMORY.   Cultural memory and the American novel. *See* **16031**.

4020. FISCHER, KATRIN.   *'Time to tear down barriers'*: Raum, Kultur und 'indianische' Identität im Kriminalroman. Essen: Blaue Eule, 2003. pp. 421. (Arbeiten zur Amerikanistik, 34.) Rev. by Carmen Birkle in Amst (49:3) 2004, 447–9.

4021. FISHER, CARL.   The Robinsonade: an intercultural history of an idea. *In* (pp. 129–39) **8537**.

4022. GEORGE, KATHLEEN.   Winter's tales: reflections on the novelistic stage. *See* **13028**.

4023. GOETSCH, PAUL.   Reader figures in narrative. Style (38:2) 2004, 188–202.

4024. GRABES, HERBERT.   Turning words on the page into 'real' people. Style (38:2) 2004, 221–35.

4025. GUNN, JAMES.   The readers of hard science fiction. *In* (pp. 81–93) **4027**.

4026. —— Touchstones. *In* (pp. 301–9) **4027**.

4027. —— CANDELARIA, MATTHEW (eds).   Speculations on speculation: theories of science fiction. Lanham, MD; London: Scarecrow Press, 2005. pp. xix, 374. Rev. by Mark Decker in Extrapolation (46:3) 2005, 400–3; by Darren Harris-Fain in Extrapolation (46:3) 2005, 403–5.

4028. HALEVI-WISE, YAEL.   Interactive fictions: scenes of storytelling in the novel. (Bibl. 2004, 4160.) Rev. by Matt DelConte in PartA (3:1) 2005, 173–7.

4029. HALLIGAN, MARION.   Where truth lies. Meanjin (64:1/2) 2005, 95–100.

4030. HARRISON, STEPHANIE (ed.).   Adaptations: from short story to big screen: 35 great stories that have inspired great films. *See* **13251**.

4031. HOFFMAN, MICHAEL J.; MURPHY, PATRICK D. (eds).   Essentials of the theory of fiction. (Bibl. 1996, 4190.) Durham, NC; London: Duke UP, 2005. pp. lvii, 511. (Third ed.: first ed. 1988.)

4032. JAMES, EDWARD; MENDLESOHN, FARAH (eds).   The Cambridge companion to science fiction. (Bibl. 2004, 4164.) Rev. by Karen Sayer in Foundation (92) 2004, 108–11; by Will Slocombe in Eng (54:208) 2005, 80–4.

4033. JAMESON, FREDRIC.   Archaeologies of the future: the desire called utopia and other science fictions. London; New York: Verso, 2005. pp. xvi, 431. Rev. by John Duda in MLN (120:5) 2005, 1245–9.

4034. JOHNSON, PETER.   Moral philosophers and the novel: a study of Winch, Nussbaum, and Rorty. Basingstoke; New York: Palgrave Macmillan, 2004. pp. viii, 203.

4035. JOHNSON, SARAH L.   Historical fiction: a guide to the genre. Westport, CT: Libraries Unlimited, 2005. pp. xxi, 813. (Genreflecting advisory series.)

4036. Joshi, S. T. Establishing the canon of weird fiction. JFA (14:3) 2004, 333–41.

4037. Kennedy, George A. Fictitious authors and imaginary novels in French, English, and American fiction from the 18th to the start of the 21st century. Lewiston, NY; Lampeter: Mellen Press, 2004. pp. xi, 304. (Studies in comparative literature, 64.)

4038. Kilgore, Douglas. Astrofuturism: science, race, and visions of utopia in space. Philadelphia: Pennsylvania UP, 2003. pp. 294. Rev. by Joseph Milicia in NYRSF (18:1) 2005, 20–1.

4039. King, Amy M. Bloom: the botanical vernacular in the English novel. (Bibl. 2004, 4167.) Rev. by Kathleen McCormack in VIJ (32) 2004, 242–5; by Mark Storey in RES (56:225) 2005, 467–8.

4040. Lee, Richard. On the strength of the sentence: aesthetics, nuance, and narrative effect. ShSt (12:2) 2004, 84–95.

4041. Li, Weiping. Transformation and controversy: a reflection on the characters in English novels. FLS (115) 2005, 85–90. (In Chinese.)

4042. Luckhurst, Roger. Science fiction. Oxford; Malden, MA: Polity Press in assn with Blackwell, 2005. pp. vii, 305. (Cultural history of literature.) Rev. by Farah Mendlesohn in NYRSF (18:1) 2005, 16–20; by Edward James in Foundation (94) 2005, 137–42.

4043. McFarlane, Brian. Change is not a choice. *See* **13304**.

4044. Martin, Graham Dunstan. An inquiry into the purposes of speculative fiction – fantasy and truth. (Bibl. 2003, 4029.) Rev. by Mark A. Heberle in MarvT (19:1) 2005, 142–5.

4045. Millbank, John. Fictioning things: gift and narratives. ReLit (37:3) 2005, 1–35.

4046. Novak, Maximillian E.; Fisher, Carl. *Crusoe's* fictional predecessors. *In* (pp. 14–16) **8537**.

4047. —— —— (eds). Approaches to teaching Defoe's *Robinson Crusoe*. *See* **8537**.

4048. Novy, Marianne. Reading adoption: family and difference in fiction and drama. Ann Arbor: Michigan UP, 2005. pp. viii, 292. Rev. by Margaret Homans in TSWL (24:2) 2005, 348–50.

4049. Panshin, Alexei; Panshin, Cory. Science fiction and the dimension of myth. *In* (pp. 219–34) **4027**.

4050. Pettersson, Bo. The many faces of unreliable narration: a cognitive narratological reorientation. *In* (pp. 59–88) **3888**.

4051. Priestman, Martin (ed.). The Cambridge companion to crime fiction. (Bibl. 2004, 4176.) Rev. by Fred Isaac in JPC (38:4) 2005, 777–8.

4052. Rege, Josna E. Colonial karma: self, action, and nation in the Indian English novel. Basingstoke; New York: Palgrave Macmillan, 2004. pp. xiii, 208.

4053. Richards, Dana. One must be masterful: fiction and reality. *See* **10866**.

4054. ROSSHOLM, GÖRAN (ed.). Essays on fiction and perspective. New York; Frankfurt: Lang, 2004. pp. 355.

4055. SCAGGS, JOHN. Crime fiction. London; New York: Routledge, 2005. pp. viii, 170. (New critical idiom.)

4056. SCHLOBIN, ROGER C. Character, the fantastic, and the failure of contemporary literary theory. See **15007.**

4057. SLUNEČKOVÁ, LENKA. Syntactic constancy of the object between Czech and English in fiction and technical writing: preliminary notes. In (pp. 197–207) **1369.**

4058. SMILEY, JANE. Thirteen ways of looking at the novel. New York: Knopf, 2005. pp. x, 591.

4059. SMITH, KAREN PATRICIA. Tradition, transformation, and the bold emergence: fantastic legacy and Pullman's His Dark Materials. In (pp. 135–51) **18952.**

4060. SMITH, SHARRON; O'CONNOR, MAUREEN. Canadian fiction: a guide to reading interests. Foreword by Catherine Sheldrick Ross. Westport, CT: Libraries Unlimited, 2005. pp. xxii, 423. (Genreflecting advisory series.)

4061. SPARK, DEBRA. Curious attractions: essays on fiction writing. Ann Arbor: Michigan UP, 2005. pp. vi, 175.

4062. STABLEFORD, BRIAN. Historical dictionary of fantasy literature. Lanham, MD; London: Scarecrow Press, 2005. pp. lxv, 499. (Historical dictionaries of literature and the arts, 5.)

4063. STAM, ROBERT. Literature through film: realism, magic, and the art of adaptation. See **13396.**

4064. STANZEL, FRANZ K. The 'complementary story': outline of a reader-oriented theory of the novel. Style (38:2) 2004, 203–20.

4065. STEVENS, LAURA M. Reading the hermit's manuscript: The Female American and female Robinsonades. In (pp. 140–51) **8537.**

4066. SUGIYAMA, MICHELLE SCALISE. Reverse-engineering narrative: evidence of special design. In (pp. 177–96) **14807.**

4067. TER HORST, ROBERT. The fortunes of the novel: a study in the transposition of a genre. New York; Frankfurt: Lang, 2003. pp. 303. (Studies on Cervantes and his times, 8.) Rev. by Ana María Laguna in Scriblerian (37:2 /38:1) 2005, 142.

4068. TURCHI, PETER. Maps of the imagination: the writer as cartographer. San Antonio, TX: Trinity UP, 2004. pp. 245.

4069. VAN DOVER, J. K. We must have certainty: four essays on the detective story. Selinsgrove, PA: Susquehanna UP, 2005. pp. 220.

4070. WALLACE, DIANA. Uncanny stories: the ghost story as female gothic. GothS (6:1) 2004, 57–68.

4071. WELCH, SHANNON. Notes from the stupid tent. Iris (51) 2005, 33–6. (Women in fiction.)

4072. WILAMOVÁ, SIRMA. On expressing negative politeness in English fictional discourse. Ostrava: Univ. of Ostrava, 2005. pp. 158.

4073. WISKER, GINA. Horror fiction: an introduction. London; New York: Continuum, 2005. pp. 294. (Continuum studies in literary genre.)

4074. WISZNIOWSKA, MARTA. Feasting in drama. *In* (pp. 294–303) **3756.**

4075. WOLFE, GARY K. Coming to terms. *In* (pp. 13–22) **4027.**

4076. WOLOCH, ALEX. The one *vs* the many: minor characters and the space of the protagonist in the novel. (Bibl. 2004, 4191.) Rev. by John Mullan in LRB (27:9) 2005, 30–1; by Deidre Lynch in VS (47:2) 2005, 281–2; by Eric Hayot in Mod/Mod (12:2) 2005, 339–41; by Jesse Matz in MLQ (66:3) 2005, 400–3.

4077. YORK, R. A. The extension of life: fiction and history in the American novel. (Bibl. 2003, 4064.) Rev. by Judie Newman in MLR (100:3) 2005, 801–2.

LITERATURE FOR CHILDREN

4078. BENES, PETER (ed.); BENES, JANE MONTAGUE (assoc. ed.). The worlds of children, 1620–1920. Boston, MA: Boston Univ., 2004. pp. 243. (Dublin Seminar for New England Folklife Annual Proceedings: 2002.) Rev. by Marilyn S. Blackwell in VH (73:2) 2005, 190–2.

4079. BOTTOMS, JANET. 'To read aright': representations of Shakespeare for children. *See* **5861.**

4080. CHAPLEAU, SEBASTIEN. New voices in children's literature criticism. Lichfield: Pied Piper, 2004. pp. 131. Rev. by Ruth Mirtz in LU (29:3) 2005, 445–9; by Claudia Nelson in CLAQ (30:2) 2005, 232–4.

4081. CLARK, BEVERLY LYON. Kiddie lit: the cultural construction of children's literature in America. (Bibl. 2004, 4195.) Rev. by Ilana Nash in WRB (22:1) 2004, 15; by Bettina Kümmerling-Meibauer in LU (29:1) 2005, 112–16; by Michael Newton in TLS, 9 Sept. 2005, 27.

4082. FORDYCE, RACHEL (comp.). Dissertations of note. ChildLit (31) 2003, 215–26.

4083. —— Dissertations of note. ChildLit (32) 2004, 270–84.

4084. GILLESPIE, JOHN T. The children's and young adult literature handbook: a research and reference guide. Westport, CT: Libraries Unlimited, 2005. pp. viii, 393. (Children's and young adult literature reference.)

4085. GOODENOUGH, ELIZABETH (ed.). Secret spaces of childhood. Ann Arbor: Michigan UP, 2003. pp. viii, 354. Rev. by James Holt McGavran, Jr, in CLAQ (29:4) 2004, 368–70.

4086. GREENWAY, BETTY (ed.). Twice-told children's tales: the influence of childhood reading on writers for adults. London; New York: Routledge, 2005. pp. xi, 247. (Children's literature and culture, 35.)

4087. GUPTA, SUMAN. Sociological speculations on the professions of children's literature. LU (29:3) 2005, 299–323.

4088. KIRK, CONNIE ANN. Companion to American children's picture books. Westport, CT; London: Greenwood Press, 2005. pp. xxi, 396.

4089. LUNDIN, ANNE. Constructing the canon of children's literature: beyond library walls and ivory towers. (Bibl. 2004, 4202.) Rev. by Kathy Piehl in CLAQ (30:4) 2005, 428–30.

4090. LUPACK, BARBARA TEPA (ed.). Adapting the Arthurian legends for children: essays on Arthurian juvenilia. (Bibl. 2004, 4203.) Rev. by Kevin J. Harty in Arthuriana (15:2) 2005, 76–7.

4091. LURIE, ALISON.   Boys and girls forever: children's classics from Cinderella to Harry Potter. (Bibl. 2004, 4204.) Rev. by Jerry Griswold in ChildLit (32) 2004, 235–8; by Adrienne Kertzer in CanL (186) 2005, 146–8.

4092. MILLBANK, JOHN.   Fictioning things: gift and narratives. See **4045**.

4093. NATOV, RONI.   The poetics of childhood. (Bibl. 2003, 4081.) Rev. by Heather Scutter in ChildLit (32) 2004, 239–45; by Leo Zanderer in LU (29:1) 2005, 102–6; by Juliet McMaster in VicR (31:1) 2005, 62–3.

4094. NIKOLAJEVA, MARIA.   Aesthetic approaches to children's literature. Lanham, MD; London: Scarecrow Press, 2005. pp. xx, 313.

4095. O'SULLIVAN, EMER.   Comparative children's literature. London; New York: Routledge, 2005. pp. 205.

4096. REYNOLDS, KIMBERLEY (ed.).   Children's literature and childhood in performance. Lichfield: Pied Piper, 2003. pp. 148. (NCRCL papers, 9.) Rev. by Lucy Rollin in CLAQ (30:1) 2005, 118–20.

4097. ROCKMAN, CONNIE C. (ed.).   The ninth book of junior authors and illustrators. New York; Dublin: Wilson, 2004. pp. xiii, 583.

4098. STANTON, JOSEPH.   The important books: children's picture books as art and literature. Lanham, MD; London: Scarecrow Press, 2005. pp. 88.

4099. WEINSTEIN, AMY.   Once upon a time: illustrations from fairytales, fables, primers, pop-ups, and other children's books. See **133**.

POETRY

4100. ARMSTRONG, ISOBEL.   The first post: Victorian poetry and post-War criticism. See **14690**.

4101. BATCHELOR, RHONDA.   Ex libris: too many books. See **357**.

4102. BRUNS, GERALD L.   The material of poetry: sketches for a philosophical poetics. Athens; London: Georgia UP, 2005. pp. xxi, 143. (Georgia Southern Univ.: Jack N. and Addie D. Averitt lecture series, 13.)

4103. BUTSCHER, EDWARD.   Poets on poets and poetry. GaR (57:2) 2003, 412–25 (review-article).

4104. CARPER, THOMAS; ATTRIDGE, DEREK.   Meter and meaning: an introduction to rhythm in poetry. (Bibl. 2003, 4110.) Rev. by Tom Barney in LLit (14:1) 2005, 93–6; by John Gouws in NQ (52:1) 2005, 130–1; by Heather Knowles-Smith in Style (39:1) 2005, 92–5.

4105. CHERRY, KELLY.   History, passion, freedom, death, and hope: prose about poetry. Tampa, FL: Tampa UP, 2005. pp. xiv, 193.

4106. EDWARDS, DAVID L.   Poets and God: Chaucer, Shakespeare, Herbert, Milton, Wordsworth, Coleridge, Blake. London: Darton, Longman & Todd, 2005. pp. xv, 256. Rev. by John Whale in TLS, 15 Apr. 2005, 27.

4107. FREEMAN, MARGARET H.   Poetry as power: the dynamics of cognitive poetics as a scientific and literary paradigm. In (pp. 31–57) **3888**.

4108. GANDER, FORREST.   A faithful existence: reading, memory, and transcendence. See **16638**.

4109. GROSHOLZ, EMILY.   The uses of periodicity in English verse. HR (58:2) 2005, 259–74.

4110. HELLER, MICHAEL. Uncertain poetries: essays on poets, poetry, and poetics. Great Wilbraham, Cambridge: Salt, 2005. pp. xvi, 247.

4111. HIRSCH, EDWARD. The work of lyric: night and day. GaR (57:2) 2003, 368–80.

4112. HOOKER, JEREMY. Nostalgia and the kiss of life. *See* **7881**.

4113. HÜHN, PETER; KIEFER, JENS. The narratological analysis of lyric poetry: studies in English poetry from the 16th to the 20th century. Trans. by Alastair Matthews. Berlin; New York: Mouton de Gruyter, 2005. pp. viii, 259. (Narratologia, 7.)

4114. HURLEY, MICHAEL D. The audible reading of poetry revisited. *See* **11307**.

4115. JONES, CHRIS. Knight or wight in Keats's *La Belle Dame*? An ancient ditty reconsidered. *See* **11516**.

4116. KARR, MARY. Facing altars: poetry and prayer. Poetry (187:2) 2005, 125–36.

4117. KENNER, ROB. Word's worth. Poetry (187:3) 2005, 221–4. (The view from here.)

4118. LECERCLE, JEAN-JACQUES. Parody as cultural memory. *See* **18381**.

4119. LENNARD, JOHN. The poetry handbook: a guide to reading poetry for pleasure and practical criticism. (Bibl. 1996, 4398.) Oxford; New York: OUP, 2005. pp. xxv, 418. (Second ed.: first ed. 1996.)

4120. LIDDELOW, EDEN. The memory poets. Meanjin (64:1/2) 2005, 192–203.

4121. LOGAN, WILLIAM. The state with the prettiest name. Parnassus (28:1/2) 2005, 433–53. (Florida.)

4122. —— The undiscovered country: poetry in the age of tin. New York: Columbia UP, 2005. pp. 382.

4123. LUNDQUIST, ROBERT. The essence of, and feeling thought: reflections on the poetic, and the analytic process. AmJP (65:3) 2005, 283–91.

4124. McCONKEY, JAMES. A song of one's own. *See* **17933**.

4125. MAZZARO, JEROME. Unlocking the heart: sincerity and the English sonnet. Philadelphia, PA: XLibris, 2004. pp. 197.

4126. MOTION, ANDREW. All in the ear. TLS, 25 Nov. 2005, 13. (Poetry reading.)

4127. PAGLIA, CAMILLE. Break, blow, burn. New York: Pantheon, 2005. pp. xvii, 247. Rev. by Phoebe Pettingell in NewL (88:2) 2005, 33–4; by Robert McDowell in HR (58:3) 2005, 507–12.

4128. PHILLIPS, CARL. Coin of the realm: essays on the life and art of poetry. (Bibl. 2004, 4252.) Rev. by Edward Butscher in GaR (59:1) 2005, 167–80.

4129. PLUMLY, STANLEY. Argument & song: sources & silences in poetry. (Bibl. 2004, 4256.) Rev. by David Haglund in EC (55:1) 2005, 71–80.

4130. PUGH, CHRISTINA. No experience necessary. Poetry (186:3) 2005, 243–7.

4131. PUGHE, THOMAS. Réinventer la nature: vers une éco-poétique. *See* **11314**.

4132. REGAN, STEPHEN. Robert Frost and the American sonnet. *See* **16613**.

4133. SAVANT, JOHN.   Follow that metaphor: what faith, jazz & poetry have in common. *See* **2460.**

4134. SHAWCROSS, JOHN T.   Works of love or enmity: do not let our minor poets disappear. CEAF (34:1) 2005.

4135. SLAVITT, DAVID R.   *Re* verse: essays on poetry and poets. Evanston, IL: Northwestern UP, 2005. pp. 215.

4136. STOTHARD, PETER.   Reading rooms. TLS, 9 Sept. 2005, 13. (Poetry readings.)

4137. WATERS, WILLIAM ADDISON.   Poetry's touch: on lyric address. (Bibl. 2004, 4277.) Rev. by David Haglund in EC (55:1) 2005, 71–80.

4138. WILLIAMS, C. K.   The music of poetry and the music of mind. LitIm (7:1) 2005, 19–29.

PROSE

4139. ATKINS, G. DOUGLAS.   Tracing the essay: through experience to truth. Athens; London: Georgia UP, 2005. pp. ix, 180.

4140. BARBERET, JOHN.   Messages in bottles: a comparative formal approach to castaway narratives. *In* (pp. 111–21) **8537.**

4141. BLOOM, LYNN Z.   Once more to the essay canon. *In* (pp. 90–111) **3749.**

4142. CURRELI, MARIO (ed.).   Scrittori inglesi a Pisa: viaggi, sogni, visioni dal Trecento al Duemila. Pisa: ETS, 2005. pp. 380. (Percorsi: collana del Dipartimento di Anglistica dell'Univ. di Pisa.)

4143. DANIELL, DAVID.   The Bible in English. (Bibl. 2004, 4288.) Rev. by Cameron A. MacKenzie in Albion (36:3) 2004, 513–14; by John N. King in LitH (14:2) 2005, 84.

4144. GLAISYER, NATASHA; PENNELL, SARA (eds).   Didactic literature in England, 1500–1800: expertise constructed. (Bibl. 2004, 5557.) Rev. by David Stymeist in RQ (57:3) 2004, 1132–4.

4145. GUALTIERI, CLAUDIA.   Re-reading the exotic in British colonial travel writing. *In* (pp. 172–81) **3690.**

4146. IYEIRI, YOKO.   'God forbid!': a historical study of the verb *forbid* in different versions of the English Bible. *See* **1686.**

4147. KENT-DRURY, ROXANNE; SAYRE, GORDON.   *Robinson Crusoe*'s parodic intertextuality. *In* (pp. 48–54) **8537.**

4148. KEWES, PAULINA.   History and its uses: introduction. HLQ (68:1/2) 2005, 1–31.

4149. LEVY, F. J.   Afterword. HLQ (68:1/2) 2005, 415–27. (English historiography.)

4150. NEVALA, MINNA.   Address in early English correspondence: insights into historical socio-pragmatics. *See* **2185.**

4151. NEWMAN, SALLY.   The archival traces of desire: Vernon Lee's failed sexuality and the interpretation of letters in lesbian history. *See* **11582.**

4152. NOVAK, MAXIMILLIAN E.; FISHER, CARL (eds).   Approaches to teaching Defoe's *Robinson Crusoe*. *See* **8537.**

4153. SIEGEL, KRISTI (ed.).   Gender, genre, and identity in women's travel writing. (Bibl. 2004, 4300.) Rev. by Helen M. Buss in Biography (28:3) 2005, 444–7.

4154. SMITH, CAROLINE J.   Living the life of a domestic goddess: chick lit's response to domestic-advice manuals. See **16472.**

4155. TODOROV, TZVETAN.   Poetry without verse. Trans. by Catherine Porter. APR (34:6) 2005, 9–13.

BIOGRAPHY AND AUTOBIOGRAPHY

4156. AMBROSIUS, LLOYD E. (ed.).   Writing biography: historians & their craft. (Bibl. 2004, 4304.) Rev. by David Watson in LitH (14:2) 2005, 75–6; by Malcolm Wagstaff in Auto/Biography (13:3) 2005, 270–2.

4157. AMIOT-JOUENNE, PASCALE (ed.).   L'autobiographie irlandaise: voix communes, voix singulières. Caen: Presses Universitaires de Caen, 2004. pp. 311. Rev. by Carle Bonafous-Murat in EtIr (30:1) 2005, 218–19.

4158. BARANCIK, SUE.   Guide to collective biographies for children and young adults. Lanham, MD; London: Scarecrow Press, 2005. pp. viii, 447.

4159. BELL, HAZEL K.   Indexing biographies and other stories of human lives. See **1071.**

4160. BENTON, MICHAEL.   Literary biomythography. Auto/Biography (13:3) 2005, 206–26.

4161. BRIEN, DONNA LEE.   True tales that nurture: auto/biographical storytelling. AF (19) 2004, 84–95.

4162. BURROW, COLIN.   Who wouldn't buy it? See **5868.**

4163. BUTTE, GEORGE.   I know that I know that I know: reflections on Paul John Eakin's *What Are We Reading When We Read Autobiography?* With a reply by Paul John Eakin. Narrative (13:3) 2005, 299–311. (Dialogue.) (*Responds to* bibl. 2004, 17722.)

4164. CURRELI, MARIO (ed.).   Scrittori inglesi a Pisa: viaggi, sogni, visioni dal Trecento al Duemila. See **4142.**

4165. DONALDSON, IAN.   Biographical uncertainty. EC (54:4) 2004, 305–22. (Critical opinion.)

4166. ENDER, EVELYNE.   Architexts of memory: literature, science, and autobiography. Ann Arbor: Michigan UP, 2005. pp. viii, 305.

4167. GRUBGELD, ELIZABETH.   Anglo-Irish autobiography: class, gender, and the forms of narrative. (Bibl. 2004, 4309.) Rev. by Denis Sampson in CJIS (30:2) 2004, 85; by Heather Bryant Jordan in NewHR (9:2) 2005, 152–6; by Brian Dillon in ILS (25:1) 2005, 23–4.

4168. HOBBS, CATHERINE L.   The elements of autobiography and life narratives. London; New York: Pearson Longman, 2005. pp. xvi, 143. (Elements of composition.)

4169. INGRAM, SUSAN.   Zarathustra's sisters: women's autobiography and the shaping of cultural history. (Bibl. 2004, 4312.) Rev. by Kristin Bisoshi in SEEJ (49:4) 2005, 682–3.

4170. JACOBSON, JOANNE.   Mr Secrets: Henry Adams and the breakdown of the exemplary tradition in American autobiography. *In* (pp. 206–21) **9887.**

4171. LEE, HERMIONE.   Virginia Woolf's nose: essays on biography. Princeton, NJ; Oxford: Princeton UP, 2005. pp. viii, 141. Rev. by Linda Simon in Biography (28:2) 2005, 309–11.

4172. LOCATELLI, CARLA.   Is s/he my gaze? (Feminist) possibilities for autobiographical co(n)texts. *In* (pp. 3–18) **12577.**

4173. MATTHEWS, ANNE, *et al.*   Leading men: authorities on the Revolutionary era say how the Founding Fathers became culture heroes. ASch (74:2) 2005, 126–30.

4174. POPKIN, JEREMY D.   History, historians, & autobiography. Chicago, IL: Dee, 2005. pp. x, 339.

4175. RAK, JULIE.   Are memoirs autobiography? A consideration of genre and public identity. Genre (37:3/4) 2004, 483–504.

4176. RISHOI, CHRISTY.   From girl to woman: American women's coming-of-age narratives. (Bibl. 2004, 4316.) Rev. by Richard S. Lowry in AL (77:1) 2005, 184–6; by Anya Jabour in AmS (46:2) 2005, 188–9.

4177. ROLLYSON, CARL.   A higher form of cannibalism? Adventures in the art and politics of biography. Chicago, IL: Dee, 2005. pp. ix, 197.

4178. TRIDGELL, SUSAN.   Understanding our selves: the dangerous art of biography. New York; Frankfurt: Lang, 2004. pp. 234. (European connections, 12.) Rev. by David McCooey in Biography (28:4) 2005, 677–80.

4179. WACHTER, PHYLLIS E.; SCHULTZ, WILLIAM TODD (comps).   Annual bibliography of works about life writing, 2004–2005. Biography (28:4) 2005, 558–676.

RELATED STUDIES

4180. AGOZZINO, MARIA TERESA.   *Ysbryd y werin*: an overview of Celtic folklore scholarship. FHist (22) 2005, 13–33 (review-article).

4181. CORRELL, TIMOTHY CORRIGAN.   Believers, sceptics, and charlatans: evidential rhetoric, the fairies, and fairy healers in Irish oral narrative and belief. Folklore (116:1) 2005, 1–18.

4182. CULLEN, JIM.   The American Dream: a short history of an idea that shaped a nation. Oxford; New York: OUP, 2003. pp. x, 214. Rev. by Michael Schudson in AmLH (16:3) 2004, 566–73.

4183. DELACAMPAGNE, ARIANE; DELACAMPAGNE, CHRISTIAN.   Here be dragons: a fantastic bestiary. Princeton, NJ; Oxford: Princeton UP, 2003. pp. 199. Rev. by Judith Kellogg in MarvT (19:1) 2005, 137–40.

4184. DONNELLY, JAMES S., JR, *et al.* (eds).   Encyclopedia of Irish history and culture. Farmington Hills, MI: Macmillan Reference USA, 2004. 2 vols. pp. xliii, 1084. Rev. by Robert G. Lowery in ILS (25:1) 2005, 11.

4185. DUPRÉ, LOUIS.   The Enlightenment and the intellectual foundations of modern culture. New Haven, CT; London: Yale UP, 2004. pp. xiv, 397. Rev. by Ricardo Miguel Alfonso in Atl (27:1) 2005, 139–43.

4186. JEFFREY, DAVID LYLE.   Houses of the Interpreter: reading Scripture, reading culture. Waco, TX: Baylor Univ., 2003. pp. x, 288. (Provost.) Rev. by George L. Scheper in ChrisL (54:1) 2004, 123–7.

4187. KERMODE, FRANK.   Yearning for the 'utile'. LRB (27:12) 2005, 21–2 (review-article). (John Carey on the arts.)

4188. SLOCUM, KAY BRAINERD.   Liturgies in honour of Thomas Becket. Toronto; Buffalo, NY; London: Toronto UP, 2004. pp. xii, 379.

LITERARY THEORY

4189. DAVIS, LLOYD.   Sexual morality and critical traditions. *In* (pp. 219–29) **6000.**

4190. ELLIS, FRANK HALE.   The ABC of criticism: aspects of craft and creation in the critical enterprise. Bethesda, MD: Academica Press, 2004. pp. x, 236.

4191. GRABES, HERBERT.   The canon *pro* and *contra*: 'The canon is dead – long live pick and mix.' *See* **3787.**

4192. —— Constructing a usable literary past: literary history and cultural memory. YREAL (21) 2005, 129–43.

4193. HABIB, M. A. R.   A history of literary criticism: from Plato to the present. Oxford; Malden, MA: Blackwell, 2005. pp. ix, 838.

4194. MARTIN, THOMAS L.   Poiesis and possible worlds: a study in modality and literary theory. Toronto; Buffalo, NY; London: Toronto UP, 2004. pp. x, 196.

OLD ENGLISH

GENERAL

4195. ALTVATER, FRANCES, *et al.* (comps). The year's work in Old English studies 2002. OEN (37:2) 2004, 5–196.

4196. AMODIO, MARK C. Writing the oral tradition: oral poetics and literate culture in medieval England. Notre Dame, IN: Notre Dame UP, 2004. pp. xvii, 298. (Poetics of orality and literacy.) Rev. by Michael Matto in TMR, Sept. 2005; by R. L. Streng in TFSB (61:1) 2005, 22–3.

4197. —— (ed.). New directions in oral theory. Tempe: Arizona Center for Medieval and Renaissance Studies, 2005. pp. x, 341. (Medieval & Renaissance texts & studies, 287.)

4198. —— O'KEEFFE, KATHERINE O'BRIEN (eds). Unlocking the wordhord: Anglo-Saxon studies in memory of Edward B. Irving, Jr. (Bibl. 2004, 4344.) Rev. by Peter Dendle in MLR (100:3) 2005, 758–9.

4199. BECKETT, KATHARINE SCARFE. Anglo-Saxon perceptions of the Islamic world. (Bibl. 2004, 4347.) Rev. by Josephine Bloomfield in Envoi (11:1) 2005 for 2002, 33–4; by Charles Burnett in JR (85:3) 2005, 523–4; by Suzanne Conklin Akbari in NQ (52:2) 2005, 238–9; by Karen Louise Jolly in Spec (80:3) 2005, 967–70.

4200. BIGGAM, C. P. (ed.). From earth to art: the many aspects of the plant-world in Anglo-Saxon England. *See* **1773**.

4201. BREDEHOFT, THOMAS A. Secondary stress in compound Germanic names in Old English verse. JEL (31:3) 2003, 199–220.

4202. CAVILL, PAUL (ed.). The Christian tradition in Anglo-Saxon England: approaches to current scholarship and teaching. (Bibl. 2004, 4355.) Rev. by Robin Norris in NQ (52:4) 2005, 515–17.

4203. CORNETT, MICHAEL. New books across the disciplines. *See* **4415**.

4204. CRONAN, DENNIS. Poetic meanings in the Old English poetic vocabulary. EngS (84:5) 2003, 397–425.

4205. CUBITT, CATHERINE (ed.). Court culture in the early Middle Ages: proceedings of the first Alcuin conference. Turnhout: Brepols, 2003. pp. xiv, 290. (Studies in the early Middle Ages, 3.) Rev. by Pamela O'Neill in Parergon (22:1) 2005, 215–17.

4206. DONOGHUE, DANIEL. Old English literature: a short introduction. (Bibl. 2004, 4364.) Rev. by Liesl Smith in TMR, Feb. 2005.

4207. FOYS, MARTIN K. *Circolwyrde* 2004: new electronic resources for Anglo-Saxon studies. OEN (38:1) 2004, 34–42.

4208. FULK, R. D.; CAIN, CHRISTOPHER M. A history of Old English literature. With a chapter on saints' lives by Rachel S. Anderson. (Bibl. 2004, 4369.) Rev. by Peter Dendle in TMR, July 2005.

4209. HARBUS, ANTONINA; POOLE, RUSSELL (eds). Verbal encounters: Anglo-Saxon and Old Norse studies for Roberta Frank. *See* **1786**.

4210. JOHNSON, DAVID FRAME; TREHARNE, ELAINE M. (eds). Readings in medieval texts: interpreting Old and Middle English literature. Oxford; New York: OUP, 2005. pp. ix, 400, (plates) 8.

4211. KARKOV, CATHERINE E.; BROWN, GEORGE HARDIN (eds). Anglo-Saxon styles. (Bibl. 2003, 4291.) Rev. by Christine Rauer in MLR (100:3) 2005, 757–8; by Fred C. Robinson in JEGP (104:2) 2005, 283–5.

4212. KEYNES, SIMON. Between Bede and the *Chronicle*: London, BL, Cotton Vespasian B.vi, fols 104–9. *In* (pp. 47–67) **4220.**

4213. KRYGIER, MARCIN; SIKORSKA, LILIANA (eds). For the loue of Inglis lede. *See* **4445.**

4214. LEES, CLARE A. Analytical survey 7: actually existing Anglo-Saxon studies. NML (7) 2005, 223–52.

4215. MITCHELL, BRUCE. The relation between Old English alliterative verse and Ælfric's alliterative prose. *In* (pp. 349–62) **4221.**

4216. MURDOCH, BRIAN; READ, MALCOLM (eds). Early Germanic literature and culture. Rochester, NY: Camden House, 2004. pp. vi, 334. (Studies in German literature, linguistics, and culture.) (Camden House history of German literature, 1.)

4217. NEVILLE, JENNIFER. Leaves of glass: plant-life in Old English poetry. *In* (pp. 287–300) **1773.**

4218. O'DONNELL, DANIEL PAU. O captain! My captain! Using technology to guide readers through an electronic edition. *See* **1124.**

4219. O'KEEFFE, KATHERINE O'BRIEN. Deaths and transformations: thinking through the 'end' of Old English verse. *In* (pp. 149–78) **4197.**

4220. —— ORCHARD, ANDY (eds). Latin literature and English lore: studies in Anglo-Saxon literature for Michael Lapidge: vol. I. Toronto; Buffalo, NY; London: Toronto UP, 2005. pp. xvii, 460. (Toronto Old English series.)

4221. —— —— Latin literature and English lore: studies in Anglo-Saxon literature for Michael Lapidge: vol. II. Toronto; Buffalo, NY; London: Toronto UP, 2005. pp. xvii, 431. (Toronto Old English series.)

4222. PASTORE PASSARO, MARIA C. Representation of women in Classical, medieval and Renaissance texts. Lewiston, NY; Lampeter: Mellen Press, 2005. pp. xiv, 215. (Studies in Renaissance literature, 27.)

4223. POLLINGTON, STEPHEN. The mead hall: the feasting tradition in Anglo-Saxon England. (Bibl. 2004, 4395.) Rev. by Alexander M. Bruce in TMR, Jan. 2005.

4224. POWELL, KATHRYN. The MANCASS C11 database: a tool for studying script and spelling in the eleventh century. *See* **1410.**

4225. —— SCRAGG, DONALD (eds). Apocryphal texts and traditions in Anglo-Saxon England. (Bibl. 2004, 4396.) Rev. by Brian Murdoch in LitTheol (18:4) 2004, 489–91; by Craig R. Davis in Envoi (11:1) 2005 for 2002, 68–73.

4226. REMLEY, PAUL G., *et al.* Bibliography for 2004. ASE (34) 2005, 263–366.

4227. ROBINSON, FRED C. *Mise en page* in Old English manuscripts and printed texts. *In* (pp. 363–75) **4221.**

4228. SCHEIL, ANDREW P. The footsteps of Israel: understanding Jews in Anglo-Saxon England. (Bibl. 2004, 4399.) Rev. by Scott DeGregorio in JEGP (104:4) 2005, 551–3.

4229. STEINER, EMILY; BARRINGTON, CANDACE (eds). The letter of the law: legal practice and literary production in medieval England. (Bibl. 2004, 4403.) Rev. by Wenxi Liu in SixCJ (34:2) 2003, 510–11.

4230. SUZUKI, SEIICHI. The metre of Old Saxon poetry: the remaking of alliterative tradition. (Bibl. 2004, 4404.) Rev. by M. J. Toswell in TMR, Oct. 2005; by Thomas A. Bredehoft in NQ (52:3) 2005, 383–4.

4231. TREHARNE, ELAINE; ROSSER, SUSAN (eds). Early medieval English texts and interpretations: studies presented to Donald G. Scragg. (Bibl. 2004, 4407.) Rev. by Bella Millett in MLR (100:3) 2005, 762–3; by Eugene Green in Spec (80:1) 2005, 346–8.

4232. TREHARNE, ELAINE M. (ed.). Old and Middle English c.890–c.1400: an anthology. (Bibl. 2004, 4408.) Rev. by Antonina Harbus in Parergon (22:1) 2005, 288–90; by Sarah Downey in NQ (52:4) 2005, 517–18.

4233. WELLS, DAVID A. The Central Franconian Rhyming Bible ('Mittelfränkische Reimbibel'), an early twelfth-century German verse homiliary: a thematic and exegetical commentary, with the text and a translation into English. (Bibl. 2004, 4409.) Rev. by Annette Volfing in MLR (100:3) 2005, 855–6; by Nigel Harris in MÆ (74:1) 2005, 153–4.

4234. WITHERS, BENJAMIN C.; WILCOX, JONATHAN (eds). Naked before God: uncovering the body in Anglo-Saxon England. Morgantown: West Virginia UP, 2003. pp. xii, 315. (Medieval European studies, 3.) Rev. by Josephine Bloomfield in Envoi (11:1) 2005 for 2002, 93–9; by Elizabeth Coatsworth in Spec (80:3) 2005, 1001–3.

4235. ZACHER, SAMANTHA. The rewards of poetry: 'homiletic' verse in Cambridge, Corpus Christi College 201. SELIM (12) 2003/04, 83–108.

RELATED STUDIES

4236. CLERMONT-FERRAND, MEREDITH. Anglo-Saxon propaganda in the Bayeux Tapestry. Lewiston, NY; Lampeter: Mellen Press, 2004. pp. xv, 153, (plates) 16. Rev. by K. A. Laity in ELN (43:1) 2005, 84–9.

4237. GOFFART, WALTER. Bede's *uera lex historiae* explained. ASE (34) 2005, 111–16.

4238. McFADDEN, BRIAN. Authority and discourse in the *Liber monstrorum*. Neophilologus (89:3) 2005, 473–93.

4239. McTURK, RORY (ed.). A companion to Old Norse–Icelandic literature and culture. Oxford; Malden, MA: Blackwell, 2005. pp. xiii, 567. (Blackwell companions to literature and culture, 31.) Rev. by Tom Shippey in TLS, 8 July 2005, 8.

4240. PIZARRO, J. M. Poetry as rumination: the model for Bede's Cædmon. Neophilologus (89:3) 2005, 469–72.

4241. ROSS, MARGARET CLUNIES. A history of Old Norse poetry and poetics. Woodbridge, Suffolk; Rochester, NY: Brewer, 2005. pp. x, 283.

4242. SOLOPOV, ALEXEI. The imperial context of place-names in Roman Britain. JEPNS (37) 2004/05, 5–18.

4243. STORY, JOANNA. The Frankish annals of Lindisfarne and Kent. ASE (34) 2005, 59–109.

AUTHORS AND ANONYMOUS WORKS

Ælfric

4244. BECKETT, KATHARINE SCARFE. Worcester sauce: Malchus in Anglo-Saxon England. In (pp. 212–31) 4221.

4245. BIGGS, FREDERICK M. Ælfric's Andrew and the Apocrypha. JEGP (104:4) 2005, 473–94.

4246. —— Ælfric's comments about the Passio Thomae. NQ (52:1) 2005, 5–8.

4247. BJORK, ROBERT E. The symbolic use of Job in Ælfric's homily on Job, Christ II, and the Phoenix. In (pp. 315–30) 4221.

4248. CANNON, CHRISTOPHER. Between the Old and the Middle of English. See 1385.

4249. CLAYTON, MARY. Ælfric's De auguriis and Cambridge, Corpus Christi College 178. In (pp. 376–94) 4221.

4250. DEKKER, KEES. Pentecost and linguistic self-consciousness in Anglo-Saxon England: Bede and Ælfric. JEGP (104:3) 2005, 345–72.

4251. GNEUSS, HELMUT. The homiliary of the Taunton fragments. See 4345.

4252. HEAD, PAULINE. Cennan, 'to cause to be born'/'to cause to know': Incarnation as revelation in Old English literature. In (pp. 55–75) 1786.

4253. HILL, JOYCE. Ælfric's Colloquy: the Antwerp/London version. In (pp. 331–48) 4221.

4254. MITCHELL, BRUCE. The relation between Old English alliterative verse and Ælfric's alliterative prose. In (pp. 349–62) 4221.

4255. O'KEEFFE, KATHERINE O'BRIEN. Deaths and transformations: thinking through the 'end' of Old English verse. In (pp. 149–78) 4197.

4256. —— ORCHARD, ANDY (eds). Latin literature and English lore: studies in Anglo-Saxon literature for Michael Lapidge: vol. II. See 4221.

4257. RUFF, CARIN. Desipere in loco: style, memory, and the teachable moment. In (pp. 91–103) 1786.

4258. SZABO, VICKI ELLEN. 'Bad to the bone'? The unnatural history of monstrous medieval whales. See 4366.

4259. TINTI, FRANCESCA (ed.). Pastoral care in late Anglo-Saxon England. Woodbridge, Suffolk; Rochester, NY: Boydell Press, 2005. pp. viii, 152. (Anglo-Saxon studies, 6.)

4260. UPCHURCH, ROBERT K. For pastoral care and political gain: Ælfric of Eynsham's preaching on marital celibacy. Traditio (59) 2004, 39–78.

4261. —— Virgin spouses as model Christians: the legend of Julian and Basilissa in Ælfric's Lives of Saints. ASE (34) 2005, 197–217.

Saint Aldhelm

4262. BECKETT, KATHARINE SCARFE. Worcester sauce: Malchus in Anglo-Saxon England. *In* (pp. 212–31) **4221**.

4263. HERREN, MICHAEL W. Aldhelm the theologian. *In* (pp. 68–89) **4220**.

4264. OSBORN, MARIJANE. 'Skep' (*Beinenkorb, *beoleap*) as a culture-specific solution to Exeter Book Riddle 17. *See* **4373**.

4265. REMLEY, PAUL G. Aldhelm as Old English poet: *Exodus*, Asser, and the *Dicta Ælfredi*. *In* (pp. 90–108) **4220**.

4266. RUFF, CARIN. *Desipere in loco*: style, memory, and the teachable moment. *In* (pp. 91–103) **1786**.

4267. —— The place of metrics in Anglo-Saxon Latin education: Aldhelm and Bede. JEGP (104:2) 2005, 149–70.

4268. RUSCHE, PHILIP G. Isidore's *Etymologiae* and the Canterbury Aldhelm *scholia*. JEGP (104:4) 2005, 437–55.

4269. WINTERBOTTOM, MICHAEL. Faricius of Arezzo's *Life of St Aldhelm*. *In* (pp. 109–31) **4220**.

Alfred, King of England (849–899)

4270. DISCENZA, NICOLE. The King's English: strategies of translation in the Old English Boethius. Albany: New York State UP, 2005. pp. viii, 224.

4271. GODDEN, MALCOLM. Alfred, Asser, and Boethius. *In* (pp. 326–48) **4220**.

4272. GRAHAM, TIMOTHY. The opening of King Alfred's preface to the Old English *Pastoral Care*: Oxford, Bodleian Library, MS Hatton 20. OEN (38:1) 2004, 43–50.

4273. IRVINE, SUSAN. Fragments of Boethius: the reconstruction of the Cotton manuscript of the Alfredian text. ASE (34) 2005, 169–81.

4274. KEESEE, NEAL K. Tolkien, King Alfred, and Boethius: Platonist views of evil in *The Lord of the Rings*. *See* **19823**.

4275. PAPAHAGI, ADRIAN. Another source for the Old English Dict of Cato 73. *See* **4332**.

4276. REMLEY, PAUL G. Aldhelm as Old English poet: *Exodus*, Asser, and the *Dicta Ælfredi*. *In* (pp. 90–108) **4220**.

4277. REUTER, TIMOTHY (ed.). Alfred the Great: papers from the eleventh-centenary conferences. (Bibl. 2004, 4466.) Rev. by I. J. Kirby in Spec (80:3) 2005, 958–60.

4278. ROGERS, NICHOLAS. Henry VI and the proposed canonisation of King Alfred. *In* (pp. 211–20) **4488**.

4279. ROUSE, ROBERT ALLEN. The idea of Anglo-Saxon England in Middle English romance. *See* **4554**.

4280. SZARMACH, PAUL E. Alfred's *Soliloquies* in London, BL, Cotton Tiberius A.iii (art. 9g, fols 50v–51v). *In* (pp. 153–79) **4221**.

Andreas

4281. DOCKRAY-MILLER, MARY. The *eadgiþ* erasure: a gloss on the Old English *Andreas*. ANQ (18:1) 2005, 3–7.

Anglo-Saxon Chronicle

4282. DUMVILLE, DAVID; KEYNES, SIMON (gen. eds). The *Anglo-Saxon Chronicle*: a collaborative edition: vol. 7, MS E: a semi-diplomatic edition with introduction and indices. Ed. by Susan Irvine. Woodbridge, Suffolk; Rochester, NY: Brewer, 2004. pp. clxxvii, 174. Rev. by Elaine Treharne in TMR, July 2005; by Richard Marsden in NQ (52:3) 2005, 385–6.

4283. KRIES, SUSANNE. English–Danish rivalry and the mutilation of Alfred in the eleventh-century *Chronicle* poem *The Death of Alfred*. JEGP (104:1) 2005, 31–53.

Apollonius of Tyre

4284. MORINI, CARLA. The first English love romance without 'love'! The Old English *Apollonius of Tyre*. SELIM (12) 2003/04, 109–25.

The Battle of Brunanburh

4285. KRIES, SUSANNE. English–Danish rivalry and the mutilation of Alfred in the eleventh-century *Chronicle* poem *The Death of Alfred*. *See* **4283**.

The Battle of Maldon

4286. HALBROOKS, JOHN. Byrhtnoth's great-hearted mirth; or, Praise and blame in *The Battle of Maldon*. PQ (82:3) 2003, 235–55.

Beowulf

4287. AMODIO, MARK C. Res(is)ting the singer: towards a non-performative Anglo-Saxon oral poetics. *In* (pp. 179–208) **4197**.

4288. BAMMESBERGER, ALFRED. The coastguard's maxim reconsidered (*Beowulf*, lines 287b–289). ANQ (18:2) 2005, 3–6.

4289. —— Old English *cuþe folme* in *Beowulf*, line 1303a. Neophilologus (89:4) 2005, 625–7.

4290. —— Old English *sum* in *Beowulf*, l. 271b. NM (106:1) 2005, 3–5.

4291. BIGGS, FREDERICK M. The politics of succession in *Beowulf* and Anglo-Saxon England. Spec (80:3) 2005, 709–41.

4292. FRANK, ROBERTA. Three 'cups' and a funeral in *Beowulf*. *In* (pp. 407–20) **4220**.

4293. FULK, R. D. Afloat in semantic space: Old English *sund* and the nature of Beowulf's exploit with Breca. JEGP (104:4) 2005, 456–72.

4294. —— Six cruces in *Beowulf* (lines 31, 83, 404, 445, 1198, and 3074–5). *In* (pp. 349–67) **4220**.

4295. —— Six cruces in the Finnsburg fragment and episode. *See* **4338**.

4296. —— Some contested readings in the *Beowulf* manuscript. RES (56:224) 2005, 192–223.

4297. GRIFFITH, M. S. Verses quite like *cwen to gebeddan* in *The Metres of Boethius*. *See* **4360**.

4298. HAINES, SIMON. Poetry and philosophy from Homer to Rousseau: romantic souls, realist lives. Basingstoke; New York: Palgrave Macmillan, 2005. pp. xiii, 215. Rev. by Rosamund Dalziell in Meanjin (64:3) 2005, 171–6.

4299. HARDER, BERNIE. A dialogic reading of oral literature: Harry Robinson's *Write It on Your Heart* and *Beowulf*. *In* (pp. 47–59) **9168**.

4300. HOWE, NICHOLAS.   *Beowulf* in the house of Dickens. *In* (pp. 421–39) **4220.**

4301. JOY, EILEEN A.   James W. Earl's *Thinking about Beowulf*: ten years later. HAge (8) 2005.

4302. KIM, SUSAN M.   'As I once did with Grendel': boasting and nostalgia in *Beowulf.* MP (103:1) 2005, 4–27.

4303. LOCKETT, LESLIE.   The role of Grendel's arm in feud, law, and the narrative strategy of *Beowulf. In* (pp. 368–88) **4220.**

4304. MOMMA, HARUKO.   The education of Beowulf and the affair of the leisure class. *In* (pp. 163–82) **1786.**

4305. MULLALLY, ERIN.   Hrethel's heirloom: kinship, succession, and weaponry in *Beowulf. In* (pp. 228–44) **5103.**

4306. NELSON, MARIE.   *Beowulf*'s boast words. Neophilologus (89:2) 2005, 299–310.

4307. ORCHARD, ANDY.   A critical companion to *Beowulf.* (Bibl. 2004, 4523.) Rev. by Nicholas Howe in Spec (80:1) 2005, 290–3.

4308. —— Reading *Beowulf* now and then. SELIM (12) 2003/04, 49–81.

4309. SHARMA, MANISH.   Metalepsis and monstrosity: the boundaries of narrative structure in *Beowulf.* SP (102:3) 2005, 247–79.

4310. SHIPPEY, TOM.   The Merov(ich)ingian again: *dramatio memoriae* and the *usus scholarum. In* (pp. 389–406) **4220.**

4311. STANLEY, ERIC.   *Beowulf*: lordlessness in ancient times is the theme, as much as the glory of kings, if not more. NQ (52:3) 2005, 267–81.

4312. STAVER, RUTH JOHNSTON.   A companion to *Beowulf.* Westport, CT; London: Greenwood Press, 2005. pp. xvi, 227.

4313. WHITE, JUDY ANNE.   Hero-ego in search of self: a Jungian reading of *Beowulf.* (Bibl. 2004, 4531.) Rev. by James W. Earl in JEGP (104:4) 2005, 553–5.

Byrhtferth

4314. BAKER, PETER S.   More diagrams by Byrhtferth of Ramsey. *In* (pp. 53–73) **4221.**

4315. RUFF, CARIN.   *Desipere in loco*: style, memory, and the teachable moment. *In* (pp. 91–103) **1786.**

Cædmon's Hymn

4316. AMODIO, MARK C.   Res(is)ting the singer: towards a non-performative Anglo-Saxon oral poetics. *In* (pp. 179–208) **4197.**

4317. DEKKER, KEES.   Pentecost and linguistic self-consciousness in Anglo-Saxon England: Bede and Ælfric. *See* **4250.**

Charters

4318. HOOKE, DELLA.   Trees in the Anglo-Saxon landscape: the charter evidence. *In* (pp. 17–39) **1773.**

4319. LOWE, KATHRYN A.   *Mearcella* in S 703 and the etymology of Childrey Brook (Berkshire). *See* **2025.**

Christ I

4320. HEAD, PAULINE.   *Cennan*, 'to cause to be born'/'to cause to know': Incarnation as revelation in Old English literature. *In* (pp. 55–75) **1786.**

Christ and Satan

4321. LABRIOLA, ALBERT C.   The begetting and exaltation of the Son: the Junius Manuscript and Milton's *Paradise Lost*. In (pp. 22–32) **7738**.

Cynewulf

4322. BJORK, ROBERT E.   The symbolic use of Job in Ælfric's homily on Job, *Christ II*, and the *Phoenix*. In (pp. 315–30) **4221**.

4323. COTTER, JAMES FINN.   Hopkins and Cynewulf: *The Wreck of the Deutschland*, *The Windhover*, *The Blessed Virgin Compared to the Air We Breathe*, and the *Christ*. See **11298**.

4324. DiNAPOLI, ROBERT.   Odd characters: runes in Old English poetry. In (pp. 145–61) **1786**.

4325. HARBUS, ANTONINA.   Articulate contact in *Juliana*. In (pp. 183–200) **1786**.

4326. HILL, THOMAS D.   The failing torch: the Old English *Elene*, 1256–1259. NQ (52:2) 2005, 155–60.

4327. VACCARO, CHRISTOPHER.   'Inbryrded breostsefa': compunction in line 841a of Cynewulf's *Elene*. NQ (52:2) 2005, 160–1.

4328. WRIGHT, CHARLES D.   The persecuted Church and the *mysterium lunae*: Cynewulf's *Ascension*, lines 252b–272 (*Christ II*, lines 691b–711). In (pp. 293–314) **4221**.

Daniel

4329. SHARMA, MANISH.   Nebuchadnezzar and the defiance of measure in the Old English *Daniel*. EngS (86:2) 2005, 103–26.

Deor

4330. POOLE, RUSSELL.   Claiming kin skaldic-style. In (pp. 269–84) **1786**.

Devotional Works

4331. FRANTZEN, ALLEN J.   Spirituality and devotion in the Anglo-Saxon penitentials. EMS (22) 2005, 117–28.

Dicts of Cato

4332. PAPAHAGI, ADRIAN.   Another source for the Old English Dict of Cato 73. NQ (52:1) 2005, 8–10.

The Dream of the Rood

4333. FJALLDAL, MAGNÚS.   A lot of learning is a dang'rous thing: the Ruthwell Cross runes and their Icelandic interpreters. StudMed (14) 2005, 30–50.

4334. HECKMAN, CHRISTINA M.   *Imitatio* in early medieval spirituality: *The Dream of the Rood*, Anselm, and militant Christology. EMS (22) 2005, 141–53.

4335. McGILLIVRAY, MURRAY.   *Dream of the Rood* 9–12 and the Christmas liturgy. NQ (52:1) 2005, 1–2.

Exodus

4336. ANLEZARK, DANIEL.   Connecting the patriarchs: Noah and Abraham in the Old English *Exodus*. JEGP (104:2) 2005, 171–88.

4337. REMLEY, PAUL G.   Aldhelm as Old English poet: *Exodus*, Asser, and the *Dicta Ælfredi*. In (pp. 90–108) **4220**.

The Fight at Finnsburh

4338. FULK, R. D.   Six cruces in the Finnsburg fragment and episode. MÆ (74:2) 2005, 191–204.

The Fortunes of Men

4339. DESKIS, SUSAN E.   Exploring text and discourse in the Old English gnomic poems: the problem of narrative. *See* **4354.**

Genesis A

4340. OLSEN, KARIN.   'Him *þæs grim lean becom*': the theme of infertility in *Genesis A*. *In* (pp. 127–43) **1786.**

Genesis B

4341. BAMMESBERGER, ALFRED.   *Freo* 'woman' in *Genesis*, line 457a. *See* **1838.**

4342. ERICKSEN, JANET SCHRUNK.   Legalizing the Fall of Man. MÆ (74:2) 2005, 205–20.

4343. LABRIOLA, ALBERT C.   The begetting and exaltation of the Son: the Junius Manuscript and Milton's *Paradise Lost*. *In* (pp. 22–32) **7738.**

Gospels

4344. ESTEBAN SEGURA, MARIA LAURA.   The punctuation system of the West Saxon version of the Gospel according to Saint John. LFil (21) 2005, 29–44.

Homilies

4345. GNEUSS, HELMUT.   The homiliary of the Taunton fragments. NQ (52:4) 2005, 440–2.

4346. HAINES, DOROTHY.   Courtroom drama and the homiletic monologues of the Vercelli Book. *In* (pp. 105–23) **1786.**

4347. KELLY, RICHARD J. (ed. and trans.).   The Blickling Homilies. London; New York: Continuum, 2003. pp. lvi, 232, (plates) 4. Rev. by Jonathan Wilcox in Spec (80:2) 2005, 604–7.

4348. PAPAHAGI, ADRIAN.   *(Ge)wyrd*: emendations to three anonymous Old English homilies and saints' lives. NM (106:3) 2005, 311–14.

4349. ROWLEY, SHARON M.   'A *wese\n/dan nacodnisse and þa ecan þistru*': language and mortality in the homily for Doomsday in Cambridge, Corpus Christi College MS 41. EngS (84:6) 2003, 493–510.

4350. SCRAGG, DONALD.   A late Old English Harrowing of Hell homily from Worcester and Blickling Homily VII. *In* (pp. 197–211) **4221.**

Judith

4351. BECKETT, KATHARINE SCARFE.   Worcester sauce: Malchus in Anglo-Saxon England. *In* (pp. 212–31) **4221.**

4352. MULLALLY, ERIN.   The cross-gendered gift: weaponry in the Old English *Judith*. Exemplaria (17:2) 2005, 255–84.

Laws

4353. OLIVER, LISI (ed.).   The laws of Æthelbert: a student edition. OEN (38:1) 2004, 51–72.

Maxims I

4354. DESKIS, SUSAN E.   Exploring text and discourse in the Old English gnomic poems: the problem of narrative. JEGP (104:3) 2005, 326–44.

Medical and Scientific Texts

4355. BRENNESSEL, BARBARA; DROUT, MICHAEL D. C.; GRAVEL, ROBYN.   A reassessment of the efficacy of Anglo-Saxon medicine. ASE (34) 2005, 183–95.

4356. D'ARONCO, MARIA AMALIA.   Anglo-Saxon plant pharmacy and the Latin medical tradition. *In* (pp. 133–51) **1773**.

4357. HALL, ALARIC.   Calling the shots: the Old English remedy *Gif hors ofscoten sie* and Anglo-Saxon *elf-shot*. NM (106:2) 2005, 195–209.

4358. RUSCHE, PHILIP G.   Dioscorides' *De materia medica* and late Old English herbal glossaries. *In* (pp. 181–94) **1773**.

Metres of Boethius

4359. DISCENZA, NICOLE.   The King's English: strategies of translation in the Old English Boethius. *See* **4270**.

4360. GRIFFITH, M. S.   Verses quite like *cwen to gebeddan* in *The Metres of Boethius*. ASE (34) 2005, 145–67.

4361. IRVINE, SUSAN.   Fragments of Boethius: the reconstruction of the Cotton manuscript of the Alfredian text. *See* **4273**.

Old English Martyrology

4362. LARSON, WENDY R.   Who is the master of this narrative? Maternal patronage of the cult of St Margaret. *In* (pp. 94–134) **4427**.

Otherworld Visions

4363. JACKSON, PETER.   Osbert of Clare and the *Vision of Leofric*: the transformation of an Old English narrative. *In* (pp. 275–92) **4221**.

The Phoenix

4364. BAMMESBERGER, ALFRED.   Old English *gefreogum* in *The Phoenix*, line 29b. Neophilologus (89:1) 2005, 115–17.

4365. BJORK, ROBERT E.   The symbolic use of Job in Ælfric's homily on Job, *Christ II*, and the *Phoenix*. *In* (pp. 315–30) **4221**.

Physiologus

4366. SZABO, VICKI ELLEN.   'Bad to the bone'? The unnatural history of monstrous medieval whales. HAge (8) 2005.

Prayers

4367. COOPER, TRACEY-ANNE.   The monastic origins of Tovie the Proud's adoration of the Cross. NQ (52:4) 2005, 437–40.

The Rewards of Piety

4368. ZACHER, SAMANTHA.   The rewards of poetry: 'homiletic' verse in Cambridge, Corpus Christi College 201. *See* **4235**.

Riddles

4369. AFROS, ELENA.   Linguistic ambiguities in some Exeter Book riddles. NQ (52:4) 2005, 431–7.

4370. —— Syntactic variaton in Riddles 30A and 30B. NQ (52:1) 2005, 2–5.

4371. DiNapoli, Robert. Odd characters: runes in Old English poetry. *In* (pp. 145–61) **1786**.

4372. Orchard, Andy. Enigma variations: the Anglo-Saxon riddle tradition. *In* (pp. 284–304) **4220**.

4373. Osborn, Marijane. 'Skep' (*Beinenkorb*, **beoleap*) as a culture-specific solution to Exeter Book Riddle 17. ANQ (18:1) 2005, 7–18.

The Ruin

4374. Peebles, Katie Lyn. Renovating ruins: the construction of Anglo-Saxon cultural heritage. MidF (31:1) 2005, 5–15.

Rune Poem

4375. DiNapoli, Robert. Odd characters: runes in Old English poetry. *In* (pp. 145–61) **1786**.

4376. Hooke, Della. Trees in the Anglo-Saxon landscape: the charter evidence. *In* (pp. 17–39) **1773**.

Saints' Lives

4377. Beckett, Katharine Scarfe. Worcester sauce: Malchus in Anglo-Saxon England. *In* (pp. 212–31) **4221**.

4378. Lees, Clare A. Vision and place in the Old English life of Mary of Egypt. OENS (33) 2005, 57–78.

4379. Norris, Robin. *Vitas matrum*: Mary of Egypt as female confessor. OENS (33) 2005, 79–109.

4380. Olsen, K. E.; Harbus, A.; Hofstra, T. (eds). Miracles and the miraculous in medieval Germanic and Latin literature: Germania Latina v. Louvain; Dudley, MA: Peeters, 2004. pp. vi, 211. (Mediaevalia Groningana, 6.)

4381. Orchard, Andy. Rhetoric and style in the Old English life of Mary of Egypt. OENS (33) 2005, 31–55.

4382. Papahagi, Adrian. (Ge)wyrd: emendations to three anonymous Old English homilies and saints' lives. See **4348**.

4383. Søndergaard, Leif; Hansen, Rasmus Thorning (eds). Monsters, marvels and miracles: imaginary journeys and landscapes in the Middle Ages. See **4483**.

4384. Tkacz, Catherine Brown. Byzantine theology in the Old English *De Transitu Mariae Ægypticae*. OENS (33) 2005, 9–29.

Solomon and Saturn

4385. Hill, Thomas D. The 'palmtwigede' Pater Noster: horticultural semantics and the Old English *Solomon and Saturn I*. MÆ (74:1) 2005, 1–9.

4386. Powell, Kathryn. Orientalist fantasy in the poetic dialogues of *Solomon and Saturn*. ASE (34) 2005, 117–43.

The Wanderer

4387. Beaston, Lawrence. The Wanderer's courage. Neophilologus (89:1) 2005, 119–37.

4388. GANZE, RONALD J. From *anhaga* to *snottor*: the Wanderer's Kierkegaardian epiphany. Neophilologus (89:4) 2005, 629–40.

Widsith

4389. POOLE, RUSSELL. Claiming kin skaldic-style. *In* (pp. 269–84) **1786**.

Wulfstan

4390. PONS-SANZ, SARA M. An etymological note on OE *of līfe forrǣdan*. *See* **1869**.

4391. —— Friends and relatives in need of an explanation: Gr *anagkaîos*, L *necessarius*, and PGmc **nauð-*. *See* **1868**.

4392. TOWNEND, MATTHEW (ed.). Wulfstan, Archbishop of York: the proceedings of the second Alcuin Conference. Turnhout: Brepols, 2004. pp. 548. (Studies in the early Middle Ages, 10.) Rev. by John Hines in TMR, July 2005; by Melanie Heyworth in Parergon (22:2) 2005, 257–9.

MIDDLE ENGLISH AND FIFTEENTH CENTURY

GENERAL

4393. ADAMS, GILLIAN.   In the hands of children. *See* **193**.

4394. AERS, DAVID.   Sanctifying signs: making Christian tradition in late medieval England. Notre Dame, IN: Notre Dame UP, 2004. pp. xiii, 281. Rev. by John C. Hirsh in MÆ (74:2) 2005, 343–4.

4395. AKBARI, SUZANNE CONKLIN.   Seeing through the veil: optical theory and medieval allegory. Toronto; Buffalo, NY; London: Toronto UP, 2004. pp. x, 354. Rev. by John North in NQ (52:4) 2005, 525–7; by Norman Klassen in MÆ (74:2) 2005, 333–4.

4396. ALLEN, ELIZABETH.   False fables and exemplary truth in later Middle English literature. Basingstoke; New York: Palgrave Macmillan, 2005. pp. viii, 225. (New Middle Ages.)

4397. ALLEN, VALERIE.   Waxing red: shame and the body, shame and the soul. *In* (pp. 191–210) **4463**.

4398. ALTMANN, BARBARA K.; CARROLL, CARLETON W. (eds).   The court reconvenes: courtly literature across the disciplines: selected papers from the Ninth Triennial Congress of the International Courtly Literature Society, University of British Columbia, 25–31 July, 1998. (Bibl. 2004, 4610.) Rev. by Angus J. Kennedy in MÆ (74:2) 2005, 334–6.

4399. AMODIO, MARK C.   Writing the oral tradition: oral poetics and literate culture in medieval England. *See* **4196**.

4400. —— (ed.).   New directions in oral theory. *See* **4197**.

4401. AMTOWER, LAUREL; KEHLER, DOROTHEA (comps).   The single woman in medieval and early modern England. (Bibl. 2003, 4476.) Rev. by Lissa Beauchamp in SCN (63:1/2) 2005, 60–3; by Theodora A. Jankowski in RQ (58:2) 2005, 718–20.

4402. BAWCUTT, PRISCILLA.   Scottish manuscript miscellanies from the fifteenth to the seventeenth century. *See* **200**.

4403. BENSON, PAMELA JOSEPH; KIRKHAM, VICTORIA (eds).   Strong voices, weak history: early women writers & canons in England, France, & Italy. *See* **5094**.

4404. BERNAU, ANKE; EVANS, RUTH; SALIH, SARA (eds).   Medieval virginities. (Bibl. 2004, 4615, where scholar details incorrect.) Rev. by Mary Swan in MLR (100:1) 2005, 186–7; by Bella Millett in JEGP (104:4) 2005, 549–51.

4405. BILDHAUER, BETTINA; MILLS, ROBERT (eds).   The monstrous Middle Ages. (Bibl. 2003, 4481.) Rev. by Ruth Evans in LitTheol (18:4) 2004, 487–9; by Carolyne Larrington in TMR, Sept. 2005; by Annie Sutherland in RES (56:224) 2005, 317–18; by Mary Scrafton in Parergon (22:2) 2005, 194–6; by Paolo Matteucci in Comitatus (36) 2005, 264–6.

4406. BINSKI, PAUL; PANAYOTOVA, STELLA (eds).   The Cambridge illuminations: ten centuries of book production in the medieval West. *See* **202**.

4407. BLUMENFELD-KOSINSKI, RENATE; ROBERTSON, DUNCAN; WARREN, NANCY BRADLEY (eds). The vernacular spirit: essays on medieval religious literature. (Bibl. 2004, 4616.) Rev. by Thomas J. Heffernan in SAC (26) 2004, 363–6.

4408. BØRCH, MARIANNE (ed.). Text and voice: the rhetoric of authority in the Middle Ages. Odense: UP of Southern Denmark, 2004. pp. 272.

4409. BURROW, J. A. Gestures and looks in medieval narrative. (Bibl. 2004, 4622.) Rev. by Mary Theresa Hall in SixCJ (34:4) 2003, 1155–7; by Helen Cooper in YLS (18) 2004, 157–61; by Sarah Stanbury in SAC (26) 2004, 367–9.

4410. CANNON, CHRISTOPHER. Between the Old and the Middle of English. See **1385**.

4411. CHEWNING, SUSANNAH MARY (ed.). Intersections of sexuality and the divine in medieval culture: the Word made flesh. Aldershot; Burlington, VT: Ashgate, 2005. pp. xiii, 213.

4412. CLARK, LINDA (ed.). Authority and subversion. Woodbridge, Suffolk; Rochester, NY: Boydell Press, 2003. pp. 191. (Fifteenth century, 3.) Rev. by Lisa Ford in TMR, Dec. 2004.

4413. COHEN, JEFFREY J. Medieval identity machines. (Bibl. 2004, 4915.) Rev. by Karma Lochrie in Spec (80:3) 2005, 853–5.

4414. CORNETT, MICHAEL. New books across the disciplines. JMEMS (35:1) 2005, 159–84.

4415. —— New books across the disciplines. JMEMS (35:2) 2005, 429–51.

4416. DALRYMPLE, ROGER (ed.). Middle English literature: a guide to criticism. (Bibl. 2004, 4628.) Rev. by Suzanne M. Yeager in NQ (52:3) 2005, 390–1.

4417. DAMROSCH, DAVID (gen. ed.). The Longman anthology of world literature: vol. B, The medieval era. Ed. by David L. Pike, et al. Harlow; New York: Longman, 2004. pp. xxxviii, 1354.

4418. D'ARCENS, LOUISE; FEROS RUYS, JUANITA (eds). 'Maistresse of my wit': medieval women, modern scholars. (Bibl. 2004, 4630.) Rev. by Richard Utz in TMR, Feb. 2005.

4419. D'ARCY, ANNE MARIE; FLETCHER, ALAN J. (eds). Studies in late medieval and early Renaissance texts in honour of John Scattergood: 'the key of all good remembrance'. Dublin; Portland, OR: Four Courts Press, 2005. pp. 416.

4420. DAVENPORT, TONY. Medieval narrative: an introduction. Oxford; New York: OUP, 2004. pp. viii, 305. Rev. by Richard Trim in EREA (3:2) 2005.

4421. DINSHAW, CAROLYN; WALLACE, DAVID (eds). The Cambridge companion to medieval women's writing. (Bibl. 2004, 4632.) Rev. by Anat Gilboa in SixCJ (36:2) 2005, 513; by Mary C. Erler in JEGP (104:2) 2005, 291–4; by Kathleen Ashley in Spec (80:1) 2005, 212–14.

4422. DI ROCCO, EMILIA. Letteratura e legge nel Trecento inglese: Chaucer, Gower e Langland. (Bibl. 2003, 4502.) Rev. by James H. McGregor in Spec (80:4) 2005, 1262–3.

4423. DYAS, DEE; EDDEN, VALERIE; ELLIS, ROGER (eds). Approaching medieval English anchoritic and mystical texts. Woodbridge, Suffolk; Rochester, NY: Brewer, 2005. pp. xvi, 213. (Christianity and culture.)

4424. EATON, R. D.　From *inwit* to *conscience* in late Middle English literature. *See* **1850.**

4425. EDWARDS, A. S. G.　John Stow and Middle English literature. *In* (pp. 109–18) **5746.**

4426. ERLER, MARY C.　Women, reading, and piety in late medieval England. (Bibl. 2004, 4634.) Rev. by Sandy Bardsley in SixCJ (34:4) 2003, 1151–2; by Anne Clark Bartlett in SAC (26) 2004, 389–91; by Joel T. Rosenthal in JBS (43:4) 2004, 506–13; by David N. Bell in JEGP (104:1) 2005, 129–30.

4427. —— KOWALESKI, MARYANNE (eds).　Gendering the master narrative: women and power in the Middle Ages. Ithaca, NY; London: Cornell UP, 2003. pp. ix, 269. Rev. by Joel T. Rosenthal in JBS (43:4) 2004, 506–13.

4428. FARMER, SHARON; PASTERNACK, CAROL BRAUN (eds).　Gender and difference in the Middle Ages. (Bibl. 2004, 4635.) Rev. by Robyn Cadwallader in Parergon (22:1) 2005, 227–9.

4429. FEDERICO, SYLVIA.　New Troy: fantasies of empire in the late Middle Ages. (Bibl. 2003, 4507.) Rev. by Matthew Giancarlo in Spec (80:1) 2005, 219–22.

4430. FENSTER, THELMA; SMAIL, DANIEL LORD (eds).　Fama: the politics of talk and reputation in medieval Europe. (Bibl. 2004, 4636.) Rev. by John Watkins in CLIO (34:1/2) 2004, 139–44.

4431. FOWLER, ELIZABETH.　Literary character: the human figure in early English writing. (Bibl. 2004, 4637.) Rev. by Maura Nolan in YLS (18) 2004, 165–72; by Alfred David in SAC (26) 2004, 391–4; by Seth Lerer in MP (102:2) 2004, 244–8.

4432. FRADENBURG, L. O. ARANYE.　Simply marvelous. SAC (26) 2004, 1–27.

4433. GADD, IAN; GILLESPIE, ALEXANDRA (eds).　John Stow (1525–1605) and the making of the English past. *See* **5746.**

4434. GILLESPIE, ALEXANDRA.　Poets, printers, and early English *Sammelbände*. *See* **852.**

4435. GOLDIE, MATTHEW BOYD.　Middle English literature: a historical sourcebook. Oxford; Malden, MA: Blackwell, 2003. pp. xxxviii, 301. Rev. by Sarah Downey in NQ (52:4) 2005, 527–8.

4436. HANNA, RALPH.　London literature, *c*.1300–1380. Cambridge; New York: CUP, 2005. pp. xxi, 359. (Cambridge studies in medieval literature.)

4437. —— Middle English books and Middle English literary history. *See* **4585.**

4438. HOLSINGER, BRUCE.　Lollard ekphrasis: situated aesthetics and literary history. *See* **4642.**

4439. JENKINS, JACQUELINE; LEWIS, KATHERINE J. (eds).　St Katherine of Alexandria: texts and contexts in Western medieval Europe. (Bibl. 2004, 4650.) Rev. by Janice Pinder in Parergon (22:2) 2005, 226–8; by Mathilde van Dijk in Spec (80:4) 2005, 1309–11.

4440. JOHNSON, DAVID FRAME; TREHARNE, ELAINE M. (eds).　Readings in medieval texts: interpreting Old and Middle English literature. *See* **4210.**

4441. JOHNSON, RICHARD FREEMAN.   Saint Michael the Archangel in medieval English legend. Woodbridge, Suffolk; Rochester, NY: Boydell Press, 2005. pp. xii, 174.

4442. KABIR, ANANYA JAHANARA; WILLIAMS, DEANNE (eds).   Postcolonial approaches to the European Middle Ages: translating cultures. Cambridge; New York: CUP, 2005. pp. xii, 298. (Cambridge studies in medieval literature, 54.)

4443. KENNEDY, RUTH.   The Evangelist in Robert Thornton's devotional book: organizing principles at the level of the quire. JEBS (8) 2005, 71–95.

4444. KRUG, REBECCA.   Reading families: women's literate practice. (Bibl. 2004, 4653.) Rev. by Jennifer Summit in SAC (26) 2004, 406–9.

4445. KRYGIER, MARCIN; SIKORSKA, LILIANA (eds).   For the loue of Inglis lede. New York; Frankfurt: Lang, 2004. pp. 172. (Medieval English mirror, 1.)

4446. LAVEZZO, KATHY (ed.).   Imagining a medieval English nation. (Bibl. 2004, 4654.) Rev. by Chris Jones in Comitatus (36) 2005, 245–50.

4447. LEUPIN, ALEXANDRE.   Fiction and Incarnation: rhetoric, theology, and literature in the Middle Ages. Trans. by David Laatsch. (Bibl. 2004, 4655.) Rev. by Rosemary Dunn in Parergon (22:1) 2005, 255–7.

4448. LIU, YIN.   Richard Beauchamp and the uses of romance. *See* **4564.**

4449. LOW, ANTHONY.   Aspects of subjectivity: society and individuality from the Middle Ages to Shakespeare and Milton. (Bibl. 2004, 4656.) Rev. by Matthew Pincombe in RES (56:227) 2005, 782–3.

4450. MCCARTHY, CONOR.   Marriage in medieval England: law, literature, and practice. Woodbridge, Suffolk; Rochester, NY: Boydell Press, 2004. pp. 185. Rev. by Emma Lipton in TMR, July 2005.

4451. MCCRACKEN, PEGGY.   The curse of Eve, the wound of the hero: blood, gender, and medieval literature. (Bibl. 2004, 4657.) Rev. by Josephine Bloomfield in Envoi (10:2) 2003 for 2001, 147–50.

4452. MACDONALD, ALASDAIR A.; DEKKER, KEES (eds).   Rhetoric, royalty, and reality: essays on the literary culture of medieval and early modern Scotland. Louvain; Dudley, MA: Peeters, 2004. pp. xi, 224. (Mediaevalia Groningana, ns 7.)

4453. MATSUDA, TAKAMI (ed.).   *Codices Keionenses*: essays on Western manuscripts and early printed books in Keio University Library. *See* **430.**

4454. MEYERSON, MARK D.; THIERY, DANIEL; FALK, OREN (eds).   'A great effusion of blood?': interpreting medieval violence. (Bibl. 2004, 4661.) Rev. by Anna Klosowska in TMR, June 2005; by Dianne Hall in Parergon (22:2) 2005, 241–3.

4455. MOLL, RICHARD J.   Before Malory: reading Arthur in later medieval England. (Bibl. 2004, 4662.) Rev. by H. L. Spencer in RES (56:225) 2005, 450–1; by Marilyn Corrie in MÆ (74:1) 2005, 131–2; by John Spence in NQ (52:4) 2005, 523–4; by Jörg O. Fichte in JEGP (104:4) 2005, 568–70; by Glenn Wright in Parergon (22:2) 2005, 243–6.

4456. MORTIMER, NIGEL.   John Lydgate's *Fall of Princes*: narrative tragedy in its literary and political contexts. *See* **4875.**

4457. MURDOCH, BRIAN. The medieval popular Bible: expansions of Genesis in the Middle Ages. (Bibl. 2004, 4664.) Rev. by John Barton in LitTheol (18:3) 2004, 362–4; by H. L. Spencer in RES (56:224) 2005, 315–17; by James M. Dean in Spec (80:4) 2005, 1337–8.

4458. NEWMAN, BARBARA. God and the goddesses: vision, poetry, and belief in the Middle Ages. (Bibl. 2004, 4665.) Rev. by Sara S. Poor in JAAR (73:2) 2005, 563–6; by Rachel Fulton in MP (102:3) 2005, 413–17.

4459. O'DONNELL, DANIEL PAU. O captain! My captain! Using technology to guide readers through an electronic edition. See **1124**.

4460. OLSON, LINDA; KERBY-FULTON, KATHRYN (eds). Voices in dialogue: reading women in the Middle Ages. Notre Dame, IN: Notre Dame UP, 2005. pp. xvii, 508. Rev. by Carolyne Larrington in TLS, 20 May 2005, 4.

4461. PASTORE PASSARO, MARIA C. Representation of women in Classical, medieval and Renaissance texts. See **4222**.

4462. PERFETTI, LISA. Women & laughter in medieval comic literature. (Bibl. 2004, 4668.) Rev. by Rosalind Brown-Grant in MLR (100:3) 2005, 749.

4463. —— (ed.). The representation of women's emotions in medieval and early modern culture. Gainesville: Florida UP, 2005. pp. 222.

4464. PETERS, CHRISTINE. Patterns of piety: women, gender and religion in late medieval and Reformation England. (Bibl. 2004, 4934.) Rev. by Carole Levin in RQ (58:1) 2005, 329–30.

4465. PETRINA, ALESSANDRA. Cultural politics in fifteenth-century England: the case of Humphrey, Duke of Gloucester. (Bibl. 2004, 4669.) Rev. by Kenneth Bartlett in RQ (58:1) 2005, 319–20.

4466. PHILLIPS, KIM M. Medieval maidens: young women and gender in England, 1270–1540. (Bibl. 2004, 4670.) Rev. by Amy J. Froide in Albion (36:3) 2004, 494–6; by Elisabeth Dutton in NQ (52:4) 2005, 521–2.

4467. PITARD, DERRICK G. A selected bibliography for Lollard studies. In (pp. 251–319) **4482**.

4468. POLLARD, A. J. Imagining Robin Hood: the late medieval stories in historical context. London; New York: Routledge, 2004. pp. xvi, 272, (plates) 12.

4469. REED, TERESA P. Shadows of Mary: reading the Virgin Mary in medieval texts. (Bibl. 2004, 4673.) Rev. by Robyn Cadwallader in Parergon (22:1) 2005, 270–1.

4470. RICHARDSON, GAVIN. Sex and secrecy in medieval antifeminist proverbs. See **3455**.

4471. RIDDY, FELICITY. Looking closely: authority and intimacy in the late medieval urban home. In (pp. 212–28) **4427**.

4472. RITT, NIKOLAUS; SCHENDL, HERBERT (eds). Rethinking Middle English: linguistic and literary approaches. See **1412**.

4473. ROBERTS, ANNA KLOSOWSKA. Queer love in the Middle Ages. Basingstoke; New York: Palgrave Macmillan, 2005. pp. ix, 195. (New Middle Ages.)

4474. ROGERS, NICHOLAS. Henry VI and the proposed canonisation of King Alfred. In (pp. 211–20) **4488**.

4475. RUUD, JAY. Encyclopedia of medieval literature. New York: Facts on File, 2005. pp. xviii, 734.

4476. SALISBURY, EVE; DONAVIN, GEORGIANA; PRICE, MERRALL LLEWELYN (eds). Domestic violence in medieval texts. (Bibl. 2004, 4676.) Rev. by Elizabeth Robertson in SAC (26) 2004, 421–4; by Elizabeth Archibald in Envoi (11:1) 2005 for 2002, 81–93.

4477. SARGENT, MICHAEL G. Mystical writings and dramatic texts in late medieval England. See **4513**.

4478. SAUNDERS, CORINNE; LE SAUX, FRANÇOISE; THOMAS, NEIL (eds). Writing war: medieval literary responses to warfare. (Bibl. 2004, 4678.) Rev. by Andrew Breeze in MLR (100:3) 2005, 759–62.

4479. SHEPARD, ALAN; POWELL, STEPHEN D. (eds). Fantasies of Troy: Classical tales and the social imaginary in medieval and early modern Europe. Toronto: Centre for Reformation and Renaissance Studies, 2004. pp. xi, 306. (Centre for Reformation and Renaissance Studies: essays and studies, 5.) Rev. by Charles Russell Stone in Comitatus (36) 2005, 227–9; by Jennifer Richards in RQ (58:4) 2005, 1386–7.

4480. SIMPSON, JAMES. Not the last word. JMEMS (35:1) 2005, 111–19. (Response to reviews of *Reform and Cultural Revolution*.)

4481. SMITH, D. VANCE. Arts of possession: the Middle English household imaginary. (Bibl. 2004, 4682.) Rev. by Matthew Boyd Goldie in YLS (18) 2004, 183–8; by Elizabeth Robertson in Spec (80:4) 2005, 1366–8.

4482. SOMERSET, FIONA; HAVENS, JILL C.; PITARD, DERRICK G. (eds). Lollards and their influence in late medieval England. Preface by Anne Hudson. Woodbridge, Suffolk; Rochester, NY: Boydell Press, 2003. pp. x, 344. Rev. by Katherine C. Little in YLS (18) 2004, 189–93; by Andrew Galloway in Spec (80:1) 2005, 326–30.

4483. SØNDERGAARD, LEIF; HANSEN, RASMUS THORNING (eds). Monsters, marvels and miracles: imaginary journeys and landscapes in the Middle Ages. Odense: UP of Southern Denmark, 2005. pp. 210.

4484. STALEY, LYNN. Languages of power in the age of Richard II. University Park: Pennsylvania State UP, 2005. pp. xiv, 394. Rev. by Robert Barrett in TMR, Sept. 2005.

4485. STEIN, ROBERT M.; PRIOR, SANDRA PIERSON (eds). Reading medieval culture: essays in honor of Robert W. Hanning. Notre Dame, IN: Notre Dame UP, 2005. pp. ix, 505.

4486. STEINBERG, THEODORE L. Reading the Middle Ages: an introduction to medieval literature. (Bibl. 2003, 4558.) Rev. by John C. Hirsh in Spec (80:1) 2005, 332–4.

4487. STEINER, EMILY. Documentary culture and the making of medieval English literature. (Bibl. 2004, 4683.) Rev. by Christopher Baswell in YLS (18) 2004, 193–9; by Eileen A. Joy in SixCJ (36:2) 2005, 519–21; by Joyce Coleman in NQ (52:2) 2005, 240–1; by Míċeál F. Vaughan in JEGP (104:2) 2005, 294–6.

4488. STRATFORD, JENNY (ed.).   The Lancastrian court: proceedings of the 2001 Harlaxton Symposium. Stamford: Tyas, 2003. pp. xii, 271. (Harlaxton medieval studies, ns 13.)

4489. STROHM, PAUL.   *Politique*: languages of statecraft between Chaucer and Shakespeare. Notre Dame, IN: Notre Dame UP, 2005. pp. 298. (Conway lectures in medieval studies.)

4490. VALDÉS MIYARES, RUBÉN.   Sturdy stories: medieval narrative into popular ballad. SELIM (12) 2003/04, 143–59.

4491. WALLACE, DAVID.   Oxford English literary history. JMEMS (35:1) 2005, 13–23 (review-article).

4492. WATTS, JOHN.   Was there a Lancastrian court? *In* (pp. 253–71) **4488.**

4493. WILLIAMS, DEANNE.   The French fetish from Chaucer to Shakespeare. Cambridge; New York: CUP, 2004. pp. xiv, 283. (Cambridge studies in Renaissance literature and culture, 47.) Rev. by A. Kent Hieatt in RQ (58:3) 2005, 1037–8.

4494. WOOD, DIANA (ed.).   Women and religion in medieval England. (Bibl. 2004, 4691.) Rev. by Fiona J. Griffiths in TMR, Feb. 2005.

4495. ZEIKOWITZ, RICHARD E.   Homoeroticism and chivalry: discourses in male same-sex desire in the fourteenth century. (Bibl. 2004, 4692.) Rev. by Allen J. Frantzen in NQ (52:2) 2005, 241–3; by Ruth Mazo Karras in Spec (80:1) 2005, 352–4.

DRAMA

General Studies

4496. BUTTERWORTH, PHILIP.   Magic on the early English stage. Cambridge; New York: CUP, 2005. pp. xxii, 295. Rev. by Emma Smith in TLS, 9 Dec. 2005, 28.

4497. COLETTI, THERESA.   Mary Magdalene and the drama of saints: theater, gender, and religion in late medieval England. (Bibl. 2004, 4693.) Rev. by Peter Happé in CompDr (38:4) 2004/05, 447–50; by Donnalee Dox in TMR, Jan. 2005; by Kevin Babbitt in TJ (57:2) 2005, 331–2; by Katherine L. Jansen in MÆ (74:2) 2005, 350–2; by Katharine Goodland in RQ (58:3) 2005, 1023–5; by Stacy Nisperos in Comitatus (36) 2005, 212–14.

4498. DAVIDSON, CLIFFORD.   'Corpus Christi Play' and the Feast of Corpus Christi. RORD (44) 2005, 1–37.

4499. DILLON, JANETTE.   Chariots and cloud machines: gods and goddesses on early English stages. *In* (pp. 111–29) **5268.**

4500. DUBRUCK, EDELGARD E.   The current state of research on late medieval drama, 2002–2004: survey, bibliography, and reviews. FCS (30) 2005, 1–38.

4501. EMMERSON, RICHARD K.   Dramatic history: on the diachronic and synchronic in the study of early English drama. JMEMS (35:1) 2005, 39–66 (review-article).

4502. GOODLAND, KATHARINE.   'Veniance, Lord, apon thaym fall': maternal mourning, divine justice, and tragedy in the Corpus Christi plays. MedRen (18) 2005, 166–92.

4503. —— 'Vs for to wepe no man may lett': accommodating female grief in the medieval English Lazarus plays. ETh (8:1) 2005, 69–94.

4504. GRANTLEY, DARRYLL. English dramatic interludes, 1300–1580: a reference guide. (Bibl. 2004, 4700.) Rev. by Claire Sponsler in ShQ (56:2) 2005, 216–18.

4505. HAPPÉ, PETER. Cyclic form and the English mystery plays: a comparative study of the English and biblical cycles and their Continental and iconographic counterparts. Amsterdam; Atlanta, GA: Rodopi, 2004. pp. 349. (Ludus, 7.) Rev. by Daniel Wakelin in MÆ (74:2) 2005, 349–50; by Barbara D. Palmer in Spec (80:4) 2005, 1298–300.

4506. —— 'Erazed in the booke': the mystery cycles and reform. In (pp. 15–33) **5268.**

4507. KAZIK, JOANNA. The Blessed Virgin's physical and spiritual intactness in the English mystery plays. In (pp. 91–9) **3756.**

4508. KERMODE, LLOYD EDWARD; SCOTT-WARREN, JASON; VAN ELK, MARTINE (eds). Tudor drama before Shakespeare, 1485–1590: new directions for research, criticism, and pedagogy. See **5268.**

4509. LANCASHIRE, ANNE. London civic theatre: city drama and pageantry from Roman times to 1558. (Bibl. 2004, 4708.) Rev. by Clifford Davidson in CompDr (37:2) 2003, 241–7; by Lukas Erne in SStud (33) 2005, 285–8; by Darryll Grantley in ETh (8:1) 2005, 122–5; by Gordon Kipling in ShQ (56:3) 2005, 362–5.

4510. MILLING, JANE; THOMSON, PETER (eds). The Cambridge history of British theatre: vol. 1, Origins to 1660. Cambridge; New York: CUP, 2004. pp. xxix, 540. Rev. by Frederick Tollini in RQ (58:4) 2005, 1430–1.

4511. NORMINGTON, KATIE. Gender and medieval drama. Woodbridge, Suffolk; Rochester, NY: Brewer, 2004. pp. 168. (Gender in the Middle Ages.) Rev. by Victor I. Scherb in TMR, July 2005; by Darryll Grantley in TRI (30:3) 2005, 298–9.

4512. OWENS, MARGARET E. Stages of dismemberment: the fragmented body in medieval and early modern drama. Newark: Delaware UP, 2005. pp. 332.

4513. SARGENT, MICHAEL G. Mystical writings and dramatic texts in late medieval England. ReLit (37:2) 2005, 77–98.

4514. SCOVILLE, CHESTER N. Saints and the audience in Middle English biblical drama. Toronto; Buffalo, NY; London: Toronto UP, 2004. pp. 140. Rev. by Michael Chemers in CompDr (38:4) 2004/05, 460–2; by Thomas Pettitt in TMR, July 2005.

4515. SHEPHERD, SIMON. Voice, writing, noise …; or, Is Herod Balinese? PRes (8:1) 2003, 74–82.

4516. SOMERSET, ALAN. Some new thoughts on an old question: 'professional' touring theater outside London before 1590. In (pp. 131–40) **5268.**

4517. SPONSLER, CLAIRE. Ritual imports: performing medieval drama in America. Ithaca, NY; London: Cornell UP, 2004. pp. viii, 235. Rev. by David Klausner in TMR, Sept. 2005.

4518. STOKES, JAMES. The lost playing places of Lincolnshire. CompDr (37:3/4) 2003/04, 275–95.

4519. —— Women and performance: evidences of universal cultural suffrage in medieval and early modern Lincolnshire. *In* (pp. 25–43) **5225**.

4520. TWYCROSS, MEG; CARPENTER, SARAH. Masks and masking in medieval and early Tudor England. (Bibl. 2004, 4713.) Rev. by Matthew C. Hansen in SixCJ (34:2) 2003, 477–8; by Clifford Davidson in CompDr (37:2) 2003, 241–7.

4521. WATKINS, JOHN. Bedevilling the histories of medieval and early modern drama. MP (101:1) 2003, 68–78 (review-article).

Separate Anonymous Works

Chester Cycle

4522. GOODLAND, KATHARINE. 'Us for to wepe no man may lett': resistant female grief in the medieval Lazarus plays. *In* (pp. 90–118) **4463**.

4523. GROVES, BEATRICE. Hal as self-styled redeemer: the Harrowing of Hell and *Henry IV Part 1. See* **6403**.

Croxton Plays

4524. NISSE, RUTH. Defining acts: drama and the politics of interpretation in late medieval England. Notre Dame, IN: Notre Dame UP, 2004. pp. x, 226. Rev. by Julie Paulson in TMR, Sept. 2005.

Digby Plays

4525. GOODLAND, KATHARINE. 'Us for to wepe no man may lett': resistant female grief in the medieval Lazarus plays. *In* (pp. 90–118) **4463**.

4526. SMITH, D. K. 'To passe the see in shortt space': mapping the world in the Digby *Mary Magdalene*. MedRen (18) 2005, 193–214.

Mankind

4527. KENDRICK, LAURA. 'In bourde and in pleye': *Mankind* and the problem of comic derision in medieval English religious plays. EA (58:3) 2005, 261–75.

N-Town Plays

4528. GOODLAND, KATHARINE. 'Us for to wepe no man may lett': resistant female grief in the medieval Lazarus plays. *In* (pp. 90–118) **4463**.

Towneley Cycle

4529. ABATE, MICHELLE ANN. Oversight as insight: reading *The Second Shepherds' Play* as *The Second Shepherd's Play*. ETh (8:1) 2005, 95–108.

4530. CAWSEY, KATHY. Tutivillus and the 'kyrkchaterars': strategies of control in the Middle Ages. SP (102:4) 2005, 434–51.

4531. EDMINSTER, WARREN. The preaching fox: festive subversion in the plays of the Wakefield Master. London; New York: Routledge, 2005. pp. xiii, 230. (Studies in medieval history and culture.) Rev. by Rick McDonald in RMER (59:2) 2005; by Clifford Davidson in BJJ (12) 2005, 287–91.

4532. GOODLAND, KATHARINE. 'Us for to wepe no man may lett': resistant female grief in the medieval Lazarus plays. *In* (pp. 90–118) **4463**.

4533. NISSE, RUTH. Defining acts: drama and the politics of interpretation in late medieval England. *See* **4524**.

4534. PURDON, LIAM O.   The Wakefield Master's dramatic art: a drama of spiritual understanding. (Bibl. 2004, 4725.) Rev. by Shearle Furnish in JEGP (104:4) 2005, 566–8; by James H. Morey in Spec (80:1) 2005, 305–6.

Wisdom

4535. NISSE, RUTH.   Defining acts: drama and the politics of interpretation in late medieval England. *See* **4524**.

York Cycle

4536. GEORGE, MICHAEL W.   Religion, sexuality, and representation in the York 'Joseph's Troubles' pageant. *In* (pp. 9–17) **4411**.

4537. GOODLAND, KATHARINE.   'Us for to wepe no man may lett': resistant female grief in the medieval Lazarus plays. *In* (pp. 90–118) **4463**.

4538. GROENEVELD, LEANNE.   Mourning, heresy, and resurrection in the York Corpus Christi cycle. CanRCL (30:1) 2003, 1–22.

4539. GUSICK, BARBARA I.   Christ's transformation of Zacchaeus in the York Cycle's *Entry into Jerusalem*. FCS (30) 2005, 68–94.

4540. NISSE, RUTH.   Defining acts: drama and the politics of interpretation in late medieval England. *See* **4524**.

4541. SCOVILLE, CHESTER.   But *owthir in frith or felde*: the rural in the York Cycle. CompDr (37:2) 2003, 175–87.

4542. WILLIAMS, GWENO; FINDLAY, ALISON; HODGSON-WRIGHT, STEPHANIE. Payments, permits and punishments: women performers and the politics of place. *In* (pp. 45–67) **5225**.

ROMANCE

General Studies

4543. ARCHIBALD, ELIZABETH.   Did knights have baths? The absence of bathing in Middle English romance. *In* (pp. 101–15) **4555**.

4544. BLACK, NANCY B.   Medieval narratives of accused queens. (Bibl. 2004, 4736.) Rev. by Jane Gilbert in MLR (100:4) 2005, 1114–15; by Julia C. Dietrich in NWSAJ (17:3) 2005, 207–8; by Claudia Bornholdt in JEGP (104:4) 2005, 545–7; by Barbara N. Sargent-Baur in Spec (80:3) 2005, 835–7.

4545. BREWER, DEREK.   Some notes on 'ennobling love' and its successor in medieval romance. *In* (pp. 117–33) **4555**.

4546. CANNON, CHRISTOPHER.   The grounds of English literature. Oxford; New York: OUP, 2004. pp. viii, 237.

4547. COOPER, HELEN.   The English romance in time: transforming motifs from Geoffrey of Monmouth to the death of Shakespeare. (Bibl. 2004, 4737.) Rev. by Richard McCabe in RES (56:224) 2005, 318–20; by Richard J. Moll in TMR, Sept. 2005; by Susan Crane in MÆ (74:1) 2005, 130–1; by Alain Bony in EREA (3:1) 2005.

4548. —— Thomas of Erceldoune: romance as prophecy. *In* (pp. 171–87) **4555**.

4549. DAVENPORT, TONY.   Chronicle and romance: the story of Ine and Æthelburgh. *In* (pp. 27–40) **4555**.

4550. FIELD, ROSALIND.   The king over the water: exile-and-return revisited. *In* (pp. 41–53) **4555**.

4551. GOODRICH, PETER H.; THOMPSON, RAYMOND H. (eds). Merlin: a casebook. (Bibl. 2003, 4635.) Rev. by C. W. Sullivan, III, in JFA (15:3) 2004, 279–80.

4552. HENG, GERALDINE. Empire of magic: medieval romance and the politics of cultural fantasy. (Bibl. 2004, 4741.) Rev. by Laurie A. Finke in Arthuriana (15:2) 2005, 71–2; by Helen Moore in TLS, 8 July 2005, 5–6.

4553. MCDONALD, NICOLA (ed.). Pulp fictions of medieval England: essays in popular romance. (Bibl. 2004, 4745.) Rev. by Robin Gilbank in Eng (54:209) 2005, 169–73; by Ivana Djordjević in NQ (52:3) 2005, 393–4.

4554. ROUSE, ROBERT ALLEN. The idea of Anglo-Saxon England in Middle English romance. Woodbridge, Suffolk; Rochester, NY: Brewer, 2005. pp. viii, 180. (Studies in medieval romance.)

4555. SAUNDERS, CORINNE (ed.). Cultural encounters in the romance of medieval England. Woodbridge, Suffolk; Rochester, NY: Brewer, 2005. pp. x, 193. (Studies in medieval romance.)

4556. WARNES, CHRISTOPHER. Avatars of Amadis: magical realism as postcolonial romance. See **11948**.

4557. WEISL, ANGELA JANE. The persistence of medievalism: narrative adventures in contemporary culture. (Bibl. 2004, 4750.) Rev. by Thomas Goodmann in Spec (80:3) 2005, 996–7.

Separate Anonymous Works

Alexander Romances

4558. GRADY, FRANK. Contextualizing Alexander and Dindimus. YLS (18) 2004, 81–106.

4559. SCATTERGOOD, JOHN. Validating the high life in Of Arthour and of Merlin and Kyng Alisaunder. See **4582**.

Athelston

4560. BRADBURY, NANCY MASON. Beyond the kick: women's agency in Athelston. In (pp. 149–58) **4555**.

4561. YOUNG, HELEN. Athelston and English law: Plantagenet practice and Anglo-Saxon precedent. Parergon (22:1) 2005, 95–118.

Gamelyn

4562. EDWARDS, A. S. G. A new text of the Canterbury Tales? In (pp. 121–8) **4419**.

4563. VÁZQUEZ, NILA. The need for 're-editing' Gamelyn. IJES (5:2) 2005, 161–73.

Guy of Warwick

4564. LIU, YIN. Richard Beauchamp and the uses of romance. MÆ (74:2) 2005, 271–87.

Havelok the Dane

4565. FALETRA, MICHAEL. The ends of romance: dreaming the nation in the Middle English Havelok. Exemplaria (17:2) 2005, 347–80.

4566. GARNER, LORI ANN.   The role of proverbs in Middle English narrative. *In* (pp. 255–77) **4197.**

4567. LINDSTRÖM, BENGT.   A note on anagrammatic corruption in *Havelok*. NQ (52:3) 2005, 295–6.

4568. MARVIN, JULIA.   Havelok in the prose *Brut* tradition. *See* **4718.**

4569. ROUSE, ROBERT.   English identity and the law in *Havelok the Dane, Horn Childe and Maiden Rimnild* and *Beues of Hamtoun*. *In* (pp. 69–83) **4555.**

Horn Childe and Maiden Rimnild

4570. HOLFORD, M. L.   A local source for *Horn Child and Maiden Rimnild*. MÆ (74:1) 2005, 34–40.

4571. ROUSE, ROBERT.   English identity and the law in *Havelok the Dane, Horn Childe and Maiden Rimnild* and *Beues of Hamtoun*. *In* (pp. 69–83) **4555.**

Ipomadon

4572. SÁNCHEZ MARTÍ, JORDI.   Longleat House MS 257: a description. *See* **312.**

4573. —— Wynkyn de Worde's editions of *Ipomydon*: a reassessment of the evidence. Neophilologus (89:1) 2005, 153–63.

King Horn

4574. BREMMER, ROLF H., JR; LAKER, STEPHEN.   Earliest Middle English *ne*, 'than'. *See* **1700.**

4575. SOBECKI, SEBASTIAN I.   The 2000 Saracens of *King Horn*. NQ (52:4) 2005, 443–5.

The King of Tars

4576. CALKIN, SIOBHAIN BLY.   Marking religion on the body: Saracens, categorization, and *The King of Tars*. JEGP (104:2) 2005, 219–38.

4577. —— Saracens and the making of English identity: the Auchinleck Manuscript. London; New York: Routledge, 2005. pp. xii, 299. (Studies in medieval history and culture.)

Morte Arthure (Alliterative)

4578. DEMARCO, PATRICIA.   An Arthur for the Ricardian age: crown, nobility, and the alliterative *Morte Arthure*. Spec (80:2) 2005, 464–93.

4579. JEFFERSON, JUDITH A.; PUTTER, AD.   Alliterative patterning in the *Morte Arthure*. SP (102:4) 2005, 415–33.

Octavian

4580. WRIGHT, GLENN.   The fabliau ethos in the French and English *Octavian* romances. MP (102:4) 2005, 478–500.

Of Arthour and of Merlin

4581. CALKIN, SIOBHAIN BLY.   Saracens and the making of English identity: the Auchinleck Manuscript. *See* **4577.**

4582. SCATTERGOOD, JOHN.   Validating the high life in *Of Arthour and of Merlin* and *Kyng Alisaunder*. EC (54:4) 2004, 323–50.

Richard Coer de Lyon

4583. AKBARI, SUZANNE CONKLIN. The hunger for national identity in *Richard Coer de Lion*. *In* (pp. 198–227) **4485**.

The Seege of Troye

4584. TROYER, PAMELA LUFF. Smiting high culture in the 'fondement': *The Seege of Troye* as medieval burlesque. *In* (pp. 117–31) **4479**.

The Siege of Jerusalem

4585. HANNA, RALPH. Middle English books and Middle English literary history. MP (102:2) 2004, 157–78.

4586. —— LAWTON, DAVID (eds). The siege of Jerusalem. (Bibl. 2004, 4780.) Rev. by George R. Keiser in JEGP (104:3) 2005, 402–4.

Sir Bevis of Hampton

4587. DJORDJEVIĆ, IVANA. Original and translation: Bevis's mother in Anglo-Norman and Middle English. *In* (pp. 11–26) **4555**.

4588. —— Versification and translation in *Sir Beves of Hampton*. MÆ (74:1) 2005, 41–59.

4589. ROUSE, ROBERT. English identity and the law in *Havelok the Dane, Horn Childe and Maiden Rimnild* and *Beues of Hamtoun*. *In* (pp. 69–83) **4555**.

Sir Gowther

4590. CARTLIDGE, NEIL. 'Therof seyus clerkus': slander, rape and *Sir Gowther*. *In* (pp. 135–47) **4555**.

Sir Orfeo

4591. CARTLIDGE, NEIL. Sir Orfeo in the Otherworld: courting chaos? SAC (26) 2004, 195–226.

4592. CONRAD-O'BRIAIN, HELEN. *Sir Orfeo's* poetic mirror of polity. *In* (pp. 76–90) **4419**.

Sir Tristrem

4593. HARDMAN, PHILLIPA. The true romance of *Tristrem and Ysoude*. *In* (pp. 85–99) **4555**.

4594. JONES, TIMOTHY S. 'Oublïe ai chevalerie': Tristan, Malory, and the outlaw-knight. *In* (pp. 79–90) **3576**.

The Sowdone of Babylone

4595. SÁNCHEZ MARTÍ, JORDI. *The Sowdoun of Babyloyne*: a description of the manuscript. SELIM (12) 2003/04, 181–9.

Torrent of Portyngale

4596. DALRYMPLE, ROGER. *Torrent of Portyngale* and the literary giants. *In* (pp. 159–70) **4555**.

The Weddynge of Sir Gawen and Dame Ragnell

4597. MINNIS, ALASTAIR. 'Dante in Inglissh': what *Il convivio* really did for Chaucer. *See* **5017**.

4598. VAN BAKER, MICHAEL. The dame and the knight: marriage, sovereignty, and transformation. Parabola (29:1) 2004, 11–18.

Ywain and Gawain

4599. FINDON, JOANNE. The other story: female friendship in the Middle English *Ywain and Gawain*. Parergon (22:1) 2005, 71–94.

POETRY
General Studies

4600. BOFFEY, JULIA (ed.). Fifteenth-century English dream visions: an anthology. (Bibl. 2004, 4811.) Rev. by Louise M. Bishop in TMR, June 2005; by Donald C. Baker in ELN (42:3) 2005, 68–70.

4601. CAIE, GRAHAM D. 'I do not wish to be called auctour, but the pore compilatour': the plight of the medieval vernacular poet. Misc (29) 2004, 9–21.

4602. CARLSON, DAVID R. Chaucer's jobs. *See* **4938**.

4603. CLUTTERBUCK, CHARLOTTE. Encounters with God in medieval and early modern English poetry. Aldershot; Burlington, VT: Ashgate, 2004. pp. viii, 226.

4604. EATON, R. D. Sin and sensibility: the *conscience* of Chaucer's Prioress. *See* **1821**.

4605. FRANTZEN, ALLEN J. Spirituality and devotion in the Anglo-Saxon penitentials. *See* **4331**.

4606. INOUE, NORIKO. A new theory of alliterative a-verses. YLS (18) 2004, 107–32.

4607. JEFFERSON, JUDITH A.; PUTTER, AD. The distribution of infinitives in -*e* and -*en* in some Middle English alliterative poems. *See* **1563**.

4608. KEISER, GEORGE R. A Middle English rosemary treatise in verse and prose. *See* **270**.

4609. —— Verse introductions to Middle English medical treatises. *See* **4703**.

4610. LIU, JIN. Chaucer's dream poetry and the medieval tradition of dream vision. *See* **4953**.

4611. MOONEY, LINNE R.; ARN, MARY-JO (eds). *The Kingis Quair* and other prison poems. *See* **4819**.

4612. SINISI, LUCIA. Urbanization and pollution in an Irish (?) town in the 14th century. SELIM (12) 2003/04, 160–78.

4613. SPEARING, A. C. Textual subjectivity: the encoding of subjectivity in medieval narratives and lyrics. Oxford; New York: OUP, 2005. pp. viii, 273.

4614. STEWART, DANA E. The arrow of love: optics, gender, and subjectivity in medieval love poetry. (Bibl. 2004, 4808.) Rev. by Simon Gilson in Spec (80:2) 2005, 679–80.

Separate Anonymous Works

The Assembly of Ladies

4615. PEARSALL, DEREK. *The Flower and the Leaf* and *The Assembly of Ladies*: a revisitation. *In* (pp. 259–69) **4419**.

The Book of Penance

4616. Trudel, Guy.   The Middle English *Book of Penance* and the readers of the *Cursor Mundi. See* **4622.**

Carols

4617. Faulkes, Anthony.   A new medieval carol text? NQ (52:4) 2005, 445.

4618. Hirsh, John C. (ed.).   Medieval lyric: Middle English lyrics, ballads, and carols. Oxford; Malden, MA: Blackwell, 2005. pp. xiv, 220.

The Charter of Christ

4619. Steiner, Emily.   Lollardy and the legal document. *In* (pp. 155–74) **4482.**

Christis Kirk on the Grene

4620. Harker, C. Marie.   *Chrystis Kirk on the Grene* and *Peblis to the Ploy*: the economy of gender. *In* (pp. 31–46) **3754.**

The Crowned King

4621. Pearsall, Derek.   *Crowned King*: war and peace in 1415. *In* (pp. 163–72) **4488.**

Cursor Mundi

4622. Trudel, Guy.   The Middle English *Book of Penance* and the readers of the *Cursor Mundi*. MÆ (74:1) 2005, 10–33.

Debate Poems

4623. Pickering, Oliver.   Stanzaic verse in the Auchinleck Manuscript: *The Alphabetical Praise of Women. In* (pp. 287–304) **4419.**

The Floure and the Leafe

4624. Pearsall, Derek.   *The Flower and the Leaf* and *The Assembly of Ladies*: a revisitation. *In* (pp. 259–69) **4419.**

The Hermit and the Outlaw

4625. Green, Richard Firth.   The hermit and the outlaw: new evidence for Robin Hood's death? *In* (pp. 51–9) **3576.**

The Hunting of the Hare

4626. Green, Richard Firth.   *The Hunting of the Hare*: an edition. *In* (pp. 129–47) **4419.**

Hymns

4627. Kennedy, Ruth (ed.).   Three alliterative saints' hymns: late Middle English stanzaic poems. (Bibl. 2004, 4820.) Rev. by Lawrence Warner in Parergon (22:1) 2005, 248–50; by Cynthia Ho in TMR, Sept. 2005; by Robert K. Upchurch in JEGP (104:4) 2005, 564–6.

The King and the Hermit

4628. Furrow, Melissa.   A fabliau called a romance: where and when, how and why, and then so what? NQ (52:3) 2005, 293–5.

Knyghthode and Bataile

4629. Wakelin, Daniel.   Scholarly scribes and the creation of *Knyghthode and Bataile*. EngMS (12) 2005, 26–45.

The Libelle of Englyshe Polycye

4630. LADD, ROGER A.   From 'sonne of marchaundy' to 'obscurely bred': the nine lives of Richard Whittington. ELN (43:1) 2005, 12–33.

Lyrics

4631. HIRSH, JOHN C. (ed.).   Medieval lyric: Middle English lyrics, ballads, and carols. *See* **4618.**

4632. MORGAN, NIGEL.   An SS collar in the devotional context of the shield of the Five Wounds. *In* (pp. 147–62) **4488.**

4633. PHILLIPS, HELEN.   Remembering Edward I. *In* (pp. 270–86) **4419.**

Metrical Chronicle

4634. COOPER, HELEN.   Lancelot, Roger Mortimer and the date of the Auchinleck Manuscript. *In* (pp. 91–9) **4419.**

4635. MOLL, RICHARD J.   Ebrauke and the politics of Arthurian geography. Arthuriana (15:4) 2005, 65–71.

Mum and the Sothsegger

4636. COLE, ANDREW.   William Langland and the invention of Lollardy. *In* (pp. 37–58) **4482.**

4637. HOROBIN, SIMON.   The dialect and authorship of *Richard the Redeless* and *Mum and the Sothsegger*. *See* **4647.**

The Owl and the Nightingale

4638. BREMMER, ROLF H., JR; LAKER, STEPHEN.   Earliest Middle English *ne*, 'than'. *See* **1700.**

Palladius on Husbondrie

4639. EDWARDS, A. S. G.   Duke Humfrey's Middle English Palladius manuscript. *In* (pp. 68–77) **4488.**

Peblis to the Ploy

4640. HARKER, C. MARIE.   *Chrystis Kirk on the Grene* and *Peblis to the Ploy*: the economy of gender. *In* (pp. 31–46) **3754.**

Pierce the Ploughman's Crede

4641. BARR, HELEN.   Wycliffite representations of the third estate. *In* (pp. 197–216) **4482.**

4642. HOLSINGER, BRUCE.   Lollard ekphrasis: situated aesthetics and literary history. JMEMS (35:1) 2005, 67–89 (review-article).

The Plowman's Tale

4643. PATTERSON, PAUL J.   Reforming Chaucer: margins and religion in an apocryphal *Canterbury Tale*. BH (8) 2005, 11–36.

4644. WALKER, GREG.   The textual archaeology of *The Plowman's Tale*. *In* (pp. 375–401) **4419.**

Poema Morale

4645. HILL, BETTY.   The writing of the septenary couplet. NQ (52:3) 2005, 296.

The Proverbs of Alfred

4646. ROUSE, ROBERT ALLEN. The idea of Anglo-Saxon England in Middle English romance. *See* **4554.**

Richard the Redeless

4647. HOROBIN, SIMON. The dialect and authorship of *Richard the Redeless* and *Mum and the Sothsegger.* YLS (18) 2004, 133–52.

Robin Hood and the Potter

4648. OHLGREN, THOMAS H. Merchant adventure in *Robin Hood and the Potter. In* (pp. 69–78) **3576.**

Saints' Lives

4649. CALKIN, SIOBHAIN BLY. Saracens and the making of English identity: the Auchinleck Manuscript. *See* **4577.**

4650. KENNEDY, RUTH. The Evangelist in Robert Thornton's devotional book: organizing principles at the level of the quire. *See* **4443.**

4651. REAMES, SHERRY L. (ed.); BLALOCK, MARTHA G.; LARSON, WENDY R. (asst eds). Middle English legends of women saints. (Bibl. 2003, 4710.) Rev. by Elizabeth Robertson in Spec (80:3) 2005, 957–8.

4652. SCAHILL, JOHN. Middle English saints' legends. Woodbridge, Suffolk; Rochester, NY: Brewer, 2005. pp. 209.

Satirical Verse

4653. SCASE, WENDY. *Satire on the Retinues of the Great* (MS Harley 2253): unpaid bills and the politics of purveyance. *In* (pp. 305–20) **4419.**

South English Legendary

4654. LARSON, WENDY R. Who is the master of this narrative? Maternal patronage of the cult of St Margaret. *In* (pp. 94–134) **4427.**

4655. THOMPSON, ANNE B. Everyday saints and the art of narrative in the *South English Legendary.* (Bibl. 2004, 4848.) Rev. by Joanne Findon in TMR, Jan. 2005; by James H. Morey in Spec (80:2) 2005, 682–4.

The Tale of Beryn

4656. ADAMS, JENNY. Exchequers and balances: anxieties of exchange in *The Tale of Beryn.* SAC (26) 2004, 267–97.

Thomas of Erceldoune

4657. COOPER, HELEN. Thomas of Erceldoune: romance as prophecy. *In* (pp. 171–87) **4555.**

Wynnere and Wastoure

4658. OWLEY, STEVEN A. *Wynnere and Wastoure.* Exp (63:4) 2005, 201–3.

PROSE
General Studies

4659. ACKER, PAUL. A Middle English prognostication by winds in Columbia University, Plimpton MS 260. JEBS (8) 2005, 261–7.

4660. BARR, HELEN. Wycliffite representations of the third estate. *In* (pp. 197–216) **4482.**

4661. CALLE MARTÍN, JAVIER.   Punctuation practice in a 15th-century arithmetical treatise (MS Bodley 790). *See* **1512.**

4662. EDWARDS, A. S. G. (ed.).   A companion to Middle English prose. Woodbridge, Suffolk; Rochester, NY: Brewer, 2004. pp. 334.

4663. HANNA, RALPH.   English biblical texts before Lollardy and their fate. *In* (pp. 141–53) **4482.**

4664. LEWIS, LUCY.   The Tavistock Boethius: one of the earliest examples of provincial printing. *In* (pp. 1–14) **880.**

4665. POPE, NANCY P.   A Middle English satirical letter in Brogyntyn MS II.1. *See* **301.**

Separate Anonymous Works

Ancrene Wisse / Ancrene Riwle

4666. CHEWNING, SUSANNAH MARY.   'Mi bodi henge/wið þi bodi': the paradox of sensuality in *Þe Wohunge of Ure Lauerd. In* (pp. 183–96) **4411.**

4667. EATON, R. D.   From *inwit* to *conscience* in late Middle English literature. *See* **1850.**

4668. RENEVEY, DENIS.   Figuring household space in *Ancrene Wisse* and *The Doctrine of the Hert.* SPELL (17) 2005, 69–84.

4669. WADA, YOKO (ed.).   A companion to *Ancrene Wisse.* (Bibl. 2004, 4868.)

4670. WATSON, NICHOLAS.   'With the heat of the hungry heart': empowerment and *Ancrene Wisse. In* (pp. 52–70) **4427.**

4671. WOGAN-BROWNE, JOCELYN.   Powers of record, powers of example: hagiography and women's history. *In* (pp. 71–93) **4427.**

The Ayenbite of Inwyt

4672. BREMMER, ROLF H., JR; LAKER, STEPHEN.   Earliest Middle English *ne*, 'than'. *See* **1700.**

The Book of Good Maners

4673. RUTKOWSKA, HANNA.   Selected orthographic features in English editions of the *Book of Good Maners* (1487–1507). SELIM (12) 2003/04, 127–42.

The Book of Priuy Counselling

4674. TAYLOR, CHERYL.   Paradox upon paradox: using and abusing language in *The Cloud of Unknowing* and related texts. *See* **4683.**

Book to a Mother

4675. RICE, NICOLE R.   Devotional literature and lay spiritual authority: *imitatio clerici* in *Book to a Mother.* JMEMS (35:2) 2005, 187–216.

Chronicles

4676. EWAN, ELIZABETH.   The dangers of manly women: late medieval perceptions of female heroism in Scotland's Second War of Independence. *In* (pp. 3–18) **3754.**

4677. GILLESPIE, ALEXANDRA.   Stow's 'owlde' manuscripts of London chronicles. *In* (pp. 57–67) **5746.**

4678. GIVEN-WILSON, CHRIS.   Chronicles: the writing of history in medieval England. (Bibl. 2004, 4873.) Rev. by Nicholas Vincent in TLS, 4 Feb. 2005, 24.

4679. McLAREN, MARY-ROSE. The London chronicles of the fifteenth century: a revolution in English writing. (Bibl. 2004, 4876.) Rev. by Jeremy Catto in Albion (36:3) 2004, 504–6.

4680. MARX, WILLIAM (ed.). An English chronicle, 1377–1461: a new edition, edited from Aberystwyth, National Library of Wales MS 21068 and Oxford, Bodleian Library MS Lyell 34. (Bibl. 2004, 4877.) Rev. by Lisa M. Ruch in TMR, Jan. 2005; by Richard J. Moll in JEGP (104:3) 2005, 409–10.

4681. WALTER, JOHN PAUL. The Arthurian material in Holkham Hall MS 669. ANQ (18:4) 2005, 15–20.

The Cloud of Unknowing

4682. GRISÉ, C. ANNETTE. The mixed life and lay piety in mystical texts printed in pre-Reformation England. See **4916**.

4683. TAYLOR, CHERYL. Paradox upon paradox: using and abusing language in *The Cloud of Unknowing* and related texts. Parergon (22:2) 2005, 31–51.

The Crafte of Nombrynge

4684. CALLE MARTÍN, JAVIER; MIRANDA GARCÍA, ANTONIO. Editing Middle English punctuation: the case of MS Egerton 2622 (ff. 136–152). IJES (5:2) 2005, 27–44.

The Doctrine of the Hert

4685. RENEVEY, DENIS. Figuring household space in *Ancrene Wisse* and *The Doctrine of the Hert*. See **4668**.

The Equatorie of the Planetis

4686. ARCH, JENNIFER. A case against Chaucer's authorship of the *Equatorie of the Planetis*. ChauR (40:1) 2005, 59–79.

The Fifteen Places Mary Visited after Christ's Ascension

4687. SCHWAMB, SARA. Introduction to Lambeth MS 546, fols 1r–7r: *The Fifteen Places Mary Visited after Christ's Ascension*. ANQ (18:4) 2005, 20–30.

Gilte Legende

4688. SAUER, MICHELLE M. The legend of St Juliana from Lambeth MS 72. ANQ (18:4) 2005, 9–15.

4689. TRACY, LARISSA (introd. and trans.). Women of the *Gilte Legende*: a selection of Middle English saints' lives. (Bibl. 2004, 4880.) Rev. by Lawrence M. Clopper in Spec (80:1) 2005, 344–6.

Homilies

4690. BLUMREICH, KATHLEEN MARIE (ed.). The Middle English *Mirror*: an edition based on Bodleian Library, MS Holkham Misc. 40. (Bibl. 2004, 4881.) Rev. by Rosemary Dunn in Parergon (22:1) 2005, 197–9; by Kantik Ghosh in RES (56:227) 2005, 779–80; by Jocelyn Wogan-Browne in Spec (80:2) 2005, 518–20.

4691. DUNCAN, THOMAS G.; CONNOLLY, MARGARET (eds). The Middle English *Mirror*: sermons from Advent to Sexagesima. Edited from Glasgow, University Library, Hunter 250, with a parallel text of the Anglo-Norman *Miroir* edited from the Nottingham, University Library, Mi LM 4. Heidelberg: Winter, 2003.

pp. lxxi, 190. (Middle English texts, 34.) Rev. by Simon Horobin in JEBS (8) 2005, 278–80.

4692. WATERS, CLAIRE M. Angels and earthly creatures: preaching, performance, and gender in the later Middle Ages. (Bibl. 2004, 4886.) Rev. by Bradley Warren in TMR, Jan. 2005; by Lawrence Besserman in Spec (80:4) 2005, 1393–5.

Jack Upland

4693. SOMERSET, FIONA. Here, there, and everywhere? Wycliffite conceptions of the Eucharist and Chaucer's 'other' Lollard joke. *In* (pp. 127–38) **4482.**

Katherine Group

4694. FROMER, JULIE E. Spectators of martyrdom: corporeality and sexuality in the *Liflade ant te Passiun of Seinte Margarete. In* (pp. 89–106) **4411.**

4695. WOGAN-BROWNE, JOCELYN. Powers of record, powers of example: hagiography and women's history. *In* (pp. 71–93) **4427.**

Letters

4696. MANN, CATHERINE. Clothing bodies, dressing rooms: fashioning fecundity in the Lisle letters. Parergon (22:1) 2005, 137–57.

4697. RAUMOLIN-BRUNBERG, HELENA. Language change in adulthood: historical letters as evidence. *See* **2878.**

Medical and Scientific Texts

4698. ALONSO ALMEIDA, FRANCISCO. All gathered together: on the construction of scientific and technical books in 15th-century England. IJES (5:2) 2005, 1–25.

4699. CARRILLO LINARES, Mᵃ JOSÉ. Middle English *Antidotarium Nicholai*: evidence for linguistic distribution and dissemination in the vernacular. IJES (5:2) 2005, 71–92.

4700. GARRIDO ANES, EDURNE. Geographical and dialectal distribution of Platearius' *Liber de simplici medicina* in England. IJES (5:2) 2005, 93–114.

4701. JONES, PETER MURRAY. Surgical narrative in Middle English. ANQ (18:3) 2005, 3–7.

4702. KEISER, GEORGE R. A Middle English rosemary treatise in verse and prose. *See* **270.**

4703. —— Verse introductions to Middle English medical treatises. EngS (84:4) 2003, 301–17.

4704. MATHESON, LISTER M. *Médecin sans frontières?* The European dissemination of John of Burgundy's plague treatise. ANQ (18:3) 2005, 17–28.

4705. OLSAN, LEA T. The language of charms in a Middle English recipe collection. ANQ (18:3) 2005, 29–35.

4706. RODRÍGUEZ-ÁLVAREZ, ALICIA; DOMÍNGUEZ-RODRÍGUEZ, Mᵃ VICTORIA. A Middle English text revised by a Renaissance reader: John Wotton's annotations to British Library MS Sloane 249 (ff. 180v–205v). IJES (5:2) 2005, 45–70.

4707. TAAVITSAINEN, IRMA; PAHTA, PÄIVI (eds). Medical and scientific writing in late medieval English. (Bibl. 2004, 4894.) Rev. by Isabel Moskowich-Spiegel Fandiño and Begoña Crespo in NM (106:1) 2005, 97–103.

4708. TAVORMINA, M. TERESA. The twenty-jordan series: an illustrated Middle English uroscopy text. ANQ (18:3) 2005, 40–64.

4709. VOIGTS, LINDA EHRSAM. The Master of the King's Stillatories. In (pp. 233–52) **4488.**

The Myroure of Oure Ladye

4710. JUSTICE, STEVEN. 'General words': response to Elizabeth Schirmer. In (pp. 377–94) **4460.**

4711. OLSON, LINDA; KERBY-FULTON, KATHRYN (eds). Voices in dialogue: reading women in the Middle Ages. See **4460.**

4712. SCHIRMER, ELIZABETH. Reading lesson at Syon Abbey: the Myroure of Oure Ladye and the mandates of vernacular theology. In (pp. 345–76) **4460.**

Peterborough Chronicle

4713. BRITTON, DEREK. Orm's wikenn and compounds with -wican in annal 1137 of the Peterborough Chronicle. NQ (52:1) 2005, 10–11.

4714. CANNON, CHRISTOPHER. Between the Old and the Middle of English. See **1385.**

The Pilgrimage of the Lyfe of the Manhode

4715. WALLS, KATHRYN. 'A prophetique dreame of the churche': William Baspoole's Laudian reception of the medieval Pilgrimage of the Lyfe of the Manhode. In (pp. 245–76) **6872.**

Prose Brut

4716. BASWELL, CHRISTOPHER. Troy, Arthur, and the languages of 'Brutis Albyoun'. In (pp. 170–97) **4485.**

4717. COOPER, HELEN. Lancelot, Roger Mortimer and the date of the Auchinleck Manuscript. In (pp. 91–9) **4419.**

4718. MARVIN, JULIA. Havelok in the prose Brut tradition. SP (102:3) 2005, 280–306.

4719. O'ROURKE, JASON; TAKAMIYA, TOSHIYUKI. Two hitherto unrecorded fragments of the Brut. NQ (52:2) 2005, 162–3.

Saints' Lives

4720. SCAHILL, JOHN. Middle English saints' legends. See **4652.**

A Talkyng of þe Loue of God

4721. SAUER, MICHELLE M. Cross-dressing souls: same-sex desire and the mystical tradition in A Talkyng of the Loue of God. In (pp. 157–81) **4411.**

A Tretise of Miraclis Pleyinge

4722. KENDRICK, LAURA. 'In bourde and in pleye': Mankind and the problem of comic derision in medieval English religious plays. See **4527.**

Wooing Group

4723. CHEWNING, SUSANNAH MARY. 'Mi bodi henge / wið þi bodi': the paradox of sensuality in Þe Wohunge of Ure Lauerd. In (pp. 183–96) **4411.**

RELATED STUDIES

4724. ANDERSON, ROBERTA; BELLENGER, DOMINIC AIDAN (eds). Medieval worlds: a sourcebook. London; New York: Routledge, 2003. pp. xx, 328. Rev. by Elizabeth S. Sklar in Arthuriana (14:4) 2004, 75–7.

4725. ARONSTEIN, SUSAN. Becoming Welsh: counter-colonialism and the negotiation of native identity in *Peredur vab Efrawc*. Exemplaria (17:1) 2005, 135–68.

4726. AUGSPACH, ELIZABETH A. The garden as woman's space in twelfth- and thirteenth-century literature. Lewiston, NY; Lampeter: Mellen Press, 2004. pp. iv, 174. (Studies in medieval literature, 27.)

4727. BENNETT, GILLIAN. William of Norwich and the expulsion of the Jews. Folklore (116:3) 2005, 311–14.

4728. BINSKI, PAUL. Becket's crown: art and imagination in gothic England, 1170–1300. New Haven, CT; London: Yale UP, 2004. pp. 343. Rev. by Anne Duggan in TLS, 8 July 2005, 7.

4729. BIRKHOLZ, DANIEL. The king's two maps: cartography and culture in thirteenth-century England. London; New York: Routledge, 2004. pp. xxxv, 254. (Studies in medieval history and culture, 22.) Rev. by Daniel K. Connolly in TMR, Oct. 2005.

4730. BLACKER, JEAN (ed.). The Anglo-Norman verse prophecies of Merlin. Arthuriana (15:1) 2005, 1–125.

4731. BOUET, PIERRE; LEVY, BRIAN; NEVEUX, FRANÇOIS (eds). The Bayeux Tapestry: embroidering the facts of history. Caen: Presses Universitaires de Caen, 2004. pp. 426, (plates) 212. Rev. by Judith Collard in Parergon (22:2) 2005, 198–200.

4732. BREEN, KATHARINE. Returning home from Jerusalem: Matthew Paris's first map of Britain in its manuscript context. Representations (89) 2005, 59–93.

4733. BRYANT, NIGEL (comp. and trans.). The legend of the Grail. (Bibl. 2004, 4908.) Rev. by Don Hoffman in Arthuriana (15:2) 2005, 65–6.

4734. CLERMONT-FERRAND, MEREDITH. Anglo-Saxon propaganda in the Bayeux Tapestry. *See* **4236**.

4735. DELIYANNIS, DEBORAH MAUSKOPF (ed.). Historiography in the Middle Ages. Leiden; Boston, MA: Brill, 2003. pp. vi, 464. Rev. by Graeme Dunphy in MLR (100:2) 2005, 468–9.

4736. DOBSON, BARRIE. Henry VI and the University of Cambridge. *In* (pp. 53–67) **4488**.

4737. DOVER, CAROL (ed.). A companion to the Lancelot–Grail cycle. Woodbridge, Suffolk; Rochester, NY: Brewer, 2003. pp. xiii, 267. (Arthurian studies, 54.) Rev. by Helen Moore in TLS, 8 July 2005, 5–6.

4738. DRESSLER, RACHEL. 'Those effigies which belonged to the English nation': antiquarianism, nationalism and Charles Alfred Stothard's *Monumental Effigies of Great Britain*. *See* **9839**.

4739. ERLER, MARY. Widows in retirement: region, patronage, spirituality, reading at the Gaunts, Bristol. ReLit (37:2) 2005, 51–75.

4740. FORD, PATRICK K.   Performance and literacy in medieval Welsh poetry. MLR (100:4) 2005, xxx–xlviii. (Presidential Address of the Modern Humanities Research Assn: 2005.)

4741. GOLDBERG, P. J. P.   Medieval England: a social history, 1250–1550. Oxford; New York: OUP, 2004. pp. 310. Rev. by Sara M. Butler in TMR, July 2005.

4742. GRIFFIN, JUSTIN E.   The Grail procession: the legend, the artifacts, and the possible sources of the story. Jefferson, NC; London: McFarland, 2004. pp. ix, 188.

4743. HALL, THOMAS N.   Preaching at Winchester in the early twelfth century. JEGP (104:2) 2005, 189–218.

4744. HAYES, ELIZABETH R.   The evolution of visual, literary, and performing arts from tribal cultures through the Middle Ages. Herriman, UT: Blue Ribbon, 2004. pp. xii, 226.

4745. HIATT, ALFRED.   The making of medieval forgeries: false documents in fifteenth-century England. (Bibl. 2004, 4923.) Rev. by A. S. G. Edwards in MÆ (74:1) 2005, 160–1; by Suzanne Conklin Akbari in NQ (52:3) 2005, 391–3; by Kathryn A. Lowe in SHARP (14:1/2) 2005, 14–15; by Bryan P. Davis in RQ (58:1) 2005, 321–2.

4746. HOGENBIRK, MARJOLEIN.   Intertextuality and Gauvain. Arthuriana (15:2) 2005, 13–25.

4747. KAEUPER, RICHARD W.   William Marshal, Lancelot, and the issue of chivalric identity. EMS (22) 2005, 1–19.

4748. KROLL, NORMA.   Power and conflict in medieval ritual and plays: the re-invention of drama. SP (102:4) 2005, 452–83.

4749. LACY, NORRIS J.   The uses of Middle Dutch Arthuriana. Arthuriana (15:2) 2005, 3–12.

4750. LE SAUX, F. H. M.   A companion to Wace. Woodbridge, Suffolk; Rochester, NY: Brewer, 2005. pp. 305.

4751. LOCKHART, RUDOLF A. ELIOTT.   Hugh of St Victor and twelfth-century English monastic reading. *In* (pp. 1–17) **19**.

4752. MARKS, RICHARD; WILLIAMSON, PAUL (eds).   Gothic: art for England 1400–1547. London: V&A, 2003. pp. 496. (Exhibition catalogue.) Rev. by Larry Silver in SixCJ (36:2) 2005, 465–6.

4753. MAZOUR-MATUSEVICH, YELENA.   Writing medieval history: an interview with Aaron Gurevich. JMEMS (35:1) 2005, 121–57.

4754. MOULTON, IAN FREDERICK (ed.).   Reading and literacy in the Middle Ages and Renaissance. Turnhout: Brepols; Abingdon: Marston, 2004. pp. xviii, 193. (Arizona studies in the Middle Ages and the Renaissance, 8.) Rev. by Antonina Harbus in Parergon (22:1) 2005, 263–5; by Phyllis R. Brown in RQ (58:2) 2005, 729–31.

4755. MURPHY, JAMES J.   Latin rhetoric and education in the Middle Ages and Renaissance. Aldershot; Burlington, VT: Ashgate, 2005. 1 vol. (various pagings). (Variorum collected studies.)

4756. NEDERMAN, CARY J.   John of Salisbury. Tempe: Arizona Center for Medieval and Renaissance Studies, 2005. pp. ix, 100. (Medieval & Renaissance texts & studies, 288.)

4757. NEEL, CAROL (ed.).   Medieval families: perspectives on marriage, household, and children. Toronto; Buffalo, NY; London: Toronto UP for the Medieval Academy of America, 2004. pp. vi, 436. (Medieval Academy reprints for teaching, 40.) Rev. by Linda E. Mitchell in TMR, Sept. 2005.

4758. NEWMAN, BARBARA.   Did goddesses empower women? The case of Dame Nature. In (pp. 135–55) **4427.**

4759. OGGINS, ROBIN S.   The kings and their hawks: falconry in medieval England. New Haven, CT; London: Yale UP, 2004. pp. xvi, 251, (plates) 8.

4760. REES JONES, SARAH.   Learning and literacy in medieval England and abroad. Turnhout: Brepols, 2003. pp. vi, 222. (Utrecht studies in medieval literacy, 3.) Rev. by Melissa Raine in Parergon (22:1) 2005, 272–4; by Andrew Galloway in Spec (80:2) 2005, 659–61.

4761. RUSSELL, D. W. (ed.).   La Vie seinte Osith, virge et martire (MS BL Addit. 70513, ff. 134va–146vb). Trans. by Jane Zatta. Revised and annotated by Jocelyn Wogan-Browne. PLL (41:3/4) 2005, 339–444.

4762. SMITH, WILLIAM H.   A unique English Cisioianus. ANQ (18:2) 2005, 9–15.

4763. WALTERS, LORI J.   Reconfiguring Wace's Round Table: Walewein and the rise of the national vernaculars. Arthuriana (15:2) 2005, 39–58.

4764. WEISS, JUDITH.   Ineffectual monarchs: portrayals of regal and imperial power in Ipomedon, Robert le Diable and Octavian. In (pp. 55–68) **4555.**

4765. WILLIAMS, STEVEN J.   The Secret of Secrets: the scholarly career of a pseudo-Aristotelian text in the Latin Middle Ages. Ann Arbor: Michigan UP, 2003. pp. xiv, 481. Rev. by Juanita Feros Ruys in Parergon (22:2) 2005, 262–4.

4766. WOGAN-BROWNE, JOCELYN.   The Life of St Osith: introduction. PLL (41:3/4) 2005, 300–5.

4767. ZATTA, JANE DICK.   The Vie seinte Osith: hagiography and politics in Anglo-Norman England. PLL (41:3/4) 2005, 306–38.

AUTHORS

George Ashby

4768. MOONEY, LINNE R.; ARN, MARY-JO (eds).   The Kingis Quair and other prison poems. See **4819.**

Blind Harry (Henry the Minstrel)

4769. MILFULL, INGE B.   War and truce: women in The Wallace. In (pp. 19–30) **3754.**

Osbern Bokenham

4770. EDWARDS, A. S. G.   Duke Humfrey's Middle English Palladius manuscript. In (pp. 68–77) **4488.**

4771. HOROBIN, SIMON.   The angle of oblivioun: a lost medieval manuscript discovered in Walter Scott's collection. See **260.**

John Capgrave

4772. LUCAS, PETER J. An Englishman in Rome: Capgrave's 1450-jubilee guide, *The Solace of Pilgrimes. In* (pp. 201–17) **4419.**

William Caxton

4773. ADAMS, TRACY. 'Noble, wyse and grete lordes, gentilmen and marchauntes': Caxton's prologues as conduct books for merchants. Parergon (22:2) 2005, 53–76.

4774. AMOS, MARK ADDISON. The gentrification of Eve: sexuality, speech, and self-regulation in noble conduct literature. *In* (pp. 19–36) **4411.**

4775. BARTLETT, ANNE CLARK. Translation, self-representation, and statecraft: Lady Margaret Beaufort and Caxton's *Blanchardyn and Eglantine* (1489). EMS (22) 2005, 53–66.

4776. BORDALEJO, BÁRBARA. The text of Caxton's second edition of the *Canterbury Tales. See* **4984.**

4777. COOPER, LISA H. Urban utterances: merchants, artisans, and the alphabet in Caxton's *Dialogues in French and English.* NML (7) 2005, 127–61.

4778. DANE, JOSEPH A. 'Wanting the first blank': frontispiece to the Huntington copy of Caxton's *Recuyell of the Historyes of Troye.* HLQ (67:2) 2004, 315–25.

4779. HANHAM, ALISON. Who made William Caxton's phrase-book? RES (56:227) 2005, 712–29.

4780. KATO, TAKAKO. Towards the digital Winchester: editing the Winchester manuscript of Malory's *Morte Darthur. See* **4889.**

4781. RUTKOWSKA, HANNA. Selected orthographic features in English editions of the *Book of Good Maners* (1487–1507). *See* **4673.**

4782. SIMPSON, JAMES. Consuming ethics: Caxton's *History of Reynard the Fox. In* (pp. 321–36) **4419.**

4783. TOKUNAGA, SATOKO. Early English printing and the hands of compositors. *See* **5036.**

4784. WANG, YU-CHIAO. Caxton's romances and their early Tudor readers. HLQ (67:2) 2004, 173–88.

4785. WEINBERG, S. CAROLE. Caxton, Anthony Woodville, and the Prologue to the *Morte Darthur. See* **4893.**

Charles of Orleans

4786. MOONEY, LINNE R.; ARN, MARY-JO (eds). *The Kingis Quair* and other prison poems. *See* **4819.**

4787. SUMMERS, JOANNA. Late medieval prison writing and the politics of autobiography. *See* **4927.**

Sir John Clanvowe

4788. SYMONS, DANA M. (ed.). Chaucerian dream visions and complaints. (Bibl. 2004, 4977.) Rev. by Kathryn L. Lynch in TMR, May 2005.

Gavin Douglas

4789. GUY-BRAY, STEPHEN. Embracing Troy: Surrey's *Aeneid. In* (pp. 177–92) **4479.**

William Dunbar

4790. CONLEE, JOHN W. (ed.). William Dunbar: the complete works. (Bibl. 2004, 4981.) Rev. by Fritz Kemmler in TMR, Mar. 2005.

4791. LYALL, RODERICK J. Writing towards the centre, reading around the periphery: the example of Scottish literature. See **3846**.

4792. STRONG, DAVID. Supra-natural creation in Dunbar's *The Goldyn Targe*. PQ (82:2) 2003, 149–66.

Edward of Norwich, Second Duke of York (1373?–1415)

4793. DODMAN, TREVOR. Hunting to teach: class, pedagogy, and maleness in *The Master of Game* and *Sir Gawain and the Green Knight*. See **5083**.

4794. KEEN, MAURICE. Hoo sto ho sto mon amy. LRB (27:24) 2005, 17–18 (review-article). (*The Master of Game*.)

John Gower (1325?–1408)

4795. BRATCHER, JAMES T. The function of the jeweled bridle in Gower's 'Tale of Rosiphelee'. ChauR (40:1) 2005, 107–10.

4796. CAIE, GRAHAM D. 'I do not wish to be called auctour, but the pore compilatour': the plight of the medieval vernacular poet. See **4601**.

4797. ECHARD, SIÂN (ed.). A companion to Gower. (Bibl. 2004, 4989.) Rev. by María Bullón-Fernández in Envoi (11:1) 2005 for 2002, 46–56; by Elliot Kendall in TLS, 11 Mar. 2005, 30; by Andrew Breeze in MLR (100:3) 2005, 759–62; by Simon Horobin in JEBS (8) 2005, 281–3; by Anthony P. Bale in MÆ (74:2) 2005, 348–9.

4798. FOX, HILARY E. 'Min herte is growen into ston': ethics and activity in John Gower's *Confessio Amantis*. Comitatus (36) 2005, 15–40.

4799. MCKITTERICK, ROSAMOND; BINSKI, PAUL. History and literature: sacred and secular. *In* (pp. 235–95) **202**.

4800. NOWLIN, STEELE. Narratives of incest and incestuous narrative: memory, process, and the *Confessio Amantis*'s 'middel weie'. JMEMS (35:2) 2005, 217–44.

4801. OESTERLEN, EVE-MARIA. Why bodies matter in mouldy tales: material (re)turns in *Pericles, Prince of Tyre*. See **6675**.

4802. TARANTINO, ELISABETTA. The Dante anecdote in Gower's *Confessio Amantis*, Book VII. ChauR (39:4) 2005, 420–35.

4803. WATT, DIANE. Amoral Gower: language, sex, and politics. (Bibl. 2004, 5002.) Rev. by Graham N. Drake in TMR, Jan. 2005; by Karma Lochrie in GLQ (11:2) 2005, 313–15; by George Shuffelton in JEGP (104:4) 2005, 561–3; by Denise Baker in Spec (80:4) 2005, 1395–7.

4804. YEAGER, R. F. John Gower's audience: the ballades. ChauR (40:1) 2005, 81–105.

John Hardyng

4805. FINKE, LAURIE A.; SCHICHTMAN, MARTIN B. King Arthur and the myth of history. Gainesville: Florida UP, 2004. pp. xiii, 262. Rev. by Dorsey Armstrong in Arthuriana (15:2) 2005, 68–71.

4806. HIATT, ALFRED.   Beyond a border: the maps of Scotland in John Hardyng's *Chronicle*. *In* (pp. 78–94) **4488.**

4807. —— Stow, Grafton, and fifteenth-century historiography. *In* (pp. 45–55) **5746.**

4808. LACY, NORRIS J. (ed.).   The fortunes of King Arthur. *See* **3836.**

4809. MOLL, RICHARD J.   Ebrauke and the politics of Arthurian geography. *See* **4635.**

Robert Henryson

4810. D'ARCY, ANNE MARIE.   'Into the kirk wald not hir self present': leprosy, blasphemy and heresy in Henryson's *The Testament of Cresseid*.   *In* (pp. 100–20) **4419.**

4811. HILL, THOMAS D.   *Stet verbum regis*: why Henryson's husbandman is not a king. EngS (86:2) 2005, 127–32.

4812. MCGINLEY, KEVIN J.   The 'fenȝeit' and the feminine: Robert Henryson's *Orpheus and Eurydice* and the gendering of poetry. *In* (pp. 74–85) **3754.**

4813. TINKER, EMMA.   An ornithological note on Henryson's *The Preaching of the Swallow*. NQ (52:2) 2005, 173–4.

Walter Hilton

4814. GRISÉ, C. ANNETTE.   The mixed life and lay piety in mystical texts printed in pre-Reformation England. *See* **4916.**

4815. KENNEDY, RUTH.   The Evangelist in Robert Thornton's devotional book: organizing principles at the level of the quire. *See* **4443.**

Thomas Hoccleve

4816. YEAGER, R. F.   Death is a lady: *The Regement of Princes* as gendered political commentary. SAC (26) 2004, 147–93.

John Irlande (*fl.*1455–1490)

4817. BOSE, MISHTOONI.   Vernacular philosophy and the making of orthodoxy in the fifteenth century. *See* **4912.**

4818. CAVANAGH, DERMOT.   Uncivil monarchy: Scotland, England and the reputation of James IV. *In* (pp. 146–61) **5187.**

James I, King of Scotland (1394–1437)

4819. MOONEY, LINNE R.; ARN, MARY-JO (eds).   *The Kingis Quair* and other prison poems. Kalamazoo, MI: Medieval Inst. in assn with the Univ. of Rochester for TEAMS, 2005. pp. viii, 206. (Middle English texts.)

4820. ROBERTSON, ELIZABETH.   '*Raptus*' and the poetics of married love in Chaucer's Wife of Bath's Tale and James I's *Kingis Quair*. *In* (pp. 302–23) **4485.**

4821. SUMMERS, JOANNA.   Late medieval prison writing and the politics of autobiography. *See* **4927.**

Julian of Norwich

4822. DIETRICH, JULIA.   Women and authority in the rhetorical economy of the late Middle Ages. *In* (pp. 21–43) **2410.**

4823. DUTTON, ELISABETH.   Augustine Baker and two manuscripts of Julian of Norwich's *Revelation of Love*. NQ (52:3) 2005, 329–37.

4824. FORBES, CHERYL.   Julian of Norwich and those ambiguous Starbridge women. *In* (pp. 187–97) **17081**.

4825. ROMAN, CHRISTOPHER.   Domestic mysticism in Margery Kempe and Dame Julian of Norwich: the transformation of Christian spirituality in the late Middle Ages. *See* **4838**.

4826. WICHER, ANDRZEJ.   The 'infantile' aspects of the 14th c. English mysticism: an introductory study. *In* (pp. 283–93) **3756**.

Margery Kempe

4827. ARNOLD, JOHN H.; LEWIS, KATHERINE J. (eds).   A companion to *The Book of Margery Kempe*. Woodbridge, Suffolk; Rochester, NY: Brewer, 2004. pp. xxiv, 246.

4828. DONNELLY, COLLEEN.   Menopausal life as imitation of art: Margery Kempe and the lack of sorority. WWr (12:3) 2005, 419–32.

4829. GERTZ-ROBINSON, GENELLE.   Stepping into the pulpit? Women's preaching in *The Book of Margery Kempe* and *The Examination of Anne Askew*. With a response by David Wallace. *In* (pp. 459–91) **4460**.

4830. McAVOY, LIZ HERBERT.   Authority and the female body in the writings of Julian of Norwich and Margery Kempe. (Bibl. 2004, 5034.) Rev. by Shannon Gayk in TMR, Mar. 2005.

4831. —— Virgin, mother, whore: the sexual spirituality of Margery Kempe. *In* (pp. 121–38) **4411**.

4832. MITCHELL, MAREA.   *The Book of Margery Kempe*: scholarship, community, and criticism. New York; Frankfurt: Lang, 2005. pp. xiv, 157.

4833. NEWMAN, BARBARA.   What did it mean to say 'I saw'? The clash between theory and practice in medieval visionary culture. Spec (80) 2005, 1–43.

4834. OLSON, LINDA; KERBY-FULTON, KATHRYN (eds).   Voices in dialogue: reading women in the Middle Ages. *See* **4460**.

4835. POWELL, RAYMOND A.   Margery Kempe: an exemplar of late medieval English piety. CathHR (89:1) 2003, 1–23.

4836. RAINE, MELISSA.   'Fals flesch': food and the embodied piety of Margery Kempe. NML (7) 2005, 101–26.

4837. RIDDY, FELICITY.   Text and self in *The Book of Margery Kempe*. *In* (pp. 435–57) **4460**.

4838. ROMAN, CHRISTOPHER.   Domestic mysticism in Margery Kempe and Dame Julian of Norwich: the transformation of Christian spirituality in the late Middle Ages. Lewiston, NY; Lampeter: Mellen Press, 2005. pp. iii, 236. (Mediaeval studies, 24.)

4839. WATSON, NICHOLAS.   The making of *The Book of Margery Kempe*. *In* (pp. 395–434, 453–7) **4460**.

William Langland

4840. AERS, DAVID.   Sanctifying signs: making Christian tradition in late medieval England. *See* **4394**.

4841. BARR, HELEN. Wycliffite representations of the third estate. *In* (pp. 197–216) **4482**.

4842. BENSON, C. DAVID. Public *Piers Plowman*: modern scholarship and late medieval English culture. (Bibl. 2004, 5042.) Rev. by Lawrence Warner in Parergon (22:1) 2005, 195–7; by A. V. C. Schmidt in RES (56:226) 2005, 662–3; by Donald C. Baker in ELN (42:3) 2005, 68–70; by Russell A. Peck in Spec (80:3) 2005, 831–2.

4843. BOWERS, JOHN M. Two professional readers of Chaucer and Langland: Scribe D and the HM 114 scribe. *See* **203**.

4844. BURROW, J. A. Lady Meed and the power of money. MÆ (74:1) 2005, 113–18.

4845. CLUTTERBUCK, CHARLOTTE. Encounters with God in medieval and early modern English poetry. *See* **4603**.

4846. COLE, ANDREW. William Langland and the invention of Lollardy. *In* (pp. 37–58) **4482**.

4847. DESKIS, SUSAN E.; HILL, THOMAS D. 'The longe man ys seld wys': proverbial characterization and Langland's Long Will. YLS (18) 2004, 73–9.

4848. ECONOMOU, GEORGE D. Chaucer and Langland: a fellowship of makers. *In* (pp. 290–301) **4485**.

4849. GRADY, FRANK. Contextualizing *Alexander and Dindimus*. *See* **4558**.

4850. HOROBIN, SIMON. 'In London and opelond': the dialect and circulation of the C version of *Piers Plowman*. MÆ (74:2) 2005, 248–69.

4851. —— MOONEY, LINNE R. A *Piers Plowman* manuscript by the Hengwrt/ Ellesmere scribe and its implications for London Standard English. SAC (26) 2004, 65–112.

4852. KIM, MARGARET. The politics of consuming worldly goods: negotiating Christian discipline and feudal power in *Piers Plowman*. Traditio (59) 2004, 339–68.

4853. MANN, JILL. The nature of Need revisited. YLS (18) 2004, 3–29.

4854. MINNIS, ALASTAIR J. Piers' protean pardon: the letter and spirit of Langland's theology of indulgences. *In* (pp. 218–40) **4419**.

4855. PEARSALL, DEREK. *Crowned King*: war and peace in 1415. *In* (pp. 163–72) **4488**.

4856. QUINN, WILLIAM A. Harriet Monroe as queen-critic of Chaucer and Langland (*viz.* Ezra Pound). *See* **4962**.

4857. ROBERTSON, ELIZABETH; SHEPHERD, STEPHEN H. A. (eds). *Piers Plowman*: the Donaldson translation, select authoritative Middle English text, sources and backgrounds, criticism. New York; London: Norton, 2004. pp. 608. (Norton critical eds.)

4858. ROGERS, WILLIAM ELFORD. Interpretation in *Piers Plowman*. (Bibl. 2004, 5056.) Rev. by James J. Paxson in YLS (18) 2004, 172–5.

4859. SCHMIDT, A. V. C. *Ars* or *scientia*? Reflections on editing *Piers Plowman*. YLS (18) 2004, 31–54.

4860. SCOTT, ANNE M. *Piers Plowman* and the poor. (Bibl. 2004, 5059.) Rev. by Stephen Medcalf in TLS, 28 Jan. 2005, 12; by Helen Barr in MÆ (74:2) 2005, 342–3.

4861. SHUFFELTON, GEORGE. *Piers Plowman* and the case of the missing book. YLS (18) 2004, 55–72.

4862. STEINER, EMILY. *Piers Plowman*, diversity, and the medieval political aesthetic. Representations (91) 2005, 1–25.

4863. TRIVEDI, KALPEN. Annual bibliography 2003. YLS (18) 2004, 201–18.

4864. WARNER, LAWRENCE. John But and the other works that Will wrought (*Piers Plowman* A XII 101–2). NQ (52:1) 2005, 13–18.

Laȝamon

4865. FINKE, LAURIE A.; SCHICHTMAN, MARTIN B. King Arthur and the myth of history. See **4805**.

4866. WATSON, JONATHAN. Writing out 'Óðinn's Storm': the literary reception of an oral-derived template in the two versions of Laȝamon's *Brut*. In (pp. 209–236) **4197**.

Nicholas Love

4867. NEWMAN, BARBARA. What did it mean to say 'I saw'? The clash between theory and practice in medieval visionary culture. See **4833**.

John Lydgate

4868. BOFFEY, JULIA. Chaucer's *Fortune* in the 1530s: some sixteenth-century recycling. In (pp. 53–64) **4419**.

4869. —— John Mychell and the printing of Lydgate in the 1530s. HLQ (67:2) 2004, 251–60.

4870. EDWARDS, A. S. G. Duke Humfrey's Middle English Palladius manuscript. In (pp. 68–77) **4488**.

4871. —— John Stow and Middle English literature. In (pp. 109–18) **5746**.

4872. GILLESPIE, ALEXANDRA. Introduction: bibliography and early Tudor texts. See **13**.

4873. LARSON, WENDY R. Who is the master of this narrative? Maternal patronage of the cult of St Margaret. In (pp. 94–134) **4427**.

4874. MORGAN, NIGEL. An SS collar in the devotional context of the shield of the Five Wounds. In (pp. 147–62) **4488**.

4875. MORTIMER, NIGEL. John Lydgate's *Fall of Princes*: narrative tragedy in its literary and political contexts. Oxford: Clarendon Press; New York: OUP, 2005. pp. xv, 360. (Oxford English monographs.)

4876. PEARSALL, DEREK. The apotheosis of John Lydgate. JMEMS (35:1) 2005, 25–38 (review-article).

4877. PERKINS, NICHOLAS. Representing advice in Lydgate. In (pp. 173–91) **4488**.

4878. PETRINA, ALESSANDRA. John Lydgate's *The Fall of Princes* and the politics of translation. In (pp. 213–23) **3690**.

4879. SÁNCHEZ MARTÍ, JORDI. Longleat House MS 257: a description. See **312**.

Sir Thomas Malory

4880. ARMSTRONG, DORSEY. Gender and the chivalric community of Malory's *Morte d'Arthur.* (Bibl. 2004, 5091.) Rev. by Ralph Norris in MLR (100:2) 2005, 477–9; by Kathleen Kelly in JEGP (104:4) 2005, 570–2; by Fiona Tolhurst in Spec (80:4) 2005, 1229–31.

4881. BATT, CATHERINE. Malory's *Morte Darthur*: remaking Arthurian tradition. (Bibl. 2004, 5095.) Rev. by Dhira B. Mahoney in Encomia (24/25) 2002/03, 10–12; by Martin B. Shichtman in SAC (26) 2004, 360–3; by Raluca L. Radulescu in MLR (100:4) 2005, 1081–2.

4882. CHRISTENSEN, PETER G. Clemence Housman's attack on King Arthur in *The Life of Sir Aglovale de Galis. See* **17072.**

4883. FINKE, LAURIE A.; SCHICHTMAN, MARTIN B. King Arthur and the myth of history. *See* **4805.**

4884. GORDON, SARAH. Kitchen knights in medieval French and English narrative: Rainouart, Lancelot, Gareth. Lit (16:2) 2005, 189–212.

4885. HARDYMENT, CHRISTINA. Malory: the life and times of King Arthur's chronicler. London: HarperCollins, 2005. pp. 634.

4886. HODGES, KENNETH. Guinevere's politics in Malory's *Morte Darthur.* JEGP (104:1) 2005, 54–79.

4887. HODGES, KENNETH L. Forging chivalric communities in Malory's *Le Morte d'Arthur.* Basingstoke; New York: Palgrave Macmillan, 2005. pp. 208. (Studies in Arthurian and courtly cultures.)

4888. JONES, TIMOTHY S. 'Oublië ai chevalerie': Tristan, Malory, and the outlaw-knight. *In* (pp. 79–90) **3576.**

4889. KATO, TAKAKO. Towards the digital Winchester: editing the Winchester manuscript of Malory's *Morte Darthur.* IJES (5:2) 2005, 175–92.

4890. LACY, NORRIS J. (ed.). The fortunes of King Arthur. *See* **3836.**

4891. MOLL, RICHARD J. Ebrauke and the politics of Arthurian geography. *See* **4635.**

4892. RADULESCU, RALUCA. The gentry context for Malory's *Morte Darthur.* (Bibl. 2004, 5124.) Rev. by Tracy Adams in Parergon (22:1) 2005, 268–9; by Maura B. Nolan in Spec (80:2) 2005, 658–9.

4893. WEINBERG, S. CAROLE. Caxton, Anthony Woodville, and the Prologue to the *Morte Darthur.* SP (102:1) 2005, 45–65.

4894. WHEELER, BONNIE (ed.). Arthurian studies in honour of P. J. C. Field. (Bibl. 2004, 5131.) Rev. by Dorsey Armstrong in TMR, Apr. 2005.

4895. WHETTER, K. S.; RADULESCU, RALUCA L. (eds). Re-viewing *Le Morte Darthur*: texts and contexts, characters and themes. Woodbridge, Suffolk; Rochester, NY: Brewer, 2005. pp. x, 165. (Arthurian studies, 60.)

'Sir John Mandeville'

4896. BASSNETT, SUSAN. Travelling and translating. WLWE (40:2) 2004, 66–76.

4897. SEYMOUR, M. C. (ed.). The defective version of *Mandeville's Travels.* (Bibl. 2004, 5137.) Rev. by Iain Macleod Higgins in SAC (26) 2004, 426–9.

4898. SØNDERGAARD, LEIF; HANSEN, RASMUS THORNING (eds). Monsters, marvels and miracles: imaginary journeys and landscapes in the Middle Ages. *See* **4483**.

4899. TZANAKI, ROSEMARY. Mandeville's medieval audiences: a study on the reception of *The Book of Sir John Mandeville* (1371–1550). (Bibl. 2004, 5138.) Rev. by M. G. Aune in SixCJ (35:4) 2004, 1124–6; by Suzanne Conklin Akbari in NQ (52:2) 2005, 239–40.

4900. VERNER, LISA. The epistemology of the monstrous in the Middle Ages. London; New York: Routledge, 2005. pp. 173. (Studies in medieval history and culture, 33.)

Henry Medwall

4901. KITCH, AARON. Medwall's 'condycion': *Fulgens and Lucrece* and the new Tudor drama. CEl (68) 2005, 1–8.

John Mirk

4902. GOODLAND, KATHARINE. 'Veniance, Lord, apon thaym fall': maternal mourning, divine justice, and tragedy in the Corpus Christi plays. *See* **4502**.

Thomas Norton (*fl*.1477)

4903. MASSON, CYNTHEA. Queer copulation and the pursuit of divine conjunction in two Middle English alchemical poems. *In* (pp. 37–48) **4411**.

Orm

4904. BRITTON, DEREK. Orm's *wikenn* and compounds with *-wican* in annal 1137 of the Peterborough Chronicle. *See* **4713**.

Paston Family

4905. CASTOR, HELEN. Blood & roses: the Paston family in the fifteenth century. London: Faber & Faber, 2004. pp. xvii, 347, (plates) 16. Rev. by Helen Cooper in LRB (27:15) 2005, 12–13.

4906. COOPER, HELEN. Family fortunes. LRB (27:15) 2005, 12–13 (review-article).

4907. ELLIS, STEVE. Framing the father: Chaucer and Virginia Woolf. *See* **4945**.

4908. LIU, YIN. Richard Beauchamp and the uses of romance. *See* **4564**.

4909. ROSENTHAL, JOEL T. Telling tales: sources and narration in late medieval England. (Bibl. 2004, 5151.) Rev. by Sally Mapstone in RES (56:225) 2005, 448–50; by Carl Lindahl in JBS (44:1) 2005, 364–6; by Linda E. Mitchell in Spec (80:4) 2005, 1363–4.

4910. WATT, DIANE (trans.). The Paston women: selected letters. Woodbridge, Suffolk; Rochester, NY: Brewer, 2004. pp. x, 178. (Library of medieval women.) Rev. by Brian Gastle in TMR, Sept. 2005.

Reginald Pecock

4911. BOSE, MISHTOONI. Reginald Pecock's vernacular voice. *In* (pp. 217–36) **4482**.

4912. —— Vernacular philosophy and the making of orthodoxy in the fifteenth century. NML (7) 2005, 73–99.

George Ripley (d.1490)

4913. MASSON, CYNTHEA. Queer copulation and the pursuit of divine conjunction in two Middle English alchemical poems. *In* (pp. 37–48) **4411**.

Anthony Woodville, Earl Rivers (1442?–1483)

4914. WEINBERG, S. CAROLE. Caxton, Anthony Woodville, and the Prologue to the *Morte Darthur. See* **4893**.

Richard Rolle

4915. DE LA CRUZ CABANILLAS, ISABEL. The language of the extant versions of Rolle's *Ego Dormio.* EngS (84:6) 2003, 511–20.

4916. GRISÉ, C. ANNETTE. The mixed life and lay piety in mystical texts printed in pre-Reformation England. JEBS (8) 2005, 97–123.

4917. MCILROY, CLAIRE ELIZABETH. The English prose treatises of Richard Rolle. (Bibl. 2004, 5155.) Rev. by Andrew Breeze in MLR (100:3) 2005, 759–62; by Cheryl Taylor in Parergon (22:1) 2005, 259–61; by Simon Horobin in JEBS (8) 2005, 290–2.

4918. POWELL, RAYMOND A. Margery Kempe: an exemplar of late medieval English piety. *See* **4835**.

4919. SUTHERLAND, ANNIE. Biblical text and spiritual experience in the English epistles of Richard Rolle. RES (56:227) 2005, 695–711.

Stephen Scrope

4920. MCKITTERICK, ROSAMOND; BINSKI, PAUL. History and literature: sacred and secular. *In* (pp. 235–95) **202**.

Richard Spalding (*fl. c.*1399)

4921. PUTTER, AD. Weak *e* and the metre of Richard Spalding's *Alliterative Katherine Hymn.* NQ (52:3) 2005, 288–92.

William Thorpe (d.1407?)

4922. AERS, DAVID. The *Testimony* of William Thorpe: reflections on self, sin and salvation. *In* (pp. 21–34) **4419**.

4923. ASTON, MARGARET. Lollards and the Cross. *In* (pp. 99–113) **4482**.

4924. REX, RICHARD. Thorpe's *Testament*: a conjectural emendation. MÆ (74:1) 2005, 109–13.

John Trevisa

4925. BASWELL, CHRISTOPHER. Troy, Arthur, and the languages of 'Brutis Albyoun'. *In* (pp. 170–97) **4485**.

Thomas Usk

4926. PATTERSON, PAUL J. Reforming Chaucer: margins and religion in an apocryphal *Canterbury Tale. See* **4643**.

4927. SUMMERS, JOANNA. Late medieval prison writing and the politics of autobiography. Oxford: Clarendon Press; New York: OUP, 2004. pp. viii, 229. (Oxford English monographs.) Rev. by Lucy Lewis in LSE (35) 2004, 193–6; by Sheila Delany in NQ (52:3) 2005, 394–5; by Fiona Somerset in MÆ (74:2) 2005, 347–8.

John Walton

4928. LEWIS, LUCY. The Tavistock Boethius: one of the earliest examples of provincial printing. *In* (pp. 1–14) **880.**

William Worcester (1415–1482)

4929. BREEZE, ANDREW. William Worcestre's *Liber cronicum Alfredi regis,* 'Greeff Island', and 'le Foorn'. NQ (52:3) 2005, 287–8.

4930. WAKELIN, DANIEL. William Worcester writes a history of his reading. NML (7) 2005, 53–71.

John Wyclif

4931. BOSE, MISHTOONI. Vernacular philosophy and the making of orthodoxy in the fifteenth century. *See* **4912.**

4932. GHOSH, KANTIK. The Wycliffite heresy: authority and the interpretation of texts. (Bibl. 2004, 5170.) Rev. by Richard Rex in SixCJ (36:1) 2005, 201–2.

GEOFFREY CHAUCER
General Scholarship and Criticism

4933. ARCH, JENNIFER. A case against Chaucer's authorship of the *Equatorie of the Planetis. See* **4686.**

4934. BOITANI, PIERO; MANN, JILL (eds). The Cambridge companion to Chaucer. (Bibl. 2004, 5173.) Rev. by Scott Lightsey in TMR, Jan. 2005; by Mary Theresa Hall in SixCJ (36:2) 2005, 514.

4935. BOWERS, JOHN M. Two professional readers of Chaucer and Langland: Scribe D and the HM 114 scribe. *See* **203.**

4936. BRASWELL, MARY FLOWERS. The Chaucer scholarship of Mary Eliza Haweis (1852–1898). ChauR (39:4) 2005, 402–19.

4937. CAIE, GRAHAM D. 'I do not wish to be called auctour, but the pore compilatour': the plight of the medieval vernacular poet. *See* **4601.**

4938. CARLSON, DAVID R. Chaucer's jobs. Basingstoke; New York: Palgrave Macmillan, 2004. pp. 168. (New Middle Ages.)

4939. COX, CATHERINE S. The Judaic Other in Dante, the *Gawain*-poet, and Chaucer. Gainesville: Florida UP, 2005. pp. x, 239.

4940. DANE, JOSEPH A. In search of Stow's Chaucer. *In* (pp. 145–55) **5746.**

4941. D'ARCY, ANNE MARIE; FLETCHER, ALAN J. (eds). Studies in late medieval and early Renaissance texts in honour of John Scattergood: 'the key of all good remembrance'. *See* **4419.**

4942. DELANY, SHEILA (ed.). Chaucer and the Jews: sources, contexts, meanings. (Bibl. 2004, 5177.) Rev. by Steven F. Kruger in SAC (26) 2004, 378–81; by John C. Hirsh in MÆ (74:1) 2005, 133–4.

4943. EDWARDS, A. S. G. John Stow and Middle English literature. *In* (pp. 109–18) **5746.**

4944. EDWARDS, ROBERT R. Chaucer and Boccaccio: antiquity and modernity. (Bibl. 2004, 5178.) Rev. by Warren Ginsberg in SAC (26) 2004, 381–5.

4945. ELLIS, STEVE. Framing the father: Chaucer and Virginia Woolf. NML (7) 2005, 35–52.

4946. —— (ed.).   Chaucer: an Oxford guide. Oxford; New York: OUP, 2005. pp. xxiv, 644.

4947. GANIM, JOHN M.   Chaucer and free love. *In* (pp. 344–63) **4485.**

4948. GRAY, DOUGLAS (ed.).   The Oxford companion to Chaucer. (Bibl. 2004, 5182.) Rev. by Michael P. Kuczynski in TMR, Mar. 2005; by Suzanne Conklin Akbari in NQ (52:1) 2005, 114–15; by R. F. Yeager in MÆ (74:2) 2005, 344–6.

4949. HAINES, SIMON.   Poetry and philosophy from Homer to Rousseau: romantic souls, realist lives. *See* **4298.**

4950. JOHNSON, JAMES D.   Identifying Chaucer allusions, 1991–2000: an annotated bibliography. ChauR (39:4) 2005, 436–55.

4951. JONES, TERRY, *et al.*   Who murdered Chaucer? A medieval mystery. (Bibl. 2004, 5185.) Rev. by Glending Olson in Spec (80:3) 2005, 900–1.

4952. KNAPP, PEGGY A.   Aesthetic attention and the Chaucerian text. ChauR (39:3) 2005, 241–58.

4953. LIU, JIN.   Chaucer's dream poetry and the medieval tradition of dream vision. FLS (116) 2005, 112–17. (In Chinese.)

4954. LIVINGSTON, MICHAEL.   A sixth hand in Cambridge, Trinity College, MS R.3.19. *See* **1529.**

4955. LYNCH, KATHRYN L. (ed.).   Chaucer's cultural geography. (Bibl. 2004, 5190.) Rev. by Jeffrey J. Cohen in SAC (26) 2004, 409–11.

4956. MCKITTERICK, ROSAMOND; BINSKI, PAUL.   History and literature: sacred and secular. *In* (pp. 235–95) **202.**

4957. MCTURK, RORY.   Chaucer and the Norse and Celtic worlds. Aldershot; Burlington, VT: Ashgate, 2005. pp. ix, 218.

4958. MITCHELL, JOHN ALLAN.   Ethics and exemplary narrative in Chaucer and Gower. (Bibl. 2004, 5193.) Rev. by Georgiana Donavin in TMR, Aug. 2005.

4959. PEARSALL, DEREK.   John Stow and Thomas Speght as editors of Chaucer: a question of class. *In* (pp. 119–25) **5746.**

4960. PERKINS, NICHOLAS.   Representing advice in Lydgate. *In* (pp. 173–91) **4488.**

4961. PRENDERGAST, THOMAS A.   Chaucer's dead body: from corpse to corpus. (Bibl. 2004, 5197.) Rev. by Joel Fredell in TMR, Aug. 2005.

4962. QUINN, WILLIAM A.   Harriet Monroe as queen-critic of Chaucer and Langland (*viz.* Ezra Pound). StudMed (14) 2005, 200–16.

4963. RICHMOND, VELMA BOURGEOIS.   Chaucer as children's literature: retellings from the Victorian and Edwardian eras. (Bibl. 2004, 5200.) Rev. by Gillian Adams in CLAQ (30:1) 2005, 131–2.

4964. —— Edward Burne-Jones's Chaucer portraits in the Kelmscott Chaucer. ChauR (40:1) 2005, 1–38.

4965. SCALA, ELIZABETH.   Absent narratives, manuscript textuality, and literary structure in late medieval England. (Bibl. 2004, 5203.) Rev. by Larry Scanlon in SAC (26) 2004, 424–6; by Karma Lochrie in MP (103:1) 2005, 98–101.

4966. STEINBERG, GLENN A.   Spenser's *Shepheardes Calender* and the Elizabethan reception of Chaucer. *See* **5722.**

4967. WATSON, NICHOLAS.   Chaucer's public Christianity. ReLit (37:2) 2005, 99–114.

4968. YEAGER, R. F.   Death is a lady: *The Regement of Princes* as gendered political commentary. *See* **4816**.

4969. —— John Gower's audience: the ballades. *See* **4804**.

Separate Works

Boece

4970. LEWIS, LUCY.   The Tavistock Boethius: one of the earliest examples of provincial printing. *In* (pp. 1–14) **880**.

4971. MACHAN, TIM WILLIAM; MINNIS, A. J. (eds).   Sources of the *Boece*. Athens; London: Georgia UP, 2005. pp. xiv, 311. (Chaucer library.)

4972. MILLER, MARK.   Philosophical Chaucer: love, sex, and agency in the *Canterbury Tales*. *See* **5016**.

The Book of the Duchess

4973. BURROW, J. A.   Politeness and privacy: Chaucer's *Book of the Duchess*. *In* (pp. 65–75) **4419**.

4974. HOROWITZ, DEBORAH.   An aesthetic of permeability: three transcapes of *The Book of the Duchess*. ChauR (39:3) 2005, 259–79.

4975. RAYBIN, DAVID; FEIN, SUSANNA.   Chaucer and aesthetics. ChauR (39:3) 2005, 225–33.

4976. SEYMOUR, M. C.   Chaucer's *Book of the Duchess*: a proposal. MÆ (74:1) 2005, 60–70.

Canterbury Tales

4977. ADAMS, JENNY.   Exchequers and balances: anxieties of exchange in *The Tale of Beryn*. *See* **4656**.

4978. ARNER, TIMOTHY D.   No joke: transcendent laughter in the *Teseida* and the Miller's Tale. SP (102:2) 2005, 143–58.

4979. ASKINS, WILLIAM.   All that glisters: the historical setting of the Tale of Sir Thopas. *In* (pp. 271–89) **4485**.

4980. ASTELL, ANN W.   Nietzsche, Chaucer, and the sacrifice of art. ChauR (39:3) 2005, 323–40.

4981. BELLAMY, ELIZABETH JANE.   Desires and disavowals: speculations on the aftermath of Stephen Greenblatt's *Psychoanalysis and Renaissance Culture*. *See* **14699**.

4982. BIGGS, FREDERICK M.   The Miller's Tale and *Heilevan Beersele*. RES (56:226) 2005, 497–523.

4983. BODDEN, M. C.   *Via erotica / via mystica*: a *tour de force* in the Merchant's Tale. *In* (pp. 51–73) **4411**.

4984. BORDALEJO, BÁRBARA.   The text of Caxton's second edition of the *Canterbury Tales*. IJES (5:2) 2005, 133–48.

4985. CARTER, SUSAN.   Duessa: Spenser's Loathly Lady. *See* **5685**.

4986. CAWSEY, KATHY.   Tutivillus and the 'kyrkchaterars': strategies of control in the Middle Ages. *See* **4530**.

4987. CORREALE, ROBERT M. (gen. ed.); HAMEL, MARY (assoc. ed.).   Sources and analogues of the *Canterbury Tales*: vol. 1, The frame, the Cook's Tale, the Clerk's Tale, the Franklin's Tale, the Friar's Tale, the Monk's Tale, the Nun's Priest's Tale, the Pardoner's Prologue and Tale, the Parson's Tale, the Reeve's Tale, the Second Nun's Prologue and Tale, the Squire's Tale, the Tale of Melibee. (Bibl. 2004, 5228.) Rev. by Helen Phillips in SAC (26) 2004, 372–5; by Jill Mann in JEGP (104:1) 2005, 103–28.

4988. EATON, R. D.   Sin and sensibility: the *conscience* of Chaucer's Prioress. *See* **1821**.

4989. ECONOMOU, GEORGE D.   Chaucer and Langland: a fellowship of makers. *In* (pp. 290–301) **4485**.

4990. EDWARDS, A. S. G.   A new text of the *Canterbury Tales*? *In* (pp. 121–8) **4419**.

4991. ERNE, LUKAS.   Words in space: the reproduction of texts and the semiotics of the page. SPELL (17) 2005, 99–118.

4992. FEICHTINGER, BARBARA.   Change and continuity in pagan and Christian (invective) thought on women and marriage from Antiquity to the Middle Ages. *In* (pp. 182–209) **5031**.

4993. FINLAYSON, JOHN.   Art and morality in Chaucer's Friar's Tale and the *Decameron*, Day One, Story One. Neophilologus (89:1) 2005, 139–52.

4994. FINLEY, WILLIAM K.; ROSENBLUM, JOSEPH (eds).   Chaucer illustrated: five hundred years of the *Canterbury Tales* in pictures. (Bibl. 2004, 5238.) Rev. by Bert Dillon in PBSA (99:2) 2005, 317–19.

4995. FRADENBURG, L. O. ARANYE.   Simply marvelous. *See* **4432**.

4996. GILLES, SEALY; TOMASCH, SYLVIA.   Professionalizing Chaucer: John Matthews Manly, Edith Rickert, and the *Canterbury Tales* as cultural capital. *In* (pp. 364–83) **4485**.

4997. GINSBERG, WARREN.   'Gli scogli neri e il niente che c'è': Dorigen's black rocks and Chaucer's translation of Italy. *In* (pp. 387–408) **4485**.

4998. GRACE, DOMINICK.   Telling differences: Chaucer's *Tale of Melibee* and Renaud de Louens' *Livre de Mellibee et Prudence*. PQ (82:4) 2003, 367–400.

4999. HAMAGUCHI, KEIKO.   Domesticating Amazons in the Knight's Tale. SAC (26) 2004, 331–54.

5000. —— Transgressing the borderline of gender: Zenobia in the Monk's Tale. ChauR (40:2) 2005, 183–205.

5001. HARDING, WENDY (ed.).   Drama, narrative and poetry in the *Canterbury Tales*. (Bibl. 2004, 5247.) Rev. by Elizabeth Scala in TMR, Feb. 2005.

5002. HEFFERNAN, CAROL F.   The Orient in Chaucer and medieval romance. (Bibl. 2004, 5250.) Rev. by Helen Moore in TLS, 8 July 2005, 5–6.

5003. HEFFERNAN, CAROL FALVO.   Chaucer's Miller's Tale and Reeve's Tale, Boccaccio's *Decameron*, and the French fabliaux. Italica (81:3) 2004, 311–24.

5004. HODGES, LAURA F.   Chaucer and clothing: clerical and academic costume in the General Prologue to the *Canterbury Tales*. Woodbridge, Suffolk; Rochester, NY: Brewer, 2005. pp. xiv, 316. (Chaucer studies, 34.)

5005. HOROBIN, S. C. P.   Pennies, pence and pans: some Chaucerian misreadings. EngS (84:5) 2003, 426–32.

5006. KISOR, YVETTE.   Moments of silence, acts of speech: uncovering the incest motif in the Man of Law's Tale. ChauR (40:2) 2005, 141–62.

5007. KLITGÅRD, EBBE.   Chaucer reception and translation in Denmark. ChauR (40:2) 2005, 207–17.

5008. KOLVE, V. A.; OLSON, GLENDING (eds).   The *Canterbury Tales*: fifteen tales and the General Prologue: authoritative text, sources and backgrounds, criticism. (Bibl. 1990, 3203.) New York; London: Norton, 2005. pp. xix, 600. (Norton critical eds.) (Second ed.: first ed. 1989.)

5009. KOWALIK, BARBARA.   Genre and gender in Chaucer's Knight's Tale. *In* (pp. 100–10) **3756**.

5010. KROCHALIS, JEANNE.   'And riden in Belmarye': Chaucer's General Prologue, line 57. ANQ (18:4) 2005, 3–8.

5011. LAMPERT, LISA.   Gender and Jewish difference from Paul to Shakespeare. (Bibl. 2004, 5261.) Rev. by M. Lindsay Kaplan in SStud (33) 2005, 277–84; by Matthew Biberman in ShY (15) 2005, 397–404; by John C. Hirsh in MÆ (74:1) 2005, 133–4; by Marilyn Francus in SRASP (28) 2005, 111–13.

5012. LUCAS, ANGELA M.   'But if a man be vertuous withal': has Aurelius in Chaucer's Franklin's Tale 'lerned gentillesse aright'? *In* (pp. 181–200) **4419**.

5013. LYNCH, KATHRYN L.   The three noble kinsmen: Chaucer, Shakespeare, Fletcher. *In* (pp. 72–91) **5103**.

5014. McCLELLAN, WILLIAM.   'Ful pale face': Agamben's biopolitical theory and the sovereign subject in Chaucer's Clerk's Tale. Exemplaria (17:1) 2005, 103–34.

5015. MANN, JILL.   Chaucer's sources and analogues revisited. JEGP (104:1) 2005, 103–28 (review-article).

5016. MILLER, MARK.   Philosophical Chaucer: love, sex, and agency in the *Canterbury Tales*. Cambridge; New York: CUP, 2004. pp. x, 289. (Cambridge studies in medieval literature, 55.) Rev. by H. L. Spencer in RES (56:227) 2005, 780–1; by Thomas Joseph O'Donnell in Comitatus (36) 2005, 261–4.

5017. MINNIS, ALASTAIR.   'Dante in Inglissh': what *Il convivio* really did for Chaucer. EC (55:2) 2005, 97–116. (F. W. Bateson Memorial Lecture.)

5018. MITCHELL, J. ALLAN.   Chaucer's Clerk's Tale and the question of ethical monstrosity. SP (102:1) 2005, 1–26.

5019. NISSE, RUTH.   Defining acts: drama and the politics of interpretation in late medieval England. *See* **4524**.

5020. PAKKALA-WECKSTRÖM, MARI.   The dialogue of love, marriage and *maistrie* in Chaucer's *Canterbury Tales*. Helsinki: Soc. Néophilologique, 2005. pp. 265. (Mémoires de la Soc. Néophilologique de Helsinki, 67.)

5021. PAPPANO, MARGARET AZIZA.   'Leve brother': fraternalism and craft identity in the Miller's Prologue and Tale. *In* (pp. 248–70) **4485**.

5022. PATTERSON, PAUL J.   Reforming Chaucer: margins and religion in an apocryphal *Canterbury Tale*. *See* **4643**.

5023. PITARD, DERRICK G. Sowing difficulty: the Parson's Tale, vernacular commentary, and the nature of Chaucerian dissent. SAC (26) 2004, 299–330.

5024. PUGH, TISON. Queering genres, battering males: the Wife of Bath's narrative violence. JNT (33:2) 2003, 115–42.

5025. ROBERTSON, ELIZABETH. '*Raptus*' and the poetics of married love in Chaucer's Wife of Bath's Tale and James I's *Kingis Quair. In* (pp. 302–23) **4485.**

5026. ROBINSON, PETER. The identification and use of authorial variants in the Miller's Tale. IJES (5:2) 2005, 115–32.

5027. SÁNCHEZ MARTÍ, JORDI. Longleat House MS 257: a description. *See* **312.**

5028. SCOTT-MACNAB, DAVID. 'Of prikyng and of huntyng for the hare': General Prologue to the *Canterbury Tales*, I 191. JEGP (104:3) 2005, 373–84.

5029. SHERIDAN, CHRISTIAN. May in the marketplace: commodificaton and textuality in the Merchant's Tale. SP (102:1) 2005, 27–44.

5030. SMITH, WARREN S. The Wife of Bath and Dorigen debate Jerome. *In* (pp. 243–69) **5031.**

5031. —— (ed.). Satiric advice on women and marriage: from Plautus to Chaucer. Ann Arbor: Michigan UP, 2005. pp. xiv, 295.

5032. SOMERSET, FIONA. Here, there, and everywhere? Wycliffite conceptions of the Eucharist and Chaucer's 'other' Lollard joke. *In* (pp. 127–38) **4482.**

5033. SØNDERGAARD, LEIF; HANSEN, RASMUS THORNING (eds). Monsters, marvels and miracles: imaginary journeys and landscapes in the Middle Ages. *See* **4483.**

5034. STEIN, ROBERT M.; PRIOR, SANDRA PIERSON (eds). Reading medieval culture: essays in honor of Robert W. Hanning. *See* **4485.**

5035. TAYLOR, KARLA. Social aesthetics and the emergence of civic discourse from the Shipman's Tale to Melibee. ChauR (39:3) 2005, 298–322.

5036. TOKUNAGA, SATOKO. Early English printing and the hands of compositors. IJES (5:2) 2005, 149–60.

5037. TOVEY, BARBARA. Chaucer's dialectic: how the establishment theology is subjected to scrutiny in five *Canterbury Tales*. IJPP (31:3) 2004, 235–99.

5038. TRAVIS, PETER W. The body of the Nun's Priest; or, Chaucer's disseminal genius. *In* (pp. 231–47) **4485.**

5039. TRIGG, STEPHANIE. Walking through cathedrals: scholars, pilgrims, and medieval tourists. NML (7) 2005, 9–33.

5040. TWU, KRISTA SUE-LO. Chaucer's vision of the Tree of Life: crossing the road with the Rood in the Parson's Tale. ChauR (39:4) 2005, 341–78.

5041. VAN BAKER, MICHAEL. The dame and the knight: marriage, sovereignty, and transformation. *See* **4598.**

5042. VÁZQUEZ, NILA. The need for 're-editing' *Gamelyn. See* **4563.**

5043. WALLING, AMANDA. 'In hir tellyng difference': gender, authority, and interpretation in the Tale of Melibee. ChauR (40:2) 2005, 163–81.

5044. WILSBACHER, GREG. Lumiansky's paradox: ethics, aesthetics and Chaucer's Prioress's Tale. ColLit (32:4) 2005, 1–28.

5045. WRIGHT, EDMOND.   Faith and narrative: a reading of the Franklin's Tale. PartA (3:1) 2005, 19–42.

The House of Fame

5046. BELLAMY, ELIZABETH JANE.   Slanderous Troys: between fame and rumor. In (pp. 215–35) **4479**.

5047. MINNIS, ALASTAIR.   'Dante in Inglissh': what *Il convivio* really did for Chaucer. See **5017**.

The Legend of Good Women

5048. FAULKNER, PETER.   The story of Alcestis in William Morris and Ted Hughes. See **11745**.

5049. HAGEDORN, SUZANNE C.   Abandoned women: rewriting the Classics in Dante, Boccaccio, & Chaucer. (Bibl. 2004, 5289.) Rev. by Mathilde Skoie in TMR, Jan. 2005; by Michael A. Calabrese in JEGP (104:3) 2005, 400–2; by Jamie C. Fumo in Spec (80:4) 2005, 1291–3.

5050. WILLIAMSON, ANNE.   'Save his own soul he hath no star': thoughts arising from *The Dream of Fair Women*. See **20234**.

The Romaunt of the Rose

5051. MILLER, MARK.   Philosophical Chaucer: love, sex, and agency in the *Canterbury Tales*. See **5016**.

Short Poems

5052. BOFFEY, JULIA.   Chaucer's *Fortune* in the 1530s: some sixteenth-century recycling. In (pp. 53–64) **4419**.

5053. O'CONNELL, BRENDAN.   *Adam Scriveyn* and the falsifiers of Dante's *Inferno*: a new interpretation of Chaucer's *Wordes*. ChauR (40:1) 2005, 39–57.

5054. THOMPSON, JOHN J.   Patch and repair and making do in manuscripts and texts associated with John Stow. In (pp. 353–61) **4419**.

A Treatise on the Astrolabe

5055. ARCH, JENNIFER.   A case against Chaucer's authorship of the *Equatorie of the Planetis*. See **4686**.

Troilus and Criseyde

5056. BURROW, J. A.   Politeness and privacy: Chaucer's *Book of the Duchess*. In (pp. 65–75) **4419**.

5057. CELLAI, ANTONELLA.   Da *truce-breaker* a *match-maker*: le metamorfosi di Pandaro da Omero a Dryden. LProv (116/117) 2003, 53–60.

5058. GARNER, LORI ANN.   The role of proverbs in Middle English narrative. In (pp. 255–77) **4197**.

5059. GIANCARLO, MATTHEW.   The structure of fate and the devising of history in Chaucer's *Troilus and Criseyde*. SAC (26) 2004, 227–66.

5060. GINSBERG, WARREN.   Aesthetics *sine nomine*. ChauR (39:3) 2005, 234–40.

5061. HILL, JOHN M.   The countervailing aesthetic of joy in *Troilus and Criseyde*. ChauR (39:3) 2005, 280–97.

5062. Howes, Laura L.   Chaucer's Criseyde: the betrayer betrayed. *In* (pp. 324–43) **4485**.

5063. Mitchell, J. Allan.   Romancing ethics in Boethius, Chaucer, and Levinas: Fortune, moral luck, and erotic adventure. CL (57:2) 2005, 101–16.

5064. O'Brien, Timothy.   Brother as problem in the *Troilus*. PQ (82:2) 2003, 125–48.

5065. Pugh, Tison.   Christian revelation and the cruel game of courtly love in *Troilus and Criseyde*. ChauR (39:4) 2005, 379–401.

5066. Revard, Carter.   Four fabliaux from London, British Library MS Harley 2253, translated into English verse. *See* **306**.

GAWAIN-POET
General Scholarship and Criticism

5067. Cox, Catherine S.   The Judaic Other in Dante, the *Gawain*-poet, and Chaucer. *See* **4939**.

Separate Works

Cleanness

5068. Søndergaard, Leif; Hansen, Rasmus Thorning (eds).   Monsters, marvels and miracles: imaginary journeys and landscapes in the Middle Ages. *See* **4483**.

Pearl

5069. Berry, Craig; Hayton, Heather (eds).   Translating desire in medieval and early modern literature. Tempe: Arizona Center for Medieval and Renaissance Studies, 2005. pp. xv, 254. (Medieval & Renaissance texts & studies, 294.)

5070. Cox, Catherine S.   'My lemman swete': gender and passion in *Pearl*. *In* (pp. 75–86) **4411**.

5071. Edmondson, George.   *Pearl*: the shadow of the object, the shape of the law. SAC (26) 2004, 29–63.

5072. Fletcher, Alan J.   *Pearl* and the limits of history. *In* (pp. 148–70) **4419**.

5073. Kline, Daniel T.   Resisting the father in *Pearl*. *In* (pp. 1–29) **5069**.

5074. Machan, Tim William.   Writing the failure of speech in *Pearl*. *In* (pp. 279–305) **4197**.

5075. Meyer, Ann R.   Medieval allegory and the building of the New Jerusalem. (Bibl. 2004, 5319.) Rev. by Amanda Luyster in Arthuriana (15:4) 2005, 73–5.

5076. Newman, Barbara.   The artifice of eternity: speaking of Heaven in three medieval poems. ReLit (37:1) 2005, 1–24.

5077. Wicher, Andrzej.   The 'infantile' aspects of the 14th c. English mysticism: an introductory study. *In* (pp. 283–93) **3756**.

St Erkenwald

5078. Thijms, Annemarie.   The sacrament of baptism in *St Erkenwald*: the perfect transformation of the Trajan legend. Neophilologus (89:2) 2005, 311–27.

5079. TURVILLE-PETRE, THORLAC.   *St Erkenwald* and the crafty chronicles. *In* (pp. 362–74) **4419**.

Sir Gawain and the Green Knight

5080. ASHTON, GAIL.   The perverse dynamics of *Sir Gawain and the Green Knight*. Arthuriana (15:3) 2005, 51–74.

5081. COSTANTINI, ROBERTO.   La problematica del segno in *Sir Gawain and the Green Knight*. SCrit (18:1) 2003, 29–74.

5082. —— Semiosi e amor cortese in *Sir Gawain and the Green Knight*. SCrit (18:3) 2003, 387–417.

5083. DODMAN, TREVOR.   Hunting to teach: class, pedagogy, and maleness in *The Master of Game* and *Sir Gawain and the Green Knight*. Exemplaria (17:2) 2005, 413–44.

5084. FRADENBURG, L. O. ARANYE.   Simply marvelous. *See* **4432**.

5085. LACY, NORRIS J.   Medieval McGuffins: the Arthurian model. Arthuriana (15:4) 2005, 53–64. (Round Table.)

5086. MORSE, CHARLOTTE C.   Scenes of farewell in the Middle Ages. *In* (pp. 241–58) **4419**.

5087. STOKES, MYRA.   Gawain the good. *In* (pp. 337–52) **4419**.

SIXTEENTH CENTURY
GENERAL

5088. ABATE, CORINNE S. (ed.).   Privacy, domesticity, and women in early modern England. (Bibl. 2004, 5331.) Rev. by Margaret J. Oakes in SixCJ (35:4) 2004, 1127–9; by Margaret Lael Mikesell in SNL (54:4) 2004/05, 93–6; by Helen Hackett in WWr (12:2) 2005, 311–13; by Sally Parkin in Parergon (22:2) 2005, 183–5.

5089. ANDERSON, JUDITH H.   Translating investments: metaphor and the dynamic of cultural change in Tudor–Stuart England. *See* **2210.**

5090. BAKER, DAVID J.; MALEY, WILLY (eds).   British identities and English Renaissance literature. (Bibl. 2004, 5334.) Rev. by Erick Kelemen in SixCJ (34:4) 2003, 1157–8.

5091. BAWCUTT, PRISCILLA.   Scottish manuscript miscellanies from the fifteenth to the seventeenth century. *See* **200.**

5092. BECKER, LUCINDA.   Death and the early modern Englishwoman. (Bibl. 2004, 5335.) Rev. by Sylvia Brown in MLR (100:3) 2005, 777–8; by Susanne Woods in CLIO (34:3) 2005, 369–76.

5093. BELLAMY, ELIZABETH JANE.   Desires and disavowals: speculations on the aftermath of Stephen Greenblatt's *Psychoanalysis and Renaissance Culture.* *See* **14699.**

5094. BENSON, PAMELA JOSEPH; KIRKHAM, VICTORIA (eds).   Strong voices, weak history: early women writers & canons in England, France, & Italy. Ann Arbor: Michigan UP, 2005. pp. viii, 380.

5095. BERRY, PHILIPPA; TUDEAU-CLAYTON, MARGARET (eds).   Textures of Renaissance knowledge. (Bibl. 2004, 5337.) Rev. by Andrew Hadfield in NQ (52:3) 2005, 412–14; by Bernhard Klein in SJ (141) 2005, 267–9.

5096. BERTRAM, BENJAMIN.   The time is out of joint: skepticism in Shakespeare's England. Newark: Delaware UP, 2004. pp. 224. Rev. by Robert A. Logan in RQ (58:4) 2005, 1441–3.

5097. BETTERIDGE, THOMAS.   The Henrician Reformation and mid-Tudor culture. JMEMS (35:1) 2005, 91–109 (review-article).

5098. BETTERIDGE, TOM.   Literature and politics in the English Reformation. Manchester; New York: Manchester UP, 2004. pp. vii, 253. (Politics, culture and society in early modern Britain.)

5099. BIBERMAN, MATTHEW.   Masculinity, anti-Semitism and early modern English literature: from the satanic to the effeminate Jew. (Bibl. 2004, 5338.) Rev. by B. J. Sokol in RES (56:227) 2005, 783–5; by Thomas Moisan in RQ (58:4) 2005, 1433–5.

5100. BLAINE, MARLIN E.   The poet's monument: assessing the national literary tradition from Elizabethan times to the Restoration. 1650–1850 (10) 2004, 265–83.

5101. BRAYMAN HACKEL, HEIDI.   Reading material in early modern England: print, gender, and literacy. *See* **780.**

5102. BROWN, GEORGIA. Redefining Elizabethan literature. Cambridge; New York: CUP, 2004. pp. viii, 261. Rev. by Lorna Hutson in TLS, 19 & 26 Aug. 2005, 13; by Michael G. Brennan in NQ (52:4) 2005, 532–3; by Judith Haber in RQ (58:4) 2005, 1437–8.

5103. BRUCE, YVONNE (ed.). Images of matter: essays on British literature of the Middle Ages and Renaissance: proceedings of the Eighth Citadel Conference on Literature, Charleston, South Carolina, 2002. Newark: Delaware UP; London: Assoc. UPs, 2005. pp. 283.

5104. BUSHNELL, REBECCA. Green desire: imagining early modern English gardens. (Bibl. 2004, 5344.) Rev. by Vin Nardizzi in MLQ (66:3) 2005, 393–6; by Martin Elsky in RQ (58:1) 2005, 330–1.

5105. CAMPBELL, GORDON (ed.). The Oxford dictionary of the Renaissance. Oxford; New York: OUP, 2003. pp. xlvi, 862. Rev. by Bernhard Klein in SJ (141) 2005, 267–9.

5106. CARPI, DANIELA (ed.). Property law in Renaissance literature. New York; Frankfurt: Lang, 2005. pp. xvi, 226. (Anglo-amerikanische Studien, 28.)

5107. CARTWRIGHT, KENT. Early modern English literature without *Hamlet*. HLQ (67:4) 2004, 633–49 (review-article).

5108. CAVANAGH, DERMOT. Uncivil monarchy: Scotland, England and the reputation of James IV. *In* (pp. 146–61) **5187**.

5109. CEFALU, PAUL. Moral identity in early modern English literature. Cambridge; New York: CUP, 2004. pp. x, 225. Rev. by Margaret Maurer in RQ (58:4) 2005, 1439–41.

5110. CHEDGZOY, KATE. In the lesbian archive. GLQ (11:3) 2005, 457–67 (review-article).

5111. CLARK, SANDRA. Women and crime in the street literature of early modern England. (Bibl. 2004, 5347.) Rev. by Elfi Bettinger in SJ (141) 2005, 258–61.

5112. CLAYTON, FREDERICK W.; TUDEAU-CLAYTON, MARGARET. Mercury, boy yet and the 'harsh' words of *Love's Labour's Lost*. See **6526**.

5113. CLEGG, CYNDIA SUSAN. 'The aucthor of this book': attributing authorship, 1580–1640. PCP (40:2) 2005, 27–37.

5114. COCKCROFT, ROBERT. Rhetorical affect in early modern writing: Renaissance passions reconsidered. (Bibl. 2004, 5349.) Rev. by Christy Desmet in MLR (100:3) 2005, 779–80; by Lenore Kitts in Comitatus (36) 2005, 210–12.

5115. COLÓN SEMENZA, GREGORY M. Sport, politics, and literature in the English Renaissance. (Bibl. 2004, 5351.) Rev. by David E. Phillips in SixCJ (36:2) 2005, 628–9; by Amy Boesky in RQ (58:2) 2005, 727–9.

5116. COOK, JAMES. Encyclopedia of Renaissance literature. New York: Facts on File, 2005. pp. 480.

5117. CORMACK, BRADIN. Practicing law and literature in early modern studies. MP (101:1) 2003, 79–91 (review-article).

5118. CORNETT, MICHAEL. New books across the disciplines. *See* **4414**.

5119. —— New books across the disciplines. *See* **4415**.

5120. CRAWFORD, JULIE. Marvelous Protestantism: monstrous births in post-Reformation England. Baltimore, MD; London: Johns Hopkins UP, 2005. pp. x, 270.

5121. CROFT, PAULINE (ed.). Patronage, culture and power: the early Cecils. New Haven, CT; London: Yale UP for the Paul Mellon Centre for Studies in British Art and the Yale Center for British Art, 2002. pp. xxi, 308. (Studies in British art, 8.) Rev. by Sara Nair James in SixCJ (35:3) 2004, 954–5.

5122. CURRAN, JOHN E., JR. Roman invasions: the British history, Protestant anti-Romanism, and the historical imagination in England, 1530–1660. (Bibl. 2004, 5359.) Rev. by Manfred Weidhorn in SixCJ (34:3) 2003, 913–14.

5123. DAMROSCH, DAVID (gen. ed.). The Longman anthology of world literature: vol. C, The early modern period. Ed. by Jane Tylus and David Damrosch. Harlow; New York: Longman, 2004. pp. xxv, 902.

5124. D'ARCY, ANNE MARIE; FLETCHER, ALAN J. (eds). Studies in late medieval and early Renaissance texts in honour of John Scattergood: 'the key of all good remembrance'. See **4419.**

5125. DAVIS, ALEX. Chivalry and romance in the English Renaissance. (Bibl. 2004, 5360.) Rev. by Helen Moore in TLS, 8 July 2005, 5–6; by Mary Theresa Hall in SixCJ (36:1) 2005, 175–6.

5126. DAYBELL, JAMES (ed.). Women and politics in early modern England, 1450–1700. (Bibl. 2004, 5361.) Rev. by Sybil M. Jack in Parergon (22:2) 2005, 212–14.

5127. DEMERS, PATRICIA. Early modern England. Toronto; Buffalo, NY; London: Toronto UP, 2005. pp. x, 363. (Women's writing in English.) Rev. by Elizabeth Scott-Baumann in TLS, 9 Sept. 2005, 27.

5128. DOBRANSKI, STEPHEN B. Readers and authorship in early modern England. Cambridge; New York: CUP, 2005. pp. xiii, 226. Rev. by Harold Love in TLS, 15 July 2005, 24.

5129. DOERKSEN, DANIEL W.; HODGKINS, CHRISTOPHER (eds). Centered on the Word: literature, Scripture, and the Tudor–Stuart middle way. See **6872.**

5130. DORAN, SUSAN. The politics of Renaissance Europe. In (pp. 21–52) **5954.**

5131. —— FREEMAN, THOMAS S. (eds). The myth of Elizabeth. (Bibl. 2004, 5364.) Rev. by Ronald H. Fritze in SixCJ (36:1) 2005, 271–3.

5132. ENTERLINE, LYNN; HILLMAN, DAVID. Other selves, other bodies. See **21023.**

5133. FERGUSON, MARGARET W. Dido's daughters: literacy, gender, and empire in early modern England and France. (Bibl. 2004, 5367.) Rev. by Jessica Munns in MLR (100:2) 2005, 472–3.

5134. FERNIE, EWAN, et al. (eds). Reconceiving the Renaissance: a critical reader. Oxford; New York: OUP, 2005. pp. ix, 436.

5135. FORTIER, MARK. The culture of equity in early modern England. Aldershot; Burlington, VT: Ashgate, 2005. pp. viii, 217.

5136. FOWLER, ALASTAIR. Renaissance realism: narrative images in literature and art. (Bibl. 2004, 5368.) Rev. by Lisa Regan in SixCJ (35:4) 2004, 1210–11.

5137. GERITZ, ALBERT J.   Recent studies in More (1990–2003). *See* **5565**.

5138. GREENBLATT, STEPHEN.   Renaissance self-fashioning: from More to Shakespeare. (Bibl. 1989, 3006.) Chicago, IL; London: Chicago UP, 2005. pp. xvii, 321. (Second ed.: first ed. 1980.)

5139. GUIBBORY, ACHSAH.   Recent studies in the English Renaissance. SELit (45:1) 2005, 213–65.

5140. GUTIERREZ, NANCY.   'Shall she famish then?': female food refusal in early modern England. (Bibl. 2003, 5131.) Rev. by Lesel Dawson in SixCJ (36:1) 2005, 156–7.

5141. GUY-BRAY, STEPHEN.   Homoerotic space: the poetics of loss in Renaissance literature. (Bibl. 2004, 5374.) Rev. by Todd W. Reeser in SixCJ (34:4) 2003, 1255–6.

5142. HADFIELD, ANDREW; HAMMOND, PAUL (eds).   Shakespeare and Renaissance Europe. *See* **5954**.

5143. HAMLIN, WILLIAM M.   Tragedy and skepticism in Shakespeare's England. Basingstoke; New York: Palgrave Macmillan, 2005. pp. xiii, 306. (Early modern literature in history.)

5144. HEALY, THOMAS.   Queene and country. *See* **5699**.

5145. HEITSCH, DOROTHY; VALLÉE, JEAN-FRANÇOIS (eds).   Printed voices: the Renaissance culture of dialogue. (Bibl. 2004, 5377.) Rev. by Christopher Braider in RQ (58:3) 2005, 981–3.

5146. HILL, W. SPEED (ed.).   New ways of looking at old texts III: papers of the Renaissance English Text Society, 1997–2001. *See* **587**.

5147. HÖFELE, ANDREAS; VON KOPPENFELS, WERNER (eds).   Renaissance go-betweens: cultural exchange in early modern Europe. Berlin; New York: Mouton de Gruyter, 2005. pp. ix, 289. (Spectrum literature, 2.)

5148. IVIC, CHRISTOPHER; WILLIAMS, GRANT (eds).   Forgetting in early modern English literature and culture: Lethe's legacies. London; New York: Routledge, 2004. pp. x, 195. (Routledge studies in Renaissance literature and culture, 3.) Rev. by Christopher Martin in MLR (100:2) 2005, 479–80.

5149. IYENGAR, SUJATA.   Shades of difference: mythologies of skin colour in early modern England. Philadelphia: Pennsylvania UP, 2005. pp. x, 307.

5150. JOHNSTONE, NATHAN.   The Protestant Devil: the experience of temptation in early modern England. JBS (43:2) 2004, 173–205.

5151. KALLENDORF, HILAIRE.   Exorcism and its texts: subjectivity in early modern literature of England and Spain. (Bibl. 2004, 5379.) Rev. by Michaela Valente in SixCJ (36:2) 2005, 634–5; by John D. Cox in ShY (15) 2005, 442–6; by James Sharpe in CathHR (91:3) 2005, 526–7; by Isaías Lerner in RQ (58:2) 2005, 667–9.

5152. KENDRICK, CHRISTOPHER.   Utopia, carnival, and commonwealth in Renaissance England. Toronto; Buffalo, NY; London: Toronto UP, 2004. pp. vi, 382. Rev. by Ivan Cañadas in Parergon (22:2) 2005, 267–8.

5153. KEWES, PAULINA (ed.).   Plagiarism in early modern England. (Bibl. 2004, 5381.) Rev. by Bruce Whiteman in ECS (38:2) 2005, 333–6; by Marilyn Randall in SHARP (14:1/2) 2005, 16; by Éliane Cuvelier in EA (58:2) 2005, 204–6.

5154. KING, JOHN N.   Thomas Bentley's *Monument of Matrons*: the earliest anthology of English women's texts. *In* (pp. 216–38) **5094**.

5155. ——— Voices of the English Reformation: a sourcebook. Philadelphia: Pennsylvania UP, 2004. pp. ix, 394. Rev. by Adam Smyth in TLS, 5 Aug. 2005, 29; by Peter Happé in BJJ (12) 2005, 273–9.

5156. KINNEY, ARTHUR.   Harriett Hawkins's Renaissance. *In* (pp. 30–41) **5167**.

5157. KNOPPERS, LAURA LUNGER; LANDES, JOAN B. (eds).   Monstrous bodies / political monstrosities in early modern Europe. (Bibl. 2004, 5382.) Rev. by Ruth Gilbert in BHM (79:2) 2005, 327–8; by Emma Smith in RES (56:224) 2005, 320–2; by Javier Moscoso in RQ (58:3) 2005, 1008–10.

5158. KUCHAR, GARY.   Divine subjection: the rhetoric of sacramental devotion in early modern England. Pittsburgh, PA: Duquesne UP, 2005. pp. xii, 297. (Medieval & Renaissance literary studies.)

5159. LOEWENSTEIN, DAVID; MUELLER, JANEL (eds).   The Cambridge history of early modern English literature. (Bibl. 2004, 5385.) Rev. by Kent Cartwright in HLQ (67:4) 2004, 633–49; in BJJ (12) 2005, 293–301.

5160. LÓPEZ-PELÁEZ CASELLAS, JESÚS.   The neo-Stoic revival in English literature of the sixteenth and seventeenth centuries: an approach. SEDERI (14) 2004, 93–115.

5161. McCOY, RICHARD C.   Alterations of state: sacred kingship in the English Reformation. (Bibl. 2004, 5388.) Rev. by Glen Bowman in SixCJ (34:4) 2003, 1175–6.

5162. MacDONALD, ALASDAIR A.; DEKKER, KEES (eds).   Rhetoric, royalty, and reality: essays on the literary culture of medieval and early modern Scotland. *See* **4452**.

5163. MacDONALD, JOYCE GREEN.   Women and race in early modern texts. (Bibl. 2004, 5389.) Rev. by Bernadette Andrea in SixCJ (35:4) 2004, 1144–6.

5164. MALCOLMSON, CRISTINA; SUZUKI, MIHOKO (eds).   Debating gender in early modern England, 1500–1700. (Bibl. 2004, 5393.) Rev. by Aida Patient in SixCJ (34:4) 2003, 1222–3.

5165. MARSHALL, CYNTHIA.   The shattering of the self: violence, subjectivity, and early modern texts. (Bibl. 2004, 5395.) Rev. by James Hirsh in CompDr (38:2/3) 2004, 321–4; by Jean-Louis Claret in EREA (2:1) 2004; by Christopher Baker in SixCJ (36:2) 2005, 582–3; by Patricia A. Cahill in MP (103:1) 2005, 109–13.

5166. MAYER, JEAN-CHRISTOPHE (ed.).   The struggle for the succession in late Elizabethan England: politics, polemics and cultural representations. Montpellier: Univ. Paul-Valéry Montpellier III, 2004. pp. xviii, 432. (Astraea, 11.) Rev. by Norman Jones in RQ (58:3) 2005, 1018–20.

5167. MICHIE, ALLEN; BUCKLEY, ERIC (eds).   Style: essays on Renaissance and Restoration language and culture in memory of Harriett Hawkins. Newark: Delaware UP; London: Assoc. UPs, 2005. pp. 296.

5168. MIKESELL, MARGARET; SEEFF, ADELE (eds).   Culture and change: attending to early modern women. (Bibl. 2004, 5396.) Rev. by Carolyn D. Williams in MLR (100:3) 2005, 749–50.

5169. MONTA, SUSANNAH BRIETZ. Martyrdom and literature in early modern England. Cambridge; New York: CUP, 2005. pp. viii, 245. Rev. by Alison Shell in TLS, 15 July 2005, 25; by Lissa Beauchamp in SCN (63:3/4) 2005, 158–61.

5170. MOULTON, IAN FREDERICK. Studies in early modern sexuality. HLQ (67:3) 2004, 481–7 (review-article).

5171. MÜLLER, MARION URSULA. 'These savage beasts become domestick': the discourse of the passions in early modern England with special reference to non-fictional texts. Trier: WVT, 2004. pp. xx, 234. Rev. by Christian Schmitt-Kilb in JSBC (12:1) 2005, 82–4.

5172. MULRYNE, J. R.; GOLDRING, ELIZABETH (eds). Court festivals of the European Renaissance: art, politics and performance. Aldershot; Burlington, VT: Ashgate, 2002. pp. xxii, 401. Rev. by Mara Wade in RQ (58:1) 2005, 310–11.

5173. MUNRO, IAN. The figure of the crowd in early modern London: the city and its double. Basingstoke; New York: Palgrave Macmillan, 2005. pp. 255. (Early modern cultural studies.)

5174. NORTH, MARCY L. The anonymous Renaissance: cultures of discretion in Tudor–Stuart England. (Bibl. 2004, 5399.) Rev. by Robert J. Griffin in PBSA (99:2) 2005, 337–9; by Karen Nelson in SixCJ (36:1) 2005, 298–300; by Evelyn B. Tribble in SStud (33) 2005, 294–8.

5175. OSTOVICH, HELEN; SAUER, ELIZABETH (eds); SMITH, MELISSA (asst ed.). Reading early modern women: an anthology of texts in manuscript and print, 1550–1700. (Bibl. 2004, 5400.) Rev. by Erica Longfellow in EJES (9:3) 2005, 325–7; by Karen L. Edwards in CamQ (34:2) 2005, 192–5.

5176. PARR, ANTHONY. Time and the satyr. See **112.**

5177. PASTORE PASSARO, MARIA C. Representation of women in Classical, medieval and Renaissance texts. See **4222.**

5178. PELTONEN, MARKKU. 'Civilized with death': civility, duelling and honour in Elizabethan England. In (pp. 51–67) **5187.**

5179. PENDERGAST, JOHN. Religion, allegory, and literacy in early modern England, 1560–1640: the control of the word. Aldershot; Burlington, VT: Ashgate, 2005. pp. 208.

5180. PERRY, NANDRA. Imitatio and identity: Thomas Rogers, Philip Sidney, and the Protestant self. See **5628.**

5181. PHILLIPPY, PATRICIA. Women, death, and literature in post-Reformation England. (Bibl. 2004, 5405.) Rev. by Raymond B. Waddington in SixCJ (35:4) 2004, 1155–7; by Susanne Woods in CLIO (34:3) 2005, 369–76; by Ann Lecercle in EA (58:1) 2005, 108–9.

5182. PINCOMBE, MIKE (ed.). Travels and translations in the sixteenth century: selected papers from the Second International Conference of the Tudor Symposium (2000). (Bibl. 2004, 5406.) Rev. by Michael G. Brennan in NQ (52:3) 2005, 397–8; by Jonathan Burton in RQ (58:1) 2005, 322–4.

5183. QUILLIGAN, MAUREEN. Incest and agency in Elizabeth's England. Philadelphia: Pennsylvania UP, 2005. pp. 281. Rev. by Elizabeth Scott-Baumann in TLS, 16 Sept. 2005, 31.

5184. RAMAN, SHANKAR. Framing 'India': the colonial imaginary in early modern culture. (Bibl. 2004, 5407.) Rev. by Sanjay Subrahmanyam in SixCJ (34:4) 2003, 1232-3.

5185. RAY, SID. Holy estates: marriage and monarchy in Shakespeare and his contemporaries. *See* **6061**.

5186. RICHARDS, JENNIFER. Rhetoric and courtliness in early modern literature. (Bibl. 2004, 5409.) Rev. by Thomas G. Olsen in SixCJ (35:4) 2004, 1149-50; by Richard Dutton in Rhetorica (22:4) 2004, 404-7.

5187. —— (ed.). Early modern civil discourses. Basingstoke; New York: Palgrave Macmillan, 2003. pp. x, 206. (Early modern literature in history.) Rev. by Ben Lowe in LitH (14:1) 2005, 85-6; by Michael G. Brennan in NQ (52:3) 2005, 410-12.

5188. ROMERO ALLUÉ, MILENA (ed.). Qui è l'inferno e quivi il paradiso: giardini, paradisi e paradossi nella letteratura inglese del Seicento. Udine: Forum, 2005. pp. 312. (Giano.)

5189. ROSS, CHARLES (ed.). Elizabethan literature and the law of fraudulent conveyance: Sidney, Spenser, and Shakespeare. (Bibl. 2004, 6272.) Rev. by Catherine M. S. Alexander in MLR (100:2) 2005, 482-4; by Karen J. Cunningham in CLIO (34:3) 2005, 347-52; by Dana E. Aspinall in SixCJ (36:2) 2005, 468-9; by B. J. Sokol and Mary Sokol in NQ (52:3) 2005, 403-4.

5190. SALOMON, DAVID A. *Corpus mysticum*: text as body/body as text. *In* (pp. 141-55) **4411**.

5191. SANFORD, RHONDA LEMKE. Maps and memory in early modern England: a sense of place. (Bibl. 2004, 5412.) Rev. by Hardin Aasand in SixCJ (34:3) 2003, 891-3.

5192. SCHABERT, INA; BOENKE, MICHAELA (eds). Imaginationen des Anderen im 16. und 17. Jahrhundert. (Bibl. 2004, 5413.) Rev. by Maria Snyder in SixCJ (36:2) 2005, 573-4.

5193. SCHOFIELD, SCOTT. According to 'the common receiued opinion': Munday's Brute in *The Triumphs of Re-United Britannia* (1605). *In* (pp. 253-68) **4479**.

5194. SCOTT-WARREN, JASON. Early modern English literature. Oxford; Malden, MA: Polity Press in assn with Blackwell, 2005. pp. vi, 325. (Cultural history of literature.)

5195. SHARPE, KEVIN; ZWICKER, STEVEN N. (eds). Reading, society and politics in early modern England. (Bibl. 2004, 5418.) Rev. by Peter Clark in Albion (36:3) 2004, 500-2; by J. Christopher Warner in CLIO (34:3) 2005, 364-9; by Jeannine E. Olson in SixCJ (36:2) 2005, 529-30.

5196. SHEEN, ERICA; HUTSON, LORNA (eds). Literature, politics and law in Renaissance England. Basingstoke; New York: Palgrave Macmillan, 2005. pp. viii, 242. (Language, discourse, society.)

5197. SHEPARD, ALAN; POWELL, STEPHEN D. (eds). Fantasies of Troy: Classical tales and the social imaginary in medieval and early modern Europe. *See* **4479**.

5198. SHRANK, CATHY. Civil tongues: language, law and Reformation. *In* (pp. 19–34) **5187.**

5199. —— Writing the nation in Reformation England, 1530–1580. Oxford; New York: OUP, 2004. pp. vi, 291. Rev. by Bart van Es in TLS, 1 Apr. 2005, 33; by Christine Coch in RQ (58:3) 2005, 1022–3.

5200. SIMPSON, JAMES. Not the last word. *See* **4480.**

5201. SNOOK, EDITH. Women, reading, and the cultural politics of early modern England. Aldershot; Burlington, VT: Ashgate, 2005. pp. viii, 188. (Women and gender in the early modern world.)

5202. SPILLER, ELIZABETH. Science, reading, and Renaissance literature: the art of making knowledge, 1580–1670. (Bibl. 2004, 5900.) Rev. by Andrew Hadfield in NQ (52:3) 2005, 412–14; by Nicole Howard in Isis (96:2) 2005, 273–5; by Karen L. Edwards in RQ (58:3) 2005, 1004–6; by Mary Floyd-Wilson in SpenR (36:3) 2005, 3–5.

5203. STROHM, PAUL. *Politique*: languages of statecraft between Chaucer and Shakespeare. *See* **4489.**

5204. SULLIVAN, CERI. The rhetoric of credit: merchants in early modern writing. (Bibl. 2004, 5423.) Rev. by Ken Jackson in SixCJ (34:3) 2003, 860–1.

5205. SUZUKI, MIHOKO. Subordinate subjects: gender, the political nation, and literary form in England, 1588–1688. (Bibl. 2004, 5424.) Rev. by Richardine Woodall in SixCJ (36:1) 2005, 166–8; by Carole Levin in SStud (33) 2005, 313–14; by Constance Jordan in MP (103:1) 2005, 105–8; by Sara Jayne Steen in SpenR (36:2) 2005, 3–5.

5206. TOTARO, REBECCA. Suffering in paradise: the bubonic plague in English literature from More to Milton. Pittsburgh, PA: Duquesne UP, 2005. pp. xiv, 242. (Medieval & Renaissance literary studies.)

5207. TRAUB, VALERIE. The renaissance of lesbianism in early modern England. (Bibl. 2004, 5426.) Rev. by Anna Viele in SixCJ (34:4) 2003, 1167–8; by Kate Chedgzoy in GLQ (11:3) 2005, 457–67.

5208. TREVOR, DOUGLAS. The poetics of melancholy in early modern England. Cambridge; New York: CUP, 2004. pp. xii, 252. (Cambridge studies in Renaissance literature and culture, 48.) Rev. by Katharine Craik in TLS, 6 May 2005, 28; by Thomas P. Anderson in SCN (63:3/4) 2005, 171–5; by Richard C. McCoy in RQ (58:4) 2005, 1443–4; by William E. Engel in SpenR (36:3) 2005, 5–7.

5209. TRILL, SUZANNE. Early modern women's writing in the Edinburgh Archives, *c.*1550–1740: a preliminary checklist. *In* (pp. 201–25) **3754.**

5210. TURNER, JAMES GRANTHAM. Schooling sex: libertine literature and erotic education in Italy, France, and England, 1534–1685. (Bibl. 2004, 5427.) Rev. by Daniel T. Lochman in SixCJ (36:1) 2005, 263–5.

5211. WALKER, GREG. Writing under tyranny: English literature and the Henrician Reformation. Oxford; New York: OUP, 2005. pp. x, 556.

5212. WALLACE, DAVID. Oxford English literary history. *See* **4491.**

5213. WATSON, ROBERT N.; DICKEY, STEPHEN. Wherefore art thou Tereu? Juliet and the legacy of rape. *See* **6704.**

5214. WILLIAMS, DEANNE. The French fetish from Chaucer to Shakespeare. See 4493.

5215. WOOLF, DANIEL R. From hystories to the historical: five transitions in thinking about the past, 1500–1700. See 5633.

5216. WOOLFSON, JONATHAN (ed.). Reassessing Tudor Humanism. (Bibl. 2004, 5431.) Rev. by Ben Lowe in SixCJ (34:4) 2003, 1219–20; by Fred Schurink in NQ (52:3) 2005, 396–7.

DRAMA AND THE THEATRE

5217. ARCHER, IAN W. Discourses of history in Elizabethan and early Stuart London. See 6706.

5218. BARBOUR, RICHMOND. Before Orientalism: London's theatre of the East 1576–1626. (Bibl. 2004, 5434.) Rev. by Lucy Munro in TLS, 28 Jan. 2005, 11; by Brian Singleton in TRI (30:2) 2005, 192–3.

5219. BERGERON, DAVID M. Pageants, masques, and history. In (pp. 41–56) 5964.

5220. BLAYNEY, PETER W. M. The alleged popularity of playbooks. See 770.

5221. BOYD, BRIAN (ed.). Words that count: essays on early modern authorship in honor of MacDonald P. Jackson. (Bibl. 2004, 5436.) Rev. by Ann Baynes Coiro in RQ (58:3) 2005, 1035–7; by Hugh Craig in ShQ (56:4) 2005, 496–8.

5222. BRAUNMULLER, A. R.; HATTAWAY, MICHAEL (eds). The Cambridge companion to English Renaissance drama. (Bibl. 2004, 5437.) Rev. by Arnold W. Preussner in SixCJ (36:1) 2005, 200; by Peggy J. Huey in MSAN (25:1) 2005, 7–10.

5223. BROWN, PAMELA ALLEN. Better a shrew than a sheep: women, drama, and the culture of jest in early modern England. (Bibl. 2004, 5438.) Rev. by Margaret Dupuis in CompDr (38:1) 2004, 120–3; by Tom Rutter in MLR (100:3) 2005, 778–9; by Indira Ghose in MedRen (18) 2005, 223–7.

5224. —— PAROLIN, PETER. Introduction. In (pp. 1–21) 5225.

5225. —— —— (eds). Women players in England, 1500–1660: beyond the all-male stage. Aldershot; Burlington, VT: Ashgate, 2005. pp. xvii, 329. (Studies in performance and early modern drama.)

5226. BURKS, DEBORAH G. Horrid spectacle: violation in the theater of early modern England. (Bibl. 2004, 5440.) Rev. by Christopher J. Wheatley in SCN (63:1/2) 2005, 24–7; by Paul Dean in RES (56:226) 2005, 664–5; by John Rooks in SRASP (28) 2005, 114–15; by Alberto Cacicedo in RQ (58:1) 2005, 333–4.

5227. BURTON, JONATHAN. Traffic and turning: Islam and English drama, 1579–1624. Newark: Delaware UP; London: Assoc. UPs, 2005. pp. 319.

5228. BUTLER, MICHELLE M. Baleus Prolocutor and the establishment of the prologue in sixteenth-century drama. In (pp. 94–109) 5268.

5229. BUTTERWORTH, PHILIP. Magic on the early English stage. See 4496.

5230. CAÑADAS, IVAN. The public theaters of Golden Age Madrid and Tudor-Stuart London: class, gender, and festive community. Aldershot; Burlington, VT: Ashgate, 2005. pp. viii, 233. (Studies in performance and early modern drama.)

5231. CAPUTO, NICOLETTA. A 'deformed' Christianity: ethical transubstantiation in English Reformation plays. *In* (pp. 63–74) 3724.

5232. CARNEGIE, DAVID. Early modern plays and performance. *See* 6145.

5233. CAVANAGH, DERMOT. Language and politics in the sixteenth-century history play. (Bibl. 2004, 5445.) Rev. by Michael Hicks in LitH (14:2) 2005, 83.

5234. CAVE, RICHARD ALLEN. Italian perspectives on late Tudor and early Stuart theatre. ETh (8:2) 2005, 109–31.

5235. CERASANO, S. P. Edward Alleyn, the new model actor, and the rise of the celebrity in the 1590s. MedRen (18) 2005, 47–58.

5236. —— The geography of Henslowe's diary. *See* 5484.

5237. DEBAX, JEAN-PAUL. Techniques de persuasion dans les interludes protestants anglais du XVIe siècle. *See* 5664.

5238. DILLON, JANETTE. Chariots and cloud machines: gods and goddesses on early English stages. *In* (pp. 111–29) 5268.

5239. DOLLIMORE, JONATHAN. Radical tragedy: religion, ideology, and power in the drama of Shakespeare and his contemporaries. *See* 5908.

5240. DUTTON, RICHARD. Recent studies in Tudor and Stuart drama. SELit (45:2) 2005, 481–523.

5241. —— FINDLAY, ALISON; WILSON, RICHARD (eds). Region, religion, and patronage: Lancastrian Shakespeare. *See* 5914.

5242. EMMERSON, RICHARD K. Dramatic history: on the diachronic and synchronic in the study of early English drama. *See* 4501.

5243. FARMER, ALAN B.; LESSER, ZACHARY. The popularity of playbooks revisited. *See* 824.

5244. —— —— Structures of popularity in the early modern book trade. *See* 825.

5245. FORKER, CHARLES R. Royal carnality and illicit desire in the English history plays of the 1590s. MedRen (17) 2005, 99–131.

5246. FORSE, JAMES H. Performance equals preference: how acting companies performing at court reflected Elizabeth's court structure. SRASP (28) 2005, 97–109.

5247. GEORGE, DAVID. The playhouse at Prescot and the 1592–94 Plague. *In* (pp. 227–42) 5914.

5248. GIESKES, EDWARD. 'Honesty and vulgar praise': the Poets' War and the literary field. MedRen (18) 2005, 75–103.

5249. GREENFIELD, PETER. Regional performance in Shakespeare's time. *In* (pp. 243–51) 5914.

5250. GROVES, BEATRICE. Memory, composition, and the relationship of *King John* to *The Troublesome Raigne of King John*. *See* 6451.

5251. GURR, ANDREW. Bears and players: Philip Henslowe's double acts. *See* 5486.

5252. —— Henry Carey's peculiar letter. *See* 6169.

5253. HABERMANN, INA. Staging slander and gender in early modern England. (Bibl. 2004, 5456.) Rev. by Rosemary Kegl in SStud (33) 2005, 259–64; by Ingrid Hotz-Davies in SJ (141) 2005, 261–3.

5254. HAPPÉ, PETER. 'Erazed in the booke': the mystery cycles and reform. *In* (pp. 15–33) **5268**.

5255. HARRIS, JONATHAN GIL; KORDA, NATASHA (eds). Staged properties in early modern English drama. (Bibl. 2004, 5459.) Rev. by David Carnegie in HLQ (67:3) 2004, 437–56; by Peter C. Herman in CompDr (38:4) 2004/05, 451–5; by Patrick Neilson in TJ (57:1) 2005, 145–7; by David Bevington in MP (103:1) 2005, 101–5; by Joachim Frenk in SJ (141) 2005, 263–5.

5256. HEALY, THOMAS. Drama, Ireland and the question of civility. *In* (pp. 131–45) **5187**.

5257. HIRSCHFELD, HEATHER ANNE. Joint enterprises: collaborative drama and the institutionalization of the English Renaissance theater. (Bibl. 2004, 5464.) Rev. by Brian Walsh in RQ (58:1) 2005, 345–7.

5258. HISCOCK, ANDREW. 'What's Hecuba to him ...': Trojan heroes and rhetorical selves in Shakespeare's *Hamlet*. *In* (pp. 161–75) **4479**.

5259. HOENSELAARS, A. J. Shakespeare and the early modern history play. *In* (pp. 25–40) **5964**.

5260. HOLLAND, PETER; ORGEL, STEPHEN (eds). From script to stage in early modern England. Basingstoke; New York: Palgrave Macmillan, 2004. pp. xiii, 251. Rev. by Leslie Thomson in ShQ (56:3) 2005, 368–70.

5261. HUEBERT, RONALD. The performance of pleasure in English Renaissance drama. (Bibl. 2004, 5466.) Rev. by Kevin Curran in RenSt (18:4) 2004, 626–8.

5262. HUTSON, LORNA. Rethinking the 'spectacle of the scaffold': juridical epistemologies and English revenge tragedy. *See* **6781**.

5263. HYLAND, PETER. *Look about You*, anonymity, and the value of theatricality. RORD (44) 2005, 65–74.

5264. ICHIKAWA, MARIKO. '*Maluolio within*': acting on the threshold between onstage and offstage spaces. *See* **6803**.

5265. JACKSON, KEN. Separate theaters: Bethlem ('Bedlam') Hospital and the Shakespearean stage. *See* **5985**.

5266. KATHMAN, DAVID. Citizens, innholders, and playhouse builders, 1543–1622. RORD (44) 2005, 38–64.

5267. —— How old were Shakespeare's boy actors? ShS (58) 2005, 220–46.

5268. KERMODE, LLOYD EDWARD; SCOTT-WARREN, JASON; VAN ELK, MARTINE (eds). Tudor drama before Shakespeare, 1485–1590: new directions for research, criticism, and pedagogy. Basingstoke; New York: Palgrave Macmillan, 2004. pp. vi, 271.

5269. KERWIN, WILLIAM. Beyond the body: the boundaries of medicine and early English Renaissance drama. Amherst: Massachusetts UP, 2005. pp. viii, 290. (Massachusetts studies in early modern culture.)

5270. KEWES, PAULINA. Contemporary Europe in Elizabethan and early Stuart drama. *In* (pp. 150–92) **5954**.

5271. LESSER, ZACHARY. Renaissance drama and the politics of publication: readings in the English book trade. Cambridge; New York: CUP, 2004. pp. xii, 244. Rev. by Michael G. Brennan in RES (56:225) 2005, 452–3; by Jason Scott-Warren in TLS, 18 Nov. 2005, 32.

5272. LEVIN, RICHARD. Frailty, thy name is wanton widow. SNL (55:1) 2005, 5–6.

5273. LOPEZ, JEREMY. Theatrical convention and audience response in early modern drama. (Bibl. 2004, 5478.) Rev. by Alan Dessen in MedRen (18) 2005, 252–7.

5274. LOW, JENNIFER. Manhood and the duel: masculinity in early modern drama and culture. (Bibl. 2004, 5480.) Rev. by Zachary A. Dorsey in TJ (57:1) 2005, 147–8; by Stephen Cohen in ShQ (56:1) 2005, 108–10; by Goran V. Stanivukovic in CLIO (34:4) 2005, 458–65; by Helen Wilcox in MedRen (18) 2005, 227–32.

5275. MACLEAN, SALLY-BETH. A family tradition: dramatic patronage by the Earls of Derby. In (pp. 205–26) 5914.

5276. MCRAE, ANDREW. Renaissance drama. London; New York: Arnold, 2003. pp. 180. (Contexts.) Rev. by Clare McManus in RenSt (18:3) 2004, 498–501; by Brett D. Hirsch in Parergon (22:2) 2005, 237–9.

5277. MADELAINE, RICHARD. 'The dark and vicious place': the location of sexual transgression and its punishment on the early modern English stage. Parergon (22:1) 2005, 159–83.

5278. MAGNUSSON, LYNNE. Scoff power in Love's Labour's Lost and the Inns of Court: language in context. See 6528.

5279. MARSALEK, KAREN SAWYER. 'Doctrine evangelicall' and Erasmus's Paraphrases in The Resurrection of Our Lord. In (pp. 35–66) 5268.

5280. MARTIN, RANDALL. Catilines and Machiavels: reading Catholic resistance in 3 Henry VI. In (pp. 105–15) 5915.

5281. MENON, MADHAVI. Wanton words: rhetoric and sexuality in English Renaissance drama. (Bibl. 2004, 5484.) Rev. by Marlene Clark in RQ (58:1) 2005, 332–3; by Bruce Danner in ShQ (56:4) 2005, 493–6.

5282. MILLING, JANE; THOMSON, PETER (eds). The Cambridge history of British theatre: vol. 1, Origins to 1660. See 4510.

5283. NARDO, DON. The Globe Theater. See 6204.

5284. OWENS, MARGARET E. Stages of dismemberment: the fragmented body in medieval and early modern drama. See 4512.

5285. PALMER, BARBARA D. Early modern mobility: players, payments, and patrons. ShQ (56:3) 2005, 259–305.

5286. PANEK, JENNIFER. Widows and suitors in early modern English comedy. (Bibl. 2004, 5488.) Rev. by Ros King in TLS, 28 Jan. 2005, 33; by Linda Anderson in RQ (58:4) 2005, 1427–8.

5287. POLITO, MARY. Governmental arts in early Tudor England. Aldershot; Burlington, VT: Ashgate, 2005. pp. 153. (Studies in performance and early modern drama.)

5288. POLLARD, TANYA. Drugs and theater in early modern England. Oxford; New York: OUP, 2005. pp. vii, 211. Rev. by Jerome de Groot in TLS, 21 Oct. 2005, 30; by Tiffany Stern in RES (56:227) 2005, 788–90.

5289. POTTER, URSULA. Performing arts in the Tudor classroom. In (pp. 143–65) 5268.

5290. PUGLIATTI, PAOLA. Beggary and the theatre in early modern England. (Bibl. 2004, 5491.) Rev. by Maurice Hunt in Albion (36:3) 2004, 510–11; by Charles Whitney in CLIO (34:3) 2005, 360–4; by Lars Engle in SStud (33) 2005, 305–8.

5291. ROMOTSKY, SALLY ROBERTSON. Henry of Monmouth and the gown-of-needles. *See* **6428.**

5292. SALKELD, DUNCAN. New allusions to London 'shewes' and playhouses, 1575–1605. ETh (8:2) 2005, 101–8.

5293. SLIGHTS, WILLIAM W. E. My heart upon my sleeve: early modern interiority, anatomy, and villainy. DalR (85:2) 2005, 163–79.

5294. SOMERSET, ALAN. Some new thoughts on an old question: 'professional' touring theater outside London before 1590. *In* (pp. 131–40) **5268.**

5295. STOCK, ANGELA. Stow's *Survey* and the London playwrights. *In* (pp. 89–98) **5746.**

5296. STOKES, JAMES. Women and performance: evidences of universal cultural suffrage in medieval and early modern Lincolnshire. *In* (pp. 25–43) **5225.**

5297. TASSI, MARGUERITE A. The scandal of images: iconoclasm, eroticism, and painting in early modern English drama. Selinsgrove, PA: Susquehanna UP; London: Assoc. UPs, 2005. pp. 259. (Apple–Zimmerman series in early modern culture.) Rev. by Ernest B. Gilman in RQ (58:4) 2005, 1431–3.

5298. TRIBBLE, EVELYN. Distributing cognition in the Globe. ShQ (56:2) 2005, 135–55.

5299. BEN-TSUR, DALIA. Early ramifications of theatrical iconoclasm: the conversion of Catholic biblical plays into Protestant drama. *See* **5772.**

5300. VANHOUTTE, JACQUELINE. Strange communion: motherland and masculinity in Tudor plays, pamphlets, and politics. (Bibl. 2004, 5505.) Rev. by Mike Pincombe in RenSt (18:4) 2004, 616–18.

5301. VITKUS, DANIEL. Turning Turk: English theater and the multicultural Mediterranean, 1570–1630. (Bibl. 2004, 5506.) Rev. by Lucy Munro in TLS, 28 Jan. 2005, 11; by Elizabeth Klett in TJ (57:3) 2005, 541–2.

5302. WALEN, DENISE A. Constructions of female homoeroticism in early modern drama. Basingstoke; New York: Palgrave Macmillan, 2005. pp. x, 230. (Early modern cultural studies.)

5303. WALL, WENDY. Staging domesticity: household work and English identity in early modern drama. (Bibl. 2004, 5507.) Rev. by Julia Matthews in SixCJ (34:3) 2003, 839–41; by Dana E. Aspinall in SNL (55:3) 2005, 76.

5304. WATKINS, JOHN. Bedevilling the histories of medieval and early modern drama. *See* **4521.**

5305. WEIMANN, ROBERT; BRUSTER, DOUGLAS. Prologues to Shakespeare's theatre: performance and liminality in early modern drama. London; New York: Routledge, 2004. pp. xi, 189. Rev. by Michael Caines in TLS, 7 Jan. 2005, 27.

5306. WESTFALL, SUZANNE. 'The useless dearness of the diamond': patronage theatre and household. *In* (pp. 32–49) **5914.**

5307. WILLIAMS, GWENO; FINDLAY, ALISON; HODGSON-WRIGHT, STEPHANIE. Payments, permits and punishments: women performers and the politics of place. *In* (pp. 45–67) **5225.**

5308. WINKELMAN, MICHAEL.   Marriage relationships in Tudor political drama. Aldershot; Burlington, VT: Ashgate, 2004. pp. xii, 234. (Studies in performance and early modern drama.)

FICTION

5309. McMORRAN, WILL.   The inn and the traveller: digressive topographies in the early modern European novel. (Bibl. 2004, 5515.) Rev. by Joseph F. Bartolomeo in ECF (17:2) 2005, 288–90.

5310. RELIHAN, CONSTANCE CAROLINE.   Cosmographical glasses: geographic discourse, gender, and Elizabethan fiction. Kent, OH; London: Kent State UP, 2004. pp. xvii, 148. Rev. by M. G. Aune in RQ (58:4) 2005, 1435–6.

POETRY

5311. BLEVINS, JACOB.   Catullan consciousness and the early modern lyric in England: from Wyatt to Donne. (Bibl. 2004, 5520.) Rev. by Roger Kuin in RQ (58:4) 2005, 1438–9.

5312. CERASANO, S. P.   Edward Alleyn, the new model actor, and the rise of the celebrity in the 1590s. See **5235.**

5313. DENBO, MICHAEL ROY.   Editing a Renaissance commonplace book: the Holgate Miscellany. In (pp. 65–73) **587.**

5314. DUFFY, EAMON.   Bare ruined choirs: remembering Catholicism in Shakespeare's England. In (pp. 40–57) **5915.**

5315. ELLIS, JIM.   Sexuality and citizenship: metamorphosis in Elizabethan erotic verse. (Bibl. 2004, 5527.) Rev. by Ian Frederick Moulton in HLQ (67:3) 2004, 481–7; by Andrew Smyth in SixCJ (35:4) 2004, 1248–9.

5316. GOY-BLANQUET, DOMINIQUE.   Elizabethan historiography and Shakespeare's sources. In (pp. 57–70) **5964.**

5317. HAMLIN, HANNIBAL.   Psalm culture and early modern English literature. (Bibl. 2004, 5529.) Rev. by Timothy R. Vande Brake in CSR (34:4) 2005, 558–9; by Michael G. Brennan in NQ (52:1) 2005, 115–17; by Nancy Rosenfeld in RQ (58:1) 2005, 327–9.

5318. HAMMONS, PAMELA S.   The gendered imagination of property in sixteenth- and seventeenth-century English women's verse. CLIO (34:4) 2005, 395–418.

5319. LAVOIE, CHANTEL.   Poems by Eminent Ladies: the encyclopedic anthology of 1755. 1650–1850 (9) 2003, 207–36.

5320. LUCAS, SCOTT.   Coping with providentialism: trauma, identity, and the failure of the English Reformation. In (pp. 255–73) **5103.**

5321. MAY, STEVEN W.; RINGLER, WILLIAM A., JR.   Elizabethan poetry: a bibliography and first-line index of English verse, 1559–1603. London: Thoemmes Press; New York: Continuum, 2004. 3 vols. pp. xx, 2337. Rev. by Paul J. Voss in BJJ (12) 2005, 259–66.

5322. NEWLYN, EVELYN S.   A methodology for reading against the culture: anonymous, women poets, and the Maitland Quarto manuscript (c.1586). In (pp. 89–103) **3754.**

5323. NORBROOK, DAVID.   Poetry and politics in the English Renaissance.
(Bibl. 2004, 5539.) Rev. by Abdulla Al-Dabbagh in SixCJ (35:4) 2004, 1203–4.

5324. SMITH, ROSALIND.   Sonnets and the English woman writer, 1560–1621: the
politics of absence. Basingstoke; New York: Palgrave Macmillan, 2005. pp. xii,
169. (Early modern literature in history.) Rev. by Elizabeth Scott-Baumann in
TLS, 9 Dec. 2005, 28.

5325. VALLARO, CRISTINA.   La simbologia lunare nei canzonieri elisabettiani.
Milan: ISU Univ. Cattolica, 2004. pp. 217.

5326. WARLEY, CHRISTOPHER.   Sonnet sequences and social distinction
in Renaissance England. Cambridge; New York: CUP, 2005. pp. xi, 240.
(Cambridge studies in Renaissance literature and culture, 49.)

5327. WORDEN, BLAIR.   Historians and poets. See 5657.

PROSE

5328. ALMOND, PHILIP C.   The Witches of Warboys: a bibliographical note.
NQ (52:2) 2005, 192–3.

5329. —— (comp.).   Demonic possession and exorcism in early modern England:
contemporary texts and their cultural contexts. Cambridge; New York: CUP,
2004. pp. x, 405. Rev. by Hilaire Kallendorf in RQ (58:2) 2005, 669–72.

5330. ARCHER, IAN W.   John Stow, citizen and historian. In (pp. 13–26) 5746.

5331. BEER, ANNA.   Ralegh's history of her world. WWr (12:1) 2005, 29–42.
(Lady Ralegh.)

5332. BJORKLUND, NANCY BASLER.   'A godly wyfe is an helper': Matthew Parker
and the defense of clerical marriage. SixCJ (34:2) 2003, 347–65.

5333. CRESSY, DAVID.   Book burning in Tudor and Stuart England. See 803.

5334. DAYBELL, JAMES.   Recent studies in sixteenth-century letters. ELR (35:2)
2005, 331–62.

5335. DUFFY, EAMON.   Bare ruined choirs: remembering Catholicism in
Shakespeare's England. In (pp. 40–57) 5915.

5336. EULER, CARRIE.   Heinrich Bullinger, marriage, and the English
Reformation: The Christen State of Matrimonye in England, 1540–53. See 5416.

5337. EVETT, DAVID.   Luther, Cranmer, service and Shakespeare. In (pp.
87–109) 6872.

5338. GILLESPIE, ALEXANDRA.   Stow's 'owlde' manuscripts of London
chronicles. In (pp. 57–67) 5746.

5339. HEAL, FELICITY.   Appropriating history: Catholic and Protestant
polemics and the national past. See 5435.

5340. HUDSON, NICHOLAS.   The alphabet of nature: writing as trope in early
modern scientific and philosophical discourse. 1650–1850 (9) 2003, 167–87.

5341. MUSVIK, VICTORIA.   'And the King of Barbary's envoy had to stand in the
yard': the perception of Elizabethan court festivals in Russia at the beginning
of the seventeenth century. In (pp. 225–40) 5172.

5342. NARVESON, KATE.   Publishing the sole-talk of the soule: genre in early
Stuart piety. In (pp. 110–26) 6872.

5343. NEVALA, MINNA.   Accessing politeness axes: forms of address and terms of reference in early English correspondence. JPrag (36:12) 2004, 2125–60.

5344. OAKLEY-BROWN, LIZ.   Framing Robin Hood: temporality and textuality in Anthony Munday's Huntington plays. *In* (pp. 113–28) **3576.**

5345. RANDALL, DAVID.   Recent studies in print culture: news, propaganda, and ephemera. HLQ (67:3) 2004, 457–72 (review-article).

5346. RAUMOLIN-BRUNBERG, HELENA.   Language change in adulthood: historical letters as evidence. *See* **2878.**

5347. RAYMOND, JOAD.   Pamphlets and pamphleteering in early modern Britain. (Bibl. 2004, 5570.) Rev. by Timothy Raylor in SCN (62:3/4) 2004, 290–4; by Felicity Heal in RES (55:219) 2004, 272–3; by Alexandra Halasz in RQ (57:3) 2004, 1131–2; by David Randall in HLQ (67:3) 2004, 457–72; by Katherine Romack in CLIO (34:3) 2005, 352–6; by Kristen Post Walton in SixCJ (36:2) 2005, 532–3.

5348. SCHNEIDER, GARY.   The culture of epistolarity: vernacular letters and letter writing in early modern England, 1500–1700. Newark: Delaware UP, 2005. pp. 388.

5349. SHRANK, CATHY.   'These fewe scribbled rules': representing scribal intimacy in early modern print. HLQ (67:2) 2004, 295–314.

5350. STEWART, ALAN; WOLFE, HEATHER (eds).   Letterwriting in Renaissance England. Washington, DC: Folger Shakespeare Library, 2004. pp. 214.

5351. WALSHAM, ALEXANDRA.   Unclasping the book? Post-Reformation English Catholicism and the vernacular Bible. JBS (42:2) 2003, 141–66.

5352. WARKENTIN, GERMAINE (ed.); PARSONS, JOHN CARMI (asst ed.).   *The Queen Majesty's Passage* & related documents. Toronto: Centre for Reformation and Renaissance Studies, 2004. pp. 158. (Tudor and Stuart texts.) Rev. by Lisa Hopkins in NQ (52:2) 2005, 247–8.

5353. WHITAKER, CURTIS.   Baptisms and burials: the presence of the Book of Common Prayer in Herbert's nature poetry. *See* **7486.**

5354. WOMERSLEY, DAVID.   Against the teleology of technique. *See* **5385.**

RELATED STUDIES

5355. BARRY, JOHN.   Richard Stanihurst's *De rebus in Hibernia gestis.* RenSt (18:1) 2004, 1–18.

5356. FEINGOLD, MORDECHAI.   A conjurer and a quack? The lives of John Dee and Simon Forman. HLQ (68:3) 2005, 545–59 (review-article).

5357. —— Giordano Bruno in England, revisited. HLQ (67:3) 2004, 329–46.

5358. HUNTER, JERRY.   Taliesin at the court of Henry VIII: aspects of the writings of Elis Gruffydd. THSC (10) 2004, 41–56.

5359. KAUFMAN, PETER IVER.   Thinking of the laity in late Tudor England. Notre Dame, IN: Notre Dame UP, 2004. pp. xi, 175. Rev. by Renee Bricker in RQ (58:3) 2005, 1015–17.

5360. KELLAR, CLARE.   Scotland, England, and the Reformation, 1534–61. Oxford: Clarendon Press; New York: OUP, 2003. pp. xi, 257. Rev. by Richard D. Culbertson in RQ (58:1) 2005, 324–6.

5361. MARKS, RICHARD; WILLIAMSON, PAUL (eds). Gothic: art for England 1400–1547. *See* **4752.**

5362. MOULTON, IAN FREDERICK (ed.). Reading and literacy in the Middle Ages and Renaissance. *See* **4754.**

5363. MURPHY, JAMES J. Latin rhetoric and education in the Middle Ages and Renaissance. *See* **4755.**

5364. SCHURINK, FRED. An Elizabethan grammar school exercise book. BLR (18:2) 2003, 174–96.

5365. SHEPARD, ALEXANDRA. Meanings of manhood in early modern England. Oxford; New York: OUP, 2003. pp. x, 292. (Oxford studies in social history.) Rev. by Ivan Cañadas in Parergon (22:1) 2005, 278–9; by Judith Haber in RQ (58:2) 2005, 723–5.

5366. SZÓNYI, GYÖRGY E. John Dee's occultism: magical exaltation through powerful signs. Albany: New York State UP, 2004. pp. xviii, 362. (SUNY series in Western esoteric traditions.) Rev. by Mordechai Feingold in HLQ (68:3) 2005, 545–59.

5367. WILLIAMS, GRUFFYDD ALED. The poetic debate of Edmwnd Prys and Wiliam Cynwal. RenSt (18:1) 2004, 33–54.

5368. WOOLF, DANIEL. The social circulation of the past: English historical culture 1500–1730. (Bibl. 2004, 5600.) Rev. by David Cressy in Albion (36:3) 2004, 515–17.

LITERARY THEORY

5369. ALEXANDER, GAVIN (ed.). Sidney's *The Defence of Poesy* and selected Renaissance literary criticism. London; New York: Penguin, 2004. pp. lxxxviii, 452. (Penguin classics.)

5370. COATALEN, GUILLAUME. 'Lô a timorous correction': unrecorded extracts from Spenser and Harington and negative criticism of *The Faerie Queene* in a folio from the Bodleian Library. *See* **5687.**

5371. PHILLIPS, ELAINE ANDERSON. Richardson reads the Renaissance: the use of Renaissance narrative theory in the novels and prefaces. *See* **8953.**

5372. WATSON, ELIZABETH SEE. George Puttenham as comedic artificer. *See* **5616.**

AUTHORS

Roger Ascham

5373. ALLEN, VALERIE. Playing soldiers: tournament and toxophily in late medieval England. *In* (pp. 35–52) **4419.**

5374. MEDINE, PETER E. (ed.). *Toxophilus* (1545). (Bibl. 2004, 5604.) Rev. by Matthew Woodcock in SixCJ (35:4) 2004, 1192–3.

Anne Askew

5375. BEILIN, ELAINE V. A woman for all seasons: the reinvention of Anne Askew. *In* (pp. 341–64) **5094.**

5376. GERTZ-ROBINSON, GENELLE. Stepping into the pulpit? Women's preaching in *The Book of Margery Kempe* and *The Examination of Anne Askew*. With a response by David Wallace. *In* (pp. 459–91) **4460**.

5377. HICKERSON, MEGAN L. Gospelling sisters 'goinge up and downe': John Foxe and disorderly women. *See* **5436**.

William Baldwin

5378. LUCAS, SCOTT. Coping with providentialism: trauma, identity, and the failure of the English Reformation. *In* (pp. 255–73) **5103**.

John Bale

5379. BUTLER, MICHELLE M. Baleus Prolocutor and the establishment of the prologue in sixteenth-century drama. *In* (pp. 94–109) **5268**.

5380. GERTZ-ROBINSON, GENELLE. Still martyred after all these years: generational suffering in Milton's *Areopagitica*. *See* **7677**.

5381. HICKERSON, MEGAN L. Gospelling sisters 'goinge up and downe': John Foxe and disorderly women. *See* **5436**.

5382. MACCOLL, ALAN. The construction of England as a Protestant 'British' nation in the sixteenth century. RenSt (18:4) 2004, 582–608.

5383. SCHWYZER, PHILIP. Literature, nationalism, and memory in early modern England and Wales. Cambridge; New York: CUP, 2004. pp. xi, 194. Rev. by Thomas Healy in TLS, 24 June 2005, 25.

5384. SHRANK, CATHY. Civil tongues: language, law and Reformation. *In* (pp. 19–34) **5187**.

5385. WOMERSLEY, DAVID. Against the teleology of technique. HLQ (68:1/2) 2005, 95–108.

Thomas Bastard (1565 or 6–1618)

5386. NICHOLLS, MARK. The authorship of *Thomas Bastard's Oxford Libel*. NQ (52:2) 2005, 186–9.

Richard Becon

5387. HADFIELD, ANDREW. Tacitus and the reform of Ireland in the 1590s. *In* (pp. 115–30) **5187**.

John Bourchier, Second Baron Berners (1467–1533)

5388. BORO, JOYCE. Lord Berners and his books: a new survey. HLQ (67:2) 2004, 236–49.

Elizabeth Bourne (*fl.*1570–1590)

5389. DAYBELL, JAMES. Elizabeth Bourne (*fl.*1570s–1580s): a new Elizabethan woman poet. NQ (52:2) 2005, 176–8.

George Buchanan (1506–1582)

5390. CARROLL, WILLIAM C. 'Two truths are told': afterlives and histories of Macbeths. *See* **6536**.

5391. FERRADOU, CARINE. Jean-Baptiste; ou, La remise en cause des autorités politiques et religieuses dans *Baptiste*, tragédie néo-latine de George Buchanan (1577). Anglophonia (17) 2005, 51–62.

5392. GREEN, ROGER P. H. Classical voices in Buchanan's hexameter Psalm paraphrases. RenSt (18:1) 2004, 55–89.

5393. HADFIELD, ANDREW. *Hamlet*'s country matters: the 'Scottish play' within the play. *In* (pp. 87–103) **6561**.

5394. WILLIAMSON, ARTHUR H. An empire to end empire: the dynamic of early modern British expansion. *See* **5655**.

William Byrd (1542 or 3–1623)

5395. COREN, PAMELA. Gurney's solace: Shakespeare, Jonson and Byrd. *See* **16844**.

5396. HARLEY, JOHN. 'My Ladye Nevell' revealed. MusL (86:1) 2005, 1–15.

5397. HULSE, LYNN. 'Musique which pleaseth myne eare': Robert Cecil's musical patronage. *In* (pp. 139–58) **5121**.

William Calverley (d.1572)

5398. BOFFEY, JULIA. Chaucer's *Fortune* in the 1530s: some sixteenth-century recycling. *In* (pp. 53–64) **4419**.

William Camden

5399. HARRIS, OLIVER. Stow and the contemporary antiquarian network. *In* (pp. 27–35) **5746**.

Edmund Campion

5400. FIELITZ, SONJA. Learned pate and golden fool: a Jesuit source for *Timon of Athens*. *In* (pp. 179–96) **5915**.

5401. KILROY, GERARD. Edmund Campion: memory and transcription. Aldershot; Burlington, VT: Ashgate, 2005. pp. x, 261.

5402. —— Requiem for a prince: rites of memory in *Hamlet*. *In* (pp. 143–60) **5915**.

5403. MARTIN, RANDALL. Catilines and Machiavels: reading Catholic resistance in *3 Henry VI*. *In* (pp. 105–15) **5915**.

5404. MAYER, JEAN-CHRISTOPHE. 'This Papist and his poet': Shakespeare's Lancastrian kings and Robert Parsons's *Conference about the Next Succession*. *In* (pp. 116–29) **5915**.

5405. MIOLA, ROBERT S. Jesuit drama in early modern England. *In* (pp. 71–86) **5915**.

William Cecil, Lord Burghley

5406. BOWDEN, CAROLINE. The library of Mildred Cooke Cecil, Lady Burghley. *See* **362**.

5407. CROFT, PAULINE. Mildred, Lady Burghley: the matriarch. *In* (pp. 283–300) **5121**.

5408. —— (ed.). Patronage, culture and power: the early Cecils. *See* **5121**.

5409. DUNN, KEVIN. Representing counsel: *Gorboduc* and the Elizabethan Privy Council. *See* **5595**.

5410. KNOWLES, JAMES. 'To raise a house of better frame': Jonson's Cecilian entertainments. *In* (pp. 181–95) **5121**.

5411. SMITH, A. G. R.   Lord Burghley and his household biographers: John Clapham and Sir Michael Hickes. *In* (pp. 248–63) **5121.**

5412. SUTTON, JAMES M.   The retiring patron: William Cecil and the cultivation of retirement, 1590–98. *In* (pp. 159–79) **5121.**

Henry Chettle

5413. KUMARAN, ARUL.   Patronage, print, and an early modern 'pamphlet moment'. *See* **5460.**

5414. MCCLUSKEY, PETER M.   Sir Edmond (*sic*) Tilney, *Sir Thomas More*, and the Netherlandic immigrant community. *See* **6709.**

Sir John Conway (d.1603)

5415. DAYBELL, JAMES.   Elizabeth Bourne (*fl.*1570s–1580s): a new Elizabethan woman poet. *See* **5389.**

Miles Coverdale (1488–1568)

5416. EULER, CARRIE.   Heinrich Bullinger, marriage, and the English Reformation: *The Christen State of Matrimonye* in England, 1540–53. SixCJ (34:2) 2003, 367–93.

Thomas Cranmer

5417. EVETT, DAVID.   Luther, Cranmer, service and Shakespeare. *In* (pp. 87–109) **6872.**

Sir John Davies (1569–1626)

5418. TARLINSKAJA, MARINA.   Who did NOT write *A Lover's Complaint*. *See* **6520.**

John Davies of Hereford (1565–1618)

5419. O'CALLAGHAN, MICHELLE.   'Now thou may'st speak freely': entering the public sphere in 1614. *In* (pp. 63–79) **6860.**

Thomas Deloney

5420. CRUPI, CHARLES W.   Reading nascent capitalism in Part II of Thomas Heywood's *If You Know Not Me, You Know Nobody*. *See* **7503.**

Richard Edwards (1523?–1566)

5421. JOHNSTON, MARK ALBERT.   Playing with the beard: courtly and commercial economies in Richard Edwards's *Damon and Pithias* and John Lyly's *Midas*. ELH (72:1) 2005, 79–103.

Elizabeth I, Queen of England (1533–1603)

5422. FLEMING, MORNA R.   An unequal correspondence: epistolary and poetic exchanges between Mary Queen of Scots and Elizabeth of England. *In* (pp. 104–19) **3754.**

5423. LEVIN, CAROLE; CARNEY, JO ELDRIDGE; BARRETT-GRAVES, DEBRA (eds). Elizabeth I: always her own free woman. (Bibl. 2004, 5384.) Rev. by Jeffery R. Hankins in SixCJ (36:2) 2005, 473–5; by Tom MacFaul in NQ (52:2) 2005, 248–9; by Betty S. Travitsky in RQ (58:2) 2005, 707–9.

5424. MARKLEY, ROBERT.   Riches, power, trade and religion: the Far East and the English imagination, 1600–1720. *See* **7714.**

5425. MAY, STEVEN W.   Queen Elizabeth's *Future Foes*: editing manuscripts with the first-line index of Elizabethan verse (a future friend). *In* (pp. 1–12) **587**.

5426. PRYOR, FELIX (comp.).   Elizabeth I: her life in letters. (Bibl. 2004, 5655.) Rev. by Mary Hill Cole in SixCJ (36:2) 2005, 622–3.

5427. ZIEGLER, GEORGIANNA (comp.).   Elizabeth I: then and now. *See* **489**.

George Ferrers (1500?–1579)

5428. LUCAS, SCOTT.   Coping with providentialism: trauma, identity, and the failure of the English Reformation. *In* (pp. 255–73) **5103**.

Giles Fletcher the Elder (1546–1611)

5429. COGLEY, RICHARD W.   'The most vile and barbarous nation of all the world': Giles Fletcher the Elder's *The Tartars; or, Ten Tribes* (*ca* 1610). RQ (58:3) 2005, 781–814.

Richard Fox (1447/8–1528)

5430. COLLETT, BARRY (ed.).   Female monastic life in early Tudor England: with an edition of Richard Fox's translation of the Benedictine rule for women, 1517. (Bibl. 2004, 5661.) Rev. by Anna Seregina in SixCJ (34:3) 2003, 800–1; by Guyonne Leduc in EA (58:2) 2005, 206–8.

John Foxe (1516–1587)

5431. BEILIN, ELAINE V.   A woman for all seasons: the reinvention of Anne Askew. *In* (pp. 341–64) **5094**.

5432. ESCOBEDO, ANDREW.   Nationalism and historical loss in Renaissance England: Foxe, Dee, Spenser, Milton. (Bibl. 2004, 5665.) Rev. by Marshall Grossman in CLIO (34:3) 2005, 342–7; by Lauren Silberman in RQ (58:1) 2005, 334–6; by Deborah E. Harkness in SpenR (36:2) 2005, 2–3.

5433. FERNANDES, ISABELLE.   Martyrs, pouvoir et pouvoirs du martyre dans *The Acts and Monuments* de John Foxe. Anglophonia (17) 2005, 63–73.

5434. GERTZ-ROBINSON, GENELLE.   Still martyred after all these years: generational suffering in Milton's *Areopagitica*. *See* **7677**.

5435. HEAL, FELICITY.   Appropriating history: Catholic and Protestant polemics and the national past. HLQ (68:1/2) 2005, 109–32.

5436. HICKERSON, MEGAN L.   Gospelling sisters 'goinge up and downe': John Foxe and disorderly women. SixCJ (35:4) 2004, 1035–51.

5437. HIGHLEY, CHRISTOPHER; KING, JOHN N. (eds).   John Foxe and his world. (Bibl. 2004, 5667.) Rev. by Susan Wabuda in SixCJ (34:2) 2003, 470–1; by Peter Marshall in CathHR (91:1) 2005, 167–8.

5438. KING, JOHN N.   Guides to reading Foxe's *Book of Martyrs*. HLQ (68:1/2) 2005, 133–50.

5439. LOADES, DAVID (ed.).   John Foxe at home and abroad. Aldershot; Burlington, VT: Ashgate, 2004. pp. xx, 297. Rev. by Marsha S. Robinson in RQ (58:2) 2005, 713–15.

5440. MACCOLL, ALAN.   The construction of England as a Protestant 'British' nation in the sixteenth century. *See* **5382**.

5441. MONTA, SUSANNAH BRIETZ.   *The Book of Sir Thomas More* and laughter of the heart. *See* **6710**.

5442. PATTERSON, PAUL J.   Reforming Chaucer: margins and religion in an apocryphal *Canterbury Tale*. *See* **4643**.

5443. RIORDAN, MICHAEL; RYRIE, ALEC.   Stephen Gardiner and the making of a Protestant villain. SixCJ (34:4) 2003, 1039–63.

5444. WOMERSLEY, DAVID.   Against the teleology of technique. *See* **5385**.

Abraham Fraunce

5445. DE LA ZUNINO GARRIDO, MARÍA.   Boscán and Garcilaso as rhetorical models in the English Renaissance: the case of Abraham Fraunce's *The Arcadian Rhetorike*. Atl (27:2) 2005, 119–34.

William Fulbeck (1560–1603?)

5446. GOODRICH, PETER.   *Amici curiae*: lawful manhood and other juristic performances in Renaissance England. *In* (pp. 23–49) **5196**.

George Gascoigne

5447. DORAN, SUSAN.   The politics of Renaissance Europe. *In* (pp. 21–52) **5954**.

5448. GAGGERO, CHRISTOPHER.   Pleasure unreconciled to virtue: George Gascoigne and didactic drama. *In* (pp. 168–93) **5268**.

5449. POPE, JON C.   The printing of 'this written book': G.T. and H.W.'s editorial disputes in *The Adventures of Master F.J.* RenP (2003) 45–53.

5450. SMYTH, ADAM.   'It were far better be a *Toad*, or a *Serpant*, then a Drunkard': writing about drunkenness. *In* (pp. 193–210) **6942**.

5451. ZURCHER, AMELIA A.   Ethics and the politic agent of early seventeenth-century prose romance. *See* **7926**.

Sir Arthur Gorges

5452. GIBSON, JONATHAN.   Civil war in 1614: Lucan, Gorges and Prince Henry. *In* (pp. 161–76) **6860**.

Richard Grafton (d.1572?)

5453. FREEMAN, JANET ING.   'Lyes' and 'hyghe treason' in 1570: John Stow annotates Grafton's *Abridgement of the Chronicles*. *See* **5744**.

5454. GADD, IAN; FERGUSON, MERAUD GRANT.   'For his paynes': John Stow and the Stationers. *In* (pp. 37–44) **5746**.

5455. HIATT, ALFRED.   Stow, Grafton, and fifteenth-century historiography. *In* (pp. 45–55) **5746**.

Robert Greene

5456. ARDOLINO, FRANK.   Greene's use of the history of Oxford in *The Honourable History of Friar Bacon and Friar Bungay*. ANQ (18:2) 2005, 20–5.

5457. BUTLER, AARON.   The gift of the magus: mystical glasses in Renaissance drama. SRASP (28) 2005, 46–56.

5458. GODMAN, MAUREEN.   'Plucking a crow' in *The Comedy of Errors*. *See* **6278**.

5459. GUSTAFSON, KEVIN L.   Homosociality, imitation, and gendered reading in Robert Greene's *Ciceronis Amor*. PQ (82:3) 2003, 277–300.

5460. KUMARAN, ARUL.   Patronage, print, and an early modern 'pamphlet moment'. ExRC (31:1) 2005, 59–88.

5461. McCarthy, Penny. Some *quises* and *quems*: Shakespeare's true debt to Nashe. *See* **6010**.

5462. Shepherd, Simon. Voice, writing, noise ...; or, Is Herod Balinese? *See* **4515**.

5463. Wells, Marion. Mistress Taleporter and the triumph of time: slander and old wives' tales in *The Winter's Tale*. *See* **6837**.

5464. Wilkinson, Katherine. A source for *The City Wit*. *See* **7269**.

Richard Hakluyt

5465. Armstrong, Catherine. The bookseller and the pedlar: the spread of knowledge of the New World in early modern England, 1580–1640. *In* (pp. 15–29) **880**.

5466. Borge, Francisco J. Richard Hakluyt, promoter of the New World: the navigational origins of the English nation. SEDERI (13) 2003, 1–9.

5467. Brayman Hackel, Heidi; Mancall, Peter C. Richard Hakluyt the Younger's notes for the East India Company in 1601: a transcription of Huntington Library Manuscript EL 2360. HLQ (67:3) 2004, 423–36.

5468. Davies, Rosalind. Intervention in the cloth trade: Richard Hakluyt, the new draperies and the Cockayne Project of 1614. *In* (pp. 113–24) **6860**.

Edward Hall

5469. Cavanagh, Dermot. Uncivil monarchy: Scotland, England and the reputation of James IV. *In* (pp. 146–61) **5187**.

Sir John Harington (1561–1612)

5470. Coatalen, Guillaume. 'Lô a timorous correction': unrecorded extracts from Spenser and Harington and negative criticism of *The Faerie Queene* in a folio from the Bodleian Library. *See* **5687**.

5471. Everson, Jane E. Translating the Pope and the Apennines: Harington's version of the *Orlando furioso*. MLR (100:3) 2005, 645–58.

5472. Kilroy, Gerard. Edmund Campion: memory and transcription. *See* **5401**.

Thomas Harman (*fl.*1567)

5473. Dionne, Craig; Mentz, Steve (eds). Rogues and early modern culture. (Bibl. 2004, 5713.) Rev. by Sandra Clark in TLS, 18 Mar. 2005, 25; by Michael Denbo in RQ (58:2) 2005, 725–7.

Thomas Harriot

5474. Hopkins, Lisa. *Doctor Faustus* and the Spanish Netherlands. *See* **5533**.

William Harrison (1535–1593)

5475. MacColl, Alan. The construction of England as a Protestant 'British' nation in the sixteenth century. *See* **5382**.

Gabriel Harvey

5476. Bregman, Alvan. A Gabriel Harvey manuscript brought to light. BC (54:1) 2005, 61–81.

5477. Gustafson, Kevin L.   Homosociality, imitation, and gendered reading in Robert Greene's *Ciceronis Amor. See* **5459**.

5478. Kumaran, Arul.   Patronage, print, and an early modern 'pamphlet moment'. *See* **5460**.

5479. Popper, Nicholas.   The English *polydaedali*: how Gabriel Harvey read late Tudor London. JHI (66:3) 2005, 351–81.

5480. Steggle, Matthew.   The names of Gabriel Harvey: cabbalistic, Russian, and fencing sources. NQ (52:2) 2005, 185–6.

5481. Wolfe, Jessica.   Humanism, machinery, and Renaissance literature. (Bibl. 2004, 5719.) Rev. by Andrew Hadfield in TLS, 4 Feb. 2005, 23; by Ira Clark in SCN (63:1/2) 2005, 14–17; by Frederika H. Jacobs in Isis (96:2) 2005, 277–8; by Robert Goulding in RQ (58:3) 2005, 1051–3; by Henry S. Turner in SpenR (36:2) 2005, 5–8.

William Haughton

5482. Stock, Angela.   Stow's *Survey* and the London playwrights. *In* (pp. 89–98) **5746**.

Stephen Hawes

5483. Griffiths, Jane.   The matter of invention in Hawes' *Passetyme of Pleasure*. SEDERI (13) 2003, 101–10.

Philip Henslowe

5484. Cerasano, S. P.   The geography of Henslowe's diary. ShQ (56:3) 2005, 328–53.

5485. ——   Henslowe's 'curious' diary. MedRen (17) 2005, 72–85.

5486. Gurr, Andrew.   Bears and players: Philip Henslowe's double acts. ShB (22:4) 2004, 31–41.

Sir William Herbert (d.1593)

5487. Hadfield, Andrew.   Tacitus and the reform of Ireland in the 1590s. *In* (pp. 115–30) **5187**.

Raphael Holinshed

5488. Chadelat, Jean-Marc.   'In God's name I'll ascend the regal throne': le sacerdoce et la royauté dans *Richard II*. *In* (pp. 113–51) **6505**.

5489. Hadfield, Andrew.   *Hamlet*'s country matters: the 'Scottish play' within the play. *In* (pp. 87–103) **6561**.

5490. Hoenselaars, Ton.   Shakespeare's *Richard II* in the European mirror. *In* (pp. 87–100) **6505**.

5491. MacColl, Alan.   The construction of England as a Protestant 'British' nation in the sixteenth century. *See* **5382**.

5492. Winter, Guillaume (ed.).   Autour de *Richard II* de William Shakespeare. *See* **6505**.

Richard Hooker

5493. Breteau, Jean-Louis.   Autorité de l'Écriture et autorité ecclésiastique dans l'Église de l'Angleterre: l'héritage de Richard Hooker. Anglophonia (17) 2005, 107–21.

5494. HILL, W. SPEED.   Richard Hooker and the rhetoric of history. *In* (pp. 75–84) **587**.

5495. KIRBY, W. J. TORRANCE.   Richard Hooker, reformer and Platonist: a reassessment of his thought. Aldershot; Burlington, VT: Ashgate, 2004. pp. xi, 138.

5496. MOHAMED, FEISAL G.   Renaissance thought on the celestial hierarchy: the decline of a tradition? *See* **5712**.

5497. ROUX, LOUIS.   Foi et raison dans l'œuvre de William Chillingworth. *See* **7318**.

5498. SIMUT, CORNELIU C.   The doctrine of salvation in the sermons of Richard Hooker. Berlin; New York: Mouton de Gruyter, 2005. pp. xiv, 350.

5499. VOAK, NIGEL.   Richard Hooker and reformed theology: a study of reason, will and grace. (Bibl. 2004, 5734.) Rev. by W. J. Torrance Kirby in SixCJ (36:1) 2005, 261–3.

Richard Jones (*fl.*1564–1613)

5500. MELNIKOFF, KIRK.   Jones's pen and Marlowe's socks: Richard Jones, print culture, and the beginnings of English dramatic literature. *See* **5545**.

Thomas Kyd

5501. KLINE, DANIEL T.   The circulation of the letter in Kyd's *The Spanish Tragedy*. *In* (pp. 229–47) **5268**.

William Lambarde (1536–1601)

5502. ADRIAN, JOHN M.   Itineraries, perambulations, and surveys: the intersections of chorography and cartography in the sixteenth century. *In* (pp. 29–46) **5103**.

5503. GORDON, ANDREW.   Overseeing and overlooking: John Stow and the surveying of the city. *In* (pp. 81–8) **5746**.

5504. HARRIS, OLIVER.   Stow and the contemporary antiquarian network. *In* (pp.27–35) **5746**.

Thomas Legge

5505. KEWES, PAULINA.   Jewish history and Christian Providence in Elizabethan England: the contexts of Thomas Legge's *Solymitana clades* (The Destruction of Jerusalem), *c.*1579–88. *In* (pp. 228–66) **5167**.

John Leland

5506. ADRIAN, JOHN M.   Itineraries, perambulations, and surveys: the intersections of chorography and cartography in the sixteenth century. *In* (pp. 29–46) **5103**.

5507. BREEZE, ANDREW.   William Worcestre's *Liber cronicum Alfredi regis*, 'Greeff Island', and 'le Foorn'. *See* **4929**.

5508. HARRIS, OLIVER.   'Motheaten, mouldye, and rotten': the early custodial history and dissemination of John Leland's manuscript remains. BLR (18:5) 2005, 460–501.

5509. —— Stow and the contemporary antiquarian network. *In* (pp. 27–35) **5746**.

Sir David Lindsay

5510. DEBAX, JEAN-PAUL. Techniques de persuasion dans les interludes protestants anglais du XVIe siècle. *See* **5664.**

5511. EPP, GARRETT P. J. Chastity in the stocks: women, sex, and marriage in *Ane Satyre of the Thrie Estaitis*. *In* (pp. 61–73) **3754.**

5512. WILLIAMS, JANET HADLEY. Women fictional and historic in Sir David Lyndsay's poetry. *In* (pp. 47–60) **3754.**

John Lyly

5513. ALWES, DEREK B. Sons and authors in Elizabethan England. (Bibl. 2004, 5749.) Rev. by Nandini Das in RQ (58:3) 2005, 1034–5.

5514. JOHNSTON, MARK ALBERT. Playing with the beard: courtly and commercial economies in Richard Edwards's *Damon and Pithias* and John Lyly's *Midas*. *See* **5421.**

5515. SCRAGG, LEAH. John Lyly and the politics of language. EC (55:1) 2005, 17–38.

Christopher Marlowe

5516. BIGLIAZZI, SILVIA. Transubstantiating the performance: towards a mimetic narrative in *Hamlet's* Hecuba scene. *In* (pp. 44–54) **3724.**

5517. BOEHRER, BRUCE. Disorder in the house of God: disrupted worship in Shakespeare and others. *See* **6731.**

5518. CARVER, GORDON. The Elizabethan erotic narrative: sex(y) reading. *See* **6818.**

5519. CHENEY, PATRICK (ed.). The Cambridge companion to Christopher Marlowe. (Bibl. 2004, 5762.) Rev. by Victoria Price in TRI (30:2) 2005, 191–2; by Robert A. Logan in RQ (58:2) 2005, 731–3.

5520. ELIAS, MICHAEL. Dido's dilemma: service to the Crown or the heart that lies beneath? MSAN (25:1) 2005, 5–6.

5521. ERNE, LUKAS. Biography, mythography, and criticism: the life and works of Christopher Marlowe. MP (103:1) 2005, 28–50.

5522. FLETCHER, ANGUS. *Doctor Faustus* and the Lutheran aesthetic. ELR (35:2) 2005, 187–209.

5523. FLOYD-WILSON, MARY. English ethnicity and race in early modern drama. (Bibl. 2004, 5769.) Rev. by Bernadette Andrea in SixCJ (35:4) 2004, 1144–6; by Michael Schoenfeldt in SStud (33) 2005, 236–9.

5524. GATES, DANIEL. Unpardonable sins: the hazards of performative language in the tragic cases of Francesco Spiera and *Doctor Faustus*. CompDr (38:1) 2004, 59–81.

5525. GÓMEZ LARA, MANUEL J. Ambiguous devices: the use of dramatic emblems in Marlowe's *Edward II* (1592). SEDERI (15) 2005, 103–13.

5526. HADFIELD, ANDREW. Poor but clever. TLS, 25 Mar. 2005, 25 (review-article).

5527. HARRAWOOD, MICHAEL. Overreachers: hyperbole, the 'circle in the water', and force in *1 Henry 6*. *See* **6438.**

5528. HILLMAN, RICHARD. The tragic Channel-crossings of George Chapman: part II, *The Revenge of Bussy D'Ambois*, *The Tragedy of Chabot*. *See* **7311**.

5529. HOENSELAARS, A. J. Shakespeare and the early modern history play. *In* (pp. 25–40) **5964**.

5530. HONAN, PARK. Christopher Marlowe: poet & spy. Oxford; New York: OUP, 2005. pp. xv, 421.

5531. HONIGMANN, E. A. J. Shakespeare, *Sir Thomas More* and asylum seekers. *See* **6707**.

5532. HOPKINS, LISA. A Christopher Marlowe chronology. Basingstoke; New York: Palgrave Macmillan, 2005. pp. xviii, 208. (Author chronologies.)

5533. —— *Doctor Faustus* and the Spanish Netherlands. ShY (15) 2005, 33–48.

5534. HUNT, MAURICE. 'Forward backward' time and the Apocalypse in *Hamlet*. *See* **6332**.

5535. HUTCHINGS, MARK. 'And almost to the very walles of *Rome*': *2 Tamburlaine*, II.i.9. NQ (52:2) 2005, 190–2.

5536. JACKSON, MACD. P. Francis Meres and the cultural contexts of Shakespeare's Rival Poet sonnets. *See* **6718**.

5537. KECK, DAVID. Marlowe and Ortelius's map. NQ (52:2) 2005, 189–90.

5538. KEEFER, MICHAEL. 'Fairer than the evening air': Marlowe's Gnostic Helen of Troy and the tropes of belatedness and historical meditation. *In* (pp. 39–62) **4479**.

5539. KENDALL, ROY. Christopher Marlowe and Richard Baines: journeys through the Elizabethan underground. (Bibl. 2004, 5778.) Rev. by Constance Brown Kuriyama in MSAN (25:2) 2005, 16–19.

5540. KNUTSON, ROSLYN L. Marlowe, company ownership, and the role of Edward II. MedRen (18) 2005, 37–46.

5541. LOCKWOOD, TOM. Edmond Malone and early modern textual culture. *See* **8820**.

5542. LUNNEY, RUTH. Marlowe and the popular tradition: innovation in the English drama before 1595. (Bibl. 2004, 5783.) Rev. by Michael Yorke Jones in TN (57:1) 2003, 74; by Julie Jackson in TJ (57:2) 2005, 327–8; by Bruce E. Brandt in MSAN (25:2) 2005, 15–16.

5543. MCCREA, SCOTT. The case for Shakespeare: the end of the authorship question. *See* **6011**.

5544. MACFIE, PAMELA ROYSTON. *All Ovids Elegies*, the *Amores*, and the allusive close of Marlowe's *Hero and Leander*. RenP (2004) 1–16.

5545. MELNIKOFF, KIRK. Jones's pen and Marlowe's socks: Richard Jones, print culture, and the beginnings of English dramatic literature. SP (102:2) 2005, 184–209.

5546. MIOLA, ROBERT S. Jesuit drama in early modern England. *In* (pp. 71–86) **5915**.

5547. MOORE, ROGER E. 'I'll rouse my senses, and awake myself': Marlowe's *The Jew of Malta* and the Renaissance Gnostic tradition. ReLit (37:3) 2005, 37–58.

5548. PETERS, JULIE STONE. Theater and book in the history of memory: materializing Mnemosyne in the age of print. MP (102:2) 2004, 179–206.

5549. RIGGS, DAVID. The world of Christopher Marlowe. (Bibl. 2004, 5790.) Rev. by Andrew Hadfield in TLS, 25 Mar. 2005, 25; by Michael Dirda in BkW, 9 Jan. 2005, 15; by Constance Brown Kuriyama in MSAN (25:2) 2005, 16–19.

5550. SCHRAY, KATERYNA A. R. 'Is this your crown?': conquest and coronation in *Tamburlaine I*, Act II scene 4. CEl (68) 2005, 19–26.

5551. SEMLER, L. E. Marlovian therapy: the chastisement of Ovid in *Hero and Leander*. ELR (35:2) 2005, 159–86.

5552. SHEPARD, ALAN. Marlowe's soldiers: rhetorics of masculinity in the age of the Armada. (Bibl. 2004, 5793.) Rev. by Richard F. Hardin in SixCJ (34:3) 2003, 792–3; by Jennifer A. Low in CompDr (38:1) 2004, 113–16; by Mario DiGangi in ETh (8:1) 2005, 136–9.

5553. SHEPHERD, SIMON. Voice, writing, noise …; or, Is Herod Balinese? See **4515**.

5554. THOMSON, LESLIE. Marlowe's staging of meaning. MedRen (18) 2005, 19–36.

5555. VAN DIJKHUIZEN, JAN FRANS. An Arab in Venice: Hafid Bouazza translates *Othello* and the *Massacre at Paris. See **6666**.

5556. VICKERS, BRIAN. Idle worship. See **6102**.

5557. WHITE, ROBERT. The cultural impact of the Massacre of St Bartholomew's Day. *In* (pp. 183–99) **5187**.

Queen Mary Stuart

5558. FLEMING, MORNA R. An unequal correspondence: epistolary and poetic exchanges between Mary Queen of Scots and Elizabeth of England. *In* (pp. 104–19) **3754**.

Francis Meres (1565–1647)

5559. JACKSON, MACD. P. Francis Meres and the cultural contexts of Shakespeare's Rival Poet sonnets. See **6718**.

Sir Thomas More

5560. BORE, ISABELLE. Vérité et liberté chez Sir Thomas More (1478–1535). Moreana (41:159) 2004, 64–74.

5561. BOSWELL, JACKSON C. References and allusions to Thomas More: 1641–1700 (part III). Moreana (41:160) 2004, 4–39.

5562. CAVANAGH, DERMOT. Uncivil monarchy: Scotland, England and the reputation of James IV. *In* (pp. 146–61) **5187**.

5563. COUSINS, A. D. Humanism, female education, and myth: Erasmus, Vives, and More's *To Candidus*. JHI (65:2) 2004, 213–30.

5564. CRESPO CANDEIAS VELEZ RELVAS, MARÍA DE JESÚS. The literary construction of a monstrous portrait – *King Richard III* by Thomas More and William Shakespeare. See **6507**.

5565. GERITZ, ALBERT J. Recent studies in More (1990–2003). ELR (35:1) 2005, 123–55.

5566. Höfele, Andreas. Making history memorable: More, Shakespeare and Richard III. YREAL (21) 2005, 187–203.

5567. Keane, Robert. Thomas More as a young lawyer. Moreana (41:160) 2004, 40–71.

5568. Kendrick, Christopher. The imperial laboratory: discovering forms in *The New Atlantis*. See 7205.

5569. Lewis, John. 'Sacrilege toward the individual': the anti-pride of Thomas More's *Utopia* and *Anthem*'s radical alternative. In (pp. 172–89) 19013.

5570. Talvet, Jüri. Between dreams and reality: the message and the image of Renaissance Humanism. SEDERI (14) 2004, 137–52.

5571. Trousson, Raymond. Sciences, techniques et utopies: du paradis à l'enfer. Paris: L'Harmattan, 2003. pp. 230. Rev. by Micheline Hugues in RLC (79:1) 2005, 86–7.

5572. van Es, Bart. Out of season. TLS, 10 June 2005, 12 (review-article).

5573. Vickers, Brian. A rage for order. TLS, 10 June 2005, 13–15 (review-article). (Utopianism.)

5574. Wegemer, Gerard B.; Smith, Stephen W. (eds). A Thomas More source book. (Bibl. 2004, 5830.) Rev. by John A. Gueguen in Moreana (41:159) 2004, 95–8; by Bart van Es in TLS, 10 June 2005, 12; by Andrew Tucker in BJJ (12) 2005, 266–70.

5575. Yoran, Hanan. More's *Utopia* and Erasmus' No-place. ELR (35:1) 2005, 3–30.

Thomas Morley (1557–1603?)

5576. Domínguez Romero, Elena. Thomas Morley's *First Book of Madrigals to Four Voices*: a pastoral romance. SEDERI (13) 2003, 45–53.

5577. Hulse, Lynn. 'Musique which pleaseth myne eare': Robert Cecil's musical patronage. In (pp. 139–58) 5121.

Anthony Munday

5578. Bergeron, David M. Pageants, masques, and history. In (pp. 41–56) 5964.

5579. Hamilton, Donna B. Anthony Munday and the Catholics, 1560–1633. Aldershot; Burlington, VT: Ashgate, 2005. pp. xxvi, 268. Rev. by Emma Smith in TLS, 25 Nov. 2005, 28.

5580. McCluskey, Peter M. Sir Edmond (*sic*) Tilney, *Sir Thomas More*, and the Netherlandic immigrant community. See 6709.

5581. Monta, Susannah Brietz. *The Book of Sir Thomas More* and laughter of the heart. See 6710.

5582. Moore, Helen. Succeeding Stow: Anthony Munday and the 1618 *Survey of London*. In (pp. 99–108) 5746.

5583. Oakley-Brown, Liz. Framing Robin Hood: temporality and textuality in Anthony Munday's Huntington plays. In (pp. 113–28) 3576.

5584. Schofield, Scott. According to 'the common receiued opinion': Munday's Brute in *The Triumphs of Re-United Britannia* (1605). In (pp. 253–68) 4479.

Thomas Nashe

5585. CARVER, GORDON. The Elizabethan erotic narrative: sex(y) reading. *See* **6818.**

5586. DUNCAN-JONES, KATHERINE. City limits: Nashe's *Choise of Valentines* and Jonson's *Famous Voyage*. RES (56:224) 2005, 247–62.

5587. FLECK, ANDREW. The limitations of narrative: Nashe's appropriation of Ovidian decorum in *The Unfortunate Traveller*. NQ (52:2) 2005, 182–5.

5588. HADFIELD, ANDREW. Introduction: Shakespeare and Renaissance Europe. *In* (pp. 1–20) **5954.**

5589. HUTCHINGS, MARK. Anti-theatrical prejudice and *1 Honest Whore*, II.i.324–326. *See* **7354.**

5590. HYMAN, WENDY. Authorial self-consciousness in Nashe's *The Vnfortunate Traveller*. SELit (45:1) 2005, 23–41.

5591. KUMARAN, ARUL. Patronage, print, and an early modern 'pamphlet moment'. *See* **5460.**

5592. McCARTHY, PENNY. Some *quis*es and *quem*s: Shakespeare's true debt to Nashe. *See* **6010.**

5593. POPPER, NICHOLAS. The English *polydaedali*: how Gabriel Harvey read late Tudor London. *See* **5479.**

5594. STEGGLE, MATTHEW. The *Manipulus florum* in *An Almond for a Parrat*. NQ (52:2) 2005, 178–82.

Thomas Norton (1532–1584)

5595. DUNN, KEVIN. Representing counsel: *Gorboduc* and the Elizabethan Privy Council. ELR (33:3) 2003, 279–308.

5596. KOBAYASHI, JUNJI. *Gorboduc* and the Inner Temple revels of Christmas. *See* **5630.**

5597. REILLY, TERRY. 'This is the case': *Gorboduc* and early modern English legal discourse concerning inheritance. *In* (pp. 195–210) **5268.**

5598. WINSTON, JESSICA. Expanding the political nation: *Gorboduc* at the Inns of Court and succession revisited. *See* **5632.**

Anne Cecil de Vere, Countess of Oxford

5599. CROFT, PAULINE. Mildred, Lady Burghley: the matriarch. *In* (pp. 283–300) **5121.**

5600. PAYNE, HELEN. The Cecil women at court. *In* (pp. 265–81) **5121.**

Edward de Vere, Earl of Oxford

5601. ANDERSON, MARK. 'Shakespeare' by another name: the life of Edward de Vere, Earl of Oxford, the man who was Shakespeare. Foreword by Derek Jacobi. *See* **5846.**

5602. MALIM, RICHARD (ed.). Great Oxford: essays on the life and work of Edward de Vere, 17th Earl of Oxford, 1550–1604. Tunbridge Wells: Parapress, 2004. pp. 362. Rev. by Brian Vickers in TLS, 19 & 26 Aug. 2005, 6–8.

5603. NELSON, ALAN H. Monstrous adversary: the life of Edward de Vere, 17th Earl of Oxford. (Bibl. 2004, 5850.) Rev. by Steven W. May in ShQ (56:2) 2005, 214–16.

5604. VICKERS, BRIAN. Idle worship. *See* **6102**.

George Peele

5605. ARDOLINO, FRANK. The Protestant context of George Peele's 'pleasant conceited' *Old Wives Tale*. MedRen (18) 2005, 146–65.

5606. BRATCHER, JAMES T. *Loach* in the Peele jestbook. NQ (52:2) 2005, 227.

5607. HADFIELD, ANDREW. '*Suum cuique*': natural law in *Titus Andronicus*, I.i.284. *See* **6780**.

Mary Herbert, Countess of Pembroke

5608. BENNETT, LYN. Women writing of divinest things: rhetoric and the poetry of Pembroke, Wroth and Lanyer. (Bibl. 2004, 5857.) Rev. by Megan Matchinske in RQ (58:4) 2005, 1424–7.

5609. BENSON, PAMELA JOSEPH. The stigma of Italy undone: Aemilia Lanyer's canonization of Lady Mary Sidney. *In* (pp. 146–75) **5094**.

Robert Persons (Parsons) (1546–1610)

5610. MAYER, JEAN-CHRISTOPHE. 'This Papist and his poet': Shakespeare's Lancastrian kings and Robert Parsons's *Conference about the Next Succession*. *In* (pp. 116–29) **5915**.

'John Pickering' (Sir John Puckering) (*fl.*1567)

5611. GEORGE, J.-A. 'A pestelaunce on the crabyd queane': the hybrid nature of John Pikeryng's *Horestes*. SEDERI (14) 2004, 65–76.

George Puttenham

5612. FRITZE, RONALD. 'His evel life, his troublesome behavior': George Puttenham and his marital problems. Archives (29:110) 2004, 38–49.

5613. PENDER, STEPHEN. The open use of living: prudence, decorum, and the 'square man'. *See* **2432**.

5614. POWELL, JASON. Puttenham's *Arte of English Poesie* and Thomas Wyatt's diplomacy. NQ (52:2) 2005, 174–6.

5615. SUTTON, JAMES M. The retiring patron: William Cecil and the cultivation of retirement, 1590–98. *In* (pp. 159–79) **5121**.

5616. WATSON, ELIZABETH SEE. George Puttenham as comedic artificer. RenP (2003) 55–69.

Sir Walter Ralegh (*c.*1552–1618)

5617. BAJETTA, CARLO M. Sir Walter Ralegh ed Elisabetta I: poesie per tre occasioni. R/R/R (9/10) 2003/04, 71–86.

5618. BEER, ANNA. Sir Walter Ralegh's *Dialogue betweene a Counsellor of State and a Justice of Peace*. *In* (pp. 127–41) **6860**.

5619. GIBSON, JONATHAN. Civil war in 1614: Lucan, Gorges and Prince Henry. *In* (pp. 161–76) **6860**.

5620. GRAVES, ROY NEIL. Raleigh's *Moral Advice*. Exp (63:4) 2005, 204–8.

5621. HOLMES, JOHN. The Guiana projects: imperial and colonial ideologies in Ralegh and Purchas. LitH (14:2) 2005, 1–13.

5622. MAROTTI, ARTHUR F. A response to Michael Rudick. *In* (pp. 143–6) **587**.

5623. RUDICK, MICHAEL. Editing Ralegh's poems historically. *In* (pp. 133–42) **587.**

5624. VALLARO, CRISTINA. La simbologia lunare nei canzonieri elisabettiani. *See* **5325.**

John Redford

5625. PETTIGREW, TODD H.J. Sex, sin, and scarring: syphilis in Redford's *Wit and Science. In* (pp. 213–27) **5268.**

5626. SCHERB, VICTOR I. Playing at maturity in John Redford's *Wit and Science.* SELit (45:2) 2005, 271–97.

Barnabe Rich

5627. KUMARAN, ARUL. Patronage, print, and an early modern 'pamphlet moment'. *See* **5460.**

Thomas Rogers (d.1616)

5628. PERRY, NANDRA. *Imitatio* and identity: Thomas Rogers, Philip Sidney, and the Protestant self. ELR (35:3) 2005, 365–406.

Thomas Sackville, First Earl of Dorset

5629. DUNN, KEVIN. Representing counsel: *Gorboduc* and the Elizabethan Privy Council. *See* **5595.**

5630. KOBAYASHI, JUNJI. *Gorboduc* and the Inner Temple revels of Christmas. SStudT (41) 2003, 25–43.

5631. REILLY, TERRY. 'This is the case': *Gorboduc* and early modern English legal discourse concerning inheritance. *In* (pp. 195–210) **5268.**

5632. WINSTON, JESSICA. Expanding the political nation: *Gorboduc* at the Inns of Court and succession revisited. ETh (8:1) 2005, 11–34.

5633. WOOLF, DANIEL R. From hystories to the historical: five transitions in thinking about the past, 1500–1700. HLQ (68:1/2) 2005, 33–70.

Robert Cecil, Earl of Salisbury

5634. CROFT, PAULINE (ed.). Patronage, culture and power: the early Cecils. *See* **5121.**

5635. HULSE, LYNN. 'Musique which pleaseth myne eare': Robert Cecil's musical patronage. *In* (pp. 139–58) **5121.**

Robert Saltwood (*fl.*1518–1538)

5636. BOFFEY, JULIA. John Mychell and the printing of Lydgate in the 1530s. *See* **4869.**

5637. GILLESPIE, ALEXANDRA. Introduction: bibliography and early Tudor texts. *See* **13.**

Sir Philip Sidney

5638. BRENNAN, MICHAEL G.; KINNAMON, NOEL J. A Sidney chronology, 1554–1654. (Bibl. 2004, 5881.) Rev. by John Gouws in NQ (52:2) 2005, 249–51.

5639. CRAIG, MARTHA. Negotiating sex: the poetics of feminization in Sidney's *Arcadia.* ExRC (31:1) 2005, 89–106.

5640. FORSYTH, V. L. Polybius's histories: an overlooked source for Sidney's *Arcadia.* SidJ (21:2) 2003, 59–65.

5641. GLIMP, DAVID. Increase and multiply: governing cultural reproduction in early modern England. (Bibl. 2004, 5887.) Rev. by Paul Stevens in SStud (33) 2005, 240–5; by Anthony Miller in Parergon (22:1) 2005, 231–3.

5642. GOLDRING, ELIZABETH. The funeral of Sir Philip Sidney and the politics of Elizabethan festival. In (pp. 199–224) **5172.**

5643. GRIFFITHS, JANE. The matter of invention in Hawes' *Passetyme of Pleasure. See* **5483.**

5644. HOWE, SARAH. 'Pregnant images of life': visual art and representation in *Arcadia* and *The Faerie Queene. See* **5703.**

5645. KASKE, CAROL. Spenser's *Amoretti* and *Epithalamion*: a psalter of love. In (pp. 28–49) **6872.**

5646. KENNEDY, WILLIAM J. The site of Petrarchism: early modern national sentiment in Italy, France, and England. (Bibl. 2004, 5891.) Rev. by Patricia Phillippy in CLIO (34:1/2) 2004, 148–52; by Jennifer Petrie in MLR (100:2) 2005, 587–8; by Sarah M. Dunnigan in TMR, July 2005.

5647. LOCKWOOD, TOM. New allusions to Jonson and Sidney. *See* **7563.**

5648. MACK, MICHAEL. Sidney's poetics: imitating creation. Washington, DC: Catholic Univ. of America Press, 2005. pp. 216. Rev. by Theodore L. Steinberg in RQ (58:4) 2005, 1448–9.

5649. MAZZOLA, ELIZABETH. Favorite sons: the politics and poetics of the Sidney family. (Bibl. 2004, 5896.) Rev. by Catherine Canino in SixCJ (36:2) 2005, 598–9; by John Gouws in NQ (52:2) 2005, 249–51.

5650. PERRY, NANDRA. *Imitatio* and identity: Thomas Rogers, Philip Sidney, and the Protestant self. *See* **5628.**

5651. PHILLIPS, ELAINE ANDERSON. Richardson reads the Renaissance: the use of Renaissance narrative theory in the novels and prefaces. *See* **8953.**

5652. RAY, ROBERT H. The admiration of Sir Philip Sidney by Lovelace and Carew: new seventeenth-century allusions. ANQ (18:1) 2005, 18–21.

5653. SMITH, JEREMY L. Music and late Elizabethan politics: the identities of Oriana and Diana. JAMS (58:3) 2005, 508–57.

5654. SUSSMAN, ANNE. Histor, history, and narrative memory in Sidney's *Arcadia*. SidJ (21:2) 2003, 39–49.

5655. WILLIAMSON, ARTHUR H. An empire to end empire: the dynamic of early modern British expansion. HLQ (68:1/2) 2005, 227–56.

5656. WILSON, LUKE. Renaissance tool abuse and the legal history of the sudden. In (pp. 121–45) **5196.**

5657. WORDEN, BLAIR. Historians and poets. HLQ (68:1/2) 2005, 71–93.

5658. ZURCHER, AMELIA A. Ethics and the politic agent of early seventeenth-century prose romance. *See* **7926.**

Robert Sidney, Earl of Leicester

5659. ARNOLD, MARGARET J. An unpublished letter of Mary Wroth. *See* **7921.**

5660. BRENNAN, MICHAEL G. 'Your lordship's to do you all humble service': Rowland Whyte's correspondence with Robert Sidney, Viscount Lisle and First Earl of Leicester. SidJ (21:2) 2003, 1–37.

John Skelton

5661. CASTRO CARRACEDO, JUAN MANUEL. *Pium vestrum Catullum Britannum*: the influence of Catullus' poetry on John Skelton. SEDERI (14) 2004, 3–16.

5662. —— 'To lerne you to dye when ye wyll': John Skelton and the *ars moriendi* tradition. SEDERI (15) 2005, 5–21.

5663. CAVANAGH, DERMOT. Uncivil monarchy: Scotland, England and the reputation of James IV. *In* (pp. 146–61) **5187.**

5664. DEBAX, JEAN-PAUL. Techniques de persuasion dans les interludes protestants anglais du XVIe siècle. Anglophonia (17) 2005, 25–33.

5665. GILLESPIE, ALEXANDRA. Introduction: bibliography and early Tudor texts. *See* **13.**

5666. GRIFFITHS, JANE. A contradiction in terms: Skelton's 'effecte energiall' in *A Replycacion*. RenSt (17:1) 2003, 55–68.

5667. —— Text and authority: John Stow's 1568 edition of Skelton's *Workes*. *In* (pp. 127–34) **5746.**

5668. —— What's in a name? The transmission of 'John Skelton, Laureate' in manuscript and print. HLQ (67:2) 2004, 215–35.

Robert Southwell

5669. BROWNLOW, FRANK. Richard Topcliffe: Elizabeth's enforcer and the representation of power in *King Lear*. *In* (pp. 161–78) **5915.**

5670. COUSINS, A. D.; WEBB, R. J. Southwell's *The Presentation*. Exp (64:1) 2005, 2–3.

5671. PILARZ, SCOTT R. Robert Southwell and the mission of literature, 1561–1595: writing reconciliation. (Bibl. 2004, 5918.) Rev. by Alison A. Chapman in RQ (58:2) 2005, 712–13.

5672. WOODS, SUSANNE. Lanyer and Southwell: a Protestant woman's re-vision of St Peter. *In* (pp. 73–86) **6872.**

Edmund Spenser

5673. ANON. (comp.). Articles: abstracts and notices. SpenR (36:3) 2005, 10–17.

5674. ADELMAN, JANET. Revaluing the body in *The Faerie Queene* I. SpenR (36:1) 2005, 15–25. (Hugh Maclean Memorial Lecture.)

5675. ALKON, GABRIEL. Refrain and the limits of poetic power in Spenser, Herbert, Hardy, and Stevens. WHR (58:2) 2004, 106–37.

5676. BATES, ROBIN E. 'The Queene is defrauded of the intent of the law': Spenser's advocation of Civil Law in *A View of the State of Ireland*. PLL (41:2) 2005, 123–45.

5677. BELLAMY, ELIZABETH JANE. Slanderous Troys: between fame and rumor. *In* (pp. 215–35) **4479.**

5678. —— CHENEY, PATRICK; SCHOENFELDT, MICHAEL (eds). Imagining death in Spenser and Milton. (Bibl. 2004, 5927.) Rev. by Tom Rutter in MLR (100:3) 2005, 774–7.

5679. BERGER, HARRY, JR. Resisting translation: Britomart in Book 3 of Spenser's *Faerie Queene*. *In* (pp. 207–50) **5069.**

5680. BERRY, CRAIG; HAYTON, HEATHER (eds). Translating desire in medieval and early modern literature. *See* **5069.**

5681. BRITLAND, KAREN. Circe's cup: wine and women in early modern drama. *In* (pp. 109–25) **6942.**

5682. BROWN, TED. Metapoetry in Edmund Spenser's *Amoretti*. PQ (82:4) 2003, 401–17.

5683. BURLINSON, CHRISTOPHER; ZURCHER, ANDREW. 'Secretary to the Lord Grey Lord Deputie here': Edmund Spenser's Irish papers. Library (6:1) 2005, 30–75.

5684. CARSCALLEN, JAMES. How Troy came to Spenser. *In* (pp. 15–38) **4479.**

5685. CARTER, SUSAN. Duessa: Spenser's Loathly Lady. CEl (68) 2005, 9–18.

5686. CELOVSKY, LISA. Early modern masculinities and *The Faerie Queene*. ELR (35:2) 2005, 210–47.

5687. COATALEN, GUILLAUME. 'Lô a timorous correction': unrecorded extracts from Spenser and Harington and negative criticism of *The Faerie Queene* in a folio from the Bodleian Library. RES (56:227) 2005, 730–48.

5688. DESAI, R. W. England, the Indian boy, and the spice trade in *A Midsummer Night's Dream*. *In* (pp. 141–57) **6096.**

5689. DUTTON, RICHARD. *Volpone* and beast fable: early modern analogic reading. *See* **7548.**

5690. ERICKSON, WAYNE. Amoret and Scudamour woo and wed: two courtly histories and a stalemate. RenP (2003) 71–82.

5691. ESOLEN, ANTHONY. Highways and byways: a response to Donald Cheney. Connotations (13:1/2) 2003/04, 1–4. (*Responds to* bibl. 2004, 5940.)

5692. FELCH, SUSAN M. Doubt and the hermeneutics of delight. Cresset (68:4) 2005, 12–15.

5693. FITZPATRICK, JOAN. Shakespeare, Spenser and the contours of Britain: reshaping the Atlantic archipelago. *See* **5932.**

5694. —— Shakespeare's *Titus Andronicus* and Bandello's *Novelle* as sources for the Munera episode in Spenser's *Faerie Queene*, Book 5, canto 2. NQ (52:2) 2005, 196–8.

5695. FREEMAN, LOUISE GILBERT. Vision, metamorphosis, and the poetics of allegory in the *Mutabilitie Cantos*. SELit (45:1) 2005, 65–93.

5696. GORJI, MINA. Clare's 'Merry England'. *See* **10438.**

5697. HADFIELD, ANDREW. Tacitus and the reform of Ireland in the 1590s. *In* (pp. 115–30) **5187.**

5698. HEALY, THOMAS. Drama, Ireland and the question of civility. *In* (pp. 131–45) **5187.**

5699. —— Queene and country. TLS, 15 Apr. 2005, 24 (review-article).

5700. HELFER, REBECA. Falling into history: trials of empire in Spenser's *Faerie Queene*. *In* (pp. 237–52) **4479.**

5701. HENRY, LORENA. Guiding the heavenly causes: faithfulness, fate and prophecy in *The Faerie Queene*. *In* (pp. 50–72) **6872.**

5702. HOLMER, JOAN OZARK. Desdemona, woman warrior: 'O, these men, these men!' (4.3.59). *See* **6651.**

5703. HOWE, SARAH. 'Pregnant images of life': visual art and representation in *Arcadia* and *The Faerie Queene*. CamQ (34:1) 2005, 33–53.

5704. HUNT, MAURICE. 'Forward backward' time and the Apocalypse in *Hamlet. See* **6332**.

5705. KANE, PAUL. Spenser's use of the Book of Tobit in Book II of *The Faerie Queene*. SRASP (28) 2005, 25–35.

5706. KASKE, CAROL. Spenser's *Amoretti* and *Epithalamion*: a psalter of love. *In* (pp. 28–49) **6872**.

5707. MCCABE, RICHARD A. Parody, sympathy and self: a response to Donald Cheney. Connotations (13:1/2) 2003/04, 5–22. (*Responds to* bibl. 2004, 5940.)

5708. MACCOLL, ALAN. The construction of England as a Protestant 'British' nation in the sixteenth century. *See* **5382**.

5709. MCKEOWN, ADAM. Looking at Britomart looking at pictures. SELit (45:1) 2005, 43–63.

5710. MELEHY, HASSAN. Antiquities of Britain: Spenser's *Ruines of Time*. SP (102:2) 2005, 159–83.

5711. MILLER, ANTHONY. The proem to *The Faerie Queene*, Book II: Spenser, Pliny, and undiscovered worlds. CML (25:2) 2005, 1–7.

5712. MOHAMED, FEISAL G. Renaissance thought on the celestial hierarchy: the decline of a tradition? JHI (65:4) 2004, 559–82.

5713. MORGAN, GERALD. 'Add faith vnto your force': the perfecting of Spenser's Knight of Holiness in faith and humility. RenSt (18:3) 2004, 449–74.

5714. NUTTALL, A. D. Spenser and Elizabethan alienation. EC (55:3) 2005, 209–25.

5715. PAOLUCCI, ANNE. The women in Dante's *Divine Comedy* and Spenser's *Faerie Queen* (*sic*). Preface by Frank D. Grande. Dover, DE: Griffon House for the Bagehot Council, 2005. pp. viii, 196.

5716. PARRY, JOSEPH. Petrarch's mourning, Spenser's Scudamour, and Britomart's gift of death. CLS (42:1) 2005, 24–49.

5717. PUGH, SYRITHE. Spenser and Ovid. Aldershot; Burlington, VT: Ashgate, 2005. pp. 302. Rev. by Andrew Hadfield in TLS, 15 Apr. 2005, 29; by Richard A. McCabe in RES (56:227) 2005, 786–7.

5718. SCHWYZER, PHILIP. Literature, nationalism, and memory in early modern England and Wales. *See* **5383**.

5719. SHAHANI, GITANJALI (comp.). Articles: abstracts and notices. SpenR (36:2) 2005, 9–14.

5720. SHEPARD, ALAN; POWELL, STEPHEN D. (eds). Fantasies of Troy: Classical tales and the social imaginary in medieval and early modern Europe. *See* **4479**.

5721. SHRANK, CATHY. Civil tongues: language, law and Reformation. *In* (pp. 19–34) **5187**.

5722. STEINBERG, GLENN A. Spenser's *Shepheardes Calender* and the Elizabethan reception of Chaucer. ELR (35:1) 2005, 31–51.

5723. SUTTON, JAMES M. The retiring patron: William Cecil and the cultivation of retirement, 1590–98. *In* (pp. 159–79) **5121**.

5724. TARLINSKAJA, MARINA. Who did NOT write *A Lover's Complaint*. *See* **6520**.

5725. WARNER, J. CHRISTOPHER. The Augustinian epic, Petrarch to Milton. Ann Arbor: Michigan UP, 2005. pp. 270.

5726. WEATHERBY, HAROLD L. Warren's Willie Talos: reflections on the name. *See* **20000**.

5727. WHEATLEY, CHLOE. Abridging the *Antiquitee of Faery lond*: new paths through old matter in *The Faerie Queene*. RQ (58:3) 2005, 857-80.

5728. WILLIAMSON, ARTHUR H. An empire to end empire: the dynamic of early modern British expansion. *See* **5655**.

5729. WOLFE, JESSICA. Spenser, Homer, and the mythography of strife. RQ (58:4) 2005, 1220-88.

5730. WOODCOCK, MATTHEW. Fairy in *The Faerie Queene*: Renaissance self-fashioning and Elizabethan myth-making. (Bibl. 2004, 6016.) Rev. by Richard Danson Brown in MLR (100:3) 2005, 763-4; by Tom MacFaul in NQ (52:3) 2005, 402-3; by Joel Davis in RQ (58:2) 2005, 734-6; by Mary Ellen Lamb in SpenR (36:3) 2005, 7-10; by Anthony Low in BJJ (12) 2005, 279-84.

5731. WOODS, SUSANNE. Lanyer and Southwell: a Protestant woman's re-vision of St Peter. *In* (pp. 73-86) **6872**.

William Stanley, Sixth Earl of Derby (1561?-1642)

5732. MCCREA, SCOTT. The case for Shakespeare: the end of the authorship question. *See* **6011**.

William Stewart (1481?-1550?)

5733. EWAN, ELIZABETH. The dangers of manly women: late medieval perceptions of female heroism in Scotland's Second War of Independence. *In* (pp. 3-18) **3754**.

John Stow

5734. ADRIAN, JOHN M. Itineraries, perambulations, and surveys: the intersections of chorography and cartography in the sixteenth century. *In* (pp. 29-46) **5103**.

5735. ARCHER, IAN W. Discourses of history in Elizabethan and early Stuart London. *See* **6706**.

5736. —— John Stow, citizen and historian. *In* (pp. 13-26) **5746**.

5737. BALE, ANTHONY. Stow's medievalism and antique Judaism in early modern London. *In* (pp. 69-80) **5746**.

5738. BOWERS, RICK. Dick Whittington, Stow's *Survey*, and 'Catte Streete'. ELN (43:1) 2005, 33-9.

5739. DANE, JOSEPH A. In search of Stow's Chaucer. *In* (pp. 145-55) **5746**.

5740. DRIVER, MARTHA W. Stow's books bequeathed: some notes on William Browne (1591-c.1643) and Peter Le Neve (1661-1729). *In* (pp. 135-43) **5746**.

5741. DUFFY, EAMON. Bare ruined choirs: remembering Catholicism in Shakespeare's England. *In* (pp. 40-57) **5915**.

5742. DUNCAN-JONES, KATHERINE. Afterword: Stow's remains. *In* (pp. 157-63) **5746**.

5743. EDWARDS, A. S. G.   John Stow and Middle English literature. *In* (pp. 109–18) **5746**.

5744. FREEMAN, JANET ING.   'Lyes' and 'hyghe treason' in 1570: John Stow annotates Grafton's *Abridgement of the Chronicles*. Library (6:3) 2005, 251–73.

5745. GADD, IAN; FERGUSON, MERAUD GRANT.   'For his paynes': John Stow and the Stationers. *In* (pp. 37–44) **5746**.

5746. —— GILLESPIE, ALEXANDRA (eds).   John Stow (1525–1605) and the making of the English past. London: British Library, 2004. pp. xiv, 192. Rev. by Sue Powell in JEBS (8) 2005, 286–7; by G. H. Martin in Library (6:3) 2005, 344–6.

5747. GILLESPIE, ALEXANDRA.   Introduction. *In* (pp. 1–11) **5746**.

5748. —— Stow's 'owlde' manuscripts of London chronicles. *In* (pp. 57–67) **5746**.

5749. GORDON, ANDREW.   Overseeing and overlooking: John Stow and the surveying of the city. *In* (pp. 81–8) **5746**.

5750. GRIFFITHS, JANE.   Text and authority: John Stow's 1568 edition of Skelton's *Workes*. *In* (pp. 127–34) **5746**.

5751. HARRIS, OLIVER.   Stow and the contemporary antiquarian network. *In* (pp. 27–35) **5746**.

5752. HIATT, ALFRED.   Stow, Grafton, and fifteenth-century historiography. *In* (pp. 45–55) **5746**.

5753. MOORE, HELEN.   Succeeding Stow: Anthony Munday and the 1618 *Survey of London*. *In* (pp. 99–108) **5746**.

5754. PEARSALL, DEREK.   John Stow and Thomas Speght as editors of Chaucer: a question of class. *In* (pp. 119–25) **5746**.

5755. STOCK, ANGELA.   Stow's *Survey* and the London playwrights. *In* (pp. 89–98) **5746**.

5756. THOMPSON, JOHN J.   Patch and repair and making do in manuscripts and texts associated with John Stow. *In* (pp. 353–61) **4419**.

John Stubbs

5757. PRESCOTT, ANNE LAKE.   Getting a record: Stubbs, Singleton, and a 1579 almanac. SidJ (21:2) 2003, 51–7.

Henry Howard, Earl of Surrey

5758. EDWARDS, A. S. G.   Manuscripts of the verse of Henry Howard, Earl of Surrey. HLQ (67:2) 2004, 283–93.

5759. —— Surrey's Martial epigram: scribes and transmission. EngMS (12) 2005, 74–82.

5760. GUY-BRAY, STEPHEN.   Embracing Troy: Surrey's *Aeneid*. *In* (pp. 177–92) **4479**.

5761. PÉREZ FERNÁNDEZ, JOSÉ MARÍA.   'Wyatt resteth here': Surrey's republican elegy. RenSt (18:2) 2004, 208–38.

Richard Tarleton

5762. DÖRING, TOBIAS.   Writing performance: how to elegize Elizabethan actors. *See* **6157**.

Edmund Tilney

5763. McCluskey, Peter M.   Sir Edmond (*sic*) Tilney, *Sir Thomas More*, and the Netherlandic immigrant community. *See* **6709.**

Richard Tottel

5764. Pérez Fernández, José María.   'Wyatt resteth here': Surrey's republican elegy. *See* **5761.**

5765. Thompson, John J.   Patch and repair and making do in manuscripts and texts associated with John Stow. *In* (pp. 353–61) **4419.**

William Turner (d.1568)

5766. Rydén, Mats.   William Turner as botanist and plant-name scholar. *In* (pp. 249–62) **1773.**

William Tyndale

5767. Dorgeloh, Heidrun.   Conjunction in sentence and discourse: sentence-initial *and* and discourse structure. *See* **1677.**

5768. Snare, Gerald.   Reading Tyndale's Bible. JMEMS (35:2) 2005, 289–325.

5769. —— William Tyndale among the demons. RenP (2003) 33–44.

Nicholas Udall

5770. Ardolino, Frank R.   'Sweete mistresse where as I loue you nothing at all': indeterminacy and ambiguity in *Roister Doister.* ExRC (31:1) 2005, 19–36.

Richard Verstegan (Richard Rowlands)

5771. Hamilton, Donna B.   Richard Verstegan and Catholic resistance: the encoding of antiquarianism and love. *In* (pp. 87–104) **5915.**

Lewis Wager

5772. Ben-Tsur, Dalia.   Early ramifications of theatrical iconoclasm: the conversion of Catholic biblical plays into Protestant drama. PartA (3:1) 2005, 43–56.

Thomas Watson

5773. Vallaro, Cristina.   La simbologia lunare nei canzonieri elisabettiani. *See* **5325.**

George Whetstone

5774. Moore, Helen.   Of marriage, morals and civility. *In* (pp. 35–50) **5187.**

Isabella Whitney

5775. Ellinghausen, Laurie.   Literary property and the single woman in Isabella Whitney's *A Sweet Nosgay.* SELit (45:1) 2005, 1–22.

Thomas Whythorne

5776. Heale, Elizabeth.   Autobiography and authorship in Renaissance verse: chronicles of the self. (Bibl. 2004, 6049.) Rev. by Rudolph P. Almasy in SixCJ (36:1) 2005, 267–9.

Thomas Wilson (1525?–1581)

5777. Schmitt-Kilb, Christian.   '*Never was the Albion Nation without Poetrie*': Poetik, Rhetorik und Nation im England der frühen Neuzeit. *See* **7343.**

Sir Thomas Wyatt

5778. BRIGDEN, SUSAN; WOOLFSON, JONATHAN. Thomas Wyatt in Italy. RQ (58:2) 2005, 464–511.

5779. PÉREZ FERNÁNDEZ, JOSÉ MARÍA. 'Wyatt resteth here': Surrey's republican elegy. *See* 5761.

5780. POWELL, JASON. 'For Caesar's I am': Henrician diplomacy and representations of King and country in Thomas Wyatt's poetry. SixCJ (36:2) 2005, 415–31.

5781. —— Puttenham's *Arte of English Poesie* and Thomas Wyatt's diplomacy. *See* 5614.

5782. —— Thomas Wyatt's poetry in embassy: Egerton 2711 and the production of literary manuscripts abroad. HLQ (67:2) 2004, 261–82.

5783. ROE, JOHN. Shakespeare, sonnets, and the 51st Psalm. *In* (pp. 197–206) 3756.

WILLIAM SHAKESPEARE
Editions and Textual Criticism

5784. ANON. Shakespeare in the nineteenth century. BC (54:3) 2005, 335–56 (review-article).

5785. —— (reviser). Henry VI, part one; Henry VI, part two; Henry VI, part three. Ed. by Lawrence V. Ryan, *et al*. With new and updated critical essays and a revised bibliography. *See* 6433.

5786. —— Love's labor's lost. Ed. by John Arthos. With new and updated critical essays and a revised bibliography. *See* 6521.

5787. —— The tragedy of Titus Andronicus; The life of Timon of Athens. Ed. by Sylvan Barnet and Maurice Charney. With new and updated critical essays and a revised bibliography. *See* 6777.

5788. BERTINETTI, PAOLO (ed. and trans.). Amleto. *See* 6301.

5789. BEST, MICHAEL. 'Is this a vision? Is this a dream?': finding new dimensions in Shakespeare's texts. TextT (14:1) 2005, 1–12.

5790. BEVINGTON, DAVID M. (ed.). Antony and Cleopatra. *See* 6255.

5791. BILLINGS, TIMOTHY. Squashing the 'shard-borne beetle' crux: a hard case with a few pat readings. *See* 6532.

5792. BÖGELS, THEO. 'Fit for the pocket': Thomas Johnson's edition of *The Tempest. See* 6743.

5793. BUTLER, MARTIN (ed.). Cymbeline. *See* 6290.

5794. CARROLL, WILLIAM C. (ed.). The two gentlemen of Verona. *See* 6811.

5795. CARSON, CHRISTIE. Digitizing performance history: where do we go from here? *See* 1103.

5796. CHANDLER, DAVID. The 'salt-fish' crux in *The Merry Wives of Windsor. See* 6614.

5797. CHARTIER, ROGER. Crossing borders in early modern Europe: sociology of texts and literature. Trans. by Maurice Elton. *See* 6525.

5798. COOK, HARDY M. Unnoticed variant reading in Q1 *Lucrece*, 1594. *See* 6680.

5799. DUTTON, RICHARD. 'Methinks the truth should live from age to age': the dating and contexts of *Henry V*. See **6418.**

5800. EDGECOMBE, RODNEY STENNING. Feste's 'leman' in *Twelfth Night*. See **6800.**

5801. —— Three proposed emendations. ShY (15) 2005, 405–14.

5802. ERNE, LUKAS. Words in space: the reproduction of texts and the semiotics of the page. See **4991.**

5803. —— KIDNIE, MARGARET JANE (eds). Textual performances: the modern reproduction of Shakespeare's drama. (Bibl. 2004, 6076.) Rev. by Tom Lockwood in Library (6:3) 2005, 346–8; by Richard Rowland in CamQ (34:1) 2005, 79–85; by Arthur F. Kinney in HLQ (68:3) 2005, 561–6; by Suzanne Gossett in ShQ (56:4) 2005, 479–81; by Sarah Werner in PRes (10:3) 2005, 109–13.

5804. EVANS, G. BLAKEMORE. 'The shard-borne [-born] beetle', *Macbeth*, 3.2.42–43. See **6543.**

5805. FOAKES, R. A. Performance and text: *King Lear*. See **6464.**

5806. GRIVELET, MICHEL, et al. (gen. ed.). Tragicomédies: II, *Périclès, Le Conte d'hiver, La Tempête*. Poésies: *Vénus et Adonis, Le Viol de Lucrèce*, sonnets. Ed. and trans. by Victor Bourgy. (Bibl. 2004, 6186, where details incomplete.) Rev. by Ruth Morse in TLS, 14 Feb. 2003, 31.

5807. HILSKÝ, MARTIN (ed. and trans.). William Shakespeare, *Král Lear/King Lear*. Afterword by Bohuslav Mánek. See **6467.**

5808. HINTEN, MARVIN D. Shakespeare's *Pericles*. See **6672.**

5809. HUNT, MAURICE. 'Forward backward' time and the Apocalypse in *Hamlet*. See **6332.**

5810. ICHIKAWA, MARIKO. '*Maluolio within*': acting on the threshold between onstage and offstage spaces. See **6803.**

5811. JANSOHN, CHRISTA. The Shakespeare apocrypha: a reconsideration. See **6389.**

5812. KAMPS, IVO; RABER, KAREN (eds). *Measure for Measure*: texts and contexts. See **6584.**

5813. KINNEY, ARTHUR F. Editing instability. HLQ (68:3) 2005, 561–6 (review-article).

5814. MCEACHERN, CLAIRE (ed.). The tragedy of King Lear. See **6477.**

5815. MENZER, PAUL. 'Come upon your Q': *Richard III*, cue-line variants, and memorial error. See **6514.**

5816. MILES, ROBERT. Trouble in the republic of letters: the reception of the Shakespeare forgeries. See **8736.**

5817. MOWAT, BARBARA A.; WERSTINE, PAUL (eds). Titus Andronicus. See **6786.**

5818. MUELLER, MARTIN. *The Nameless Shakespeare*. TextT (14:1) 2005, 61–70. (Internet ed.)

5819. MURPHY, ANDREW. Shakespeare goes to Scotland: a brief history of Scottish editions. In (pp. 157–71) **6561.**

5820. ORGEL, STEPHEN.   Imagining Shakespeare: a history of texts and visions. (Bibl. 2004, 6097.) Rev. by Ann Thompson in CLIO (34:3) 2005, 386–9; by Stuart Sillars in ShQ (56:2) 2005, 240–3; by Gabriele Rippl in SJ (141) 2005, 233–9.

5821. PROUDFOOT, RICHARD.   'Is there more toyle?': editing Shakespeare for the twenty-first century. SStudT (42) 2004, 1–27.

5822. RAFFEL, BURTON (ed.).   Othello. With an essay by Harold Bloom. See **6657.**

5823. ——   The taming of the shrew. With an essay by Harold Bloom. See **6738.**

5824. RASMUSSEN, ERIC.   The year's contributions to Shakespeare studies: 3, Editions and textual studies. ShS (57) 2004, 335–44.

5825. ——   The year's contributions to Shakespeare studies: 3, Editions and textual studies. ShS (58) 2005, 343–57.

5826. —— PROUDFOOT, G. R. (eds).   The two noble kinsmen. See **6817.**

5827. SERPIERI, ALESSANDRO.   The translator as editor: the Quartos of Hamlet. In (pp. 167–83) **5975.**

5828. SHERBO, ARTHUR.   The appendix to Edmond Malone's 1790 Shakespeare, the 1821 Boswell–Malone Shakespeare, and Elizabethan language. PBSA (99:2) 2005, 295–308.

5829. ——   James Boswell's editing of, and contributions to, the 1821 Boswell–Malone Shakespeare. See **8413.**

5830. SILLARS, STUART.   Seeing, studying, performing: Bell's Edition of Shakespeare and performative reading. PRes (10:3) 2005, 18–27.

5831. STERN, TIFFANY.   Making Shakespeare: from stage to page. (Bibl. 2004, 6108.) Rev. by Tobias Döring in SJ (141) 2005, 274–5; by Sarah Werner in PRes (10:3) 2005, 109–13.

5832. STEWART, STANLEY.   The short happy life of the 'Old Corrector': John Payne Collier. See **10539.**

5833. TAUNTON, NINA; HART, VALERIE.   King Lear, King James and the Gunpowder Treason of 1605. See **6482.**

5834. TAYLOR, GARY.   The cultural politics of Maybe. In (pp. 242–58) **5915.**

5835. THOMPSON, ANN; McMULLAN, GORDON (eds).   In Arden: editing Shakespeare: essays in honour of Richard Proudfoot. (Bibl. 2004, 6111.) Rev. by Richard Knowles in ShQ (56:4) 2005, 498–501.

5836. WATTS, CEDRIC.   The Tempest, IV.i.123–124: wise or wife? See **6771.**

5837. WELLS, STANLEY; TAYLOR, GARY (gen. eds).   The complete works. (Bibl. 1989, 3473.) Oxford; New York: OUP, 2005. pp. lxxv, 1344. (Second ed.: first ed. 1986.)

5838. WEST, ANTHONY JAMES.   The Shakespeare First Folio: the history of the book: vol. 2, A new worldwide census of First Folios. (Bibl. 2004, 6116.) Rev. by Arthur Sherbo in PBSA (99:1) 2005, 171–5; by William Proctor Williams in NQ (52:1) 2005, 120–1.

5839. WILLIAMS, GEORGE WALTON.   Scene individable: the battle of Birnam Wood. See **6576.**

General Scholarship and Criticism

5840. ACKROYD, PETER. Shakespeare: the biography. London: Chatto & Windus, 2005. pp. xiii, 546. Rev. by Peter Holland in TLS, 28 Oct. 2005, 24–5; by Cynthia L. Haven in BkW, 18 Dec. 2005, 13.

5841. ALEXANDER, CATHERINE M. S. (ed.). Shakespeare and language. Cambridge; New York: CUP, 2004. pp. viii, 294. Rev. by Héloïse Sénéchal in TLS, 9 Sept. 2005, 26; by Hardin Aasand in RQ (58:3) 2005, 1046–8.

5842. —— Shakespeare and politics. Cambridge; New York: CUP, 2004. pp. viii, 268. Rev. by John Bienz in RQ (58:3) 2005, 1045–6.

5843. ALMEIDA FLOR, JOÃO. Shakespeare in the Bay of Portugal: a tribute to Luis Cardim (1879–1958). In (pp. 243–54) **5874.**

5844. ANDERSON, LINDA. A place in the story: servants and service in Shakespeare's plays. Newark: Delaware UP, 2005. pp. 339.

5845. —— LULL, JANIS (eds). 'A certain text': close readings and textual studies on Shakespeare and others in honor of Thomas Clayton. (Bibl. 2004, 6119.) Rev. by Christopher Baker in SixCJ (35:4) 2004, 1236–7.

5846. ANDERSON, MARK. 'Shakespeare' by another name: the life of Edward de Vere, Earl of Oxford, the man who was Shakespeare. Foreword by Derek Jacobi. New York: Gotham, 2005. pp. xxxvi, 598, (plates) 6.

5847. ANDREWS, RICHARD. Shakespeare and Italian comedy. In (pp. 123–49) **5954.**

5848. ARCHER, JOHN MICHAEL. Citizen Shakespeare: freemen, city wives, and aliens in the language of the plays. Basingstoke; New York: Palgrave Macmillan, 2005. pp. xii, 211. (Early modern cultural studies.)

5849. ASQUITH, CLARE. The Catholic Bard: Shakespeare & the 'old religion'. Cweal (132:12) 2005, 10–14.

5850. —— Shadowplay: the hidden beliefs and coded politics of William Shakespeare. New York: PublicAffairs, 2005. pp. xvii, 348. Rev. by Jesse Lander in Cweal (132:13) 2005, 25–6; by Harold Love in TLS, 14 Oct. 2005, 29; by Philip Crispin in ANCW (193:18) 2005, 28–30.

5851. ATKINS, ERIC W. References to Jonson in scholarship on Shakespeare. See **7533.**

5852. BASSNETT, SUSAN. Engendering anew: Shakespeare, gender and translation. In (pp. 53–67) **5975.**

5853. BAXTER, JOHN. J. V. Cunningham's Shakespeare glosses. See **15982.**

5854. BENATTI, ROBIN; MATERZANINI, FRANCESCA (trans). Shakespeare politico: drammi storici, drammi romani, tragedie. By Ekkehart Krippendorff. Rome: Fazi, 2005. pp. x, 346. (Le terre/scritture, 115.) (Trans. of bibl. 1992, 4822.)

5855. BERGERON, DAVID M. Pageants, masques, and history. In (pp. 41–56) **5964.**

5856. BERLEY, MARC (ed.). Reading the Renaissance: ideas and idioms from Shakespeare to Milton. (Bibl. 2004, 6125.) Rev. by Stephen Smith in SixCJ (35:4) 2004, 1167–9.

5857. BICKS, CAROLINE. Midwiving subjects in Shakespeare's England. (Bibl. 2004, 6127.) Rev. by Mary Elizabeth Fissell in BHM (79:1) 2005, 125–6; by Theresa Krier in CLIO (34:3) 2005, 356–60.

5858. BIRUS, HENDRIK. 'William! Stern der schönsten Höhe ...': Goethes Shakespeare. SJ (141) 2005, 34–50.

5859. BLINN, HANSJÜRGEN; SCHMIDT, WOLF GERHARD. Shakespeare-deutsch: Bibliographie der Übersetzungen und Bearbeitungen: zugleich Bestandsnachweis der Shakespeare-Übersetzungen der Herzogin-Anna-Amalia-Bibliothek Weimar. Berlin: Schmidt, 2003. pp. 279. Rev. by Sabine Schülting in SJ (141) 2005, 251–3.

5860. BOLTZ, INGEBORG. Verzeichnis der Shakespeare-Inszenierungen und Bibliographie der Kritiken: Spielzeit 2003/2004. See **6137**.

5861. BOTTOMS, JANET. 'To read aright': representations of Shakespeare for children. ChildLit (32) 2004, 1–14.

5862. BRENNAN, MICHAEL G. English contact with Europe. In (pp. 53–97) **5954**.

5863. BRIGGS, JULIA. Virginia Woolf reads Shakespeare; or, Her silence on Master William. See **20318**.

5864. BRÖNNIMANN, WERNER. Think-along edition: the bilingual *Studienausgabe* of Shakespeare. In (pp. 184–98) **5975**.

5865. BROWN, SARAH ANNES. The prequel as palinode: Mary Cowden Clarke's *Girlhood of Shakespeare's Heroines*. See **10450**.

5866. BRUSTER, DOUGLAS. Shakespeare and the question of culture: early modern literature and the cultural turn. (Bibl. 2004, 6135.) Rev. by Crystal Bartolovich in CLIO (34:4) 2005, 466–72.

5867. BRYDON, DIANA; MAKARYK, IRENA R. (eds). Shakespeare in Canada: a world elsewhere. (Bibl. 2004, 6136.) Rev. by Graham Harley in LRC (11:6) 2003, 5–7; by Jessica Slights in ShQ (55:4) 2004, 486–8; by Louise Harrington in BJCS (17:1) 2004, 155–6; by Jenn Stephenson in TJ (57:2) 2005, 322–3; by Herbert Weil in SNL (55:1) 2005, 16.

5868. BURROW, COLIN. Who wouldn't buy it? LRB (27:2) 2005, 9–11 (review-article). (Shakespeare biography and cultural materialism.)

5869. BURWICK, FREDERICK. Coleridge on Shakespeare, Goethe and Schiller. See **10469**.

5870. BUTLER, COLIN. The practical Shakespeare: the plays in practice and on the page. Athens: Ohio UP, 2005. pp. 205.

5871. CALBI, MAURIZIO. Approximate bodies: gender and power in early modern drama and anatomy. See **7651**.

5872. CALVO, CLARA. Shakespeare and Cervantes in 1916: the politics of language. In (pp. 78–94) **6000**.

5873. CARVALHO HOMEM, RUI. Translating Shakespeare for the twenty-first century: introduction. In (pp. 1–24) **5874**.

5874. —— HOENSELAARS, TON (eds). Translating Shakespeare for the twenty-first century. Amsterdam; Atlanta, GA: Rodopi, 2004. pp. vii, 269. (DQR studies in literature, 35.) Rev. by Jonathan Hope in TLS, 19 & 26 Aug. 2005, 10–11.

5875. CAVELL, STANLEY. Disowning knowledge in seven plays of Shakespeare. (Bibl. 1993, 3963.) Cambridge; New York: CUP, 2003. pp. xvi, 250. (Revised ed.: first ed. 1993.) (Orig. pub. as *Disowning Knowledge in Six Plays of Shakespeare*.) Rev. by Gilles Monsarrat in EA (58:1) 2005, 107–8.

5876. CEFALU, PAUL. Revisionist Shakespeare: transitional ideologies in texts and contexts. Basingstoke; New York: Palgrave Macmillan, 2004. pp. 212.

5877. CHARNEY, MAURICE. Shakespeare's eloquence. *In* (pp. 99–112) 5167.

5878. CHAUDHURI, SUKANTA. Shakespeare's India. *In* (pp. 158–67) 6096.

5879. CHENEY, PATRICK GERARD. Shakespeare, national poet-playwright. Cambridge; New York: CUP, 2004. pp. xv, 319. Rev. by Christopher Burlinson in RES (56:226) 2005, 667–9; by Richard Dutton in ShQ (56:3) 2005, 371–4; by Bridget Gellert Lyons in RQ (58:4) 2005, 1446–8; by Jeanne A. Roberts in SpenR (36:3) 2005, 2–3.

5880. CIAVOLELLA, MASSIMO; COLEMAN, PATRICK (eds). Culture and authority in the baroque. Toronto; Buffalo, NY; London: Toronto UP for the Medieval Academy of America, 2005. pp. vi, 255. (UCLA Clark Memorial Library series.)

5881. CLAYTON, TOM; BROCK, SUSAN; FORÉS, VICENTE (eds). Shakespeare and the Mediterranean: the selected proceedings of the International Shakespeare Association World Congress, Valencia, 2001. (Bibl. 2004, 6143.) Rev. by Hardin Aasand in RQ (58:2) 2005, 740–2.

5882. COHEN, DEREK. Searching Shakespeare: studies in culture and authority. (Bibl. 2004, 6144.) Rev. by Jonathan Baldo in SStud (33) 2005, 214–17; by Gretchen E. Minton in ShQ (56:4) 2005, 507–9.

5883. COOK, ANN JENNALIE. J. Leeds Barroll, III: a tribute. MedRen (17) 2005, 21–6.

5884. COREN, PAMELA. Gurney's solace: Shakespeare, Jonson and Byrd. *See* 16844.

5885. CRAWFORD, ROBERT. The Bard: Ossian, Burns, and the shaping of Shakespeare. *In* (pp. 124–40) 6561.

5886. DA ROCHA AFONSO, MARIA JOÃO. From words to action: translating Shakespeare for the Portuguese stage. *In* (pp. 163–80) 5874.

5887. DAS, SISIR KUMAR. Shakespeare in Indian languages. *In* (pp. 47–73) 6096.

5888. DÁVIDHÁZI, PÉTER. Weimar, Shakespeare and the birth of Hungarian literary history. SJ (141) 2005, 98–118.

5889. DAVIES, MICHAEL. The Transubstantial Bard: Shakespeare and Catholicism. *In* (pp. 26–43) 3724.

5890. DAVIS, LLOYD. Sexual morality and critical traditions. *In* (pp. 219–29) 6000.

5891. —— (ed.). Shakespeare matters: history, teaching, performance. (Bibl. 2004, 6150.) Rev. by David Reinheimer in SixCJ (35:4) 2004, 1239–40; by Madhavi Menon in ShQ (56:2) 2005, 233–5.

5892. DAVIS, PHILIP. 'The future in the instant': Hazlitt's *Essay* and Shakespeare. *In* (pp. 43–55) 11245.

5893. DAWKINS, PETER. The Shakespeare enigma. London: Polair, 2004. pp. 477. Rev. by Brian Vickers in TLS, 19 & 26 Aug. 2005, 6–8.

5894. DELABASTITA, DIRK. Cross-language comedy in Shakespeare. Humor (18:2) 2005, 161–84.

5895. —— 'If I know the letters and the language': translation as a dramatic device in Shakespeare's plays. In (pp. 31–52) **5975.**

5896. —— Notes on Shakespeare in Dutch translation: historical perspectives. In (pp. 99–116) **5874.**

5897. —— Shakespeare and translation: a guide to further reading. In (pp. 289–306) **5975.**

5898. DE LEO, MADDALENA. Shakespeare and the Brontës: a comment. BrSt (30:2) 2005, 169–70.

5899. DEL SAPIO GARBERO, MARIA. Il bene ritrovato: le figlie di Shakespeare dal King Lear ai romances. Rome: Bulzoni, 2005. (Piccola biblioteca shakespeariana, 35.)

5900. DÉPRATS, JEAN-MICHEL. Translating Shakespeare's stagecraft. In (pp. 133–47) **5975.**

5901. —— Translation at the crossroads of the past and present. In (pp. 65–78) **5874.**

5902. DEVECMON, WILLIAM C. In re Shakespeare's 'legal acquirements': notes by an unbeliever therein. Union, NJ: Lawbook Exchange, 2004. pp. iii, 51.

5903. DE VOS, JOZEF. Discussing Ten oorlog: an interview with Tom Lanoye. ShY (15) 2005, 317–28.

5904. DÍAZ FERNÁNDEZ, JOSÉ RAMÓN. Shakespeare film and television derivatives: a bibliography. In (pp. 169–89) **13273.**

5905. —— Toward a survey of Shakespeare in Latin America. In (pp. 293–325) **5995.**

5906. DICKSON, ANDREW. The Rough Guide to Shakespeare: the plays, the poems, the life. Ed. by Jo Staines. London: Haymarket, 2005. pp. xi, 532. (Rough Guides.) Rev. by Robert Shore in TLS, 10 June 2005, 10.

5907. DISTILLER, NATASHA. South Africa, Shakespeare, and postcolonial culture. Lewiston, NY; Lampeter: Mellen Press, 2005. pp. iii, 301.

5908. DOLLIMORE, JONATHAN. Radical tragedy: religion, ideology, and power in the drama of Shakespeare and his contemporaries. (Bibl. 1990, 3804.) Durham, NC; London: Duke UP, 2004. pp. xcix, 312. (Third ed.: first ed. 1984.) Rev. by Jacob Blevins in Intertexts (8:2) 2004, 201–3; by R. V. Young in BJJ (12) 2005, 255–9.

5909. DROUET, PASCALE. Le vagabond dans l'Angleterre de Shakespeare; ou, L'art de contrefaire à la ville et à la scène. (Bibl. 2004, 6154.) Rev. by Sophie Chiari-Lasserre in CEl (66) 2004, 81–3; by Jean-Marie Maguin in EA (58:3) 2005, 356–8.

5910. DUFFIN, ROSS W. Shakespeare's songbook. Foreword by Stephen Orgel. (Bibl. 2004, 6155.) Rev. by William Lyons in TLS, 8 Apr. 2005, 20.

5911. DUNCAN-JONES, KATHERINE. Afterword: Stow's remains. *In* (pp. 157–63) **5746.**

5912. DUROT-BOUCÉ, ELIZABETH. Tours et détours: William Henry Ireland, de Shakespeare au gothique. *See* **8733.**

5913. DUTTON, RICHARD. Shakespeare and Lancaster. *In* (pp. 143–68) **5914.**

5914. —— FINDLAY, ALISON; WILSON, RICHARD (eds). Region, religion, and patronage: Lancastrian Shakespeare. Manchester; New York: Manchester UP, 2003. pp. xiii, 258. Rev. by Verena Olejniczak Lobsien in SJ (141) 2005, 239–43; by Park Honan in NQ (52:3) 2005, 404–6.

5915. —— —— —— Theatre and religion: Lancastrian Shakespeare. Basingstoke; New York: Palgrave Macmillan, 2003. pp. xiii, 267. Rev. by Geoff Ridden in LitH (14:2) 2005, 81–2; by Verena Olejniczak Lobsien in SJ (141) 2005, 239–43; by Park Honan in NQ (52:3) 2005, 404–6.

5916. —— HOWARD, JEAN E. (eds). A companion to Shakespeare's works: vol. 1, The tragedies. (Bibl. 2004, 6158.) Rev. by Jorge Luis Bueno Alonso in SEDERI (14) 2004, 249–64.

5917. —— —— A companion to Shakespeare's works: vol. 2, The histories. (Bibl. 2004, 6159.) Rev. by Jorge Luis Bueno Alonso in SEDERI (14) 2004, 249–64.

5918. —— —— A companion to Shakespeare's works: vol. 3, The comedies. (Bibl. 2004, 6160.) Rev. by Jorge Luis Bueno Alonso in SEDERI (14) 2004, 249–64.

5919. —— —— A companion to Shakespeare's works: vol. 4, The poems, problem comedies, late plays. (Bibl. 2004, 6161.) Rev. by Jorge Luis Bueno Alonso in SEDERI (14) 2004, 249–64.

5920. DYER, TINA. Metaphysics and the mask: symbol of the Wildean aesthetic. *See* **12383.**

5921. EDWARDS, PAUL. Drift: performing the relics of intention. TheatreA (56) 2003, 1–53.

5922. ELLIS, DAVID. Biographical uncertainty and Shakespeare. EC (55:3) 2005, 193–208 (review-article). (Critical opinion.)

5923. ERNE, LUKAS. Shakespeare as literary dramatist. (Bibl. 2004, 6165.) Rev. by Lois Kim in SixCJ (36:1) 2005, 195–7; by Douglas A. Brooks in SStud (33) 2005, 221–36; by F. W. Brownlow in ELN (42:4) 2005, 80–2; by Gerald Downs in ShY (15) 2005, 383–95; by Richard Rowland in CamQ (34:1) 2005, 79–85; by Sonia Massai in SJ (141) 2005, 243–5; by Andrew Murphy in MedRen (18) 2005, 271–7.

5924. EVETT, DAVID. Discourses of service in Shakespeare's England. Basingstoke; New York: Palgrave Macmillan, 2005. pp. viii, 286.

5925. FABISZAK, JACEK; GIBIŃSKA, MARTA; NAWROCKA, EWA (eds). Czytanie Szekspira. (Reading Shakespeare.) Gdańsk: Słowo/Obraz Terytoria, 2004. pp. 632.

5926. FALLON, ROBERT THOMAS. A theatergoer's guide to Shakespeare's characters. (Bibl. 2004, 6167.) Rev. by Daniel Leary in AmBR (26:3) 2005, 31, 36.

5927. FERNIE, EWAN. Introduction: Shakespeare, spirituality and contemporary criticism. *In* (pp. 1–27) **5928.**

5928. —— (ed.). Spiritual Shakespeares. London; New York: Routledge, 2005. pp. xix, 241. (Accents on Shakespeare.)

5929. FIELDS, BERTRAM. Players: the mysterious identity of William Shakespeare. New York: Regan, 2005. pp. xii, 308, (plates) 8.

5930. FINDLAY, ALISON; DUTTON, RICHARD. Introduction. In (pp. 1–31) 5914.

5931. FINN, PATRICK. The politics of culture: the play's the thing. In (pp. 7–21) 13273.

5932. FITZPATRICK, JOAN. Shakespeare, Spenser and the contours of Britain: reshaping the Atlantic archipelago. Hatfield: UP of Hertfordshire, 2004. pp. x, 182. Rev. by Tom MacFaul in NQ (52:4) 2005, 533–4; by Curtis Perry in RQ (58:2) 2005, 733–4; by Virginia Mason Vaughan in SpenR (36:1) 2005, 4–6.

5933. FLEISSNER, ROBERT F. Shakespeare and Africa: the Dark Lady of his sonnets revamped and other Africa-related associations. Philadelphia, PA: XLibris, 2005. pp. 130.

5934. FOAKES, R. A. Shakespeare and violence. (Bibl. 2004, 6170.) Rev. by Katherine West Scheil in TheatreS (46:1) 2005, 161–3; by Susan Zimmerman in MLR (100:4) 2005, 1087–8; by Nicholas R. Moschovakis in ShQ (56:2) 2005, 235–7; by Duncan Salkeld in NQ (52:1) 2005, 118–19; by Ricardo Quinones in MedRen (18) 2005, 282–5.

5935. FORKER, CHARLES R. How did Shakespeare come by his books? ShY (14) 2004, 109–20.

5936. —— Royal carnality and illicit desire in the English history plays of the 1590s. See 5245.

5937. FRANSSEN, PAUL. The (absent) Dutch Shakespeare cult. ShY (15) 2005, 211–32.

5938. GARBER, MARJORIE. Shakespeare after all. New York: Pantheon, 2004. pp. xii, 989. Rev. by Anston Bosman in ShQ (56:3) 2005, 376–9; by Eric Rasmussen in CommRev (3:4) 2005, 51–3; by John Mulryan in Cithara (45:1) 2005, 44–5.

5939. GILLESPIE, STUART. Shakespeare's reading of modern European literature. In (pp. 98–122) 5954.

5940. GODSHALK, W. L. Shakespeare and the problem of literary character. PsyArt (9) 2005.

5941. GONZÁLEZ DÍAZ, VICTORINA. Adjective comparison in Renaissance English. See 1660.

5942. GOTTSCHALL, JONATHAN; WILSON, DAVID SLOAN (eds). The literary animal: evolution and the nature of narrative. Forewords by E. O. Wilson and Frederick Crews. See 14807.

5943. GOY-BLANQUET, DOMINIQUE. Elizabethan historiography and Shakespeare's sources. In (pp. 57–70) 5964.

5944. —— Shakespeare's early history plays: from chronicle to stage. (Bibl. 2004, 6183.) Rev. by Lawrence Manley in ShQ (55:4) 2004, 466–9; by Fritz Levy in CompDr (38:2/3) 2004, 329–32; by Mark Bayer in LitH (14:2) 2005, 80–1; by Enno Ruge in SJ (141) 2005, 245–9; by Gilles Monsarrat in EA (58:3) 2005, 354–5; by Thomas A. Pendleton in SNL (55:3) 2005, 68.

5945. GREENBLATT, STEPHEN. Will in the world: how Shakespeare became Shakespeare. (Bibl. 2004, 6185.) Rev. by John Paul Spiro in UC (24) 2004, 116–19; by Thomas A. Pendleton in SNL (54:4) 2004/05, 107–8; by Franco Marenco in Indice (2005:11) 18; by Colin Burrow in LRB (27:2) 2005, 9–11; by Alastair Fowler in TLS, 4 Feb. 2005, 3–5; by Sarah Kennedy in Shen (55:1) 2005, 203–6; by Andrew Hadfield in TexP (19:2) 2005, 408–12; by Rebecca Gillis in PartA (3:2) 2005, 189–95; by Joan Bridgman in ContRev (287:1675) 2005, 116–17; by David Ellis in EC (55:3) 2005, 193–208; by Lois Potter in ShQ (56:3) 2005, 374–6; by John B. Breslin in ANCW (192:10) 2005, 17–18; by Daniel Leary in AmBR (26:5) 2005, 21, 26; by Maurice Charney in SNL (55:2) 2005, 60; by Eric Rasmussen in CommRev (3:4) 2005, 51–3.

5946. GREENE, THOMAS M. Poetry, signs, and magic. Newark: Delaware UP, 2005. pp. 327.

5947. GREINER, NORBERT. Shakespeare im Schatten der Klassik. SJ (141) 2005, 81–97.

5948. GUTTAL, VIJAYA. Translation and performance of Shakespeare in Kannada. *In* (pp. 106–19) **6096**.

5949. HABIB, IMTIAZ. Shakespeare's spectral Turks: the postcolonial poetics of a mimetic narrative. *See* **6650**.

5950. HABICHT, WERNER. Bildnisse aus der Geschichte der deutschen Shakespeare-Rezeption: ein Album in Birmingham. SJ (141) 2005, 150–7.

5951. HADFIELD, ANDREW. Introduction: Shakespeare and Renaissance Europe. *In* (pp. 1–20) **5954**.

5952. —— Shakespeare and Renaissance politics. London: Arden Shakespeare, 2004. pp. xii, 315. (Arden critical companions.) Rev. by Constance Jordan in ShQ (56:4) 2005, 487–9.

5953. —— Shakespeare, Spenser, and the Matter of Britain. (Bibl. 2004, 6188.) Rev. by Thomas Healy in TLS, 15 Apr. 2005, 24; by Tom MacFaul in NQ (52:1) 2005, 117–18.

5954. —— HAMMOND, PAUL (eds). Shakespeare and Renaissance Europe. London: Arden Shakespeare, 2004. pp. xxix, 314. (Arden Shakespeare companions.) Rev. by Lisa Hopkins in NQ (52:4) 2005, 536–7.

5955. HAMBURGER, MAIK. Translating and copyright. *In* (pp. 148–66) **5975**.

5956. HAMLIN, WILLIAM M. Tragedy and skepticism in Shakespeare's England. *See* **5143**.

5957. HAMMERSCHMIDT-HUMMEL, HILDEGARD (ed.). Die Shakespeare-Illustration (1594–2000): bildkünstlerische Darstellungen zu den Dramen William Shakespeares: Katalog, Geschichte, Funktion und Deutung; mit Künstlerlexikon, klassifizierter Bibliographie und Registern. Wiesbaden: Harrassowitz, 2003. 3 vols. pp. 1259. Rev. by Gabriele Rippl in SJ (141) 2005, 233–9.

5958. HAMMOND, PAUL. Figuring sex between men from Shakespeare to Rochester. (Bibl. 2004, 6189.) Rev. by Alan Stewart in SStud (33) 2005, 264–8; by Nick Kneale in MLR (100:4) 2005, 1084–6.

5959. HARMON, A. G.   Eternal bonds, true contracts: law and nature in Shakespeare's problem plays. (Bibl. 2004, 6191.) Rev. by Jonathan Hart in RQ (58:3) 2005, 1043–5.

5960. HARRIS, JONATHAN GIL.   Sick economies: drama, mercantilism and disease in Shakespeare's England. (Bibl. 2004, 6192.) Rev. by Joyce Boro in TMR, Sept. 2005; by Pramod K. Nayar in SixCJ (36:2) 2005, 631–2; by Byron Nelson in SCN (63:1/2) 2005, 47–9; by Katherine Rowe in SStud (33) 2005, 268–71; by Stephen Deng in ShY (15) 2005, 447–53; by Ernest B. Gilman in RQ (58:2) 2005, 736–7.

5961. HART, JONATHAN.   Columbus, Shakespeare, and the interpretation of the New World. (Bibl. 2004, 6193.) Rev. by Peter C. Herman in CLS (42:2) 2005, 330–3.

5962. HASSEL, RUDOLPH CHRIS, JR.   Shakespeare's religious language: a dictionary. See **1957.**

5963. HATTAWAY, MICHAEL.   The Shakespearean history play. In (pp. 3–24) **5964.**

5964. —— (ed.).   The Cambridge companion to Shakespeare's history plays. Cambridge; New York: CUP, 2002. pp. xvii, 283. (Cambridge companions to literature.) Rev. by Douglas Bruster in ShQ (55:3) 2004, 328–30.

5965. HAWKES, TERENCE.   The Prince's Choice. In (pp. 267–78) **5167.**

5966. HAYS, MICHAEL L.   Shakespearean tragedy as chivalric romance: rethinking Macbeth, Hamlet, Othello, and King Lear. (Bibl. 2004, 6763.) Rev. by Julia Matthews in SixCJ (36:2) 2005, 489–91.

5967. HEALY, THOMAS.   Queene and country. See **5699.**

5968. HIRSH, JAMES.   Shakespeare and the history of soliloquies. (Bibl. 2004, 6199.) Rev. by Robert C. Evans in CompDr (38:1) 2004, 123–7; by Paul J. Hecht in ShB (22:4) 2004, 149–51; by Margaret Maurer in ShQ (56:4) 2005, 504–7.

5969. HOENSELAARS, A. J.   Shakespeare and the early modern history play. In (pp. 25–40) **5964.**

5970. —— (ed.).   Shakespeare's history plays: performance, translation and adaptation in Britain and abroad. Foreword by Dennis Kennedy. Cambridge; New York: CUP, 2004. pp. xiv, 287. Rev. by Rachel Wifall in RQ (58:3) 2005, 1048–9.

5971. HOENSELAARS, TON.   Introduction. In (pp. 1–27) **5975.**

5972. ——   Shakespeare and the Low Countries: an introduction. ShY (15) 2005, 1–8.

5973. ——   Shakespeare's histories and European cultural identity. LittPr (15:30) 2005, 67–78.

5974. ——   'There is tremendous poetry in killings': traditions of Shakespearean translation and adaptation in the Low Countries. In (pp. 79–98) **5874.**

5975. —— (ed.).   Shakespeare and the language of translation. London: Arden Shakespeare, 2004. pp. xiv, 346. (Shakespeare and language.) Rev. by Jonathan Hope in TLS, 19 & 26 Aug. 2005, 10–11; by Jorge Luis Bueno Alonso in Atl (27:2) 2005, 169–76.

5976. —— Rijser, David. From Homer to Shakespeare: an interview with H. J. de Roy van Zuydewijn. ShY (15) 2005, 299–316.

5977. Holland, Peter. Dramatizing the dramatist. See 13042.

5978. Hope, Jonathan. Shakespeare's grammar. London: Arden Shakespeare, 2003. pp. xiii, 210. Rev. by Jean-Paul Debax in EA (58:2) 2005, 200–2.

5979. —— Thou art translated. TLS, 19 & 26 Aug. 2005, 10–11 (review-article).

5980. Hopkins, Lisa. Beginning Shakespeare. Manchester; New York: Manchester UP, 2005. pp. viii, 212. (Beginnings.)

5981. Hunt, Maurice. Shakespeare's religious allusiveness: its play and tolerance. (Bibl. 2004, 6209.) Rev. by John S. Mebane in RQ (58:3) 2005, 1042–3.

5982. Hyland, Peter. Look about You, anonymity, and the value of theatricality. See 5263.

5983. Ilsemann, Hartmut. Some statistical observations on speech lengths in Shakespeare's plays. SJ (141) 2005, 158–68.

5984. Im, Yeeyon. The pitfalls of intercultural discourse: the case of Yukio Ninagawa. ShB (22:4) 2004, 7–30.

5985. Jackson, Ken. Separate theaters: Bethlem ('Bedlam') Hospital and the Shakespearean stage. Newark: Delaware UP, 2005. pp. 309. Rev. by Monica Calabritto in ShQ (56:4) 2005, 484–7.

5986. Jackson, Russell. Jocza Savits: organic Shakespeare for the folk. In (pp. 140–51) 6000.

5987. James, Brenda; Rubinstein, William D. Truth will out: unmasking the real Shakespeare. Harlow: Pearson Education, 2005. pp. xxiv, 360. Rev. by Alan H. Nelson in TLS, 25 Nov. 2005, 28; by MacDonald P. Jackson in SNL (55:2) 2005, 40.

5988. Johnová, Lucie. Patterns of crossdressing in Shakespeare's comedies. In (pp. 65–70) 3753.

5989. Joseph, Miriam. Shakespeare's use of the arts of language. Philadelphia, PA: Dry, 2005. pp. xiv, 423.

5990. Kapadia, Parmita. Shakespeare transposed: the British stage on the post-colonial screen. In (pp. 42–56) 13273.

5991. Karremann, Isabel; Roder, Carolin. Meaning by critics: Klassikerverehrung als Ausschlusspolitik. SJ (141) 2005, 119–32.

5992. Keller, James R.; Stratyner, Leslie (eds). Almost Shakespeare: reinventing his works for cinema and television. See 13273.

5993. Kirby, David. Give me life coarse and rank. See 12327.

5994. Kishi, Tetsuo; Bradshaw, Graham. Shakespeare in Japan. London; New York: Continuum, 2005. pp. xii, 153.

5995. Kliman, Bernice W.; Santos, Rick J. (eds). Latin American Shakespeares. Madison, NJ: Fairleigh Dickinson UP, 2005. pp. 347.

5996. Knowles, Ric. Shakespeare and Canada: essays on production, translation and adaptation. (Bibl. 2004, 6219.) Rev. by W. B. Worthen in CanTR (121) 2005, 86–7.

5997. Ko, Yu Jin. Mutability and division on Shakespeare's stage. Newark: Delaware UP, 2004. pp. 223. Rev. by Linda McJannet in RQ (58:3) 2005, 1040–2.

5998. Korda, Natasha. Shakespeare's domestic economies: gender and property in early modern England. (Bibl. 2004, 6221.) Rev. by Phyllis Rackin in ShQ (56:1) 2005, 113–16.

5999. Kujawińska-Courtney, Krystyna. Shakespeare's sources in past and present. In (pp. 122–9) **3756.**

6000. Lambert, Ladina Bezzola; Engler, Balz (eds). Shifting the scene: Shakespeare in European culture. Newark: Delaware UP, 2004. pp. 308.

6001. Lanier, Douglas. Shakespeare and modern popular culture. (Bibl. 2004, 6222.) Rev. by Maria Cristina Fumagalli in JSBC (12:1) 2005, 79–81; by Eric S. Mallin in ShQ (56:1) 2005, 101–4.

6002. Laroque, François. Shakespeare's imaginary geography. In (pp. 193–219) **5954.**

6003. Lehmann, Courtney; Starks, Lisa S. (eds). Spectacular Shakespeare: critical theory and popular cinema. (Bibl. 2004, 6225.) Rev. by Ramona Wray in ShQ (55:4) 2004, 494–6.

6004. León Alfar, Cristina. Fantasies of female evil: the dynamics of gender and power in Shakespearean tragedy. (Bibl. 2004, 6226.) Rev. by Frances Teague in MLR (100:2) 2005, 484–5; by Cristina Malcolmson in ShQ (56:1) 2005, 110–12.

6005. Levenson, Jill L. Shakespeare in drama since 1990: vanishing act. See **13067.**

6006. Levith, Murray J. Shakespeare in China. (Bibl. 2004, 6227.) Rev. by Andrew Schonebaum in ShY (15) 2005, 432–5.

6007. Lewis, Peter B. Wittgenstein, Tolstoy, and Shakespeare. PhilL (29:2) 2005, 241–55.

6008. Lupton, Julia Reinhard. Citizen-saints: Shakespeare and political theology. Chicago, IL; London: Chicago UP, 2005. pp. xi, 277.

6009. McAlindon, Tom. Shakespeare minus 'theory'. (Bibl. 2004, 6230.) Rev. by John Lee in MLR (100:3) 2005, 768–70.

6010. McCarthy, Penny. Some *quis*es and *quem*s: Shakespeare's true debt to Nashe. ShY (14) 2004, 175–92.

6011. McCrea, Scott. The case for Shakespeare: the end of the authorship question. Westport, CT; London: Praeger, 2005. pp. xiv, 280. Rev. by Brian Vickers in TLS, 19 & 26 Aug. 2005, 6–8.

6012. McDonald, Russ (ed.). Shakespeare: an anthology of criticism and theory, 1945–2000. (Bibl. 2004, 6231.) Rev. by Adrian Streete in NQ (52:3) 2005, 409–10.

6013. Makaryk, Irena R. Shakespeare in the undiscovered bourn: Les Kurbas, Ukrainian Modernism, and early Soviet cultural politics. Toronto; Buffalo, NY; London: Toronto UP, 2004. pp. xx, 257. Rev. by Banụta Rubess in LRC (12:7) 2004, 8–9; by Spencer Golub in TJ (57:3) 2005, 546–7; by Oleh S. Ilnytzkyj in SlavR (64:4) 2005, 896–7.

6014. MALEY, WILLY. Nation, state, and empire in English Renaissance literature: Shakespeare to Milton. (Bibl. 2004, 6234.) Rev. by Rebecca Ann Bach in SpenR (36:1) 2005, 6–9.

6015. —— MURPHY, ANDREW. Introduction: then with Scotland first begin. *In* (pp. 1–19) **6561**.

6016. —— —— (eds). Shakespeare and Scotland. *See* **6561**.

6017. MALIM, RICHARD (ed.). Great Oxford: essays on the life and work of Edward de Vere, 17th Earl of Oxford, 1550–1604. *See* **5602**.

6018. MAROTTI, ARTHUR F. Shakespeare and Catholicism. *In* (pp. 218–41) **5915**.

6019. MARRAPODI, MICHELE (ed.). Shakespeare, Italy and intertextuality. Manchester; New York: Manchester UP, 2004. pp. ix, 278. Rev. by Paul Dean in RES (56:227) 2005, 790–2.

6020. MARTINDALE, CHARLES; TAYLOR, A. B. (eds). Shakespeare and the Classics. (Bibl. 2004, 6238.) Rev. by Adrian Poole in TLS, 29 July 2005, 10–11; by Joost Daalder in RES (56:226) 2005, 669–71; by Owen Williams in ShQ (56:4) 2005, 481–4; by Michael Anderson in TRI (30:3) 2005, 304.

6021. MARTINEAU, JANE (ed.). Shakespeare in art. (Bibl. 2003, 5881.) Rev. by Gabriele Rippl in SJ (141) 2005, 233–9.

6022. MATEI-CHESNOIU, MONICA. 'The Globe': Romanian poetry and Shakespeare's histories. *In* (pp. 327–43) **12868**.

6023. MAYER, JEAN-CHRISTOPHE. 'This Papist and his poet': Shakespeare's Lancastrian kings and Robert Parsons's *Conference about the Next Succession*. *In* (pp. 116–29) **5915**.

6024. MEAGHER, JOHN C. Pursuing Shakespeare's dramaturgy: some contexts, resources, and strategies in his playmaking. (Bibl. 2004, 6239.) Rev. by Thomas Fulton in RQ (58:1) 2005, 344–5.

6025. METZIDAKIS, STAMOS; YOUNG, REGINA M. Hugo, Shakespeare et l'enseignement des langues vivantes. NCFrS (31:1/2) 2002/03, 9–26.

6026. MILLER, DAVID LEE. Dreams of the burning child: sacrificial sons and the father's witness. (Bibl. 2004, 6240.) Rev. by Judith Haber in CLIO (34:3) 2005, 338–41; by Suzanne Verderber in SStud (33) 2005, 289–94.

6027. MILWARD, PETER. Shakespeare's Jesuit schoolmasters. *In* (pp. 58–70) **5915**.

6028. MODENESSI, ALFREDO MICHEL. 'A double tongue within your mask': translating Shakespeare in/to Spanish-speaking Latin America. *In* (pp. 240–54) **5975**.

6029. MORSE, RUTH. Barbarian! TLS, 19 & 26 Aug. 2005, 9 (review-article). (French reception of Shakespeare.)

6030. —— Children's hours: Shakespeare, the Lambs, and French education. *In* (pp. 193–204) **6000**.

6031. —— The year's contributions to Shakespeare studies: 1, Critical studies. ShS (57) 2004, 299–325.

6032. —— The year's contributions to Shakespeare studies: 1, Critical studies. ShS (58) 2005, 308–34.

6033. Moss, Stephanie; Peterson, Kaara L. (eds).   Disease, diagnosis, and cure on the early modern stage. (Bibl. 2004, 6243.) Rev. by Samuel Glen Wong in RQ (58:2) 2005, 737–9; by Frédéric Delord in CEl (67) 2005, 87–91.

6034. Muirden, James.   Shakespeare well-versed: a rhyming guide to all his plays. New York: Walker, 2004. pp. 224.

6035. Murphy, Andrew.   Shakespeare among the workers. ShS (58) 2005, 107–17.

6036. —— Shakespeare in print: a history and chronology of Shakespeare publishing. (Bibl. 2004, 6244.) Rev. in BC (54:3) 2005, 335–56; by Catherine S. Cox in SixCJ (36:2) 2005, 508–9; by Sonia Massai in Library (6:2) 2005, 196–8; by Zachary Lesser in ShY (15) 2005, 415–21; by William Proctor Williams in NQ (52:3) 2005, 408–9; by R. A. Foakes in MedRen (18) 2005, 265–71; by Carlo M. Bajetta in Bibliofilia (107:2) 2005, 183–5.

6037. Murray, Barbara A. (ed.).   Shakespeare adaptations from the Restoration: five plays. Madison, NJ: Fairleigh Dickinson UP, 2005. pp. lxxxiii, 556.

6038. Naughton, John (ed.).   Shakespeare & the French poet: including an interview with Yves Bonnefoy. Chicago, IL; London: Chicago UP, 2004. pp. xix, 283. Rev. by John Taylor in HR (58:1) 2005, 161–6.

6039. Neely, Carol Thomas.   Distracted subjects: madness and gender in Shakespeare and early modern culture. (Bibl. 2004, 6245.) Rev. by Jeanne A. Roberts in ShY (15) 2005, 439–42; by Julie Robin Solomon in BHM (79:3) 2005, 576–7; by Tanya Pollard in RQ (58:3) 2005, 1028–30; by Monica Calabritto in ShQ (56:4) 2005, 484–7.

6040. Nelson, Alan H.   Shakespeare and the bibliophiles: from the earliest years to 1616. *In* (pp. 49–73) **19**.

6041. Nordlund, Marcus.   The problem of romantic love: Shakespeare and evolutionary psychology. *In* (pp. 107–25) **14807**.

6042. O'Neil, Catherine.   With Shakespeare's eyes: Pushkin's creative appropriation of Shakespeare. (Bibl. 2003, 5900.) Rev. by Ivan Eubanks in SEEJ (48:1) 2004, 111–13; by Helen Galbraith in MLR (100:3) 2005, 891–2; by Brett Cooke in SlavR (64:1) 2005, 223–4.

6043. Orkin, Martin.   Local Shakespeares: proximations and power. London; New York: Routledge, 2005. pp. x, 220.

6044. Palfrey, Simon.   Doing Shakespeare. London: Arden Shakespeare, 2005. pp. xiv, 300. Rev. by Emma Smith in TLS, 15 Apr. 2005, 29.

6045. Palmer, Daryl W.   Writing Russia in the age of Shakespeare. (Bibl. 2004, 6254.) Rev. by Richmond Barbour in RQ (58:3) 2005, 1038–40.

6046. Parker, Barbara L.   Plato's *Republic* and Shakespeare's Rome: a political study of the Roman works. (Bibl. 2004, 6500.) Rev. by Arthur F. Kinney in RQ (58:1) 2005, 342–3.

6047. Paster, Gail Kern.   Humoring the body: emotions and the Shakespearean stage. Chicago, IL; London: Chicago UP, 2004. pp. xv, 274. Rev. by Katharine Craik in TLS, 7 Jan. 2005, 23; by Ralph Berry in RES (56:226) 2005,

665-7; by Alberto Cacicedo in RQ (58:3) 2005, 1032-4; by Frédéric Delord in CEl (67) 2005, 87-91; by Loren M. Blinde in Comitatus (36) 2005, 274-6.

6048. PAULIN, ROGER. The critical reception of Shakespeare in Germany 1682-1914: native literature and foreign genius. Hildesheim: Olms, 2003. pp. viii, 532. (Anglistische und amerikanistische Texte und Studien, 11.) Rev. by Sabine Schülting in SJ (141) 2005, 251-3; by Andreas Höfele in ShQ (56:4) 2005, 489-91.

6049. PAYNE, MICHAEL (ed.). The Greenblatt reader. *See* **14960.**

6050. PFISTER, MANFRED. 'In states unborn and accents yet unknown': Shakespeare and the European canon. *In* (pp. 41-63) **6000.**

6051. PIRES, MARIA JOÃO. A palimpsest, or an image of a mutilated statue: the experience of translating Shakespeare. *In* (pp. 181-91) **5874.**

6052. PLATT, PETER G. 'Believing and not believing': Shakespeare and the archaeology of wonder. *In* (pp. 12-29) **5880.**

6053. POOLE, ADRIAN. A. C. Bradley's *Shakespearean Tragedy.* EC (55:1) 2005, 58-70. (New impressions, 9.)

6054. —— Confundering the past. TLS, 29 July 2005, 10-11 (review-article). (Shakespeare's Classical allusions.)

6055. —— Shakespeare and the Victorians. (Bibl. 2004, 6265.) Rev. by Susan Carlson in ShQ (55:4) 2004, 483-6; by Julia Thomas in SStud (33) 2005, 299-305; by Matthew Reynolds in EC (55:1) 2005, 80-8.

6056. POTTER, LOIS. Having our Will: imagination in recent Shakespeare biographies. ShS (58) 2005, 1-8.

6057. PROCHÁZKA, MARTIN; PILNÝ, ONDŘEJ (eds). Time refigured: myths, foundation texts and imagined communities. *See* **12868.**

6058. PURCELL, JANE. Not of an age, but for all time: Shakespeare at the Huntington. San Marino, CA: Huntington Library Press, 2005. pp. 85. (Huntington Library pubs.)

6059. RACKIN, PHYLLIS. Shakespeare and women. Oxford; New York: OUP, 2005. pp. 168. (Oxford Shakespeare topics.)

6060. —— Women's roles in the Elizabethan history plays. *In* (pp. 71-85) **5964.**

6061. RAY, SID. Holy estates: marriage and monarchy in Shakespeare and his contemporaries. Selinsgrove, PA: Susquehanna UP, 2004. pp. 227. (Apple-Zimmerman series in early modern culture.) Rev. by Tita French Baumlin in RQ (58:4) 2005, 1428-30; by Jane Donawerth in ShQ (56:4) 2005, 491-3.

6062. REISS, BENJAMIN. Bardolatry in Bedlam: Shakespeare, psychiatry, and cultural authority in nineteenth-century America. ELH (72:4) 2005, 769-97.

6063. REYNOLDS, BRYAN. Performing transversally: reimagining Shakespeare and the critical future. (Bibl. 2004, 6267.) Rev. by Thomas Cartelli in TJ (57:2) 2005, 329-31.

6064. RHODES, NEIL. Shakespeare and the origins of English. (Bibl. 2004, 6268.) Rev. by Fred Schurink in NQ (52:4) 2005, 539-40.

6065. RICHMOND, HUGH MACRAE. Dramatists against theory: the affective dramaturgy of Cinthio, Lope de Vega, and William Shakespeare. ShB (22:4) 2004, 43–53.

6066. RITCHIE, FIONA. Elizabeth Montagu: 'Shakespear's poor little critick'? *See* **8836.**

6067. ROBERTS, SASHA. Reading Shakespeare's poems in early modern England. (Bibl. 2003, 5918.) Rev. by Holly A. Crocker in ShQ (56:2) 2005, 224–6.

6068. RUPP, SUSANNE. Fremde zeitgenossen Klassiker. SJ (141) 2005, 133–49.

6069. SAHEL, PIERRE. Shakespeare: esquisses de modes républicains. EREA (1:2) 2003, 30–3.

6070. SAWYER, ROBERT. Victorian appropriations of Shakespeare: George Eliot, A. C. Swinburne, Robert Browning, and Charles Dickens. (Bibl. 2003, 5926.) Rev. by Matt Kozusko in SAtlR (70:2) 2005, 157–60.

6071. SCHONEVALD, CORNELIS W. (introd. and trans.). Arnoldus Pannevis: *Shakspere: a Critical Contribution* (1863). *In* (pp. 123–35) **9237.**

6072. SCOTT, JILL. Electra after Freud: myth and culture. Ithaca, NY; London: Cornell UP, 2005. pp. vii, 200. (Cornell studies in the history of psychiatry.) Rev. by Josh Cohen in TLS, 9 Sept. 2005, 24.

6073. SEDDON, DEBORAH. Shakespeare's orality: Solomon Plaatje's Setswana translations. ESA (47:2) 2004, 77–95.

6074. SERPIERI, ALESSANDRO. Translating Shakespeare: a brief survey of some problematic areas. *In* (pp. 27–49) **5874.**

6075. —— Translation and performance. *In* (pp. 258–81) **6000.**

6076. SHAPIRO, JAMES. 1599: a year in the life of William Shakespeare. London; Boston, MA: Faber & Faber, 2005. pp. xxiv, 429, (plates) 8. Rev. by Stephen Orgel in TLS, 19 & 26 Aug. 2005, 11; by Michael Dobson in LRB (27:20) 2005, 7–8; by Cynthia L. Haven in BkW, 18 Dec. 2005, 13.

6077. —— Toward a new biography of Shakespeare. ShS (58) 2005, 9–14.

6078. SHAW, INES SENA. *Histórias de Shakespeare*: propaganda in the guise of entertaining love stories. *In* (pp. 196–215) **5995.**

6079. SHURBANOV, ALEXANDER. The Shakespearean sound in translation. *In* (pp. 239–57) **6000.**

6080. —— The translatability of Shakespearean texts into an unrelated language/culture. *In* (pp. 51–64) **5874.**

6081. —— SOKOLOVA, BOIKA. Translating Shakespeare under Communism: Bulgaria and beyond. *In* (pp. 82–97) **5975.**

6082. ŠKANDEROVÁ, IVONA. Shakespeare's plays in Pilsen theatres. *In* (pp. 163–9) **3734.**

6083. SNYDER, SUSAN. Shakespeare: a wayward journey. (Bibl. 2004, 6287.) Rev. by Manfred Weidhorn in SixCJ (34:4) 2003, 1242–3.

6084. SOKOL, B. J.; SOKOL, MARY. Shakespeare, law, and marriage. (Bibl. 2004, 6288.) Rev. by Catherine M. S. Alexander in MLR (100:2) 2005, 482–4; by Susan W. Ahern in SixCJ (36:2) 2005, 506–8; by Stephen Cohen in ShY (15) 2005, 436–9; by Carol Thomas Neely in RQ (58:1) 2005, 338–9.

6085. SORELIUS, GUNNAR (ed.).   Shakespeare and Scandinavia: a collection of Nordic studies. (Bibl. 2004, 6289.) Rev. by Christopher Smith in Scandinavica (42:2) 2003, 286–7; by Christa Jansohn in ShQ (56:1) 2005, 106–8.

6086. STARNAWSKI, JERZY.   Literatura angielska w Bibliotece Narodowej 1921–1929: kulisy w świetle archiwum Stanisława Kota. (English literature in the National Library [series] 1921–1929 in the light of Stanisław Kot's archive.) In (pp. 227–37) **3756**.

6087. STEWART, STANLEY.   David Hume's 'Shakespeare'. Cithara (45:1) 2005, 13–27.

6088. STŘÍBRNÝ, ZDENĚK.   Proud času: stati o Shakespearovi. (The stream of time: essays on Shakespeare.) Prague: Karolinum, 2005. pp. 408.

6089. SUKHANOVA, EKATERINA.   Voicing the distant: Shakespeare and Russian Modernist poetry. (Bibl. 2004, 6293.) Rev. by Marina von Hirsch in AmBR (26:4) 2005, 31; by Irena R. Makaryk in SlavR (64:4) 2005, 935–6.

6090. TALVET, JÜRI.   Between dreams and reality: the message and the image of Renaissance Humanism. See **5570**.

6091. TAYLOR, GARY.   The cultural politics of Maybe. In (pp. 242–58) **5915**.

6092. TAYLOR, JOHN.   Bonnefoy and Shakespeare. HR (58:1) 2005, 161–6 (review-article).

6093. THOMPSON, AYANNA.   Suture, Shakespeare, and race; or, What is our cultural debt to the Bard? In (pp. 57–72) **13273**.

6094. TIFFANY, GRACE.   Borges and Shakespeare, Shakespeare and Borges. In (pp. 145–65) **5995**.

6095. TOLLINI, FREDERICK.   The Shakespeare productions of Max Reinhardt. Lewiston, NY; Lampeter: Mellen Press, 2004. pp. xiv, 242. (Studies in theatre arts, 31.)

6096. TRIVEDI, POONAM; BARTHOLOMEUSZ, DENNIS (eds).   India's Shakespeare: translation, interpretation, and performance. Newark: Delaware UP, 2005. pp. 303. (International studies in Shakespeare and his contemporaries.)

6097. TUCKER, KENNETH.   Shakespeare and Jungian typology: a reading of the plays. Jefferson, NC; London: McFarland, 2003. pp. 169. Rev. by Emily Detmer-Goebel in KenPR (19) 2004, 66–7.

6098. VAN DOREN, MARK.   Shakespeare. Foreword by David Lehman. New York: New York Review, 2005. pp. xxiii, 302. (New York Review books classics.)

6099. VELZ, JOHN W.   On Bards, Bibles, and bears. SNL (54:4) 2004/05, 87–8.

6100. VERMA, RAJIVA.   Shakespeare in Hindi cinema. In (pp. 269–90) **6096**.

6101. VICKERS, BRIAN.   'Counterfeiting' Shakespeare: evidence, authorship, and John Ford's Funerall Elegye. (Bibl. 2004, 6298.) Rev. by John Lee in SixCJ (34:4) 2003, 1158–60; by Katherine Duncan-Jones in MLR (100:1) 2005, 197–8; by Jeffrey Kahan in ShY (15) 2005, 427–9.

6102. —— Idle worship. TLS, 19 & 26 Aug. 2005, 6–8 (review-article). (Attribution.)

6103. VON SCHWERIN-HIGH, FRIEDERIKE.   Shakespeare, reception and translation: Germany and Japan. London; New York: Continuum, 2004. pp. vii, 253.

6104. WALLACE, NATHAN. Shakespeare biography and the theory of reconciliation in Edward Dowden and James Joyce. *See* **10837**.

6105. WATSON, DAVID. Shakespeare: the discovery of America. ESA (47:2) 2004, 25–40.

6106. WATTS, CEDRIC. The lady and her horsekeeper and Shakespeare. NQ (52:2) 2005, 208–13.

6107. WEIL, JUDITH. Service and dependency in Shakespeare's plays. Cambridge; New York: CUP, 2005. pp. ix, 210.

6108. WEIMANN, ROBERT; BRUSTER, DOUGLAS. Prologues to Shakespeare's theatre: performance and liminality in early modern drama. *See* **5305**.

6109. WELLS, STANLEY. Looking for sex in Shakespeare. (Bibl. 2004, 6304.) Rev. by Jeff Wax in TJ (57:2) 2005, 328–9.

6110. —— ORLIN, LENA COWEN (eds). Shakespeare: an Oxford guide. (Bibl. 2003, 5956.) Rev. by Katherine Acheson in ColLit (32:3) 2005, 203–6.

6111. WESTFALL, SUZANNE. 'The useless dearness of the diamond': patronage theatre and household. *In* (pp. 32–49) **5914**.

6112. WHITE, PAUL WHITFIELD; WESTFALL, SUZANNE R. (eds). Shakespeare and theatrical patronage in early modern England. (Bibl. 2004, 6306.) Rev. by Janet M. Spencer in SixCJ (34:4) 2003, 1169–70.

6113. WIGGINS, MARTIN. Shakespeare Jesuited: the plagiarisms of 'Pater Clarcus'. SevC (20:1) 2005, 1–21. (*Innocentia purpurata*.)

6114. WILKES, G. A. Shakespeare studies in Australia: some reflections. AUMLA (104) 2005, 1–8.

6115. WILLIAMSON, MARILYN L. (ed.). *As You Like It, Much Ado about Nothing*, and *Twelfth Night; or, What You Will*: an annotated bibliography of Shakespeare studies 1673–2001. (Bibl. 2004, 7083.) Rev. by Laury Magnus in SNL (54:4) 2004/05, 109–10.

6116. WILSON, CHRISTOPHER R.; CALORE, MICHELA. Music in Shakespeare: a dictionary. *See* **1978**.

6117. WILSON, RICHARD. Introduction: a torturing hour – Shakespeare and the martyrs. *In* (pp. 1–39) **5915**.

6118. —— The management of mirth: Shakespeare *via* Bourdieu. *In* (pp. 50–67) **5914**.

6119. —— Secret Shakespeare: studies in theatre, religion and resistance. (Bibl. 2004, 6307.) Rev. by Ros King in TLS, 18 Mar. 2005, 26; by Geoff Ridden in LitH (14:2) 2005, 81–2; by Thomas Merriam in NQ (52:1) 2005, 119–20; by Peter Milward in RelArts (9:1/2) 2005, 135–40.

6120. WISZNIOWSKA, MARTA. Feasting in drama. *In* (pp. 294–303) **3756**.

6121. WRIGHT, NANCY E.; FERGUSON, MARGARET W.; BUCK, A. R. (eds). Women, property, and the letters of the law in early modern England. *See* **6964**.

6122. YANNI, MARA. Shakespeare and the Greeks: a hundred years of negotiations. ShY (14) 2004, 193–214.

6123. ZARO, JUAN J. Translating from exile: Léon Felipe's Shakespeare *Paraphrases*. *In* (pp. 92–111) **5995**.

6124. ZIMMERMAN, SUSAN.   The early modern corpse in Shakespeare's theatre. Edinburgh: Edinburgh UP, 2005. pp. vii, 214.

6125. ZYSSET, SYLVIA.   Unstopping our mouths: Shakespeare in Swiss-German *Mundart. In* (pp. 152–64) **6000**.

Productions

6126. AEBISCHER, PASCALE.   Shakespeare's violated bodies: stage and screen performance. (Bibl. 2004, 6315.) Rev. by Genevieve Condon in WS (34:1) 2005, 106–7; by Kathryn Sloan in TJ (57:4) 2005, 778–80; by Ann Thompson in CLIO (35:1) 2005, 103–7; by Frédéric Delord in CEl (67) 2005, 87–91; by Jeremy Lopez in ShQ (56:4) 2005, 501–4.

6127. —— ESCHE, EDWARD J.; WHEALE, NIGEL (eds).   Remaking Shakespeare: performance across media, genres, and cultures. (Bibl. 2004, 6317.) Rev. by Stephen J. Phillips in NQ (52:4) 2005, 537–9.

6128. ANDEREGG, MICHAEL.   Cinematic Shakespeare. (Bibl. 2004, 6319.) Rev. by Paula Marantz Cohen in MichQR (44:3) 2005, 533–40.

6129. BARROLL, LEEDS.   Shakespeare and the second Blackfriars Theater. SStud (33) 2005, 156–70.

6130. BERGER, HARRY, JR.   Acts of silence, acts of speech: how to do things with Othello and Desdemona. *See* **6636**.

6131. BERKOWITZ, JOEL.   Shakespeare on the American Yiddish stage. (Bibl. 2004, 6323.) Rev. by Dorothy Chansky in NYH (84:3) 2003, 344–6; by Michael Shapiro in CompDr (37:3/4) 2003/04, 434–7.

6132. BESNAULT, MARIE-HÉLÈNE.   Historical legacy and fiction: the poetical reinvention of King Richard III. *In* (pp. 106–25) **5964**.

6133. BIRD, ALAN.   The theatre at Wynnstay: some further observations. *See* **8095**.

6134. BLOOM, GINA.   Words made of breath: gender and vocal agency in *King John. See* **6450**.

6135. BOGDANOV, MICHAEL.   Shakespeare, the director's cut: vol. 1, Essays on Shakespeare's plays. Edinburgh: Capercaillie, 2003. pp. vii, 159.

6136. BOLAM, ROBYN.   *Richard II*: Shakespeare and the languages of the stage. *In* (pp. 141–57) **5964**.

6137. BOLTZ, INGEBORG.   Verzeichnis der Shakespeare-Inszenierungen und Bibliographie der Kritiken: Spielzeit 2003/2004. SJ (141) 2005, 205–29.

6138. BROWN, JOHN RUSSELL.   Shakespeare dancing: a theatrical study of the plays. Basingstoke; New York: Palgrave Macmillan, 2005. pp. viii, 210. Rev. by Samantha Ellis in TLS, 21 Jan. 2005, 28.

6139. BUCHANAN, JUDITH.   Shakespeare on film. London; New York: Pearson Longman, 2005. pp. x, 288. (Inside film.)

6140. BUHLER, STEPHEN M.   Shakespeare in the cinema: ocular proof. (Bibl. 2004, 6330.) Rev. by Sheila J. Nayar in SixCJ (34:1) 2003, 265–7.

6141. BURNETT, MARK THORNTON.   Local *Macbeth* / global Shakespeare: Scotland's screen destiny. *In* (pp. 189–206) **6561**.

6142. ——   Writing Shakespeare in the global economy. ShS (58) 2005, 185–98.

6143. BURT, RICHARD (ed.). Shakespeare after mass media. (Bibl. 2004, 6333.) Rev. by Michael Bristol in ShQ (55:4) 2004, 491–4.

6144. —— BOOSE, LYNDA E. (eds). Shakespeare, the movie II: popularizing the plays on film, TV, video, and DVD. (Bibl. 2003, 5984.) Rev. by Sabine Schülting in SJ (141) 2005, 275–6.

6145. CARNEGIE, DAVID. Early modern plays and performance. HLQ (67:3) 2004, 437–56 (review-article).

6146. CARSON, CHRISTIE. Digitizing performance history: where do we go from here? See **1103**.

6147. CERASANO, S. P. The geography of Henslowe's diary. See **5484**.

6148. CHILTON, NEIL. Conceptions of a beautiful crisis: Henry James's reading of The Tempest. See **11388**.

6149. CIEŚLAK, MAGDALENA. Popularising Shakespeare: Franco Zeffirelli's Hamlet. In (pp. 36–46) **3756**.

6150. COX, EMMA. Negotiating cultural narratives: all-Aboriginal Shakespearean dreaming. See **6621**.

6151. CROWL, SAMUEL. Shakespeare at the cineplex: the Kenneth Branagh era. (Bibl. 2004, 6347.) Rev. by Robert C. Evans in CompDr (37:3/4) 2003/04, 417–19; by Mark Thornton Burnett in ShQ (56:1) 2005, 104–6.

6152. CRYSTAL, DAVID. Pronouncing Shakespeare: the Globe experiment. Cambridge; New York: CUP, 2005. pp. xviii, 187.

6153. DÉPRATS, JEAN-MICHEL. Translating Shakespeare's stagecraft. In (pp. 133–47) **5975**.

6154. DE VOS, JOZEF. Directing Shakespeare on the late twentieth-century stage: the case of Franz Marijnen. ShY (15) 2005, 267–84.

6155. DOBSON, MICHAEL. The British personality of the millennium: British Shakespeares, amateur and professional, in the new century. In (pp. 113–28) **6000**.

6156. —— Writing about [Shakespearian] performance. ShS (58) 2005, 160–8.

6157. DÖRING, TOBIAS. Writing performance: how to elegize Elizabethan actors. ShS (58) 2005, 60–71.

6158. ESCOLME, BRIDGET. Talking to the audience: Shakespeare, performance, self. London; New York: Routledge, 2005. pp. xii, 192.

6159. FLAHERTY, KATE. Theatre and metatheatre in Hamlet. See **6321**.

6160. FOAKES, R. A. 'Armed at point exactly': the ghost in Hamlet. See **6322**.

6161. —— Performance and text: King Lear. See **6464**.

6162. FULLER, DAVID. The Bogdanov version: the English Shakespeare Company Wars of the Roses. See **6401**.

6163. GABY, ROSE. 'Here's a marvellous convenient place for our rehearsal': Shakespeare in Australian space. ADS (46) 2005, 124–38.

6164. GAGNON, CHANTAL. Le Shakespeare québécois des années 1990. See **6750**.

6165. GERRITSEN, JOHAN. De Witt, Van Buchell, the Swan, and the second Globe: an assessment of the evidence. See **6997**.

6166. GODMAN, MAUREEN.   'Plucking a crow' in *The Comedy of Errors*. See **6278**.

6167. GREEN, MELISSA.   Tribal Shakespeare: the Federal Theatre Project's 'Voodoo Macbeth' (1936). See **6549**.

6168. GREER, DAVID.   Music of Global interest. NQ (52:2) 2005, 216–19.

6169. GURR, ANDREW.   Henry Carey's peculiar letter. ShQ (56:1) 2005, 51–75.

6170. —— The Shakespeare Company, 1594–1642. (Bibl. 2004, 6362.) Rev. by William Proctor Williams in NQ (52:2) 2005, 253–4; by David Kathman in ShQ (56:3) 2005, 360–2; by Frederick Tollini in RQ (58:2) 2005, 742–4.

6171. GUTTAL, VIJAYA.   Translation and performance of Shakespeare in Kannada. *In* (pp. 106–19) **6096**.

6172. HALIO, JAY L.   A Midsummer Night's dream. See **6625**.

6173. HAMPTON-REEVES, STUART.   Theatrical afterlives. *In* (pp. 229–44) **5964**.

6174. HATCHUEL, SARAH.   Shakespeare: from stage to screen. (Bibl. 2004, 6365.) Rev. by Robert C. Evans in CompDr (38:4) 2004/05, 455–9; by Kathryn Sloan in TJ (57:4) 2005, 778–80; by William Green in SNL (55:2) 2005, 43–4.

6175. HELMBOLD, ANITA.   'Take a soldier, take a king': the (in)separability of king and conflict in Branagh's *Henry V*. See **6421**.

6176. HOENSELAARS, A. J. (ed.).   Shakespeare's history plays: performance, translation and adaptation in Britain and abroad. Foreword by Dennis Kennedy. See **5970**.

6177. HOENSELAARS, TON.   'Out-ranting the enemy leader': *Henry V* and/as World War II propaganda. *In* (pp. 215–34) **9237**.

6178. HOLMES, JONATHAN.   Merely players? Actors' accounts of performing Shakespeare. (Bibl. 2004, 6371.) Rev. by Bridget Mary Aitchison in ADS (46) 2005, 143–5.

6179. ICHIKAWA, MARIKO.   '*Maluolio within*': acting on the threshold between onstage and offstage spaces. See **6803**.

6180. JACKSON, RUSSELL.   Staging Birnam Wood in the 1840s: a discovery at the Folger Shakespeare Library. See **6551**.

6181. JENSEN, MICHAEL P.   Olivier's *Richard III* on radio. See **6510**.

6182. JONES, MARIA.   Shakespeare's culture in modern performance. (Bibl. 2004, 6380.) Rev. by M. J. Jardine in LitH (14:2) 2005, 79–80; by Stephen J. Phillips in NQ (52:4) 2005, 537–9.

6183. KAABER, LARS.   Staging Shakespeare's *Hamlet*: a director's interpreting text through performance. See **6335**.

6184. KELLY, PHILIPPA.   Finding *King Lear*'s female parts. See **6470**.

6185. —— Performing Australian identity: gendering *King Lear*. See **6471**.

6186. —— See what breeds about her heart: *King Lear*, feminism, and performance. See **6472**.

6187. KIEFER, FREDERICK.   Shakespeare's visual theatre: staging the personified characters. (Bibl. 2004, 6382.) Rev. by Katherine West Scheil in MLR (100:3) 2005, 765–6; by Douglas W. Hayes in SixCJ (36:2) 2005, 516–17; by Jeremy Lopez in

ShY (15) 2005, 430–2; by Stuart Sillars in ShQ (56:2) 2005, 240–3; by Joachim Frenk in SJ (141) 2005, 263–7.

6188. KINNEY, ARTHUR F. Shakespeare by stages: an historical introduction. (Bibl. 2003, 6032.) Rev. by David Olive in MLR (100:4) 2005, 1086–7.

6189. KNAPP, JEFFREY. What is a co-author? See **6341.**

6190. LAMBERT, LADINA BEZZOLA; ENGLER, BALZ (eds). Shifting the scene: Shakespeare in European culture. See **6000.**

6191. LEGGATT, ALEXANDER. King Lear. See **6474.**

6192. LEHMANN, COURTNEY. Shakespeare remains: theater to film, early modern to postmodern. (Bibl. 2004, 6386.) Rev. by Dana E. Aspinall in SixCJ (34:4) 2003, 1177–8; by Stephen M. Buhler in ETh (8:1) 2005, 125–9.

6193. LI, RURU. Shashibiya: staging Shakespeare in China. Hong Kong: Hong Kong UP; London: Eurospan, 2003. pp. 314. Rev. by Richard Fotheringham in ADS (46) 2005, 139–43; by Alexander C. Y. Huang in ATJ (22:2) 2005, 371–4.

6194. LYNCH, JACK. King Lear and 'the taste of the age', 1681–1838. See **6476.**

6195. McDONALD, RUSS. Look to the lady: Sarah Siddons, Ellen Terry, and Judi Dench on the Shakespearean stage. Athens; London: Georgia UP, 2005. pp. xviii, 172. (Georgia Southern Univ.: Jack N. and Addie D. Averitt lecture series, 12.) Rev. by Katherine Duncan-Jones in TLS, 1 July 2005, 20.

6196. McMILLIN, SCOTT. Shakespeare and the Chamberlain's Men in 1598. MedRen (17) 2005, 205–15.

6197. MAJUMDAR, SAROTTAMA. That sublime 'old gentleman': Shakespeare's plays in Calcutta, 1775–1930. In (pp. 260–8) **6096.**

6198. MARGOLIES, DAVID. King Lear: Kozintsev's social translation. In (pp. 230–8) **6000.**

6199. MARSHALL, GAIL; POOLE, ADRIAN (eds). Victorian Shakespeare: vol. 1, Theatre, drama and performance. Foreword by Stanley Wells. (Bibl. 2004, 6393.) Rev. by Peter Holbrook in TLS, 18 Feb. 2005, 26; by Asa Briggs in LitH (14:2) 2005, 90–1; by Matthew Reynolds in EC (55:1) 2005, 80–8.

6200. MARSHALL, KELLI. 'It doth forget to do the thing it should': Kenneth Branagh, Love's Labour's Lost, and (mis)interpreting the musical genre. See **6529.**

6201. MASON, PAMELA. Henry V: 'the quick forge and working house of thought'. In (pp. 177–92) **5964.**

6202. MENZER, PAUL. 'Come upon your Q': Richard III, cue-line variants, and memorial error. See **6514.**

6203. MORSE, RUTH. Monsieur Macbeth: from Jarry to Ionesco. See **6562.**

6204. NARDO, DON. The Globe Theater. San Diego, CA: Blackbirch Press, 2005. pp. 48. (Building world landmarks.)

6205. NELSON, ROBIN. Live or wired? Technologizing the event. In (pp. 303–16) **3974.**

6206. OCCHIOGROSSO, FRANK (ed.). Shakespeare in performance: a collection of essays. (Bibl. 2004, 6403.) Rev. by David Carnegie in HLQ (67:3) 2004, 437–56; by David Roberts in ShQ (56:3) 2005, 366–8; by Michael Raab in SJ (141) 2005, 270–2.

6207. O'RAWE, DES. Venice in film: the postcard and the palimpsest. *See* **6655**.

6208. ORMSBY, ROBERT. Making Shakespeare work in the twenty-first century: an interview with R. H. Thomson. *See* **6696**.

6209. O'SHEA, JOSÉ ROBERTO. Early Shakespearean stars performing in Brazilian skies: João Caetano and national theater. *In* (pp. 25–36) **5995**.

6210. PEMBLE, JOHN. Shakespeare goes to Paris: how the Bard conquered France. London: Hambledon & London, 2005. pp. xix, 240, (plates) 8. Rev. by Ruth Morse in TLS, 19 & 26 Aug. 2005, 9.

6211. PETTENGILL, RICHARD. Pitfalls of cinematic aspiration: the reception of Peter Sellars's *The Merchant of Venice*. *See* **6609**.

6212. PIESSE, A. J. *King John*: changing perspectives. *In* (pp. 126–40) **5964**.

6213. PRESCOTT, PAUL. Doing all that becomes a man: the reception and afterlife of the Macbeth actor, 1744–1889. *See* **6565**.

6214. PURCELL, STEPHEN. A shared experience: Shakespeare and popular theatre. PRes (10:3) 2005, 74–84.

6215. RIPLEY, JOHN. Sociology and soundscape: Herbert Beerbohm Tree's 1908 *Merchant of Venice*. *See* **6611**.

6216. ROGERS, REBECCA. How Scottish was 'the Scottish play'? *Macbeth*'s national identity in the eighteenth century. *In* (pp. 104–23) **6561**.

6217. ROMANSKA, MAGDA. NecrOphelia: death, femininity and the making of modern aesthetics. *See* **6361**.

6218. ROTHWELL, KENNETH SPRAGUE. A history of Shakespeare on screen: a century of film and television. (Bibl. 2003, 6073.) Cambridge; New York: CUP, 2004. pp. xvii, 380. (Second ed.: first ed. 1999.) Rev. by Robert C. Evans in CompDr (38:4) 2004/05, 455–9.

6219. ROWE, KATHERINE. The politics of sleepwalking: American Lady Macbeths. *See* **6569**.

6220. RUTTER, CAROL CHILLINGTON. Remind me: how many children had Lady Macbeth? *See* **6570**.

6221. SCHEIL, KATHERINE WEST. The taste of the town: Shakespearean comedy and the early eighteenth-century theater. (Bibl. 2004, 6416.) Rev. by Jean MacIntyre in SixCJ (35:4) 2004, 1142–3; by Rebecca Rogers in MLR (100:3) 2005, 767–8; by Gefen Bar-On in CEl (67) 2005, 94–5; by Don-John Dugas in Scriblerian (37:2/38:1) 2005, 147–8.

6222. SCHUCH, ELKE. '*I exceed my sex*': Inszenierungen von Geschlecht in Shakespeares Dramen: Text und Aufführung. Heidelberg: Winter, 2003. pp. xiv, 345, (plates) 6. Rev. by Ingrid Hotz-Davies in SJ (141) 2005, 261–3.

6223. SCULLION, ADRIENNE. Citz Scotland where it did? Shakespeare in production at the Citizens' Theatre, Glasgow, 1970–74. *In* (pp. 172–88) **6561**.

6224. SENGUPTA, DEBJANI. Playing the canon: Shakespeare and the Bengali actress in nineteenth-century Calcutta. *In* (pp. 242–59) **6096**.

6225. SHEPPARD, PHILIPPA. Latino elements in Baz Luhrmann's *Romeo + Juliet*. *In* (pp. 242–62) **5995**.

6226. —— 'Sigh no more ladies' – the song in *Much Ado about Nothing*: Shakespeare and Branagh deliver aural pleasure. *See* **6634**.

6227. SHIRLEY, FRANCES A. (ed.). *Troilus and Cressida. See* **6797**.

6228. SILVERSTONE, CATHERINE. Shakespeare live: reproducing Shakespeare at the 'new' Globe Theatre. TexP (19:1) 2005, 31–50.

6229. SMITH, EMMA. The year's contributions to Shakespeare studies: 2, Shakespeare in performance. ShS (57) 2004, 325–35.

6230. —— The year's contributions to Shakespeare studies: 2, Shakespeare in performance. ShS (58) 2005, 334–42.

6231. SMYTH, ADAM. A new record of the 1613 Globe fire during a performance of Shakespeare's *King Henry VIII. See* **6449**.

6232. STURGESS, KIM C. Shakespeare and the American nation. (Bibl. 2004, 6428.) Rev. by Simon Barker in LitH (14:2) 2005, 95–6.

6233. TAYLOR, NANCY. Women direct Shakespeare in America: productions from the 1990s. Madison, NJ: Fairleigh Dickinson UP, 2005. pp. 303.

6234. TRIBBLE, EVELYN. Distributing cognition in the Globe. *See* **5298**.

6235. TRIVEDI, POONAM. 'Folk Shakespeare': the performance of Shakespeare in traditional Indian theater forms. *In* (pp. 171–92) **6096**.

6236. —— BARTHOLOMEUSZ, DENNIS (eds). India's Shakespeare: translation, interpretation, and performance. *See* **6096**.

6237. TULLOCH, JOHN. Shakespeare and Chekhov in production and reception: theatrical events and their audiences. Iowa City: Iowa UP, 2005. pp. xv, 310. (Studies in theatre history & culture.)

6238. WEIL, HERBERT. Canadian Shakespeare. SNL (55:1) 2005, 13, 16 (review-article).

6239. WEST, RUSSELL. Spatial representations and the Jacobean stage: from Shakespeare to Webster. (Bibl. 2004, 6440.) Rev. by Garrett A. Sullivan, Jr, in ShQ (55:4) 2004, 464–6.

6240. WILDER, LINA PERKINS. Toward a Shakespearean 'memory theater': Romeo, the apothecary, and the performance of memory. *See* **6705**.

6241. WILKINSON, JANE. The cripples at the gate: Orson Welles's 'woodoo' *Macbeth. See* **6574**.

6242. WILLIAMS, DEANNE. Mick Jagger Macbeth. *See* **6575**.

6243. WORTHEN, W. B. Shakespeare and the force of modern performance. (Bibl. 2004, 6443.) Rev. by Stephen J. Phillips in NQ (52:4) 2005, 535–6; by Ric Knowles in MedRen (18) 2005, 257–65.

6244. YANNI, MARA. Shakespeare and the Greeks: a hundred years of negotiations. *See* **6122**.

Separate Works

All's Well That Ends Well

6245. BAMFORD, KAREN. Foreign affairs: the search for the lost husband in Shakespeare's *All's Well That Ends Well*. ETh (8:2) 2005, 57–72.

6246. BARKER, SIMON (ed.). Shakespeare's problem plays: *All's Well That Ends Well, Measure for Measure, Troilus and Cressida*. Basingstoke; New York: Palgrave Macmillan, 2005. pp. ix, 237. (New casebooks.)

6247. BERRY, CRAIG; HAYTON, HEATHER (eds). Translating desire in medieval and early modern literature. See **5069**.

6248. HUNTER, DIANNE. Miraculous daughters in Shakespeare's late romances. PsyArt (9) 2005.

6249. MARSH, NICHOLAS. Shakespeare: three problem plays. Basingstoke; New York: Palgrave Macmillan, 2003. pp. xi, 280. (Analysing texts.) Rev. by Barbara J. Baines in MedRen (18) 2005, 285–91.

6250. MUKHERJI, SUBHA. Women, law, and dramatic realism in early modern England. ELR (35:2) 2005, 248–72.

6251. RYAN, KIERNAN. 'Where hope is coldest': *All's Well That Ends Well*. In (pp. 28–49) **5928.**

6252. TRULL, MARY. 'Odious ballads': fallen women's laments in *All's Well That Ends Well*. In (pp. 133–54) **5069**.

6253. VENET, GISÈLE. *Twelfth Night* et *All's Well That Ends Well*: deux comédies que tout oppose, ou deux moments d'une même esthétique? See **6810**.

Antony and Cleopatra

6254. BATTISTI, SUSANNA. Metamorfosi del teatro: gli adattamenti shakespeariani di John Dryden. See **7405**.

6255. BEVINGTON, DAVID M. (ed.). Antony and Cleopatra. (Bibl. 1993, 3868.) Cambridge; New York: CUP, 2005. pp. xviii, 285. (New Cambridge Shakespeare.) (Second ed.: first ed. 1990.)

6256. BILLINGS, TIMOTHY. Squashing the 'shard-borne beetle' crux: a hard case with a few pat readings. See **6532**.

6257. BRITLAND, KAREN. Circe's cup: wine and women in early modern drama. In (pp. 109–25) **6942**.

6258. CARVALHO HOMEM, RUI. Gipsy queens: Portuguese Cleopatras and the fascination of opprobrium. In (pp. 225–41) **5874**.

6259. DASENBROCK, REED WAY. Imitation *versus* contestation: Walcott's postcolonial Shakespeare. See **19939**.

6260. FANEGO, TERESA. 'Fare thee well, dame': Shakespeare's forms of address and their socio-affective role. SEDERI (15) 2005, 23–42.

6261. FUSINI, NADIA. Donne fatali: Ofelia, Desdemona, Cleopatra. See **6323**.

6262. HOLLAND, NORMAN N. 'The barge she sat in': psychoanalysis and diction. PsyArt (9) 2005.

6263. LEINWAND, THEODORE B. *Coniugium interruptum* in Shakespeare and Webster. ELH (72:1) 2005, 239–57.

6264. LEVIN, RICHARD. More jibes at Shakespeare in 1606, and the date of *Antony and Cleopatra*. NQ (52:2) 2005, 207–8.

6265. MATAR, NABIL; STOECKEL, RUDOLPH. Europe's Mediterranean frontier: the Moor. In (pp. 220–52) **5954**.

6266. METTS, ROSE M. Antony's women. CEACrit (66:2/3) 2004, 92–104.

6267. MILLER, ANTHONY.   Varieties of power in *Antony and Cleopatra*. SSE (30) 2004, 42–59.

6268. MIOLA, ROBERT S.   Shakespeare's Ancient Rome: difference and identity. *In* (pp. 193–213) **5964**.

6269. O'SHEA, JOSÉ ROBERTO.   From printed text to performance text: Brazilian translations of Shakespearean drama. *In* (pp. 145–59) **5874**.

6270. PARKER, PATRICIA.   Barbers and Barbary: early modern cultural semantics. RenD (ns 33) 2004, 201–44.

As You Like It

6271. BELSEY, CATHERINE.   Remembering as re-inscription – with a difference. *See* **3475**.

6272. DOMÍNGUEZ ROMERO, ELENA.   Some considerations on the pastourelle in Shakespeare's *As You Like It*. SEDERI (14) 2004, 199–206.

6273. ENOS, CAROL.   Catholic exiles in Flanders and *As You Like It*; or, What if you don't like it at all? *In* (pp. 130–42) **5915**.

6274. GABY, ROSE.   'Here's a marvellous convenient place for our rehearsal': Shakespeare in Australian space. *See* **6163**.

6275. KISHI, TETSUO.   'Our language of love': Shakespeare in Japanese translation. *In* (pp. 68–81) **5975**.

6276. POWELL, TAMARA; SHATTUCK, SIM.   Looking for liberation and lesbians in Shakespeare's cross-dressing comedies. *See* **6813**.

6277. SOULE, LESLEY WADE.   *As You Like It*. Basingstoke; New York: Palgrave Macmillan, 2005. pp. vii, 175. (Shakespeare handbooks.)

The Comedy of Errors

6278. GODMAN, MAUREEN.   'Plucking a crow' in *The Comedy of Errors*. ETh (8:1) 2005, 53–68.

6279. KISHI, TETSUO.   'Our language of love': Shakespeare in Japanese translation. *In* (pp. 68–81) **5975**.

6280. RAMAN, SHANKAR.   Marking time: memory and market in *The Comedy of Errors*. ShQ (56:2) 2005, 176–205.

6281. WHITWORTH, CHARLES WALTERS (ed.).   The comedy of errors. (Bibl. 2004, 6495.) Rev. by Matthew C. Hansen in SixCJ (35:4) 2004, 1174–6; by Gilles Monsarrat in EA (58:1) 2005, 105–6.

Coriolanus

6282. FERREIRA DA ROCHA, ROBERTO.   Hero or villain: a Brazilian *Coriolanus* during the period of the military dictatorship. *In* (pp. 37–53) **5995**.

6283. GEORGE, DAVID (ed.).   Coriolanus. (Bibl. 2004, 6497.) Rev. by Ros King in TLS, 18 Feb. 2005, 31.

6284. MIOLA, ROBERT S.   Shakespeare's Ancient Rome: difference and identity. *In* (pp. 193–213) **5964**.

6285. PEQUIGNEY, JOSEPH.   'What the age might call sodomy' and homosexuality in certain studies of Shakespeare's plays. *See* **6697**.

6286. STEIBLE, MARY.   *Coriolanus*: a guide to the play. Westport, CT; London: Greenwood Press, 2004. pp. 144. (Greenwood guides to Shakespeare.)

6287. West, Michael; Silberstein, Myron. The controversial eloquence of Shakespeare's Coriolanus – an anti-Ciceronian orator? MP (102:3) 2005, 307–31.

Cymbeline

6288. Bevington, David.   Shakespeare's biography in his plays. See **6668**.

6289. Billings, Timothy.   Squashing the 'shard-borne beetle' crux: a hard case with a few pat readings. See **6532**.

6290. Butler, Martin (ed.).   Cymbeline. Cambridge; New York: CUP, 2005. pp. xvi, 269. (New Cambridge Shakespeare.)

6291. Edgecombe, Rodney Stenning.   Three proposed emendations. See **5801**.

6292. Foakes, R. A.   Shakespeare's other historical plays. In (pp. 214–28) **5964**.

6293. Holland, Peter.   Staging Europe in Shakespeare. In (pp. 21–40) **6000**.

6294. Jones-Davies, Margaret.   *Cymbeline* and the sleep of faith. In (pp. 197–217) **5915**.

6295. Malick, Javed.   Appropriating Shakespeare freely: Parsi Theater's first Urdu play *Khurshid*. In (pp. 92–105) **6096**.

6296. O'Shea, José Roberto.   From printed text to performance text: Brazilian translations of Shakespearean drama. In (pp. 145–59) **5874**.

6297. Powell, Tamara; Shattuck, Sim.   Looking for liberation and lesbians in Shakespeare's cross-dressing comedies. See **6813**.

6298. Schwartz, Murray M.   Between fantasy and imagination: a psychological exploration of *Cymbeline*. PsyArt (9) 2005.

Hamlet

6299. Aasand, Hardin L. (ed.).   Stage directions in *Hamlet*: new essays and new directions. (Bibl. 2004, 6514.) Rev. by David Carnegie in HLQ (67:3) 2004, 437–56; by Matthew C. Hansen in SixCJ (35:4) 2004, 1174–6; by Kevin J. Wetmore, Jr, in TheatreS (46:1) 2005, 163–7; by David Roberts in ShQ (56:3) 2005, 366–8.

6300. Agarez Medeiros, Helena.   The translator's visibility: the debate over a 'royal translation' of *Hamlet*. In (pp. 67–77) **6000**.

6301. Bertinetti, Paolo (ed. and trans.).   Amleto. Turin: Einaudi, 2005. pp. xxii, 408. (Einaudi tascabili: Teatro, 1370.) (English and Italian texts.)

6302. Bigliazzi, Silvia.   Transubstantiating the performance: towards a mimetic narrative in *Hamlet*'s Hecuba scene. In (pp. 44–54) **3724**.

6303. Borchmeyer, Dieter.   Das Alte und das Neue auf eine überschwengliche Weise verbunden: Schiller und Shakespeare im Lichte Goethes. SJ (141) 2005, 17–33.

6304. Boyd, Brian.   Literature and evolution: a bio-cultural approach. See **21002**.

6305. Byles, Joanna Montgomery.   Tragic alternatives: eros and superego revenge in *Hamlet*. PsyArt (9) 2005.

6306. Campbell, Erin E.   'Sad generations seeking water': the social construction of madness in O(phelia) and Q(uentin Compson). See **16396**.

6307. CANTOR, PAUL ARTHUR. Shakespeare, *Hamlet.* (Bibl. 2004, 6527.) Rev. by Willy Maley in TRI (30:2) 2005, 202–3.

6308. CATHCART, CHARLES. Borrowings and the authorial domain: Gostanzo, Polonius, and Marston's Gonzago. *See* **7614**.

6309. CHANDLER, DAVID. Another Lucy poem about a glow-worm. *See* **12465**.

6310. CHANDRASHEKAR, LAXMI. 'A sea change into something rich and strange': Ekbal Ahmed's *Macbeth* and *Hamlet. In* (pp. 193–203) **6096**.

6311. CIEŚLAK, MAGDALENA. Popularising Shakespeare: Franco Zeffirelli's *Hamlet. In* (pp. 36–46) **3756**.

6312. CREASY, MATTHEW. Shakespeare burlesque in *Ulysses. See* **17263**.

6313. DÁVIDHÁZI, PÉTER. Camel, weasel, whale: the cloud-scene in *Hamlet* as a Hungarian parable. *In* (pp. 95–110) **6000**.

6314. DELANEY, BILL. Shakespeare's *Hamlet.* Exp (63:2) 2005, 66–8.

6315. DEMASTES, WILLIAM W. Hamlet in his world: Shakespeare anticipates/ assaults Cartesian dualism. JDTC (20:1) 2005, 27–39.

6316. EDGECOMBE, RODNEY STENNING. Hadrian's '*animula vagula*' and *Hamlet.* ANQ (18:2) 2005, 18–20.

6317. FANEGO, TERESA. 'Fare thee well, dame': Shakespeare's forms of address and their socio-affective role. *See* **6260**.

6318. FEIJÓ, ANTÓNIO M. Practically speaking: on translating *Hamlet. In* (pp. 193–202) **5874**.

6319. FERNIE, EWAN. The last act: presentism, spirituality and the politics of *Hamlet. In* (pp. 186–211) **5928**.

6320. —— Shakespeare and the prospect of presentism. ShS (58) 2005, 169–84.

6321. FLAHERTY, KATE. Theatre and metatheatre in *Hamlet.* SSE (31) 2005, 3–20.

6322. FOAKES, R. A. 'Armed at point exactly': the ghost in *Hamlet.* ShS (58) 2005, 34–47.

6323. FUSINI, NADIA. Donne fatali: Ofelia, Desdemona, Cleopatra. Rome: Bulzoni, 2005. pp. 100. (Piccola biblioteca shakespeariana, 35.)

6324. GERVIN, MARY A. The monodrama *Maud*: Tennyson's little *Hamlet. See* **12144**.

6325. GRIFFITHS, HUW (ed.). Shakespeare: *Hamlet.* Basingstoke; New York: Palgrave Macmillan, 2005. pp. xii, 178. (Readers' guides to essential criticism.)

6326. HADFIELD, ANDREW. *Hamlet*'s country matters: the 'Scottish play' within the play. *In* (pp. 87–103) **6561**.

6327. HAMBURGER, MAIK. 'If it be now': the knocking of Fate: reading Shakespeare for translation. *In* (pp. 117–28) **5874**.

6328. HAMPEL, SHARON. 'Who is this King of Glory?': Psalm 24 and reconciliation in *Hamlet.* ShY (14) 2004, 215–35.

6329. HISCOCK, ANDREW. 'What's Hecuba to him …': Trojan heroes and rhetorical selves in Shakespeare's *Hamlet. In* (pp. 161–75) **4479**.

6330. Huang, Alexander C. Y.   Impersonation, autobiography, and cross-cultural adaptation: Lee Kuo-Hsiu's *Shamlet*. ATJ (22:1) 2005, 122–37.

6331. Huelin, Scott.   Reading, writing, and memory in *Hamlet*. ReLit (37:1) 2005, 25–44.

6332. Hunt, Maurice.   'Forward backward' time and the Apocalypse in *Hamlet*. CompDr (38:4) 2004/05, 379–99.

6333. —— Impregnating Ophelia. Neophilologus (89:4) 2005, 641–63.

6334. Husain, Adrian A.   Politics and genre in *Hamlet*. Foreword by John Bayley. Oxford; New York: OUP, 2004. pp. xiv, 49.

6335. Kaaber, Lars.   Staging Shakespeare's *Hamlet*: a director's interpreting text through performance. Lewiston, NY; Lampeter: Mellen Press, 2005. pp. xii, 513. (Studies in performance, 1.)

6336. Kane, Paul.   Hamlet in Elysium. SRASP (27) 2004, 51–61.

6337. Katrizky, Peg.   Pickelhering and Hamlet in Dutch art: the English comedians of Robert Browne, John Green, and Robert Reynolds. ShY (15) 2005, 113–40.

6338. Kearney, Richard.   Spectres of *Hamlet*. *In* (pp. 157–85) **5928.**

6339. Kelly, Aaron; Salter, David.   'The time is out of joint': *Withnail and I* and historical melancholia. *In* (pp. 99–112) **13273.**

6340. Kilroy, Gerard.   Requiem for a prince: rites of memory in *Hamlet*. *In* (pp. 143–60) **5915.**

6341. Knapp, Jeffrey.   What is a co-author? Representations (89) 2005, 1–29.

6342. Kottman, Paul A.   The limits of mimesis: risking confession in Shakespeare's *Hamlet*. SStudT (42) 2004, 42–70.

6343. Krause, Thomas.   A picture in little is worth a thousand words: debasement in *Hamlet* and *Measure for Measure*. SRASP (28) 2005, 57–96.

6344. Lee, John.   Kipling's Shakespearean *Traffics and Discoveries*. *See* **17471.**

6345. Levin, Richard.   Frailty, thy name is wanton widow. *See* **5272.**

6346. —— Hamlet's dramatic soliloquies. *In* (pp. 113–34) **5167.**

6347. Lieblein, Leanore.   'Cette belle langue': the 'tradaptation' of Shakespeare in Quebec. *In* (pp. 255–69) **5975.**

6348. Lin, Shen.   A mirror up to 'human' nature: the case of the Chinese translator Liang Shi Qiu. *In* (pp. 98–113) **5975.**

6349. Malcolm, Jody.   Horatio: the first CSI. *In* (pp. 113–21) **13273.**

6350. Mesa Villar, José María.   Musings from Ophelia's watery voyage: images of female submission in Shakespeare's and Millais' drowning maiden. SEDERI (14) 2004, 227–37.

6351. Minier, Marta.   Shakespeare translation and taboo: a case study in retranslation. Gramma (12) 2004, 73–87.

6352. Nettle, Daniel.   What happens in *Hamlet*? Exploring the psychological foundations of drama. *In* (pp. 56–75) **14807.**

6353. Oremland, Jerome.   Death and the fear of finiteness in *Hamlet*. San Francisco, CA: Lake Street, 2005. pp. viii, 147.

6354. Paglia, Camille.   'Stay, illusion': ambiguity in *Hamlet*. *In* (pp. 117–30) **3748.**

6355. PETERS, JULIE STONE. Theater and book in the history of memory: materializing Mnemosyne in the age of print. *See* **5548**.

6356. PUJANTE, ÁNGEL LUIS; GREGOR, KEITH. The four neoclassical Spanish *Hamlets*: assimilation and revision. SEDERI (15) 2005, 129–41.

6357. PURINTON, MARJEAN D. Shakespeare's Ghost and Felicia Hemans's *The Vespers of Palermo*: nineteenth-century readings of the page and feminist meanings for the stage. *See* **11262**.

6358. RAGG, EDWARD. Good-bye major man: reading Stevens without 'Stevensian'. *See* **19679**.

6359. RASMUS, AGNIESZKA. Shakespeare's Horatio: crossing the dramatic boundaries. *In* (pp. 188–96) **3756**.

6360. ROE, JOHN. Shakespeare, sonnets, and the 51st Psalm. *In* (pp. 197–206) **3756**.

6361. ROMANSKA, MAGDA. NecrOphelia: death, femininity and the making of modern aesthetics. PRes (10:3) 2005, 35–53.

6362. —— Ontology and eroticism: two bodies of Ophelia. WS (34:6) 2005, 485–513.

6363. ROWLAND, SUSAN. Jung, *Wolf Solent* and myth. *See* **18923**.

6364. RUTTER, TOM. Fit Hamlet, fat Hamlet, and the problems of aristocratic labour. CEI (68) 2005, 27–32.

6365. SATŌ, SABURO. The father–son relationship in Tōson Shimazaki's *The Broken Commandment* and William Shakespeare's *Hamlet*. CLS (41:4) 2004, 501–8.

6366. SCHLICHTMANN, SILKE. Deutsch Werden mit Tasso und *Hamlet*: Rahel Levin Varnhagens Goethe-und-Shakespeare-Lektüren als Akkulturationsversuche. SJ (141) 2005, 51–69.

6367. SERPIERI, ALESSANDRO. The translator as editor: the Quartos of *Hamlet*. *In* (pp. 167–83) **5975**.

6368. SILHOL, ROBERT. On Hamlet's 'To be or not to be' soliloquy. PsyArt (9) 2005.

6369. SMITH, KAY H. 'Hamlet, Part Eight, the Revenge'; or, Sampling Shakespeare in a postmodern world. ColLit (31:4) 2004, 135–49.

6370. SMITH, PETER J. 'Under Western eyes': Sulaynam Al-Bassam's *The Al-Hamlet Summit* in an age of terrorism. ShB (22:4) 2004, 65–77.

6371. SPINRAD, PHOEBE S. The fall of the sparrow and the map of Hamlet's mind. MP (102:4) 2005, 453–77.

6372. STALLYBRASS, PETER, *et al.* Hamlet's tables and the technologies of writing in Renaissance England. ShQ (55:4) 2004, 379–419.

6373. STAUFFER, ZAHR SAID. The politicisation of Shakespeare in Arabic in Youssef Chahine's film trilogy. ESA (47:2) 2004, 41–55.

6374. TEAGUE, FRANCES. *Mr Hamlet of Broadway.* ShS (57) 2004, 249–57.

6375. TRONCH-PÉREZ, JESÚS. The unavenging prince: a nineteenth-century Mexican stage adaptation of *Hamlet*. *In* (pp. 54–70) **5995**.

6376. VÉLEZ NÚÑEZ, RAFAEL. Melancholic sounds: singing madness in Restoration drama. *See* **7295**.

6377. VERDAGUER, ISABEL. Shakespeare's 'poem unlimited' in eighteenth-century Spain. *In* (pp. 129–43) **5874.**

6378. WILCOX, AGNES. Denmark is a prison, you are there. JMMLA (38:1) 2005, 101–6.

6379. YOUNG, ALAN R. *Hamlet* and the visual arts, 1709–1900. (Bibl. 2004, 6585.) Rev. by Christie Carson in MLR (100:1) 2005, 194–6; by Gabriele Rippl in SJ (141) 2005, 233–9.

Julius Caesar

6380. CORA ALONSO, JESÚS. 'This dream is all amiss interpreted': *Julius Caesar*, Shakespeare's alchemical tragedy. SEDERI (14) 2004, 17–51.

6381. MCGOWAN, MARGARET M. Caesar's cloak: diversion as an art of persuasion in sixteenth-century writing. RenSt (18:3) 2004, 437–48.

6382. MIOLA, ROBERT S. Shakespeare's Ancient Rome: difference and identity. *In* (pp. 193–213) **5964.**

6383. MITTELBACH, JENS. Die Kunst des Widerspruchs: Ambiguität als Darstellungsprinzip in Shakespeares *Henry V* and *Julius Caesar. See* **6425.**

6384. ORKIN, MARTIN. 'I am the tusk of an elephant' – *Macbeth, Titus* and *Caesar* in Johannesburg. *In* (pp. 270–86) **5975.**

6385. OSTROWSKI, WITOLD. Shakespeare's presence in *Dear Brutus* by J. M. Barrie. *In* (pp. 176–82) **3756.**

6386. PHOON, ADRIAN. 'A vision fair and fortunate': ideology, politics and selfhood in *Julius Caesar.* SSE (30) 2004, 21–41.

6387. SCOTT, AMY. 'Romans, countrymen, and lovers': performing politics, sovereign amity and masculinity in *Julius Caesar.* RenP (2003) 99–117.

6388. SHEPHERD, SIMON. Voice, writing, noise …; or, Is Herod Balinese? *See* **4515.**

King Edward III

6389. JANSOHN, CHRISTA. The Shakespeare apocrypha: a reconsideration. EngS (84:4) 2003, 318–29.

6390. LULL, JANIS. Plantagenets, Lancastrians, Yorkists, and Tudors: *1–3 Henry VI, Richard III, Edward III. In* (pp. 89–105) **5964.**

King Henry IV

6391. BAKER, DAVID J. 'Stands Scotland where it did?': Shakespeare on the march. *In* (pp. 20–36) **6561.**

6392. BARNABY, ANDREW. Imitation as originality in Gus Van Sant's *My Own Private Idaho. In* (pp. 22–41) **13273.**

6393. BULMAN, JAMES C. *Henry IV, Parts 1* and *2. In* (pp. 158–76) **5964.**

6394. CAMPILLO ARNÁIZ, LAURA. Spanish translations of culture-bound elements in *The First Part of Henry IV*: a historical perspective. SEDERI (13) 2003, 23–31.

6395. CHEDGZOY, KATE. The civility of early modern Welsh women. *In* (pp. 162–82) **5187.**

6396. CLARET, JEAN-LOUIS. Shakespeare *fuit hic*: reflets en quête de miroir. EREA (2:1) 2004, 32–40.

6397. DAVIES, MICHAEL.   Falstaff's lateness: Calvinism and the Protestant hero in *Henry IV*. RES (56:225) 2005, 351–78.

6398. EDELMAN, CHARLES.   Shakespeare and the invention of the epic theatre: working with Brecht. ShS (58) 2005, 130–6.

6399. —— Shakespeare's *Henry IV, Part 1*. Exp (64:1) 2005, 5–7.

6400. ELLIS, DAVID.   Falstaff and the problems of comedy. CamQ (34:2) 2005, 95–108.

6401. FULLER, DAVID.   The Bogdanov version: the English Shakespeare Company *Wars of the Roses*. LitFQ (33:2) 2005, 118–41.

6402. GRINNELL, RICHARD W.   Witchcraft, race, and the rhetoric of barbarism in *Othello* and *1 Henry IV*. See **6649**.

6403. GROVES, BEATRICE.   Hal as self-styled redeemer: the Harrowing of Hell and *Henry IV Part 1*. ShS (57) 2004, 236–48.

6404. HARMON, A. G.   Shakespeare's carved saints. See **6490**.

6405. JONES-DAVIES, MARGARET.   Defacing the icon of the king: *Richard II* and the issues of iconoclasm. *In* (pp. 101–12) **6505**.

6406. KELLER, JAMES R.   Discretion and valor: Prince Hal's *Platoon*. See **13713**.

6407. KELLEY, GREG.   Tall tales from Cheapside: Falstaff's lying legacy in American Southern literature. See **9311**.

6408. MCBRIDE, CHARLOTTE.   A natural drink for an English man: national stereotyping in early modern culture. *In* (pp. 181–91) **6942**.

6409. MERRIAM, THOMAS.   Anomalous verse in *Henry IV* and *Henry V*. NQ (52:2) 2005, 200–2.

6410. PLAW, AVERY.   Prince Harry: Shakespeare's critique of Machiavelli. IJPP (33:1) 2005, 19–43.

6411. RHODES, NEIL.   Wrapped in the strong arms of the Union: Shakespeare and King James. *In* (pp. 37–52) **6561**.

6412. SCHECKNER, PETER.   Roth's Falstaff: transgressive humor in *Sabbath's Theater*. See **19176**.

6413. TURNER, WALT.   Coins, cons, and the caduceus: the making of a sovereign in Shakespeare's Henry plays. SRASP (27) 2004, 1–10.

King Henry V

6414. BAKER, DAVID J.   'Stands Scotland where it did?': Shakespeare on the march. *In* (pp. 20–36) **6561**.

6415. BILLINGS, TIMOTHY.   Two new sources for Shakespeare's bawdy French in *Henry V*. NQ (52:2) 2005, 202–4.

6416. BLACKSTONE, MARY A.   Lancashire, Shakespeare and the construction of cultural neighbourhoods in sixteenth-century England. *In* (pp. 186–204) **5914**.

6417. DELABASTITA, DIRK.   *Henry V* in the Low Countries: English, Dutch, and the other languages. ShY (15) 2005, 233–50.

6418. DUTTON, RICHARD.   'Methinks the truth should live from age to age': the dating and contexts of *Henry V*. HLQ (68:1/2) 2005, 173–204.

6419. ELLIS, DAVID.   Falstaff and the problems of comedy. See **6400**.

6420. FULLER, DAVID. The Bogdanov version: the English Shakespeare Company *Wars of the Roses. See* **6401.**

6421. HELMBOLD, ANITA. 'Take a soldier, take a king': the (in)separability of king and conflict in Branagh's *Henry V.* LitFQ (33:4) 2005, 280–9.

6422. HOENSELAARS, TON. 'Out-ranting the enemy leader': *Henry V* and/as World War II propaganda. *In* (pp. 215–34) **9237.**

6423. MASON, PAMELA. *Henry V:* 'the quick forge and working house of thought'. *In* (pp. 177–92) **5964.**

6424. MERRIAM, THOMAS. Anomalous verse in *Henry IV* and *Henry V. See* **6409.**

6425. MITTELBACH, JENS. Die Kunst des Widerspruchs: Ambiguität als Darstellungsprinzip in Shakespeares *Henry V* and *Julius Caesar.* Trier: WVT, 2003. pp. viii, 275. (Jenaer Studien zur Anglistik und Amerikanistik, 5.) Rev. by Peter Paul Schnierer in SJ (141) 2005, 272–4.

6426. PLAW, AVERY. Prince Harry: Shakespeare's critique of Machiavelli. *See* **6410.**

6427. RHODES, NEIL. Wrapped in the strong arms of the Union: Shakespeare and King James. *In* (pp. 37–52) **6561.**

6428. ROMOTSKY, SALLY ROBERTSON. Henry of Monmouth and the gown-of-needles. Intertexts (8:2) 2004, 155–72.

6429. RUITER, DAVID. Harry's (in)human face. *In* (pp. 50–72) **5928.**

6430. SCHECKNER, PETER. Roth's Falstaff: transgressive humor in *Sabbath's Theater. See* **19176.**

6431. SCHWYZER, PHILIP. Literature, nationalism, and memory in early modern England and Wales. *See* **5383.**

6432. TURNER, WALT. Coins, cons, and the caduceus: the making of a sovereign in Shakespeare's Henry plays. *See* **6413.**

King Henry VI

6433. ANON. (reviser). Henry VI, part one; Henry VI, part two; Henry VI, part three. Ed. by Lawrence V. Ryan, *et al.* With new and updated critical essays and a revised bibliography. New York: Signet Classics, 2005. pp. lx, 625. (Signet Classics Shakespeare.) (Second ed.: first ed. 1967.)

6434. CRESPO CANDEIAS VELEZ RELVAS, MARÍA DE JESÚS. The literary construction of a monstrous portrait – *King Richard III* by Thomas More and William Shakespeare. *See* **6507.**

6435. DICKSON, LISA. The king is dead: mourning the nation in the three parts of Shakespeare's *Henry VI.* CanRCL (30:1) 2003, 31–53.

6436. FITTER, CHRIS. Emergent Shakespeare and the politics of protest: *2 Henry VI* in historical contexts. ELH (72:1) 2005, 129–58.

6437. FULLER, DAVID. The Bogdanov version: the English Shakespeare Company *Wars of the Roses. See* **6401.**

6438. HARRAWOOD, MICHAEL. Overreachers: hyperbole, the 'circle in the water', and force in *1 Henry 6.* ELR (33:3) 2003, 309–27.

6439. LULL, JANIS. Plantagenets, Lancastrians, Yorkists, and Tudors: *1–3 Henry VI, Richard III, Edward III. In* (pp. 89–105) **5964.**

6440. MARTIN, RANDALL. Catilines and Machiavels: reading Catholic resistance in 3 *Henry VI. In* (pp. 105–15) **5915.**

6441. RICH, JENNIFER A. Gender and the market in *Henry VI, 1. In* (pp. 206–27) **5103.**

6442. ROSSINI, MANUELA S. The sexual/textual impossibility of female heroism in the first tetralogy. ShY (14) 2004, 45–78.

6443. TATSPAUGH, PATRICIA. Propeller's staging of *Rose Rage.* MedRen (17) 2005, 239–54.

6444. TAYLOR, MICHAEL (ed.). Henry VI, part one. (Bibl. 2004, 6662.) Rev. by Randall Martin in ShQ (56:2) 2005, 218–20.

King Henry VIII

6445. CHADELAT, JEAN-MARC. 'In God's name I'll ascend the regal throne': le sacerdoce et la royauté dans *Richard II. In* (pp. 113–51) **6505.**

6446. FOAKES, R. A. Shakespeare's other historical plays. *In* (pp. 214–28) **5964.**

6447. HILLMAN, RICHARD. The tragic Channel-crossings of George Chapman: part II, *The Revenge of Bussy D'Ambois, The Tragedy of Chabot. See* **7311.**

6448. MERRIAM, THOMAS. The palm of martyrdom, the crown of victory. NQ (52:2) 2005, 213–14.

6449. SMYTH, ADAM. A new record of the 1613 Globe fire during a performance of Shakespeare's *King Henry VIII.* NQ (52:2) 2005, 214–16.

King John

6450. BLOOM, GINA. Words made of breath: gender and vocal agency in *King John.* SStud (33) 2005, 125–55.

6451. GROVES, BEATRICE. Memory, composition, and the relationship of *King John* to *The Troublesome Raigne of King John.* CompDr (38:2/3) 2004, 277–90.

6452. PIESSE, A. J. *King John*: changing perspectives. *In* (pp. 126–40) **5964.**

6453. THORET, YVES. Princess Constance in Shakespeare's *King John*: from distress to despair. PsyArt (9) 2005.

King Lear

6454. BERTRAM, BENJAMIN. The time is out of joint: skepticism in Shakespeare's England. *See* **5096.**

6455. BOTTINELLI, JENNIFER J. Watching Lear: resituating the gaze at the intersection of film and drama in Kristian Levring's *The King Is Alive. See* **13623.**

6456. BOYLE, CATHERINE. Nicanor Parra's transcription of *King Lear*: the transfiguration of the literary composition. *In* (pp. 112–29) **5995.**

6457. BROWNLOW, FRANK. Richard Topcliffe: Elizabeth's enforcer and the representation of power in *King Lear. In* (pp. 161–78) **5915.**

6458. BUCK, A. R. Cordelia's estate: women and the law of property from Shakespeare to Nahum Tate. *In* (pp. 183–97) **6964.**

6459. CALVO, CLARA. Rewriting Lear's untender daughter: Fanny Price as a Regency Cordelia in Jane Austen's *Mansfield Park*. *See* **9958**.

6460. DAUGHERTY, DIANE. The pendulum of intercultural performance: *Kathakali King Lear* at Shakespeare's Globe. ATJ (22:1) 2005, 52–72.

6461. DUTTON, RICHARD. Jonson, Shakespeare and the exorcists. *See* **7547**.

6462. EDGECOMBE, RODNEY STENNING. O'Connor's *A Good Man Is Hard to Find*. *See* **18556**.

6463. ESTOK, SIMON C. Shakespeare and ecocriticism: an analysis of 'home' and 'power' in *King Lear*. AUMLA (103) 2005, 15–41.

6464. FOAKES, R. A. Performance and text: *King Lear*. MedRen (17) 2005, 86–98.

6465. —— Shakespeare's other historical plays. *In* (pp. 214–28) **5964**.

6466. GUERNSEY-SHAW, JULIA C. The royal we; the divine I: narcissitic (*sic*) imbalance in the worlds of *King Lear* and *Paradise Lost*. PsyArt (9) 2005.

6467. HILSKÝ, MARTIN (ed. and trans.). William Shakespeare, *Král Lear / King Lear*. Afterword by Bohuslav Mánek. Brno: Atlantis, 2005. pp. 376.

6468. IOPPOLO, GRACE. 'A jointure more or less': re-measuring *The True Chronicle History of King Leir and His Three Daughters*. *See* **7011**.

6469. JONES-DAVIES, MARGARET. Defacing the icon of the king: *Richard II* and the issues of iconoclasm. *In* (pp. 101–12) **6505**.

6470. KELLY, PHILIPPA. Finding *King Lear's* female parts. ShY (14) 2004, 19–44.

6471. —— Performing Australian identity: gendering *King Lear*. TJ (57:2) 2005, 205–27.

6472. —— See what breeds about her heart: *King Lear*, feminism, and performance. RenD (ns 33) 2004, 137–57.

6473. KOLOSOV, JACQUELINE. 'Is this the promised end?': witness in *King Lear* and apocalyptic poetry of the twentieth century. Intertexts (8:2) 2004, 189–99.

6474. LEGGATT, ALEXANDER. *King Lear*. (Bibl. 1994, 4454.) Manchester; New York: Manchester UP, 2004. pp. viii, 216. (Shakespeare in performance.) (Second ed.: first ed. 1991.)

6475. LIEBLEIN, LEANORE. '*Cette belle langue*': the 'tradaptation' of Shakespeare in Quebec. *In* (pp. 255–69) **5975**.

6476. LYNCH, JACK. *King Lear* and 'the taste of the age', 1681–1838. 1650–1850 (10) 2004, 286–303.

6477. MCEACHERN, CLAIRE (ed.). The tragedy of King Lear. London; New York: Pearson Longman, 2005. pp. xxiv, 264. (Longman cultural eds.)

6478. MARGOLIES, DAVID. *King Lear*: Kozintsev's social translation. *In* (pp. 230–8) **6000**.

6479. RAY, ROBERT H. Uses of the royal plural in *King Lear*. CEl (67) 2005, 43–4.

6480. SCHECKNER, PETER. Roth's Falstaff: transgressive humor in *Sabbath's Theater*. *See* **19176**.

6481. SCHWYZER, PHILIP. Literature, nationalism, and memory in early modern England and Wales. *See* **5383**.

6482. TAUNTON, NINA; HART, VALERIE. *King Lear,* King James and the Gunpowder Treason of 1605. RenSt (17:4) 2003, 695–715.

6483. VAN DIJKHUIZEN, JAN FRANS. Demonic possession and gender identity in *King Lear* and *Macbeth.* ShY (14) 2004, 79–91.

King Richard II

6484. BATSON, BEATRICE (ed.). Shakespeare's second historical tetralogy: some Christian features. (Bibl. 2004, 6718.) Rev. by Maurice Hunt in CompDr (38:2/3) 2004, 325–7.

6485. BOLAM, ROBYN. *Richard II*: Shakespeare and the languages of the stage. *In* (pp. 141–57) **5964.**

6486. CHADELAT, JEAN-MARC. 'In God's name I'll ascend the regal throne': le sacerdoce et la royauté dans *Richard II. In* (pp. 113–51) **6505.**

6487. FULLER, DAVID. The Bogdanov version: the English Shakespeare Company *Wars of the Roses. See* **6401.**

6488. GARBIN, LIDIA. 'Not fit to tie his brogues': Shakespeare and Scott. *In* (pp. 141–56) **6561.**

6489. GOY-BLANQUET, DOMINIQUE. Droit des hommes, droit divin: histoires du sacre: *from Edward the Confessor to James VI & I,* de Saint Louis à Charles V ou VI. *In* (pp. 43–56) **6505.**

6490. HARMON, A. G. Shakespeare's carved saints. SELit (45:2) 2005, 315–31.

6491. HOENSELAARS, TON. Shakespeare's *Richard II* in the European mirror. *In* (pp. 87–100) **6505.**

6492. JONES-DAVIES, MARGARET. Defacing the icon of the king: *Richard II* and the issues of iconoclasm. *In* (pp. 101–12) **6505.**

6493. JOUGHIN, JOHN J. The inauguration of modern subjectivity: Shakespeare's 'lyrical tragedy' *Richard II.* EREA (2:2) 2004, 22–34.

6494. LAROQUE, FRANÇOIS. Temps et contretemps dans *Richard II. In* (pp. 27–41) **6505.**

6495. MATHOLÉ, PAUL. Milton's use of 'unking'd': an allusion to *Richard II. See* **7720.**

6496. RHODES, NEIL. Wrapped in the strong arms of the Union: Shakespeare and King James. *In* (pp. 37–52) **6561.**

6497. ROGER, VINCENT. 'That sweet way I was in to despair': le chemin de croix de Richard II. *In* (pp. 57–70) **6505.**

6498. RUITER, DAVID. Shakespeare's festive history: feasting, festivity, fasting, and Lent in the second Henriad. (Bibl. 2004, 6736.) Rev. by Maria Carrig in SixCJ (36:1) 2005, 154–5; by Enno Ruge in SJ (141) 2005, 245–9.

6499. SCHULER, ROBERT M. De-coronation and demonic meta-ritual in *Richard II.* Exemplaria (17:1) 2005, 169–214.

6500. —— Magic mirrors in *Richard II.* CompDr (38:2/3) 2004, 151–81.

6501. SIEMON, JAMES R. Word against word: Shakespearean utterance. (Bibl. 2004, 6738.) Rev. by Michael D. Bristol in SStud (33) 2005, 308–12.

6502. TURNER, WALT. Coins, cons, and the caduceus: the making of a sovereign in Shakespeare's Henry plays. *See* **6413.**

6503. WILSON, RICHARD. 'A stringless instrument': *Richard II* and the defeat of poetry. *In* (pp. 13–26) **6505.**

6504. WINTER, GUILLAUME. '*I cannot see*': vision et visibilité dans *Richard II*. *In* (pp. 71–86) **6505.**

6505. —— (ed.). Autour de *Richard II* de William Shakespeare. Arras: Presses Universitaires d'Artois, 2005. pp. 158. (Lettres et civilisations étrangères.)

King Richard III

6506. BESNAULT, MARIE-HÉLÈNE. Historical legacy and fiction: the poetical reinvention of King Richard III. *In* (pp. 106–25) **5964.**

6507. CRESPO CANDEIAS VELEZ RELVAS, MARÍA DE JESÚS. The literary construction of a monstrous portrait – *King Richard III* by Thomas More and William Shakespeare. SEDERI (13) 2003, 183–9.

6508. HÖFELE, ANDREAS. Making history memorable: More, Shakespeare and Richard III. *See* **5566.**

6509. HUTCHINGS, MARK. *Richard III* and *The Changeling*. NQ (52:2) 2005, 229–30.

6510. JENSEN, MICHAEL P. Olivier's *Richard III* on radio. SNL (54:4) 2004/05, 101–2.

6511. LOPEZ, JEREMY. Time and talk in *Richard III* i.iv. SELit (45:2) 2005, 299–314.

6512. LULL, JANIS. Plantagenets, Lancastrians, Yorkists, and Tudors: *1–3 Henry VI, Richard III, Edward III*. *In* (pp. 89–105) **5964.**

6513. MARCHE, STEPHEN. Mocking dead bones: historical memory and the theater of the dead in *Richard III*. CompDr (37:1) 2003, 37–57.

6514. MENZER, PAUL. 'Come upon your Q': *Richard III*, cue-line variants, and memorial error. ShY (14) 2004, 121–56.

6515. OLSON, GRETA. Richard III's animalistic criminal body. PQ (82:3) 2003, 301–24.

6516. ROBSON, MARK. Shakespeare's words of the future: promising *Richard III*. TexP (19:1) 2005, 13–30.

6517. ROSSINI, MANUELA S. The sexual/textual impossibility of female heroism in the first tetralogy. *See* **6442.**

6518. TEMPERA, MARIANGELA. Looking for Riccardo: two Italian versions of *Richard III*. *In* (pp. 315–26) **12868.**

A Lover's Complaint

6519. DUBROW, HEATHER. 'Lending soft audience to my sweet design': shifting roles and shifting readings of Shakespeare's *A Lover's Complaint*. ShS (58) 2005, 23–33.

6520. TARLINSKAJA, MARINA. Who did NOT write *A Lover's Complaint*. ShY (15) 2005, 343–82.

Love's Labour's Lost

6521. ANON. (reviser). Love's labor's lost. Ed. by John Arthos. With new and updated critical essays and a revised bibliography. New York: Signet Classics, 2004. pp. lxxiii, 178. (Signet Classics Shakespeare.) (Third ed.: first ed. 1965.)

6522. BERRY, PHILIPPA. 'Salving the mail': perjury, grace and the disorder of things in *Love's Labour's Lost*. *In* (pp. 94–108) **5928.**

6523. CAMPBELL, JULIE D. 'Merry, nimble, stirring spirit[s]': academic, salon and *commedia dell'arte* influence on the *innamorate* of *Love's Labour's Lost*. *In* (pp. 145–70) **5225.**

6524. CARVALHO HOMEM, RUI. The feast and the scraps: translating *Love's Labour's Lost* into Portuguese. *In* (pp. 114–29) **5975.**

6525. CHARTIER, ROGER. Crossing borders in early modern Europe: sociology of texts and literature. Trans. by Maurice Elton. BH (8) 2005, 37–50.

6526. CLAYTON, FREDERICK W.; TUDEAU-CLAYTON, MARGARET. Mercury, boy yet and the 'harsh' words of *Love's Labour's Lost*. ShS (57) 2004, 209–24.

6527. KRIMS, MARVIN. Love's lost labor in *Love's Labour's Lost*. PsyArt (9) 2005.

6528. MAGNUSSON, LYNNE. Scoff power in *Love's Labour's Lost* and the Inns of Court: language in context. ShS (57) 2004, 196–208.

6529. MARSHALL, KELLI. 'It doth forget to do the thing it should': Kenneth Branagh, *Love's Labour's Lost*, and (mis)interpreting the musical genre. LitFQ (33:2) 2005, 83–91.

6530. MODENESSI, ALFREDO MICHEL. 'A double tongue within your mask': translating Shakespeare in/to Spanish-speaking Latin America. *In* (pp. 240–54) **5975.**

6531. WHITE, ROBERT. The cultural impact of the Massacre of St Bartholomew's Day. *In* (pp. 183–99) **5187.**

Macbeth

6532. BILLINGS, TIMOTHY. Squashing the 'shard-borne beetle' crux: a hard case with a few pat readings. ShQ (56:4) 2005, 434–47.

6533. BLACKBURN, TOM. *MacBird!* and *Macbeth*: topicality and imitation in Barbara Garson's satirical pastiche. ShS (57) 2004, 137–44.

6534. BORCHMEYER, DIETER. Das Alte und das Neue auf eine überschwengliche Weise verbunden: Schiller und Shakespeare im Lichte Goethes. *See* **6303.**

6535. BURNETT, MARK THORNTON. Local *Macbeth*/global Shakespeare: Scotland's screen destiny. *In* (pp. 189–206) **6561.**

6536. CARROLL, WILLIAM C. 'Two truths are told': afterlives and histories of Macbeths. ShS (57) 2004, 69–80.

6537. CHAMBERLAIN, STEPHANIE. Fantasizing infanticide: Lady Macbeth and the murdering mother in early modern England. ColLit (32:3) 2005, 72–91.

6538. CHANDRASHEKAR, LAXMI. 'A sea change into something rich and strange': Ekbal Ahmed's *Macbeth* and *Hamlet*. *In* (pp. 193–203) **6096.**

6539. DELANEY, BILL. Shakespeare's *Macbeth*. Exp (63:4) 2005, 209–11.

6540. DELONG, ANNE. 'What are these?': hunting for witches in *Macbeth*. SRASP (27) 2004, 23–34.

6541. DISTILLER, NATASHA. 'The Zulu Macbeth': the value of an 'African Shakespeare'. ShS (57) 2004, 159–68. (Welcome Msomi's *uMabatha*.)

6542. DUCASSÉ-TURNER, MILAGRO. Gods on earth: usurping kingly and godly authority in Shakespeare's *Macbeth* and Webster's *The Duchess of Malfi.* Anglophonia (17) 2005, 35–49.

6543. EVANS, G. BLAKEMORE. 'The shard-borne [-born] beetle', *Macbeth*, 3.2.42–43. ANQ (18:4) 2005, 31–4.

6544. FANEGO, TERESA. 'Fare thee well, dame': Shakespeare's forms of address and their socio-affective role. *See* **6260.**

6545. FENDT, GENE. Banquo: a false *faux ami*? NQ (52:2) 2005, 204–6.

6546. FOWLER, ELIZABETH. *Macbeth* and the rhetoric of political forms. *In* (pp. 67–86) **6561.**

6547. GAAKEER, JEANNE. Strange matters: *Macbeth* and Dutch criminology. ShY (15) 2005, 251–66.

6548. GOY-BLANQUET, DOMINIQUE. Droit des hommes, droit divin: histoires du sacre: *from Edward the Confessor to James VI & I*, de Saint Louis à Charles V ou VI. *In* (pp. 43–56) **6505.**

6549. GREEN, MELISSA. Tribal Shakespeare: the Federal Theatre Project's 'Voodoo Macbeth' (1936). UC (24) 2004, 56–62.

6550. HIGHLEY, CHRISTOPHER. The place of Scots in the Scottish play: *Macbeth* and the politics of language. *In* (pp. 53–66) **6561.**

6551. JACKSON, RUSSELL. Staging Birnam Wood in the 1840s: a discovery at the Folger Shakespeare Library. TN (57:2) 2003, 107–11.

6552. KELLER, J. GREGORY. The moral thinking of *Macbeth.* PhilL (29:1) 2005, 41–56.

6553. KINNEY, ARTHUR F. Macbeth's knowledge. ShS (57) 2004, 11–26.

6554. KRONTIRIS, TINA. Translation as appropriation: Vassilis Rotas, Shakespeare and Modern Greek. ShS (58) 2005, 208–19.

6555. LEINWAND, THEODORE B. *Coniugium interruptum* in Shakespeare and Webster. *See* **6263.**

6556. LI, RURU. 'A drum, a drum – Macbeth doth come': when Birnam Wood moved to China. ShS (57) 2004, 169–85.

6557. MCCLURE, J. DERRICK. Scots for Shakespeare. *In* (pp. 217–39) **5975.**

6558. MCCOY, RICHARD C. 'The grace of grace' and double-talk in *Macbeth.* ShS (57) 2004, 27–37.

6559. MCLUSKIE, KATHLEEN. Humane statute and the gentle weal: historical reading and historical allegory. ShS (57) 2004, 1–10.

6560. MALEY, WILLY; MURPHY, ANDREW. Introduction: then with Scotland first begin. *In* (pp. 1–19) **6561.**

6561. —— —— (eds). Shakespeare and Scotland. Manchester; New York: Manchester UP, 2004. pp. viii, 211.

6562. MORSE, RUTH. Monsieur Macbeth: from Jarry to Ionesco. ShS (57) 2004, 112–25.

6563. ORKIN, MARTIN. 'I am the tusk of an elephant' – *Macbeth*, *Titus* and *Caesar* in Johannesburg. *In* (pp. 270–86) **5975.**

6564. PALFREY, SIMON. Macbeth and Kierkegaard. ShS (57) 2004, 96–111.

6565. PRESCOTT, PAUL. Doing all that becomes a man: the reception and afterlife of the Macbeth actor, 1744–1889. ShS (57) 2004, 81–95.

6566. RAFFEL, BURTON (introd. and notes). Macbeth. With an essay by Harold Bloom. New Haven, CT; London: Yale UP, 2005. pp. xli, 210. (Annotated Shakespeare.)

6567. ROE, JOHN. Shakespeare, sonnets, and the 51st Psalm. In (pp. 197–206) **3756**.

6568. ROGERS, REBECCA. How Scottish was 'the Scottish play'? Macbeth's national identity in the eighteenth century. In (pp. 104–23) **6561**.

6569. ROWE, KATHERINE. The politics of sleepwalking: American Lady Macbeths. ShS (57) 2004, 126–36.

6570. RUTTER, CAROL CHILLINGTON. Remind me: how many children had Lady Macbeth? ShS (57) 2004, 38–53.

6571. SHOHET, LAUREN. The banquet of Scotland (PA). See **20773**.

6572. TAMBLING, JEREMY. Levinas and Macbeth's 'strange dreams of death'. EC (54:4) 2004, 351–72.

6573. VAN DIJKHUIZEN, JAN FRANS. Demonic possession and gender identity in King Lear and Macbeth. See **6483**.

6574. WILKINSON, JANE. The cripples at the gate: Orson Welles's 'woodoo' Macbeth. Rome: Bulzoni, 2004. pp. 168. (Piccola biblioteca shakespeariana, 34.)

6575. WILLIAMS, DEANNE. Mick Jagger Macbeth. ShS (57) 2004, 145–58.

6576. WILLIAMS, GEORGE WALTON. Scene individable: the battle of Birnam Wood. SNL (55:2) 2005, 33, 36.

6577. WILLIAMS, SIMON. Taking Macbeth out of himself: Davenant, Garrick, Schiller and Verdi. ShS (57) 2004, 54–68.

6578. WOODBRIDGE, LINDA. Shakespeare and magical grammar. In (pp. 84–98) **5167**.

Measure for Measure

6579. BARKER, SIMON (ed.). Shakespeare's problem plays: All's Well That Ends Well, Measure for Measure, Troilus and Cressida. See **6246**.

6580. CHO, SUNG-WON. Renaissance nun vs Korean gisaeng: chastity and female celibacy in Measure for Measure and Chun-hyang Jeon. CLS (41:4) 2004, 565–83.

6581. GOMES DA TORRE, M. The translation of proper names in Measure for Measure. In (pp. 203–15) **5874**.

6582. JOHNOVÁ, LUCIE. Dark tones and corrupt relationships in Measure for Measure. In (pp. 73–7) **3734**.

6583. KAMARALLI, ANNA. Writing about motive: Isabella, the Duke and moral authority. ShS (58) 2005, 48–59.

6584. KAMPS, IVO; RABER, KAREN (eds). Measure for Measure: texts and contexts. Basingstoke: Macmillan; Boston, MA: Bedford Books of St Martin's Press, 2004. pp. xvi, 378. (Bedford Shakespeare.)

6585. KRAUSE, THOMAS. A picture in little is worth a thousand words: debasement in Hamlet and Measure for Measure. See **6343**.

6586. McBride, Charlotte. A natural drink for an English man: national stereotyping in early modern culture. *In* (pp. 181–91) **6942**.

6587. Marsh, Nicholas. Shakespeare: three problem plays. *See* **6249**.

6588. Mukherji, Subha. Women, law, and dramatic realism in early modern England. *See* **6250**.

6589. Panek, Jennifer. Why were there stewed prunes in Shakespearean brothels? ELN (42:3) 2005, 18–21.

6590. Zaller, Robert. 'Send the head to Angelo': capital punishment in *Measure for Measure*. UC (24) 2004, 63–71.

6591. Zurcher, Amelia A. Ethics and the politic agent of early seventeenth-century prose romance. *See* **7926**.

The Merchant of Venice

6592. Ardolino, Frank. 'Lord, how art thou chang'd!': the incarnation of Launcelot Gobbo. SNL (55:2) 2005, 55–6.

6593. Asquith, Clare. The Catholic Bard: Shakespeare & the 'old religion'. *See* **5849**.

6594. Baker, William; Vickers, Brian (eds). *The Merchant of Venice*. London: Thoemmes Press; New York: Continuum, 2005. pp. xli, 437. (Shakespeare: the critical tradition.)

6595. Bartholomeusz, Dennis. Shylock's shoes: the art of localization. *In* (pp. 227–41) **6096**.

6596. Critchley, Simon; McCarthy, Tom. Universal Shylockery: money and morality in *The Merchant of Venice*. Diacritics (34:1) 2004, 3–17.

6597. Drakakis, John. Jews, bastards, and black rams (and women): representations of 'otherness' in Shakespearean texts. *See* **6778**.

6598. Edelman, Charles (ed.). The merchant of Venice. (Bibl. 2004, 6797.) Rev. by Grace Ioppolo in MLR (100:1) 2005, 196–7; by Stephen J. Phillips in NQ (52:4) 2005, 535–6.

6599. Gallagher, Lowell. Waiting for Gobbo. *In* (pp. 73–93) **5928**.

6600. Halio, Jay L. Shylock: Shakespeare's bad Jew. *In* (pp. 245–54) **5103**.

6601. Hirsch, Brett D. 'In the likeness of a Jew': Kabbalah and *The Merchant of Venice*. BJJ (12) 2005, 119–40.

6602. Hirschfeld, Heather. Compulsions of the Renaissance. SStud (33) 2005, 109–14.

6603. Lal, Ananda. Re-creating *The Merchant of Venice* on the Indian stage: a director's note. *In* (pp. 218–26) **6096**.

6604. Landau, Aaron. 'Rouse up a brave mind': *The Merchant of Venice* and social uprising in the 1590s. RenP (2003) 119–47.

6605. McCullough, Christopher. *The Merchant of Venice*. Basingstoke; New York: Palgrave Macmillan, 2005. pp. 175. (Shakespeare handbooks.)

6606. Mahon, John W.; Mahon, Ellen Macleod (eds). *The Merchant of Venice*: new critical essays. (Bibl. 2004, 6805.) Rev. by Michelle Ephraim in ShQ (55:4) 2004, 475–9.

6607. Minton, Gretchen E. A Polynesian Shakespeare film: the Maori *Merchant of Venice*. UC (24) 2004, 45–55.

6608. MONSARRAT, GILLES. Shylock and mercy. CEl (67) 2005, 1–13.

6609. PETTENGILL, RICHARD. Pitfalls of cinematic aspiration: the reception of Peter Sellars's *The Merchant of Venice*. PRes (10:3) 2005, 54–64.

6610. POWELL, TAMARA; SHATTUCK, SIM. Looking for liberation and lesbians in Shakespeare's cross-dressing comedies. *See* **6813**.

6611. RIPLEY, JOHN. Sociology and soundscape: Herbert Beerbohm Tree's 1908 *Merchant of Venice*. ShQ (56:4) 2005, 385–410.

6612. STEVENS, PAUL. Heterogenizing imagination: globalization, *The Merchant of Venice*, and the work of literary criticism. NLH (36:3) 2005, 425–37.

6613. TETI, DENNIS. The unholy sacrifice: the Catholic theology of Shakespeare's *Merchant of Venice*. IJPP (33:1) 2005, 45–91.

The Merry Wives of Windsor

6614. CHANDLER, DAVID. The 'salt-fish' crux in *The Merry Wives of Windsor*. ELN (42:3) 2005, 1–14.

6615. COCHRAN, PETER. One ton per square foot: the antecedents of *The Vision of Judgement*. *See* **12048**.

6616. EDGECOMBE, RODNEY STENNING. 'The salt fish is an old coat' in *The Merry Wives of Windsor* 1.1. UC (24) 2004, 34–5.

6617. GABY, ROSE. 'Here's a marvellous convenient place for our rehearsal': Shakespeare in Australian space. *See* **6163**.

6618. KELLEY, GREG. Tall tales from Cheapside: Falstaff's lying legacy in American Southern literature. *See* **9311**.

6619. LANDRETH, DAVID. Once more into the preech: the merry wives' English pedagogy. ShQ (55:4) 2004, 420–49.

A Midsummer Night's Dream

6620. CLARKE, BRUCE. Paradox and the form of metamorphosis: systems theory in *A Midsummer Night's Dream*. Intertexts (8:2) 2004, 173–87.

6621. COX, EMMA. Negotiating cultural narratives: all-Aboriginal Shakespearean dreaming. Southerly (64:3) 2004, 15–27.

6622. DAVIS, TRACY C. 'Do you believe in fairies?': the hiss of dramatic license. *See* **15345**.

6623. DESAI, R. W. England, the Indian boy, and the spice trade in *A Midsummer Night's Dream*. *In* (pp. 141–57) **6096**.

6624. GABY, ROSE. 'Here's a marvellous convenient place for our rehearsal': Shakespeare in Australian space. *See* **6163**.

6625. HALIO, JAY L. A Midsummer Night's dream. (Bibl. 1998, 5759.) Manchester; New York: Manchester UP, 2003. pp. xii, 208. (Shakespeare in performance.) (Second ed.: first ed. 1994.) Rev. by Clare McManus in RenSt (18:3) 2004, 498–501.

6626. JOUGHIN, JOHN J. Bottom's secret ... *In* (pp. 130–56) **5928**.

6627. KEINÄNEN, NELY (introd.). Juhannusyön uni. (A Midsummer Night's dream.) Trans. by Matti Rossi. Helsinki: Werner Söderström Osakeyhtiö, 2005. pp. 135.

6628. KENNEDY, JUDITH B. On the sources of the Pyramus and Thisbe playlet. SNL (55:1) 2005, 9–10, 18–20, 32.

6629. PANJA, SHORMISHTHA. An Indian (mid)summer: *Bagro Basant Hai.* In (pp. 204–17) **6096.**

6630. SAVAGE, ROGER. Checklists for Philostrate. In (pp. 294–307) **5172.**

Much Ado about Nothing

6631. CORPORAAL, MARGUÉRITE. Women, wit, and honor: a comparative study of *Much Ado about Nothing* and Jan Jansz Starter's *Timbre de Cardone ende Fenicie Van Messine.* ShY (15) 2005, 141–64.

6632. DRAKAKIS, JOHN. Jews, bastards, and black rams (and women): representations of 'otherness' in Shakespearean texts. See **6778.**

6633. FINDLAY, ALISON. 'Adam's sons are my brethren': reading Beatrice's feminism, past and present. ShY (14) 2004, 1–18.

6634. SHEPPARD, PHILIPPA. 'Sigh no more ladies' – the song in *Much Ado about Nothing*: Shakespeare and Branagh deliver aural pleasure. LitFQ (33:2) 2005, 92–100.

Othello

6635. ABRAHAMS, EILEEN. 'I nothing know': Emilia's rhetoric of self-resistance in *Othello.* SEDERI (14) 2004, 179–88.

6636. BERGER, HARRY, JR. Acts of silence, acts of speech: how to do things with Othello and Desdemona. RenD (ns 33) 2004, 3–35.

6637. BROWN, ERIC C. Cinema in the round: self-reflexivity in Tim Blake Nelson's *O.* In (pp. 73–85) **13273.**

6638. CALBI, MAURIZIO. Approximate bodies: gender and power in early modern drama and anatomy. See **7651.**

6639. —— 'Civil monsters': race, eroticism and the body in early modern literature and culture. SEDERI (13) 2003, 11–21.

6640. COLLINGTON, PHILIP D. Othello the traveller. ETh (8:2) 2005, 73–100.

6641. COLÓN SEMENZA, GREGORY M. Shakespeare after Columbine: teen violence in Tim Blake Nelson's *O.* See **20748.**

6642. CORPORAAL, MARGUÉRITE. Women, speech and subjectivity in Shakespeare's *Othello*: a comparative analysis. ShY (14) 2004, 93–107.

6643. DJORDJEVIC, IGOR. *Goodnight Desdemona (Good Morning Juliet)*: from Shakespearean tragedy to postmodern satyr play. See **17948.**

6644. DRÁBEK, PAVEL. 'There's Magicke in the web of it': the occult dimension of Shakespeare's *Othello.* In (pp. 43–50) **3734.**

6645. DRAKAKIS, JOHN. Jews, bastards, and black rams (and women): representations of 'otherness' in Shakespearean texts. See **6778.**

6646. ERICKSON, PETER; HUNT, MAURICE (eds). Approaches to teaching Shakespeare's *Othello.* New York: Modern Language Assn of America, 2005. pp. ix, 244. (Approaches to teaching world literature.)

6647. FERGUSON, FRANCES. Envy rising. In (pp. 132–48) **9217.**

6648. FUSINI, NADIA. Donne fatali: Ofelia, Desdemona, Cleopatra. See **6323.**

6649. GRINNELL, RICHARD W.   Witchcraft, race, and the rhetoric of barbarism in *Othello* and *1 Henry IV*. UC (24) 2004, 72–80.

6650. HABIB, IMTIAZ.   Shakespeare's spectral Turks: the postcolonial poetics of a mimetic narrative. ShY (14) 2004, 237–69.

6651. HOLMER, JOAN OZARK.   Desdemona, woman warrior: 'O, these men, these men!' (4.3.59). MedRen (17) 2005, 132–64.

6652. KARREMANN, ISABEL.   One and one is two, three is potency: the dynamics of the erotic triangle in *Othello*. SEDERI (13) 2003, 111–21.

6653. LEINWAND, THEODORE B.   *Coniugium interruptum* in Shakespeare and Webster. *See* **6263**.

6654. MATAR, NABIL; STOECKEL, RUDOLPH.   Europe's Mediterranean frontier: the Moor. *In* (pp. 220–52) **5954**.

6655. O'RAWE, DES.   Venice in film: the postcard and the palimpsest. LitFQ (33:3) 2005, 224–32.

6656. PASSOS, JOSÉ LUIZ.   *Othello* and Hugo in Machado de Assis. *In* (pp. 166–82) **5995**.

6657. RAFFEL, BURTON (ed.).   Othello. With an essay by Harold Bloom. New Haven, CT; London: Yale UP, 2005. pp. xxxix, 268. (Annotated Shakespeare.)

6658. RONK, MARTHA.   Desdemona's self-presentation. ELR (35:1) 2005, 52–72.

6659. ROSS, MELANIE H.   Conceiving jealousy: Othello's imitated pregnancy. FMLS (41:1) 2005, 1–17.

6660. SCHALKWYK, DAVID.   Race, body, and language in Shakespeare's sonnets and plays. ESA (47:2) 2004, 5–23.

6661. SCHREINER, SUSAN E.   Appearances and reality in Luther, Montaigne, and Shakespeare. JR (83:3) 2003, 345–80.

6662. SCHWAB, ROXANNE Y.   'Filth, thou liest': the spousal abuse of Emilia in *Othello*. PsyArt (9) 2005.

6663. SEGAN, SAUNDRA.   The pressure to do great things and the impulse to resist it: the case of Iago in *Othello*. PsyArt (9) 2005.

6664. SMITH, BRUCE R.   Female impersonation in early modern ballads. *In* (pp. 281–304) **5225**.

6665. TAYLOR, MARK.   Shakespeare's kisses. SRASP (28) 2005, 3–24.

6666. VAN DIJKHUIZEN, JAN FRANS.   An Arab in Venice: Hafid Bouazza translates *Othello* and the *Massacre at Paris*. ShY (15) 2005, 285–97.

6667. WHITE, R. S.   Sex, lies, videotape – and Othello. *In* (pp. 86–98) **13273**.

Pericles

6668. BEVINGTON, DAVID.   Shakespeare's biography in his plays. Intertexts (8:2) 2004, 105–16.

6669. CHESNOIU, MONICA MATEI.   *Pericles' 'mille periclis'*: Shakespeare and the Falckenburgk Latin verse narrative. ShY (14) 2004, 157–73.

6670. DEWAR-WATSON, SARAH.   Shakespeare's dramatic odysseys: Homer as a tragicomic model in *Pericles* and *The Tempest*. CML (25:1) 2005, 23–40.

6671. GOSSETT, SUZANNE (ed.).   Pericles. (Bibl. 2004, 6911.) Rev. by Lee Bliss in ShQ (56:3) 2005, 354–6.

6672. HINTEN, MARVIN D. Shakespeare's *Pericles*. Exp (63:3) 2005, 130–1.

6673. HUNTER, DIANNE. Miraculous daughters in Shakespeare's late romances. *See* **6248**.

6674. JACKSON, MACDONALD P. Defining Shakespeare: *Pericles* as test case. (Bibl. 2004, 6912.) Rev. by Hugh Craig in ShQ (55:4) 2004, 462–4; by Gilles Monsarrat in EA (58:3) 2005, 355–6.

6675. OESTERLEN, EVE-MARIA. Why bodies matter in mouldy tales: material (re)turns in *Pericles, Prince of Tyre*. UC (24) 2004, 36–44.

6676. WARREN, ROGER (ed.). A reconstructed text of *Pericles, Prince of Tyre*. Text prepared by Gary Taylor and MacD. P. Jackson. (Bibl. 2004, 6918.) Rev. by Lee Bliss in ShQ (56:3) 2005, 354–6.

6677. ZURCHER, AMELIA. Untimely monuments: Stoicism, history, and the problem of utility in *The Winter's Tale* and *Pericles*. *See* **6838**.

The Phoenix and the Turtle

6678. BAXTER, JOHN. J. V. Cunningham's Shakespeare glosses. *See* **15982**.

The Rape of Lucrece

6679. CARVER, GORDON. The Elizabethan erotic narrative: sex(y) reading. *See* **6818**.

6680. COOK, HARDY M. Unnoticed variant reading in Q1 *Lucrece*, 1594. NQ (52:2) 2005, 193–5.

6681. DUBROW, HEATHER. Mourning becomes electric: the politics of grief in Shakespeare's *Lucrece*. CanRCL (30:1) 2003, 23–30.

6682. HYLAND, PETER. An introduction to Shakespeare's poems. (Bibl. 2004, 6921.) Rev. by MacD. P. Jackson in Parergon (22:1) 2005, 242–3; by Patrick Cheney in ShQ (56:2) 2005, 220–4.

6683. JOHNSON, CHRISTOPHER. Appropriating Troy: ekphrasis in Shakespeare's *The Rape of Lucrece*. *In* (pp. 193–212) **4479**.

6684. MIOLA, ROBERT S. Shakespeare's Ancient Rome: difference and identity. *In* (pp. 193–213) **5964**.

Romeo and Juliet

6685. BERRY, PHILIPPA. Between idolatry and astrology: modes of temporal repetition in *Romeo and Juliet*. *In* (pp. 68–83) **5914**.

6686. BOLTON, MATTHEW J. Shakespeare's *Romeo and Juliet*. Exp (63:4) 2005, 208–9.

6687. BULLA, GUIDO. Il verso e la tragedia: forme del linguaggio in *Romeo and Juliet*. Rome: Bulzoni, 2004. pp. 226. (Piccola biblioteca shakespeariana, 33.)

6688. DA CUNHA RESENDE, AIMARA. Text, context, and audience: two versions of *Romeo and Juliet* in Brazilian popular culture. *In* (pp. 270–89) **5995**.

6689. DJORDJEVIC, IGOR. *Goodnight Desdemona (Good Morning Juliet)*: from Shakespearean tragedy to postmodern satyr play. *See* **17948**.

6690. ERNE, LUKAS. Words in space: the reproduction of texts and the semiotics of the page. *See* **4991**.

6691. ISENBERG, NANCY. Accommodating Shakespeare to ballet: John Cranko's *Romeo and Juliet* (Venice, 1958). *In* (pp. 129–39) **6000**.

6692. KISHI, TETSUO.   'Our language of love': Shakespeare in Japanese translation. *In* (pp. 68–81) **5975.**

6693. LIEBLEIN, LEANORE.   *'Cette belle langue'*: the 'tradaptation' of Shakespeare in Quebec. *In* (pp. 255–69) **5975.**

6694. MODENESSI, ALFREDO MICHEL.   Cantinflas's *Romeo y Julieta*: the rogue and Will. *In* (pp. 219–41) **5995.**

6695. NOGUEIRA DINIZ, THAÏS FLORES.   Shakespeare parodied: *Romeo and Juliet*. *In* (pp. 263–9) **5995.**

6696. ORMSBY, ROBERT.   Making Shakespeare work in the twenty-first century: an interview with R. H. Thomson. CanTR (123) 2005, 81–8.

6697. PEQUIGNEY, JOSEPH.   'What the age might call sodomy' and homosexuality in certain studies of Shakespeare's plays. Intertexts (8:2) 2004, 117–34.

6698. PURINTON, MARJEAN D.   Shakespeare's Ghost and Felicia Hemans's *The Vespers of Palermo*: nineteenth-century readings of the page and feminist meanings for the stage. *See* **11262.**

6699. RACZ, GREGORY J.   Strategies of deletion in Pablo Neruda's *Romeo y Julieta*. *In* (pp. 71–91) **5995.**

6700. SHEPPARD, PHILIPPA.   Latino elements in Baz Luhrmann's *Romeo +Juliet*. *In* (pp. 242–62) **5995.**

6701. SOHMER, STEVE.   Shakespeare's time-riddles in *Romeo and Juliet* solved. ELR (35:3) 2005, 407–28.

6702. TREVOR, DOUGLAS.   Love, humoralism, and 'soft' psychoanalysis. SStud (33) 2005, 87–94.

6703. TRIVEDI, HARISH.   Colonizing love: *Romeo and Juliet* in modern Indian disseminations. *In* (pp. 74–91) **6096.**

6704. WATSON, ROBERT N.; DICKEY, STEPHEN.   Wherefore art thou Tereu? Juliet and the legacy of rape. RQ (58:1) 2005, 127–56.

6705. WILDER, LINA PERKINS.   Toward a Shakespearean 'memory theater': Romeo, the apothecary, and the performance of memory. ShQ (56:2) 2005, 156–75.

Sir Thomas More

6706. ARCHER, IAN W.   Discourses of history in Elizabethan and early Stuart London. HLQ (68:1/2) 2005, 205–26.

6707. HONIGMANN, E. A. J.   Shakespeare, *Sir Thomas More* and asylum seekers. ShS (57) 2004, 225–35.

6708. JANSOHN, CHRISTA.   The Shakespeare apocrypha: a reconsideration. *See* **6389.**

6709. MCCLUSKEY, PETER M.   Sir Edmond (*sic*) Tilney, *Sir Thomas More*, and the Netherlandic immigrant community. ShY (15) 2005, 49–64.

6710. MONTA, SUSANNAH BRIETZ.   *The Book of Sir Thomas More* and laughter of the heart. SixCJ (34:1) 2003, 107–21.

Sonnets

6711. BRANDT, LINE; BRANDT, PER AAGE.   Cognitive poetics and imagery. *See* **18227.**

6712. DELANEY, BILL.   Shakespeare's *Macbeth*. See **6539**.

6713. DUFFY, EAMON.   Bare ruined choirs: remembering Catholicism in Shakespeare's England. *In* (pp. 40–57) **5915**.

6714. EDMONDSON, PAUL; WELLS, STANLEY.   Shakespeare's sonnets. Oxford; New York: OUP, 2004. pp. xiv, 194. (Oxford Shakespeare topics.) Rev. by Adam Smyth in TLS, 29 Apr. 2005, 31; by James Schiffer in ShQ (56:4) 2005, 509–11.

6715. FREINKEL, LISA.   The Shakespearean fetish. *In* (pp. 109–29) **5928**.

6716. GREEN, MARTIN.   The pronunciation of *Wriothesley*. See **2061**.

6717. GUTSCH, JÜRGEN (ed.).   '... lesen, wie kraß schön du bist konkret': William Shakespeare, Sonett 18, vermittelt durch deutsche Übersetzer in 154 + 1 Versionen. Dozwil: Signathur, 2003. pp. 180. Rev. by Wolfgang G. Müller in SJ (141) 2005, 253–5.

6718. JACKSON, MACD. P.   Francis Meres and the cultural contexts of Shakespeare's Rival Poet sonnets. RES (56:224) 2005, 224–46. (Sonnets 78–86.)

6719. KUIPER, KONRAD.   Shakespeare's Sonnet 116. Exp (64:1) 2005, 7–9.

6720. MOORE, JAMES.   Shakespeare: a new image. (Bibl. 2004, 6960.) Rev. by William Proctor Williams in NQ (52:2) 2005, 252–3.

6721. PETERS, ROGER.   William Shakespeare's sonnet philosophy. Kaponga, New Zealand: Quaternary, 2005. 4 vols. pp. xxiii, 560; 374; 488; 284.

6722. POINTNER, FRANK ERIK.   Bawdy and soul: a revaluation of Shakespeare's sonnets. Heidelberg: Winter, 2003. pp. 226. (Anglistische Forschungen, 321.) Rev. by John Lee in MLR (100:3) 2005, 768–70.

6723. ROE, JOHN.   Shakespeare, sonnets, and the 51st Psalm. *In* (pp. 197–206) **3756**.

6724. SCHALKWYK, DAVID.   Love and service in *Twelfth Night* and the sonnets. See **6809**.

6725. —— Race, body, and language in Shakespeare's sonnets and plays. See **6660**.

6726. STAPLETON, M. L.   Making the woman of him: Shakespeare's Man Right Fair as sonnet lady. TSLL (46:3) 2004, 271–95.

6727. WINNICK, R. H.   Anagrammatic patterns in Shakespeare's Sonnet 69. NQ (52:2) 2005, 198–200.

6728. WOOD, JANE.   Elizabeth Barrett Browning and Shakespeare's Sonnet 130. See **10256**.

The Taming of the Shrew

6729. BAILEY, AMANDA.   Livery and its discontents: 'braving it' in *The Taming of the Shrew*. RenD (ns 33) 2004, 87–135.

6730. BALIZET, ARIANE M.   Teen scenes: recognizing Shakespeare in teen film. *In* (pp. 122–36) **13273**.

6731. BOEHRER, BRUCE.   Disorder in the house of God: disrupted worship in Shakespeare and others. CompDr (38:1) 2004, 83–103.

6732. CONAWAY, CHARLES.   Shakespeare, molly house culture, and the eighteenth-century stage. CompDr (38:4) 2004/05, 401–23.

6733. —— 'Thou'rt the man': David Garrick, William Shakespeare, and the masculinization of the eighteenth-century stage. *See* **8645**.

6734. DASH, IRENE G. Double vision: *Kiss Me Kate*. SNL (55:1) 2005, 3–4, 19, 22–9.

6735. FREE, MARY. Strange bedfellows: 'the Churching of Women' and *The Taming of the Shrew*. RenP (2003) 83–97.

6736. JONES, MELISSA. 'An aweful rule': safe schools, hard canons, and Shakespeare's loose heirs. *In* (pp. 137–54) **13273**.

6737. LEVIN, RICHARD. What was the life that Petruchio lately led? SNL (55:2) 2005, 33, 36–8, 58.

6738. RAFFEL, BURTON (ed.). The taming of the shrew. With an essay by Harold Bloom. New Haven, CT; London: Yale UP, 2005. pp. xxxvii, 174. (Annotated Shakespeare.)

6739. STAPLETON, M. L. Making the woman of him: Shakespeare's Man Right Fair as sonnet lady. *See* **6726**.

The Tempest

6740. BATTISTI, SUSANNA. Metamorfosi del teatro: gli adattamenti shakespeariani di John Dryden. *See* **7405**.

6741. BEVINGTON, DAVID. Shakespeare's biography in his plays. *See* **6668**.

6742. BISHOP, TOM. The masque and Shakespeare's scepticism. SStudT (42) 2004, 28–41.

6743. BÖGELS, THEO. 'Fit for the pocket': Thomas Johnson's edition of *The Tempest*. ShY (15) 2005, 165–78.

6744. BOLTON, MATTHEW. Shakespeare's *The Tempest*. Exp (64:1) 2005, 4.

6745. CHILTON, NEIL. Conceptions of a beautiful crisis: Henry James's reading of *The Tempest*. *See* **11388**.

6746. DEWAR-WATSON, SARAH. Shakespeare's dramatic odysseys: Homer as a tragicomic model in *Pericles* and *The Tempest*. *See* **6670**.

6747. DEWEESE, DAN. Prospero's pharmacy: Peter Greenaway and the critics play Shakespeare's mimetic game. *In* (pp. 155–68) **13273**.

6748. EVETT, DAVID. Luther, Cranmer, service and Shakespeare. *In* (pp. 87–109) **6872**.

6749. FRASSINELLI, PIER PAOLO. Shakespeare and transculturation: Aimé Césaire's *A Tempest*. ESA (47:2) 2004, 57–75.

6750. GAGNON, CHANTAL. Le Shakespeare québécois des années 1990. TRC (24:1/2) 2003, 58–75.

6751. GANDARA RAUEN, MARARIDA. Guilherme Schiffer Durães's Caliban: from canonical text to resistance. *In* (pp. 130–42) **5995**.

6752. GOLDBERG, JONATHAN. *Tempest* in the Caribbean. (Bibl. 2004, 6995.) Rev. by Peter Hulme in SStud (33) 2005, 252–9.

6753. GONZÁLEZ CAMPOS, MIGUEL ÁNGEL. The portrayal of treason in *The Tempest*: the fourfold role of a Machiavellian duke. SEDERI (14) 2004, 207–16.

6754. GOZZI, FRANCESCO. Shakespeare as Paraclitus: Transubstantiation in Joyce and T. S. Eliot. *In* (pp. 88–94) **3724**.

6755. HENKE, HOLGER. Ariel's ethos: on the moral economy of Caribbean experience. CultC (56) 2004, 33–63.

6756. LEE, JOHN. Kipling's Shakespearean *Traffics and Discoveries*. *See* **17471.**

6757. McCOMBE, JOHN P. 'Suiting the action to the word': the Clarendon *Tempest* and the evolution of a narrative silent Shakespeare. LitFQ (33:2) 2005, 142–55.

6758. MATAR, NABIL; STOECKEL, RUDOLPH. Europe's Mediterranean frontier: the Moor. *In* (pp. 220–52) **5954.**

6759. NELSON, ROBIN. Live or wired? Technologizing the event. *In* (pp. 303–16) **3974.**

6760. PESTA, DUKE. 'This rough magic I here abjure': Shakespeare's *The Tempest* and the fairy-tale body. JFA (15:1) 2004, 49–60.

6761. RHODES, NEIL. Shakespeare the barbarian. *In* (pp. 99–114) **5187.**

6762. SAVAGE, ROGER. Checklists for Philostrate. *In* (pp. 294–307) **5172.**

6763. SHULLENBERGER, WILLIAM. The profession of virginity in *A Maske Presented at Ludlow Castle*. *In* (pp. 77–94) **7717.**

6764. SOKOL, B. J. A brave new world of knowledge: Shakespeare's *The Tempest* and early modern epistemology. (Bibl. 2003, 6551.) Rev. by Scott Maisano in MLR (100:3) 2005, 773–4.

6765. SUTTON, JAMES M. The retiring patron: William Cecil and the cultivation of retirement, 1590–98. *In* (pp. 159–79) **5121.**

6766. TERANDO, LORENA. Traces of Shakespeare's *Tempest* in Cuba's Carpentier. *In* (pp. 183–95) **5995.**

6767. THIERFELDER, BILL. Wordsworth's *Ode: Intimations of Immortality*, Shakespeare's *The Tempest* 5.1, and Vaughan's *The Retreat*. *See* **12519.**

6768. TONNING, JUDITH E. 'Like this insubstantial pageant, faded': eschatology and theatricality in *The Tempest*. LitTheol (18:4) 2004, 371–82.

6769. VIEIRA, FÁTIMA. The gender of spirits: Ariel and the Portuguese audience. *In* (pp. 217–23) **5874.**

6770. WALLACE, NATHAN. Shakespeare biography and the theory of reconciliation in Edward Dowden and James Joyce. *See* **10837.**

6771. WATTS, CEDRIC. *The Tempest*, IV.i.123–124: *wise* or *wife*? NQ (52:2) 2005, 213.

Timon of Athens

6772. BERTRAM, BENJAMIN. The time is out of joint: skepticism in Shakespeare's England. *See* **5096.**

6773. DARCY, ROBERT. Shakespeare's empty plot: the epicenotaph in *Timon of Athens*. RenD (ns 33) 2004, 159–79.

6774. FIELITZ, SONJA. Learned pate and golden fool: a Jesuit source for *Timon of Athens*. *In* (pp. 179–96) **5915.**

6775. JOWETT, JOHN. Timon and mining. SEDERI (14) 2004, 77–92.

6776. PIERCE, ROBERT B. From anecdotal philosophy to drama: Shakespeare's Apemantus as Cynic. CML (25:2) 2005, 77–88.

Titus Andronicus

6777. ANON. (reviser). The tragedy of Titus Andronicus; The life of Timon of Athens. Ed. by Sylvan Barnet and Maurice Charney. With new and updated critical essays and a revised bibliography. (Bibl. 1964, 2688.) New York: Signet Classics, 2005. pp. lx, 404. (Signet Classics Shakespeare.) (Second ed.: first ed. 1964.)

6778. DRAKAKIS, JOHN. Jews, bastards, and black rams (and women): representations of 'otherness' in Shakespearean texts. SEDERI (13) 2003, 55–75.

6779. FITZPATRICK, JOAN. Shakespeare's *Titus Andronicus* and Bandello's *Novelle* as sources for the Munera episode in Spenser's *Faerie Queene*, Book 5, canto 2. See **5694.**

6780. HADFIELD, ANDREW. 'Suum cuique': natural law in *Titus Andronicus*, 1.i.284. NQ (52:2) 2005, 195–6.

6781. HUTSON, LORNA. Rethinking the 'spectacle of the scaffold': juridical epistemologies and English revenge tragedy. Representations (89) 2005, 30–58.

6782. KAHAN, JEFFREY. A further note on Semiramis. See **7636.**

6783. MARTÍN RODRÍGUEZ, ANTONIO MARÍA. Fuentes clásicas en *Titus Andronicus* de Shakespeare. León: Univ. de León, Secretariado Publicaciones y Medios Audiovisuales, 2003. Rev. by José Manuel González in RAEI (18) 2005, 309–10.

6784. MATAR, NABIL; STOECKEL, RUDOLPH. Europe's Mediterranean frontier: the Moor. In (pp. 220–52) **5954.**

6785. MIOLA, ROBERT S. Shakespeare's Ancient Rome: difference and identity. In (pp. 193–213) **5964.**

6786. MOWAT, BARBARA A.; WERSTINE, PAUL (eds). Titus Andronicus. New York: Washington Square Press, 2005. pp. lii, 267. (New Folger Library Shakespeare.)

6787. ORKIN, MARTIN. 'I am the tusk of an elephant' – *Macbeth*, *Titus* and *Caesar* in Johannesburg. In (pp. 270–86) **5975.**

6788. RHODES, NEIL. Shakespeare the barbarian. In (pp. 99–114) **5187.**

6789. TAYLOR, QUENTIN. 'To order well the state': the politics of *Titus Andronicus*. IJPP (32:2) 2005, 125–50.

Troilus and Cressida

6790. BARKER, SIMON (ed.). Shakespeare's problem plays: *All's Well That Ends Well, Measure for Measure, Troilus and Cressida*. See **6246.**

6791. BATTISTI, SUSANNA. Metamorfosi del teatro: gli adattamenti shakespeariani di John Dryden. See **7405.**

6792. BRITLAND, KAREN. Circe's cup: wine and women in early modern drama. In (pp. 109–25) **6942.**

6793. CELLAI, ANTONELLA. Da *truce-breaker* a *match-maker*: le metamorfosi di Pandaro da Omero a Dryden. See **5057.**

6794. D'AGOSTINO, NEMI (introd.). Troilo e Cressida. Trans. by Francesco Binni. Milan: Garzanti, 2005. pp. xlv, 265. (Second ed.: first ed. 1994.)

6795. KAHAN, JEFFREY. Shakespeare's Hector and Heywood's *The Rape of Lucrece*. ANQ (18:2) 2005, 25–6.

6796. MARSH, NICHOLAS. Shakespeare: three problem plays. *See* **6249**.

6797. SHIRLEY, FRANCES A. (ed.). *Troilus and Cressida*. Cambridge; New York: CUP, 2005. pp. xxi, 258. (Shakespeare in production.)

6798. YACHNIN, PAUL. 'The perfection of ten': populuxe art and artisanal value in *Troilus and Cressida*. ShQ (56:3) 2005, 306–27.

Twelfth Night

6799. CLARE, JANET. The 'complexion' of *Twelfth Night*. ShS (58) 2005, 199–207.

6800. EDGECOMBE, RODNEY STENNING. Feste's 'leman' in *Twelfth Night*. SNL (55:2) 2005, 43.

6801. EDMONDSON, PAUL. *Twelfth Night*. Basingstoke; New York: Palgrave Macmillan, 2005. pp. x, 181. (Shakespeare handbooks.)

6802. FORD, JOHN R. Changeable taffeta: re-dressing the bears in *Twelfth Night*. UC (24) 2004, 3–14.

6803. ICHIKAWA, MARIKO. '*Maluolio within*': acting on the threshold between onstage and offstage spaces. MedRen (18) 2005, 123–45.

6804. KISHI, TETSUO. 'Our language of love': Shakespeare in Japanese translation. *In* (pp. 68–81) **5975**.

6805. LECERCLE, ANNE. Country house, Catholicity and the crypt(ic) in *Twelfth Night*. *In* (pp. 84–100) **5914**.

6806. PEQUIGNEY, JOSEPH. 'What the age might call sodomy' and homosexuality in certain studies of Shakespeare's plays. *See* **6697**.

6807. POULSEN, RACHEL. Women performing homoerotic desire in English and Italian comedy: *La calandria*, *Gl'ingannati* and *Twelfth Night*. *In* (pp. 171–91) **5225**.

6808. POWELL, TAMARA; SHATTUCK, SIM. Looking for liberation and lesbians in Shakespeare's cross-dressing comedies. *See* **6813**.

6809. SCHALKWYK, DAVID. Love and service in *Twelfth Night* and the sonnets. ShQ (56:1) 2005, 76–100.

6810. VENET, GISÈLE. *Twelfth Night* et *All's Well That Ends Well*: deux comédies que tout oppose, ou deux moments d'une même esthétique? EA (58:3) 2005, 276–92.

The Two Gentlemen of Verona

6811. CARROLL, WILLIAM C. (ed.). The two gentlemen of Verona. London: Arden Shakespeare, 2004. pp. xix, 315. (Arden Shakespeare: third series.) Rev. by Margaret Maurer in ShQ (56:3) 2005, 357–9.

6812. EDGECOMBE, RODNEY STENNING. Three proposed emendations. *See* **5801**.

6813. POWELL, TAMARA; SHATTUCK, SIM. Looking for liberation and lesbians in Shakespeare's cross-dressing comedies. UC (24) 2004, 25–33.

6814. RIVLIN, ELIZABETH. Mimetic service in *The Two Gentlemen of Verona*. ELH (72:1) 2005, 105–28.

The Two Noble Kinsmen

6815. FUSINI, NADIA (introd.). I due nobili congiunti. Trans. by Giorgio Melchiori and Miranda Melchiori. Milan: Mondadori, 2005. pp. xxxiii, 249. (Oscar classici, 620.)

6816. LYNCH, KATHRYN L. The three noble kinsmen: Chaucer, Shakespeare, Fletcher. In (pp. 72–91) **5103.**

6817. RASMUSSEN, ERIC; PROUDFOOT, G. R. (eds). The two noble kinsmen. Oxford; New York: OUP for the Malone Soc., 2005. pp. xvi, 95. (Malone Soc. reprints, 169.)

Venus and Adonis

6818. CARVER, GORDON. The Elizabethan erotic narrative: sex(y) reading. ExRC (31:1) 2005, 107–34.

6819. MENON, MADHAVI. Spurning teleology in Venus and Adonis. GLQ (11:4) 2005, 491–519.

The Winter's Tale

6820. BEVINGTON, DAVID. Shakespeare's biography in his plays. See **6668.**

6821. COLDIRON, A. E. B. ''Tis rigor and not law': trials of women as trials of patriarchy in The Winter's Tale. RenP (2004) 29–68.

6822. COTTRILL, CHRISTINA M. 'There's some ill planet reigns': telescopic vision, the heavens and The Winter's Tale. SRASP (28) 2005, 36–45.

6823. DOBSON, MICHAEL. The British personality of the millennium: British Shakespeares, amateur and professional, in the new century. In (pp. 113–28) **6000.**

6824. DROUET, PASCALE. Breaking boundaries: tyranny and roguery in The Winter's Tale. CEl (67) 2005, 15–22.

6825. FANEGO, TERESA. 'Fare thee well, dame': Shakespeare's forms of address and their socio-affective role. See **6260.**

6826. FLECK, ANDREW. Vulgar fingers of the multitude: Shakespeare, Jonson, and the transformation of news from the Low Countries. ShY (15) 2005, 89–111.

6827. HALL, JOAN LORD. The Winter's Tale: a guide to the play. Westport, CT; London: Greenwood Press, 2005. pp. x, 210. (Greenwood guides to literature.)

6828. HOPKINS, BROOKE. 'Every man kills the thing he loves': object use and potential space in The Winter's Tale. PsyArt (9) 2005.

6829. JOUGHIN, JOHN J. Bottom's secret … In (pp. 130–56) **5928.**

6830. MALAGI, R. A. Toward a terrestrial Divine Comedy: a study of The Winter's Tale and Shakuntalam. In (pp. 123–40) **6096.**

6831. MORAN, ANDREW. Synaesthesia and eating in The Winter's Tale. RelArts (9:1/2) 2005, 38–61.

6832. PARKER, PATRICIA. Temporal gestation, legal contracts, and the promissory economies of The Winter's Tale. In (pp. 25–49) **6964.**

6833. REYNOLDS, SIMON. Pregnancy and imagination in The Winter's Tale and Heliodorus' Aithiopika. EngS (84:5) 2003, 433–47.

6834. SCHWARTZ, MURRAY M. Loss and transformation in The Winter's Tale: part I, Leontes' jealousy. PsyArt (9) 2005.

6835. —— Loss and transformation in *The Winter's Tale*: part II, Transformations. PsyArt (9) 2005.

6836. VAUGHT, JENNIFER. Masculinity and affect in Shakespeare's *Winter's Tale*: men of feeling from the Renaissance through the Enlightenment. 1650–1850 (10) 2004, 305–25.

6837. WELLS, MARION. Mistress Taleporter and the triumph of time: slander and old wives' tales in *The Winter's Tale*. ShS (58) 2005, 247–59.

6838. ZURCHER, AMELIA. Untimely monuments: Stoicism, history, and the problem of utility in *The Winter's Tale* and *Pericles*. ELH (70:4) 2003, 903–27.

SEVENTEENTH CENTURY

GENERAL

6839. ABRAMS, M. H.; GREENBLATT, STEPHEN (gen. eds). The Norton anthology of English literature: vol. 1C, The Restoration and the eighteenth century. Ed. by Lawrence Lipking. (Bibl. 1995, 2902.) New York; London: Norton, 2003. pp. xxvi, 2045–888, 70. (Seventh ed.: first ed. 1962.) Rev. by Lisa Berglund in AJ (15) 2004, 331–65.

6840. AMORY, HUGH. Bibliography and the book trades: studies in the print culture of early New England. Ed. by David D. Hall. See **754**.

6841. ANDERSON, JUDITH H. Translating investments: metaphor and the dynamic of cultural change in Tudor–Stuart England. See **2210**.

6842. BAKER, JENNIFER J. Securing the commonwealth: debt, speculation, and writing in the making of Early America. Baltimore, MD; London: Johns Hopkins UP, 2005. pp. x, 218.

6843. BALLASTER, ROS (ed.). Fables of the East: selected tales, 1662–1785. Oxford; New York: OUP, 2005. pp. vii, 277.

6844. BARBOUR, REID. Literature and religious culture in seventeenth-century England. (Bibl. 2004, 7116.) Rev. by Mark Haverland in JR (83:2) 2003, 285–6; by Hannibal Hamlin in SixCJ (34:2) 2003, 485–7; by Holly Faith Nelson in SCN (63:3/4) 2005, 161–4.

6845. BAUER, RALPH. The cultural geography of Colonial American literatures: empire, travel, modernity. (Bibl. 2004, 7119.) Rev. by Debra Boyle in ECS (38:2) 2005, 367–71; by Susan Scott Parrish in EAL (40:3) 2005, 545–53.

6846. BAWCUTT, PRISCILLA. Scottish manuscript miscellanies from the fifteenth to the seventeenth century. See **200**.

6847. BELLAMY, ELIZABETH JANE. Desires and disavowals: speculations on the aftermath of Stephen Greenblatt's *Psychoanalysis and Renaissance Culture*. See **14699**.

6848. BLAINE, MARLIN E. The poet's monument: assessing the national literary tradition from Elizabethan times to the Restoration. See **5100**.

6849. BOWERBANK, SYLVIA. Speaking for nature: women and ecologies of early modern England. (Bibl. 2004, 7130.) Rev. by Joan Blythe in MQ (39:2) 2005, 107–12.

6850. BRAYMAN HACKEL, HEIDI. Reading material in early modern England: print, gender, and literacy. See **780**.

6851. BROSS, KRISTINA. Dry bones and Indian sermons: praying Indians in Colonial America. (Bibl. 2004, 7133.) Rev. by Phillip H. Round in EAL (40:2) 2005, 375–85.

6852. BROWN, GEORGIA. Redefining Elizabethan literature. See **5102**.

6853. BRUCE, YVONNE (ed.). Images of matter: essays on British literature of the Middle Ages and Renaissance: proceedings of the Eighth Citadel Conference on Literature, Charleston, South Carolina, 2002. See **5103**.

6854. CAMPBELL, GORDON (ed.). The Oxford dictionary of the Renaissance. See **5105**.

6855. CARPI, DANIELA (ed.). Property law in Renaissance literature. *See* **5106.**

6856. CARTWRIGHT, KENT. Early modern English literature without *Hamlet*. *See* **5107.**

6857. CEFALU, PAUL. Moral identity in early modern English literature. *See* **5109.**

6858. CHEDGZOY, KATE. In the lesbian archive. *See* **5110.**

6859. CLEGG, CYNDIA SUSAN. 'The aucthor of this book': attributing authorship, 1580–1640. *See* **5113.**

6860. CLUCAS, STEPHEN; DAVIES, ROSALIND (eds). The crisis of 1614 and the Addled Parliament: literary and historical perspectives. Aldershot; Burlington, VT: Ashgate, 2003. pp. xi, 213. Rev. by David L. Smith in SevC (20:1) 2005, 145–6; by Sybil M. Jack in Parergon (22:2) 2005, 203–4; by Johann Sommerville in CLIO (34:3) 2005, 317–32.

6861. COOK, JAMES. Encyclopedia of Renaissance literature. *See* **5116.**

6862. CORMACK, BRADIN. Practicing law and literature in early modern studies. *See* **5117.**

6863. CORNETT, MICHAEL. New books across the disciplines. *See* **4415.**

6864. CRAWFORD, JULIE. Marvelous Protestantism: monstrous births in post-Reformation England. *See* **5120.**

6865. CROFT, PAULINE (ed.). Patronage, culture and power: the early Cecils. *See* **5121.**

6866. DAMROSCH, DAVID (gen. ed.). The Longman anthology of world literature: vol. C, The early modern period. Ed. by Jane Tylus and David Damrosch. *See* **5123.**

6867. —— The Longman anthology of world literature: vol. D, The seventeenth and eighteenth centuries. Ed. by April Alliston. Harlow; New York: Longman, 2004. pp. xxvi, 689.

6868. DAVIDSON, JENNY. Hypocrisy and the politics of politeness: manners and morals from Locke to Austen. (Bibl. 2004, 7150.) Rev. by Paddy Bullard in TLS, 8 Apr. 2005, 26; by Adam Potkay in Scriblerian (37:2 / 38:1) 2005, 151–3.

6869. DEMERS, PATRICIA. Early modern England. *See* **5127.**

6870. DILLON, ELIZABETH MADDOCK. The gender of freedom: fictions of liberalism and the literary public sphere. (Bibl. 2004, 7154.) Rev. by Bruce Burgett in EAL (40:2) 2005, 391–5; by Caroline Levander in Legacy (22:2) 2005, 208–9.

6871. DOBRANSKI, STEPHEN B. Readers and authorship in early modern England. *See* **5128.**

6872. DOERKSEN, DANIEL W.; HODGKINS, CHRISTOPHER (eds). Centered on the Word: literature, Scripture, and the Tudor–Stuart middle way. Newark: Delaware UP, 2004. pp. 367. Rev. by Jacob Blevins in SCN (62:3/4) 2004, 182–6; by Susan M. Felch in ChrisL (54:2) 2005, 289–93; by Andrew Barnaby in RQ (58:2) 2005, 716–18.

6873. ENTERLINE, LYNN; HILLMAN, DAVID. Other selves, other bodies. *See* **21023.**

6874. EZELL, MARGARET J. M. Eclectic circulation: the functional dynamics of manuscript and electronic literary cultures. *In* (pp. 27–35) **587.**

6875. —— Looking-glass histories. JBS (43:3) 2004, 317–38.

6876. FERNIE, EWAN, *et al.* (eds). Reconceiving the Renaissance: a critical reader. *See* **5134.**

6877. FORTIER, MARK. The culture of equity in early modern England. *See* **5135.**

6878. GILL, CATIE. Women in the seventeenth-century Quaker community: a literary study of political identities, 1650–1700. Aldershot; Burlington, VT: Ashgate, 2005. pp. xii, 243. (Women and gender in the early modern world.)

6879. GILLESPIE, KATHARINE. Domesticity and Dissent in the seventeenth century: English women writers and the public sphere. Cambridge; New York: CUP, 2004. pp. xii, 272. Rev. by Jerome S. Dees in SCN (63:1/2) 2005, 20–4; by Tita French Baumlin in RQ (58:1) 2005, 349–51; by Joan E. Hartman in CLIO (35:1) 2005, 107–11; by James Fitzmaurice in JAAR (73:4) 2005, 1209–12.

6880. GÓMEZ LARA, MANUEL. Discourses on health and leisure and modern constructions of holidays at the Restoration spas. *In* (pp. 202–27) **5167.**

6881. GREENE, JODY. The trouble with ownership: literary property and authorial liability in England, 1660–1730. Princeton, NJ; Oxford: Princeton UP, 2005. pp. 272. (Material texts.) Rev. by Harold Love in TLS, 7 Oct. 2005, 28.

6882. GUIBBORY, ACHSAH. Recent studies in the English Renaissance. *See* **5139.**

6883. HAGER, ALAN (ed.). The age of Milton: an encyclopedia of major 17th-century British and American authors. (Bibl. 2004, 7168.) Rev. by John Mulryan in SixCJ (36:2) 2005, 572–3.

6884. HAMLIN, WILLIAM M. Tragedy and skepticism in Shakespeare's England. *See* **5143.**

6885. HAVENS, EARLE. English manuscript culture and the ambiguous triumph of print: seventy years of the Osborn Collection, 1934–2004. *See* **400.**

6886. HILL, W. SPEED (ed.). New ways of looking at old texts III: papers of the Renaissance English Text Society, 1997–2001. *See* **587.**

6887. HINNANT, CHARLES HASKELL. *Moll Flanders*, *Roxana*, and first-person female narratives: models and prototypes. *See* **8519.**

6888. HÖFELE, ANDREAS; VON KOPPENFELS, WERNER (eds). Renaissance go-betweens: cultural exchange in early modern Europe. *See* **5147.**

6889. HOXBY, BLAIR. Mammon's music: literature and economics in the age of Milton. (Bibl. 2004, 7175.) Rev. by Warren Chernaik in MLR (100:3) 2005, 783–5; by Carl Wennerlind in SevC (20:1) 2005, 147–8.

6890. HUME, ROBERT D. 'Satire' in the reign of Charles II. MP (102:3) 2005, 332–71.

6891. IVIC, CHRISTOPHER; WILLIAMS, GRANT (eds). Forgetting in early modern English literature and culture: Lethe's legacies. *See* **5148.**

6892. IYENGAR, SUJATA. Shades of difference: mythologies of skin colour in early modern England. *See* **5149.**

6893. JOHNSTONE, NATHAN. The Protestant Devil: the experience of temptation in early modern England. *See* **5150.**

6894. KAHN, VICTORIA. Wayward contracts: the crisis of political obligation in England, 1640–1674. (Bibl. 2004, 7178.) Rev. by Michael Mendle in RQ (58:3) 2005, 1053–4.

6895. KENDRICK, CHRISTOPHER. Utopia, carnival, and commonwealth in Renaissance England. *See* **5152.**

6896. KING, JOHN N. Voices of the English Reformation: a sourcebook. *See* **5155.**

6897. KINNEY, ARTHUR. Harriett Hawkins's Renaissance. *In* (pp. 30–41) **5167.**

6898. KNOPPERS, LAURA LUNGER (ed.). Puritanism and its discontents. (Bibl. 2004, 7182.) Rev. by Donald K. McKim in SixCJ (35:4) 2004, 1237–9.

6899. KNOTT, SARAH; TAYLOR, BARBARA (eds). Women, gender and Enlightenment. *See* **8016.**

6900. KNOWLES, JAMES. Crack kisses not staves: sexual politics and court masques in 1613–1614. *In* (pp. 143–60) **6860.**

6901. KUCHAR, GARY. Divine subjection: the rhetoric of sacramental devotion in early modern England. *See* **5158.**

6902. LEITZ, ROBERT C., III; COPE, KEVIN L. Imagining the sciences: expressions of new knowledge in the 'long' eighteenth century. *See* **8019.**

6903. LONGFELLOW, ERICA. Women and religious writing in early modern England. Cambridge; New York: CUP, 2004. pp. ix, 241. Rev. by Maureen Bell in TLS, 17 June 2005, 24; by Frances M. Malpezzi in SCN (63:3/4) 2005, 141–3; by Megan Matchinske in RQ (58:4) 2005, 1424–7.

6904. LÓPEZ-PELÁEZ CASELLAS, JESÚS. The neo-Stoic revival in English literature of the sixteenth and seventeenth centuries: an approach. *See* **5160.**

6905. LUDINGTON, CHARLES C. 'Be sometimes to your country true': the politics of wine in England, 1660–1714. *In* (pp. 89–106) **6942.**

6906. MCCOLLUM, SARAH C. Some current publications. Restoration (29:1) 2005, 65–78.

6907. MACDONALD, ALASDAIR A.; DEKKER, KEES (eds). Rhetoric, royalty, and reality: essays on the literary culture of medieval and early modern Scotland. *See* **4452.**

6908. MCDOWELL, NICHOLAS. The English Radical imagination: culture, religion, and revolution, 1630–1660. (Bibl. 2004, 7189.) Rev. by Austin Woolrych in LitH (14:1) 2005, 88–9; by N. H. Keeble in MLR (100:3) 2005, 781–2; by Derek Hirst in JBS (44:2) 2005, 368–9; by John McWilliams in NQ (52:1) 2005, 123–5; by Jacques Coulardeau in EREA (3:1) 2005.

6909. MCKEON, MICHAEL. Recent studies in the Restoration and eighteenth century. SELit (45:3) 2005, 707–82.

6910. MCRAE, ANDREW. Literature, satire, and the early Stuart State. (Bibl. 2004, 7192.) Rev. by Johann Sommerville in CLIO (34:3) 2005, 317–32; by Melissa Mohr in SCN (63:1/2) 2005, 34–7; by Janet Hadley Williams in Parergon (22:1) 2005, 261–3; by Kirk Combe in NQ (52:1) 2005, 122–3; by Gary D. Hamilton in RQ (58:1) 2005, 347–9.

6911. McWilliams, John. New England's crises and cultural memory: literature, politics, history, religion, 1620–1860. Cambridge; New York: CUP, 2004. pp. xii, 366. (Cambridge studies in American literature and culture, 142.) Rev. by Douglas Anderson in SAtlR (70:2) 2005, 132–4.

6912. Michie, Allen; Buckley, Eric (eds). Style: essays on Renaissance and Restoration language and culture in memory of Harriett Hawkins. *See* **5167.**

6913. Monta, Susannah Brietz. Martyrdom and literature in early modern England. *See* **5169.**

6914. Moulton, Ian Frederick. Studies in early modern sexuality. *See* **5170.**

6915. Mowry, Melissa M. The bawdy politic in Stuart England, 1660–1714: political pornography and prostitution. Aldershot; Burlington, VT: Ashgate, 2004. pp. viii, 173. (Women and gender in the early modern world.) Rev. by Shannon Reed in RQ (58:4) 2005, 1421–2.

6916. Müller, Marion Ursula. 'These savage beasts become domestick': the discourse of the passions in early modern England with special reference to non-fictional texts. *See* **5171.**

6917. Munro, Ian. The figure of the crowd in early modern London: the city and its double. *See* **5173.**

6918. Nace, Nicholas D. Some current publications. Restoration (29:2) 2005, 65–79.

6919. Paster, Gail Kern; Rowe, Katherine; Floyd-Wilson, Mary (eds). Reading the early modern passions: essays in the cultural history of emotion. (Bibl. 2004, 7204.) Rev. by Katharine Craik in TLS, 7 Jan. 2005, 23; by Stephen Pender in RQ (58:3) 2005, 1030–2.

6920. Pastore Passaro, Maria C. Representation of women in Classical, medieval and Renaissance texts. *See* **4222.**

6921. Peltonen, Markku. 'Civilized with death': civility, duelling and honour in Elizabethan England. *In* (pp. 51–67) **5187.**

6922. Pendergast, John. Religion, allegory, and literacy in early modern England, 1560–1640: the control of the word. *See* **5179.**

6923. Persels, Jeff; Ganim, Russell (eds). Fecal matters in early modern literature and art: studies in scatology. (Bibl. 2004, 5786.) Rev. by Carla Freccero in RQ (58:3) 2005, 980–1; by Nicolas Buté in CEl (67) 2005, 91–2.

6924. Picciotto, Joanna. Reforming the garden: the experimentalist Eden and *Paradise Lost. See* **7735.**

6925. —— Scientific investigations: experimentalism and paradisal return. *In* (pp. 36–57) **6958.**

6926. Prescott, Sarah. Women, authorship, and literary culture, 1690–1740. (Bibl. 2004, 7209.) Rev. by Sasha Roberts in MLR (100:4) 2005, 1091–3.

6927. Rankin, Deana. Between Spenser and Swift: English writing in seventeenth-century Ireland. Cambridge; New York: CUP, 2005. pp. xiii, 294.

6928. Ray, Sid. Holy estates: marriage and monarchy in Shakespeare and his contemporaries. *See* **6061.**

6929. RIBEIRO, AILEEN. Fashion and fiction: dress in art and literature in Stuart England. New Haven, CT; London: Yale UP, 2005. pp. ix, 387.

6930. RICHARDS, JENNIFER (ed.). Early modern civil discourses. *See* **5187.**

6931. RICHETTI, JOHN. The Cambridge history of English literature, 1660–1780. Cambridge; New York: CUP, 2005. pp. xviii, 945. (New Cambridge history of English literature.)

6932. ROUND, PHILLIP H. The return of the native: recent scholarship in the literature of Christianization and contact. EAL (40:2) 2005, 375–85 (review-article).

6933. ROUX, LOUIS. Foi et raison dans l'œuvre de William Chillingworth. *See* **7318.**

6934. SAUER, ELIZABETH. 'Paper-contestations' and textual communities in England, 1640–1675. Toronto; Buffalo, NY; London: Toronto UP, 2005. pp. viii, 199. (Studies in book and print culture.)

6935. SAUER, ELIZABETH M. The experience of defeat: Milton and some female contemporaries. *In* (pp. 133–52) **7717.**

6936. SCHOFIELD, SCOTT. According to 'the common receiued opinion': Munday's Brute in *The Triumphs of Re-United Britannia* (1605). *In* (pp. 253–68) **4479.**

6937. SCOTT-WARREN, JASON. Early modern English literature. *See* **5194.**

6938. SHEEN, ERICA; HUTSON, LORNA (eds). Literature, politics and law in Renaissance England. *See* **5196.**

6939. SHEPARD, ALAN; POWELL, STEPHEN D. (eds). Fantasies of Troy: Classical tales and the social imaginary in medieval and early modern Europe. *See* **4479.**

6940. SMYTH, ADAM. 'It were far better be a *Toad*, or a *Serpant*, then a Drunkard': writing about drunkenness. *In* (pp. 193–210) **6942.**

6941. —— 'Profit and delight': printed miscellanies in England, 1640–1682. (Bibl. 2004, 7223.) Rev. by A. H. De Quehen in SCN (63:1/2) 2005, 17–20; by Douglas Alan Brooks in RQ (58:2) 2005, 747–9.

6942. —— (ed.). A pleasing sinne: drink and conviviality in seventeenth-century England. Woodbridge, Suffolk; Rochester, NY: Brewer, 2004. pp. xxv, 214. (Studies in Renaissance literature, 14.) Rev. by Jeremy Black in NQ (52:4) 2005, 540–1; by Mark Taylor in RQ (58:3) 2005, 1013–15.

6943. SNOOK, EDITH. Women, reading, and the cultural politics of early modern England. *See* **5201.**

6944. SPENCER, JANE. Literary relations: kinship and the canon 1660–1830. Oxford; New York: OUP, 2005. pp. 268.

6945. STAUB, SUSAN C. Nature's cruel stepdames: murderous women in the street literature of seventeenth-century England. Pittsburgh, PA: Duquesne UP, 2004. pp. x, 356. (Medieval & Renaissance literary studies.)

6946. STEPHANSON, RAYMOND. The yard of wit: male creativity and sexuality, 1650–1750. (Bibl. 2004, 7225.) Rev. by Linda Zionkowski in ECF (18:1) 2005, 153–5; by Harry M. Solomon in Scriblerian (37:2 / 38:1) 2005, 101–3; by George E. Haggerty in JHS (14:3) 2005, 347–52.

6947. STEVENS, LAURA M.   The poor Indians: British missionaries, Native Americans, and Colonial sensibility. Philadelphia: Pennsylvania UP, 2004. pp. 264. (Early American studies.) Rev. by Phillip H. Round in EAL (40:2) 2005, 375–85.

6948. TOTARO, REBECCA.   Suffering in paradise: the bubonic plague in English literature from More to Milton. See **5206**.

6949. TREVOR, DOUGLAS.   The poetics of melancholy in early modern England. See **5208**.

6950. TRILL, SUZANNE.   Early modern women's writing in the Edinburgh Archives, c.1550–1740: a preliminary checklist. In (pp. 201–25) **3754**.

6951. TRUDEL, JEAN-LOUIS.   Looking for little green men. See **14293**.

6952. TURNER, JAMES GRANTHAM.   Libertine literature forty years on: part 1, From Aretino to The School of Venus. BC (54:1) 2005, 29–51. (Adds to bibl. 1963, 938.)

6953. ——   Libertines and Radicals in early modern London: sexuality, politics, and literary culture, 1630–1685. (Bibl. 2004, 7230.) Rev. by Robert A. Erickson in ECF (17:2) 2005, 269–76; by Melissa Mowry in JBS (44:1) 2005, 178–86.

6954. ULLYOT, MICHAEL.   The fall of Troynovant: exemplarity after the death of Henry, Prince of Wales. In (pp. 269–90) **4479**.

6955. VAN DELFT, LOUIS.   Frammento e anatomia: rivoluzione scientifica e creazione letteraria. Ed. by Carmelina Imbroscio. Trans. from French by Francesca Longo. Bologna: Il Mulino, 2004. pp. 278, (plates) 26. (Scorciatoie.) Rev. by Arielle Saiber in RQ (58:3) 2005, 990–2.

6956. VICKERS, BRIAN.   A rage for order. See **5573**.

6957. VON SNEIDERN, MAJA-LISA.   Savage indignation: colonial discourse from Milton to Swift. Newark: Delaware UP, 2005. pp. 204.

6958. WALL, CYNTHIA (ed.).   A concise companion to the Restoration and eighteenth century. Oxford; Malden, MA: Blackwell, 2005. pp. x, 284. (Blackwell concise companions to literature and culture.)

6959. WATKINS, JOHN A.   Representing Elizabeth in Stuart England: literature, history, sovereignty. (Bibl. 2004, 7233.) Rev. by Clifton W. Potter, Jr, in SixCJ (34:4) 2003, 1162–4.

6960. WILLIS, PATRICIA.   Marianne Moore and the seventeenth century. In (pp. 40–55) **18316**.

6961. WOMERSLEY, DAVID.   Introduction. In (pp. 9–26) **8091**.

6962. —— (ed.); BULLARD, PADDY; WILLIAMS, ABIGAIL (asst eds).   'Cultures of Whiggism': new essays on English literature and culture in the long eighteenth century. See **8091**.

6963. WOOLF, DANIEL R.   From hystories to the historical: five transitions in thinking about the past, 1500–1700. See **5633**.

6964. WRIGHT, NANCY E.; FERGUSON, MARGARET W.; BUCK, A. R. (eds). Women, property, and the letters of the law in early modern England. Toronto; Buffalo, NY; London: Toronto UP, 2004. pp. x, 316. Rev. by Nancy M. Bunker in SCN (63:1/2) 2005, 53–7; by Tim Stretton in DalR (85:1) 2005, 143–5; by Mihoko Suzuki in RQ (58:3) 2005, 1025–8.

6965. WYNNE-DAVIES, MARION. Suicide at the Elephant and Castle, or did the lady vanish? Alternative endings for early modern women writers. *In* (pp. 121–42) **5914.**

DRAMA AND THE THEATRE

6966. ARCHER, IAN W. Discourses of history in Elizabethan and early Stuart London. *See* **6706.**

6967. ASTINGTON, JOHN H. A Jacobean ghost, and other stories. MedRen (17) 2005, 37–54.

6968. —— John Rhodes: draper, bookseller and man of the theatre. TN (57:2) 2003, 82–8.

6969. BANERJEE, RITA. *Women Pleas'd* and *Swetnam the Woman-Hater Arraigned by Women*: John Fletcher's participation in the Swetnam debate and the date of his play. *See* **7445.**

6970. BERGERON, DAVID M. Pageants, masques, and history. *In* (pp. 41–56) **5964.**

6971. BERRY, HERBERT. Building playhouses, the accession of James I, and the Red Bull. MedRen (18) 2005, 61–74.

6972. BLAYNEY, PETER W. M. The alleged popularity of playbooks. *See* **770.**

6973. BROWN, PAMELA ALLEN; PAROLIN, PETER. Introduction. *In* (pp. 1–21) **5225.**

6974. —— —— (eds). Women players in England, 1500–1660: beyond the all-male stage. *See* **5225.**

6975. BROWNING, LOGAN D. A conversation with Sir Frank Kermode. *See* **14720.**

6976. BURTON, JONATHAN. Traffic and turning: Islam and English drama, 1579–1624. *See* **5227.**

6977. BUTTERWORTH, PHILIP. Magic on the early English stage. *See* **4496.**

6978. CALBI, MAURIZIO. Approximate bodies: gender and power in early modern drama and anatomy. *See* **7651.**

6979. CALVI, LISANNA. Kingship and tragedy (1660–1715). Verona: QuiEdit, 2005. pp. 212. (Uniedit.)

6980. CAÑADAS, IVAN. The public theaters of Golden Age Madrid and Tudor-Stuart London: class, gender, and festive community. *See* **5230.**

6981. CARNEGIE, DAVID. Early modern plays and performance. *See* **6145.**

6982. CATHCART, CHARLES. Authorship, indebtedness, and the Children of the King's Revels. *See* **7540.**

6983. CAVE, RICHARD ALLEN. Italian perspectives on late Tudor and early Stuart theatre. *See* **5234.**

6984. CHOWDHURY, AHSAN. 'A fearful blazing star': signs of the Exclusion Crisis in Robert Knox's *An Historical Relation of the Island Ceylon* (1681). *See* **7098.**

6985. DAWSON, MARK S. Gentility and the comic theatre of late Stuart London. Cambridge; New York: CUP, 2005. pp. xvi, 300. (Cambridge social and cultural histories, 5.) Rev. by Michael Caines in TLS, 21 Oct. 2005, 34.

6986. DEBAX, JEAN-PAUL. Techniques de persuasion dans les interludes protestants anglais du xvie siècle. *See* **5664.**

6987. DOLLIMORE, JONATHAN. Radical tragedy: religion, ideology, and power in the drama of Shakespeare and his contemporaries. *See* **5908.**

6988. DONOHUE, JOSEPH (ed.). The Cambridge history of British theatre: vol. 2, 1660 to 1895. Cambridge; New York: CUP, 2004. pp. xci, 481.

6989. DUTTON, RICHARD. Jonson, Shakespeare and the exorcists. *See* **7547.**

6990. —— 'Methinks the truth should live from age to age': the dating and contexts of *Henry V. See* **6418.**

6991. —— Recent studies in Tudor and Stuart drama. *See* **5240.**

6992. —— FINDLAY, ALISON; WILSON, RICHARD (eds). Region, religion, and patronage: Lancastrian Shakespeare. *See* **5914.**

6993. EDELMAN, CHARLES. Shakespeare's *Henry IV, Part 1. See* **6399.**

6994. FARMER, ALAN B.; LESSER, ZACHARY. The popularity of playbooks revisited. *See* **824.**

6995. —— —— Structures of popularity in the early modern book trade. *See* **825.**

6996. FORSE, JAMES H. Performance equals preference: how acting companies performing at court reflected Elizabeth's court structure. *See* **5246.**

6997. GERRITSEN, JOHAN. De Witt, Van Buchell, the Swan, and the second Globe: an assessment of the evidence. ShY (15) 2005, 9–31.

6998. GIESKES, EDWARD. 'Honesty and vulgar praise': the Poets' War and the literary field. *See* **5248.**

6999. GONZÁLEZ DÍAZ, VICTORINA. Adjective comparison in Renaissance English. *See* **1660.**

7000. GORDON, ANDREW. 'If my sign could speak': the signboard and the visual culture of early modern London. ETh (8:1) 2005, 35–51.

7001. GOUGH, MELINDA J. Courtly *comédiantes*: Henrietta Maria and amateur women's stage plays in France and England. *In* (pp. 193–215) **5225.**

7002. GREENFIELD, PETER. Regional performance in Shakespeare's time. *In* (pp. 243–51) **5914.**

7003. GURR, ANDREW. Bears and players: Philip Henslowe's double acts. *See* **5486.**

7004. HANSON, ELIZABETH. There's meat and money too: rich widows and allegories of wealth in Jacobean city comedy. *See* **7219.**

7005. HISCOCK, ANDREW. 'What's Hecuba to him ...': Trojan heroes and rhetorical selves in Shakespeare's *Hamlet. In* (pp. 161–75) **4479.**

7006. HODGKINS, CHRISTOPHER. Plays out of season: Puritanism, antitheatricalism, and Parliament's 1642 closing of the theaters. *In* (pp. 298–318) **6872.**

7007. HOLLAND, PETER; ORGEL, STEPHEN (eds). From script to stage in early modern England. *See* **5260.**

7008. HUGHES, DEREK. Aphra Behn and the Restoration theatre. *In* (pp. 29–45) **7242.**

7009. HUTSON, LORNA. Rethinking the 'spectacle of the scaffold': juridical epistemologies and English revenge tragedy. *See* **6781**.

7010. ICHIKAWA, MARIKO. *'Maluolio within'*: acting on the threshold between onstage and offstage spaces. *See* **6803**.

7011. IOPPOLO, GRACE. 'A jointure more or less': re-measuring *The True Chronicle History of King Leir and His Three Daughters*. MedRen (17) 2005, 165–79.

7012. JACKSON, KEN. Separate theaters: Bethlem ('Bedlam') Hospital and the Shakespearean stage. *See* **5985**.

7013. JENSEN, PHEBE. Recusancy, festivity and community: the Simpsons at Gowlthwaite Hall. *In* (pp. 101–20) **5914**.

7014. JOHNSON, NORA. The actor as playwright in early modern drama. (Bibl. 2004, 7466.) Rev. by Tracey Hill in RenSt (18:2) 2004, 348–51; by Emily R. Isaacson in SixCJ (36:1) 2005, 193–5; by A. R. Braunmuller in SStud (33) 2005, 271–7; by Robert A. Logan in MSAN (25:1) 2005, 10–11; by Kirk Melnikoff in MedRen (18) 2005, 247–52.

7015. KATHMAN, DAVID. Citizens, innholders, and playhouse builders, 1543–1622. *See* **5266**.

7016. —— How old were Shakespeare's boy actors? *See* **5267**.

7017. KERWIN, WILLIAM. Beyond the body: the boundaries of medicine and early English Renaissance drama. *See* **5269**.

7018. KEWES, PAULINA. Contemporary Europe in Elizabethan and early Stuart drama. *In* (pp. 150–92) **5954**.

7019. LAGAE, DENIS. *'Here is a sight indeed'*: l'ostension dans la comédie de la Restauration (1660–1700). EA (58:3) 2005, 293–307.

7020. LESSER, ZACHARY. Renaissance drama and the politics of publication: readings in the English book trade. *See* **5271**.

7021. LLOYD, WILLIAM. John Webster and *The London Prodigal*: new sources for *The Devil's Law-Case*. *See* **7904**.

7022. LONG, WILLIAM B. Dulwich MS XX, *The Telltale*: clues to provenance. MedRen (17) 2005, 180–204.

7023. MACLEAN, SALLY-BETH. A family tradition: dramatic patronage by the Earls of Derby. *In* (pp. 205–26) **5914**.

7024. MADELAINE, RICHARD. 'The dark and vicious place': the location of sexual transgression and its punishment on the early modern English stage. *See* **5277**.

7025. MARLOW, CHRISTOPHER. Scholarly interiority in the *Parnassus* trilogy. DalR (85:2) 2005, 275–84.

7026. MEHL, DIETER; STOCK, ANGELA; ZWIERLEIN, ANNE-JULIA (eds). Plotting early modern London: new essays on Jacobean city comedy. (Bibl. 2004, 7294.) Rev. by Leeds Barroll in RQ (58:3) 2005, 1050–1.

7027. MILHOUS, JUDITH; HUME, ROBERT D. Murder in Elizabeth Barry's dressing room. *See* **7133**.

7028. MILLING, JANE; THOMSON, PETER (eds). The Cambridge history of British theatre: vol. 1, Origins to 1660. *See* **4510**.

7029. MUKHERJI, SUBHA. Women, law, and dramatic realism in early modern England. *See* **6250**.

7030. MUNRO, LUCY. Children of the Queen's Revels: a Jacobean theatre repertory. Cambridge; New York: CUP, 2005. pp. xiii, 267.

7031. NARDO, DON. The Globe Theater. *See* **6204**.

7032. O'BRIEN, JOHN. Drama: genre, gender, theater. *In* (pp. 183–201) **6958**.

7033. O'CALLAGHAN, MICHELLE. Tavern societies, the Inns of Court, and the culture of conviviality in early seventeenth-century London. *In* (pp. 37–51) **6942**.

7034. OWENS, MARGARET E. Stages of dismemberment: the fragmented body in medieval and early modern drama. *See* **4512**.

7035. PAROLIN, PETER. The Venetian theater of Aletheia Talbot, Countess of Arundel. *In* (pp. 219–39) **5225**.

7036. POOLE, WILLIAM; THORP, JENNIFER. Women among the prisoners: New College fragments of a new Jacobean play. TLS, 25 Nov. 2005, 12–13.

7037. PORTILLO, RAFAEL. Staging Restoration dramas: practical aspects of their performance. SEDERI (15) 2005, 63–80.

7038. ROACH, JOSEPH. The global parasol: accessorizing the four corners of the world. *In* (pp. 93–106) **8039**.

7039. ROBERTS, JEANNE ADDISON. Revenge tragedy and Elizabeth Cary's *Mariam*. *See* **7304**.

7040. ROUYER-DANEY, MARIE-CLAIRE. Quelle légitimité pour la 'petite comédie' georgienne? *See* **8112**.

7041. SALKELD, DUNCAN. New allusions to London 'shewes' and playhouses, 1575–1605. *See* **5292**.

7042. STRAZNICKY, MARTA. Privacy, playreading, and women's closet drama, 1550–1700. (Bibl. 2004, 7311.) Rev. by Elizabeth Scott-Baumann in TLS, 18 Mar. 2005, 29; by Nancy M. Bunker in SCN (63:3/4) 2005, 146–50; by Victoria E. Price in TRI (30:3) 2005, 299–300.

7043. TASSI, MARGUERITE A. The scandal of images: iconoclasm, eroticism, and painting in early modern English drama. *See* **5297**.

7044. TOSI, LAURA. 'Then rose the seed of chaos': masque and antimasque in *The Dunciad in Four Books*. *See* **8913**.

7045. TRIBBLE, EVELYN. Distributing cognition in the Globe. *See* **5298**.

7046. WALEN, DENISE A. Constructions of female homoeroticism in early modern drama. *See* **5302**.

7047. WATKINS, JOHN. Bedevilling the histories of medieval and early modern drama. *See* **4521**.

7048. WATTS, CEDRIC. The lady and her horsekeeper and Shakespeare. *See* **6106**.

7049. WEBSTER, JEREMY W. Performing libertinism in Charles II's court: politics, drama, sexuality. Basingstoke; New York: Palgrave Macmillan, 2005. pp. 251.

7050. WEST, WILLIAM N. Theatres and encyclopedias in early modern Europe. (Bibl. 2004, 7317.) Rev. by Julian Yates in SStud (33) 2005, 315–21; by Ty Buckman in MedRen (18) 2005, 243–7.

7051. WESTFALL, SUZANNE. 'The useless dearness of the diamond': patronage theatre and household. *In* (pp. 32–49) **5914**.

7052. WILLIAMS, GWENO; FINDLAY, ALISON; HODGSON-WRIGHT, STEPHANIE. Payments, permits and punishments: women performers and the politics of place. *In* (pp. 45–67) **5225**.

7053. WOODBRIDGE, LINDA; BEEHLER, SHARON (eds). Women, violence, and English Renaissance literature: essays honoring Paul Jorgensen. (Bibl. 2004, 7321.) Rev. by Susan Ahern in RQ (58:2) 2005, 722–3.

FICTION

7054. RELIHAN, CONSTANCE CAROLINE. Cosmographical glasses: geographic discourse, gender, and Elizabethan fiction. *See* **5310**.

LITERATURE FOR CHILDREN

7055. BOTTIGHEIMER, RUTH B. The book on the bookseller's shelf and the book in the English child's hand. *In* (pp. 3–28) **8171**.

7056. MARKS, SYLVIA KASEY. Writing for the rising generation: British fiction for young people 1672–1839. (Bibl. 2004, 7324.) Rev. by Naomi Wood in StudN (37:3) 2005, 359–60.

POETRY

7057. ACHILLEOS, STELLA. The *Anacreontea* and a tradition of refined male sociability. *In* (pp. 21–35) **6942**.

7058. BAKER, CHRISTOPHER. Porphyro's rose: Keats and T. S. Eliot's *The Metaphysical Poets*. *See* **16242**.

7059. BLAND, MARK. Francis Beaumont's verse letters to Ben Jonson and 'the Mermaid Club'. *See* **7224**.

7060. CLARKE, SUSAN A. 'Bright Heir t' th' Bird Imperial': Richard Lovelace's *The Falcon* in context. *See* **7607**.

7061. —— Royalists write the death of Lord Hastings: post-regicide funerary propaganda. Parergon (22:2) 2005, 113–30.

7062. CONWAY, ALISON. 'Let us be govern'd by an English c—t': reading Nell Gwyn. Restoration (29:1) 2005, 47–63.

7063. CORP, EDWARD, *et al*. A court in exile: the Stuarts in France, 1689–1718. Cambridge; New York: CUP, 2004. pp. xvi, 386. Rev. by Eric N. Lindquist in RQ (58:4) 2005, 1419–21.

7064. CRAIK, KATHARINE A. John Taylor's pot-poetry. *See* **7863**.

7065. CURTH, LOUISE HILL; CASSIDY, TANYA M. 'Health, strength and happiness': medical constructions of wine and beer in early modern England. *In* (pp. 143–59) **6942**.

7066. DÖRING, TOBIAS. Writing performance: how to elegize Elizabethan actors. *See* **6157**.

7067. Hammons, Pamela S.   The gendered imagination of property in sixteenth- and seventeenth-century English women's verse. *See* **5318**.

7068. Harries, Byron.   John Owen the epigrammatist: a literary and historical context. *See* **7809**.

7069. Jones, Angela McShane.   Roaring Royalists and ranting brewers: the politicisation of drink and drunkenness in political broadside ballads from 1640 to 1689. *In* (pp. 69–87) **6942**.

7070. Keblusek, Marika.   Wine for comfort: drinking and the Royalist exile experience, 1642–1660. *In* (pp. 55–68) **6942**.

7071. Keith, Jennifer.   Poetry and the feminine from Behn to Cowper. Newark: Delaware UP; London: Assoc. UPs, 2005. pp. 227.

7072. Lavoie, Chantel.   *Poems by Eminent Ladies*: the encyclopedic anthology of 1755. *See* **5319**.

7073. McWilliams, John.   An echo of an anonymous Royalist broadside poem of 1643 in Marvell's *An Horatian Ode upon Cromwell's Return from Ireland*. *See* **7628**.

7074. May, Steven W.; Ringler, William A., Jr.   Elizabethan poetry: a bibliography and first-line index of English verse, 1559–1603. *See* **5321**.

7075. Morris, Amy M. E.   Popular measures: poetry and church order in seventeenth-century Massachusetts. Newark: Delaware UP, 2005. pp. 282.

7076. Roper, Alan.   Aeneas and Agathocles in the Exclusion Crisis. *See* **7515**.

7077. —— Doctor Balack and Bishop Boloch: nomenclature in Restoration parallel poems. *See* **7425**.

7078. Roston, Murray.   Donne and the meditative tradition. *See* **7390**.

7079. Semler, L. E.   Creative adoption in *Eliza's Babes* (1652): Puritan refigurations of Sibbes, Herrick, and Herbert. *In* (pp. 319–45) **6872**.

7080. Smith, Bruce R.   Female impersonation in early modern ballads. *In* (pp. 281–304) **5225**.

7081. Smith, Rosalind.   Sonnets and the English woman writer, 1560–1621: the politics of absence. *See* **5324**.

7082. Warley, Christopher.   Sonnet sequences and social distinction in Renaissance England. *See* **5326**.

7083. Williams, Abigail.   Poetry and the creation of a Whig literary culture, 1681–1714. Oxford; New York: OUP, 2005. pp. 303. Rev. by Kevin Sharpe in TLS, 15 July 2005, 28–9.

7084. Worden, Blair.   Historians and poets. *See* **5657**.

PROSE

7085. Almond, Philip C. (comp.).   Demonic possession and exorcism in early modern England: contemporary texts and their cultural contexts. *See* **5329**.

7086. Arcara, Stefania.   Mystical picaresque: the 'Great Tryals' of Quaker prophetesses. *In* (pp. 43–53) **3690**.

7087. ARMSTRONG, CATHERINE. The bookseller and the pedlar: the spread of knowledge of the New World in early modern England, 1580–1640. *In* (pp. 15–29) **880**.

7088. BANKS, DAVID. On the historical origins of nominalized process in scientific text. *See* **2809**.

7089. BANNET, EVE TAVOR. Empire of letters: letter manuals and transatlantic correspondence, 1680–1820. Cambridge; New York: CUP, 2005. pp. xxiii, 347.

7090. —— 'Secret history'; or, Talebearing inside and outside the secretorie. HLQ (68:1/2) 2005, 375–96.

7091. BEER, ANNA. Ralegh's history of her world. *See* **5331**.

7092. BELL, MAUREEN. Offensive behaviour in the English book trade, 1641–1700. *In* (pp. 61–79) **937**.

7093. BRANCH, LORI. The rejection of liturgy, the rise of free prayer, and modern religious subjectivity. Restoration (29:1) 2005, 1–28.

7094. BROWN, LAURA FEITZINGER. Brawling in church: noise and the rhetoric of lay behavior in early modern England. *See* **7466**.

7095. BULLARD, PADDY. The latitude of Whiggism: Tillotson, Burnet, and Lord William Russell in Whig historiography, 1675–1775. *In* (pp. 299–329) **8091**.

7096. BURNS, WILLIAM E. Astrology and politics in seventeenth-century England: King James II and the almanac men. *See* **785**.

7097. CALKINS, SUSANNA. Colonial whips, royal writs and the Quaker challenge: Elizabeth Hooton's voyages through New England in the seventeenth century. Journeys (5:2) 2004, 72–92.

7098. CHOWDHURY, AHSAN. 'A fearful blazing star': signs of the Exclusion Crisis in Robert Knox's *An Historical Relation of the Island Ceylon* (1681). Restoration (29:2) 2005, 1–20.

7099. CLUCAS, STEPHEN. Robert Cotton's *A Short View of the Life of Henry the Third*, and its presentation in 1614. *In* (pp. 177–89) **6860**.

7100. COGLEY, RICHARD W. The ancestry of the American Indians: Thomas Thorowgood's *Iewes in America* (1650) and *Jews in America* (1660). ELR (35:2) 2005, 304–30.

7101. COLCLOUGH, DAVID. 'Better becoming a senate of Venice'? The 'Addled Parliament' and Jacobean debates on freedom of speech. *In* (pp. 51–61) **6860**.

7102. —— Freedom of speech, libel and the law in early Stuart England. *In* (pp. 170–88) **5196**.

7103. CRESSY, DAVID. Book burning in Tudor and Stuart England. *See* **803**.

7104. —— Remembrancers of the Revolution: histories and historiographies of the 1640s. HLQ (68:1/2) 2005, 257–68.

7105. CURTH, LOUISE HILL. The medical content of English almanacs, 1640–1700. JHM (60:3) 2005, 255–82.

7106. —— CASSIDY, TANYA M. 'Health, strength and happiness': medical constructions of wine and beer in early modern England. *In* (pp. 143–59) **6942**.

7107. DACOME, LUCIA. Noting the mind: commonplace books and the pursuit of the self in eighteenth-century Britain. JHI (65:4) 2004, 603–25.

7108. DEMETRIOU, EROULLA. Michael Du Val and Count Gondomar: an approximation towards the authorship of *The Spanish–English Rose; or, The English–Spanish Pomgranet* (c.1623). SEDERI (14) 2004, 53–64.

7109. DREHER, UTE. Sex, sermons and ornithology: Thomas Webbe, Edward Stokes and the Wiltshire Ranters. SRASP (27) 2004, 62–78.

7110. DUREL, HENRI. La Conférence de Hampton Court (janvier 1604); ou, L'autorité de Jacques Ier sur l'Église anglicane. *See* 7525.

7111. DZELZAINIS, MARTIN. History and ideology: Milton, the Levellers, and the Council of State in 1649. *See* 7672.

7112. FALLON, ROBERT THOMAS (ed.). The Christian soldier: religious tracts published for soldiers on both sides during and after the English Civil Wars, 1642–1648. (Bibl. 2004, 7376.) Rev. by Anthony Low in BJJ (12) 2005, 279–84.

7113. FOX, CHRISTOPHER. Getting Gotheridge: notes on Swift's grandfather and a new letter from Thomas Swift. *See* 9062.

7114. GREENBERG, STEPHEN. Plague, the printing press, and public health in seventeenth-century London. *See* 861.

7115. HALLAM, H. A. N. The anonymous pamphleteer: a checklist of the writings of Edward Stephens (1633–1706). BLR (18:5) 2005, 502–31.

7116. HAWLEY, JUDITH (gen. ed.). Literature and science, 1660–1834: vol. 5, Fauna. Ed. by David Clifford. (Bibl. 2004, 7385.) Rev. by Ashton Nichols in WordsC (35:4) 2004, 208–10.

7117. —— Literature and science, 1660–1834: vol. 6, Astronomy. Ed. by Rob Iliffe. (Bibl. 2004, 7386.) Rev. by Ashton Nichols in WordsC (35:4) 2004, 208–10.

7118. —— Literature and science, 1660–1834: vol. 7, Natural philosophy. Ed. by Rob Iliffe. (Bibl. 2004, 7387.) Rev. by Ashton Nichols in WordsC (35:4) 2004, 208–10.

7119. —— Literature and science, 1660–1834: vol. 8, Chemistry. Ed. by Brian Dolan. (Bibl. 2004, 7388.) Rev. by Ashton Nichols in WordsC (35:4) 2004, 208–10.

7120. HEAL, FELICITY. Appropriating history: Catholic and Protestant polemics and the national past. *See* 5435.

7121. HUDSON, NICHOLAS. The alphabet of nature: writing as trope in early modern scientific and philosophical discourse. *See* 5340.

7122. HUNTER, LYNETTE. Letters of Dorothy Moore, 1612–64: the friendships, marriage, and intellectual life of a seventeenth-century woman. Aldershot; Burlington, VT: Ashgate, 2004. pp. lviii, 138. (Early modern Englishwoman, 1500–1750: Contemporary eds.) Rev. by Ellen J. Jenkins in SCN (63:3/4) 2005, 221–3.

7123. HUTCHINGS, MARK. Anti-theatrical prejudice and *1 Honest Whore*, II.i.324–326. *See* 7354.

7124. JENKINSON, MATTHEW T. A new author for the 'observations' in *Rebels No Saints* (1661)? NQ (52:3) 2005, 311–14.

7125. JOHN, JUDITH GERO. I have been dying to tell you: early advice books for children. *See* 7527.

7126. KEARNS, JUDITH. Fashioning innocence: rhetorical construction of character in the *Memoirs* of Anne, Lady Halkett. TSLL (46:3) 2004, 340–62.

7127. KIETZMAN, MARY JO. The self-fashioning of an early modern Englishwoman: Mary Carleton's lives. (Bibl. 2004, 7396.) Rev. by Tim Reinke-Williams in SCN (63:3/4) 2005, 144–6; by Margaret J. Arnold in RQ (58:2) 2005, 720–2.

7128. KNIGHTS, MARK. Representation and misrespresentation in later Stuart Britain: partisanship and political culture. Oxford; New York: OUP, 2005. pp. xvi, 431.

7129. LEE, C. D. The authorship of *Letters Writ by a Turkish Spy* – the Oxford connection. BLR (18:4) 2004, 333–64.

7130. LUPTON, JULIA REINHARD. Rights, commandments, and the literature of citizenship. MLQ (66:1) 2005, 21–54.

7131. MCELLIGOTT, JASON. Roger Morrice and the reputation of the *Eikon Basilike* in the 1680s. *See* 7317.

7132. MCGEE, J. SEARS. Francis Rous and 'scabby or itchy children': the problem of toleration in 1645. HLQ (67:3) 2004, 401–22.

7133. MILHOUS, JUDITH; HUME, ROBERT D. Murder in Elizabeth Barry's dressing room. YLG (79:3/4) 2005, 149–74.

7134. NARVESON, KATE. Publishing the sole-talk of the soule: genre in early Stuart piety. *In* (pp. 110–26) 6872.

7135. NAYAR, PRAMOD K. Marvelous excesses: English travel writing and India, 1608–1727. JBS (44:2) 2005, 213–38.

7136. NEUMAN, MEREDITH MARIE. Beyond narrative: the conversion plot of John Dane's *A Declaration of Remarkable Providences*. EAL (40:2) 2005, 251–77.

7137. NEVALA, MINNA. Accessing politeness axes: forms of address and terms of reference in early English correspondence. *See* 5343.

7138. NEVITT, MARCUS. John Selden among the Quakers: antifeminism and the seventeenth-century tithes controversy. *In* (pp. 189–208) 5196.

7139. OGBORN, MILES; WITHERS, CHARLES W. J. Travel, trade, and empire: knowing other places, 1660–1800. *In* (pp. 13–35) 6958.

7140. PARNHAM, DAVID. The nurturing of righteousness: Sir Henry Vane on freedom and discipline. JBS (42:1) 2003, 1–34.

7141. PEACEY, JASON. Politicians and pamphleteers: propaganda during the English Civil Wars and Interregnum. (Bibl. 2004, 7414.) Rev. by David Randall in HLQ (67:3) 2004, 457–72; by Nicole Greenspan in SHARP (14:1/2) 2005, 18; by Dosia Reichardt in Parergon (22:2) 2005, 251–2.

7142. PETERS, KATE. Print culture and the early Quakers. Cambridge; New York: CUP, 2005. pp. xiii, 273. (Cambridge studies in early modern British history.)

7143. PINCUS, STEVEN C. A. Whigs, political economy, and the Revolution of 1688–89. *In* (pp. 62–85) 8091.

7144. RANDALL, DAVID. Recent studies in print culture: news, propaganda, and ephemera. *See* 5345.

2005] PROSE 379

7145. RAUMOLIN-BRUNBERG, HELENA. Language change in adulthood: historical letters as evidence. *See* **2878**.

7146. RAYMOND, JOAD. 'The language of the public': print, politics, and the book trade in 1614. *In* (pp. 95–112) **6860**.

7147. REID, JENNIFER I. M. Worse than beasts: an anatomy of melancholy and the literature of travel in seventeenth- and eighteenth-century England. *See* **7290**.

7148. RYKEN, LELAND. Milton's Sonnet 14 and Puritan funeral sermons for women. *In* (pp. 136–48) **7738**.

7149. SALE, CAROLYN. The 'Roman hand': women, writing and the law in the *Att.-Gen. v. Chatterton* and the letters of the Lady Arbella Stuart. ELH (70:4) 2003, 929–61.

7150. SCHNEIDER, GARY. The culture of epistolarity: vernacular letters and letter writing in early modern England, 1500–1700. *See* **5348**.

7151. SCOTT, JONATHAN. Commonwealth principles: Republican writing of the English Revolution. Cambridge; New York: CUP, 2004. pp. xii, 402. Rev. by Jerome de Groot in TLS, 13 May 2005, 11.

7152. SHERMAN, SANDRA. Impotence and capital: the debate over imported beverages in the seventeenth and eighteenth centuries. 1650–1850 (9) 2003, 123–51.

7153. SÖNMEZ, MARGARET J.-M. A study of request markers in English family letters from 1623 to 1660. EJES (9:1) 2005, 9–19.

7154. SPURR, JOHN. 'A special kindness for dead bishops': the Church, history, and testimony in seventeenth-century Protestantism. HLQ (68:1/2) 2005, 313–34.

7155. STEWART, ALAN. Instigating treason: the life and death of Henry Cuffe, secretary. *In* (pp. 50–70) **5196**.

7156. —— WOLFE, HEATHER (eds). Letterwriting in Renaissance England. *See* **5350**.

7157. STOKER, DAVID. Norwich 'publishing' in the seventeenth century. *In* (pp. 31–46) **880**.

7158. STUBBLEFIELD, JAY. 'very worthely sett in printe': writing the Virginia Company of London. RenP (2003) 167–84.

7159. SUMMIT, JENNIFER. Writing home: Hannah Wolley, the Oxinden letters, and household epistolary practice. *In* (pp. 201–18) **6964**.

7160. TAYLOR, NANCY (ed.). Cousins in love: the letters of Lydia DuGard, 1665–1672: with a new edition of *The Marriages of Cousin Germans* by Samuel DuGard. Tempe: Arizona Center for Medieval and Renaissance Studies, 2003. pp. xii, 218. (Medieval & Renaissance texts & studies, 268.) (Renaissance English Text Soc., 7:28.) Rev. by Jennie Batchelor in NQ (52:2) 2005, 259–60.

7161. VILLANI, STEFANO (ed.). A true account of the great tryals and cruel sufferings undergone by those two faithful servants of God Katherine Evans and Sarah Cheevers. Pisa: Scuola Normale Superiore, 2003. pp. xiv, 366. (Pubblicazioni della Classe di Lettere e Filosofia, Scuola Normale Superiore, Pisa, 29.) Rev. by Julie D. Campbell in SCN (63:1/2) 2005, 57–9.

7162. WEBER, A. S. Women's early modern medical almanacs in historical context. ELR (33:3) 2003, 358–402.

BIOGRAPHY AND AUTOBIOGRAPHY

7163. BEDDARD, R. A. The sources of Anthony Wood's life of Nicholas Hill. See **7918**.

7164. BOOY, DAVID (ed.). Autobiographical writings by early Quaker women. Aldershot; Burlington, VT: Ashgate, 2004. pp. xviii, 211. (Early modern Englishwoman, 1500–1750: Contemporary eds.)

7165. BOTONAKI, EFFIE. Seventeenth-century English women's autobiographical writings: disclosing enclosures. Lewiston, NY; Lampeter: Mellen Press, 2004. pp. iv, 239. (Studies in British literature, 88.)

7166. BROWNLEY, MARTINE WATSON. Denzil Holles and the stylistic development of the early English memoir. In (pp. 135–49) **5167**.

7167. DOLAN, FRANCES E. Reading, work, and Catholic women's biographies. See **7300**.

7168. MARTIN, RANDALL. Henry Goodcole, visitor of Newgate: crime, conversion, and patronage. SevC (20:2) 2005, 153–84.

7169. MULLAN, DAVID GEORGE. Scottish women's religious narrative, 1660–1720: constructing the evangelical self. In (pp. 178–91) **3754**.

7170. —— (ed.). Women's life writing in early modern Scotland: writing the evangelical self, c.1670–1730. (Bibl. 2003, 6896.) Rev. by Lynda Payne in SixCJ (36:1) 2005, 163–4; by Dolly MacKinnon in Parergon (22:1) 2005, 265–7.

7171. PRITCHARD, ALLAN. English biography in the seventeenth century: a critical survey. Toronto; Buffalo, NY; London: Toronto UP, 2005. pp. 297.

7172. SMITH, A. G. R. Lord Burghley and his household biographers: John Clapham and Sir Michael Hickes. In (pp. 248–63) **5121**.

7173. WISEMAN, SUE. Martyrdom in a merchant world: law and martyrdom in the Restoration memoirs of Elizabeth Jekyll and Mary Love. In (pp. 209–35) **5196**.

RELATED STUDIES

7174. COLCLOUGH, DAVID. Freedom of speech in early Stuart England. Cambridge; New York: CUP, 2005. pp. xiv, 293. (Ideas in context.) Rev. by David Hawkes in TLS, 19 & 26 Aug. 2005, 31.

7175. DOWNIE, J. A. Public and private: the myth of the bourgeois public sphere. In (pp. 58–79) **6958**.

7176. FEINGOLD, MORDECHAI. A conjurer and a quack? The lives of John Dee and Simon Forman. See **5356**.

7177. HARVEY, KAREN. The history of masculinity, circa 1650–1800. JBS (44:2) 2005, 296–311.

7178. HUNTER, MICHAEL; MONEY, DAVID. Robert Boyle's first encomium: two Latin poems by Samuel Collins (1647). SevC (20:2) 2005, 223–41.

7179. MALCOLM, NOEL. Thomas Harrison and his 'ark of studies': an episode in the history of the organization of knowledge. SevC (19:2) 2004, 196–232.

7180. Moulton, Ian Frederick (ed.). Reading and literacy in the Middle Ages and Renaissance. *See* **4754**.

7181. Ó Baoill, Colm. 'Neither out nor in': Scottish Gaelic women poets 1650–1750. *In* (pp. 136–52) **3754**.

7182. O'Brien, John. Harlequin Britain: pantomime and entertainment, 1690–1760. (Bibl. 2004, 7454.) Rev. by Jason Shaffer in TJ (57:2) 2005, 341–2.

7183. Ryan, Salvador. Steadfast saints or malleable models? Seventeenth-century Irish hagiography revisited. CathHR (91:2) 2005, 251–77.

7184. Shepard, Alexandra. Meanings of manhood in early modern England. *See* **5365**.

7185. Sullivan, Vickie B. Machiavelli, Hobbes, and the formation of a liberal republicanism in England. Cambridge; New York: CUP, 2004. pp. x, 284. Rev. by Cary J. Nederman in RQ (58:1) 2005, 356–8.

7186. Vaisey, David. 'Overtravelled with the librarie businesse'. BC (52:1) 2003, 46–57.

LITERARY THEORY

7187. Alexander, Gavin (ed.). Sidney's *The Defence of Poesy* and selected Renaissance literary criticism. *See* **5369**.

7188. Lynch, Jack. *King Lear* and 'the taste of the age', 1681–1838. *See* **6476**.

7189. Phillips, Elaine Anderson. Richardson reads the Renaissance: the use of Renaissance narrative theory in the novels and prefaces. *See* **8953**.

7190. Trolander, Paul; Tenger, Zaynep. Addison and the personality of the critic. *In* (pp. 175–99) **1285**.

7191. Walls, Kathryn. 'A prophetique dreame of the churche': William Baspoole's Laudian reception of the medieval *Pilgrimage of the Lyfe of the Manhode*. *In* (pp. 245–76) **6872**.

AUTHORS

Robert Ashley

7192. Whitlock, Keith. The Robert Ashley founding bequest to the Middle Temple Library and John Donne's library. *See* **7401**.

Mary Astell

7193. Kolbrener, William. 'Forced into an interest': High Church politics and feminine agency in the works of Mary Astell. 1650–1850 (10) 2004, 3–31.

7194. O'Neill, Eileen. Early modern women philosophers and the history of philosophy. *See* **7791**.

7195. Perry, Ruth. Mary Astell and Enlightenment. *In* (pp. 357–70) **8016**.

7196. Richardson, Leslie. Leaving her father's house: Astell, Locke, and Clarissa's body politic. StudECC (34) 2005, 151–71.

7197. Taylor, E. Derek; New, Melvyn (eds). Mary Astell and John Norris: letters concerning the love of God. Aldershot; Burlington, VT: Ashgate, 2004. pp. vii, 263. (Early modern Englishwoman, 1500–1750: Contemporary eds.)

John Aubrey

7198. BEDDARD, R. A.   The sources of Anthony Wood's life of Nicholas Hill. *See* **7918.**

7199. PURDON, JOHN JAMES.   John Aubrey's 'discourse in paper'. EC (55:3) 2005, 226–47.

Henry Austin (*fl.*1613)

7200. CARVER, GORDON.   The Elizabethan erotic narrative: sex(y) reading. *See* **6818.**

Francis Bacon (1561–1626)

7201. ASH, ERIC H.   Power, knowledge, and expertise in Elizabethan England. Baltimore, MD; London: Johns Hopkins UP, 2004. pp. viii, 265. Rev. by Deborah E. Harkness in RQ (58:4) 2005, 1416–17.

7202. DEUTSCH, HELEN.   The body's moments: visible disability, the essay and the limits of sympathy. PrSt (27:1/2) 2005, 11–26.

7203. DUREL, HENRI.   La Conférence de Hampton Court (janvier 1604); ou, L'autorité de Jacques Ier sur l'Église anglicane. *See* **7525.**

7204. JAMES-CAVAN, KATHLEEN.   '[A]ll in me is nature': the values of deformity in William Hay's *Deformity: an Essay. See* **8702.**

7205. KENDRICK, CHRISTOPHER.   The imperial laboratory: discovering forms in *The New Atlantis.* ELH (70:4) 2003, 1021–42.

7206. LEWIS, RHODRI.   'The best Mnemonicall Expedient': John Beale's art of memory and its uses. SevC (20:1) 2005, 113–44.

7207. LINDEN, STANTON J. (ed.).   The alchemy reader: from Hermes Trismegistus to Isaac Newton. Cambridge; New York: CUP, 2003. pp. xi, 260. Rev. by Eugene R. Cunnar in SCN (62:1/2) 2004, 62–4; by David Hawkes in CLIO (35:1) 2005, 75–86.

7208. LUND, ROGER.   Laughing at cripples: ridicule, deformity and the argument from design. *See* **8021.**

7209. MCCREA, SCOTT.   The case for Shakespeare: the end of the authorship question. *See* **6011.**

7210. PICCIOTTO, JOANNA.   Scientific investigations: experimentalism and paradisal return. *In* (pp. 36–57) **6958.**

7211. STEWART, ALAN.   Purging troubled humours: Bacon, Northampton and the anti-duelling campaign of 1613–1614. *In* (pp. 81–91) **6860.**

7212. TROUSSON, RAYMOND.   Sciences, techniques et utopies: du paradis à l'enfer. *See* **5571.**

7213. VICKERS, BRIAN.   Idle worship. *See* **6102.**

7214. —— A rage for order. *See* **5573.**

7215. WAKELY, MARIA; REES, GRAHAM.   Folios fit for a king: James I, John Bill, and the King's Printers, 1616–1620. *See* **1013.**

Daniel Baker

7216. PERRY, LORI A. DAVIS.   The literary model for Elizabeth Singer Rowe's *History of Joseph. See* **8975.**

Jane Barker

7217. HINNANT, CHARLES HASKELL.   *Moll Flanders, Roxana,* and first-person female narratives: models and prototypes. *See* **8519.**

7218. SWENSON, RIVKA.   Representing modernity in Jane Barker's Galesia trilogy: Jacobite allegory and the patch-work aesthetic. StudECC (34) 2005, 55–80.

Lording Barry

7219. HANSON, ELIZABETH.   There's meat and money too: rich widows and allegories of wealth in Jacobean city comedy. ELH (72:1) 2005, 209–38.

7220. PANEK, JENNIFER.   Why were there stewed prunes in Shakespearean brothels? *See* **6589.**

Richard Baxter

7221. CLARK, MICHAEL P. (ed.).   The Eliot tracts: with letters from John Eliot to Thomas Thorowgood and Richard Baxter. *See* **7435.**

7222. LIM, PAUL CHANG-HA.   In pursuit of purity, unity, and liberty: Richard Baxter's Puritan ecclesiology in its seventeenth-century context. Leiden; Boston, MA: Brill, 2004. pp. xix, 263. (Studies in the history of Christian thought, 112.) Rev. by Carrie A. Hintz in RQ (58:2) 2005, 715–16.

7223. O'HARAE, ALISON.   Theology, genre, and romance in Richard Baxter and Harriet Beecher Stowe. *See* **12112.**

Francis Beaumont (1584–1616)

7224. BLAND, MARK.   Francis Beaumont's verse letters to Ben Jonson and 'the Mermaid Club'. EngMS (12) 2005, 139–79.

7225. LEVIN, RICHARD.   More jibes at Shakespeare in 1606, and the date of *Antony and Cleopatra.* *See* **6264.**

Beaumont and Fletcher

7226. BLISS, LEE (ed.).   A king and no king. Manchester; New York: Manchester UP, 2004. pp. ix, 194. (Revels plays.) Rev. by Elliot Kendall in TLS, 7 Oct. 2005, 31.

7227. PARKER, PATRICIA.   Barbers and Barbary: early modern cultural semantics. *See* **6270.**

7228. TUCKER, KENNETH.   An obscure poem by Robert Herrick and the unlikely popularity of the plays of Beaumont and Fletcher. *See* **7498.**

Aphra Behn

7229. AHERN, STEPHEN.   'Glorious ruine': romantic excess and the politics of sensibility in Behn's *Love-Letters.* Restoration (29:1) 2005, 29–45.

7230. BALLASTER, ROS.   'The story of the heart': *Love-Letters between a Noble-Man and His Sister. In* (pp. 135–50) **7242.**

7231. BATCHELOR, JENNIE; KAPLAN, CORA (eds).   British women's writing in the long eighteenth century: authorship, politics, and history. *See* **7936.**

7232. BEACH, ADAM R.   Anti-colonist discourse, tragicomedy, and the 'American' Behn. CompDr (38:2/3) 2004, 213–33.

7233. BIGNAMI, MARIALUISA. What the writer said: self-reflexive statements in early British fiction. Textus (18:1) 2005, 121–32.

7234. BOWLES, EMILY. Frances Brooke's erotic–didactic garden: desire, shame, and sensibility in *The Excursion*. See **8419**.

7235. BURKE, HELEN M. The Cavalier myth in *The Rover*. In (pp. 118–34) **7242**.

7236. CHALMERS, HERO. Royalist women writers, 1650–1689. Oxford: Clarendon Press; New York: OUP, 2004. pp. xii, 228. (Oxford English monographs.) Rev. by Elizabeth J. Scott-Baumann in TLS, 8 July 2005, 29; by Sarah Skwire in RES (56:226) 2005, 676–7; by Erica Longfellow in EJES (9:3) 2005, 325–7.

7237. COPELAND, NANCY. Staging gender in Behn and Centlivre: women's comedy and the theatre. (Bibl. 2004, 7502.) Rev. by Helen Burke in RECTR (19:1) 2004, 70–3.

7238. CORSE, TAYLOR. Seventeenth-century Naples and Aphra Behn's *The Rover*. Restoration (29:2) 2005, 41–51.

7239. COTTEGNIES, LINE. Aphra Behn's French translations. In (pp. 221–34) **7242**.

7240. FROHOCK, RICHARD. Heroes of empire: the British imperial protagonist in America, 1596–1764. Newark: Delaware UP, 2004. pp. 227.

7241. HUGHES, DEREK. Aphra Behn and the Restoration theatre. In (pp. 29–45) **7242**.

7242. —— TODD, JANET (eds). The Cambridge companion to Aphra Behn. Cambridge; New York: CUP, 2004. pp. xxii, 248. (Cambridge companions to literature.) Rev. by Elizabeth J. Scott-Baumann in TLS, 22 July 2005, 9.

7243. KROLL, RICHARD. 'Tales of love and gallantry': the politics of *Oroonoko*. HLQ (67:4) 2004, 573–605.

7244. LAUDIEN, HEIDI. Aphra Behn: pastoral poet. WWr (12:1) 2005, 43–58.

7245. LIPKING, JOANNA. 'Others', slaves, and colonists in *Oroonoko*. In (pp. 166–87) **7242**.

7246. MCMURRAN, MARY HELEN. Aphra Behn from both sides: translation in the Atlantic world. StudECC (34) 2005, 1–23.

7247. MARKLEY, ROBERT. Behn and the unstable traditions of social comedy. In (pp. 98–117) **7242**.

7248. MUNNS, JESSICA. Pastoral and lyric: Astrea in Arcadia. In (pp. 204–20) **7242**.

7249. O'DONNELL, MARY ANN. Aphra Behn: the documentary record. In (pp. 1–11) **7242**.

7250. OWEN, SUSAN J. Behn's dramatic response to Restoration politics. In (pp. 68–82) **7242**.

7251. —— Drink, sex and power in Restoration comedy. In (pp. 127–39) **6942**.

7252. PEARSON, JACQUELINE. The short fiction (excluding *Oroonoko*). In (pp. 188–203) **7242**.

7253. RAYLOR, TIMOTHY. Willmore's 'prince': a note on Behn's *The Rover*, I.ii. NQ (52:3) 2005, 327–9.

7254. ROSENTHAL, LAURA J. *Oroonoko*: reception, ideology, and narrative strategy. In (pp. 151–65) **7242**.

7255. STAVES, SUSAN. Behn, women, and society. In (pp. 12–28) **7242**.

7256. TODD, JANET; HUGHES, DEREK. Tragedy and tragicomedy. *In* (pp. 83–97) **7242**.

7257. VILLEGAS LÓPEZ, SONIA. Aphra Behn's sentimental history: the case study of *Agnes de Castro; or, The Force of Generous Love* (1688). SEDERI (14) 2004, 239–46.

7258. WANDLESS, WILLIAM H. Narrative pain and the moral sense: toward an ethics of suffering in the long eighteenth century. LitMed (24:1) 2005, 51–69.

7259. WIDMAYER, ANNE F. The politics of adapting Aphra Behn's *Oroonoko*. CompDr (37:2) 2003, 189–223.

7260. ZOOK, MELINDA S. The political poetry of Aphra Behn. *In* (pp. 46–67) **7242**.

Thomas Betterton

7261. ROACH, JOSEPH. The global parasol: accessorizing the four corners of the world. *In* (pp. 93–106) **8039**.

William Bradford

7262. ANDERSON, DOUGLAS. William Bradford's books: *Of Plimmoth Plantation* and the printed word. (Bibl. 2004, 7519.) Rev. by Julie Sievers in LibC (40:4) 2005, 570–2.

Anne Bradstreet

7263. GORDON, CHARLOTTE. Mistress Bradstreet: the untold life of America's first poet. London; Boston, MA: Little, Brown, 2005. pp. xiii, 337, (plates) 8.

7264. HARDE, ROXANNE. 'Then soul and body shall unite': Anne Bradstreet's theology of embodiment. SPAS (8) 2004, 1–50.

Richard Brathwait

7265. GOODRICH, PETER. *Amici curiae*: lawful manhood and other juristic performances in Renaissance England. *In* (pp. 23–49) **5196**.

Alexander Brome (1620–1666)

7266. GEE, SOPHIE. The sewers: ordure, effluence, and excess in the eighteenth century. *In* (pp. 101–20) **6958**.

7267. KEBLUSEK, MARIKA. Wine for comfort: drinking and the Royalist exile experience, 1642–1660. *In* (pp. 55–68) **6942**.

Richard Brome

7268. STEGGLE, MATTHEW. Richard Brome: place and politics on the Caroline stage. Manchester; New York: Manchester UP, 2004. pp. 222. (Revels plays companion library.) Rev. in BJJ (12) 2005, 293–301; by Nicholas Robins in TLS, 17 June 2005, 27; by Paulina Kewes in RES (56:226) 2005, 672–4.

7269. WILKINSON, KATHERINE. A source for *The City Wit*. NQ (52:2) 2005, 230–2.

Christopher Brooke

7270. O'CALLAGHAN, MICHELLE. 'Now thou may'st speak freely': entering the public sphere in 1614. *In* (pp. 63–79) **6860**.

Sir Thomas Browne (1605–1682)

7271. CORLESS-SMITH, MARTIN. That purple piece of silk between Sebald and Browne; or, How we spin our literary shrouds. DQ (40:1) 2005, 27–39.

7272. FULLER, WILLIAM. Restatement of trysts. See 7893.

7273. HUEBERT, RONALD. The private opinions of Sir Thomas Browne. SELit (45:1) 2005, 117–34.

7274. LEAHY, MARK. Plantation and thicket: a double (sight) reading of Sir Thomas Browne's *Garden of Cyrus*. PRes (10:2) 2005, 111–21.

7275. PRESTON, CLAIRE. Thomas Browne and the writing of early modern science. Cambridge; New York: CUP, 2005. pp. xiv, 250. Rev. by Andrew Hadfield in TLS, 21 Oct. 2005, 29; by R. H. Robbins in RES (56:227) 2005, 792–5; by Allison B. Kavey in RQ (58:4) 2005, 1408–9.

7276. YOSHINAKA, TAKASHI. The politics of Traducianism and Robert Herrick. See 7499.

William Browne of Tavistock

7277. DRIVER, MARTHA W. Stow's books bequeathed: some notes on William Browne (1591–c.1643) and Peter Le Neve (1661–1729). *In* (pp. 135–43) 5746.

7278. O'CALLAGHAN, MICHELLE. 'Now thou may'st speak freely': entering the public sphere in 1614. *In* (pp. 63–79) 6860.

John Bunyan

7279. AUSTIN, MICHAEL. The figural logic of the sequel and the unity of *The Pilgrim's Progress*. SP (102:4) 2005, 484–509.

7280. BERTSCH, JANET. Storytelling in the works of Bunyan, Grimmelshausen, Defoe, and Schnabel. Rochester, NY: Camden House, 2004. pp. 152. (Studies in German literature, linguistics, and culture.)

7281. DAVIES, MICHAEL. Graceful reading: theology and narrative in the works of John Bunyan. (Bibl. 2004, 7530.) Rev. by Maxine Hancock in SevC (19:2) 2004, 286–8; by Dora Rice Hawthorne in JR (85:2) 2005, 361–2.

7282. HOFMEYR, ISABEL. The portable Bunyan: a transnational history of *The Pilgrim's Progress*. (Bibl. 2004, 7534.) Rev. by John Lemly in AfSR (47:3) 2004, 230–1; by Galen K. Johnson in ChrisL (54:2) 2005, 287–9; by Anne Fuchs in RAL (36:1) 2005, 126–7; by Stephanie Newell in MLQ (66:2) 2005, 255–8.

7283. LIEBERT, ELISABETH. *Samson Agonistes* and spiritual autobiography. See 7710.

7284. LYNCH, BETH. John Bunyan and the language of conviction. Woodbridge, Suffolk; Rochester, NY: Brewer, 2004. pp. xiii, 183. (Studies in Renaissance literature, 15.)

7285. MANIQUIS, ROBERT. Teaching *The Pilgrim's Progress* and *Robinson Crusoe*; or, From filthy mire to the glory of things. *In* (pp. 25–36) 8537.

7286. ROSENFELD, NANCY. *The Man of Mode*: the mode of man. See 7439.

7287. WILLIAMS, J. R. 'Suffer the little children to come unto me': T. F. Powys's child-men in a landscape of redemption. See 18928.

Gilbert Burnet

7288. BULLARD, PADDY. The latitude of Whiggism: Tillotson, Burnet, and Lord William Russell in Whig historiography, 1675–1775. *In* (pp. 299–329) **8091.**

7289. STARKIE, ANDREW. Contested histories of the English Church: Gilbert Burnet and Jeremy Collier. *See* **7325.**

Robert Burton

7290. REID, JENNIFER I. M. Worse than beasts: an anatomy of melancholy and the literature of travel in seventeenth- and eighteenth-century England. Aurora, CO: Davies, 2004. pp. vii, 143. (Contexts and consequences.)

7291. SCHMIDT, JEREMY. Melancholy and the therapeutic language of moral philosophy in seventeenth-century thought. JHI (65:4) 2004, 583–601.

7292. SHERBERT, GARY. 'Hieroglyphics of sleep and pain': Djuna Barnes's anatomy of melancholy. *See* **15330.**

7293. TIBURI, MARCIA. Saturn's body: melancholy and method in the *Anatomy of Melancholy*. SEDERI (13) 2003, 209–18.

7294. TILMOUTH, CHRISTOPHER. Burton's 'turning picture': argument and anxiety in *The Anatomy of Melancholy*. RES (56:226) 2005, 524–49.

7295. VÉLEZ NÚÑEZ, RAFAEL. Melancholic sounds: singing madness in Restoration drama. SEDERI (13) 2003, 219–27.

Samuel Butler (1612–1680)

7296. ACHINSTEIN, SHARON. 'When civil fury first grew high': politics and incivility in Restoration England. *In* (pp. 85–98) **5187.**

Thomas Carew

7297. FOREY, MARGARET. Manuscript evidence and the author of *Aske Me No More*: William Strode, not Thomas Carew. *See* **7853.**

7298. RAY, ROBERT H. The admiration of Sir Philip Sidney by Lovelace and Carew: new seventeenth-century allusions. *See* **5652.**

Mary Carleton (1642?–1673)

7299. WAGNER, GERALDINE. The staged self in Mary Carleton's autobiographical narratives. CLCWeb (7:3) 2005.

Elizabeth Cary, Viscountess Falkland

7300. DOLAN, FRANCES E. Reading, work, and Catholic women's biographies. ELR (33:3) 2003, 328–57.

7301. HELLER, JENNIFER L. Space, violence, and bodies in Middleton and Cary. *See* **7645.**

7302. OSTMAN, HEATHER E. Backbiters, flatterers, and monarchs: domestic politics in *The Tragedy of Mariam*. *In* (pp. 183–205) **5103.**

7303. POITEVIN, KIMBERLY WOOSLEY. 'Counterfeit colour': making up race in Elizabeth Cary's *The Tragedy of Mariam*. TSWL (24:1) 2005, 13–34.

7304. ROBERTS, JEANNE ADDISON. Revenge tragedy and Elizabeth Cary's *Mariam*. RenP (2003) 149–66.

7305. SWAN, JESSE G. Towards a textual history of the 1680 folio *The History of the Life, Reign and Death of Edward II* (attributed to Elizabeth Cary, Lady

Falkland): understanding the collateral 1680 octavo *The History of the Most Unfortunate Prince. In* (pp. 177–90) **587**.

7306. WOLFE, HEATHER.   A family affair: the life and letters of Elizabeth Cary, Lady Falkland. *In* (pp. 97–108) **587**.

7307. WYNNE-DAVIES, MARION.   Suicide at the Elephant and Castle, or did the lady vanish? Alternative endings for early modern women writers. *In* (pp. 121–42) **5914**.

John Caryll

7308. SUAREZ, MICHAEL F.   A crisis in English public life: the Popish Plot, *Naboth's Vineyard* (1679), and mock-biblical satire's exemplary redress. HLQ (67:4) 2004, 529–52.

George Chapman

7309. CATHCART, CHARLES.   Borrowings and the authorial domain: Gostanzo, Polonius, and Marston's Gonzago. *See* **7614**.

7310. GOSSETT, SUZANNE.   Marston, collaboration, and *Eastward Ho! See* **7617**.

7311. HILLMAN, RICHARD.   The tragic Channel-crossings of George Chapman: part II, *The Revenge of Bussy D'Ambois, The Tragedy of Chabot.* CEl (67) 2005, 23–31.

7312. HOENSELAARS, A. J.   Shakespeare and the early modern history play. *In* (pp. 25–40) **5964**.

7313. JACKSON, MacD. P.   Francis Meres and the cultural contexts of Shakespeare's Rival Poet sonnets. *See* **6718**.

7314. O'CALLAGHAN, MICHELLE.   'Now thou may'st speak freely': entering the public sphere in 1614. *In* (pp. 63–79) **6860**.

7315. SMITH, STAN.   Epic *logos*: on first looking into several Homers. *See* **11535**.

Charles I, King of England

7316. AINSWORTH, DAVID.   Spiritual reading in Milton's *Eikonoklastes. See* **7654**.

7317. McELLIGOTT, JASON.   Roger Morrice and the reputation of the *Eikon Basilike* in the 1680s. Library (6:2) 2005, 119–32.

William Chillingworth (1602–1644)

7318. ROUX, LOUIS.   Foi et raison dans l'œuvre de William Chillingworth. Anglophonia (17) 2005, 207–15.

Edward Hyde, Earl of Clarendon

7319. SEAWARD, PAUL.   Clarendon, Tacitism, and the civil wars of Europe. HLQ (68:1/2) 2005, 289–311.

7320. WOMERSLEY, DAVID.   Confessional politics in Defoe's *Journal of the Plague Year. In* (pp. 237–56) **8091**.

John Cleveland

7321. GRIFFIN, JULIA B.   'Twixt treason and convenience: some images of Thomas Wentworth, First Earl of Strafford. *In* (pp. 153–80) **5103**.

Anne Clifford,
Countess of Dorset, Pembroke and Montgomery

7322. CHAN, MARY; WRIGHT, NANCY E.   Marriage, identity, and the pursuit of property in seventeenth-century England: the cases of Anne Clifford and Elizabeth Wiseman. *In* (pp. 162–82) **6964**.

7323. SALZMAN, PAUL.   Early modern (aristocratic) women and textual property. *In* (pp. 281–95) **6964**.

Jeremy Collier

7324. GELINEAU, DAVID.   Dryden's *Cymon and Iphigenia*: the 'Vigour of the Worse' prevailing. *See* **7416**.

7325. STARKIE, ANDREW.   Contested histories of the English Church: Gilbert Burnet and Jeremy Collier. HLQ (68:1/2) 2005, 335–51.

Elizabeth Colville,
Lady Colville of Culross (Elizabeth Melville)

7326. EVANS, DEANNA DELMAR.   Holy terror and love divine: the passionate voice in Elizabeth Melville's *Ane Godlie Dreame*. *In* (pp. 153–61) **3754**.

7327. LAROCHE, REBECCA.   Elizabeth Melville and her friends: seeing *Ane Godlie Dreame* through political lenses. CLIO (34:3) 2005, 277–95.

7328. REID-BAXTER, JAMIE.   Elizabeth Melville, Lady Culross: 3500 new lines of verse. *In* (pp. 195–200) **3754**.

William Congreve

7329. BIGNAMI, MARIALUISA.   What the writer said: self-reflexive statements in early British fiction. *See* **7233**.

Anne Conway (1631–1679)

7330. HUTTON, SARAH.   Authority and the Word: Henry More, William Penn and the *logos*. *See* **7782**.

Thomas Coryate

7331. O'CALLAGHAN, MICHELLE.   Tavern societies, the Inns of Court, and the culture of conviviality in early seventeenth-century London. *In* (pp. 37–51) **6942**.

John Cotgrave (*fl.*1655)

7332. SMYTH, ADAM.   'It were far better be a *Toad*, or a *Serpant*, then a Drunkard': writing about drunkenness. *In* (pp. 193–210) **6942**.

John Cotton

7333. DYRNESS, WILLIAM A.   Reformed theology and visual culture: the Protestant imagination from Calvin to Edwards. *See* **8563**.

7334. GORDIS, LISA M.   Opening Scripture: Bible reading and interpretive authority in Puritan New England. (Bibl. 2004, 7569.) Rev. by Evan Haefeli in JR (84:3) 2004, 460–2; by Roger Pooley in MLR (100:2) 2005, 481–2.

Richard Crashaw

7335. WALL, JOHN N.   Crashaw, Catholicism, and Englishness: defining religious identity. RenP (2004) 107–26.

7336. WILLIAMS, GEORGE WALTON.   Addendum. RenP (2004) 127–9.

Thomas Creech

7337. GURR, JENS MARTIN. 'Let me suppose thee for a ship a-while': nautical metaphors and contemporary politics in eighteenth-century translations of Horace's Ode I, xiv. *See* 9069.

Helkiah Crooke (1576–1635)

7338. CALBI, MAURIZIO. 'Civil monsters': race, eroticism and the body in early modern literature and culture. *See* 6639.

John Crowne

7339. MURRAY, BARBARA A. (ed.). Shakespeare adaptations from the Restoration: five plays. *See* 6037.

Samuel Daniel

7340. DUBROW, HEATHER. 'Lending soft audience to my sweet design': shifting roles and shifting readings of Shakespeare's *A Lover's Complaint*. *See* 6519.

7341. PITCHER, JOHN. Samuel Daniel's gifts of books to Lord Chancellor Egerton. MedRen (17) 2005, 216–38.

7342. RHODES, NEIL. Shakespeare the barbarian. *In* (pp. 99–114) 5187.

7343. SCHMITT-KILB, CHRISTIAN. 'Never was the Albion Nation without Poetrie': Poetik, Rhetorik und Nation im England der frühen Neuzeit. Frankfurt: Klostermann, 2004. pp. 235. (Zeitsprünge: Forschungen zur frühen Neuzeit, 8:1/2.) Rev. by Daniel Dornhofer in JSBC (11:2) 2004, 233–4.

7344. TARLINSKAJA, MARINA. Who did NOT write *A Lover's Complaint*. *See* 6520.

Charles Darby ('C.D.') (d.1709)

7345. SMYTH, ADAM. 'It were far better be a *Toad*, or a *Serpant*, then a *Drunkard*': writing about drunkenness. *In* (pp. 193–210) 6942.

Sir William Davenant

7346. BALLASTER, ROS. Performing *Roxane*: the Oriental woman as the sign of luxury in eighteenth-century fictions. *In* (pp. 165–77) 7941.

7347. BÖGELS, THEO. 'Fit for the pocket': Thomas Johnson's edition of *The Tempest*. *See* 6743.

7348. HOENSELAARS, TON; VAN MEURS, FRANK. The Haarlem manuscript of *Hartogh van Savoij*: an eighteenth-century Dutch translation of *The Tempest; or, The Enchanted Island*. *See* 7417.

7349. HOLBERTON, EDWARD. 'Soe Honny from the Lyon came': the 1657 wedding-masques for the Protector's daughters. *See* 7626.

7350. THOMAS, CHAD. Negotiating the Interregnum: the political works of Davenant and Tatham. 1650–1850 (10) 2004, 225–44.

7351. WILLIAMS, SIMON. Taking Macbeth out of himself: Davenant, Garrick, Schiller and Verdi. *See* 6577.

Thomas Dekker

7352. CRUPI, CHARLES W. Reading nascent capitalism in Part II of Thomas Heywood's *If You Know Not Me, You Know Nobody*. *See* 7503.

7353. GIESKES, EDWARD.   'Honesty and vulgar praise': the Poets' War and the literary field. See 5248.

7354. HUTCHINGS, MARK.   Anti-theatrical prejudice and *1 Honest Whore*, II.i.324–326. NQ (52:2) 2005, 220–1.

7355. KORDA, NATASHA.   The case of Moll Frith: women's work and the 'all-male stage'. *In* (pp. 71–87) 5225.

7356. MIOLA, ROBERT S.   Jesuit drama in early modern England. *In* (pp. 71–86) 5915.

7357. NICOL, DAVID.   Interrogating the Devil: social and demonic pressure in *The Witch of Edmonton*. CompDr (38:4) 2004/05, 425–45.

7358. SMITH, AMY L.   Performing cross-class clandestine marriage in *The Shoemaker's Holiday*. SELit (45:2) 2005, 333–55.

Sir John Denham

7359. BROWN, LAURA.   Oceans and floods: fables of global perspective. *In* (pp. 107–20) 8039.

7360. CARSON, ANNE ELIZABETH.   The hunted stag and the beheaded king. SELit (45:3) 2005, 537–56.

7361. CLARKE, SUSAN A.   Royalists write the death of Lord Hastings: post-regicide funerary propaganda. See 7061.

7362. GRIFFIN, JULIA B.   'Twixt treason and convenience: some images of Thomas Wentworth, First Earl of Strafford. *In* (pp. 153–80) 5103.

7363. KEBLUSEK, MARIKA.   Wine for comfort: drinking and the Royalist exile experience, 1642–1660. *In* (pp. 55–68) 6942.

John Donne (1572–1631)

7364. ALBRECHT, ROBERTA.   Alchemical augmentation and primordial fire in Donne's *The Dissolution*. SELit (45:1) 2005, 95–115.

7365. BACH, REBECCA ANN.   (Re)placing John Donne in the history of sexuality. ELH (72:1) 2005, 259–89.

7366. CLUTTERBUCK, CHARLOTTE.   Encounters with God in medieval and early modern English poetry. See 4603.

7367. COLCLOUGH, DAVID (ed.).   John Donne's professional lives. (Bibl. 2004, 7618.) Rev. by Raymond-Jean Frontain in SCN (62:3/4) 2004, 176–9; by Alex Davis in MLR (100:1) 2005, 199–200.

7368. CORRENTE, MARCELLO (introd. and trans.).   Liriche d'amore e *Sonetti sacri*. Milan: Quercia fiorita, 2005. pp. cvi, 244. (English poetry, 1.)

7369. DOERKSEN, DANIEL W.   Discerning God's voice, God's hand: Scripturalist moderation in Donne's *Devotions*. *In* (pp. 148–72) 6872.

7370. EMSLEY, SARAH.   Is Emily Dickinson a Metaphysical poet? See 10776.

7371. FELCH, SUSAN M.   Doubt and the hermeneutics of delight. See 5692.

7372. FLETCHER, ANGUS.   Living magnets, Paracelsian corpses, and the psychology of grace in Donne's religious verse. ELH (72:1) 2005, 1–22.

7373. FLORÉN, CELIA (ed.).   John Donne: a complete concordance of the poems. Hildesheim; New York: Olms-Weidmann, 2004. 2 vols. pp. 1027. (Alpha–omega, C: Englische Autoren, 5.)

7374. FRONTAIN, RAYMOND-JEAN. 'The man which have affliction seene': Donne, Jeremiah, and the fashioning of lamentation. *In* (pp. 127–47) **6872**.

7375. GREENE, THOMAS M. Poetry, signs, and magic. *See* **5946**.

7376. HARRIES, BYRON. John Owen the epigrammatist: a literary and historical context. *See* **7809**.

7377. HARVEY, ANDREW. Crossing wits: Donne, Herbert, and sacramental rhetoric. RenP (2004) 69–83.

7378. HESTER, M. THOMAS; SORLIEN, ROBERT PARKER; FLYNN, DENNIS (eds). John Donne's marriage letters in the Folger Shakespeare Library. Washington, DC: Folger Shakespeare Library, 2005. pp. 110.

7379. JONES, HESTER. Graham and the numinous: the 'centre aloneness' and the 'unhailed water'. *In* (pp. 160–83) **16793**.

7380. KRŪMINIENĖ, JADVYGA. John Donne's sermons: paradox as a fundamental structural device. *In* (pp. 101–8) **3734**.

7381. MCDUFFIE, FELECIA WRIGHT. 'To our bodies turn we then': body as word and sacrament in the works of John Donne. London; New York: Continuum, 2005. pp. xvi, 175.

7382. MCLEOD, RANDALL. Obliterature: reading a censored text of Donne's *To His Mistress Going to Bed*. EngMS (12) 2005, 83–138.

7383. MANSOUR, WISAM. Gender ambivalence in Donne's *Valediction: Forbidding Mourning*. ELN (42:4) 2005, 19–23.

7384. MICHIE, ALLEN. 'New philosophy calls all in doubt': chaos theory and the fractal poetics of John Donne. *In* (pp. 150–77) **5167**.

7385. MOUSLEY, ANDY. Transubstantiating love: John Donne and cultural criticism. *In* (pp. 55–62) **3724**.

7386. NELSON, BYRON. 'The King shall be his friend': John Donne's sermons about King James. SRASP (27) 2004, 35–50.

7387. PANDO CANTELLI, MARÍA J. ' … and often Absences / Withdrew our Soules and made us Carcasses': the destructive power of the female figure in Donne's *Nocturnall* and Quevedo's love poetry. SEDERI (13) 2003, 155–62.

7388. PAPAZIAN, MARY ARSHAGOUNI (ed.). John Donne and the Protestant Reformation: new perspectives. (Bibl. 2004, 7638.) Rev. by Christopher Baker in SixCJ (36:2) 2005, 637–9; by Robert Ellrodt in EA (58:2) 2005, 208–10.

7389. ROBERTS, JOHN R. John Donne: an annotated bibliography of modern criticism, 1979–1995. (Bibl. 2004, 7643.) Rev. in BJJ (12) 2005, 293–301; by Donald R. Dickson in SCN (63:3/4) 2005, 168–9.

7390. ROSTON, MURRAY. Donne and the meditative tradition. ReLit (37:1) 2005, 45–68.

7391. RYERSE, BARBARA. Browning's *Christmas-Eve and Easter-Day*: formal verse satire and the Donnean influence. *See* **10266**.

7392. SCODEL, JOSHUA. 'None's slave': some versions of liberty in Donne's *Satires 1* and *4*. ELH (72:2) 2005, 363–85.

7393. SHAMI, JEANNE. John Donne and conformity in crisis in the late Jacobean pulpit. (Bibl. 2004, 7646.) Rev. by Daniel W. Doerksen in ChrisL (54:1) 2004, 138–41; by Robert C. Evans in SixCJ (36:2) 2005, 488–9; by Peter McCullough in

RES (56:226) 2005, 671–2; by Dennis Flynn in EC (55:2) 2005, 173–7; by Byron Nelson in SCN (63:3/4) 2005, 135–7.

7394. —— Love and power: the rhetorical motives of John Donne's 1622 sermon to the Virginia Company. RenP (2004) 85–106.

7395. —— Squint-eyed, left-handed, half-deaf: *imperfect senses* and John Donne's interpretive middle way. *In* (pp. 173–92) **6872**.

7396. STEGGLE, MATTHEW, *et al.* Jonson and his era: overviews of modern research. *See* **7586**.

7397. STEVENSON, WINIFRED. Donne's nocturnal. SevC (19:2) 2004, 178–82.

7398. STIRLING, KIRSTEN. 'Imagined corners': space, time and iconoclasm in John Donne's Last Judgement *Holy Sonnets.* WI (21:3) 2005, 244–51.

7399. STRINGER, GARY A. Words, artifacts, and the editing of Donne's *Elegies. In* (pp. 13–26) **587**.

7400. WHALEN, ROBERT. The poetry of immanence: sacrament in Donne and Herbert. (Bibl. 2004, 7651.) Rev. by Jeffrey Powers-Beck in GHJ (26:1/2) 2002/03, 117–19; by Jonathan Nauman in SCN (63:1/2) 2005, 7–14.

7401. WHITLOCK, KEITH. The Robert Ashley founding bequest to the Middle Temple Library and John Donne's library. SEDERI (14) 2004, 153–75.

Michael Drayton

7402. VALLARO, CRISTINA. La simbologia lunare nei canzonieri elisabettiani. *See* **5325**.

William Drummond of Hawthornden (1585–1649)

7403. BOEHRER, BRUCE. Disorder in the house of God: disrupted worship in Shakespeare and others. *See* **6731**.

John Dryden

7404. ACHINSTEIN, SHARON. 'When civil fury first grew high': politics and incivility in Restoration England. *In* (pp. 85–98) **5187**.

7405. BATTISTI, SUSANNA. Metamorfosi del teatro: gli adattamenti shakespeariani di John Dryden. Bari: Adriatica, 2005. pp. 172. (Biblioteca di studi inglesi, 75.)

7406. BEACH, ADAM R. Anti-colonist discourse, tragicomedy, and the 'American' Behn. *See* **7232**.

7407. BÖGELS, THEO. 'Fit for the pocket': Thomas Johnson's edition of *The Tempest. See* **6743**.

7408. BROWN, LAURA. Oceans and floods: fables of global perspective. *In* (pp. 107–20) **8039**.

7409. CALDWELL, TANYA. Meanings of *All for Love,* 1677–1813. CompDr (38:2/3) 2004, 183–211.

7410. CELLAI, ANTONELLA. Da *truce-breaker* a *match-maker*: le metamorfosi di Pandaro da Omero a Dryden. *See* **5057**.

7411. CHOWDHURY, AHSAN. 'A fearful blazing star': signs of the Exclusion Crisis in Robert Knox's *An Historical Relation of the Island Ceylon* (1681). *See* **7098**.

7412. D'ADDARIO, CHRISTOPHER. Dryden and the historiography of exile: Milton and Virgil in Dryden's late period. HLQ (67:4) 2004, 553–72.

7413. DEWAR-WATSON, SARAH. Dryden's *Aeneis* 2.718–41. Exp (64:1) 2005, 17–19.

7414. GEE, SOPHIE. The invention of the wasteland: civic narrative and Dryden's *Annus Mirabilis*. ECL (29:1) 2005, 82–108.

7415. —— The sewers: ordure, effluence, and excess in the eighteenth century. *In* (pp. 101–20) **6958.**

7416. GELINEAU, DAVID. Dryden's *Cymon and Iphigenia*: the 'Vigour of the Worse' prevailing. SP (102:2) 2005, 210–32.

7417. HOENSELAARS, TON; VAN MEURS, FRANK. The Haarlem manuscript of *Hartogh van Savoij*: an eighteenth-century Dutch translation of *The Tempest; or, The Enchanted Island*. ShY (15) 2005, 179–210.

7418. LEWIS, JAYNE; NOVAK, MAXIMILLIAN E. (eds). Enchanted ground: reimagining John Dryden. (Bibl. 2004, 7688.) Rev. by James S. Baumlin in RQ (58:4) 2005, 1451–2.

7419. MORA, MARÍA JOSÉ. Type-casting in the Restoration theatre: Dryden's *All for Love*, 1677–1704. Atl (27:2) 2005, 75–86.

7420. NEILL, MICHAEL. 'An artificiall following of nature': Dryden, Etherege, and perfection of art. *In* (pp. 181–201) **5167.**

7421. NESVET, REBECCA. Parallel histories: Dryden's Plutarch and religious toleration. RES (56:225) 2005, 424–37.

7422. RAWSON, CLAUDE; SANTESSO, AARON (eds). John Dryden (1631–1700): his politics, his plays, and his poets. A tercentenary celebration held at Yale University 6–7 October, 2000. (Bibl. 2004, 7698.) Rev. by Carolyn D. Williams in RECTR (19:1) 2004, 79–80; by Jerome Donnelly in SCN (63:1/2) 2005, 27–31; by Cedric D. Reverand, II, in Scriblerian (37:2 / 38:1) 2005, 103–5.

7423. ROACH, JOSEPH. The global parasol: accessorizing the four corners of the world. *In* (pp. 93–106) **8039.**

7424. ROPER, ALAN. Aeneas and Agathocles in the Exclusion Crisis. *See* **7515.**

7425. —— Doctor Balack and Bishop Boloch: nomenclature in Restoration parallel poems. ELN (43:1) 2005, 39–48.

7426. THOMPSON, PEGGY. 'I hope, you wou'd not offer violence to me': the trope of insincere resistance in Dryden's *The Kind Keeper*. Restoration (29:2) 2005, 21–40.

7427. WALLS, KATHRYN. 'Adam-wits' in *Absalom and Achitophel*. NQ (52:3) 2005, 337–8.

7428. ZWICKER, STEVEN N. 'What every literate man once knew': tracing readers in early modern England. *In* (pp. 75–90) **19.**

7429. —— (ed.). The Cambridge companion to John Dryden. (Bibl. 2004, 7715.) Rev. by Kirk Combe in NQ (52:4) 2005, 544–6; by Jennifer Brady in RQ (58:1) 2005, 354–6.

Thomas D'Urfey

7430. FISK, DEBORAH PAYNE (ed.). Four Restoration libertine plays. *See* **7436.**

7431. GÓMEZ, CARLOS J. Farcical innocuousness *versus* morality and satire in the comedies of Thomas Durfey. SEDERI (13) 2003, 77–86.

7432. MORA, MARÍA JOSÉ. The political is personal: the attack on Shadwell in *Sir Barnaby Whigg.* SEDERI (15) 2005, 115–28.

7433. MURRAY, BARBARA A. (ed.). Shakespeare adaptations from the Restoration: five plays. *See* **6037.**

7434. VÉLEZ NÚÑEZ, RAFAEL. Melancholic sounds: singing madness in Restoration drama. *See* **7295.**

John Eliot (1604–1690)

7435. CLARK, MICHAEL P. (ed.). The Eliot tracts: with letters from John Eliot to Thomas Thorowgood and Richard Baxter. Westport, CT; London: Praeger, 2003. pp. vi, 452. (Contributions in American history, 199.) Rev. by Phillip H. Round in EAL (40:2) 2005, 375–85; by William J. Scheick in SCN (63:3/4) 2005, 196–8.

Sir George Etherege

7436. FISK, DEBORAH PAYNE (ed.). Four Restoration libertine plays. Oxford; New York: OUP, 2005. pp. liv, 414. (Oxford English drama.) (Etherege, *The Man of Mode*; D'Urfey, *A Fond Husband*; Shadwell, *The Libertine*; Otway, *Friendship in Fashion.*) Rev. by Michael Caines in TLS, 29 July 2005, 28.

7437. KACHUR, B. A. Etherege & Wycherley. (Bibl. 2004, 7718.) Rev. by David Roberts in NQ (52:4) 2005, 543–4.

7438. NEILL, MICHAEL. 'An artificiall following of nature': Dryden, Etherege, and perfection of art. *In* (pp. 181–201) **5167.**

7439. ROSENFELD, NANCY. *The Man of Mode*: the mode of man. McNR (42) 2004, 20–40.

John Evelyn

7440. EMMERSON, J. McL. Dan Fleming and John Evelyn: two seventeenth-century book collectors. *See* **386.**

7441. HARRIS, FRANCES; HUNTER, MICHAEL (eds). John Evelyn and his milieu. (Bibl. 2004, 7727.) Rev. by Christopher Baker in SCN (63:3/4) 2005, 191–4; by Lee Piepho in RQ (58:2) 2005, 744–7; by Laura York in Comitatus (36) 2005, 250–2.

Sir Richard Fanshawe

7442. GRIFFIN, JULIA B. 'Twixt treason and convenience: some images of Thomas Wentworth, First Earl of Strafford. *In* (pp. 153–80) **5103.**

Nicholas Ferrar

7443. DYCK, PAUL. 'So rare a use': scissors, reading, and devotion at Little Gidding. *See* **7472.**

7444. RANSOME, JOYCE. Monotessaron: the harmonies of Little Gidding. SevC (20:1) 2005, 22–52.

John Fletcher (1579–1625)

7445. BANERJEE, RITA. *Women Pleas'd* and *Swetnam the Woman-Hater Arraigned by Women*: John Fletcher's participation in the Swetnam debate and the date of his play. RORD (44) 2005, 103–15.

7446. BYRNE, PETER. 'Where appetite directs': tragic heroism's recovery in Rochester's *Valentinian*. PCP (40:1) 2005, 158–77.

7447. LIVINGSTON, MEG POWERS. *The Tragedy of Sir John Van Olden Barnavelt*: a re-examination of Fletcher and Massinger's sources. ShY (15) 2005, 65–88.

7448. LYNCH, KATHRYN L. The three noble kinsmen: Chaucer, Shakespeare, Fletcher. *In* (pp. 72–91) **5103**.

7449. MCBRIDE, CHARLOTTE. A natural drink for an English man: national stereotyping in early modern culture. *In* (pp. 181–91) **6942**.

7450. RASMUSSEN, ERIC; PROUDFOOT, G. R. (eds). The two noble kinsmen. *See* **6817**.

Emanuel Ford

7451. STANIVUKOVIC, GORAN (ed.). The most pleasant history of Ornatus and Artesia. (Bibl. 2004, 7749.) Rev. by Helen Moore in TLS, 8 July 2005, 5–6.

John Ford (1586–c.1640)

7452. HOPKINS, LISA. Staging passion in Ford's *The Lover's Melancholy*. SELit (45:2) 2005, 443–59.

7453. NICOL, DAVID. Interrogating the Devil: social and demonic pressure in *The Witch of Edmonton*. *See* **7357**.

Constance Aston Fowler (b.1621)

7454. ALDRICH-WATSON, DEBORAH. Notes on editing *The Verse Miscellany of Constance Aston Fowler: a Diplomatic Edition*. *In* (pp. 157–65) **587**.

Joseph Glanvill (1636–1680)

7455. FUNAKAWA, KAZUHIKO. The metamorphoses of the scholar-gipsy. *See* **9931**.

John Goodwin (c.1594–1665)

7456. KNAPP, HENRY M. John Owen's interpretation of Hebrews 6:4–6: eternal perseverance of the saints in Puritan exegesis. *See* **7810**.

Robert Gould

7457. MARTIN, SUSAN M. Robert Gould's attacks on the London stage, 1689 and 1709: the two versions of *The Playhouse: a Satyr*. PQ (82:1) 2003, 59–86.

John Hall (1627–1656)

7458. CLARKE, SUSAN A. Royalists write the death of Lord Hastings: post-regicide funerary propaganda. *See* **7061**.

James Harrington (1611–1677)

7459. HUGUES, GÉRARD. Les origines harringtoniennes de la Constitution américaine. EREA (1:2) 2003, 46–51.

7460. LEVILLAIN, CHARLES-ÉDOUARD. L'Angleterre de la Restauration au miroir de la 'vraie liberté' (1660–1672): la rencontre entre républicanismes anglais et hollandais à travers les écrits de Pieter de la Court. EREA (1:2) 2003, 34–45.

Sir John Hayward

7461. WOMERSLEY, DAVID. Against the teleology of technique. *See* 5385.

Richard Head (1637?–1686?)

7462. STEGGLE, MATTHEW. Richard Head's *The Floating Island* (1673) plagiarizes Thomas Powell. NQ (52:3) 2005, 325–7.

George Herbert

7463. ALKON, GABRIEL. Refrain and the limits of poetic power in Spenser, Herbert, Hardy, and Stevens. *See* 5675.

7464. BALIZET, ARIANE M. 'A Jewish choice': the Judaic past and present in the poetry of George Herbert. GHJ (26:1/2) 2002/03, 46–64.

7465. BLAISE, ANNE-MARIE MILLER. 'Sweetnesse readie penn'd': Herbert's theology of beauty. GHJ (27:1/2) 2003/04, 1–21.

7466. BROWN, LAURA FEITZINGER. Brawling in church: noise and the rhetoric of lay behavior in early modern England. SixCJ (34:4) 2003, 955–72.

7467. CLARKE, ELIZABETH. George Herbert and Cambridge scholars. GHJ (27:1/2) 2003/04, 43–52.

7468. COOLEY, RONALD W. 'Full of all knowledg': George Herbert's *Country Parson* and early modern social discourse. (Bibl. 2004, 7774.) Rev. by Cristina Malcolmson in GHJ (26:1/2) 2002/03, 111–16; by Gayle Gaskill in RQ (58:1) 2005, 351–2.

7469. CRUICKSHANK, FRANCES. Herbert's *Jordan (1)*. Exp (64:1) 2005, 12–14.

7470. DAVIDSON, ADELE. The Temple's left column: George Herbert in 'Acrostick Land'. TLS, 9 Dec. 2005, 12–13.

7471. DYCK, PAUL. Locating the Word: the textual church and George Herbert's *Temple*. In (pp. 224–44) 6872.

7472. —— 'So rare a use': scissors, reading, and devotion at Little Gidding. GHJ (27:1/2) 2003/04, 67–81.

7473. GOEGLEIN, TIMOTHY S. A sense of the sacred. Poetry (186:1) 2005, 53–5.

7474. GOLL, PAULETTE S. Recent hymnal and musical adaptations of George Herbert. GHJ (26:1/2) 2002/03, 94–102.

7475. HARVEY, ANDREW. Crossing wits: Donne, Herbert, and sacramental rhetoric. *See* 7377.

7476. JUDGE, JEANNIE SARGENT. Accepting the flesh: George Herbert and the sacrament of Holy Communion. *In* (pp. 136–52) 5103.

7477. KILGORE, ROBERT. Reading ourselves in *Redemption*. GHJ (26:1/2) 2002/03, 1–14.

7478. MCDOWELL, SEAN. Finding readers: Herbert's appeals to the passions. GHJ (26:1/2) 2002/03, 65–82.

7479. MALCOLMSON, CRISTINA. George Herbert: a literary life. (Bibl. 2004, 7781.) Rev. by Daniel W. Doerksen in GHJ (27:1/2) 2003/04, 119–23.

7480. MILLER, GREG. Self-parody and pastoral praise: George Herbert's *Memoriae matris sacrum*. GHJ (26:1/2) 2002/03, 15–34.

7481. OAKES, MARGARET J.   'To be thy praise, / And be my salvation': the double function of praise in *The Temple*. TSLL (47:2) 2005, 120–38.

7482. SCOTT, DAVID.   Priest as poet. *See* **11541.**

7483. SEMLER, L. E.   Creative adoption in *Eliza's Babes* (1652): Puritan refigurations of Sibbes, Herrick, and Herbert. *In* (pp. 319–45) **6872.**

7484. TURNBULL, MARGARET.   George Herbert and John Jewel: *Vanitie (1)*, *The Agonie*, and *Divinitie*. GHJ (26:1/2) 2002/03, 83–93.

7485. VENDLER, HELEN.   Invisible listeners: lyric intimacy in Herbert, Whitman, and Ashbery. Princeton, NJ; Oxford: Princeton UP, 2005. pp. 144. Rev. by Angela Leighton in TLS, 16 Dec. 2005, 26.

7486. WHITAKER, CURTIS.   Baptisms and burials: the presence of the Book of Common Prayer in Herbert's nature poetry. GHJ (27:1/2) 2003/04, 82–104.

7487. WILCHER, ROBERT.   The darkened scribe and the blessed man: changing uses of allusion in the work of Henry Vaughan. *See* **7885.**

7488. WILCOX, HELEN.   Herbert's 'enchanting language': the poetry of a Cambridge orator. GHJ (27:1/2) 2003/04, 53–66.

7489. WOLBERG, KRISTINE.   George Herbert's *The Country Parson* and Stefano Guazzo's *The Civile Conversation*. GHJ (27:1/2) 2003/04, 105–18.

7490. WOOD, CHAUNCEY.   Herbert's biblically titled poems. GHJ (26:1/2) 2002/03, 35–45.

7491. —— Herbert's *The Pearl* and the *Commentary* by Franciscus Lucas Brugensis. GHJ (27:1/2) 2003/04, 32–42.

Edward, Lord Herbert of Cherbury

7492. OVER, WILLIAM.   Race, culture, and openness: an early modern precedent. PartA (3:2) 2005, 1–22.

Robert Herrick (1591–1674)

7493. ACHILLEOS, STELLA.   The *Anacreontea* and a tradition of refined male sociability. *In* (pp. 21–35) **6942.**

7494. BROWN, CEDRIC C.   Sons of beer and sons of Ben: drink as a social marker in seventeenth-century England. *In* (pp. 3–20) **6942.**

7495. JOHNSON, WILLIAM C.   *In vino – et in amore – veritas*: transformational animation in Herrick's 'sack' poems. PLL (41:1) 2005, 89–108.

7496. PRESTWICH, NATALIE K.   Ghostly metaphysicality: a manuscript variant of Robert Herrick's *The Apparition*. NQ (52:2) 2005, 232–3.

7497. SEMLER, L. E.   Creative adoption in *Eliza's Babes* (1652): Puritan refigurations of Sibbes, Herrick, and Herbert. *In* (pp. 319–45) **6872.**

7498. TUCKER, KENNETH.   An obscure poem by Robert Herrick and the unlikely popularity of the plays of Beaumont and Fletcher. KenPR (19) 2004, 50–7.

7499. YOSHINAKA, TAKASHI.   The politics of Traducianism and Robert Herrick. SevC (19:2) 2004, 183–95.

Peter Heylyn

7500. MARKLEY, ROBERT.   Riches, power, trade and religion: the Far East and the English imagination, 1600–1720. *See* **7714.**

7501. MAYHEW, ROBERT. British geography's republic of letters: mapping an imagined community, 1600–1800. JHI (65:2) 2004, 251–75.

Thomas Heywood

7502. CREASER, SHARON. Public and private performance of guilt in Thomas Heywood's *A Woman Killed with Kindness*. DalR (85:2) 2005, 285–94.

7503. CRUPI, CHARLES W. Reading nascent capitalism in Part II of Thomas Heywood's *If You Know Not Me, You Know Nobody*. TSLL (46:3) 2004, 296–323.

7504. HOLBROOK, PETER. An earthy muse. TLS, 17 June 2005, 25 (review-article). (*King Edward the Fourth*.)

7505. HOWARD, JEAN E. Staging the absent woman: the theatrical evocation of Elizabeth Tudor in Heywood's *If You Know Not Me, You Know Nobody, Part 1*. In (pp. 263–80) **5225**.

7506. KAHAN, JEFFREY. Shakespeare's Hector and Heywood's *The Rape of Lucrece*. See **6795**.

7507. LADD, ROGER A. From 'sonne of marchaundy' to 'obscurely bred': the nine lives of Richard Whittington. See **4630**.

7508. MUKHERJI, SUBHA. 'Unmanly indignities': adultery, evidence and judgement in Heywood's *A Woman Killed with Kindness*. In (pp. 71–99) **5196**.

7509. PARKER, PATRICIA. Barbers and Barbary: early modern cultural semantics. See **6270**.

7510. ROWLAND, RICHARD. 'Speaking some words, but of no importance'? Stage directions, Thomas Heywood, and *Edward IV*. MedRen (18) 2005, 104–22.

7511. —— (ed.). The first and second parts of King Edward IV. Manchester; New York: Manchester UP, 2005. pp. xiii, 318. (Revels plays.) Rev. by Peter Holbrook in TLS, 17 June 2005, 25.

7512. SMYTH, ADAM. 'It were far better be a *Toad*, or a *Serpant*, then a Drunkard': writing about drunkenness. In (pp. 193–210) **6942**.

Thomas Hobbes (1588–1679)

7513. ROBERTSON, RANDY. Swift's *Leviathan* and the end of licensing. See **9086**.

7514. ROGERS, G. A. J.; SCHUHMANN, KARL (eds). *Leviathan*: a critical edition. London; New York: Continuum, 2003. 2 vols. pp. 271; vii, 567. Rev. by Noel Malcolm in TLS, 3 Dec. 2004, 3–4; by Lodi Nauta in RQ (58:2) 2005, 701–3.

Thomas Hoy (1659–1718?)

7515. ROPER, ALAN. Aeneas and Agathocles in the Exclusion Crisis. RES (56:226) 2005, 550–76.

Anna Hume (*fl*.1644)

7516. DUNNIGAN, SARAH M. Daughterly desires: representing and reimagining the feminine in Anna Hume's *Triumphs*. In (pp. 120–35) **3754**.

Anne Hutchinson

7517. LaPlante, Eve. American Jezebel: the uncommon life of Anne Hutchinson, the woman who defied the Puritans. San Francisco, CA: HarperSanFrancisco, 2004. pp. xxi, 312. Rev. by Mel Freilicher in AmBR (26:2) 2005, 29.

Lucy Hutchinson

7518. Miller, Shannon. Maternity, marriage, and contract: Lucy Hutchinson's response to patriarchal theory in Order and Disorder. SP (102:3) 2005, 340–77.

7519. Norbrook, David. 'But a copy': textual authority and gender in editions of The Life of John Hutchinson. In (pp. 109–30) 587.

7520. —— 'Words more than civil': Republican civility in Lucy Hutchinson's The Life of John Hutchinson. In (pp. 68–84) 5187.

Elinor James (c.1649–1719)

7521. Landau, Leya. Street sisters. TLS, 9 Dec. 2005, 8–9 (review-article).

7522. McDowell, Paula (sel. and introd.). Elinor James. Aldershot; Burlington, VT: Ashgate, 2005. pp. xxviii, 293. (Early modern Englishwoman, II: Printed writings, 1641–1700, 3:11.) Rev. by Leya Landau in TLS, 9 Dec. 2005, 8–9; by Gillian Wright in SHARP (14:4) 2005, 12.

James I and VI,
King of England and Scotland (1566–1625)

7523. Colclough, David. Freedom of speech, libel and the law in early Stuart England. In (pp. 170–88) 5196.

7524. Croft, Pauline. King James. Basingstoke; New York: Palgrave Macmillan, 2003. pp. vii, 214. Rev. by Clifton W. Potter, Jr, in SixCJ (35:4) 2004, 1215–16; by Craig Allan Horton in Parergon (22:1) 2005, 213–15.

7525. Durel, Henri. La Conférence de Hampton Court (janvier 1604); ou, L'autorité de Jacques Ier sur l'Église anglicane. Anglophonia (17) 2005, 187–96.

7526. Goy-Blanquet, Dominique. Droit des hommes, droit divin: histoires du sacre: from Edward the Confessor to James VI & I, de Saint Louis à Charles V ou VI. In (pp. 43–56) 6505.

7527. John, Judith Gero. I have been dying to tell you: early advice books for children. LU (29:1) 2005, 52–64.

7528. Jones-Davies, Margaret. Defacing the icon of the king: Richard II and the issues of iconoclasm. In (pp. 101–12) 6505.

7529. Rhodes, Neil. Wrapped in the strong arms of the Union: Shakespeare and King James. In (pp. 37–52) 6561.

7530. —— Richards, Jennifer; Marshall, Joseph (eds). King James VI and I: selected writings. (Bibl. 2004, 7817.) Rev. by Johann Sommerville in CLIO (34:3) 2005, 317–32; by Sally Mapstone in NQ (52:1) 2005, 121–2.

7531. Wakely, Maria; Rees, Graham. Folios fit for a king: James I, John Bill, and the King's Printers, 1616–1620. See 1013.

7532. Winter, Guillaume (ed.). Autour de Richard II de William Shakespeare. See 6505.

Ben Jonson

7533. ATKINS, ERIC W.   References to Jonson in scholarship on Shakespeare. BJJ (12) 2005, 203–16.

7534. BAKER, DAVID J.   'The allegory of a China shop': Jonson's *Entertainment at Britain's Burse*. ELH (72:1) 2005, 159–80.

7535. BLAND, MARK.   Ben Jonson and the legacies of the past. HLQ (67:3) 2004, 371–400.

7536. —— Francis Beaumont's verse letters to Ben Jonson and 'the Mermaid Club'. *See* **7224**.

7537. —— The James A. Riddell collection of Jonson's 1616 and 1640 *Workes*. HLQ (67:3) 2004, 489–503.

7538. BOEHRER, BRUCE.   Disorder in the house of God: disrupted worship in Shakespeare and others. *See* **6731**.

7539. BUCCOLA, REGINA.   'The top of woman! All her sex in abstract!': Ben Jonson directs the boy actor in *The Devil Is an Ass*. ETh (8:2) 2005, 11–34.

7540. CATHCART, CHARLES.   Authorship, indebtedness, and the Children of the King's Revels. SELit (45:2) 2005, 357–74.

7541. CLARE, JANET.   The 'complexion' of *Twelfth Night*. *See* **6799**.

7542. COOPER, JOHN R.   Voice in Ben Jonson's tetrameter lyrics. BJJ (12) 2005, 93–118.

7543. COREN, PAMELA.   Gurney's solace: Shakespeare, Jonson and Byrd. *See* **16844**.

7544. CORONATO, ROCCO.   Jonson *versus* Bakhtin: carnival and the grotesque. (Bibl. 2004, 7834.) Rev. by Ronald Knowles in MLR (100:1) 2005, 198–9.

7545. DÖRING, TOBIAS.   Writing performance: how to elegize Elizabethan actors. *See* **6157**.

7546. DUNCAN-JONES, KATHERINE.   City limits: Nashe's *Choise of Valentines* and Jonson's *Famous Voyage*. *See* **5586**.

7547. DUTTON, RICHARD.   Jonson, Shakespeare and the exorcists. ShS (58) 2005, 15–22.

7548. —— *Volpone* and beast fable: early modern analogic reading. HLQ (67:3) 2004, 347–70.

7549. —— (ed.).   Epicene; or, The silent woman. (Bibl. 2004, 7839.) Rev. by Matthew Steggle in NQ (52:2) 2005, 255–7.

7550. ELLIS, ANTHONY.   Senescence in Jonson's *Alchemist*: magic, mortality, and the debasement of (the Golden) Age. BJJ (12) 2005, 23–44.

7551. ERNE, LUKAS.   Words in space: the reproduction of texts and the semiotics of the page. *See* **4991**.

7552. FLECK, ANDREW.   Vulgar fingers of the multitude: Shakespeare, Jonson, and the transformation of news from the Low Countries. *See* **6826**.

7553. GAGGERO, CHRISTOPHER.   Civic Humanism and gender politics in Jonson's *Catiline*. SELit (45:2) 2005, 401–24.

7554. GIESKES, EDWARD.   'Honesty and vulgar praise': the Poets' War and the literary field. *See* **5248**.

7555. GOSSETT, SUZANNE. Marston, collaboration, and *Eastward Ho!* See **7617**.

7556. HUTSON, LORNA. Liking men: Ben Jonson's closet opened. ELH (71:4) 2004, 1065–96.

7557. JACKSON, MACD. P. Francis Meres and the cultural contexts of Shakespeare's Rival Poet sonnets. See **6718**.

7558. JONES, JENNIFER. Machiavellianism in Jonson's *Sejanus* and *Catiline.* SRASP (27) 2004, 11–22.

7559. KNIGHT, STEPHEN. 'Meere English flocks': Ben Jonson's *The Sad Shepherd* and the Robin Hood tradition. *In* (pp. 129–44) **3576**.

7560. KNOWLES, JAMES. Crack kisses not staves: sexual politics and court masques in 1613–1614. *In* (pp. 143–60) **6860**.

7561. —— 'To raise a house of better frame': Jonson's Cecilian entertainments. *In* (pp. 181–95) **5121**.

7562. LOCKWOOD, TOM. Ben Jonson in the Romantic age. Oxford; New York: OUP, 2005. pp. xi, 257.

7563. —— New allusions to Jonson and Sidney. NQ (52:2) 2005, 227–9.

7564. LOEWENSTEIN, JOSEPH. Ben Jonson and possessive authorship. (Bibl. 2004, 7848.) Rev. by Claire M. Busse in SixCJ (34:4) 2003, 1152–3; by Matthew Greenfield in MP (102:2) 2004, 264–7; by Sonia Massai in SJ (141) 2005, 243–5.

7565. LOXLEY, JAMES. Performatives and performativity: Ben Jonson makes his excuses. RenD (ns 33) 2004, 63–85.

7566. MCGEE, C. E. 'The Ferret and the Coney': an oddity of editorial annotation. BJJ (12) 2005, 165–9.

7567. MARTIN, PATRICK; FINNIS, JOHN. A gunpowder priest? *Benedicam dominum* – Ben Jonson's strange 1605 inscription. TLS, 4 Nov. 2005, 12–13.

7568. MARTIN, RANDALL. Stepping into risky business: Jonson's canine ventures in *Every Man out of His Humor.* BJJ (12) 2005, 1–21.

7569. MATOS, TIMOTHY L. Jonson's *Epicœne.* Exp (64:1) 2005, 9–12.

7570. MAUS, KATHARINE EISAMAN. Idol and gift in *Volpone.* ELR (35:3) 2005, 429–53.

7571. MESKILL, LYNN SERMIN. Exorcising the Gorgon of terror: Jonson's *Masque of Queenes.* ELH (72:1) 2005, 181–207.

7572. MULRYAN, JOHN. Jonson's epigrams and the adages of Erasmus: a holistic analysis. BJJ (12) 2005, 73–92.

7573. NOE, MARK. The real and the preferable: Perelman's structures of reality in Jonson's *Bartholomew Fair.* RhR (24:4) 2005, 421–37.

7574. O'CALLAGHAN, MICHELLE. Tavern societies, the Inns of Court, and the culture of conviviality in early seventeenth-century London. *In* (pp. 37–51) **6942**.

7575. OUELLETTE, ANTHONY J. *The Alchemist* and the emerging adult private playhouse. SELit (45:2) 2005, 375–99.

7576. PASTOOR, CHARLES. The Puritan audience in Jonson's *Bartholomew Fair* and Shirley's *The Bird in a Cage.* ELN (43:1) 2005, 1–12.

7577. PEARSON, JACQUELINE. The least certain of boundaries: gendered bodies and gendered spaces in early modern drama. SEDERI (13) 2003, 163–81.

7578. PELLICER, JUAN CHRISTIAN. Apollo and Mercury in Ben Jonson's poem to Shakespeare: an allusive paraphrase of Horace's *utile dulci*. NQ (52:2) 2005, 223–4.

7579. POSTLEWAIT, THOMAS. Constructing events in theatre history: a matter of credibility. *In* (pp. 33–52) **3974**.

7580. PUGH, SYRITHE. 'Rosmarine' in the *Masque of Blackness*: Jonson's herbal *medicamina faciei*? NQ (52:2) 2005, 221–3.

7581. RIBES TRAVER, PURIFICACIÓN. Araquistáin's 1929 version of *Volpone*. SEDERI (15) 2005, 81–100.

7582. SALKELD, DUNCAN. Literary traces in Bridewell and Bethlem, 1602–1624. RES (56:225) 2005, 379–85.

7583. SAVAGE, ROGER. Checklists for Philostrate. *In* (pp. 294–307) **5172**.

7584. SHARGEL, RAPHAEL. A stewed comedy: chaos and authority in *The Staple of News*. BJJ (12) 2005, 45–72.

7585. SHEA, COLLEEN. 'This truest glass': Ben Jonson's verse epistles and the construction of the ideal patron. SEDERI (13) 2003, 199–208.

7586. STEGGLE, MATTHEW, *et al.* Jonson and his era: overviews of modern research. BJJ (12) 2005, 171–202 (review-article).

7587. TOSI, LAURA. 'Then rose the seed of chaos': masque and antimasque in *The Dunciad in Four Books*. See **8913**.

7588. WOOD, MARCUS. Black bodies and satiric limits in the long eighteenth century. *In* (pp. 55–70) **9305**.

7589. WOOLLAND, BRIAN (ed.). Jonsonians: living traditions. (Bibl. 2004, 7878.) Rev. by Lukas Erne in MLR (100:2) 2005, 480–1; by Matthew Steggle in NQ (52:2) 2005, 255–7.

7590. ZUCKER, ADAM. The social logic of Ben Jonson's *Epicoene*. RenD (ns 33) 2004, 37–62.

Thomas Killigrew the Elder (1612–1683)

7591. CORSE, TAYLOR. Seventeenth-century Naples and Aphra Behn's *The Rover*. See **7238**.

7592. KEBLUSEK, MARIKA. Wine for comfort: drinking and the Royalist exile experience, 1642–1660. *In* (pp. 55–68) **6942**.

Henry King (1592–1669)

7593. CARSON, ANNE ELIZABETH. The hunted stag and the beheaded king. See **7360**.

John Lacy (d.1681)

7594. PRIETO PABLOS, JUAN ANTONIO. Audience deception and farce in John Lacy's *Sir Hercules Buffoon*. Atl (27:1) 2005, 65–78.

Aemilia Lanyer

7595. BENSON, PAMELA JOSEPH. The stigma of Italy undone: Aemilia Lanyer's canonization of Lady Mary Sidney. *In* (pp. 146–75) **5094**.

7596. ROBERTS, WENDY MILLER. Gnosis in Aemilia Lanyer's *Salve Deus Rex Judaeorum*. RMER (59:2) 2005.

7597. WOODS, SUSANNE. Lanyer and Southwell: a Protestant woman's re-vision of St Peter. *In* (pp. 73–86) **6872**.

Jane Lead (1624–1704)

7598. KEMP, THERESA D. 'Here must a beheading go before': the antirationalist androgynist theosophy of Jane Lead's *Revelation of Revelations*. CLIO (34:3) 2005, 251–75.

Nathaniel Lee

7599. BALLASTER, ROS. Performing *Roxane*: the Oriental woman as the sign of luxury in eighteenth-century fictions. *In* (pp. 165–77) **7941**.

Sir Nicholas Le Strange

7600. BROWN, PAMELA ALLEN. Jesting rights: women players in the manuscript jestbook of Sir Nicholas Le Strange. *In* (pp. 305–14) **5225**.

Sir Roger L'Estrange

7601. DUNAN-PAGE, ANNE. Les Non-Conformistes anglais pendant la Restauration: entre autorité divine et autorité ecclésiastique. *See* **7671**.

7602. MÜLLER, ANJA. Picturing Æsops: re-visions of *Æsop's Fables* from L'Estrange to Richardson. *See* **107**.

John Locke (1632–1704)

7603. MANKIN, ROBERT. Locke's education of the personality. EA (58:4) 2005, 387–401.

7604. MÜLLER, ANJA. Picturing Æsops: re-visions of *Æsop's Fables* from L'Estrange to Richardson. *See* **107**.

7605. SHAPIRO, IAN (ed.). *Two Treatises of Government* and *A Letter Concerning Toleration*. With essays by John Dunn, Ruth Grant and Ian Shapiro. New Haven, CT; London: Yale UP, 2003. pp. xv, 358. (Rethinking the Western tradition.) Rev. by Matthew Simpson in Scriblerian (37:2/38:1) 2005, 168–9.

7606. YOLTON, JOHN W. The two intellectual worlds of John Locke: man, person, and spirits in the *Essay*. Ithaca, NY; London: Cornell UP, 2004. pp. ix, 180. Rev. by Gustavo Costa in RQ (58:2) 2005, 705–7.

Richard Lovelace

7607. CLARKE, SUSAN A. 'Bright Heir t' th' Bird Imperial': Richard Lovelace's *The Falcon* in context. RES (56:224) 2005, 263–75.

7608. MCDOWELL, NICHOLAS. Urquhart's Rabelais: translation, patronage, and cultural politics. *See* **7874**.

7609. RAY, ROBERT H. The admiration of Sir Philip Sidney by Lovelace and Carew: new seventeenth-century allusions. *See* **5652**.

M.P. (Martin Parker) (d.1656?)

7610. HEPWORTH, DAVID. Appendix: written epitaphs of Robin Hood. *In* (pp. 188–9) **3576**.

Sir George Mackenzie (1636–1691)

7611. BEESEMYER, IRENE BASEY.   Sir George Mackenzie's *Aretina* of 1660: a Scot's assault on Restoration politics. ScSR (4:1) 2003, 41–68.

John Marston (1575?–1634)

7612. BRITLAND, KAREN.   Circe's cup: wine and women in early modern drama. *In* (pp. 109–25) **6942**.

7613. CATHCART, CHARLES.   Authorship, indebtedness, and the Children of the King's Revels. *See* **7540**.

7614. —— Borrowings and the authorial domain: Gostanzo, Polonius, and Marston's Gonzago. CompDr (37:2) 2003, 159–74.

7615. CROSSAN, GREG.   'That wolf-howled, witch-prayed, owl-sung fool': Beddoes and the play of words. *See* **10088**.

7616. GIESKES, EDWARD.   'Honesty and vulgar praise': the Poets' War and the literary field. *See* **5248**.

7617. GOSSETT, SUZANNE.   Marston, collaboration, and *Eastward Ho!* RenD (ns 33) 2004, 181–200.

7618. YEARLING, REBECCA.   False facial hair and early modern boy actors: a correction. NQ (52:2) 2005, 219–20.

Andrew Marvell

7619. ANDERSON, THOMAS P.   'We cannot say hee's dead': writing royal effigies in Marvell's poetry. ELR (35:3) 2005, 507–31.

7620. BURROWS, JOHN.   Andrew Marvell and the 'painter satires': a computational approach to their authorship. MLR (100:2) 2005, 281–97.

7621. CARSON, ANNE ELIZABETH.   The hunted stag and the beheaded king. *See* **7360**.

7622. CHERNAIK, WARREN.   Was Marvell a Republican? SevC (20:1) 2005, 77–96.

7623. EDGECOMBE, RODNEY STENNING.   Two echoes of Marvell in Byron's *Mazeppa*. *See* **10305**.

7624. GREENE, THOMAS M.   Poetry, signs, and magic. *See* **5946**.

7625. HAAN, ESTELLE.   Andrew Marvell's Latin poetry: from text to context. Brussels: Latomus, 2003. pp. 356. (Latomus, 275.) Rev. by David Norbrook in RES (56:226) 2005, 675–6.

7626. HOLBERTON, EDWARD.   'Soe Honny from the Lyon came': the 1657 wedding-masques for the Protector's daughters. SevC (20:1) 2005, 97–112.

7627. —— The textual transmission of Marvell's *A Letter to Doctor Ingelo*: the Longleat manuscript. EngMS (12) 2005, 233–53.

7628. McWILLIAMS, JOHN.   An echo of an anonymous Royalist broadside poem of 1643 in Marvell's *An Horatian Ode upon Cromwell's Return from Ireland*. NQ (52:3) 2005, 315–17.

7629. MILLER, ANTHONY.   Marvell's *First Anniversary* and Ammianus Marcellinus. NQ (52:3) 2005, 317–18.

7630. PARKER, IAN C.   Marvell and the 'Tygress fell'. NQ (52:3) 2005, 318–24.

7631. SMITH, NIGEL (ed.). The poems of Andrew Marvell. (Bibl. 2003, 7235.) Rev. by Warren Chernaik in MLR (100:3) 2005, 782–3.

7632. SULLIVAN, CERI. Wreaths in Marvell's *The Garden*. NQ (52:3) 2005, 314–15.

7633. VON MALTZAHN, NICHOLAS. Andrew Marvell and the prehistory of Whiggism. *In* (pp. 31–61) **8091**.

7634. —— An Andrew Marvell chronology. Basingstoke; New York: Palgrave Macmillan, 2005. pp. xii, 317. (Author chronologies.)

Philip Massinger

7635. JOWITT, CLAIRE. Piracy and court scandals in Massinger's *The Unnatural Combat* (1624–25?). CEl (67) 2005, 33–41.

7636. KAHAN, JEFFREY. A further note on Semiramis. ANQ (18:2) 2005, 27–8.

7637. LIVINGSTON, MEG POWERS. *The Tragedy of Sir John Van Olden Barnavelt*: a re-examination of Fletcher and Massinger's sources. See **7447**.

7638. MIOLA, ROBERT S. Jesuit drama in early modern England. *In* (pp. 71–86) **5915**.

Cotton Mather

7639. CEPPI, ELISABETH. Come when you are called: radicalized servitude and the division of Puritan labor. Lit (16:2) 2005, 213–31.

7640. LIEBERT, ELISABETH. *Samson Agonistes* and spiritual autobiography. See **7710**.

7641. MULFORD, CARLA. Pox and 'hell-fire': Boston's smallpox controversy, the New Science, and early modern liberalism. *In* (pp. 7–27) **1244**.

Increase Mather

7642. DAYAN, COLIN. Legal terrors. Representations (92) 2005, 42–80.

7643. JOHNSON, CHRISTOPHER. 'Periwigged heralds': epistemology and intertextuality in early American cometography. JHI (65:3) 2004, 399–419.

Thomas Middleton

7644. BAWCUTT, N. W. The assassination of Alessandro de' Medici in early seventeenth-century English drama. See **7869**.

7645. HELLER, JENNIFER L. Space, violence, and bodies in Middleton and Cary. SELit (45:2) 2005, 425–41.

7646. HUTCHINGS, MARK. Anti-theatrical prejudice and *1 Honest Whore*, II.i.324–326. See **7354**.

7647. KORDA, NATASHA. The case of Moll Frith: women's work and the 'all-male stage'. *In* (pp. 71–87) **5225**.

7648. PANEK, JENNIFER. Why were there stewed prunes in Shakespearean brothels? See **6589**.

7649. ROSSINI, MANUELA. The gendered spatiology of Middleton's *A Chaste Maid in Cheapside*. SPELL (17) 2005, 85–97.

7650. TAYLOR, GARY. The cultural politics of Maybe. *In* (pp. 242–58) **5915**.

Middleton and Rowley

7651. CALBI, MAURIZIO. Approximate bodies: gender and power in early modern drama and anatomy. London; New York: Routledge, 2005. pp. xxii, 168.

7652. HUTCHINGS, MARK. *Richard III* and *The Changeling. See* **6509.**

John Milton (1608–1674)

7653. ACHINSTEIN, SHARON. Literature and Dissent in Milton's England. (Bibl. 2004, 7970.) Rev. by Albert C. Labriola in JR (84:3) 2004, 508–9; by John C. Lassiter in SixCJ (36:2) 2005, 524–5; by P. G. Stanwood in SCN (63:3/4) 2005, 164–8.

7654. AINSWORTH, DAVID. Spiritual reading in Milton's *Eikonoklastes.* SELit (45:1) 2005, 157–89.

7655. BENET, DIANA TREVIÑO. Adam's evil conscience and Satan's surrogate Fall. MQ (39:1) 2005, 2–15.

7656. BLYTHE, JOAN. Cain and Abel in *Paradise Regained*: fratricide, regicide, and cultural equity. *In* (pp. 70–82) **7738.**

7657. BOESKY, AMY. Samson and surrogacy. *In* (pp. 153–66) **7717.**

7658. BRATCHER, JAMES T. The speaker's occasion and the death of Pan in Eliot's *Journey of the Magi. See* **16245.**

7659. BROWN, JAMES C. Le Milton de Toland. EREA (1:2) 2003, 64–70.

7660. BRYSON, MICHAEL. The tyranny of Heaven: Milton's rejection of God as king. (Bibl. 2004, 7981.) Rev. by Catherine Gimelli Martin in RQ (58:1) 2005, 352–4.

7661. CALLOWAY, KATHERINE. Beyond parody: Satan as Aeneas in *Paradise Lost.* MQ (39:2) 2005, 82–92.

7662. CAMPBELL, W. GARDNER. Hierarchy, alterity, and freedom in *Paradise Lost. In* (pp. 50–69) **7738.**

7663. CLUTTERBUCK, CHARLOTTE. Encounters with God in medieval and early modern English poetry. *See* **4603.**

7664. COUDERT, ALLISON P.; SHOULSON, JEFFREY S. (eds). *Hebraica veritas?* Christian Hebraists and the study of Judaism in early modern Europe. *See* **7839.**

7665. CUMMINS, JULIET, *et al.* (ed.). Milton and the ends of time. (Bibl. 2004, 7995.) Rev. by Robert Appelbaum in CLIO (34:3) 2005, 381–5; by Jean Pironon in EA (58:1) 2005, 111–12.

7666. D'ADDARIO, CHRISTOPHER. Dryden and the historiography of exile: Milton and Virgil in Dryden's late period. *See* **7412.**

7667. DICKSON, DONALD R.; NELSON, HOLLY FAITH (eds). Of Paradise and light: essays on Henry Vaughan and John Milton in honor of Alan Rudrum. (Bibl. 2004, 8001.) Rev. by Ernest W. Sullivan, II, in RQ (58:3) 2005, 1057–8.

7668. DOBRANSKI, STEPHEN B. Milton's ideal readers. *In* (pp. 191–207) **7738.**

7669. —— Pondering Satan's shield in *Paradise Lost.* ELR (35:3) 2005, 490–506.

7670. DOWLING, PAUL M. *Paradise Lost* and politics gained: Milton rewrites Scripture. Cithara (44:2) 2005, 16–31.

7671. DUNAN-PAGE, ANNE. Les Non-Conformistes anglais pendant la Restauration: entre autorité divine et autorité ecclésiastique. Anglophonia (17) 2005, 275–87.

7672. DZELZAINIS, MARTIN. History and ideology: Milton, the Levellers, and the Council of State in 1649. HLQ (68:1/ 2) 2005, 269–87.

7673. ENTZMINGER, ROBERT L. The power and the glory: *Paradise Regained* and the toleration controversy. In (pp. 83–102) **7738.**

7674. FLEMING, JAMES DOUGAL. Composing 1629. In (pp. 149–64) **7738.**

7675. FORSYTH, NEIL. The Satanic epic. (Bibl. 2004, 8016.) Rev. by John Mulryan in Cithara (43:1) 2003, 49–50; by Claire Colebrook in EJES (9:1) 2005, 98–102; by Michael Lieb in MQ (39:2) 2005, 104–6; by Beverley Sherry in AUMLA (104) 2005, 160–3.

7676. FURMAN-ADAMS, WENDY; TUFTE, VIRGINIA JAMES. Saying it with flowers: Jane Giraud's ecofeminist *Paradise Lost* (1846). In (pp. 223–53) **7717.**

7677. GERTZ-ROBINSON, GENELLE. Still martyred after all these years: generational suffering in Milton's *Areopagitica*. ELH (70:4) 2003, 963–87.

7678. GOODERHAM, DAVID. Fantasizing it as it is: religious language in Philip Pullman's trilogy *His Dark Materials*. See **18942.**

7679. GREEN, MANDY. The virgin in the garden: Milton's Ovidian Eve. MLR (100:4) 2005, 903–22.

7680. GREENE, THOMAS M. Poetry, signs, and magic. See **5946.**

7681. GROSSMAN, MARSHALL. The genders of God and the redemption of the flesh in *Paradise Lost*. In (pp. 95–114) **7717.**

7682. —— The rhetoric of feminine priority and the ethics of form in *Paradise Lost*. ELR (33:3) 2003, 424–43.

7683. GUERNSEY-SHAW, JULIA C. The royal we; the divine I: narcissitic (*sic*) imbalance in the worlds of *King Lear* and *Paradise Lost*. See **6466.**

7684. GUIBBORY, ACHSAH. 'The Jewish Question' and 'the Woman Question' in *Samson Agonistes*: gender, religion, and nation. In (pp. 184–203) **7717.**

7685. HALE, JOHN K. Milton's Cambridge Latin: performing in the genres, 1625–1632. Tempe: Arizona Center for Medieval and Renaissance Studies, 2005. pp. xii, 305. (Medieval & Renaissance texts & studies, 289.)

7686. HAO, TIANHU. Ku Hung-Ming, an early reader of Milton. MQ (39:2) 2005, 93–100.

7687. HARVEY, A. D. Hyperion's cousins: epic poetry in the style of Milton, c.1818. See **11515.**

7688. HASKIN, DAYTON. George Eliot as a 'Miltonist': marriage and Milton in *Middlemarch*. In (pp. 207–22) **7717.**

7689. HATLEN, BURTON. Pullman's *His Dark Materials*, a challenge to the fantasies of J. R. R. Tolkien and C. S. Lewis, with an epilogue on Pullman's neo-Romantic reading of *Paradise Lost*. In (pp. 75–94) **18952.**

7690. HAUSKNECHT, GINA. The gender of civic virtue. In (pp. 19–33) **7717.**

7691. HENRIKSEN, ERIN M. The Passion in *Poems of Mr John Milton*: Milton's poetics of omission and supplement. In (pp. 165–79) **7738.**

7692. HERMAN, PETER C. Destabilizing Milton: *Paradise Lost* and the poetics of incertitude. Basingstoke; New York: Palgrave Macmillan, 2005. pp. 230.

7693. HILTNER, KEN. Milton and ecology. (Bibl. 2004, 8027.) Rev. by Joan Blythe in MQ (39:2) 2005, 107–12; by Šárka Kühnová in NQ (52:3) 2005, 414–15; by Jean Pironon in EA (58:3) 2005, 358–9.

7694. ITTZÉS, GÁBOR. Milton's sun in the zodiac. NQ (52:3) 2005, 307–10.

7695. JENKINS, HUGH. 'The revolt[ing] Welsh'? Milton and 'the dark corners of the land'. In (pp. 103–15) **7738**.

7696. JONES, EDWARD. The loyalty and subsidy returns of 1641 and 1642: what they can tell us about the Milton family. In (pp. 234–47) **7738**.

7697. KEAN, MARGARET (ed.). John Milton's *Paradise Lost*: a sourcebook. London; New York: Routledge, 2005. pp. 173. (Routledge guides to literature.)

7698. KELLEY, MARK R.; LIEB, MICHAEL; SHAWCROSS, JOHN T. (eds). Milton and the grounds of contention. (Bibl. 2004, 8039.) Rev. by W. Scott Howard in SCN (63:1/2) 2005, 43–7.

7699. KERRIGAN, WILLIAM. Complicated monsters: essence and metamorphosis in Milton. TSLL (46:3) 2004, 324–39.

7700. KILBOURN, RUSSELL J. A. American Frankenstein: modernity's monstrous progeny. See **13450**.

7701. KILGOUR, MAGGIE. 'Thy perfect image viewing': poetic creation and Ovid's Narcissus in *Paradise Lost*. SP (102:3) 2005, 307–39.

7702. KING, JOHN N. Milton and the bishops: ecclesiastical controversy and the early poems. In (pp. 277–97) **6872**.

7703. KLINGE, MARKUS. Milton's balcony in *Areopagitica*, II, 524. NQ (52:3) 2005, 298–304.

7704. KNOTT, JOHN R. Milton's wild garden. SP (102:1) 2005, 66–82.

7705. KRANIDAS, THOMAS. Milton and the rhetoric of zeal. Pittsburgh, PA: Duquesne UP, 2005. pp. xvi, 255. (Medieval & Renaissance literary studies.) Rev. by James Egan in SCN (63:3/4) 2005, 152–8.

7706. LABRIOLA, ALBERT C. The begetting and exaltation of the Son: the Junius Manuscript and Milton's *Paradise Lost*. In (pp. 22–32) **7738**.

7707. LEASURE, T. ROSS. The Belial tradition revisited: situating the lesser demon in the works of Palladinus, Salandra, Vondel and Milton. Cithara (44:2) 2005, 3–15.

7708. —— Jacobus Palladinus, the Belial tradition, and Milton's lesser demon. Cithara (43:1) 2003, 37–45.

7709. LEHNHOF, KENT R. Uncertainty and 'the sociable Spirit': Raphael's role in *Paradise Lost*. In (pp. 33–49) **7738**.

7710. LIEBERT, ELISABETH. *Samson Agonistes* and spiritual autobiography. Parergon (22:2) 2005, 131–57.

7711. LOW, LISA. Woolf's allusion to *Comus* in *The Voyage Out*. In (pp. 254–70) **7717**.

7712. LUXON, THOMAS H. Single imperfection: Milton, marriage, and friendship. Pittsburgh, PA: Duquesne UP, 2005. pp. xvi, 215. (Medieval & Renaissance literary studies.)

7713. McDOWELL, NICHOLAS. Ideas of Creation in the writings of Richard Overton the Leveller and *Paradise Lost.* JHI (66:1) 2005, 59–78.

7714. MARKLEY, ROBERT. Riches, power, trade and religion: the Far East and the English imagination, 1600–1720. RenSt (17:3) 2003, 494–516.

7715. MARTIN, CATHERINE GIMELLI. Dalila, misogyny, and Milton's Christian liberty of divorce. *In* (pp. 53–74) 7717.

7716. —— Introduction: Milton's gendered subjects. *In* (pp. 1–15) 7717.

7717. —— (ed.). Milton and gender. Cambridge; New York: CUP, 2004. pp. xiii, 277.

7718. MATHEWS, ALICE. Eve's 'sweet converse': conversational patterns in *Paradise Lost.* 1650–1850 (9) 2003, 153–66.

7719. MATHIS, GILLES. Quand (re)dire c'est (re)faire: stratégies citationnelles dans le *Paradis perdu.* EREA (2:1) 2004, 5–31.

7720. MATHOLÉ, PAUL. Milton's use of 'unking'd': an allusion to *Richard II.* NQ (52:3) 2005, 304–7.

7721. MATTISON, ANDREW. 'Thine own inventions': the environs of imagination in *Paradise Lost* 7 and 8. MQ (39:1) 2005, 23–44.

7722. MAYER, JOSEPH G. Between two pillars: the hero's plight in *Samson Agonistes* and *Paradise Regained.* Lanham, MD; London: UP of America, 2004. pp. viii, 266. Rev. by Joseph Wittreich in RQ (58:3) 2005, 1055–6.

7723. MICROS, MARIANNE. 'A world of my own': John Milton and Margaret Cavendish's reflections of Paradise. Cithara (43:1) 2003, 3–24.

7724. MILLER, CHRISTOPHER. Staying out late: Anne Finch's poetics of evening. *See* 9126.

7725. MILLER, SHANNON. Maternity, marriage, and contract: Lucy Hutchinson's response to patriarchal theory in *Order and Disorder. See* 7518.

7726. MINER, EARL (ed.); MOECK, WILLIAM; JABLONSKI, STEVEN EDWARD (asst eds). *Paradise Lost,* 1668–1968: three centuries of commentary. (Bibl. 2004, 8056.) Rev. by John Mulryan in SCN (63:1/2) 2005, 41–3; by Robert C. Evans in BJJ (12) 2005, 284–7.

7727. MINTZ, SUSANNAH B. Threshold poetics: Milton and intersubjectivity. (Bibl. 2004, 8057.) Rev. by Tom Rutter in MLR (100:3) 2005, 774–7.

7728. MORRISON, SARAH R. Truth or consequences: Johnson's *Life of Milton* and the moral biographer's dilemma. *In* (pp. 220–33) 7738.

7729. MULFORD, CARLA. Pox and 'hell-fire': Boston's smallpox controversy, the New Science, and early modern liberalism. *In* (pp. 7–27) 1244.

7730. MULRYAN, JOHN. Satan's headache: the perils and pains of giving birth to a bad idea. MQ (39:1) 2005, 16–22.

7731. MYERS, BENJAMIN. Milton's *Paradise Lost,* Book 11. Exp (64:1) 2005, 14–17.

7732. NARDO, ANNA K. George Eliot's dialogue with John Milton. *See* 10943.

7733. PARRY, GRAHAM; RAYMOND, JOAD (eds). Milton and the terms of liberty. (Bibl. 2004, 8063.) Rev. by Mary A. Papazian in SixCJ (34:4) 2003, 1138–40.

7734. PHILLIPS, MICHAEL. Blake's annotations in context. *See* 8380.

7735. PICCIOTTO, JOANNA. Reforming the garden: the experimentalist Eden and *Paradise Lost*. ELH (72:1) 2005, 23–78.

7736. POOLE, WILLIAM. Milton and the idea of the Fall. Cambridge; New York: CUP, 2005. pp. ix, 240.

7737. PRUITT, KRISTIN A. Gender and the power of relationship: 'united as one individual soul' in *Paradise Lost*. (Bibl. 2004, 8070.) Rev. by Matthew Steggle in SixCJ (36:2) 2005, 554–6; by David V. Urban in ANQ (18:4) 2005, 53–6.

7738. —— DURHAM, CHARLES W. (eds). Milton's legacy. Selinsgrove, PA: Susquehanna UP; London: Assoc. UPs, 2005. pp. 257.

7739. QUIGLEY, BRENDAN. The distant hero of *Samson Agonistes*. ELH (72:3) 2005, 529–51.

7740. RAUWERDA, ANTJE M. 'Angelicdevilish' combinations: Milton's Satan and Salman Rushdie's *The Satanic Verses*. See **19276**.

7741. REVARD, STELLA P. From metanoia to apocalypse: *Paradise Lost* and the apocryphal *Lives of Adam and Eve*. JEGP (104:1) 2005, 80–102.

7742. REYNOLDS, DAVID. Christ's: a Cambridge college over five centuries. London: Pan Macmillan, 2005. pp. xvi, 265, (plates) 8. Rev. by Elisabeth Leedham-Green in TLS, 24 June 2005, 29.

7743. RIBEIRO, NUNO MANUEL DIAS PINTO. The Second Coming: prophecy and utopian thought in John Milton (1608–74) and António Vieira (1608–97). SEDERI (13) 2003, 191–8.

7744. ROGERS, JOHN. Transported touch: the fruit of marriage in *Paradise Lost*. In (pp. 115–32) **7717**.

7745. ROSEN, DAVID. Maturity and poetic style. Raritan (24:4) 2005, 81–97 (review-article).

7746. ROSENFELD, NANCY. *The Man of Mode*: the mode of man. See **7439**.

7747. ROVIRA, JAMES. Gathering the scattered body of Milton's *Areopagitica*. Ren (57:2) 2005, 87–102.

7748. RYKEN, LELAND. Milton's Sonnet 14 and Puritan funeral sermons for women. In (pp. 136–48) **7738**.

7749. SAUER, ELIZABETH M. The experience of defeat: Milton and some female contemporaries. In (pp. 133–52) **7717**.

7750. SCOTT, CAROLE. Pullman's enigmatic ontology: revamping old traditions in *His Dark Materials*. In (pp. 95–105) **18952**.

7751. SHAWCROSS, JOHN T. The arms of the family: the significance of John Milton's relatives and associates. (Bibl. 2004, 8084.) Rev. by John McWilliams in MLR (100:2) 2005, 485–6; by Pitt Harding in SAtlR (70:2) 2005, 144–7.

7752. —— A 'new' bibliographical item and its accompanying art work. MQ (39:1) 2005, 45–8.

7753. —— Rethinking Milton studies: time present and time past. Newark: Delaware UP, 2005. pp. 241. Rev. by John Mulryan in Cithara (44:2) 2005, 49–50.

7754. SHOHET, LAUREN. Reading dark materials. In (pp. 22–36) **18952**.

7755. —— Subjects and objects in *Lycidas*. TSLL (47:2) 2005, 101–19.

7756. SHULLENBERGER, WILLIAM. Nietzsche for girls. In (pp. 116–35) **7738**.

7757. —— The profession of virginity in *A Maske Presented at Ludlow Castle*. *In* (pp. 77–94) **7717**.

7758. —— Tragedy in translation: the Lady's Echo song. ELR (33:3) 2003, 403–23.

7759. SNART, JASON. Blake's Milton: did Blake own and annotate the 1732 Bentley edition of Milton's *Paradise Lost? See* **8390**.

7760. SOBOLEV, DENNIS. *Contra* Milton. EngS (84:6) 2003, 530–44.

7761. STACKHOUSE, AMY D. The damnation of excessive praise. *In* (pp. 180–90) **7738**.

7762. STARNAWSKI, JERZY. Literatura angielska w Bibliotece Narodowej 1921–1929: kulisy w świetle archiwum Stanisława Kota. (English literature in the National Library [series] 1921–1929 in the light of Stanisław Kot's archive.) *In* (pp. 227–37) **3756**.

7763. STEVENSON, KAY GILLILAND. Beyond 'no end': the shape of *Paradise Lost*, x. RenP (2004) 131–9.

7764. STUTZ, CHAD P. No 'sombre Satan': C. S. Lewis, Milton, and representations of the diabolical. *See* **17796**.

7765. TALBOT, JOHN. Auden's Horatian mosaic. *See* **15244**.

7766. THEIS, JEFFREY S. Milton's principles of architecture. ELR (35:1) 2005, 102–22.

7767. TOGASHI, GO. Milton and the Presbyterian opposition, 1649–1650: the engagement controversy and *The Tenure of Kings and Magistrates*, second edition (1649). MQ (39:2) 2005, 59–81.

7768. TOSI, LAURA. 'Then rose the seed of chaos': masque and antimasque in *The Dunciad in Four Books. See* **8913**.

7769. TOURNU, CHRISTOPHE. République et républicanisme chez Milton. EREA (1:2) 2003, 52–63.

7770. TRUBOWITZ, RACHEL. 'I was his nursling once': nation, lactation, and the Hebraic in *Samson Agonistes. In* (pp. 167–83) **7717**.

7771. TURNER, JAMES GRANTHAM. The aesthetics of divorce: 'masculinism', idolatry, and poetic authority in *Tetrachordon* and *Paradise Lost*. *In* (pp. 34–52) **7717**.

7772. ULREICH, JOHN C. Two great world systems: Galileo, Milton and the problem of truth. Cithara (43:1) 2003, 25–36.

7773. URBAN, DAVID V. 'Out of his treasurie things new and old': Milton's parabolic householder in *The Doctrine and Discipline of Divorce* and *De doctrina Christiana. In* (pp. 208–19) **7738**.

7774. WARNER, J. CHRISTOPHER. The Augustinian epic, Petrarch to Milton. *See* **5725**.

7775. WEINFIELD, HENRY. Skepticism and poetry in Milton's infernal conclave. SELit (45:1) 2005, 191–212.

7776. WELLENS, OSKAR. A unique bibliophile edition of Milton's sonnets. MQ (39:2) 2005, 101–3.

7777. WILCHER, ROBERT. The darkened scribe and the blessed man: changing uses of allusion in the work of Henry Vaughan. *See* **7885**.

7778. WILLIAMS, FREDERICK. Milton and Aesculapius: a footnote. NQ (52:3) 2005, 298.

7779. ZWICKER, STEVEN N. 'What every literate man once knew': tracing readers in early modern England. *In* (pp. 75–90) **19**.

Mary Southworth Mollineux (1651?–1695)

7780. ACHINSTEIN, SHARON. 'When civil fury first grew high': politics and incivility in Restoration England. *In* (pp. 85–98) **5187**.

Gertrude More (1606–1633)

7781. WYNNE-DAVIES, MARION. Suicide at the Elephant and Castle, or did the lady vanish? Alternative endings for early modern women writers. *In* (pp. 121–42) **5914**.

Henry More

7782. HUTTON, SARAH. Authority and the Word: Henry More, William Penn and the *logos*. Anglophonia (17) 2005, 253–61.

Margaret Cavendish, Duchess of Newcastle

7783. BOYLE, DEBORAH. Margaret Cavendish's nonfeminist natural philosophy. Configurations (12:2) 2004, 195–227.

7784. CARSON, ANNE ELIZABETH. The hunted stag and the beheaded king. *See* **7360**.

7785. CHALMERS, HERO. Royalist women writers, 1650–1689. *See* **7236**.

7786. CLUCAS, STEPHEN (ed.). A princely brave woman: essays on Margaret Cavendish, Duchess of Newcastle. (Bibl. 2004, 8113.) Rev. by Michael R. Lynn in SixCJ (36:2) 2005, 477–8.

7787. COTTEGNIES, LINE; WEITZ, NANCY (eds). Authorial conquests: essays on genre in the writings of Margaret Cavendish. (Bibl. 2004, 8114.) Rev. by Jacqueline Pearson in MLR (100:3) 2005, 780–1.

7788. CRAWFORD, JULIE. 'Pleaders, atturneys, petitioners and the like': Margaret Cavendish and the dramatic petition. *In* (pp. 241–60) **5225**.

7789. FITZMAURICE, JAMES (ed.). Sociable letters. Peterborough, Ont.; Orchard Park, NY: Broadview Press, 2004. pp. 336. (Broadview eds.) Rev. by Sarah R. Moreman in SCN (63:1/2) 2005, 37–41.

7790. MICROS, MARIANNE. 'A world of my own': John Milton and Margaret Cavendish's reflections of Paradise. *See* **7723**.

7791. O'NEILL, EILEEN. Early modern women philosophers and the history of philosophy. Hypatia (20:3) 2005, 185–97.

7792. SALZMAN, PAUL. Early modern (aristocratic) women and textual property. *In* (pp. 281–95) **6964**.

7793. WILSON, MIRANDA. Building a perfect silence: the use of Renaissance architecture in Margaret Cavendish's *Bell in Campo*. 1650–1850 (10) 2004, 245–64.

7794. WORSLEY, LUCY. Building a family: William Cavendish, First Duke of Newcastle, and the construction of Bolsover and Nottingham Castles. *See* **7797**.

7795. Wu, Hui. The paradigm of Margaret Cavendish: reading women's alternative rhetorics in a global context. *In* (pp. 171–85) **2457**.

William Cavendish, Duke of Newcastle

7796. Crawford, Julie. 'Pleaders, atturneys, petitioners and the like': Margaret Cavendish and the dramatic petition. *In* (pp. 241–60) **5225**.

7797. Worsley, Lucy. Building a family: William Cavendish, First Duke of Newcastle, and the construction of Bolsover and Nottingham Castles. SevC (19:2) 2004, 233–59.

John Norris

7798. Taylor, E. Derek; New, Melvyn (eds). Mary Astell and John Norris: letters concerning the love of God. *See* **7197**.

John Ogilby

7799. Müller, Anja. Picturing Æsops: re-visions of *Æsop's Fables* from L'Estrange to Richardson. *See* **107**.

'Orinda' (Katherine Philips)

7800. Chalmers, Hero. Royalist women writers, 1650–1689. *See* **7236**.

7801. Hageman, Elizabeth H. Treacherous accidents and the abominable printing of Katherine Philips's *1664 Poems*. *In* (pp. 85–95) **587**.

Dorothy Osborne

7802. Crangle, Sara. Epistolarity, audience, selfhood: the letters of Dorothy Osborne to William Temple. WWr (12:3) 2005, 433–51.

7803. Parker, Kenneth (ed.). Dorothy Osborne: letters to Sir William Temple, 1652–54: observations on love, literature, politics, and religion. (Bibl. 2004, 8145.) Rev. by Diane Willen in SixCJ (34:4) 2003, 1125–6.

Thomas Otway

7804. Edgecombe, Rodney Stenning. Otway's *Windsor Castle* and Pope's *Windsor-Forest*. ANQ (18:1) 2005, 22–4.

7805. Fisk, Deborah Payne (ed.). Four Restoration libertine plays. *See* **7436**.

Sir Thomas Overbury

7806. Beecher, Donald (ed.). Characters: together with poems, news, edicts, and paradoxes based on the eleventh edition of *A Wife Now the Widow of Sir Thomas Overbury*. (Bibl. 2004, 8148.) Rev. by Robert C. Evans in SixCJ (36:1) 2005, 216–17; by Élisabeth Soubrenie in EA (58:2) 2005, 202–4.

7807. Bellany, Alastair. The politics of court scandal in early modern England: news culture and the Overbury affair, 1603–1666. (Bibl. 2004, 8149.) Rev. by David L. Smith in SixCJ (34:3) 2003, 844–5.

Richard Overton

7808. McDowell, Nicholas. Ideas of Creation in the writings of Richard Overton the Leveller and *Paradise Lost*. *See* **7713**.

John Owen (1616–1683)

7809. HARRIES, BYRON.   John Owen the epigrammatist: a literary and historical context. RenSt (18:1) 2004, 19–32.

7810. KNAPP, HENRY M.   John Owen's interpretation of Hebrews 6:4–6: eternal perseverance of the saints in Puritan exegesis. SixCJ (34:1) 2003, 29–52.

Julia Palmer (*fl.*1671–1673)

7811. BURKE, VICTORIA E.; CLARKE, ELIZABETH.   Julia Palmer's *Centuries*: the politics of editing and anthologizing early modern women's manuscript compilations. *In* (pp. 47–64) **587**.

William Penn

7812. HUTTON, SARAH.   Authority and the Word: Henry More, William Penn and the *logos*. *See* **7782**.

Samuel Pepys

7813. ROACH, JOSEPH.   Public intimacy: the prior history of 'it'. *In* (pp. 15–30) **3985**.

7814. ROBERTSON, RANDY.   Censors of the mind: Samuel Pepys and the Restoration licensers. DalR (85:2) 2005, 181–94.

7815. TOMALIN, CLAIRE.   Samuel Pepys: the unequalled self. (Bibl. 2004, 8158.) Rev. by D. E. Richardson in SewR (111:4) 2003, cviii–cxvi; by Elspeth Findlay in SevC (19:2) 2004, 288–9.

7816. WEBSTER, JEREMY W.   Rochester's easy king: rereading the (sexual) politics of the scepter lampoon. *See* **7834**.

William Percy (1575–1648)

7817. NICHOLLS, MARK.   The authorship of *Thomas Bastard's Oxford Libel*. *See* **5386**.

John Philips (1676–1709)

7818. PELLICER, JUAN CHRISTIAN.   'A dry consumptive smoaking sot': Ned Ward's epigram on John Philips? *See* **9112**.

Mary Pix

7819. VILLEGAS LÓPEZ, SONIA.   Narrative levels in *The Inhumane Cardinal* (1696) by Mary Pix. SEDERI (13) 2003, 229–36.

Thomas Powell (1572?–1635?)

7820. STEGGLE, MATTHEW.   Richard Head's *The Floating Island* (1673) plagiarizes Thomas Powell. *See* **7462**.

Vavasor Powell (1617–1670)

7821. COULTON, BARBARA.   The poet and the preacher: Henry Vaughan and Vavasor Powell in their place and time. *See* **7879**.

Samuel Purchas

7822. ARMSTRONG, CATHERINE.   The bookseller and the pedlar: the spread of knowledge of the New World in early modern England, 1580–1640. *In* (pp. 15–29) **880**.

7823. HOLMES, JOHN.   The Guiana projects: imperial and colonial ideologies in Ralegh and Purchas. *See* 5621.

Edward Ravenscroft (1654?–1707)

7824. MURRAY, BARBARA A. (ed.).   Shakespeare adaptations from the Restoration: five plays. *See* 6037.

John Wilmot, Earl of Rochester

7825. BYRNE, PETER.   'Where appetite directs': tragic heroism's recovery in Rochester's *Valentinian*. *See* 7446.

7826. ELLENZWEIG, SARAH.   The faith of unbelief: Rochester's *Satyre*, Deism, and religious freethinking in seventeenth-century England. JBS (44:1) 2005, 27–45.

7827. FISHER, NICHOLAS.   Jacob Tonson and the Earl of Rochester. Library (6:2) 2005, 133–60.

7828. JOHNSON, JAMES WILLIAM.   A profane wit: the life of John Wilmot, Earl of Rochester. (Bibl. 2004, 8178.) Rev. by Peter Porter in TLS, 9 Dec. 2005, 16–17; by Harold Love in SCN (63:3/4) 2005, 137–41.

7829. MILHOUS, JUDITH; HUME, ROBERT D.   Murder in Elizabeth Barry's dressing room. *See* 7133.

7830. NARAIN, MONA.   Libertine spaces and the female body in the poetry of Rochester and Ned Ward. ELH (72:3) 2005, 553–76.

7831. RAYLOR, TIMOTHY.   Willmore's 'prince': a note on Behn's *The Rover*, I.ii. *See* 7253.

7832. ROSENFELD, NANCY.   *The Man of Mode*: the mode of man. *See* 7439.

7833. SANCHEZ, MELISSA E.   Libertinism and romance in Rochester's poetry. ECS (38:3) 2005, 441–59.

7834. WEBSTER, JEREMY W.   Rochester's easy king: rereading the (sexual) politics of the scepter lampoon. ELN (42:4) 2005, 1–19.

Alexander Ross (1591–1654)

7835. WARNER, J. CHRISTOPHER.   The Augustinian epic, Petrarch to Milton. *See* 5725.

Mary Rowlandson

7836. MACNEIL, DENISE.   Mary Rowlandson and the foundational mythology of the American frontier hero. WS (34:8) 2005, 625–53.

William Rowley

7837. NICOL, DAVID.   Interrogating the Devil: social and demonic pressure in *The Witch of Edmonton*. *See* 7357.

John Selden

7838. BARBOUR, REID.   John Selden: measures of the Holy Commonwealth in seventeenth-century England. (Bibl. 2004, 8195.) Rev. by William Tighe in SixCJ (36:2) 2005, 633–4; by Daniel Woolf in LitH (14:2) 2005, 85–6.

7839. COUDERT, ALLISON P.; SHOULSON, JEFFREY S. (eds).   *Hebraica veritas?* Christian Hebraists and the study of Judaism in early modern Europe.

Philadelphia: Pennsylvania UP, 2004. pp. x, 316. (Jewish culture and contexts.)
Rev. by Norman Simms in Parergon (22:2) 2005, 206–8.

7840. NEVITT, MARCUS.   John Selden among the Quakers: antifeminism and
the seventeenth-century tithes controversy. In (pp. 189–208) 5196.

Thomas Shadwell

7841. FISK, DEBORAH PAYNE (ed.).   Four Restoration libertine plays.
See 7436.

7842. JERNIGAN, DANIEL.   Serious Money becomes 'business by other means':
Caryl Churchill's metatheatrical subject. See 15792.

7843. MORA, MARÍA JOSÉ.   The political is personal: the attack on Shadwell in
Sir Barnaby Whigg. See 7432.

Thomas Shelton

7844. CHARTIER, ROGER.   Crossing borders in early modern Europe: sociology
of texts and literature. Trans. by Maurice Elton. See 6525.

Thomas Shepard

7845. LIEBERT, ELISABETH.   Samson Agonistes and spiritual autobiography.
See 7710.

James Shirley

7846. BAWCUTT, N. W.   The assassination of Alessandro de' Medici in early
seventeenth-century English drama. See 7869.

7847. PASTOOR, CHARLES.   The Puritan audience in Jonson's Bartholomew Fair
and Shirley's The Bird in a Cage. See 7576.

Richard Sibbes (1577–1635)

7848. SEMLER, L. E.   Creative adoption in Eliza's Babes (1652): Puritan
refigurations of Sibbes, Herrick, and Herbert. In (pp. 319–45) 6872.

Algernon Sidney

7849. LEVILLAIN, CHARLES-ÉDOUARD.   L'Angleterre de la Restauration au
miroir de la 'vraie liberté' (1660–1672): la rencontre entre républicanismes
anglais et hollandais à travers les écrits de Pieter de la Court. See 7460.

Lillias Skene (1626 or 7–1697)

7850. DESBRISAY, GORDON.   Lilias Skene: a Quaker poet and her 'cursed self'.
In (pp. 162–77) 3754.

Captain John Smith (1580–1631)

7851. PETERS, JILL.   The role of Pocahontas and Sacagawea in the creation of
new American mythology. MidF (31:1) 2005, 16–26.

Thomas Southerne

7852. WIDMAYER, ANNE F.   The politics of adapting Aphra Behn's Oroonoko.
See 7259.

William Strode

7853. FOREY, MARGARET.   Manuscript evidence and the author of Aske Me
No More: William Strode, not Thomas Carew. EngMS (12) 2005, 180–200.

Joseph Swetnam ('Thomas Tel-Troth')

7854. BANERJEE, RITA. *Women Pleas'd* and *Swetnam the Woman-Hater Arraigned by Women*: John Fletcher's participation in the Swetnam debate and the date of his play. *See* 7445.

7855. FINDLAY, ALISON. 'Adam's sons are my brethren': reading Beatrice's feminism, past and present. *See* 6633.

Josuah Sylvester (1563–1618)

7856. BANDERIER, GILLES. Enjeux linguistiques et idéologiques des traductions de Du Bartas (1579–1650). NM (106:3) 2005, 337–48.

Nahum Tate

7857. BUCK, A. R. Cordelia's estate: women and the law of property from Shakespeare to Nahum Tate. *In* (pp. 183–97) **6964**.

7858. CALVO, CLARA. Rewriting Lear's untender daughter: Fanny Price as a Regency Cordelia in Jane Austen's *Mansfield Park*. *See* **9958**.

7859. MURRAY, BARBARA A. (ed.). Shakespeare adaptations from the Restoration: five plays. *See* **6037**.

John Tatham (*fl.*1632–1664)

7860. THOMAS, CHAD. Negotiating the Interregnum: the political works of Davenant and Tatham. *See* **7350**.

Edward Taylor

7861. JOHNSON, KIMBERLY. Edward Taylor's 'menstruous cloth': self-feminization and the problem of assurance. SPAS (8) 2004, 51–79.

7862. SCHEICK, WILLIAM J. Taylor's *Meditation 1.7*. Exp (63:2) 2005, 68–71.

John Taylor (1580–1653)

7863. CRAIK, KATHARINE A. John Taylor's pot-poetry. SevC (20:2) 2005, 185–203.

Sir William Temple

7864. CRANGLE, SARA. Epistolarity, audience, selfhood: the letters of Dorothy Osborne to William Temple. *See* **7802**.

7865. VON MALTZAHN, NICHOLAS. Andrew Marvell and the prehistory of Whiggism. *In* (pp. 31–61) **8091**.

Alice Thornton (b.1627)

7866. ANSELMENT, RAYMOND A. Seventeenth-century manuscript sources of Alice Thornton's life. SELit (45:1) 2005, 135–55.

7867. LEAR, ANNE. Thank God for haemorrhoids! Illness and identity in a seventeenth-century woman's autobiography. WWr (12:3) 2005, 337–45.

Robert Tofte

7868. VALLARO, CRISTINA. La simbologia lunare nei canzonieri elisabettiani. *See* **5325**.

Cyril Tourneur

7869. BAWCUTT, N. W. The assassination of Alessandro de' Medici in early seventeenth-century English drama. RES (56:225) 2005, 412–23.

7870. HIRSCHFELD, HEATHER.   Compulsions of the Renaissance. *See* **6602**.

Aurelian Townshend

7871. GOUGH, MELINDA J.   'Not as myself': the queen's voice in *Tempe Restored*. MP (101:1) 2003, 48–67.

Thomas Traherne

7872. BLEVINS, JACOB.   Finding felicity through the 'Pythagorean eye': Pythagoreanism in the work of Thomas Traherne. CML (25:1) 2005, 41–51.

Sir Samuel Tuke (d.1674)

7873. HOPKINS, PAUL M. S. (ed.).   The adventures of Sir Samuel Tuke: full authentic text of Tuke's play and suggestions for staging *The Adventures of Five Hours*. Woodford Halse, Northants.: Ituri, 2003. pp. 142. Rev. by Carolyn D. Williams in RECTR (19:1) 2004, 77–8.

Sir Thomas Urquhart

7874. MCDOWELL, NICHOLAS.   Urquhart's Rabelais: translation, patronage, and cultural politics. ELR (35:2) 2005, 273–303.

James Ussher (1581–1656)

7875. GRIBBEN, CRAWFORD.   Rhetoric, fiction and theology: James Ussher and the death of Jesus Christ. SevC (20:1) 2005, 53–76.

Sir John Vanbrugh

7876. HAMMOND, BREAN (ed.).   *The Relapse* and other plays. Oxford; New York: OUP, 2004. pp. xli, 380. (Oxford world's classics.)

Henry Vaughan

7877. BURROW, COLIN.   Henry Vaughan's *The Queer*: a note on queries. NQ (52:3) 2005, 310–11.

7878. CAREY, JOHN.   Henry Vaughan's poetry: pointful vagueness and the merging of contraries. *In* (pp. 69–83) **5167**.

7879. COULTON, BARBARA.   The poet and the preacher: Henry Vaughan and Vavasor Powell in their place and time. Scintilla (9) 2005, 155–74.

7880. DICKSON, DONALD R.   Henry Vaughan's medical library. Scintilla (9) 2005, 189–209.

7881. HOOKER, JEREMY.   Nostalgia and the kiss of life. Scintilla (9) 2005, 9–24.

7882. HUTTON, CLARK.   Images of time and eternity in the religious poetry of Henry Vaughan. Comitatus (36) 2005, 142–56.

7883. THIERFELDER, BILL.   Wordsworth's *Ode: Intimations of Immortality*, Shakespeare's *The Tempest* 5.1, and Vaughan's *The Retreat*. *See* **12519**.

7884. WEST, PHILIP.   *Silex Scintillans* and the 'public'. Scintilla (9) 2005, 70–82.

7885. WILCHER, ROBERT.   The darkened scribe and the blessed man: changing uses of allusion in the work of Henry Vaughan. Scintilla (9) 2005, 38–52.

Edmund Waller

7886. HOLBERTON, EDWARD.   'Soe Honny from the Lyon came': the 1657 wedding-masques for the Protector's daughters. *See* **7626**.

7887. RAYLOR, TIMOTHY. Waller's Machiavellian Cromwell: the imperial argument of *A Panegyrick to My Lord Protector.* RES (56:225) 2005, 386–411.

Izaak Walton

7888. BEDDARD, R. A. Anthony Wood and Izaak Walton: an exchange between two seventeenth-century biographers. BLR (18:4) 2004, 301–32.

7889. CLARKE, ELIZABETH. George Herbert and Cambridge scholars. *See* 7467.

7890. CLARKE, SUSAN A. 'Bright Heir t' th' Bird Imperial': Richard Lovelace's *The Falcon* in context. *See* 7607.

7891. MILLER, JOHN J. Reading as pastoral experience in Walton's *Compleat Angler.* Reader (53) 2005, 24–44.

7892. SMITH, NICHOLAS D. An annotated copy of the third Hawkins edition of Izaak Walton's *The Complete Angler.* YLG (79:1/2) 2004, 70–7.

William Walwyn (1600–1681)

7893. FULLER, WILLIAM. Restatement of trysts. ChiR (50:2–4) 2004/05, 241–59.

John Webster

7894. ANDERSON, THOMAS P. 'We cannot say hee's dead': writing royal effigies in Marvell's poetry. *See* 7619.

7895. BARKER, ROBERTA. 'Another voyage': death as social performance in the major tragedies of John Webster. ETh (8:2) 2005, 35–56.

7896. BLAU, HERBERT. Art and crisis: homeland security and the Noble Savage. *See* 15293.

7897. BOTELHO, KEITH M. 'Into a Russian winter': Russian extremes in *The Duchess of Malfi.* ELN (42:3) 2005, 14–18.

7898. CALBI, MAURIZIO. Approximate bodies: gender and power in early modern drama and anatomy. *See* 7651.

7899. DUCASSÉ-TURNER, MILAGRO. Gods on earth: usurping kingly and godly authority in Shakespeare's *Macbeth* and Webster's *The Duchess of Malfi.* *See* 6542.

7900. GUNBY, DAVID; CARNEGIE, DAVID; JACKSON, MACDONALD P. (eds). The Devil's law-case; A cure for a cuckold; Appius and Virginia. Cambridge; New York: CUP, 2003. pp. xxxi, 644. (Works of John Webster: an old-spelling critical ed., 2.) Rev. by Richard Grinnell in SixCJ (35:4) 2004, 1148–9.

7901. HABERMANN, INA. 'She has that in her belly will dry up your ink': femininity as challenge in the 'equitable drama' of John Webster. *In* (pp. 100–20) **5196**.

7902. INGRAM, JILL PHILLIPS. The 'noble lie': casuistry and Machiavellianism in *The Duchess of Malfi.* ExRC (31:1) 2005, 135–60.

7903. LEINWAND, THEODORE B. *Coniugium interruptum* in Shakespeare and Webster. *See* 6263.

7904. LLOYD, WILLIAM. John Webster and *The London Prodigal*: new sources for *The Devil's Law-Case.* RORD (44) 2005, 75–102.

7905. MUKHERJI, SUBHA. Women, law, and dramatic realism in early modern England. See 6250.

7906. VÉLEZ NÚÑEZ, RAFAEL. Melancholic sounds: singing madness in Restoration drama. See 7295.

Leonard Wheatcroft (1627–1707)

7907. BROWN, CEDRIC C. Sons of beer and sons of Ben: drink as a social marker in seventeenth-century England. In (pp. 3–20) 6942.

Roger Williams (1604?–1683)

7908. HERRMANN, FRÉDÉRIC. 'Israël selon la chair' et 'Israël selon l'esprit': philo-sémitisme et réforme chez Roger Williams. Anglophonia (17) 2005, 223–33.

Gerrard Winstanley

7909. BOROT, LUC. Le prophète et l'autorité scripturaire: Winstanley et les premiers Quakers comme continuateurs de la révélation biblique. Anglophonia (17) 2005, 263–73.

John Winthrop the Elder (1588–1649)

7910. BREMER, FRANCIS J. John Winthrop: America's forgotten Founding Father. (Bibl. 2004, 8263.) Rev. by Tom Webster in SevC (20:2) 2005, 300–2.

7911. GOLDMAN, ERIC. Bringing out the beast in Melville's *Billy Budd*: the dialogue of Darwinian and 'holy' lexicons on board the *Bellipotent*. See 11684.

7912. SCHWEITZER, IVY. John Winthrop's 'model' of American affiliation. EAL (40:3) 2005, 441–69.

George Wither

7913. BROWNING, ROB. 'To serve my purpose': interpretive agency in George Wither's *A Collection of Emblems*. In (pp. 47–71) 5103.

7914. O'CALLAGHAN, MICHELLE. 'Now thou may'st speak freely': entering the public sphere in 1614. In (pp. 63–79) 6860.

7915. —— Taking liberties: George Wither's *A Satyre*, libel and the law. In (pp. 146–69) 5196.

Hannah Wolley (c.1622–c.1674)

7916. SUMMIT, JENNIFER. Writing home: Hannah Wolley, the Oxinden letters, and household epistolary practice. In (pp. 201–18) 6964.

Anthony Wood

7917. BEDDARD, R. A. Anthony Wood and Izaak Walton: an exchange between two seventeenth-century biographers. See 7888.

7918. —— The sources of Anthony Wood's life of Nicholas Hill. Archives (29:111) 2004, 1–11.

Sir Henry Wotton (1568–1639)

7919. CURZON, GERALD. Wotton and his worlds: spying, science, and Venetian intrigues. Philadelphia, PA: XLibris, 2003. pp. 341. Rev. by Dennis Flynn in SCN (63:1/2) 2005, 4–7.

7920. PAROLIN, PETER. The Venetian theater of Aletheia Talbot, Countess of Arundel. In (pp. 219–39) 5225.

Lady Mary Wroth

7921. ARNOLD, MARGARET J.   An unpublished letter of Mary Wroth. ELR (35:3) 2005, 454–8.

7922. GOSSETT, SUZANNE.   The ethics of post-mortem editing. *In* (pp. 147–55) **587.**

7923. MILLER, SHANNON.   Textual crimes and punishment in Mary Wroth's *Urania.* JMEMS (35:2) 2005, 385–427.

7924. MUNROE, JENNIFER.   'In this strang Labourinth, how shall I turne?': needlework, gardens, and writing in Mary Wroth's *Pamphilia to Amphilanthus.* TSWL (24:1) 2005, 35–55.

7925. TRULL, MARY.   'Philargus' house is not in all places': marriage, privacy, and the overheard lament in Mary Wroth's *Urania.* ELR (35:3) 2005, 459–89.

7926. ZURCHER, AMELIA A.   Ethics and the politic agent of early seventeenth-century prose romance. ELR (35:1) 2005, 73–101.

William Wycherley

7927. MARKLEY, ROBERT.   Riches, power, trade and religion: the Far East and the English imagination, 1600–1720. *See* **7714.**

7928. OWEN, SUSAN J.   Drink, sex and power in Restoration comedy. *In* (pp. 127–39) **6942.**

EIGHTEENTH CENTURY
GENERAL

7929. ANON. (comp.).   Recent articles. Scriblerian (37:2/38:1) 2005, 1–90.

7930. ABRAMS, M. H.; GREENBLATT, STEPHEN (gen. eds).   The Norton anthology of English literature: vol. 1C, The Restoration and the eighteenth century. Ed. by Lawrence Lipking. *See* **6839**.

7931. AMORY, HUGH.   Bibliography and the book trades: studies in the print culture of early New England. Ed. by David D. Hall. *See* **754**.

7932. BAINES, PAUL.   The long 18th century. London; New York: Arnold, 2004. pp. xii, 188. (Contexts.) Rev. by David A. Brewer in Scriblerian (37:2/38:1) 2005, 128–9.

7933. BAKER, JENNIFER J.   Securing the commonwealth: debt, speculation, and writing in the making of Early America. *See* **6842**.

7934. BALLASTER, ROS (ed.).   Fables of the East: selected tales, 1662–1785. *See* **6843**.

7935. BATCHELOR, JENNIE.   Dress, distress and desire: clothing and the female body in eighteenth-century literature. Basingstoke; New York: Palgrave Macmillan, 2005. pp. ix, 216.

7936. —— KAPLAN, CORA (eds).   British women's writing in the long eighteenth century: authorship, politics, and history. Basingstoke; New York: Palgrave Macmillan, 2005. pp. 193.

7937. BAYLEY, JOHN.   The power of delight: a lifetime in literature: essays 1962–2002. Selected by Leo Carey. New York; London: Norton, 2005. pp. xvii, 677. Rev. by Clive James in TLS, 27 May 2005, 3–4; by James Wood in LRB (27:20) 2005, 9–10.

7938. BENCHIMOL, ALEX.   Remaking the Romantic period: cultural materialism, Cultural Studies and the radical public sphere. *See* **14700**.

7939. BENEDICT, BARBARA M.   Readers, writers, reviewers, and the professionalization of literature. *In* (pp. 3–23) **8014**.

7940. BERG, MAXINE; EGER, ELIZABETH.   The rise and fall of the luxury debates. *In* (pp. 7–27) **7941**.

7941. —— —— (eds).   Luxury in the eighteenth century: debates, desires and delectable goods. Basingstoke; New York: Palgrave Macmillan, 2003. pp. xii, 259, (plates) 24. Rev. by Joan Thirsk in LitH (14:1) 2005, 91–2; by James E. Evans in Scriblerian (37:2/38:1) 2005, 153–4.

7942. BODE, CHRISTOPH; RENNHAK, KATHARINA (eds).   Romantic voices, Romantic poetics: Selected papers from the Regensburg conference of the German Society of English Romanticism. *See* **9193**.

7943. BOTTING, FRED; TOWNSHEND, DALE (eds).   Gothic: critical concepts in literary and cultural studies. London; New York: Routledge, 2004. 4 vols. pp. 1552. (Critical concepts in literary and cultural studies.)

7944. BRANT, CLARE.   Fume and perfume: some eighteenth-century uses of smell. JBS (43:4) 2004, 444–63.

7945. BREWER, DAVID A.   The afterlife of character, 1726–1825. Philadelphia: Pennsylvania UP, 2005. pp. 259. (Material texts.)

7946. BROWN, HILARY.   Benedikte Naubert (1756–1819) and her relations to English culture. Leeds: Maney for the Modern Humanities Research Assn and the Inst. of Germanic Studies, Univ. of London, 2005. pp. 161. (MHRA texts and dissertations, 63.) (Bithell series of dissertations, 27.)

7947. BULLARD, PADDY.   Just good manners. TLS, 8 Apr. 2005, 26 (review-article).

7948. BUTTE, GEORGE.   I know that you know that I know: narrating subjects from Moll Flanders to Marnie. (Bibl. 2004, 8294.) Rev. by Susan Fraiman in ECF (17:2) 2005, 278–81.

7949. CANFIELD, J. DOUGLAS.   The baroque in English neoclassical literature. (Bibl. 2004, 8295.) Rev. by Tom Rutter in MLR (100:3) 2005, 774–7.

7950. CARDWELL, M. JOHN.   Arts and arms: literature, politics, and patriotism during the Seven Years War. Manchester; New York: Manchester UP, 2004. pp. xi, 306. Rev. by Bob Harris in BJECS (28:2) 2005, 286–7; by Jeremy Black in NQ (52:1) 2005, 127–8.

7951. CAREY, BRYCCHAN.   British Abolitionism and the rhetoric of sensibility: writing, sentiment, and slavery, 1760–1807. Basingstoke; New York: Palgrave Macmillan, 2005. pp. viii, 240. (Palgrave studies in the Enlightenment, Romanticism and the cultures of print.)

7952. CARTER, PHILIP.   Tears and the man. *In* (pp. 156–73) **8016**.

7953. CARTER, SOPHIE.   Purchasing power: representing prostitution in eighteenth-century English popular print culture. Aldershot; Burlington, VT: Ashgate, 2004. pp. ix, 211. (British art and visual culture since 1750: new readings.) Rev. by Deborah Simonton in BJECS (28:2) 2005, 288–9.

7954. CAVALIERO, RODERICK.   *Italia Romantica*: English Romantics and Italian freedom. *See* **9215**.

7955. CHANDLER, JAMES; GILMARTIN, KEVIN.   Introduction: engaging the eidometropolis. *In* (pp. 1–41) **9217**.

7956. —— —— (eds).   Romantic metropolis: the urban scene of British culture, 1780–1840. *See* **9217**.

7957. CHEEK, PAMELA.   Sexual antipodes: Enlightenment globalization and the placing of sex. Stanford, CA: Stanford UP, 2003. pp. xi, 246. Rev. by Robert A. Erickson in ECF (17:2) 2005, 269–76; by Betty Joseph in CLS (42:2) 2005, 313–16.

7958. CHICO, TITA.   Designing women: the dressing room in eighteenth-century English literature and culture. Lewisburg, PA: Bucknell UP, 2005. pp. 302. (Bucknell studies in eighteenth-century literature and culture.)

7959. CLARK, ANNA.   Women in eighteenth-century British politics. *In* (pp. 570–86) **8016**.

7960. CLARKE, NORMA.   Bluestocking fictions: devotional writings, didactic literature and the imperative of female improvement. *In* (pp. 460–73) **8016**.

7961. CLERY, E. J.   The feminization debate in eighteenth-century England: literature, commerce and luxury. Basingstoke; New York: Palgrave Macmillan,

2004. pp. xi, 234. (Palgrave studies in the Enlightenment, Romanticism and the cultures of print.) Rev. by Michael Caines in TLS, 29 July 2005, 11.

7962. COHEN, MICHÈLE. 'To think, to compare, to combine, to methodise': girls' education in Enlightenment Britain. *In* (pp. 224–42) **8016**.

7963. CONNELL, PHILIP. Death and the author: Westminster Abbey and the meanings of the literary monument. ECS (38:4) 2005, 557–85.

7964. CRACIUN, ADRIANA. British women writers and the French Revolution: citizens of the world. Basingstoke; New York: Palgrave Macmillan, 2005. pp. xii, 225. (Palgrave studies in the Enlightenment, Romanticism and the cultures of print.)

7965. CRONIN, RICHARD. Literary scene. *In* (pp. 289–96) **10060**.

7966. DAMROSCH, DAVID (gen. ed.). The Longman anthology of world literature: vol. D, The seventeenth and eighteenth centuries. Ed. by April Alliston. *See* **6867**.

7967. DAVIS, PAUL. Bransonism. *See* **8715**.

7968. DE MONTLUZIN, EMILY LORRAINE. Attributions of authorship in the *Gentleman's Magazine*, 1745–1754: a supplement to the *Union List. See* **1188**.

7969. —— Attributions of authorship in the *Gentleman's Magazine*, 1755–64: a supplement to the *Union List. See* **1189**.

7970. D'HAEN, THEO. 'Nilotic mud': British Romantic writers and the colonies. *In* (pp. 51–63) **9237**.

7971. —— *et al.* (eds). Configuring Romanticism: essays offered to C. C. Barfoot. *See* **9237**.

7972. DOUTHWAITE, JULIA V. The wild girl, natural man, and the monster: dangerous experiments in the age of Enlightenment. (Bibl. 2004, 8311.) Rev. by Yves Citton in ECS (38:2) 2005, 381–5.

7973. DOWNES, PAUL. Democracy, revolution, and monarchism in early American literature. (Bibl. 2004, 8312.) Rev. by Debra Boyle in ECS (38:2) 2005, 367–71.

7974. EGER, ELIZABETH. 'The noblest commerce of mankind': conversation and community in the Bluestocking Circle. *In* (pp. 288–305) **8016**.

7975. ELLIS, MARKMAN. Trade. *In* (pp. 415–24) **10060**.

7976. ERKKILÄ, BETSY. Mixed bloods and other crosses: rethinking American literature from the Revolution to the Culture Wars. Philadelphia: Pennsylvania UP, 2005. pp. xii, 272.

7977. ERWIN, TIMOTHY. Parody and prostitution. HLQ (68:4) 2005, 677–83 (review-article).

7978. FESTA, LYNN. Cosmetic differences: the changing faces of England and France. *See* **8991**.

7979. FLEMING, CHRIS; O'CARROLL, JOHN. Romanticism. *See* **9254**.

7980. FRANK, FREDERICK S. Guide to the gothic III: an annotated bibliography of criticism, 1994–2003: vol. II. Lanham, MD; London: Scarecrow Press, 2005. pp. xviii, 604. Rev. by Edward J. Ingebretsen in GothS (7:2) 2005, 207–10.

7981. FULFORD, TIM. 'Getting and spending': the Orientalization of satire in Romantic London. *In* (pp. 11–29) **9305**.

7982. —— LEE, DEBBIE; KITSON, PETER J. Literature, science and exploration in the Romantic era: bodies of knowledge. *See* **9262**.

7983. GILMOUR, IAN. Out of bounds. *See* **854**.

7984. GÓMEZ LARA, MANUEL. Discourses on health and leisure and modern constructions of holidays at the Restoration spas. *In* (pp. 202–27) **5167**.

7985. GORING, PAUL. The rhetoric of sensibility in eighteenth-century culture. Cambridge; New York: CUP, 2005. pp. xi, 222.

7986. GOULD, PHILIP. The African slave trade and Abolitionism: rereading antislavery literature, 1776–1800. *In* (pp. 201–19) **1244**.

7987. —— Barbaric traffic: commerce and anti-slavery in the eighteenth-century Atlantic world. Cambridge, MA; London: Harvard UP, 2003. pp. viii, 258. Rev. by David Raybin in AAR (38:4) 2004, 718–20; by Jared Gardner in EAL (40:1) 2005, 199–202; by Jonathan Elmer in AmLH (17:1) 2005, 160–70.

7988. GREENE, JODY. The trouble with ownership: literary property and authorial liability in England, 1660–1730. *See* **6881**.

7989. HALLOCK, THOMAS. From the fallen tree: frontier narratives, environmental politics, and the roots of a national pastoral, 1749–1826. (Bibl. 2004, 8319.) Rev. by Lawrence Buell in JAH (91:3) 2004, 1008–9; by David Curtis Skaggs in NwOH (75:2) 2004, 175–6; by Barbara Ryan in AL (77:1) 2005, 200–2; by Larry F. Kutchen in EAL (40:1) 2005, 163–71; by Michael Ziser in ECS (39:1) 2005, 120–30; by Christoph Irmscher in CanL (186) 2005, 173–4; by Jennifer Hughes Westerman in ISLE (12:1) 2005, 283–4.

7990. HAMMILL, FAYE. Literary culture and female authorship in Canada 1760–2000. Amsterdam; Atlanta, GA: Rodopi, 2003. pp. xxiv, 245. (Cross/cultures: readings in the post-colonial literatures in English, 63.) Rev. by Maria Truchan-Tataryn in CanL (183) 2004, 132–4; by B. F. R. Edwards in SHARP (14:1/2) 2005, 14.

7991. HANEY, DAVID P. Recent work in Romanticism and religion: from witness to critique. *See* **9281**.

7992. HARRIS, SHARON M. Executing race: early American women's narratives of race, society, and the law. Columbus: Ohio State UP, 2005. pp. x, 240.

7993. HARROW, SHARON. Adventures in domesticity: gender and colonial adulteration in eighteenth-century British literature. (Bibl. 2004, 8321.) Rev. by Alison Stenton in TLS, 22 Apr. 2005, 27.

7994. HARVEY, KAREN. Reading sex in the eighteenth century: bodies and gender in English erotic culture. Cambridge; New York: CUP, 2004. pp. ix, 261. (Cambridge social and cultural histories, 3.)

7995. HASLETT, MOYRA. Pope to Burney, 1714–1779: Scriblerians to Bluestockings. (Bibl. 2003, 7542.) Rev. by A. F. T. Lurcock in NQ (52:3) 2005, 416–18; by Heather King in Scriblerian (37:2/38:1) 2005, 124–6.

7996. HAVENS, EARLE. English manuscript culture and the ambiguous triumph of print: seventy years of the Osborn Collection, 1934–2004. *See* **400**.

7997. HAWES, CLEMENT. The British eighteenth century and global critique. Basingstoke; New York: Palgrave Macmillan, 2005. pp. xix, 257.

7998. HAYWOOD, IAN. The revolution in popular literature: print, politics, and the people, 1790–1860. (Bibl. 2004, 8328.) Rev. by Stephanie Kuduk Weiner in NineL (59:4) 2005, 529–31; by Noah Heringman in SELit (45:4) 2005, 961–1020.

7999. HEPWORTH, DAVID. Appendix: written epitaphs of Robin Hood. *In* (pp. 188–9) **3576.**

8000. HERINGMAN, NOAH (ed.). Romantic science: the literary forms of natural history. (Bibl. 2004, 8330.) Rev. by Martin Halliwell in ERR (16:3) 2005, 373–80.

8001. HEWITT, ELIZABETH. Correspondence and American literature, 1787–1865. Cambridge; New York: CUP, 2004. pp. x, 230. (Cambridge studies in American literature and culture, 146.)

8002. HITCHCOCK, TIM. The streets: literary beggars and the realities of eighteenth-century London. *In* (pp. 80–100) **6958.**

8003. HOEVELER, DIANE LONG. The secularization of suffering: toward a theory of gothic subjectivity. WordsC (35:3) 2004, 113–17.

8004. HOLDEN, PHILIP; RUPPEL, RICHARD J. (eds). Imperial desire: dissident sexualities and colonial literature. (Bibl. 2004, 8332.) Rev. by Ellen Burton Harrington in Conradiana (36:3) 2004, 251–61; by Alfred J. López in SAtlR (70:3) 2005, 134–9.

8005. HOOPER, GLENN (ed.). Landscape and empire 1770–2000. Aldershot; Burlington, VT: Ashgate, 2005. pp. xi, 265.

8006. ISHAM, HOWARD. Image of the sea: oceanic consciousness in the Romantic century. *See* **9299.**

8007. JARVIS, ROBIN. The Romantic period: the intellectual and cultural context of English literature, 1789–1830. *See* **9303.**

8008. JONES, STEVEN E. (ed.). The satiric eye: forms of satire in the Romantic period. *See* **9305.**

8009. JORDAN, SARAH. The anxieties of idleness: idleness in eighteenth-century British literature and culture. (Bibl. 2004, 8335.) Rev. by Paul Baines in MLR (100:2) 2005, 487–8.

8010. JOSEPH, BETTY. Reading the East India Company, 1720–1840: colonial currencies of gender. Chicago, IL; London: Chicago UP, 2004. pp. xiv, 220. (Women in culture and society.) Rev. by Pablo Mukherjee in MLR (100:3) 2005, 802–3; by Teresa Hubel in CanL (185) 2005, 160–1.

8011. KALTER, BARRETT. DIY gothic: Thomas Gray and the medieval revival. *See* **8690.**

8012. KAMRATH, MARK L.; HARRIS, SHARON M. (eds). Periodical literature in eighteenth-century America. *See* **1244.**

8013. KEEN, PAUL (ed.). Revolutions in Romantic literature: an anthology of print culture, 1780–1832. (Bibl. 2004, 8340.) Rev. by Gregory Dart in TLS, 7 Jan. 2005, 22.

8014. KEYMER, THOMAS; MEE, JON (eds). The Cambridge companion to English literature 1740–1830. Cambridge; New York: CUP, 2004. pp. xv, 308. Rev. by Rebecca Rees in RES (56:225) 2005, 453–5; by Peter Brier in HLQ (68:4) 2005, 691–7.

8015. KIPP, JULIE. Romanticism, maternity, and the body politic. Cambridge; New York: CUP, 2003. pp. xiii, 237. (Cambridge studies in Romanticism, 57.) Rev. by Susanne Scholz in JSBC (11:2) 2004, 235–7; by Clare Hanson in MLR (100:4) 2005, 1097–8; by Marjean D. Purinton in ERR (16:3) 2005, 380–4; by Jacqueline M. Labbe in NineL (60:1) 2005, 98–101.

8016. KNOTT, SARAH; TAYLOR, BARBARA (eds). Women, gender and Enlightenment. Basingstoke; New York: Palgrave Macmillan, 2005. pp. xxi, 769.

8017. KUTCHEN, LARRY F. The neo-Turnerian frontier. EAL (40:1) 2005, 163–71 (review-article).

8018. LEE, ANTHONY W. Mentoring relationships in the life and writings of Samuel Johnson: a study in the dynamics of eighteenth-century literary mentoring. *See* **8768**.

8019. LEITZ, ROBERT C., III; COPE, KEVIN L. Imagining the sciences: expressions of new knowledge in the 'long' eighteenth century. New York: AMS Press, 2004. pp. xvi, 361. (AMS studies in the eighteenth century, 43.) Rev. by Andrew Rodgerson in BJECS (28:2) 2005, 297–8.

8020. LUDINGTON, CHARLES C. 'Be sometimes to your country true': the politics of wine in England, 1660–1714. *In* (pp. 89–106) **6942**.

8021. LUND, ROGER. Laughing at cripples: ridicule, deformity and the argument from design. ECS (39:1) 2005, 91–114.

8022. MCDONAGH, JOSEPHINE. Child murder and British culture, 1720–1900. (Bibl. 2004, 8349.) Rev. by Christine L. Krueger in SR (43:4) 2004, 670–4; by Charlotte Sussman in NineL (59:3) 2004, 404–8; by Marion Shaw in RES (56:224) 2005, 333–5; by Sophia Andres in VPR (38:3) 2005, 337–9; by Georges Lamoine in EA (58:2) 2005, 218–19.

8023. MCILVANNEY, LIAM; RYAN, RAY (eds). Ireland and Scotland: culture and society, 1700–2000. Dublin; Portland, OR: Four Courts Press, 2005. pp. 284.

8024. MCKEON, MICHAEL. Recent studies in the Restoration and eighteenth century. *See* **6909**.

8025. MCWILLIAMS, JOHN. New England's crises and cultural memory: literature, politics, history, religion, 1620–1860. *See* **6911**.

8026. MAKDISI, SAREE. Literature, national identity, and empire. *In* (pp. 61–79) **8014**.

8027. MANNING, SUSAN. Sensibility. *In* (pp. 80–99) **8014**.

8028. MARSHALL, DAVID. The frame of art: fictions of aesthetic experience, 1750–1815. Baltimore, MD; London: Johns Hopkins UP, 2005. pp. 259. (Parallax.)

8029. MARTINY, ERIK. 'There I could never be a boy': Frank O'Hara and the cult of the child. *See* **18601**.

8030. MASON, NICHOLAS. 'The quack has become God': puffery, print, and the 'death' of literature in Romantic-era Britain. *See* **1271**.

8031. MAY, JAMES E. Scribleriana transferred: manuscripts and books at auction and in dealer's catalogues, 2002–2003. Scriblerian (37:2/38:1) 2005, 172–6.

8032. MOSKAL, JEANNE; WOODEN, SHANNON R. (eds). Teaching British women writers, 1750–1900. New York; Frankfurt: Lang, 2005. pp. ix, 235.

8033. MOULTON, IAN FREDERICK. Studies in early modern sexuality. *See* **5170.**

8034. MOWRY, MELISSA M. The bawdy politic in Stuart England, 1660–1714: political pornography and prostitution. *See* **6915.**

8035. MUDGE, BRADFORD K. (ed.). When flesh becomes word: an anthology of early eighteenth-century libertine literature. (Bibl. 2004, 8360.) Rev. by Elizabeth J. Scott-Baumann in TLS, 28 Jan. 2005, 13; by Joseph Pappa in Scriblerian (37:2 / 38:1) 2005, 160–1.

8036. MURPHY, JAMES H. Ireland: a social, cultural and literary history, 1791–1891. (Bibl. 2003, 7572.) Rev. by Sara L. Maurer in VS (47:3) 2005, 466–8.

8037. NASH, RICHARD. Wild Enlightenment: the borders of human identity in the eighteenth century. (Bibl. 2004, 8363.) Rev. by James A. Steintrager in ECS (38:4) 2005, 681–6; by Peter Hulme in ECF (17:2) 2005, 276–8.

8038. NUSSBAUM, FELICITY A. The limits of the human: fictions of anomaly, race, and gender in the long eighteenth century. (Bibl. 2004, 8366.) Rev. by James A. Steintrager in ECS (38:4) 2004, 681–6; by Caroline Breashears in Scriblerian (37:2 / 38:1) 2005, 154–5.

8039. —— (ed.). The global eighteenth century. Baltimore, MD; London: Johns Hopkins UP, 2003. pp. xiv, 385. Rev. by Kathleen Wilson in JBS (44:1) 2005, 194–203; by James Thompson in SAtlR (70:1) 2005, 196–8; by Matthew Dimmock in MLR (100:3) 2005, 751.

8040. OSSELTON, N. E. Bishop Lowth converted: an English grammar for Catholics in the late eighteenth century. *See* **1428.**

8041. PAGE, JUDITH W. Imperfect sympathies: Jews and Judaism in British Romantic literature and culture. *See* **9371.**

8042. PARKER, FRED. Scepticism and literature: an essay on Pope, Hume, Sterne, and Johnson. (Bibl. 2004, 9138.) Rev. by John P. Zomchick in MLR (100:3) 2005, 785–7; by Freya Johnston in CamQ (34:2) 2005, 196–9.

8043. PEACOCK, JAMES. Who was John Bartram? Literary and epistolary representations of the Quaker. Symbiosis (9:1) 2005, 29–43.

8044. PERRY, RUTH. Novel relations: the transformation of kinship in English literature and culture, 1748–1818. (Bibl. 2004, 8374.) Rev. by Norma Clarke in TLS, 17 June 2005, 24; by Catherine Gallagher in LRB (27:21) 2005, 26–7.

8045. PIRONON, JEAN; WAGNER, JACQUES (eds). Formes littéraires du théologico-politique de la Renaissance au XVIIIe siècle: Angleterre et Europe: actes du colloque international, 19–21 septembre 2002. (Bibl. 2004, 8380.) Rev. by Alexis Tadié in RLC (79:1) 2005, 95–6.

8046. PITCHER, EDWARD W. R. (comp.). The *New American Magazine* (Woodbridge, New Jersey, January 1758 – March 1760): an annotated catalogue of the literary contents with an appendix on *The Instructor* (New York, March 6 – May 10, 1755). *See* **1307.**

8047. PORTER, ROY. Flesh in the age of reason. Foreword by Simon Schama. (Bibl. 2004, 8709.) Rev. by Arthur J. Weitzman in Scriblerian (37:2/38:1) 2005, 159–60.

8048. PRICKETT, STEPHEN. Narrative, religion, and science: fundamentalism *versus* irony, 1700–1999. (Bibl. 2004, 8386.) Rev. by Eric Ziolkowski in JR (83:3) 2003, 507–9.

8049. PROCHÁZKA, MARTIN; HRBATA, ZDENĚK. Romantismus a romantismy: pojmy, proudy, kontexty. (Romanticism and romanticisms: concepts, currents, contexts.) *See* 9386.

8050. PUNTER, DAVID; BYRON, GLENNIS. The gothic. (Bibl. 2004, 8387.) Rev. by Jerrold E. Hogle in GothS (6:2) 2004, 252–5.

8051. REGAN, STEPHEN (ed.). Irish writing: an anthology of Irish literature in English 1789–1939. Oxford; New York: OUP, 2004. pp. lxiv, 549. (Oxford world's classics.) Rev. by Claude Fierobe in EtIr (30:1) 2005, 220.

8052. REID, CHRISTOPHER. Speaking candidly: rhetoric, politics, and the meaning of candour in the later eighteenth century. BJECS (28:1) 2005, 67–82.

8053. REMAK, HENRY H. H. West European Romanticism: definition and scope. *See* 9392.

8054. REYNOLDS, MARGARET. The Sappho history. (Bibl. 2004, 8392.) Rev. by Alison Chapman in MLR (100:3) 2005, 898–9.

8055. RIBEIRO, ALVARO, *et al.* The Tinker legacy: the Yale 'school' of eighteenth-century studies. *See* 14983.

8056. RICHARDSON, ALAN. Reading practices. *In* (pp. 397–405) 10060.

8057. RICHETTI, JOHN. The Cambridge history of English literature, 1660–1780. *See* 6931.

8058. RINTOUL, SUZANNE. Gothic anxieties: struggling with a definition. *See* 21108.

8059. RIZZO, BETTY. Male oratory and female prate: 'then hush and be an angel quite'. *See* 3197.

8060. ROBERTSON, JOHN. Women and Enlightenment: a historiographical conclusion. *In* (pp. 692–704) 8016.

8061. ROBINSON, ALAN. Imagining London, 1770–1900. (Bibl. 2004, 8393.) Rev. by Eveline Kilian in JSBC (12:1) 2005, 86–8; by Jeremy Tambling in Dickensian (101:1) 2005, 64–6.

8062. ROE, NICHOLAS (ed.). Romanticism: an Oxford guide. *See* 9399.

8063. ROUND, PHILLIP H. The return of the native: recent scholarship in the literature of Christianization and contact. *See* 6932.

8064. RUDMAN, JOSEPH. Unediting, de-editing, and editing in non-traditional authorship attribution studies: with an emphasis on the canon of Daniel Defoe. *See* 8542.

8065. RUWE, DONELLE (ed.). Culturing the child, 1690–1914: essays in memory of Mitzi Myers. *See* 8171.

8066. SCHELLENBERG, BETTY A. The professionalization of women writers in eighteenth-century Britain. Cambridge; New York: CUP, 2005. pp. x, 250. Rev. by Emily Hodgson Anderson in HLQ (68:4) 2005, 685–90.

8067. SCRIVENER, MICHAEL. Literature and politics. *In* (pp. 43–60) **8014.**

8068. SHA, RICHARD C. Romanticism and the sciences of perversion. *See* **9412.**

8069. SOPER, KATE. Feminism and Enlightenment legacies. *In* (pp. 705–15) **8016.**

8070. SPACKS, PATRICIA MEYER. Privacy: concealing the eighteenth-century self. (Bibl. 2004, 8409.) Rev. by Clare Brant in MLR (100:4) 2005, 1093–5; by David Oakleaf in ECF (18:1) 2005, 134–6; by Jacqueline Pearson in MP (103:1) 2005, 131–4.

8071. SPENCER, JANE. Literary relations: kinship and the canon 1660–1830. *See* **6944.**

8072. STAUFFER, ANDREW M. Anger, revolution, and Romanticism. *See* **9419.**

8073. STAVES, SUSAN. Gendering texts: 'the abuse of title pages': men writing as women. *In* (pp. 162–82) **6958.**

8074. STEVENS, LAURA M. The poor Indians: British missionaries, Native Americans, and Colonial sensibility. *See* **6947.**

8075. STRACHAN, JOHN (gen. ed.). British satire: vol. 4, Gifford and the Della Cruscans. Ed. by John Strachan. *See* **11060.**

8076. THORN, JENNIFER (ed.). Writing British infanticide: child-murder, gender, and print, 1722–1859. (Bibl. 2003, 7610.) Rev. by Charlotte Sussman in NineL (59:3) 2004, 404–8; by Deborah A. Symonds in ECF (17:3) 2005, 558–62.

8077. TOBIN, BETH FOWKES. Colonizing nature: the tropics in British arts and letters, 1760–1820. Philadelphia: Pennsylvania UP, 2005. pp. xvi, 255. Rev. by Kitty Scoular Datta in TLS, 10 June 2005, 11.

8078. TOBIN, ROBERT D. The emancipation of the flesh: the legacy of Romanticism in the homosexual rights movement. RomNet (36/37) 2004/05.

8079. TREADWELL, JAMES. Autobiographical writing and British literature, 1783–1834. Oxford; New York: OUP, 2005. pp. xi, 256. Rev. by David Womersley in TLS, 22 July 2005, 8–9.

8080. TRILL, SUZANNE. Early modern women's writing in the Edinburgh Archives, c.1550–1740: a preliminary checklist. *In* (pp. 201–25) **3754.**

8081. UNDERWOOD, TED. The work of the sun: literature, science, and political economy, 1760–1860. Basingstoke; New York: Palgrave Macmillan, 2005. pp. x, 240.

8082. VALDÉS MIYARES, J. RUBÉN. The prejudices of education: educational aspects of the Scottish Enlightenment. Atl (27:2) 2005, 101–18.

8083. VICINUS, MARTHA. Intimate friends: women who loved women, 1778–1928. Chicago, IL; London: Chicago UP, 2004. pp. xxxii, 314. Rev. by Katherine Binhammer in VicR (30:2) 2004, 109–13; by Laura Doan in NineL (59:4) 2005, 526–9; by Caroline Gonda in TSWL (24:1) 2005, 157–9.

8084. VON SNEIDERN, MAJA-LISA. Savage indignation: colonial discourse from Milton to Swift. *See* **6957.**

8085. WALL, CYNTHIA (ed.). A concise companion to the Restoration and eighteenth century. *See* **6958.**

8086. WHITE, R. S.   Natural rights and the birth of Romanticism in the 1790s. Basingstoke; New York: Palgrave Macmillan, 2005. pp. x, 277.

8087. WILLIAMS, ABIGAIL.   Patronage and Whig literary culture in the early eighteenth century. *In* (pp. 149–72) **8091.**

8088. WILPUTTE, EARLA A.   Parody in Eliza Haywood's *A Letter from H— G—g, Esq*. See **8712.**

8089. WOMERSLEY, DAVID.   Introduction. *In* (pp. 9–26) **8091.**

8090. —— Revising the life. TLS, 22 July 2005, 8–9 (review-article). (Autobiographical literature.)

8091. —— (ed.); BULLARD, PADDY; WILLIAMS, ABIGAIL (asst eds).   'Cultures of Whiggism': new essays on English literature and culture in the long eighteenth century. Newark: Delaware UP, 2005. pp. 370.

8092. WRIGHT, EAMON.   British women writers and race, 1788–1818: narrations of modernity. Basingstoke; New York: Palgrave Macmillan, 2005. pp. xvii, 205.

8093. ZAGARRI, ROSEMARIE.   American women's rights before Seneca Falls. *In* (pp. 667–91) **8016.**

DRAMA AND THE THEATRE

8094. ARENS, KATHERINE.   Castrati and the masquerade of the eighteenth century: *Farinelli* and Sitwell. 1650–1850 (9) 2003, 237–68.

8095. BIRD, ALAN.   The theatre at Wynnstay: some further observations. TN (59:1) 2005, 53–5.

8096. BRATTON, JACKY.   New readings in theatre history. (Bibl. 2004, 8433.) Rev. by Richard Schoch in NineL (59:4) 2005, 531–3; by David Mayer in TheatreS (46:1) 2005, 144–7; by Jan McDonald in TRI (30:1) 2005, 90–1; by Susan Bennett in NCT (32:1) 2005, 90–3.

8097. BURKE, HELEN M.   Riotous performances: the struggle for hegemony in the Irish theatre, 1712–1784. (Bibl. 2004, 8435.) Rev. by Susan M. Martin in Scriblerian (37:2 /38:1) 2005, 148–9; by John Greene in YES (35) 2005, 324–5.

8098. CALVI, LISANNA.   Kingship and tragedy (1660–1715). See **6979.**

8099. COX, JEFFREY N.; GAMER, MICHAEL (eds).   The Broadview anthology of Romantic drama. See **9462.**

8100. DONOHUE, JOSEPH (ed.).   The Cambridge history of British theatre: vol. 2, 1660 to 1895. See **6988.**

8101. DURING, SIMON.   'The temple lives': the Lyceum and Romantic show business. *In* (pp. 204–24) **9217.**

8102. EDWARDS, ADRIAN.   Provincial theatre in Britain, 1773–1808: the Burney playbills examined. TN (57:3) 2003, 136–42.

8103. FITZGERALD-HUME, ELIZABETH.   Rights and riots: footmen's riots at Drury Lane 1737. TN (59:1) 2005, 41–52.

8104. GARDNER, VIV.   *The Diary of an Actress*: an introduction. NCT (32:1) 2005, 2–14. (Documents of performance.)

8105. HARRIS, SUSAN CANNON.   Outside the box: the female spectator, *The Fair Penitent*, and the Kelly Riots of 1747. See **8977.**

8106. LAGAE, DENIS. *'Here is a sight indeed'*: l'ostension dans la comédie de la Restauration (1660–1700). *See* **7019.**

8107. MILHOUS, JUDITH; HUME, ROBERT D. Arthur Bedford's (?) *A Serious Advertisement* (1705) and the early history of theatre in Bristol. TN (57:1) 2003, 2–10.

8108. NATHANS, HEATHER S. Early American theatre from the Revolution to Thomas Jefferson: into the hands of the people. (Bibl. 2004, 8448.) Rev. by Bruce McConachie in NCT (31:2) 2004, 85–9; by Odai Johnson in TJ (57:1) 2005, 133–4; by Jeffrey H. Richards in SAtlR (70:3) 2005, 151–4.

8109. NUSSBAUM, FELICITY. Actresses and the economics of celebrity, 1700–1800. *In* (pp. 148–68) **3985.**

8110. O'BRIEN, JOHN. Drama: genre, gender, theater. *In* (pp. 183–201) **6958.**

8111. ROGERS, REBECCA. How Scottish was 'the Scottish play'? *Macbeth's* national identity in the eighteenth century. *In* (pp. 104–23) **6561.**

8112. ROUYER-DANEY, MARIE-CLAIRE. Quelle légitimité pour la 'petite comédie' georgienne? EA (58:3) 2005, 308–22.

8113. RUSSELL, GILLIAN. Theatrical culture. *In* (pp. 100–18) **8014.**

8114. SAGGINI, FRANCESCA. Memories beyond the pale: the eighteenth-century actress between stage and closet. RECTR (19:1) 2004, 43–63.

8115. SHEVELOW, KATHRYN. Charlotte: being a true account of an actress's flamboyant adventures in eighteenth-century London's wild and wicked theatrical world. *See* **8465.**

8116. WANKO, CHERYL. Roles of authority: thespian biography and celebrity in eighteenth-century Britain. *See* **8273.**

8117. WEST, SHEARER. Siddons, celebrity and regality: portraiture and the body of the ageing actress. *In* (pp. 191–213) **3985.**

FICTION

8118. AUGUSTIN, SABINE. Eighteenth-century female voices: education and the novel. New York; Frankfurt: Lang, 2005. pp. ix, 231. (Trierer Studien zur Literatur, 42.)

8119. BACKSCHEIDER, PAULA R.; INGRASSIA, CATHERINE (eds). A companion to the eighteenth-century English novel and culture. Oxford; Malden, MA: Blackwell, 2005. pp. xiii, 550. (Blackwell companions to literature and culture, 30.)

8120. BALLASTER, ROS. Performing *Roxane*: the Oriental woman as the sign of luxury in eighteenth-century fictions. *In* (pp. 165–77) **7941.**

8121. BARCHAS, JANINE. Graphic design, print culture, and the eighteenth-century novel. (Bibl. 2004, 8456.) Rev. by Richard Quaintance in WI (20:4) 2004, 323; by Paul J. Korshin in Library (6:1) 2005, 95–7.

8122. BENEDICT, BARBARA. Identity and quest: experimental experience and the eighteenth-century novel. ECN (4) 2004, 1–38.

8123. BLACKWELL, MARK R. The gothic: moving in the world of novels. *In* (pp. 144–61) **6958.**

8124. BONY, ALAIN.   Leonora, Lydia et les autres: étude sur le (nouveau) roman anglais du XVIIIe siècle. Lyons: Presses Universitaires de Lyon, 2004. pp. 394. (Champ anglophone.) Rev. by Madeleine Descargues-Grant in EA (58:3) 2005, 359–61.

8125. BROWN, MARSHALL.   The gothic text. Stanford, CA: Stanford UP, 2005. pp. xx, 111, 280. Rev. by C. C. Wharram in GothS (7:2) 2005, 203–5.

8126. COTTOM, DANIEL.   I think; therefore, I am Heathcliff. ELH (70:4) 2003, 1067–88.

8127. DAVIDSON, CATHY N.   Revolution and the word: the rise of the novel in America. Oxford; New York: OUP, 2004. pp. xv, 458.

8128. DICKIE, SIMON.   *Joseph Andrews* and the great laughter debate. *See* **8606**.

8129. FITZGERALD, LAUREN.   Female gothic and the institutionalization of Gothic Studies. *See* **14783**.

8130. ——   The gothic villain and the vilification of the plagiarist: the case of *The Castle Spectre*. *See* **8794**.

8131. FRANK, FREDERICK S.   Guide to the gothic III: an annotated bibliography of criticism, 1994–2003: vol. I. Lanham, MD; London: Scarecrow Press, 2005. pp. xviii, 583. Rev. by Edward J. Ingebretsen in GothS (7:2) 2005, 207–10.

8132. GEVIRTZ, KAREN BLOOM.   Life after death: widows and the English novel. Newark: Delaware UP, 2005. pp. 218.

8133. GRIFFIN, ROBERT J.   The text in motion: eighteenth-century *Roxana*s. *See* **8517**.

8134. HAGGERTY, GEORGE.   The horrors of Catholicism: religion and sexuality in gothic fiction. RomNet (36/37) 2004/05.

8135. HORNER, AVRIL (ed.).   European gothic: a spirited exchange, 1760–1960. (Bibl. 2004, 8474.) Rev. by Claude Fierobe in EtIr (28:1) 2003, 202–3; by Diane Long Hoeveler in WordsC (35:4) 2004, 179–82.

8136. HUDSON, NICHOLAS.   Social rank, 'the rise of the novel', and Whig histories of eighteenth-century fiction. ECF (17:4) 2005, 563–98.

8137. JOHNSON, NANCY E.   The English Jacobin novel on rights, property, and the law: critiquing the contract. Basingstoke; New York: Palgrave Macmillan, 2004. pp. 215.

8138. KILFEATHER, SIOBHÁN.   Terrific register: the gothicization of atrocity in Irish Romanticism. *See* **11656**.

8139. LOGAN, LISA M.   'The ladies in particular': constructions of femininity in the *Gentlemen and Ladies Town and Country Magazine* and the *Lady's Magazine; and Repository of Entertaining Knowledge*. *In* (pp. 277–306) **1244**.

8140. LYNCH, DEIDRE SHAUNA.   The novel: novels in the world of moving goods. *In* (pp. 121–43) **6958**.

8141. MCEVOY, EMMA.   'Really, though secretly, a Papist': G. K. Chesterton's and John Meade Falkner's rewritings of the gothic. *See* **15776**.

8142. MCMASTER, JULIET.   Reading the body in the eighteenth-century novel. (Bibl. 2004, 8481.) Rev. by Allan Ingram in MLR (100:2) 2005, 486–7; by Yael Shapira in PartA (3:1) 2005, 168–73.

8143. MEINER, CARSTEN. L'individualité romanesque au xviiie siècle: une lecture foucaldienne. ECF (18:1) 2005, 1–26.

8144. MULLAN, JOHN. Psychology. In (pp. 377–86) **10060**.

8145. NEILL, NATALIE. 'The trash with which the press now groans': *Northanger Abbey* and the gothic best sellers of the 1790s. See **10028**.

8146. O'BRIEN, KAREN. History and the novel in eighteenth-century Britain. HLQ (68:1/2) 2005, 397–413.

8147. PALMERI, FRANK. Satire, history, novel: narrative forms, 1665–1815. (Bibl. 2004, 8485.) Rev. by Vincent Carretta in Scriblerian (37:2 / 38:1) 2005, 109–11.

8148. POLLAK, ELLEN. Incest and the English novel, 1684–1814. (Bibl. 2004, 7322.) Rev. by Margaret Case Croskery in ECN (4) 2004, 244–9; by Alison Conway in ECF (17:3) 2005, 551–4; by Ros Ballaster in CLIO (34:4) 2005, 480–6; by William Donaghue in Scriblerian (37:2/38:1) 2005, 113–15.

8149. PRIOR, KAREN SWALLOW. Hannah More, the didactic tradition, and the rise of the English novel. See **8845**.

8150. RICHARDSON, LESLIE. Leaving her father's house: Astell, Locke, and Clarissa's body politic. See **7196**.

8151. SACHS, JONATHAN. From Roman to *roman*: the Jacobin novel and the Roman legacy in the 1790s. See **8703**.

8152. SAMUELS, SHIRLEY (ed.). A companion to American fiction, 1780–1865. Oxford; Malden, MA: Blackwell, 2004. pp. xv, 470.

8153. SHEVLIN, ELEANOR F. The titular claims of female surnames in eighteenth-century fiction. In (pp. 256–80) **6964**.

8154. STABLER, JANE. Literary influences. In (pp. 41–50) **10060**.

8155. STARR, G. GABRIELLE. Lyric generations: poetry and the novel in the long eighteenth century. (Bibl. 2004, 8493.) Rev. by Don Bialostosky in WordsC (35:4) 2004, 171–2; by Marshall Brown in MP (102:2) 2004, 271–5.

8156. THOMPSON, HELEN. Ingenuous subjection: compliance and power in the eighteenth-century domestic novel. Philadelphia: Pennsylvania UP, 2005. pp. 278.

8157. TIERNEY-HYNES, REBECCA. Shaftesbury's *Soliloquy*: authorship and the psychology of romance. See **8996**.

8158. TOWNSHEND, DALE. Gothic panoptics and the persistence of torturous enjoyment, 1764–1820. Genre (37:3/4) 2004, 395–432.

8159. WAGNER, TAMARA S. Longing: narratives of nostalgia in the British novel, 1740–1890. Lewisburg, PA: Bucknell UP, 2004. pp. 297.

8160. WATT, JAMES. Gothic. In (pp. 119–35) **8014**.

8161. WEYLER, KAREN A. Intricate relations: sexual and economic desire in American fiction, 1789–1814. Iowa City: Iowa UP, 2004. pp. x, 269. Rev. by Stephen Carl Arch in EAL (40:3) 2005, 561–4.

8162. WOOD, LISA. Modes of discipline: women, conservatism, and the novel after the French Revolution. (Bibl. 2004, 8496.) Rev. by Kate Williams in MLR (100:3) 2005, 790–1; by Marjean D. Purinton in ERR (16:3) 2005, 380–4.

8163. WRIGHT, ANGELA. 'To live the life of hopeless recollection': mourning and melancholia in female gothic, 1780–1800. GothS (6:1) 2004, 19–29.

8164. ZUNSHINE, LISA.   Bastards and foundlings: illegitimacy in eighteenth-century England. Columbus: Ohio State UP, 2005. pp. xi, 228.

8165. —— The spectral hospital: eighteenth-century philanthropy and the novel. ECL (29:1) 2005, 1–22.

LITERATURE FOR CHILDREN

8166. BOTTIGHEIMER, RUTH B.   The book on the bookseller's shelf and the book in the English child's hand. *In* (pp. 3–28) **8171.**

8167. BRIGGS, JULIA.   'Delightful task!': women, children, and reading in the mid-eighteenth century. *In* (pp. 67–82) **8171.**

8168. DAWSON, MUIR.   Two children's books illustrated by Bewick, with notes on printing from the original blocks. BC (54:3) 2005, 375–88.

8169. O'MALLEY, ANDREW.   The making of the modern child: children's literature and childhood in the late eighteenth century. London; New York: Routledge, 2003. pp. ix, 189. (Children's literature and culture, 28.) Rev. by Ruth B. Bottigheimer in ChildLit (32) 2004, 222–5.

8170. ROWE, KAREN E.   Virtue in the guise of vice: the making and unmaking of morality from fairy tale fantasy. *In* (pp. 29–66) **8171.**

8171. RUWE, DONELLE (ed.).   Culturing the child, 1690–1914: essays in memory of Mitzi Myers. Lanham, MD; London: Scarecrow Press for the Children's Literature Assn, 2005. pp. xiv, 266. Rev. by Marilynn Olson in CLAQ (30:3) 2005, 338–40.

POETRY

8172. ASHLEY, LEONARD R. N.; CONTI, CHRISTI.   An anonymous poem to Alexander Pope from South Carolina (1737). *See* **8870.**

8173. BACKSCHEIDER, PAULA R.   Eighteenth-century women poets and their poetry: inventing agency, inventing genre. Baltimore, MD; London: Johns Hopkins UP, 2005. pp. xvii, 514.

8174. BAINBRIDGE, SIMON.   British poetry and the Revolutionary and Napoleonic Wars: visions of conflict. (Bibl. 2004, 8501.) Rev. by Beth Darlington in SR (43:4) 2004, 667–70; by Michael Wiley in WordsC (35:4) 2004, 156–8; by Philip Shaw in BJ (32:2) 2004, 157–8; by Malcolm Kelsall in MLR (100:3) 2005, 795–6; by Steven Stryer in EC (55:2) 2005, 178–84.

8175. BELLORINI, MARIAGRAZIA.   'First follow Nature': riflessioni e note sulla semantica del giardino nella poesia e nella cultura inglese del Settecento. Milan: ISU Univ. Cattolica, 2004. pp. 122.

8176. CIAVOLELLA, MASSIMO; COLEMAN, PATRICK (eds).   Culture and authority in the baroque. *See* **5880.**

8177. CLYMER, LORNA.   Philosophical tours of the universe in British poetry, 1700–1729; or, The soaring muse. *In* (pp. 30–62) **5880.**

8178. CORP, EDWARD, *et al.*   A court in exile: the Stuarts in France, 1689–1718. *See* **7063.**

8179. CRAWFORD, RACHEL.   Forms of sublimity: the garden, the georgic, and the nation. *In* (pp. 226–46) **6958.**

8180. FANNING, CHRISTOPHER.   The Scriblerian sublime. *See* **8884.**

8181. GOODRIDGE, JOHN; KEEGAN, BRIDGET. Clare and the traditions of labouring-class verse. *In* (pp. 280–95) **8014**.

8182. HARVEY, A. D. Hyperion's cousins: epic poetry in the style of Milton, *c*.1818. *See* **11515**.

8183. HAUT, ASIA. Reading Flora: Erasmus Darwin's *The Botanic Garden*, Henry Fuseli's illustrations, and various literary responses. *See* **8497**.

8184. HUNTER, J. PAUL. Poetry: the poetry of occasions. *In* (pp. 202–25) **6958**.

8185. JARVIS, SIMON. Mock as screen and optic. *See* **8890**.

8186. JUNG, SANDRO. Collins's *Ode to Evening*. *See* **8480**.

8187. KEEGAN, BRIDGET. Romantic labouring-class pastoral as eco-queer camp. *See* **9697**.

8188. KEITH, JENNIFER. The formal challenges of antislavery poetry. StudECC (34) 2005, 97–124.

8189. —— Poetry and the feminine from Behn to Cowper. *See* **7071**.

8190. KING, KATHRYN R. Effeminate pacifists and war-mongering women: thoughts on war and peace in the long eighteenth century. 1650–1850 (9) 2003, 3–21.

8191. KORD, SUSANNE. Women peasant poets in eighteenth-century England, Scotland, and Germany: milkmaids on Parnassus. (Bibl. 2004, 8523.) Rev. by Donna Landry in ECS (38:3) 2005, 535–8.

8192. LANDRY, DONNA. 'But were they any good?': milkmaids on Parnassus; or, Political aesthetics. ECS (38:3) 2005, 535–8 (review-article).

8193. LAVOIE, CHANTEL. *Poems by Eminent Ladies*: the encyclopedic anthology of 1755. *See* **5319**.

8194. MCNEIL, DAVID. Collage and social theories: an examination of Bowles's 'Medley' prints of the 1720 South Sea Bubble. WI (20:4) 2004, 283–98.

8195. MEE, JON. Blake and the poetics of Enthusiasm. *In* (pp. 194–210) **8014**.

8196. MILLER, CHRISTOPHER. Staying out late: Anne Finch's poetics of evening. *See* **9126**.

8197. PETERSON, LELAND D. A letter to the editor on the occasion of his correspondence about Swift's *The Beasts' Confession to the Priest*. *See* **9082**.

8198. PITTOCK, MURRAY G. H. Robert Fergusson and the Romantic ode. *See* **8601**.

8199. RENNIE, NEIL. The Point Venus 'scene', Tahiti, 14 May 1769. *In* (pp. 239–50) **8039**.

8200. RICHARDSON, JOHN. Modern warfare in early eighteenth-century poetry. SELit (45:3) 2005, 557–77.

8201. RUMBOLD, VALERIE; MCGEARY, THOMAS. *Folly*, session poems, and the preparations for Pope's *Dunciad*s. *See* **8626**.

8202. SAGLIA, DIEGO. The aesthetics of the present: commerce, empire and technology in late eighteenth-century women's poetry. *See* **8988**.

8203. STABILE, SUSAN M. Memory's daughters: the material culture of remembrance in eighteenth-century America. Ithaca, NY; London: Cornell UP, 2004. pp. xiii, 284. Rev. by Martin Brückner in EAL (40:2) 2005, 387–90;

by Angela Vietto in Legacy (22:1) 2005, 71–2; by Gayle R. Davis in JAH (92:3) 2005, 960–1.

8204. STEEDMAN, CAROLYN.   Poetical maids and cooks who wrote. ECS (39:1) 2005, 1–27.

8205. STRACHAN, JOHN (gen. ed.).   British satire: vol. 1, Collected satires i: shorter satires. Ed. by Nicholas Mason. London; Brookfield, VT: Pickering & Chatto, 2003. pp. xxxii, 313. Rev. by Marcus Wood in WordsC (35:4) 2004, 162–4; by Bernard Beatty in BJ (32:2) 2004, 153–5.

8206. —— British satire: vol. 2, Collected satires ii: extracts from longer satires. Ed. by David Walker. London; Brookfield, VT: Pickering & Chatto, 2003. pp. xviii, 310. Rev. by Marcus Wood in WordsC (35:4) 2004, 162–4; by Bernard Beatty in BJ (32:2) 2005, 153–5.

8207. —— British satire: vol. 3, Collected satires iii: complete longer satires. Ed. by Benjamin Colbert. London; Brookfield, VT: Pickering & Chatto, 2003. pp. xviii, 463. Rev. by Marcus Wood in WordsC (35:4) 2003, 162–4; by Bernard Beatty in BJ (32:2) 2004, 153–5.

8208. TERRY, RICHARD.   Pope and plagiarism. See **8912**.

8209. THORMÄHLEN, MARIANNE.   Anne Brontë's *Sacred Harmony*: a discovery. See **10147**.

8210. TWOMBLY, DAVID J.   Newtonian schemes: an unknown poetic satire from 1728. BJECS (28:2) 2005, 251–72.

8211. WHITE, JONATHAN.   The 'slow but sure Poyson': the representation of gin and its drinkers, 1736–1751. See **8257**.

8212. WILLIAMS, ABIGAIL.   Poetry and the creation of a Whig literary culture, 1681–1714. See **7083**.

PROSE

8213. BANDER, ELAINE.   From interior to exterior worlds: Anne Elliot goes Hollywood. See **9945**.

8214. BANNET, EVE TAVOR.   Empire of letters: letter manuals and transatlantic correspondence, 1680–1820. See **7089**.

8215. —— 'Secret history'; or, Talebearing inside and outside the secretorie. See **7090**.

8216. BERTELSEN, LARS KIEL.   The Claude glass: a modern metaphor between word and image. Trans. by Stacey M. Cozart. See **8865**.

8217. BLAND, CAROLINE; CROSS, MÁIRE (eds).   Gender and politics in the age of letter-writing, 1750–2000. Aldershot; Burlington, VT: Ashgate, 2003. pp. ix, 280.

8218. BRANT, CLARE.   'The tribunal of the public': eighteenth-century letters and the politics of vindication. *In* (pp. 15–28) **8217**.

8219. BROWN, STEPHEN.   James Tytler's misadventures in the late eighteenth-century Edinburgh book trade. *In* (pp. 47–63) **880**.

8220. BULLARD, PADDY.   The latitude of Whiggism: Tillotson, Burnet, and Lord William Russell in Whig historiography, 1675–1775. *In* (pp. 299–329) **8091**.

8221. CARROLL, WILLIAM C.   'Two truths are told': afterlives and histories of Macbeths. *See* **6536**.

8222. CESERANI, GIOVANNA.   Narrative, interpretation, and plagiarism in Mr Robertson's 1778 *History of Ancient Greece*. JHI (66:3) 2005, 413–36.

8223. CHAMPION, JUSTIN.   '*Anglia libera*': Commonwealth politics in the early years of George I. *In* (pp. 86–107) **8091**.

8224. CHERNOCK, ARIANNE.   Extending the 'right of election': men's arguments for women's political representation in late Enlightenment Britain. *In* (pp. 587–609) **8016**.

8225. COX, JOHN D.   Traveling south: travel narratives and the construction of American identity. Athens; London: Georgia UP, 2005. pp. 252.

8226. ELIAS, A. C., JR.   Consolation for the Christian: a new sermon by Matthew Pilkington. SwSt (20) 2005, 132–42.

8227. GELLES, EDITH B.   'Remember the ladies': politics in the letters of Abigail Adams. *In* (pp. 67–75) **8217**.

8228. HELENIAK, KATHRYN MOORE.   An English gentleman's encounter with Islamic architecture: Henry Swinburne's *Travels through Spain* (1779). BJECS (28:2) 2005, 181–200.

8229. HIGGINS, IAN.   Remarks on *Cato's Letters*. *In* (pp. 127–46) **8091**.

8230. HOWE, JOHN R.   Language and political meaning in Revolutionary America. Amherst: Massachusetts UP, 2004. pp. xii, 281. Rev. by Peter S. Onuf in JAH (91:4) 2005, 1428–9; by Jacquelyn C. Miller in JSH (71:3) 2005, 669–70.

8231. HYARD, ALEXANDRA.   Adam Smith et le 'républicanisme'. EREA (1:2) 2003, 87–96.

8232. ITALIA, IONA.   The rise of literary journalism in the eighteenth century: anxious employment. London; New York: Routledge, 2005. pp. x, 248. (Routledge studies in eighteenth-century literature, 3.)

8233. KRENTZ, CHRISTOPHER.   Duncan Campbell and the discourses of deafness. *See* **8524**.

8234. LEMAY, J. A. LEO.   Deborah Franklin, Lord Loudoun, and Franklin's *Autobiography*. *See* **8635**.

8235. LOGAN, LISA M.   'Dear matron —': constructions of women in eighteenth-century American periodical columns. *See* **1260**.

8236. MCKENZIE, ANDREA.   Martyrs in low life? Dying 'game' in Augustan England. JBS (42:2) 2003, 167–205.

8237. MILHOUS, JUDITH; HUME, ROBERT D.   Arthur Bedford's (?) *A Serious Advertisement* (1705) and the early history of theatre in Bristol. *See* **8107**.

8238. MINKEMA, KENNETH P.; STOUT, HARRY S.   The Edwardsean tradition and the anti-slavery debate, 1740–1865. *See* **8577**.

8239. MOODY, JOYCELYN.   Naming and proclaiming the self: Black feminist literary history-making. *In* (pp. 107–20) **2457**.

8240. NAYAR, PRAMOD K.   Marvelous excesses: English travel writing and India, 1608–1727. *See* **7135**.

8241. O'BRIEN, KAREN.   History and the novel in eighteenth-century Britain. *See* **8146**.

8242. OGBORN, MILES; WITHERS, CHARLES W. J.   Travel, trade, and empire: knowing other places, 1660–1800. *In* (pp. 13–35) **6958**.

8243. REID, CHAD.   'Widely read by American patriots': the *New-York Weekly Journal* and the influence of *Cato's Letters* on Colonial America. *In* (pp. 109–42) **1244**.

8244. REID, CHRISTOPHER.   Character construction in the eighteenth-century House of Commons: evidence from the Cavendish diary (1768–74). *See* **2447**.

8245. REID, JENNIFER I. M.   Worse than beasts: an anatomy of melancholy and the literature of travel in seventeenth- and eighteenth-century England. *See* **7290**.

8246. RENDALL, JANE.   'Friends of liberty & virtue': women Radicals and transatlantic correspondence, 1789–1848. *In* (pp. 77–92) **8217**.

8247. RIX, ROBERT (ed.).   A political dictionary explaining the true meaning of words. Aldershot: Ashgate Variorum, 2004. pp. xxxi, 114.

8248. SAYRE, ROBERT.   On the borders of the adventure novel: narratives of 18th-century travel in Indian territory. EREA (3:1) 2005, 10–20.

8249. SEBASTIANI, SILVIA.   'Race', women and progress in the Scottish Enlightenment. *In* (pp. 75–96) **8016**.

8250. SHERMAN, SANDRA.   Impotence and capital: the debate over imported beverages in the seventeenth and eighteenth centuries. *See* **7152**.

8251. SMITH, TANIA SONA.   *The Lady's Rhetorick* (1707): the tip of the iceberg of women's rhetorical education in Enlightenment France and Britain. Rhetorica (22:4) 2004, 349–73.

8252. TIEKEN-BOON VAN OSTADE, INGRID.   Eighteenth-century English letters: in search of the vernacular. LFil (21) 2005, 113–46.

8253. —— Of social networks and linguistic influence: the language of Robert Lowth and his correspondents. *See* **3206**.

8254. VAN STRIEN, KEES.   Daniel Bellamy Jr, parish priest and Shandean traveller. EngS (84:6) 2003, 521–9.

8255. WHELAN, TIMOTHY.   'I have *confessed myself a devil*': Crabb Robinson's confrontation with Robert Hall, 1798–1800. *See* **11849**.

8256. WHITE, DANIEL E.   'With Mrs Barbauld it is different': Dissenting heritage and the devotional taste. *In* (pp. 474–92) **8016**.

8257. WHITE, JONATHAN.   The 'slow but sure Poyson': the representation of gin and its drinkers, 1736–1751. JBS (42:1) 2003, 35–64.

BIOGRAPHY AND AUTOBIOGRAPHY

8258. ANDREWS, WILLIAM L. (gen. ed.).   North Carolina slave narratives: the lives of Moses Roper, Lunsford Lane, Moses Grandy & Thomas H. Jones. Ed. by David A. Davis, *et al.* Chapel Hill; London: North Carolina UP, 2003. pp. 279. (John Hope Franklin series in African American history and culture.) Rev. by Mary Jo Festle in JSH (71:1) 2005, 153–4.

8259. BAIESI, SERENA (ed.).   Pioniere in Australia: diari, lettere memoriali del periodo coloniale 1770–1850. Naples: Liguori, 2005. pp. 216.

8260. Booy, David (ed.). Autobiographical writings by early Quaker women. *See* **7164**.

8261. Breashears, Caroline. Scandalous categories: classifying the memoirs of unconventional women. PQ (82:2) 2003, 187–212.

8262. Colley, Linda. The narrative of Elizabeth Marsh: Barbary, sex, and power. *In* (pp. 138–50) **8039**.

8263. Harris, Jennifer. Seeing the light: re-reading James Albert Ukawsaw Gronniosaw. ELN (42:4) 2005, 43–57.

8264. Hindmarsh, D. Bruce. The Evangelical conversion narrative: spiritual autobiography in early modern England. Oxford; New York: OUP, 2005. pp. x, 384.

8265. Jones, Vivien. Luxury, satire and prostitute narratives. *In* (pp. 178–89) **7941**.

8266. Junod, Karen. Drawing pictures in words: the anecdote as spatial form in biographies of Hogarth. SPELL (17) 2005, 119–34.

8267. Lawson-Pebbles, Robert. Style wars: the problems of writing military autobiography in the eighteenth century. *In* (pp. 61–80) **14645**.

8268. May, Cedrick. John Marrant and the narrative construction of an early Black Methodist evangelical. AAR (38:4) 2004, 553–70.

8269. Mullan, David George. Scottish women's religious narrative, 1660–1720: constructing the evangelical self. *In* (pp. 178–91) **3754**.

8270. Pierce, Yolanda. Hell without fires: slavery, Christianity, and the antebellum spiritual narrative. Foreword by Stephen W. Angell and Anthony B. Pinn. *See* **9820**.

8271. Porterfield, Amanda. American religious biography. RAC (15:2) 2005, 245–53 (review-article).

8272. Wagner, Corinna. Loyalist propaganda and the scandalous life of Tom Paine: 'Hypocritical monster!' *See* **8855**.

8273. Wanko, Cheryl. Roles of authority: thespian biography and celebrity in eighteenth-century Britain. Lubbock: Texas Tech UP, 2003. pp. ix, 258. Rev. by Shearer West in Biography (27:3) 2004, 609–11; by Calhoun Winton in Albion (36:2) 2004, 310–11; by John O'Brien in Scriblerian (37:2/38:1) 2005, 146–7.

RELATED STUDIES

8274. Allan, David. The Scottish Enlightenment and the politics of provincial culture: the Perth Literary and Antiquarian Society, *ca* 1784–1790. ECL (27:3) 2003, 1–30.

8275. Black, Jeremy. A subject for taste: culture in eighteenth-century England. London: Hambledon & London, 2005. pp. xix, 272, (plates) 8. Rev. by Michael Caines in TLS, 23 Sept. 2005, 31.

8276. Dawson, Deidre; Morère, Pierre (eds). Scotland and France in the Enlightenment. Lewisburg, PA: Bucknell UP; London: Assoc. UPs, 2004. pp. 348. (Studies in eighteenth-century Scotland.) Rev. by Thomas Ahnert in BJECS (28:2) 2005, 292–3.

8277. DOWNIE, J. A.   Public and private: the myth of the bourgeois public sphere. *In* (pp. 58–79) **6958**.

8278. EGLIN, JOHN.   The imaginary autocrat: Beau Nash and the invention of Bath. London: Profile, 2005. pp. xii, 292. Rev. by E. S. Turner in LRB (27:14) 2004, 30–1; by Timothy Mowl in TLS, 8 July 2005, 32.

8279. FINN, MARGOT C.   The character of credit: personal debt in English culture, 1740–1914. Cambridge; New York: CUP, 2003. pp. xii, 362. (Cambridge social and cultural histories, 1.) Rev. by Deborah Valenze in JBS (44:2) 2005, 378–80; by Paul Johnson in JVC (10:2) 2005, 309–13; by Susan Mitchell Sommers in Historian (67:2) 2005, 351–2.

8280. GITELMAN, LISA; PINGREE, GEOFFREY B. (eds).   New media 1740–1915. Cambridge, MA; London: MIT Press, 2003. pp. xxxiii, 271. (Media in transition.) Rev. by Andrew Dewdney in EJES (9:2) 2005, 209–14; by Richard Menke in VS (48:1) 2005, 201–3.

8281. HARVEY, KAREN.   The history of masculinity, *circa* 1650–1800. *See* **7177**.

8282. HOOCK, HOLGER.   The king's artists: the Royal Academy of Arts and the politics of British culture, 1760–1840. Oxford; New York: OUP, 2003. pp. xvi, 367. (Oxford historical monographs.) Rev. by Morton D. Paley in Romanticism (10:2) 2004, 260–2.

8283. JUSTER, SUSAN.   Doomsayers: Anglo-American prophecy in the age of Revolution. Philadelphia: Pennsylvania UP, 2003. pp. xi, 276. (Early American studies.) Rev. by Colin Bonwick in JAStud (38:1) 2004, 147–8.

8284. LICHTENWALNER, SHAWNA THORP.   'In the eye of the light': ancient Druids and international influences. WordsC (36:1) 2005, 9–11.

8285. MOLINEUX, CATHERINE.   Hogarth's fashionable slaves: moral corruption in eighteenth-century London. ELH (72:2) 2005, 495–520.

8286. Ó BAOILL, COLM.   'Neither out nor in': Scottish Gaelic women poets 1650–1750. *In* (pp. 136–52) **3754**.

8287. SHERMAN, SANDRA.   *The Wealth of Nations* in the 1790s. StudECC (34) 2005, 81–96.

8288. SWEET, ROSEMARY.   Antiquaries: the discovery of the past in eighteenth-century Britain. London: Hambledon & London, 2004. pp. xxi, 473, (plates) 24. Rev. by R. C. Richardson in LitH (14:1) 2005, 93–5.

8289. TURNER, E. S.   Paddling in the gravy. LRB (27:14) 2005, 30–1 (review-article). (Richard 'Beau' Nash.)

8290. VAISEY, DAVID.   'Overtravelled with the librarie businesse'. *See* **7186**.

8291. WILLIAMS, HYWEL.   Francophone, anglophone and *gallois*-phone: the politics of cultural identity, 1763–2003. THSC (10) 2004, 133–43.

8292. BAR-YOSEF, EITAN.   The Holy Land in English culture 1799–1917: Palestine and the question of Orientalism. Oxford: Clarendon Press; New York: OUP, 2005. pp. ix, 319. (Oxford English monographs.)

LITERARY THEORY

8293. CHANDLER, ANNE.   The 'seeds of order and taste': Wollstonecraft, the *Analytical Review*, and critical idiom. *See* **9132**.

8294. GOLINELLI, GILBERTA.   The concept of genius and its metamorphoses in eighteenth-century English criticism. Textus (18:1) 2005, 189–204.

8295. JARVIS, SIMON.   Criticism, taste, aesthetics. *In* (pp. 24–42) **8014.**

8296. JONES, PETER (ed.).   Elements of criticism. By Henry Home, Lord Kames. Indianapolis, IN: Liberty Fund, 2005. pp. xxi, 821.

8297. LYNCH, JACK.   *King Lear* and 'the taste of the age', 1681–1838. *See* **6476.**

8298. MANOLESCU, BETH INNOCENTI.   Kames's legal career and writings as precedents for *Elements of Criticism*. Rhetorica (23:3) 2005, 239–59.

8299. PHILLIPS, MARK SALBER.   Criticism: literary history and literary historicism. *In* (pp. 247–65) **6958.**

8300. RITCHIE, FIONA.   Elizabeth Montagu: 'Shakespear's poor little critick'? *See* **8836.**

8301. SIMPSON, DAVID.   The limits of cosmopolitanism and the case for translation. *See* **9878.**

8302. TIERNEY-HYNES, REBECCA.   Shaftesbury's *Soliloquy*: authorship and the psychology of romance. *See* **8996.**

8303. TROLANDER, PAUL; TENGER, ZAYNEP.   Addison and the personality of the critic. *In* (pp. 175–99) **1285.**

8304. TROTT, NICOLA.   Wordsworth and the parodic school of criticism. *In* (pp. 71–97) **9305.**

8305. VAUGHT, JENNIFER.   Masculinity and affect in Shakespeare's *Winter's Tale*: men of feeling from the Renaissance through the Enlightenment. *See* **6836.**

8306. WATERS, MARY A.   British women writers and the profession of literary criticism, 1789–1832. Basingstoke; New York: Palgrave Macmillan, 2004. pp. viii, 225. (Palgrave studies in the Enlightenment, Romanticism and the cultures of print.)

AUTHORS

Hannah Adams (1755–1831)

8307. SCHMIDT, GARY D.   A passionate usefulness: the life and literary labors of Hannah Adams. (Bibl. 2004, 8617.) Rev. by Michael Everton in Legacy (22:2) 2005, 203–4.

John Adams (1704–1740)

8308. FRANKLIN, BENJAMIN, V.   The other John Adams, 1705–1740. (Bibl. 2003, 7836.) Rev. by John Gatta in MLR (100:3) 2005, 788–9.

Joseph Addison

8309. ALVAREZ, DAVID.   'Poetical cash': Joseph Addison, antiquarianism, and aesthetic value. ECS (38:3) 2005, 509–31.

8310. ASCARI, MAURIZIO.   The role of Addison's dream visions and Oriental tales in the nascent poetics of short fiction. Textus (18:1) 2005, 11–23.

8311. BANNET, EVE TAVOR.   'Epistolary commerce' in *The Spectator*. *In* (pp. 220–47) **1285.**

8312. BASTOS DA SILVA, JORGE.   Cato's ghosts: Pope, Addison, and opposition cultural politics. SLI (38:1) 2005, 95–115.

8313. BATCHELOR, ROBERT. Concealing the bounds: imagining the British nation through China. *In* (pp. 79–92) **8039.**

8314. BOWERS, TERENCE. Universalizing sociability: *The Spectator*, civic enfranchisement, and the rule(s) of the public sphere. *In* (pp. 150–74) **1285.**

8315. CAREY, BRYCCHAN. 'Accounts of savage nations': *The Spectator* and the Americas. *In* (pp. 129–49) **1285.**

8316. CONAWAY, CHARLES. 'Thou'rt the man': David Garrick, William Shakespeare, and the masculinization of the eighteenth-century stage. *See* **8645.**

8317. FERRARI, ROBERTA. In search of a new aesthetics: Addison, Fielding and the 'challenge' of travel writing. Textus (18:1) 2005, 77–92.

8318. GOODMAN, KEVIS. Georgic modernity and British Romanticism: poetry and the mediation of history. (Bibl. 2004, 8624.) Rev. by John Axcelson in WordsC (35:4) 2004, 170–1; by Emily Rohrbach in EREA (3:2) 2005.

8319. HAAN, ESTELLE. Twin Augustans: Addison, Hannes, and Horatian intertexts. NQ (52:3) 2005, 338–46.

8320. _____ *Vergilius redivivus*: studies in Joseph Addison's Latin poetry. Philadelphia, PA: American Philosophical Soc., 2005. pp. xiv, 210. (Transactions of the American Philosophical Soc., 95:2.)

8321. HENDERSON, CHRISTINE DUNN; YELLIN, MARK E. (eds). *Cato: a Tragedy and selected essays.* Foreword by Forrest McDonald. (Bibl. 2004, 8626.) Rev. by Melvyn New in Scriblerian (37:2 /38:1) 2005, 145–6.

8322. JUSTICE, GEORGE. *The Spectator* and distance education. *In* (pp. 265–99) **1285.**

8323. KLEIN, LAWRENCE E. Joseph Addison's Whiggism. *In* (pp. 108–26) **8091.**

8324. KRAFT, ELIZABETH. Wit and *The Spectator*'s ethics of desire. *See* **1250.**

8325. MCCREA, BRIAN. The virtue of repetition: Mr Spectator trains Benjamin Franklin. *In* (pp. 248–64) **1285.**

8326. MACKIE, ERIN SKYE. Being too positive about the public sphere. *In* (pp. 81–104) **1285.**

8327. MERRITT, JULIETTE. Originals, copies, and the iconography of femininity in *The Spectator*. *In* (pp. 41–58) **1285.**

8328. MOUNT, KEVIN. Woman in white meets man in black. *See* **15711.**

8329. MÜLLER, ANJA. Putting the child into discourse: framing children in *The Spectator*. *In* (pp. 59–80) **1285.**

8330. NEWMAN, DONALD J. (ed.). *The Spectator*: emerging discourses. *See* **1285.**

8331. OSELL, TEDRA. Tatling women in the public sphere: rhetorical femininity and the English essay periodical. *See* **1293.**

8332. POLLY, GREG. Leviathan of letters. *In* (pp. 105–28) **1285.**

8333. RICHARDSON, ANNIE. From the moral mound to the material maze: Hogarth's *Analysis of Beauty*. *In* (pp. 119–34) **7941.**

8334. TROLANDER, PAUL; TENGER, ZAYNEP. Addison and the personality of the critic. *In* (pp. 175–99) **1285.**

8335. WALMSLEY, PETER.   Death and the nation in *The Spectator*.   *In* (pp. 200–19) **1285.**

8336. WILLIAMS, ABIGAIL.   Patronage and Whig literary culture in the early eighteenth century. *In* (pp. 149–72) **8091.**

Mark Akenside

8337. ROUNCE, ADAM.   Akenside's clamors for liberty. *In* (pp. 216–33) **8091.**

Penelope Aubin

8338. BACKSCHEIDER, PAULA R.   Crusoe among the travelers. *In* (pp. 69–77) **8537.**

8339. GOLLAPUDI, APARNA.   Virtuous voyages in Penelope Aubin's fiction. SELit (45:3) 2005, 669–90.

James Austen (1765–1819)

8340. SELWYN, DAVID.   Poetry. *In* (pp. 59–67) **10060.**

Mrs (Anna Letitia) Barbauld (1743–1825)

8341. BIRNS, NICHOLAS.   'Thy world, Columbus!': Barbauld and global space, 1803, *1811*, 1812, 2003. ERR (16:5) 2005, 545–62.

8342. BRADSHAW, PENNY.   The limits of Barbauld's feminism: re-reading *The Rights of Woman*. ERR (16:1) 2005, 23–37.

8343. LEVINE, WILLIAM.   The eighteenth-century jeremiad and progress-piece traditions in Anna Barbauld's *Eighteen Hundred and Eleven*. WWr (12:2) 2005, 177–86.

8344. PASCOE, JUDITH.   'Unsex'd females': Barbauld, Robinson, and Smith. *In* (pp. 211–26) **8014.**

8345. ROE, NICHOLAS.   Politics. *In* (pp. 357–65) **10060.**

8346. VARGO, LISA.   The Aikins and the Godwins: notions of conflict and stoicism in Anna Barbauld and Mary Shelley. *See* **11991.**

8347. WHITE, DANIEL E.   'With Mrs Barbauld it is different': Dissenting heritage and the devotional taste. *In* (pp. 474–92) **8016.**

William Bartram

8348. NICHOLS, ASHTON.   Roaring alligators and burning tygers: poetry and science from William Bartram to Charles Darwin. PAPS (149:3) 2005, 304–15.

James Beattie

8349. MAJOR, EMMA.   Femininity and national identity: Elizabeth Montagu's trip to France. *See* **8835.**

8350. ROBINSON, ROGER J. (ed.).   The correspondence of James Beattie. London: Thoemmes Press; New York: Continuum, 2004. 4 vols. pp. 1300.

8351. TANKARD, PAUL.   Samuel Johnson's 'history of memory'. *See* **8778.**

William Beckford

8352. GRAHAM, KENNETH.   'Painting the eyes of the Circassians': Samuel Henley's mistranslations in *Vathek*. *See* **8714.**

Richard Bentley

8353. MORRISON, ROBERT.   Chatterton at the races: De Quincey, Cottle, Southey, and the *Battle of Hastynges*. *See* **8469.**

George Berkeley

8354. FABRICANT, CAROLE. George Berkeley the islander: some reflections on utopia, race, and tar-water. *In* (pp. 263–78) **8039.**

Isaac Bickerstaff

8355. THOMSON, PETER. Celebrity and rivalry: David [Garrick] and Goliath [Quin]. *In* (pp. 127–47) **3985.**

Sir Richard Blackmore (d.1729)

8356. CLYMER, LORNA. Philosophical tours of the universe in British poetry, 1700–1729; or, The soaring muse. *In* (pp. 30–62) **5880.**

Hugh Blair

8357. HOLMES, DAVID G. Say what? Rediscovering Hugh Blair and the racialization of language, culture, and pedagogy in eighteenth-century rhetoric. *In* (pp. 203–13) **2457.**

8358. MCILVANNEY, LIAM. Hugh Blair, Robert Burns, and the invention of Scottish literature. *See* **8455.**

8359. SCHMIDT, WOLF GERHARD (ed.). 'Homer des Nordens' und 'Mutter der Romantik': James Macphersons *Ossian* und seine Rezeption in der deutschsprachigen Literatur: 3, Kommentierte Neuausgabe deutscher Übersetzungen der *Fragments of Ancient Poetry* (1766), der *Poems of Ossian* (1782) sowie der Vorreden und Abhandlungen von Hugh Blair und James Macpherson. *See* **8815.**

William Blake (1757–1827)

8360. BEER, JOHN. William Blake: a literary life. Basingstoke; New York: Palgrave Macmillan, 2005. pp. xi, 250. (Literary lives.) Rev. by Michael O'Neill in TLS, 2 Dec. 2005, 32.

8361. BROGLIO, RON. Criticism from inside the poem: MOOs and Blake's *Milton*. TextT (13:2) 2004, 83–90.

8362. EAVES, MORRIS (ed.). The Cambridge companion to William Blake. (Bibl. 2003, 7882.) Rev. by W. H. Stevenson in EC (55:3) 2005, 270–5.

8363. GRAVES, ROY NEIL. Blake's *London*. Exp (63:3) 2005, 131–6.

8364. GREEN, MATTHEW J. A. Visionary materialism in the early works of William Blake: the intersection of Enthusiasm and empiricism. Basingstoke; New York: Palgrave Macmillan, 2005. pp. x, 218.

8365. HALMI, NICHOLAS. Northrop Frye's *Fearful Symmetry*. EC (55:2) 2005, 159–72. (New impressions, 10.)

8366. —— (ed.). Northrop Frye's *Fearful Symmetry: a Study of William Blake*. *See* **14818.**

8367. HARLEY, ALEXIS. *America: a Prophecy*: when Blake meets *Blade Runner*. *See* **13477.**

8368. HOWE, SARAH. General and invariable ideas of nature: Joshua Reynolds and his critical descendants. *See* **8929.**

8369. JANOWITZ, ANNE. The artifactual sublime: making London poetry. *In* (pp. 246–60) **9217.**

8370. JASPER, DAVID. The sacred desert: religion, literature, art, and culture. *See* **3815**.

8371. LARRISSY, EDWARD. Blake's Orient. Romanticism (11:1) 2005, 1–13.

8372. MAKDISI, SAREE. Blake's metropolitan Radicalism. *In* (pp. 113–31) **9217**.

8373. —— William Blake and the impossible history of the 1790s. (Bibl. 2004, 8700.) Rev. by Kenneth Johnston in WordsC (35:4) 2004, 210–15; by Dennis M. Welch in EngS (86:1) 2005, 91–2; by Robin Jarvis in LitH (14:2) 2005, 86–9.

8374. MATTHEWS, SUSAN. Rouzing the faculties to act: Pullman's Blake for children. *In* (pp. 125–34) **18952**.

8375. MEE, JON. Blake and the poetics of Enthusiasm. *In* (pp. 194–210) **8014**.

8376. NICHOLS, ASHTON. Roaring alligators and burning tygers: poetry and science from William Bartram to Charles Darwin. *See* **8348**.

8377. PALEY, MORTON D. The traveller in the evening: the last works of William Blake. (Bibl. 2004, 8704.) Rev. by Sheila A. Spector in WordsC (35:4) 2004, 164–7; by Angus Whitehead in CamQ (34:1) 2005, 65–71; by Stephen L. Carr in SR (44:3) 2005, 450–1.

8378. PERRY, SEAMUS. Old Druid time. *See* **19124**.

8379. PETERFREUND, STUART. Dissent and ontological space in Romantic science and literature. WordsC (36:2) 2005, 59–65.

8380. PHILLIPS, MICHAEL. Blake's annotations in context. ERR (16:1) 2005, 93–5.

8381. —— The printing of Blake's *Illustrations of the Book of Job*. PrQ (22:2) 2005, 138–59.

8382. PIERCE, JOHN B. The wond'rous art: William Blake and writing. (Bibl. 2003, 7916.) Rev. by Jeremy Tambling in MLR (100:2) 2005, 488–9.

8383. PUDVA, FEDERICA. *The Devil's party*: Jim Morrison e William Blake. AngP (2:1/2) 2005, 119–38.

8384. RAWLINSON, NICK. William Blake's comic vision. Basingstoke; New York: Palgrave Macmillan, 2003. pp. xiii, 292. Rev. by Kathleen Lundeen in Blake (38:2) 2004, 85–7; by Brian Wilkie in MLR (100:1) 2005, 200–1; by Robin Jarvis in LitH (14:2) 2005, 86–9.

8385. RIX, ROBERT W. Blake's *Auguries of Innocence*, *The French Revolution*, and *London*. Exp (64:1) 2005, 23–5.

8386. SCHNEIDER, MATTHEW. The anxiety of innocence in Blake and Kierkegaard. ERR (16:3) 2005, 351–9.

8387. SCHOCK, PETER A. Romantic Satanism: myth and the historical moment in Blake, Shelley, and Byron. (Bibl. 2004, 8712.) Rev. by Paul M. Curtis in BJ (32:1) 2004, 63–5.

8388. SCOTT, CAROLE. Pullman's enigmatic ontology: revamping old traditions in *His Dark Materials*. *In* (pp. 95–105) **18952**.

8389. SŁAWEK, TADEUSZ. From rags (of memory) to riches (of literature). *See* **10183**.

8390. SNART, JASON. Blake's Milton: did Blake own and annotate the 1732 Bentley edition of Milton's *Paradise Lost*? ERR (16:1) 2005, 79–91.

8391. TAMBLING, JEREMY.   Blake's night thoughts. Basingstoke; New York: Palgrave Macmillan, 2005. pp. x, 202.

8392. VELDHOEN, BART.   J. R. R. Tolkien, philologist and holist. *See* **19853**.

8393. WEINER, STEPHANIE KUDUK.   Republican politics and English poetry, 1789–1874. *See* **9732**.

8394. WEIR, DAVID.   Brahma in the West: William Blake and the Oriental renaissance. (Bibl. 2003, 7934.) Rev. by Kathryn Freeman in CLIO (34:1/2) 2004, 180–4.

8395. WESTERWEEL, BART.   Some reflections on William Blake and the emblem. *In* (pp. 11–25) **9237**.

8396. WHITEHEAD, ANGUS.   New information concerning Mrs Enoch, William and Catherine Blake's 'fellow inhabitant' at 17 South Molton Street. NQ (52:4) 2005, 460–3.

8397. —— A reference to William Blake and James Parker, printsellers, in *Bailey's British Directory* (1785). NQ (52:1) 2005, 32–5.

8398. WRIGHT, JULIA M.   Blake, nationalism, and the politics of alienation. (Bibl. 2004, 8717.) Rev. by David Baulch in RomNet (36/37) 2004/05; by Jack Bushnell in SR (44:2) 2005, 274–7.

8399. ZENG, FANGRONG.   Ethics in Blake's poetry. FLS (116) 2005, 20–7. (In Chinese.)

Susanna Blamire (1747–1794)

8400. MAYCOCK, CHRISTOPHER.   A passionate poet: Susanna Blamire, 1747–94: a biography. (Bibl. 2004, 8718.) Rev. by Jennie Batchelor in NQ (52:3) 2005, 419–20.

Ann Eliza Bleecker

8401. HARRIS, SHARON M.   The *New-York Magazine*: cultural repository. *In* (pp. 339–64) **1244**.

Henry St John, Viscount Bolingbroke

8402. BATCHELOR, ROBERT.   Concealing the bounds: imagining the British nation through China. *In* (pp. 79–92) **8039**.

8403. MONOD, PAUL.   *Tom Jones* and the crisis of Whiggism in mid-Hanoverian England. *In* (pp. 268–96) **8091**.

Sir Brooke Boothby

8404. ZOONEVELD, JACQUES.   Sir Brooke Boothby: Rousseau's roving baronet friend. Voorburg: Nieuwe Haagsche, 2003. pp. 542. Rev. by Georges Lamoine in EA (58:3) 2005, 361–2.

James Boswell

8405. BELL, ROBERT H.   Boswell's anatomy of folly. SewR (111:4) 2003, 578–94.

8406. FRASER, RUSSELL.   Boswell the retailer of phrases. SewR (111:4) 2003, 603–9 (review-article).

8407. HATZBERGER, WILLIAM F.   Boswell's *London Journal*, Lord Eglinton, and the politics of preferment. 1650–1850 (10) 2004, 173–88.

8408. LYALL, RODERICK J. Writing towards the centre, reading around the periphery: the example of Scottish literature. *See* **3846.**

8409. O'MARA, RICHARD. London and Boswell. SewR (111:4) 2003, 595–602.

8410. PITTOCK, MURRAY. Johnson, Boswell, and their circle. *In* (pp. 157–72) **8014.**

8411. REED, JOSEPH W. The Pottles at Glen Cove: education of a country mouse. YLG (77:3/4) 2003, 143–65. (Isham Boswell Collection at Long Island.)

8412. SHERBO, ARTHUR. The appendix to Edmond Malone's 1790 *Shakespeare*, the 1821 Boswell–Malone *Shakespeare*, and Elizabethan language. *See* **5828.**

8413. —— James Boswell's editing of, and contributions to, the 1821 Boswell–Malone *Shakespeare*. PBSA (99:1) 2005, 71–111.

8414. WATERHOUSE, WILLIAM C. Boswell, Joseph Warton, and Servius. NQ (52:3) 2005, 374.

8415. WOOD, MARCUS. Black bodies and satiric limits in the long eighteenth century. *In* (pp. 55–70) **9305.**

John Boyle, Fifth Earl of Orrery

8416. FRÓES, JOÃO. 'A part omitted' from Swift's *Sentiments of a Church-of-England Man*. *See* **9065.**

Hugh Henry Brackenridge

8417. HASELSTEIN, ULLA. Collateral advantages: Hugh Henry Brackenridge's *Modern Chivalry*. YREAL (19) 2003, 307–23.

Jane Brereton (1685–1740)

8418. PRESCOTT, SARAH. The Cambrian muse: Welsh identity and Hanoverian loyalty in the poems of Jane Brereton. ECS (38:4) 2005, 587–603.

Frances Brooke

8419. BOWLES, EMILY. Frances Brooke's erotic–didactic garden: desire, shame, and sensibility in *The Excursion*. ECN (4) 2004, 139–62.

Christopher Bullock (1690?–1724)

8420. CONAWAY, CHARLES. Shakespeare, molly house culture, and the eighteenth-century stage. *See* **6732.**

Edmund Burke (1729–1797)

8421. BLACKWELL, MARK. The sublimity of taste in Edmund Burke's *A Philosophical Enquiry into the Origin of Our Ideas of the Sublime and Beautiful*. PQ (82:3) 2003, 325–47.

8422. BOLTON, BETSY. Imperial sensibilities, colonial ambivalence: Edmund Burke and Frances Burney. *See* **8445.**

8423. BROMWICH, DAVID. Burke and the argument from human nature. *In* (pp. 37–58) **8425.**

8424. BULLARD, PADDY. The meaning of the 'sublime and beautiful': Shaftesburian contexts and rhetorical issues in Edmund Burke's *Philosophical Enquiry*. RES (56:224) 2005, 169–91. (*Review of English Studies* prize essay.)

8425. CROWE, IAN (ed.). An imaginative Whig: reassessing the life and thought of Edmund Burke. Columbia; London: Missouri UP, 2005. pp. vi, 247.

8426. DEANE, SEAMUS. Burke and Tocqueville: new worlds, new beings. B2 (31:1) 2004, 1–23.

8427. DIMOCK, JAMES PATRICK. Rediscovering the heroic Conservatism of Richard M. Weaver. *See* **20019.**

8428. FABRICANT, CAROLE. Colonial sublimities and sublimations: Swift, Burke, and Ireland. *See* **9059.**

8429. FROHNEN, BRUCE. Burke and the conundrum of international human rights. *In* (pp. 175–202) **8425.**

8430. GIBBONS, LUKE. Edmund Burke and Ireland: aesthetics, politics and the colonial sublime. (Bibl. 2004, 8747.) Rev. by Andrew Keanie in WordsC (35:4) 2004, 177–8; by Julia Wright in CJIS (30:2) 2004, 76–7; by David J. Denby in ECS (38:2) 2005, 385–91; by Evan Gottlieb in ERR (16:5) 2005, 627–33; by Tadhg O'Sullivan in YES (35) 2005, 330–1.

8431. HARRIS, IAN C. *The Case of the Suffering Clergy of France*: a short study in bibliography, history, and textual criticism. YLG (79:3/4) 2005, 103–18.

8432. HUHN, TOM. Imitation and society: the persistence of mimesis in the work of Burke, Hogarth, and Kant. University Park: Pennsylvania State UP, 2004. pp. 215. Rev. by G. Gabrielle Starr in ECL (29:3) 2005, 97–101.

8433. KAROUNOS, MICHAEL. The theory of the dynamic erotic. *See* **8942.**

8434. LEE, YOON SUN. Nationalism and irony: Burke, Scott, Carlyle. (Bibl. 2004, 8753.) Rev. by Barton Swaim in TLS, 1 Apr. 2005, 24–5; by Evan Gottlieb in ERR (16:5) 2005, 627–33; by Simon Bainbridge in NineL (60:2) 2005, 241–4.

8435. LOCK, F. P. Burke and religion. *In* (pp. 19–36) **8425.**

8436. PAPPIN, JOSEPH L., III. Edmund Burke and the Thomistic foundations of natural law. *In* (pp. 203–27) **8425.**

8437. SARAFIANOS, ARIS. Pain, labor, and the sublime: medical gymnastics and Burke's aesthetics. Representations (91) 2005, 58–83.

8438. SCHMIDGEN, WOLFRAM. Reembodying the aesthetic. MLQ (66:1) 2005, 55–84.

8439. SEGALL, KIMBERLY WEDEVEN. Pursuing ghosts: the traumatic sublime in J. M. Coetzee's *Disgrace*. *See* **15838.**

8440. WHELAN, FREDERICK G. Burke, India, and Orientalism. *In* (pp. 127–57) **8425.**

8441. WOLF, PHILIPP. The anachronism of modern cultural memories, and an ethics of literary memory. YREAL (21) 2005, 331–48.

Mrs W. Burke

8442. BATCHELOR, JENNIE. The claims of literature: women applicants to the Royal Literary Fund, 1790–1810. *See* **8856.**

Fanny Burney (Mme d'Arblay)

8443. ANDERSON, EMILY HODGSON. Staged insensibility in Burney's *Cecilia, Camilla,* and *The Wanderer*: how a playwright writes novels. ECF (17:4) 2005, 629–48.

8444. BAX, RANDY. Traces of Johnson in the language of Fanny Burney. IJES (5:1) 2005, 159–81.

8445. BOLTON, BETSY. Imperial sensibilities, colonial ambivalence: Edmund Burke and Frances Burney. ELH (72:4) 2005, 871–99.

8446. KLEKAR, CYNTHIA. 'Her gift was compelled': gender and the failure of the 'gift' in *Cecilia*. ECF (18:1) 2005, 107–26.

8447. KOEHLER, MARTHA J. Models of reading: paragons and parasites in Richardson, Burney, and Laclos. *See* **8945**.

8448. LANDAU, LEYA. 'The middle state': Italian opera in Frances Burney's *Cecilia*. ECF (17:4) 2005, 649–82.

8449. RIZZO, BETTY (ed.). The early journals and letters of Fanny Burney: vol. 4, The Streatham years: part II, 1780–1781. Montreal; Buffalo, NY; London: McGill-Queen's UP, 2003. pp. xix, 569. Rev. by David Roberts in NQ (52:3) 2005, 418–19.

Robert Burns

8450. CRAWFORD, ROBERT. The Bard: Ossian, Burns, and the shaping of Shakespeare. *In* (pp. 124–40) **6561**.

8451. DORNAN, STEPHEN. Thomas Dermody, Robert Burns and the Killeigh cycle. *See* **8556**.

8452. GAILLET-DE CHEZELLES, FLORENCE. Voyage et initiation poétique: l'aventure de Keats en 1818. *See* **11513**.

8453. MCGINTY, J. WALTER. Robert Burns and religion. (Bibl. 2004, 8777.) Rev. by Robert Crawford in ReLit (37:1) 2005, 127–30.

8454. MCILVANNEY, LIAM. Burns the Radical: poetry and politics in late eighteenth-century Scotland. (Bibl. 2004, 8778.) Rev. by Ian Duncan in SHogg (15) 2004, 179–82; by Alan Riach in MLR (100:4) 2005, 1095–7.

8455. —— Hugh Blair, Robert Burns, and the invention of Scottish literature. ECL (29:2) 2005, 25–46.

8456. MCMURTREY, LEAH. Robert Burns and Jesse Stuart: the spark that ignited the inferno. KenEB (54:2/3) 2005, 66–71.

8457. MILNE, ANNE. Dogs and the 'talking animal syndrome' in Janet Little's *From Snipe, a Favourite Dog, to His Master* (1791). *See* **8799**.

George Campbell

8458. MCGREEVY, MICHAEL WALLACE. Approaching experiential discourse iconicity from the field. TextB (25:1) 2005, 67–105.

Elizabeth Carter

8459. CLARKE, NORMA. Bluestocking fictions: devotional writings, didactic literature and the imperative of female improvement. *In* (pp. 460–73) **8016**.

8460. HAMPSHIRE, GWEN (ed.). Elizabeth Carter, 1717–1806: an edition of some unpublished letters. Newark: Delaware UP, 2005. pp. 227.

Susannah Centlivre (Susannah Carroll)

8461. O'BRIEN, JOHN (ed.). The wonder: a woman keeps a secret. Peterborough, Ont.; Orchard Park, NY: Broadview Press, 2004. pp. 147. (Broadview literary texts.) Rev. by Kathleen James-Cavan in Scriblerian (37:2/38:1) 2005, 142–3.

Hester Chapone

8462. STRAIGHT, JULIE. Religious controversy in Hester Chapone's *Letters on the Improvement of the Mind*. NCC (27:4) 2005, 315–34.

Charlotte Charke

8463. PULLEN, KIRSTEN. Actresses and whores: on stage and in society. *See* **3993**.

8464. SAGGINI, FRANCESCA. Memories beyond the pale: the eighteenth-century actress between stage and closet. *See* **8114**.

8465. SHEVELOW, KATHRYN. Charlotte: being a true account of an actress's flamboyant adventures in eighteenth-century London's wild and wicked theatrical world. New York: Holt, 2005. pp. xii, 433. Rev. by Stephen Kuehler in GLRW (12:5) 2005, 39–40.

Thomas Chatterton

8466. DOLAN, JOHN. The third great text-finder: Joseph E. Smith Jr as colleague of Chatterton and Macpherson. AUMLA (104) 2005, 9–40.

8467. JONES, ROBERT. Thomas Chatterton and the experience of defeat. Romanticism (11:1) 2005, 41–54.

8468. MILES, ROBERT. Forging a Romantic identity: Herbert Croft's *Love and Madness* and W. H. Ireland's Shakespeare MS. *See* **8493**.

8469. MORRISON, ROBERT. Chatterton at the races: De Quincey, Cottle, Southey, and the *Battle of Hastynges*. NQ (52:1) 2005, 51–2.

Philip Dormer Stanhope, Earl of Chesterfield

8470. DEAN, ANN C. Authorship, print, and public in Chesterfield's *Letters to His Son*. SELit (45:3) 2005, 691–706.

8471. MAYO, CHRISTOPHER. Manners and manuscripts: the editorial manufacture of Lord Chesterfield in *Letters to His Son*. PBSA (99:1) 2005, 37–69.

Charles Churchill

8472. ROUNCE, ADAM. Stuarts without end: Wilkes, Churchill, and anti-Scottishness. *See* **9121**.

8473. TWOMBLY, DAVID J. The revenant Charles Churchill: a haunting of literary history. SP (102:1) 2005, 83–109.

Colley Cibber

8474. GOLLAPUDI, APARNA. Seeing is believing: performing reform in Colley Cibber's *Love's Last Shift*. RECTR (19:1) 2004, 1–21.

8475. THOMSON, PETER. Celebrity and rivalry: David [Garrick] and Goliath [Quin]. *In* (pp. 127–47) **3985**.

John Cleland

8476. FOWLER, PATSY S.; JACKSON, ALAN (eds). Launching *Fanny Hill*: essays on the novel and its influence. (Bibl. 2003, 8008.) Rev. by Clive Probyn in ECF (18:1) 2005, 149–51; by Todd C. Parker in Scriblerian (37:2/38:1) 2005, 137–9.

8477. GLADFELDER, HAL. Obscenity, censorship, and the eighteenth-century novel: the case of John Cleland. WordsC (35:3) 2004, 134–41.

8478. JONES, VIVIEN. Luxury, satire and prostitute narratives. *In* (pp. 178–89) **7941.**

Catharine Cockburn (Catharine Trotter)

8479. O'NEILL, EILEEN. Early modern women philosophers and the history of philosophy. *See* **7791.**

William Collins (1721–1759)

8480. JUNG, SANDRO. Collins's *Ode to Evening.* Exp (64:1) 2005, 19–23.

8481. —— Unnoticed echoes of Collins's *Ode to Evening* in Mary Whateley's *Elegy on the Uses of Poetry.* ANQ (18:4) 2005, 34–6.

George Colman the Elder (1732–1794)

8482. ZUNSHINE, LISA. Bastard daughters and foundling heroines: rewriting illegitimacy for the eighteenth-century stage. *See* **9028.**

John Gilbert Cooper

8483. JUNG, SANDRO. John Gilbert Cooper's revisions of *The Tomb of Shakespear: a Vision.* ANQ (18:2) 2005, 37–40.

8484. —— John Gilbert Cooper's *The Tomb of Shakespear*: an edition. ANQ (18:2) 2005, 30–7.

Hannah Cowley

8485. WALLIS, MICK. Translating bodies: Siddons, Cowley and the stage sublime. PRes (10:1) 2005, 68–80.

William Cowper

8486. DUFFY, CIAN. *On the Ice-Islands Seen Floating in the Germanic Ocean*: Cowper's source for the poem. NQ (52:1) 2005, 22–5.

8487. FULFORD, TIM. 'Getting and spending': the Orientalization of satire in Romantic London. *In* (pp. 11–29) **9305.**

8488. GROTH, HELEN. Literary nostalgia and early Victorian photographic discourse. *See* **9687.**

George Crabbe

8489. GROTH, HELEN. Literary nostalgia and early Victorian photographic discourse. *See* **9687.**

8490. RAY, MARTIN. Thomas Hardy: four notes. *See* **11155.**

'J. Hector St John de Crèvecœur'
(Michel-Guillaume Jean de Crèvecœur)

8491. PEACOCK, JAMES. Who was John Bartram? Literary and epistolary representations of the Quaker. *See* **8043.**

8492. SCHUELLER, MALINI JOHAR; WATTS, EDWARD (eds). Messy beginnings: postcoloniality and Early American Studies. *See* **9925.**

Sir Herbert Croft

8493. MILES, ROBERT. Forging a Romantic identity: Herbert Croft's *Love and Madness* and W. H. Ireland's Shakespeare MS. ECF (17:4) 2005, 599–627.

Henry Cromwell (1659–1728)

8494. ROGERS, PAT. Pope's friend Henry Cromwell. NQ (52:3) 2005, 359–60.

Mary Darwall (Mary Whateley)

8495. JUNG, SANDRO. Unnoticed echoes of Collins's *Ode to Evening* in Mary Whateley's *Elegy on the Uses of Poetry*. See **8481**.

Erasmus Darwin

8496. GEORGE, SAM. Linnaeus in letters and the cultivation of the female mind: 'Botany in an English dress'. See **8866**.

8497. HAUT, ASIA. Reading Flora: Erasmus Darwin's *The Botanic Garden*, Henry Fuseli's illustrations, and various literary responses. WI (20:4) 2004, 240–56.

8498. MOORE, LISA L. Queer gardens: Mary Delany's flowers and friendships. See **8549**.

8499. PAGE, MICHAEL. The Darwin before Darwin: Erasmus Darwin, visionary science, and Romantic poetry. PLL (41:2) 2005, 146–69.

Mary Davys

8500. WAKELY, ALICE. Mary Davys and the politics of epistolary form. *In* (pp. 257–67) **8091**.

Daniel Defoe

8501. ALMAGRO JIMÉNEZ, MANUEL. 'Father to my story': writing *Foe*, de-authorizing (De)Foe. See **15818**.

8502. BACKSCHEIDER, PAULA R. Crusoe among the travelers. *In* (pp. 69–77) **8537**.

8503. BALLASTER, ROS. Performing *Roxane*: the Oriental woman as the sign of luxury in eighteenth-century fictions. *In* (pp. 165–77) **7941**.

8504. BARBERET, JOHN. Messages in bottles: a comparative formal approach to castaway narratives. *In* (pp. 111–21) **8537**.

8505. BEESEMYER, IRENE BASEY. Crusoe the *isolato*: Daniel Defoe wrestles with solitude. 1650–1850 (10) 2004, 79–102.

8506. BENZONI, PIETRO. Il senso della fine in *Robinson Crusoe* di Daniel Defoe. SCrit (20:1) 2005, 101–26.

8507. BERTSCH, JANET. Storytelling in the works of Bunyan, Grimmelshausen, Defoe, and Schnabel. See **7280**.

8508. BIGNAMI, MARIALUISA. What the writer said: self-reflexive statements in early British fiction. See **7233**.

8509. BRAVERMAN, RICHARD. *Robinson Crusoe* and *Gulliver's Travels*: some pedagogical frameworks. *In* (pp. 37–47) **8537**.

8510. CALDER, MARTIN. Encounters with the Other: a journey to the limits of language through works by Rousseau, Defoe, Prévost and Graffigny. Amsterdam; Atlanta, GA: Rodopi, 2003. pp. 312. (Faux titre, 234.) Rev. by Michael Cardy in MLR (100:3) 2005, 820; by Katherine Astbury in BJECS (28:1) 2005, 125.

8511. CAPOFERRO, RICCARDO. Defoe: guida al *Robinson Crusoe*. Rome: Carocci, 2003. pp. 109. (Le bussole, 113.) Rev. by Laura Giovannelli in Scriblerian (37:2/38:1) 2005, 133–4.

8512. DE MICHELIS, LIDIA. Daniel Defoe and the aesthetics of discovery. Textus (18:1) 2005, 107–20.

8513. FAN, KIT. Imagined places: Robinson Crusoe and Elizabeth Bishop. Biography (28:1) 2005, 43–53.

8514. FISHER, CARL. The Robinsonade: an intercultural history of an idea. *In* (pp. 129–39) **8537.**

8515. GANZ, MELISSA J. *Moll Flanders* and English marriage law. ECF (17:2) 2005, 157–82.

8516. GLADFELDER, HAL. Obscenity, censorship, and the eighteenth-century novel: the case of John Cleland. *See* **8477.**

8517. GRIFFIN, ROBERT J. The text in motion: eighteenth-century *Roxanas.* ELH (72:2) 2005, 387–406.

8518. HAGGERTY, GEORGE E. Thank God it's Friday: the construction of masculinity in *Robinson Crusoe. In* (pp. 78–87) **8537.**

8519. HINNANT, CHARLES HASKELL. *Moll Flanders, Roxana,* and first-person female narratives: models and prototypes. ECN (4) 2004, 39–72.

8520. HUDSON, NICHOLAS. Social rank, 'the rise of the novel', and Whig histories of eighteenth-century fiction. *See* **8136.**

8521. JOSEPH, BETTY. Reading the East India Company, 1720–1840: colonial currencies of gender. *See* **8010.**

8522. KENT-DRURY, ROXANNE; SAYRE, GORDON. *Robinson Crusoe's* parodic intertextuality. *In* (pp. 48–54) **8537.**

8523. KITSI-MITAKOU, KATERINA. Whoring, incest, duplicity, or the 'self-polluting' erotics of Daniel Defoe's *Moll Flanders. In* (pp. 79–94) **12579.**

8524. KRENTZ, CHRISTOPHER. Duncan Campbell and the discourses of deafness. PrSt (27:1/2) 2005, 39–52.

8525. LAMB, JONATHAN. The crying of lost things. *See* **8652.**

8526. LUNDIN, ANNE. *Robinson Crusoe* and children's literature. *In* (pp. 198–206) **8537.**

8527. MADDOCKS, MELVIN. The ungarnished plate of Daniel Defoe. SewR (111:4) 2003, 615–20 (review-article).

8528. MANIQUIS, ROBERT. Teaching *The Pilgrim's Progress* and *Robinson Crusoe*; or, From filthy mire to the glory of things. *In* (pp. 25–36) **8537.**

8529. MARKLEY, ROBERT. Riches, power, trade and religion: the Far East and the English imagination, 1600–1720. *See* **7714.**

8530. MARSHALL, DAVID. Autobiographical acts in *Robinson Crusoe.* ELH (71:4) 2004, 899–920.

8531. MAURER, SHAWN LISA. 'I wou'd be a *man–woman': Roxana's* Amazonian threat to the ideology of marriage. TSLL (46:3) 2004, 363–86.

8532. MAYER, ROBERT. *Robinson Crusoe* in Hollywood. *In* (pp. 169–74) **8537.**

8533. NOVAK, MAXIMILLIAN E.; FISHER, CARL. The critical reputation of *Robinson Crusoe* and its status as a novel. *In* (pp. 7–12) **8537.**

8534. —— —— Publishing history and modern editions. *In* (pp. 3–5) **8537.**

8535. —— —— *Crusoe's* fictional predecessors. *In* (pp. 14–16) **8537.**

8536. —— —— *Robinson Crusoe* as international text: translation, circulation, and adaptation. *In* (pp. 16–18) **8537.**

8537. —— —— (eds). Approaches to teaching Defoe's *Robinson Crusoe.* New York: Modern Language Assn of America, 2005. pp. xxii, 243.

8538. OGBORN, MILES; WITHERS, CHARLES W. J.   Travel, trade, and empire: knowing other places, 1660–1800. *In* (pp. 13–35) **6958.**

8539. RICHETTI, JOHN J.   The life of Daniel Defoe. Oxford; Malden, MA: Blackwell, 2005. pp. xi, 406. (Blackwell critical biographies.)

8540. ROGERS, PAT.   Defoe and the expiring peerage. SP (102:4) 2005, 510–36.

8541. ROTHMAN, IRVING N.; BOWERMAN, R. MICHAEL (eds).   The political history of the Devil. (Bibl. 2004, 8885.) Rev. by Geoffrey Sill in Scriblerian (37:2 / 38:1) 2005, 117–19; by Élisabeth Détis in EA (58:2) 2005, 212–13.

8542. RUDMAN, JOSEPH.   Unediting, de-editing, and editing in non-traditional authorship attribution studies: with an emphasis on the canon of Daniel Defoe. PBSA (99:1) 2005, 5–36.

8543. SCHONHORN, MANUEL.   Weber, Watt, and restraint: *Robinson Crusoe* and the critical tradition. *In* (pp. 55–60) **8537.**

8544. SILL, GEOFFREY.   Myths of modern individualism: Defoe, Franklin, and Whitman. *In* (pp. 61–8) **8537.**

8545. STEVENS, LAURA M.   Reading the hermit's manuscript: *The Female American* and female Robinsonades. *In* (pp. 140–51) **8537.**

8546. WHEELER, ROXANN.   *Robinson Crusoe* and early eighteenth-century racial ideology. *In* (pp. 88–95) **8537.**

8547. WOMERSLEY, DAVID.   Confessional politics in Defoe's *Journal of the Plague Year. In* (pp. 237–56) **8091.**

8548. ZIMMERMAN, EVERETT.   Contexts for *Crusoe*: colonial adventure and social disintegration. *In* (pp. 152–60) **8537.**

Mary Delany

8549. MOORE, LISA L.   Queer gardens: Mary Delany's flowers and friendships. ECS (39:1) 2005, 49–70.

John Dennis

8550. DONNELLY, PHILLIP J.   Enthusiastic poetry and rationalized Christianity: the poetic theory of John Dennis. ChrisL (54:2) 2005, 235–64.

8551. GERRARD, CHRISTINE.   Pope, *Peri Bathous*, and the Whig sublime. *In* (pp. 200–15) **8091.**

8552. LOWERRE, KATHRYN.   Dramatick opera and theatrical reform: Dennis's *Rinaldo and Armida* and Motteux's *The Island Princess.* TN (59:1) 2005, 23–40.

8553. PRESCOTT, SARAH.   Elizabeth Singer Rowe: gender, Dissent, and Whig poetics. *In* (pp. 173–99) **8091.**

8554. SIKES, ALAN.   'Snip snip here, snip snip there, and a couple of tra la las': the castrato and the nature of sexual difference. *See* **8620.**

8555. TROLANDER, PAUL; TENGER, ZAYNEP.   Addison and the personality of the critic. *In* (pp. 175–99) **1285.**

Thomas Dermody (1775–1802)

8556. DORNAN, STEPHEN.   Thomas Dermody, Robert Burns and the Killeigh cycle. ScSR (6:1) 2005, 9–21.

John Dunton

8557. BERRY, HELEN. Crimes of conscience: the last will and testament of John Dunton. *In* (pp. 81–101) **937.**

8558. PRESCOTT, SARAH. Elizabeth Singer Rowe: gender, Dissent, and Whig poetics. *In* (pp. 173–99) **8091.**

Jonathan Edwards (1703–1758)

8559. BROWN, ROBERT E. The Bible. *In* (pp. 87–102) **8571.**

8560. —— Jonathan Edwards and the Bible. (Bibl. 2004, 8899.) Rev. by Stephen J. Stein in JR (83:3) 2003, 462–4; by William Breitenback in JAH (90:3) 2003, 993–4; by Michael J. McClymond in CHist (72:2) 2003, 416–18.

8561. CRISP, OLIVER D. Jonathan Edwards and the metaphysics of sin. Aldershot; Burlington, VT: Ashgate, 2005. pp. vi, 146.

8562. DAYAN, COLIN. Legal terrors. *See* **7642.**

8563. DYRNESS, WILLIAM A. Reformed theology and visual culture: the Protestant imagination from Calvin to Edwards. Cambridge; New York: CUP, 2004. pp. xv, 339. Rev. by Graham Parry in SCN (63:1/2) 2005, 1–4.

8564. GUELZO, ALLEN C. Freedom of the will. *In* (pp. 115–29) **8571.**

8565. GURA, PHILIP. Jonathan Edwards: America's evangelical. New York: Hill & Wang, 2005. pp. xv, 284.

8566. JENSON, ROBERT W. Christology. *In* (pp. 72–86) **8571.**

8567. KIMMACH, WILSON H. The sermons: concept and execution. *In* (pp. 243–57) **8571.**

8568. KLING, DAVID W.; SWEENEY, DOUGLAS A. (eds). Jonathan Edwards at home and abroad: historical memories, cultural movements, global horizons. (Bibl. 2004, 8905.) Rev. by William Breitenback in JAH (91:4) 2005, 1426.

8569. LEE, SANG HYUN. God's relation to the world. *In* (pp. 59–71) **8571.**

8570. —— Grace and justification by faith alone. *In* (pp. 130–46) **8571.**

8571. —— (ed.). The Princeton companion to Jonathan Edwards. Princeton, NJ; Oxford: Princeton UP, 2005. pp. xxviii, 331.

8572. McDERMOTT, GERALD R. The eighteenth-century American culture war: Thomas Jefferson and Jonathan Edwards on religion and religions. LittPr (15:29) 2005, 48–63.

8573. —— Mission and Native Americans. *In* (pp. 258–73) **8571.**

8574. MARSDEN, GEORGE M. Jonathan Edwards: a life. (Bibl. 2004, 8908.) Rev. by John J. Bombaro in CathHR (89:4) 2003, 812–14; by Michael G. Ditmore in ChrisL (54:1) 2004, 135–8; by Avihu Zakai in JAH (90:4) 2004, 1423–4.

8575. MILLER, PERRY. Jonathan Edwards. Introd. by John F. Wilson. Lincoln; London: Nebraska UP, 2005. pp. xix, 348.

8576. MINKEMA, KENNETH P. Jonathan Edwards: a theological life. *In* (pp. 1–15) **8571.**

8577. —— STOUT, HARRY S. The Edwardsean tradition and the anti-slavery debate, 1740–1865. JAH (92:1) 2005, 47–74.

8578. NIEBUHR, RICHARD R. Being and consent. *In* (pp. 34–43) **8571.**

8579. NOLL, MARK. Edwards' theology after Edwards. *In* (pp. 292–308) **8571.**

8580. PAUW, AMY PLANTINGA. The Trinity. *In* (pp. 44–58) **8571.**

8581. PIGGIN, STUART; COOKE, DIANNE. Keeping alive the heart in the head: the significance of 'eternal language' in the aesthetics of Jonathan Edwards and S. T. Coleridge. LitTheol (18:4) 2004, 383–414.

8582. PORTERFIELD, AMANDA. American religious biography. *See* **8271.**

8583. SMITH, JOHN E. Religious affections and the 'sense of the heart'. *In* (pp. 103–14) **8571.**

8584. STEIN, STEPHEN J. Eschatology. *In* (pp. 226–42) **8571.**

8585. SWEENEY, DOUGLAS A. The Church. *In* (pp. 167–89) **8571.**

8586. THUESEN, PETER J. Edwards' intellectual background. *In* (pp. 16–33) **8571.**

8587. WILSON, JOHN F. History. *In* (pp. 210–25) **8571.**

8588. WILSON, STEPHEN A. Virtue reformed: rereading Jonathan Edwards's ethics. Leiden; Boston, MA: Brill, 2005. pp. xxv, 406. (Brill's studies in intellectual history, 132.)

8589. ZAKAI, AVIHU. Jonathan Edwards's philosophy of history: the re-enchantment of the world in the age of Enlightenment. (Bibl. 2004, 8917, where title incorrect.) Rev. by George M. Marsden in JAH (91:1) 2004, 217–18; by Michael J. McClymond in JR (85:1) 2005, 121–3.

Olaudah Equiano

8590. BUGG, JOHN. 'Master of their language': education and exile in Mary Shelley's *Frankenstein*. *See* **11963.**

8591. CARRETTA, VINCENT. Questioning the identity of Olaudah Equiano, or Gustavus Vassa, the African. *In* (pp. 226–35) **8039.**

8592. EARLEY, SAMANTHA MANCHESTER. Writing from the center or the margins? Olaudah Equiano's writing life reassessed. AfSR (46:3) 2003, 1–16.

8593. ELMER, JONATHAN. The Black Atlantic archive. AmLH (17:1) 2005, 160–70 (review-article).

8594. PUDALOFF, ROSS J. No change without purchase: Olaudah Equiano and the economies of self and market. EAL (40:3) 2005, 499–527.

8595. RICHARD, JESSICA. 'A paradise of my own creation': *Frankenstein* and the improbable romance of Polar exploration. *See* **11984.**

8596. WILEY, MICHAEL. Consuming Africa: geography and identity in Olaudah Equiano's *Interesting Narrative*. SR (44:2) 2005, 165–79.

8597. YOUNGQUIST, PAUL. The Afro Futurism of DJ Vassa. ERR (16:2) 2005, 181–92.

Margaretta V. Faugeres (1771–1801)

8598. HARRIS, SHARON M. The *New-York Magazine*: cultural repository. *In* (pp. 339–64) **1244.**

Elizabeth Graeme Fergusson (1737–1801)

8599. OUSTERHOUT, ANNE M. The most learned woman in America: a life of Elizabeth Graeme Fergusson. University Park: Pennsylvania State UP, 2004. pp. xx, 391. Rev. by Rochelle Raineri Zuck in Legacy (22:1) 2005, 70–1.

Robert Fergusson

8600. CRAWFORD, ROBERT (ed.). 'Heaven-taught Fergusson', Robert Burns's favourite Scottish poet: poems and essays. (Bibl. 2003, 8092.) Rev. by Rhona Brown in ScSR (4:2) 2003, 144–5; by Alan Riach in MLR (100:4) 2005, 1095–7.

8601. PITTOCK, MURRAY G. H. Robert Fergusson and the Romantic ode. BJECS (28:1) 2005, 55–66.

Henry Fielding

8602. BELSEY, CATHERINE. Remembering as re-inscription – with a difference. See **3475**.

8603. BERNARD, NATHALIE. Fielding auteur/*auctor*: du garant à l'inventeur dans *The Journal of a Voyage to Lisbon* (1755). EREA (3:1) 2005, 4–9.

8604. CAMPBELL, JILL. Fielding's style. ELH (72:2) 2005, 407–28.

8605. COLEY, WILLIAM B. (ed.). Contributions to *The Champion* and related writings. Oxford: Clarendon Press; New York: OUP, 2003. pp. cxxvi, 687. (Wesleyan ed. of the works of Henry Fielding.) Rev. by Jeremy Black in NQ (52:1) 2005, 125; by Brian McCrea in Scriblerian (37:2 / 38:1) 2005, 93–6; by Guyonne Leduc in EA (58:2) 2005, 214–15.

8606. DICKIE, SIMON. *Joseph Andrews* and the great laughter debate. StudECC (34) 2005, 271–332.

8607. FERRARI, ROBERTA. In search of a new aesthetics: Addison, Fielding and the 'challenge' of travel writing. See **8317**.

8608. FÜGER, WILHELM. Limits of the narrator's knowledge in Fielding's *Joseph Andrews*: a contribution to a theory of negated knowledge in fiction. Style (38:3) 2004, 278–89.

8609. GRIMM, REINHOLD. Fielding's *Tom Jones* and the European novel since Antiquity: Fielding's *Tom Jones* as a final joinder. New York; Frankfurt: Lang, 2005. pp. 134. (Analysen und Dokumente, 50.)

8610. HARWEG, ROLAND. Are Fielding's Shamela and Richardson's Pamela one and the same person? A contribution to the problem of the number of fictive worlds. See **8939**.

8611. INGRASSIA, CATHERINE (ed.). Anti-Pamela; or, Feign'd innocence detected; An Apology for the life of Mrs Shamela Andrews. See **8707**.

8612. JUSTICE, GEORGE. *Rasselas* in 'the rise of the novel'. See **8764**.

8613. LAMB, JONATHAN. The crying of lost things. See **8652**.

8614. McGRANE, LAURA. Fielding's fallen oracles: print culture and the elusiveness of common sense. MLQ (66:2) 2005, 173–96.

8615. MONOD, PAUL. *Tom Jones* and the crisis of Whiggism in mid-Hanoverian England. *In* (pp. 268–96) **8091**.

8616. RAWSON, CLAUDE. Squeezum before Thrasher: how the novels of Henry Fielding were presaged by his now neglected plays. TLS, 21 Jan. 2005, 3–4 (review-article).

8617. RIBBLE, FREDERICK G. New light on Henry Fielding from the Malmesbury Papers. MP (103:1) 2005, 51–94.

8618. RIZZO, BETTY. The Devil in *Tom Jones*. 1650–1850 (10) 2004, 103–24.

8619. Sabor, Peter.   Richardson, Henry Fielding, and Sarah Fielding. *In* (pp. 139–56) **8014**.

8620. Sikes, Alan.   'Snip snip here, snip snip there, and a couple of tra la las': the castrato and the nature of sexual difference. StudECC (34) 2005, 197–229.

8621. Stevenson, John Allen.   The real history of Tom Jones. Basingstoke; New York: Palgrave Macmillan, 2005. pp. x, 225. Rev. by Thomas Keymer in TLS, 15 July 2005, 25.

8622. Teynor, Hilary.   A Partridge in the family tree: fixity, mobility, and community in *Tom Jones*. ECF (17:3) 2005, 349–72.

8623. Wandless, William H.   Narrative pain and the moral sense: toward an ethics of suffering in the long eighteenth century. *See* **7258**.

8624. Wolf, Amy.   Bernard Mandeville, Henry Fielding's *Amelia*, and the necessities of plot. ECN (4) 2004, 73–102.

Sarah Fielding

8625. Sabor, Peter.   Richardson, Henry Fielding, and Sarah Fielding. *In* (pp. 139–56) **8014**.

Thomas Fitzgerald (1694 or 5–1752)

8626. Rumbold, Valerie; McGeary, Thomas.   *Folly*, session poems, and the preparations for Pope's *Dunciad*s. RES (56:226) 2005, 577–610.

Samuel Foote

8627. Anderson, Misty G.   'Our purpose is the same': Whitefield, Foote, and the theatricality of Methodism. StudECC (34) 2005, 125–49.

8628. Moody, Jane.   Stolen identities: character, mimicry and the invention of Samuel Foote. *In* (pp. 65–89) **3985**.

James Fordyce (1720–1796)

8629. Straight, Julie.   Religious controversy in Hester Chapone's *Letters on the Improvement of the Mind*. *See* **8462**.

Hannah Webster Foster

8630. Schweitzer, Ivy.   Foster's *Coquette*: resurrecting friendship from the tomb of marriage. AQ (61:2) 2005, 1–32.

Benjamin Franklin

8631. Allen, Brooke.   Benjamin Franklin's triumph of reason. HR (58:1) 2005, 133–42 (review-article).

8632. Isaacson, Walter.   Benjamin Franklin: an American life. Waterville, ME: Thorndike, 2004. pp. 907. Rev. by Barbara B. Oberg in JAH (91:2) 2004, 606; by Brooke Allen in HR (58:1) 2005, 133–42.

8633. Jacobson, Joanne.   Mr Secrets: Henry Adams and the breakdown of the exemplary tradition in American autobiography. *In* (pp. 206–21) **9887**.

8634. Kamrath, Mark L.   American Indian oration and discourses of the Republic in eighteenth-century American periodicals. *In* (pp. 143–78) **1244**.

8635. Lemay, J. A. Leo.   Deborah Franklin, Lord Loudoun, and Franklin's *Autobiography*. HLQ (67:4) 2004, 607–21.

8636. LUPTON, CHRISTINA. Two texts told twice: poor Richard, Pastor Yorick, and the case of the word's return. *See* **9037.**

8637. McCREA, BRIAN. The virtue of repetition: Mr Spectator trains Benjamin Franklin. *In* (pp. 248–64) **1285.**

8638. OLSON, LESTER C. Benjamin Franklin's vision of American community: a study in rhetorical iconology. (Bibl. 2004, 8954.) Rev. by S. Michael Halloran in RSQ (35:4) 2005, 115–22; by David T. Morgan in JAH (92:2) 2005, 588–9.

8639. PORTERFIELD, AMANDA. American religious biography. *See* **8271.**

8640. SCHUELLER, MALINI JOHAR; WATTS, EDWARD (eds). Messy beginnings: postcoloniality and Early American Studies. *See* **9925.**

8641. SILL, GEOFFREY. Myths of modern individualism: Defoe, Franklin, and Whitman. *In* (pp. 61–8) **8537.**

8642. STROUT, CUSHING. A man for all seasons. SewR (111:4) 2003, 610–15 (review-article).

8643. WOOD, GORDON S. The Americanization of Benjamin Franklin. (Bibl. 2004, 8955.) Rev. by Jack Fruchtman, Jr, in ECInt (18:3) 2004, 35–9; by Brooke Allen in HR (58:1) 2005, 133–42; by Nian-Sheng Huang in JAH (92:1) 2005, 199–200.

Philip Freneau

8644. LINK, ERIC CARL. Lactantius, teleology, and American literature. MidQ (46:2) 2005, 169–86.

David Garrick (1717–1779)

8645. CONAWAY, CHARLES. 'Thou'rt the man': David Garrick, William Shakespeare, and the masculinization of the eighteenth-century stage. RECTR (19:1) 2004, 22–42.

8646. PRESCOTT, PAUL. Doing all that becomes a man: the reception and afterlife of the Macbeth actor, 1744–1889. *See* **6565.**

8647. RUSSELL, GILLIAN. Theatrical culture. *In* (pp. 100–18) **8014.**

8648. SCHOCH, RICHARD W. 'A supplement to public laws': Arthur Murphy, David Garrick, and *Hamlet, with Alterations*. *See* **8849.**

8649. THOMSON, PETER. Celebrity and rivalry: David [Garrick] and Goliath [Quin]. *In* (pp. 127–47) **3985.**

8650. WILLIAMS, SIMON. Taking Macbeth out of himself: Davenant, Garrick, Schiller and Verdi. *See* **6577.**

John Gay

8651. GREGORI, FLAVIO. The 'audacious' art of walking: the metropolis and the proto-*flâneur* in John Gay's *Trivia*. SAtlR (70:1) 2005, 71–96.

8652. LAMB, JONATHAN. The crying of lost things. ELH (71:4) 2004, 949–67.

8653. McKENZIE, ANDREA. Martyrs in low life? Dying 'game' in Augustan England. *See* **8236.**

8654. ROGERS, PAT. Macheath and the gaol-breakers. LitH (14:2) 2005, 14–36.

Edward Gibbon

8655. BARBOUR, JOHN D. The value of solitude: the ethics and spirituality of aloneness in autobiography. *See* **12179.**

8656. MILLER, ANTHONY.   Corrections to the Womersley text of Gibbon's *Decline and Fall*. NQ (52:3) 2005, 374–6.

8657. MILLER, STEPHEN.   The achievement of Gibbon. SewR (111:4) 2003, 562–77.

8658. NORMAN, BRIAN.   The influence of Switzerland on the life and writing of Edward Gibbon. (Bibl. 2004, 8965.) Rev. by Joy Charnley in MLR (100:2) 2005, 473–4.

William Gilpin

8659. BERTELSEN, LARS KIEL.   The Claude glass: a modern metaphor between word and image. Trans. by Stacey M. Cozart. *See* **8865**.

8660. BROGLIO, RON.   The Romantic cow: animals as technology. WordsC (36:2) 2005, 48–52.

8661. DUCKWORTH, ALISTAIR M.   Landscape. *In* (pp. 278–88) **10060**.

8662. KINSLEY, ZOË.   Dorothy Richardson's manuscript travel journals (1761–1801) and the possibilities of picturesque aesthetics. *See* **8930**.

8663. ORESTANO, FRANCESCA.   *Picturesque: a transformation*: William Gilpin's aesthetics and Ann Radcliffe's visual imagination. Textus (18:1) 2005, 39–60.

8664. WICKMAN, MATTHEW.   Terror's abduction of experience: a gothic history. *See* **8926**.

William Godwin ('Edward Baldwin') (1756–1836)

8665. À COURT, FRANCIS.   *Magnifique, mais ce n'est pas Daguerre*: some notes on the life of Tom Wedgwood. CLB (123) 2003, 78–90.

8666. AYERS, ELAINE M.   Repeating 'a half-told and mangled tale': reading *Caleb Williams* through Emily Melvile. ELN (42:4) 2005, 24–43.

8667. BOTTOMS, JANET.   'To read aright': representations of Shakespeare for children. *See* **5861**.

8668. BOUR, ISABELLE.   Sensibility as epistemology in *Caleb Williams*, *Waverley*, and *Frankenstein*. SELit (45:4) 2005, 813–27.

8669. CHEVALIER, NOEL.   The Liberty Tree and the Whomping Willow: political justice, magical science, and Harry Potter. *See* **19202**.

8670. CLEMIT, PAMELA.   William Godwin and James Watt's copying machine: wet transfer copies in the Abinger papers. BLR (18:5) 2005, 532–60.

8671. —— William Godwin's papers in the Abinger deposit: an unmapped country. BLR (18:3) 2004, 253–63.

8672. HOGSETTE, DAVID S.   Textual surveillance, social codes, and sublime voices: the tyranny of narrative in *Caleb Williams* and *Wieland*. RomNet (38/39) 2005.

8673. JARRELLS, ANTHONY S.   Britain's bloodless revolutions: 1688 and the Romantic reform of literature. Basingstoke; New York: Palgrave Macmillan, 2005. pp. ix, 229. (Palgrave studies in the Enlightenment, Romanticism and the cultures of print.)

8674. KLANCHER, JON.   Discriminations; or, Romantic cosmopolitanisms in London. *In* (pp. 65–82) **9217**.

8675. MARKLEY, A. A. 'The success of gentleness': homosocial desire and the homosexual personality in the novels of William Godwin. RomNet (36/37) 2004/05.

8676. O'SHAUGHNESSY, DAVID. Kotzebue and Thompson's *The Stranger*: a new source for Godwin's *St Leon*. NQ (52:4) 2005, 452–6.

8677. PFAU, THOMAS. Romantic moods: paranoia, trauma, and melancholy, 1790–1840. Baltimore, MD; London: Johns Hopkins UP, 2005. pp. xii, 572.

8678. REITZ, CAROLINE. Detecting the nation: fictions of detection and the imperial venture. (Bibl. 2004, 8982.) Rev. by Jon Barnes in TLS, 28 Jan. 2005, 33; by Kathy Alexis Psomiades in VS (48:1) 2005, 155–7.

8679. SACHS, JONATHAN. From Roman to *roman*: the Jacobin novel and the Roman legacy in the 1790s. *See* **8703**.

8680. SCRIVENER, MICHAEL. Trials in Romantic-era writing: modernity, guilt, and the scene of justice. WordsC (35:3) 2004, 128–33.

8681. STEEDMAN, CAROLYN. Servants and their relationship to the unconscious. *See* **8791**.

8682. TAYLOR, BARBARA. Feminists *versus* gallants: manners and morals in Enlightenment Britain. *In* (pp. 30–52) **8016**.

8683. WHELAN, TIMOTHY. 'I have *confessed myself a devil*': Crabb Robinson's confrontation with Robert Hall, 1798–1800. *See* **11849**.

8684. WU, DUNCAN. Godwin and Hazlitt estranged. *See* **11254**.

Oliver Goldsmith (1730?–1774)

8685. KRISHNAN, R. S. Exotic travels, traveling exotics: satire and nationalism in Goldsmith and Hamilton. LJH (30:1) 2005, 5–16.

8686. NICHOLS, ASHTON. Roaring alligators and burning tygers: poetry and science from William Bartram to Charles Darwin. *See* **8348**.

8687. NÜNNING, VERA. Unreliable narration and the historical variability of values and norms: *The Vicar of Wakefield* as a test case of a cultural-historical narratology. Style (38:2) 2004, 236–52.

James Grainger

8688. FROHOCK, RICHARD. Heroes of empire: the British imperial protagonist in America, 1596–1764. *See* **7240**.

Thomas Gray

8689. EDGECOMBE, RODNEY STENNING. St John Chrysostom's *Homilies on Romans* and Gray's *Elegy*. ANQ (18:2) 2005, 28–9.

8690. KALTER, BARRETT. DIY gothic: Thomas Gray and the medieval revival. ELH (70:4) 2003, 989–1019.

John Gregory (1724–1773)

8691. MORAN, MARY CATHERINE. Between the savage and the civil: Dr John Gregory's natural history of femininity. *In* (pp. 8–29) **8016**.

8692. STRAIGHT, JULIE. Religious controversy in Hester Chapone's *Letters on the Improvement of the Mind*. *See* **8462**.

Dr Alexander Hamilton (1712–1756)

8693. BEYERS, CHRIS.   Race, power, and sociability in Alexander Hamilton's *Records of the Tuesday Club*. SoLJ (38:1) 2005, 21–42.

Elizabeth Hamilton (1758–1816)

8694. KRISHNAN, R. S.   Exotic travels, traveling exotics: satire and nationalism in Goldsmith and Hamilton. *See* **8685**.

8695. MELLOR, ANNE K.   Romantic Orientalism begins at home: Elizabeth Hamilton's *Translations of the Letters of a Hindoo Rajah*. SR (44:2) 2005, 151–64.

8696. RENDALL, JANE.   'Women that would plague me with rational conversation': aspiring women and Scottish Whigs, *c*.1790–1830. *In* (pp. 326–47) **8016**.

George Hardinge (1743–1816)

8697. JONES, ROBERT.   Thomas Chatterton and the experience of defeat. *See* **8467**.

John Hawkesworth

8698. RENNIE, NEIL.   The Point Venus 'scene', Tahiti, 14 May 1769. *In* (pp. 239–50) **8039**.

8699. WIDMAYER, ANNE F.   The politics of adapting Aphra Behn's *Oroonoko*. *See* **7259**.

Sir John Hawkins (1719–1789)

8700. SMITH, NICHOLAS D.   An annotated copy of the third Hawkins edition of Izaak Walton's *The Complete Angler*. *See* **7892**.

William Hay (1695–1755)

8701. DEUTSCH, HELEN.   The body's moments: visible disability, the essay and the limits of sympathy. *See* **7202**.

8702. JAMES-CAVAN, KATHLEEN.   '[A]ll in me is nature': the values of deformity in William Hay's *Deformity: an Essay*. PrSt (27:1/2) 2005, 27–38.

Mary Hays

8703. SACHS, JONATHAN.   From Roman to *roman*: the Jacobin novel and the Roman legacy in the 1790s. StudN (37:3) 2005, 253–72.

8704. TAYLOR, BARBARA.   Feminists *versus* gallants: manners and morals in Enlightenment Britain. *In* (pp. 30–52) **8016**.

8705. WALKER, GINA LURIA.   Mary Hays (1759–1843): an enlightened quest. *In* (pp. 493–518) **8016**.

Eliza Haywood

8706. BOWLES, EMILY.   Frances Brooke's erotic–didactic garden: desire, shame, and sensibility in *The Excursion*. *See* **8419**.

8707. INGRASSIA, CATHERINE (ed.).   Anti-Pamela; or, Feign'd innocence detected; An apology for the life of Mrs Shamela Andrews. Peterborough, Ont.; Orchard Park, NY: Broadview Press, 2004. pp. 336. (Broadview literary texts.) Rev. by Brian McCrea in Scriblerian (37:2 / 38:1) 2005, 136–7.

8708. KRAMNICK, JONATHAN BRODY. Locke, Haywood, and consent. ELH (72:2) 2005, 453–70.

8709. MERRITT, JULIETTE. Beyond spectacle: Eliza Haywood's female spectators. Toronto; Buffalo, NY; London: Toronto UP, 2004. pp. 154. Rev. by Paula Backscheider in ECF (18:1) 2005, 141–3; by Helen Thompson in Scriblerian (37:2 / 38:1) 2005, 143–5.

8710. PETTIT, ALEXANDER; CROSKERY, MARGARET CASE; PATCHIAS, ANNA C. (eds). *Fantomima* and other works. Peterborough, Ont.; Orchard Park, NY: Broadview Press, 2004. pp. 283. (Broadview literary texts.) Rev. by Helen Thompson in Scriblerian (37:2 /38:1) 2005, 143–5.

8711. SPEDDING, PATRICK. A note on the ornament usage of Henry Woodfall. *See* **180.**

8712. WILPUTTE, EARLA A. Parody in Eliza Haywood's *A Letter from H— G—g, Esq.* ECF (17:2) 2005, 207–30.

Elizabeth Helme (d.1814?)

8713. BATCHELOR, JENNIE. The claims of literature: women applicants to the Royal Literary Fund, 1790–1810. *See* **8856.**

Samuel Henley (1740–1815)

8714. GRAHAM, KENNETH. 'Painting the eyes of the Circassians': Samuel Henley's mistranslations in *Vathek*. Textus (18:1) 2005, 173–88.

Aaron Hill

8715. DAVIS, PAUL. Bransonism. LRB (27:6) 2005, 23–4 (review-article). (Biography of Hill.)

8716. GERRARD, CHRISTINE. Aaron Hill: the Muses' projector, 1685–1750. (Bibl. 2004, 9015.) Rev. by Paul Davis in LRB (27:6) 2005, 23–4; by Kirk Combe in NQ (52:1) 2005, 126–7.

8717. —— Pope, *Peri Bathous*, and the Whig sublime. *In* (pp. 200–15) **8091.**

Benjamin Hoadly

8718. GIBSON, WILLIAM. Benjamin Hoadly: myth and archives. Archives (29:111) 2004, 12–22.

Thomas Holcroft

8719. PATERSON, MARGOT. The name of the poet is Brandes. RECTR (19:1) 2004, 64–7.

8720. SACHS, JONATHAN. From Roman to *roman*: the Jacobin novel and the Roman legacy in the 1790s. *See* **8703.**

8721. TROOST, LINDA. The noble peasant. *In* (pp. 145–53) **3576.**

Francis Hopkinson

8722. SHUFFELTON, FRANK. Thomas Jefferson, Francis Hopkinson, and the representation of the *Notes on the State of Virginia*. *In* (pp. 255–76) **1244.**

John Hughes (1677–1720)

8723. CLYMER, LORNA. Philosophical tours of the universe in British poetry, 1700–1729; or, The soaring muse. *In* (pp. 30–62) **5880.**

David Hume (1711–1776)

8724. GAULL, MARILYN. Romans and Romanticism. *See* **12482**.

8725. KNOX-SHAW, PETER. Philosophy. *In* (pp. 346–56) **10060**.

Richard Hurd

8726. BANDIERA, LAURA (ed. and trans.). Lettere sulla cavalleria e il romance. Parma: Monte Univ. Parma, 2005. pp. 267. (Humanitas et scientia.)

8727. COHEN, MICHÈLE. 'Manners' make the man: politeness, chivalry, and the construction of masculinity, 1750–1830. *See* **9965**.

Francis Hutcheson

8728. STANCO, MICHELE. Hutcheson's 'idea' of beauty and the formation of taste in early eighteenth-century Britain. Textus (18:1) 2005, 25–38.

Gilbert Imlay

8729. MAZZEO, TILAR J. The impossibility of being Anglo-American: the rhetoric of emigration and transatlanticism in British Romantic culture, 1791–1833. *See* **8980**.

Elizabeth Inchbald

8730. BODE, CHRISTOPH. Unfit for an English stage? Inchbald's *Lovers' Vows* and Kotzebue's *Das Kind der Liebe*. ERR (16:3) 2005, 297–309.

8731. JENKINS, ANNIBEL. I'll tell you what: the life of Elizabeth Inchbald. (Bibl. 2004, 9028.) Rev. by Jennifer Golightly in RECTR (19:1) 2004, 74–6; by Lance Wilcox in 1650–1850 (10) 2004, 385–8.

8732. SAGGINI, FRANCESCA. The art of fine drama: Inchbald's *Remarks for the British Theatre* and the aesthetic experience of the late eighteenth-century theatre-goer. Textus (18:1) 2005, 133–52.

William Henry Ireland

8733. DUROT-BOUCÉ, ELIZABETH. Tours et détours: William Henry Ireland, de Shakespeare au gothique. M/M (19:2) 2005, 57–66.

8734. KAHAN, JEFFREY (ed.). The poetry of W. H. Ireland, 1801–1815, including the poet's imitations, satires, romantic verses, and commentaries on Coleridge, Wordsworth, Southey, and others. Lewiston, NY; Lampeter: Mellen Press, 2004. pp. xiv, 375. (Studies in British literature, 85.)

8735. MILES, ROBERT. Forging a Romantic identity: Herbert Croft's *Love and Madness* and W. H. Ireland's Shakespeare MS. *See* **8493**.

8736. —— Trouble in the republic of letters: the reception of the Shakespeare forgeries. SR (44:3) 2005, 317–40.

Thomas Jefferson

8737. BROWNE, STEPHEN HOWARD. Jefferson's call for nationhood: the first inaugural address. *See* **2233**.

8738. GLASBERG, ELENA. The intimate sphere: national strategies of mapping and embodiment. Genre (36:3/4) 2003, 251–70.

8739. HOLLAND, SHARON P. The last word on racism: new directions for a critical race theory. *See* **16417**.

8740. McDermott, Gerald R. The eighteenth-century American culture war: Thomas Jefferson and Jonathan Edwards on religion and religions. *See* **8572.**

8741. Porterfield, Amanda. American religious biography. *See* **8271.**

8742. Shuffelton, Frank. Thomas Jefferson, Francis Hopkinson, and the representation of the *Notes on the State of Virginia*. *In* (pp. 255–76) **1244.**

8743. Valsania, Maurizio. 'Our original barbarism': man *vs* nature in Thomas Jefferson's moral experience. JHI (65:4) 2004, 627–45.

8744. Whitesell, David R. Thomas Jefferson and the book arts. PrH (24:2) 2005, 3–24.

8745. Zhu, Chungeng. Ezra Pound's Confucianism. *See* **18905.**

Charles Johnson (1679–1748)

8746. Conaway, Charles. Shakespeare, molly house culture, and the eighteenth-century stage. *See* **6732.**

Dr Samuel Johnson (1709–1784)

8747. Bax, Randy. Traces of Johnson in the language of Fanny Burney. *See* **8444.**

8748. Bell, Robert H. Boswell's anatomy of folly. *See* **8405.**

8749. Brack, O. M., Jr (ed.). A commentary on Mr Pope's principles of morality, or *Essay on Man*: a translation from the French. New Haven, CT; London: Yale UP, 2004. pp. lvi, 440. (Yale ed. of the works of Samuel Johnson, 17.) Rev. by H. J. Jackson in TLS, 11 Nov. 2005, 3–4.

8750. —— Carlile, Susan. Samuel Johnson's contributions to Charlotte Lennox's *The Female Quixote*. *See* **8788.**

8751. Chambers, Claire. 'The absolute essentialness of conversations': a discussion with Amitav Ghosh. *See* **16664.**

8752. Chapin, Chester. Samuel Johnson and the argument against prophecy. Cithara (45:1) 2005, 28–38.

8753. —— Samuel Johnson on education and the English class structure. 1650–1850 (9) 2003, 189–206.

8754. Clingham, Greg. Johnson, writing, and memory. (Bibl. 2004, 9039.) Rev. by Steven Scherwatzky in ECF (17:2) 2005, 290–4.

8755. Fraser, Russell. Boswell the retailer of phrases. *See* **8406.**

8756. Guerra, Lia. Unexpected symmetries: Samuel Johnson and Mary Wollstonecraft on the Northern Road. Textus (18:1) 2005, 93–106.

8757. Hall, Dennis. Signs of life in the eighteenth century: Dr Johnson and the invention of popular culture. KenPR (19) 2004, 12–16.

8758. Hitchings, Henry. Dr Johnson's *Dictionary*: the extraordinary story of the book that defined the world. London: Murray, 2005; New York: Farrar, Straus, & Giroux, 2005. pp. viii, 278. (Pub. in US as *Defining the world: the extraordinary story of Dr Johnson's 'Dictionary'*.) Rev. by Thomas Keymer in TLS, 15 Apr. 2005, 10; by Jonathan Yardley in BkW, 13 Nov. 2005, 2.

8759. Howe, Sarah. General and invariable ideas of nature: Joshua Reynolds and his critical descendants. *See* **8929.**

8760. HUDSON, NICHOLAS. Samuel Johnson and the making of modern England. (Bibl. 2004, 9042.) Rev. by Steven Scherwatzky in ECF (17:2) 2005, 290–4; by A. F. T. Lurcock in NQ (52:1) 2005, 128–9.

8761. JACKSON, H. J. Big and little matters: discrepancies in the genius of Samuel Johnson. TLS, 11 Nov. 2005, 3–4 (review-article).

8762. JOHNSTON, FREYA. Samuel Johnson and the art of sinking, 1709–1791. Oxford; New York: OUP, 2005. pp. xv, 265. Rev. by H. J. Jackson in TLS, 11 Nov. 2005, 3–4.

8763. JUNG, SANDRO. David Mallet and Lord Bolingbroke. See **8819**.

8764. JUSTICE, GEORGE. *Rasselas* in 'the rise of the novel'. ECN (4) 2004, 217–31.

8765. KEYMER, THOMAS. Meaning exuberant. TLS, 15 Apr. 2005, 10 (review-article). (*Dictionary.*)

8766. KOLB, GWIN J.; DEMARIA, ROBERT, JR (eds). Johnson on the English language. New Haven, CT; London: Yale UP, 2005. pp. xlviii, 506. (Yale ed. of the works of Samuel Johnson, 18.) Rev. by H. J. Jackson in TLS, 9 Dec. 2005, 29.

8767. LEDERER, RICHARD. No harmless drudge: a quatrimillenial celebration. See **1933**.

8768. LEE, ANTHONY W. Mentoring relationships in the life and writings of Samuel Johnson: a study in the dynamics of eighteenth-century literary mentoring. Lewiston, NY; Lampeter: Mellen Press, 2005. pp. xviii, 276. (Studies in British literature, 95.)

8769. LYNCH, JACK. Samuel Johnson, unbeliever. ECL (29:3) 2005, 1–19.

8770. —— MCDERMOTT, ANNE (eds). Anniversary essays on Johnson's dictionary. See **1934**.

8771. MAYHEW, ROBERT J. Landscape, literature, and English religious culture, 1660–1800: Samuel Johnson and languages of natural description. (Bibl. 2004, 9053.) Rev. by Bruce Redford in BJECS (28:1) 2005, 134–5; by Chris Fitter in NQ (52:3) 2005, 420–2.

8772. MORRISON, SARAH R. Truth or consequences: Johnson's *Life of Milton* and the moral biographer's dilemma. *In* (pp. 220–33) **7738**.

8773. PITTOCK, MURRAY. Johnson, Boswell, and their circle. *In* (pp. 157–72) **8014**.

8774. RUDD, NIALL (ed.). The Latin poems. Lewisburg, PA: Bucknell UP, 2005. pp. 153.

8775. SAIRIO, ANNI. 'Sam of Streatham Park': a linguistic study of Dr Johnson's membership in the Thrale family. EJES (9:1) 2005, 21–35.

8776. SERTOLI, GIUSEPPE (ed.). Rasselas principe d'Abissinia. Trans. by G. Miglietta. Venice: Marsilio, 2005. pp. 351. (Letteratura universale.) (Elsinore.)

8777. SHERBO, ARTHUR. More Johnsoniana from the *Gentleman's Magazine*. NQ (52:3) 2005, 376–7.

8778. TANKARD, PAUL. Samuel Johnson's 'history of memory'. SP (102:1) 2005, 110–42.

Sir William Jones

8779. BEWELL, ALAN. William Jones and cosmopolitan natural history. ERR (16:2) 2005, 167–80.

8780. CANNON, GARLAND; FRANKLIN, MICHAEL J. A Cymmrodor claims kin in Calcutta: an assessment of Sir William Jones as philologer, polymath, and pluralist. THSC (11) 2005, 50–69.

8781. FRANKLIN, MICHAEL J. 'I burn with a desire of seeing Shiraz': a new letter from Sir William Jones to Harford Jones. RES (56:227) 2005, 749–57.

8782. ROCHER, ROSANE. Sir William Jones as a satirist: an ethic epistle to the Second Earl Spencer. THSC (11) 2005, 70–104.

George Keate (1729–1797)

8783. GOULDING, CHRISTOPHER. *Avalanche*: antedating the entry in the *Oxford English Dictionary*. See **1813**.

Hugh Kelly

8784. SHEVLIN, ELEANOR F. The titular claims of female surnames in eighteenth-century fiction. *In* (pp. 256–80) **6964**.

Mary Leapor

8785. GREENE, RICHARD; MESSENGER, ANN (eds). The works of Mary Leapor. (Bibl. 2004, 9068.) Rev. by Donna Landry in ECS (38:3) 2005, 535–8.

8786. MEYER, MICHAEL. Mary Leapor: the female body and the body of her texts. 1650–1850 (10) 2004, 63–78.

Sophia Lee

8787. WRIGHT, ANGELA. 'To live the life of hopeless recollection': mourning and melancholia in female gothic, 1780–1800. See **8163**.

Charlotte Lennox

8788. BRACK, O. M., JR; CARLILE, SUSAN. Samuel Johnson's contributions to Charlotte Lennox's *The Female Quixote*. YLG (77:3/4) 2003, 166–73.

8789. CARLILE, SUSAN. Expanding the feminine: reconsidering Charlotte Lennox's age and *The Life of Harriot Stuart*. ECN (4) 2004, 103–37.

8790. HOWARD, SUSAN KUBICA. Seeing Colonial America and writing home about it: Charlotte Lennox's *Euphemia*, epistolarity, and the feminine picturesque. StudN (37:3) 2005, 273–91.

8791. STEEDMAN, CAROLYN. Servants and their relationship to the unconscious. JBS (42:3) 2003, 316–50.

M. G. Lewis

8792. BREWER, WILLIAM D. Transgendering in Matthew Lewis's *The Monk*. GothS (6:2) 2004, 192–207.

8793. DORNAN, STEPHEN. Thomas Dermody, Robert Burns and the Killeigh cycle. See **8556**.

8794. FITZGERALD, LAUREN. The gothic villain and the vilification of the plagiarist: the case of *The Castle Spectre*. GothS (7:1) 2005, 5–17.

8795. —— The sexuality of authorship in *The Monk*. RomNet (36/37) 2004/05.

8796. HOGLE, JERROLD E.   *Christabel* as gothic: the abjection of instability. *See* **10491**.

8797. MACDONALD, D. L.   'A dreadful dreadful dream': transvaluation, realization, and literalization of *Clarissa* in *The Monk*. *See* **8947**.

8798. WICKMAN, MATTHEW.   Terror's abduction of experience: a gothic history. *See* **8926**.

Janet Little

8799. MILNE, ANNE.   Dogs and the 'talking animal syndrome' in Janet Little's *From Snipe, a Favourite Dog, to His Master* (1791). ScSR (4:1) 2003, 69–81.

Evan Lloyd (1734–1776)

8800. DURING, SIMON.   'The temple lives': the Lyceum and Romantic show business. *In* (pp. 204–24) **9217**.

George Lyttelton, First Baron Lyttelton

8801. MONOD, PAUL.   *Tom Jones* and the crisis of Whiggism in mid-Hanoverian England. *In* (pp. 268–96) **8091**.

Catharine Macaulay (1731–1791)

8802. HUTTON, SARAH.   Liberty, equality and God: the religious roots of Catherine (*sic*) Macaulay's feminism. *In* (pp. 538–50) **8016**.

8803. O'BRIEN, KAREN.   Catharine Macaulay's histories of England: a female perspective on the history of liberty. *In* (pp. 523–37) **8016**.

James Macpherson (1736–1796)

8804. BYSTYDZIEŃSKA, GRAŻYNA.   The landscape in grey: the role of nature in the Ossianic epics. *In* (pp. 29–35) **3756**.

8805. CRAWFORD, ROBERT.   The Bard: Ossian, Burns, and the shaping of Shakespeare. *In* (pp. 124–40) **6561**.

8806. DANE, JOSEPH A.; DJANANOVA, SVETLANA.   The typographical gothic: a cautionary note on the title page to Percy's *Reliques of Ancient English Poetry*. *See* **8857**.

8807. DOLAN, JOHN.   The third great text-finder: Joseph E. Smith Jr as colleague of Chatterton and Macpherson. *See* **8466**.

8808. GASKILL, HOWARD (ed.).   The reception of 'Ossian' in Europe. London; New York: Continuum, 2004. pp. lxviii, 452. (Athlone critical traditions, 5.)

8809. GIOVANNELLI, LAURA.   From substantial body into evanescent ghost: the world of James Macpherson's Ossianic 'fragments'. *In* (pp. 75–87) **3724**.

8810. LAMPORT, FRANCIS.   Ossian and Ossianism in Britain and Germany: a review-article. MLR (100:3) 2005, 740–6 (review-article).

8811. LEERSSEN, JOEP.   On the Celtic roots of a Romantic theme. *In* (pp. 1–10) **9237**.

8812. MAC CRAITH, MÍCHEÁL.   Wrestling with the form: the genesis of Macpherson's *Fragments*. *In* (pp. 344–65) **12868**.

8813. MOORE, DAFYDD (ed.).   Ossian and Ossianism. (Bibl. 2004, 9087.) Rev. by Francis Lamport in MLR (100:3) 2005, 740–6.

8814. PURSER, JOHN. Erik Chisholm and Macpherson's *Night Song of the Bards*. ScSR (6:1) 2005, 43–58.

8815. SCHMIDT, WOLF GERHARD (ed.). 'Homer des Nordens' und 'Mutter der Romantik': James Macphersons *Ossian* und seine Rezeption in der deutschsprachigen Literatur: 3, Kommentierte Neuausgabe deutscher Übersetzungen der *Fragments of Ancient Poetry* (1766), der *Poems of Ossian* (1782) sowie der Vorreden und Abhandlungen von Hugh Blair und James Macpherson. Berlin; New York: Mouton de Gruyter, 2003. pp. xiv, 850. Rev. by Francis Lamport in MLR (100:3) 2005, 740–6.

8816. —— GASKILL, HOWARD (eds). 'Homer des Nordens' und 'Mutter der Romantik': James Macphersons *Ossian* und seine Rezeption in der deutschsprachigen Literatur: 4, Kommentierte Neuausgabe wichtiger Texte zur deutschen Rezeptione. Berlin; New York: Mouton de Gruyter, 2003. pp. xvi, 850. Rev. by Francis Lamport in MLR (100:3) 2005, 740–6.

8817. SEBASTIANI, SILVIA. 'Race', women and progress in the Scottish Enlightenment. *In* (pp. 75–96) **8016**.

David Mallet

8818. CLYMER, LORNA. Philosophical tours of the universe in British poetry, 1700–1729; or, The soaring muse. *In* (pp. 30–62) **5880**.

8819. JUNG, SANDRO. David Mallet and Lord Bolingbroke. ANQ (18:1) 2005, 24–8.

Edmond Malone

8820. LOCKWOOD, TOM. Edmond Malone and early modern textual culture. YLG (79:1/2) 2004, 53–69.

8821. SHERBO, ARTHUR. The appendix to Edmond Malone's 1790 *Shakespeare*, the 1821 Boswell–Malone *Shakespeare*, and Elizabethan language. *See* **5828**.

8822. —— James Boswell's editing of, and contributions to, the 1821 Boswell–Malone *Shakespeare*. *See* **8413**.

Bernard Mandeville

8823. DEW, BEN. Spurs to industry in Bernard Mandeville's *Fable of the Bees*. BJECS (28:2) 2005, 151–65.

8824. HUNDERT, EDWARD. Mandeville, Rousseau and the political economy of fantasy. *In* (pp. 28–40) **7941**.

8825. KNOX-SHAW, PETER. Philosophy. *In* (pp. 346–56) **10060**.

8826. LAMB, JONATHAN. The crying of lost things. *See* **8652**.

8827. PELTONEN, MARKKU. The duel in early modern England: civility, politeness and honour. (Bibl. 2004, 9093.) Rev. by Goran V. Stanivukovic in CLIO (34:4) 2005, 458–65; by Brett F. Parker in SCN (63:3/4) 2005, 198–9.

8828. WOLF, AMY. Bernard Mandeville, Henry Fielding's *Amelia*, and the necessities of plot. *See* **8624**.

Mary de la Rivière Manley

8829. BOWLES, EMILY. Frances Brooke's erotic–didactic garden: desire, shame, and sensibility in *The Excursion*. *See* **8419**.

8830. HERMAN, RUTH. The business of a woman: the political writings of Delarivier Manley. (Bibl. 2003, 8279.) Rev. by Ros Ballaster in RES (56:224) 2005, 323–5.

8831. NOVÁKOVÁ, SOŇA. Sex and politics: Delarivier Manley's *New Atalantis*. *In* (pp. 121–6) 3753.

William Mason

8832. JUNG, SANDRO. William Mason and Count Francesco Algarotti: two new letters. ANQ (18:1) 2005, 29–31.

William Massey (1691–1764?)

8833. HOLFORD-STREVENS, LEOFRANC. The first translation of Aulus Gellius. NQ (52:3) 2005, 370–4.

Elizabeth Montagu

8834. EGER, ELIZABETH. Luxury, industry and charity: Bluestocking culture displayed. *In* (pp. 190–204) 7941.

8835. MAJOR, EMMA. Femininity and national identity: Elizabeth Montagu's trip to France. ELH (72:4) 2005, 901–18.

8836. RITCHIE, FIONA. Elizabeth Montagu: 'Shakespear's poor little critick'? ShS (58) 2005, 72–82.

Lady Mary Wortley Montagu

8837. DOCKER, JOHN. The Enlightenment and genocide. JNT (33:3) 2003, 292–314.

8838. MERRILL, YVONNE. The role of language in the construction of Mary Wortley Montagu's rhetorical identity. *In* (pp. 44–62) 2410.

Edward Moore

8839. ZUNSHINE, LISA. Bastard daughters and foundling heroines: rewriting illegitimacy for the eighteenth-century stage. *See* 9028.

Hannah More ('Z')

8840. CAIRNIE, JULIE. The ambivalence of Ann Yearsley: laboring and writing, submission and resistance. *See* 9156.

8841. COMITINI, PATRICIA. Vocational philanthropy and British women's writing, 1790–1810: Wollstonecraft, More, Edgeworth, Wordsworth. *See* 9134.

8842. DAVIDSON, JULIE E. William Roberts's dating of Hannah More's memoirs. NQ (52:3) 2005, 377–80.

8843. DENLINGER, ELIZABETH CAMPBELL. Before Victoria: extraordinary women of the British Romantic era. Foreword by Lyndall Gordon. New York: New York Public Library / Columbia UP, 2005. pp. xii, 188. Rev. by Donelle Ruwe in NCC (27:4) 2005, 383–5.

8844. ORR, CLARISSA CAMPBELL. Aristocratic feminism, the learned governess, and the republic of letters. *In* (pp. 306–25) 8016.

8845. PRIOR, KAREN SWALLOW. Hannah More, the didactic tradition, and the rise of the English novel. 1650–1850 (9) 2003, 41–78.

8846. PURINTON, MARJEAN. Gender, nationalism, and science in Hannah More's pedagogical plays for children. *In* (pp. 113–36) 8171.

8847. STOTT, ANNE.   Hannah More: the first Victorian. (Bibl. 2004, 9112.)
Rev. by Nancy LoPatin-Lummis in Albion (36:3) 2004, 539–41; by Judy Simons in
MLR (100:1) 2005, 203–5; by Harriet Devine Jump in WWr (12:2) 2005, 321–8.

Peter Motteux

8848. LOWERRE, KATHRYN.   Dramatick opera and theatrical reform: Dennis's
Rinaldo and Armida and Motteux's *The Island Princess. See* **8552**.

Arthur Murphy

8849. SCHOCH, RICHARD W.   'A supplement to public laws': Arthur Murphy,
David Garrick, and *Hamlet, with Alterations.* TJ (57:1) 2005, 21–32.

Ann Murry (*fl.*1778–1799)

8850. RAUCH, ALAN.   *Mentoria*: women, children, and the structures of science.
NCC (27:4) 2005, 335–51.

Mr (John) Oldmixon (1673–1742)

8851. ROGERS, PAT (ed.).   The letters, life, and works of John Oldmixon.
Lewiston, NY; Lampeter: Mellen Press, 2004. pp. v, 161. (Studies in British
literature, 91.) Rev. by John Baird in TLS, 22 July 2005, 28–9.

James Orr (1770–1816)

8852. BARANIUK, CAROL.   James Orr: Ulster Scot and poet of the 1798
Rebellion. ScSR (6:1) 2005, 22–32.

Thomas Paine (1737–1809)

8853. EVERTON, MICHAEL.   'The would-be author and the real bookseller':
Thomas Paine and eighteenth-century printing ethics. EAL (40:1) 2005,
79–110.

8854. MAKDISI, SAREE.   Blake's metropolitan Radicalism. *In* (pp. 113–31) **9217**.

8855. WAGNER, CORINNA.   Loyalist propaganda and the scandalous life of Tom
Paine: 'Hypocritical monster!' BJECS (28:1) 2005, 97–115.

Eliza Parsons

8856. BATCHELOR, JENNIE.   The claims of literature: women applicants to the
Royal Literary Fund, 1790–1810. WWr (12:3) 2005, 505–21.

Thomas Percy

8857. DANE, JOSEPH A.; DJANANOVA, SVETLANA.   The typographical gothic:
a cautionary note on the title page to Percy's *Reliques of Ancient English Poetry.*
ECL (29:3) 2005, 76–96.

8858. RIX, ROBERT.   'Letters in a strange character': runes, rocks and
Romanticism. ERR (16:5) 2005, 589–611.

Ambrose Philips

8859. CHAMPION, JUSTIN.   '*Anglia libera*': Commonwealth politics in the early
years of George I. *In* (pp. 86–107) **8091**.

Letitia Pilkington

8860. ELIAS, A. C., JR.   Consolation for the Christian: a new sermon by Matthew
Pilkington. *See* **8226**.

John Pinkerton (1758–1826)

8861. MAYHEW, ROBERT. British geography's republic of letters: mapping an imagined community, 1600–1800. *See* **7501.**

Hester Lynch Piozzi (Mrs Thrale)

8862. SAIRIO, ANNI. 'Sam of Streatham Park': a linguistic study of Dr Johnson's membership in the Thrale family. *See* **8775.**

8863. STEEDMAN, CAROLYN. Servants and their relationship to the unconscious. *See* **8791.**

Anne Plumptre (1760–1818)

8864. CHANDLER, DAVID. Coleridge satirized by Anne Plumptre. NQ (52:1) 2005, 40–2.

James Plumptre (1770–1832)

8865. BERTELSEN, LARS KIEL. The Claude glass: a modern metaphor between word and image. Trans. by Stacey M. Cozart. WI (20:3) 2004, 182–90.

Richard Polwhele (1760–1838)

8866. GEORGE, SAM. Linnaeus in letters and the cultivation of the female mind: 'Botany in an English dress'. BJECS (28:1) 2005, 1–18.

8867. HAUT, ASIA. Reading Flora: Erasmus Darwin's *The Botanic Garden*, Henry Fuseli's illustrations, and various literary responses. *See* **8497.**

8868. JONES, VIVIEN. Advice and Enlightenment: Mary Wollstonecraft and sex education. *In* (pp. 140–55) **8016.**

8869. PASCOE, JUDITH. 'Unsex'd females': Barbauld, Robinson, and Smith. *In* (pp. 211–26) **8014.**

Alexander Pope

8870. ASHLEY, LEONARD R. N.; CONTI, CHRISTI. An anonymous poem to Alexander Pope from South Carolina (1737). SoCR (38:1) 2005, 20–32.

8871. BASTOS DA SILVA, JORGE. Cato's ghosts: Pope, Addison, and opposition cultural politics. *See* **8312.**

8872. BATCHELOR, ROBERT. Concealing the bounds: imagining the British nation through China. *In* (pp. 79–92) **8039.**

8873. BELLORINI, MARIAGRAZIA. *'First follow Nature'*: riflessioni e note sulla semantica del giardino nella poesia e nella cultura inglese del Settecento. *See* **8175.**

8874. BRACK, O. M., JR (ed.). A commentary on Mr Pope's principles of morality, or *Essay on Man*: a translation from the French. *See* **8749.**

8875. BROICH, ULRICH. Alexander Pope, the ideal of the hero, Ovid, and Menippean satire. SLI (38:1) 2005, 179–96.

8876. BROWN, DENNIS. *The Rape of the Lock*: desire between couple(t)s – a counselling intervention. CritS (16:3) 2004, 1–16.

8877. BROWN, LAURA. Oceans and floods: fables of global perspective. *In* (pp. 107–20) **8039.**

8878. DAVIDSON, PETER. Pope's recusancy. SLI (38:1) 2005, 63–76.

8879. DEUTSCH, HELEN. Bolingbroke's laugh: Alexander Pope's *Epistle to Bolingbroke* and the rhetoric of embodied exemplarity. SLI (38:1) 2005, 137–61.

8880. EDGECOMBE, RODNEY STENNING. Horace's *Odes* 4.2 and Pope's *Essay on Criticism*. ANQ (18:1) 2005, 21–2.

8881. —— Otway's *Windsor Castle* and Pope's *Windsor-Forest*. See **7804**.

8882. —— Pope's *An Essay on Criticism*. Exp (63:4) 2005, 212–13.

8883. EDWARDS, CHRISTOPHER. From Pope to Swift: a book from Swift's library. See **9058**.

8884. FANNING, CHRISTOPHER. The Scriblerian sublime. SELit (45:3) 2005, 647–67.

8885. GARDNER, KEVIN J. Timon's potlatch: generosity, prodigality, and the English country house in Pope's *Epistle to Burlington*. CEACrit (67:1) 2004, 25–37.

8886. GEE, SOPHIE. The sewers: ordure, effluence, and excess in the eighteenth century. *In* (pp. 101–20) **6958**.

8887. GERRARD, CHRISTINE. Pope, *Peri Bathous*, and the Whig sublime. *In* (pp. 200–15) **8091**.

8888. GREGORI, FLAVIO. Introduction: Pope on the margins and in the center. SLI (38:1) 2005, i–xliv.

8889. HAMMOND, BREAN S. *The Dunciad* and the city: Pope and heterotopia. SLI (38:1) 2005, 219–32.

8890. JARVIS, SIMON. Mock as screen and optic. CritQ (46:3) 2004, 1–19.

8891. JONES, TOM. Pope and Berkeley: the language of poetry and philosophy. Basingstoke; New York: Palgrave Macmillan, 2005. pp. viii, 203.

8892. KAIROFF, CLAUDIA THOMAS. Living on the margin: Alexander Pope and the rural ideal. SLI (38:1) 2005, 15–38.

8893. LIU, YU. The importance of the Chinese connection: the origin of the English garden. ECL (27:3) 2003, 70–98.

8894. MCCABE, RICHARD A. Parody, sympathy and self: a response to Donald Cheney. See **5707**.

8895. MACPHERSON, SANDRA. Sex at Twickenham. See **8985**.

8896. NICHOLSON, COLIN. The mercantile bard: commerce and conflict in Pope. SLI (38:1) 2005, 77–94.

8897. NOGGLE, JAMES. Taste and temporality in *An Epistle to Burlington*. SLI (38:1) 2005, 117–35.

8898. ORESTANO, FRANCESCA. Bust story: Pope at Stowe; or, The politics and myths of landscape gardening. SLI (38:1) 2005, 39–61.

8899. PRITCHARD, JONATHAN. Pope, John Rackett, and the slave trade. SELit (45:3) 2005, 579–601.

8900. ROGERS, PAT. The maypole in the Strand: Pope and the politics of revelry. BJECS (28:1) 2005, 83–95.

8901. —— Notes on Pope's correspondence. NQ (52:3) 2005, 351–5.

8902. —— Pope and the Moore family. NQ (52:3) 2005, 355–9.

8903. —— Pope's cardinal virtues and the coronation of 1727: a possible link. Scriblerian (37:2 / 38:1) 2005, 90–3.

8904. —— Pope's friend Henry Cromwell. *See* **8494**.

8905. —— The symbolic design of *Windsor-Forest*: iconography, pageant, and prophecy in Pope's early work. (Bibl. 2004, 9148.) Rev. by Richard Eversole in Scriblerian (37:2/38:1) 2005, 123–4.

8906. RUMBOLD, VALERIE; MCGEARY, THOMAS. *Folly*, session poems, and the preparations for Pope's *Dunciads*. *See* **8626**.

8907. RUPP, SUSANNE. Fremde zeitgenossen Klassiker. *See* **6068**.

8908. SMALLWOOD, PHILIP. Reconstructing criticism: Pope's *Essay on Criticism* and the logic of definition. (Bibl. 2003, 8331.) Rev. in Scriblerian (37:2/38:1) 2005, 129–30; by Jennifer Snead in ECS (38:2) 2005, 349–55.

8909. SNEAD, JENNIFER. No exit? Recent publications on Pope. ECS (38:2) 2005, 349–55 (review-article).

8910. SPENCER, JANE. 'Mighty mother': Pope and the maternal. SLI (38:1) 2005, 163–78.

8911. TALBOT, JOHN. Auden's Horatian mosaic. *See* **15244**.

8912. TERRY, RICHARD. Pope and plagiarism. MLR (100:3) 2005, 593–608.

8913. TOSI, LAURA. 'Then rose the seed of chaos': masque and antimasque in *The Dunciad in Four Books*. SLI (38:1) 2005, 197–218.

8914. VENDLER, HELEN. Poets thinking: Pope, Whitman, Dickinson, Yeats. (Bibl. 2004, 9162.) Rev. by Fiona Green in TLS, 7 Oct. 2005, 13.

8915. WEINBROT, HOWARD D. Menippean satire reconsidered: from Antiquity to the eighteenth century. Baltimore, MD; London: Johns Hopkins UP, 2005. pp. xvi, 375.

8916. WOODMAN, THOMAS. Pope and the paradoxical centrality of the satirist. SLI (38:1) 2005, 1–13.

George Psalmanazar

8917. KEEVAK, MICHAEL. The pretended Asian: George Psalmanazar's eighteenth-century Formosan hoax. Detroit, MI: Wayne State UP, 2004. pp. x, 182. Rev. by Nick Groom in RES (56:224) 2005, 325–7.

Ann Radcliffe

8918. BLACKWELL, MARK R. The gothic: moving in the world of novels. *In* (pp. 144–61) **6958**.

8919. CARBONI, PIERRE. '*A romance interspersed with pieces of poetry*': la citation poétique et les marges sublimes du discours dans les romans d'Ann Radcliffe. EREA (2:1) 2004, 47–53.

8920. CLOSE, ANNE. Notorious: Mary Robinson and the gothic. *See* **8963**.

8921. ELIA, ADRIANO. Sublime and word-painting in Ann Radcliffe's *The Mysteries of Udolpho*. Textus (18:1) 2005, 61–76.

8922. NEILL, NATALIE. 'The trash with which the press now groans': *Northanger Abbey* and the gothic best sellers of the 1790s. *See* **10028**.

8923. ORESTANO, FRANCESCA. *Picturesque: a transformation*: William Gilpin's aesthetics and Ann Radcliffe's visual imagination. *See* **8663**.

8924. SMITH, ANDREW. Love, Freud, and the female gothic: Bram Stoker's *The Jewel of Seven Stars*. *See* **12102**.

8925. WENNERSTROM, COURTNEY. Cosmopolitan bodies and dissected sexualities: anatomical mis-stories in Ann Radcliffe's *Mysteries of Udolpho*. ERR (16:2) 2005, 193–207.

8926. WICKMAN, MATTHEW. Terror's abduction of experience: a gothic history. YJC (18:1) 2005, 179–206.

Clara Reeve

8927. COYKENDALL, ABBY. Gothic genealogies, the family romance, and Clara Reeve's *The Old English Baron*. ECF (17:3) 2005, 443–80.

8928. WICKMAN, MATTHEW. Terror's abduction of experience: a gothic history. *See* **8926**.

Sir Joshua Reynolds

8929. HOWE, SARAH. General and invariable ideas of nature: Joshua Reynolds and his critical descendants. Eng (54:208) 2005, 1–13.

Dorothy Richardson (1748–1819)

8930. KINSLEY, ZOË. Dorothy Richardson's manuscript travel journals (1761–1801) and the possibilities of picturesque aesthetics. RES (56:226) 2005, 611–31.

Samuel Richardson

8931. BRIGGS, JULIA. 'Delightful task!': women, children, and reading in the mid-eighteenth century. *In* (pp. 67–82) **8171**.

8932. BROWN, MURRAY L. T. C. Duncan Eaves, Ben D. Kimpel, and the life: a brief and apologetic memoir. 1650–1850 (9) 2003, 327–37. (*Discusses* bibl. 1971, 6052.)

8933. BRÜCKMANN, PATRICIA. 'Men, Women and Poles': Samuel Richardson and the romance of a Stuart princess. ECL (27:3) 2003, 31–52.

8934. BUDD, ADAM. Mourn not a change: the moralizing consolations of Samuel Richardson. TLS, 8 Apr. 2005, 14.

8935. EASTON, CELIA A. Austen's urban redemption: rejecting Richardson's view of the city. *See* **9976**.

8936. EPSTEIN, WILLIAM H. Remembering the past: Eaves and Kimpel's *Richardson* and the uses of literary biography. 1650–1850 (9) 2003, 285–306. (*Discusses* bibl. 1971, 6052.)

8937. FLYNN, CAROL HOULIHAN. The uses and abuses of biography: incendiary information. 1650–1850 (9) 2003, 308–26. (*Discusses* bibl. 1971, 6052.)

8938. FRAIL, ROBERT J. Realism in Samuel Richardson and the abbé Prévost. Lewiston, NY; Lampeter: Mellen Press, 2005. pp. vi, 198. (Studies in comparative literature, 65.)

8939. HARWEG, ROLAND. Are Fielding's Shamela and Richardson's Pamela one and the same person? A contribution to the problem of the number of fictive worlds. Style (38:3) 2004, 290–301.

8940. HOW, JAMES. Epistolary spaces: English letter-writing from the foundation of the Post Office to Richardson's *Clarissa*. (Bibl. 2003, 8362.) Rev. by Allan Ingram in MLR (100:3) 2005, 787–8.

8941. JUSTICE, GEORGE. *Rasselas* in 'the rise of the novel'. *See* **8764**.

8942. KAROUNOS, MICHAEL. The theory of the dynamic erotic. 1650–1850 (9) 2003, 107–22.

8943. KEYMER, THOMAS. Parliamentary printing, paper credit, and corporate fraud: a new episode in Richardson's early career. ECF (17:2) 2005, 183–206.

8944. —— SABOR, PETER. *Pamela* in the marketplace: literary controversy and print culture in eighteenth-century Britain and Ireland. Cambridge; New York: CUP, 2005. pp. x, 295.

8945. KOEHLER, MARTHA J. Models of reading: paragons and parasites in Richardson, Burney, and Laclos. Lewisburg, PA: Bucknell UP, 2005. pp. 328.

8946. LIPSEDGE, KAREN. Representations of the domestic parlour in Samuel Richardson's *Clarissa*, 1747–48. ECF (17:3) 2005, 391–423.

8947. MACDONALD, D. L. 'A dreadful dreadful dream': transvaluation, realization, and literalization of *Clarissa* in *The Monk*. GothS (6:2) 2004, 157–71.

8948. MACPHERSON, SANDRA. Sex at Twickenham. *See* **8985**.

8949. MÜLLER, ANJA. Picturing Æsops: re-visions of *Æsop's Fables* from L'Estrange to Richardson. *See* **107**.

8950. PARK, JULIE. 'I shall enter her heart': fetishizing feeling in *Clarissa*. StudN (37:4) 2005, 371–93.

8951. PARKE, CATHERINE N. 'Definitive', 'exhaustive', and 'rather old-fashioned': scholarly biography on the cusp of critical change. 1650–1850 (9) 2003, 339–56. (*Discusses* bibl. 1971, 6052.)

8952. PASCOE, JUDITH. Before I read *Clarissa* I was nobody: aspirational reading and Samuel Richardson's great novel. HR (56:2) 2003, 239–53.

8953. PHILLIPS, ELAINE ANDERSON. Richardson reads the Renaissance: the use of Renaissance narrative theory in the novels and prefaces. 1650–1850 (10) 2004, 327–47.

8954. RICHARDSON, LESLIE. Leaving her father's house: Astell, Locke, and Clarissa's body politic. *See* **7196**.

8955. SABOR, PETER. Richardson, Henry Fielding, and Sarah Fielding. *In* (pp. 139–56) **8014**.

8956. SIMS, CLARE. Christian sin and mimetic contagion: repentance in Samuel Richardson's *Clarissa*. Anthropoetics (10:2) 2004/05.

8957. WANDLESS, WILLIAM H. Narrative pain and the moral sense: toward an ethics of suffering in the long eighteenth century. *See* **7258**.

8958. WEBSTER, JEREMY W. Sentimentalizing patriarchy: patriarchal anxiety and filial obligation in *Sir Charles Grandison*. ECF (17:3) 2005, 425–42.

8959. WEINBROT, HOWARD D. Menippean satire reconsidered: from Antiquity to the eighteenth century. *See* **8915**.

8960. ZIAS, HEATHER. Who can believe? Sentiment *vs* cynicism in Richardson's *Clarissa*. ECL (27:3) 2003, 99–123.

J. Robinson (*fl.*1792)

8961. GOUDIE, SEAN X. The West Indies, commerce, and a play for US empire: recovering J. Robinson's *The Yorker's Stratagem* (1792). EAL (40:1) 2005, 1–35.

Mary Robinson (1758–1800)

8962. BYRNE, PAULA.   Perdita: the literary, theatrical, scandalous life of Mary Robinson. New York: Random House, 2004. pp. xviii, 445, (plates) 8. Rev. by Nora Crook in TLS, 7 Jan. 2005, 32; by Meryle Secrest in BkW, 14 Aug. 2005, 9.

8963. CLOSE, ANNE.   Notorious: Mary Robinson and the gothic. GothS (6:2) 2004, 172–91.

8964. CRACIUN, ADRIANA.   British women writers and the French Revolution: citizens of the world. *See* **7964**.

8965. CROOK, NORA.   That woman has an ear. TLS, 7 Jan. 2005, 32 (review-article).

8966. DAVENPORT, HESTER.   The prince's mistress: a life of Mary Robinson. Stroud: Sutton, 2004. pp. xiv, 274, (plates) 8. Rev. by Nora Crook in TLS, 7 Jan. 2005, 32; by Alix Nathan in WWr (12:2) 2005, 313–15.

8967. DENLINGER, ELIZABETH CAMPBELL.   Before Victoria: extraordinary women of the British Romantic era. Foreword by Lyndall Gordon. *See* **8843**.

8968. GARNAI, AMY.   'One victim from the last despair': Mary Robinson's Marie Antoinette. WWr (12:3) 2005, 381–98.

8969. GORDON, FELICIA.   *Filles publiques* or public women: the actress as citizen: Marie Madeleine Jodin (1741–90) and Mary Darby Robinson (1758–1800). *In* (pp. 610–29) **8016**.

8970. KLANCHER, JON.   Discriminations; or, Romantic cosmopolitanisms in London. *In* (pp. 65–82) **9217**.

8971. PASCOE, JUDITH.   'Unsex'd females': Barbauld, Robinson, and Smith. *In* (pp. 211–26) **8014**.

8972. SETZER, SHARON M. (ed.).   *A Letter to the Women of England* and *The Natural Daughter*. Peterborough, Ont.; Orchard Park, NY: Broadview Press, 2003. pp. 336. (Broadview literary texts.) Rev. by Claire Grogan in ECF (17:2) 2005, 305–6.

8973. SHAFFER, JULIE A. (ed.).   Walsingham; or, The pupil of nature. Peterborough, Ont.; Orchard Park, NY: Broadview Press, 2003. pp. 559. (Broadview literary texts.) Rev. by Claire Grogan in ECF (17:2) 2005, 305–6.

8974. STELZIG, EUGENE.   'Spirit divine! With thee I'll wander': Mary Robinson and Coleridge in poetic dialogue. WordsC (35:3) 2004, 118–22.

Elizabeth Singer Rowe

8975. PERRY, LORI A. DAVIS.   The literary model for Elizabeth Singer Rowe's *History of Joseph*. NQ (52:3) 2005, 349–51.

8976. PRESCOTT, SARAH.   Elizabeth Singer Rowe: gender, Dissent, and Whig poetics. *In* (pp. 173–99) **8091**.

Nicholas Rowe

8977. HARRIS, SUSAN CANNON.   Outside the box: the female spectator, *The Fair Penitent*, and the Kelly Riots of 1747. TJ (57:1) 2005, 33–55.

8978. WILSON, BRETT.   Jane Shore and the Jacobites: Nicholas Rowe, the Pretender, and the national she-tragedy. ELH (72:4) 2005, 823–43.

Susanna Rowson

8979. DILLON, ELIZABETH MADDOCK. *Slaves in Algiers*: race, Republican genealogies, and the global stage. AmLH (16:3) 2004, 407–36.

8980. MAZZEO, TILAR J. The impossibility of being Anglo-American: the rhetoric of emigration and transatlanticism in British Romantic culture, 1791–1833. ERR (16:1) 2005, 59–78.

Benjamin Rush

8981. KNOTT, SARAH. Benjamin Rush's ferment: Enlightenment medicine and female citizenship in Revolutionary America. *In* (pp. 649–66) **8016.**

Ignatius Sancho

8982. GOULD, PHILIP. The African slave trade and Abolitionism: rereading antislavery literature, 1776–1800. *In* (pp. 201–19) **1244.**

Sarah Scott

8983. BOWLES, EMILY. Frances Brooke's erotic–didactic garden: desire, shame, and sensibility in *The Excursion*. See **8419.**

8984. VAN SANT, ANN. Historicizing domestic relations: Sarah Scott's use of the 'household family'. ECF (17:3) 2005, 373–90.

Edward Sellon (1818?–1866)

8985. MACPHERSON, SANDRA. Sex at Twickenham. ELH (72:2) 2005, 471–93.

Anna Seward

8986. BRIDEOAKE, FIONA. 'Extraordinary female affection': the Ladies of Llangollen and the endurance of queer community. RomNet (36/37) 2004/05.

8987. HAUT, ASIA. Reading Flora: Erasmus Darwin's *The Botanic Garden*, Henry Fuseli's illustrations, and various literary responses. See **8497.**

8988. SAGLIA, DIEGO. The aesthetics of the present: commerce, empire and technology in late eighteenth-century women's poetry. Textus (18:1) 2005, 205–20.

Anthony Ashley Cooper, Third Earl of Shaftesbury

8989. BULLARD, PADDY. The meaning of the 'sublime and beautiful': Shaftesburian contexts and rhetorical issues in Edmund Burke's *Philosophical Enquiry*. See **8424.**

8990. DACOME, LUCIA. Noting the mind: commonplace books and the pursuit of the self in eighteenth-century Britain. See **7107.**

8991. FESTA, LYNN. Cosmetic differences: the changing faces of England and France. StudECC (34) 2005, 25–54.

8992. HUHN, TOM. Imitation and society: the persistence of mimesis in the work of Burke, Hogarth, and Kant. See **8432.**

8993. MCGRANE, LAURA. Fielding's fallen oracles: print culture and the elusiveness of common sense. See **8614.**

8994. MEE, JON. Blake and the poetics of Enthusiasm. *In* (pp. 194–210) **8014.**

8995. PETERSON, LELAND D. A letter to the editor on the occasion of his correspondence about Swift's *The Beasts' Confession to the Priest*. See **9082.**

8996. TIERNEY-HYNES, REBECCA. Shaftesbury's *Soliloquy*: authorship and the psychology of romance. ECS (38:4) 2004, 605–21.

Thomas Sheridan (1719–1788)

8997. GLENN, CHERYL. Unspoken: a rhetoric of silence. *See* **2317**.

8998. HARRIS, SUSAN CANNON. Outside the box: the female spectator, *The Fair Penitent*, and the Kelly Riots of 1747. *See* **8977**.

Christopher Smart

8999. GURR, JENS MARTIN. 'Let me suppose thee for a ship a-while': nautical metaphors and contemporary politics in eighteenth-century translations of Horace's Ode I, xiv. *See* **9069**.

9000. PAULSON, RONALD. Hogarth's harlot: sacred parody in Enlightenment England. (Bibl. 2004, 9226.) Rev. by Martha F. Bowden in Scriblerian (37:2/38:1) 2005, 106–8.

Charlotte Smith

9001. FLETCHER, LORAINE (ed.). Emmeline: the orphan of the castle. (Bibl. 2004, 9231.) Rev. by Mary Anne Schofield in ECF (17:2) 2005, 301–2.

9002. KELLEY, THERESA M. Romantic histories: Charlotte Smith and *Beachy Head*. NineL (59:3) 2004, 281–314.

9003. LABBE, JACQUELINE M. Charlotte Smith: Romanticism, poetry, and the culture of gender. (Bibl. 2004, 9234.) Rev. by Jennie Batchelor in NQ (52:1) 2005, 136–7.

9004. NORDIUS, JANINA. 'A kind of living death': gothicizing the colonial encounter in Charlotte Smith's *The Old Manor House*. EngS (86:1) 2005, 40–50.

9005. PASCOE, JUDITH. 'Unsex'd females': Barbauld, Robinson, and Smith. *In* (pp. 211–26) **8014**.

9006. STANTON, JUDITH PHILLIPS (ed.). The collected letters of Charlotte Smith. (Bibl. 2004, 9238.) Rev. by Mary A. Favret in WordsC (35:4) 2004, 186–8; by Brent Raycroft in StudN (37:2) 2005, 248–51; by Mary Anne Schofield in ECF (17:2) 2005, 301–2.

9007. THIERFELDER, BILL. Smith's *Elegiac Sonnets*. Exp (64:1) 2005, 28–30.

Tobias Smollett

9008. BRACK, O. M., JR (ed.). The history and adventures of the renowned Don Quixote. Introd. and notes by Martin C. Battestin. (Bibl. 2004, 9244.) Rev. by Julie Candler Hayes in HLQ (67:4) 2004, 651–68; by Paddy Bullard in TLS, 8 Apr. 2005, 32; by Joseph Kronick in Scriblerian (37:2/38:1) 2005, 141–2.

9009. GOTTLIEB, EVAN. 'Fools of prejudice': sympathy and national identity in the Scottish Enlightenment and *Humphry Clinker*. ECF (18:1) 2005, 81–106.

9010. HAYES, JULIE CANDLER. Tobias Smollett and the translators of the *Quixote*. HLQ (67:4) 2004, 651–68 (review-article).

9011. MCINELLY, BRETT C. Domestic and colonial space in *Humphry Clinker*. 1650–1850 (10) 2004, 125–44.

9012. MCKEON, MICHAEL. Aestheticising the critique of luxury: Smollett's *Humphry Clinker*. *In* (pp. 57–67) **7941**.

John Gabriel Stedman (1744–1797)

9013. KLARER, MARIO. Humanitarian pornography: John Gabriel Stedman's *Narrative of a Five Years Expedition against the Revolted Negroes of Surinam* (1796). NLH (36:4) 2005, 559–87.

Anne Steele (1717–1778)

9014. WATSON, J. R.; CHO, NANCY. Anne Steele's drowned fiancé. BJECS (28:1) 2005, 117–21.

Sir Richard Steele

9015. BANNET, EVE TAVOR. 'Epistolary commerce' in *The Spectator*. *In* (pp. 220–47) **1285**.

9016. BOWERS, TERENCE. Universalizing sociability: *The Spectator*, civic enfranchisement, and the rule(s) of the public sphere. *In* (pp. 150–74) **1285**.

9017. CAREY, BRYCCHAN. 'Accounts of savage nations': *The Spectator* and the Americas. *In* (pp. 129–49) **1285**.

9018. CONAWAY, CHARLES. 'Thou'rt the man': David Garrick, William Shakespeare, and the masculinization of the eighteenth-century stage. *See* **8645**.

9019. JUSTICE, GEORGE. *The Spectator* and distance education. *In* (pp. 265–99) **1285**.

9020. MCCREA, BRIAN. The virtue of repetition: Mr Spectator trains Benjamin Franklin. *In* (pp. 248–64) **1285**.

9021. MACKIE, ERIN SKYE. Being too positive about the public sphere. *In* (pp. 81–104) **1285**.

9022. MERRITT, JULIETTE. Originals, copies, and the iconography of femininity in *The Spectator*. *In* (pp. 41–58) **1285**.

9023. MÜLLER, ANJA. Putting the child into discourse: framing children in *The Spectator*. *In* (pp. 59–80) **1285**.

9024. NEWMAN, DONALD J. (ed.). *The Spectator*: emerging discourses. *See* **1285**.

9025. POLLY, GREG. Leviathan of letters. *In* (pp. 105–28) **1285**.

9026. ROACH, JOSEPH. Public intimacy: the prior history of 'it'. *In* (pp. 15–30) **3985**.

9027. WALMSLEY, PETER. Death and the nation in *The Spectator*. *In* (pp. 200–19) **1285**.

9028. ZUNSHINE, LISA. Bastard daughters and foundling heroines: rewriting illegitimacy for the eighteenth-century stage. MP (102:4) 2005, 501–33.

Laurence Sterne

9029. APROBERTS, RUTH. The historian as Shandean humorist: Carlyle and Frederick the Great. *In* (pp. 15–26) **10393**.

9030. CAZZATO, LUIGI. Laurence Sterne and hs paradoxical aesthetics of the new. Textus (18:1) 2005, 153–72.

9031. DE VOOGD, PETER; NEUBAUER, JOHN (eds). The reception of Laurence Sterne in Europe. (Bibl. 2004, 9257.) Rev. by Fred Bridgham in EJES (9:2) 2005, 215–18.

9032. GERARD, W. B. 'All that the heart wishes': changing views toward sentimentality reflected in visualizations of Sterne's Maria, 1773–1888. StudECC (34) 2005, 231–69.

9033. HOLLANDS, HOWARD. Drawing a blank: picturing nothing on the page. *See* **14336.**

9034. JACK, IAN; PARNELL, TIM (eds). *A Sentimental Journey* and other writings. Oxford; New York: OUP, 2003. pp. xliv, 262. (Oxford world's classics.) (New ed.: first ed. 1968.) Rev. by Melvyn New in Scriblerian (37:2/38:1) 2005, 134–6.

9035. KEYMER, THOMAS. Sterne and Romantic autobiography. *In* (pp. 173–93) **8014.**

9036. LESLIE, JOHN C. Music's sentimental role in *Tristram Shandy.* PLL (41:1) 2005, 55–66.

9037. LUPTON, CHRISTINA. Two texts told twice: poor Richard, Pastor Yorick, and the case of the word's return. EAL (40:3) 2005, 471–98.

9038. MACKENZIE, SCOTT R. *Homunculus economicus*: Laurence Sterne's labour theory of literary value. ECF (18:1) 2005, 49–80.

9039. SIMPSON, M. CARLETON. Participation and immersion in Walton and Calvino. PhilL (29:2) 2005, 321–36.

9040. STEWART, CAROL. The Anglicanism of *Tristram Shandy*: Latitudinarianism at the limits. BJECS (28:2) 2005, 239–50.

9041. TADIÉ, ALEXIS. Sterne's whimsical theatres of language: orality, gesture, literacy. (Bibl. 2004, 9274.) Rev. by John Valdimir Price in NQ (52:1) 2005, 129–30; by Pierre Dubois in EA (58:2) 2005, 215–18.

9042. VAN STRIEN, KEES. Daniel Bellamy Jr, parish priest and Shandean traveller. *See* **8254.**

Jonathan Swift

9043. ANON. Bibliography. *In* (pp. 284–364) **9084.**

9044. —— (comp.). Recent books and articles received. SwSt (20) 2005, 179–88.

9045. BALTES, SABINE. Father Time: the emblematic and iconographic context of 'The Epistle Dedicatory to His Royal Highness Prince Posterity' in Swift's *Tale.* SwSt (20) 2005, 41–50.

9046. —— Swiftian material culture. *In* (pp. 273–83) **9084.**

9047. BASTOS DA SILVA, JORGE. A Lusitanian dish: Swift to Portuguese taste. *In* (pp. 79–92) **9084.**

9048. BRAVERMAN, RICHARD. *Robinson Crusoe* and *Gulliver's Travels*: some pedagogical frameworks. *In* (pp. 37–47) **8537.**

9049. BRIGGS, PETER M. John Graunt, Sir William Petty, and Swift's *Modest Proposal.* ECL (29:2) 2005, 3–24.

9050. BUISSON, FRANÇOISE. Gulliver sauvé des eaux: dilution et résurrection du voyage dans *Water Music* de T. Coraghessan Boyle. *See* **15550.**

9051. BURKE, JOHN J., JR. Jonathan Swift's crimes against humanity: truth or fiction? 1650–1850 (10) 2004, 205–16 (review-article).

9052. CARPENTER, ANDREW. *A Tale of a Tub* as an Irish text. SwSt (20) 2005, 30–40.

9053. CHAMOSA GONZÁLEZ, JOSÉ LUIS. Swift's horses in the land of the *caballeros. In* (pp. 57–78) **9084.**

9054. CHILD, PAUL W. Once more into the breech: Jonathan Swift and excremental medicine. SwSt (20) 2005, 82–101.

9055. DÜRING, MICHAEL. Detecting Swift in the Czech lands. *In* (pp. 214–23) **9084.**

9056. —— From Russian '*Sviftovedenie*' to the Soviet school of Swift criticism: the Dean's fate in Russia. *In* (pp. 170–213) **9084.**

9057. —— No Swift beyond Gulliver: notes on the Polish reception. *In* (pp. 156–69) **9084.**

9058. EDWARDS, CHRISTOPHER. From Pope to Swift: a book from Swift's library. SwSt (20) 2005, 174–8.

9059. FABRICANT, CAROLE. Colonial sublimities and sublimations: Swift, Burke, and Ireland. ELH (72:2) 2005, 309–37.

9060. FANNING, CHRISTOPHER. The Scriblerian sublime. *See* **8884.**

9061. FILIPOVA, FILIPINA. Swift's impact in Bulgaria. *In* (pp. 238–47) **9084.**

9062. FOX, CHRISTOPHER. Getting Gotheridge: notes on Swift's grandfather and a new letter from Thomas Swift. SwSt (20) 2005, 10–29.

9063. —— (ed.). The Cambridge companion to Jonathan Swift. (Bibl. 2004, 9287.) Rev. by J. A. Downie in ECF (18:1) 2005, 139–41; by Charles Hinnant in Scriblerian (37:2 / 38:1) 2005, 96–8.

9064. FRANKLIN, MICHAEL J. Lemuel self-translated; or, Being an ass in Houyhnhnmland. MLR (100:1) 2005, 1–19.

9065. FRÓES, JOÃO. 'A part omitted' from Swift's *Sentiments of a Church-of-England Man.* SwSt (20) 2005, 124–31.

9066. GEE, SOPHIE. The sewers: ordure, effluence, and excess in the eighteenth century. *In* (pp. 101–20) **6958.**

9067. GRAEBER, WILHELM. Swift's first voyages to Europe: his impact on eighteenth-century France. *In* (pp. 5–16) **9084.**

9068. GREGORI, FLAVIO. The Italian reception of Swift. *In* (pp. 17–56) **9084.**

9069. GURR, JENS MARTIN. 'Let me suppose thee for a ship a-while': nautical metaphors and contemporary politics in eighteenth-century translations of Horace's Ode I, xiv. SwSt (20) 2005, 70–81.

9070. HARTMANN, NILS. Swiftian presence in Scandinavia: Denmark, Norway, Sweden. *In* (pp. 142–55) **9084.**

9071. HARTVIG, GABRIELLA. The Dean in Hungary. *In* (pp. 224–37) **9084.**

9072. HORNERO CORISCO, ANA Mᴬ. *Gulliver's Travels* on the screen: Spanish film versions. SwSt (20) 2005, 111–23.

9073. KEITHLEY, WALTHER H. Jonathan Swift, a Grub Street hack, and the problem of the popularization of science in *A Tale of a Tub.* SwSt (20) 2005, 51–69.

9074. KRAKE, ASTRID; REAL, HERMANN J.; SPIECKERMANN, MARIE-LUISE. The Dean's voyages into Germany. *In* (pp. 93–141) **9084.**

9075. LYNALL, GREGORY. Swift's caricatures of Newton: 'Taylor', 'Conjurer' and 'Workman in the Mint'. BJECS (28:1) 2005, 19–32.

9076. MAY, JAMES E.   Swift and Swiftiana offered, sold, and acquired, 2002–2005. SwSt (20) 2005, 143–73.

9077. MENZIES, RUTH.   Re-writing *Gulliver's Travels*: the demise of a genre? EREA (3:1) 2005, 87–93.

9078. MUDURE, MIHAELA.   From the infantile to the subversive: Swift's Romanian adventures. *In* (pp. 248–72) **9084**.

9079. OGBORN, MILES; WITHERS, CHARLES W. J.   Travel, trade, and empire: knowing other places, 1660–1800. *In* (pp. 13–35) **6958**.

9080. PARRINDER, PATRICK.   Entering dystopia, entering *Erewhon*. *See* **10283**.

9081. PASSMANN, DIRK F.; VIENKEN, HEINZ J.   The library and reading of Jonathan Swift: a bio-bibliographical handbook: part 1, Swift's library in four volumes. (Bibl. 2004, 9307.) Rev. by Robin Alston in Library (6:1) 2005, 93–5.

9082. PETERSON, LELAND D.   A letter to the editor on the occasion of his correspondence about Swift's *The Beasts' Confession to the Priest*. SwSt (20) 2005, 102–10.

9083. REAL, HERMANN J.   Introduction. *In* (pp. 1–4) **9084**.

9084. —— (ed.).   The reception of Jonathan Swift in Europe. London: Thoemmes Press; New York: Continuum, 2005. pp. xxxii, 378. (Athlone critical traditions.)

9085. REID, JENNIFER I. M.   Worse than beasts: an anatomy of melancholy and the literature of travel in seventeenth- and eighteenth-century England. *See* **7290**.

9086. ROBERTSON, RANDY.   Swift's *Leviathan* and the end of licensing. PCP (40:2) 2005, 38–55.

9087. STARKIE, ANDREW.   Contested histories of the English Church: Gilbert Burnet and Jeremy Collier. *See* **7325**.

9088. SUSSMAN, CHARLOTTE.   The colonial afterlife of political arithmetic: Swift, demography, and mobile populations. CultC (56) 2004, 96–126.

9089. SUVIN, DARKO.   To Laputa and back: a missing chapter of *Gulliver's Travels*. *In* (pp. 11–31) **3690**.

9090. TWOMBLY, DAVID J.   Newtonian schemes: an unknown poetic satire from 1728. *See* **8210**.

9091. WEINBROT, HOWARD D.   Menippean satire reconsidered: from Antiquity to the eighteenth century. *See* **8915**.

Catherine Talbot (1721–1770)

9092. CLARKE, NORMA.   Bluestocking fictions: devotional writings, didactic literature and the imperative of female improvement. *In* (pp. 460–73) **8016**.

Isaac Teale (d.1764)

9093. WOOD, MARCUS.   Black bodies and satiric limits in the long eighteenth century. *In* (pp. 55–70) **9305**.

John Thelwall ('John Beaufort') (1764–1834)

9094. GRAVIL, RICHARD.   The Somerset sound; or, The darling child of speech. *See* **10485**.

9095. JAMES, FELICITY. Agreement, dissonance, dissent: the many conversations of *This Lime-Tree Bower*. *See* **10493**.

Isaiah Thomas (1749–1831)

9096. REED, BEVERLY J. Exhibiting the fair sex: the *Massachusetts Magazine* and the bodily order of the American woman. *In* (pp. 227–54) **1244**.

James Thomson (1700–1748)

9097. KINSLEY, ZOË. Landscapes 'dynamically in motion': revisiting issues of structure and agency in Thomson's *The Seasons*. PLL (41:1) 2005, 3–25.

John Toland (1670–1722)

9098. BROWN, JAMES C. Le Milton de Toland. *See* **7659**.

9099. BROWNLEY, MARTINE WATSON. Denzil Holles and the stylistic development of the early English memoir. *In* (pp. 135–49) **5167**.

Jacob Tonson the Elder (1656–1736)

9100. FISHER, NICHOLAS. Jacob Tonson and the Earl of Rochester. *See* **7827**.

John Horne Tooke

9101. MILLER, CHRISTOPHER. Shelley's uncertain Heaven. *See* **12021**.

9102. SHERBO, ARTHUR. From the sale catalogue of the library of Samuel Rogers. *See* **11852**.

Melesina (Chenevix) St George Trench (1768–1827)

9103. KITTREDGE, KATHARINE. The poetry of Melesina Trench: a growing skill at sorrow. BJECS (28:2) 2005, 201–13.

Royall Tyler

9104. BRANCA, R. RENE. Melodrama, convention, and rape. AmDr (14:1) 2005, 32–45.

Horace Walpole

9105. BICKHAM, TROY. 'A conviction of the reality of things': material culture, North American Indians and empire in eighteenth-century Britain. ECS (39:1) 2005, 29–47.

9106. COYKENDALL, ABBY. Gothic genealogies, the family romance, and Clara Reeve's *The Old English Baron*. *See* **8927**.

9107. FRANK, FREDERICK S. (ed.). *The Castle of Otranto: a Gothic Story* and *The Mysterious Mother: a Tragedy*. Peterborough, Ont.; Orchard Park, NY: Broadview Press, 2003. pp. 357. (Broadview literary texts.) Rev. by George E. Haggerty in GothS (7:1) 2005, 110–12.

9108. HATOOKA, KEITA. Inu-tachi no chinmoku: *Mason & Dixon* ni okeru hyosho no kanosei. (The silence of the dogs: the possibility of representation in *Mason & Dixon*.) *See* **18985**.

Sir Robert Walpole

9109. CHAMPION, JUSTIN. 'Anglia libera': Commonwealth politics in the early years of George I. *In* (pp. 86–107) **8091**.

Edward Ward (1667–1731)

9110. FITZGERALD-HUME, ELIZABETH. Rights and riots: footmen's riots at Drury Lane 1737. *See* **8103**.

9111. NARAIN, MONA. Libertine spaces and the female body in the poetry of Rochester and Ned Ward. *See* **7830**.

9112. PELLICER, JUAN CHRISTIAN. 'A dry consumptive smoking sot': Ned Ward's epigram on John Philips? NQ (52:3) 2005, 346–9.

Joseph Warton

9113. WATERHOUSE, WILLIAM C. Boswell, Joseph Warton, and Servius. *See* **8414**.

Isaac Watts

9114. PRESCOTT, SARAH. Elizabeth Singer Rowe: gender, Dissent, and Whig poetics. *In* (pp. 173–99) **8091**.

John Wesley

9115. HINDMARSH, D. BRUCE. The Evangelical conversion narrative: spiritual autobiography in early modern England. *See* **8264**.

9116. PETERFREUND, STUART. Dissent and ontological space in Romantic science and literature. *See* **8379**.

9117. YAMAGUCHI, MIHO. Elizabeth Prentiss' faith in suffering and perplexity about the Wesleyan and the higher life doctrines: on *Stepping Heavenward*. *See* **11833**.

Phillis Wheatley

9118. BOREN, MARK EDELMAN. A fiery furnace and a sugar train: metaphors that challenge the legacy of Phillis Wheatley's *On Being Brought from Africa to America*. CEACrit (67:1) 2004, 38–56.

9119. BROWN, GILLIAN. Thinking in the future perfect: consent, childhood, and minority rights. *See* **1161**.

George Whitefield (1714–1770)

9120. HINDMARSH, D. BRUCE. The Evangelical conversion narrative: spiritual autobiography in early modern England. *See* **8264**.

John Wilkes

9121. ROUNCE, ADAM. Stuarts without end: Wilkes, Churchill, and anti-Scottishness. ECL (29:3) 2005, 20–43.

Edward Williams ('Iolo Morganwg') (1746–1826)

9122. CONSTANTINE, MARY-ANN. Iolo Morganwg, Coleridge, and the Bristol lectures, 1795. *See* **10476**.

Helen Maria Williams

9123. FRANKLIN, CAROLINE. Romantic patriotism as feminist critique of empire: Helen Maria Williams, Sydney Owenson and Germaine de Staël. *In* (pp. 551–64) **8016**.

9124. KENNEDY, DEBORAH. Helen Maria Williams and the age of revolution. (Bibl. 2004, 9352.) Rev. by Richard Matlak in WordsC (35:4) 2004, 188–91.

9125. SAGLIA, DIEGO. The aesthetics of the present: commerce, empire and technology in late eighteenth-century women's poetry. *See* **8988**.

Anne Finch, Countess of Winchilsea

9126. MILLER, CHRISTOPHER. Staying out late: Anne Finch's poetics of evening. SELit (45:3) 2005, 603–23.

Jane Cave Winscom (1754–1813)

9127. McKIM, A. ELIZABETH. Making poetry of pain: the headache poems of Jane Cave Winscom. LitMed (24:1) 2005, 93–108.

John Wolcot ('Peter Pindar')

9128. COLBERT, BENJAMIN. Petrio-pindarics: John Wolcot and the Romantics. ERR (16:3) 2005, 311–28.

Mary Wollstonecraft

9129. BLAIR, KIRSTIE. Spasmodic affections: poetry, pathology, and the Spasmodic hero. *See* **10249**.

9130. BRADSHAW, PENNY. The limits of Barbauld's feminism: re-reading *The Rights of Woman*. *See* **8342**.

9131. BUGG, JOHN. 'Master of their language': education and exile in Mary Shelley's *Frankenstein*. *See* **11963**.

9132. CHANDLER, ANNE. The 'seeds of order and taste': Wollstonecraft, the *Analytical Review*, and critical idiom. ERR (16:1) 2005, 1–21.

9133. CHANEY, CHRISTINE. The rhetorical strategies of 'tumultuous emotions': Wollstonecraft's *Letters Written in Sweden*. JNT (34:3) 2004, 277–303.

9134. COMITINI, PATRICIA. Vocational philanthropy and British women's writing, 1790–1810: Wollstonecraft, More, Edgeworth, Wordsworth. Aldershot; Burlington, VT: Ashgate, 2005. pp. viii, 168.

9135. DENLINGER, ELIZABETH CAMPBELL. Before Victoria: extraordinary women of the British Romantic era. Foreword by Lyndall Gordon. *See* **8843**.

9136. GONZÁLEZ FERNÁNDEZ, MARÍA FE (trans. and notes). Vindicación dos dereitos da muller. Introd. by María Jesús Lorenzo Modia. Pontes, Corunna: Sotelo Blanco, 2004. pp. 388. (Letras das mulleres, 2.) Rev. by Manuela Palacios González in Atl (27:1) 2005, 151–6.

9137. GORDON, LYNDALL. Vindication: a life of Mary Wollstonecraft. London: HarperCollins, 2005. pp. x, 562. Rev. by Brenda Maddox in BkW, 3 July 2005, 4.

9138. GUERRA, LIA. Unexpected symmetries: Samuel Johnson and Mary Wollstonecraft on the Northern Road. *See* **8756**.

9139. HARRIS, SHARON M. The *New-York Magazine*: cultural repository. *In* (pp. 339–64) **1244**.

9140. HOEVELER, DIANE LONG. The construction of the female gothic posture: Wollstonecraft's *Mary* and gothic feminism. GothS (6:1) 2004, 30–44.

9141. JONES, VIVIEN. Advice and Enlightenment: Mary Wollstonecraft and sex education. *In* (pp. 140–55) **8016**.

9142. KINSLEY, ZOË. Dorothy Richardson's manuscript travel journals (1761–1801) and the possibilities of picturesque aesthetics. *See* **8930**.

9143. MAZZEO, TILAR J. The impossibility of being Anglo-American: the rhetoric of emigration and transatlanticism in British Romantic culture, 1791–1833. *See* **8980.**

9144. O'NEILL, EILEEN. Early modern women philosophers and the history of philosophy. *See* **7791.**

9145. SCHOR, ESTHER. Further vindications. TLS, 11 Feb. 2005, 4–5 (review-article).

9146. TAUCHERT, ASHLEY. Mary Wollstonecraft and the accent of the feminine. (Bibl. 2004, 9373.) Rev. by Eleanor Ty in ECF (17:2) 2005, 294–8; by Susan Allen Ford in ERR (16:1) 2005, 120–7.

9147. TAYLOR, BARBARA. Feminists *versus* gallants: manners and morals in Enlightenment Britain. *In* (pp. 30–52) **8016.**

9148. —— Mary Wollstonecraft and the feminist imagination. (Bibl. 2004, 9374.) Rev. by Melinda Zook in Historian (67:1) 2005, 170–1; by Heidi Thomson in MLR (100:3) 2005, 789–90; by Josephine McDonagh in TexP (19:1) 2005, 202–8; by Susan Allen Ford in ERR (16:1) 2005, 120–7.

9149. TODD, JANET. Rebel daughters: Ireland in conflict 1798. (Bibl. 2004, 9375.) Rev. by Harriet Devine Jump in WWr (12:2) 2005, 321–8.

9150. —— (ed.). The collected letters of Mary Wollstonecraft. (Bibl. 2004, 9376.) Rev. by Eleanor Ty in ECF (17:2) 2005, 294–8.

9151. TOMASELLI, SYLVANA. Civilization, patriotism and enlightened histories of woman. *In* (pp. 117–35) **8016.**

9152. WACH, HOWARD M. A Boston vindication: Margaret Fuller and Caroline Dall read Mary Wollstonecraft. *See* **11036.**

9153. WALKER, GINA LURIA. Mary Hays (1759–1843): an enlightened quest. *In* (pp. 493–518) **8016.**

9154. ZAGARRI, ROSEMARIE. American women's rights before Seneca Falls. *In* (pp. 667–91) **8016.**

Henry Woodfall (d.1747)

9155. SPEDDING, PATRICK. A note on the ornament usage of Henry Woodfall. *See* **180.**

Ann Yearsley

9156. CAIRNIE, JULIE. The ambivalence of Ann Yearsley: laboring and writing, submission and resistance. NCC (27:4) 2005, 353–64.

Edward Young

9157. BROWN, LAURA. Oceans and floods: fables of global perspective. *In* (pp. 107–20) **8039.**

9158. ODELL, D. W. Young's *Night Thoughts*: Christian rationalism or fideism? ELN (43:1) 2005, 48–59.

NINETEENTH CENTURY

GENERAL

9159. ABRAMS, ROBERT E.   Landscape and ideology in American renaissance literature: topographies of skepticism. (Bibl. 2004, 9382.) Rev. by Jennifer L. Hughes in NCP (32:1) 2005, 254–7.

9160. ADAMS, JAMES ELI.   The function of journals at the present time. *See* **20988**.

9161. ALDRICH, ROBERT.   Colonialism and homosexuality. London; New York: Routledge, 2003. pp. xii, 436, (plates) 15. Rev. by Kathleen Wilson in JBS (44:1) 2005, 194–203.

9162. ALEXANDER, CHRISTINE.   Defining and representing literary juvenilia. *In* (pp. 70–97) **9164**.

9163. —— Nineteenth-century juvenilia: a survey. *In* (pp. 11–30) **9164**.

9164. —— MCMASTER, JULIET (eds).   The child writer from Austen to Woolf. Cambridge; New York: CUP, 2005. pp. xv, 312. (Cambridge studies in nineteenth-century literature and culture, 47.)

9165. ALEXANDER, LYNN M.   Women, work, and representation: needlewomen in Victorian art and literature. (Bibl. 2004, 9384.) Rev. by Shani D'Cruze in Albion (36:3) 2004, 535–6.

9166. ALLEN, RICK; ASSAEL, BRENDA.   City of vision: Lynda Nead's *Victorian Babylon*. With a response by Lynda Nead. JVC (8:2) 2003, 305–21. (Roundtable.)

9167. ANDERSON, AMANDA.   Victorian Studies and the two modernities. *See* **14687**.

9168. ANDERSON, MARK CRONLUND; BLAYER, IRENE MARIA F. (eds). Interdisciplinary and cross-cultural narratives in North America. New York; Frankfurt: Lang, 2005. pp. 173. (Studies on themes and motifs in literature, 73.)

9169. ARAC, JONATHAN.   The emergence of American literary narrative, 1820–1860. Cambridge, MA; London: Harvard UP, 2005. pp. 267.

9170. ARDIS, ANN L.; LEWIS, LESLIE W. (eds).   Women's experience of modernity, 1875–1945. (Bibl. 2004, 9388.) Rev. by Susan McCabe in StudN (37:2) 2005, 237–40; by Priscilla Wald in Mod/Mod (12:4) 2005, 729–31; by Morag Shiach in YES (35) 2005, 353–4.

9171. ARMSTRONG, CHARLES I.   Romantic organicism: from idealist origins to ambivalent afterlife. (Bibl. 2004, 9389.) Rev. by Michael John Kooy in NQ (52:1) 2005, 137–9; by Robert Mitchell in RomNet (38/39) 2005.

9172. ASHTON, SUSANNA.   Collaborators in literary America, 1870–1920. Basingstoke; New York: Palgrave Macmillan, 2003. pp. 223. Rev. by Michael Anesko in JAH (91:2) 2004, 646–7.

9173. ATTRIDGE, STEVE.   Nationalism, imperialism, and identity in late Victorian culture. (Bibl. 2004, 9391.) Rev. by V. G. Kiernan in LitH (14:1) 2005, 96–7; by Nicholas Daly in VS (47:2) 2005, 305–7.

9174. AUGST, THOMAS. The clerk's tale: young men and moral life in nineteenth-century America. (Bibl. 2004, 9392.) Rev. by Timothy B. Spears in JAH (91:4) 2005, 1457–8.

9175. BADIA, JANET; PHEGLEY, JENNIFER (eds). Reading women: literary figures and cultural icons from the Victorian age to the present. See **12549**.

9176. BAINES, PAUL. The long 18th century. See **7932**.

9177. BAUER, RALPH. Laying claim to the literary borderlands: the contested grounds of Hispanism in the US. AmLH (16:3) 2004, 487–95 (review-article).

9178. BAYLEY, JOHN. The power of delight: a lifetime in literature: essays 1962–2002. Selected by Leo Carey. See **7937**.

9179. BAYM, NINA. American women of letters and the nineteenth-century sciences: styles of affiliation. (Bibl. 2004, 9395.) Rev. by Stephanie Browner in AmLH (16:3) 2004, 509–19.

9180. BEAUMONT, MATTHEW. Utopia Ltd: ideologies of social dreaming in England, 1870–1900. Leiden; Boston, MA: Brill, 2005. pp. x, 214. (Historical materialism, 7.)

9181. BECKETT, SANDRA. Recycling Red Riding Hood in the Americas. In (pp. 7–28) **9168**.

9182. BEER, JOHN. Post-Romantic consciousness: Dickens to Plath. (Bibl. 2004, 9396.) Rev. by Corinna Russell in BJ (32:2) 2004, 161–2; by Tamara S. Wagner in DickQ (22:2) 2005, 117–19.

9183. BELL, BILL. Bound for Botany Bay; or, What did the nineteenth-century convict read? In (pp. 151–75) **937**.

9184. BELLORINI, MARIAGRAZIA (ed.). The Ring and the Book di Robert Browning: poesia e dramma. See **10257**.

9185. BENCHIMOL, ALEX. Remaking the Romantic period: cultural materialism, Cultural Studies and the radical public sphere. See **14700**.

9186. BENEDICT, BARBARA M. Readers, writers, reviewers, and the professionalization of literature. In (pp. 3–23) **8014**.

9187. BENNETT, MICHAEL. Democratic discourses: the radical Abolition movement and antebellum American literature. New Brunswick, NJ: Rutgers UP, 2005. pp. x, 223. Rev. by Sylvia J. Cook in SPC (28:2) 2005, 196–8.

9188. BERGLUND, MICHAEL H. Looking back to look ahead: homosexuality and the postmodern gothic in American literature. PoeS (36) 2003, 110–17 (review-article).

9189. BIRNBAUM, MICHELE. Race, work, and desire in American literature, 1860–1930. (Bibl. 2004, 9405.) Rev. by Paul Giles in RES (56:224) 2005, 338–9.

9190. BLACK, DANIEL P. Literary subterfuge: early African American writing and the trope of the mask. CLAJ (48:4) 2005, 387–403.

9191. BLAIR, JENNIFER, et al. (ed.). ReCalling early Canada: reading the political in literary and cultural production. Edmonton: Alberta UP, 2005. pp. xlvi, 412, (plates) 8.

9192. BLOTNER, JOSEPH. Robert Penn Warren, Cleanth Brooks, and the Southern literary tradition. See **19980**.

9193. BODE, CHRISTOPH; RENNHAK, KATHARINA (eds). Romantic voices, Romantic poetics: Selected papers from the Regensburg conference of the German Society of English Romanticism. Trier: WVT, 2005. pp. 211. (Studien zur englischen Romantik, ns 1.)

9194. BOONE, TROY. Youth of darkest England: working-class children at the heart of Victorian empire. London; New York: Routledge, 2005. pp. 235. (Children's literature and culture, 34.)

9195. BOTTALICO, MICHELE; CHIALANT, MARIA TERESA (eds). L'impulso autobiografico: Inghilterra, Stati Uniti, Canada … e altrove. See **12577.**

9196. BOTTING, FRED; TOWNSHEND, DALE (eds). Gothic: critical concepts in literary and cultural studies. See **7943.**

9197. BOYD, ANNE E. Writing for immortality: women and the emergence of high literary culture in America. Baltimore, MD; London: Johns Hopkins UP, 2004. pp. x, 305. Rev. by Martha Saxton in JAH (92:3) 2005, 1003–4; by Mary Rigsby in TSWL (24:2) 2005, 355–6; by Felicia L. Carr in Legacy (22:2) 2005, 199–200.

9198. BRAKE, LAUREL; CODELL, JULIE F. (eds). Encounters in the Victorian press: editors, authors, readers. See **1160.**

9199. BRAZ, ALBERT. The false traitor: Louis Riel in Canadian culture. Toronto; Buffalo, NY; London: Toronto UP, 2003. pp. xi, 245. Rev. by Warren Cariou in LRC (11:5) 2003, 8–9; by Peter Noble in BJCS (17:2) 2004, 253–4; by Clint Evans in CanL (186) 2005, 115–17.

9200. BREWER, DAVID A. The afterlife of character, 1726–1825. See **7945.**

9201. BRICKHOUSE, ANNA. Transamerican literary relations and the nineteenth-century public sphere. Cambridge; New York: CUP, 2004. pp. xii, 329. (Cambridge studies in American literature and culture, 145.) Rev. by Rachel Adams in NineL (60:1) 2005, 87–90.

9202. BRINKS, ELLEN. Gothic masculinity: effeminacy and the supernatural in English and German Romanticism. (Bibl. 2003, 8612.) Rev. by Steven Bruhm in WordsC (35:4) 2004, 183–4.

9203. BROWN, GILLIAN. Thinking in the future perfect: consent, childhood, and minority rights. See **1161.**

9204. BROWN, HILARY. Benedikte Naubert (1756–1819) and her relations to English culture. See **7946.**

9205. BROWN, SARAH ANNES. Devoted sisters: representation of the sister relationship in nineteenth-century British and American literature. (Bibl. 2003, 8616.) Rev. by Susan Fraiman in VS (48:1) 2005, 177–9.

9206. BRYDEN, INGA. Reinventing King Arthur: the Arthurian legends in Victorian culture. Aldershot; Burlington, VT: Ashgate, 2005. pp. 171. (Nineteenth century.)

9207. CAMPBELL, CLAIRE. 'Our dear north country': regional identity and national meaning in Ontario's Georgian Bay. JCanStud (37:4) 2002/03, 68–91.

9208. CAMPBELL, MATTHEW. Victorian Ireland? JVC (10:2) 2005, 297–303 (review-article).

9209. CAPORALE BIZZINI, SILVIA. We, the 'other Victorians': considering the heritage of 19th-century thought. Alicante: Univ. de Alicante, 2003. pp. 213. (Monografías, Univ. de Alicante.) Rev. by José Ángel García Landa in Atl (27:1) 2005, 111–15.

9210. CAREY, BRYCCHAN. British Abolitionism and the rhetoric of sensibility: writing, sentiment, and slavery, 1760–1807. See 7951.

9211. CARPENTER, MARY WILSON. Imperial Bibles, domestic bodies: women, sexuality, and religion in the Victorian market. Athens: Ohio UP, 2003. pp. xxii, 206. Rev. by Emma Major in MLR (100:2) 2005, 492; by Anya Clayworth in ELT (48:1) 2005, 82–5.

9212. CARROLL, JOSEPH. Literary Darwinism: evolution, human nature, and literature. (Bibl. 2004, 9416.) Rev. by Jonathan Greenberg in Novel (38:1) 2004, 117–20.

9213. CARRUTHERS, GERARD; RAWES, ALAN (eds). English Romanticism and the Celtic world. (Bibl. 2003, 8622.) Rev. by Fiona Stafford in WordsC (35:4) 2004, 178–9; by Ashley Chantler in BJ (32:1) 2004, 66–8; by Suzanne Gilbert in MLR (100:3) 2005, 798–9.

9214. CASTRONOVO, RUSS. The pit and the gothic chiasmus. PoeS (36) 2003, 118–21 (review-article).

9215. CAVALIERO, RODERICK. *Italia Romantica*: English Romantics and Italian freedom. London; New York: Tauris, 2005. pp. 256. Rev. by Esther Schor in TLS, 25 Nov. 2005, 10–11; by Stephen Hebron in KSR (19) 2005, 150–7.

9216. CHANDLER, JAMES; GILMARTIN, KEVIN. Introduction: engaging the eidometropolis. In (pp. 1–41) 9217.

9217. —— —— (eds). Romantic metropolis: the urban scene of British culture, 1780–1840. Cambridge; New York: CUP, 2005. pp. xiii, 291.

9218. CHURA, PATRICK. Vital contact: downclassing journeys in American literature from Herman Melville to Richard Wright. London; New York: Routledge, 2005. pp. ix, 240. (Literary criticism and cultural theory.)

9219. CLYMER, JEFFORY A. Naturalism's histories. MFS (51:1) 2005, 183–91 (review-article).

9220. COHEN, WILLIAM A.; JOHNSON, RYAN (eds). Filth: dirt, disgust, and modern life. Minneapolis; London: Minnesota UP, 2005. pp. xxxvii, 317. Rev. by Christopher Lane in VS (48:1) 2005, 185–8.

9221. COLCLOUGH, STEPHEN. 'A grey goose quill and an album': the manuscript book and text transmission, 1800–1850. In (pp. 153–73) 19.

9222. COLE, NATALIE B. Dickens and the act of gardening. See 10661.

9223. COOK, MATT. London and the culture of homosexuality, 1885–1914. Cambridge; New York; Melbourne: CUP, 2003. pp. xiv, 223. (Cambridge studies in nineteenth-century literature and culture, 39.) Rev. by Karen Tongson in Novel (38:1) 2004, 103–6; by Matthew Bradley in MLR (100:2) 2005, 474–5; by Roger Luckhurst in ELT (48:2) 2005, 209–14; by Charles Upchurch in JBS (44:2) 2005, 397–8; by Leland Monk in VS (47:4) 2005, 599–601; by Michael Seeney in Wildean (26) 2005, 80–2.

9224. Coviello, Peter. Intimacy in America: dreams of affiliation in antebellum literature. Minneapolis; London: Minnesota UP, 2005. pp. xii, 229.

9225. Craciun, Adriana. Fatal women of Romanticism. (Bibl. 2004, 9424.) Rev. by Diane Long Hoeveler in GothS (6:1) 2004, 134–7.

9226. Cronin, Richard. Literary scene. In (pp. 289–96) **10060**.

9227. Daehnke, Joel. In the work of their hands is their prayer: cultural narrative and redemption on the American frontiers, 1830–1930. (Bibl. 2004, 9426.) Rev. by Blake Allmendinger in AL (77:1) 2005, 202–3.

9228. Daly, Nicholas. Literature, technology, and modernity, 1860–2000. (Bibl. 2004, 9427.) Rev. by Matthew Beaumont in TexP (19:2) 2005, 373–9; by John M. Picker in VS (47:4) 2005, 597–8.

9229. Damrosch, David (gen. ed.). The Longman anthology of world literature: vol. E, The nineteenth century. Ed. by Marshall Brown. Harlow; New York: Longman, 2004. pp. xxiv, 977.

9230. Danahay, Martin A. Gender at work in Victorian culture: literature, art and masculinity. Aldershot; Burlington, VT: Ashgate, 2005. pp. xi, 180, (plates) 8.

9231. Davis, Leith; Duncan, Ian; Sorensen, Janet (eds). Scotland and the borders of Romanticism. (Bibl. 2004, 9429.) Rev. by Sharon Ragaz in SHogg (15) 2004, 175–9; by Robert Crawford in Romanticism (11:1) 2005, 114–15; by Michael O'Neill in RES (56:224) 2005, 327–9; by Evan Gottlieb in ERR (16:5) 2005, 627–33; by Yann Tholoniat in EREA (3:2) 2005.

9232. Dawson, Alma; Van Fleet, Connie (eds). African American literature: a guide to reading interests. Westport, CT: Libraries Unlimited, 2004. pp. xx, 470. (Genreflecting advisory series.)

9233. Delano, Sterling F. Brook Farm: the dark side of utopia. Cambridge, MA; London: Belknap Press of Harvard UP, 2004. pp. xvii, 428. Rev. by Leigh E. Schmidt in JAH (92:1) 2005, 213–14; by Robert N. Hudspeth in MaHR (7) 2005, 120–31.

9234. de Montluzin, Emily Lorraine. The *Anti-Jacobin Review* after Gifford: contributions by identified authors, 1807–21. See **1187**.

9235. Demoor, Marysa (ed.). Marketing the author: authorial personae, narrative selves, and self-fashioning, 1880–1930. (Bibl. 2004, 9434.) Rev. by Michelle Tusan in Biography (28:4) 2005, 688–90; by Ann L. Ardis in CLIO (35:1) 2005, 121–5.

9236. D'haen, Theo. 'Nilotic mud': British Romantic writers and the colonies. In (pp. 51–63) **9237**.

9237. —— *et al.* (eds). Configuring Romanticism: essays offered to C. C. Barfoot. Amsterdam; Atlanta, GA: Rodopi, 2003. pp. vii, 306. (Costerus, ns 147.)

9238. Diamond, Michael. Victorian sensations; or, The spectacular, the shocking, and the scandalous in nineteenth-century Britain. (Bibl. 2004, 9437.) Rev. by Mark Hampton in JVC (10:1) 2005, 143–9; by Anya Clayworth in Wildean (26) 2005, 75–8.

9239. DONOGHUE, DENIS. The American classics: a personal essay. New Haven, CT; London: Yale UP, 2005. pp. 295. Rev. by William H. Pritchard in TLS, 9 Sept. 2005, 24.

9240. DUPERRAY, MAX. Le promeneur londonien au XIXe siècle: une excursion dans l'obscur. See **10606.**

9241. EBBATSON, ROGER. An imaginary England: nation, landscape and literature, 1840-1920. Ed. by Ann Donahue. Aldershot; Burlington, VT: Ashgate, 2005. pp. 232. Rev. by Ralph Pite in THJ (21) 2005, 158-61.

9242. EDWARDS, JUSTIN. Gothic Canada: reading the spectre of a national literature. Edmonton: Alberta UP, 2005. pp. xxxiv, 194. Rev. by Anne Burke in PJCL (44) 2005, 46-8.

9243. EDWARDS, JUSTIN D.; IVISON, DOUGLAS (eds). Downtown Canada: writing Canadian cities. Toronto; Buffalo, NY; London: Toronto UP, 2005. pp. viii, 227.

9244. ELMER, JONATHAN. The Black Atlantic archive. See **8593.**

9245. ERKKILÄ, BETSY. Mixed bloods and other crosses: rethinking American literature from the Revolution to the Culture Wars. See **7976.**

9246. —— Revolution in the renaissance. ESQ (49:1-3) 2003, 17-32.

9247. ESTERHAMMER, ANGELA. The improviser's disorder: spontaneity, sickness, and social deviance in late Romanticism. ERR (16:3) 2005, 329-40.

9248. ESTEVE, MARY. The aesthetics and politics of the crowd in American literature. (Bibl. 2004, 9447.) Rev. by John Plotz in Novel (37:3) 2004, 353-5; by Trenton Hickman in StudN (37:2) 2005, 242-4; by Richard Salmon in MLR (100:4) 2005, 1078-9.

9249. EVANS, BRAD. Before cultures: the ethnographic imagination in American literature, 1865-1920. Chicago, IL; London: Chicago UP, 2005. pp. x, 244.

9250. EVERETT, GLENN. Electronic resources for Victorian researchers – 2005 and beyond. See **1108.**

9251. FANUZZI, ROBERT. Abolition's public sphere. (Bibl. 2004, 9451.) Rev. by Aaron Ogletree in AAR (38:3) 2004, 541-3.

9252. FELDMAN, DAVID, et al. Catherine Hall's *Civilising Subjects.* With a response by Catherine Hall. JVC (9:2) 2004, 235-58 (review-article).

9253. FERENS, DOMINIKA; KOCIATKIEWICZ, JUSTYNA; KLIMEK-DOMINIAK, ELŻBIETA (eds). Traveling subjects: American journeys in space and time. See **12672.**

9254. FLEMING, CHRIS; O'CARROLL, JOHN. Romanticism. Anthropoetics (11:1) 2005.

9255. FLINT, KATE. Recent studies in the nineteenth century. SELit (44:4) 2004, 873-945.

9256. —— Why 'Victorian'? Response. See **21034.**

9257. FLOYD, JANET; FORSTER, LAUREL (eds). The recipe reader: narrative, contexts, traditions. Aldershot; Burlington, VT: Ashgate, 2003. pp. ix, 246. Rev. by Alison Ryley in SHARP (14:1/2) 2005, 13.

9258. FRANK, FREDERICK S. Guide to the gothic III: an annotated bibliography of criticism, 1994-2003: vol. I. See **8131.**

9259. FRAWLEY, MARIA H. Invalidism and identity in nineteenth-century Britain. (Bibl. 2004, 9457.) Rev. by Jill Rappoport in NineL (59:3) 2004, 412–15; by E. M. Palmegiano in JBS (44:2) 2005, 390–1; by Martin Wallen in Isis (96:3) 2005, 444–5.

9260. FRENCH, SCOT. The rebellious slave: Nat Turner in American memory. Boston, MA: Houghton Mifflin, 2004. pp. x, 379. Rev. by Mary Kemp Davis in JAH (91:4) 2005, 1460–1.

9261. FULFORD, TIM. 'Getting and spending': the Orientalization of satire in Romantic London. In (pp. 11–29) **9305.**

9262. —— LEE, DEBBIE; KITSON, PETER J. Literature, science and exploration in the Romantic era: bodies of knowledge. Cambridge; New York: CUP, 2004. pp. xvii, 324. (Cambridge studies in Romanticism, 60.) Rev. by Diego Saglia in NineL (60:1) 2005, 94–8.

9263. GALLAGHER, CATHERINE. Theoretical answers to interdisciplinary questions or interdisciplinary answers to theoretical questions? See **21038.**

9264. GALLET, RENÉ. Romantisme et postromantisme: de Wordsworth à Pater. Paris: L'Harmattan, 2004. pp. 223. Rev. by Bénédicte Coste in CVE (61) 2005, 347; by Alain Jumeau in EA (58:4) 2005, 500–1.

9265. GARDNER, SARAH E. Blood & irony: Southern White women's narratives of the Civil War, 1861–1937. Chapel Hill; London: North Carolina UP, 2004. pp. x, 341. Rev. by Karen L. Cox in JAH (91:4) 2005, 1474–5; by Betina Entzminger in SoLJ (38:1) 2005, 147–50; by Jane Turner Censer in JSH (71:2) 2005, 456–7.

9266. GIBBONS, PETER. Early castings for a canon: some 1920s perceptions of New Zealand literary achievements. JNZL (23:1) 2005, 98–108.

9267. GILLMAN, SUSAN. Blood talk: American race melodrama and the culture of the occult. (Bibl. 2003, 8676.) Rev. by Jeffrey W. Miller in AL (77:1) 2005, 190–1; by Shawn Michelle Smith in MFS (51:1) 2005, 207–10.

9268. —— The new, newest thing: have American Studies gone imperial? See **10594.**

9269. GILMOUR, IAN. Out of bounds. See **854.**

9270. GOLDMAN, PAUL. Beyond decoration: the illustrations of John Everett Millais. See **75.**

9271. GOLDSWORTHY, KERRYN. Going global. Meanjin (64:3) 2005, 103–8 (review-article).

9272. GONZÁLEZ, GILBERT G. Culture of empire: American writers, Mexico, and Mexican immigrants, 1880–1930. Austin: Texas UP, 2004. pp. viii, 245. Rev. by Mauricio Tenorio in JAH (92:1) 2005, 237–8.

9273. GOODLAD, LAUREN M. E. Victorian literature and the Victorian State: character and governance in a liberal society. (Bibl. 2004, 9464.) Rev. by Janice Carlisle in DickQ (21:3) 2004, 189–92; by Josephine M. Guy in ELT (48:4) 2005, 468–72.

9274. GORDON, JOHN. Physiology and the literary imagination: Romantic to modern. (Bibl. 2004, 12514.) Rev. by Clark Lawlor in BHM (78:3) 2004, 726–7.

9275. GOTTSCHALL, JONATHAN; WILSON, DAVID SLOAN (eds). The literary animal: evolution and the nature of narrative. Forewords by E. O. Wilson and Frederick Crews. *See* **14807.**

9276. GOULD, MARTY. Flirting with disaster: sexual play in the Victorian periodical. *See* **1212.**

9277. GREVEN, DAVID. Men beyond desire: manhood, sex, and violation in American literature. Basingstoke; New York: Palgrave Macmillan, 2005. pp. xii, 294.

9278. HAMILTON, PAUL. Metaromanticism: aesthetics, literature, theory. (Bibl. 2004, 9473.) Rev. by Paul H. Fry in CLIO (34:1/2) 2004, 175–80; by James O'Rourke in SR (43:4) 2004, 653–7; by Patrick Hogan in MLR (100:3) 2005, 794–5; by Richard Eldridge in ERR (16:3) 2005, 389–95; by Simon Swift in SoHR (39:4) 2005, 378–81.

9279. HAMLIN, CHRISTOPHER. Good and intimate filth. *In* (pp. 3–29) **9220.**

9280. HAMMILL, FAYE. Literary culture and female authorship in Canada 1760–2000. *See* **7990.**

9281. HANEY, DAVID P. Recent work in Romanticism and religion: from witness to critique. ChrisL (54:2) 2005, 265–82 (review-article).

9282. HARPHAM, GEOFFREY GALT. Things and theory. Raritan (25:2) 2005, 134–45 (review-article).

9283. HARRIS, SHARON M. Executing race: early American women's narratives of race, society, and the law. *See* **7992.**

9284. —— Whose renaissance? Women writers in the era of the American renaissance. ESQ (49:1–3) 2003, 59–80.

9285. HARRIS, W. C. *E pluribus unum*: nineteenth-century American literature and the Constitutional paradox. Iowa City: Iowa UP, 2005. pp. x, 314.

9286. HELLER, DANA. Anatomies of rape. *See* **12724.**

9287. HELLER, TAMAR; MORAN, PATRICIA (eds). Scenes of the apple: food and the female body in nineteenth- and twentieth-century women's writing. (Bibl. 2004, 9481.) Rev. by Kathryn R. Kent in Gastronomica (5:2) 2005, 108–9; by Sarah Sceats in TSWL (24:2) 2005, 351–3.

9288. HERINGMAN, NOAH. Recent studies in the nineteenth century. SELit (45:4) 2005, 961–1020 (review-article).

9289. HETHERINGTON, CAROL; PETERSSON, IRMTRAUD (comps). Annual bibliography of studies in Australian literature: 2004. *See* **21055.**

9290. HEWITT, ELIZABETH. Correspondence and American literature, 1787–1865. *See* **8001.**

9291. HEYWOOD, CHRISTOPHER. A history of South African literature. *See* **12727.**

9292. HOAGWOOD, TERENCE ALLAN; LEDBETTER, KATHRYN. 'Colour'd shadows': contexts in publishing, printing, and reading nineteenth-century British women writers. Basingstoke; New York: Palgrave Macmillan, 2005. pp. xi, 198. Rev. by Andrew Piper in SHARP (14:4) 2005, 14–15.

9293. HOEVELER, DIANE LONG. The secularization of suffering: toward a theory of gothic subjectivity. *See* **8003.**

9294. HOLMES, MARTHA STODDARD.   Fictions of affliction: physical disability in Victorian culture. (Bibl. 2004, 9484.) Rev. by Matthew Bolton in VS (47:3) 2005, 483–5.

9295. HOMESTEAD, MELISSA J.   American women authors and literary property, 1822–1869. Cambridge; New York: CUP, 2005. pp. xi, 272.

9296. HOOPER, GLENN (ed.).   Landscape and empire 1770–2000. See **8005.**

9297. HUDSPETH, ROBERT N. (ed.).   'Born with knives in their brain': recent writing on American Transcendentalism. MaHR (7) 2005, 120–31 (review-article).

9298. IRWIN, ROBERT.   Omar's metamorphosis. See **11017.**

9299. ISHAM, HOWARD.   Image of the sea: oceanic consciousness in the Romantic century. New York; Frankfurt: Lang, 2004. pp. xxiii, 415. Rev. by George J. Leonard in WordsC (35:4) 2004, 207.

9300. JACKSON, CASSANDRA.   Barriers between us: interracial sex in nineteenth-century American literature. Bloomington: Indiana UP, 2004. pp. 146. (Blacks in the diaspora.)

9301. JACKSON, H. J.   Romantic readers: the evidence of marginalia. New Haven, CT; London: Yale UP, 2005. pp. xvii, 366.

9302. JARRETT, GENE.   'Entirely *black* verse from him would succeed': minstrel Realism and William Dean Howells. See **11342.**

9303. JARVIS, ROBIN.   The Romantic period: the intellectual and cultural context of English literature, 1789–1830. Harlow; New York: Longman, 2004. pp. x, 219. (Longman literature in English.) Rev. by Sharon Ruston in Romanticism (11:1) 2005, 122–5.

9304. JONES, JENNY ROBIN.   Writers in residence: a journey with pioneer New Zealand writers. (Bibl. 2004, 9488.) Rev. by Michael Caines in TLS, 29 Apr. 2005, 30.

9305. JONES, STEVEN E. (ed.).   The satiric eye: forms of satire in the Romantic period. Basingstoke; New York: Palgrave Macmillan, 2003. pp. 231. Rev. by Kenneth R. Johnston in WordsC (34:4) 2003, 211–15; by Malcolm Kelsall in BJ (32:1) 2004, 65–6; by Michael Scrivener in Criticism (46:1) 2004, 151–65; by Susan Eilenberg in CLIO (34:4) 2005, 486–91.

9306. JOSEPH, BETTY.   Reading the East India Company, 1720–1840: colonial currencies of gender. See **8010.**

9307. JUSTUS, JAMES H.   Fetching the Old Southwest: humorous writing from Longstreet to Twain. See **12248.**

9308. KANG, NANCY.   'As if I had entered a Paradise': fugitive slave narratives and cross-border literary history. See **10419.**

9309. KAPLAN, MORRIS.   Sodom on the Thames: sex, love, and scandal in Wilde times. See **12398.**

9310. KEACH, WILLIAM.   Arbitrary power: Romanticism, language, politics. (Bibl. 2004, 9492.) Rev. by Richard Cronin in WordsC (35:4) 2004, 160–1; by Richard Marggraf Turley in Eng (54:209) 2005, 157–61; by Jane Stabler in RES (56:224) 2005, 329–31.

9311. KELLEY, GREG. Tall tales from Cheapside: Falstaff's lying legacy in American Southern literature. NCarF (52:1) 2005, 25–38.

9312. KELSEY, PENELOPE. Natives, nation, narration: reading Roanoke in the American renaissance. ESQ (49:1–3) 2003, 149–60.

9313. KER, IAN. Catholic revival in English literature, 1845–1961: Newman, Hopkins, Belloc, Chesterton, Greene, Waugh. (Bibl. 2004, 9494.) Rev. by Cyrus P. Olsen, III, in LitTheol (18:4) 2004, 496–8; by Mary Gerhart in JR (85:3) 2005, 533–4.

9314. KEYMER, THOMAS; MEE, JON (eds). The Cambridge companion to English literature 1740–1830. See **8014.**

9315. KIPP, JULIE. Romanticism, maternity, and the body politic. See **8015.**

9316. KLEIN, JÜRGEN. Æsthetics of coldness: the Romantic scene and a glimpse at Baudelaire. 1650–1850 (9) 2003, 79–105.

9317. KLIMASMITH, BETSY. At home in the city: urban domesticity in American literature and culture, 1850–1930. Hanover, NH; London: UP of New England; Durham: New Hampshire UP, 2005. pp. xii, 293. (Becoming modern.)

9318. KUCICH, JOHN J. Ghostly communion: cross-cultural Spiritualism in nineteenth-century American literature. Hanover, NH: Dartmouth College Press, 2004. pp. xxxii, 190. (Re-encounters with colonialism – new perspectives on the Americas.)

9319. KUTCHEN, LARRY F. The neo-Turnerian frontier. See **8017.**

9320. LANE, CHRISTOPHER. Hatred & civility: the antisocial life in Victorian England. (Bibl. 2004, 9501.) Rev. by Ilana M. Blumberg in NineL (59:3) 2004, 419–22; by John Plotz in VS (47:2) 2005, 288–91; by Nicola Bradbury in MLR (100:4) 2005, 1100–1; by Sean Grass in Conradiana (37:3) 2005, 293–5.

9321. LAURITSEN, JOHN. Hellenism and homoeroticism in Shelley and his circle. JHo (49:3/4) 2005, 357–76.

9322. LEARY, PATRICK. Googling the Victorians. See **1118.**

9323. LEDBETTER, KATHRYN. Bonnets and rebellions: imperialism in *The Lady's Newspaper*. See **1253.**

9324. LEE, DEBBIE. Slavery and the Romantic imagination. (Bibl. 2004, 9505.) Rev. by Claire Emilie Martin and David Shafer in ECS (38:2) 2005, 355–60.

9325. LEE, MAURICE S. Slavery, philosophy, and American literature, 1830–1860. Cambridge; New York: CUP, 2005. pp. viii, 223. (Cambridge studies in American literature and culture, 148.) Rev. by Howard Temperley in TLS, 23 & 30 Dec. 2005, 29.

9326. LEE, SOHUI. '[O]ur American kinsman': British nationalism and book reviews of American literature in the 1840s. RomNet (38/39) 2005.

9327. LEVINE, GEORGE. Dying to know: scientific epistemology and narrative in Victorian England. (Bibl. 2004, 9509.) Rev. by Thomas Dixon in JVC (9:2) 2004, 279–84.

9328. LHAMON, W. T., JR (ed.). Jump Jim Crow: lost plays, lyrics, and street prose of the first Atlantic popular culture. (Bibl. 2004, 9510.) Rev. by Rosemarie K. Bank in JAH (91:2) 2004, 624–5; by David Carlyon in TJ (57:1) 2005, 136–7.

9329. LINK, ERIC CARL. The vast and terrible drama: American literary naturalism in the late nineteenth century. (Bibl. 2004, 9511.) Rev. by Jeffory A. Clymer in MFS (51:1) 2005, 183–91; by Leonard Cassuto in ALR (38:1) 2005, 77–8; by Michelle Ann Abate in HC (42:4) 2005, 19–20.

9330. LLOYD, ROSEMARY. Shimmering in a transformed light: writing the still life. Ithaca, NY; London: Cornell UP, 2005. pp. xvi, 173.

9331. LOUIS, MARGOT K. Gods and mysteries: the revival of paganism and the remaking of mythography through the nineteenth century. *See* **12496**.

9332. LYE, COLLEEN. America's Asia: racial form and American literature, 1893–1945. Princeton, NJ; Oxford: Princeton UP, 2005. pp. x, 342. Rev. by Mari Yoshihara in JAH (92:3) 2005, 1032–3; by Chris Vials in JAAS (8:2) 2005, 227–30.

9333. MCCAULEY, ELIZABETH ANNE, *et al.* Gondola days: Isabella Stewart Gardner and the Palazzo Barbaro circle. *See* **11429**.

9334. MCCAW, NEIL (ed.). Writing Irishness in nineteenth-century British culture. (Bibl. 2004, 9512.) Rev. by Matthew Campbell in JVC (10:2) 2005, 297–303.

9335. MCHENRY, ELIZABETH. Forgotten readers: recovering the lost history of African American literary societies. (Bibl. 2004, 9514.) Rev. by Christine Pawley in LQ (73:3) 2003, 351–3; by Keith E. Byerman in JAH (90:4) 2004, 1495–6; by Heidi L. M. Jacobs in ColLit (32:1) 2005, 191–3; by Joycelyn Moody in MLQ (66:1) 2005, 143–7.

9336. MCILVANNEY, LIAM; RYAN, RAY (eds). Ireland and Scotland: culture and society, 1700–2000. *See* **8023**.

9337. MCMASTER, JULIET. What Daisy knew: the epistemology of the child writer. *In* (pp. 51–69) **9164**.

9338. MCWILLIAMS, JOHN. New England's crises and cultural memory: literature, politics, history, religion, 1620–1860. *See* **6911**.

9339. MAJEWSKI, KAREN. Traitors and true Poles: narrating a Polish American identity, 1880–1939. (Bibl. 2004, 9519.) Rev. by Aleksandra Fleszar and Arna Bronstein in SEEJ (47:4) 2003, 708–9; by Adam Walaszek in JAH (91:1) 2004, 276.

9340. MAKDISI, SAREE. Literature, national identity, and empire. *In* (pp. 61–79) **8014**.

9341. MANNING, SUSAN. Sensibility. *In* (pp. 80–99) **8014**.

9342. MARGOLIS, STACEY. The public life of privacy in nineteenth-century American literature. Durham, NC; London: Duke UP, 2005. pp. 235. (New Americanists.)

9343. MARSHALL, DAVID. The frame of art: fictions of aesthetic experience, 1750–1815. *See* **8028**.

9344. MARSHALL, GAIL; POOLE, ADRIAN (eds). Victorian Shakespeare: vol. 2, Literature and culture. Foreword by Nina Auerbach. (Bibl. 2004, 9521.) Rev. by Peter Holbrook in TLS, 18 Feb. 2005, 26; by Asa Briggs in LitH (14:2) 2005, 90–1; by Matthew Reynolds in EC (55:1) 2005, 80–8.

9345. MARTIN, RONALD E. The languages of difference: American writers and anthropologists reconfigure the primitive, 1878–1940. Newark: Delaware UP, 2005. pp. 280.

9346. MARTINY, ERIK. 'There I could never be a boy': Frank O'Hara and the cult of the child. See 18601.

9347. MASON, JENNIFER. Civilized creatures: urban animals, Sentimental culture, and American literature, 1850–1900. Baltimore, MD; London: Johns Hopkins UP, 2005. pp. x, 229. (Animals, history, culture.)

9348. MASON, NICHOLAS. 'The quack has become God': puffery, print, and the 'death' of literature in Romantic-era Britain. See 1271.

9349. MAUNDER, ANDREW; MOORE, GRACE (eds). Victorian crime, madness and sensation. (Bibl. 2004, 9524.) Rev. by Kelly Grovier in TLS, 18 Mar. 2005, 29; by Michèle Mendelssohn in ELT (48:4) 2005, 466–8.

9350. MELTZER, MITCHELL. Secular revelations: the Constitution of the United States and classic American literature. Cambridge, MA; London: Harvard UP, 2005. pp. x, 192.

9351. MIEDER, WOLFGANG; BRYAN, GEORGE B. A dictionary of Anglo-American proverbs and proverbial phrases found in literary sources of the nineteenth and twentieth centuries. See 3452.

9352. MILDER, ROBERT. 'A literature for the time'. ESQ (49:1–3) 2003, 193–207.

9353. MITCHELL, SALLY. Reading class. VLC (33:1) 2005, 329–37 (review-article).

9354. —— Victorian 'companions': forward to the past? See 21091.

9355. MORGENTALER, GOLDIE. Consider the blonde head severed: subverting beauty in Victorian literature. Gramma (11) 2003, 95–106.

9356. MORTENSEN, PETER. British Romanticism and Continental influences: writing in an age of europhobia. (Bibl. 2004, 9528.) Rev. by James Vigus in ColB (ns 25) 2005, 90–5.

9357. MOSKAL, JEANNE; WOODEN, SHANNON R. (eds). Teaching British women writers, 1750–1900. See 8032.

9358. MOUNT, NICK. The expatriate origins of Canadian literature. In (pp. 237–55) 9191.

9359. —— When Canadian literature moved to New York. Toronto; Buffalo, NY; London: Toronto UP, 2005. pp. x, 217. (Studies in book and print culture.) Rev. by Dennis Duffy in LRC (13:9) 2005, 6–7.

9360. NALBANTIAN, SUZANNE. Memory in literature: from Rousseau to neuroscience. Basingstoke; New York: Palgrave Macmillan, 2003. pp. x, 185. Rev. by Patricia Feito in VWM (66) 2004, 30–1.

9361. NELSON, JAMES G. 'A delightful companion': Leonard Smithers and the Decadents. See 12404.

9362. NERAD, JULIE CARY. A darker woods: African American writers in the American renaissance. ESQ (49:1–3) 2003, 107–28.

9363. NEWMAN, LANCE. Our common dwelling: Henry Thoreau, Transcendentalism, and the class politics of nature. See 12206.

9364. NICHOLS, HEIDI L. The fashioning of middle-class America: *Sartain's Union Magazine of Literature and Art* and antebellum culture. (Bibl. 2004, 9532.) Rev. by Mantri Sivananda in JAC (28:1) 2005, 159.

9365. OLWELL, VICTORIA. 'It spoke itself': women's genius and eccentric politics. See **10989**.

9366. ORESTANO, FRANCESCA (ed.). La parola e lo sguardo nella letteratura inglese tra Ottocento e modernismo. Bari: Adriatica, 2005. pp. 420. (Biblioteca di studi inglesi, 74.)

9367. OULTON, CAROLYN W. DE LA L. Literature and religion in mid-Victorian England: from Dickens to Eliot. (Bibl. 2003, 8765.) Rev. by Mark Knight in JVC (8:2) 2003, 334–8; by Margaret Flanders Darby in DickQ (22:4) 2005, 259–61.

9368. OWEN, ALEX. The place of enchantment: British occultism and the culture of the modern. Chicago, IL; London: Chicago UP, 2004. pp. xiv, 355, (plates) 8. Rev. by Christine Ferguson in VicR (31:1) 2005, 64–6; by Rene Kolar in Historian (67:3) 2005, 579–80.

9369. PACE, JOEL; SCOTT, MATTHEW E. (eds). Wordsworth in American literary culture. See **12508**.

9370. PACKARD, CHRIS. Queer cowboys, and other erotic male friendships in nineteenth-century American literature. Basingstoke; New York: Palgrave Macmillan, 2005. pp. viii, 144. Rev. by James Polchin in GLRW (12:6) 2005, 42–3.

9371. PAGE, JUDITH W. Imperfect sympathies: Jews and Judaism in British Romantic literature and culture. Basingstoke; New York: Palgrave Macmillan, 2004. pp. xiv, 257. Rev. by Emily A. Bernhard Jackson in WordsC (35:4) 2004, 205–6.

9372. PALMGREN, JENNIFER A.; HOLLOWAY, LORRETTA M. (eds). Beyond Arthurian romances: the reach of Victorian medievalism. Basingstoke; New York: Palgrave Macmillan, 2005. pp. xiv, 252.

9373. PARHAM, JOHN. Green man Hopkins: Gerard Manley Hopkins and Victorian ecological criticism. See **11311**.

9374. PEER, LARRY H. The year's work in Romanticism studies. Prism(s) (13) 2005, 114–19.

9375. PERKINS, DAVID. Romanticism and animal rights. (Bibl. 2004, 9544.) Rev. by Christopher Strathman in ERR (16:3) 2005, 395–8.

9376. PERKINS, MAUREEN. Thoroughly modern mulatta: rethinking 'Old World' stereotypes in a 'New World' setting. See **10424**.

9377. PETERSON, LESLEY; ROBERTSON, LESLIE. An annotated bibliography of nineteenth-century juvenilia. *In* (pp. 269–303) **9164**.

9378. PHEGLEY, JENNIFER. Educating the proper woman reader: Victorian family literary magazines and the cultural health of the nation. See **1303**.

9379. —— 'I should no more think of dictating ... what kinds of books she should read': images of women readers in Victorian family literary magazines. *In* (pp. 105–28) **12549**.

9380. PHILLIPS, LAWRENCE. Introduction: the swarming streets: twentieth-century literary representations of London. *In* (pp. 1–6) **14254**.

9381. PHILLIPS, WM M. Nightmares of anarchy: language and cultural change, 1870–1914. (Bibl. 2004, 9549.) Rev. by Arthur Redding in SAtlR (70:3) 2005, 144–8.

9382. PIACENTINO, ED. Southwest humor's *magnum opus*. SAH (12) 2005, 121–30 (review-article).

9383. PICKER, JOHN M. Victorian soundscapes. (Bibl. 2004, 9550.) Rev. by John Gardiner in DickQ (21:4) 2004, 252–6; by Jonathan H. Grossman in MP (102:2) 2004, 285–9; by Peter Bailey in VicR (31:1) 2005, 67–70; by Phyllis Weliver in NineL (60:2) 2005, 262–5.

9384. PIONKE, ALBERT D. Plots of opportunity: representing conspiracy in Victorian England. (Bibl. 2004, 9552.) Rev. by Chris R. Vanden Bossche in VS (48:1) 2005, 183–5.

9385. PREIS-SMITH, AGATA; PARYZ, MAREK (eds). The poetics of America: explorations in the literature and culture of the United States. Warsaw: Univ. of Warsaw, 2004. pp. 257.

9386. PROCHÁZKA, MARTIN; HRBATA, ZDENĚK. Romantismus a romantismy: pojmy, proudy, kontexty. (Romanticism and romanticisms: concepts, currents, contexts.) Prague: Karolinum, 2005. pp. 419.

9387. QUAYUM, M. A. Saul Bellow and American Transcendentalism. *See* 15451.

9388. REDFIELD, MARC. The politics of aesthetics: nationalism, gender, Romanticism. (Bibl. 2004, 9561.) Rev. by David L. Clark in SR (44:2) 2005, 261–70.

9389. REGAN, STEPHEN (ed.). Irish writing: an anthology of Irish literature in English 1789–1939. *See* 8051.

9390. REISNER, GAVRIEL. The death-ego and the vital self: romances of desire in literature and psychoanalysis. (Bibl. 2004, 11488.) Rev. by Barbara Schapiro in AI (62:3) 2005, 373–80.

9391. REISNER, ROSALIND. Jewish American literature: a guide to reading interests. *See* 12879.

9392. REMAK, HENRY H. H. West European Romanticism: definition and scope. Prism(s) (13) 2005, 81–111.

9393. REVELLI, GIORGETTA (ed.). Da Ulisse a …: la città e il mare, dalla Liguria al mondo: atti del convegno internazionale (Imperia, 7–9 ottobre 2004). Pisa: ETS, 2005. pp. 672. (Memorie e atti di convegni, 29.)

9394. REVIE, LINDA L. The Niagara companion: explorers, artists and writers at the Falls from discovery through the twentieth century. Waterloo, Ont.: Wilfrid Laurier UP, 2003. pp. x, 212. Rev. by Christoph Irmscher in CanL (186) 2005, 173–4.

9395. RICHARDS, ELIZA. Gender and the poetics of reception in Poe's circle. *See* 11823.

9396. RICHARDSON, ALAN. Reading practices. *In* (pp. 397–405) 10060.

9397. RINTOUL, SUZANNE. Gothic anxieties: struggling with a definition. *See* 21108.

9398. ROE, NICHOLAS. Politics. *In* (pp. 357–65) 10060.

9399. —— (ed.). Romanticism: an Oxford guide. Oxford; New York: OUP, 2005. pp. xxv, 743. Rev. by Clive Marsland in KSR (19) 2005, 171–4.

9400. ROMINE, SCOTT. Playing like a man: noncompetitive manhood and frontier humor. SAH (11) 2004, 38–56.

9401. ROSENDALE, STEVEN (ed.). American radical and reform writers. Detroit, MI: Gale Research, 2005. pp. xxii, 502. (Dictionary of literary biography, 303.)

9402. ROWLINSON, MATTHEW. Theory of Victorian Studies: anachronism and self-reflexivity. See 21115.

9403. RUGGIERI, FRANCA (ed.). Dal vittorianesimo al modernismo: la cultura letteraria inglese (1830–1950). Rome: Carocci, 2005. pp. 491. (Studi superiori, 476.)

9404. RUWE, DONELLE (ed.). Culturing the child, 1690–1914: essays in memory of Mitzi Myers. See 8171.

9405. RYAN, SUSAN M. The grammar of good intentions: race and the antebellum culture of benevolence. (Bibl. 2004, 9575.) Rev. by Lori D. Ginzberg in JAH (91:2) 2004, 625–6.

9406. ST CLAIR, WILLIAM. The reading nation in the Romantic period. (Bibl. 2004, 9577.) Rev. by Gary Dyer in WordsC (35:4) 2004, 197–9; by Peter Cochran in BJ (32:2) 2004, 149–51; by Jack Gumpert Wasserman in BJ (32:2) 2004, 151–3; by Ian Gilmour in LRB (27:2) 2005, 26–8; by Ricardo Miguel Alfonso in Atl (27:2) 2005, 227–31; by Andrew Elfenbein in VS (47:3) 2005, 457–9; by Tom Lockwood in BJECS (28:2) 2005, 301–2; by Robert Morrison in EC (55:3) 2005, 275–83; by Noah Heringman in SELit (45:4) 2005, 961–1020; by Stephen Colclough in SHARP (14:4) 2005, 17–18; by Diego Saglia in NineL (60:2) 2005, 237–41; by Seamus Perry in KSR (19) 2005, 163–8.

9407. SCHAFFER, TALIA. The importance of being greedy: connoisseurship and domesticity in the writings of Elizabeth Robins Pennell. In (pp. 105–26) 9257.

9408. SCHMIDT, BERNARD. American literary personalism: emergence and decline. Lewiston, NY; Lampeter: Mellen Press, 2004. pp. vii, 138. (Studies in American literature, 70.)

9409. SCHOR, ESTHER. Among the lemon trees. TLS, 25 Nov. 2005, 10–11 (review-article). (Italian travel.)

9410. SCRIVENER, MICHAEL. Literature and politics. In (pp. 43–60) 8014.

9411. —— Trials in Romantic-era writing: modernity, guilt, and the scene of justice. See 8680.

9412. SHA, RICHARD C. Romanticism and the sciences of perversion. WordsC (36:2) 2005, 43–8.

9413. SHRIMPTON, NICHOLAS. Bradley and the Aesthetes. EC (55:4) 2005, 309–31.

9414. SIEGEL, JONAH. Haunted museum: longing, travel, and the art–romance tradition. Princeton, NJ; Oxford: Princeton UP, 2005. pp. xv, 285. (Princeton paperbacks.)

9415. SILVA GRUESZ, KIRSTEN. Ambassadors of culture: the transamerican origins of Latino writing. (Bibl. 2004, 9590.) Rev. by Ralph Bauer in AmLH (16:3) 2004, 487–95; by Ivonne M. García in AmP (15:1) 2005, 114–16.

9416. SOFER, NAOMI Z. Making the 'America of art': cultural nationalism and nineteenth-century women writers. Columbus: Ohio State UP, 2005. pp. viii, 286.

9417. SORISIO, CAROLYN. Fleshing out America: race, gender, and the politics of the body in American literature, 1833–1879. (Bibl. 2004, 9594.) Rev. by Shirley Samuels in NineL (59:3) 2004, 409–12.

9418. SPENCER, JANE. Literary relations: kinship and the canon 1660–1830. See **6944.**

9419. STAUFFER, ANDREW M. Anger, revolution, and Romanticism. Cambridge; New York: CUP, 2005. pp. x, 221. (Cambridge studies in Romanticism, 62.) Rev. by Robert Mitchell in ERR (16:5) 2005, 633–6; by Andrew Franta in SR (44:3) 2005, 445–9.

9420. STEELE, JEFFREY. Crises of relationship: developing relational models for the study of the American renaissance. ESQ (49:1–3) 2003, 33–43.

9421. STONEMAN, PATSY. Introduction. In (pp. 1–13) **10222.**

9422. SWIENCICKI, JILL. Sew it seams: (a)mending civic rhetorics for our classrooms and for rhetorical history. In (pp. 55–73) **2318.**

9423. TAKETANI, ETSUKO. US women writers and the discourses of colonialism, 1825–1861. (Bibl. 2003, 8813.) Rev. by Jeanne Boydston in JAH (91:2) 2004, 623–4; by Shelley Streeby in Legacy (22:1) 2005, 74–5.

9424. TAYLOR, ANDREW. What do we see when we look at the sea? The sea in post-Romantic Australian, British and American writing. In (pp. 367–77) **9393.**

9425. TAYLOR, CLARE L. Women, writing, and fetishism, 1890–1950: female cross-gendering. (Bibl. 2004, 9600.) Rev. by Lynette Felber in MFS (51:1) 2005, 228–31.

9426. TAYLOR, MILES; WOLFF, MICHAEL (eds). The Victorians since 1901: histories, representations, and revisions. Basingstoke; New York: Palgrave Macmillan, 2004. pp. xv, 295. Rev. by Neil McCaw in LitH (14:2) 2005, 69–73.

9427. THOMAS, DAVID WAYNE. Cultivating Victorians: liberal culture and the aesthetic. (Bibl. 2004, 9601.) Rev. by Julia F. Saville in NineL (59:3) 2004, 415–18; by Jonah Siegel in VS (47:2) 2005, 309–11; by Neil McCaw in LitH (14:2) 2005, 69–73.

9428. THOMAS, JULIA. Pictorial Victorians: the inscription of values in word and image. See **127.**

9429. THROSBY, CORIN. Flirting with fame: Byron's anonymous female fans. See **10339.**

9430. TOBIN, BETH FOWKES. Colonizing nature: the tropics in British arts and letters, 1760–1820. See **8077.**

9431. TOBIN, ROBERT D. The emancipation of the flesh: the legacy of Romanticism in the homosexual rights movement. See **8078.**

9432. TRACHTENBERG, ALAN. Shades of Hiawatha: staging Indians, making Americans, 1880–1930. (Bibl. 2004, 9602.) Rev. by Frank Van Nuys in JAH (92:3) 2005, 1008.

9433. TREADWELL, JAMES. Autobiographical writing and British literature, 1783–1834. *See* **8079**.

9434. TRUDEL, JEAN-LOUIS. Looking for little green men. *See* **14293**.

9435. TURNER, MARK W. Backward glances: cruising the queer streets of New York and London. London: Reaktion, 2003. pp. 191. Rev. by Leland Monk in VS (47:4) 2005, 599–601.

9436. UNDERWOOD, TED. The work of the sun: literature, science, and political economy, 1760–1860. *See* **8081**.

9437. VALDÉS MIYARES, J. RUBÉN. The prejudices of education: educational aspects of the Scottish Enlightenment. *See* **8082**.

9438. VAN NOY, RICK. Surveying the interior: literary cartographers and the sense of place. (Bibl. 2004, 9605.) Rev. by Barbara Ryan in AL (77:1) 2005, 200–2.

9439. VERNON, JAMES. Historians and the Victorian Studies question: response. *See* **21136**.

9440. VICINUS, MARTHA. Intimate friends: women who loved women, 1778–1928. *See* **8083**.

9441. VOGEL, TODD. Rewriting White: race, class, and cultural capital in nineteenth-century America. (Bibl. 2004, 9607.) Rev. by Bridget T. Heneghan in JAH (92:2) 2005, 620–1; by Tim Engles in MELUS (30:3) 2005, 247–51.

9442. WALLEN, MARTIN J. City of health, fields of disease: revolutions in the poetry, medicine, and philosophy of Romanticism. (Bibl. 2004, 9611.) Rev. by Tim Fulford in ColB (ns 26) 2005, 75–8.

9443. WATSON, J. R. Romanticism and war: a study of British Romantic-period writers and the Napoleonic Wars. (Bibl. 2004, 9613.) Rev. by Michael Wiley in WordsC (35:4) 2004, 156–8; by Philip Shaw in BJ (32:2) 2004, 157–8.

9444. WEINSTEIN, CINDY. Family, kinship, and sympathy in nineteenth-century American literature. Cambridge; New York: CUP, 2004. pp. x, 243. (Cambridge studies in American literature and culture, 147.) Rev. by Charlene Avallone in Leviathan (7:2) 2005, 55–9.

9445. WHYTE, WILLIAM. The intellectual aristocracy revisited. JVC (10:1) 2005, 15–45.

9446. WIESEPAPE, BETTY HOLLAND. Lone Star chapters: the story of Texas literary clubs. (Bibl. 2004, 9614.) Rev. by Crista DeLuzio in JSH (71:2) 2005, 490–1.

9447. WILCZYŃSKI, MAREK. A week on the rivers, summer on the lakes: notes on the poetics of American Romantic travelogue. *In* (pp. 39–45) **12672**.

9448. WILSON, ERIC G. The spiritual history of ice: Romanticism, science, and the imagination. (Bibl. 2004, 9615.) Rev. by Daniel E. White in GothS (6:1) 2004, 152–5; by Martin Halliwell in ERR (16:3) 2005, 373–80.

9449. WILSON, LESLIE PERRIN. 'No worthless books': Elizabeth Peabody's Foreign Library, 1840–52. PBSA (99:1) 2005, 113–52.

9450. WOMERSLEY, DAVID. Revising the life. *See* **8090**.

9451. WRIGHT, EAMON. British women writers and race, 1788–1818: narrations of modernity. *See* **8092**.

9452. YOUNGQUIST, PAUL. Monstrosities: bodies and British Romanticism. (Bibl. 2004, 9619.) Rev. by Jeffrey Longacre in ColLit (32:4) 2005, 229–31; by Kathryn Pratt in SAtlR (70:2) 2005, 174–7.

9453. ZAGARRI, ROSEMARIE. American women's rights before Seneca Falls. In (pp. 667–91) **8016.**

9454. ZHOU, XIAOJING; NAJMI, SAMINA (eds). Form and transformation in Asian American literature. Seattle; London: Washington UP, 2005. pp. 296. (Scott and Laurie Oki series in Asian American studies.)

DRAMA AND THE THEATRE

9455. ALLEN, CAROL DAWN. Peculiar passages: Black women playwrights, 1875 to 2000. New York; Frankfurt: Lang, 2005. pp. 295.

9456. ANDREWS, MATTHEW. Still fervent: Phoebe Brand at 96: the last of the Group Theatre and of the first generation of American Stanislavsky System actors. THS (25) 2005, 125–48.

9457. BELLORINI, MARIAGRAZIA (ed.). *The Ring and the Book* di Robert Browning: poesia e dramma. *See* **10257.**

9458. BENNETT, BRIDGET. Sacred theatres: Shakers, Spiritualists, theatricality, and the Indian in the 1830s and 1840s. TDR (49:3) 2005, 114–34.

9459. BIRD, KYM. Redressing the past: the politics of early English Canadian women's drama 1880–1920. Montreal; Buffalo, NY; London: McGill-Queen's UP, 2004. pp. xii, 269. Rev. by Meghan Brodie in TJ (57:2) 2005, 325–7.

9460. BOTTLE, TED. Coventry's forgotten theatre: the Theatre Royal, Smithford Street, which became the Empire Theatre of Varieties; including glimpses of other Coventry venues of entertainment and the workings of the English provincial theatre during the nineteenth century. Westbury, Wilts.: Badger Press, 2004. pp. xiv, 183. Rev. by Graeme Cruickshank in TN (59:1) 2005, 57.

9461. BRATTON, JACKY. The celebrity of Edmund Kean: an institutional story. In (pp. 90–106) **3985.**

9462. COX, JEFFREY N.; GAMER, MICHAEL (eds). The Broadview anthology of Romantic drama. Peterborough, Ont.; Orchard Park, NY: Broadview Press, 2003. pp. xxiv, 432. (Broadview anthologies of English literature.) Rev. by Catherine Burroughs in RomNet (29/30) 2003.

9463. CRONIN-JORTNER, MAURA L. Expansion, expulsion, and domination: Jonathan's spatial tactics on the Jacksonian stage. JADT (17:1) 2005, 61–78. ('Jonathan' as precursor of 'Uncle Sam'.)

9464. DASSORI, EMMA. Performing the Woman Question: the emergence of anti-suffrage drama. ATQ (19:4) 2005, 301–17.

9465. DAVIS, TRACY C. 'Do you believe in fairies?': the hiss of dramatic license. *See* **15345.**

9466. DAWSON, MARK S. Gentility and the comic theatre of late Stuart London. *See* **6985.**

9467. DONOHUE, JOSEPH. Fantasies of empire: the Empire Theatre of Varieties and the licensing controversy of 1894. Iowa City: Iowa UP, 2005. pp. xi, 290. (Studies in theatre history & culture.)

9468. —— (ed.). The Cambridge history of British theatre: vol. 2, 1660 to 1895. *See* **6988**.

9469. DURING, SIMON. 'The temple lives': the Lyceum and Romantic show business. *In* (pp. 204–24) **9217**.

9470. EDWARDS, ADRIAN. Provincial theatre in Britain, 1773–1808: the Burney playbills examined. *See* **8102**.

9471. ELTIS, SOS. Private lives and public spaces: reputation, celebrity and the late Victorian actress. *In* (pp. 169–88) **3985**.

9472. EMELJANOW, VICTOR, *et al.* (comps). Romantic and Revolutionary theatre, 1789–1860. Ed. by Donald Roy. (Bibl. 2004, 8439.) Rev. by Barry Daniels in TheatreS (45:2) 2004, 310–11.

9473. ERDMAN, ANDREW L. Blue vaudeville: sex, morals and the mass marketing of amusement, 1895–1915. (Bibl. 2004, 9633.) Rev. by Leigh Woods in TheatreS (46:1) 2005, 132–4; by Kathryn J. Oberdeck in JAH (92:1) 2005, 244–5.

9474. FITZSIMMONS, LINDA. The Theatre Royal, York, in the 1840s. NCT (31:1) 2004, 18–25.

9475. FOULKES, RICHARD. Lewis Carroll and the Victorian theatre: theatricals in a quiet life. *See* **10400**.

9476. FRICK, JOHN W. Theatre, culture and Temperance reform in nineteenth-century America. (Bibl. 2004, 9640.) Rev. by Rosemarie K. Bank in TheatreS (45:2) 2004, 288–90; by Bruce McConachie in NCT (31:2) 2004, 85–9; by Louis James in NCT (31:2) 2004, 80–2; by Scott C. Martin in JAH (91:2) 2004, 625; by Elizabeth Reitz Mullenix in TJ (57:1) 2005, 135–6.

9477. FRISKEN, AMANDA. Victoria Woodhull's sexual revolution: political theatre and the popular press in nineteenth-century America. Philadelphia: Pennsylvania UP, 2004. pp. ix, 225. Rev. by Patricia Okker in Legacy (22:2) 2005, 211–12; by Paulette Kilmer in JoH (30:4) 2005, 217.

9478. GANDOLFI, ROBERTA. La prima regista: Edith Craig fra rivoluzione della scena e cultura. (Bibl. 2003, 8856.) Rev. by Massimo Bacigalupo in Indice (2005:3) 28.

9479. GAULL, MARILYN. Pantomime as satire: mocking a broken charm. *In* (pp. 207–24) **9305**.

9480. GOODALL, JANE R. Performance and evolution in the age of Darwin: out of the natural order. (Bibl. 2004, 9642.) Rev. by Andréa J. Onstad in TJ (57:2) 2005, 340–1; by Joseph Roach in ModDr (48:1) 2005, 208–10.

9481. GORDON-CLARK, JANETTE. From Melbourne to Broadway: the career of Eleanor Carey. NCT (30:1) 2003, 11–25.

9482. GOULD, MARTY. Anticipation, transformation, accommodation: the Great Exhibition on the London stage. *See* **12130**.

9483. HOLLAND, PETER. Dramatizing the dramatist. *See* **13042**.

9484. HUGHES, GILLIAN. James Hogg and the theatre. *See* **11278**.

9485. KELLY, VERONICA. Early Australian high comedy to 1890: performing the colonial bourgeois self. Southerly (64:3) 2004, 58–77.

9486. KERSHAW, BAZ (ed.). The Cambridge history of British theatre: vol. 3, Since 1895. Cambridge; New York: CUP, 2004. pp. xxxiv, 562.

9487. KING, DONALD C. The theatres of Boston: a stage and screen history. Jefferson, NC; London: McFarland, 2005. pp. xi, 266.

9488. LEWIS, ROBERT M. (ed.). From traveling show to vaudeville: theatrical spectacle in America, 1830–1910. (Bibl. 2004, 9651.) Rev. by Annemarie Bean in TJ (57:1) 2005, 137–8.

9489. LOCKWOOD, TOM. Ben Jonson in the Romantic age. See **7562**.

9490. LÓPEZ RODRÍGUEZ, MIRIAM; NARBONA CARRIÓN, MARIA DOLORES. Women's contribution to nineteenth-century American theatre. Valencia: Biblioteca Javier Coy d'estudis nord-americans, Univ. de València, 2004. pp. 184. Rev. by Felicia Hardison Londré in THS (25) 2005, 200–2.

9491. McALLISTER, MARVIN. White people do not know how to behave at entertainments designed for ladies & gentlemen of colour: William Brown's African & American theater. (Bibl. 2004, 9653.) Rev. by Craig Steven Wilder in JAH (91:2) 2004, 615–16; by Nikki Taylor in JAAH (89:2) 2004, 185–7; by John Rogers Harris in TheatreS (46:1) 2005, 130–2.

9492. MEER, SARAH. Uncle Tom mania: slavery, minstrelsy, and transatlantic culture in the 1850s. See **12110**.

9493. MILLER, RENATA KOBETTS. Child-killers and the competition between late Victorian theater and the novel. MLQ (66:2) 2005, 197–226.

9494. OCKMAN, CAROL; SILVER, KENNETH E. Sarah Bernhardt: the art of high drama. New York: Jewish Museum, New York, under the auspices of the Jewish Theological Seminary of America; New Haven, CT: Yale UP, 2005. pp. xv, 216.

9495. PEDLEY, CATHERINE. Maria Marten; or, The Murder in the Red Barn: the theatricality of provincial life. NCT (31:1) 2004, 26–38.

9496. POOLE, RALPH J. Indecent ingénues: David Belasco's and Mae West's delegitimization and refashioning of American melodrama. See **15432**.

9497. POSTLEWAIT, THOMAS. Constructing events in theatre history: a matter of credibility. In (pp. 33–52) **3974**.

9498. POWELL, KERRY (ed.). The Cambridge companion to Victorian and Edwardian theatre. (Bibl. 2004, 9664.) Rev. by Stephen Watt in CompDr (38:1) 2004, 110–13.

9499. RINEAR, DAVID L. Stage, page, scandals, and vandals: William E. Burton and nineteenth-century American theatre. Carbondale: Southern Illinois UP, 2004. pp. xvi, 283. (Theater in the Americas.) Rev. by Heather S. Nathans in THS (25) 2005, 202–4.

9500. ROBINSON, JOANNE. Mapping performance culture: locating the spectator in theatre history. NCT (31:1) 2004, 3–17.

9501. SENELICK, LAURENCE. Consuming passions: eating and the stage at the fin de siècle. Gastronomica (5:2) 2005, 43–9.

9502. SHELTON, LEWIS E. Ideas of the theatre: the five directorial perspectives of the American stage. Bethesda, MD: Academica Press, 2005. pp. xii, 262.

9503. STETZ, MARGARET D. Gender and the London theatre, 1880–1920. High Wycombe: Rivendale Press in assn with Bryn Mawr College Library, 2004. pp. 141, (plates) 8. Rev. by Katherine E. Kelly in ELT (48:4) 2005, 464–6.

9504. STOKES, JOHN. The French actress and her English audience. Cambridge; New York: CUP, 2005. pp. x, 224. Rev. by John Glavin in VS (47:4) 2005, 623–4.

9505. TETENS, KRISTAN. 'A grand informal Durbar': Henry Irving and the coronation of Edward VII. *See* **13121**.

9506. VANDEVELDE, KAREN. Modernisation and national representation in late 19th-century Dublin theatres. EtIr (29:1) 2004, 25–40.

9507. VOSKUIL, LYNN M. Acting naturally: Victorian theatricality and authenticity. Charlottesville; London: Virginia UP, 2004. pp. xi, 268. (Victorian literature and culture.) Rev. by Samantha Ellis in TLS, 29 Apr. 2005, 30.

9508. ZITER, EDWARD. The Orient on the Victorian stage. (Bibl. 2004, 9676.) Rev. by Joseph McLaughlin in NCT (31:2) 2004, 82–5; by John M. MacKenzie in VS (47:2) 2005, 307–8.

FICTION

9509. ALLEN, EMILY. Theater figures: the production of the nineteenth-century British novel. (Bibl. 2004, 9679.) Rev. by Mary Jean Corbett in WordsC (35:4) 2004, 172–4; by Marcie Frank in RomNet (36/37) 2004/05; by William A. Davis in VPR (38:1) 2005, 106–8.

9510. ANDRES, SOPHIA. The Pre-Raphaelite art of the Victorian novel: narrative challenges to visual gendered boundaries. Columbus: Ohio State UP, 2005. pp. xxvii, 208.

9511. ARCHIMEDES, SONDRA M. Gendered pathologies: the female body and biomedical discourse in the nineteenth-century English novel. London; New York: Routledge, 2005. pp. vii, 202. (Literary criticism and cultural theory.)

9512. AUCHINCLOSS, LOUIS. Writers and personality. Columbia; London: South Carolina UP, 2005. pp. 125. Rev. by Catharine Savage Brosman in Chronicles (29:10) 2005, 36–7.

9513. BERGMAN, JILL; BERNARDI, DEBRA (eds). Our sisters' keepers: nineteenth-century benevolence literature by American women. Tuscaloosa; London: Alabama UP, 2005. pp. xii, 299. (Studies in American literary realism and naturalism.)

9514. BERNARD, CATHERINE. Habitations of the past: of shrines and haunted houses. YREAL (21) 2005, 161–72.

9515. BIGELOW, GORDON. Fiction, famine, and the rise of economics in Victorian Britain and Ireland. (Bibl. 2004, 9690.) Rev. by Robert Brazeau in VicR (30:1) 2004, 113–16; by Francis O'Gorman in RES (56:225) 2005, 463–5.

9516. BILSTON, SARAH. The awkward age in women's popular fiction, 1850–1900: girls and the transition to womanhood. (Bibl. 2004, 9692.) Rev. by Catherine Maxwell in RES (56:225) 2005, 461–3.

9517. BLAIR, JENNIFER. The knowledge of 'sex' and the lattice of the confessional: the nun's tales and early North American popular discourse. *In* (pp. 173–210) **9191**.

9518. BRETON, ROB. Ghosts in the machine: plotting in Chartist and working-class fiction. VS (47:4) 2005, 557–75.

9519. BROOKS, PETER.   Realist vision. New Haven, CT; London: Yale UP, 2005. pp. 255. Rev. by Andrew Starner in ASch (74:3) 2005, 140; by Keith Miller in TLS, 14 Oct. 2005, 34.

9520. BROWN, BILL.   A sense of things: the object matter of American literature. (Bibl. 2004, 9695.) Rev. by Douglas Mao in CLIO (34:1/2) 2004, 217–24; by William Gleason in WinP (39:4) 2004, 295–300; by Lori Merish in Novel (38:1) 2004, 111–13; by Geoffrey Galt Harpham in Raritan (25:2) 2005, 134–45.

9521. BROWN, HARRY J.   Injun Joe's ghost: the Indian mixed-blood in American writing. (Bibl. 2004, 9696.) Rev. by J. Randolph Cox in DNR (74:1) 2005, 33–4; by Ray B. Browne in JAC (28:1) 2005, 141; by Margo Lukens in AICRJ (29:2) 2005, 139–41.

9522. BROWN, MARSHALL.   The gothic text. See 8125.

9523. BROWN, SARAH ANNES.   The double taboo: lesbian incest in the nineteenth century. NCS (18) 2004, 81–98.

9524. BURSTEIN, MIRIAM ELIZABETH.   Reviving the Reformation: Victorian women witers and the Protestant historical novel. WWr (12:1) 2005, 73–84.

9525. BUZARD, JAMES.   Disorienting fiction: the autoethnographic work of nineteenth-century British novels. Princeton, NJ; Oxford: Princeton UP, 2005. pp. vi, 320.

9526. CALDWELL, JANIS McLARREN.   Literature and medicine in nineteenth-century Britain: from Mary Shelley to George Eliot. Cambridge; New York: CUP, 2004. pp. xi, 201. (Cambridge studies in nineteenth-century literature and culture.) Rev. by Sharon Ruston in TLS, 23 Sept. 2005, 27; by Nicholas Birns in LitMed (24:2) 2005, 318–21; by Lillan R. Furst in NineL (60:2) 2005, 244–7.

9527. CARENS, TIMOTHY L.   Outlandish English subjects in the Victorian domestic novel. Basingstoke; New York: Palgrave Macmillan, 2005. pp. x, 198.

9528. CARLISLE, JANICE.   Common scents: comparative encounters in high Victorian fiction. (Bibl. 2004, 9697.) Rev. by John Gardiner in DickQ (21:4) 2004, 252–6.

9529. CHAKRAVARTY, GAUTAM.   The Indian Mutiny and the British imagination. Cambridge; New York: CUP, 2005. pp. xi, 242. (Cambridge studies in nineteenth-century literature and culture, 43.) Rev. by Andrew Rudd in TLS, 18 Mar. 2005, 29; by Maya Jasanoff in LRB (27:14) 2005, 9–10; by Shuchi Kapila in VS (48:1) 2005, 157–9.

9530. CHRISTENSEN, ALLAN CONRAD.   Nineteenth-century narratives of contagion: our feverish contact. London; New York: Routledge, 2005. pp. ix, 350. (Routledge studies in nineteenth-century literature, 1.)

9531. CLAUSSON, NILS.   Degeneration, *fin-de-siècle* gothic, and the science of detection: Arthur Conan Doyle's *The Hound of the Baskervilles* and the emergence of the modern detective story. See 10842.

9532. COTTOM, DANIEL.   I think; therefore, I am Heathcliff. See 8126.

9533. COX, J. RANDOLPH.   Premiums in dime novels. DNR (74:5) 2005, 190–3.

9534. CUDDY, LOIS A.; ROCHE, CLAIRE M. (eds).   Evolution and eugenics in American literature and culture, 1880–1940: essays on ideological conflict and complicity. (Bibl. 2004, 9703.) Rev. by Seth Bovey in ALR (38:1) 2005, 78–9.

9535. DAGBOVIE, PERO GAGLO. Black women historians from the late 19th century to the dawning of the Civil Rights Movement. JAAH (89:3) 2004, 241–61.

9536. DALZIELL, TANYA. Settler romances and the Australian girl. *See* 14118.

9537. DAVIDSON, CATHY N. Revolution and the word: the rise of the novel in America. *See* 8127.

9538. DAY, VOX. C. S. Lewis and the problem of religion in science fiction and fantasy. *In* (pp. 219–28) 17727.

9539. DEANE, BRADLEY. The making of the Victorian novelist: anxieties of authorship in the mass market. (Bibl. 2004, 9705.) Rev. by Daniel Hack in VS (47:3) 2005, 473–5.

9540. DELLAMORA, RICHARD. Friendship's bonds: democracy and the novel in Victorian England. Philadelphia: Pennsylvania UP, 2004. pp. 252. Rev. by John Plotz in NineL (60:1) 2005, 101–5.

9541. DEVLIN, ATHENA. Between profits and primitivism: shaping White middle-class masculinity in the United States, 1880–1917. London; New York: Routledge, 2005. pp. xi, 174. (Literary criticism and cultural theory.)

9542. DUFFY, CIAN. 'His *canaille* of an audience': Thomas De Quincey and the revolution of reading. *See* 10605.

9543. FASICK, LAURA. Professional men and domesticity in the mid-Victorian novel. (Bibl. 2003, 8921.) Rev. by Allen J. Salerno in VS (47:3) 2005, 475–7.

9544. FITZGERALD, LAUREN. Female gothic and the institutionalization of Gothic Studies. *See* 14783.

9545. FLAVIN, MICHAEL. Gambling in the nineteenth-century English novel: 'A leprosy is o'er the land.' (Bibl. 2003, 8928.) Rev. by Liz Rosdeitcher in VS (47:2) 2005, 287–8.

9546. FLINT, KATE. Re-visiting *A Literature of Their Own*. JVC (10:2) 2005, 289–96. (Re-evaluation.) (*Discusses* bibl. 1977, 6050.)

9547. FOLKS, JEFFREY J. In a time of disorder: form and meaning in Southern fiction from Poe to O'Connor. (Bibl. 2004, 9714.) Rev. by John D. Cox in FOR (3) 2005, 122–3.

9548. FRANK, FREDERICK S. Guide to the gothic III: an annotated bibliography of criticism, 1994–2003: vol. II. *See* 7980.

9549. FREELAND, NATALKA. The dustbins of history: waste management in late Victorian utopias. *In* (pp. 225–49) 9220.

9550. FULLER, SOPHIE; LOSSEFF, NICKY (eds). The idea of music in Victorian fiction. Aldershot; Burlington, VT: Ashgate, 2004. pp. xx, 297. (Music in nineteenth-century Britain.) Rev. by Donna S. Parsons in VS (48:1) 2005, 175–7.

9551. GATES, SONDRA SMITH. The edge of possibility: Susan Warner and the world of Sunday school fiction. *See* 12285.

9552. GIORCELLI, CRISTINA. Da Irving – a Hawthorne, a Poe – a Irving: alle origini del fantastico nella letteratura statunitense. LAm (24:101) 2004, 23–52.

9553. GOLDEN, CATHERINE J. Images of the woman reader in Victorian British and American fiction. Gainesville: Florida UP, 2003. pp. xvi, 287. Rev. by Katherine Malone in ELT (48:1) 2005, 79–82; by Diana C. Archibald in DickQ (22:2) 2005, 119–21; by Jennifer Phegley in VS (48:1) 2005, 171–3.

9554. GOODMAN, SUSAN. Civil wars: American novelists and manners, 1880–1940. (Bibl. 2004, 9716.) Rev. by Claire Preston in MLR (100:1) 2005, 207–8.

9555. GRIFFIN, SUSAN M. Anti-Catholicism and nineteenth-century fiction. (Bibl. 2004, 9718.) Rev. by James H. Murphy in VIJ (32) 2004, 219–22; by Maria LaMonaca in VS (47:3) 2005, 463–5; by Susan E. Hill in JR (85:4) 2005, 701–2; by Thomas Butler in ReLit (37:3) 2005, 141–4.

9556. GRIMES, HILARY. The haunted self: visions of the ghost and the woman at the *fin-de-siècle*. See **12059**.

9557. HACK, DANIEL. The material interests of the Victorian novel. Charlottesville; London: Virginia UP, 2005. pp. xi, 226. (Victorian literature and culture.)

9558. HAGGERTY, GEORGE. The horrors of Catholicism: religion and sexuality in gothic fiction. See **8134**.

9559. HALLDÉN, RUTH. Radikaler & Viktorianer. Stockholm: Atlantis, 2004. pp. 178. Rev. by Christina Sjöholm in GissJ (41:1) 2005, 34–6.

9560. HANCOCK, STEPHEN. The Romantic sublime and middle-class subjectivity in the Victorian novel. London; New York: Routledge, 2005. pp. ix, 204. (Literary criticism and cultural theory.)

9561. HAPGOOD, LYNNE. Margins of desire: the suburbs in fiction and culture, 1880–1925. Manchester; New York: Manchester UP, 2005. pp. vi, 264. Rev. by Andrew Radford in EJES (9:3) 2005, 329–31.

9562. HENEGHAN, BRIDGET T. Whitewashing America: material culture and race in the antebellum imagination. (Bibl. 2004, 9722.) Rev. by Neil Kamil in JAH (91:4) 2005, 1458–9; by Robert E. May in AmS (46:1) 2005, 159–60.

9563. HOBERMAN, RUTH. Constructing the turn-of-the-century shopper: narratives about purchased objects in the *Strand* magazine, 1891–1910. VPR (37:1) 2004, 1–17.

9564. HODDER, KAREN. *Jane Eyre* and subversive influences. *In* (pp. 39–52) **10222**.

9565. HUNT, PAUL. Serial fiction in the *Otago Witness*, 1851–1906. BSANZB (27:3/4) 2003, 94–103.

9566. ISHIZUKA, HIROKO. Victorian no Chichukai. (The Victorians in the Mediterranean.) Tokyo: Kaibunsha, 2004. pp. iv, 259. Rev. by Mitsuharu Matsuoka in GissJ (41:1) 2005, 30–4.

9567. JAMES, CLIVE. Starting with sludge: a literary education: from the fiction of Biggles to Braddon's brute facts. See **14179**.

9568. JASANOFF, MAYA. Secret signals in lotus flowers. LRB (27:14) 2005, 9–10 (review-article). (Indian Mutiny in fiction.)

9569. JAY, ELISABETH. The enemy within: the housekeeper in Victorian fiction. CVE (61) 2005, 247–60.

9570. JEFFERS, THOMAS L. Apprenticeships: the *Bildungsroman* from Goethe to Santayana. Basingstoke; New York: Palgrave Macmillan, 2005. pp. 246.

9571. JONES, PAUL CHRISTIAN. Unwelcome voices: subversive fiction in the antebellum South. Knoxville: Tennessee UP, 2005. pp. x, 225.

9572. JOYCE, SIMON. Capital offenses: geographies of class and crime in Victorian London. (Bibl. 2004, 9731.) Rev. by Sascha Auerbach in VIJ (32) 2004, 215–19.

9573. KAPPLER, MARY ELLEN. Playing 'theayter': dramatic performance in the late Victorian fictional slum. VicR (29:2) 2003, 1–18.

9574. KAYE, RICHARD A. The flirt's tragedy: desire without end in Victorian and Edwardian fiction. (Bibl. 2004, 9732.) Rev. by James Najarian in StudN (37:2) 2005, 223–31.

9575. KERN, STEPHEN. A cultural history of causality: science, murder novels, and systems of thought. (Bibl. 2004, 9734.) Rev. by Colin Burrow in LRB (27:18) 2005, 23–4.

9576. KESTNER, JOSEPH A. Sherlock's sisters: the British female detective, 1864–1913. (Bibl. 2004, 9735.) Rev. by Alisa Clapp-Itnyre in VIJ (32) 2004, 229–33; by Edward S. Lauterbach in ELT (48:2) 2005, 224–6; by Lynn M. Alexander in TSWL (24:1) 2005, 162–4.

9577. KICKHAM, LISBET. Protestant women novelists and Irish society 1879–1922. Lund: Dept of English, Lund Univ., 2004. pp. 192. (Lund studies in English, 106.) Rev. by Mary Jean Corbett in NineL (60:2) 2005, 266–9.

9578. KILFEATHER, SIOBHÁN. Terrific register: the gothicization of atrocity in Irish Romanticism. See **11656**.

9579. KNIGHT, STEPHEN. Crime fiction, 1800–2000: detection, death, diversity. (Bibl. 2004, 9738.) Rev. by Susan Rowland in MLR (100:4) 2005, 1076–7; by Jason David Hall in Clues (23:3) 2005, 77–8.

9580. KRASNER, JAMES. Accumulated lives: metaphor, materiality, and the homes of the elderly. See **17688**.

9581. KRUGER, DANIEL J.; FISHER, MARYANNE; JOBLING, IAN. Proper hero dads and dark hero cads: alternate mating strategies exemplified in British Romantic literature. In (pp. 225–43) **14807**.

9582. LAMB, ROBERT PAUL; THOMPSON, G. R. (eds). A companion to American fiction, 1865–1914. Oxford; Malden, MA: Blackwell, 2004. pp. 576. (Blackwell companions to literature and culture, 35.)

9583. LAW, GRAHAM. Savouring of the Australian soil? On the sources and affiliations of colonial newspaper fiction. See **1252**.

9584. LEHAN, RICHARD. Realism and naturalism: the novel in an age of transition. Madison; London: Wisconsin UP, 2005. pp. xxxiv, 312.

9585. LEMENAGER, STEPHANIE. Manifest and other destinies: territorial fictions of the nineteenth-century United States. Lincoln; London: Nebraska UP, 2004. pp. viii, 285. (Postwestern horizons.)

9586. LEVANDER, CAROLINE. Consenting fictions, fictions of consent. AmLH (16:2) 2004, 318–28 (review-article).

9587. LEVERENZ, DAVID. Paternalism incorporated: fables of American fatherhood, 1865–1940. (Bibl. 2004, 9744.) Rev. by K. A. Cuordileone in JAH (91:3) 2004, 1033–4.

9588. LEVINE, CAROLINE. The serious pleasures of suspense: Victorian realism and narrative doubt. (Bibl. 2003, 8970.) Rev. by Peter Garrett in MLR (100:2) 2005, 490–1; by Thomas Recchio in ColLit (32:3) 2005, 182–92; by Rosemarie Bodenheimer in MLQ (66:3) 2005, 404–6; by Johanna M. Smith in CLIO (35:1) 2005, 111–15; by Pam Morris in NineL (60:2) 2005, 258–62.

9589. LINDNER, CHRISTOPH. Fictions of commodity culture: from the Victorian to the postmodern. (Bibl. 2003, 8972.) Rev. by Peter Stoneley in MLR (100:3) 2005, 804–5; by Matthew Beaumont in RES (56:224) 2005, 335–7.

9590. MCEVOY, EMMA. 'Really, though secretly, a Papist': G. K. Chesterton's and John Meade Falkner's rewritings of the gothic. See 15776.

9591. MCLAUGHLIN, KEVIN. Paperwork: fiction and mass mediacy in the paper age. Philadelphia: Pennsylvania UP, 2005. pp. 181. (Critical authors & issues.)

9592. MAYER, NANCY. Finding herself alone: Emily Dickinson, Victorian women novelists, and the female subject. See 10795.

9593. MERISH, LORI. Representing the 'deserving poor': the 'sentimental seamstress' and the feminization of poverty in antebellum America. In (pp. 49–79) 9513.

9594. MILLER, RENATA KOBETTS. Child-killers and the competition between late Victorian theater and the novel. See 9493.

9595. MOFFAT, KIRSTINE. The demon drink: Prohibition novels 1882–1924. JNZL (23:1) 2005, 139–61.

9596. MORGAN, WILLIAM M. Questionable charity: gender, humanitarianism, and complicity in US literary realism. (Bibl. 2004, 9749.) Rev. by Carrie Tirado Bramen in JAH (92:3) 2005, 1011–12.

9597. MORRIS, PAM. Imagining inclusive society in nineteenth-century novels: the code of sincerity in the public sphere. Baltimore, MD; London: Johns Hopkins UP, 2004. pp. x, 261. Rev. by Mark M. Hennelly, Jr, in DickQ (22:3) 2005, 186–9.

9598. MUKHERJEE, UPAMANYU PABLO. Crime and empire: the colony in nineteenth-century fictions of crime. (Bibl. 2004, 9750.) Rev. by V. G. Kiernan in LitH (14:1) 2005, 75–80; by Robert Burroughs in JVC (10:2) 2005, 319–23.

9599. OKKER, PATRICIA. Social stories: the magazine novel in nineteenth-century America. (Bibl. 2004, 9754.) Rev. by Katherine Henry in AmP (15:1) 2005, 112–14; by Melissa J. Homestead in Legacy (22:1) 2005, 84–6.

9600. PAL-LAPINSKI, PIYA. The exotic woman in nineteenth-century British fiction and culture: a reconsideration. Durham: New Hampshire UP, 2004. pp. xx, 156. (Becoming modern.)

9601. PARAVISINI-GEBERT, LIZABETH. 'He of the trees': nature, environment, and creole religiosities in Caribbean literature. In (pp. 182–96) 12632.

9602. PARRINDER, PATRICK. Entering dystopia, entering Erewhon. See 10283.

9603. PATERSON, KATHERINE. Why historical fiction? VH (73:1) 2005, 5–15.

9604. PATTERSON, MARTHA H. Beyond the Gibson Girl: reimagining the American New Woman, 1895–1915. Urbana: Illinois UP, 2005. pp. xii, 230.

9605. PEPRNÍK, MICHAL. The place of the Other: the dark forest. In (pp. 339–46) **3696.**

9606 PETTITT, CLARE. Patent inventions: intellectual property and the Victorian novel. (Bibl. 2004, 9760.) Rev. by Trey Philpotts in DickQ (22:1) 2005, 51–4.

9607. PHEGLEY, JENNIFER. Domesticating the sensation novelist: Ellen Price Wood as author and editor of the *Argosy Magazine*. See **1302.**

9608. POTTER, FRANZ J. The history of gothic publishing, 1800–1835: exhuming the trade. See **965.**

9609. PRICKETT, STEPHEN. Victorian fantasy. (Bibl. 1982, 6823.) Waco, TX: Baylor UP, 2005. pp. xvii, 288. (Second ed.: first ed. 1979.)

9610. QUAMEN, HARVEY N. Unnatural interbreeding: H. G. Wells's *A Modern Utopia* as species and genre. See **20060.**

9611. RAIMON, EVE ALLEGRA. The 'tragic mulatta' revisited: race and nationalism in nineteenth-century antislavery fiction. New Brunswick, NJ: Rutgers UP, 2004. pp. x, 202. Rev. by Susan M. Ryan in JAH (92:3) 2005, 988–9.

9612. RICHARDSON, ANGELIQUE. Love and eugenics in the late nineteenth century: rational reproduction and the New Woman. (Bibl. 2004, 9766.) Rev. by Thomas Recchio in ColLit (32:3) 2005, 182–92; by Naomi Hetherington in TexP (19:2) 2005, 385–8.

9613. ROBINSON, SOLVEIG C. Expanding a 'limited orbit': Margaret Oliphant, *Blackwood's Edinburgh Magazine*, and the development of a critical voice. See **11768.**

9614. RODENSKY, LISA. The crime in mind: criminal responsibility and the Victorian novel. (Bibl. 2004, 9767.) Rev. by Thomas Recchio in ColLit (32:3) 2005, 182–92; by Anthea Trodd in NineL (60:1) 2005, 113–16.

9615. SAMUELS, SHIRLEY (ed.). A companion to American fiction, 1780–1865. See **8152.**

9616. SIEGEL, DANIEL. The failure of condescension. VLC (33:2) 2005, 395–414.

9617. SINGH, G. Q. D. Leavis and the novel. EngS (84:4) 2003, 355–71.

9618. SMAJIC, SRDJAN. The trouble with ghost-seeing: vision, ideology, and genre in the Victorian ghost story. ELH (70:4) 2003, 1107–35.

9619. STEIN, ATARA. The Byronic hero in film, fiction, and television. See **10337.**

9620. SURRIDGE, LISA ANNE. Bleak houses: marital violence in Victorian fiction. Athens: Ohio UP, 2005. pp. xiv, 271.

9621. SWENSON, KRISTINE. Medical women and Victorian fiction. Columbia; London: Missouri UP, 2005. pp. ix, 233. Rev. by Nicholas Birns in VS (47:3) 2005, 481–3.

9622. THOMPSON, COREY. Did Melville write *The Death Craft*? See **11707.**

9623. TOWHEED, SHAFQUAT. Determining 'fluctuating opinions': Vernon Lee, popular fiction, and theories of reading. *See* **11583.**

9624. TOWNSHEND, DALE. Gothic panoptics and the persistence of torturous enjoyment, 1764–1820. *See* **8158.**

9625. TRACEY, KAREN. Stories of the poorhouse. *In* (pp. 23–48) **9513.**

9626. UHSADEL, KATHARINA. Antonia Byatts *Quartet* in der Tradition des englischen Bildungsroman. *See* **15649.**

9627. WAGNER, TAMARA S. Longing: narratives of nostalgia in the British novel, 1740–1890. *See* **8159.**

9628. WARNE, VANESSA; COLLIGAN, COLETTE. The man who wrote a New Woman novel: Grant Allen's *The Woman Who Did* and the gendering of New Woman authorship. *See* **9922.**

9629. WARREN, JOYCE W. Women, money, and the law: nineteenth-century fiction, gender, and the courts. Iowa City: Iowa UP, 2005. pp. viii, 373.

9630. WATT, JAMES. Gothic. *In* (pp. 119–35) **8014.**

9631. WEBER, JEAN JACQUES. Cognitive poetics and literary criticism: types of resolution in the Condition-of-England novel. EJES (9:2) 2005, 131–41.

9632. WEIERMAN, KAREN WOODS. One nation, one blood: interracial marriage in American fiction, scandal, and law, 1820–1870. Amherst: Massachusetts UP, 2005. pp. x, 214.

9633. WEVERS, LYDIA. Reading on the farm: a study of the Brancepeth Farm library. BSANZB (28:1/2) 2004, 184–94.

9634. WEYLER, KAREN A. Intricate relations: sexual and economic desire in American fiction, 1789–1814. *See* **8161.**

9635. WHITE, EVA ROA. Emigration as emancipation: portrayals of the immigrant Irish girl in nineteenth-century fiction. NewHR (9:1) 2005, 95–108.

9636. WORTHINGTON, HEATHER. The rise of the detective in early nineteenth-century popular fiction. Basingstoke; New York: Palgrave Macmillan, 2005. pp. x, 203. (Crime files.)

9637. YOUNG, LAUREL. Dorothy L. Sayers and the New Woman detective novel. *See* **19333.**

9638. YOUNG, PAUL. Economy, empire, extermination: the Christmas Pudding, the Crystal Palace and the narrative of capitalist progress. LitH (14:1) 2005, 14–30.

9639. ZIEGER, SUSAN. 'How far am I responsible?': women and morphinomania in late nineteenth-century Britain. *See* **11836.**

LITERATURE FOR CHILDREN

9640. BOTTIGHEIMER, RUTH B. The book on the bookseller's shelf and the book in the English child's hand. *In* (pp. 3–28) **8171.**

9641. DAWSON, MUIR. Two children's books illustrated by Bewick, with notes on printing from the original blocks. *See* **8168.**

9642. DE ROSA, DEBORAH C. Domestic Abolitionism and juvenile literature, 1830–1865. (Bibl. 2003, 9044.) Rev. by Patricia Demers in LU (29:1) 2005, 106–9;

by Lesley Ginsberg in Legacy (22:1) 2005, 76–7; by Paula T. Connolly in CLAQ (30:4) 2005, 440–2.

9643. —— (comp.). Into the mouths of babes: an anthology of children's Abolitionist literature. Westport, CT; London: Praeger, 2005. pp. xix, 390. Rev. by Paula T. Connolly in CLAQ (30:4) 2005, 440–2.

9644. FAHS, ALICE; WAUGH, JOAN (eds). The memory of the Civil War in American culture. Chapel Hill; London: North Carolina UP, 2004. pp. 286. (Civil War America.) Rev. by Robert Tracy McKenzie in JAH (92:2) 2005, 617–18; by Richard D. Starnes in JSH (71:4) 2005, 911–12.

9645. GALWAY, ELIZABETH. Poetical patriotism: Canadian children's poetry and nationalist discourse in the late Victorian period. VIJ (32) 2004, 37–62.

9646. GUNN, JAMES. *Harry Potter* as schooldays novel. In (pp. 145–55) **19221**.

9647. LUCAS, ANN LAWSON (ed.). The presence of the past in children's literature. (Bibl. 2003, 9055.) Rev. by Susan Stan in CLAQ (29:4) 2004, 375–9.

9648. LUNDIN, ANNE. *Robinson Crusoe* and children's literature. In (pp. 198–206) **8537**.

9649. —— WIEGAND, WAYNE A. (eds). Defining print culture for youth: the cultural work of children's literature. (Bibl. 2003, 9057.) Rev. by Don Latham in LQ (74:2) 2004, 215–17.

9650. MCCULLOCH, FIONA. The fictional role of childhood in Victorian and early twentieth-century children's literature. (Bibl. 2004, 9787.) Rev. by Anne Lundin in LU (29:3) 2005, 442–5.

9651. MANLOVE, COLIN NICHOLAS. From Alice to Harry Potter: children's fantasy in England. (Bibl. 2004, 9788.) Rev. by Leona Fisher in CLAQ (30:2) 2005, 212–15.

9652. PARRIS, BRANDY. Difficult sympathy in the Reconstruction-era animal stories of *Our Young Folks*. ChildLit (31) 2003, 25–49.

9653. PASSET, JOANNE E. Freethought children's literature and the construction of religious identity in late nineteenth-century America. BH (8) 2005, 107–29.

9654. ROWE, KAREN E. Virtue in the guise of vice: the making and unmaking of morality from fairy tale fantasy. In (pp. 29–66) **8171**.

9655. RUWE, DONELLE (ed.). Culturing the child, 1690–1914: essays in memory of Mitzi Myers. See **8171**.

9656. RUWE, DONELLE R. Satirical birds and natural bugs: J. Harris' chapbooks and the aesthetic of children's literature. In (pp. 115–37) **9305**.

9657. SCHACKER, JENNIFER. National dreams: the remaking of fairy tales in nineteenth-century England. (Bibl. 2004, 9793.) Rev. by Yuko Ashitagawa in MLR (100:1) 2005, 202–3; by Phillippa Bennett in NineL (60:1) 2005, 90–4.

9658. SINGH, RASHNA B. Goodly is our heritage: children's literature, empire, and the certitude of character. (Bibl. 2004, 9794.) Rev. by Troy Boone in CLAQ (30:2) 2005, 224–7.

9659. SORBY, ANGELA. Schoolroom poets: childhood and the place of American poetry, 1865–1917. Durham: New Hampshire UP, 2005. pp. xlv, 233. (Becoming modern.) Rev. by Joseph T. Thomas, Jr, in CLAQ (30:4) 2005, 443–7.

9660. STONELEY, PETER.   Consumerism and American girls' literature, 1860–1940. (Bibl. 2004, 9795.) Rev. by Kathleen Chamberlain in DNR (74:2) 2005, 63–5; by Stephanie Spencer in LitH (14:2) 2005, 92–3.

9661. TIGGES, WIM.   A glorious thing: the Byronic hero as chief. *In* (pp. 153–72) **9237.**

POETRY

9662. APPLEWHITE, JAMES.   The mind's lyric and the spaces of nature: Wordsworth and Stevens. *See* **19642.**

9663. ARTELLE, STEVEN.   'Orient dreams': urbanity and the post-Confederation literary culture of Ottawa. *In* (pp. 32–49) **9243.**

9664. BACKÈS, JEAN-LOUIS.   Le poème narratif dans l'Europe romantique. Paris: PUF, 2003. pp. 268. (Écriture.) Rev. by Jean-Yves Masson in RLC (78:1) 2004, 113–16.

9665. BAKER, CHRISTOPHER.   Porphyro's rose: Keats and T. S. Eliot's *The Metaphysical Poets*. *See* **16242.**

9666. BEHRENDT, STEPHEN C.   Irish women poets of the Romantic period: a different sort of Other. WWr (12:2) 2005, 153–75.

9667. ——— Mourning, myth, merchandising: the public death of Princess Charlotte. CanRCL (30:1) 2003, 75–95.

9668. BENNETT, PAULA BERNAT.   A muse of their own: the satirical poetry of nineteenth-century feminists. SAH (11) 2004, 63–72.

9669. ——— Poets in the public sphere: the emancipatory project of American women's poetry, 1800–1900. (Bibl. 2004, 9801.) Rev. by Vivian R. Pollak in MLQ (66:1) 2005, 132–6.

9670. BENTLEY, D. M. R.   The Confederation Group of Canadian poets, 1880–1897. Toronto; Buffalo, NY; London: Toronto UP, 2004. pp. xiv, 411. Rev. by W. J. Keith in LRC (12:8) 2004, 23–4.

9671. BLAIR, KIRSTIE.   Spasmodic affections: poetry, pathology, and the Spasmodic hero. *See* **10249.**

9672. BOOS, FLORENCE S.   'Spasm' and class: W. E. Aytoun, George Gilfillan, Sydney Dobell, and Alexander Smith. *See* **10818.**

9673. BORKOWSKA, EWA.   At the threshold of mystery: poetic encounters with other(ness). New York; Frankfurt: Lang, 2005. pp. 240. (Literary and cultural theory, 18.)

9674. BRENNAN, CATHERINE.   Angers, fantasies and ghostly fears: nineteenth-century women from Wales and English-language poetry. Cardiff: UP of Wales, 2003. pp. viii, 237. Rev. by Stephanie Forward in MLR (100:3) 2005, 791–2.

9675. BRISTOW, JOSEPH (ed.).   The *fin-de-siècle* poem: English literary culture and the 1890s. Columbus: Ohio State UP, 2005. pp. xxxi, 352.

9676. BUFFONI, FRANCO (ed. and trans.).   Poeti romantici inglesi. Milan: Mondadori, 2005. pp. cxl, 821. (Oscar grandi classici, 99.)

9677. COHEN, MICHAEL.   E. C. Stedman and the invention of Victorian poetry. *See* **9865.**

9678. CRYER, MAX. 'Hear our voices, we entreat': the extraordinary story of New Zealand's national anthems. Foreword by Dame Kiri Te Kanawa. Auckland: Exisle, 2004. pp. 140, (plates) 4.

9679. DERESIEWICZ, WILLIAM. Jane Austen and the Romantic poets. *See* **9973.**

9680. EASLEY, ALEXIS. *Tait's Edinburgh Magazine* in the 1830s: dialogues on gender, class, and reform. *See* **1194.**

9681. FAVRET, MARY A. Everyday war. *See* **9980.**

9682. FORBES, DEBORAH. Sincerity's shadow: self-consciousness in British Romantic and mid-twentieth-century American poetry. (Bibl. 2004, 9811.) Rev. by Reena Sastri in EC (55:4) 2005, 381–8.

9683. FRANKEL, NICHOLAS. 'A wreath for the brows of time': the books of the Rhymers' Club as material texts. *In* (pp. 131–57) **9675.**

9684. GOODRIDGE, JOHN; KEEGAN, BRIDGET. Clare and the traditions of labouring-class verse. *In* (pp. 280–95) **8014.**

9685. GORDON, DAVID J. Imagining the end of life in post-Enlightenment poetry: voices against the void. Gainesville: Florida UP, 2005. pp. 169.

9686. GRAY, JANET. Race and time: American women's poetics from antislavery to racial modernity. (Bibl. 2004, 9814.) Rev. by Keith D. Leonard in Legacy (22:1) 2005, 81–3; by Laurel Bollinger in TSWL (24:2) 2005, 346–8.

9687. GROTH, HELEN. Literary nostalgia and early Victorian photographic discourse. NCC (25:3) 2003, 199–217.

9688. HOLMES, JOHN. Dante Gabriel Rossetti and the late Victorian sonnet sequence: sexuality, belief and the self. *See* **11870.**

9689. HORNE, PHILIP. Henry James among the poets. *See* **11410.**

9690. HUGHES, LINDA K. Women poets and contested spaces in *The Yellow Book*. *See* **1236.**

9691. JACKSON-HOULSTON, C. M. 'With Mike Hunt I have travelled over the town': the norms of 'deviance' in sub-respectable nineteenth-century song. CVE (61) 2005, 211–25.

9692. JANOWITZ, ANNE. The artifactual sublime: making London poetry. *In* (pp. 246–60) **9217.**

9693. JOUKOVSKY, NICHOLAS A. Keats, Shelley, and *The Troubadour*. *See* **1241.**

9694. KAHAN, JEFFREY (ed.). The poetry of W. H. Ireland, 1801–1815, including the poet's imitations, satires, romantic verses, and commentaries on Coleridge, Wordsworth, Southey, and others. *See* **8734.**

9695. KAYLOR, MICHAEL M. 'In thy cedarn prison thou waitest': Johnson's *Ionica* and Uranian intertextuality. *In* (pp. 79–85) **3734.**

9696. KAYLOR, MICHAEL MATTHEW. 'The divine friend, unknown, most desired': the problematic Uranian poets. *In* (pp. 71–6) **3753.**

9697. KEEGAN, BRIDGET. Romantic labouring-class pastoral as eco-queer camp. RomNet (36/37) 2004/05.

9698. LAIRD, HOLLY. The death of the author by suicide: *fin-de-siècle* poets and the construction of identity. *In* (pp. 69–100) **9675.**

9699. LaPorte, Charles. Spasmodic poetics and Clough's apostasies. *See* **10455.**

9700. Lehman, David (ed.). Great American prose poems: from Poe to the present. (Bibl. 2003, 9095.) Rev. by John Taylor in MichQR (44:2) 2005, 362–81.

9701. Loeffelholz, Mary. From school to salon: reading nineteenth-century American women's poetry. (Bibl. 2004, 9821.) Rev. by Faith Barrett in Legacy (22:2) 2005, 196–7.

9702. Lootens, Tricia. Between treasuries and the Web: compendious Victorian poetry anthologies in transition. VS (47:4) 2005, 577–96 (review-article).

9703. McCormack, Jerusha. Engendering tragedy: toward a definition of 1890s poetry. *In* (pp. 47–68) **9675.**

9704. McNees, Eleanor. *Punch* and the Pope: three decades of anti-Catholic caricature. *See* **1269.**

9705. Mader, D. H. The Greek mirror: the Uranians and their use of Greece. JHo (49:3/4) 2005, 377–420.

9706. Mason, Emma. 'Some kind friends': Scott's *Harold the Dauntless* (HM 1937) and Frederick Locker-Lampson. *See* **11936.**

9707. Matthews, Samantha. Poetical remains: poets' graves, bodies, and books in the nineteenth century. (Bibl. 2004, 9826.) Rev. by Robert Douglas-Fairhurst in TLS, 24 June 2005, 25; by Guy Cuthbertson in RES (56:224) 2005, 337–8; by John Morton in EC (55:2) 2005, 184–92; by Marc Porée in EREA (3:2) 2005.

9708. Mee, Jon. Romanticism, Enthusiasm and regulation: poetics and the policing of culture in the Romantic period. (Bibl. 2003, 9105.) Rev. by Adam Potkay in WordsC (35:4) 2004, 158–9; by Michael Tomko in SR (44:2) 2005, 278–83; by Michael John Kooy in NQ (52:1) 2005, 137–9.

9709. Mencher, M. B. Lawrence and sex. *See* **17618.**

9710. Mortimer, Anthony (ed.). From Wordsworth to Stevens: essays in honour of Robert Rehder. *See* **12503.**

9711. Paulin, Tom (foreword). Rhyming weavers, and other country poets of Antrim and Down. Ed. by John Hewitt. (Bibl. 1974, 7609.) Belfast: Blackstaff Press, 2004. pp. xiv, 191. (Second ed.: first ed. 1974.)

9712. Petrino, Elizabeth A. Late bloomer: the gentian as sign or symbol in the work of Dickinson and her contemporaries. *See* **10798.**

9713. Revelli, Giorgetta (ed.). Da Ulisse a ...: il viaggio nelle terre d'oltremare: atti del convegno internazionale (Imperia, 9–11 ottobre 2003). *See* **14479.**

9714. Riede, David G. Allegories of one's own mind: melancholy in Victorian poetry. Columbus: Ohio State UP, 2005. pp. ix, 226.

9715. Rosenberg, John D. Elegy for an age: the presence of the past in Victorian literature. London: Anthem Press, 2005. pp. 292. (Anthem nineteenth-century studies.) Rev. by Roger Ebbatson in TRB (8:4) 2005, 309–11.

9716. RUDY, JASON R. Rhythmic intimacy, Spasmodic epistemology. *See* **10820**.

9717. SCHEINBERG, CYNTHIA. Women's poetry and religion in Victorian England: Jewish identity and Christian culture. (Bibl. 2004, 9836.) Rev. by Joanne E. Myers in JR (84:4) 2004, 673–5; by James Najarian in VicR (30:1) 2004, 100–3.

9718. SHIRES, LINDA. Hardy and nineteenth-century poetry and politics. *In* (pp. 255–78) **11140**.

9719. SLINN, E. WARWICK. Victorian poetry as cultural critique: the politics of performative language. (Bibl. 2003, 9124.) Rev. by Andrew Stauffer in JPRS (14:1) 2005, 91–3.

9720. SMITH, CHRIS. The name and nature of poetry. *See* **17068**.

9721. STAUFFER, ANDREW M. Dante Gabriel Rossetti and the burdens of Nineveh. *See* **11878**.

9722. STRACHAN, JOHN (gen. ed.). British satire: vol. 1, Collected satires i: shorter satires. Ed. by Nicholas Mason. *See* **8205**.

9723. —— British satire: vol. 2, Collected satires ii: extracts from longer satires. Ed. by David Walker. *See* **8206**.

9724. —— British satire: vol. 3, Collected satires iii: complete longer satires. Ed. by Benjamin Colbert. *See* **8207**.

9725. TAYLOR, JOHN. Two cultures of the prose poem. MichQR (44:2) 2005, 362–81 (review-article).

9726. THORMÄHLEN, MARIANNE. Anne Brontë's *Sacred Harmony*: a discovery. *See* **10147**.

9727. TROTT, NICOLA. Wordsworth and the parodic school of criticism. *In* (pp. 71–97) **9305**.

9728. TUCKER, HERBERT F. Glandular omnism and beyond: the Victorian Spasmodic epic. *See* **10255**.

9729. VINCENT, PATRICK H. The Romantic poetess: European culture, politics, and gender, 1820–1840. Hanover, NH; London: UP of New England, 2004. pp. 296. (Becoming modern.) (New nineteenth-century studies.) Rev. by Mary Anne Nunn in TSWL (24:2) 2005, 358–60; by Alison Chapman in NineL (60:2) 2005, 247–50.

9730. VRÁNKOVÁ, KAMILA. Variations and transformations of the 'Lenore' motif in European ballads. *In* (pp. 171–6) **3734**.

9731. WEBBY, ELIZABETH. Images of Europe in two nineteenth-century Australian illustrated magazines. *See* **1360**.

9732. WEINER, STEPHANIE KUDUK. Republican politics and English poetry, 1789–1874. Basingstoke; New York: Palgrave Macmillan, 2005. pp. viii, 220. (Palgrave studies in nineteenth-century writing and culture.)

PROSE

9733. BEN-AARON, DIANA. Given and news: evaluation in newspaper stories about national anniversaries. *See* **2802**.

9734. AMIGONI, DAVID. Carving coconuts, the philosophy of drawing rooms, and the politics of dates: Grant Allen, popular scientific journalism, evolution, and culture in the *Cornhill Magazine*. *In* (pp. 251–61) **1226.**

9735. ANDERSON, ANNE. Oscar's enemy ... and neighbour: 'Arry' Quilter and the 'Gospel of Intensity'. *See* **12363.**

9736. BANKS, DAVID. The case of Perrin and Thomson: an example of the use of a mini-corpus. ESpP (24:2) 2005, 201–11.

9737. BANNET, EVE TAVOR. Empire of letters: letter manuals and transatlantic correspondence, 1680–1820. *See* **7089.**

9738. BEETHAM, MARGARET. Of recipe books and reading in the nineteenth century: Mrs Beeton and her cultural consequences. *In* (pp. 15–30) **9257.**

9739. BELCHEM, JOHN. Radical language, meaning and identity in the age of the Chartists. *See* **2816.**

9740. BERGMAN, JILL; BERNARDI, DEBRA (eds). Our sisters' keepers: nineteenth-century benevolence literature by American women. *See* **9513.**

9741. BLAND, CAROLINE; CROSS, MÁIRE (eds). Gender and politics in the age of letter-writing, 1750–2000. *See* **8217.**

9742. BUCHANAN, LINDAL. Regendering delivery: the fifth canon and antebellum women rhetors. *See* **2236.**

9743. BURLEY, STEPHEN. Hazlitt and John Stoddart: brothers-in-law or brothers at war? *See* **11231.**

9744. COX, JOHN D. Traveling south: travel narratives and the construction of American identity. *See* **8225.**

9745. CRAMER, JANET M. Cross purposes: publishing practices and social priorities of nineteenth-century US missionary women. JoH (30:3) 2004, 123–30.

9746. DALRYMPLE, WILLIAM. Fanny Parkes and changing British attitudes to India in the mid-nineteenth century. Journeys (5:2) 2004, 1–18.

9747. DEAN, JANET. Nameless outrages: narrative authority, rape rhetoric, and the Dakota Conflict of 1862. AL (77:1) 2005, 93–122.

9748. ELLERAY, MICHELLE. Crossing the beach: a Victorian tale adrift in the Pacific. VS (47:2) 2005, 164–73.

9749. FISH, CHERYL J. Black and White women's travel narratives: antebellum explorations. (Bibl. 2004, 9862.) Rev. by Etsuko Taketani in JAH (91:4) 2005, 1454–5; by Daphne Mary Lamothe in Meridians (6:1) 2005, 216–22; by Edlie Wong in AAR (39:3) 2005, 467–8.

9750. FLOYD, JANET; FORSTER, LAUREL. The recipe in its cultural contexts. *In* (pp. 1–11) **9257.**

9751. FORD-SMITH, ALICE. Confessions: the Midlands execution broadside trade. *In* (pp. 153–67) **880.**

9752. FRANEY, LAURA E. Victorian travel writing and imperial violence: British writing on Africa, 1855–1902. (Bibl. 2004, 9865.) Rev. by V. G. Kiernan in LitH (14:1) 2005, 75–80; by Robert Burroughs in JVC (10:2) 2005, 319–23.

9753. FYFE, AILEEN. Commerce and philanthropy: the Religious Tract Society and the business of publishing. *See* **838.**

9754. GASSMAN, RICHARD.　The first American tourist guidebooks: authorship and the print culture of the 1820s. *See* **846**.

9755. GOHRISCH, JANA.　Bürgerliche Gefühlsdispositionen in der englischen Prosa des 19. Jahrhunderts. Heidelberg: Winter, 2005. pp. 522. (Anglistische Forschungen, 340.)

9756. GOODAY, GRAEME J. N.　'I never will have the electric light in my house': Alice Gordon and the gendered periodical representation of a contentious new technology. *In* (pp. 173–85) **1226**.

9757. GUIGENO, VINCENT.　Engineering the words: Robert Louis Stevenson and the Bell Rock lighthouse. *See* **12068**.

9758. HAMPTON, MARK.　Rethinking the 'New Journalism', 1850s–1930s. *See* **1219**.

9759. HAYWOOD, CHANTA M.　Prophesying daughters: Black women preachers and the Word, 1823–1913. Columbia; London: Missouri UP, 2003. pp. xiii, 144. Rev. by Diane Batts Morrow in JAStud (38:3) 2004, 521–2; by Dolan Hubbard in CLIO (34:4) 2005, 472–5.

9760. HENDERSON, JENNIFER.　Settler feminism and race making in Canada. *See* **11477**.

9761. HENSON, LOUISE, *et al.* (eds).　Culture and science in the nineteenth-century media. *See* **1226**.

9762. JOHNSON, NAN.　Parlor rhetoric and the performance of gender in postbellum America. *In* (pp. 107–28) **2318**.

9763. JOHNSTON, ANNA.　Missionary writing and empire, 1800–1860. (Bibl. 2004, 9879.) Rev. by Mark Knight in LitTheol (18:3) 2004, 364–6; by V. G. Kiernan in LitH (14:1) 2005, 75–80.

9764. KEATES, JONATHAN.　Guides of old: *vade mecum* to where the ladies' orchestra used to be. TLS, 15 July 2005, 12–13.

9765. KING, AMY M.　Re-orienting the scientific frontier: Victorian tide pools and literary realism. VS (47:2) 2005, 153–63.

9766. KOBAK, ANNETTE.　Leader of the breed. TLS, 15 July 2005, 7 (review-article). (Lady Hester Stanhope.)

9767. LLOYD, DAVID.　The indigent sublime: specters of Irish hunger. *See* **10382**.

9768. LUCKHURST, ROGER.　W. T. Stead's occult economies. *In* (pp. 125–35) **1226**.

9769. McCORKLE, BEN.　Harbingers of the printed page: nineteenth-century theories of delivery as remediation. *See* **2389**.

9770. McINTYRE, REBECCA C.　Promoting the gothic South. SoCult (11:2) 2005, 33–61.

9771. MEIR, NATALIE KAPETANIOS.　'A fashionable dinner is arranged as follows': Victorian dining taxonomies. VLC (33:1) 2005, 133–48.

9772. MINKEMA, KENNETH P.; STOUT, HARRY S.　The Edwardsean tradition and the anti-slavery debate, 1740–1865. *See* **8577**.

9773. MOODY, JOYCELYN.　Naming and proclaiming the self: Black feminist literary history-making. *In* (pp. 107–20) **2457**.

9774. MOZER, HADLEY J. 'I WANT a hero': advertising for an epic hero in *Don Juan. See* **10322**.

9775. NEWLYN, ANDREA K. Redefining 'rudimentary' narrative: women's nineteenth-century manuscript cookbooks. *In* (pp. 31–51) **9257**.

9776. O'DONNELL, KEVIN E.; HOLLINGSWORTH, HELEN. Seekers of scenery: travel writing from southern Appalachia, 1840–1900. Knoxville: Tennessee UP, 2004. pp. xix, 385. Rev. by Katherine Ledford in Now (21:1) 2005, 30; by John Inscoe in AppalJ (32:4) 2005, 489–91.

9777. PUTZI, JENNIFER. Capturing identity in ink: the captivities of Olive Oatman. WAL (39:2) 2004, 177–99.

9778. RENDALL, JANE. 'Friends of liberty & virtue': women Radicals and transatlantic correspondence, 1789–1848. *In* (pp. 77–92) **8217**.

9779. RICHARD, JESSICA. 'A paradise of my own creation': *Frankenstein* and the improbable romance of Polar exploration. *See* **11984**.

9780. RITVO, HARRIET. Narratives of nature: response. VS (47:2) 2005, 188–93.

9781. —— The view from the hills: environment and technology in Victorian periodicals. *In* (pp. 165–72) **1226**.

9782. ROYSTER, JACQUELINE JONES; SIMPKINS, ANN MARIE MANN (eds). Calling cards: theory and practice in studies of race, gender, and culture. *See* **2457**.

9783. SCOTT, GRANT F. Sacred relics: a discovery of new Severn letters. ERR (16:3) 2005, 283–95.

9784. SHILLUE, EDITH. Natural language, scientific discourse and auto-ethnographic representation in nineteenth-century Ireland. EtIr (30:1) 2005, 131–49.

9785. SIMPKINS, ANN MARIE MANN. Rhetorical tradition(s) and the reform writing of Mary Ann Shadd Cary. *In* (pp. 229–41) **2457**.

9786. SMITH, JEFF. Lords (and ladies) of misrule: carnival, scandal, and satire in the age of Andrew Jackson. SAH (12) 2005, 52–82.

9787. SMYTHE, TED CURTIS. The Gilded Age press 1865–1900. *See* **1335**.

9788. SUMPTER, CAROLINE. Making Socialists or murdering to dissect? Natural history and child socialization in the *Labour Prophet* and *Labour Leader*. *In* (pp. 29–40) **1226**.

9789. VENEMA, KATHLEEN. Letitia Mactavish Hargrave and Hudson's Bay Company domestic politics: negotiating kinship in *Letters from the Canadian North-West. In* (pp. 145–71) **9191**.

9790. WARDROP, DANEEN. Collaboration in *Running a Thousand Miles for Freedom*: William's key and Ellen's renaming. AQ (61:3) 2005, 57–73.

9791. WARNES, ANDREW. 'Talking' recipes: *What Mrs Fisher Knows* and the African American cookbook tradition. *In* (pp. 52–71) **9257**.

9792. WARRIOR, ROBERT. The people and the word: reading Native nonfiction. Minneapolis; London: Minnesota UP, 2005. pp. xxxi, 244. (Indigenous Americas.)

9793. WEAVER, RACHAEL.   Reflecting the detectives: crime fiction and the New Journalism in late nineteenth-century Australia. *See* **9885.**

9794. WEST, ELIZABETH.   Cooper and Crummell: dialogics of race and womanhood. *In* (pp. 81–102) **2410.**

9795. WILLIS, CHRIS.   From voyeurism to feminism: Victorian and Edwardian London's streetfighting slum viragoes. *See* **18150.**

9796. WINSTON, GREG.   Stephen's schoolbooks: a portrait of geography in a young nation. *See* **17355.**

9797. ZLOTNICK, SUSAN.   Domesticating imperialism: curry and cookbooks in Victorian England. *In* (pp. 72–87) **9257.**

BIOGRAPHY AND AUTOBIOGRAPHY

9798. AMIGONI, DAVID.   Distinctively queer little morsels: imagining distinction, groups, and difference in the *DNB* and the *ODNB*. JVC (10:2) 2005, 279–88.

9799. ANDERSON, DAVID.   Down memory lane: nostalgia for the Old South in post-Civil War plantation reminiscences. JSH (71:1) 2005, 105–36.

9800. ANDREWS, WILLIAM L. (gen. ed.).   North Carolina slave narratives: the lives of Moses Roper, Lunsford Lane, Moses Grandy & Thomas H. Jones. Ed. by David A. Davis, *et al. See* **8258.**

9801. BAIESI, SERENA (ed.).   Pioniere in Australia: diari, lettere memoriali del periodo coloniale 1770–1850. *See* **8259.**

9802. BOOTH, ALISON.   Fighting for lives in the *ODNB*; or, Taking prosopography personally. *See* **20966.**

9803. —— How to make it as a woman: collective biographical history from Victoria to the present. Chicago, IL; London: Chicago UP, 2004. pp. xvi, 423. (Women in culture and society.) Rev. by Kali Israel in VS (47:3) 2005, 479–81.

9804. CHEUNG, FLOYD.   Political resistance, cultural appropriation, and the performance of manhood in Yung Wing's *My Life in China and America*. *In* (pp. 77–100) **9454.**

9805. CODELL, JULIE F.   The Victorian artist: artists' lifewritings in Britain, *ca* 1870–1910. (Bibl. 2004, 9908.) Rev. by Jason Rosenfeld in JPRS (13:2) 2004, 129–34; by Tess Cosslett in ELT (48:1) 2005, 85–7; by David Amigoni in Biography (28:2) 2005, 305–8; by Laurent Bury in EA (58:4) 2005, 503.

9806. COMER, DENISE K.   'White child is good, black child his [or her] slave': women, children, and empire in early nineteenth-century India. *See* **12036.**

9807. ETTER, WILLIAM.   Cripple, soldier, crippled soldier: Alfred Bellard's Civil War memoir. PrSt (27:1/2) 2005, 80–92.

9808. GATES, BARBARA T.   When life writing becomes death writing: the *Journal of Emily Shore*. LitMed (24:1) 2005, 70–92.

9809. GROSSMAN, MORRIS.   Carroll's platonic love. *See* **10403.**

9810. HIGGINS, DAVID MINDEN.   Romantic genius and the literary magazine: biography, celebrity, and politics. *See* **11227.**

9811. HIGGINSON, KATE.   Feminine vulnerability, (neo)colonial captivities, and rape scenes: Theresa Gowanlock, Theresa Delaney and Jessica Lynch. *In* (pp. 35–72) **9191**.

9812. HUFF, CYNTHIA.   Victorian family fictions. A/B (19:1/2) 2004, 89–99.

9813. IVES, MAURA.   Further evidence for Eliza Straffen's authorship of *Some Recollections of Jean Ingelow and Her Early Friends*. *See* **11364**.

9814. JUNOD, KAREN.   Drawing pictures in words: the anecdote as spatial form in biographies of Hogarth. *See* **8266**.

9815. KIMBERLY, CAROLINE E.   Effeminacy, masculinity, and homosocial bonds: the (un)intentional queering of John Keats. *See* **11518**.

9816. LE FAYE, DEIRDRE.   Memoirs and biographies. *In* (pp. 51–8) **10060**.

9817. MERITT, MARK.   The politics of literary biography in Charles Brown's *Life of John Keats*. SR (44:2) 2005, 207–38.

9818. MEYERS, JEFFREY.   Whitman's lives. *See* **12336**.

9819. MUKHERJEE, PABLO.   Nimrods: hunting, authority, identity. *See* **11548**.

9820. PIERCE, YOLANDA.   Hell without fires: slavery, Christianity, and the antebellum spiritual narrative. Foreword by Stephen W. Angell and Anthony B. Pinn. Gainesville: Florida UP, 2005. pp. xii, 151. (History of African American religions.) Rev. by John B. Boles in Biography (28:4) 2005, 696–8.

9821. PITE, RALPH (gen. ed.).   Lives of Victorian literary figures II: the Brownings, the Brontës, and the Rossettis by their contemporaries: vol. 1, The Brownings. Ed. by Simon Avery. *See* **10272**.

9822. ——   Lives of Victorian literary figures II: the Brownings, the Brontës, and the Rossettis by their contemporaries: vol. 2, The Brontës. Ed. by Marianna Kambani. *See* **10223**.

9823. ——   Lives of Victorian literary figures II: the Brownings, the Brontës, and the Rossettis by their contemporaries: vol. 3, The Rossettis. Ed. by Hester Jones. *See* **11883**.

9824. ——   Lives of Victorian literary figures III: Elizabeth Gaskell, the Carlyles and John Ruskin by their contemporaries: vol. 1, Elizabeth Gaskell. Ed. by Valerie Sanders. *See* **11050**.

9825. ——   Lives of Victorian literary figures III: Elizabeth Gaskell, the Carlyles and John Ruskin by their contemporaries: vol. 2, The Carlyles. Ed. by Aileen Christianson and Sheila McIntosh. *See* **10392**.

9826. ——   Lives of Victorian literary figures III: Elizabeth Gaskell, the Carlyles and John Ruskin by their contemporaries: vol. 3, John Ruskin. Ed. by Simon Grimble. *See* **11898**.

9827. POWELL, MALEA.   Princess Sarah, the civilized Indian: the rhetoric of cultural literacies in Sarah Winnemucca Hopkins's *Life among the Piutes*. *In* (pp.63–80) **2410**.

9828. RUSSELL, PENNY.   Wife stories: narrating marriage and self in the life of Jane Franklin. VS (48:1) 2005, 35–57.

9829. SANTAMARINA, XIOMARA.   Belabored professions: narratives of African American working womanhood. *See* **12231**.

9830. STREETS, HEATHER.   Military influence in late Victorian and Edwardian popular media: the case of Frederick Roberts. JVC (8:2) 2003, 231–56.

9831. THOMAS, SUE.   *Pringle v. Cadell* and *Wood v. Pringle*: the libel cases over *The History of Mary Prince*. JCL (40:1) 2005, 113–35.

9832. WAGNER, CORINNA.   Loyalist propaganda and the scandalous life of Tom Paine: 'Hypocritical monster!' *See* **8855**.

9833. WINEAPPLE, BRENDA.   Nathaniel Hawthorne, writer; or, The fleeing of the biographied. *In* (pp. 181–98) **11186**.

9834. ZHOU, XIAOJING; NAJMI, SAMINA (eds).   Form and transformation in Asian American literature. *See* **9454**.

RELATED STUDIES

9835. ALBERTI, SAMUEL J. M. M.   Conversaziones and the experience of science in Victorian England. JVC (8:2) 2003, 208–30.

9836. ANDERSON, NANCY FIX.   Threading lives: work, art, and pleasure in the worlds of nineteenth-century women. NCS (18) 2004, 163–9 (review-article).

9837. BRANTLINGER, PATRICK.   Dark vanishings: discourse on the extinction of primitive races, 1800–1930. Ithaca, NY; London: Cornell UP, 2003. pp. x, 248. Rev. by Ian Duncan in VS (47:1) 2004, 110–11; by Howard Malchow in Albion (36:3) 2004, 575–6; by Todd Starkweather in Symplokē (12:1/2) 2004, 303–5; by Regenia Gagnier in ELT (48:2) 2005, 227–9.

9838. CANTOR, GEOFFREY, *et al.*   Science in the nineteenth-century periodical: reading the magazine of nature. Cambridge; New York: CUP, 2004. pp. xi, 329. (Cambridge studies in nineteenth-century literature and culture, 45.) Rev. by Anne Humpherys in NineL (60:1) 2005, 105–9; by Richard Yeo in VS (48:1) 2005, 151–3.

9839. DRESSLER, RACHEL.   'Those effigies which belonged to the English nation': antiquarianism, nationalism and Charles Alfred Stothard's *Monumental Effigies of Great Britain*. StudMed (14) 2005, 143–74.

9840. FARAGO, CLAIRE, *et al.*   'Scraps as it were': binding memories. JVC (10:1) 2005, 114–22.

9841. FAULK, BARRY J.   Music hall & modernity: the late Victorian discovery of popular culture. Athens: Ohio UP, 2004. pp. xii, 244. Rev. by Keith Wilson in VS (47:4) 2005, 621–3.

9842. FINN, MARGOT C.   The character of credit: personal debt in English culture, 1740–1914. *See* **8279**.

9843. FLORA, NIRMOLINI V.   Nineteenth-century libraries in the hill stations of British North India. BSANZB (28:1/2) 2004, 52–61.

9844. FRICK, JOHN W.   Monday *The Herald*; Tuesday the Victoria: (re)packaging, and (re)presenting the celebrated and the notorious on the popular stage. NCT (30:1) 2003, 26–37.

9845. GARDNER, VIV.   Mapping performance culture: 2, Reading the street. NCT (31:1) 2004, 58–80. (Documents of performance.)

9846. GITELMAN, LISA; PINGREE, GEOFFREY B. (eds).   New media 1740–1915. *See* **8280**.

9847. HAMPTON, MARK.   Visions of the press in Britain, 1850–1950. Urbana: Illinois UP, 2004. pp. ix, 218. Rev. by E. M. Palmegiano in VS (47:4) 2005, 614–15.

9848. HOBERMAN, RUTH.   'A thought in the huge bald forehead': depictions of women in the British Musuem Reading Room, 1857–1929. In (pp. 168–91) **12549**.

9849. HOOCK, HOLGER.   The king's artists: the Royal Academy of Arts and the politics of British culture, 1760–1840. See **8282**.

9850. JUSTER, SUSAN.   Doomsayers: Anglo-American prophecy in the age of Revolution. See **8283**.

9851. KOVEN, SETH.   Slumming: sexual and social politics in Victorian London. Princeton, NJ; Oxford: Princeton UP, 2004. pp. xvii, 399. Rev. by Ruth Livesey in NineL (60:1) 2005, 116–20.

9852. MAYER, DAVID.   George Cruikshank, *The First Appearance of William Shakespeare on the Stage of the Globe with Part of His Dramatic Company in 1564*. NCT (30:1) 2003, 53–64. (Documents of performance.)

9853. MOON, KRYSTYN R.   Yellowface: creating the Chinese in American popular music and performance, 1850s–1920s. New Brunswick, NJ: Rutgers UP, 2005. pp. xi, 220. Rev. by Shannon Steen in TJ (57:3) 2005, 529–31.

9854. O'BRIEN, MICHAEL.   Conjectures of order: intellectual life and the American South, 1810–1860. Chapel Hill; London: North Carolina UP, 2004. 2 vols. pp. xviii, 1353; xi, 591–1354. Rev. by Richard E. Nicholls in ASch (74:1) 2005, 122–6; by Paul D. H. Quigley in SoCult (11:2) 2005, 101–4.

9855. PHELAN, JOSEPH.   The British reception of Pierre-Jean Béranger. RLC (79:1) 2005, 5–20.

9856. PORTER, BERNARD.   Absent-minded imperialists: empire, society, and culture in Britain. Oxford; New York: OUP, 2004. pp. xxii, 475. Rev. by David Page in KJ (79:313) 2005, 60.

9857. RODEN, FREDERICK S.   Same-sex desire in Victorian religious culture. (Bibl. 2004, 9936.) Rev. by Mark Knight in JVC (8:2) 2003, 334–8.

9858. VAISEY, DAVID.   'Overtravelled with the librarie businesse'. See **7186**.

9859. WILLIAMS, HYWEL.   Francophone, anglophone and *gallois*-phone: the politics of cultural identity, 1763–2003. See **8291**.

9860. YOSEF, EITAN BAR-.   The Holy Land in English culture 1799–1917: Palestine and the question of Orientalism. See **8292**.

LITERARY THEORY

9861. ANGER, SUZY.   Victorian interpretation. See **10904**.

9862. ATHERTON, CAROL.   Defining literary criticism: scholarship, authority, and the possession of literary knowledge, 1880–2002. Basingstoke; New York: Palgrave Macmillan, 2005. pp. viii, 221.

9863. BRASWELL, MARY FLOWERS.   The Chaucer scholarship of Mary Eliza Haweis (1852–1898). See **4936**.

9864. CHANDLER, DAVID.   The early development of the 'Lake School' idea. See **12466**.

9865. COHEN, MICHAEL. E. C. Stedman and the invention of Victorian poetry. VP (43:2) 2005, 165–88.

9866. DRYDEN, LINDA. The Hardys and William Mathie Parker. See 11118.

9867. JARVIS, SIMON. Criticism, taste, aesthetics. In (pp. 24–42) 8014.

9868. KIJINSKI, JOHN L. Respectable reading in the late nineties: H. D. Traill's Literature. See 1245.

9869. LAZIER, BENJAMIN. Abject academy. In (pp. 277–301) 9220.

9870. LYNCH, DEIDRE SHAUNA. Cult of Jane Austen. In (pp. 111–20) 10060.

9871. LYNCH, JACK. King Lear and 'the taste of the age', 1681–1838. See 6476.

9872. MOODY, JOYCELYN. Naming and proclaiming the self: Black feminist literary history-making. In (pp. 107–20) 2457.

9873. OLSEN, STEIN HAUGOM. Progress in literary studies. See 14947.

9874. PEPRNÍK, MICHAL. The making of American national literature: the war over J. F. Cooper in 19th-century criticism. In (pp. 72–82) 1368.

9875. SAVILLE, JULIA F. The poetic imaging of Michael Field. In (pp. 178–206) 9675.

9876. SCHOUTEN, ERICA. The 'encyclopaedic god-professor': John Macmillan Brown and the discipline of English in colonial New Zealand. JNZL (23:1) 2005, 109–23.

9877. SICHERT, MARGIT. Implanting literary history in cultural memory: Robert Chambers' History of the English Language and Literature. YREAL (21) 2005, 97–127.

9878. SIMPSON, DAVID. The limits of cosmopolitanism and the case for translation. ERR (16:2) 2005, 141–52.

9879. SPEVACK, MARVIN (ed.). Isaac D'Israeli on books: pre-Victorian essays on the history of literature. (Bibl. 2004, 9961.) Rev. by Jacqueline Belanger in LibH (21:1) 2005, 76–8.

9880. TROTT, NICOLA. Critical responses, 1830–1970. In (pp. 92–100) 10060.

9881. —— Wordsworth and the parodic school of criticism. In (pp. 71–97) 9305.

9882. TURLEY, RICHARD MARGGRAF. 'Amorous cavaliers': Keats, Barry Cornwall, and Francis Jeffrey. See 11537.

9883. WALDRON, MARY. Critical responses, early. In (pp. 83–91) 10060.

9884. WATERS, MARY A. British women writers and the profession of literary criticism, 1789–1832. See 8306.

AUTHORS

Francis Adams

9885. WEAVER, RACHAEL. Reflecting the detectives: crime fiction and the New Journalism in late nineteenth-century Australia. ALS (22:1) 2005, 61–72.

Henry Adams

9886. DECKER, WILLIAM MERRILL. A martyr to the disease of omniscience. In (pp. 315–44) 9887.

9887. —— HARBERT, EARL N. (eds). Henry Adams & the need to know. Boston: Massachusetts Historical Soc., 2005. pp. xv, 383. (Massachusetts Historical Soc. studies in American history and culture, 8.)

9888. FOJAS, CAMILLA. American cosmopolis: the World's Columbian Exposition and Chicago across the Americas. CLS (42:2) 2005, 264–87.

9889. HORI, TOMOHIRO. The Victorian sage, autobiography, and the questions of genre and interpretation: on some Carlylean motifs in The Education of Henry Adams. StAL (41) 2004, 19–37.

9890. JACOBSON, JOANNE. Mr Secrets: Henry Adams and the breakdown of the exemplary tradition in American autobiography. In (pp. 206–21) 9887.

9891. LAFAYETTE, PIERRE. Henry Adams: travel as episteme. In (pp. 222–35) 9887.

9892. LEVENSON, J. C. Writing history in the age of Darwin. Raritan (23:3) 2004, 115–48.

9893. MAZUR, ZYGMUNT. Historical process and revision in Thomas Pynchon's V. In (pp. 143–52) 3756.

9894. ORR, JOHN C. 'I measured her as they did with pigs': Henry Adams as Other. In (pp. 273–99) 9887.

9895. VANDERSEE, CHARLES. Henry Adams's unwritten American travels. In (pp. 236–72) 9887.

9896. WEINSTEIN, CINDY. From true woman to New Woman to virgin. In (pp. 300–14) 9887.

9897. WILLS, GARRY. Henry Adams and the making of America. Boston, MA: Houghton Mifflin, 2005. pp. viii, 467. Rev. by Edwin M. Yoder, Jr, in BkW, 18 Sept. 2005, 13.

Jane Addams

9898. BROWN, VICTORIA BISSELL. The education of Jane Addams. Philadelphia: Pennsylvania UP, 2004. pp. viii, 421. (Politics and culture in modern America.) Rev. by Linda Schott in JAH (91:4) 2005, 1484; by Casey Nelson Blake in Raritan (25:2) 2005, 153–67.

9899. CHINN, SARAH E. 'To reveal the humble immigrant parents to their own children': immigrant women, their American daughters, and the Hull-House Labor Museum. In (pp. 227–48) 9513.

9900. ELAHI, BABAK. The heavy garments of the past: Mary and Frieda Antin in The Promised Land. See 15175.

9901. JOSLIN, KATHERINE. Jane Addams: a writer's life. Urbana: Illinois UP, 2004. pp. x, 306. Rev. by Grace Farrell in Legacy (22:2) 2005, 205–6.

9902. SALAZAR, JAMES. Character's conduct: the democratic habits of Jane Addams's 'charitable effort'. In (pp. 249–81) 9513.

Louisa M. Alcott

9903. DOYLE, CHRISTINE. Singing Mignon's song: German literature and culture in the March trilogy. ChildLit (31) 2003, 50–70.

9904. ETTER, WILLIAM. Cripple, soldier, crippled soldier: Alfred Bellard's Civil War memoir. See 9807.

9905. FOOTE, STEPHANIE. Resentful *Little Women*: gender and class feeling in Louisa May Alcott. ColLit (32:1) 2005, 63–85.

9906. JACOBSON, KRISTIN J. The neodomestic American novel: the politics of home in Barbara Kingsolver's *The Poisonwood Bible*. See **17446**.

9907. KENT, KATHRYN R. Making girls into women: American women's writing and the rise of lesbian identity. (Bibl. 2004, 9971.) Rev. by Richard S. Lowry in AL (77:1) 2005, 184–6; by Dana Luciano in GLQ (11:2) 2005, 327–30; by Susan McCabe in GLQ (11:1) 2005, 119–34.

9908. OLWELL, VICTORIA. 'It spoke itself': women's genius and eccentric politics. See **10989**.

9909. PHILLIPS, ANNE K.; EISELEIN, GREGORY (eds). Little women. New York; London: Norton, 2003. pp. 352. (Norton critical eds.) Rev. by Ruth Morse in TLS, 1 July 2005, 26.

9910. ROBINSON, LAURA. Remodeling *An Old-Fashioned Girl*: troubling girlhood in Ann-Marie MacDonald's *Fall on Your Knees*. See **17954**.

9911. ROSS, CHERI LOUISE. Louisa May Alcott's (con)temporary periodical fiction: the thrillers live on. JPC (38:5) 2005, 911–23.

9912. SHEALY, DANIEL. Louisa May Alcott's juvenilia. *In* (pp. 222–36) **9164**.

9913. —— (ed.). Alcott in her own time: a biographical chronicle of her life, drawn from recollections, interviews, and memoirs by family, friends, and associates. Iowa City: Iowa UP, 2005. pp. xxix, 240. (Writers in their own time.) Rev. by Roberta Seelinger Trites in CLAQ (30:3) 2005, 341–4.

9914. SHOWALTER, ELAINE (ed.). Little women; Little men; Jo's boys. New York: Library of America, 2005. pp. 1092. (Library of America, 157.) Rev. by Ruth Morse in TLS, 1 July 2005, 26.

9915. SIMONS, JUDY. Behind the mask: the writing life of Louisa May Alcott. *In* (pp. 133–43) **12577**.

9916. WADSWORTH, SARAH A. Social reading, social work, and the social function of literacy in Louisa May Alcott's *May Flowers*. *In* (pp. 149–67) **12549**.

Sidney Arthur Alexander (1866–1948)

9917. FRANKLIN, J. JEFFREY. The life of the Buddha in Victorian England. ELH (72:4) 2005, 941–74.

Horatio Alger, Jr

9918. AMANO, KYOKO. Alger's shadows in Jane Smiley's *A Thousand Acres*. See **19474**.

9919. GORMAN, ANITA. Great expectations: contrasting goals for women and men in the novels of Alger and Libbey. DNR (74:2) 2005, 43–52.

Grant Allen ('Cecil Power', 'Olive Pratt Rayner')

9920. GREENSLADE, WILLIAM; RODGERS, TERENCE (eds). Grant Allen: literature and cultural politics at the *fin de siècle*. Aldershot; Burlington, VT: Ashgate, 2005. pp. viii, 252.

9921. MORTON, PETER. The busiest man in England: Grant Allen and the writing trade, 1875–1900. Basingstoke; New York: Palgrave Macmillan, 2005. pp. xv, 251.

9922. WARNE, VANESSA; COLLIGAN, COLETTE. The man who wrote a New Woman novel: Grant Allen's *The Woman Who Did* and the gendering of New Woman authorship. VLC (33:1) 2005, 21–46.

James Lane Allen (1849–1925)

9923. BERKE, AMY. Darwinism and the spiritual impulse in the works of Ellen Glasgow and James Lane Allen. *See* **16708**.

Joseph A. (Joseph Alexander) Altsheler (1862–1919)

9924. MCILVAINE, ROBERT M. The serial fiction of Joseph A. Altsheler. DNR (74:5) 2005, 176–83.

William Apess (b.1798)

9925. SCHUELLER, MALINI JOHAR; WATTS, EDWARD (eds). Messy beginnings: postcoloniality and Early American Studies. New Brunswick, NJ: Rutgers UP, 2003. pp. vii, 267. Rev. by Jeanne Boydston in AmQ (57:4) 2005, 1223–9.

9926. WARRIOR, ROBERT. The people and the word: reading Native nonfiction. *See* **9792**.

Sir Edwin Arnold

9927. FRANKLIN, J. JEFFREY. The life of the Buddha in Victorian England. *See* **9917**.

Matthew Arnold

9928. CERVO, NATHAN. Three Victorian 'medieval' poems: *Dover Beach, The Windhover,* and *The Higher Pantheism. See* **12136**.

9929. CRICK, BRIAN; DISANTO, MICHAEL (sels and introds). Literary criticism of Matthew Arnold. Harleston, Norfolk: Edgeways, 2004. pp. xxiv, 291. Rev. by Matthew Beaumont in RES (56:226) 2005, 682–4.

9930. DENISOFF, DENNIS. Oscar Wilde, commodity, culture. *In* (pp. 119–42) **12414**.

9931. FUNAKAWA, KAZUHIKO. The metamorphoses of the scholar-gipsy. EC (55:2) 2005, 117–35.

9932. HADLEY, ELAINE. On a darkling plain: Victorian liberalism and the fantasy of agency. VS (48:1) 2005, 92–102.

9933. HARRISON, ANTONY H. Victorian culture wars: Alexander Smith, Arthur Hugh Clough, and Matthew Arnold in 1853. VP (42:4) 2004, 509–20.

9934. KENNY, ANTHONY. For love of Fausta: Arthur Hugh Clough and the other Arnold. *See* **10454**.

9935. KOKERNOT, WALTER H. 'Where ignorant armies clash by night' and the Sikh rebellion: a contemporary source for Matthew Arnold's night-battle imagery. VP (43:1) 2005, 99–108.

9936. LAPORTE, CHARLES. Spasmodic poetics and Clough's apostasies. *See* **10455**.

9937. LOUIS, MARGOT K. Gods and mysteries: the revival of paganism and the remaking of mythography through the nineteenth century. *See* **12496**.

9938. MACILWEE, MICHAEL. Saul Bellow and Norman Mailer. *See* **15449**.

9939. MUHLESTEIN, DANIEL K. From Arnold to Eagleton to Oehlschlaeger: 'sweetness and light' in a postmodern world. LitB (24:1/2) 2004, 267–95.

9940. PEASE, ALLISON. Aestheticism and aesthetic theory. *In* (pp. 96–118) **12414**.

9941. RIMMER, MARY. Hardy, Victorian culture and provinciality. *In* (pp. 135–55) **11140**.

9942. XIAO, BIN. Morality in Matthew Arnold's literary criticism. FLS (114) 2005, 125–30. (In Chinese.)

Thomas Arnold the Younger (1823–1900)

9943. BERGONZI, BERNARD. A Victorian wanderer: the life of Thomas Arnold the Younger. Oxford; New York: OUP, 2003. pp. ix, 274. Rev. by Alain Jumeau in EA (58:2) 2005, 229–30; by Susan Morgan in VS (48:1) 2005, 161–4.

Jane Austen

9944. AUERBACH, EMILY. Searching for Jane Austen. Madison; London: Wisconsin UP, 2004. pp. xiii, 344.

9945. BANDER, ELAINE. From interior to exterior worlds: Anne Elliot goes Hollywood. Persuasions (26) 2004, 136–45.

9946. BATCHELOR, JENNIE; KAPLAN, CORA (eds). British women's writing in the long eighteenth century: authorship, politics, and history. *See* **7936**.

9947. BEVERLEY, JO. Gold diggers of 1813. *In* (pp. 33–40) **9971**.

9948. BLACKWELL, MARK R. The gothic: moving in the world of novels. *In* (pp. 144–61) **6958**.

9949. BLANK, ANTJE. Dress. *In* (pp. 234–51) **10060**.

9950. BONAPARTE, FELICIA. Conjecturing possibilities: reading and misreading texts in Jane Austen's *Pride and Prejudice*. StudN (37:2) 2005, 141–61.

9951. BOYLE, NICHOLAS. Sacred and secular scriptures: a Catholic approach to literature. (Bibl. 2004, 10001.) Rev. by Michael D. Hurley in TLS, 11 Feb. 2005, 27; by Gregory Wolfe in Cweal (132:14) 2005, 34–6.

9952. BRASSARD, GENEVIÈVE. 'The sacred impulse of maternal devotion': Austen's critique of domesticity and motherhood in *Lady Susan*. WS (34:1) 2005, 27–48.

9953. BROWNSTEIN, RACHEL M. Endless imitation: Austen's and Byron's juvenilia. *In* (pp. 122–37) **9164**.

9954. BYRNE, PAULA. Jane Austen and the theatre. (Bibl. 2004, 10002.) Rev. by Marjean D. Purinton in NCT (31:1) 2004, 83–6.

9955. —— Manners. *In* (pp. 297–305) **10060**.

9956. —— 'The unmeaning luxuries of Bath': urban pleasures in Jane Austen's world. Persuasions (26) 2004, 13–26.

9957. CAINES, MICHAEL. Political persuasions: a thoroughgoing Tory like her prime ministerial fans? TLS, 4 Mar. 2005, 3–4 (review-article).

9958. CALVO, CLARA. Rewriting Lear's untender daughter: Fanny Price as a Regency Cordelia in Jane Austen's *Mansfield Park*. ShS (58) 2005, 83–94.

9959. CANUEL, MARK. Jane Austen and the importance of being wrong. SR (44:2) 2005, 123–50.

9960. CARROLL, JOSEPH. Human nature and literary meaning: a theoretical model illustrated with a critique of *Pride and Prejudice*. *In* (pp. 76–106) **14807**.

9961. CASAL, ELVIRA. More distinguished in his domestic virtues: Captain Wentworth comes home. *Persuasions* (26) 2004, 146–55.

9962. CASS, JEFFREY. Lost in translation: Caroline Percy's 'unwounded ear' and Voltaire's Orientalist intertext in *Patronage*. *See* **10889**.

9963. CHAN, MARY M. Insignificant dwarves and Scotch giants: height, perception, and power in Jane Austen. *Persuasions* (26) 2004, 89–97.

9964. CLARK, ROBERT; DUTTON, GERRY. Agriculture. *In* (pp. 185–93) **10060**.

9965. COHEN, MICHÈLE. 'Manners' make the man: politeness, chivalry, and the construction of masculinity, 1750–1830. JBS (44:2) 2005, 312–29.

9966. COPELAND, EDWARD. Money. *In* (pp. 317–26) **10060**.

9967. COSSY, VALÉRIE; SAGLIA, DIEGO. Translations. *In* (pp. 169–81) **10060**.

9968. CRONIN, RICHARD. Literary scene. *In* (pp. 289–96) **10060**.

9969. —— MCMILLAN, DOROTHY. *Emma*, Harriet Martin, and parlour boarders. NQ (52:1) 2005, 19–22.

9970. —— —— (eds). Emma. Cambridge; New York: CUP, 2005. pp. lxxvii, 600. (Cambridge ed. of the works of Jane Austen.)

9971. CRUSIE, JENNIFER (ed.); YEFFETH, GLENN (asst ed.). Flirting with *Pride and Prejudice*: fresh perspectives on the original chick-lit masterpiece. Dallas, TX: BenBella, 2005. pp. 230. (Smart pop.)

9972. CYR, MARC. Bad morality, truth, and Mrs Smith in *Persuasion*. ECN (4) 2004, 193–216.

9973. DERESIEWICZ, WILLIAM. Jane Austen and the Romantic poets. New York: Columbia UP, 2004. pp. x, 211. Rev. by Michael Caines in TLS, 15 July 2005, 28.

9974. DOODY, MARGARET ANNE. Jane Austen, that disconcerting 'child'. *In* (pp. 101–21) **9164**.

9975. DUCKWORTH, ALISTAIR M. Landscape. *In* (pp. 278–88) **10060**.

9976. EASTON, CELIA A. Austen's urban redemption: rejecting Richardson's view of the city. *Persuasions* (26) 2004, 121–35.

9977. ELLIS, MARKMAN. Trade. *In* (pp. 415–24) **10060**.

9978. EMSLEY, SARAH BAXTER. Jane Austen's philosophy of the virtues. Basingstoke; New York: Palgrave Macmillan, 2005. pp. x, 202.

9979. ENGELHARDT, MOLLY. The manner of reading: Jane Austen and the semiotics of dance. *Persuasions* (26) 2004, 237–48.

9980. FAVRET, MARY A. Everyday war. ELH (72:3) 2005, 605–33.

9981. FERGUS, JAN. Biography. *In* (pp. 3–11) **10060**.

9982. FIEDLER, ELIZABETH. A devoted reticence: the art of telling and not telling in Jane Austen's *Persuasion*. *Persuasions* (26) 2004, 159–69.

9983. FORD, SUSAN ALLEN. Learning romance from Scott and Byron: Jane Austen's natural sequel. *Persuasions* (26) 2004, 72–88.

9984. GALPERIN, WILLIAM H. The historical Austen. (Bibl. 2004, 10017.) Rev. by Harriet Kramer Linkin in ERR (16:5) 2005, 640–5; by Kathryn Sutherland in NCC (27:4) 2005, 390–5; by Deborah Elise White in SR (44:3) 2005, 439–45.

9985. GAY, PENNY. Jane Austen and the theatre. (Bibl. 2004, 10019.) Rev. by Marjean D. Purinton in NCT (31:1) 2004, 83–6; by Christopher Nagle in CompDr (38:1) 2004, 128–33; by Kathryn Sutherland in NCC (27:4) 2005, 390–5.

9986. —— Pastimes. *In* (pp. 337–45) **10060.**

9987. GAYLIN, ANN. Eavesdropping in the novel from Austen to Proust. (Bibl. 2004, 10021.) Rev. by Laura Mooneyham White in NCFrS (33:1/2) 2004/05, 178–9; by Clare Brant in MLR (100:4) 2005, 1093–5.

9988. GEVIRTZ, KAREN BLOOM. Life after death: widows and the English novel. *See* **8132.**

9989. GILSON, DAVID. Jane Austen and Europe. BC (52:1) 2003, 31–45.

9990. —— Later publishing history, with illustrations. *In* (pp. 121–59) **10060.**

9991. GRAHAM, PETER W. Why Lyme Regis? Persuasions (26) 2004, 27–40.

9992. HEYDT-STEVENSON, JILL. Jane Austen: comedies of the flesh. Basingstoke; New York: Palgrave Macmillan, 2005. pp. x, 275.

9993. HUDSON, NICHOLAS. Social rank, 'the rise of the novel', and Whig histories of eighteenth-century fiction. *See* **8136.**

9994. IRVINE, ROBERT P. Jane Austen. London; New York: Routledge, 2005. pp. viii, 190.

9995. JONES, CHRIS. Landownership. *In* (pp. 269–77) **10060.**

9996. JONES, VIVIEN. Reading for England: Austen, taste, and female patriotism. ERR (16:2) 2005, 221–30.

9997. —— (ed.). Selected letters. Oxford; New York: OUP, 2004. pp. li, 294. (Oxford world's classics.)

9998. KAROUNOS, MICHAEL. Ordination and revolution in *Mansfield Park*. SELit (44:4) 2004, 715–36.

9999. KELLY, DAVID. *Emma*, Cher, and the maze of unknowing. *See* **13519.**

10000. KELLY, GARY. Education and accomplishments. *In* (pp. 252–61) **10060.**

10001. KENDRICK, BETH. 'Does this petticoat make me look fat?': having it all in Jane Austen's time and today. *In* (pp. 7–12) **9971.**

10002. KENNEY, THERESA. 'As she was not really Mrs Croft': playing the Admiral's wife in Bath. Persuasions (26) 2004, 51–61.

10003. KEYMER, THOMAS. Rank. *In* (pp. 387–96) **10060.**

10004. KIRKHAM, MARGARET. Portraits. *In* (pp. 68–79) **10060.**

10005. KNOX-SHAW, PETER. Jane Austen and the Enlightenment. (Bibl. 2004, 10035.) Rev. by Michael Caines in TLS, 4 Mar. 2005, 3–4.

10006. —— Philosophy. *In* (pp. 346–56) **10060.**

10007. KROEBER, KARL. Jane Austen's *Northanger Abbey*: self-reflexive satire and biopoetics. *In* (pp. 99–114) **9305.**

10008. LAMONT, CLAIRE. Domestic architecture. *In* (pp. 225–33) **10060.**

10009. LANE, MAGGIE. Food. *In* (pp. 262–8) **10060.**

10010. LECERCLE, JEAN-JACQUES. Jane Austen meets Dickens: a response to Thierry Labica. *See* **16864.**

10011. LE FAYE, DEIRDRE. Letters. *In* (pp. 33–40) **10060.**

10012. —— Memoirs and biographies. *In* (pp. 51–8) **10060.**

10013. LIEBREGTS, PETER. Images of an imaginist: two film versions of Jane Austen's *Emma*. *In* (pp. 277–99) **9237**.

10014. LYNCH, DEIDRE SHAUNA. Cult of Jane Austen. *In* (pp. 111–20) **10060**.

10015. —— Sequels. *In* (pp. 160–8) **10060**.

10016. MACDONALD, GINA; MACDONALD, ANDREW (eds). Jane Austen on screen. (Bibl. 2004, 10043.) Rev. by Sarah Cardwell in MLR (100:3) 2005, 793–4.

10017. MCMASTER, JULIET. Illustrating Jane's juvenilia. Persuasions (26) 2004, 195–211.

10018. MANDAL, ANTHONY. Language. *In* (pp. 23–32) **10060**.

10019. MAX, D. T. The literary Darwinists. NYTM, 6 Nov. 2005, 74–9.

10020. MEZEI, KATHY. Domestic space and the idea of home in auto/biographical practices. *In* (pp. 81–95) **12750**.

10021. MILES, ROBERT. Jane Austen. Plymouth: Northcote House in assn with the British Council, 2003. pp. x, 175. (Writers and their work.) Rev. by Margaret Forsyth in WWr (12:2) 2005, 328–30.

10022. MILLER, CHRISTOPHER R. Jane Austen's aesthetics and ethics of surprise. Narrative (13:3) 2005, 238–60.

10023. MILLER, D. A. Jane Austen; or, The secret of style. (Bibl. 2004, 10050.) Rev. by Celia A. Easton in GLQ (11:1) 2005, 151–3; by Jacqueline Foertsch in SAtlR (70:2) 2005, 140–3.

10024. MORRISON, ROBERT (ed.). Jane Austen's *Pride and Prejudice*: a sourcebook. London; New York: Routledge, 2005. pp. xviii, 172. (Routledge guides to literature.)

10025. MULLAN, JOHN. Psychology. *In* (pp. 377–86) **10060**.

10026. MURPHY, OLIVIA. Books, bras and Bridget Jones: reading adaptions of *Pride and Prejudice*. SSE (31) 2005, 21–38.

10027. NAFISI, AZAR. Reading *Lolita* in Tehran: a memoir in books. *See* **18463**.

10028. NEILL, NATALIE. 'The trash with which the press now groans': *Northanger Abbey* and the gothic best sellers of the 1790s. ECN (4) 2004, 163–92.

10029. NEWTON, K. M. Revisions of Scott, Austen, and Dickens in *Daniel Deronda*. *See* **10944**.

10030. OLSEN, KIRSTIN. All things Austen: an encyclopedia of Austen's world. Westport, CT; London: Greenwood Press, 2005. 2 vols. pp. xxii, 804. Rev. by John D. Baird in TLS, 16 Sept. 2005, 24.

10031. PALMER, SALLY. Anne takes the cure: *Persuasion* and the spa. Persuasions (26) 2004, 111–20.

10032. PIKOULIS, JOHN. Reading and writing in *Persuasion*. MLR (100:1) 2005, 20–36.

10033. PUCCI, SUZANNE R.; THOMPSON, JAMES (eds). Jane Austen and Co.: remaking the past in contemporary culture. (Bibl. 2004, 10067.) Rev. by Robert G. Dryden in StudN (37:3) 2005, 342–5.

10034. RAJAN, RAJESWARI SUNDER. Critical responses, recent. *In* (pp. 101–10) **10060.**

10035. RAVEN, JAMES. Book production. *In* (pp. 194–203) **10060.**

10036. REGIS, PAMELA. 'Her happiness was from within': courtship and the interior world in *Perusasion.* Persuasions (26) 2004, 62–71.

10037. RESNICK, LAURA. *Bride and Prejudice. In* (pp. 87–96) **9971.**

10038. RICHARDSON, ALAN. Reading practices. *In* (pp. 397–405) **10060.**

10039. ROBERTS, WARREN. Nationalism and empire. *In* (pp. 327–36) **10060.**

10040. ROE, NICHOLAS. Politics. *In* (pp. 357–65) **10060.**

10041. ROGERS, PAT. Transport. *In* (pp. 425–33) **10060.**

10042. ROHRBACH, EMILY. Austen's later subjects. SELit (44:4) 2004, 737–52.

10043. SELWYN, DAVID. Consumer goods. *In* (pp. 215–24) **10060.**

10044. —— Poetry. *In* (pp. 59–67) **10060.**

10045. SIMMONS, JAMES R., JR. Did Willoughby join the Navy? Patrick O'Brian's thirty-year homage to Jane Austen. Persuasions (26) 2004, 170–5.

10046. SMITH, MURIEL. Jane Austen, Pemberley, and Chatsworth. NQ (52:4) 2005, 451.

10047. SODEMAN, MELISSA. Domestic mobility in *Persuasion* and *Sanditon.* SELit (45:4) 2005, 787–812.

10048. SOUTER, KAY TORNEY. Heads and arms and legs enough: Jane Austen and sibling dynamics. Persuasions (26) 2004, 176–87.

10049. SOUTHAM, BRIAN. Professions. *In* (pp. 366–76) **10060.**

10050. STABLER, JANE. Cities. *In* (pp. 204–14) **10060.**

10051. —— Literary influences. *In* (pp. 41–50) **10060.**

10052. STEARNS, PRECIOUS MCKENZIE. Lady Bertram's lapdog: the Empire rests in *Mansfield Park.* NQ (52:4) 2005, 450–1.

10053. STURROCK, JUNE. Dandies, beauties, and the issue of good looks in *Persuasion.* Persuasions (26) 2004, 41–50.

10054. SUTHERLAND, JOHN. Some nabob: the sometimes useful errors of Edward Said. *See* **15032.**

10055. SUTHERLAND, KATHRYN. Chronology of composition and publication. *In* (pp. 12–22) **10060.**

10056. —— Jane Austen and the invention of the serious modern novel. *In* (pp. 244–62) **8014.**

10057. —— Jane Austen's textual lives: from Aeschylus to Bollywood. Oxford; New York: OUP, 2005. pp. xix, 387.

10058. TAKEI, AKIKO. 'Your complexion is so improved!': a diagnosis of Fanny Price's 'dis-ease'. ECF (17:4) 2005, 683–700.

10059. TANDON, BHARAT. Jane Austen and the morality of conversation. (Bibl. 2004, 10080.) Rev. by Robert G. Dryden in StudN (37:3) 2005, 342–5.

10060. TODD, JANET (ed.). Jane Austen in context. Cambridge; New York: CUP, 2005. pp. xxx, 467. (Cambridge ed. of the works of Jane Austen.)

10061. TROTT, NICOLA. Critical responses, 1830–1970. *In* (pp. 92–100) **10060.**

10062. WALDRON, MARY. Critical responses, early. *In* (pp. 83–91) **10060.**

10063. WANDLESS, WILLIAM H.   Narrative pain and the moral sense: toward an ethics of suffering in the long eighteenth century. *See* **7258**.

10064. WATT-EVANS, LAWRENCE.   World at war. *In* (pp. 27–32) **9971**.

10065. WELLS, JULIETTE.   'In music she had always used to feel alone in the world': Jane Austen, solitude, and the artistic woman. Persuasions (26) 2004, 98–110.

10066. WHEELER, MICHAEL.   Religion. *In* (pp. 406–14) **10060**.

10067. WHELEHAN, IMELDA.   Sex and the single girl: Helen Fielding, Erica Jong and Helen Gurley Brown. *See* **16473**.

10068. WILLIAMS, J. R.   'Suffer the little children to come unto me': T. F. Powys's child-men in a landscape of redemption. *See* **18928**.

10069. WILTSHIRE, JOHN.   Medicine, illness and disease. *In* (pp. 306–16) **10060**.

10070. —— (ed.).   Mansfield Park. Cambridge; New York: CUP, 2005. pp. lxxxvi, 738. (Cambridge ed. of the works of Jane Austen.)

10071. WINTERS, JILL.   The secret life of Mary. *In* (pp. 159–64) **9971**.

10072. WOOLF, DANIEL.   Jane Austen and history revisited: the past, gender, and memory from the Restoration to *Persuasion*. Persuasions (26) 2004, 217–36.

10073. ZETTEL, SARAH.   Times and tenors; or, What the movies have done, and failed to do, to *Pride and Prejudice*. *In* (pp. 97–103) **9971**.

10074. ZUNSHINE, LISA.   Bastards and foundlings: illegitimacy in eighteenth-century England. *See* **8164**.

William Edmondstoune Aytoun

10075. BOOS, FLORENCE S.   'Spasm' and class: W. E. Aytoun, George Gilfillan, Sydney Dobell, and Alexander Smith. *See* **10818**.

Walter Bagehot

10076. HAJDENKO-MARSHALL, CATHERINE.   Le républicanisme paradoxal de Walter Bagehot (1826–1877). EREA (1:2) 2003, 97–104.

10077. ROACH, JOSEPH.   Public intimacy: the prior history of 'it'. *In* (pp. 15–30) **3985**.

Joanna Baillie

10078. BEHRENDT, STEPHEN C.   An urn, a teapot, and the archaeology of Romantic reading. CEACrit (67:2) 2005, 1–14.

10079. HEWITT, REGINA.   Scott, Baillie, and the bewitching of social relations. ERR (16:3) 2005, 341–50.

10080. MURRAY, JULIE.   Governing economic man: Joanna Baillie's theatre of utililty. ELH (70:4) 2003, 1043–65.

10081. MYERS, VICTORIA.   Joanna Baillie: speculations on legal cruelty. WordsC (35:3) 2004, 123–7.

Charles Wolcott Balestier (1861–1891)

10082. TOWHEED, SHAFQUAT.   Rudyard Kipling's literary property, international copyright law and *The Naulahka*. *See* **17491**.

E. J. (Edmund James) Banfield (b.1825)

10083. TAYLOR, CHERYL. Threshold to fulfillment: the Barrier Reef writings of E. J. Banfield and Jean Devanny. Antipodes (18:1) 2004, 18–23.

Sabine Baring-Gould

10084. LEVORATO, ALESSANDRA. Language and gender in the fairy-tale tradition: a linguistic analysis of old and new story telling. (Bibl. 2004, 10119.) Rev. by Clare Walsh in LLit (14:2) 2005, 196–9; by Jeana Jorgensen in MarvT (19:2) 2005, 316–19.

Natalie Clifford Barney

10085. TEDESCHINI LALLI, BIANCAMARIA. Americane europee in due guerre mondiali. In (pp. 95–115) **12589.**

10086. WELLS-LYNN, AMY. The intertextual, sexually coded Rue Jacob: a geocritical approach to Djuna Barnes, Natalie Barney, and Radclyffe Hall. See **15334.**

Thomas Haynes Bayly (1797–1839)

10087. RAY, MARTIN. Thomas Hardy's *The Trumpet-Major*: the source of 'Upon the Hill He Turned'. See **11156.**

Thomas Lovell Beddoes

10088. CROSSAN, GREG. 'That wolf-howled, witch-prayed, owl-sung fool': Beddoes and the play of words. JTLBS (11) 2005, 25–30.

10089. JOSHUA, ESSAKA. Lionel and Anthony von Rothschild at Göttingen University. JTLBS (11) 2005, 31–7.

10090. —— Thomas Lovell Beddoes and William John Hamilton. JTLBS (11) 2005, 17–24.

'Cuthbert Bede' (The Rev. Edward Bradley)

10091. VERNIER, PETER. Oscar's drawing of 'Little Mr Bouncer'. See **12434.**

Edward Bellamy

10092. SAXTON, A. In dubious battle. See **19630.**

Walter Besant

10093. NASH, ANDREW. Walter Besant's *All Sorts and Conditions of Men* and Robert Louis Stevenson's *The Strange Case of Dr Jekyll and Mr Hyde*. NQ (52:4) 2005, 494–7.

10094. WOOD, JOHN. *Christina*: Shaw's new ending for Ibsen's *A Doll's House*. See **19422.**

Ambrose Bierce ('Dod Grile')

10095. BUTSCHER, EDWARD. Culture and literature: three collections of letters. GaR (59:3) 2005, 691–706 (review-article).

10096. DUBAN, JAMES; SALLFORS, SOLOMON. A phenomenal occurrence at Owl Creek Bridge: the presence of Emanuel Swedenborg and Henry James, Sr. ELN (42:3) 2005, 33–8.

10097. JOSHI, S. T.; SCHULTZ, DAVID E. (eds). A much misunderstood man: selected letters of Ambrose Bierce. Columbus: Ohio State UP, 2003. 1 CD-ROM. Rev. by Edward Butscher in GaR (59:3) 2005, 691–706.

Robert Montgomery Bird

10098. ROBERTS-MILLER, PATRICIA. Robert Montgomery Bird and the rhetoric of the improbable cause. RSQ (35:1) 2005, 73–90.

Robert Blatchford

10099. MUTCH, DEBORAH. The *Merrie England* triptych: Robert Blatchford, Edward Fay and the didactic use of *Clarion* fiction. See **1283.**

Marguerite, Countess of Blessington (1789–1849)

10100. HAWKINS, ANN R. Marketing gender and nationalism: Blessington's *Gems of Beauty/L'Écrin* and the mid-century book trade. WWr (12:2) 2005, 225–40.

10101. JUMP, HARRIET DEVINE (gen. ed.). Silver fork novels, 1826–1841: vol. 4, *The Victims of Society* (1837). Ed. by Ann R. Hawkins and Jeraldine R. Kraver. London; Brookfield, VT: Pickering & Chatto, 2005. pp. xli, 327. Rev. by Lauren Gillingham in TLS, 23 & 30 Dec. 2005, 30.

'Rolf Boldrewood' (Thomas Alexander Browne) (1826–1915)

10102. D'ARCENS, LOUISE. Inverse invasions: medievalism and colonialism in Rolf Boldrewood's *A Sydney-Side Saxon*. Parergon (22:2) 2005, 159–82.

'Sherwood Bonner' (Catherine McDowell)

10103. McKEE, KATHRYN. Writing region from the hub: Sherwood Bonner's travel letters and questions of postbellum US Southern identity. Legacy (22:2) 2005, 126–43.

Edwin Booth

10104. WATERMEIER, DANIEL J. Edwin Booth goes West: 1852–1856. THS (25) 2005, 77–105.

James Skipp Borlase ('J. J. G. Bradley') (b.1839)

10105. LAW, GRAHAM. Imagined local communities: three Victorian newspaper novelists. *In* (pp. 185–203) **880.**

10106. SUSSEX, LUCY. 'Bobbing around': James Skipp Borlase, Adam Lindsay Gordon, and surviving in the literary market of Australia, 1860s. VPR (37:4) 2003, 98–110.

George Borrow

10107. CHANDLER, DAVID. Lindley Williams Hubbell, Borrovian. See **17088.**

10108. DAKYNS, ANDREW G. Schooldays of George H. Borrow (1803–81) & James M. Wilson (1836–1931): a comparison. GBB (29) 2004, 97–104.

10109. FULTON, HELEN. George Borrow and the Oldest Animals in *Wild Wales*. THSC (10) 2004, 23–40.

10110. GÓMEZ ALFARO, ANTONIO. Some positive and negative views of Borrow's work from nineteenth-century travellers to Spain. Trans. by Ann Ridler. GBB (31) 2005, 45–58.

10111. HITCHCOCK, RICHARD. John Walker, Geroge Borrow and gypsies in Spain. GBB (31) 2005, 58–64.

10112. HUNTER-RUTTER, KATHLEEN. Another distinguished Borrovian: Theodore Roosevelt. GBB (30) 2005, 63–7.

10113. KABELL, INGE.   George Borrow and Finland (part 1). GBB (29) 2004, 32–51.

10114. —— George Borrow and Finland (part 2). GBB (30) 2005, 43–55.

10115. —— George Borrow and Finland (part 3). GBB (31) 2005, 31–42.

10116. MISSLER, PETER.   The case of the underpriced Testaments. GBB (29) 2004, 17–31.

10117. —— A partial judgement. GBB (30) 2005, 30–42. (Spanish reception of *The Bible in Spain*.)

10118. MURPHY, MARTIN.   The Hamaxobii and their mobile homes. GBB (31) 2005, 42–5.

10119. PRICE, DAVID.   George on the Net. GBB (31) 2005, 98–103.

10120. RIDLER, ANN.   Censorship and *The Sleeping Bard*. GBB (29) 2004, 62–5.

10121. —— An early review of *Wild Wales*. GBB (31) 2005, 69–70.

10122. —— Mary Borrow's account book and the family's visit to the Isle of Man in 1855. GBB (29) 2004, 88–97.

10123. —— Some unexpected references to Borrow. GBB (29) 2004, 51–3.

10124. ROBERTSON, IAN.   Wry aspersions in the *Rye*. GBB (31) 2005, 66–9. (Reference to Richard Ford in draft appendix to *The Romany Rye*.)

10125. SHEPHEARD, RICHARD.   A coat of green: George Borrow and Horncastle horsefair (part 1). GBB (30) 2005, 8–29.

10126. —— A coat of green: George Borrow and Horncastle horsefair (part 2). GBB (31) 2005, 12–31.

10127. —— 'Live and let live': a miniature of Coke of Norfolk. GBB (29) 2004, 57–62.

10128. WILKINS-JONES, CLIVE.   *Gweledigaethau uffernol*: George Borrow, Goronwy Owen and the vision of Hell. GBB (31) 2005, 81–97.

10129. WOODERSON, PETER.   George Borrow and bees. GBB (29) 2004, 53–7.

Dion Boucicault

10130. CHILES, KATY L.   Blackened Irish and brownfaced Amerindians: constructions of American Whiteness in Dion Boucicault's *The Octoroon*. NCT (31:2) 2004, 28–50.

10131. DUBOST, THIERRY.   Boucicault, Friel et Kilroy: étude en do bémol et majeur. EtIr (30:1) 2005, 67–81.

William Lisle Bowles

10132. VINCENT, PATRICK H.   'Switzerland no more': Turner, Wordsworth and the changed landscape of Revolution. *See* **12523**.

Thomas Bracken (1843–1898)

10133. CRYER, MAX.   'Hear our voices, we entreat': the extraordinary story of New Zealand's national anthems. Foreword by Dame Kiri Te Kanawa. *See* **9678**.

10134. HEENAN, ASHLEY.   *God Defend New Zealand*: a history of the national anthem. Christchurch, New Zealand: School of Music, Univ. of Canterbury,

2004. pp. 160. (Canterbury series of bibliographies, catalogues, and source documents in music, 11.)

Mary Elizabeth Braddon (Mrs Maxwell)

10135. HASSAN, NARIN. 'Hothouse flowers and despair': reading the Victorian garden in M. E. Braddon's *The Doctor's Wife*. Mosaic (38:4) 2005, 67–81.

10136. HEILMANN, ANN. Emma Bovary's sisters: infectious desire and female reading appetites in Mary Braddon and George Moore. VicR (29:1) 2003, 31–48.

10137. HODDER, KAREN. *Jane Eyre* and subversive influences. *In* (pp. 39–52) 10222.

10138. HOUSTON, NATALIE M. (ed.). Lady Audley's secret. Peterborough, Ont.; Orchard Park, NY: Broadview Press, 2003. pp. 510. (Broadview literary texts.) Rev. by Lisa Hopkins in GothS (6:1) 2004, 145.

10139. LODGE, MARY JO. From madness to melodramas to musicals: the women of *Lady Audley's Secret* and *Sweeney Todd*. TheatreA (56) 2003, 78–96.

10140. MALCOLM, GABRIELLE. Mary Braddon, literary critic: introduction to a 'costly' edition of *Little Dorrit*. Dickensian (101:1) 2005, 15–26.

10141. MANGHAM, ANDREW. 'Murdered at the breast': maternal violence and the self-made man in popular Victorian culture. CritS (16:1) 2004, 20–34.

10142. NAŁĘCZ-WOJTCZAK, JOLANTA. Facing evil: the motif of temptation in some ghost and vampire stories. *In* (pp. 159–66) 3756.

Amelia Bristow (b.1783)

10143. KILFEATHER, SIOBHÁN. Terrific register: the gothicization of atrocity in Irish Romanticism. *See* 11656.

Anne Brontë

10144. BELLAMY, JOAN. *The Tenant of Wildfell Hall*: what Anne Brontë knew and what modern readers don't. BrSt (30:3) 2005, 255–7.

10145. KREILKAMP, IVAN. Petted things: *Wuthering Heights* and the animal. *See* 10203.

10146. SUMMERS, MARY. Anne Brontë: educating parents. (Bibl. 2004, 10171.) Rev. by Emma Liggins in WWr (12:2) 2005, 316–18.

10147. THORMÄHLEN, MARIANNE. Anne Brontë's *Sacred Harmony*: a discovery. BrSt (30:2) 2005, 93–102. (Anthology of religious verse.)

Branwell Brontë

10148. NEUFELDT, VICTOR A. The child is parent to the author: Branwell Brontë. *In* (pp. 173–87) 9164.

Charlotte Brontë

10149. ANON. Illustrations. *In* (pp. 15–22) 10222.

10150. —— (ed.). The foundling: a tale of our own times by Captain Tree. London: Hesperus Press, 2004. pp. 112. Rev. by Bob Duckett in BrSt (30:3) 2005, 267–8.

10151. —— The spell. Foreword by Nicola Baker. London: Hesperus Press, 2005. pp. ix, 136. (Hesperus classics.) Rev. by Bob Duckett in BrSt (30:3) 2005, 267–8.

10152. ALEXANDER, CHRISTINE. Autobiography and juvenilia: the fractured self in Charlotte Brontë's early manuscripts. *In* (pp. 154–72) **9164.**

10153. ARMSTRONG, MARY A. Reading a head: *Jane Eyre*, phrenology, and the homoerotics of legibility. VLC (33:1) 2005, 107–32.

10154. BERGLUND, BIRGITTA. In defence of Madame Beck. BrSt (30:3) 2005, 185–211.

10155. CAMPBELL, IAN. The Brontës and power. BrSt (30:1) 2005, 1–6.

10156. CONDÉ, MARY. As cold as ice: *The Underpainter*. *In* (pp. 57–64) **19900.**

10157. CROUCH, KRISTIN. 'Inside out': the creative process of Shared Experience theatre. *See* **21296.**

10158. EELLS, EMILY. The mystery of *Kitty Bell*: a possible solution? BrSt (30:2) 2005, 113–23.

10159. GARGANO, ELIZABETH. The education of Brontë's new *nouvelle Héloïse* in *Shirley*. SELit (44:4) 2004, 779–803.

10160. GLEN, HEATHER. Charlotte Brontë: the imagination in history. (Bibl. 2004, 10182.) Rev. by Richard J. Dunn in StudN (37:2) 2005, 246–8; by Josephine McDonagh in TexP (19:1) 2005, 202–8; by Alain Jumeau in EA (58:2) 2005, 224–5.

10161. GODFREY, ESTHER. *Jane Eyre*, from governess to girl bride. SELit (45:4) 2005, 853–71.

10162. HADLEY, TESSA. Seated alone with a book ... *See* **11407.**

10163. HAGER, KELLY. Brontë for kids. *See* **14332.**

10164. HAGUE, ANGELA. Fiction, intuition, and creativity: studies in Brontë, James, Woolf, and Lessing. (Bibl. 2003, 9460.) Rev. by N. H. Reeve in MLR (100:4) 2005, 1077–8.

10165. HATELEY, ERICA. The end of *The Eyre Affair*: *Jane Eyre*, parody, and popular culture. *See* **21201.**

10166. HODDER, KAREN. *Jane Eyre* and subversive influences. *In* (pp. 39–52) **10222.**

10167. HODGE, JON. *Villette's* compulsory education. SELit (45:4) 2005, 899–916.

10168. KEES, LARA FREEBURG. 'Sympathy' in *Jane Eyre*. SELit (45:4) 2005, 873–97.

10169. KINSER, BRENT E. A not so 'simple story': Jane Welsh Carlyle and Charlotte Brontë's *Shirley*. MidQ (46:2) 2005, 152–68.

10170. KLAUS, H. GUSTAV. Mrs Rochester and Mr Cooper: alternative visions of class, history and rebellion in the 'hungry forties'. LitH (14:1) 2005, 1–13.

10171. KNIGHT, CHARMIAN. Thornfield Hall revisited. *In* (pp. 63–73) **10222.**

10172. LESCART, ALAIN. All women are *grisettes* in *Villette*. BrSt (30:2) 2005, 103–11.

10173. LOSANO, ANTONIA. Reading women / reading pictures: textual and visual reading in Charlotte Brontë's fiction and nineteenth-century painting. *In* (pp. 27–52) **12549.**

10174. NEWMAN, BETH. Subjects on display: psychoanalysis, social expectation, and Victorian femininity. (Bibl. 2004, 10194.) Rev. by Dianne F. Sadoff in VS (47:4) 2005, 619–21; by Laura Green in TSWL (24:2) 2005, 357–8.

10175. PESCHIER, DIANA. Nineteenth-century anti-Catholic discourses: the case of Charlotte Brontë. Basingstoke; New York: Palgrave Macmillan, 2005. pp. x, 198.

10176. PHILLIPS, HELEN. Robin Hood, the prioress of Kirklees, and Charlotte Brontë. In (pp. 154–66) **3576.**

10177. PHILPOTT, HELEN. 'Something dangerous in her nature': madwomen in *Jane Eyre* and *The Woman in White*. In (pp. 23–37) **10222.**

10178. PIONKE, ALBERT D. Reframing the Luddites: materialist and idealist models of self in Charlotte Brontë's *Shirley*. VicR (30:2) 2004, 81–102.

10179. PLASA, CARL. Charlotte Brontë. (Bibl. 2004, 10200.) Rev. by Sarah Fermi in BrSt (30:1) 2005, 89–90.

10180. ROGERS, PHILIP. Fraudulent closure in *Villette*'s 'Faubourg Clotilde'. BrSt (30:2) 2005, 125–30.

10181. RUIJSSENAARS, ERIC. The Brussels Tahon photograph redated. BrSt (30:1) 2005, 61–5.

10182. SEELYE, JOHN D. Jane Eyre's American daughters: from *The Wide, Wide World* to *Anne of Green Gables*: a study of marginalized maidens and what they mean. Newark: Delaware UP, 2005. pp. 368.

10183. SŁAWEK, TADEUSZ. From rags (of memory) to riches (of literature). YREAL (21) 2005, 239–58.

10184. SORAYA GARCÍA SÁNCHEZ, MARÍA. Talking about women, history, and writing with Michèle Roberts. See **19089.**

10185. STARZYK, LAWRENCE J. Charlotte Brontë's *The Professor*: the appropriation of images. JNT (33:2) 2003, 143–62.

10186. STYCZYŃSKA, ADELA. Character studies in Charlotte Brontë's *Shirley*. In (pp. 238–49) **3756.**

10187. TORGERSON, BETH. Ailing women in the age of cholera: illness in *Shirley*. VicR (30:2) 2004, 1–31.

10188. TRACY, THOMAS. 'Reader, I buried him': apocalypse and empire in *Jane Eyre*. CritS (16:2) 2004, 59–77.

10189. VANDEN BOSSCHE, CHRIS R. What did *Jane Eyre* do? Ideology, agency, class and the novel. Narrative (13:1) 2005, 46–66.

10190. WILSON, CHERYL A. Female reading communities in *Jane Eyre*. BrSt (30:2) 2005, 131–9.

10191. WILTSHIRE, IRENE. Speech in *Wuthering Heights*: Joseph's dialect and Charlotte's emendations. See **10209.**

Emily Brontë

10192. ALLEN, MAGGIE. Emily Brontë and the influence of the German Romantic poets. BrSt (30:1) 2005, 7–10.

10193. BEAUMONT, MATTHEW. Heathcliff's great hunger: the cannibal Other in *Wuthering Heights*. JVC (9:2) 2004, 137–63.

10194. CAESAR, JUDITH. Brontë's *Wuthering Heights*. Exp (63:3) 2005, 149–51.

10195. CAMPBELL, IAN. The Brontës and power. *See* **10155.**

10196. CORY, ABBIE L. 'Out of my brother's power': gender, class, and rebellion in *Wuthering Heights*. WS (34:1) 2005, 1–26.

10197. COTTOM, DANIEL. I think; therefore, I am Heathcliff. *See* **8126.**

10198. DAWSON, TERENCE. The effective protagonist in the nineteenth-century British novel: Scott, Brontë, Eliot, Wilde. *See* **11912.**

10199. DE LEO, MADDALENA. Shakespeare and the Brontës: a comment. *See* **5898.**

10200. FERMI, SARAH. Emily Brontë: a theory. BrSt (30:1) 2005, 71–4.

10201. GEERKEN, INGRID. 'The dead are not annihilated': mortal regret in *Wuthering Heights*. JNT (34:3) 2004, 373–406.

10202. HAGER, KELLY. Brontë for kids. *See* **14332.**

10203. KREILKAMP, IVAN. Petted things: *Wuthering Heights* and the animal. YJC (18:1) 2005, 87–110.

10204. MCSWEENEY, KERRY. Dream-representation in *Wuthering Heights*, *Crime and Punishment*, and *War and Peace*. Symposium (59:3) 2005, 163–78.

10205. SIMPSON, KATRINA. *Wuthering Heights* – a personal interpretation. BrSt (30:1) 2005, 69–70.

10206. SPENCER, LUKE. Sylvia Plath, Ted Hughes and *Wuthering Heights*: some uses of memory. *In* (pp. 75–85) **10222.**

10207. TYTLER, GRAEME. The parameters of reason in *Wuthering Heights*. BrSt (30:3) 2005, 231–42.

10208. VAN DER MEER, CAROLYNE. Interrogating Brontë sequels: Anna L'Estrange, *The Return to Wuthering Heights*. BrSt (30:1) 2005, 41–52.

10209. WILTSHIRE, IRENE. Speech in *Wuthering Heights*: Joseph's dialect and Charlotte's emendations. BrSt (30:1) 2005, 19–29.

The Rev. Patrick Brontë

10210. GREEN, DUDLEY (ed.). The letters of the Reverend Patrick Brontë. Foreword by Asa Briggs. Stroud: Nonsuch, 2005. pp. 382.

10211. WALKER, MICHAEL. William Morgan, BD, 1782–1858. *See* **11740.**

The Brontës

10212. ALEXANDER, CHRISTINE. Play and apprenticeship: the culture of family magazines. *In* (pp. 31–50) **9164.**

10213. —— SMITH, MARGARET (eds). Oxford companion to the Brontës. (Bibl. 2004, 10227.) Rev. by Alain Jumeau in EA (58:2) 2005, 223–4; by Ellen Bayuk Rosenman in VS (48:1) 2005, 193–5.

10214. BAUMAN, SUSAN R. In the market for fame: the Victorian publication history of the Brontë poems. VicR (30:1) 2004, 44–71.

10215. BENTON, MICHAEL. Literary biomythography. *See* **4160.**

10216. DUCKETT, BOB. The working classes read Brontë: some examples. BrSt (30:2) 2005, 163–6.

10217. EAGLETON, TERRY. Myths of power: a Marxist study of the Brontës. Basingstoke; New York: Palgrave Macmillan, 2005. pp. xxxix, 148.

10218. ENGLAND, RICHARD.   Undisputed sovereignty. Meanjin (64:1/2) 2005, 270–9.

10219. FERMI, SARAH.   The young Brontës, Lord Wilton, and the Manor of Oxenhope. BrSt (30:1) 2005, 11–18.

10220. HEYWOOD, CHRISTOPHER.   The mark 'Bronte' on Frederic Montagu's *Gleanings in Craven. See* **11731.**

10221. KNIGHT, CHARMIAN.   Who's afraid of the Brontë sisters? *In* (pp. 53–62) **10222.**

10222. —— STONEMAN, PATSY (eds).   The Brontë influence. Haworth, W. Yorks.: Brontë Soc., 2004. pp. 87. (Brontë Soc. occasional pubs, 8.) Rev. by Valerie Smith in BrSt (30:3) 2005, 269–71.

10223. PITE, RALPH (gen. ed.).   Lives of Victorian literary figures II: the Brownings, the Brontës, and the Rossettis by their contemporaries: vol. 2, The Brontës. Ed. by Marianna Kambani. London; Brookfield, VT: Pickering & Chatto, 2004. pp. xli, 436.

10224. SELLARS, JANE.   The artist in her studio: the influence of the Brontës on women artists. BrSt (30:3) 2005, 243–54.

10225. STONEMAN, PATSY.   Introduction. *In* (pp. 1–13) **10222.**

10226. TORGERSON, BETH.   Reading the Brontë body: disease, desire, and the constraints of culture. Basingstoke; New York: Palgrave Macmillan, 2005. pp. x, 180.

10227. TWINN, FRANCES.   The portrait of Haworth in *The Life of Charlotte Brontë.* BrSt (30:2) 2005, 151–61.

10228. WHITEHEAD, STEPHEN.   Henry Bonnell: guardian of the relics of passion. BrSt (30:1) 2005, 31–40.

Charles Brockden Brown

10229. AMFREVILLE, MARC.   Charles Brockden Brown's cultural paradox. LAm (24:101) 2004, 5–21.

10230. BARNARD, PHILIP; KAMRATH, MARK L.; SHAPIRO, STEPHEN (eds). Revising Charles Brockden Brown: culture, politics, and sexuality in the Early Republic. (Bibl. 2004, 10244.) Rev. by Bryan Waterman in EAL (40:1) 2005, 173–91.

10231. CODY, MICHAEL.   Charles Brockden Brown and *The Literary Magazine*: cultural journalism in the Early American Republic. (Bibl. 2004, 10249.) Rev. by Bryan Waterman in EAL (40:1) 2005, 173–91.

10232. COMMENT, KRISTIN M.   Charles Brockden Brown's *Ormond* and lesbian possibility in the Early Republic. EAL (40:1) 2005, 57–78.

10233. ELLIS, SCOTT.   Charles Brockden Brown's *Ormond*, property exchange, and the literary marketplace in the Early American Republic. StudN (37:1) 2005, 1–19.

10234. GIBBONS, LUKE.   Ireland, America, and gothic memory: transatlantic terror in the Early Republic. B2 (31:1) 2004, 25–47.

10235. HARRIS, JENNIFER.   At one with the land: the domestic remove – Charles Brockden Brown's *Wieland* and matters of belonging. CRAS (33:3) 2003, 189–210.

10236. HOGSETTE, DAVID S. Textual surveillance, social codes, and sublime voices: the tyranny of narrative in *Caleb Williams* and *Wieland*. *See* **8672**.

10237. KAFER, PETER. Charles Brockden Brown's Revolution and the birth of American gothic. (Bibl. 2004, 10254.) Rev. by Bryan Waterman in EAL (40:1) 2005, 173–91; by Mark L. Kamrath in JAH (92:1) 2005, 203–4.

10238. KAZANJIAN, DAVID. The colonizing trick: national culture and imperial citizenship in Early America. (Bibl. 2004, 10256.) Rev. by Russ Castronovo in AL (77:1) 2005, 179–81.

10239. LEWIS, PAUL. Attaining masculinity: Charles Brockden Brown and woman warriors of the 1790s. EAL (40:1) 2005, 37–55.

10240. ROWE, KATHERINE. The politics of sleepwalking: American Lady Macbeths. *See* **6569**.

10241. SLAWINSKI, SCOTT. Validating bachelorhood: audience, patriarchy, and Charles Brockden Brown's editorship of the *Monthly Magazine* and *American Review*. London; New York: Routledge, 2005. pp. ix, 128.

10242. STRODE, TIMOTHY FRANCIS. The ethics of exile: colonialism in the fictions of Charles Brockden Brown and J. M. Coetzee. London; New York: Routledge, 2005. pp. ix, 253. (Literary criticism and cultural theory.)

10243. WATERMAN, BRYAN. Charles Brockden Brown, revised and expanded. EAL (40:1) 2005, 173–91 (review-article).

Thomas Edward Brown (1830–1897)

10244. DAKYNS, ANDREW G. Schooldays of George H. Borrow (1803–81) & James M. Wilson (1836–1931): a comparison. *See* **10108**.

William Wells Brown (1815–1884)

10245. DICKERSON, VANESSA D. Performing Blackness: Carlyle and *The Nigger Question*. *In* (pp. 151–8) **10393**.

10246. JAMES, JENNIFER. 'Civil' War wounds: William Wells Brown, violence, and the domestic narrative. AAR (39:1/2) 2005, 39–54.

10247. NABERS, DEAK. The problem of revolution in the age of slavery: *Clotel*, fiction, and the government of man. Representations (91) 2005, 84–108.

10248. THOMAS-KROUSE, ONDRA. Dancing to transgress. *See* **12114**.

Elizabeth Barrett Browning

10249. BLAIR, KIRSTIE. Spasmodic affections: poetry, pathology, and the Spasmodic hero. VP (42:4) 2004, 473–90.

10250. JAMES, DAVID. Realism, late Modernist abstraction, and Sylvia Townsend Warner's fictions of impersonality. *See* **19978**.

10251. MONTWIELER, KATHERINE. Domestic politics: gender, protest, and Elizabeth Barrett Browning's *Poems before Congress*. TSWL (24:2) 2005, 291–317.

10252. PHELAN, JOE. Dear Alibel. TLS, 11 Feb. 2005, 5 (review-article). (E.B.B.'s correspondence with her sister.)

10253. TAYLOR, BEVERLY. Childhood writings of Elizabeth Barrett Browning: 'At four I first mounted Pegasus.' *In* (pp. 138–53) **9164**.

10254. THORNE-MURPHY, LESLEE. Prostitute rescue, rape, and poetic inspiration in Elizabeth Barrett Browning's *Aurora Leigh*. WWr (12:2) 2005, 241–57.

10255. TUCKER, HERBERT F. Glandular omnism and beyond: the Victorian Spasmodic epic. VP (42:4) 2004, 429–50.

10256. WOOD, JANE. Elizabeth Barrett Browning and Shakespeare's Sonnet 130. NQ (52:1) 2005, 77–9.

Robert Browning

10257. BELLORINI, MARIAGRAZIA (ed.). *The Ring and the Book* di Robert Browning: poesia e dramma. Milan: ISU Univ. Cattolica, 2004. pp. 464.

10258. BROWN, STEPHEN. *Hugh Selwyn Mauberley* as Pound's *Sordello*. *In* (pp. 9–20) **3756**.

10259. EDGECOMBE, RODNEY STENNING. O'Connor's *A Good Man Is Hard to Find*. *See* **18556**.

10260. GENTRY, LARRY. The dramatic monologue as confession: Robert Browning's *Fra Lippo Lippi* and *A Forgiveness*. TPB (42) 2005, 6–15.

10261. GRIBBLE, JENNIFER. Subject and power in *Porphyria's Lover*. SSE (29) 2003, 17–29.

10262. GRIFFIN, JULIA B. 'Twixt treason and convenience: some images of Thomas Wentworth, First Earl of Strafford. *In* (pp. 153–80) **5103**.

10263. HAWLIN, STEFAN; BURNETT, T. A. J. (eds). The poetical works of Robert Browning: vol. 9, *The Ring and the Book*, Books IX–XII. Oxford: Clarendon Press; New York: OUP, 2004. pp. ix, 408. (Oxford English texts.) Rev. by Peter McDonald in NQ (52:1) 2005, 142–3.

10264. KING, ROMA A., JR, *et al.* (gen. eds). The complete works of Robert Browning, with variant readings & annotations: vol. 14. Ed. by John C. Berkey, *et al.* Athens: Ohio UP; Waco, TX: Baylor Univ., 2003. pp. xxvi, 463. Rev. by John Greenfield in VPR (38:3) 2005, 341–3.

10265. PHELAN, JOE. Robert Browning and colonialism. JVC (8:1) 2003, 80–107.

10266. RYERSE, BARBARA. Browning's *Christmas-Eve and Easter-Day*: formal verse satire and the Donnean influence. VicR (29:1) 2003, 49–69.

10267. SAVILLE, JULIA F. The poetic imaging of Michael Field. *In* (pp. 178–206) **9675**.

10268. STARZYK, LAWRENCE J. Browning's *Childe Roland*: the visionary poetic. VN (107) 2005, 11–18.

10269. TUCKER, HERBERT F. James's Browning inside-out. *See* **11458**.

10270. VITA, PAUL. Returning the look: Victorian writers and the Paris morgue. *See* **10759**.

The Brownings

10271. MARTENS, BRITTA. 'Hardly shall I tell my joys and sorrows': Robert Browning's engagement with Elizabeth Barrett Browning's poetics. VP (43:1) 2005, 75–97.

10272. PITE, RALPH (gen. ed.). Lives of Victorian literary figures II: the Brownings, the Brontës, and the Rossettis by their contemporaries: vol. 1, The Brownings. Ed. by Simon Avery. London; Brookfield, VT: Pickering & Chatto, 2004. pp. l, 424.

Mary Brunton

10273. SUTHERLAND, KATHRYN. Jane Austen and the invention of the serious modern novel. *In* (pp. 244–62) **8014.**

John Baldwin Buckstone

10274. CRONIN-JORTNER, MAURA L. In soldier's clothes: Adah Isaacs Menken goes to war. *See* **11717.**

Sir Edward Coley Burne-Jones (1833–1898)

10275. RICHMOND, VELMA BOURGEOIS. Edward Burne-Jones's Chaucer portraits in the Kelmscott Chaucer. *See* **4964.**

Frances Hodgson Burnett

10276. MEREDITH, MARGARET EILEEN. *The Secret Garden: temenos* for individuation: a Jungian appreciation of themes in the novel by Frances Hodgson Burnett. Toronto; Buffalo, NY; London: Toronto UP, 2005. pp. 159. (Studies in Jungian psychology by Jungian analysts.)

10277. STOKES, SALLY SIMS. Noel Streatfeild's secret gardens. *See* **19717.**

John Burroughs

10278. SCHUYLER, DAVID. Coming home with John Burroughs. NYH (84:1) 2003, 89–102 (review-article).

Sir Richard Burton

10279. KENNEDY, DANE. The highly civilized man: Richard Burton and the Victorian world. Cambridge, MA; London: Harvard UP, 2005. pp. 354.

10280. MARZOLPH, ULRICH; VAN LEEUWEN, RICHARD (eds); WASSOUF, HASSAN (asst ed.). The Arabian Nights encyclopedia. *See* **11788.**

10281. MONTICELLI, RITA. Autobiografia e *camouflage* nella letteratura di viaggio di Richard F. Burton. *In* (pp. 145–64) **12577.**

Samuel Butler (1835–1902)

10282. HAACK, SUSAN. The ideal of intellectual integrity, in life and literature. NLH (36:3) 2005, 359–73.

10283. PARRINDER, PATRICK. Entering dystopia, entering *Erewhon.* CritS (17:1) 2005, 6–21.

Anne Isabella Milbanke Byron, Baroness Byron (1792–1860)

10284. COONEY, BRIAN C. 'Words of deeper sorrow': Byronic ambiguity in the separation poems of Lord and Lady Byron. *See* **10301.**

George Gordon Noel, Lord Byron

10285. ADDISON, CATHERINE. Gender and race in Byron's *The Island* and Mitford's *Christina.* Antipodes (18:1) 2004, 72–6.

10286. —— Heritage and innovation in Byron's narrative stanzas. BJ (32:1) 2004, 9–20.

10287. ALLEN, BROOKE.   Byron: revolutionary, libertine and friend. HR (56:2) 2003, 369–76 (review-article).

10288. BENTON, MICHAEL.   Literary biomythography. *See* **4160**.

10289. BONE, DRUMMOND (ed.).   The Cambridge companion to Byron. Cambridge; New York: CUP, 2004. pp. xx, 305. (Cambridge companions to literature.)

10290. BROWNSTEIN, RACHEL M.   Endless imitation: Austen's and Byron's juvenilia. *In* (pp. 122–37) **9164**.

10291. BUFFONI, FRANCO (ed. and trans.).   Manfred. Milan: Mondadori, 2005. pp. xliii, 110. (Oscar classici, 617.)

10292. CARDWELL, RICHARD (ed.).   The reception of Byron in Europe: vol. 1, Southern Europe, France and Romania. London: Thoemmes Press; New York: Continuum, 2004. pp. lv, 233. (Athlone critical traditions.)

10293. —— The reception of Byron in Europe: vol. 2, Northern, Central, and Eastern Europe. London: Thoemmes Press; New York: Continuum, 2004. pp. vii, 235–500. (Athlone critical traditions.)

10294. CARMINATI, MARIA NELLA, *et al.*   The visual impact of *ottava rima*. BJ (32:1) 2004, 39–44.

10295. CHEEKE, STEPHEN.   Byron and place: history, translation, nostalgia. (Bibl. 2004, 10313.) Rev. by Peter W. Graham in WordsC (35:4) 2004, 174–5; by Alan Rawes in BJ (32:1) 2004, 59–60; by Moyra Haslett in MLR (100:3) 2005, 796–8; by Marc Porée in EREA (3:2) 2005.

10296. CLUBBE, JOHN.   Byron, Sully, and the power of portraiture. Aldershot; Burlington, VT: Ashgate, 2005. pp. xxi, 343, (plates) 8. (Nineteenth century.) Rev. by Frances Wilson in TLS, 29 July 2005, 32.

10297. COCHRAN, PETER.   The draught fermenting on the chimney-piece. BJ (32:2) 2004, 125–30. (Correspondence with Annabella Byron.)

10298. —— One ton per square foot: the antecedents of *The Vision of Judgement*. *See* **12048**.

10299. —— (ed.); REES, MICHAEL (trans.).   Lord Byron's life in Italy. By Teresa Guiccioli. Newark: Delaware UP, 2005. pp. xvii, 700.

10300. COLLIGAN, COLETTE.   The unruly copies of Byron's *Don Juan*: harems, underground print culture, and the age of mechanical reproduction. NineL (59:4) 2005, 433–62.

10301. COONEY, BRIAN C.   'Words of deeper sorrow': Byronic ambiguity in the separation poems of Lord and Lady Byron. CEACrit (66:2/3) 2004, 63–75.

10302. CREGAN-REID, VYBARR.   Water defences: the arts of swimming in nineteenth-century culture. *See* **10669**.

10303. DOKOU, CHRISTINA.   Postmodernity is a beach: the diachronic ethics of Lord Byron. BLFSEB (3:6) 2005, 143–60.

10304. DOUGLASS, PAUL.   What Lord Byron learned from Lady Caroline Lamb. *See* **11555**.

10305. EDGECOMBE, RODNEY STENNING.   Two echoes of Marvell in Byron's *Mazeppa*. NQ (52:1) 2005, 45.

10306. FAFLAK, JOEL. Romanticism and the pornography of talking. *See* **12477.**

10307. FELLUGA, DINO FRANCO. The perversity of poetry: Romantic ideology and the popular male poet of genius. Albany: New York State UP, 2005. pp. xi, 208.

10308. FORD, SUSAN ALLEN. Learning romance from Scott and Byron: Jane Austen's natural sequel. *See* **9983.**

10309. FULFORD, TIM. 'Getting and spending': the Orientalization of satire in Romantic London. *In* (pp. 11–29) **9305.**

10310. GARDNER, JOHN. The death of Byron's Doge in *Marino Faliero.* NQ (52:1) 2005, 45–8.

10311. GEORGE, LAURA. Reification and the dandy: *Beppo*, Byron, and other queer things. RomNet (36/37) 2004/05.

10312. GILMOUR, IAN. Little mania. *See* **11556.**

10313. GRIMES, KYLE. Verbal jujitsu: William Hone and the tactics of satirical conflict. *In* (pp. 173–84) **9305.**

10314. HAWLEY, MICHELLE. Harriet Beecher Stowe and Lord Byron: a case of celebrity justice in the Victorian public sphere. *See* **12108.**

10315. HOPPS, GAVIN. Inhabiting a place beyond 'to be or not to be': the playful devotions of Byron and Coleridge. *See* **10492.**

10316. HUGHES, LINDA K. Alexander Smith and the bisexual poetics of *A Life-Drama. See* **12043.**

10317. KAO, SHE-RU. Byron's Cain: a disqualified champion of justice. BJ (32:2) 2004, 131–5.

10318. KUCICH, GREG. Keats, Shelley, Byron, and the Hunt circle. *In* (pp. 263–79) **8014.**

10319. LANGAN, CELESTE. Venice. *In* (pp. 261–85) **9217.**

10320. MÁNEK, BOHUSLAV. Early Czech translation of Byron's lyrical poems and the beginnings of Romanticism in Czech literature. *In* (pp. 101–9) **1373.**

10321. MELANEY, WILLIAM D. Ambiguous difference: ethical concern in Byron's *Manfred.* NLH (36:3) 2005, 461–75.

10322. MOZER, HADLEY J. 'I WANT a hero': advertising for an epic hero in *Don Juan.* SR (44:2) 2005, 239–60.

10323. MULVIHILL, JAMES. *The Love Song of J. Alfred Prufrock* and Byron's speaker in *Don Juan. See* **16289.**

10324. MUSSAPI, ROBERTO (ed. and trans.). I ragazzi che amavano il vento. *See* **12022.**

10325. NEWEY, VINCENT. Rival cultures: Charles Dickens and the Byronic legacy. *See* **10721.**

10326. O'NEIL, CATHERINE. Byron's sea in Pushkin and Lermontov. BJ (32:2) 2004, 101–13.

10327. —— Poets as dramatists: Pushkin and Byron's historical drama *Marino Faliero, Doge of Venice.* SEEJ (47:4) 2003, 589–608.

10328. PAPE, WALTER. Empathized with immediacy: improvisation, Romantic folk song and Goethe's concept of the 'born poet'. ERR (16:3) 2005, 361–72.

10329. RAVELHOFER, BARBARA.   Oral poetry and the printing press in Byron's *The Giaour* (1813). Romanticism (11:1) 2005, 23–40.

10330. RAY, MARTIN.   Thomas Hardy: four notes. *See* **11155.**

10331. RIGBY, MAIR.   'Prey to some cureless disquiet': Polidori's queer vampyre at the margins of Romanticism. *See* **11829.**

10332. SCHARNHORST, GARY.   Byron and Bret Harte. *See* **11180.**

10333. SCHMIDT, ARNOLD A.   Bligh, Christian, Murray, and Napoleon: Byronic mutiny from London to the South Seas. BJ (32:1) 2004, 21–30.

10334. SPENCE, GORDON.   The supernatural in *Manfred*. BJ (32:1) 2004, 1–8.

10335. STARNAWSKI, JERZY.   Literatura angielska w Bibliotece Narodowej 1921–1929: kulisy w świetle archiwum Stanisława Kota. (English literature in the National Library [series] 1921–1929 in the light of Stanisław Kot's archive.) *In* (pp. 227–37) **3756.**

10336. STAUFFER, ANDREW M.   Byron, the pyramids, and 'uncertain paper'. WordsC (36:1) 2005, 11–15.

10337. STEIN, ATARA.   The Byronic hero in film, fiction, and television. Carbondale: Southern Illinois UP, 2004. pp. 260. Rev. by David A. Janssen in GothS (7:2) 2005, 219–21.

10338. STRAND, ERIC.   Byron's *Don Juan* as a global allegory. SR (43:4) 2004, 503–36.

10339. THROSBY, CORIN.   Flirting with fame: Byron's anonymous female fans. BJ (32:2) 2004, 115–23.

10340. WAINWRIGHT, STEVEN P.; WILLIAMS, CLARE.   Biography and vulnerability: loss, dying and death in the Romantic paintings of J. M. W. Turner (1775–1851). *See* **12232.**

10341. WILSON, FRANCES.   Portrait of the artist as an icon. TLS, 29 July 2005, 32 (review-article).

10342. ZANI, STEVEN.   Clubfoot, caul and controversy: Byron biography and the foundation of genius. BJ (32:1) 2004, 31–8.

10343. ZUCKER, MARILYN SLUTZKY.   Lord Orlando, Lord Byron. *See* **20444.**

George Washington Cable

10344. GERMANA, MICHAEL.   Real change: George Washington Cable's *The Grandissimes* and the crime of '73. AQ (61:3) 2005, 75–108.

10345. HASPEL, PAUL.   Gothicism in Rebel gray: postbellum evolution of the Southern gothic in the early fiction of George Washington Cable. SDR (43:1/2) 2005, 88–104.

10346. SILVA, REINALDO.   The ethnic garden in Portuguese American writing. *See* **19909.**

10347. WAGNER, BRYAN.   Disarmed and dangerous: the strange history of Bras-Coupé. Representations (92) 2005, 117–51.

Hall Caine

10348. HAMMOND, MARY.   Hall Caine and the melodrama on page, stage and screen. NCT (31:1) 2004, 39–57.

Alice Mona Caird ('G. Noel Hatton')

10349. HEILMANN, ANN.   Medea at the *fin de siècle*: revisionist uses of Classical myth in Mona Caird's *The Daughters of Danaus*. VicR (31:1) 2005, 21–39.

10350. —— New Woman strategies: Sarah Grand, Olive Schreiner, Mona Caird. *See* **11092**.

10351. RICHARDSON, ANGELIQUE.   Eugenics and freedom at the *fin de siècle*. *In* (pp. 275–86) **1226**.

10352. ROSENBERG, TRACEY S.   A challenge to Victorian motherhood: Mona Caird and Gertrude Atherton. WWr (12:3) 2005, 485–504.

10353. SURRIDGE, LISA.   Narrative time, history, and feminism in Mona Caird's *The Daughters of Danaus*. WWr (12:1) 2005, 127–41.

10354. ŽABICKA, AGNIESZKA.   Female gothic motifs in Mona Caird's *The Wing of Azrael*. VicR (31:1) 2005, 5–20.

Maria, Lady Callcott (1745–1842)

10355. COMER, DENISE K.   'White child is good, black child his [or her] slave': women, children, and empire in early nineteenth-century India. *See* **12036**.

Thomas Campbell

10356. MAZZEO, TILAR J.   The impossibility of being Anglo-American: the rhetoric of emigration and transatlanticism in British Romantic culture, 1791–1833. *See* **8980**.

Jane Welsh Carlyle

10357. CAMPBELL, IAN.   Geraldine Jewsbury: Jane Welsh Carlyle's 'best friend'? *In* (pp. 185–95) **10393**.

10358. CHAMBERLAIN, KATHY.   A 'creative adventure': Jane Welsh Carlyle's 'simple story'. *In* (pp. 230–9) **10393**.

10359. CHRISTIANSON, AILEEN.   Jane Welsh Carlyle's travel narratives: 'portable perspectives'. *In* (pp. 209–18) **10393**.

10360. FIELDING, KENNETH J.; SORENSEN, DAVID R. (eds).   Jane Carlyle: newly selected letters. (Bibl. 2004, 10352.) Rev. by Sylvère Monod in EA (58:2) 2005, 220–2.

10361. KINSER, BRENT E.   A not so 'simple story': Jane Welsh Carlyle and Charlotte Brontë's *Shirley*. *See* **10169**.

10362. RUSSELL, PENNY.   Wife stories: narrating marriage and self in the life of Jane Franklin. *See* **9828**.

10363. TARR, RODGER L.   'The Victorian lady' – Jane Welsh Carlyle and the psycho-feminist myth: a retrospective. *In* (pp. 196–208) **10393**.

Thomas Carlyle

10364. APROBERTS, RUTH.   The historian as Shandean humorist: Carlyle and Frederick the Great. *In* (pp. 15–26) **10393**.

10365. BRETON, ROB.   The stones of happiness: Ruskin and working-class culture. *See* **11889**.

10366. CAMPBELL, IAN.   The Brontës and power. *See* **10155**.

10367. CRAIG, CAIRNS.   Carlyle and Symbolism. *In* (pp. 102–12) **10393**.

10368. DeLaura, David. Carlyle and the 'insane' fine arts. *In* (pp. 27–39) **10393.**

10369. Dickerson, Vanessa D. Performing Blackness: Carlyle and *The Nigger Question. In* (pp. 151–8) **10393.**

10370. Donovan, David. Spiritual selfhood and the modern idea: Thomas Carlyle and T. S. Eliot. Philadelphia, PA: XLibris, 2004. pp. 237.

10371. Edwards, Owen Dudley. 'True Thomas': Carlyle, Young Ireland, and the legacy of millenialism. *In* (pp. 60–76) **10393.**

10372. Engel, Mark. Collating Carlyle: patterns of revision in *Heroes, Sartor Resartus*, and *The French Revolution. In* (pp. 240–7) **10393.**

10373. Fielding, Kenneth J. Justice to Carlyle's memory: the later Carlyle. *In* (pp. 1–14) **10393.**

10374. Groves, David. Carlyle, Dr James Browne, and the 'mystical blackguard' Werner. NQ (52:4) 2005, 469–71.

10375. Hill, Marylu. The 'magical speculum': vision and truth in Carlyle's early histories. *In* (pp. 83–90) **10393.**

10376. Hori, Tomohiro. The Victorian sage, autobiography, and the questions of genre and interpretation: on some Carlylean motifs in *The Education of Henry Adams. See* **9889.**

10377. Jumeau, Alain. Translating Carlyle's French Revolution: a French perspective. *In* (pp. 77–82) **10393.**

10378. Keane, Patrick J. Emerson, Romanticism, and intuitive reason: the transatlantic 'light of all our day'. *See* **10982.**

10379. Kinser, Brent. Mark Twain, Thomas Carlyle, and shooting Niagara. *In* (pp. 113–24) **10393.**

10380. Kinser, Brent E. A not so 'simple story': Jane Welsh Carlyle and Charlotte Brontë's *Shirley. See* **10169.**

10381. Lawton, Lesley. 'Celestial hieroglyphs': exegetical authority in Thomas Carlyle's *Sartor Resartus.* Anglophonia (17) 2005, 381–90.

10382. Lloyd, David. The indigent sublime: specters of Irish hunger. Representations (92) 2005, 152–85.

10383. Morelli, Henriette M. 'An incarnated word': a revisionary reading of 'The Insurrection of Women' in Thomas Carlyle's *The French Revolution.* WS (34:7) 2005, 533–50.

10384. Schlicke, Paul. Hazlitt, Horne, and *The Spirit of the Age. See* **11250.**

10385. Sorensen, David R. 'A Scotch Proudhon': Carlyle, Herzen, and the French Revolutions of 1789 and 1848. *In* (pp. 40–59) **10393.**

10386. Taylor, Andrew. 'The same old sausage': Thomas Carlyle and the James family. *In* (pp. 125–36) **10393.**

10387. Vanden Bossche, Chris R. Cedric the Saxon and the Haiti Duke of Marmalade: race in *Past and Present. In* (pp. 137–50) **10393.**

10388. Wendling, Ronald C. Prophet and friend: the reflective politics of Carlyle and Coleridge. *In* (pp. 91–101) **10393.**

The Carlyles

10389. ASHTON, ROSEMARY. The uses of German literature in the Carlyles' courtship. *In* (pp. 170–84) **10393**.

10390. CLARKE, NORMA. 'Wonderful worlds up yonder': Rousseau and the erotics of teaching and learning. *In* (pp. 219–29) **10393**.

10391. MCINTOSH, SHEILA. The Carlyles and 'phantasm aristocracy'. *In* (pp. 159–69) **10393**.

10392. PITE, RALPH (gen. ed.). Lives of Victorian literary figures III: Elizabeth Gaskell, the Carlyles and John Ruskin by their contemporaries: vol. 2, The Carlyles. Ed. by Aileen Christianson and Sheila McIntosh. London; Brookfield, VT: Pickering & Chatto, 2005. pp. xliv, 470.

10393. SORENSEN, DAVID R.; TARR, RODGER L. (eds). The Carlyles at home and abroad. Aldershot; Burlington, VT: Ashgate, 2004. pp. xii, 255. Rev. by Francis O'Gorman in TLS, 21 Jan. 2005, 28; by Marion Shaw in RES (56:227) 2005, 799–801.

Edward Carpenter (1844–1929)

10394. DOTY, MARK. Form, eros, and the unspeakable: Whitman's stanzas. *See* **12308**.

'Lewis Carroll' (Charles Lutwidge Dodgson)

10395. ALEXANDER, CHRISTINE. Play and apprenticeship: the culture of family magazines. *In* (pp. 31–50) **9164**.

10396. BILLONE, AMY. The boy who lived: from Carroll's Alice and Barrie's Peter Pan to Rowling's Harry Potter. ChildLit (32) 2004, 178–202.

10397. DEMAKOS, MATTHEW. Accountably and unaccountably shy. Carrollian (14) 2004, 9–42.

10398. DOCHERTY, JOHN. A Christmas Carroll. Carrollian (14) 2004, 3–8.

10399. FIRTICH, NIKOLAI. Worldbackwards: Lewis Carroll, Aleksei Kruchenykh and Russian alogism. SEEJ (48:4) 2004, 593–606.

10400. FOULKES, RICHARD. Lewis Carroll and the Victorian theatre: theatricals in a quiet life. Aldershot; Burlington, VT: Ashgate, 2005. pp. xi, 224.

10401. GARDNER, MARTIN. A Gardner's bouquet: new annotations. KnLet (75) 2005, 1–6.

10402. GEER, JENNIFER. 'All sorts of pitfalls and surprises': competing views of idealized girlhood in Lewis Carroll's Alice books. ChildLit (31) 2003, 1–24.

10403. GROSSMAN, MORRIS. Carroll's platonic love. KnLet (75) 2005, 11–14.

10404. LECERCLE, JEAN-JACQUES. Parody as cultural memory. *See* **18381**.

10405. LOCKWOOD, DAVID. Pictorial puzzles from *Alice*. Carrollian (14) 2004, 43–61.

10406. LOVETT, CHARLIE. Lewis Carroll among his books: a descriptive catalogue of the private library of Charles L. Dodgson. Jefferson, NC; London: McFarland, 2005. pp. vii, 375.

10407. MORRIS, FRANKIE. Artist of Wonderland: the life, political cartoons, and illustrations of Tenniel. *See* **103**.

10408. —— Researching *Artist of Wonderland*. *See* **104**.

10409. SMITH, WENDY. The abuses of enchantment: why some children's classics give parents the creeps. *See* **14355.**

10410. WOOLF, JENNY. Sounds and sense: the looking-glass secrets of Lewis Carroll's bank account. TLS, 11 Feb. 2005, 14–15.

Mary Carshore (Mrs W. S. Carshore)

10411. GIBSON, MARY ELLIS. Poems of Mary Carshore: the Indian legacy of L.E.L. and Tom Moore. VIJ (32) 2004, 63–79.

Henry Francis Cary (1772–1844)

10412. CRISAFULLI, EDOARDO. The vision of Dante: Cary's translation of *The Divine Comedy.* Market Harborough: Troubadour, 2003. pp. xi, 348. (Troubadour Italian studies.) Rev. by Alison Milbank in MLR (100:3) 2005, 838–9.

Sir Roger Casement (1864–1916)

10413. MCDIARMID, LUCY. The Irish art of controversy. *See* **16824.**

10414. Ó SÍOCHÁIN, SÉAMAS; O'SULLIVAN, MICHAEL (eds). The eyes of another race: Roger Casement's Congo report and 1903 diary. Dublin: University College Dublin Press, 2003. pp. xvi, 350, (plates) 8. Rev. by Brian Dolan in Journeys (5:2) 2004, 95–8.

James Casey (1824–1909)

10415. FOLEY, JOHN. The historical origins of Flann O'Brien's Jem Casey. *See* **18542.**

Sir George Tomkyns Chesney

10416. RIEDER, JOHN. Science fiction, colonialism, and the plot of invasion. *See* **14263.**

Charles W. Chesnutt

10417. CASH, WILEY. 'Those folks downstairs believe in ghosts': the eradication of folklore in the literature of Charles W. Chesnutt. CLAJ (49:2) 2005, 184–204.

10418. HOLMES, DAVID G. Revisiting racialized voice: African American ethos in language and literature. Carbondale: Southern Illinois UP, 2004. pp. xi, 131. Rev. by Keith D. Miller in RhR (24:3) 2005, 348–50.

10419. KANG, NANCY. 'As if I had entered a Paradise': fugitive slave narratives and cross-border literary history. AAR (39:3) 2005, 431–57.

10420. KOY, CHRISTOPHER E. The mule as metaphor in the fiction of Charles Waddell Chesnutt. *In* (pp. 93–100) **3734.**

10421. LOGAN, SHIRLEY WILSON. 'To get an education and teach my people': rhetoric for social change. *In* (pp. 36–52) **2318.**

10422. PETRIE, PAUL R. Conscience and purpose: fiction and social consciousness in Howells, Jewett, Chesnutt, and Cather. Tuscaloosa; London: Alabama UP, 2005. pp. xvii, 234. (Studies in American literary realism and naturalism.)

10423. WONHAM, HENRY B. Playing the races: ethnic caricature and American literary realism. (Bibl. 2004, 10417.) Rev. by Kelly Richardson in SAH (third series) (11) 2004, 97–9.

Lydia Maria Child

10424. PERKINS, MAUREEN. Thoroughly modern mulatta: rethinking 'Old World' stereotypes in a 'New World' setting. Biography (28:1) 2005, 104–16.

10425. SWEET, NANCY F. Dissent and the daughter in *A New England Tale* and *Hobomok*. See **11953**.

Kate Chopin

10426. BRADLEY, PATRICIA L. *The Birth of Tragedy* and *The Awakening*: influences and intertextualities. SoLJ (37:2) 2005, 40–61.

10427. MARGRAF, ERIK. Kate Chopin's *The Awakening* as a naturalistic novel. ALR (37:2) 2005, 93–116.

10428. PARVULESCU, ANCA. To die laughing and to laugh at dying: revisiting *The Awakening*. NLH (36:3) 2005, 477–95.

10429. STEIN, ALLEN F. Women and autonomy in Kate Chopin's short fiction. New York; Frankfurt: Lang, 2005. pp. 156. (Modern American literature: new approaches, 45.)

10430. WIEGAND, WAYNE. Collecting contested titles: the experience of five small public libraries in the rural Midwest, 1893–1956. See **480**.

John Clare

10431. BATE, JONATHAN. John Clare: a biography. (Bibl. 2004, 10433.) Rev. by Michael O'Neill in WordsC (35:4) 2004, 194–6; by Lawrence Lipking in Parnassus (28:1/2) 2005, 74–99; by Greg Crossan in JCSJ (24) 2005, 87–90; by Colin Fleming in MR (28:3) 2005, 190–1.

10432. —— (ed.). 'I am': the selected poetry of John Clare. (Bibl. 2004, 10434.) Rev. by Michael O'Neill in WordsC (35:4) 2004, 194–6; by Lawrence Lipking in Parnassus (28:1/2) 2005, 74–99.

10433. —— Selected poems. London; Boston, MA: Faber & Faber, 2004. pp. 288. Rev. by R. K. R. Thornton in JCSJ (24) 2005, 80–6.

10434. COLCLOUGH, STEPHEN. 'Designated in print as "Mr John Clare"': the annuals and the field of reading, 1827–1835. JCSJ (24) 2005, 52–68.

10435. DAWSON, P. M. S. The making of Clare's *Poems Descriptive of Rural Life and Scenery* (1820). RES (56:224) 2005, 276–312.

10436. FAUBERT, MICHELLE. Cure, classification, and John Clare. VLC (33:1) 2005, 269–91.

10437. GOODRIDGE, JOHN; KEEGAN, BRIDGET. Clare and the traditions of labouring-class verse. *In* (pp. 280–95) **8014**.

10438. GORJI, MINA. Clare's 'Merry England'. JCSJ (24) 2005, 5–24.

10439. HEYES, BOB. Selling John Clare: the poet in the marketplace. JCSJ (24) 2005, 31–40.

10440. LIPKING, LAWRENCE. Visions of Clare. Parnassus (28:1/2) 2005, 74–99 (review-article).

10441. MABEY, RICHARD. Nature cure. London: Chatto & Windus, 2005. pp. 244. Rev. by Peter Reynolds in JCSJ (24) 2005, 90–2.

10442. MACFARLANE, ROBERT. A road of one's own: past and present artists of the randomly motivated walk. See **19461**.

10443. MACRAE, ALISDAIR.   Exile in British poetry. *In* (pp. 113–23) **14479**.

10444. ROBINSON, ERIC; POWELL, DAVID (eds).   John Clare: major works. Ed. by Tom Paulin. (Bibl. 1986, 7873.) Oxford; New York: OUP, 2004. pp. xxxiv, 531. (Oxford world's classics.) (Revised ed.: first ed. 1984.) (Orig. pub. as *John Clare*.) Rev. by R. K. R. Thornton in JCSJ (24) 2005, 78–80.

10445. —— —— DAWSON, P. M. S. (eds).   Poems of the middle period, 1822–1837: vol. 5. (Bibl. 2004, 10444.) Rev. by Mina Gorji in RES (56:225) 2005, 455–7; by Jonathan Bate in NQ (52:1) 2005, 131–4; by Kevin De Ornellas in ISLE (12:1) 2005, 250–1.

10446. SCHREY, MICK.   On the occasion inspiring *Song to Liberty*, an unsung Scottish anthem by John Clare: part II. JCSJ (24) 2005, 41–51.

10447. TREHANE, EMMA.   'Emma and Johnny': the friendship between Eliza Emmerson and John Clare. JCSJ (24) 2005, 69–77.

Marcus Clarke

10448. BIRNS, NICHOLAS.   Receptacle or reversal? Globalization down under in Marcus Clarke's *His Natural Life*. ColLit (32:2) 2005, 127–45.

10449. MOORE, TONY.   Urban iconoclast. Meanjin (64:1/2) 2005, 204–13.

Mary Cowden Clarke (1809–1898)

10450. BROWN, SARAH ANNES.   The prequel as palinode: Mary Cowden Clarke's *Girlhood of Shakespeare's Heroines*. ShS (58) 2005, 95–106.

Henry Ebenezer Clay (1844–1896)

10451. KINSELLA, JOHN.   Henry Clay: racist or not? VIJ (32) 2004, 9–35.

Arthur Hugh Clough

10452. HARRISON, ANTONY H.   Victorian culture wars: Alexander Smith, Arthur Hugh Clough, and Matthew Arnold in 1853. *See* **9933**.

10453. KENNY, ANTHONY.   Arthur Hugh Clough: a poet's life. London; New York: Continuum, 2005. pp. vi, 298.

10454. ——   For love of Fausta: Arthur Hugh Clough and the other Arnold. TLS, 7 Oct. 2005, 14–15.

10455. LAPORTE, CHARLES.   Spasmodic poetics and Clough's apostasies. VP (42:4) 2004, 521–36.

Frances Power Cobbe (1822–1904)

10456. HENRY, PEACHES.   The worthwhile life of a heterodox spinster – Frances Power Cobbe. A/B (19:1/2) 2004, 71–88.

10457. HUGHES, KATHRYN.   What she fancied. TLS, 23 Sept. 2005, 13 (review-article).

10458. WILLIAMSON, LORI.   Power and protest: Frances Power Cobbe and Victorian society. London; New York: Rivers Oram, 2005. pp. viii, 277. Rev. by Lori Hughes in TLS, 23 Sept. 2005, 13.

Richard Cobbold

10459. SHEPHEARD, RICHARD.   A coat of green: George Borrow and Horncastle horsefair (part 1). *See* **10125**.

Samuel Taylor Coleridge

10460. À COURT, FRANCIS. *Magnifique, mais ce n'est pas Daguerre*: some notes on the life of Tom Wedgwood. *See* **8665**.

10461. BARR, MARK L. The lyric dispensation: Coleridge, Mosaic law, and equivocal authority in *The Eolian Harp*. SR (44:3) 2005, 293–316.

10462. BARTH, J. ROBERT. Coleridge on beauty: beauty, love, and the 'beauty-making power'. Romanticism (11:1) 2005, 14–22.

10463. BAULCH, DAVID. Several hundred pages of promise: the phantom of the gothic in Peacock's *Nightmare Abbey* and Coleridge's *Biographia Literaria*. ColB (ns 25) 2005, 71–7.

10464. BAULCH, DAVID M. The 'perpetual exercise of an interminable quest': the *Biographia Literaria* and the Kantian revolution. SR (43:4) 2004, 557–81.

10465. BERKELEY, RICHARD. The anxiety of pantheism: hidden dimensions of Coleridge's transcendental deduction. Prism(s) (13) 2005, 1–25.

10466. BLACKWELL, MARK R. The gothic: moving in the world of novels. *In* (pp. 144–61) **6958**.

10467. BLADES, JOHN. Wordsworth and Coleridge: *Lyrical Ballads*. *See* **12461**.

10468. BRETT, R. L, *et al.* (ed.). Wordsworth and Coleridge: *Lyrical Ballads*. Introd. by Nicholas Roe. *See* **12463**.

10469. BURWICK, FREDERICK. Coleridge on Shakespeare, Goethe and Schiller. SJ (141) 2005, 70–80.

10470. —— De Quincey and animal magnetism. *See* **10604**.

10471. CARTWRIGHT, KEITH. Weave a circle round him thrice: Komunyakaa's Hoodoo balancing act. *See* **17514**.

10472. CHANDLER, DAVID. Coleridge satirized by Anne Plumptre. *See* **8864**.

10473. —— The early development of the 'Lake School' idea. *See* **12466**.

10474. CHRISTIE, WILLIAM. Coleridge and Wordsworth in *Pandaemonium*. *See* **13703**.

10475. COLBERT, BENJAMIN. Petrio-pindarics: John Wolcot and the Romantics. *See* **9128**.

10476. CONSTANTINE, MARY-ANN. Iolo Morganwg, Coleridge, and the Bristol lectures, 1795. NQ (52:1) 2005, 42–4.

10477. CURRELI, MARIO. Leitmotifs from Coleridge and Wagner in *Nostromo* and beyond. *See* **15871**.

10478. DOUGHERTY, MICHELLE RUGGABER. Virgil's Alecto as a possible model for Coleridge's Geraldine. NQ (52:4) 2005, 473–4.

10479. FAFLAK, JOEL. Romanticism and the pornography of talking. *See* **12477**.

10480. FARINA, JONATHAN V. Superstitious marginalia: Coleridge and *Waverley*. WordsC (36:1) 2005, 29–32.

10481. FERGUSON, FRANCES. Envy rising. *In* (pp. 132–48) **9217**.

10482. FLEISSNER, ROBERT F. Auden's *As I Walked Out One Evening*. *See* **15236**.

10483. GARRATT, EDMUND. The early friendship of Captain James Burney and Charles Lamb. *See* **11557.**

10484. GOH, ROBBIE B. H. (M)othering the nation: guilt, sexuality and the commercial state in Coleridge's gothic poetry. JNT (33:3) 2003, 270–91.

10485. GRAVIL, RICHARD. The Somerset sound; or, The darling child of speech. ColB (ns 26) 2005, 1–21.

10486. GREENE, THOMAS M. Poetry, signs, and magic. *See* **5946.**

10487. GREGORY, ALAN P. R. Coleridge and the conservative imagination. (Bibl. 2003, 9779.) Rev. by James Vigus in ColB (ns 26) 2005, 85–9.

10488. HALMI, NICHOLAS. Greek myths, Christian mysteries, and the tautegorical symbol. WordsC (36:1) 2005, 6–8.

10489. —— MAGNUSON, PAUL; MODIANO, RAIMONDA (eds). Coleridge's poetry and prose: authoritative texts, criticism. (Bibl. 2004, 10486.) Rev. by John Beer in Romanticism (11:1) 2005, 119–20.

10490. HIPOLITO, JEFFREY. 'Conscience the ground of consciousness': the moral epistemology of Coleridge's *Aids to Reflection*. JHI (65:3) 2004, 455–74.

10491. HOGLE, JERROLD E. *Christabel* as gothic: the abjection of instability. GothS (7:1) 2005, 18–28.

10492. HOPPS, GAVIN. Inhabiting a place beyond 'to be or not to be': the playful devotions of Byron and Coleridge. ColB (ns 25) 2005, 15–39.

10493. JAMES, FELICITY. Agreement, dissonance, dissent: the many conversations of *This Lime-Tree Bower*. ColB (ns 26) 2005, 37–57.

10494. KEANE, PATRICK J. Emerson, Romanticism, and intuitive reason: the transatlantic 'light of all our day'. *See* **10982.**

10495. KEYMER, THOMAS. Sterne and Romantic autobiography. *In* (pp. 173–93) **8014.**

10496. LARKIN, PETER. *Frost at Midnight* – some Coleridgean intertwinings. ColB (ns 26) 2005, 22–36.

10497. LEVY, MICHELLE. Discovery and the domestic affections in Coleridge and Shelley. SELit (44:4) 2004, 693–713.

10498. LUNA, ALINA M. Visual perversity: a re-articulation of maternal instinct. Lanham, MD: Lexington, 2004. pp. ix, 109.

10499. MCCOMBE, JOHN P. 'Oh, I see …': *The Birds* and the culmination of Hitchcock's hyper-Romantic vision. *See* **13474.**

10500. MAGNUSON, PAUL. The Lake School: Wordsworth and Coleridge. *In* (pp. 227–43) **8014.**

10501. MANNING, PETER J. Manufacturing the Romantic image: Hazlitt and Coleridge lecturing. *In* (pp. 227–45) **9217.**

10502. MAY, TIM. The Pantisocrats in College Street. *See* **12050.**

10503. MAZZEO, TILAR J. The impossibility of being Anglo-American: the rhetoric of emigration and transatlanticism in British Romantic culture, 1791–1833. *See* **8980.**

10504. MEURS, NORA. Resisting the silence: Coleridge's courtship of the sublime. ColB (ns 25) 2005, 40–5.

10505. MITCHELL, ROBERT. Adam Smith and Coleridge on the love of systems. ColB (ns 25) 2005, 54–60.

10506. MORRISON, ROBERT. De Quincey on *Mount Pleasant*: William Roscoe and *Confessions of an English Opium-Eater*. See **10635**.

10507. MULLEN, PETER. The religious opinions of Samuel Taylor Coleridge. CLB (123) 2003, 91–100.

10508. NATARAJAN, UTTARA. Hazlitt, Lamb, and the philosophy of familiarity. See **11243**.

10509. O'NEILL, MICHAEL. The gleam of those words: Coleridge and Shelley. KSR (19) 2005, 76–96.

10510. OSER, LEE. Tolkien and Coleridge: an encounter. ALSCN (11:4) 2005, 14–15.

10511. PERRY, SEAMUS. The little horror show. See **12510**.

10512. —— The Romantic matter of fact. WordsC (35:3) 2004, 103–7.

10513. —— Samuel Taylor Coleridge. (Bibl. 2004, 10510.) Rev. by Heidi Thomson in ColB (ns 26) 2005, 79–84.

10514. PETERFREUND, STUART. Dissent and ontological space in Romantic science and literature. See **8379**.

10515. PIGGIN, STUART; COOKE, DIANNE. Keeping alive the heart in the head: the significance of 'eternal language' in the aesthetics of Jonathan Edwards and S. T. Coleridge. See **8581**.

10516. POLGA, KIT. Dickens and the morality of imagination. See **10732**.

10517. POTKAY, ADAM. Coleridge's joy. WordsC (35:3) 2004, 107–13.

10518. PROCHÁZKA, MARTIN. Between hoax and ideology: theory and illusions of imagination in Chapter XIII of Coleridge's *Biographia Literaria*. *In* (pp. 119–32) **9193**.

10519. RIEM NATALE, ANTONELLA. The one life: Coleridge and Hinduism. Jaipur: Rawat, 2005. pp. xiv, 410.

10520. ROUSSEAU, G. S.; HAYCOCK, DAVID BOYD. Coleridge's choleras: *cholera morbus*, Asiatic cholera, and dysentery in early nineteenth-century England. BHM (77:2) 2003, 298–331.

10521. RULE, PHILIP C. Coleridge and Newman: the centrality of conscience. (Bibl. 2004, 10516.) Rev. by Ian Ker in VS (48:1) 2005, 190–1.

10522. SCHLUTZ, ALEXANDER. The dangers of imagination: Coleridgean dreams and nightmares. ColB (ns 25) 2005, 46–53.

10523. SONODA, AKIKO. Coleridge's later poetry and the rise of literary annuals. ColB (ns 26) 2005, 58–74.

10524. STELZIG, EUGENE. 'Spirit divine! With thee I'll wander': Mary Robinson and Coleridge in poetic dialogue. See **8974**.

10525. TAUSSIG, GURION. Coleridge and the idea of friendship, 1789–1804. (Bibl. 2004, 10519.) Rev. by David Vallins in MLR (100:1) 2005, 201–2.

10526. THOMAS, SOPHIE. Seeing things ('as they are'): Coleridge, Schiller, and the play of semblance. SR (43:4) 2004, 537–55.

10527. TOMLINSON, RICHARD S. Pivotal points in Coleridge's *Opus Maximum*. CLB (130) 2005, 43–55.

10528. Trott, Nicola. Wordsworth and the parodic school of criticism. *In* (pp. 71–97) **9305**.

10529. Ulmer, William A. Virtue of necessity: Coleridge's Unitarian moral theory. MP (102:3) 2005, 372–404.

10530. VanWinkle, Matthew. Fluttering on the grate: revision in *Frost at Midnight*. SR (43:4) 2004, 583–98.

10531. Vickers, Neil. Coleridge and the doctors, 1795–1806. (Bibl. 2004, 10527.) Rev. by Michael O'Neill in TLS, 13 May 2005, 11; by Alfred I. Tauber in JHM (60:3) 2005, 367–9; by Allan Ingram in BHM (79:4) 2005, 315–17; by Tim Fulford in ColB (ns 26) 2005, 75–8; by Michael John Kooy in EREA (3:2) 2005.

10532. Vincent, Patrick H. 'Switzerland no more': Turner, Wordsworth and the changed landscape of Revolution. *See* **12523**.

10533. Wedd, Mary. *The Pains of Sleep*. ColB (ns 25) 2005, 1–14.

10534. Wendling, Ronald C. Prophet and friend: the reflective politics of Carlyle and Coleridge. *In* (pp. 91–101) **10393**.

10535. Wilson, Eric G. Coleridge's melancholia: an anatomy of Limbo. (Bibl. 2004, 10531.) Rev. by Tim Davis in SoHR (39:4) 2005, 389–92.

10536. Wu, Duncan. The road to Nether Stowey. *In* (pp. 83–97) **11245**.

John Payne Collier (1789–1883)

10537. Anon. Shakespeare in the nineteenth century. *See* **5784**.

10538. Freeman, Arthur; Freeman, Janet Ing. John Payne Collier: scholarship and forgery in the nineteenth century. (Bibl. 2004, 10538.) Rev. in BC (54:3) 2005, 335–56; by Jeffrey Kahan in LitIm (7:2) 2005, 263–8; by R. A. Foakes in PBSA (99:2) 2005, 319–21; by K. K. Ruthven in ShY (15) 2005, 421–7; by Tom Lockwood in Library (6:3) 2005, 350–2; by A. S. G. Edwards in SHARP (14:3) 2005, 6–7; by Stanley Stewart in BJJ (12) 2005, 233–54.

10539. Stewart, Stanley. The short happy life of the 'Old Corrector': John Payne Collier. BJJ (12) 2005, 233–54 (review-article).

John Churton Collins (1848–1908)

10540. Olsen, Stein Haugom. Progress in literary studies. *See* **14947**.

Wilkie Collins (1824–1889)

10541. Baker, William (ed.). The public face of Wilkie Collins: the collected letters: vol. 1, Letters 1831–1864. London; Brookfield, VT: Pickering & Chatto, 2005. pp. xciv, 334.

10542. —— The public face of Wilkie Collins: the collected letters: vol. 2, Letters 1865–1873. London; Brookfield, VT: Pickering & Chatto, 2005. pp. 430.

10543. —— The public face of Wilkie Collins: the collected letters: vol. 3, Letters 1874–1883. London; Brookfield, VT: Pickering & Chatto, 2005. pp. 455.

10544. —— The public face of Wilkie Collins: the collected letters: vol. 4, Letters 1884–1889. London; Brookfield, VT: Pickering & Chatto, 2005. pp. 456.

10545. Blumberg, Ilana. Collins's *Moonstone*: the Victorian novel as sacrifice, theft, gift and debt. StudN (37:2) 2005, 162–86.

10546. Edgecombe, Rodney Stenning. Dickens and the comedy of abbreviation. *See* **10676**.

10547. EMRYS, A. B.   *Laura*, Vera, and Wilkie: deep sensation roots of a *noir* novel. *See* **15719.**

10548. GLADDEN, SAMUEL LYNDON.   Spectacular deceptions: closets, secrets, and identity in Wilkie Collins's *Poor Miss Finch*. VLC (33:2) 2005, 467–86.

10549. HARRINGTON, ELLEN.   Failed detectives and dangerous females: Wilkie Collins, Arthur Conan Doyle, and the detective short story. JSSE (45) 2005, 13–28.

10550. JACKSON, NOEL B.   Rethinking the cultural divide: Walter Pater, Wilkie Collins, and the legacies of Wordsworthian aesthetics. *See* **11780.**

10551. PHILPOTT, HELEN.   'Something dangerous in her nature': madwomen in *Jane Eyre* and *The Woman in White*. *In* (pp. 23–37) **10222.**

10552. PYKETT, LYN.   Wilkie Collins. Oxford; New York: OUP, 2005. pp. xvii, 254. (Oxford world's classics.) (Authors in context.)

10553. STRAHAN, LINDA.   There's a hole in the (Inspector) Bucket: the Victorian police in fact and fiction. *See* **10748.**

10554. WAGNER, TAMARA.   Victorian fictions of the nerves: telepathy and depression in Wilkie Collins's *The Two Destinies*. VIJ (32) 2004, 189–213.

James Collinson (1825–1881)

10555. BENTLEY, D. M. R.   The principal Pre-Raphaelite pictures of James Collinson. VicR (30:1) 2004, 21–43.

Anna Julia Cooper

10556. GLASS, KATHY L.   Tending to the roots: Anna Julia Cooper's sociopolitical thought and activism. Meridians (6:1) 2005, 23–55.

10557. WEST, ELIZABETH.   Cooper and Crummell: dialogics of race and womanhood. *In* (pp. 81–102) **2410.**

J. Fenimore Cooper

10558. FINGER, ROLAND.   The reassurance of sororicide. PCP (40:1) 2005, 117–37.

10559. LOGES, MAX L.   Cooper's *The Prairie*. Exp (63:2) 2005, 74–6.

10560. MASTERS, JOSHUA J.   Reading the book of nature, inscribing the savage mind: George Catlin and the textualization of the American West. AmS (46:2) 2005, 63–89.

10561. PEPRNÍK, MICHAL.   Cooper's Indians: typology and function. *In* (pp. 127–33) **3734.**

10562. ——   The making of American national literature: the war over J. F. Cooper in 19th-century criticism. *In* (pp. 72–82) **1368.**

10563. ——   Moravian origins of J. F. Cooper's Indians. *In* (pp. 75–92) **3939.**

10564. ——   The recoil effect of retaliation: Leatherstocking's unerring arm of (divine?) justice. *In* (pp. 153–7) **3753.**

10565. RUSSO, JOHN PAUL.   Isle of the Dead: a Classical topos in J. Fenimore Cooper and Sheridan Le Fanu. LAm (24:101) 2004, 53–102.

10566. VERHOEVEN, WIL.   Ecology as requiem: nature, nationhood and history in Francis Parkman's *History of the American Forest*. *In* (pp. 137–52) **9237.**

10567. VINCENT, PATRICK H. 'Natural arabesques': James Fenimore Cooper's Republican ideal on the Léman. SPELL (16) 2003, 37–50.

Thomas Cooper (1805–1892)

10568. KLAUS, H. GUSTAV. Mrs Rochester and Mr Cooper: alternative visions of class, history and rebellion in the 'hungry forties'. See 10170.

'Barry Cornwall' (Bryan Waller Procter)

10569. TURLEY, RICHARD MARGGRAF. 'Amorous cavaliers': Keats, Barry Cornwall, and Francis Jeffrey. See 11537.

10570. —— Bright stars and bosom-friends: John Keats and Barry Cornwall. See 11538.

William Johnson Cory (1823–1892)

10571. KAYLOR, MICHAEL M. 'In thy cedarn prison thou waitest': Johnson's *Ionica* and Uranian intertextuality. In (pp. 79–85) 3734.

Joseph Cottle

10572. MAY, TIM. The Pantisocrats in College Street. See 12050.

10573. MORRISON, ROBERT. Chatterton at the races: De Quincey, Cottle, Southey, and the *Battle of Hastynges*. See 8469.

Palmer Cox (1840–1924)

10574. MARGERUM, EILEEN. Palmer Cox: telling stories to produce modern children. In (pp. 89–107) 9168.

Hannah Crafts

10575. GATES, HENRY LOUIS, JR; ROBBINS, HOLLIS (eds). In search of Hannah Crafts: critical essays on *The Bondwoman's Narrative*. (Bibl. 2004, 10591.) Rev. by Elaine Showalter and English Showalter in LRB (27:16) 2005, 9–10; by Shirley Wilson Logan in Legacy (22:2) 2005, 209–10.

10576. HASLAM, JASON. 'The strange ideas of right and justice': prison, slavery and other horrors in *The Bondwoman's Narrative*. GothS (7:1) 2005, 29–40.

10577. SHOWALTER, ELAINE; SHOWALTER, ENGLISH. Every single one matters. LRB (27:16) 2005, 9–10 (review-article).

Stephen Crane

10578. FAGG, JOHN. Arcane subjects / urbane tones: Stephen Crane's Sullivan County sketches. StCS (13:2) 2004, 10–20.

10579. —— Stephen Crane and the literary sketch: genre and history in *Sailing Day Scenes* and *Coney Island's Failing Days*. ALR (38:1) 2005, 1–17.

10580. KUGA, SHUNJI. Feminine domesticity and the feral city: Stephen Crane's *George's Mother*, *Maggie*, and *A Detail*. StCS (13:2) 2004, 21–31.

10581. LAWSON, ANDREW. The red badge of class: Stephen Crane and the industrial army. LitH (14:2) 2005, 53–68.

10582. LINK, ERIC CARL. Lactantius, teleology, and American literature. See 8644.

10583. MASUZAKI, KOU. Stephen Crane no suramu hyosho to kangoku: imin kyofu to 19 seiki-matsu hanzaisha-ron. (Stephen Crane's representation of the slums and prison: immigrants as criminals in 1890s crime discourse.) StAL (41) 2004, 19–35.

10584. SCHAEFER, MICHAEL. Stephen Crane in the time of shock and awe: teaching *The Red Badge of Courage* during the Iraq War. StCS (13:2) 2004, 2–9.

10585. ZHANG, FANGFANG. A reinterpretation of the hero model in *The Red Badge of Courage*. FLS (115) 2005, 128–32. (In Chinese.)

Isabella Valancy Crawford

10586. DEVEREUX, CECILY. The search for a livable past: Frye, Crawford, and the healing link. *In* (pp. 281–300) **9191.**

Thomas Crofton Croker (1798–1854)

10587. GOLIGHTLY, KAREN B. Transforming the Other: the merrow of Croker's *Fairy Legends* and the 'little Jewess' of *Daniel Deronda*. *See* **10922.**

Margaret Cullen (d.1837)

10588. RENDALL, JANE. 'Women that would plague me with rational conversation': aspiring women and Scottish Whigs, *c*.1790–1830. *In* (pp. 326–47) **8016.**

Charles Darwin (1809–1882)

10589. CALDWELL, JANIS MCLARREN. Literature and medicine in nineteenth-century Britain: from Mary Shelley to George Eliot. *See* **9526.**

10590. DAVIS, WHITNEY. Decadence and the organic metaphor. *See* **2269.**

10591. LEVINE, GEORGE. Darwin's romance. Raritan (25:2) 2005, 50–77.

10592. PAGETTI, CLAUDIO. Autobiografie darwiniane: *collecting* e *recollecting*. *In* (pp. 71–83) **12577.**

Rebecca Harding Davis

10593. WOMACK, WHITNEY A. Reforming women's reform literature: Rebecca Harding Davis's rewriting of the industrial novel. *In* (pp. 105–31) **9513.**

Richard Harding Davis

10594. GILLMAN, SUSAN. The new, newest thing: have American Studies gone imperial? AmLH (17:1) 2005, 196–214 (review-article).

10595. MILLER, CHAR. Proving ground: Richard Harding Davis in the American West. SRev (90:1) 2005, 13–28.

10596. SEELYE, JOHN D. War games: Richard Harding Davis and the new imperialism. (Bibl. 2004, 10631.) Rev. by Thomas Schoonover in JAH (91:1) 2004, 273–4; by Susan Gillman in AmLH (17:1) 2005, 196–214.

Sir Humphry Davy

10597. PETERFREUND, STUART. Dissent and ontological space in Romantic science and literature. *See* **8379.**

J. W. De Forest

10598. ETTER, WILLIAM. Cripple, soldier, crippled soldier: Alfred Bellard's Civil War memoir. *See* **9807.**

Martin R. Delany

10599. ADELEKE, TUNDE. Without regard to race: the other Martin Robison Delany. Jackson; London: Mississippi UP, 2003. pp. xxxiii, 274. Rev. by Tony Martin in JAH (92:1) 2005, 215–16.

10600. BROWN, KIMBERLY NICHELE. Sniffing the 'calypso magnolia': unearthing the Caribbean presence in the South (response to John Lowe). SCR (22:1) 2005, 81–6.

10601. LOWE, JOHN. 'Calypso magnolia': the Caribbean side of the South. SCR (22:1) 2005, 54–80.

James De Mille

10602. KOLINSKÁ, KLÁRA. 'All that they saw was the message itself': textual calamities in Flaubert and De Mille. *In* (pp. 87–92) **3734**.

Thomas De Quincey

10603. BURT, E. S. Hospitality in autobiography: Levinas *chez* De Quincey. ELH (71:4) 2004, 867–97.

10604. BURWICK, FREDERICK. De Quincey and animal magnetism. WordsC (36:1) 2005, 32–40.

10605. DUFFY, CIAN. 'His *canaille* of an audience': Thomas De Quincey and the revolution of reading. SR (44:1) 2005, 7–22.

10606. DUPERRAY, MAX. Le promeneur londonien au xixe siècle: une excursion dans l'obscur. CVE (61) 2005, 135–45.

10607. FAFLAK, JOEL. Romanticism and the pornography of talking. *See* **12477**.

10608. FREY, ANNE. De Quincey's imperial systems. SR (44:1) 2005, 41–61.

10609. JAGOE, EVA-LYNN ALICIA. Degrading forms of pantomime: Englishness and shame in De Quincey. SR (44:1) 2005, 23–40.

10610. LINDOP, GREVEL (gen. ed.). The works of Thomas De Quincey: vol. 1, Writings, 1799–1820. Ed. by Barry Symonds. (Bibl. 2004, 104799.) Rev. by Charles Z. Rzepka in SR (44:1) 2005, 81–7.

10611. —— The works of Thomas De Quincey: vol. 2, *Confessions of an English Opium-Eater* 1821–1856. Ed. by Grevel Lindop. (Bibl. 2004, 104800.) Rev. by Charles Z. Rzepka in SR (44:1) 2005, 81–7.

10612. —— The works of Thomas De Quincey: vol. 3, Articles and translations from the *London Magazine, Blackwood's Magazine* and others 1821–1824. Ed. by Frederick Burwick. (Bibl. 2004, 104801.) Rev. by Charles Z. Rzepka in SR (44:1) 2005, 81–7.

10613. —— The works of Thomas De Quincey: vol. 4, Articles and translations from the *London Magazine; Walladmor* 1824–1825. Ed. by Frederick Burwick. (Bibl. 2004, 104802.) Rev. by Charles Z. Rzepka in SR (44:1) 2005, 81–7.

10614. —— The works of Thomas De Quincey: vol. 5, Articles from the *Edinburgh Saturday Post* 1827–1828. Ed. by David Groves. (Bibl. 2004, 104803.) Rev. by Charles Z. Rzepka in SR (44:1) 2005, 81–7.

10615. —— The works of Thomas De Quincey: vol. 6, Articles from the *Edinburgh Evening Post, Blackwood's Edinburgh Magazine* and the *Edinburgh*

Literary Gazette 1826-1829. Ed. by David Groves and Grevel Lindop. (Bibl. 2004, 104804.) Rev. by Charles Z. Rzepka in SR (44:1) 2005, 81-7.

10616. —— The works of Thomas De Quincey: vol. 7, Articles from the *Edinburgh Literary Gazette* and *Blackwood's Magazine* 1829-1831. Ed. by Robert Morrison. (Bibl. 2004, 104805.) Rev. by Charles Z. Rzepka in SR (44:1) 2005, 81-7.

10617. —— The works of Thomas De Quincey: vol. 8, Articles from *Blackwood's Edinburgh Magazine* and *The Gallery of Portraits*; *Klosterheim; or, The Masque* 1831-2. Ed. by Robert Morrison. (Bibl. 2003, 9927.) Rev. by Nicholas Halmi in WordsC (35:4) 2004, 201-3; by Daniel Brown in SR (44:1) 2005, 87-100.

10618. —— The works of Thomas De Quincey: vol. 9, Articles from *Blackwood's Edinburgh Magazine* and *Tait's Edinburgh Magazine* 1832-8. Ed. by Grevel Lindop, Robert Morrison and Barry Symonds. (Bibl. 2003, 9928.) Rev. by Nicholas Halmi in WordsC (35:4) 2004, 201-3; by Daniel Brown in SR (44:1) 2005, 87-100.

10619. —— The works of Thomas De Quincey: vol. 10, Articles from *Tait's Edinburgh Magazine* 1834-8. Ed. by Alina Clej. London; Brookfield, VT: Pickering & Chatto, 2003. pp. xvi, 435. (Pickering masters.) Rev. by Nicholas Halmi in WordsC (35:4) 2004, 201-3; by Michael Wheeler in SR (44:1) 2005, 100-12.

10620. —— The works of Thomas De Quincey: vol. 11, Articles from *Tait's Edinburgh Magazine* and *Blackwood's Magazine* 1838-41. Ed. by Julian North. London; Brookfield, VT: Pickering & Chatto, 2003. pp. x, 722. (Pickering masters.) Rev. by Nicholas Halmi in WordsC (35:4) 2004, 201-3; by Michael Wheeler in SR (44:1) 2005, 100-12.

10621. —— The works of Thomas De Quincey: vol. 12, Articles from *Blackwood's Edinburgh Magazine* 1840-1. Ed. by Grevel Lindop. (Bibl. 2003, 9929.) Rev. by Nicholas Halmi in WordsC (35:4) 2004, 201-3; by Daniel Brown in SR (44:1) 2005, 87-100.

10622. —— The works of Thomas De Quincey: vol. 13, Articles from *Blackwood's Edinburgh Magazine* and the *Encyclopaedia Britannica* 1841-2. Ed. by Grevel Lindop and John Whale. (Bibl. 2003, 9930.) Rev. by Nicholas Halmi in WordsC (35:4) 2004, 201-3; by Daniel Brown in SR (44:1) 2005, 87-100.

10623. —— The works of Thomas De Quincey: vol. 14, Articles from *Blackwood's Edinburgh Magazine* 1842-3. Ed. by John Whale. (Bibl. 2003, 9931.) Rev. by Nicholas Halmi in WordsC (35:4) 2004, 201-3; by Daniel Brown in SR (44:1) 2005, 87-100.

10624. —— The works of Thomas De Quincey: vol. 15, Articles from *Blackwood's Edinburgh Magazine* and *Tait's Edinburgh Magazine* 1844-6. Ed. by Frederick Burwick. London; Brookfield, VT: Pickering & Chatto, 2003. pp. x, 754. (Pickering masters.) Rev. by Nicholas Halmi in WordsC (35:4) 2004, 201-3; by Michael Wheeler in SR (44:1) 2005, 100-12.

10625. —— The works of Thomas De Quincey: vol. 16, Articles from *Tait's Edinburgh Magazine, MacPhail's Edinburgh Ecclesiastical Journal*, the *Glasgow Athenaeum Album* the *North British Review* and *Blackwood's Edinburgh*

Magazine 1842–3. Ed. by John Whale. London; Brookfield, VT: Pickering & Chatto, 2003. pp. xviii, 751. (Pickering masters.) Rev. by Nicholas Halmi in WordsC (35:4) 2004, 201–3; by Michael Wheeler in SR (44:1) 2005, 100–12.

10626. —— The works of Thomas De Quincey: vol. 17, Articles from *Hogg's Instructor* and *Tait's Edinburgh Magazine* 1850–2. Ed. by Edmund Baxter. (Bibl. 2003, 9932.) Rev. by Nicholas Halmi in WordsC (35:4) 2004, 201–3; by Daniel Brown in SR (44:1) 2005, 87–100.

10627. —— The works of Thomas De Quincey: vol. 18, 1853–8. Ed. by Edmund Baxter. (Bibl. 2003, 9933.) Rev. by Nicholas Halmi in WordsC (35:4) 2004, 201–3; by Daniel Brown in SR (44:1) 2005, 87–100.

10628. —— The works of Thomas De Quincey: vol. 19, Autobiographic sketches. Ed. by Daniel Sanjiv Roberts. London; Brookfield, VT: Pickering & Chatto, 2003. pp. xx, 499. (Pickering masters.) Rev. by Nicholas Halmi in WordsC (35:4) 2004, 201–3; by Michael Wheeler in SR (44:1) 2005, 100–12.

10629. —— The works of Thomas De Quincey: vol. 20, Prefaces &c. to the collected editions, published addenda, marginalia, manuscript addenda, undatable manuscripts. Ed. by Frederick Burwick. London; Brookfield, VT: Pickering & Chatto, 2003. pp. xv, 509. (Pickering masters.) Rev. by Nicholas Halmi in WordsC (35:4) 2004, 201–3; by Michael Wheeler in SR (44:1) 2005, 100–12.

10630. —— The works of Thomas De Quincey: vol. 21, Transcripts of unlocated manuscripts; index. Ed. by Grevel Lindop. London; Brookfield, VT: Pickering & Chatto, 2003. pp. ix, 377. (Pickering masters.) Rev. by Nicholas Halmi in WordsC (35:4) 2004, 201–3; by Michael Wheeler in SR (44:1) 2005, 100–12.

10631. MCDONAGH, JOSEPHINE. De Quincey, Malthus and the anachronism-effect. SR (44:1) 2005, 63–80.

10632. MANNING, PETER J. Manufacturing the Romantic image: Hazlitt and Coleridge lecturing. *In* (pp. 227–45) **9217**.

10633. MILLIGAN, BARRY. Morphine-addicted doctors, the English opium-eater, and embattled medical authority. VLC (33:2) 2005, 541–53.

10634. MORRISON, ROBERT. Chatterton at the races: De Quincey, Cottle, Southey, and the *Battle of Hastynges*. *See* **8469**.

10635. —— De Quincey on *Mount Pleasant*: William Roscoe and *Confessions of an English Opium-Eater*. NQ (52:1) 2005, 54–6.

10636. —— *De Quincey's Revenge*: David Macbeth Moir and *Confessions of an English Opium-Eater*. *See* **11729**.

10637. ROBERTS, DANIEL SANJIV. 'A nugget of pure truth': Woolf's debt to De Quincey. *See* **20407**.

Charles Dickens

10638. ALLAN, JANICE M. (ed.). Charles Dickens's *Bleak House*: a sourcebook. London; New York: Routledge, 2004. pp. xiii, 162. (Routledge guides to literature.)

10639. ALTER, ROBERT. Imagined cities: urban experience and the language of the novel. New Haven, CT; London: Yale UP, 2005. pp. xiii, 175, (plates) 8.

10640. ANDREWS, MALCOLM.   The 'set' for Charles Dickens's public readings. DickQ (21:4) 2004, 211–24.

10641. ARMSTRONG, MARY.   Multiplicities of longing: the queer desires of *Bleak House* and *Little Dorrit*. NCS (18) 2004, 59–79.

10642. BALCERZAK, SCOTT.   Dickensian orphan as child star: Freddie Bartholomew and the commodity of cute in MGM's *David Copperfield* (1935). See **13706**.

10643. BELSEY, CATHERINE.   Remembering as re-inscription – with a difference. See **3475**.

10644. BENTON, MICHAEL.   Literary biomythography. See **4160**.

10645. BOWN, NICOLA; BURDETT, CAROLYN; THURSCHWELL, PAMELA (eds). The Victorian supernatural. (Bibl. 2004, 10657.) Rev. by Jill Galvan in NineL (59:3) 2004, 423–6; by Helen Sword in Mod/Mod (12:2) 2005, 341–2; by James Finley in VPR (38:1) 2005, 108–10; by Michèle Mendelssohn in VicR (31:1) 2005, 70–3; by Sylvère Monod in EA (58:2) 2005, 236–7.

10646. BRATTIN, JOEL J.   The failure of plot in *Little Dorrit*. Dickensian (101:2) 2005, 111–15.

10647. BRIDGHAM, ELIZABETH.   The *Dickens Quarterly* checklist. DickQ (21:4) 2004, 264–8.

10648. ——   The *Dickens Quarterly* checklist. DickQ (22:1) 2005, 55–8.

10649. ——   The *Dickens Quarterly* checklist. DickQ (22:2) 2005, 123–6.

10650. ——   The *Dickens Quarterly* checklist. DickQ (22:4) 2005, 274–8.

10651. BROOKS, DIANNE.   The beautiful English boy: Mark Lester and *Oliver!* In (pp. 114–30) **13342**.

10652. BRUNS, JOHN.   Get out of gaol free; or, How to read a comic plot. JNT (35:1) 2005, 25–59.

10653. CAMPBELL, ELIZABETH A.   Fortune's wheel: Dickens and the iconography of women's time. (Bibl. 2004, 10658.) Rev. by David Paroissien in DickQ (21:4) 2004, 249–52; by George J. Worth in VPR (38:1) 2005, 119–20; by Hilary M. Schor in Dickensian (101:2) 2005, 162–4; by Robert L. Patten in StudN (37:4) 2005, 477–84.

10654. CAMUS, MARIANNE.   Gender and madness in the novels of Charles Dickens. (Bibl. 2004, 10659.) Rev. by Rick Allen in DickQ (22:2) 2005, 114–16.

10655. CASTILLO, LARISA TOKMAKOFF.   Between 'the cup and the lip': retroactive constructions of inheritance in *Our Mutual Friend*.   In (pp. 43–63) **14737**.

10656. CHIALANT, MARIA TERESA.   Tra confessione e autobiografia: tre casi vittoriani. In (pp. 165–87) **12577**.

10657. CLARK, NICHOLAS.   Dickens, Eric Crozier and Benjamin Britten: an opera that might have been. Dickensian (101:1) 2005, 27–8.

10658. CLAYTON, JAY.   Charles Dickens in cyberspace: the afterlife of the nineteenth century in postmodern culture. (Bibl. 2004, 10663.) Rev. by John Gardiner in DickQ (21:2) 2004, 114–17; by John Plunkett in NineL (59:4) 2005, 543–7; by Priscilla L. Walton in ConLit (46:1) 2005, 134–8.

10659. CLEERE, EILEEN. 'Implicit faith in the deception': misanthropy, natural history and *The Old Curiosity Shop*. DSA (35) 2005, 45–62.

10660. CLEMM, SABINE. 'Amidst the heterogeneous masses': Charles Dickens's *Household Words* and the Great Exhibition of 1851. NCC (27:3) 2005, 207–30.

10661. COLE, NATALIE B. Dickens and the act of gardening. DickQ (22:4) 2005, 242–54.

10662. COOKE, SIMON. Anxious travelers: a contextual reading of *The Signalman*. DickQ (22:2) 2005, 101–8.

10663. CORDERY, GARETH. Harry Furniss and the 'Boom in Boz' (part one). DickQ (21:2) 2004, 90–103.

10664. —— Harry Furniss and the 'Boom in Boz' (part two). DickQ (21:3) 2004, 143–56.

10665. —— A special relationship: Stiggins in England and America (part one). DickQ (22:3) 2005, 135–52. (Harry Furniss's use of Dickens's character in anti-Prohibition cartoons.)

10666. —— A special relationship: Stiggins in England and America (part two). DickQ (22:4) 2005, 224–41.

10667. CRAIG, RANDALL. Fictional license: the case of (and in) *Great Expectations*. DSA (35) 2005, 109–32.

10668. CREGAN-REID, VYBARR. Drowning in early Dickens. TexP (19:1) 2005, 71–91.

10669. —— Water defences: the arts of swimming in nineteenth-century culture. CritS (16:3) 2004, 33–47.

10670. DEUTSCHENDORF, BRIAN. Dickens's *Oliver Twist*. Exp (63:3) 2005, 146–9.

10671. DEVRIES, DUANE. Bibliographies, catalogues, collections, and bibliographical and textual studies of Dickens's works. New York: AMS Press, 2004. pp. lxix, 809. (AMS studies in the nineteenth century, 22.) (General studies of Charles Dickens and his writings and collected eds of his works, 1.) Rev. by Leon Litvack in Dickensian (100:2) 2004, 155–7; by David Paroissien in DickQ (22:2) 2005, 109–13.

10672. DOCHERTY, JOHN. A Christmas Carroll. See **10398**.

10673. DREW, JOHN M. L. Dickens the journalist. (Bibl. 2004, 10670.) Rev. by Rick Allen in DickQ (21:4) 2004, 246–8; by Beryl Gray in RES (56:225) 2005, 457–60.

10674. DUPERRAY, MAX. Le promeneur londonien au XIXe siècle: une excursion dans l'obscur. See **10606**.

10675. EASSON, ANGUS; BROWN, MARGARET (eds). The letters of Charles Dickens: supplement v. Dickensian (101:2) 2005, 134–58.

10676. EDGECOMBE, RODNEY STENNING. Dickens and the comedy of abbreviation. DickQ (22:2) 2005, 80–91.

10677. —— Dickens, Hunt and the waiter in *Somebody's Luggage*. VN (107) 2005, 25–8.

10678. EELLS, EMILY. From word to image: illustrating *Great Expectations*. NCC (25:3) 2003, 219–39.

10679. EYSELL, JOANNE. A medical companion to Dickens's fiction. New York; Frankfurt: Lang, 2005. pp. 274. (European univ. studies, XIV: Anglo-Saxon language and literature, 417.)

10680. FERGUSON, FRANCES. Envy rising. *In* (pp. 132–48) **9217.**

10681. —— On terrorism and morals: Dickens's *A Tale of Two Cities*. PartA (3:2) 2005, 49–74.

10682. FITZPATRICK, TONY. The trisected society: social welfare in early Victorian fiction. PartA (3:2) 2005, 23–47.

10683. FONTANA, ERNEST. Darwinian sexual selection and Dickens's *Our Mutual Friend*. DickQ (22:1) 2005, 36–42.

10684. FRANK, LAWRENCE. Victorian detective fiction and the nature of evidence: the scientific investigations of Poe, Dickens, and Doyle. (Bibl. 2004, 10682.) Rev. by Simon A. Cole in Isis (95:3) 2004, 510–11; by Kenneth Thompson in VS (47:4) 2005, 609–11.

10685. FRIEDMAN, STANLEY. Dickens' fictions: tapestries of conscience. (Bibl. 2003, 9966.) Rev. by David Parker in DickQ (21:3) 2004, 183–5; by Marisa Sestito in MLR (100:2) 2005, 489–90.

10686. GARNETT, ROBERT R. Recent Dickens studies: 2003. DSA (35) 2005, 335–95.

10687. GERVAIS, DAVID. J. C. Powys's Dostoievsky. *See* **18917.**

10688. GILBERT, PAMELA K. Medical mapping: the Thames, the body, and *Our Mutual Friend*. *In* (pp. 78–102) **9220.**

10689. GINSBURG, MICHAL PELED. Dickens and the scene of recognition. PartA (3:2) 2005, 75–97.

10690. GLAVIN, JOHN (ed.). Dickens on screen. (Bibl. 2004, 10684.) Rev. by Cara Lane in DickQ (22:1) 2005, 45–8; by Robert L. Patten in StudN (37:4) 2005, 477–84.

10691. GOODIN, GEORGE. Margins of conversation in the dialogue of Dickens. DickQ (21:3) 2004, 170–82.

10692. GRIBBLE, JENNIFER. Why the Good Samaritan was a bad economist: Dickens' parable for hard times. LitTheol (18:4) 2004, 427–41.

10693. HEARN, MICHAEL PATRICK (introd. and notes). The annotated *Christmas Carol: A Christmas Carol in Prose*. (Bibl. 2004, 10691.) Rev. by Richard J. Dunn in DickQ (21:2) 2004, 121–4.

10694. HENSON, LOUISE. 'In the natural course of physical things': ghosts and science in Charles Dickens's *All the Year Round*. *In* (pp. 113–23) **1226.**

10695. HILLARD, MOLLY CLARK. Dangerous exchange: fairy footsteps, goblin economies, and *The Old Curiosity Shop*. DSA (35) 2005, 63–86.

10696. HOLLINGTON, MICHAEL. Nickleby, *flânerie*, reverie: the view from Cheerybles'. DSA (35) 2005, 21–43.

10697. HORI, MASAHIRO. Investigating Dickens' style: a collocational analysis. Basingstoke; New York: Palgrave Macmillan, 2004. pp. xviii, 251. Rev. by Lynda C. Mugglestone in DickQ (22:3) 2005, 179–81.

10698. HOWE, NICHOLAS. *Beowulf* in the house of Dickens. *In* (pp. 421–39) **4220.**

10699. HUETT, LORNA. Among the unknown public: *Household Words, All the Year Round* and the mass-market weekly periodical in the mid-nineteenth century. *See* **1232.**

10700. HUGHES, JIM. Those who passed through: Charles Dickens. NYH (84:2) 2003, 205–9.

10701. JAMES, ELIZABETH. Charles Dickens. Oxford; New York: OUP, 2004. pp. 128. (British Library writers' lives.) Rev. by Natalie McKnight in DickQ (22:1) 2005, 48–50.

10702. JAMES, SIMON J. (ed.). Collected works of George Gissing on Charles Dickens: vol. 2, Charles Dickens: a critical study. Afterword by David Parker. *See* **11076.**

10703. JOHN, JULIET. Fagin, the Holocaust and mass culture; or, *Oliver Twist* on screen. DickQ (22:4) 2005, 204–23.

10704. JOHNSON, GREG. Modern writers, modern lives. *See* **20973.**

10705. JOHNSON, MICHAEL K. Not telling the story the way it happened: Alfonso Cuarón's *Great Expectations*. *See* **13598.**

10706. KELLY, RICHARD (ed.). A Christmas carol. (Bibl. 2004, 10698.) Rev. by David Paroissien in DickQ (22:4) 2005, 268–9.

10707. KLOTZ, MICHAEL. Two Dickens rooms in *The Yellow Wall-Paper*. *See* **16689.**

10708. LANDAU, AARON. *Great Expectations*, romance, and capital. DSA (35) 2005, 157–77.

10709. LECERCLE, JEAN-JACQUES. Jane Austen meets Dickens: a response to Thierry Labica. *See* **16864.**

10710. LE RESTE, ANNE-CLAIRE. Intertextualizing *The Princess Casamassima*: realism and reference(s). *See* **11423.**

10711. LITVACK, LEON. *The Dickensian*: editors, contributors and readers, 1905–2005. DickQ (22:2) 2005, 68–79.

10712. LOCK, CHARLES. *Owen Glendower* and the dashing of expectations. *See* **18921.**

10713. MCCARTHY, PATRICK J. The Empire strikes back: Dickens on the rioting colonists. NCP (32:2) 2005, 209–17 (review-article).

10714. MAGNET, MYRON. Dickens and the social order. Wilmington, DE: ISI, 2004. pp. xvi, 266.

10715. MALCOLM, GABRIELLE. Mary Braddon, literary critic: introduction to a 'costly' edition of *Little Dorrit*. *See* **10140.**

10716. MEYER, SUSAN. Antisemitism and social critique in Dickens's *Oliver Twist*. VLC (33:1) 2005, 239–52.

10717. MOORE, GRACE. Dickens and empire: discourses of class, race, and colonialism in the works of Charles Dickens. (Bibl. 2004, 10711.) Rev. by Brian Gasser in RES (56:227) 2005, 802–4; by David Paroissien in DickQ (22:3) 2005, 181–5; by Patrick J. McCarthy in NCP (32:2) 2005, 209–17.

10718. MORGENTALER, GOLDIE. Dickens and the scattered identity of Silas Wegg. DickQ (22:2) 2005, 92–100.

10719. MUKHERJEE, ANKHI.   Missed encounters: repetition, rewriting, and contemporary returns to Charles Dickens's *Great Expectations*. ConLit (46:1) 2005, 108–33.

10720. NELSON, DALE.   Little Nell and Frodo the halfling. *See* **19834.**

10721. NEWEY, VINCENT.   Rival cultures: Charles Dickens and the Byronic legacy. BJ (32:2) 2004, 85–100.

10722. —— The scriptures of Charles Dickens: novels of ideology, novels of the self. (Bibl. 2004, 10715.) Rev. by Natalie Bell Cole in DickQ (22:1) 2005, 43–5.

10723. NEWTON, K. M.   Revisions of Scott, Austen, and Dickens in *Daniel Deronda*. *See* **10944.**

10724. NIXON, JUDE V.   'Lost in the vast worlds of wonder': Dickens and science. DSA (35) 2005, 267–333.

10725. NOONKESTER, MYRON C.   Dickens's *Bleak House*. Exp (64:1) 2005, 35–8.

10726. OHI, KEVIN.   Autobiography and *David Copperfield*'s temporalities of loss. VLC (33:2) 2005, 435–49.

10727. OULTON, CAROLYN.   'My undisciplined heart': romantic friendship in *David Copperfield*. DickQ (21:3) 2004, 157–69.

10728. PAROISSIEN, DAVID.   Monsters in the classroom: Dickens's case against industrialised education. Dickensian (101:2) 2005, 101–10.

10729. —— *Oliver Twist*: an annotated bibliography, supplement I: 1984–2004. DSA (35) 2005, 397–519.

10730. PAYNE, DAVID.   The reenchantment of nineteenth-century fiction: Dickens, Thackeray, George Eliot, and serialization. Basingstoke; New York: Palgrave Macmillan, 2005. pp. xiii, 206. (Palgrave studies in nineteenth-century writing and culture.)

10731. PHILPOTTS, TREY.   The companion to *Little Dorrit*. (Bibl. 2004, 10724.) Rev. by Rodney Stenning Edgecombe in MLR (100:4) 2005, 1098–9; by Sara Thornton in EA (58:3) 2005, 366–7.

10732. POLGA, KIT.   Dickens and the morality of imagination. DickQ (22:3) 2005, 172–8.

10733. RIDENHOUR, JAMIESON.   'In that boney light': the Bakhtinian gothic of *Our Mutual Friend*. DickQ (22:3) 2005, 153–71.

10734. ROSE, NATALIE.   Flogging and fascination: Dickens and the fragile will. VS (47:4) 2005, 505–33.

10735. ROTUNNO, LAURA.   The long history of 'in short': Mr Micawber, letter-writers, and literary men. VLC (33:2) 2005, 415–33.

10736. ROWLAND, PETER.   No sich a person? The hunt for Fagin. Dickensian (101:2) 2005, 132–3.

10737. SCHARNHORST, GARY (introd.).   Kate Field's *An Evening with Charles Dickens*: a reconstructed lecture. *See* **11009.**

10738. SCHLICKE, PAUL.   Revisions to *Sketches by Boz*. Dickensian (101:1) 2005, 29–38.

10739. —— 'Risen like a rocket': the impact of *Sketches by Boz*. DickQ (22:1) 2005, 3–18.

10740. SCHMIDT, GERALD.   George Gissing's psychology of 'female imbecility'.
See **11082.**

10741. SICHER, EFRAIM.   Rereading the city, rereading Dickens: representation,
the novel, and urban realism. (Bibl. 2004, 10742.) Rev. by David Seed in MLR
(100:1) 2005, 205–6; by Robert L. Patten in StudN (37:4) 2005, 477–84.

10742. SIEGEL, DANIEL.   The *Dickens Quarterly* checklist. DickQ (21:2) 2004,
132–4.

10743. —— The *Dickens Quarterly* checklist. DickQ (21:3) 2004, 198–200.

10744. SIMS, JENNIFER S.   Dickens's *A Tale of Two Cities.* Exp (63:4) 2005,
219–22.

10745. SMITH, GRAHAME.   Dickens and the dream of cinema. (Bibl. 2004, 10747.)
Rev. by David Paroissien in DickQ (21:2) 2004, 125–7; by David Seed in MLR
(100:1) 2005, 205–6; by Paul Schlicke in RES (56:225) 2005, 460–1.

10746. SOTO VÁZQUEZ, ADOLFO LUIS.   Charles Dickens makes fun of idiolects
in *Martin Chuzzlewit.* RAEI (18) 2005, 261–73.

10747. STOLTE, TYSON.   Mightier than the sword: aggression of the written
word in *Great Expectations.* DSA (35) 2005, 179–208.

10748. STRAHAN, LINDA.   There's a hole in the (Inspector) Bucket: the Victorian
police in fact and fiction. Clues (23:3) 2005, 57–62.

10749. TAKEI, AKIKO.   Benevolence or manipulation? The treatment of Mr Dick.
Dickensian (101:2) 2005, 116–31.

10750. TAMBLING, JEREMY.   Opium, wholesale, resale, and for export: on
Dickens and China (part two). DickQ (21:2) 2004, 104–13.

10751. TATUM, KAREN ELIZABETH.   'Something covered with an old blanket':
Nancy and other dead mothers in *Oliver Twist.* AmJP (65:3) 2005, 239–60.

10752. TIPPER, KAREN.   A Dickens of a Wilde paper: a comparison and contrast
of their respective tours of America. See **12431.**

10753. TRACY, ROBERT.   Time in *Bleak House.* DickQ (21:4) 2004, 225–34.

10754. TROSS, RUTH.   Dickens and the crime of literacy. DickQ (21:4) 2004,
235–45.

10755. UCHIDA, MASAKO.   The activities of the Chancery Reform Association
and Dickens's writing of *A December Vision*: part II. Dickensian (101:1) 2005,
46–56.

10756. VANFASSE, NATHALIE.   The poetics of social deviance in *Our Mutual
Friend* by Charles Dickens. CVE (61) 2005, 227–43.

10757. —— 'The reader's passport': parcours géographique et
détours littéraires dans *Pictures from Italy* (1846) de Charles Dickens.
EREA (3:1) 2005, 34–41.

10758. —— Récits de voyage, fiction et voyageurs fictifs dans *American Notes*
de Charles Dickens. EREA (3:1) 2005, 34–42.

10759. VITA, PAUL.   Returning the look: Victorian writers and the Paris morgue.
NCC (25:3) 2003, 241–56.

10760. WESTLAND, ELLA.   Dickens's *Dombey* and the storied sea. DSA (35)
2005, 87–108.

10761. WILKINSON, IAN. Performance and control: the carnivalesque city and its people in Charles Dickens's *Sketches by Boz*. DSA (35) 2005, 1–19.

10762. WILLIAMS, LEE. Telling as denouement in Charles Dickens's *Great Expectations* and Roberto Arlt's *El juguete rabioso* (*Mad Toy*). DickQ (22:1) 2005, 19–35.

10763. WILSON, PETER. The corpus of Jinglese: a syntactic profile of an idiolectal 'system of stenography'. CritS (16:3) 2004, 78–93.

10764. WOOD, JAMES HUNTER. Interventional narratology: form and function of the narrative medical write-up. LitMed (24:2) 2005, 283–96.

10765. ZANGEN, BRITTA. Our daughters must be wives: marriageable young women in the novels of Dickens, Eliot, and Hardy. New York; Frankfurt: Lang, 2005. pp. 391. (Feministische Forschungen, 2.) Rev. by Holly Furneaux in GER (36) 2005, 81–2.

10766. ZEMKA, SUE. Chronometrics of love and money in *Great Expectations*. DSA (35) 2005, 133–56.

Emily Dickinson

10767. BAKER, DAVID. Elegy and eros: configuring grief. See **12294**.

10768. BORUS, AUDREY. A student's guide to Emily Dickinson. Berkeley Heights, NJ: Enslow, 2005. pp. 152. (Understanding literature.)

10769. BRANTLEY, RICHARD E. Experience and faith: the late Romantic imagination of Emily Dickinson. Basingstoke; New York: Palgrave Macmillan, 2004. pp. xi, 275.

10770. BRUNAZZI, ELIZABETH. A conversation with Claire Malroux, contemporary French translator of Emily Dickinson. EDISB (16:1) 2004, 2–3, 22.

10771. BUSHELL, SALLY. Meaning in Dickinson's manuscripts: intending the unintentional. EDJ (14:1) 2005, 24–61.

10772. COOLEY, CAROLYN LINDLEY. The music of Dickinson's poems and letters: a study of imagery and form. (Bibl. 2004, 10762.) Rev. by Emily Seelbinder in EDISB (15:2) 2003, 27–8.

10773. D'ARIENZO, DARIA. Looking at Emily. EDISB (17:2) 2005, 4–5.

10774. DEPPMAN, JED. To own the art within the soul: Emily Dickinson and creative writing. EDISB (17:1) 2005, 1–2.

10775. —— Trying to think with Emily Dickinson. EDJ (14:1) 2005, 84–103.

10776. EMSLEY, SARAH. Is Emily Dickinson a Metaphysical poet? CRAS (33:3) 2003, 249–65.

10777. ESDALE, LOGAN. Dickinson's epistolary 'naturalness'. EDJ (14:1) 2005, 1–23.

10778. FARR, JUDITH; CARTER, LOUISE. The gardens of Emily Dickinson. (Bibl. 2004, 10764.) Rev. by Sheila Coghill in EDISB (16:2) 2004, 30–2; by Evelyn C. White in GLRW (12:2) 2005, 35–6; by Alfred Habegger in NineL (59:4) 2005, 536–9; by Elizabeth A. Petrino in Legacy (22:2) 2005, 214–16.

10779. FINNERTY, PÁRAIC. The daisy and the dandy: Emily Dickinson and Oscar Wilde. Symbiosis (9:1) 2005, 63–87.

10780. FREEMAN, MARGARET H. Poetry as power: the dynamics of cognitive poetics as a scientific and literary paradigm. *In* (pp. 31–57) **3888.**

10781. GAILEY, AMANDA. How anthologists made Dickinson a tolerable American woman writer. EDJ (14:1) 2005, 62–83.

10782. GILBERT, SANDRA M. The supple suitor: death, women, feminism, and (assisted or unassisted) suicide. TSWL (24:2) 2005, 247–55.

10783. HABEGGER, ALFRED. Some notes on the Emily Dickinson Collection at Sophia University in Tokyo. EDISB (15:2) 2003, 18–20.

10784. HALLEN, CYNTHIA L. The ways of possibility: Emily Dickinson and Dag Hammarskjöld. EDISB (17:1) 2005, 4–7.

10785. HART, ELLEN LOUISE. Poets against the war. EDISB (15:2) 2003, 8–9, 33.

10786. HEGINBOTHAM, ELEANOR ELSON. Reading the fascicles of Emily Dickinson: dwelling in possibilities. (Bibl. 2003, 10053.) Rev. by Dorothy Huff Oberhaus in EDISB (15:2) 2003, 26–7.

10787. HOWARD, ROBERT. 'Out of sound — out of sight': Emily Dickinson and the poetics of trauma. PsyArt (9) 2005.

10788. HUBBARD, MELANIE. 'Turn it, a little': the influence of the daguerreotype and the stereograph on Emily Dickinson's use of manuscript variants. Mosaic (38:1) 2005, 115–32.

10789. JACKSON, VIRGINIA. Dickinson undone. Raritan (24:4) 2005, 128–48. (Electronic archive Radical Scatters.)

10790. —— Dickinson's misery: a theory of lyric reading. Princeton, NJ; Oxford: Princeton UP, 2005. pp. xvii, 298.

10791. KIRK, CONNIE ANN. 'To stay behind — with just the toys': Gilbert Dickinson's living treasures in the Evergreens. EDISB (15:2) 2003, 12–13, 34–5.

10792. LOEFFELHOLZ, MARY. Dickinson's *Decoration*. ELH (72:3) 2005, 663–89.

10793. MCDOWELL, MARTA. Emily Dickinson's gardens: a celebration of a poet and a gardener. Boston, MA: McGraw-Hill, 2005. pp. vi, 218. Rev. by Cheryl Langdell in EDISB (17:1) 2005, 18–19.

10794. MARTIN, WENDY (ed.). The Cambridge companion to Emily Dickinson. (Bibl. 2004, 10777.) Rev. by Olivier Buteux in EREA (1:1) 2003; by Amanda Gailey in ALR (37:2) 2005, 183–6.

10795. MAYER, NANCY. Finding herself alone: Emily Dickinson, Victorian women novelists, and the female subject. RomNet (38/39) 2005.

10796. —— Reloading that gun: reading an old poem as if it matters. HR (57:4) 2005, 537–49.

10797. MITCHELL, DOMHNALL. Measures of possibility: Emily Dickinson's manuscripts. Amherst: Massachusetts UP, 2005. pp. xv, 425.

10798. PETRINO, ELIZABETH A. Late bloomer: the gentian as sign or symbol in the work of Dickinson and her contemporaries. EDJ (14:1) 2005, 104–25.

10799. POLLAK, VIVIAN R. (ed.). A historical guide to Emily Dickinson. (Bibl. 2004, 10781.) Rev. by Marcy L. Tanter in EDISB (16:1) 2004, 17–18; by Elizabeth A. Petrino in Legacy (22:2) 2005, 214–16.

10800. SRIKANTH, REDDY. 'All we secure of beauty is its evanescences': the ratio, the rainbow, and Dickinson's theory of value. DQ (39:4) 2005, 66–76.

10801. THOMPSON-RIZZO, PATRICIA. *Gone-to-Kansas*: a reading of Dickinson's L182. RSA (14) 2003, 17–35.

10802. ZHANG, XUEMEI. Emily Dickinson's redefining Transcendentalist view of nature. FLS (116) 2005, 64–70. (In Chinese.)

Benjamin Disraeli

10803. CLAUSSON, NILS. 'Picturesque emotion' or 'great Asian mystery'? Disraeli's *Tancred* as an ironic *Bildungsroman*. CritS (16:1) 2004, 1–19.

10804. FITZPATRICK, TONY. The trisected society: social welfare in early Victorian fiction. See **10682**.

10805. HIBBERT, CHRISTOPHER. Disraeli: a personal history. London: HarperCollins, 2004. pp. xii, 401, (plates) 24. Rev. by Richard Whittington-Egan in ContRev (287:1674) 2005, 54–5.

10806. NICOLAY, CLAIRE. The anxiety of 'Mosaic' influence: Thackeray, Disraeli, and Anglo-Jewish assimilation in the 1840s. See **12168**.

10807. SCHWARZ, DANIEL R. (gen. ed.). The early novels of Benjamin Disraeli: vol. 1, *Vivian Gray* (1826–7). Ed. by Michael Sanders. London; Brookfield, VT: Pickering & Chatto, 2004. pp. lxv, 689. (Pickering masters.) Rev. by William M. Kuhn in TLS, 26 Nov. 2004, 24.

10808. —— The early novels of Benjamin Disraeli: vol. 2, *The Young Duke* (1831). Ed. by Miles A. Kimball. London; Brookfield, VT: Pickering & Chatto, 2004. pp. xix, 327. (Pickering masters.)

10809. —— The early novels of Benjamin Disraeli: vol. 3, *Contarini Fleming* (1832). Ed. by Charles Richmond. London; Brookfield, VT: Pickering & Chatto, 2004. pp. xix, 310. (Pickering masters.)

10810. —— The early novels of Benjamin Disraeli: vol. 4, *The Wondrous Tale of Alroy* (1833). Ed. by Geoffrey Harvey. London; Brookfield, VT: Pickering & Chatto, 2004. pp. xx, 269. (Pickering masters.)

10811. —— The early novels of Benjamin Disraeli: vol. 5, *Henrietta Temple* (1837). Ed. by Jeraldine R. Kraver and Ann R. Hawkins. London; Brookfield, VT: Pickering & Chatto, 2004. pp. xxvi, 360. (Pickering masters.)

10812. —— The early novels of Benjamin Disraeli: vol. 6, *Venetia* (1837). Ed. by Ann R. Hawkins and Jeraldine R. Kraver. London; Brookfield, VT: Pickering & Chatto, 2004. pp. xxii, 446. (Pickering masters.)

10813. SPEVACK, MARVIN. Benjamin Disraeli and the Athenaeum Club. NQ (52:1) 2005, 68–70.

10814. WEBER, JEAN JACQUES. Cognitive poetics and literary criticism: types of resolution in the Condition-of-England novel. See **9631**.

10815. WIEBE, M. G., *et al.* (eds). Benjamin Disraeli letters: vol. 7, 1857–1859. Toronto; Buffalo, NY; London: Toronto UP, 2004. pp. lxvi, 578. Rev. by Robert O'Kell in VS (47:1) 2004, 117–19.

Ella Hepworth Dixon

10816. FEHLBAUM, VALERIE. As she knew him: as Ella Hepworth Dixon knew Oscar Wilde. See **12385**.

10817. —— Ella Hepworth Dixon: the story of a modern woman. Aldershot; Burlington, VT: Ashgate, 2005. pp. xii, 203. (Nineteenth century.)

Sydney Dobell

10818. BOOS, FLORENCE S. 'Spasm' and class: W. E. Aytoun, George Gilfillan, Sydney Dobell, and Alexander Smith. VP (42:4) 2004, 553–83.

10819. MASON, EMMA. Rhythmic numinousness: Sydney Dobell and 'the Church'. VP (42:4) 2004, 537–51.

10820. RUDY, JASON R. Rhythmic intimacy, Spasmodic epistemology. VP (42:4) 2004, 451–72.

Mary Abigail Dodge (Gail Hamilton) (1833–1896)

10821. KREGER, ERIKA M. The nineteenth-century female humorist as 'iconoclast in the temple': Gail Hamilton and the myth of reviewers' disapproval of women's comic-ironic writings. SAH (11) 2004, 5–38.

Mary Mapes Dodge (1830–1905)

10822. GAMMON, SUSAN R. Heroism reconsidered: negotiating autonomy in *St Nicholas* magazine (1873–1914). *In* (pp. 179–98) **8171**.

Alfred Domett (1811–1887)

10823. STAFFORD, JANE. Immeasurable abysses and living books: oral literature and Victorian poetics in Alfred Domett's *Ranolf and Amohia*. BSANZB (28:1/2) 2004, 161–71.

Charles M. Doughty

10824. DELMAS, CATHERINE. Parcours et détours de Charles Doughty en Arabie Déserte. EREA (3:1) 2005, 49–54.

Frederick Douglass

10825. BURNS, MARK K. 'A slave in form but not in fact': subversive humor and the rhetoric of irony in *Narrative of the Life of Frederick Douglass*. SAH (12) 2005, 83–96.

10826. FEE, FRANK E., JR. Intelligent union of Black with White: Frederick Douglass and the Rochester press, 1847–48. JoH (31:1) 2005, 32–45.

10827. HAMILTON, CYNTHIA S. Models of agency: Frederick Douglass and *The Heroic Slave*. PAAS (114:1) 2004, 87–136.

10828. LEE, MAURICE S. The old and the new: double consciousness and the literature of slavery. See **10984**.

10829. LOGAN, SHIRLEY WILSON. 'To get an education and teach my people': rhetoric for social change. *In* (pp. 36–52) **2318**.

10830. MATZKE, JASON P. The John Brown way: Frederick Douglass and Henry David Thoreau on the use of violence. MassR (46:1) 2005, 62–75.

10831. MOSES, WILSON JEREMIAH. Creative conflict in African American thought: Frederick Douglass, Alexander Crummell, Booker T. Washington,

2005]   AUTHORS   581

W. E. B. Du Bois, and Marcus Garvey. Cambridge; New York: CUP, 2004. pp. xviii, 308. Rev. by Jonathan M. Hansen in JAH (92:2) 2005, 648–9.

10832. ROEMER, KENNETH M. A 'touching man' brings Aacqu close. *See* **18666.**

10833. STAUFFER, JOHN. Frederick Douglass and the aesthetics of freedom. Raritan (25:1) 2005, 114–36.

10834. TUHKANEN, MIKKO. The optical trade: from slave-breaking in Frederick Douglass's *Narrative* to self-breaking in Richard Wright's *Black Boy*. AmS (46:2) 2005, 91–116.

10835. WALLACE, ROBERT K. Douglass and Melville: anchored together in a neighborly style. *See* **11711.**

10836. —— Douglass and Melville: 'in neighborly style and anchored together'. *See* **11712.**

Edward Dowden

10837. WALLACE, NATHAN. Shakespeare biography and the theory of reconciliation in Edward Dowden and James Joyce. ELH (72:4) 2005, 799–822.

Ernest Dowson

10838. ADAMS, JAD. Hideous absinthe: a history of the devil in a bottle. *See* **12126.**

Sir Arthur Conan Doyle

10839. BEHEREC, MARC A. The Devil, the terror, and the horror: the Whateley twins' further debts to folklore and fiction. *See* **17855.**

10840. CHILDERS, JOSEPH W. Foreign matter: imperial filth. *In* (pp. 201–21) **9220.**

10841. CLAUSSON, NILS. The case of the anomalous narrative: gothic 'surmise' and trigonometric 'proof' in Arthur Conan Doyle's *The Musgrave Ritual*. VN (107) 2005, 5–10.

10842. —— Degeneration, *fin-de-siècle* gothic, and the science of detection: Arthur Conan Doyle's *The Hound of the Baskervilles* and the emergence of the modern detective story. JNT (35:1) 2005, 60–87.

10843. —— The importance of being Gwendolen Fairfax: Arthur Conan Doyle's *The Voice of Science* & Oscar Wilde's *The Importance of Being Earnest*. *See* **12373.**

10844. COOKE, CATHERINE. Mrs Hudson: a legend in her own lodging-house. BSJ (55:2) 2005, 13–23.

10845. DIERKES, JOSEPH E. Mary Sutherland: identifying the crime and the villain. BSJ (55:4) 2005, 23–5. (*A Case of Identity*.)

10846. ELLIOTT, M. J. In our absence. BSJ (55:4) 2005, 6–10.

10847. FERRY, FRANCIS T. A London general practitioner and a dying detective. BSJ (55:4) 2005, 16–22.

10848. GENOVA, JOHN. Sydney Paget's successor: the life of Arthur Twidle. *See* **68.**

10849. GOODMAN, JEFFREY. Defending author-essentialism. PhilL (29:1) 2005, 200–8.

10850. HARRINGTON, ELLEN.   Failed detectives and dangerous females: Wilkie Collins, Arthur Conan Doyle, and the detective short story. *See* **10549.**

10851. HARRIS, BRUCE.   Bootlaces? BSJ (55:1) 2005, 46–8.

10852. HILL, GIDEON.   The richest man in horseracing. BSJ (55:3) 2005, 30–3. (*Silver Blaze*.)

10853. HYDE, JAY.   Arthur, Jack, and Jill. BSJ (55:1) 2005, 49–52. (Doyle and Jack the Ripper.)

10854. HYDER, WILLIAM.   Lestrade: a fair cop. BSJ (55:2) 2005, 39–46.

10855. JENSEN, JENS BYSKOV.   A memory for crime. BSJ (55:4) 2005, 11–15. (*The Adventure of the Three Garridebs*; *The Red-Headed League*.)

10856. KELLOGG, RICHARD L.   Whatever happened to Edward Rucastle? BSJ (55:1) 2005, 54–6. (*The Copper Beeches*.)

10857. KENNY, KEVIN.   The Molly Maguires and *The Valley of Fear*. BSJ (55:2) 2005, 24–31.

10858. KLINGER, LESLIE S.   Game over? BSJ (55:3) 2005, 6–11.

10859. —— (ed.).   The new annotated Sherlock Holmes. With additional research by Patricia J. Chui. Introd. by John le Carré. New York; London: Norton, 2005. 2 vols. pp. lxvii, 1878. Rev. by Daniel Stashower in BkW, 5 Dec. 2004, 8; by Jon Barnes in TLS, 7 Jan. 2005, 16.

10860. MCBRATNEY, JOHN.   Racial and criminal types: Indian ethnography and Sir Arthur Conan Doyle's *The Sign of Four*. VLC (33:1) 2005, 149–67.

10861. MENEGALDO, GILLES; NAUGRETTE, JEAN-PIERRE (eds).   R. L. Stevenson & A. Conan Doyle – aventures de la fiction: actes du colloque de Cerisy. Rennes: Terre de Brume, 2003. pp. 428, (plates) 16. (Terres fantastiques: Essais.) Rev. by François Gallix in EA (58:2) 2005, 231–2.

10862. MEYER, CHARLES A.   An investigation into the Greek interpreter. BSJ (55:1) 2005, 43–5.

10863. PENNINGTON, JOHN.   'Eliminate all other factors': fantastic hesitation in Arthur Conan Doyle's *Hound of the Baskervilles*. JFA (15:2) 2004, 132–43.

10864. PLEGER, DAVID.   Thereby hangs a tale. BSJ (55:3) 2005, 34–7. (*The Adventure of the Speckled Band*.)

10865. RADFORD, JOHN.   Dr Watson to 1878. BSJ (55:1) 2005, 38–42.

10866. RICHARDS, DANA.   One must be masterful: fiction and reality. BSJ (55:4) 2005, 26–32.

10867. SINGLETON, PAUL.   The whole art in the blood. BSJ (55:3) 2005, 20–9.

10868. STINSON, REGINA.   A quite exceptional woman. BSJ (55:3) 2005, 38–41.

10869. STINSON, SAM.   The Tracy connection. BSJ (55:2) 2005, 53–5.

10870. STOCK, RANDALL.   The trail of the semi-solitary manuscript. BSJ (55:4) 2005, 46–54. (*The Adventure of the Solitary Cyclist*.)

10871. TAYLOR-IDE, JESSE OAK.   Ritual and the liminality of Sherlock Holmes in *The Sign of Four* and *The Hound of the Baskervilles*. ELT (48:1) 2005, 55–70.

10872. WALSH, WILLIAM R.   The missing boat. BSJ (55:2) 2005, 47–51. (*The Adventure of the Bruce-Partington Plans*.)

William Henry Drummond (b.1854)

10873. CARTER, ADAM. Anthropomorphism and trope in the national ode. *In* (pp. 117–44) **9191**.

George du Maurier (1834–1896)

10874. ANOLIK, RUTH BIENSTOCK. The scandal of the Jew: reflexive transgressiveness in du Maurier's *Trilby*. PartA (3:2) 2005, 99–127.

10875. BRISTOW, JOSEPH. 'Dirty pleasure': Trilby's filth. *In* (pp. 155–81) **9220**.

10876. DALY, NICHOLAS. The woman in white: Whistler, Hiffernan, Courbet, du Maurier. Mod/Mod (12:1) 2005, 1–25.

10877. VITA, PAUL. Returning the look: Victorian writers and the Paris morgue. *See* **10759**.

Paul Laurence Dunbar

10878. JARRETT, GENE. 'We must write like the white men': race, realism, and Dunbar's anomalous first novel. Novel (37:3) 2004, 303–25.

Sara Jeannette Duncan

10879. FIAMENGO, JANICE. 'Baptized with tears and sighs': Sara Jeannette Duncan and the rhetoric of feminism. *In* (pp. 257–80) **9191**.

Toru Dutt

10880. LOOTENS, TRICIA. Alien homelands: Rudyard Kipling, Toru Dutt, and the poetry of empire. *In* (pp. 285–310) **9675**.

Edith Eaton ('Sui Sin Far')

10881. CHEUNG, FLOYD. Political resistance, cultural appropriation, and the performance of manhood in Yung Wing's *My Life in China and America*. *In* (pp. 77–100) **9454**.

10882. GRASSO, LINDA M. Inventive desperation: anger, violence, and belonging in Mary Wilkins Freeman's and Sui Sin Far's murderous mother stories. *See* **11026**.

10883. SHIH, DAVID. The seduction of origins: Sui Sin Far and the race for tradition. *In* (pp. 48–76) **9454**.

Winnifred Babcock Eaton ('Onoto Watanna')

10884. FERENS, DOMINIKA. Winnifred Eaton / Onoto Watanna: establishing ethnographic authority. *In* (pp. 30–47) **9454**.

10885. MOSER, LINDA TRINH; ROONEY, ELIZABETH (eds). *A Half Caste* and other writings. (Bibl. 2004, 10863.) Rev. by Janice Brown in CanL (184) 2005, 128–9; by Jennifer Putzi in Legacy (22:1) 2005, 91–4.

10886. SHIH, DAVID. The self and generic convention: Winifred Eaton's *Me: a Book of Remembrance*. *In* (pp. 41–59) **12775**.

Emily Eden

10887. POON, ANGELIA. Seeing double: performing English identity and imperial duty in Emily Eden's *Up the Country* and Harriet Martineau's *British Rule in India*. WWr (12:3) 2005, 453–70.

Maria Edgeworth

10888. BRUNDAN, KATY.   Cosmopolitan complexities in Maria Edgeworth's *Ennui*. StudN (37:2) 2005, 123–40.

10889. CASS, JEFFREY.   Lost in translation: Caroline Percy's 'unwounded ear' and Voltaire's Orientalist intertext in *Patronage*. ANQ (18:1) 2005, 42–6.

10890. COMITINI, PATRICIA.   Vocational philanthropy and British women's writing, 1790–1810: Wollstonecraft, More, Edgeworth, Wordsworth. *See* **9134**.

10891. EGENOLF, SUSAN B.   Maria Edgeworth in blackface: *Castle Rackrent* and the Irish Rebellion of 1798. ELH (72:4) 2005, 845–69.

10892. EGER, ELIZABETH; Ó GALLCHOIR, CLÍONA (eds).   The parent's assistant: moral tales for young people. London; Brookfield, VT: Pickering & Chatto, 2003. pp. xxiii, 322. (Novels and selected works of Maria Edgeworth, 10.) (Pickering masters.) Rev. by Hugh Parry in JTLBS (11) 2005, 39–43.

10893. —— —— BUTLER, MARILYN (eds).   Popular tales; Early lessons; Whim for whim. London; Brookfield, VT: Pickering & Chatto, 2003. pp. xix, 476. (Novels and selected works of Maria Edgeworth, 12.) (Pickering masters.) Rev. by Hugh Parry in JTLBS (11) 2005, 39–43.

10894. FLANAGAN, CHRISTINA.   Edgeworth's *Ennui*. Exp (63:2) 2005, 72–3.

10895. KILFEATHER, SIOBHÁN (ed.).   Belinda. London; Brookfield, VT: Pickering & Chatto, 2003. pp. xlvi, 441. (Novels and selected works of Maria Edgeworth, 2.) (Pickering masters.) Rev. by Hugh Parry in JTLBS (11) 2005, 39–43.

10896. KIPP, JULIE.   Romanticism, maternity, and the body politic. *See* **8015**.

10897. MANLY, SUSAN (ed.).   Practical education. London; Brookfield, VT: Pickering & Chatto, 2003. pp. xxv, 515. (Novels and selected works of Maria Edgeworth, 11.) (Pickering masters.) Rev. by Hugh Parry in JTLBS (11) 2005, 39–43.

10898. MONTWIELER, KATHERINE.   Reading disease: the corrupting performance of Edgeworth's *Belinda*. WWr (12:3) 2005, 347–68.

10899. MURPHY, SHARON.   Maria Edgeworth and romance. Dublin; Portland, OR: Four Courts Press, 2004. pp. 208. Rev. by Ciara Ní Bhroin in ILS (25:1) 2005, 20.

10900. Ó GALLCHOIR, CLÍONA.   Maria Edgeworth: women, Enlightenment and nation. Dublin: University College Dublin Press, 2005. pp. xi, 221.

Pierce Egan the Elder (1772–1849)

10901. BERMINGHAM, ANN.   Urbanity and the spectacle of art. *In* (pp. 151–76) **9217**.

10902. MANNING, PETER J.   Manufacturing the Romantic image: Hazlitt and Coleridge lecturing. *In* (pp. 227–45) **9217**.

'George Eliot' (Mary Ann Evans)

10903. AMANO, MIYUKI.   The widening vision and undying hope in *The Spanish Gypsy*. GER (36) 2005, 63–72.

10904. ANGER, SUZY.   Victorian interpretation. Ithaca, NY; London: Cornell UP, 2005. pp. 232.

10905. BATES, TIMOTHY. George Eliot's eclectic use of names in *Daniel Deronda*. GEGHLS (48/49) 2005, 39–52.

10906. BIRCH, DINAH. 'School-time': George Eliot and education. GER (36) 2005, 7–16. (Thirty-third George Eliot Memorial Lecture: 2004.)

10907. BLAKE, KATHLEEN. Between economies in *The Mill on the Floss*: loans *versus* gifts; or, Auditing Mr Tulliver's accounts. VLC (33:1) 2005, 219–37.

10908. BORNSTEIN, GEORGE. The colors of Zion: Black, Jewish, and Irish nationalisms at the turn of the century. *See* **20482.**

10909. —— A forgotten alliance: Africans, Americans, Zionists and Irish. TLS, 4 Mar. 2005, 12–13.

10910. CARROLL, ALICIA. Dark smiles: race and desire in George Eliot. (Bibl. 2004, 10889.) Rev. by Michael Davis in GEGHLS (48/49) 2005, 135–7.

10911. CHISHTY-MUJAHID, NADYA. Scarred and healed identities: fallenness, morality, and the issue of personal autonomy in *Adam Bede* and *Ruth*. VicR (30:2) 2004, 58–80.

10912. CHRISTIANSON, FRANK. Christian evaluation and moral action in George Eliot's *Middlemarch*. LitB (24:1/2) 2004, 239–52.

10913. COLÓN, SUSAN. 'One function in particular': professionalism and specialization in *Daniel Deronda*. StudN (37:3) 2005, 292–307.

10914. CULLER, JONATHAN. The Hertzian sublime. *See* **14748.**

10915. DA SOUSA CORREA, DELIA. George Eliot, music and Victorian culture. (Bibl. 2004, 10895.) Rev. by Lee Orr in NCS (18) 2004, 183–96.

10916. DAWSON, TERENCE. The effective protagonist in the nineteenth-century British novel: Scott, Brontë, Eliot, Wilde. *See* **11912.**

10917. DOLIN, TIM. George Eliot. Oxford; New York: OUP, 2005. pp. xviii, 284. (Oxford world's classics.) (Authors in context.) Rev. by Margaret Harris in GER (36) 2005, 76–7.

10918. FAUBERT, MICHELLE. A possible source for George Eliot's Edward Casaubon. ANQ (18:2) 2005, 46–52.

10919. GALLAGHER, CATHERINE. George Eliot: immanent Victorian. Representations (90) 2005, 61–74.

10920. GATENS, MOIRA. Freedom and determinism in *Middlemarch*; or, Dorothea, the lunatic. SSE (29) 2003, 31–8.

10921. GIARDETTI, MELORA. How does your garden grow? Plants, gardens, and doctrines in George Eliot's *Silas Marner.* GEGHLS (48/49) 2005, 27–32.

10922. GOLIGHTLY, KAREN B. Transforming the Other: the merrow of Croker's *Fairy Legends* and the 'little Jewess' of *Daniel Deronda*. GEGHLS (48/49) 2005, 53–63.

10923. GOODLAD, LAUREN M. E. Towards a Victorianist's theory of androgynous experiment. *See* **16557.**

10924. GREEN, LAURA. 'I recognized myself in her': identifying with the reader in George Eliot's *The Mill on the Floss* and Simone de Beauvoir's *Memoirs of a Dutiful Daughter.* TSWL (24:1) 2005, 57–79.

10925. HASKIN, DAYTON. George Eliot as a 'Miltonist': marriage and Milton in *Middlemarch. In* (pp. 207–22) **7717.**

10926. HAWES, DONALD.   Articles on George Eliot in 2004: a selective survey. GEGHLS (48/49) 2005, 110–18.

10927. HERTZ, NEIL.   George Eliot's pulse. (Bibl. 2004, 10908.) Rev. by Lisa Hinrichsen in EC (54:4) 2004, 406–11.

10928. HILL, SUSAN E.   Rethinking the translator's invisibility: George Eliot, authority, and the politics of translation. *In* (pp. 75–89) **12978**.

10929. HOLLANDER, RACHEL.   *Daniel Deronda* and the ethics of alterity. Lit (16:1) 2005, 75–99.

10930. HUDSPITH, BARBARA.   Adam's mourning and the Herculean task in *Adam Bede*. CanRCL (30:1) 2003, 97–116.

10931. HUGHES, LINDA K.   Constructing fictions of authorship in George Eliot's *Middlemarch*, 1871–1872. VPR (38:2) 2005, 158–79.

10932. HUNTER, CERI.   Moving beyond signs: the crisis of language in *Daniel Deronda*. GER (36) 2005, 17–23.

10933. JUMEAU, ALAIN.   Fallen women in George Eliot's early novels. CVE (61) 2005, 275–84.

10934. KITSI-MITAKOU, KATERINA.   Aquatic spaces and women's places: a comparative reading of George Eliot's *The Mill on the Floss* and Alexandros Papadiamantis' Ἡ Φόνισσα. BMGS (29:2) 2005, 187–202.

10935. LUSTIG, T. J.   Sunspots and blindspots in *The Europeans*. *See* **11428**.

10936. McCORMACK, KATHLEEN.   George Eliot's English travels: composite characters and coded communications. London; New York: Routledge, 2005. pp. 193. (Context and genre in English literature.)

10937. McKAY, BRENDA.   George Eliot and Victorian attitudes to racial diversity, colonialism, Darwinism, class, gender, and Jewish culture and prophecy. (Bibl. 2004, 10918.) Rev. by Avrom Fleishman in GEGHLS (48/49) 2005, 119–21.

10938. McMASTER, JULIET.   Choosing a model: George Eliot's 'prentice hand. *In* (pp. 188–99) **9164**.

10939. McMULLEN, BONNIE SHANNON.   Legitimate plots, private lots in *Felix Holt* and *Daniel Deronda*. GER (36) 2005, 39–45.

10940. MAERTZ, GREGORY (ed.).   Middlemarch: a study of provincial life. Peterborough, Ont.; Orchard Park, NY: Broadview Press, 2004. pp. 739. (Broadview literary texts.) Rev. by Margaret Harris in GER (36) 2005, 76–7.

10941. MAZAHERI, JOHN.   Religion and work in *Adam Bede*. GEGHLS (48/49) 2005, 64–74.

10942. MUELLER, MONIKA.   George Eliot US: transatlantic literary and cultural perspectives. Madison, NJ: Fairleigh Dickinson UP, 2005. pp. 291. Rev. by Laura Green in VS (48:1) 2005, 169–71.

10943. NARDO, ANNA K.   George Eliot's dialogue with John Milton. Columbia; London: Missouri UP, 2003. pp. xii, 278. Rev. by Graham Handley in GER (36) 2005, 74–5.

10944. NEWTON, K. M.   Revisions of Scott, Austen, and Dickens in *Daniel Deronda*. DSA (35) 2005, 241–66.

10945. ORMOND, LEONÉE.   George Eliot and the Victorian art world. GER (36) 2005, 25–38.

2005]   AUTHORS   587

10946. Paris, Bernard J.   Rereading George Eliot: changing responses to her experiments in life. (Bibl. 2004, 10926.) Rev. by William Baker in StudN (37:1) 2005, 115–18.

10947. Payne, David.   The reenchantment of nineteenth-century fiction: Dickens, Thackeray, George Eliot, and serialization. See **10730**.

10948. Plasa, Carl.   George Eliot's 'confectionery business': sugar and slavery in *Brother Jacob*. Lit (16:3) 2005, 285–309.

10949. Purdy, Dwight.   The ethic of sympathy in Conrad's *Lord Jim* and Eliot's *Mill on the Floss*. See **15912**.

10950. Purdy, Dwight H.   'The one poor word' in *Middlemarch*. SELit (44:4) 2004, 805–21.

10951. ——— The wit of biblical allusion in *The Mill on the Floss*. SP (102:2) 2005, 233–46.

10952. Roden, Frederick S.   Eppie's queer daddy: spiritual fatherhood in *Silas Marner*. GEGHLS (48/49) 2005, 33–8.

10953. Sabbagh, Omar.   Aspects of 'indefiniteness' in George Eliot's *Middlemarch*. GER (36) 2005, 46–52.

10954. Sacks, Glenda.   The shock of the new: allegory and realism in *Adam Bede*. GEGHLS (48/49) 2005, 75–102.

10955. Solie, Ruth.   Music in other words: Victorian conversations. Berkeley; London: California UP, 2004. pp. 223. (California studies in 19th-century music, 12.) Rev. by Donna Parsons in VS (47:3) 2005, 468–70.

10956. Staveley, Helene.   Caught between the serpent and the swan: George Eliot's alien maids. GEGHLS (46/47) 2004, 64–78.

10957. van Zuylen, Marina.   Monomania: the flight from everyday life in literature and art. Ithaca, NY; London: Cornell UP, 2005. pp. x, 238. Rev. by Rebecca N. Mitchell in GER (36) 2005, 83–4.

10958. Willis, Martin.   Clairvoyance, economics and authorship in George Eliot's *The Lifted Veil*. JVC (10:2) 2005, 184–209.

10959. Winter, Richard.   Romantic love as a spiritual companionship? A Buddhist re-reading of George Eliot. GER (36) 2005, 53–62.

10960. Zangen, Britta.   Our daughters must be wives: marriageable young women in the novels of Dickens, Eliot, and Hardy. See **10765**.

Ebenezer Elliott

10961. Easley, Alexis.   *Tait's Edinburgh Magazine* in the 1830s: dialogues on gender, class, and reform. See **1194**.

Charles Isaac Elton (1839–1900)

10962. Shaw, John.   *Luriana, Lurilee* revisited: i, *A Garden Song*: Leonard Woolf's manuscript copy: the 'right version' of the poem. NQ (52:1) 2005, 89–93.

10963. ——— *Luriana, Lurilee* revisited: ii, More poems by Charles Elton. NQ (52:1) 2005, 93–4.

'Embe' (Marianna Burgess)

10964. GOULD, JANICE.   Telling stories to the seventh generation: resisting the assimilationist narrative of *Stiya*. *In* (pp. 9–20) **12725**.

Ralph Waldo Emerson

10965. BELKNAP, ROBERT E.   The list: the uses and pleasures of cataloguing. New Haven, CT; London: Yale UP, 2004. pp. xviii, 252.

10966. BELLOT, MARC.   Ralph Waldo Emerson: parcours de l'œuvre en prose. Neuilly: Atlande, 2003. pp. 223. (Clefs concours: Civilisation américaine.) Rev. by Yves Carlet in EREA (1:2) 2003.

10967. BUELL, LAWRENCE.   Emerson. (Bibl. 2004, 10952.) Rev. by Robert E. Burkholder in JAH (92:3) 2005, 986–7; by Philip Joseph in AmS (46:1) 2005, 158–9; by William Rossi in ISLE (12:1) 2005, 270–3; by Robert N. Hudspeth in MaHR (7) 2005, 120–31.

10968. CLEMENTE, VINCE.   Like Whitman, 'fed and bred under the Italian dispensation'. *See* **15806**.

10969. COLE, RACHEL.   The reality effect: Emerson's speakers and the phenomenon of personality. YJC (18:1) 2005, 67–86.

10970. CROUSE, JAMIE S.   'If they have a moral power': Margaret Fuller, Transcendentalism, and the question of women's moral nature. *See* **11030**.

10971. ESDALE, LOGAN.   Dickinson's epistolary 'naturalness'. *See* **10777**.

10972. FIELD, SUSAN.   Open to influence: Ralph Waldo Emerson and Audre Lorde on loss. ATQ (19:1) 2005, 5–22.

10973. FORD, MAX.   Trust yourself: Emerson and Dylan. *In* (pp. 127–42) **16207**.

10974. FRESONKE, KRIS.   West of Emerson: the design of Manifest Destiny. (Bibl. 2004, 10959.) Rev. by Charles W. Mignon in GPQ (24:3) 2004, 211–12; by Martin Kevorkian in AmS (46:2) 2005, 177–8.

10975. GOODSPEED-CHADWICK, JULIE ELAINE.   The 19 September 1838 letter from George Bailey Loring (1817–1891) to James Russell Lowell (1819–1891). *See* **11619**.

10976. GROSSMAN, JAY.   Reconstituting the American renaissance: Emerson, Whitman, and the politics of representation. (Bibl. 2004, 10963.) Rev. by Mary Kupice Cayton in JAH (91:2) 2004, 631–2; by Claudette Fillard in EA (58:2) 2005, 240–2.

10977. HANLON, CHRISTOPHER.   Eloquence and *Invisible Man*. *See* **16330**.

10978. HECKERL, DAVID K.   'Nature will not be disposed of': Emerson against historicism. CRAS (35:1) 2005, 109–21 (review-article).

10979. HOELLER, HILDEGARD.   Self-reliant women in Frances Harper's writings. *See* **11172**.

10980. HURTH, ELISABETH.   Between faith and unbelief: Ralph Waldo Emerson on man and God. Amst (48:4) 2003, 483–95.

10981. JOHNSON, MARK.   'Keep looking': Mary Oliver's Emersonian project. *See* **18607**.

10982. KEANE, PATRICK J. Emerson, Romanticism, and intuitive reason: the transatlantic 'light of all our day'. Columbia; London: Missouri UP, 2005. pp. xv, 555.

10983. LARSON, KERRY. Emerson's strange equality. NineL (59:3) 2004, 315–39.

10984. LEE, MAURICE S. The old and the new: double consciousness and the literature of slavery. ESQ (49:1–3) 2003, 95–105.

10985. LUNDIN, ROGER. From nature to experience: the American search for cultural authority. Lanham, MD; Oxford: Rowman & Littlefield, 2005. pp. xiii, 263. (American intellectual culture.)

10986. MAYNARD, W. BARKSDALE. Emerson's 'Wyman lot': forgotten context for Thoreau's house at Walden. See **12204.**

10987. MONTEIRO, GEORGE. An Emerson letter re-edited. ANQ (18:2) 2005, 45–6.

10988. MORTON, HEATHER. Democracy, self-reviews and the 1855 Leaves of Grass. See **12337.**

10989. OLWELL, VICTORIA. 'It spoke itself': women's genius and eccentric politics. AL (77:1) 2005, 33–63.

10990. QUINN, GERARD. The crooked straightness of Frost and Emerson. See **16611.**

10991. QUINN, JUSTIN. American errancy: empire, sublimity & modern poetry. See **14474.**

10992. SACKS, KENNETH S. Understanding Emerson: 'the American scholar' and his struggle for self-reliance. (Bibl. 2004, 10981.) Rev. by Russell B. Goodman in JAH (91:1) 2004, 240–1; by Martin Kevorkian in AmS (46:2) 2005, 177–8.

10993. SAITO, NAOKO. The gleam of light: moral perfectionism and education in Dewey and Emerson. New York: Fordham UP, 2005. pp. xiv, 210. (American philosophy, 16.)

10994. SPECQ, FRANÇOIS. Thoreau's flowering of facts and the truth of experience. See **12212.**

10995. TAYLOR, ANDREW. 'The same old sausage': Thomas Carlyle and the James family. In (pp. 125–36) **10393.**

10996. WALLS, LAURA DASSOW. Emerson's life in science: the culture of truth. (Bibl. 2004, 10986.) Rev. by Russell B. Goodman in JAH (91:1) 2004, 240–1; by William Rossi in ISLE (12:1) 2005, 270–3.

10997. WATSON, DAVID. Shakespeare: the discovery of America. See **6105.**

10998. ZHANG, XUEMEI. Emily Dickinson's redefining Transcendentalist view of nature. See **10802.**

Augusta Jane Evans (Augusta Evans Wilson) (1835–1909)

10999. ASHWORTH, SUZANNE M. Reading mind, reading body: Augusta Jane Evans's Beulah and the physiology of reading. In (pp. 77–104) **12549.**

11000. TRUBEY, ELIZABETH FEKETE. Emancipating the lettered slave: sentiment and slavery in Augusta Evans's St Elmo. AL (77:1) 2005, 123–50.

John Meade Falkner

11001. McEvoy, Emma. 'Really, though secretly, a Papist': G. K. Chesterton's and John Meade Falkner's rewritings of the gothic. *See* **15776.**

Marianne Farningham (1834–1909)

11002. Forsyth, Margaret. Looking for grandmothers: working-class women poets and 'herstory'. WWr (12:2) 2005, 259–69.

Frederic W. Farrar

11003. Dakyns, Andrew G. Schooldays of George H. Borrow (1803–81) & James M. Wilson (1836–1931): a comparison. *See* **10108.**

Edward Francis Fay

11004. Mutch, Deborah. The *Merrie England* triptych: Robert Blatchford, Edward Fay and the didactic use of *Clarion* fiction. *See* **1283.**

Eliza Fenwick

11005. Chatterjee, Ranita. Sapphic subjectivity and gothic desires in Eliza Fenwick's *Secresy* (1795). GothS (6:1) 2004, 45–56.

Sir Samuel Ferguson

11006. Patten, Eve. Samuel Ferguson and the culture of nineteenth-century Ireland. Dublin; Portland, OR: Four Courts Press, 2004. pp. 207. Rev. by Ciara Hogan in ILS (24:2) 2005, 12.

'Fanny Fern' (Sara Payson (Willis) Parton)

11007. Weyler, Karen A. Literary labors and intellectual prostitution: Fanny Fern's defense of working women. SAtlR (70:2) 2005, 96–131.

Susan Ferrier

11008. Shields, Juliet. From family roots to the routes of empire: national tales and the domestication of the Scottish Highlands. *See* **11098.**

Kate Field (1838–1896)

11009. Scharnhorst, Gary (introd.). Kate Field's *An Evening with Charles Dickens*: a reconstructed lecture. DickQ (21:2) 2004, 71–89.

'Michael Field' (Katharine Bradley and Edith Cooper)

11010. Banash, David. To the Other: the animal and desire in Michael Field's *Whym Chow: Flame of Love. In* (pp. 195–205) **14258.**

11011. Ehnenn, Jill. Looking strategically: feminist and queer aesthetics in Michael Field's *Sight and Song.* VP (43:1) 2005, 109–54.

11012. Lysack, Krista. Aesthetic consumption and the cultural production of Michael Field's *Sight and Song.* SELit (45:4) 2005, 935–60.

11013. Morley, Rachel N. A new sketch of Edith Cooper ('Michael Field'). NQ (52:1) 2005, 81–2.

11014. Parejo Vadillo, Ana. Immaterial poetics: A. Mary F. Robinson and the *fin-de-siècle* poem. *In* (pp. 231–60) **9675.**

11015. Saville, Julia F. The poetic imaging of Michael Field. *In* (pp. 178–206) **9675.**

11016. THAIN, MARION. 'Damnable Aestheticism' and the turn to Rome: John Gray, Michael Field, and a poetics of conversion. *In* (pp. 311–36) **9675.**

Edward FitzGerald

11017. IRWIN, ROBERT. Omar's metamorphosis. TLS, 23 & 30 Dec. 2005, 10–11 (review-article).

Eliza Dawson Fletcher (1770–1858)

11018. RENDALL, JANE. 'Women that would plague me with rational conversation': aspiring women and Scottish Whigs, *c.*1790–1830. *In* (pp. 326–47) **8016.**

Eliza Lee Cabot Follen (1787–1860)

11019. TEMPLIN, MARY. 'Dedicated to works of beneficence': charity as model for a domesticated economy in antebellum women's panic fiction. *In* (pp. 80–104) **9513.**

Mary Hallock Foote

11020. KARELL, LINDA. The postmodern author on stage: *Fair Use* and Wallace Stegner. *See* **19576.**

11021. MILLER, DARLIS A. Mary Hallock Foote: author–illustrator of the American West. (Bibl. 2004, 11012.) Rev. by Karen S. Langlois in PacHR (72:4) 2003, 643–4.

Richard Ford (1796–1858)

11022. ROBERTSON, IAN. Richard Ford 1796–1858: hispanophile, connoisseur and critic. Norwich: Russell, 2004. pp. 381, (plates) 16. Rev. by Anthony H. Clarke in GBB (29) 2004, 74–6.

11023. —— Wry aspersions in the *Rye*. *See* **10124.**

John Monk Foster (1858–1930)

11024. LAW, GRAHAM. Imagined local communities: three Victorian newspaper novelists. *In* (pp. 185–203) **880.**

Mary E. Wilkins Freeman

11025. BERNARDI, DEBRA. 'The right to be let alone': Mary Wilkins Freeman and the right to a 'private share'. *In* (pp. 135–56) **9513.**

11026. GRASSO, LINDA M. Inventive desperation: anger, violence, and belonging in Mary Wilkins Freeman's and Sui Sin Far's murderous mother stories. ALR (38:1) 2005, 18–31.

James Anthony Froude

11027. MARKUS, JULIA. J. Anthony Froude: the last undiscovered great Victorian: a biography. New York: Scribner, 2005. pp. 340, (plates) 8.

Margaret Fuller

11028. BIRKLE, CARMEN. Travelogues of independence: Margaret Fuller and Henry David Thoreau. Amst (48:4) 2003, 497–512.

11029. CLEMENTE, VINCE. Like Whitman, 'fed and bred under the Italian dispensation'. *See* **15806.**

11030. CROUSE, JAMIE S. 'If they have a moral power': Margaret Fuller, Transcendentalism, and the question of women's moral nature. ATQ (19:4) 2005, 259–79.

11031. DE JONG, MARY. Margaret Fuller, prescient and present. NCP (32:1) 2005, 227–41 (review-article).

11032. JONES, MARION AVRILYN. 'An exalted and sensitive existence': Margaret Fuller's account of the Seeress of Prevost as feminist hagiography in *Summer on the Lakes, in 1843*. SPAS (8) 2004, 81–102.

11033. KOLK, HEIDI. Tropes of suffering and postures of authority in Margaret Fuller's European travel letters. Biography (28:3) 2005, 377–413.

11034. LAWRENCE, KATHLEEN. Osmond's complaint: Gilbert Osmond's mother and the cultural context of James's *The Portrait of a Lady*. See **11422**.

11035. NEWMAN, LANCE. Margaret Fuller's *Summer on the Lakes in 1843* and the condition of America. RomNet (38/39) 2005.

11036. WACH, HOWARD M. A Boston vindication: Margaret Fuller and Caroline Dall read Mary Wollstonecraft. MaHR (7) 2005, 3–35.

Elizabeth Gaskell

11037. BLAIR, EMILY. 'The wrong side of the tapestry': Elizabeth Gaskell's *Wives and Daughters*. VLC (33:2) 2005, 585–97.

11038. BOIKO, KAREN. Reading and (re)writing class: Elizabeth Gaskell's *Wives and Daughters*. VLC (33:1) 2005, 85–106.

11039. BRASS, DANIEL. Defining pastoral in *North and South*. SSE (30) 2004, 60–78.

11040. CHISHTY-MUJAHID, NADYA. Scarred and healed identities: fallenness, morality, and the issue of personal autonomy in *Adam Bede* and *Ruth*. See **10911**.

11041. CHRISTENSEN, ALLAN C. 'Ruth … sick for home': the Keatsian imagination in the novel of Elizabeth Gaskell. *In* (pp. 105–22) **9237**.

11042. FITZPATRICK, TONY. The trisected society: social welfare in early Victorian fiction. See **10682**.

11043. HANDLEY, GRAHAM. An Elizabeth Gaskell chronology. Basingstoke; New York: Palgrave Macmillan, 2005. pp. 288.

11044. JACKSON, JEFFREY E. Elizabeth Gaskell and the dangerous edge of things: epigraphs in *North and South* and Victorian publishing practices. PCP (40:2) 2005, 56–72.

11045. KIESEL, ALYSON J. Meaning and misinterpretation in *Cranford*. ELH (71:4) 2004, 1001–17.

11046. MALTON, SARA A. Illicit inscriptions: reframing forgery in Elizabeth Gaskell's *Ruth*. VLC (33:1) 2005, 187–202.

11047. MARKOVITS, STEFANIE. *North and South*, East and West: Elizabeth Gaskell, the Crimean War, and the Condition of England. NineL (59:4) 2005, 463–93.

11048. MARTIN-BERNARD, FRANÇOISE. Récits de voyage dans *Sylvia's Lovers* d'Elizabeth Gaskell (1863): tours et détours de la narration. EREA (3:1) 2005, 42–8.

11049. NILES, LISA.   Malthusian menopause: aging and sexuality in Elizabeth Gaskell's *Cranford*. VLC (33:1) 2005, 293–310.

11050. PITE, RALPH (gen. ed.).   Lives of Victorian literary figures III: Elizabeth Gaskell, the Carlyles and John Ruskin by their contemporaries: vol. 1, Elizabeth Gaskell. Ed. by Valerie Sanders. London; Brookfield, VT: Pickering & Chatto, 2005. pp. xliii, 375.

11051. SCHAFFER, TALIA.   Craft, authorial anxiety, and *The Cranford Papers*. VPR (38:2) 2005, 221–39.

11052. SEELYE, JOHN D.   Jane Eyre's American daughters: from *The Wide, Wide World* to *Anne of Green Gables*: a study of marginalized maidens and what they mean. *See* **10182**.

11053. TWINN, FRANCES.   The portrait of Haworth in *The Life of Charlotte Brontë*. *See* **10227**.

11054. VÉGSŐ, ROLAND.   *Mary Barton* and the dissembled dialogue. JNT (33:2) 2003, 163–83.

11055. WEBB, IGOR.   Reading *Mary Barton*. LitIm (7:1) 2005, 43–65.

11056. WOMACK, WHITNEY A.   Reforming women's reform literature: Rebecca Harding Davis's rewriting of the industrial novel. *In* (pp. 105–31) **9513**.

11057. WYNNE, DEBORAH.   Hysteria repeating itself: Elizabeth Gaskell's *Lois the Witch*. WWr (12:1) 2005, 85–97.

Myron Bartlett Gibson (b.1858)

11058. APOL, LAURA.   Shooting bears, saving butterflies: ideology of the environment in Gibson's *Herm and I* (1894) and Klass's *California Blue* (1994). ChildLit (31) 2003, 90–115.

William Gifford

11059. GAMER, MICHAEL.   'Bell's poetics': *The Baviad*, the Della Cruscans, and the book of *The World*. *In* (pp. 31–53) **9305**.

11060. STRACHAN, JOHN (gen. ed.).   British satire: vol. 4, Gifford and the Della Cruscans. Ed. by John Strachan. London; Brookfield, VT: Pickering & Chatto, 2003. pp. xxxvii, 384. Rev. by Marcus Wood in WordsC (35:4) 2004, 162–4; by Bernard Beatty in BJ (32:2) 2004, 153–5.

W. S. (William Schwenck) Gilbert (1836–1911)

11061. BRISTOW, JOSEPH.   Biographies: Oscar Wilde – the man, the life, the legend. *In* (pp. 6–35) **12414**.

11062. CREASY, MATTHEW.   Shakespeare burlesque in *Ulysses*. *See* **17263**.

Anne Gilchrist

11063. CAVITCH, MAX.   Audience terminable and interminable: Anne Gilchrist, Walt Whitman, and the achievement of disinhibited reading. VP (43:2) 2005, 249–61.

George Gilfillan (1813–1878)

11064. BOOS, FLORENCE S.   'Spasm' and class: W. E. Aytoun, George Gilfillan, Sydney Dobell, and Alexander Smith. *See* **10818**.

George Gissing

11065. ANON. Gissing returns to Manchester. GissJ (41:3) 2005, 19–21.

11066. ALLEN, M. D.   Eduard Bertz's Rugby, Tennessee. GissJ (41:1) 2005, 1–12.

11067. CHIALANT, MARIA TERESA.   Tra confessione e autobiografia: tre casi vittoriani. *In* (pp. 165–87) **12577.**

11068. COUSTILLAS, PIERRE.   The correspondence between Clara Collet and Morley Roberts (fourth and last instalment). See **11545.**

11069. —— George Gissing: the definitive bibliography. High Wycombe: Rivendale Press, 2005. pp. xxxv, 604, (plates) 24. Rev. by D. J. Taylor in TLS, 27 May 2005, 29; by Bouwe Postmus in GissJ (41:2) 2005, 26–30; by Richard Whittington-Egan in ContRev (287:1676) 2005, 157–9.

11070. —— Three companions in one: in turn Daniele Cristofaro takes the plunge and fully identifies Coriolano Paparazzo. GissJ (41:3) 2005, 22–32 (review-article).

11071. CRISTOFARO, DANIELE.   George Robert Gissing: il viaggio desiderato, Calabria 1897. Cosenza: Pellegrini, 2005. pp. 167. (Viaggi, 1.) Rev. by Pierre Coustillas in GissJ (41:3) 2005, 22–32.

11072. DEVINE, CHRISTINE.   Class in turn-of-the-century novels of Gissing, James, Hardy, and Wells. Aldershot; Burlington, VT: Ashgate, 2005. pp. 158. (Nineteenth century.)

11073. HARSH, CONSTANCE.   The text of *Eve's Ransom*: insights from the *Illustrated London News* serialization. GissJ (41:3) 2005, 1–9.

11074. HAYDOCK, JAMES.   Portraits in charcoal: George Gissing's women. Bloomington, IN: AuthorHouse, 2004. pp. 316. Rev. by Pierre Coustillas in GissJ (41:2) 2005, 30–4.

11075. JAMES, SIMON J.   Unsettled accounts: money and narrative in the novels of George Gissing. (Bibl. 2004, 11066.) Rev. by Emma Liggins in ELT (48:1) 2005, 97–100; by John Sloan in NineL (59:4) 2005, 547–50.

11076. —— (ed.).   Collected works of George Gissing on Charles Dickens: vol. 2, Charles Dickens: a critical study. Afterword by David Parker. Grayswood, Surrey: Grayswood Press, 2004. pp. 274. Rev. by Bouwe Postmus in GissJ (41:1) 2005, 27–30; by Christine Huguet in CVE (61) 2005, 338–40.

11077. KOMIYA, AYAKA.   Gissing, Tolstoi, and the Victorian vegetarian movement. GissJ (41:2) 2005, 18–25.

11078. MESSENGER, NIGEL.   'The dung-heap and the flower': Gissing's *Nether World*. CVE (61) 2005, 303–15.

11079. MITCHELL, MARGARET E.   Gissing's moral mischief: prostitutes and narrative resolution. StudN (37:4) 2005, 411–29.

11080. NOONKESTER, MYRON C.   Dickens's *Bleak House*. See **10725.**

11081. PEARSON, RICHARD.   George Gissing and the ethnographer's 'I': civilisation in *The Nether World* and *Eve's Ransom*. CritS (16:1) 2004, 35–51.

11082. SCHMIDT, GERALD.   George Gissing's psychology of 'female imbecility'. StudN (37:3) 2005, 329–41.

11083. SLOAN, JOHN; COUSTILLAS, PIERRE.   *Demos*: a review in *The State*. GissJ (41:1) 2005, 26–7.

11084. SPIERS, JOHN. For flag and fortune? The colonial edition, 1843–1972: a Gissing perspective. GissJ (41:3) 2005, 9–18 (review-article).

11085. VILLA, LUISA. Gissing, le folle e la modernità urbana: transgressione, carnevale e crisi dell'autorità paterna. NCorr (133) 2004, 127–64.

11086. WHITTINGTON-EGAN, RICHARD. Gissing games. ContRev (287:1676) 2005, 157–9 (review-article).

11087. WILLIS, CHRIS. From voyeurism to feminism: Victorian and Edwardian London's streetfighting slum viragoes. See **18150.**

William Ewart Gladstone

11088. BEBBINGTON, D. W. The mind of Gladstone: religion, Homer, and politics. (Bibl. 2004, 11075.) Rev. by Walter L. Arnstein in VS (47:4) 2005, 625–6.

Adam Lindsay Gordon (1833–1870)

11089. SUSSEX, LUCY. 'Bobbing around': James Skipp Borlase, Adam Lindsay Gordon, and surviving in the literary market of Australia, 1860s. See **10106.**

Mrs (Catherine Grace Frances) Gore (1799–1861)

11090. JUMP, HARRIET DEVINE (gen. ed.). Silver fork novels, 1826–1841: vol. 6, *Cecil; or, The Adventures of a Coxcomb* (1841). Ed. by Andrea Hibbard and Edward Copeland. London; Brookfield, VT: Pickering & Chatto, 2005. pp. xl, 440. Rev. by Lauren Gillingham in TLS, 23 & 30 Dec. 2005, 30.

'Sarah Grand' (Frances Elizabeth Clarke)

11091. CHIRICO, MIRIAM. Social critique and comedic reconciliation in Shaw's *You Never Can Tell. See* **19385.**

11092. HEILMANN, ANN. New Woman strategies: Sarah Grand, Olive Schreiner, Mona Caird. Manchester; New York: Manchester UP, 2004. pp. xii, 292. Rev. by Naomi Hetherington in TexP (19:2) 2005, 385–8.

11093. RICHARDSON, ANGELIQUE. Eugenics and freedom at the *fin de siècle*. *In* (pp. 275–86) **1226.**

Anne MacVicar Grant (1755–1838)

11094. PERKINS, PAM. Paradises lost: Anne Grant and late eighteenth-century idealizations of America. EAL (40:2) 2005, 315–40.

Rosa Graul (*fl.*1897)

11095. PASSET, JOANNE E. Reading *Hilda's Home*: gender, print culture, and the dissemination of utopian thought in late nineteenth-century America. LibC (40:3) 2005, 307–23.

John Gray (1866–1934)

11096. THAIN, MARION. 'Damnable Aestheticism' and the turn to Rome: John Gray, Michael Field, and a poetics of conversion. *In* (pp. 311–36) **9675.**

Anna Katharine Green

11097. NICKERSON, CATHERINE ROSS (introd.). *That Affair Next Door* and *Lost Man's Lane*. Durham, NC; London: Duke UP, 2003. pp. 445. Rev. by Jennifer Putzi in Legacy (22:1) 2005, 91–4.

Sarah Green (*fl.*1790–1825)

11098. SHIELDS, JULIET.   From family roots to the routes of empire: national tales and the domestication of the Scottish Highlands. ELH (72:4) 2005, 919–40.

Grace Greenwood (1823–1904)

11099. GARRETT, PAULA K.   A splinter off the 'sound old theological block': Grace Greenwood's revision of the American jeremiad. SAH (12) 2005, 17–43.

Sutton E. Griggs

11100. BECKHAM, JACK M., II.   Griggs's *Imperium in Imperio.* Exp (63:2) 2005, 85–7.

11101. DAVIDSON, ADENIKE MARIE.   Double leadership, double trouble: critiquing double consciousness and racial uplift in Sutton Griggs's *Imperium in Imperio.* CLAJ (48:2) 2004, 127–55.

11102. LOGAN, SHIRLEY WILSON.   'To get an education and teach my people': rhetoric for social change. *In* (pp. 36–52) **2318.**

Sir Henry Rider Haggard

11103. KAUFMAN, HEIDI.   *King Solomon's Mines?* African Jewry, British imperialism, and H. Rider Haggard's diamonds. VLC (33:2) 2005, 517–39.

11104. LIBBY, ANDREW.   Revisiting the sublime: terrible women and the aesthetics of misogyny in H. Rider Haggard's *King Solomon's Mines* and *She.* CEACrit (67:1) 2004, 1–14.

John Thomas Haines (1799?–1843)

11105. CRONIN-JORTNER, MAURA L.   In soldier's clothes: Adah Isaacs Menken goes to war. *See* **11717.**

Fitz-Greene Halleck (1790–1867)

11106. BERGLUND, MICHAEL H.   Looking back to look ahead: homosexuality and the postmodern gothic in American literature. *See* **9188.**

J. O. Halliwell-Phillipps

11107. ANON.   Shakespeare in the nineteenth century. *See* **5784.**

Janet Thomson Hamilton (1795–1873)

11108. FORSYTH, MARGARET.   Looking for grandmothers: working-class women poets and 'herstory'. *See* **11002.**

Thomas Hardy

11109. ALKON, GABRIEL.   Refrain and the limits of poetic power in Spenser, Herbert, Hardy, and Stevens. *See* **5675.**

11110. ANDERSON, JORDAN.   'The architecture of the grave'. HarSJ (1:1) 2005, 24–31.

11111. ASQUITH, MARK.   Thomas Hardy, metaphysics and music. Basingstoke; New York: Palgrave Macmillan, 2005. pp. ix, 234.

11112. BENDER, TODD K.   Competing cultural domains, borderlands and spatial/temporal thresholds in Hardy, Conrad, and D. H. Lawrence. YREAL (21) 2005, 173–83.

11113. CLARK, INDY. 'The misfortune of ruins': Hardy and Stonehenge. HarSJ (1:1) 2005, 18–23.

11114. CORNWELL, NEIL. 'A Dorset yokel's knuckles': Thomas Hardy and *Lolita*. *See* **18453**.

11115. DAVIS, W. EUGENE. Folk songs in the shearing-supper scene: John Schlesinger's movie version of *Far from the Madding Crowd*. HaR (7) 2004, 79–85.

11116. DEVINE, CHRISTINE. Class in turn-of-the-century novels of Gissing, James, Hardy, and Wells. *See* **11072**.

11117. DOWNEY, GLEN R. Chess and social game playing in *A Pair of Blue Eyes*. HaR (6) 2003, 105–46.

11118. DRYDEN, LINDA. The Hardys and William Mathie Parker. Bibliotheck (ns 1:2) 2004, 25–38.

11119. EBBATSON, ROGER. Hardy and class. *In* (pp. 111–34) **11140**.

11120. EFRON, ARTHUR. Experiencing *Tess of the d'Urbervilles*: a Deweyan account. Amsterdam; Atlanta, GA: Rodopi, 2005. pp. xiii, 248. (Value inquiry books, 162.) (Studies in Pragmatism and values.) Rev. by Robert Schweik in ELT (48:3) 2005, 359–63; by Claire Seymour in HarSJ (1:2) 2005, 50–3.

11121. EVERETT, BARBARA. Larkin and the doomsters: walking 'down life's sunless hill' with Hardy and Barbara Pym. *See* **18979**.

11122. FINCHAM, ANTHONY. Hardy, death and the psychosomatic. THJ (21) 2005, 58–93.

11123. GREENSLADE, WILLIAM (ed.). Thomas Hardy's 'Facts' notebook. (Bibl. 2004, 11106.) Rev. by Guy Cuthbertson in RES (56:225) 2005, 468–70; by Michael Irwin in HarSJ (1:1) 2005, 48–50.

11124. HARRISON, DeSALES. The end of the mind: the edge of the intelligible in Hardy, Stevens, Larkin, Plath, and Glück. (Bibl. 2004, 11110.) Rev. by Angus Cleghorn in WSJ (29:2) 2005, 319–20.

11125. HOLLAND, NORMAN N. 'The barge she sat in': psychoanalysis and diction. *See* **6262**.

11126. HUGHES, JOHN. Tennyson revisited: Hardy's *After a Journey*. THJ (21) 2005, 152–7.

11127. —— Visual inspiration in Hardy's fiction. *In* (pp. 229–54) **11140**.

11128. IRWIN, MICHAEL. Hardy and the 'Baby' poems. *See* **16883**.

11129. KEARNEY, ANTHONY. Hardy and Jowett: fact and fiction in *Jude the Obscure*. THJ (21) 2005, 103–8.

11130. —— Thomas Hardy and Samuel Smiles: biography, fiction and the self-help debate. HarSJ (1:1) 2005, 32–40.

11131. KIM, DONGUK. 'Memorable little scenes': colour symbolism, hat imagery and Victorian culture in *A Pair of Blue Eyes*. THJ (21) 2005, 125–34.

11132. KNOWLES, RONALD. Carnival and tragedy in Thomas Hardy's novels. THJ (21) 2005, 109–24.

11133. —— A tragic pattern: *The Convergence of the Twain* and Hardy's fiction. HarSJ (1:1) 2005, 41–6.

11134. LOCK, CHARLES. Hardy and the critics. *In* (pp. 14–37) **11140**.

11135. LOWMAN, ROGER. Thomas Hardy's *The Dorsetshire Labourer* and Wessex. Lewiston, NY; Lampeter: Mellen Press, 2005. pp. xiv, 260. (Studies in British literature, 96.)

11136. LUCAS, JOHN. Trade terms. TLS, 25 Feb. 2005, 9 (review-article). (Hardy's professionalism.)

11137. McCARTY, STEVE. 'That we can talk of another time': Boldwood's madness and Victorian law. THJ (21) 2005, 94–102.

11138. McEATHRON, SCOTT (ed.). Thomas Hardy's *Tess of the d'Urbervilles*: a sourcebook. London; New York: Routledge, 2005. pp. vi, 194. (Routledge guides to literature.)

11139. MALLETT, PHILLIP. 'The immortal puzzle': Hardy and sexuality. *In* (pp. 181–202) **11140**.

11140. —— (ed.). Palgrave advances in Thomas Hardy studies. Basingstoke; New York: Palgrave Macmillan, 2004. pp. xiv, 314. (Palgrave advances.) Rev. by Simon Gatrell in CamQ (34:2) 2005, 181–4.

11141. MARTIN, SHIRLEY A. 'He knew psychoanalysis': Thomas Hardy and the paradox of degeneracy in *Tess of the d'Urbervilles*. PsyArt (9) 2005.

11142. MILLGATE, MICHAEL. Thomas Hardy: a biography revisited. (Bibl. 2004, 11132.) Rev. by John Lucas in TLS, 25 Feb. 2005, 9; by Keith Wilson in LRC (13:5) 2005, 6–7.

11143. MORGAN, ROSEMARIE. Editing Hardy. *In* (pp. 90–110) **11140**.

11144. —— A Hardy hymn. HaR (6) 2003, 93–6.

11145. NEILL, EDWARD. 'Heavenly bodies?': feminism and fiction(s) in *Two on a Tower* (1882). THJ (21) 2005, 143–51.

11146. NEMESVARI, RICHARD. Collaboration or compromise? From screenplay to screen in the Ian Sharp production of *Tess of the d'Urbervilles*. HaR (7) 2004, 65–78.

11147. —— Hardy and his readers. *In* (pp. 38–74) **11140**.

11148. NEWBY, MARK. He hath wrought folly in Wessex: Hardy's use of biblical narrative in *Tess of the d'Urbervilles*. Eng (54:209) 2005, 135–45.

11149. NISHIMURA, SATOSHI. Language, violence, and irrevocability: speech acts in *Tess of the d'Urbervilles*. StudN (37:2) 2005, 208–22.

11150. PASTORE, STEPHEN. The cat and the canard. HarSJ (1:2) 2005, 47–9.

11151. PETTIT, CHARLES P. C. The unique achievement of *Far from the Madding Crowd*. HaR (7) 2004, 118–43.

11152. PITE, RALPH. Hardy and biography. *In* (pp. 75–89) **11140**.

11153. RADFORD, ANDREW. Hardy's Tess, Jane Harrison and the twilight of a goddess. THJ (21) 2005, 27–57.

11154. RAY, MARTIN. The Bodleian manuscript of *Poems of the Past and the Present*. HaR (6) 2003, 99–104.

11155. —— Thomas Hardy: four notes. NQ (52:4) 2005, 491–3.

11156. —— Thomas Hardy's *The Trumpet-Major*: the source of 'Upon the Hill He Turned'. HarSJ (1:2) 2005, 33–4.

11157. RICHARDSON, ANGELIQUE. Hardy and science: a chapter of accidents. *In* (pp. 156–80) **11140**.

11158. RIMMER, MARY. Hardy, Victorian culture and provinciality. *In* (pp. 135–55) **11140**.

11159. ROBSON, PETER. Thomas Hardy and *The Outlandish Knight*. HarSJ (1:2) 2005, 29–32.

11160. ROGERS, SHANNON. The whole left behind: omitted scenes in Polanski's *Tess*. *See* **13816**.

11161. SCHWEIK, ROBERT. A note on some modern critical views of the relationship of *The Well-Beloved* to the Victorian art context. HaR (7) 2004, 99–117.

11162. SEEBER, HANS ULRICH. The retrospective attitude in poems by Edward Thomas and Andrew Motion. *See* **19777**.

11163. SEYMOUR, CLAIRE. 'Absalom's place': Gerald Finzi and Thomas Hardy. HarSJ (1:2) 2005, 38–46.

11164. SHIRES, LINDA. Hardy and nineteenth-century poetry and politics. *In* (pp. 255–78) **11140**.

11165. VARCOE, STEPHEN. Some thoughts on singing the poems of Thomas Hardy. HarSJ (1:2) 2005, 35–7.

11166. WANG, GUIQIN. A statistical analysis of the research papers on Hardy from 1980 to 2004 in Chinese journals. FLS (116) 2005, 153–61. (In Chinese.)

11167. WARD, JOHN POWELL. Hardy's aesthetics and twentieth-century poetry. *In* (pp. 279–302) **11140**.

11168. WHITEHEAD, JAMES S. Hardy and Englishness. *In* (pp. 203–28) **11140**.

11169. WILSON, KEITH; BRADY, KRISTIN (eds). *The Fiddler of the Reels* and other stories, 1888–1900. London; New York: Penguin, 2003. pp. lvi, 339. (Penguin classics.)

11170. WITTENBERG, JUDITH BRYANT. Thomas Hardy and Augustus John. THJ (21) 2005, 135–42.

11171. ZANGEN, BRITTA. Our daughters must be wives: marriageable young women in the novels of Dickens, Eliot, and Hardy. *See* **10765**.

Frances Ellen Watkins Harper

11172. HOELLER, HILDEGARD. Self-reliant women in Frances Harper's writings. ATQ (19:3) 2005, 205–20.

11173. LOGAN, SHIRLEY WILSON. 'To get an education and teach my people': rhetoric for social change. *In* (pp. 36–52) **2318**.

11174. NOVAK, TERRY D. Frances Harper's poverty relief mission in the African American community. *In* (pp. 213–26) **9513**.

11175. PETRINO, ELIZABETH A. 'We are rising as a people': Frances Harper's radical views on class and racial equality in *Sketches of Southern Life*. ATQ (19:2) 2005, 133–53.

11176. ROBISON, LORI. An 'imperceptible infusion' of blood: *Iola Leroy*, racial identity, and Sentimental discourse. Genre (37:3/4) 2004, 433–60.

11177. RYAN, SUSAN M. *The Bostonians* and the Civil War. *See* **11451**.

11178. SANBORN, GEOFFREY. Mother's milk: Frances Harper and the circulation of blood. ELH (72:3) 2005, 691–715.

Joel Chandler Harris

11179. GRIFFIN, REBECCA. Courtship contests and the meaning of conflict in the folklore of slaves. *See* **3491**.

Bret Harte

11180. SCHARNHORST, GARY. Byron and Bret Harte. BJ (32:1) 2004, 45–50.

11181. —— Nabokov and Bret Harte: an overlooked allusion in *Lolita*. *See* **18467**.

Julian Hawthorne

11182. WINEAPPLE, BRENDA. Nathaniel Hawthorne, writer; or, The fleeing of the biographied. *In* (pp. 181–98) **11186**.

Nathaniel Hawthorne

11183. ANDERSON, DOUGLAS. *The Blithedale Romance* and post-heroic life. NineL (60:1) 2005, 32–56.

11184. BAYM, NINA. Revisiting Hawthorne's feminism. *In* (pp. 107–24) **11186**.

11185. BELL, MILLICENT. Hawthorne and the real. *In* (pp. 1–21) **11186**.

11186. —— (ed.). Hawthorne and the real: bicentennial essays. Columbus: Ohio State UP, 2005. pp. ix, 228.

11187. BELLIS, PETER J. Writing revolution: aesthetics and politics in Hawthorne, Whitman, and Thoreau. (Bibl. 2004, 11175.) Rev. by James Emmett Ryan in SAtlR (70:3) 2005, 158–61.

11188. BENOIT, RAYMOND. Hawthorne and his kinsman, Frank Lloyd Wright. NHR (31:1) 2005, 50–5.

11189. BOONE, N. S. *The Minister's Black Veil* and Hawthorne's ethical refusal of reciprocity: a Levinasian parable. Ren (57:3) 2005, 165–76.

11190. BUELL, LAWRENCE. Hawthorne and the problem of 'American' fiction: the example of *The Scarlet Letter*. *In* (pp. 70–87) **11186**.

11191. COLACURCIO, MICHAEL J. 'Red man's grave': art and destiny in Hawthorne's *Main-Street*. NHR (31:2) 2005, 1–18.

11192. COOK, JONATHAN A. The biographical background to *Rappaccini's Daughter*. NHR (31:2) 2005, 34–73.

11193. DANIELS, CINDY LOU. Hawthorne's Pearl: woman–child of the future. ATQ (19:3) 2005, 221–36.

11194. DAVIS, CLARK. Hawthorne's shyness: ethics, politics, and the question of engagement. Baltimore, MD; London: Johns Hopkins UP, 2005. pp. x, 188.

11195. DAVIS, DAVID A. The myth of Hester Prynne. NHR (31:1) 2005, 29–43.

11196. DUNNE, MICHAEL. Nathaniel Hawthorne's Calvinist humor. SAH (12) 2005, 1–16.

11197. FANG, WENKAI. Hawthorne's aesthetic modernity. FLS (115) 2005, 133–8. (In Chinese.)

11198. GILL, JO. The influence of Nathaniel Hawthorne's *The Scarlet Letter* on Sylvia Plath's *Daddy*. *See* **18819**.

11199. GILMORE, MICHAEL T. Hawthorne and politics (again): words and deeds in the 1850s. *In* (pp. 22–39) **11186**.

11200. GIORCELLI, CRISTINA.   Da Irving – a Hawthorne, a Poe – a Irving: alle origini del fantastico nella letteratura statunitense. *See* **9552.**

11201. GOLLIN, RITA K.   Estranged allegiances in Hawthorne's unfinished romances. *In* (pp. 159–80) **11186.**

11202. —— 'The fairest hope of heaven': Hawthorne on immortality. NHR (31:2) 2005, 74–89.

11203. GRIFFIN, EDWARD M.   Dancing around the maypole, ripping up the flag: the Merry Mount caper and issues in American history and art. *See* **17872.**

11204. HOEVELER, DIANE LONG.   Beatrice Cenci in Hawthorne, Melville and her Atlantic-rim contexts. RomNet (38/39) 2005.

11205. KOPLEY, RICHARD.   The threads of *The Scarlet Letter*: a study of Hawthorne's transformative art. (Bibl. 2003, 10532.) Rev. by Leland S. Person in NHR (31:1) 2005, 56–9.

11206. LEVERENZ, DAVID.   Working women and creative doubles: getting to *The Marble Faun*. *In* (pp. 144–58) **11186.**

11207. LIGGERA, J.   Hawthorne coins a term in *The Scarlet Letter*. NHR (31:1) 2005, 44–9. ('Lurid playfulness'.)

11208. LOMAN, ANDREW.   'Somewhat on the community system': Fourierism in the works of Nathaniel Hawthorne. London; New York: Routledge, 2005. pp. xxiv, 159.

11209. LUSTIG, T. J.   Sunspots and blindspots in *The Europeans*. *See* **11428.**

11210. MCFARLAND, PHILIP.   Hawthorne in Concord. (Bibl. 2004, 11210.) Rev. by Gerald T. Cobb in ANCW (192:5) 2005, 22–3; by K. P. Stich in NHR (31:2) 2005, 138–41.

11211. MAYER, DAVID R.   Artemisia Gentileschi as artist model for Miriam in Hawthorne's *The Marble Faun*. NHR (31:2) 2005, 19–33.

11212. MILLINGTON, RICHARD (ed.).   The Cambridge companion to Nathaniel Hawthorne. Cambridge; New York: CUP, 2004. pp. xviii, 285. (Cambridge companions to literature.)

11213. MORGAN, ELIZABETH.   Mary and modesty. *See* **15779.**

11214. MUIRHEAD, KIMBERLY FREE.   Nathaniel Hawthorne's *The Scarlet Letter*: a critical resource guide and comprehensive bibliography of literary criticism, 1950–2000. Lewiston, NY; Lampeter: Mellen Press, 2004. pp. cxv, 513. (Studies in American literature, 73.)

11215. PERSON, LELAND S.   Hawthorne's early tales: male authorship, domestic violence, and female readers. *In* (pp. 125–43) **11186.**

11216. PÉTILLON, PIERRE-YVES.   *La Lettre écarlate*; ou, La double exposition. EA (58:4) 2005, 416–27.

11217. PROCHÁZKA, MARTIN.   Apocalypticism in American cultural history: 2, Revelations of the Other. LittPr (15:30) 2005, 79–106.

11218. RAMDYA, KAVITA.   Hawthorne's resistance to and appropriation of Sentimental writing in *The Scarlet Letter*. McNR (42) 2004, 41–60.

11219. RASKIN, ANNIE.   Hawthorne and the daguerreotype – portraits gleaned from the sun. MiE, Spring 2005, 5–15.

11220. REYNOLDS, LARRY J.   The challenge of cultural relativity: the case of Hawthorne. ESQ (49:1–3) 2003, 129–47.

11221. —— 'Strangely ajar with the human race': Hawthorne, slavery, and the question of moral responsibility. *In* (pp. 40–69) 11186.

11222. ROSENBLUM, ANDREW E.   The idea of another: Hawthorne's 'friend of friends', dissociation, and *The Blithedale Romance*. NHR (31:1) 2005, 1–28.

11223. ROWE, JOHN CARLOS.   Nathaniel Hawthorne and transnationality. *In* (pp. 88–106) 11186.

11224. STECKER, ROBERT.   The interaction of ethical and aesthetic value. BJA (45:2) 2005, 138–50.

11225. SWEETING, ADAM W.   Preserving the renaissance: literature and public memory in the homes of Longfellow, Hawthorne, and Poe. See 11617.

11226. WINEAPPLE, BRENDA.   Nathaniel Hawthorne, writer; or, The fleeing of the biographied. *In* (pp. 181–98) 11186.

Benjamin Robert Haydon

11227. HIGGINS, DAVID MINDEN.   Romantic genius and the literary magazine: biography, celebrity, and politics. London; New York: Routledge, 2005. pp. 224. (Routledge studies in Romanticism, 6.)

William Stephens Hayward

11228. BRIGHTWELL, GERRI.   The case of the household spy: public service and domestic service in Hayward's *The Mysterious Countess*. Clues (23:3) 2005, 63–73.

William Hazlitt

11229. BERMINGHAM, ANN.   Urbanity and the spectacle of art. *In* (pp. 151–76) 9217.

11230. BROMWICH, DAVID.   Disinterested imagining and impersonal feeling. *In* (pp. 17–29) 11245.

11231. BURLEY, STEPHEN.   Hazlitt and John Stoddart: brothers-in-law or brothers at war? CLB (122) 2003, 52–63.

11232. BURWICK, FREDERICK.   Schelling and Hazlitt on disinterestedness and freedom. *In* (pp. 137–50) 11245.

11233. DAVIS, PHILIP.   'The future in the instant': Hazlitt's *Essay* and Shakespeare. *In* (pp. 43–55) 11245.

11234. GRAYLING, A. C.   'A nature towards one another': Hazlitt and the inherent disinterestedness of moral agency. *In* (pp. 151–9) 11245.

11235. HAMILTON, PAUL.   Hazlitt and the 'kings of speech'. *In* (pp. 68–80) 11245.

11236. HIGGINS, DAVID MINDEN.   Romantic genius and the literary magazine: biography, celebrity, and politics. See 11227.

11237. HOWE, SARAH.   General and invariable ideas of nature: Joshua Reynolds and his critical descendants. See 8929.

11238. KLANCHER, JON.   Discriminations; or, Romantic cosmopolitanisms in London. *In* (pp. 65–82) 9217.

11239. MANNING, PETER J. Manufacturing the Romantic image: Hazlitt and Coleridge lecturing. *In* (pp. 227–45) **9217**.

11240. MILNES, TIM. 'Darkening knowledge': Hazlitt and Bentham on the limits of empiricism. *In* (pp. 125–36) **11245**.

11241. MULVIHILL, JAMES. Hazlitt and the idea of identity. *In* (pp. 30–42) **11245**.

11242. NATARAJAN, UTTARA. Circle of sympathy: Shelley's Hazlitt. *In* (pp. 112–22) **11245**.

11243. —— Hazlitt, Lamb, and the philosophy of familiarity. CLB (124) 2003, 110–18.

11244. —— Introduction: Hazlitt's *Essay on the Principles of Human Action* – 1805–2005. *In* (pp. 1–14) **11245**.

11245. —— PAULIN, TOM; WU, DUNCAN (eds). Metaphysical Hazlitt: bicentenary essays. London; New York: Routledge, 2005. pp. xviii, 188. (Routledge studies in Romanticism, 5.)

11246. OLDFIELD, SYBIL. 'What were the leaders of the Revolution to do?': Hazlitt on Revolutionary terror in his *Life of Napoleon*. CLB (132) 2005, 104–9.

11247. PAULIN, TOM. One impulse: Hazlitt, Wordsworth and *The Principles of Human Action*. *In* (pp. 98–111) **11245**.

11248. —— A voluptuous eye: William Hazlitt's voyage through France and Italy. TLS, 7 Jan. 2005, 11–12.

11249. ROACH, JOSEPH. Public intimacy: the prior history of 'it'. *In* (pp. 15–30) **3985**.

11250. SCHLICKE, PAUL. Hazlitt, Horne, and *The Spirit of the Age*. SELit (45:4) 2005, 829–51.

11251. WHALE, JOHN. Hazlitt and the selfishness of passion. *In* (pp. 56–67) **11245**.

11252. WOOD, GILLEN D'ARCY. Cockney Mozart: the Hunt circle, the King's Theatre, and *Don Giovanni*. *See* **11362**.

11253. —— Crying game: operatic strains in Wordsworth's lyrical ballads. *See* **12528**.

11254. WU, DUNCAN. Godwin and Hazlitt estranged. CLB (129) 2005, 2–8.

11255. —— Hazlitt, Francis Place, and the Bentham circle: new findings. CLB (132) 2005, 94–103.

11256. —— Hazlitt's *Essay on the Principles of Human Action*: a bibliographical note. *In* (pp. xv–xviii) **11245**.

11257. —— The road to Nether Stowey. *In* (pp. 83–97) **11245**.

11258. —— William Hazlitt (1737–1820), the Priestley circle, and *The Theological Repository*: a brief survey and bibliography. RES (56:227) 2005, 758–66.

Felicia Dorothea Hemans

11259. DYMOND, ERICA JOAN. Hemans's *The Child's Last Sleep*. Exp (63:4) 2005, 213–16.

11260. ESTERHAMMER, ANGELA. The cosmopolitan *improvvisatore*: spontaneity and performance in Romantic poetics. *See* **12476**.

11261. LECERCLE, JEAN-JACQUES. Parody as cultural memory. *See* **18381**.

11262. Purinton, Marjean D.   Shakespeare's Ghost and Felicia Hemans's *The Vespers of Palermo*: nineteenth-century readings of the page and feminist meanings for the stage. Intertexts (8:2) 2004, 135–54.

11263. Saglia, Diego.   Mediterranean unrest: 1820s verse tragedies and revolutions in the South. *See* **11959.**

11264. Vincent, Patrick H.   The Romantic poetess: European culture, politics, and gender, 1820–1840. *See* **9729.**

W. E. Henley

11265. Chandran, K. Narayana.   T. S. Eliot and W. E. Henley: a source for the 'water-dripping song' in *The Waste Land*. *See* **16252.**

11266. van Bronswijk, R.   Driving the darkness: W. E. Henley's *The Song of the Sword* as uneasy battle cry. EngS (84:4) 2003, 330–46.

Thomas Wentworth Higginson

11267. Loeffelholz, Mary.   Dickinson's *Decoration*. *See* **10792.**

Barbara Hofland

11268. Behrendt, Stephen C.   Women without men: Barbara Hofland and the economics of widowhood. ECF (17:3) 2005, 481–508.

James Hogg (1770–1835)

11269. Alker, Sharon; Nelson, Holly Faith.   'Ghastly in the moonlight': Wordsworth, Hogg and the anguish of war. SHogg (15) 2004, 76–89.

11270. Brewster, Scott.   Borderline experience: madness, mimicry and Scottish gothic. GothS (7:1) 2005, 79–86.

11271. Garside, Peter.   Hogg and the Blackwoodian novel. SHogg (15) 2004, 5–20.

11272. Groves, David.   The genesis of 'Gil-Martin': James Hogg, *Colonel Cloud*, and 'the madman in the *Mercury*'. NQ (52:4) 2005, 467–9.

11273. —— James Hogg on the death of a friend. NQ (52:4) 2005, 471–2.

11274. Hughes, Gillian.   Hogg and the *Monthly Musical and Literary Magazine*. SHogg (15) 2004, 120–5.

11275. —— Interim index. SHogg (15) 2004, 100–14. (Letters.)

11276. —— James Hogg, and Edinburgh's triumph over Napoleon. ScSR (4:1) 2003, 98–111.

11277. —— James Hogg and *The Metropolitan*. Bibliotheck (ns 1:2) 2004, 7–23.

11278. —— James Hogg and the theatre. SHogg (15) 2004, 53–66.

11279. —— (ed.).   Altrive tales: collected among the peasantry of Scotland and from foreign adventurers. (Bibl. 2004, 11266.) Rev. by Penny Fielding in ScSR (6:1) 2005, 120–3.

11280. Jackson, Richard D.   Border line business: aspects of James Hogg's *The Three Perils of Woman*. SHogg (15) 2004, 115–20.

11281. Killick, Tim.   Hogg and the collection of short fiction in the 1820s. SHogg (15) 2004, 21–31.

11282. Lincoln, Andrew.   The mercenary, the savage, and the civilized war: Scott and *A Legend of the Wars of Montrose*. *See* **11935.**

11283. MACK, DOUGLAS (ed.). The queen's wake. Edinburgh: Edinburgh UP, 2004. pp. 470. (Collected works of James Hogg, 14.) Rev. by Graham Tulloch in SHogg (15) 2004, 163–6.

11284. —— MACK, WILMA (eds). *Tales of Fathers and Daughters* no. 2. SHogg (15) 2004, 126–62.

11285. MACK, DOUGLAS S. Hogg and angels. SHogg (15) 2004, 90–8.

11286. PITTOCK, MURRAY G. H. Hogg's gothic and the transformation of genre: towards a Scottish Romanticism. SHogg (15) 2004, 67–75.

11287. —— Sources and dates for the Jacobite song: II. *See* **3577**.

11288. TULLOCH, GRAHAM. Writing 'by advice': *Ivanhoe* and *The Three Perils of Man. See* **11946**.

William Hone

11289. GRIMES, KYLE. Verbal jujitsu: William Hone and the tactics of satirical conflict. *In* (pp. 173–84) **9305**.

11290. GROVIER, KELLY. The dumpling one. TLS, 13 May 2005, 25 (review-article).

11291. WILSON, BEN. The laughter of triumph: William Hone and the fight for the free press. London; Boston, MA: Faber & Faber, 2005. pp. x, 452. Rev. by Kelly Grovier in TLS, 13 May 2005, 25.

Thomas Hood

11292. BUTTERWORTH, ROBERT D. Hood's *Stanzas ('Farewell, Life ...').* Exp (64:1) 2005, 30–2.

Gerard Manley Hopkins

11293. BERGONZI, BERNARD. Hopkins, tradition and the individual talent. HopQ (31:1–4) 2004, 1–10.

11294. BROWN, DANIEL. Gerard Manley Hopkins. Plymouth: Northcote House in assn with the British Council, 2004. pp. xi, 123. (Writers and their work.)

11295. —— Hopkins and the problem of singularity. HopQ (31:1–4) 2004, 83–96.

11296. CERVO, NATHAN. Three Victorian 'medieval' poems: *Dover Beach, The Windhover*, and *The Higher Pantheism. See* **12136**.

11297. COTTER, JAMES FINN. Hopkins and Augustine. HopQ (31:1–4) 2004, 127–41.

11298. —— Hopkins and Cynewulf: *The Wreck of the Deutschland, The Windhover, The Blessed Virgin Compared to the Air We Breathe*, and the *Christ.* VP (43:1) 2005, 19–34.

11299. DAU, DUC. The caress of God's breath in Gerard Manley Hopkins. SSE (31) 2005, 39–60.

11300. DOWNES, DAVID ANTHONY. The Hopkins Society: the making of a world-class poet. Ren (57:4) 2005, 244–98.

11301. FEENEY, JOSEPH J. Scarlet geraniums and the 'mother of muses': Gerard Manley Hopkins in Wales 1874–1877. HopQ (31:1–4) 2004, 181–93.

11302. FENNELL, FRANCIS L., JR. Appropriating Hopkins. Ren (57:4) 2005, 323–32.

11303. GALLET, RENÉ. Hopkins's sense of divine action. HopQ (31:1–4) 2004, 69–81.

11304. GOEGLEIN, TIMOTHY S. A sense of the sacred. See **7473**.

11305. HERRINGTON, ELDRID. Hopkins and Whitman. EC (55:1) 2005, 39–57.

11306. HIGGINS, LESLEY. 'To prove him with hard questions': degrees of answerability in Hopkins's writing. HopQ (31:1–4) 2004, 97–125.

11307. HURLEY, MICHAEL D. The audible reading of poetry revisited. BJA (44:4) 2004, 393–407.

11308. MÁNEK, BOHUSLAV. The Czech reception of G. M. Hopkins's poetry. In (pp. 115–20) **3753**.

11309. MOORE, MICHAEL D. 'A world undone': earth and utterance in Hopkins. HopQ (31:1–4) 2004, 143–56.

11310. NIXON, JUDE V. '[A] virginal tongue hold': Hopkins's *The Wreck of the Deutschland* and Muriel Spark's *The Girls of Slender Means*. See **19553**.

11311. PARHAM, JOHN. Green man Hopkins: Gerard Manley Hopkins and Victorian ecological criticism. NCC (25:3) 2003, 257–76.

11312. PHILLIPS, CATHERINE. 'Believe me very sincerely yours': Gerard Manley Hopkins as letter-writer. HopQ (31:1–4) 2004, 157–65.

11313. PLOTKIN, CARY. Ametaphoricity and presence in Hopkins's poetics. HopQ (31:1–4) 2004, 43–68.

11314. PUGHE, THOMAS. Réinventer la nature: vers une éco-poétique. EA (58:1) 2005, 68–81.

11315. QUINN, PETER. The instinct toward mercy: what Hopkins has to teach Darwin. Cweal (132:12) 2005, 15–18.

11316. SALMON, RACHEL. Poetry and religious work: defamiliarizing Hopkins's *The Wreck of the Deutschland*. HopQ (31:1–4) 2004, 11–30.

11317. SCHMID, SABINE. 'Keeping the sources pure': the making of George Mackay Brown. See **15591**.

11318. SCOTT, DAVID. Priest as poet. See **11541**.

11319. SHIMANE, KUNIO. Ecstasy and exultation: *The May Magnificat*. HopQ (31:1–4) 2004, 167–79.

11320. SOBOLEV, DENNIS. Contra Milton. See **7760**.

11321. —— Semantic counterpoint, Hopkins, and *The Wreck of the Deutschland*. SELit (44:4) 2004, 823–47.

11322. TALBOT, JOHN. Auden's Horatian mosaic. See **15244**.

11323. THORNTON, R. K. R. 'What can I but enumerate old themes?' HopQ (31:1–4) 2004, 31–41.

11324. WHITEFORD, PETER. What were Felix Randal's 'fatal four disorders'? RES (56:225) 2005, 438–46.

11325. WINTERS, SARAH FIONA. Christina Rossetti's poetic vocation. See **11864**.

Pauline Elizabeth Hopkins

11326. BUSSEY, SUSAN HAYS. Whose will be done? Self-determination in Pauline Hopkins's *Hagar's Daughter*. AAR (39:3) 2005, 299–313.

11327. DeLaMotte, Eugenia. 'Collusions of the mystery': ideology and the gothic in *Hagar's Daughter.* GothS (6:1) 2004, 69–79.

11328. Wallinger, Hanna. Pauline E. Hopkins: a literary biography. Athens; London: Georgia UP, 2005. pp. xi, 368.

Richard Hengist Horne

11329. Schlicke, Paul. Hazlitt, Horne, and *The Spirit of the Age. See* 11250.

Julia Ward Howe

11330. Porterfield, Amanda. American religious biography. *See* 8271.

11331. Williams, Gary (ed.). The hermaphrodite. Lincoln; London: Nebraska UP, 2004. pp. xlvi, 208. (Legacies of nineteenth-century American women writers.) Rev. by Renée Bergland in Legacy (22:2) 2005, 197–9.

11332. Ziegler, Valarie H. Diva Julia: the public romance and private agony of Julia Ward Howe. (Bibl. 2004, 11310.) Rev. by Amanda Porterfield in RAC (15:2) 2005, 245–53.

W. D. Howells

11333. Abeln, Paul. William Dean Howells and the ends of Realism. London; New York: Routledge, 2005. pp. vii, 165. (Studies in major literary authors, 36.)

11334. Brilli, Attilio (ed.). Panforte di Siena. Ospedaletto Pisa: Pacini, 2005. pp. 86.

11335. Claybaugh, Amanda. The autobiography of a substitute: trauma, history, Howells. YJC (18:1) 2005, 45–65.

11336. —— A broken teacup. LRB (27:19) 2005, 35–6 (review-article). (Biography of Howells.)

11337. Davidson, Rob. The Master and the Dean: the literary criticism of Henry James and William Dean Howells. *See* 11395.

11338. Frank, Armin Paul; Lohse, Rolf (eds). Internationality in American fiction: Henry James, William Dean Howells, William Faulkner, Toni Morrison. *See* 16406.

11339. Godspeed-Chadwick, Julie. Howells' *Editha*: a reevaluation. ShSt (12:2) 2004, 63–70.

11340. Goodman, Susan; Dawson, Carl. William Dean Howells: a writer's life. Berkeley; London: California UP, 2005. pp. 519, (plates) 16. Rev. by William P. Kelly in ASch (74:3) 2005, 133–5; by Amanda Claybaugh in LRB (27:19) 2005, 35–6.

11341. Irmscher, Christoph. 'Pearly light': Genoa in the nineteenth-century American imagination. *In* (pp. 285–301) 9393.

11342. Jarrett, Gene. 'Entirely *black* verse from him would succeed': minstrel Realism and William Dean Howells. NineL (59:4) 2005, 494–525.

11343. —— 'We must write like the white men': race, realism, and Dunbar's anomalous first novel. *See* 10878.

11344. Lustig, T. J. Sunspots and blindspots in *The Europeans. See* 11428.

11345. Petrie, Paul R. Conscience and purpose: fiction and social consciousness in Howells, Jewett, Chesnutt, and Cather. *See* 10422.

11346. SEHULSTER, PATRICIA J. The unanswerable Woman Question in William Dean Howells's *A Hazard of New Fortunes*. ATQ (19:2) 2005, 115–31.

11347. TEOREY, MATTHEW. 'I write very deliberately indeed': four uncollected interviews with W. D. Howells. ALR (37:2) 2005, 159–79.

11348. WETZEL-SAHM, BIRGIT. New England versions of the *femme fatale*: Howells' deviating responses to Turgenev. *In* (pp. 111–34) **16406**.

John Richard Desborus Huggins

11349. STRACHAN, JOHN. 'Trimming the "Muse of Satire"': J. R. D. Huggins and the poetry of hair-cutting. *In* (pp. 185–206) **9305**.

Thomas Hughes (1822–1896)

11350. ALLEN, M. D. Eduard Bertz's Rugby, Tennessee. *See* **11066**.

11351. RIDLER, ANN. Some unexpected references to Borrow. *See* **10123**.

Fergus Hume

11352. WEAVER, RACHAEL. Reflecting the detectives: crime fiction and the New Journalism in late nineteenth-century Australia. *See* **9885**.

Mrs Margaret Wolfe (Hamilton) Hungerford ('The Duchess') (1855?–1897)

11353. FLEMING, BRENDAN. *Mrs Gardiner: a Comedy in One Act* (1888): a play by George Moore. *See* **18301**.

Leigh Hunt

11354. ANDERSON, DOUGLAS A. (introd.). The rebellion of the beasts; or, The ass is dead! Long live the ass!!! Chicago, IL: Wicker Park Press, 2004. pp. xv, 151. Rev. by Nicholas Roe in WordsC (35:4) 2004, 191–3.

11355. EBERLE-SINATRA, MICHAEL. Leigh Hunt and the London literary scene: a reception history of his major works, 1805–1828. London; New York: Routledge, 2005. pp. ix, 175. (Routledge studies in Romanticism, 3.)

11356. EDGECOMBE, RODNEY STENNING. Dickens, Hunt and the waiter in *Somebody's Luggage*. *See* **10677**.

11357. HALLIDAY, IAIN. 'Our love on one side, our dictionary on the other': Leigh Hunt's *A Jar of Honey from Mount Hybla* (1847). *In* (pp. 77–88) **9237**.

11358. JONES, JOHN. How did he get it done? LRB (27:18) 2005, 32–3 (review-article). (Biographies of Hunt.)

11359. KUCICH, GREG. Keats, Shelley, Byron, and the Hunt circle. *In* (pp. 263–79) **8014**.

11360. LINDOP, GREVEL. Out of gaol. TLS, 8 Apr. 2005, 24–5 (review-article).

11361. ROE, NICHOLAS. Fiery heart: the first life of Leigh Hunt. London: Pimlico, 2005. pp. xvi, 428, (plates) 8. Rev. by Grevel Lindop in TLS, 8 Apr. 2005, 24; by John Jones in LRB (27:18) 2005, 32–3; by Stephen Hebron in KSR (19) 2005, 150–7.

11362. WOOD, GILLEN D'ARCY. Cockney Mozart: the Hunt circle, the King's Theatre, and *Don Giovanni*. SR (44:3) 2005, 367–97.

Jean Ingelow

11363. GEER, JENNIFER. 'Many worlds more': feminine imagination in Jean Ingelow's *Gladys and Her Island* and *Mopsa the Fairy*. VIJ (32) 2004, 167–88.

11364. IVES, MAURA. Further evidence for Eliza Straffen's authorship of *Some Recollections of Jean Ingelow and Her Early Friends*. NQ (52:1) 2005, 79–80.

Washington Irving

11365. ANTHONY, DAVID. 'Gone distracted': *Sleepy Hollow*, gothic masculinity, and the panic of 1819. EAL (40:1) 2005, 111–44.

11366. BURN, STEPHEN J. Kennedy's *Roscoe*. See **17395.**

11367. FERGUSON, ROBERT A. Rip Van Winkle and the generational divide in American culture. EAL (40:3) 2005, 529–44.

11368. GIORCELLI, CRISTINA. Da Irving – a Hawthorne, a Poe – a Irving: alle origini del fantastico nella letteratura statunitense. *See* **9552.**

11369. HORWITZ, HOWARD. Rip Van Winkle and legendary national memory. WHR (58:2) 2004, 34–47.

11370. HUGHES, ROBERT. Sleepy Hollow: fearful pleasures and the nightmare of history. AQ (61:3) 2005, 1–26.

11371. IRMSCHER, CHRISTOPH. 'Pearly light': Genoa in the nineteenth-century American imagination. *In* (pp. 285–301) **9393.**

Helen Hunt Jackson

11372. GONZALEZ, JOHN M. The warp of Whiteness: domesticity and empire in Helen Hunt Jackson's *Ramona*. AmLH (16:3) 2004, 437–65.

11373. IRWIN, ROBERT MCKEE. The legend of Lola Casanova: on the borders of Border Studies. Aztlan (30:2) 2005, 35–64.

Harriet Jacobs

11374. LOVROD, MARIE. Shifting contexts, shaping experiences: child abuse survivor narratives and educating for empire. *See* **11980.**

11375. MOORE, GENEVA COBB. A Freudian reading of Harriet Jacobs's *Incidents in the Life of a Slave Girl*. SoLJ (38:1) 2005, 3–20.

11376. YELLIN, JEAN FAGAN. Harriet Jacobs: a life. (Bibl. 2004, 11352.) Rev. by Jennifer Fleischner in Legacy (22:1) 2005, 78–80.

Alice James

11377. DUQUETTE, ELIZABETH. 'A new claim for the family renown': Alice James and the picturesque. ELH (72:3) 2005, 717–45.

G. P. R. (George Payne Rainsford) James (1801?–1860)

11378. FLYNN, MICHAEL J. The transatlantic grudges of William Makepeace Thackeray and G. P. R. James. *See* **12166.**

Henry James (1843–1916)

11379. ANKER, RICHARD. 'Figures trop réelles pour durer': Blanchot avec James. EREA (3:2) 2005, 96–104.

11380. ARMSTRONG, PAUL B. Play and the politics of reading: the social uses of Modernist form. Ithaca, NY; London: Cornell UP, 2005. pp. xv, 207. Rev. by Richard Greaves in RES (56:227) 2005, 805–7.

11381. BARTEL, KIM. Unmoored from 'the shore of the real': Henry James, Roderick Hudson, and the advent of the modern in nineteenth-century painting. HJR (26:2) 2005, 168–88.

11382. BENOIT, RAYMOND. Pynchon's *Lot 49* on James's *Jolly Corner*. See **18982**.

11383. BESSIÈRE, JEAN. L'énigmaticité de Henry James, en passant par la réception française de son œuvre. EREA (3:2) 2005, 87–95.

11384. BRAM, CHRISTOPHER. Queer monster. Meanjin (62:2) 2003, 11–22.

11385. BRIGGS, JULIA. The conversation behind the conversation: speaking the unspeakable in Virginia Woolf. See **20315**.

11386. BRUNS, JOHN. Baffling doom: dialogue, laughter, and comic perception in Henry James. TSLL (47:1) 2005, 1–30.

11387. CHEN, PING. Language, reality, and desire: *The Bostonians* and the distorted reality. FLS (116) 2005, 56–63. (In Chinese.)

11388. CHILTON, NEIL. Conceptions of a beautiful crisis: Henry James's reading of *The Tempest*. HJR (26:3) 2005, 218–28.

11389. CLAGGETT, SHALYN. Narcissism and the conditions of self-knowledge in James's *The Jolly Corner*. HJR (26:2) 2005, 189–200.

11390. COSLOVI, MARINA. James and Vittore Carpaccio: the horizontal and vertical in art. RSA (15/16) 2004/05, 31–44.

11391. COULSON, VICTORIA. Teacups and love letters: Constance Fenimore Woolson and Henry James. See **12445**.

11392. COUSINEAU, THOMAS J. Ritual unbound: reading sacrifice in Modernist fiction. (Bibl. 2004, 11370.) Rev. by Katherine I. Baxter in ELT (48:4) 2005, 492–5.

11393. CUTTING, ANDREW. Death in Henry James. Basingstoke; New York: Palgrave Macmillan, 2005. pp. ix, 198.

11394. DAUGHERTY, SARAH B. *The Wings of the Dove* and the critics. LitB (24:1/2) 2004, 174–81.

11395. DAVIDSON, ROB. The Master and the Dean: the literary criticism of Henry James and William Dean Howells. Columbia; London: Missouri UP, 2005. pp. xi, 298.

11396. DEMOOR, MARYSA. From epitaph to obituary: the death politics of T. S. Eliot and Ezra Pound. See **16261**.

11397. DESPOTOPOULOU, ANNA. The monster and the atom: representation of London in James and Conrad. CamQ (34:2) 2005, 131–46.

11398. DEVINE, CHRISTINE. Class in turn-of-the-century novels of Gissing, James, Hardy, and Wells. See **11072**.

11399. EVERETT, BARBARA. The last turn: Henry James and the spirits of the English country house. TLS, 23 & 30 Dec. 2005, 16–18.

11400. FLANNERY, DENIS. The appalling Mrs Luna: sibling love, queer attachment, and Henry James's *The Bostonians*. HJR (26:1) 2005, 1–19.

11401. —— The powers of apostrophe and the boundaries of mourning: Henry James, Alan Hollinghurst, and Toby Litt. HJR (26:3) 2005, 293–305.

11402. FRANK, ARMIN PAUL. James's *The American*: a tragedy of intercultural bafflement. *In* (pp. 19–110) 16406.

11403. —— LOHSE, ROLF (eds). Internationality in American fiction: Henry James, William Dean Howells, William Faulkner, Toni Morrison. *See* 16406.

11404. FRANKE, WILLIAM. Varieties and valences of unsayability. *See* 15877.

11405. FURBANK, P. N. On the historical novel. *See* 16802.

11406. GILBERT, GEOFF. Before Modernism was: modern history and the constituency of writing. *See* 12694.

11407. HADLEY, TESSA. Seated alone with a book ... HJR (26:3) 2005, 229–36.

11408. HARALSON, ERIC. Henry James and queer modernity. (Bibl. 2003, 10716.) Rev. by Lisa Tyler in HemR (24:1) 2004, 114–17; by Jonathan Warren in HJR (26:1) 2005, 105–7; by John Dudley in AL (77:1) 2005, 188–9; by Jesse Matz in Mod/Mod (12:1) 2005, 192–3; by Nick Kneale in MLR (100:4) 2005, 1099–1100; by Wendy Graham in StudN (37:3) 2005, 355–7; by Ellis Hanson in SAtlR (70:3) 2005, 127–32.

11409. HARDEN, EDGAR F. A Henry James chronology. Basingstoke; New York: Palgrave Macmillan, 2005. pp. xi, 235. (Author chronologies.)

11410. HORNE, PHILIP. Henry James among the poets. HJR (26:1) 2005, 68–81.

11411. HUTCHISON, HAZEL. James's spectacles: distorted vision in *The Ambassadors*. HJR (26:1) 2005, 39–51.

11412. IONESCU, ANDREEA. The reception of Henry James's letters throughout the 20th century. EREA (3:2) 2005, 111–18.

11413. IRMSCHER, CHRISTOPH. 'Pearly light': Genoa in the nineteenth-century American imagination. *In* (pp. 285–301) 9393.

11414. JÖTTKANDT, SIGI. Acting beautifully: Henry James and the ethical aesthetic. Albany: New York State UP, 2005. pp. xvii, 177. (SUNY series in psychoanalysis and culture.)

11415. KALUPAHANA, CHAMIKA. 'Les beaux jours sont passés': staging Whiteness and postcolonial ambivalence in *The Europeans* by Henry James. CRAS (33:2) 2003, 119–38.

11416. KREIGER, GEORGIA. *East Angels*: Constance Fenimore Woolson's revision of Henry James's *The Portrait of a Lady*. *See* 12447.

11417. KREISEL, DEANNA K. What Maxie knew: the gift and Oedipus in *What Maisie Knew* and *Rushmore*. Mosaic (38:2) 2005, 1–17.

11418. KRESS, JILL M. The figure of consciousness: William James, Henry James, and Edith Wharton. (Bibl. 2004, 11395.) Rev. by Renée Tursi in StudN (37:1) 2004, 101–4; by Constance E. Holmes in EWR (20:2) 2004, 2, 32.

11419. KURNICK, DAVID. 'Horrible impossible': Henry James's awkward stage. HJR (26:1) 2005, 109–29. (Leon Edel Prize essay.)

11420. LANSDOWN, RICHARD. 'What at bottom do men live for?': how Henry James widened the scope of F. R. Leavis's criticism. *See* 14873.

11421. LAPAIRE, JEAN-RÉMI. Coordination et cognition. *See* 2708.

11422. LAWRENCE, KATHLEEN. Osmond's complaint: Gilbert Osmond's mother and the cultural context of James's *The Portrait of a Lady*. HJR (26:1) 2005, 52–67.

11423. LE RESTE, ANNE-CLAIRE. Intertextualizing *The Princess Casamassima*: realism and reference(s). EREA (3:2) 2005, 19–32.

11424. LEWIS, PERICLES. Christopher Newman's haircloth shirt: worldly asceticism, conversion, and *auto-machia* in *The American*. StudN (37:3) 2005, 308–28.

11425. ——— 'The reality of the unseen': shared fictions and religious experience in the ghost stories of Henry James. AQ (61:2) 2005, 33–66.

11426. LOCK, CHARLES. Hardy and the critics. *In* (pp. 14–37) **11140**.

11427. LOSANO, ANTONIA. *East Lynne, The Turn of the Screw*, and the female *Doppelgänger* in governess fiction. *See* **12442**.

11428. LUSTIG, T. J. Sunspots and blindspots in *The Europeans*. EREA (3:2) 2005, 6–18.

11429. MCCAULEY, ELIZABETH ANNE, *et al*. Gondola days: Isabella Stewart Gardner and the Palazzo Barbaro circle. Boston, MA: Isabella Stewart Gardner Museum, 2004. pp. xviii, 297. (Exhibition catalogue.) Rev. by Susan M. Griffin in HJR (26:3) 2005, 306–8.

11430. MACHLAN, ELIZABETH BOYLE. 'There are plenty of houses': architecture and genre in *The Portrait of a Lady*. StudN (37:4) 2005, 394–410.

11431. MCMASTER, JULIET. What Daisy knew: the epistemology of the child writer. *In* (pp. 51–69) **9164**.

11432. MAMOLI ZORZI, ROSELLA (ed.). Beloved boy: letters to Hendrik C. Andersen, 1899–1915. Introd. by Millicent Bell. Afterword by Elena di Majo. (Bibl. 2004, 11401.) Rev. by Sean O'Toole in CEAF (34:1) 2005.

11433. MILLER, J. HILLIS. Literature as conduct: speech acts in Henry James. New York: Fordham UP, 2005. pp. xiii, 350.

11434. ——— What is a kiss? Isabel's moments of decision. CI (31:3) 2005, 722–46.

11435. MITCHELL, LEE CLARK. 'To suffer like chopped limbs': the dispossessions of *The Spoils of Poynton*. HJR (26:1) 2005, 20–38.

11436. MONTEIRO, GEORGE. Henry James' Californian. ALR (38:1) 2005, 47–57.

11437. MOSELEY, MERRITT. Henry James and novelistic impersonation. SewR (113:2) 2005, 298–308. (State of letters.)

11438. NAFISI, AZAR. Reading *Lolita* in Tehran: a memoir in books. *See* **18463**.

11439. NIKOLOPOULOU, KALLIOPI. Autospectrography: on Henry James's *The Turn of the Screw*. JML (28:1) 2004, 1–24.

11440. NORMAN, WILL. *The Real Life of Sebastian Knight* and two stories by Henry James. *See* **18466**.

11441. OHI, KEVIN. *The Author of 'Beltraffio'*: the exquisite boy and Henry James's equivocal aestheticism. ELH (72:3) 2005, 747–67.

11442. PAVANS, JEAN. Henry James, théâtre et narration: 'le divin principe du scénario'. EREA (3:2) 2005, 33–42.

11443. PERSON, LELAND S. Henry James and the suspense of masculinity. (Bibl. 2004, 11413.) Rev. by Eric Haralson in HJR (26:2) 2005, 201–4; by John Dudley in AL (77:1) 2005, 188–9; by Nick Kneale in RES (56:227) 2005, 804–5.

11444. PETTY, LESLIE. The political is personal: the feminist lesson of Henry James's *The Bostonians*. WS (34:5) 2005, 377–403.

11445. PIGEON, ELAINE. Queer impressions: Henry James's art of fiction. London; New York: Routledge, 2005. pp. ix, 184.

11446. PITTOCK, MALCOLM. The Decadence of *The Turn of the Screw*. EC (55:4) 2005, 332–51.

11447. RIGHTER, WILLIAM. American memory in Henry James: void and value. (Bibl. 2004, 11419.) Rev. by Stanley Weintraub in ELT (48:1) 2005, 104–8.

11448. RIVKIN, JULIE. Writing the gay '80s with Henry James: David Leavitt's *A Place I've Never Been* and Alan Hollinghurst's *The Line of Beauty*. See **17044**.

11449. ROBINSON, ALAN. Social spaces in some early tales by Henry James. SPELL (17) 2005, 163–77.

11450. ROSS, MELANIE H. 'The mirror with a memory': tracking consciousness in the preface to *The Golden Bowl*. HJR (26:3) 2005, 246–55.

11451. RYAN, SUSAN M. *The Bostonians* and the Civil War. HJR (26:3) 2005, 265–72.

11452. SANNER, KRISTIN. 'Wasn't all history full of the destruction of precious things?': missing mothers, feminized fathers, and the purchase of freedom in Henry James's *The Portrait of a Lady*. HJR (26:2) 2005, 147–67.

11453. SCHOR, HILARY M. Reading knowledge: curiosity in *The Golden Bowl*. HJR (26:3) 2005, 237–45.

11454. SHAHEEN, AARON. 'The social dusk of that mysterious democracy': race, sexology, and the New Woman in Henry James's *The Bostonians*. ATQ (19:4) 2005, 281–99.

11455. STOKES, JOHN. The French actress and her English audience. See **9504**.

11456. SYMINGTON, MICÉALA. From realist to 'avant-garde': Henry James in France. EREA (3:2) 2005, 105–10.

11457. TEYSSANDIER, HUBERT. Voices of the unseen: Benjamin Britten's reading of *The Turn of the Screw*. EREA (3:2) 2005, 43–9.

11458. TUCKER, HERBERT F. James's Browning inside-out. HJR (26:3) 2005, 210–17.

11459. UGO, RUBEO. Taking the 'organic' view: the vertical/horizontal crux in Henry James's *The American Scene*. RSA (15/16) 2004/05, 7–30.

11460. VALTAT-COMET, NELLY. From novella to opera: Dominick Argento's *The Aspern Papers*. EREA (3:2) 2005, 50–66.

11461. WAKANA, MAYA HIGASHI. Society in self, self in society: survival in *The Wings of the Dove*. TSLL (47:1) 2005, 31–60.

11462. WALTON, JAMES. *The Liar* and Le Fanu. ShSt (12:2) 2004, 97–104.

11463. WERNSMAN, MARIJANE R. DAVIS.   The figure in the carpet of *Honeysuckle Cottage*: P. G. Wodehouse and Henry James. HJR (26:1) 2005, 99–104.

11464. WONHAM, HENRY B.   Amerigo's miraculous metamorphosis; or, The logic of ethnic caricature in *The Golden Bowl*. HJR (26:2) 2005, 130–46.

11465. WOOD, MICHAEL.   The museum of what happens. HJR (26:3) 2005, 256–64. (*The Sacred Fount* and *Pale Fire*.)

11466. ZACHARIAS, GREG.   Henry James cartoons. HJR (26:3) 2005, 273–81.

Henry James, Sr (1811–1882)

11467. COLE, RACHEL.   The reality effect: Emerson's speakers and the phenomenon of personality. *See* **10969**.

11468. DUBAN, JAMES; SALLFORS, SOLOMON.   A phenomenal occurrence at Owl Creek Bridge: the presence of Emanuel Swedenborg and Henry James, Sr. *See* **10096**.

William James (1842–1910)

11469. HART, HENRY.   Charles Simic's dark nights of the soul. *See* **19457**.

11470. HAWKINS, STEPHANIE L.   Building the 'blue' race: miscegenation, mysticism, and the language of cognitive evolution in Jean Toomer's *The Blue Meridian*. *See* **19865**.

11471. ——   The science of superstition: Gertrude Stein, William James, and the formation of belief. *See* **19587**.

11472. LUNDIN, ROGER.   From nature to experience: the American search for cultural authority. *See* **10985**.

11473. MEHNE, PHILLIP.   '*Making it strange*': Bewusstsein, Erfahrung und Sprache bei Gertrude Stein und Lyn Hejinian. *See* **19591**.

11474. REDMOND, JOHN.   Muldoon and Pragmatism. *In* (pp. 96–109) **18404**.

The Jameses

11475. TAYLOR, ANDREW.   'The same old sausage': Thomas Carlyle and the James family. *In* (pp. 125–36) **10393**.

Anna Jameson

11476. ESTERHAMMER, ANGELA.   The cosmopolitan *improvvisatore*: spontaneity and performance in Romantic poetics. *See* **12476**.

11477. HENDERSON, JENNIFER.   Settler feminism and race making in Canada. Toronto; Buffalo, NY; London: Toronto UP, 2003. pp. x, 288. Rev. by Marie-Thérèse Blanc in CanL (184) 2005, 138–9.

11478. MONTICELLI, RITA.   In praise of art and literature: intertextuality, translations and migrations of knowledge in Anna Jameson's travel writings. PrSt (27:3) 2005, 299–312.

Richard Jefferies

11479. CUTHBERTSON, GUY.   Leonard Bast and Edward Thomas. *See* **16553**.

11480. FULLAGAR, BRIAN.   Further thoughts on Richard Jefferies and Henry Williamson. HWSJ (41) 2005, 17–38.

11481. STEWART, RICHARD.   Henry Williamson's debt to Richard Jefferies. *See* **20232**.

11482. WILLIAMSON, ANNE. A purple thread: an examination of W. H. Hudson, naturalist and author, in relation to HW. See 17090.

Douglas Jerrold

11483. HALE, FREDERICK. 'The brains of the Right' emergent: Douglas Jerrold and *The Oxford Fortnightly*. BLR (18:4) 2004, 379–400.

11484. SLATER, MICHAEL. Douglas Jerrold: 1803–1857. (Bibl. 2004, 11445.) Rev. by Patrick J. McCarthy in NCP (32:1) 2005, 242–9.

11485. WESTLAND, ELLA. Dickens's *Dombey* and the storied sea. See 10760.

Sarah Orne Jewett

11486. ELBERT, MONIKA. Women's charity *vs* scientific philanthropy in Sarah Orne Jewett. *In* (pp. 157–89) 9513.

11487. HELLER, TERRY. Eunice and the jade gods: Jewett's religious rhetoric in *A Country Doctor*. Legacy (22:2) 2005, 158–75.

11488. HSU, HSUAN L. Literature and regional production. AmLH (17:1) 2005, 36–69.

11489. PETRIE, PAUL R. Conscience and purpose: fiction and social consciousness in Howells, Jewett, Chesnutt, and Cather. See 10422.

11490. ZAPĘDOWSKA, MAGDA. An Arcadia in Maine: the pastoral in Sarah Orne Jewett's Dunnet Landing sketches. *In* (pp. 57–70) 12672.

Geraldine Jewsbury

11491. CAMPBELL, IAN. Geraldine Jewsbury: Jane Welsh Carlyle's 'best friend'? *In* (pp. 185–95) 10393.

11492. ROBERTS, LEWIS C. 'The production of a female hand': professional writing and the career of Geraldine Jewsbury. WWr (12:3) 2005, 399–418.

Maria Jane Jewsbury (Mrs Fletcher)

11493. LOW, DENNIS. Gold and silver fishes in a vase: a portrait of Wordsworth and Maria Jane Jewsbury. See 12497.

11494. SAGLIA, DIEGO. Other homes: exoticism and domesticity in Maria Jane Jewsbury's *Oceanides*. WWr (12:2) 2005, 205–23.

Ellen Johnston

11495. FORSYTH, MARGARET. Looking for grandmothers: working-class women poets and 'herstory'. See 11002.

C. I. (Christian Isobel) Johnstone (1781–1857)

11496. MONNICKENDAM, ANDREW. Eating your words: plate and nation in Meg Dods's *The Cook and Housewife's Manual* (1826). ScSR (6:1) 2005, 33–42.

Ernest Charles Jones (1819–1869)

11497. TAYLOR, MILES. Ernest Jones, Chartism, and the romance of politics, 1819–1869. Oxford; New York: OUP, 2003. pp. viii, 277, (plates) 8. Rev. by James Epstein in JVC (9:2) 2004, 264–70.

'Junius Redivivus' (William Bridges Adams) (1797–1872)

11498. COX, CHARLES. *A Tale of Tucuman*: a Tennyson reference of 1831. See 12139.

Charles Kean

11499. JACKSON, RUSSELL.   Staging Birnam Wood in the 1840s: a discovery at the Folger Shakespeare Library. *See* **6551**.

John Keats

11500. BAJETTA, CARLO M.   Redeeming the vagrant: Wordsworth's *Peter Bell* and its revisions. *In* (pp. 54–65) **3690**.

11501. BAKER, CHRISTOPHER.   Porphyro's rose: Keats and T. S. Eliot's *The Metaphysical Poets*. *See* **16242**.

11502. BALL, NORMAN.   The swoon of the unknown soulmate. NewR (12:2) 2005, 166–9.

11503. BAMFORD, CHRISTOPHER.   Negative capability. Parabola (30:2) 2005, 14–20.

11504. BECCONE, SIMONA.   'The principle of beauty in all things': l'esperienza estetica come deautomatizzazione della percezione in John Keats. SCrit (20:2) 2005, 197–224.

11505. BEHRENDT, STEPHEN C.   An urn, a teapot, and the archaeology of Romantic reading. *See* **10078**.

11506. BINELLI, ANDREA.   *Ode on a Grecian Urn* di John Keats; ovvero, La natura dialogica e transtemporale della bellezza. SCrit (18:3) 2003, 439–54.

11507. CAMAIORA CONTI, LUISA.   Keats's *La Belle Dame sans Merci*: the story of two versions. AngP (2:1/2) 2005, 9–30.

11508. CHRISTENSEN, ALLAN C.   'Ruth ... sick for home': the Keatsian imagination in the novel of Elizabeth Gaskell. *In* (pp. 105–22) **9237**.

11509. COLÓN, CHRISTINE.   Revising Keats's *The Eve of St Agnes*: the shift from dreams to reality in Adelaide Procter's *A Legend of Provence*. *See* **11835**.

11510. EDGECOMBE, RODNEY STENNING.   Keats's *Ode on a Grecian Urn* and Theognis' *Elegies* 1.15–18. NQ (52:4) 2005, 463.

11511. —— Ovid's Golden Age and Keats's ode *To Autumn*. NQ (52:1) 2005, 50–1.

11512. FERMANIS, PORSCHA.   Stadial theory, Robertson's *History of America*, and *Hyperion*. KSR (19) 2005, 21–31.

11513. GAILLET-DE CHEZELLES, FLORENCE.   Voyage et initiation poétique: l'aventure de Keats en 1818. EREA (3:1) 2005, 27–33.

11514. HARRISON, ANTONY H.   Victorian culture wars: Alexander Smith, Arthur Hugh Clough, and Matthew Arnold in 1853. *See* **9933**.

11515. HARVEY, A. D.   Hyperion's cousins: epic poetry in the style of Milton, c.1818. KSR (19) 2005, 32–8.

11516. JONES, CHRIS.   Knight or wight in Keats's *La Belle Dame*? An ancient ditty reconsidered. KSR (19) 2005, 39–49.

11517. JOUKOVSKY, NICHOLAS A.   Keats, Shelley, and *The Troubadour*. *See* **1241**.

11518. KIMBERLY, CAROLINE E.   Effeminacy, masculinity, and homosocial bonds: the (un)intentional queering of John Keats. RomNet (36/37) 2004/05.

11519. KUCICH, GREG. Keats, Shelley, Byron, and the Hunt circle. *In* (pp. 263–79) **8014**.

11520. LA CASSAGNÈRE, CHRISTIAN (ed.). Keats; ou, Le sortilège des mots. (Bibl. 2004, 11481.) Rev. by Joanny Moulin in EREA (2:1) 2004.

11521. LEERSSEN, JOEP. On the Celtic roots of a Romantic theme. *In* (pp. 1–10) **9237**.

11522. LINDOP, GREVEL. Out of gaol. *See* **11360**.

11523. LUO, YIHUA. Keats' poetry and his moral consciousness. FLS (115) 2005, 51–7. (In Chinese.)

11524. MERITT, MARK. The politics of literary biography in Charles Brown's *Life of John Keats*. *See* **9817**.

11525. MUSSAPI, ROBERTO (ed. and trans.). I ragazzi che amavano il vento. *See* **12022**.

11526. PAYLING, CATHERINE. An echo and a light unto eternity: the founding of the Keats–Shelley Memorial House. KSR (19) 2005, 50–63.

11527. PITTOCK, MURRAY G. H. Robert Fergusson and the Romantic ode. *See* **8601**.

11528. PLUMLY, STANLEY. Cold pastoral. VQR (81:4) 2005, 146–78.

11529. RABB, MARGARET. Exquisite harmonies. *See* **16897**.

11530. ROHRBACH, EMILY. Representing time and gender: Keats's prose, Keats's poetics. EREA (2:2) 2004, 86–92.

11531. ROSEN, DAVID. Maturity and poetic style. *See* **7745**.

11532. SCOTT, GRANT F. Sacred relics: a discovery of new Severn letters. *See* **9783**.

11533. —— Severn *redivivus*. TLS, 18 Mar. 2005, 13. (Severn's album.)

11534. SCOTT, HEIDI. Keats's *Ode to a Nightingale*. Exp (63:3) 2005, 139–41.

11535. SMITH, STAN. Epic *logos*: on first looking into several Homers. EREA (2:2) 2004, 2–13.

11536. TOBIN, THOMAS J. (ed.). Worldwide Pre-Raphaelitism. *See* **11754**.

11537. TURLEY, RICHARD MARGGRAF. 'Amorous cavaliers': Keats, Barry Cornwall, and Francis Jeffrey. NQ (52:1) 2005, 48–50.

11538. —— Bright stars and bosom-friends: John Keats and Barry Cornwall. NQ (52:4) 2005, 464–6.

11539. WHALE, JOHN C. John Keats. Basingstoke; New York: Palgrave Macmillan, 2005. pp. x, 164. (Critical issues.) Rev. by Clive Marsland in KSR (19) 2005, 171–4.

John Keble

11540. BLAIR, KIRSTIE (ed.). John Keble in context. (Bibl. 2004, 11497.) Rev. by Joe Phelan in TLS, 18 Feb. 2005, 26.

11541. SCOTT, DAVID. Priest as poet. Scintilla (9) 2005, 134–40.

John Philip Kemble (1757–1823)

11542. SCULLION, ADRIENNE. *Politesse* and the woman at risk: the social comedies of Marie-Thérèse De Camp. *See* **11543**.

Marie Thérèse Kemble (1774–1838)

11543. SCULLION, ADRIENNE. *Politesse* and the woman at risk: the social comedies of Marie-Thérèse De Camp. CompDr (38:2/3) 2004, 235–58.

Henry Kendall

11544. MCCANN, ANDREW. The obstinacy of the sacred. Antipodes (19:2) 2005, 152–8.

'Clover King' (Clara Collet)

11545. COUSTILLAS, PIERRE. The correspondence between Clara Collet and Morley Roberts (fourth and last instalment). GissJ (41:1) 2005, 13–26.

Grace King

11546. HEIDARI, MELISSA WALKER (ed.). To find my own peace: Grace King in her journals, 1886–1910. (Bibl. 2004, 11504.) Rev. by Susanne B. Dietzel in JSH (71:2) 2005, 475–6.

Charles Kingsley

11547. FITZPATRICK, TONY. The trisected society: social welfare in early Victorian fiction. See **10682.**

11548. MUKHERJEE, PABLO. Nimrods: hunting, authority, identity. MLR (100:4) 2005, 923–39.

11549. NÜNNING, VERA. Fictions of collective memory. See **3511.**

Mary Kingsley

11550. GUALTIERI, CLAUDIA. Re-reading the exotic in British colonial travel writing. *In* (pp. 172–81) **3690.**

William Kirby

11551. DUFFY, DENNIS. The robber baron of Canadian literature. See **814.**

11552. STACEY, ROBERT DAVID. Romance, pastoral romance, and the nation in history: William Kirby's *The Golden Dog* and Philippe-Joseph Aubert de Gaspé's *Les Anciens Canadiens*. *In* (pp. 91–116) **9191.**

Caroline M. Kirkland ('Mrs Mary Clavers')

11553. ALIAGA-BUCHENAU, ANA-ISABEL. 'The magic circle': women and community formation of a frontier village in Caroline Kirkland's *New Home – Who'll Follow?* CritS (16:3) 2004, 62–77.

Lady Caroline Lamb

11554. DOUGLASS, PAUL. Lady Caroline Lamb: a biography. (Bibl. 2004, 11514.) Rev. by Ian Gilmour in LRB (27:10) 2005, 31–2.

11555. —— What Lord Byron learned from Lady Caroline Lamb. ERR (16:3) 2005, 273–81.

11556. GILMOUR, IAN. Little mania. LRB (27:10) 2005, 31–2 (review-article).

Charles Lamb

11557. GARRATT, EDMUND. The early friendship of Captain James Burney and Charles Lamb. CLB (122) 2003, 64–70.

11558. NATARAJAN, UTTARA. Hazlitt, Lamb, and the philosophy of familiarity. See **11243.**

11559. WU, DUNCAN.   Yasuhiko Ozawa: a Japanese Elian. CLB (123) 2003, 101–5.

Mary Lamb

11560. HITCHCOCK, SUSAN TYLER.   Mad Mary Lamb: lunacy and murder in literary London. New York; London: Norton, 2005. pp. 333, (plates) 16.

The Lambs

11561. BOTTOMS, JANET.   'To read aright': representations of Shakespeare for children. *See* **5861**.

11562. BURTON, SARAH.   A double life: a biography of Charles and Mary Lamb. (Bibl. 2003, 10885.) Rev. by D. E. Wickham in CLB (132) 2005, 110–14.

11563. —— Toothache and gumboil: biographical dilemmas. CLB (124) 2003, 119–31.

11564. MORSE, RUTH.   Children's hours: Shakespeare, the Lambs, and French education. *In* (pp. 193–204) **6000**.

Letitia Elizabeth Landon (L.E.L.)

11565. FERNANDEZ, JEAN.   Graven images: the woman writer, the Indian poetess, and imperial aesthetics in L.E.L.'s *Hindoo Temples and Palaces at Madura*. VP (43:1) 2005, 35–52.

11566. GIBSON, MARY ELLIS.   Poems of Mary Carshore: the Indian legacy of L.E.L. and Tom Moore. *See* **10411**.

11567. JUMP, HARRIET DEVINE (gen. ed.).   Silver fork novels, 1826–1841: vol. 2, *Romance and Reality* (1831). Ed. by Cynthia Lawford. London; Brookfield, VT: Pickering & Chatto, 2005. pp. xxxix, 524. Rev. by Lauren Gillingham in TLS, 23 & 30 Dec. 2005, 30.

11568. NÍ FHLATHÚIN, MÁIRE.   India and women's poetry of the 1830s: femininity and the picturesque in the poetry of Emma Roberts and Letitia Elizabeth Landon. WWr (12:2) 2005, 187–204.

11569. VINCENT, PATRICK H.   The Romantic poetess: European culture, politics, and gender, 1820–1840. *See* **9729**.

Andrew Lang

11570. BRAZZELLI, NICOLETTA.   Andrew Lang e Robert Louis Stevenson: cronaca di un'amicizia letteraria. *See* **12064**.

11571. SHAW, JOHN.   *Luriana, Lurilee* revisited: II, More poems by Charles Elton. *See* **10963**.

Millicent Langton (*fl.*1865)

11572. FORSYTH, MARGARET.   Looking for grandmothers: working-class women poets and 'herstory'. *See* **11002**.

George A. (George Alfred) Lawrence (1827–1876)

11573. MUKHERJEE, PABLO.   Nimrods: hunting, authority, identity. *See* **11548**.

Caroline Woolmer Leakey ('Oline Keese')

11574. ELLIOTT, DORICE WILLIAMS.   Convict servants and middle-class mistresses. *See* **12279**.

Edward Lear

11575. Muschio, Carla (ed. and trans.). *Senza senso.* Viterbo: Nuovi Equilibri, 2005. pp. 174. (Fiabesca grande.)

Hannah Farnham Sawyer Lee (1780–1865)

11576. Templin, Mary. 'Dedicated to works of beneficence': charity as model for a domesticated economy in antebellum women's panic fiction. *In* (pp. 80–104) **9513.**

'Vernon Lee' (Violet Paget)

11577. Colby, Vineta. Vernon Lee: a literary biography. (Bibl. 2004, 11543.) Rev. by Linda Lappin in KR (27:3) 2005, 148–55.

11578. Fraser, Hilary. Evelyn De Morgan, Vernon Lee, and assimilation from without. JPRS (14:1) 2005, 75–90.

11579. Kandola, Sondeep. Vernon Lee: New Woman? WWr (12:3) 2005, 471–84.

11580. Kane, Mary Patricia. Spurious ghosts: the fantastic tales of Vernon Lee. (Bibl. 2004, 11546.) Rev. by Christa Zorn in VIJ (32) 2004, 226–9; by Patricia Pulham in NineL (59:4) 2005, 550–2.

11581. Lappin, Linda. The ardent pen of Vernon Lee. KR (27:3) 2005, 148–55 (review-article).

11582. Newman, Sally. The archival traces of desire: Vernon Lee's failed sexuality and the interpretation of letters in lesbian history. JHS (14:1/2) 2005, 51–75.

11583. Towheed, Shafquat. Determining 'fluctuating opinions': Vernon Lee, popular fiction, and theories of reading. NineL (60:2) 2005, 199–236.

11584. Zorn, Christa. Vernon Lee: aesthetics, history, and the Victorian female intellectual. (Bibl. 2003, 10906.) Rev. by Elyse Blankly in Albion (36:3) 2004, 536–8; by Sarah Bilston in ELT (48:1) 2005, 75–9; by Catherine A. Wiley in VPR (38:1) 2005, 117–18.

Sheridan Le Fanu

11585. Crossan, Greg. Proverbs and proverbial sayings in J. S. Le Fanu's *The Wyvern Mystery.* NQ (52:4) 2005, 480–5.

11586. Davis, Michael. Gothic's enigmatic signifier: the case of J. Sheridan Le Fanu's *Carmilla.* GothS (6:2) 2004, 223–35.

11587. Manara, Franck. Une eau fantastique: lecture de *The Haunted Baronet* de Joseph Sheridan Le Fanu. EtIr (29:2) 2004, 121–34.

11588. Nałęcz-Wojtczak, Jolanta. Facing evil: the motif of temptation in some ghost and vampire stories. *In* (pp. 159–66) **3756.**

11589. Russo, John Paul. Isle of the Dead: a Classical topos in J. Fenimore Cooper and Sheridan Le Fanu. *See* **10565.**

11590. Sage, Victor. Le Fanu's gothic: the rhetoric of darkness. Basingstoke; New York: Palgrave Macmillan, 2004. pp. viii, 233. Rev. by Nicholas Daly in GothS (6:2) 2004, 255–6; by Gaïd Girard in EtIr (29:2) 2004, 200–1; by Elke D'hoker in BELL (ns 3) 2005, 208–10; by Julian Wolfreys in CamQ (34:2) 2005, 177–81.

11591. Saler, Benson; Ziegler, Charles A. Dracula and Carmilla: monsters and the mind. *See* **12100.**

11592. Walton, James. *The Liar* and Le Fanu. *See* **11462.**

Amy Levy

11593. Beckman, Linda Hunt. Amy Levy: urban poetry, poetic innovation, and the *fin-de-siècle* woman poet. *In* (pp. 207–30) **9675.**

11594. Hetherington, Naomi. New Woman, 'new boots': Amy Levy as child journalist. *In* (pp. 254–68) **9164.**

G. H. Lewes

11595. Hughes, Linda K. Constructing fictions of authorship in George Eliot's *Middlemarch*, 1871–1872. *See* **10931.**

11596. Rylance, Rick. 'The disturbing anarchy of investigation': psychological debate and the Victorian periodical. *In* (pp. 239–50) **1226.**

11597. Scholtes, Joann. Additions and corrections to G. H. Lewes's primary bibliography. GEGHLS (48/49) 2005, 8–18.

11598. Wagner-Lawlor, Jennifer A. 'Who acts John Bull?': speculating on English national character and modern morality. *See* **12131.**

Henry Clay Lewis

11599. Martin, Gretchen. A Louisiana swamp doctor's diagnosis: romantic fatality and the frontier roots of realism. SoLJ (37:2) 2005, 17–39.

Laura Jean Libbey (1862–1924)

11600. Cummins, Donna Aycock. Who is Laura Jean Libbey? DNR (74:6) 2005, 241–61.

11601. Gorman, Anita. Great expectations: contrasting goals for women and men in the novels of Alger and Libbey. *See* **9919.**

11602. Masteller, Jean Carwile. Serial romance: Laura Jean Libbey and nineteenth-century story papers. DNR (74:6) 2005, 205–40.

Isabella Lickbarrow

11603. Parrish, Constance (ed.). Collected poems. Grasmere: Wordsworth Trust, 2004. pp. ix, 248. Rev. by Mary Wedd in CLB (130) 2005, 56–8.

Abraham Lincoln

11604. Jang, Jeong U. Thymotic misprision of self-evident truth. MidQ (47:1) 2005, 81–96.

11605. Schwartz, Barry. The new Gettysburg Address: fusing history and memory. Poetics (33:1) 2005, 63–79.

11606. Tackach, James. Abraham Lincoln's election jeremiad: the second inaugural address. SPAS (8) 2004, 147–69.

George Lippard

11607. Faflik, David. The case for *Charles Anderson Chester.* Book (65) 2005, 5–6.

T. H. (Thomas Henry) Lister (1800–1842)

11608. Jump, Harriet Devine (gen. ed.).   Silver fork novels, 1826–1841: vol. 1, *Granby: a Novel* (1826). Ed. by Clare Bainbridge. London; Brookfield, VT: Pickering & Chatto, 2005. pp. xli, 399. Rev. by Lauren Gillingham in TLS, 23 & 30 Dec. 2005, 30.

J. G. Lockhart

11609. Swaim, Barton.   Murray, Lockhart, Croker, and the *Quarterly*. Bibliotheck (ns 1:1) 2004, 27–38.

Henry Wadsworth Longfellow

11610. Calhoun, Charles C.   Longfellow: a rediscovered life. (Bibl. 2004, 11563.) Rev. by Patrick J. Walsh in Chronicles (29:3) 2005, 37.

11611. Calhoun, Joshua.   Democracy in American poetry: Longfellow, Whitman, and the 'tyranny of the majority'. SAtlR (70:1) 2005, 21–45.

11612. Eigenbrod, Renate.   Evangeline, Hiawatha and a Jewish cemetery: hi/stories of interconnected and multiple displacements. WLWE (40:1) 2002/03, 101–14.

11613. Frank, Armin Paul; Maas, Christel-Maria.   Transnational Longfellow: a project of American national poetry. New York; Frankfurt: Lang, 2005. pp. 168. (Interamericana, 5.)

11614. Gartner, Matthew.   Poetry lessons: Longfellow's cultivation of a readership. SPC (28:2) 2005, 49–75.

11615. Higgins, Andrew C.   Longfellow's *Snow-Flakes*. Exp (63:4) 2005, 216–19.

11616. Irmscher, Christoph.   'Pearly light': Genoa in the nineteenth-century American imagination. *In* (pp. 285–301) **9393**.

11617. Sweeting, Adam W.   Preserving the renaissance: literature and public memory in the homes of Longfellow, Hawthorne, and Poe. AmS (46:1) 2005, 23–43.

Augustus Baldwin Longstreet

11618. Justus, James H.   Fetching the Old Southwest: humorous writing from Longstreet to Twain. *See* **12248**.

James Russell Lowell

11619. Goodspeed-Chadwick, Julie Elaine.   The 19 September 1838 letter from George Bailey Loring (1817–1891) to James Russell Lowell (1819–1891). ANQ (18:1) 2005, 46–50.

Edward Bulwer Lytton, Baron Lytton (1803–1873)

11620. Bachman, Maria K.   Bulwer-Lytton's *Pelham*: the disciplinary dandy and the art of government. TSLL (47:2) 2005, 167–87.

11621. Christensen, Allan Conrad (ed.).   The subverting vision of Bulwer Lytton: bicentenary reflections. (Bibl. 2004, 11575.) Rev. by Anthea Trodd in TLS, 25 Feb. 2005, 28.

11622. Dyer, Gary R.   Reading as a criminal in early nineteenth-century fiction. *See* **11915**.

11623. JUMP, HARRIET DEVINE (gen. ed.). Silver fork novels, 1826–1841: vol. 3, *Godolphin: a Novel* (1833). Ed. by Harriet Devine Jump. London; Brookfield, VT: Pickering & Chatto, 2005. pp. xxxvi, 364. Rev. by Lauren Gillingham in TLS, 23 & 30 Dec. 2005, 30.

11624. LEVIN, YAEL. Conrad, Freud, and Derrida on Pompeii: a paradigm of disappearance. *See* **15893**.

11625. MITCHELL, LESLIE. Bulwer-Lytton: the rise and fall of a Victorian man of letters. (Bibl. 2004, 11583.) Rev. by Stan Walker in Albion (36:3) 2004, 549–50; by Juliet John in JVC (10:2) 2005, 304–9.

11626. MURRAY, OSWYN (ed.). Athens: its rise and fall; with views of the literature, philosophy, and social life of the Athenian people. (Bibl. 2004, 11585.) Rev. by Anthea Trodd in TLS, 25 Feb. 2005, 28.

11627. PARRINDER, PATRICK. Entering dystopia, entering *Erewhon*. *See* **10283**.

11628. WAGNER-LAWLOR, JENNIFER A. 'Who acts John Bull?': speculating on English national character and modern morality. *See* **12131**.

11629. WYSE, BRUCE. Mesmeric machinery, textual production and simulacra in Bulwer-Lytton's *The Haunted and the Haunters; or, The House and the Brain*. VicR (30:2) 2004, 32–57.

Rosina Bulwer Lytton, Baroness Lytton (1802–1882)

11630. JUMP, HARRIET DEVINE (gen. ed.). Silver fork novels, 1826–1841: vol. 5, *Cheveley; or, The Man of Honour* (1839). Ed. by Marie Mulvey-Roberts. London; Brookfield, VT: Pickering & Chatto, 2005. pp. xxxv, 536. Rev. by Lauren Gillingham in TLS, 23 & 30 Dec. 2005, 30.

Louisa S. McCord

11631. FOUGHT, LEIGH. Southern womanhood and slavery: a biography of Louisa S. McCord, 1810–1879. Columbia; London: Missouri UP, 2003. pp. xiv, 216.

George MacDonald

11632. ATTEBERY, BRIAN. High Church *versus* Broad Church: Christian myth in George MacDonald and C. S. Lewis. NYRSF (18:3) 2005, 14–17.

11633. GAARDEN, BONNIE. Cosmic and psychological redemption in George MacDonald's *Lilith*. StudN (37:1) 2005, 20–36.

11634. GRAY, WILLIAM. A source for the trampling scene in *Jekyll and Hyde*. *See* **12067**.

11635. KING, SHELLEY. 'Without Lyra we would understand neither the New nor the Old Testament': exegesis, allegory, and reading *The Golden Compass*. *In* (pp. 106–24) **18952**.

11636. LOBDELL, JARED C. The rise of Tolkienian fantasy. *See* **19829**.

11637. MANLOVE, COLIN. MacDonald's shorter fairy tales: journeys into the mind. SEVEN (22) 2005, 11–28.

11638. MOONEY, RODNEY. Journey through *A Wrinkle in Time* and explore the world of 'sacred idleness'. *See* **17685**.

11639. PHILLIPS, MICHAEL R.   George MacDonald. Minneapolis, MN: Bethany House, 2005. pp. 398.

11640. SHELEY, ERIN.   From Eden to eternity: the timescales of Genesis in George MacDonald's *The Golden Key* and *Lilith*. CLAQ (29:4) 2004, 329–44.

Richard Robert Madden (1798–1886)

11641. SWEENEY, FIONNGHUALA.   Atlantic countercultures and the networked text: Juan Francisco Manzano, R. R. Madden and the Cuban slave narrative. FMLS (40:4) 2004, 401–14.

Mrs General Mainwaring

11642. HERMAN, JEANETTE.   Men and women of feeling: conventions of sensibility and sentimentality in the *sati* debate and Mainwaring's *The Suttee*. CLS (42:2) 2005, 223–63.

Charles Mair

11643. GRUBISIC, KATIA.   'Savage nations roam o'er native wilds': Charles Mair and the ecological Indian. StudCanL (30:1) 2005, 58–82.

James Clarence Mangan

11644. CHUTO, JACQUES; VAN DE KAMP, PETER; SHANNON-MANGAN, ELLEN (eds).   Selected prose of James Clarence Mangan. Foreword by A. Norman Jeffares. Dublin; Portland, OR: Irish Academic Press, 2004. pp. xi, 357. (Bicentenary ed.) Rev. by Claude Fierobe in EtIr (30:1) 2005, 216–17.

11645. —— *et al.* (eds).   Selected poems of James Clarence Mangan. Foreword by Terence Brown. (Bibl. 2004, 11608.) Rev. by Claude Fierobe in EtIr (28:2) 2003, 175; by Denis Donoghue in LRB (27:6) 2005, 21–2.

11646. DEANE, SEAMUS.   Joyce the Irishman. *In* (pp. 28–48) **17244**.

11647. DONOGHUE, DENIS.   I hate thee, Djaun Bool. LRB (27:6) 2005, 21–2 (review-article). (Editions of Mangan.)

11648. RYDER, SEAN (ed.).   Selected writings. (Bibl. 2004, 11609.) Rev. by Denis Donoghue in LRB (27:6) 2005, 21–2.

11649. VAN DE KAMP, PETER.   Hands off! Joyce and the Mangan in the Mac. *In* (pp. 183–213) **9237**.

11650. WHEATLEY, DAVID (ed.).   Poems. (Bibl. 2004, 11610.) Rev. by Denis Donoghue in LRB (27:6) 2005, 21–2.

Harriet Martineau

11651. EASLEY, ALEXIS.   *Tait's Edinburgh Magazine* in the 1830s: dialogues on gender, class, and reform. *See* **1194**.

11652. FRAWLEY, MARIA.   Behind the scenes of history: Harriet Martineau and *The Lowell Offering*. VPR (38:2) 2005, 141–57.

11653. LOGAN, DEBORAH.   Fighting a war of words: Harriet Martineau in the *National Anti-Slavery Standard*. VPR (37:1) 2004, 46–71.

11654. LOGAN, DEBORAH ANNA.   The hour and the woman: Harriet Martineau's 'somewhat remarkable' life. (Bibl. 2004, 11615.) Rev. by Karen Kurt Teal in VPR (37:1) 2004, 97–8; by Linda H. Peterson in VIJ (32) 2004, 238–42.

11655. POON, ANGELIA. Seeing double: performing English identity and imperial duty in Emily Eden's *Up the Country* and Harriet Martineau's *British Rule in India*. *See* **10887**.

C. R. Maturin

11656. KILFEATHER, SIOBHÁN. Terrific register: the gothicization of atrocity in Irish Romanticism. B2 (31:1) 2004, 49–71.

Henry Mayhew

11657. BOONE, TROY. Youth of darkest England: working-class children at the heart of Victorian empire. *See* **9194**.

11658. HAYWARD, SALLY. 'Those who cannot work': an exploration of disabled men and masculinity in Henry Mayhew's *London Labour and the London Poor*. PrSt (27:1/2) 2005, 53–71.

11659. PIKE, DAVID L. Sewage treatments: vertical space and waste in nineteenth-century Paris and London. *In* (pp. 51–77) **9220**.

11660. RIVERS, BRYAN. Rossetti's *Jenny*. *See* **11874**.

L. T. Meade

11661. REIMER, MAVIS. Worlds of girls: educational reform and fictional form in L. T. Meade's school stories. *In* (pp. 199–217) **8171**.

Herman Melville

11662. ARMSTRONG, PHILIP. 'Leviathan is a skein of networks': translations of nature and culture in *Moby-Dick*. ELH (71:4) 2004, 1039–63.

11663. —— What animals mean, in *Moby-Dick*, for example. TexP (19:1) 2005, 93–111.

11664. BACIGALUPO, MASSIMO. 'Mannahatta': città insulare in Whitman e Melville. *In* (pp. 331–51) **9393**.

11665. BALL, DAVID M. Toward an archaeology of American Modernism: reconsidering prestige and popularity in the American renaissance. *See* **12284**.

11666. BANERJEE, MITA. Civilizational critique in Herman Melville's *Typee, Omoo*, and *Mardi*. Amst (48:2) 2003, 207–25.

11667. BARNUM, JILL. Melville, Lorenz Oken, and biology: engaging the 'long now'. Leviathan (7:2) 2005, 41–6.

11668. BEAUCHAMP, GORMAN. The scorpion's suicide: Claggart's death in *Billy Budd*. MelSE (129) 2005, 7–10.

11669. BELKNAP, ROBERT E. The list: the uses and pleasures of cataloguing. *See* **10965**.

11670. BELLIS, PETER. Discipline and the lash in Melville's *White-Jacket*. Leviathan (7:2) 2005, 25–40.

11671. BERTHOLD, DENNIS. 'The Italian turn of thought': Risorgimento politics in *Clarel*. NineL (59:3) 2004, 340–71.

11672. CAPPUCCI, PAUL R. Down from the crow's nest: Herman Melville's *Battle-Pieces and Aspects of the War*. WLA (17:1/2) 2005, 162–9.

11673. CHRISTODOULOU, A. C. The demigod Taji: commentary on an episode from Melville's *Mardi*. Leviathan (7:2) 2005, 3–24.

11674. CURRELI, MARIO. Leitmotifs from Coleridge and Wagner in *Nostromo* and beyond. *See* **15871.**

11675. DELBANCO, ANDREW. Melville: his world and work. New York: Knopf, 2005. pp. xxiii, 415. Rev. by Michael Dirda in BkW, 25 Sept. 2005, 15.

11676. DENEEN, PATRICK J.; ROMANCE, JOSEPH (eds). Democracy's literature: politics and fiction in America. *See* **14121.**

11677. DJELAL, JUANA CELIA. The shape of the whale: flukes and other tales. Leviathan (7:2) 2005, 47–53.

11678. DOWLING, PAUL M. Robert E. Lee and Melville's politics in *Battle-Pieces and Aspects of War.* MelSE (128) 2005, 1–2, 18–23.

11679. DRYDEN, EDGAR A. Monumental Melville: the formation of a literary career. (Bibl. 2004, 11633.) Rev. by William Lansing Brown in AmBR (26:2) 2005, 26.

11680. DUGGAN, ROBERT A., JR. 'Sleep no more' again: Melville's rewriting of Book x of Wordsworth's *Prelude.* RomNet (38/39) 2005.

11681. DUMM, THOMAS L. Who is Ishmael? MassR (46:3) 2005, 398–414.

11682. EDELMAN, LEE. Unknowing Barbara. *See* **14765.**

11683. GIESENKIRCHEN, MICHAELA. 'Still half bleeding with the blue of the sea': Goethe's theory of colors in *Moby-Dick.* Leviathan (7:1) 2005, 3–18.

11684. GOLDMAN, ERIC. Bringing out the beast in Melville's *Billy Budd*: the dialogue of Darwinian and 'holy' lexicons on board the *Bellipotent.* StudN (37:4) 2005, 430–42.

11685. GUNN, GILES B. (ed.). A historical guide to Herman Melville. Oxford; New York: OUP, 2005. pp. viii, 262. (Historical guides to American authors.)

11686. HECHT, ROGER. Rents in the landscape: the Anti-Rent War in Melville's *Pierre.* ATQ (19:1) 2005, 37–50.

11687. HEFLIN, WILSON. Herman Melville's whaling years. Ed. by Mary K. Bercaw Edwards and Thomas Farel Heffernan. (Bibl. 2004, 11641.) Rev. by R. D. Madison in MelSE (128) 2005, 15–17.

11688. HELMREICH, STEFAN. Cetology now: a sketch for the twenty-first century. MelSE (129) 2005, 10–12.

11689. HOEVELER, DIANE LONG. Beatrice Cenci in Hawthorne, Melville and her Atlantic-rim contexts. *See* **11204.**

11690. JOHNSON, CLAUDIA DURST. Understanding Melville's short fiction: a student's casebook to issues, sources, and historical documents. Westport, CT; London: Greenwood Press, 2005. pp. 248. (Literature in context.)

11691. KAMUF, PEGGY. 'J' is for just a minute: it's Miller time when it shimmers. *In* (pp. 197–209) **14737.**

11692. LEE, MAURICE S. The old and the new: double consciousness and the literature of slavery. *See* **10984.**

11693. McCLENDON, AARON. 'for not in words can it be spoken': John Sullivan Dwight's Transcendental music theory and Herman Melville's *Pierre; or, The Ambiguities.* ATQ (19:1) 2005, 23–36.

11694. MANHEIM, DAN. Melville's *Benito Cereno.* Exp (63:3) 2005, 151–4.

11695. MIZUKI, KEIKO. Melville no *The Piazza* to the Catskill Mountain House to fukei-ga. (Melville's *The Piazza*, the Catskill Mountain House, and American landscape painting.) StAL (41) 2004, 73–97.

11696. PARDES, ILANA. Remapping Jonah's voyage: Melville's *Moby-Dick* and Kitto's *Cyclopedia of Biblical Literature*. CL (57:2) 2005, 135–57.

11697. PRESTON, TODD. *Moby-Dick* and John Singleton Copley's *Watson and the Shark*. MelSE (129) 2005, 1–7.

11698. PROCHÁZKA, MARTIN. Apocalypticism in American cultural history: 2, Revelations of the Other. See **11217.**

11699. REIGELMAN, MILTON. Melville's *Mardi* as literary Pompidou Center. KenPR (19) 2004, 58–62.

11700. SABIA, DAN. *Billy Budd* and the politics of prudence. *In* (pp. 9–30) **14121.**

11701. SALAZAR, JAMES. Philanthropic taste: race and character in *The Confidence-Man*. Leviathan (7:1) 2005, 55–74.

11702. SCHEEL, EUGENE. Melville's poem recalls an elusive target. MelSE (128) 2005, 3–5.

11703. SEED, DAVID. Policing the Cold War frontier: *The Bedford Incident*. See **19027.**

11704. SESNIC, JELENA. Melville and his Medusæ: a reading of *Pierre*. Leviathan (7:1) 2005, 41–54.

11705. SINGER, ALAN. Aesthetic corrigibility: Bartleby and the character of the aesthetic. JNT (33:3) 2003, 231–69.

11706. STUCKEY, STERLING. Atufal, Aranda's skeleton, and *Moby-Dick*. MassR (46:3) 2005, 367–97.

11707. THOMPSON, COREY. Did Melville write *The Death Craft*? ANQ (18:2) 2005, 41–5.

11708. THOMPSON, COREY EVAN. Melville, Ishmael, teaching and whaling. ANQ (18:4) 2005, 36–9.

11709. —— Melville's *The Apple-Tree Table*. Exp (64:1) 2005, 38–41.

11710. WALIGORA-DAVIS, NICOLE A. The ghetto: illness and the formation of the 'suspect' in American polity. FMLS (40:2) 2004, 182–203.

11711. WALLACE, ROBERT K. Douglass and Melville: anchored together in a neighborly style. New Bedford, MA: Spinner, 2005. pp. xii, 147.

11712. —— Douglass and Melville: 'in neighborly style and anchored together'. MelSE (supp.) 2005, 3–9.

11713. WATSON, DAVID. Shakespeare: the discovery of America. See **6105.**

11714. WEINSTEIN, CINDY. We are family: Melville's *Pierre*. Leviathan (7:1) 2005, 19–40.

11715. WELTON, MARTIN. Once more with feeling. PRes (10:1) 2005, 100–12. (Stage adaptation of *Moby-Dick*.)

11716. YU, JIANHUA; YANG, JINCAI. The grotesque form of *Mardi* as an adventure into the novel. FLS (115) 2005, 121–7. (In Chinese.)

Adah Isaacs Menken

11717. CRONIN-JORTNER, MAURA L. In soldier's clothes: Adah Isaacs Menken goes to war. NCT (31:2) 2004, 51–72.

11718. SENTILLES, RENÉE M. Performing Menken: Adah Isaacs Menken and the birth of American celebrity. (Bibl. 2004, 11678.) Rev. by Charles L. Ponce de Leon in JAH (91:2) 2004, 629–30; by Kim Marra in TheatreS (46:1) 2005, 139–42.

George Meredith

11719. HARSH, CONSTANCE. The ambivalently modern master: hedges against the modern in Meredith's *The Amazing Marriage*. ELT (48:4) 2005, 436–58.

11720. JONES, ANNA MARIA. Eugenics by way of aesthetics: sexual selection, cultural consumption, and the cultivated reader in *The Egoist*. Lit (16:1) 2005, 101–28.

Alice Meynell

11721. PRINS, YOPIE. Patmore's law, Meynell's rhythm. *In* (pp. 261–84) **9675.**

John Stuart Mill

11722. CAPALDI, NICHOLAS. John Stuart Mill: a biography. (Bibl. 2004, 11686.) Rev. by James N. Jordan in IJPP (32:3) 2005, 307–13.

11723. SHERWOOD, MARION. 'Mr Tennyson's singular genius': the reception of *Poems* (1832). *See* **12159.**

H. M. (Henry M.) Milner

11724. CRONIN-JORTNER, MAURA L. In soldier's clothes: Adah Isaacs Menken goes to war. *See* **11717.**

S. Weir Mitchell

11725. KNIGHT, DENISE D. 'All the facts of the case': Gilman's lost letter to Dr S. Weir Mitchell. *See* **16690.**

Mary Russell Mitford

11726. ADDISON, CATHERINE. Gender and race in Byron's *The Island* and Mitford's *Christina*. *See* **10285.**

11727. KILLICK, TIM. Mary Russell Mitford and the topography of short fiction. JSSE (43) 2004, 11–28.

11728. SAGLIA, DIEGO. Mediterranean unrest: 1820s verse tragedies and revolutions in the South. *See* **11959.**

David Macbeth Moir (1798–1851)

11729. MORRISON, ROBERT. *De Quincey's Revenge*: David Macbeth Moir and *Confessions of an English Opium-Eater*. NQ (52:1) 2005, 53–4.

Mrs Molesworth ('Ennis Graham')

11730. GRIMES, HILARY. The haunted self: visions of the ghost and the woman at the *fin-de-siècle*. *See* **12059.**

Frederic Montagu (*fl.*1838)

11731. HEYWOOD, CHRISTOPHER. The mark 'Bronte' on Frederic Montagu's *Gleanings in Craven*. BLR (18:5) 2005, 576–84.

Susanna Moodie

11732. DELGADO, ANA BEATRIZ. Paradigms of Canadian literary biography: who will write our history? *See* **14585.**

Thomas Moore (1779–1852)

11733. BURNETT, PAULA. Walcott's intertextual method: non-Greek naming in *Omeros*. *See* **19936.**

11734. DYER, GARY. Intercepted letters, men of information: Moore's *Twopenny Post-Bag* and *Fudge Family in Paris*. *In* (pp. 151–71) **9305.**

11735. GIBSON, MARY ELLIS. Poems of Mary Carshore: the Indian legacy of L.E.L. and Tom Moore. *See* **10411.**

11736. STRACHAN, JOHN (gen. ed.). British satire: vol. 5, The satires of Thomas Moore. Ed. by Jane Moore. London; Brookfield, VT: Pickering & Chatto, 2003. pp. xxxvi, 555. Rev. by Marcus Wood in WordsC (35:4) 2004, 162–4; by Bernard Beatty in BJ (32:2) 2004, 153–5.

Lady Morgan (Sydney Owenson)

11737. ABBATE BADIN, DONATELLA. Lady Morgan and the Italian female Other. *In* (pp. 32–42) **3690.**

11738. FRANKLIN, CAROLINE. Romantic patriotism as feminist critique of empire: Helen Maria Williams, Sydney Owenson and Germaine de Staël. *In* (pp. 551–64) **8016.**

11739. FREEMAN, KATHRYN. 'Eternally disunited': gender, empire, and epistemology in Sydney Owenson's *The Missionary*. WordsC (36:1) 2005, 21–8.

William Morgan (1782–1858)

11740. WALKER, MICHAEL. William Morgan, BD, 1782–1858. BrSt (30:3) 2005, 213–30.

William Morris (1834–1896)

11741. BENNETT, PHILLIPPA. Rediscovering the topography of wonder: Morris, Iceland and the last romances. JWMS (16:2/3) 2005, 31–48.

11742. BIZUP, JOSEPH. Manufacturing culture: vindications of early Victorian industry. Charlottesville; London: Virginia UP, 2003. pp. xii, 229. (Victorian literature and culture.) Rev. by Elaine Freedgood in NineL (59:4) 2005, 533–6; by Daniel Siegel in ELT (48:4) 2005, 472–6.

11743. BOOS, FLORENCE S. Dystopian violence: William Morris and the nineteenth-century peace movement. JPRS (14:1) 2005, 15–35.

11744. —— William Morris's *Our Country Right or Wrong*: a critical edition. JPRS (14:1) 2005, 36–56.

11745. FAULKNER, PETER. The story of Alcestis in William Morris and Ted Hughes. JWMS (16:2/3) 2005, 56–79.

11746. GAGNIER, REGENIA. Morris's ethics, cosmopolitanism, and globalisation. JWMS (16:2/3) 2005, 9–30.

11747. GANIM, JOHN M. Chaucer and free love. *In* (pp. 344–63) **4485.**

11748. GOPEN, GEORGE D. The music of the mind: structure and substance in William Morris's *The Water of the Wondrous Isles*. JWMS (16:2/3) 2005, 92–102.

11749. ORCHARD, ANDY.   Reading *Beowulf* now and then. *See* **4308.**

11750. PINKNEY, TONY.   Kinetic utopias: H. G. Wells's *A Modern Utopia* and William Morris's *News from Nowhere. See* **20059.**

11751. —— (ed.).   We met Morris: interviews with William Morris, 1885–96. Reading: Spire Books in assn with the William Morris Soc., 2005. pp. 144. Rev. by Marcus Waithe in TLS, 14 Oct. 2005, 34.

11752. PRESCOTT, LYNDA.   Evelyn Waugh, Morris, and the ideal of craftsmanship. *See* **20014.**

11753. RICHMOND, VELMA BOURGEOIS.   Edward Burne-Jones's Chaucer portraits in the Kelmscott Chaucer. *See* **4964.**

11754. TOBIN, THOMAS J. (ed.).   Worldwide Pre-Raphaelitism. Albany: New York State UP, 2005. pp. xi, 326. (SUNY series: Studies in the long nineteenth century.) Rev. by Norman Kelvin in VS (47:3) 2005, 470–3; by Peter Faulkner in JWMS (16:2/3) 2005, 148–52.

11755. WHITLA, WILLIAM.   William Morris's translation of Homer's *Iliad*, I.1–214. JPRS (13:2) 2004, 75–121.

Arthur Morrison

11756. WILLIS, CHRIS.   From voyeurism to feminism: Victorian and Edwardian London's streetfighting slum viragoes. *See* **18150.**

Anna Cora Mowatt

11757. BRANCA, R. RENE.   Melodrama, convention, and rape. *See* **9104.**

Anne Mozley (1809–1891)

11758. JORDAN, ELLEN.   Sister as journalist: the almost anonymous career of Anne Mozley. VPR (37:3) 2004, 315–41.

John Muir (1838–1914)

11759. LEWIS, COREY LEE.   Reading the trail: exploring the literature and natural history of the California Crest. *See* **12780.**

Neil Munro ('Hugh Foulis')

11760. OSBORNE, BRIAN D.   Conrad and Neil Munro: notes on a literary acquaintance. *See* **15905.**

John Henry Newman

11761. BARR, COLIN.   Paul Cullen, John Henry Newman, and the Catholic University of Ireland, 1845–1865. (Bibl. 2004, 11743.) Rev. by Paul A. Townend in JMH (77:2) 2005, 425–7.

11762. DOCHERTY, THOMAS.   Newman, Ireland, and universality. B2 (31:1) 2004, 73–92.

11763. TURNER, FRANK M.   John Henry Newman: the challenge to evangelical religion. (Bibl. 2004, 11752.) Rev. by Jouett L. Powell in CHist (72:2) 2003, 413–14; by W. R. Ward in JMH (76:3) 2004, 680–1.

Caroline Norton

11764. BELLAMY, JOAN.   *The Tenant of Wildfell Hall*: what Anne Brontë knew and what modern readers don't. *See* **10144.**

11765. LATANÉ, DAVID E., JR. Two letters from Caroline Norton to Charles Molloy Westmacott. NQ (52:1) 2005, 65–8.

Mrs Harriet P. H. Nowell ('May Mannering')

11766. JOHNSON, DEIRDRE A. Harriet P. Hardy Nowell: a brief biography. DNR (74:3) 2005, 90–5.

Mrs (Margaret) Oliphant (1828–1897)

11767. MOUTON, MICHELLE. Margaret Oliphant and John Stuart Mill: disinterested politicians and the 1865 General Election. DSA (35) 2005, 209–39.

11768. ROBINSON, SOLVEIG C. Expanding a 'limited orbit': Margaret Oliphant, *Blackwood's Edinburgh Magazine*, and the development of a critical voice. VPR (38:2) 2005, 199–220.

Amelia Opie

11769. KING, SHELLEY; PIERCE, JOHN B. (eds). *The Father and Daughter* with *Dangers of Coquetry*. Peterborough, Ont.; Orchard Park, NY: Broadview Press, 2003. pp. 377. (Broadview literary texts.) Rev. by Deborah Kennedy in ECF (17:2) 2005, 307–9.

'Ouida' (Marie Louise de la Ramée)

11770. POLLOCK, MARY SANDERS. Ouida's rhetoric of empathy: a case study in Victorian anti-vivisection narrative. *In* (pp. 135–59) **14258**.

11771. WALKER, CHARLOTTE ZOË. FETCH! *Solid Objects, A Dog of Flanders*, and the short story. *In* (pp. 194–201) **14204**.

'Our Nig' (Harriet E. Wilson) (1825–1900)

11772. FOREMAN, P. GABRIELLE; PITTS, REGINALD H. (eds). Our Nig; or, Sketches from the life of a free Black. London; New York: Penguin, 2005. pp. liii, 103. (Penguin classics.) Rev. by Eric Gardner in AAR (38:4) 2004, 715–18.

11773. SANTAMARINA, XIOMARA. Belabored professions: narratives of African American working womanhood. *See* **12231**.

David Pae (1828–1884)

11774. LAW, GRAHAM. Imagined local communities: three Victorian newspaper novelists. *In* (pp. 185–203) **880**.

H. B. Richenda (Helena Beatrice Richenda) Parham

11775. REEVE, PHYLLIS. *Plantation Printer's Pie*: grandmother and the Multigraph. *See* **174**.

Francis Parkman

11776. VERHOEVEN, WIL. Ecology as requiem: nature, nationhood and history in Francis Parkman's *History of the American Forest*. *In* (pp. 137–52) **9237**.

Walter Pater

11777. BANN, STEPHEN (ed.). The reception of Walter Pater in Europe. London; New York: Continuum, 2004. pp. xxvi, 295. (Athlone critical traditions, 4.)

11778. COATES, JOHN. Pater and the Lacedaemonian ideal. CVE (61) 2005, 41–66.

11779. DAWSON, GOWAN.   Walter Pater's *Marius the Epicurean* and the discourse of science in *Macmillan's Magazine*: 'a creature of the nineteenth century'. ELT (48:1) 2005, 38–54.

11780. JACKSON, NOEL B.   Rethinking the cultural divide: Walter Pater, Wilkie Collins, and the legacies of Wordsworthian aesthetics. MP (102:2) 2004, 207–34.

11781. JÖTTKANDT, SIGI.   Effectively equivalent: Walter Pater, 'Sebastian van Storck', and the ethics of metaphor. NineL (60:2) 2005, 163–98.

11782. KANDOLA, SONDEEP.   Vernon Lee: New Woman? *See* **11579.**

11783. KREUTZIGER, JOSEPH.   Darwin's temporal aesthetics: a brief stretch in time from Pater to Woolf. *See* **20376.**

11784. LEIGHTON, ANGELA.   Pater's music. JPRS (14:2) 2005, 67–79.

11785. SAVILLE, JULIA F.   The poetic imaging of Michael Field. *In* (pp. 178–206) **9675.**

11786. SCHWEIK, ROBERT.   A note on some modern critical views of the relationship of *The Well-Beloved* to the Victorian art context. *See* **11161.**

Coventry Patmore

11787. PRINS, YOPIE.   Patmore's law, Meynell's rhythm. *In* (pp. 261–84) **9675.**

John Payne (1842–1916)

11788. MARZOLPH, ULRICH; VAN LEEUWEN, RICHARD (eds); WASSOUF, HASSAN (asst ed.).   The Arabian Nights encyclopedia. Santa Barbara, CA: ABC-CLIO, 2004. 2 vols. pp. xxvii, 921. Rev. by Thomas Geider in MarvT (19:2) 2005, 322–5.

Elizabeth Palmer Peabody

11789. WILSON, LESLIE PERRIN.   'No worthless books': Elizabeth Peabody's Foreign Library, 1840–52. *See* **9449.**

Thomas Love Peacock

11790. BAULCH, DAVID.   Several hundred pages of promise: the phantom of the gothic in Peacock's *Nightmare Abbey* and Coleridge's *Biographia Literaria*. *See* **10463.**

11791. BAULCH, DAVID M.   The 'perpetual exercise of an interminable quest': the *Biographia Literaria* and the Kantian revolution. *See* **10464.**

Elizabeth Stuart Phelps ('H. Trusta')

11792. BERGMAN, JILL.   'Oh the poor women!': Elizabeth Stuart Phelps's motherly benevolence. *In* (pp. 190–212) **9513.**

11793. WEGENER, FREDERICK.   'Few things more womanly or more noble': Elizabeth Stuart Phelps and the advent of the woman doctor in America. Legacy (22:1) 2005, 1–17.

Richard Phillips of Leamington (*fl.*1871)

11794. FRANKLIN, J. JEFFREY.   The life of the Buddha in Victorian England. *See* **9917.**

Catherine Louisa Pirkis (1839–1910)

11795. MILLER, ELIZABETH CAROLYN. Trouble with she-dicks: private eyes and public women in *The Adventures of Loveday Brooke, Lady Detective*. VLC (33:1) 2005, 47–65.

George Dibdin Pitt (1799–1855)

11796. LODGE, MARY JO. From madness to melodramas to musicals: the women of *Lady Audley's Secret* and *Sweeney Todd*. See **10139**.

Ann Plato (*fl*.1841)

11797. XAVIER, SILVIA. Engaging George Campbell's 'sympathy' in the rhetoric of Charlotte Forten and Ann Plato, African American women of the antebellum North. See **2523**.

Edgar Allan Poe

11798. BEIDLER, PHILIP D. Mythopoetic justice: democracy and the death of Edgar Allan Poe. MidQ (46:3) 2005, 252–67.

11799. CARTER, CATHERINE. 'Not a woman': the murdered muse in *Ligeia*. PoeS (36) 2003, 45–57.

11800. CASTRONOVO, RUSS. Death to the American renaissance: history, Heidegger, Poe. ESQ (49:1–3) 2003, 179–92.

11801. CURRELI, MARIO. Leitmotifs from Coleridge and Wagner in *Nostromo* and beyond. See **15871**.

11802. DELANEY, BILL. Poe's *The Cask of Amontillado*. Exp (64:1) 2005, 33–5.

11803. FAHERTY, DUNCAN. 'A certain unity of design': Edgar Allan Poe's *Tales of the Grotesque and Arabesque* and the terrors of Jacksonian democracy. EAPR (6:2) 2005, 4–21.

11804. FOLKS, JEFFREY J. Edgar Allan Poe and Elias Canetti: illuminating the sources of terror. SoLJ (37:2) 2005, 1–16.

11805. FRANK, ADAM. Valdemar's tongue, Poe's telegraphy. ELH (72:3) 2005, 635–62.

11806. FREEDMAN, WILLIAM. *Berenice* and the art of incorporative exclusion. PoeS (36) 2003, 68–75.

11807. GAMPER, MICHAEL. 'Er lasst sich nicht lesen': physiognomy and the city. In (pp. 150–60) **3884**.

11808. GETZ, JOHN. Edith Wharton and the ghost of Poe: *Miss Mary Pask* and *Mr Jones*. See **20118**.

11809. GIORCELLI, CRISTINA. Da Irving – a Hawthorne, a Poe – a Irving: alle origini del fantastico nella letteratura statunitense. See **9552**.

11810. GRIMSTAD, PAUL. C. Auguste Dupin and Charles S. Peirce: an abductive affinity. EAPR (6:2) 2005, 22–30.

11811. GRIMSTAD, PAUL C. Algorithm – genre – *linguisterie*: 'creative distortion' in *Count Zero* and *Nova Express*. JML (27:4) 2004, 82–92.

11812. HARRIS, PAUL A. Poe-tic mathematics: detecting topology in *The Purloined Letter*. PoeS (36) 2003, 18–31.

11813. HARRISON, RUTH M. Poe Möbius: an exploration of Poe's fractal universe. PoeS (36) 2003, 32–44.

11814. HECKER, WILLIAM F. (ed.). Private Perry and Mister Poe: the West Point poems, 1831. Baton Rouge: Louisiana State UP, 2005. pp. lxxv, 165. Rev. by Benjamin F. Fisher in EAPR (6:2) 2005, 47–9.

11815. HUTCHISSON, JAMES M. Poe. Jackson; London: Mississippi UP, 2005. pp. xvii, 290. (Willie Morris books in memoir and biography.) Rev. by Kevin J. Hayes in EAPR (6:2) 2005, 43–6.

11816. KENNEDY, J. GERALD. 'A mania for composition': Poe's *annus mirabilis* and the violence of nation-building. AmLH (17:1) 2005, 1–35.

11817. KENYON, JOSEPH P. Auber and Avernus: Poe's use of myth and ritual in *Ulalume*. PoeS (36) 2003, 58–67.

11818. MORISI, EVE CÉLIA. Poe's *To One in Paradise*. Exp (63:3) 2005, 141–4.

11819. PEEPLES, SCOTT. The afterlife of Edgar Allan Poe. (Bibl. 2004, 11848.) Rev. by Alexander Hammond in EAPR (6:2) 2005, 39–42.

11820. POLLIN, BURTON. Poe and Ray Bradbury: a persistent influence and interest. EAPR (6:2) 2005, 31–8.

11821. POLLIN, BURTON R. Music and Edgar Allan Poe: a fourth annotated checklist. PoeS (36) 2003, 77–100.

11822. RAMBOUSEK, JIŘÍ. Unpublished translations of Poe's *The Raven* by František Nevrla. *In* (pp. 249–56) **1370.**

11823. RICHARDS, ELIZA. Gender and the poetics of reception in Poe's circle. Cambridge; New York: CUP, 2004. pp. xvii, 238. (Cambridge studies in American literature and culture.) (Cf. bibl. 1999, 11741.).

11824. —— Outsourcing *The Raven*: retroactive origins. VP (43:2) 2005, 205–21.

11825. SWEENEY, SUSAN ELIZABETH. The magnifying glass: spectacular distance in Poe's *Man of the Crowd* and beyond. PoeS (36) 2003, 3–17.

11826. SWEETING, ADAM W. Preserving the renaissance: literature and public memory in the homes of Longfellow, Hawthorne, and Poe. *See* **11617.**

11827. VEEL, KRISTIN. The irreducibility of space: labyrinths, cities, cyberspace. *See* **2506.**

John Polidori

11828. BISHOP, FRANKLIN CHARLES (ed.). *The Vampyre* and other writings. Manchester: Carcanet Press, 2005. (Fyfield.)

11829. RIGBY, MAIR. 'Prey to some cureless disquiet': Polidori's queer vampyre at the margins of Romanticism. RomNet (36/37) 2004/05.

John Poole (1786?–1872)

11830. CREASY, MATTHEW. Shakespeare burlesque in *Ulysses*. *See* **17263.**

Eliza Potter

11831. SANTAMARINA, XIOMARA. Black hairdresser and social critic: Eliza Potter and the labors of femininity. AL (77:1) 2005, 151–77.

Mrs Campbell Praed

11832. MCCANN, ANDREW. Unknown Australia: Rosa Praed's vanished race. ALS (22:1) 2005, 37–50.

E. (Elizabeth) Prentiss (1818–1878)

11833. YAMAGUCHI, MIHO.   Elizabeth Prentiss' faith in suffering and perplexity about the Wesleyan and the higher life doctrines: on *Stepping Heavenward*. LitTheol (18:4) 2004, 415–26.

Thomas Pringle

11834. COLCLOUGH, STEPHEN.   'Designated in print as "Mr John Clare" ': the annuals and the field of reading, 1827–1835. See **10434**.

Adelaide Anne Procter

11835. COLÓN, CHRISTINE.   Revising Keats's *The Eve of St Agnes*: the shift from dreams to reality in Adelaide Procter's *A Legend of Provence*. WWr (12:2) 2005, 271–90.

Richard Pryce (1864–1942)

11836. ZIEGER, SUSAN.   'How far am I responsible?': women and morphinomania in late nineteenth-century Britain. VS (48:1) 2005, 59–81.

Charles Reade

11837. BURY, LAURENT.   Le paradoxe de la comédienne: Peg Woffington selon Charles Reade. CVE (61) 2005, 27–39.

George W. M. Reynolds

11838. EELLS, EMILY.   The mystery of *Kitty Bell*: a possible solution? See **10158**.

John Hamilton Reynolds

11839. BAJETTA, CARLO M.   Redeeming the vagrant: Wordsworth's *Peter Bell* and its revisions. *In* (pp. 54–65) **3690**.

11840. CLYMER, LORNA.   Philosophical tours of the universe in British poetry, 1700–1729; or, The soaring muse. *In* (pp. 30–62) **5880**.

11841. PERRY, SEAMUS.   The little horror show. See **12510**.

Major (John) Richardson (1796–1852)

11842. BEASLEY, DAVID.   The Canadian Don Quixote: the life and works of Major John Richardson, Canada's first novelist. Simcoe, Ont.; Buffalo, NY: Davus, 2004. pp. ix, 341.

Anne Thackeray Ritchie

11843. APLIN, JOHN.   Three Tennyson letters to Anne Thackeray. See **12132**.

Sir Charles G. D. Roberts

11844. CARTER, ADAM.   Anthropomorphism and trope in the national ode. *In* (pp. 117–44) **9191**.

11845. CAVELL, RICHARD.   'An ordered absence': defeatured topologies in Canadian literature. *In* (pp. 14–31) **9243**.

Emma Roberts (1794?–1840)

11846. NÍ FHLATHÚIN, MÁIRE.   India and women's poetry of the 1830s: femininity and the picturesque in the poetry of Emma Roberts and Letitia Elizabeth Landon. See **11568**.

Henry Crabb Robinson

11847. STELZIG, EUGENE. A cultural tourist in Romantic Germany: Henry Crabb Robinson as nineteenth-century life writer. Biography (28:4) 2005, 515–33.

11848. STOCKHORST, STEFANIE. Henry Crabb Robinsons doppeltes Deutschlandbild: Funktionsweise deutsch–englischer Literaturbeziehungen um 1800. WB (51:2) 2005, 254–69.

11849. WHELAN, TIMOTHY. 'I have *confessed myself a devil*': Crabb Robinson's confrontation with Robert Hall, 1798–1800. CLB (121) 2003, 2–25.

Mary Robinson (1857–1944)

11850. PAREJO VADILLO, ANA. Immaterial poetics: A. Mary F. Robinson and the *fin-de-siècle* poem. *In* (pp. 231–60) **9675**.

Joseph Rocchietti

11851. ALBRIGHT, CAROL BONOMO; DI FABIO, ELVIRA G. (eds). Republican ideals in the selected literary works of Italian American Joseph Rocchietti, 1835/1845. (Bibl. 2004, 11892.) Rev. by Giuliana Minghelli in ItalA (23:1) 2005, 106–7.

Samuel Rogers (1763–1855)

11852. SHERBO, ARTHUR. From the sale catalogue of the library of Samuel Rogers. NQ (52:1) 2005, 25–32.

William Roscoe (1753–1831)

11853. MORRISON, ROBERT. De Quincey on *Mount Pleasant*: William Roscoe and *Confessions of an English Opium-Eater. See* **10635**.

11854. RUWE, DONELLE R. Satirical birds and natural bugs: J. Harris' chapbooks and the aesthetic of children's literature. *In* (pp. 115–37) **9305**.

11855. WHALE, JOHN. The making of a city of culture: William Roscoe's Liverpool. ECL (29:2) 2005, 91–107.

Christina Rossetti

11856. BLAIR, EMILY. 'The wrong side of the tapestry': Elizabeth Gaskell's *Wives and Daughters. See* **11037**.

11857. BOWLES, NOELLE. A chink in the armour: Christina Rossetti's *The Prince's Progress*, *A Royal Princess*, and Victorian medievalism. WWr (12:1) 2005, 115–26.

11858. D'ALESSANDRO, JEAN M. ELLIS. Christina Rossetti: the Italian heritage. Pisa: ETS, 2004. pp. 212. (Poiesis e critica mitica, 33.)

11859. HARRISON, ANTONY H. (ed.). The letters of Christina Rossetti: vol. 4, 1887–1894. (Bibl. 2004, 11904.) Rev. by Amanda Hubbard in RES (56:226) 2005, 684–6.

11860. KABITOGLOU, EKATERINI DOUKA. Europa in Wonderland: *Goblin Market* or Sappho's gymnasium? Misc (30) 2004, 51–69.

11861. KOOISTRA, LORRAINE JANZEN. Christina Rossetti and illustration: a publishing history. (Bibl. 2004, 11907.) Rev. by Paul Goldman in Library (6:1) 2005, 101–3.

11862. LYSACK, KRISTA. Goblin markets: Victorian women shoppers at Liberty's Oriental Bazaar. NCC (27:2) 2005, 139–65.

11863. ROGERS, SCOTT. The edge of sisterhood in Christina Rossetti's *The Convent Threshold*. JPRS (14:2) 2005, 30–42.

11864. WINTERS, SARAH FIONA. Christina Rossetti's poetic vocation. WWr (12:2) 2005, 291–307.

Dante Gabriel Rossetti

11865. BENTLEY, D. M. R. Dante Gabriel Rossetti's *Lady Lilith* and *Sibylla Palmifera*: 'body's beauty', and 'soul's beauty'. JPRS (13:2) 2004, 64–74.

11866. BUMA, MICHAEL. Rossetti's *Sudden Light*. Exp (63:3) 2005, 154–9.

11867. D'ALESSANDRO, JEAN M. ELLIS. Christina Rossetti: the Italian heritage. *See* 11858.

11868. FERRAND, AUDE. Revisiting *Beatrix*: intertextuality, tradition and modernity in Evelyn Waugh's *Brideshead Revisited*. *See* 20011.

11869. FERRARI, ROBERTO C. To the Rossettis, from the Solomons: five unpublished letters. NQ (52:1) 2005, 70–5.

11870. HOLMES, JOHN. Dante Gabriel Rossetti and the late Victorian sonnet sequence: sexuality, belief and the self. Aldershot; Burlington, VT: Ashgate, 2005. pp. viii, 189. (Nineteenth century.)

11871. McGANN, JEROME (ed.). Collected poetry and prose. (Bibl. 2004, 11922.) Rev. by Yann Tholoniat in EREA (2:2) 2004; by Laurent Bury in EA (58:4) 2005, 502–3.

11872. MARSHIK, CELIA. The case of *Jenny*: Dante Gabriel Rossetti and the censorship dialectic. VLC (33:2) 2005, 557–84.

11873. RIVERS, BRYAN. 'Jenny's cage-bird': symbolic realism in D. G. Rossetti's *Jenny*. NQ (52:1) 2005, 75–7.

11874. —— Rossetti's *Jenny*. Exp (63:2) 2005, 82–5.

11875. ROUSSILLON, LAURENCE. '*All now is still*': de la citation à l'œuvre dans *Ruggiero and Angelica* de Dante Gabriel Rossetti. EREA (2:1) 2004, 41–6.

11876. SCHWEIK, ROBERT. A note on some modern critical views of the relationship of *The Well-Beloved* to the Victorian art context. *See* 11161.

11877. STARZYK, LAWRENCE J. 'The peril of pleasure unavoidable': Rossetti and the verbal incarnation of the visual. JPRS (14:2) 2005, 5–16.

11878. STAUFFER, ANDREW M. Dante Gabriel Rossetti and the burdens of Nineveh. VLC (33:2) 2005, 369–94.

11879. TINKLER-VILLANI, VALERIA. Victorian Shelley: perspectives on a Romantic poet. *In* (pp. 89–104) 9237.

11880. TOBIN, THOMAS J. (ed.). Worldwide Pre-Raphaelitism. *See* 11754.

William Michael Rossetti

11881. FERRARI, ROBERTO C. To the Rossettis, from the Solomons: five unpublished letters. *See* 11869.

The Rossettis

11882. BENTLEY, D. M. R. The principal Pre-Raphaelite pictures of James Collinson. *See* 10555.

11883. PITE, RALPH (gen. ed.). Lives of Victorian literary figures II: the Brownings, the Brontës, and the Rossettis by their contemporaries: vol. 3, The Rossettis. Ed. by Hester Jones. London; Brookfield, VT: Pickering & Chatto, 2004. pp. xxxix, 432.

11884. THIRLWELL, ANGELA. William and Lucy: the other Rossettis. (Bibl. 2004, 11930.) Rev. by Peter Stansky in ELT (48:3) 2005, 367–70; by Julie L'Enfant in JPRS (14:1) 2005, 95–8.

María Amparo Ruiz de Burton (1832–1895)

11885. DE LA LUZ MONTES, AMELIA MARÍA; GOLDMAN, ANNE ELIZABETH (eds). María Amparo Ruiz de Burton: critical and pedagogical perspectives. (Bibl. 2004, 11934.) Rev. by Ella Maria Diaz in Legacy (22:2) 2005, 202–3.

John Ruskin

11886. ANDERSON, ANNE. Oscar's enemy ... and neighbour: 'Arry' Quilter and the 'Gospel of Intensity'. See **12363**.

11887. BENNETT, PHILLIPPA. Rediscovering the topography of wonder: Morris, Iceland and the last romances. See **11741**.

11888. BIZUP, JOSEPH. Manufacturing culture: vindications of early Victorian industry. See **11742**.

11889. BRETON, ROB. The stones of happiness: Ruskin and working-class culture. JVC (10:2) 2005, 210–28.

11890. DAY, BRIAN J. The moral intuition of Ruskin's *Storm-Cloud*. SELit (45:4) 2005, 917–33.

11891. HANSON, DAVID C. Precocity and the economy of the evangelical self in John Ruskin's juvenilia. *In* (pp. 200–21) **9164**.

11892. HILTON, TIM (introd.). *Praeterita* and *Dilecta*. New York: Knopf, 2005. pp. xli, 564. (Everyman's library.)

11893. LEE, ALAN. Colour and pictorial representation. BJA (45:1) 2005, 49–63.

11894. LENG, ANDREW. Collectors in crisis: the Ruskins' posthumous Turners. NCC (27:3) 2005, 231–43.

11895. PANAYOTOVA, STELLA. A Ruskinian project with a Cockerellian flavour. BC (54:3) 2005, 357–74.

11896. PAROISSIEN, DAVID. Monsters in the classroom: Dickens's case against industrialised education. See **10728**.

11897. PEASE, ALLISON. Aestheticism and aesthetic theory. *In* (pp. 96–118) **12414**.

11898. PITE, RALPH (gen. ed.). Lives of Victorian literary figures III: Elizabeth Gaskell, the Carlyles and John Ruskin by their contemporaries: vol. 3, John Ruskin. Ed. by Simon Grimble. London; Brookfield, VT: Pickering & Chatto, 2005. pp. xliv, 470.

11899. SHIRES, LINDA. Hardy and nineteenth-century poetry and politics. *In* (pp. 255–78) **11140**.

11900. SPATES, JAMES L.; BURD, VAN AKIN. Ruskin in Milan: a chapter from *Dark Star,* Helen Gill Viljoen's unpublished biography of John Ruskin. JPRS (13:2) 2004, 17–62.

11901. WAINWRIGHT, STEVEN P.; WILLIAMS, CLARE. Biography and vulnerability: loss, dying and death in the Romantic paintings of J. M. W. Turner (1775–1851). See **12232**.

Mary Anne Sadlier

11902. HOWES, MARJORIE. Discipline, sentiment, and the Irish American public: Mary Ann Sadlier's popular fiction. EI (40:1/2) 2005, 140–69.

Olive Schreiner

11903. HEILMANN, ANN. New Woman strategies: Sarah Grand, Olive Schreiner, Mona Caird. See **11092**.

11904. SIMON, LEWIS. White women writers and their African invention. See **16100**.

Sir Walter Scott

11905. BEIDERWELL, BRUCE; McCORMICK, ANITA HEMPHILL. The making and unmaking of a children's classic: the case of Scott's *Ivanhoe.* In (pp. 165–77) **8171**.

11906. BOUR, ISABELLE. Sensibility as epistemology in *Caleb Williams, Waverley,* and *Frankenstein.* See **8668**.

11907. BROWN, IAIN GORDON. Cabinet reshuffle: the fate of Sir Walter Scott's furniture – and his father's. TLS, 8 Apr. 2005, 15.

11908. —— (ed.). Abbotsford and Sir Walter Scott: the image and the influence. Edinburgh: Soc. of Antiquaries of Scotland, 2003. pp. xvii, 173. Rev. by Penny Fielding in ScSR (5:1) 2004, 134–5.

11909. CARRUTHERS, GERARD; LUMSDEN, ALISON (eds). Reliquiæ Trotcosienses; or, The gabions of the late Jonathan Oldbuck Esq. of Monkbarns. Introd. by David Hewitt. Edinburgh: Edinburgh UP in assn with the Abbotsford Library Project Trust, 2004. pp. xxii, 143. Rev. by J. H. Alexander in SHogg (15) 2004, 166–71.

11910. COOPER, JOAN GARDEN. Scott's critique of the English treason law in *Waverley.* ScSR (4:2) 2003, 17–36.

11911. D'ARCENS, LOUISE. Inverse invasions: medievalism and colonialism in Rolf Boldrewood's *A Sydney-Side Saxon. See* **10102**.

11912. DAWSON, TERENCE. The effective protagonist in the nineteenth-century British novel: Scott, Brontë, Eliot, Wilde. Aldershot; Burlington, VT: Ashgate, 2004. pp. vi, 300. (Nineteenth century.) Rev. by Mark W. Turner in GER (36) 2005, 78–80.

11913. DIGGLE, JAMES. Some literary allusions in Scott's *The Antiquary.* NQ (52:4) 2005, 466–7.

11914. DUNCAN, IAN. Edinburgh, capital of the nineteenth century. *In* (pp. 45–64) **9217**.

11915. DYER, GARY R. Reading as a criminal in early nineteenth-century fiction. WordsC (35:3) 2004, 141–6.

11916. EASLEY, ALEXIS.   *Tait's Edinburgh Magazine* in the 1830s: dialogues on gender, class, and reform. *See* **1194**.

11917. ELBERT, MONIKA.   Nature, magic, and history: forging a national identity in Stowe. *See* **12106**.

11918. ELPHINSTONE, MARGARET.   What force made men act so? A question of historical fiction. *See* **16341**.

11919. FARINA, JONATHAN V.   Superstitious marginalia: Coleridge and *Waverley*. *See* **10480**.

11920. FELLUGA, DINO FRANCO.   The perversity of poetry: Romantic ideology and the popular male poet of genius. *See* **10307**.

11921. FERGUSON, STUART.   At the grave of the Gentile constitution: Walter Scott, Georg Lukács and Romanticism. SR (44:3) 2005, 423–37.

11922. —— Walter Scott and the construction of historical knowledge: a Lukácsian perspective. AUMLA (103) 2005, 43–63.

11923. FORD, SUSAN ALLEN.   Learning romance from Scott and Byron: Jane Austen's natural sequel. *See* **9983**.

11924. FURBANK, P. N.   On the historical novel. *See* **16802**.

11925. GARBIN, LIDIA.   'Not fit to tie his brogues': Shakespeare and Scott. *In* (pp. 141–56) **6561**.

11926. GUNN, DIARMID.   Walter Scott to John Buchan: the handing over of a baton? *See* **15605**.

11927. HALL, STEFAN THOMAS.   Awkward silences in Scott's *Waverley*. ScSR (4:1) 2003, 82–97.

11928. HEWITT, REGINA.   Scott, Baillie, and the bewitching of social relations. *See* **10079**.

11929. HOROBIN, SIMON.   The angle of oblivioun: a lost medieval manuscript discovered in Walter Scott's collection. *See* **260**.

11930. INCORVATI, RICK.   Darsie Latimer's 'little solidity'; or, The case for homosexuality in Scott's *Redgauntlet*. RomNet (36/37) 2004/05.

11931. JONES, CATHERINE.   Literary memory: Scott's Waverley novels and the psychology of narrative. Lewisburg, PA: Bucknell UP; London: Assoc. UPs, 2003. pp. 249. Rev. by Ina Ferris in WordsC (35:4) 2004, 175–7; by Fiona Stafford in RES (56:226) 2005, 681–2.

11932. KIPP, JULIE.   Back to the future: Walter Scott on the politics of radical reform in Ireland and Scotland. ERR (16:2) 2005, 231–42.

11933. —— Romanticism, maternity, and the body politic. *See* **8015**.

11934. LAMONT, CLAIRE.   Scott and eighteenth-century imperialism: India and the Scottish Highlands. *In* (pp. 35–50) **9237**.

11935. LINCOLN, ANDREW.   The mercenary, the savage, and the civilized war: Scott and *A Legend of the Wars of Montrose*. ScSR (4:2) 2003, 37–47.

11936. MASON, EMMA.   'Some kind friends': Scott's *Harold the Dauntless* (HM 1937) and Frederick Locker-Lampson. HLQ (67:4) 2004, 623–31.

11937. MAY, CHAD T.   'The horrors of my tale': trauma, the historical imagination, and Sir Walter Scott. PCP (40:1) 2005, 98–116.

11938. MONNICKENDAM, ANDREW. Eating your words: plate and nation in Meg Dods's *The Cook and Housewife's Manual* (1826). *See* **11496.**

11939. NEWTON, K. M. Revisions of Scott, Austen, and Dickens in *Daniel Deronda. See* **10944.**

11940. NÜNNING, VERA. Fictions of collective memory. *See* **3511.**

11941. PROCHÁZKA, MARTIN. The 'neutral ground' of history? Tully-Veolan in *Waverley* as a zone of contact. *In* (pp. 143–53) **3734.**

11942. PURSER, JOHN. Erik Chisholm and Macpherson's *Night Song of the Bards. See* **8814.**

11943. REID, JULIA. The *Academy* and *Cosmopolis*: evolution and culture in Robert Louis Stevenson's periodical encounters. *In* (pp. 263–73) **1226.**

11944. SCRIVENER, MICHAEL. Trials in Romantic-era writing: modernity, guilt, and the scene of justice. *See* **8680.**

11945. STARNAWSKI, JERZY. Literatura angielska w Bibliotece Narodowej 1921–1929: kulisy w świetle archiwum Stanisława Kota. (English literature in the National Library [series] 1921–1929 in the light of Stanisław Kot's archive.) *In* (pp. 227–37) **3756.**

11946. TULLOCH, GRAHAM. Writing 'by advice': *Ivanhoe* and *The Three Perils of Man*. SHogg (15) 2004, 32–52.

11947. TYTLER, GRAEME. Lavater's influence on Sir Walter Scott: a tacit assumption? *In* (pp. 109–20) **3884.**

11948. WARNES, CHRISTOPHER. Avatars of Amadis: magical realism as postcolonial romance. JCL (40:3) 2005, 7–20.

Mary Seacole (1805–1881)

11949. MERCER, LORRAINE. I shall make no excuse: the narrative odyssey of Mary Seacole. JNT (35:1) 2005, 1–24.

Catharine Maria Sedgwick

11950. FINGER, ROLAND. The reassurance of sororicide. *See* **10558.**

11951. INSKO, JEFFREY. Anachronistic imaginings: *Hope Leslie's* challenge to historicism. AmLH (16:2) 2004, 179–207.

11952. LUCIANO, DANA. Voicing removal: mourning (as) history in *Hope Leslie*. WHR (58:2) 2004, 48–67.

11953. SWEET, NANCY F. Dissent and the daughter in *A New England Tale* and *Hobomok*. Legacy (22:2) 2005, 107–25.

11954. TEMPLIN, MARY. 'Dedicated to works of beneficence': charity as model for a domesticated economy in antebellum women's panic fiction. *In* (pp. 80–104) **9513.**

11955. TUTHILL, MAUREEN. Land and the narrative site in Sedgwick's *Hope Leslie*. ATQ (19:2) 2005, 95–113.

11956. VANDETTE, EMILY. 'It should be a family thing': family, nation, and Republicanism in Catharine Maria Sedgwick's *A New-England Tale* and *The Linwoods*. ATQ (19:1) 2004, 51–74.

Luis Senarens ('Noname') (1863–1939)

11957. BERREY, SARA. Frank Reade Jr's dirigibles and speaking trumpets: how dime novels dream technology. DNR (74:4) 2005, 115–49.

Anna Sewell

11958. GAVIN, ADRIENNE E. Dark horse: a life of Anna Sewell. Stroud: Sutton, 2004. pp. x, 276, (plates) 8. Rev. by Naomi Wood in CLAQ (29:4) 2004, 373–5.

Richard Lalor Sheil (1791–1851)

11959. SAGLIA, DIEGO. Mediterranean unrest: 1820s verse tragedies and revolutions in the South. Romanticism (11:1) 2005, 99–113.

Mary Shelley

11960. ANOLIK, RUTH BIENSTOCK. Reviving the golem, revisiting *Frankenstein*: cultural negotiations in Ozick's *The Puttermesser Papers* and Piercy's *He, She, and It*. In (pp. 139–59) **12895.**

11961. BOUR, ISABELLE. Sensibility as epistemology in *Caleb Williams, Waverley,* and *Frankenstein*. See **8668.**

11962. BRAYLEY, ANDREW. Mary Shelley and Italy. In (pp. 78–88) **3690.**

11963. BUGG, JOHN. 'Master of their language': education and exile in Mary Shelley's *Frankenstein*. HLQ (68:4) 2005, 655–66.

11964. CHAMBERS, ROSS. The queer and the creepy: Western fictions of artificial life. PCP (40:1) 2005, 19–35.

11965. CHEVALIER, NOEL. The Liberty Tree and the Whomping Willow: political justice, magical science, and Harry Potter. See **19202.**

11966. CRAGWALL, JASPER. The Shelleys' enthusiasm. See **12002.**

11967. DAVIDSON, BRETT. *The War of the Worlds* considered as a modern myth. See **20043.**

11968. EBERLE-SINATRA, MICHAEL. Readings of homosexuality in Mary Shelley's *Frankenstein* and four film adaptations. GothS (7:2) 2005, 185–202.

11969. FULLER, SARAH CANFIELD. Reading the cyborg in Mary Shelley's *Frankenstein*. JFA (14:2) 2003, 217–27.

11970. GIORELLO, GIULIO. Prometeo, Ulisse, Gilgameš: figure del mito. See **17280.**

11971. GLADDEN, SAMUEL LYNDON. Mary Shelley's editions of *The Collected Poems of Percy Bysshe Shelley*: the editor as subject. SR (44:2) 2005, 181–205.

11972. GRACE, DOMINICK. Frankenstein, motherhood, and Phyllis Gotlieb's *O Master Caliban! See* **16762.**

11973. HOEVELER, DIANE LONG. Screen-memories and fictionalized autobiography: Mary Shelley's *Mathilda* and *The Mourner*. NCC (27:4) 2005, 365–81.

11974. KILBOURN, RUSSELL J. A. American Frankenstein: modernity's monstrous progeny. See **13450.**

11975. KILGOUR, MAGGIE. 'One immortality': the shaping of the Shelleys in *The Last Man*. ERR (16:5) 2005, 563–88.

11976. KROEG, SUSAN M. From 'this shore, renowned for its hospitality' to 'the detested shore of Ireland' in *Frankenstein*. ELN (42:3) 2005, 21–8.

11977. LANGE, DIRK.   Warum will Frankensteins Monster sterben? Selbstmord im englischen Roman des 19. Jahrhunderts. Heidelberg: Winter, 2005. pp. 346. (Anglistische Forschungen, 352.)

11978. LEVY, MICHELLE.   Discovery and the domestic affections in Coleridge and Shelley. *See* **10497.**

11979. LOKKE, KARI E.   Tracing women's Romanticism: gender, history and transcendence. London; New York: Routledge, 2004. pp. vii, 199. (Routledge studies in Romanticism, 4.)

11980. LOVROD, MARIE.   Shifting contexts, shaping experiences: child abuse survivor narratives and educating for empire. Meridians (5:2) 2005, 30–56.

11981. NESVET, REBECCA.   'Have you thought of a story?': Galland's Scheherazade and Mary Shelley's 1831 *Frankenstein*. WWr (12:3) 2005, 369–80.

11982. O'LEARY, CRYSTAL L.   Transcending monstrous flesh: a revision of the hero's mythic quest. *See* **19063.**

11983. PETKOU, PANAGIOTA.   Getting dirty with the body: abjection in Mary Shelley's *Frankenstein*. Gramma (11) 2003, 31–8.

11984. RICHARD, JESSICA.   'A paradise of my own creation': *Frankenstein* and the improbable romance of Polar exploration. NCC (25:4) 2003, 295–314.

11985. RUEKBERG, BEN.   A possible Copernicus–Frankenstein connection. NQ (52:1) 2005, 39.

11986. RUSTON, SHARON.   Resurrecting *Frankenstein*. KSR (19) 2005, 97–116.

11987. SCHOR, ESTHER (ed.).   The Cambridge companion to Mary Shelley. (Bibl. 2004, 12026.) Rev. by Alison Lumsden in BJECS (28:1) 2005, 141–2.

11988. SITES, MELISSA.   Chivalry and utopian domesticity in Mary Shelley's *The Fortunes of Perkin Warbeck*. ERR (16:5) 2005, 525–43.

11989. SMITH, ALLAN LLOYD.   'This thing of darkness': racial discourse in Mary Shelley's *Frankenstein*. GothS (6:2) 2004, 208–22.

11990. VARENNE, CAROLINE.   La quête romantique de trois voyageurs: *History of a Six Weeks' Tour* de Mary Shelley. EREA (3:1) 2005, 21–6.

11991. VARGO, LISA.   The Aikins and the Godwins: notions of conflict and stoicism in Anna Barbauld and Mary Shelley. Romanticism (11:1) 2005, 84–98.

11992. VIDAL, RICARDA.   Man's creation of man: from the cruel nature of de Sade and Mary Shelley to F. T. Marinetti's mechanical son. Prism(s) (13) 2005, 27–46.

11993. WRIGHT, PETER.   Intertextuality, generic shift and ideological transformation in the internationalising of *Doctor Who*. *See* **14066.**

Percy Bysshe Shelley

11994. BACIGALUPO, MASSIMO.   Yeats, Boccaccio, and Leopardi. *See* **20481.**

11995. BAJETTA, CARLO M.   Redeeming the vagrant: Wordsworth's *Peter Bell* and its revisions. *In* (pp. 54–65) **3690.**

11996. BERRY, AMANDA.   Some of my best friends are Romanticists: Shelley and the queer project in Romanticism. RomNet (36/37) 2004/05.

11997. BIERI, JAMES.   Percy Bysshe Shelley: a biography: exile of unfulfilled reknown, 1816–1822. Newark: Delaware UP, 2005. pp. 441. Rev. by Sharon Ruston in TLS, 14 Oct. 2005, 26.

11998. —— Percy Bysshe Shelley: a biography: youth's unextinguished fire, 1792–1816. Newark: Delaware UP, 2004. pp. 457.

11999. COCHRAN, PETER. One ton per square foot: the antecedents of *The Vision of Judgement*. See **12048.**

12000. COLBERT, BENJAMIN. Petrio-pindarics: John Wolcot and the Romantics. See **9128.**

12001. —— Shelley's eye: travel writing and aesthetic vision. Aldershot; Burlington, VT: Ashgate, 2004. pp. xi, 259. (Nineteenth century.)

12002. CRAGWALL, JASPER. The Shelleys' enthusiasm. HLQ (68:4) 2005, 631–53.

12003. CROSSAN, GREG. 'That wolf-howled, witch-prayed, owl-sung fool': Beddoes and the play of words. See **10088.**

12004. D'HAEN, THEO. 'Nilotic mud': British Romantic writers and the colonies. *In* (pp. 51–63) **9237.**

12005. DUFFY, CIAN. Shelley and the revolutionary sublime. Cambridge; New York: CUP, 2005. pp. xiv, 260. (Cambridge studies in Romanticism, 63.)

12006. ELLIS, JONATHAN. 'A curious cat': Elizabeth Bishop and the Spanish Civil War. See **15490.**

12007. FROSCH, THOMAS R. 'More than ever can be spoken': unconscious fantasy in Shelley's Jane Williams poems. SP (102:3) 2005, 378–413.

12008. GIORELLO, GIULIO. Prometeo, Ulisse, Gilgameš: figure del mito. See **17280.**

12009. GLADDEN, SAMUEL LYNDON. Mary Shelley's editions of *The Collected Poems of Percy Bysshe Shelley*: the editor as subject. See **11971.**

12010. GOSLEE, NANCY. Shelley's cosmopolitan 'discourse': Ancient Greek manners and modern liberty. WordsC (36:1) 2005, 2–5.

12011. HAMILTON, PAUL. Hazlitt and the 'kings of speech'. *In* (pp. 68–80) **11245.**

12012. HITT, CHRISTOPHER. Shelley's unwriting of Mont Blanc. TSLL (47:2) 2005, 139–66.

12013. HOEVELER, DIANE LONG. Beatrice Cenci in Hawthorne, Melville and her Atlantic-rim contexts. See **11204.**

12014. —— Screen-memories and fictionalized autobiography: Mary Shelley's *Mathilda* and *The Mourner*. See **11973.**

12015. JOUKOVSKY, NICHOLAS A. Keats, Shelley, and *The Troubadour*. See **1241.**

12016. KILGOUR, MAGGIE. 'One immortality': the shaping of the Shelleys in *The Last Man*. See **11975.**

12017. KIPP, JULIE. Romanticism, maternity, and the body politic. See **8015.**

12018. KNOTTENBELT, E. M. Romantic residues? Virgil's *Aeneid* 'in such a tongue as the people understandeth' or in a 'language really spoken by men'. *In* (pp. 235–57) **9237.**

12019. KUCICH, GREG. Keats, Shelley, Byron, and the Hunt circle. *In* (pp. 263–79) **8014.**

12020. LAURITSEN, JOHN.   Hellenism and homoeroticism in Shelley and his circle. *See* **9321.**

12021. MILLER, CHRISTOPHER.   Shelley's uncertain Heaven. ELH (72:3) 2005, 577–603.

12022. MUSSAPI, ROBERTO (ed. and trans.).   I ragazzi che amavano il vento. Milan: Feltrinelli, 2005. pp. 117. (Universale economica.) (Classici, 2132.)

12023. NATARAJAN, UTTARA.   Circle of sympathy: Shelley's Hazlitt. *In* (pp. 112–22) **11245.**

12024. NICKSON, RICHARD.   Telling the truth and spreading slander. *See* **19403.**

12025. O'NEILL, MICHAEL.   The gleam of those words: Coleridge and Shelley. *See* **10509.**

12026. PAYLING, CATHERINE.   An echo and a light unto eternity: the founding of the Keats–Shelley Memorial House. *See* **11526.**

12027. PERRY, SEAMUS.   The little horror show. *See* **12510.**

12028. ROSSINGTON, MICHAEL.   Commemorating the relic: the beginnings of the Bodleian Shelley collections. BLR (18:3) 2004, 264–75.

12029. RUSTON, SHARON.   Shelley and vitality. Basingstoke; New York: Palgrave Macmillan, 2005. pp. xiii, 229. Rev. by Nora Crook in TLS, 2 Sept. 2005, 26–7; by Clark Lawlor in KSR (19) 2005, 175–8.

12030. SCHWENGER, PETER.   Gothic optics. GothS (7:1) 2005, 102–9.

12031. SCRIVENER, MICHAEL.   Trials in Romantic-era writing: modernity, guilt, and the scene of justice. *See* **8680.**

12032. SMITH, DAVID V.   *Der Dichter spricht*: Shelley, Rousseau and the perfect society. KSR (19) 2005, 117–31.

12033. TINKLER-VILLANI, VALERIA.   Victorian Shelley: perspectives on a Romantic poet. *In* (pp. 89–104) **9237.**

12034. WELLENS, OSKAR.   The first Dutch performance of *The Cenci* (1819). KSR (19) 2005, 142–9.

12035. WILSON, ERIC GLENN.   Shelley and the poetics of glaciers. WordsC (36:2) 2005, 53–6.

Mary Martha Sherwood

12036. COMER, DENISE K.   'White child is good, black child his [or her] slave': women, children, and empire in early nineteenth-century India. ERR (16:1) 2005, 39–58.

William Gilmore Simms ('Frank Cooper')

12037. ALLEN, THOMAS M.   South of the American renaissance. AmLH (16:3) 2004, 496–508 (review-article).

12038. BUSICK, SEAN R.   A sober desire for history: William Gilmore Simms as historian. Columbia; London: South Carolina UP, 2005. pp. xii, 143.

12039. GUILDS, JOHN CALDWELL; HUDSON, CHARLES (eds).   An early and strong sympathy: the Indian writings of William Gilmore Simms. (Bibl. 2004, 12076.) Rev. by Thomas M. Allen in AmLH (16:3) 2004, 496–508; by Miriam H. Schacht in SAIL (17:1) 2005, 107–10.

12040. KERKERING, JOHN D. American renaissance poetry and the *topos* of positionality: *genius mundi* and *genius loci* in Walt Whitman and William Gilmore Simms. *See* **12325**.

Alexander Smith (1830–1867)

12041. BOOS, FLORENCE S. 'Spasm' and class: W. E. Aytoun, George Gilfillan, Sydney Dobell, and Alexander Smith. *See* **10818**.

12042. HARRISON, ANTONY H. Victorian culture wars: Alexander Smith, Arthur Hugh Clough, and Matthew Arnold in 1853. *See* **9933**.

12043. HUGHES, LINDA K. Alexander Smith and the bisexual poetics of *A Life-Drama*. VP (42:4) 2004, 491–508.

Effie Waller Smith

12044. ENGELHARDT, ELIZABETH. Nature-loving souls and Appalachian Mountains: the promise of feminist ecocriticism. *In* (pp. 337–52) **12822**.

Joseph Smith (1805–1844)

12045. DOLAN, JOHN. The third great text-finder: Joseph E. Smith Jr as colleague of Chatterton and Macpherson. *See* **8466**.

Robert Southey

12046. BESHERO-BONDAR, ELISA E. British conquistadors and Aztec priests: the horror of Southey's *Madoc*. PQ (82:1) 2003, 87–113.

12047. CHANDLER, DAVID. The early development of the 'Lake School' idea. *See* **12466**.

12048. COCHRAN, PETER. One ton per square foot: the antecedents of *The Vision of Judgement*. KSR (19) 2005, 64–75.

12049. CONSTANTINE, MARY-ANN. Iolo Morganwg, Coleridge, and the Bristol lectures, 1795. *See* **10476**.

12050. MAY, TIM. The Pantisocrats in College Street. NQ (52:4) 2005, 456–60.

12051. MORRISON, ROBERT. Chatterton at the races: De Quincey, Cottle, Southey, and the *Battle of Hastynges*. *See* **8469**.

12052. PHILLIPS, MARK SALBER. Criticism: literary history and literary historicism. *In* (pp. 247–65) **6958**.

12053. PRATT, LYNDA (gen. ed.). Robert Southey: poetical works 1793–1810: vol. 1, *Joan of Arc*. Ed. by Lynda Pratt. London; Brookfield, VT: Pickering & Chatto, 2004. pp. lv, 526. (Pickering masters.) Rev. by A. R. Kidwai in BJ (32:2) 2004, 159–61; by Peter J. Kitson in RomNet (36/37) 2004/05.

12054. —— Robert Southey: poetical works 1793–1810: vol. 2, *Madoc*. Ed. by Lynda Pratt with the assistance of Carol Bolton and Paul Jarman. London; Brookfield, VT: Pickering & Chatto, 2004. pp. xxxii, 592. (Pickering masters.) Rev. by A. R. Kidwai in BJ (32:2) 2004, 159–61; by Peter J. Kitson in RomNet (36/37) 2004/05.

12055. —— Robert Southey: poetical works 1793–1810: vol. 3, *Thalaba the Destroyer*. Ed. by Tim Fulford with the assistance of Daniel E. White and Carol Bolton. London; Brookfield, VT: Pickering & Chatto, 2004. pp. xxxvi, 354. (Pickering masters.) Rev. by A. R. Kidwai in BJ (32:2) 2004, 159–61; by Peter J. Kitson in RomNet (36/37) 2004/05.

12056. —— Robert Southey: poetical works 1793–1810: vol. 4, *The Curse of Kehama*. Ed. by Daniel Sanjiv Roberts. London; Brookfield, VT: Pickering & Chatto, 2004. pp. xxix, 412. (Pickering masters.) Rev. by A. R. Kidwai in BJ (32:2) 2004, 159–61; by Peter J. Kitson in RomNet (36/37) 2004/05.

12057. —— Robert Southey: poetical works 1793–1810: vol. 5, Selected shorter poems *c*.1793–1810. Ed. by Lynda Pratt. London; Brookfield, VT: Pickering & Chatto, 2004. pp. xli, 531. (Pickering masters.) Rev. by A. R. Kidwai in BJ (32:2) 2004, 159–61; by Peter J. Kitson in RomNet (36/37) 2004/05.

12058. VANDER MOTTEN, J. P.   Robert Southey, Charles Watkin Williams Wynn and *The Miser's Mansion. In* (pp. 65–75) **9237.**

William T. Stead

12059. GRIMES, HILARY.   The haunted self: visions of the ghost and the woman at the *fin-de-siècle*. VN (107) 2005, 1–4.

12060. LUCKHURST, ROGER.   W. T. Stead's occult economies. *In* (pp. 125–35) **1226.**

Edmund Clarence Stedman (1833–1908)

12061. LOEFFELHOLZ, MARY.   Edmund Clarence Stedman's Black Atlantic. VP (43:2) 2005, 189–204.

Sir Leslie Stephen

12062. BOOTH, ALISON.   Fighting for lives in the *ODNB*; or, Taking prosopography personally. *See* **20966.**

Robert Louis Stevenson

12063. BOONE, TROY.   Youth of darkest England: working-class children at the heart of Victorian empire. *See* **9194.**

12064. BRAZZELLI, NICOLETTA.   Andrew Lang e Robert Louis Stevenson: cronaca di un'amicizia letteraria. LProv (118) 2003, 7–21.

12065. DRYDEN, LINDA.   The modern gothic and literary doubles: Stevenson, Wilde, and Wells. (Bibl. 2004, 12120.) Rev. by Martin Willis in GothS (6:1) 2004, 137–40.

12066. DURY, RICHARD (ed.).   Strange case of Dr Jekyll and Mr Hyde. Edinburgh: Edinburgh UP, 2004. pp. lxii, 199. (Collected works of Robert Louis Stevenson.) Rev. by Richard D. Jackson in SHogg (15) 2004, 173–5; by Harold Orel in ELT (48:3) 2005, 363–6.

12067. GRAY, WILLIAM.   A source for the trampling scene in *Jekyll and Hyde*. NQ (52:4) 2005, 493–4.

12068. GUIGENO, VINCENT.   Engineering the words: Robert Louis Stevenson and the Bell Rock lighthouse. YLG (80:1/2) 2005, 57–64. (*Records of a Family of Engineers.*)

12069. HARMAN, CLAIRE.   Myself and the other fellow: a life of Robert Louis Stevenson. New York: HarperCollins, 2005. pp. xix, 503, (plates) 16.

12070. JOLLY, ROSLYN.   Light work: R.L.S., the family business and the guilt of the writer. TLS, 28 Jan. 2005, 14–15.

12071. MCCULLOCH, FIONA.   'Playing double': performing childhood in *Treasure Island*. ScSR (4:2) 2003, 66–81.

12072. MACRAE, ALISDAIR. Exile in British poetry. *In* (pp. 113–23) **14479.**

12073. MENEGALDO, GILLES; NAUGRETTE, JEAN-PIERRE (eds). R. L. Stevenson & A. Conan Doyle – aventures de la fiction: actes du colloque de Cerisy. *See* **10861.**

12074. NASH, ANDREW. Walter Besant's *All Sorts and Conditions of Men* and Robert Louis Stevenson's *The Strange Case of Dr Jekyll and Mr Hyde. See* **10093.**

12075. O'HAGAN, ANDREW. In his hot head. LRB (27:4) 2005, 10–12 (review-article). (Biography of Stevenson.)

12076. PARFECT, RALPH. Robert Louis Stevenson's *The Clockmaker* and *The Scientific Ape*: two unpublished fables. ELT (48:4) 2005, 387–96.

12077. REID, JULIA. The *Academy* and *Cosmopolis*: evolution and culture in Robert Louis Stevenson's periodical encounters. *In* (pp. 263–73) **1226.**

12078. —— Robert Louis Stevenson and the 'romance of anthropology'. JVC (10:1) 2005, 46–71.

12079. SPILA, CRISTIANO. La strategia del finale in *The Strange Case of Dr Jekyll and Mr Hyde* di R. L. Stevenson. SCrit (19:3) 2004, 171–88.

12080. STEVENSON, SHERYL. The uncanny case of Dr Rivers and Mr Prior: dynamics of transference in *The Eye in the Door. In* (pp. 219–32) **15309.**

12081. STURGIS, MATTHEW. Hauf a laddie. TLS, 11 Mar. 2005, 8 (review-article).

12082. WEST, CHRIS. Perverting science fiction: thinking the alien within the genre. Foundation (94) 2005, 100–17.

12083. WICOMB, ZOË. Setting, intertextuality and the resurrection of the postcolonial author. JPW (41:2) 2005, 144–55.

Maria W. Stewart (1803–1879)

12084. CARLACIO, JAMI L. Speaking with and to me: discursive positioning and the unstable categories of race, class, and gender. *In* (pp. 121–32) **2457.**

Bram Stoker

12085. BARTEL, ELKE. From archfiend to *Angel*: Dracula's political dimensions. SPC (27:3) 2005, 15–25.

12086. BURKE, MARY. Eighteenth- and nineteenth-century sources for Bram Stoker's gypsies. ANQ (18:1) 2005, 54–9.

12087. DALBY, RICHARD; HUGHES, WILLIAM. Bram Stoker: a bibliography. Westcliff-on-Sea: Desert Island, 2004. pp. 184. (Desert Island *Dracula* library.) Rev. by Elizabeth Miller in JFA (15:4) 2004, 380–2.

12088. DERN, JOHN A. The revenant of Vienna: a critical comparison of Carol Reed's film *The Third Man* and Bram Stoker's novel *Dracula. See* **13819.**

12089. FERNÁNDEZ RETAMAR, ROBERTO. On Dracula, the West, America, and other inventions. BSch (35:3) 2005, 22–9.

12090. FRY, CAROL L.; EDWARDS, CARLA. The new naturalism: primal screams in Abraham Stoker's *Dracula*. MidQ (47:1) 2005, 40–54.

12091. GIBSON, MATTHEW. Bram Stoker and the Treaty of Berlin (1878). GothS (6:2) 2004, 236–51.

12092. GLADDEN, SAMUEL LYNDON.   *Dracula*'s earnestness: Stoker's debt to Wilde. ELN (42:4) 2005, 62–75.

12093. HARSE, KATIE.   'Sick of Count Dracula': Scott, Carter, Rice and the response to Stoker's authority. *See* **19348.**

12094. INGELBIEN, RAPHAËL.   Gothic genealogies: *Dracula*, *Bowen's Court*, and Anglo-Irish psychology. ELH (70:4) 2003, 1089–1105.

12095. LAWTON, HENRY.   Dracula rising: our continuing fascination with vampire fantasies. M/M (19:2) 2005, 14–21.

12096. McGUNNIGLE, CHRISTOPHER.   My own vampire: the metamorphosis of the queer monster in Francis Ford Coppola's *Bram Stoker's Dracula*. *See* **13489.**

12097. MILLER, ELIZABETH (ed.).   Bram Stoker's *Dracula*: a documentary volume. Detroit, MI: Gale Research, 2005. pp. xxxi, 480. (Dictionary of literary biography, 304.) Rev. by Carol A. Senf in GothS (7:2) 2005, 211–13.

12098. MURRAY, PAUL.   From the shadow of Dracula: a life of Bram Stoker. (Bibl. 2004, 12146.) Rev. by Paul Murray in JFA (15:4) 2004, 379–80.

12099. PRESCOTT, CHARLES E.; GIORGIO, GRACE A.   Vampiric affinities: Mina Harker and the paradox of femininity in Bram Stoker's *Dracula*. VLC (33:2) 2005, 487–515.

12100. SALER, BENSON; ZIEGLER, CHARLES A.   Dracula and Carmilla: monsters and the mind. PhilL (29:1) 2005, 218–27.

12101. SAUDO, NATHALIE.   *I was glad to see her paleness and her illness*: la redoutable bonne santé dans *Dracula*. EA (58:4) 2005, 402–15.

12102. SMITH, ANDREW.   Love, Freud, and the female gothic: Bram Stoker's *The Jewel of Seven Stars*. GothS (6:1) 2004, 80–9.

12103. THIELE, DAVID.   *Dracula* and Whitmania: 'the pass-word primeval'. ELT (48:2) 2005, 188–205.

12104. ZLOTNICK, SUSAN.   Domesticating imperialism: curry and cookbooks in Victorian England. *In* (pp. 72–87) **9257.**

John Augustus Stone

12105. BRANCA, R. RENE.   Melodrama, convention, and rape. *See* **9104.**

Harriet Beecher Stowe

12106. ELBERT, MONIKA.   Nature, magic, and history: forging a national identity in Stowe. WWr (12:1) 2005, 99–113.

12107. GALLAGHER, NOELLE.   The bagging factory and the breakfast factory: industrial labor and sentimentality in Harriet Beecher Stowe's *Uncle Tom's Cabin*. NCC (27:2) 2005, 167–87.

12108. HAWLEY, MICHELLE.   Harriet Beecher Stowe and Lord Byron: a case of celebrity justice in the Victorian public sphere. JVC (10:2) 2005, 229–56.

12109. LEE, MAURICE S.   The old and the new: double consciousness and the literature of slavery. *See* **10984.**

12110. MEER, SARAH.   Uncle Tom mania: slavery, minstrelsy, and transatlantic culture in the 1850s. Athens; London: Georgia UP, 2005. pp. viii, 332.

12111. MILLER, ELISE.   The 'maw of Western culture': James Baldwin and the anxieties of influence. *See* **15274.**

12112. O'HARAE, ALISON.   Theology, genre, and romance in Richard Baxter and Harriet Beecher Stowe. ReLit (37:1) 2005, 69–91.

12113. SHACKELFORD, LYNNE P.   Stowe's *Uncle Tom's Cabin.* Exp (63:3) 2005, 144–6.

12114. THOMAS-KROUSE, ONDRA.   Dancing to transgress. LHR (19:1) 2004, 27–39.

12115. TRUBEY, ELIZABETH FEKETE.   'Success is sympathy': *Uncle Tom's Cabin* and the woman reader. *In* (pp. 53–76) **12549.**

12116. WEINSTEIN, CINDY (ed.).   The Cambridge companion to Harriet Beecher Stowe. (Bibl. 2004, 12166.) Rev. by Oscar Hernandez in WS (34:1) 2005, 107.

12117. WHITE, BARBARA A.   The Beecher sisters. (Bibl. 2004, 12167.) Rev. by A. Cheree Carlson in JAH (92:1) 2005, 217.

G. S. (George Slythe) Street (1867–1936)

12118. HARRIS, WENDELL V.   George Slythe Street: avant-garde anachronism. ELT (48:3) 2005, 285–304.

Ruth Stuart

12119. REYNOLDS, CLAIRE E.   Ruth McEnery Stuart: 'featherbed resistance' and 'a dozen proofs of woman's superiority'. CEACrit (67:2) 2005, 43–61.

R. S. Surtees

12120. MUKHERJEE, PABLO.   Nimrods: hunting, authority, identity. *See* **11548.**

Algernon Charles Swinburne

12121. KEARNEY, ANTHONY.   Hardy and Jowett: fact and fiction in *Jude the Obscure. See* **11129.**

12122. LOUIS, MARGOT K.   Gods and mysteries: the revival of paganism and the remaking of mythography through the nineteenth century. *See* **12496.**

12123. McGANN, JEROME J.; SLIGH, CHARLES L. (eds).   Algernon Charles Swinburne: major poems and selected prose. New Haven, CT; London: Yale UP, 2004. pp. xxx, 498. Rev. by Rikky Rooksby in VP (43:2) 2005, 266–74.

12124. MEYERS, TERRY L.   A manuscript of Swinburne's *The Garden of Proserpine.* YLG (80:1/2) 2005, 45–55.

John Addington Symonds

12125. AMIGONI, DAVID.   Distinctively queer little morsels: imagining distinction, groups, and difference in the *DNB* and the *ODNB. See* **9798.**

Arthur Symons

12126. ADAMS, JAD.   Hideous absinthe: a history of the devil in a bottle. London; New York: Tauris, 2004. pp. x, 294, (plates) 16. Rev. by Karl Beckson in ELT (48:1) 2005, 124–6.

12127. DANIEL, ANNE MARGARET.   Arthur Symons and *The Savoy.* LitIm (7:2) 2005, 165–93.

12128. TOOMEY, DEIRDRE.   'Amaryllis in the shade': the Municipal Gallery revisited. *See* **20525.**

Jane Taylor (1783–1824)

12129. CURRAN, STUART. Jane Taylor's satire on satire. *In* (pp. 139–50) **9305.**

Tom Taylor (1817–1880)

12130. GOULD, MARTY. Anticipation, transformation, accommodation: the Great Exhibition on the London stage. VicR (29:2) 2003, 19–39.

12131. WAGNER-LAWLOR, JENNIFER A. 'Who acts John Bull?': speculating on English national character and modern morality. VicR (29:2) 2003, 64–96.

Alfred, Lord Tennyson

12132. APLIN, JOHN. Three Tennyson letters to Anne Thackeray. TRB (8:4) 2005, 287–90.

12133. ARMSTRONG, JOHN. Beautiful thing. Meanjin (62:2) 2003, 5–9.

12134. BRATCHER, JAMES T. Tennyson's 'hendecasyllabics', Catullus' '*basationes*', and a parody of Ezra Pound. NQ (52:1) 2005, 100–1.

12135. CAWS, MARY ANN; JOSEPH, GERHARD. Naming and not naming: Tennyson and Mallarmé. VP (43:1) 2005, 1–18.

12136. CERVO, NATHAN. Three Victorian 'medieval' poems: *Dover Beach*, *The Windhover*, and *The Higher Pantheism*. VN (107) 2005, 28–30.

12137. CERVO, NATHAN A. Tennyson's *The Higher Pantheism*. Exp (63:2) 2005, 76–8.

12138. CHANEY, CAREY. St Peter, Blue Mesa, 'ruins', and archaic forms in Willa Cather's *The Professor's House*. See **15726.**

12139. COX, CHARLES. A *Tale of Tucuman*: a Tennyson reference of 1831. TRB (8:4) 2005, 291–9.

12140. DAY, AIDAN. Tennyson's scepticism. Basingstoke; New York: Palgrave Macmillan, 2005. pp. ix, 225.

12141. EBBATSON, ROGER. Shadows of three dead men: *In the Garden at Swainston*. TRB (8:4) 2005, 270–86.

12142. FISHER, DEVON. In graceful service to the queen (bee): the politics of the hive in Tennyson's *The Princess*. VIJ (32) 2004, 107–28.

12143. GAULL, MARILYN. Romans and Romanticism. See **12482.**

12144. GERVIN, MARY A. The monodrama *Maud*: Tennyson's little *Hamlet*. CLAJ (48:3) 2005, 274–89.

12145. HARDY, ANNE. Tennyson, Millais, and the depiction of mood in *Mariana* and *St Agnes Eve*. TRB (8:4) 2005, 211–25.

12146. HORNE, PHILIP. Henry James among the poets. See **11410.**

12147. HUGHES, JOHN. Tennyson revisited: Hardy's *After a Journey*. See **11126.**

12148. KOOISTRA, LORRAINE JANZEN. The illustrated *Enoch Arden* and Victorian visual culture. JPRS (14:2) 2005, 43–66.

12149. LEDBETTER, KATHRYN. Protesting success: Tennyson's 'indecent exposure' in the periodicals. VP (43:1) 2005, 53–73.

12150. LEIMBERG, INGE. 'Across the pale parabola of joy': Wodehouse parodist. See **20274.**

12151. LOVELACE, J. TIMOTHY. The secret of the gods in Tennyson's *Tiresias*. VIJ (32) 2004, 97–105.

12152. MARCHESI, MARIA SERENA. '*There shall no sign be given*': il soprannaturale cristiano in *The Holy Grail* di Tennyson. AngP (2:1/2) 2005, 31–58.

12153. MARKLEY, A. A. Stateliest measures: Tennyson and the literature of Greece and Rome. Toronto; Buffalo, NY; London: Toronto UP, 2004. pp. x, 238. Rev. by Jason R. Rudy in VS (47:3) 2005, 459–61; by Norman Vance in TRB (8:4) 2005, 307–9; by Cornelia D. J. Pearsall in NineL (60:2) 2005, 250–3.

12154. MAZZENO, LAURENCE W. Alfred Tennyson: the critical legacy. (Bibl. 2004, 12199.) Rev. by John Morton in TLS, 25 Mar. 2005, 30; by Marion Shaw in TRB (8:4) 2005, 301–4; by Kathryn Ledbetter in VS (48:1) 2005, 192–3.

12155. NÜNNING, VERA. Fictions of collective memory. See **3511**.

12156. O'GORMAN, FRANCIS. Tennyson's *The Lotus-Eaters* and the politics of the 1830s. VicR (30:1) 2004, 1–20.

12157. PERRY, SEAMUS. Alfred Tennyson. Plymouth: Northcote House in assn with the British Council, 2004. pp. xviii, 190. (Writers and their work.) Rev. by Joe Phelan in TLS, 18 Nov. 2005, 30.

12158. PITE, RALPH (gen. ed.). Lives of Victorian literary figures I: Eliot, Dickens, and Tennyson by their contemporaries: vol. 3, Alfred, Lord Tennyson. Ed. by Matthew Bevis. (Bibl. 2004, 12204.) Rev. by Seamus Perry in TRB (8:2) 2003, 146–8; by Dinah Birch in TLS, 19 Sept. 2003, 6–7.

12159. SHERWOOD, MARION. 'Mr Tennyson's singular genius': the reception of *Poems* (1832). TRB (8:4) 2005, 251–69.

12160. SMALL, HELEN. Tennyson and late style. TRB (8:4) 2005, 226–50.

12161. WILLIAMSON, ANNE. 'Save his own soul he hath no star': thoughts arising from *The Dream of Fair Women*. See **20234**.

12162. YOUNG-ZOOK, MONICA M. Sons and lovers: Tennyson's fraternal paternity. VLC (33:2) 2005, 451–66.

William Makepeace Thackeray

12163. BEAUMONT, JOHN. Thackeray in 'Pattledom'. NQ (52:4) 2005, 474–6.

12164. EDGECOMBE, R. S. Alfred de Musset, Thackeray, and Louis Gallet. ELN (42:3) 2005, 28–33.

12165. FISHER, JUDITH L. Thackeray's skeptical narrative and the 'perilous trade' of authorship. (Bibl. 2004, 12222.) Rev. by Nicholas Dames in VS (47:2) 2005, 283–4; by Margaret Godbey O'Brien in VPR (38:3) 2005, 339–41; by Sara Thornton in EA (58:2) 2005, 225–6.

12166. FLYNN, MICHAEL J. The transatlantic grudges of William Makepeace Thackeray and G. P. R. James. NQ (52:4) 2005, 476–8.

12167. HARDEN, EDGAR F. (ed.). *The Snobs of England* and *Punch's Prize Novelists*. Ann Arbor: Michigan UP, 2005. pp. viii, 255.

12168. NICOLAY, CLAIRE. The anxiety of 'Mosaic' influence: Thackeray, Disraeli, and Anglo-Jewish assimilation in the 1840s. NCC (25:2) 2003, 119–45.

12169. PALMERI, FRANK. Cruikshank, Thackeray, and the Victorian eclipse of satire. SELit (44:4) 2004, 753–77.

12170. PAYNE, DAVID. The reenchantment of nineteenth-century fiction: Dickens, Thackeray, George Eliot, and serialization. *See* **10730.**

12171. SIMPSON, M. CARLETON. Participation and immersion in Walton and Calvino. *See* **9039.**

12172. SUTHERLAND, JOHN. Some nabob: the sometimes useful errors of Edward Said. *See* **15032.**

12173. THOMAS, DEBORAH A. Thackeray, capital punishment, and the demise of Jos Sedley. VLC (33:1) 2005, 1–20.

12174. ZLOTNICK, SUSAN. Domesticating imperialism: curry and cookbooks in Victorian England. *In* (pp. 72–87) **9257.**

Ernest Lawrence Thayer

12175. BARAGONA, ALAN. By the numbers: a tale without words. Aethlon (23:1) 2005, 117–27.

'Rowland Thirlmere' (John Walker) (1861–1932)

12176. HITCHCOCK, RICHARD. John Walker, Geroge Borrow and gypsies in Spain. *See* **10111.**

Benjamin Thompson (1776?–1816)

12177. O'SHAUGHNESSY, DAVID. Kotzebue and Thompson's *The Stranger*: a new source for Godwin's *St Leon*. *See* **8676.**

James Thomson ('B.V.') (1834–1882)

12178. JANOWITZ, ANNE. The artifactual sublime: making London poetry. *In* (pp. 246–60) **9217.**

Henry David Thoreau

12179. BARBOUR, JOHN D. The value of solitude: the ethics and spirituality of aloneness in autobiography. Charlottesville; London: Virginia UP, 2004. pp. 237. (Studies in religion and culture.) Rev. by Nicholas Paige in Biography (28:4) 2005, 681–3.

12180. BELKNAP, ROBERT E. The list: the uses and pleasures of cataloguing. *See* **10965.**

12181. BIRKLE, CARMEN. Travelogues of independence: Margaret Fuller and Henry David Thoreau. *See* **11028.**

12182. BRAIN, J. WALTER. Three Thoreau haunts at Walden Woods. ConS (ns 12/13) 2004/05, 139–62.

12183. CASADO DA ROCHA, ANTONIO. 'Live thus deliberately': authenticity and narrative ethics in *Walden*. ConS (ns 12/13) 2004/05, 305–21.

12184. CLEMENTE, VINCE. Like Whitman, 'fed and bred under the Italian dispensation'. *See* **15806.**

12185. CONRAD, RANDALL. 'I heard a very loud sound': Thoreau processes the spectacle of sudden, violent death. ATQ (19:2) 2005, 81–94.

12186. —— Realizing resistance: Thoreau and the first of August, 1846, at Walden. ConS (ns 12/13) 2004/05, 165–93.

12187. DEAN, BRADLEY P. Another 'new' Thoreau letter. TSB (252) 2005, 8.

12188. —— Rediscovery at Walden: the history of Thoreau's bean-field. ConS (ns 12/13) 2004/05, 87–127.

12189. —— Science, poetry, and 'order among the clouds': Thoreau and Luke Howard. TSB (253) 2005, 1–5.

12190. DOLIS, JOHN. Tracking Thoreau: double-crossing nature and technology. Madison, NJ: Fairleigh Dickinson UP, 2005. pp. 231.

12191. GROSS, ROBERT A. Faith in the boardinghouse: new views of Thoreau family religion. TSB (250) 2005, 1–5.

12192. HARAD, ALYSSA (notes). *Walden; or, Life in the Woods* and *On the Duty of Civil Disobedience*. London; New York: Pocket Books, 2004. pp. xx, 455.

12193. HARTMAN, STEVEN. 'Invading *Walden*': part 1, An exchange between Walter Harding and Wallace Stegner. TSB (251) 2005, 1–7.

12194. —— 'Invading *Walden*': part 2, The Thoreauvian dilemmas of Wallace Stegner's *On a Darkling Plain*. *See* **19575.**

12195. —— 'The life excited': faces of Thoreau in *Walden*. ConS (ns 12/13) 2004/05, 341–60.

12196. HILTNER, KEN. Ripeness: Thoreau's critique of technological modernity. ConS (ns 12/13) 2004/05, 323–38.

12197. HODDER, ALAN. In the nick of time: Thoreau's 'present' experiment as a colloquy of East and West. RelArts (9:3/4) 2005, 235–57.

12198. HUDSPETH, ROBERT N. Additions to the Thoreau bibliography. TSB (250) 2005, 14–16.

12199. —— Additions to the Thoreau bibliography. TSB (251) 2005, 14–15.

12200. —— Additions to the Thoreau bibliography. TSB (252) 2005, 15–16.

12201. —— Additions to the Thoreau bibliography. TSB (253) 2005, 14–16.

12202. MALACHUK, DANIEL S. Transcendentalism, perfectionism, and *Walden*. ConS (ns 12/13) 2004/05, 283–303.

12203. MATZKE, JASON P. The John Brown way: Frederick Douglass and Henry David Thoreau on the use of violence. *See* **10830.**

12204. MAYNARD, W. BARKSDALE. Emerson's 'Wyman lot': forgotten context for Thoreau's house at Walden. ConS (ns 12/13) 2004/05, 61–84.

12205. MICELI, THOMAS J. The profitability of Thoreau's Walden experiment. TSB (251) 2005, 7–9.

12206. NEWMAN, LANCE. Our common dwelling: Henry Thoreau, Transcendentalism, and the class politics of nature. Basingstoke; New York: Palgrave Macmillan, 2005. pp. xv, 255. Rev. by Laura Dassow Walls in TSB (251) 2005, 10–11.

12207. OTTERBERG, HENRIK. Hound, bay horse, and turtle-dove: obscurity and authority in Thoreau's *Walden*. ConS (ns 12/13) 2004/05, 221–80.

12208. PALMER, SCOTT. Why go straight? Stepping out with Henry David Thoreau's *Walking* and Edward Thomas' *The Icknield Way*. ISLE (12:1) 2005, 115–29.

12209. QUINN, PAUL. Strummed by winds. TLS, 7 Jan. 2005, 13.

12210. ROBINSON, DAVID M.   Natural life: Thoreau's worldly Transcendentalism. (Bibl. 2004, 12266.) Rev. by Kent C. Ryden in ASch (74:1) 2005, 132–4; by Stephen Germic in JAH (92:3) 2005, 988.

12211. ROOT, ROBERT.   The everlastingly great look of the sky: Thoreau and E. B. White at Walden Pond. ConS (ns 12/13) 2004/05, 371–87.

12212. SPECQ, FRANÇOIS.   Thoreau's flowering of facts and the truth of experience. SPELL (16) 2003, 51–66.

12213. SPERBER, MICHAEL.   Henry David Thoreau: cycles and psyche. Higganum, CT: Higganum Hill, 2004. pp. xii, 160.

12214. TALLEY, SHARON.   Following Thoreau's 'tracks in the sand': tactile impressions in *Cape Cod*. AI (62:1) 2005, 7–34.

12215. WALLS, LAURA DASSOW.   *Walden* as feminist manifesto. ConS (ns 12/13) 2004/05, 363–9.

Mary Tighe

12216. LINKIN, HARRIET KRAMER (ed.).   The collected poems and journals of Mary Tighe. Lexington: Kentucky UP, 2005. pp. xxxvi, 345. Rev. by Maureen E. Mulvihill in ILS (25:1) 2005, 19–20; by Nora Crook in TLS, 2 Dec. 2005, 28.

Henry Timrod

12217. CISCO, WALTER BRIAN.   Henry Timrod: a biography. (Bibl. 2004, 12279.) Rev. by Clyde Wilson in Chronicles (29:5) 2005, 40.

'Graham R. Tomson' (Rosamund Marriott Watson)

12218. HUGHES, LINDA K.   A woman on the Wilde side: masks, perversity, and print culture's role in poems by 'Graham R. Tomson'/Rosamund Marriott Watson. *In* (pp. 101–30) **9675**.

Catharine Parr Traill

12219. DELGADO, ANA BEATRIZ.   Paradigms of Canadian literary biography: who will write our history? *See* **14585**.

12220. FLOYD, JANET.   'I am a *gleaner*': Catharine Parr Traill and *Forest Gleanings*. BJCS (17:1) 2004, 93–104.

Richard Trench

12221. MIEDER, WOLFGANG (ed.).   Proverbs and their lessons. *See* **3451**.

Sarah Trimmer

12222. GRENBY, M. O.   'A conservative woman doing radical things': Sarah Trimmer and *The Guardian of Education*. *In* (pp. 137–61) **8171**.

Anthony Trollope

12223. BLYTHE, HELEN LUCY.   *The Fixed Period* (1882): euthanasia, cannibalism, and colonial extinction in Trollope's Antipodes. NCC (25:2) 2003, 161–80.

12224. LEDBETTER, KATHRYN.   Protesting success: Tennyson's 'indecent exposure' in the periodicals. *See* **12149**.

12225. McCOURT, JOHN.   An 'I' for an 'E', an Ireland for England: Trollope's Hiberno-English in *An Eye for an Eye*. EtIr (29:1) 2004, 7–23.

12226. ROBINSON, ALAN.   Social spaces in some early tales by Henry James. *See* **11449**.

12227. ROWE, JOHN CARLOS. Mark Twain's critique of globalization (old and new) in *Following the Equator: a Journey around the World* (1897). See **12269**.

Frances Trollope

12228. COTUGNO, CLARE. 'Stay away from Paris!': Frances Trollope rewrites America. VPR (38:2) 2005, 240–57.

12229. VITA, PAUL. Returning the look: Victorian writers and the Paris morgue. See **10759**.

Sojourner Truth

12230. BRUMMETT, BARRY. Rhetorical homologies: form, culture, experience. See **2234**.

12231. SANTAMARINA, XIOMARA. Belabored professions: narratives of African American working womanhood. Chapel Hill; London: North Carolina UP, 2005. pp. xiv, 222.

Joseph M. W. Turner

12232. WAINWRIGHT, STEVEN P.; WILLIAMS, CLARE. Biography and vulnerability: loss, dying and death in the Romantic paintings of J. M. W. Turner (1775–1851). Auto/Biography (13:1) 2005, 16–32.

'Mark Twain' (Samuel L. Clemens)

12233. AVALOS, JULIO C., JR. 'An agony of pleasurable suffering': masochism and maternal deprivation in Mark Twain. AI (62:1) 2005, 35–58.

12234. BRAHM, GABRIEL NOAH; ROBINSON, FORREST G. The jester and the sage: Twain and Nietzsche. NineL (60:2) 2005, 137–62.

12235. CAMFIELD, GREGG. In the mirror of the imagination: Mark Twain's Kipling. AQ (61:1) 2005, 85–107.

12236. CANTOR, PAUL A. Yankee go home: Twain's postcolonial romance. *In* (pp. 31–60) **14121**.

12237. COULOMBE, JOSEPH L. Mark Twain and the American West. (Bibl. 2003, 11610.) Rev. by Jason G. Horn in WAL (39:2) 2004, 237–40; by Stephen Railton in ISLE (12:1) 2005, 266–7.

12238. DENEEN, PATRICK J.; ROMANCE, JOSEPH (eds). Democracy's literature: politics and fiction in America. See **14121**.

12239. FISHKIN, SHELLEY FISHER. Mark Twain and the Jews. AQ (61:1) 2005, 137–66.

12240. FULTON, JOE B. The lost manuscript conclusion to Mark Twain's *Corn-Pone Opinions*: an editorial history and an edition of the restored text. ALR (37:3) 2005, 238–58.

12241. GILLMAN, SUSAN. In Twain's times. AQ (61:1) 2005, 7–39.

12242. GUSSOW, ADAM. Beaten boys and frantic pets: a close reading of *Tom Sawyer* reveals why Mark Twain isn't nearly as funny as he thinks he is. ASch (74:4) 2005, 94–9.

12243. HURM, GERD. Rewriting the vernacular Mark Twain: the aesthetics and politics of orality in Samuel Clemens's fictions. Trier: WVT, 2003. pp. xi, 282. (Mosaic, 18.) Rev. by Henry B. Wonham in ALR (38:1) 2005, 90–4.

12244. HURT, MATTHEW. Twain's *Adventures of Huckleberry Finn*. Exp (64:1) 2005, 41–4.

12245. IRMSCHER, CHRISTOPH. 'Pearly light': Genoa in the nineteenth-century American imagination. *In* (pp. 285–301) **9393.**

12246. ISHIHARA, TSUYOSHI. Mark Twain in Japan: the cultural reception of an American icon. Columbia; London: Missouri UP, 2005. pp. xix, 178.

12247. JACKSON, ROBERT. Seeking the region in American literature and culture: modernity, dissidence, innovation. Baton Rouge: Louisiana State UP, 2005. pp. x, 174. (Southern literary studies.)

12248. JUSTUS, JAMES H. Fetching the Old Southwest: humorous writing from Longstreet to Twain. Columbia; London: Missouri UP, 2004. pp. xiii, 591. Rev. by Johanna Nicol Shields in JAH (92:3) 2005, 982; by Jerry Elijah Brown in SoCR (38:1) 2005, 244–6; by Ed Piacentino in SAH (third series) (12) 2005, 121–30.

12249. KANE, CAROLYN. Birthplace of controversy: the history of a house. Twainian (60:4) 2004, 1–4.

12250. —— Birthplace of controversy: the history of a house: part 2. Twainian (61:1) 2005, 1–4.

12251. KAPLAN, FRED. The singular Mark Twain: a biography. (Bibl. 2004, 12323.) Rev. by Joseph Csicsila in SAH (third series) (11) 2004, 94–7; by Charles L. Crow in WAL (39:2) 2004, 240–1.

12252. KINSER, BRENT. Mark Twain, Thomas Carlyle, and shooting Niagara. *In* (pp. 113–24) **10393.**

12253. KOY, CHRISTOPHER E. The misunderstood conclusion of Mark Twain's *Pudd'nhead Wilson*. *In* (pp. 93–100) **3753.**

12254. KRAUTH, LELAND. Mark Twain & Company: six literary relations. (Bibl. 2004, 12325.) Rev. by John Bird in SAH (third series) (11) 2004, 93–4; by Jason G. Horn in WAL (39:2) 2004, 237–40; by Peter Stoneley in StudN (37:3) 2005, 357–8.

12255. LEONARD, JAMES S. (ed.). About Mark Twain. MTJ (42:1) 2004, 1–48. (Bibliography.) (*Adds to* bibl. 1977, 8163.)

12256. LYSTRA, KAREN. Dangerous intimacy: the untold story of Mark Twain's final years. Berkeley; London: California UP, 2004. pp. xxi, 342. Rev. by Michael Gorra in TLS, 30 Apr. 2004, 3–4; by Victor Strandberg in AL (77:1) 2005, 186–7; by Gregg Camfield in NineL (59:4) 2005, 540–3; by Forrest G. Robinson in JAH (92:1) 2005, 236–7; by Richard Lowry in AmS (46:2) 2005, 184–5.

12257. MESSENT, PETER. Mark Twain, manhood, the Henry H. Rogers friendship, and *Which Was the Dream?* AQ (61:1) 2005, 57–84.

12258. MINTZ, STEVEN. Huck's raft: a history of American childhood. (Bibl. 2004, 12339.) Rev. by Joyce Carol Oates in TLS, 11 Mar. 2005, 9; by Judith Sealander in JAH (92:3) 2005, 945–6.

12259. MORGAN, ELIZABETH. Paddling against ethics: Huck Finn as moral quagmire. *In* (pp. 171–80) **3748.**

12260. NISSEN, AXEL. A tramp at home: *Huckleberry Finn*, romantic friendship, and the homeless man. NineL (60:1) 2005, 57–86.

12261. OBENZINGER, HILTON. Better dreams: political satire and Twain's final 'exploding' novel. AQ (61:1) 2005, 167–84.

12262. OBER, K. PATRICK. The body in the cave: Dr Joseph McDowell's influence on Mark Twain. MTJ (41:2) 2003, 4–15.

12263. —— Mark Twain and medicine: 'any mummery will cure'. (Bibl. 2004, 12340.) Rev. by Justin Kaplan in BHM (78:4) 2004, 902–3.

12264. ORTH, RALPH H. George Gregory Smith and Mark Twain: Florence, 1903–1904. MTJ (41:2) 2003, 27–36.

12265. O'SHEA, MARY B. Crazy from the heat: Southern boys and coming of age. In (pp. 83–97) **13342**.

12266. POWERS, RON. Mark Twain: a life. New York: Free Press, 2005. pp. xi, 722. Rev. by Michael Patrick Hearn in BkW, 9 Oct. 2005, 4–5.

12267. QUIRK, TOM (ed.). The portable Mark Twain. London; New York: Penguin, 2004. pp. liv, 583.

12268. ROBINSON, FORREST G. The general and the Maid: Mark Twain on Ulysses S. Grant and Joan of Arc. AQ (61:1) 2005, 41–56.

12269. ROWE, JOHN CARLOS. Mark Twain's critique of globalization (old and new) in *Following the Equator: a Journey around the World* (1897). AQ (61:1) 2005, 109–35.

12270. SALAMO, LIN; FISCHER, VICTOR; FRANK, MICHAEL B. (eds). Mark Twain's helpful hints for good living: a handbook for the damned human race. Berkeley; London: California UP, 2004. pp. xiv, 207. (Jumping frogs, 2.)

12271. SCOTT, KEVIN MICHAEL. 'There's more honor': reinterpreting Tom and the evasion in *Huckleberry Finn*. StudN (37:2) 2005, 187–207.

12272. SLOAN, KAREN. Twain's *Adventures of Huckleberry Finn*. Exp (63:3) 2005, 159–64.

12273. SMITH, DAVID LIONEL. Mark Twain, pretexts, iconoclasm. AQ (61:1) 2005, 185–95.

12274. TROMBLEY, LAURA SKANDERA. 'She wanted to kill': Jean Clemens and postictal psychosis. ALR (37:3) 2005, 225–37.

12275. WIEGAND, WAYNE. Collecting contested titles: the experience of five small public libraries in the rural Midwest, 1893–1956. See **480**.

12276. ZIFF, LARZER. Mark Twain. Oxford; New York: OUP, 2004. pp. 126. Rev. by Jan Wordby Gertlund in JSH (71:4) 2005, 916–17.

12277. ZUCKERT, CATHERINE H. Tom Sawyer, potential president. In (pp. 61–78) **14121**.

Jones Very

12278. GOODSPEED-CHADWICK, JULIE ELAINE. The 19 September 1838 letter from George Bailey Loring (1817–1891) to James Russell Lowell (1819–1891). See **11619**.

Mary Theresa Vidal

12279. ELLIOTT, DORICE WILLIAMS. Convict servants and middle-class mistresses. Lit (16:2) 2005, 163–87.

Priscilla Wakefield

12280. KROEG, SUSAN M. Class mobility: Priscilla Wakefield's *A Family Tour through the British Empire* (1804). KenPR (19) 2004, 24–9.

Mrs Humphry Ward (Mary Augusta Arnold)

12281. BOUGHTON, GILLIAN E. Dr Arnold's granddaughter: Mary Augusta Ward. *In* (pp. 237–53) **9164**.

12282. WILT, JUDITH. Behind her times: transition England in the novels of Mary Arnold Ward. Charlottesville; London: Virginia UP, 2005. pp. 242. (Victorian literature and culture.) Rev. by John Sutherland in TLS, 16 Dec. 2005, 30.

Charles Dudley Warner

12283. FAGG, JOHN. Arcane subjects / urbane tones: Stephen Crane's Sullivan County sketches. *See* **10578**.

Susan Warner

12284. BALL, DAVID M. Toward an archaeology of American Modernism: reconsidering prestige and popularity in the American renaissance. ESQ (49:1–3) 2003, 161–77.

12285. GATES, SONDRA SMITH. The edge of possibility: Susan Warner and the world of Sunday school fiction. AQ (60:4) 2004, 1–31.

12286. ROWE, JOHN CARLOS. Religious transnationalism in the American renaissance: Susan Warner's *Wide, Wide World*. ESQ (49:1–3) 2003, 45–57.

12287. SEELYE, JOHN D. Jane Eyre's American daughters: from *The Wide, Wide World* to *Anne of Green Gables*: a study of marginalized maidens and what they mean. *See* **10182**.

William Hale White ('Mark Rutherford')

12288. CHIALANT, MARIA TERESA. Tra confessione e autobiografia: tre casi vittoriani. *In* (pp. 165–87) **12577**.

Walt Whitman

12289. ACKERMAN, DIANE. Panes of glass. VQR (81:2) 2005, 16–18.

12290. ALEXANDER, MEENA. In Whitman's country. VQR (81:2) 2005, 186–92.

12291. ALLEN, MICHAEL. *Pax Hibernica / pax Americana*: rhyme and reconciliation in Muldoon. *In* (pp. 62–95) **18404**.

12292. ASPIZ, HAROLD. So long! Walt Whitman's poetry of death. (Bibl. 2004, 12373.) Rev. by Nick Selby in MLR (100:2) 2005, 493–4.

12293. BACIGALUPO, MASSIMO. 'Mannahatta': città insulare in Whitman e Melville. *In* (pp. 331–51) **9393**.

12294. BAKER, DAVID. Elegy and eros: configuring grief. VQR (81:2) 2005, 207–20.

12295. BELKNAP, ROBERT E. The list: the uses and pleasures of cataloguing. *See* **10965**.

12296. BERGMAN, HERBERT; NOVERR, DOUGLAS A.; RECCHIA, EDWARD J. (eds). The journalism: vol. 2, 1846–1848. (Bibl. 2004, 12377.) Rev. by Jason Stacy in AL (77:1) 2005, 183–4.

12297. BLAKE, DAVID HAVEN. Reading Whitman, growing up rock 'n' roll. VQR (81:2) 2005, 34–47.

12298. BLAKEMORE, STEVEN; NOBLE, JON. Whitman and 'the Indian problem': the texts and contexts of *Song of the Redwoood-Tree*. WWQR (22:2/3) 2004/05, 108–25.

12299. CALHOUN, JOSHUA. Democracy in American poetry: Longfellow, Whitman, and the 'tyranny of the majority'. See **11611**.

12300. CAMBONI, MARINA. Walt Whitman e la lingua del Mondo Nuovo: con tre testi di Walt Whitman. Rome: Edizioni di Storia e Letteratura, 2005. pp. xiv, 118. (Biblioteca di studi americani, 29.)

12301. CAVITCH, MAX. Audience terminable and interminable: Anne Gilchrist, Walt Whitman, and the achievement of disinhibited reading. See **11063**.

12302. CLEMENTE, VINCE. Like Whitman, 'fed and bred under the Italian dispensation'. See **15806**.

12303. COLLIER, MICHAEL. On Whitman's *To a Locomotive in Winter*. VQR (81:2) 2005, 202–5.

12304. COVIELLO, PETER (ed.). Memoranda during the war. Oxford; New York: OUP, 2004. pp. liv, 176, (plates) 10. Rev. by Ted Genoways in WWQR (23:1/2) 2005, 61–3.

12305. COX, MICHAEL W. Whitman's *The Sleepers*. Exp (63:2) 2005, 78–82.

12306. CREELEY, ROBERT. Reflections on Whitman in age. VQR (81:2) 2005, 261–74.

12307. CUSHMAN, STEPHEN. Whitman and patriotism. VQR (81:2) 2005, 163–77.

12308. DOTY, MARK. Form, eros, and the unspeakable: Whitman's stanzas. VQR (81:2) 2005, 66–78.

12309. DOUNIA, CHRISTINA. Walt Whitman: enas ishiros progonos tou Andrea Empirikou. (Walt Whitman: an important predecessor of Andreas Empirikos.) Syncrise (15) 2004, 80–96.

12310. EPSTEIN, DANIEL MARK. Lincoln and Whitman: parallel lives in Civil War Washington. (Bibl. 2004, 12383.) Rev. by Jay Grossman in JAH (92:1) 2005, 223; by Kenneth M. Price in WWQR (23:1/2) 2005, 64–5.

12311. FELDMAN, MARK B. Remembering a convulsive war: Whitman's *Memoranda during the War* and the therapeutics of display. WWQR (23:1/2) 2005, 1–25.

12312. FOLSOM, ED. 'This heart's geography's map': the photographs of Walt Whitman. VQR (81:2) 2005, 6–7.

12313. —— An unrecorded Whitman interview. WWQR (22:2/3) 2004/05, 129–31.

12314. —— 'What a filthy Presidentiad!': Clinton's Whitman, Bush's Whitman, and Whitman's America. VQR (81:2) 2005, 96–113.

12315. —— PRICE, KENNETH M. Re-scripting Walt Whitman: an introduction to his life and work. Oxford; Malden, MA: Blackwell, 2005. pp. xv, 156. (Blackwell introductions to literature.)

12316. FORD, MAX. Trust yourself: Emerson and Dylan. *In* (pp. 127–42) **16207**.

12317. GANNON, THOMAS C. Reading Boddo's body: crossing the borders of race and sexuality in Whitman's *Half-Breed*. WWQR (22:2/3) 2004/05, 87–107.

12318. GENOWAYS, TED. Inventing Walt Whitman. VQR (81:2) 2005, 1–3.

12319. GERHARDT, CHRISTINE. Managing the wilderness: Walt Whitman's Southern landscapes. FMLS (40:2) 2004, 225–35.

12320. GEWIRTZ, ISAAC. I am with you: Walt Whitman's *Leaves of Grass* (1855–2005). New York: New York Public Library, 2005. pp. 52.

12321. GOODBY, JOHN. Whitman's influence on Dylan Thomas and the use of *sidle* as noun. See **19767**.

12322. GREENSPAN, EZRA (ed.). *Song of Myself*: a sourcebook and critical edition. London; New York: Routledge, 2005. pp. xiii, 210.

12323. HERRINGTON, ELDRID. Hopkins and Whitman. See **11305**.

12324. HIRSHFIELD, JANE. Section 26 of *Song of Myself* and Whitman's listening. VQR (81:2) 2005, 48–9.

12325. KERKERING, JOHN D. American renaissance poetry and the *topos* of positionality: *genius mundi* and *genius loci* in Walt Whitman and William Gilmore Simms. VP (43:2) 2005, 223–48.

12326. KILLINGSWORTH, M. JIMMIE. Walt Whitman and the earth: a study in ecopoetics. Iowa City: Iowa UP, 2004. pp. 224. (Iowa Whitman.)

12327. KIRBY, DAVID. Give me life coarse and rank. VQR (81:2) 2005, 244–57.

12328. KUUSISTO, STEPHEN. Walt Whitman's *Specimen Days* and the discovery of the disability memoir. PrSt (27:1/2) 2005, 155–62.

12329. LAPORTE, CHARLES. Spasmodic poetics and Clough's apostasies. See **10455**.

12330. LOGAN, WILLIAM. Prisoner, fancy-man, rowdy, lawyer, physician, priest: Whitman's brags. VQR (81:2) 2005, 19–33.

12331. MCLEAN, ANDREW M. 'Breathing in': Liddy, the Irish and American poet. See **17825**.

12332. MARTIN, DOUG. A study of Walt Whitman's mimetic prosody: free-bound and full circle. Lewiston, NY; Lampeter: Mellen Press, 2004. pp. viii, 174. (Studies in American literature, 69.)

12333. MARTIN, ROBERT K. Newton Arvin: literary critic and lewd person. See **14905**.

12334. MAZUR, KRYSTYNA. Poetry and repetition: Walt Whitman, Wallace Stevens, John Ashbery. London; New York: Routledge, 2005. pp. xxi, 180. (Literary criticism and cultural theory.)

12335. MENKE, RICHARD. Media in America, 1881: Garfield, Guiteau, Bell, Whitman. CI (31:3) 2005, 638–64.

12336. MEYERS, JEFFREY. Whitman's lives. AR (63:4) 2005, 755–87.

12337. MORTON, HEATHER. Democracy, self-reviews and the 1855 *Leaves of Grass*. VQR (81:2) 2005, 229–43.

12338. NAYLOR, NATALIE A.   Walter Whitman at school: education and teaching in the nineteenth century. NYH (86:1) 2005, 7–27.

12339. OUTKA, PAUL.   (De)composing Whitman. ISLE (12:1) 2005, 41–60.

12340. PRICE, KENNETH M.   Whitman in selected anthologies: the politics of his afterlife. VQR (81:2) 2005, 147–62.

12341. REHDER, ROBERT.   Williams and Moore: wasps, a gentian and real toads. See **20217**.

12342. REYNOLDS, DAVID S.   Walt Whitman. Oxford; New York: OUP, 2005. pp. x, 159. (Lives and legacies.)

12343. SELBY, NICK (ed.).   The poetry of Walt Whitman: a reader's guide to essential criticism. (Bibl. 2004, 12405.) Rev. by Donald D. Kummings in WWQR (22:2/3) 2004/05, 138–40.

12344. SERRANO, RICHARD.   Beyond the length of an average penis: reading across traditions in the poetry of Timothy Liu. In (pp. 190–208) **9454**.

12345. SILL, GEOFFREY.   Myths of modern individualism: Defoe, Franklin, and Whitman. In (pp. 61–8) **8537**.

12346. SNEDIKER, MICHAEL.   Whitman on the verge: on the desires of solitude. AQ (61:3) 2005, 27–56.

12347. SOODIK, NICHOLAS.   A tribe called text: Whitman and representing the American Indian body. WWQR (22:2/3) 2004/05, 67–86.

12348. SYCHTERZ, JEFF.   'Silently watch(ing) the dead': the modern disillusioned war poet and the crisis of representation in Whitman's *Drum-Taps*. Discourse (25:3) 2003, 9–29.

12349. TAYSON, RICHARD.   The casualties of Walt Whitman. VQR (81:2) 2005, 79–95.

12350. —— Manly love: Whitman, Ginsberg, Monette. GLRW (12:5) 2005, 23–6.

12351. TELL, CAROL.   Considering classroom communities: Ciaran Carson and Paul Muldoon. See **15701**.

12352. THIELE, DAVID.   *Dracula* and Whitmania: 'the pass-word primeval'. See **12103**.

12353. THOMAS, M. WYNN.   Transatlantic connections: Whitman US, Whitman UK. Iowa City: Iowa UP, 2005. pp. xvii, 289. (Iowa Whitman.) Rev. by William Pannapacker in WWQR (23:1/2) 2005, 65–9.

12354. TRETHEWEY, NATASHA.   On Whitman, Civil War memory, and my South. VQR (81:2) 2005, 50–7.

12355. TURNER, MARK W.   Backward glances: cruising the queer streets of New York and London. See **9435**.

12356. VENDLER, HELEN.   Invisible listeners: lyric intimacy in Herbert, Whitman, and Ashbery. See **7485**.

12357. WARDROP, DANEEN.   Civil War nursing narratives, Whitman's *Memoranda during the War*, and eroticism. WWQR (23:1/2) 2005, 26–47.

12358. WATSON, DAVID.   Shakespeare: the discovery of America. See **6105**.

12359. WILHITE, KEITH.   His mind was full of absences: Whitman at the scene of writing. ELH (71:4) 2004, 921–48.

12360. WORTHEN, JOHN. 'Wild turkeys': some versions of America by D. H. Lawrence. *See* **17637.**

John Greenleaf Whittier

12361. IANNONE, CAROL. John Greenleaf Whittier's Civil War. Mod Age (47:2) 2005, 132–8.

12362. WINCHELL, MARK ROYDEN. Understanding Whittier; or, Warren in the aftermath of Modernism. *See* **20001.**

Oscar Wilde

12363. ANDERSON, ANNE. Oscar's enemy … and neighbour: 'Arry' Quilter and the 'Gospel of Intensity'. Wildean (27) 2005, 39–54.

12364. ANGER, SUZY. Victorian interpretation. *See* **10904.**

12365. AQUIEN, PASCAL. Oscar Wilde, *The Picture of Dorian Gray*: pour une poétique du roman. Nantes: Éditions du Temps, 2004. pp. 191. (Lectures d'une œuvre.) (Variations sur un texte.) Rev. by Alain Jumeau in EA (58:3) 2005, 368–9.

12366. BERAN, ZDENĔK. *Teleny* and the question of *fin de siècle* sexuality. *In* (pp. 27–33) **3734.**

12367. BRISTOW, JOSEPH. Biographies: Oscar Wilde – the man, the life, the legend. *In* (pp. 6–35) **12414.**

12368. —— (ed.). Wilde writings: contextual conditions. (Bibl. 2004, 12418.) Rev. by Lucie Sutherland in JVC (10:1) 2005, 149–54; by Nicholas Frankel in JPRS (14:1) 2005, 107–11.

12369. BUMA, MICHAEL. *The Picture of Dorian Gray*; or, The embarrassing orthodoxy of Oscar Wilde. VN (107) 2005, 18–25.

12370. CARROLL, JOSEPH. Aestheticism, homoeroticism, and Christian guilt in *The Picture of Dorian Gray*. PhilL (29:2) 2005, 286–304.

12371. CHADWICK, PETER. Oscar Wilde: the artist as psychologist. Wildean (27) 2005, 2–11.

12372. CHAN, LEO TAK-HUNG. The poetics of recontextualization: intertextuality in a Chinese adaptive translation of *The Picture of Dorian Gray*. CLS (41:4) 2004, 464–81.

12373. CLAUSSON, NILS. The importance of being Gwendolen Fairfax: Arthur Conan Doyle's *The Voice of Science* & Oscar Wilde's *The Importance of Being Earnest*. Wildean (27) 2005, 37–8.

12374. COPPA, FRANCESCA. Performance theory and performativity. *In* (pp. 72–95) **12414.**

12375. CRAFT, CHRISTOPHER. Come see about me: enchantment of the double in *The Picture of Dorian Gray*. Representations (91) 2005, 109–36.

12376. DANIEL, ANNE MARGARET. Wilde the writer. *In* (pp. 36–71) **12414.**

12377. DAWSON, TERENCE. The effective protagonist in the nineteenth-century British novel: Scott, Brontë, Eliot, Wilde. *See* **11912.**

12378. DELLAMORA, RICHARD. Friendship's bonds: democracy and the novel in Victorian England. *See* **9540.**

12379. DENISOFF, DENNIS. Oscar Wilde, commodity, culture. *In* (pp. 119–42) **12414.**

12380. DIBB, GEOFF. Oscar Wilde's lecture tour of the United Kingdom 1883/1884. Wildean (27) 2005, 29–36.

12381. DICKINSON, PETER. Oscar Wilde: reading the life after the life. Biography (28:3) 2005, 414–32.

12382. DOODY, NOREEN. Oscar Wilde: nation and empire. *In* (pp. 246–66) **12414.**

12383. DYER, TINA. Metaphysics and the mask: symbol of the Wildean aesthetic. Wildean (27) 2005, 64–71.

12384. ELTIS, SOS. Private lives and public spaces: reputation, celebrity and the late Victorian actress. *In* (pp. 169–88) **3985.**

12385. FEHLBAUM, VALERIE. As she knew him: as Ella Hepworth Dixon knew Oscar Wilde. Wildean (26) 2005, 41–50.

12386. FENDALL, JEFF. Imagining Salomé. Wildean (26) 2005, 72–4.

12387. FERNANDES, ANA RAQUEL. Il ritratto avvelenato. *In* (pp. 154–60) **14322.**

12388. FINNERTY, PÁRAIC. The daisy and the dandy: Emily Dickinson and Oscar Wilde. *See* **10779.**

12389. FISHER, TREVOR. Douglas and Wilde: a voice from the past. Wildean (26) 2005, 82–5 (review-article).

12390. FRANKEL, NICHOLAS. On the dates of composition and completion for Wilde's *Salome* and *Lady Windermere's Fan.* NQ (52:4) 2005, 488–90.

12391. FREEMAN, NICHOLAS. 'Nothing of the wild wood'? Pan, paganism and spiritual confusion in E. F. Benson's *The Man Who Went Too Far. See* **15468.**

12392. FRYER, JONATHAN. Oscar Wilde: Liberal martyr? Wildean (26) 2005, 23–6.

12393. GLADDEN, SAMUEL LYNDON. *Dracula's* earnestness: Stoker's debt to Wilde. *See* **12092.**

12394. GLENDENING, JOHN. Track of the Sphinx: H. G. Wells, the modern universe, and the decay of Aestheticism. *See* **20048.**

12395. GUY, JOSEPHINE M. Oscar Wilde's 'self-plagiarism': some new manuscript evidence. NQ (52:4) 2005, 485–8.

12396. HUGHES, LINDA K. A woman on the Wilde side: masks, perversity, and print culture's role in poems by 'Graham R. Tomson'/Rosamund Marriott Watson. *In* (pp. 101–30) **9675.**

12397. KANDOLA, SONDEEP. Vernon Lee: New Woman? *See* **11579.**

12398. KAPLAN, MORRIS. Sodom on the Thames: sex, love, and scandal in Wilde times. Ithaca, NY; London: Cornell UP, 2005. pp. 314.

12399. KAYE, RICHARD A. Gay Studies/queer theory and Oscar Wilde. *In* (pp. 189–223) **12414.**

12400. LAPAIRE, JEAN-RÉMI. Coordination et cognition. *See* **2708.**

12401. LIU, MAOSHENG. The coincidence of hedonism and Aestheticism in Oscar Wilde: a case study of *The Picture of Dorian Gray.* FLS (116) 2005, 85–90. (In Chinese.)

12402. MCKENNA, NEIL. The secret life of Oscar Wilde. (Bibl. 2004, 12448.) Rev. by Charles Kaiser in BkW, 3 July 2005, 3; by Michael Hattersley in GLRW (12:5) 2005, 37–9.

12403. MAO, DOUGLAS. Auden and son: environment, evolution, exhibition. *See* **15240.**

12404. NELSON, JAMES G. 'A delightful companion': Leonard Smithers and the Decadents. Wildean (26) 2005, 11–22.

12405. NIEDERHOFF, BURKHARD. Parody, paradox and play in *The Importance of Being Earnest.* Connotations (13:1/2) 2003/04, 32–55.

12406. NUNOKAWA, JEFF. Tame passions of Wilde: the styles of manageable desire. (Bibl. 2004, 12456.) Rev. by Lucie Sutherland in JVC (10:1) 2005, 149–54.

12407. O'MALLEY, PATRICK R. Religion. *In* (pp. 167–88) **12414.**

12408. PEACOCK, ALAN. Oscar and the 'dismal science'. Wildean (26) 2005, 69–71.

12409. PEASE, ALLISON. Aestheticism and aesthetic theory. *In* (pp. 96–118) **12414.**

12410. PERRELLA, SILVIO (foreword). Il critico come artista; L'anima dell'uomo sotto il socialismo. Trans. by Alessandro Ceni. Milan: Feltrinelli, 2005. pp. 223. (English and Italian texts.)

12411. PITTOCK, MALCOLM. The Decadence of *The Turn of the Screw.* *See* **11446.**

12412. RABY, PETER. Wilde: the remarkable rocket. *In* (pp. 31–47) **3985.**

12413. RIQUELME, JOHN PAUL. *Stephen Hero* and *A Portrait of the Artist as a Young Man*: transforming the nightmare of history. *In* (pp. 103–21) **17244.**

12414. RODEN, FREDERICK S. (ed.). Palgrave advances in Oscar Wilde studies. Basingstoke; New York: Palgrave Macmillan, 2004. pp. xxxix, 275. (Palgrave advances.) Rev. by Anya Clayworth in Wildean (26) 2005, 75–8.

12415. ROGERS, WILLIAM W.; WARD, ROBERT DAVID; MACINERNEY, DOROTHY MCLEOD. Aesthetic messenger: Oscar Wilde lectures in Memphis, 1882. THQ (63:4) 2004, 250–65.

12416. ROSE, D. C. Some trouble with Henri; or, The difficulty of knowing Lautrec. Wildean (27) 2005, 12–20.

12417. ROWLAND, PETER. Waugh on the Wilde side. *See* **20016.**

12418. SALE, ROGER. Being earnest. HR (56:3) 2003, 475–84.

12419. SCHNITZER, CAROL. Oscar Wilde in prison. Wildean (26) 2005, 64–8.

12420. —— Prison confession: an analysis of *De Profundis.* Wildean (27) 2005, 72–7.

12421. SCHWEIK, ROBERT. A note on some modern critical views of the relationship of *The Well-Beloved* to the Victorian art context. *See* **11161.**

12422. SHILLINGLAW, ANN. Wilde's *The Remarkable Rocket.* Exp (63:4) 2005, 222–5.

12423. SIMOND, ANNE-MARIE (ed.). Salomé, drame en un acte. Lausanne: Héron, 2003. pp. 176. (Bilingual ed.) Rev. by Pascal Aquien in EA (57:3) 2004, 367–8.

12424. SMALL, IAN (gen. ed.). The complete works of Oscar Wilde: vol. 3, *The Picture of Dorian Gray*: the 1890 and 1891 texts. Ed. by Joseph Bristow. Oxford; New York: OUP, 2005. pp. lxxvii, 465. Rev. by Anya Clayworth in Wildean (27) 2005, 78–81.

12425. SMITH, PHILIP.   Philosophical approaches to interpretation of Oscar Wilde. *In* (pp. 143–66) **12414.**

12426. SNIDER, CLIFTON.   Synchronicity and the trickster in *The Importance of Being Earnest*. Wildean (27) 2005, 55–63.

12427. STETZ, MARGARET.   Exhibiting the late Victorians. JPRS (13:2) 2004, 122–8.

12428. STETZ, MARGARET DIANE.   Oscar Wilde and feminist criticism. *In* (pp. 224–45) **12414.**

12429. STOKES, JOHN.   The French actress and her English audience. *See* **9504.**

12430. TADIÉ, ALEXIS.   'An age of surfaces': le langage de la comédie dans *The Importance of Being Earnest* d'Oscar Wilde. EA (58:3) 2005, 323–35.

12431. TIPPER, KAREN.   A Dickens of a Wilde paper: a comparison and contrast of their respective tours of America. Wildean (26) 2005, 51–63.

12432. TOOKEY, HELEN.   'The fiend that smites with a look': the monstrous/menstruous woman and the danger of the gaze in Oscar Wilde's *Salomé*. LitTheol (18:1) 2004, 23–37.

12433. URBANOVÁ, LUDMILA.   On phatic function of language. *In* (pp. 271–7) **1369.**

12434. VERNIER, PETER.   Oscar's drawing of 'Little Mr Bouncer'. Wildean (26) 2005, 2–10.

12435. WALSHE, ÉIBHEAR.   The first gay Irishman? Ireland and the Wilde trials. EI (40:3/4) 2005, 38–57.

12436. WEINTRAUB, STANLEY.   Reggie Turner, forgotten Edwardian novelist. *See* **19881.**

12437. WILSON, STEPHEN CLIFFORD.   Oscar Wilde and Arthur Cruttenden: inside and outside Reading Gaol. NQ (52:1) 2005, 82–4.

Ruth Wills (*fl.*1861)

12438. FORSYTH, MARGARET.   Looking for grandmothers: working-class women poets and 'herstory'. *See* **11002.**

Harriette Wilson (1786–1846)

12439. WILSON, FRANCES.   The courtesan's revenge: Harriette Wilson, the woman who blackmailed the king. (Bibl. 2003, 11791.) Rev. by Harriet Devine Jump in WWr (12:2) 2005, 321–8.

Eliza Winstanley (1818–1882)

12440. ELLIOTT, DORICE WILLIAMS.   Convict servants and middle-class mistresses. *See* **12279.**

'John Strange Winter'
(Henrietta Eliza Vaughan Palmer Stannard) (1856–1911)

12441. YOUNGKIN, MOLLY.   'Independent in thought and expression, kindly and tolerant in tone': Henrietta Stannard, *Golden Gates*, and gender controversies in *fin-de-siècle* periodicals. *See* **1367.**

Mrs Henry Wood

12442. LOSANO, ANTONIA. *East Lynne, The Turn of the Screw*, and the female *Doppelgänger* in governess fiction. NCS (18) 2004, 99–116.

12443. PHEGLEY, JENNIFER. Domesticating the sensation novelist: Ellen Price Wood as author and editor of the *Argosy Magazine*. See **1302**.

Constance Fenimore Woolson

12444. BREHM, VICTORIA; DEAN, SHARON L. (eds). Constance Fenimore Woolson: selected stories and travel narratives. Knoxville: Tennessee UP, 2004. pp. xxvi, 342.

12445. COULSON, VICTORIA. Teacups and love letters: Constance Fenimore Woolson and Henry James. HJR (26:1) 2005, 82–98.

12446. HALL, CAROLYN. An elaborate pretense for the Major: making up the face of the postbellum nation. Legacy (22:2) 2005, 144–57.

12447. KREIGER, GEORGIA. *East Angels*: Constance Fenimore Woolson's revision of Henry James's *The Portrait of a Lady*. Legacy (22:1) 2005, 18–29.

Dorothy Wordsworth

12448. CHRISTIE, WILLIAM. Coleridge and Wordsworth in *Pandaemonium*. See **13703**.

12449. COMITINI, PATRICIA. Vocational philanthropy and British women's writing, 1790–1810: Wollstonecraft, More, Edgeworth, Wordsworth. See **9134**.

12450. MARKS, CLIFFORD J. 'My dear, dear Sister': sustaining the 'I' in *Tintern Abbey*. See **12500**.

12451. WOOF, PAMELA. The solitary poet at home. See **12530**.

William Wordsworth

12452. AGATHOCLEOUS, TANYA. Wordsworth at the panoramas: the sublime spectacle of the world. Genre (36:3/4) 2003, 295–316.

12453. ALDERMAN, NIGEL. Unity sublime: *The Excursion*'s social self. YJC (18:1) 2005, 21–43.

12454. ALKER, SHARON; NELSON, HOLLY FAITH. 'Ghastly in the moonlight': Wordsworth, Hogg and the anguish of war. See **11269**.

12455. APPLEWHITE, JAMES. The mind's lyric and the spaces of nature: Wordsworth and Stevens. See **19642**.

12456. BACIGALUPO, MASSIMO. William Wordsworth: *Il preludio* e i suoi lettori. PoesiaM (198) 2005, 52–68.

12457. BAJETTA, CARLO M. Redeeming the vagrant: Wordsworth's *Peter Bell* and its revisions. *In* (pp. 54–65) **3690**.

12458. BAKER, JOHN HAYDN. Browning and Wordsworth. (Bibl. 2004, 12485.) Rev. by Joe Phelan in TLS, 24 June 2005, 28.

12459. BAUER, PEARL CHAOZON. An unpublished letter from William Wordsworth to C. H. Parry. NQ (52:4) 2005, 472–3.

12460. BLACKWELL, MARK R. The gothic: moving in the world of novels. *In* (pp. 144–61) **6958**.

12461. BLADES, JOHN. Wordsworth and Coleridge: *Lyrical Ballads*. Basingstoke; New York: Palgrave Macmillan, 2004. pp. xi, 291. (Analysing texts.)

12462. Boly, John.   Beloved mentors: Seamus Heaney's poems of vocation. *See* **16936**.

12463. Brett, R. L, *et al.* (ed.).   Wordsworth and Coleridge: *Lyrical Ballads*. Introd. by Nicholas Roe. (Bibl. 1992, 8349.) London; New York: Routledge, 2005. pp. xxix, 403. (Routledge classics.) (New ed.: first pub. 1968.)

12464. Bushell, Sally.   Wordsworthian composition: the micro-*Prelude*. SR (44:3) 2005, 399–421.

12465. Chandler, David.   Another Lucy poem about a glow-worm. NQ (521:1) 2005, 37–8.

12466. —— The early development of the 'Lake School' idea. NQ (52:1) 2005, 35–7.

12467. Cheuse, Alan.   Reflections on dialogue: 'How d'yuh get t'Eighteent' Avenoo and Sixty-Sevent' Street?' *See* **14104**.

12468. Christie, William.   Coleridge and Wordsworth in *Pandaemonium*. *See* **13703**.

12469. Collier, Michael.   On Whitman's *To a Locomotive in Winter*. *See* **12303**.

12470. Culler, Jonathan.   The Hertzian sublime. *See* **14748**.

12471. Deboo, James.   Wordsworth and the stripping of the altars. RelArts (8:3) 2004, 323–43.

12472. Duggan, Robert A., Jr.   'Sleep no more' again: Melville's rewriting of Book x of Wordsworth's *Prelude*. *See* **11680**.

12473. Eakin, Paul John.   Living autobiographically. *See* **14587**.

12474. Earle, Bo.   World legislation: the form and function of a Romantic cosmopolitanism. ERR (16:2) 2005, 209–20.

12475. Elam, Helen Regueiro; Ferguson, Frances (eds).   The Wordsworthian Enlightenment: Romantic poetry and the ecology of reading: essays in honor of Geoffrey Hartman. Baltimore, MD; London: Johns Hopkins UP, 2005. pp. vi, 374.

12476. Esterhammer, Angela.   The cosmopolitan *improvvisatore*: spontaneity and performance in Romantic poetics. ERR (16:2) 2005, 153–65.

12477. Faflak, Joel.   Romanticism and the pornography of talking. NCC (27:1) 2005, 77–97.

12478. Fosso, Kurt.   Buried communities: Wordsworth and the bonds of mourning. (Bibl. 2004, 12506.) Rev. by Bruce Matsunaga in ANQ (18:4) 2005, 59–62.

12479. François, Anne-Lise.   'O happy living things': Frankenfoods and the bounds of Wordsworthian natural piety. Diacritics (33:2) 2003, 42–70.

12480. Frey, Anne.   De Quincey's imperial systems. *See* **10608**.

12481. Gaull, Marilyn.   Pantomime as satire: mocking a broken charm. *In* (pp. 207–24) **9305**.

12482. —— Romans and Romanticism. WordsC (36:1) 2005, 15–20.

12483. Gravil, Richard.   The Somerset sound; or, The darling child of speech. *See* **10485**.

12484. Grovier, Kelly. 'Shades of the prison-house': 'Walking' Stewart, Michel Foucault and the making of Wordsworth's 'two consciousnesses'. SR (44:3) 2005, 341–66.

12485. Hamilton, Paul. Hazlitt and the 'kings of speech'. *In* (pp. 68–80) **11245**.

12486. Harvey, Melinda. Re-educating the Romantic: sex and the nature-poet in J. M. Coetzee's *Disgrace*. *See* **15831**.

12487. Hewitt, Rachel. Wordsworth's Irish friend. TLS, 30 Sept. 2005, 15. (William Rowan Hamilton, Astronomer Royal.)

12488. Higgins, David Minden. Romantic genius and the literary magazine: biography, celebrity, and politics. *See* **11227**.

12489. Jackson, Geoffrey (ed.). Sonnet series and itinerary poems, 1820–1845. (Bibl. 2004, 12526.) Rev. by David Simpson in WordsC (35:4) 2004, 152–3; by Duncan Wu in RES (56:224) 2005, 331–3.

12490. Jackson, Noel B. Rethinking the cultural divide: Walter Pater, Wilkie Collins, and the legacies of Wordsworthian aesthetics. *See* **11780**.

12491. James, Felicity. Agreement, dissonance, dissent: the many conversations of *This Lime-Tree Bower*. *See* **10493**.

12492. Jarrells, Anthony S. Britain's bloodless revolutions: 1688 and the Romantic reform of literature. *See* **8673**.

12493. Keane, Patrick J. Emerson, Romanticism, and intuitive reason: the transatlantic 'light of all our day'. *See* **10982**.

12494. Keymer, Thomas. Sterne and Romantic autobiography. *In* (pp. 173–93) **8014**.

12495. Knottenbelt, E. M. Romantic residues? Virgil's *Aeneid* 'in such a tongue as the people understandeth' or in a 'language really spoken by men'. *In* (pp. 235–57) **9237**.

12496. Louis, Margot K. Gods and mysteries: the revival of paganism and the remaking of mythography through the nineteenth century. VS (47:3) 2005, 329–61.

12497. Low, Dennis. Gold and silver fishes in a vase: a portrait of Wordsworth and Maria Jane Jewsbury. ColB (ns 25) 2005, 61–70.

12498. Magnuson, Paul. The Lake School: Wordsworth and Coleridge. *In* (pp. 227–43) **8014**.

12499. Markley, A. A. Wordsworth's *Ruth*. Exp (64:1) 2005, 26–8.

12500. Marks, Clifford J. 'My dear, dear Sister': sustaining the 'I' in *Tintern Abbey*. CEACrit (66:2/3) 2004, 47–62.

12501. Matlak, Richard E. Deep distresses: William Wordsworth, John Wordsworth, Sir George Beaumont: 1800–1808. Newark: Delaware UP; London: Assoc. UPs, 2003. pp. 201. Rev. by Paul F. Betz in WordsC (35:4) 2004, 154–6; by Kenneth R. Johnston in SR (44:2) 2005, 283–8; by J. R. Watson in Romanticism (11:1) 2005, 121–2.

12502. Morrison, Robert. De Quincey on *Mount Pleasant*: William Roscoe and *Confessions of an English Opium-Eater*. *See* **10635**.

12503. Mortimer, Anthony (ed.). From Wordsworth to Stevens: essays in honour of Robert Rehder. New York; Frankfurt: Lang, 2005. pp. 347.

12504. NEWMAN, STEVE.   Representation, violence, and the fate of culture: an interview with Geoffrey Hartman. *See* **14934.**

12505. NICHOLS, ASHTON.   Roaring alligators and burning tygers: poetry and science from William Bartram to Charles Darwin. *See* **8348.**

12506. NUSS, MELYNDA.   'Look in my face': the dramatic ethics of *The Borderers*. SR (43:4) 2004, 599–621.

12507. OREL, HAROLD (ed.).   William Wordsworth: interviews and recollections. Basingstoke; New York: Palgrave Macmillan, 2005. pp. xii, 199.

12508. PACE, JOEL; SCOTT, MATTHEW E. (eds).   Wordsworth in American literary culture. Basingstoke; New York: Palgrave Macmillan, 2005. pp. xix, 248. Rev. by Paul Giles in RES (56:227) 2005, 797–8.

12509. PAULIN, TOM.   One impulse: Hazlitt, Wordsworth and *The Principles of Human Action*. *In* (pp. 98–111) **11245.**

12510. PERRY, SEAMUS.   The little horror show. TLS, 21 Jan. 2005, 5 (review-article). (*Peter Bell*.)

12511. —— The Romantic matter of fact. *See* **10512.**

12512. PETERFREUND, STUART.   Dissent and ontological space in Romantic science and literature. *See* **8379.**

12513. PFAU, THOMAS.   Romantic moods: paranoia, trauma, and melancholy, 1790–1840. *See* **8677.**

12514. PUGHE, THOMAS.   Réinventer la nature: vers une éco-poétique. *See* **11314.**

12515. REHDER, ROBERT.   Williams and Moore: wasps, a gentian and real toads. *See* **20217.**

12516. ROBINSON, JEFFREY CANE.   Wordsworth, day by day: reading his work into poetry now. Barrytown, NY: Station Hill Press, 2005. pp. 160.

12517. RYAN, ROBERT M.   Wordsworthian science in the 1870s. WordsC (36:2) 2005, 57–9.

12518. SOULE, GEORGE.   *The Prelude* and the French Revolution. CLB (129) 2005, 9–19.

12519. THIERFELDER, BILL.   Wordsworth's *Ode: Intimations of Immortality*, Shakespeare's *The Tempest* 5.1, and Vaughan's *The Retreat*. Exp (63:3) 2005, 136–8.

12520. TROTT, NICOLA.   Wordsworth and the parodic school of criticism. *In* (pp. 71–97) **9305.**

12521. TURNER, JOHN.   'Hauntings from the infirmity of love': Wordsworth and the illusion of pastoral. SR (43:4) 2004, 623–51.

12522. VESPA, JACK.   Georgic inquisitiveness, pastoral meditation, Romantic reflexivity: *Nutting* and the figure of Wordsworth as poet. Genre (38:1/2) 2005, 1–44.

12523. VINCENT, PATRICK H.   'Switzerland no more': Turner, Wordsworth and the changed landscape of Revolution. SPELL (17) 2005, 135–51.

12524. WARD, JOHN POWELL.   Wordsworth's eldest son: John Wordsworth and the Intimations Ode. WordsC (36:2) 2005, 66–80.

12525. WEDD, MARY R.   Romantic presentations of the Lake District: the Lake District of *The Prelude* Book IV. CLB (121) 2003, 26–42.

12526. WESTENDORP, TJEBBE A.   Phantoms of delight: lines composed by William Wordsworth. *In* (pp. 27–33) **9237.**

12527. WILLIAMS, J. R.   'Suffer the little children to come unto me': T. F. Powys's child-men in a landscape of redemption. *See* **18928.**

12528. WOOD, GILLEN D'ARCY.   Crying game: operatic strains in Wordsworth's lyrical ballads. ELH (71:4) 2004, 969–1000. (Translations of libretti.)

12529. WOOD, MARCUS.   Black bodies and satiric limits in the long eighteenth century. *In* (pp. 55–70) **9305.**

12530. WOOF, PAMELA.   The solitary poet at home. CLB (130) 2005, 28–42.

12531. WU, DUNCAN.   The road to Nether Stowey. *In* (pp. 83–97) **11245.**

Mabel E. Wotton

12532. ROCHELSON, MERI-JANE.   The friendship of Israel Zangwill and Mabel E. Wotton: 'Faithfully yours, Margaret'. *See* **12536.**

Frances Wright

12533. BRANCA, R. RENE.   Melodrama, convention, and rape. *See* **9104.**

12534. CAMPBELL, KARLYN KOHRS.   Theory emerging from practice: the rhetorical theory of Frances Wright. *In* (pp. 125–41) **2410.**

Charlotte M. Yonge

12535. SCHAFFER, TALIA.   Taming the tropics: Charlotte Yonge takes on Melanesia. VS (47:2) 2005, 204–14.

Israel Zangwill

12536. ROCHELSON, MERI-JANE.   The friendship of Israel Zangwill and Mabel E. Wotton: 'Faithfully yours, Margaret'. ELT (48:3) 2005, 305–23.

TWENTIETH CENTURY

GENERAL

12537. ANON. (comp.).   Annual bibliography of Commonwealth literature 2004: South Africa. Introd. by Crystal Warren. *See* **20542**.

12538. ADÉÈKÓ, ADÉLÉKÈ.   Symptoms of the present in Ato Quayson's *Calibrations. See* **20989**.

12539. AITKEN, KELLEY; GOYETTE, SUE; SCOTT, BARBARA (eds).   First writes. *See* **753**.

12540. ALDAMA, FREDERICK LUIS.   Brown on brown: Chicano/a representations of gender, sexuality, and ethnicity. Austin: Texas UP, 2005. pp. 176.

12541. ALDRICH, ROBERT.   Colonialism and homosexuality. *See* **9161**.

12542. ALEXANDER, CHRISTINE; MCMASTER, JULIET (eds).   The child writer from Austen to Woolf. *See* **9164**.

12543. ALLEN, CHADWICK.   Blood narrative: indigenous identity in American Indian and Maori literary and activist texts. (Bibl. 2004, 12582.) Rev. by James O. Gump in PacHR (72:4) 2003, 668–9.

12544. ALLMENDINGER, BLAKE.   Imagining the African American West. Lincoln; London: Nebraska UP, 2005. pp. xix, 161. (Race and ethnicity in the American West.)

12545. ANDERSON, SARAH A.   The place to go: the 135th Street Branch Library and the Harlem renaissance. LQ (73:4) 2003, 383–421.

12546. ARANA, R. VICTORIA; RAMEY, LAURI (eds).   Black British writing. Basingstoke; New York: Palgrave Macmillan, 2004. pp. viii, 178.

12547. ARNDT, SUSAN.   Dynamics of African feminism: defining and classifying African feminist literatures. Trans. by Isabel Cole. Trenton, NJ: Africa World Press; London: Turnaround, 2004. pp. 234. Rev. by Pia Thielmann in RAL (36:2) 2005, 156–7.

12548. ASHTON, SUSANNA.   Collaborators in literary America, 1870–1920. *See* **9172**.

12549. BADIA, JANET; PHEGLEY, JENNIFER (eds).   Reading women: literary figures and cultural icons from the Victorian age to the present. Toronto; Buffalo, NY; London: Toronto UP, 2005. pp. x, 297. (Studies in book and print culture.)

12550. BAILEY NURSE, DONNA.   What's a Black critic to do? Interviews, profiles, and reviews of Black writers. Toronto: Insomniac Press, 2003. pp. 208. Rev. by Eric Gardner in AAR (38:4) 2004, 736–7; by Leslie Sanders in CanL (185) 2005, 174–5.

12551. BALDICK, CHRIS.   The modern movement: 1910–1940. Oxford; New York: OUP, 2004. pp. xvii, 477. (Oxford English literary history, 10.) Rev. by Richard Greaves in RES (56:226) 2005, 688–9.

12552. BAMFORTH, IAIN (ed.).   The body in the library: a literary anthology of modern medicine. (Bibl. 2004, 12591.) Rev. by Jacalyn Duffin in BHM (79:1) 2005, 175–6.

12553. BARR, MARLEEN S. (ed.).   Envisioning the future: science fiction and the next millennium. (Bibl. 2004, 12594.) Rev. by Sherryl Vint in Extrapolation (46:1) 2005, 144–9.

12554. BAUER, RALPH.   Laying claim to the literary borderlands: the contested grounds of Hispanism in the US. See **9177**.

12555. BAYLEY, JOHN.   The power of delight: a lifetime in literature: essays 1962–2002. Selected by Leo Carey. See **7937**.

12556. BEHLAU, ULRIKE; REITZ, BERNHARD (eds).   Jewish women's writing of the 1990s and beyond in Great Britain and the United States. Trier: WVT, 2004. pp. 337. (MUSE: Mainz Univ. studies in English, 5.)

12557. BELL, ELEANOR.   Questioning Scotland: literature, nationalism, postmodernism. Basingstoke; New York: Palgrave Macmillan, 2004. pp. xi, 194. Rev. by Gavin Miller in ScSR (6:1) 2005, 118–20.

12558. BENNETT, JUDA.   Writing into the prison–industrial complex. In (pp. 203–16) **12821**.

12559. BEPLATE, JUSTIN.   Express or exploit. TLS, 23 & 30 Dec. 2005, 13–14 (review-article). (Anglo-Irish literature.)

12560. BERGFELDER, TIM; STREET, SARAH (eds).   The Titanic in myth and memory: representations in visual and verbal culture. See **13826**.

12561. BERGLUND, MICHAEL H.   Looking back to look ahead: homosexuality and the postmodern gothic in American literature. See **9188**.

12562. BERGMAN, DAVID.   The violet hour: the Violet Quill and the making of gay culture. (Bibl. 2004, 12603.) Rev. by Gary L. Atkins in JAH (92:1) 2005, 307–8.

12563. BERGNER, GWEN.   Taboo subjects: race, sex, and psychoanalysis. Minneapolis; London: Minnesota UP, 2005. pp. xxxii, 209.

12564. BIRBALSINGH, FRANK (ed.).   Guyana and the Caribbean: reviews, essays and interviews. Chichester: Dido Press, 2004. pp. 313. Rev. by Matthew Mead in JPW (41:1) 2005, 125–7.

12565. BIRGY, PHILIPPE.   Une terrible beauté: les modernistes anglais à l'épreuve de la critique girardienne. Toulouse: Presses Universitaires du Mirail, 2005. pp. 249. (Interlangues: Littératures.) Rev. by Françoise Besson in Anglophonia (17) 2005, 485–8.

12566. BLOCH, AVITAL H.; UMANSKY, LAURI (eds).   Impossible to hold: women and culture in the 1960s. New York; London: New York UP, 2005. pp. viii, 342. (American history and culture.)

12567. BLOOM, JAMES D.   Gravity fails: the comic Jewish shaping of America (Bibl. 2004, 12610.) Rev. by Christie Davis in Humor (18:1) 2005, 116–17.

12568. BLOTNER, JOSEPH.   Robert Penn Warren, Cleanth Brooks, and the Southern literary tradition. See **19980**.

12569. BOELHOWER, WILLIAM; DAVIS, ROCÍO G.; BIRKLE, CARMEN (eds).   Sites of ethnicity: Europe and the Americas. (Bibl. 2004, 12613.) Rev. by María Lourdes López Ropero in Atl (27:2) 2005, 209–13.

12570. BOND, BRIAN.   The unquiet Western Front: Britain's role in literature and history. (Bibl. 2004, 12616.) Rev. by John Horne in JMH (77:2) 2005, 429–30.

12571. BORKOWSKA, EWA (ed.). In the space of arts: interdisciplinarity, identity and (post)modernity. Katowice: Silesia UP, 2004. pp. 273.

12572. BORNHOLDT, JENNY; O'BRIEN, GREGORY (eds). The colour of distance: New Zealand writers in France, French writers in New Zealand. Wellington: Victoria UP, 2005. pp. 247, (plates) 24.

12573. BORNSTEIN, GEORGE. The colors of Zion: Black, Jewish, and Irish nationalisms at the turn of the century. See 20482.

12574. —— A forgotten alliance: Africans, Americans, Zionists and Irish. See 10909.

12575. BÖSS, MICHAEL; MAHER, EAMON (eds). Engaging modernity: readings of Irish politics, literature, and culture at the turn of the century. (Bibl. 2004, 12617.) Rev. by Anne Goarzin in EtIr (28:2) 2003, 181–3.

12576. BOTTALICO, MICHELE. Scrivere un'altra storia: tendenze divergenti nella scrittura autoreferenziale chicana. In (pp. 85–103) 12577.

12577. —— CHIALANT, MARIA TERESA (eds). L'impulso autobiografico: Inghilterra, Stati Uniti, Canada ... e altrove. Naples: Liguori, 2005. pp. 301. (Critica e letteratura, 63.)

12578. BRAZ, ALBERT. The false traitor: Louis Riel in Canadian culture. See 9199.

12579. BREEN, MARGARET SÖNSER; PETERS, FIONA (eds). Genealogies of identity: interdisciplinary readings on sex and sexuality. Amsterdam; Atlanta, GA: Rodopi, 2005. pp. xv, 266. (At the interface/Probing the boundaries.)

12580. BROOKER, PETER. Bohemia in London: the social scene of early Modernism. (Bibl. 2004, 12625.) Rev. by John Sloan in RES (56:224) 2005, 346–9; by Matthew Gaughan in CamQ (34:1) 2005, 72–4.

12581. —— THACKER, ANDREW (eds). Geographies of Modernism: literatures, cultures, spaces. London; New York: Routledge, 2005. pp. 181.

12582. BROWDY DE HERNANDEZ, JENNIFER (ed.). Women writing resistance: essays from Latin America and the Caribbean. Preface by Elizabeth Martinez. Cambridge, MA: South End Press, 2003. pp. xii, 241. Rev. by Jill Bystydzienski in NWSAJ (17:3) 2005, 203–4.

12583. BROWN, NICHOLAS. Utopian generations: the political horizon of twentieth-century literature. Princeton, NJ; Oxford: Princeton UP, 2005. pp. viii, 235. (Translation/transnation.)

12584. BROWN, RICHARD DANSON; GUPTA, SUMAN (eds). Aestheticism & Modernism: debating twentieth-century literature 1900–1960. London; New York: Routledge in assn with the Open UP, 2005. pp. vi, 445. (Twentieth-century literature: texts and debates.)

12585. BROYARD, ANATOLE (ed.). Furoreggiava Kafka: ricordi del Greenwich Village. Milan: Bonnard, 2005. pp. 184. (Il piacere di leggere.)

12586. BUMA, MICHAEL. Rossetti's Sudden Light. See 11866.

12587. CALDER, ALISON; WARDHAUGH, ROBERT (eds). History, literature, and the writing of the Canadian prairies. Winnipeg: Manitoba UP, 2005. pp. v, 310.

12588. CAMBIAGHI, MARA. 'Moving times – new words': the sixties on both sides of the Channel. *In* (pp. 296–312) **12868.**

12589. CAMBONI, MARINA; SACERDOTI MARIANI, GIGLIOLA; TEDESCHINI LALLI, BIANCAMARIA (eds). *Words at war*: parole di guerra e cultura di pace nel 'primo secolo delle guerre mondiali'. Florence: Le Monnier, 2005. pp. x, 154.

12590. CAMPBELL, CLAIRE. 'Our dear north country': regional identity and national meaning in Ontario's Georgian Bay. *See* **9207.**

12591. CAPORALE BIZZINI, SILVIA. We, the 'other Victorians': considering the heritage of 19th-century thought. *See* **9209.**

12592. CARROLL, ANNE ELIZABETH. Word, image, and the New Negro: representation and identity in the Harlem renaissance. Bloomington: Indiana UP, 2005. pp. xiv, 275. (Blacks in the diaspora.)

12593. CASTILLO, DEBRA A. Redreaming America: toward a bilingual American culture. Albany: New York State UP, 2005. pp. 232. (SUNY series in Latin American and Iberian thought and culture.)

12594. CASTRONOVO, DAVID. Beyond the gray flannel suit: books from the 1950s that made American culture. (Bibl. 2004, 12645.) Rev. by Jay Martin in AR (63:2) 2005, 397–8; by R. H. W. Dillard in SewR (113:2) 2005, 337–43; by Robert Emmet Long in ANCW (192:3) 2005, 16–17.

12595. CAUGHIE, PAMELA L. Passing as Modernism. *See* **13180.**

12596. CAWELTI, JOHN G. Mystery, violence, and popular culture: essays. Madison; London: Wisconsin UP/Popular Press, 2004. pp. xiv, 410. Rev. by Marshall W. Fishwick in JAC (28:1) 2005, 144.

12597. CHAKKALAKAL, TESS. 'Making a collection': James Weldon Johnson and the mission of African American literature. *See* **17213.**

12598. CHAMBERS, ROSS. Untimely interventions: AIDS writing, testimonial, and the rhetoric of haunting. Ann Arbor: Michigan UP, 2004. pp. xxxiv, 415. Rev. by Jean-Pierre Boulé in MLR (100:3) 2005, 756–7.

12599. CHEN, AIMIN. On the presentation of Chinese culture in the Chinese American women literature. FLS (116) 2005, 71–4. (In Chinese.)

12600. CHEN, TINA. Double agency: acts of impersonation in Asian American literature and culture. Stanford, CA: Stanford UP, 2005. pp. xxvi, 245. (Asian America.)

12601. CHEN, TINA MAI. Introduction: thinking through embeddedness: globalization, culture, and the popular. CultC (58) 2004, 1–29.

12602. CHEVIGNY, BELL GALE. 'All I have, a lament and a boast': why prisoners write. *In* (pp. 246–71) **12821.**

12603. CHLEBEK, DIANA (comp.). Annual bibliography of Commonwealth literature 2004: Canada 2003–04. *See* **20553.**

12604. CHRISMAN, LAURA. Postcolonial contraventions: cultural readings of race, imperialism, and transnationalism. Manchester; New York: Manchester UP, 2003. pp. viii, 200. Rev. by Apollo O. Amoko in RAL (36:1) 2005, 128–9; by Cristina Sandru in Eng (54:209) 2005, 162–9; by Angela Smith in YES (35) 2005, 343–4.

12605. CHUH, KANDICE. Imagine otherwise: on Asian Americanist critique. Durham, NC; London: Duke UP, 2003. pp. xii, 215. Rev. by Kyoo Lee in Comparatist (29) 2005, 153–5.

12606. CHURA, PATRICK. Vital contact: downclassing journeys in American literature from Herman Melville to Richard Wright. *See* **9218.**

12607. CIRILLO, NANCY. Anthologizing the Caribbean; or, Squaring beaches, bananas, and Nobel laureates. *In* (pp. 222–46) **3749.**

12608. CLARK, WILLIAM BEDFORD; GRIMSHAW, JAMES A., JR. A conversation with Lewis P. Simpson. *See* **19460.**

12609. CLEARY, JOE. Toward a materialist–formalist history of twentieth-century Irish literature. B2 (31:1) 2004, 207–41.

12610. CLIFF, BRIAN; WALSHE, ÉIBHEAR (eds). Representing the Troubles: texts and images, 1970–2000. Dublin; Portland, OR: Four Courts Press, 2004. pp. 160. Rev. by Paula Murphy in ILS (25:1) 2005, 18–19.

12611. CLYMER, JEFFORY A. America's culture of terrorism: violence, capitalism, and the written word. (Bibl. 2004, 12652.) Rev. by Robert Justin Goldstein in JAH (91:2) 2004, 647–8.

12612. —— Naturalism's histories. *See* **9219.**

12613. COCCHIARALE, MICHAEL; EMMERT, SCOTT D. (eds). Upon further review: sports in American literature. (Bibl. 2004, 12653.) Rev. by Tony Jackson in Aethlon (23:1) 2005, 193.

12614. COHEN, ROBERT. 'The piano has been drinking': on the art of the rant. GaR (59:2) 2005, 233–53.

12615. COLE, SARAH. Modernism, male friendship, and the First World War. (Bibl. 2004, 12655.) Rev. by Adrian Caesar in MLR (100:4) 2004, 1102–3; by Andrzej Gasiorek in LitH (14:1) 2005, 97–9; by Hilda D. Spear in Eng (54:208) 2005, 69–72; by Chiara Briganti in ELT (48:3) 2005, 342–5; by Nick Kneale in RES (56:226) 2005, 686–7.

12616. COMENTALE, EDWARD P. Modernism, cultural production, and the British avant-garde. Cambridge; New York: CUP, 2004. pp. x, 261. Rev. by Steve Ferebee in VWM (67) 2005, 30–1.

12617. CONNOR, STEVEN (ed.). The Cambridge companion to postmodernism. Cambridge; New York: CUP, 2004. pp. xii, 237. Rev. by Marshall W. Fishwick in JAC (28:1) 2005, 156.

12618. COOK, MATT. London and the culture of homosexuality, 1885–1914. *See* **9223.**

12619. COOPER, JOHN XIROS. Modernism and the culture of market society. Cambridge; New York: CUP, 2004. pp. x, 289. Rev. by Gary Day in TLS, 23 Sept. 2005, 27; by Patricia Laurence in ELT (48:3) 2005, 356–9; by Nicholas Daly in Mod/Mod (12:3) 2005, 533–5.

12620. CORNELL, M. DORETTA. Mother of all the living: reinterpretations of Eve in contemporary literature. CC (54:4) 2005, 91–107.

12621. DALEY, YVONNE. Vermont writers: a state of mind. Castleton, VT: Castleton State College; Hanover, NH: Wesleyan UP, 2005. pp. xix, 330.

12622. DAMROSCH, DAVID (gen. ed.). The Longman anthology of world literature: vol. F, The twentieth century. Ed. by Djelal Kadir and Ursula K. Heise. Harlow; New York: Longman, 2004. pp. xxvi, 1158.

12623. DAVIS, CAROLINE. The politics of postcolonial publishing: Oxford University Press's Three Crowns series 1962–1976. See **805**.

12624. DAVIS, GEOFFREY. Voices of justice and reason: apartheid and beyond in South African literature. Amsterdam; Atlanta, GA: Rodopi, 2003. pp. xxx, 376. (Cross/cultures: readings in the post-colonial literatures in English, 61.) Rev. by Sam Durrant in RAL (36:1) 2005, 114–19.

12625. DAVIS, STEVEN L. Texas literary outlaws: six writers in the sixties and beyond. (Bibl. 2004, 12665.) Rev. by Tom Pilkington in GPQ (25:4) 2005, 261–2.

12626. DAWAHARE, ANTHONY. Nationalism, Marxism, and African American literature between the wars: a new Pandora's box. (Bibl. 2004, 12666.) Rev. by Joseph McLaren in RAL (36:1) 2005, 136–7; by Jon Woodson in MELUS (30:3) 2005, 256–8.

12627. DAWSON, ALMA; VAN FLEET, CONNIE (eds). African American literature: a guide to reading interests. See **9232**.

12628. DAWSON, LESEL. Menstruation, misogyny, and the cure for love. WS (34:6) 2005, 461–84.

12629. DAYMOND, M. J., et al. (eds). Women writing Africa: the southern region. (Bibl. 2004, 12667.) Rev. by Daniel P. Kunene in RAL (36:2) 2005, 147–8.

12630. DE COURTIVRON, ISABELLE (ed.). Lives in translation: bilingual writers on identity and creativity. Basingstoke; New York: Palgrave Macmillan, 2003. pp. 171. Rev. by Adele King in WLWE (40:2) 2004, 126–30.

12631. DEKOVEN, MARIANNE. Utopia limited: the sixties and the emergence of the postmodern. Durham, NC; London: Duke UP, 2004. pp. xix, 362. (Post-contemporary interventions.) Rev. by Thomas Carmichael in MFS (51:1) 2005, 236–9; by J. Robert Kent in AmS (46:1) 2005, 179–80; by Marshall W. Fishwick in JAC (28:1) 2005, 162.

12632. DELOUGHREY, ELIZABETH M.; HANDLEY, GEORGE B.; GOSSON, RENÉE K. (eds). Caribbean literature and the environment: between nature and culture. Charlottesville; London: Virginia UP, 2005. pp. xii, 303. (New World studies.)

12633. DELROSSO, JEANA. Writing Catholic women: contemporary international Catholic girlhood narratives. Basingstoke; New York: Palgrave Macmillan, 2005. pp. x, 203.

12634. DE NOOY, JULIANA. Twins in contemporary literature and culture: look twice. Basingstoke; New York: Palgrave Macmillan, 2005. pp. xviii, 198.

12635. DICKSTEIN, MORRIS. The mirror in the roadway: literature and the real world. Princeton, NJ; Oxford: Princeton UP, 2005. pp. xv, 280.

12636. DILLARD, R. H. W. Notes from after the deluge. See **14758**.

12637. DINOVA, JOANNE R. Spiraling webs of relation: movements toward an indigenist criticism. London; New York: Routledge, 2005. pp. ix, 214. (Indigenous peoples and politics.)

12638. DISTILLER, NATASHA. English and the African renaissance. ESA (47:2) 2004, 115–30.

12639. DOYLE, JAMES. Progressive heritage: the evolution of a politically radical literary tradition in Canada. (Bibl. 2004, 12684.) Rev. by Roxanne Rimstead in CanL (184) 2005, 126–8.

12640. DOYLE, LAURA; WINKIEL, LAURA (eds). Geomodernisms: race, Modernism, modernity. Bloomington: Indiana UP, 2005. pp. ix, 354.

12641. DROWNE, KATHLEEN MORGAN. Spirits of defiance: national Prohibition and Jazz Age literature, 1920–1933. Columbus: Ohio State UP, 2005. pp. xii, 189.

12642. DUBEY, MADHU. Signs and cities: Black literary postmodernism. (Bibl. 2004, 12686.) Rev. by Scott Saul in MLQ (66:2) 2005, 269–72; by Daylanne K. English in ConLit (46:2) 2005, 358–62.

12643. DUEÑAS VINUESA, MARÍA. Border Studies: an annotated list of cultural and academic Web sources. RAEI (16) 2003, 339–53.

12644. DUNCAN, PATTI. Tell this silence: Asian American women writers and the politics of speech. (Bibl. 2004, 12688.) Rev. by Deborah M. Mix in MFS (51:1) 2005, 204–7; by Patricia P. Chu in TCL (51:3) 2005, 385–90.

12645. DUNN, CAROLYN. The trick is going home: secular spiritualism in Native American women's literature. *In* (pp. 189–202) **12725.**

12646. DWORKIN, CRAIG. Textual prostheses. *See* **155.**

12647. DYBSKA, ANETA. Afrocentrism: back to the center. *In* (pp. 317–25) **12672.**

12648. EBBATSON, ROGER. An imaginary England: nation, landscape and literature, 1840–1920. Ed. by Ann Donahue. *See* **9241.**

12649. EBEST, RON. Private histories: the writing of Irish Americans, 1900–1935. Notre Dame, IN: Notre Dame UP, 2005. pp. xi, 319.

12650. EDWARDS, BRENT HAYES. The practice of diaspora: literature, translation, and the rise of Black internationalism. (Bibl. 2004, 12690.) Rev. by Bennetta Jules-Rosette in RAL (36:2) 2005, 153–5; by Abdoulaye Gueye in AfSR (48:1) 2005, 199–202; by Kimberly Lamm in ColLit (32:4) 2005, 217–27.

12651. EDWARDS, JUSTIN. Gothic Canada: reading the spectre of a national literature. *See* **9242.**

12652. EDWARDS, JUSTIN D. Gothic passages: racial ambiguity and the American gothic. (Bibl. 2004, 12691.) Rev. by Russ Castronovo in PoeS (36) 2003, 118–21; by Jeffrey Andrew Weinstock in JFA (16:2) 2005, 165–9.

12653. —— IVISON, DOUGLAS (eds). Downtown Canada: writing Canadian cities. *See* **9243.**

12654. EK, AULI. Race and masculinity in contemporary American prison narratives. London; New York: Routledge, 2005. pp. ix, 148. (Studies in African American history and culture.)

12655. ELMER, JONATHAN. The Black Atlantic archive. *See* **8593.**

12656. EMIG, RAINER. Alien sex fiends: the metaphoricity of sexuality in postmodernity. EJES (9:3) 2005, 271–85.

12657. ENGLISH, DAYLANNE K.   Unnatural selections: eugenics in American Modernism and the Harlem renaissance. (Bibl. 2004, 12693.) Rev. by Johnny Williams in JAAH (90:4) 2005, 434–6; by Katherine Castles in JSH (71:3) 2005, 727–8.

12658. ENGLISH, JAMES F.   The economy of prestige: prizes, awards, and the circulation of cultural value. See 819.

12659. ERDAL, JENNIE.   Ghosting. See 821.

12660. ERKKILÄ, BETSY.   Mixed bloods and other crosses: rethinking American literature from the Revolution to the Culture Wars. See 7976.

12661. ERTLER, KLAUS-DIETER; LÖSCHNIGG, MARTIN (eds).   Canada in the sign of migration and trans-culturalism: from multi- to trans-culturalism. New York; Frankfurt: Lang, 2004. pp. 219. (Canadiana, 1.)

12662. ESPOSITO, EDOARDO (ed.).   Le letterature straniere nell'Italia dell'*entre-deux-guerres*: atti del Convegno di Milano, 26–27 febbraio e 1 marzo 2003. Lecce: Pensa MultiMedia, 2004. pp. 317. (Quaderni per leggere: Strumenti, 1:1.)

12663. ESTY, JOSHUA.   A shrinking island: Modernism and national culture in England. (Bibl. 2004, 12695.) Rev. by Martin Puchner in Mod/Mod (12:2) 2005, 352–3; by Erica L. Johnson in WSA (11) 2005, 186–92; by Jonathan Goodwin in MFS (51:3) 2005, 690–2; by Richard Greaves in RES (56:224) 2005, 340–1; by Raphaël Ingelbien in BELL (ns 3) 2005, 205–7.

12664. EVANS, BRAD.   Before cultures: the ethnographic imagination in American literature, 1865–1920. See 9249.

12665. EVANS, PATRICK.   Good keen men: weighing the cultural nationalists. HN (10:3/4) 2005, 10–16.

12666. ——— Whipping up a local culture: masochism and the cultural nationalists. Landfall (209) 2005, 137–52.

12667. EZELL, MARGARET J. M.   Eclectic circulation: the functional dynamics of manuscript and electronic literary cultures. In (pp. 27–35) 587.

12668. EZENWA-OHAETO.   Winging words: interviews with Nigerian writers. Ibadan: Kraft, 2003. pp. 172. Rev. by J. Roger Kurtz in WLT (79:3/4) 2005, 83.

12669. FABRE, GENEVIÈVE; BENESCH, KLAUS (eds).   African diasporas in the New and Old Worlds: consciousness and imagination. Amsterdam; Atlanta, GA: Rodopi, 2004. pp. xxi, 358. (Cross/cultures: readings in the post-colonial literatures in English, 69.) Rev. by Adele King in WLWE (40:2) 2005, 126–30.

12670. FARRELL, FRANK B.   Why does literature matter? (Bibl. 2004, 12701.) Rev. by Thomas Docherty in MLR (100:2) 2005, 467.

12671. FELSKI, RITA.   Literature after feminism. (Bibl. 2004, 12702.) Rev. by Meg Gardiner in Iris (47) 2003, 89–90; by Cristanne Miller in TCL (51:3) 2005, 373–7.

12672. FERENS, DOMINIKA; KOCIATKIEWICZ, JUSTYNA; KLIMEK-DOMINIAK, ELŻBIETA (eds).   Traveling subjects: American journeys in space and time. Cracow: Rabid, 2004. pp. 351.

12673. FERNÁNDEZ RODRÍGUEZ, CAROLINA.   The thematic tradition in Black British literature and its poetic representation. RAEI (16) 2003, 55–71.

12674. FERRALL, CHARLES; MILLAR, PAUL; SMITH, KEREN (eds). East by south: China in the Australasian imagination. Wellington: Victoria UP, 2005. pp. 439.

12675. FISCHER, HEINZ-D.; FISCHER, ERIKA J. Complete bibliographical manual of books about the Pulitzer Prizes, 1935–2003: monographs and anthologies on the coveted awards. Munich: Saur, 2004. pp. xxiv, 416. (Pulitzer Prize archive, 18.)

12676. FLANNERY, KATHRYN THOMS. Feminist literacies, 1968–75. Urbana: Illinois UP, 2005. pp. xxii, 254.

12677. FLOYD, JANET; FORSTER, LAUREL (eds). The recipe reader: narrative, contexts, traditions. *See* **9257.**

12678. FOLEY, BARBARA. Spectres of 1919: class and nation in the making of the New Negro. (Bibl. 2004, 12706.) Rev. by Jeffrey W. Miller in AL (77:1) 2005, 190–1.

12679. FRASER, RUSSELL. Moderns worth keeping. New Brunswick, NJ: Transaction, 2005. pp. xi, 195.

12680. FRAWLEY, OONA. Irish pastoral: nostalgia and twentieth-century Irish literature. Dublin; Portland, OR: Irish Academic Press, 2005. pp. vii, 206.

12681. FREDERICK, RHONDA D. 'Colón man a come': mythographies of Panama Canal migration. Lanham, MD: Lexington, 2005. pp. xxvi, 237. (Caribbean studies.)

12682. FRENCH, SCOT. The rebellious slave: Nat Turner in American memory. *See* **9260.**

12683. FROULA, CHRISTINE. Virginia Woolf and the Bloomsbury avant-garde: war, civilization, modernity. *See* **20354.**

12684. FRYKHOLM, AMY JOHNSON. Rapture culture: Left Behind in Evangelical America. (Bibl. 2004, 12720.) Rev. by Marshall W. Fishwick in JPC (38:5) 2005, 967–9.

12685. FULLER, DANIELLE. Writing the everyday: women's textual communities in Atlantic Canada. Montreal; Buffalo, NY; London: McGill-Queen's UP, 2004. pp. xi, 298.

12686. GALLAGHER, SUSAN VANZANTEN. Truth and reconciliation: the confessional mode in South African literature. (Bibl. 2004, 12721.) Rev. by Michael Battle in JR (84:2) 2004, 341–2.

12687. GARDINER, DAVID. 'The last summer': James Liddy's *Arena*. *See* **17823.**

12688. GARDNER, SARAH E. Blood & irony: Southern White women's narratives of the Civil War, 1861–1937. *See* **9265.**

12689. GARRITY, JANE. Step-daughters of England: British women Modernists and the national imaginary. (Bibl. 2004, 12724.) Rev. by Kristin Bluemel in ELT (48:1) 2005, 114–18; by Miranda B. Hickman in MFS (51:3) 2005, 693–6.

12690. GBEMISOLA, ADEOTI. The military in Nigeria's postcolonial literature: an overview. RAEI (16) 2003, 111–27.

12691. GEORGE, OLAKUNLE. Relocating agency: modernity and African letters. (Bibl. 2004, 12725.) Rev. by Sanya Osha in CLS (42:1) 2005, 100–4.

12692. GIBBONS, PETER. Early castings for a canon: some 1920s perceptions of New Zealand literary achievements. See **9266.**

12693. GIKANDI, SIMON. Africa and the epiphany of Modernism. In (pp. 31–50) **12640.**

12694. GILBERT, GEOFF. Before Modernism was: modern history and the constituency of writing. Basingstoke; New York: Palgrave Macmillan, 2004. pp. xviii, 222. (Language, discourse, society.) Rev. by Janine M. Utell in Mod/Mod (12:3) 2005, 515–17.

12695. GILROY, PAUL. After empire: melancholia or convivial culture? London; New York: Routledge, 2004. pp. xiv, 183. Rev. by Bhikhu Parekh in TLS, 9 Sept. 2005, 32.

12696. GIUNTA, EDVIGE (ed.). Writing with an accent: contemporary Italian American women authors. (Bibl. 2004, 12730.) Rev. by Ilaria Serra in Italica (82:1) 2005, 144–5.

12697. GLAJAR, VALENTINA; RADULESCU, DOMNICA (eds). Vampirettes, wretches, and Amazons: Western representations of East European women. Boulder, CO: East European Monographs; Lublin: Maria Curie-Skłodowska Univ., 2004. pp. vi, 252. Rev. by Moira Dimauro-Jackson in Comparatist (29) 2005, 157–8.

12698. GLASS, LOREN. Authors Inc.: literary celebrity in the modern United States, 1880–1980. (Bibl. 2004, 12731.) Rev. by Suzanne del Gizzo in HemR (24:1) 2004, 117–21; by Ronald Weber in JAH (92:2) 2005, 654.

12699. GOH, ROBBIE B. H.; WONG, SHAWN (eds). Asian diasporas: cultures, identities, representations. Hong Kong: Hong Kong UP, 2004. pp. vi, 208.

12700. GOLDBLATT, ROY. As plain as the nose on your face: the nose as the organ of othering. See **19146.**

12701. GOLDSWORTHY, KERRYN. Going global. See **9271.**

12702. GONZÁLEZ, GILBERT G. Culture of empire: American writers, Mexico, and Mexican immigrants, 1880–1930. See **9272.**

12703. GOODHEART, EUGENE. The cult of the ego: the self in modern literature. (Bibl. 1969, 2162.) New Brunswick, NJ: Transaction, 2005. pp. xviii, 225. (Second ed.: first ed. 1968.)

12704. GOPAL, PRIYAMVADA. Literary radicalism in India: gender, nation and the transition to independence. London; New York: Routledge, 2005. pp. xii, 177. (Routledge research in postcolonial literatures, 11.)

12705. GOTTSCHALL, JONATHAN; WILSON, DAVID SLOAN (eds). The literary animal: evolution and the nature of narrative. Forewords by E. O. Wilson and Frederick Crews. See **14807.**

12706. GRANDT, JÜRGEN E. Kinds of blue: the jazz aesthetic in African American narrative. Kent: Ohio State UP, 2004. pp. xix, 160.

12707. GREENWOOD, EMILY. Classics and the Atlantic Triangle: Caribbean readings of Greece and Rome via Africa. FMLS (40:4) 2004, 365–76.

12708. GREGSON, IAN. Postmodern literature. London; New York: Arnold, 2004. pp. xvii, 187. (Contexts.)

12709. GRUESSER, JOHN CULLEN. Confluences: postcolonialism, African American literary studies, and the Black Atlantic. Athens; London: Georgia UP, 2005. pp. xi, 177.

12710. GUNDY, JEFF. New maps of the territories: on Mennonite writing. GaR (57:4) 2003, 870–87 (review-article).

12711. GUNEW, SNEJA. 'Mouthwork': food and language as the corporeal home for the unhoused diasporic body in South Asian women's writing. JCL (40:2) 2005, 93–103.

12712. HABELL-PALLÁN, MICHELLE. Loca motion: the travels of Chicana and Latina popular culture. New York; London: New York UP, 2005. pp. x, 310.

12713. HADDOX, THOMAS F. Fears and fascinations: representing Catholicism in the American South. New York: Fordham UP, 2005. pp. ix, 225.

12714. HAMILTON, RICHARD PAUL; BREEN, MARGARET SÖNSER (eds). This thing of darkness: perspectives on evil and human wickedness. Amsterdam; Atlanta, GA: Rodopi, 2004. pp. xv, 159. (At the interface / Probing the boundaries.) Rev. by Claire Colebrook in EJES (9:1) 2005, 98–102.

12715. HAMILTON, STEPHEN (comp.). Annual bibliography of Commonwealth literature 2004: New Zealand. *See* **20566**.

12716. HAMMILL, FAYE. Literary culture and female authorship in Canada 1760–2000. *See* **7990**.

12717. HAMMOND, ANDREW. The Balkans and the West: constructing the European Other, 1945–2003. Aldershot; Burlington, VT: Ashgate, 2004. pp. xxiii, 236. Rev. by Tomislav Z. Longinovic in SlavR (64:4) 2005, 887–8.

12718. HARGREAVES, TRACY. Androgyny in modern literature. Basingstoke; New York: Palgrave Macmillan, 2005. pp. ix, 202.

12719. HARRIS-LOPEZ, TRUDIER. South of tradition: essays on African American literature. (Bibl. 2004, 12750.) Rev. by Jessica Williams in ColLit (32:1) 2005, 188–90; by Debra Walker King in SoLJ (37:2) 2005, 145–51; by Jennifer Denise Williams in MFS (51:3) 2005, 686–9; by Jean C. Griffith in SCR (22:1) 2005, 130–2.

12720. HARRISON-KAHAN, LORI. 'Drunk with the fiery rhythms of jazz': Anzia Yezierska, hybridity, and the Harlem renaissance. *See* **20531**.

12721. HARVEY, A. D. On the literary front. *See* **15606**.

12722. HAYTOCK, JENNIFER ANNE. At home, at war: domesticity and World War I in American literature. Athens: Ohio UP, 2003. pp. xviii, 147.

12723. HEER, JEET; WORCESTER, KENT (eds). Arguing comics: literary masters on a popular medium. *See* **87**.

12724. HELLER, DANA. Anatomies of rape. AmLH (16:2) 2004, 329–49 (review-article).

12725. HERNÁNDEZ-AVILA, INÉS (ed.). Reading Native American women: critical/creative representations. Lanham, MD; Toronto; Oxford: AltaMira Press, 2005. pp. ix, 275. (Contemporary Native American communities, 15.)

12726. HETHERINGTON, CAROL; PETERSSON, IRMTRAUD (comps). Annual bibliography of studies in Australian literature: 2004. *See* **21055**.

12727. HEYWOOD, CHRISTOPHER. A history of South African literature. Cambridge; New York: CUP, 2004. pp. xiv, 296. Rev. by Sophie Elmhirst in TLS, 14 Oct. 2005, 35; by Andrew van der Vlies in RES (56:226) 2005, 691–3; by Laura Wright in AfSR (48:3) 2005, 202–4.

12728. HIGONNET, MARGARET R. The 2005 ACLA Presidential Address: whose can(n)on? World War I and literary empires. CL (57:3) 2005, vi–xviii.

12729. HOBSON, FRED. *The Silencing of Emily Mullen* and other essays. Baton Rouge: Louisiana State UP, 2005. pp. xii, 217.

12730. HOGUE, W. LAWRENCE. The African American male, writing and difference: a polycentric approach to African American literature, criticism, and history. (Bibl. 2003, 12091.) Rev. by Miguel A. Segovia in AAR (38:4) 2004, 737–40.

12731. HOLLRAH, PATRICE E. M. 'The old lady trill, the victory yell': the power of women in Native American literature. (Bibl. 2004, 20534.) Rev. by Jo-Ann Episkenew in CanL (186) 2005, 142–3.

12732. HOOPER, GLENN (ed.). Landscape and empire 1770–2000. *See* 8005.

12733. HOPKINS, RICHARD. Book signing: the view from both sides of the table. *See* 404.

12734. HUNGERFORD, AMY. The Holocaust of texts: genocide, literature, and personification. (Bibl. 2004, 12772.) Rev. by Daniel T. O'Hara in JML (26:3/4) 2003, 154–8; by David Brauner in YES (35) 2005, 349–51; by Michael J. Kessler in ReLit (37:3) 2005, 113–15.

12735. HUSSAIN, YASMIN. Writing diaspora: South Asian women, culture, and ethnicity. Aldershot; Burlington, VT: Ashgate, 2005. pp. 148. (Studies in migration and diaspora.)

12736. HUTTON, CLARE (ed.). The Irish book in the twentieth century. *See* 892.

12737. IKIN, VAN; JORGENSEN, DARREN (comps). Annual bibliography of Commonwealth literature 2004: Australia. *See* 20569.

12738. IRELE, F. ABIOLA; GIKANDI, SIMON (eds). The Cambridge history of African and Caribbean literature. (Bibl. 2004, 12778.) Rev. by Gaurav Desai in RAL (36:3) 2005, 158–9; by Christopher L. Miller in AfSR (48:2) 2005, 181–3; by Sameer Rahim in TLS, 23 & 30 Dec. 2005, 29.

12739. IRVINE, DEAN (ed.). Canadian Modernists meet. Ottawa: Ottawa UP, 2005. pp. xv, 363. (Re-appraisals: Canadian writers, 29.)

12740. IZZO, DAVID GARRETT. Christopher Isherwood encyclopedia. *See* 17161.

12741. JAFFE, AARON. Modernism and the culture of celebrity. Cambridge; New York: CUP, 2004. pp. xi, 248.

12742. JARRAWAY, DAVID R. Going the distance: dissident subjectivity in Modernist American literature. (Bibl. 2003, 12112.) Rev. by Paulette Gergen Lane in JML (26:3/4) 2003, 169–72; by Daniel Morris in WCWR (25:1) 2005, 97–100.

12743. JOHNSON, DAVID (ed.). The popular & the canonical: debating twentieth-century literature 1940–2000. London; New York: Routledge in assn with the Open UP, 2005. pp. vi, 452.

12744. JOHNSON, GREG. Modern writers, modern lives. *See* **20973.**

12745. JOHNSTON, ALLAN. Consumption, addiction, vision, energy: political economies and utopian visions in the writings of the Beat Generation. ColLit (32:2) 2005, 103–26.

12746. JONES, LAWRENCE. Picking up the traces: the making of a New Zealand literary culture, 1932–1945. (Bibl. 2004, 12791.) Rev. by Bruce King in JPW (41:1) 2005, 113–23.

12747. JOUSNI, STÉPHANE; GOARZIN, ANNE (eds). Voix et langues dans la littérature irlandaise. Rennes: Presses Universitaires de Rennes, 2003. pp. 162. (Interférences.) Rev. by Françoise Canon-Roger in EtIr (30:1) 2005, 224–5.

12748. JOVANOVICH, WILLIAM. The temper of the West: a memoir. (Bibl. 2004, 12793.) Rev. by William Cloonan in SAtlR (70:1) 2005, 151–4.

12749. JUHASZ, SUZANNE. A desire for women: relational psychoanalysis, writing, and relationships between women. (Bibl. 2003, 12124.) Rev. by Susan Fraiman in AL (77:1) 2005, 206–8.

12750. KADAR, MARLENE, *et al.* (eds). Tracing the autobiographical. Waterloo, Ont.: Wilfrid Laurier UP, 2005. pp. viii, 276. (Life writing.)

12751. KANG, NANCY. 'As if I had entered a Paradise': fugitive slave narratives and cross-border literary history. *See* **10419.**

12752. KAPLAN, E. ANN. Trauma culture: the politics of terror and loss in media and literature. New Brunswick, NJ: Rutgers UP, 2005. pp. viii, 192.

12753. KELLEY, GREG. Tall tales from Cheapside: Falstaff's lying legacy in American Southern literature. *See* **9311.**

12754. KELLMAN, STEVEN G. (ed.). Switching languages: translingual writers reflect on their craft. (Bibl. 2003, 12130.) Rev. by Martha J. Cutter in ColLit (32:2) 2005, 199–201; by Daniel Pantano in Style (39:1) 2005, 95–7.

12755. KEOWN, MICHELLE. Postcolonial Pacific writing: representations of the body. London; New York: Routledge, 2005. pp. xiv, 237. (Routledge research in postcolonial literatures, 9.) Rev. by Chris Prentice in JNZL (23:2) 2005, 109–17.

12756. KERBEL, SORREL (ed.); EMANUEL, MURIEL; PHILLIPS, LAURA (asst eds). Jewish writers of the twentieth century. (Bibl. 2004, 12801.) Rev. by Alice Nakhimowsky in SEEJ (49:2) 2005, 326–7.

12757. KEREN, MICHAEL. The citizen's voice: twentieth-century politics and literature. Calgary, Alta: Calgary UP, 2003. pp. 173. Rev. by Modris Eksteins in LRC (12:6) 2004, 11–12.

12758. KERESZTESI, RITA. Strangers at home: American ethnic Modernism between the World Wars. Lincoln; London: Nebraska UP, 2005. pp. xxii, 224.

12759. KHOO, TSEEN-LING. Banana bending: Asian Australian and Asian Canadian literatures. Montreal; Buffalo, NY; London: McGill-Queen's UP, 2003. pp. viii, 223. Rev. by Radhika Mohanram in ALS (22:1) 2005, 122–3.

12760. KING, BRUCE. Kiwi nationalism and identity. JPW (41:1) 2005, 113–23 (review-article).

12761. KING, BRUCE ALVIN. The internationalization of English literature. (Bibl. 2004, 12802.) Rev. by C. L. Innes in RAL (36:4) 2005, 240–1.

12762. KINGSBURY, CELIA M. 'In close touch with her government': women and the domestic science movement in World War One propaganda. *In* (pp. 88–101) **9257**.

12763. KIRK, JOHN. Twentieth-century writing and the British working class. Cardiff: UP of Wales, 2003. pp. viii, 224. Rev. by Simon Kövesi in EJES (9:1) 2005, 102–5; by Clive Behagg in LitH (14:2) 2005, 93; by Alf Louvre in YES (35) 2005, 351–2.

12764. KIRK, STEPHEN. Scribblers: stalking the authors of Appalachia. Winston-Salem, NC: Blair, 2004. pp. 248. Rev. by Reneé Critcher in Now (21:1) 2005, 30–1.

12765. KLAUS, H. GUSTAV; KNIGHT, STEPHEN (eds). 'To hell with culture': anarchism in twentieth-century British literature. Cardiff: UP of Wales, 2005. pp. ix, 214. Rev. by Bharat Tandon in TLS, 7 Oct. 2005, 30.

12766. KLIMASMITH, BETSY. At home in the city: urban domesticity in American literature and culture, 1850–1930. *See* **9317**.

12767. KOVAL, RAMONA (ed.). Tasting life twice: conversations with remarkable writers. Sydney: ABC for the Australian Broadcasting Corporation, 2005. pp. vii, 357.

12768. KRUPNICK, MARK. Jewish writing and the deep places of the imagination. Ed. by Jean K. Carney and Mark Shechner. Madison; London: Wisconsin UP, 2005. pp. xvii, 363.

12769. KUGELMASS, JACK (ed.). Key texts in American Jewish culture. New Brunswick, NJ: Rutgers UP, 2003. pp. vii, 308. Rev. by Andrew Gordon in AJH (92:1) 2004, 135–8.

12770. LALLA, BARBARA. Creole and respec' in the development of Jamaican literary discourse. *See* **3127**.

12771. LAMBERT, GREGG. The return of baroque in modern culture. London; New York: Continuum, 2004. pp. 168.

12772. LAROCQUE-POIRIER, JOANNE. John Buchan's legacy: the Governor-General's Literary Awards. *See* **15609**.

12773. LAURENCE, PATRICIA. Lily Briscoe's Chinese eyes: Bloomsbury, Modernism, and China. (Bibl. 2004, 12809.) Rev. by Diane Gillespie in VWM (66) 2004, 31–2; by Randi Saloman in WSA (11) 2005, 216–19; by Urmila Seshagiri in MFS (51:3) 2005, 699–703; by Lidan Lin in Mod/Mod (12:4) 2005, 705–11.

12774. LAWLOR, WILLIAM T. (ed.). Beat culture: lifestyles, icons, and impact. Santa Barbara, CA: ABC-CLIO, 2005. pp. liv, 392.

12775. LAWRENCE, KEITH; CHEUNG, FLOYD (eds). Recovered legacies: authority and identity in early Asian American literature. Philadelphia, PA: Temple UP, 2005. pp. xii, 308. (Asian American history and culture.)

12776. LEAK, JEFFREY B. Racial myths and masculinity in African American literature. Knoxville: Tennessee UP, 2005. pp. 160.

12777. LEE, JAMES KYUNG-JIN. Urban triage: race and the fictions of multiculturalism. Minneapolis; London: Minnesota UP, 2004. pp. xxx, 254. (Critical American studies.) Rev. by Anita Mannur in JAAS (8:1) 2005, 106–9; by Andrew P. Hoberek in TCL (51:3) 2005, 378–84.

12778. LEMBERT, ALEXANDRA. The heritage of Hermes: alchemy in contemporary British literature. Berlin; Cambridge, MA: Galda & Wilch, 2004. pp. ii, 261. (Leipzig explorations in literature and culture, 10.)

12779. LEONARD, FRANCES; CEARLEY, RAMONA (eds). Conversations with Texas writers. Introd. by Joe Holley. Austin: Texas UP, 2005. pp. ix, 422. (Jack and Doris Smothers series in Texas history, life, and culture, 16.) Rev. by Twister Marquiss in TBR (25:1/2) 2005, 19.

12780. LEWIS, COREY LEE. Reading the trail: exploring the literature and natural history of the California Crest. Reno: Nevada UP, 2005. pp. xiv, 241. (Environmental arts and humanities.)

12781. LEWIS, LEON (ed.). Robert M. Young: essays on the films. See **13950**.

12782. LEWIS, NATHANIEL. Unsettling the literary West: authenticity and authorship. (Bibl. 2004, 12814.) Rev. by J. David Stevens in GPQ (24:3) 2004, 213; by Blake Allmendinger in AL (77:1) 2005, 202–3; by Gregory Wright in SAIL (17:1) 2005, 122–4; by Jan Goggans in PacHR (74:4) 2005, 663–4.

12783. LI, GUICANG. Review of the national perspective on Chinese American identity. FLS (114) 2005, 52–7. (In Chinese.)

12784. LINETT, MAREN. Introduction: Modernism's Jews / Jewish Modernisms. MFS (51:2) 2005, 249–57.

12785. LIU, YABIN. Culture representation in postcolonial literatures. FLS (114) 2005, 114–20. (In Chinese.)

12786. LIU, YU. A review of American eco-literature and ecocriticism. See **14887**.

12787. LLOYD, DAVID. The indigent sublime: specters of Irish hunger. See **10382**.

12788. LLOYD, ROSEMARY. Shimmering in a transformed light: writing the still life. See **9330**.

12789. LOOMBA, ANIA, et al. (eds). Postcolonial Studies and beyond. Durham, NC; London: Duke UP, 2005. pp. x, 499.

12790. LÓPEZ ROPERO, LOURDES. Diaspora: concept, context, and its application in the study of new literatures. RAEI (16) 2003, 215–25.

12791. LOUIS, WM ROGER (ed.). Yet more adventures with Britannia: personalities, politics, and culture in Britain. London; New York: Tauris, 2005. pp. x, 419. Rev. by Michael Howard in TLS, 18 Nov. 2005, 24.

12792. LOWE, JOHN. 'Pulling in the natural environment': an interview with Pinkie Gordon Lane. See **17566**.

12793. —— (ed.). Bridging Southern cultures: an interdisciplinary approach. Baton Rouge: Louisiana State UP, 2005. pp. xiii, 317. (Southern literary studies.)

12794. LYE, COLLEEN. America's Asia: racial form and American literature, 1893–1945. See **9332**.

12795. MCCANN, ANDREW. The obstinacy of the sacred. See **11544**.

12796. MCGILL, LISA D. Constructing Black selves: Caribbean American narratives and the second generation. New York; London: New York UP, 2005. pp. ix, 318. (Nation of newcomers.)

12797. McGraw, Eliza R. L.   Two covenants: representations of Southern Jewishness. Baton Rouge: Louisiana State UP, 2005. pp. x, 194. (Southern literary studies.)

12798. McIlvanney, Liam; Ryan, Ray (eds).   Ireland and Scotland: culture and society, 1700–2000. *See* **8023.**

12799. McKinley, James Conrad (ed.).   Southern excursions: views on Southern letters in my time. (Bibl. 2004, 12828.) Rev. by Sam Pickering in SoCult (10:3) 2004, 99–102.

12800. McLeod, John.   Postcolonial London: rewriting the metropolis. (Bibl. 2004, 12829.) Rev. by Bénédicte Ledent in EJES (9:3) 2005, 327–9.

12801. McMaster, Juliet.   What Daisy knew: the epistemology of the child writer. *In* (pp. 51–69) **9164.**

12802. McPherson, Tara.   Reconstructing Dixie: race, gender, and nostalgia in the imagined South. (Bibl. 2004, 12831.) Rev. by Jeffrey W. Miller in AL (77:1) 2005, 190–1; by Hollis Griffin in VLT (55) 2005, 68–70; by Harriet Pollack in SCR (22:1) 2005, 139–41.

12803. MacSkimming, Roy.   The perilous trade: publishing Canada's writers. *See* **922.**

12804. Marazzi, Martino.   Voices of Italian America: a history of early Italian American literature with a critical anthology. Trans. by Ann Goldstein. (Bibl. 2004, 12837.) Rev. by Ilaria Serra in ItalA (23:2) 2005, 238–9.

12805. Marcus, Laura; Nicholls, Peter (eds).   The Cambridge history of twentieth-century English literature. (Bibl. 2004, 12838.) Rev. by John Sutherland in TLS, 4 Mar. 2005, 28.

12806. Marino, John B.   The Grail legend in modern literature. Woodbridge, Suffolk; Rochester, NY: Brewer, 2004. pp. vi, 165. (Arthurian studies, 59.) Rev. by K. Sarah-Jane Murray in TMR, Sept. 2005.

12807. Martin, Ronald E.   The languages of difference: American writers and anthropologists reconfigure the primitive, 1878–1940. *See* **9345.**

12808. Martinez, Manuel Luis.   Countering the counterculture: rereading postwar dissent from Jack Kerouac to Tomás Rivera. (Bibl. 2004, 12840.) Rev. by Robert Bennett in ColLit (32:2) 2005, 177–84.

12809. Martin-Rodriguez, Manuel M.   Life in search of readers: reading (in) Chicano/a literature. (Bibl. 2004, 12841.) Rev. by Lee Bebout in MFS (51:3) 2005, 669–72.

12810. Marx, John.   Postcolonial literature and the Western literary canon. *In* (pp. 83–96) **14876.**

12811. Marzola, Alessandra (ed.).   Guerra e identità: percorsi nella letteratura inglese del Novecento. Rome: Carocci, 2005. pp. 228. (Lingue e letterature Carocci, 500.)

12812. Matthews, Steven.   Modernism. London; New York: Arnold, 2004. pp. 192. (Contexts.)

12813. Mazza, Cris.   Finding the chic in lit. *In* (pp. 155–69) **3749.**

12814. Meredith, James H. (ed.).   Understanding the literature of World War I: a student casebook to issues, sources & historical documents.

Westport, CT; London: Greenwood Press, 2004. pp. xix, 183. (Literature in context.)
Rev. by Thomas Coakley in WLA (17:1/2) 2005, 343–5.

12815. MERMANN-JOZWIAK, ELISABETH. Postmodern vernaculars: Chicana literature and postmodern rhetoric. New York; Frankfurt: Lang, 2005. pp. viii, 147.

12816. MEYERS, JEFFREY. George Orwell and the art of writing. *See* **18688.**

12817. MEZU, ROSE URE (ed.). A history of Africana women's literature: essays on poetry, gender, religion, feminism, aesthetics, politics, moral values, African tradition & diaspora. Baltimore, MD: Black Academy Press, 2004. pp. 364.

12818. MICHAELS, WALTER BENN. The shape of the signifier: 1967 to the end of history. (Bibl. 2004, 12847.) Rev. by Samuel Cohen in TCL (51:1) 2005, 98–104; by Robin J. Sowards in MinnR (63/64) 2005, 225–38.

12819. MIEDER, WOLFGANG; BRYAN, GEORGE B. A dictionary of Anglo-American proverbs and proverbial phrases found in literary sources of the nineteenth and twentieth centuries. *See* **3452.**

12820. MILLER, CRISTANNE. Cultures of Modernism: Marianne Moore, Mina Loy, & Elsa Lasker-Schüler: gender and literary community in New York and Berlin. *See* **18318.**

12821. MILLER, D. QUENTIN (ed.). Prose and cons: essays on prison literature in the United States. Jefferson, NC; London: McFarland, 2005. pp. viii, 280.

12822. MILLER, DANNY L.; HATFIELD, SHARON; NORMAN, GURNEY (eds). An American vein: critical readings in Appalachian literature. Athens: Ohio UP, 2005. pp. xvii, 400. Rev. by Michael Pringle in RMER (59:2) 2005.

12823. MINOGUE, SALLY. Portrait of the artist: Ivor Gurney as modern maker. *See* **16847.**

12824. MODJESKA, DRUSILLA. PNG writing, writing PNG. Meanjin (62:3) 2003, 46–54. (Focus on Papua New Guinea.)

12825. MORARU, CHRISTIAN. Memorious discourse: reprise and representation in postmodernism. Madison, NJ: Fairleigh Dickinson UP, 2005. pp. 282.

12826. MORGAN, BILL. The Beat Generation in San Francisco: a literary tour. Introd. by Lawrence Ferlinghetti. San Francisco, CA: City Lights, 2003. pp. xv, 232.

12827. MORGAN, STACY I. Rethinking social realism: African American art and literature, 1930–1953. Athens; London: Georgia UP, 2004. pp. x, 356. Rev. by David Krasner in JAH (91:4) 2005, 1517–18; by 'BioDun J. Ogundayo in AAR (39:3) 2005, 475–7; by Bill V. Mullen in SAtlR (70:3) 2005, 141–4.

12828. MORTENSON, ERIK. Capturing the fleeting moment: photography in the work of Allen Ginsberg. *See* **16698.**

12829. MOSS, LAURA (ed.). Is Canada postcolonial? Unsettling Canadian literature. (Bibl. 2004, 12852.) Rev. by Faye Hammill in BJCS (17:2) 2004, 256.

12830. MOYA, PAULA M. L. 'This is not your country!': nation and belonging in Latina/o literature. AmLH (17:1) 2005, 183–95 (review-article).

12831. NADELL, MARTHA JANE. Enter the New Negroes: images of race in American culture. Cambridge, MA; London: Harvard UP, 2004. pp. xii, 199. Rev. by Michelle D. Commander in JPC (38:6) 2005, 1104–5.

12832. NALBANTIAN, SUZANNE. Memory in literature: from Rousseau to neuroscience. *See* **9360**.

12833. NEUMAN, KLAUS. 'Thinking the forbidden concept': refugees as immigrants and exiles. Antipodes (19:1) 2005, 6–11.

12834. NEW, W. H. Grandchild of empire: about irony, mainly in the Commonwealth. Vancouver: Ronsdale Press, 2003. pp. 92. (Garnett Sedgewick Memorial Lectures: 2002.)

12835. NEWELL, STEPHANIE. Literary culture in colonial Ghana: how to play the game of life. (Bibl. 2004, 12861.) Rev. by Ray Kea in AfSR (46:3) 2003, 160–3.

12836. NGAI, SIANNE. The cuteness of the avant-garde. *See* **19595**.

12837. NIELSEN, ALDON LYNN. The future of an allusion: the color of modernity. *In* (pp. 17–30) **12640**.

12838. —— Integral music: languages of African American innovation. Tuscaloosa; London: Alabama UP, 2004. pp. 218. (Modern and contemporary poetics.)

12839. NJEGOSH, TATIANA PETROVICH. Cultura e razza nel rinascimento di Harlem: identità e creatività come *mongrelization*. *In* (pp. 156–74) **14377**.

12840. OCHNER, NOBUKO; RIDGEWAY, WILLIAM N. (eds). Confluence: studies from East to West in honor of V. H. Viglielmo. Honolulu: Hawai'i UP, 2005. pp. xiv, 272.

12841. O'CONNELL, NICHOLAS. On sacred ground: the spirit of place in Pacific Northwest literature. (Bibl. 2004, 12866.) Rev. by Harold P. Simonson in PacHR (73:3) 2004, 498–9; by Nancy Pagh in WAL (39:2) 2004, 236–7.

12842. Ó DRISCEOIL, DONAL. 'The best banned in the land': censorship and Irish writing since 1950. YES (35) 2005, 146–60.

12843. O'DWYER, ELLA. The rising of the moon: the language of power. (Bibl. 2003, 12209.) Rev. by Gregory Dobbins in ILS (24:2) 2005, 7–8.

12844. OLSTER, STACEY MICHELE. The trash phenomenon: contemporary literature, popular culture, and the making of the American century. Athens; London: Georgia UP, 2003. pp. x, 299.

12845. O'NEILL, ANGELINE. Distinguishing the map from the territory. *In* (pp. 247–63) **3749**.

12846. ORESTANO, FRANCESCA (ed.). La parola e lo sguardo nella letteratura inglese tra Ottocento e modernismo. *See* **9366**.

12847. OSTEEN, MARK. Introduction: Blue notes toward a new jazz discourse. Genre (37:1) 2004, 1–46.

12848. OWEN, ALEX. The place of enchantment: British occultism and the culture of the modern. *See* **9368**.

12849. PANOFSKY, RUTH. Barometers of change: Presidents Hugh Eayrs and John Gray of the Macmillan Company of Canada. *See* **951**.

12850. PAPAYANIS, MARILYN ADLER. Writing in the margins: the ethics of expatriation from Lawrence to Ondaatje. *See* **17621**.

12851. PARINI, JAY (ed.). British writers: supplement x. New York: Scribner's Sons, 2004. pp. lvi, 455.

12852. —— British writers: supplement XI. New York: Scribner's Sons, 2005. pp. lvi, 456.

12853. PARKER, ROBERT DALE. The invention of Native American literature. (Bibl. 2004, 12874.) Rev. by Lori Burlingame in GPQ (24:1) 2004, 64; by Bud Hirsch in SAIL (17:1) 2005, 93–8.

12854. PELAN, REBECCA. Two Irelands: literary feminisms North and South. Syracuse, NY: Syracuse UP, 2005. pp. xxxiv, 203. (Irish studies.)

12855. PERERA, S. W. (comp.). Annual bibliography of Commonwealth literature 2004: Sri Lanka. See **20584**.

12856. PÉREZ FIRMAT, GUSTAVO. Tongue ties: logo-eroticism in Anglo-Hispanic literature. (Bibl. 2004, 12884.) Rev. by Ralph Rodriguez in CLS (42:2) 2005, 316–20.

12857. PHILLIPS, LAWRENCE. Introduction: the swarming streets: twentieth-century literary representations of London. *In* (pp. 1–6) **14254**.

12858. PINSKER, SANFORD. The revisionist memory. GaR (57:3) 2003, 635–41 (review-article).

12859. PLATE, LIEDEKE. Intermedial Woolf: text, image, and in-between. *See* **20399**.

12860. PLEASANTS, BEN. Visceral Bukowski: inside the sniper landscapes of L.A. writers. *See* **15616**.

12861. PODDAR, PREM; JOHNSON, DAVID (eds). A historical companion to postcolonial thought in English. New York: Columbia UP, 2005. pp. xxvii, 574, (plates) 6.

12862. POPLAWSKI, PAUL (ed.). Encyclopedia of literary Modernism. (Bibl. 2004, 12896.) Rev. by John Wrighton in Eng (54:208) 2005, 72–6.

12863. PORTER, JOY; ROEMER, KENNETH M. (eds). The Cambridge companion to Native American literature. Cambridge; New York: CUP, 2005. pp. xviii, 343.

12864. POWELL, JOHN (ed.). Dictionary of literary influences: the twentieth century, 1914–2000. (Bibl. 2004, 12897.) Rev. by John Wrighton in Eng (54:208) 2005, 72–6.

12865. PREIS-SMITH, AGATA; PARYZ, MAREK (eds). The poetics of America: explorations in the literature and culture of the United States. *See* **9385**.

12866. PRIEBE, RICHARD K. Literature, community, and violence: reading African literature in the West, post-9/11. RAL (36:2) 2005, 46–58.

12867. PRINCE, VALERIE SWEENEY. Burnin' down the house: home in African American literature. New York: Columbia UP, 2004. pp. x, 153.

12868. PROCHÁZKA, MARTIN; PILNÝ, ONDŘEJ (eds). Time refigured: myths, foundation texts and imagined communities. Prague: Litteraria Pragensia Books, 2005. pp. 383.

12869. PRYOR, WILLIAM. The living memes and jeans of Bloomsbury and neo-paganism. *See* **20403**.

12870. QUANTIC, DIANE D.; HAFEN, P. JANE (eds). A Great Plains reader. Lincoln; London: Nebraska UP, 2003. pp. xxii, 730. Rev. by Debbie A. Hanson in WF (64:1/2) 2005, 136–8.

12871. QUAYSON, ATO. Calibrations: reading for the social. (Bibl. 2004, 12903.) Rev. by Deepika Bahri in MFS (51:1) 2005, 222–5.

12872. QUAYUM, M. A. Saul Bellow and American Transcendentalism. *See* **15451.**

12873. RABAN, JONATHAN. Thinking about documentary: notes toward a lecture. *See* **15090.**

12874. RAINEY, LAWRENCE (ed.). Modernism: an anthology. Oxford; Malden, MA: Blackwell, 2005. pp. xxxii, 1181. (Blackwell anthologies.)

12875. RAPHAEL-HERNANDEZ, HEIKE (ed.). Blackening Europe: the African American presence. Foreword by Paul Gilroy. (Bibl. 2004, 12908.) Rev. by Jeffrey Geiger in MELUS (30:1) 2005, 254–7.

12876. REDSHAW, THOMAS DILLON. 'We done our best when we were let': James Liddy's *Arena*, 1963–1965. *See* **17827.**

12877. REED, CHRISTOPHER. Bloomsbury rooms: Modernism, subculture, and domesticity. New Haven, CT; London: Yale UP for the Bard Graduate Center for Studies in the Decorative Arts, Design, and Culture, 2004. pp. viii, 314. Rev. by Randy Gener in VWM (66) 2004, 32–3.

12878. REGAN, STEPHEN (ed.). Irish writing: an anthology of Irish literature in English 1789–1939. *See* **8051.**

12879. REISNER, ROSALIND. Jewish American literature: a guide to reading interests. Westport, CT: Libraries Unlimited, 2004. pp. xviii, 339. (Genreflecting advisory series.)

12880. REVELLI, GIORGETTA (ed.). Da Ulisse a …: la città e il mare, dalla Liguria al mondo: atti del convegno internazionale (Imperia, 7–9 ottobre 2004). *See* **9393.**

12881. REVIE, LINDA L. The Niagara companion: explorers, artists and writers at the Falls from discovery through the twentieth century. *See* **9394.**

12882. REYNIER, CHRISTINE. La citation *in absentia* à l'œuvre dans *Atonement* de Ian McEwan. *See* **17971.**

12883. RICCIARDI, CATERINA; VELLUCCI, SABRINA (eds). Miti americani oggi. Reggio Emilia: Diabasis, 2005. pp. 343. (I muri bianchi.)

12884. RIEMENSCHNEIDER, DIETER. Global fantasy – glocal imagination: the new literatures in English and their fantastic imagiNations. JPW (41:1) 2005, 14–25.

12885. RIQUELME, JOHN PAUL. Introduction to *Reading Modernism, after Hugh Kenner (1923–2003)*. *See* **14984.**

12886. RODRÍGUEZ, MARÍA CRISTINA. What women lose: exile and the construction of imaginary homelands in novels by Caribbean writers. New York; Frankfurt: Lang, 2005. pp. xxii, 200. (Caribbean studies, 6.)

12887. ROSEN, ALAN. Sounds of defiance: the Holocaust, multilingualism, and the problem of English. Lincoln; London: Nebraska UP, 2005. pp. xiv, 248.

12888. ROSENBAUM, S. P. Georgian Bloomsbury. (Bibl. 2004, 12922.) Rev. by Molly Youngkin in ELT (48:2) 2005, 232–5.

12889. ROSENDALE, STEVEN (ed.). American radical and reform writers. *See* **9401.**

12890. ROSNER, VICTORIA.   Modernism and the architecture of private life. *See* **20409.**

12891. ROUSSEAU, GEORGE S.   Nervous acts: essays on literature, culture, and sensibility. Basingstoke; New York: Palgrave Macmillan, 2004. pp. xii, 395.

12892. ROYSTER, JACQUELINE JONES; SIMPKINS, ANN MARIE MANN (eds). Calling cards: theory and practice in studies of race, gender, and culture. *See* **2457.**

12893. RUBIN, DEREK (ed.).   Who we are: on being (and not being) a Jewish American writer. New York: Schocken, 2005. pp. xix, 345.

12894. RUBIN, LOIS E.   Coming of age: the creative development of seven Jewish women writers and their characters. *In* (pp. 45–57) **12895.**

12895. —— (ed.).   Connections and collisions: identities in contemporary Jewish American women's writing. Newark: Delaware UP, 2005. pp. 260.

12896. RUGGIERI, FRANCA (ed.).   Dal vittorianesimo al modernismo: la cultura letteraria inglese (1830–1950). *See* **9403.**

12897. RUSSO, JOHN PAUL.   The future without a past: the humanities in a technological society. *See* **16045.**

12898. RYAN, JUDITH; WALLACE-CRABBE, CHRIS (eds).   Imagining Australia: literature and culture in the new New World. (Bibl. 2004, 12927.) Rev. by Kerryn Goldsworthy in Meanjin (64:3) 2005, 103–8.

12899. RYAN, JUDYLYN S.   Spirituality as ideology in Black women's film and literature. Charlottesville; London: Virginia UP, 2005. pp. xi, 193.

12900. RYAN, MARIE-LAURE (ed.).   Narrative across media: the languages of storytelling. (Bibl. 2004, 12928.) Rev. by Jennifer Bay in MFS (51:3) 2005, 721–4.

12901. SABIN, MARGERY.   Anthologies of modern Indian literature. CE (68:1) 2005, 90–106 (review-article).

12902. SALMON, CATHERINE.   Crossing the abyss: erotica and the intersection of evolutionary psychology and literary studies. *In* (pp. 244–57) **14807.**

12903. SALSKA, AGNIESZKA (ed.).   Historia literatury amerykańskiej xx wieku. (A history of twentieth-century American literature.) Cracow: Universitas, 2003. 2 vols. pp. 667, (plates) 16; 814, (plates) 20.

12904. SAMPIETRO, LUIGI.   Divagazioni americane. *In* (pp. 51–63) **12662.**

12905. SARAT, AUSTIN; DOUGLAS, LAWRENCE; UMPHREY, MARTHA MERRILL (eds).   Law on the screen. *See* **13368.**

12906. SAWAYA, FRANCESCA.   Modern women, modern work: domesticity, professionalism, and American writing, 1890–1950. (Bibl. 2004, 12935.) Rev. by Anne E. Boyd in Legacy (22:1) 2005, 88–9; by Susan Albertine in JAH (91:4) 2005, 1515–16.

12907. SCAFE, SUZANNE (comp.).   Annual bibliography of Commonwealth literature 2004: the Caribbean. *See* **20588.**

12908. SCHMIDT, BERNARD.   American literary personalism: emergence and decline. *See* **9408.**

12909. SCHUDSON, MICHAEL.   American dreams. AmLH (16:3) 2004, 566–73 (review-article).

12910. Schwarz, A. B. Christa. Gay voices of the Harlem renaissance. (Bibl. 2004, 12939.) Rev. by Mason Stokes in AmLH (17:1) 2005, 171–82.

12911. Seaman, Donna. Writers on the air: conversations about books. Philadelphia, PA: Dry, 2005. pp. xvi, 467.

12912. Shackleton, Mark; Supinen, Veera (eds). First and other nations: articles based on the Canada seminar 'First Nations: Symbolic Representations', at the University of Helsinki, March 1–2, 2002. Helsinki: Renvall Inst., 2005. pp. v, 170. (Renvall Inst. pubs, 20.)

12913. Shamsie, Muneeza. Annual bibliography of Commonwealth literature 2004: Pakistan 2001–04. See **20589**.

12914. Shankar, S. Midnight's orphans; or, A postcolonialism worth its name. See **19279**.

12915. Shannon, Drew Patrick. The lightly attached web: the fictional Virginia Woolf. See **20418**.

12916. Shepard, Deborah (ed.). Between the lives: partners in art. Auckland: Auckland UP, 2005. pp. ix, 246. Rev. by Bridie Lonie in Landfall (210) 2005, 179–84.

12917. Sherry, Vincent. The Great War and the language of Modernism. (Bibl. 2004, 12947.) Rev. by Meg Albrinck in Novel (37:3) 2004, 360–2; by Leonard Diepeveen in ELT (48:3) 2005, 339–42.

12918. Sherry, Vincent B. Liberal measures: language, Modernism, and the Great War. In (pp. 9–23) **12946**.

12919. —— (ed.). The Cambridge companion to the literature of the First World War. Cambridge; New York: CUP, 2005. pp. xviii, 322. (Cambridge companions to literature.) Rev. by Guy Cuthbertson in RES (56:227) 2005, 801–2.

12920. Shiach, Morag. Modernism, labour, and selfhood in British literature and culture, 1890–1930. (Bibl. 2004, 12948.) Rev. by Gary Day in TLS, 23 Sept. 2005, 27; by Lisa Hager in ELT (48:3) 2005, 352–6.

12921. Shu, Yuan. Globalization and 'Asian values': teaching and theorizing Asian American literature. ColLit (32:1) 2005, 86–102.

12922. Shumway, David R. Modern love: romance, intimacy, and the marriage crisis. (Bibl. 2004, 12950.) Rev. by Eva Illouz in MFS (51:1) 2005, 243–6; by Andrew Hoberek in SAtlR (70:1) 2005, 161–5.

12923. Sim, Stuart (ed.). The Routledge companion to postmodernism. (Bibl. 1999,1948.) London; New York: Routledge, 2005. pp. xiv, 349. (Routledge companions.) (Second ed.: first ed. 1999.) (Orig. pub. as *The Routledge Critical Dictionary of Postmodern Thought*.)

12924. Skerl, Jennie (ed.). Reconstructing the Beats. (Bibl. 2004, 12953.) Rev. by Robert Bennett in ColLit (32:2) 2005, 177–84; by Jonah Raskin in AmS (46:2) 2005, 197–8.

12925. Smethurst, James Edward. The Black Arts Movement: literary nationalism in the 1960s and 1970s. Chapel Hill; London: North Carolina UP, 2005. pp. xv, 471. (John Hope Franklin series in African American history and culture.) Rev. by Gene Jarrett in AmQ (57:4) 2005, 1243–51.

12926. SMITH, ANDREW. Migrancy, hybridity, and postcolonial literary studies. *In* (pp. 241–61) **14876.**

12927. SMITH, ANNA; WEVERS, LYDIA (eds). On display: new essays in Cultural Studies. (Bibl. 2004, 12955.) Rev. by Ruth Brown in WLWE (40:1) 2002/03, 147–8.

12928. SMITH, JOHN; COHN, DEBORAH (eds). Look away! The US South in New World Studies. Durham, NC; London: Duke UP, 2004. pp. xii, 521. (New Americanists.) Rev. by David A. Davis in SoCult (11:3) 2005, 104–8; by Harilaos Stecopoulos in AmQ (57:4) 2005, 1201–10.

12929. SMITH, STAN. Epic *logos*: on first looking into several Homers. *See* **11535.**

12930. SPAHR, JULIANA. Connected disconnection and localized globalism in Pacific multilingual literature. *See* **19731.**

12931. SPILLERS, HORTENSE J. Black, white, and in color: essays in American literature and culture. (Bibl. 2003, 12287.) Rev. by Kimberly Lamm in ColLit (32:4) 2005, 217–27.

12932. STAVANS, ILAN. Conversations with Ilan Stavans. Tucson: Arizona UP, 2005. pp. 216.

12933. STELLA, REGIS. Untying the cultural knot. Meanjin (62:3) 2003, 178–82.

12934. STEPHAN, HALINA (ed.). Living in translation: Polish writers in America. Amsterdam; Atlanta, GA: Rodopi, 2003. pp. 382. (Studies in Slavic literature and poetics, 38.) Rev. by Andrej Karcz in SlavR (63:4) 2004, 859–61; by Elwira M. Grossman in MLR (100:3) 2005, 894–6; by Todd Armstrong in SEEJ (49:4) 2005, 695–7.

12935. STONEMAN, PATSY. Introduction. *In* (pp. 1–13) **10222.**

12936. SUGARS, CYNTHIA (ed.). Unhomely states: theorizing English Canadian postcolonialism. (Bibl. 2004, 12966.) Rev. by Alison Struselis in JPW (41:1) 2005, 128–30.

12937. SWENSON, JEFFERY. In good company: the Midwestern literary community and the short fiction of Ruth Suckow and Hamlin Garland. *See* **19728.**

12938. SWORD, HELEN. Ghostwriting Modernism. (Bibl. 2004, 12969.) Rev. by Daniel T. O'Hara in JML (26:3/4) 2003, 154–8; by Stephen J. Burn in JJQ (40:3) 2003, 611–13.

12939. TALIB, ISMAIL S. (comp.). Annual bibliography of Commonwealth literature 2004: Malaysia and Singapore. *See* **20592.**

12940. TAYLOR, ANDREW. What do we see when we look at the sea? The sea in post-Romantic Australian, British and American writing. *In* (pp. 367–77) **9393.**

12941. TAYLOR, DOUGLAS. Prison slang and the poetics of imprisonment. *In* (pp. 233–45) **12821.**

12942. TEMPLE, CHRISTEL N. Literary Pan-Africanism: history, contexts, and criticism. Durham, NC: Carolina Academic Press, 2005. pp. viii, 200.

12943. THAROOR, SHASHI. Bookless in Baghdad: reflections on writing and writers. New York: Arcade, 2005. pp. x, 277.

12944. THOMPSON, CLIFFORD, *et al.* (eds). World authors, 1995–2000. New York; Dublin: Wilson, 2003. pp. xv, 872.

12945. THORMÄHLEN, MARIANNE. A bibliography of Modernism. *In* (pp. 252–73) 12946.

12946. —— (ed.). Rethinking Modernism. Basingstoke; New York: Palgrave Macmillan, 2003. pp. xiv, 286. Rev. by Alan Munton in YES (35) 2005, 354–6.

12947. TIGHE, CARL. Writing and responsibility. London; New York: Routledge, 2005. pp. vi, 165.

12948. TRASK, MICHAEL. Cruising Modernism: class and sexuality in American literature and social thought. (Bibl. 2004, 12981.) Rev. by Justus Nieland in Mod/Mod (12:2) 2005, 350–1.

12949. TURNER, CATHERINE. Marketing Modernism between the two World Wars. (Bibl. 2004, 12983.) Rev. by Wim Van Mierlo in Library (6:3) 2005, 356–8; by Aaron Zacks in LibC (40:1) 2005, 106–7; by Craig Monk in YES (35) 2005, 352–3.

12950. TURNER, JOYCE MOORE. Caribbean crusaders and the Harlem renaissance. Introd. by Franklin W. Knight. Urbana: Illinois UP, 2005. pp. xxii, 291.

12951. TUTTLE, JON. How you get that story: Heisenberg's Uncertainty Principle and the literature of the Vietnam War. *See* 16808.

12952. TY, ELEANOR. The politics of the visible in Asian North American narratives. (Bibl. 2004, 12984.) Rev. by Angela Laflen in MFS (51:1) 2005, 201–4.

12953. VAN STRALEN, HANS. Choices and conflict: essays on literature and existentialism. New York; Frankfurt: Lang, 2005. pp. 241. (New comparative poetics, 16.)

12954. VICINUS, MARTHA. Intimate friends: women who loved women, 1778–1928. *See* 8083.

12955. WAGGONER, ERIC G. Radical rhetoric, American iconography, and *The Autobiography of Mother Jones*. AppalJ (32:2) 2005, 192–200.

12956. WALKER, ALICE. In search of our mothers' gardens: womanist prose. Orlando, FL: Harcourt, 2004. pp. xviii, 397. (Harvest.)

12957. WALTERS, WENDY W. At home in diaspora: Black international writing. Minneapolis; London: Minnesota UP, 2005. pp. xxv, 177. (Critical American studies.)

12958. WALTJE, JÖRG. Blood obsession: vampires, serial murder, and the popular imagination. New York; Frankfurt: Lang, 2005. pp. 157.

12959. WANJALA, CHRIS L.; WANJALA, ALEX NELUNGO. Annual bibliography of Commonwealth literature 2004: Central and East Africa – a personal overview. *See* 20593.

12960. WARNES, ANDREW. Hunger overcome? Food and resistance in twentieth-century African American literature. (Bibl. 2004, 12997.) Rev. by Tiffany A. Flowers in JAAH (90:1/2) 2005, 177–8.

12961. WASHINGTON, TERESA N. Our mothers, our powers, our texts: manifestations of Ajé in Africana literature. Bloomington: Indiana UP, 2005. pp. x, 332.

12962. WEDDE, IAN. Making ends meet: essays and talks 1992–2004. Wellington: Victoria UP, 2005. pp. 368. Rev. by Stephen Turner in JNZL (23:2) 2005, 101–8.

12963. WEISS, BETTINA. Tangible voice-throwing: empowering corporeal discourses in African women's writing of Southern Africa. New York; Frankfurt: Lang, 2004. pp. 269. (European univ. studies, XIV: Anglo-Saxon language and literature, 408.)

12964. WHELAN, KEVIN. The revisionist debate in Ireland. B2 (31:1) 2004, 179–205.

12965. WHYTE, WILLIAM. The intellectual aristocracy revisited. See 9445.

12966. WICOMB, ZOË. Setting, intertextuality and the resurrection of the postcolonial author. See 12083.

12967. WILLIAMS, MARK (ed.). Writing at the edge of the universe: essays from the 'Creative Writing in New Zealand' conference, University of Canterbury, August 2003. (Bibl. 2004, 13008.) Rev. by Wystan Curnow in Landfall (209) 2005, 210–12.

12968. WINDUO, STEVEN. Transition and transformation. See 20253.

12969. WOLF, PHILIPP. The anachronism of modern cultural memories, and an ethics of literary memory. See 8441.

12970. WOUDHUYSEN, H. R. A good morning's work. TLS, 30 Sept. 2005, 29. (Sale of a collection of author-portraits.)

12971. WRIGHT, MICHELLE M. Becoming Black: creating identity in the African diaspora. Durham, NC; London: Duke UP, 2004. pp. ix, 280. Rev. by Rebecca Wanzo in RAL (36:2) 2005, 155–6.

12972. WROBEL, DAVID M. Movement and adjustment in twentieth-century Western writing. PacHR (72:3) 2003, 393–404.

12973. WYATT-BROWN, BERTRAM. Hearts of darkness: wellsprings of a Southern literary tradition. (Bibl. 2003, 12337.) Rev. by Karen Michele Chandler in SCR (22:1) 2005, 141–2.

12974. YAO, STEVEN G. Translation and the languages of Modernism: gender, politics, language. (Bibl. 2004, 13012.) Rev. by Christopher Bush in Mod/Mod (12:1) 2005, 190–1; by Yunte Huang in Comparatist (29) 2005, 163–4.

12975. ZABEL, DARCY A. The (underground) railroad in African American literature. New York; Frankfurt: Lang, 2004. pp. 229. (African American literature and culture, 6.)

12976. ZANDY, JANET. Hands: physical labor, class, and cultural work. (Bibl. 2004, 13016.) Rev. by Joseph Entin in AmQ (57:4) 2005, 1211–21.

12977. ZHOU, XIAOJING; NAJMI, SAMINA (eds). Form and transformation in Asian American literature. See 9454.

12978. ZIOLKOWSKI, ERIC (ed.). Literature, religion, and East/West comparison: essays in honor of Anthony C. Yu. Newark: Delaware UP; London: Assoc. UPs, 2005. pp. xiv, 295.

12979. Ziolkowski, Margaret.   Alien visions: the Chechens and the Navajos in Russian and American literature. Newark: Delaware UP, 2005. pp. 239.

THEATRE

12980. Abbotson, Susan C. W.   Masterpieces of 20th-century American drama. Westport, CT; London: Greenwood Press, 2005. pp. 227. (Greenwood introduces literary masterpieces.)

12981. Allen, Carol Dawn.   Peculiar passages: Black women playwrights, 1875 to 2000. See **9455**.

12982. Amkpa, Awam.   Theatre and postcolonial desires. (Bibl. 2004, 13026.) Rev. by James Gibbs in RAL (36:2) 2005, 146–7; by Frances Harding in TRI (30:1) 2005, 96–7.

12983. Apple, Jacki.   A different world: a personal history of Franklin Furnace. TDR (49:1) 2005, 36–54.

12984. Aston, Elaine.   Feminist views on the English stage: women playwrights, 1990–2000. (Bibl. 2004, 13028.) Rev. by Alicia Tycer in TheatreS (46:1) 2005, 153–5; by Jill Dolan in TRI (30:1) 2005, 98–9.

12985. Barranger, Milly S.   Margaret Webster: a life in the theater. (Bibl. 2004, 13031.) Rev. by Yvonne Shafer in THS (25) 2005, 206–7.

12986. Bass, George Houston; Jones, Rhett S.   Rites and reason: a theatre that lets the people speak. LHR (19:1) 2004, 3–26.

12987. Bay-Cheng, Sarah.   Following the gaze: the influence (and problems) of feminist film theory in theater criticism. *In* (pp. 162–71) **13058**.

12988. Bennett, Susan.   Performing Ireland: tourism and the Abbey Theatre. CJIS (30:2) 2004, 30–7.

12989. ——   Theatre/tourism. TJ (57:3) 2005, 407–28.

12990. Bial, Henry.   Acting Jewish: negotiating ethnicity on the American stage & screen. Ann Arbor: Michigan UP, 2005. pp. viii, 195.

12991. Bird, Kym.   Redressing the past: the politics of early English Canadian women's drama 1880–1920. See **9459**.

12992. Black, Cheryl.   The women of Provincetown, 1915–1922. (Bibl. 2004, 13036.) Rev. by Marcia Noe in AmDr (14:1) 2005, 115–20.

12993. Blatanis, Konstantinos.   Popular culture icons in contemporary American drama. (Bibl. 2004, 13038.) Rev. by Robert Baker-White in ModDr (48:1) 2003, 215–17.

12994. Bollen, Jonathan.   Remembering masculinities in the theatre of war. ADS (46) 2005, 3–19.

12995. Boon, Richard; Plastow, Jane (eds).   Theatre and empowerment: community drama on the world stage. (Bibl. 2004, 13040.) Rev. by Loren Kruger in TJ (57:3) 2005, 548–50.

12996. Bottoms, Stephen J.   Playing underground: a critical history of the 1960s off-off-Broadway movement. (Bibl. 2004, 13042.) Rev. by Michael Paller in TDR (49:3) 2005, 194–6; by Philip C. Kolin in TJ (57:4) 2005, 780–1; by Wendell Stone in THS (25) 2005, 211–14.

12997. BOURGAULT, LOUISE M.   Playing for life: performance in Africa in the age of AIDS. Durham, NC: Carolina Academic Press, 2003. pp. xxvii, 315. Rev. by Mary Jo Arnoldi in RAL (36:1) 2005, 121–2; by Loren Kruger in TJ (57:3) 2005, 548–50.

12998. BOWER, MARTHA GILMAN.   'Color struck' under the gaze: ethnicity and the pathology of being in the plays of Johnson, Hurston, Childress, Hansberry, and Kennedy. (Bibl. 2004, 13043.) Rev. by Robert L. Tener in AAR (38:4) 2004, 729–31.

12999. BREWER, MARY F.   Staging Whiteness. Middletown, CT: Wesleyan UP, 2005. pp. xvi, 236.

13000. BROWN, IAN.   Thrawn themes and dramatic experiment: W. Gordon Smith and the paradoxes of creative iconoclasm. See **19495.**

13001. BULL, JOHN STANLEY (ed.).   British and Irish dramatists since World War II: fourth series. Detroit, MI: Gale Research, 2005. pp. xix, 461. (Dictionary of literary biography, 310.)

13002. CALLENS, JOHAN (trans.).   The Wooster Group and its traditions. New York; Frankfurt: Lang, 2004. pp. 290. (Dramaturgies, 13.)

13003. CARR, C.   The fiery Furnace: performance in the '80s, war in the '90s. TDR (49:1) 2005, 19–28. (Franklin Furnace.)

13004. CASEY, MARYROSE.   Creating frames: contemporary indigenous theatre 1967–1990. St Lucia: Queensland UP, 2004. pp. xxvii, 372. Rev. by Bernadette Brennan in Southerly (64:3) 2004, 198–201; by Michelle Evans in ALS (22:1) 2005, 117–19; by Alan Filewod in TRI (30:1) 2005, 100–1.

13005. CHANSKY, DOROTHY.   Composing ourselves: the Little Theatre movement and the American audience. Carbondale: Southern Illinois UP, 2004. pp. xv, 293. (Theater in the Americas.) Rev. by Marcia Noe in AmDr (14:1) 2005, 115–20; by Katie N. Johnson in TJ (57:1) 2005, 138–40; by Michael A. Rothmayer in THS (25) 2005, 204–6; by Pam Cobrin in TDR (49:4) 2005, 192–3; by Beate Hein Bennett in TRI (30:3) 2005, 300–1.

13006. CLARKE, DENISE.   Memory from the deep rodeo barrel. CanTR (124) 2005, 22–4. (Canadian theatre.)

13007. COHEN-CRUZ, JAN.   Local acts: community-based performance in the United States. New Brunswick, NJ: Rutgers UP, 2005. pp. xii, 212. (Rutgers series on the public life of the arts.)

13008. COLEMAN, TERRY.   Olivier. New York: Holt, 2005. pp. x, 595, (plates) 16.

13009. CONTEH-MORGAN, JOHN; OLANIYAN, TEJUMOLA (eds).   African drama and performance. (Bibl. 2004, 13053.) Rev. by Esiaba Irobi in TJ (57:4) 2005, 770–1.

13010. COTSELL, MICHAEL.   The theater of trauma: American Modernist drama and the psychological struggle for the American mind, 1900–1930. New York; Frankfurt: Lang, 2005. pp. xv, 377.

13011. CRAIG, CAROLYN CASEY.   Women Pulitzer playwrights: biographical profiles and analyses of the plays. Jefferson, NC; London: McFarland, 2004. pp. viii, 339.

13012. CURRY, J. K. The National Black Theatre Festival: a one-stop tour. ThSym (13) 2005, 95–104.

13013. DASH, IRENE G. Double vision: *Kiss Me Kate*. See **6734**.

13014. DASYLVA, ADEMOLA. Dapo Adelugba on theatre practice in Nigeria. Introd. by Dotun Ogundeji. (Bibl. 2004, 13055.) Rev. by Reuben Abati in RAL (35:4) 2004, 142–8.

13015. DEAN, JOAN FITZPATRICK. Riot and great anger: stage censorship in twentieth-century Ireland. Madison; London: Wisconsin UP, 2004. pp. xiii, 261. (Irish studies in literature and culture.) Rev. by Chris Morash in ModDr (48:1) 2005, 202–4; by Kathleen A. Heininge in ILS (24:2) 2005, 20–1.

13016. DE GIACOMO, ALBERT J.; FRIDDLE, JONAS. Frank J. Hugh O'Donnell (1894–1976): toward a Ministry of Arts and a Federation of Irish Amateur Drama. See **18588**.

13017. DENKERT, DARCIE. A fine romance. New York: Watson-Guptill, 2005. pp. 360. (Stage and film musicals.)

13018. DOYLE, MARY AGNES. Crossing the Jordan: genealogy, geography, genre, gender. See **13458**.

13019. ENGLISH, JAMES F. The economy of prestige: prizes, awards, and the circulation of cultural value. See **819**.

13020. FAHY, THOMAS; KING, KIMBALL (eds). Captive audience: prison and captivity in contemporary theater. (Bibl. 2003, 12400.) Rev. by William Hutchings in SAtlR (70:3) 2005, 132–4.

13021. FOLEY, IMELDA. The girls in the big picture: gender in contemporary Ulster theatre. (Bibl. 2004, 13075.) Rev. by Martine Pelletier in EtIr (29:1) 2004, 167–8; by Helen Lojek in ILS (24:2) 2005, 18.

13022. FOSDICK, SCOTT. From discussion leader to consumer guide: a century of theater criticism in Chicago newspapers. JoH (30:2) 2004, 91–7.

13023. FRANK, HAIKE. Role-play in South African theatre. Bayreuth: Breitinger, 2004. pp. 375. (Bayreuth African studies, 70.) Rev. by Brian Crow in RAL (36:2) 2005, 144–5.

13024. FRAYLING, CHRISTOPHER. Mad, bad and dangerous? The scientist and the cinema. London: Reaktion, 2005. pp. 239.

13025. FRAZEE, CATHERINE. Disability pride with disability performance. CanTR (122) 2005, 10–12.

13026. FREY, HEATHER FITZSIMMONS. Dramaturgy and a collective theatre. CanTR (123) 2005, 73–8.

13027. GALE, MAGGIE B.; GARDNER, VIV (eds). Auto/biography and identity: women, theatre, and performance. Manchester; New York: Manchester UP, 2004. pp. xii, 260.

13028. GEORGE, KATHLEEN. Winter's tales: reflections on the novelistic stage. Newark: Delaware UP, 2005. pp. 231.

13029. GEWIRTZ, ARTHUR; KOLB, JAMES J. (eds). Experimenters, rebels, and disparate voices: the theatre of the 1920s celebrates American diversity. (Bibl. 2003, 12409.) Rev. by Margaret F. Savilonis in TJ (57:4) 2005, 766–7.

13030. GRACE, SHERRILL (introd.). Voice of her own. Toronto: Playwrights Canada Press, 2003. pp. viii, 142.

13031. GRAHAM-JONES, JEAN. 'The truth is ... my soul is with you': documenting a tale of two Evitas. TheatreS (46:1) 2005, 67–78.

13032. GREELEY, LYNNE. Whatever happened to the cultural feminists? Martha Boesing and At the Foot of the Mountain. TheatreS (46:1) 2005, 49–65.

13033. GRIFFIN, GABRIELE. Contemporary Black and Asian women playwrights in Britain. (Bibl. 2004, 13088.) Rev. by Nandi Bhatia in ModDr (48:1) 2005, 206–8; by Yvonne Brewster in TRI (30:1) 2005, 99–100.

13034. HARBIN, BILLY J.; MARRA, KIM; SCHANKE, ROBERT A. (eds). The gay & lesbian theatrical legacy: a biographical dictionary of major figures in American stage history in the pre-Stonewall era. Ann Arbor: Michigan UP, 2005. pp. 428. (Triangulations.)

13035. HARRISON, PAUL CARTER; WALKER, VICTOR LEO, II; EDWARDS, GUS (eds). Black theatre: ritual performance in the African diaspora. (Bibl. 2004, 13095.) Rev. by Annemarie Bean in RAL (36:1) 2005, 122–4.

13036. HAWKINS, JOAN. When taste politics meet terror: the Critical Art Ensemble on trial. CTHEORY (158) 2005.

13037. HEPTONSTALL, GEOFFREY. Otherwise engaged: the theatre of Jonathan Miller. ContRev (287:1676) 2005, 165–70.

13038. HERBST, JUDITH KATHERINE. The Keswick Theatre. Portsmouth, NH: Arcadia, 2004. pp. 127. (Images of America.)

13039. HILL, ERROL G.; HATCH, JAMES V. A history of African American theatre. (Bibl. 2004, 13101.) Rev. by Harry Elam in TheatreS (46:1) 2005, 127–9; by Miriam Chirico in ELN (42:4) 2005, 83–95; by N. Graham Nesmith in TDR (49:1) 2005, 168–71; by Harvey Young in TJ (57:4) 2005, 761–2.

13040. HIRSCH, FOSTER. Harold Prince and the American musical theatre. New York: Applause, 2005. pp. xv, 269. (Second ed.: first ed. 1989.)

13041. HISCHAK, THOMAS S. Through the screen door: what happened to the Broadway musical when it went to Hollywood. *See* **13260**.

13042. HOLLAND, PETER. Dramatizing the dramatist. ShS (58) 2005, 137–47. (Plays featuring Shakespeare as a character.)

13043. —— 'Some of you may have seen him': Laurence Olivier's celebrity. *In* (pp. 214–32) **3985**.

13044. HOUCHIN, JOHN H. Censorship of the American theatre in the twentieth century. Cambridge; New York: CUP, 2003. pp. ix, 332. (Cambridge studies in American theatre and drama, 16.) Rev. by Miriam Chirico in ELN (41:4) 2004, 74–80; by D. Quentin Miller in AL (77:1) 2005, 196–8; by Barry B. Witham in TheatreS (46:1) 2005, 136–7; by Melissa Dana Gibson in TJ (57:4) 2005, 775–7.

13045. HOUSTON, ANDREW. Deep-mapping a morning on 3A: the found and the fabricated of the Weyburn Project. CanTR (121) 2005, 32–40.

13046. INNES, CHRISTOPHER. Shifting the frame – Modernism in the theatre. *In* (pp. 204–12) **12946**.

13047. JACKSON, ANTHONY; LEV-ALADGEM, SHULAMITH. Rethinking audience participation: audiences in alternative and educational theatre. *In* (pp. 207–36) 3974.

13048. JACKSON, JULIE. Theatrical space and place in the presentational aesthetic of director Frank Joseph Galati. *See* 19620.

13049. JOHNSON, E. PATRICK. Appropriating Blackness: performance and the politics of authenticity. (Bibl. 2003, 12431.) Rev. by Cleo House, Jr, in TJ (57:4) 2005, 762–3.

13050. JONES, JOHN BUSH. Our musicals, ourselves: a social history of the American musical theater. (Bibl. 2004, 13109.) Rev. by Warren Hoffman in TJ (57:2) 2005, 338–9; by Mary Jo Lodge in THS (25) 2005, 195–7.

13051. KEENAN, THOMAS. The Theatre Guild archive at the Beinecke. *See* 410.

13052. KENNEDY, DENNIS. The director, the spectator and the Eiffel Tower. TRI (30:1) 2005, 36–48.

13053. KENTON, EDNA. The Provincetown Players and the Playwrights' Theatre, 1915–1922. Ed. by Travis Bogard and Jackson R. Bryer. (Bibl. 2004, 13113.) Rev. by Brenda Murphy in EOR (27) 2005, 176–9.

13054. KERSHAW, BAZ (ed.). The Cambridge history of British theatre: vol. 3, Since 1895. *See* 9486.

13055. KIERNANDER, ADRIAN. What's a man to do? Images of rural Australian masculinities in three plays of the 1950s: *Reedy River, The Bastard Country* and *Lola Montez*. ADS (46) 2005, 38–57.

13056. KING, DONALD C. The theatres of Boston: a stage and screen history. *See* 9487.

13057. KLEIN, CHRISTINA. Cold War Orientalism: Asia in the middlebrow imagination, 1945–1961. (Bibl. 2004, 13116.) Rev. by Shannon Steen in TJ (57:3) 2005, 529–31.

13058. KNOPF, ROBERT (ed.). Theater and film: a comparative anthology. New Haven, CT; London: Yale UP, 2005. pp. xii, 440.

13059. KNOWLES, RIC; TOMPKINS, JOANNE; WORTHEN, W. B. (eds). Modern drama: defining the field. (Bibl. 2004, 13118.) Rev. by Martin Harries in TRI (30:2) 2005, 200–1.

13060. KNOWLES, RICHARD PAUL. Reading the material theatre. (Bibl. 2004, 13119.) Rev. by Jill Dolan in TJ (57:4) 2005, 781–2.

13061. KOLINSKÁ, KLÁRA. 'What happened to the naming in this strange place?': remapping the space of Ontario in the (con)texts of Native Canadian theatre. *In* (pp. 176–89) 12868.

13062. KRAMER, RICHARD E. The Washington Square Players: art for art's sake. THS (25) 2005, 149–72.

13063. KRASNER, DAVID (ed.). A companion to twentieth-century American drama. Oxford; Malden, MA: Blackwell, 2005. pp. xviii, 576. (Blackwell companions to literature and culture, 29.)

2005] THEATRE 703

13064. KUPPERS, PETRA. Disability and contemporary performance: bodies on edge. London; New York: Routledge, 2004. pp. x, 176. Rev. by Ann M. Fox in TRI (30:1) 2005, 101–2.

13065. KUSTOW, MICHAEL. Peter Brook: a biography. London: Bloomsbury, 2005. pp. xvi, 334, (plates) 16. Rev. by Randall Stevenson in TLS, 1 July 2005, 20.

13066. LEE, JOSEPHINE. Asian American (im)mobility: perspectives on the *College Plays 1937–1955. In* (pp. 120–40) **12775.**

13067. LEVENSON, JILL L. Shakespeare in drama since 1990: vanishing act. ShS (58) 2005, 148–59.

13068. LO, JACQUELINE. Staging nation: English-language theatre in Malaysia and Singapore. Hong Kong: Hong Kong UP, 2004. pp. x, 227. Rev. by William Peterson in ADS (46) 2005, 162–5; by Eng-Beng Lim in TJ (57:3) 2005, 536–8.

13069. MCCONACHIE, BRUCE. American theater in the culture of the Cold War: producing and contesting containment, 1947–1962. (Bibl. 2004, 13132.) Rev. by Dorothy Chansky in TJ (57:3) 2005, 531–2; by Ann C. Hall in TRI (30:3) 2005, 296–7.

13070. MCMANUS, DONALD. No kidding! Clown as protagonist in twentieth-century theater. (Bibl. 2004, 13136.) Rev. by Joel Schechter in TheatreS (45:2) 2004, 315–17.

13071. MAKEHAM, PAUL. Performing the city. TRI (30:2) 2005, 150–60.

13072. MARTIN, BRADFORD D. The theater is in the street: politics and performance in sixties America. (Bibl. 2004, 13142.) Rev. by Wini Breines in JAH (92:3) 2005, 1064–5.

13073. MATHEWS, P. J. Revival: the Abbey Theatre, Sinn Féin, the Gaelic League, and the Co-operative Movement. (Bibl. 2004, 13143.) Rev. by Paul Delaney in CJIS (30:2) 2004, 81–2.

13074. MAURIN, FRÉDÉRIC (ed.). Peter Sellars. Paris: CNRS, 2003. pp. 447. (Arts du spectacle: voies de la création théâtrale, 22.) Rev. by Jane Baldwin in TJ (56:2) 2004, 326–7.

13075. MENDELSOHN, JUDITH. One Yellow Rabbit's High Performance Rodeo, 1987–2005: a chronology. CanTR (124) 2005, 25–34.

13076. MESZAROS, BETH. Infernal sound cues: aural geographies and the politics of noise. ModDr (48:1) 2005, 118–31.

13077. MILNE, GEOFFREY. Theatre Australia (un)limited: Australian theatre since the 1950s. Amsterdam; Atlanta, GA: Rodopi, 2004. pp. xiv, 444, (plates) 14. (Australian playwrights, 10.) Rev. by Maryrose Casey in ADS (46) 2005, 159–62; by Helen Thomson in TRI (30:2) 2005, 199–200.

13078. MOE, CHRISTIAN H.; PARKER, SCOTT J.; MCCALMON, GEORGE. Creating historical drama: a guide for communities, theatre groups, and playwrights. Foreword by Romulus Linney. *See* **20608.**

13079. MORROW, MARTIN. Wild theatre: the history of One Yellow Rabbit. (Bibl. 2004, 13150.) Rev. by David Fancy in TRC (24:1/2) 2003, 218–20.

13080. MOST, ANDREA. Making Americans: Jews and the Broadway musical. (Bibl. 2004, 13151.) Rev. by Bruce Kirle in TJ (57:2) 2005, 336–7; by David Krasner in ModDr (48:1) 2005, 217–19; by Jeffrey Shandler in JAH (92:1) 2005, 267; by Harley Erdman in TRI (30:2) 2005, 196–7.

13081. MÜNDEL, INGRID.   Radical storytelling: performance process in popular Canadian theatre. TRC (24:1/2) 2003, 147–70.

13082. NELSON, EMMANUEL S. (ed.).   African American dramatists: an A to Z guide. Westport, CT; London: Greenwood Press, 2004. pp. 527.

13083. NESMITH, N. GRAHAM.   Lloyd Richards: reminiscence of a theatre life and beyond. AAR (39:3) 2005, 281–98. (Interview.)

13084. NESTERUK, PETER.   Ritual and identity in late twentieth-century American drama. JDTC (19:2) 2005, 43–69.

13085. NICHOLSON, STEVE.   The censorship of British drama, 1900–1968: vol. 1, 1900–1932. (Bibl. 2004, 13153.) Rev. by Nadine Holdsworth in ModDr (48:1) 2005, 204–6; by Melissa Dana Gibson in TJ (57:4) 2005, 775–7.

13086. NOONAN, JULIE A.   *Little Shop of Horrors*: re-visioning the future through pastiche and science fiction. See **13637**.

13087. O'DONNELL, DAVID; TWEDDLE, BRONWYN.   Naked Samoans: Pacific Island voices in the theatre of Aotearoa / New Zealand. PRes (8:1) 2003, 51–60.

13088. O'REILLY, ANNE F.   Sacred play: soul-journeys in contemporary Irish theatre. Dublin: Carysfort Press, 2004. pp. 336. Rev. by Helen Lojek in ILS (25:1) 2005, 14.

13089. O'TOOLE, FINTAN.   Critical moments: Fintan O'Toole on modern Irish theatre. Ed. by Julia Furay and Redmond O'Hanlon. (Bibl. 2004, 13154.) Rev. by Martine Pelletier in EtIr (29:2) 2004, 204–5.

13090. PALLER, MICHAEL.   Gentlemen callers: Tennessee Williams, homosexuality, and mid-twentieth-century Broadway drama. See **20195**.

13091. PARR, BRUCE.   The misfit male body in Adelaide theatre, 1959. ADS (46) 2005, 20–37.

13092. PATTERSON, MICHAEL.   Strategies of political theatre: post-war British playwrights. (Bibl. 2004, 13157.) Rev. by David Richard Jones in TJ (57:1) 2005, 144–5.

13093. PLOTKINS, MARILYN J.   The American Repertory Theatre reference book: the Brustein years. Westport, CT; London: Praeger, 2005. pp. xi, 282.

13094. RAVENHILL, MARK.   A tear in the fabric: the James Bulger murder and new theatre writing in the nineties. See **19029**.

13095. RICHARDS, SHAUN (ed.).   The Cambridge companion to twentieth-century Irish drama. (Bibl. 2004, 13166.) Rev. by Émile-Jean Dumay in EtIr (30:1) 2005, 223; by Christina Hunt Mahony in ILS (24:2) 2005, 18.

13096. RIFKIND, CANDIDA.   Modernism's Red stage: theatre and the Left in the 1930s. *In* (pp. 181–204) **12739**.

13097. RIVELLINO, STEVEN.   Bright lights, big changes: transatlantic theatre at the turn of the century. Philadelphia, PA: XLibris, 2004. pp. 207.

13098. SANT, TONI.   Franklin Furnace and Martha Wilson: on a mission to make the world safe for avantgarde art. TDR (49:1) 2005, 29–35, 55–9, 80–5, 104–10.

13099. SAVRAN, DAVID.   The death of the avantgarde. TDR (49:3) 2005, 10–42. (Wooster Group.)

13100. —— A queer sort of materialism: recontextualizing American theater. (Bibl. 2004, 13172.) Rev. by Peter Hays in AL (77:1) 2005, 198–200; by Ilka Saal in TDR (49:3) 2005, 187–91.

13101. SCOTT, SHELLEY. Bodies, form and nature: three Canadian plays and reproductive choice in the 1990s. BJCS (17:2) 2004, 197–209.

13102. —— Enacting *This Is for You, Anna*: re-enacting the collective process. CanTR (121) 2005, 41–5.

13103. SEBESTA, JUDITH. From celluloid to stage: the 'movical', *The Producers*, and the postmodern. *See* **13716**.

13104. SENELICK, LAURENCE. Consuming passions: eating and the stage at the *fin de siècle*. *See* **9501**.

13105. SHALSON, LARA. Creating community, constructing criticism: the Women's One World festival 1980–1981. TT (15:2) 2005, 221–39.

13106. SHELTON, LEWIS E. Ideas of the theatre: the five directorial perspectives of the American stage. *See* **9502**.

13107. SHIMAKAWA, KAREN. National abjection: the Asian American body onstage. (Bibl. 2004, 13181.) Rev. by Lucy Mae San Pablo Burns in JAAS (7:1) 2004, 73–8; by Esther Kim Lee in TJ (57:1) 2005, 154–5; by Carol Fisher Sorgenfrei in TRI (30:2) 2005, 193–4.

13108. SHIMIZU, CELINE PARREÑAS. The bind of representation: performing and consuming hypersexuality in *Miss Saigon*. TJ (57:2) 2005, 247–65.

13109. SHTEIR, RACHEL. Notes on New York theater criticism. Theater (35:3) 2005, 74–85.

13110. SIMON, JOHN IVAN. John Simon on theater: criticism, 1974–2003. Introd. by Jack O'Brien. New York: Applause, 2005. pp. 837.

13111. SMITH, ANNA DEVEARE, *et al.* A forum on Black theatre. The questions: what is a Black play? And/or what is playing Black? TJ (57:4) 2005, 571–616.

13112. SMITH, WENDY. Miller's tale: the playwright drew a line between reaching out and selling out. *See* **18253**.

13113. SOMERSET-WARD, RICHARD. An American theatre: the story of Westport Country Playhouse, 1931–2005. Foreword by Joanne Woodward and Paul Newman. New Haven, CT; London: Yale UP, 2005. pp. 304.

13114. STERNLICHT, SANFORD. Masterpieces of modern British and Irish drama. Westport, CT; London: Greenwood Press, 2005. pp. 111. (Greenwood introduces literary masterpieces.)

13115. STETZ, MARGARET D. Gender and the London theatre, 1880–1920. *See* **9503**.

13116. STOKES, JOHN. The French actress and her English audience. *See* **9504**.

13117. STONE, WENDELL C. Caffe Cino: the birthplace of off-off-Broadway. Carbondale: Southern Illinois UP, 2005. pp. xiii, 227. (Theater in the Americas.)

13118. TAXIDOU, OLGA. Tragedy, modernity, and mourning. Edinburgh: Edinburgh UP, 2004. pp. 215. Rev. by Ian Ruffell in TRI (30:2) 2005, 190–1.

13119. TAYLOR, DIANA. The archive and the repertoire: performing cultural memory in the Americas. Durham, NC; London: Duke UP, 2003. pp. xx, 326. Rev. by Lisa Wylam in TRI (30:2) 2005, 197–8.

13120. TEAGUE, FRANCES. *Mr Hamlet of Broadway. See* **6374**.

13121. TETENS, KRISTAN. 'A grand informal Durbar': Henry Irving and the coronation of Edward VII. JVC (8:2) 2003, 257–91.

13122. TRIST, PETER; TAKAKU, WILLIAM. Living legends, dying stages. Meanjin (62:3) 2003, 113–22.

13123. UKAEGBU, VICTOR. Performing postcolonially: contextual changes in the adaptations of Wole Soyinka's *Death and the King's Horseman* and Femi Osofisan's *Once upon Four Robbers. See* **19547**.

13124. ULLOM, JEFFREY. The landmark years of the Humana Festival. THS (25) 2005, 23–42.

13125. WALKER, JULIA A. Expressionism and Modernism in the American theatre: bodies, voices, words. Cambridge; New York: CUP, 2005. pp. xii, 300. (Cambridge studies in American theatre and drama, 21.)

13126. WALLACE, CLARE. Responsibility and postmodernity: Mark Ravenhill and 1990s British drama. *In* (pp. 269–75) **3734**.

13127. WALSH, DAVID; PLATT, LEN. Musical theater and American culture. Westport, CT; London: Praeger, 2003. pp. xiii, 200. Rev. by Mary Jo Lodge in THS (25) 2005, 195–7.

13128. WARRINGTON, LISA. Brave 'New World': Asian voices in the theatre of Aotearoa. ADS (46) 2005, 98–116.

13129. WEHLE, PHILIPPA. A wild man of the theatre: Josh Fox and his International WOW Company. TheatreForum (27) 2005, 63–5.

13130. WEITZ, ERIC (ed.). The power of laughter: comedy and contemporary Irish theatre. Dublin: Carysfort Press, 2004. pp. xii, 192. Rev. by Kathleen A. Heininge in ILS (24:2) 2005, 20.

13131. WERTHEIM, ALBERT. Staging the war: American drama and World War II. (Bibl. 2004, 13201.) Rev. by Maria Beach in TJ (57:3) 2005, 532–3; by John Frick in TDR (49:2) 2005, 166–9.

13132. WINKIEL, LAURA. Cabaret Modernism: Vorticism and racial spectacle. *In* (pp. 206–24) **12640**.

13133. BEN-ZVI, LINDA. The Provincetown Players: the success that failed. *See* **18653**.

CINEMA

General

13134. ABEL, RICHARD (ed.). Encyclopedia of early cinema. London; New York: Routledge, 2005. pp. xxx, 791.

13135. ABERTH, JOHN. A knight at the movies: medieval history on film. (Bibl. 2004, 13211.) Rev. by Donald L. Hoffman in Envoi (10:2) 2003 for 2001, 97–100; by Dean Swinford in JFV (56:4) 2004, 54–6; by Stephen M. Buhler in QRFV (22:3) 2005, 292–6.

13136. ALBION, ALEXIS. Wanting to be James Bond. *In* (pp. 202–20) **16517**.

13137. ALEISS, ANGELA. Making the White man's Indian: Native Americans and Hollywood movies. Westport, CT; London: Praeger, 2005. pp. xix, 211.

13138. ANKER, ROY M. Catching light: looking for God in the movies. (Bibl. 2004, 13215.) Rev. by Conrad Ostwalt in Cresset (69:1) 2005, 47–8.

13139. ARONSTEIN, SUSAN. Hollywood knights: Arthurian cinema and the politics of nostalgia. Basingstoke; New York: Palgrave Macmillan, 2005. pp. vii, 264. (Studies in Arthurian and courtly cultures.)

13140. AVILA, ERIC. Popular culture in the age of White flight: fear and fantasy in suburban Los Angeles. Berkeley; London: California UP, 2004. pp. 308. (American crossroads, 13.) Rev. by Scott Harvey Tang in JAH (92:2) 2005, 679–80.

13141. AYERS, BRENDA (ed.). The emperor's old groove: decolonizing Disney's Magic Kingdom. (Bibl. 2004, 13218.) Rev. by Elinor Levy in WF (64:1/2) 2005, 135–6.

13142. AZZARO, GABRIELE. Four-letter films: taboo language in movies. See **1722**.

13143. BAETENS, JAN. Novelization, a contaminated genre? Trans. by Pieter Verrmeulen. See **4008**.

13144. BAINBRIDGE, CAROLINE; YATES, CANDIDA. Cinematic symptoms of masculinity in transition: memory, history and mythology in contemporary film. See **20624**.

13145. BARKAWI, TARAK. Globalization, culture, and war: on the popular mediation of 'small wars'. CultC (58) 2004, 115–47.

13146. BARON, LAWRENCE. Projecting the Holocaust into the present: the changing focus of contemporary Holocaust cinema. Lanham, MD; Oxford: Rowman & Littlefield, 2005. pp. x, 307.

13147. BARRA, ALLEN. Dashiell Hammett. See **16866**.

13148. BARTON, BRUCE. Imagination in transition: Mamet's move to film. See **18068**.

13149. BARTON, RUTH. Irish national cinema. (Bibl. 2004, 13226.) Rev. by Maria Pramaggiore in FilmQ (59:1) 2005, 57–9.

13150. BARTOV, OMER. The 'Jew' in cinema: from *The Golem* to *Don't Touch My Holocaust*. Bloomington: Indiana UP, 2005. pp. xv, 374. (Helen and Martin Schwartz lectures in Jewish studies.)

13151. BECK, JERRY. Outlaw animation: cutting-edge cartoons from the Spike & Mike Festivals. New York: Abrams, 2003. pp. 159.

13152. BECKMAN, KAREN. Vanishing women: magic, film, and feminism. (Bibl. 2004, 13228.) Rev. by Francesca Coppa in TJ (57:2) 2005, 342–4.

13153. BELLIN, JOSHUA DAVID. Framing monsters: fantasy film and social alienation. Carbondale: Southern Illinois UP, 2005. pp. xii, 240.

13154. BIAL, HENRY. Acting Jewish: negotiating ethnicity on the American stage & screen. See **12990**.

13155. BIESEN, SHERI CHINEN. Blackout: World War II and the origins of *film noir*. Baltimore, MD; London: Johns Hopkins UP, 2005. pp. xii, 243.

13156. BIGSBY, CHRISTOPHER (ed.). Remembering Arthur Miller. See **18231**.

13157. BLAKESLEY, DAVID (ed.).   The terministic screen: rhetorical perspectives on film. (Bibl. 2003, 12576.) Rev. by John Muckelbauer in JACJ (23:4) 2003, 901–7; by Dean Rader in CE (67:6) 2005, 636–50.

13158. BLESSING, KIMBERLY A.; TUDICO, PAUL J. (eds).   Movies and the meaning of life: philosophers take on Hollywood. Chicago, IL: Open Court, 2005. pp. xvi, 302.

13159. BODNAR, JOHN.   Blue-collar Hollywood: liberalism, democracy, and working people in American film. (Bibl. 2004, 13239.) Rev. by Robert Brent Toplin in JAH (91:2) 2004, 677–8; by Victor Cohen in AmS (46:1) 2005, 173–4.

13160. BOGLE, DONALD.   Bright boulevards, bold dreams: the story of Black Hollywood. New York: One World Ballantine, 2005. pp. xiv, 411. Rev. by Abby McGanney Nolan in BkW, 27 Feb. 2005, 5; by Charles Michael Smith in GLRW (12:3) 2005, 45–6; by Patrick McGilligan in Cineaste (30:4) 2005, 73–4.

13161. BOGUE, RONALD.   Deleuze on cinema. London; New York: Routledge, 2003. pp. x, 231. (Deleuze and the arts.) Rev. by Jill Marsden in BJA (45:1) 2005, 97–101.

13162. BOHN, WILLARD.   Marvelous encounters: Surrealist responses to film, art, poetry, and architecture. See **14367.**

13163. BONDANELLA, PETER.   Hollywood Italians: dagos, palookas, Romeos, wise guys, and Sopranos. (Bibl. 2004, 13241.) Rev. by Matt Warman in TLS, 1 July 2005, 31.

13164. BONILA, PAUL C.   Is there more to Hollywood lowbrow than meets the eye? QRFV (22:1) 2005, 17–24.

13165. BORDWELL, DAVID; THOMPSON, KRISTIN.   Film art: an introduction. (Bibl. 1981, 9291.) Boston, MA: McGraw-Hill, 2004. pp. xx, 532. (Seventh ed.: first ed. 1979.)

13166. BRADLEY, EDWIN M.   The first Hollywood sound shorts, 1926–1931. Jefferson, NC; London: McFarland, 2005. pp. viii, 551.

13167. BRIEFEL, AVIVA.   Monster pains: masochism, menstruation, and identification in the horror film. FilmQ (58:3) 2005, 16–27.

13168. BRITTON, WESLEY.   Beyond Bond: spies in fiction and film. Westport, CT; London: Praeger, 2005. pp. xiv, 267.

13169. BRODE, DOUGLAS.   From Walt to Woodstock: how Disney created the counterculture. (Bibl. 2004, 13247.) Rev. by Marshall W. Fishwick in JAC (28:1) 2005, 137.

13170. BRODERICK, MICK.   Septic tanks downunder: representing American soldiers as 'other' in Australian cinema. PS (24:2/3) 2005, 94–108.

13171. BRONFEN, ELIZABETH.   Home in Hollywood: the imaginary geography of cinema. New York: Columbia UP, 2004. pp. 310. Rev. by Sam B. Girgus in AmS (46:2) 2005, 194.

13172. BROTTMAN, MIKITA.   Offensive films. Nashville, TN: Vanderbilt UP, 2005. pp. ix, 205.

13173. BUHLE, PAUL; WAGNER, DAVE.   Hide in plain sight: the Hollywood blacklistees in film and television, 1950–2002. (Bibl. 2004, 13248.) Rev. by John

Sbardellati in PacHR (73:3) 2004, 522–3; by Sam B. Girgus in JAH (91:3) 2004, 1082; by Jeff Smith in FilmQ (58:2) 2004/05, 54–6.

13174. BUKATMAN, SCOTT.   Matters of gravity: special effects and supermen in the 20th century. (Bibl. 2004, 13250.) Rev. by Stephen Burt in ColLit (32:1) 2005, 166–76.

13175. BUSCOMBE, EDWARD.   Cinema today. London: Phaidon, 2003. pp. 512.

13176. BUTLER, ANDREW M.   Between the 'deaths' of science fiction: a skeptical view of the possibility for anti-genres. JFA (15:3) 2004, 208–16.

13177. BUTLER, MARGARET.   Film and community, Britain and France: from *La Règle du jeu* to *Room at the Top*. London; New York: Tauris, 2004. pp. xi, 252.

13178. CAPUTI, JANE.   Goddesses and monsters: women, myth, power, and popular culture. Madison; London: Wisconsin UP/Popular Press, 2004. pp. x, 468. Rev. by Linda S. Coleman in JAC (28:3) 2005, 321–3.

13179. CARDULLO, BERT.   In search of cinema: writings on international film art. Foreword by Richard Gilman. Montreal; Buffalo, NY; London: McGill-Queen's UP, 2004. pp. xvii, 351.

13180. CAUGHIE, PAMELA L.   Passing as Modernism. Mod/Mod (12:3) 2005, 385–406.

13181. CAWELTI, JOHN G.   Mystery, violence, and popular culture: essays. *See* **12596**.

13182. CHAMBERS, ROSS.   The queer and the creepy: Western fictions of artificial life. *See* **11964**.

13183. CHAPMAN, JAMES.   Bond and Britishness. *In* (pp. 129–43) **16517**.

13184. CLIFF, BRIAN; WALSHE, ÉIBHEAR (eds).   Representing the Troubles: texts and images, 1970–2000. *See* **12610**.

13185. COLLINS, FELICITY; DAVIS, THERESE.   Australian cinema after Mabo. Cambridge; New York: CUP, 2004. pp. vii, 204. Rev. by Felicity Plunkett in AF (19) 2004, 262–72.

13186. COLLINS, PETER C.; O'CONNOR, JOHN E. (eds).   Hollywood's West: the American frontier in film, television, and history. Lexington: Kentucky UP, 2005. pp. xii, 373.

13187. COMENTALE, EDWARD P.; WATT, STEPHEN; WILLMAN, SKIP (eds).   Ian Fleming and James Bond: the cultural politics of 007. *See* **16517**.

13188. CONNOLLY, MAEVE.   Sighting an Irish avant-garde in the intersection of local and international film cultures. B2 (31:1) 2004, 243–65.

13189. CONNOR, STEVEN (ed.).   The Cambridge companion to postmodernism. *See* **12617**.

13190. CONRICH, IAN.   Global pressure and the political state: New Zealand's cinema of crisis. PS (24:2/3) 2005, 140–50.

13191. —— Kiwi gothic: New Zealand's cinema of a perilous paradise. *In* (pp. 114–27) **13374**.

13192. COOK, PAM.   Screening the past: memory and nostalgia in cinema. London; New York: Routledge, 2005. pp. xiii, 246.

13193. CORKIN, STANLEY.   Cowboys as cold warriors: the western and US history. (Bibl. 2004, 13262.) Rev. by Abraham Hoffman in PacHR (74:2) 2005, 321–2.

13194. COURTNEY, SUSAN.   Hollywood fantasies of miscegenation: spectacular narratives of gender and race. Princeton, NJ; Oxford: Princeton UP, 2004. pp. xxi, 373.

13195. COX, STEPHEN.   The *Titanic* and the art of myth. CritR (15:3/4) 2003, 403–34.

13196. CREED, BARBARA.   Pandora's box: essays in film theory. Melbourne: Australian Centre for the Moving Image, 2004. pp. xi, 144.

13197. CROYDEN, MARGARET.   Conversations with Peter Brook, 1970–2000. (Bibl. 2003, 12620.) Rev. by Jenny Koralek in Parabola (28:3) 2003, 111–13.

13198. CRUSIE, JENNIFER (ed.); YEFFETH, GLENN (asst ed.).   Flirting with *Pride and Prejudice*: fresh perspectives on the original chick-lit masterpiece. *See* **9971**.

13199. DALLE VACCHE, ANGELA (ed.).   The visual turn: classical film theory and art history. (Bibl. 2004, 13266.) Rev. by Valérie Orlando in QRFV (21:4) 2004, 356–61.

13200. DALZIELL, TANYA; HUGHES-D'AETH, TONY.   Thematising the global: recent Australian film. PS (24:2/3) 2005, 109–21.

13201. DANIEL, TRENTON.   Hollywood confidential part 2: a conversation with Zeb Ejiro, Ajoke Jacobs, Timde Kelani, and Aquila Njamah. Transition (95) 2004, 110–28.

13202. DAVIS, BLAIR.   Horror meets *noir*: the evolution of cinematic style, 1931–1958. *In* (pp. 191–212) **13250**.

13203. DAY, BARRY.   Coward on film: the cinema of Noël Coward. Foreword by Sir John Mills. *See* **15951**.

13204. DEACY, CHRISTOPHER.   Faith in film: religious themes in contemporary cinema. Aldershot; Burlington, VT: Ashgate, 2005. pp. ix, 170.

13205. DELTCHEVA, ROUMIANA.   Eastern women in Western chronotopes: the representation of East European women in Western films after 1989. *In* (pp. 161–85) **12697**.

13206. DENKERT, DARCIE.   A fine romance. *See* **13017**.

13207. DE NOOY, JULIANA.   Twins in contemporary literature and culture: look twice. *See* **12634**.

13208. DEROSE, MARIA.   Redefining women's power through feminist science fiction. *See* **14122**.

13209. DESAI, JIGNA.   Beyond Bollywood: the cultural politics of South Asian diasporic film. London; New York: Routledge, 2004. pp. x, 280. Rev. by Corey K. Creekmur in FilmQ (59:1) 2005, 49–51.

13210. DE VALCK, MARIJKE; HAGENER, MALTE (eds).   Cinephilia: movies, love and memory. Amsterdam: Amsterdam UP, 2005. pp. 236. (Film culture in transition.)

13211. DÍAZ FERNÁNDEZ, JOSÉ RAMÓN.   Shakespeare film and television derivatives: a bibliography. *In* (pp. 169–89) **13273**.

13212. DIFFRIENT, DAVID SCOTT.   A film is being beaten: notes on the shock cut and the material violence of horror. *In* (pp. 52–81) **13250**.

13213. DIKA, VERA.   Recycled culture in contemporary art and film: the uses of nostalgia. Cambridge; New York: CUP, 2003. pp. xi, 241. (Cambridge studies in film.) Rev. by J. E. Smyth in FilmQ (58:3) 2005, 69–70.

13214. DIMENDBERG, EDWARD.   *Film noir* and the spaces of modernity. (Bibl. 2004, 13273.) Rev. by Adrian Martin in Cineaste (30:2) 2005, 69–70.

13215. DIXON, WHEELER WINSTON.   Lost in the fifties: recovering phantom Hollywood. Carbondale: Southern Illinois UP, 2005. pp. xiv, 209.

13216. —— Straight: constructions of heterosexuality in the cinema. (Bibl. 2004, 13274.) Rev. by Jeff Bennett in FilmQ (58:4) 2005, 71–2.

13217. —— Visions of the apocalypse: spectacles of destruction in American cinema. London: Wallflower, 2003. pp. xiii, 169, (plates) 8. Rev. by Richard Ascarate in FilmQ (59:1) 2005, 72–3.

13218. DONALD, RALPH.   From 'knockout punch' to 'home run': masculinity's 'dirty dozen' sports metaphors in American combat films. FilmH (35:1) 2005, 20–8.

13219. DONALSON, MELVIN.   Black directors in Hollywood. (Bibl. 2004, 13276.) Rev. by Ed Guerrero in FilmQ (58:4) 2005, 54–6.

13220. DONIGER, WENDY.   The woman who pretended to be who she was: myths of self-imitation. *See* **3751**.

13221. DOVEY, LINDIWE.   South African cinema in exile. *See* **13849**.

13222. DRAGON, ZOLTÁN.   Adaptation as intermedial dialogue; or, Tennessee Williams goes to Hollywood. *In* (pp. 187–92) **3734**.

13223. DRIVER, MARTHA W.; RAY, SID (eds).   The medieval hero on screen: representations from *Beowulf* to *Buffy*. (Bibl. 2004, 13278.) Rev. by María José Gómez Calderón in SELIM (12) 2003/04, 209–14; by Christine Mains in JFA (15:4) 2004, 377–9; by Bettina Bildhauer in TLS, 1 Apr. 2005, 33; by Susan Aronstein in Arthuriana (15:2) 2005, 67–8.

13224. DUNNE, MICHAEL.   American film musical themes and forms. (Bibl. 2004, 13280.) Rev. by Charlene Etkind in FilmH (35:2) 2005, 94–5.

13225. EARLY, EMMETT.   The war veteran in film. Jefferson, NC; London: McFarland, 2003. pp. xi, 278.

13226. EBERWEIN, ROBERT (ed.).   The war film. New Brunswick, NJ: Rutgers UP, 2005. pp. viii, 236. (Rutgers depth of field series.) Rev. by Dean R. Cooledge in LitFQ (33:4) 2005, 322–4.

13227. EHRLICH, MATTHEW C.   Journalism in the movies. (Bibl. 2004, 13281.) Rev. by Johanna Cleary in JMCQ (82:1) 2005, 220–1; by Michael Dillon in AmJ (22:1) 2005, 123–4.

13228. ELLIOTT, EMORY.   Cultural memory and the American novel. *See* **16031**.

13229. FAHY, THOMAS (ed.).   Considering Aaron Sorkin: essays on the politics, poetics, and sleight of hand in the films and television series. *See* **19531**.

13230. FEENEY, MARK. Nixon at the movies: a book about belief. Chicago, IL; London: Chicago UP, 2004. pp. xiii, 422. Rev. by James O. Tate in Chronicles (29:8) 2005, 31–2; by Nicholas Evan Sarantakes in JAH (92:3) 2005, 1067–8.

13231. FOSTER, GWENDOLYN AUDREY. Performing Whiteness: postmodern re/constructions in the cinema. (Bibl. 2004, 13290.) Rev. by Arne Lunde in FilmQ (58:1) 2004, 73–4.

13232. FRANCESCHINA, JOHN (ed.). They started talking. By Frank Tuttle. Boalsburg, PA: BearManor Media, 2005. pp. vi, 224.

13233. FRIGERIO, FRANCESCA. 'A filmless London': *flânerie* and urban culture in Dorothy Richardson's articles for *Close Up*. In (pp. 19–31) **14254**.

13234. GABBARD, KRIN. Black magic: White Hollywood and African American culture. (Bibl. 2004, 13294.) Rev. by Jans B. Wager in LitFQ (33:3) 2005, 246–8.

13235. GADD, TIM. Human–animal affiliation in modern popular film. In (pp. 247–59) **14258**.

13236. GASHER, MIKE. Hollywood north: the feature film industry in British Columbia. (Bibl. 2004, 13298.) Rev. by Jerry Wasserman in CanL (185) 2005, 150–2.

13237. GATES, PHILIPPA. Manhunting: the female detective in the serial-killer film. See **20642**.

13238. GATEWARD, FRANCES. In love and trouble: teenage boys and interracial romance. In (pp. 157–82) **13342**.

13239. GERSTNER, DAVID A.; STAIGER, JANET (eds). Authorship and film. (Bibl. 2004, 13301.) Rev. by John Belton in FilmQ (58:3) 2005, 60–2; by Charles R. Warner in JPFT (33:3) 2005, 174–5.

13240. GERTEL, ELLIOT B. Over the top Judaism: precedents and trends in the depiction of Jewish beliefs and observances in film and television. (Bibl. 2003, 12654.) Rev. by Michael Gesin in JPC (38:4) 2005, 772–3.

13241. GIBBS, JOHN; PYE, DOUGLAS (eds). Style and meaning: studies in the detailed analysis of film. Manchester; New York: Manchester UP, 2005. pp. xiii, 250.

13242. GLAJAR, VALENTINA; RADULESCU, DOMNICA (eds). Vampirettes, wretches, and Amazons: Western representations of East European women. See **12697**.

13243. GODARD, JEAN LUC; ISHAGHPOUR, YOUSSEF. Cinema: the archeology of film and the memory of a century. Trans. by John Howe. Oxford; New York: Berg, 2005. pp. 143.

13244. GRAINGE, PAUL (ed.). Memory and popular film. (Bibl. 2004, 13303.) Rev. by Dava L. Simpson in JPC (38:4) 2005, 788–90; by John Streamas in AmS (46:1) 2005, 174–5.

13245. GRANT, BARRY KEITH; SHARRETT, CHRISTOPHER (eds). Planks of reason: essays on the horror film. (Bibl. 1986, 9966.) Lanham, MD; London: Scarecrow Press, 2004. pp. xv, 416. (Revised ed.: first ed. 1984.)

13246. GREENE, DOYLE. Mexploitation cinema: a critical history of Mexican vampire, wrestler, ape-man, and similar films, 1957–1977. Jefferson, NC; London: McFarland, 2005. pp. x, 192.

13247. GRIEVESON, LEE; SONNET, ESTHER; STANFIELD, PETER (eds). Mob culture: hidden histories of the American gangster film. New Brunswick, NJ: Rutgers UP, 2005. pp. xii, 311.

13248. GUGLER, JOSEF. African film: re-imagining a continent. Oxford: Currey; Portsmouth, NH: Heinemann, 2003. pp. xiii, 202. Rev. by Sheila Petty in AfSR (47:3) 2004, 233–4; by Kevin D. Smith in FilmQ (58:3) 2005, 59–60.

13249. GUNN, DREWEY WAYNE. The gay male sleuth in print and film: a history and annotated bibliography. *See* **14153**.

13250. HANTKE, STEFFEN (ed.). Horror film: creating and marketing fear. Jackson; London: Mississippi UP, 2004. pp. xiii, 261.

13251. HARRISON, STEPHANIE (ed.). Adaptations: from short story to big screen: 35 great stories that have inspired great films. New York: Three Rivers Press, 2005. pp. xix, 619.

13252. HAUSLADEN, GARY J.; STARRS, PAUL F. L.A. *noir.* JCG (23:1) 2005, 43–69.

13253. HEDLING, ERIK. Political Modernism and the quest for Film Studies. *In* (pp. 213–20) **12946**.

13254. HEFFERNAN, KEVIN. Ghouls, gimmicks, and gold: horror films and the American movie business, 1953–1968. (Bibl. 2004, 13317.) Rev. by David Sanjek in JAH (92:2) 2005, 677–8.

13255. HEPBURN, ALLAN. Intrigue: espionage and culture. *See* **14164**.

13256. HERZBERG, BOB. Shooting scripts: from pulp western to film. *See* **14166**.

13257. HERZOGENRATH, BERND. Let's get physical: Heidegger's cyborg and the vicissitudes of the machine/body. Gramma (11) 2003, 56–66.

13258. HILLIS, KEN. Film noir and the American Dream: the dark side of enlightenment. VLT (55) 2005, 3–18.

13259. HILLS, MATT. The pleasures of horror. *See* **3803**.

13260. HISCHAK, THOMAS S. Through the screen door: what happened to the Broadway musical when it went to Hollywood. Lanham, MD; London: Scarecrow Press, 2004. pp. ix, 311.

13261. HOBERMAN, J. The dream life: movies, media, and the mythology of the sixties. (Bibl. 2004, 13321.) Rev. by Greg Taylor in FilmQ (58:4) 2004, 58–60; by Andre Millard in JPC (38:3) 2005, 591–3.

13262. HOLMLUND, CHRIS; WYATT, JUSTIN (eds). Contemporary American independent film: from the margins to the mainstream. *See* **20646**.

13263. HOPKINS, LISA. Screening the gothic. Austin: Texas UP, 2005. pp. xvi, 170.

13264. HUGHES, HOWARD. Once upon a time in the Italian West: the filmgoers' guide to spaghetti westerns. London; New York: Tauris, 2004. pp. xxii, 266.

13265. JACKSON, LAUREN. The film connection: twenty years of contacts between the film cultures of New Zealand and Germany. Illusions (37) 2005, 9–15.

13266. JAFFE, AARON. James Bond, meta-brand. *In* (pp. 87–106) **16517**.

13267. JAMES, DAVID E. (ed.).   Stan Brakhage: filmmaker. Philadelphia, PA: Temple UP, 2005. pp. vi, 240. (Wide angle.)

13268. JENKINS, TRICIA.   'Potential lesbians at two o'clock': the hetero-sexualization of lesbianism in the recent teen film. JPC (38:3) 2005, 491–504.

13269. JOHN, JULIET.   Fagin, the Holocaust and mass culture; or, *Oliver Twist* on screen. *See* 10703.

13270. JOHNSON, MICHAEL.   Cowboys, cooks, comics: African American characters in westerns of the 1930s. QRFV (22:3) 2005, 225–35.

13271. KAPLAN, E. ANN.   Trauma culture: the politics of terror and loss in media and literature. *See* 12752.

13272. KEATING, NICOLE MARIE.   Mamma's boy: counting on ghosts, sending smoke signals, and finding surrogate fathers in contemporary film. *In* (pp. 246–63) 13342.

13273. KELLER, JAMES R.; STRATYNER, LESLIE (eds).   Almost Shakespeare: reinventing his works for cinema and television. Jefferson, NC; London: McFarland, 2004. pp. vi, 197.

13274. KELLEY, BEVERLY MERRILL.   Reelpolitik II: political ideologies in '50s and '60s films. (Bibl. 2004, 13334.) Rev. by Kevin Dvorak in FilmH (35:2) 2005, 92–3.

13275. KIM, SUE J.   Apparatus: Theresa Hak Kyung and the politics of form. *See* 15757.

13276. KING, DONALD C.   The theatres of Boston: a stage and screen history. *See* 9487.

13277. KING, GEOFF.   American independent cinema. Bloomington: Indiana UP, 2005. pp. 294.

13278. KIRBY, DAVID A.; GAITHER, LAURA A.   Genetic coming of age: genomics, enhancement, and identity in film. NLH (36:2) 2005, 263–82.

13279. KIRK, JOHN.   Twentieth-century writing and the British working class. *See* 12763.

13280. KITSES, JIM.   Horizons west: directing the western from John Ford to Clint Eastwood. London: British Film Inst., 2004. pp. 342. Rev. by Clive Sinclair in TLS, 21 Jan. 2005, 17; by Jared Rapfogel in Cineaste (30:4) 2005, 68–70.

13281. KNOPF, ROBERT (ed.).   Theater and film: a comparative anthology. *See* 13058.

13282. KOWALSKI, DEAN A.   Classic questions & contemporary film: an introduction to philosophy. Boston, MA: McGraw-Hill, 2005. pp. xiv, 530.

13283. KUGELMASS, JACK (ed.).   Key texts in American Jewish culture. *See* 12769.

13284. LACEY, NICK.   Introduction to film. Basingstoke; New York: Palgrave Macmillan, 2005. pp. xvi, 336.

13285. LAWN, JENNIFER; BEATTY, BRONWYN.   Getting to Wellywood: national branding and the globalisation of the New Zealand film industry. PS (24:2/3) 2005, 122–39.

13286. LAWRENCE, JOHN SHELTON.   Filmography. *In* (pp. 300–21) 13186.

13287. LAWTON, HENRY. Dracula rising: our continuing fascination with vampire fantasies. *See* **12095**.

13288. LENDRUM, ROB. The super Black Macho, one baaad mutha: Black superhero masculinity in 1970s mainstream comic books. *See* **96**.

13289. LEVI, ROSS D. The celluloid courtroom: a history of legal cinema. Westport, CT; London: Praeger, 2005. pp. xxi, 168.

13290. LEWERENZ, SPENCER; NICOLOSI, BARBARA (eds). Behind the screen: Hollywood insiders on faith, film, and culture. Grand Rapids, MI: Baker, 2005. pp. 216.

13291. LINDNER, CHRISTOPH. Why size matters. *In* (pp. 224–37) **16517**.

13292. LOBRUTTO, VINCENT. Becoming film literate: the art and craft of motion pictures. Foreword by Jan Harlan. Westport, CT; London: Praeger, 2005. pp. xviii, 384.

13293. LOISELLE, ANDRÉ. Stage-bound: feature film adaptations of Canadian and Québécois drama. *See* **3983**.

13294. LOTT, M. RAY. The American martial arts film. (Bibl. 2004, 13352.) Rev. by Douglas MacLeod in FilmH (35:1) 2005, 89–90.

13295. LOUGHLIN, GERARD. Alien sex: the body and desire in cinema and theology. Oxford; Malden, MA: Blackwell, 2004. pp. xxx, 306. (Challenges in contemporary theology.) Rev. by M. Gail Hammer in JR (85:3) 2005, 508–9; by Richard Cooper in JAAR (73:4) 2005, 1238–40.

13296. LOY, R. PHILIP. Westerns in a changing America, 1955–2000. (Bibl. 2004, 13353.) Rev. by Scott C. Zeman in JPC (38:6) 2005, 1132–3.

13297. LUCIA, CYNTHIA. Framing female lawyers: women on trial in film. Austin: Texas UP, 2005. pp. xii, 269. Rev. by Yvonne Tasker in Cineaste (31:1) 2005, 79–80.

13298. LUKINBEAL, CHRIS. Cinematic landscapes. JCG (23:1) 2005, 3–22.

13299. LYDEN, JOHN C. Film as religion: myths, morals, and rituals. (Bibl. 2004, 13357.) Rev. by Kent Brintnall in FilmQ (58:4) 2004, 60–1.

13300. MCCABE, SUSAN. Cinematic Modernism: Modernist poetry and film. *See* **14444**.

13301. MCCALL, JOHN C. Hollywood confidential: the unlikely rise of Nigerian video film. Transition (95) 2004, 98–109.

13302. —— Juju and justice at the movies: vigilantes in Nigerian popular videos. AfSR (47:3) 2004, 51–67.

13303. MCCRISKEN, TREVOR B.; PEPPER, ANDREW. American history and contemporary Hollywood film. New Brunswick, NJ: Rutgers UP, 2005. pp. xii, 227.

13304. MCFARLANE, BRIAN. Change is not a choice. Meanjin (62:2) 2003, 112–19. (Film adaptation.)

13305. —— Down the garden path. Meanjin (62:4) 2003, 126–33. (Personal response to British cinema.)

13306. MCGINN, COLIN. The power of movies: how screen and mind interact. New York: Pantheon, 2005. pp. viii, 210.

13307. MAGISTRALE, TONY. Abject terrors: surveying the modern and postmodern horror film. New York; Frankfurt: Lang, 2005. pp. xviii, 213.

13308. MALTBY, RICHARD. Hollywood cinema. (Bibl. 2004, 13365.) Rev. by Howard Libov in JFV (56:4) 2004, 52–4.

13309. MARSHALL, KELLI. 'It doth forget to do the thing it should': Kenneth Branagh, *Love's Labour's Lost*, and (mis)interpreting the musical genre. See **6529**.

13310. MASSOOD, PAULA J. Black city cinema: African American urban experiences in film. (Bibl. 2004, 13373.) Rev. by Jennifer Fuller in FilmQ (57:4) 2004, 48–9.

13311. MATHESON, SUE. The West – hardboiled: adaptations of *film noir* elements, existentialism, and ethics in John Wayne's westerns. JPC (38:5) 2005, 888–910.

13312. MAYER, ROBERT. *Robinson Crusoe* in Hollywood. In (pp. 169–74) **8537.**

13313. MELNYK, GEORGE. One hundred years of Canadian cinema. Toronto; Buffalo, NY; London: Toronto UP, 2004. pp. x, 361. Rev. by Jerry White in DalR (85:1) 2005, 147–8.

13314. MIDDLETON, JOYCE IRENE. Toni Morrison and 'race matters' rhetoric: reading race and Whiteness in visual culture. In (pp. 243–53) **2457.**

13315. MITCHNER, LESLIE. 'Oy vey! Is it a crisis or is it just me?' CinJ (44:3) 2005, 82–6.

13316. MITCHUM, PETRINE DAY; PAVIA, AUDREY. Hollywood hoofbeats: trails blazed across the silver screen. Irvine, CA: BowTie Press, 2005. pp. 216.

13317. MIZEJEWSKI, LINDA. Hardboiled & high heeled: the woman detective in popular culture. (Bibl. 2004, 13383.) Rev. by William B. Covey in MFS (51:1) 2005, 239–43; by Natalie Hevener Kaufman in Clues (23:3) 2005, 75–6.

13318. MOREY, ANNE. Hollywood outsiders: the adaptation of the film industry, 1913–1934. Minneapolis; London: Minnesota UP, 2003. pp. x, 242. (Commerce and mass culture.) Rev. by Chuck Maland in FilmQ (58:3) 2005, 66–7.

13319. MORRIS, NIGEL. 'Talk to me in your language': broadcasting and the context of Wales on film. JSBC (12:1) 2005, 9–23.

13320. MORRISON, AIMÉE. It's more than a game: cinematic videogaming in the 1980s. TextT (13:1) 2004, 113–34.

13321. MOSELEY, MERRITT. Henry James and novelistic impersonation. See **11437.**

13322. NACHBAR, JACK; MERLOCK, RAY. Bibliography: trail dust. Books about western movies: selected classics and works since 1980. In (pp. 322–44) **13186.**

13323. NERONI, HILARY. The violent woman: femininity, narrative, and violence in contemporary American cinema. Albany: New York State UP, 2005. pp. xiv, 203. (SUNY series in feminist criticism and theory.)

13324. NEVINS, FRANCIS M. An afficionado's view: the Latino dimension of the Hopalong Cassidy films. BR (27:2) 2003, 143–58.

13325. NICHOLSON, HEATHER NORRIS (ed.). Screening culture: constructing image and identity. (Bibl. 2003, 12765.) Rev. by Roy Todd in BJCS (17:2) 2004, 252–3.

13326. NOCHIMSON, MARTHA P.   Waddaya lookin' at? Rereading the gangster film through *The Sopranos*. *In* (pp. 185–204) **13247**.

13327. NOONAN, BONNIE.   Women scientists in fifties science fiction films. Jefferson, NC; London: McFarland, 2005. pp. ix, 225.

13328. O'DONNELL, PATRICK.   James Bond, cyborg–aristocrat. *In* (pp. 55–68) **16517**.

13329. OKADA, JUN.   The PBS and NAATA connection: comparing the public spheres of Asian American film and video. VLT (55) 2005, 39–51.

13330. ONEGA, SUSANA; GUTLEBEN, CHRISTIAN (eds).   Refracting the canon in contemporary British literature and film. *See* **3879**.

13331. O'PRAY, MICHAEL.   Film, form, and phantasy: Adrian Stokes and film aesthetics. Basingstoke; New York: Palgrave Macmillan, 2004. pp. xiv, 252.

13332. PELIZZON, V. PENELOPE; WEST, NANCY M.   Multiple indemnity: *film noir*, James M. Cain, and adaptations of a tabloid case. Narrative (13:3) 2005, 211–37.

13333. PETRO, PATRICE.   Whose crisis is it? CinJ (44:3) 2005, 86–9. (Crisis in Film Studies publishing.)

13334. PETROLLE, JEAN; WEXMAN, VIRGINIA WRIGHT (eds).   Women and experimental filmmaking. Urbana: Illinois UP, 2005. pp. x, 300.

13335. PFAFF, FRANÇOISE (ed.).   Focus on African films. (Bibl. 2004, 13397.) Rev. by Carmela Garritano in AfSR (48:2) 2005, 179–81.

13336. PHILLIPS, KENDALL R.   Projected fears: horror films and American culture. Westport, CT; London: Praeger, 2005. pp. 227.

13337. PICART, CAROLINE JOAN S.   Remaking the Frankenstein myth on film: between laughter and horror. (Bibl. 2004, 13399.) Rev. by John W. Howard, III, in WL (28:2) 2005, 42–3.

13338. PINSKY, MARK I.   The Gospel according to Disney: faith, trust, and pixie dust. (Bibl. 2004, 13401.) Rev. by Kelly J. Baker in JPC (38:4) 2005, 763–4.

13339. PIZZATO, MARK.   Theatres of human sacrifice: from ancient ritual to screen violence. Albany: New York State UP, 2005. pp. ix, 265. (SUNY series in psychoanalysis and culture.)

13340. PLUNKETT, FELICITY.   B[l]acktracking towards Australia: *Australian Film after Mabo*. AF (19) 2004, 262–72 (review-article).

13341. POLLOCK, MARY S.; RAINWATER, CATHERINE (eds).   Figuring animals: essays on animal images in art, literature, philosophy, and popular culture. *See* **14258**.

13342. POMERANCE, MURRAY; GATEWARD, FRANCES (eds).   Where the boys are: cinemas of masculinity and youth. Detroit, MI: Wayne State UP, 2005. pp. 421. (Contemporary approaches to film and television.)

13343. POSTER, JAMIE.   Code orange: career fear and publishing. CinJ (44:3) 2005, 89–92.

13344. RA'AD, BASEM L.   Subliminal filmic reflections of ancient Eastern Mediterranean civilizations. QRFV (22:4) 2005, 371–7.

13345. RADER, DEAN.   Composition, visual culture, and the problems of class. *See* **20668.**

13346. RAND, YARDENA.   Wild open spaces: why we love westerns. Manville, RI: Maverick Spirit Press, 2005. pp. xii, 192.

13347. RAYNER, JONATHAN.   Conflict and conspiracy: public and personal memory in Australian film. PS (24:2/3) 2005, 82–93.

13348. —— 'Terror Australia': areas of horror in the Australian cinema. *In* (pp. 89–113) **13374.**

13349. REID, MARK A.   Black lenses, Black voices: African American film now. *See* **20669.**

13350. RENZI, THOMAS C. (ed.).   H. G. Wells: six scientific romances adapted for film. *See* **20061.**

13351. RHODES, GARY D.; SPRINGER, JOHN PARRIS (eds).   Docufictions: essays on the intersection of documentary and fictional filmmaking. Jefferson, NC; London: McFarland, 2005. pp. x, 294.

13352. RICH, NATHANIEL.   San Francisco *noir*: the city in *film noir* from 1940 to the present. New York: Little Bookroom, 2005. pp. 167.

13353. RICHTER, DAVID H.   Your cheatin' art: double dealing in cinematic narrative. Narrative (13:1) 2005, 11–28.

13354. ROBB, DAVID L.   Operation Hollywood: how the Pentagon shapes and censors the movies. Amherst, NY: Prometheus, 2004. pp. 384. Rev. by John Shelton Lawrence in JAC (28:3) 2005, 329–30.

13355. ROBERTS, TERRI.   Momentum is key: translating *Sweeney* to the silver screen. *See* **19518.**

13356. ROCKETT, KEVIN; HILL, JOHN (eds).   National cinema and beyond. Dublin; Portland, OR: Four Courts Press, 2004. pp. 170. (Studies in Irish film, 1.)

13357. ROLLINS, PETER C.; O'CONNOR, JOHN E. (eds).   Hollywood's Indian: the portrayal of the Native American in film. (Bibl. 2004, 13422.) Rev. by R. David Edmunds in JAH (86:1) 1999, 333–4.

13358. —— —— Hollywood's West: the American frontier in film, television, and history. Lexington: Kentucky UP, 2005. pp. xii, 373.

13359. ROMANO, FREDERICK V.   The boxing filmography: American features, 1920–2003. (Bibl. 2004, 13424.) Rev. by Ron Briley in FilmH (35:2) 2005, 99–100.

13360. ROMBES, NICHOLAS.   Avant-garde realism. CTHEORY (135) 2005.

13361. ROOF, JUDITH.   Living the James Bond lifestyle. *In* (pp. 71–86) **16517.**

13362. ROTH, ELAINE.   Momophobia: incapacitated mothers and their adult children in 1990s films. QRFV (22:2) 2005, 189–202.

13363. ROTHMAN, WILLIAM (ed.).   Cavell on film. Albany: New York State UP, 2005. pp. xxvii, 399. (SUNY series: Horizons of cinema.)

13364. RÜCK, STEFANIE.   'Good Queen Bess': the mnemonic construction of Queen Elizabeth I. YREAL (21) 2005, 205–23.

13365. RUFFLES, TOM. Ghost images: cinema of the afterlife. Jefferson, NC; London: McFarland, 2004. pp. x, 269.

13366. RYAN, JUDYLYN S. Spirituality as ideology in Black women's film and literature. *See* **12899.**

13367. SÁNCHEZ-ESCALONILLA, ANTONIO. The hero as a visitor in Hell: the descent into death in film structure. JPFT (32:4) 2005, 149–56.

13368. SARAT, AUSTIN; DOUGLAS, LAWRENCE; UMPHREY, MARTHA MERRILL (eds). Law on the screen. Stanford, CA: Stanford UP, 2005. pp. xi, 264. (Amherst series in law, jurisprudence, and social thought.)

13369. SCHAEFER, ERIC. Dirty little secrets: scholars, archivists, and dirty movies. MovIm (5:2) 2005, 79–105.

13370. SCHATZ, THOMAS. *Stagecoach* and Hollywood's A-western renaissance. *In* (pp. 21–47) **13776.**

13371. SCHECHTER, HAROLD. Savage pastimes: a cultural history of violent entertainment. *See* **3917.**

13372. SCHNEIDER, STEVEN JAY (ed.). Horror film and psychoanalysis: Freud's worst nightmare. (Bibl. 2004, 13430.) Rev. by Roz Kaveney in TLS, 28 Jan. 2005, 20.

13373. —— New Hollywood violence. *See* **20676.**

13374. —— WILLIAMS, TONY (eds). Horror international. Detroit, MI: Wayne State UP, 2005. pp. xi, 384. (Contemporary approaches to film and television.)

13375. SCHOBER, ADRIAN. Possessed child narratives in literature and film: contrary states. *See* **14272.**

13376. SCHWARTZ, RONALD. Neo-*noir*: the new *film noir* style from *Psycho* to *Collateral*. Lanham, MD; London: Scarecrow Press, 2005. pp. xiv, 157.

13377. SEED, DAVID. Brainwashing: the fictions of mind control: a study of novels and films since World War II. *See* **14273.**

13378. SHADOIAN, JACK. Dreams & dead ends: the American gangster film. (Bibl. 2003, 12828.) Rev. by Jeff Evans in JPC (38:3) 2005, 583–4.

13379. SHAPIRO, HARRY. Shooting stars: drugs, Hollywood, and the movies. London: Serpent's Tail, 2003. pp. v, 314. Rev. by Jon Garvie in TLS, 11 Nov. 2005, 27.

13380. SHARRY, TIMOTHY. Bad boys and Hollywood hype: gendered conflict in juvenile delinquency film. *In* (pp. 21–40) **13342.**

13381. SHELTON, BOB. A cultural study of the art film. Lewiston, NY; Lampeter: Mellen Press, 2003. 2 vols. pp. 883.

13382. SHERMAN, FRASER A. *The Wizard of Oz* catalog: L. Frank Baum's novel, its sequels, their adaptations for stage, television, movies, radio, music videos, comic books, commercials, and more. *See* **15363.**

13383. SHIEL, MARK; FITZMAURICE, TONY (eds). Screening the city. London; New York: Verso, 2003. pp. vi, 312. Rev. by Mariana Mogilevich in FilmQ (57:4) 2004, 69–70.

13384. SHORT, SUE. Cyborg cinema and contemporary subjectivity. Basingstoke; New York: Palgrave Macmillan, 2005. pp. xi, 247.

13385. SILVER, ALAIN; URSINI, JAMES. L.A. *noir*: the city as character. Santa Monica, CA: Santa Monica Press, 2005. pp. 173.

13386. SIMMON, SCOTT. The invention of the western film: a cultural history of the genre's first half-century. (Bibl. 2004, 13441.) Rev. by Chuck Maland in FilmQ (58:1) 2004, 68–70; by Sam B. Girgus in AmS (46:1) 2005, 171–2; by Nicola McDonald in Mod/Mod (12:4) 2005, 733–5.

13387. SIMPSON, PAUL. The Rough Guide to kids' movies. London: Haymarket, 2004. pp. x, 303. (Rough Guides reference guides.)

13388. SJOGREN, BRITTA. Into the vortex: female voice and paradox in film. Urbana: Illinois UP, 2005. pp. 248.

13389. SLOCUM, J. DAVID. Cinema and the civilizing process: rethinking violence in the World War II combat film. CinJ (44:3) 2005, 35–63.

13390. —— (ed.). Terrorism, media, liberation. New Brunswick, NJ: Rutgers UP, 2005. pp. ix, 353. (Rutgers depth of field series.)

13391. SMITH, ANGELA MARIE. Impaired and ill at ease: New Zealand's cinematics of disability. PS (24:2/3) 2005, 64–81.

13392. SMITH, KAY H. 'Hamlet, Part Eight, the Revenge'; or, Sampling Shakespeare in a postmodern world. *See* **6369**.

13393. SMOODIN, ERIC. How I learned to stop worrying and love the crisis in publishing. CinJ (44:3) 2005, 95–8.

13394. SOBCHACK, VIVIAN. Carnal thoughts: embodiment and moving image culture. Berkeley; London: California UP, 2004. pp. xii, 328.

13395. SOLLORS, WERNER. Hemingway, *film noir*, and the emergence of a twentieth-century American style. *See* **16993**.

13396. STAM, ROBERT. Literature through film: realism, magic, and the art of adaptation. Oxford; Malden, MA: Blackwell, 2005. pp. xvii, 388. Rev. by Thomas Leitch in LitFQ (33:3) 2005, 233–45; by James Naremore in Cineaste (31:1) 2005, 75–6.

13397. —— RAENGO, ALESSANDRA (eds). A companion to literature and film. (Bibl. 2004, 13453.) Rev. by Thomas Leitch in LitFQ (33:3) 2005, 233–45; by James Naremore in Cineaste (31:1) 2005, 75–6.

13398. —— —— Literature and film: a guide to the theory and practice of film adaptation. *See* **20681**.

13399. STANFIELD, PETER. 'American as chop suey': invocations of gangsters in Chinatown, 1920–1936. *In* (pp. 238–62) **13247**.

13400. —— Walking the streets: Black gangsters and the 'abandoned city' in the 1970s Blaxploitation cycle. *In* (pp. 281–300) **13247**.

13401. STARR, CHARLIE W. *The Silver Chair* and the silver screen: C. S. Lewis on myth, fairy tale and film. *In* (pp. 3–23) **17727**.

13402. STEIN, ATARA. The Byronic hero in film, fiction, and television. *See* **10337**.

13403. STINSON, SAM. The Tracy connection. *See* **10869**.

13404. SUID, LAWRENCE H.; HAVERSTICK, DOLORES A. Stars and stripes on screen: a comprehensive guide to portrayals of American military on film.

Lanham, MD; London: Scarecrow Press, 2005. pp. xxi, 419. Rev. by Robert Fyne in FilmH (35:2) 2005, 103.

13405. SUTHERLAND, KATHRYN. Jane Austen's textual lives: from Aeschylus to Bollywood. *See* **10057.**

13406. SWEET, MATTHEW. Shepperton Babylon: the lost worlds of British cinema. London; Boston, MA: Faber & Faber, 2005. pp. 388.

13407. TATAR, MARIA. Secrets beyond the door: the story of Bluebeard and his wives. Princeton, NJ; Oxford: Princeton UP, 2004. pp. xii, 247.

13408. TAUB, MICHAEL (ed.). Films about Jewish life and culture. Lewiston, NY; Lampeter: Mellen Press, 2005. pp. x, 120.

13409. TELOTTE, J. P. Annual bibliography of Film Studies – 2003. PS (24:1) 2004, 82–107.

13410. —— Annual bibliography of Film Studies – 2004. PS (25:1) 2005, 76–95.

13411. TEVIS, RAY; TEVIS, BRENDA. The image of librarians in cinema, 1917–1999. Jefferson, NC; London: McFarland, 2005. pp. ix, 230.

13412. THOMSON, DAVID. The whole equation: a history of Hollywood. New York: Knopf, 2005. pp. x, 402. Rev. by Paula Marantz Cohen in TLS, 15 July 2005, 18.

13413. TIBBETTS, JOHN C. Composers in the movies: studies in musical biography. Foreword by Simon Callow. New Haven, CT; London: Yale UP, 2005. pp. xvi, 365.

13414. TURNER, MATTHEW. Cowboys and comedy: the simultaneous deconstruction and reinforcement of generic conventions in western parody. *In* (pp. 218–35) **13186.**

13415. VOIGTS-VIRCHOW, ECKART (ed.). Janespotting and beyond: British heritage retrovisions since the mid-1990s. Tübingen: Narr, 2004. pp. 212.

13416. VON DOVIAK, SCOTT. Hick flicks: the rise and fall of redneck cinema. Foreword by Chris Gore. Jefferson, NC; London: McFarland, 2005. pp. x, 222. Rev. by Jay Morong in FilmH (35:2) 2005, 101–3.

13417. WAGER, JANS B. Dames in the driver's seat: rereading *film noir*. Austin: Texas UP, 2005. pp. 190.

13418. WALKER, JANET. Trauma cinema: documenting incest and the Holocaust. Berkeley; London: California UP, 2005. pp. xxii, 251.

13419. WALSH, RICHARD. Finding St Paul in film. New York: Clark, 2005. pp. v, 218.

13420. —— Reading the Gospels in the dark: portrayals of Jesus in film. (Bibl. 2004, 13464.) Rev. by Melanie J. Wright in LitTheol (18:3) 2004, 366–8.

13421. WALTJE, JÖRG. Blood obsession: vampires, serial murder, and the popular imagination. *See* **12958.**

13422. WARTENBERG, THOMAS E.; CURRAN, ANGELA (eds). The philosophy of film: introductory text and readings. Oxford; Malden, MA: Blackwell, 2005. pp. xii, 308.

13423. WELSCH, JANICE R.; ADAMS, J. Q. Multicultural films: a reference guide. Westport, CT; London: Greenwood Press, 2005. pp. xvii, 231.

13424. WILLIAMS, JUAN. Black political power in film and television. *See* **14060**.

13425. WILSON, RONALD W. Gang busters: the Kefauver Crime Committee and the syndicate films of the 1950s. *In* (pp. 67–89) **13247**.

13426. WITHAM, BARRY B. The Federal Theatre Project: a case study. (Bibl. 2004, 13469.) Rev. by Jeffrey H. Richards in CompDr (37:3/4) 2003/04, 438–40; by Kurt Eisen in ModDr (48:1) 2005, 213–14; by Rena Fraden in TheatreS (46:1) 2005, 134–5; by Lionel Kelly in RES (56:225) 2005, 476–8.

13427. WOLFE, CARY. Animal rites: American culture, the discourse of species, and posthumanist theory. Foreword by W. J. T. Mitchell. *See* **3962**.

13428. WORLEY, ALEC. Empires of the imagination: a critical survey of fantasy cinema from Georges Méliès to *The Lord of the Rings*. Foreword by Brian Sibley. Jefferson, NC; London: McFarland, 2005. pp. viii, 296.

13429. WYLLIE, BARBARA. Nabokov at the movies: film perspectives in fiction. *See* **18479**.

13430. YANOW, SCOTT. Jazz on film: the complete story of the musicians & music onscreen. San Francisco, CA: Backbeat, 2004. pp. vi, 314.

13431. YOUNG, SUZIE. Snapping up schoolgirls: legitimation crisis in recent Canadian horror. *In* (pp. 235–56) **13374**.

13432. ZETTEL, SARAH. Times and tenors; or, What the movies have done, and failed to do, to *Pride and Prejudice*. *In* (pp. 97–103) **9971**.

13433. ZIMMERMAN, STEVE; WEISS, KEN. Food in the movies. Jefferson, NC; London: McFarland, 2005. pp. ix, 306.

Individual Films

10 Things I Hate about You (1999)

13434. BADIA, JANET. 'One of those people like Anne Sexton or Sylvia Plath': the pathologized woman reader in literary and popular culture. *In* (pp. 236–54) **12549**.

13435. BALIZET, ARIANE M. Teen scenes: recognizing Shakespeare in teen film. *In* (pp. 122–36) **13273**.

13436. JONES, MELISSA. 'An aweful rule': safe schools, hard canons, and Shakespeare's loose heirs. *In* (pp. 137–54) **13273**.

2001: a Space Odyssey (1968)

13437. NAREMORE, JAMES. Love and death in *AI: Artificial Intelligence*. *See* **20691**.

The Age of Innocence (1993)

13438. NICHOLLS, MARK. Male melancholia and Martin Scorsese's *The Age of Innocence*. FilmQ (58:1) 2004, 25–35.

Aladdin (1992)

13439. MALLAN, KERRY; McGILLIS, RODERICK. Between a frock and a hard place: camp aesthetics and children's culture. CRAS (35:1) 2005, 1–19.

Alien Films (1979–1997)

13440. Boyle, Brenda M.   Monstrous bodies, monstrous sex: queering *Alien Resurrection*. GothS (7:2) 2005, 158–71.

13441. Gallardo C., Ximena; Smith, C. Jason.   Alien woman: the making of Lt Ellen Ripley. (Bibl. 2004, 13491.) Rev. by Matthew Kapell in Extrapolation (46:1) 2005, 142–4; by Stacie L. Hanes in JFA (16:2) 2005, 155–7.

13442. Russell, Lorena.   Queer gothic and heterosexual panic in the ass-end of space. GothS (7:2) 2005, 143–57.

All about Eve (1950)

13443. Corber, Robert J.   Cold War *femme*: lesbian visibility in Joseph L. Mankiewicz's *All about Eve*. GLQ (11:1) 2005, 1–22.

American Beauty (1999)

13444. Hole, George T.   *American Beauty*: look closer. In (pp. 153–68) **13158**.

13445. Potkay, Adam.   The joy of *American Beauty*. Raritan (25:1) 2005, 69–86.

13446. Tripp, Daniel.   'Wake up!': narratives of masculine epiphany in millennial cinema. QRFV (22:2) 2005, 181–8.

American Pie (1999)

13447. Schneider, Steven Jay.   Jerkus interruptus: the terrible trials of masturbating boys in recent Hollywood cinema. In (pp. 377–93) **13342**.

The American President (1995)

13448. Downing, Spencer.   Handling the truth: Sorkin's liberal vision. In (pp. 127–45) **19531**.

13449. Nein, John.   The republic of Sorkin: a view from the cheap seats. In (pp. 193–209) **19531**.

American Psycho (2000)

13450. Kilbourn, Russell J. A.   American Frankenstein: modernity's monstrous progeny. Mosaic (38:3) 2005, 167–84.

Angels with Dirty Faces (1938)

13451. Shannon, Christopher.   Public enemies, local heroes: the Irish American gangster film in classic Hollywood cinema. See **13722**.

Another Day in Paradise (1998)

13452. Mahadevan, Sadhir.   'Perfect childhoods': Larry Clark puts boys on screen. In (pp. 98–113) **13342**.

Apocalypse Now (1979)

13453. Oziewicz, M.   A personal voyage of discovery in F. F. Coppola's *Apocalypse Now*: réchauffé *Heart of Darkness*. In (pp. 205–16) **12672**.

Arsenic and Old Lace (1944)

13454. Haslam, Jason.   'A secret proclamation': queering the gothic parody of *Arsenic and Old Lace*. GothS (7:2) 2005, 127–42.

Ashpet: an American Cinderella (1990)

13455. GRUNER, ELISABETH ROSE. Saving 'Cinderella': history and story in *Ashpet* and *Ever After*. See **13559.**

The Bad News Bears (1976)

13456. MOSHER, JERRY. Survival of the fattest: contending with the fat boy in children's ensemble films. *In* (pp. 61–82) **13342.**

The Ballad of Gregorio Cortez (1982)

13457. CONWAY, CECELIA. *Ballad of Gregorio Cortez*: a traditional tale for postmodern times. *In* (pp. 112–32) **13950.**

The Ballad of Little Jo (1993)

13458. DOYLE, MARY AGNES. Crossing the Jordan: genealogy, geography, genre, gender. TheatreA (56) 2003, 67–77.

Bamboozled (2000)

13459. BARLOWE, JAMIE. 'You must never be a misrepresented people': Spike Lee's *Bamboozled*. CRAS (33:1) 2003, 1–15.

13460. EPP, MICHAEL H. Raising minstrelsy: humour, satire and the stereotype in *The Birth of a Nation* and *Bamboozled*. CRAS (33:1) 2003, 17–35.

13461. KEELING, KARA. Passing for human: *Bamboozled* and digital humanism. WP (15:1) 2005, 237–50.

Banana Split (1991)

13462. MARCHETTI, GINA. Pursuits of hapa-ness: Kip Fulbeck's boyhood among ghosts. *In* (pp. 279–96) **13342.**

The Band Wagon (1953)

13463. SILVA, ARTURO. Vincente Minnelli's dream of Tony Hunter's *Band Wagon*'s 'Girl Hunt'. FilCr (30:1) 2005, 2–20.

Beauty and the Beast (1991)

13464. STEEVES, H. PETER. Yep, Gaston's gay: Disney and the beauty of a beastly love. PCR (16:1) 2005, 125–45.

beDevil (1993)

13465. SUMMERHAYES, CATHERINE. Haunting secrets: Tracey Moffatt's *beDevil*. FilmQ (58:1) 2004, 14–24.

The Bedford Incident (1965)

13466. SEED, DAVID. Policing the Cold War frontier: *The Bedford Incident*. See **19027.**

Being John Malkovich (1999)

13467. OTT, WALTER. It's my heeeeaaaad! Sex and death in *Being John Malkovich*. *In* (pp. 61–76) **13158.**

13468. YOUNG, WILLIAM. Otherwise than *Being John Malkovich*: incarnating the name of God. LitTheol (18:1) 2004, 95–108.

The Big Lebowski (1998)

13469. COMER, TODD A. 'This aggression will not stand': myth, war, and ethics in *The Big Lebowski*. SubStance (107) 2005, 98–117.

13470. Cook, James L.   Reproaching the military hero *sans peur*. See **3737**.

Big Night (1996)

13471. DeAngelis, Rose; Anderson, Donald R.   Gastronomic *miscuglio*: foodways in Italian American narrative. See **14120**.

Bill and Ted's Excellent Adventure (1989)

13472. Troyer, John; Marchiselli, Chani.   Slack, slacker, slackest: homosocial bonding practices in contemporary dude cinema. *In* (pp. 264–76) **13342**.

Bird (1988)

13473. McCombe, John P.   Reinventing Bird: the evolving image of Charlie Parker on film. See **13745**.

The Birds (1963)

13474. McCombe, John P.   'Oh, I see …': *The Birds* and the culmination of Hitchcock's hyper-Romantic vision. CinJ (44:3) 2005, 64–80.

The Bitter Ash (1963)

13475. Enemark, Brett.   The city as Other in Larry Kent's film *The Bitter Ash*. WCL (39:2) 2005, 237–43.

The Black Stallion (1979)

13476. Addison, Lindsay McLean.   The Black Stallion in print and film. *In* (pp. 163–75) **14258**.

Blade Runner (1982)

13477. Harley, Alexis.   *America: a Prophecy*: when Blake meets *Blade Runner*. SSE (31) 2005, 61–75.

13478. Morris, Robyn.   Re-visioning representations of difference in Larissa Lai's *When Fox Is a Thousand* and Ridley Scott's *Blade Runner*. See **17557**.

13479. Nishime, LeiLani.   The mulatto cyborg: imagining a multiracial future. CinJ (44:2) 2005, 34–49.

13480. Park, Jane Chi Hyun.   Stylistic crossings: cyberpunk impulses in *anime*. See **16680**.

13481. Wilson, Eric G.   Moviegoing and golem-making: the case of *Blade Runner*. JFV (57:3) 2005, 31–43.

The Blair Witch Project (1999)

13482. Higley, Sarah L.; Weinstock, Jeffrey Andrew (eds).   Nothing that is: millennial cinema and the *Blair Witch* controversies. (Bibl. 2004, 13535.) Rev. by Carl Boehm in JFA (15:4) 2004, 369–71.

The Bloody Child (1996)

13483. Petrolle, Jean.   Allegory, politics, and the avant-garde. *In* (pp. 93–104) **13334**.

Bloody Mama (1970)

13484. Strunk, Mary Elizabeth.   Mother Barker: film star and public enemy no. 1. *In* (pp. 146–62) **13247**.

Blue in the Face (1995)

13485. ARDOLINO, FRANK. A name, a number, and a picture: the cinematic memorialization of Jackie Robinson. *See* **13549**.

Boys Don't Cry (1999)

13486. DANDO, CHRISTINA. Range wars: the Plains frontier of *Boys Don't Cry*. JCG (23:1) 2005, 91–113.

13487. HANRAHAN, REBECCA. Popping it in: gender identity in *Boys Don't Cry*. *In* (pp. 77–93) **13158**.

Boyz N the Hood (1991)

13488. REGESTER, CHARLENE. The feminization and victimization of the African American athlete in *Boyz N the Hood*, *Cooley High*, and *Cornbread, Earl and Me*. *In* (pp. 333–49) **13342**.

Bram Stoker's Dracula (1992)

13489. MCGUNNIGLE, CHRISTOPHER. My own vampire: the metamorphosis of the queer monster in Francis Ford Coppola's *Bram Stoker's Dracula*. GothS (7:2) 2005, 172–84.

13490. SAUDO, NATHALIE. *I was glad to see her paleness and her illness*: la redoutable bonne santé dans *Dracula*. *See* **12101**.

Brazil (1985)

13491. WHEELER, BEN. Reality is what you can get away with: fantastic imaginings, rebellion and control in Terry Gilliam's *Brazil*. CritS (17:1) 2005, 95–108.

Breaking the Waves (1996)

13492. SHILOH, ILANA. Lars von Trier: *Breaking the Waves*; *Dancer in the Dark*; *Dogville*. MLS (35:1) 2005, 84–8.

Bride of Frankenstein (1935)

13493. EBERLE-SINATRA, MICHAEL. Readings of homosexuality in Mary Shelley's *Frankenstein* and four film adaptations. *See* **11968**.

Brighton Rock (1947)

13494. CHIBNALL, STEVE. *Brighton Rock*. London; New York: Tauris, 2005. pp. 130. (Turner classic movies: British film guides.)

Broken Arrow (1950)

13495. HEARNE, JOANNA. The 'ache for home': assimilation and separatism in Anthony Mann's *Devil's Doorway*. *In* (pp. 126–59) **13186**.

Bugsy (1991)

13496. RIZZO, SERGIO. Learning from Las Vegas: Hollywood narrates the simulacrum. *See* **13504**.

Bulworth (1998)

13497. SWIRSKI, PETER. *Bulworth* and the new American Left. JAC (28:3) 2005, 293–301.

Busman's Honeymoon (1940)

13498. GORMAN, ANITA G.; MATEER, LESLIE R.   The medium is the message: *Busman's Honeymoon* as play, novel, and film. *See* **19328.**

Calamity Jane (1953)

13499. BATES, ANNA LOUISE.   Calamity Jane and the social construction of gender in the 1930s and 1950s. PCR (16:2) 2005, 69–81.

Calendar (1993)

13500. NELSON, TOLLOF.   Passing time in intercultural cinema: the exilic experience of the time-passer in Atom Egoyan's *Calendar* (1993). SubStance (106) 2005, 129–44.

The Cape Town Affair (1967)

13501. HEUMANN, JOSEPH K.; MURRAY, ROBIN L.   *Cape Town Affair*: right-wing *noir*, South African style. JuC (47) 2005.

Casablanca (1942)

13502. PONTUSO, JAMES F. (ed.).   Political philosophy comes to Rick's: *Casablanca* and American civic culture. Lanham, MD: Lexington, 2005. pp. 200.

13503. SINGER, BARNETT.   *Casablanca* in its time – and ours. ContRev (287:1677) 2005, 233–7.

Casino (1995)

13504. RIZZO, SERGIO.   Learning from Las Vegas: Hollywood narrates the simulacrum. PCR (16:2) 2005, 131–43.

Caught (1949)

13505. DEUTELBAUM, MARSHALL.   Leonora's place: the spatial logic of *Caught*. AQ (60:5) 2005, 87–96.

13506. STUDLAR, GAYLYN.   Max Op(h)uls fashions femininity. *See* **13635.**

Caught (1996)

13507. MCLAUGHLIN, THOMAS.   Space and sexuality in *Caught*.   *In* (pp. 206–18) **13950.**

Chariots of Fire (1981)

13508. JONES, GLEN.   'Down on the floor and give me ten sit-ups': British sports feature film. *See* **13587.**

Charlie's Angels (2000)

13509. COON, DAVID ROGER.   Two steps forward, one step back: the selling of *Charlie's Angels*. JPFT (33:1) 2005, 2–11.

Chasing Amy (1997)

13510. WALLS, JERRY L.   Flying without a map: *Chasing Amy* and the quest for satisfying relationships. *In* (pp. 137–50) **13158.**

Chimes at Midnight (1965)

13511. BARNABY, ANDREW.   Imitation as originality in Gus Van Sant's *My Own Private Idaho*. *In* (pp. 22–41) **13273.**

13512. BELL, ROBERT H. Rereading Orson Welles's *Chimes at Midnight*. SRev (89:4) 2004, 566–76.

Christmas in Connecticut (1945)

13513. SIGLER, CAROLYN. 'I'll be home for Christmas': misrule and the paradox of gender in World War II-era Christmas films. *See* 13735.

Cimarron (1931)

13514. SMYTH, J. E. The new Western history in 1931: RKO and the challenge of *Cimarron*. *In* (pp. 37–64) 13186.

Citizen Kane (1941)

13515. NAREMORE, JAMES (ed.). Orson Welles's *Citizen Kane*: a casebook. (Bibl. 2004, 13568.) Rev. by Peter Lambert in TLS, 1 Apr. 2005, 20.

13516. SZÉPÁL, LÍVIA. The modern American city in *Citizen Kane*: an unconventional history. *In* (pp. 243–8) 3734.

A Civil Action (1998)

13517. WALDMAN, DIANE. A case for corrective criticism: *A Civil Action*. *In* (pp. 201–30) 13368.

The Client (1994)

13518. O'SHEA, MARY B. Crazy from the heat: Southern boys and coming of age. *In* (pp. 83–97) 13342.

Clueless (1995)

13519. KELLY, DAVID. *Emma*, Cher, and the maze of unknowing. SSE (29) 2003, 3–15.

The Color Purple (1985)

13520. WHITT, JAN. What happened to Celie and Idgie? 'Apparitional lesbians' in American film. SPC (27:3) 2005, 43–57.

Coming Home (1978)

13521. BOYLE, BRENDA M. Phantom pains: disability, masculinity and the normal in Vietnam War representations. PrSt (27:1/2) 2005, 93–107.

Contact (1997)

13522. KEITH, HEATHER; FESMIRE, STEVEN. Our place in the cosmos: faith and belief in *Contact*. *In* (pp. 17–31) 13158.

Cooley High (1975)

13523. REGESTER, CHARLENE. The feminization and victimization of the African American athlete in *Boyz N the Hood*, *Cooley High*, and *Cornbread, Earl and Me*. *In* (pp. 333–49) 13342.

Cornbread, Earl and Me (1975)

13524. REGESTER, CHARLENE. The feminization and victimization of the African American athlete in *Boyz N the Hood*, *Cooley High*, and *Cornbread, Earl and Me*. *In* (pp. 333–49) 13342.

Cortile Cascino (1962)

13525. FISCHER, CRAIG. *NBC White Paper, Cortile Cascino*, and the assault on the familiar. *In* (pp. 43–57) 13950.

Crazy in Alabama (1999)

13526. O'SHEA, MARY B.   Crazy from the heat: Southern boys and coming of age. *In* (pp. 83–97) **13342.**

Crimes and Misdemeanors (1989)

13527. CONRAD, MARK T.   The indifferent universe: Woody Allen's *Crimes and Misdemeanors. In* (pp. 113–24) **13158.**

Cruel Intentions (1999)

13528. BENSON-ALLOTT, CAETLIN.   The 'mechanical truth' behind *Cruel Intentions*: desire, AIDS, and the MTV Movie Awards' 'Best Kiss'. QRFV (22:4) 2005, 341–58.

Cruising (1980)

13529. DAVIDSON, GUY.   Contagious relations: simulation, paranoia, and the postmodern condition in William Friedkin's *Cruising* and Felice Picano's *The Lure*. GLQ (11:1) 2005, 23–64.

The Crying Game (1992)

13530. LOCKETT, CHRISTOPHER.   Terror and rebirth: Cathleen ni Houlihan, from Yeats to *The Crying Game*. LitFQ (33:4) 2005, 290–305.

13531. MORIEL, LIORA.   Passing and the performance of gender, race, and class acts: a theoretical framework. *See* **17584.**

Dance, Fools, Dance (1931)

13532. SONNET, ESTHER.   Ladies love brutes: reclaiming female pleasures in the lost history of Hollywood gangster cycles, 1929–1931. *In* (pp. 93–119) **13247.**

Dancer in the Dark (2000)

13533. SHILOH, ILANA.   Lars von Trier: *Breaking the Waves*; *Dancer in the Dark*; *Dogville. See* **13492.**

Dances with Wolves (1990)

13534. KELLER, ALEXANDRA.   Historical discourse and American identity in westerns since the Reagan era. *In* (pp. 239–60) **13186.**

Dangerous Liaisons (1988)

13535. CARDULLO, BERT.   Fiction into film: notes on one paradigmatic scene and two emblematic adaptations. *See* **13831.**

Dark City (1998)

13536. TRIPP, DANIEL.   'Wake up!': narratives of masculine epiphany in millennial cinema. *See* **13446.**

13537. WILSON, DAVID H.   The pathological machine: *Dark City*'s translation of Schreber's *Memoirs*. JFA (15:2) 2004, 153–64.

Daughters of the Dust (1991)

13538. DEMPSEY, ANNA.   Nurturing nature and the cinematic experience: the American landscape and the rural female community. *See* **13711.**

13539. MACHIORLATTI, JENNIFER A.   Revisiting Julie Dash's *Daughters of the Dust*: Black feminist narrative and diasporic recollection. SAtlR (70:1) 2005, 97–116.

Dead End (1937)

13540. CLAVARON, YVES; DIETERLE, BERNARD (eds).   La mémoire des villes. *See* **20330**.

Dead Man Walking (1995)

13541. REINELT, JANELLE.   The ambivalence of Catholic compassion. JDTC (20:1) 2005, 103–12.

Death and the Maiden (1994)

13542. KAMIR, ORIT.   Cinematic judgment and jurisprudence: a woman's memory, recovery, and justice in a post-traumatic society (a study of Polanski's *Death and the Maiden*). *In* (pp. 27–81) **13368**.

The Deer Hunter (1978)

13543. CHONG, SYLVIA SHIN HUEY.   Restaging the War: *The Deer Hunter* and the primal scene of violence. CinJ (44:2) 2005, 89–106.

Devil in a Blue Dress (1995)

13544. SHAPIRO, MICHAEL J.   The racial–spatial order and the law: *Devil in a Blue Dress*. *In* (pp. 82–105) **13368**.

13545. SHEFRIN, ELANA.   *Le noir et le blanc*: hybrid myths in *Devil in a Blue Dress* and *L.A. Confidential*. *See* **13626**.

Devil's Doorway (1950)

13546. HEARNE, JOANNA.   The 'ache for home': assimilation and separatism in Anthony Mann's *Devil's Doorway*. *In* (pp. 126–59) **13186**.

Diamonds Are Forever (1971)

13547. ALLEN, DENNIS W.   'Alimentary, Dr Leiter': anal anxiety in *Diamonds Are Forever*. *In* (pp. 24–41) **16517**.

Diner (1982)

13548. HOFFMAN, EMILY.   Now ask me what's on the flip side: trivia, validation, and narrative in Barry Levinson's *Diner*. SPC (27:3) 2005, 27–42.

Do the Right Thing (1989)

13549. ARDOLINO, FRANK.   A name, a number, and a picture: the cinematic memorialization of Jackie Robinson. JPFT (33:3) 2005, 151–9.

Dominick and Eugene (1988)

13550. PITOFSKY, ALEX.   'Don't let anybody hurt me': working-class masculinity in *Dominick and Eugene*. *In* (pp. 149–60) **13950**.

The Doom Generation (1995)

13551. HART, KYLO-PATRICK R.   *Auteur/bricoleur/provocateur*: Gregg Araki and postpunk style in *The Doom Generation*. JFV (55:1) 2003, 30–8.

Double Indemnity (1944)

13552. MANON, HUGH S.   Some like it cold: fetishism in Billy Wilder's *Double Indemnity*. CinJ (44:4) 2005, 18–43.

Drums along the Mohawk (1939)

13553. POAGUE, LELAND.   That past, this present: historicizing John Ford, 1939. *In* (pp. 82–112) **13776**.

Dude, Where's My Car? (2000)

13554. TROYER, JOHN; MARCHISELLI, CHANI.   Slack, slacker, slackest: homo-social bonding practices in contemporary dude cinema. *In* (pp. 264–76) **13342.**

Emma (1996)

13555. LIEBREGTS, PETER.   Images of an imaginist: two film versions of Jane Austen's *Emma*. *In* (pp. 277–99) **9237.**

The English Patient (1996)

13556. HSU, HSUAN.   Post-nationalism and the cinematic apparatus in Minghella's adaptation of Ondaatje's *The English Patient*. *In* (pp. 49–61) **18634.**

13557. TÖTÖSY DE ZEPETNEK, STEVEN.   Ondaatje's *The English Patient* and questions of history. *In* (pp. 115–31) **18634.**

Eve's Bayou (1997)

13558. ELLISON, MARY.   Echoes of Africa in *To Sleep with Anger* and *Eve's Bayou*. *See* **13827.**

Ever After (1998)

13559. GRUNER, ELISABETH ROSE.   Saving 'Cinderella': history and story in *Ashpet* and *Ever After*. ChildLit (31) 2003, 142–54.

Evita (1996)

13560. GRAHAM-JONES, JEAN.   'The truth is … my soul is with you': documenting a tale of two Evitas. *See* **13031.**

The Exorcist (1973)

13561. ARNZEN, MICHAEL.   'There is only one': the restoration of the repressed in *The Exorcist*: the version you've never seen. *In* (pp. 99–116) **13250.**

Extremities (1986)

13562. STILLING, ROGER JAMES.   Love, death, and healing: some psychoanalytic themes in *Extremities*. *In* (pp. 133–48) **13950.**

Eyes Wide Shut (1999)

13563. ARNOLD, DANA; IVERSEN, MARGARET (eds).   Art and thought. Oxford; Malden, MA: Blackwell, 2003. pp. x, 224. (New interventions in art history, 1.) Rev. by Katerina Reed-Tsocha in BJA (45:2) 2005, 200–2.

Far from the Madding Crowd (1967)

13564. DAVIS, W. EUGENE.   Folk songs in the shearing-supper scene: John Schlesinger's movie version of *Far from the Madding Crowd*. *See* **11115.**

Fargo (1996)

13565. LUHR, WILLIAM G. (ed.).   The Coen Brothers' *Fargo*. (Bibl. 2004, 13616.) Rev. by R. Barton Palmer in FilmQ (58:4) 2005, 57–8.

Fast Times at Ridgemont High (1982)

13566. SCHNEIDER, STEVEN JAY.   Jerkus interruptus: the terrible trials of masturbating boys in recent Hollywood cinema. *In* (pp. 377–93) **13342.**

Fear and Loathing in Las Vegas (1998)

13567. RIZZO, SERGIO. Learning from Las Vegas: Hollywood narrates the simulacrum. *See* **13504.**

A Few Good Men (1992)

13568. MILLS, FIONA. Depictions of the US military: only 'a few good men' need apply. *In* (pp. 101–14) **19531.**

13569. NEIN, JOHN. The republic of Sorkin: a view from the cheap seats. *In* (pp. 193–209) **19531.**

13570. RINGELBERG, KIRSTIN. His Girl Friday (and every day): brilliant women put to poor use. *In* (pp. 91–100) **19531.**

Field of Dreams (1989)

13571. REISING, R. W. 'BOB'. From the big top to the big leagues: Burt Lancaster's baseball odysseys (oddities?). JPC (38:3) 2005, 552–63.

Fight Club (1999)

13572. NIEMI, ALISON. Film as religious experience: myths and models in mass entertainment. *See* **13664.**

13573. TRIPP, DANIEL. 'Wake up!': narratives of masculine epiphany in millennial cinema. *See* **13446.**

13574. WESTERFELHAUS, ROBERT; BROOKEY, ROBERT ALAN. At the unlikely confluence of conservative religion and popular culture: *Fight Club* as heteronormative ritual. TPQ (24:3/4) 2004, 302–26.

13575. WHITEHOUSE, GLENN. Unimaginable variations: Christian responsibility in the cinema of broken identity. LitTheol (18:3) 2004, 321–50.

13576. ZAVODNY, JOHN. I am Jack's wasted life: *Fight Club* and personal identity. *In* (pp. 47–60) **13158.**

Firecreek (1968)

13577. COSTELLO, MATTHEW J. Rewriting *High Noon*: transformations in American popular political culture during the Cold War, 1952–1968. *In* (pp. 175–97) **13186.**

Floating Life (1996)

13578. MESSAGE, KYLIE. Clara Law's *Floating Life* (interview). *In* (pp. 311–23) **12674.**

Fort Apache (1948)

13579. McDONOUGH, KATHLEEN A. *Wee Willie Winkie* goes west: the influence of the British Empire genre on Ford's cavalry trilogy. *In* (pp. 99–114) **13186.**

Frankenstein (1931)

13580. EBERLE-SINATRA, MICHAEL. Readings of homosexuality in Mary Shelley's *Frankenstein* and four film adaptations. *See* **11968.**

A Free Soul (1931)

13581. SONNET, ESTHER. Ladies love brutes: reclaiming female pleasures in the lost history of Hollywood gangster cycles, 1929–1931. *In* (pp. 93–119) **13247.**

Fried Green Tomatoes at the Whistle Stop Café (1991)

13582. WHITT, JAN.   What happened to Celie and Idgie? 'Apparitional lesbians' in American film. *See* **13520**.

Full Metal Jacket (1987)

13583. GRUBEN, PATRICIA.   Practical joker: the invention of a protagonist in *Full Metal Jacket*. LitFQ (33:4) 2005, 270–9.

Gattaca (1997)

13584. JOWETT, LORNA.   Remasculinisation in *Gattaca* and *The Matrix*. Foundation (92) 2004, 51–63.

Get on the Bus (1996)

13585. BRUMMETT, BARRY.   Rhetorical homologies: form, culture, experience. *See* **2234**.

Giant (1956)

13586. BAXTER, MONIQUE JAMES.   *Giant* helps America recognize the cost of discrimination: a lesson of World War II. *In* (pp. 160–72) **13186**.

The Girl with Brains in Her Feet (1997)

13587. JONES, GLEN.   'Down on the floor and give me ten sit-ups': British sports feature film. FilmH (35:2) 2005, 29–40.

The Glass Key (1942)

13588. STUDLAR, GAYLYN.   A gunsel is being beaten: gangster masculinity and the homoerotics of the crime film, 1941–1942. *In* (pp. 120–45) **13247**.

The Godfather (1972–1990)

13589. BLACK, RONALD J.   The American Dream as paradox in *The Godfather*. *See* **18978**.

Godzilla (1998)

13590. TAYLER, CHRISTOPHER.   It's alive! LRB (27:3) 2005, 23–4 (review-article).

13591. TSUTSUI, WILLIAM.   Godzilla on my mind: fifty years of the king of monsters. (Bibl. 2004, 13645.) Rev. by Christopher Tayler in LRB (27:3) 2005, 23–4.

Goldfinger (1964)

13592. HOVEY, JAIME.   Lesbian bondage; or, Why dykes like 007. *In* (pp. 42–54) **16517**.

13593. JENKINS, TRICIA.   James Bond's 'Pussy' and Anglo-American Cold War sexuality. *See* **16521**.

Good Morning, Vietnam (1987)

13594. FELLERS, CARLA.   'What a wonderful world': the rhetoric of the official and the unofficial in *Good Morning, Vietnam*. WLA (17:1/2) 2005, 232–41.

The Goonies (1985)

13595. MOSHER, JERRY.   Survival of the fattest: contending with the fat boy in children's ensemble films. *In* (pp. 61–82) **13342**.

Great Expectations (1946)

13596. EELLS, EMILY. From word to image: illustrating *Great Expectations*. See **10678**.

13597. JOHNSON, MICHAEL K. Not telling the story the way it happened: Alfonso Cuarón's *Great Expectations*. See **13598**.

Great Expectations (1998)

13598. JOHNSON, MICHAEL K. Not telling the story the way it happened: Alfonso Cuarón's *Great Expectations*. LitFQ (33:1) 2005, 62–78.

13599. MUKHERJEE, ANKHI. Missed encounters: repetition, rewriting, and contemporary returns to Charles Dickens's *Great Expectations*. See **10719**.

Groundhog Day (1993)

13600. SPENCE, JAMES H. What Nietzsche could teach you: eternal return in *Groundhog Day*. In (pp. 273–87) **13158**.

Guns Don't Argue (1957)

13601. STRUNK, MARY ELIZABETH. Mother Barker: film star and public enemy no. 1. In (pp. 146–62) **13247**.

The Haunting (1999)

13602. HATTENHAUER, DARRYL. Stephen Spielberg's *The Haunting*: a reconsideration of David Self's script. In (pp. 251–66) **17181**.

Heaven & Earth (1993)

13603. KILLMEIER, MATTHEW A.; KWOK, GLORIA. A people's history of empire; or, The imperial recuperation of Vietnam? Countermyths and myths in *Heaven and Earth*. JCI (29:3) 2005, 256–72.

Hell Drivers (1957)

13604. GIRELLI, ELISABETTA. Transnational maleness: the Italian immigrant in *Hell Drivers*. CinJ (44:4) 2005, 44–56.

High Noon (1952)

13605. BLAKE, MICHAEL F. Code of honor: the making of three great American westerns – *High Noon*, *Shane*, and *The Searchers*. Lanham, MD: Taylor Trade, 2003. pp. xvi, 260.

13606. COSTELLO, MATTHEW J. Rewriting *High Noon*: transformations in American popular political culture during the Cold War, 1952–1968. In (pp. 175–97) **13186**.

13607. PETCH, SIMON. Trampling out the vintage: revenge and resentment in *High Noon*. SSE (29) 2003, 57–68.

Honeymoon in Vegas (1992)

13608. RIZZO, SERGIO. Learning from Las Vegas: Hollywood narrates the simulacrum. See **13504**.

Hoosiers (1986)

13609. BRILEY, RON. Basketball's great White hope and Ronald Reagan's America: *Hoosiers*. FilmH (35:1) 2005, 12–19.

The Horse Whisperer (1998)

13610. BRUMMETT, BARRY. Rhetorical homologies: form, culture, experience. *See* **2234**.

House of Games (1987)

13611. McINTIRE-STRASBURG, JEFFREY O. Performing pedagogy: teaching and confidence games in David Mamet's *House of Games* and *The Spanish Prisoner*. JMMLA (38:1) 2005, 31–7.

Housekeeping (1987)

13612. CARDULLO, BERT. Fiction into film: notes on one paradigmatic scene and two emblematic adaptations. *See* **13831**.

If... (1968)

13613. SINKER, MARK. *If...* London: British Film Inst., 2004. pp. 88. (BFI film classics.) Rev. by Richard Armstrong in Cineaste (30:3) 2005, 83–4.

Imitation of Life (1934)

13614. ZARAGOZA CRUZ, OMAYRA. Orchestra seats: passing in cinema. WP (15:1) 2005, 211–36.

Imitation of Life (1959)

13615. NIU, GRETA AI-YU. Performing white triangles: Joan Riviere's *Womanliness as a Masquerade* and *Imitation of Life* (1959). QRFV (22:2) 2005, 135–44.

The Innocents (1961)

13616. TREDY, DENNIS. Shadows of shadows: techniques of ambiguity in three film adaptations of *The Turn of the Screw*: J. Clayton's *The Innocents* (1961), D. Curtis's *The Turn of the Screw* (1974), and A. Aloy's *Presence of Mind* (1999). EREA (3:2) 2005, 67–86.

JFK (1991)

13617. VON BOTHMER, BERNARD. Oliver Stone's *JFK*: political assassination, Kennedy, and Vietnam. WLA (17:1/2) 2005, 242–51.

Johnny Eager (1942)

13618. STUDLAR, GAYLYN. A gunsel is being beaten: gangster masculinity and the homoerotics of the crime film, 1941–1942. *In* (pp. 120–45) **13247**.

Kids (1995)

13619. MAHADEVAN, SADHIR. 'Perfect childhoods': Larry Clark puts boys on screen. *In* (pp. 98–113) **13342**.

The Killing (1956)

13620. HARPER, COSSAR. The revenge of the repressed: homosexuality as Other in *The Killing*. QRFV (22:2) 2005, 145–54.

The Killing Fields (1984)

13621. GRAY, SPALDING. Swimming to Cambodia. New York: Theatre Communications Group, 2005. pp. xvi, 133.

The King and I (1956)

13622. HOUSTON, KERR. 'Siam not so small!': maps, history, and gender in *The King and I*. CamOb (59) 2005, 73–117.

The King Is Alive (2000)

13623. BOTTINELLI, JENNIFER J. Watching Lear: resituating the gaze at the intersection of film and drama in Kristian Levring's *The King Is Alive*. LitFQ (33:2) 2005, 101–9.

King of Kings (1961)

13624. TORRY, ROBERT. The wrath of God: Hollywood epics and American Cold War policy. See **13814**.

Kiss Me Deadly (1955)

13625. PRITTS, NATE. The dingus and the great whatsit: motivating strategies in cinema. See **13650**.

L.A. Confidential (1997)

13626. SHEFRIN, ELANA. *Le noir et le blanc*: hybrid myths in *Devil in a Blue Dress* and *L.A. Confidential*. LitFQ (33:3) 2005, 172–81.

Ladies Love Brutes (1930)

13627. SONNET, ESTHER. Ladies love brutes: reclaiming female pleasures in the lost history of Hollywood gangster cycles, 1929–1931. *In* (pp. 93–119) **13247**.

The Last Temptation of Christ (1988)

13628. MIDDLETON, DARREN J. N. Celluloid synoptics: viewing the gospels of Marty and Mel together. *In* (pp. 71–81) **20763**.

13629. ORTIZ, GAYE W. 'Passion'-ate women: the female presence in *The Passion of the Christ*. *In* (pp. 109–20) **20763**.

13630. RILEY, ROBIN. Film, faith, and cultural conflict: the case of Martin Scorsese's *The Last Temptation of Christ*. (Bibl. 2004, 13697.) Rev. by Darren J. N. Middleton in SoHR (39:1) 2005, 93–6.

Laura (1944)

13631. EMRYS, A. B. *Laura*, Vera, and Wilkie: deep sensation roots of a *noir* novel. See **15719**.

Lawrence of Arabia (1962)

13632. RAW, LAURENCE. T. E. Lawrence, the Turks, and the Arab revolt in the cinema: Anglo-American and Turkish representations. LitFQ (47:2) 2004, 252–61.

A League of Their Own (1992)

13633. DANIELS, DAYNA B. You throw like a girl: sport and misogyny on the silver screen. FilmH (35:1) 2005, 29–38.

Leaving Las Vegas (1995)

13634. RIZZO, SERGIO. Learning from Las Vegas: Hollywood narrates the simulacrum. See **13504**.

Letter from an Unknown Woman (1948)

13635. STUDLAR, GAYLYN.   Max Op(h)uls fashions femininity. AQ (60:5) 2005, 65–86.

The Little Mermaid (1989)

13636. MALLAN, KERRY; MCGILLIS, RODERICK.   Between a frock and a hard place: camp aesthetics and children's culture. *See* **13439**.

The Little Shop of Horrors (1960)

13637. NOONAN, JULIE A.   *Little Shop of Horrors*: re-visioning the future through pastiche and science fiction. TheatreA (56) 2003, 113–29.

The Loneliness of the Long Distance Runner (1962)

13638. HUGHSON, JOHN.   The loneliness of the angry young sportsman. FilmH (35:2) 2005, 41–8.

Lone Star (1996)

13639. ARREOLA, DANIEL D.   Forget the Alamo: the border as place in John Sayles' *Lone Star.* JCG (23:1) 2005, 23–42.

13640. HANDLEY, GEORGE B.   Oedipus in the Americas: *Lone Star* and the reinvention of American Studies. FMLS (40:2) 2004, 160–81.

13641. SULTZE, KIMBERLY.   Challenging legends, complicating border lines: the concept of '*frontera*' in John Sayles's *Lone Star. In* (pp. 261–80) **13186**.

Lord of the Flies (1963)

13642. MOSHER, JERRY.   Survival of the fattest: contending with the fat boy in children's ensemble films. *In* (pp. 61–82) **13342**.

Lost Highway (1997)

13643. ROCHE, DAVID.   The death of the subject in David Lynch's *Lost Highway* and *Mulholland Drive.* EREA (2:2) 2004, 42–52.

A Lost Lady (1934)

13644. SCHUETH, MICHAEL.   Taking liberties: Willa Cather and the 1934 film adaptation of *A Lost Lady. In* (pp. 113–24) **15749**.

Ma Barker's Killer Brood (1960)

13645. STRUNK, MARY ELIZABETH.   Mother Barker: film star and public enemy no. 1. *In* (pp. 146–62) **13247**.

Mad Max Films (1979–1985)

13646. THOMPSON, STACY.   Tentative utopias. *See* **17677**.

Magnolia (1999)

13647. DILLMAN, JOANNE CLARKE.   Twelve characters in search of a televisual text: *Magnolia* masquerading as a soap opera. JPFT (33:3) 2005, 142–50.

Malice (1993)

13648. COKAL, SUSANN.   In plain view and the dark unknown: narratives of the feminine body in *Malice. In* (pp. 37–60) **19531**.

13649. GROSS, ROBERT F.   Mannerist *noir*: *Malice. In* (pp. 19–35) **19531**.

The Maltese Falcon (1941)

13650. PRITTS, NATE. The dingus and the great whatsit: motivating strategies in cinema. MidQ (47:1) 2005, 68–80.

13651. STUDLAR, GAYLYN. A gunsel is being beaten: gangster masculinity and the homoerotics of the crime film, 1941–1942. *In* (pp. 120–45) **13247.**

The Manchurian Candidate (1962)

13652. OHI, KEVIN. Of Red queens and garden clubs: *The Manchurian Candidate*, Cold War paranoia, and the historicity of the homosexual. CamOb (58) 2005, 149–83.

Mansfield Park (1999)

13653. SUTHERLAND, JOHN. Some nabob: the sometimes useful errors of Edward Said. *See* **15032.**

The Man Who Came to Dinner (1942)

13654. SIGLER, CAROLYN. 'I'll be home for Christmas': misrule and the paradox of gender in World War II-era Christmas films. *See* **13735.**

The Man with the Golden Arm (1955)

13655. SIMMONS, JEROLD. Challenging the Production Code: *The Man with the Golden Arm*. JPFT (33:1) 2005, 39–48.

Mary Poppins (1964)

13656. COCKIN, KATHARINE. Inventing the suffragettes: anachronism, gnosticism and corporeality in contemporary fiction. *See* **16469.**

Mary Shelley's Frankenstein (1994)

13657. EBERLE-SINATRA, MICHAEL. Readings of homosexuality in Mary Shelley's *Frankenstein* and four film adaptations. *See* **11968.**

The Matrix (1999–)

13658. ANGEL, MARIA. Brainfood: rationality, aesthetics and economies of affect. *See* **16902.**

13659. CLOVER, JOSHUA. *The Matrix*. London: British Film Inst., 2004. pp. 95. (BFI modern classics.) Rev. by Anna Thomson in TLS, 3 June 2005, 27.

13660. GRAU, CHRISTOPHER (ed.). Philosophers explore *The Matrix*. Oxford; New York: OUP, 2005. pp. xvi, 336.

13661. HASLAM, JASON. Coded discourse: romancing the (electronic) shadow in *The Matrix*. ColLit (32:3) 2005, 92–115.

13662. IRWIN, WILLIAM (ed.). More *Matrix* and philosophy: *Revolutions* and *Reloaded* decoded. Chicago, IL: Open Court, 2005. pp. xiii, 226. (Popular culture and philosophy, 11.) Rev. by Rebecca Housel in JAC (28:3) 2005, 326.

13663. JOWETT, LORNA. Remasculinisation in *Gattaca* and *The Matrix*. *See* **13584.**

13664. NIEMI, ALISON. Film as religious experience: myths and models in mass entertainment. CritR (15:3/4) 2003, 435–46.

13665. PARK, JANE CHI HYUN. Stylistic crossings: cyberpunk impulses in *anime*. *See* **16680.**

13666. SHUSTERMAN, RONALD. Thinking by numbers; or, Cultural memory after the 'end' of art. YREAL (21) 2005, 365–78.

13667. TRIPP, DANIEL. 'Wake up!': narratives of masculine epiphany in millennial cinema. *See* **13446**.

13668. WHITEHOUSE, GLENN. Unimaginable variations: Christian responsibility in the cinema of broken identity. *See* **13575**.

Memento (2000)

13669. BAUR, MICHAEL. We all need mirrors to remind us who we are: inherited meaning and inherited selves in *Memento*. *In* (pp. 94–110) **13158**.

13670. LITTLE, WILLIAM G. Surviving *Memento*. Narrative (13:1) 2005, 67–83.

13671. WHITEHOUSE, GLENN. Unimaginable variations: Christian responsibility in the cinema of broken identity. *See* **13575**.

Midnight in the Garden of Good and Evil (1997)

13672. JUNCKER, CLARA. Simulacrum Savannah: midnight in the garden of good and evil. *See* **15470**.

Miracle on 34th Street (1947)

13673. SIGLER, CAROLYN. 'I'll be home for Christmas': misrule and the paradox of gender in World War II-era Christmas films. *See* **13735**.

The Misfits (1961)

13674. GOLDSTEIN, LAURENCE. Finishing the picture: Arthur Miller, 1915–2005. *See* **18244**.

13675. —— *The Misfits* and American culture. *In* (pp. 109–34) **18234**.

Mr Arkadin / Confidential Report (1955)

13676. RORABACK, ERIK S. Cinematic movement within Orson Welles's *Mr Arkadin / Confidential Report* (1955) for a newly armed eye. *In* (pp. 229–35) **3734**.

Mr Smith Goes to Washington (1939)

13677. RINGELBERG, KIRSTIN. His Girl Friday (and every day): brilliant women put to poor use. *In* (pp. 91–100) **19531**.

13678. SMOODIN, ERIC. 'Everyone went wild over it': film audiences, political cinema, and *Mr Smith Goes to Washington*. *In* (pp. 231–52) **13368**.

Monsoon Wedding (2000)

13679. SHARPE, JENNY. Gender, nation, and globalization in *Monsoon Wedding* and *Dilwale Dulhania Le Jayenge*. Meridians (6:1) 2005, 58–81.

Moulin Rouge (1952)

13680. O'CONNOR, ROBERT. Baz Luhrmann's *Moulin Rouge!* Orpheus again descending. *See* **20737**.

Mulholland Falls (1996)

13681. SONNET, ESTHER; STANFIELD, PETER. 'Good evening gentlemen; can I check your hats please?': masculinity, dress, and the retro gangster cycles of the 1990s. *In* (pp. 163–84) **13247**.

Murder in Harlem (1935)

13682. BERNSTEIN, MATTHEW. Oscar Micheaux and Leo Frank: cinematic justice across the color line. FilmQ (57:4) 2004, 8–21.

My Beautiful Laundrette (1986)

13683. GERAGHTY, CHRISTINE. *My Beautiful Laundrette.* London; New York: Tauris, 2005. pp. 108. (Turner classic movies: British film guides.)

My Own Private Idaho (1991)

13684. BARNABY, ANDREW. Imitation as originality in Gus Van Sant's *My Own Private Idaho. In* (pp. 22–41) **13273.**

13685. TINKCOM, MATTHEW. Out West: Gus Van Sant's *My Own Private Idaho. In* (pp. 233–45) **13342.**

The Natural (1984)

13686. HUNTER, LATHAM. 'What's natural about it?': a baseball movie as introduction to key concepts in Cultural Studies. FilmH (35:2) 2005, 71–7.

Ninotchka (1939)

13687. RADULESCU, DOMNICA. Amazons, wretches, and vampirettes: essentialism and beyond in the representation of East European women. *In* (pp. 23–59) **12697.**

Nixon (1995)

13688. WITCHER, RUSS. A textual analysis of movie director Oliver Stone's *Nixon.* Lewiston, NY; Lampeter: Mellen Press, 2004. pp. viii, 97. (Studies in the history and criticism of film, 9.)

Nora (2000)

13689. MEANEY, GERARDINE. *Nora.* Cork: Cork UP in assn with the Film Inst. of Ireland, 2004. pp. 86. (Ireland into film, 9.) Rev. by Carol Shloss in JJLS (19:1) 2005, 13.

Nothing but a Man (1964)

13690. DICK, BRUCE; VOGEL, MARK. Demanding dignity: *Nothing but a Man. In* (pp. 58–73) **13950.**

Notorious (1946)

13691. PRITTS, NATE. The dingus and the great whatsit: motivating strategies in cinema. *See* **13650.**

Notting Hill (1998)

13692. TAYLOR, CHRISTOPHER JOHN. The language of film: corpora and statistics in the search for authenticity: *Notting Hill* (1998) – a case study. Misc (30) 2004, 71–85.

O Brother, Where Art Thou? (2000)

13693. WEINLICH, BARBARA P. 'Odyssey, where art thou?': myth and mythmaking in the twenty-first century. CML (25:2) 2005, 89–108.

Oklahoma! (1955)

13694. AIKIN, ROGER CUSHING. Was Jud Jewish? Property, ethnicity, and gender in *Oklahoma!* QRFV (22:3) 2005, 277–83.

Oliver! (1968)

13695. BROOKS, DIANNE.   The beautiful English boy: Mark Lester and *Oliver! In* (pp. 114–30) **13342.**

The Omega Man (1971)

13696. MURRAY, ROBIN L.; HEUMANN, JOSEPH K.   Environmental nostalgia in eco-disaster movies of the early 1970s. CEACrit (67:2) 2005, 15–28.

Orlando (1992)

13697. NEWMAN, HERTA.   Orlando: fantasy fiction and film. *See* **20394.**

13698. NYMAN, MICKI.   Positioning Orlando as subject in Lacan's Imaginary. *See* **20395.**

Out of Rosenheim (1987)

13699. DEMPSEY, ANNA.   Nurturing nature and the cinematic experience: the American landscape and the rural female community. *See* **13711.**

Out of Sight (1998)

13700. HOLMLUND, CHRIS.   Postfeminism from A to G. *See* **20771.**

The Outlaw Josey Wales (1976)

13701. HASPEL, PAUL.   Studies in outlawry: the strange career of Josey Wales. *See* **15709.**

Pale Rider (1985)

13702. HEUMANN, JOSEPH K.; MURRAY, ROBIN L.   *Pale Rider*: environmental politics, Eastwood style. JuC (47) 2005.

Pandaemonium (2000)

13703. CHRISTIE, WILLIAM.   Coleridge and Wordsworth in *Pandaemonium*. SSE (31) 2005, 109–20.

Peeping Tom (1960)

13704. ZIMMER, CATHERINE.   The camera's eye: *Peeping Tom* and technological perversion. *In* (pp. 35–51) **13250.**

Performance (1970)

13705. WILLIAMS, DEANNE.   Mick Jagger Macbeth. *See* **6575.**

The Personal History, Adventures, Experience, and Observation of David Copperfield, the Younger (1935)

13706. BALCERZAK, SCOTT.   Dickensian orphan as child star: Freddie Bartholomew and the commodity of cute in MGM's *David Copperfield* (1935). LitFQ (33:1) 2005, 51–61.

Philadelphia (1993)

13707. FARMER, BRETT.   The fabulous sublimity of gay diva worship. CamOb (59) 2005, 164–95.

π (1998)

13708. KLAVER, ELIZABETH.   *Proof, π,* and *Happy Days*: the performance of mathematics. *See* **15233.**

The Piano (1993)

13709. BIHLMEYER, JAIME. The (un)speakable FEMININITY in mainstream movies: Jane Campion's *The Piano*. CinJ (44:2) 2005, 68–88.

Pickup on South Street (1953)

13710. HEUMANN, JOSEPH K.; MURRAY, ROBIN L. *Cape Town Affair*: right-wing *noir*, South African style. *See* **13501**.

Places in the Heart (1984)

13711. DEMPSEY, ANNA. Nurturing nature and the cinematic experience: the American landscape and the rural female community. JCG (23:1) 2005, 115–37.

The Plainsman (1936)

13712. BATES, ANNA LOUISE. Calamity Jane and the social construction of gender in the 1930s and 1950s. *See* **13499**.

Platoon (1986)

13713. KELLER, JAMES R. Discretion and valor: Prince Hal's *Platoon*. LitFQ (33:2) 2005, 110–17.

Pleasantville (1998)

13714. REITAN, ERIC. *Pleasantville*, Aristotle, and the meaning of life. *In* (pp. 213–27) **13158**.

Presence of Mind (1999)

13715. TREDY, DENNIS. Shadows of shadows: techniques of ambiguity in three film adaptations of *The Turn of the Screw*: J. Clayton's *The Innocents* (1961), D. Curtis's *The Turn of the Screw* (1974), and A. Aloy's *Presence of Mind* (1999). *See* **13616**.

The Producers (1968)

13716. SEBESTA, JUDITH. From celluloid to stage: the 'movical', *The Producers*, and the postmodern. TheatreA (56) 2003, 97–112.

The Professionals (1966)

13717. HOWE, WINONA. Almost angels, almost feminists: women in *The Professionals*. *In* (pp. 198–217) **13186**.

Prospero's Books (1991)

13718. DEWEESE, DAN. Prospero's pharmacy: Peter Greenaway and the critics play Shakespeare's mimetic game. *In* (pp. 155–68) **13273**.

Psycho (1960)

13719. LUNA, ALINA M. Visual perversity: a re-articulation of maternal instinct. *See* **10498**.

13720. SKERRY, PHILIP J. The shower scene in Hitchcock's *Psycho*: creating cinematic suspense and terror. Lewiston, NY; Lampeter: Mellen Press, 2005. pp. viii, 409. (Studies in the history and criticism of film, 11.)

The Public Enemy (1931)

13721. MALTBY, RICHARD. Why boys go wrong: gangsters, hoodlums, and the natural history of delinquent careers. *In* (pp. 41–66) **13247**.

13722. SHANNON, CHRISTOPHER.   Public enemies, local heroes: the Irish American gangster film in classic Hollywood cinema. NewHR (9:4) 2005, 48–64.

Pulp Fiction (1994)

13723. SILBERSTEIN, MICHAEL.   Grace, fate, and accident in *Pulp Fiction*. *In* (pp. 257–72) **13158**.

Queen of the Mob (1940)

13724. STRUNK, MARY ELIZABETH.   Mother Barker: film star and public enemy no. 1. *In* (pp. 146–62) **13247**.

The Racketeer (1929)

13725. SONNET, ESTHER.   Ladies love brutes: reclaiming female pleasures in the lost history of Hollywood gangster cycles, 1929–1931. *In* (pp. 93–119) **13247**.

Radiance (1998)

13726. ADAH, ANTHONY.   Agential mortality: death, corporeality, and identity in *Radiance* (1997). PS (24:2/3) 2005, 35–47.

Radio Flyer (1992)

13727. ARDOLINO, FRANK.   A name, a number, and a picture: the cinematic memorialization of Jackie Robinson. *See* **13549**.

Raging Bull (1980)

13728. HAYES, KEVIN J. (ed.).   Martin Scorsese's *Raging Bull*. Cambridge; New York: CUP, 2005. pp. xi, 164. (Cambridge film handbooks.)

Rebel without a Cause (1955)

13729. FRASCELLA, LAWRENCE; WEISEL, AL.   Live fast, die young: the wild ride of making *Rebel without a Cause*. New York: Simon & Schuster, 2005. pp. ix, 372.

The Reckless Moment (1949)

13730. PAUL, WILLIAM.   Off the deep end far from heaven: social topography in *The Reckless Moment*. AQ (60:5) 2005, 43–63.

Red River (1948)

13731. SPRINGER, JOHN PARRIS.   Beyond the river: women and the role of the feminine in Howard Hawks's *Red River*. *In* (pp. 115–25) **13186**.

Regeneration (1997)

13732. WESTMAN, KARIN E.   Generation not regeneration: screening out class, gender, and cultural change in the film of *Regeneration*. *In* (pp. 162–74) **15309**.

The Remains of the Day (1993)

13733. GIBSON, SARAH.   English journeys: the tourist, the guidebook, and the motorcar in *The Remains of the Day*. Journeys (5:2) 2004, 43–71.

13734. SUMERA, ADAM.   *The Remains of the Day*: Kazuo Ishiguro's novel and James Ivory's film adaptation. *In* (pp. 250–7) **3756**.

Remember the Night (1940)

13735. SIGLER, CAROLYN.   'I'll be home for Christmas': misrule and the paradox of gender in World War II-era Christmas films. JAC (28:4) 2005, 345–56.

Reunion (1989)

13736. GRIMES, CHARLES.   Process and history in Harold Pinter's *Reunion* screenplay. *See* **18796**.

Rio Grande (1950)

13737. MCDONOUGH, KATHLEEN A.   *Wee Willie Winkie* goes west: the influence of the British Empire genre on Ford's cavalry trilogy. *In* (pp. 99–114) **13186**.

RoboCop (1987)

13738. NISHIME, LEILANI.   The mulatto cyborg: imagining a multiracial future. *See* **13479**.

Rocky (1976–)

13739. ELMWOOD, VICTORIA A.   'Just some bum from the neighborhood': the resolution of post-Civil Rights tension and heavyweight public sphere discourse in *Rocky* (1976). FilmH (35:2) 2005, 49–59.

13740. MOTLEY, CLAY.   Fighting for manhood: *Rocky* and turn-of-the-century antimodernism. FilmH (35:2) 2005, 60–6.

The Rocky Horror Picture Show (1975)

13741. EBERLE-SINATRA, MICHAEL.   Readings of homosexuality in Mary Shelley's *Frankenstein* and four film adaptations. *See* **11968**.

Romeo Must Die (2000)

13742. BELTRÁN, MARY C.   The new Hollywood racelessness: only the fast, furious, (and multiracial) will survive. CinJ (44:2) 2005, 50–67.

Roosters (1993)

13743. MARTIN, HOLLY E.   Stereotypes collide: *machismo* and *marianismo* in *Roosters*. *In* (pp. 191–205) **13950**.

Rosemary's Baby (1968)

13744. VALERIUS, KARYN.   *Rosemary's Baby*, gothic pregnancy, and fetal subjects. ColLit (32:3) 2005, 116–35.

Round Midnight (1986)

13745. MCCOMBE, JOHN P.   Reinventing Bird: the evolving image of Charlie Parker on film. PS (25:1) 2005, 22–37.

Rushmore (1998)

13746. KREISEL, DEANNA K.   What Maxie knew: the gift and Oedipus in *What Maisie Knew* and *Rushmore*. *See* **11417**.

Safe (1995)

13747. BOUCHARD, DANIELLE; DESAI, JIGNA.   'There's nothing more debilitating than travel': locating US empire in Todd Haynes' *Safe*. QRFV (22:4) 2005, 359–70.

13748. GROSSMAN, JULIE.   The trouble with Carol: the costs of feeling good in Todd Haynes's *Safe* and the American cultural landscape. OV (2:3) 2005.

Saving Private Ryan (1998)

13749. O'CONNELL, AARON B.   Saving Private Lynch: a hyperreal hero in an age of postmodern warfare. WLA (17:1/2) 2005, 33–52.

Schindler's List (1993)

13750. WEISSMAN, GARY. Fantasies of witnessing: postwar efforts to experience the Holocaust. Ithaca, NY; London: Cornell UP, 2004. pp. xiii, 266. Rev. by Michael E. Staub in JAH (92:2) 2005, 671.

Scream (1996–)

13751. WEE, VALERIE. The *Scream* trilogy, 'hyperpostmodernism', and the late nineties teen slasher film. JFV (57:3) 2005, 44–59.

The Searchers (1956)

13752. BLAKE, MICHAEL F. Code of honor: the making of three great American westerns – *High Noon*, *Shane*, and *The Searchers*. See **13605**.

13753. RUSHTON, RICHARD. The perversion of *The Silence of the Lambs* and the dilemma of *The Searchers*: on psychoanalytic 'reading'. See **13764**.

13754. ZESCH, SCOTT. The search for Alice Todd. JWest (44:2) 2005, 73–80.

The Secret Garden (1949)

13755. STOKES, SALLY SIMS. Noel Streatfeild's secret gardens. See **19717**.

The Servant (1963)

13756. PREVITI, SIMONA. Dioniso vestito da servo: la contaminazione della casa da Maugham a Losey. *In* (pp. 93–103) **14322**.

sex, lies, and videotape (1989)

13757. WHITE, R. S. Sex, lies, videotape – and Othello. *In* (pp. 86–98) **13273**.

Shadowlands (1993)

13758. BAGGETT, DAVID. Rats in God's laboratory: *Shadowlands* and the problem of evil. *In* (pp. 125–36) **13158**.

Shakespeare-Wallah (1965)

13759. KAPADIA, PARMITA. Shakespeare transposed: the British stage on the post-colonial screen. *In* (pp. 42–56) **13273**.

Shane (1953)

13760. BLAKE, MICHAEL F. Code of honor: the making of three great American westerns – *High Noon*, *Shane*, and *The Searchers*. See **13605**.

The Shawshank Redemption (1994)

13761. YOUNG, WILLIE. The *Shawshank Redemption* and the hope for escape. *In* (pp. 184–98) **13158**.

She Wore a Yellow Ribbon (1949)

13762. MCDONOUGH, KATHLEEN A. *Wee Willie Winkie* goes west: the influence of the British Empire genre on Ford's cavalry trilogy. *In* (pp. 99–114) **13186**.

Short Eyes (1979)

13763. CRUTCHFIELD, JOHN. From cell to celluloid: a dramaturgical note on Miguel Piñero's *Short Eyes*. *In* (pp. 87–111) **13950**.

The Silence of the Lambs (1991)

13764. RUSHTON, RICHARD. The perversion of *The Silence of the Lambs* and the dilemma of *The Searchers*: on psychoanalytic 'reading'. PsCS (10:3) 2005, 252–68.

Silent Running (1972)

13765. MURRAY, ROBIN L.; HEUMANN, JOSEPH K.   Environmental nostalgia in eco-disaster movies of the early 1970s. *See* **13696**.

A Simple Plan (1998)

13766. HILL, JANE.   Ambition and ideology: intertextual clues to *A Simple Plan*'s view of the American Dream. PS (24:1) 2004, 62–70.

Small Faces (1996)

13767. CLANDFIELD, PETER; LLOYD, CHRISTOPHER.   The 'wee men' of Glasgow grow up: boyhood and urban space in *Small Faces*. *In* (pp. 183–202) **13342**.

Song of the South (1946)

13768. SPERB, JASON.   'Take a frown, turn it upside down': Splash Mountain, Walt Disney World, and the cultural de-rac[e]-ination of Disney's *Song of the South* (1946). JPC (38:5) 2005, 924–38.

A Song to Remember (1945)

13769. TIBBETTS, JOHN C.   Whose Chopin? Politics and patriotism in *A Song to Remember* (1945). AmS (46:1) 2005, 115–40.

South Park: Bigger Longer & Uncut (1999)

13770. GARDINER, JUDITH KEGAN.   Why Saddam is gay: masculinity politics in *South Park – Bigger, Longer, and Uncut*. QRFV (22:1) 2005, 51–62.

Soylent Green (1973)

13771. MURRAY, ROBIN L.; HEUMANN, JOSEPH K.   Environmental nostalgia in eco-disaster movies of the early 1970s. *See* **13696**.

The Spanish Prisoner (1997)

13772. MCINTIRE-STRASBURG, JEFFREY O.   Performing pedagogy: teaching and confidence games in David Mamet's *House of Games* and *The Spanish Prisoner. See* **13611**.

Spanking the Monkey (1994)

13773. SCHNEIDER, STEVEN JAY.   Jerkus interruptus: the terrible trials of masturbating boys in recent Hollywood cinema. *In* (pp. 377–93) **13342**.

The Spitfire Grill (1996)

13774. DEMPSEY, ANNA.   Nurturing nature and the cinematic experience: the American landscape and the rural female community. *See* **13711**.

Stagecoach (1939)

13775. GRANT, BARRY KEITH.   Introduction: spokes in the wheels. *In* (pp. 1–20) **13776**.

13776. —— (ed.).   John Ford's *Stagecoach*. Cambridge; New York: CUP, 2003. pp. xii, 243. (CUP film handbooks.) Rev. by Matthew Bernstein in FilmQ (58:1) 2004, 70–1.

13777. MALAND, CHARLES J.   'Powered by a Ford'? Dudley Nichols, authorship, and cultural ethos in *Stagecoach*. *In* (pp. 48–81) **13776**.

13778. POAGUE, LELAND.   That past, this present: historicizing John Ford, 1939. *In* (pp. 82–112) **13776**.

13779. ROTHMAN, WILLIAM.   *Stagecoach* and the quest for selfhood. *In* (pp. 158–77) **13776**.

13780. SCHATZ, THOMAS.   *Stagecoach* and Hollywood's A-western renaissance. *In* (pp. 21–47) **13776**.

13781. STUDLAR, GAYLYN.   'Be a proud, glorified dreg': class, gender, and frontier democracy in *Stagecoach*. *In* (pp. 132–57) **13776**.

13782. TELOTTE, J. P.   'A little bit savage': *Stagecoach* and racial representation. *In* (pp. 113–31) **13776**.

Stand by Me (1986)

13783. MOSHER, JERRY.   Survival of the fattest: contending with the fat boy in children's ensemble films. *In* (pp. 61–82) **13342**.

Star Trek (1986–)

13784. GERAGHTY, LINCOLN.   The American jeremiad and *Star Trek*'s Puritan legacy. JFA (14:2) 2003, 228–45.

Star Wars (1977–)

13785. ABRAMS, JEROLD J.   A technological galaxy: Heidegger and the philosophy of technology in *Star Wars*. *In* (pp. 107–19) **13794**.

13786. ARP, ROBERT.   'If droids could think …': droids as slaves and persons. *In* (pp. 120–31) **13794**.

13787. BARAD, JUDITH.   The aspiring Jedi's handbook of virtue. *In* (pp. 57–68) **13794**.

13788. BORTOLIN, MATTHEW.   The dharma of *Star Wars*. Boston, MA: Wisdom, 2005. pp. xiv, 205.

13789. BROWN, CHRISTOPHER M.   'A wretched hive of scum and villainy': *Star Wars* and the problem of evil. *In* (pp. 69–79) **13794**.

13790. CAMERON, BRIAN K.   'What is thy bidding, my master?': *Star Wars* and the Hegelian struggle for recognition. *In* (pp. 159–67) **13794**.

13791. COOKE, ELIZABETH F.   'Be mindful of the living force': environmental ethics in *Star Wars*. *In* (pp. 80–92) **13794**.

13792. COX, ALEXANDER.   *Star Wars*: decoding the spectacle of myth. Foundation (92) 2004, 17–30.

13793. DECKER, KEVIN S.   By any means necessary: tyranny, democracy, republic and empire. *In* (pp. 168–80) **13794**.

13794. —— EBERL, JASON T. (eds).   *Star Wars* and philosophy: more powerful than you can possibly imagine. Chicago, IL: Open Court, 2005. pp. xvi, 227. (Popular culture and philosophy, 12.)

13795. DEES, RICHARD H.   Moral ambiguity in a black-and-white universe. *In* (pp. 39–53) **13794**.

13796. DONNELLY, JEROME.   Humanizing technology: flesh and machine in Aristotle and *The Empire Strikes Back*. *In* (pp. 181–91) **13794**.

13797. EBERL, JASON T. 'You cannot escape your destiny' (or can you?): freedom and predestination in the Skywalker family. *In* (pp. 3–15) **13794**.

13798. FADER, SHANTI. 'A certain point of view': lying Jedi, honest Sith, and the viewers who love them. *In* (pp. 192–204) **13794**.

13799. GERAGHTY, LINCOLN. Creating and comparing myth in twentieth-century science fiction: *Star Trek* and *Star Wars*. LitFQ (33:3) 2005, 191–200.

13800. HANLEY, RICHARD. Send in the clones: the ethics of future wars. *In* (pp. 93–103) **13794**.

13801. JONES, JAN-ERIK. 'Size matters not': the Force as the causal power of the Jedi. *In* (pp. 132–43) **13794**.

13802. KENNY, GLENN (ed.). A galaxy not so far away: writers and artists on twenty-five years of *Star Wars*. London: Allison & Busby, 2003. pp. xxxi, 222. Rev. by Steven J. Corvi in JPC (38:5) 2005, 961–3.

13803. LAWLER, JAMES. The Force is with us: Hegel's philosophy of spirit strikes back at the Empire. *In* (pp. 144–56) **13794**.

13804. LONG, JOSEPH W. Religious pragmatism through the eyes of Luke Skywalker. *In* (pp. 205–12) **13794**.

13805. ROBINSON, WALTER (RITOKU). The Far East of *Star Wars*. *In* (pp. 29–38) **13794**.

13806. STEPHENS, WILLIAM O. Stoicism in the stars: Yoda, the Emperor, and the Force. *In* (pp. 16–28) **13794**.

13807. WETMORE, KEVIN J., JR. The Empire triumphant: race, religion and rebellion in the *Star Wars* films. Jefferson, NC; London: McFarland, 2005. pp. ix, 214.

Strange Days (1995)

13808. HAIRSTON, ANDREA. Driving Mr Lenny: notes on race and gender as a transport to another reality, another dimension. Foundation (92) 2004, 5–16.

Street Scene (1931)

13809. CLAVARON, YVES; DIETERLE, BERNARD (eds). La mémoire des villes. *See* **20330**.

Suture (1993)

13810. THOMPSON, AYANNA. *Suture*, Shakespeare, and race; or, What is our cultural debt to the Bard? *In* (pp. 57–72) **13273**.

Talent for the Game (1991)

13811. MILLER, EUGENE L. California dreamin': *Talent for the Game*. *In* (pp. 180–90) **13950**.

The Tango Lesson (1997)

13812. VOLLMER, ULRIKE. Towards an ethics of seeing: Sally Potter's *The Tango Lesson*. LitTheol (19:1) 2005, 74–85.

The Tenant (1976)

13813. MAZIERSKA, EWA. The autobiographical effect in the cinema of Roman Polanski. *See* **20768**.

The Ten Commandments (1956)

13814. TORRY, ROBERT.   The wrath of God: Hollywood epics and American Cold War policy. AQ (61:2) 2005, 67–86.

The Terror of Tiny Town (1938)

13815. MILLER, CYNTHIA J.   Tradition, parody, and adaptation: Jed Buell's unconventional West. *In* (pp. 65–80) **13186**.

Tess (1979)

13816. ROGERS, SHANNON.   The whole left behind: omitted scenes in Polanski's *Tess*. HaR (7) 2004, 86–98.

Thelma & Louise (1991)

13817. OLEKSY, ELŻBIETA H.   Action heroines in Polish and American film. *In* (pp. 167–75) **3756**.

The Thin Red Line (1998)

13818. WALSH, SUSIE.   Friendly fire: epistolary voice-over in Terrence Malick's *The Thin Red Line*. LitFQ (33:4) 2005, 306–12.

The Third Man (1949)

13819. DERN, JOHN A.   The revenant of Vienna: a critical comparison of Carol Reed's film *The Third Man* and Bram Stoker's novel *Dracula*. LitFQ (33:1) 2005, 4–11.

A Thousand Acres (1997)

13820. KELLY, PHILIPPA.   Finding *King Lear*'s female parts. See **6470**.

13821. O'DAIR, SHARON.   Horror or realism? Filming 'toxic discourse' in Jane Smiley's *A Thousand Acres*. See **19477**.

Three Seasons (1999)

13822. BACHOLLE-BOŠKOVIĆ, MICHÈLE.   Vietnamese cinema: new voices from abroad. ConnR (27:1) 2005, 67–79.

13823. DUONG, LAN.   Manufacturing authenticity: the feminine ideal in Tony Bui's *Three Seasons*. AmerJ (31:2) 2005, 1–19.

The Time Machine (1960)

13824. MENEGALDO, GILLES.   L'inscription de l'histoire et la vision du futur dans *The Time Machine* de H. G. Wells et son adaptation filmique par George Pal. See **20053**.

The Tin Star (1957)

13825. COSTELLO, MATTHEW J.   Rewriting *High Noon*: transformations in American popular political culture during the Cold War, 1952–1968. *In* (pp. 175–97) **13186**.

Titanic (1997)

13826. BERGFELDER, TIM; STREET, SARAH (eds).   The *Titanic* in myth and memory: representations in visual and verbal culture. London; New York: Tauris, 2004. pp. xiv, 241, (plates) 8.

To Sleep with Anger (1990)

13827. ELLISON, MARY.   Echoes of Africa in *To Sleep with Anger* and *Eve's Bayou*. AAR (39:1/2) 2005, 213–29.

Tombstone (1993)

13828. KELLER, ALEXANDRA.   Historical discourse and American identity in westerns since the Reagan era. *In* (pp. 239–60) **13186**.

Tortilla Flat (1942)

13829. FOWLER, CHARLES RAYMOND.   Adapting Steinbeck: *Tortilla Flat* in the information age – an interview with screenwriter Bill U'Ren. *See* **19609**.

Traffic (2000)

13830. SHAW, DEBORAH.   'You are alright, but …': individual and collective representations of Mexicans, Latinos, Anglo-Americans and African Americans in Steven Soderbergh's *Traffic*. QRFV (22:3) 2005, 211–23.

Trainspotting (1996)

13831. CARDULLO, BERT.   Fiction into film: notes on one paradigmatic scene and two emblematic adaptations. LJH (30:2) 2005, 5–20.

Triumph of the Spirit (1989)

13832. BOYD, ZOHARA; HOROWITZ, ROSEMARY.   Memory and history in *Triumph of the Spirit*. *In* (pp. 161–79) **13950**.

Trouble in Paradise (1932)

13833. TODD, DREW.   Decadent heroes: dandyism and masculinity in Art Deco Hollywood. JPFT (32:4) 2005, 168–81.

The Truman Show (1998)

13834. BLESSING, KIMBERLY A.   Deceit and doubt: the search for truth in *The Truman Show* and Descartes's *Meditations*. *In* (pp. 3–16) **13158**.

13835. CUNNINGHAM, DOUGLAS A.   A theme park built for one: the new utopianism *vs* Disney design in *The Truman Show*. CritS (17:1) 2005, 109–30.

13836. GOLDMAN, PETER.   Consumer society and its discontents: *The Truman Show* and *The Day of the Locust*. Anthropoetics (10:2) 2004/05.

Ulysses (1967)

13837. NORRIS, MARGOT.   *Ulysses. See* **17322**.

Uncivilised (1936)

13838. HOORN, JEANETTE.   White *lubra* / White savage: *pituri* and colonialist fantasy in Charles Chauvel's *Uncivilised* (1936). PS (24:2/3) 2005, 48–63.

Union Pacific (1939)

13839. TELOTTE, J. P.   'A little bit savage': *Stagecoach* and racial representation. *In* (pp. 113–31) **13776**.

The Untouchables (1987)

13840. SONNET, ESTHER; STANFIELD, PETER.   'Good evening gentlemen; can I check your hats please?': masculinity, dress, and the retro gangster cycles of the 1990s. *In* (pp. 163–84) **13247**.

Velvet Goldmine (1998)

13841. COPPA, FRANCESCA.   Performance theory and performativity. *In* (pp. 72–95) **12414**.

Vertigo (1958)

13842. GUNNING, TOM; PIPPIN, ROBERT B.   The desire and pursuit of the hole: cinema's obscure object of desire. *In* (pp. 261–81) **3702**.

Warlock (1959)

13843. COSTELLO, MATTHEW J.   Rewriting *High Noon*: transformations in American popular political culture during the Cold War, 1952–1968. *In* (pp. 175–97) **13186**.

Wee Willie Winkie (1937)

13844. MCDONOUGH, KATHLEEN A.   *Wee Willie Winkie* goes west: the influence of the British Empire genre on Ford's cavalry trilogy. *In* (pp. 99–114) **13186**.

What Ever Happened to Baby Jane? (1962)

13845. RUSSELL, LORENA.   Queering consumption and production in *What Ever Happened to Baby Jane? In* (pp. 213–26) **13250**.

Withnail and I (1986)

13846. JACKSON, KEVIN.   *Withnail & I.* London: British Film Inst., 2004. pp. 95. (BFI modern classics.)

13847. KELLY, AARON; SALTER, DAVID.   'The time is out of joint': *Withnail and I* and historical melancholia. *In* (pp. 99–112) **13273**.

The Wizard of Oz (1939)

13848. BELLIN, JOSHUA DAVID.   'I don't know how it works': *The Wizard of Oz* and the technology of alienation. AQ (60:4) 2004, 65–97.

A World Apart (1988)

13849. DOVEY, LINDIWE.   South African cinema in exile. JPW (41:2) 2005, 189–99.

Young Mr Lincoln (1939)

13850. POAGUE, LELAND.   That past, this present: historicizing John Ford, 1939. *In* (pp. 82–112) **13776**.

13851. WEXMAN, VIRGINIA WRIGHT.   'Right and wrong: that's [not] all there is to it!': *Young Mr Lincoln* and American law. CinJ (44:3) 2005, 20–34.

Directors

'Woody Allen' (Allen Stewart Konigsberg)

13852. BLAKE, RICHARD A.   Street smart: the New York of Lumet, Allen, Scorsese, and Lee. Lexington: Kentucky UP, 2005. pp. xv, 335, (plates) 16.

Roy Ward Baker

13853. MAYER, GEOFF.   Roy Ward Baker. Manchester; New York: Manchester UP, 2004. pp. 224. (British film makers.) Rev. by David Lancaster in FilmH (35:2) 2005, 93–4.

William Beaudine, Sr (1892–1970)

13854. MARSHALL, WENDY L. William Beaudine: from silents to television. Lanham, MD; London: Scarecrow Press, 2005. pp. xviii, 387. (Filmmakers, 116.)

John Boorman

13855. BOORMAN, JOHN. Adventures of a suburban boy. (Bibl. 2004, 13955.) Rev. by David Lancaster in FilmH (35:1) 2005, 85–6.

Tim Burton

13856. FRAGA, KRISTAN (ed.). Tim Burton: interviews. Jackson; London: Mississippi UP, 2005. pp. xl, 192. (Conversations with filmmakers.)

13857. MCMAHAN, ALISON. The films of Tim Burton: animating live action in contemporary Hollywood. London; New York: Continuum, 2005. pp. xiii, 262.

Jane Campion

13858. RUESCHMANN, EVA. Out of place: reading (post)colonial landscapes as gothic space in Jane Campion's films. PS (24:2/3) 2005, 8–21.

John Carpenter

13859. CONRICH, IAN; WOODS, DAVID (eds). The cinema of John Carpenter: the technique of terror. London: Wallflower, 2004. pp. x, 219. (Directors' cuts.) Rev. by J. Robert Craig in JFA (16:1) 2005, 62–4.

Charlie Chaplin

13860. DAVIS, THERESE. First sight: blindness, cinema and unrequited love. JNT (33:1) 2003, 48–62.

13861. HAYES, KEVIN J. Charlie Chaplin: interviews. Jackson; London: Mississippi UP, 2005. pp. xl, 150. (Conversations with filmmakers.)

13862. INGE, M. THOMAS. Jay Gatsby and the Little Tramp: F. Scott Fitzgerald and Charlie Chaplin. *See* **16493**.

13863. WRANOVICS, JOHN. Chaplin and Agee: the untold story of the tramp, the writer, and the lost screenplay. *See* **15092**.

Bill Condon

13864. GRUNDMANN, ROY. Sex, science, and the biopic: an interview with Bill Condon. Cineaste (30:2) 2005, 11.

Merian C. Cooper

13865. VAZ, MARK COTTA. Living dangerously: the adventures of Merian C. Cooper, creator of *King Kong.* New York: Villard, 2005. pp. 478. Rev. by Thomas Doherty in Cineaste (31:1) 2005, 72–3.

Francis Ford Coppola

13866. PHILLIPS, GENE D.; HILL, RODNEY (eds). Francis Ford Coppola: interviews. Jackson; London: Mississippi UP, 2004. pp. xxxvi, 190. (Conversations with filmmakers.)

Roger Corman

13867. Dixon, Wheeler Winston. Filmmaking 'for the fun of it': an interview with Jack Hill. *See* **13880.**

David Cronenberg

13868. Dee, Jonathan. David Cronenberg's body language. NYTM, 18 Sept. 2005, 74–9.

13869. Hantke, Steffen. Spectacular optics: the deployment of special effects in David Cronenberg's films. FilCr (29:2) 2004/05, 34–52.

13870. Pospíšil, Tomáš. Attractive ambiguities: epistemological uncertainty of the films of David Cronenberg. *In* (pp. 217–22) **3734.**

Terence Davies

13871. Everett, Wendy. Terence Davies. Manchester; New York: Manchester UP, 2004. pp. ix, 246. (British film makers.)

Cecil B. DeMille

13872. Costa de Beauregard, Raphaëlle. Authority, Protestantism and Cecil B. DeMille's early silent films (1913–1923). Anglophonia (17) 2005, 399–407.

Walt Disney

13873. Merritt, Russell. Lost on pleasure islands: storytelling in Disney's Silly Symphonies. FilmQ (59:1) 2005, 4–17.

Thomas Dixon (1864–1946)

13874. Slide, Anthony. American racist: the life and films of Thomas Dixon. (Bibl. 2004, 13976.) Rev. by Daniel Bernardi in JAH (92:2) 2005, 644; by Patrick McGilligan in Cineaste (30:2) 2005, 71–2.

John Ford (b.1894)

13875. Cowie, Peter. John Ford and the American West. New York: Abrams, 2004. pp. 224. Rev. by Clive Sinclair in TLS, 21 Jan. 2005, 17.

13876. Grant, Barry Keith (ed.). John Ford's *Stagecoach. See* **13776.**

Peter Greenaway

13877. Badt, Karin. Peter Greenaway holds court: an interview at the Venice Film Festival. FilCr (29:2) 2004/05, 53–66.

Monte Hellman

13878. Dixon, Wheeler Winston. An interview with Monte Hellman. QRFV (22:3) 2005, 263–75.

George Roy Hill

13879. Horton, Andrew. The films of George Roy Hill. Foreword by Paul Newman. Jefferson, NC; London: McFarland, 2005. pp. x, 210.

Jack Hill

13880. Dixon, Wheeler Winston. Filmmaking 'for the fun of it': an interview with Jack Hill. FilCr (29:3) 2005, 46–59.

Sir Alfred Hitchcock

13881. DRUMIN, WILLIAM A. Thematic and methodological foundations of Alfred Hitchcock's artistic vision. Lewiston, NY; Lampeter: Mellen Press, 2004. pp. vi, 432. (Studies in the history and criticism of film, 8.)

13882. HAEFFNER, NICHOLAS. Alfred Hitchcock. London; New York: Pearson Longman, 2005. pp. ix, 125.

13883. LACY, NORRIS J. Medieval McGuffins: the Arthurian model. *See* **5085.**

13884. McGILLIGAN, PATRICK. Alfred Hitchcock: a life in darkness and light. (Bibl. 2004, 13987.) Rev. by Marshall Deutelbaum in FilmQ (58:1) 2004, 56–8.

13885. MAGISTRALE, TONY. Abject terrors: surveying the modern and postmodern horror film. *See* **13307.**

13886. POMERANCE, MURRAY. An eye for Hitchcock. (Bibl. 2004, 13990.) Rev. by Jason Landrum in JAC (28:1) 2005, 133.

13887. SINGER, IRVING. Three philosophical filmmakers: Hitchcock, Welles, Renoir. (Bibl. 2004, 13992.) Rev. by Kate Khatib in MLN (120:5) 2005, 1256–9.

13888. STRAUSS, MARC RAYMOND. Alfred Hitchcock's silent films. Jefferson, NC; London: McFarland, 2004. pp. vii, 215.

13889. YANAL, ROBERT J. Hitchcock as philosopher. Jefferson, NC; London: McFarland, 2005. pp. ix, 206.

James Ivory

13890. LONG, ROBERT EMMET (ed.). James Ivory in conversation: how Merchant Ivory makes its movies. Foreword by Janet Maslin. Berkeley; London: California UP, 2005. pp. xi, 339.

Derek Jarman

13891. BROPHY, SARAH. Witnessing AIDS: writing, testimony, and the work of mourning. *See* **17425.**

13892. DILLON, STEVEN. Derek Jarman and lyric film: the mirror and the sea. (Bibl. 2004, 13995.) Rev. by Jim Nawrocki in GLRW (12:3) 2005, 39–40.

Jim Jarmusch

13893. HIRSCHBERG, LYNN. The last of the indies. NYTM, 31 July 2005, 18–21, 44.

Neil Jordan

13894. McILROY, BRIAN. Irish horror: Neil Jordan and the Anglo-Irish gothic. *In* (pp. 128–40) **13374.**

Elia Kazan

13895. SCHICKEL, RICHARD. Elia Kazan: a biography. London: HarperCollins, 2005. pp. xxxi, 510.

Stanley Kubrick

13896. COCKS, GEOFFREY. The wolf at the door: Stanley Kubrick, history, & the Holocaust. New York; Frankfurt: Lang, 2004. pp. xii, 338, (plates) 4. (Contemporary film, television, and video, 1.)

13897. KUBERSKI, PHILIP. Plumbing the abyss: Stanley Kubrick's bathrooms. AQ (60:4) 2004, 139–60.

13898. MAGISTRALE, TONY. Abject terrors: surveying the modern and postmodern horror film. *See* **13307.**

Spike Lee

13899. AFTAB, KALEEM. Spike Lee: that's my story and I'm sticking to it. London: Vintage; New York: Norton, 2005. pp. viii, 324.

13900. BLAKE, RICHARD A. Street smart: the New York of Lumet, Allen, Scorsese, and Lee. *See* **13852.**

13901. HOUSTON, KERR. Athletic iconography in Spike Lee's early feature films. AAR (38:4) 2004, 637–49.

Joseph Losey

13902. GARDNER, COLIN. Joseph Losey. Manchester; New York: Manchester UP, 2004. pp. xi, 315. (British film makers.) Rev. by David Lancaster in FilmH (35:1) 2005, 88–9.

George Lucas

13903. HEARN, MARCUS. The cinema of George Lucas. Foreword by Ron Howard. New York: Abrams, 2005. pp. 263.

Sidney Lumet

13904. BLAKE, RICHARD A. Street smart: the New York of Lumet, Allen, Scorsese, and Lee. *See* **13852.**

David Lynch

13905. JOHNSON, JEFF. Pervert in the pulpit: morality in the works of David Lynch. (Bibl. 2004, 14004.) Rev. by David Lancaster in FilmH (35:2) 2005, 100–1.

13906. RODLEY, CHRIS (ed.). Lynch on Lynch. London; Boston, MA: Faber & Faber, 2005. pp. xiii, 322. (Revised ed.: first ed. 1997.)

Leo McCarey

13907. GEHRING, WES D. Leo McCarey: from Marx to McCarthy. Lanham, MD; London: Scarecrow Press, 2005. pp. xxii, 304. (Filmmakers, 117.)

J. P. McGowan

13908. MCGOWAN, JOHN J. J. P. McGowan: biography of a Hollywood pioneer. Jefferson, NC; London: McFarland, 2005. pp. ix, 220.

Terrence Malick

13909. MORRISON, JAMES; SCHUR, THOMAS. The films of Terrence Malick. (Bibl. 2004, 14006.) Rev. by Jon Long in QRFV (22:1) 2005, 83–90.

Michael Mann

13910. WILDERMUTH, MARK E. Blood in the moonlight: Michael Mann and information age cinema. Jefferson, NC; London: McFarland, 2005. pp. xi, 211.

Radley Metzger

13911. SCHAEFER, ERIC. Dirty little secrets: scholars, archivists, and dirty movies. *See* **13369.**

Russ Meyer

13912. McDonough, Jimmy. Big bosoms and square jaws: the biography of Russ Meyer, king of the sex film. New York: Crown, 2005. pp. 463.

13913. Schaefer, Eric. Dirty little secrets: scholars, archivists, and dirty movies. *See* **13369.**

Oscar Micheaux

13914. McGilligan, Patrick. Me and Oscar Micheaux: an interview with LeRoy Collins. FilmQ (57:4) 2004, 2–7.

13915. Munby, Jonathan. The underworld films of Oscar Micheaux and Ralph Cooper: toward a genealogy of the Black screen gangster. *In* (pp. 263–80) **13247.**

13916. Zaragoza Cruz, Omayra. Orchestra seats: passing in cinema. *See* **13614.**

Phillip Noyce

13917. Petzke, Ingo. Phillip Noyce: backroads to Hollywood. Sydney: Pan Macmillan, 2004. pp. xxix, 392.

Max Ophüls

13918. Amiel, Vincent. Nature and artifice in Max Ophuls' cinema. AQ (60:5) 2005, 149–58.

13919. Bacher, Lutz. The lost *Ballad*: Max Ophuls' last Hollywood project. AQ (60:5) 2005, 97–126.

13920. Bourget, Jean-Loup. Ophuls and Renoir. AQ (60:5) 2005, 127–48.

13921. White, Susan. Max Ophüls: an introduction. AQ (60:5) 2005, 1–13.

Alan J. Pakula

13922. Brown, Jared. Alan J. Pakula: his films and his life. New York: Back Stage, 2005. pp. 416.

Sam Peckinpah

13923. Engel, Leonard (ed.). Sam Peckinpah's West: new perspectives. (Bibl. 2003, 13591.) Rev. by David Cremean in TBR (24:4) 2004/05, 12–13.

13924. Murray, Gabrielle. This wounded cinema, this wounded life: violence and utopia in the films of Sam Peckinpah. (Bibl. 2004, 14010.) Rev. by Robert Fyne in JAC (28:3) 2005, 341.

Sidney Poitier

13925. Goudsouzian, Aram. Sidney Poitier: man, actor, icon. (Bibl. 2004, 14011, where title incomplete.) Rev. by Gerald R. Butters, Jr, in AmS (46:2) 2005, 201.

Roman Polanski

13926. Cronin, Paul (ed.). Roman Polanski: interviews. Jackson; London: Mississippi UP, 2005. pp. xxvii, 211. (Conversations with filmmakers.)

Sally Potter

13927. Lucia, Cynthia. Saying *Yes* to taking risks: an interview with Sally Potter. Cineaste (30:4) 2005, 24–30.

Michael Powell

13928. MOOR, ANDREW.   Powell & Pressburger: a cinema of magic spaces. London; New York: Tauris, 2005. pp. xii, 250. (Cinema and society.)

Emeric Pressburger

13929. MOOR, ANDREW.   Powell & Pressburger: a cinema of magic spaces. *See* 13928.

Gaylene Preston

13930. FRANCES, HELEN.   Facts, fairytales, and the politics of storytelling: an interview with Gaylene Preston. Cineaste (30:4) 2005, 36–41.

Sam Raimi

13931. MUIR, JOHN KENNETH.   The unseen force: the films of Sam Raimi. New York: Applause, 2004. pp. ix, 342.

Yvonne Rainer

13932. LEVIN, PATRICIA.   Yvonne Rainer's avant-garde melodramas. *In* (pp. 149–75) 13334.

13933. TURIM, MAUREEN.   The violence of desire in avant-garde films. *In* (pp. 71–90) 13334.

Ken Russell

13934. TIBBETTS, JOHN C.   Elgar's ear: a conversation with Ken Russell. QRFV (22:1) 2005, 37–49.

John Schlesinger

13935. MANN, WILLIAM J.   Edge of midnight: the life of John Schlesinger. New York: Watson-Guptill, 2005. pp. xii, 268, (plates) 16.

Budd Schulberg

13936. BAER, WILLIAM.   On the waterfront: a conversation with Budd Schulberg. SoCR (36:2) 2004, 27–42.

Martin Scorsese

13937. BLAKE, RICHARD A.   Street smart: the New York of Lumet, Allen, Scorsese, and Lee. *See* 13852.

13938. NICHOLLS, MARK.   Scorsese's men: melancholia and the Mob. London; Sterling, VA: Pluto Press, 2004. pp. xvi, 191.

Ridley Scott

13939. KNAPP, LAURENCE F.; KULAS, ANDREA F. (eds).   Ridley Scott: interviews. Jackson; London: Mississippi UP, 2005. pp. xxxi, 237. (Conversations with filmmakers.)

Steven Spielberg

13940. POMERANCE, MURRAY.   The man-boys of Steven Spielberg. *In* (pp. 132–54) 13342.

George Stevens

13941. MOSS, MARILYN ANN.   Giant: George Stevens, a life on film. Madison; London: Wisconsin UP, 2004. pp. xii, 327.

Oliver Stone

13942. Crowdus, Gary.   Dramatizing issues that historians don't address: an interview with Oliver Stone. Cineaste (30:2) 2005, 12–23.

Frank Tuttle

13943. Franceschina, John (ed.).   They started talking. By Frank Tuttle. *See* **13232.**

Orson Welles (1915–1985) (director)

13944. Conrad, Peter.   Orson Welles: the stories of his life. (Bibl. 2004, 14030.) Rev. by James Naremore in FilmQ (58:1) 2004, 71–3; by Sidney Gottlieb in Cineaste (30:2) 2005, 66–8.

13945. Garis, Robert.   The films of Orson Welles. (Bibl. 2004, 14031.) Rev. by Sidney Gottlieb in Cineaste (30:2) 2005, 66–8.

13946. Heyer, Paul.   The medium and the magician: Orson Welles, the radio years, 1934–1952. Lanham, MD; Oxford: Rowman & Littlefield, 2005. pp. xvi, 255.

13947. Walters, Ben.   Welles. London: Haus, 2004. pp. 178. (Life & times.)

Wim Wenders

13948. Mariniello, Silvestra.   Experience and memory in the films of Wim Wenders. Trans. by James Cisneros. SubStance (106) 2005, 159–79.

Robert M. Young (b.1924)

13949. Arnold, Edwin T.   Interview with Robert M. Young. *In* (pp. 9–42) **13950.**

13950. Lewis, Leon (ed.).   Robert M. Young: essays on the films. Jefferson, NC; London: McFarland, 2005. pp. viii, 263.

Fred Zinnemann

13951. Miller, Gabriel (ed.).   Fred Zinnemann: interviews. Jackson; London: Mississippi UP, 2005. pp. xxxviii, 161. (Conversations with filmmakers.)

RADIO, TELEVISION, INTERACTIVE MEDIA

13952. Adams, Michael.   Meaningful interposing: a countervalent form. *See* **1547.**

13953. Adare, Sierra S.   'Indian' stereotypes in TV science fiction: First Nations' voices speak out. Austin: Texas UP, 2005. pp. xviii, 142.

13954. Akass, Kim; McCabe, Janet (eds).   Reading *Sex and the City.* London; New York: Tauris, 2004. pp. 288. Rev. by Eve Blachman in JAC (28:1) 2005, 151–2.

13955. Allrath, Gaby; Gymnich, Marion (eds).   Narrative strategies in television series. Basingstoke; New York: Palgrave Macmillan, 2005. pp. xi, 231.

13956. Atkins, Barry.   More than a game: the computer game as fictional form. Manchester; New York: Manchester UP, 2003. pp. 176. Rev. by Derek A. Burrill in CLAQ (29:4) 2004, 382–4.

13957. BARTEL, ELKE.   From archfiend to *Angel*: Dracula's political dimensions. *See* **12085.**

13958. BATTIS, JES.   Blood relations: chosen families in *Buffy the Vampire Slayer* and *Angel*. Jefferson, NC; London: McFarland, 2005. pp. ix, 190.

13959. BOOKER, M. KEITH.   Science fiction television. (Bibl. 2004, 14049.) Rev. by Roz Kaveney in TLS, 5 Aug. 2005, 18; by Tim Prchal in JAC (28:2) 2005, 250.

13960. BRITTON, PIERS D.; BARKER, SIMON J.   Reading between designs: visual imagery and the generation of meaning in *The Avengers, The Prisoner*, and *Doctor Who*. Austin: Texas UP, 2003. pp. xiii, 251. Rev. by Kevin Donnelly in MedH (10:3) 2004, 219–21.

13961. BRITTON, WESLEY.   Beyond Bond: spies in fiction and film. *See* **13168.**

13962. —— Spy television. (Bibl. 2004, 14054.) Rev. by Fred Isaac in JAC (28:1) 2005, 153.

13963. BROOK, VINCENT.   Something ain't kosher here: the rise of the 'Jewish' sitcom. (Bibl. 2003, 13642.) Rev. by Grace Russo Bullaro in FilmQ (58:2) 2005, 61–2; by Elliot B. Gertel in JudQ (54:3/4) 2005, 264–71.

13964. CALLENS, JOHAN.   Remediation in David Mamet's *The Water Engine*. *See* **18071.**

13965. CASSIDY, MARSHA F.   What women watched: daytime television in the 1950s. Austin: Texas UP, 2005. pp. x, 264. (Louann Atkins Temple women and culture series, 10.)

13966. CAWELTI, JOHN G.   Mystery, violence, and popular culture: essays. *See* **12596.**

13967. CAZEAUX, CLIVE.   Phenomenology and radio drama. *See* **20800.**

13968. CHAOULI, MICHEL.   How interactive can fiction be? CI (31:3) 2005, 599–617.

13969. COLLINS, PETER C.; O'CONNOR, JOHN E. (eds).   Hollywood's West: the American frontier in film, television, and history. *See* **13186.**

13970. CONOLLY, L. W.   G.B.S. & the BBC: *Saint Joan*, 1929. *See* **19386.**

13971. CONRAD, ROXANNE LONGSTREET.   Mirror/mirror: a parody. *In* (pp. 169–82) **20809.**

13972. COON, DAVID ROGER.   Two steps forward, one step back: the selling of *Charlie's Angels*. *See* **13509.**

13973. CREEBER, GLEN (ed.).   Fifty key television programmes. London; New York: Arnold, 2004. pp. xvii, 282. Rev. by David Pierson in JPC (38:6) 2005, 1125–6.

13974. DELTCHEVA, ROUMIANA.   Eastern women in Western chronotopes: the representation of East European women in Western films after 1989. *In* (pp. 161–85) **12697.**

13975. DEROSE, MARIA.   Redefining women's power through feminist science fiction. *See* **14122.**

13976. DÍAZ FERNÁNDEZ, JOSÉ RAMÓN.   Shakespeare film and television derivatives: a bibliography. *In* (pp. 169–89) **13273.**

13977. DOHERTY, THOMAS. Cold War, cool medium: television, McCarthyism, and American culture. (Bibl. 2004, 14068.) Rev. by Vincent Brook in AmS (46:2) 2005, 195–6; by Christine Becker in FilmQ (59:1) 2005, 54–6.

13978. DOWNING, SPENCER. Handling the truth: Sorkin's liberal vision. *In* (pp. 127–45) **19531.**

13979. EARLY, FRANCES; KENNEDY, KATHLEEN (eds). Athena's daughters: television's new women warriors. Foreword by Rhonda V. Wilcox. Syracuse, NY: Syracuse UP, 2003. pp. xvi, 175. (Television series.) Rev. by James Brian Wagaman in JPC (38:4) 2005, 790–1.

13980. FAHY, THOMAS. Athletes, grammar geeks, and porn stars: the liberal education of *Sports Night*. *In* (pp. 61–76) **19531.**

13981. —— (ed.). Considering Aaron Sorkin: essays on the politics, poetics, and sleight of hand in the films and television series. *See* **19531.**

13982. FINN, PATRICK. The politics of culture: the play's the thing. *In* (pp. 7–21) **13273.**

13983. FISCHER, CRAIG. *NBC White Paper, Cortile Cascino*, and the assault on the familiar. *In* (pp. 43–57) **13950.**

13984. GANS-BORISKIN, RACHEL TISINGER. The Bushlet administration: terrorism and war on *The West Wing*. JAC (28:1) 2005, 100–13.

13985. GARRETT, LAURA K. Women of *The West Wing*: gender stereotypes in the political fiction. *In* (pp. 179–92) **19531.**

13986. GATES, PHILIPPA; GILLIS, STACY. Screening L. M. Montgomery: heritage, nostalgia and national identity. *See* **18289.**

13987. GERAGHTY, LINCOLN. The American jeremiad and *Star Trek*'s Puritan legacy. *See* **13784.**

13988. —— Creating and comparing myth in twentieth-century science fiction: *Star Trek* and *Star Wars*. *See* **13799.**

13989. GERTEL, ELLIOT B. Jews on the small screen. JudQ (54:3/4) 2005, 264–71 (review-article).

13990. GRAY, HERMAN S. Cultural moves: African Americans and the politics of representation. Berkeley; London: California UP, 2005. pp. viii, 249. (American crossroads, 15.)

13991. GREENE, RICHARD; VERNEZZE, PETER (eds). *The Sopranos* and philosophy: I kill therefore I am. (Bibl. 2004, 14080.) Rev. by Rebecca A. Housel in JPC (38:3) 2005, 586–8.

13992. GREVEN, DAVID. The fantastic powers of the other sex: male mothers in fantastic fiction. JFA (14:3) 2004, 301–17.

13993. HALL, ANN C. Giving propaganda a good name: *The West Wing*. *In* (pp. 115–26) **19531.**

13994. HEINECKEN, DAWN. The warrior women of television: a feminist cultural analysis of the female body in popular media. New York; Frankfurt: Lang, 2003. pp. 187. (Intersections in communications and culture, 7.) Rev. by Peggy Davis in JPC (38:3) 2005, 576–7.

13995. HELLER, DANA. Sex and the series: Paris, New York, and the post-national romance. AmS (46:2) 2005, 145–69.

13996. HEYER, PAUL. The medium and the magician: Orson Welles, the radio years, 1934–1952. *See* **13946**.

13997. HILMES, MICHELE. The bad object: television in the American academy. CinJ (45:1) 2005, 111–16.

13998. —— (ed.); JACOBS, JASON (assoc. ed.). The television history book. London: British Film Inst., 2003. pp. xii, 163. Rev. by Marshall W. Fishwick in JAC (28:1) 2005, 163.

13999. HUGHES, WILLIAM C. James Agee, *Omnibus*, and Mr Lincoln: the culture of liberalism and the challenge of television, 1952–1953. *See* **15086**.

14000. HUNT, DARRELL M. Channeling Blackness: studies on television and race in America. New York: OUP, 2005. pp. ix, 320. (Media and African Americans.) Rev. by Jean Humez in JPFT (33:2) 2005, 126–7.

14001. INGLIS, KEN. Aunty's story. Meanjin (62:2) 2003, 162–72. (Australian radio station ABC.)

14002. INNESS, SHERRIE A. (ed.). Action chicks: new images of tough women in popular culture. (Bibl. 2004, 14089.) Rev. by Carol-Ann Farkas in JPC (38:3) 2005, 585–6.

14003. JANCOVICH, MARK; LYONS, JAMES (eds). Quality popular television: cult TV, the industry and fans. (Bibl. 2004, 14091.) Rev. by Alison McCracken in AmS (46:2) 2005, 200; by Margaret Tally in JAC (28:1) 2005, 150.

14004. JIWANI, YASMIN. The Eurasian female hero(ine): Sydney Fox as relic hunter. JPFT (32:4) 2005, 182–91.

14005. JOHN, JULIET. Fagin, the Holocaust and mass culture; or, *Oliver Twist* on screen. *See* **10703**.

14006. JOHNSON-SMITH, JAN. American science fiction TV: *Star Trek*, *Stargate* and beyond. London; New York: Tauris, 2005. pp. vii, 308. (Popular television genres.) Rev. by Roz Kaveney in TLS, 5 Aug. 2005, 18; by David Moyle in Extrapolation (46:2) 2005, 280–3.

14007. JOWETT, LORNA. Sex and the slayer: a Gender Studies primer for the *Buffy* fan. Middletown, CT: Wesleyan UP, 2005. pp. 241.

14008. KEESEY, DOUGLAS. A phantom fly and frightening fish: the unconscious speaks in *Sports Night*. *In* (pp. 77–90) **19531**.

14009. KELLER, JAMES R.; STRATYNER, LESLIE (eds). Almost Shakespeare: reinventing his works for cinema and television. *See* **13273**.

14010. KLINE, SUSAN L. Interactive media systems: influence strategies in television home shopping. TextB (25:2) 2005, 201–31.

14011. KOCELA, CHRISTOPHER. Unmade men: *The Sopranos* after Whiteness. PMC (15:2) 2005.

14012. LANDY, MARCIA. *Monty Python's Flying Circus*. Detroit, MI: Wayne State UP, 2005. pp. viii, 120. (Contemporary approaches to film and television.)

14013. LAWRENCE, JOHN SHELTON. *The Lone Ranger*: adult legacies of a juvenile western. *In* (pp. 81–96) **13186**.

14014. LEITCH, THOMAS. Perry Mason. Detroit, MI: Wayne State UP, 2005. pp. vii, 129. (TV milestones.)

14015. LIEBREGTS, PETER. Images of an imaginist: two film versions of Jane Austen's *Emma*. *In* (pp. 277–99) **9237.**

14016. McCAW, NEIL. Those other villagers: policing Englishness in Caroline Graham's *The Killings at Badger's Drift*. *In* (pp. 13–28) **14191.**

14017. MALCOLM, JODY. Horatio: the first CSI. *In* (pp. 113–21) **13273.**

14018. MARINUCCI, MIMI. Television, Generation X, and Third Wave Feminism: a contextual analysis of *The Brady Bunch*. JPC (38:3) 2005, 505–24.

14019. MASCARO, THOMAS A. Shades of black on *Homicide: Life on the Street*: advances and retreats in portrayals of African American women. JPFT (33:2) 2005, 56–67.

14020. MIKLITSCH, ROBERT. Gen-X TV: political–libidinal structures of feeling in *Melrose Place*. JFV (55:1) 2003, 16–29.

14021. MITCHELL, DANIELLE. Producing containment: the rhetorical construction of difference in *Will & Grace*. *See* **20826.**

14022. MORGAN-ZAYACHEK, EILEEN. Losing their day jobs: the Radio Éireann Players as a permanent repertory company. TheatreS (46:1) 2005, 31–48.

14023. MORRISON, AIMÉE. It's more than a game: cinematic videogaming in the 1980s. *See* **13320.**

14024. MURPHY, OLIVIA. Books, bras and Bridget Jones: reading adaptions of *Pride and Prejudice*. *See* **10026.**

14025. NADEL, ALAN. Television in Black-and-White America: race and national identity. Lawrence: Kansas UP, 2005. pp. 224. (Culture America.)

14026. NEAME, CHRISTOPHER. A take on British TV drama: stories from the golden years. Lanham, MD; London: Scarecrow Press, 2004. pp. xix, 153. (Filmmakers, 112.)

14027. NEIN, JOHN. The republic of Sorkin: a view from the cheap seats. *In* (pp. 193–209) **19531.**

14028. NELSON, ROBIN. Live or wired? Technologizing the event. *In* (pp. 303–16) **3974.**

14029. NEMESVARI, RICHARD. Collaboration or compromise? From screenplay to screen in the Ian Sharp production of *Tess of the d'Urbervilles*. *See* **11146.**

14030. NEWCOMB, HORACE. Studying television: same questions, different contexts. CinJ (45:1) 2005, 107–11.

14031. NEWMAN, DONALD J. Jacques Derrida visits Cicely: the deconstruction of *Northern Exposure*. PCR (16:2) 2005, 45–58.

14032. NOCHIMSON, MARTHA P. Waddaya lookin' at? Rereading the gangster film through *The Sopranos*. *In* (pp. 185–204) **13247.**

14033. OKUDA, TED; MULQUEEN, JACK. The golden age of Chicago children's television. Chicago, IL: Lake Claremont Press, 2004. pp. xviii, 249.

14034. OZERSKY, JOSH. Archie Bunker's America: TV in an era of change, 1968–1978. Foreword by Mark Crispin Miller. Carbondale: Southern Illinois UP, 2003. pp. xxii, 194. Rev. by Michael Curtin in JAH (91:1) 2004, 334–5.

14035. PAXTON, NATHAN A. Virtue from vice: duty, power, and *The West Wing*. *In* (pp. 147–77) **19531.**

14036. PIERSON, DAVID.   Turner Network Television's made-for-TV western films: engaging audiences through genres and themes. *In* (pp. 281–99) **13186.**

14037. PONDILLO, BOB.   Racial discourse and censorship on NBC-TV, 1948–1960. JPFT (33:2) 2005, 102–14.

14038. RADER, DEAN.   Composition, visual culture, and the problems of class. *See* **20668.**

14039. RIKER, MARTIN.   Fiction and the boob tube. *See* **14264.**

14040. ROLLINS, PETER C.; O'CONNOR, JOHN E. (eds).   Hollywood's West: the American frontier in film, television, and history. *See* **13358.**

14041. SAPORITO, SHERILYN.   Sartre and *The Sopranos*: Italian American identity in the media and real life. MiE, Spring 2005, 47–59.

14042. SCHECHTER, HAROLD.   Savage pastimes: a cultural history of violent entertainment. *See* **3917.**

14043. SHARRETT, CHRISTOPHER.   *The Rifleman*. Detroit, MI: Wayne State UP, 2005. pp. x, 129. (Contemporary approaches to film and television.) (TV milestones.)

14044. SHERMAN, FRASER A.   *The Wizard of Oz* catalog: L. Frank Baum's novel, its sequels, their adaptations for stage, television, movies, radio, music videos, comic books, commercials, and more. *See* **15363.**

14045. SHORT, SUE.   The Federation and Borg value-systems in *Star Trek*. Foundation (92) 2004, 31–50.

14046. SPAISE, TERRY L.   Necrophilia and SM: the deviant side of *Buffy the Vampire Slayer*. JPC (38:4) 2005, 744–62.

14047. STANTON, WILLIAM.   The invisible theatre of radio drama. CritQ (46:4) 2004, 94–107.

14048. STEIN, ATARA.   The Byronic hero in film, fiction, and television. *See* **10337.**

14049. TAGLIAMONTE, SALI; ROBERTS, CHRIS.   So weird; so cool; so innovative: the use of intensifiers in the television series *Friends*. *See* **1647.**

14050. TAVINOR, GRANT.   Videogames and interactive fiction. *See* **20837.**

14051. TELOTTE, J. P.   Disney in science fiction land. JPFT (33:1) 2005, 12–20.

14052. THORBURN, DAVID; JENKINS, HENRY (eds); SEAWELL, BRAD (assoc. ed.).   Rethinking media change: the aesthetics of transition. *See* **24.**

14053. THORNHAM, SUE; PURVIS, TONY.   Television drama: theories and identities. Basingstoke; New York: Palgrave Macmillan, 2005. pp. xii, 212.

14054. TIESSEN, PAUL.   Dorothy Livesay, the 'housewife', and the radio in 1951: Modernist embodiments of audience. *In* (pp. 205–28) **12739.**

14055. TREDY, DENNIS.   Shadows of shadows: techniques of ambiguity in three film adaptations of *The Turn of the Screw*: J. Clayton's *The Innocents* (1961), D. Curtis's *The Turn of the Screw* (1974), and A. Aloy's *Presence of Mind* (1999). *See* **13616.**

14056. TURNER, CHRIS.   Planet Simpson: how a cartoon masterpiece defined a generation. New York: Da Capo Press, 2004. pp. xiv, 450. Rev. by Robert W. Smith in JPC (38:6) 2005, 1128–30.

14057. Voigts-Virchow, Eckart (ed.). Janespotting and beyond: British heritage retrovisions since the mid-1990s. See **13415**.

14058. Wasko, Janet (ed.). A companion to television. Oxford; Malden, MA: Blackwell, 2005. pp. xv, 627. (Blackwell companions in cultural studies, 10.)

14059. Whitt, Jan. Frank's Place: coming home to a place we'd never been before. JPFT (33:2) 2005, 80–7.

14060. Williams, Juan. Black political power in film and television. JPFT (33:2) 2005, 98–101.

14061. Winnington, G. Peter (introd.). Mervyn Peake's two radio plays for Christmas. See **18755**.

14062. Wittebols, James H. Watching M*A*S*H, watching America: a social history of the 1972–1983 television series. Jefferson, NC; London: McFarland, 2003. pp. xi, 272. Rev. by Robert W. Smith in JPC (38:3) 2005, 595–6.

14063. Wlodarz, Joe. Maximum insecurity: genre trouble and closet erotics. CamOb (58) 2005, 59–105. (Television show Oz.)

14064. Wolf, Mark J. P.; Perron, Bernard (eds). The video game theory reader. London; New York: Routledge, 2003. pp. xxii, 343. Rev. by Guy Reynolds in QRFV (22:3) 2005, 285–7.

14065. Woodman, Brian J. Escaping genre's village: fluidity and genre mixing in television's The Prisoner. JPC (38:5) 2005, 939–56.

14066. Wright, Peter. Intertextuality, generic shift and ideological transformation in the internationalising of Doctor Who. Foundation (92) 2004, 64–90.

14067. Zettel, Sarah. Times and tenors; or, What the movies have done, and failed to do, to Pride and Prejudice. In (pp. 97–103) **9971**.

14068. Zunshine, Lisa. Bastards and foundlings: illegitimacy in eighteenth-century England. See **8164**.

14069. Zurawik, David. The Jews of primetime. (Bibl. 2004, 14169.) Rev. by Elliot B. Gertel in JudQ (54:3/4) 2005, 264–71.

FICTION

14070. Aarons, Victoria. What happened to Abraham? Reinventing the covenant in American Jewish fiction. Newark: Delaware UP, 2005. pp. 181.

14071. Abbott, Megan E. The street was mine: White masculinity in hardboiled fiction and film noir. (Bibl. 2004, 14170.) Rev. by Erin A. Smith in StudN (37:2) 2005, 235–7.

14072. Abernathy, Jeff. To hell and back: race and betrayal in the Southern novel. (Bibl. 2004, 14172.) Rev. by Gary M. Ciuba in AAR (38:4) 2004, 733–5; by Betina Entzminger in ColLit (32:2) 2005, 201–4; by Warren J. Carson in SoLJ (37:2) 2005, 152–5.

14073. Adams, David. Colonial odysseys: empire and epic in the Modernist novel. (Bibl. 2004, 14175.) Rev. by Amar Acheraïou in Conradiana (36:3) 2004, 262–9; by Erica L. Johnson in WSA (11) 2005, 186–92; by Gregory Castle in ELT (48:4) 2005, 500–3; by Jed Esty in Mod/Mod (12:3) 2005, 519–21; by Steve Ferebee in VWM (67) 2005, 30–1.

14074. ADAMS, RACHEL. 'Going to Canada': the politics and poetics of Northern exodus. YJC (18:2) 2005, 409–33.

14075. ALLEN, EDDIE B., JR. Low road: the life and legacy of Donald Goines. *See* **16731.**

14076. ALMEIDA, ROCHELLE. The politics of mourning: grief-management in cross-cultural fiction. Madison, NJ: Fairleigh Dickinson UP, 2004. pp. 239.

14077. ANDERSON, GEORGE PARKER (ed.). American mystery and detective writers. Detroit, MI: Gale Research, 2005. pp. xxii, 475. (Dictionary of literary biography, 306.)

14078. ARMITT, LUCIE. Fantasy fiction: an introduction. London; New York: Continuum, 2005. pp. ix, 229. Rev. by W. A. Senior in JFA (16:2) 2005, 162–4.

14079. ASHLEY, MIKE. Transformations: the story of the science-fiction magazines from 1950 to 1970. Liverpool: Liverpool UP, 2005. pp. ix, 393. (Liverpool science fiction texts and studies, 30.) (History of the science fiction magazine, 2.) Rev. by Michael Saler in TLS, 13 May 2005, 30–1.

14080. ATTEBERY, BRIAN. Science fiction, parables, and parabolas. *See* **16717.**

14081. AUCHINCLOSS, LOUIS. Writers and personality. *See* **9512.**

14082. BELL, BERNARD W. The contemporary African American novel: its folk roots and modern literary branches. Amherst: Massachusetts UP, 2004. pp. xxviii, 490. Rev. by Christopher De Santis in AmBR (27:1) 2005, 18–19; by Dolan Hubbard in CLAJ (49:2) 2005, 242–6.

14083. BENDER, BERT. Evolution and 'the sex problem': American narratives during the eclipse of Darwinism. Kent, OH; London: Kent State UP, 2004. pp. xvi, 389.

14084. BENTLEY, NICK (ed.). British fiction of the 1990s. London; New York: Routledge, 2005. pp. x, 244.

14085. BERNARD, CATHERINE. Habitations of the past: of shrines and haunted houses. *See* **9514.**

14086. BEVERLY, WILLIAM. On the lam: narratives of flight in J. Edgar Hoover's America. Jackson; London: Mississippi UP, 2003. pp. xvii, 236. Rev. by D. Quentin Miller in AL (77:1) 2005, 196–8.

14087. BONE, MARTYN. The postsouthern sense of place in contemporary fiction. Baton Rouge: Louisiana State UP, 2005. pp. xvi, 275. (Southern literary studies.)

14088. BOTSHON, LISA; GOLDSMITH, MEREDITH (eds). Middlebrow moderns: popular American women writers of the 1920s. (Bibl. 2004, 14197.) Rev. by Martha Patterson in Legacy (21:1) 2004, 104–5.

14089. BRENNAN, ZOE. The older woman in recent fiction. Jefferson, NC; London: McFarland, 2005. pp. vii, 187. Rev. by Tim Charest in WS (34:3/4) 2005, 349–50.

14090. BRITTON, WESLEY. Beyond Bond: spies in fiction and film. *See* **13168.**

14091. BRODERICK, DAMIEN. Transreal nostalgia in a time of singularity. JFA (16:1) 2005, 21–36.

14092. BRODSKY, G. W. STEPHEN. Prester John's workbook: Joseph Conrad, Edmund Candler, John Towson, and some imperial Others. *See* **15860.**

14093. BROOKS, PETER.   Realist vision. *See* **9519.**

14094. BROWNE, RAY B.   Murder on the reservation: American Indian crime fiction: aims and achievements. (Bibl. 2004, 14200.) Rev. by Ken Dvorak in JPC (38:5) 2005, 965–6; by Marshall W. Fishwick in JAC (28:2) 2005, 242–3; by Nancy Ellen Talburt in Clues (23:3) 2005, 76–7; by Lisa Berglund in DRM (25:1) 2005, 1, 8, 12.

14095. BRUNNHUBER, NICOLE.   The faces of Janus: English-language fiction by German-speaking exiles in Great Britain, 1933–45. New York; Frankfurt: Lang, 2005. pp. 240. (Exil-Studien, 8.)

14096. BULLARD, PADDY.   In the world of Nora Barnacle: the tradition of the Irish short story. TLS, 13 May 2005, 21–2 (review-article).

14097. BURGESS, MICHAEL; VASSILAKOS, JILL H.   Murder in retrospect: a selective guide to historical mystery fiction. Westport, CT: Libraries Unlimited, 2005. pp. xi, 410.

14098. BURTON, ROB.   Cheerleading and charting the cosmopolis: London as linear narrative and contested space. *In* (pp. 131–7) **14254.**

14099. BUTLER, ANDREW M.   Between the 'deaths' of science fiction: a skeptical view of the possibility for anti-genres. *See* **13176.**

14100. BYERMAN, KEITH.   Remembering the past in contemporary African American fiction. Chapel Hill; London: North Carolina UP, 2005. pp. viii, 228.

14101. CAMINERO-SANTANGELO, BYRON.   African fiction and Joseph Conrad: reading postcolonial intertextuality. *See* **15863.**

14102. CARLITO, M. DELORES.   Cuban American fiction in English: an annotated bibliography of primary and secondary sources. Lanham, MD; London: Scarecrow Press, 2005. pp. 129.

14103. CHERRY, KELLY.   What comes next: women writing women in contemporary short fiction. *In* (pp. 128–36) **14204.**

14104. CHEUSE, ALAN.   Reflections on dialogue: 'How d'yuh get t'Eighteent' Avenoo and Sixty-Sevent' Street?' AR (63:2) 2005, 222–33.

14105. CHILDS, PETER.   Contemporary novelists: British fiction since 1970. (Bibl. 2004, 14210.) Rev. by Katharine Begg in TLS, 8 Apr. 2005, 33.

14106. CHIVERS, SALLY.   From old woman to older woman: contemporary culture and women's narratives. (Bibl. 2003, 13871.) Rev. by Tanis MacDonald in CanL (186) 2005, 122–3.

14107. CLONTZ, TED L.   Wilderness city: the post-World War II American novel from Algren to Wideman. London; New York: Routledge, 2005. pp. ix, 169. (Literary criticism and cultural theory.)

14108. CLUTE, JOHN.   Canary fever. JFA (15:3) 2004, 217–27.

14109. COALE, SAMUEL CHASE.   Paradigms of paranoia: the culture of conspiracy in contemporary American fiction. Tuscaloosa; London: Alabama UP, 2005. pp. 258.

14110. COLAVINCENZO, MARC.   'Trading magic for fact, fact for magic': myth and mythologizing in postmodern Canadian historical fiction. Amsterdam; Atlanta, GA: Rodopi, 2003. pp. xxii, 239. Rev. by Judith Leggatt in CanL (186) 2005, 126–7.

14111. COLLETTA, LISA. Dark humor and social satire in the modern British novel. (Bibl. 2004, 14213.) Rev. by Julia Paolitto in RES (56:224) 2005, 343–5; by John Morreall in Humor (18:1) 2005, 118–20.

14112. CONROY, MARK. Muse in the machine: American fiction and mass publicity. (Bibl. 2004, 14214.) Rev. by Anne Longmuir in Genre (38:1/2) 2005, 193–6.

14113. COUTURIER, MAURICE. The subjects in and out of the text. *See* **14743**.

14114. COX, J. RANDOLPH. Premiums in dime novels. *See* **9533**.

14115. CROWE, CHRIS. More than a game: sports literature for young adults. (Bibl. 2004, 14216.) Rev. by Jim Beggs in CLAQ (30:2) 2005, 221–4.

14116. CUNNINGHAM, SOPHIE. Alien star. Meanjin (62:1) 2003, 100–13.

14117. DAGBOVIE, PERO GAGLO. Black women historians from the late 19th century to the dawning of the Civil Rights Movement. *See* **9535**.

14118. DALZIELL, TANYA. Settler romances and the Australian girl. Crawley: Western Australia UP, 2004. pp. ix, 178.

14119. DAY, VOX. C. S. Lewis and the problem of religion in science fiction and fantasy. *In* (pp. 219–28) **17727**.

14120. DEANGELIS, ROSE; ANDERSON, DONALD R. Gastronomic *miscuglio*: foodways in Italian American narrative. ItalA (23:1) 2005, 48–68.

14121. DENEEN, PATRICK J.; ROMANCE, JOSEPH (eds). Democracy's literature: politics and fiction in America. Lanham, MD; Oxford: Rowman & Littlefield, 2005. pp. vi, 238.

14122. DEROSE, MARIA. Redefining women's power through feminist science fiction. Extrapolation (46:1) 2005, 66–89.

14123. DEVLIN, ATHENA. Between profits and primitivism: shaping White middle-class masculinity in the United States, 1880–1917. *See* **9541**.

14124. DICKSON-CARR, DARRYL. The Columbia guide to contemporary African American fiction. New York: Columbia UP, 2005. pp. xiv, 257. (Columbia guides to literature since 1945.)

14125. DISCH, THOMAS M. On SF. Ann Arbor: Michigan UP, 2005. pp. 271.

14126. DIZER, JOHN T. How I started collecting books. *See* **379**.

14127. DORE, FLORENCE. The novel and the obscene: sexual subjects in American Modernism. Stanford, CA: Stanford UP, 2005. pp. xii, 167.

14128. DUDLEY, JOHN. A man's game: masculinity and the anti-aesthetics of American literary naturalism. Tuscaloosa; London: Alabama UP, 2004. pp. viii, 222. Rev. by Jeffory A. Clymer in MFS (51:1) 2005, 183–91; by Caren J. Town in ALR (38:1) 2005, 89–90.

14129. DURHAM, CAROLYN A. Literary globalism: Anglo-American fiction set in France. Lewisburg, PA: Bucknell UP, 2005. pp. 265.

14130. EKELUND, BO G.; BÖRJESSON, MIKAEL. Comparing literary worlds: an analysis of the spaces of fictional universes in the work of two US prose fiction debut cohorts, 1940 and 1955. Poetics (33:5/6) 2005, 343–68.

14131. Emrys, A. B.   Does formula matter? Why popular fiction is essential to narrative studies. Storytelling (4:1) 2004, 1–13.

14132. Farr, Cecilia Konchar.   Reading Oprah: how Oprah's Book Club changed the way America reads. Albany: New York State UP, 2005. pp. 164. Rev. by Trysh Travis in SHARP (14:4) 2005, 13; by Beth Luey in PubRQ (21:4) 2005, 102–3; by Lisa Tyler in JMMLA (38:1) 2005, 137–9.

14133. Ferrebe, Alice.   Masculinity in male-authored fiction 1950–2000: keeping it up. Basingstoke; New York: Palgrave Macmillan, 2005. pp. ix, 221.

14134. Fleissner, Jennifer.   Women, compulsion, modernity: the moment of American naturalism. (Bibl. 2004, 14237.) Rev. by Jeffory A. Clymer in MFS (51:1) 2005, 183–91; by Marjorie Pryse in TSWL (24:1) 2005, 164–6; by Melanie Dawson in Legacy (22:2) 2005, 200–1.

14135. Flesch, Juliet.   From Australia with love: a history of modern Australian popular romance novels. Fremantle, W. Australia: Curtin Univ., 2004. pp. 320. Rev. by Toni Johnson-Woods in ALS (22:1) 2005, 119–20.

14136. Ford, Susan Allen.   Stately homes of England: Robert Barnard's country house mysteries. See **15319**.

14137. Forrest, Katherine V. (ed.).   Lesbian pulp fiction: the sexually intrepid world of lesbian paperback novels, 1950–1965. San Francisco, CA: Cleis Press, 2005. pp. 413.

14138. Freeman, Alan.   Imagined worlds: fiction by Scottish women, 1900–1935. New York; Frankfurt: Lang, 2005. pp. 247. (Scottish studies international, 36.)

14139. Freier, Mary P.   Information ethics in the detective novel. See **20866**.

14140. Furst, Lilian R.   Random destinations: escaping the Holocaust and starting life anew. Basingstoke; New York: Palgrave Macmillan, 2005. pp. xviii, 213.

14141. Gallego, Mar.   Passing novels in the Harlem renaissance: identity politics and textual strategies. (Bibl. 2004, 14245.) Rev. by Yupei Zhou in AAR (38:4) 2004, 720–3.

14142. Gannon, Charles E.   Rumors of war and infernal machines: technomilitary agenda-setting in American and British speculative fiction. Lanham, MD; Oxford: Rowman & Littlefield, 2005. pp. 311.

14143. Gelder, Ken.   Popular fiction: the logics and practices of a literary field. London; New York: Routledge, 2004. pp. 179.

14144. Gelly, Christophe.   De William Faulkner à James Hadley Chase: appropriation et mutation du genre policier. See **16409**.

14145. Ghosh, Bishnupriya.   When borne across: literary cosmopolitics in the contemporary Indian novel. (Bibl. 2004, 14247.) Rev. by Andrew Teverson in MFS (51:3) 2005, 703–6.

14146. Goeller, Alison D.   The politics of food in Italian American women's autobiography. See **14595**.

14147. Goldie, Terry.   Pink snow: homotextual possibilities in Canadian fiction. (Bibl. 2004, 14248.) Rev. by Jes Battis in CanL (186) 2005, 140–1.

14148. GRACE, SHERRILL. Inventing Tom Thomson: from biographical fictions to fictional autobiographies and reproductions. Montreal; Buffalo, NY; London: McGill-Queen's UP, 2004. pp. xiii, 234, (plates) 4. Rev. by David P. Silcox in LRC (12:10) 2004, 6–7.

14149. GRAYSON, SANDRA M. Visions of the third millennium: Black science fiction novelists write the future. (Bibl. 2004, 14253.) Rev. by Ronald Dorris in CLAJ (48:2) 2004, 240–3.

14150. GREEN, JEREMY. Late postmodernism: American fiction at the millennium. Basingstoke; New York: Palgrave Macmillan, 2005. pp. xii, 246.

14151. GREVEN, DAVID. The fantastic powers of the other sex: male mothers in fantastic fiction. See **13992**.

14152. GRIBBEN, CRAWFORD. Rapture fictions and the changing evangelical condition. LitTheol (18:1) 2004, 77–94.

14153. GUNN, DREWEY WAYNE. The gay male sleuth in print and film: a history and annotated bibliography. Lanham, MD; London: Scarecrow Press, 2005. pp. vi, 328.

14154. HACKETT, ROBIN. Sapphic primitivism: productions of race, class, and sexuality in key works of modern fiction. (Bibl. 2004, 14255.) Rev. by Erica L. Johnson in WSA (11) 2005, 186–92.

14155. HAHN, TORSTEN. Risk communication and paranoid hermeneutics: towards a distinction between 'medical thrillers' and 'mind-control thrillers' in narrations on biocontrol. NLH (36:2) 2005, 187–204.

14156. HAND, ELIZABETH. The beckoning fair ones: some thoughts on muses. JFA (15:3) 2004, 192–207.

14157. HAPGOOD, LYNNE. Margins of desire: the suburbs in fiction and culture, 1880–1925. See **9561**.

14158. HARRIS-FAIN, DARREN. Understanding contemporary American science fiction: the age of maturity, 1970–2000. Columbia; London: South Carolina UP, 2005. pp. xi, 220. (Understanding contemporary American literature.)

14159. HARRISON, BRADY. Agent of empire: William Walker and the imperial self in American literature. (Bibl. 2004, 14259.) Rev. by Andrew Burstein in AmS (46:2) 2005, 179–80; by Amy S. Greenberg in CWH (51:4) 2005, 436–8.

14160. HAWLITSCHKA, KATJA. Detection, deconstruction, and academic death sentences: female scholars reading the mysteries of high and low culture. Clues (23:3) 2005, 15–29.

14161. HEBBAR, RESHMI J. Modeling minority women: heroines in African and Asian American fiction. London; New York: Routledge, 2005. pp. xxvii, 152. (Studies in Asian Americans.)

14162. HEGERFELDT, ANNE C. Lies that tell the truth: magic realism seen through contemporary fiction from Britain. Amsterdam; Atlanta, GA: Rodopi, 2005. pp. 383. (Costerus, ns 155.) Rev. by Luc Herman in BELL (ns 3) 2005, 207–8.

14163. HELMS, GABRIELE.   Challenging Canada: dialogism and narrative techniques in Canadian novels. Montreal; Buffalo, NY; London: McGill-Queen's UP, 2003. pp. x, 212. Rev. by Gordon Bölling in CanL (184) 2005, 136–8.

14164. HEPBURN, ALLAN.   Intrigue: espionage and culture. New Haven, CT; London: Yale UP, 2005. pp. xvii, 327. Rev. by Robert Carver in TLS, 14 Oct. 2005, 28; by Wesley Wark in LRC (13:7) 2005, 10–11.

14165. HERMAN, PETER C.   Shadows on the Hudson: Isaac Bashevis Singer and the problem of post-Holocaust Judaism. StudAJL (24) 2005, 158–79.

14166. HERZBERG, BOB.   Shooting scripts: from pulp western to film. Jefferson, NC; London: McFarland, 2005. pp. vii, 204.

14167. HESTERMANN, SANDRA.   Meeting the Other – encountering oneself: Paradigmen der Selbst- und Fremddarstellung in ausgewählten anglo-indischen und indisch-englischen Kurzgeschichten. New York; Frankfurt: Lang, 2003. pp. 322. (Neue Studien zur Anglistik und Amerikanistik, 28.) Rev. by Dieter Riemenschneider in WLWE (39:2) 2002/03, 149–51.

14168. HO, JENNIFER ANN.   Consumption and identity in Asian American coming-of-age novels. London; New York: Routledge, 2005. pp. ix, 202. (Studies in Asian Americans.)

14169. HOBEREK, ANDREW.   The twilight of the middle class:post-World War II American fiction and white-collar work. Princeton, NJ; Oxford: Princeton UP, 2005. pp. x, 158.

14170. HOBERMAN, RUTH.   Constructing the turn-of-the-century shopper: narratives about purchased objects in the *Strand* magazine, 1891–1910. *See* **9563.**

14171. HOLLINGER, VERONICA; GORDON, JOAN (eds).   Edging into the future: science fiction and contemporary cultural transformation. (Bibl. 2004, 14266.) Rev. by Farah Mendlesohn in JFA (13:3) 2003, 313–23.

14172. HONEYMAN, SUSAN.   Elusive childhood: impossible representations in modern fiction. Athens: Ohio UP, 2005. pp. viii, 184.

14173. HORSLEY, LEE.   Twentieth-century crime fiction. Oxford; New York: OUP, 2005. pp. xii, 313.

14174. HORSTKOTTE, MARTIN.   The postmodern fantastic in contemporary British fiction. (Bibl. 2004, 14269.) Rev. by Iuliu Ratiu in Extrapolation (46:2) 2005, 270–3; by Nicholas Ruddick in JFA (16:1) 2005, 75–8.

14175. HOWELLS, CORAL ANN.   Contemporary Canadian women's fiction: refiguring identities. Basingstoke; New York: Palgrave Macmillan, 2003. pp. x, 230. Rev. by Heidi Slettedahl Macpherson in BJCS (17:2) 2004, 259–61; by Cynthia Sugars in CanL (184) 2005, 144–5.

14176. HULL, ELIZABETH ANNE.   Science fiction as a manifestation of culture in America. FLS (116) 2005, 41–7.

14177. HUME, KATHRYN.   Narrative speed in contemporary fiction. Narrative (13:2) 2005, 105–24.

14178. HUNT, PAUL.   Serial fiction in the *Otago Witness*, 1851–1906. *See* **9565.**

14179. JAMES, CLIVE.   Starting with sludge: a literary education: from the fiction of Biggles to Braddon's brute facts. TLS, 16 Dec. 2005, 14–15.

14180. JASANOFF, MAYA. Secret signals in lotus flowers. *See* **9568.**

14181. JEFFERS, THOMAS L. Apprenticeships: the *Bildungsroman* from Goethe to Santayana. *See* **9570.**

14182. JOHNSON, GEORGE M. Dynamic psychology in Modernist British fiction. Basingstoke; New York: Palgrave Macmillan, 2005. pp. xxix, 240.

14183. JONES, GEORGE FENWICK. Of *inquits*. ELN (43:1) 2005, 77–83.

14184. KAMINSKY, STUART. Behind the mystery: top mystery writers. Cohasset, MA: Hot House Press, 2005. pp. vii, 237.

14185. KAPELL, MATTHEW; BECKER, SUZANNE. Patriarchy, the Christian romance novel, and the 'ecosystem of sex'. PCR (16:1) 2005, 147–55.

14186. KELLER, YVONNE. 'Was it right to love her brother's wife so passionately?': lesbian pulp novels and US lesbian identity, 1950–1965. AmQ (57:2) 2005, 385–410.

14187. KELLY, AARON. The thriller and Northern Ireland since 1969: utterly resigned terror. Aldershot; Burlington, VT: Ashgate, 2004. pp. viii, 213. (Studies in European cultural transition, 28.)

14188. KELMAN, SUANNE. The glittering prizes: the struggle between merit and Mammon continues, ten years after the birth of the Giller. LRC (11:9) 2003, 7–9.

14189. KENNELL, VICKI R. *Pygmalion* as narrative bridge between the centuries. *See* **19397.**

14190. KICKHAM, LISBET. Protestant women novelists and Irish society 1879–1922. *See* **9577.**

14191. KIM, JULIE H. (ed.). Race and religion in the postcolonial British detective story. Jefferson, NC; London: McFarland, 2005. pp. viii, 244.

14192. KING, JEANNETTE. The Victorian Woman Question in contemporary feminist fiction. Basingstoke; New York: Palgrave Macmillan, 2005. pp. ix, 210.

14193. KING, ROSEMARY A. Border confluences: borderland narratives from the Mexican War to the present. (Bibl. 2004, 14295.) Rev. by Luz Elena Ramirez in Comparatist (29) 2005, 148–51.

14194. KORT, WESLEY A. Place and space in modern fiction. (Bibl. 2004, 14300.) Rev. by Rebecca Garcia Lucas in ReLit (37:3) 2005, 145–7.

14195. KOSHY, SUSAN. Sexual naturalization: Asian Americans and miscegenation. Stanford, CA: Stanford UP, 2004. pp. x, 208. (Asian America.)

14196. KRUK, LAURIE. The voice is the story: conversations with Canadian writers of short fiction. (Bibl. 2004, 14304.) Rev. by Paul Denham in CanL (185) 2005, 163–4.

14197. LAMB, ROBERT PAUL; THOMPSON, G. R. (eds). A companion to American fiction, 1865–1914. *See* **9582.**

14198. LAMONT, VICTORIA; NEWELL, DIANNE. House opera: frontier mythology and subversion of domestic discourse in mid-twentieth-century women's space opera. Foundation (95) 2005, 71–88.

14199. LANTERS, JOSÉ. 'We are a different people': life writing, representation, and the Travellers. *See* **14608.**

14200. Latham, Sean. 'Am I a snob?': Modernism and the novel. (Bibl. 2004, 14308.) Rev. by Ruth Saxton in VWM (66) 2004, 28–9; by Catherine Turner in StudN (37:1) 2005, 104–6; by Alyssa J. O'Brien in ELT (48:3) 2005, 348–52.

14201. Leader, Zachary (ed.). On modern British fiction. (Bibl. 2004, 14309.) Rev. by Jeffrey Meyers in StudN (37:1) 2004, 107–9.

14202. Leavis, L. R. Current literature 2001: 1, New writing: novels and short stories. See **20881**.

14203. Ledent, Bénédicte. A new wor(l)d order: language in the fiction of the new Caribbean diaspora. RAEI (16) 2003, 191–200.

14204. Lee, Maurice A. (ed.). Writers on writing: the art of the short story. Westport, CT; London: Praeger, 2005. pp. xxii, 247. (Contributions to the study of world literature, 128.) Rev. by Ronny Noor in ShSt (ns 12:2) 2004, 109–13.

14205. Lehan, Richard. Realism and naturalism: the novel in an age of transition. See **9584**.

14206. Lendrum, Rob. The super Black Macho, one baaad mutha: Black superhero masculinity in 1970s mainstream comic books. See **96**.

14207. Lohafer, Susan. Reading for storyness: preclosure theory, empirical poetics, and culture in the short story. Baltimore, MD; London: Johns Hopkins UP, 2003. pp. 191. Rev. by Michael Trussler in WasRCPSF (38:1) 2003, ii–viii.

14208. Luo, Shiping. British postwar novels: postcolonial experimentalism. FLS (111) 2005, 147–53 (review-article). (In Chinese.)

14209. Lynch, Deidre Shauna. Sequels. In (pp. 160–8) **10060**.

14210. McCann, Sean; Szalay, Michael. Do you believe in magic? Literary thinking after the New Left. See **18056**.

14211. McDonald, Ronan. Strategies of silence: colonial strains in short stories of the Troubles. YES (35) 2005, 249–63.

14212. McGlamery, Gayla. The three tropographies of Ronald Wright's *A Scientific Romance*. See **20470**.

14213. McGurl, Mark. The program era: pluralisms of postwar American fiction. See **15350**.

14214. McLean, Patricia. 'Man Alone': the demise of a cultural icon in the fiction of Maurice Gee. See **16654**.

14215. McNeer, Rebecca. 'What might be true': the diverse relationships of Australian novels to fact. Antipodes (18:1) 2004, 68–71.

14216. Maltby, Paul. The visionary moment: a postmodern critique. (Bibl. 2004, 14324.) Rev. by Daniel T. O'Hara in JML (26:3/4) 2003, 154–8.

14217. Mardorossian, Carine M. Reclaiming difference: Caribbean women rewrite postcolonialism. Charlottesville; London: Virginia UP, 2005. pp. x, 187. (New World studies.)

14218. Marie, Caroline. '*The strangest transformation took place*': parcours, détours et bifurcations dans *Orlando* de Virginia Woolf. See **20392**.

14219. Markley, Robert. Dying planet: Mars in science and the imagination. Durham, NC; London: Duke UP, 2005. pp. 444.

14220. Markowitz, Judith A.   The gay detective novel: lesbian and gay main characters and themes in mystery fiction. Foreword by Katherine V. Forrest. Jefferson, NC; London: McFarland, 2004. pp. ix, 302.

14221. Matthews, Pamela.   Southern hauntology: a response to Patricia Yaeger's *Ghosts and Shattered Bodies.* SCR (22:1) 2005, 109–13.

14222. Mendlesohn, Farah.   *Conjunctions 39* and liminal fantasy. JFA (15:3) 2004, 228–39.

14223. Menzies, Ruth.   Re-writing *Gulliver's Travels*: the demise of a genre? *See* **9077**.

14224. Mergenthal, Silvia.   A fast-forward version of England: constructions of Englishness in contemporary fiction. Heidelberg: Winter, 2003. pp. 205. (Anglistische Forschungen, 314.) Rev. by Ina Habermann in JSBC (11:1) 2004, 94–6.

14225. Micali, Simona.   La trama del mondo: contaminazione tra linguaggio e realtà nel romanzo postmoderno. *In* (pp. 298–312) **14322**.

14226. Millar, Paul.   'Canton bromides': the Chinese presence in twentieth-century New Zealand fiction. *In* (pp. 156–72) **12674**.

14227. Miller, P. Andrew.   Mutants, metaphor, and marginalism: what x-actly do the X-Men stand for? JFA (13:3) 2003, 282–90.

14228. Moffat, Kirstine.   The demon drink: Prohibition novels 1882–1924. *See* **9595**.

14229. Mohr, Dunja M.   Worlds apart: dualism and transgression in contemporary female dystopias. Jefferson, NC; London: McFarland, 2005. pp. xi, 312. (Critical explorations in science fiction and fantasy, 1.)

14230. Monda, Andrea; Simonelli, Saverio.   Gli anelli della fantasia. Milan: Frassinelli, 2004. pp. xii, 290.

14231. Monteith, Sharon; Newman, Jenny; Wheeler, Pat (eds). Contemporary British & Irish fiction: an introduction through interviews. London; New York: Arnold, 2004. pp. xi, 180.

14232. Morrison, Jago.   Contemporary fiction. (Bibl. 2003, 14034.) Rev. by Julie Mullaney in MLR (100:4) 2005, 1107–8.

14233. Morrow, James.   Once upon a time in the future: science fiction and the storytelling movement. NYRSF (16:9) 2004, 17–19.

14234. Most, Glenn W.   *Urban blues* e gialli metropolitani. Bel (60:5) 2005, 527–41.

14235. Murat, Jean-Christophe.   Community-centred *versus* subject-centred representation in the narrative fiction of the 1940s. EREA (2:2) 2004, 35–41.

14236. Murphy, Graham J.   Ideas and inhabitations. *See* **21309**.

14237. Nesbitt, Jennifer Poulos.   Narrative settlements: geographies of British women's fiction between the wars. Toronto; Buffalo, NY; London: Toronto UP, 2005. pp. viii, 146.

14238. Newman, Judie.   Black Atlantic or Black Athena? Neo-slave narratives in contemporary fiction. FLS (111) 2005, 64–71.

14239. NG, ANDREW HOCK-SOON.   Dimensions of monstrosity in contemporary narratives: theory, psychoanalysis, postmodernism. Basingstoke; New York: Palgrave Macmillan, 2004. pp. viii, 229.

14240. NOBLE, JEAN BOBBY.   Masculinities without men? Female masculinity in twentieth-century fictions. (Bibl. 2004, 14347.) Rev. by Marc A. Ouellette in CanL (186) 2005, 171–2.

14241. NYMAN, JOPI.   Postcolonial animal tale from Kipling to Coetzee. New Delhi: Atlantic, 2003. pp. vi, 176. Rev. by John Simons in LitH (14:2) 2005, 95.

14242. O'GORMAN, FARRELL.   Peculiar crossroads: Flannery O'Connor, Walker Percy, and Catholic vision in postwar Southern fiction. See **18573.**

14243. PAES DE BARROS, DEBORAH.   Fast cars and bad girls: nomadic subjects and women's road stories. New York; Frankfurt: Lang, 2004. pp. 208. (Travel writing across the disciplines, 9.) Rev. by Frances Hennessey in WS (34:6) 2005, 517–20.

14244. PARAVISINI-GEBERT, LIZABETH.   'He of the trees': nature, environment, and creole religiosities in Caribbean literature. *In* (pp. 182–96) **12632.**

14245. PARKER, EMMA.   Introduction: 'the proper stuff of fiction': defending the domestic, reappraising the parochial. EAS (57) 2004, 1–15.

14246. PARRINDER, PATRICK.   Entering dystopia, entering *Erewhon.* See **10283.**

14247. PATERSON, KATHERINE.   Why historical fiction? See **9603.**

14248. PATTERSON, MARTHA H.   Beyond the Gibson Girl: reimagining the American New Woman, 1895–1915. See **9604.**

14249. PEACH, LINDEN.   The contemporary Irish novel. (Bibl. 2004, 14353.) Rev. by Sylvie Mikowski in EtIr (29:2) 2004, 202–3; by Thomas Mansell in YES (35) 2005, 340–1.

14250. PECK, DALE.   Hatchet jobs: writings on contemporary fiction. (Bibl. 2004, 14354.) Rev. by Myles Weber in GaR (59:2) 2005, 422–7; by Sean McCann in CommRev (3:3) 2005, 41–5.

14251. PENNY, SARAH.   A literary *vox pop.* JPW (41:2) 2005, 212–21.

14252. PETTY, ANNE C.   Dragons of fantasy. Cold Spring Harbor, NY: Cold Spring Press, 2004. pp. 311. Rev. by Jonathan Evans in JFA (15:4) 2004, 372–3.

14253. PHELAN, JAMES.   Living to tell about it: a rhetoric and ethics of character narration. Ithaca, NY; London: Cornell UP, 2005. pp. xiv, 236. Rev. by Pekka Tammi in PartA (3:2) 2005, 200–6.

14254. PHILLIPS, LAWRENCE (ed.).   The swarming streets: twentieth-century literary representations of London. Amsterdam; Atlanta, GA: Rodopi, 2004. pp. vi, 227. (Costerus, ns 154.) Rev. by Bénédicte Ledent in EJES (9:3) 2005, 327–9.

14255. PHILLIPSON, ALLAN.   Dollarman *vs The Lord of the Rings*: the battle of nature and progress. See **20727.**

14256. PILINOVSKY, HELEN.   Borderlands: the who, what, when, where, and why of the interstitial arts. JFA (15:3) 2004, 240–2.

14257. Polak, Iva. Postcolonial imagination and postcolonial theory: indigenous Canadian and Australian literature fighting for (postcolonial) space. *In* (pp. 135–42) **3734.**

14258. Pollock, Mary S.; Rainwater, Catherine (eds). Figuring animals: essays on animal images in art, literature, philosophy, and popular culture. Basingstoke; New York: Palgrave Macmillan, 2005. pp. xi, 292.

14259. Rainey, Lawrence. Eliot among the typists: writing *The Waste Land*. *See* **16296.**

14260. Reilly, Patrick. The dark landscape of modern fiction. (Bibl. 2004, 14363.) Rev. by Sophie Ratcliffe in RES (56:224) 2005, 345–6.

14261. Renger, Nicola. Mapping and historiography in contemporary Canadian literature in English. New York; Frankfurt: Lang, 2005. pp. 406. (European univ. studies, XIV: Anglo-Saxon language and literature, 418.)

14262. Richards, Gary. Lovers and beloveds: sexual otherness in Southern fiction, 1936–1961. Baton Rouge: Louisiana State UP, 2005. pp. x, 243. (Southern literary studies.)

14263. Rieder, John. Science fiction, colonialism, and the plot of invasion. Extrapolation (46:3) 2005, 373–94.

14264. Riker, Martin. Fiction and the boob tube. DQ (39:3) 2005, 96–104.

14265. Rodriguez, Ralph E. Brown gumshoes: detective fiction and the search for Chicana/o identity. Austin: Texas UP, 2005. pp. xv, 183. (CMAS history, culture, & society.)

14266. Roudeau, Cécile. À quoi rêvent les vieilles filles? Éros au féminin; ou, La débandade du roman domestique en Amérique. EREA (1:1) 2003, 26–35.

14267. Rück, Stefanie. 'Good Queen Bess': the mnemonic construction of Queen Elizabeth I. *See* **13364.**

14268. Salgueiro Seabra Ferreira, Maria Aline. I am the Other: literary negotiations of human cloning. Westport, CT; London: Praeger, 2004. pp. 304. (Contributions to the study of science fiction and fantasy, 85.)

14269. Saloman, Randi. 'Here again is the usual door': the modernity of Virginia Woolf's *Street Haunting*. *See* **20415.**

14270. Sceats, Sarah. Regulation and creativity: the use of recipes in contemporary fiction. *In* (pp. 169–86) **9257.**

14271. Schanoes, Veronica. Critical theory, academia, and interstitiality. JFA (15:3) 2004, 243–7.

14272. Schober, Adrian. Possessed child narratives in literature and film: contrary states. Basingstoke; New York: Palgrave Macmillan, 2004. pp. xi, 206. (Crime files.)

14273. Seed, David. Brainwashing: the fictions of mind control: a study of novels and films since World War II. Kent, OH; London: Kent State UP, 2004. pp. xxvi, 325.

14274. —— (ed.). A companion to science fiction. Oxford; Malden, MA: Blackwell, 2005. pp. xvi, 612. (Blackwell companions to literature and culture, 34.)

14275. SHOWALTER, ELAINE.   Faculty towers: the academic novel and its discontents. Philadelphia: Pennsylvania UP, 2005. pp. 143. Rev. by Ruth Morse in TLS, 16 Sept. 2005, 24.

14276. SICHER, EFRAIM.   The Holocaust novel. London; New York: Routledge, 2005. pp. 224. (Genres in context.)

14277. SIMATEI, TIROP.   Colonial violence, postcolonial violations: violence, landscape, and memory in Kenyan fiction. RAL (36:2) 2005, 85–94.

14278. SIMPSON, HYACINTH M.   The Jamaican short story: oral and related influences. JCarL (4:1) 2005, 11–30.

14279. SIMPSON, PETER (ed.).   Nine New Zealand novellas. Auckland: Reed, 2005. pp. 395. (*Supplements* bibl. 2003, 14113.)

14280. SPAULDING, A. TIMOTHY.   Re-forming the past: history, the fantastic, and the postmodern slave narrative. Columbus: Ohio State UP, 2005. pp. x, 148.

14281. SPURGEON, SARA L.   Exploding the western: myths of empire on the postmodern frontier. College Station: Texas A&M UP, 2005. pp. x, 168. (Tarleton State Univ. Southwestern studies in the humanities, 19.)

14282. SQUIER, SUSAN MERRILL.   Liminal lives: imagining the human at the frontiers of biomedicine. Durham, NC; London: Duke UP, 2004. pp. xvi, 350. Rev. by Lennard J. Davis in LitMed (24:2) 2005, 315–18.

14283. STAFFORD, JANE.   Going native: how the New Zealand settler became indigenous. See **16831**.

14284. STANFORD, ANN FOLWELL.   Bodies in a broken world: women novelists of color and the politics of medicine. (Bibl. 2004, 14386.) Rev. by J. Elizabeth Clark in LitMed (24:1) 2005, 142–5; by Delese Wear in NWSAJ (17:3) 2005, 205–6.

14285. STEIN, ATARA.   The Byronic hero in film, fiction, and television. See **10337**.

14286. STEIN, MARK.   Black British literature: novels of transformation. Columbus: Ohio State UP, 2004. pp. xviii, 243.

14287. STERNLICHT, SANFORD V.   The tenement saga: the Lower East Side and early Jewish American writers. Madison; London: Wisconsin UP, 2004. pp. xv, 171.

14288. STRAHAN, LINDA.   There's a hole in the (Inspector) Bucket: the Victorian police in fact and fiction. See **10748**.

14289. STRAND, ERIC.   Gandhian communalism and the Midnight Children's Conference. See **19281**.

14290. SULLIVAN, KATHLEEN.   Women characters in baseball literature: a critical study. Jefferson, NC; London: McFarland, 2005. pp. ix, 196.

14291. TIFFIN, HELEN.   'Man fitting the landscape': nature, culture, and colonialism. *In* (pp. 199–212) **12632**.

14292. TROUT, STEVEN (ed.).   American prose writers of World War I: a documentary volume. See **14553**.

14293. TRUDEL, JEAN-LOUIS.   Looking for little green men. NYRSF (18:3) 2005, 1, 6–11.

14294. TURCHI, PETER; BARRETT, ANDREA (eds). The story behind the story: 26 writers and how they work. Introd. by Richard Russo. New York; London: Norton, 2004. pp. 479.

14295. UHSADEL, KATHARINA. Antonia Byatts *Quartet* in der Tradition des englischen Bildungsroman. *See* **15649**.

14296. WALKER, DAVID. Godless heathen: China in the American bestseller. *In* (pp. 136–55) **12674**.

14297. WALL, CHERYL A. Worrying the line: Black women writers, lineage, and literary tradition. Chapel Hill; London: North Carolina UP, 2005. pp. xii, 309. (Gender and American culture.) Rev. by Suzanne W. Jones in TSWL (24:2) 2005, 341–3.

14298. WALLACE, DIANA. The woman's historical novel: British women writers, 1900–2000. Basingstoke; New York: Palgrave Macmillan, 2005. pp. xiii, 269. Rev. by David James in Mod/Mod (12:3) 2005, 531–3.

14299. WARNES, CHRISTOPHER. The hermeneutics of vagueness: magical realism in current literary critical discourse. *See* **15047**.

14300. WASSON, SARA. 'A network of inscrutable canyons': wartime London's sensory landscapes. *In* (pp. 77–95) **14254**.

14301. WEATHERBY, H. L.; CORE, GEORGE (eds). Place in American fiction: excursions and explorations. (Bibl. 2004, 14411.) Rev. by Robert Buffington in SewR (113:1) 2005, 123–6; by Bryan Moore in ArkR (36:3) 2005, 222–3.

14302. WEBER, JEAN JACQUES. Cognitive poetics and literary criticism: types of resolution in the Condition-of-England novel. *See* **9631**.

14303. WEINBAUM, BATYA. Early US sci fi: post-nationalist exploration for Jews in outer space? StudAJL (24) 2005, 180–201.

14304. WEINSTEIN, LEE. In search of *The Eye of Argon*. NYRSF (17:3) 2004, 1, 6–8.

14305. WEINSTEIN, PHILIP. Unknowing: the work of Modernist fiction. Ithaca, NY; London: Cornell UP, 2005. pp. x, 308.

14306. WELLS, LYNN. Allegories of telling: self-referential narrative in contemporary British fiction. Amsterdam; Atlanta, GA: Rodopi, 2003. pp. vii, 182. (Costerus, ns 146.) Rev. by Jean-Michel Ganteau in EtBr (25) 2003, 193–5.

14307. WHITE, ROBERTA. A studio of one's own: fictional women painters and the art of fiction. Madison, NJ: Fairleigh Dickinson UP, 2005. pp. 257.

14308. WHITEHEAD, ANNE. Trauma fiction. Edinburgh: Edinburgh UP, 2004. pp. vii, 184. Rev. by Laura Beadling in MFS (51:3) 2005, 710–13.

14309. WIEGAND, WAYNE. Collecting contested titles: the experience of five small public libraries in the rural Midwest, 1893–1956. *See* **480**.

14310. WILLIAMS, DAVID. Imagined nations: reflections on media in Canadian fiction. (Bibl. 2003, 14156.) Rev. by Kathryn Grafton in CanL (183) 2004, 178–9.

14311. WILLS, CLAIR. The aesthetics of Irish neutrality during the Second World War. *See* **18032**.

14312. WISKER, GINA. Demisting the mirror: contemporary British women's horror. *See* **17030**.

14313. WOLEDGE, ELIZABETH.   From slash to the mainstream: female writers and gender-blending men. Extrapolation (46:1) 2005, 50–65.

14314. WONG, MITALI P.; HASAN, ZIA.   The fiction of South Asians in North America and the Caribbean: a critical study of English-language works since 1950. Jefferson, NC; London: McFarland, 2004. pp. ix, 145.

14315. WOOD, JAMES.   The irresponsible self: on laughter and the novel. (Bibl. 2004, 14418.) Rev. by Andrew Harrison in StudN (37:4) 2005, 497–9.

14316. WYATT, JEAN.   Risking difference: identification, race, and community in contemporary fiction and feminism. (Bibl. 2004, 14419.) Rev. by Greg Forter in MFS (51:3) 2005, 717–20; by J. Brooks Bouson in TSWL (24:1) 2005, 173–7; by Aimee Pozorski in PsCS (10:3) 2005, 338–40.

14317. YAEGER, PATRICIA.   Ghosts and shattered bodies; or, What does it mean to still be haunted by Southern literature? SCR (22:1) 2005, 87–108.

14318. YEFFETH, GLENN (ed.).   The anthology at the end of the universe: leading science fiction authors on Douglas Adams' *The Hitchhiker's Guide to the Galaxy*. *See* **15081.**

14319. YOUNG, LAUREL.   Dorothy L. Sayers and the New Woman detective novel. *See* **19333.**

14320. YOUSAF, NAHEM; MONTEITH, SHARON.   Making an impression: new immigrant fiction in the contemporary South. FMLS (40:2) 2004, 214–24.

14321. ZACKODNIK, TERESA C.   The mulatta and the politics of race. Jackson; London: Mississippi UP, 2004. pp. xxxii, 235.

14322. ZANOTTI, PAOLO (ed.).   Contaminazioni: quaderni di Synapsis IV: atti della Scuola Europea di Studi Comparati, Bertinoro, 14–21 settembre 2003. Florence: Le Monnier, 2005. pp. 332. (Cartografie dell'immaginario: Saggi di letterature comparate.)

LITERATURE FOR CHILDREN

14323. ANON.   Cyclopedia of young adult authors. Pasadena, CA: Salem Press, 2005. pp. xiv, 756.

14324. ALSTON, ANN.   Your room or mine? Spatial politics in children's literature. NRCLL (11:1) 2005, 15–31.

14325. BENES, REBECCA C.   Native American picture books of change: the art of historic children's editions. Santa Fe: Museum of New Mexico Press, 2004. pp. xvi, 168. Rev. by David L. Russell in LU (29:1) 2005, 133–5; by Susan Gardner in CLAQ (30:3) 2005, 333–7; by Naomi R. Caldwell in AICRJ (29:4) 2005, 148–9.

14326. DE GOLDI, KATE.   Blaming Tolkien. NZBooks (15:1) 2005, 22–3.

14327. FOX, DANA L.; SHORT, KATHY G. (eds).   Stories matter: the complexity of cultural authenticity in children's literature. (Bibl. 2004, 14442.) Rev. by Paula T. Connolly in LU (29:1) 2005, 109–12; by Meena G. Khorana in CLAQ (30:2) 2005, 215–19.

14328. FOX, GEOFF.   News from the Front: the Great War (1914–1918) in literature for young readers. NRCLL (11:2) 2005, 175–88.

14329. GANGI, JANE M.   Inclusive aesthetics and social justice: the vanguard of small, multicultural presses. *See* **1038.**

14330. GORTON, DON. Literature of hope for GLBT youth. GLRW (12:6) 2005, 20–3.

14331. GUNN, JAMES. *Harry Potter* as schooldays novel. *In* (pp. 145–55) **19221.**

14332. HAGER, KELLY. Brontë for kids. CLAQ (30:3) 2005, 314–32.

14333. HALE, ELIZABETH; WINTERS, SARAH FIONA (eds). Marvellous codes: the fiction of Margaret Mahy. *See* **18044.**

14334. HINTZ, CARRIE; OSTRY, ELAINE (eds). Utopian and dystopian writing for children and young adults. (Bibl. 2004, 14448.) Rev. by C. W. Sullivan, III, in CLAQ (29:4) 2004, 384–6; by Anita Tarr in LU (29:1) 2005, 116–20.

14335. HOGAN, WALTER. Humor in young adult literature: a time to laugh. Lanham, MD; London: Scarecrow Press, 2005. pp. xvii, 223. (Scarecrow studies in young adult literature, 14.)

14336. HOLLANDS, HOWARD. Drawing a blank: picturing nothing on the page. PRes (9:2) 2004, 24–33.

14337. HUNT, PETER. Alternative worlds in fantasy fiction – revisited. NRCLL (11:2) 2005, 163–74.

14338. —— Joan Aiken, British children's fantasy fiction and the meaning of the mainstream. *See* **15097.**

14339. JAMES, CYNTHIA. From orature to literature in Jamaican and Trinidadian children's folk traditions. *See* **3678.**

14340. KERTZER, ADRIENNE. Circular journeys and glass bridges: the geography of postmemory. *In* (pp. 205–21) **12750.**

14341. LOFTS, W. O. G.; ADLEY, DEREK. *Scoops*: the first British science-fiction boys' paper. *See* **1259.**

14342. LUNDIN, ANNE. *Robinson Crusoe* and children's literature. *In* (pp. 198–206) **8537.**

14343. MCGILLIS, RODERICK. Luxuriant and prurient chaos: life's a fantasy on Primrose Lane. JFA (14:2) 2003, 255–64.

14344. MARCHANT, JENNIFER. 'An advocate, a defender, an intimate': Kristeva's imaginary father in fictional girl–animal relationships. CLAQ (30:1) 2005, 3–15.

14345. MARTIN, MICHAEL J. Experience and expectations: the dialogic narrative of adolescent Holocaust literature. CLAQ (29:4) 2004, 315–28.

14346. MOLIN, PAULETTE F. American Indian themes in young adult literature. Lanham, MD; London: Scarecrow Press, 2005. pp. xvii, 183. (Scarecrow studies in young adult literature, 17.) Rev. by John E. Smelcer in AICRJ (29:4) 2005, 124–5.

14347. O'KEEFE, DEBORAH. Readers in Wonderland: the liberating worlds of fantasy fiction from Dorothy to Harry Potter. (Bibl. 2004, 4206.) Rev. by Adrienne Kertzer in CanL (186) 2005, 146–8.

14348. PARIS, MICHAEL. Over the top: the Great War and juvenile literature in Britain. Westport, CT; London: Praeger, 2004. pp. xxii, 191.

14349. PATTEE, AMY S. Mass-market mortification: the developmental appropriateness of teen magazines and the embarrassing story standard. *See* **1298.**

14350. Pavonetti, Linda M. (ed.). Children's literature remembered: issues, trends, and favorite books. (Bibl. 2004, 14475.) Rev. by Kathy Piehl in CLAQ (29:4) 2004, 379–82; by Lee N. McLaird in SHARP (14:1/2) 2005, 17.

14351. Reynolds, Kimberley. Frightening fiction: beyond horror. NRCLL (11:2) 2005, 151–61.

14352. —— (ed.). Modern children's literature: an introduction. Basingstoke; New York: Palgrave Macmillan, 2005. pp. x, 278.

14353. Schall, Lucy. Teen genre connections: from booktalking to booklearning. Westport, CT: Libraries Unlimited, 2005. pp. xvii, 318.

14354. Smith, Katharine Capshaw. Children's literature of the Harlem renaissance. (Bibl. 2004, 14486.) Rev. by Nancy D. Tolson in LU (29:3) 2005, 453–7.

14355. Smith, Wendy. The abuses of enchantment: why some children's classics give parents the creeps. ASch (74:4) 2005, 126–31.

14356. Sorby, Angela. Schoolroom poets: childhood and the place of American poetry, 1865–1917. See **9659**.

14357. Tigges, Wim. A glorious thing: the Byronic hero as chief. In (pp. 153–72) **9237**.

14358. Watson, Victor. Has children's literature come of age? NRCLL (11:2) 2005, 117–28.

14359. Wyile, Andrea Schwenke. The value of singularity in first- and restricted third-person engaging narration. ChildLit (31) 2003, 116–41.

14360. Yampbell, Cat. Judging a book by its cover: publishing trends in young adult literature. See **1028**.

POETRY

14361. Aji, Hélène. The subject in the structure: issues of procedure in contemporary American poetry. See **19579**.

14362. Alim, H. Samy. On some serious next millennium rap ishhh: Pharoahe Monch, Hip Hop poetics, and the internal rhymes of Internal Affairs. JEL (31:1) 2003, 60–84.

14363. Altieri, Charles. The fate of the imaginary in twentieth-century American poetry. AmLH (17:1) 2005, 70–94.

14364. Baker, Robert. The extravagant: crossings of modern poetry and modern philosophy. Notre Dame, IN: Notre Dame UP, 2005. pp. 405.

14365. Ballerini, Luigi; Vangelisti, Paul (eds and trans). Nuova poesia americana. Milan: Mondadori, 2005. pp. xxi, 385. (Oscar poesia del Novecento, 68.)

14366. Becker, Jeff. Twenty-five Blue Canary years. See **17822**.

14367. Bohn, Willard. Marvelous encounters: Surrealist responses to film, art, poetry, and architecture. Lewisburg, PA: Bucknell UP, 2005. pp. 252.

14368. Borkowska, Ewa. At the threshold of mystery: poetic encounters with other(ness). See **9673**.

14369. Boruch, Marianne. In the blue pharmacy: essays on poetry and other transformations. San Antonio, TX: Trinity UP, 2005. pp. x, 218.

14370. Bosselaar, Laure-Anne (ed.). Thomas Lux: an interview. *See* **17916**.

14371. Braune, Bev. Who is the reader? And how many of us are there? Antipodes (19:2) 2005, 216–19.

14372. Brearton, Fran. For father read mother: Muldoon's antecedents. *In* (pp. 45–61) **18404**.

14373. Buntz, Veit. 'Hammered out of artillery shells': the discourse of trauma in Vietnam veterans' poetry. Amst (48:2) 2003, 227–48.

14374. Butling, Pauline; Rudy, Susan. Writing in our time: Canada's radical poetries in English (1957–2003). Waterloo, Ont.: Wilfrid Laurier UP, 2005. pp. xvii, 290. Rev. by Frank Davey in CanP (56) 2005, 120–32; by Meredith Quartermain in LRC (13:10) 2005, 17.

14375. Butscher, Edward. Mirrors: American poetry pure and impure. GaR (59:1) 2005, 167–80 (review-article).

14376. Camboni, Marina. 'Disarmonia perfetta': polilinguismo e transnazionalismo nella poesia sperimentale contemporanea. *In* (pp. 9–33) **14377**.

14377. —— Morresi, Renata (eds). Incontri transnazionali: modernità, poesia, sperimentazione, polilinguismo. Florence: Le Monnier, 2005. pp. 290.

14378. Campbell, Matthew (ed.). The Cambridge companion to contemporary Irish poetry. (Bibl. 2004, 14510.) Rev. by Mary O'Donoghue in JJLS (19:2) 2005, 17.

14379. Caplan, David. Questions of possibility: contemporary poetry and poetic form. Oxford; New York: OUP, 2005. pp. viii, 165.

14380. Clark, Kevin. Poetic modernism and the Oceanic divide. GaR (59:2) 2005, 403–9 (review-article).

14381. Clark, Steve; Ford, Mark (eds). Something we have that they don't: British and American poetic relations since 1925. (Bibl. 2004, 14513.) Rev. by Fiona Green in TLS, 7 Oct. 2005, 13.

14382. Clarke, Cheryl. 'After Mecca': women poets and the Black Arts Movement. New Brunswick, NJ: Rutgers UP, 2005. pp. xi, 206. Rev. by Gene Jarrett in AmQ (57:4) 2005, 1243–51.

14383. Cooley, Dennis. Documents in the postmodern long prairie poem. *In* (pp. 175–211) **12587**.

14384. Costello, Bonnie. Shifting ground: reinventing landscape in modern American poetry. (Bibl. 2004, 14516.) Rev. by William Hogan in JML (27:4) 2004, 129–32; by Chris Beyers in ColLit (32:2) 2005, 195–8; by Pat Righelato in MLR (100:4) 2005, 1106–7; by Mark A. Roberts in ISLE (12:1) 2005, 269–70.

14385. Coyle, Michael. Jazz songbooks and Modernist tradition. Genre (37:1) 2004, 65–83.

14386. Davidson, Ian. Visual poetry as performance. *See* **15814**.

14387. Davidson, Michael. Guys like us: citing masculinity in Cold War poetics. (Bibl. 2004, 14518.) Rev. by Fiona Paton in AmQ (57:1) 2005, 289–96; by Edward Brunner in TCL (51:1) 2005, 105–9.

14388. de Toledano, Ralph. Erato in the throes. Chronicles (29:6) 2005, 42–3.

14389. Dowson, Jane; Entwistle, Alice. A history of twentieth-century British women's poetry. Cambridge; New York: CUP, 2005. pp. xxi, 381.

14390. Elia, Adriano. Carmen figuratum – calligrams – concrete poetry: shaping the ad. *In* (pp. 144–57) **3690**.

14391. Evans, David. The flash and dazzle of sports poetry. Aethlon (22:2) 2005, 1–14.

14392. Finch, Annie. The body of poetry: essays on women, form, and the poetic self. Ann Arbor: Michigan UP, 2005. pp. xii, 177. (Poets on poetry.)

14393. Flajšar, Jiří. Issues of form in contemporary American poetry. *In* (pp. 51–6) **3734**.

14394. Fletcher, Angus. A new theory for American poetry: democracy, the environment, and the future of imagination. (Bibl. 2004, 14533.) Rev. by Heather Krebs in ISLE (12:1) 2005, 255–6.

14395. Frantzen, Allen J. Bloody good: chivalry, sacrifice, and the Great War. (Bibl. 2004, 14765.) Rev. by Andrzej Gasiorek in LitH (14:1) 2005, 97–9.

14396. Fredman, Stephen (ed.). A concise companion to twentieth-century American poetry. Oxford; Malden, MA: Blackwell, 2005. pp. 258. (Blackwell concise companions to literature and culture.)

14397. Gioia, Dana. Disappearing ink: poetry at the end of print culture. *See* **20921**.

14398. —— Disappearing ink: poetry at the end of print culture. *See* **20922**.

14399. Golding, Alan C. *The Dial, The Little Review*, and the dialogics of Modernism. *See* **1210**.

14400. Gordon, David J. Imagining the end of life in post-Enlightenment poetry: voices against the void. *See* **9685**.

14401. Gray, Jeffrey. Mastery's end: travel and postwar American poetry. Athens; London: Georgia UP, 2005. pp. xiv, 288.

14402. Gundy, Jeff. Taste and the open door. GaR (57:1) 2003, 159–75 (review-article).

14403. Gupta, Suman. In search of genius: T. S. Eliot as publisher. *See* **16272**.

14404. Gwiazda, Piotr. 'Nothing else left to read': poetry and audience in Adrienne Rich's *An Atlas of the Difficult World. See* **19066**.

14405. Halliday, Mark. The arrogance of poetry. GaR (57:2) 2003, 214–37.

14406. Hamilton, Craig A. Toward a cognitive rhetoric of Imagism. Style (38:4) 2004, 468–90.

14407. Hamilton, David. The common writer. SoHR (39:3) 2005, 226–33. (*Black Mountain Review.*)

14408. Hand, Elizabeth. The beckoning fair ones: some thoughts on muses. *See* **14156**.

14409. Hardy, Henry; Holmes, Jennifer. *Old Croaker*: a new T. S. Eliot poem – by Maurice Bowra. TLS, 16 Sept. 2005, 14–15.

14410. Harrell, D. Fox. Algebra of identity: skin of wind, skin of streams, skin of shadows, skin of vapor. CTHEORY, 12 Oct. 2005.

14411. HARRIS, TIMOTHY. Elsewhere. *See* **18217**.

14412. HARTMAN, ANNE. Confessional counterpublics in Frank O'Hara and Allen Ginsberg. *See* **18600**.

14413. HARTNETT, STEPHEN JOHN. Incarceration nation: investigative prison poems of hope and terror. Lanham, MD; Toronto; Oxford: AltaMira Press, 2003. pp. xiii, 181. (Crossroads in qualitative inquiry.)

14414. HAUGHTON, HUGH (sel.). Second World War poems. London; Boston, MA: Faber & Faber, 2004. pp. xli, 334. Rev. by Lynn Parker in IGSJ (11) 2005, 127–8.

14415. HECKER, WILLIAM. Finding Wilfred Owen's forwarding address: moving beyond the World War One paradigm. *See* **18708**.

14416. HEDEEN, PAUL M.; MYERS, D. G. (eds). Unrelenting readers: the new poet–critics. Ashland, OR: Story Line Press, 2004. pp. 355.

14417. HENNESSY, CHRISTOPHER. Outside the lines: talking with contemporary gay poets. Ann Arbor: Michigan UP, 2005. pp. viii, 216.

14418. —— Ten ways of looking at gay poetry. GLRW (12:5) 2005, 10–12.

14419. HENRY, BRIAN; ZAWACKI, ANDREW (eds). The Verse book of interviews: 27 poets on language, craft & culture. Amherst, MA: Verse Press, 2005. pp. 342.

14420. HILLRINGHOUSE, MARK. The New York School poets. LitR (48:4) 2005, 146–79.

14421. HODGES, HUGH. Walk good: West Indian oratorical traditions in Bob Marley's *Uprising*. JCL (40:2) 2005, 43–63.

14422. JANOWITZ, ANNE. The artifactual sublime: making London poetry. *In* (pp. 246–60) **9217**.

14423. JENKINS, LEE M. The language of Caribbean poetry: boundaries of expression. Gainesville: Florida UP, 2004. pp. x, 232.

14424. JOHNSON, DON. Playing through the dark: 'blindness' as a vehicle for transcendence in selected sports poems. Aethlon (23:1) 2005, 1–7.

14425. —— The sporting muse: a critical study of poetry about athletes and athletics. (Bibl. 2004, 14569.) Rev. by Jerry Teller in Aethlon (22:2) 2005, 180–1.

14426. KANE, DANIEL. All poets welcome: the Lower East Side poetry scene in the 1960s. (Bibl. 2004, 14577.) Rev. by Michael Robbins in ChiR (51:3) 2005, 169–72.

14427. KASDORF, JULIA. Same, same! Pleasures and purposes of metaphor. *See* **2364**.

14428. KELL, SUSAN; ROSIER, PAT (comps). Women's Studies Association (N.Z.) Conference 2003: collected papers and presentations. Wellington: Women's Studies Association (N.Z.), 2004. pp. 252.

14429. KENDALL, TIM; MCDONALD, PETER (eds). Paul Muldoon: critical essays. *See* **18404**.

14430. KINDSETH, TIM. The wide, wide world of chapbooks. AmBR (26:3) 2005, 1, 4.

14431. KINSELLA, JOHN.   Can there be a radical 'Western' pastoral ...? LitR (48:2) 2005, 120–33.

14432. KIRCHWEY, KARL.   'And the half-true rhyme is love': modern verse drama and the Classics. *See* **16946.**

14433. KIRSCH, ADAM.   Friendly chats. *See* **17509.**

14434. —— The wounded surgeon: confession and transformation in six American poets: Robert Lowell, Elizabeth Bishop, John Berryman, Randall Jarrell, Delmore Schwartz, and Sylvia Plath. New York; London: Norton, 2005. pp. xv, 299.

14435. KITCHEN, JUDITH.   Anthologizing – the good, the bad, and the indifferent. GaR (57:4) 2003, 849–69 (review-article).

14436. KNOTTENBELT, E. M.   Romantic residues? Virgil's *Aeneid* 'in such a tongue as the people understandeth' or in a 'language really spoken by men'. *In* (pp. 235–57) **9237.**

14437. KONG, YING.   Cinematic techniques in Modernist poetry. *See* **19669.**

14438. LOGAN, WILLIAM.   Prisoner, fancy-man, rowdy, lawyer, physician, priest: Whitman's brags. *See* **12330.**

14439. LONGENBACH, JAMES.   The dream of Modernism. *See* **16779.**

14440. LONGLEY, EDNA.   'Altering the past': Northern Irish poetry and modern canons. YES (35) 2005, 1–17.

14441. —— 'Modernism', poetry, and Ireland. *In* (pp. 160–79) **12946.**

14442. LOPEZ, TONY.   Graham and the 1940s. *In* (pp. 26–42) **16793.**

14443. LYON, PHILIPPA (ed.).   Twentieth-century war poetry. Basingstoke; New York: Palgrave Macmillan, 2005. pp. viii, 188. (Readers' guides to essential criticism.)

14444. McCABE, SUSAN.   Cinematic Modernism: Modernist poetry and film. Cambridge; New York: CUP, 2004. pp. x, 284.

14445. McCOMBE, JOHN P.   'Eternal jazz': jazz historiography and the persistence of the resurrection myth. Genre (37:1) 2004, 85–108.

14446. McGOWAN, PHILIP.   Anne Sexton and Middle Generation poetry: the geography of grief. *See* **19370.**

14447. McHALE, BRIAN.   The obligation toward the difficult whole: postmodernist long poems. (Bibl. 2004, 14595.) Rev. by Brian Reed in ConLit (46:2) 2005, 340–5; by Joseph Conte in AmBR (26:5) 2005, 10–11.

14448. MACKEY, NATHANIEL.   Paracritical hinge: essays, talks, notes, interviews. Madison; London: Wisconsin UP, 2005. pp. viii, 382. (Contemporary North American poetry.) Rev. by Richard Deming in TCL (51:2) 2005, 249–58.

14449. McLEAN, ANDREW M.   'Breathing in': Liddy, the Irish and American poet. *See* **17825.**

14450. MADER, D. H.   The Greek mirror: the Uranians and their use of Greece. *See* **9705.**

14451. MANHIRE, BILL (sel. and introd.).   121 New Zealand poems. Auckland: Godwit, 2005. pp. 256 (unnumbered).

14452. Marx, Edward.   The idea of a colony: cross-culturalism in modern poetry. (Bibl. 2004, 14599.) Rev. by Jeffrey Twitchell-Waas in VIJ (32) 2004, 234–8.

14453. Mellors, Anthony.   Late Modernist poetics: from Pound to Prynne. Manchester; New York: Manchester UP, 2005. pp. 230. (Angelaki humanities.)

14454. Middleton, Christopher.   A retrospective sketch. See **18221**.

14455. Middleton, Peter.   Distant reading: performance, readership, and consumption in contemporary poetry. See **20930**.

14456. —— How to read a reading of a written poem. OT (20:1) 2005, 7–34.

14457. Miller, Wayne.   Chapbooks: democratic ephemera. AmBR (26:3) 2005, 1, 6.

14458. Milovanovič, Čelica.   A Classicist reads some modern poetry. CML (25:1) 2005, 129–37.

14459. Morgan, Marcyliena.   Hip Hop women shredding the veil: race and class in popular feminist identity. SAQ (104:3) 2005, 425–44.

14460. Mortimer, Anthony (ed.).   From Wordsworth to Stevens: essays in honour of Robert Rehder. See **12503**.

14461. Nelson, Cary.   The economic challenges to anthologies. In (pp. 170–85) **3749**.

14462. —— Martial lyrics: the vexed history of the wartime poem card. AmLH (16:2) 2004, 263–89.

14463. Newcomb, John Timberman.   Would poetry disappear? American verse and the crisis of modernity. (Bibl. 2004, 14610.) Rev. by David Bergman in AL (77:1) 2005, 192–4.

14464. Newman, Michael.   Rap as literacy: a genre analysis of Hip Hop ciphers. TextB (25:3) 2005, 399–436.

14465. Nixon, Mark.   'A brief glow in the dark': Samuel Beckett's presence in modern Irish poetry. See **15408**.

14466. Notley, Alice.   Coming after: essays on poetry. Ann Arbor: Michigan UP, 2005. pp. vii, 182. (Poets on poetry.)

14467. Nyberg, Lennart.   'The imagination': a twentieth-century itinerary. In (pp. 40–54) **12946**.

14468. Oliver, Stephen.   The poet as fraud: a composite. See **18608**.

14469. Parisi, Joseph.   Poetry and the embarrassment of riches. CommRev (3:3) 2005, 15–21.

14470. Peng, Yu.   The therapeutic value of confessional poems. See **17879**.

14471. Perry, Imani.   Prophets of the Hood: politics and poetics in Hip Hop. Durham, NC; London: Duke UP, 2004. pp. x, 236. Rev. by James Bryant in JPC (38:6) 2005, 1099–1100.

14472. Petrescu, Ioana; Brewer, Naomi (eds).   Heart of the matter: an introduction to eighteen South Australian poets. Adelaide: Lythrum Press, 2004. pp. 240.

14473. Pfefferle, W. T. (comp.).   Poets on place: tales and interviews from the road. Foreword by David St John. Logan: Utah State UP, 2005. pp. xvii, 294.

14474. QUINN, JUSTIN. American errancy: empire, sublimity & modern poetry. Dublin: University College Dublin Press, 2005. pp. vi, 186.

14475. QUINN, WILLIAM A. Harriet Monroe as queen-critic of Chaucer and Langland (*viz.* Ezra Pound). *See* **4962**.

14476. RADER, DEAN; GOULD, JANICE (eds). Speak to me words: essays on contemporary American Indian poetry. (Bibl. 2003, 14404.) Rev. by Kimberly Roppolo in GPQ (24:3) 2004, 214–15; by Molly McGlennen in SAIL (17:1) 2005, 104–7.

14477. RAMAZANI, JAHAN; ELLMANN, RICHARD; O'CLAIR, ROBERT (eds). The Norton anthology of modern and contemporary poetry. (Bibl. 2004, 14625.) Rev. by Judith Kitchen in GaR (57:4) 2003, 849–69.

14478. REES-JONES, DERYN (ed.). Consorting with angels: essays on modern women poets. Newcastle upon Tyne: Bloodaxe, 2005. pp. 298.

14479. REVELLI, GIORGETTA (ed.). Da Ulisse a …: il viaggio nelle terre d'oltremare: atti del convegno internazionale (Imperia, 9–11 ottobre 2003). Pisa: ETS, 2004. pp. 594. (Memorie e atti di convegni, 25.)

14480. ROBERSON, JOANIE. Inventing a female New Zealand: constructs of place, culture and literature in New Zealand women's poetry. *In* (pp. 186–91) **14428**.

14481. ROBINSON, JEFFREY CANE. Wordsworth, day by day: reading his work into poetry now. *See* **12516**.

14482. ROBINSON, PETER. Twentieth-century poetry: selves and situations. Oxford; New York: OUP, 2005. pp. vi, 287. Rev. by Angela Leighton in TLS, 11 Nov. 2005, 22.

14483. RUEFLE, MARY. On sentimentality. WeBr (57) 2005, 44–59.

14484. SADOFF, IRA. On the margins. APR (34:6) 2005, 49–54. (Avant-garde US poetry.)

14485. —— Trafficking in the radiant: the spiritualization of American poetry. APR (34:4) 2005, 11–14.

14486. SÁNCHEZ-FLAVIAN, PATRICIA. Language and politicized spaces in US Latino prison poetry: 1970–1990. BR (27:2) 2003, 114–24.

14487. SCHULTZ, SUSAN M. A poetics of impasse in modern and contemporary American poetry. Tuscaloosa; London: Alabama UP, 2005. pp. viii, 247. (Modern and contemporary poetics.)

14488. SEEBER, HANS ULRICH. The retrospective attitude in poems by Edward Thomas and Andrew Motion. *See* **19777**.

14489. SHAPIRO, HARVEY (ed.). Poets of World War II. (Bibl. 2003, 14425.) Rev. by Ron Smith in GaR (57:4) 2003, 839–48.

14490. SMITH, RON. War and poets. GaR (57:4) 2003, 839–48 (review-article).

14491. SMITH, STAN. The disconsolate chimera: T. S. Eliot and the fixation of Modernism. *In* (pp. 180–203) **12946**.

14492. —— Irish poetry and the construction of modern identity: Ireland between fantasy and history. Dublin; Portland, OR: Irish Academic Press, 2005. pp. x, 238.

14493. SOLE, KELWYN. 'The deep thoughts the one in need falls into': quotidian experience and the perspectives of poetry in postliberation South Africa. *In* (pp. 182–205) **12789**.

14494. SOMERS-WILLETT, SUSAN B. A. Slam poetry and the cultural politics of performing identity. JMMLA (38:1) 2005, 51–73.

14495. SPIEGELMAN, WILLARD. How poets see the world: the art of description in contemporary poetry. Oxford; New York: OUP, 2005. pp. xi, 238. Rev. by Stephen Cushman in TCL (51:2) 2005, 244–8.

14496. STARNINO, CARMINE. A lover's quarrel: essays and reviews. Erin, Ont.: Porcupine's Quill, 2004. pp. 265. Rev. by W. J. Keith in CanP (56) 2005, 133–41.

14497. STOUT, JANIS P. Coming out of war: poetry, grieving, and the culture of the World Wars. Tuscaloosa; London: Alabama UP, 2005. pp. xxii, 270.

14498. SWEET, DAVID LeHARDY. Savage sight, constructed noise: poetic adaptations of painterly techniques in the French and American avant-gardes. (Bibl. 2004, 14643.) Rev. by David Huntsperger in MLQ (66:3) 2005, 406–10; by William Cloonan in SAtlR (70:3) 2005, 119–22.

14499. SYCHTERZ, JEFF. 'Silently watch(ing) the dead': the modern disillusioned war poet and the crisis of representation in Whitman's *Drum-Taps*. *See* **12348**.

14500. TAYLOR, HENRY. The publishing legacy of Leslie E. Phillabaum. *See* **1003**.

14501. TAYLOR, JOHN. Two cultures of the prose poem. *See* **9725**.

14502. THERNSTROM, MELANIE. A woman of verse. *See* **1343**.

14503. THORMÄHLEN, MARIANNE. Modernism and the Georgians. *In* (pp. 77–94) **12946**.

14504. TILLINGHAST, RICHARD. Poetry and what is real. Ann Arbor: Michigan UP, 2004. pp. ix, 186. (Poets on poetry.)

14505. TOBIN, DANIEL. The need for routes: genealogy and Irish American poetry. EtIr (28:2) 2003, 51–78.

14506. TURCO, LEWIS. Oswego poems and poets: Murabito and Davis. *See* **21261**.

14507. WALDMAN, ANNE; BIRMAN, LISA (eds). Civil disobediences: poetics and politics in action. (Bibl. 2004, 14651.) Rev. by Paul Martinez-Pompa in InR (27:1) 2005, 246–9.

14508. WALDROP, ROSMARIE. Dissonance (if you are interested). Tuscaloosa; London: Alabama UP, 2005. pp. xii, 313. (Modern and contemporary poetics.)

14509. WALKER, FELICIA R.; KUYKENDALL, VIECE. Manifestations of nommo in *Def Poetry*. JBlaS (36:2) 2005, 229–47.

14510. WARD, JOHN POWELL. Hardy's aesthetics and twentieth-century poetry. *In* (pp. 279–302) **11140**.

14511. WESTOVER, JEFFREY W. The colonial moment: discoveries and settlements in modern American poetry. (Bibl. 2004, 14652.) Rev. by Cristanne Miller in Mod/Mod (12:3) 2005, 542–3.

14512. WILENTZ, SEAN; MARCUS, GREIL. The rose & the briar: death, love, and liberty in the American ballad. *See* **3596**.

14513. WOOTTEN, WILLIAM. Pleasure and joy. *See* **19339**.

PROSE

14514. BEN-AARON, DIANA. Given and news: evaluation in newspaper stories about national anniversaries. *See* **2802.**

14515. BARTHOLOMEW, MICHAEL. In search of H. V. Morton. London: Methuen, 2004. pp. xxii, 248. Rev. by Kitty Hauser in LRB (27:6) 2005, 28–9.

14516. BESEMERES, MARY. Anglos abroad: memoirs of immersion in a foreign language. Biography (28:1) 2005, 27–42.

14517. BLAND, CAROLINE; CROSS, MÁIRE (eds). Gender and politics in the age of letter-writing, 1750–2000. *See* **8217.**

14518. BLEW, MARY CLEARMAN; DRUKER, PHIL (eds). Forged in fire: essays by Idaho writers. Moscow: Idaho UP, 2004. pp. 272. (Elemental Idaho.)

14519. BORM, JAN. Wilfred Thesiger au désert des déserts: écriture et réception de *Arabian Sands* (1959). EREA (3:1) 2005, 62–6.

14520. BOYNTON, ROBERT S. The new New Journalism: conversations with America's best nonfiction writers on their craft. New York: Vintage, 2005. pp. xxxiv, 456. Rev. by David Hayes in CrN (27) 2005, 130–2; by Julia M. Klein in ColJR (43:6) 2005, 59–60.

14521. BRAZZELLI, NICOLETTA. In and out of Africa: women's travel writing and autobiography in the thirties. *In* (pp. 89–98) **3690.**

14522. COCKIN, KATHARINE. Slinging the ink about: Ellen Terry and women's suffrage agitation. *In* (pp. 201–11) **8217.**

14523. CORNETT, SHERYL. 'Wilderness is preservation': an interview with Jan DeBlieu. NCLR (14) 2005, 83–95.

14524. COX, STEPHEN. The *Titanic* and the art of myth. *See* **13195.**

14525. DIEMERT, BRIAN. Uncontainable metaphor: George F. Kennan's 'X' article and Cold War discourse. *See* **2834.**

14526. FEATHERSTONE, KERRY. A problematic subject: Afghanistan in two contemporary travel accounts. EREA (3:1) 2005, 75–80.

14527. FLOYD, JANET. Simple, honest food: Elizabeth David and the construction of nation in cookery writing. *In* (pp. 127–43) **9257.**

14528. —— FORSTER, LAUREL. The recipe in its cultural contexts. *In* (pp. 1–11) **9257.**

14529. FORSTER, LAUREL. Liberating the recipe: a study of the relationship between food and feminism in the early 1970s. *In* (pp. 147–68) **9257.**

14530. GERMANO, WILLIAM. Final thoughts. *See* **1078.**

14531. HAMPTON, MARK. Rethinking the 'New Journalism', 1850s–1930s. *See* **1219.**

14532. HAUSER, KITTY. Bowling along. LRB (27:6) 2005, 28–9 (review-article). (H. V. Morton's travel writing.)

14533. HAY, JOHN. Mind the gap: the education of a nature writer. Reno: Nevada UP, 2004. pp. 121. (Environmental arts and humanities.)

14534. HAYWOOD, CHANTA M. Prophesying daughters: Black women preachers and the Word, 1823–1913. *See* **9759.**

14535. HOFFER, PETER CHARLES. Past imperfect: facts, fictions, and fraud in the writing of American history. New York: PublicAffairs, 2004. pp. xiv, 287. Rev. by Wallace B. Eberhard in JoH (30:4) 2005, 217–19.

14536. JOLLY, MARGARETTA. Corresponding in the sex and gender revolution: desire, education and feminist letters, 1970–2000. *In* (pp. 253–70) **8217.**

14537. KEATES, JONATHAN. Guides of old: *vade mecum* to where the ladies' orchestra used to be. *See* **9764.**

14538. MAHER, SUSAN NARAMORE. Deep mapping history: Wallace Stegner's *Wolf Willow* and William Least Heat-Moon's *PrairyErth: a Deep Map. See* **19577.**

14539. MEMSHAW, MICHAEL. Travel, travel writing, and the literature of travel. SCR (22:2) 2005, 2–10.

14540. MONTGOMERIE, DEBORAH. Love in time of war: letter writing in the Second World War. Auckland: Auckland UP, 2005. pp. 146. (AUP studies in cultural and social history, 1.)

14541. O'DONNELL, KEVIN E.; HOLLINGSWORTH, HELEN. Seekers of scenery: travel writing from southern Appalachia, 1840–1900. *See* **9776.**

14542. OLDFIELD, SYBIL (ed.). Afterwords: letters on the death of Virginia Woolf. New Brunswick, NJ: Rutgers UP, 2005. pp. xxxii, 221. Rev. by Gina Vitello in TLS, 27 May 2005, 26–7; by Stephen Barkway in VWB (20) 2005, 44–8.

14543. PELIZZON, V. PENELOPE; WEST, NANCY M. Multiple indemnity: *film noir*, James M. Cain, and adaptations of a tabloid case. *See* **13332.**

14544. PHELAN, JAMES. Living to tell about it: a rhetoric and ethics of character narration. *See* **14253.**

14545. POSNER, DAVID M. Rhetoric, redemption, and fraud: what we do when we end books. *See* **1088.**

14546. PRICE, JOHN. Not just any land: a personal and literary journey into the American grasslands. (Bibl. 2004, 14688.) Rev. by Elizabeth Schultz in AmS (46:1) 2005, 183–4.

14547. REED, JOSEPH W. The Pottles at Glen Cove: education of a country mouse. *See* **8411.**

14548. RETIEF, GLEN. Heartfelt horrors: Africa, racial difference and the quest for moral enlightenment in Conrad's *Heart of Darkness* and Rian Malan's *My Traitor's Heart. See* **15914.**

14549. SCHIAVINI, CINZIA. Writing the land: horizontality, verticality, and deep travel in William Least Heat-Moon's *PrairyErth*. RSA (15/16) 2004/05, 93–113.

14550. SCHOENFELDT, MICHAEL. First impressions and last thoughts: the importance of scholarly introductions. *See* **1091.**

14551. STIERSTORFER, KLAUS (ed.). Return to postmodernism: theory – travel writing – autobiography. Festschrift in honour of Ihab Hassan. *See* **15028.**

14552. TONELLO, FABRIZIO. Il giornalismo americano. Rome: Carocci, 2005. pp. 144. (Le bussole, 174.)

14553. TROUT, STEVEN (ed.). American prose writers of World War I: a documentary volume. Detroit, MI: Gale Research, 2005. pp. xxiv, 497. (Dictionary of literary biography, 316.)

14554. URE, JOHN. In search of nomads: an Anglo-American obsession from Hester Stanhope to Bruce Chatwin. (Bibl. 2004, 14698.) Rev. by Jeremy Swift in TLS, 17 Dec. 2004, 30.

14555. WARRIOR, ROBERT. The people and the word: reading Native nonfiction. *See* **9792**.

14556. WETHERELL, RODNEY. Sage of the suburbs. Meanjin (62:2) 2003, 129–36.

14557. WINSTON, GREG. Stephen's schoolbooks: a portrait of geography in a young nation. *See* **17355**.

14558. WOOD, JAMES HUNTER. Interventional narratology: form and function of the narrative medical write-up. *See* **10764**.

14559. XIAO, ZHONGHUA; MCENERY, ANTHONY. Two approaches to genre analysis: three genres in Modern American English. *See* **3034**.

BIOGRAPHY AND AUTOBIOGRAPHY

14560. AGUILERA LINDE, MAURICIO D. Hemingway and gender: biography revisited. *See* **16962**.

14561. ALABI, ADETAYO. Telling our stories: continuities and divergences in Black autobiographies. Basingstoke; New York: Palgrave Macmillan, 2005. pp. x, 185.

14562. ALTIERI, CHARLES. Autobiography and the limits of moral criticism. A/B (19:1/2) 2004, 156–75.

14563. ALTSCHULER, GLENN C.; RAUCHWAY, ERIC. Presidential biography and the great commoner complex. AmLH (16:2) 2004, 363–74 (review-article).

14564. AMIGONI, DAVID. Distinctively queer little morsels: imagining distinction, groups, and difference in the *DNB* and the *ODNB*. *See* **9798**.

14565. ARAPOGLOU, ELEFTHERIA. Identity configuration and ideological manipulation in Nicholas Gage's *A Place for Us*. MELUS (30:3) 2005, 71–93.

14566. BARRETT, MARVIN. Touched by Aldous Huxley. *See* **17145**.

14567. BENTON, MICHAEL. Literary biography: the Cinderella of literary studies. JAE (39:3) 2005, 44–57.

14568. BLOOM, LYNN Z. Women's confinement as women's liberation: World War II civilian internees in South Pacific camps. *In* (pp. 129–43) **14645**.

14569. BOARDMAN, KATHLEEN A.; WOODS, GIOIA (eds). Western subjects: autobiographical writing in the North American West. (Bibl. 2004, 14705.) Rev. by Kyle T. Bulthuis in PacNQ (96:4) 2005, 217–18; by Jennie A. Camp in RMER (59:2) 2005.

14570. BOMBERY, VICTORIA. Blood, rebellion, and motherhood in the political imagination of indigenous people. *In* (pp. 21–37) **12725**.

14571. BOOTH, ALISON. Fighting for lives in the *ODNB*; or, Taking prosopography personally. *See* **20966**.

14572. —— How to make it as a woman: collective biographical history from Victoria to the present. *See* **9803**.

14573. BOSTRIDGE, MARK (ed.). Lives for sale; biographers' tales. London; New York: Continuum, 2004. pp. xvi, 220.

14574. BRADY, VERONICA. After life with Judith Wright. *See* **20455**.

14575. BRISTOW, JOSEPH. Biographies: Oscar Wilde – the man, the life, the legend. *In* (pp. 6–35) **12414**.

14576. BROSMAN, CATHARINE SAVAGE. Autobiography and the complications of postmodernism and feminism. SewR (113:1) 2005, 96–107.

14577. BROWN, MURRAY L. T. C. Duncan Eaves, Ben D. Kimpel, and the life: a brief and apologetic memoir. *See* **8932**.

14578. BUNYAN, SCOTT. The space of the prison: the last bastion of morality? *In* (pp. 174–99) **12821**.

14579. BURKE, MARY. Negotiating the bi-vocal discourses of 'Catholic' and 'Protestant', 'Nationalist' and 'Loyalist': Irish traveller identity as 'third space'. *See* **18020**.

14580. COLE, KEVIN L.; WEINS, LEAH. Religion, idealism, and African American autobiography in the Northern Plains: Era Bell Thompson's *American Daughter*. GPQ (23:4) 2003, 219–29.

14581. CONNIFF, BRIAN. The prison writer as ideologue: George Jackson and the Attica rebellion. *In* (pp. 147–73) **12821**.

14582. COUSER, G. THOMAS. Vulnerable subjects: ethics and life writing. (Bibl. 2004, 14713.) Rev. by Terry Martin in Auto/Biography (13:2) 2005, 176–7.

14583. CROWE, CHRISTINE. Giving pain a place in the world: Aboriginal women's bodies in Australian stolen generations autobiographical narratives. *In* (pp. 189–204) **12750**.

14584. DAS, SANTANU. 'The impotence of sympathy': touch and trauma in the memoirs of First World War nurses. TexP (19:2) 2005, 239–62.

14585. DELGADO, ANA BEATRIZ. Paradigms of Canadian literary biography: who will write our history? PrSt (27:3) 2005, 330–43.

14586. DOLMAGE, JAY. Between the valley and the field: metaphor and disability. *See* **17984**.

14587. EAKIN, PAUL JOHN. Living autobiographically. Biography (28:1) 2005, 1–14.

14588. EGAN, SUSANNA; HELMS, GABRIELE. Generations of the Holocaust in Canadian auto/biography. *In* (pp. 31–51) **14629**.

14589. EPSTEIN, WILLIAM H. Remembering the past: Eaves and Kimpel's *Richardson* and the uses of literary biography. *See* **8936**.

14590. FIELDING, KENNETH J. Justice to Carlyle's memory: the later Carlyle. *In* (pp. 1–14) **10393**.

14591. FLYNN, CAROL HOULIHAN. The uses and abuses of biography: incendiary information. *See* **8937**.

14592. FREADMAN, RICHARD. Recognition and autobiography. PartA (3:1) 2005, 133–61.

14593. GALE, MAGGIE B.; GARDNER, VIV (eds). Auto/biography and identity: women, theatre, and performance. *See* **13027**.

14594. GERSHENOWITZ, DEBORAH A. Negotiating voices: biography and the curious triangle between subject, author and editor. OHR (32:2) 2005, 71–6.

14595. GOELLER, ALISON D. The politics of food in Italian American women's autobiography. PrSt (27:3) 2005, 235–47.

14596. GOLDMAN, LAWRENCE. No smoking dons: the *ODNB* and the new structures of knowledge. TLS, 4 Feb. 2005, 12–13 (review-article).

14597. GRACE, SHERRILL. Inventing Tom Thomson: from biographical fictions to fictional autobiographies and reproductions. *See* **14148**.

14598. GROSSMAN, MORRIS. Carroll's platonic love. *See* **10403**.

14599. GUDMUNDSDÓTTIR, GUNNTHÓRUNN. Borderlines: autobiography and fiction in postmodern life writing. Amsterdam; Atlanta, GA: Rodopi, 2003. pp. viii, 294. (Postmodern studies, 33.) Rev. by Ursula Fanning in MLR (100:1) 2005, 191–3.

14600. HERRERO, M. DOLORES. Snake dreaming: the life-giving and life-taking powers of the snake. ALS (22:1) 2005, 73–89.

14601. HOFFMAN, BETTINA. On the battlefield and home front: American women writing their lives on the Vietnam War. *In* (pp. 202–17) **14645**.

14602. HOLDEN, PHILIP. Other modernities: national autobiography and globalization. Biography (28:1) 2005, 89–103.

14603. JACKLIN, MICHAEL. Collaboration and closure: negotiating indigenous mourning protocols in Australian life writing. Antipodes (19:2) 2005, 184–91.

14604. JOLLY, MARGARETTA. Myths of unity: remembering the Second World War through letters and their editing. *In* (pp. 144–70) **14645**.

14605. KERTZER, ADRIENNE. Circular journeys and glass bridges: the geography of postmemory. *In* (pp. 205–21) **12750**.

14606. KINCAID, ANDREW. Memory and the city: urban renewal and literary memoirs in contemporary Dublin. ColLit (32:2) 2005, 16–42.

14607. KRUPAT, ARNOLD. Representing Cherokee dispossession. *See* **15852**.

14608. LANTERS, JOSÉ. 'We are a different people': life writing, representation, and the Travellers. NewHR (9:2) 2005, 25–41.

14609. LE FAYE, DEIRDRE. Memoirs and biographies. *In* (pp. 51–8) **10060**.

14610. LOEB, JEFFREY. The African American autobiography of the Vietnam War. *In* (pp. 218–35) **14645**.

14611. LOPEZ, TIFFANY ANA. Critical witnessing in Latino/a and African American prison narratives. *In* (pp. 62–77) **12821**.

14612. MCDONALD-RISSANEN, MARY. Veils and gaps: the private worlds of Amy Andrew and L. M. Montgomery, 1910–1914. *In* (pp. 154–69) **18288**.

14613. MCNEILL, LAURIE. Writing lives in death: Canadian death notices as auto/biography. *In* (pp. 187–205) **14629**.

14614. MARTÍN JUNQUERA, IMELDA. From *Black Elk Speaks* to *Lakota Woman*: reflections upon modern collaborative Native American autobiography. LittPr (15:30) 2005, 58–64.

14615. MATTHEWS, S. LEIGH. 'The precarious perch' of the 'decent woman': spatial (de)constructions of gender in women's prairie memoirs. *In* (pp. 141–74) **12587**.

14616. MEYERS, JEFFREY. Whitman's lives. *See* **12336**.

14617. MILLER, D. QUENTIN.   'On the outside looking in': White readers of nonwhite prison narratives. *In* (pp. 15–32) **12821.**

14618. MILLER, LYNN C.; TAYLOR, JACQUELINE; CARVER, M. HEATHER (eds). Voices made flesh: performing women's autobiography. (Bibl. 2004, 14736.) Rev. by Tanis MacDonald in CanL (186) 2005, 122–3.

14619. PARKE, CATHERINE N.   'Definitive', 'exhaustive', and 'rather old-fashioned': scholarly biography on the cusp of critical change. *See* **8951.**

14620. PARKER, DAVID.   Narratives of autonomy and narratives of relationality in auto/biography. A/B (19:1/2) 2004, 137–55.

14621. PERKINS, MAUREEN.   The role of colour and 'ethnic' autobiography: Fanon, Capécia and difference. Auto/Biography (13:1) 2005, 1–15.

14622. PHU, THY.   Decapitated forms: Theresa Hak Kyung Cha's visual text and the politics of visibility. Mosaic (38:1) 2005, 17–36.

14623. PIEDMONT-MARTON, ELISABETH.   Writing against the Vietnam War in two Gulf War memoirs: Anthony Swofford's *Jarhead* and Joel Turnipseed's *Baghdad Express. In* (pp. 257–72) **14645.**

14624. PITE, RALPH.   Hardy and biography. *In* (pp. 75–89) **11140.**

14625. POLETTI, ANNA.   Self-publishing in the global and local: situating life writing in zines. Biography (28:1) 2005, 183–92.

14626. POTTER, LOIS.   Having our Will: imagination in recent Shakespeare biographies. *See* **6056.**

14627. PRYS-WILLIAMS, BARBARA.   Twentieth-century autobiography. Cardiff: UP of Wales, 2004. pp. xi, 188. (Writing Wales in English.) (CREW series of critical and scholarly studies.) Rev. by Timothy Dow Adams in Biography (28:2) 2005, 314–16; by Brian Roberts in Auto/Biography (13:2) 2005, 177–9.

14628. RAK, JULIE.   The digital queer: weblogs and Internet identity. *See* **20979.**

14629. —— (ed.).   Auto/biography in Canada: critical directions. Waterloo, Ont.: Wilfrid Laurier UP, 2005. pp. viii, 264. (Life writing.) (Cultural studies.)

14630. RATEKIN, THOMAS.   Allon White tracks down himself: criticism as autobiography in *Too Close to the Bone. See* **14980.**

14631. RAVENSCROFT, ALISON.   Recasting indigenous lives along the lines of Western desire: editing, autobiography, and the colonizing project. A/B (19:1/2) 2004, 189–202.

14632. REDMAN, C. MARTIN.   Sons writing fathers in auto/biography. A/B (19:1/2) 2004, 129–36.

14633. ROSE, MARILYN.   The literary archive and the telling of Modernist lives: retrieving Anne Marriott. *In* (pp. 231–49) **12739.**

14634. SCHEFFLER, JUDITH.   Imprisoned mothers and sisters: dealing with loss through writing and solidarity. *In* (pp. 111–28) **12821.**

14635. SHAFFER, TERI.   Cambodian American autobiography: testimonial discourse. *In* (pp. 144–67) **9454.**

14636. SHARISTANIAN, JANET.   Subjectivity and creativity in feminist literary biography. Proteus (20:2) 2003, 22–8.

14637. SMITH, THOMAS R. Generating selves: issues of self-representation. A/B (19:1/2) 2004, 59–70.

14638. SPATES, JAMES L.; BURD, VAN AKIN. Ruskin in Milan: a chapter from *Dark Star*, Helen Gill Viljoen's unpublished biography of John Ruskin. *See* **11900**.

14639. SRIKANTH, RAJINI. Abraham Verheses doctors autobiography in his own country. *In* (pp. 125–43) **9454**.

14640. STEWART, VICTORIA. 'War memoirs of the dead': writing and remembrance in the First World War. LitH (14:2) 2005, 37–52.

14641. STIERSTORFER, KLAUS (ed.). Return to postmodernism: theory – travel writing – autobiography. Festschrift in honour of Ihab Hassan. *See* **15028**.

14642. THOMAS, KEITH. How it strikes a contemporary. TLS, 16 Dec. 2005, 6–7 (review-article). (Obituaries.)

14643. TOBIN, ROBERT. 'Tracing again the tiny snail track': Southern Protestant memoir since 1950. YES (35) 2005, 171–85.

14644. VERNON, ALEX. No genre's land: the problem of genre in war memoirs and military autobiographies. *In* (pp. 1–40) **14645**.

14645. —— (ed.). Arms and the self: war, the military, and autobiographical writing. Kent, OH; London: Kent State UP, 2005. pp. x, 305.

14646. VICE, SUE. Children writing the Holocaust. Basingstoke; New York: Palgrave Macmillan, 2004. pp. vi, 212.

14647. WALLY, JOHANNES. Selected twentieth-century Anglo-Irish autobiographies: theory and patterns of self-representation. (Bibl. 2004, 14756.) Rev. by Denis Sampson in CJIS (30:2) 2004, 85.

14648. WATKHAOLARM, PIMYUPA. Think in Thai, write in English: *Thainess* in Thai English literature. *See* **15085**.

14649. WHITLOCK, GILLIAN. Disciplining the child: recent British academic memoir. A/B (19:1/2) 2004, 46–58.

14650. ZANI, STEVEN. Clubfoot, caul and controversy: Byron biography and the foundation of genius. *See* **10342**.

14651. ZHOU, XIAOJING; NAJMI, SAMINA (eds). Form and transformation in Asian American literature. *See* **9454**.

RELATED STUDIES

14652. BINKIEWICZ, DONNA M. Federalizing the muse: United States arts policy and the National Endowment for the Arts, 1965–1980. Chapel Hill; London: North Carolina UP, 2004. pp. xii, 295. Rev. by Alice Goldfarb Marquis in JAH (92:2) 2005, 692.

14653. BRANTLINGER, PATRICK. Dark vanishings: discourse on the extinction of primitive races, 1800–1930. *See* **9837**.

14654. COUPE, LAURENCE. Kenneth Burke on myth: an introduction. London; New York: Routledge, 2005. pp. ix, 206. (Theorists of myth.)

14655. CROSS, GARY. The cute and the cool: wondrous innocence and modern American children's culture. *See* **20981**.

14656. DENVIR, GEARÓID. From Inis Fraoigh to Innisfree ... and back again? Sense of place in poetry in Irish since 1950. YES (35) 2005, 107–30.

14657. DINERSTEIN, JOEL. Swinging the machine: modernity, technology, and African American culture between the World Wars. Amherst: Massachusetts UP, 2003. pp. xiii, 415. Rev. by Betty Parker Duff in JPC (38:3) 2005, 579–81.

14658. FINN, MARGOT C. The character of credit: personal debt in English culture, 1740–1914. *See* **8279.**

14659. FREEMAN, SUZANNE. End of discussion: why I'm leaving my book group. ASch (74:1) 2005, 138–42.

14660. FYNSK, CHRISTOPHER. The claim of language: a case for the humanities. Minneapolis; London: Minnesota UP, 2004. pp. xvi, 106.

14661. GARDNER, VIV. Mapping performance culture: 2, Reading the street. *See* **9845.**

14662. GITELMAN, LISA; PINGREE, GEOFFREY B. (eds). New media 1740–1915. *See* **8280.**

14663. GLASS, DEREK. Goethe in English: a bibliography of the translations in the twentieth century. Ed. by Matthew Bell and Martin H. Jones. Leeds: Maney for the Modern Humanities Research Assn and the English Goethe Soc., 2005. pp. xix, 345. Rev. by John L. Flood in TLS, 7 Oct. 2005, 28; by Ian Cooper in BJECS (28:2) 2005, 294–5.

14664. HAMPTON, MARK. Visions of the press in Britain, 1850–1950. *See* **9847.**

14665. HIRSCH, JERROLD. Portrait of America: a cultural history of the Federal Writers' Project. Chapel Hill; London: North Carolina UP, 2003. pp. xii, 293. (Cf. bibl. 1985, 9413.) Rev. by Christine Bold in JAH (91:3) 2004, 1071–2; by Simon J. Bronner in WF (63:4) 2004, 347–9; by Charles C. Alexander in JSH (71:1) 2005, 198–200.

14666. HOBERMAN, RUTH. 'A thought in the huge bald forehead': depictions of women in the British Musuem Reading Room, 1857–1929. *In* (pp. 168–91) **12549.**

14667. KAEUPER, RICHARD W. William Marshal, Lancelot, and the issue of chivalric identity. *See* **4747.**

14668. KEARNEY, RICHARD. Strangers, gods, and monsters: interpreting otherness. London; New York: Routledge, 2003. pp. iii, 294. Rev. by Bradley A. Johnson in LitTheol (18:2) 2004, 229–31.

14669. MARTIN, JACQUELINE; SEFFRIN, GEORGIA; WISSLER, ROD. The festival is a theatrical event. *In* (pp. 91–110) **3974.**

14670. MOON, KRYSTYN R. Lee Tung Foo and the making of a Chinese American vaudevillian, 1900s–1920s. JAAS (8:1) 2005, 23–48.

14671. —— Yellowface: creating the Chinese in American popular music and performance, 1850s–1920s. *See* **9853.**

14672. Ó CONCHUBHAIR, BRIAN. The novel in Irish since 1950: from national narrative to counter-narrative. YES (35) 2005, 212–31.

14673. PORTER, BERNARD. Absent-minded imperialists: empire, society, and culture in Britain. *See* **9856.**

14674. SCHRUM, KELLY. Some wore bobby sox: the emergence of teenage girls' culture, 1920–1945. Basingstoke; New York: Palgrave Macmillan, 2004. pp. xii, 209. (Girls' history & culture.) Rev. by Susan J. Matt in JAH (92:1) 2005, 282–4.

14675. TARAS, DAVID; BAKARDJIEVA, MARIA; PANNEKOEK, FRITS (eds). How Canadians communicate. Calgary, Alta: Calgary UP, 2003. pp. 332. Rev. by David Hutchison in BJCS (17:2) 2004, 251–2.

14676. TATE, GREG (ed.). Everything but the burden: what White people are taking from Black culture. New York: Broadway, 2003. pp. viii, 260. Rev. by Marcia Alesan Dawkins in JPC (38:3) 2005, 577–9.

14677. THOMPSON, GRAHAM. The business of America: the cultural production of a post-war nation. London; Sterling, VA: Pluto Press, 2004. pp. ix, 189. Rev. by David W. Noble in AmQ (57:2) 2005, 555–60.

14678. WARHOL, ROBYN R. Having a good cry: effeminate feelings and pop-culture forms. Columbus: Ohio State UP, 2003. pp. xx, 148. (Theory and interpretation of narrative.) Rev. by Beverly Lyon Clark in Novel (37:3) 2004, 363–4.

14679. WILLIAMS, HYWEL. Francophone, anglophone and *gallois*-phone: the politics of cultural identity, 1763–2003. *See* **8291**.

14680. WOOD, JULIETTE. Folk narrative research in Wales at the beginning of the twentieth century: the influence of John Rhŷs (1840–1916). Folklore (116:3) 2005, 325–41.

14681. WOOD, RALPH C. Contending for the faith: the Church's engagement with culture. Waco, TX: Baylor Univ., 2003. pp. xii, 218. (Interpreting Christian texts and traditions.) Rev. by David V. Urban in ChrisL (54:1) 2004, 141–5.

14682. YOSEF, EITAN BAR-. The Holy Land in English culture 1799–1917: Palestine and the question of Orientalism. *See* **8292**.

LITERARY THEORY

14683. ANON. (comp.). Barbara Johnson: list of publications. Diacritics (34:1) 2004, 98–100.

14684. AHEARN, BARRY. Kenner, Eliot, and language. Mod/Mod (12:3) 2005, 487–91.

14685. ALLEN, VALERIE. Playing soldiers: tournament and toxophily in late medieval England. *In* (pp. 35–52) **4419**.

14686. ALTIERI, CHARLES. Autobiography and the limits of moral criticism. *See* **14562**.

14687. ANDERSON, AMANDA. Victorian Studies and the two modernities. VS (47:2) 2005, 195–203.

14688. APTER, EMILY. Saidian humanism. B2 (31:2) 2004, 35–53.

14689. ARMAND, LOUIS. Solicitations: essays on criticism and culture. Prague: Litteraria Pragensia Books, 2005. pp. 331.

14690. ARMSTRONG, ISOBEL. The first post: Victorian poetry and post-War criticism. JVC (8:2) 2003, 292–304.

14691. ATHERTON, CAROL. Defining literary criticism: scholarship, authority, and the possession of literary knowledge, 1880–2002. *See* **9862.**

14692. ATTRIDGE, DEREK. Deconstruction today. *See* **15819.**

14693. BADMINGTON, NEIL. From *Critical Practice* to cultural criticism: an interview with Catherine Belsey. TexP (19:1) 2005, 1–12.

14694. BAETENS, JAN. Novelization, a contaminated genre? Trans. by Pieter Verrmeulen. *See* **4008.**

14695. BAHRI, DEEPIKA. Feminism in/and postcolonialism. *In* (pp. 199–220) **14876.**

14696. BAY-CHENG, SARAH. Following the gaze: the influence (and problems) of feminist film theory in theater criticism. *In* (pp. 162–71) **13058.**

14697. BECKER-LECKRONE, MEGAN. Julia Kristeva and literary theory. Basingstoke; New York: Palgrave Macmillan, 2005. pp. xiv, 215. (Transitions.)

14698. BEHDAD, ALI. Edward Said: the founder of postcolonial discursivity. AmerJ (31:1) 2005, 10–16.

14699. BELLAMY, ELIZABETH JANE. Desires and disavowals: speculations on the aftermath of Stephen Greenblatt's *Psychoanalysis and Renaissance Culture.* CLIO (34:3) 2005, 297–315.

14700. BENCHIMOL, ALEX. Remaking the Romantic period: cultural materialism, Cultural Studies and the radical public sphere. TexP (19:1) 2005, 51–70.

14701. BENEDETTI, CARLA. The empty cage: inquiry into the mysterious disappearance of the author. Trans. by William J. Hartley. Ithaca, NY; London: Cornell UP, 2005. pp. xi, 232.

14702. BENNETT, LYN. Boundaries and frontiers: metaphor and the rhetoric of interdisciplinarity in literary studies. Genre (37:3/4) 2004, 505–29.

14703. BERNARD, ANNA. My mother the hero: Edward Said's *Out of Place: a Memoir* as feminist text. AmerJ (31:1) 2005, 16–19.

14704. BEWES, TIMOTHY. The novel as an absence: Lukács and the event of postmodern fiction. *See* **15248.**

14705. BEYERS, CHRIS. Critical studies in a post-theoretical age: three books sort of about Wallace Stevens. *See* **19646.**

14706. BHABHA, HOMI K.; MITCHELL, W. J. T. (eds). Edward Said: continuing the conversation. Chicago, IL; London: Chicago UP, 2005. pp. 171.

14707. BILGRAMI, AKEEL. Interpreting a distinction. CI (31:2) 2005, 389–98.

14708. BLOOM, HAROLD (ed.). Deconstruction and criticism. London; New York: Continuum, 2004. pp. x, 208.

14709. BLOOM, LYNN Z. Once more to the essay canon. *In* (pp. 90–111) **3749.**

14710. BLOTNER, JOSEPH. Robert Penn Warren, Cleanth Brooks, and the Southern literary tradition. *See* **19980.**

14711. BOER, ROLAND. Terry Eagleton and the vicissitudes of Christology. CulL (8) 2005.

14712. BOGUE, RONALD. Deleuze on cinema. *See* **13161.**

14713. —— Deleuze on literature. *See* **3711.**

14714. BORTOLUSSI, MARISA; DIXON, PETER. Psychonarratology: foundations for the empirical study of literary response. (Bibl. 2004, 14826.) Rev. by Nilli Diengott in Narrative (12:3) 2004, 306–16.

14715. BOVÉ, PAUL. Continuing the conversation. CI (31:2) 2005, 399–405 (review-article). (Said and US cultural imperialism.)

14716. BRANDIST, CRAIG; SHEPHERD, DAVID; TIHANOV, GALIN (eds). The Bakhtin circle: in the master's absence. Manchester; New York: Manchester UP, 2004. pp. 286.

14717. BRENNAN, TIMOTHY. From development to globalization: Postcolonial Studies and globalization theory. In (pp. 120–38) 14876.

14718. BRESLIN, PAUL. Derek Walcott's 'reversible world': centers, peripheries, and the scale of nature. See 19935.

14719. BROWN, STEPHEN. Attuned to the moon. See 18844.

14720. BROWNING, LOGAN D. A conversation with Sir Frank Kermode. SELit (45:2) 2005, 461–79.

14721. BRUNS, GERALD. The Newton of Modernism. Mod/Mod (12:3) 2005, 477–81.

14722. BUELL, LAWRENCE. The future of environmental criticism: environmental crisis and literary imagination. See 21005.

14723. —— Hawthorne and the problem of 'American' fiction: the example of The Scarlet Letter. In (pp. 70–87) 11186.

14724. —— Theorizing the national in a spirit of due reluctance. YREAL (19) 2003, 177–99.

14725. BUTLER, CHRISTOPHER. Dylan and the academics. In (pp. 51–70) 16207.

14726. BUTLER, JUDITH. Betrayal's felicity. Diacritics (34:1) 2004, 82–7. (Barbara Johnson.)

14727. —— Undoing gender. London; New York: Routledge, 2004. pp. viii, 273. Rev. by H. N. Lukes in GLQ (11:4) 2005, 632–4; by Atticus Schoch Zavaletta in Comparatist (29) 2005, 152–3.

14728. CARBY, HAZEL V. African American intellectuals symposium. JAAH (88:1) 2003, 78–81.

14729. CARRILLO ROWE, AIMEE. Be longing: toward a feminist politics of relation. See 19065.

14730. CARROLL, CLARE; KING, PATRICIA (eds). Ireland and postcolonial theory. (Bibl. 2004, 3871.) Rev. by Sylvie Mikowski in EtIr (29:1) 2004, 171–2.

14731. CARROLL, JOSEPH. Human nature and literary meaning: a theoretical model illustrated with a critique of Pride and Prejudice. In (pp. 76–106) 14807.

14732. CASTILLO, LARISA TOKMAKOFF. Between 'the cup and the lip': retroactive constructions of inheritance in Our Mutual Friend. In (pp. 43–63) 14737.

14733. CHAMBERS, ROSS. The queer and the creepy: Western fictions of artificial life. See 11964.

14734. CHANDLER, JAMES; GILMARTIN, KEVIN. Introduction: engaging the eidometropolis. *In* (pp. 1–41) **9217.**

14735. CHRISMAN, LAURA. Nationalism and Postcolonial Studies. *In* (pp. 183–98) **14876.**

14736. CLAVIEZ, THOMAS. Afterword: American Studies – the state of affairs and the affairs of State. YREAL (19) 2003, 325–41.

14737. COHEN, BARBARA; KUJUNDŽIĆ, DRAGAN (eds). Provocations to reading: J. Hillis Miller and the democracy to come. New York: Fordham UP, 2005. pp. xxi, 313.

14738. COHEN, TOM. 'J'; or, Hillis *le mal*. *In* (pp. 83–94) **14737.**

14739. CONNELL, LIAM. Global narratives: globalisation and literary studies. *See* **16384.**

14740. COOK, ANN JENNALIE. J. Leeds Barroll, III: a tribute. *See* **5883.**

14741. COOK, MALCOLM. The *Modern Language Review*: the first hundred years. *See* **1181.**

14742. COUTURIER, MAURICE. Objection, what subject? *See* **16319.**

14743. —— The subjects in and out of the text. CritW (46:3) 2005, 179–90.

14744. CREED, BARBARA. Pandora's box: essays in film theory. *See* **13196.**

14745. CSICSILA, JOSEPH. Canons by consensus: critical trends and American literature anthologies. Foreword by Tom Quirk. *See* **3739.**

14746. CUDDY-KEANE, MELBA. From fan-mail to readers' letters: locating John Farrelly. *See* **20336.**

14747. CULLER, JONATHAN. The genius of Barbara Johnson. Diacritics (34:1) 2004, 74–6.

14748. —— The Hertzian sublime. MLN (120:5) 2005, 969–85.

14749. DAULATZAI, SOHAIL. Blood of a slave, heart of a king: Edward Said as b-boy. AmerJ (31:1) 2005, 24–7.

14750. DELANY, SAMUEL R. Science fiction and 'literature'; or, The conscience of the king. *In* (pp. 95–117) **4027.**

14751. DENHAM, ROBERT D. Northrop Frye: religious visionary and architect of the spiritual world. Charlottesville; London: Virginia UP, 2004. pp. xiv, 373.

14752. —— Thou art that: Woolylamb Hormone, Northcote Fricassee, and chap named Denim. *See* **16894.**

14753. —— (ed.). Northrop Frye's notebooks and lectures on the Bible and other religious texts. Toronto; Buffalo, NY; London: Toronto UP, 2003. pp. lvii, 740. (Collected works of Northrop Frye, 13.) Rev. by John Ayre in LRC (12:5) 2004, 30–1; by Barbara Pell in CanL (184) 2005, 122–3.

14754. —— (sel.). Northrop Frye unbuttoned: wit and wisdom from the notebooks and diaries. Frankfurt, KY: Gnomon, 2004. pp. ix, 326.

14755. DENISOFF, DENNIS. Oscar Wilde, commodity, culture. *In* (pp. 119–42) **12414.**

14756. DEVEREUX, CECILY. The search for a livable past: Frye, Crawford, and the healing link. *In* (pp. 281–300) **9191.**

14757. DI LEO, JEFFREY R. (ed.). On anthologies: politics and pedagogy. *See* **3749.**

14758. DILLARD, R. H. W. Notes from after the deluge. SewR (113:2) 2005, 337–43 (review-article). (New Literary History and the decline of 'literary theory'.)

14759. DiNOVA, JOANNE R. Spiraling webs of relation: movements toward an indigenist criticism. *See* **12637.**

14760. DOKOU, CHRISTINA. Postmodernity is a beach: the diachronic ethics of Lord Byron. *See* **10303.**

14761. DOUGLAS-FAIRHURST, ROBERT. I. A. Richards's *Practical Criticism.* EC (54:4) 2004, 373–89. (New impressions, 8.)

14762. DOWNING, DAVID B. Theorizing the discipline and the disciplining of theory. *In* (pp. 342–70) **3749.**

14763. EAGLETON, TERRY. After theory. (Bibl. 2004, 14894.) Rev. by L. M. Findlay in DalR (85:1) 2005, 138–9.

14764. EASTHOPE, ANTONY; MCGOWAN, KATE (eds). A critical and cultural theory reader. (Bibl. 1993, 11104.) Toronto; Buffalo, NY; London: Toronto UP, 2004. pp. xii, 287. (Second ed.: first ed. 1992.)

14765. EDELMAN, LEE. Unknowing Barbara. Diacritics (34:1) 2004, 89–93. (Barbara Johnson.)

14766. ELIAS, CAMELIA. The fragment: towards a history and poetics of a performative genre. *See* **3762.**

14767. ELLIS, DAVID. Biographical uncertainty and Shakespeare. *See* **5922.**

14768. EMBRY, CHARLES R.; COOPER, BARRY (eds). Philosophy, literature, and politics: essays honoring Ellis Sandoz. Columbia; London: Missouri UP, 2005. pp. xiv, 354.

14769. EMRYS, A. B. Does formula matter? Why popular fiction is essential to narrative studies. *See* **14131.**

14770. ERKKILÄ, BETSY. Revolution in the renaissance. *See* **9246.**

14771. ERLL, ASTRID; NÜNNING, ANSGAR. Where literature and memory meet: towards a systematic approach to the concepts of memory used in literary studies. YREAL (21) 2005, 261–94.

14772. ERNE, LUKAS. Biography, mythography, and criticism: the life and works of Christopher Marlowe. *See* **5521.**

14773. ESONWANNE, UZOMA. Critique and extension: Said and Freud. RAL (36:3) 2005, 98–111.

14774. EVANS, DYLAN. From Lacan to Darwin. *In* (pp. 38–55) **14807.**

14775. EVANS, MARGARET CARPENTER. Rosemond Tuve: a life of the mind. (Bibl. 2004, 14905.) Rev. by Kathleen Swaim in GHJ (27:1/2) 2003/04, 123–6; by Amelia Zurcher in SpenR (36:1) 2005, 2–4.

14776. FENG, XIANGUANG. Major theories of ontology of 20th-century Western Marxist criticism. FLS (114) 2005, 100–9. (In Chinese.)

14777. FERGUSON, STUART. Walter Scott and the construction of historical knowledge: a Lukácsian perspective. *See* **11922.**

14778. FERNIE, EWAN. Introduction: Shakespeare, spirituality and contemporary criticism. *In* (pp. 1–27) **5928.**

14779. —— Shakespeare and the prospect of presentism. *See* **6320.**

14780. —— (ed.). Spiritual Shakespeares. *See* **5928.**

14781. FINKE, LAURIE. The hidden curriculum. *In* (pp. 395–404) **3749.**

14782. FISHKIN, SHELLEY FISHER. Crossroads of cultures: the transnational turn in American Studies – Presidential Address to the American Studies Association, November 12, 2004. AmQ (57:1) 2005, 17–57.

14783. FITZGERALD, LAUREN. Female gothic and the institutionalization of Gothic Studies. GothS (6:1) 2004, 8–18.

14784. FLINT, KATE. Re-visiting *A Literature of Their Own*. *See* **9546.**

14785. —— Why 'Victorian'? Response. *See* **21034.**

14786. FLORBY, GUNILLA. Postscript: so what about postmodernism? Fredric Jameson *vs* Linda Hutcheon. *In* (pp. 239–51) **12946.**

14787. FLUCK, WINFRIED. American culture and modernity: a twice-told tale. YREAL (19) 2003, 65–80.

14788. FORD, SARAH. Listening to the ghosts: the 'New Southern Studies': a response to Michael Kreyling. SCR (22:1) 2005, 19–25.

14789. FREEDMAN, ARIELA. On the Ganges side of Modernism: Raghubir Singh, Amitav Ghosh, and the postcolonial modern. *In* (pp. 114–29) **12640.**

14790. FREEMAN, MARGARET H. Poetry as power: the dynamics of cognitive poetics as a scientific and literary paradigm. *In* (pp. 31–57) **3888.**

14791. FROMM, HAROLD. Muses, spooks, neurons, and the rhetoric of 'freedom'. NLH (36:2) 2005, 147–59. (Consciousness and critical response.)

14792. —— The new Darwinism in the humanities: part II, Back to nature, again. HR (56:2) 2003, 315–27.

14793. FROULA, CHRISTINE. Hugh Kenner's Modernism and ours. Mod/Mod (12:3) 2005, 471–5.

14794. FUCHS, ELINOR. Theorizing *Salesman*. *In* (pp. 219–35) **18234.**

14795. GAILEY, AMANDA. How anthologists made Dickinson a tolerable American woman writer. *See* **10781.**

14796. GAIROLA, RAHUL. Queering Orientalism: sexual otherness and Asian American Studies. AmerJ (31:1) 2005, 27–31.

14797. GALLAGHER, CATHERINE. Theoretical answers to interdisciplinary questions or interdisciplinary answers to theoretical questions? *See* **21038.**

14798. GANGULY, KEYA. Temporality and postcolonial critique. *In* (pp. 162–79) **14876.**

14799. GARDNER-CORBETT, COLENA. Escaping the colonizer's whip: the binary discipline. *See* **17427.**

14800. GELLEY, ALEXANDER. On the line. *In* (pp. 117–27) **14737.**

14801. GIKANDI, SIMON. Poststructuralism and postcolonial discourse. *In* (pp. 97–119) **14876.**

14802. GIRI, B. P. Edward Said and Asian American / postcolonial diaspora studies. AmerJ (31:1) 2005, 31–4.

14803. GOLDSTEIN, PHILIP. Black feminism and the canon: Faulkner's *Absalom, Absalom!* and Morrison's *Beloved* as gothic romances. *See* **16412.**

14804. GOODLAD, LAUREN M. E. Towards a Victorianist's theory of androgynous experiment. *See* **16557.**

14805. GOPAL, PRIYAMVADA.   Reading subaltern history. *In* (pp. 139–61) **14876.**

14806. GORAK, JAN (ed.).   Northrop Frye on modern culture. Toronto; Buffalo, NY; London: Toronto UP, 2003. pp. xlix, 409. (Collected works of Northrop Frye, 11.) Rev. by Graham Good in CanL (183) 2004, 125–7; by John Ayre in LRC (12:5) 2004, 30–1.

14807. GOTTSCHALL, JONATHAN; WILSON, DAVID SLOAN (eds).   The literary animal: evolution and the nature of narrative. Forewords by E. O. Wilson and Frederick Crews. Evanston, IL: Northwestern UP, 2005. pp. xxvi, 304. (Rethinking theory.)

14808. GOURGOURIS, STATHIS.   Transformation, not transcendence. B2 (31:2) 2004, 55–79.

14809. GRABBE, HANS-JÜRGEN.   50 Jahre Deutsche Gesellschaft für Amerikastudien. Amst (48:2) 2003, 159–84.

14810. GRAFF, RICHARD; WALZER, ARTHUR E.; ATWILL, JANET M. (eds).   The viability of the rhetorical tradition. *See* **2324.**

14811. GREENBERG, GERALD S.   Poststructuralism and communication: an annotated bibliography. Lanham, MD; London: Scarecrow Press, 2005. pp. xii, 231.

14812. GUNN, JAMES.   The readers of hard science fiction. *In* (pp. 81–93) **4027.**

14813. —— CANDELARIA, MATTHEW (eds).   Speculations on speculation: theories of science fiction. *See* **4027.**

14814. GUPTA, SUMAN.   Sociological speculations on the professions of children's literature. *See* **4087.**

14815. HAFFENDEN, JOHN.   William Empson: among the mandarins. *See* **16345.**

14816. HÄGGLUND, MARTIN.   The necessity of discrimination: disjoining Derrida and Levinas. Diacritics (34:1) 2004, 40–71.

14817. HALMI, NICHOLAS.   Northrop Frye's *Fearful Symmetry*. *See* **8365.**

14818. —— (ed.).   Northrop Frye's *Fearful Symmetry: a Study of William Blake*. Toronto; Buffalo, NY; London: Toronto UP, 2004. pp. xlix, 516. (Collected works of Northrop Frye, 14.)

14819. HANDLEY, GEORGE B.   Oedipus in the Americas: *Lone Star* and the reinvention of American Studies. *See* **13640.**

14820. HARDING, JASON.   Seven types of torment. TLS, 1 July 2005, 4–6 (review-article).

14821. HAROOTUNIAN, HARRY.   Conjunctural traces: Said's 'inventory'. CI (31:2) 2005, 431–42.

14822. HARPHAM, GEOFFREY GALT.   Things and theory. *See* **9282.**

14823. HARRISON, NICHOLAS.   Postcolonial criticism: history, theory, and the work of fiction. (Bibl. 2004, 14967.) Rev. by Peter Hallward in TLS, 11 Feb. 2005, 33; by Richard Ruppel in SAtlR (70:3) 2005, 154–8.

14824. HARTMAN, GEOFFREY; O'HARA, DANIEL T. (eds).   The Geoffrey Hartman reader. New York: Fordham UP, 2004. pp. ix, 458.

14825. HAWES, CLEMENT.   The British eighteenth century and global critique. *See* **7997.**

14826. Hawkes, Terence.	Structuralism and semiotics. (Bibl. 1980, 2344.) London; New York: Routledge, 2003. pp. 208. (New accents.) (Second ed.: first ed. 1977.) Rev. by Karl Simms in LLit (14:2) 2005, 195–6.

14827. Hawkins, Joan.	When taste politics meet terror: the Critical Art Ensemble on trial. *See* **13036.**

14828. Haynes, Christine.	Reassessing 'genius' in studies of authorship: the state of the discipline. *See* **875.**

14829. Hedeen, Paul M.; Myers, D. G. (eds).	Unrelenting readers: the new poet–critics. *See* **14416.**

14830. Hegeman, Susan.	The 'culture' of American Studies. YREAL (19) 2003, 47–63.

14831. Hempfer, Klaus W.	Some problems concerning a theory of fiction(ality). Style (38:3) 2004, 302–24.

14832. Herbrechter, Stefan; Callus, Ivan (eds).	Discipline and practice: the (ir)resistibility of theory. (Bibl. 2004, 14975.) Rev. by Juuso Aarnio in EJES (9:2) 2005, 218–20.

14833. Herman, David (ed.).	Narrative theory and the cognitive sciences. (Bibl. 2004, 14977.) Rev. by Jean Jacques Weber in BELL (ns 2) 2004, 347–9.

14834. —— Jahn, Manfred; Ryan, Marie-Laure (eds).	Routledge encyclopedia of narrative theory. London; New York: Routledge, 2005. pp. xxix, 718.

14835. Herman, Luc; Vervaeck, Bart.	Handbook of narrative analysis. *See* **21054.**

14836. Herman, Peter C. (ed.).	Historicizing theory. (Bibl. 2004, 14978.) Rev. by Hugh Grady in CLIO (35:1) 2005, 144–52.

14837. Hite, Molly.	We think back through Carolyn Heilbrun if we are women. *See* **15967.**

14838. Hornung, Alfred.	Transnational American Studies: response to the Presidential Address. AmQ (57:1) 2005, 67–73.

14839. Huang, Yunxia; He, Changsheng.	'Baroque' buried in oblivion: a survey of baroque literature studies. FLS (114) 2005, 155–60. (In Chinese.)

14840. Huddart, David.	Post-colonial piracy: anxiety and interdisciplinarity. CritS (16:2) 2004, 7–27.

14841. Huggan, Graham.	(Not) reading *Orientalism*. RAL (36:3) 2005, 124–36.

14842. Hume, Robert D.	Construction and legitimation in literary history. *See* **21059.**

14843. Hunter, Latham.	'What's natural about it?': a baseball movie as introduction to key concepts in Cultural Studies. *See* **13686.**

14844. Irvine, Craig A.	The other side of silence: Levinas, medicine, and literature. LitMed (24:1) 2005, 8–18.

14845. Johansen, Jørgen Dines.	Theory and/*vs* interpretation in literary studies. *In* (pp. 241–66) **3888.**

14846. JOHNSON, BARBARA E.   Allegory and psychoanalysis. JAAH (88:1) 2003, 66–70.

14847. JOHNSON, MARK.   'Keep looking': Mary Oliver's Emersonian project. *See* **18607.**

14848. JONES, ANNE GOODWYN.   'The tools of the master': Southernists in theoryland. *In* (pp. 172–96) **12793.**

14849. JÖTTKANDT, SIGI.   Effectively equivalent: Walter Pater, 'Sebastian van Storck', and the ethics of metaphor. *See* **11781.**

14850. JOUGHIN, JOHN J.; MALPAS, SIMON (eds).   The New Aestheticism. Manchester; New York: Manchester UP, 2003. pp. vi, 242. Rev. by Joanny Moulin in EREA (1:2) 2003.

14851. JOY, EILEEN A.   James W. Earl's *Thinking about Beowulf*: ten years later. *See* **4301.**

14852. JOYCE, CHRIS.   Meeting in meaning: philosophy and theory in the work of F. R. Leavis. ModAge (47:3) 2005, 240–9.

14853. JUSTICE, GEORGE.   *Rasselas* in 'the rise of the novel'. *See* **8764.**

14854. KAHANE, CLAIRE.   The re-vision of rage: Flannery O'Connor and me. *See* **18564.**

14855. KAMUF, PEGGY.   'J' is for just a minute: it's Miller time when it shimmers. *In* (pp. 197–209) **14737.**

14856. KAPLAN, AMY.   A call for a truce. AmLH (17:1) 2005, 141–7. (Leo Marx's *The Machine in the Garden*.)

14857. KATES, JOSHUA.   Essential history: Jacques Derrida and the development of deconstruction. Evanston, IL: Northwestern UP, 2005. pp. xxix, 318. (Northwestern Univ. studies in phenomenology and existential philosophy.)

14858. KAYE, RICHARD A.   Gay Studies/queer theory and Oscar Wilde. *In* (pp. 189–223) **12414.**

14859. KENNER, ROB.   Word's worth. *See* **4117.**

14860. KERMODE, FRANK.   Pleasure and change: the aesthetics of canon. Ed. by Robert Alter. (Bibl. 2004, 15021.) Rev. by Adam Smyth in TLS, 27 May 2005, 26.

14861. KEUSS, JEFF.   George Steiner and the Minotaur at the heart of love: a review of *Real Presences*. LitTheol (18:3) 2004, 351–7 (review-article).

14862. KILCUP, KAREN L.   The poetry and prose of recovery work. *In* (pp. 112–38) **3749.**

14863. KIMBERLY, CAROLINE E.   Effeminacy, masculinity, and homosocial bonds: the (un)intentional queering of John Keats. *See* **11518.**

14864. KINDT, TOM; MÜLLER, HANS-HARALD (eds).   What is narratology? Questions and answers regarding the status of a theory. Berlin; New York: Mouton de Gruyter, 2003. pp. x, 368. (Narratologia, 1.) Rev. by David Gorman in Style (38:3) 2004, 392–6.

14865. KING, RICHARD H.   'Perception at the pitch of passion': Alfred Kazin in retrospect. AmLH (16:3) 2004, 558–65 (review-article).

14866. KINNEY, ARTHUR.   Harriett Hawkins's Renaissance. *In* (pp. 30–41) **5167.**

14867. KNIGHT, CHRISTOPHER J. Uncommon readers: Denis Donoghue, Frank Kermode, George Steiner and the tradition of the common reader. (Bibl. 2004, 15025.) Rev. by Brian Conniff in ChrisL (54:2) 2005, 301–5; by Graham Good in CanL (185) 2005, 161–3.

14868. KORANG, KWAKU LARBI. A man for all seasons and climes? Reading Edward Said from and for our African place. RAL (36:3) 2005, 23–52.

14869. KORITZ, AMY. Urban form *vs* human function in the 1920s: Lewis Mumford and John Dos Passos. *See* **16124**.

14870. KREYLING, MICHAEL. Toward 'a New Southern Studies'. SCR (22:1) 2005, 4–18.

14871. KRUGER, DANIEL J.; FISHER, MARYANNE; JOBLING, IAN. Proper hero dads and dark hero cads: alternate mating strategies exemplified in British Romantic literature. *In* (pp. 225–43) **14807**.

14872. LACAPRA, DOMINICK. History in transit: experience, identity, critical theory. Ithaca, NY; London: Cornell UP, 2004. pp. ix, 274. Rev. by Michael Bernard-Donals in CLIO (34:4) 2005, 505–11.

14873. LANSDOWN, RICHARD. 'What at bottom do men live for?': how Henry James widened the scope of F. R. Leavis's criticism. TLS, 29 Apr. 2005, 14.

14874. LAZARUS, NEIL. Introducing Postcolonial Studies. *In* (pp. 1–16) **14876**.

14875. —— Representations of the intellectual in *Representations of the Intellectual*. RAL (36:3) 2005, 112–23.

14876. —— (ed.). The Cambridge companion to postcolonial literary studies. Cambridge; New York: CUP, 2004. pp. xlv, 301. (Cambridge companions to literature.) Rev. by Sameer Rahim in TLS, 4 Mar. 2005, 26–7.

14877. LEMKE, SIEGLINDE. Theories of American culture in the name of the vernacular. YREAL (19) 2003, 155–74.

14878. LEONARD, PHILIP. Nationality between poststructuralism and postcolonial theory: a new cosmopolitanism. Basingstoke; New York: Palgrave Macmillan, 2005. pp. vi, 198.

14879. LI, GUICANG. Review of the national perspective on Chinese American identity. *See* **12783**.

14880. LI, KEHE; ZHANG, WEIJIA. A comparative study of the 'blankness' in Chinese and Western aesthetics. FLS (111) 2005, 100–6. (In Chinese.)

14881. LICONA, ADELA C. (B)orderlands' rhetorics and representations: the transformative potential of feminist third-space scholarship and zines. NWSAJ (17:2) 2005, 104–29.

14882. —— CARRILLO ROWE, AIMEE. After words: feminist praxis as a bridge between theory and practice. *See* **15179**.

14883. LINETT, MAREN. Introduction: Modernism's Jews / Jewish Modernisms. *See* **12784**.

14884. LING, JINQI. Before and after *Orientalism*. AmerJ (31:1) 2005, 42–7.

14885. LIPSITZ, GEORGE. Our America. AmLH (17:1) 2005, 135–40. (Leo Marx's *The Machine in the Garden*.)

14886. LIU, JIANJUN. The current nature of literary ethical criticism. FLS (111) 2005, 21–3. (In Chinese.)

14887. LIU, YU. A review of American eco-literature and ecocriticism. FLS (111) 2005, 154–9 (review-article). (In Chinese.)

14888. LJUNGBERG, CHRISTINA. Models of reading: diagrammatic aspects of literary texts. *In* (pp. 105–25) **3888.**

14889. LOMBARDY, ANTHONY. Allen Tate and the metaphysics of metaphor. *See* **19749.**

14890. LONG, MARK C. Ecocriticism *as* a practice of reading. Reader (53) 2005, 4–23.

14891. LOVE, GLEN A. Practical ecocriticism: literature, biology and the environment. (Bibl. 2004, 15050.) Rev. by Jonathan Levin in ISLE (12:1) 2005, 256–7.

14892. LURIE, PETER. Querying the Modernist canon: historical consciousness and the sexuality of suffering in Faulkner and Hart Crane. *See* **16426.**

14893. LYNCH, DEIDRE SHAUNA. Cult of Jane Austen. *In* (pp. 111–20) **10060.**

14894. MCCALLUM, PAMELA. Textual form and cultural affect: William Empson's double-plot and Raymond Williams's structure of feeling. FLS (111) 2005, 32–9.

14895. MACCANNELL, JULIET. 'J' for *jouissance*. *In* (pp. 3–13) **14737.**

14896. MCCORMACK, W. J. Yeats's politics since 1943: approaches and reproaches. *See* **20511.**

14897. MCINTURFF, KATE. 'The heritage of perception': nation and deracination in early Conrad criticism. *See* **15898.**

14898. MCKAY, ROBERT. 'Identifying with the animals': language, subjectivity, and the animal politics of Margaret Atwood's *Surfacing*. *In* (pp. 207–27) **14258.**

14899. MCKENZIE, TIM. 'I shall win at the odds' – George Steiner's wager on the meaning of meaning: a review of *Real Presences*. LitTheol (18:3) 2004, 357–62.

14900. MACKILLOP, IAN; STORER, RICHARD (eds). F. R. Leavis: essays and documents. London; New York: Continuum, 2005. pp. vi, 314.

14901. MACLACHLAN, IAN (ed.). Jacques Derrida: critical thought. Aldershot; Burlington, VT: Ashgate, 2004. pp. xii, 166.

14902. MCLEAN, PATRICIA. The Prior family drama: a Kristevan reading of *In My Father's Den*. *See* **16655.**

14903. MARCHANT, JENNIFER. 'An advocate, a defender, an intimate': Kristeva's imaginary father in fictional girl–animal relationships. *See* **14344.**

14904. MARKLEY, ROBERT. Harriett Hawkins and the criticism of the 1970s: interpretation, theory, and iconoclasm. *In* (pp. 42–54) **5167.**

14905. MARTIN, ROBERT K. Newton Arvin: literary critic and lewd person. AmLH (16:2) 2004, 290–317.

14906. MARX, LEO. On recovering the 'Ur' theory of American Studies. AmLH (17:1) 2005, 118–34.

14907. —— On recovering the 'Ur' theory of American Studies. YREAL (19) 2003, 3–17.

14908. MAY, VIVIAN M.; FERRI, BETH A. Fixated on ability: questioning ableist metaphors in feminist theories of resistance. PrSt (27:1/2) 2005, 120–40.

14909. MAZRUI, ALI A. The re-invention of Africa: Edward Said, V. Y. Mudimbe, and beyond. RAL (36:3) 2005, 68–82.

14910. MEDOVARSKI, ANDREA. Unstable post(-)colonialities: speculations through punctuation. WLWE (39:2) 2005, 84–100.

14911. MEISTER, JAN CHRISTOPH (ed.); KINDT, TOM; SCHERNUS, WILHELM (asst eds). Narratology beyond literary criticism: mediality, disciplinarity. *See* **21087**.

14912. MENCHER, M. B. Lawrence and sex. *See* **17618**.

14913. MEYER, KINERETH. William Carlos Williams, *Paterson*, and the cultural uses of pastoral. *See* **20215**.

14914. MIALL, DAVID S. Beyond interpretation: the cognitive significance of reading. *In* (pp. 129–56) **3888**.

14915. MICHIE, ALLEN; BUCKLEY, ERIC (eds). Style: essays on Renaissance and Restoration language and culture in memory of Harriett Hawkins. *See* **5167**.

14916. MILDER, ROBERT. 'A literature for the time'. *See* **9352**.

14917. MILLER, ELISE. The 'maw of Western culture': James Baldwin and the anxieties of influence. *See* **15274**.

14918. MIRRLEES, TANNER. Cognitive mapping; or, The resistant element in the work of Fredric Jameson: a response to Jason Berger. CulL (8) 2005.

14919. MISHRA, VIJAY; HODGE, BOB. What was postcolonialism? NLH (36:3) 2005, 375–402.

14920. MITCHELL, MAREA. *The Book of Margery Kempe*: scholarship, community, and criticism. *See* **4832**.

14921. MITCHELL, PAUL. Reading (and) the late poems of Sylvia Plath. *See* **18826**.

14922. MITCHELL, SALLY. Reading class. *See* **9353**.

14923. —— Victorian 'companions': forward to the past? *See* **21091**.

14924. MITCHELL, W. J. T. Secular divination: Edward Said's humanism. CI (31:2) 2005, 462–71.

14925. MOHANTY, CHANDRA TALPADE. Feminism without borders: decolonizing theory, practicing solidarity. Durham, NC; London: Duke UP, 2003. pp. viii, 300. Rev. by Sunera Thobani in Hypatia (20:3) 2005, 221–4.

14926. MORETTI, FRANCO. Graphs, maps, trees: abstract models for a literary history. London; New York: Verso, 2005. pp. 119.

14927. MORTIMER, MILDRED. Edward Said and Assia Djebar: a contrapuntal reading. RAL (36:3) 2005, 53–67.

14928. MORTON, STEPHEN. Gayatri Chakravorty Spivak. (Bibl. 2004, 15095.) Rev. by Lindsey Moore in TexP (18:1) 2004, 131–40; by Bronagh Clarke in BJCS (17:2) 2004, 257.

14929. MUFTI, AAMIR R. Critical secularism: a reintroduction for perilous times. B2 (31:2) 2004, 1–9.

14930. —— Global comparativism. CI (31:2) 2005, 472–89.

14931. MUHLESTEIN, DANIEL K. From Arnold to Eagleton to Oehlschlaeger: 'sweetness and light' in a postmodern world. *See* **9939**.

14932. NAAS, MICHAEL. Taking on the tradition: Jacques Derrida and the legacies of deconstruction. (Bibl. 2004, 15103.) Rev. by Deborah Elise White in CLIO (34:1/2) 2004, 235–43.

14933. NEMESVARI, RICHARD. Hardy and his readers. *In* (pp. 38–74) **11140**.

14934. NEWMAN, STEVE. Representation, violence, and the fate of culture: an interview with Geoffrey Hartman. JML (26:3/4) 2003, 103–22.

14935. NGAI, MAE M. Transnationalism and the transformation of the 'Other': response to the Presidential Address. AmQ (57:1) 2005, 59–65.

14936. NGUYEN-VO, THU-HUONG. *Orientalism*: entrances and exits. AmerJ (31:1) 2005, 51–4.

14937. NIE, ZHENZHAO. On literary ethical criticism. FLS (111) 2005, 8–11. (In Chinese.)

14938. NIU, GRETA AI-YU. Performing white triangles: Joan Riviere's *Womanliness as a Masquerade* and *Imitation of Life* (1959). *See* **13615**.

14939. NIXON, ROB. Environmentalism and postcolonialism. *In* (pp. 233–51) **12789**.

14940. NORMENT, NATHANIEL, JR. Addison Gayle Jr, 'the consummate black critic' 1932–1991. CLAJ (48:4) 2005, 353–86.

14941. NORRIS, MARGOT. The voice and the void: Hugh Kenner's Joyce. Mod/Mod (12:3) 2005, 483–6.

14942. NÜNNING, ANSGAR. Where historiographic metafiction and narratology meet: towards an applied cultural narratology. *See* **3874**.

14943. NYBERG, LENNART. 'The imagination': a twentieth-century itinerary. *In* (pp. 40–54) **12946**.

14944. ODOM, GLENN. Finding the Zumbah: an analysis of infelicity in *Speech Acts in Literature*. *In* (pp. 30–42) **14737**.

14945. O'GRADY, JEAN; NING, WANG (eds). Northrop Frye: Eastern and Western perspectives. (Bibl. 2003, 14959.) Rev. by Graham Good in CanL (183) 2004, 156–8.

14946. —— STAINES, DAVID (eds). Northrop Frye on Canada. Toronto; Buffalo, NY; London: Toronto UP, 2003. pp. xlviii, 741. (Collected works of Northrop Frye, 12.) Rev. by John Ayre in LRC (12:5) 2004, 30–1.

14947. OLSEN, STEIN HAUGOM. Progress in literary studies. NLH (36:3) 2005, 341–58.

14948. ORR, LEONARD. Modernism and the issue of periodization. CLCWeb (7:1) 2005.

14949. ORTOLANO, GUY. Human science or a human face? Social history and the 'two cultures' controversy. *See* **19503**.

14950. OSSIP, KATHLEEN. The nervousness of Yvor Winters. *See* **20255**.

14951. OWEN, SUE. *The Abuse of Literacy* and the feeling heart: the trials of Richard Hoggart. CamQ (34:2) 2005, 147–76.

14952. PARHAM, JOHN. Green man Hopkins: Gerard Manley Hopkins and Victorian ecological criticism. *See* **11311**.

14953. PARK, CLARA CLAIBORNE. Artist of empire: Kipling and *Kim*. *See* **17482**.

14954. PARKER, EMMA. Lost in translation: gender and the figure of the translator in contemporary queer fiction. *In* (pp. 118–25) **3724**.

14955. PARRY, BENITA. The institutionalization of Postcolonial Studies. *In* (pp. 66–80) **14876**.

14956. —— Postcolonial Studies: a materialist critique. (Bibl. 2004, 15117.) Rev. by Cristina Sandru in Eng (54:209) 2005, 162–9; by Priyamvada Gopal in TexP (19:2) 2005, 389–94.

14957. PATAI, DAPHNE; CORRAL, WILL (eds). Theory's empire: an anthology of dissent. New York: Columbia UP, 2005. pp. ix, 725.

14958. PATKE, RAJEEV S. Benjamin and Bakhtin: the possibility of conversation. JNT (33:1) 2003, 12–32.

14959. PAYNE, MICHAEL. What difference has theory made? From Freud to Adam Phillips. ColLit (32:2) 2005, 1–15.

14960. —— (ed.). The Greenblatt reader. Oxford; Malden, MA: Blackwell, 2005. pp. vii, 318.

14961. PEASE, DONALD. American literary studies and American cultural studies in the times of the national emergency: J's paradoxes. *In* (pp. 159–94) **14737**.

14962. PEASE, DONALD E. The place of theory in American Cultural Studies: the case of Gene Wise. YREAL (19) 2003, 19–35.

14963. PEQUIGNEY, JOSEPH. 'What the age might call sodomy' and homosexuality in certain studies of Shakespeare's plays. *See* **6697**.

14964. PERLOFF, MARJORIE. Hugh Kenner and the invention of Modernism. Mod/Mod (12:3) 2005, 465–9.

14965. PERRY, SEAMUS. The Romantic matter of fact. *See* **10512**.

14966. PETRILLI, SUSAN; PONZIO, AUGUSTO. Views in literary semiotics. *See* **3885**.

14967. PHELAN, JAMES; RABINOWITZ, PETER J. (eds). A companion to narrative theory. Oxford; Malden, MA: Blackwell, 2005. pp. xvi, 571. (Blackwell companions to literature and culture, 33.)

14968. PIER, JOHN (ed.). The dynamics of narrative form: studies in Anglo-American narratology. Berlin; New York: Mouton de Gruyter, 2004. pp. 272. (Narratologia, 4.)

14969. PILINOVSKY, HELEN. Borderlands: the who, what, when, where, and why of the interstitial arts. *See* **14256**.

14970. POLVINEN, MERJA (ed.). Cognition and literary interpretation in practice. Introd. by Harri Veivo. Afterword by Bo Pettersson. *See* **3888**.

14971. POOLE, ADRIAN. A. C. Bradley's *Shakespearean Tragedy*. *See* **6053**.

14972. PUGHE, THOMAS. Réinventer la nature: vers une éco-poétique. *See* **11314**.

14973. PULITANO, ELVIRA. Toward a Native American critical theory. (Bibl. 2004, 15135.) Rev. by Renate Eigenbrod in GPQ (24:4) 2004, 302–3; by Scott Andrews in AL (77:1) 2005, 204–5; by James H. Cox in AIQ (29:1/2) 2005, 316–21; by Deanna Reder in AIQ (29:1/2) 2005, 322–4; by Barbara K. Robins in AIQ

(29:1/2) 2005, 325–30; by Dean Rader in AIQ (29:1/2) 2005, 330–3; by Chris Teuton in AIQ (29:1/2) 2005, 334–7; by Jesse Peters in AIQ (29:1/2) 2005, 337–9.

14974. QIAO, GUOQIANG.   A peep into literary ethical criticism. FLS (111) 2005, 24–7. (In Chinese.)

14975. QUAYSON, ATO.   Incessant particularities: *Calibrations* as close reading. *See* **21105.**

14976. RABAN, JONATHAN.   Thinking about documentary: notes toward a lecture. *See* **15090.**

14977. RACEVSKIS, KARLIS.   Edward Said and Michel Foucault: affinities and dissonances. RAL (36:3) 2005, 83–97.

14978. RAJAN, RAJESWARI SUNDER.   Critical responses, recent. *In* (pp. 101–10) **10060.**

14979. RAMNARAYAN, AKHILA.   Veiled wor(l)ds: the postcolonial feminist and the question of where. *In* (pp. 159–70) **2457.**

14980. RATEKIN, THOMAS.   Allon White tracks down himself: criticism as autobiography in *Too Close to the Bone.* CEACrit (67:2) 2005, 62–75.

14981. REDFIELD, MARC.   War on terror. *In* (pp. 128–58) **14737.**

14982. REGARD, FRÉDÉRIC.   Autobiography as linguistic incompetence: notes on Derrida's readings of Joyce and Cixous. *See* **17332.**

14983. RIBEIRO, ALVARO, *et al.*   The Tinker legacy: the Yale 'school' of eighteenth-century studies. YLG (80:1/2) 2005, 23–43. (Round-table discussion.)

14984. RIQUELME, JOHN PAUL.   Introduction to *Reading Modernism, after Hugh Kenner (1923–2003).* Mod/Mod (12:3) 2005, 459–63.

14985. ⸻   Kenner, Beckett, 'irrational' 'man', and the obligation to express. Mod/Mod (12:3) 2005, 499–503.

14986. ROBERTS, ANDREW MICHAEL.   Conrad and the territory of ethics. *See* **15916.**

14987. ROBERTS, JESSICA FORBES.   A prayer for mourning: seduction and trauma in Carolivia Herron's *Thereafter Johnnie. See* **17012.**

14988. ROBILLARD, DOUGLAS, JR (ed.).   The critical response to Flannery O'Connor. *See* **18577.**

14989. RODDEN, JOHN (ed.).   Irving Howe and the critics: celebrations and attacks. Lincoln; London: Nebraska UP, 2005. pp. xxii, 237.

14990. ⸻   The worlds of Irving Howe: the critical legacy. Boulder, CO: Paradigm, 2005. pp. xxv, 353.

14991. RODEN, FREDERICK S. (ed.).   Palgrave advances in Oscar Wilde studies. *See* **12414.**

14992. ROHR, SUSANNE.   Pragmaticism – a new approach to literary and cultural analysis. YREAL (19) 2003, 293–305.

14993. ROORDA, RANDALL.   Wonderful world: comic frames, dissolution of scene, the temper of ecocriticism. *See* **15552.**

14994. ROVIRA, JAMES.   Gathering the scattered body of Milton's *Areopagitica. See* **7747.**

14995. ROWLINSON, MATTHEW.   Theory of Victorian Studies: anachronism and self-reflexivity. *See* **21115.**

14996. RUDRUM, DAVID. From narrative representation to narrative use: towards the limits of definition. Narrative (13:2) 2005, 195–204.

14997. —— Living alone: solipsism in *Heart of Darkness. See* **15918.**

14998. RUSH, FRED (ed.). The Cambridge companion to critical theory. Cambridge; New York: CUP, 2004. pp. xx, 376.

14999. RUSSO, JOHN PAUL. The future without a past: the humanities in a technological society. *See* **16045.**

15000. SAID, EDWARD. Humanism and democratic criticism. New York: Columbia UP, 2004. pp. xvii, 154. Rev. by Paul Bové in CI (31:2) 2005, 399–405.

15001. SALIH, SARA; BUTLER, JUDITH (eds). The Judith Butler reader. Oxford; Malden, MA: Blackwell, 2004. pp. viii, 374. Rev. by Carla Freccero in GLQ (11:2) 2005, 311–13.

15002. SALMON, CATHERINE. Crossing the abyss: erotica and the intersection of evolutionary psychology and literary studies. *In* (pp. 244–57) **14807.**

15003. SCANLAN, ROBERT. The late plays of Arthur Miller. *In* (pp. 180–90) **18234.**

15004. SCHANOES, VERONICA. Critical theory, academia, and interstitiality. *See* **14271.**

15005. SCHEINER, CORINNE. *Teleiopoiesis, telepoesis,* and the practice of comparative literature. *See* **21120.**

15006. SCHLAEGER, JÜRGEN. *Ars memoriae,* collective memory and neurobiology. YREAL (21) 2005, 295–304.

15007. SCHLOBIN, ROGER C. Character, the fantastic, and the failure of contemporary literary theory. JFA (13:3) 2003, 258–70.

15008. SCHONHORN, MANUEL. Weber, Watt, and restraint: *Robinson Crusoe* and the critical tradition. *In* (pp. 55–60) **8537.**

15009. SEAMON, ROGER. Why Poe? Why not Peirce? *See* **3920.**

15010. SELL, ROGER D. Literature, cultural memory, scholarship. YREAL (21) 2005, 349–64.

15011. SHALSON, LARA. Creating community, constructing criticism: the Women's One World festival 1980–1981. *See* **13105.**

15012. SHEN, DAN. Broadening the horizon: on J. Hillis Miller's ananarratology. *In* (pp. 14–29) **14737.**

15013. —— Narratology in China and in the West. FLS (114) 2005, 110–13. (In Chinese.)

15014. SHRIMPTON, NICHOLAS. Bradley and the Aesthetes. *See* **9413.**

15015. SHU, YUAN. Globalization and 'Asian values': teaching and theorizing Asian American literature. *See* **12921.**

15016. SIEMENS, R. G. 'What two crownes shall they be?': 'lower' criticism, 'higher' criticism, and the impact of the electronic scholarly edition. *In* (pp. 37–46) **587.**

15017. SIMPSON, M. CARLETON. Participation and immersion in Walton and Calvino. *See* **9039.**

15018. SINGH, G. Q. D. Leavis and the novel. *See* **9617.**

15019. SMITH, ANDREW. Migrancy, hybridity, and postcolonial literary studies. *In* (pp. 241–61) **14876.**

15020. SMITH, PHILIP. Philosophical approaches to interpretation of Oscar Wilde. *In* (pp. 143–66) **12414**.

15021. SNEDEKER, GEORGE. The politics of critical theory: language/discourse/ society. Lanham, MD; London: UP of America, 2004. pp. xxi, 104. Rev. by Martha Gimenez in CulL (8) 2005.

15022. SNEDIKER, MICHAEL. Hart Crane's smile. *See* **15959**.

15023. SPILLERS, HORTENSE J. A tale of three Zoras: Barbara Johnson and Black women writers. Diacritics (34:1) 2004, 94–7 (review-article).

15024. SPIVAK, GAYATRI CHAKRAVORTY. Death of a discipline. (Bibl. 2004, 15206.) Rev. by John Mowitt in CLIO (34:1/2) 2004, 121–9; by Emily Apter in CL (57:3) 2005, 201–6; by Christopher Bush in CL (57:3) 2005, 207–13; by Jane Gallop in CL (57:3) 2005, 214–18; by Eric Hayot in CL (57:3) 2005, 219–26; by Haun Saussy in CL (57:3) 2005, 234–8; by Corinne Scheiner in CL (57:3) 2005, 239–45; by Steven G. Yao in CL (57:3) 2005, 246–55.

15025. STANITZEK, GEORG. Texts and paratexts in media. CI (32:1) 2005, 27–42.

15026. STEELE, JEFFREY. Crises of relationship: developing relational models for the study of the American renaissance. *See* **9420**.

15027. STETZ, MARGARET DIANE. Oscar Wilde and feminist criticism. *In* (pp. 224–45) **12414**.

15028. STIERSTORFER, KLAUS (ed.). Return to postmodernism: theory – travel writing – autobiography. Festschrift in honour of Ihab Hassan. Heidelberg: Winter, 2005. pp. 414. (Anglistische Forschungen, 354.)

15029. SULLIVAN, NIKKI. A critical introduction to queer theory. Edinburgh: Edinburgh UP, 2003. pp. vii, 232. Rev. by Margaret Morrison in GLQ (11:2) 2005, 316–18.

15030. SUSSMAN, HENRY. The afterlife of Judaism: the Zohar, Benjamin, Miller. *In* (pp. 95–116) **14737**.

15031. —— The task of the critic: poetics, philosophy, and religion. New York: Fordham UP, 2005. pp. xi, 292. Rev. by Beryl Schlossman in MLN (120:5) 2005, 1249–51.

15032. SUTHERLAND, JOHN. Some nabob: the sometimes useful errors of Edward Said. TLS, 18 Mar. 2005, 12.

15033. TEW, PHILIP. Across the prairies, and beyond the postmodern: A. L. Kennedy, Linda Hutcheon, and realizing the contemporary. *See* **17389**.

15034. TOBIN, ROBERT D. The emancipation of the flesh: the legacy of Romanticism in the homosexual rights movement. *See* **8078**.

15035. TOTTEN, GARY. Zitkala-Ša and the problem of regionalism: nations, narratives, and critical traditions. *See* **20536**.

15036. TRIFONAS, PETER PERICLES; PETERS, MICHAEL A. (eds). Deconstructing Derrida: tasks for the new humanities. Basingstoke; New York: Palgrave Macmillan, 2005. pp. vi, 224.

15037. TROTT, NICOLA. Critical responses, 1830–1970. *In* (pp. 92–100) **10060**.

15038. TROTTER, DAVID. The New Historicism and the psychopathology of everyday modern life. *In* (pp. 30–48) **9220.**

15039. UTELL, JANINE. Virtue in scraps, *mysterium* in fragments: Robert Graves, Hugh Kenner, and Ezra Pound. *See* **16805.**

15040. VEIVO, HARRI; KNUUTTILA, TARJA. Modelling, theorising and interpretation in cognitive literary studies. *In* (pp. 283–305) **3888.**

15041. VINE, STEVE (ed.). Literature in psychoanalysis: a reader. Basingstoke; New York: Palgrave Macmillan, 2005. pp. x, 232.

15042. WAESE, REBECCA. 'Mystory' in Allison Muri's *the hystery of the broken fether*. *See* **21262.**

15043. WALKER, ALISON TARA. Destabilizing order, challenging history: Octavia Butler, Deleuze and Guattari, and affective beginnings. *See* **15639.**

15044. WANG, GUIQIN. A statistical analysis of the research papers on Hardy from 1980 to 2004 in Chinese journals. *See* **11166.**

15045. WANG, LABAO. From structure to exchange: on Ian Reid's postcolonial theory of narrative exchanges. FLS (111) 2005, 107–13. (In Chinese.)

15046. WANG, NING. Environmental ethics of literature: the significance of ecocriticism. FLS (111) 2005, 18–20. (In Chinese.)

15047. WARNES, CHRISTOPHER. The hermeneutics of vagueness: magical realism in current literary critical discourse. JPW (41:1) 2005, 1–13.

15048. WEBER, JEAN JACQUES. A new paradigm for literary studies; or, The teething troubles of cognitive poetics. *See* **21141.**

15049. WICKE, JENNIFER. Hugh Kenner's pound of flesh. Mod/Mod (12:3) 2005, 493–7.

15050. WILLIAMS, DANIEL. 'Insularly English'? Raymond Williams, nation and race. JSBC (12:1) 2005, 55–66.

15051. WILLIAMS, JEFFREY J. Anthology disdain. *In* (pp. 207–21) **3749.**

15052. WILLIAMS, JENNIFER H. Hillis's charity. *In* (pp. 64–79) **14737.**

15053. WINCHELL, MARK ROYDEN. Leslie Fiedler, ahead of the herd. SoR (41:2) 2005, 403–16.

15054. WINTER, SARAH. Cultural politics and the sociology of the university. *See* **21144.**

15055. WOLFE, CARY. Animal rites: American culture, the discourse of species, and posthumanist theory. Foreword by W. J. T. Mitchell. *See* **3962.**

15056. WOLFE, GARY K. Coming to terms. *In* (pp. 13–22) **4027.**

15057. WOLFREYS, JULIAN. Occasional deconstructions. Albany: New York State UP, 2004. pp. viii, 373.

15058. —— 'A self-referential density': *Glyph* and the 'theory' thing. *See* **21198.**

15059. —— (ed.); THOMAS, HARUN KARIM (asst ed.). Glossalalia: an alphabet of critical keywords. *See* **1979.**

15060. WOOD, JAMES HUNTER. Interventional narratology: form and function of the narrative medical write-up. *See* **10764.**

15061. WRIGHT, TERRY. Religion and literature from the modern to the postmodern: Scott, Steiner and Detweiler. LitTheol (19:1) 2005, 3–21.

15062. YOUNG, R. V. Harold Bloom: the critic as gnostic. ModAge (47:1) 2005, 19–29.

15063. ZELEZA, PAUL TIYAMBE. The politics and poetics of exile: Edward Said in Africa. RAL (36:3) 2005, 1–22.

15064. ZIOLKOWSKI, JAN M. Metaphilology. JEGP (104:2) 2005, 239–72 (review-article).

15065. ZOU, JIANJUN. The independent and compatible character of ethical literary criticism. FLS (116) 2005, 7–13. (In Chinese.)

15066. —— Three dimensional index: literary ethical criticism. FLS (111) 2005, 28–31. (In Chinese.)

AUTHORS

Edward Abbey

15067. ROMESBURG, ROD. Deterministic chaos in Ed Abbey's *Desert Solitaire.* WAL (39:2) 2004, 200–19.

Reza Abdoh

15068. CHAMBERS, JONATHAN. 'To question and reconstruct': Reza Abdoh's *The Hip-Hop Waltz of Eurydice.* TheatreA (56) 2003, 54–66.

Walter Abish

15069. ORBÁN, KATALIN. Ethical diversions: the post-Holocaust narratives of Pynchon, Abish, DeLillo, and Spiegelman. *See* **18991.**

Chinua Achebe

15070. GARCÍA RAMÍREZ, PAULA. Aetiological values in Achebe's stories for children. RAEI (16) 2003, 93–109.

15071. PULITANO, ELVIRA. 'In vain I tried to tell you': crossreading strategies in global literatures. WLWE (39:2) 2002/03, 52–70.

15072. PURCELL, WILLIAM F. The missionary as ambivalent metaphor in Chinua Achebe's *Sugar Baby.* NCL (35:5) 2005, 4–6.

15073. SALLAH, TIJAN M.; OKONJO-IWEALA, NGOZI. Chinua Achebe, teacher of light: a biography. (Bibl. 2004, 15342.) Rev. by Abdoulaye S. Saine in AfSR (48:2) 2005, 173–4.

15074. WILKINS, KAROL M. Providing higher education through Achebe and Hurston's cultural roots. *See* **17143.**

Kathy Acker

15075. HARDIN, MICHAEL (ed.). Devouring institutions. San Diego, CA: San Diego State UP, 2004. pp. xvi, 271. (Hyperbole.) Rev. by Ryan Smith in AmBR (26:5) 2005, 27.

Peter Ackroyd

15076. CARTIER, SOPHIE. Peter Ackroyd's representation of the past: London as a site of memory. EtBr (29) 2005, 123–32.

15077. —— La représentation de Londres chez Peter Ackroyd: l'origine comme parcours des possibles. EtBr (28) 2005, 21–32.

15078. NG, ANDREW HOCK-SOON. 'At the threshold of eternity': religious inversion in Peter Ackroyd's *Hawksmoor*. *In* (pp. 138–63) **14191**.

Oscar Zeta Acosta

15079. ALDAMA, FREDERICK LUIS. Postethnic narrative criticism: magicorealism in Oscar 'Zeta' Acosta, Ana Castillo, Julie Dash, Hanif Kureishi, and Salman Rushdie. (Bibl. 2004, 15372.) Rev. by John S. Christie in MFS (51:1) 2005, 225–8; by Rafael E. Saumell in MELUS (30:1) 2005, 243–5.

Douglas Adams

15080. WEBB, NICK. Wish you were here: the official biography of Douglas Adams. New York: Ballantine, 2005. pp. xiv, 346, (plates) 16.

15081. YEFFETH, GLENN (ed.). The anthology at the end of the universe: leading science fiction authors on Douglas Adams' *The Hitchhiker's Guide to the Galaxy*. Dallas, TX: BenBella, 2005. pp. 199.

Robert Adamson

15082. MCCOOEY, DAVID. Opaque lucidity. *See* **16914**.

Fleur Adcock

15083. ZAMORANO LLENA, CARMEN. The salvage from postmodernism: nomadic subjectivity in contemporary women's poetry in the British Isles. EREA (2:2) 2004, 93–101.

Gary Adelman (b.1935)

15084. ADELMAN, GARY. Old age and Beckett: a partial autobiography. *See* **15375**.

'Paul Adirex' (Pōngphon 'Adirēksān)

15085. WATKHAOLARM, PIMYUPA. Think in Thai, write in English: *Thainess* in Thai English literature. WorldE (24:2) 2005, 145–58.

James Agee

15086. HUGHES, WILLIAM C. James Agee, *Omnibus*, and Mr Lincoln: the culture of liberalism and the challenge of television, 1952–1953. Lanham, MD; London: Scarecrow Press, 2004. pp. xiv, 169. (Studies and documentation in the history of popular entertainment, 7.)

15087. LOFARO, MICHAEL A.; DAVIS, HUGH (eds). James Agee rediscovered: the journals of *Let Us Now Praise Famous Men* and other new manuscripts. Knoxville: Tennessee UP, 2005. pp. xlv, 437.

15088. MAHARIDGE, DALE. Close enough to hurt: second read. ColJR (43:5) 2005, 54–7.

15089. —— WILLIAMSON, MICHAEL. And their children after them: the legacy of *Let Us Now Praise Famous Men*: James Agee, Walker Evans, and the rise and fall of cotton in the South. Foreword by Carl Mydans. New York: Seven Stories Press, 2004. pp. xxiv, 262, (plates) 80.

15090. RABAN, JONATHAN. Thinking about documentary: notes toward a lecture. MichQR (44:4) 2005, 554–69.

15091. Sragow, Michael (ed.). *Let Us Now Praise Famous Men, A Death in the Family*, & shorter fiction. New York: Library of America, 2005. pp. 818, (plates) 61. (Library of America, 159.) Rev. by Michael Dirda in BkW, 23 Oct. 2005, 15.

15092. Wranovics, John. Chaplin and Agee: the untold story of the tramp, the writer, and the lost screenplay. Basingstoke; New York: Palgrave Macmillan, 2005. pp. xxx, 256.

Agha Shahid Ali (b.1949)

15093. Chiu, Jeannie. Melancholy and human rights in *A Nostalgist's Map of America* and *Midnight's Children*. See **19267**.

Rukhsana Ahmad

15094. Schlote, Christiane. Confrontational sites: cultural conflicts, social inequality and sexual politics in the work of Rukhsana Ahmad. EAS (57) 2004, 85–103.

Ama Ata Aidoo

15095. Frías, María. An interview with Ama Ata Aidoo: 'I learnt my first feminist lessons in Africa.' RAEI (16) 2003, 317–35.

15096. Osei-Nyame, Kwadwo, Jr. Images of London in African literature: Ama Ata Aidoo's *Our Sister Killjoy* and Dambudzo Marechera's *The Black Insider*. In (pp. 175–97) **14254**.

Joan Aiken

15097. Hunt, Peter. Joan Aiken, British children's fantasy fiction and the meaning of the mainstream. Foundation (95) 2005, 23–8.

Zoë Akins (b.1886)

15098. Kreizenbeck, Alan. Zoë Akins: Broadway playwright. (Bibl. 2004, 15391.) Rev. by Tice L. Miller in THS (25) 2005, 193–5.

Rabih Alameddine

15099. Hout, Syrine C. Memory, home, and exile in contemporary anglophone Lebanese fiction. CritW (46:3) 2005, 219–33.

Edward Albee

15100. Bottoms, Stephen (ed.). The Cambridge companion to Edward Albee. Cambridge; New York: CUP, 2005. pp. xxi, 263. (Cambridge companions to literature.)

15101. Cohen, Patricia. Guild seminar: race & politics in theater. Dramatist (7:4) 2005, 6–15.

15102. Mann, Bruce J. (ed.). Edward Albee: a casebook. (Bibl. 2004, 15396.) Rev. by Natka Bianchini in TheatreS (46:1) 2005, 137–9.

15103. Nesteruk, Peter. Ritual and identity in late twentieth-century American drama. See **13084**.

Lyle Victor Albert (b.1960)

15104. Houston, Andrew. Lyle Victor Albert's after shave: *Scraping the Surface* through theatre anthropology. CanTR (122) 2005, 34–40.

Laurie Alberts

15105. ALBERTS, LAURIE. Between revolutions: an American romance with Russia. Columbia; London: Missouri UP, 2005. pp. 133.

Brian Aldiss

15106. EDELSON, MARIA. The motif of the island and the theme of destructive creation in *Moreau's Other Island* by Brian Aldiss. *In* (pp. 47–54) **3756**.

15107. HORSTKOTTE, MARTIN. The worlds of the fantastic Other in postmodern English fiction. *See* **19215**.

Meena Alexander

15108. ALEXANDER, MEENA. In Whitman's country. *See* **12290**.

Sherman Alexie

15109. CARROLL, KATHLEEN L. Ceremonial tradition as form and theme in Sherman Alexie's *The Lone Ranger and Tonto Fistfight in Heaven*: a performance-based approach to Native American literature. JMMLA (38:1) 2005, 74–84.

15110. CLAVIEZ, THOMAS. Cosmopolitanism and its discontents: the politics of Sherman Alexie's *Reservation Blues* and Leslie Marmon Silko's *Almanac of the Dead*. LittPr (15:30) 2005, 17–27.

15111. GRASSIAN, DANIEL. Understanding Sherman Alexie. Columbia; London: South Carolina UP, 2005. pp. 211. (Understanding contemporary American literature.)

15112. JAMES, MEREDITH K. Literary and cinematic reservation in selected works of Native American author Sherman Alexie. Lewiston, NY; Lampeter: Mellen Press, 2005. pp. v, 95. (Native American studies, 18.)

15113. MARTÍNEZ FALQUINA, SILVIA. From the monologic eye to healing polyphonies: dialogic re/vision in Native American narratives. RAEI (16) 2003, 239–53.

Edna Alford

15114. LALONDE, JEREMY. Narrative community in Edna Alford's *A Sleep Full of Dreams*. StudCanL (29:2) 2004, 84–101.

Nelson Algren

15115. DUMAS, FRÉDÉRIC. Éros est mort à Chicago: Nelson Algren accuse *Playboy*. EREA (1:1) 2003, 69–75.

15116. HORVATH, BROOKE. Understanding Nelson Algren. Columbia; London: South Carolina UP, 2005. pp. 227. (Understanding contemporary American literature.)

15117. SIMMONS, JEROLD. Challenging the Production Code: *The Man with the Golden Arm*. *See* **13655**.

Dick Allen (b.1939)

15118. DAVIS, COURTNEY. Poet of American transitions: an interview with Dick Allen. ConnR (27:1) 2005, 169–78.

Paula Gunn Allen

15119. EPPERT, CLAUDIA. Leslie Silko's *Ceremony*: rhetorics of ethical reading and composition. *See* **19447**.

Rewi Alley (b.1897)

15120. McKinnon, Dugal. Other notes: Jack Body's *Alley*.   *In* (pp. 262–86) **12674**.

Margery Allingham (1904–1966)

15121. Jones, Julia. 'A fine, sturdy piece of work […]': Margery Allingham's book reviews for *Time & Tide* 1938–1944. Clues (23:1) 2004, 9–18.

15122. Kinsman, Margaret. 'Old age ain't no place for sissies': a look at Allingham's portrayal of the older woman. Clues (23:1) 2004, 19–26.

15123. Perriam, Geraldine. Sex, *Sweet Danger* and the fairy tale. Clues (23:1) 2004, 41–8.

15124. Rowland, Susan. Margery Allingham's gothic: genre as cultural criticism. Clues (23:1) 2004, 27–39.

15125. Rowlands, Alison. Contextualizing magic and witchcraft in the novels of Margery Allingham: the examples of *Sweet Danger* and *Look to the Lady*. Clues (23:1) 2004, 49–60.

15126. Spring, Michelle. Marriage and class in Margery Allingham's *Sweet Danger*. Clues (23:1) 2004, 61–72.

15127. van Hoeven, Marianne (ed.). Margery Allingham: 100 years of a great mystery writer. Foreword by Sara Paretsky. Thorndon, Suffolk: Lucas, 2004. pp. xxiv, 312. Rev. by Chris Willis in Clues (23:1) 2004, 89–90.

15128. Woods, Paula M. The final novels in Allingham's Campion series: speculations on authorial intentions. Clues (23:1) 2004, 81–8.

15129. Wyllie, Andrew. Presences and absences in Margery Allingham's *The Tiger in the Smoke*. Clues (23:1) 2004, 73–9.

Dorothy Allison

15130. Allison, Dorothy. Between fiction and real life: the reality of our work. *In* (pp. 229–37) **2410**.

15131. Blouch, Christine; Vickroy, Laurie (eds). Critical essays on the works of American author Dorothy Allison. Lewiston, NY; Lampeter: Mellen Press, 2005. pp. vii, 164. (Studies in American literature, 71.)

15132. Christopher, Renny. 'Shotgun strategies': working-class literature and violence. *In* (pp. 113–28) **15131**.

15133. Ehrhardt, Julia C. Meeting at a barbecue: Zora Neale Hurston, Dorothy Allison and apocalyptic literary miscegenation. *In* (pp. 71–90) **15131**.

15134. Friedel, Tania. The transformational power of shame: masturbation, religion, and White trash myths in *Bastard out of Carolina*.   *In* (pp. 29–54) **15131**.

15135. Henke, Suzette A. 'A child is being beaten': Dorothy Allison's testimony of trauma in *Bastard out of Carolina*.   *In* (pp. 9–28) **15131**.

15136. Kraus, Carolyn. Embracing pariahdom: the bastard theme in Dorothy Allison's *Bastard out of Carolina*.   *In* (pp. 91–111) **15131**.

15137. Vickroy, Laurie. Vengeance is fleeting: masculine transgressions in Dorothy Allison's *Bastard out of Carolina*.   *In* (pp. 55–70) **15131**.

15138. VINT, SHERRYL. The burden of surviving: the ambiguous body in Dorothy Allison's fiction. *In* (pp. 129–57) 15131.

Kenneth Allott (b.1912)

15139. CRAIK, ROGER. Two influences on L. P. Hartley's *The Go-Between*. *See* 16915.

Julia Alvarez

15140. ALVAREZ, JULIA. The writing life. BkW, 11 Sept. 2005, 10.

15141. HICKMAN, TRENTON. Coffee and colonialism in Julia Alvarez's *A Cafecito Story*. *In* (pp. 70–82) 12632.

15142. IRIZARRY, YLCE. The ethics of writing the Caribbean: Latina narrative as *testimonio*. Lit (16:3) 2005, 263–84.

15143. JOHNSON, KELLI LYON. Julia Alvarez: writing a new place on the map. Albuquerque: New Mexico UP, 2005. pp. xix, 180.

15144. —— 'The terrible moral disinheritance of exile': asymptosy and disintegration in Julia Alvarez's *In the Name of Salomé*. JCarL (4:1) 2005, 149–61.

15145. LIROLA, MARÍA. Reflections on some syntactical processes and their communicative implications in two short stories written by Julia Alvarez: *My English* and *A Genetics of Justice*. RAEI (16) 2003, 201–13.

15146. LOVELADY, STEPHANIE. Walking backwards: coming of age in *My Ántonia* and *How the García Girls Lost Their Accents*. *See* 15735.

Kingsley Amis ('Robert Markham', 'William Tanner')

15147. BURNETT, ARCHIE. Allusions and echoes in Kingsley Amis's letters. NQ (52:4) 2005, 507–10.

Martin Amis

15148. FORTIN-TOURNÈS, ANNE-LAURE. Martin Amis: le postmodernisme en question. Rennes: Presses Universitaires de Rennes, 2003. pp. 132. (Interférences.) Rev. by Jean-Michel Ganteau in EtBr (26) 2004, 202–5.

15149. LAROSE, NICOLE. Reading *The Information* on Martin Amis's London. CritW (46:2) 2005, 160–76.

A. R. Ammons

15150. BARBARESE, J. T. Theology for atheists: reading Ammons. JML (26:3/4) 2003, 73–83.

15151. BURAK, DAVID; GILBERT, ROGER (eds). Considering the radiance: essays on the poetry of A. R. Ammons. New York; London: Norton, 2005. pp. 365. Rev. by Peter Campion in TCL (51:4) 2005, 491–4.

Rudolfo Anaya

15152. MATERASSI, MARIO. It was doubles: strategies of sense production in Rudolfo Anaya's *The Man Who Found a Pistol*. JSwest (47:2) 2005, 249–58.

15153. SOTELO, SUSAN BAKER. Chicano detective fiction: a critical study of five novelists. Jefferson, NC; London: McFarland, 2005. pp. ix, 225.

Maggie Anderson (b.1948)

15154. ANON. (comp.). A Maggie Anderson bibliography. IMR (21) 2005, 43–4.

15155. BIZZARO, PATRICK. Representations of truth in Maggie Anderson's poetry: 'beautiful nostalgia', education and permanence. IMR (21) 2005, 20–6.

15156. DYER, JOYCE. Confluences: fluidity in the art and vision of Maggie Anderson. IMR (21) 2005, 27–34.

15157. LANG, JOHN. Maggie Anderson. IMR (21) 2005, 2.

15158. LONG, KATE. The spaces between: a conversation. IMR (21) 2005, 35–42.

15159. MANN, JEFF. 'A beloved place and people': landscape and folk culture in the poetry of Maggie Anderson. IMR (21) 2005, 10–19.

Sherwood Anderson

15160. BUECHSEL, MARK PETER. The mystery of identity: the journey from constructedness to essence in Sherwood Anderson's *Poor White*. MidAmerica (30) 2003, 54–64.

15161. DUNNE, ROBERT. A new book of the grotesques: contemporary approaches to Sherwood Anderson's early fiction. Kent, OH; London: Kent State UP, 2005. pp. xvii, 134.

15162. GNIADEK, MELISSA. The art of becoming: Sherwood Anderson, Frank Sargeson and the grotesque aesthetic. JNZL (23:2) 2005, 21–35.

15163. SKLAR, HOWARD. Believable fictions: the moral implications of story-based emotions. *In* (pp. 157–82) **3888**.

Gail Anderson-Dargatz (b.1963)

15164. MACPHERSON, HEIDI SLETTEDAHL. Coyote as culprit: 'her-story' and the feminist fantastic in Gail Anderson-Dargatz's *The Cure for Death by Lightning. In* (pp. 87–100) **12587**.

15165. —— Coyote as culprit: the coyote aesthetics of Gail Anderson-Dargatz's *The Cure for Death by Lightning*. BJCS (17:2) 2004, 175–85.

Maya Angelou

15166. BARNWELL, CHERRON A. Singin' de Blues, writing Black female survival in *I Know Why the Caged Bird Sings*. LHR (19:2) 2005, 48–60.

15167. COLE-LEONARD, NATASHA. Maya Angelou's *Hallelujah! The Welcome Table: a Lifetime of Memories with Recipes* as evocative text; or, 'Ain't' Jemima's recipes. LHR (19:2) 2005, 66–9.

15168. DEGOUT, YASMIN Y. The poetry of Maya Angelou: liberation ideology and technique. LHR (19:2) 2005, 36–47.

15169. HENKE, SUZETTE A. Maya Angelou's *Caged Bird* as trauma narrative. LHR (19:2) 2005, 22–35.

15170. MANORA, YOLANDA M. 'What you looking at me for? I didn't come to stay': displacement, disruption and Black female subjectivity in Maya Angelou's *I Know Why the Caged Bird Sings*. WS (34:5) 2005, 359–75.

15171. NERO, CLARENCE. A discursive trifecta: community, education, and language in *I Know Why the Caged Bird Sings*. LHR (19:2) 2005, 61–5.

15172. TRAYLOR, ELEANOR W. Maya Angelou writing life, inventing literary genre. LHR (19:2) 2005, 8–21.

Tina McElroy Ansa

15173. Okonkwo, Christopher. Of caul and response: *Baby of the Family*, Ansa's neglected metafiction of the veil of Blackness. CLAJ (49:2) 2005, 144–67.

David Antin

15174. Allison, Raphael C. David Antin's pragmatist technophobia. JML (28:4) 2005, 110–34.

Mary Antin

15175. Elahi, Babak. The heavy garments of the past: Mary and Frieda Antin in *The Promised Land*. ColLit (32:4) 2005, 29–49.

Kofi Anyidoho

15176. Okunoye, Oyeniyi. 'We too sing': Kofi Anyidoho and Ewe poetic traditions in *Elegy for the Revolution*. JCL (40:1) 2005, 91–111.

Gloria Anzaldúa

15177. Bost, Suzanne. Gloria Anzaldúa's *mestiza* pain: Mexican sacrifice, Chicana embodiment, and feminist politics. Aztlan (30:2) 2005, 5–34.

15178. Fishkin, Shelley Fisher. Crossroads of cultures: the transnational turn in American Studies – Presidential Address to the American Studies Association, November 12, 2004. *See* **14782.**

15179. Licona, Adela C.; Carrillo Rowe, Aimee. After words: feminist praxis as a bridge between theory and practice. NWSAJ (17:2) 2005, 130–5.

15180. Pérez, Emma. Gloria Anzaldúa: *la gran nueva mestiza* theorist, writer, activist–scholar. NWSAJ (17:2) 2005, 1–10.

15181. Ramsdell, Lea. Language and identity politics: the linguistic autobiographies of Latinos in the United States. *See* **19103.**

15182. Saldaña Portillo, María Josefina. Revolutionary imagination in the Americas and the age of development. Durham, NC; London: Duke UP, 2003. pp. xiii, 366. (Latin America otherwise.) Rev. by Elliott Young in Symposium (59:3) 2005, 187–9.

Lisa Appignanesi (b.1946)

15183. Besemeres, Mary. The family in exile, between languages: Eva Hoffman's *Lost in Translation*, Lisa Appignanesi's *Losing the Dead*, Anca Vlasopolos's *No Return Address*. *See* **17037.**

Jeffrey Archer (b.1940)

15184. Archer, Jeffrey. A prison diary: vol. 3, Heaven. Basingstoke: Macmillan; New York: St Martin's Press, 2005. pp. 473.

Rae Armantrout

15185. von Hallberg, Robert. Lyric thinking. *See* **15577.**

Simon Armitage

15186. Armitage, Simon. Rock of ages. *In* (pp. 105–26) **16207.**

Jeannette Armstrong

15187. LUTZ, HARTMUT.   Construction, identity, representation: First Nations peoples as selves and others. *In* (pp. 1–19) **12912.**

Harriette Arnow

15188. ALLEN, JESSICA D.   'The borrower is servant to the lender' (Proverbs 22:7): slavery, freedom, and stewardship in Harriette Simpson Arnow's *The Dollmaker.* KenEB (54:2/3) 2005, 72–6.

15189. ARNOW, THOMAS L.   On being Harriette Arnow's son. AppalJ (32:4) 2005, 460–7.

15190. BILLIPS, MARTHA.   The writer and the land: Harriette Simpson Arnow and the genesis of her novel *Between the Flowers.* AppalJ (32:4) 2005, 468–82.

Oscar Asche (1871–1936)

15191. SINGLETON, BRIAN.   Oscar Asche, Orientalism, and British musical comedy. (Bibl. 2004, 15472.) Rev. by Howard McNaughton in ADS (46) 2005, 148–50.

John Ashbery

15192. CASPER, ROBERT N.   Interview with John Ashbery. Jubilat (9) 2004, 44–50.

15193. DIMAKOPOULOU, STAMATINA.   The poetics of vision and the redemption of the subject in John Ashbery's *Self-Portrait in a Convex Mirror.* EREA (2:2) 2004, 60–5.

15194. FARRELL, MICHAEL.   Counting and comparing personal etc. pronouns in and between Ryan's *Pure and Applied* and Ashbery's *Wakefulness. See* **19284.**

15195. MAZUR, KRYSTYNA.   Poetry and repetition: Walt Whitman, Wallace Stevens, John Ashbery. *See* **12334.**

15196. RICHIE, EUGENE (ed.).   Selected prose. Ann Arbor: Michigan UP, 2004. pp. 326. (Poets on poetry.) Rev. by John Yau in APR (34:3) 2005, 45–50.

15197. SHAPIRO, MICHAEL (ed.).   From the critic's workbench: essays in literature and semiotics. By Marianne Shapiro. New York; Frankfurt: Lang, 2005. pp. xii, 522. (Berkeley insights in linguistics and semiotics, 58.)

15198. SUÁREZ-TOSTE, ERNESTO.   'The tension is in the concept': John Ashbery's surrealism. Style (38:1) 2004, 1–15.

15199. VENDLER, HELEN.   Invisible listeners: lyric intimacy in Herbert, Whitman, and Ashbery. *See* **7485.**

15200. YAU, JOHN.   The poet as art critic. APR (34:3) 2005, 45–50 (review-article).

Daisy Ashford

15201. MCMASTER, JULIET.   What Daisy knew: the epistemology of the child writer. *In* (pp. 51–69) **9164.**

Gertrude Atherton

15202. KINNEY, ARTHUR F.   The other Dorothy Parkers. *In* (pp. 114–26) **18738.**

15203. PIEP, KARSTEN H.   War as feminist utopia in Dorothy Canfield Fisher's *Home Fires in France* and Gertrude Atherton's *The White Morning. See* **15673.**

15204. ROSENBERG, TRACEY S. A challenge to Victorian motherhood: Mona Caird and Gertrude Atherton. *See* **10352.**

Dame Eileen Atkins (b.1934)

15205. CZARNECKI, KRISTIN KOMMERS. Filming feminism: *A Room of One's Own* on Masterpiece Theater. *See* **20340.**

Margaret Atwood

15206. ATWOOD, MARGARET. My life in science-fiction. Cycnos (22:2) 2005, 155–64.

15207. BARZILAI, SHULI. The Bluebeard syndrome in Atwood's *Lady Oracle*: fear and femininity. MarvT (19:2) 2005, 249–73.

15208. BIDIVILLE, ANNICK. Margaret Atwood's *The Edible Woman*: from body representations to feminist theories. NMAS (34) 2005, 4–15.

15209. BLACKFORD, HOLLY. Haunted housekeeping: fatal attractions of servant and mistress in twentieth-century female gothic literature. *See* **20115.**

15210. DIMARCO, DANETTE. Paradice lost, paradise regained: *homo faber* and the makings of a new beginning in *Oryx and Crake*. PLL (41:2) 2005, 170–95.

15211. DUNNING, STEPHEN. Margaret Atwood's *Oryx and Crake*: the terror of the therapeutic. CanL (186) 2005, 86–101.

15212. EAGLETON, MARY. What's the matter? Authors in Carol Shields' short fiction. *See* **19433.**

15213. EDWARDSON, RYAN. 'Kicking Uncle Sam out of the peaceable kingdom': English Canadian 'new nationalism' and Americanization. JCanStud (37:4) 2002/03, 131–50.

15214. HAROLD, JAMES. Narrative engagement with *Atonement* and *The Blind Assassin*. *See* **17963.**

15215. HOWELLS, CORAL ANN. Margaret Atwood. (Bibl. 2000, 15095.) Basingstoke; New York: Palgrave Macmillan, 2005. pp. x, 213. (Second ed.: first ed. 1996.)

15216. LABUDOVÁ, KATARÍNA. From retrospective to reconstruction of the 'auto/biographical' subject in *Cat's Eye* by Margaret Atwood. *In* (pp. 109–14) **3734.**

15217. LJUNGBERG, CHRISTINA. Models of reading: diagrammatic aspects of literary texts. *In* (pp. 105–25) **3888.**

15218. LÓPEZ RÚA, PAULA. The manipulative power of word-formation devices in Margaret Atwood's *Oryx and Crake*. RAEI (18) 2005, 149–65.

15219. MCKAY, ROBERT. 'Identifying with the animals': language, subjectivity, and the animal politics of Margaret Atwood's *Surfacing*. *In* (pp. 207–27) **14258.**

15220. MASSOURA, KIRIAKI. 'I look at it and see my life entire': language, third-eye vision and painting in Margaret Atwood's *Cat's Eye*. BJCS (17:2) 2004, 210–22.

15221. MORGAN, ELIZABETH. Mary and modesty. *See* **15779.**

15222. OATES-INDRUCHOVÁ, LIBORA. Initiation motives in Margaret Atwood's *The Robber Bride*. *In* (pp. 127–34) **3753.**

15223. STOREY, FRANÇOISE; STOREY, JEFF.   History and allegory in Margaret Atwood's *Oryx and Crake*. Cycnos (22:2) 2005, 129–38.

15224. STRATTON, FLORENCE.   There is no Bentham Street in Calgary: panoptic discourses and Thomas King's *Medicine River*. See **17442**.

15225. THOMPSON, STACY.   Tentative utopias. See **17677**.

15226. TOLAN, FIONA.   Guilt and innocence in the community and the self: an examination of mutual responsibility in Margaret Atwood's *Surfacing*. BJCS (17:1) 2004, 105–16.

15227. TRUSSLER, MICHAEL.   Where do things come from? We never know: an interview with Margaret Atwood. WasRCPSF (38:1) 2003, 223–33.

15228. VICKROY, LAURIE.   Seeking symbolic immortality: visualizing trauma in *Cat's Eye*. Mosaic (38:2) 2005, 129–43.

15229. VIVIANI, AGLAIA.   'There are two islands, at least': la Circe postcoloniale di Margaret Atwood. LProv (121) 2004, 61–7.

15230. WARKENTIN, GERMAINE.   Mapping Wonderland: the city of Toronto as seen through its writers' eyes. See **19968**.

15231. WILSON, SHARON ROSE (ed.).   Margaret Atwood's textual assassinations: recent poetry and fiction. (Bibl. 2004, 15502.) Rev. by Annette Kern-Stähler in CanL (186) 2005, 190–2.

15232. WRIGHT, LAURA.   National photographic: images of sensibility and the nation in Margaret Atwood's *Surfacing* and Nadine Gordimer's *July's People*. Mosaic (38:1) 2005, 75–92.

David Auburn

15233. KLAVER, ELIZABETH.   *Proof*, π, and *Happy Days*: the performance of mathematics. JMMLA (38:1) 2005, 5–22.

W. H. Auden

15234. BURT, STEPHEN; BROOKS-MOTL, HANNAH (eds).   Randall Jarrell on W. H. Auden. New York: Columbia UP, 2005. pp. xiv, 178. Rev. by Jon Tribble in BkW, 3 July 2005, 3–4.

15235. EPSTEIN, JOSEPH.   Vin Audenaire. HR (56:1) 2003, 57–72.

15236. FLEISSNER, ROBERT F.   Auden's *As I Walked Out One Evening*. Exp (64:1) 2005, 48–50.

15237. KIRSCH, ARTHUR.   Auden and Christianity: a spiritual biography. New Haven, CT; London: Yale UP, 2005. pp. 240. Rev. by Edward T. Wheeler in Cweal (132:18) 2005, 34–5; by Robert Bové in ANCW (193:14) 2005, 34–5.

15238. —— (ed.).   The sea and the mirror: a commentary on Shakespeare's *The Tempest*. (Bibl. 2004, 15511.) Rev. by Pascal Aquien in EREA (2:1) 2004; by Stan Smith in RES (56:225) 2005, 478–80.

15239. KOHN, ROBERT E.   The fivesquare *Amsterdam* of Ian McEwan. See **17967**.

15240. MAO, DOUGLAS.   Auden and son: environment, evolution, exhibition. Paideuma (32:1–3) 2003, 301–49.

15241. NEMEROV, ALEXANDER.   The flight of form: Auden, Bruegel, and the turn to abstraction in the 1940s. CI (31:4) 2005, 780–810.

15242. ROBERTS, BETH ELLEN.   W. H. Auden and the Jews. JML (28:3) 2005, 87–108.

15243. SMITH, STAN (ed.).   The Cambridge companion to W. H. Auden. Cambridge; New York: CUP, 2004. pp. xxi, 261. (Cambridge companions to literature.)

15244. TALBOT, JOHN.   Auden's Horatian mosaic. CML (25:2) 2005, 9–28.

15245. TIPPINS, SHERILL.   February House. Boston, MA: Houghton Mifflin, 2005. pp. xiv, 317. Rev. by Peter Parker in TLS, 23 Sept. 2005, 25; by Martha E. Stone in GLRW (12:4) 2005, 41–2.

Paul Auster

15246. BARBOUR, JOHN D.   Solitude, writing, and fathers in Paul Auster's *The Invention of Solitude*. A/B (19:1/2) 2004, 19–32.

15247. —— The value of solitude: the ethics and spirituality of aloneness in autobiography. See **12179.**

15248. BEWES, TIMOTHY.   The novel as an absence: Lukács and the event of postmodern fiction. Novel (38:1) 2004, 5–20.

15249. DUPERRAY, ANNICK.   Paul Auster: les ambiguïtés de la negation. Paris: Belin, 2003. pp. 125. (Voix américaines.) Rev. by François Gavillon in EREA (1:2) 2003.

15250. LJUNGBERG, CHRISTINA.   Constructing new 'realities': the performative function of maps in contemporary fiction. See **19906.**

15251. MASIERO MARCOLIN, PIA.   Notes on/in Paul Auster's *Oracle Night*. RSA (14) 2003, 181–96.

15252. MORRIS, MAY (ed. and trans.).   Purgatory. Rome: Leconte, 2005. pp. 153. (Storie: the write side.) (Includes interview with the author.)

15253. NIGIANNI, BETTY.   Corporeality and the metropolis: dissolving the body in Paul Auster's *The New York Trilogy*. Gramma (11) 2003, 139–49.

15254. PORTER, ROGER J.   Finding the father: autobiography as bureau of missing persons. See **16757.**

15255. ROGER, CATHERINE.   The ego, the self and the subject in Paul Auster's fictions. EREA (2:2) 2004, 72–7.

15256. VALLAS, SOPHIE.   'All the others inside me': les enjeux ambigus de la citation dans 'The Book of Memory' (The Invention of Solitude) de Paul Auster. EREA (2:1) 2004, 76–83.

Mary Austin

15257. BLACKBIRD, CHELSEA; NELSON, BARNEY (eds).   Mary Austin's Southwest: an anthology of her literary criticism. Salt Lake City: Utah UP, 2005. pp. ix, 302.

15258. KLIMASMITH, BETSY.   Naturist as tourist: Mary Austin's 'automobile eye view' in *The Land of Journeys' Ending*. WAL (39:1) 2004, 54–78.

15259. LAPE, NOREEN GROOVER (introd.).   One-smoke stories. Athens, OH: Swallow Press, 2003. pp. lxvi, 177. Rev. by Jennie A. Camp in RMER (59:1) 2005.

15260. PAES DE BARROS, DEBORAH. Fast cars and bad girls: nomadic subjects and women's road stories. *See* **14243**.

15261. REED, MAUREEN E. A woman's place: women writing New Mexico. Albuquerque: New Mexico UP, 2005. pp. xi, 355.

15262. SALZER, MAUREEN. Native presence and survivance in early twentieth-century translations by Natalie Curtis Burlin and Mary Austin. WAL (39:1) 2004, 79–103.

15263. SCHAEFER, HEIKE. Mary Austin's regionalism: reflections on gender, genre, and geography. (Bibl. 2004, 15532.) Rev. by Betsy Klimasmith in Legacy (22:2) 2005, 206–8.

15264. VIEHMANN, MARTHA L. A rain song for America: Mary Austin, American Indians, and American literature and culture. WAL (39:1) 2004, 5–35.

Alan Ayckbourn ('Roland Allen')

15265. CAMPOS, LILIANE. Rewriting the plot: re-creations in contemporary British comedy. *See* **15464**.

Jimmy Santiago Baca

15266. ALDAMA, FREDERICK LUIS. An interview with Jimmy Santiago Baca. MELUS (30:3) 2005, 113–27.

Richard Bach

15267. COOPER, KEN. Flight of ideas: *Jonathan Livingston Seagull* and the new economy. MFS (51:1) 2005, 158–82.

Karle Wilson Baker (1878–1960)

15268. JACKSON, SARAH R. Texas woman of letters, Karle Wilson Baker. College Station: Texas A&M UP, 2005. pp. xvi, 236. (Sam Rayburn series on rural life, 8.)

Nicholson Baker

15269. RAMBEAU, ERIC. Le sexe sans le soufre: lecture de deux romans de Nicholson Baker. EREA (1:1) 2003, 84–91.

James Baldwin

15270. DAVIS, NICHOLAS K. Go tell it on the stage: *Blues for Mr Charlie* as dialectical drama. JADT (17:2) 2005, 30–42.

15271. LEE, SUSANNA. The jazz harmonies of connection and disconnection in *Sonny's Blues*. Genre (37:2) 2004, 285–99.

15272. MCWILLIAMS, WILSON CAREY. *Go Tell It on the Mountain*: James Baldwin and the politics of faith. *In* (pp. 153–70) **14121**.

15273. MILLER, D. QUENTIN. 'On the outside looking in': White readers of nonwhite prison narratives. *In* (pp. 15–32) **12821**.

15274. MILLER, ELISE. The 'maw of Western culture': James Baldwin and the anxieties of influence. AAR (38:4) 2004, 625–36.

15275. MORENO, RENEE M. Bombs and bullshit: interventions in a very dangerous time. *In* (pp. 33–45) **2457**.

15276. NABERS, DEAK.   Past using: James Baldwin and Civil Rights law in the 1960s. YJC (18:2) 2005, 221–42.

15277. NORMAN, BRIAN.   Reading a 'closet screenplay': Hollywood, James Baldwin's Malcolms and the threat of historical irrelevance. AAR (39:1/2) 2005, 103–18.

15278. ROBINSON, ANGELO R.   The other proclamation in James Baldwin's *Go Tell It on the Mountain*. CLAJ (48:3) 2005, 336–51.

15279. WEN, PATRICK.   The terror of neutrality: civil rights, tortured quietism, and the tactical disengagement of Flannery O'Connor. See **18582**.

David Ballantyne (1924–1986)

15280. REID, BRYAN.   After the fireworks: a life of David Ballantyne. (Bibl. 2004, 15550.) Rev. by Jennifer Lawn in JNZL (23:2) 2005, 92–100.

J. G. Ballard

15281. HUBBLE, NICK.   Five English disaster novels, 1951–1972. See **20473**.

15282. POCOBELLI, ADRIAN.   'Pre-uterine claims': cultural contexts and iconographic parallels in Ballard's *The Atrocity Exhibition*. NYRSF (17:2) 2004, 18–21.

Edwin Balmer (1883–1959)

15283. STEELE, ALLEN M.   Doomsday 1933: *When Worlds Collide* reconsidered. See **20472**.

Asha Bandele

15284. DAWKINS, LAURA.   'A scream that is not female and that is not male': imprisonment and African American gender identity in asha bandele's *The Prisoner's Wife*. In (pp. 81–94) **12821**.

Biyi Bandele-Thomas (b.1967)

15285. KEHINDE, AYO.   A parable of the African condition: the interface of postmodernism and postcolonialism in Biyi Bandele-Thomas's fiction. RAEI (16) 2003, 177–90.

15286. WIDMAYER, ANNE F.   The politics of adapting Aphra Behn's *Oroonoko*. See **7259**.

John Banville

15287. D'HOKER, ELKE.   Visions of alterity: representation in the works of John Banville. Amsterdam; Atlanta, GA: Rodopi, 2004. pp. 243. (Costerus, ns 151.) Rev. by Françoise Canon-Roger in EtIr (30:1) 2005, 223–4.

15288. DUFFY, BRIAN.   Banville's other ghost: Samuel Beckett's presence in John Banville's *Eclipse*. EtIr (28:1) 2003, 85–106.

15289. JOUSNI, STÉPHANE.   Écrire Dublin après Joyce. See **17292**.

15290. MCNAMEE, BRENDAN.   Sacred chaos: form and the immediate in John Banville's *Mefisto*. CritW (46:3) 2005, 205–18.

15291. POWELL, KERSTI TARIEN.   'Not a son but a survivor': Beckett … Joyce … Banville. See **15412**.

Amiri Baraka (LeRoi Jones)

15292. BARAKA, AMIRI.   Short story and poetry. In (pp. 3–6) **14204**.

15293. BLAU, HERBERT. Art and crisis: homeland security and the Noble Savage. PAJ (75) 2003, 6–19.

Joan Barfoot

15294. MILTON, PAUL. Rewriting White flight: suburbia in Gerald Lynch's *Troutstream* and Joan Barfoot's *Dancing in the Dark*. *In* (pp. 166–82) **9243**.

Howard Barker

15295. BARKER, HOWARD. Death, the one and the art of theatre. London; New York: Routledge, 2005. pp. 105.

15296. LAMB, CHARLES. The theatre of Howard Barker. London; New York: Routledge, 2005. pp. 228.

15297. RABEY, DAVID IAN. Two against nature: rehearsing and performing Howard Barker's production of his play *The Twelfth Battle of Isonzo*. TRI (30:2) 2005, 175–89.

Pat Barker

15298. BARTLETT, CARINA. Bringing the house down: Pat Barker, Sarah Daniels, and the dramatic dialogue. *In* (pp. 87–100) **15309**.

15299. BRANNIGAN, JOHN. The small world of Kelly Brown: home and dereliction in *Union Street*. *In* (pp. 3–13) **15309**.

15300. BROPHY, SARAH. Working-class women, labor, and the problem of community in *Union Street* and *Liza's England*. *In* (pp. 24–39) **15309**.

15301. BROWN, DENNIS. The Regeneration Trilogy: total war, masculinities, anthropologies, and the talking cure. *In* (pp. 187–202) **15309**.

15302. DUCKWORTH, ALISTAIR M. Two borrowings in Pat Barker's *Regeneration*. JML (27:3) 2004, 63–7.

15303. JOANNOU, MAROULA. Pat Barker and the languages of region and class. EAS (57) 2004, 41–54.

15304. JOHNSON, PATRICIA E. Embodying losses in Pat Barker's Regeneration Trilogy. CritW (46:4) 2005, 307–19.

15305. JOLLY, MARGARETTA. Toward a masculine maternal: Pat Barker's bodily fictions. *In* (pp. 235–54) **15309**.

15306. KRASNER, JAMES. Accumulated lives: metaphor, materiality, and the homes of the elderly. *See* **17688**.

15307. MONTEITH, SHARON. Screening *The Man Who Wasn't There*: the Second World War and 1950s cinema. *In* (pp. 115–27) **15309**.

15308. —— YOUSAF, NAHEM. *Double Vision*: regenerative or traumatized pastoral? *In* (pp. 283–99) **15309**.

15309. —— et al. (ed.). Critical perspectives on Pat Barker. Columbia; London: South Carolina UP, 2005. pp. xxiii, 314.

15310. NUNN, HEATHER; BIRESSI, ANITA. In the shadow of monstrosities: memory, violence, and childhood in *Another World*. *In* (pp. 255–65) **15309**.

15311. PAUL, RONALD. In pastoral fields: the Regeneration Trilogy and classic First World War fiction. *In* (pp. 147–61) **15309**.

15312. STEVENSON, SHERYL. The uncanny case of Dr Rivers and Mr Prior: dynamics of transference in *The Eye in the Door*. *In* (pp. 219–32) **15309**.

15313. —— With the listener in mind: talking about the Regeneration Trilogy with Pat Barker. *In* (pp. 175–84) **15309**.

15314. SUMMERS-BREMNER, ELUNED.   Family at war: memory, sibling rivalry, and the nation in *Border Crossing* and *Another World*. *In* (pp. 266–82) **15309**.

15315. WATERMAN, DAVID.   Le miroir de la societé: la violence institutionelle chez Anthony Burgess, Doris Lessing et Pat Barker. Ravenna: Longo, 2003. pp. 132. (Interprete.) Rev. by Vanessa Guignery in EA (58:2) 2005, 239–40.

15316. WEISS, RUDOLF.   *Mise-en-abyme* in Pat Barker's *Regeneration*. *In* (pp. 189–94) **3753**.

15317. WESTMAN, KARIN E.   Generation not regeneration: screening out class, gender, and cultural change in the film of *Regeneration*. *In* (pp. 162–74) **15309**.

15318. WHEELER, PAT.   Transgressing masculinities: *The Man Who Wasn't There*. *In* (pp. 128–43) **15309**.

Robert Barnard

15319. FORD, SUSAN ALLEN.   Stately homes of England: Robert Barnard's country house mysteries. Clues (23:4) 2005, 3–14.

Djuna Barnes

15320. BAY-CHENG, SARAH.   The transcendental realism of American verse drama. JADT (17:2) 2005, 17–29.

15321. CHAIT, SANDRA.   Site also of angst and spiritual search. *In* (pp. 150–69) **15847**.

15322. COPELAND, DAVID.   The innocent children of *Nightwood* and Hayford Hall. *In* (pp. 116–32) **15847**.

15323. FARFAN, PENNY.   *The Antiphon* as parody: Djuna Barnes and the literary tradition. JADT (17:1) 2005, 46–60.

15324. GROBBEL, MICHAELA M.   Enacting past and present: the memory theaters of Djuna Barnes, Ingeborg Bachmann, and Marguerite Duras. (Bibl. 2004, 15579.) Rev. by Karen Kaivola in Biography (28:2) 2005, 311–14.

15325. HERRING, PHILLIP F.; STUTMAN, OSIAS (eds).   The collected poems; with notes toward the memoirs. Madison; London: Wisconsin UP, 2005. pp. xix, 285, (plates) 22.

15326. KAUP, MONIKA.   The neobaroque in Djuna Barnes. Mod/Mod (12:1) 2005, 85–110.

15327. PARSONS, DEBORAH.   Djuna Barnes. Plymouth: Northcote House in assn with the British Council, 2003. pp. viii, 104. (Writers and their work.) Rev. by Ian F. A. Bell in JAStud (38:3) 2004, 524–5.

15328. PODNIEKS, ELIZABETH; CHAIT, SANDRA (eds).   Hayford Hall: hangovers, erotics, and Modernist aesthetics. *See* **15847**.

15329. SÁNCHEZ-PARDO, ESTHER.   Cultures of the death drive: Melanie Klein and Modernist melancholia. *See* **20416**.

15330. SHERBERT, GARY.   'Hieroglyphics of sleep and pain': Djuna Barnes's anatomy of melancholy. CanRCL (30:1) 2003, 117–44.

15331. STRANGE, MARTINA. 'Melancholia, melancholia': changing black bile into black ink in Djuna Barnes's *Nightwood*. *In* (pp. 133–49) **15847**.

15332. TRUBOWITZ, LARA. In search of 'the Jew' in Djuna Barnes's *Nightwood*: Jewishness, antisemitism, structure, and style. MFS (51:2) 2005, 311–34.

15333. VANDIVERE, JULIE. Framed liminalities: Antonia White's *Beyond the Glass* and Emily Coleman's *The Shutter of Snow*. *In* (pp. 46–69) **15847**.

15334. WELLS-LYNN, AMY. The intertextual, sexually coded Rue Jacob: a geocritical approach to Djuna Barnes, Natalie Barney, and Radclyffe Hall. SCR (22:3) 2005, 78–112.

Julian Barnes ('Dan Kavanagh')

15335. GOODE, MIKE. Knowing seizures: Julian Barnes, Jean-Paul Sartre, and the erotics of the postmodern condition. TexP (19:1) 2005, 149–71.

15336. GUIGNERY, VANESSA. Réécritures du Déluge et de l'arche de Noé dans la fiction contemporaine de langue anglaise (Coover, Findley, Winterson, Roberts et Barnes). *See* **19088**.

15337. RUBINSON, GREGORY J. The fiction of Rushdie, Barnes, Winterson, and Carter: breaking cultural and literary boundaries in the work of four postmodernists. *See* **19277**.

15338. SEMINO, ELENA. Representing characters' speech and thought in narrative fiction: a study of *England, England* by Julian Barnes. Style (38:4) 2004, 428–51.

15339. WILSON, KEITH. Julian Barnes and the marginalisation of metropolitanism: the suburban centre in *Metroland* and *Letters from London*. *In* (pp. 153–67) **14254**.

Wilton Barnhardt (b.1960)

15340. BARNHARDT, WILTON. Behind the story. *In* (pp. 194–6) **14294**.

Andrea Barrett

15341. BARRETT, ANDREA. Behind the story. *In* (pp. 298–300) **14294**.

J. M. Barrie

15342. BILLONE, AMY. The boy who lived: from Carroll's Alice and Barrie's Peter Pan to Rowling's Harry Potter. *See* **10396**.

15343. BIRCH, DINAH. His greatest pretend. LRB (27:17) 2005, 27–8 (review-article).

15344. CHANEY, LISA. Hide-and-seek with angels: a life of J. M. Barrie. London: Hutchinson, 2005. pp. 402, (plates) 16. Rev. by Dinah Birch in LRB (27:17) 2005, 27–8; by Claire Harman in TLS, 16 Sept. 2005, 3–4.

15345. DAVIS, TRACY C. 'Do you believe in fairies?': the hiss of dramatic license. TJ (57:1) 2005, 57–81.

15346. HARMAN, CLAIRE. 'I am youth. I am joy': intimacy and transitoriness in the life and work of J. M. Barrie. TLS, 16 Sept. 2005, 3–4 (review-article).

15347. LAPAIRE, JEAN-RÉMI. Coordination et cognition. *See* **2708**.

15348. OSTROWSKI, WITOLD. Shakespeare's presence in *Dear Brutus* by J. M. Barrie. *In* (pp. 176–82) **3756**.

15349. Young, Timothy. My heart in company: the work of J. M. Barrie and the birth of Peter Pan. New Haven, CT: Beinecke Rare Book & Manuscript Library, Yale Univ., 2005. pp. 89.

John Barth

15350. McGurl, Mark. The program era: pluralisms of postwar American fiction. CI (32:1) 2005, 102–29.

15351. Shackelford, Laura. Narrative subjects meet their limits: John Barth's *Click* and the remediation of hypertext. ConLit (46:2) 2005, 275–310.

15352. Wald, Priscilla. What's in a cell? John Moore's spleen and the language of bioslavery. *See* **15935**.

Donald Barthelme

15353. Nealon, Jeffrey T. Disastrous aesthetics: irony, ethics, and gender in Barthelme's *Snow White*. TCL (51:2) 2005, 123–41.

Frederick Barthelme

15354. Hughes, John C. The novels and short stories of Frederick Barthelme: a literary critical analysis. Lewiston, NY; Lampeter: Mellen Press, 2005. pp. v, 146. (Studies in American literature, 75.)

Neil Bartlett

15355. Dickinson, Peter. Oscar Wilde: reading the life after the life. *See* **12381**.

John Barton (b.1928)

15356. May, Robert G. 'Moving from place to face': landscape and longing in the poetry of John Barton. StudCanL (30:1) 2005, 245–69.

Hamilton Basso (1904–1964)

15357. Perry, Keith. The Kingfish in fiction: Huey P. Long and the modern American novel. (Bibl. 2004, 15616.) Rev. by Bryan Giemza in SoCult (11:1) 2005, 96–9.

Blanche Edith Baughan

15358. Calder, Alex. Blending and belonging: Blanche Baughan and scenic New Zealand. JNZL (23:1) 2005, 174–85.

Frank Baum

15359. Canaan, Howard. The pressures of history and fiction in Geoff Ryman's *Was*. *See* **19286**.

15360. Cox, J. Randolph. *Aunt Jane's Nieces on Tour*: a probably phantom title. DNR (74:5) 2005, 187–90.

15361. Matthews, Gareth B. Platform 9¾: the idea of a different reality. *In* (pp. 175–85) **19194**.

15362. Pickrell, Alan. L. Frank Baum's *Aunt Jane's Nieces*: pseudonyms can pay off. DNR (74:5) 2005, 163–75.

15363. Sherman, Fraser A. *The Wizard of Oz* catalog: L. Frank Baum's novel, its sequels, their adaptations for stage, television, movies, radio, music videos, comic books, commercials, and more. Jefferson, NC; London: McFarland, 2005. pp. ix, 275.

15364. VELLUCCI, SABRINA.   La meravigliose illusioni del Mago di Oz. *In* (pp. 163–76) **12883.**

Richard Bausch (b.1945)

15365. TAYLOR, ART.   An interview with Richard Bausch. CaroQ (57:1) 2005, 69–75.

George Baxt (b.1923)

15366. KINNEY, ARTHUR F.   The other Dorothy Parkers. *In* (pp. 114–26) **18738.**

Charles Baxter

15367. BAXTER, CHARLES.   Behind the story. *In* (pp. 78–82) **14294.**

James K. Baxter

15368. DENNISON, JOHN.   *Ko te Pakeha te teina*: Baxter's cross-cultural poetry. JNZL (23:2) 2005, 36–46. ('The European is the younger sibling.')

15369. MILLAR, PAUL.   'Nobody would have given tuppence for our chances': James K. Baxter & J. C. Sturm. *In* (pp. 136–65) **12916.**

John Bayley (b.1925)

15370. JAMES, CLIVE.   A fabulous marketplace: who says that book reviews should never be collected in a book? TLS, 27 May 2005, 3–4.

Peter S. Beagle

15371. MATHESON, SUE.   Psychic transformation and the regeneration of language in Peter S. Beagle's *The Last Unicorn*. LU (29:3) 2005, 416–26.

Ann Beattie

15372. RAMAL, RANDY.   Love, self-deception, and the moral 'must'. PhilL (29:2) 2005, 379–93.

Samuel Beckett

15373. ACKERLEY, C. J.; GONTARSKI, S. E.   The Grove companion to Samuel Beckett: a reader's guide to his works, life, and thought. (Bibl. 2004, 15633.) Rev. by Patrick Johnstone in TexP (19:2) 2005, 402–7.

15374. ACKERLEY, CHRIS.   Inorganic form: Samuel Beckett's nature. AUMLA (104) 2005, 79–101.

15375. ADELMAN, GARY.   Old age and Beckett: a partial autobiography. NER (26:3) 2005, 138–48.

15376. ALBRIGHT, DANIEL.   Beckett and aesthetics. (Bibl. 2004, 15636.) Rev. by Thomas Mansell in YES (35) 2005, 338–40.

15377. BATTY, MARK.   Staged dialogues with authorship: Pinter and Beckett as directors. *See* **18790.**

15378. BENNETT, BENJAMIN.   All theater is revolutionary theater. *See* **16244.**

15379. BERNARD, CATHERINE.   L'art de l'aporie: penser l'impensable avec Adorno et Benjamin. EA (58:1) 2005, 31–41.

15380. BRADBY, DAVID.   'A joke which still goes on' – *Le Kid, Eleuthéria, Waiting for Godot*. JBecS (13:1) 2003, 63–72.

15381. BRATER, ENOCH.   The globalization of Beckett's *Godot*. CompDr (37:2) 2003, 145–58.

15382. BURKMAN, KATHERINE H. The contamination of birth by sex and death in the plays of Beckett and Pinter. *See* **18792.**

15383. CASCETTA, ANNAMARIA; PEJÀ, LAURA. Winnie and the tradition of the actor: from the old Italian style theatre to the experimental stage. Trans. by Mark Pietralunga. JBecS (13:1) 2003, 73–97.

15384. CRANE, RALPH J. After Beckett: the influence of Samuel Beckett on the fiction of J. G. Farrell. NewHR (9:1) 2005, 109–16.

15385. DI ROCCO, EMILIA. Beckett e Dante. SCrit (20:3) 2005, 403–22.

15386. DOUGLAS-FAIRHURST, ROBERT. Old bags and 'the old style': a new source for Beckett's *Happy Days*? NQ (52:4) 2005, 502–5.

15387. DUFFY, BRIAN. Banville's other ghost: Samuel Beckett's presence in John Banville's *Eclipse*. *See* **15288.**

15388. FERRINI, JEAN-PIERRE. Dante et Beckett. Preface by Jacqueline Risset. Paris: Hermann, 2003. pp. xvii, 240. (Savoir: lettres.) Rev. by Mary Bryden in BecC (27:2) 2004, 16–17.

15389. FLETCHER, JOHN. About Beckett: the playwright and the work. (Bibl. 2004, 15652.) Rev. by W. B. Worthen in JBecS (13:1) 2003, 130–4.

15390. GENDRON, SARAH. 'A cogito for the dissolved self': writing, presence, and the subject in the work of Samuel Beckett, Jacques Derrida, and Gilles Deleuze. JML (28:1) 2004, 47–64.

15391. GIULIETTI, MARGHERITA. Visual and vocal ventures in *Eh Joe*'s telerhythms. JBecS (13:1) 2003, 112–26.

15392. GRAVER, LAWRENCE. Samuel Beckett, *Waiting for Godot*. (Bibl. 2004, 15657.) Rev. by Willy Maley in TRI (30:2) 2005, 202–3.

15393. HADFIELD, ANDREW. Beckett and Dylan Thomas. NQ (52:4) 2005, 505–6.

15394. HOROWITZ, EVAN. *Endgame*: beginning to end. JML (27:4) 2004, 121–8.

15395. HOUPPERMANS, SJEF. Samuel Beckett & compagnie. Amsterdam; Atlanta, GA: Rodopi, 2003. pp. 153. (Faux titre, 235.) Rev. by William Cloonan in JBecS (13:1) 2003, 151–3; by Jean-Michel Rabaté in BecC (27:1) 2004, 20–1.

15396. HUTCHINGS, WILLIAM. Samuel Beckett's *Waiting for Godot*: a reference guide. Westport, CT; London: Praeger, 2005. pp. xvi, 167.

15397. INNES, CHRISTOPHER. Shifting the frame – Modernism in the theatre. *In* (pp. 204–12) **12946.**

15398. KENNEDY, SEÁN. A note on Mr Nidder. JBecS (13:1) 2003, 127–9.

15399. KENNER, HUGH. Flaubert, Joyce, and Beckett: the stoic comedians. Normal, IL: Dalkey Archive Press, 2005. pp. xviii, 106.

15400. KLAVER, ELIZABETH. *Proof*, π, and *Happy Days*: the performance of mathematics. *See* **15233.**

15401. KNOWLSON, JAMES. Images of Beckett. (Bibl. 2004, 15666.) Rev. by Chris Ackerley in JBecS (13:1) 2003, 142–50.

15402. LAWLEY, PAUL. *Endgame* in the subjunctive. JBecS (13:1) 2003, 1–11.

15403. LEVY, ERIC P. The literary depiction of ontological shock. MidQ (46:2) 2005, 107–22.

15404. Loevlie, Elisabeth Marie.   Literary silences in Pascal, Rousseau, and Beckett. (Bibl. 2004, 15671.) Rev. by Mary Bryden in MLR (100:3) 2005, 836–7.

15405. McKee, Al.   Buster's hat. FilmQ (57:4) 2004, 31–4. (Beckett and Keaton's collaboration on *Film* (1965).)

15406. Marchesini, Manuela.   *Signorina Rosina*: Pizzuto e Beckett; ovvero, La scrittura come pittogramma. SCrit (18:2) 2003, 183–202.

15407. Mayer, Aric Dain.   Consciousness and being in equilibrium: good company for Beckett and Merleau-Ponty. JBecS (13:1) 2003, 34–62.

15408. Nixon, Mark.   'A brief glow in the dark': Samuel Beckett's presence in modern Irish poetry. YES (35) 2005, 43–57.

15409. Oppenheim, Lois (ed.).   Palgrave advances in Samuel Beckett studies. Basingstoke; New York: Palgrave Macmillan, 2004. pp. xii, 262. (Palgrave advances.) Rev. by Patrick Johnstone in TexP (19:2) 2005, 402–7.

15410. Perloff, Marjorie.   'In love with hiding': Samuel Beckett's war. IowaR (35:1) 2005, 76–103.

15411. Popova, Yanna.   'Little is left to tell': Beckett's theater of mind, *Ohio Impromptu*, and the new cognitive turn in analyzing drama. Style (38:4) 2004, 452–67.

15412. Powell, Kersti Tarien.   'Not a son but a survivor': Beckett … Joyce … Banville. YES (35) 2005, 199–211.

15413. Reid, James H.   Proust, Beckett, and narration. (Bibl. 2004, 15684.) Rev. by Chris Ackerley in JBecS (13:1) 2003, 142–50.

15414. Restivo, Giuseppina.   Directing Beckett's *Endgame* in Italy: cultural mediations and reinventions. JBecS (13:1) 2003, 98–111.

15415. Riquelme, John Paul.   Kenner, Beckett, 'irrational' 'man', and the obligation to express. *See* **14985**.

15416. Wang, Shanshan.   On waiting in *Waiting for Godot*. FLS (114) 2005, 88–92. (In Chinese.)

15417. Weller, Shane.   A taste for the negative: Beckett and nihilism. Oxford: Legenda, 2005. pp. xii, 212.

15418. Willmott, Glenn.   Sheila Watson, aboriginal discourse, and cosmopolitan Modernism. *In* (pp. 101–16) **12739**.

15419. Wilson, Susan.   Metaphysical fabrication and its *Catastrophe*. JBecS (13:1) 2003, 12–33.

15420. Worth, Katharine.   Ambiguous strength: women alone in Beckett's *Human Wishes*. *In* (pp. 304–8) **3756**.

15421. Wynands, Sandra.   Visuality and incongruity in Samuel Beckett's *Catastrophe*. ReLit (37:3) 2005, 81–102.

15422. Yeoh, Gilbert.   Beckett's persistent humanism: ethics and epistemology in *Molloy*. AUMLA (103) 2005, 109–35.

Sybille Bedford

15423. Bedford, Sybille.   Quicksands: a memoir. New York: Counterpoint, 2005. pp. 370. Rev. by Rosemary Hill in LRB (27:16) 2005, 13; by Caroline Moorehead in TLS, 19 & 26 Aug. 2005, 29.

15424. HILL, ROSEMARY.　Patrician poverty. LRB (27:16) 2005, 13 (review-article). (Memoirs.)

15425. LEWIS, TESS.　Truth and consequences: the writings of Sybille Bedford. HR (56:3) 2003, 496–506.

15426. MOOREHEAD, CAROLINE.　The shimmer of memory. TLS, 19 & 26 Aug. 2005, 29 (review-article).

Sir Max Beerbohm

15427. HALL, N. JOHN.　Max Beerbohm: a kind of a life. (Bibl. 2004, 15700.) Rev. by Alexandra Mullen in HR (56:2) 2003, 391–9.

15428. MULLEN, ALEXANDRA.　Max Beerbohm: spectator sport. HR (56:2) 2003, 391–9 (review-article).

15429. ROWLAND, PETER.　Waugh on the Wilde side. See **20016**.

Mark Behr

15430. GUARDUCCI, MARIA PAOLA.　The age of deception: childhood in South African contemporary literature. *In* (pp. 182–92) **3690**.

S. N. Behrman

15431. DUGAN, LAWRENCE.　Holden and the Lunts. See **19294**.

David Belasco

15432. POOLE, RALPH J.　Indecent ingénues: David Belasco's and Mae West's delegitimization and refashioning of American melodrama. Amst (48:4) 2003, 513–36.

Esther G. Belin

15433. BERGLUND, JEFF.　'Planting the seeds of revolution': an interview with poet Esther Belin (Diné). SAIL (17:1) 2005, 62–72.

Betty Louise Bell (b.1949)

15434. KROUSE, SUSAN APPLEGATE.　Transforming images: the scholarship of American Indian women. *In* (pp. 47–59) **2457**.

Marvin Bell

15435. RUBIN, STAN SANVEL.　'The truth of the darkness': a conversation with Marvin Bell. AtlR (11:2) 2005, 94–100.

Saul Bellow

15436. ASSADI, JAMAL.　From possession to exorcism: acting and interpretation in Bellow's *Henderson the Rain King.* SBJ (20:1) 2004, 33–46.

15437. BIRKERTS, SVEN.　*Humboldt's Gift.* VQR (81:3) 2005, 148–60.

15438. CHAVKIN, ALLAN; CHAVKIN, NANCY FEYL.　Skepticism and the depth of life in Saul Bellow's *The Old System.* SBJ (19:1) 2003, 23–9.

15439. CODDE, PHILIPPE.　'[H]ere on strange contingencies': *The Adventures of Augie March* and prewar French existentialism. SBJ (20:1) 2004, 20–32.

15440. CRONIN, GLORIA L.; HALL, BLAINE.　Selected annotated critical bibliography 1999. SBJ (19:1) 2003, 108–16.

15441. —— ——　Selected annotated critical bibliography 2000. SBJ (19:2) 2003, 55–100.

15442. FREEZE, ERIC.　Reading *Ravelstein.* SBJ (19:2) 2003, 19–30.

15443. Freidrich, Marianne M.   'Something to remember me by': from early fragments to finished story. SBJ (19:1) 2003, 44–51.

15444. Griffith, Michael.   Jostling with the actual: my summer with Saul Bellow. SoR (41:4) 2005, 726–36.

15445. Halio, Jay.   Unraveling Bellow through *Ravelstein*. SBJ (19:2) 2003, 31–5.

15446. Liu, Wensong.   Bellow's representation of economic power relations in marriage. SBJ (20:1) 2004, 72–86.

15447. —— Power relations between intellectual couples in three Saul Bellow novels. SBJ (19:1) 2003, 52–77.

15448. Macilwee, Michael.   *Henderson the Rain King*: translations between Conrad and Hemingway. SBJ (20:1) 2004, 47–71.

15449. —— Saul Bellow and Norman Mailer. SBJ (19:1) 2003, 3–22.

15450. Muhlestein, Dan.   Presence, absence, and commodity fetish in *Ravelstein*. SBJ (20:1) 2004, 5–19.

15451. Quayum, M. A.   Saul Bellow and American Transcendentalism. New York; Frankfurt: Lang, 2004. pp. x, 288. (Twentieth-century American Jewish writers.)

15452. Radulescu, Domnica.   Amazons, wretches, and vampirettes: essentialism and beyond in the representation of East European women. *In* (pp. 23–59) **12697**.

15453. Salzberg, Joel.   The importance of being Saul Bellow: narcissistic narrative and the parodic impulse in *Ravelstein*. SBJ (19:2) 2003, 36–52.

15454. Sánchez Canales, Gustavo.   Life, death and Aristophanes' concept of Eros in Saul Bellow's *Ravelstein*. SBJ (19:2) 2003, 8–18.

15455. Scotchie, Joe.   Saul Bellow: an appreciation. SoCR (38:1) 2005, 60–1.

15456. Shere, Jeremy.   '[G]loving the knuckles': reading Bellow's *The Adventures of Augie March* as a response to the question of postwar, American Jewish culture. SBJ (20:1) 2004, 87–101.

15457. Siegel, Ben.   Saul Bellow as novelist, biographer, and subject. SBJ (19:2) 2003, 3–7.

15458. Steed, J. P.   'Can death be funny?': humor, the Holocaust, and Bellow's *The Bellarosa Connection*. SBJ (19:1) 2003, 30–44.

15459. Wood, James.   The Jewish King James Version; or, Saul Bellow: not exactly English but biblically English. TLS, 5 Aug. 2005, 12–13.

Stephen Vincent Benét

15460. Drabeck, Bernard A.   *Scratch* revisited. *See* **18012**.

15461. Milgram, Shoshana.   *Anthem* in the context of related literary works: 'We are not like our brothers.' *In* (pp. 119–70) **19013**.

David Benioff

15462. Scarpino, Cinzia.   After *The 25th Hour*: perspectives on David Benioff's novel. RSA (15/16) 2004/05, 115–38.

Alan Bennett

15463. BENNETT, ALAN. Untold stories. London; Boston, MA: Faber & Faber, 2005. pp. xiii, 658, (plates) 24.

15464. CAMPOS, LILIANE. Rewriting the plot: re-creations in contemporary British comedy. EA (58:3) 2005, 336–48.

15465. MEDDEMMEN, JOHN. L'estro comico della lingua inglese in italiano: a proposito di Alan Bennett. SCrit (18:1) 2003, 91–122.

Arnold Bennett

15466. HARVEY, A. D. On the literary front. See **15606**.

Gwendolyn Bennett

15467. WHALAN, MARK. 'The only real white democracy' and the language of liberation: the Great War, France, and African American culture in the 1920s. See **16163**.

E. F. (Edward Frederic) Benson (1867–1940)

15468. FREEMAN, NICHOLAS. 'Nothing of the wild wood'? Pan, paganism and spiritual confusion in E. F. Benson's *The Man Who Went Too Far*. LitTheol (19:1) 2005, 22–33.

Eric Bentley (b.1916)

15469. PETERS, SALLY. Eric Bentley on Bernard Shaw: an interview. See **19409**.

John Berendt (b.1939)

15470. JUNCKER, CLARA. Simulacrum Savannah: midnight in the garden of good and evil. LitFQ (33:3) 2005, 182–90.

Lucia Berlin (1936–2004)

15471. ANON. (introd.). Love, Lucia: Lucia Berlin's letters to August Kleinzahler. LRB (27:15) 2005, 33–4.

James Berry

15472. LOGAN, MAWUENA KOSSI. The diasporic griot: James Berry and his fiction for the young. CLAQ (30:2) 2005, 179–93.

Wendell Berry

15473. BERRY, WENDELL. My conversation with Gurney Norman. See **18514**.

15474. BRYSON, J. SCOTT. The west side of any mountain: place, space, and ecopoetry. See **18204**.

15475. DEWEESE-BOYD, IAN; DEWEESE-BOYD, MARGARET. 'Flying the flag of Rough Branch': rethinking post-September 11 patriotism through the writings of Wendell Berry. AppalJ (32:2) 2005, 214–32.

15476. SMITH, KIMBERLY K. Wendell Berry and the Agrarian tradition: a common grace. Lawrence: Kansas UP, 2003. pp. x, 270. (American political thought.) Rev. by John E. Miller in JAStud (38:3) 2004, 532–3.

John Berryman

15477. COLEMAN, PHILIP. 'The politics of praise': John Berryman's engagement with W. B. Yeats. EtIr (28:2) 2003, 11–27.

15478. SMITH, ERNEST. Colossal departures: figuring the lost father in Berryman's and Plath's poetry. CanRCL (30:1) 2003, 145–59.

Ursula Bethell

15479. WHITEFORD, PETER (ed.). Vibrant with words: the letters of Ursula Bethell. Wellington: Victoria UP, 2005. pp. xxviii, 370.

Sir John Betjeman

15480. DARLEY, GILLIAN. The undesired result. LRB (27:7) 2005, 27–9 (review-article). (Biography of Betjeman.)

15481. HILLIER, BEVIS. Betjeman: the bonus of laughter. (Bibl. 2004, 15744.) Rev. by Gillian Darley in LRB (27:7) 2005, 27–9; by William H. Pritchard in HR (58:3) 2005, 481–8.

15482. PRITCHARD, WILLIAM H. Betjeman's way. HR (58:3) 2005, 481–8 (review-article).

Doris Betts

15483. EADS, MARTHA GREENE. Sex, money, and food as spiritual signposts in Doris Betts's *Sharp Teeth of Love*. ChrisL (54:1) 2004, 31–49.

Laurence Binyon

15484. JANOWITZ, ANNE. The artifactual sublime: making London poetry. *In* (pp. 246–60) **9217.**

Carmel Bird (b.1940)

15485. RODRÍGUEZ SALAS, GERARDO. The tide that riffles back: spiral femininity in Carmen Bird's *Cape Grimm*. Antipodes (19:1) 2005, 85–90.

Sandra Birdsell

15486. FILIPCZAK, DOROTA. Not wanted in the canon: Canadian literature in the wilderness. *In* (pp. 55–64) **3756.**

Elizabeth Bishop

15487. BROGAN, JACQUELINE VAUGHT. 'Inessential houses' in Stevens and Bishop. *See* **19648.**

15488. CHIASSON, DAN. One kind of everything. Agni (62) 2005, 227–36.

15489. COSTELLO, BONNIE. A response to Frank J. Kearful. Connotations (13:1/2) 2003/04, 89–92. (*Responds to* bibl. 2004, 15759.)

15490. ELLIS, JONATHAN. 'A curious cat': Elizabeth Bishop and the Spanish Civil War. JML (27:1/2) 2003, 137–48.

15491. FAN, KIT. Imagined places: Robinson Crusoe and Elizabeth Bishop. *See* **8513.**

15492. GRAF, ANASTASIA. Representing the Other: a conversation among Mikhail Bakhtin, Elizabeth Bishop, and Wisława Szymborska. CL (57:1) 2005, 84–99.

15493. MARKS, HERBERT. Elizabeth Bishop's art of memory. LitIm (7:2) 2005, 197–223.

15494. MATERER, TIMOTHY. Mirrored lives: Elizabeth Bishop and James Merrill. TCL (51:2) 2005, 179–209.

15495. Nesme, Axel. The lyrical object in Elizabeth Bishop's poetry. EREA (2:2) 2004, 53–9.

15496. Rieke, Alison. 'Plunder' or 'accessibility to experience': consumer culture and Marianne Moore's Modernist self-fashioning. *See* **18327.**

15497. Rognoni, Francesco. In un mondo di libri crollato: attorno a *Visits to St Elizabeths* di Elizabeth Bishop. NCorr (131) 2003, 85–91.

15498. Rosenbaum, Susan. Elizabeth Bishop and the miniature museum. JML (28:2) 2005, 61–99.

15499. Rotella, Guy. Castings: monuments and monumentality in poems by Elizabeth Bishop, Robert Lowell, James Merrill, Derek Walcott, and Seamus Heaney. (Bibl. 2004, 15765.) Rev. by Jeff Westover in TCL (51:2) 2005, 259–62.

15500. Schweizer, Harold. With sabbath eyes: the particular and the claims of history in Elizabeth Bishop's *Poem*. JML (28:2) 2005, 49–60.

15501. Sircy, Jonathan. Bishop's *One Art*. Exp (63:4) 2005, 241–4.

15502. Spivack, Kathleen. Conceal/reveal: passion and restraint in the work of Elizabeth Bishop; or, Why we care about Elizabeth Bishop's poetry. MassR (46:3) 2005, 496–510.

15503. Upton, Lee. Defensive measures: the poetry of Niedecker, Bishop, Glück, and Carson. Lewisburg, PA: Bucknell UP, 2005. pp. 144.

15504. Walker, Cheryl. God and Elizabeth Bishop: meditations on religion and poetry. Basingstoke; New York: Palgrave Macmillan, 2005. pp. xi, 157.

John Peale Bishop

15505. Bratcher, James T. Tennyson's 'hendecasyllabics', Catullus' '*basationes*', and a parody of Ezra Pound. *See* **12134.**

Algernon Blackwood

15506. Thompson, Terry W. Blackwood's *The Listener*. Exp (64:1) 2005, 44–8.

Clark Blaise

15507. Blaise, Clark. The justice-dealing machine. *In* (pp. 221–5) **14204.**

15508. Porter, Roger J. Finding the father: autobiography as bureau of missing persons. *See* **16757.**

William J. (William James) Blake (1894–1968)

15509. Harris, Margaret (ed.). Dearest Munx: the letters of Christina Stead and William J. Blake. *See* **19570.**

William Peter Blatty

15510. Arnzen, Michael. 'There is only one': the restoration of the repressed in *The Exorcist*: the version you've never seen. *In* (pp. 99–116) **13250.**

Alan Bleasdale

15511. John, Juliet. Fagin, the Holocaust and mass culture; or, *Oliver Twist* on screen. *See* **10703.**

Lawrence Block

15512. CHAPMAN, JULIE M. The burglar who sought, evaluated, and used information: applying the information literacy standards to Lawrence Block's Bernie Rhodenbarr mysteries. Clues (24:1) 2005, 55–63.

Libbie Block

15513. DEUTELBAUM, MARSHALL. Leonora's place: the spatial logic of *Caught*. *See* **13505**.

Edmund Blunden

15514. DUCKWORTH, ALISTAIR M. Two borrowings in Pat Barker's *Regeneration*. *See* **15302**.

15515. FLETCHER, CHRISTOPHER. Edmund Blunden's *Young Fieldmouse*: a source for Philip Larkin's *The Mower*? *See* **17574**.

Robert Bly

15516. GENOWAYS, TED (introd.). Robert Bly and James Wright: a correspondence. VQR (81:1) 2005, 104–31.

Louise Bogan

15517. KINZIE, MARY. Louise Bogan in her prose. APR (34:2) 2005, 15–23.

15518. —— (ed.). A poet's prose: selected writings of Louise Bogan; with the uncollected poems. Athens: Swallow Press/Ohio UP, 2005. pp. xxxv, 394. Rev. by Danielle Chapman in Poetry (186:5) 2005, 450–2.

Eavan Boland

15519. CLUTTERBUCK, CATRIONA. Eavan Boland and the politics of authority in Irish poetry. YES (35) 2005, 72–90.

15520. KOLOSOV, JACQUELINE. 'Is this the promised end?': witness in *King Lear* and apocalyptic poetry of the twentieth century. *See* **6473**.

15521. ZAMORANO LLENA, CARMEN. The salvage from postmodernism: nomadic subjectivity in contemporary women's poetry in the British Isles. *See* **15083**.

Dermot Bolger

15522. KURDI, MÁRIA. Interview with Dermot Bolger. EtIr (28:1) 2003, 7–22.

Ruskin Bond

15523. BANDYOPADHYAY, DEBASHIS. The past unearthed: new reading of Ruskin Bond's supernatural tales. CLAQ (30:1) 2005, 53–71.

Paul Bonin-Rodriguez

15524. BONIN-RODRIGUEZ, PAUL. Introduction: artist's statement. TPQ (24:2) 2004, 182–4.

15525. COREY, FREDERICK C. A letter to Paul. TPQ (24:2) 2004, 185–90.

15526. DILLARD, SCOTT. Acceptance and resistance in *Memory's Caretaker*. TPQ (24:2) 2004, 191–5.

15527. DOLAN, JILL. Redemption, doubt, benediction. TPQ (24:2) 2004, 196–200.

15528. GENTILE, JOHN S. Telling the untold tales: *Memory's Caretaker*. TPQ (24:2) 2004, 201–4.

15529. MENCHACA, DENISE A.   Memory's vigil: witnessing departures in Paul Bonin-Rodriguez's *Memory's Caretaker*. TPQ (24:2) 2004, 205–8.

Arna Bontemps
15530. THOMPSON, MARK CHRISTIAN.   Voodoo Fascism: Fascist ideology in Arna Bontemps's *Drums at Dusk*. MELUS (30:3) 2005, 155–77.

Marianne Boruch
15531. BORUCH, MARIANNE.   In the blue pharmacy: essays on poetry and other transformations. *See* **14369**.

Herman Charles Bosman
15532. GRAY, STEPHEN.   Life sentence: a biography of Herman Charles Bosman. Cape Town: Human & Rousseau, 2005. pp. 382, (plates) 16.

Robert Boswell (b.1953)
15533. BOSWELL, ROBERT.   Behind the story. *In* (pp. 464–70) **14294**.

Elizabeth Bowen
15534. CORCORAN, NEIL.   Elizabeth Bowen: the enforced return. (Bibl. 2004, 15809.) Rev. by Anthony Radice in ContRev (287:1675) 2005, 115–16; by Shannon Wells-Lassagne in EREA (3:1) 2005; by Sarah Savitt in CamQ (34:2) 2005, 188–92.

15535. INGELBIEN, RAPHAËL.   Gothic genealogies: *Dracula*, *Bowen's Court*, and Anglo-Irish psychology. *See* **12094**.

15536. MCNAMEE, BRENDAN.   Some post-feminist thoughts on Elizabeth Bowen's *The Last September*. NCL (35:2) 2005, 8–9.

15537. RAU, PETRA.   The common frontier: fictions of alterity in Elizabeth Bowen's *The Heat of the Day* and Graham Greene's *The Ministry of Fear*. LitH (14:1) 2005, 31–55.

15538. SUMMERS-BREMNER, ELUNED.   Heart(h) and home: Elizabeth Bowen's Irishness. EtIr (29:2) 2004, 135–50.

15539. WILLS, CLAIR.   The aesthetics of Irish neutrality during the Second World War. *See* **18032**.

B. M. Bower (1874–1940)
15540. LAMONT, VICTORIA.   Cattle branding and the traffic in women in early twentieth-century westerns by women. *See* **17959**.

George Bowering
15541. GRACE, SHERRILL.   Calling out the McLean boys: George Bowering's *Shoot* and the autobiography of British Columbia history. CanL (184) 2005, 11–25.

Edgar Bowers
15542. HECKER, WILLIAM.   Finding Wilfred Owen's forwarding address: moving beyond the World War One paradigm. *See* **18708**.

Jane Bowles
15543. TIPPINS, SHERILL.   February House. *See* **15245**.

Paul Bowles

15544. CARR, VIRGINIA SPENCER. Paul Bowles: a life. New York: Scribner, 2004. pp. xv, 409. Rev. by Jim Nawrocki in GLRW (12:2) 2004, 43.

15545. PAPAYANIS, MARILYN ADLER. Writing in the margins: the ethics of expatriation from Lawrence to Ondaatje. *See* 17621.

15546. TIPPINS, SHERILL. February House. *See* 15245.

Louise Morey Bowman

15547. CAMPBELL, WANDA. Moonlight and morning: women's early contributions to Canadian Modernism. *In* (pp. 79–99) 12739.

Martin Boyd

15548. NIALL, BRENDA. Martin Boyd: a life. (Bibl. 1988, 6977.) Carlton South, Vic.: Melbourne UP, 2004. pp. x, 268, (plates) 24. (New ed.: first ed. 1988.) Rev. by Gerard Windsor in TLS, 29 Oct. 2004, 25.

T. Coraghessan Boyle

15549. BOYLE, T. C. The writing life. BkW, 26 June 2005, 10.

15550. BUISSON, FRANÇOISE. Gulliver sauvé des eaux: dilution et résurrection du voyage dans *Water Music* de T. Coraghessan Boyle. EREA (3:1) 2005, 81–6.

15551. CLERICUZIO, ALESSANDRO. Messico–Stati Uniti, una frontiera di tortillas: T. C. Boyle, John Sayles, Sam Shepard. *In* (pp. 295–304) 12883.

15552. ROORDA, RANDALL. Wonderful world: comic frames, dissolution of scene, the temper of ecocriticism. Reader (53) 2005, 76–110.

Malcolm Bradbury

15553. STIERSTORFER, KLAUS. 'Postmortemism': Malcolm Bradbury's legacy in *To the Hermitage*. EA (58:2) 2005, 154–65.

Ray Bradbury

15554. ELLER, JONATHAN R.; TOUPONCE, WILLIAM F. Ray Bradbury: the life of fiction. (Bibl. 2004, 15828.) Rev. by David Moyle in Extrapolation (46:2) 2005, 274–80.

15555. HARLOW, MORGAN. Martian legacy: Ray Bradbury's *The Martian Chronicles*. WLA (17:1/2) 2005, 311–14.

15556. MORGAN, SPEER; SOWIENSKI, RICHARD; SOMERVILLE, KRISTINE (introds). Ray Bradbury's letters to Rupert Hart-Davis. MR (27:3) 2004, 119–63.

15557. POLLIN, BURTON. Poe and Ray Bradbury: a persistent influence and interest. *See* 11820.

15558. WELLER, SAM. The Bradbury chronicles: the life of Ray Bradbury. New York: Morrow, 2005. pp. 384.

David Bradley

15559. ENTZMINGER, BETINA. Snow job: the whitening of history in William Faulkner's *Absalom! Absalom!* and David Bradley's *The Chaneysville Incident*. *See* 16404.

Dionne Brand

15560. FRASER, KAYA. Language to light on: Dionne Brand and the rebellious word. StudCanL (30:1) 2005, 291–308.

15561. MEZEI, KATHY. Domestic space and the idea of home in auto/biographical practices. *In* (pp. 81–95) **12750**.

15562. QUIGLEY, ELLEN. Picking the deadlock of legitimacy: Dionne Brand's 'noise like the world cracking'. CanL (186) 2005, 48–67.

Edward Kamau Brathwaite

15563. WILLIAMS, EMILY ALLEN (ed.). The critical response to Kamau Brathwaite. Westport, CT; London: Praeger, 2004. pp. xi, 326. (Critical responses in arts and letters, 41.)

Maeve Brennan

15564. BOURKE, ANGELA. Maeve Brennan: homesick at *The New Yorker*. (Bibl. 2004, 15838.) Rev. by Audrey S. Eyler in ILS (24:2) 2005, 3–4.

Kenneth Brewer (b.1941)

15565. WATANABE, SANDY. An authentic voice: a conversation with Ken Brewer. WebS (22:1) 2004, 2–18.

Breyten Breytenbach

15566. COULLIE, JUDITH LÜTGE; JACOBS, J. U. (eds). A.k.a. Breyten Breytenbach: critical approaches to his writings and paintings. Amsterdam; Atlanta, GA: Rodopi, 2004. pp. xxii, 336. (Cross/cultures: readings in the postcolonial literatures in English, 75.) Rev. by Laura Wright in AfSR (48:2) 2005, 177–9.

Robert Bridges

15567. VICKERY, JOHN B. Bridges and Housman as elegists: the modern threshold. ELT (48:4) 2005, 404–19.

André Brink

15568. JOSEPH-VILAIN, MÉLANIE. Le théâtre dans *Looking on Darkness* d'André Brink: le roman d'un acteur. EREA (2:1) 2003, 108–14.

Vera Brittain

15569. DAS, SANTANU. 'The impotence of sympathy': touch and trauma in the memoirs of First World War nurses. *See* **14584**.

15570. PETERSON, ANDREA. The female subject and the First World War: the case of Vera M. Brittain, VAD London / 268, BRCS. *In* (pp. 104–28) **14645**.

Joseph Brodsky (b.1940)

15571. ANON. Selected recent acquisitions briefly noted. *See* **345**.

15572. REYNOLDS, ANDREW. Returning the ticket: Joseph Brodsky's *August* and the end of the Petersburg text? SlavR (64:2) 2005, 307–32.

15573. SHTERN, LUDMILA. Brodsky: a personal memoir. Fort Worth, TX: Baskerville, 2004. pp. 386.

15574. SMITH, G. S. Joseph Brodsky: summing up. LitIm (7:3) 2005, 399–410.

15575. WEISSBORT, DANIEL. From Russian with love: Joseph Brodsky in English: pages from a journal, 1996–97. London: Anvil Press Poetry, 2004. pp. 253. (Poetica, 35.) Rev. by Ekaterina Sukhanova in AmBR (26:6) 2005, 14.

Louis Bromfield

15576. WATERMAN, JANE.   Louis Bromfield and the idea of the middle. MidAmerica (30) 2003, 73–84.

William Bronk

15577. VON HALLBERG, ROBERT.   Lyric thinking. TriQ (120) 2005, 171–93.

Rupert Brooke

15578. BIDNEY, MARTIN.   Peace and pathos in the sea epiphanies of Rupert Brooke: contours of narcissistic desire. ELT (48:3) 2005, 324–38.

15579. HOLMES, JOHN.   Dante Gabriel Rossetti and the late Victorian sonnet sequence: sexuality, belief and the self. *See* **11870**.

Christine Brooke-Rose

15580. RAO, ELEONORA.   Masks of the self: autobiographical signatures in the feminine. *In* (pp. 189–99) **12577**.

Bertram Brooker (1888–1955)

15581. BETTS, GREGORY.   A philosophy of the verb: Bertram Brooker's early Canadian mystical–Modernist verse. StudCanL (30:1) 2005, 135–59.

Anita Brookner

15582. WILLIAMS-WANQUET, EILEEN.   Art and life in the novels of Anita Brookner: reading for life, subversive re-writing to live. (Bibl. 2004, 15857.) Rev. by Alain Blayac in EtBr (28) 2005, 149–50.

Gwendolyn Brooks

15583. CUMMINGS, ALLISON.   Public subjects: race and the critical reception of Gwendolyn Brooks, Erica Hunt, and Harryette Mullen. Frontiers (26:2) 2005, 3–36.

15584. DEBO, ANNETTE.   Reflecting violence in the warpland: Gwendolyn Brooks's *Riot*. AAR (39:1/2) 2005, 143–52.

15585. EDWARDS, PAUL.   Drift: performing the relics of intention. *See* **5921**.

15586. FRANCINI, ANTONELLA.   Sonnet *vs* sonnet: the fourteen lines in African American poetry. *See* **17999**.

15587. FRAZIER, VALERIE.   Domestic epic warfare in *Maud Martha*. AAR (39:1/2) 2005, 133–41.

Allan Brown (b.1934)

15588. ANON.   An interview with Allan Brown. PJCL (44) 2005, 43–4.

Carlyle Brown

15589. LEWIS, BARBARA.   Caught on rails: the traveling Black performer as prey. ThSym (13) 2005, 68–84.

George Mackay Brown (b.1921)

15590. MURRAY, ROWENA; MURRAY, BRIAN. Interrogation of silence: the writings of George Mackay Brown. London: Murray, 2004. pp. xi, 306. Rev. by Berthold Schoene in ScSR (6:1) 2005, 131–3.

15591. SCHMID, SABINE. 'Keeping the sources pure': the making of George Mackay Brown. New York; Frankfurt: Lang, 2003. pp. 310. (European connections, 7.)

Larry Brown

15592. HAWKINS, GARY. Just one more: Larry Brown (1951–2004). OxAm (49) 2005, 138–43.

Rebecca Brown (b.1956)

15593. BLAIR, JENNIFER. The glove of shame and the touch of Rebecca Brown's *Gifts of the Body*. GLQ (11:4) 2005, 521–45.

Sterling A. Brown

15594. ANTONUCCI, MICHAEL A. 'Crash down home Blues': Sterling D. Plumpp, Sterling A. Brown and Blues poetics. *See* **18841.**

Joseph Bruchac (b.1942)

15595. BRUCHAC, JOSEPH. At the end of Ridge Road. Minneapolis, MN: Milkweed, 2005. pp. 143. (Credo.)

Louise Stevens Bryant (b.1885)

15596. ROAZEN, PAUL. Eugene O'Neill and Louise Bryant: new documents. *See* **18650.**

Winifred Bryher
(Annie Winifred Ellerman, 'Bryher') (b.1894)

15597. CAMBONI, MARINA. Bryher fra barbarie e modernità. *In* (pp. 1–26) **12589.**

15598. MCCABE, SUSAN (introd.). Visa for Avalon: a novel. Ashfield, MA: Paris Press, 2004. pp. xxii, 157. Rev. by Ariela Freedman in Mod/Mod (12:3) 2005, 523–5.

15599. WILLIS, PATRICIA C. A Modernist epithalamium: Marianne Moore's *Marriage. See* **18331.**

John Buchan (1875–1940)

15600. BARLOW, GILLIAN F. Of spats and moccasins: reflections on archiving and curating the John Buchan papers in Canada. JBJ (32) 2005, 31–4.

15601. CRAIK, ROGER. Two influences on L. P. Hartley's *The Go-Between. See* **16915.**

15602. GALBRAITH, J. WILLIAM. The Canadian impact of John Buchan's appointment as Governor-General: catalyst to sovereignty. JBJ (32) 2005, 53–9.

15603. GORMAN, DANIEL. Race and the late Victorian imperial world-view: *A Lodge in the Wilderness* and *Prester John*. JBJ (32) 2005, 41–8.

15604. GUNARATNE, MAHASARA. John Buchan: his writing influenced our formative years. JBJ (32) 2005, 21–3.

15605. GUNN, DIARMID. Walter Scott to John Buchan: the handing over of a baton? JBJ (32) 2005, 5–19.

15606. HARVEY, A. D. On the literary front. TLS, 14 Jan. 2005, 12–13.

15607. HASLETT, MICHAEL. Is Francis Galliard a French Canadian version of the young John Buchan? JBJ (32) 2005, 49–52.

15608. HENSHAW, PETER. John Buchan and the invention of postcolonial literature. JBJ (32) 2005, 35–40.

15609. LAROCQUE-POIRIER, JOANNE. John Buchan's legacy: the Governor-General's Literary Awards. JBJ (32) 2005, 60–2.

Pearl S. Buck

15610. WACKER, GRANT. Pearl S. Buck and the waning of the missionary impulse. CHist (72:4) 2003, 852–74.

Ernest Buckler

15611. PURDHAM, MEDRIE. The hunger to be seen: *The Mountain and the Valley*'s Modernist new eyes. In (pp. 305–30) **12739**.

Christopher Buckley

15612. GONZÁLEZ, RAY. The psyche at risk: on the work of Larry Lewis: an interview with editor and poet Christopher Buckley. See **17810**.

Vincent Buckley

15613. ROWE, NOEL. How to gossip with angels: Australian poetry after the gods. Antipodes (19:2) 2005, 177–83.

Sally Buckner (b.1931)

15614. BLACKBURN, CHARLES, JR (ed.). 2004 North Carolina Writers Conference honors Sally Buckner. PemM (37) 2005, 264–76.

Charles Bukowski

15615. ABENI, DAMIANO (ed. and trans.). Sotto un sole di sigarette e cetrioli. Rome: Minimum Fax, 2005. pp. 225. (Sotterranei, 82.)

15616. PLEASANTS, BEN. Visceral Bukowski: inside the sniper landscapes of L.A. writers. Northville, MI: Sun Dog Press, 2004. pp. 231.

Carlos Bulosan

15617. PONCE, MARTIN JOSEPH. On becoming socially articulate: transnational Bulosan. JAAS (8:1) 2005, 49–80.

Edward Bunker (b.1933)

15618. CUNNELL, HOWARD. Condemned men: compulsive masculinity and the convict ethic in the writing of Edward Bunker. In (pp. 95–110) **12821**.

Anthony Burgess

15619. BISWELL, ANDREW. The real life of Anthony Burgess. London: Picador, 2005. pp. 434, (plates) 16. Rev. by Hal Jensen in TLS, 18 Nov. 2005, 3–4.

15620. JANÁK, PETR. Fungování vícejazyčnosti v *Mechanickém pomeranč*. (The use of multilingualism in *A Clockwork Orange*.) JazA (42:1/2) 2005, 8–25.

15621. WATERMAN, DAVID. Le miroir de la societé: la violence institutionelle chez Anthony Burgess, Doris Lessing et Pat Barker. See **15315**.

Thomas Burke (1887–1945)

15622. WITCHARD, ANNE. Thomas Burke, the 'laureate of Limehouse': a new biographical outline. ELT (48:2) 2005, 164–87.

John Burnside

15623. BREWSTER, SCOTT. Borderline experience: madness, mimicry and Scottish gothic. *See* **11270**.

15624. DÓSA, ATTILA. Poets and other animals: an interview with John Burnside. ScSR (4:1) 2003, 9–23.

Edgar Rice Burroughs

15625. COHEN, MATT (ed.). Brother men: the correspondence of Edgar Rice Burroughs and Herbert T. Weston. Durham, NC; London: Duke UP, 2005. pp. x, 310.

15626. LUPOFF, RICHARD A. Master of adventure: the worlds of Edgar Rice Burroughs. Foreword by Michael Moorcock. Preface by Henry Hardy Heins. With an essay by Phillip R. Burger. (Bibl. 1965, 8060.) Lincoln; London: Nebraska UP, 2005. pp. xl, 307. (Bison frontiers of imagination.) (Second ed.: first ed. 1965.) (Orig. pub. as *Edgar Rice Burroughs, Master of Adventure*.) Rev. by Jon Barnes in TLS, 9 Sept. 2005, 27.

William Burroughs

15627. GRIFFITHS, ERIC. Junk junkie: William Burroughs reappraised. TLS, 22 July 2005, 11–13.

15628. GRIMSTAD, PAUL C. Algorithm – genre – *linguisterie*: 'creative distortion' in *Count Zero* and *Nova Express*. *See* **11811**.

15629. HARRIS, OLIVER. William Burroughs and the secret of fascination. (Bibl. 2004, 15899.) Rev. by Regina Weinreich in AmBR (25:3) 2004, 25; by Douglas Haynes in TexP (19:1) 2005, 195–201.

15630. VRBANČIĆ, MARIO. Burroughs's phantasmic maps. NLH (36:2) 2005, 313–25.

Katharine Newlin Burt (b.1882)

15631. LAMONT, VICTORIA. Cattle branding and the traffic in women in early twentieth-century westerns by women. *See* **17959**.

Frederick Busch

15632. BUSCH, FREDERICK. Deaths. *In* (pp. 159–66) **14204**.

Sharon Butala

15633. KAYE, FRANCES W. The tantalizing possibility of living on the Plains. *In* (pp. 25–42) **12587**.

Jack Butler (b.1944)

15634. CROWDER, ASHBY BLAND. Butler's *Subplot*. Exp (63:3) 2005, 186–9.

Octavia Butler

15635. BALFOUR, LAWRIE. Vexed genealogy: Octavia Butler and political memories of slavery. *In* (pp. 171–90) **14121**.

15636. Escoda Agustí, Clara. The relationship between community and subjectivity in Octavia E. Butler's *Parable of the Sower.* Extrapolation (46:3) 2005, 351–9.

15637. Hampton, Gregory J. Migration and capital of the body: Octavia Butler's *Parable of the Sower.* CLAJ (49:1) 2005, 56–73.

15638. Thompson, Stacy. Tentative utopias. *See* **17677**.

15639. Walker, Alison Tara. Destabilizing order, challenging history: Octavia Butler, Deleuze and Guattari, and affective beginnings. Extrapolation (46:1) 2005, 103–19.

Robert Olen Butler

15640. Trussler, Michael. Everything must resonate: an interview with Robert Olen Butler. WasRCPSF (38:1) 2003, 241–50.

Mary Butts

15641. Rives, Rochelle. Problem space: Mary Butts, Modernism, and the etiquette of placement. Mod/Mod (12:4) 2005, 607–27.

A. S. Byatt

15642. Cambiaghi, Mara. 'Moving times – new words': the sixties on both sides of the Channel. *In* (pp. 296–312) **12868**.

15643. Campbell, Jane. A. S. Byatt and the heliotropic imagination. Waterloo, Ont.: Wilfrid Laurier UP, 2004. pp. x, 310. Rev. by Thelma Shinn Richard in MFS (51:3) 2005, 696–9.

15644. Cao, Li. *Possession*: historical truth and the pleasure of the text. FLS (116) 2005, 75–84. (In Chinese.)

15645. Fort, Camille. '*In the presence of absence*': la remémoration dans *The Conjugial Angel* d'A. S. Byatt. EtBr (29) 2005, 111–22.

15646. Martínez Alfaro, María Jesús. A tapestry of riddling links: universal contiguity in A. S. Byatt's *Arachne.* JSSE (45) 2005, 145–61.

15647. Martinière, Nathalie. Pseudo-citations: présence/absence de l'hypotexte dans *Possession* de A. S. Byatt. EREA (2:1) 2004, 100–7.

15648. Sorensen, Sue. A. S. Byatt and the life of the mind: a response to June Sturrock. Connotations (13:1/2) 2003/04, 180–90. (*Responds to* bibl. 2004, 15925.)

15649. Uhsadel, Katharina. Antonia Byatts *Quartet* in der Tradition des englischen Bildungsroman. Heidelberg: Winter, 2005. pp. 192. (Anglistische Forschungen, 357.)

Kathryn Stripling Byer

15650. Buckner, Sally. *Wake*: a triptych in words. PemM (37) 2005, 281–3.

15651. Chappell, Fred. Windy-voices: Kathryn Stripling Byer's poetry. Shen (55:1) 2005, 64–82.

15652. Harvley-Felder, Irene. Word choice. OurS (73:5) 2005, 46–53.

John Cage

15653. Armand, Louis. Solicitations: essays on criticism and culture. *See* **14689**.

15654. CESARE, T. NIKKI.   The fall of babble: an ontogenesic experiment on the fragmentation of language. PRes (9:1) 2004, 20–35.

15655. HOLLANDS, HOWARD.   Drawing a blank: picturing nothing on the page. *See* **14336**.

15656. THOMPSON, CHRIS.   Voicing Joyce: crossmess parzels from Cage to Beuys. *See* **17345**.

Abraham Cahan

15657. BLAIR, SARA.   Whose modernism is it? Abraham Cahan, fictions of Yiddish, and the contest of modernity. MFS (51:2) 2005, 258–84.

15658. HOFFMAN, WARREN.   The rise (and fall) of David Levinsky: performing Jewish American heterosexuality. MFS (51:2) 2005, 393–415.

15659. STEED, J. P.   Joke-making Jews, jokes making Jews: humor and identity in Abraham Cahan's *Yekl*. JSSE (43) 2004, 45–58.

James M. Cain

15660. PELIZZON, V. PENELOPE; WEST, NANCY M.   Multiple indemnity: *film noir*, James M. Cain, and adaptations of a tabloid case. *See* **13332**.

Eleanor Cameron

15661. ATTEBERY, BRIAN.   Eleanor Cameron: the theory and practice of fantasy. JFA (16:2) 2005, 96–109.

Alistair Campbell

15662. MacKENZIE, JOY.   'My way is to be with you': Meg & Alistair Te Ariki Campbell. *In* (pp. 186–209) **12916**.

15663. WATTIE, NELSON.   Alistair Te Ariki Campbell and the community of readers. PNZ (31) 2005, 82–90.

Maria Campbell

15664. SUZACK, CHERYL.   Law stories as life stories: Jeannette Lavell, Yvonne Bédard and *Halfbreed*. *In* (pp. 117–41) **12750**.

Meg Campbell (b.1937)

15665. MacKENZIE, JOY.   'My way is to be with you': Meg & Alistair Te Ariki Campbell. *In* (pp. 186–209) **12916**.

Roy Campbell

15666. PECHEY, GRAHAM.   'Pharaoh's sjambok': Roy Campbell and the lexicon of emigration. JPW (41:2) 2005, 200–11.

Wilfred Campbell

15667. CARTER, ADAM.   Anthropomorphism and trope in the national ode. *In* (pp. 117–44) **9191**.

Edmund Candler (1874–1926)

15668. BRODSKY, G. W. STEPHEN.   Prester John's workbook: Joseph Conrad, Edmund Candler, John Towson, and some imperial Others. *See* **15860**.

15669. CORKILL, RACHAEL A.   Conrad and Edmund Candler: a neglected correspondence. *See* **15868**.

15670. COWASJEE, SAROS (ed.).   A Raj collection. *See* **19571**.

15671. FURBANK, P. N.   Anglo-Indian dialogues: the Raj, the historical novel and misunderstandings between the races. *See* **19572.**

Dorothy Canfield (Dorothy Canfield Fisher)

15672. CUMMINS, JUNE.   Understood Betsy, understood nation: Dorothy Canfield Fisher and Willa Cather queer America. ChildLit (32) 2004, 15–40.

15673. PIEP, KARSTEN H.   War as feminist utopia in Dorothy Canfield Fisher's *Home Fires in France* and Gertrude Atherton's *The White Morning*. WS (34:2) 2005, 159–89.

Dorothy Cannell (b.1943)

15674. OVERMIER, JUDITH ANN.   'Muddling along': a reality check for information literacy. Clues (24:1) 2005, 35–43.

Moya Cannon

15675. CUSICK, CHRISTINE.   'Our language was tidal': Moya Cannon's poetics of place. NewHR (9:1) 2005, 59–76.

Truman Capote

15676. CLARKE, GERALD (ed.).   Too brief a treat: the letters of Truman Capote. (Bibl. 2004, 15945.) Rev. by Colm Tóibín in LRB (27:8) 2005, 8–10; by James O. Tate in Chronicles (29:3) 2005, 30–2; by Shelton Waldrep in GLQ (11:4) 2005, 637–40; by Gerald Weales in GaR (59:2) 2005, 395–402.

15677. HICKMAN, TRENTON.   'The last to see them alive': panopticism, the supervisory gaze, and catharsis in Capote's *In Cold Blood*. StudN (37:4) 2005, 464–76.

15678. PRICE, REYNOLDS (introd.).   The complete stories of Truman Capote. New York: Random House, 2004. pp. xv, 300. Rev. by James O. Tate in Chronicles (29:3) 2005, 30–2.

15679. RICCIARDI, CATERINA.   Tiffany: Fifth Avenue, Via del Babuino. *In* (pp. 181–293) **12883.**

15680. TATE, JAMES O.   Beautiful terror. Chronicles (29:3) 2005, 30–2 (review-article).

15681. TÓIBÍN, COLM.   In his pink negligée. LRB (27:8) 2005, 8–10 (review-article). (Editions of Capote.)

15682. TREDY, DENNIS.   Shadows of shadows: techniques of ambiguity in three film adaptations of *The Turn of the Screw*: J. Clayton's *The Innocents* (1961), D. Curtis's *The Turn of the Screw* (1974), and A. Aloy's *Presence of Mind* (1999). *See* **13616.**

15683. WEALES, GERALD.   'Mille tenderesse, T'. GaR (59:2) 2005, 395–402 (review-article).

Philip Caputo

15684. BURNS, ROBERT W.   'More frail and mortal': the wound of fear in Philip Caputo's *In the Forest of the Laughing Elephant*. WLA (17:1/2) 2005, 102–7.

Peter Carey

15685. INNES, LYN.   Resurrecting Ned Kelly. SSE (29) 2003, 69–78.

15686. MUKHERJEE, ANKHI. Missed encounters: repetition, rewriting, and contemporary returns to Charles Dickens's *Great Expectations*. *See* **10719**.

15687. RUBIK, MARGARETE. Provocative and unforgettable: Peter Carey's short fiction – a cognitive approach. EJES (9:2) 2005, 169–84.

15688. RYAN-FAZILLEAU, SUE. Bob's dreaming: playing with reader expectations in Peter Carey's *Oscar and Lucinda*. RMER (59:1) 2005.

15689. WEBBY, ELIZABETH. Books and covers: reflections on some recent Australian novels. *See* **131**.

A. A. (Aaron Albert) Carr (b.1963)

15690. RAINWATER, CATHERINE. Who may speak for the animals? Deep ecology in Linda Hogan's *Power* and A. A. Carr's *Eye Killers*. *In* (pp. 261–80) **14258**.

Caleb Carr (b.1955)

15691. LINK, ALEX. City limits: fixing New York in Caleb Carr's *The Alienist*. Clues (23:3) 2005, 31–41.

Emily Carr

15692. CREAN, SUSAN (ed.). Opposite contraries: the unknown journals of Emily Carr and other writings. (Bibl. 2004, 15956.) Rev. by Linda M. Morra in CanL (183) 2004, 114–15.

15693. STEWART, JANICE. Cultural appropriations and identificatory practices in Emily Carr's 'Indian stories'. Frontiers (26:2) 2005, 59–72.

Marina Carr

15694. LEENEY, CATHY; MCMULLAN, ANNA (eds). The theatre of Marina Carr: 'before rules was made'. (Bibl. 2004, 15960.) Rev. by Martine Pelletier in EtIr (29:1) 2004, 166–7; by Natalie Harrower in TheatreS (46:1) 2005, 149–53; by Jill Dolan in TRI (30:1) 2005, 98–9; by John P. Harrington in ILS (24:2) 2005, 21–2.

Hayden Carruth

15695. GRIFFIN, SHAUN T. From sorrow's well: on Hayden Carruth's resolute poetics. BRev (24:6) 2004, 27–8.

15696. MILOVANOVIČ, ČELICA. A Classicist reads some modern poetry. *See* **14458**.

Anne Carson (b.1950)

15697. HENRIKSEN, LINE. The verse novel as a hybrid genre: monstrous bodies in Anne Carson's *Autobiography of Red* and Les Murray's *Fredy Neptune*. BELL (ns 3) 2005, 35–47.

15698. UPTON, LEE. Defensive measures: the poetry of Niedecker, Bishop, Glück, and Carson. *See* **15503**.

Ciaran Carson

15699. GIBBONS, DAVID. Gained in the translation? *The Inferno of Dante Alighieri* by Ciaran Carson. Culture (17) 2003, 173–88.

15700. MCCARTHY, CONOR. Ciaran Carson's labyrinths. Eng (54:209) 2005, 99–116.

15701. TELL, CAROL.   Considering classroom communities: Ciaran Carson and Paul Muldoon. YES (35) 2005, 91–106.

Jo Carson (b.1946)

15702. TURPIN, ANITA J.   Family journeys in Jo Carson's *Daytrips*. *In* (pp. 231–8) **12822.**

Catherine Carswell

15703. NASH, ANDREW.   The publication of Catherine Carswell's novels. Bibliotheck (ns 1:1) 2004, 7–26.

Angela Carter

15704. BROOKE, PATRICIA.   Lyons and tigers and wolves – oh my! Revisionary fairy tales in the work of Angela Carter. CritS (16:1) 2004, 67–88.

15705. HARSE, KATIE.   'Sick of Count Dracula': Scott, Carter, Rice and the response to Stoker's authority. *See* **19348.**

15706. HORNER, AVRIL; ZLOSNIK, SUE.   Skin chairs and other domestic horrors: Barbara Comyns and the female gothic tradition. *See* **15851.**

15707. RUBINSON, GREGORY J.   The fiction of Rushdie, Barnes, Winterson, and Carter: breaking cultural and literary boundaries in the work of four postmodernists. *See* **19277.**

15708. SIMON, JULIA.   Rewriting the body: desire, gender and power in selected novels by Angela Carter. New York; Frankfurt: Lang, 2004. pp. xv, 280. (Neue Studien zur Anglistik und Amerikanistik, 90.)

Forrest Carter

15709. HASPEL, PAUL.   Studies in outlawry: the strange career of Josey Wales. QRFV (22:2) 2005, 155–67.

15710. McGURL, MARK.   Learning from *Little Tree*: the political education of the counterculture. YJC (18:2) 2005, 243–67.

Claire Carvalho

15711. MOUNT, KEVIN.   Woman in white meets man in black. PRes (9:2) 2004, 7–14. (*Paging Danger.*)

Raymond Carver

15712. BETHEA, ARTHUR F.   Carver's *Rhodes*. Exp (63:2) 2005, 114–17.

15713. CORNWELL, GARETH.   Mediated desire and American disappointment in the stories of Raymond Carver. CritW (46:4) 2005, 344–56.

15714. GOMEZ-VEGA, IBIS.   Urban violence and failed myths in Raymond Carver's *What We Talk about When We Talk about Love*. ShSt (12:2) 2004, 71–83.

15715. STULL, W. L.; CARROLL, M. P. (eds and trans).   Tell it all. Rome: Leconte, 2005. pp. 161. (Storie: the write side.)

15716. TRUSSLER, MICHAEL.   The voice tells according to its urgency: a letter from Timothy Findley. *See* **16477.**

15717. TYSDAL, DAN.   Inarticulation and the figure of enjoyment: Raymond Carver's minimalism meets David Foster Wallace's *A Radically Condensed History of Postindustrial Life*. WasRCPSF (38:1) 2003, 66–83.

15718. WRIGLESWORTH, CHAD. Raymond Carver and Alcoholics Anonymous: the narrative under the 'surface of things'. RelArts (8:4) 2004, 458–78.

Vera Caspary

15719. EMRYS, A. B. *Laura*, Vera, and Wilkie: deep sensation roots of a *noir* novel. Clues (23:3) 2005, 5–13.

Neal Cassady

15720. MOORE, DAVE (ed.). Collected letters, 1944–1967. Introd. by Carolyn Cassady. London; New York: Penguin, 2004. pp. xxii, 490.

Ana Castillo

15721. CAMINERO-SANTANGELO, MARTA. 'The pleas of the desperate': collective agency *versus* magical realism in Ana Castillo's *So Far from God*. TSWL (24:1) 2005, 81–103.

15722. JIRÓN-KING, SHIMBERLEE. The second Tower of Babel: Ana Castillo's Borgesian precursors in *The Mixquiahala Letters*. PQ (82:4) 2003, 419–40.

15723. SPURGEON, SARA L. Ana Castillo. Boise, ID: Boise State Univ., 2004. pp. 56. (Boise State Univ. Western writers, 163.)

Willa Cather

15724. BRADLEY, JENNIFER L. To entertain, to educate, to elevate: Cather and the commodification of manners at the *Home Monthly*. *In* (pp. 37–65) **15749**.

15725. BUCKER, PARK. 'That kitchen with the shining windows': Willa Cather's *Neighbour Rosicky* and the *Woman's Home Companion*. *In* (pp. 66–112) **15749**.

15726. CHANEY, CAREY. St Peter, Blue Mesa, 'ruins', and archaic forms in Willa Cather's *The Professor's House*. WCPMN (48:3) 2005, 62–3.

15727. CUMMINS, JUNE. Understood Betsy, understood nation: Dorothy Canfield Fisher and Willa Cather queer America. *See* **15672**.

15728. DYCK, REGINALD. Willa Cather's reluctant New Woman pioneer. GPQ (23:3) 2003, 161–73.

15729. GIANNONE, RICHARD. Music, silence, and the spirituality of Willa Cather. Ren (57:2) 2005, 123–50.

15730. GUSTAFSON, NEIL. Willa Cather and Hamlin Garland: parallel early lives. WCPMN (49:1) 2005, 9–11.

15731. HILL, DAVID. The quotidian sublime: cognitive perspectives on identity-formation in Willa Cather's *My Ántonia*. AQ (61:3) 2005, 109–27.

15732. LEWIS, NGHANA. We shall pave the way: Willa Cather and Lillian Smith's aesthetics of Civil Rights politics. AQ (60:4) 2004, 33–64.

15733. LINDEMANN, MARILEE (ed.). The Cambridge companion to Willa Cather. Cambridge; New York: CUP, 2004. pp. xx, 229. (Cambridge companions to literature.)

15734. LINDNER, CHRISTOPH. Willa Cather, Daniel Liebeskind, and the creative destruction of Manhattan. JAC (28:1) 2005, 114–21.

15735. LOVELADY, STEPHANIE. Walking backwards: coming of age in *My Ántonia* and *How the García Girls Lost Their Accents*. MLS (35:1) 2005, 28–37.

15736. MIDDLETON, JoANN.   Cather studies 2003. WCPMN (49:1) 2005, 15–17.

15737. MILLER, ROBERT K.   Gloves full of gold: violations of the gift cycle in *My Mortal Enemy. In* (pp. 188–206) **15749.**

15738. MULLINS, MARIE.   Alexandra's dreams: 'the mightiest of all lovers' in Willa Cather's *O Pioneers!* GPQ (25:3) 2005, 147–59.

15739. O'FARRELL, MARY ANN.   Words to do with things: reading about Willa Cather and material culture. *In* (pp. 207–17) **15749.**

15740. PAYNE, SARAH.   Reconstructions of literary settings in North America's prairie regions: a cross-cultural comparison of Red Cloud, Nebraska, and Neepawa, Manitoba. *In* (pp. 213–33) **12587.**

15741. PETRIE, PAUL R.   Conscience and purpose: fiction and social consciousness in Howells, Jewett, Chesnutt, and Cather. *See* **10422.**

15742. RADULESCU, DOMNICA.   Amazons, wretches, and vampirettes: essentialism and beyond in the representation of East European women. *In* (pp. 23–59) **12697.**

15743. RAINE, ANNE.   Object lessons: nature education, museum science, and ethnographic tourism in *The Professor's House. In* (pp. 125–43) **15749.**

15744. ROMINES, ANN.   Willa Cather: a life with quilts. *In* (pp. 15–36) **15749.**

15745. RYDER, MARY R.   'Looking for love in all the wrong places': voyeurism in Cather's 1920s fiction. WCPMN (49:1) 2005, 3–8.

15746. SCHUETH, MICHAEL.   Taking liberties: Willa Cather and the 1934 film adaptation of *A Lost Lady. In* (pp. 113–24) **15749.**

15747. SMITH, JENNIFER A.   Cather's *Death Comes for the Archbishop.* Exp (63:2) 2005, 90–3.

15748. STOUT, JANIS P.   Brown and White at the dance: another word on Cather and race. WCPMN (49:2) 2005, 37–9.

15749. —— (ed.).   Willa Cather and material culture: real-world writing, writing the real world. Tuscaloosa; London: Alabama UP, 2005. pp. viii, 240. (Studies in American literary realism and naturalism.) Rev. by Catharine Randall in RMER (59:2) 2005; by Joseph Urgo in SAtlR (70:2) 2005, 182–6; by Steven Trout in GPQ (25:4) 2005, 260.

15750. TROUT, STEVEN.   From *The Namesake* to *One of Ours*: Willa Cather on war. ALR (37:2) 2005, 117–40.

15751. ——   Seeing the rattlesnake in Willa Cather's *My Ántonia.* ISLE (12:1) 2005, 99–114.

15752. WALLACE, HONOR McKITRICK.   'An orgy of acquisition': the female consumer, infidelity, and commodity culture in *A Lost Lady* and *The Professor's House. In* (pp. 144–55) **15749.**

15753. WILLIAMS, DEBORAH LINDSAY.   'Fragments of their desire': Willa Cather and the alternative aesthetic tradition of Native American women. *In* (pp. 156–70) **15749.**

15754. WILSON, ANNA.   Canonical relations: Willa Cather, America, and *The Professor's House.* TSLL (47:1) 2005, 61–74.

15755. WILSON, SARAH.   Material objects as sites of cultural mediation in *Death Comes for the Archbishop. In* (pp. 171–87) **15749.**

Theresa Hak Kyung Cha

15756. FRIEDMAN, SUSAN STANFORD. Modernism in a transnational landscape: spatial poetics, postcolonialism, and gender in Césaire's *Cahier/Notebook* and Cha's *Dictée*. Paideuma (32:1–3) 2003, 39–74.

15757. KIM, SUE J. Apparatus: Theresa Hak Kyung and the politics of form. JAAS (8:2) 2005, 143–69.

15758. PARK, JOSEPHINE NOCK-HEE. 'What of the partition': *Dictée*'s boundaries and the American epic. ConLit (46:2) 2005, 213–42.

Raymond Chandler

15759. DEFINO, DEAN. Lead birds and falling beams. See **16867**.

15760. SMITH, MICHELLE DENISE. Guns, lies, and ice: the Canadian pulp magazine industry and the crime fiction of Raymond Chandler and Niel Perrin. DNR (74:1) 2005, 3–17.

15761. SOLLORS, WERNER. Hemingway, *film noir*, and the emergence of a twentieth-century American style. See **16993**.

Vikram Chandra

15762. ALEXANDRU, MARIA-SABINA. 'Virtual reality on infinite bandwidth': Vikram Chandra interviewed. JCL (40:2) 2005, 5–21.

Joy Chant (b.1945)

15763. ENGLAND, RICHARD. Undisputed sovereignty. See **10218**.

Evelina Chao

15764. CHAO, EVELINA. Yeh Yeh's house. New York: St Martin's Press, 2004. pp. 287.

Fred Chappell

15765. CLABOUGH, CASEY. Fred Chappell's Cthulhu appropriations: *Dagon*. See **17857**.

15766. CLABOUGH, CASEY HOWARD. Experimentation and versatility: the early novels and short fiction of Fred Chappell. Macon, GA: Mercer UP, 2005. pp. 182. Rev. by John Lang in AppalJ (33:1) 2005, 120–2.

Suzy McKee Charnas

15767. WULF, ELIZABETH. Becoming heroic: alternative female heroes in Suzy McKee Charnas' *The Conqueror's Child*. Extrapolation (46:1) 2005, 120–32.

James Hadley Chase

15768. GELLY, CHRISTOPHE. De William Faulkner à James Hadley Chase: appropriation et mutation du genre policier. See **16409**.

Bruce Chatwin

15769. SMITH, THOMAS R. Blurring distinctions: autobiography and identity in Bruce Chatwin's *The Songlines*. BuR (47:2) 2004, 90–103.

15770. VISCONTI, LAURA. *Bruce Chatwin on Patagonia*: tortuosi sentieri alla ricerca dei miti. *In* (pp. 305–16) **12883**.

John Cheever

15771. MATHEWS, PETER. A farewell to goodbyes: reconciling the past in Cheever's *Goodbye, My Brother*. JSSE (43) 2004, 107–20.

Kelly Cherry

15772. CHERRY, KELLY. What comes next: women writing women in contemporary short fiction. *In* (pp. 128–36) **14204**.

G. K. Chesterton

15773. BODI, RUSS. G. K. Chesterton's Midwestern legacy. MidAmerica (30) 2003, 112–22.

15774. GILL, RICHARD. Chesterton's realism. Ren (57:3) 2005, 203–17.

15775. GOEGLEIN, TIMOTHY S. A sense of the sacred. *See* **7473**.

15776. MCEVOY, EMMA. 'Really, though secretly, a Papist': G. K. Chesterton's and John Meade Falkner's rewritings of the gothic. LitTheol (18:1) 2004, 49–61.

15777. PEARCE, JOSEPH. Man and Everyman: assembling the fragments. *See* **17775**.

15778. SCHWARTZ, ADAM. The third spring: G. K. Chesterton, Graham Greene, Christopher Dawson, and David Jones. Washington, DC: Catholic Univ. of America Press, 2005. pp. xv, 416. Rev. by Jay P. Corrin in CathHR (91:4) 2005, 837–9.

Tracy Chevalier

15779. MORGAN, ELIZABETH. Mary and modesty. ChrisL (54:2) 2005, 209–33.

Erskine Childers

15780. PIPER, LEONARD. Dangerous waters: the life and death of Erskine Childers. London; New York: Hambledon & London, 2003. pp. x, 261. Rev. by Francis M. Carroll in ILS (24:2) 2005, 32.

Alice Childress

15781. LEWIS, NGHANA. Neo-slave drama: narratives of resistance in Alice Childress's *Wedding Band*. JADT (17:1) 2005, 79–95.

William Childress

15782. CHILDRESS, WILLIAM. An Ozark odyssey: the journey of a father and son. Carbondale: Southern Illinois UP, 2005. pp. xii, 181, (plates) 12.

Frank Chin

15783. KIM, DANIEL Y. Writing manhood in black and yellow: Ralph Ellison, Frank Chin, and the literary politics of identity. *See* **16336**.

15784. MAEDA, DARYL J. Black Panthers, Red Guards, and Chinamen: constructing Asian American identity through performing Blackness, 1969–1972. AmQ (57:4) 2005, 1079–1103.

Marilyn Chin

15785. TAMMARO, THOM; GARAAS-JOHNSON, KRISTIN. The rigorous Muse: a conversation with poet Marilyn Chin. BRev (24:2) 2004, 17–20.

Ping Chong

15786. KURAHASHI, YUKO. Search for home and identity: Ping Chong and Michael Rohd's *Undesirable Elements – Berlin.* JMMLA (38:1) 2005, 85–100.

Wayson Choy (b.1939)

15787. LIM, HUAI-YANG. 'There's nothing more to know': silences, secrets, and ghosts in Wayson Choy's *Paper Shadows: a Chinatown Childhood.* A/B (19:1/2) 2004, 249–57.

Agatha Christie ('Mary Westmacott')

15788. EAMES, ANDREW. The 8:55 to Baghdad: from London to Iraq on the trail of Agatha Christie. Woodstock, NY: Overlook Press, 2005. pp. 403.

15789. KNEPPER, MARTY S. The curtain falls: Agatha Christie's last novels. Clues (23:4) 2005, 69–84.

Chrystos (b.1946)

15790. LOVROD, MARIE. Shifting contexts, shaping experiences: child abuse survivor narratives and educating for empire. *See* **11980.**

Louis H. Chu

15791. CHANG, JULIANA. Melancholic remains: domestic and national secrets in Fae Myenne Ng's *Bone. See* **18505.**

Caryl Churchill

15792. JERNIGAN, DANIEL. *Serious Money* becomes 'business by other means': Caryl Churchill's metatheatrical subject. CompDr (38:2/3) 2004, 291–313.

15793. ORLICH, ILEANA. Mad voices in the forest: Caryl Churchill's configurations of women in pre-post-Communist Romania. *In* (pp. 215–28) **12697.**

15794. RADULESCU, DOMNICA. Amazons, wretches, and vampirettes: essentialism and beyond in the representation of East European women. *In* (pp. 23–59) **12697.**

Sir Winston Churchill (1874–1965)

15795. REYNOLDS, DAVID. In command of history: Churchill fighting and writing the Second World War. London: Allen Lane, 2004. pp. xxvi, 645, (plates) 16. Rev. by Valerie Holman in SHARP (14:1/2) 2005, 18–19.

John Ciardi

15796. ALFIER, JEFFREY C. Recall roster. WLA (17:1/2) 2005, 315–21. (*The Pilot in the Jungle.*)

15797. CLEMENTE, VINCE. Some lines – lifelines – in John Ciardi. SoCR (36:2) 2004, 71–82.

Sandra Cisneros

15798. KOLÁŘ, STANISLAV. Cisneros' house of imagination and reality. SPFFOU (220) 2005, 27–40. (Studia anglica.)

Amy Clampitt

15799. SPIEGELMAN, WILLARD (ed.). Love, Amy: the selected letters of Amy Clampitt. New York: Columbia UP, 2005. pp. xxiv, 304.

Tom Clancy

15800. GREENBERG, MARTIN H. (ed.).   The Tom Clancy companion. Introd. by Larry Bond. (Bibl. 1993, 12032.) New York: Berkley, 2005. pp. xiv, 431. (Second ed.: first ed. 1992.)

15801. WALKER, DAVID.   Godless heathen: China in the American bestseller. *In* (pp. 136–55) **12674**.

Austin Clarke (1896–1974)

15802. CARMONA RODRÍGUEZ, PEDRO M.   Men don't have nothing like virginity: migration, refraction, and Black masculine performance in Austin Clarke's *The Question*. RAEI (16) 2003, 21–34.

15803. FARRELL, TYLER.   Austin Clarke and the consolations of Irish Catholicism. NewHR (9:4) 2005, 113–28.

15804. STOLAR, BATIA BOE.   Building and living the immigrant city: Michael Ondaatje's and Austin Clarke's Toronto. *In* (pp. 122–41) **9243**.

Ann Cleeves (b.1954)

15805. WEDGE, PHILIP.   *High Island Blues*: the sport of birding in the novels of Ann Cleeves. Aethlon (23:1) 2005, 29–36.

Vince Clemente

15806. CLEMENTE, VINCE.   Like Whitman, 'fed and bred under the Italian dispensation'. VIA (16:1) 2005, 35–43.

Michelle Cliff

15807. RICHARDS, CONSTANCE S.   Nationalism and the development of identity in postcolonial fiction: Zoë Wicomb and Michelle Cliff. *See* **20156**.

15808. TOLAND-DIX, SHIRLEY.   Re-negotiating racial identity: the challenge of migration and return in Michelle Cliff's *No Telephone to Heaven*. SLI (37:2) 2004, 37–52.

Lucille Clifton

15809. HOLLADAY, HILARY.   Wild blessings: the poetry of Lucille Clifton. Baton Rouge: Louisiana State UP, 2004. pp. xv, 224. (Southern literary studies.)

15810. KRINER, TIFFANY EBERLE.   Conjuring hope in a body: Lucille Clifton's eschatology. ChrisL (54:2) 2005, 185–208.

15811. LUPTON, MARY JANE.   'Remember my name': Lucille Clifton's Crazy Horse poems. ZNHF (18) 2004, 77–83.

Joshua Clover

15812. ALTIERI, CHARLES.   Some problems with being contemporary: aging critics, younger poets and the new century. *See* **18389**.

Constance Clyde (b.1872)

15813. LAWLESS, DAPHNE.   The trans-Tasman boomerang: the dialectic of convention and individuality in *A Pagan's Love* (1905). JNZL (23:1) 2005, 124–38.

Bob Cobbing (b.1920)

15814. DAVIDSON, IAN.   Visual poetry as performance. PRes (9:2) 2004, 99–107.

Andrei Codrescu

15815. OLSON, KIRBY. Andrei Codrescu and the myth of America. Jefferson, NC; London: McFarland, 2005. pp. vi, 207.

Jonathan Coe

15816. BENDINELLI, ALICE. Il paradosso della visione in *What a Carve Up!* di Jonathan Coe. LProv (121) 2004, 51–9.

15817. —— Scopofilia, tra desiderio e sguardo: il luogo dell'identità in *What a Carve Up!* di Jonathan Coe. LProv (118) 2003, 61–76.

J. M. Coetzee

15818. ALMAGRO JIMÉNEZ, MANUEL. 'Father to my story': writing *Foe*, de-authorizing (De)Foe. RAEI (18) 2005, 7–24.

15819. ATTRIDGE, DEREK. Deconstruction today. EA (58:1) 2005, 42–52.

15820. —— J. M. Coetzee and the ethics of reading: literature in the event. Chicago, IL; London: Chicago UP, 2004. pp. xv, 225. Rev. by Andrew van der Vlies in TLS, 29 July 2005, 29; by Peter D. McDonald in LRB (27:20) 2005, 24–5; by Patrick Hayes in JPW (41:2) 2005, 240–2.

15821. CANEPARI-LABIB, MICHELA. Old myths – modern empires: power, language, and identity in J. M. Coetzee's work. New York; Frankfurt: Lang, 2005. pp. 314.

15822. CONNELL, LIAM. Global narratives: globalisation and literary studies. *See* **16384**.

15823. COOPER, PAMELA. Metamorphosis and sexuality: reading the strange passions of *Disgrace*. RAL (36:4) 2005, 22–39.

15824. DURRANT, SAM. Postcolonial narrative and the work of mourning: J. M. Coetzee, Wilson Harris, and Toni Morrison. (Bibl. 2004, 16112.) Rev. by Barbara Eckstein in MFS (51:3) 2005, 714–17.

15825. FAN, KIT. Imagined places: Robinson Crusoe and Elizabeth Bishop. *See* **8513**.

15826. FIORELLA, LUCIA. '*I am far from being a master*': Lacan, Derrida e il *Master of Petersburg* di J. M. Coetzee. SCrit (19:2) 2004, 297–316.

15827. —— Il silenzio di Dio nel *Master of Petersburg* di J. M. Coetzee. LProv (121) 2004, 69–85.

15828. FLANERY, PATRICK DENMAN. (Re-)marking Coetzee & Costello: *The* (textual) *Lives of Animals*. ESA (47:1) 2004, 61–84.

15829. FRANSSEN, PAUL. Fleeing from the burning city: Michael K, vagrancy and empire. EngS (84:5) 2003, 453–63.

15830. GUARDUCCI, MARIA PAOLA. The age of deception: childhood in South African contemporary literature. *In* (pp. 182–92) **3690**.

15831. HARVEY, MELINDA. Re-educating the Romantic: sex and the nature-poet in J. M. Coetzee's *Disgrace*. SSE (31) 2005, 94–108.

15832. HELGESSON, STEFAN. Writing in crisis: ethics and history in Gordimer, Ndebele, and Coetzee. *See* **16752**.

15833. HERRON, TOM. The dog man: becoming animal in Coetzee's *Disgrace*. TCL (51:4) 2005, 467–90.

15834. LEUSMANN, HARALD. Moral labyrinths in J. M. Coetzee's *Elizabeth Costello*. NCL (35:4) 2005, 7–9.

15835. McDONALD, PETER D. Stony ground. LRB (27:20) 2005, 24–5 (review-article).

15836. MUNRO, BRENNA MOREMI. Queer democracy: J. M. Coetzee and the racial politics of gay identity in the new South Africa. JCPS (10:1) 2003, 209–25.

15837. NKOSI, LEWIS. Luster's lost quarter: reading South African identities (William Faulkner and J. M. Coetzee). See **16436**.

15838. SEGALL, KIMBERLY WEDEVEN. Pursuing ghosts: the traumatic sublime in J. M. Coetzee's *Disgrace*. RAL (36:4) 2005, 40–54.

15839. SPLENDORE, PAOLA. Vagrants and angels of death in two contemporary South African novels. *In* (pp. 255–63) **3690**.

15840. STRODE, TIMOTHY FRANCIS. The ethics of exile: colonialism in the fictions of Charles Brockden Brown and J. M. Coetzee. See **10242**.

15841. URBANOVÁ, LUDMILA. On phatic function of language. *In* (pp. 271–7) **1369**.

15842. WARNER, MARINA. Angels & engines: the culture of apocalypse. See **3954**.

15843. ZIMBLER, JARAD. Under local eyes: the South African publishing context of J. M. Coetzee's *Foe*. ESA (47:1) 2004, 47–59.

Emily Holmes Coleman

15844. CHAIT, SANDRA. Site also of angst and spiritual search. *In* (pp. 150–69) **15847**.

15845. LEE, AMY. Emily Holmes Coleman. RCF (25:1) 2005, 116–38.

15846. PODNIEKS, ELIZABETH. 'They sat and roared': Hayford Hall's performance in the diary of Emily Coleman. *In* (pp. 89–115) **15847**.

15847. —— CHAIT, SANDRA (eds). Hayford Hall: hangovers, erotics, and Modernist aesthetics. Carbondale: Southern Illinois UP, 2005. pp. xi, 223.

15848. VANDIVERE, JULIE. Framed liminalities: Antonia White's *Beyond the Glass* and Emily Coleman's *The Shutter of Snow*. *In* (pp. 46–69) **15847**.

R. G. Collingwood

15849. SKAGESTAD, PETER. Collingwood and Berlin: a comparison. JHI (66:1) 2005, 99–112.

Wayde Compton (b.1972)

15850. LOWRY, GLEN. Cultural citizenship and writing post-colonial Vancouver: Daphne Marlatt's *Ana Historic* and Wayde Compton's *Bluesprint*. See **18105**.

Barbara Comyns (b.1909)

15851. HORNER, AVRIL; ZLOSNIK, SUE. Skin chairs and other domestic horrors: Barbara Comyns and the female gothic tradition. GothS (6:1) 2004, 90–102.

Robert J. Conley

15852. KRUPAT, ARNOLD. Representing Cherokee dispossession. SAIL (17:1) 2005, 16–41.

Joseph Conrad

15853. ACHERAÏOU, AMAR. 'Action is consolatory': the dialectics of action and thought in *Nostromo*. Conradian (29:2) 2004, 49–58.

15854. —— Going beyond limits: de-territorialization in Conrad's novels. Conradiana (37:3) 2005, 173–84.

15855. ARMSTRONG, PAUL B. Play and the politics of reading: the social uses of Modernist form. See **11380**.

15856. ARROSTI, ELISABETTA. Conrad's Hirsch: the rehabilitation parable of a modern Wandering Jew. AngP (2:1/2) 2005, 59–71.

15857. BALDWIN, DEBRA ROMANICK. The horror and the human: the politics of dehumanization in *Heart of Darkness* and Primo Levi's *Se questo è un uomo*. Conradiana (37:3) 2005, 185–204.

15858. BENDER, TODD K. Competing cultural domains, borderlands and spatial/temporal thresholds in Hardy, Conrad, and D. H. Lawrence. *See* **11112**.

15859. BRICE, XAVIER. Ford Madox Ford and the composition of *Nostromo*. Conradian (29:2) 2004, 75–95.

15860. BRODSKY, G. W. STEPHEN. Prester John's workbook: Joseph Conrad, Edmund Candler, John Towson, and some imperial Others. Conradiana (37:1/2) 2005, 23–55.

15861. BRUYNS, WILLEM F. J. A Dutch naval officer on the Berau River in the 1870s. Conradian (30:1) 2005, 132–43.

15862. CAIRNEY, CHRISTOPHER. Pushkin, Mickiewicz, and 'the Horse of Stone' in *Nostromo*. Conradian (29:2) 2004, 110–15.

15863. CAMINERO-SANTANGELO, BYRON. African fiction and Joseph Conrad: reading postcolonial intertextuality. Albany: New York State UP, 2005. pp. x, 172.

15864. CARABINE, KEITH. 'A very charming old gentleman': Conrad, Count Szembek, and *Il Conde*. Conradiana (37:1/2) 2005, 57–77.

15865. —— STAPE, J. H. Family letters: Conrad to a sister-in-law, and Jessie Conrad on Conrad's death. Conradian (30:1) 2005, 127–31.

15866. COLLITS, TERRY. Anti-heroics and epic failures: the case of *Nostromo*. Conradian (29:2) 2004, 1–13.

15867. COOPER, BRENDA. Weary sons of Conrad: White fiction against the grain of Africa's dark heart. (Bibl. 2004, 16147.) Rev. by Robert E. Livingston in RAL (36:1) 2005, 134–5.

15868. CORKILL, RACHAEL A. Conrad and Edmund Candler: a neglected correspondence. Conradiana (37:1/2) 2005, 11–22.

15869. CURRELI, MARIO. Conrad and Scola: transposing the heart of darkness into film. *In* (pp. 126–36) **3724**.

15870. —— Invading other people's territory: *The Inheritors.* Conradiana (37:1/2) 2005, 79–100.

15871. —— Leitmotifs from Coleridge and Wagner in *Nostromo* and beyond. Conradian (29:2) 2004, 96–109.

15872. —— Within the Tides; ovvero, 'Quattro diverse maniere di raccontare una storia'. AngP (2:1/2) 2005, 77–100.

15873. DESPOTOPOULOU, ANNA. The monster and the atom: representation of London in James and Conrad. *See* **11397.**

15874. DRYDEN, LINDA. H. G. Wells and Joseph Conrad: a literary friendship. Wellsian (28) 2005, 2–13.

15875. DUTHEIL DE LA ROCHÈRE, MARTINE HENNARD. Body politics: Conrad's anatomy of empire in *Heart of Darkness.* Conradiana (36:3) 2004, 185–205.

15876. EPSTEIN, HUGH. *The Rover*: a post-skeptical novel? Conradiana (37:1/2) 2005, 101–18.

15877. FRANKE, WILLIAM. Varieties and valences of unsayability. PhilL (29:2) 2005, 489–97.

15878. HAND, RICHARD J. The theatre of Joseph Conrad: reconstructed fictions. Basingstoke; New York: Palgrave Macmillan, 2005. pp. xvii, 192.

15879. HAWTHORN, JEREMY. Artful dodges in mental territory: self-deception in Conrad's fiction. Conradiana (37:3) 2005, 205–31.

15880. —— The use of *coon* in Conrad: British slang or racist slur? Conradian (30:1) 2005, 111–17.

15881. HUBBARD, DOLAN. Du Bois, Conrad and the luminous darkness. *See* **16159.**

15882. HUTCHINGS, MARK. Golding's Conrad inheritance. *See* **16736.**

15883. İÇÖZ, NURSEL. Conrad and ambiguity: social commitment and ideology in *Heart of Darkness* and *Nostromo.* Conradiana (37:3) 2005, 245–74.

15884. ITALIA, PAUL G. 'No joke!': the mediation of ironic humour in Conrad's *Lord Jim.* Conradiana (36:3) 2004, 207–24.

15885. KIMMEL, MICHAEL. From metaphor to the 'mental sketchpad': literary macrostructure and compound image schemas in *Heart of Darkness.* MetS (20:3) 2005, 199–238.

15886. KNOWLES, OWEN; STAPE, J. H. The rationale of punctuation in Conrad's *Blackwood's* fictions. Conradian (30:1) 2005, 1–45.

15887. KOZAK, WOJCIECH. Beyond the rational: Joseph Conrad's portrayal of the sea. *In* (pp. 81–92) **12868.**

15888. KRAJKA, WIESŁAW. A return to the roots: Conrad, Poland and East-Central Europe. Boulder, CO: East European Monographs; Lublin: Maria Curie-Skłodowska Univ., 2004. pp. vii, 308. (East European monographs, 658.) (Conrad: Eastern and Western perspectives, 13.)

15889. KRISHNAN, SANJAY. Seeing the animal: colonial space and movement in Joseph Conrad's *Lord Jim.* Novel (37:3) 2004, 326–51.

15890. LACKEY, MICHAEL. The moral conditions for genocide in Joseph Conrad's *Heart of Darkness.* ColLit (32:1) 2005, 20–41.

15891. Le Boulicaut, Yannick.   Shores in Joseph Conrad's works. Conradiana (37:3) 2005, 233–44.

15892. Leps, Marina.   *'A personal note in the margin of the public page'*: A Personal Record di Joseph Conrad. *In* (pp. 223–32) **12577.**

15893. Levin, Yael.   Conrad, Freud, and Derrida on Pompeii: a paradigm of disappearance. PartA (3:1) 2005, 81–99.

15894. Lin, Lidan.   The center cannot hold: ambiguous narrative voices in Wu's *The Journey West* and Conrad's *Heart of Darkness*. Comparatist (29) 2005, 63–81.

15895. Lobb, Edward.   Waugh among the Modernists: allusion and theme in *A Handful of Dust*. *See* **20013.**

15896. Machosky, Brenda.   A poetics at the limit of the subject: Nancy's philosophy of singular being in Conrad's *The Secret Sharer*. EREA (2:2) 2004, 112–17.

15897. Macilwee, Michael.   *Henderson the Rain King*: translations between Conrad and Hemingway. *See* **15448.**

15898. McInturff, Kate.   'The heritage of perception': nation and deracination in early Conrad criticism. Conradiana (37:3) 2005, 275–92.

15899. Michael, Marion C.; Daniell, Steven J.   Conrad in the British Museum Reading Room. Conradiana (36:3) 2004, 245–50.

15900. Miller, C. Brook.   Holroyd's man: tradition, fetishization, and the United States in *Nostromo*. Conradian (29:2) 2004, 14–30.

15901. Monod, Sylvère.   Joseph Conrad's polyglot wordplay. MLR (100:4:supp.) 2005, 222–34.

15902. —— Re-reading *Il Conde*. Conradian (30:1) 2005, 118–26.

15903. Moore, Gene M. (ed.).   Joseph Conrad's *Heart of Darkness*: a casebook. (Bibl. 2004, 16186.) Rev. by Martin Bock in ELT (48:4) 2005, 476–9.

15904. Okuda, Yoko.   *Under Western Eyes* and Sōseki's *Kokoro*. Conradian (30:1) 2005, 59–70.

15905. Osborne, Brian D.   Conrad and Neil Munro: notes on a literary acquaintance. Conradian (30:1) 2005, 81–7.

15906. Oziewicz, M.   A personal voyage of discovery in F. F. Coppola's *Apocalypse Now*: réchauffé *Heart of Darkness*. *In* (pp. 205–16) **12672.**

15907. Paccaud-Huguet, Josiane.   The remains of Kurtz's day: Joseph Conrad and historical correctness. Conradiana (36:3) 2004, 167–84.

15908. Panichas, George A.   Joseph Conrad: his moral vision. Macon, GA: Mercer UP, 2005. pp. xviii, 165.

15909. Pedot, Richard.   *Heart of Darkness* de Joseph Conrad: le sceau de l'inhumain. Paris: Éditions du temps, 2003. pp. 160. Rev. by Sylvère Monod in EA (57:4) 2004, 505–6.

15910. Piechota, Marcin.   The first Conrad translation: *An Outcast of the Islands* in Polish. Conradian (30:1) 2005, 88–96.

15911. Prescott, Lynda.   Autobiography as evasion: Joseph Conrad's *A Personal Record*. JML (28:1) 2004, 177–88.

15912. Purdy, Dwight. The ethic of sympathy in Conrad's *Lord Jim* and Eliot's *Mill on the Floss*. Conradiana (37:1/2) 2005, 119–31.

15913. Rawson, Claude. Tribal drums and the dull tom-tom: thoughts on Modernism and the savage in Conrad and Eliot. In (pp. 95–111) **12946**.

15914. Retief, Glen. Heartfelt horrors: Africa, racial difference and the quest for moral enlightenment in Conrad's *Heart of Darkness* and Rian Malan's *My Traitor's Heart*. Conradiana (36:3) 2004, 225–43.

15915. Rhodes, Neil. Shakespeare the barbarian. In (pp. 99–114) **5187**.

15916. Roberts, Andrew Michael. Conrad and the territory of ethics. Conradiana (37:1/2) 2005, 133–46.

15917. Ross, Stephen. Conrad and empire. (Bibl. 2004, 16203.) Rev. by Amar Acheraïou in Conradiana (36:3) 2004, 269–75; by Wendell V. Harris in ELN (42:3) 2005, 71–4; by Michael John DiSanto in DalR (85:3) 2005, 479–80.

15918. Rudrum, David. Living alone: solipsism in *Heart of Darkness*. PhilL (29:2) 2005, 409–27.

15919. Schenkel, Elmar. The city and the sea: Genoa and the Mediterranean in Joseph Conrad's novel *Suspense: a Napoleonic Novel*. In (pp. 303–11) **9393**.

15920. Schnauder, Ludwig. Free will and determinism in *Nostromo*. Conradian (29:2) 2004, 59–74.

15921. Schneider, Lissa. Conrad's narratives of difference: not exactly tales for the boys. (Bibl. 2003, 16096.) Rev. by Ellen Burton Harrington in Conradiana (36:3) 2004, 251–61; by Tom Henthorne in StudN (37:1) 2005, 118–20; by Lorrie Clark in ELT (48:4) 2005, 479–82.

15922. Shidara, Yasuko. *The Shadow-Line*'s 'sympathetic doctor': Dr William Willis in Bangkok, 1888. Conradian (30:1) 2005, 97–110.

15923. Soane, Bev. The colony at the heart of empire: domestic space in *The Secret Agent*. Conradian (30:1) 2005, 46–58.

15924. Stape, J. H. *The End of the Tether* and Victor Hugo's *Les Travailleurs de la mer*. Conradian (30:1) 2005, 71–80.

15925. —— (ed.); Busza, Andrew (asst ed.). Notes on life and letters. (Bibl. 2004, 16209.) Rev. by Allan H. Simmons in ELT (48:2) 2005, 229–32; by Susan Jones in RES (56:225) 2005, 470–2.

15926. Stubbs, Michael. Conrad in the computer: examples of quantitative stylistic methods. LLit (14:1) 2005, 5–24.

15927. Voitkovska, Ludmilla. Conrad in Russia: a discipline *in absentia*. Conradiana (37:1/2) 2005, 147–64.

15928. —— Homecoming in *Nostromo*. Conradian (29:2) 2004, 31–48.

David Constantine (b.1944)

15929. Constantine, David. A living language. See **20916**.

'Murray Constantine' (Katharine Burdekin)

15930. Payne, Kenneth. Accessing utopia through 'altered states of consciousness' in Katharine Burdekin's *The End of This Day's Business*. NCL (35:3) 2005, 3–5.

15931. ——— 'Debased and impure': Christianity and Christian resistance in Katharine Burdekin's *Swastika Night*. NCL (35:1) 2005, 8–10.

15932. ——— Grania, 'a mad woman ... doomed to attempt the impossible': imagining utopia in Katharine Burdekin's *The End of This Day's Business*. LJH (30:2) 2005, 33–42.

George Cram Cook (1873–1924)

15933. NOE, MARCIA; MARLOWE, ROBERT LLOYD. *Suppressed Desires* and *Tickless Time*: an intertextual critique of modernity. See 16714.

15934. BEN-ZVI, LINDA (introd. and notes). The road to the temple: a biography of George Cram Cook. By Susan Glaspell. See 16716.

Robin Cook

15935. WALD, PRISCILLA. What's in a cell? John Moore's spleen and the language of bioslavery. NLH (36:2) 2005, 205–25.

Grace MacGowan Cooke (1863–1944)

15936. ENGELHARDT, ELIZABETH S. D. (introd.). The power and the glory. Boston, MA: Northeastern UP, 2003. pp. xxxii, 373. Rev. by Jennifer Putzi in Legacy (22:1) 2005, 91–4.

Dennis Cooley

15937. MCLENNAN, ROB. Fielding quotations: an interview with Dennis Cooley. Rampike (14:1) 2005, 40–4.

Dennis Cooper

15938. AARON, MICHELE. (Fill-in-the) blank fiction: Dennis Cooper's cinematics and the complicitous reader. JML (27:3) 2004, 115–27.

15939. BEWES, TIMOTHY. The novel as an absence: Lukács and the event of postmodern fiction. See 15248.

15940. STOREY, MARK. 'And as things fell apart': the crisis of postmodern masculinity in Bret Easton Ellis's *American Psycho* and Dennis Cooper's *Frisk*. See 16322.

J. California Cooper

15941. WEAVER, JAMES. Rehabilitative storytelling: the narrator–narratee relationship in J. California Cooper's *Family*. MELUS (30:1) 2005, 109–34.

Robert Coover

15942. GUIGNERY, VANESSA. Réécritures du Déluge et de l'arche de Noé dans la fiction contemporaine de langue anglaise (Coover, Findley, Winterson, Roberts et Barnes). See 19088.

15943. HIDALGO DOWNING, LAURA. Reading R. Coover's *Quenby and Ola, Swede and Carl*: an empirical study on reference and story interpretation. EJES (9:2) 2005, 155–68.

15944. KUŠNÍR, JAROSLAV. Parody of western in American literature: Doctorow's *Welcome to Hard Times*, and R. Coover's *Ghost Town*. In (pp. 101–8) 3753.

Edwin Corley (b.1931)

15945. KINNEY, ARTHUR F. The other Dorothy Parkers. In (pp. 114–26) 18738.

Patricia Cornwell

15946. FEOLE, GLENN L.; LASSETER, DON. The complete Patricia Cornwell companion. New York: Berkley, 2005. pp. xiii, 353.

Lucha Corpi (b.1945)

15947. BICKFORD, DONNA M. A praxis of parataxis: epistemology and dissonance in Lucha Corpi's detective fiction. Meridians (5:2) 2005, 89–103.

15948. LIBRETTI, TIM. Detecting empire from inside-out and outside-in: the politics of detection in the fiction of Elizabeth George and Lucha Corpi. *In* (pp. 71–95) **14191.**

15949. SOTELO, SUSAN BAKER. Chicano detective fiction: a critical study of five novelists. *See* **15153.**

Kia Corthron

15950. ANDERSON, LISA M. Violence, tragedy, and race in Kia Corthron's *Wake Up, Lou Rizer*. JDTC (19:2) 2005, 71–84.

Sir Noel Coward (1899–1973)

15951. DAY, BARRY. Coward on film: the cinema of Noël Coward. Foreword by Sir John Mills. Lanham, MD; London: Scarecrow Press, 2005. pp. xviii, 181.

15952. GALE, MAGGIE B. The many masks of Clemence Dane. *In* (pp. 48–61) **3985.**

James Gould Cozzens

15953. KINDER, JOHN M. The Good War's 'raw chunks': Norman Mailer's *The Naked and the Dead* and James Gould Cozzens's *Guard of Honor*. *See* **18055.**

Edward Gordon Craig

15954. CARROLL-HORROCKS, BETH. A working relationship: the Dorothy Nevile Lees papers relating to Edward Gordon Craig and *The Mask*, at the Harvard Theatre Collection. *See* **1171.**

Hart Crane

15955. COLLIER, MICHAEL. On Whitman's *To a Locomotive in Winter*. *See* **12303.**

15956. COMBS, ROBERT. Affinities between the poetry of Hart Crane and the plays of Eugene O'Neill. *See* **18639.**

15957. LURIE, PETER. Querying the Modernist canon: historical consciousness and the sexuality of suffering in Faulkner and Hart Crane. *See* **16426.**

15958. REHDER, ROBERT. Stevens, Williams, Crane, and the motive for metaphor. *See* **19681.**

15959. SNEDIKER, MICHAEL. Hart Crane's smile. Mod/Mod (12:4) 2005, 629–58.

Robert Creeley

15960. HOLLENBERG, DONNA. 'Dancing edgeways': Robert Creeley's role in Denise Levertov's post-war transition. Ren (58:1) 2005, 5–16.

15961. MOSSIN, ANDREW. 'In thicket': Charles Olson, Frances Boldereff, Robert Creeley and the crisis of masculinity at mid-century. *See* **18615.**

2005]   AUTHORS   867

Michael Crichton

15962. HAHN, TORSTEN. Risk communication and paranoid hermeneutics: towards a distinction between 'medical thrillers' and 'mind-control thrillers' in narrations on biocontrol. *See* **14155**.

15963. MILBURN, COLIN. Nano/splatter: disintegrating the postbiological body. NLH (36:2) 2005, 283–311.

15964. PETHES, NICOLAS. Terminal men: biotechnological experimentation and the reshaping of 'the human' in medical thrillers. NLH (36:2) 2005, 161–85.

15965. WHITLARK, JAMES. Horrifying 'boredom' in Michael Crichton's fictions. JFA (13:3) 2003, 226–38.

Caresse Crosby (Mary Phelps Jacob) (1892–1970)

15966. HAMALIAN, LINDA. The Cramoisy queen: a life of Caresse Crosby. Carbondale: Southern Illinois UP, 2005. pp. xiii, 247.

'Amanda Cross' (Carolyn G. Heilbrun)

15967. HITE, MOLLY. We think back through Carolyn Heilbrun if we are women. TSWL (24:2) 2005, 269–74.

15968. HOLST-WARHAFT, GAIL. Death unmanned. TSWL (24:2) 2005, 275–82.

15969. KRESS, SUSAN. The mysterious life of Kate Fansler. TSWL (24:2) 2005, 257–64.

15970. REGALDO, MARIANA. The excitement of the chase: information literacy in the Kate Fansler novels by Amanda Cross. Clues (24:1) 2005, 44–53.

15971. WOODWARD, KATHLEEN. Performing age, performing gender: the legacy of Carolyn Heilbrun. TSWL (24:2) 2005, 283–90.

Thomas Rain Crowe (b.1949)

15972. CROWE, THOMAS RAIN. Zoro's field: my life in the Appalachian woods. Foreword by Christopher Camuto. Athens; London: Georgia UP, 2005. pp. xiv, 221.

Aleister Crowley

15973. OWEN, ALEX. The place of enchantment: British occultism and the culture of the modern. *See* **9368**.

John Crowley (b.1942)

15974. CUNNINGHAM, RODGER. The wolves of Aegypt: John Crowley's Appalachians. *In* (pp. 350–70) **12822**.

15975. WOLFE, GARY. Peter Straub and John Crowley in conversation: ICFA 26, March 18, 2005. Ed. and transcribed by Sherryl Vint. *See* **19716**.

Chris Crutcher

15976. SOMMERS, MICHAEL A. Chris Crutcher. New York: Rosen Central, 2005. pp. 112. (Library of author biographies.)

Countee Cullen

15977. SÁNCHEZ-PARDO, ESTHER. Cultures of the death drive: Melanie Klein and Modernist melancholia. *See* **20416**.

e. e. cummings

15978. Marano, Salvatore.   Still life with a machine: e. e. cummings's typewriter poems. RSA (14) 2003, 120–38.

15979. Vernyik, Zénó.   'decomposing in the mouth of New York': spatial New York City in E. E. Cummings' *Tulips and Chimneys*. *In* (pp. 261–7) **3734**.

Nancy Cunard

15980. Marcus, Jane.   Hearts of darkness: White women write race. (Bibl. 2004, 16272.) Rev. by Bonnie Kime Scott in VWM (66) 2004, 29–30; by Tuzyline Jita Allan in WSA (11) 2005, 201–4; by Jeanne Perreault in TSWL (24:1) 2005, 168–70.

15981. Morresi, Renata.   'I treni misti vanno molto lontano': polilinguismo, utopia e sperimentazione nell'opera di Nancy Cunard. *In* (pp. 204–24) **14377**.

J. V. (James Vincent) Cunningham (b.1911)

15982. Baxter, John.   J. V. Cunningham's Shakespeare glosses. EC (55:4) 2005, 285–308. (Critical opinion.)

Michael Cunningham (b.1952)

15983. Aimone, Laura Francesca.   In the footsteps of Virginia Woolf: *The Hours* by Michael Cunningham. SPACVW (13) 2005, 159–64.

15984. Spohrer, Erika.   Seeing stars: commodity stardom in Michael Cunningham's *The Hours* and Virginia Woolf's *Mrs Dalloway*. AQ (61:2) 2005, 113–32.

Allen Curnow ('Whim Wham')

15985. Sturm, Terry (ed.).   Whim Wham's New Zealand: the best of Whim Wham 1937–1988. Auckland: Random House, 2005. pp. 317.

Dymphna Cusack

15986. Ryan, J. S.   Dymphna Cusack (1902–1981), cultural historian, controversialist and opponent of social injustice: her New England threshing floor. AF (19) 2004, 109–34.

Cyril Dabydeen

15987. Dabydeen, Cyril.   Shaping the environment: sugar plantation; or, Life after indentured labor. *In* (pp. 58–69) **12632**.

15988. —— The short story as process – not what it means. *In* (pp. 153–8) **14204**.

Roald Dahl

15989. Tal, Eve.   Deconstructing the peach: *James and the Giant Peach* as postmodern fairy tale. JFA (14:2) 2003, 265–76.

Blanche d'Alpuget

15990. Yu, Ouyang.   How post are they colonial: an enquiry into Christopher Koch, Blanche d'Alpuget and Bruce Grant's representation of Chinese in recent 'Asian writing'. *In* (pp. 243–61) **12674**.

'Clemence Dane' (Winifred Ashton)

15991. GALE, MAGGIE B. The many masks of Clemence Dane. *In* (pp. 48–61) **3985.**

Achmat Dangor

15992. RASTOGI, PALLAVI. From South Asia to South Africa: locating other postcolonial diasporas. *See* **16380.**

Mark Z. Danielewski

15993. SLOCOMBE, WILL. 'This is not for you': nihilism and the house that Jacques built. MFS (51:1) 2005, 88–109.

Jim Daniels

15994. LANPHIER-WILLSON, JULIANN. Daniels's *Digger Laps at the Bowl.* Exp (63:4) 2005, 248–52.

Sarah Daniels

15995. BARTLETT, CARINA. Bringing the house down: Pat Barker, Sarah Daniels, and the dramatic dialogue. *In* (pp. 87–100) **15309.**

Edwidge Danticat

15996. BRAZIEL, JANA EVANS. Défilée's diasporic daughters: revolutionary narratives of *Ayiti* (Haiti), *nanchon* (nation), and *dyaspora* (diaspora) in Edwidge Danticat's *Krik? Krak!* SLI (37:2) 2004, 77–96.

15997. HONG, TERRY. Honor, hope, and redemption: a talk with Edwidge Danticat about her latest novel, *The Dew Breaker.* BRev (24:5) 2004, 21.

15998. SMITH, KATHARINE CAPSHAW. Splintered families, enduring connections: an interview with Edwidge Danticat. CLAQ (30:2) 2005, 194–205.

Olive Tilford Dargan ('Fielding Burke')

15999. ACKERMAN, KATHY CANTLEY. The heart of revolution: the radical life and novels of Olive Dargan. (Bibl. 2004, 16304.) Rev. by Nancy Carol Joyner in AppH (33:1) 2005, 74–6.

Helen Darville ('Helen Demidenko') (b.1971)

16000. MEYER, TESS. Stereotypes and the autobiography of a fictional author: Helen Demidenko's ethnic performance in the light of her short story *Other Places.* WLWE (40:2) 2004, 40–51.

Guy Davenport

16001. COZY, DAVID. Guy Davenport. RCF (25:3) 2005, 42–85.

Kiana Davenport

16002. MARINELLI, SARA. Irreversible contagion: leprosy and ethnicity in *Shark Dialogs* by Kiana Davenport. *In* (pp. 193–201) **3690.**

16003. SPENCER, STEPHEN. Cultural hybridity in Kiana Davenport's *Shark Dialogs.* Storytelling (5:1) 2005, 21–8.

Joy Davidman

16004. KING, DON W. Fire and ice: C. S. Lewis and the love poetry of Joy Davidman and Ruth Pitter. *See* **17751.**

16005. SIBLEY, BRIAN. Through the shadowlands: the love story of C. S. Lewis and Joy Davidman. *See* **17791**.

Donald Davidson

16006. CHODAT, ROBERT. Real toads and imaginary gardens: Freud and Davidson on meaning and metaphor. SPELL (16) 2003, 23–35.

Ian Davidson (b.1957)

16007. JARVIS, MATTHEW. The politics of place in the poetry of Ian Davidson. WWrE (10) 2005, 144–59.

Donald Davie

16008. WILMER, CLIVE. Song and stone: Donald Davie reappraised. TLS, 6 May 2005, 12–14.

16009. —— (ed.). Modernist essays: Yeats, Pound, Eliot. By Donald Davie. *See* **20528**.

Dan Davin

16010. MCNEISH, JAMES. Dance of the peacocks: New Zealanders in exile in the time of Hitler and Mao Tse-tung. (Bibl. 2004, 16318.) Rev. by Jack Ross in WLWE (39:2) 2002/03, 143–6.

Christopher Dawson

16011. SCHWARTZ, ADAM. The third spring: G. K. Chesterton, Graham Greene, Christopher Dawson, and David Jones. *See* **15778**.

Robert Day (b.1941)

16012. WHITEHEAD, FRED. The glittering eye of the narrator: an interview with Robert Day. NewLet (71:1) 2004/05, 124–33.

John F. Deane (b.1943)

16013. DE LUCA, CHIARA. John F. Deane, gli strumenti dell'arte. PoesiaM (194) 2005, 58–64.

Seamus Deane

16014. ARROWSMITH, AIDAN. Photographic memories: nostalgia and Irish diaspora writing. TexP (19:2) 2005, 297–322.

16015. GOARZIN, ANNE. Traversées en eaux troubles: *Reading in the Dark* de Seamus Deane et *Grace Notes* de Bernard Mac Laverty. EtIr (29:1) 2004, 41–53.

16016. HERRON, TOM. Derry *is* Donegal: thresholds, vectors, limits in Seamus Deane's *Reading in the Dark*. EtIr (29:2) 2004, 165–83.

16017. KERRIGAN, JOHN. Paul Muldoon's transits: muddling through after *Madoc*. *In* (pp. 125–49) **18404**.

16018. MCCARTHY, CONOR. Seamus Deane: between Burke and Adorno. YES (35) 2005, 232–48.

Paul De Kruif (1890–1971)

16019. GROSS, ROBERT F. Fighting disease, seducing cavalrymen, and achieving modernity: *Yellow Jack*. *See* **17074**.

Samuel R. Delany

16020. DELANY, SAMUEL R. The motion of light in water: sex and science fiction writing in the East Village. Minneapolis; London: Minnesota UP, 2004. pp. 572.

16021. TUCKER, JEFFREY ALLEN. A sense of wonder: Samuel R. Delany, race, identity and difference. (Bibl. 2004, 16328.) Rev. by Valerie Holliday in Extrapolation (46:3) 2005, 395–9.

16022. WEST, CHRIS. Perverting science fiction: thinking the alien within the genre. See 12082.

Mazo de la Roche

16023. KIRK, HEATHER. Caroline Clement: the hidden life of Mazo de la Roche's collaborator. CanL (184) 2005, 46–67.

Nicholas Delbanco (b.1942)

16024. DELBANCO, NICHOLAS. Anywhere out of the world: essays on travel, writing, death. New York: Columbia UP, 2005. pp. 193. Rev. by Gregory Norminton in TLS, 13 May 2005, 31.

Don DeLillo

16025. BASU, BIMAN. Reading the techno-ethnic Other in Don DeLillo's *White Noise*. AQ (61:2) 2005, 87–111.

16026. BOXALL, PETER. Don DeLillo: the possibilities of fiction. London; New York: Routledge, 2005. pp. 224.

16027. CONSONNINI, STEFANIA. '*The shot heard around the world*': baseball e cospirazioni narrative in *Underworld* di DeLillo. NCorr (134) 2004, 319–42.

16028. DENEEN, PATRICK J. The American mystery deepens: hearing Tocqueville in Don DeLillo's *White Noise*. In (pp. 207–34) **14121**.

16029. DEPIETRO, THOMAS (ed.). Conversations with Don DeLillo. Jackson; London: Mississippi UP, 2005. pp. xiv, 183. (Literary conversations.)

16030. DÍEZ COBO, ROSA MARIA. '*The never-ending neon*': storia e terrore di un'epoca terminale. NCorr (136) 2005, 253–68.

16031. ELLIOTT, EMORY. Cultural memory and the American novel. YREAL (21) 2005, 225–37.

16032. GHELLI, FRANCESCO. *Hantise* e contaminazione: sulle *ghost stories* e le case stregate. In (pp. 115–30) **14322**.

16033. IACOLI, GIULIO. *CorpoReality show*: elegia e deformazione del mondo in Don DeLillo, *The Body Artist*. NCorr (136) 2005, 339–56.

16034. IULI, M. CRISTINA. Sottrarre strati di coscienza? Identità e intermedialità in *Libra*. NCorr (136) 2005, 323–38.

16035. LANDON, RICHARD. Sport fiction and the untellable: cliché and language in Don DeLillo's *End Zone*. Aethlon (23:1) 2005, 71–80.

16036. LECLAIR, TOM. *Mao II* ed io. NCorr (136) 2005, 323–38.

16037. LONGMUIR, ANNE. The language of history: Don DeLillo's *The Names* and the Iranian hostage crisis. CritW (46:2) 2005, 105–22.

16038. MCGOWAN, TODD. The obsolescence of mystery and the accumulation of waste in Don DeLillo's *Underworld*. CritW (46:2) 2005, 123–45.

16039. MANSUTTI, PAMELA. *'Using the whole picture'*: il doppio sogno cinematografico di *Americana*. NCorr (136) 2005, 233–52.

16040. MARTINS, SUSANA S. *White Noise* and everyday technologies. AmS (46:1) 2005, 87–113.

16041. MICALI, SIMONA. La trama del mondo: contaminazione tra linguaggio e realtà nel romanzo postmoderno. *In* (pp. 298–312) **14322**.

16042. ORBÁN, KATALIN. Ethical diversions: the post-Holocaust narratives of Pynchon, Abish, DeLillo, and Spiegelman. *See* **18991**.

16043. OSTEEN, MARK. Echo chamber: undertaking *The Body Artist*. StudN (37:1) 2005, 64–81.

16044. PACKER, MATTHEW J. 'At the dead center of things' in Don DeLillo's *White Noise*: mimesis, violence, and religious awe. MFS (51:3) 2005, 648–66.

16045. RUSSO, JOHN PAUL. The future without a past: the humanities in a technological society. Columbia; London: Missouri UP, 2005. pp. x, 313.

16046. VARSAVA, JERRY A. The 'saturated self': Don DeLillo on the problem of rogue capitalism. ConLit (46:1) 2005, 78–107.

16047. VERVENNE, JASMINE. *Ratner's Star*: a 'piece of mathematics'? BELL (ns 3) 2005, 49–56.

16048. ZHU, XINFU. The ecological consciousness in *White Noise*. FLS (115) 2005, 109–14. (In Chinese.)

16049. ZIEGLER, ROBERT. Mourning and creation in Don DeLillo's *The Body Artist*. NCL (35:3) 2005, 7–10.

Charles de Lint (b.1951)

16050. MAINS, CHRISTINE. Old World, New World, Otherworld: Celtic and Native American influences in Charles de Lint's *Moonheart* and *Forests of the Heart*. Extrapolation (46:3) 2005, 338–50.

Floyd Dell

16051. WAKESBERG, SI. Concerning Floyd Dell. BRev (25:1) 2005, 18.

William Demby

16052. BIGGERS, JEFF. William Demby has not left the building: postcard from Tuscany. BRev (24:1) 2004, 12.

Barbara Deming

16053. MCDANIEL, JUDITH. Shaping the sixties: the emergence of Barbara Deming. *In* (pp. 196–216) **12566**.

C. J. (Clarence James) Dennis (1876–1938)

16054. BUTTERSS, PHILIP. Gadding about: C. J. Dennis and the *Gadfly*. Southerly (64:3) 2004, 158–71.

Jeff Derksen (b.1958)

16055. MANCINI, DONATO. We were signifying like crazy! Jeff Derksen's relational poetics of hyper-referential humour. WCL (39:1) 2005, 59–70.

Toi Derricotte (b.1941)

16056. DERRICOTTE, TOI. Seeing and re-seeing: an exchange between Yusef Komunyakaa and Toi Derricotte. *See* **17518**.

Anita Desai

16057. KHAN, NYLA ALI. The fiction of nationality in an era of transnationalism. London; New York: Routledge, 2005. pp. vii, 123. (Literary criticism and cultural theory.)

16058. RAJA, IRA. Ageing subjects, agentic bodies: appetite, modernity and the middle class in two Indian short stories in English. *See* **16704**.

16059. VOLNÁ, LUDMILA. Anita Desai's *Fasting, Feasting* and the condition of women. CLCWeb (7:3) 2005.

Shashi Deshpande

16060. MAJUMDAR, SAIKAT. The fiction of 'subaltern pasts': Shashi Deshpande and Sunetra Gupta. RAEI (16) 2003, 227–37.

Robert Dessaix (b.1944)

16061. CUMMINS, IAN. Love and death. Meanjin (64:1/2) 2005, 38–44 (review-article). (Dessaix's work on Turgenev.)

16062. ENGLAND, RICHARD. Undisputed sovereignty. *See* **10218**.

Sarah Dessen

16063. GLENN, WENDY J. Sarah Dessen: from burritos to box office. Lanham, MD; London: Scarecrow Press, 2005. pp. xiv, 147. (Scarecrow studies in young adult literature, 16.)

Jean Devanny

16064. TAYLOR, CHERYL. Threshold to fulfillment: the Barrier Reef writings of E. J. Banfield and Jean Devanny. *See* **10083**.

Bernard Augustine De Voto (1897–1955)

16065. GRAULICH, MELODY. Cultural criticism, *circa* 1974. *See* **19573**.

Herbert I. E. Dhlomo

16066. WENZEL, JENNIFER. Voices of spectral and textual ancestors: reading Tiyo Soga alongside H. I. E. Dhlomo's *The Girl Who Killed to Save*. RAL (36:1) 2005, 51–73.

Philip K. Dick ('Richard Phillips') (1928–1982)

16067. BILSON, FRED. The colonialists' fear of colonisation and the alternate worlds of Ward Moore, Philip K. Dick and Keith Roberts. *See* **18333**.

16068. SALER, MICHAEL. Partial recall. TLS, 5 Aug. 2005, 10 (review-article).

16069. TRON, DANIEL. La reconstruction de l'histoire de Philip K. Dick au cinéma coréen contemporain. Cycnos (22:2) 2005, 39–54.

16070. WILSON, ERIC G. Moviegoing and golem-making: the case of *Blade Runner*. *See* **13481**.

Christopher Dickey

16071. DICKEY, CHRISTOPHER. Firebombings: from my father's wars to mine. *See* **16079**.

James Dickey

16072. ANDERSON, JOHN. The triumph of trying: James Dickey's mystical journey through *The Zodiac*. JDN (22:1) 2005, 25–32.

16073. BARNETT, PAMELA E. James Dickey's *Deliverance*: Southern, White, suburban male nightmare or dream come true? FMLS (40:2) 2004, 145–59.

16074. BLUNK, JONATHAN. Praise the winters gone: introduction to a selection of ten letters by James Wright. *See* **20450**.

16075. BOWEN, SCOTT. Reading the verse of Orion. JDN (22:1) 2005, 1–16.

16076. CHAPMAN, WAYNE. Dickey *redivivus* at Clemson, 1966–1986. SoCR (37:2) 2005, 78–92.

16077. CLABOUGH, CASEY. Elements of Dickey's fiction. SoCR (37:2) 2005, 29–33.

16078. DICKEY, BRONWEN. The truth as a 'lie': James Dickey and the spirit of poetic revelation. SoCR (37:2) 2005, 19–23.

16079. DICKEY, CHRISTOPHER. Firebombings: from my father's wars to mine. SoCR (36:2) 2004, 5–17.

16080. DICKEY, KEVIN. Comments on *The Sheep Child* and *The Bee*. SoCR (37:2) 2005, 45–8.

16081. EISIMINGER, SKIP. A year with James Dickey. SoCR (37:2) 2005, 24–9.

16082. FRANK, BERNHARD. Dickey's *Passengers*. Exp (64:1) 2005, 54–6.

16083. GECKLE, GEORGE. Dickey inside out. JDN (21:2) 2005, 4–9.

16084. HAVIRD, DAVID. Revising holy writ: James Dickey at Mid-Week Manna. JDN (22:1) 2005, 17–24.

16085. LANE, JOHN. On the Chattooga. SoCR (37:2) 2005, 34–8. (Setting of *Deliverance*.)

16086. SHAW, DENISE. Rape, murder, and masculinity in *Deliverance*. JDN (22:1) 2005, 33–45.

16087. SLOVIC, SCOTT. Visceral Faulkner: fiction and the tug of the organic world. *In* (pp. 115–32) **16453**.

16088. STANDRIDGE, JANICE. Researching Dickey's *Falling*. SoCR (37:2) 2005, 92–7.

16089. STENDER, JESSICA. Dickey's *The Eagle's Mile* in the making. SoCR (37:2) 2005, 98–104.

16090. VAN NESS, GORDON (ed.). The one voice of James Dickey: his letters and life, 1942–1969. (Bibl. 2003, 16273.) Rev. by Susan Meyers in SoCR (38:1) 2005, 249–51.

16091. —— The one voice of James Dickey: his letters and life, 1970–1997. Columbia; London: Missouri UP, 2005. pp. xv, 554. Rev. by Joyce Morrow Pair in JDN (22:1) 2005, 46–50.

16092. WALKER, SUE. Woman as nature / nature as woman: interiority and exteriority, psychic life, the environment, and the deep ecology of James Dickey. SoCR (37:2) 2005, 38–43.

Joan Didion

16093. DIDION, JOAN. The year of magical thinking. New York: Knopf, 2005. pp. 227.

16094. SCATAMACCHIA, CRISTINA. Horizontal and vertical themes in Joan Didion's memoir *Where I Was From*. RSA (15/16) 2004/05, 69–91.

Pietro di Donato

16095. MacKenzie, Gina Masucci.   Under-writing: forming an American minority literature. JML (26:3/4) 2003, 1–11.

'Isak Dinesen' (Karen Blixen)

16096. Brazzelli, Nicoletta.   In and out of Africa: women's travel writing and autobiography in the thirties. *In* (pp. 89–98) **3690.**

16097. Hansen, Frantz Leander.   The aristocratic universe of Karen Blixen: destiny and the denial of fate. Brighton; Portland, OR: Sussex Academic Press, 2003. pp. ix, 165. Rev. by Susan Brantly in SS (76:3) 2004, 429–31.

16098. Lokke, Kari E.   Tracing women's Romanticism: gender, history and transcendence. *See* **11979.**

16099. Sabo, Anne G.   Revamped woman and the untruth of truth: unraveling the antifeminism of Nietzsche and Dinesen. Lit (16:1) 2005, 41–73.

16100. Simon, Lewis.   White women writers and their African invention. Gainesville: Florida UP, 2003. pp. viii, 263. Rev. by Lezlie Margaret Hall in MFS (51:1) 2005, 232–5.

Diane di Prima

16101. Farland, Maria.   'Total system, total solution, total apocalypse': sex oppression, systems of property, and 1970s women's liberation fiction. *See* **17231.**

Chitra Banerjee Divakaruni (b.1956)

16102. Hong, Terry.   Responding with hope to 9/11: a talk with Chitra Banerjee Divakaruni about her latest novel, *Queen of Dreams.* BRev (24:6) 2004, 5.

Stephen Dobyns

16103. Dobyns, Stephen.   Behind the story. *In* (pp. 244–8) **14294.**

16104. Gregson, Ian.   Making something real with words: the dog named fear, and the dog named Jasper, in the writings of Stephen Dobyns. Eng (54:208) 2005, 49–58.

E. L. Doctorow

16105. Eichelberger, Julia.   Spiritual regeneration in E. L. Doctorow's *Heist* and *City of God.* StudAJL (24) 2005, 82–94.

16106. Girardin, Sophie.   *The Book of Daniel* de E. L. Doctorow: la citation comme stratégie de rupture. EREA (2:1) 2004, 84–91.

16107. —— E. L. Doctorow's *The Book of Daniel*: a writer-in-process. EREA (2:2) 2004, 78–85.

16108. Kušnír, Jaroslav.   Parody of western in American literature: Doctorow's *Welcome to Hard Times*, and R. Coover's *Ghost Town*. *In* (pp. 101–8) **3753.**

Emma Donoghue (b.1969)

16109. Palmer, Paulina.   Lesbian transformations of gothic and fairy tale. *See* **16634.**

Hilda Doolittle ('H.D.')

16110. FREEDMAN, ARIELA. Zeppelin fictions and the British home front. *See* **20047**.

16111. GLASER, BRIAN BRODHEAD. H.D.'s *Helen in Egypt*: aging and the unconscious. JML (28:4) 2005, 91–109.

16112. HATLEN, BURTON. From the transcendental to the immanent sublime: the poetry of William Carlos Williams, 1913–1917. *See* **20212**.

16113. KORG, JACOB. Winter love: Ezra Pound and H.D. (Bibl. 2004, 16398.) Rev. by E. P. Walkiewicz in ELT (48:4) 2005, 485–9.

16114. SIMPSON, KATHRYN. Pearl-diving: inscriptions of desire and creativity in H.D. and Woolf. JML (27:4) 2004, 37–58.

16115. SVENSSON, LARS-HÅKAN. Modernism and the Classical tradition: the examples of Pound and H.D. *In* (pp. 112–31) **12946**.

16116. TRYPHONOPOULOS, DEMETRES. 'Fragments of a faith forgotten': Ezra Pound, H.D. and the occult tradition. *See* **18898**.

Ariel Dorfman

16117. MCCLENNEN, SOPHIA A. The diasporic subject in Ariel Dorfman's *Heading South, Looking North*. MELUS (30:1) 2005, 169–88.

16118. RAMSDELL, LEA. Language and identity politics: the linguistic autobiographies of Latinos in the United States. *See* **19103**.

Michael Dorris

16119. MATCHIE, TOM. Collaboration in the works of Erdrich and Michael Dorris: a study in the process of writing. *In* (pp. 147–57) **16372**.

John Dos Passos

16120. CARR, VIRGINIA SPENCER. Dos Passos: a life. Foreword by Donald Pizer. Evanston, IL: Northwestern UP, 2004. pp. xxi, 624.

16121. GUÉTIN, NICOLE. Éros et les romanciers des années trente. *See* **19614**.

16122. HOCK, STEPHEN. 'Stories told sideways out of the big mouth': John Dos Passos's Bazinian camera eye. LitFQ (33:1) 2005, 20–7.

16123. KOCH, STEPHEN. The breaking point: Hemingway, Dos Passos, and the murder of José Robles. *See* **16982**.

16124. KORITZ, AMY. Urban form *vs* human function in the 1920s: Lewis Mumford and John Dos Passos. AmS (45:2) 2004, 101–23.

16125. PACKER, MATTHEW J. Mimetic desire in John Dos Passos's *USA* trilogy. PLL (41:2) 2005, 215–31.

16126. PAUL, RONALD. In pastoral fields: the Regeneration Trilogy and classic First World War fiction. *In* (pp. 147–61) **15309**.

Lord Alfred Douglas

16127. FISHER, TREVOR. Douglas and Wilde: a voice from the past. *See* **12389**.

16128. SCHNITZER, CAROL. Prison confession: an analysis of *De Profundis*. *See* **12420**.

Rita Dove

16129. DUNGY, CAMILLE T. Interview with Rita Dove. Callaloo (28:4) 2005, 1027–40.

16130. FRANCINI, ANTONELLA. Sonnet *vs* sonnet: the fourteen lines in African American poetry. See **17999**.

16131. SPIEGELMAN, WILLARD. Rita Dove, dancing. VQR (81:1) 2005, 228–34.

Roddy Doyle

16132. DOCHERTY, THOMAS. Newman, Ireland, and universality. See **11762**.

16133. JACKLEIN, CHARLOTTE. Rebel songs and hero pawns: music in *A Star Called Henry*. NewHR (9:4) 2005, 129–43.

16134. McGLYNN, MARY. Pregnancy, privacy, and domesticity in *The Snapper*. NewHR (9:1) 2005, 141–56.

Margaret Drabble

16135. DRABBLE, MARGARET. Only correct: a reluctant combatant on the Orientalist battlefield. TLS, 29 July 2005, 12–13.

16136. LIN, LIDAN. Spatial narrative and postfeminist fiction: Margaret Drabble's *The Radiant Way*. EngS (86:1) 2005, 51–70.

16137. YU, YI-LIN. Mother, she wrote: matrilineal narrative in contemporary women's writing. New York; Frankfurt: Lang, 2004. pp. xii, 237.

Michael Dransfield

16138. ARMAND, LOUIS. Solicitations: essays on criticism and culture. See **14689**.

Ruth Draper

16139. ROSE, MARGARET. Lauro de Bosis e Ruth Draper: un intreccio letterario, politico e sentimentale. *In* (pp. 151–9) **12662**.

Theodore Dreiser

16140. GROSS, ANDREW S. Cars, postcards, and patriotism: tourism and national politics in the United States, 1893–1929. PCP (40:1) 2005, 77–97.

16141. HAKUTANI, YOSHINOBU (ed.). Theodore Dreiser's uncollected magazine articles, 1897–1902. (Bibl. 2003, 16351.) Rev. by Nadjia Amrane in EA (58:3) 2005, 373–4.

16142. JURAS, UWE. Pleasing to the 'I': the culture of personality and its representations in Theodore Dreiser and F. Scott Fitzgerald. New York; Frankfurt: Lang, 2005. pp. xiv, 440. (Mainzer Studien zur Amerikanistik, 50.)

16143. LINK, ERIC CARL. Lactantius, teleology, and American literature. See **8644**.

16144. LOVING, JEROME. The last Titan: a life of Theodore Dreiser. Berkeley; London: California UP, 2005. pp. xvi, 480, (plates) 32. Rev. by Sally E. Parry in AmBR (26:5) 2005, 1, 5; by Stephen C. Brennan in DreiS (36:1) 2005, 55–60.

16145. MARKOV, NINA. Class, culture, and capital in *Sister Carrie*. DreiS (36:1) 2005, 3–27.

16146. PACKER-KINLAW, DONNA. Dreiser–Mencken letters. See **18181**.

16147. Ricciardi, Caterina.   Tiffany: Fifth Avenue, Via del Babuino. *In* (pp. 181–293) **12883**.

16148. Rusch, Frederic E.; Pizer, Donald (eds).   Theodore Dreiser: interviews. Urbana: Illinois UP, 2004. pp. xiv, 371. Rev. by Roger W. Smith in DreiS (36:1) 2005, 63–6.

16149. Smith, Roger W.   A Dreiser checklist, 2004. DreiS (36:1) 2005, 49–54.

16150. Totten, Gary.   Dreiser and the writing market: new letters on the publication history of *Jennie Gerhardt*. DreiS (36:1) 2005, 28–48.

16151. von Bardeleben, Renate (ed.).   A traveler at forty. Urbana: Illinois UP, 2004. pp. xii, 991. (Dreiser ed.)

Richard Dresser (b.1951)

16152. Bohr, Dennis.   From script to screen: adaptation of Richard Dresser's *Below the Belt*. *In* (pp. 219–38) **13950**.

Rosalyn Drexler ('Julia Sorel')

16153. Geis, Deborah R.   In Willy Loman's garden: contemporary re-visions of *Death of a Salesman*. *In* (pp. 202–18) **18234**.

W. E. B. Du Bois

16154. Balfour, Lawrie.   Representative women: slavery, citizenship, and feminist theory in Du Bois's *Damnation of Women*. Hypatia (20:3) 2005, 127–48.

16155. Brody, Jennifer DeVere.   The blackness of Blackness ...: reading the typography of *Invisible Man*. See **16327**.

16156. Brown, Gillian.   Thinking in the future perfect: consent, childhood, and minority rights. See **1161**.

16157. Fisher, Rebecka Rutledge.   Cultural artifacts and the narrative of history: W. E. B. Du Bois and the exhibiting of culture at the 1900 Paris Exposition Universelle. MFS (51:4) 2005, 741–74.

16158. Holmes, David G.   Revisiting racialized voice: African American ethos in language and literature. See **10418**.

16159. Hubbard, Dolan.   Du Bois, Conrad and the luminous darkness. ZNHF (18) 2004, 60–76.

16160. Judy, Ronald A. T.   America and powerless potentialities. YREAL (19) 2003, 129–54.

16161. Moses, Wilson Jeremiah.   Creative conflict in African American thought: Frederick Douglass, Alexander Crummell, Booker T. Washington, W. E. B. Du Bois, and Marcus Garvey. See **10831**.

16162. Oliver, Lawrence J.   W. E. B. Du Bois' *The Quest of the Silver Fleece* and contract realism. ALR (38:1) 2005, 32–46.

16163. Whalan, Mark.   'The only real white democracy' and the language of liberation: the Great War, France, and African American culture in the 1920s. MFS (51:4) 2005, 775–800.

Louis Dudek

16164. Tremblay, Tony.   'A widening of the northern coterie': the cross-border cultural politics of Ezra Pound, Marshall McLuhan, and Louis Dudek. *In* (pp. 153–77) **12739**.

John Dufresne (b.1948)

16165. WILLIAMS, TOM. 'It's my job to imagine': an interview with John Dufresne. ArkR (36:2) 2005, 101–11.

Henry Dumas

16166. SCHULTHEIS, PATRICIA. Henry Dumas: truths, poetry, and memory. ChattR (25:4) 2005, 25–37.

Daphne du Maurier

16167. BLACKFORD, HOLLY. Haunted housekeeping: fatal attractions of servant and mistress in twentieth-century female gothic literature. See 20115.

16168. FRANK, BERNHARD. Du Maurier's *Rebecca*. Exp (63:4) 2005, 239–41.

16169. KNIGHT, CHARMIAN. Thornfield Hall revisited. *In* (pp. 63–73) 10222.

16170. PYRHÖNEN, HETA. Bluebeard's accomplice: *Rebecca* as a masochistic fantasy. Mosaic (38:3) 2005, 149–65.

David James Duncan

16171. SEXTON, ZAC. The rhythm of rivers: an interview with David James Duncan. BRev (23:2) 2003, 3, 8–9.

Lois Duncan

16172. CASIL, AMY STERLING. Lois Duncan. New York: Rosen Central, 2005. pp. 112. (Library of author biographies.)

Robert Duncan

16173. BERTHOLF, ROBERT J. (ed.). Letters: poems 1953–1956. Chicago, IL: Flood, 2003. pp. xv, 71. Rev. by Jeff Hamilton in ChiR (51:1/2) 2005, 242–9.

16174. —— GELPI, ALBERT (eds). The letters of Robert Duncan and Denise Levertov. (Bibl. 2004, 16473.) Rev. by Peter O'Leary in ChiR (51:1/2) 2005, 232–9.

16175. BLOCK, ED, JR. Mystery, myth, and presence: concord and conflict in the correspondence of Denise Levertov and Robert Duncan. Ren (58:1) 2005, 63–89.

16176. FINKELSTEIN, NORMAN. Late Duncan: from poetry to scripture. TCL (51:3) 2005, 341–72.

16177. HAMILTON, JEFF. *Letters*, abroad and back. ChiR (51:1/2) 2005, 242–9 (review-article).

16178. KEENAGHAN, ERIC. Vulnerable households: Cold War containment and Robert Duncan's queered nation. JML (28:4) 2005, 57–90.

16179. O'LEARY, PETER. Duncan, Levertov, and the age of correspondences. ChiR (51:1/2) 2005, 232–9 (review-article).

16180. RODRÍGUEZ HERRERA, JOSÉ. Linguistic *versus* organic, sfumato *versus* chiaroscuro: some aesthetic differences between Denise Levertov and Robert Duncan. See 17704.

Douglas Dunn

16181. SKINNER, JONATHAN. Nationalist poets and 'barbarian poetry': Scotland's Douglas Dunn and Montserrat's Howard Fergus. FMLS (40:4) 2004, 377–88.

John Gregory Dunne

16182. DIDION, JOAN. The year of magical thinking. *See* **16093.**

16183. KICH, MARTIN. *Playland* by John Gregory Dunne. NCL (35:4) 2005, 9–12.

Edward John Plunkett, Lord Dunsany

16184. GOODRICH, PETER. Mannerism and the macabre in H. P. Lovecraft's Dunsanian *Dream-Quest. See* **17860.**

Rachel Blau DuPlessis

16185. CAMBONI, MARINA. 'Disarmonia perfetta': polilinguismo e transnazionalismo nella poesia sperimentale contemporanea. *In* (pp. 9–33) **14377.**

16186. DUPLESSIS, RACHEL BLAU. 'Lexicon's mixage': on multi-lingual strategies in my poetry. *In* (pp. 51–69) **14377.**

Lawrence Durrell

16187. DIBOLL, MICHAEL V. Lawrence Durrell's *Alexandria Quartet* in its Egyptian contexts. Lewiston, NY; Lampeter: Mellen Press, 2004. pp. xxxii, 359. (Studies in British literature, 84.)

16188. PAPAYANIS, MARILYN ADLER. Writing in the margins: the ethics of expatriation from Lawrence to Ondaatje. *See* **17621.**

16189. PHILIPPE, MURIELLE. *Reflections on a Marine Venus* (1953): le détour par Rhodes dans la trilogie des îles de Lawrence Durrell. EREA (3:1) 2005, 55–61.

16190. RASHIDI, LINDA STUMP. (Re)constructing reality: complexity in Lawrence Durrell's *Alexandria Quartet.* New York; Frankfurt: Lang, 2005. pp. xii, 143. (Studies in twentieth-century British literature, 7.)

16191. STEINBERG, THEODORE LOUIS. Twentieth-century epic novels. Newark: Delaware UP, 2005. pp. 247.

Stuart Dybek (b.1942)

16192. SEAMAN, DONNA. A conversation with Stuart Dybek. TriQ (123) 2005, 15–25.

Eva Emery Dye (1855–1947)

16193. BROWNE, SHERI BARTLETT. Eva Emery Dye: romance with the West. (Bibl. 2004, 16493.) Rev. by Richard W. Etulain in JAH (92:1) 2005, 234–5.

Geoff Dyer

16194. BROOKER, JOE. Shades of the eighties: *The Colour of Memory. In* (pp. 139–52) **14254.**

Wilma Dykeman

16195. ENGELHARDT, ELIZABETH. Nature-loving souls and Appalachian Mountains: the promise of feminist ecocriticism. *In* (pp. 337–52) **12822.**

16196. GANTT, PATRICIA. Casting a long shadow: *The Tall Woman. In* (pp. 91–103) **12822.**

'Bob Dylan' (Robert Zimmerman)

16197. BAYLES, MARTHA. The strange career of folk music. *See* **3530.**

16198. BOUCHER, DAVID. Images and distorted facts: politics, poetry and protest in the songs of Bob Dylan. *In* (pp. 134–69) **16199.**

16199. —— BROWNING, GARY (eds). The political art of Bob Dylan. Basingstoke; New York: Palgrave Macmillan, 2004. pp. xii, 178.

16200. BROWN, RICHARD. Bob Dylan's critique of judgement: 'thinkin' about the law'. *In* (pp. 35–54) **16199**.

16201. —— Highway 61 and other American states of mind. *In* (pp. 193–220) **16207**.

16202. BROWNING, GARY. Dylan and Lyotard: is it happening? *In* (pp. 105–33) **16199**.

16203. BUTLER, CHRISTOPHER. Dylan and the academics. *In* (pp. 51–70) **16207**.

16204. CHEYETTE, BRYAN. On the 'D' train: Bob Dylan's conversions. *In* (pp. 221–52) **16207**.

16205. CORCORAN, NEIL. Death's honesty. *In* (pp. 143–74) **16207**.

16206. —— Introduction: writing aloud. *In* (pp. 7–23) **16207**.

16207. —— (ed.). 'Do you, Mr Jones?': Bob Dylan with the poets and professors. London: Chatto & Windus, 2002. pp. 378. Rev. by Geoff Ward in CamQ (33:3) 2004, 261–9.

16208. CRAIK, ROGER. Weldon Kees and Bob Dylan's *Idiot Wind*. *See* **17376**.

16209. CROTTY, PATRICK. Bob Dylan's last words. *In* (pp. 307–33) **16207**.

16210. CUSHING, JAMES. Prisoners in a world of mystery: Bob Dylan and his chronicler. ARSCJ (36:1) 2005, 45–9.

16211. DAY, AIDAN. Looking for nothing: Dylan now. *In* (pp. 275–93) **16207**.

16212. DYLAN, BOB. Chronicles: vol. 1. New York: Simon & Schuster, 2004. pp. 293. Rev. by Richard Williams in TLS, 12 Nov. 2004, 8–9; by Jeff Wiederkehr in AmBR (26:3) 2005, 37–9; by Bill McGarvey in ANCW (192:2) 2005, 31–2.

16213. —— Younger than that now: the collected interviews with Bob Dylan. New York: Thunder's Mouth Press; London: Orion, 2004. pp. 294.

16214. FORD, MAX. Trust yourself: Emerson and Dylan. *In* (pp. 127–42) **16207**.

16215. GAMBLE, ANDREW. The drifter's escape. *In* (pp. 12–34) **16199**.

16216. GREENLAW, LAVINIA. Big brass bed: Bob Dylan and delay. *In* (pp. 71–80) **16207**.

16217. JONES, MICHAEL. Judas and the many 'betrayals' of Bob Dylan. *In* (pp. 55–78) **16199**.

16218. KARLIN, DANIEL. Bob Dylan's names. *In* (pp. 27–49) **16207**.

16219. MARQUSEE, MIKE. Wicked messenger: Bob Dylan and the 1960s. New York: Seven Stories Press, 2005. pp. vii, 367. (Second ed.: first ed. 2003.) (Orig. pub. as *Chimes of Freedom*.)

16220. RICKS, CHRISTOPHER. Dylan's visions of sin. (Bibl. 2004, 16498.) Rev. by Matt Stefon in JPC (38:5) 2005, 983–4.

16221. RILEY, TIM. Another side of Bob Dylan. WLT (79:3/4) 2005, 8–12.

16222. ROE, NICHOLAS. Playing time. *In* (pp. 81–104) **16207**.

16223. STEEN, GERARD. Can discourse properties of metaphor affect metaphor recognition? *See* **2487**.

16224. THURSCHWELL, PAMELA. 'A different baby blue'. *In* (pp. 253–73) **16207**.

16225. WHEELER, SUSAN. Jokerman. *In* (pp. 175–91) **16207**.

16226. WILDE, LAWRENCE. The cry of humanity: Dylan's expressionist period. *In* (pp. 79–104) **16199.**

16227. WILENTZ, SEAN. American recordings: on *Love and Theft* and the minstrel boy. *In* (pp. 295–305) **16207.**

Terry Eagleton (b.1943)

16228. DICKINSON, PETER. Oscar Wilde: reading the life after the life. *See* **12381.**

16229. MCNEILL, DOUGAL. Sounding the future: Marxism and the plays of Terry Eagleton. CulL (8) 2005.

Mignon Good Eberhart (b.1899)

16230. CYPERT, RICK. America's Agatha Christie: Mignon Good Eberhart, her life and works. Selinsgrove, PA: Susquehanna UP, 2005. pp. 319.

Dorothy Edwards (1903–1934)

16231. STEVENSON, LUCY. Two drafts of an unpublished story by Dorothy Edwards. WWrE (10) 2005, 160–89.

John Ehle

16232. BOGGESS, CAROL. Interview with John Ehle. AppalJ (33:1) 2005, 32–51.

W. D. Ehrhart

16233. KICH, MARTIN (introd. and notes). *The Outer Banks*: poems of Muriel Rukeyser and W. D. Ehrhart. *See* **19254.**

Loren Eiseley

16234. WISNER, WILLIAM H. The perilous self: Loren Eiseley and the reticence of autobiography. SewR (113:1) 2005, 84–95.

'M. Barnard Eldershaw'
(Flora Eldershaw and Marjorie Barnard)

16235. DEVER, MARYANNE. 'A friendship that is grown on paper': reflections on editing Marjorie Barnard's letters to Nettie Palmer. Antipodes (19:1) 2005, 13–19.

T. S. Eliot

16236. AHEARN, BARRY. Kenner, Eliot, and language. *See* **14684.**

16237. ALKALAY-GUT, KAREN. The dream life of Ms Dog: Anne Sexton's revolutionary use of pop culture. *See* **19367.**

16238. ASHTON, DORE. Was this angel necessary? *See* **19643.**

16239. BACIGALUPO, MASSIMO. Autobiografia e modernismo in America: il caso Pound. *In* (pp. 261–81) **12577.**

16240. BADENHAUSEN, RICHARD. T. S. Eliot and the art of collaboration. Cambridge; New York: CUP, 2004. pp. xi, 256.

16241. BAJETTA, CARLO M. T. S. Eliot: nota bibliografica. LT (5) 2005, 36–40.

16242. BAKER, CHRISTOPHER. Porphyro's rose: Keats and T. S. Eliot's *The Metaphysical Poets*. JML (27:1/2) 2003, 57–62.

16243. BAY-CHENG, SARAH. The transcendental realism of American verse drama. *See* **15320.**

16244. BENNETT, BENJAMIN. All theater is revolutionary theater. Ithaca, NY; London: Cornell UP, 2005. pp. x, 241.

16245. BRATCHER, JAMES T. The speaker's occasion and the death of Pan in Eliot's *Journey of the Magi.* NQ (52:4) 2005, 497–8.

16246. BROOKER, JEWEL SPEARS. Dialectic and impersonality in T. S. Eliot. Part A (3:2) 2005, 129–51.

16247. —— To murder and create: ethics and aesthetics in Levinas, Pound, and Eliot. *In* (pp. 55–76) **12946.**

16248. —— (ed.). T. S. Eliot: the contemporary reviews. (Bibl. 2004, 16513.) Rev. by Richard Badenhausen in ELT (48:3) 2005, 370–5; by Wallace Martin in JML (28:4) 2005, 176–9; by James Olney in SAtlR (66:3) 2005, 139–41; by Mª Lourdes López Ropero in RAEI (18) 2005, 311–13; by Nancy D. Hargrove in SAtlR (70:2) 2005, 147–50.

16249. BROWN, DENNIS. The Regeneration Trilogy: total war, masculinities, anthropologies, and the talking cure. *In* (pp. 187–202) **15309.**

16250. CASELLA, STEFANO M. 'Empty silences': T. S. Eliot and Eugenio Montale. RSA (14) 2003, 67–91.

16251. CASELLA, STEFANO MARIA. L'immaginario iniziatico e mistico nei *Four Quartets* di T. S. Eliot. *In* (pp. 91–119) **3891.**

16252. CHANDRAN, K. NARAYANA. T. S. Eliot and W. E. Henley: a source for the 'water-dripping song' in *The Waste Land.* ELN (43:1) 2005, 59–62.

16253. CHINITZ, DAVID E. T. S. Eliot and the cultural divide. (Bibl. 2003, 16447.) Rev. by Ronald Bush in Mod/Mod (12:1) 2005, 198–200; by Richard Greaves in RES (56:225) 2005, 472–4; by Jayme Stayer in TCL (51:4) 2005, 504–11.

16254. CLAVARON, YVES; DIETERLE, BERNARD (eds). La mémoire des villes. *See* **20330.**

16255. COMENTALE, EDWARD P. Modernism, cultural production, and the British avant-garde. *See* **12616.**

16256. COPLEY, J. H. Plurilingualism and the mind of Europe in T. S. Eliot and Dante. YER (22:1) 2005, 2–24.

16257. CRAIG, CAIRNS. Carlyle and Symbolism. *In* (pp. 102–12) **10393.**

16258. CUDA, ANTHONY J. The use of memory: Seamus Heaney, T. S. Eliot, and the unpublished epigraph to *North. See* **16941.**

16259. —— Who stood over Eliot's shoulder? MLQ (66:3) 2005, 329–64.

16260. D'AMBROSIO, VINNI MARIE. Meeting Eliot and Hodgson in *Five-Finger Exercises.* YER (22:2) 2005, 7–14.

16261. DEMOOR, MARYSA. From epitaph to obituary: the death politics of T. S. Eliot and Ezra Pound. Biography (28:2) 2005, 255–75.

16262. DENTE, CARLA. RSC 1999: enter guilt on the stage of conscience: *The Family Reunion* by T. S. Eliot. *In* (pp. 137–49) **3724.**

16263. DONG, HONGCHUAN. Jiuye poets' reception of T. S. Eliot: a probe into the historical context. FLS (111) 2005, 120–7. (In Chinese.)

16264. DONOVAN, DAVID. Spiritual selfhood and the modern idea: Thomas Carlyle and T. S. Eliot. *See* **10370.**

16265. Douglas-Fairhurst, Robert.   Old bags and 'the old style': a new source for Beckett's *Happy Days*? *See* **15386**.

16266. Ellmann, Maud.   Writing like a rat. CritQ (46:4) 2004, 59–76.

16267. Fornero, Caterina.   Chess is the game wherein I'll catch the conscience of the king: the metaphor of the game of chess in T. S. Eliot's *The Waste Land*. YER (22:2) 2005, 2–6.

16268. Ghose, Zulfikar.   Christopher Middleton and 'the bare bone of creation'. *See* **18216**.

16269. Gill, Joanna.   'My Sweeney, Mr Eliot': Anne Sexton and the 'impersonal theory of poetry'. *See* **19369**.

16270. Goeglein, Timothy S.   A sense of the sacred. *See* **7473**.

16271. Gozzi, Francesco.   Shakespeare as Paraclitus: Transubstantiation in Joyce and T. S. Eliot. *In* (pp. 88–94) **3724**.

16272. Gupta, Suman.   In search of genius: T. S. Eliot as publisher. JML (27:1/2) 2003, 26–35.

16273. Hardy, Henry; Holmes, Jennifer.   *Old Croaker*: a new T. S. Eliot poem – by Maurice Bowra. *See* **14409**.

16274. Hargrove, Nancy D.   T. S. Eliot and opera in Paris, 1910–1911. YER (21:3) 2004, 2–20.

16275. Innes, Christopher.   Shifting the frame – Modernism in the theatre. *In* (pp. 204–12) **12946**.

16276. Johnson, Loretta.   T. S. Eliot's bawdy verse: Lulu, Bolo and more ties. JML (27:1/2) 2003, 14–25.

16277. Kehoe, Deborah P.   Early reflections in a 'nothing place': three Gethsemani poems. *See* **18198**.

16278. Levy, Eric P.   The literary depiction of ontological shock. *See* **15403**.

16279. Liu, Tian.   The time subject and elements' variations in *Four Quartets*. FLS (115) 2005, 97–102. (In Chinese.)

16280. Lobb, Edward.   Waugh among the Modernists: allusion and theme in *A Handful of Dust*. *See* **20013**.

16281. Longenbach, James.   The dream of Modernism. *See* **16779**.

16282. Longley, Edna.   'Altering the past': Northern Irish poetry and modern canons. *See* **14440**.

16283. Lowe, Peter.   Prufrock in St Petersburg: the presence of Dostoyevsky's *Crime and Punishment* in T. S. Eliot's *The Love Song of J. Alfred Prufrock*. JML (28:3) 2005, 1–24.

16284. Mallinson, Jane.   A modern mode of epiphany. *In* (pp. 173–81) **9237**.

16285. Marshall, Ashley.   T. S. Eliot on the limits of criticism: the anomalous 'experiment' of 1929. MLR (100:3) 2005, 609–20.

16286. Mellor, Leo.   Words from the bombsites: debris, Modernism and literary salvage. CritQ (46:4) 2004, 77–90.

16287. Miller, James E., Jr.   T. S. Eliot: the making of an American poet, 1888–1922. University Park: Pennsylvania State UP, 2005. pp. xx, 468.

16288. Moody, A. David.   Kipling in Eliot and in Pound: a measure of their difference. *In* (pp. 153–8) **3756**.

16289. MULVIHILL, JAMES. *The Love Song of J. Alfred Prufrock* and Byron's speaker in *Don Juan*. NQ (52:1) 2005, 101.

16290. MUSACCHIO, GEORGE. C. S. Lewis, T. S. Eliot, and the Anglican Psalter. *See* **17769.**

16291. NESME, AXEL. Intertextual 'tissue preserved': a reading of Ezra Pound's *Hugh Selwyn Mauberley*. *See* **18882.**

16292. NYBERG, LENNART. 'The imagination': a twentieth-century itinerary. *In* (pp. 40–54) **12946.**

16293. POLLARD, CHARLES W. New World Modernisms: T. S. Eliot, Derek Walcott, and Kamau Brathwaite. (Bibl. 2004, 16556.) Rev. by Laurence A. Breiner in TCL (51:1) 2005, 110–13.

16294. PONDROM, CYRENA N. T. S. Eliot: the performativity of gender in *The Waste Land*. Mod/Mod (12:3) 2005, 425–41.

16295. POTTER, LOIS. Robin Hood and the fairies: Alfred Noyes' *Sherwood*. *In* (pp. 167–80) **3576.**

16296. RAINEY, LAWRENCE. Eliot among the typists: writing *The Waste Land*. Mod/Mod (12:1) 2005, 27–84.

16297. —— Revisiting *The Waste Land*. New Haven, CT; London: Yale UP, 2005. pp. xiv, 205. Rev. by Michael Tyrell in CommRev (4:2) 2005, 50–3.

16298. —— (ed.). The annotated *Waste Land*, with T. S. Eliot's contemporary prose. New Haven, CT; London: Yale UP for the Paul Mellon Centre for Studies in British Art, 2005. pp. vi, 270.

16299. RAWSON, CLAUDE. Tribal drums and the dull tom-tom: thoughts on Modernism and the savage in Conrad and Eliot. *In* (pp. 95–111) **12946.**

16300. RICKS, CHRISTOPHER. Decisions and revisions in T. S. Eliot. London: British Library/Faber & Faber, 2003. pp. xii, 100. (Panizzi Lectures: 2002.)

16301. ROSEN, DAVID. Maturity and poetic style. *See* **7745.**

16302. SANESI, ROBERTO (ed. and trans.). Opere: vol. 1, 1904–1939. Milan: Bompiani, 2005. pp. xxxv, 1659. (Classici stranieri.) (Second ed.: first ed. 1992.)

16303. SANSOM, IAN. Listen: W. S. Graham. *In* (pp. 11–23) **16793.**

16304. SCHUCHARD, RONALD. Did Eliot know Hulme? Final answer. JML (27:1/2) 2003, 63–9.

16305. SHARPE, PETER. The ground of our beseeching: metaphor and the poetics of meditation. Selinsgrove, PA: Susquehanna UP, 2004. pp. 391. Rev. by Charles M. Murphy in WSJ (29:2) 2005, 317–18.

16306. SINGH, SUKHBIR. Rewriting the American wasteland: John Updike's *The Centaur. See* **19896.**

16307. SMITH, STAN. Constitutions of silence: Mr Eliot's second revolution. Paideuma (32:1–3) 2003, 15–38.

16308. —— The disconsolate chimera: T. S. Eliot and the fixation of Modernism. *In* (pp. 180–203) **12946.**

16309. SNEDIKER, MICHAEL. Hart Crane's smile. *See* **15959.**

16310. SORUM, EVE. Masochistic Modernisms: a reading of Eliot and Woolf. JML (28:3) 2005, 25–43.

16311. SPENCER, MICHAEL D. The garden in T. S. Eliot's *Four Quartets*. Cithara (44:2) 2005, 32–45.

16312. SUMMERS-BREMNER, ELUNED. Unreal city and dream deferred: psychogeographies of Modernism in T. S. Eliot and Langston Hughes. *In* (pp. 262–80) **12640**.

16313. TADIÉ, BENOÎT. The room of infinite possibilities: Joyce, Flaubert, and the historical imagination. *See* **17343**.

16314. WANG, XIAOLIN. T. S. Eliot's influence on Jiuye poets. FLS (111) 2005, 114–19. (In Chinese.)

16315. WHITEHEAD, ANNE. Tony Harrison, the Gulf War and the poetry of protest. *See* **16911**.

16316. WILLIAMS, DAVID A. 'Several centers': T. S. Eliot's wartime agenda of cultural unity and diversity. YER (22:2) 2005, 15–23.

16317. WILMER, CLIVE (ed.). Modernist essays: Yeats, Pound, Eliot. By Donald Davie. *See* **20528**.

16318. WOLF, PHILIPP. The anachronism of modern cultural memories, and an ethics of literary memory. *See* **8441**.

Stanley Elkin

16319. COUTURIER, MAURICE. Objection, what subject? EREA (2:2) 2004, 14–21.

Rosemary Ellerbeck ('Anna L'Estrange')

16320. VAN DER MEER, CAROLYNE. Interrogating Brontë sequels: Anna L'Estrange, *The Return to Wuthering Heights*. *See* **10208**.

Bret Easton Ellis

16321. ALLADAYE, RENÉ. De Bateman à Bacon: surface et profondeur dans deux romans de Bret Easton Ellis. EREA (1:1) 2003, 92–8.

16322. STOREY, MARK. 'And as things fell apart': the crisis of postmodern masculinity in Bret Easton Ellis's *American Psycho* and Dennis Cooper's *Frisk*. CritW (47:1) 2005, 57–72.

Zoila Ellis (b.1957)

16323. CANEPARI-LABIB, MICHELA. Linguistic hybridity and fragmented identities in Belizean literature. *In* (pp. 109–19) **3690**.

Ralph Ellison

16324. ALLEN, DANIELLE. Ralph Ellison on the tragicomedy of citizenship. Raritan (23:3) 2004, 56–74.

16325. BLAIR, SARA. Ralph Ellison, photographer. Raritan (24:4) 2005, 15–44.

16326. BORSHUK, MICHAEL. 'So black, so blue': Ralph Ellison, Louis Armstrong and the Bebop aesthetic. Genre (37:2) 2004, 261–83.

16327. BRODY, JENNIFER DEVERE. The blackness of Blackness ...: reading the typography of *Invisible Man*. TJ (57:4) 2005, 679–98.

16328. CALLAHAN, JOHN F. (ed.). Ralph Ellison's *Invisible Man*: a casebook. (Bibl. 2004, 16583.) Rev. by Robert Butler in AAR (39:3) 2005, 477–8.

16329. EDDY, BETH. The rites of identity: the religious naturalism and cultural criticism of Kenneth Burke and Ralph Ellison. (Bibl. 2004, 16585.) Rev. by Jeremy Biles in JR (85:1) 2005, 186–8.

16330. HANLON, CHRISTOPHER. Eloquence and *Invisible Man*. ColLit (32:4) 2005, 74–98.

16331. HOBSON, CHRISTOPHER Z. *Invisible Man* and African American radicalism in World War II. AAR (39:3) 2005, 355–76.

16332. —— Ralph Ellison, *Juneteenth*, and African American prophecy. MFS (51:3) 2005, 617–47.

16333. JACKSON, LAWRENCE. Ralph Ellison: emergence of genius. (Bibl. 2004, 16591.) Rev. by Raymond A. Mazurek in ColLit (32:2) 2005, 170–6.

16334. JENSEN, PAMELA K. Ralph Ellison's *Invisible Man*. In (pp. 117–51) **14121**.

16335. JUA, ROSELYNE M. Ralph Ellison and the paradox of *Juneteenth*. JBlaS (35:3) 2005, 310–26.

16336. KIM, DANIEL Y. Writing manhood in black and yellow: Ralph Ellison, Frank Chin, and the literary politics of identity. Stanford, CA: Stanford UP, 2005. pp. xxviii, 286. (Asian America.)

16337. RICHARDSON, RICHÉ. 'A house set off from the rest': Ralph Ellison's rural geography. FMLS (40:2) 2004, 126–44.

16338. WARREN, KENNETH W. So black and blue: Ralph Ellison and the occasion of criticism. (Bibl. 2004, 16603.) Rev. by Raymond A. Mazurek in ColLit (32:2) 2005, 170–6.

16339. WEBER, MYLES. Consuming silences: how we read authors who don't publish. *See* **19297**.

James Ellroy

16340. WOLFE, PETER. Like hot knives to the brain: James Ellroy's search for himself. Lanham, MD: Lexington, 2005. pp. xv, 266.

Margaret Elphinstone

16341. ELPHINSTONE, MARGARET. What force made men act so? A question of historical fiction. ScSR (4:2) 2003, 121–30.

Ben Elton (b.1959)

16342. CAMPOS, LILIANE. Rewriting the plot: re-creations in contemporary British comedy. *See* **15464**.

Buchi Emecheta

16343. NIERAGDEN, GÖRAN. Otherness at work: the non-indigenous English novel. BELL (ns 3) 2005, 57–65.

16344. PERREGAUX, MYRIAM. The city as gendered space: a reading of three literary texts in the light of feminist geography. *See* **17690**.

William Empson

16345. HAFFENDEN, JOHN. William Empson: among the mandarins. Oxford; New York: OUP, 2005. pp. xxi, 695, (plates) 16. Rev. by Frank Kermode in LRB (27:10) 2005, 3–5; by Michael Dirda in BkW, 19 June 2005, 15; by John Harding in TLS, 1 July 2005, 4–6.

16346. KERMODE, FRANK. The savage life. LRB (27:10) 2005, 3–5 (review-article).

Marian Engel

16347. VERDUYN, CHRISTL; GARAY, KATHLEEN (eds). Marian Engel: life in letters. Toronto; Buffalo, NY; London: Toronto UP, 2004. pp. xxxi, 295, (plates) 8.

Eve Ensler (b.1953)

16348. ENSLER, EVE. 'The first time …': my nightmare happened. Dramatist (7:5) 2005, 12–13.

16349. HALL, KIM Q. Queerness, disability, and *The Vagina Monologues*. Hypatia (20:1) 2005, 99–119.

16350. STRIFF, ERIN. Realism and *Realpolitik* in Eve Ensler's *The Vagina Monologues*. JADT (17:2) 2005, 71–85.

16351. UHRY, ALFRED. Guild roundtable: playwrights on Broadway. Dramatist (7:5) 2005, 6–11.

16352. VLACHOU, OLGA. Negotiating the difference between Ensler's *The Vagina Monologues* and its Greek translation. Gramma (12) 2004, 59–71.

Leslie Epstein

16353. EPSTEIN, LESLIE. Coming home. *In* (pp. 64–75) **12893**.

Louise Erdrich

16354. BARTON, GAY. Family as character in Erdrich's novels. *In* (pp. 77–82) **16372**.

16355. BROWN, ALANNA KATHLEEN. 'Patterns and waves generation to generation': *The Antelope Wife*. *In* (pp. 88–94) **16372**.

16356. BROZZO, SHIRLEY. Food for thought: a postcolonial study of food imagery in Louise Erdrich's *Antelope Wife*. SAIL (17:1) 2005, 1–15.

16357. CHICK, NANCY L. Does power travel in the bloodlines? A genealogical red herring. *In* (pp. 83–7) **16372**.

16358. COUSER, G. THOMAS. Tracing the trickster: Nanapush, Ojibwe oral tradition, and *Tracks*. *In* (pp. 58–65) **16372**.

16359. DIANA, VANESSA HOLFORD. Reading *The Beet Queen* from a feminist perspective. *In* (pp. 175–82) **16372**.

16360. HORNE, DEE. A postcolonial reading of *Tracks*. *In* (pp. 191–200) **16372**.

16361. HOULIHAN, PATRICK E. 'This ain't real estate': a Bakhtinian approach to *The Bingo Palace*. *In* (pp. 201–9) **16372**.

16362. JACOBS, CONNIE A. A history of the Turtle Mountain Band of Chippewa Indians. *In* (pp. 23–31) **16372**.

16363. KATANSKI, AMELIA V. Track Fleur: the Ojibwe roots of Erdrich's novels. *In* (pp. 66–76) **16372**.

16364. LISCHKE, UTE. '*Blitzkuchen*': an exploration of story-telling in Louise Erdrich's *The Antelope Wife*. *In* (pp. 61–72) **9168**.

16365. McNAB, DAVID T. Of bears and birds: the concept of history in Erdrich's autobiographical writings. *In* (pp. 32–41) **16372**.

16366. —— Story-telling and transformative spaces in Louise Erdrich's *The Blue Jay's Dance, The Birchbark House*, and *The Last Report on the Miracles at Little No Horse. In* (pp. 73–88) **9168.**

16367. McWilliams, John. Doubling the last survivor: *Tracks* and American narratives of lost wilderness. *In* (pp. 158–69) **16372.**

16368. Martínez Falquina, Silvia. From the monologic eye to healing polyphonies: dialogic re/vision in Native American narratives. *See* **15113.**

16369. Matchie, Tom. Collaboration in the works of Erdrich and Michael Dorris: a study in the process of writing. *In* (pp. 147–57) **16372.**

16370. Rosenthal, Caroline. Narrative deconstructions of gender in works by Audrey Thomas, Daphne Marlatt, and Louise Erdrich. (Bibl. 2004, 16618.) Rev. by Nancy Gillespie in BJCS (17:2) 2004, 263–4.

16371. Ruppert, James. Identity indexes in *Love Medicine* and *Jacklight. In* (pp. 170–4) **16372.**

16372. Sarris, Greg; Jacobs, Connie A.; Giles, James R. (eds). Approaches to teaching the works of Louise Erdrich. New York: Modern Language Assn of America, 2004. pp. ix, 261. (Approaches to teaching world literature.)

16373. Scarberry-García, Susan. Beneath creaking oaks: spirits and animals in *Tracks. In* (pp. 42–50) **16372.**

16374. Stokes, Karah. Sisters, lovers, magdalens, and martyrs: Ojibwe two-sisters stories in *Love Medicine. In* (pp. 51–7) **16372.**

16375. Treuer, David. Smartberries: interpreting Louise Erdrich's *Love Medicine*. AICRJ (29:1) 2005, 21–36.

16376. Winter, Kari J. Gender as a drag in *The Beet Queen. In* (pp. 183–90) **16372.**

16377. Zazula, Piotr. 'Riding scars you can't get lost': traveling women in Louise Erdrich's *Jacklight. In* (pp. 121–34) **12672.**

Martín Espada

16378. Barillas, William. Music is all we have: an interview with poet Martín Espada. BRev (23:5) 2003, 3, 26.

16379. Salgado, César A. About Martín Espada: a profile. Ploughshares (31:1) 2005, 203–8.

Ahmed Essop

16380. Rastogi, Pallavi. From South Asia to South Africa: locating other postcolonial diasporas. MFS (51:3) 2005, 536–60.

Jeffrey Eugenides

16381. Collado-Rodríguez, Francisco. Back to myth and ethical compromise: García Márquez's traces on Jeffrey Eugenides's *The Virgin Suicides*. Atl (27:2) 2005, 27–40.

Frederick Exley

16382. Saracino, Maria Antonietta. Elogio della sconfitta: *A Fan's Notes* di Frederick Exley. Àcoma (31) 2005, 39–45.

John Fante (b.1909)

16383. BARONE, DENNIS.   'Beating the marbles game': the hagiography of John Fante. VIA (15:2) 2004, 11–25.

Nuruddin Farah

16384. CONNELL, LIAM.   Global narratives: globalisation and literary studies. CritS (16:2) 2004, 78–95.

16385. NGABOH-SMART, FRANCIS.   Beyond empire and nation: postnational arguments in the fiction of Nuruddin Farah and B. Kojo Laing. Amsterdam; Atlanta, GA: Rodopi, 2004. pp. xxi, 168. (Cross/cultures: readings in the postcolonial literatures in English, 70.) Rev. by Tobias Robert Klein in WLWE (40:2) 2004, 147–8; by Julia Praud in RAL (36:1) 2005, 130–1.

Walter Farley

16386. ADDISON, LINDSAY MCLEAN.   The Black Stallion in print and film. In (pp. 163–75) **14258**.

J. G. (James Gordon) Farrell (b.1935)

16387. CRANE, RALPH J.   After Beckett: the influence of Samuel Beckett on the fiction of J. G. Farrell. See **15384**.

16388. ROSS, MICHAEL L.   Passage to Krishnapur: J. G. Farrell's comic vision of India. JCL (40:3) 2005, 63–79.

James T. (James Thomas) Farrell (1904–1979)

16389. ONKEY, LAUREN.   James Farrell's Studs Lonigan trilogy and the anxieties of race. EI (40:3/4) 2005, 104–18.

William Faulkner

16390. ANDERSON, ERIC GARY.   Environed blood: ecology and violence in *The Sound and the Fury* and *Sanctuary*. In (pp. 30–46) **16453**.

16391. ATKINSON, TED.   Faulkner and the Great Depression: aesthetics, ideology, and cultural politics. Athens; London: Georgia UP, 2005. pp. xi, 271.

16392. BAUER, MARGARET DONOVAN.   William Faulkner's legacy: 'what shadow, what stain, what mark'. Gainesville: Florida UP, 2005. pp. 255.

16393. BERNER, SETH.   Collecting Faulkner. In (pp. 153–67) **16453**.

16394. BLOSHTEYN, MARIA R.   'Anguish for the sake of anguish' – Faulkner and his Dostoevskian allusion. FJ (19:2) 2004, 69–90.

16395. BLOTNER, JOSEPH.   Faulkner: a biography. Jackson; London: Mississippi UP, 2005. pp. xv, 778.

16396. CAMPBELL, ERIN E.   'Sad generations seeking water': the social construction of madness in O(phelia) and Q(uentin Compson). FJ (20:1/2) 2004, 53–69.

16397. COSS, DAVID L.   Sutpen's sentient house. JFA (15:2) 2004, 101–18.

16398. COVEY, MEGAN.   A yellow rose for Emily. NCL (35:3) 2005, 14–16.

16399. DAVIS, THADIOUS M.   Games of property: law, race, gender, and Faulkner's *Go Down, Moses*. (Bibl. 2004, 16649.) Rev. by Marilyn Mobley McKenzie in Novel (38:1) 2004, 121–3; by Jason Gary Horn in AL (77:1) 2005,

194–6; by Doreen Fowler in SoLJ (38:1) 2005, 135–41; by Steven B. Canaday in JSH (71:1) 2005, 210–11; by Thomas Bonner, Jr, in SCR (22:1) 2005, 114–16.

16400. DE SANTIS, CHRISTOPHER C. Pseudo-history *versus* social critique: Faulkner's Reconstruction. SoQ (43:1) 2005, 9–27.

16401. DIMITRI, CARL J. *Go Down, Moses* and *Intruder in the Dust*: from negative to positive liberty. FJ (19:1) 2003, 11–26.

16402. DOBBS, CYNTHIA. 'Ruin or landmark?': Black bodies as *lieux de mémoire* in *The Sound and the Fury*. FJ (20:1/2) 2004, 35–51.

16403. ENSRUD, BARBARA. Faulkner's taste for wine. OxAm (49) 2005, 132–3.

16404. ENTZMINGER, BETINA. Snow job: the whitening of history in William Faulkner's *Absalom! Absalom!* and David Bradley's *The Chaneysville Incident*. SPC (28:2) 2005, 99–119.

16405. FISHER-WIRTH, ANN. William Faulkner, Peter Matthiessen, and the environmental imagination. *In* (pp. 47–60) **16453**.

16406. FRANK, ARMIN PAUL; LOHSE, ROLF (eds). Internationality in American fiction: Henry James, William Dean Howells, William Faulkner, Toni Morrison. New York; Frankfurt: Lang, 2005. pp. 272. (Interamericana, 3.)

16407. FULTON, LORIE WATKINS. Justice as he saw it: Gavin Stevens in *Knight's Gambit*. FJ (19:2) 2004, 25–48.

16408. GAYLORD, JOSHUA. The radiance of the fake: *Pylon*'s postmodern narrative of disease. FJ (20:1/2) 2004, 177–95.

16409. GELLY, CHRISTOPHE. De William Faulkner à James Hadley Chase: appropriation et mutation du genre policier. EREA (2:1) 2004, 69–75.

16410. GETTY, LAURA J. Faulkner's *A Rose for Emily*. Exp (63:4) 2005, 230–4.

16411. GOBETTI, NORMAN. Pavese e Vittorini, traduttori di William Faulkner. Indice (2005:12) 31.

16412. GOLDSTEIN, PHILIP. Black feminism and the canon: Faulkner's *Absalom, Absalom!* and Morrison's *Beloved* as gothic romances. FJ (20:1/2) 2004, 133–47.

16413. GWIN, MINROSE C. Racial wounding and the aesthetics of the middle voice in *Absalom, Absalom!* and *Go Down, Moses*. FJ (20:1/2) 2004, 21–33.

16414. HAMBLIN, ROBERT W.; ABADIE, ANN J. (eds). Faulkner in the twenty-first century: Faulkner and Yoknapatawpha, 2000. (Bibl. 2004, 16656.) Rev. by James G. Watson in SCR (22:1) 2005, 122–4.

16415. HANDLEY, GEORGE B. Oedipus in the Americas: *Lone Star* and the reinvention of American Studies. *See* **13640**.

16416. HANNON, CHARLES. Faulkner and the discourses of culture. Baton Rouge: Louisiana State UP, 2005. pp. x, 195. (Southern literary studies.) Rev. by D. Matthew Ramsey in ArkR (36:3) 2005, 224–5.

16417. HOLLAND, SHARON P. The last word on racism: new directions for a critical race theory. SAQ (104:3) 2005, 403–23.

16418. HORTON, MERRILL. Faulkner, Balzac, and the word. FJ (19:2) 2004, 91–106.

16419. JACKSON, ROBERT. Seeking the region in American literature and culture: modernity, dissidence, innovation. *See* **12247**.

16420. KING, SALLY WOLFF. 'He liked to call me padre': Bishop Duncan Gray remembers Faulkner. SoQ (43:1) 2005, 80–106. (Interview.)

16421. KOCH, MARKUS. The hand writing beyond the wall: Faulkner and an American cultural cringe. *In* (pp. 135–85) **16406.**

16422. KOON, BILL. 'If you lived in Clay': the small towns of Eudora Welty and William Faulkner. *See* **20078.**

16423. KRIEWALD, GARY L. The widow of Windsor and the spinster of Jefferson: a possible source for Faulkner's Emily Grierson. FJ (19:1) 2003, 3–10.

16424. LABATT, BLAIR. Faulkner the storyteller. Tuscaloosa; London: Alabama UP, 2005. pp. xviii, 263.

16425. LAWRENCE, KEITH. Moral sentiment and redemption in Faulkner's 'borrowed gothic', *Requiem for a Nun.* LitB (24:1/2) 2004, 63–79.

16426. LURIE, PETER. Querying the Modernist canon: historical consciousness and the sexuality of suffering in Faulkner and Hart Crane. FJ (20:1/2) 2004, 149–76.

16427. McHANEY, THOMAS. Welty's *Home by Dark/Yalobusha County/1936* in the jacket designs of two novels about slavery. *See* **20083.**

16428. McHANEY, THOMAS L. The ecology of Uncle Ike: teaching *Go Down, Moses* with Janisse Ray's *Ecology of a Cracker Childhood.* *In* (pp. 98–114) **16453.**

16429. MARK, REBECCA. As they lay dying; or, Why we should teach, write, and read Eudora Welty instead of, alongside of, because of, as often as William Faulkner. *See* **20085.**

16430. MATTHEWS, JOHN T. Recalling the West Indies: from Yoknapatawpha to Haiti and back. AmLH (16:2) 2004, 238–62.

16431. MERIWETHER, JAMES B. (ed.). Essays, speeches, & public letters; updated, with material never before collected in one volume. (Bibl. 1967, 8490.) New York: Modern Library, 2004. pp. xxiv, 352. (Second ed.: first ed. 1965.) Rev. by Clyde Wilson in Chronicles (29:6) 2005, 32–3; by Marc Smirnoff in OxAm (48) 2005, 130–2.

16432. MESSMER, MARIETTA. Intra-American internationality: Morrison responding to Faulkner. *In* (pp. 187–242) **16406.**

16433. MILLER, NATHANIEL A. 'Felt, not seen not heard': Quentin Compson, Modernist suicide and Southern history. StudN (37:1) 2005, 37–49.

16434. MORTON, CLAY. *A Rose for Emily*: oral plot, typographic story. Storytelling (5:1) 2005, 7–18.

16435. NELSON, LISA K. Masculinity, menace, and American mythologies of race in Faulkner's anti-heroes. FJ (19:2) 2004, 49–68.

16436. NKOSI, LEWIS. Luster's lost quarter: reading South African identities (William Faulkner and J. M. Coetzee). JPW (41:2) 2005, 166–78.

16437. PEEK, CHARLES A. Faulkner's myth and the 'peculiar institution': shaping Yoknapatawpha. FLS (114) 2005, 16–24.

16438. PETTEY, HOMER B. Perception and the destruction of being in *As I Lay Dying.* FJ (19:1) 2003, 27–46.

16439. PITAVY, FRANÇOIS. Is Faulkner green? The wilderness as aporia. *In* (pp. 81–97) **16453.**

16440. RICHARDSON, DANIEL C. Bridging the gulf: an analysis of a Brazilian translation of Faulkner's *The Wild Palms*. FJ (19:1) 2003, 61–76.

16441. ROMANCE, JOSEPH. Patriots and philosophers: the idea of obligation and race in William Faulkner's *Intruder in the Dust*. *In* (pp. 79–96) **14121.**

16442. ROVIT, EARL; WALDHORN, ARTHUR (eds). Hemingway and Faulkner in their time. London; New York: Continuum, 2005. pp. 200. Rev. by Joseph Fruscione in HemR (25:1) 2005, 139–41.

16443. SCHREIBER, EVELYN JAFFE. 'Memory believes before knowing remembers': the insistence of the past and Lacan's unconscious desire in *Light in August*. FJ (20:1/2) 2004, 71–84.

16444. SHARPE, PETER. Bonds that shackle: memory, violence, and freedom in *The Unvanquished*. FJ (20:1/2) 2005, 85–110.

16445. SILLS, CARYL K. Patterns of victimization in *Light in August*. Mosaic (38:2) 2005, 163–79.

16446. SLOVIC, SCOTT. Visceral Faulkner: fiction and the tug of the organic world. *In* (pp. 115–32) **16453.**

16447. SMIRNOFF, MARC. Faulkner as racist. OxAm (48) 2005, 130–2 (review-article).

16448. SUMMERSGILL, TRAVIS. William Faulkner's visit to Nagano. *In* (pp. 217–33) **12840.**

16449. TEBBETTS, TERRELL. *Sanctuary*, marriage, and the status of women in 1920s America. FJ (19:1) 2003, 47–60.

16450. TICHI, CECELIA. 'Old Man': shackles, chains, and water water everywhere. *In* (pp. 3–14) **16453.**

16451. URGO, JOSEPH R. William Faulkner's map of the unseen world, Yoknapatawpha County. LitB (24:1/2) 2004, 40–62.

16452. —— ABADIE, ANN J. (eds). Faulkner and his contemporaries: Faulkner and Yoknapatawpha, 2002. (Bibl. 2004, 16701.) Rev. by Ted Atkinson in ArkR (36:1) 2005, 55–6.

16453. —— —— Faulkner and the ecology of the South. Jackson; London: Mississippi UP, 2005. pp. xxiv, 173.

16454. VISSER, IRENE. Faulkner's mendicant Madonna: the light of *Light in August*. LitTheol (18:1) 2004, 38–48.

16455. WAINWRIGHT, MICHAEL. The enemy within: Faulkner's Snopes Trilogy. *In* (pp. 61–80) **16453.**

16456. WEINSTEIN, PHILIP. The land's turn. *In* (pp. 15–29) **16453.**

16457. WILHELM, RANDALL S. Faulkner's big picture book: word and image in *The Marionettes*. FJ (19:2) 2004, 3–24.

16458. WULFMAN, CLIFFORD E. The poetics of ruptured mnemosis: telling encounters in William Faulkner's *Absalom, Absalom!* FJ (20:1/2) 2004, 111–32.

16459. WYATT-BROWN, BERTRAM. William Faulkner: art, alienation, and alcohol. *In* (pp. 77–99) **12793.**

Raymond Federman

16460. CRAWFORD, BRIAN D. The value of a gambler's promise: self-imprisonment and writing survival in Raymond Federman's *Double or Nothing*. *In* (pp. 33–61) **12821**.

Ross Feld (b.1947)

16461. STEPHENS, M. G. Ross Feld. RCF (25:2) 2005, 84–130.

Alison Fell

16462. MENZIES, RUTH. Re-writing *Gulliver's Travels*: the demise of a genre? *See* **9077**.

Howard A. Fergus

16463. SKINNER, JONATHAN. Nationalist poets and 'barbarian poetry': Scotland's Douglas Dunn and Montserrat's Howard Fergus. *See* **16181**.

Rachel Ferguson (b.1893)

16464. KNIGHT, CHARMIAN. Who's afraid of the Brontë sisters? *In* (pp. 53–62) **10222**.

Lawrence Ferlinghetti

16465. EMBLIDGE, DAVID M. City Lights Bookstore: 'a finger in the dike'. *See* **818**.

16466. GONZÁLEZ, RAY. Tracing the public surface: an interview with Lawrence Ferlinghetti. BRev (23:2) 2003, 13, 18.

Arthur Davison Ficke

16467. CHURCHILL, SUZANNE W. The lying game: *Others* and the great Spectra hoax of 1917. *See* **16924**.

Leslie Fiedler

16468. BIRNBAUM, MILTON. Two of a kind? ModAge (47:2) 2005, 167–70 (review-article). (Fiedler and Aldous Huxley.)

Helen Fielding (b.1958)

16469. COCKIN, KATHARINE. Inventing the suffragettes: anachronism, gnosticism and corporeality in contemporary fiction. CritS (16:3) 2004, 17–32.

16470. HANSON, CLARE. Fiction, feminism and femininity from the eighties to the noughties. EAS (57) 2004, 16–27.

16471. MURPHY, OLIVIA. Books, bras and Bridget Jones: reading adaptions of *Pride and Prejudice*. *See* **10026**.

16472. SMITH, CAROLINE J. Living the life of a domestic goddess: chick lit's response to domestic-advice manuals. WS (34:8) 2005, 671–99.

16473. WHELEHAN, IMELDA. Sex and the single girl: Helen Fielding, Erica Jong and Helen Gurley Brown. EAS (57) 2004, 28–40.

Eva Figes (b.1932)

16474. CORONA, DANIELA. Al di qua del paradiso: memoria spaziale e confini del rifugio in *Little Eden*. *In* (pp. 45–61) **12577**.

Timothy Findley

16475. FILIPCZAK, DOROTA. Not wanted in the canon: Canadian literature in the wilderness. *In* (pp. 55–64) **3756.**

16476. GUIGNERY, VANESSA. Réécritures du Déluge et de l'arche de Noé dans la fiction contemporaine de langue anglaise (Coover, Findley, Winterson, Roberts et Barnes). *See* **19088.**

16477. TRUSSLER, MICHAEL. The voice tells according to its urgency: a letter from Timothy Findley. WasRCPSF (38:1) 2003, 267–9.

Nikky Finney

16478. BURRISS, THERESA L. Claiming a space: the Affrilachian Poets. *In* (pp. 315–36) **12822.**

M. F. K. (Mary Frances Kennedy) Fisher (b.1908)

16479. LEVY, PAUL. Cooking wolf. TLS, 25 Feb. 2005, 10 (review-article). (Fisher's gastroprose.)

16480. REARDON, JOAN. Poet of the appetites: the lives and loves of M. F. K. Fisher. (Bibl. 2004, 16735.) Rev. by Paul Levy in TLS, 25 Feb. 2005, 10; by Josephine Woll in Gastronomica (5:2) 2005, 106–7.

Rudolph Fisher

16481. MCCANN, PAUL. Music and the marketplace: jazz and the Great Depression in the short stories of Rudolph Fisher and Langston Hughes. SPC (28:2) 2005, 77–98.

F. Scott Fitzgerald

16482. ABRAMSON, EDWARD A. Aliens, stereotypes, and social change: the Jews and Hollywood in F. Scott Fitzgerald's fiction. StudAJL (24) 2005, 116–36.

16483. ADAMS, JAD. Hideous absinthe: a history of the devil in a bottle. *See* **12126.**

16484. BERMAN, RONALD. Modernity and progress: Fitzgerald, Hemingway, Orwell. Tuscaloosa; London: Alabama UP, 2005. pp. 123.

16485. BEVILACQUA, WINIFRED FARRANT. '... and the long secret extravaganza was played out': *The Great Gatsby* and carnival in a Bakhtinian perspective. Connotations (13:1/2) 2003/04, 111–29.

16486. BONNET, MICHÈLE. La femme-fleur et la femme-cheval dans *Tender Is the Night*: le double visage d'Éros; ou, L'écriture d'une imposture. EREA (1:1) 2003, 36–45.

16487. BUCKER, PARK (comp.). The Matthew J. and Arlyn Bruccoli Collection of F. Scott Fitzgerald at the University of South Carolina: an illustrated catalogue. Columbia; London: South Carolina UP, 2004. pp. 299. Rev. by William L. Butts in MSS (57:1) 2005, 49–52.

16488. CERVO, NATHAN A. Fitzgerald's *The Great Gatsby*. Exp (63:3) 2005, 169–70.

16489. CHURCHWELL, SARAH. '$4000 a screw': the prostituted art of F. Scott Fitzgerald and Ernest Hemingway. EurJAC (24:2) 2005, 105–29.

16490. COKAL, SUSANN. Caught in the wrong story: psychoanalysis and narrative structure in *Tender Is the Night*. TSLL (47:1) 2005, 75–100.

16491. CURNUTT, KIRK (ed.). A historical guide to F. Scott Fitzgerald. (Bibl. 2004, 16742.) Rev. by Paula Byrne in TLS, 18 Mar. 2005, 26; by Catherine Kunce in RMER (59:1) 2005.

16492. GIBB, THOMAS. Fitzgerald's *The Great Gatsby*. Exp (63:2) 2005, 96–8.

16493. INGE, M. THOMAS. Jay Gatsby and the Little Tramp: F. Scott Fitzgerald and Charlie Chaplin. SPC (28:1) 2005, 60–9.

16494. JAMES, PEARL. History and masculinity in F. Scott Fitzgerald's *This Side of Paradise*. MFS (51:1) 2005, 1–33.

16495. JURAS, UWE. Pleasing to the 'I': the culture of personality and its representations in Theodore Dreiser and F. Scott Fitzgerald. See 16142.

16496. NAFISI, AZAR. Reading *Lolita* in Tehran: a memoir in books. See 18463.

16497. PLATH, JAMES. On a fairy's wing: hints of Fitzgerald in Hemingway's *The Butterfly and the Tank*. See 16987.

16498. RICCIARDI, CATERINA. Tiffany: Fifth Avenue, Via del Babuino. In (pp. 181–293) 12883.

16499. RIELLY, EDWARD J. F. Scott Fitzgerald: a biography. Westport, CT; London: Greenwood Press, 2005. pp. xviii, 131. (Greenwood biographies.)

16500. SWEETMAN, CHARLES. Sheltering assets and reorganizing debts: Fitzgerald's declaration of emotional bankruptcy in *The Crack-Up*. Proteus (20:2) 2003, 10–14.

16501. WEST, JAMES L. W., III. The perfect hour: the romance of F. Scott Fitzgerald and Ginevra King, his first love. New York: Random House, 2005. pp. xx, 211.

16502. WILL, BARBARA. *The Great Gatsby* and the obscene word. ColLit (32:4) 2005, 125–44.

Penelope Fitzgerald

16503. FLOWER, DEAN. A completely determined human being. HR (57:4) 2005, 581–92.

16504. WOLFE, PETER. Understanding Penelope Fitzgerald. Columbia; London: South Carolina UP, 2004. pp. viii, 332. (Understanding contemporary British literature.)

Zelda Fitzgerald

16505. WAGNER-MARTIN, LINDA. Zelda Sayre Fitzgerald: an American woman's life. Basingstoke; New York: Palgrave Macmillan, 2004. pp. 251. Rev. by Regina Weinreich in AmBR (26:5) 2005, 5.

Fannie Flagg

16506. DUNNE, MICHAEL. Bakhtin eats some *Fried Green Tomatoes*: dialogic elements in Fannie Flagg's famous novel. SPC (28:1) 2005, 25–36.

16507. WHITT, JAN. What happened to Celie and Idgie? 'Apparitional lesbians' in American film. See 13520.

Richard Flanagan (b.1961)

16508. SCHWENGER, PETER. Gothic optics. See 12030.

16509. WALLHEAD, CELIA.   To voice or not to voice the Tasmanian Aborigines: novels by Matthew Kneale and Richard Flanagan. RAEI (16) 2003, 283–95.

16510. WEBBY, ELIZABETH.   Books and covers: reflections on some recent Australian novels. *See* **131**.

Charles Macomb Flandrau (1871–1938)

16511. HAEG, LARRY.   In Gatsby's shadow: the story of Charles Macomb Flandrau. Iowa City: Iowa UP, 2004. pp. xviii, 273. Rev. by Martha E. Stone in GLRW (12:3) 2005, 41–2.

James Elroy Flecker

16512. GIBBS, ALAN.   Gustav Holst and Gregynog. THSC (10) 2004, 163–74. (Musical setting of *The Gates of Damascus*.)

Ian Fleming

16513. ALBION, ALEXIS.   Wanting to be James Bond. *In* (pp. 202–20) **16517**.

16514. ALLEN, DENNIS W.   'Alimentary, Dr Leiter': anal anxiety in *Diamonds Are Forever*. *In* (pp. 24–41) **16517**.

16515. CHAPMAN, JAMES.   Bond and Britishness. *In* (pp. 129–43) **16517**.

16516. COMENTALE, EDWARD P.   Fleming's company man: James Bond and the management of Modernism. *In* (pp. 3–23) **16517**.

16517. —— WATT, STEPHEN; WILLMAN, SKIP (eds).   Ian Fleming and James Bond: the cultural politics of 007. Bloomington: Indiana UP, 2005. pp. xxiii, 281.

16518. HALLORAN, VIVIAN.   Tropical Bond. *In* (pp. 158–77) **16517**.

16519. HOVEY, JAIME.   Lesbian bondage; or, Why dykes like 007. *In* (pp. 42–54) **16517**.

16520. JAFFE, AARON.   James Bond, meta-brand. *In* (pp. 87–106) **16517**.

16521. JENKINS, TRICIA.   James Bond's 'Pussy' and Anglo-American Cold War sexuality. JAC (28:3) 2005, 309–17.

16522. LINDNER, CHRISTOPH.   Why size matters. *In* (pp. 224–37) **16517**.

16523. MATHESON, SUE.   Primitive masculinity/ 'sophisticated' stomach: gender, appetite, and power in the novels of Ian Fleming. CEACrit (67:1) 2004, 15–24.

16524. O'DONNELL, PATRICK.   James Bond, cyborg–aristocrat. *In* (pp. 55–68) **16517**.

16525. OWENS, CRAIG N.   The Bond market. *In* (pp. 107–25) **16517**.

16526. PATTON, BRIAN.   Shoot back in anger: Bond and the 'angry young man'. *In* (pp. 144–57) **16517**.

16527. ROOF, JUDITH.   Living the James Bond lifestyle. *In* (pp. 71–86) **16517**.

16528. WATT, STEPHEN.   007 and 9/11: specters and structures of feeling. *In* (pp. 238–59) **16517**.

16529. WILLMAN, SKIP.   The Kennedys, Fleming, and Cuba. *In* (pp. 178–201) **16517**.

Jonathan Safran Foer (b.1977)

16530. FOER, JONATHAN SAFRAN.   The writing life. BkW, 8 May 2005, 10.

Horton Foote

16531. CASTLEBERRY, MARION (ed.). Genesis of an American playwright. (Bibl. 2004, 16767.) Rev. by John D. Anderson in TT (15:2) 2005, 246–7.

16532. PORTER, LAURIN. Orphans' home: the voice and vision of Horton Foote. (Bibl. 2004, 16768.) Rev. by Gerald C. Wood in SoLJ (37:2) 2005, 156–9.

16533. WATSON, CHARLES S. Horton Foote: a literary biography. (Bibl. 2004, 16770.) Rev. by Gerald C. Wood in SoLJ (37:2) 2005, 156–9.

Shelby Foote

16534. PANABAKER, JAMES. Shelby Foote and the art of history: two gates to the city. Knoxville: Tennessee UP, 2004. pp. xviii, 238.

Esther Forbes

16535. RUBIN, JOAN SHELLEY. Silver linings: print and gentility in the world of Johnny Tremain. PAAS (113:1) 2003, 37–52.

'Ford Madox Ford' (Ford Madox Hueffer)

16536. BRICE, XAVIER. Ford Madox Ford and the composition of Nostromo. See **15859**.

16537. CURRELI, MARIO. Invading other people's territory: The Inheritors. See **15870**.

16538. DE GIOVANNI, FLORA. 'Some sort of common bond': the avant-garde and the arts. In (pp. 134–43) **3690**.

16539. FREEDMAN, ARIELA. Zeppelin fictions and the British home front. See **20047**.

16540. HAMPSON, ROBERT; SAUNDERS, MAX (eds). Ford Madox Ford's modernity. Amsterdam; Atlanta, GA: Rodopi for the Ford Madox Ford Soc., 2003. pp. x, 313. (International Ford Madox Ford studies, 2.) Rev. by Alistair Davies in ELT (48:4) 2005, 482–5.

16541. HASLAM, SARA (ed.). Ford Madox Ford and the city. Amsterdam; Atlanta, GA: Rodopi for the Ford Madox Ford Soc., 2005. pp. 249. (International Ford Madox Ford studies, 4.)

16542. —— SAUNDERS, MAX (introds). Denver: an unpublished essay by Ford Madox Ford. TLS, 30 Sept. 2005, 14–15.

16543. HOFFMANN, KAREN A. 'Am I no better than a eunuch?': narrating masculinity and empire in Ford Madox Ford's The Good Soldier. JML (27:3) 2004, 30–46.

16544. PHILLIPS, LAWRENCE. Introduction: the swarming streets: twentieth-century literary representations of London. In (pp. 1–6) **14254**.

16545. STANNARD, MARTIN. Reformations: Ford Madox Ford and Transubstantiation. In (pp. 104–17) **3724**.

16546. TROY, MICHELE K. Double trouble: the Hueffer brothers and the artistic temperament. JML (26:3/4) 2003, 28–46.

16547. WIESENFARTH, JOSEPH. Ford Madox Ford and the regiment of women: Violet Hunt, Jean Rhys, Stella Bowen, Janice Biala. Madison; London: Wisconsin UP, 2005. pp. xvi, 217, (plates) 16. Rev. by Mark Crees in TLS, 25 Nov. 2005, 29.

Richard Ford (b.1944)

16548. FORD, RICHARD. A short story. *In* (pp. 178–85) **14204**.

Richard Foreman

16549. SELLAR, TOM. Magic disappearances: Richard Foreman. Theater (35:2) 2005, 19–25. (Interview.)

Leon Forrest

16550. WILLIAMS, DANA A. 'In the light of likeness-transformed': the literary art of Leon Forrest. Columbus: Ohio State UP, 2005. pp. xviii, 155.

E. M. Forster

16551. ARMSTRONG, PAUL B. Play and the politics of reading: the social uses of Modernist form. *See* **11380**.

16552. CUCULLU, LOIS. Expert Modernists, matricide, and modern culture: Woolf, Forster, Joyce. Basingstoke; New York: Palgrave Macmillan, 2004. pp. ix, 233. Rev. by Emer Nolan in Mod/Mod (12:3) 2005, 505–9.

16553. CUTHBERTSON, GUY. Leonard Bast and Edward Thomas. NQ (52:1) 2005, 87–9.

16554. FORDONSKI, KRZYSZTOF. The shaping of the double vision: the symbolic systems of the Italian novels of Edward Morgan Forster. New York; Frankfurt: Lang, 2005. pp. 144. (European univ. studies, XIV: Anglo-Saxon language and literature, 414.)

16555. FRIEDMAN, SUSAN STANFORD. Paranoia, pollution, and sexuality: affiliations between E. M. Forster's *A Passage to India* and Arundhati Roy's *The God of Small Things*. *In* (pp. 245–61) **12640**.

16556. FROULA, CHRISTINE. Truth on trial: quantum physics, Western Enlightenment, and *A Passage to India*. EA (58:1) 2005, 15–30.

16557. GOODLAD, LAUREN M. E. Towards a Victorianist's theory of androgynous experiment. VS (47:2) 2005, 215–29.

16558. GRABES, HERBERT. Turning words on the page into 'real' people. *See* **4024**.

16559. GRMELOVÁ, ANNA. Beyond the traditional: an attempt to reassess E. M. Forster's fiction. *In* (pp. 45–50) **3753**.

16560. ISHIZUKA, HIROKO. Victorian no Chichukai. (The Victorians in the Mediterranean.) *See* **9566**.

16561. MAJEED, JAVED. Bathos, architecture and knowing India: E. M. Forster's *A Passage to India* and nineteenth-century British ethnology and the romance quest. JCL (40:1) 2005, 21–36.

16562. MARCH-RUSSELL, PAUL. 'IMAGINE IF YOU CAN': love, time and the impossibility of utopia in E. M. Forster's *The Machine Stops*. CritS (17:1) 2005, 56–71.

16563. MILGRAM, SHOSHANA. *Anthem* in the context of related literary works: 'We are not like our brothers.' *In* (pp. 119–70) **19013**.

16564. ROSS, MICHAEL L. Passage to Krishnapur: J. G. Farrell's comic vision of India. *See* **16388**.

16565. RUSSELL, RICHARD RANKIN.   E. M. Forster's Leonard Bast: a source for Virginia Woolf's Septimus Smith. ELN (42:3) 2005, 52–67.

16566. SHAHEEN, MOHAMMAD.   E. M. Forster and the politics of imperialism. Basingstoke; New York: Palgrave Macmillan, 2004. pp. xiii, 209.

16567. SMITH, GRAHAM.   Sinclair Lewis's snapshots of Gopher Prairie. See **17814**.

16568. WATSON, GEORGE.   Forever Forster: Edward Morgan Forster (1879–1970). HR (55:4) 2003, 626–32.

16569. WHITE, LESLIE.   Vital disconnection in *Howards End*. TCL (51:1) 2005, 43–63.

Margaret Forster (b.1938)

16570. YU, YI-LIN.   Mother, she wrote: matrilineal narrative in contemporary women's writing. See **16137**.

John Fowles

16571. DRAZIN, CHARLES (ed.).   The journals: vol. 1. (Bibl. 2004, 16809.) Rev. by Dennis Drabelle in BkW, 5 June 2005, 2.

16572. IYER, PICO.   Unravelling Ariadne's thread (with John Fowles). Brick (75) 2005, 118–26.

16573. PEDOT, RICHARD.   My tongue did things by itself: story-telling/story-writing in *Conversation with a Cupboard Man* (Ian McEwan). See **17969**.

Janet Frame

16574. CRONIN, JAN.   Contexts of exploration: Janet Frame's *The Rainbirds*. JCL (40:1) 2005, 5–19.

16575. —— 'Encircling tubes of being': New Zealand as a hypothetical site in Janet Frame's *A State of Siege*. JNZL (23:2) 2005, 79–91.

16576. OETTLI-VAN DELDEN, SIMONE.   Surfaces of strangeness: Janet Frame and the rhetoric of madness. (Bibl. 2003, 16809.) Rev. by Jennifer Lawn in WLWE (39:2) 2002/03, 140–3.

16577. SUTHERLAND, KATHERINE G.   Land of their graves: maternity, mourning, and nation in Janet Frame, Sara Suleri, and Arundhati Roy. CanRCL (30:1) 2003, 201–16.

'Miles Franklin' (Stella Maria Miles Franklin, 'Brent of Bin Bin', 'Mrs Ogniblat l'Artsau')

16578. BRUNTON, PAUL (ed.).   The diaries of Miles Franklin. (Bibl. 2004, 16824.) Rev. by Sandra Knowles in Southerly (64:3) 2004, 212–17.

Michael Frayn

16579. ANON.   In conversation: Michael Frayn and Richard Nelson. Dramatist (7:5) 2005, 38–43.

16580. BARNETT, DAVID.   Reading and performing uncertainty: Michael Frayn's *Copenhagen* and the postdramatic theatre. TRI (30:2) 2005, 139–49.

16581. KLEMM, DAVID E.   'The darkness inside the human soul': uncertainty in theological humanism and Michael Frayn's play *Copenhagen*. LitTheol (18:3) 2004, 292–307.

16582. PETTERSSON, BO. The many faces of unreliable narration: a cognitive narratological reorientation. *In* (pp. 59–88) **3888.**

Charles Frazier (b.1950)

16583. HOLT, KAREN C. Frazier's *Cold Mountain.* Exp (63:2) 2005, 118–21.

16584. MEROLA, NICOLE M. Reading (in) the Blue Ridge Mountains: the bioregional imperative of *Cold Mountain.* Reader (53) 2005, 45–75.

16585. WAY, ALBERT. 'A world properly put together': environmental knowledge in Charles Frazier's *Cold Mountain.* SoCult (10:4) 2004, 33–54.

Angelika Fremd (b.1944)

16586. FACHINGER, PETRA. German mothers, New World daughters: Angelika Fremd's *Heartland* and Sigrid Nunez's *A Feather on the Breath of God. See* **18528.**

Esther Freud (b.1963)

16587. HANSON, CLARE. Fiction, feminism and femininity from the eighties to the noughties. *See* **16470.**

Elsa von Freytag-Loringhoven (1874–1927)

16588. MCKIBLE, ADAM. 'Life is real and life is earnest': Mike Gold, Claude McKay, and the Baroness Elsa von Freytag-Loringhoven. *See* **16732.**

Bruce Jay Friedman (b.1930)

16589. FOWLER, NICK. Bruce Jay Friedman: making sense of entropy. AR (63:1) 2005, 151–62.

Brian Friel

16590. DUBOST, THIERRY. Boucicault, Friel et Kilroy: étude en do bémol et majeur. *See* **10131.**

16591. GERMANOU, MARIA. An American in Ireland: the representation of the American in Brian Friel's plays. CompDr (38:2/3) 2004, 259–76.

16592. JĘDRZEJEWSKI, JAN. Brian Friel's *Translations*: a dangerous masterpiece? *In* (pp. 82–90) **3756.**

16593. LACHMAN, MICHAŁ. Story telling in Brian Friel's *Faith Healer*: landscape without land. *In* (pp. 130–42) **3756.**

16594. LYSANDROU, YVONNE. The English language and 'proregression': language conflict and stasis as reflected in Brian Friel's *Translations.* WLWE (39:2) 2005, 116–31.

16595. RICHARDS, SHAUN. Irish Studies and the adequacy of theory: the case of Brian Friel. YES (35) 2005, 264–78.

Alma Fritchley (b.1954)

16596. VIZCAYA ECHANO, MARTA. Gender and ethnic otherness in selected novels by Ann Granger, Cath Staincliffe, and Alma Fritchley. *In* (pp. 189–210) **14191.**

Robert Frost

16597. BENTLEY, GREG. Robert Frost's *Dust of Snow* and the erotics of subjectivity. RFR (14) 2004, 60–8.

16598. BORROFF, MARIE. Another look at Robert Frost's *Birches*. LitIm (7:1) 2005, 69–80.

16599. BUXTON, RACHEL. Never quite showing his hand: Robert Frost and Paul Muldoon. *In* (pp. 26–44) **18404.**

16600. DAVIS, ALICIA. Frost bibliography 2003–2004. RFR (14) 2004, 126–9.

16601. DAVIS, MATTHEW. The laconic response: Spartan and Athenian mindsets in Robert Frost's *Mending Wall*. LitIm (7:3) 2005, 289–305.

16602. FERRY, ANNE. Frost's design. LitIm (7:3) 2005, 313–29.

16603. GRIEVE-CARLSON, GARY. 'Just showing off to the devil': *A Masque of Reason* and the meaning of human suffering. CEACrit (67:1) 2004, 57–67.

16604. HAGLUND, DAVID. 'Puke or prude': Frost and Stevens in the literary market place of 1922. RFR (14) 2004, 46–59.

16605. JOST, WALTER. Rhetorical investigations: studies in ordinary language criticism. *See* **2701.**

16606. LINK, ERIC CARL. Lactantius, teleology, and American literature. *See* **8644.**

16607. MACARTHUR, MARIT J. Digging up the cellar hole: Old Home Week and *The Generations of Men*. RFR (14) 2004, 98–102.

16608. MONTEIRO, GEORGE. Early Ransom, early Frost. RFR (14) 2004, 91–7.

16609. PACK, ROBERT. Belief and uncertainty in the poetry of Robert Frost. (Bibl. 2004, 16851.) Rev. by Robert Bernard Hass in RFR (14) 2004, 116–20.

16610. PATON, PRISCILLA. Abandoned New England: landscape in the works of Homer, Frost, Hopper, Wyeth, and Bishop. (Bibl. 2004, 16853.) Rev. by Elizabeth Johns in JAH (91:2) 2004, 663.

16611. QUINN, GERARD. The crooked straightness of Frost and Emerson. RFR (14) 2004, 86–90.

16612. REDMOND, JOHN. Muldoon and Pragmatism. *In* (pp. 96–109) **18404.**

16613. REGAN, STEPHEN. Robert Frost and the American sonnet. RFR (14) 2004, 13–35.

16614. SANDERS, DAVID. Frost's *North of Boston*, its language, its people, and its poet. JML (27:1/2) 2003, 70–8.

16615. SOCHER, ABRAHAM P. Shades of Frost: a hidden source for Nabokov's *Pale Fire*. *See* **18474.**

16616. SPENCER, MATTHEW (introd.). Elected friends: Robert Frost & Edward Thomas to one another. Foreword by Michael Hofmann. Afterword by Christopher Ricks. (Bibl. 2004, 16859.) Rev. by Lesley Lee Francis in RFR (14) 2004, 103–8.

16617. SPURR, DAVID. Architecture in Frost and Stevens. JML (28:3) 2005, 72–86.

16618. SYKES, JENNIE. Robert Frost and William Carlos Williams: replying to Greek and Latin with the bare hands? RFR (14) 2004, 36–45.

16619. WESTOVER, JEFF. National forgetting and remembering in the poetry of Robert Frost. TSLL (46:2) 2004, 213–44.

16620. ZAPF, HUBERT. Robert Frost: an ecological perspective. RFR (14) 2004, 69–85.

Athol Fugard

16621. Raji, Wumi. Africanizing *Antigone*: postcolonial discourse and strategies of indigenizing a Western classic. RAL (36:4) 2005, 135–54.

Charles Fuller

16622. Richardson, Riché. Charles Fuller's Southern specter and the geography of Black masculinity. AL (77:1) 2005, 7–32.

Henry Blake Fuller

16623. Salska, Agnieszka. An American *la vie de Bohème*: Henry Blake Fuller's portrait of the *fin-de-siècle* artist in Chicago. In (pp. 207–17) **3756.**

William Gaddis

16624. Anon. An addendum to *Buddhist Duality in William Gaddis's 'Carpenter's Gothic'*. CritW (46:3) 2005, 301–2. (*Adds to* bibl. 2004, 16872.)

Neil Gaiman

16625. Ekman, Stefan. Down, out and invisible in London and Seattle. Foundation (94) 2005, 64–74.

16626. Gaiman, Neil. The knight at the door. *See* **20280.**

16627. Olson, Steven P. Neil Gaiman. New York: Rosen Central, 2005. pp. 112. (Library of graphic novelists.)

16628. Schiff, Len. Into the stratosphere: *TSR* talks with Neil Gaiman. SondR (12:1) 2005, 39–41.

Ernest J. Gaines

16629. Doyle, Mary Ellen. Voices from the quarters: the fiction of Ernest J. Gaines. (Bibl. 2004, 16877.) Rev. by John Lowe in MFS (51:3) 2005, 683–6.

16630. Gaines, Ernest J. Writing *A Lesson before Dying*. SoR (41:4) 2005, 770–7.

16631. Raynard, Claudine. *The Autobiography of Miss Jane Pittman*: generic twists and trappings. EA (58:4) 2005, 440–55.

Mary Gaitskill (b.1954)

16632. Schapiro, Barbara. Trauma and sadomasochistic narrative: Mary Gaitskill's *The Dentist*. Mosaic (38:2) 2005, 37–52.

Zona Gale

16633. Ehrhardt, Julia C. Writers of conviction: the personal politics of Zona Gale, Dorothy Canfield Fisher, Rose Wilder Lane, and Josephine Herbst. (Bibl. 2004, 16884.) Rev. by Jennifer Parchesky in Legacy (22:2) 2005, 213–14.

Ellen Galford

16634. Palmer, Paulina. Lesbian transformations of gothic and fairy tale. EAS (57) 2004, 139–53.

Tess Gallagher

16635. Stull, W. L.; Carroll, M. P. (eds and trans). Tell it all. *See* **15715.**

Janice Galloway

16636. McGlynn, Mary. Janice Galloway's alienated spaces. ScSR (4:2) 2003, 82–97.

James Galvin

16637. TREDINNICK, MARK. The land's wild music: encounters with Barry Lopez, Peter Matthiessen, Terry Tempest Williams, & James Galvin. San Antonio, TX: Trinity UP, 2005. pp. xiii, 338.

Forrest Gander (b.1956)

16638. GANDER, FORREST. A faithful existence: reading, memory, and transcendence. Washington, DC: Shoemaker & Hoard, 2005. pp. 149.

Jack Gantos

16639. GANTOS, JACK. Evidence of books not yet written. LU (29:1) 2005, 1–5.

Cristina Garcia

16640. IRIZARRY, YLCE. The ethics of writing the Caribbean: Latina narrative as *testimonio*. *See* **15142**.

Erle Stanley Gardner

16641. LEITCH, THOMAS. Perry Mason. *See* **14014**.

Alex Garland (b.1970)

16642. STEPHENSON, WILLIAM. Island of the assassins: cannabis, spectacle, and terror in Alex Garland's *The Beach*. CritW (46:4) 2005, 369–81.

Hamlin Garland

16643. GUSTAFSON, NEIL. Willa Cather and Hamlin Garland: parallel early lives. *See* **15730**.

16644. MARTIN, QUENTIN E. Agricultural awakenings: Hamlin Garland's *A Little Norsk* and *The Land of the Straddle-Bug*. ALR (37:2) 2005, 141–58.

16645. SWENSON, JEFFERY. In good company: the Midwestern literary community and the short fiction of Ruth Suckow and Hamlin Garland. *See* **19728**.

Alan Garner

16646. HINE, MARY E.; POPE, ROB; WALLER, ALISON. Rewriting Mahy's *The Tricksters*: exploring sense of place and fictional space through adaptation and imitation. *In* (pp. 234–54) **18044**.

Helen Garner

16647. ROONEY, BRIGID. The sinner, the prophet, and the Pietà: sacrifice and the sacred in Helen Garner's narratives. Antipodes (19:2) 2005, 159–65.

Barbara Garson (b.1941)

16648. BLACKBURN, TOM. *MacBird!* and *Macbeth*: topicality and imitation in Barbara Garson's satirical pastiche. *See* **6533**.

David Gascoyne

16649. MELLOR, LEO. Words from the bombsites: debris, Modernism and literary salvage. *See* **16286**.

Frank Gaspar (b.1946)

16650. SILVA, REINALDO. The ethnic garden in Portuguese American writing. *See* **19909**.

William Gass
16651. FOGEL, STANLEY. William H. Gass. RCF (25:2) 2005, 7–45.

Tim Gautreaux
16652. PIACENTINO, ED. Second chances: patterns of failure and redemption in Tim Gautreaux's *Same Place, Same Things*. SoLJ (38:1) 2005, 115–33.

Maggie Gee
16653. SEARS, JOHN. 'Making sorrow speak': Maggie Gee's novels. EAS (57) 2004, 55–67.

Maurice Gee
16654. MCLEAN, PATRICIA. 'Man Alone': the demise of a cultural icon in the fiction of Maurice Gee. WLWE (39:2) 2002/03, 101–15.
16655. —— The Prior family drama: a Kristevan reading of *In My Father's Den*. JNZL (23:2) 2005, 62–78.
16656. PETRIE, DUNCAN. From the cinema of poetry to the cinema of unease: Brad McGann's *In My Father's Den*. *See* 20715.

Martha Gellhorn
16657. MOOREHEAD, CAROLINE. Gellhorn: a twentieth-century life. (Bibl. 2003, 16912.) Rev. by Rose Marie Burwell in HemR (25:1) 2005, 132–8.

Nikki Gemmell (b.1967)
16658. GEMMELL, NIKKI. The identity trap. Meanjin (64:1/2) 2005, 296–301.

Elizabeth George (b.1949)
16659. KOPPELMAN, KATE. Deliver us to evil: religion as abject Other in Elizabeth George's *A Great Deliverance*. *In* (pp. 96–117) **14191**.
16660. LIBRETTI, TIM. Detecting empire from inside-out and outside-in: the politics of detection in the fiction of Elizabeth George and Lucha Corpi. *In* (pp. 71–95) **14191**.

Merrill Joan Gerber
16661. GERBER, MERRILL JOAN. Gut feelings: a writer's truths and minute inventions. (Bibl. 2004, 16916.) Rev. by Janet Carey Eldred in CE (66:6) 2004, 652–62.
16662. —— A short history of a short story: a writer's beginnings. *In* (pp. 32–3) **14204**.

Zulfikar Ghose
16663. ALDAMA, FREDERICK LUIS. Crafting against the grain: an interview with Zulfikar Ghose. CEACrit (66:1) 2003, 57–68.

Amitav Ghosh
16664. CHAMBERS, CLAIRE. 'The absolute essentialness of conversations': a discussion with Amitav Ghosh. JPW (41:1) 2005, 26–39.
16665. FREEDMAN, ARIELA. On the Ganges side of Modernism: Raghubir Singh, Amitav Ghosh, and the postcolonial modern. *In* (pp. 114–29) **12640**.

16666. GABRIEL, SHARMANI PATRICIA. The heteroglossia of home: re-'routing' the boundaries of national identity in Amitav Ghosh's *The Shadow Lines*. JPW (41:1) 2005, 40–53.

16667. GHOSH, BISHNUPRIYA. On grafting the vernacular: the consequences of postcolonial spectrology. B2 (31:2) 2004, 197–218.

16668. GOPAL, PRIYAMVADA. Reading subaltern history. *In* (pp. 139–61) **14876.**

16669. KHAN, NYLA ALI. The fiction of nationality in an era of transnationalism. *See* **16057.**

16670. ROMANIK, BARBARA. Transforming the colonial city: science and the practice of dwelling in *The Calcutta Chromosome*. Mosaic (38:3) 2005, 41–57.

16671. SINGH, SUJALA. Who can save the subaltern? Knowledge and power in Amitav Ghosh's *The Circle of Reason*. CritS (16:2) 2004, 45–58.

Kaye Gibbons

16672. GIBBONS, KAYE. Don't try this at home: dangerous secrets about writing for a living. OxAm (48) 2005, 26–8.

Stella Gibbons

16673. KNIGHT, CHARMIAN. Who's afraid of the Brontë sisters? *In* (pp. 53–62) **10222.**

16674. SCHNELLER, BEVERLY. A neglected author: Stella Gibbons. ALSCN (11:2) 2005, 12.

Miles Gibson (b.1947)

16675. COCKIN, KATHARINE. Inventing the suffragettes: anachronism, gnosticism and corporeality in contemporary fiction. *See* **16469.**

Richard Gibson (b.1931)

16676. GIBSON, RICHARD. Richard Wright's *Island of Hallucination* and the 'Gibson Affair'. *See* **20463.**

William Gibson

16677. FAIR, BENJAMIN. Stepping razor in orbit: postmodern identity and political alternatives in William Gibson's *Neuromancer*. CritW (46:2) 2005, 92–103.

16678. HASLAM, JASON. Coded discourse: romancing the (electronic) shadow in *The Matrix*. *See* **13661.**

16679. NAYAR, PRAMOD K. The sublime in William Gibson. NCL (35:3) 2005, 12–14.

16680. PARK, JANE CHI HYUN. Stylistic crossings: cyberpunk impulses in *anime*. WLT (79:3/4) 2005, 60–3.

Ellen Gilchrist

16681. GILCHRIST, ELLEN. The writing life. Jackson; London: Mississippi UP, 2005. pp. xiii, 211.

16682. HOOPER, BRAD. The fiction of Ellen Gilchrist. Westport, CT; London: Praeger, 2005. pp. 167.

Charlotte Perkins Gilman (Mrs Stetson)

16683. DAVIS, CYNTHIA J. Love and economics: Charlotte Perkins Gilman on 'the Woman Question'. ATQ (19:4) 2005, 243–58.

16684. —— KNIGHT, DENISE D. (eds). Charlotte Perkins Gilman and her contemporaries: literary and intellectual contexts. (Bibl. 2004, 16944.) Rev. by Catherine J. Golden in ALR (38:1) 2005, 84–6; by Beverly A. Hume in Legacy (22:1) 2005, 86–7.

16685. GOLDEN, CATHERINE. *The Yellow Wall-Paper* and Joseph Henry Hatfield's original magazine illustrations. ANQ (18:2) 2005, 53–63.

16686. GOLDEN, CATHERINE J. (ed.). Charlotte Perkins Gilman's *The Yellow Wall-Paper*: a sourcebook and critical edition. London; New York: Routledge, 2004. pp. xvi, 166. (Routledge guides to literature.)

16687. GROSSMAN, JULIE. The trouble with Carol: the costs of feeling good in Todd Haynes's *Safe* and the American cultural landscape. *See* **13748.**

16688. HOCHMAN, BARBARA. The reading habit and *The Yellow Wallpaper*. In (pp. 129–48) **12549.**

16689. KLOTZ, MICHAEL. Two Dickens rooms in *The Yellow Wall-Paper*. NQ (52:4) 2005, 490–1.

16690. KNIGHT, DENISE D. 'All the facts of the case': Gilman's lost letter to Dr S. Weir Mitchell. ALR (37:3) 2005, 259–77.

16691. —— DAVIS, CYNTHIA J. (eds). Approaches to teaching Gilman's *The Yellow Wall-Paper and Herland*. (Bibl. 2004, 16953.) Rev. by Beverly A. Hume in Legacy (22:1) 2005, 86–7.

16692. SEITLER, DANA (introd.). The crux. Durham, NC; London: Duke UP, 2003. pp. 171. Rev. by Jennifer Putzi in Legacy (22:1) 2005, 91–4.

16693. SUTTON-RAMSPECK, BETH. Raising the dust: the literary housekeeping of Mary Ward, Sarah Grand, and Charlotte Perkins Gilman. (Bibl. 2004, 16958.) Rev. by Eileen Cleere in VS (47:3) 2005, 477–9; by Mary Titus in TSWL (24:2) 2005, 353–5.

Allen Ginsberg

16694. EMBLIDGE, DAVID M. City Lights Bookstore: 'a finger in the dike'. *See* **818.**

16695. HARTMAN, ANNE. Confessional counterpublics in Frank O'Hara and Allen Ginsberg. *See* **18600.**

16696. HUNGERFORD, AMY. Postmodern supernaturalism: Ginsberg and the search for a supernatural language. YJC (18:2) 2005, 269–98.

16697. MOORE, DAVE (ed.). Collected letters, 1944–1967. Introd. by Carolyn Cassady. *See* **15720.**

16698. MORTENSON, ERIK. Capturing the fleeting moment: photography in the work of Allen Ginsberg. ChiR (51:1/2) 2005, 215–31.

16699. QUINN, JUSTIN. Coteries, landscape and the sublime in Allen Ginsberg. JML (27:1/2) 2003, 193–206.

16700. RASKIN, JONAH. American scream: Allen Ginsberg's *Howl* and the making of the Beat Generation. (Bibl. 2004, 16969.) Rev. by Manuel Luis

Martinez in JAH (92:1) 2005, 287–8; by Edward Butscher in GaR (59:1) 2005, 167–80.

16701. SPANGLER, JASON.   Ginsberg: chronicling depressions great and small. SPC (28:2) 2005, 149–68.

16702. TAYSON, RICHARD.   Manly love: Whitman, Ginsberg, Monette. *See* **12350**.

Dana Gioia

16703. GIOIA, DANA.   'Lonely impulse of delight': one reader's childhood. SoR (41:1) 2005, 44–50.

Githa Hariharan

16704. RAJA, IRA.   Ageing subjects, agentic bodies: appetite, modernity and the middle class in two Indian short stories in English. JCL (40:1) 2005, 73–89.

Diane Glancy

16705. GLANCY, DIANE.   In-between places: essays. *See* **3786**.

16706. —— Migration and stasis in the art of short fiction; or, Some words as experiment. *In* (pp. 214–20) **14204**.

16707. KRUPAT, ARNOLD.   Representing Cherokee dispossession. *See* **15852**.

Ellen Glasgow

16708. BERKE, AMY.   Darwinism and the spiritual impulse in the works of Ellen Glasgow and James Lane Allen. EGN (54) 2005, 7–10.

16709. DOWNS, CATHY.   Sex, art, and anarchy in Glasgow's *Descendant*. EGN (54) 2005, 3–6, 10.

16710. DROWNE, KATHLEEN.   The flapper figure in Ellen Glasgow's 1920s fiction. EGN (55) 2005, 3–6.

16711. MATTHEWS, PAMELA R. (ed.).   Perfect companionship: Ellen Glasgow's selected correspondence with women. Charlottesville; London: Virginia UP, 2005. pp. xlvi, 324. Rev. by Catherine Rainwater in EGN (55) 2005, 7–8.

Susan Glaspell

16712. BLACK, CHERYL.   Making queer new things: queer identities in the life and dramaturgy of Susan Glaspell. JDTC (20:1) 2005, 49–64.

16713. MARSH, KELLY A.   Dear husbands and other 'girls' stuff': the *Trifles* in *Legally Blonde*. *See* **20723**.

16714. NOE, MARCIA; MARLOWE, ROBERT LLOYD.   *Suppressed Desires* and *Tickless Time*: an intertextual critique of modernity. AmDr (14:1) 2005, 1–14.

16715. BEN-ZVI, LINDA.   Susan Glaspell: a life. Oxford; New York: OUP, 2005. pp. xvi, 476.

16716. —— (introd. and notes).   The road to the temple: a biography of George Cram Cook. By Susan Glaspell. Jefferson, NC; London: McFarland, 2005. pp. viii, 356.

Molly Gloss

16717. ATTEBERY, BRIAN.   Science fiction, parables, and parabolas. Foundation (95) 2005, 7–22.

Louise Glück

16718. BIDART, FRANK. Louise Glück. *In* (pp. 23–5) **16724.**

16719. BRESLIN, PAUL. *Thanatos turannos*: the poetry of Louise Glück. *In* (pp. 90–130) **16724.**

16720. BURT, STEPHEN. 'The dark garage with the garbage': Louise Glück's structures. *In* (pp. 74–89) **16724.**

16721. COSTELLO, BONNIE. *Meadowlands*: trustworthy speakers. *In* (pp. 48–62) **16724.**

16722. DIEHL, JOANNE FEIT. 'From one world to another': voice in *Vita Nova*. *In* (pp. 151–64) **16724.**

16723. —— An interview with Louise Glück. *In* (pp. 183–9) **16724.**

16724. —— (ed.). On Louise Glück: change what you see. Ann Arbor: Michigan UP, 2005. pp. 194. (Under discussion.)

16725. GILBERT, SANDRA M. The lamentations of the new. *In* (pp. 131–5) **16724.**

16726. GREGERSON, LINDA. The sower against gardens. *In* (pp. 28–47) **16724.**

16727. LONGENBACH, JAMES. Louise Glück's nine lives. *In* (pp. 136–50) **16724.**

16728. UPTON, LEE. Defensive measures: the poetry of Niedecker, Bishop, Glück, and Carson. *See* **15503.**

16729. WILLIAMSON, ALAN. Splendor and mistrust. *In* (pp. 63–73) **16724.**

16730. YENSER, STEPHEN. Louise Glück's new life. *In* (pp. 165–82) **16724.**

Donald Goines (1937–1974)

16731. ALLEN, EDDIE B., JR. Low road: the life and legacy of Donald Goines. New York: St Martin's Press, 2004. pp. xv, 208.

'Michael Gold' (Irwin Granich)

16732. MCKIBLE, ADAM. 'Life is real and life is earnest': Mike Gold, Claude McKay, and the Baroness Elsa von Freytag-Loringhoven. AmP (15:1) 2005, 56–73.

Nora Gold

16733. PANOFSKY, RUTH. Close to the bone: the fiction of Nora Gold. *In* (pp. 61–70) **12895.**

William Golding

16734. FORT, CAMILLE. Dérives de la parole: les récits de William Golding. Paris: L'Harmattan, 2003. pp. 426. (Aire anglophone.) Rev. by Alain Blayac in EtBr (26) 2004, 197–8; by Michel Morel in EA (58:2) 2005, 243–4.

16735. GIOVANNELLI, LAURA. 'Moving, always moving': self-obliteration and nomadism in Wiliam Golding's *The Paper Men*. *In* (pp. 158–71) **3690.**

16736. HUTCHINGS, MARK. Golding's Conrad inheritance. ELN (42:4) 2005, 75–9.

16737. MEDCALF, STEPHEN. Island skies: William Golding reappraised. TLS, 2 Sept. 2005, 12–13.

16738. RÁČKOVÁ, PATRICIA. The angel with a hoof: metamorphosis in Golding's *The Spire*. *In* (pp. 159–64) **3753.**

16739. REGARD, FRÉDÉRIC. 'Nothing more to say': William Golding's *Egyptian Journal* and the fate of the Orientalist. EA (58:2) 2005, 141–53.

Rebecca Goldstein

16740. LEVINSON, MELANIE. 'Wayfinding': (re)constructing Jewish identity in *Mazel* and *Lovingkindness*. *In* (pp. 110–19) **12895.**

Jewelle Gomez (b.1948)

16741. ANON. It's in her blood. Iris (49) 2004, 18–22. (Interview.)

Maud Gonne

16742. JEFFARES, A. NORMAN. Iseult Gonne. YA (16) 2005, 197–278.

16743. MCCOOLE, SINÉAD. No ordinary women: Irish female activists in the revolutionary years, 1900–1923. Dublin: O'Brien Press, 2004. pp. 288. Rev. by James F. Knapp in ELT (48:2) 2005, 220–3.

16744. STEELE, KAREN (ed.). Maud Gonne's Irish Nationalist writings, 1895–1946. (Bibl. 2004, 17001.) Rev. by Anne Magny in EtIr (29:1) 2004, 163–4.

Jovita González Mireles (1904–1983)

16745. KAUP, MONIKA. The unsustainable *hacienda*: the rhetoric of progress in Jovita González and Eve Raleigh's *Caballero*. *See* **19001.**

Lorna Goodison

16746. HODGES, HUGH. Start-over: possession rites and healing rituals in the poetry of Lorna Goodison. RAL (36:2) 2005, 19–32.

Allegra Goodman

16747. CRONIN, GLORIA L. Seasons of our (dis)content; or, Orthodox women in Walden: Allegra Goodman's *Kaaterskill Falls*. *In* (pp. 120–36) **12895.**

16748. SCHOETT-KRISTENSEN, LENE. Allegra Goodman's *Kaaterskill Falls*: a liturgical novel. StudAJL (24) 2005, 22–41.

Mitchell Goodman (1925–1997)

16749. MACGOWAN, CHRISTOPHER. Making it free: Mitchell Goodman's radical Williams. *See* **20214.**

Nadine Gordimer

16750. BARRETT, SUSAN. 'What I say will not be understood': intertextuality as a subversive force in Nadine Gordimer's *Burger's Daughter*. EREA (2:1) 2004, 115–21.

16751. DIALA, ISIDORE. Interrogating mythology: the Mandela myth and Black empowerment in Nadine Gordimer's post-apartheid writing. Novel (38:1) 2004, 41–56.

16752. HELGESSON, STEFAN. Writing in crisis: ethics and history in Gordimer, Ndebele, and Coetzee. Scottsville: KwaZulu-Natal UP, 2004. pp. xii, 274. Rev. by Derek Attridge in RAL (36:3) 2005, 154–5.

16753. WRIGHT, LAURA. National photographic: images of sensibility and the nation in Margaret Atwood's *Surfacing* and Nadine Gordimer's *July's People*. *See* **15232.**

Caroline Gordon

16754. LEROY-FRAZIER, JILL. Saving Southern history in Caroline Gordon's *Penhally*. SoLJ (38:1) 2005, 62–75.

Mary Gordon (b.1949)

16755. MEZEI, KATHY. Domestic space and the idea of home in auto/biographical practices. *In* (pp. 81–95) **12750**.

16756. MORGAN, ELIZABETH. Mary and modesty. *See* **15779**.

16757. PORTER, ROGER J. Finding the father: autobiography as bureau of missing persons. A/B (19:1/2) 2004, 100–17.

16758. PRENATT, DIANE. Simulation and authentic self: issues of identity in works by Flannery O'Connor and Mary Gordon. *See* **18576**.

Sir Edmund Gosse

16759. LEE, HERMIONE. Writing Victorian lives and Victorian life-writing: Gosse's *Father and Son* revisited. JVC (8:1) 2003, 108–18.

16760. NEWTON, MICHAEL (ed.). Father and son. Oxford; New York: OUP, 2004. pp. xlv, 241. (Oxford world's classics.)

16761. OLSEN, STEIN HAUGOM. Progress in literary studies. *See* **14947**.

Phyllis Gotlieb (b.1926)

16762. GRACE, DOMINICK. Frankenstein, motherhood, and Phyllis Gotlieb's *O Master Caliban!* Extrapolation (46:1) 2005, 90–102.

Hiromi Goto

16763. DARIAS BEAUTELL, EVA. Hiromi Goto's *Chorus of Mushrooms*: cultural difference, visibility and the Canadian tradition. RAEI (16) 2003, 35–53.

Barbara Gowdy

16764. GORDON, NETA. Sign and symbol in Barbara Gowdy's *The White Bone*. CanL (185) 2005, 76–90.

William Goyen

16765. EPISCOPO, GIUSEPPE. 'Mise en cruauté': le forme della crudeltà nella narrativa di Federigo Tozzi, William Goyen e J. Rudolfo Wilcock. SCrit (20:1) 2005, 27–70.

16766. RZEPA, AGNIESZKA. Homesickness in *The House of Breath*: travel, home, memory. *In* (pp. 345–51) **12672**.

Patricia Grace

16767. FRESNO CALLEJA, PALOMA. Imagin(ing) the nation through Maori eyes/I's. RAEI (16) 2003, 73–91.

Caroline Graham (b.1931)

16768. McCAW, NEIL. Those other villagers: policing Englishness in Caroline Graham's *The Killings at Badger's Drift*. *In* (pp. 13–28) **14191**.

Eleanor Graham (1896–1984)

16769. TUCKER, NICHOLAS. Missing parents in the family story. NRCLL (11:2) 2005, 189–93.

Jorie Graham

16770. BACIGALUPO, MASSIMO. Novità su W. B. Yeats. Con testi di Richard Murphy, Seamus Heaney e Jorie Graham. *See* **20480**.

16771. BEDIENT, CALVIN. Toward a Jorie Graham lexicon. *In* (pp. 275–91) **16773**.

16772. BURT, STEPHEN. 'Tell them *no*': Jorie Graham's poems of adolescence. *In* (pp. 257–74) **16773**.

16773. GARDNER, THOMAS (ed.). Jorie Graham: essays on the poetry. Madison; London: Wisconsin UP, 2005. pp. viii, 305. (Contemporary North American poetry.)

16774. GINGRICH-PHILBROOK, CRAIG. Ambition *vs* inflation in the poetry of Jorie Graham: a lesson for autoperformance. TPQ (25:1) 2005, 27–42.

16775. HAMERA, JUDITH. Regions of likeness: the poetry of Jorie Graham, dance, and citational solidarity. TPQ (25:1) 2005, 14–26.

16776. HOGUE, CYNTHIA. The speaking subject in/me: gender and ethical subjectivity in the poetry of Jorie Graham. *In* (pp. 238–56) **16773**.

16777. INGRAM, CLAUDIA. 'Fission and fusion both liberate energy': James Merrill, Jorie Graham, and the metaphoric imagination. *See* **18189**.

16778. KARAGUEUZIAN, CATHERINE SONA. No image there and the gaze remains: the visual in the work of Jorie Graham. London; New York: Routledge, 2005. pp. ix, 212. (Studies in major literary authors.)

16779. LONGENBACH, JAMES. The dream of Modernism. Paideuma (32:1–3) 2003, 5–14.

16780. —— The place of Jorie Graham. *In* (pp. 206–18) **16773**.

16781. SHEPHERD, REGINALD. On Jorie Graham's *Erosion*: poetry, perception, politics. LitIm (7:3) 2005, 371–89.

16782. SPIEGELMAN, WILLARD. Jorie Graham listening. *In* (pp. 219–37) **16773**.

16783. STRINE, MARY S. Jorie Graham's subversive poetics: appetites of mind, empire-building, and the spaces of lyric performativity. TPQ (25:1) 2005, 3–13.

16784. VON HALLBERG, ROBERT. Lyric thinking. *See* **15577**.

W. S. (William Sydney) Graham (b.1918)

16785. FRANCIS, MATTHEW. Syntax gram and the magic typewriter: W. S. Graham's automatic writing. *In* (pp. 86–105) **16793**.

16786. —— (ed.). New collected poems. London; Boston, MA: Faber & Faber, 2004. pp. xxiv, 387. Rev. by Brian Kim Stefans in BosR (30:2) 2005, 51–2.

16787. GREEN, FIONA. Achieve further through elegy. *In* (pp. 132–57) **16793**.

16788. JONES, HESTER. Graham and the numinous: the 'centre aloneness' and the 'unhailed water'. *In* (pp. 160–83) **16793**.

16789. LOPEZ, TONY. Graham and the 1940s. *In* (pp. 26–42) **16793**.

16790. MORGAN, EDWIN. The poetry of W. S. Graham. *In* (pp. 186–94) **16793**.

16791. PIETTE, ADAM. 'Roaring between the lines': W. S. Graham and the white threshold of line-breaks. *In* (pp. 44–62) **16793**.

16792. PITE, RALPH. Abstract, real and particular: Graham and painting. *In* (pp. 65–83) **16793**.

16793. —— JONES, HESTER (eds). W. S. Graham: speaking towards you. Liverpool: Liverpool UP, 2004. pp. viii, 205. (Liverpool English texts and studies, 43.)

16794. ROBINSON, PETER. Dependence in the poetry of W. S. Graham. *In* (pp. 108–29) **16793**.

16795. SANSOM, IAN. *Listen*: W. S. Graham. *In* (pp. 11–23) **16793.**

Kenneth Grahame

16796. SULLIVAN, C. W., III. 'Chops, ... cheese, new bread, great swills of beer': food and home in Kenneth Grahame's *The Wind in the Willows.* JFA (15:2) 2004, 144–52.

Judy Grahn

16797. RAVAL, SHILPA. The three faces of Helen: 1970s and 1980s feminist revisions of the myth of Helen of Troy. *See* **19371.**

Ann Granger (b.1939)

16798. VIZCAYA ECHANO, MARTA. Gender and ethnic otherness in selected novels by Ann Granger, Cath Staincliffe, and Alma Fritchley. *In* (pp. 189–210) **14191.**

Bruce Alexander Grant

16799. YU, OUYANG. How post are they colonial: an enquiry into Christopher Koch, Blanche d'Alpuget and Bruce Grant's representation of Chinese in recent 'Asian writing'. *In* (pp. 243–61) **12674.**

Robert Graves

16800. BREARTON, FRAN. For father read mother: Muldoon's antecedents. *In* (pp. 45–61) **18404.**

16801. DUCKWORTH, ALISTAIR M. Two borrowings in Pat Barker's *Regeneration. See* **15302.**

16802. FURBANK, P. N. On the historical novel. Raritan (23:3) 2004, 94–114.

16803. PETTER, CHRIS; ROBERTS, LINDA; ROSE, SPENCER. The Robert Graves diary (1935–39). TextT (14:1) 2005, 71–8.

16804. ROSENFELD, NANCY. Trees, kings, and muses: Robert Graves's battle of the trees and Jotham's parable of the trees. PLL (41:2) 2005, 196–214.

16805. UTELL, JANINE. Virtue in scraps, *mysterium* in fragments: Robert Graves, Hugh Kenner, and Ezra Pound. JML (27:1/2) 2003, 99–104.

16806. YOUNG, TIMOTHY. The Robert Graves collection of William S. Reese. YLG (77:3/4) 2003, 174–6.

Alasdair Gray

16807. BÖHNKE, DIETMAR. Shades of Gray: science fiction, history and the problem of postmodernism in the work of Alasdair Gray. Berlin; Cambridge, MA: Galda & Wilch, 2004. pp. xxi, 316. (Leipzig explorations in literature and culture, 11.)

Amlin Gray (b.1946)

16808. TUTTLE, JON. How you get that story: Heisenberg's Uncertainty Principle and the literature of the Vietnam War. JPC (38:6) 2005, 1088–98.

Terence Gray (Wei Wu Wei) (1895–1987)

16809. CORNWELL, PAUL. American drama at the Cambridge Festival Theatre, 1928–1935. *See* **18640.**

Paul Green

16810. ROPER, JOHN HERBERT.   Paul Green: playwright of the real South. (Bibl. 2003, 17038.) Rev. by Gerald C. Wood in SoLJ (37:2) 2005, 156–9; by Frederick J. Rubeck in JSH (71:1) 2005, 200–1; by Cecelia Moore in NCHR (82:2) 2005, 256–8.

Alvin Greenberg

16811. PINSKER, SANFORD.   The revisionist memory. See 12858.

Joanne Greenberg ('Hannah Green')

16812. MAROVITZ, SANFORD E.   'A mensh fights back' in Joanne Greenberg's fiction. In (pp. 179–96) 12895.

Graham Greene

16813. BOSCO, MARK.   Graham Greene's Catholic imagination. Oxford; New York: OUP, 2005. pp. viii, 205. (American Academy of Religion: Academy series.)

16814. CHIBNALL, STEVE.   Brighton Rock. See 13494.

16815. GUNBY, INGRID.   Tales from the crypt: wartime London in Graham Swift's Shuttlecock. In (pp. 97–109) 14254.

16816. MEMSHAW, MICHAEL.   Travel, travel writing, and the literature of travel. See 14539.

16817. RAU, PETRA.   The common frontier: fictions of alterity in Elizabeth Bowen's The Heat of the Day and Graham Greene's The Ministry of Fear. See 15537.

16818. SCHWARTZ, ADAM.   The third spring: G. K. Chesterton, Graham Greene, Christopher Dawson, and David Jones. See 15778.

16819. SHERRY, NORMAN.   The life of Graham Greene: vol. 3, 1955–1991. London: Cape, 2004. pp. xxxiii, 906, (plates) 24. Rev. by Sunil Iyengar in BkW, 3 Oct. 2004, 13; by Bernard Bergonzi in Cweal (131:18) 2004, 28–30; by Ann M. Begley in ANCW (191:10) 2004, 33–5.

16820. WESELIŃSKI, ANDRZEJ.   'Leopard' images in Graham Greene's fiction. In (pp. 275–82) 3756.

Walter Greenwood

16821. ROSS, STEPHEN.   Authenticity betrayed: the 'idiotic folk' of Love on the Dole. CultC (56) 2004, 189–209.

Robert O. Greer (b.1944)

16822. KENNEY, JAY.   Renaissance man, western writer: an interview with Robert Greer. BRev (25:4) 2005, 13–15.

Augusta, Lady Gregory

16823. HILL, JUDITH.   Lady Gregory: an Irish life. Stroud: Sutton, 2005. pp. xii, 420.

16824. MCDIARMID, LUCY.   The Irish art of controversy. Ithaca, NY; London: Cornell UP, 2005. pp. xvii, 280. Rev. by Marc C. Conner in ILS (25:1) 2005, 13–14.

16825. PETHICA, JAMES. *Upon a House Shaken*: the struggle for Coole Park 1907–1912. *See* **20519**.

Zane Grey

16826. PAULY, THOMAS H. Zane Grey: his life, his adventures, his women. Urbana: Illinois UP, 2005. pp. xi, 385.

'Grey Owl' (Archibald Stansfield Belaney)

16827. BRAZ, ALBERT. The modern Hiawatha: Grey Owl's construction of his aboriginal self. *In* (pp. 53–68) **14629**.

John Howard Griffin (1920–1980)

16828. BONAZZI, ROBERT (introd.). Scattered shadows: a memoir of blindness and vision. Maryknoll, NY: Orbis, 2004. pp. 230. Rev. by Patricia Hampl in Cweal (132:15) 2005, 34–5.

Ann Warren Griffith

16829. YASZEK, LISA. Domestic satire as social commentary in mid-century women's media landscape sf. Foundation (95) 2005, 29–39.

Judith Grossman (b.1937)

16830. GROSSMAN, JUDITH. Behind the story. *In* (pp. 179–80) **14294**.

Edith Searle Grossmann

16831. STAFFORD, JANE. Going native: how the New Zealand settler became indigenous. JNZL (23:1) 2005, 162–73.

Frederick Philip Grove (Felix Paul Greve) (1879–1948)

16832. CAVELL, RICHARD. 'An ordered absence': defeatured topologies in Canadian literature. *In* (pp. 14–31) **9243**.

16833. HJARTARSON, PAUL; KULBA, TRACY (eds). The politics of cultural mediation: Baroness Elsa von Freytag-Loringhoven and Felix Paul Greve. Edmonton: Alberta UP, 2003. pp. xiii, 212. Rev. by Markus M. Müller in BJCS (17:2) 2004, 261–2; by Rosmarin Heidenreich in CanL (184) 2005, 140–2.

Davis Grubb (b.1919)

16834. DOUGLASS, THOMAS E. Before the Appalachian literary renaissance, there was Davis Grubb's *The Voices of Glory*. AppH (33:3) 2005, 83–91.

Barbara Guest

16835. MORRISON, RUSTY. An echoing after the object. DQ (39:3) 2005, 83–93.

Joseph Guinan (1863–1932)

16836. MAUME, PATRICK. A pastoral vision: the novels of Canon Joseph Guinan. NewHR (9:4) 2005, 79–98.

Romesh Gunesekera

16837. MANNUR, ANITA. Feeding desire: food, domesticity, and challenges to hetero-patriarchy. JCPS (10:1) 2003, 34–51.

Thom Gunn

16838. FORESTER, C. Q. Re-experiencing Thom Gunn. GLRW (12:5) 2005, 14–19.

16839. HAMMER, LANGDON. Two formalists. ASch (74:1) 2005, 51–8.

16840. HAVEN, CYNTHIA L. 'No giants': an interview with Thom Gunn. GaR (59:1) 2005, 104–22.

16841. SACKS, OLIVER. Remembering Thom Gunn. Brick (76) 2005, 55–62.

Sunetra Gupta

16842. MAJUMDAR, SAIKAT. The fiction of 'subaltern pasts': Shashi Deshpande and Sunetra Gupta. See **16060**.

A. R. Gurney

16843. GROSS, ROBERT F. Forms of restraint: high comic renunciation in three plays by A. R. Gurney. JDTC (20:1) 2005, 7–26.

Ivor Gurney

16844. COREN, PAMELA. Gurney's solace: Shakespeare, Jonson and Byrd. IGSJ (11) 2005, 7–24.

16845. HIPP, DANIEL. The poetry of shell shock: wartime trauma and healing in Wilfred Owen, Ivor Gurney and Siegfried Sassoon. See **18709**.

16846. LANCASTER, PHILIP, et al. (comps). Bibliography update. IGSJ (11) 2005, 119–26.

16847. MINOGUE, SALLY. Portrait of the artist: Ivor Gurney as modern maker. IGSJ (11) 2005, 25–42.

16848. THORNTON, R. K. R. (ed.). On having a genius in the family: Winifred Gurney's memories of Ivor. IGSJ (11) 2005, 60–118.

Woody Guthrie

16849. CHEYETTE, BRYAN. On the 'D' train: Bob Dylan's conversions. In (pp. 221–52) **16207**.

16850. RILEY, TIM. Another side of Bob Dylan. See **16221**.

Marilyn Hacker

16851. BIGGS, MARY. Bread and brandy: food and drink in the poetry of Marilyn Hacker. TSWL (24:1) 2005, 129–50.

Charlie Haffner

16852. CHRISTENSEN, MATTHEW J. Cannibals in the postcolony: Sierra Leone's intersecting hegemonies in Charlie Haffner's slave revolt drama *Amistad Kata-Kata*. RAL (36:1) 2005, 1–19.

Jessica Hagedorn

16853. WERRLEIN, DEBRA T. Legacies of the 'innocent' frontier: failed memory and the infantilized Filipina expatriate in Jessica Hagedorn's *Dogeaters*. JAAS (7:1) 2004, 27–50.

Kimiko Hahn (b.1955)

16854. ZHOU, XIAOJING. Two hat softeners 'in the trade confession': John Yau and Kimiko Hahn. In (pp. 168–89) **9454**.

Robert Hahn (b.1938)

16855. HAHN, ROBERT. Running out of time: a memoir. SoR (41:1) 2005, 131–41.

John Haines (b.1924)

16856. MURRAY, JOHN A.	Fables and distances: a conversation with Alaska writer John Haines. BRev (24:4) 2004, 13–14.

'Katherine Hale'
(Amelia Beers Warnock, Mrs John W. Garvin) (1878–1956)

16857. CAMPBELL, WANDA.	Moonlight and morning: women's early contributions to Canadian Modernism. In (pp. 79–99) 12739.

16858. WALBOHM, SAMARA.	Katherine Hale: 'but now another one has come'. CanP (56) 2005, 65–86.

Donald Hall

16859. DAVIS, TODD F.; WOMACK, KENNETH.	Reading the ethics of mourning in the poetry of Donald Hall. CanRCL (30:1) 2003, 161–78.

James W. (James Wilson) Hall (b.1947)

16860. FISTER, BARBARA.	Copycat crimes: crime fiction and the marketplace of anxieties. See 18931.

Radclyffe Hall

16861. WELLS-LYNN, AMY.	The intertextual, sexually coded Rue Jacob: a geocritical approach to Djuna Barnes, Natalie Barney, and Radclyffe Hall. See 15334.

Marion Halligan

16862. DOOLEY, GILLIAN.	An interview with Marion Halligan. Antipodes (18:1) 2004, 5–7.

Sam Hamill (b.1943?)

16863. HAMILL, SAM.	A monk's tale. VQR (81:2) 2005, 129–45.

Patrick Hamilton

16864. LECERCLE, JEAN-JACQUES.	Jane Austen meets Dickens: a response to Thierry Labica. Connotations (13:1/2) 2003/04, 145–8. (Responds to bibl. 2004, 17125.)

Oscar Hammerstein, II

16865. AIKIN, ROGER CUSHING.	Was Jud Jewish? Property, ethnicity, and gender in Oklahoma! See 13694.

Dashiell Hammett

16866. BARRA, ALLEN.	Dashiell Hammett. AH (56:4) 2005, 21. (History now.)

16867. DEFINO, DEAN.	Lead birds and falling beams. JML (27:4) 2004, 73–81. (Hard-boiled genre.)

16868. DELANEY, BILL.	Hammett's The Maltese Falcon. Exp (63:3) 2005, 167–9.

16869. HEISE, THOMAS.	'Going blood-simple like the natives': contagious urban spaces and modern power in Dashiell Hammett's Red Harvest. MFS (51:3) 2005, 485–512.

16870. METRESS, CHRISTOPHER. Reading the *rara avis*: seventy-five years of *Maltese Falcon* criticism. Clues (23:2) 2005, 65–77.

16871. NOLAN, TOM. Hammett and Macdonald. Clues (23:2) 2005, 51–63.

16872. PELTIER, JOSIANE. Economic discourse in *The Maltese Falcon*. Clues (23:2) 2005, 21–30.

16873. RIVETT, JULIE M. On Samuel Spade and Samuel Dashiell Hammett: a granddaughter's perspective. Clues (23:2) 2005, 11–20.

16874. WHITING, FREDERICK. Bodies of evidence: post-war detective fiction and the monstrous origins of the sexual psychopath. See **19561**.

Peter Handke

16875. PARK, CHRISTINE COHEN. Close comfort? Sons as their mothers' memoirists. See **17235**.

Barbara Hanrahan

16876. MASGRAU-PEYA, ELISENDA. Towards a poetics of the 'unhomed': the house in Katherine Mansfield's *Prelude* and Barbara Hanrahan's *The Scent of Eucalyptus*. See **18086**.

Lorraine Hansberry

16877. ARDOLINO, FRANK. Hansberry's *A Raisin in the Sun*. Exp (63:3) 2005, 181–3.

16878. GILL, GLENDA. Sean Combs' 2004 Broadway portrayal of Walter Lee Younger in Lorraine Hansberry's *A Raisin in the Sun*: a historical assessment. JADT (17:3) 2005, 57–76.

16879. NESMITH, N. GRAHAM. Lloyd Richards: reminiscence of a theatre life and beyond. See **13083**.

16880. WILKERSON, MARGARET B. The *Theatre Journal* auto/archive: Margaret B. Wilkerson. TJ (57:4) 2005, 783–8.

J. O. de Graft Hanson (b.1932)

16881. KLOBAH, MAHOUMBAH. Sowing the seeds of knowledge in children's literature: sociocultural values in J. O. de Graft Hanson's *The Golden Oware Counters*. CLAQ (30:2) 2005, 152–63.

Florence Emily Hardy (1881–1937)

16882. DRYDEN, LINDA. The Hardys and William Mathie Parker. See **11118**.

16883. IRWIN, MICHAEL. Hardy and the 'Baby' poems. THJ (21) 2005, 9–26.

16884. PITE, RALPH. Hardy and biography. *In* (pp. 75–89) **11140**.

Frank (Francis Joseph) Hardy (1917–1994)

16885. ADAMS, PAUL; LEE, CHRISTOPHER (eds). Frank Hardy & the literature of commitment. Carlton, Vic.: Vulgar Press, 2003. pp. 291. Rev. by Teri Merlyn in ALS (22:1) 2005, 121.

16886. CERCE, DANICA. Frank Hardy: social analyst or man of letters? Antipodes (19:1) 2005, 70–4.

David Hare

16887. ANON. The trenchancy of Shaw's eight words. See **19379**.

16888. DICKINSON, PETER. Oscar Wilde: reading the life after the life. *See* 12381.

Joy Harjo

16889. BRYSON, J. SCOTT. The west side of any mountain: place, space, and ecopoetry. *See* 18204.

16890. LEMAY, SHAWNA. Women writing horses. PJCL (44) 2005, 39–42.

16891. ROOT, WILLIAM PITT. About Joy Harjo: a profile. Ploughshares (30:4) 2004/05, 180–5.

Robert Harling (b.1951)

16892. UHRY, ALFRED. Guild roundtable: playwrights on Broadway. *See* 16351.

William Harmon (b.1938)

16893. CARPENTER, BRIAN. Up late with William Harmon. PemM (37) 2005, 20–5.

16894. DENHAM, ROBERT D. Thou art that: Woolylamb Hormone, Northcote Fricassee, and chap named Denim. PemM (37) 2005, 34–49. (*Uneeda Review.*)

16895. MCFEE, MICHAEL. 'To account for it': William Harmon's *Where Scars Come From.* PemM (37) 2005, 15–19.

16896. MORGAN, ROBERT. Concord Constructivist and Yankee doodler: the poetry of William Harmon. PemM (37) 2005, 9–14.

16897. RABB, MARGARET. Exquisite harmonies. PemM (37) 2005, 31–3.

16898. RUTLEDGE, BRENNAN. William Harmon: a bibliography. PemM (37) 2005, 52–64.

Jonathan Harr (b.1948)

16899. WALDMAN, DIANE. A case for corrective criticism: *A Civil Action.* *In* (pp. 201–30) 13368.

Claire Harris

16900. WILLIAMS, EMILY ALLEN. Triadic revelations of exilic identity: Claire Harris's *Fables from the Women's Quarters, Dipped in Shadow,* and *She.* SLI (37:2) 2004, 53–75.

Frank Harris

16901. KINSER, BRENT E. A not so 'simple story': Jane Welsh Carlyle and Charlotte Brontë's *Shirley. See* 10169.

Thomas Harris

16902. ANGEL, MARIA. Brainfood: rationality, aesthetics and economies of affect. TexP (19:2) 2005, 323–48.

16903. FULLER, STEPHEN M. Deposing an American cultural totem: Clarice Starling and postmodern heroism in Thomas Harris's *Red Dragon, The Silence of the Lambs,* and *Hannibal.* JPC (38:5) 2005, 819–33.

Wilson Harris

16904. DELOUGHREY, ELIZABETH M.; HANDLEY, GEORGE B.; GOSSON, RENÉE K. (eds). Caribbean literature and the environment: between nature and culture. *See* 12632.

16905. Harris, Wilson. Theatre of the arts. *In* (pp. 261–8) **12632.**

16906. Jackson, Shona N. Subjection and resistance in the transformation of Guyana's mytho-colonial landscape. *In* (pp. 85–98) **12632.**

16907. Maes-Jelinek, Hena. From living nature to borderless culture in Wilson Harris's work. *In* (pp. 247–60) **12632.**

16908. Upstone, Sara. Anancy as trickster: magical space in the fiction of Wilson Harris. WLWE (40:2) 2004, 23–39.

Jamie Harrison

16909. Schaffer, Rachel. A hilarious prairie occurrence: uses of humor in Jamie Harrison's Blue Deer mysteries. Clues (23:4) 2005, 15–24.

Kathryn Harrison

16910. Harrison, Kathryn. Seeking rapture: scenes from a woman's life. New York: Random House, 2003. pp. 186.

Tony Harrison

16911. Whitehead, Anne. Tony Harrison, the Gulf War and the poetry of protest. TexP (19:2) 2005, 349–72.

Carla Harryman

16912. Hinton, Laura. To write within situations of contradiction: an introduction to the cross-genre writings of Carla Harryman. PMC (16:1) 2005.

Josephine Hart

16913. Stothard, Peter. Reading rooms. *See* **4136.**

Kevin Hart

16914. McCooey, David. Opaque lucidity. Meanjin (62:1) 2003, 44–51 (review-article).

L. P. Hartley

16915. Craik, Roger. Two influences on L. P. Hartley's *The Go-Between.* NCL (35:4) 2005, 4–5.

16916. Ingersoll, Earl G. Intertextuality in L. P. Hartley's *The Go-Between* and Ian McEwan's *Atonement.* FMLS (40:3) 2004, 241–58.

Elisabeth Harvor

16917. Compton, Anne. The theatre of the body: extreme states in Elisabeth Harvor's poetry. CanL (183) 2004, 13–27. (Interviews.)

Gustav Hasford

16918. Gruben, Patricia. Practical joker: the invention of a protagonist in *Full Metal Jacket. See* **13583.**

Jon Hassler

16919. Plut, Joseph. Conversation with Jon Hassler: *Grand Opening.* Ren (57:3) 2005, 219–36.

Mildred Haun

16920. Jensen, Arden. The granny-woman speaks: Mildred Haun's *The Hawk's Done Gone* as parable. TPB (42) 2005, 40–8.

16921. RUBIN, RACHEL. 'What ain't called Melungeons is called hillbillies': Southern Appalachia's in-between people. *See* **17936.**

Ehud Havazelet (b.1956)

16922. HAVAZELET, EHUD. Behind the story. *In* (pp. 221–4) **14294.**

John Hawkes

16923. REGNAULD, ARNAUD. L'érotisme dans *Virginie*; ou, Le décentrement du sens. EREA (1:1) 2003, 76–83.

Elijah Hay

16924. CHURCHILL, SUZANNE W. The lying game: *Others* and the great Spectra hoax of 1917. AmP (15:1) 2005, 23–41.

George Campbell Hay

16925. BYRNE, MICHEL (ed.). Collected poems and songs of George Campbell Hay (Deòrsa Mac Iain Dheòrsa). Edinburgh: Edinburgh UP, 2003. pp. xxxiii, 713. Rev. by Meg Bateman in ScSR (2:2) 2001, 150–1.

Robert Hayden

16926. FRANCINI, ANTONELLA. Sonnet *vs* sonnet: the fourteen lines in African American poetry. *See* **17999.**

David Haynes (b.1955)

16927. HAYNES, DAVID. Behind the story. *In* (pp. 278–9) **14294.**

John Hayward (1905–1965)

16928. BADENHAUSEN, RICHARD. T. S. Eliot and the art of collaboration. *See* **16240.**

Bessie Head

16929. PATKE, RAJEEV S. Method and madness in *A Question of Power* and *Wide Sargasso Sea*. JCarL (4:1) 2005, 185–93.

16930. SAMPLE, MAXINE (ed.). Critical essays on Bessie Head. (Bibl. 2003, 17154.) Rev. by Robert Cancel in AfSR (48:1) 2005, 195–6; by Femi Ojo-Ade in RAL (36:1) 2005, 127–8.

16931. TALAHITE, ANISSA. Cape gooseberries and giant cauliflowers: transplantation, hybridity, and growth in Bessie Head's *A Question of Power*. Mosaic (38:4) 2005, 141–56.

Seamus Heaney

16932. ALLISON, JONATHAN. *Friendship's Garland* and the manuscripts of Seamus Heaney's *Fosterage*. YES (35) 2005, 58–71.

16933. BACIGALUPO, MASSIMO. Novità su W. B. Yeats. Con testi di Richard Murphy, Seamus Heaney e Jorie Graham. *See* **20480.**

16934. —— (ed. and trans.). Fuori campo. Novara: Interlinea, 2005. pp. 90. (Lyra, 21.)

16935. BERENSMEYER, INGO. Identity or hybridization? Mapping Irish culture in Seamus Heaney and Paul Muldoon. EtIr (28:1) 2003, 65–83.

16936. BOLY, JOHN. Beloved mentors: Seamus Heaney's poems of vocation. Genre (38:1/2) 2005, 145–78.

16937. BOUCHARD, LARRY D. Contingent gifts: dramatizing patterns of integrity in Sophocles' *Philoctetes* and Seamus Heaney's *The Cure at Troy*. *In* (pp. 41–62) **12978.**

16938. COLLINS, FLOYD. Seamus Heaney: the crisis of identity. Newark: Delaware UP; London: Assoc. UPs, 2003. pp. 246. Rev. by Rachel Buxton in YES (35) 2005, 341–2.

16939. CORCORAN, BRENDAN. Seamus Heaney: retreat from the global? IE (27:2) 2005, 23–33.

16940. CROWDER, ASHBY BLAND. Heaney's *Docker*. Exp (63:2) 2005, 117–18.

16941. CUDA, ANTHONY J. The use of memory: Seamus Heaney, T. S. Eliot, and the unpublished epigraph to *North*. JML (28:4) 2005, 152–75.

16942. HEININGER, JOSEPH. Making a Dantean poetic: Seamus Heaney's *Ugolino*. NewHR (9:2) 2005, 50–64.

16943. HILLAN, SOPHIA. Wintered into wisdom: Michael McLaverty, Seamus Heaney, and the Northern word-hoard. *See* **18011.**

16944. JAMES, STEPHEN. Seamus Heaney's sway. TCL (51:3) 2005, 263–84.

16945. KENNEDY, DAVID. 'Tell-tale skins' and 'repeatable codes': historical bodies and mythic readings in Seamus Heaney's 'bog poems'. Eng (54:208) 2005, 35–47.

16946. KIRCHWEY, KARL. 'And the half-true rhyme is love': modern verse drama and the Classics. Parnassus (28:1/2) 2005, 254–81 (review-article).

16947. KRUCZKOWSKA, JOANNA. Seamus Heaney on Zbigniew Herbert: affinities. *In* (pp. 111–21) **3756.**

16948. O'BRIEN, EUGENE. Seamus Heaney: searches for answers. London; Sterling, VA: Pluto Press, 2003. pp. ix, 213. Rev. by Patrick Hicks in NewHR (8:4) 2004, 159–60.

16949. OLDCORN, ANTHONY (ed. and trans.). *Attraversamenti*: con nuovi inediti e un'intervista al poeta. Milan: Scheiwiller, 2005. pp. 98. (PlayOn, 15.)

16950. O'SULLIVAN, MICHAEL. 'Bare life' and the garden politics of Roethke and Heaney. *See* **19108.**

16951. TYLER, MEG. A singing contest: conventions of sound in the poetry of Seamus Heaney. London; New York: Routledge, 2005. pp. xiv, 214.

Anthony Hecht

16952. FORD, MARK. He used to notice such things. TLS, 18 Feb. 2005, 27–8 (review-article).

16953. HAMMER, LANGDON. Two formalists. *See* **16839.**

Larry Heinemann

16954. HEINEMANN, LARRY. Black Virgin Mountain: a return to Vietnam. New York: Doubleday, 2005. pp. 243.

Robert A. Heinlein

16955. WEST, CHRIS. Perverting science fiction: thinking the alien within the genre. *See* **12082.**

Lyn Hejinian

16956. MEHNE, PHILLIP. *'Making it strange'*: Bewusstsein, Erfahrung und Sprache bei Gertrude Stein und Lyn Hejinian. *See* **19591.**

16957. SANDLER, STEPHANIE. Arkadii Dragomoshchenko, Lyn Hejinian, and the persistence of Romanticism. ConLit (46:1) 2005, 18–45.

Joseph Heller

16958. CACICEDO, ALBERTO. 'You must remember this': trauma and memory in *Catch-22* and *Slaughterhouse-Five.* CritW (46:4) 2005, 357–68.

16959. MAUS, DEREK. Series and systems: Russian and American dystopian satires of the Cold War. CritS (17:1) 2005, 72–94.

Lillian Hellman

16960. MARTINSON, DEBORAH. Lillian Hellman: a life with foxes and scoundrels. New York: Counterpoint, 2005. pp. xvi, 448, (plates) 16.

Ernest Hemingway

16961. ADAMS, JAD. Hideous absinthe: a history of the devil in a bottle. *See* **12126.**

16962. AGUILERA LINDE, MAURICIO D. Hemingway and gender: biography revisited. Atl (27:2) 2005, 15–26.

16963. AKO, EDWARD O. Ernest Hemingway, Derek Walcott, and old men of the sea. CLAJ (48:2) 2004, 200–12.

16964. ARNELL, CARLA A. Earthly men and otherworldly women: gender types and religious types in Jeanette Winterson's *Atlantic Crossing* and other short fiction. *See* **20257.**

16965. AZEVEDO, MILTON M. *Addio, adieu, adiós: A Farewell to Arms* in three Romance languages. HemR (25:1) 2005, 22–42.

16966. BARLOON, JIM. Very short stories: the miniaturization of war in Hemingway's *In Our Time.* HemR (24:2) 2005, 5–17.

16967. BERMAN, RONALD. Modernity and progress: Fitzgerald, Hemingway, Orwell. *See* **16484.**

16968. BITTNER, JOHN. *Vie hors série, fin dramatique*: the Paris press coverage of the death of Ernest Hemingway. HemR (24:2) 2005, 73–86.

16969. BREDENDICK, NANCY. *Death in the Afternoon* as seen by Tomás Orts-Ramos (Uno al Sesgo). HemR (24:2) 2005, 41–61.

16970. CALLOWAY, KATHERINE. *'Pulvis et umbra sumus'*: Horace in Hemingway's *The Sun Also Rises.* HemR (25:1) 2005, 120–31.

16971. CHURCHWELL, SARAH. '$4000 a screw': the prostituted art of F. Scott Fitzgerald and Ernest Hemingway. *See* **16489.**

16972. CIRINO, MARK. 'You don't know the Italian language well enough': the bilingual dialogue of *A Farewell to Arms.* HemR (25:1) 2005, 43–62.

16973. COOK, JAMES L. Reproaching the military hero *sans peur. See* **3737.**

16974. DEFAZIO, ALBERT J., III (ed.). Dear Papa, Dear Hotch: the correspondence of Ernest Hemingway and A. E. Hotchner. Preface by A. E. Hotchner. Columbia; London: Missouri UP, 2005. pp. xxv, 382.

16975. —— GREGG, PATRICK.   Current bibliography: annotated. HemR (24:2) 2005, 106–12.

16976. DOW, WILLIAM.   The perils of irony in Hemingway's *The Sun Also Rises*. EA (58:2) 2005, 178–92.

16977. EBY, CARL.   'He felt the change so that it hurt him all through': sodomy and transvestic hallucination in Hemingway. HemR (25:1) 2005, 77–95.

16978. FANTINA, RICHARD.   Ernest Hemingway: machismo and masochism. Basingstoke; New York: Palgrave Macmillan, 2004. pp. 206.

16979. HEMINGWAY, VALERIE.   Running with the bulls: my years with the Hemingways. (Bibl. 2004, 17219.) Rev. by Maureen Connelly in HemR (24:2) 2005, 102–5; by Catharine Savage Brosman in Chronicles (29:8) 2005, 29–30.

16980. JUSTICE, HILARY K.   Music at the Finca Vigia: a preliminary catalog of Hemingway's audio collection. HemR (25:1) 2005, 96–108.

16981. KERN, ALFRED.   About literary wars. WLA (17:1/2) 2005, 146–61.

16982. KOCH, STEPHEN.   The breaking point: Hemingway, Dos Passos, and the murder of José Robles. New York: Counterpoint, 2005. pp. xi, 308. Rev. by Matthew Stewart in HemR (25:1) 2005, 142–5; by Tim Davis in ANCW (192:19) 2005, 25–6.

16983. MACILWEE, MICHAEL.   *Henderson the Rain King*: translations between Conrad and Hemingway. See **15448**.

16984. MANDEL, MIRIAM B. (ed.).   A companion to Hemingway's *Death in the Afternoon*. Rochester, NY: Camden House, 2004. pp. xix, 339. (Studies in American literature and culture: literary criticism in perspective.) Rev. by Arthur Waldhorn in HemR (24:2) 2005, 94–102.

16985. MONTGOMERY, PAUL.   Hemingway and Guy Hickock in Italy: the *Brooklyn Eagle* articles. HemR (25:1) 2005, 112–19.

16986. OTT, MARK P.   Nick Adams at a windy cross roads: echoes of past and future fictions in Ernest Hemingway's *Che ti dice la patria?* HemR (24:2) 2005, 18–27.

16987. PLATH, JAMES.   On a fairy's wing: hints of Fitzgerald in Hemingway's *The Butterfly and the Tank*. JSSE (43) 2004, 75–85.

16988. RANKIN, PAUL.   Hemingway's *Hills Like White Elephants*. Exp (63:4) 2005, 234–7.

16989. ROBINSON, DANIEL.   'My true occupation is that of a writer': Hemingway's passport correspondence. HemR (24:2) 2005, 87–93.

16990. ROVIT, EARL; WALDHORN, ARTHUR (eds).   Hemingway and Faulkner in their time. See **16442**.

16991. SCHMIGALLE, GÜNTHER.   'How people go to hell': pessimism, tragedy, and affinity to Schopenhauer in *The Sun Also Rises*. HemR (25:1) 2005, 7–21.

16992. SEALS, MARC.   Trauma theory and Hemingway's lost Paris manuscripts. HemR (24:2) 2005, 62–72.

16993. SOLLORS, WERNER.   Hemingway, *film noir*, and the emergence of a twentieth-century American style. YREAL (21) 2005, 45–55.

16994. STRYCHACZ, THOMAS.   Hemingway's theaters of masculinity. (Bibl. 2004, 17251.) Rev. by Suzanne Del Gizzo in MFS (51:3) 2005, 679–83; by Robert W. Trogdon in StudN (37:3) 2005, 367–9.

2005] AUTHORS 925

16995. TRABER, DANIEL S. Performing the feminine in *A Farewell to Arms*. HemR (24:2) 2005, 28–40.

16996. VERNON, ALEX. Soldiers once and still: Ernest Hemingway, James Salter & Tim O'Brien. (Bibl. 2004, 17253.) Rev. by Mark A. Heberle in MFS (51:1) 2005, 197–200.

16997. VOELLER, CAREY. 'He only looked sad the same way I felt': the textual confessions of Hemingway's hunters. HemR (25:1) 2005, 63–76.

16998. WRYNN, SUSAN. News from the Hemingway Collection. HemR (24:1) 2004, 127–8.

16999. —— News from the Hemingway Collection. HemR (24:2) 2005, 113–15.

17000. —— News from the Hemingway Collection. HemR (25:1) 2005, 151–5.

17001. YU, DONGYUN. Desire, writing and the contradiction of eco-ethics: on Hemingway's hunting works. FLS (115) 2005, 58–64. (In Chinese.)

Essex Hemphill

17002. SERRANO, RICHARD. Beyond the length of an average penis: reading across traditions in the poetry of Timothy Liu. *In* (pp. 190–208) **9454**.

Alice Corbin Henderson

17003. RUDNICK, LOIS. Modernism in the high desert: the multivocal ecology of Alice Corbin Henderson's *Red Earth*. WAL (39:1) 2004, 37–53.

Josephine Gattuso Hendin

17004. ANTONUCCI, CLARA. Scrittura e memoria: i luoghi del sé nella creatività italoamericana. *In* (pp. 105–18) **12577**.

Beth Henley

17005. BRYER, JACKSON R. Expressing 'the misery and confusion truthfully': an interview with Beth Henley. AmDr (14:1) 2005, 87–109.

17006. PLUNKA, GENE A. The plays of Beth Henley: a critical study. Jefferson, NC; London: McFarland, 2005. pp. 228.

Sir A. P. (Alan Patrick) Herbert (1890–1971)

17007. ROPER, MICHAEL. Between manliness and masculinity: the 'war generation' and the psychology of fear in Britain, 1914–1950. *See* **19430**.

Frank Herbert

17008. ROSSIGNOL, BENOÎT. Figures de l'historien dans le cycle de *Dune* de Frank Herbert. Cycnos (22:2) 2005, 67–83.

Jerry Herman (b.1933)

17009. BEAN, MATT. An apple and an orange: comparing *Sunday in the Park with George* and *La Cage aux folles*. *See* **19507**.

Michelle Herman

17010. HERMAN, MICHELLE. The middle of everything: memoirs of motherhood. Lincoln; London: Nebraska UP, 2005. pp. 214.

Michael Herr

17011. ADAMS, JON. Envelope please: upholding masculinity in Michael Herr's *Dispatches* and David Rabe's *Streamers*. SPC (28:2) 2005, 169–91.

Carolivia Herron

17012. ROBERTS, JESSICA FORBES. A prayer for mourning: seduction and trauma in Carolivia Herron's *Thereafter Johnnie*. Callaloo (28:4) 2005, 1060–73.

Karen Hesse

17013. OLIPHANT-INGHAM, ROSEMARY. Karen Hesse. Lanham, MD; London: Scarecrow Press, 2005. pp. xii, 95. (Scarecrow studies in young adult literature, 19.)

Dorothy Hewett

17014. BENNETT, BRUCE. A romantic for all generations: Dorothy Hewett. A/B (19:1/2) 2004, 222–38.

Georgette Heyer ('Stella Martin', Mrs Ronald Rougier)

17015. KLOESTER, JENNIFER. Georgette Heyer's Regency world. Oxford; Portsmouth, NH: Heinemann, 2005. pp. 382. Rev. by Laura Baggaley in TLS, 9 Dec. 2005, 29.

Carl Hiaasen

17016. SMITH, JULIE A. Sensory experience as consciousness in literary representations of animal minds. *In* (pp. 231–46) **14258**.

Aidan Higgins

17017. HIGGINS, AIDAN. Windy arbours: collected criticism. Normal, IL: Dalkey Archive Press, 2005. pp. 308. (Irish literature.)

Patricia Highsmith ('Claire Morgan')

17018. MEAKER, MARIJANE. Highsmith: a romance of the 1950s: a memoir. (Bibl. 2003, 17278.) Rev. by David Jarraway in GLQ (11:2) 2005, 319–21.

17019. WILSON, ANDREW. Beautiful shadow: a life of Patricia Highsmith. (Bibl. 2003, 17280.) Rev. by David Jarraway in GLQ (11:2) 2005, 319–21.

Tomson Highway

17020. KLEIN, VERENA. Healing the Native Canadian soul: three accounts of spiritual homecoming. LittPr (15:30) 2005, 35–50.

17021. SHACKLETON, MARK. Interview with Tomson Highway. *In* (pp. 92–100) **12912**.

17022. VOUTILAINEN, EMMA. The queer Queen of Heaven: queer in Tomson Highway's *Kiss of the Fur Queen*. *In* (pp. 101–14) **12912**.

17023. WASSERMAN, JERRY. 'God of the whiteman! God of the Indian! God Al-fucking-mighty!': the residential school legacy in two Canadian plays. JCanStud (39:1) 2005, 23–48.

Oscar Hijuelos

17024. SOCOLOVSKY, MAYA. From rumba to funeral march: remembering Cuba in Oscar Hijuelos's *A Simple Habana Melody (from When the World Was Good)*. SAtlR (70:1) 2005, 117–47.

Barry Hill (b.1943)

17025. HILL, BARRY. Crossing cultures. Meanjin (62:4) 2003, 116–20.

Geoffrey Hill

17026. KILGORE, JENNIFER. Tropes of memory in *The Orchards of Syon*. EtBr (29) 2005, 41–51.

17027. KOOY, MICHAEL JOHN. Word and image in the later work of Geoffrey Hill. WI (20:3) 2004, 191–205.

17028. LYON, JOHN M. 'What are you incinerating?': Geoffrey Hill and popular culture. Eng (54:209) 2005, 85–98.

Susan Hill

17029. SCULLION, VAL. Gothic transformations and musical appropriations in Susan Hill's novel *The Bird of Night*. GothS (7:1) 2005, 53–63.

17030. WISKER, GINA. Demisting the mirror: contemporary British women's horror. EAS (57) 2004, 154–70.

Chester Himes

17031. BELL, KEVIN. Assuming the position: fugitivity and futurity in the work of Chester Himes. MFS (51:4) 2005, 846–72.

Rolando Hinojosa

17032. SOTELO, SUSAN BAKER. Chicano detective fiction: a critical study of five novelists. *See* **15153**.

Edward Hoagland

17033. DOYLE, BRIAN; MYERS, JASON. The essay as jazz, butterfly, knuckleball: an interview with Edward Hoagland. Agni (62) 2005, 133–55.

Russell Hoban

17034. COCKRELL, AMANDA. On this enchanted ground: reflections of a Cold War childhood in Russell Hoban's *Riddley Walker* and Walter M. Miller's *A Canticle for Leibowitz*. JFA (15:1) 2004, 20–36.

Ralph Hodgson (1871–1962)

17035. D'AMBROSIO, VINNI MARIE. Meeting Eliot and Hodgson in *Five-Finger Exercises. See* **16260**.

Alice Hoffman

17036. SEXTON, MEGAN. Alice Hoffman: an interview. FiveP (9:3) 2005, 51–62.

Eva Hoffman

17037. BESEMERES, MARY. The family in exile, between languages: Eva Hoffman's *Lost in Translation*, Lisa Appignanesi's *Losing the Dead*, Anca Vlasopolos's *No Return Address*. A/B (19:1/2) 2004, 239–48.

17038. FANETTI, SUSAN. Translating self into liminal space: Eva Hoffman's acculturation in/to a postmodern world. WS (34:5) 2005, 405–19.

17039. MARÇAIS, DOMINIQUE. Language and identity in Eva Hoffman's *Lost in Translation. In* (pp. 63–8) **12577**.

Linda Hogan

17040. COOK, BARBARA J. (ed.). From the center of tradition: critical perspectives on Linda Hogan. (Bibl. 2003, 17314.) Rev. by Vanessa Hall in WAL (39:1) 2004, 129–30; by Donelle N. Dreese in MELUS (30:1) 2005, 240–2.

17041. DIRENC, DILEK.   From a new paradise to a new earth: European myths and New World alternatives converse in Linda Hogan's *Power*. LittPr (15:30) 2005, 51–7.

17042. RAINWATER, CATHERINE.   Who may speak for the animals? Deep ecology in Linda Hogan's *Power* and A. A. Carr's *Eye Killers*. *In* (pp. 261–80) **14258.**

Alan Hollinghurst

17043. FLANNERY, DENIS.   The powers of apostrophe and the boundaries of mourning: Henry James, Alan Hollinghurst, and Toby Litt. *See* **11401.**

17044. RIVKIN, JULIE.   Writing the gay '80s with Henry James: David Leavitt's *A Place I've Never Been* and Alan Hollinghurst's *The Line of Beauty*. HJR (26:3) 2005, 282–92.

Winifred Holtby

17045. KNIGHT, CHARMIAN.   Thornfield Hall revisited. *In* (pp. 63–73) **10222.**

17046. SAKAMOTO, TADANOBU.   A new relation between the narrator and the reader in *Jacob's Room*. *See* **20413.**

Ann Hood (b.1956)

17047. WILLIAMS, ELLY.   Ann Hood: an interview. FiveP (9:1) 2005, 69–91.

Christopher Hope

17048. NIERAGDEN, GÖRAN.   Otherness at work: the non-indigenous English novel. *See* **16343.**

Nalo Hopkinson

17049. REID, MICHELLE.   Crossing the boundaries of the 'Burn': Canadian multiculturalism and Caribbean hybridity in Nalo Hopkinson's *Brown Girl in the Ring*. Extrapolation (46:3) 2005, 297–314.

17050. WOOD, SARAH.   'Serving the spirits': emergent identities in Nalo Hopkinson's *Brown Girl in the Ring*. Extrapolation (46:3) 2005, 315–26.

Nick Hornby

17051. KESKINEN, MIKKO.   Single, long-playing, and compilation: the formats of audio and amorousness in Nick Hornby's *High Fidelity*. CritW (47:1) 2005, 3–21.

Janette Turner Hospital

17052. CARR, RICHARD.   'Just enough religion to make us hate': the case of *Tourmaline* and *Oyster*. *See* **19705.**

17053. HOSPITAL, JANETTE TURNER.   Giacometti's foot and Proust's madeleine: the short story of desire. *In* (pp. 77–82) **14204.**

17054. LOVELL, SUE.   Janette Turner Hospital's *The Last Magician* in 'an expanded field'. AUMLA (104) 2005, 121–49.

Silas House (b.1971)

17055. BLYTHE, HAL; SWEET, CHARLIE; RAHIMZADEH, KEVIN.   Water imagery in *Clay's Quilt*. NCL (35:1) 2005, 14–16.

A. E. Housman

17056. ALBANO, GIUSEPPE. Housman's fluid dynamics. HSJ (31) 2005, 127–43.

17057. BECKETT, LORNA. *Two Cities* – the true author. HSJ (31) 2005, 146–8. (Miscellanea.)

17058. BREEN, JENNIFER. And asunder to remain. TLS, 4 Feb. 2005, 13. (*Oh Were He and I Together.*)

17059. BREEZE, ANDREW. Ashes under Uricon. HSJ (31) 2005, 37–40.

17060. KOPFF, E. CHRISTIAN. Conservatism and creativity in A. E. Housman. ModAge (47:3) 2005, 229–39.

17061. LEACH, COLIN. A. E. Housman and Classical scholarship, then and now. HSJ (31) 2005, 59–62.

17062. MALONE, RICHARD. Etiquette in Pandemonium: Grant Richards and the early American editions of A. E. Housman's *A Shropshire Lad*. HSJ (31) 2005, 53–8.

17063. NAIDITCH, P. G. Additional problems in the life and writings of A. E. Housman. Los Angeles, CA: Sam:Johnson, 2005. pp. 210. Rev. by J. H. C. Leach in TLS, 1 July 2005, 30; by Colin Leach in HSJ (31) 2005, 152–3.

17064. —— The extant portion of the library of A. E. Housman: part IV, Non-Classical materials. HSJ (31) 2005, 154–80.

17065. PAGE, JIM. 'Mutilated by music': a look at Housman and the composers. HSJ (31) 2005, 89–101.

17066. PLOWDEN, GEOFFREY. Housman's blottings. HSJ (31) 2005, 149–50. (Miscellanea.)

17067. —— Parodies. HSJ (31) 2005, 148–9. (Miscellanea.)

17068. SMITH, CHRIS. The name and nature of poetry. HSJ (31) 2005, 7–14. (Housman Lecture.)

17069. TAIT, MICHAEL S. Hell-fire and the beauties of Shropshire: the poetry of A. E. Housman. HSJ (31) 2005, 41–52.

17070. TAROZZI, BIANCA (ed. and trans.). *Un ragazzo dello Shropshire* e altre poesie. Florence: Lettere, 2005. pp. 222. (Nuovo melograno, 62.)

17071. VICKERY, JOHN B. Bridges and Housman as elegists: the modern threshold. *See* **15567.**

Clemence Housman

17072. CHRISTENSEN, PETER G. Clemence Housman's attack on King Arthur in *The Life of Sir Aglovale de Galis*. HSJ (31) 2005, 63–88.

Laurence Housman

17073. HART, LINDA. Laurence Housman in search of a biographer. HSJ (31) 2005, 15–36.

Sidney Howard

17074. GROSS, ROBERT F. Fighting disease, seducing cavalrymen, and achieving modernity: *Yellow Jack*. JADT (16:1) 2004, 17–36.

Susan Howatch

17075. EDWARDS, ELIZABETH. The 'hidden' agenda: feminist perspectives in the Starbridge novels. *In* (pp. 168–86) **17081.**

17076. FORBES, CHERYL. Julian of Norwich and those ambiguous Starbridge women. *In* (pp. 187–97) **17081.**

17077. GAMBLE, SARAH. Romance, desire, and history: the shifting narratives of *Penmarric*. *In* (pp. 53–71) **17081.**

17078. GILL, GAYLE HAMILTON. Alternate languages and abused powers: the sexual, psychic, and spiritual in Howatch's ecclesiastical novels. *In* (pp. 122–40) **17081.**

17079. HUTTAR, CHARLES A. Searching for the elusive truth: the unity of Susan Howatch's career. *In* (pp. 38–52) **17081.**

17080. JOHNSON, BRUCE. One story, one voice, one love: the use of convention and repetition in Howatch's fiction. *In* (pp. 17–37) **17081.**

17081. —— HUTTAR, CHARLES A. (eds). Scandalous truths: essays by and about Susan Howatch. Selinsgrove, PA: Susquehanna UP; London: Assoc. UPs, 2005. pp. 293.

17082. KUPERSMITH, WILLIAM; WAPLES, JAN S. *Scandalous Risks*: sex, scandal, and spirituality in the sixties. *In* (pp. 198–218) **17081.**

17083. LUX, ELAINE. The expanding 'I' in *Absolute Truths*. *In* (pp. 72–99) **17081.**

17084. SHULLENBERGER, BONNIE. The lady is the Other: women and spirituality in Howatch's Church of England fiction. *In* (pp. 141–67) **17081.**

17085. SPROLES, KARYN Z. Reading, faith, and the analytic process of the Starbridge novels. *In* (pp. 100–21) **17081.**

Fanny Howe

17086. MORRISON, RUSTY. An echoing after the object. *See* **16835.**

CJ Hribal

17087. HRIBAL, CJ. Behind the story. *In* (pp. 261–4) **14294.**

Lindley Williams Hubbell (b.1901)

17088. CHANDLER, DAVID. Lindley Williams Hubbell, Borrovian. GBB (29) 2004, 6–10.

Andrew Hudgins

17089. DOWLING, GREGORY. Living outside the blast: Andrew Hudgins's *After the Lost War*. RSA (14) 2003, 139–57.

W. H. Hudson ('Henry Harford')

17090. WILLIAMSON, ANNE. A purple thread: an examination of W. H. Hudson, naturalist and author, in relation to HW. HWSJ (41) 2005, 39–51.

Oliver Madox Hueffer ('Jane Wardle') (1877–1931)

17091. TROY, MICHELE K. Double trouble: the Hueffer brothers and the artistic temperament. *See* **16546.**

Langston Hughes

17092. COOK, DANA (comp.). Meeting Hughes: first encounters & initial impressions. LHR (19:1) 2004, 50–4.

17093. DE SANTIS, CHRISTOPHER C. (ed.).   Langston Hughes: a documentary volume. Detroit, MI: Gale Research, 2005. pp. xxxii, 458. (Dictionary of literary biography, 315.)

17094. LUO, LIANGGONG.   Langston Hughes' humor. FLS (114) 2005, 25–31. (In Chinese.)

17095. MCCANN, PAUL.   Music and the marketplace: jazz and the Great Depression in the short stories of Rudolph Fisher and Langston Hughes. See **16481**.

17096. MILLER, R. BAXTER.   Reinvention and globalization in Hughes's stories. MELUS (30:1) 2005, 69–83.

17097. RAMPERSAD, ARNOLD (gen. ed.).   The collected works of Langston Hughes: vol. 11, Works for children and young adults: poetry, fiction, and other writing. Ed. by Dianne Johnson. Columbia; London: Missouri UP, 2003. pp. xvi, 393. Rev. by Donna Akiba Sullivan Harper in JAAH (89:4) 2004, 371–2; by R. Baxter Miller in AAR (38:4) 2004, 727–9; by the same in MELUS (30:1) 2005, 246–9.

17098. SCOTT, WILLIAM.   *Motivos* of translation: Nicolás Guillén and Langston Hughes. CRNew (5:2) 2005, 35–71.

17099. SUMMERS-BREMNER, ELUNED.   Unreal city and dream deferred: psychogeographies of Modernism in T. S. Eliot and Langston Hughes. *In* (pp. 262–80) **12640**.

Ted Hughes

17100. CLARK, HEATHER.   Tracking the thought-fox: Sylvia Plath's revision of Ted Hughes. See **18815**.

17101. FAULKNER, PETER.   The story of Alcestis in William Morris and Ted Hughes. See **11745**.

17102. GORDON, JOHN.   Being Sylvia being Ted being Dylan: Plath's *The Snowman on the Moor*. See **18820**.

17103. HIBBETT, RYAN.   Imagining Ted Hughes: authorship, authenticity, and the symbolic work of *Collected Poems*. TCL (51:4) 2005, 414–36.

17104. PEEL, ROBIN.   The ideological apprenticeship of Sylvia Plath. See **18827**.

17105. POLLAK, VIVIAN R.   Moore, Plath, Hughes, and *The Literary Life*. See **18323**.

17106. SPENCER, LUKE.   Sylvia Plath, Ted Hughes and *Wuthering Heights*: some uses of memory. *In* (pp. 75–85) **10222**.

17107. UPTON, LEE.   'I / Have a self to recover': the restored *Ariel*. See **18838**.

Keri Hulme

17108. PULITANO, ELVIRA.   'In vain I tried to tell you': crossreading strategies in global literatures. See **15071**.

17109. RAUWERDA, ANTJE M.   The White whipping boy: Simon in Keri Hulme's *The Bone People*. JCL (40:2) 2005, 23–42.

T. E. Hulme

17110. COMENTALE, EDWARD P.   Modernism, cultural production, and the British avant-garde. *See* **12616.**

17111. SCHUCHARD, RONALD.   Did Eliot know Hulme? Final answer. *See* **16304.**

17112. TROTTER, DAVID.   Modernism, anti-mimesis, and the professionalization of English society. *In* (pp. 24–39) **12946.**

Emyr Humphreys

17113. GREEN, DIANE.   'The first interpreter': Emyr Humphreys's use of titles and epigraphs. WWrE (10) 2005, 98–120.

17114. —— Welsh writing and postcoloniality: the strategic use of the Blodeuwedd myth in Emyr Humphreys's novels. RAEI (16) 2003, 129–46.

Barry Humphries

17115. DAVIDSON, JIM.   The multiple lives of Barry Humphries. Meanjin (62:2) 2003, 220–8 (review-article).

Erica Hunt (b.1955)

17116. CUMMINGS, ALLISON.   Public subjects: race and the critical reception of Gwendolyn Brooks, Erica Hunt, and Harryette Mullen. *See* **15583.**

Violet Hunt

17117. FREEDMAN, ARIELA.   Zeppelin fictions and the British home front. *See* **20047.**

17118. WIESENFARTH, JOSEPH.   Ford Madox Ford and the regiment of women: Violet Hunt, Jean Rhys, Stella Bowen, Janice Biala. *See* **16547.**

Fannie Hurst

17119. NIU, GRETA AI-YU.   Performing white triangles: Joan Riviere's *Womanliness as a Masquerade* and *Imitation of Life* (1959). *See* **13615.**

Zora Neale Hurston

17120. BOON, KEVIN ALEXANDER.   Zora Neale Hurston's *Their Eyes Were Watching God* as Aristotelian tragedy: Janie's flaw, Tea Cake's defects, and the illusion of romantic love. ZNHF (18) 2004, 21–6.

17121. BOYD, VALERIE.   Wrapped in rainbows: the life of Zora Neale Hurston. (Bibl. 2003, 17388.) Rev. by Greg Johnson in GaR (57:1) 2003, 176–85; by Elizabeth Robeson in JSH (71:4) 2005, 934–5.

17122. BRITT, BRIAN.   Contesting history and identity in modern fiction about Moses. *In* (pp. 90–105) **12978.**

17123. BROWN, KIMBERLY NICHELE.   Sniffing the 'calypso magnolia': unearthing the Caribbean presence in the South (response to John Lowe). *See* **10600.**

17124. CHEN, GUANGXING.   Carnivalism in *Their Eyes Were Watching God*. FLS (114) 2005, 32–8. (In Chinese.)

17125. CHU, PATRICIA E.   Modernist (pre)occupations: Haiti, Primitivism, and anticolonial nationalism. *In* (pp. 170–86) **12640.**

17126. CONLEE, LYNN. The uncanny world of Zora Neale Hurston. ZNHF (18) 2004, 50–9.

17127. DAVIS, HUGH. *She Rock*: a 'new' story by Zora Neale Hurston. ZNHF (18) 2004, 14–20.

17128. EHRHARDT, JULIA C. Meeting at a barbecue: Zora Neale Hurston, Dorothy Allison and apocalyptic literary miscegenation. *In* (pp. 71–90) **15131**.

17129. EMERY, AMY FASS. The zombie in/as the text: Zora Neale Hurston's *Tell My Horse*. AAR (39:3) 2005, 327–36.

17130. GYIMAH, MIRIAM C. Setting the word on fire: treatment of the tongue in *Jonah's Gourd Vine* and *Their Eyes Were Watching God*. ZNHF (18) 2004, 36–43.

17131. HAGOOD, TAYLOR. Dramatic deception and Black identity in *The First One* and *Riding the Goat*. AAR (39:1/2) 2005, 55–66.

17132. HOFFMAN-JEEP, LYNDA. Creating ethnography: Zora Neale Hurston and Lydia Cabrera. AAR (39:3) 2005, 337–53.

17133. HOLMES, DAVID G. Revisiting racialized voice: African American ethos in language and literature. *See* **10418**.

17134. KANTHAK, JOHN F. Legacy of dysfunction: family systems in Zora Neale Hurston's *Jonah's Gourd Vine*. JML (28:2) 2005, 113–29.

17135. LOWE, JOHN. 'Calypso magnolia': the Caribbean side of the South. *See* **10601**.

17136. MUKUNDI, PAUL M. Looking beyond the horizon at all times at all places: the triumphant African woman in Zora Neale Hurston's *Their Eyes Were Watching God*, Mariama Bâ's *So Long a Letter* and Margaret Ogola's *The River and the Source*. ZNHF (18) 2004, 84–92.

17137. PATTERSON, TIFFANY RUBY. Zora Neale Hurston and a history of Southern life. Philadelphia, PA: Temple UP, 2005. pp. 229. (Critical perspectives on the past.)

17138. RODRIGUEZ, SUSANNAH. Universal harmony and the trickster in the works of Zora Neale Hurston and Lydia Cabrera. ZNHF (18) 2004, 1–13.

17139. SPILLERS, HORTENSE J. A tale of three Zoras: Barbara Johnson and Black women writers. *See* **15023**.

17140. VALKEAKARI, TUIRE. 'Luxuriat(ing) in Milton's syllables': writer as reader in Zora Neale Hurston's *Dust Tracks on a Road*. *In* (pp. 192–214) **12549**.

17141. WEATHERS, GLENDA B. Biblical trees, biblical deliverance: literary landscapes of Zora Neale Hurston and Toni Morrison. AAR (39:1/2) 2005, 201–12.

17142. WEST, M. GENEVIEVE. Zora Neale Hurston and American literary culture. Gainesville: Florida UP, 2005. pp. xv, 300.

17143. WILKINS, KAROL M. Providing higher education through Achebe and Hurston's cultural roots. ZNHF (18) 2004, 44–9.

17144. WRIGHT, MELANIE JANE. Moses in America: the cultural uses of biblical narrative. (Bibl. 2003, 17409.) Rev. by Brian Britt in JR (84:1) 2004, 166–8.

Aldous Huxley

17145. BARRETT, MARVIN.   Touched by Aldous Huxley. Parabola (28:4) 2003, 90–4 (review-article).

17146. BIRNBAUM, MILTON.   Two of a kind? *See* **16468**.

17147. IZZO, DAVID GARRETT.   Aldous Huxley. RCF (25:3) 2005, 86–136.

17148. MARCH-RUSSELL, PAUL.   'IMAGINE IF YOU CAN': love, time and the impossibility of utopia in E. M. Forster's *The Machine Stops*. *See* **16562**.

17149. MILGRAM, SHOSHANA.   *Anthem* in the context of related literary works: 'We are not like our brothers.' *In* (pp. 119–70) **19013**.

17150. MURRAY, NICHOLAS.   Aldous Huxley: a biography. New York: Dunne / St Martin's Press, 2003. pp. 496, (plates) 16. Rev. by Marvin Barrett in Parabola (28:4) 2003, 90–4; by Milton Birnbaum in ModAge (47:2) 2005, 167–70.

17151. POSNER, RICHARD A.   Orwell *versus* Huxley: economics, technology, privacy, and satire. *In* (pp. 183–211) **18680**.

17152. ROSENHAN, CLAUDIA.   An attribution in Huxley's short story *Chawdron* via Lawrence and Ludovici. NQ (52:1) 2005, 95–7.

Elspeth Huxley

17153. LASSNER, PHYLLIS.   Colonial strangers: women writing at the end of the British Empire. (Bibl. 2004, 17435.) Rev. by Kristin Bluemel in Mod/Mod (12:1) 2005, 186–8; by Margaret D. Stetz in TSWL (24:1) 2005, 166–8; by Lisa Colletta in WS (34:5) 2005, 425–7.

David Henry Hwang

17154. COHEN, PATRICIA.   Guild seminar: race & politics in theater. *See* **15101**.

17155. PATRICK, ANNE E.   David Henry Hwang's *Golden Child* and the ambiguities of Christian (and post-Christian) missions. *In* (pp. 260–72) **12978**.

Douglas Hyde

17156. BORNSTEIN, GEORGE.   The colors of Zion: Black, Jewish, and Irish nationalisms at the turn of the century. *See* **20482**.

'Robin Hyde' (Iris Guiver Wilkinson)

17157. STAFFORD, JANE.   Robin Hyde's *Dragon Rampant* and 1930s travel writing. *In* (pp. 190–216) **12674**.

William Inge

17158. JOHNSON, JEFF.   William Inge and the subversion of gender: rewriting stereotypes in the plays, novels, and screenplays. Foreword by Jackson R. Bryer. Jefferson, NC; London: McFarland, 2005. pp. vii, 192.

John Irving (b.1942)

17159. REILLY, CHARLIE.   A conversation with John Irving. Onthebus (19/20) 2005, 106–13.

Christopher Isherwood

17160. COLLETTA, LISA (ed.). Kathleen and Christopher: Christopher Isherwood's letters to his mother. Minneapolis; London: Minnesota UP, 2005. pp. xx, 185, (plates) 16.

17161. IZZO, DAVID GARRETT. Christopher Isherwood encyclopedia. Jefferson, NC; London: McFarland, 2005. pp. 190.

17162. PARKER, PETER. Isherwood: a life revealed. New York: Random House, 2004. pp. xiii, 815. Rev. by John Sutherland in LRB (26:11) 2004, 23–4; by Edmund White in TLS, 4 June 2004, 3–4; by Andrew Monnickendam in Atl (27:1) 2005, 145–50; by Jim Marks in BkW, 13 Feb. 2005, 5; by Chris Freeman in GLRW (12:2) 2005, 41–2.

Kazuo Ishiguro

17163. GIBSON, SARAH. English journeys: the tourist, the guidebook, and the motorcar in *The Remains of the Day*. See **13733**.

17164. PÉGON, CLAIRE. L'art de la fugue chez K. Ishiguro. Toulouse: Presses Universitaires du Mirail, 2004. pp. 175. (Interlangues: Littératures.) Rev. by Christine Reynier in EtBr (27) 2004, 185–6.

17165. SIM, WAI-CHEW. Kazuo Ishiguro. RCF (25:1) 2005, 80–115.

17166. STAMIROWSKA, KRYSTYNA. Revisiting a foreign land: *The Unconsoled* and *When We Were Orphans* by Kazuo Ishiguro. In (pp. 218–26) **3756**.

17167. SUMERA, ADAM. *The Remains of the Day*: Kazuo Ishiguro's novel and James Ivory's film adaptation. In (pp. 250–7) **3756**.

17168. TRIMM, RYAN S. Inside job: professionalism and postimperial communities in *The Remains of the Day*. Lit (16:2) 2005, 135–61.

17169. VEYRET, PAUL. The strange case of the disappearing Chinamen: memory and desire in Kazuo Ishiguro's *The Remains of the Day* and *When We Were Orphans*. EtBr (29:2) 2005, 159–72.

17170. VINET, DOMINIQUE. Revisiting the memory of guilt in Ishiguro's *When We Were Orphans*. EtBr (29) 2005, 133–42.

17171. ZINCK, PASCAL. The palimpsest of memory in Kazuo Ishiguro's *When We Were Orphans*. EtBr (29) 2005, 145–58.

Arturo Islas

17172. ALDAMA, FREDERICK LUIS. Dancing with ghosts: a critical biography of Arturo Islas. Berkeley; London: California UP, 2005. pp. xix, 188.

Shirley Jackson

17173. BLACKFORD, HOLLY. Haunted housekeeping: fatal attractions of servant and mistress in twentieth-century female gothic literature. See **20115**.

17174. CASTRICANO, JODEY. Shirley Jackson's *The Haunting of Hill House* and the strange question of trans-subjectivity. GothS (7:1) 2005, 87–101.

17175. DOWNEY, DARA; JONES, DARRYL. King of the castle: Shirley Jackson and Stephen King. In (pp. 214–36) **17181**.

17176. EGAN, JAMES. Comic–satiric–fantastic–gothic: interactive modes in Shirley Jackson's narratives. In (pp. 34–51) **17181**.

17177. HAGUE, ANGELA.   'A faithful anatomy of our times': reassessing Shirley Jackson. Frontiers (26:2) 2005, 73–96.

17178. HATTENHAUER, DARRYL.   Stephen Spielberg's *The Haunting*: a reconsideration of David Self's script. *In* (pp. 251–66) **17181**.

17179. HOEVELER, DIANE LONG.   Life lessons in Shirley Jackson's late fiction: ethics, cosmology, eschatology. *In* (pp. 267–80) **17181**.

17180. MURPHY, BERNICE M.   'The people of the village have always hated us': Shirley Jackson's New England gothic. *In* (pp. 104–26) **17181**.

17181. —— (ed.).   Shirley Jackson: essays on the literary legacy. Jefferson, NC; London: McFarland, 2005. pp. viii, 296.

C. L. R. James

17182. NIELSEN, ALDON LYNN.   The future of an allusion: the color of modernity. *In* (pp. 17–30) **12640**.

17183. WEBB, CONSTANCE.   Not without love: memoirs. (Bibl. 2004, 17471.) Rev. by Donald E. Pease in JML (26:3/4) 2003, 123–7.

Clive James (b.1939)

17184. BENNETT, BRUCE.   Clive James, humour and empire. JCL (40:3) 2005, 37–45.

17185. JAMES, CLIVE.   Starting with sludge: a literary education: from the fiction of Biggles to Braddon's brute facts. *See* **14179**.

M. R. James

17186. NAŁĘCZ-WOJTCZAK, JOLANTA.   Facing evil: the motif of temptation in some ghost and vampire stories. *In* (pp. 159–66) **3756**.

Storm Jameson

17187. BRIGANTI, CHIARA.   'Thou art full of stirs, a tumultuous city': Storm Jameson and London in the 1920s. *In* (pp. 61–75) **14254**.

Edna Jaques

17188. RIFKIND, CANDIDA.   Too close to home: middlebrow anti-Modernism and the sentimental poetry of Edna Jaques. JCanStud (39:1) 2005, 90–114.

Randall Jarrell

17189. BERGMAN, DAVID.   Disturbing Randall Jarrell. AmLH (16:2) 2004, 350–62 (review-article).

17190. BURT, STEPHEN.   R. P. Blackmur and Randall Jarrell on literary magazines: an exchange. *See* **1166**.

17191. —— BROOKS-MOTL, HANNAH (eds).   Randall Jarrell on W. H. Auden. *See* **15234**.

17192. CHIASSON, DAN.   Randall Jarrell's persons. Raritan (24:3) 2005, 121–30 (review-article).

Robinson Jeffers

17193. GELPI, ALBERT (sel.).   The wild god of the world: an anthology of Robinson Jeffers. Stanford, CA: Stanford UP, 2003. pp. x, 204.

'Gish Jen' (Lillian Gen)

17194. MADSEN, DEBORAH L.   American exceptionalism and multiculturalism: myths and realities. SPELL (16) 2003, 177–88.

Jerry B. Jenkins

17195. FARRINGTON, HOLLY.   Have you been Left Behind? Jenkins, LaHaye and the Second Coming of Christian science fiction. See **17550**.

17196. LAHAYE, TIM; JENKINS, JERRY B.; SWANSON, SANDI L.   The authorized *Left Behind* handbook. See **17551**.

17197. STANDAERT, MICHAEL.   Skipping towards Armageddon: the politics and propaganda of the *Left Behind* novels and the LaHaye empire. See **17553**.

Mike Jenkins (b.1953)

17198. PIKOULIS, JOHN.   'Some kind o' beginnin' ': Mike Jenkins and the voices of Cwmtaff. WWrE (10) 2005, 121–43.

Humphrey Jennings

17199. JACKSON, KEVIN.   Humphrey Jennings. London: Picador, 2004. pp. xiii, 448, (plates) 8. Rev. by Paul Laity in LRB (27:5) 2005, 18–20.

17200. LAITY, PAUL.   Damsons and custard. LRB (27:5) 2005, 18–20 (review-article). (Socialist realism.)

Ruth Prawer Jhabvala

17201. KAPADIA, PARMITA.   Shakespeare transposed: the British stage on the post-colonial screen. *In* (pp. 42–56) **13273**.

Meiling Jin (b.1956)

17202. PERREGAUX, MYRIAM.   The city as gendered space: a reading of three literary texts in the light of feminist geography. See **17690**.

Rita Joe

17203. MCDONALD-RISSANEN, MARY.   Imaging the past: Atlantic Canada and popular representations. *In* (pp. 148–57) **12912**.

B. S. Johnson

17204. COE, JONATHAN.   Like a fiery elephant: the story of B. S. Johnson. (Bibl. 2004, 17492.) Rev. by Michael Dirda in BkW, 5 June 2005, 15; by George Garrett in HC (42:4) 2005, 18–19.

17205. TEW, PHILIP.   'My doingthings': London according to B. S. Johnson. *In* (pp. 111–29) **14254**.

17206. ZSIZSMANN, ÉVA.   Mapping memory in B. S. Johnson's *The Unfortunates*. *In* (pp. 177–83) **3734**.

Charles Johnson (b.1948)

17207. KEIZER, ARLENE R.   Black subjects: identity formation in the contemporary narrative of slavery. (Bibl. 2004, 17495.) Rev. by Keith E. Byerman in JAH (92:3) 2005, 1071–2.

17208. MCWILLIAMS, JIM (ed.).   Passing the three gates: interviews with Charles Johnson. Seattle; London: Washington UP, 2004. pp. xxxii, 335. Rev. by Marc C. Conner in AAR (39:3) 2005, 481–3.

17209. STORHOFF, GARY.   Understanding Charles Johnson. Columbia; London: South Carolina UP, 2004. pp. 255. (Understanding contemporary American literature.)

Colin Johnson (Mudrooroo Narogin)

17210. OBOE, ANNALISA (ed.).   Mongrel signatures: reflections on the work of Mudrooroo. Amsterdam; Atlanta, GA: Rodopi, 2003. pp. xxi, 236. (Cross/cultures, 64.) Rev. by Nicholas Birns in Antipodes (18:1) 2004, 89–91.

Georgia Douglas Johnson

17211. O'BRIEN, C. C.   Cosmopolitanism in Georgia Douglas Johnson's anti-lynching literature. AAR (38:4) 2004, 571–87.

17212. STEPHENS, JUDITH L.   Art, activism, and uncompromising attitude in Georgia Douglas Johnson's lynching plays. AAR (39:1/2) 2005, 87–102.

James Weldon Johnson

17213. CHAKKALAKAL, TESS.   'Making a collection': James Weldon Johnson and the mission of African American literature. SAQ (104:3) 2005, 521–41.

17214. MORIEL, LIORA.   Passing and the performance of gender, race, and class acts: a theoretical framework. See **17584**.

17215. NOWLIN, MICHAEL.   James Weldon Johnson's *Black Manhattan* and the kingdom of American culture. AAR (39:3) 2005, 315–25.

17216. SPAULDING, A. TIMOTHY.   The cultural matrix of ragtime in James Weldon Johnson's *The Autobiography of an Ex-Colored Man*. Genre (37:2) 2004, 225–43.

Josephine W. Johnson

17217. GRAVES, MARK.   Josephine W. Johnson: the second short-story collection and beyond. MidAmerica (30) 2003, 85–93.

Mike Johnson

17218. SARTI EVANS, ANTONELLA.   Mike Johnson: la maledizione de Lear. LProv (119/120) 2004, 111–19.

Jennifer Johnston

17219. GALLIX, FRANÇOIS; GUIGNERY, VANESSA; RIHOIT, CATHERINE.   Jennifer Johnston at the Sorbonne, 19 November 2004. EtBr (28) 2005, 115–41. (Interview.)

17220. ROSSLYN, FELICITY.   'The nonsense about our Irishness': Jennifer Johnston. EAS (57) 2004, 104–22.

Wayne Johnston

17221. ANDREWS, JENNIFER.   Reading risk in *The Navigator of New York*. JCL (40:1) 2005, 37–56.

David Jones (1895–1974)

17222. MELLOR, LEO.   Words from the bombsites: debris, Modernism and literary salvage. See **16286**.

17223. SCHWARTZ, ADAM.   The third spring: G. K. Chesterton, Graham Greene, Christopher Dawson, and David Jones. See **15778**.

2005] AUTHORS 939

Diana Wynne Jones

17224. MENDLESOHN, FARAH. Diana Wynne Jones: children's literature and the fantastic tradition. London; New York: Routledge, 2005. pp. xxxiii, 240. (Children's literature and culture, 36.)

Edward P. Jones

17225. McHANEY, THOMAS. Welty's *Home by Dark/Yalobusha County/1936* in the jacket designs of two novels about slavery. *See* **20083.**

Gayl Jones

17226. CLABOUGH, CASEY. Afrocentric recolonizations: Gayl Jones's 1990s fiction. ConLit (46:2) 2005, 243–74.

17227. DAVIS, AMANDA J. To build a nation: Black women writers, Black nationalism, and violent reduction of wholeness. Frontiers (26:3) 2005, 24–53.

17228. ESCODA AGUSTÍ, CLARA. Strategies of subversion: the deconstruction of madness in *Eva's Man*, *Corregidora*, and *Beloved*. Atl (27:1) 2005, 29–38.

17229. YOUNG, HERSHINI BHANA. Inheriting the criminalized Black body: race, gender, and slavery in *Eva's Man*. AAR (39:3) 2005, 377–93.

James Jones

17230. ABEL, JONATHAN E. Canon and censor: how war wounds bodies of writing. *See* **19876.**

Erica Jong

17231. FARLAND, MARIA. 'Total system, total solution, total apocalypse': sex oppression, systems of property, and 1970s women's liberation fiction. YJC (18:2) 2005, 381–407.

17232. WHELEHAN, IMELDA. Sex and the single girl: Helen Fielding, Erica Jong and Helen Gurley Brown. *See* **16473.**

June Jordan

17233. LEVI, JAN HELLER; MILES, SARA (eds). Directed by desire: the collected poems of June Jordan. Port Townsend, WA: Copper Canyon Press, 2005. pp. xxix, 649. Rev. by Darryl Lorenzo Wellington in BkW, 18 Dec. 2005, 12.

17234. RICH, ADRIENNE. The witness takes a stand. BosR (30:2) 2005, 49–50.

Gabriel Josipovici

17235. PARK, CHRISTINE COHEN. Close comfort? Sons as their mothers' memoirists. A/B (19:1/2) 2004, 118–28.

17236. PERNOT, DOMINIQUE. Memory as deranged and immemorial in Josipovici's work. EtBr (29) 2005, 83–96.

James Joyce

17237. ALTER, ROBERT. Imagined cities: urban experience and the language of the novel. *See* **10639.**

17238. ANASTASI, WILLIAM. Jarry and Joyce. *In* (pp. 44–52) **17303.**

17239. ARMAND, LOUIS. Solicitations: essays on criticism and culture. *See* **14689.**

17240. ARMSTRONG, PAUL B. Play and the politics of reading: the social uses of Modernist form. *See* **11380.**

17241. ARNOLD, BRUCE. The scandal of *Ulysses*: the life and afterlife of a twentieth-century masterpiece. (Bibl. 2004, 17550.) Rev. by Alison Armstrong in ILS (25:1) 2005, 15; by Michael H. Epp in JJLS (19:1) 2005, 4.

17242. ATTRIDGE, DEREK. Joyce and the making of Modernism: the question of technique. *In* (pp. 149–59) 12946.

17243. —— Reading Joyce. *In* (pp. 1–27) 17244.

17244. —— (ed.). The Cambridge companion to James Joyce. (Bibl. 1996, 19021.) Cambridge; New York: CUP, 2004. pp. xviii, 290. (Cambridge companions to literature.) (Second ed.: first ed. 1990.) Rev. by Mary Lowe-Evans in JJLS (19:2) 2005, 10–11.

17245. —— James Joyce's *Ulysses*: a casebook. (Bibl. 2004, 17552.) Rev. by Heyward Ehrlich in JJLS (19:1) 2005, 7–8.

17246. BALSAMO, GIAN. Joyce's messianism: Dante, negative existence, and the messianic self. Columbia; London: South Carolina UP, 2004. pp. viii, 180.

17247. —— The necropolitan journey: Dante's negative poetics in James Joyce's *The Dead*. JJQ (40:4) 2003, 763–81.

17248. BEPLATE, JUSTIN. Joyce, Bergson, and the memory of words. MLR (100:2) 2005, 298–312.

17249. —— No mistakes: are Joyce's failings merely failures of discovery? TLS, 29 Apr. 2005, 3–4 (review-article).

17250. BERMAN, JESSICA. Modernism's possible geographies. *In* (pp. 281–96) 12640.

17251. BORNSTEIN, GEORGE. The colors of Zion: Black, Jewish, and Irish nationalisms at the turn of the century. See 20482.

17252. BROCKMAN, WILLIAM S. Collecting Joyce. *In* (pp. 273–84) 17274.

17253. —— Current JJ checklist (92). JJQ (40:3) 2003, 565–84.

17254. —— Current JJ checklist (93). JJQ (40:4) 2003, 783–96.

17255. BROOKER, JOSEPH. Joyce's critics: transitions in reading and culture. (Bibl. 2004, 17569.) Rev. by Justin Beplate in TLS, 29 Apr. 2005, 3–4; by John Gordon in ELT (48:4) 2005, 495–9; by Emer Nolan in Mod/Mod (12:3) 2005, 505–9.

17256. BUTLER, CHRISTOPHER. Joyce the Modernist. *In* (pp. 67–86) 17244.

17257. CARAHER, BRIAN G. Trieste, Dublin, Galway: Joyce, journalism, 1912. *In* (pp. 132–50) 17274.

17258. CASTLE, GREGORY. Coming of age in the age of empire: Joyce's Modernist *Bildungsroman*. JJQ (40:4) 2003, 665–90.

17259. CLAVARON, YVES; DIETERLE, BERNARD (eds). La mémoire des villes. See 20330.

17260. CONLEY, TIM. 'Are you to have all the pleasure quizzing on me?': *Finnegans Wake* and literary cognition. JJQ (40:4) 2003, 711–27.

17261. —— *Samizdat* odyssey: *Ulysses* above the 42nd parallel. *In* (pp. 139–51) 12739.

17262. CORNWELL, NEIL. 'A Dorset yokel's knuckles': Thomas Hardy and *Lolita*. See 18453.

17263. CREASY, MATTHEW. Shakespeare burlesque in *Ulysses*. EC (55:2) 2005, 136–58.

17264. CUCULLU, LOIS. Expert Modernists, matricide, and modern culture: Woolf, Forster, Joyce. *See* **16552.**

17265. DASENBROCK, REED WAY. Infinity, the 'terribly burned' Bruno, and *Ulysses*. *In* (pp. 28–41) **17274.**

17266. DEANE, SEAMUS. Joyce the Irishman. *In* (pp. 28–48) **17244.**

17267. DING, YUN. Simultaneity and the stream of consciousness in *Ulysses*. FLS (116) 2005, 100–4. (In Chinese.)

17268. DOCHERTY, THOMAS. Newman, Ireland, and universality. *See* **11762.**

17269. DONOVAN, STEPHEN. 'Short but to the point': newspaper typography in 'Aeolus'. JJQ (40:3) 2003, 519–41.

17270. DRISCOLL, CATHERINE. *Felix culpa*: sex, sin, and discourse in Joyce's fiction. *In* (pp. 171–86) **17274.**

17271. EARLE, DAVID M. 'Green eyes, I see you. Fang, I feel': the symbol of absinthe in *Ulysses*. JJQ (40:4) 2003, 691–709.

17272. EHRLICH, HEYWARD. Joyce, Yeats and Kabbalah. *In* (pp. 60–87) **17274.**

17273. EPSTEIN, EDMUND L. (ed.). A skeleton key to *Finnegans Wake*: unlocking James Joyce's masterwork. By Joseph Campbell and Henry Morton Robinson. (Bibl. 1947, 3561.) Novato, CA: New World Library, 2005. pp. xxvi, 402. (New ed.: first ed. 1947.)

17274. FOGARTY, ANNE; MARTIN, TIMOTHY (eds). Joyce on the threshold. Gainesville: Florida UP, 2005. pp. 299. (Florida James Joyce.)

17275. FRASER, JENNIFER MARGARET. Rite of passage in the narratives of Dante and Joyce. (Bibl. 2004, 17588.) Rev. by Heather Webb in Italica (82:1) 2005, 126–7.

17276. FRAWLEY, OONA (ed.). A new & complex sensation: essays on Joyce's *Dubliners*. Dublin: Lilliput Press, 2004. pp. xv, 251. Rev. by Blake Hobby in JJLS (19:2) 2005, 19–20.

17277. GANA, NOURI. Horizons of desire, horizons of mourning: Joyce's *Dubliners*. EtIr (28:1) 2003, 25–43.

17278. GIBSON, ANDREW. 'An Irish bull in an English chinashop': 'Oxen' and the cultural politics of the anthology. *In* (pp. 91–109) **17274.**

17279. GILBERT, GEOFF. Words, flies, ~~Jews~~, Joyce, *Joint*: Wyndham Lewis and the unpublishing of obscenity. *See* **17815.**

17280. GIORELLO, GIULIO. Prometeo, Ulisse, Gilgameš: figure del mito. Milan: Cortina, 2005. pp. xiii, 250. (Scienza e idee, 121.)

17281. GOLDMAN, JONATHAN E. Joyce, the propheteer. Novel (38:1) 2004, 84–102.

17282. GOZZI, FRANCESCO. Shakespeare as Paraclitus: Transubstantiation in Joyce and T. S. Eliot. *In* (pp. 88–94) **3724.**

17283. GUNN, IAN; HART, CLIVE; BECK, HARALD. James Joyce's Dublin: a topographical guide to the Dublin of *Ulysses*: with 121 illustrations. (Bibl. 2004, 17599.) Rev. by Phillip Herring in JJLS (19:1) 2005, 23–4.

17284. Guo, Jun.   Hidden historical–political rhetoric: take two stories from *Dubliners* for examples. FLS (111) 2005, 52–9. (In Chinese.)

17285. Guth, Ryan K.   Experiencing technical difficulties: a reader's negotiation with the compositional method of *Ulysses*, episode 12. JJQ (40:4) 2003, 753–62.

17286. Hagena, Katharina.   Towers of babble and silence. In (pp. 187–99) **17274.**

17287. Harris, Claudia W.   Caught in the nets: James Joyce's intimate portraits. LitB (24:1/2) 2004, 134–55.

17288. Hayes, Christa-Maria Lerm.   Joyce in art: visual art inspired by James Joyce. Foreword by Fritz Senn. Afterword by James Elkins. Dublin: Lilliput Press, 2004. pp. xi, 415. Rev. by Justin Beplate in TLS, 15 Apr. 2005, 28; by Archie K. Loss in JJLS (19:1) 2005, 18; by Alison Armstrong in ILS (24:2) 2005, 9–10.

17289. Howes, Marjorie.   Joyce, colonialism, and nationalism. In (pp. 254–71) **17244.**

17290. Johnsen, William A.   Violence and Modernism: Ibsen, Joyce and Woolf. (Bibl. 2004, 17607.) Rev. by Keri Elizabeth Ames in ELT (48:1) 2005, 111–14; by Celia Marshik in WSA (11) 2005, 220–4.

17291. Johnson, Jeri.   Joyce and feminism. In (pp. 196–212) **17244.**

17292. Jousni, Stéphane.   Écrire Dublin après Joyce. EtIr (29:1) 2004, 73–84.

17293. Kenner, Hugh.   Flaubert, Joyce, and Beckett: the stoic comedians. See **15399.**

17294. Killeen, Terence.   Ulysses unbound: a reader's companion to James Joyce's *Ulysses*. Bray, Co. Wicklow: Wordwell in assn with the National Library of Ireland, 2004. pp. ix, 258. Rev. by Robert F. Garratt in JJLS (19:1) 2005, 17.

17295. Klein, Axel.   'The distant music mournfully murmereth …': the influence of James Joyce on Irish composers. ALyr (14) 2004, 71–94.

17296. Knowlton, Eloise.   Showings forth: *Dubliners*, photography, and the rejection of realism. Mosaic (38:1) 2005, 133–50.

17297. Koch, Markus.   The hand writing beyond the wall: Faulkner and an American cultural cringe. In (pp. 135–85) **16406.**

17298. Lawrence, Karen R.   Bloom in circulation: who's he when he's not at home? In (pp. 15–27) **17274.**

17299. Leckie, Barbara.   The simple case of adultery. JJQ (40:4) 2003, 729–52.

17300. Leonard, Garry.   *Dubliners.* In (pp. 87–102) **17244.**

17301. Lernout, Geert; Van Mierlo, Wim (eds).   The reception of James Joyce in Europe. (Bibl. 2004, 17623.) Rev. by Justin Beplate in TLS, 29 Apr. 2005, 3–4; by John Nash in RES (56:226) 2005, 689–91; by Ida Klitgard in SoCR (38:1) 2005, 226–8.

17302. Levine, Jennifer.   *Ulysses.* In (pp. 122–48) **17244.**

17303. Levy, Aaron; Rabaté, Jean-Michel (eds).   William Anastasi's Pataphysical Society: Jarry, Joyce, Duchamp, and Cage. Introd. by Osvaldo Romberg. Philadelphia, PA: Slought, 2005. pp. 113. (Contemporary artists, 3.)

17304. Li, Rucheng.   Joyce's aesthetic pursuit reflected in *A Portrait of the Artist as a Young Man*. FLS (115) 2005, 91–6. (In Chinese.)

17305. LINGUANTI, ELSA. La percezione del tempo in letteratura e la sfida della simultaneità nell'episodio delle 'Sirene' nell'*Ulysses* di Joyce. AngP (2:1/2) 2005, 101–18.

17306. LOWE-EVANS, MARY. Freddy Malins: a fool for Chrissake! *In* (pp. 42–59) **17274.**

17307. MCAULIFFE, JODY. Lucia Joyce as Cordelia and the Fool. JML (28:3) 2005, 170–82 (review-article).

17308. MACCABE, COLIN. Bloomsday 2004. CritQ (46:3) 2004, 79–81.

17309. MCDONALD, RUSSELL. Who speaks for Fergus? Silence, homophobia, and the anxiety of Yeatsian influence in Joyce. TCL (51:4) 2005, 391–413.

17310. MAHAFFEY, VICKI. Joyce's shorter works. *In* (pp. 172–95) **17244.**

17311. MAMIGONIAN, MARC A.; TURNER, JOHN NOEL. Annotations for *Stephen Hero*. JJQ (40:3) 2003, 347–518.

17312. MASHECK, JOSEPH. Jarry–Joyce–Duchamp in an Anastasian illumination. *In* (pp. 12–23) **17303.**

17313. MATHEWS, P. J. 'A.E.I.O.U': Joyce and the *Irish Homestead*. *In* (pp. 151–68) **17274.**

17314. MELCHIORI, GIORGIO. Joyce e l'eternità da Dante a Vico. Bel (60:6) 2005, 617–33.

17315. MILESI, LAURENT (ed.). James Joyce and the difference of language. Cambridge; New York: CUP, 2003. pp. xiii, 232. Rev. by John McCourt in StudN (37:1) 2005, 111–15; by Paul K. Saint-Amour in SAtlR (70:1) 2005, 189–93.

17316. MULLIN, KATHERINE. James Joyce, sexuality, and social purity. (Bibl. 2004, 17648.) Rev. by John Nash in RES (56:225) 2005, 474–5; by John Paul Riquelme in JJLS (19:2) 2005, 2–4; by Richard Rankin Russell in StudN (37:4) 2005, 491–3.

17317. NASH, JOHN. Reading Joyce in English. *In* (pp. 110–31) **17274.**

17318. NORBURN, ROGER. A James Joyce chronology. Basingstoke; New York: Palgrave Macmillan, 2004. pp. xiv, 231. (Author chronologies.) Rev. by David Pierce in JML (28:3) 2005, 162–9.

17319. NØRGAARD, NINA. Systemic functional linguistics and literary analysis: a Hallidayan approach to Joyce, a Joycean approach to Halliday. (Bibl. 2004, 17654.) Rev. by Liesbet Heyvaert in BELL (ns 2) 2004, 342–4.

17320. NORRIS, MARGOT. *Finnegans Wake*. *In* (pp. 149–71) **17244.**

17321. —— Suspicious readings of Joyce's *Dubliners*. (Bibl. 2004, 17656.) Rev. by Thomas Docherty in YES (35) 2005, 336–7.

17322. —— *Ulysses*. Cork: Cork UP in assn with the Film Inst. of Ireland, 2004. pp. 102. (Ireland into film, 8.) Rev. by Susan Bazargan in JJLS (19:2) 2005, 6.

17323. —— The voice and the void: Hugh Kenner's Joyce. *See* **14941.**

17324. OCHSHORN, KATHLEEN. Who's modern now? Shaw, Joyce, and Ibsen's *When We Dead Awaken*. *See* **19404.**

17325. O'CONNOR, ULICK (ed.). The Joyce we knew: memoirs of Joyce. Dingle, Co. Kerry: Brandon, 2004. pp. 126.

17326. Ó GRÁDA, CORMAC. Lost in Little Jerusalem: Leopold Bloom and Irish Jewry. JML (27:4) 2004, 17–26.

17327. O'NEILL, PATRICK. Extending the text: textuality and transtextuality. *In* (pp. 255–72) **17274**.

17328. POTTER, RACHEL. 'Can my daughter of 18 read this book?': *Ulysses* and obscenity. CritQ (46:4) 2004, 22–37.

17329. POWELL, KERSTI TARIEN. 'Not a son but a survivor': Beckett ... Joyce ... Banville. *See* **15412**.

17330. RABATÉ, JEAN-MICHEL. Joyce the Parisian. *In* (pp. 49–66) **17244**.

17331. —— (ed.). Palgrave advances in James Joyce studies. Basingstoke; New York: Palgrave Macmillan, 2004. pp. xviii, 293. (Palgrave advances.) Rev. by Emer Nolan in Mod/Mod (12:3) 2005, 505–9.

17332. REGARD, FRÉDÉRIC. Autobiography as linguistic incompetence: notes on Derrida's readings of Joyce and Cixous. TexP (19:2) 2005, 283–95.

17333. RIQUELME, JOHN PAUL. *Stephen Hero* and *A Portrait of the Artist as a Young Man*: transforming the nightmare of history. *In* (pp. 103–21) **17244**.

17334. RORABACK, ERIK S. Para-baroque conceptual intersections & interventions: *Finnegans Wake, Gravity's Rainbow* and *The Writing of the Disaster*. HJS (5:2) 2004/05.

17335. SAINT-AMOUR, PAUL K. Ride 'em cowpoyride: literary property metadiscourse in *Ulysses*. *In* (pp. 229–54) **17274**.

17336. SCHNEIDER, ERIK. Towards *Ulysses*: some unpublished Joyce documents from Trieste. JML (27:4) 2004, 1–16.

17337. SHLOSS, CAROL LOEB. Lucia Joyce: to dance in the wake. (Bibl. 2004, 17683.) Rev. by Finn Fordham in Mod/Mod (12:2) 2005, 357–8; by Jody McAuliffe in JML (28:3) 2005, 170–82.

17338. SIMONS, JEFFREY; TEJEDOR CABRERA, JOSÉ MARÍA (eds). Silver-powdered olivetrees: reading Joyce in Spain. Seville: Secretariado de Pubs de la Univ. de Sevilla, 2003. pp. 295. (Literatura, 74.) Rev. by Antonio Ballesteros González in Atl (27:2) 2005, 151–6; by Lelia Menéndez in JJLS (19:1) 2005, 21–2.

17339. SINDING, MICHAEL. *Genera mixta*: conceptual blending and mixed genres in *Ulysses*. NLH (36:4) 2005, 589–619.

17340. SLOTE, SAM. *Gillet lit le Joyce dans la Woolf*: genre in *Orlando* and *Ulysses*. *See* **20429**.

17341. STEINBERG, ERWIN R.; HALLSTEIN, CHRISTIAN W. Probing silences in Joyce's *Ulysses* and the question of authorial intention. JJQ (40:3) 2003, 543–54.

17342. STREIT, WOLFGANG. Joyce/Foucault: sexual confessions. Ann Arbor: Michigan UP, 2004. pp. 229.

17343. TADIÉ, BENOÎT. The room of infinite possibilities: Joyce, Flaubert, and the historical imagination. EA (58:2) 2005, 131–40.

17344. THIHER, ALLEN. Fiction refracts science: Modernist writers from Proust to Borges. Columbia; London: Missouri UP, 2005. pp. xii, 297.

17345. THOMPSON, CHRIS. Voicing Joyce: crossmess parzels from Cage to Beuys. PRes (8:1) 2003, 5–22.

17346. TÓIBÍN, COLM. Reading the city. Brick (76) 2005, 35–43.

17347. VALENTE, JOSEPH. Joyce and sexuality. *In* (pp. 213–33) **17244**.

17348. VALTAT, JEAN-CHRISTOPHE. Culture et figures de la relativité: *Le Temps retrouvé, Finnegans Wake*. Paris: Champion, 2004. pp. 320. (Bibliothèque de littérature générale et comparée, 43.) Rev. by Yves-Michel Ergal in RLC (79:1) 2005, 101–2.

17349. VAN DE KAMP, PETER. Hands off! Joyce and the Mangan in the Mac. In (pp. 183–213) **9237**.

17350. VAN HULLE, DIRK. Textual awareness: a genetic study of late manuscripts by Joyce, Proust, and Mann. Ann Arbor: Michigan UP, 2004. pp. xi, 219. (Editorial theory and literary criticism.)

17351. WALLACE, NATHAN. Shakespeare biography and the theory of reconciliation in Edward Dowden and James Joyce. See **10837**.

17352. WELCH, ROBERT. Walking from the dark: Giordano Bruno and James Joyce. (Based on a lecture given at Newman House, Dublin.) In (pp. 267–74) **3756**.

17353. WICHT, WOLFGANG. 'Bleibtreustrasse 34, Berlin, W. 15' (*U* 4.199), once again. JJQ (40:4) 2003, 797–811.

17354. WICKE, JENNIFER. Joyce and consumer culture. In (pp. 234–53) **17244**.

17355. WINSTON, GREG. Stephen's schoolbooks: a portrait of geography in a young nation. EtIr (30:1) 2005, 83–99.

17356. WU, QINGJUN. The defamiliarized language in *Ulysses*. FLS (116) 2005, 95–9. (In Chinese.)

17357. ZINGG, GISELA. Hiberno-English in Joyce's *Ulysses*. SPELL (17) 2005, 195–206.

Rachel Kadish (b.1969)

17358. KADISH, RACHEL. The *davka* method. In (pp. 277–92) **12893**.

Cynthia Kadohata

17359. CONNER, KRISTA. Western literature at century's end: sketches in Generation X, Los Angeles, and the post-Civil Rights novel. PacHR (72:3) 2003, 405–13.

Winston C. Kam

17360. MIKI, ROY. *Inside the Black Egg*: cultural practice, citizenship, and belonging in a globalizing nation. Mosaic (38:3) 2005, 1–19.

Sarah Kane

17361. CAMPBELL, ALYSON. Experiencing Kane: an affective analysis of Sarah Kane's 'experiential' theatre in performance. ADS (46) 2005, 80–97.

17362. LUCKHURST, MARY. Infamy and dying young: Sarah Kane, 1971–1999. In (pp. 107–24) **3985**.

17363. VIVAN, ITALA. A cultural analysis of Sarah Kane's rewriting of the myth of Phaedra as a fearful symmetry of impossible love. Culture (17) 2003, 87–100.

Farida Karodia

17364. RASTOGI, PALLAVI. From South Asia to South Africa: locating other postcolonial diasporas. See **16380**.

Sam Kashner

17365. KASHNER, SAM. When I was cool: my life at the Jack Kerouac School: a memoir. (Bibl. 2004, 17723.) Rev. by Mike Golden in AmBR (26:2) 2005, 12–14.

Dori Katz

17366. GOLDENBERG, MYRNA. Identity, memory, and authority: an introduction to Holocaust poems by Hilary Tham, Myra Sklarew, and Dori Katz. See **19761.**

Moises Kaufman

17367. BAGLIA, JAY; FOSTER, ELISSA. Performing the 'really' real: cultural criticism, representation, and commodification in *The Laramie Project*. JDTC (19:2) 2005, 127–45.

Patrick Kavanagh (1904–1967)

17368. LAIRD, NICK. Not a damn thing. LRB (27:16) 2005, 26–7 (review-article). (*Collected Poems.*)

17369. QUINN, ANTOINETTE (ed.). Collected poems. London: Allen Lane, 2004. pp. xxxv, 298. Rev. by Nick Laird in LRB (27:16) 2005, 26–7.

Guy Gavriel Kay

17370. COBB, CHRISTOPHER. Guy Gavriel Kay and the psychology of history. Foundation (94) 2005, 87–99.

Jackie Kay (b.1961)

17371. HÁCOVÁ, PAVLÍNA. The poet as cultural dentist: ethnicity in the poetry of Jackie Kay. *In* (pp. 63–7) **3734.**

17372. NIERAGDEN, GÖRAN. Otherness at work: the non-indigenous English novel. See **16343.**

Elia Kazan

17373. PARKER, BRIAN. Elia Kazan and *Sweet Bird of Youth*. See **20196.**

17374. SCHICKEL, RICHARD. Elia Kazan: a biography. See **13895.**

Weldon Kees

17375. ARMILLAS-TISEYRA, MAGALI. Interview: Kathleen Rooney. See **21279.**

17376. CRAIK, ROGER. Weldon Kees and Bob Dylan's *Idiot Wind*. NCL (35:1) 2005, 5–6.

17377. REIDEL, JAMES. Vanished act: the life and art of Weldon Kees. (Bibl. 2004, 17741.) Rev. by Raymond Nelson in GPQ (24:4) 2004, 300–1; by Rod Phillips in WAL (39:2) 2004, 241–3.

17378. YAU, JOHN. At the movies with Weldon Kees and Frank O'Hara. APR (34:5) 2005, 11–17.

Nora Okja Keller

17379. NAJMI, SAMINA. Decolonizing the *Bildungsroman*: narratives of war and womanhood in Nora Okja Keller's *Comfort Woman*. *In* (pp. 209–30) **9454.**

William Melvin Kelley

17380. ANDERSON, ERIC GARY. The real live, invisible languages of *A Different Drummer*: a response to Trudier Harris. SCR (22:1) 2005, 48–53.

17381. HARRIS, TRUDIER. William Melvin Kelley's real live, invisible South. SCR (22:1) 2005, 26–47.

Éamon Kelly (b.1914)

17382. KELLY, ÉAMON. Éamon Kelly: the storyteller. Douglas Village, Cork: Mercier Press, 2004. pp. 351.

James Kelman

17383. HAGEMANN, SUSANNE. Postcolonial translation studies and James Kelman's *Translated Accounts*. ScSR (6:1) 2005, 74–83.

17384. KLAUS, H. GUSTAV. James Kelman. Plymouth: Northcote House in assn with the British Council, 2004. pp. x, 111. (Writers and their work.)

17385. MURPHY, TERENCE PATRICK. Durational realism? Voice-over narrative in James Kelman's *'An Old Pub near the Angel' and Other Stories*. JNT (33:3) 2003, 335–56.

17386. ZDERADIČKOVÁ, OLGA. Scottish national identity in the works of James Kelman. *In* (pp. 195–200) **3753**.

Thomas Keneally

17387. RYAN, J. S. 'The great gaol by the sea' – the developing lore and associations of one such place of incarceration, Trial Bay Jail, New South Wales. AF (20) 2005, 182–96.

A. L. Kennedy

17388. SUMMERS-BREMNER, ELUNED. 'Fiction with a thread of Scottishness in its truth': the paradox of the national in A. L. Kennedy. EAS (57) 2004, 123–38.

17389. TEW, PHILIP. Across the prairies, and beyond the postmodern: A. L. Kennedy, Linda Hutcheon, and realizing the contemporary. WasRCPSF (38:1) 2003, 51–65.

Adrienne Kennedy

17390. BARNETT, CLAUDIA. 'An evasion of ontology': being Adrienne Kennedy. TDR (49:3) 2005, 157–86.

17391. KENNEDY, ADRIENNE. Paragraphs, passages, and pages that changed my life. Theater (35:3) 2005, 6–19.

17392. KOLIN, PHILIP C. Understanding Adrienne Kennedy. Columbia; London: South Carolina UP, 2005. pp. xii, 222. (Understanding contemporary American literature.) Rev. by Beth Schachter in TJ (57:4) 2005, 763–5; by Annette J. Saddik in CLAJ (49:1) 2005, 103–6.

17393. KUMAR, NITA N. Dramatic trans-formations: the surrealism of being Black and female in Adrienne Kennedy's *The Owl Answers*. JADT (17:2) 2005, 59–70.

Thomas E. Kennedy (b.1944)

17394. HERRIGES, GREG. The making of Thomas E. Kennedy: *Copenhagen Quartet*. SoCR (38:1) 2005, 85–96.

William Kennedy

17395. BURN, STEPHEN J.   Kennedy's *Roscoe*. Exp (63:4) 2005, 247–8.

17396. O'DONNELL, BRENNAN.   Francis Phelan in Purgatory: William Kennedy's Catholic imagination in *Ironweed*. ChrisL (54:1) 2004, 51–71.

Brendan Kennelly

17397. MCDONALD, MARIANNE.   Rebel women: Brendan Kennelly's versions of Irish tragedy. NewHR (9:3) 2005, 123–36.

Jane Kenyon

17398. CRAMER, STEVEN.   Home alone: self and relation in part 1 of *The Boat of Quiet Hours*. *In* (pp. 160–8) **17404.**

17399. DAVIS, TODD F.; WOMACK, KENNETH.   Reading the ethics of mourning in the poetry of Donald Hall. *See* **16859.**

17400. HALL, DONALD.   The best day the worst day: life with Jane Kenyon. Boston, MA: Houghton Mifflin, 2005. pp. 258.

17401. HARRIS, JUDITH.   Discerning cherishment in Jane Kenyon's poetry: a psychoanalytic approach. *In* (pp. 191–202) **17404.**

17402. KENYON, JANE.   Seven letters to Alice Mattison. *In* (pp. 23–31) **17404.**

17403. PERILLO, LUCIA.   Notes from the other side. *In* (pp. 247–50) **17404.**

17404. PESEROFF, JOYCE (ed.).   Simply lasting: writers on Jane Kenyon. Saint Paul, MN: Graywolf Press, 2005. pp. xvi, 280.

17405. PRIDE, MIKE.   Still present. *In* (pp. 94–109) **17404.**

17406. RECTOR, LIAM.   Remembering Jane Kenyon. *In* (pp. 74–82) **17404.**

17407. STRONGIN, LYNN.   A faith that blessed through sorrow: meditations on Jane Kenyon's poetry. *In* (pp. 212–23) **17404.**

Jack Kerouac

17408. BRINKLEY, DOUGLAS (ed.).   Windblown world: the journals of Jack Kerouac, 1947–1954. New York: Viking, 2004. pp. xliv, 387. Rev. by Rob Johnson in AmBR (26:6) 2005, 13–15.

17409. GILL, R. B.   Kerouac and the comic dilemma. SPC (27:3) 2005, 87–98.

17410. HAYES, KEVIN J. (ed.).   Conversations with Jack Kerouac. Jackson; London: Mississippi UP, 2005. pp. xxi, 100. (Literary conversations.)

17411. MAHER, PAUL, JR.   Kerouac: the definitive biography. Foreword by David Amram. (Bibl. 2004, 17768.) Rev. by Ron Butlin in TLS, 29 July 2005, 28.

17412. MOORE, DAVE (ed.).   Collected letters, 1944–1967. Introd. by Carolyn Cassady. *See* **15720.**

17413. STERRITT, DAVID.   Screening the Beats: media culture and the Beat sensibility. (Bibl. 2004, 17770.) Rev. by Greg Taylor in FilmQ (58:4) 2004, 74.

17414. STUART, ANGUS F.   The geography of solitude: inner space and the sense of place. *See* **18202.**

Philip Kerr

17415. SCAGGS, JOHN.   Missing persons and multicultural identity: the case of Philip Kerr's *Berlin Noir*. *In* (pp. 119–37) **14191.**

Susan Kerslake

17416. FENNELL, FRANCIS L., JR. Appropriating Hopkins. *See* **11302**.

Joseph Kesselring (1902–1967)

17417. HASLAM, JASON. 'A secret proclamation': queering the gothic parody of *Arsenic and Old Lace*. *See* **13454**.

John Oliver Killens

17418. MURRAY, ROLLAND. How the conjure-man gets busy: cultural nationalism, masculinity, and performativity. YJC (18:2) 2005, 299–321.

Joyce Kilmer (1886–1918)

17419. POLLIN, BURTON R. Kilmer's *Trees*. Exp (63:4) 2005, 227–30.

Thomas Kilroy

17420. DUBOST, THIERRY. Boucicault, Friel et Kilroy: étude en do bémol et majeur. *See* **10131**.

Richard E. Kim (b.1932)

17421. LAWRENCE, KEITH. Toshio Mori, Richard Kim, and the masculine ideal. *In* (pp. 207–28) **12775**.

Ronyoung Kim

17422. THOMA, PAMELA. Representing Korean American female subjects, negotiating multiple Americas, and reading beyond the ending in Ronyoung Kim's *Clay Walls*. *In* (pp. 265–93) **12775**.

Jamaica Kincaid

17423. BOUSON, J. BROOKS. Jamaica Kincaid: writing memory, writing back to the mother. Albany: New York State UP, 2005. pp. ix, 242.

17424. BRAZIEL, JANA EVANS. 'Caribbean genesis': language, gardens, worlds (Jamaica Kincaid, Derek Walcott, Édouard Glissant). *In* (pp. 110–26) **12632**.

17425. BROPHY, SARAH. Witnessing AIDS: writing, testimony, and the work of mourning. Toronto; Buffalo, NY; London: Toronto UP, 2004. pp. x, 271, (plates) 8. (Cultural spaces.) Rev. by G. Thomas Couser in Biography (28:2) 2005, 295–7.

17426. DAVIDSON, DIANA. Writing AIDS in Antigua: tensions between public activisms in Jamaica Kincaid's *My Brother*. JCPS (10:1) 2003, 121–44.

17427. GARDNER-CORBETT, COLENA. Escaping the colonizer's whip: the binary discipline. CLAJ (49:1) 2005, 74–92.

17428. SIMON, LOUIS. Triumph of ambivalence: Jamaica Kincaid's *The Autobiography of My Mother*. JCarL (4:1) 2005, 31–7.

17429. WEBER, JEAN JACQUES. From 'bad' to 'worse': pragmatic scales and the (de)construction of cultural models. LLit (14:1) 2005, 45–63.

Laurie R. King

17430. TAYLOR, RHONDA HARRIS. 'It's about who controls the information': mystery antagonists and information literacy. Clues (24:1) 2005, 7–17.

Stephen King ('Richard Bachman')

17431. CAHILL, BRYON. Stephen King: Hallowe'en's answer to Santa Claus. Writing (28:2) 2005, 8–13. (Interview.)

17432. DOWNEY, DARA; JONES, DARRYL. King of the castle: Shirley Jackson and Stephen King. *In* (pp. 214–36) **17181.**

17433. STRENGELL, HEIDI. Dissecting Stephen King: from the gothic to literary naturalism. Madison; London: Wisconsin UP, 2005. pp. ix, 308.

17434. VINCENT, BEV. The road to *The Dark Tower*: exploring Stephen King's *magnum opus*. New York: New American Library, 2004. pp. ix, 350.

Thomas King

17435. BENITO SÁNCHEZ, JESÚS; MANZANAS CALVO, ANA MARÍA. Re-citing master narratives: Thomas King's *Green Grass, Running Water* and the politics of enunciation. LittPr (15:30) 2005, 28–34.

17436. DAVIDSON, ARNOLD E.; WALTON, PRISCILLA L.; ANDREWS, JENNIFER (eds). Border crossings: Thomas King's cultural inversions. (Bibl. 2004, 17796.) Rev. by Marlene Goldman in CanL (183) 2004, 117–18; by Valerie Alia in BJCS (17:2) 2004, 254–5; by Penny van Toorn in MLR (100:4) 2005, 1105–6.

17437. HIRSCH, BUD. 'Stay calm, be brave, wait for signs': sign-offs and send-ups in the fiction of Thomas King. WAL (39:2) 2004, 145–75.

17438. KING, THOMAS. The truth about stories: a native narrative. (Bibl. 2004, 17798.) Rev. by Warren Cariou in LRC (12:4) 2004, 23–4.

17439. KLEIN, VERENA. Healing the Native Canadian soul: three accounts of spiritual homecoming. *See* **17020.**

17440. SARKOWSKY, KATJA. Churches, museums, and the return of the buffalo: spatial art in Thomas King's *Truth and Bright Water*. *In* (pp. 53–69) **12912.**

17441. SCHORCHT, BLANCA. Storied voices in Native American texts: Harry Robinson, Thomas King, James Welch, and Leslie Marmon Silko. (Bibl. 2003, 17720.) Rev. by Ellen L. Arnold in SAIL (17:1) 2005, 90–3.

17442. STRATTON, FLORENCE. There is no Bentham Street in Calgary: panoptic discourses and Thomas King's *Medicine River*. CanL (185) 2005, 11–27.

Karen King-Aribisala

17443. KING-ARIBISALA, KAREN. My sister – the short story. *In* (pp. 74–6) **14204.**

Donald Kingsbury (b.1929)

17444. BARBOUR, DOUGLAS. Archive fever in the technological far future histories *Appleseed*, *Permanence* and *Psychohistorical Crisis*. *See* **21181.**

Hugh Kingsmill (1889–1949)

17445. PLOWDEN, GEOFFREY. Parodies. *See* **17067.**

Barbara Kingsolver

17446. JACOBSON, KRISTIN J. The neodomestic American novel: the politics of home in Barbara Kingsolver's *The Poisonwood Bible*. TSWL (24:1) 2005, 105–27.

17447. JUSSAWALLA, FEROZA. Reading and teaching Barbara Kingsolver's *Poisonwood Bible* as postcolonial. RAEI (16) 2003, 165–75.

Maxine Hong Kingston

17448. DE CUSATIS, FELICE. 'The making of more Americans': il 'mito americano' in *China Men* di Maxine Hong Kingston. *In* (pp. 71–85) **12883.**

17449. DOUGLAS, CHRISTOPHER. Reading ethnography: the Cold War social science of Jade Snow's *Fifth Chinese Daughter* and *Brown v. Board of Education*. In (pp. 101–24) **9454**.

17450. EPERJESI, JOHN R. The imperialist imaginary: visions of Asia and the Pacific in American culture. Foreword by Donald E. Pease. *See* **18518**.

17451. NARCISI, LARA. Wittman's transitions: multivocality and the play of *Tripmaster Monkey*. MELUS (30:3) 2005, 95–111.

17452. SABINE, MAUREEN ALICE. Maxine Hong Kingston's broken book of life: an intertextual study of *The Woman Warrior* and *China Men*. (Bibl. 2004, 17812.) Rev. by Shameem Black in TSWL (24:2) 2005, 345–6.

Galway Kinnell

17453. NICKSON, RICHARD. Telling the truth and spreading slander. *See* **19403**.

John Kinsella (b.1963)

17454. ARMAND, LOUIS. Solicitations: essays on criticism and culture. *See* **14689**.

17455. KINSELLA, JOHN. *Poetics recidivous* and the de-poetics of lightning, herbicides, and pesticides. ColoR (32:2) 2005, 83–108.

Thomas Kinsella

17456. HARMON, MAURICE. Thomas Kinsella: jousting with evil. YES (35) 2005, 18–30.

W. P. Kinsella

17457. MORSE, DONALD E. W. P. Kinsella's postmodern metafictional fantasy *Shoeless Joe*. JFA (15:4) 2004, 309–19.

17458. REISING, R. W. 'BOB'. From the big top to the big leagues: Burt Lancaster's baseball odysseys (oddities?). *See* **13571**.

Rudyard Kipling

17459. ANNIS, GEOFFREY. *The Light That Failed* and *Captains Courageous*: studies in endurance. KJ (79:314) 2005, 31–46.

17460. BANDYOPADHYAY, DEBASHIS. The past unearthed: new reading of Ruskin Bond's supernatural tales. *See* **15523**.

17461. BUFFONI, FRANCO (introd. and trans.). Poesie. Milan: Nuages, 2005. pp. 143. (Classici illustrati.) (Second ed.: first ed. 1993.)

17462. CAMFIELD, GREGG. In the mirror of the imagination: Mark Twain's Kipling. *See* **12235**.

17463. CARAHER, BRIAN G. Trieste, Dublin, Galway: Joyce, journalism, 1912. In (pp. 132–50) **17274**.

17464. CROOKSHANK, JOHN. *Ford o' Kabul River*. KJ (79:314) 2005, 29–30.

17465. DÍAZ DE CHUMACEIRO, CORA L. A note on Rudyard Kipling's loss of brother John: *Little Tobrah*. PsyArt (9) 2005.

17466. DILLINGHAM, WILLIAM B. Bacon and eggs: Kipling's calling. KJ (79:313) 2005, 34–46.

17467. —— Rudyard Kipling: hell and heroism. Basingstoke; New York: Palgrave Macmillan, 2005. pp. xi, 383.

17468. HAGIIOANNU, ANDREW. The man who would be Kipling: the colonial fiction and the frontiers of exile. (Bibl. 2004, 17826.) Rev. by Patrick Brantlinger in ELT (48:1) 2005, 88–91.

17469. JOHNSON, ALAN. The savage city: locating colonial modernity. NCC (25:4) 2003, 315–32.

17470. KRAJKA, WIESŁAW. Just So Stories by Rudyard Kipling as a mythological–aesthetic foundation text for children. In (pp. 93–105) 12868.

17471. LEE, JOHN. Kipling's Shakespearean Traffics and Discoveries. SStudT (41) 2003, 1–24.

17472. LOOTENS, TRICIA. Alien homelands: Rudyard Kipling, Toru Dutt, and the poetry of empire. In (pp. 285–310) 9675.

17473. MCBRATNEY, JOHN. Imperial subjects, imperial space: Rudyard Kipling's fiction of the native-born. (Bibl. 2004, 17833.) Rev. by Ted Holt in JVC (9:2) 2004, 284–9.

17474. MAIDMENT, RICHARD. Kipling and the Chronicle. KJ (79:313) 2005, 9–19.

17475. MALLETT, PHILLIP. Rudyard Kipling: a literary life. (Bibl. 2004, 17834.) Rev. by Ted Holt in JVC (9:2) 2004, 284–9; by D. H. Stewart in ELT (48:2) 2005, 252–3.

17476. MANGUEL, ALBERTO. From a Reader's Diary: Kim. Brick (74) 2004, 55–64.

17477. MARSH, DARREN. Two unpublished letters of Rudyard Kipling. NQ (52:1) 2005, 84–7.

17478. MOHANRAM, RADHIKA. Dermographia: written on the skin; or, How the Irish became White in India. EJES (9:3) 2005, 251–70.

17479. MONTEFIORE, JANET. archy experiences a seizure and The Rhyme of the Three Captains. KJ (79:314) 2005, 47–52.

17480. MOODY, A. DAVID. Kipling in Eliot and in Pound: a measure of their difference. In (pp. 153–8) 3756.

17481. MORAN, NEIL K. Kipling and Afghanistan: a study of the young author as journalist writing on the Afghan Border Crisis of 1884–1885. Jefferson, NC; London: McFarland, 2005. pp. ix, 233.

17482. PARK, CLARA CLAIBORNE. Artist of empire: Kipling and Kim. HR (55:4) 2003, 537–61.

17483. PINNEY, THOMAS. Some reflections on Kipling's letters. KJ (79:314) 2005, 10–22.

17484. —— (ed.). The letters of Rudyard Kipling: vol. 5, 1920–30. Basingstoke; New York: Palgrave Macmillan, 2003. pp. viii, 584.

17485. —— The letters of Rudyard Kipling: vol. 6, 1931–36. Basingstoke; New York: Palgrave Macmillan, 2003. pp. ix, 527.

17486. POWICI, CHRISTOPHER. 'Who are the Bandar-log?': questioning animals in Rudyard Kipling's Mowgli stories and Ursula Le Guin's Buffalo Gals, Won't You Come Out Tonight. In (pp. 177–94) 14258.

17487. PRICKETT, STEPHEN. Victorian fantasy. *See* **9609.**

17488. RIVES, MAX. Kipling and France. KJ (79:313) 2005, 20–7.

17489. STOCKWELL, PETER. Texture and identification. EJES (9:2) 2005, 143–53.

17490. STRACK, DANIEL C. Who are the bridge-builders? Metaphor, metonymy, and the architecture of empire. Style (39:1) 2005, 37–54.

17491. TOWHEED, SHAFQUAT. Rudyard Kipling's literary property, international copyright law and *The Naulahka.* ELT (48:4) 2005, 420–35.

17492. VAN BRONSWIJK, R. Driving the darkness: W. E. Henley's *The Song of the Sword* as uneasy battle cry. *See* **11266.**

17493. WIGGINS, DEBORAH E. The residue of Victorian idealism: Rudyard Kipling and the Imperial War Graves Commission. KJ (79:313) 2005, 47–57.

17494. WISEMAN, T. P. Horace, Faunus, and Kipling: an address given to the Horatian Society. KJ (79:314) 2005, 23–8.

17495. ZHENG, YUN. The identity dilemma: a reading of Kipling's short story *On the City Wall.* FLS (115) 2005, 103–8. (In Chinese.)

Bharti Kirchner

17496. ANDRE, SUSAN. The Zen of pastry and cross-cultural bytes: an interview with Bharti Kirchner. BRev (24:1) 2004, 13.

Russell Kirk

17497. PERSON, JAMES E., JR. The achievement of Russell Kirk. ModAge (47:4) 2005, 344–9 (review-article).

Roy Kiyooka

17498. CHIVERS, SALLY. 'This is my memory, a fact': the many mediations of *Mothertalk: Life Stories of May Kiyoshi Kiyooka.* *In* (pp. 69–87) **14629.**

David Klass

17499. APOL, LAURA. Shooting bears, saving butterflies: ideology of the environment in Gibson's *Herm and I* (1894) and Klass's *California Blue* (1994). *See* **11058.**

A. M. Klein

17500. BENTLEY, D. M. R. 'New styles of architecture, a change of heart'? The architexts of A. M. Klein and F. R. Scott. *In* (pp. 17–58) **12739.**

17501. BICK, ANGELA. 'Speak to one another with psalms': the unity of A. M. Klein's Psalter. CanP (56) 2005, 9–26.

August Kleinzahler

17502. ANON. (introd.). Love, Lucia: Lucia Berlin's letters to August Kleinzahler. *See* **15471.**

17503. KLEINZAHLER, AUGUST. Cutty, One Rock: low characters and strange places, gently explained. New York: Farrar, Straus, & Giroux, 2004. pp. 155.

Irena Klepfisz

17504. BACHMANN, MONICA. Split worlds and intersecting metaphors: representations of Jewish and lesbian identity in the works of Irena Klepfisz. *In* (pp. 197–214) **12895.**

Damon Francis Knight (1922–2002)

17505. SLEIGHT, GRAHAM. Putting the pieces back together again: making sense of Damon Knight's *Humpty Dumpty*. NYRSF (17:1) 2004, 1, 8–10.

John Knoepfle

17506. STEWART, ROBERT. Keep you from hunger: an interview with John Knoepfle. NewLet (71:2) 2005, 50–4.

Elizabeth Knox

17507. ENGLAND, RICHARD. Undisputed sovereignty. See **10218**.

C. J. Koch

17508. YU, OUYANG. How post are they colonial: an enquiry into Christopher Koch, Blanche d'Alpuget and Bruce Grant's representation of Chinese in recent 'Asian writing'. In (pp. 243–61) **12674**.

Kenneth Koch

17509. KIRSCH, ADAM. Friendly chats. TLS, 25 Nov. 2005, 9 (review-article). (New York Poets.)

Ron Koertge (b.1940)

17510. BLASINGAME, JAMES. Interview with Ron Koertge. JAAL (48:6) 2005, 526–7.

Joy Kogawa

17511. DARIAS BEAUTELL, EVA. Hiromi Goto's *Chorus of Mushrooms*: cultural difference, visibility and the Canadian tradition. See **16763**.

17512. RAO, ELEONORA. 'This is my own, my native land': paradoxes of exile in Joy Kogawa's *Obasan*. In (pp. 233–43) **3690**.

Yusef Komunyakaa

17513. ANDERSON, T. J.; HARRIS, TRUDIER; WARD, JERRY W. A finer form: T. J. Anderson and Yusef Komunyakaa in conversation. Callaloo (28:3) 2005, 584–91.

17514. CARTWRIGHT, KEITH. Weave a circle round him thrice: Komunyakaa's Hoodoo balancing act. Callaloo (28:3) 2005, 851–63.

17515. COLLINS, MICHAEL. Komunyakaa, collaboration, and the Wishbone: an interview. Callaloo (28:3) 2005, 620–34.

17516. —— On the phone with composer Bill Banfield: an interview. Callaloo (28:3) 2005, 635–42.

17517. —— Yusef Komunyakaa: a bibliography. Callaloo (28:3) 2005, 883–6.

17518. DERRICOTTE, TOI. Seeing and re-seeing: an exchange between Yusef Komunyakaa and Toi Derricotte. Callaloo (28:3) 2005, 513–18.

17519. DOWDY, MICHAEL C. Working in the space of disaster: Yusef Komunyakaa's dialogues with America. Callaloo (28:3) 2005, 812–23.

17520. FEINSTEIN, SASCHA. Yusef Komunyakaa's *Testimony* and the humanity of Charlie Parker. Callaloo (28:3) 2005, 757–62.

17521. FRANCINI, ANTONELLA. Notes on translating Yusef Komunyakaa's poetry into Italian. Callaloo (28:3) 2005, 707–12.

17522. —— Sonnet *vs* sonnet: the fourteen lines in African American poetry. *See* **17999.**

17523. GOLDSTEIN, LAURENCE. Madame Nhu, woman and warrior: a reading of *Le Xuan, Beautiful Spring.* Callaloo (28:3) 2005, 764–70.

17524. HECKER, WILLIAM. Finding Wilfred Owen's forwarding address: moving beyond the World War One paradigm. *See* **18708.**

17525. JAKUBIAK, KATARZYNA. Between a failure and a new creation: (re)reading Yusef Komunyakaa's *The Beast & Burden* in the light of Paul Gilroy's *Black Atlantic.* Callaloo (28:3) 2005, 865–81.

17526. —— *Nienaturalny stan jednoro żca*: translating Komunyakaa's *Unicorn* into Polish. Callaloo (28:3) 2005, 721–4.

17527. JAŘAB, JOSEF. Translating Yusef Komunyakaa into Czech: a personal confession. Callaloo (28:3) 2005, 691–6.

17528. LEONARD, KEITH. Yusef Komunyakaa's Blues: the postmodern music of *Neon Vernacular.* Callaloo (28:3) 2005, 824–49.

17529. MEJER, VALERIE. On awareness. Callaloo (28:3) 2005, 716–17.

17530. MITRANO, G. F. A conversation with Yusef Komunyakaa. Callaloo (28:3) 2005, 521–30.

17531. PAVLIĆ, ED. Open the unusual door: visions from the dark window in Yusef Komunyakaa's early poems. Callaloo (28:3) 2005, 780–96.

17532. RAMSEY, WILLIAM M. Knowing their place: three Black writers and the postmodern South. SoLJ (37:2) 2005, 119–39.

17533. ROCHA, FLAVIA. Man talking to a mirror: on the attempt to translate Yusef Komunyakaa's vibrant verbal landscape into the mild undulations of Brazilian Portuguese. Callaloo (28:3) 2005, 725–7.

17534. SALAS, ANGELA M. *Talking Dirty to the Gods* and the infinitude of language; or, Mr Komunyakaa's cabinet of wonder. Callaloo (28:3) 2005, 798–811.

17535. TABACZYNSKI, MICHAL. Rhythm that survives, rhythm that saves. Callaloo (28:3) 2005, 701–2.

17536. TRETHEWEY, NATASHA. On close reading: Yusef Komunyakaa's *White Lady.* Callaloo (28:3) 2005, 775–7.

Jerzy Kosinski

17537. KOLÁŘ, STANISLAV. Animal imagery in Kosinski's *The Painted Bird* and Spiegelman's *Maus. In* (pp. 87–92) **3753.**

17538. MORIEL, LIORA. Passing and the performance of gender, race, and class acts: a theoretical framework. *See* **17584.**

Robert Kroetsch

17539. BROWN, RUSSELL MORTON. Robert Kroetsch, Marshall McLuhan, and Canada's prairie postmodernism: the Aberhart effect. *In* (pp. 101–40) **12587.**

Dorothy Meserve Kunhardt (b.1901)

17540. KUNHARDT, PHILIP B., JR. The dreaming game: a portrait of a passionate life. New York: Riverhead, 2004. pp. xx, 348.

Stanley Kunitz

17541. Lentine, Genine (ed.). The wild braid: a poet reflects on a century in the garden. New York; London: Norton, 2005. pp. 144. (Interviews.)

Frank Kuppner (b.1951)

17542. Dósa, Attila. Extracts from a longer interview with Frank Kuppner. ScSR (6:1) 2005, 84–100.

Hanif Kureishi

17543. Ferretter, Luke. Hanif Kureishi and the politics of comedy. SSE (29) 2003, 87–102.

17544. Nieragden, Göran. Otherness at work: the non-indigenous English novel. *See* **16343.**

17545. Thomas, Susie (ed.). Hanif Kureishi. Basingstoke; New York: Palgrave Macmillan, 2005. pp. 191. (Readers' guides to essential criticism.)

Katherine Kurtz

17546. Kurtz, Katherine; Reginald, Robert (eds). Codex Derynianus ii: being a comprehensive guide to the peoples, places & things of the Derynye & the human worlds of the xi kingdoms. (Bibl. 1998, 17231.) Nevada City, CA: Underwood, 2005. pp. 353. (Second ed.: first ed. 1998.)

Tony Kushner

17547. Dickinson, Peter. Travels with Tony Kushner and David Beckham, 2002–2004. TJ (57:3) 2005, 429–50.

17548. Kushner, Tony. Bard College: April 14, 2004. Dramatist (7:4) 2005, 24–8.

17549. Sparks, Julie. Playwrights' progress: the evolution of the play cycle, from Shaw's 'Pentateuch' to *Angels in America*. *See* **19416.**

Tim F. LaHaye

17550. Farrington, Holly. Have you been Left Behind? Jenkins, LaHaye and the Second Coming of Christian science fiction. Foundation (94) 2005, 127–31 (review-article).

17551. LaHaye, Tim; Jenkins, Jerry B.; Swanson, Sandi L. The authorized *Left Behind* handbook. Wheaton, IL: Tyndale House, 2005. pp. 335.

17552. Shuck, Glenn W. Marks of the Beast: the *Left Behind* novels and the struggle for evangelical identity. New York; London: New York UP, 2005. pp. xiii, 273.

17553. Standaert, Michael. Skipping towards Armageddon: the politics and propaganda of the *Left Behind* novels and the LaHaye empire. Brooklyn, NY: Soft Skull Press, 2005. pp. 256.

Larissa Lai

17554. Lai, Larissa. Future Asians: migrant speculations, repressed history & cyborg hope. WCL (38:2) 2004, 168–75.

17555. Lee, Tara. Mutant bodies in Larissa Lai's *Salt Fish Girl*: challenging the alliance between science and capital. WCL (38:2) 2004, 94–109.

17556. MANSBRIDGE, JOANNA. Abject origins: uncanny strangers and figures of fetishism in Larissa Lai's *Salt Fish Girl*. WCL (38:2) 2004, 121–33.

17557. MORRIS, ROBYN. Re-visioning representations of difference in Larissa Lai's *When Fox Is a Thousand* and Ridley Scott's *Blade Runner*. WCL (38:2) 2004, 69–86.

17558. —— 'Sites of articulation': an interview with Larissa Lai. WCL (38:2) 2004, 21–30.

Alexander Laing (b.1903)

17559. LYNCH, LISA. Strange germs and hopeful monsters: Alexander Laing's 1930s American biotechnology tales. NLH (36:2) 2005, 247–61.

B. Kojo Laing

17560. NGABOH-SMART, FRANCIS. Beyond empire and nation: postnational arguments in the fiction of Nuruddin Farah and B. Kojo Laing. See **16385.**

Philip Lamantia (b.1927)

17561. CAPLES, GARRETT. *In memoriam*: high poet: Philip Lamantia (23 October 1927 – 7 March 2005). ChiR (51:1/2) 2005, 302–5.

17562. FRATTALI, STEVEN. Hypodermic light: the poetry of Philip Lamantia and the question of Surrealism. New York; Frankfurt: Lang, 2005. pp. 144. (Studies in modern poetry, 15.)

Janet Lambert

17563. THOMPSON, ANNE B. Rereading fifties teen romance: reflections on Janet Lambert. LU (29:3) 2005, 373–96.

Anne Lamott

17564. LAMOTT, ANNE. Plan B: further thoughts on faith. New York: Riverhead, 2005. pp. 320.

Patrick Lane

17565. LANE, PATRICK. There is a season: a memoir in a garden. Toronto: McClelland & Stewart, 2004. pp. 309.

Pinkie Gordon Lane

17566. LOWE, JOHN. 'Pulling in the natural environment': an interview with Pinkie Gordon Lane. AAR (39:1/2) 2005, 17–38.

Ring Lardner (1885–1933)

17567. BLOOM, JONATHAN. Revision as transformation: the making and re-making of V. S. Pritchett's *You Make Your Own Life*. See **18935.**

17568. LARDNER, KATE. Shut up he explained: the memoir of a blacklisted kid. New York: Ballantine, 2004. pp. 272.

Philip Larkin

17569. BOONE, N. S. Larkin's *Toads*. Exp (64:1) 2005, 52–4.

17570. BOOTH, JAMES. Philip Larkin: the poet's plight. Basingstoke; New York: Palgrave Macmillan, 2005. pp. xi, 230.

17571. BURKE, MICHAEL. How cognition can augment stylistic analysis. EJES (9:2) 2005, 185–95.

17572. COOPER, STEPHEN. Philip Larkin: subversive writer. Brighton; Portland, OR: Sussex Academic Press, 2004. pp. xi, 208.

17573. EVERETT, BARBARA. Larkin and the doomsters: walking 'down life's sunless hill' with Hardy and Barbara Pym. See **18979**.

17574. FLETCHER, CHRISTOPHER. Edmund Blunden's *Young Fieldmouse*: a source for Philip Larkin's *The Mower*? NQ (52:1) 2005, 102–3.

17575. KIRSCH, ADAM. Green selfconscious spurts. TLS, 13 May 2005, 9–10 (review-article). (Juvenilia.)

17576. LOPEZ, TONY. Graham and the 1940s. *In* (pp. 26–42) **16793**.

17577. MCNAMEE, BRENDAN. Larkin's *Sad Steps*. Exp (63:2) 2005, 102–5.

17578. SOCCIO, ANNA ENRICHETTA. Philip Larkin e l'impossibilità dell'essere: una nota su *Poetry of Departures*. LProv (121) 2004, 45–50.

Nella Larsen

17579. BERNARD, EMILY. Unlike many others: exceptional White characters in Harlem renaissance fiction. See **19789**.

17580. DEFALCO, AMELIA. Jungle creatures and dancing apes: modern primitivism and Nella Larsen's *Quicksand*. Mosaic (38:2) 2005, 19–35.

17581. DOYLE, LAURA. Liberty, race, and Larsen in Atlantic modernity: a New World genealogy. *In* (pp. 51–76) **12640**.

17582. FRANCIS, TERRI. Embodied fictions, melancholy migrations: Josephine Baker's cinematic celebrity. MFS (51:4) 2005, 824–45.

17583. JENKINS, CANDICE M. Decoding essentialism: cultural authenticity and the Black bourgeoisie in Nella Larsen's *Passing*. MELUS (30:3) 2005, 129–54.

17584. MORIEL, LIORA. Passing and the performance of gender, race, and class acts: a theoretical framework. WP (15:1) 2005, 167–210.

17585. THAGGERT, MIRIAM. Racial etiquette: Nella Larsen's *Passing* and the Rhinelander Case. Meridians (5:2) 2005, 1–29.

17586. THOMPSON, CARLYLE VAN. 'Making a way outta no way': the dangerous business of racial masquerade in Nella Larsen's *Passing*. WP (15:1) 2005, 79–104.

P. J. Laska

17587. BIGGERS, JEFF. The Tao of Appalachia: an interview with P. J. Laska. BRev (24:4) 2004, 15–16.

Evelyn Lau

17588. CASTELAO, ISABEL. Rediscovering the poet: Evelyn Lau. StudCanL (29:2) 2004, 163–76. (Interview.)

James Laughlin

17589. BARNHISEL, GREGORY. James Laughlin, New Directions, and the remaking of Ezra Pound. Amherst: Massachusetts UP, 2005. pp. x, 272.

17590. GLASSGOLD, PETER (ed.). Byways: a memoir. Preface by Guy Davenport. New York: New Directions, 2005. pp. xxiv, 323. Rev. by Michael Dirda in BkW, 27 Mar. 2005, 15; by Irving Malin in HC (42:3) 2005, 18.

Margaret Laurence

17591. DUDEK, DEBRA.   A timeless imagined prairie: return and regeneration in Margaret Laurence's Manawaka novels. *In* (pp. 235–58) **12587**.

17592. FILIPCZAK, DOROTA.   Not wanted in the canon: Canadian literature in the wilderness. *In* (pp. 55–64) **3756**.

17593. PAYNE, SARAH.   Reconstructions of literary settings in North America's prairie regions: a cross-cultural comparison of Red Cloud, Nebraska, and Neepawa, Manitoba. *In* (pp. 213–33) **12587**.

17594. RIEGEL, CHRISTIAN.   Writing grief: Margaret Laurence and the work of mourning. Winnipeg: Manitoba UP, 2003. pp. 192. Rev. by Helen M. Buss in GPQ (25:3) 2005, 199–200.

17595. STOVEL, NORA FOSTER (ed.).   Heart of a stranger. (Bibl. 2004, 17920.) Rev. by Wendy Roy in CanL (183) 2004, 145–6.

17596. STRATTON, FLORENCE.   There is no Bentham Street in Calgary: panoptic discourses and Thomas King's *Medicine River*. *See* **17442**.

Arthur Laurents

17597. PUCCIO, PAUL M.   *Anyone* can still whistle. *See* **19517**.

Ann Lauterbach

17598. LAUTERBACH, ANN.   The night sky: writings on the poetics of experience. New York: Viking, 2005. pp. x, 261.

D. H. Lawrence

17599. BARON, HELEN (ed.).   Paul Morel. (Bibl. 2004, 17925.) Rev. by Peter Balbert in ELT (48:2) 2005, 239–44; by Pierre Vitoux in EA (58:2) 2005, 237–9.

17600. BELL, MICHAEL.   D. H. Lawrence and the meaning of Modernism. *In* (pp. 132–48) **12946**.

17601. BENDER, TODD K.   Competing cultural domains, borderlands and spatial/temporal thresholds in Hardy, Conrad, and D. H. Lawrence. *See* **11112**.

17602. BILSING, TRACY E.   'To every man the war is himself': D. H. Lawrence, the battle of the sexes, and the Great War. CEACrit (66:2/3) 2004, 76–91.

17603. BOULTON, JAMES T. (ed.).   Late essays and articles. (Bibl. 2004, 17928.) Rev. by Mark Crees in TLS, 18 Mar. 2005, 11; by Peter Balbert in ELT (48:3) 2005, 375–8.

17604. BRADSHAW, DAVID.   Red trousers: *Lady Chatterley's Lover* and John Hargrave. EC (55:4) 2005, 352–73.

17605. BURNS, ROBERT W.   'More frail and mortal': the wound of fear in Philip Caputo's *In the Forest of the Laughing Elephant*. *See* **15684**.

17606. CHAUDHURI, AMIT.   D. H. Lawrence and 'difference'. (Bibl. 2004, 17931.) Rev. by Michael H. Whitworth in RES (56:224) 2005, 341–3.

17607. COMELLINI, CARLA.   D. H. Lawrence and the arts: painting, sculpture and the cinema. *In* (pp. 120–33) **3690**.

17608. CREES, MARK.   Another animal. TLS, 18 Mar. 2005, 11 (review-article).

17609. CUSHMAN, KEITH; INGERSOLL, EARL G. (eds).   D. H. Lawrence: new worlds. (Bibl. 2003, 17863.) Rev. by Margaret Storch in YES (35) 2005, 359–63.

17610. EDWARDS, DUANE. The objectivity of D. H. Lawrence's *The Woman Who Rode Away*. SoHR (39:3) 2005, 205–22.

17611. FERGUSON, FRANCES. Pornography, the theory: what Utilitarianism did to action. (Bibl. 2004, 17935.) Rev. by Denise Gigante in NineL (60:1) 2005, 120–3.

17612. FERRALL, CHARLES. Unlikely *Blutbrüderschaft*: Mansfield and D. H. Lawrence. *In* (pp. 60–74) **18084.**

17613. GRANOFSKY, RONALD. D. H. Lawrence and survival: Darwinism in the fiction of the transitional period. Montreal; Buffalo, NY; London: McGill-Queen's UP, 2003. pp. xii, 212. Rev. by Bruce Clarke in StudN (37:3) 2005, 352–4.

17614. INGERSOLL, EARL G. Intertextuality in L. P. Hartley's *The Go-Between* and Ian McEwan's *Atonement*. See **16916.**

17615. LEON, CAROL E. Movement and belonging: lines, places and spaces of travel. New York; Frankfurt: Lang, 2004. pp. vi, 260. (Travel writing across the disciplines, 11.)

17616. LEVY, ERIC P. The literary depiction of ontological shock. See **15403.**

17617. MCDONALD, PETER D. The politics of obscenity: *Lady Chatterley's Lover* and the apartheid State. ESA (47:1) 2004, 31–46.

17618. MENCHER, M. B. Lawrence and sex. EngS (84:4) 2003, 347–54.

17619. NASH, ANDREW. *At the Gates*: new commentaries on a lost text by D. H. Lawrence. RES (56:227) 2005, 767–76.

17620. NAVA, YOLANDA. Letters from the D. H. Lawrence papers: 1922–1930. Palacio (110:1) 2005, 16–19.

17621. PAPAYANIS, MARILYN ADLER. Writing in the margins: the ethics of expatriation from Lawrence to Ondaatje. Nashville, TN: Vanderbilt UP, 2005. pp. xv, 277.

17622. PIAZZA, ANTONELLA. Lawrence's Mexican encounters: *The Plumed Serpent* (1926). *In* (pp. 224–32) **3690.**

17623. POLLNITZ, CHRISTOPHER. The censorship and transmission of D. H. Lawrence's *Pansies*: the Home Office and the 'foul-mouthed fellow'. JML (28:3) 2005, 44–71.

17624. —— Editing D. H. Lawrence's *Collected Poems*: the composite typescript and base-text. BSANZB (28:3) 2004, 78–96.

17625. REEVE, N. H. Reading late Lawrence. (Bibl. 2004, 17947.) Rev. by Margaret Storch in YES (35) 2005, 359–63.

17626. —— WORTHEN, JOHN (eds). Introductions and reviews. (Bibl. 2004, 17948.) Rev. by Mark Crees in TLS, 18 Mar. 2005, 11.

17627. ROBERTS, NEIL. D. H. Lawrence, travel and cultural difference. Basingstoke; New York: Palgrave Macmillan, 2004. pp. xii, 195.

17628. ROSENHAN, CLAUDIA. An attribution in Huxley's short story *Chawdron* via Lawrence and Ludovici. See **17152.**

17629. RUDMAN, MARK. On the road, touch and go, with D. H. Lawrence. APR (34:4) 2005, 41–9.

17630. SAGAR, KEITH (introd.).   D. H. Lawrence's paintings. London: Chaucer, 2003. pp. 160. Rev. by Judith Ruderman in ELT (48:2) 2005, 244–8.

17631. SCHERR, BARRY J.   D. H. Lawrence today: literature, culture, politics. (Bibl. 2004, 17951.) Rev. by Matthew Leone in ELT (48:3) 2005, 378–82.

17632. SEELOW, DAVID.   Radical Modernism and sexuality: Freud, Reich, D. H. Lawrence & beyond. Basingstoke; New York: Palgrave Macmillan, 2005. pp. ix, 162.

17633. SKELTON, PHILIP.   'A slobbery affair' and 'stinking mongrelism': individualism, postmodernity and D. H. Lawrence's *Kangaroo*. EngS (84:6) 2003, 545–57.

17634. STEELE, BRUCE (ed.).   *Psychoanalysis and the Unconscious* and *Fantasia of the Unconscious*. Cambridge; New York: CUP, 2004. pp. liv, 300. (Cambridge ed. of the letters and works of D. H. Lawrence.) Rev. by John Lyon in RES (56:227) 2005, 807–9.

17635. WALLACE, JEFF.   D. H. Lawrence, science and the posthuman. Basingstoke; New York: Palgrave Macmillan, 2005. pp. xi, 264.

17636. WOOD, JAMES.   The Jewish King James Version; or, Saul Bellow: not exactly English but biblically English. See **15459**.

17637. WORTHEN, JOHN.   'Wild turkeys': some versions of America by D. H. Lawrence. EurJAC (24:2) 2005, 91–103.

17638. —— HARRISON, ANDREW (eds).   D. H. Lawrence's *Sons and Lovers*: a casebook. Oxford; New York: OUP, 2005. pp. xii, 305. (Casebooks in criticism.)

T. E. Lawrence

17639. BROWN, MALCOLM (ed.).   T. E. Lawrence in war and peace: an anthology of the military writings of Lawrence of Arabia. London: Greenhill, 2005. pp. 320, (plates) 16.

17640. RAW, LAURENCE.   T. E. Lawrence, the Turks, and the Arab revolt in the cinema: Anglo-American and Turkish representations. See **13632**.

17641. REILLY, TERRY.   T. E. Lawrence: writing the military life from Homer to high Modernism. *In* (pp. 81–103) **14645**.

17642. WOUDHUYSEN, H. R.   Not lonely, but alone. TLS, 8 July 2005, 27. (Correspondence.)

Henry Lawson

17643. HAWORTH, ROBERT.   Chris Kempster, musician, 1933–2004: a true native voice. See **3556**.

17644. ROWE, NOEL.   The misty ways of Asia. *In* (pp. 70–86) **12674**.

17645. TEJEDOR, JOSÉ MARÍA.   Henry Lawson's nihilism in *The Union Buries Its Dead*. Atl (27:2) 2005, 87–100.

David Leavitt

17646. RIVKIN, JULIE.   Writing the gay '80s with Henry James: David Leavitt's *A Place I've Never Been* and Alan Hollinghurst's *The Line of Beauty*. See **17044**.

'John le Carré' (David John Cornwell)

17647. BRUCCOLI, MATTHEW J.; BAUGHMAN, JUDITH S. (eds). Conversations with John le Carré. Jackson; London: Mississippi UP, 2004. pp. xvi, 180.

17648. HINDERSMANN, JOST. 'The right side lost but the wrong side won': John le Carré's spy novels before and after the end of the Cold War. Clues (23:4) 2005, 25–37.

Tom LeClair (b.1944)

17649. ISAACS, NEIL. Who is Tom LeClair and why is he playing these games with us? Aethlon (22:2) 2005, 35–42.

Chang-rae Lee

17650. CARROLL, HAMILTON. Traumatic patriarchy: reading gendered nationalisms in Chang-rae Lee's *A Gesture Life*. MFS (51:3) 2005, 592–616.

17651. HONG, TERRY. Flying aloft with Chang-rae Lee: a conversation. BRev (24:5) 2004, 23–4.

17652. LEE, YOUNG-OAK. Gender, race, and the nation in *A Gesture Life*. CritW (46:2) 2005, 146–59.

Dennis Lee

17653. WARKENTIN, GERMAINE. Mapping Wonderland: the city of Toronto as seen through its writers' eyes. See **19968**.

Ursula K. Le Guin

17654. ATTEBERY, BRIAN. Science fiction, parables, and parabolas. See **16717**.

17655. BURNS, TONY. Science and politics in *The Dispossessed*: Le Guin and the 'science wars'. *In* (pp. 195–215) **17659**.

17656. CADDEN, MIKE. Ursula K. Le Guin beyond genre: fiction for children and adults. London; New York: Routledge, 2005. pp. xvi, 203. (Children's literature and culture, 33.) Rev. by David Bratman in Mythprint (42:9) 2005, 10–11.

17657. CURTIS, CLAIRE P. Ambiguous choices: skepticism as a grounding for utopia. *In* (pp. 265–82) **17659**.

17658. DAVIS, LAURENCE. The dynamic and revolutionary utopia of Ursula K. Le Guin. *In* (pp. 3–36) **17659**.

17659. —— STILLMAN, PETER (eds). The new utopian politics of Ursula K. Le Guin's *The Dispossessed*. Afterword by Ursula K. Le Guin. Lanham, MD; Oxford: Rowman & Littlefield, 2005. pp. xxvii, 324.

17660. ELLIOTT, WINTER. Breaching invisible walls: individual anarchy in *The Dispossessed*. *In* (pp. 149–64) **17659**.

17661. FERNS, CHRIS. Future conditional or future perfect? *The Dispossessed* and permanent revolution. *In* (pp. 249–62) **17659**.

17662. HAMMER, EVERETT L. The gap in the wall: partnership, physics, and politics in *The Dispossessed*. *In* (pp. 219–31) **17659**.

17663. KHADER, JAMIL. Race matters: people of color, ideology, and the politics of erasure and reversal in Ursula Le Guin's *The Left Hand of Darkness* and Mary Doria Russell's *The Sparrow*. JFA (16:2) 2005, 110–27.

17664. Loy, David R.; Goodhew, Linda. The dharma of dragons and dæmons: Buddhist themes in modern fantasy. *See* **19830.**

17665. O'Connor, Patrick. Fabulous historians: Ursula Le Guin and Angélica Gorodischer. JFA (16:2) 2005, 128–41.

17666. Petersen, Zina. Balancing act: Ursula Kroeber Le Guin. *In* (pp. 65–77) **12566.**

17667. Plaw, Avery. Empty hands: communication, pluralism, and community in Ursula K. Le Guin's *The Dispossessed*. *In* (pp. 283–304) **17659.**

17668. Powici, Christopher. 'Who are the Bandar-log?': questioning animals in Rudyard Kipling's Mowgli stories and Ursula Le Guin's *Buffalo Gals, Won't You Come Out Tonight*. *In* (pp. 177–94) **14258.**

17669. Reynolds, Andrew. Ursula K. Le Guin, Herbert Marcuse, and the fate of utopia in the postmodern. *In* (pp. 75–94) **17659.**

17670. Rigsby, Ellen M. Time and the measure of the political animal. *In* (pp. 167–80) **17659.**

17671. Rodgers, Jennifer. Fulfillment as a function of time; or, The ambiguous process of utopia. *In* (pp. 181–94) **17659.**

17672. Sabia, Dan. Individual and community in Le Guin's *The Dispossessed*. *In* (pp. 111–28) **17659.**

17673. Somay, Bülent. From ambiguity to self-reflexivity: revolutionizing fantasy space. *In* (pp. 233–47) **17659.**

17674. Spencer, Douglas. The alien comes home: getting past the twin planets of possession and austerity in Le Guin's *The Dispossessed*. *In* (pp. 95–108) **17659.**

17675. Stillman, Peter G. *The Dispossessed* as ecological political theory. *In* (pp. 55–73) **17659.**

17676. Stow, Simon. Worlds apart: Ursula K. Le Guin and the possibility of method. *In* (pp. 37–51) **17659.**

17677. Thompson, Stacy. Tentative utopias. PsCS (10:3) 2005, 269–85.

17678. Tunick, Mark. The need for walls: privacy, community, and freedom in *The Dispossessed*. *In* (pp. 129–47) **17659.**

Dennis Lehane

17679. Fister, Barbara. Copycat crimes: crime fiction and the marketplace of anxieties. *See* **18931.**

17680. Morrey, Douglas. 'The acorn don't fall far from the tree': genealogy and eternal return in *Mystic River*. *See* **20745.**

Rosamond Lehmann

17681. Bacher, Lutz. The lost *Ballad*: Max Ophuls' last Hollywood project. *See* **13919.**

17682. Knight, Charmian. Thornfield Hall revisited. *In* (pp. 63–73) **10222.**

17683. Pollard, Wendy. Rosamond Lehmann and her critics: the vagaries of literary reception. (Bibl. 2004, 17996.) Rev. by Lucy Carlyle in TLS, 25 Mar. 2005, 30; by Lynne M. Thomas in SHARP (14:4) 2005, 16.

Fritz Leiber

17684. KILLUS, JAMES. Sleeping in Fritz Leiber's bed. NYRSF (16:9) 2004, 1, 8–11.

Madeleine L'Engle

17685. MOONEY, RODNEY. Journey through *A Wrinkle in Time* and explore the world of 'sacred idleness'. NRCLL (11:1) 2005, 73–86.

Doris Lessing ('Jane Somers')

17686. BREVET, ANNE-LAURE. Flights of memory: digression and allusion in Doris Lessing's *Memoirs of a Survivor*. EtBr (29) 2005, 25–40.

17687. DOOLEY, GILLIAN. The post-war novel in crisis: three perspectives. *See* **18423**.

17688. KRASNER, JAMES. Accumulated lives: metaphor, materiality, and the homes of the elderly. LitMed (24:2) 2005, 209–30.

17689. LESSING, DORIS. Time bites: views and reviews. London; New York: Fourth Estate, 2004. pp. vii, 376. Rev. by Elaine Showalter in TLS, 12 Nov. 2004, 27; by Stephen Wade in ContRev (287:1674) 2005, 52–3.

17690. PERREGAUX, MYRIAM. The city as gendered space: a reading of three literary texts in the light of feminist geography. SPELL (17) 2005, 179–94.

17691. ROSENFELD, AARON S. *Re-membering the future*: Doris Lessing's 'experiment in autobiography'. CritS (17:1) 2005, 40–55.

17692. WATERMAN, DAVID. Le miroir de la societé: la violence institutionelle chez Anthony Burgess, Doris Lessing et Pat Barker. *See* **15315**.

Julius Lester

17693. LESTER, JULIUS. On writing for children & other people. New York: Dial, 2004. pp. 159. Rev. by Millie Jackson and Gary Schmidt in LU (29:3) 2005, 450–3.

Meridel Le Sueur

17694. OBERMUELLER, ERIN V. Reading the body in Meridel Le Sueur's *The Girl*. Legacy (22:1) 2005, 47–62.

Jonathan Lethem

17695. LETHEM, JONATHAN. *The Disappointment Artist* and other essays. New York: Doubleday, 2005. pp. 149. Rev. by Henry Hitchings in TLS, 16 Sept. 2005, 30.

17696. —— The writing life. BkW, 6 Feb. 2005, 5.

Ada Leverson

17697. RABY, PETER. Wilde: the remarkable rocket. *In* (pp. 31–47) **3985**.

Denise Levertov

17698. BEEBE, ANN. Levertov's *Making Peace*. Exp (63:3) 2005, 176–9.

17699. BLOCK, ED, JR. Mystery, myth, and presence: concord and conflict in the correspondence of Denise Levertov and Robert Duncan. *See* **16175**.

17700. GIORCELLI, CRISTINA. Le ali del mito. *In* (pp. 29–43) **12883**.

17701. HOLLENBERG, DONNA. 'Dancing edgeways': Robert Creeley's role in Denise Levertov's post-war transition. *See* **15960**.

17702. LACEY, PAUL A. Denise Levertov as teacher. Ren (58:1) 2005, 91–106.

17703. O'LEARY, PETER. Duncan, Levertov, and the age of correspondences. See **16179**.

17704. RODRÍGUEZ HERRERA, JOSÉ. Linguistic *versus* organic, sfumato *versus* chiaroscuro: some aesthetic differences between Denise Levertov and Robert Duncan. Ren (58:1) 2005, 41–61.

17705. SCHLOESSER, STEPHEN. 'Not behind but within': *sacramentum et res.* Ren (58:1) 2005, 17–39.

Aurora Levins Morales (b.1954)

17706. CRISTIAN, RÉKA MÓNIKA. Border stories and post-nationalist American identities: reading Aurora Levins Morales and Bharati Mukherjee. *In* (pp. 35–42) **3734**.

Larry Levis

17707. BUCKLEY, CHRISTOPHER; LONG, ALEXANDER (eds). A condition of the spirit: the life and work of Larry Levis. (Bibl. 2004, 18022.) Rev. by Ray González and Christopher Buckley in BRev (25:2) 2005, 12–14.

Andrea Levy (b.1956)

17708. FISCHER, SUSAN ALICE. Andrea Levy's London novels. *In* (pp. 199–213) **14254**.

Alun Lewis

17709. HARBINSON, CHRISTOPHER. Alun Lewis's *Song (on Seeing Dead Bodies Floating off the Cape)* and Ovid's 'Ceyx and Alcyone'. NQ (52:1) 2005, 103–5.

C. Day Lewis ('Nicholas Blake')

17710. BALCON, JILL (ed.). Selected poems. London: Enitharmon Press, 2004. pp. 216. Rev. by William Wootten in TLS, 3 June 2005, 6–7.

17711. WOOTTEN, WILLIAM. How selfhood begins. TLS, 3 June 2005, 6–7 (review-article).

C. S. (Clive Staples) Lewis ('N. W. Clerk') (1898–1963)

17712. ABANES, RICHARD. Harry Potter, Narnia, and *The Lord of the Rings.* See **19191**.

17713. ALOI, PEG. The last of the bibliophiles: Narnia's enduring impact on the pagan community. *In* (pp. 205–18) **17727**.

17714. ANACKER, GAYNE J. Narnia and the moral imagination. *In* (pp. 130–42) **17720**.

17715. ARTHUR, SARAH. Walking through the wardrobe: a devotional quest into *The Lion, the Witch, and the Wardrobe.* Wheaton, IL: Tyndale House, 2005. pp. xxiii, 189.

17716. ATTEBERY, BRIAN. High Church *versus* Broad Church: Christian myth in George MacDonald and C. S. Lewis. See **11632**.

17717. BAJETTA, CARLO M. Più magico di Harry Potter: Lewis al cinema. LT (9) 2005, 69–77.

17718. BARKMAN, ADAM. The shame of glad surrender stood confessed: C. S. Lewis and confession. CSL (36:4) 2005, 1–17.

17719. BASSHAM, GREGORY. Some dogs go to Heaven: Lewis on animal salvation. *In* (pp. 273–85) **17720.**

17720. —— WALLS, JERRY L. (eds). *The Chronicles of Narnia and philosophy: the lion, the witch, and the worldview.* Chicago, IL: Open Court, 2005. pp. xvi, 302. (Popular culture and philosophy, 15.)

17721. BELL, ROBERT H. Inside the wardrobe: is 'Narnia' a Christian allegory? Cweal (132:22) 2005, 12–14.

17722. BROWN, DEVIN. Inside Narnia: a guide to exploring *The Lion, the Witch, and the Wardrobe.* Grand Rapids, MI: Baker, 2005. pp. 255.

17723. —— Work, vocation, and the good life in Narnia. *In* (pp. 79–93) **17720.**

17724. BUMBAUGH, DAVID E. *The Horse and His Boy*: the theology of Bree. *In* (pp. 243–52) **17727.**

17725. CAILLAVA, MARIE-CATHERINE. A knight in the mud. *In* (pp. 267–79) **17727.**

17726. CAREY, JACQUELINE. Heathen eye for the Christian guy. *In* (pp. 159–64) **17727.**

17727. CAUGHEY, SHANNA (ed.). Revisiting Narnia: fantasy, myth, and religion in C. S. Lewis's *Chronicles.* Dallas, TX: BenBella, 2005. pp. x, 310. (Smart pop.)

17728. CLEVELAND, TIMOTHY. Different worlds, different bodies: personal identity in Narnia. *In* (pp. 180–92) **17720.**

17729. COMO, JAMES. Believing Narnia. *In* (pp. 77–89) **17727.**

17730. DALTON, RUSSELL W. Aslan is on the move: images of Providence in *The Chronicles of Narnia.* *In* (pp. 129–45) **17727.**

17731. DAURIO, JANICE. Is it good to be bad? Immoralism in Narnia. *In* (pp. 119–29) **17720.**

17732. DAVIS, BILL. Extreme makeover: moral education and the encounter with Aslan. *In* (pp. 106–18) **17720.**

17733. DORSETT, LYLE. Seeking the secret place: the spiritual formation of C. S. Lewis. Grand Rapids, MI: Brazos Press, 2004. pp. 182. Rev. by Joseph Williams in SEVEN (22) 2005, 103–4.

17734. DOWNING, DAVID C. Into the region of awe: mysticism in C. S. Lewis. Downers Grove, IL: InterVarsity Press, 2005. pp. 207. Rev. by Joe R. Christopher in Mythprint (42:10) 2005, 10–11; by Dale Nelson in CSL (36:5) 2005, 15.

17735. —— Into the wardrobe: C. S. Lewis and the Narnia chronicles. San Francisco, CA: Jossey-Bass, 2005. pp. xvii, 238. Rev. by Jorge Crespo in CSL (36:6) 2005, 7.

17736. DULLES, AVERY CARDINAL. C. S. Lewis: the case for apologetics. CSL (36:1) 2005, 1–9.

17737. DURIEZ, COLIN. A field guide to Narnia. (Bibl. 2004, 18030.) Rev. by Donald T. Williams in Mythprint (42:2) 2005, 11.

17738. —— Narnia in the modern world: rehabilitating a lost consciousness. *In* (pp. 297–310) **17727.**

17739. —— Tolkien and C. S. Lewis: the gift of friendship. *See* **19809.**

17740. FIFE, ERNELLE. Reading J. K. Rowling magically: creating C. S. Lewis's 'good reader'. *In* (pp. 137–58) **19214.**

17741. FORTUNATI, GIUSEPPE.   Narnia e Narni: dalla storia al fantastico. Preface by Carlo M. Bajetta. Isola Rizza, Verona: Heos, 2005. pp. 112.

17742. FRY, KARIN.   No longer a friend of Narnia: gender in Narnia. *In* (pp. 155–66) **17720.**

17743. GARCIA, LAURA.   Worth dying for: Narnian lessons on heroism and altruism. *In* (pp. 67–78) **17720.**

17744. GIARDINA, NATASHA.   Elusive prey: searching for traces of Narnia in the jungles of the psyche. *In* (pp. 33–43) **17727.**

17745. GILCHRIST, K. J.   A morning after war: C. S. Lewis and WWI. New York; Frankfurt: Lang, 2005. pp. xv, 225. Rev. by Joe R. Christopher in Mythprint (42:9) 2005, 12–13.

17746. HAMBLET, WENDY C.   Beasts, heroes, and monsters: configuring the moral imaginary. *In* (pp. 143–54) **17720.**

17747. HATLEN, BURTON.   Pullman's *His Dark Materials*, a challenge to the fantasies of J. R. R. Tolkien and C. S. Lewis, with an epilogue on Pullman's neo-Romantic reading of *Paradise Lost.*   *In* (pp. 75–94) **18952.**

17748. HOOPER, WALTER (ed.).   Collected letters: vol. 2, Books, broadcasts, and war, 1931–1949. (Bibl. 2004, 18036.) Rev. by Don W. King in ChrisL (54:1) 2004, 128–33.

17749. JACOBS, ALAN.   The Narnian: the life and imagination of C. S. Lewis. San Francisco, CA: HarperSanFrancisco, 2005. pp. xxvi, 342. Rev. by David Weber in Cresset (69:2) 2005, 55–7.

17750. KAWANO, ROLAND M.   C. S. Lewis: always a poet. (Bibl. 2004, 18038.) Rev. by Joe R. Christopher in Mythprint (42:2) 2005, 13–14.

17751. KING, DON W.   Fire and ice: C. S. Lewis and the love poetry of Joy Davidman and Ruth Pitter. SEVEN (22) 2005, 60–88.

17752. KINGHORN, KEVIN.   Virtue epistemology: why Uncle Andrew couldn't hear the animals speak. *In* (pp. 15–26) **17720.**

17753. KORT, WESLEY A.   *The Chronicles of Narnia*: where to start. *In* (pp. 103–11) **17727.**

17754. LEIBER, JUSTIN.   Mrs Coulter *vs* C. S. Lewis. *In* (pp. 163–70) **18973.**

17755. LINDSLEY, ART.   C. S. Lewis's case for Christ: insights from reason, imagination, and faith. Downers Grove, IL: InterVarsity Press, 2005. pp. 216.

17756. LOBDELL, JARED.   The scientifiction novels of C. S. Lewis: space and time in the Ransom stories. (Bibl. 2004, 18042.) Rev. by Joe R. Christopher in Mythprint (42:4) 2005, 3–5.

17757. LOVELL, STEVEN.   Breaking the spell of skepticism: Puddleglum *versus* the Green Witch. *In* (pp. 41–52) **17720.**

17758. MCBRIDE, SAM.   Coming of age in Narnia. *In* (pp. 59–71) **17727.**

17759. MCSPORRAN, CATHY.   Daughters of Lilith: witches and wicked women in *The Chronicles of Narnia. In* (pp. 191–204) **17727.**

17760. MAMATAS, NICK.   Greek delight: what if C. S. Lewis had been Eastern Orthodox? *In* (pp. 173–80) **17727.**

17761. MARKOS, LOUIS A.   Redeeming postmodernism: at play in the fields of Narnia. *In* (pp. 229–41) **17727.**

17762. Matthews, Gareth B. Platform 9¾: the idea of a different reality. *In* (pp. 175–85) **19194**.

17763. —— Plato in Narnia. *In* (pp. 169–79) **17720**.

17764. Menuge, Angus. Why Eustace almost deserved his name: Lewis's critique of modern secularism. *In* (pp. 193–203) **17720**.

17765. Miskech, Peter. Two Lewis letters from *Time and Tide*. CSL (36:1) 2005, 12–13.

17766. Monda, Andrea; Gulisano, Paolo. Il mondo di Narnia. Milan: San Paolo, 2005. pp. 182. (Dimensioni dello spirito.)

17767. —— Simonelli, Saverio. Gli anelli della fantasia. *See* **14230**.

17768. Mosteller, Tim. The Tao of Narnia. *In* (pp. 94–105) **17720**.

17769. Musacchio, George. C. S. Lewis, T. S. Eliot, and the Anglican Psalter. SEVEN (22) 2005, 45–59.

17770. Myers, Doris T. Bareface: a guide to C. S. Lewis's last novel. (Bibl. 2004, 18045.) Rev. by Mary R. Bowman in JMMLA (38:1) 2005, 134–6; by Peter J. Schakel in SEVEN (22) 2005, 104–7.

17771. Nelson, Dale. Wagner, Holst, Sibelius: Lewis's interest in three composers. CSL (36:3) 2005, 12–15.

17772. Newkirk, Ingrid. Would the modern-day C. S. Lewis be a PETA protester? *In* (pp. 165–71) **17727**.

17773. Palma, Robert J. C. S. Lewis's use of analogy in theological understanding. SEVEN (22) 2005, 89–102.

17774. Pearce, Joseph. C. S. Lewis and the Catholic Church. (Bibl. 2004, 18047.) Rev. by David Thomas in CSR (34:2) 2005, 272–5.

17775. —— Man and Everyman: assembling the fragments. Chronicles (29:3) 2005, 20–2.

17776. —— Narnia and Middle-earth: when two worlds collide. *In* (pp. 113–27) **17727**.

17777. Peterson, Michael; Peterson, Adam. Time keeps on ticking, or does it? The significance of time in *The Chronicles of Narnia*. *In* (pp. 204–17) **17720**.

17778. Reichenbach, Bruce R. At any rate there's no humbug here: truth and perspective. *In* (pp. 53–64) **17720**.

17779. Reppert, Victor. The Green Witch and the great debate: freeing Narnia from the spell of the Lewis–Anscombe legend. *In* (pp. 260–72) **17720**.

17780. Rhodes, Milton L. Mere worship: C. S. Lewis and the art of adoration. CSL (36:3) 2005, 8–10.

17781. Rialti, Edoardo (ed. and trans.). C. S. Lewis: come un fulmine a ciel sereno: saggi e racconti. Afterword by Carlo M. Bajetta. Genoa: Marietti, 2005. pp. xvi, 222. (Saggistica.)

17782. —— C. S. Lewis: prima che faccia notte. Preface by Thomas Howard. Milan: Biblioteca Univ. Rizzoli, 2005. pp. 144. (Libri dello spirito cristiano.)

17783. Rogers, Jonathan. The world according to Narnia: Christian meaning in C. S. Lewis's beloved *Chronicles*. New York: Time Warner, 2005. pp. xix, 182.

17784. SAMMONS, MARTHA C. *The Chronicles of Narnia*: for adults only? *In* (pp. 73–6) **17727.**

17785. SANCHEZ, HELEN. Christ according to the 'gospel' of Aslan. CSL (36:6) 2005, 1–7.

17786. SCHAKEL, PETER J. The 'correct' order for reading *The Chronicles of Narnia*. *In* (pp. 91–102) **17727.**

17787. —— The way into Narnia: a reader's guide. Grand Rapids, MI: Eerdmans, 2005. pp. x, 202.

17788. SCHALL, JAMES V. The beginning of the real story. *In* (pp. 147–58) **17727.**

17789. SENNETT, JAMES F. Worthy of a better god: religious diversity and salvation in *The Chronicles of Narnia*. *In* (pp. 231–44) **17720.**

17790. SENOR, THOMAS D. Trusting Lucy: believing the incredible. *In* (pp. 27–40) **17720.**

17791. SIBLEY, BRIAN. Through the shadowlands: the love story of C. S. Lewis and Joy Davidman. Grand Rapids, MI: Revell, 2005. pp. 205.

17792. SMITH, MARK EDDY. Aslan's call: finding our way to Narnia. Downers Grove, IL: InterVarsity Press, 2005. pp. 127.

17793. STABB, SALLY D. 'Most right and proper, I'm sure …': manners and politeness in *The Chronicles of Narnia*. *In* (pp. 281–95) **17727.**

17794. STARR, CHARLIE. C. S. Lewis's vision of Heaven. CSL (36:3) 2005, 1–6.

17795. STARR, CHARLIE W. *The Silver Chair* and the silver screen: C. S. Lewis on myth, fairy tale and film. *In* (pp. 3–23) **17727.**

17796. STUTZ, CHAD P. No 'sombre Satan': C. S. Lewis, Milton, and representations of the diabolical. RelArts (9:3/4) 2005, 208–34.

17797. TALIAFERRO, CHARLES; TRAUGHBER, RACHEL. The Atonement in Narnia. *In* (pp. 245–59) **17720.**

17798. THORSON, STEPHEN. Bibliographic notes – update 2005: part 1. CSL (36:5) 2005, 1–15. (*Adds to* bibl. 1996, 19719.)

17799. —— C. S. Lewis bibliography – update 2005: part 2. CSL (36:6) 2005, 8–17. (*Adds to* bibl. 1996, 19719.)

17800. TREXLER, ROBERT. New C. S. Lewis books for 2005. CSL (36:4) 2005, 16–19.

17801. VANDER ELST, PHILIP. C. S. Lewis: a short introduction. London; New York: Continuum, 2005. pp. 114. (Continuum icons.)

17802. VAUS, WILL. Mere theology: a guide to the thought of C. S. Lewis. Foreword by Douglas Gresham. (Bibl. 2004, 18056.) Rev. by Donald T. Williams in Mythprint (42:4) 2005, 5.

17803. WATT-EVANS, LAWRENCE. On the origins of evil. *In* (pp. 25–32) **17727.**

17804. WEBB, STEPHEN H. Aslan's voice: C. S. Lewis and the magic of sound. *In* (pp. 3–14) **17720.**

17805. WIELENBERG, ERIK J. Aslan the terrible: painful encounters with absolute goodness. *In* (pp. 221–30) **17720.**

17806. WOOD, NAOMI. God in the details: narrative voice and belief in *The Chronicles of Narnia*. *In* (pp. 45–58) **17727.**

17807. Zambreno, Mary Frances.   A reconstructed image: medieval time and space in *The Chronicles of Narnia*. *In* (pp. 253–66) **17727**.

17808. Zeitel, Sarah.   Why I love Narnia: a liberal, feminist agnostic tells all. *In* (pp. 181–90) **17727**.

Gwyneth Lewis (b.1959)

17809. McElroy, Ruth.   'For a mothertongue is a treasure but not a God': Gwyneth Lewis and the dynamics of language in contemporary Welsh poetry. JSBC (12:1) 2005, 39–53.

Larry Lewis

17810. González, Ray.   The psyche at risk: on the work of Larry Lewis: an interview with editor and poet Christopher Buckley. BRev (25:2) 2005, 12–14 (review-article).

Sinclair Lewis

17811. Allen, Brooke.   Sinclair Lewis: the bard of discontents. HR (56:1) 2003, 191–200.

17812. Gross, Andrew S.   Cars, postcards, and patriotism: tourism and national politics in the United States, 1893–1929. *See* **16140**.

17813. Schwartz, Frederic D.   Time machine: November/December 1930: Lewis wins the Nobel. AH (56:6) 2005, 84.

17814. Smith, Graham.   Sinclair Lewis's snapshots of Gopher Prairie. WI (20:1) 2004, 22–7.

Wyndham Lewis

17815. Gilbert, Geoff.   Words, flies, ~~Jews~~, Joyce, *Joint*: Wyndham Lewis and the unpublishing of obscenity. CritQ (46:4) 2004, 1–21.

17816. Innes, Christopher.   Shifting the frame – Modernism in the theatre. *In* (pp. 204–12) **12946**.

17817. Trotter, David.   Modernism, anti-mimesis, and the professionalization of English society. *In* (pp. 24–39) **12946**.

17818. Winkiel, Laura.   Cabaret Modernism: Vorticism and racial spectacle. *In* (pp. 206–24) **12640**.

Leslie Li (b.1945)

17819. Li, Leslie.   Daughter of heaven: a memoir with earthly recipes. New York: Arcade, 2005. pp. xix, 274.

Mary Liddell (*fl.*1926)

17820. op de Beeck, Nathalie.   'The first picture book for modern children': Mary Liddell's *Little Machinery* and the fairy tale of modernity. ChildLit (32) 2004, 41–83.

James Liddy (b.1934)

17821. Arkins, Brian.   James Liddy's Ireland: Corca Bascinn, Coolgreany, Avondale. Sionnach (1:1) 2005, 41–55.

17822. Becker, Jeff.   Twenty-five *Blue Canary* years. Sionnach (1:1) 2005, 98–106.

17823. GARDINER, DAVID. 'The last summer': James Liddy's *Arena*. Sionnach (1:1) 2005, 71–86.

17824. LIDDY, JAMES. The doctor's house: an authobiography. Cliffs of Moher, Co. Clare: Salmon, 2004. pp. 142. Rev. by Tyler Farrell in ILS (25:1) 2005, 29–30; by David Gardiner in NewHR (9:3) 2005, 153–5.

17825. MCLEAN, ANDREW M. 'Breathing in': Liddy, the Irish and American poet. Sionnach (1:1) 2005, 88–97.

17826. REDSHAW, THOMAS DILLON. By James Liddy: a descriptive checklist, 1962–2004. Sionnach (1:1) 2005, 108–39.

17827. —— 'We done our best when we were let': James Liddy's *Arena*, 1963–1965. SoCR (38:1) 2005, 97–117.

17828. TOBIN, DANIEL. 'Figures in the set': James Liddy and the sublime. Sionnach (1:1) 2005, 57–65.

17829. WALL, EAMONN. James Liddy: editor and poet. Sionnach (1:1) 2005, 32–40.

Tim Lilburn (b.1950)

17830. MAILLET, GREGORY. In a boat on the river nowhere writing home: the spiritual poetic of Tim Lilburn. StudCanL (30:1) 2005, 226–44.

Wendy Lill

17831. WASSERMAN, JERRY. 'God of the whiteman! God of the Indian! God Al-fucking-mighty!': the residential school legacy in two Canadian plays. *See* **17023**.

Megan Lindholm ('Robin Hobb')

17832. EKMAN, STEFAN. Down, out and invisible in London and Seattle. *See* **16625**.

Norman Lindsay (1879–1969)

17833. FORSYTH, HANNAH. Sex, seduction, and sirens in love: Norman Lindsay's women. Antipodes (19:1) 2005, 58–66.

17834. HOLT, PATRICIA. 'It's enough to drive a bloke mad': Norman Lindsay's art and literature. BSANZB (27:1/2) 2003, 62–81.

Timothy Liu (b.1965)

17835. SERRANO, RICHARD. Beyond the length of an average penis: reading across traditions in the poetry of Timothy Liu. *In* (pp. 190–208) **9454**.

Penelope Lively

17836. WILLIAMS-WANQUET, EILEEN. The geography of memory in the novels of Penelope Lively. EtBr (29) 2005, 97–110.

Dorothy Livesay

17837. TIESSEN, PAUL. Dorothy Livesay, the 'housewife', and the radio in 1951: Modernist embodiments of audience. *In* (pp. 205–28) **12739**.

Margot Livesey

17838. LIVESEY, MARGOT. Behind the story. *In* (pp. 51–2) **14294**.

Caroline Lockhart

17839. CLAYTON, JOHN.   Caroline Lockhart (1871–1962). Legacy (22:1) 2005, 63–7. (*Legacy* profiles.)

David Lodge

17840. WILAMOVÁ, SIRMA.   Grammatical realizations of the avoidance strategy as a significant negative politeness strategy in English discourse. *In* (pp. 295–305) **1369.**

Sandra Tsing Loh

17841. CONNER, KRISTA.   Western literature at century's end: sketches in Generation X, Los Angeles, and the post-Civil Rights novel. *See* **17359.**

Jack London

17842. EPERJESI, JOHN R.   The imperialist imaginary: visions of Asia and the Pacific in American culture. Foreword by Donald E. Pease. *See* **18518.**

H. Kingsley Long

17843. BRYCE-WUNDER, SYLVIA.   Of hard men and hairies: *No Mean City* and modern Scottish urban fiction. *See* **17919.**

Michael Longley

17844. BERTONI, ROBERTO; PILLONCA, GIOVANNI (eds).   Lucciole alla cascata. Turin: Trauben, 2005. pp. 109. (Collana di poesia irlandese, 9.)

17845. DRUMMOND, GAVIN.   The difficulty of we: the epistolary poems of Michael Longley and Derek Mahon. YES (35) 2005, 31–42.

Anita Loos

17846. BEAUCHAMP, CARI; LOOS, MARY ANITA.   Anita Loos rediscovered: film treatments and fiction. (Bibl. 2004, 18100.) Rev. by J. E. Smyth in MovIm (5:1) 2005, 161–4.

Barry Lopez

17847. SHAPIRO, MICHAEL.   The big rhythm: a conversation with Barry Lopez on the McKenzie River. MichQR (44:4) 2005, 582–610.

17848. TREDINNICK, MARK.   The land's wild music: encounters with Barry Lopez, Peter Matthiessen, Terry Tempest Williams, & James Galvin. *See* **16637.**

Audre Lorde (Gamba Adisa)

17849. DURÁN, ISABEL.   The body as cultural critique in American autobiography. SAtlR (70:1) 2005, 46–70.

17850. FIELD, SUSAN.   Open to influence: Ralph Waldo Emerson and Audre Lorde on loss. *See* **10972.**

17851. KEMP, YAKINI B.   Writing power: identity complexities and the exotic in Audre Lorde's writing. SLI (37:2) 2004, 21–36.

17852. OBOURN, MEGAN.   Audre Lord: trauma theory and liberal multiculturalism. MELUS (30:3) 2005, 219–45.

Bret Lott

17853. LOTT, BRET. Before we get started: a practical memoir of the writer's life. New York: Ballantine, 2005. pp. 210. Rev. by Jonathan Yardley in BkW, 23 Jan. 2005, 2.

Adrian C. Louis

17854. FAST, ROBIN RILEY. 'We'll always survive!': the challenges of home in the poetry of Adrian C. Louis. AICRJ (29:3) 2005, 101–20.

H. P. Lovecraft

17855. BEHEREC, MARC A. The Devil, the terror, and the horror: the Whateley twins' further debts to folklore and fiction. LovS (44) 2004, 23–5.

17856. BOUCHARD,ALEXANDRE;LACROIX,LOUIS-PIERRESMITH. Necronomicon: a note. LovS (44) 2004, 107–12.

17857. CLABOUGH, CASEY. Fred Chappell's Cthulhu appropriations: *Dagon*. LovS (44) 2004, 113–18.

17858. COLAVITO, JASON. The cult of alien gods: H. P. Lovecraft and extra-terrestrial pop culture. Amherst, NY: Prometheus, 2005. pp. 398, (plates) 8.

17859. EVANS, TIMOTHY H. A last defence against the dark: folklore, horror, and the uses of tradition in the works of H. P. Lovecraft. JFR (42:1) 2005, 99–135.

17860. GOODRICH, PETER. Mannerism and the macabre in H. P. Lovecraft's Dunsanian *Dream-Quest*. JFA (15:1) 2004, 37–48.

17861. McROY, JAY. There goes the neighborhood: chaotic apocalypse and monstrous genesis in H. P. Lovecraft's *The Street*, *The Horror at Red Hook*, and *He*. JFA (13:4) 2003, 335–51.

17862. MARTEN, ROBERT D. The Pickman models. LovS (44) 2004, 42–80.

17863. SMITH, DON G. H. P. Lovecraft in popular culture: the works and their adaptations in film, television, comics, music, and games. Jefferson, NC; London: McFarland, 2005. pp. ix, 173.

17864. WAUGH, ROBERT H. 'Hey, yew, why don't ye say somethin'?': Lovecraft's dramatic monologues. LovS (44) 2004, 81–106.

Maud Hart Lovelace

17865. MILLS, CLAUDIA. Diversity in Deep Valley: encountering the 'other' in the Betsy-Tacy series. ChildLit (32) 2004, 84–111.

Amy Lowell

17866. MUNICH, ADRIENNE; BRADSHAW, MELISSA (eds). Amy Lowell, American modern. (Bibl. 2004, 18120.) Rev. by Susan McCabe in Legacy (22:1) 2005, 89–90.

17867. YOSHIHARA, MARI. Embracing the East: White women and American Orientalism. (Bibl. 2004, 18124.) Rev. by Gina Marchetti in PacHR (73:2) 2004, 299–304.

Robert Lowell (1917–1977)

17868. BIDART, FRANK; GEWANTER, DAVID (eds); HARRISON, DESALES (asst ed.). Collected poems. (Bibl. 2004, 18127.) Rev. by Robyn Creswell in Raritan (24:3) 2005, 104–20; by Willard Spiegelman in KR (27:1) 2005, 134–69.

17869. CLARKE, COLIN A. 'Only man is miserable': the evolving view of imprisonment in Robert Lowell's poetry. *In* (pp. 131–46) **12821**.

17870. CRESWELL, ROBYN. Reimagining Robert Lowell. Raritan (24:3) 2005, 104–20 (review-article).

17871. GRAY, JEFFREY. Fear of flying: Robert Lowell and travel. PLL (41:1) 2005, 26–54.

17872. GRIFFIN, EDWARD M. Dancing around the maypole, ripping up the flag: the Merry Mount caper and issues in American history and art. Ren (57:3) 2005, 177–202. (Joseph M. Schwartz Memorial Essay: 2005.)

17873. HAMILTON, SASKIA (ed.). The letters of Robert Lowell. New York: Farrar, Straus, & Giroux, 2005. pp. xxxi, 852. Rev. by Craig Raine in TLS, 9 Sept. 2005, 3–5; by Adam Kirsch in Poetry (186:3) 2005, 248–54; by Phoebe Pettingell in NewL (88:3) 2005, 49–50; by Frank Kermode in LRB (27:18) 2005, 10–11; by Daniel M. Murtaugh in Cweal (132:15) 2005, 29–30; by William Logan in VQR (81:4) 2005, 269–84; by Charles Nicol in BkW, 21 Aug. 2005, 12.

17874. JAMES, STEPHEN. Energy and enervation: the poetry of Robert Lowell. CamQ (34:2) 2005, 109–29.

17875. KERMODE, FRANK. A hammer in his hands. LRB (27:18) 2005, 10–11 (review-article). (Letters.)

17876. KOŚĆ, GRZEGORZ. Robert Lowell: uncomfortable epigone of the *grands maîtres*. New York; Frankfurt: Lang, 2005. pp. vii, 338. (Polish studies in English language and literature, 12.)

17877. LOGAN, WILLIAM. The most contemptible moth: Lowell in letters. VQR (81:4) 2005, 269–84 (review-article).

17878. MURTAUGH, DANIEL M. A large soul. Cweal (132:15) 2005, 29–30 (review-article).

17879. PENG, YU. The therapeutic value of confessional poems. FLS (111) 2005, 79–85. (In Chinese.)

17880. RAINE, CRAIG. Dear rivals: from Robert Lowell to his dear friends, lovers, fellow poets and posterity. TLS, 9 Sept. 2005, 3–5 (review-article).

17881. SPIEGELMAN, WILLARD. The achievement of Robert Lowell. KR (27:1) 2005, 134–69 (review-article).

Lois Lowry

17882. LATHAM, DON. Discipline and its discontents: a Foucauldian reading of *The Giver*. ChildLit (32) 2004, 134–51.

Malcolm Lowry

17883. HAMA, MARK L. 'Whatever I do, it shall be deliberately': the Consul's political epiphany in *Under the Volcano*. SCR (22:2) 2005, 59–77.

17884. KUHLKEN, PAM FOX. 'Absolutamente necesario': the express train in Malcolm Lowry's *Under the Volcano*, chapter twelve. Mod/Mod (12:2) 2005, 209–28.

17885. SCHAEFFER, PIERRE. Éruptions et irruptions: de quleques avatars de la citation dans *Under the Volcano* de Malcolm Lowry. EREA (2:1) 2004, 92–100.

17886. TIESSEN, PAUL. Dorothy Livesay, the 'housewife', and the radio in 1951: Modernist embodiments of audience. *In* (pp. 205–28) **12739**.

Robert Lowry (b.1919)

17887. REIDEL, JAMES. Robert Lowry. RCF (25:2) 2005, 46–83.

Mina Loy

17888. FEINSTEIN, AMY. Goy interrupted: Mina Loy's unfinished novel and mongrel Jewish fiction. MFS (51:2) 2005, 335–53.

17889. MILLER, CRISTANNE. Cultures of Modernism: Marianne Moore, Mina Loy, & Elsa Lasker-Schüler: gender and literary community in New York and Berlin. *See* **18318**.

17890. —— Feminist location and Mina Loy's *Anglo-Mongrels and the Rose*. Paideuma (32:1–3) 2003, 75–94.

17891. POZORSKI, AIMEE L. Eugenicist mistress & ethnic mother: Mina Loy and Futurism, 1913–1917. MELUS (30:3) 2005, 41–69.

Craig Lucas (b.1951)

17892. ORLOFF, RICH. In conversation with Craig Lucas. Dramatist (7:5) 2005, 14–17.

Charles Ludlam

17893. EDWARDS, PAUL. Drift: performing the relics of intention. *See* **5921**.

Mabel Dodge Luhan

17894. REED, MAUREEN E. A woman's place: women writing New Mexico. *See* **15261**.

17895. ROSENHAN, CLAUDIA. An attribution in Huxley's short story *Chawdron* via Lawrence and Ludovici. *See* **17152**.

Glenna Luschei (b.1935)

17896. BACKER, SARA. My squandered youth. PemM (37) 2005, 159–60.

17897. BLY, ROBERT. Walking on the mountain. PemM (37) 2005, 154.

17898. BRANDT, ABIGAIL. La Luz. PemM (37) 2005, 131–2.

17899. DICKSON, RAY CLARK. A literary Venus. PemM (37) 2005, 152–3.

17900. FIELD, EDWARD. A gift the dying give us. PemM (37) 2005, 133.

17901. FRUMKIN, GENE. The happy traveler. PemM (37) 2005, 139–40.

17902. HAINES, JOHN. For Glenna, a backward glance. PemM (37) 2005, 144–5.

17903. HOYT, SARNIA. The years of our squandered youth. PemM (37) 2005, 161–2.

17904. LAWSON, PAUL. La Luschei. PemM (37) 2005, 150–1.

17905. McKINNON, KAREN. Albuquerque memoir. PemM (37) 2005, 146.

17906. MECHEM, JAMES. Charmed. PemM (37) 2005, 142–3.

17907. NOYES, STANLEY. Glenna and Glinda. PemM (37) 2005, 164–6.

17908. RETI, INGRID. Profile of the poet. PemM (37) 2005, 141.

17909. SCOTT, RODGER. Glenna Luschei, poet and maker of books. PemM (37) 2005, 155–6.

17910. SHER, STEVEN. Glenna Luschei: the poets' matchmaker. PemM (37) 2005, 123.

17911. SHERIDAN, DIANA KEELING. An introduction to California. PemM (37) 2005, 134–6.

17912. SIMON, MARJORIE. A vignette. PemM (37) 2005, 149.

17913. STEPHENSON, SHELBY. Glenna Luschei: an appreciation. PemM (37) 2005, 163.

17914. SULLIVAN, KEVIN. Her embrace that extends to us all. PemM (37) 2005, 147–8.

17915. YUDOVIN, DANA. The blonde goddess is a poet! PemM (37) 2005, 138.

Thomas Lux (b.1946)

17916. BOSSELAAR, LAURE-ANNE (ed.). Thomas Lux: an interview. FiveP (9:2) 2005, 55–79.

Gerald Lynch (b.1953)

17917. MILTON, PAUL. Rewriting White flight: suburbia in Gerald Lynch's *Troutstream* and Joan Barfoot's *Dancing in the Dark*. In (pp. 166–82) **9243.**

Robert McAlmon

17918. WILLIS, PATRICIA C. A Modernist epithalamium: Marianne Moore's *Marriage*. See **18331.**

Alexander McArthur

17919. BRYCE-WUNDER, SYLVIA. Of hard men and hairies: *No Mean City* and modern Scottish urban fiction. ScSR (4:1) 2003, 112–25.

Rose Macaulay

17920. MELLOR, LEO. Words from the bombsites: debris, Modernism and literary salvage. See **16286.**

17921. SMITH, STAN. 'The answer would appear to be a lemon': Rose Macaulay's Civil War. Eng (54:208) 2005, 15–34.

James McAuley

17922. ACKLAND, MICHAEL. Polemics anonymous: James McAuley's *nom de plume* contributions from *Hermes* to *Quadrant*. Southerly (64:3) 2004, 180–90.

17923. ROWE, NOEL. How to gossip with angels: Australian poetry after the gods. See **15613.**

James McBride (b.1957)

17924. PARK, CHRISTINE COHEN. Close comfort? Sons as their mothers' memoirists. See **17235.**

17925. RAMSEY, WILLIAM M. Knowing their place: three Black writers and the postmodern South. See **17532.**

Norman MacCaig

17926. DELMAIRE, DOMINIQUE. Self and otherness in Norman MacCaig's poetry. EREA (2:2) 2004, 102–11.

17927. FAZZINI, MARCO. Traduzione, rifacimento e scrittura creativa: il castello dei destini incrociati. In (pp. 107–16) **14377.**

2005] AUTHORS

Cormac McCarthy

17928. CURTIS, DIANA. McCarthy's *Blood Meridian*. Exp (63:2) 2005, 112–14.

Robbie McCauley

17929. GRIFFITHS, JENNIFER. Between women: trauma witnessing and the legacy of interracial rape in Robbie McCauley's *Sally's Rape*. Frontiers (26:3) 2005, 1–23.

Rebecca McClanahan

17930. PINSKER, SANFORD. The revisionist memory. *See* **12858.**

Nellie L. McClung

17931. MACPHERSON, MARGARET. Nellie McClung: voice for the voiceless. Montreal: XYZ, 2003. pp. 184. (Quest library.) Rev. by Janice Fiamengo in CanL (186) 2005, 182–4.

17932. ROY, WENDY. 'The ensign of the mop and the dustbin': the maternal and the material in autobiographical writings by Laura Goodman and Nellie McClung. *In* (pp. 247–62) **14629.**

James McConkey

17933. MCCONKEY, JAMES. A song of one's own. APR (34:2) 2005, 39–40.

17934. —— The telescope in the parlor: essays on life and literature. *See* **3850.**

John McCrae

17935. HOLMES, NANCY. *In Flanders Fields* – Canada's official poem: breaking faith. StudCanL (30:1) 2005, 11–33.

Sharyn McCrumb (b.1948)

17936. RUBIN, RACHEL. 'What ain't called Melungeons is called hillbillies': Southern Appalachia's in-between people. FMLS (40:3) 2004, 259–78.

Carson McCullers

17937. GLEESON-WHITE, SARAH. Strange bodies: gender and identity in the novels of Carson McCullers. (Bibl. 2004, 18192.) Rev. by Will Brantley in MFS (51:3) 2005, 676–8.

17938. GONZÁLEZ GROBA, CONSTANTE. Ivan Ilych in the Jim Crow South: Carson McCullers and Leo Tolstoy. LitB (24:1/2) 2004, 117–33.

17939. TIPPINS, SHERILL. February House. *See* **15245.**

'Hugh MacDiarmid' (C. M. Grieve)

17940. MCCULLOCH, MARGERY PALMER (introd.). For the vernacular circle (*The Bulletin* January 1938): the re-emergence of a long-lost contribution to the *Scott and Scotland* controversy. *See* **18391.**

17941. MANSON, JOHN. Further notes on Hugh MacDiarmid's poems. Bibliotheck (ns 1:2) 2004, 39–44.

17942. —— Hugh MacDiarmid's *First* and *Second Hymn to Lenin*. Bibliotheck (ns 1:1) 2004, 39–54.

17943. O'CONNOR, LAURA. Neighborly hostility and literary creoles: the example of Hugh MacDiarmid. PMC (15:2) 2005.

17944. ROBICHAUD, PAUL. MacDiarmid and Muir: Scottish Modernism and the nation as anthropological site. JML (28:4) 2005, 135–51.

Martin McDonagh

17945. GRENE, NICHOLAS.   Ireland in two minds: Martin McDonagh and Conor McPherson. YES (35) 2005, 298–311.

17946. WALLACE, CLARE.   'Pastiche soup', bad taste, biting irony and Martin McDonagh. LittPr (15:29) 2005, 3–38.

Ann-Marie MacDonald

17947. BAETZ, JOEL.   Tales from the Canadian crypt: Canadian ghosts, the cultural uncanny, and the necessity of haunting in Ann-Marie MacDonald's *Fall on Your Knees.* StudCanL (29:2) 2004, 62–83.

17948. DJORDJEVIC, IGOR.   *Goodnight Desdemona (Good Morning Juliet)*: from Shakespearean tragedy to postmodern satyr play. CompDr (37:1) 2003, 89–115.

17949. FROST, COREY.   Intersections of gender and ethnic performativity in Ann-Marie MacDonald's *Fall on Your Knees.* CRAS (35:2) 2005, 195–213.

17950. GEORGIS, DINA.   *Falling for jazz:* desire, dissonance, and racial collaboration. CRAS (35:2) 2005, 215–29.

17951. GORDON, NETA.   Twin tales: narrative profusion and genealogy in *Fall on Your Knees.* CRAS (35:2) 2005, 159–76.

17952. LOCKHART, MELANIE LEE.   'Taking them to the moon in a station wagon': an interview with Ann-Marie MacDonald. CRAS (35:2) 2005, 139–57.

17953. PARRO, GABRIELLA.   'Who's your father, dear?': haunted bloodlines and miscegenation in Ann-Marie MacDonald's *Fall on Your Knees.* CRAS (35:2) 2005, 177–93.

17954. ROBINSON, LAURA.   Remodeling *An Old-Fashioned Girl*: troubling girlhood in Ann-Marie MacDonald's *Fall on Your Knees.* CanL (186) 2005, 30–45.

17955. SALAH, TRISH.   What memory wants: broken tongue, stranger fugue in *Fall on Your Knees.* CRAS (35:2) 2005, 231–49.

'Ross Macdonald' (Kenneth Millar)

17956. KREYLING, MICHAEL.   The novels of Ross Macdonald. Columbia; London: South Carolina UP, 2005. pp. x, 185.

17957. NOLAN, TOM.   Hammett and Macdonald. *See* **16871**.

Jo McDougall

17958. HOOPER, MONIKA; STEWART, JENNIFER.   'I'm always looking at fields': an interview with Jo McDougall. ArkR (36:2) 2005, 124–32.

Frances McElrath

17959. LAMONT, VICTORIA.   Cattle branding and the traffic in women in early twentieth-century westerns by women. Legacy (22:1) 2005, 30–46.

Ian McEwan

17960. BIRRER, DORYJANE.   'What are novelists for?': writing and rewriting reality from Woolf to McEwan. *See* **20311**.

17961. FINNEY, BRIAN.   Briony's stand against oblivion: the making of fiction in Ian McEwan's *Atonement.* JML (27:3) 2004, 68–82.

17962. Hadley, Elaine. On a darkling plain: Victorian liberalism and the fantasy of agency. *See* **9932.**

17963. Harold, James. Narrative engagement with *Atonement* and *The Blind Assassin*. PhilL (29:1) 2005, 130–45.

17964. Hidalgo, Pilar. Memory and storytelling in Ian McEwan's *Atonement*. CritW (46:2) 2005, 82–91.

17965. Ingersoll, Earl G. City of endings: Ian McEwan's *Amsterdam*. MidQ (46:2) 2005, 123–38.

17966. —— Intertextuality in L. P. Hartley's *The Go-Between* and Ian McEwan's *Atonement*. *See* **16916.**

17967. Kohn, Robert E. The fivesquare *Amsterdam* of Ian McEwan. CritS (16:1) 2004, 89–106.

17968. Long, Jiang. The child within and magic time. FLS (114) 2005, 70–6. (In Chinese.)

17969. Pedot, Richard. My tongue did things by itself: story-telling/story-writing in *Conversation with a Cupboard Man* (Ian McEwan). JSSE (45) 2005, 135–43.

17970. Reynier, Christine. *Atonement* de Ian McEwan; ou, Le désir d'expiation d'un écrivain. EtBr (28) 2005, 101–14.

17971. —— La citation *in absentia* à l'œuvre dans *Atonement* de Ian McEwan. EREA (2:1) 2004, 61–8.

Gwendolyn MacEwen

17972. Wood, Brent. No-man's land: mythic crisis in Gwendolyn MacEwen's *The T. E. Lawrence Poems*. StudCanL (29:2) 2004, 141–62.

Ronald E. McFarland (b.1942)

17973. McFarland, Ron. For the birds. WebS (22:2) 2005, 48–60.

Leslie McFarlane (b.1902)

17974. Greenwald, Marilyn S. The secret of the Hardy Boys: Leslie McFarlane and the Stratemeyer Syndicate. (Bibl. 2004, 18207.) Rev. by Paul Parsons in JoH (30:3) 2004, 160; by Gabrielle Halko in AmJ (22:1) 2005, 119–20; by Chris McGee in CLAQ (30:4) 2005, 430–4.

Michael McFee

17975. Morgan, Robert. Coming down from Pisgah: a memoir of Michael McFee. AppH (33:2) 2005, 23–5.

17976. Powell, Tara. Ringing his being: an overview of Michael McFee's career. AppH (33:2) 2005, 9–13.

17977. West, Robert M. 'This is Paradise': Michael McFee's poems about Heaven. AppH (33:2) 2005, 30–5.

John McGahern

17978. Burrow, Colin. No way out. LRB (27:20) 2005, 26–7 (review-article). (Memoirs.)

17979. Holland, Siobhán. Marvellous fathers in the fiction of John McGahern. YES (35) 2005, 186–98.

17980. McGahern, John.   Memoir. London; Boston, MA: Faber & Faber, 2005. pp. 272. Rev. by Colin Burrow in LRB (27:20) 2005, 26–7.

17981. Maher, Eamon.   John McGahern and his Irish readers. NewHR (9:2) 2005, 125–36.

17982. —— John McGahern: from the local to the universal. (Bibl. 2004, 18209.) Rev. by Maguy Pernot-Deschamps in EtIr (29:1) 2004, 166; by Brad Kent in CJIS (30:2) 2004, 74.

Patrick MacGill (b.1890)

17983. McGonigal, James.   Literacy, technology and memory in three Scots Irish novels. EtIr (30:1) 2005, 19–35.

Campbell McGrath (b.1962)

17984. Dolmage, Jay.   Between the valley and the field: metaphor and disability. PrSt (27:1/2) 2005, 108–19.

Thomas McGrath

17985. Dussol, Vincent.   Modalités d'une négociation: le trèfle et la faucille chez Thomas McGrath (1916–1990). EtIr (28:2) 2003, 29–50.

17986. Sheldon, Glenn.   Thomas McGrath: another Agrarian revolt. MidAmerica (30) 2003, 100–11.

Fiona McGregor (b.1965)

17987. Davidson, Guy.   Minor literature, microculture: Fiona McGregor's *Chemical Palace*. Southerly (64:3) 2004, 140–53.

Medbh McGuckian

17988. Mallot, J. Edward.   Medbh McGuckian's poetic techtonics. EI (40:3/4) 2005, 240–55.

17989. Schrage-Früh, Michaela.   An interview with Medbh McGuckian. ConLit (46:1) 2005, 1–17.

Frank McGuinness

17990. Kiberd, Declan.   Frank McGuinness and the sons of Ulster. YES (35) 2005, 279–97.

17991. Lojek, Helen.   Spatial metaphors in Frank McGuinness's *Gates of Gold*. EtIr (29:2) 2004, 151–64.

17992. Lojek, Helen Heusner.   Contexts for Frank McGuinness's drama. (Bibl. 2004, 18221.) Rev. by Chris Morash in TLS, 21 Jan. 2005, 18; by John P. Harrington in ILS (24:2) 2005, 21.

Eduardo Machado

17993. Ortiz, Ricardo.   Fables of (Cuban) exile: special periods and queer moments in Eduardo Machado's Floating Island plays. ModDr (48:1) 2005, 132–62.

Christopher McIlroy

17994. McIlroy, Christopher.   Behind the story. *In* (pp. 144–5) **14294.**

William McIlvanney

17995. McGonigal, James.   Literacy, technology and memory in three Scots Irish novels. *See* **17983**.

Kevin McIlvoy (b.1953)

17996. McIlvoy, Kevin.   Behind the story. *In* (pp. 350–2) **14294**.

Colin MacInnes

17997. Bentley, Nick.   Translating English: youth, race and nation in Colin MacInnes's *City of Spades* and *Absolute Beginners*. Connotations (13:1/2) 2003/04, 149–69.

Charles E. Mack (1888–1934)

17998. Whalan, Mark.   'The only real white democracy' and the language of liberation: the Great War, France, and African American culture in the 1920s. *See* **16163**.

Claude McKay

17999. Francini, Antonella.   Sonnet *vs* sonnet: the fourteen lines in African American poetry. RSA (14) 2003, 37–66.

18000. McKible, Adam.   'Life is real and life is earnest': Mike Gold, Claude McKay, and the Baroness Elsa von Freytag-Loringhoven. *See* **16732**.

Alecia McKenzie (b.1960)

18001. McKenzie, Alecia.   The joys of the brief encounter. *In* (pp. 7–8) **14204**.

Nathaniel Mackey

18002. Lavery, Matthew A.   The ontogeny and phylogeny of Mackey's *Song of the Andoumboulou*. AAR (38:4) 2004, 683–94.

18003. Mackey, Nathaniel.   Paracritical hinge: essays, talks, notes, interviews. *See* **14448**.

Patricia McKillip

18004. Mains, Christine.   Bridging world and story: Patricia McKillip's reluctant heroes. JFA (16:1) 2005, 37–48.

18005. ——   Having it all: the female hero's quest for love and power in Patricia McKillip's *Riddle-Master* trilogy. Extrapolation (46:1) 2005, 23–35.

18006. Pilinovsky, Helen.   The mother of all witches: Baba Yaga and Brume in Patricia McKillip's *In the Forests of Serre*. Extrapolation (46:1) 2005, 36–49.

Reginald McKnight

18007. Champion, Laurie.   Search for identity in Reginald McKnight's short fiction. ShSt (12:1) 2004, 79–90.

18008. Murray, Rolland.   Diaspora by bus: Reginald McKnight, postmodernism, and transatlantic subjectivity. ConLit (46:1) 2005, 46–77.

Bernard Mac Laverty

18009. Goarzin, Anne.   Traversées en eaux troubles: *Reading in the Dark* de Seamus Deane et *Grace Notes* de Bernard Mac Laverty. *See* **16015**.

Michael McLaverty

18010. ALLISON, JONATHAN. *Friendship's Garland* and the manuscripts of Seamus Heaney's *Fosterage. See* **16932.**

18011. HILLAN, SOPHIA. Wintered into wisdom: Michael McLaverty, Seamus Heaney, and the Northern word-hoard. NewHR (9:3) 2005, 86–106.

Archibald MacLeish

18012. DRABECK, BERNARD A. *Scratch* revisited. AMacJ, Summer 2005, 48–59.

18013. ELLIS, HELEN E. Archibald MacLeish: lessons in aging. AMacJ, Summer 2005, 25–33.

18014. OICKLE, ALVIN F. Archibald MacLeish, teacher: a greeting of the spirit. AMacJ, Summer 2005, 64–70.

18015. PORTER, DAVID. Our need for the art of MacLeish. AMacJ, Summer 2005, 19–24.

18016. RIGOLOT, CAROL. Blood brothers: Archibald MacLeish and Saint-John Perse. AMacJ, Summer 2005, 34–47.

Hugh MacLennan

18017. ARMSTRONG, CHRISTOPHER J. Postcolonial historicity: Halifax, region, and empire in *Barometer Rising* and *The Nymph and the Lamp. In* (pp. 50–64) **9243.**

18018. COLEMAN, ANNE. I'll tell you a secret: a memory of seven summers. Toronto: McClelland & Stewart, 2004. pp. 235.

Alistair MacLeod

18019. BAER, WILLIAM. A lesson in the art of storytelling: an interview with Alistair MacLeod. MichQR (44:2) 2005, 334–52.

Bryan MacMahon

18020. BURKE, MARY. Negotiating the bi-vocal discourses of 'Catholic' and 'Protestant', 'Nationalist' and 'Loyalist': Irish traveller identity as 'third space'. EtIr (29:2) 2004, 59–74.

James McMichael

18021. ARCHAMBEAU, ROBERT. Caging the demon: James McMichael and the poetics of restraint. ChiR (51:3) 2005, 141–54.

Patricia McMullan (1913–1995)

18022. GIEMZA, BRYAN (introd.). *Cottie Mourns: a Comedy of Sea Island Folk* by Patricia McMullan. NCLR (14) 2005, 7–9.

Larry McMurtry

18023. DAIGREPONT, LLOYD M. Passion, romance and *agape* in Larry McMurtry's *Lonesome Dove.* LJH (30:2) 2005, 43–61.

18024. MILLER-PURRENHAGE, JOHN. 'Kin to nobody': the disruption of genealogy in Larry McMurtry's *Lonesome Dove.* CritW (47:1) 2005, 73–89.

18025. SOLOMON, DEBORAH. Cowboy culture. NYTM, 29 May 2005, 17. (Interview.)

Terrence McNally

18026. COHEN, PATRICIA. Guild seminar: race & politics in theater. See 15101.

18027. EADS, MARTHA GREENE. Conversion tactics in Terrence McNally's and Paul Rudnick's gay gospels. ModDr (48:1) 2005, 163–85.

Louis MacNeice

18028. ALLISON, JONATHAN. Louis MacNeice, travel, and the sea. In (pp. 69–77) 14479.

18029. BROWN, RICHARD DANSON. Neutrality and commitment: MacNeice, Yeats, Ireland and the Second World War. JML (28:3) 2005, 109–29.

18030. CIOMPI, FAUSTO. L'ultimo MacNeice. AngP (2:1/2) 2005, 139–68.

18031. TAIT, PETER. Littleton Powys, 1874–1955: headmaster, Sherborne Preparatory School. See 18929.

18032. WILLS, CLAIR. The aesthetics of Irish neutrality during the Second World War. B2 (31:1) 2004, 119–45.

Conor McPherson (b.1971)

18033. GRENE, NICHOLAS. Ireland in two minds: Martin McDonagh and Conor McPherson. See 17945.

Sindiwe Magona

18034. KOYANA, SIPHOKAZI (ed.). Sindiwe Magona: the first decade. Scottsville: KwaZulu-Natal UP, 2004. pp. xii, 207.

Jayanta Mahapatra

18035. DAS, LIZA; BHUSHAN, BRAJ. From hard poetics to situated reading: a cognitive–empirical study of imagery and graded figurative language. In (pp. 219–36) 3888.

Derek Mahon

18036. BOISSEAU, MARYVONNE. Traduire/travestir: Derek Mahon détourne Molière. EtIr (30:1) 2005, 55–66.

18037. DRUMMOND, GAVIN. The difficulty of we: the epistolary poems of Michael Longley and Derek Mahon. See 17845.

18038. FARRELL, L. J. Poetic presage and epistemological terror: an alternative conception of the past. IE (27:2) 2005, 34–9.

18039. KERRIGAN, JOHN. Paul Muldoon's transits: muddling through after Madoc. In (pp. 125–49) 18404.

18040. NIXON, MARK. 'A brief glow in the dark': Samuel Beckett's presence in modern Irish poetry. See 15408.

Margaret Mahy

18041. COHOON, LORINDA B. Pirate parenting in Margaret Mahy's middle-grade readers. In (pp. 84–109) 18044.

18042. DUDER, TESSA. Margaret Mahy, a writer's life. Auckland: HarperCollins, 2005. pp. 336, (plates) 16.

18043. FEINGOLD, RUTH P. Gardening in Eden: Margaret Mahy's postcolonial ghosts and the New Zealand landscape. In (pp. 210–33) 18044.

18044. HALE, ELIZABETH; WINTERS, SARAH FIONA (eds). Marvellous codes: the fiction of Margaret Mahy. Wellington: Victoria UP, 2005. pp. 264.

18045. HEBLEY, DIANE. 'A fertility and felicity and ferocity of invention': New Zealand landscapes in Margaret Mahy's young adult novels. *In* (pp. 187–209) **18044.**

18046. HESTER, SAM. The wobble in the symmetry: the narrator's role in *The Catalogue of the Universe*. *In* (pp. 168–86) **18044.**

18047. HINE, MARY E.; POPE, ROB; WALLER, ALISON. Rewriting Mahy's *The Tricksters*: exploring sense of place and fictional space through adaptation and imitation. *In* (pp. 234–54) **18044.**

18048. MARQUIS, CLAUDIA. Ariadne 'down under': Margaret Mahy's *The Tricksters*. *In* (pp. 62–83) **18044.**

18049. SAUNDERS, KATHY. Setting free: Margaret Mahy and disability. *In* (pp. 110–29) **18044.**

18050. SCALLY, LISA. 'Telling stories of desire': the power of authorship in *The Changeover* and *The Amber Spyglass*. *In* (pp. 130–47) **18044.**

18051. SMITH, ANNA. Contagious knowledge: Margaret Mahy and the adolescent novel. *In* (pp. 44–61) **18044.**

18052. WALLER, ALISON. 'Solid all the way through': Margaret Mahy's ordinary witches. *In* (pp. 21–43) **18044.**

18053. WALLS, KATHRYN. 'True-seeming lyes' in Margaret Mahy's fiction. *In* (pp. 148–67) **18044.**

Norman Mailer

18054. JUNCKER, CLARA. Real Marilyns. SPELL (16) 2003, 129–42 (review-article).

18055. KINDER, JOHN M. The Good War's 'raw chunks': Norman Mailer's *The Naked and the Dead* and James Gould Cozzens's *Guard of Honor*. MidQ (46:2) 2005, 187–202.

18056. McCANN, SEAN; SZALAY, MICHAEL. Do you believe in magic? Literary thinking after the New Left. YJC (18:2) 2005, 435–68.

18057. MACILWEE, MICHAEL. Saul Bellow and Norman Mailer. *See* **15449.**

18058. ROSCHER, JENNIFER. The ambivalence of *The Executioner's Song*: postmodern captivity from Death Row. *In* (pp. 217–32) **12821.**

18059. SHI, YAFANG. On the author's absence in *The Executioner's Song*. FLS (114) 2005, 44–51. (In Chinese.)

18060. WHALEN-BRIDGE, JOHN. Murderous desire in *Lolita* (with related thoughts on Mailer's *An American Dream*). *See* **18477.**

Robert Majzels (b.1950)

18061. BENEVENTI, DOMENIC. Lost in the city: the Montreal novels of Régine Robin and Robert Majzels. *In* (pp. 104–21) **9243.**

Bernard Malamud

18062. HUNTER, LATHAM. 'What's natural about it?': a baseball movie as introduction to key concepts in Cultural Studies. *See* **13686.**

18063. KOLÁŘ, STANISLAV. Faith against skepticism, emotionality against rationalism: Bernard Malamud's *Angel Levine* and *The Silver Crown*. CLIN (8:1/2) 2005, 27–37.

18064. STEED, JASON. Malamud's *God's Grace* and the theme of reversal; or, Old joke, better version. StudAJL (24) 2005, 103–15.

18065. VLADAŘOVÁ, HELENA. Bernard Malamud (1914–1986): a quest of *A New Life. In* (pp. 181–8) **3753.**

David Malouf

18066. BYRON, MARK. Crossing borders of the self in the fiction of David Malouf. SSE (31) 2005, 76–93.

18067. SEMPRUCH, JUSTYNA. Philosophical encounters with identity: David Malouf's *Remembering Babylon*. Antipodes (19:1) 2005, 44–50.

David Mamet

18068. BARTON, BRUCE. Imagination in transition: Mamet's move to film. New York; Frankfurt: Lang, 2005. pp. 245. (Dramaturgies, 5.)

18069. BIGSBY, CHRISTOPHER (ed.). The Cambridge companion to David Mamet. (Bibl. 2004, 18284.) Rev. by Kimball King in SAtlR (70:2) 2005, 155–7.

18070. BREWER, GAYLORD. Mamet's divided magics: communion and duplicity in *The Shawl, The Cryptogram*, and other works. AmDr (14:2) 2005, 16–38.

18071. CALLENS, JOHAN. Remediation in David Mamet's *The Water Engine*. AmDr (14:2) 2005, 39–55.

18072. CHARNEY, MAURICE. Parody – and self-parody in David Mamet. Connotations (13:1/2) 2003/04, 77–88.

18073. KANE, LESLIE (ed.). The art of crime: the plays and films of Harold Pinter and David Mamet. *See* **18797.**

18074. PEARCE, HOWARD. David Mamet's *Old Neighborhood*: journey and geography. AmDr (14:1) 2005, 46–62.

Manjula Padmanabhan

18075. RAMACHANDRAN, AYESHA. New World, no world: seeking utopia in Padmanabhan's *Harvest*. TRI (30:2) 2005, 161–74.

Emily Mann

18076. MARTIN, CAROL. In defense of democracy: celebrating Emily Mann. WP (14:2) 2005, 111–16.

Phillip Mann (b.1942)

18077. MANN, PHILLIP. Inter aliens: the impact of China on the creation of the science fiction novel *The Eye of the Queen. In* (pp. 324–55) **12674.**

Olivia Manning

18078. BRAYBROOKE, NEVILLE; BRAYBROOKE, JUNE. Olivia Manning: a life. Ed. by Francis King. London: Chatto & Windus, 2004. pp. xvii, 301, (plates) 16.

18079. STEINBERG, THEODORE LOUIS. Twentieth-century epic novels. *See* **16191.**

'Katherine Mansfield'
(Kathleen Mansfield Beauchamp, 'Julian Mark')

18080. BENNETT, ANDREW. Katherine Mansfield. Plymouth: Northcote House in assn with the British Council, 2004. pp. xi, 98. (Writers and their work.)

18081. CAMPBELL, DUNCAN. 'What lies beneath these strange rich surfaces?': *chinoiserie* in Thorndon. *In* (pp. 173–89) **12674**.

18082. CORSI, MARCELLA. Il fascino perentorio dei *Poems* di Katherine Mansfield. LProv (119/120) 2004, 75–85.

18083. FERRALL, CHARLES. Unlikely *Blutbrüderschaft*: Mansfield and D. H. Lawrence. *In* (pp. 60–74) **18084**.

18084. —— STAFFORD, JANE (eds). Katherine Mansfield's men: perspectives from the 2004 Katherine Mansfield Birthplace lecture series. Wellington, New Zealand: Katherine Mansfield Birthplace Soc. in assn with Steele Roberts, 2004. pp. 154.

18085. GAMBARO, ELISA. Immagini di spazialità dei racconti di Elsa Morante e Katherine Mansfield. Culture (17) 2003, 155–72.

18086. MASGRAU-PEYA, ELISENDA. Towards a poetics of the 'unhomed': the house in Katherine Mansfield's *Prelude* and Barbara Hanrahan's *The Scent of Eucalyptus*. Antipodes (18:1) 2004, 60–6.

18087. MATHEWS, PETER. Myth and unity in Mansfield's *At the Bay*. JNZL (23:2) 2005, 47–61.

18088. MORRIS, PAUL. Mansfield and her magician. *In* (pp. 75–95) **18084**.

18089. NAKANO, EIKO. Intuition and intellect: Henri Bergson's influence on Katherine Mansfield's representations of places. WLWE (40:1) 2002/03, 86–100.

18090. O'SULLIVAN, VINCENT. What we mostly don't say about Katherine Mansfield. *In* (pp. 96–105) **18084**.

18091. RICKETTS, HARRY. John Middleton Murry: keeper of the flame. *In* (pp. 106–23) **18084**.

18092. STAFFORD, JANE. The boyfriends. *In* (pp. 27–46) **18084**.

18093. STEAD, C. K. Men and Mansfield in *Mansfield*. *In* (pp. 124–40) **18084**.

18094. UTELL, JANINE. A fatal place: the ritual encounters with death in the fiction of Katherine Mansfield. CEACrit (66:1) 2003, 22–31.

18095. WILLIAMS, MARK. The Pa man: Sir Harold Beauchamp. *In* (pp. 13–26) **18084**.

18096. —— Sentimental racism. *In* (pp. 29–45) **12674**.

18097. WOODS, JOANNA. Tall (and short) dark strangers: K.M. and foreign men. *In* (pp. 47–59) **18084**.

Dambudzo Marechera

18098. OSEI-NYAME, KWADWO, JR. Images of London in African literature: Ama Ata Aidoo's *Our Sister Killjoy* and Dambudzo Marechera's *The Black Insider*. *In* (pp. 175–97) **14254**.

18099. VEIT-WILD, FLORA. The grotesque body of the postcolony: Sony Labou Tansi and Dambudzo Marechera. RLC (79:2) 2005, 227–39.

Donald Margulies

18100. BOSSLER, GREGORY.   In conversation with Donald Margulies. Dramatist (7:5) 2005, 18–21.

18101. GEIS, DEBORAH R.   In Willy Loman's garden: contemporary re-visions of *Death of a Salesman*. *In* (pp. 202–18) **18234**.

David Markson

18102. DEMPSEY, PETER.   Novelist of shreds and patches: the fiction of David Markson. HC (42:4) 2005, 1–13.

Daphne Marlatt

18103. CHIVERS, SALLY.   'This is my memory, a fact': the many mediations of *Mothertalk: Life Stories of May Kiyoshi Kiyooka*. *In* (pp. 69–87) **14629**.

18104. EGAN, SUSANNA.   The shifting grounds of exile and home in Daphne Marlatt's *Steveston*. *In* (pp. 97–115) **12750**.

18105. LOWRY, GLEN.   Cultural citizenship and writing post-colonial Vancouver: Daphne Marlatt's *Ana Historic* and Wayde Compton's *Bluesprint*. Mosaic (38:3) 2005, 21–39.

John P. Marquand

18106. WHIPPLE, ROBERT D., JR (ed.).   Essays on the literature of American novelist John P. Marquand (1893–1960). Lewiston, NY; Lampeter: Mellen Press, 2004. pp. x, 123. (Studies in American literature, 72.)

Don Marquis (1878–1937)

18107. MONTEFIORE, JANET.   *archy experiences a seizure* and *The Rhyme of the Three Captains*. *See* **17479**.

18108. TISCHLER, ALYSON.   A rose is a pose: Steinian Modernism and mass culture. *See* **19597**.

Anne Marriott

18109. ROSE, MARILYN.   The literary archive and the telling of Modernist lives: retrieving Anne Marriott. *In* (pp. 231–49) **12739**.

Ngaio Marsh

18110. SARTI EVANS, ANTONELLA.   Ngaio Marsh: l'immedesimazione totale: quando Shakespeare 'uccide'. LProv (118) 2003, 41–60.

Paule Marshall

18111. BALESTRA, GIANFRANCA.   Spanning the distance between the Americas: Paule Marshall's *The Chosen Place, the Timeless People*. Culture (17) 2003, 101–12.

18112. BENJAMIN, SHANNA GREENE.   Weaving the web of reintegration: locating Aunt Nancy in *Praisesong for the Widow*. MELUS (30:1) 2005, 49–67.

Yann Martel

18113. COLE, STEWART.   Believing in tigers: anthropomorphism and incredulity in Yann Martel's *Life of Pi*. StudCanL (29:2) 2004, 22–36.

18114. DWYER, JUNE.   Yann Martel's *Life of Pi* and the evolution of the shipwreck narrative. MLS (35:2) 2005, 8–21.

18115. STRATTON, FLORENCE. 'Hollow at the core': deconstructing Yann Martel's *Life of Pi*. StudCanL (29:2) 2004, 5–21.

Jane Martin

18116. ULLOM, JEFFREY. The landmark years of the Humana Festival. *See* **13124**.

Michael Martone

18117. MARTONE, MICHAEL. Behind the story. *In* (pp. 403–4) **14294**.

John Masefield

18118. ERRINGTON, PHILIP W. John Masefield, the 'Great Auk' of English literature: a bibliography. New Castle, DE: Oak Knoll Press; London: British Library, 2004. pp. xiv, 907. Rev. by Paul W. Nash in Library (6:2) 2005, 209–10; by Clive Hurst in BC (54:2) 2005, 309–10.

18119. POWELL, NEIL. Down to the seas again. TLS, 3 June 2005, 7 (review article).

Philip Mason ('Philip Woodruff')

18120. FURBANK, P. N. Anglo-Indian dialogues: the Raj, the historical novel and misunderstandings between the races. *See* **19572**.

R. A. K. Mason

18121. BARROWMAN, RACHEL. Mason: the life of R. A. K. Mason. (Bibl. 2004 18327.) Rev. by Bruce King in JPW (41:1) 2005, 113–23.

Edgar Lee Masters

18122. LOPATE, PHILIP (introd.). Last stands: notes from memory. Afterword by Hilary Masters. Dallas, TX: Southern Methodist UP, 2004. pp. xiv, 216 (plates) 2.

Hilary Masters

18123. LOPATE, PHILIP (introd.). Last stands: notes from memory. Afterword by Hilary Masters. *See* **18122**.

William Matthews

18124. BELL, MARVIN. On *Mingus at the Showplace*. PInt (9) 2005, 143.

18125. BROWN, KURT. CHOPS: on the early poems of William Matthews. PInt (9) 2005, 144–5.

18126. BUCKLEY, CHRISTOPHER. On *Sad Stories Told in Bars: the Reader's Digest Version*. PInt (9) 2005, 147–8.

18127. COX, MARK. On *A Night at the Opera*. PInt (9) 2005, 150–1.

18128. DAVISON, PETER. Losing William Matthews. PInt (9) 2005, 152.

18129. FROST, CAROL. On *Mingus in Shadow*. PInt (9) 2005, 154.

18130. JACKSON, RICHARD. William Matthews' lovable weather. PInt (9) 2005, 134–41.

18131. JARMAN, MARK. 'The issue was a human life': William Matthews' *The Search Party*. PInt (9) 2005, 159–60.

18132. KUMIN, MAXINE. On *Four Poems about Jamaica*. PInt (9) 2005, 164–5.

18133. LEVINE, PHILIP. Remembering Mingus and Matthews: on *Mingus at the Half Note*. PInt (9) 2005, 167.

18134. LONG, ALEXANDER. On *Masterful.* PInt (9) 2005, 169.

18135. MARGOLIS, GARY. On *The Dream.* PInt (9) 2005, 171.

18136. MATTHEWS, SEBASTIAN. Why I love *Dancing to Reggae Music.* PInt (9) 2005, 173.

18137. PAUL, BRADLEY. King of the one-liners: Bill Matthews and the volta. PInt (9) 2005, 174–5.

18138. PAUL, KARRI HARRISON. Cloudy mirror, a poetry of reversal: on *Mingus in Shadow.* PInt (9) 2005, 155–6.

18139. PLUMLY, STANLEY. On *Spring Snow.* PInt (9) 2005, 177–9.

18140. RIVARD, DAVID. The game is the same, it's just up on another level: *In Memory of the Utah Stars.* PInt (9) 2005, 181–2.

18141. SMITH, ARTHUR. Leonardo's horses: on *Men in Dark Suits.* PInt (9) 2005, 184.

18142. STERN, GERALD. Nowhere, USA: on *Morningside Heights, July.* PInt (9) 2005, 186.

18143. WIER, DARA. On *Funeral Homes.* PInt (9) 2005, 188.

Peter Matthiessen

18144. FISHER-WIRTH, ANN. William Faulkner, Peter Matthiessen, and the environmental imagination. *In* (pp. 47–60) **16453.**

18145. TREDINNICK, MARK. The land's wild music: encounters with Barry Lopez, Peter Matthiessen, Terry Tempest Williams, & James Galvin. *See* **16637.**

18146. WATSON, JAMES G. Man writing: the Watson trilogy: Peter Matthiessen in archive. TSLL (46:2) 2004, 245–70.

Robin Maugham (b.1916)

18147. PREVITI, SIMONA. Dioniso vestito da servo: la contaminazione della casa da Maugham a Losey. *In* (pp. 93–103) **14322.**

W. Somerset Maugham

18148. MEYERS, JEFFREY. Somerset Maugham: a life. (Bibl. 2004, 18333.) Rev. by Troy J. Bassett in ELT (48:2) 2005, 236–9; by Christopher Tayler in LRB (27:17) 2005, 19–22; by Robert L. Calder in StudN (37:3) 2005, 360–3.

18149. TAYLER, CHRISTOPHER. I only want the OM. LRB (27:17) 2005, 19–22 (review-article).

18150. WILLIS, CHRIS. From voyeurism to feminism: Victorian and Edwardian London's streetfighting slum viragoes. VicR (29:1) 2003, 70–86.

William Maxwell (b.1908)

18151. BAXTER, CHARLES; COLLIER, MICHAEL; HIRSCH, EDWARD (eds). A William Maxwell portrait: memories and appreciations. New York; London: Norton, 2004. pp. 234. Rev. by Michael Gorra in TLS, 27 May 2005, 11.

18152. BURCKHARDT, BARBARA. William Maxwell: a literary life. Urbana: Illinois UP, 2005. pp. xiv, 308, (plates) 8. Rev. by Michael Gorra in TLS, 27 May 2005, 11; by Chris Lehmann in BkW, 20 Mar. 2005, 8–9.

18153. COLLIER, MICHAEL. The dog gets to Dover: William Maxwell as a correspondent. GaR (57:4) 2003, 765–74.

18154. Gorra, Michael. During the day. TLS, 27 May 2005, 11 (review-article).

F. B. Maynard

18155. Schaub, Danielle. Autobiographical story cycles as a vehicle for enlightenment: Fredelle Bruser Maynard's *Raisins and Almonds* and *The Tree of Life*. PrSt (27:3) 2005, 313–29.

Zakes Mda

18156. Barnard, Rita. On laughter, the grotesque, and the South African transition: Zakes Mda's *Ways of Dying*. Novel (37:3) 2004, 277–302.

18157. Splendore, Paola. Vagrants and angels of death in two contemporary South African novels. *In* (pp. 255–63) **3690**.

18158. Williams, Elly. An interview with Zakes Mda. MR (28:2) 2005, 62–79.

Pablo Medina (b.1948)

18159. Medina, Pablo. Behind the story. *In* (pp. 306–7) **14294**.

18160. —— The mark of exile. BosR (30:2) 2005, 48.

Mark Medoff

18161. Zachary, Samuel J. (comp.). The dramaturgy of Mark Medoff: five plays dealing with deafness and social issues. Foreword by Mark Medoff. Lewiston, NY; Lampeter: Mellen Press, 2004. pp. xxvii, 428. (Studies in theatre arts, 27.)

Charles L. Mee

18162. Reilly, Kara. A collage reality (re)made: the postmodern dramaturgy of Charles L. Mee. AmDr (14:2) 2005, 56–69.

18163. Schlueter, Jen. Staging Versailles: Charles Mee and the re-presentation of history. JADT (17:3) 2005, 5–23.

Peter Meinke

18164. Milovanovič, Čelica. A Classicist reads some modern poetry. *See* **14458**.

Samuel Menashe

18165. Ricks, Christopher (ed.). New and selected poems. New York: Library of America, 2005. pp. xxxviii, 191. (American poets project.)

H. L. Mencken

18166. Anon. Mencken's many identities. Menckeniana (165) 2003, 1–3.

18167. Combs, Norris K. Uncle Joe and Mr Mencken. Menckeniana (166) 2003, 2–5.

18168. Crowther, Hal. Money, media, mythology: Mencken and the maiming of America. Menckeniana (167) 2003, 1–13.

18169. Dorbin, Jerry. The Goldberg variations. Menckeniana (174) 2005, 5–6.

18170. Fitzpatrick, Vincent. H. L. Mencken. (Bibl. 2004, 18357.) Rev. by S. L. Harrison in Menckeniana (171) 2004, 11.

18171. HARRISON, S. L. Mencken's pseudonymous writings. Menckeniana (165) 2003, 4–11.

18172. —— Misquoting Mencken. Menckeniana (171) 2004, 9–10.

18173. —— (ed.). A.k.a. H. L. Mencken: a selection of his pseudonymous writings. Miami, FL: Wolf Den, 2005. pp. viii, 184. Rev. by Gloria Monday in Menckeniana (172) 2004, 13.

18174. HEITMAN, DANNY. *Minority Report* reexamined. Menckeniana (173) 2005, 1–12.

18175. HENLEY, ANN. Sara Haardt: flower of the Sahara. Menckeniana (175) 2005, 5–14.

18176. JEFFERS, THOMAS L. A fresh life for Mencken. HR (55:4) 2003, 605–16 (review-article).

18177. JOSHI, S. T. Mencken and terrorism. Menckeniana (173) 2005, 13–15.

18178. —— Mencken bibliography addenda. Menckeniana (165) 2003, 12–16.

18179. LEWIS, NGHANA TAMU. The rhetoric of mobility, the politics of consciousness: Julia Mood Peterkin and the case of a White Black writer. *See* **18774**.

18180. OWENS, GWINN. Mencken: the family man? Menckeniana (169) 2004, 3–7.

18181. PACKER-KINLAW, DONNA. Dreiser–Mencken letters. Menckeniana (172) 2004, 1–9.

18182. RODGERS, MARION ELIZABETH. The American iconoclast. Menckeniana (176) 2005, 2–10.

18183. —— Mencken: the American iconoclast. Oxford; New York: OUP, 2005. pp. ix, 662.

18184. TEACHOUT, TERRY. The Mencken who matters. Menckeniana (168) 2003, 1–14.

18185. —— The skeptic: the life of H. L. Mencken. (Bibl. 2004, 18361.) Rev. by Thomas L. Jeffers in HR (55:4) 2003, 605–16; by Vincent Fitzpatrick in Menckeniana (166) 2003, 10–14.

18186. THOMPSON, GEORGE H. The art of collecting H. L. Mencken. Menckeniana (169) 2004, 8–10.

Louise Meriwether

18187. DAVIS, AMANDA J. To build a nation: Black women writers, Black nationalism, and violent reduction of wholeness. *See* **17227**.

James Merrill

18188. HAMMER, LANGDON. Life into art: James Merrill's *16.ix.65*. LitIm (7:3) 2005, 278–85.

18189. INGRAM, CLAUDIA. 'Fission and fusion both liberate energy': James Merrill, Jorie Graham, and the metaphoric imagination. TCL (51:2) 2005, 142–78.

18190. MATERER, TIMOTHY. Mirrored lives: Elizabeth Bishop and James Merrill. *See* **15494**.

Thomas Merton

18191. ANDERSON, JOHN. The triumph of trying: James Dickey's mystical journey through *The Zodiac*. *See* **16072.**

18192. BARBOUR, JOHN D. The ethics of intercultural travel: Thomas Merton's Asian pilgrimage and Orientalism. Biography (28:1) 2005, 15–26.

18193. —— Thomas Merton's pilgrimage and Orientalism. *In* (pp. 243–59) **12978.**

18194. —— The value of solitude: the ethics and spirituality of aloneness in autobiography. *See* **12179.**

18195. BELCASTRO, DAVID JOSEPH. An obscure theology misread: 2003 bibliographic review. MerA (17) 2004, 256–85 (review-article).

18196. ELIE, PAUL. The life you save may be your own: an American pilgrimage. (Bibl. 2004, 18373.) Rev. by David Joseph Belcastro in MerA (17) 2004, 256–64.

18197. JASPER, DAVID. The sacred desert: religion, literature, art, and culture. *See* **3815.**

18198. KEHOE, DEBORAH P. Early reflections in a 'nothing place': three Gethsemani poems. MerA (17) 2004, 61–75.

18199. KRAMER, VICTOR A. 'A very disciplined person' from Nelson County: an interview with Canon A. M. Allchin about Merton. Ed. and trans. by Glenn Crider. MerA (17) 2004, 235–55.

18200. LEIGH, DAVID. Firewatch in the belly of the whale: imagery of fire, water, and place in *The Sign of Jonas*. MerA (17) 2004, 153–65.

18201. MONTALDO, JONATHAN (introd.); HART, PATRICK (foreword). Thomas Merton's Gethsemani: landscapes of paradise. With an essay by Monica Weis. Lexington: Kentucky UP, 2005. pp. xviii, 157.

18202. STUART, ANGUS F. The geography of solitude: inner space and the sense of place. MerA (17) 2004, 76–87.

18203. SZABO, LYNN R. (ed.). In the dark before dawn: new selected poems of Thomas Merton. Preface by Kathleen Norris. New York: New Directions, 2005. pp. xxxiv, 253. Rev. by James S. Torrens in ANCW (192:16) 2005, 22–3.

W. S. Merwin

18204. BRYSON, J. SCOTT. The west side of any mountain: place, space, and ecopoetry. Iowa City: Iowa UP, 2005. pp. 156.

18205. CLERMONT-FERRAND, MEREDITH. An interview with William Stanley Merwin. ConnR (27:1) 2005, 25–36.

18206. KING, KENNETH. W. S. Merwin's house abroad: the troubadour as householder. KenPR (19) 2004, 17–23.

18207. MERWIN, W. S. Summer doorways: a memoir. Washington, DC: Shoemaker & Hoard, 2005. pp. 216.

18208. —— Unframed originals: recollections. Washington, DC: Shoemaker & Hoard, 2005. pp. xvi, 236.

John Metcalf

18209. METCALF, JOHN. An aesthetic underground: a literary memoir. (Bibl. 2003, 18409.) Rev. by Bronwyn Drainie in LRC (11:5) 2003, 12–13.

Anne Michaels (b.1958)

18210. WARKENTIN, GERMAINE.   Mapping Wonderland: the city of Toronto as seen through its writers' eyes. *See* **19968**.

Oscar Micheaux

18211. ALLMENDINGER, BLAKE.   Imagining the African American West. *See* **12544**.

18212. MCGILLIGAN, PATRICK.   Me and Oscar Micheaux: an interview with LeRoy Collins. *See* **13914**.

James A. Michener

18213. MAY, STEPHEN J.   Michener: a writer's journey. Foreword by Valerie Hemingway. Norman: Oklahoma UP, 2005. pp. xx, 339.

Christopher Middleton (b.1926)

18214. ANON.   Christopher Middleton: bibliography, 1962–2002. ChiR (51:1/2) 2005, 132–7.

18215. ENDRES, CLIFFORD.   Travelling in Turkey with Christopher M. ChiR (51:1/2) 2005, 101–11.

18216. GHOSE, ZULFIKAR.   Christopher Middleton and 'the bare bone of creation'. ChiR (51:1/2) 2005, 49–58.

18217. HARRIS, TIMOTHY.   Elsewhere. ChiR (51:1/2) 2005, 71–5. (European Modernism.)

18218. KLEINZAHLER, AUGUST.   Dance of the intellect. ChiR (51:1/2) 2005, 41–8.

18219. KOCIEJOWSKI, MARIUS.   C.M.: a portrait. ChiR (51:1/2) 2005, 80–9.

18220. LEVIN, GABRIEL.   Middleton in Asia Minor. ChiR (51:1/2) 2005, 112–24.

18221. MIDDLETON, CHRISTOPHER.   A retrospective sketch. ChiR (51:1/2) 2005, 11–16.

China Miéville

18222. AICHELE, GEORGE.   Dark conceptions; or, The birth of a messiah in *King Rat* and the Gospel of Luke. Foundation (95) 2005, 62–70.

18223. FREEDMAN, CARL.   To the Perdido Street station: the representation of revolution in China Miéville's *Iron Council*. Extrapolation (46:2) 2005, 235–48.

Emma Bell Miles

18224. BROSI, GEORGE.   Emma Bell Miles: bibliography. AppH (33:4) 2005, 25.

18225. ——   The heart-wrenching life of Emma Bell Miles. AppH (33:4) 2005, 11–21.

Josephine Miles (b.1911)

18226. MULLER, ERIK.   Josephine Miles. Boise, ID: Boise State Univ., 2005. pp. 48. (Boise State Univ. Western writers, 164.)

Edna St Vincent Millay ('Nancy Boyd')

18227. BRANDT, LINE; BRANDT, PER AAGE.   Cognitive poetics and imagery. EJES (9:2) 2005, 117–30.

18228. Schürer, Norbert.   Millay's *What Lips My Lips Have Kissed, and Where, and Why.* Exp (63:2) 2005, 94–6.

Arthur Miller

18229. Benziman, Galia.   Success, law, and the law of success: reevaluating *Death of a Salesman*'s treatment of the American Dream. SAtlR (70:2) 2005, 20–40.

18230. Bigsby, Christopher.   Arthur Miller: a critical study. Cambridge; New York: CUP, 2005. pp. x, 514.

18231. —— (ed.).   Remembering Arthur Miller. London: Methuen in assn with the Arthur Miller Centre for American Studies, 2005. pp. 305.

18232. Brater, Enoch.   A conversation with Arthur Miller. *In* (pp. 244–55) **18234.**

18233. ——   Early days, early works: Arthur Miller at the University of Michigan. *In* (pp. 1–16) **18234.**

18234. —— (ed.).   Arthur Miller's America: theater & culture in a time of change. Ann Arbor: Michigan UP, 2005. pp. xii, 268. (Theater: theory/text/performance.)

18235. Centola, Steven R.   Arthur Miller and the art of the possible. AmDr (14:1) 2005, 63–86.

18236. Cohn, Ruby.   Manipulating Miller. *In* (pp. 191–201) **18234.**

18237. Denison, Patricia D.   *All My Sons*: competing contexts and comparative scales. *In* (pp. 46–59) **18234.**

18238. Desafy-Grignard, Christiane.   Jewishness and Judaism revisited in two short stories by Arthur Miller: *Monte Sant' Angelo* and *I Don't Need You Any More.* JSSE (43) 2004, 87–106.

18239. Dunkleberger, Amy.   A student's guide to Arthur Miller. Berkeley Heights, NJ: Enslow, 2005. pp. 160. (Understanding literature.)

18240. Ferran, Peter W.   *The American Clock*: 'epic vaudeville'. *In* (pp. 153–63) **18234.**

18241. Fuchs, Elinor.   Theorizing *Salesman*. *In* (pp. 219–35) **18234.**

18242. Gagliano, Frank.   The *Timebends* world: prospect for performance. *In* (pp. 17–22) **18234.**

18243. Geis, Deborah R.   In Willy Loman's garden: contemporary re-visions of *Death of a Salesman*. *In* (pp. 202–18) **18234.**

18244. Goldstein, Laurence.   Finishing the picture: Arthur Miller, 1915–2005. MichQR (44:2) 2005, 209–15.

18245. ——   *The Misfits* and American culture. *In* (pp. 109–34) **18234.**

18246. McCormick, Frank.   'Like a diamond shining in the dark': Ben's role in *Death of a Salesman*. NCL (35:2) 2005, 11–12.

18247. Mann, Bruce J.   Teaching the unseen presence in Miller's plays. *In* (pp. 36–45) **18234.**

18248. Marino, Stephen A.   Language and metaphor in Arthur Miller's *After the Fall*. SAtlR (70:2) 2005, 41–56.

18249. OTTEN, TERRY. The temptation of innocence in the dramas of Arthur Miller. (Bibl. 2004, 18403.) Rev. by Gregory W. Lanier in CompDr (37:1) 2003, 132–5; by Richard Tharp in TJ (57:1) 2005, 141–2.

18250. QUIGLEY, AUSTIN E. Setting the scene: *Death of a Salesman* and *After the Fall*. In (pp. 60–77) **18234.**

18251. SCANLAN, ROBERT. The late plays of Arthur Miller. In (pp. 180–90) **18234.**

18252. SELL, MIKE. Arthur Miller and the drama of American liberalism. In (pp. 23–35) **18234.**

18253. SMITH, WENDY. Miller's tale: the playwright drew a line between reaching out and selling out. ASch (74:2) 2005, 121–5.

18254. SOFER, ANDREW. From technology to trope: *The Archbishop's Ceiling* and Miller's prismatic drama. In (pp. 94–108) **18234.**

18255. TALLACK, DOUGLAS. 'Moving inward as well as north': the historical imagination in Arthur Miller's *The Crucible* and *Timebends*. FLS (114) 2005, 8–15.

18256. THOMPSON, TERRY W. Miller's *Death of a Salesman*. Exp (63:4) 2005, 244–7.

18257. ZINMAN, TOBY. 'Vaudeville at the edge of the cliff'. In (pp. 164–73) **18234.**

Henry Miller

18258. GUÉTIN, NICOLE. Éros et les romanciers des années trente. See **19614.**

May Miller

18259. HAGOOD, TAYLOR. Dramatic deception and Black identity in *The First One* and *Riding the Goat*. See **17131.**

Walter M. Miller, Jr

18260. COCKRELL, AMANDA. On this enchanted ground: reflections of a Cold War childhood in Russell Hoban's *Riddley Walker* and Walter M. Miller's *A Canticle for Leibowitz*. See **17034.**

Ralph J. Mills (b.1931)

18261. JOHNSTON, DEVIN. Quiet attention: some reflections on the poetry and prose of Ralph J. Mills, Jr, with an interview. ChiR (50:2–4) 2004/05, 157–69.

Hope Mirrlees (1887–1978)

18262. BRIGGS, JULIA. 'Printing hope': Virginia Woolf, Hope Mirrlees, and the iconic imagery of *Paris*. See **20316.**

Rohinton Mistry

18263. BAHRI, DEEPIKA. Native intelligence: aesthetics, politics, and postcolonial literature. (Bibl. 2003, 18448.) Rev. by Bishnupriya Ghosh in MFS (51:1) 2005, 214–17.

18264. JOSEPH, CLARA A. B. Language in contact and literatures in conflict: text, context, and pedagogy. WorldE (24:2) 2005, 131–43.

Jacquelyn Mitchard

18265. ANON. Interview with Jacquelyn Mitchard. WAR (51:3) 2005, 9.

Gary Mitchell

18266. RUSSELL, RICHARD RANKIN. 'Loyal to the truth': Gary Mitchell's aesthetic loyalism in *As the Beast Sleeps* and *The Force of Change*. ModDr (48:1) 2005, 186–201.

Joseph Mitchell (b.1908)

18267. RUNDUS, RAYMOND J. Joseph Mitchell reconsidered. SewR (113:1) 2005, 62–83.

Margaret Mitchell

18268. HOLLAND, SHARON P. The last word on racism: new directions for a critical race theory. *See* **16417.**

18269. STEWART, MART. Teaching *Gone with the Wind* in the Socialist Republic of Vietnam. SoCult (11:3) 2005, 9–34.

W. O. (William Ormond) Mitchell (b.1914)

18270. FILIPCZAK, DOROTA. Not wanted in the canon: Canadian literature in the wilderness. *In* (pp. 55–64) **3756.**

Nancy Mitford

18271. NICULESCU, EMIL. The link between Ronald (*sic*) Pym and 'La Petite Dormeuse' in *Lolita*. *See* **18465.**

18272. THOMPSON, LAURA. Life in a cold climate: Nancy Mitford – a portrait of a contradictory woman. (Bibl. 2003, 18462.) Rev. by Alain Blayac in EA (58:1) 2005, 112–13.

Drusilla Modjeska

18273. HOPKINS, LEKKIE. Finding voice as a postparadigmatic researcher and biographer: writing the self and writing the Other. A/B (19:1/2) 2004, 176–88.

Monique Mojica

18274. LYYTINEN, MARIA. Deconstructing the Pocahontas myth: Monique Mojica's *Princess Pocahontas and the Blue Spots*. *In* (pp. 70–91) **12912.**

Paul Monette

18275. DURÁN, ISABEL. The body as cultural critique in American autobiography. *See* **17849.**

18276. KERMODE, LLOYD EDWARD. Using up words in Paul Monette's AIDS elegy. CanRCL (30:1) 2003, 217–46.

18277. TAYSON, RICHARD. Manly love: Whitman, Ginsberg, Monette. *See* **12350.**

Harriet Monroe

18278. NEWCOMB, JOHN TIMBERMAN. *Poetry*'s opening door: Harriet Monroe and American Modernism. *See* **1284.**

John Montague

18279. REDSHAW, THOMAS DILLON (ed.). Well dreams: essays on John Montague. (Bibl. 2004, 18456.) Rev. by Tyler Farrell in ILS (24:2) 2005, 24–5; by Jefferson Holdridge in SoCR (38:1) 2005, 232–5.

L. M. Montgomery

18280. ALEXANDER, JOY. 'I hear what you say': soundings in L. M. Montgomery's life writing. *In* (pp. 210–21) **18288.**

18281. CAVERT, MARY BETH. Nora, Maud, and Isabel: summoning voices in diaries and memories. *In* (pp. 106–25) **18288.**

18282. DEVEREUX, CECILY. 'See my Journal for the full story': fictions of truth in *Anne of Green Gables* and L. M. Montgomery's journals. *In* (pp. 241–57) **18288.**

18283. DUFFY, DENNIS. The robber baron of Canadian literature. *See* **814.**

18284. EPPERLY, ELIZABETH R. Visual drama: capturing life in L. M. Montgomery's scrapbooks. *In* (pp. 189–209) **18288.**

18285. FIAMENGO, JANICE. '… the refuge of my sick spirit …': L. M. Montgomery and the shadows of depression. *In* (pp. 170–86) **18288.**

18286. GAMMEL, IRENE. 'I loved Herman Leard madly': L. M. Montgomery's confession of desire. *In* (pp. 129–53) **18288.**

18287. —— Life writing as masquerade: the many faces of L. M. Montgomery. *In* (pp. 3–15) **18288.**

18288. —— (ed.). The intimate life of L. M. Montgomery. Toronto; Buffalo, NY; London: Toronto UP, 2005. pp. xii, 305. Rev. by Raymond E. Jones in CLAQ (30:4) 2005, 437–40; by K. L. Poe in Biography (28:4) 2005, 690–3.

18289. GATES, PHILIPPA; GILLIS, STACY. Screening L. M. Montgomery: heritage, nostalgia and national identity. BJCS (17:2) 2004, 186–96.

18290. LISTER, JENNIFER H. The 'secret' diary of Maud Montgomery, aged 28¼. *In* (pp. 88–105) **18288.**

18291. McDONALD-RISSANEN, MARY. Veils and gaps: the private worlds of Amy Andrew and L. M. Montgomery, 1910–1914. *In* (pp. 154–69) **18288.**

18292. PRYCER, MELISSA. The hectic flush: the fiction and reality of consumption in L. M. Montgomery's life. *In* (pp. 258–72) **18288.**

18293. ROBINSON, LAURA. Remodeling *An Old-Fashioned Girl*: troubling girlhood in Ann-Marie MacDonald's *Fall on Your Knees*. *See* **17954.**

18294. RUBIO, MARY; WATERSTON, ELIZABETH. Untangling the web: L. M. Montgomery's later journals and fiction, 1929–1939. *In* (pp. 273–90) **18288.**

18295. SEELYE, JOHN D. Jane Eyre's American daughters: from *The Wide, Wide World* to *Anne of Green Gables*: a study of marginalized maidens and what they mean. *See* **10182.**

18296. TIESSEN, PAUL; TIESSEN, HILDI FROESE. Epistolary performance: writing Mr Weber. *In* (pp. 222–38) **18288.**

Marion Montgomery

18297. JORDAN, MICHAEL M. (ed.). On matters Southern: essays about literature and culture, 1964–2000. By Marion Montgomery. Foreword by Eugene D. Genovese. *See* **3819.**

Anne Moody

18298. ANDREWS, WILLIAM L. In search of a common identity: the self and the South in four Mississippi autobiographies. *In* (pp. 39–56) **12793.**

Brian Moore ('Michael Bryan')

18299. ARROWSMITH, AIDAN. Photographic memories: nostalgia and Irish diaspora writing. *See* **16014.**

George Moore

18300. BASSETT, TROY J. Circulating morals: George Moore's attack on late Victorian literary censorship. PCP (40:2) 2005, 73–89.

18301. FLEMING, BRENDAN. *Mrs Gardiner: a Comedy in One Act* (1888): a play by George Moore. ELT (48:3) 2005, 259–67.

18302. HEILMANN, ANN. Emma Bovary's sisters: infectious desire and female reading appetites in Mary Braddon and George Moore. *See* **10136.**

18303. —— LLEWELLYN, MARK. What Kitty knew: George Moore's John Norton, multiple personality, and the psychopathology of late-Victorian sex crime. NineL (59:3) 2004, 372–403.

18304. LLEWELLYN, MARK. Masculinity, materialism and the introjected self in George Moore's *Mike Fletcher*: 'I'm weary of playing at Faust.' ELT (48:2) 2005, 131–46.

18305. MAYS, J. C. C. (ed.). *Diarmuid and Grania*: manuscript materials. *See* **20515.**

18306. RUSSELL, RICHARD RANKIN. Escaping the examined life in George Moore's *Home Sickness*. JSSE (45) 2005, 29–45.

Marianne Moore

18307. BERGER, CHARLES. The 'not-native' Moore: hybridity and heroism in the thirties. *In* (pp. 150–64) **18316.**

18308. FRIEDLANDER, BENJAMIN. Marianne Moore today. *In* (pp. 222–39) **18316.**

18309. GREEN, FIONA. 'The magnitude of their root systems': *An Octopus* and national character. *In* (pp. 137–49) **18316.**

18310. GREGORY, ELIZABETH. 'Combat cultural': Marianne Moore and the mixed brow. *In* (pp. 208–21) **18316.**

18311. HUBBARD, STACY CARSON. Mannerist Moore: poetry, painting, photography. *In* (pp. 113–36) **18316.**

18312. LADINO, JENNIFER K. Rewriting nature tourism in 'an age of violence': tactical collage in Marianne Moore's *An Octopus*. TCL (51:3) 2005, 285–315.

18313. LEADER, JENNIFER. 'Certain axioms rivaling scriptures': Marianne Moore, Reinhold Niebuhr, and the ethics of engagement. TCL (51:3) 2005, 316–40.

18314. LEAVELL, LINDA. Kirkwood and kindergarten: a Modernist's childhood. *In* (pp. 25–39) **18316.**

18315. —— Marianne Moore, her family, and their language. PAPS (147:2) 2003, 140–9.

18316. —— MILLER, CRISTANNE; SCHULZE, ROBIN G. (eds). Critics and poets on Marianne Moore: 'a right good salvo of barks'. Lewisburg: Bucknell UP; London: Assoc. UPs, 2005. pp. 266.

18317. MEYER, KIMBERLY. Where feeling dwells: on reading Marianne Moore. GaR (57:2) 2003, 256–65.

18318. MILLER, CRISTANNE. Cultures of Modernism: Marianne Moore, Mina Loy, & Elsa Lasker-Schüler: gender and literary community in New York and Berlin. Ann Arbor: Michigan UP, 2005. pp. xii, 267, (plates) 8.

18319. —— 'What is war for?': Moore's development of an ethical poetry. *In* (pp. 56–73) **18316.**

18320. NARDI, PAOLA A. Taking the Potomac cowbirdlike: history through space in Marianne Moore. RSA (14) 2003, 93–119.

18321. NYBERG, LENNART. 'The imagination': a twentieth-century itinerary. *In* (pp. 40–54) **12946.**

18322. O'CONNOR, LAURA. Flamboyant reticence: an Irish *incognita*. *In* (pp. 165–83) **18316.**

18323. POLLAK, VIVIAN R. Moore, Plath, Hughes, and *The Literary Life*. AmLH (17:1) 2005, 95–117.

18324. QIAN, ZHAOMING. Marianne Moore and *The Tao of Painting*. Paideuma (32:1–3) 2003, 245–63.

18325. —— The Modernist response to Chinese art: Pound, Moore, Stevens. (Bibl. 2004, 18478.) Rev. by Lidan Lin in Mod/Mod (12:1) 2005, 196–8.

18326. REHDER, ROBERT. Williams and Moore: wasps, a gentian and real toads. *See* **20217.**

18327. RIEKE, ALISON. 'Plunder' or 'accessibility to experience': consumer culture and Marianne Moore's Modernist self-fashioning. JML (27:1/2) 2003, 149–70.

18328. SCHULZE, ROBIN G. 'Injudicious gardening': Marianne Moore, gender, and the hazards of domestication. *In* (pp. 74–89) **18316.**

18329. WHITE, HEATHER CASS. Relentless accuracy and a capacity for fact: authorship in Marianne Moore and Gertrude Stein. *In* (pp. 98–112) **18316.**

18330. WILLIS, PATRICIA. Marianne Moore and the seventeenth century. *In* (pp. 40–55) **18316.**

18331. WILLIS, PATRICIA C. A Modernist epithalamium: Marianne Moore's *Marriage*. Paideuma (32:1–3) 2003, 265–99.

18332. WILSON, ELIZABETH. El Greco's daughter: necessary deflection in Marianne Moore's *For February 14th* and *Saint Valentine*. *In* (pp. 192–207) **18316.**

Ward Moore

18333. BILSON, FRED. The colonialists' fear of colonisation and the alternate worlds of Ward Moore, Philip K. Dick and Keith Roberts. Foundation (94) 2005, 50–63.

Frank Moorhouse

18334. MOORHOUSE, FRANK. Tales of history and imagination. Meanjin (64:3) 2005, 97–102.

Shani Mootoo

18335. GARVEY, JOHANNA X. K. Complicating categories: 'race' and sexuality in Caribbean women's fiction. JCPS (10:1) 2003, 94–120.

18336. HOVING, ISABEL. Moving the Caribbean landscape: *Cereus Blooms at Night* as a re-imagination of the Caribbean environment. *In* (pp. 154–68) **12632.**

18337. MAY, VIVIAN M. Dislocation and desire in Shani Mootoo's *Cereus Blooms at Night.* SLI (37:2) 2004, 97–122.

18338. PIRBHAI, MIRIAM. Sexuality as (counter)discourse and hybridity as healing practice in Shani Mootoo's *Cereus Blooms at Night.* JCarL (4:1) 2005, 174–84.

Pat Mora

18339. CHRISTIAN, B. MARIE. Many ways to remember: layered time in Mora's *House of Houses.* MELUS (30:1) 2005, 135–48.

Cherríe Moraga

18340. SOTO, SANDRA K. Cherríe Moraga's going brown: 'reading like a queer'. GLQ (11:2) 2005, 237–63.

Edwin Morgan

18341. FABI, SAURO. Sperimentazione e comunicatività: poesia concreta, poesia visiva e il modello degli *Emergent Poems* di Edwin Morgan. *In* (pp. 92–106) **14377.**

18342. FAZZINI, MARCO. Traduzione, rifacimento e scrittura creativa: il castello dei destini incrociati. *In* (pp. 107–16) **14377.**

Marlo Morgan

18343. EUSTACE, JOHN. An unsettling affair: territorial anxieties and the *Mutant Message.* JCL (40:2) 2005, 65–91.

Toshio Mori

18344. ARAKAWA, SUZANNE. Suffering male bodies: representations of dissent and displacement in the internment-themed narratives of John Okada and Toshio Mori. *In* (pp. 183–206) **12775.**

18345. LAWRENCE, KEITH. Toshio Mori, Richard Kim, and the masculine ideal. *In* (pp. 207–28) **12775.**

Willie Morris (1934–1999)

18346. ANDREWS, WILLIAM L. In search of a common identity: the self and the South in four Mississippi autobiographies. *In* (pp. 39–56) **12793.**

Jim Morrison

18347. DAVIS, STEPHEN. Jim Morrison: life, death, legend. (Bibl. 2004, 18508.) Rev. by Mark Kidel in TLS, 28 Jan. 2005, 29.

18348. PUDVA, FEDERICA. *The Devil's party*: Jim Morrison e William Blake. *See* **8383.**

Toni Morrison

18349. BERNARD, EMILY. Unlike many others: exceptional White characters in Harlem renaissance fiction. *See* **19789.**

18350. CLOSSER, RALEEN. Morrison's *Sula.* Exp (63:2) 2005, 111.

18351. COLLINS, MICHAEL. On the phone with composer Bill Banfield: an interview. *See* **17516.**

18352. COONRADT, NICOLE M.   To be loved: Amy Denver and human need – bridges to understanding in Toni Morrison's *Beloved*. ColLit (32:4) 2005, 168–87.

18353. DAUTERICH, EDWARD.   Hybrid expression: orality and literacy in *Jazz* and *Beloved*. MidQ (47:1) 2005, 26–39.

18354. DICKSON-CARR, DARRYL.   The projection of the beast: subverting mythologies in Toni Morrison's *Jazz*. CLAJ (49:2) 2005, 168–83.

18355. ESCODA AGUSTÍ, CLARA.   Strategies of subversion: the deconstruction of madness in *Eva's Man*, *Corregidora*, and *Beloved*. See **17228**.

18356. FRANK, ARMIN PAUL; LOHSE, ROLF (eds).   Internationality in American fiction: Henry James, William Dean Howells, William Faulkner, Toni Morrison. See **16406**.

18357. FULTON, LORIE WATKINS.   Hiding fire and brimstone in lacy groves: the twinned trees of *Beloved*. AAR (39:1/2) 2005, 189–99.

18358. GAUTHIER, MARNI.   The other side of *Paradise*: Toni Morrison's (un)making of mythic history. AAR (39:3) 2005, 395–414.

18359. GOLDSTEIN, PHILIP.   Black feminism and the canon: Faulkner's *Absalom, Absalom!* and Morrison's *Beloved* as gothic romances. See **16412**.

18360. HAYES, ELIZABETH T.   The named and the nameless: Morrison's 124 and Naylor's 'the other place' as semiotic *chorae*. AAR (38:4) 2004, 669–81.

18361. HOLLAND, SHARON P.   The last word on racism: new directions for a critical race theory. See **16417**.

18362. JACKSON, ROBERT.   Seeking the region in American literature and culture: modernity, dissidence, innovation. See **12247**.

18363. JAGGI, MAYA.   An interview with Toni Morrison. Brick (76) 2005, 97–103.

18364. LESEUR, GETA.   'Sweet desolation' and seduction in Toni Morrison's *Jazz*. PCR (16:1) 2005, 21–30.

18365. MESSMER, MARIETTA.   Intra-American internationality: Morrison responding to Faulkner. *In* (pp. 187–242) **16406**.

18366. MIDDLETON, JOYCE IRENE.   Toni Morrison and 'race matters' rhetoric: reading race and Whiteness in visual culture. *In* (pp. 243–53) **2457**.

18367. OKONKWO, CHRISTOPHER N.   A critical divination: reading Sula as *ogbanje-abiku*. AAR (38:4) 2004, 651–68.

18368. O'REILLY, ANDREA.   Toni Morrison and motherhood: a politics of the heart. (Bibl. 2004, 18525.) Rev. by Vanessa K. Valdés in MELUS (30:3) 2005, 259–61.

18369. ROMERO, CHANETTE.   Creating the beloved community: religion, race, and nation in Toni Morrison's *Paradise*. AAR (39:3) 2005, 415–30.

18370. SATHYARAJ, V.; NEELAKANTAN, G.   'Dragon daddies and false-hearted men': patriarchy in Toni Morrison's *Love*. NCL (35:5) 2005, 2–4.

18371. SHIFFMAN, SMADAR.   Someone else's dream? An approach to twentieth-century fantastic fiction. JFA (13:4) 2003, 352–67.

18372. THOMAS, GRISELDA. If you see my scars, you will feel my pain: the significance of scarification in the private narrative fiction of Black women writers. *See* **19969.**

18373. VEGA-GONZÁLEZ, SUSANA. Toni Morrison's *Love* and the trickster paradigm. RAEI (18) 2005, 275–89.

18374. WARDI, ANISSA JANINE. A laying-on of hands: Toni Morrison and the materiality of *Love.* MELUS (30:3) 2005, 201–18.

18375. WASHINGTON, TERESA N. The mother–daughter *Àjé* relationship in Toni Morrison's *Beloved.* AAR (39:1/2) 2005, 171–88.

18376. WATSON, REGINALD. The power of the 'milk' and motherhood: images of deconstruction and reconstruction in Toni Morrison's *Beloved* and Alice Walker's *The Third Life of Grange Copeland.* CLAJ (48:2) 2004, 156–82.

18377. WEATHERS, GLENDA B. Biblical trees, biblical deliverance: literary landscapes of Zora Neale Hurston and Toni Morrison. *See* **17141.**

18378. WEINSTOCK, JEFFREY ANDREW. Ten minutes for seven letters: reading *Beloved*'s epitaph. AQ (61:3) 2005, 129–52.

18379. WICOMB, ZOË. Setting, intertextuality and the resurrection of the postcolonial author. *See* **12083.**

John Mortimer

18380. BUCHANAN, BRAD. A nice point of blood: race and religion in *Rumpole's Return.* *In* (pp. 29–50) **14191.**

J. B. (John Bingham) Morton ('Beachcomber') (1893–1979)

18381. LECERCLE, JEAN-JACQUES. Parody as cultural memory. YREAL (21) 2005, 31–44.

Walter Mosley

18382. FORD, ELISABETH V. Miscounts, loopholes, and flashbacks: strategic evasion in Walter Mosley's detective fiction. Callaloo (28:4) 2005, 1074–90.

18383. MOSLEY, WALTER. The writing life. BkW, 20 Nov. 2005, 10.

18384. SHAPIRO, MICHAEL J. The racial–spatial order and the law: *Devil in a Blue Dress.* *In* (pp. 82–105) **13368.**

Thylias Moss

18385. HAMMER, LANGDON. Invisible things: Thylias Moss and Charles Simic. *See* **19456.**

Andrew Motion

18386. SEEBER, HANS ULRICH. The retrospective attitude in poems by Edward Thomas and Andrew Motion. *See* **19777.**

Stuart Moulthrop

18387. VEEL, KRISTIN. The irreducibility of space: labyrinths, cities, cyberspace. *See* **2506.**

Mourning Dove (Humishuma, Christine Quintasket)

18388. DYMOND, JUSTINE. Modernism(s) inside out: history, space, and modern American Indian subjectivity in *Cogewea, the Half-Blood.* *In* (pp. 297–312) **12640.**

Jennifer Moxley

18389. ALTIERI, CHARLES. Some problems with being contemporary: aging critics, younger poets and the new century. Paideuma (32:1–3) 2003, 387–412.

Malcolm Muggeridge

18390. WALSH, PATRICK J. Malcolm Muggeridge: a modern pilgrim. ModAge (47:2) 2005, 181–4.

Edwin Muir

18391. McCULLOCH, MARGERY PALMER (introd.). For the vernacular circle (*The Bulletin* January 1938): the re-emergence of a long-lost contribution to the *Scott and Scotland* controversy. ScSR (6 :1) 2005, 59–73. (Muir and MacDiarmid on Scots English as a literary language.)

18392. ROBICHAUD, PAUL. MacDiarmid and Muir: Scottish Modernism and the nation as anthropological site. *See* **17944**.

18393. SCHMID, SABINE. 'Keeping the sources pure': the making of George Mackay Brown. *See* **15591**.

Bharati Mukherjee

18394. CRISTIAN, RÉKA MÓNIKA. Border stories and post-nationalist American identities: reading Aurora Levins Morales and Bharati Mukherjee. *In* (pp. 35–42) **3734**.

18395. RASTOGI, PALLAVI. Telling twice-told tales all over again: literary and historical subversion in Bharati Mukherjee's *The Holder of the World*. *In* (pp. 268–84) **9454**.

18396. RAY, BRIAN. Metempsychosis in Bharati Mukherjee's *Jasmine*. NCL (35:2) 2005, 4–6.

Paul Muldoon

18397. ALLEN, MICHAEL. *Pax Hibernica / pax Americana*: rhyme and reconciliation in Muldoon. *In* (pp. 62–95) **18404**.

18398. BERENSMEYER, INGO. Identity or hybridization? Mapping Irish culture in Seamus Heaney and Paul Muldoon. *See* **16935**.

18399. BOYLESTON, J. MATTHEW. To sing the magic words that raise the dead: form and allusion in Paul Muldoon's *Incantata*. SoCR (38:1) 2005, 128–35.

18400. BREARTON, FRAN. For father read mother: Muldoon's antecedents. *In* (pp. 45–61) **18404**.

18401. BURT, STEPHEN. 'Thirteen or fourteen': Paul Muldoon's poetics of adolescence. *In* (pp. 6–25) **18404**.

18402. BUXTON, RACHEL. Never quite showing his hand: Robert Frost and Paul Muldoon. *In* (pp. 26–44) **18404**.

18403. CAMPBELL, MATTHEW. Muldoon's remains. *In* (pp. 170–88) **18404**.

18404. KENDALL, TIM; McDONALD, PETER (eds). Paul Muldoon: critical essays. Liverpool: Liverpool UP, 2004. pp. viii, 192. (Liverpool English texts and studies, 41.) Rev. by Guinn Batten in ILS (25:1) 2005, 28–9.

18405. KERRIGAN, JOHN. Paul Muldoon's transits: muddling through after *Madoc*. *In* (pp. 125–49) **18404**.

18406. LARRISSY, EDWARD. Muldoon's betweenness. Eng (54:209) 2005, 117–33.

18407. LYON, JOHN. 'All that': Muldoon and the vanity of interpretation. *In* (pp. 110–24) **18404**.

18408. O'LEARY, TIMOTHY. Foucault, Dewey, and the experience of literature. NLH (36:4) 2005, 543–57.

18409. REDMOND, JOHN. Muldoon and Pragmatism. *In* (pp. 96–109) **18404**.

18410. TELL, CAROL. Considering classroom communities: Ciaran Carson and Paul Muldoon. *See* **15701**.

18411. WHEATLEY, DAVID. 'All art is a collaboration': Paul Muldoon as librettist. *In* (pp. 150–69) **18404**.

John Mulgan

18412. O'SULLIVAN, VINCENT. Long journey to the border: a life of John Mulgan. (Bibl. 2004, 18555.) Rev. by Jack Ross in WLWE (39:2) 2002/03, 143–6.

Harryette Mullen

18413. CUMMINGS, ALLISON. Public subjects: race and the critical reception of Gwendolyn Brooks, Erica Hunt, and Harryette Mullen. *See* **15583**.

18414. MIX, DEBORAH. Tender revisions: Harryette Mullen's *Trimmings* and *S*PeRM**K*T.* AL (77:1) 2005, 65–92.

John Munonye

18415. PURCELL, WILLIAM F. Contested translations: the gospel *versus* foreign missionaries in John Munonye's *Obi.* ChrisL (54:1) 2004, 15–29.

Alice Munro

18416. DAWSON, CARRIE. Skinned: taxidermy and pedophilia in Alice Munro's *Vandals.* CanL (184) 2005, 69–83.

18417. MAY, CHARLES. Why does Alice Munro write short stories? WasRCPSF (38:1) 2003, 16–28.

18418. SOPER-JONES, ELLA. Wilderness stations: peregrination and homesickness in Alice Munro's *Open Secrets.* WasRCPSF (38:1) 2003, 29–50.

18419. SUTTON, BRIAN. Munro's *How I Met My Husband.* Exp (63:2) 2005, 107–10.

H. H. Munro ('Saki')

18420. GIBSON, BRIAN. Saki's dependent dissidence: exploring *The East Wing.* ELN (42:3) 2005, 39–52.

18421. MAXEY, RUTH. 'Children are given us to discourage our better instincts': the paradoxical treatment of children in Saki's short fiction. JSSE (45) 2005, 47–62.

Iris Murdoch

18422. ANTONACCIO, MARIA. Iris Murdoch's secular theology of culture. LitTheol (18:3) 2004, 271–91.

18423. DOOLEY, GILLIAN. The post-war novel in crisis: three perspectives. AUMLA (104) 2005, 103–19.

18424. —— (ed.). From a tiny corner in the house of fiction: conversations with Iris Murdoch. (Bibl. 2004, 18589.) Rev. by Margaret Moan Rowe in StudN (37:3) 2005, 351–2.

18425. FAN, LINGMEI. *A Severed Head* and Jean-Paul Sartre's existentialism. FLS (116) 2005, 91–4. (In Chinese.)

18426. HE, WEIWEN. *The Unicorn*: pursuit of truth and beauty in a world of contingency. FLS (111) 2005, 45–51. (In Chinese.)

18427. NICOL, BRAN. Iris Murdoch: the retrospective fiction. (Bibl. 2001, 5266.) Basingstoke; New York: Palgrave Macmillan, 2004. pp. xviii, 201. (Second ed.: first ed. 1999.)

18428. WIDDOWS, HEATHER. The moral vision of Iris Murdoch. Aldershot; Burlington, VT: Ashgate, 2005. pp. vii, 182.

Richard Murphy

18429. BACIGALUPO, MASSIMO. Novità su W. B. Yeats. Con testi di Richard Murphy, Seamus Heaney e Jorie Graham. *See* **20480.**

Albert Murray

18430. MAGUIRE, ROBERTA S. *The Seven League Boots*: Albert Murray's 'Swing' poetics. Genre (37:2) 2004, 245–59.

Les A. Murray

18431. CATALANO, GARY. Les Murray's ark. Meanjin (62:1) 2003, 10–18.

18432. HENRIKSEN, LINE. The verse novel as a hybrid genre: monstrous bodies in Anne Carson's *Autobiography of Red* and Les Murray's *Fredy Neptune*. *See* **15697.**

18433. MCCREDDEN, LYN. The impossible infinite: Les Murray, poetry, and the sacred. Antipodes (19:2) 2005, 166–71.

18434. PETERSSON, IRMTRAUD. 'Odysseus from the outback': *Fredy Neptune* in German and its critical reception. ALS (22:1) 2005, 1–28.

18435. —— EICHHORN, THOMAS. Translating *Fredy Neptune*: interview with Thomas Eichhorn. ALS (22:1) 2005, 29–36.

John Middleton Murry (1889–1957)

18436. RICKETTS, HARRY. John Middleton Murry: keeper of the flame. *In* (pp. 106–23) **18084.**

Rosalie Muspratt ('Jasper John') (1906–1976)

18437. NAŁĘCZ-WOJTCZAK, JOLANTA. Facing evil: the motif of temptation in some ghost and vampire stories. *In* (pp. 159–66) **3756.**

Walter Dean Myers

18438. BURSHTEIN, KAREN. Walter Dean Myers. New York: Rosen Central, 2004. pp. 112.

Eileen Myles

18439. TENNANT-MOORE, HANNAH. Eileen Myles' song of the self. GLRW (12:5) 2005, 20–2.

Anton Myrer

18440. COOK, JAMES L. Reproaching the military hero *sans peur*. *See* **3737.**

Vladimir Nabokov

18441. ALEXANDER, VICTORIA N. Nabokov, teleology, and insect mimicry. NabSt (7) 2002/03, 177–213.

18442. ANDREU, ALAIN. *Look at the Harlequins!* Dyslexia and aphasia, a vision through the looking glass. Trans. by Curt Robinson. Nabokovian (55) 2005, 13–20.

18443. —— The tattoo is a Tahitian *vahine* (*Lolita*, part II, chapter 22). Nabokovian (54) 2005, 64–7.

18444. BABIKOV, ANDREY. *The Event* and the main thing in Nabokov's theory of drama. NabSt (7) 2002/03, 151–76.

18445. BASSO, ANN MCCAULEY. Nabokov's *Lolita*. Exp (63:4) 2005, 237–9.

18446. BONTILA, MARIA-RUXANDA. Photograph reading in *Signs and Symbols*. Nabokovian (55) 2005, 44–8.

18447. BOYD, BRIAN. 'Afternote': annotations to *Ada*: 24, Part I chapter 24. Nabokovian (55) 2005, 56–65.

18448. —— Annotations to *Ada*: 24, Part I chapter 24. Nabokovian (54) 2005, 68–92.

18449. —— Annotations to *Ada*: 25, Part I chapter 25. Nabokovian (55) 2005, 66–91.

18450. CAPONI, PAOLO. La commercializzazione di *Lolita*: sulla circolazione dei testi nell'era del mercato globale. Acme (58:1) 2005, 411–19.

18451. CONLEY, TIM. History and denial in Nabokov's *Conversation Piece, 1945*. JSSE (45) 2005, 113–21.

18452. CONNOLLY, JULIAN W. (ed.). The Cambridge companion to Nabokov. Cambridge; New York: CUP, 2005. pp. xxiii, 258. (Cambridge companions to literature.)

18453. CORNWELL, NEIL. 'A Dorset yokel's knuckles': Thomas Hardy and *Lolita*. Nabokovian (54) 2005, 54–64.

18454. CURTIN, ADRIAN; SHRAYER, MAXIM D. Netting the butterfly man: the significance of Vladimir Nabokov in W. G. Sebald's *The Emigrants*. RelArts (9:3/4) 2005, 258–83.

18455. DE LA DURANTAYE, LELAND. Vladimir Nabokov and Sigmund Freud; or, A particular problem. AI (62:1) 2005, 59–73.

18456. DOLININ, ALEXANDER. What happened to Sally Horner? A real-life source for Vladimir Nabokov's *Lolita*. TLS, 9 Sept. 2005, 11–12.

18457. DRAGUNOIU, DANA. Vladimir Nabokov's *Ada*: art, deception, ethics. ConLit (46:2) 2005, 311–39.

18458. JENKINS, JENNIFER L. Searching high and Lo: unholy quests for Lolita. TCL (51:2) 2005, 210–43.

18459. KUZMANOVICH, ZORAN. 'Just as it was, or perhaps a little more perfect': notes on Nabokov's sources. NabSt (7) 2002/03, 13–32.

18460. LARMOUR, DAVID H. J. (ed.). Discourse & ideology in Nabokov's prose. (Bibl. 2004, 18617.) Rev. by Stephen H. Blackwell in SlavR (62:3) 2003, 634–6.

18461. MAAR, MICHAEL. The two *Lolitas*. Trans. by Perry Anderson. London; New York: Verso, 2005. pp. 107.

18462. MELLO, JANSY. Time before and time after in Nabokov's novels. Nabokovian (55) 2005, 20–9.

18463. NAFISI, AZAR. Reading *Lolita* in Tehran: a memoir in books. New York: Random House, 2003. pp. 347. Rev. by Margaret Atwood in LRC (11:7) 2003, 5–6.

18464. NAIMAN, ERIC. Perversion in *Pnin* (reading Nabokov preposterously). NabSt (7) 2002/03, 89–117.

18465. NICULESCU, EMIL. The link between Ronald (*sic*) Pym and 'La Petite Dormeuse' in *Lolita*. Nabokovian (54) 2005, 51–3.

18466. NORMAN, WILL. *The Real Life of Sebastian Knight* and two stories by Henry James. Nabokovian (55) 2005, 7–13.

18467. SCHARNHORST, GARY. Nabokov and Bret Harte: an overlooked allusion in *Lolita*. Nabokovian (54) 2005, 53–4.

18468. SHAPIRO, GAVRIEL. *La Veneziana* revisited. Nabokovian (55) 2005, 48–55.

18469. —— (ed.). Nabokov at Cornell. (Bibl. 2004, 18627.) Rev. by David Rampton in SlavR (63:2) 2004, 446–7.

18470. SHAPIRO, MICHAEL (ed.). From the critic's workbench: essays in literature and semiotics. By Marianne Shapiro. See **15197**.

18471. SHIGETOSHI, MOROSAKA. The haunted graph: *signifiant* studies of Nakajima, Borges, and Nabokov. CLS (41:4) 2005, 520–45.

18472. SKLYARENKO, ALEXEY. *Ada* as a Russian fairy tale spun by the Phoenix and sung by the Sirin. Nabokovian (55) 2005, 29–44.

18473. —— Some dreams of Alexander Blok as enacted in *Ada* by Van Veen and *vice versa*. Trans. by Sergey Karpukhin. Nabokovian (54) 2005, 16–51.

18474. SOCHER, ABRAHAM P. Shades of Frost: a hidden source for Nabokov's *Pale Fire*. TLS, 1 July 2005, 13–14.

18475. TADEVOSYAN, MARGARIT. *The Road to Nowhere*, a road to *Glory*: Vladimir Nabokov and Aleksandr Grin. MLR (100:2) 2005, 429–43.

18476. TROUSDALE, RACHEL. 'Faragod bless them': Nabokov, spirits, and electricity. NabSt (7) 2002/03, 119–28.

18477. WHALEN-BRIDGE, JOHN. Murderous desire in *Lolita* (with related thoughts on Mailer's *An American Dream*). NabSt (7) 2002/03, 75–88.

18478. WOOD, MICHAEL. The museum of what happens. See **11465**.

18479. WYLLIE, BARBARA. Nabokov at the movies: film perspectives in fiction. Jefferson, NC; London: McFarland, 2003. pp. x, 298. Rev. by Eric Naiman in SEEJ (48:4) 2004, 694–6.

18480. ZWART, JANE. Nabokov's primer: letters and numbers in *The Real Life of Sebastian Knight*. PQ (82:2) 2003, 213–34.

V. S. Naipaul

18481. CHAMBERS, CLAIRE. 'The absolute essentialness of conversations': a discussion with Amitav Ghosh. See **16664**.

18482. DOOLEY, GILLIAN. The post-war novel in crisis: three perspectives. See **18423**.

18483. KELLER, ISABELLE. L'écriture de la vérité révélée; ou, Le récit impossible dans *Among the Believers: an Islamic Journey* de V. S. Naipaul. EREA (3:1) 2005, 67–74.

18484. KHAN, NYLA ALI. The fiction of nationality in an era of transnationalism. *See* **16057.**

18485. VARELA-ZAPATA, JÉSUS. Narratives of displacement: V. S. Naipaul's Indians in exile. RAEI (16) 2003, 269–81.

R. K. Narayan

18486. SHANKAR, S. Midnight's orphans; or, A postcolonialism worth its name. *See* **19279.**

Ogden Nash

18487. PARKER, DOUGLAS M. Ogden Nash: the life and work of America's laureate of light verse. Foreword by Dana Gioia. Chicago, IL: Dee, 2005. pp. xiv, 316. Rev. by Jonathan Yardley in BkW, 8 May 2005, 2; by William H. Pritchard in TLS, 4 Nov. 2005, 7.

Michael Nava

18488. SOTELO, SUSAN BAKER. Chicano detective fiction: a critical study of five novelists. *See* **15153.**

Gloria Naylor

18489. HAYES, ELIZABETH T. The named and the nameless: Morrison's 124 and Naylor's 'the other place' as semiotic *chorae*. *See* **18360.**

18490. IVEY, ADRIANE L. Beyond sacrifice: Gloria Naylor rewrites the Passion. MELUS (30:1) 2005, 85–108.

18491. LAMOTHE, DAPHNE. Gloria Naylor's *Mama Day*: bridging roots and routes. AAR (39:1/2) 2005, 155–69.

Phyllis Reynolds Naylor

18492. JONES, CAROLINE. For adults only? Searching for subjectivity in Phyllis Reynolds Naylor's Alice Series. CLAQ (30:1) 2005, 16–31.

Njabulo S. Ndebele

18493. HELGESSON, STEFAN. Writing in crisis: ethics and history in Gordimer, Ndebele, and Coetzee. *See* **16752.**

Barbara Neely

18494. HATHAWAY, ROSEMARY V. The signifyin(g) detective: Barbara Neely's Blanche White, undercover in plain sight. CritW (46:4) 2005, 320–32.

John G. Neihardt

18495. HOLLOWAY, BRIAN. Interpreting the legacy: John Neihardt and *Black Elk Speaks*. Boulder: Colorado UP, 2003. pp. xiv, 220. Rev. by Dale Stover in GPQ (24:1) 2004, 61–2; by Frances W. Kaye in SAIL (17:1) 2005, 98–101.

18496. MARTÍN JUNQUERA, IMELDA. From *Black Elk Speaks* to *Lakota Woman*: reflections upon modern collaborative Native American autobiography. *See* **14614.**

Antonya Nelson (b.1961)

18497. FEITELL, MERRILL. About Antonya Nelson: a profile. Ploughshares (31:2/3) 2005, 221–5.

18498. NELSON, ANTONYA. Behind the story. *In* (pp. 32–3) **14294**.

Marilyn Nelson (b.1946)

18499. FLYNN, RICHARD; HAGER, KELLY; THOMAS, JOSEPH T., JR. It could be verse: the 2005 *Lion and the Unicorn* Award for Excellence in North American Poetry. LU (29:3) 2005, 427–41.

Richard Nelson (b.1950)

18500. ANON. In conversation: Michael Frayn and Richard Nelson. *See* **16579**.

E. (Edith) Nesbit (1858–1924)

18501. BAVIDGE, JENNY. Treasure seekers in the city: London in the novels of E. Nesbit. *In* (pp. 45–59) **14254**.

18502. NOIMANN, CHAMUTAL. 'Poke your finger into the soft round dough': the absent father and political reform in Edith Nesbit's *The Railway Children*. CLAQ (30:4) 2005, 368–85.

18503. PRICKETT, STEPHEN. Victorian fantasy. *See* **9609**.

Susan Neville (b.1951)

18504. NEVILLE, SUSAN. Behind the story. *In* (pp. 321–3) **14294**.

Fae Myenne Ng (b.1956)

18505. CHANG, JULIANA. Melancholic remains: domestic and national secrets in Fae Myenne Ng's *Bone*. MFS (51:1) 2005, 110–33.

Ngũgĩ wa Thiong'o

18506. AMOKO, APOLLO O. The resemblance of colonial mimicry: a revisionary reading of Ngũgĩ wa Thiong'o's *The River Between*. RAL (36:1) 2005, 34–50.

18507. NICHOLLS, BRENDON. The topography of 'woman' in Ngũgĩ's *Weep Not, Child*. JCL (40:3) 2005, 81–101.

Grace Nichols

18508. BRINGAS LÓPEZ, ANA. Representations of Black women in Grace Nichols's poetry: from otherness to empowerment. RAEI (16) 2003, 3–19.

Norman Nicholson

18509. FLETCHER, CHRISTOPHER. Norman Nicholson's *The Blackberry* – a fruitful source for Sylvia Plath? *See* **18816**.

Sir Harold Nicolson

18510. ROSE, NORMAN. Harold Nicolson. London: Cape, 2005. pp. xiii, 384, (plates) 8. Rev. by Richard Mullen in ContRev (287:1677) 2005, 244–5.

Lorine Niedecker

18511. UPTON, LEE. Defensive measures: the poetry of Niedecker, Bishop, Glück, and Carson. *See* **15503**.

Anaïs Nin

18512. TOOKEY, HELEN. Anaïs Nin, fictionality and femininity: playing a thousand roles. (Bibl. 2003, 18714.) Rev. by Jim Stewart in Mod/Mod (12:2) 2005, 359–60.

Gurney Norman

18513. BAYENS, LEAH. The death of the double-minded man; or, Thinking like a mountain: evangelicalism, counter-culture, and strip-mining in *Divine Right's Trip* and *Kinfolks*. AppH (33:3) 2005, 32–8.

18514. BERRY, WENDELL. My conversation with Gurney Norman. AppH (33:3) 2005, 19–21.

18515. BROSI, GEORGE. Gurney Norman. AppH (33:3) 2005, 9–14.

18516. MCCLANAHAN, ED. The story of the story. AppH (33:3) 2005, 26–8.

Frank Norris

18517. BERTE, LEIGH ANN LITWILLER. Mapping *The Octopus*: Frank Norris' naturalist geography. ALR (37:3) 2005, 202–24.

18518. EPERJESI, JOHN R. The imperialist imaginary: visions of Asia and the Pacific in American culture. Foreword by Donald E. Pease. Hanover, NH; London: UP of New England, 2005. pp. xiii, 194.

18519. HSU, HSUAN L. Literature and regional production. *See* 11488.

18520. MCELRATH, JOSEPH R., JR; CRISLER, JESSE S. Frank Norris: a life. Urbana: Illinois UP, 2005. pp. xxii, 492.

Kathleen Norris (b.1947)

18521. OBUCHOWSKI, MARY DEJONG. *The Virgin of Bennington*: Eastern or Midwestern? MidAmerica (30) 2003, 94–9.

Kathleen Thompson Norris (1880–1966)

18522. THORNTON, EDITH. 'Innocence' consumed: packaging Edith Wharton with Kathleen Norris in *Pictorial Review* magazine, 1920–21. *See* 20136.

Mary Norton

18523. O'MALLEY, ANDREW. Mary Norton's 'Borrowers' series and the myth of the paternalist past. ChildLit (31) 2003, 71–89.

Alice Notley (b.1945)

18524. NOTLEY, ALICE. Coming after: essays on poetry. *See* 14466.

Louis Nowra

18525. PELAN, REBECCA. Identity performance in Northern Ireland and Australia: *The Belle of the Belfast City* and *Radiance*. *See* 19037.

Sir Alfred Noyes

18526. POTTER, LOIS. Robin Hood and the fairies: Alfred Noyes' *Sherwood*. *In* (pp. 167–80) 3576.

Bruce Nugent (1906–1987)

18527. GOESER, CAROLINE. The case of *Ebony and Topaz*: racial and sexual hybridity in Harlem renaissance illustrations. *See* 1208.

Sigrid Nunez

18528. FACHINGER, PETRA. German mothers, New World daughters: Angelika Fremd's *Heartland* and Sigrid Nunez's *A Feather on the Breath of God*. CritW (46:3) 2005, 253–66.

Elizabeth Nuñez-Harrell

18529. RAHMING, MELVIN B. Theorizing spirit: the critical challenge of Elizabeth Nuñez's *When Rocks Dance* and *Beyond the Limbo Silence*. SLI (37:2) 2004, 1–19.

Nkem Nwankwo (b.1936)

18530. LYNN, THOMAS J. Tricksters don't walk the dogma: Nkem Nwankwo's *Danda*. ColLit (32:3) 2005, 1–20.

Flora Nwapa

18531. SILKÜ, REZZAN KOCAÖNER. Postcolonial feminist discourse in Flora Nwapa's *Women Are Different*. WLWE (40:1) 2002/03, 125–35.

Robert Nye

18532. MUÑOZ VALDIVIESO, SOFÍA. Postmodern recreations of the Renaissance: Robert Nye's fictional biographies of William Shakespeare. SEDERI (15) 2005, 43–62.

Joyce Carol Oates

18533. COLOGNE-BROOKES, GAVIN. Dark eyes on America: the novels of Joyce Carol Oates. Baton Rouge: Louisiana State UP, 2005. pp. xii, 282.

18534. CRUISE, JAMES. *Where Are You Going, Where Have You Been?* and Cold War hermeneutics. SCR (22:2) 2005, 95–109.

18535. JUNCKER, CLARA. Real Marilyns. *See* **18054**.

18536. MUZAFFAR, HANAN. Violence as proof of existence: Joyce Carol Oates and the construction of Shelley the schizoid. AmJP (65:2) 2005, 189–96.

18537. SCHILLING, TIMOTHY P. The shape of our despair: the fiction of Joyce Carol Oates. Cweal (132:13) 2005, 21–3.

18538. THURSCHWELL, PAMELA. 'A different baby blue'. *In* (pp. 253–73) **16207**.

Achy Obejas (b.1956)

18539. JOHNSON, KELLI LYON. Lost in El Olvido: translation and collective memory in Achy Obejas's *Days of Awe*. BR (27:1) 2003, 34–44.

Patrick O'Brian

18540. SIMMONS, JAMES R., JR. Did Willoughby join the Navy? Patrick O'Brian's thirty-year homage to Jane Austen. *See* **10045**.

18541. TOLSTOY, NIKOLAI. Patrick O'Brian: the making of the novelist, 1914–1949. London: Arrow, 2005. pp. xv, 512, (plates) 16.

'Flann O'Brien' (Brian O'Nolan, 'Myles na gCopaleen')

18542. FOLEY, JOHN. The historical origins of Flann O'Brien's Jem Casey. NQ (52:1) 2005, 97–9.

18543. JOUSNI, STÉPHANE. Écrire Dublin après Joyce. *See* **17292**.

18544. MURPHY, NEIL. Flann O'Brien. RCF (25:3) 2005, 7–41.

Tim O'Brien

18545. DALEY, CHRIS. The 'atrocious privilege': bearing witness to war and atrocity in O'Brien, Levi, and Remarque. *In* (pp. 182–201) **14645**.

18546. FARRELL, SUSAN. Tim O'Brien and gender: a defense of *The Things They Carried*. CEACrit (66:1) 2003, 1–21.

18547. KAUFMANN, MICHAEL. The solace of bad form: Tim O'Brien's postmodernist revisions of Vietnam in *Speaking of Courage*. CritW (46:4) 2005, 333–43.

18548. SMITH, PATRICK A. Tim O'Brien: a critical companion. Westport, CT; London: Greenwood Press, 2005. pp. xi, 181. (Critical companions to popular contemporary writers.)

18549. TUTTLE, JON. How you get that story: Heisenberg's Uncertainty Principle and the literature of the Vietnam War. *See* **16808**.

Sean O'Casey

18550. HARRIS, PETER JAMES. Sean O'Casey's letters and autobiographies: reflections of a radical ambivalence. Trier: WVT, 2004. pp. 193. (Schriftenreihe Literaturwissenschaft, 66.) Rev. by Paul O'Brien in ILS (24:2) 2005, 17.

18551. MURRAY, CHRISTOPHER. Sean O'Casey, writer at work: a biography. Dublin: Gill & Macmillan, 2004. pp. xvi, 590, (plates) 32. Rev. by Paul O'Brien in CJIS (30:2) 2004, 75–6.

Edwin O'Connor

18552. DUFFY, CHARLES F. A family of his own: a life of Edwin O'Connor. (Bibl. 2004, 18721.) Rev. by James Silas Rogers in ILS (25:1) 2005, 23.

Flannery O'Connor

18553. BOSCO, MARK. Consenting to love: autobiographical roots of *Good Country People*. SoR (41:2) 2005, 283–95.

18554. CARUSO, TERESA (ed.). 'On the subject of the feminist business': re-reading Flannery O'Connor. (Bibl. 2004, 18728.) Rev. by Sheila Coghill in FOR (3) 2005, 110–14.

18555. DOBROTT, GRETCHEN. A promising future: Flannery O'Connor in Spain. FOR (3) 2005, 73–5.

18556. EDGECOMBE, RODNEY STENNING. O'Connor's *A Good Man Is Hard to Find*. Exp (64:1) 2005, 56–8.

18557. FEITH, MICHEL. The stained-glass man: word and icon in Flannery O'Connor's *Parker's Back*. JSSE (45) 2005, 95–111.

18558. FOLKS, JEFFREY J. Flannery O'Connor in her letters: 'a refugee from deep thought'. ModAge (47:2) 2005, 176–80.

18559. HADDOX, THOMAS F. The city reconsidered: problems and possibilities of urban community in *A Stroke of Good Fortune* and *The Artificial Nigger*. FOR (3) 2005, 4–18.

18560. HARDY, DONALD E. Collocational analysis as a stylistic discovery procedure: the case of Flannery O'Connor's *eyes*. Style (38:4) 2004, 410–27.

18561. —— Narrating knowledge in Flannery O'Connor's fiction. (Bibl. 2004, 18747.) Rev. by Sura P. Rath in SCR (22:1) 2005, 129–30.

18562. JACKSON, ROBERT. Seeking the region in American literature and culture: modernity, dissidence, innovation. *See* **12247**.

18563. JORDAN, MICHAEL M. Flannery O'Connor's writing: a guide for the perplexed. ModAge (47:1) 2005, 48–57.

18564. KAHANE, CLAIRE. The re-vision of rage: Flannery O'Connor and me. MassR (46:3) 2005, 439–61.

18565. LAKE, CHRISTINA BIEBER. The incarnational art of Flannery O'Connor. Macon, GA: Mercer UP, 2005. pp. 258.

18566. LAWLER, PETER AUGUSTINE. A story about nothing: two kinds of nihilists and one kind of Christian in Flannery O'Connor's *Good Country People*. *In* (pp. 97–116) **14121**.

18567. LEWIS, HELEN MATTHEWS. GSCW in the 1940s: Mary Flannery was there too. FOR (3) 2005, 49–58. (O'Connor's schooldays.)

18568. LOTT, BRET. The dirt at Andalusia. FOR (3) 2005, 1–3.

18569. MCDERMOTT, JOHN V. Blame *versus* blameful corruption in Flannery O'Connor's *The Comforts of Home*. NCL (35:5) 2005, 6–7.

18570. MAGEE, ROSEMARY M.; WRIGHT, EMILY. A good guide: a final conversation with Sally Fitzgerald. FOR (3) 2005, 19–38. (Fitzgerald's work as editor and translator.)

18571. MOSER, BARRY. From where it is to where it ain't: illustration as an act of vision. FOR (3) 2005, 76–83.

18572. MURPHY, JOSEPH C. Strange capabilities: grace, space, and Modernism in the short fiction of Flannery O'Connor and Leo Tolstoy. LitB (24:1/2) 2004, 216–38.

18573. O'GORMAN, FARRELL. Peculiar crossroads: Flannery O'Connor, Walker Percy, and Catholic vision in postwar Southern fiction. Baton Rouge: Louisiana State UP, 2004. pp. ix, 259. (Southern literary studies.) Rev. by J. Robert Baker in ChrisL (54:1) 2004, 111–21; by Gary M. Ciuba in FOR (3) 2005, 115–17.

18574. PETERS, JASON. O'Connor's *Wise Blood*. Exp (63:3) 2005, 179–81.

18575. —— The source of Flannery O'Connor's 'flung' fish in *The Violent Bear It Away*. ANQ (18:4) 2005, 48–53.

18576. PRENATT, DIANE. Simulation and authentic self: issues of identity in works by Flannery O'Connor and Mary Gordon. FOR (3) 2005, 39–48.

18577. ROBILLARD, DOUGLAS, JR (ed.). The critical response to Flannery O'Connor. Westport, CT; London: Praeger, 2004. pp. xxiii, 317. (Critical responses in arts and letters, 43.)

18578. SIMPSON, MELISSA. Flannery O'Connor: a biography. Westport, CT; London: Greenwood Press, 2005. pp. xii, 125. (Greenwood biographies.)

18579. SRIGLEY, SUSAN. Flannery O'Connor's sacramental art. Notre Dame, IN: Notre Dame UP, 2004. pp. xii, 195. Rev. by George Kilcourse in ANCW (192:16) 2005, 18–19; by Louis A. DelFra in ReLit (37:3) 2005, 152–3.

18580. STEED, J. P. 'Through our laughter we are involved': Bergsonian humor in Flannery O'Connor's fiction. MidQ (46:3) 2005, 299–313.

18581. Sun, Lili. A sinners' world where a good man is hard to find: Flannery O'Connor's view of Original Sin in her short stories. FLS (111) 2005, 86–91. (In Chinese.)

18582. Wen, Patrick. The terror of neutrality: civil rights, tortured quietism, and the tactical disengagement of Flannery O'Connor. SPC (28:2) 2005, 121–47.

18583. Whitt, Margaret Earley. 1963, a pivotal year: Flannery O'Connor and the Civil Rights Movement. FOR (3) 2005, 59–72.

18584. Wood, Ralph C. Flannery O'Connor and the Christ-haunted South. (Bibl. 2004, 18759.) Rev. by J. Robert Baker in ChrisL (54:1) 2004, 111–21; by Sarah Gordon in FOR (3) 2005, 102–9.

18585. —— Flannery O'Connor's witness to the gospel of life. ModAge (47:4) 2005, 321–9.

Joseph O'Connor (b.1963)

18586. Estévez-Saá, José Manuel. An interview with Joseph O'Connor. ConLit (46:2) 2005, 160–75.

Clifford Odets

18587. Herr, Christopher J. Clifford Odets and American political theatre. (Bibl. 2004, 18764.) Rev. by Kurt A. Edwards in TJ (57:1) 2005, 140–1.

Frank J. Hugh O'Donnell (1894–1976)

18588. De Giacomo, Albert J.; Friddle, Jonas. Frank J. Hugh O'Donnell (1894–1976): toward a Ministry of Arts and a Federation of Irish Amateur Drama. NewHR (9:1) 2005, 24–38.

Peadar O'Donnell

18589. Kerwin, William. Rhythms of the political: Peadar O'Donnell's rural fiction. NewHR (9:2) 2005, 111–24.

Bernard O'Dowd

18590. Bongiorno, Frank. Reputation of a romantic. Meanjin (62:2) 2003, 137–51.

Dennis O'Driscoll

18591. O'Driscoll, Dennis. The Library of Adventure. NewHR (9:1) 2005, 9–23.

Seán O'Faoláin (b.1900)

18592. Chaussinand, Christelle. Fenêtres sur couples: trois nouvelles de Seán O'Faoláin. EtIr (28:1) 2003, 45–64.

18593. McCaffrey, Lawrence J. Seán O'Faoláin and Irish identity. NewHR (9:4) 2005, 144–56.

18594. Shovlin, Frank. The struggle for form: Seán O'Faoláin's autobiographies. YES (35) 2005, 161–70.

Chris Offutt (b.1958)

18595. Offutt, Chris. Telling stories in my head. *In* (pp. 169–72) **14204.**

Liam O'Flaherty

18596. Levy, Eric P. The literary depiction of ontological shock. *See* **15403.**

18597. PHILLIPS, TERRY.   A study in grotesques: transformations of the human in the writing of Liam O'Flaherty. GothS (7:1) 2005, 41–52.

Timothy O'Grady (b.1951)

18598. ARROWSMITH, AIDAN.   Photographic memories: nostalgia and Irish diaspora writing. *See* **16014.**

Andrew O'Hagan (b.1968)

18599. MCGONIGAL, JAMES.   Literacy, technology and memory in three Scots Irish novels. *See* **17983.**

Frank O'Hara

18600. HARTMAN, ANNE.   Confessional counterpublics in Frank O'Hara and Allen Ginsberg. JML (28:4) 2005, 40–56.

18601. MARTINY, ERIK.   'There I could never be a boy': Frank O'Hara and the cult of the child. CamQ (34:1) 2005, 23–32.

18602. YAU, JOHN.   At the movies with Weldon Kees and Frank O'Hara. *See* **17378.**

18603. —— The poet as art critic. *See* **15200.**

John Okada

18604. ARAKAWA, SUZANNE.   Suffering male bodies: representations of dissent and displacement in the internment-themed narratives of John Okada and Toshio Mori. *In* (pp. 183–206) **12775.**

Ben Okri

18605. MCCABE, DOUGLAS.   'Higher realities': New Age spirituality in Ben Okri's *The Famished Road.* RAL (36:4) 2005, 1–21.

Mary Oliver

18606. BRYSON, J. SCOTT.   The west side of any mountain: place, space, and ecopoetry. *See* **18204.**

18607. JOHNSON, MARK.   'Keep looking': Mary Oliver's Emersonian project. MassR (46:1) 2005, 78–98.

Stephen Oliver (b.5 Dec. 1950)

18608. OLIVER, STEPHEN.   The poet as fraud: a composite. Antipodes (19:1) 2005, 22–9.

Lance Olsen (b.1956)

18609. PETROVIC, PAUL.   Between visibility and invisibility: Baudrillard, Jean-Luc Marion, and Lance Olsen's *Girl Imagined by Chance.* Extrapolation (46:2) 2005, 249–58.

Tillie Olsen

18610. WEBER, MYLES.   Consuming silences: how we read authors who don't publish. *See* **19297.**

Charles Olson

18611. BRAM, SHAHAR.   Charles Olson and Alfred North Whitehead: an essay on poetry. Trans. by Batya Stein. Lewisburg, PA: Bucknell UP, 2004. pp. 164.

18612. GRIEVE-CARLSON, GARY.   Trying to read Charles Olson's *The Distances*. MLS (35:2) 2005, 56–69.

18613. HOLLENBERG, DONNA.   'Dancing edgeways': Robert Creeley's role in Denise Levertov's post-war transition. *See* **15960.**

18614. LAVERY, MATTHEW A.   The ontogeny and phylogeny of Mackey's *Song of the Andoumboulou*. *See* **18002.**

18615. MOSSIN, ANDREW.   'In thicket': Charles Olson, Frances Boldereff, Robert Creeley and the crisis of masculinity at mid-century. JML (28:4) 2005, 13–39.

Mary O'Malley

18616. WALL, EAMONN.   From Macchu Picchu to Inis Mór: the poetry of Mary O'Malley. SoCR (38:1) 2005, 118–27.

Michael Ondaatje

18617. BOLLAND, JOHN.   Michael Ondaatje's *Anil's Ghost*: civil wars, mystics, and rationalists. StudCanL (29:2) 2004, 102–21.

18618. CAMPBELL-HALL, DEVON.   Dangerous artisans: anarchic labour in Michael Ondaatje's *The English Patient* and *Anil's Ghost* and Arundhati Roy's *The God of Small Things*. WLWE (40:1) 2002/03, 42–55.

18619. COOK, VICTORIA.   Exploring transnational identities in Ondaatje's *Anil's Ghost*. *In* (pp. 6–15) **18634.**

18620. CURRAN, BEVERLEY.   Ondaatje's *The English Patient* and altered states of narrative. *In* (pp. 16–26) **18634.**

18621. FARRIER, DAVID.   Gesturing towards the local: intimate histories in *Anil's Ghost*. JPW (41:1) 2005, 83–93.

18622. GOLDMAN, MARLENE.   Representations of Buddhism in Ondaatje's *Anil's Ghost*. *In* (pp. 27–37) **18634.**

18623. HASWELL, JANIS; EDWARDS, ELAINE.   The English patient and his narrator: 'opener of the ways'. StudCanL (29:2) 2004, 122–40.

18624. HILGER, STEPHANIE M.   Ondaatje's *The English Patient* and rewriting history. *In* (pp. 38–48) **18634.**

18625. HSU, HSUAN.   Post-nationalism and the cinematic apparatus in Minghella's adaptation of Ondaatje's *The English Patient*. *In* (pp. 49–61) **18634.**

18626. LOWRY, GLEN.   The representation of 'race' in Ondaatje's *In the Skin of a Lion*. *In* (pp. 62–72) **18634.**

18627. SAKLOFSKE, JON.   The motif of the collector and implications of historical appropriation in Ondaatje's novels. *In* (pp. 73–82) **18634.**

18628. SANGHERA, SANDEEP.   Touching the language of citizenship in Ondaatje's *Anil's Ghost*. *In* (pp. 83–91) **18634.**

18629. SIEMERLING, WINFRIED.   Oral history and the writing of the Other in Ondaatje's *In the Skin of a Lion*. *In* (pp. 92–103) **18634.**

18630. SOLECKI, SAM.   Ragas of longing: the poetry of Michael Ondaatje. (Bibl. 2004, 18811.) Rev. by Gillian Roberts in LitTheol (19:1) 2005, 89–91.

18631. STOLAR, BATIA BOE.   Building and living the immigrant city: Michael Ondaatje's and Austin Clarke's Toronto. *In* (pp. 122–41) **9243.**

18632. SUMMERS-BREMNER, ELUNED. Reading Ondaatje's poetry. *In* (pp. 104–14) **18634.**

18633. TÖTÖSY DE ZEPETNEK, STEVEN. Ondaatje's *The English Patient* and questions of history. *In* (pp. 115–31) **18634.**

18634. —— (ed.). Comparative cultural studies and Michael Ondaatje's writing. West Lafayette, IN: Purdue UP, 2005. pp. 147. (Comparative cultural studies.)

18635. WARKENTIN, GERMAINE. Mapping Wonderland: the city of Toronto as seen through its writers' eyes. *See* **19968.**

Eugene O'Neill

18636. ALEXANDER, DORIS. Eugene O'Neill's last plays: separating art from autobiography. Athens; London: Georgia UP, 2005. pp. ix, 246.

18637. BARLOW, JUDITH E. Influence, echo and coincidence: O'Neill and the Provincetown's women writers. EOR (27) 2005, 22–8.

18638. BLACK, STEPHEN A. *Mourning Becomes Electra* at 74. EOR (27) 2005, 115–25.

18639. COMBS, ROBERT. Affinities between the poetry of Hart Crane and the plays of Eugene O'Neill. EOR (27) 2005, 51–60.

18640. CORNWELL, PAUL. American drama at the Cambridge Festival Theatre, 1928–1935. EOR (27) 2005, 61–75.

18641. DUGAN, LAWRENCE. The Tyrone anthology: authority in the last act of *Long Day's Journey into Night*. CompDr (37:3/4) 2003/04, 379–95.

18642. FRANK, GLENDA. Fractured comedy: a glimpse into Eugene O'Neill's tragic constructs. EOR (27) 2005, 135–51.

18643. GARVEY, SHEILA HICKEY. O'Neill's bridge. EOR (27) 2005, 98–114.

18644. KING, WILLIAM DAVIES. Oresteian structures in *The Iceman Cometh*. EOR (27) 2005, 126–34.

18645. McCOWN, CYNTHIA. All the wrong dreams: *Marco Millions* and the acquisitive instinct. EOR (27) 2005, 152–62.

18646. MANUEL, CARME. A ghost in the Expressionist jungle of O'Neill's *The Emperor Jones*. AAR (39:1/2) 2005, 67–85.

18647. PORTER, LAURIN. 'The end of the quest': freedom and selfhood in O'Neill's late plays. EOR (27) 2005, 163–71.

18648. PORTER, THOMAS E. The *magna mater*: the maternal goddess in O'Neill's plays. EOR (27) 2005, 41–50.

18649. RICHTER, ROBERT A. Eugene O'Neill and 'dat ole davil sea': maritime influences in the life and works of Eugene O'Neill. Mystic, CT: Mystic Seaport, 2004. pp. 160. Rev. by Kurt Eisen in EOR (27) 2005, 172–5.

18650. ROAZEN, PAUL. Eugene O'Neill and Louise Bryant: new documents. EOR (27) 2005, 29–40.

18651. SHEA, LAURA. O'Neill, the Theatre Guild, and *A Moon for the Misbegotten*. EOR (27) 2005, 76–97.

18652. STEFANELLI, MARIA ANITA. Satiri e capriole sotto gli olmi di O'Neill. LAm (24:101) 2004, 121–42.

18653. BEN-ZVI, LINDA. The Provincetown Players: the success that failed. EOR (27) 2005, 9–21.

George Oppen

18654. BURT, STEPHEN.   Shipwrecked singular. TLS, 15 Apr. 2005, 25 (review-article).

18655. ESTEVE, MARY.   Shipwreck and autonomy: Rawls, Riesman, and Oppen in the 1960s. YJC (18:2) 2005, 323–49.

18656. HELLER, MICHAEL.   Speaking the estranged: Oppen's poetics of the word. ChiR (50:2–4) 2005, 137–50.

18657. NICHOLLS, PETER.   George Oppen and 'that primitive, Hegel'. Paideuma (32:1–3) 2003, 351–75.

18658. —— George Oppen: the new or the avant-garde? JML (28:4) 2005, 1–12.

Dael Orlandersmith

18659. COHEN, PATRICIA.   Guild seminar: race & politics in theater. See **15101**.

Susan Orlean

18660. ORLEAN, SUSAN.   Roads taken (and not). MichQR (44:3) 2005, 443–53.

Simon Ortiz

18661. DUNAWAY, DAVID.   An interview with Simon Ortiz, July 14, 1988. SAIL (16:4) 2004, 12–19.

18662. DUNSMORE, ROGER.   Simon Ortiz and the lyricism of continuance: 'for the sake of the people, for the sake of the land'. SAIL (16:4) 2004, 20–8.

18663. HAFEN, P. JANE.   'Story speaks for us': centering the voice of Simon Ortiz. SAIL (16:4) 2004, 61–7.

18664. HOLLRAH, PATRICE.   Resistance and continuance through cultural connections in Simon J. Ortiz's Out There Somewhere. SAIL (16:4) 2004, 79–88.

18665. MOORE, DAVID L.   'The story goes its own way': Ortiz, nationalism, and the oral poetics of power. SAIL (16:4) 2004, 34–46.

18666. ROEMER, KENNETH M.   A 'touching man' brings Aacqu close. SAIL (16:4) 2004, 68–78.

18667. TOHE, LAURA.   'It was that Indian': Simon Ortiz, activist poet. SAIL (16:4) 2004, 54–6.

18668. WIDER, SARAH ANN.   Maps of the universe. SAIL (16:4) 2004, 29–33.

'George Orwell' (Eric Blair)

18669. BERMAN, RONALD.   Modernity and progress: Fitzgerald, Hemingway, Orwell. See **16484**.

18670. BETENSKY, CAROLYN.   Princes as paupers: pleasure and the imagination of powerlessness. CultC (56) 2004, 129–57.

18671. BHABHA, HOMI K.   Doublespeak and the minority of one. In (pp. 28–37) **18680**.

18672. BURTON, PAUL.   George Orwell and the Classics. CML (25:1) 2005, 53–75.

18673. CONANT, JAMES.   Rorty and Orwell on truth. In (pp. 86–111) **18680**.

18674. CORBALLIS, TIM. Not pornography: reading Orwell's *Nineteen Eighty-Four*. Landfall (209) 2005, 65–74.

18675. CUSHMAN, THOMAS; RODDEN, JOHN (eds). George Orwell: into the twenty-first century. Boulder, CO: Paradigm, 2004. pp. x, 316.

18676. DRABBLE, MARGARET. Of beasts and men: Orwell on beastliness. *In* (pp. 38–48) **18680.**

18677. EPSTEIN, RICHARD A. Does literature work as social science? The case of George Orwell. *In* (pp. 49–69) **18680.**

18678. FEDERICO, ANNETTE. Making do: George Orwell's *Coming Up for Air*. StudN (37:1) 2005, 50–63.

18679. GLEASON, ABBOTT. Puritanism and power politics during the Cold War: George Orwell and historical objectivity. *In* (pp. 73–85) **18680.**

18680. —— GOLDSMITH, JACK; NUSSBAUM, MARTHA C. (eds). On *Nineteen Eighty-Four*: Orwell and our future. Princeton, NJ; Oxford: Princeton UP, 2005. pp. xiv, 312.

18681. HALDANE, JOHN. *Nineteen Eighty-Four*, Catholicism, and the meaning of human sexuality. *In* (pp. 261–75) **18680.**

18682. HARGER-GRINLING, VIRGINIA; JORDAAN, CHANTAL. Fifty years on: *Animal Farm* gets under the skin. JFA (14:2) 2003, 246–54.

18683. HUBBLE, NICK. Imagined and imaginary whales: George Orwell, Benedict Anderson and Salman Rushdie. WLWE (40:1) 2002/03, 29–41.

18684. KERN, ALFRED. About literary wars. *See* **16981.**

18685. LARKIN, EMMA. Finding George Orwell in Burma. London; New York: Penguin, 2005. pp. 294. Rev. by Karen Swenson in NewL (88:3) 2005, 46–7.

18686. LESSIG, LAWRENCE. On the Internet and the benign invasions of *Nineteen Eighty-Four*. *In* (pp. 212–21) **18680.**

18687. MEANS, A. L. A student's guide to George Orwell. Berkeley Heights, NJ: Enslow, 2005. pp. 176. (Understanding literature.)

18688. MEYERS, JEFFREY. George Orwell and the art of writing. KR (27:4) 2005, 92–114.

18689. —— Orwell's *Burmese Days*: a Hindi and Burmese glossary. NCL (35:3) 2005, 2–3.

18690. MILGRAM, SHOSHANA. *Anthem* in the context of related literary works: 'We are not like our brothers.' *In* (pp. 119–70) **19013.**

18691. MURAT, JEAN-CHRISTOPHE. Community-centred *versus* subject-centred representation in the narrative fiction of the 1940s. *See* **14235.**

18692. NUSSBAUM, MARTHA C. The death of pity: Orwell and American political life. *In* (pp. 279–99) **18680.**

18693. POSNER, RICHARD A. Orwell *versus* Huxley: economics, technology, privacy, and satire. *In* (pp. 183–211) **18680.**

18694. PRITCHARD, WILLIAM H. Orwell matters. HR (56:1) 2003, 183–90.

18695. REJALI, DARIUS. Whom do you trust? What do you count on? *In* (pp. 155–79) **18680.**

18696. ROSS, STEPHEN. Authenticity betrayed: the 'idiotic folk' of *Love on the Dole*. *See* **16821.**

18697. ROSSI, JOHN P. Two irascible Englishmen: Mr Waugh and Mr Orwell. JSwest (47:2) 2005, 148–52.

18698. SMITH, JIMMY DEAN. 'A stench in genteel nostrils': the filth motif in George Orwell's cultural travels. KenPR (19) 2004, 43–9.

18699. SMITH, STAN. 'The answer would appear to be a lemon': Rose Macaulay's Civil War. See 17921.

18700. SUNSTEIN, CASS R. Sexual freedom and political freedom. In (pp. 234–41) 18680.

18701. WEST, ROBIN. Sex, law, power, and community. In (pp. 242–60) 18680.

18702. ZIMBARDO, PHILIP G. Mind control in Orwell's Nineteen Eighty-Four: fictional concepts become operational realities in Jim Jones's jungle experiment. In (pp. 127–54) 18680.

John Osborne

18703. SCHLÜSSEL, ANGELIKA. Making a political statement or refusing to grow up – reflections on the situation of the academic youth in postwar British literature. AmJP (65:4) 2005, 381–403.

Femi Osofisan ('Okinba Launko')

18704. RAJI, WUMI. Africanizing Antigone: postcolonial discourse and strategies of indigenizing a Western classic. See 16621.

18705. UKAEGBU, VICTOR. Performing postcolonially: contextual changes in the adaptations of Wole Soyinka's Death and the King's Horseman and Femi Osofisan's Once upon Four Robbers. See 19547.

Wilfred Owen

18706. BROWN, DENNIS. The Regeneration Trilogy: total war, masculinities, anthropologies, and the talking cure. In (pp. 187–202) 15309.

18707. CORCORAN, NEIL. Death's honesty. In (pp. 143–74) 16207.

18708. HECKER, WILLIAM. Finding Wilfred Owen's forwarding address: moving beyond the World War One paradigm. FMLS (41:2) 2005, 136–48.

18709. HIPP, DANIEL. The poetry of shell shock: wartime trauma and healing in Wilfred Owen, Ivor Gurney and Siegfried Sassoon. Jefferson, NC; London: McFarland, 2005. pp. v, 218.

18710. PECHEY, GRAHAM. 'Pharaoh's sjambok': Roy Campbell and the lexicon of emigration. See 15666.

Louis Owens

18711. KILPATRICK, JACQUELYN (ed.). Louis Owens: literary reflections on his life and work. (Bibl. 2004, 18881.) Rev. by Rick Waters in SAIL (17:1) 2005, 110–14; by Kimberly Roppolo in GPQ (25:3) 2005, 200–1; by Lee Schweninger in AICRJ (29:2) 2005, 144–7.

Cynthia Ozick

18712. ANOLIK, RUTH BIENSTOCK. Reviving the golem, revisiting Frankenstein: cultural negotiations in Ozick's The Puttermesser Papers and Piercy's He, She and It. In (pp. 139–59) 12895.

18713. GARRETT, LEAH. Cynthia Ozick's *Envy*: a reconsideration. StudAJL (24) 2005, 60–81.

18714. KATZ, ADAM. Iconoclastic commitments: idolatry and imagination in Cynthia Ozick and Ronald Sukenick. Mosaic (38:3) 2005, 113–29.

18715. OZICK, CYNTHIA. Tradition and (or *versus*) the Jewish writer. *In* (pp. 19–23) 12893.

18716. PINSKER, SANFORD. The tortoise and the hare; or, Philip Roth, Cynthia Ozick, and the vagaries of fiction writing. VQR (81:3) 2005, 214–24.

18717. SCHOETT-KRISTENSEN, LENE. Allegra Goodman's *Kaaterskill Falls*: a liturgical novel. *See* 16748.

18718. SIVAN, MIRIAM. Crossing the abyss: language and the Holocaust in Cynthia Ozick's *The Shawl*. StudAJL (24) 2005, 42–59.

18719. —— Cynthia Ozick's golem: a messianic double. LitTheol (19:1) 2005, 47–59.

18720. WALDEN, DANIEL. Cynthia Ozick's classical feminism. *In* (pp. 35–44) 12895.

Frank G. Paci

18721. PIVATO, JOSEPH (ed.). F. G. Paci: essays on his works. (Bibl. 2003, 18978.) Rev. by Jim Zucchero in CanL (185) 2005, 177–9.

P. K. Page

18722. HULAN, SHELLEY. Canadian Modernism, P. K. Page's *Arras*, and the idea of the emotions. *In* (pp. 331–53) 12739.

18723. SWANN, JANE. Mapping the mind's 'I': vision, perception, and complicity in the early poems of P. K. Page. StudCanL (30:1) 2005, 181–97.

Ty Pak

18724. CHEUNG, KING-KOK. (Mis)interpretations and (in)justice: the 1992 Los Angeles 'riots' and 'Black–Korean conflict'. MELUS (30:3) 2005, 3–40.

Chuck Palahniuk

18725. MENDIETA, EDUARDO. Surviving American culture: on Chuck Palahniuk. PhilL (29:2) 2005, 394–408.

Grace Paley

18726. AARONS, VICTORIA. An old discussion about feminism and Judaism: faith and renewal in Grace Paley's short fiction. *In* (pp. 215–28) 12895.

18727. PALEY, GRACE. Clearing my Jewish throat. *In* (pp. 12–18) 12893.

Michael Palmer (b.1943)

18728. ROSENTHAL, SARAH. The recovery of language: an interview with Michael Palmer. DQ (40:2) 2005, 92–113.

18729. VON HALLBERG, ROBERT. Lyric thinking. *See* 15577.

Américo Paredes

18730. ABRAHAMS, ROGER D. 'I must be doing something right': Don Américo among *los (g)rinches*. WF (64:1/2) 2005, 29–38.

18731. CONWAY, CECELIA. *Ballad of Gregorio Cortez*: a traditional tale for postmodern times. *In* (pp. 112–32) 13950.

18732. LEAL, LUIS. Américo Paredes and the culmination of Chicano folklore studies. WF (64:1/2) 2005, 83–92.

18733. LÓPEZ MORÍN, JOSÉ R. The life and early works of Américo Paredes. WF (64:1/2) 2005, 7–28.

18734. OLGUÍN, B. V. Reassessing *pocho* poetics: Américo Paredes's poetry and the (trans)national question. Aztlan (30:1) 2005, 87–121.

Ruth Park

18735. ROONEY, MONIQUE. Stages of development: remembering old Sydney in Ruth Park's *Playing Beatie Bow* and *A Companion Guide to Sydney*. Southerly (64:3) 2004, 95–105.

Dorothy Parker

18736. ARNER, ROBERT D. Textual transmission and the transformation of texts: on the dialogic margins of Dorothy Parker's *The Waltz*. In (pp. 86–113) 18738.

18737. KINNEY, ARTHUR F. The other Dorothy Parkers. In (pp. 114–26) 18738.

18738. PETTIT, RHONDA S. (ed.). The critical waltz: essays on the work of Dorothy Parker. Madison, NJ: Fairleigh Dickinson UP, 2005. pp. 379.

Robert B. Parker

18739. JAMES, DEAN; FOXWELL, ELIZABETH. The Robert B. Parker companion. New York: Berkley, 2005. pp. 206.

18740. SCHMID, GEORG. Profiling the American detective: Parker's prose on the coded game of sleuth and rogue, and the tradition of the crime story. New York; Frankfurt: Lang, 2004. pp. 269.

18741. TAYLOR, RHONDA HARRIS. 'It's about who controls the information': mystery antagonists and information literacy. See 17430.

Suzan-Lori Parks

18742. FOSTER, VERNA. Suzan-Lori Parks's staging of the Lincoln myth in *The America Play* and *Topdog/Underdog*. JADT (17:3) 2005, 24–35.

18743. FRADEN, RENA. A mid-life critical crisis: chiastic criticism and encounters with the theatrical work of Suzan-Lori Parks. JADT (17:3) 2005, 36–56.

18744. SAAL, ILKA. The politics of mimicry: the minor theater of Suzan-Lori Parks. SAtlR (70:2) 2005, 57–71.

Francine Pascal

18745. THOMPSON, ANNE B. Rereading fifties teen romance: reflections on Janet Lambert. See 17563.

Kenneth Patchen

18746. NELSON, RAYMOND. Patchen's evil book. AmLH (16:3) 2004, 466–86.

Alexs D. Pate (b.1950)

18747. WADE, DEENA. Writing toward home and into exile: a profile of author Alexs D. Pate. BRev (23:1) 2003, 13–14.

Katherine Paterson

18748. McGinty, Alice B.   Katherine Paterson. New York: Rosen Central, 2005. pp. 112. (Library of author biographies.)

Alan Paton

18749. Barnard, Rita.   Oprah's Paton; or, South Africa and the globalization of suffering. ESA (47:1) 2004, 85–107.

James Patterson (b.1947) and Andrew Gross

18750. Taylor, Rhonda Harris.   'It's about who controls the information': mystery antagonists and information literacy. See **17430**.

Tom Paulin

18751. Kirchwey, Karl.   'And the half-true rhyme is love': modern verse drama and the Classics. See **16946**.

Gary Paulsen

18752. Blasingame, James.   Interview with Gary Paulsen. JAAL (48:3) 2004, 270–1.

David Payne

18753. Osborne, Virginia Nickles.   Saving the Outer Banks: discreet consumption in David Payne's *Gravesend Light*. NCLR (14) 2005, 113–22.

Mervyn Peake

18754. Mantrant, Sophie.   Mervyn Peake's Gormenghast novels: a baroque hostility to straight lines. EtBr (28) 2005, 71–82.

18755. Winnington, G. Peter (introd.).   Mervyn Peake's two radio plays for Christmas. PeakeS (9:2) 2005, 5–31.

Donn Pearce (b.1928)

18756. Alsup, Benjamin.   This was a man. Esquire (144:4) 2005, 138–47, 234. (*Cool Hand Luke*.)

Robert Newton Peck

18757. Peck, Robert Newton.   Weeds in bloom: the autobiography of an ordinary man. New York: Random House, 2005. pp. 209.

William Dudley Pelley (b.1890)

18758. Beekman, Scott.   William Dudley Pelley: a life in right-wing extremism and the occult. Syracuse, NY: Syracuse UP, 2005. pp. xvi, 269.

Elizabeth Robins Pennell (1855–1936)

18759. Schaffer, Talia.   The importance of being greedy: connoisseurship and domesticity in the writings of Elizabeth Robins Pennell. *In* (pp. 105–26) **9257**.

Walker Percy

18760. Carpenter, Brian.   A splendor never known: Walker Percy and historic preservation. SoLJ (37:2) 2005, 103–18.

18761. Desmond, John F.   Walker Percy and suicide. JSwest (47:1) 2005, 58–63.

18762. —— Walker Percy's search for community. (Bibl. 2004, 18936.) Rev. by J. Robert Baker in ChrisL (54:1) 2004, 111–21.

18763. DUNNE, SARA LEWIS. Moviegoing in the modern novel: Holden, Binx, Ignatius. SPC (28:1) 2005, 37–47.

18764. HODGES, JOHN O. William Alexander Percy's *Lanterns*: a reply from a Mississippi sharecropper's son. See **18768**.

18765. O'GORMAN, FARRELL. Peculiar crossroads: Flannery O'Connor, Walker Percy, and Catholic vision in postwar Southern fiction. See **18573**.

18766. STEWART, ARTHUR. Charles Sanders Peirce and Walker Percy, MD: interdisciplinary observations on the soul, medicine, and why realism counts. LJH (30:1) 2005, 37–51.

William Alexander Percy (1885–1942)

18767. ANDREWS, WILLIAM L. In search of a common identity: the self and the South in four Mississippi autobiographies. *In* (pp. 39–56) **12793**.

18768. HODGES, JOHN O. William Alexander Percy's *Lanterns*: a reply from a Mississippi sharecropper's son. SoQ (43:1) 2005, 29–48.

Maxwell Perkins

18769. BRUCCOLI, MATTHEW J.; BAUGHMAN, JUDITH S. (eds). The sons of Maxwell Perkins: letters of F. Scott Fitzgerald, Ernest Hemingway, Thomas Wolfe, and their editor. (Bibl. 2004, 18941.) Rev. by Kenneth Panda in HemR (24:1) 2004, 106–10; by Gordon B. Neavill in SHARP (14:3) 2005, 6; by James P. Hammersmith in SoHR (39:3) 2005, 284–7.

18770. TARR, RODGER L. (ed.). As ever yours: the letters of Max Perkins and Elizabeth Lemmon. (Bibl. 2004, 18942.) Rev. by Craig Monk in RMER (59:2) 2005.

Niel Perrin

18771. SMITH, MICHELLE DENISE. Guns, lies, and ice: the Canadian pulp magazine industry and the crime fiction of Raymond Chandler and Niel Perrin. See **15760**.

Saint-John Perse

18772. RIGOLOT, CAROL. Blood brothers: Archibald MacLeish and Saint-John Perse. See **18016**.

Fernando Pessoa (Antonio Nogueira, 'Alexander Search')

18773. RAMALHO SANTOS, IRENE. Modernist muses that matter: inspiration revisited in Pessoa and Stevens. See **19680**.

Julia Mood Peterkin

18774. LEWIS, NGHANA TAMU. The rhetoric of mobility, the politics of consciousness: Julia Mood Peterkin and the case of a White Black writer. AAR (38:4) 2004, 589–608.

'Ellis Peters' (Edith Pargeter)

18775. SONGER, MARCIA J. The ultimate penance of Brother Cadfael. Clues (23:4) 2005, 63–8.

Ann Petry

18776. CRESCENZO, MICHELE. Poor Lutie's almanac: reading and social critique in Ann Petry's *The Street*. *In* (pp. 215–35) **12549**.

18777. ERVIN, HAZEL ARNETT. The critical response to Ann Petry. Westport, CT; London: Praeger, 2005. pp. xxxii, 401. (Critical responses in arts and letters, 44.)

18778. LUCY, ROBIN. Fables of the reconstruction: Black women on the domestic front in Ann Petry's World War II fiction. CLAJ (49:1) 2005, 1–27.

Caryl Phillips

18779. YOUNG, HERSHINI BHANA. Inheriting the criminalized Black body: race, gender, and slavery in *Eva's Man*. See 17229.

Felice Picano (b.1944)

18780. DAVIDSON, GUY. Contagious relations: simulation, paranoia, and the postmodern condition in William Friedkin's *Cruising* and Felice Picano's *The Lure. See* 13529.

Samuel F. Pickering (b.1941)

18781. PICKERING, SAMUEL. On the genteel. MR (28:1) 2005, 190–210.

Marge Piercy

18782. ANOLIK, RUTH BIENSTOCK. Reviving the golem, revisiting *Frankenstein*: cultural negotiations in Ozick's *The Puttermesser Papers* and Piercy's *He, She, and It. In* (pp. 139–59) 12895.

18783. CALVERT, BRONWEN. Cyborg utopia in Marge Piercy's *Body of Glass*. Foundation (95) 2005, 52–61.

18784. KREMER, S. LILLIAN. A feminist interpretation of Jewish history and spirituality: collision and fusion in Marge Piercy's later poetry and fiction. *In* (pp. 160–78) 12895.

Doris Pilkington (b.1937)

18785. LOVROD, MARIE. Shifting contexts, shaping experiences: child abuse survivor narratives and educating for empire. *See* 11980.

Cecile Pineda

18786. BIGGERS, JEFF. Pineda unbound: an interview with Cecile Pineda. BRev (24:5) 2004, 3, 24.

Miguel Piñero

18787. CRUTCHFIELD, JOHN. From cell to celluloid: a dramaturgical note on Miguel Piñero's *Short Eyes. In* (pp. 87–111) 13950.

Robert Pinsky

18788. PASSEY, JOEL. An appetite for art: a conversation with Robert Pinsky. WebS (22:2) 2005, 2–13.

18789. PINSKY, ROBERT. Myths of the workroom. APR (34:3) 2005, 23–4.

Harold Pinter

18790. BATTY, MARK. Staged dialogues with authorship: Pinter and Beckett as directors. PinR (12) 2003/04, 48–60.

18791. BEGLEY, VARUN. The modernist as populist: Pinter's *Betrayal* and mass culture. PinR (12) 2003/04, 83–102.

18792. Burkman, Katherine H.   The contamination of birth by sex and death in the plays of Beckett and Pinter. PinR (12) 2003/04, 39–47.

18793. Connor, Kathleen; Homan, Sidney.   Tears and an actor's discovery: playing Kate in *Old Times*. PinR (12) 2003/04, 156–70.

18794. Fahey, Joseph.   An interview with Pavel Dobrusky and Peter Hackett. PinR (12) 2003/04, 178–86.

18795. Gale, Steven H.   Sharp cut: Harold Pinter's screenplays and the artistic process. (Bibl. 2003, 19088.) Rev. by Christopher C. Hudgins in PinR (12) 2003/04, 216–20; by Stephen C. Behrendt in QRFV (22:1) 2005, 93–5.

18796. Grimes, Charles.   Process and history in Harold Pinter's *Reunion* screenplay. PinR (12) 2003/04, 144–55.

18797. Kane, Leslie (ed.).   The art of crime: the plays and films of Harold Pinter and David Mamet. London; New York: Routledge, 2004. pp. x, 242. (Studies in modern drama.)

18798. Kharoubi, Liza.   'Looking back through smoke': the faces of memory in Harold Pinter's *Old Times*. EtBr (29) 2005, 53–64.

18799. Merritt, Susan Hollis.   'Hurry up please it's time': Pinter past, Pinter present, and Pinter future. PinR (12) 2003/04, 61–82.

18800. —— (comp.).   Harold Pinter bibliography: 2000–2002. PinR (12) 2003/04, 242–300.

18801. Paiva de Oliveira, Ubiratan.   The presence of music in Pinter's works. PinR (12) 2003/2004, 109–22.

18802. Previti, Simona.   Dioniso vestito da servo: la contaminazione della casa da Maugham a Losey. In (pp. 93–103) **14322**.

18803. Smith, Ian (comp.).   Pinter in the theatre. Foreword by Harold Pinter. London: Hern, 2005. pp. 234. (Interviews.) Rev. by Randall Stevenson in TLS, 24 June 2005, 28.

18804. Smith, Susan Harris.   'Pinteresque' in the popular press. PinR (12) 2003/2004, 103–8.

18805. Sofer, Andrew.   The cheese-roll under the cocktail cabinet: Pinter's object lessons. PinR (12) 2003/04, 29–38.

18806. Uchman, Jadwiga.   Harold Pinter's specific brand of the Theatre of the Absurd and his anti-totalitarian plays. In (pp. 258–66) **3756**.

18807. Wixson, Christopher.   'I'm compelled to ask you questions': interrogative comedy and Harold Pinter's *Ashes to Ashes*. PinR (12) 2003/04, 6–28.

18808. Woolf, Henry, *et al.*   Staging Pinter: from pregnant pauses to political causes: a panel. Ed. and transcribed by Susan Hollis Merritt. PinR (12) 2003/04, 123–43.

Ruth Pitter

18809. King, Don W.   Fire and ice: C. S. Lewis and the love poetry of Joy Davidman and Ruth Pitter. *See* **17751**.

Sol T. Plaatje

18810. SEDDON, DEBORAH.   Shakespeare's orality: Solomon Plaatje's Setswana translations. *See* **6073**.

David Plante

18811. PLANTE, DAVID.   American ghosts. Boston, MA: Beacon Press, 2005. pp. 288. (Memoirs.) Rev. by Ronald Wright in TLS, 9 Dec. 2005, 11.

Sylvia Plath

18812. BADIA, JANET.   'One of those people like Anne Sexton or Sylvia Plath': the pathologized woman reader in literary and popular culture. *In* (pp. 236–54) **12549**.

18813. BALDWIN, KATE A.   The radical imaginary of *The Bell Jar*. Novel (38:1) 2004, 21–40.

18814. BENTON, MICHAEL.   Literary biomythography. *See* **4160**.

18815. CLARK, HEATHER.   Tracking the thought-fox: Sylvia Plath's revision of Ted Hughes. JML (28:2) 2005, 100–12.

18816. FLETCHER, CHRISTOPHER.   Norman Nicholson's *The Blackberry* – a fruitful source for Sylvia Plath? NQ (52:4) 2005, 507.

18817. FREEMAN, MARGARET H.   The poem as complex blend: conceptual mappings of metaphor in Sylvia Plath's *The Applicant*. LLit (14:1) 2005, 25–44.

18818. GILBERT, SANDRA M.   The supple suitor: death, women, feminism, and (assisted or unassisted) suicide. *See* **10782**.

18819. GILL, JO.   The influence of Nathaniel Hawthorne's *The Scarlet Letter* on Sylvia Plath's *Daddy*. NQ (52:1) 2005, 107–8.

18820. GORDON, JOHN.   Being Sylvia being Ted being Dylan: Plath's *The Snowman on the Moor*. JML (27:1/2) 2003, 188–92.

18821. HUGHES, FRIEDA (foreword).   *Ariel*: the restored edition. A facsimile of Plath's manuscript, reinstating her original selection and arrangement. (Bibl. 2004, 18984.) Rev. by Anthony J. Cuda in AmBR (26:6) 2005, 19, 24; by Melissa Crowe in GaR (59:3) 2005, 721–6.

18822. KIRK, CONNIE ANN.   Sylvia Plath: a biography. Westport, CT; London: Greenwood Press, 2004. pp. xxiii, 135. (Greenwood biographies.)

18823. LEVIN, DANA.   The heroics of style: a study in three parts. APR (34:3) 2005, 20–2.

18824. MEYERS, JEFFREY.   Sylvia Plath: the paintings in the poems. WI (20:2) 2004, 107–22.

18825. MIDDLEBROOK, DIANE.   Her husband: Hughes and Plath: a marriage. (Bibl. 2004, 18990.) Rev. by Axel Nesme in EREA (2:1) 2004.

18826. MITCHELL, PAUL.   Reading (and) the late poems of Sylvia Plath. MLR (100:1) 2005, 37–50.

18827. PEEL, ROBIN.   The ideological apprenticeship of Sylvia Plath. JML (27:4) 2004, 59–72.

18828. PENG, YU.   The therapeutic value of confessional poems. *See* **17879**.

18829. POLLAK, VIVIAN R.   Moore, Plath, Hughes, and *The Literary Life*. *See* **18323**.

18830. Rosen, David. Maturity and poetic style. *See* **7745.**

18831. Roudeau, Cécile. Crossing the voice, crisscrossing the text: writing at the intersection of prose and poetry in Sylvia Plath's *Sunday at the Mintons*. RSA (15/16) 2004/05, 45–67.

18832. Rudman, Mark. On the road, touch and go, with D. H. Lawrence. *See* **17629.**

18833. St Clair, Pamela. In search of the self: Virginia Woolf's shadow across Sylvia Plath's page. *See* **20412.**

18834. Scott, Jill. Electra after Freud: myth and culture. *See* **6072.**

18835. Shulkes, Debra. Signs not taken for wonders: disavowing the poetic function in the writing of Sylvia Plath. *In* (pp. 155–62) **3734.**

18836. Smith, Ernest. Colossal departures: figuring the lost father in Berryman's and Plath's poetry. *See* **15478.**

18837. Spencer, Luke. Sylvia Plath, Ted Hughes and *Wuthering Heights*: some uses of memory. *In* (pp. 75–85) **10222.**

18838. Upton, Lee. 'I/Have a self to recover': the restored *Ariel*. LitR (48:4) 2005, 260–4.

18839. Wisker, Gina. Viciousness in the kitchen: Sylvia Plath's gothic. GothS (6:1) 2004, 103–17.

Sterling Plumpp (b.1940)

18840. Allen, Jeffrey Renard. 'Distinguished breakage': the jazz poetry of Sterling D. Plumpp. ArkR (36:3) 2005, 198–202.

18841. Antonucci, Michael A. 'Crash down home Blues': Sterling D. Plumpp, Sterling A. Brown and Blues poetics. ArkR (36:3) 2005, 205–11.

18842. Gibbons, Reginald. Conversations with Sterling D. Plumpp. ArkR (36:3) 2005, 182–93.

18843. Harris, Duriel E. Living Blues: an introduction to selected poems by Sterling D. Plumpp. ArkR (36:3) 2005, 177–8.

Cole Porter

18844. Brown, Stephen. Attuned to the moon. TLS, 21 Jan. 2005, 13.

Eleanor H. (Eleanor Hodgman) Porter (1868–1920)

18845. Robinson, Laura. Remodeling *An Old-Fashioned Girl*: troubling girlhood in Ann-Marie MacDonald's *Fall on Your Knees*. *See* **17954.**

Katherine Anne Porter

18846. McDermott, John V. Porter's *Rope*: the symbolic catalyst for self-strangulation. NCL (35:2) 2005, 6–7.

18847. Phillips, Jayne Anne. Guided tours of time and death. *In* (pp. 34–8) **14204.**

18848. Titus, Mary. The ambivalent art of Katherine Anne Porter. Athens; London: Georgia UP, 2005. pp. xii, 252.

18849. Unrue, Darlene Harbour. Katherine Anne Porter: the life of an artist. Jackson; London: Mississippi UP, 2005. pp. xxviii, 381. (Willie Morris books in memoir and biography.)

Charles Portis

18850. TARTT, DONNA. The great abiding pleasure of *True Grit*. Brick (76) 2005, 20–6.

Beatrix Potter

18851. KUTZER, M. DAPHNE. Beatrix Potter: writing in code. (Bibl. 2004, 19014.) Rev. by Margaret Mackey in CLAQ (30:2) 2005, 208–9.

18852. SIKORSKA, MAGDALENA. The stories illustrations tell: the creative illustrating strategy in the pictures by Beatrix Potter and Janosch. NRCLL (11:1) 2005, 1–14.

Ezra Pound

18853. AJI, HÉLÈNE. The subject in the structure: issues of procedure in contemporary American poetry. *See* **19579.**

18854. ALTIERI, CHARLES. The fate of the imaginary in twentieth-century American poetry. *See* **14363.**

18855. BACIGALUPO, MASSIMO. America in Ezra Pound's posthumous cantos. JML (27:1/2) 2003, 90–8.

18856. —— Autobiografia e modernismo in America: il caso Pound. *In* (pp. 261–81) **12577.**

18857. —— History and the American poet. RSA (14) 2003, 3–16.

18858. —— Yeats, Boccaccio, and Leopardi. *See* **20481.**

18859. BADENHAUSEN, RICHARD. T. S. Eliot and the art of collaboration. *See* **16240.**

18860. BARNHISEL, GREGORY. James Laughlin, New Directions, and the remaking of Ezra Pound. *See* **17589.**

18861. BAYES, RONALD. The 'mystery Senator' and E.P.'s release. PemM (37) 2005, 66–9.

18862. BRATCHER, JAMES T. Tennyson's 'hendecasyllabics', Catullus' '*basationes*', and a parody of Ezra Pound. *See* **12134.**

18863. BROOKER, JEWEL SPEARS. To murder and create: ethics and aesthetics in Levinas, Pound, and Eliot. *In* (pp. 55–76) **12946.**

18864. BROWN, STEPHEN. *Hugh Selwyn Mauberley* as Pound's *Sordello*. *In* (pp. 9–20) **3756.**

18865. BUSH, RONALD. Remaking Canto 74. Paideuma (32:1–3) 2003, 157–86.

18866. CASILLO, ROBERT. Ezra Pound, the *prisca theologia*, and the origin of the modern age. LAm (24:101) 2004, 103–20.

18867. DASENBROCK, REED WAY. *Paradiso ma non troppo*: the place of the lyric Dante in the late cantos of Ezra Pound. CL (57:1) 2005, 45–60.

18868. DE GIOVANNI, FLORA. 'Some sort of common bond': the avant-garde and the arts. *In* (pp. 134–43) **3690.**

18869. DEMOOR, MARYSA. From epitaph to obituary: the death politics of T. S. Eliot and Ezra Pound. *See* **16261.**

18870. FERRERO DE LUCA, MARIA COSTANZA (ed.). Ezra Pound e il *Canto dei sette laghi*. Introd. by Massimo Bacigalupo. Afterword by Alessandro Vantaggi. Reggio Emilia: Diabasis, 2004. pp. xii, 112.

18871. FISHER, MARGARET.   Great bass: undertones of continuous influence. PRes (8:1) 2003, 23–40.

18872. FROULA, CHRISTINE.   Hugh Kenner's Modernism and ours. *See* **14793.**

18873. GALLESI, LUCA.   Le origini del fascismo di Ezra Pound. Milan: Ares, 2005. pp. 305. (Poundiana, 3.)

18874. GIORELLO, GIULIO.   Prometeo, Ulisse, Gilgameš: figure del mito. *See* **17280.**

18875. HATLEN, BURTON.   From the transcendental to the immanent sublime: the poetry of William Carlos Williams, 1913–1917. *See* **20212.**

18876. HELLER, MICHAEL.   Ezra Pound's gothic designs on history. NER (26:3) 2005, 99–108.

18877. LAN, FENG.   Ezra Pound / Ming Mao: a liberal disciple of Confucius. JML (27:1/2) 2003, 79–89.

18878. MCCORMICK, JOHN.   Among decadents, heretics, and madmen. *See* **19312.**

18879. MOODY, A. DAVID.   *Directio voluntatis*: Pound's economics in the economy of *The Cantos*. Paideuma (32:1–3) 2003, 187–203.

18880. —— Kipling in Eliot and in Pound: a measure of their difference. *In* (pp. 153–8) **3756.**

18881. NADEL, IRA BRUCE.   Ezra Pound: a literary life. (Bibl. 2004, 19039.) Rev. by John Maerhofer in AmBR (26:5) 2005, 1, 6.

18882. NESME, AXEL.   Intertextual 'tissue preserved': a reading of Ezra Pound's *Hugh Selwyn Mauberley*. EREA (2:1) 2004, 54–60.

18883. PATEY, CAROLINE.   Lungomare, Rapallo: poetiche anglo-provenzali e politica culturale. *In* (pp. 65–82) **12662.**

18884. PAUL, CATHERINE E.   Italian Fascist exhibitions and Ezra Pound's move to the imperial. TCL (51:1) 2005, 64–97.

18885. PERLOFF, MARJORIE.   The search for 'prime words': Pound, Duchamp and the nominalist ethos. Paideuma (32:1–3) 2003, 205–28.

18886. POLIZZOTTI, MARK.   He do the poets in different voices. Parnassus (28:1/2) 2005, 54–71 (review-article).

18887. QIAN, ZHAOMING (ed.).   Ezra Pound and China. (Bibl. 2003, 19182.) Rev. by Robert Kern in Mod/Mod (12:1) 2005, 194–6; by Ian F. A. Bell in MLR (100:4) 2005, 1104–5.

18888. QUINN, WILLIAM A.   Harriet Monroe as queen-critic of Chaucer and Langland (*viz.* Ezra Pound). *See* **4962.**

18889. RHENISCH, HAROLD.   The genesis of Linda Rogers. *In* (pp. 50–73) **19115.**

18890. RICCIARDI, CATERINA (ed.).   Indiscrezioni; o, *Une revue de deux mondes*. Rimini: Raffaelli, 2004. pp. 118. (Quaderni poundiani, 1.)

18891. SHERRY, VINCENT B.   Liberal measures: language, Modernism, and the Great War. *In* (pp. 9–23) **12946.**

18892. SIEBURTH, RICHARD (ed.).   The *Pisan Cantos*. (Bibl. 2004, 19046.) Rev. by David Trotter in LRB (27:13) 2005, 21–3.

18893. —— Poems and translations. (Bibl. 2004, 19047.) Rev. by David Trotter in LRB (27:13) 2005, 21–3; by Mark Polizzotti in Parnassus (28:1/2) 2005, 54–71.

18894. SVENSSON, LARS-HÅKAN. Modernism and the Classical tradition: the examples of Pound and H.D. *In* (pp. 112–31) **12946.**

18895. TIFFANY, DANIEL. Kitsching *The Cantos.* Mod/Mod (12:2) 2005, 329–37.

18896. TREMBLAY, TONY. 'A widening of the northern coterie': the cross-border cultural politics of Ezra Pound, Marshall McLuhan, and Louis Dudek. *In* (pp. 153–77) **12739.**

18897. TROTTER, DAVID. Saved by the ant's fore-foot. LRB (27:13) 2005, 21–3 (review-article). (Editions of Pound.)

18898. TRYPHONOPOULOS, DEMETRES. 'Fragments of a faith forgotten': Ezra Pound, H.D. and the occult tradition. Paideuma (32:1–3) 2003, 229–44.

18899. TRYPHONOPOULOS, DEMETRES P.; ADAMS, STEPHEN J. (eds). The Ezra Pound encyclopedia. Westport, CT; London: Greenwood Press, 2005. pp. xvii, 342.

18900. UTELL, JANINE. Virtue in scraps, *mysterium* in fragments: Robert Graves, Hugh Kenner, and Ezra Pound. *See* **16805.**

18901. VON HALLBERG, ROBERT. Lyric thinking. *See* **15577.**

18902. WICKE, JENNIFER. Hugh Kenner's pound of flesh. *See* **15049.**

18903. WILMER, CLIVE (ed.). Modernist essays: Yeats, Pound, Eliot. By Donald Davie. *See* **20528.**

18904. ZHENG, JIANQING. An approach to lines 7–14 of Ezra Pound's Canto 49. NCL (35:1) 2005, 6–8.

18905. ZHU, CHUNGENG. Ezra Pound's Confucianism. PhilL (29:1) 2005, 57–72.

Anthony Powell

18906. BARBER, MICHAEL. Anthony Powell: a life. (Bibl. 2004, 19054.) Rev. by William H. Pritchard in HR (57:4) 2005, 655–62; by Stephen Wade in ContRev (287:1675) 2005, 117–18; by Derek Turner in Chronicles (29:5) 2005, 38–40.

18907. BIRNS, NICHOLAS. Understanding Anthony Powell. (Bibl. 2004, 19055.) Rev. by Christine Berberich in Mod/Mod (12:1) 2005, 200–2; by William H. Pritchard in HR (57:4) 2005, 655–62; by Derek Turner in Chronicles (29:5) 2005, 38–40.

18908. PRITCHARD, WILLIAM H. Anthony Powell and his critics. HR (57:4) 2005, 655–62 (review-article).

18909. SANDFORD, CHRISTOPHER. An enduring feast. Chronicles (29:12) 2005, 44–5.

18910. SPURLING, HILARY. Painting time: Anthony Powell's pictorial imagination. TLS, 28 Oct. 2005, 12–15.

18911. TAYLOR, D. J. A briefcase life: the full picture of Brian Howard is more than a portrait of failure. *See* **20017.**

D. A. (Douglas A.) Powell (b.1963)

18912. COOPERMAN, MATTHEW. Between the brackets: an interview with D. A. Powell. ChiR (50:2–4) 2004/05, 265–81.

Tim Powers

18913. STEIN, ATARA. Fictionalized Romantics: Byron, Shelley, and Keats as characters in contemporary genre fiction. *See* **21218**.

John Cowper Powys (1872–1963)

18914. DE WAEGENAERE, JEAN-PIERRE. Wild flowers, shrubs and trees in John Cowper Powys's novels. PowJ (14) 2004, 81–102.

18915. FAWKNER, H. W. Dysfunctional responsiveness in *A Glastonbury Romance*: John Cowper Powys, nihilism, and Christianity. PowJ (14) 2004, 103–20.

18916. FOULI, JANET. *Wood and Stone*: a reconsideration. PowJ (15) 2005, 109–28.

18917. GERVAIS, DAVID. J. C. Powys's Dostoievsky. PowJ (15) 2005, 29–44.

18918. GOODWAY, DAVID. A cult of sensations: John Cowper Powys's life-philosophy and individualist anarchism. PowJ (14) 2004, 45–80.

18919. KEITH, W. J. Beyond novel, beyond romance: reading the complete *Porius*. PowJ (14) 2004, 8–26.

18920. LINDSTEDT, EIVOR. Chroniclers and prophets: time and genre in *Porius*. PowJ (14) 2004, 27–44.

18921. LOCK, CHARLES. *Owen Glendower* and the dashing of expectations. PowJ (15) 2005, 66–86.

18922. MARKOVA, OLGA. A Russian perspective on John Cowper Powys. PowJ (14) 2004, 121–7.

18923. ROWLAND, SUSAN. Jung, *Wolf Solent* and myth. PowJ (15) 2005, 129–46.

Llewelyn Powys (1884–1939)

18924. FOSS, PETER J. An inventory of the Llewelyn Powys holdings: manuscripts of works (part two). PowJ (14) 2004, 128–64. (*Adds to* bibl. 2004, 19070.)

18925. —— (ed.). Wessex memories: country essays. (Bibl. 2004, 19069, where scholar details incomplete.) Rev. by Clinton Machann in PowJ (14) 2004, 165–7.

T. F. Powys (1875–1953)

18926. CLAYTON, HUGH. Tom il Matto and Jar le Rétameur: aspects of T. F. Powys in Italian and French. PowJ (15) 2005, 45–65.

18927. MENCHER, ELAINE (ed.). Selected early works. Harleston: Brynmill, 2003. 2 vols. pp. cxxvii, 615. (Facsimiles.) Rev. by J. Lawrence Mitchell in PowJ (15) 2005, 161–7.

18928. WILLIAMS, J. R. 'Suffer the little children to come unto me': T. F. Powys's child-men in a landscape of redemption. PowJ (15) 2005, 87–108.

The Powys Brothers

18929. TAIT, PETER. Littleton Powys, 1874–1955: headmaster, Sherborne Preparatory School. PowJ (15) 2005, 8–28.

Reynolds Price

18930. JORGENSEN, B. W.   Reading 'news from God' in Reynolds Price's *Good Hearts*. LitB (24:1/2) 2004, 201–15.

Richard Price (b.1949)

18931. FISTER, BARBARA.   Copycat crimes: crime fiction and the marketplace of anxieties. Clues (23:3) 2005, 43–56.

Christopher Priest

18932. BUTLER, ANDREW M. (ed.).   Christopher Priest: the interaction. Reading: Science Fiction Foundation, 2005. pp. 185. (Foundation studies in science fiction.)

18933. HUBBLE, NICK.   Five English disaster novels, 1951–1972. *See* **20473**.

F. T. Prince

18934. PECHEY, GRAHAM.   'Pharaoh's sjambok': Roy Campbell and the lexicon of emigration. *See* **15666**.

V. S. Pritchett

18935. BLOOM, JONATHAN.   Revision as transformation: the making and re-making of V. S. Pritchett's *You Make Your Own Life*. JSSE (45) 2005, 63–94.

18936. FLOWER, DEAN.   Pritchett unselfing himself. HR (58:2) 2005, 311–18.

J. H. Prynne

18937. FULLER, WILLIAM.   Restatement of trysts. *See* **7893**.

Philip Pullman (b.1946)

18938. BIRD, ANNE-MARIE.   Circumventing the grand narrative: dust as an alternate theological vision in Pullman's *His Dark Materials*. *In* (pp. 188–98) **18952**.

18939. DEBRANDT, DON.   His dark pharmaceuticals: drug-related themes and imagery in the *His Dark Materials* trilogy. *In* (pp. 25–37) **18973**.

18940. DOLGIN, KIM.   Coming of age in Svalbard, and beyond. *In* (pp. 71–9) **18973**.

18941. GIARDINA, NATASHA.   Kids in the kitchen? *His Dark Materials* on childhood, adulthood, and social power. *In* (pp. 139–49) **18973**.

18942. GOODERHAM, DAVID.   Fantasizing it as it is: religious language in Philip Pullman's trilogy *His Dark Materials*. ChildLit (31) 2003, 155–75.

18943. GRIBBIN, MARY; GRIBBIN, JOHN R.   The science of Philip Pullman's *His Dark Materials*. Introd. by Philip Pullman. New York: Random House, 2005. pp. xix, 203.

18944. HATLEN, BURTON.   Pullman's *His Dark Materials*, a challenge to the fantasies of J. R. R. Tolkien and C. S. Lewis, with an epilogue on Pullman's neo-Romantic reading of *Paradise Lost*. *In* (pp. 75–94) **18952**.

18945. HINES, MAUDE.   Second nature: dæmons and ideology in *The Golden Compass*. *In* (pp. 37–47) **18952**.

18946. HODGSON, DAVE.   A new Eve: evolution of sustainability across many worlds. *In* (pp. 151–61) **18973**.

18947. HOPKINS, LISA. Dyads or triads? *His Dark Materials* and the structure of the human. *In* (pp. 48–56) **18952**.

18948. KENYON, KAY. Reading by flashlight: what fantasy writers can learn from Pullman. *In* (pp. 97–107) **18973**.

18949. KING, SHELLEY. 'Without Lyra we would understand neither the New nor the Old Testament': exegesis, allegory, and reading *The Golden Compass. In* (pp. 106–24) **18952**.

18950. LEET, ANDREW. Rediscovering faith through science fiction: Pullman's *His Dark Materials. In* (pp. 174–87) **18952**.

18951. LEIBER, JUSTIN. Mrs Coulter *vs* C. S. Lewis. *In* (pp. 163–70) **18973**.

18952. LENZ, MILLICENT; SCOTT, CAROLE (eds). *His Dark Materials* illuminated: critical essays on Philip Pullman's trilogy. Detroit, MI: Wayne State UP, 2005. pp. xi, 242. (Landscapes of childhood.)

18953. LOY, DAVID R.; GOODHEW, LINDA. The dharma of dragons and dæmons: Buddhist themes in modern fantasy. *See* **19830**.

18954. MACKEY, MARGARET. *Northern Lights* and Northern readers: background knowledge, affect linking, and literary understanding. *In* (pp. 57–67) **18952**.

18955. McMULLEN, SEAN. The field naturalist's guide to dæmons. *In* (pp. 129–37) **18973**.

18956. MARKMAN, ARTHUR B. Science, technology and the danger of dæmons. *In* (pp. 61–9) **18973**.

18957. MATTHEWS, SUSAN. Rouzing the faculties to act: Pullman's Blake for children. *In* (pp. 125–34) **18952**.

18958. METZGER, ROBERT A. Philip Pullman, research scientist. *In* (pp. 49–59) **18973**.

18959. MOLONEY, DANIEL P. Show me, don't tell me: Pullman's imperfectly Christian story (and how he lost his way). *In* (pp. 171–85) **18973**.

18960. PINSENT, PAT. Unexpected allies? Pullman and the feminist theologians. *In* (pp. 199–211) **18952**.

18961. PULLMAN, PHILIP. The making and faking of Lyra's Oxford. LU (29:1) 2005, 6–8.

18962. RABE, JEAN. Letter to the editor: in praise of Mrs Coulter. *In* (pp. 89–95) **18973**.

18963. RUSSELL, MARY HARRIS. 'Eve again! Mother Eve!': Pullman's Eve variations. *In* (pp. 212–22) **18952**.

18964. SCALLY, LISA. 'Telling stories of desire': the power of authorship in *The Changeover* and *The Amber Spyglass. In* (pp. 130–47) **18044**.

18965. SCHWEIZER, BERNARD. 'And he's a-going to destroy him': religious subversion in Pullman's *His Dark Materials. In* (pp. 160–73) **18952**.

18966. SCOTT, CAROLE. Pullman's enigmatic ontology: revamping old traditions in *His Dark Materials. In* (pp. 95–105) **18952**.

18967. SHOHET, LAUREN. Reading dark materials. *In* (pp. 22–36) **18952**.

18968. SMITH, KAREN PATRICIA. Tradition, transformation, and the bold emergence: fantastic legacy and Pullman's *His Dark Materials*. *In* (pp. 135–51) **18952.**

18969. TRAVISS, KAREN. I gotta get me one of those: why dæmons might make the world a better place. *In* (pp. 81–8) **18973.**

18970. TURTLEDOVE, HARRY. Occam's razor and *The Subtle Knife*: invention in *His Dark Materials*. *In* (pp. 119–27) **18973.**

18971. WARNER, MARINA. Angels and engines: apocalypse and its aftermath, from George W. Bush to Philip Pullman. TLS, 19 & 26 Aug. 2005, 14–17.

18972. WOOD, NAOMI. Dismembered starlings and neutered minds: innocence in *His Dark Materials*. *In* (pp. 15–23) **18973.**

18973. YEFFETH, GLENN (ed.). Navigating *The Golden Compass*: religion, science, and demonology in *His Dark Materials*. Dallas, TX: BenBella, 2005. pp. 185.

18974. ZETTEL, SARAH. Dust to dust: the destruction of fantasy trope and archetype in *His Dark Materials*. *In* (pp. 39–48) **18973.**

Tom Purdom (b.1936)

18975. SCHWEITZER, DARRELL. An interview with Tom Purdom. NYRSF (18:4) 2005, 1, 10–15.

Al Purdy

18976. SOLECKI, SAM (ed.). Yours, Al: the collected letters of Al Purdy. Madeira Park, BC: Harbour, 2004. pp. 560. Rev. by George Galt in LRC (12:9) 2004, 12–13.

Philip Purser (b.1925)

18977. HOENSELAARS, TON. 'Out-ranting the enemy leader': *Henry V* and/as World War II propaganda. *In* (pp. 215–34) **9237.**

Mario Puzo (b.1920)

18978. BLACK, RONALD J. The American Dream as paradox in *The Godfather*. Storytelling (4:1) 2004, 60–70.

Barbara Pym

18979. EVERETT, BARBARA. Larkin and the doomsters: walking 'down life's sunless hill' with Hardy and Barbara Pym. TLS, 3 June 2005, 11–13.

18980. KRASNER, JAMES. Accumulated lives: metaphor, materiality, and the homes of the elderly. *See* **17688.**

Thomas Pynchon

18981. ABBAS, NIRAN (ed.). Thomas Pynchon: reading from the margins. (Bibl. 2003, 19245.) Rev. by Kathryn Hume in StudN (37:1) 2005, 99–101.

18982. BENOIT, RAYMOND. Pynchon's *Lot 49* on James's *Jolly Corner*. NCL (35:3) 2005, 10–12.

18983. CLARKE, COLIN A. Consumption on the frontier: food and sacrament in *Mason & Dixon*. *In* (pp. 77–100) **18986.**

18984. García-Caro, Pedro. 'America was the only place …': American exceptionalism and the geographic politics of Pynchon's *Mason & Dixon.* *In* (pp. 101–24) **18986.**

18985. Hatooka, Keita. Inu-tachi no chinmoku: *Mason & Dixon* ni okeru hyosho no kanosei. (The silence of the dogs: the possibility of representation in *Mason & Dixon*.) StAL (41) 2004, 53–69.

18986. Hinds, Elizabeth Jane Wall (ed.). The multiple worlds of Pynchon's *Mason & Dixon*: eighteenth-century contexts, postmodern observations. Rochester, NY: Camden House, 2005. pp. viii, 222. (Studies in American literature and culture: literary criticism in perspective.)

18987. Huehls, Mitchum. 'The space that may not be seen': the form of historicity in *Mason & Dixon.* *In* (pp. 25–46) **18986.**

18988. Lensing, Dennis M. Postmodernism at sea: the quest for longitude in Thomas Pynchon's *Mason & Dixon* and Umberto Eco's *The Island of the Day Before.* *In* (pp. 125–43) **18986.**

18989. Mattessich, Stefan. Lines of flight: discursive time and countercultural desire in the work of Thomas Pynchon. (Bibl. 2004, 19116.) Rev. by Daniel Punday in StudN (37:1) 2004, 109–11.

18990. Mazur, Zygmunt. Historical process and revision in Thomas Pynchon's *V.* *In* (pp. 143–52) **3756.**

18991. Orbán, Katalin. Ethical diversions: the post-Holocaust narratives of Pynchon, Abish, DeLillo, and Spiegelman. London; New York: Routledge, 2005. pp. ix, 209. (Literary criticism and cultural theory.)

18992. Palmeri, Frank. General Wolfe and the weavers: re-envisioning history in Pynchon's *Mason & Dixon.* *In* (pp. 184–98) **18986.**

18993. Roraback, Erik S. Para-baroque conceptual intersections & interventions: *Finnegans Wake, Gravity's Rainbow* and *The Writing of the Disaster. See* **17334.**

18994. Smith, Shawn. Pynchon and history: metahistorical rhetoric and postmodern narrative form in the novels of Thomas Pynchon. London; New York: Routledge, 2005. pp. viii, 248. (Studies in major literary authors.)

18995. Thill, Brian. The sweetness of immorality: *Mason & Dixon* and the American sins of consumption. *In* (pp. 49–75) **18986.**

'Ellery Queen' (Frederic Dannay and Manfred B. Lee)

18996. Wheat, Carolyn. The last word: the real Queen(s) of crime. Clues (23:4) 2005, 86–90.

Sir Arthur Quiller-Couch ('Q')

18997. Taylor, Miles; Wolff, Michael (eds). The Victorians since 1901: histories, representations, and revisions. *See* **9426.**

Jonathan Raban

18998. Dancygier, Barbara. Blending and narrative viewpoint: Jonathan Raban's travels through mental spaces. LLit (14:2) 2005, 99–127.

David Rabe

18999. ADAMS, JON. Envelope please: upholding masculinity in Michael Herr's *Dispatches* and David Rabe's *Streamers*. *See* **17011**.

Thomas H. Raddall

19000. ARMSTRONG, CHRISTOPHER J. Postcolonial historicity: Halifax, region, and empire in *Barometer Rising* and *The Nymph and the Lamp*. *In* (pp. 50–64) **9243**.

Eve Raleigh (d.1978)

19001. KAUP, MONIKA. The unsustainable *hacienda*: the rhetoric of progress in Jovita González and Eve Raleigh's *Caballero*. MFS (51:3) 2005, 561–91.

Ayn Rand

19002. BERLINER, MICHAEL S. Reviews of *Anthem*. *In* (pp. 55–60) **19013**.

19003. BERNSTEIN, ANDREW. *Anthem* and collectivist regression into primitivism. *In* (pp. 299–305) **19013**.

19004. BINSWANGER, HARRY. *Anthem*: an appreciation. *In* (pp. 307–10) **19013**.

19005. BOECKMANN, TORE. *Anthem* as a psychological fantasy. *In* (pp. 83–118) **19013**.

19006. BRITTING, JEFF. Adapting *Anthem*: projects that were and might have been. *In* (pp. 61–9) **19013**.

19007. —— *Anthem* and *The Individualist Manifesto*. *In* (pp. 70–80) **19013**.

19008. —— Ayn Rand. Woodstock, NY: Overlook Press, 2004. pp. 135. (Overlook illustrated lives.) Rev. by Jenny Turner in LRB (27:23) 2005, 13–16.

19009. GHATE, ONKAR. Breaking the metaphysical chains of dictatorship: free will and determinism in *Anthem*. *In* (pp. 225–54) **19013**.

19010. LEWIS, JOHN. 'Sacrilege toward the individual': the anti-pride of Thomas More's *Utopia* and *Anthem*'s radical alternative. *In* (pp. 172–89) **19013**.

19011. MAYHEW, ROBERT. *Anthem*: '38 & '46. *In* (pp. 28–54) **19013**.

19012. —— Ayn Rand and *Song of Russia*: Communism and anti-Communism in 1940s Hollywood. Lanham, MD; London: Scarecrow Press, 2005. pp. xv, 213.

19013. —— (ed.). Essays on Ayn Rand's *Anthem*. Lanham, MD: Lexington, 2005. pp. xiii, 337.

19014. MILGRAM, SHOSHANA. *Anthem* in manuscript: finding the words. *In* (pp. 3–23) **19013**.

19015. —— *Anthem* in the context of related literary works: 'We are not like our brothers.' *In* (pp. 119–70) **19013**.

19016. PEIKOFF, AMY. Freedom of disassociation in *Anthem*. *In* (pp. 285–98) **19013**.

19017. RALSTON, RICHARD E. Publishing *Anthem*. *In* (pp. 24–7) **19013**.

19018. SALMIERI, GREGORY. Prometheus' discovery: individualism and the meaning of the concept 'I' in *Anthem*. *In* (pp. 255–84) **19013**.

19019. TURNER, JENNY. As astonishing as Elvis. LRB (27:23) 2005, 13–16 (review-article).

19020. WRIGHT, DARRYL. Needs of the psyche in Ann Rand's early ethical thought. *In* (pp. 190–224) **19013**.

Alice Randall

19021. HOLLAND, SHARON P. The last word on racism: new directions for a critical race theory. *See* **16417**.

Dudley Randall (b.1914)

19022. BOYD, MELBA JOYCE. Wrestling with the muse: Dudley Randall and the Broadside Press. (Bibl. 2004, 19155.) Rev. by James Edward Smethurst in JAH (91:4) 2005, 1546.

Ian Rankin

19023. DIEMERT, BRIAN. Ian Rankin and the God of the Scots. *In* (pp. 164–88) **14191**.

19024. PLAIN, GILL. Rankin revisited: an interview with Ian Rankin. ScSR (4:1) 2003, 126–37.

John Crowe Ransom

19025. MONTEIRO, GEORGE. Early Ransom, early Frost. *See* **16608**.

Nessa Rapoport

19026. RAPOPORT, NESSA. Body of love. *In* (pp. 175–89) **12893**.

Mark Rascovich

19027. SEED, DAVID. Policing the Cold War frontier: *The Bedford Incident*. EurJAC (24:1) 2005, 47–59.

Ron Rash (b.1953)

19028. BIGGERS, JEFF. Out of Appalachia: new writing from an old region, including an interview with Gretchen Laskas and Ron Rash. BRev (23:4) 2003, 14–15.

Mark Ravenhill

19029. RAVENHILL, MARK. A tear in the fabric: the James Bulger murder and new theatre writing in the nineties. TheatreForum (26) 2005, 85–92.

19030. WALLACE, CLARE. Responsibility and postmodernity: Mark Ravenhill and 1990s British drama. *In* (pp. 269–75) **3734**.

Marjorie Kinnan Rawlings

19031. GRAHAM-BERTOLINI, ALISON. Marjorie Kinnan Rawlings and the reckoning of ideology. SoQ (43:1) 2005, 49–62.

19032. TARR, RODGER L. (ed.). The private Marjorie: the love letters of Marjorie Kinnan Rawlings to Norton S. Baskin. Gainesville: Florida UP, 2004. pp. xiv, 720.

David Ray (b.1932)

19033. MCNAMEE, GREGORY. A poetry of conscience: a conversation with David Ray. BRev (25:6) 2005, 26–7.

Liam Rector (b.1949)

19034. KANNING, SARAH. An interview by Sarah Kanning. APR (34:5) 2005, 37–41.

Ishmael Reed

19035. COOPER, LOUISE. The origins of Aton in Ishmael Reed's *Mumbo Jumbo*. NCL (35:1) 2005, 13–14.

Tova Reich

19036. KIRSCHENBAUM, BLOSSOM S. Tova Reich's fiction: perspectives on mothering. *In* (pp. 71–109) **12895.**

Christina Reid

19037. PELAN, REBECCA. Identity performance in Northern Ireland and Australia: *The Belle of the Belfast City* and *Radiance*. ADS (46) 2005, 70–9.

Paisley Rekdal

19038. HO, JENNIFER. Ambiguous movements: Paisley Rekdal's passing identity in *The Night My Mother Met Bruce Lee: Observations on Not Fitting In*. WP (15:1) 2005, 141–65.

Ruth Rendell ('Barbara Vine')

19039. KYZLINKOVÁ, LIDIA. Ruth Rendell / Barbara Vine: social thriller, ethnicity and Englishness. *In* (pp. 109–14) **3753.**

19040. PENUEL, SUZANNE. Relocating the heart of darkness in Ruth Rendell. *In* (pp. 51–70) **14191.**

Kenneth Rexroth

19041. GUTIERREZ, DONALD. Kenneth Rexroth: the poetry of luminous authenticity. Onthebus (19/20) 2005, 74–80.

Oliver Reynolds

19042. JARNIEWICZ, JERZY. The vanishing source in Oliver Reynolds' *Synopticon*. *In* (pp. 76–81) **3756.**

Charles Reznikoff

19043. COONEY, SEAMUS (ed.). The poems of Charles Reznikoff: 1918–1975. Boston, MA: Godine, 2005. pp. xiii, 445.

Jean Rhys

19044. BERMAN, JESSICA. Modernism's possible geographies. *In* (pp. 281–96) **12640.**

19045. CROUCH, KRISTIN. 'Inside out': the creative process of Shared Experience theatre. *See* **21296.**

19046. CZARNECKI, KRISTIN. 'Altered and cut to an echo': marriage and Modernism in Jean Rhys's *After Leaving Mr Mackenzie*. CEACrit (67:2) 2005, 29–42.

19047. DELL'AMICO, CAROL. Colonialism and the Modernist moment in the early novels of Jean Rhys. London; New York: Routledge, 2005. pp. xi, 141. (Studies in major literary authors.)

19048. FUMAGALLI, MARIA CRISTINA. Maryse Condé's *La Migration des cœurs*, Jean Rhys's *Wide Sargasso Sea*, and (the possibility) of creolization. JCarL (4:1) 2005, 195–213.

19049. JOHNSON, ERICA L. Home, *maison, casa*: the politics of location in works by Jean Rhys, Marguerite Duras, and Erminia Dell'Oro. Madison, NJ:

Fairleigh Dickinson UP; London: Assoc. UPs, 2003. pp. 264. Rev. by Loredana Polezzi in MLR (100:2) 2005, 588–9.

19050. KINNEY, DEBORAH A. Women, fire, and dangerous things: metatextuality and the politics of reading in Jean Rhys's *Wide Sargasso Sea*. WS (34:2) 2005, 113–31.

19051. KNIGHT, CHARMIAN. Thornfield Hall revisited. *In* (pp. 63–73) **10222.**

19052. LINETT, MAREN. 'New words, new everything': fragmentation and trauma in Jean Rhys. TCL (51:4) 2005, 437–66.

19053. PALUMBO, ANGELICA. *Wide Sargasso Sea* and the colonial drifting. *In* (pp. 202–12) **3690.**

19054. PATKE, RAJEEV S. Method and madness in *A Question of Power* and *Wide Sargasso Sea*. *See* **16929.**

19055. SIMPSON, ANNE B. Territories of the psyche: the fiction of Jean Rhys. Basingstoke; New York: Palgrave Macmillan, 2005. pp. xiv, 168.

19056. STOUCK, JORDAN. Gardening in the diaspora: place and identity in Olive Senior's poetry. *See* **19358.**

19057. SUVIN, DARKO. To Laputa and back: a missing chapter of *Gulliver's Travels*. *In* (pp. 11–31) **3690.**

19058. THOMAS, SUE. Jean Rhys writing White creole childhoods. A/B (19:1/2) 2004, 203–21.

19059. WIESENFARTH, JOSEPH. Ford Madox Ford and the regiment of women: Violet Hunt, Jean Rhys, Stella Bowen, Janice Biala. *See* **16547.**

19060. ZEIKOWITZ, RICHARD E. Writing a feminine Paris in Jean Rhys's *Quartet*. JML (28:2) 2005, 1–17.

Nino Ricci

19061. GERVAIS, MARTY. A little fire in the dark night: an interview with Nino Ricci. Rampike (14:1) 2005, 36–9.

Anne Rice ('Anne Rampling', 'A. N. Roquelaure')

19062. HARSE, KATIE. 'Sick of Count Dracula': Scott, Carter, Rice and the response to Stoker's authority. *See* **19348.**

19063. O'LEARY, CRYSTAL L. Transcending monstrous flesh: a revision of the hero's mythic quest. JFA (13:3) 2003, 239–49.

John Andrew Rice (b.1888)

19064. CHADDOCK, KATHERINE REYNOLDS. John Andrew Rice: coming to terms with self and South. SoCR (37:2) 2005, 219–27.

Adrienne Rich

19065. CARRILLO ROWE, AIMEE. Be longing: toward a feminist politics of relation. NWSAJ (17:2) 2005, 15–46.

19066. GWIAZDA, PIOTR. 'Nothing else left to read': poetry and audience in Adrienne Rich's *An Atlas of the Difficult World*. JML (28:2) 2005, 165–88.

Grant Richards (1872–1948)

19067. MALONE, RICHARD. Etiquette in Pandemonium: Grant Richards and the early American editions of A. E. Housman's *A Shropshire Lad*. *See* **17062.**

2005] AUTHORS 1041

'Anne Richardson' (Anne Richardson Roiphe)

19068. LEVINSON, MELANIE. 'Wayfinding': (re)constructing Jewish identity in *Mazel* and *Lovingkindness*. *In* (pp. 110–19) **12895.**

Dorothy Miller Richardson (1873–1957)

19069. ATTEWELL, NADINE. A risky business: going out in the fiction of Virginia Woolf and Dorothy Richardson. *In* (pp. 7–18) **14254.**

19070. FINN, HOWARD. 'In the quicksands of disintegrating faiths': Dorothy Richardson and the Quakers. LitTheol (19:1) 2005, 34–46.

19071. FRIGERIO, FRANCESCA. Cultura urbana e scrittura femminile: una rassegna di studi. Culture (17) 2003, 49–70.

19072. —— 'A filmless London': *flânerie* and urban culture in Dorothy Richardson's articles for *Close Up*. *In* (pp. 19–31) **14254.**

'Henry Handel Richardson' (Ethel Florence Lindesay Robertson)

19073. ACKLAND, MICHAEL. Henry Handel Richardson's years in Wilhelmine Germany: the 'most cultured land in Europe'? ELT (48:2) 2005, 147–63.

19074. —— Only a 'well-schooled interpreter': Henry Handel Richardson's final year at the Leipzig Conservatorium and its authorial recasting. ALS (22:1) 2005, 51–60.

Laura Riding (Laura (Riding) Jackson)

19075. DITIFECI, FRANCESCA. Laura (Riding) Jackson and *The Promise of Words*. *In* (pp. 80–94) **12589.**

19076. FRIEDMANN, ELIZABETH. A mannered grace: the life of Laura (Riding) Jackson. New York: Persea, 2005. pp. xx, 571. Rev. by Phoebe Pettingell in NewL (88:2) 2005, 34–5; by Laurel Blossom in AmBR (26:5) 2005, 1, 4.

19077. —— (ed.). The Laura (Riding) Jackson reader. New York: Persea, 2005. pp. xxi, 386. Rev. by Phoebe Pettingell in NewL (88:2) 2005, 35.

19078. NOLAN, JOHN; CLARK, ALAN J. (eds). Under the mind's watch: concerning issues of language, literature, life of contemporary bearing. New York; Frankfurt: Lang, 2004. pp. 534.

19079. OPHIR, ELLA ZOHAR. The Laura Riding question: Modernism, poetry, and truth. MLQ (66:1) 2005, 85–114.

19080. PETTER, CHRIS; ROBERTS, LINDA; ROSE, SPENCER. The Robert Graves diary (1935–39). *See* **16803.**

Lynn Riggs

19081. WEAVER, JACE (foreword). The Cherokee Night and other plays. (Bibl. 2004, 19224.) Rev. by Craig S. Womack in SAIL (17:1) 2005, 114–21.

Joan Riley

19082. ELLIS, DAVID. 'Wives and workers': the novels of Joan Riley. EAS (57) 2004, 68–84.

Alberto Ríos

19083. WOOTTEN, LESLIE A. At the kitchen table: a conversation with Alberto Ríos. BRev (23:4) 2003, 5.

Keith Roberts

19084. Bilson, Fred. The colonialists' fear of colonisation and the alternate worlds of Ward Moore, Philip K. Dick and Keith Roberts. *See* **18333.**

19085. Hubble, Nick. Five English disaster novels, 1951–1972. *See* **20473.**

Michèle Roberts

19086. Burgass, Catherine. Food for the soul: reading Mrs Ramsay's *bœuf en daube. In* (pp. 95–103) **3724.**

19087. Guignery, Vanessa. *The Book of Mrs Noah* (1987) de Michèle Roberts: un roman aux sentiers qui bifurquent. EtBr (28) 2005, 1–20.

19088. —— Réécritures du Déluge et de l'arche de Noé dans la fiction contemporaine de langue anglaise (Coover, Findley, Winterson, Roberts et Barnes). EREA (2:1) 2004, 128–33.

19089. Soraya García Sánchez, María. Talking about women, history, and writing with Michèle Roberts. Atl (27:2) 2005, 137–47.

Morley Roberts

19090. Coustillas, Pierre. The correspondence between Clara Collet and Morley Roberts (fourth and last instalment). *See* **11545.**

Elizabeth Robins ('C. E. Raimond')

19091. Farfan, Penny. Women, Modernism, and performance. Cambridge; New York: CUP, 2004. pp. xi, 173.

Eden Robinson

19092. Appleford, Rob. 'Close, very close, a *b'gwus* howls': the contingency of execution in Eden Robinson's *Monkey Beach*. CanL (184) 2005, 85–101.

19093. Visvis, Vikki. Beyond the 'talking cure': the practical joke as testimony for intergenerational trauma in Eden Robinson's *Queen of the North*. StudCanL (29:2) 2004, 37–61.

Kim Stanley Robinson

19094. Frisch, Adam J. The subjective objective in *The Years of Rice and Salt*. Foundation (94) 2005, 31–8.

Marilynne Robinson

19095. Cardullo, Bert. Fiction into film: notes on one paradigmatic scene and two emblematic adaptations. *See* **13831.**

19096. Chakrabarti, M. K. An American prophet. BosR (30:5) 2005, 55–7.

19097. Harken, Amy Lignitz; Moses, Lee Hull. Gifts of Gilead. St Louis, MO: Chalice Press, 2005. pp. 106. (Popular insights.)

19098. Ryan, Katy. Horizons of grace: Marilynne Robinson and Simone Weil. PhilL (29:2) 2005, 349–64.

19099. Silverblatt, Michael. Falling to grace. Brick (75) 2005, 104–16. (Interview.)

Luis J. Rodríguez (b.1954)

19100. Biggers, Jeff. Compassion and community: an interview with Luis J. Rodríguez. BRev (23:3) 2003, 5, 12.

Richard Rodriguez

19101. Durán, Isabel. The body as cultural critique in American autobiography. *See* **17849**.

19102. Marzán, J. A. The art of being Richard Rodriguez. BR (27:1) 2003, 45–64.

19103. Ramsdell, Lea. Language and identity politics: the linguistic autobiographies of Latinos in the United States. JML (28:1) 2004, 166–76.

19104. Saldaña Portillo, María Josefina. Revolutionary imagination in the Americas and the age of development. *See* **15182**.

Sue Roe (b.1956)

19105. Mukherjee, Ankhi. Missed encounters: repetition, rewriting, and contemporary returns to Charles Dickens's *Great Expectations*. *See* **10719**.

Theodore Roethke

19106. Hirsch, Edward (ed.). Selected poems. New York: Library of America, 2005. pp. xxv, 158. (American poets project, 15.) Rev. by Jay Parini in TLS, 16 Dec. 2005, 29.

19107. Kolosov, Jacqueline. 'Is this the promised end?': witness in *King Lear* and apocalyptic poetry of the twentieth century. *See* **6473**.

19108. O'Sullivan, Michael. 'Bare life' and the garden politics of Roethke and Heaney. Mosaic (38:4) 2005, 17–34.

19109. Sharpe, Peter. The ground of our beseeching: metaphor and the poetics of meditation. *See* **16305**.

Linda Rogers (b.1944)

19110. Brown, Allan. Worlds turned on their heads: the adult novels of Linda Rogers. *In* (pp. 107–21) **19115**.

19111. Gould, John. Making God: poetry as spiritual practice. *In* (pp. 13–37) **19115**.

19112. Hatch, Ronald B. Linda Rogers and 'children's writers'. *In* (pp. 81–106) **19115**.

19113. Rhenisch, Harold. Finding grace through music: an interview with Linda Rogers. *In* (pp. 122–57) **19115**.

19114. —— The genesis of Linda Rogers. *In* (pp. 50–73) **19115**.

19115. —— (ed.). Linda Rogers: essays on her works. Toronto; Buffalo, NY; Lancaster: Guernica, 2005. pp. 175. (Writers series, 14.)

19116. Rogers, Linda. The writing life: an autobiography. *In* (pp. 158–66) **19115**.

19117. Young, Patricia. Coming out of silence. *In* (pp. 38–49) **19115**.

Michael Rohd

19118. Kurahashi, Yuko. Search for home and identity: Ping Chong and Michael Rohd's *Undesirable Elements – Berlin*. *See* **15786**.

Jonathan Rosen (b.1963)

19119. Roach, Korri. *Eve's Apple*: a Midrashic commentary surrounding the figure of Eve. StudAJL (24) 2005, 95–102.

Thane Rosenbaum

19120. BERGER, ALAN L.   Myth, mysticism, and memory: the Holocaust in Thane Rosenbaum's *The Golems of Gotham*. StudAJL (24) 2005, 1–21.

19121. ROSENBAUM, THANE.   Law and legacy in the post-Holocaust imagination. *In* (pp. 238–48) **12893.**

Isaac Rosenberg

19122. COOK, ELIZABETH.   From Pandemonium. LRB (27:17) 2005, 23–4 (review-article).

19123. NOAKES, VIVIEN (ed.).   The poems and plays of Isaac Rosenberg. Oxford; New York: OUP, 2004. pp. xlviii, 427. Rev. by Elizabeth Cook in LRB (27:17) 2005, 23–4; by Seamus Perry in TLS, 25 Nov. 2005, 8; by Chris Walsh in EC (55:4) 2005, 389–98; by Jennifer Kilgore in EREA (3:2) 2005.

19124. PERRY, SEAMUS.   Old Druid time. TLS, 25 Nov. 2005, 8 (review-article). (Mythic quality of Rosenberg's works.)

Alan Ross (b.1922)

19125. HUGHES, DAVID (sel. and introd.).   Poems. London: Harvill Press, 2005. pp. xi, 289.

Sinclair Ross

19126. CAVELL, RICHARD.   'An ordered absence': defeatured topologies in Canadian literature. *In* (pp. 14–31) **9243.**

19127. HILL, COLIN.   As for me and my blueprint: Sinclair Ross's debt to Arthur Stringer. *In* (pp. 251–72) **12739.**

19128. STOUCK, DAVID.   As for Sinclair Ross. Toronto; Buffalo, NY; London: Toronto UP, 2005. pp. xv, 353, (plates) 24. Rev. by Stephen Henighan in TLS, 23 & 30 Dec. 2005, 12; by W. J. Keith in LRC (13:7) 2005, 24–5; by Anne Burke in PJCL (44) 2005, 48–50.

Henry Roth

19129. GIBBS, ALAN.   A means to an end: Henry Roth's self-consuming short fiction. JSSE (44) 2005, 25–36.

19130. KELLMAN, STEVEN G.   *At Times in Flight*: Henry Roth's parable of renunciation. JSSE (44) 2005, 37–48.

19131. ——   The education of Henry Roth. NER (26:3) 2005, 10–42.

19132. ——   Redemption: the life of Henry Roth. New York; London: Norton, 2005. pp. 371. Rev. by David Kirby in BkW, 21 Aug. 2005, 10.

19133. RICARD, VIRGINIA.   Against oblivion: Henry Roth's *The Surveyor*. JSSE (44) 2005, 49–63.

19134. SCHOTT-KRISTENSEN, LENE.   Writing and parricide in Henry Roth's *Final Dwarf.* JSSE (44) 2005, 65–83.

19135. SHAW, MARTÍN URDIALES.   Henry Roth's short fiction (1940–1980): a geography of loss. JSSE (44) 2005, 85–101.

19136. TURNER, SIMON.   Pieces of a man: considering *Shifting Landscape* as autobiographical critique. JSSE (44) 2005, 103–11.

19137. WEBER, MYLES.   Consuming silences: how we read authors who don't publish. *See* **19297.**

Philip Roth

19138. BRAUNER, DAVID. 'Getting in your retaliation first': narrative strategies in *Portnoy's Complaint. In* (pp. 43–57) **19173.**

19139. BRENNER, ARTHUR. Counterfactual history and Roth's purpose in *The Plot against America.* PhRSN (3:2) 2005, 17–18.

19140. CHOUARD, GÉRALDINE. Fantasmes et fantômes dans *Sabbath's Theater*, de Philip Roth (1995). EREA (1:1) 2003, 99–110.

19141. COOPER, ALAN. It can happen here; or, All in the family values: surviving *The Plot against America. In* (pp. 241–53) **19173.**

19142. DANIEL, ANNE MARGARET. Philip Roth, MVP: *Our Gang, The Breast,* and *The Great American Novel. In* (pp. 59–74) **19173.**

19143. GELDER, RACHEL. Passing and failing: reflections on the limitations of showing the passer in *The Human Stain. See* **20714.**

19144. GENTRY, MARSHALL BRUCE. Newark Maid feminism in Philip Roth's *American Pastoral. In* (pp. 160–71) **19149.**

19145. GERSTLE, ELLEN L. *The Dying Animal*: the art of obsessing, or obsessing about art? *In* (pp. 194–9) **19149.**

19146. GOLDBLATT, ROY. As plain as the nose on your face: the nose as the organ of othering. Amst (48:4) 2003, 563–76.

19147. GORDON, ANDREW. The critique of utopia in Philip Roth's *The Counterlife* and *American Pastoral. In* (pp. 151–9) **19149.**

19148. HALIO, JAY L. Eros and death in Roth's later fiction. *In* (pp. 200–6) **19149.**

19149. —— SIEGEL, BEN (eds). Turning up the flame: Philip Roth's later novels. Newark: Delaware UP, 2005. pp. 223. Rev. by Patrick Lennon in BELL (ns 3) 2005, 197–204.

19150. HEDIN, BENJAMIN. A history that never happened: Philip Roth's *The Plot against America.* GetR (18:1) 2005, 93–106.

19151. —— The measure of all things: *Patrimony. In* (pp. 143–51) **19173.**

19152. HUGHES, DARREN. The 'written world' of Philip Roth's nonfiction. *In* (pp. 255–69) **19173.**

19153. HUSBAND, JULIE. Female hysteria and sisterhood in *Letting Go* and *When She Was Good. In* (pp. 25–41) **19173.**

19154. KAPLAN, BRETT ASHLEY. Reading race and the conundrums of reconciliation in Philip Roth's *The Human Stain. In* (pp. 172–93) **19149.**

19155. LENNON, PATRICK. And Roth begat Portnoy, and Portnoy begat Roth. BELL (ns 3) 2005, 197–204 (review-article).

19156. LÉVY, PAULE; SAVIN, ADA (eds). Philip Roth. (Bibl. 2004, 19271.) Rev. by Marcienne Rocard in Anglophonia (15) 2004, 295–6; by Heiner Bus in MELUS (30:1) 2005, 258–62.

19157. LYONS, BONNIE. En-countering pastorals in *The Counterlife. In* (pp. 119–27) **19173.**

19158. —— Philip Roth's American tragedies. *In* (pp. 125–30) **19149.**

19159. MCGARRY, PASCALE. Philip Roth et l'art de mourir, *The Dying Animal.* WI (21:1) 2005, 103–7.

19160. McGurl, Mark. The program era: pluralisms of postwar American fiction. See **15350**.

19161. Maslan, Mark. The faking of the Americans: passing, trauma, and national identity in Philip Roth's *Human Stain*. MLQ (66:3) 2005, 365–89.

19162. Mellard, James M. Death, mourning, and Besse's ghost: from Philip Roth's *The Facts* to *Sabbath's Theater*. In (pp. 115–24) **19149**.

19163. Neelakantan, G. Textualizing the self: adultery, blatant fictions, and Jewishness in Philip Roth's *Deception*. In (pp. 58–67) **19149**.

19164. Omer-Sherman, Ranen. 'A little stranger in the house': madness and identity in *Sabbath's Theater*. In (pp. 169–83) **19173**.

19165. Parrish, Tim. Becoming Black: Zuckerman's bifurcating self in *The Human Stain*. In (pp. 209–23) **19173**.

19166. Parrish, Timothy L. The end of identity: Philip Roth's Jewish *American Pastoral*. In (pp. 131–50) **19149**.

19167. Pinsker, Sanford. The tortoise and the hare; or, Philip Roth, Cynthia Ozick, and the vagaries of fiction writing. See **18716**.

19168. Pozorski, Aimee. How to tell a true ghost story: *The Ghost Writer* and the case of Anne Frank. In (pp. 89–102) **19173**.

19169. Rabin, Jessica G. Still (resonant, relevant and) crazy after all these years: '*Goodbye, Columbus*' and *Five Short Stories*. In (pp. 9–23) **19173**.

19170. Rankine, Patrice D. Passing as tragedy: Philip Roth's *The Human Stain*, the Oedipus myth, and the self-made man. CritW (47:1) 2005, 101–12.

19171. Royal, Derek Parker. Pastoral dreams and national identity in *American Pastoral* and *I Married a Communist*. In (pp. 185–207) **19173**.

19172. —— Text, lives and bellybuttons: Philip Roth's *Operation Shylock* and the regeneration of subjectivity. In (pp. 68–91) **19149**.

19173. —— (ed.). Philip Roth: new perspectives on an American author. Foreword by Daniel Walden. Westport, CT; London: Praeger, 2005. pp. ix, 303. Rev. by Patrick Lennon in BELL (ns 3) 2005, 197–204.

19174. Rudnytsky, Peter L. *Goodbye, Columbus*: Roth's portrait of the narcissist as a young man. TCL (51:1) 2005, 25–42.

19175. Safer, Elaine B. *Operation Shylock*: double double Jewish trouble. In (pp. 153–67) **19173**.

19176. Scheckner, Peter. Roth's Falstaff: transgressive humor in *Sabbath's Theater*. MidQ (46:3) 2005, 220–35.

19177. Schwartz, Larry. Roth, race and Newark. CulL (8) 2005.

19178. Shechner, Mark. Up society's ass, copper: rereading Philip Roth. (Bibl. 2004, 19286.) Rev. by Jake Fuchs in AmBR (25:3) 2004, 29–31; by Patrick Lennon in BELL (ns 3) 2005, 197–204.

19179. Shostak, Debra. Philip Roth: countertexts, counterlives. (Bibl. 2004, 19287.) Rev. by Patrick Lennon in BELL (ns 3) 2005, 197–204; by Derek Parker Royal in StudAJL (24) 2005, 222–4.

19180. —— Philip Roth's fictions of self-exposure. In (pp. 31–57) **19149**.

19181. Smith, Margaret. Autobiography: false confession? In (pp. 99–114) **19149**.

19182. —— *My Life as a Man*: 'the surprises manhood brings'. *In* (pp. 75–87) **19173**.

19183. STANLEY, SANDRA KUMAMOTO. Mourning the 'greatest generation': myth and history in Philip Roth's *American Pastoral*. TCL (51:1) 2005, 1–24.

19184. TUERK, RICHARD. Caught between *The Facts* and *Deception*. *In* (pp. 129–42) **19173**.

19185. WEST, KEVIN R. Professing desire: the Kepesh novels. *In* (pp. 225–39) **19173**.

19186. WILSON, ALEXIS KATE. The ghosts of Zuckerman's past: the *Zuckerman Bound* series. *In* (pp. 103–17) **19173**.

19187. —— The travels of the American *talush*. *In* (pp. 92–8) **19149**.

Jerome Rothenberg

19188. MEILICKE, CHRISTINE A. Jerome Rothenberg's experimental poetry and Jewish tradition. Bethlehem, PA: Lehigh UP, 2005. pp. 328.

Ola Rotimi

19189. COKER, NIYI, JR. Ola Rotimi's African theatre: the development of an indigenous aesthetic. Lewiston, NY; Lampeter: Mellen Press, 2005. pp. vi, 150. (Studies in theatre arts, 32.)

Noel Rowe (b.1951)

19190. ROWE, NOEL. How to gossip with angels: Australian poetry after the gods. *See* **15613**.

J. K. Rowling

19191. ABANES, RICHARD. Harry Potter, Narnia, and *The Lord of the Rings*. Eugene, OR: Harvest House, 2005. pp. 297.

19192. ANDERSEN, KARA LYNN. Harry Potter and the susceptible child audience. CLCWeb (7:2) 2005.

19193. BAGGETT, DAVID. Magic, Muggles and moral imagination. *In* (pp. 158–71) **19194**.

19194. —— KLEIN, SHAWN E. (eds). Harry Potter and philosophy: if Aristotle ran Hogwarts. Chicago, IL: Open Court, 2004. pp. x, 243. (Popular culture and philosophy, 9.) Rev. by Rebecca Housel in JPC (38:4) 2005, 775–6.

19195. BARFIELD, STEVEN. Of young magicians and growing up: J. K. Rowling, her critics and the 'cultural infantilism' debate. *In* (pp. 175–97) **19214**.

19196. BASSHAM, GREGORY. The prophecy-driven life: fate and freedom at Hogwarts. *In* (pp. 213–26) **19194**.

19197. BEAHM, GEORGE. Muggles and magic: J. K. Rowling and the Harry Potter phenomenon. Charlottesville, VA: Hampton Roads, 2004. pp. xxi, 393, (plates) 16.

19198. BEHR, KATE. 'Same-as-difference': narrative transformations and intersecting cultures in Harry Potter. JNT (35:1) 2005, 112–32.

19199. BELSEY, CATHERINE. Remembering as re-inscription – with a difference. *See* **3475**.

19200. BILLONE, AMY. The boy who lived: from Carroll's Alice and Barrie's Peter Pan to Rowling's Harry Potter. *See* **10396**.

19201. CASTRO, ADAM-TROY. From Azkaban to Abu Ghraib: fear and Fascism in *Harry Potter and the Order of the Phoenix. In* (pp. 119–32) **19221**.

19202. CHEVALIER, NOEL. The Liberty Tree and the Whomping Willow: political justice, magical science, and Harry Potter. LU (29:3) 2005, 397–415.

19203. COOLEY, RON W. Harry Potter and the temporal prime directive: time travel, rule-breaking, and misapprehension in *Harry Potter and the Prisoner of Azkaban. In* (pp. 29–42) **19214**.

19204. COTHRAN, CASEY A. Lessons in transfiguration: allegories of male identity in Rowling's Harry Potter series. *In* (pp. 123–34) **19214**.

19205. DEAVEL, DAVID; DEAVEL, CATHERINE. A skewed reflection: the nature of evil. *In* (pp. 132–47) **19194**.

19206. DEVOS, ELISABETH. It's all about God. *In* (pp. 69–81) **19221**.

19207. EBERL, JASON T. Why Voldemort won't just die already: what wizards can teach us about personal identity. *In* (pp. 200–12) **19194**.

19208. FIFE, ERNELLE. Reading J. K. Rowling magically: creating C. S. Lewis's 'good reader'. *In* (pp. 137–58) **19214**.

19209. GAFFINKLE, RICHARD. Why killing Harry is the worst outcome for Voldemort. *In* (pp. 179–94) **19221**.

19210. GELLIS, ROBERTA. The Dursleys as social commentary. *In* (pp. 27–38) **19221**.

19211. GIBBONS, SARAH E. Death and rebirth: Harry Potter & the mythology of the phoenix. *In* (pp. 85–105) **19214**.

19212. GLADSTEIN, MIMI R. Feminism and equal opportunity: Hermione and the women of Hogwarts. *In* (pp. 49–59) **19194**.

19213. GUNN, JAMES. *Harry Potter* as schooldays novel. *In* (pp. 145–55) **19221**.

19214. HALLETT, CYNTHIA WHITNEY (ed.). Scholarly studies in Harry Potter: applying academic methods to a popular text. Lewiston, NY; Lampeter: Mellen Press, 2005. pp. xiii, 277. (Studies in British literature, 99.)

19215. HORSTKOTTE, MARTIN. The worlds of the fantastic Other in postmodern English fiction. JFA (14:3) 2004, 318–32.

19216. HSIEH, DIANA MERTZ. Dursley duplicity: the morality and psychology of self-deception. *In* (pp. 22–37) **19194**.

19217. HUEY, PEGGY J. A basilisk, a phoenix, and a philosopher's stone: Harry Potter's myths and legends. *In* (pp. 65–83) **19214**.

19218. KLEIN, SHAWN E. The Mirror of Erised: why we should heed Dumbledore's warning. *In* (pp. 92–104) **19194**.

19219. KRAUSE, MARGUERITE. Harry Potter and the end of religion. *In* (pp. 53–67) **19221**.

19220. LACKEY, MERCEDES. Harry Potter and the post-traumatic stress disorder counselor. *In* (pp. 157–62) **19221**.

19221. —— WILSON, LEAH (eds). Mapping the world of Harry Potter: science fiction and fantasy writers explore the bestselling fantasy series of all time. Dallas, TX: BenBella, 2005. pp. iv, 195.

19222. LEWIS, JONATHAN P. If yeh know where to go: vision and mapping in the wizarding world. *In* (pp. 43–64) **19214**.

19223. LIPSCOMB, BENJAMIN J. BRUXVOORT; STEWART, W. CHRISTOPHER. Magic, science, and the ethics of technology. *In* (pp. 77–91) **19194.**

19224. LONGSTER, REBECCA WHITUS. The harlequins in the Weasley twins: jesters in the court of Prince Harry (and J. K. Rowling). *In* (pp. 107–21) **19214.**

19225. MAIER, SARAH E. Educating Harry Potter: a Muggle's perspective on magic and knowledge in the wizard world of J. K. Rowling. *In* (pp. 7–27) **19214.**

19226. MATTERN, JOANNE. J. K. Rowling, author. New York: Ferguson, 2005. pp. 122. (Ferguson career biographies.)

19227. MATTHEWS, GARETH B. Platform 9¾: the idea of a different reality. *In* (pp. 175–85) **19194.**

19228. MATTHEWS, SUSAN R. *Ich bin ein Hufflepuff*: strategies for variable skill management in J. K. Rowling's Harry Potter novels. *In* (pp. 133–44) **19221.**

19229. MILLMAN, JOYCE. To Sir, with love: how fan fiction transformed Professor Snape from a greasy git to a Byronic hero … who's really, really into s/m. *In* (pp. 39–52) **19221.**

19230. MOLONEY, DANIEL P. Harry Potter and the young man's mistake: the illusion of innocence and the temptation of power. *In* (pp. 7–26) **19221.**

19231. MORRIS, TOM. The courageous Harry Potter. *In* (pp. 9–21) **19194.**

19232. NEITHARDT, LEIGH A. The problem of identity in *Harry Potter and the Sorcerer's Stone*. *In* (pp. 159–73) **19214.**

19233. PATTERSON, STEVEN W. Is ambition a virtue? Why Slytherin belongs at Hogwarts. *In* (pp. 121–31) **19194.**

19234. —— Kreacher's lament: S.P.E.W. as a parable on discrimination, indifference, and social justice. *In* (pp. 105–17) **19194.**

19235. PERRY, EVELYN M. Metaphor and metafantasy: questing for literary inheritance in J. K. Rowling's *Harry Potter and the Sorcerer's Stone*. *In* (pp. 241–75) **19214.**

19236. SILBERSTEIN, MICHAEL. Space, time, and magic. *In* (pp. 186–99) **19194.**

19237. THORSRUD, HARALD. Voldemort's agents, Malfoy's cronies, and Hagrid's chums: friendship in Harry Potter. *In* (pp. 38–48) **19194.**

19238. WALLS, JERRY L. Heaven, Hell and Harry Potter. *In* (pp. 63–76) **19194.**

19239. WANDLESS, WILLIAM. Hogwarts vs *The 'Values' Wasteland*: Harry Potter and the formation of character. *In* (pp. 217–40) **19214.**

19240. WATT-EVANS, LAWRENCE. Why Dumbledore had to die. *In* (pp. 111–18) **19221.**

19241. WEED, JENNIFER HART. Voldemort, Boethius, and the destructive effects of evil. *In* (pp. 148–57) **19194.**

19242. WELLS, MARTHA. Neville Longbottom: the hero with a thousand faces. *In* (pp. 101–9) **19221.**

19243. WYTENBROEK, LYNN (J. R.). Harry Potter and the Canadian fantasy. CanL (186) 2005, 197–9.

19244. ZETTEL, SARAH. Hermione Granger and the charge of sexism. *In* (pp. 83–99) **19221.**

Arundhati Roy

19245. CAMPBELL-HALL, DEVON. Dangerous artisans: anarchic labour in Michael Ondaatje's *The English Patient* and *Anil's Ghost* and Arundhati Roy's *The God of Small Things*. *See* **18618.**

19246. ESHELMAN, RAOUL. Checking out of the epoch: performatism in Olga Tokarczuk's *The Hotel Capital* vs late postmodernism in Ali Smith's *Hotel World* (with remarks on Arundhati Roy's *The God of Small Things* and Miloš Urban's *Sevenchurch*). *See* **21291.**

19247. FRIEDMAN, SUSAN STANFORD. Paranoia, pollution, and sexuality: affiliations between E. M. Forster's *A Passage to India* and Arundhati Roy's *The God of Small Things*. *In* (pp. 245–61) **12640.**

19248. MULLANEY, JULIE. 'Globalizing dissent'? Arundhati Roy, local and postcolonial feminisms in the transnational economy. WLWE (40:1) 2002/03, 56–70.

19249. SUTHERLAND, KATHERINE G. Land of their graves: maternity, mourning, and nation in Janet Frame, Sara Suleri, and Arundhati Roy. *See* **16577.**

Rudy v. B. (Rudy von Bitter) Rucker (b.1946)

19250. LATHAM, ROB. Long live Gonzo: an introduction to Rudy Rucker. JFA (16:1) 2005, 3–5.

19251. RUCKER, RUDY. Seek the Gnarl. JFA (16:1) 2005, 6–20.

Paul Rudnick

19252. EADS, MARTHA GREENE. Conversion tactics in Terrence McNally's and Paul Rudnick's gay gospels. *See* **18027.**

Muriel Rukeyser

19253. KAUFMAN, JANET E.; HERZOG, ANNE F.; LEVI, JAN HELLER (eds). The collected poems of Muriel Rukeyser. Pittsburgh, PA: Pittsburgh UP, 2005. pp. xli, 670. Rev. by Joshua A. Weiner in BkW, 3 July 2005, 5.

19254. KICH, MARTIN (introd. and notes). *The Outer Banks*: poems of Muriel Rukeyser and W. D. Ehrhart. NCLR (14) 2005, 31–42.

19255. PERREAULT, JEANNE. Muriel Rukeyser: egodocuments and the ethics of propaganda. *In* (pp. 143–63) **12750.**

19256. SACERDOTI MARIANI, GIGLIOLA. 'Words at war': testi e pre-testi di Muriel Rukeyser. *In* (pp. 116–39) **12589.**

19257. SCIGAJ, LEONARD M. Ecology, Egyptology, and dialectics in Muriel Rukeyser's *The Book of the Dead*. Mosaic (38:3) 2005, 131–47.

19258. SELINGER, ERIC MURPHY. Rukeyser without commitment. Parnassus (28:1/2) 2005, 124–50 (review-article).

Carol Rumens

19259. ZAMORANO LLENA, CARMEN. The salvage from postmodernism: nomadic subjectivity in contemporary women's poetry in the British Isles. *See* **15083.**

Salman Rushdie

19260. AHMAD, DOHRA. 'This fundo stuff is really something new': fundamentalism and hybridity in *The Moor's Last Sigh*. YJC (18:1) 2005, 1–20.

19261. ALMOND, IAN. Mullahs, mystics, moderates and moghuls: the many Islams of Salman Rushdie. ELH (70:4) 2003, 1137–51.

19262. BARNABY, EDWARD. Airbrushed history: photography, realism, and Rushdie's *Midnight's Children*. Mosaic (38:1) 2005, 1–16.

19263. BISWAS, AMRIT. The colonial subject and colonial discourse: Salman Rushdie's critique of Englishness in *The Satanic Verses*. WLWE (40:2) 2004, 91–105.

19264. BROUILLETTE, SARAH. Authorship as crisis in Salman Rushdie's *Fury*. JCL (40:1) 2005, 137–56.

19265. BUONAIUTO, CLAUDIA; CARIELLO, MARTA. A Western/Eastern map of London. In (pp. 99–108) **3690**.

19266. CHAMBERS, CLAIRE. 'The absolute essentialness of conversations': a discussion with Amitav Ghosh. See **16664**.

19267. CHIU, JEANNIE. Melancholy and human rights in *A Nostalgist's Map of America* and *Midnight's Children*. Lit (16:1) 2005, 25–39.

19268. DESZCZ, J. Salman Rushdie's American adventure: the theme of the journey to America in *Fury*. In (pp. 151–9) **12672**.

19269. FALCONER, RACHEL. Shape-changing in hell: metamorphosis and katabasis in Rushdie's *The Ground beneath Her Feet*. EREA (2:2) 2004, 118–27.

19270. GONZALEZ, MADELENA. Fiction after the fatwa: Salman Rushdie and the charm of catastrophe. Amsterdam; Atlanta, GA: Rodopi, 2005. pp. 266. (Costerus, ns 153.) Rev. by Claire Pégon in EREA (3:2) 2005.

19271. HUBBLE, NICK. Imagined and imaginary whales: George Orwell, Benedict Anderson and Salman Rushdie. See **18683**.

19272. KHAN, NYLA ALI. The fiction of nationality in an era of transnationalism. See **16057**.

19273. MIQUEL, CATHERINE. Quand Salman cherche à faire mauvais genre: analyse des genres dans *Fury*, de Salman Rushdie. EtBr (28) 2005, 83–100.

19274. PIPES, DANIEL. The Rushdie affair: the novel, the Ayatollah, and the West. Postscript by Konraad Elst. (Bibl. 1991, 15230.) New Brunswick, NJ: Transaction, 2003. pp. 303. (Second ed.: first ed. 1990.)

19275. RAMACHANDRAN, HEMA. Salman Rushdie's *The Satanic Verses*: hearing the postcolonial cinematic novel. JCL (40:3) 2005, 102–17.

19276. RAUWERDA, ANTJE M. 'Angelicdevilish' combinations: Milton's Satan and Salman Rushdie's *The Satanic Verses*. JPW (41:1) 2005, 94–107.

19277. RUBINSON, GREGORY J. The fiction of Rushdie, Barnes, Winterson, and Carter: breaking cultural and literary boundaries in the work of four postmodernists. Jefferson, NC; London: McFarland, 2005. pp. vii, 228.

19278. —— Revisiting *The Satanic Verses*: Rushdie's desacralizing treatment of the Koran as a literary intertext. EREA (2:1) 2004, 122–7.

19279. SHANKAR, S. Midnight's orphans; or, A postcolonialism worth its name. CultC (56) 2004, 64–95.

19280. SKINNER, JOHN. Literary moonlighting: the cultural spaces of Shashi Tharoor. *See* **19762.**

19281. STRAND, ERIC. Gandhian communalism and the Midnight Children's Conference. ELH (72:4) 2005, 975–1016.

Charles M. Russell

19282. CRISTY, RAPHAEL JAMES. Charles M. Russell: the storyteller's art. Albuquerque: New Mexico UP, 2004. pp. xx, 347. Rev. by Anne Morand in Montana (55:4) 2005, 84–5.

Mary Doria Russell (b.1950)

19283. KHADER, JAMIL. Race matters: people of color, ideology, and the politics of erasure and reversal in Ursula Le Guin's *The Left Hand of Darkness* and Mary Doria Russell's *The Sparrow*. *See* **17663.**

Gig Ryan

19284. FARRELL, MICHAEL. Counting and comparing personal etc. pronouns in and between Ryan's *Pure and Applied* and Ashbery's *Wakefulness*. Antipodes (18:1) 2004, 57–8.

Michael Ryan

19285. RIVARD, DAVID. Resistance to the unreal: Michael Ryan's *New and Selected Poems*. APR (34:3) 2005, 11–15 (review-article).

Geoff Ryman

19286. CANAAN, HOWARD. The pressures of history and fiction in Geoff Ryman's *Was*. JFA (13:3) 2003, 218–25.

V. Sackville-West

19287. BARKWAY, STEPHEN. Laughton Place: a Knole of Woolf's own? *See* **20304.**

19288. GANIM, JOHN M. Chaucer and free love. *In* (pp. 344–63) **4485.**

19289. JOHNSTON, GEORGIA. Counterfeit perversion: Vita Sackville-West's *Portrait of a Marriage*. JML (28:1) 2004, 124–37.

19290. MARES, CHERYL. Woolf and the American imaginary. *See* **20391.**

19291. ZEISS, MCKENZIE L. The political legacy of the garden: (anti)pastoral images and national identity in Virginia Woolf and Vita Sackville-West. *See* **20443.**

Nayantara Sahgal

19292. GUTTMAN, ANNA. Secularism as syncretism in Nayantara Sahgal's *Lesser Breeds*. JCL (40:3) 2005, 47–62.

Margaret St Clair (b.1911)

19293. YASZEK, LISA. Domestic satire as social commentary in mid-century women's media landscape sf. *See* **16829.**

J. D. Salinger

19294. DUGAN, LAWRENCE. Holden and the Lunts. NQ (52:4) 2005, 510–11.

19295. DUNNE, SARA LEWIS. Moviegoing in the modern novel: Holden, Binx Ignatius. *See* **18763.**

19296. LACY, ROBERT.   Sing a song of Sonny. SewR (113:2) 2005, 309–16.

19297. WEBER, MYLES.   Consuming silences: how we read authors who don't publish. Athens; London: Georgia UP, 2005. pp. 159. Rev. by R. H. W. Dillard in SewR (113:2) 2005, 337–43.

Ralph J. Salisbury

19298. KRYSL, MARILYN.   The big seminar we call time: an interview with poet, storyteller and fiction writer Ralph Salisbury. BRev (24:2) 2004, 15, 18.

Mary Jo Salter

19299. BACIGALUPO, MASSIMO.   A note on Mary Jo Salter's America. RSA (15/16) 2004/05, 145–8.

Laura Goodman Salverson

19300. ROY, WENDY.   'The ensign of the mop and the dustbin': the maternal and the material in autobiographical writings by Laura Goodman and Nellie McClung. In (pp. 247–62) **14629.**

Agnes Sam

19301. RASTOGI, PALLAVI.   From South Asia to South Africa: locating other postcolonial diasporas. See **16380.**

Sonia Sanchez

19302. KEITA, MICHELLE NZADI.   Sonia Sanchez: 'fearless about the world'. In (pp. 279–91) **12566.**

19303. LUO, LIANGGONG.   Poetic craftsmanship and spiritual freedom: an interview with Professor Sonia Sanchez. FLS (116) 2005, 1–6.

19304. WOOD, JACQUELINE.   'This thing called playwriting': an interview with Sonia Sanchez on the art of her drama. AAR (39:1/2) 2005, 119–32.

Carl Sandburg

19305. REED, BRIAN M.   Carl Sandburg's *The People, Yes*, thirties Modernism, and the problem of bad political poetry. TSLL (46:2) 2004, 181–211.

Peter Sanger (b.1943)

19306. DONALDSON, JEFFERY.   Geologist and giant: two Canadian poets and their landscapes. See **19760.**

George Santayana

19307. COREY, ELIZABETH.   A discipline of the mind and heart: Vogelin and Santayana as philosophers of experience. In (pp. 129–45) **14768.**

19308. COSTELLO, BONNIE.   Planets on tables: still life and war in the poetry of Wallace Stevens. See **19652.**

19309. HOLZBERGER, WILLIAM G. (ed.).   The letters of George Santayana: book 4, 1928–1932. Cambridge, MA; London: MIT Press, 2003. pp. lxxv, 530. (Works of George Santayana, 5:4.)

19310. —— The letters of George Santayana: book 5, 1933–1936. Cambridge, MA; London: MIT Press, 2003. pp. xlvii, 609. (Works of George Santayana, 5:5.) Rev. by John McCormick in SewR (113:1) 2005, i–iv.

19311. —— The letters of George Santayana: book 6, 1937–1940. Cambridge, MA; London: MIT Press, 2004. pp. lxxv, 618. (Works of George Santayana, 5:6.) Rev. by John McCormick in SewR (113:1) 2005, iv–vii.

19312. McCORMICK, JOHN. Among decadents, heretics, and madmen. SewR (113:1) 2005, iv–vii (review-article).

19313. —— De profundis. SewR (113:1) 2005, i–iv (review-article).

Robyn Sarah

19314. SWARD, ROBERT. A conversation with Robyn Sarah: *A Day's Grace*. Nimrod (49:1) 2005, 181–200.

Frank Sargeson

19315. GNIADEK, MELISSA. The art of becoming: Sherwood Anderson, Frank Sargeson and the grotesque aesthetic. *See* **15162**.

19316. PHILLIPSON, ALLAN. Dollarman *vs The Lord of the Rings*: the battle of nature and progress. *See* **20727**.

Ken Saro-Wiwa

19317. PRABHU, ANJALI. Reading *Calibrations*: re-reading for the social. *See* **21101**.

Siegfried Sassoon

19318. BOWEN, SUSAN. Sherston and Sassoon in France. EtBr (29) 2005, 1–14.

19319. BROWN, DENNIS. The Regeneration Trilogy: total war, masculinities, anthropologies, and the talking cure. *In* (pp. 187–202) **15309**.

19320. EGREMONT, MAX. Siegfried Sassoon: a biography. London: Picador, 2005. pp. 639. Rev. by Dominic Hibberd in TLS, 4 Nov. 2005, 6–7.

19321. HEMMINGS, ROBERT. 'The blameless physician': narrative and pain, Sassoon and Rivers. LitMed (24:1) 2005, 109–26.

19322. HIBBERD, DOMINIC. To endure their ache. TLS, 4 Nov. 2005, 6–7 (review-article). (Pacifism.)

19323. HIPP, DANIEL. The poetry of shell shock: wartime trauma and healing in Wilfred Owen, Ivor Gurney and Siegfried Sassoon. *See* **18709**.

George Saunders (b.1958)

19324. HANSEN, JOSEPH. An interview with George Saunders. DQ (40:2) 2005, 43–9.

Alexander Saxton

19325. RYDELL, ROBERT W. Grand crossings: the life and work of Alexander Saxton. PacHR (73:2) 2004, 263–86.

Dorothy L. Sayers

19326. DOWNING, CRYSTAL. The orthodoxology of Dorothy L. Sayers. SEVEN (22) 2005, 29–44.

19327. —— Writing performances: the stages of Dorothy L. Sayers. (Bibl. 2004, 19365.) Rev. by Margaret Goodman in CSL (36:3) 2005, 16.

19328. GORMAN, ANITA G.; MATEER, LESLIE R. The medium is the message: *Busman's Honeymoon* as play, novel, and film. Clues (23:4) 2005, 54–62.

19329. Harbus, Antonina. Colchester's legend on stage: *The Emperor Constantine* by Dorothy L. Sayers. ModDr (48:1) 2005, 87–107.

19330. Nurmi, Arja. 'A jolly kind of letter': *The Documents in the Case* and Dorothy L. Sayers's correspondence on trial. EJES (9:1) 2005, 53–9.

19331. Simmons, Laura K. Creed without chaos: exploring theology in the writings of Dorothy L. Sayers. Grand Rapids, MI: Baker Academic, 2005. pp. 222. Rev. by Joe R. Christopher in Mythprint (42:11) 2005, 5–6.

19332. Victoroff, Tatiana. *La création inachevée*: la poétique sacramentelle du mystère dans les années 1930. RLC (79:1) 2005, 51–73.

19333. Young, Laurel. Dorothy L. Sayers and the New Woman detective novel. Clues (23:4) 2005, 39–53.

John Sayles

19334. Clericuzio, Alessandro. Messico–Stati Uniti, una frontiera di tortillas: T. C. Boyle, John Sayles, Sam Shepard. *In* (pp. 295–304) **12883**.

Diane Schoemperlen

19335. Struthers, J. R. (Tim). Illustrated fiction: an interview with Diane Schoemperlen. WasRCPSF (38:1) 2003, 251–66.

George Schuyler

19336. Ferguson, Jeffrey B. The sage of Sugar Hill: George S. Schuyler and the Harlem renaissance. New Haven, CT; London: Yale UP, 2005. pp. xv, 303.

James Schuyler

19337. Corbett, William (ed.). Just the thing: selected letters of James Schuyler, 1951–1991. (Bibl. 2004, 19378.) Rev. by William Wootten in TLS, 9 Sept. 2005, 6; by August Kleinzahler in LRB (27:22) 2005, 21–2.

19338. Kleinzahler, August. Living on apple crumble. LRB (27:22) 2005, 21–2 (review-article). (Letters.)

19339. Wootten, William. Pleasure and joy. TLS, 9 Sept. 2005, 6 (review-article). (Letters.)

Steven Schwartz (b.1950)

19340. Schwartz, Steven. Behind the story. *In* (pp. 341–4) **14294**.

Duncan Campbell Scott

19341. Carter, Adam. Anthropomorphism and trope in the national ode. *In* (pp. 117–44) **9191**.

Mrs Evelyn Scott

19342. Franks, Jill. Oxymorons and the pathetic fallacy in *The Narrow House*: a Lacanian reading. TPB (42) 2005, 30–9.

19343. Ryan, Steven. Evelyn Scott's lost echo: the beginning and the end of a Modernist. TPB (42) 2005, 49–60.

19344. Tyrer, Pat. 'A bird alive in a snake's body': the New Woman of Evelyn Scott's *The Narrow House*. SoLJ (38:1) 2005, 43–61.

F. R. Scott

19345. Bentley, D. M. R. 'New styles of architecture, a change of heart'? The architexts of A. M. Klein and F. R. Scott. *In* (pp. 17–58) **12739**.

19346. RICHARDS, ALAN. Between tradition and counter-tradition: the poems of A. J. M. Smith and F. R. Scott in *The Canadian Mercury* (1928–1929). *See* **19480.**

Gail Scott (b.1945)

19347. LECLERC, CATHERINE. Une héritière rebelle: *Heroine* de Gail Scott et la représentation des francophones. QStud (39) 2005, 79–97.

Jody Scott

19348. HARSE, KATIE. 'Sick of Count Dracula': Scott, Carter, Rice and the response to Stoker's authority. JFA (13:3) 2003, 250–7.

Melissa Scott

19349. MURPHY, GRAHAM J. Penetrating the body-plus-virtualisation in Melissa Scott's *Trouble and Her Friends*. Foundation (95) 2005, 40–51.

Paul Scott

19350. STEINBERG, THEODORE LOUIS. Twentieth-century epic novels. *See* **16191.**

Maureen Seaton (b.1947)

19351. LEE, ESTHER. Exquisite flotsam and kismet: the making of literary collage (and collaboration): an interview with Maureen Seaton. InR (27:1) 2005, 109–20.

David Sedaris

19352. SPALDING, ESTA. An interview with David Sedaris. Brick (76) 2005, 45–51.

J.otto Seibold

19353. PARSONS, ELIZABETH. The appeal of the underdog: Mr Lunch and Left politics as entertainment. CLAQ (30:4) 2005, 354–67.

W. C. (Walter Carruthers) Sellar (b.1898) and R. J. (Robert Julian) Yeatman

19354. MILNE, LESLEY. *Universal History as Reworked by 'Satirikon'* and *1066 and All That* as parody history textbooks: a suggestion of a literary genre. MLR (100:3) 2005, 723–39.

Shyam Selvadurai (b.1965)

19355. JAYAWICKRAMA, SHARANYA. At home in the nation? Negotiating identity in Shyam Selvadurai's *Funny Boy*. JCL (40:2) 2005, 123–39.

Maurice Sendak

19356. GOLLAPUDI, APARNA. Unraveling the invisible seam: text and image in Maurice Sendak's *Higglety Pigglety Pop!* ChildLit (32) 2004, 112–33.

Olive Senior

19357. SENIOR, OLIVE. The story as *su-su*, the writer as gossip. *In* (pp. 41–50) **14204.**

19358. STOUCK, JORDAN. Gardening in the diaspora: place and identity in Olive Senior's poetry. Mosaic (38:4) 2005, 103–22.

Danzy Senna

19359. HARRISON-KAHAN, LORI. Passing for White, passing for Jewish: mixed-race identity in Danzy Senna and Rebecca Walker. MELUS (30:1) 2005, 19–48.

Robert Service

19360. SMULDERS, SHARON. 'A man in a world of men': the rough, the tough, and the tender in Robert W. Service's *Song of a Sourdough*. StudCanL (30:1) 2005, 34–57.

Vikram Seth (b.1952)

19361. SETH, VIKRAM. Two lives. New York: HarperCollins, 2005. pp. 503, (plates) 24.

19362. TRIVEDI, HARISH. Colonizing love: *Romeo and Juliet* in modern Indian disseminations. *In* (pp. 74–91) **6096**.

'Dr Seuss' (Theodor Seuss Geisel)

19363. COHEN, CHARLES D. The Seuss, the whole Seuss, and nothing but the Seuss: a visual biography of Theodor Seuss Geisel. (Bibl. 2004, 19403.) Rev. by Jill P. May in LU (29:1) 2005, 121–4.

19364. LINDEMANN, RICHARD H. F. The Dr Seuss catalog: an annotated guide to works by Theodor Geisel in all media, writings about him, and appearance of characters in the books, stories, and films. Jefferson, NC; London: McFarland, 2005. pp. ix, 245.

19365. NEL, PHILIP. Dr Seuss: American icon. (Bibl. 2004, 19405.) Rev. by Jill P. May in LU (29:1) 2005, 121–4; by George Bodmer in CLAQ (30:1) 2005, 120–2.

Stephen Sewell

19366. LEY, G. K. H. Re-reading Stephen Sewell's *Traitors*: ideology and gender in 'the Australian play'. ModDr (48:1) 2005, 108–17.

Anne Sexton

19367. ALKALAY-GUT, KAREN. The dream life of Ms Dog: Anne Sexton's revolutionary use of pop culture. ColLit (32:4) 2005, 50–73.

19368. BADIA, JANET. 'One of those people like Anne Sexton or Sylvia Plath': the pathologized woman reader in literary and popular culture. *In* (pp. 236–54) **12549**.

19369. GILL, JOANNA. 'My Sweeney, Mr Eliot': Anne Sexton and the 'impersonal theory of poetry'. JML (27:1/2) 2003, 36–56.

19370. McGOWAN, PHILIP. Anne Sexton and Middle Generation poetry: the geography of grief. Westport, CT; London: Praeger, 2004. pp. xvi, 147. (Contributions to the study of American literature, 16.)

Miranda Seymour

19371. RAVAL, SHILPA. The three faces of Helen: 1970s and 1980s feminist re-visions of the myth of Helen of Troy. CML (25:1) 2005, 1–22.

Maurice Shadbolt

19372. TEMPLE, PHILIP. Maurice Shadbolt (1932–2004). NZBooks (15:1) 2005, 4–5. (Obituary.)

Peter Shaffer

19373. DESPOTOPOULOU, ANNA.   From Dionysus to Gorgon: Peter Shaffer's revision of Classical myth and theory. CML (25:1) 2005, 85–97.

Alan Shain

19374. SHAIN, ALAN.   Disability, theatre, and power: an analysis of a one-person play. CanTR (122) 2005, 13–18.

Ntozake Shange

19375. EL-SHAYAL, DALIA.   Nonverbal theatrical elements in Ntozake Shange's *for colored girls* ... and Intissar Abdel-Fatah's *Makhadet El-Kohl (The Kohl Pillow)*. CompDr (37:3/4) 2003/04, 361–78.

John Patrick Shanley

19376. TORRE, ROMA.   The making of *Doubt*. Dramatist (8:1) 2005, 6–11. (Interview.)

19377. UHRY, ALFRED.   Guild roundtable: playwrights on Broadway. *See* **16351.**

Karl Shapiro

19378. UPDIKE, JOHN (ed.).   Selected poems. New York: Library of America, 2003. pp. xxxi, 197. (American poets project.) Rev. by Phoebe Pettingell in NewL (86:2) 2003, 28–9; by Jules Smith in TLS, 3 Sept. 2004, 24.

George Bernard Shaw

19379. ANON.   The trenchancy of Shaw's eight words. IndS (42:1/2) 2004, 13.

19380. ALBERT, SIDNEY P.   Shaw's *Republic*. Shaw (25) 2005, 82–8.

19381. BENNETT, BENJAMIN.   All theater is revolutionary theater. *See* **16244.**

19382. BERRY, PATRICK.   Teachers, capitalists, and class in *Pygmalion* and *The Millionairess*. IndS (42:3) 2004, 51–8.

19383. BERTOLINI, JOHN A.   Shaw responds to Shaw-bashing. Shaw (25) 2005, 127–34.

19384. CARPENTER, CHARLES A.   Tracking down Shaw studies: the effective use of printed and online bibliographical sources. Shaw (25) 2005, 165–78.

19385. CHIRICO, MIRIAM.   Social critique and comedic reconciliation in Shaw's *You Never Can Tell*. Shaw (25) 2005, 105–26.

19386. CONOLLY, L. W.   G.B.S. & the BBC: *Saint Joan*, 1929. TN (57:1) 2003, 11–24.

19387. ——   Shaw and BBC English. IndS (42:3) 2004, 59–63.

19388. ——   Who was Phillipa Summers? Reflections on Vivie Warren's Cambridge. Shaw (25) 2005, 89–95.

19389. DUBA, FRANK.   'The genuine pulpit article': Shaw's prefatorial practice and the preface to *Man and Superman*. Shaw (25) 2005, 221–40.

19390. DUKORE, BERNARD F.   Machiavelli, the shark, and the tinpot tragedienne. Shaw (25) 2005, 59–72.

19391. EDGECOMBE, RODNEY STENNING.   Two Verdian echoes in *Heartbreak House*. NQ (52:1) 2005, 99–100.

19392. EINSOHN, HOWARD IRA.   Economies of the gift: Shaw, Ricoeur, and the poetics of the ethical life. Shaw (25) 2005, 27–51.

19393. ELTIS, SOS. Private lives and public spaces: reputation, celebrity and the late Victorian actress. *In* (pp. 169–88) **3985.**

19394. GAHAN, PETER. Shaw shadows: rereading the texts of Bernard Shaw. Gainesville: Florida UP, 2004. pp. 316. (Florida Bernard Shaw.) Rev. by Michel W. Pharand in ELT (48:4) 2005, 459–62; by Jean Reynolds in Shaw (25) 2005, 291–3.

19395. HADDAD, ROSALIE RAHAL. Bermard Shaw : past, present, and future. IndS (43:1/2) 2005, 9–16.

19396. HEROLD, LARRY. Writing was only step one: Bernard Shaw's immersion in the premiere of *Major Barbara*. IndS (42:1/2) 2004, 35–43.

19397. KENNELL, VICKI R. *Pygmalion* as narrative bridge between the centuries. Shaw (25) 2005, 73–81.

19398. LAURENCE, DAN H. Shaw's children. Shaw (25) 2005, 22–6.

19399. LI, KAY. *Mrs Warren's Profession* in China: factors in cross-cultural adaptations. Shaw (25) 2005, 201–20.

19400. LIPSCOMB, VALERIE BARNES. 'Old gentleman': age differences as plot subversion. Shaw (25) 2005, 147–61.

19401. MCDIARMID, LUCY. The Irish art of controversy. *See* **16824.**

19402. MUKLEWICZ, SHANNON. Is *Too True to Be Good* good at all? IndS (43:1/2) 2005, 25–37.

19403. NICKSON, RICHARD. Telling the truth and spreading slander. IndS (42:1/2) 2004, 11–13.

19404. OCHSHORN, KATHLEEN. Who's modern now? Shaw, Joyce, and Ibsen's *When We Dead Awaken*. Shaw (25) 2005, 96–104.

19405. OWENS, CRAIG N. Bernard Shaw's weekly *supplément*. ModDr (48:1) 2005, 11–29.

19406. PAGLIARO, HAROLD E. Relations between the sexes in the plays of George Bernard Shaw. (Bibl. 2004, 19447.) Rev. by Bernard F. Dukore in Shaw (25) 2005, 289–91.

19407. PAPRECK, ANNIE. Shaw, baseball, and episodic history. IndS (42:1/2) 2004, 21–2.

19408. PETERS, JULIE STONE. Joan of Arc *internationale*: Shaw, Brecht, and the Law of Nations. CompDr (38:4) 2004/05, 355–77.

19409. PETERS, SALLY. Eric Bentley on Bernard Shaw: an interview. IndS (42:1/2) 2004, 3–10.

19410. —— Septuagenarian *versus* the Siren: Shaw and Molly Tompkins. IndS (43:1/2) 2005, 20–4.

19411. PFEIFFER, JOHN R. A continuing checklist of Shaviana. Shaw (25) 2005, 260–88.

19412. PHARAND, MICHEL W. Billions of letters. IndS (42:3) 2004, 64–73.

19413. —— A supplement to *Shaw* 24's selected bibliography of writings by and about Bernard Shaw concerning love, sex, marriage, women, and related topics. Shaw (25) 2005, 257–9.

19414. POSTLEWAIT, THOMAS. Constructing events in theatre history: a matter of credibility. *In* (pp. 33–52) **3974.**

19415. SCHWEIGER, HANNES. Bernard Shaw's contributions to the culture and politics of *fin-de-siècle* Vienna. Shaw (25) 2005, 135–46.

19416. SPARKS, JULIE. Playwrights' progress: the evolution of the play cycle, from Shaw's 'Pentateuch' to *Angels in America*. Shaw (25) 2005, 179–200.

19417. TUNNEY, JAY. *Cashel Byron's Profession*: a catalyst to friendship – life imitates art. Shaw (25) 2005, 52–8.

19418. WAGNER-LAWLOR, JENNIFER A. 'Who acts John Bull?': speculating on English national character and modern morality. *See* **12131**.

19419. WEARING, J. P. (ed.). Bernard Shaw and Nancy Astor. Toronto; Buffalo, NY; London: Toronto UP, 2005. pp. xl, 235. (Selected correspondence of Bernard Shaw.) Rev. by Samantha Ellis in TLS, 28 Oct. 2005, 26; by Michel W. Pharand in Shaw (25) 2005, 293–5.

19420. WEINTRAUB, STANLEY. Shaw for the here and now. Shaw (25) 2005, 11–21.

19421. —— Shaw's goddess: Lady Colin Campbell. Shaw (25) 2005, 241–56.

19422. WOOD, JOHN. *Christina*: Shaw's new ending for Ibsen's *A Doll's House*. TLS, 20 May 2005, 11–13.

Trevor Shearston (b.1946)

19423. SHEARSTON, TREVOR. Memory stone. Meanjin (62:3) 2003, 108–12.

Sam Shepard

19424. CLERICUZIO, ALESSANDRO. Messico–Stati Uniti, una frontiera di tortillas: T. C. Boyle, John Sayles, Sam Shepard. *In* (pp. 295–304) **12883**.

19425. MARSZALSKI, MARIUSZ. Sam Shepard's *Motel Chronicles* and *Hawk Moon*: a postmodern (American) traveler's scrapbook. *In* (pp. 251–8) **12672**.

19426. PRZEMECKA, IRENA. Melodrama, myth and role playing in Sam Shepard's work. *In* (pp. 183–7) **3756**.

19427. ROSEN, CAROL. Sam Shepard: a 'poetic rodeo'. Basingstoke; New York: Palgrave Macmillan, 2004. pp. xiii, 282. (Palgrave modern dramatists.)

Delia Sherman

19428. PILINOVSKY, HELEN. Interstitial arts: an interview with Delia Sherman. JFA (15:3) 2004, 248–50.

R. C. Sherriff

19429. MOORCOCK, MICHAEL. *The Hopkins Manuscript*. NYRSF (18:1) 2005, 1, 6–10.

19430. ROPER, MICHAEL. Between manliness and masculinity: the 'war generation' and the psychology of fear in Britain, 1914–1950. JBS (44:2) 2005, 343–62.

Carol Shields

19431. ATWOOD, MARGARET. A soap bubble hovering over the void: a tribute to Carol Shields. VQR (81:1) 2005, 139–42.

19432. BESNER, NEIL K. Carol Shields: the arts of a writing life. Winnipeg, Man.: Prairie Fire Press, 2003. pp. 270. Rev. by Kathy Dilks in BJCS (17:1) 2004, 156; by Faye Hammill in CanL (185) 2005, 132–4.

19433. EAGLETON, MARY.   What's the matter? Authors in Carol Shields' short fiction. CanL (186) 2005, 70–84.

19434. EDEN, EDWARD; GOERTZ, DEE (eds).   Carol Shields, narrative hunger, and the possibilities of fiction. (Bibl. 2004, 19458.) Rev. by Coral Ann Howells in BJCS (17:1) 2004, 157; by Alison Clader in GPQ (24:3) 2004, 215.

19435. MAHARAJ, ROBYN.   'The arc of a whole life': a telephone interview with Carol Shields from her home in Victoria, B.C., May 4, 2002. PrF (23:4) 2002/03, 8–11.

19436. VAN GESSEL, NINA.   Autogeology: limestone and life narrative in Carol Shields's *The Stone Diaries*. In (pp. 63–85) **12587.**

19437. WILLIAMS, DAVID.   Making stories, making selves: 'alternate versions' in *The Stone Diaries*. CanL (186) 2005, 10–28.

David Shields

19438. SHIELDS, DAVID.   Behind the story. In (pp. 60–2) **14294.**

George Shiels

19439. MCKENNA, BERNARD.   George Shiels' *The Passing Day* – the author's text with deletions and emendations. NCL (35:5) 2005, 9–11.

Ann Allen Shockley

19440. ASHFORD, TOMEIKO R.   Marginal Black feminist religiosity: Ann Shockley's construction of the divine heroine in *Say Jesus and Come to Me*. CLAJ (48:3) 2005, 290–307.

Joan Seliger Sidney (b.1942)

19441. SIDNEY, JOAN SELIGER.   Body of diminishing motion: poems and a memoir. Fort Lee, NJ: CavanKerry Press, 2004. pp. xix, 123.

Eleni Sikélianòs

19442. SIKÉLIANÒS, ELENI.   The book of Jon. San Francisco, CA: City Lights, 2004. pp. xi, 116.

Joan Silber (b.1945)

19443. SILBER, JOAN.   Behind the story. In (pp. 163–5) **14294.**

Leslie Marmon Silko

19444. CLAVIEZ, THOMAS.   Cosmopolitanism and its discontents: the politics of Sherman Alexie's *Reservation Blues* and Leslie Marmon Silko's *Almanac of the Dead. See* **15110.**

19445. DE ANGELIS, VALERIO MASSIMO.   Lo spazio del ritorno: contro-miti di iniziazione in *Ceremony* di Leslie Marmon Silko. In (pp. 103–14) **12883.**

19446. DOMINA, LYNN.   Understanding *Ceremony*: a student casebook to issues, sources, and historical documents. Westport, CT; London: Greenwood Press, 2004. pp. xiv, 167. (Literature in context.)

19447. EPPERT, CLAUDIA.   Leslie Silko's *Ceremony*: rhetorics of ethical reading and composition. JACJ (24:3) 2004, 727–54.

19448. FITZ, BREWSTER E.   Silko: writing storyteller and medicine woman. (Bibl. 2004, 19469.) Rev. by Ellen L. Arnold in MFS (51:1) 2005, 194–7.

19449. GOULD, JANICE. Telling stories to the seventh generation: resisting the assimilationist narrative of *Stiya*. *In* (pp. 9–20) **12725**.

19450. MARTÍNEZ FALQUINA, SILVIA. From the monologic eye to healing polyphonies: dialogic re/vision in Native American narratives. *See* **15113**.

19451. MOREL, PAULINE. Counter-stories and border identities: storytelling and myth as a means of identification, subversion, and survival in Leslie Marmon Silko's *Yellow Woman* and *Tony's Story. In* (pp. 29–45) **9168**.

19452. PULITANO, ELVIRA. 'In vain I tried to tell you': crossreading strategies in global literatures. *See* **15071**.

19453. REGIER, A. M. Revolutionary enunciatory spaces: Ghost Dancing, transatlantic travel, and modernist arson in *Gardens in the Dunes*. MFS (51:1) 2005, 134–57.

19454. TILLETT, REBECCA. Reality consumed by realty: the ecological costs of 'development' in Leslie Marmon Silko's *Almanac of the Dead*. EurJAC (24:2) 2005, 153–69.

Alan Sillitoe

19455. HUGHSON, JOHN. The loneliness of the angry young sportsman. *See* **13638**.

Charles Simic

19456. HAMMER, LANGDON. Invisible things: Thylias Moss and Charles Simic. ASch (74:2) 2005, 49–50.

19457. HART, HENRY. Charles Simic's dark nights of the soul. KR (27:3) 2005, 124–47.

Dan Simmons

19458. STEIN, ATARA. Fictionalized Romantics: Byron, Shelley, and Keats as characters in contemporary genre fiction. *See* **21218**.

Neil Simon

19459. SIMON, NEIL. The darkness of comedy. Dramatist (8:2) 2005, 34–7.

Lewis P. Simpson

19460. CLARK, WILLIAM BEDFORD; GRIMSHAW, JAMES A., JR. A conversation with Lewis P. Simpson. RWP (5) 2005, 37–53.

Iain Sinclair

19461. MACFARLANE, ROBERT. A road of one's own: past and present artists of the randomly motivated walk. TLS, 7 Oct. 2005, 3–4 (review-article).

19462. MURRAY, ALEX. Jack the Ripper, the dialectic of enlightenment and the search for spiritual deliverance in *White Chappell, Scarlet Tracings*. CritS (16:1) 2004, 52–66.

19463. SKINNER, SAMANTHA. 'This patron of the spurned, this perambulator of margins, this witness': Iain Sinclair as rag-picker. *In* (pp. 169–74) **14254**.

Upton Sinclair

19464. COODLEY, LAUREN (ed.). The land of orange groves and jails: Upton Sinclair's California. By Upton Sinclair. Santa Clara, CA: Santa Clara Univ.; Berkeley, CA: Heyday, 2004. pp. xiii, 215. (California legacy.)

19465. PIEP, KARSTEN H.   War as proletarian *Bildungsroman* in Upton Sinclair's *Jimmie Higgins*. WLA (17:1/2) 2005, 199–226.

19466. STECKER, ROBERT.   The interaction of ethical and aesthetic value. *See* **11224**.

Kirpal Singh

19467. SINGH, KIRPAL.   Writing tough – staying honest: challenge for a writer in Singapore. *In* (pp. 85–90) **14204**.

Sacheverell Sitwell

19468. ARENS, KATHERINE.   Castrati and the masquerade of the eighteenth century: *Farinelli* and Sitwell. *See* **8094**.

Myra Sklarew

19469. GOLDENBERG, MYRNA.   Identity, memory, and authority: an introduction to Holocaust poems by Hilary Tham, Myra Sklarew, and Dori Katz. *See* **19761**.

Peter Skrzynecki

19470. SKRZYNECKI, PETER.   The sparrow garden. St Lucia: Queensland UP, 2004. pp. xii, 235.

David R. Slavitt ('David Benjamin', 'Henry Lazarus', 'Lynn Meyer', 'Henry Sutton') (b.1935)

19471. SLAVITT, DAVID R.   Re verse: essays on poetry and poets. *See* **4135**.

Elizabeth Smart

19472. QUÉMA, ANNE.   Elizabeth Smart and Cecil Buller: engendering experimental Modernism. *In* (pp. 275–303) **12739**.

Agnes Smedley

19473. PRICE, RUTH.   The lives of Agnes Smedley. Oxford; New York: OUP, 2005. pp. xii, 498.

Jane Smiley

19474. AMANO, KYOKO.   Alger's shadows in Jane Smiley's *A Thousand Acres*. CritW (47:1) 2005, 23–39.

19475. BROWN, SARAH ANNES.   The prequel as palinode: Mary Cowden Clarke's *Girlhood of Shakespeare's Heroines*. *See* **10450**.

19476. KELLY, PHILIPPA.   Finding *King Lear*'s female parts. *See* **6470**.

19477. O'DAIR, SHARON.   Horror or realism? Filming 'toxic discourse' in Jane Smiley's *A Thousand Acres*. TexP (19:2) 2005, 263–82.

19478. SMILEY, JANE.   Thirteen ways of looking at the novel. *See* **4058**.

19479. SMITH, JULIE A.   Sensory experience as consciousness in literary representations of animal minds. *In* (pp. 231–46) **14258**.

A. J. M. (Arthur James Marshall) Smith (b.1902)

19480. RICHARDS, ALAN.   Between tradition and counter-tradition: the poems of A. J. M. Smith and F. R. Scott in *The Canadian Mercury* (1928–1929). StudCanL (30:1) 2005, 113–34.

19481. Trehearne, Brian. A. J. M. Smith's eclectic surrealism. *In* (pp. 119–38) **12739**.

Anna Deavere Smith

19482. Cho, Nancy. Beyond identity politics: national and transnational dialogues in Anna Deavere Smith's *Twilight: Los Angeles, 1992* and Chay Yew's *A Beautiful Country*. JDTC (20:1) 2005, 65–81.

19483. Feffer, Steve. Extending the breaks: *Fires in the Mirror* in the context of Hip Hop structure, style, and culture. CompDr (37:3/4) 2003/04, 397–415.

Dave Smith ('Smith Cornwell')

19484. Johnson, Mark. The dangerous poems of Dave Smith. SoLJ (38:1) 2005, 91–114.

Iain Crichton Smith

19485. Macrae, Alisdair. Exile in British poetry. *In* (pp. 113–23) **14479**.

Lee Smith

19486. Rubin, Rachel. 'What ain't called Melungeons is called hillbillies': Southern Appalachia's in-between people. *See* **17936**.

Lillian Smith

19487. Lewis, Nghana. We shall pave the way: Willa Cather and Lillian Smith's aesthetics of Civil Rights politics. *See* **15732**.

Pauline Smith

19488. Zarandona, Juan Miguel. The hybrid language and society (Afrikaans–English) of the South African postcolonial writing of Pauline Smith (1882–1959) in Spanish translation: *Anna's Marriage/La boda de Anna* (1925). RAEI (16) 2003, 297–314.

Russell Smith (b.1963)

19489. Salem-Wiseman, Lisa. Divided cities, divided selves: portraits of the artist as ambivalent urban hipster. *In* (pp. 142–65) **9243**.

Stevie Smith

19490. Huk, Romana. Stevie Smith: between the lines. Basingstoke; New York: Palgrave Macmillan, 2005. pp. ix, 331.

19491. Mallot, J. Edward. Not drowning but waving: Stevie Smith and the language of the lake. JML (27:1/2) 2003, 171–87.

19492. May, William. *The Choosers*: posthumous collections of Stevie Smith's poetry. Library (6:3) 2005, 321–38.

19493. Steward, Julie Sims. The problem of the body in Stevie Smith's body of work. SAtlR (70:2) 2005, 72–95.

Vivian Smith

19494. Rowe, Noel. How to gossip with angels: Australian poetry after the gods. *See* **15613**.

W. Gordon (William Gordon) Smith (b.1928)

19495. Brown, Ian. Thrawn themes and dramatic experiment: W. Gordon Smith and the paradoxes of creative iconoclasm. ScSR (4:2) 2003, 98–120.

William Gardner Smith (1927–1974)

19496. GIBSON, RICHARD. Richard Wright's *Island of Hallucination* and the 'Gibson Affair'. *See* **20463.**

Zadie Smith

19497. BUONAIUTO, CLAUDIA; CARIELLO, MARTA. A Western/Eastern map of London. *In* (pp. 99–108) **3690.**

19498. FURMAN, ANDREW. The Jewishness of the contemporary Gentile writer: Zadie Smith's *The Autograph Man*. MELUS (30:1) 2005, 3–17.

19499. NIERAGDEN, GÖRAN. Otherness at work: the non-indigenous English novel. *See* **16343.**

19500. PAGANONI, MARIA CRISTINA. Zadie Smith's new ethnicities. Culture (17) 2003, 113–27.

Kendrick Smithyman

19501. SIMPSON, PETER. 'Sinfonia domestica': Mary Stanley & Kendrick Smithyman. *In* (pp. 54–87) **12916.**

Dame Ethel Smyth

19502. CLEMENTS, ELICIA. Virginia Woolf, Ethel Smyth, and music: listening as a productive mode of social interaction. *See* **20332.**

C. P. Snow

19503. ORTOLANO, GUY. Human science or a human face? Social history and the 'two cultures' controversy. JBS (43:4) 2004, 482–505.

19504. REYNOLDS, DAVID. Christ's: a Cambridge college over five centuries. *See* **7742.**

Gary Snyder

19505. CHUNG, LING. Gary Snyder's American Asian shamanism. Comparatist (29) 2005, 38–62.

19506. —— Gary Snyder's seventeen T'ang poems: an anti-climax after his 'Cold Mountain poems'? TransR (69) 2005, 55–62.

Stephen Sondheim

19507. BEAN, MATT. An apple and an orange: comparing *Sunday in the Park with George* and *La Cage aux folles*. SondR (12:2) 2005, 28–9.

19508. BELL, JOHN. Carping, correcting and cutting. SondR (11:3) 2005, 24–6. (Letters.)

19509. BYRNE, CHRISTOPHER. Desperate times, desperate measures: redefining *Sweeney Todd*, and the cutthroat game of Broadway economics. SondR (12:2) 2005, 34–6.

19510. HANSON, LAURA. John Weidman: one thing led to another. *See* **20027.**

19511. HOROWITZ, MARK EDEN. Biography of a song: *Finishing the Hat*. SondR (12:1) 2005, 24–9.

19512. —— Biography of a song: *Losing My Mind*. SondR (11:4) 2005, 28–33.

19513. —— Biography of a song: *Not a Day Goes By*. SondR (12:2) 2005, 20–7.

19514. —— Biography of a song: *Send in the Clowns*. SondR (11:3) 2005, 15–20.

19515. LODGE, MARY JO. From madness to melodramas to musicals: the women of *Lady Audley's Secret* and *Sweeney Todd*. See **10139**.

19516. PERLMAN, GARY. *Pacific Overtures*: varying perspectives. SondR (11:4) 2005, 26–7.

19517. PUCCIO, PAUL M. *Anyone* can still whistle. SondR (11:4) 2005, 36.

19518. ROBERTS, TERRI. Momentum is key: translating *Sweeney* to the silver screen. SondR (12:1) 2005, 19–20.

19519. SCHIFF, LEN. Into the stratosphere: *TSR* talks with Neil Gaiman. See **16628**.

19520. —— Joss Whedon: absolute admiration for Sondheim. See **20793**.

19521. —— Vision and voice: Marc Cherry shows no desperation in his devotion to Sondheim. See **20833**.

19522. SHENTON, MARK. A London chat with Stephen Sondheim. SondR (11:3) 2005, 21–3.

19523. SKILES, CHRISTA. *Company* turns 35. SondR (11:4) 2005, 8–11.

19524. UZDIENSKI, LAUREN. Where you going? Static in Sondheim. SondR (12:2) 2005, 17–18.

Susan Sontag

19525. MANSON, AARON. Remembering Susan Sontag. LitMed (24:1) 2005, 1–4.

19526. WALIGORA-DAVIS, NICOLE A. The ghetto: illness and the formation of the 'suspect' in American polity. See **11710**.

Aaron Sorkin (b.1961)

19527. COKAL, SUSANN. In plain view and the dark unknown: narratives of the feminine body in *Malice*. *In* (pp. 37–60) **19531**.

19528. DOWNING, SPENCER. Handling the truth: Sorkin's liberal vision. *In* (pp. 127–45) **19531**.

19529. FAHY, THOMAS. Athletes, grammar geeks, and porn stars: the liberal education of *Sports Night*. *In* (pp. 61–76) **19531**.

19530. —— An interview with Aaron Sorkin. *In* (pp. 11–17) **19531**.

19531. —— (ed.). Considering Aaron Sorkin: essays on the politics, poetics, and sleight of hand in the films and television series. Jefferson, NC; London: McFarland, 2005. pp. vi, 223.

19532. GARRETT, LAURA K. Women of *The West Wing*: gender stereotypes in the political fiction. *In* (pp. 179–92) **19531**.

19533. GROSS, ROBERT F. Mannerist *noir*: *Malice*. *In* (pp. 19–35) **19531**.

19534. HALL, ANN C. Giving propaganda a good name: *The West Wing*. *In* (pp. 115–26) **19531**.

19535. KEESEY, DOUGLAS. A phantom fly and frightening fish: the unconscious speaks in *Sports Night*. *In* (pp. 77–90) **19531**.

19536. MILLS, FIONA. Depictions of the US military: only 'a few good men' need apply. *In* (pp. 101–14) **19531**.

19537. NEIN, JOHN. The republic of Sorkin: a view from the cheap seats. *In* (pp. 193–209) **19531**.

19538. PAXTON, NATHAN A. Virtue from vice: duty, power, and *The West Wing*. *In* (pp. 147–77) **19531**.

19539. RINGELBERG, KIRSTIN. His Girl Friday (and every day): brilliant women put to poor use. *In* (pp. 91–100) **19531**.

Gary Soto

19540. ORR, TAMRA. Gary Soto. New York: Rosen Central, 2005. pp. 112. (Library of author biographies.)

19541. WHITE, JULIANNE. Soto's *Oranges*. Exp (63:2) 2005, 121–4.

Ahdaf Soueif

19542. VALASSOPOULOS, ANASTASIA. Fictionalising post-colonial theory: the creative native informant? CritS (16:2) 2004, 28–44.

Raymond Souster

19543. CAIN, STEPHEN. Mapping Raymond Souster's Toronto. *In* (pp. 59–75) **12739**.

Wole Soyinka

19544. JEYIFO, BIODUN. Wole Soyinka: politics, poetics and postcolonialism. (Bibl. 2004, 19548.) Rev. by Ato Quayson in RAL (36:2) 2005, 139–41.

19545. KIRCHWEY, KARL. 'And the half-true rhyme is love': modern verse drama and the Classics. *See* **16946**.

19546. MA, JIANJUN; WANG, JIN. Rereading the Yoruban–Western cultural clash in Soyinka's *Death and the King's Horseman*. FLS (115) 2005, 161–6. (In Chinese.)

19547. UKAEGBU, VICTOR. Performing postcolonially: contextual changes in the adaptations of Wole Soyinka's *Death and the King's Horseman* and Femi Osofisan's *Once upon Four Robbers*. WLWE (40:1) 2002/03, 71–85.

Debra Spark (b.1962)

19548. SPARK, DEBRA. Behind the story. *In* (pp. 364–6) **14294**.

Muriel Spark

19549. BRIDGEMAN, TERESA. Thinking ahead: a cognitive approach to prolepsis. Narrative (13:2) 2005, 125–59.

19550. GREGSON, IAN. Muriel Spark's caricatural effects. EC (55:1) 2005, 1–16. (Critical opinion.)

19551. JELÍNKOVÁ, EMA. The concept of evil in *Symposium* and *Not to Disturb*. *In* (pp. 69–72) **3734**.

19552. KRASNER, JAMES. Accumulated lives: metaphor, materiality, and the homes of the elderly. *See* **17688**.

19553. NIXON, JUDE V. '[A] virginal tongue hold': Hopkins's *The Wreck of the Deutschland* and Muriel Spark's *The Girls of Slender Means*. Ren (57:4) 2005, 299–322.

Roberta Spear (b.1948)

19554. LEVINE, PHILIP. In the next world: the poetry of Roberta Spear. GreRR (42) 2005, 3–12.

Elizabeth Spencer

19555. ARBEIT, MARCEL.   Elizabeth Spencerová a její umění vypravěčského odstupu. (Elizabeth Spencer and her art of narrative distance.) Aluze (8) 2004, 68–71.

Jack Spicer

19556. VINCENT, JOHN EMIL.   Pinnacle of no explanation: Jack Spicer's exercise of the novel. MassR (46:2) 2005, 313–41.

Art Spiegelman

19557. KOLÁŘ, STANISLAV.   Animal imagery in Kosinski's *The Painted Bird* and Spiegelman's *Maus. In* (pp. 87–92) **3753.**

19558. MORRISON, KEVIN A.   Satirical irony in Art Spiegelman's *Maus: a Survivor's Tale.* PCR (16:2) 2005, 59–68.

19559. ORBÁN, KATALIN.   Ethical diversions: the post-Holocaust narratives of Pynchon, Abish, DeLillo, and Spiegelman. *See* **18991.**

Mickey Spillane

19560. GALE, ROBERT L.   A Mickey Spillane companion. Westport, CT; London: Greenwood Press, 2003. pp. xv, 338.

19561. WHITING, FREDERICK.   Bodies of evidence: post-war detective fiction and the monstrous origins of the sexual psychopath. YJC (18:1) 2005, 149–78.

Jean Stafford

19562. TOLES, GEORGE.   Animals drunk and sober, famished and dead in the fiction of Jean Stafford. AQ (60:4) 2004, 99–138.

William Stafford

19563. RICOU, LAURIE.   Pacifist poetics. CanL (185) 2005, 6–9.

Cath Staincliffe (b.1956)

19564. VIZCAYA ECHANO, MARTA.   Gender and ethnic otherness in selected novels by Ann Granger, Cath Staincliffe, and Alma Fritchley. *In* (pp. 189–210) **14191.**

Mary (Mary Isobel) Stanley (1919–1980)

19565. SIMPSON, PETER.   'Sinfonia domestica': Mary Stanley & Kendrick Smithyman. *In* (pp. 54–87) **12916.**

'Starhawk' (Marian Simos) (b.1950)

19566. GOLDMAN-PRICE, IRENE C.   Starhawk dreaming a post-feminist, post-Jewish world. *In* (pp. 229–50) **12895.**

Floyd Favel Starr (b.1964)

19567. APPLEFORD, ROB.   The Indian act(ing): proximate perversions in Genet's *The Blacks* and Floyd Favel Starr's *Lady of Silences* (1993, 2003). TRC (24:1/2) 2003, 109–24.

C. K. (Christian Karlson) Stead (b.1932)

19568. STEAD, C. K.   Men and Mansfield in *Mansfield. In* (pp. 124–40) **18084.**

19569. WHITE, MARGO. Mr Congeniality. Metro (290) 2005, 58–63. (Interview.)

Christina Stead (b.1902)

19570. HARRIS, MARGARET (ed.). Dearest Munx: the letters of Christina Stead and William J. Blake. Carlton, Vic.: Miegunyah Press, 2005. pp. xvii, 557.

Flora Annie Steel

19571. COWASJEE, SAROS (ed.). A Raj collection. New Delhi; Oxford: OUP, 2005. pp. l, 1031. Rev. by P. N. Furbank in TLS, 22 Apr. 2005, 19–20.

19572. FURBANK, P. N. Anglo-Indian dialogues: the Raj, the historical novel and misunderstandings between the races. TLS, 22 Apr. 2005, 19–20 (review-article).

Wallace Stegner

19573. GRAULICH, MELODY. Cultural criticism, circa 1974. AmLH (16:3) 2004, 536–42 (review-article).

19574. HARTMAN, STEVEN. 'Invading Walden': part 1, An exchange between Walter Harding and Wallace Stegner. See 12193.

19575. —— 'Invading Walden': part 2, The Thoreauvian dilemmas of Wallace Stegner's On a Darkling Plain. TSB (252) 2005, 1–7.

19576. KARELL, LINDA. The postmodern author on stage: Fair Use and Wallace Stegner. AmDr (14:2) 2005, 70–89.

19577. MAHER, SUSAN NARAMORE. Deep mapping history: Wallace Stegner's Wolf Willow and William Least Heat-Moon's PrairyErth: a Deep Map. HGP (38:1) 2005, 39–54.

Gertrude Stein

19578. ADAMS, JAD. Hideous absinthe: a history of the devil in a bottle. See 12126.

19579. AJI, HÉLÈNE. The subject in the structure: issues of procedure in contemporary American poetry. EREA (2:2) 2004, 66–71.

19580. ANDERSON, CORINNE. I am not who 'I' pretend to be: The Autobiography of Alice B. Toklas and its photographic frontispiece. Comparatist (29) 2005, 26–37.

19581. BERMAN, JESSICA. Modernism's possible geographies. In (pp. 281–96) 12640.

19582. CHODAT, ROBERT. Sense, science, and the interpretations of Gertrude Stein. Mod/Mod (12:4) 2005, 581–605.

19583. DURHAM, LESLIE ATKINS. Staging Gertrude Stein: absence, culture, and the landscape of American alternative theatre. Basingstoke; New York: Palgrave Macmillan, 2005. pp. viii, 182.

19584. DYDO, ULLA E.; RICE, WILLIAM. Gertrude Stein: the language that rises, 1923–1934. (Bibl. 2004, 19595.) Rev. by John Whittier-Ferguson in Mod/Mod (12:4) 2005, 723–6.

19585. EPP, MICHAEL. Full contact: Robert McAlmon, Gertrude Stein, and Modernist book making. PBSA (99:2) 2005, 265–93.

19586. GIESENKIRCHEN, MICHAELA. Ethnic types and problems of characterization in Gertrude Stein's Radcliff themes. ALR (38:1) 2005, 58–72.

19587. HAWKINS, STEPHANIE L. The science of superstition: Gertrude Stein, William James, and the formation of belief. MFS (51:1) 2005, 60–87.

19588. KALATA, KRISTIANNE. 'There was a world of things … and a world of words': narration of self through object in Sylvia Townsend Warner's *Scenes of Childhood*. See **19979**.

19589. KENNEDY, JAKE. Dust and the avant-garde. CLCWeb (7:2) 2005.

19590. LOCATELLI, CARLA. Gertrude Stein e la (in)rappresentabilità autobiografica. In (pp. 73–83) **14377**.

19591. MEHNE, PHILLIP. 'Making it strange': Bewusstsein, Erfahrung und Sprache bei Gertrude Stein und Lyn Hejinian. Amst (48:4) 2003, 537–61.

19592. MEYEROWITZ, PATRICIA (ed.). Look at me now and here I am: writings and lectures, 1911–1945. Introd. by Elizabeth Sprigge. London: Owen, 2004. pp. 418.

19593. MITRANO, G. F. Gertrude Stein: woman without qualities. Aldershot; Burlington, VT: Ashgate, 2005. pp. x, 202.

19594. MIX, DEBORAH. Tender revisions: Harryette Mullen's *Trimmings* and *S*PeRM**K*T*. See **18414**.

19595. NGAI, SIANNE. The cuteness of the avant-garde. CI (31:4) 2005, 811–47.

19596. NICCOLAI, GIULIA. Stein come pietra miliare. In (pp. 84–91) **14377**.

19597. TISCHLER, ALYSON. A rose is a pose: Steinian Modernism and mass culture. JML (26:3/4) 2003, 12–27.

19598. WATSON, DANA CAIRNS. Gertrude Stein and the essence of what happens. Nashville, TN: Vanderbilt UP, 2005. pp. x, 258.

19599. WHITE, HEATHER CASS. Relentless accuracy and a capacity for fact: authorship in Marianne Moore and Gertrude Stein. In (pp. 98–112) **18316**.

19600. WILL, BARBARA. Gertrude Stein and Zionism. MFS (51:2) 2005, 437–55.

John Steinbeck

19601. AGUIAR, SARAH APPLETON. 'No sanctuary': reconsidering the evil of Cathy Ames Trask. In (pp. 145–53) **19612**.

19602. ALLEGRETTI, JOSEPH. Business, sex, and ethics in *The Wayward Bus*. In (pp. 155–67) **19612**.

19603. —— John Steinbeck and the morality of roles: lessons for business ethics. In (pp. 21–31) **19612**.

19604. BAILEY, PAUL. Researching Tom Joad: John Steinbeck, journalist, 1936. ChronOkla (83:1) 2005, 68–83.

19605. BULLIVANT, STEPHEN. 'That's him. That shiny bastard': Jim Casy and Christology. StStud (16:1/2) 2005, 15–31.

19606. CASWELL, ROGER. A musical journey through John Steinbeck's *The Pearl*: emotion, engagement, and comprehension. JAAL (49:1) 2005, 62–7.

19607. DOOLEY, PATRICK K. John Steinbeck's lower-case utopia: basic human needs, a duty to share, and the good life. In (pp. 3–20) **19612**.

19608. DOWLAND, DOUGLAS. 'Macrocosm of microcosm me': Steinbeck's *Travels with Charley.* Lit (16:3) 2005, 311–31.

19609. FOWLER, CHARLES RAYMOND. Adapting Steinbeck: *Tortilla Flat* in the information age – an interview with screenwriter Bill U'Ren. StStud (16:1/2) 2005, 57–65.

19610. GEORGE, STEPHEN K. 'The disintegration of a man': moral integrity in *The Winter of Our Discontent. In* (pp. 169–82) **19612.**

19611. —— The emotional content of cruelty: an analysis of Kate in *East of Eden. In* (pp. 131–44) **19612.**

19612. —— (ed.). The moral philosophy of John Steinbeck. Lanham, MD; London: Scarecrow Press, 2005. pp. xv, 201. Rev. by Brian Railsback in StStud (16:1/2) 2005, 139–43.

19613. GORTON, TERRY. Judging Elisa Allen: reader entrapment in *The Chrysanthemums. In* (pp. 87–105) **19612.**

19614. GUÉTIN, NICOLE. Éros et les romanciers des années trente. EREA (1:1) 2003, 46–51.

19615. HAN, JOHN J. 'I want to make 'em happy': Utilitarian philosophy in Steinbeck's fiction. *In* (pp. 41–8) **19612.**

19616. HANSEN, MICHAEL D. The power of strange faces: revisiting *The Grapes of Wrath* with the postmodern ethics of Emmanuel Levinas. *In* (pp. 107–29) **19612.**

19617. HART, RICHARD E. Moral experience in *Of Mice and Men*: challenges and reflection. *In* (pp. 61–71) **19612.**

19618. HEAVILIN, BARBARA A. The existential vacuum and Ethan Allen Hawley: John Steinbeck's moral philosophy. *In* (pp. 49–58) **19612.**

19619. —— John Steinbeck's *Of Mice and Men*: a reference guide. Foreword by Charles L. Etheridge, Jr. Westport, CT; London: Praeger, 2005. pp. xi, 118. Rev. by Mimi Gladstein in StStud (16:1/2) 2005, 145–8.

19620. JACKSON, JULIE. Theatrical space and place in the presentational aesthetic of director Frank Joseph Galati. TT (15:2) 2005, 131–48.

19621. KOPECKY, PETR. The story of John Steinbeck in Communist Czechoslovakia. StStud (16:1/2) 2005, 81–90.

19622. KRAJNC, VESNA. The translation and reception of John Steinbeck in Slovenia: a bibliographic exploration. StStud (16:1/2) 2005, 179–89.

19623. LI, LUCHEN (ed.). John Steinbeck: a documentary volume. Detroit, MI: Gale Research, 2005. pp. xxviii, 447. (Dictionary of literary biography, 309.)

19624. MANNING, THOMAS; MATOS, SUZANNE; ADLER, BRIAN. Hidden treasure: the Steinbeck–Rudloe letters. StStud (16:1/2) 2005, 109–18.

19625. MANVILLE, GRETA. Bibliography: durable Steinbeck. StStud (16:1/2) 2005, 195–209.

19626. MELNIC, OANA. Following the steps of the hero: an approach to Jim Nolan's initiation journey in John Steinbeck's *In Dubious Battle*. StStud (16:1/2) 2005, 91–106.

19627. MEYER, MICHAEL J. One is the loneliest number: Steinbeck's paradoxical attraction and repulsion to isolation/solitude. SDR (43:1/2) 2005, 144–56.

19628. NEWMAN, GERALD; LAYFIELD, ELEANOR NEWMAN. A student's guide to John Steinbeck. Berkeley Heights, NJ: Enslow, 2004. pp. 176. (Understanding literature.)

19629. PARKER, ALLENE M. Of death, life, and virtue in Steinbeck's *Of Mice and Men* and *The Grapes of Wrath*. *In* (pp. 73–85) **19612**.

19630. SAXTON, A. In dubious battle. PacHR (73:2) 2004, 249–62.

19631. TIMMERMAN, JOHN H. John Steinbeck: an ethics of fiction. *In* (pp. 33–9) **19612**.

19632. WELTER, KIM. *The Wayward Bus*: Steinbeck and queer America. StStud (16:1/2) 2005, 67–79.

19633. WILLIS, LLOYD. Monstrous ecology: John Steinbeck, ecology, and American cultural politics. JAC (28:4) 2005, 357–67.

Neal Stephenson

19634. LEWIS, JONATHAN P. Opening notes: the Treaty of Utrecht, the Atlantic slave trade, and the start of Neal Stephenson's *Baroque Cycle*. NCL (35:1) 2005, 4–5.

George Sterling

19635. MATTILA, ROBERT W. George Sterling: a bibliography: including periodical contributions and manuscript material. Seattle: Book Club of Washington, 2004. 1 vol. (unpaginated).

Gerald Stern

19636. SADOFF, IRA. Dreaming creatures. APR (34:1) 2005, 45–50 (review-article).

19637. STERN, GERALD. What I can't bear losing: notes from a life. (Bibl. 2004, 19641.) Rev. by Ira Sadoff in APR (34:1) 2005, 45–50.

Richard Stern

19638. STERN, RICHARD. Becoming a writer: the forties. LitIm (7:2) 2005, 141–4.

James Stevens (1892–1971)

19639. MAGUIRE, JAMES H. James Stevens. Boise, ID: Boise State Univ., 2005. pp. 59. (Boise State Univ. Western writers, 165.)

Wallace Stevens

19640. ALKON, GABRIEL. Refrain and the limits of poetic power in Spenser, Herbert, Hardy, and Stevens. *See* **5675**.

19641. ALTIERI, CHARLES. The fate of the imaginary in twentieth-century American poetry. *See* **14363**.

19642. APPLEWHITE, JAMES. The mind's lyric and the spaces of nature: Wordsworth and Stevens. WSJ (29:1) 2005, 117–30.

19643. ASHTON, DORE. Was this angel necessary? Raritan (23:3) 2004, 24–42. (American Modernism.)

19644. BACIGALUPO, MASSIMO. Bisanzio e Florida: le rotte contrarie di W. B. Yeats e Wallace Stevens. *In* (pp. 203–13) **14479**.

19645. —— History and the American poet. *See* **18857**.

19646. BEYERS, CHRIS. Critical studies in a post-theoretical age: three books sort of about Wallace Stevens. ColLit (32:4) 2005, 200–10 (review-article).

19647. BOYAGODA, ANNA. 'Being there together': Stevens and the postcolonial imagination. WSJ (29:1) 2005, 62–71.

19648. BROGAN, JACQUELINE VAUGHT. 'Inessential houses' in Stevens and Bishop. WSJ (29:1) 2005, 25–33.

19649. BURT, STEPHEN. The absence of the poet as virile youth. WSJ (29:1) 2005, 81–90.

19650. CAMPBELL, P. MICHAEL. 'The world is my idea': similar worlds (similar ideas) in Wallace Stevens and Arthur Schopenhauer. WSJ (29:1) 2005, 156–62.

19651. CLEGHORN, ANGUS. The fictive coverings of home. WSJ (29:1) 2005, 9–17.

19652. COSTELLO, BONNIE. Planets on tables: still life and war in the poetry of Wallace Stevens. Mod/Mod (12:3) 2005, 443–58.

19653. CRITCHLEY, SIMON. Things merely are: philosophy in the poetry of Wallace Stevens. London; New York: Routledge, 2005. pp. xiii, 137. Rev. by Tom McBride in PhilL (29:2) 2005, 503–8; by Lee M. Jenkins in WSJ (29:2) 2005, 313–15.

19654. DORESKI, WILLIAM. Wallace Stevens at home in the wilderness. WSJ (29:1) 2005, 18–24.

19655. EECKHOUT, BART. How Dutch was Stevens? WSJ (29:1) 2005, 34–43.

19656. GERBER, NATALIE. Stevens' prosody: meaningful rhythms. WSJ (29:1) 2005, 178–87.

19657. GOLDFARB, LISA. Philosophical parallels: Wallace Stevens and Paul Valéry. WSJ (29:1) 2005, 163–70.

19658. —— 'Pure rhetoric of a language without words': Stevens's musical creation of belief in *Credences of Summer*. JML (27:1/2) 2003, 122–36.

19659. GOLDSTONE, ANDREW. The two voices of Wallace Stevens' blank final music. WSJ (29:2) 2005, 213–32.

19660. HAGLUND, DAVID. 'Puke or prude': Frost and Stevens in the literary market place of 1922. *See* **16604**.

19661. HART, HENRY. Charles Simic's dark nights of the soul. *See* **19457**.

19662. HATLEN, BURTON. From the transcendental to the immanent sublime: the poetry of William Carlos Williams, 1913–1917. *See* **20212**.

19663. —— Stevens' revisions of the Romantic sublime in *Esthétique du Mal*. WSJ (29:1) 2005, 131–41.

19664. HELGESON, KAREN. Anding and ending: metaphor and closure in Stevens' *An Ordinary Evening in New Haven*. WSJ (29:2) 2005, 275–303.

19665. —— Current bibliography. WSJ (29:1) 2005, 203–6.

19666. HOLANDER, STEFAN. Between categories: Modernist and postmodernist appropriations of Wallace Stevens. *In* (pp. 221–38) **12946**.

19667. JAECKLE, JEFF. 'These minutiae mean more': five editions of Wallace Stevens' *Esthétique du Mal*. WSJ (29:2) 2005, 233–48.

19668. JOHNSON, KURT A. Stevens's *The House Was Quiet and the World Was Calm*. Exp (63:2) 2005, 88–90.

19669. KONG, YING. Cinematic techniques in Modernist poetry. LitFQ (33:1) 2005, 28–40.

19670. KUBIAK, ANTHONY. Beyond the genius of the sea: the theatre of the natural unconscious. PRes (9:2) 2004, 142–50.

19671. LEGGETT, B. J. God, imagination, and the interior paramour. WSJ (29:1) 2005, 171–7.

19672. —— Late Stevens: the final fiction. Baton Rouge: Louisiana State UP, 2005. pp. xiii, 170. Rev. by David Jarraway in WSJ (29:2) 2005, 310–13.

19673. LEPPARD, NATALIE R. Stevens's *Landscape with Boat*. Exp (63:3) 2005, 164–7.

19674. MACKENZIE, GINA MASUCCI; O'HARA, DANIEL T. Reading Stevens with Lacan on the real: toward a poetics of destitution. WSJ (29:1) 2005, 72–80.

19675. MAO, DOUGLAS. Privative synecdoches. WSJ (29:1) 2005, 56–61.

19676. MAZUR, KRYSTYNA. Poetry and repetition: Walt Whitman, Wallace Stevens, John Ashbery. *See* **12334**.

19677. MIKKELSEN, ANN. 'Fat! Fat! Fat! Fat!' – Wallace Stevens's figurations of masculinity. JML (27:1/2) 2003, 105–21.

19678. OLSON, LIESL M. Wallace Stevens' commonplace. WSJ (29:1) 2005, 106–16.

19679. RAGG, EDWARD. Good-bye major man: reading Stevens without 'Stevensian'. WSJ (29:1) 2005, 98–105.

19680. RAMALHO SANTOS, IRENE. Modernist muses that matter: inspiration revisited in Pessoa and Stevens. WSJ (29:1) 2005, 44–55.

19681. REHDER, ROBERT. Stevens, Williams, Crane, and the motive for metaphor. Basingstoke; New York: Palgrave Macmillan, 2004. pp. xxv, 207. Rev. by Guy Rotella in WSJ (29:2) 2005, 315–17.

19682. ROY, AYON. From deconstruction to decreation: Wallace Stevens' notes toward a poetics of nobility. WSJ (29:2) 2005, 249–62.

19683. SHARPE, PETER. The ground of our beseeching: metaphor and the poetics of meditation. *See* **16305**.

19684. SHINBROT, VICTORIA. The lyric element and the prosaic world in *The Idea of Order at Key West*. WSJ (29:2) 2005, 263–74.

19685. SPURR, DAVID. Architecture in Frost and Stevens. *See* **16617**.

19686. SURETTE, LEON. Vaihinger and Stevens: a rumor that won't go away. WSJ (29:1) 2005, 142–55.

19687. —— Wallace Stevens, Roger Caillois and 'the pure good of theory'. Paideuma (32:1–3) 2003, 95–122.

19688. UTARD, JULIETTE. Collecting oneself: the late poetry of Wallace Stevens. WSJ (29:1) 2005, 188–97.

19689. VIRDIS, DANIELA. Giovanni Papini, Wallace Stevens e l'idea di poesia e di poeta. LProv (122) 2005, 85–96.

19690. WOODLAND, MALCOLM. 'Amen to the feelings': Wallace Stevens and the politics of emotion. WSJ (29:1) 2005, 91–7.

19691. —— Wallace Stevens and the apocalyptic mode. Iowa City: Iowa UP, 2005. pp. xvii, 256. Rev. by J. Donald Blount in WSJ (29:2) 2005, 320–3.

James Still

19692. CRUM, CLAUDE LAFIE. Constructing a marketable writer: James Still's fictional persona. AppalJ (32:4) 2005, 430–9.

Robert Stone

19693. LEVENE, MARK. Half-moments and glintings: four short stories by Robert Stone. WasRCPSF (38:1) 2003, 1–15.

Marie Stopes ('Marie Carmichael')

19694. SULLIVAN, ESTHER BETH. *Vectia*, man-made censorship, and the drama of Marie Stopes. TheatreS (46:1) 2005, 79–102.

Tom Stoppard

19695. CAMPOS, LILIANE. Rewriting the plot: re-creations in contemporary British comedy. See **15464**.

19696. JERNIGAN, DANIEL. Tom Stoppard and 'postmodern science': normalizing radical epistemologies in *Hapgood* and *Arcadia*. CompDr (37:1) 2003, 3–35.

19697. NADEL, IRA. Tom Stoppard: a life. (Bibl. 2004, 19691.) Rev. by Morton P. Levitt in JML (26:3/4) 2003, 166–8; by Myles Weber in GaR (57:3) 2003, 654–6.

19698. NADEL, IRA B. Writing the life of *Tom Stoppard*. JML (27:3) 2004, 19–29.

19699. RUSSELL, RICHARD RANKIN. 'It will make us friends': cultural reconciliation in Tom Stoppard's *Indian Ink*. JML (27:3) 2004, 1–18.

19700. SCOLNICOV, HANNA. Making ears serve for eyes: Stoppard's visual radio play. WI (20:1) 2004, 63–83.

19701. TAIT, MICHAEL S. Hell-fire and the beauties of Shropshire: the poetry of A. E. Housman. See **17069**.

19702. TUCKER, HERBERT F. History played back: in defense of Stoppard's *Coast of Utopia*. Raritan (24:4) 2005, 149–69.

David Storey

19703. WISZNIOWSKA, MARTA. Feasting in drama. *In* (pp. 294–303) **3756**.

Randolph Stow

19704. ASHCROFT, BILL. The horizontal sublime. See **20021**.

19705. CARR, RICHARD. 'Just enough religion to make us hate': the case of *Tourmaline* and *Oyster.* Antipodes (18:1) 2004, 9–15.

Lytton Strachey

19706. CAINE, BARBARA. Bombay to Bloomsbury: a biography of the Strachey family. Oxford; New York: OUP, 2005. pp. xvii, 488, (plates) 16. Rev. by Sarah Curtis in TLS, 29 July 2005, 22; by Philippa Levine in VS (48:1) 2005, 195–7.

19707. CURTIS, SARAH. Not so eminent. TLS, 29 July 2005, 22 (review-article). (Strachey family biography.)

19708. FORTUNATI, VITA. La biografia come autobiografia: il caso di Lytton Strachey. *In* (pp. 233–46) **12577**.

19709. LEVY, PAUL (ed.); MARCUS, PENELOPE (asst ed.). The letters of Lytton Strachey. London: Penguin; New York: Viking, 2005. pp. xxii, 698. Rev. by Peter Parker in TLS, 29 Apr. 2005, 24; by Ruth Yeazell in LRB (27:23) 2005, 25–6; by Sarah M. Hall, *et al.*, in VWB (20) 2005, 58–64.

19710. SÁNCHEZ-PARDO, ESTHER. Cultures of the death drive: Melanie Klein and Modernist melancholia. *See* **20416.**

19711. SHAW, JOHN. *Luriana, Lurilee* revisited: 1, *A Garden Song*: Leonard Woolf's manuscript copy: the 'right version' of the poem. *See* **10962.**

19712. TAYLOR, MILES; WOLFF, MICHAEL (eds). The Victorians since 1901: histories, representations, and revisions. *See* **9426.**

19713. YEAZELL, RUTH. Ah, la vie! LRB (27:23) 2005, 25–6 (review-article). (Letters.)

Mark Strand

19714. KARDOKAS, LAIMA. The twilight zone of experience uncannily shared by Mark Strand and Edward Hopper. Mosaic (38:2) 2005, 111–28.

The Stratemeyer Syndicate

19715. REHAK, MELANIE. Girl sleuth: Nancy Drew and the women who created her. Orlando, FL: Harcourt, 2005. pp. xviii, 364, (plates) 8.

Peter Straub

19716. WOLFE, GARY. Peter Straub and John Crowley in conversation: ICFA 26, March 18, 2005. Ed. and transcribed by Sherryl Vint. JFA (16:1) 2005, 49–61.

Noel Streatfeild

19717. STOKES, SALLY SIMS. Noel Streatfeild's secret gardens. CLAQ (29:3) 2004, 172–206.

T. S. Stribling

19718. VICKERS, KENNETH W. T. S. Stribling: a life of the Tennessee novelist. (Bibl. 2004, 19717.) Rev. by Matthew Lessig in SoQ (43:1) 2005, 151–3; by Ben Johnson in JSH (71:2) 2005, 483.

Arthur Stringer

19719. HILL, COLIN. As for me and my blueprint: Sinclair Ross's debt to Arthur Stringer. *In* (pp. 251–72) **12739.**

Francis Stuart

19720. JEFFARES, A. NORMAN. Iseult Gonne. *See* **16742.**

19721. WILLS, CLAIR. The aesthetics of Irish neutrality during the Second World War. *See* **18032.**

Jesse Stuart

19722. DICK, DAVID. Jesse Stuart: the heritage. North Middletown, KY: Plum Lick, 2005. pp. 292. Rev. by Scott Vander Ploeg in KenPR (19) 2004, 63–4.

19723. MCMURTREY, LEAH. Robert Burns and Jesse Stuart: the spark that ignited the inferno. *See* **8456.**

19724. RUBIN, RACHEL. 'What ain't called Melungeons is called hillbillies': Southern Appalachia's in-between people. *See* **17936.**

Theodore Sturgeon

19725. HARTWELL, DAVID G.   Middle high Sturgeon. NYRSF (16:5) 2004, 20-3.

J. C. (Jacqueline Cecilia) Sturm (b.1927)

19726. MILLAR, PAUL.   'Nobody would have given tuppence for our chances': James K. Baxter & J. C. Sturm. *In* (pp. 136-65) **12916**.

William Styron

19727. FRENCH, SCOT.   The rebellious slave: Nat Turner in American memory. *See* **9260**.

Ruth Suckow

19728. SWENSON, JEFFERY.   In good company: the Midwestern literary community and the short fiction of Ruth Suckow and Hamlin Garland. MidAmerica (30) 2003, 20-31.

Ronald Sukenick

19729. KATZ, ADAM.   Iconoclastic commitments: idolatry and imagination in Cynthia Ozick and Ronald Sukenick. *See* **18714**.

Sara Suleri

19730. SUTHERLAND, KATHERINE G.   Land of their graves: maternity, mourning, and nation in Janet Frame, Sara Suleri, and Arundhati Roy. *See* **16577**.

Robert Sullivan (b.1967)

19731. SPAHR, JULIANA.   Connected disconnection and localized globalism in Pacific multilingual literature. B2 (31:3) 2004, 75-100.

Toyo Suyemoto (Kawakami) (b.1916)

19732. STREAMAS, JOHN.   Toyo Suyemoto, Ansel Adams, and the landscape of justice. *In* (pp. 141-57) **12775**.

Mary Swander (b.1950)

19733. DAVIS, TODD F.   Writing back through the body: flesh and spirit in the work of Mary Swander. Mosaic (38:2) 2005, 79-94.

Graham Swift

19734. ACHESON, JAMES.   *Historia* and guilt: Graham Swift's *Waterland*. CritW (47:1) 2005, 90-100.

19735. BRYK, MARTA.   Kaleidoscopic (dis)array of Graham Swift's *Waterland*. *In* (pp. 21-8) **3756**.

19736. CRAPS, STEF.   Trauma and ethics in the novels of Graham Swift: no short-cuts to salvation. Brighton; Portland, OR: Sussex Academic Press, 2005. pp. viii, 230.

19737. GALLIX, FRANÇOIS.   Graham Swift: écrire l'imagination. Pessac: Presses Universitaires de Bordeaux, 2003. pp. 119. (Couleurs anglaises.) Rev. by Christian Gutleben in EtBr (25) 2003, 196; by Vanessa Guignery in EA (58:2) 2005, 240.

19738. GUNBY, INGRID.   Tales from the crypt: wartime London in Graham Swift's *Shuttlecock*. *In* (pp. 97-109) **14254**.

Randall Swingler

19739. CROFT, ANDY. Comrade heart: a life of Randall Swingler. (Bibl. 2004, 19735.) Rev. by Ross Bradshaw in CritS (16:1) 2004, 115–18.

J. M. Synge

19740. CARAHER, BRIAN G. Trieste, Dublin, Galway: Joyce, journalism, 1912. *In* (pp. 132–50) **17274**.

19741. FRAZIER, ADRIAN (ed.). Playboys of the Western world: production histories. Dublin: Carysfort Press, 2004. pp. xiv, 182. Rev. by J. P. Wearing in ELT (48:4) 2005, 462–4.

19742. MATHEWS, P. J. 'A.E.I.O.U': Joyce and the *Irish Homestead*. *In* (pp. 151–68) **17274**.

Arthur Sze

19743. ELSHTAIN, ERIC P. An interview with Arthur Sze. ChiR (50:2–4) 2004/05, 202–13.

Larissa Szporluk

19744. WILLIAMS, LISA. Momentous bodies: the poetry of Larissa Szporluk. HC (42:1) 2005, 1–20.

Rabindranath Tagore

19745. CHAUDHURI, SUKANTA (ed.). Selected poems. New Delhi; Oxford: OUP, 2004. pp. xxi, 449. (Oxford Tagore translations.)

19746. HOU, CHUANWEN. Tagore's theory of poetry. FLS (115) 2005, 139–45. (In Chinese.)

19747. YANG, YUZHEN. Cold reception of Tagore's works in China. FLS (114) 2005, 150–4. (In Chinese.)

Justin Tanner

19748. HORNBY, RICHARD. New York hot *versus* L.A. cool. *See* **21213**.

Allen Tate

19749. LOMBARDY, ANTHONY. Allen Tate and the metaphysics of metaphor. SoLJ (37:2) 2005, 62–80.

19750. MACE, JENNINGS. The lynching in Allen Tate's *The Swimmers*. ANQ (18:4) 2005, 42–8.

James Tate

19751. HENRY, BRIAN (ed.). On James Tate. (Bibl. 2004, 19765.) Rev. by Cliff Toliver in RMER (59:2) 2005.

Drew Hayden Taylor (b.1962)

19752. KOLINSKÁ, KLÁRA. 'What happened to the naming in this strange place?': remapping the space of Ontario in the (con)texts of Native Canadian theatre. *In* (pp. 176–89) **12868**.

19753. MOFFATT, JOHN; TAIT, SANDY. I just see myself as an old-fashioned storyteller: a conversation with Drew Hayden Taylor. CanL (183) 2004, 72–86.

Ken Taylor (b.1930)

19754. BARTLETT, JOHN.   Fire and water. Meanjin (62:1) 2003, 207–13. (Interview.)

Mildred D. Taylor

19755. HOUGHTON, GILLIAN.   Mildred Taylor. New York: Rosen Central, 2005. pp. 112. (Library of author biographies.)

Sydney Taylor (b.1904)

19756. CUMMINS, JUNE.   Leaning Left: progressive politics in Sydney Taylor's All-of-a-Kind Family series. CLAQ (30:4) 2005, 386–408.

Richard Tayson (b.1962)

19757. TAYSON, RICHARD.   The casualties of Walt Whitman. See **12349**.

Emma Tennant ('Catherine Aydy')

19758. WISKER, GINA.   Demisting the mirror: contemporary British women's horror. See **17030**.

Studs Terkel

19759. FERRAN, PETER W.   *The American Clock*: 'epic vaudeville'. *In* (pp. 153–63) **18234**.

John Terpstra

19760. DONALDSON, JEFFERY.   Geologist and giant: two Canadian poets and their landscapes. LRC (11:3) 2003, 21–4 (review-article).

Hilary Tham (b.1946)

19761. GOLDENBERG, MYRNA.   Identity, memory, and authority: an introduction to Holocaust poems by Hilary Tham, Myra Sklarew, and Dori Katz. StudAJL (24) 2005, 137–44.

Shashi Tharoor

19762. SKINNER, JOHN.   Literary moonlighting: the cultural spaces of Shashi Tharoor. RAEI (16) 2003, 255–68.

19763. THAROOR, SHASHI.   Bookless in Baghdad: reflections on writing and writers. See **12943**.

Angela Thirkell

19764. RAMSDEN, VALERIE.   The use of names in the Barsetshire novels. JATS (25) 2005, 8–10.

D. M. (Donald Michael) Thomas (b.1935)

19765. TCHERNICHOVA, VICTORIA.   Dominant narrative strategies in D. M. Thomas's *Pictures at an Exhibition*: a case study. AngP (2:1/2) 2005, 169–90.

Dylan Thomas

19766. GOLIGHTLY, VICTOR.   'Speak on a finger and thumb': Dylan Thomas, language and the deaf. WWrE (10) 2005, 73–97.

19767. GOODBY, JOHN.   Whitman's influence on Dylan Thomas and the use of *sidle* as noun. NQ (52:1) 2005, 105–7.

19768. GORDON, JOHN.   Being Sylvia being Ted being Dylan: Plath's *The Snowman on the Moor*. See **18820**.

19769. —— Dylan Thomas: the Great War and recovered memory. ANQ (18:4) 2005, 39–42.

19770. GRIFFITHS, LESLIE.   Dylan Thomas: poet of his people? THSC (11) 2005, 204–15.

19771. HADFIELD, ANDREW.   Beckett and Dylan Thomas. *See* **15393.**

19772. HEYS, ALISTAIR.   Ambivalence and antithesis: R. S. Thomas's relationship with Dylan Thomas. *See* **19780.**

19773. LOPEZ, TONY.   Graham and the 1940s. *In* (pp. 26–42) **16793.**

Edward Thomas (1878–1917)

19774. CUTHBERTSON, GUY.   Leonard Bast and Edward Thomas. *See* **16553.**

19775. HOWARTH, PETER.   Loose woven. LRB (27:15) 2005, 24–5 (review-article).

19776. PALMER, SCOTT.   Why go straight? Stepping out with Henry David Thoreau's *Walking* and Edward Thomas' *The Icknield Way*. *See* **12208.**

19777. SEEBER, HANS ULRICH.   The retrospective attitude in poems by Edward Thomas and Andrew Motion. YREAL (21) 2005, 147–59.

19778. THOMAS, R. GEORGE (ed.).   The collected poems and war diary, 1917. Introd. by Peter Sacks. London; Boston, MA: Faber & Faber, 2004. pp. xlviii, 264. Rev. by Peter Howarth in LRB (27:15) 2005, 24–5.

R. S. (Ronald Stuart) Thomas (1913–2000)

19779. DAVIES, DAMIAN WALFORD (ed.).   Echoes to the amen: essays after R. S. Thomas. Cardiff: UP of Wales, 2003. pp. xvi, 233. Rev. by Thomas Day in CamQ (34:2) 2005, 184–8.

19780. HEYS, ALISTAIR.   Ambivalence and antithesis: R. S. Thomas's relationship with Dylan Thomas. WWrE (10) 2005, 52–72.

19781. MCKENZIE, TIM.   'Green as a leaf': the religious nationalism of R. S. Thomas. WWrE (10) 2005, 32–51.

19782. THOMAS, M. WYNN.   For Wales, see landscape: early R. S. Thomas and the English topographical tradition. WWrE (10) 2005, 1–31.

Hunter S. Thompson

19783. LOVE, ROBERT.   A technical guide for editing gonzo: Hunter S. Thompson from the other end of the mojo wire. ColJR (44:1) 2005, 61–5.

Jim Thompson

19784. PAYNE, KENNETH.   *The Criminal*: Jim Thompson's counterculture vision of the American 1950s. McNR (42) 2004, 61–72.

19785. WHITING, FREDERICK.   Bodies of evidence: post-war detective fiction and the monstrous origins of the sexual psychopath. *See* **19561.**

Judith Thompson

19786. LEVIN, LAURA.   Environmental affinities: naturalism and the porous body. TRC (24:1/2) 2003, 171–86.

19787. READ, ROBYN.   Who is the stranger? The role of the monstrous in Judith Thompson's *Capture Me*. TRC (24:1/2) 2003, 187–201.

Mervyn Thompson

19788. EDMOND, MURRAY.   The terror and the pity of 1984: Mervyn Thompson's *Coaltown Blues*. Landfall (209) 2005, 13–28.

Wallace Thurman

19789. BERNARD, EMILY.   Unlike many others: exceptional White characters in Harlem renaissance fiction. Mod/Mod (12:3) 2005, 407–23.

19790. SINGH, AMRITJIT; SCOTT, DANIEL M., III (eds).   The collected writings of Wallace Thurman: a Harlem renaissance reader. (Bibl. 2004, 19823.) Rev. by Nibir K. Ghosh in MELUS (30:1) 2005, 250–3; by Mason Stokes in AmLH (17:1) 2005, 171–82.

Richard Tillinghast (b.1940)

19791. TILLINGHAST, RICHARD.   Poetry and what is real. See **14504**.

J. R. R. Tolkien

19792. ABANES, RICHARD.   Harry Potter, Narnia, and *The Lord of the Rings*. See **19191**.

19793. ALTVATER, FRANCES, *et al.* (comps).   The year's work in Old English studies 2002. See **4195**.

19794. ANDERSON, DOUGLAS A.   J. R. R. Tolkien and W. Rhys Roberts's *Gerald of Wales on the Survival of Welsh*. TolStud (2) 2005, 230–4.

19795. ——   Tales before Tolkien: the roots of modern fantasy. See **4007**.

19796. ANKENY, REBECCA.   Poem as sign in *The Lord of the Rings*. JFA (16:2) 2005, 86–95.

19797. BASSHAM, GREGORY; BRONSON, ERIC (eds).   *The Lord of the Rings* and philosophy: one book to rule them all. (Bibl. 2003, 19935.) Rev. by W. A. Senior in JFA (15:4) 2004, 386–8.

19798. BATES, BRIAN.   The real Middle-earth: exploring the magic and mystery of the Middle Ages, J. R. R. Tolkien and *The Lord of the Rings*. (Bibl. 2004, 19831.) Rev. by Brad Eden in TolStud (2) 2005, 256–7.

19799. BRATMAN, DAVID.   The year's work in Tolkien studies: 2001–2002. TolStud (2) 2005, 289–315.

19800. BRISBOIS, MICHAEL J.   Tolkien's imaginary nature: an analysis of the structure of Middle-earth. TolStud (2) 2005, 197–216.

19801. CALDECOTT, STRATFORD.   The power of the ring: the spiritual vision behind *The Lord of the Rings*. (Bibl. 2004, 19838.) New York: Crossroad, 2005. pp. vii, 151. (Revised ed.: first ed. 2003.) (Orig. pub. as *Secret Fire: the Spiritual Vision of J. R. R. Tolkien*.) Rev. by Colin Duriez in SEVEN (22) 2005, 112–14.

19802. CHANCE, JANE (ed.).   Tolkien and the invention of myth: a reader. (Bibl. 2004, 19839.) Rev. by Carol A. Leibiger in JFA (16:2) 2005, 158–61.

19803. ——   Tolkien the medievalist. (Bibl. 2004, 19840.) Rev. by Shaun F. D. Hughes in TolStud (2) 2005, 277–85.

19804. ——   SIEWERS, ALFRED K. (eds).   Tolkien's modern Middle Ages. Basingstoke; New York: Palgrave Macmillan, 2005. pp. xiv, 250. (New Middle Ages.)

19805. CROFT, JANET BRENNAN. War and the works of J. R. R. Tolkien. (Bibl. 2004, 19843.) Rev. by David Bratman in Mythprint (42:2) 2005, 10.

19806. —— (ed.). Tolkien on film: essays on Peter Jackson's *The Lord of the Rings.* See **20725.**

19807. DE GOLDI, KATE. Blaming Tolkien. See **14326.**

19808. DICKERSON, MATTHEW T. Following Gandalf: epic battles and moral victory in *The Lord of the Rings.* (Bibl. 2004, 19846.) Rev. by Joe R. Christopher in TolStud (2) 2005, 253–6.

19809. DURIEZ, COLIN. Tolkien and C. S. Lewis: the gift of friendship. Mahwah, NJ: HiddenSpring, 2003. pp. xii, 244. Rev. by Wesley A. Kort in CHist (73:1) 2004, 217–18; by Mike Foster in TolStud (2) 2005, 266–7.

19810. ERRIGO, ANGIE. The Rough Guide to *The Lord of the Rings.* London: Haymarket, 2003. pp. 304. (Rough Guides.) Rev. by David Bratman in Mythprint (41:8) 2004, 3.

19811. FLIEGER, VERLYN (ed.). Smith of Wootton Major. London: HarperCollins, 2005. pp. vi, 149.

19812. FORD, JUDY ANN. The white city: *The Lord of the Rings* as an early medieval myth of the restoration of the Roman Empire. TolStud (2) 2005, 53–73.

19813. FOREST-HILL, LYNN. Elves on the Avon: the place of medieval Warwick in J. R. R. Tolkien's vision of Middle-earth. TLS, 8 July 2005, 12–13.

19814. GARTH, JOHN. Tolkien and the Great War: the threshold of Middle-earth. (Bibl. 2004, 19857.) Rev. by W. A. Senior in JFA (15:3) 2004, 271–8; by Chad Engbers in LU (29:1) 2005, 128–33; by Brian Rosebury in TolStud (2) 2005, 268–71; by Bradley J. Birzer in SEVEN (22) 2005, 110–12.

19815. GEE, HENRY. The science of Middle-earth. Cold Spring Harbor, NY: Cold Spring Press, 2004. pp. 255.

19816. HAMMOND, WAYNE G.; SCULL, CHRISTINA. *The Lord of the Rings*: a reader's companion. Boston, MA: Houghton Mifflin, 2005. pp. lxxxii, 894. Rev. by David Bratman in Mythprint (42:12) 2005, 11–13.

19817. HATLEN, BURTON. Pullman's *His Dark Materials,* a challenge to the fantasies of J. R. R. Tolkien and C. S. Lewis, with an epilogue on Pullman's neo-Romantic reading of *Paradise Lost. In* (pp. 75–94) **18952.**

19818. HOEIM, ELIZABETH MASSA. World creation as colonization: British imperialism in *Aldarion and Erendis.* TolStud (2) 2005, 75–92.

19819. HONEGGER, THOMAS (ed.). Tolkien in translation. (Bibl. 2004, 19866.) Rev. by Janet Brennan Croft in Mythprint (42:2) 2005, 12–13; by David Bratman in SEVEN (22) 2005, 118–21.

19820. HOOKER, MARK T. Schuchart *vs* Mensink-van Warmelo: round two. Lembas-extra (2004) 75–99.

19821. —— Tolkien through Russian eyes. Zurich: Walking Tree, 2003. pp. 320. (Cormarë, 5.) Rev. by Timothy P. Wickham-Crowley in TolStud (2) 2005, 285–7.

19822. JAKOBSSON, ÁRMANN. Tolkien og hringurinn. (Tolkien and the Ring.) Reykjavík: Forlagið, 2003. pp. 254. Rev. by Shaun F. D. Hughes in MFS (50:4) 2004, 980–1014.

19823. KEESEE, NEAL K. Tolkien, King Alfred, and Boethius: Platonist views of evil in *The Lord of the Rings*. TolStud (2) 2005, 131–59.

19824. KELLS, F. MACDONALD. The culture of Middle-earth: everyday life in Tolkien's world. Carlton South, Vic.: Bread Street Press, 2004. pp. 231. Rev. by David Bratman in Mythprint (41:8) 2004, 4–5.

19825. LARSEN, KRISTINE. A definitive identification of Tolkien's 'Borgil': an astronomical and literary approach. TolStud (2) 2005, 161–70.

19826. LEIBER, JUSTIN. Mrs Coulter *vs* C. S. Lewis. *In* (pp. 163–70) **18973.**

19827. LEWIS, ALEX. The emergence of Mordor and the abode of evil in Middle-earth. Lembas-extra (2004) 41–65.

19828. LIBRÁN-MORENO, MIRYAM. Parallel lives: the sons of Denethor and the sons of Telamon. TolStud (2) 2005, 15–52.

19829. LOBDELL, JARED C. The rise of Tolkienian fantasy. Chicago, IL: Open Court, 2005. pp. 176.

19830. LOY, DAVID R.; GOODHEW, LINDA. The dharma of dragons and dæmons: Buddhist themes in modern fantasy. Boston, MA: Wisdom, 2004. pp. x, 155.

19831. MONDA, ANDREA; SIMONELLI, SAVERIO. Gli anelli della fantasia. *See* **14230.**

19832. MORRISON, RONALD D. 'I much prefer history, true or feigned': Tolkien and literary history. KenPR (19) 2004, 36–42.

19833. MORTIMER, PATCHEN. Tolkien and Modernism. TolStud (2) 2005, 113–29.

19834. NELSON, DALE. Little Nell and Frodo the halfling. TolStud (2) 2005, 245–8.

19835. NELSON, MARIE. *Beowulf*'s boast words. *See* **4306.**

19836. OSER, LEE. Tolkien and Coleridge: an encounter. *See* **10510.**

19837. PEARCE, JOSEPH. Narnia and Middle-earth: when two worlds collide. *In* (pp. 113–27) **17727.**

19838. PETTY, ANNE C. Tolkien in the land of heroes: discovering the human spirit. (Bibl. 2004, 19887.) Rev. by W. A. Senior in JFA (15:3) 2004, 271–8; by Alexandra Bolintineanu in TolStud (2) 2005, 273–7.

19839. PIRSON, RON. Two rings to corrupt them all? Lembas-extra (2004) 110–22.

19840. PORTER, LYNNETTE R. Unsung heroes of *The Lord of the Rings*: from the page to the screen. Westport, CT; London: Praeger, 2005. pp. xiv, 224.

19841. RAICHE, DONALD. Making the darkness conscious: J. R. R. Tolkien's *The Lord of the Rings*. Parabola (29:3) 2005, 95–101.

19842. RIPP, JOSEPH. Middle America meets Middle-earth: American discussion and readership of J. R. R. Tolkien's *The Lord of the Rings*, 1965–1969. BH (8) 2005, 245–86.

19843. ROSEBURY, BRIAN. Tolkien: a cultural phenomenon. (Bibl. 2004, 19891.) Rev. by Jane Chance in TolStud (2) 2005, 262–5; by Douglas A. Anderson in SEVEN (22) 2005, 114–16.

19844. Rulyova, Natalia. Piracy and narrative games: Dmitry Puchkov's translations of *The Lord of the Rings*. SEEJ (49:4) 2005, 625–38.

19845. Selling, Kim. J. R. R. Tolkien's *The Lord of the Rings*: the book, the film, and genre criticism. SSE (29) 2003, 39–56.

19846. Shippey, Tom. Indexing and poetry in *The Lord of the Rings*. Lembas-extra (2004) 66–74.

19847. Sinex, Margaret. 'Tricksy lights': literary and folkloric elements in Tolkien's passage of the Dead Marshes. TolStud (2) 2005, 93–112.

19848. Speed, Diane. Christian perspectives in *The Lord of the Rings*. SSE (30) 2004, 79–92.

19849. Stopfel, Susanne. A matter of form. Lembas-extra (2004) 100–9. (Clothes and armour in *The Lord of the Rings*.)

19850. Straubhaar, Sandra Ballif. Gilraen's linnod: function, genre, prototypes. TolStud (2) 2005, 235–44.

19851. Turner, Allan. Translating Tolkien: philological elements in *The Lord of the Rings*. New York; Frankfurt: Lang, 2005. pp. 213. (Duisburger Arbeiten zur Sprach- und Kulturwissenschaft, 59.)

19852. Tyler, J. E. A. The complete Tolkien companion. (Bibl. 2004, 19905.) Rev. by Jenny Blackford in NYRSF (16:7) 2004, 23.

19853. Veldhoen, Bart. J. R. R. Tolkien, philologist and holist. Lembas-extra (2004) 1–14.

19854. Vink, Renée. The wise woman's gospel. Lembas-extra (2004) 15–40.

19855. Wainwright, Edmund. Tolkien's mythology for England: a Middle-earth companion. (Bibl. 2004, 19906.) Rev. by Verlyn Flieger in TMR, Jan. 2005.

19856. Werber, Niels. Geo- and biopolitics of Middle-earth: a German reading of Tolkien's *The Lord of the Rings*. NLH (36:2) 2005, 227–46.

19857. West, Richard C. 'And she named her own name': being true to one's word in Tolkien's Middle-earth. TolStud (2) 2005, 1–10.

19858. Wilde, Dana. This moral core: J. R. R. Tolkien's books and Peter Jackson's films. XavR (25:1) 2005, 66–76.

19859. Zimbardo, Rose A.; Isaacs, Neil D. (eds). Understanding *The Lord of the Rings*: the best of Tolkien criticism. (Bibl. 2004, 19910.) Rev. by Walter Minkel in NYRSF (17:5) 2005, 5–6; by Greg Beatty in NYRSF (17:5) 2005, 6–7.

Charles Tomlinson

19860. Saunders, Judith P. The poetry of Charles Tomlinson: border lines. (Bibl. 2004, 19911.) Rev. by Michael Hennessy in ConLit (46:2) 2005, 346–57.

John Kennedy Toole

19861. Dunne, Sara Lewis. Moviegoing in the modern novel: Holden, Binx, Ignatius. *See* **18763**.

19862. Fletcher, Joel L. Ken and Thelma: the story of *A Confederacy of Dunces*. Gretna, LA: Pelican, 2005. pp. 216.

Jean Toomer

19863. FORD, KAREN JACKSON.   Split-gut song: Jean Toomer and the poetics of modernity. Tuscaloosa; London: Alabama UP, 2005. pp. x, 205. Rev. by C. L. Bledsoe in ArkR (36:3) 2005, 223–4.

19864. GRANT, NATHAN.   Masculinist impulses: Toomer, Hurston, Black writing, and modernity. (Bibl. 2004, 19915.) Rev. by James Coleman in SoLJ (38:1) 2005, 142–6; by Gordon Thompson in AmBR (26:3) 2005, 35, 38.

19865. HAWKINS, STEPHANIE L.   Building the 'blue' race: miscegenation, mysticism, and the language of cognitive evolution in Jean Toomer's *The Blue Meridian*. TSLL (46:2) 2004, 149–80.

19866. WILKS, JENNIFER M.   Writing home: comparative Black Modernism and form in Jean Toomer and Aimé Césaire. MFS (51:4) 2005, 801–23.

Lola Lemire Tostevin

19867. GERRY, THOMAS M. F.   'If only I were Isis': remembrance, ritual, and writing in Lola Lemire Tostevin's *Cartouches*. CanRCL (30:1) 2003, 179–99.

19868. ZOLF, RACHEL.   An interview with Lola Lemire Tostevin. WCL (38:2) 2004, 185–91.

John Tranter

19869. HENRY, BRIAN.   John Tranter's new form(alism): the terminal. Antipodes (18:1) 2004, 36–43.

19870. TRIKHA, PRADEEP.   An interview with John Tranter. Antipodes (18:1) 2004, 31–5.

'Robert Traver' (John Donaldson Voelker)

19871. SEATON, JAMES.   Law and literature: the case of *Anatomy of a Murder*. MidAmerica (30) 2003, 123–33.

Natasha Trethewey

19872. TRETHEWEY, NATASHA.   On Whitman, Civil War memory, and my South. *See* **12354**.

David Treuer

19873. STIRRUP, DAVID.   Life after death in Poverty: David Treuer's *Little*. AIQ (29:3/4) 2005, 651–72.

T. Minh-Ha (Thi Minh-Ha) Trinh (b.1952)

19874. FOSTER, GWENDOLYN AUDREY.   Experiments in ethnography. *In* (pp. 179–91) **13334**.

Quincy Troupe

19875. CASTRO, JAN GARDEN.   Quincy Troupe: an interview. APR (34:2) 2005, 49–57.

Dalton Trumbo

19876. ABEL, JONATHAN E.   Canon and censor: how war wounds bodies of writing. CLS (42:1) 2005, 74–93.

H. T. Tsiang

19877. LEE, JULIA H. The capitalist and imperialist critique in H. T. Tsiang's *And China Has Hands*. In (pp. 80–97) 12775.

Richard Walton Tully (1877–1945)

19878. BALME, CHRISTOPHER B. Selling the bird: Richard Walton Tully's *The Bird of Paradise* and the dynamics of theatrical commodification. TJ (57:1) 2005, 1–20.

Peter Turchi (b.1960)

19879. TURCHI, PETER. Behind the story. In (pp. 439–41) 14294.

Lewis Turco

19880. TURCO, LEWIS. A sheaf of leaves: literary memoirs. Scottsdale, AZ: Star Cloud Press, 2004. pp. viii, 255.

Reggie Turner (1869?–1938)

19881. WEINTRAUB, STANLEY. Reggie Turner, forgotten Edwardian novelist. ELT (48:1) 2005, 3–37.

Scott Turow

19882. MACDONALD, ANDREW F.; MACDONALD, GINA. Scott Turow: a critical companion. Westport, CT; London: Greenwood Press, 2005. pp. 259. (Critical companions to popular contemporary writers.)

Amos Tutuola

19883. RICARD, ALAIN. De Félix Couchoro (1900–1968) à Amos Tutuola (1923–1997): les marges de la marge: discours dominé et discours métissé. RLC (79:2) 2005, 179–88.

Anne Tyler

19884. ELFENBEIN, ANNA SHANNON. Living lessons: the evolving racial norm in the novels of Anne Tyler. SoQ (43:1) 2005, 63–79.

Maxine Tynes

19885. MCDONALD-RISSANEN, MARY. Imaging the past: Atlantic Canada and popular representations. In (pp. 148–57) 12912.

Louis Untermeyer (1885–1977)

19886. BRITT, BRIAN. Contesting history and identity in modern fiction about Moses. In (pp. 90–105) 12978.

John Updike

19887. BENTLEY, GREG W. Sammy's erotic experience: subjectivity and sexual difference in John Updike's *A&P*. JSSE (43) 2004, 121–41.

19888. BROWN, SARAH ANNES. The prequel as palinode: Mary Cowden Clarke's *Girlhood of Shakespeare's Heroines*. See 10450.

19889. DEAVER, KAREN. Updike's *No More Access to Her Underpants*. Exp (63:3) 2005, 183–4.

19890. DE BELLIS, JACK (ed.). John Updike: the critical responses to the Rabbit saga. Westport, CT; London: Praeger, 2005. pp. xi, 298. (Critical responses in arts and letters, 40.)

19891. DICKSTEIN, MORRIS. John Updike's secret. LitIm (7:1) 2005, 15–17.

19892. GRIMBERT, JOAN TASKER. John Updike's *Brazil*: Tristan & Iseult in Black & White, White & Black. Tristania (23) 2004, 61–73.

19893. KEENER, BRIAN. John Updike's human comedy: comic morality in *The Centaur* and the Rabbit novels. New York; Frankfurt: Lang, 2005. pp. x, 148. (Modern American literature: new approaches, 43.)

19894. MATHÉ, SYLVIE. 'Welcome to the post-Pill paradise': variations sur quelques figures d'Éros dans la fiction de John Updike (*Marry Me, Couples & The Witches of Eastwick*). EREA (1:1) 2003, 59–68.

19895. PARKS, JOHN G. The need of some imperishable bliss: John Updike's *Toward the End of Time*. Ren (57:2) 2005, 151–7.

19896. SINGH, SUKHBIR. Rewriting the American wasteland: John Updike's *The Centaur*. ANQ (18:1) 2005, 60–4.

Arthur Upfield

19897. HOWE, WINONA. Inspecting women: Arthur W. Upfield and Napoleon Bonaparte. Antipodes (18:1) 2004, 77–9.

Jane Urquhart

19898. CONDÉ, MARY. As cold as ice: *The Underpainter*. In (pp. 57–64) **19900**.

19899. FERRI, LAURA. A conversation with Jane Urquhart. In (pp. 15–41) **19900**.

19900. —— (ed.). Jane Urquhart: essays on her works. Toronto; Buffalo, NY; Lancaster: Guernica, 2005. pp. 151. (Writers series, 13.)

19901. RICCIARDI, CATERINA. *Away* and the meanings of colonization. In (pp. 65–77) **19900**.

19902. STAINES, DAVID. *The Stone Carvers*. In (pp. 43–5) **19900**.

Jean Valentine

19903. HARMS, JAMES. Jean Valentine: remnants and recognition. WeBr (56) 2005, 72–80.

Guy Vanderhaeghe

19904. WYILE, HERB. Doing the honourable thing: Guy Vanderhaeghe's *The Last Crossing*. CanL (185) 2005, 59–74.

Paul Vangelisti

19905. MOHR, BILL. Likelihood of survival: Paul Vangelisti's poetry. ChiR (51:1/2) 2005, 277–84 (review-article).

Aritha van Herk

19906. LJUNGBERG, CHRISTINA. Constructing new 'realities': the performative function of maps in contemporary fiction. SPELL (16) 2003, 159–76.

Carl Van Vechten

19907. JONES, JACQUELINE C. The unknown patron: Harold Jackman and the Harlem renaissance archives. LHR (19:1) 2004, 55–66.

19908. KELLNER, BRUCE (ed.). The splendid drunken twenties: selections from the daybooks, 1922–1930. Urbana: Illinois UP, 2003. pp. xvii, 336. Rev. by Martha E. Stone in GLRW (11:3) 2004, 40–1; by Kathleen Pfeiffer in Mod/Mod (12:1) 2005, 202–3.

Katherine Vaz (b.1955)

19909. Silva, Reinaldo.   The ethnic garden in Portuguese American writing. JAC (28:2) 2005, 191–200.

Yvonne Vera

19910. Coundouriotis, Eleni.   Self-inflicted wounds in Yvonne Vera's *Butterfly Burning.* WLT (79:3/4) 2005, 64–7.

Gore Vidal

19911. Harris, Stephen.   Gore Vidal's historical novels and the shaping of American political consciousness. Lewiston, NY; Lampeter: Mellen Press, 2005. pp. xiii, 247. (Studies in the historical novel, 4.)

19912. Peabody, Richard; Ebersole, Lucinda (eds).   Conversations with Gore Vidal. Jackson; London: Mississippi UP, 2005. pp. xxiv, 196. (Literary conversations.) Rev. by Thom Nickels in GLRW (12:6) 2005, 37–8.

Helena María Viramontes

19913. Grewe-Volpp, Christa.   'The oil was made from their bones': environmental (in)justice in Helena María Viramontes's *Under the Feet of Jesus.* ISLE (12:1) 2005, 61–78.

Gerald Vizenor

19914. Purdy, John; Hausman, Blake.   The future of print narratives and comic holotropes: a conversation with Gerald Vizenor. AIQ (29:1/2) 2005, 212–25.

Paula Vogel

19915. Geis, Deborah R.   In Willy Loman's garden: contemporary re-visions of *Death of a Salesman. In* (pp. 202–18) **18234.**

Mary Annette, Countess von Arnim ('Elizabeth') (1866–1941)

19916. Pennacchia, Maddalena.   Generare il proprio sé: scrittura e giardinaggio nella narrativa autobiografica di Elizabeth von Arnim. *In* (pp. 33–43) **12577.**

Kurt Vonnegut, Jr

19917. Cacicedo, Alberto.   'You must remember this': trauma and memory in *Catch-22* and *Slaughterhouse-Five. See* **16958.**

19918. Klinkowitz, Jerome.   The Vonnegut effect. (Bibl. 2004, 19966.) Rev. by Leonard Mustazza in SAtlR (70:2) 2005, 165–8.

19919. McInnis, Gilbert.   Evolutionary mythology in the writings of Kurt Vonnegut, Jr. CritW (46:4) 2005, 383–96.

19920. Procházka, Martin.   Apocalypticism in American cultural history: 2, Revelations of the Other. *See* **11217.**

19921. Ren, Xiaojin; He, Jiawei.   *Timequake*: a unity of incredulity to metanarratives and historiographic metafiction. FLS (116) 2005, 48–55.

Chuck Wachtel

19922. Wachtel, Chuck.   Behind the story. *In* (pp. 390–5) **14294.**

Helen Waddell

19923. BURLEIGH, DAVID (ed.). Helen Waddell's writings from Japan. Dublin; Portland, OR: Irish Academic Press, 2005. pp. xiii, 165.

Miriam Waddington (b.1917)

19924. GANZ, SHOSHANNA. The sound of every falling star: Miriam Waddington's poetry and translation of Rachel Korn's poetry. Gramma (12) 2004, 49–57.

Richard Wagamese (b.1955)

19925. KLEIN, VERENA. Healing the Native Canadian soul: three accounts of spiritual homecoming. See 17020.

Fred Wah

19926. WEAVER, ANDY. Synchronous foreignicity: Fred Wah's poetry and the recuperation of experimental texts. StudCanL (30:1) 2005, 309–25.

John Wain

19927. SCHLÜSSEL, ANGELIKA. Making a political statement or refusing to grow up – reflections on the situation of the academic youth in postwar British literature. See 18703.

Diane Wakoski

19928. BUNGE, NANCY. I wouldn't be a true intellectual if I weren't always combating the world as I see it: an interview with Diane Wakoski. Kalliope (27:1) 2005, 36–44.

19929. GILLESPIE, DEBORAH. An interview with Diane Wakoski. SoCR (38:1) 2005, 14–19.

Derek Walcott

19930. AKO, EDWARD O. Ernest Hemingway, Derek Walcott, and old men of the sea. See 16963.

19931. BAUGH, EDWARD. Of men and heroes: Walcott and the Haitian Revolution. Callaloo (28:1) 2005, 45–54.

19932. —— NEPAULSINGH, COLBERT (notes). Another Life. With a critical essay. (Bibl. 2004, 19983.) Rev. by Robert Hamner in WLWE (39:2) 2002/03, 146–8.

19933. BRAZIEL, JANA EVANS. 'Caribbean genesis': language, gardens, worlds (Jamaica Kincaid, Derek Walcott, Édouard Glissant). In (pp. 110–26) 12632.

19934. BREINER, LAURENCE A. Creole language in the poetry of Derek Walcott. Callaloo (28:1) 2005, 29–41.

19935. BRESLIN, PAUL. Derek Walcott's 'reversible world': centers, peripheries, and the scale of nature. Callaloo (28:1) 2005, 8–24.

19936. BURNETT, PAULA. Walcott's intertextual method: non-Greek naming in Omeros. Callaloo (28:1) 2005, 171–87.

19937. CAMPAGNOLI, MATTEO. Derek Walcott, nell'occhio del Ciclope. PoesiaM (196) 2005, 2–13.

19938. D'AGUIAR, FRED. 'In God we troust': Derek Walcott and God. Callaloo (28:1) 2005, 216–23.

19939. DASENBROCK, REED WAY. Imitation *versus* contestation: Walcott's postcolonial Shakespeare. Callaloo (28:1) 2005, 104–13.

19940. DOKOU, CHRISTINA. 'Fruit of the loom': new spins on Penelope in Walcott and Márquez. Syncrise (15) 2004, 153–74.

19941. ERICKSON, PETER. Artists' self-portraiture and self-exploration in Derek Walcott's *Tiepolo's Hound*. Callaloo (28:1) 2005, 224–35.

19942. FAN, KIT. Imagined places: Robinson Crusoe and Elizabeth Bishop. *See* **8513.**

19943. GRAY, JEFFREY. Walcott's traveler and the problem of witness. Callaloo (28:1) 2005, 117–28.

19944. GREENWOOD, EMILY. 'Still going on': temporal adverbs and the view of the past in Walcott's poetry. Callaloo (28:1) 2005, 132–45.

19945. HANDLEY, GEORGE. Derek Walcott's poetics of the environment in *The Bounty*. Callaloo (28:1) 2005, 201–15.

19946. ——— Triangulation and the aesthetics of temporality in *Tiepolo's Hound*. Callaloo (28:1) 2005, 236–56.

19947. HANDLEY, GEORGE B. 'The argument of the outboard motor': an interview with Derek Walcott. *In* (pp. 127–39) **12632.**

19948. ——— Interview with Derek Walcott. JCarL (4:1) 2005, 95–108.

19949. KING, JANE. 'Images of flight …': 'This time, Shabine, like you really gone!' Callaloo (28:1) 2005, 75–86.

19950. KRAUS, JOE. Through loins and coins: Derek Walcott's weaving of the West Indian Federation. Callaloo (28:1) 2005, 60–74.

19951. MACDONALD, JOYCE GREEN. Bodies, race, and performance in Derek Walcott's *A Branch of the Blue Nile*. TJ (57:2) 2005, 191–203.

19952. MACDONALD-SMYTHE, ANTONIA. The privileges of being born in … a backward and underdeveloped society: Derek Walcott's prodigal provincialism. Callaloo (28:1) 2005, 88–101.

19953. MARTYNIUK, IRENE. Playing with Europe: Derek Walcott's retelling of Homer's *Odyssey*. Callaloo (28:1) 2005, 188–99.

19954. MELAS, NATALIE. Forgettable vacations and metaphor in ruins: Walcott's *Omeros*. Callaloo (28:1) 2005, 147–68.

19955. MOFFETT, JOE W. 'Master, I was the freshest of all your readers': Derek Walcott's *Omeros* and Homer as literary origin. Lit (16:1) 2005, 1–23.

19956. WALCOTT, DEREK. Isla incognita. *In* (pp. 51–7) **12632.**

19957. WALLART, KERRY-JANE. La métaphore chez Derek Walcott: à la recherche d'une 'arrière-langue'. EA (58:4) 2005, 456–72.

Anne Waldman (b.1945)

19958. HAMILTON, ROXANNE POWER. Take everyone to heaven with us: Anne Waldman's poetry cultures. *In* (pp. 98–125) **12566.**

Alice Walker

19959. BATES, GERRI. Alice Walker: a critical companion. Westport, CT; London: Greenwood Press, 2005. pp. xi, 220. (Critical companions to popular contemporary writers.)

19960. DAVIS, AMANDA J.   To build a nation: Black women writers, Black nationalism, and violent reduction of wholeness. *See* **17227.**

19961. HOOKER, DEBORAH ANNE.   Reanimating the trope of the talking book in Alice Walker's *Strong Horse Tea.* SoLJ (37:2) 2005, 81–102.

19962. MCMILLAN, LAURIE.   Telling a critical story: Alice Walker's *In Search of Our Mothers' Gardens.* JML (28:1) 2004, 107–23.

19963. SILVA, REINALDO.   The ethnic garden in Portuguese American writing. *See* **19909.**

19964. WALKER, ALICE.   In search of our mothers' gardens: womanist prose. *See* **12956.**

19965. WANG, XIAOYING.   The art of irony in Alice Walker's *Everyday Use.* FLS (114) 2005, 39–43. (In Chinese.)

19966. WATSON, REGINALD.   The power of the 'milk' and motherhood: images of deconstruction and reconstruction in Toni Morrison's *Beloved* and Alice Walker's *The Third Life of Grange Copeland.* *See* **18376.**

19967. WHITT, JAN.   What happened to Celie and Idgie? 'Apparitional lesbians' in American film. *See* **13520.**

George F. Walker

19968. WARKENTIN, GERMAINE.   Mapping Wonderland: the city of Toronto as seen through its writers' eyes. LRC (13:10) 2005, 14–16.

Margaret Walker

19969. THOMAS, GRISELDA.   If you see my scars, you will feel my pain: the significance of scarification in the private narrative fiction of Black women writers. ZNHF (18) 2004, 27–35.

Mildred Walker

19970. PEARSON, CARMEN.   Mildred Walker (1905–1998). Legacy (22:2) 2005, 187–94. (*Legacy* profiles.)

David Foster Wallace

19971. TYSDAL, DAN.   Inarticulation and the figure of enjoyment: Raymond Carver's minimalism meets David Foster Wallace's *A Radically Condensed History of Postindustrial Life.* *See* **15717.**

Edward Lewis Wallant

19972. CODDE, PHILIPPE.   'No enemy, no betrayer, no bearded torturer': the death of God, the Holocaust, and existentialism in Wallant's *The Human Season.* ELN (43:1) 2005, 63–77.

19973. KOLÁŘ, STANISLAV.   Memories as a nightmare: E. L. Wallant's *Pawnbroker.* SlStE (1) 2005, 264–9.

Vivian Walsh

19974. PARSONS, ELIZABETH.   The appeal of the underdog: Mr Lunch and Left politics as entertainment. *See* **19353.**

Andy Warhol

19975. BERNARD, CATHERINE.   L'art de l'aporie: penser l'impensable avec Adorno et Benjamin. *See* **15379.**

Marina Warner

19976. WILLIAMS-WANQUET, EILEEN. Marina Warner's *Indigo* as ethical deconstruction and reconstruction. CritW (46:3) 2005, 267–82.

Rex Warner

19977. SUITS, THOMAS A. Rex Warner and Catullus 8. CML (25:1) 2005, 77–83.

Sylvia Townsend Warner

19978. JAMES, DAVID. Realism, late Modernist abstraction, and Sylvia Townsend Warner's fictions of impersonality. Mod/Mod (12:1) 2005, 111–31.

19979. KALATA, KRISTIANNE. 'There was a world of things ... and a world of words': narration of self through object in Sylvia Townsend Warner's *Scenes of Childhood*. TSWL (24:2) 2005, 319–39.

Robert Penn Warren

19980. BLOTNER, JOSEPH. Robert Penn Warren, Cleanth Brooks, and the Southern literary tradition. RWP (5) 2005, 55–74.

19981. BRADLEY, PATRICIA L. Robert Penn Warren's circus aesthetic and the Southern renaissance. (Bibl. 2004, 20023.) Rev. by Lesa C. Shaul in ArkR (36:1) 2005, 56–7.

19982. BURT, JOHN. A note on *Uncertain Season in High Country*. SoR (41:2) 2005, 243–9.

19983. —— Purity, panic, and Pasiphaë in *Brother to Dragons*. RWP (5) 2005, 147–70.

19984. BURT, STEPHEN. R. P. Blackmur and Randall Jarrell on literary magazines: an exchange. See **1166**.

19985. CLARK, WILLIAM BEDFORD; GRIMSHAW, JAMES A., JR. A conversation with Lewis P. Simpson. See **19460**.

19986. EALY, STEVEN D. Compactness, poetic ambiguity, and the fiction of Robert Penn Warren. *In* (pp. 146–69) **14768**.

19987. —— Corruption and innocence in Robert Penn Warren's fiction. ModAge (47:2) 2005, 139–47.

19988. FERRIS, WILLIAM R. Robert Penn Warren: 'mad for poetry'. SoCult (10:4) 2004, 8–32.

19989. FERRISS, LUCY. Robert Penn Warren and psychological pastoralism. Shen (55:3) 2005, 126–33.

19990. FURY, FRANK P. Sports, politics, and the corruption of power in Robert Penn Warren's *All the King's Men*. Aethlon (22:2) 2005, 67–73.

19991. HENDRICKS, RANDY; PERKINS, JAMES A. (eds). Three letters. SoR (41:2) 2005, 213–23.

19992. LIU, XIANGYANG. Augustinian time and Robert Penn Warren's poetry. FLS (115) 2005, 115–20. (In Chinese.)

19993. MILLER, STEPHEN. The achievement of Gibbon. See **8657**.

19994. MURPHY, PAUL. Divorcing Robert Penn Warren from the South. RWP (5) 2005, 75–86.

19995. PERKINS, JAMES A. (ed.). The Cass Mastern material: the core of Robert Penn Warren's *All the King's Men*. Baton Rouge: Louisiana State UP, 2005. pp. x, 197. (Southern literary studies.)

19996. SCHUCHARD, RONALD. The Robert Penn Warren collection at Emory University: a personal account. RWP (5) 2005, 103–29.

19997. SIMPSON, LEWIS P. Robert Penn Warren and the South. RWP (5) 2005, 33–6.

19998. SZCZESIUL, ANTHONY. Racial politics and Robert Penn Warren's poetry. (Bibl. 2004, 20035.) Rev. by Warren J. Carson in SoLJ (37:2) 2005, 152–5.

19999. WARREN, ROSANNA. Places: a memoir. SoR (41:1) 2005, 233–42.

20000. WEATHERBY, HAROLD L. Warren's Willie Talos: reflections on the name. RWP (5) 2005, 131–7.

20001. WINCHELL, MARK ROYDEN. Understanding Whittier; or, Warren in the aftermath of Modernism. RWP (5) 2005, 87–102.

Booker T. Washington

20002. BRUNDAGE, W. FITZHUGH (ed.). Booker T. Washington and Black progress: *Up from Slavery* 100 years later. Gainesville: Florida UP, 2003. pp. vii, 227. Rev. by Cary D. Wintz in JAH (91:4) 2005, 1500–1.

20003. HSU, HSUAN L. Literature and regional production. *See* **11488**.

20004. MENSON-FURR, LADRICA. Booker T. Washington, August Wilson, and the shadows in the garden. *See* **20240**.

20005. MOSES, WILSON JEREMIAH. Creative conflict in African American thought: Frederick Douglass, Alexander Crummell, Booker T. Washington, W. E. B. Du Bois, and Marcus Garvey. *See* **10831**.

Vernon Watkins

20006. GOLIGHTLY, VICTOR. 'Speak on a finger and thumb': Dylan Thomas, language and the deaf. *See* **19766**.

J. Wreford Watson ('James Wreford') (b.1915)

20007. ATKINSON, KEN. Wilderness and the Canadian mind. BJCS (16:2) 2003, 228–42.

Sheila Watson

20008. FLAHIFF, F. T. Always someone to kill the doves: a life of Sheila Watson. Edmonton, Alta: NeWest Press, 2005. pp. x, 356. Rev. by W. J. Keith in LRC (13:10) 2005, 29–30.

20009. WILLMOTT, GLENN. Sheila Watson, aboriginal discourse, and cosmopolitan Modernism. *In* (pp. 101–16) **12739**.

Evelyn Waugh

20010. BLAYAC, ALAIN. *Ars memoriae, memoria artis*: Charles Ryder's case in *Brideshead Revisited*. EtBr (29) 2005, 15–24.

20011. FERRAND, AUDE. Revisiting *Beatrix*: intertextuality, tradition and modernity in Evelyn Waugh's *Brideshead Revisited*. EtBr (28) 2005, 57–70.

20012. LE ROUX, BENOÎT. Evelyn Waugh. Paris: L'Harmattan, 2003. pp. 319. (Aire anglophone.) Rev. by Alain Blayac in EtBr (25) 2003, 199–200.

20013. LOBB, EDWARD. Waugh among the Modernists: allusion and theme in *A Handful of Dust*. Connotations (13:1/2) 2003/04, 130–44.

20014. PRESCOTT, LYNDA. Evelyn Waugh, Morris, and the ideal of craftsmanship. JWMS (16:2/3) 2005, 80–91.

20015. ROSSI, JOHN P. Two irascible Englishmen: Mr Waugh and Mr Orwell. *See* **18697**.

20016. ROWLAND, PETER. Waugh on the Wilde side. Wildean (26) 2005, 27–40.

20017. TAYLOR, D. J. A briefcase life: the full picture of Brian Howard is more than a portrait of failure. TLS, 18 Nov. 2005, 14–15. (Howard as inspiration for Waugh characters.)

20018. VILLAR FLOR, CARLOS; DAVIS, ROBERT MURRAY (eds). Waugh without end: new trends in Evelyn Waugh studies. New York; Frankfurt: Lang, 2005. pp. 291.

Richard M. Weaver

20019. DIMOCK, JAMES PATRICK. Rediscovering the heroic Conservatism of Richard M. Weaver. ModAge (47:4) 2005, 301–10.

20020. PANICHAS, GEORGE A. Restoring the meaning of Conservatism. *See* **1822**.

Francis Webb (1925–1973)

20021. ASHCROFT, BILL. The horizontal sublime. Antipodes (19:2) 2005, 141–51.

20022. BRENNAN, BERNADETTE. Recognizing the 'face of love' in Francis Webb's *The Canticle*. Antipodes (19:1) 2005, 31–8.

20023. ROWE, NOEL. How to gossip with angels: Australian poetry after the gods. *See* **15613**.

Phyllis Webb

20024. COLLIS, STEPHEN. Essay on abstraction: Phyllis Webb & the death of the lyric. WCL (38:3) 2005, 79–81, 84–7, 90–5.

20025. FARR, ROGER. The 'insurrectionary wilderness of the I': Phyllis Webb's anarchist poetics. WCL (38:3) 2005, 63–76.

Ian Wedde

20026. CRIGLINGTON, MEREDITH. White flight: escaping the illegitimate and inauthentic city in Ian Wedde's *Symmes Hole*. JNZL (23:2) 2005, 10–20.

John Weidman (b.1946)

20027. HANSON, LAURA. John Weidman: one thing led to another. SondR (11:3) 2005, 13–14. (Interview.)

James Welch

20028. LARSON, SIDNER. Colonization as subtext in James Welch's *Winter in the Blood*. AIQ (29:1/2) 2005, 274–80.

20029. LINCOLN, KENNETH. Winter naming: James Welch. AICRJ (29:3) 2005, 1–23.

20030. Lupton, Mary Jane. Interview with James Welch (1940–2003), November 17, 2001. AIQ (29:1/2) 2005, 198–211.

20031. Vernon, Irene S. 'A happiness that sleeps with sadness': an examination of 'white scabs' in *Fools Crow.* AIQ (29:1/2) 2005, 178–97.

Fay Weldon

20032. Rao, Eleonora. Masks of the self: autobiographical signatures in the feminine. *In* (pp. 189–99) **12577.**

20033. Wisker, Gina. Demisting the mirror: contemporary British women's horror. *See* **17030.**

Marjorie Welish (b.1944)

20034. Wilkinson, John. Faktura: the work of Marjorie Welish. ChiR (51:3) 2005, 115–27.

Orson Welles (1915–1985)

20035. Bell, Robert H. Rereading Orson Welles's *Chimes at Midnight. See* **13512.**

20036. Heyer, Paul. The medium and the magician: Orson Welles, the radio years, 1934–1952. *See* **13946.**

20037. Walters, Ben. Welles. *See* **13947.**

H. G. Wells

20038. Bertolini, John A. Shaw responds to Shaw-bashing. *See* **19383.**

20039. Bond, Barbara. H. G. Wells's *Tono-Bungay* as a reflection of its time. Wellsian (26) 2003, 3–11.

20040. Csala-Gáti, Katalin; Tóth, János I. The socio-biological and human-ecological notions in *The Time Machine.* Wellsian (26) 2003, 12–23.

20041. Curreli, Mario. Invading other people's territory: *The Inheritors. See* **15870.**

20042. Davidson, Brett. H. G. Wells, the artilleryman and the intersection on Putney Hill. Wellsian (26) 2003, 45–54.

20043. —— *The War of the Worlds* considered as a modern myth. Wellsian (28) 2005, 39–50.

20044. DeVine, Christine. Class in turn-of-the-century novels of Gissing, James, Hardy, and Wells. *See* **11072.**

20045. Dryden, Linda. H. G. Wells and Joseph Conrad: a literary friendship. *See* **15874.**

20046. Edelson, Maria. The motif of the island and the theme of destructive creation in *Moreau's Other Island* by Brian Aldiss. *In* (pp. 47–54) **3756.**

20047. Freedman, Ariela. Zeppelin fictions and the British home front. JML (27:3) 2004, 47–62.

20048. Glendening, John. Track of the Sphinx: H. G. Wells, the modern universe, and the decay of Aestheticism. VIJ (32) 2004, 129–66.

20049. Hammond, John R. H. G. Wells's *The Time Machine*: a reference guide. (Bibl. 2004, 20079.) Rev. by John S. Partington in Wellsian (28) 2005, 62–6.

20050. HARACK, KATRINA.   Limning the impossible: time travel, the uncanny and destructive futurity in H. G. Wells's *The Time Machine*. Wellsian (28) 2005, 28–38.

20051. KELLER, CHRIS; MILLER, TOM.   Commanding the Land Ironclads. Wellsian (26) 2003, 31–45.

20052. MÁNEK, BOHUSLAV.   A welcome guest: the Czech reception of H. G. Wells. *In* (pp. 165–373) **20055**.

20053. MENEGALDO, GILLES.   L'inscription de l'histoire et la vision du futur dans *The Time Machine* de H. G. Wells et son adaptation filmique par George Pal. Cycnos (22:1) 2005, 139–50.

20054. PARRINDER, PATRICK.   History in the science-fiction of H. G. Wells. Cycnos (22:2) 2005, 139–46.

20055. —— PARTINGTON, JOHN S. (eds).   The reception of H. G. Wells in Europe. London: Thoemmes Press; New York: Continuum, 2005. pp. xl, 419. (Athlone critical traditions.)

20056. PARTINGTON, JOHN S.   Building cosmopolis: the political thought of H. G. Wells. (Bibl. 2004, 20086.) Rev. by John R. Reed in VS (47:3) 2005, 461–3.

20057. ——   Julian Huxley's time machine: a biologist's retelling of Wells's scientific romance? Wellsian (28) 2005, 50–5.

20058. —— (ed.).   The Wellsian: selected essays on H. G. Wells. (Bibl. 2004, 20087.) Rev. by Jon Barnes in TLS, 5 Aug. 2005, 28.

20059. PINKNEY, TONY.   Kinetic utopias: H. G. Wells's *A Modern Utopia* and William Morris's *News from Nowhere*. JWMS (16:2/3) 2005, 49–55.

20060. QUAMEN, HARVEY N.   Unnatural interbreeding: H. G. Wells's *A Modern Utopia* as species and genre. VLC (33:1) 2005, 67–84.

20061. RENZI, THOMAS C. (ed.).   H. G. Wells: six scientific romances adapted for film. Lanham, MD; London: Scarecrow Press, 2004. pp. 227. (Second ed.: first ed. 1992.) Rev. by John S. Partington in Wellsian (28) 2005, 57–62.

20062. RIEDER, JOHN.   Science fiction, colonialism, and the plot of invasion. *See* **14263**.

20063. ROHMAN, CARRIE.   Burning out the animal: the failure of Enlightenment purification in H. G. Wells's *The Island of Dr Moreau*. *In* (pp. 121–34) **14258**.

20064. ROSS, WILLIAM T.   H. G. Wells's world reborn: *The Outline of History* and its companions. (Bibl. 2004, 20089.) Rev. by John S. Partington in Wellsian (26) 2003, 66–70.

20065. SMITH, DON G.   H. G. Wells on film: the utopian nightmare. (Bibl. 2004, 20090.) Rev. by John Huntington in JFA (13:3) 2003, 296–8; by John S. Partington in Wellsian (26) 2003, 59–62.

20066. SOMMERVILLE, B. D.   A tissue of moonshine: the mechanics of deception in *The Sea Lady*. Wellsian (26) 2003, 23–30.

20067. SWAFFORD, KEVIN.   Aesthetics, narrative and the critique of respectability in *The History of Mr Polly*. Wellsian (28) 2005, 14–27.

20068. WAGAR, W. WARREN.   H. G. Wells: traversing time. (Bibl. 2004, 20097.) Rev. by Nicholas Ruddick in JFA (15:2) 2004, 179–81; by Elmar Schenkel in Wellsian (28) 2005, 55–7; by John R. Reed in VS (47:3) 2005, 461–3.

20069. WRIGHT, PETER. Intertextuality, generic shift and ideological transformation in the internationalising of *Doctor Who. See* **14066.**

Irvine Welsh

20070. CARDULLO, BERT. Fiction into film: notes on one paradigmatic scene and two emblematic adaptations. *See* **13831.**

20071. JEFFERS, JENNIFER M. Rhizome national identity: 'Scatlin's psychic defense' in *Trainspotting.* JNT (35:1) 2005, 88–111.

Eudora Welty

20072. BAYNE, JOHN. Barry Moser, the robber, and Eudora Welty. EWeltyN (28:1) 2004, 19–21.

20073. CHENGGES, CATHERINE H. Checklist of Welty scholarship 2004–2005. EWeltyN (29:2) 2005, 30–5.

20074. COLE, HUNTER. Eudora on Stephen Tennant: a personal conversation. EWeltyN (29:2) 2005, 10–12.

20075. HOYT, HEATHER M. The mediating voice of humor: *The Shoe Bird* and Welty's adult texts. EWeltyN (29:1) 2005, 10–15.

20076. KAPLAN, DAVID. Segovia in San Francisco. EWeltyN (28:2) 2004, 15–19.

20077. KOJIMA, NANCY. 'She offered Virgie her Beethoven': Beethoven as metaphor in Welty's *June Recital.* EWeltyN (29:1) 2005, 18–23.

20078. KOON, BILL. 'If you lived in Clay': the small towns of Eudora Welty and William Faulkner. SoCR (37:2) 2005, 117–20.

20079. McHANEY, PEARL AMELIA. Interview with Suzanne Marrs, author of *Eudora Welty: a Biography.* EWeltyN (29:2) 2005, 6–10.

20080. —— Works by Welty: a continuing checklist. EWeltyN (29:2) 2005, 29.

20081. —— *The Yale Review* and Eudora Welty. EWeltyN (29:2) 2005, 35–6.

20082. —— (ed.). Eudora Welty: the contemporary reviews. Cambridge; New York: CUP, 2005. pp. xxv, 394. (American critical archives, 15.)

20083. McHANEY, THOMAS. Welty's *Home by Dark / Yalobusha County / 1936* in the jacket designs of two novels about slavery. EWeltyN (28:2) 2004, 30–3.

20084. —— You can go 'home by dark' again. EWeltyN (29:2) 2005, 36.

20085. MARK, REBECCA. As they lay dying; or, Why we should teach, write, and read Eudora Welty instead of, alongside of, because of, as often as William Faulkner. FJ (19:2) 2004, 107–19.

20086. MARRS, SUZANNE. Eudora Welty: a biography. Orlando, FL: Harcourt, 2005. pp. xix, 652, (plates) 16. Rev. by Jonathan Yardley in BkW, 14 Aug. 2005, 1–2; by Pam Kingsbury in ANCW (193:4) 2005, 25–6.

20087. —— One writer's imagination: the fiction of Eudora Welty. (Bibl. 2004, 20113.) Rev. by Veronica Makowsky in SoLJ (37:2) 2005, 141–4; by Sarah Ford in SCR (22:1) 2005, 137–8.

20088. MICHAELS, CINDY SHEFFIELD. Welty's words for the birds … and for children and scholars, too. EWeltyN (29:1) 2005, 6–10.

20089. MILLICHAP, JOSEPH. Eudora Welty's personal epic: autobiography, art, and Classical myth. SoLJ (38:1) 2005, 76–90.

20090. NICHOLS, DANA.   Graduates take the worn path: Welty's commencement stories. EWeltyN (29:2) 2005, 21–5.

20091. SHIMKUS, JIM.   King MacLain awakens as Finn MacCool. EWeltyN (29:1) 2005, 15–18.

20092. SNOW, MALINDA.   On the map: finding place and identity in *Delta Wedding*. EWeltyN (29:2) 2005, 25–9.

20093. ULMANOVÁ, HANA.   Eudora Welty in Czech cultural context. EWeltyN (29:1) 2005, 1–5.

20094. WEN, PATRICK.   The terror of neutrality: civil rights, tortured quietism, and the tactical disengagement of Flannery O'Connor. See **18582**.

20095. WHITT, MARGARET EARLEY.   1963, a pivotal year: Flannery O'Connor and the Civil Rights Movement. See **18583**.

Arnold Wesker

20096. WISZNIOWSKA, MARTA.   Feasting in drama. *In* (pp. 294–303) **3756**.

Don West

20097. BIGGERS, JEFF.   Let us now praise dangerous poets: memoirs of time spent with Appalachian poet-activist Don West. BRev (24:3) 2004, 5.

20098. —— BROSI, GEORGE (eds).   No lonesome road: selected prose and poems. (Bibl. 2004, 20129.) Rev. by Chris Green in AppH (33:3) 2005, 93–8.

Dorothy West

20099. SHERRARD-JOHNSON, CHERENE.   'This plague of their own locusts': space, property, and identity in Dorothy West's *The Living Is Easy*. AAR (38:4) 2004, 609–24.

Mae West

20100. POOLE, RALPH J.   Indecent ingénues: David Belasco's and Mae West's delegitimization and refashioning of American melodrama. See **15432**.

20101. PULLEN, KIRSTEN.   Actresses and whores: on stage and in society. See **3993**.

Morris L. West ('Michael East', 'Julian Morris') (b.1916)

20102. CONFOY, MARYANNE.   Morris West: literary maverick. Milton, Qld: Wiley, 2005. pp. xii, 372.

'Nathanael West' (Nathan Wallenstein Weinstein)

20103. GOLDMAN, PETER.   Consumer society and its discontents: *The Truman Show* and *The Day of the Locust*. See **13836**.

20104. IULI, MARIA CRISTINA.   Giusto il tempo di esplodere: *Miss Lonelyhearts*, il romanzo pop di Nathanael West. Bergamo: Bergamo UP/Sestante, 2005. pp. 207.

20105. NIELAND, JUSTUS.   West's deadpan: affect, slapstick, and publicity in *Miss Lonelyhearts*. Novel (38:1) 2004, 57–83.

'Rebecca West' (Mrs H. M. Andrews)

20106. BONIKOWSKI, WYATT.   The return of the soldier brings death home. MFS (51:3) 2005, 513–35.

20107. HOSPITAL, JANETTE TURNER.   West's *Survivors in Mexico*. ELT (48:1) 2005, 71–5 (review-article).

20108. PAUL, RONALD.   In pastoral fields: the Regeneration Trilogy and classic First World War fiction. *In* (pp. 147–61) **15309.**

20109. SCHWEIZER, BERNARD (ed.).   Survivors in Mexico. New Haven, CT; London: Yale UP, 2003. pp. xxx, 264. Rev. by Janette Turner Hospital in ELT (48:1) 2005, 71–5.

20110. STETZ, MARGARET DIANE.   Oscar Wilde and feminist criticism. *In* (pp. 224–45) **12414.**

20111. WINKIEL, LAURA.   Cabaret Modernism: Vorticism and racial spectacle. *In* (pp. 206–24) **12640.**

Christine Weston (b.1904)

20112. COWASJEE, SAROS (ed.).   A Raj collection. *See* **19571.**

20113. FURBANK, P. N.   Anglo-Indian dialogues: the Raj, the historical novel and misunderstandings between the races. *See* **19572.**

Edith Wharton

20114. BENERT, ANNETTE L.   Edith Wharton, Charles McKim, and the American renaissance. EWR (20:2) 2004, 10–17.

20115. BLACKFORD, HOLLY.   Haunted housekeeping: fatal attractions of servant and mistress in twentieth-century female gothic literature. Lit (16:2) 2005, 233–61.

20116. DiGIANVITTORIO, LINDSAY; SAUNDERS, JUDITH P.   Janey Archer's myopia and *The Age of Innocence*. EWR (21:1) 2005, 15–18.

20117. GALBUS, JULIA A.   Edith Wharton's material republic: *The House of Mirth*. EWR (20:2) 2004, 1–7.

20118. GETZ, JOHN.   Edith Wharton and the ghost of Poe: *Miss Mary Pask* and *Mr Jones*. EWR (21:1) 2005, 18–23.

20119. GOLDSMITH, MEREDITH.   The year of the rose: Jewish masculinity in *The House of Mirth*. MFS (51:2) 2005, 374–92.

20120. HALL, SUSAN L.   The death of love: sexuality, secrets, and settings in Wharton's *Summer*. EWR (21:2) 2005, 10–17.

20121. HORNE, PHILIP.   Henry James among the poets. *See* **11410.**

20122. KASSANOFF, JENNIE A.   Edith Wharton and the politics of race. Cambridge; New York: CUP, 2004. pp. xii, 226. (Cambridge studies in American literature and culture.) Rev. by Renée Tursi in TLS, 2 Dec. 2005, 31.

20123. McLAUGHLIN, KATE.   Edith Wharton, war correspondent. EWR (21:2) 2005, 1–10.

20124. OLIN-AMMENTORP, JULIE.   Edith Wharton's writings from the Great War. (Bibl. 2004, 20153.) Rev. by Hildegard Hoeller in ALR (38:1) 2005, 86–8; by Mary Anne Schofield in TSWL (24:1) 2005, 170–1.

20125. PEEL, ROBIN.   Apart from Modernism: Edith Wharton, politics, and fiction before World War I. Madison, NJ: Fairleigh Dickinson UP, 2005. pp. 345.

20126. —— Vulgarity, bohemia, and Edith Wharton's *The Reef*. ALR (37:3) 2005, 187–201.

20127. PENNELL, MELISSA MCFARLAND. Student companion to Edith Wharton. Westport, CT; London: Greenwood Press, 2003. pp. xii, 186. (Student companions to classic writers.)

20128. RICH, CHARLOTTE. Fictions of colonial anxiety: Edith Wharton's *The Seed of the Faith* and *A Bottle of Perrier*. JSSE (43) 2004, 59–74.

20129. SAUNDERS, JUDITH P. Evolutionary biological issues in Edith Wharton's *The Children*. ColLit (32:2) 2005, 83–102.

20130. SHAFFER-KOROS, CAROLE M. Nietzsche, German culture and Edith Wharton. EWR (20:2) 2004, 7–10.

20131. SILVA, REINALDO FRANCISCO. Eroticizing the Other in Edith Wharton's *Beatrice Palmato*. M/M (19:1) 2005, 38–45.

20132. SINGLEY, CAROL J. (ed.). Edith Wharton's *The House of Mirth*: a casebook. (Bibl. 2004, 20156.) Rev. by Phoebe Jackson in ColLit (32:4) 2005, 211–16.

20133. SOMERS, RENEE. Edith Wharton as spatial activist and analyst. London; New York: Routledge, 2005. pp. x, 172. (Studies in major literary authors.)

20134. STANSELL, ELIZABETH. Lest you mistake your mud hut for the Parthenon: echoes of Edith Wharton's *The Valley of Childish Things, and Other Emblems* in *The House of Mirth*. EWR (21:2) 2005, 17–23.

20135. TAVARES, TERESA. New Women, New Men, or what you will in Edith Wharton's *The Fruit of the Tree*. EWR (21:1) 2005, 1–15.

20136. THORNTON, EDITH. 'Innocence' consumed: packaging Edith Wharton with Kathleen Norris in *Pictorial Review* magazine, 1920–21. EurJAC (24:1) 2005, 29–45.

20137. WARE, MICHELE S. The architecture of the short story: Edith Wharton's Modernist practice. EWR (20:2) 2004, 17–23.

Thomas Wharton (b.1963)

20138. OMHOVÈRE, CLAIRE. The melting of time in Thomas Wharton's *Icefields*. *In* (pp. 43–62) **12587**.

Antonia White

20139. CHAIT, SANDRA. Site also of angst and spiritual search. *In* (pp. 150–69) **15847**.

20140. JEFFERY, SANDRA. Antonia White and the subversion of literary impotence at Hayford Hall. *In* (pp. 70–88) **15847**.

20141. PODNIEKS, ELIZABETH; CHAIT, SANDRA (eds). Hayford Hall: hangovers, erotics, and Modernist aesthetics. *See* **15847**.

20142. VANDIVERE, JULIE. Framed liminalities: Antonia White's *Beyond the Glass* and Emily Coleman's *The Shutter of Snow*. *In* (pp. 46–69) **15847**.

E. B. (Elwyn Brooks) White (1899–1985)

20143. ARONSON, DEB. E. B. White. New York: Rosen Central, 2005. pp. 112. (Library of author biographies.)

20144. ROOT, ROBERT. The everlastingly great look of the sky: Thoreau and E. B. White at Walden Pond. *See* **12211**.

Edmund White (b.1940)

20145. NAWROCKI, JIM. Makers and shakers of gay literature. GLRW (12:1) 2005, 36–7.

20146. WHITE, EDMUND. My lives. London: Bloomsbury, 2005. pp. 356. Rev. by Adam Phillips in LRB (27:21) 2005, 7–9.

Patrick White

20147. ASHCROFT, BILL. The horizontal sublime. *See* **20021.**

20148. BESTON, JOHN. Films and Patrick White. Southerly (64:3) 2004, 176–9.

20149. BRADY, VERONICA. God, history, and Patrick White. Antipodes (19:2) 2005, 172–6.

20150. HUBBER, BRIAN; SMITH, VIVIAN. Patrick White: a bibliography. Auburn, Vic.: Quiddlers Press; New Castle, DE: Oak Knoll Press, 2004. pp. xvii, 304. Rev. by Laurie Hergenhan in ALS (22:1) 2005, 114–16; by Geordie Williamson in BC (54:4) 2005, 610–11.

20151. LEON, CAROL E. Movement and belonging: lines, places and spaces of travel. *See* **17615.**

20152. WETHERELL, RODNEY. Uncheery soul. Meanjin (64:1/2) 2005, 243–54.

Edward Whittemore

20153. STEINBERG, THEODORE LOUIS. Twentieth-century epic novels. *See* **16191.**

Zoë Wicomb

20154. ATTRIDGE, DEREK. Zoë Wicomb's home truths: place, genealogy, and identity in *David's Story*. JPW (41:2) 2005, 156–65.

20155. MARAIS, MIKE. Bastards and bodies in Zoë Wicomb's *David's Story*. JCL (40:3) 2005, 21–36.

20156. RICHARDS, CONSTANCE S. Nationalism and the development of identity in postcolonial fiction: Zoë Wicomb and Michelle Cliff. RAL (36:1) 2005, 20–33.

20157. WICOMB, ZOË. Setting, intertextuality and the resurrection of the postcolonial author. *See* **12083.**

John Edgar Wideman

20158. BUNYAN, SCOTT. The space of the prison: the last bastion of morality? *In* (pp. 174–99) **12821.**

20159. MILLER, D. QUENTIN. 'On the outside looking in': White readers of nonwhite prison narratives. *In* (pp. 15–32) **12821.**

20160. RUFFIN, KIMBERLY N. Mourning in the 'second Middle Passage': visual and verbal praxis in John Edgar Wideman's *Two Cities*. CLAJ (48:4) 2005, 415–39.

20161. WALIGORA-DAVIS, NICOLE A. The ghetto: illness and the formation of the 'suspect' in American polity. *See* **11710.**

Rudy Wiebe

20162. FILIPCZAK, DOROTA.	Not wanted in the canon: Canadian literature in the wilderness. *In* (pp. 55–64) **3756.**

20163. KORKKA, JANNE.	Writing the Canadian West: Rudy Wiebe. *In* (pp. 115–29) **12912.**

20164. LJUNGBERG, CHRISTINA.	Constructing new 'realities': the performative function of maps in contemporary fiction. *See* **19906.**

20165. RYMHS, DEENA.	Auto/biographical jurisdictions: collaboration, self-representation, and the law in *Stolen Life: the Journey of a Cree Woman.* *In* (pp. 89–108) **14629.**

Diana J. (Diana Jean) Wieler (b.1961)

20166. LEFEBVRE, BENJAMIN.	From *Bad Boy* to dead boy: homophobia, adolescent problem fiction, and male bodies that matter. CLAQ (30:3) 2005, 288–313.

Elie Wiesel

20167. WEISSMAN, GARY.	Fantasies of witnessing: postwar efforts to experience the Holocaust. *See* **13750.**

20168. WIESEL, ELIE.	The writing life. BkW, 14 Aug. 2005, 10.

Richard Wilbur

20169. GRAY, JASON.	An interview with Richard Wilbur. MR (27:3) 2004, 35–48.

20170. HECKER, WILLIAM.	Finding Wilfred Owen's forwarding address: moving beyond the World War One paradigm. *See* **18708.**

20171. PRITCHARD, WILLIAM H.	A master. Cweal (132:8) 2005, 24–6 (review-article).

20172. WAI, ISABELLA.	Wilbur's *Walking to Sleep.* Exp (64:1) 2005, 50–2.

Laura Ingalls Wilder

20173. KILGORE, JOHN.	*Little House* and the culture wars. VocR (7:4) 2005.

Anne Wilkinson

20174. MEZEI, KATHY.	'And we are homesick still': home, the unhomely, and the everyday in Anne Wilkinson. StudCanL (30:1) 2005, 160–80.

C. K. (Charles Kenneth) Williams (b.1936)

20175. SADOFF, IRA.	Dreaming creatures. *See* **19636.**

Charles Williams (1886–1945)

20176. LOBDELL, JARED C. (ed.).	The detective fiction reviews of Charles Williams, 1930–1935. (Bibl. 2004, 14316.) Rev. by Mike Ripley in SEVEN (22) 2005, 117–18.

20177. WENDLING, SUSAN.	*Descent into Hell* as poem: the centrality of poetry to Charles Williams' prose. CSL (36:2) 2005, 1–9, 12–14.

Tennessee Williams

20178. BERNARD, MARK.	Punishment and the body: Boss Whalen, Michel Foucault, and *Not about Nightingales.* TWAR (7) 2005.

20179. BRAY, ROBERT.	Foreword to *His Father's House.* TWAR (7) 2005.

20180. —— *et al.* The early plays of Tennessee Williams. TWAR (7) 2005. (Panel discussion.)

20181. CAÑADAS, IVAN. The naming of Jack Straw and Peter Ochello in Tennessee Williams's *Cat on a Hot Tin Roof.* ELN (42:4) 2005, 57–62.

20182. CAVE, MARK. Fred W. Todd and the Tennessee Williams holdings at the Historic New Orleans Collection. TWAR (7) 2005.

20183. DRAGON, ZOLTÁN. Adaptation as intermedial dialogue; or, Tennessee Williams goes to Hollywood. *In* (pp. 187–92) **3734.**

20184. FALOCCO, JOE. Gardens of desire: toward a unified vision of *Garden District.* TWAR (7) 2005.

20185. FAMBROUGH, PRESTON. Williams's *The Glass Menagerie.* Exp (63:2) 2005, 100–2.

20186. FORDYCE, EHREN. Inhospitable structures: some themes and forms in Tennessee Williams. JADT (17:2) 2005, 43–58.

20187. FRAYSSE, SUZANNE. Tennessee Williams, *A Streetcar Named Desire*: une lecture nommée désir. EREA (1:1) 2003, 52–8.

20188. HALE, ALLEAN. Tennessee Williams' *Three Plays for the Lyric Theatre.* TWAR (7) 2005.

20189. HEINTZELMAN, GRETA; HOWARD, ALYCIA SMITH. Critical companion to Tennessee Williams. New York: Facts on File, 2005. pp. xi, 436. (Facts on File library of American literature.)

20190. KOLIN, PHILIP C. Tennessee Williams and sports. PCR (16:2) 2005, 5–22.

20191. —— Williams's *Sand.* Exp (63:3) 2003, 173–6.

20192. —— (ed.). The Tennessee Williams encyclopedia. (Bibl. 2004, 20200.) Rev. by John S. Bak in AmDr (14:2) 2005, 102–6; by James Foley in JPC (38:5) 2005, 969–71; by Andrew Sofer in ModDr (48:1) 2005, 219–21; by Milton L. Tarver in SAtlR (70:1) 2005, 193–6; by Tom Mitchell in THS (25) 2005, 209–11; by Nancy Tischler in TWAR (7) 2005; by Lotta M. Löfgren in SoHR (39:3) 2005, 291–7.

20193. —— The undiscovered country: the later plays of Tennessee Williams. (Bibl. 2004, 20201.) Rev. by James F. Scott in ANQ (18:1) 2005, 65–9; by Peter A. Davis in TRI (30:2) 2005, 195–6.

20194. MOSCHOVAKIS, NICK. Tennessee Williams' American Blues: from the early manuscripts through *Menagerie.* TWAR (7) 2005.

20195. PALLER, MICHAEL. Gentlemen callers: Tennessee Williams, homosexuality, and mid-twentieth-century Broadway drama. Basingstoke; New York: Palgrave Macmillan, 2005. pp. xii, 269. Rev. by Raymond-Jean Frontain in GLRW (12:6) 2005, 41–2.

20196. PARKER, BRIAN. Elia Kazan and *Sweet Bird of Youth.* TWAR (7) 2005.

Terry Tempest Williams

20197. CHANDLER, KATHERINE R. Whale song from the desert: refuge without resolution and community without homogeneity in Terry Tempest Williams's *Refuge.* WS (34:8) 2005, 655–70.

20198. —— GOLDTHWAITE, MELISSA A. (eds). Surveying the literary landscapes of Terry Tempest Williams: new critical essays. (Bibl. 2004, 20207.) Rev. by Gioia Woods in ISLE (12:1) 2005, 284–5.

20199. SLOVIC, SCOTT. There's something about your voice I cannot hear: environmental literature, public policy and ecocriticism. Southerly (64:2) 2004, 59–68.

20200. TREDINNICK, MARK. The land's wild music: encounters with Barry Lopez, Peter Matthiessen, Terry Tempest Williams, & James Galvin. See **16637.**

William Carlos Williams

20201. AHEARN, BARRY (ed.). The correspondence of William Carlos Williams & Louis Zukofsky. (Bibl. 2004, 20210.) Rev. by Daniel Bouchard in ChiR (50:2–4) 2004/05, 346–50; by Mark Scroggins in WCWR (25:1) 2005, 100–3.

20202. AJI, HÉLÈNE. The subject in the structure: issues of procedure in contemporary American poetry. See **19579.**

20203. ALTIERI, CHARLES. The fate of the imaginary in twentieth-century American poetry. See **14363.**

20204. ASHTON, DORE. Was this angel necessary? See **19643.**

20205. BAY-CHENG, SARAH. The transcendental realism of American verse drama. See **15320.**

20206. BUTSCHER, EDWARD. Culture and literature: three collections of letters. See **10095.**

20207. COPESTAKE, IAN. 'Nothing that is not true': the impact of Unitarianism on the poetry of William Carlos Williams. WCWR (25:1) 2005, 1–25.

20208. CRAWFORD, T. HUGH. Williams and the bomb: the great destroyer or the magic bullet? WCWR (25:1) 2005, 27–42.

20209. EAST, JAMES H. (ed.). The humane particulars: the collected letters of William Carlos Williams and Kenneth Burke. (Bibl. 2004, 20216.) Rev. by Edward Butscher in GaR (59:3) 2005, 691–706.

20210. FRANKE, ASTRID. William Carlos Williams and John Dewey on the public, its problems, and its poetry. YREAL (19) 2003, 269–92.

20211. FRYE, RICHARD. 'The beginning comes only with the finish of what is past': Williams as cultural critic. WCWR (25:1) 2005, 43–62.

20212. HATLEN, BURTON. From the transcendental to the immanent sublime: the poetry of William Carlos Williams, 1913–1917. Paideuma (32:1–3) 2003, 123–55.

20213. HOLLENBERG, DONNA. 'Dancing edgeways': Robert Creeley's role in Denise Levertov's post-war transition. See **15960.**

20214. MACGOWAN, CHRISTOPHER. Making it free: Mitchell Goodman's radical Williams. Paideuma (32:1–3) 2003, 377–85.

20215. Meyer, Kinereth.   William Carlos Williams, *Paterson*, and the cultural uses of pastoral. WCWR (25:1) 2005, 63–78.

20216. Rehder, Robert.   Stevens, Williams, Crane, and the motive for metaphor. *See* **19681.**

20217. —— Williams and Moore: wasps, a gentian and real toads. SPELL (16) 2003, 67–77.

20218. Schmidt, Peter.   Colonial romance: Williams's dark 'supplying female'. WCWR (25:1) 2005, 79–92.

20219. Sykes, Jennie.   Robert Frost and William Carlos Williams: replying to Greek and Latin with the bare hands? *See* **16618.**

20220. Turco, Lewis.   Oswego poems and poets: Murabito and Davis. *See* **21261.**

20221. Wallaert, Josh.   The ecopoetics of perfection: William Carlos Williams and nature in *Spring and All*. ISLE (12:1) 2005, 79–98.

Henry Williamson

20222. Brown, Andy.   'Pauper spirits'. HWSJ (39) 2003, 18–29.

20223. Burns, Walker.   Golden days. HWSJ (41) 2005, 72–80. (Stories published in *The Golden Book Magazine*.)

20224. Fullagar, Brian.   Further thoughts on Richard Jefferies and Henry Williamson. *See* **11480.**

20225. Gregory, John.   Journalism: the public face of the Norfolk farm. HWSJ (40) 2004, 5–36.

20226. —— Keeping the wolf from the door: Henry Williamson's early journalism. HWSJ (39) 2003, 66–84.

20227. Jowett, Tony.   A jaunt to Belgium. HWSJ (39) 2003, 85–96.

20228. Lewis, Peter.   Helena and Doris: calf-love in fiction and real life ('Helena Rolls' and Doris Nicholson). HWSJ (41) 2005, 81–91.

20229. —— On the trail of 'Bugg Cottages'. HWSJ (40) 2004, 37–42.

20230. Mortimer, Ian.   The Henry Williamson archive at Exeter University Library. HWSJ (41) 2005, 64–71.

20231. Shepherd, Fred.   Imaginary but true: Henry's Wakenham. HWSJ (39) 2003, 6–17.

20232. Stewart, Richard.   Henry Williamson's debt to Richard Jefferies. HWSJ (41) 2005, 8–16.

20233. Williamson, Anne.   A purple thread: an examination of W. H. Hudson, naturalist and author, in relation to HW. *See* **17090.**

20234. —— 'Save his own soul he hath no star': thoughts arising from *The Dream of Fair Women*. HWSJ (39) 2003, 30–60.

20235. Williamson, Richard.   Impressions of nature: the nature writings of Henry Williamson. HWSJ (41) 2005, 52–63.

20236. Woudhuysen, H. R.   Not lonely, but alone. *See* **17642.**

A. N. Wilson (b.1950)

20237. Levitt, Morton P. A. N. Wilson and Marcel Proust: surprising bedfellows. JML (26:3/4) 2003, 62–72.

'August Wilson' (Frederick August Kittel) (1945–2005)

20238. Elam, Harry J., Jr. The past as present in the drama of August Wilson. (Bibl. 2004, 20232.) Rev. by Steve Feffer in CompDr (38:2/3) 2004, 332–6; by Yuko Kurahashi in AAR (39:3) 2005, 479–80; by Cheryl Black in THS (25) 2005, 198–200.

20239. Hornby, Richard. New York hot *versus* L.A. cool. See **21213**.

20240. Menson-Furr, Ladrica. Booker T. Washington, August Wilson, and the shadows in the garden. Mosaic (38:4) 2005, 175–90.

20241. Nesmith, N. Graham. Lloyd Richards: reminiscence of a theatre life and beyond. See **13083**.

20242. Snodgrass, Mary Ellen. August Wilson: a literary companion. Jefferson, NC; London: McFarland, 2004. pp. ix, 266. (McFarland literary companions, 1.)

20243. Viertel, Jack. The Wilson method. Dramatist (7:5) 2005, 22–6.

Barbara Wilson (b.1950)

20244. Parker, Emma. Lost in translation: gender and the figure of the translator in contemporary queer fiction. *In* (pp. 118–25) **3724**.

Edmund Wilson

20245. Collini, Stefan. Liquored-up. LRB (27:22) 2005, 15–18 (review-article). (Biography of Wilson.)

20246. Dabney, Lewis M. Edmund Wilson: a life in literature. New York: Farrar, Straus, & Giroux, 2005. pp. xiii, 639, (plates) 16. Rev. by Stefan Collini in LRB (27:22) 2005, 15–18; by William H. Pritchard in ASch (74:4) 2005, 131–4; by Jonathan Yardley in BkW, 4 Sept. 2005, 2.

20247. Pritchard, William H. Edmund Wilson's clear light: the lucid prose and inclusive views of 'the last great critic in the English line'. ASch (74:4) 2005, 131–4 (review-article).

Ethel Wilson

20248. Cavell, Richard. 'An ordered absence': defeatured topologies in Canadian literature. *In* (pp. 14–31) **9243**.

20249. Stouck, David. Ethel Wilson: a critical biography. (Bibl. 2004, 20238.) Rev. by Verena Klein in BJCS (17:2) 2004, 267–8; by Janice Fiamengo in CanL (186) 2005, 182–4.

Robert Wilson (b.1941)

20250. Bennett, Benjamin. All theater is revolutionary theater. See **16244**.

Robert McLiam Wilson (b.1964)

20251. D'hoker, Elke. 'Ripley Irish British Bogle' and 'the new Irish': hybrid identities in the fiction of Robert McLiam Wilson. BELL (ns 3) 2005, 23–34.

20252. FARQUHARSON, DANINE.   The language of violence in Robert McLiam Wilson's *Eureka Street*. NewHR (9:4) 2005, 65–78.

Steven Edmund Winduo (b.1964)

20253. WINDUO, STEVEN.   Transition and transformation. Meanjin (62:3) 2003, 169–77.

Yvor Winters

20254. ARCHAMBEAU, ROBERT.   Caging the demon: James McMichael and the poetics of restraint. *See* **18021**.

20255. OSSIP, KATHLEEN.   The nervousness of Yvor Winters. GC (17:2) 2005, 212–22.

20256. REID, DAVID.   Rationality in the poetry of Yvor Winters. CamQ (34:1) 2005, 1–21.

Jeanette Winterson

20257. ARNELL, CARLA A.   Earthly men and otherworldly women: gender types and religious types in Jeanette Winterson's *Atlantic Crossing* and other short fiction. JSSE (45) 2005, 163–77.

20258. COKAL, SUSANN.   Expression in a diffuse landscape: contexts for Jeanette Winterson's lyricism. Style (38:1) 2004, 16–37.

20259. COPPOLA, MARIA MICAELA.   Soggetti d'arte e di scambio: la semiotica del sé nei saggi di Jeanette Winterson. *In* (pp. 283–94) **12577**.

20260. FAU, HÉLÈNE.   Libérer l' 'inretenable' retenu: le musée dans l'œuvre romanesque de Jeanette Winterson. EA (58:2) 2005, 166–77.

20261. GUIGNERY, VANESSA.   Réécritures du Déluge et de l'arche de Noé dans la fiction contemporaine de langue anglaise (Coover, Findley, Winterson, Roberts et Barnes). *See* **19088**.

20262. HANSEN, JENNIFER L.   Written on the body, written by the senses. PhilL (29:2) 2005, 365–78.

20263. MAKINEN, MERJA.   The novels of Jeanette Winterson. Basingstoke; New York: Palgrave Macmillan, 2005. pp. xii, 179. (Readers' guides to essential criticism.)

20264. MERLEAU, CHLOË TAYLOR.   Postmodern ethics and the expression of differends in the novels of Jeanette Winterson. JML (26:3/4) 2003, 84–102.

20265. PALMER, PAULINA.   Foreign bodies: the grotesque body in the fiction of Jeanette Winterson. Gramma (11) 2003, 81–93.

20266. PARKER, EMMA.   Lost in translation: gender and the figure of the translator in contemporary queer fiction. *In* (pp. 118–25) **3724**.

20267. REYNIER, CHRISTINE.   Jeanette Winterson: le miracle ordinaire. Pessac: Presses Universitaires de Bordeaux, 2004. pp. 122. (Couleurs anglaises.) Rev. by Jean-Michel Ganteau in EtBr (26) 2004, 206–8.

20268. RUBINSON, GREGORY J.   The fiction of Rushdie, Barnes, Winterson, and Carter: breaking cultural and literary boundaries in the work of four postmodernists. *See* **19277.**

20269. SMITH, ANGELA MARIE.   Fiery constellations: Winterson's *Sexing the Cherry* and Benjamin's materialist historiography. ColLit (32:3) 2005, 21–50.

20270. Tomášková, Renáta.   On language and grafting in Jeanette Winterson's fiction. *In* (pp. 261–9) **1369.**

Tim Winton

20271. Webby, Elizabeth.   Books and covers: reflections on some recent Australian novels. *See* **131.**

Owen Wister

20272. Graulich, Melody; Tatum, Stephen (eds).   Reading *The Virginian* in the New West. (Bibl. 2004, 20262.) Rev. by Forrest G. Robinson in GPQ (24:1) 2004, 59–60.

P. G. Wodehouse

20273. Connolly, Joseph.   P. G. Wodehouse. London: Haus, 2004. pp. viii, 148. Rev. by Fatema Ahmed in LRB (27:21) 2005, 31–2.

20274. Leimberg, Inge.   'Across the pale parabola of joy': Wodehouse parodist. Connotations (13:1/2) 2003/04, 56–76.

20275. McCrum, Robert.   Wodehouse: a life. (Bibl. 2004, 20264.) Rev. by Fatema Ahmed in LRB (27:21) 2005, 31–2; by Chilton Williamson, Jr, in Chronicles (29:7) 2005, 30–2; by Daniel Born in CommRev (3:4) 2005, 56.

20276. Vesterman, William.   Plum time in Neverland: the divine comedy of P. G. Wodehouse. Raritan (25:1) 2005, 92–113.

20277. Wernsman, Marijane R. Davis.   The figure in the carpet of *Honeysuckle Cottage*: P. G. Wodehouse and Henry James. *See* **11463.**

Gene Wolfe

20278. Attebery, Brian.   Science fiction, parables, and parabolas. *See* **16717.**

20279. Dupeyron-Lafay, Françoise.   Gene Wolfe's *The Fifth Head of Cerberus* (1972); or, An uncanny science fiction revision of Proust's *A la recherche du temps perdu* ... EtBr (29) 2005, 65–82.

20280. Gaiman, Neil.   The knight at the door. NYRSF (16:6) 2004, 1, 4–5. (Interview.)

20281. Palumbo, Donald.   The monomyth in Gene Wolfe's *The Book of the New Sun*. Extrapolation (46:2) 2005, 189–234.

20282. Wright, Peter.   Attending Daedalus: Gene Wolfe, artifice, and the reader. Liverpool: Liverpool UP, 2003. pp. xv, 237. (Liverpool science fiction texts and studies.) Rev. by Paul Kincaid in Foundation (92) 2004, 118–21.

Thomas Wolfe (1900–1938)

20283. Evans, Elizabeth.   Asheville, cooks, and Heinz pickles. PemM (37) 2005, 91–6. (*Welcome to Our City.*)

20284. Halliday, Shawn.   Thomas Wolfe's *River of Earth* and Modernist orality. SoCR (36:2) 2004, 97–103.

20285. Idol, John L., Jr.   Meeting the satirist: the satire of Thomas Wolfe's *O Lost*. SoCR (36:2) 2004, 90–6.

20286. Madden, David (ed.).   Thomas Wolfe's Civil War. (Bibl. 2004, 20273.) Rev. by Shawn Holliday in AppH (33:4) 2005, 76–7.

20287. SLOVIC, SCOTT. Visceral Faulkner: fiction and the tug of the organic world. *In* (pp. 115–32) **16453**.

Tobias Wolff

20288. CONTINO, PAUL J. This writer's life: irony & faith in the work of Tobias Wolff. Cweal (132:18) 2005, 18–24.

Virginia Euwer Wolff

20289. REID, SUZANNE ELIZABETH. Virginia Euwer Wolff: capturing the music of young voices. (Bibl. 2004, 20277.) Rev. by Sharon M. Scapple in CLAQ (30:2) 2005, 219–21.

Meg Wolitzer

20290. WOLITZER, MEG. The writing life. BkW, 9 Jan. 2005, 10.

Jade Snow Wong

20291. DOUGLAS, CHRISTOPHER. Reading ethnography: the Cold War social science of Jade Snow's *Fifth Chinese Daughter* and *Brown v. Board of Education*. *In* (pp. 101–24) **9454**.

Jacqueline Woodson

20292. STOVER, LOIS THOMAS. Jacqueline Woodson: the real thing. (Bibl. 2004, 20280.) Rev. by Millie Jackson and Gary Schmidt in LU (29:3) 2005, 450–3; by Sharon M. Scapple in CLAQ (30:2) 2005, 219–21.

Leonard Woolf

20293. GORDON, LYNDALL (preface). The wise virgins: a story of words, opinions and a few emotions. London: Persephone, 2003. pp. xix, 285. (Persephone books, 43.) Rev. by Sarah M. Hall in VWB (18) 2005, 54–7.

20294. OLDFIELD, SYBIL (ed.). Afterwords: letters on the death of Virginia Woolf. *See* **14542**.

20295. ONDAATJE, CHRISTOPHER. Woolf in Ceylon: an imperial journey in the shadow of Leonard Woolf, 1904–1911. Toronto: HarperCollins, 2005. pp. xi, 326.

20296. SHAW, JOHN. *Luriana, Lurilee* revisited: 1, *A Garden Song*: Leonard Woolf's manuscript copy: the 'right version' of the poem. *See* **10962**.

Virginia Woolf

20297. ADOLPH, ANDREA. Luncheon at 'The Leaning Tower': consumption and class in Virginia Woolf's *Between the Acts*. WS (34:6) 2005, 439–59.

20298. AIMONE, LAURA FRANCESCA. In the footsteps of Virginia Woolf: *The Hours* by Michael Cunningham. *See* **15983**.

20299. ALEXANDER, CHRISTINE. Play and apprenticeship: the culture of family magazines. *In* (pp. 31–50) **9164**.

20300. ALLEN, ANNETTE. Virginia Woolf's spirituality: 'We are the words; we are the music.' LitB (24:1/2) 2004, 183–200.

20301. ALTER, ROBERT. Imagined cities: urban experience and the language of the novel. *See* **10639**.

20302. AMSELLE, FRÉDÉRIQUE. Les lieux du temps: contours du moi dans l'autobiographie et le journal de Woolf. EtBr (28) 2005, 33–44.

20303. ATTEWELL, NADINE. A risky business: going out in the fiction of Virginia Woolf and Dorothy Richardson. *In* (pp. 7–18) **14254.**

20304. BARKWAY, STEPHEN. Laughton Place: a Knole of Woolf's own? VWB (19) 2005, 20–5.

20305. —— A letter from Virginia. VWB (20) 2005, 4–8.

20306. BARRETT, MICHÈLE. Virginia Woolf and pacifism. SPACVW (13) 2005, 37–41.

20307. BEAUMAN, SALLY (preface). Flush: a biography. London: Persephone, 2004. pp. xxv, 118. (Persephone books, 55.) Rev. by Stephen Barkway and Sarah M. Hall in VWB (19) 2005, 57–60.

20308. BENZEL, KATHRYN N.; HOBERMAN, RUTH (eds). Trespassing boundaries: Virginia Woolf's short fiction. (Bibl. 2004, 20296.) Rev. by Sarah M. Hall in VWB (19) 2005, 60–3.

20309. BERKMAN, JOYCE AVRECH. Doing the splits: outsider/insider as women's historian and feminist activist. SPACVW (13) 2005, 183–6.

20310. BERMAN, JESSICA. Modernism's possible geographies. *In* (pp. 281–96) **12640.**

20311. BIRRER, DORYJANE. 'What are novelists for?': writing and rewriting reality from Woolf to McEwan. SPACVW (13) 2005, 165–70.

20312. BISHOP, EDWARD L. (ed.). Jacob's room. Oxford; Malden, MA: Blackwell for the Shakespeare Head Press, 2004. pp. xxxviii, 184. (Shakespeare Head Press ed. of Virginia Woolf.) Rev. by Stuart N. Clarke and Stephen Barkway in VWB (18) 2005, 43–7.

20313. BLACK, NAOMI. Virginia Woolf as feminist. (Bibl. 2004, 20299.) Rev. by Anna Smith in WSA (11) 2005, 212–15; by Tammy Clewell in ColLit (32:3) 2005, 172–81; by Stuart N. Clarke in VWB (20) 2005, 48–51; by Anne E. Fernald in VWM (67) 2005, 28–9.

20314. BOOTH, ALISON. Fighting for lives in the *ODNB*; or, Taking prosopography personally. *See* **20966.**

20315. BRIGGS, JULIA. The conversation behind the conversation: speaking the unspeakable in Virginia Woolf. EA (58:1) 2005, 6–14.

20316. —— 'Printing hope': Virginia Woolf, Hope Mirrlees, and the iconic imagery of *Paris*. SPACVW (13) 2005, 31–6.

20317. —— Virginia Woolf: an inner life. London: Allen Lane, 2005. pp. xiv, 527. Rev. by Jim Stewart in TLS, 13 May 2005, 24; by Sally Zigmond in VWB (20) 2005, 41–4.

20318. —— Virginia Woolf reads Shakespeare; or, Her silence on Master William. ShS (58) 2005, 118–29.

20319. BURGASS, CATHERINE. Food for the soul: reading Mrs Ramsay's *bœuf en daube*. *In* (pp. 95–103) **3724.**

20320. Burian, Cornelia. Modernity's shock and beauty: trauma and the vulnerable body in Virginia Woolf's *Mrs Dalloway.* SPACVW (13) 2005, 70–5.

20321. Burnett, Paula. Walcott's intertextual method: non-Greek naming in *Omeros. See* **19936.**

20322. Bush, Christopher. Deaths of a discipline. *See* **21006.**

20323. Channing, Jill. Magical realism and gender variability in *Orlando.* VWM (67) 2005, 11–13.

20324. Chapman, Wayne K. (ed.). Virginia Woolf's illnesses. By Douglass W. Orr. Clemson, SC: Clemson Univ. Digital Press, 2004. pp. xiv, 182. Rev. by Malcolm Ingram in VWB (17) 2004, 64–7.

20325. Christ, Carol. Virginia Woolf and education. SPACVW (13) 2005, 2–10.

20326. Clark, Hilary. The traveling self in Virginia Woolf's *Evening over Sussex: Reflections in a Motor Car.* VWM (66) 2004, 6–8.

20327. Clarke, Stuart N. A letter from Virginia. VWB (19) 2005, 4–7.

20328. —— Now you see them, now you don't: Woolf's illustrated books. VWB (18) 2005, 15–19.

20329. —— Virginia Woolf's unidentified contributions to the *Nation & Athenæum.* VWB (19) 2005, 8–11.

20330. Clavaron, Yves; Dieterle, Bernard (eds). La mémoire des villes. Saint-Étienne: Univ. de Saint-Étienne, 2003. pp. 421, (plates) 8. Rev. by Chloé Conant in RLC (79:1) 2005, 87–8.

20331. Clements, Elicia. Transforming musical sounds into words: narrative method in Virginia Woolf's *The Waves.* Narrative (13:2) 2005, 160–81.

20332. —— Virginia Woolf, Ethel Smyth, and music: listening as a productive mode of social interaction. ColLit (32:3) 2005, 51–71.

20333. Clewell, Tammy. The making of a new Virginia Woolf icon. ColLit (32:3) 2005, 172–81 (review-article).

20334. Cramer, Patricia. Jane Harrison and lesbian plots: the absent lover in Virginia Woolf's *The Waves.* StudN (37:4) 2005, 443–63.

20335. Cucullu, Lois. Expert Modernists, matricide, and modern culture: Woolf, Forster, Joyce. *See* **16552.**

20336. Cuddy-Keane, Melba. From fan-mail to readers' letters: locating John Farrelly. WSA (11) 2005, 3–32.

20337. —— Virginia Woolf, the intellectual, and the public sphere. (Bibl. 2004, 20317.) Rev. by Karin Westman in Novel (38:1) 2004, 114–16; by Georgia Johnston in ELT (48:1) 2005, 118–21; by Anne Fernald in WSA (11) 2005, 205–9; by Tammy Clewell in ColLit (32:3) 2005, 172–81; by Anna Snaith in YES (35) 2005, 356–9.

20338. Curtis, Vanessa. The hidden houses of Virginia Woolf and Vanessa Bell. London: Hale, 2005. pp. 240, (plates) 24. Rev. by Frances Spalding in TLS, 1 July 2005, 30.

20339. —— A house detective at 46 Gordon Square. VWB (18) 2005, 26–30.

20340. CZARNECKI, KRISTIN KOMMERS. Filming feminism: *A Room of One's Own* on Masterpiece Theater. SPACVW (13) 2005, 177–82.

20341. DE GIOVANNI, FLORA. 'Some sort of common bond': the avant-garde and the arts. *In* (pp. 134–43) **3690.**

20342. —— Tra impersonalità e autobiografismo: la morte della madre in Virginia Woolf. *In* (pp. 247–60) **12577.**

20343. DELL, MARION. Looking for a postcard from Scarborough: Woolf's Yorkshire connections. VWB (19) 2005, 26–31.

20344. DEMOOR, MARYSA. From epitaph to obituary: the death politics of T. S. Eliot and Ezra Pound. *See* **16261.**

20345. DU, JUAN. Death and change: connotations of Virginia Woolf's *Mrs Dalloway, To the Lighthouse* and *The Waves*. FLS (115) 2005, 65–71. (In Chinese.)

20346. DYER, TINA. Beyond the mortal stain: cyclothymia, *Mrs Dalloway* and *Mrs Dalloway in Bond Street*. PsyArt (9) 2005.

20347. ELLIS, STEVE. Framing the father: Chaucer and Virginia Woolf. *See* **4945.**

20348. FARFAN, PENNY. Women, Modernism, and performance. *See* **19091.**

20349. FORBES, SHANNON. Equating performance with identity: the failure of Clarissa Dalloway's Victorian 'self' in Virginia Woolf's *Mrs Dalloway*. JMMLA (38:1) 2005, 38–50.

20350. FRATTAROLA, ANGELA. Listening for 'found sound': samples in the novels of Virginia Woolf. WSA (11) 2005, 133–59.

20351. FREEMAN, JAN. The Paris Press publication of *On Being Ill*. SPACVW (13) 2005, 141–6.

20352. FRENCH, SABINE. Peeling the gypsy. VWM (67) 2005, 8–11. (*Orlando*.)

20353. FROULA, CHRISTINE. On French and British freedoms: early Bloomsbury and the brothels of Modernism. Mod/Mod (12:4) 2005, 553–80.

20354. —— Virginia Woolf and the Bloomsbury avant-garde: war, civilization, modernity. New York: Columbia UP, 2005. pp. xvii, 428. (Gender and culture.) Rev. by Jim Stewart in TLS, 29 Apr. 2005, 31; by Vara Neverow in Mod/Mod (12:3) 2005, 527–8.

20355. GANIM, JOHN M. Chaucer and free love. *In* (pp. 344–63) **4485.**

20356. GORDON, LYNDALL. 'This loose, drifting material of life': Virginia Woolf and biography. SPACVW (13) 2005, 11–18.

20357. GORSKY, SUSAN RUBINOW. The mask/masque of food: illness and art. SPACVW (13) 2005, 50–5.

20358. HANKINS, LESLIE K. Switching sex and redirecting desire: the surrealist film *Entr'acte* and Woolf's *Orlando*. VWM (67) 2005, 25–6.

20359. HELAL, KATHLEEN M. Anger, anxiety, abstraction: Virginia Woolf's 'submerged truth'. SCR (22:2) 2005, 78–94.

2005]   AUTHORS   1113

20360. HENRY, HOLLY. Virginia Woolf and the discourse of science: the aesthetics of astronomy. (Bibl. 2004, 20342.) Rev. by David Ross in EC (54:4) 2004, 412–16; by Kathryn Neeley in Isis (96:1) 2005, 132–3; by Anna Snaith in YES (35) 2005, 356–9.

20361. HIGDON, DAVID LEON. The churchly Doris Kilman. VWM (66) 2004, 14–15.

20362. HILL, JEN. The Arctic genealogy of Clarissa Dalloway. NQ (52:4) 2005, 500–1.

20363. HIRSH, ELIZABETH. Mrs Dalloway's menopause: encrypting the female life course. SPACVW (13) 2005, 76–81.

20364. HITE, MOLLY. We think back through Carolyn Heilbrun if we are women. See **15967.**

20365. HOBERMAN, RUTH. Aesthetic taste, kitsch, and *The Years*. WSA (11) 2005, 77–98.

20366. HOLLIS, CATHERINE W. Virginia Woolf's double signature. SPACVW (13) 2005, 19–23.

20367. HUMM, MAGGIE. Modernist women and visual cultures: Virginia Woolf, Vanessa Bell, photography, and cinema. (Bibl. 2004, 20345.) Rev. by Ann Ardis in Novel (37:3) 2004, 356–7; by Tammy Clewell in ColLit (32:3) 2005, 172–81.

20368. —— Virginia Woolf and Vanessa Bell as photographers: 'the same pair of eyes, only different spectacles'. SPACVW (13) 2005, 24–30.

20369. HUNTER, DIANNE. Objects dissolving in time. SPACVW (13) 2005, 94–9.

20370. JAMES, DAVID. Realism, late Modernist abstraction, and Sylvia Townsend Warner's fictions of impersonality. See **19978.**

20371. JOHNSON, ERICA L. Writing the land: the geography of national identity in *Orlando*. SPACVW (13) 2005, 105–9.

20372. KIGHTLINGER, JENNIFER-ANN DIGREGORIO. Sex costumes: signifying sex and gender in Woolf's *The Introduction* and *The Years*. SPACVW (13) 2005, 117–22.

20373. KOLOCOTRONI, VASSILIKI. 'This curious silent unrepresented life': Greek lessons in Virginia Woolf's early fiction. MLR (100:2) 2005, 313–22.

20374. KOSTKOWSKA, JUSTYNA. Virginia Woolf's experiment in genre and politics, 1926–1931: visioning and versioning *The Waves*. Lewiston, NY; Lampeter: Mellen Press, 2005. pp. vi, 145. (Studies in British literature, 94.)

20375. KOVACEVIC, NATASA. Beyond the politics of emancipation: utopianism and radical (im)possibilities in Virginia Woolf. Lit (16:3) 2005, 333–57.

20376. KREUTZIGER, JOSEPH. Darwin's temporal aesthetics: a brief stretch in time from Pater to Woolf. SPACVW (13) 2005, 64–9.

20377. KSIEZOPOLSKI, IRENA. Props and personages: the significance of the secondary characters in *Mrs Dalloway*. VWM (66) 2004, 23–5.

20378. LAPAIRE, JEAN-RÉMI. Coordination et cognition. See **2708.**

20379. LAUFER, MATT. 'And what about the Jews?' VWM (66) 2004, 22.

20380. LAWSON, JEREMY. Atomic and surface theories of matter in *Mrs Dalloway*: a comparative study of Clarissa and Septimus. VWM (66) 2004, 13–14.

20381. LESLIE, HANNAH. A simple darting melody: birds in the works of Virginia Woolf. VWB (19) 2005, 32–40.

20382. LOW, LISA. Woolf's allusion to *Comus* in *The Voyage Out*. *In* (pp. 254–70) **7717**.

20383. LOWE, GILL (ed.). *Hyde Park Gate News*: the Stephen family newspaper. London: Hesperus Press, 2005. pp. xxii, 240.

20384. LV, HONGLING. Woolf's 'other sexes' and *The Waves*. FLS (115) 2005, 72–9. (In Chinese.)

20385. MCINTIRE, GABRIELLE. Heteroglossia, monologism, and Fascism: Bernard reads *The Waves*. Narrative (13:1) 2005, 29–45.

20386. MACKAY, MARINA. Putting the house in order: Virginia Woolf and Blitz Modernism. MLQ (66:2) 2005, 227–52.

20387. MCMILLAN, LAURIE. Telling a critical story: Alice Walker's *In Search of Our Mothers' Gardens*. See **19962**.

20388. MCNEER, REBECCA. Pointing the way to *Orlando*: literary signposts. VWM (67) 2005, 6–8.

20389. MCNEES, ELEANOR. The guidebook and the dog: Virginia Woolf and Italy. SPACVW (13) 2005, 110–16.

20390. MADDEN, MARY C. Woolf's interrogation of class in *Night and Day*. SPACVW (13) 2005, 56–63.

20391. MARES, CHERYL. Woolf and the American imaginary. SPACVW (13) 2005, 42–8.

20392. MARIE, CAROLINE. *'The strangest transformation took place'*: parcours, détours et bifurcations dans *Orlando* de Virginia Woolf. EtBr (28) 2005, 45–56.

20393. MONTEITH, SHARON; YOUSAF, NAHEM. *Double Vision*: regenerative or traumatized pastoral? *In* (pp. 283–99) **15309**.

20394. NEWMAN, HERTA. Orlando: fantasy fiction and film. VWM (67) 2005, 21–2.

20395. NYMAN, MICKI. Positioning Orlando as subject in Lacan's Imaginary. VWM (67) 2005, 19–21.

20396. OLDFIELD, SYBIL (ed.). Afterwords: letters on the death of Virginia Woolf. *See* **14542**.

20397. PARADISI, VALENTINA. *'He was a woman'*: questioni di genere in *Orlando* di Virginia Woolf. *In* (pp. 161–72) **14322**.

20398. PHILLIPS, BRIAN. Reality and Virginia Woolf. HR (56:3) 2003, 415–30.

20399. PLATE, LIEDEKE. Intermedial Woolf: text, image, and in-between. WI (20:4) 2004, 299–307.

20400. PREISSLE, ROBERT. Society's child: Orlando's son. VWM (66) 2004, 15–21.

20401. PROSE, FRANCINE (ed.). The *Mrs Dalloway* reader. (Bibl. 2004, 20393.) Rev. by Stuart N. Clarke in VWB (20) 2005, 51–2.

2005]   AUTHORS   1115

20402. PRUDENTE, TERESA. *Orlando*: the mind as phantasmagoria. VWM (67) 2005, 13–19.

20403. PRYOR, WILLIAM. The living memes and jeans of Bloomsbury and neo-paganism. SPACVW (13) 2005, 147–52.

20404. —— (ed.). Virginia Woolf & the Raverats: a different sort of friendship. (Bibl. 2004, 20394.) Rev. by Patricia Laurence in AmBR (26:3) 2005, 27, 30.

20405. REINHOLD, NATALYA (ed.). Woolf across cultures. (Bibl. 2004, 20398.) Rev. by David Adams in Mod/Mod (12:3) 2005, 525–6; by Sarah M. Hall in VWB (18) 2005, 51–4; by Pamela L. Caughie in VWM (67) 2005, 27–8.

20406. REYNIER, CHRISTINE. La citation *in absentia* à l'œuvre dans *Atonement* de Ian McEwan. *See* **17971**.

20407. ROBERTS, DANIEL SANJIV. 'A nugget of pure truth': Woolf's debt to De Quincey. NQ (52:1) 2005, 94–5.

20408. ROE, SUE. The art of making memories. VWB (20) 2005, 9–27.

20409. ROSNER, VICTORIA. Modernism and the architecture of private life. New York: Columbia UP, 2005. pp. xi, 219. (Gender and culture.)

20410. RUSSELL, RICHARD RANKIN. E. M. Forster's Leonard Bast: a source for Virginia Woolf's Septimus Smith. *See* **16565**.

20411. SAINT-AMOUR, PAUL K. Air war prophecy and interwar Modernism. CLS (42:2) 2005, 130–61.

20412. ST CLAIR, PAMELA. In search of the self: Virginia Woolf's shadow across Sylvia Plath's page. SPACVW (13) 2005, 171–6.

20413. SAKAMOTO, TADANOBU. A new relation between the narrator and the reader in *Jacob's Room*. VWB (19) 2005, 41–7.

20414. —— The significance of the old woman and her song in *Mrs Dalloway*. VWB (20) 2005, 28–32.

20415. SALOMAN, RANDI. 'Here again is the usual door': the modernity of Virginia Woolf's *Street Haunting*. Genre (38:1/2) 2005, 71–94.

20416. SÁNCHEZ-PARDO, ESTHER. Cultures of the death drive: Melanie Klein and Modernist melancholia. Durham, NC; London: Duke UP, 2003. pp. xi, 490. Rev. by Jed Deppman in Symplokē (12:1/2) 2004, 274–8.

20417. SAXTON, RUTH O. A glimpse of Vanessa Bell through two sets of letters. VWB (18) 2005, 20–5.

20418. SHANNON, DREW PATRICK. The lightly attached web: the fictional Virginia Woolf. SPACVW (13) 2005, 153–8.

20419. SHAW, JOHN. *Luriana, Lurilee* revisited: 1, *A Garden Song*: Leonard Woolf's manuscript copy: the 'right version' of the poem. *See* **10962**.

20420. SHERRY, VINCENT B. Liberal measures: language, Modernism, and the Great War. *In* (pp. 9–23) **12946**.

20421. SHIH, ELIZABETH A.; KENNEY, SUSAN M. Editing the palimpsestic text: the case of Virginia Woolf's *A Sketch of the Past*. SPACVW (13) 2005, 132–40.

20422. SIM, LORRAINE. Ailing dualisms: Woolf's revolt against rationalism in the 'real world' of influenza. SPACVW (13) 2005, 88–93.

20423. —— Virginia Woolf tracing patterns through Plato's forms. JML (28:2) 2005, 38–48.

20424. SIMPSON, KATHRYN. Economies and desire: gifts and the market in *Moments of Being: 'Slater's Pins Have No Points'*. JML (28:2) 2005, 18–37.

20425. —— The paradox of the gift: gift-giving as a disruptive force in *Mrs Dalloway in Bond Street*. WSA (11) 2005, 53–75.

20426. —— The paradox of the gift: gift-giving as a disruptive force in Woolf's writing. SPACVW (13) 2005, 82–7.

20427. —— Pearl-diving: inscriptions of desire and creativity in H.D. and Woolf. *See* **16114**.

20428. SKRBIC, NENA. Wild outbursts of freedom: reading Virginia Woolf's short fiction. (Bibl. 2004, 20410.) Rev. by Hilary Newman in VWB (18) 2005, 47–50.

20429. SLOTE, SAM. *Gillet lit le Joyce dans la Woolf*: genre in *Orlando* and *Ulysses*. JML (27:4) 2004, 27–36.

20430. SORUM, EVE. Masochistic Modernisms: a reading of Eliot and Woolf. *See* **16310**.

20431. SOUTHWORTH, HELEN. The intersecting realities and fictions of Virginia Woolf and Colette. Columbus: Ohio State UP, 2004. pp. xii, 240. Rev. by Isobel Shirlaw in TLS, 3 June 2005, 27; by Carole K. Harris in TCL (51:4) 2005, 495–503.

20432. —— 'Mixed Virginia': reconciling the 'stigma of nationality' and the sting of nostalgia in Virginia Woolf's later fiction. WSA (11) 2005, 99–132.

20433. SPOHRER, ERIKA. Seeing stars: commodity stardom in Michael Cunningham's *The Hours* and Virginia Woolf's *Mrs Dalloway*. *See* **15984**.

20434. STETZ, MARGARET DIANE. Oscar Wilde and feminist criticism. *In* (pp. 224–45) **12414**.

20435. TROMANHAUSER, VICKI. Virginia Woolf's London and the archaeology of character. *In* (pp. 33–43) **14254**.

20436. VIVIANI, AGLAIA. '*When old Queen Bess came to dine*': la figurazione di Elizabeth I nell'opera di Virginia Woolf. LProv (119/120) 2004, 87–96.

20437. VON KLEMPERER, ELIZABETH GALLAHER. 'The works of women are symbolical.' SPACVW (13) 2005, 123–8.

20438. VOROBYOVA, OLGA. *The Mark on the Wall* and literary fancy: a cognitive sketch. *In* (pp. 201–17) **3888**.

20439. WHITWORTH, MICHAEL H. Virginia Woolf. Oxford; New York: OUP, 2005. pp. xvii, 268. (Oxford world's classics.) (Authors in context.) Rev. by Julie Singleton in VWB (20) 2005, 53–7.

20440. WILSON, GREGORY A. 'This insatiable hunger for sympathy': Virginia Woolf's vision of unity in *Mrs Dalloway*. CEACrit (66:1) 2003, 32–42.

20441. WOLFE, JESSE. The sane woman in the attic: sexuality and self-authorship in *Mrs Dalloway*. MFS (51:1) 2005, 34–59.

20442. YANG, SHIZHEN. On Big Ben in *Mrs Dalloway*. FLS (115) 2005, 80–4. (In Chinese.)

20443. Zeiss, McKenzie L. The political legacy of the garden: (anti)pastoral images and national identity in Virginia Woolf and Vita Sackville-West. SPACVW (13) 2005, 100–4.

20444. Zucker, Marilyn Slutzky. Lord Orlando, Lord Byron. VWM (67) 2005, 22–5.

C. D. (Carolyn D.) Wright (b.1949)

20445. Brouwer, Joel. Comply whether a believer or not. Parnassus (28:1/2) 2005, 192–221.

Carolyne Wright (b.1949)

20446. Painter, Stephanie. Risking exile: an interview with Carolyne Wright. BRev (23:6) 2003, 20–1, 30.

Charles Wright (b.1935)

20447. Bacigalupo, Massimo. History and the American poet. See **18857**.

20448. Franzek, Phyllis. Charles Wright's half-life: elegiacally inventive. PCP (40:1) 2005, 138–57.

Dare Wright (1914–2001)

20449. Nathan, Jean. The secret life of the lonely doll: the search for Dare Wright. New York: Holt, 2004. pp. 308.

James Arlington Wright (b.1927)

20450. Blunk, Jonathan. Praise the winters gone: introduction to a selection of ten letters by James Wright. GaR (59:1) 2005, 10–18.

20451. —— (introd.). A selection of letters: a special APR supplement. APR (34:4) 2005, 23–30.

20452. Genoways, Ted (introd.). Robert Bly and James Wright: a correspondence. See **15516**.

20453. Wright, Anne. Watching the evening begin in Fano. GaR (59:1) 2005, 40–8.

20454. —— Maley, Saundra Rose (eds); Blunk, Jonathan (asst ed.). A wild perfection: the selected letters of James Wright. New York: Farrar, Straus, & Giroux, 2005. pp. xxxii, 633. Rev. by Charles Nicol in BkW, 21 Aug. 2005, 12.

Judith Wright

20455. Brady, Veronica. After life with Judith Wright. Meanjin (64:3) 2005, 109–11.

20456. Clarke, Patricia; McKinney, Meredith (eds). The equal heart and mind: letters between Judith Wright and Jack McKinney. St Lucia: Queensland UP, 2004. pp. xiii, 202, (plates) 16. Rev. by Paul Hetherington in TLS, 15 Oct. 2004, 31.

20457. Griffiths, Tom. Legend and lament. See **3492**.

20458. Ryan, J. S. 'The great gaol by the sea' – the developing lore and associations of one such place of incarceration, Trial Bay Jail, New South Wales. See **17387**.

Richard Wright (1908–1960)

20459. ANDREWS, WILLIAM L.   In search of a common identity: the self and the South in four Mississippi autobiographies. *In* (pp. 39–56) **12793**.

20460. ATTEBERRY, JEFFREY.   Entering the politics of the outside: Richard Wright's critique of Marxism and existentialism. MFS (51:4) 2005, 873–95.

20461. BERNARD, PATRICK.   Travel culture as performance in Richard Wright's *Black Power.* LHR (19:1) 2004, 40–9.

20462. DEMIRTÜRK, LALE.   Mapping the interstitial space of 'Black' and 'Western': Richard Wright's *White Man, Listen!* CLAJ (49:1) 2005, 45–55.

20463. GIBSON, RICHARD.   Richard Wright's *Island of Hallucination* and the 'Gibson Affair'. MFS (51:4) 2005, 896–920.

20464. IADONISI, RICHARD.   *I Am Nobody:* the haiku of Richard Wright. MELUS (30:3) 2005, 179–200.

20465. JANMOHAMED, ABDUL R.   The death-bound-subject: Richard Wright's archaeology of death. Durham, NC; London: Duke UP, 2005. pp. ix, 327.

20466. JONES, EDWARD P. (preface).   *Black Boy (American Hunger):* a record of childhood and youth. New York: HarperCollins, 2005. pp. x, 419. (60th anniversary ed.)

20467. REED, BRIAN D.   Wright turns the Bible left: rewriting the Christian parable in *Uncle Tom's Children.* XavR (24:2) 2004, 56–65.

20468. TUHKANEN, MIKKO.   The optical trade: from slave-breaking in Frederick Douglass's *Narrative* to self-breaking in Richard Wright's *Black Boy.* See **10834**.

20469. WALLACE, MAURICE.   Richard Wright's Black Medusa. JAAH (88:1) 2003, 71–7.

Ronald Wright (b.1948)

20470. MCGLAMERY, GAYLA.   The three tropographies of Ronald Wright's *A Scientific Romance.* CanL (185) 2005, 92–109.

Patricia Wrightson

20471. ATTEBERY, BRIAN.   Patricia Wrightson and Aboriginal myth. Extrapolation (46:3) 2005, 327–37.

Philip Wylie

20472. STEELE, ALLEN M.   Doomsday 1933: *When Worlds Collide* reconsidered. NYRSF (16:8) 2004, 1, 4–6.

John Wyndham

20473. HUBBLE, NICK.   Five English disaster novels, 1951–1972. Foundation (95) 2005, 89–103.

20474. KETTERER, DAVID.   John Wyndham and the sins of his father: damaging disclosures in court. Extrapolation (46:2) 2005, 163–88.

Lois-Ann Yamanaka (b.1961)

20475. DAVIS, ROCÍO G.   Short story cycle and Hawai'i *Bildungsroman:* writing self, place, and family in Lois-Ann Yamanaka's *Wild Meat and the Bully Burgers.* *In* (pp. 231–48) **9454**.

J. Michael Yates

20476. RHENISCH, HAROLD. The genesis of Linda Rogers. *In* (pp. 50–73) **19115.**

John Yau

20477. ZHOU, XIAOJING. Two hat softeners 'in the trade confession': John Yau and Kimiko Hahn. *In* (pp. 168–89) **9454.**

W. B. Yeats

20478. AJI, HÉLÈNE. The subject in the structure: issues of procedure in contemporary American poetry. *See* **19579.**

20479. BACIGALUPO, MASSIMO. Bisanzio e Florida: le rotte contrarie di W. B. Yeats e Wallace Stevens. *In* (pp. 203–13) **14479.**

20480. —— Novità su W. B. Yeats. Con testi di Richard Murphy, Seamus Heaney e Jorie Graham. PoesiaM (190) 2005, 46–61.

20481. —— Yeats, Boccaccio, and Leopardi. NQ (52:4) 2005, 499–500.

20482. BORNSTEIN, GEORGE. The colors of Zion: Black, Jewish, and Irish nationalisms at the turn of the century. Mod/Mod (12:3) 2005, 369–84.

20483. BROWN, RICHARD DANSON. Neutrality and commitment: MacNeice, Yeats, Ireland and the Second World War. *See* **18029.**

20484. CERULLI, GRAZIA. W. B. Yeats: a poet and his discontents. SCrit (18:1) 2003, 75–90.

20485. CHAPMAN, WAYNE K. Yeats's dislocated Rebellion poems and the Great War: the case of *The Wild Swans at Coole* and *Michael Robartes and the Dancer*. YA (16) 2005, 71–97.

20486. COLEMAN, PHILIP. 'The politics of praise': John Berryman's engagement with W. B. Yeats. *See* **15477.**

20487. CRAIG, CAIRNS. Carlyle and Symbolism. *In* (pp. 102–12) **10393.**

20488. DIRST, SHELLEY SHARP. From *The Hour-Glass* to *At the Hawk's Well*: revisions toward an idealized theater. SoCR (36:2) 2004, 120–34.

20489. EHRLICH, HEYWARD. Joyce, Yeats and Kabbalah. *In* (pp. 60–87) **17274.**

20490. FAHERTY, MICHAEL (ed.). The poetry of W. B. Yeats. Basingstoke; New York: Palgrave Macmillan, 2005. pp. viii, 177. (Readers' guides to essential criticism.)

20491. FOSTER, R. F. W. B. Yeats: a life: vol. 2, The arch-poet, 1915–1939. (Bibl. 2004, 20484.) Rev. by Daniel T. O'Hara in JML (26:3/4) 2003, 128–35; by Brian Cosgrove in CJIS (30:2) 2004, 79–81; by John Kerrigan in LRB (27:5) 2005, 7–10; by Ljiljana Ina Gjurgjan in ELT (48:2) 2005, 214–17; by Eric Ormsby in Parnassus (28:1/2) 2005, 106–22; by John Harwood in YA (16) 2005, 365–70; by Ronan McDonald in YES (35) 2005, 334–6.

20492. GALLESI, LUCA. Le origini del fascismo di Ezra Pound. *See* **18873.**

20493. GENET, JACQUELINE. Yeats et la mort. EtIr (30:1) 2005, 37–54.

20494. GOULD, WARWICK. Writing the life of the text: the case of W. B. Yeats. Misc (30) 2004, 9–34.

20495. —— (ed.). 'Gasping on the strand': Richard Ellmann's W. B. Yeats notebooks. YA (16) 2005, 279–361.

20496. —— TOOMEY, DEIRDRE (eds). Mythologies. Basingstoke; New York: Palgrave Macmillan, 2005. pp. cx, 545.

20497. GRAF, SUSAN JOHNSTON. An infant avatar: the mature occultism of W. B. Yeats. NewHR (9:4) 2005, 99–112.

20498. GRAHAM, KENNETH. Yeats and transformation. In (pp. 65–75) 3756.

20499. HASLAM, RICHARD. W. B. Yeats: snobbery as mood and mode. EtIr (29:1) 2004, 55–72.

20500. HASSETT, JOSEPH M. Crazy Jane reconsidered. YA (16) 2005, 99–112.

20501. HENNESSEY, OLIVER. 'I shall find the dark grow luminous when I understand I have nothing': Yeats's failing Vision. YER (21:2) 2004, 2–19.

20502. —— Talking with the dead: Leo Africanus, esoteric Yeats, and early modern imperialism. ELH (71:4) 2004, 1019–38.

20503. INGELBIEN, RAPHAËL. Gothic genealogies: Dracula, Bowen's Court, and Anglo-Irish psychology. See 12094.

20504. JEFFARES, A. NORMAN. Iseult Gonne. See 16742.

20505. —— WHITE, ANNA MACBRIDE; BRIDGWATER, CHRISTINA (eds). Letters to W. B. Yeats and Ezra Pound from Iseult Gonne, a girl that knew all Dante once. (Bibl. 2004, 20494.) Rev. by Eve Patten in NQ (52:1) 2005, 145–6.

20506. KELLY, JOHN S. A W. B. Yeats chronology. (Bibl. 2004, 20497.) Rev. by David Pierce in JML (28:3) 2005, 162–9.

20507. KERRIGAN, JOHN. Old, old, old, old, old. LRB (27:5) 2005, 7–10 (review-article). (Biography of Yeats.)

20508. KIRSCH, ADAM. Green selfconscious spurts. See 17575.

20509. LOCKETT, CHRISTOPHER. Terror and rebirth: Cathleen ni Houlihan, from Yeats to The Crying Game. See 13530.

20510. LONGLEY, EDNA. 'Altering the past': Northern Irish poetry and modern canons. See 14440.

20511. MCCORMACK, W. J. Yeats's politics since 1943: approaches and reproaches. YES (35) 2005, 131–45.

20512. MCDONALD, RUSSELL. Who speaks for Fergus? Silence, homophobia, and the anxiety of Yeatsian influence in Joyce. See 17309.

20513. MCNAMEE, BRENDAN. 'What then?': poststructuralism, authorial intention and W. B. Yeats. RAEI (18) 2005, 215–26.

20514. MANN, NEIL. George Yeats and Athanasius Kircher. YA (16) 2005, 163–93.

20515. MAYS, J. C. C. (ed.). Diarmuid and Grania: manuscript materials. Ithaca, NY; London: Cornell UP, 2005. pp. lxviii, 1081. (Cornell Yeats.)

20516. O'HARA, DANIEL T. Why Lacan? JML (26:3/4) 2003, 136–42 (review-article).

20517. —— Yeats with Lacan: towards the real Modernism. JML (26:3/4) 2003, 128–35 (review-article).

20518. ORMSBY, ERIC. Passionate syntax. Parnassus (28:1/2) 2005, 106–22 (review-article).

20519. PETHICA, JAMES. Upon a House Shaken: the struggle for Coole Park 1907–1912. YA (16) 2005, 3–51.

20520. PRUITT, VIRGINIA. Yeats's *Sailing to Byzantium*. Exp (63:4) 2005, 225–7.

20521. RAMAZANI, JAHAN. Self-theorizing poetry: Yeats's *ars poetica* in *'The Green Helmet' and Other Poems*. YA (16) 2005, 53–69.

20522. REGGIANI, ENRICO. *'The complimentary dream, perhaps'*: saggi su William Butler Yeats. Preface by Luisa Camaiora Conti. Milan: Europrint, 2004. pp. 182.

20523. SRI, P. S. The influence of Vedanta on Yeats's 'Supernatural Songs'. YA (16) 2005, 113–29.

20524. TEYSSANDIER, HUBERT. Voices of the unseen: Benjamin Britten's reading of *The Turn of the Screw*. See **11457**.

20525. TOOMEY, DEIRDRE. 'Amaryllis in the shade': the Municipal Gallery revisited. YA (16) 2005, 131–59.

20526. VAN BRONSWIJK, R. Driving the darkness: W. E. Henley's *The Song of the Sword* as uneasy battle cry. See **11266**.

20527. WEE, LIONEL. 'Extreme illocutionary acts' and the boosting of illocutionary force. See **2201**.

20528. WILMER, CLIVE (ed.). Modernist essays: Yeats, Pound, Eliot. By Donald Davie. Manchester: Carcanet Press, 2004. pp. xv, 247. Rev. by Roland John in Agenda (40:4) 2004, 107–10.

Chay Yew

20529. CHO, NANCY. Beyond identity politics: national and transnational dialogues in Anna Deavere Smith's *Twilight: Los Angeles, 1992* and Chay Yew's *A Beautiful Country*. See **19482**.

Anzia Yezierska

20530. FRIEDMAN, NATALIE. Marriage and the immigrant narrative: Anzia Yezierska's *Salome of the Tenements*. Legacy (22:2) 2005, 176–86.

20531. HARRISON-KAHAN, LORI. 'Drunk with the fiery rhythms of jazz': Anzia Yezierska, hybridity, and the Harlem renaissance. MFS (51:2) 2005, 416–36.

20532. MACKENZIE, GINA MASUCCI. Under-writing: forming an American minority literature. See **16095**.

Jane Yolen

20533. BAER, ELIZABETH R. A postmodern fairy tale of the Holocaust: Jane Yolen's *Briar Rose*. StudAJL (24) 2005, 145–52.

Samuel Youd ('John Christopher', 'Hilary Ford', 'William Godfrey', 'Peter Graaf', 'Peter Nichols', 'Anthony Rye') (b.1922)

20534. HUBBLE, NICK. Five English disaster novels, 1951–1972. See **20473**.

Zitkala-Ša (Gertrude Bonnin) (1876–1938)

20535. SILKÜ, ATILLA. Fiddler on the threshold: cultural hybridity in Gertrude Bonnin's *American Indian Stories*. WLWE (40:1) 2002/03, 115–24.

20536. TOTTEN, GARY. Zitkala-Ša and the problem of regionalism: nations, narratives, and critical traditions. AIQ (29:1/2) 2005, 84–123.

Louis Zukofsky

20537. AHEARN, BARRY (introd.). A selection of Louis Zukofsky's correspondence (1930–1976). ChiR (50:2–4) 2004/05, 39–50.

20538. HASS, ROBERT. Zukofsky at the outset. APR (34:5) 2005, 59–70.

20539. NIRENBERG, RICARDO. The sky over Louis Zukofsky and some others. LittPr (15:29) 2005, 64–77.

20540. WRAY, DAVID. 'cool rare air': Zukofsky's breathing with Catullus and Plautus. ChiR (50:2–4) 2004/05, 52–100.

20541. ZUKOFSKY, PAUL. Louis Zukofsky's marginalia. ChiR (50:2–4) 2004/05, 101–3.

TWENTY-FIRST CENTURY

GENERAL

20542. ANON. (comp.). Annual bibliography of Commonwealth literature 2004: South Africa. Introd. by Crystal Warren. JCL (40:4) 2005, 195–234.

20543. ADÉÈKÓ, ADÉLÉKÈ. Symptoms of the present in Ato Quayson's *Calibrations. See* **20989**.

20544. ANTONELLI, SARA. L'America come genere letterario. Àcoma (31) 2005, 46–63.

20545. ARANA, R. VICTORIA; RAMEY, LAURI (eds). Black British writing. *See* **12546**.

20546. BAILEY NURSE, DONNA. What's a Black critic to do? Interviews, profiles, and reviews of Black writers. *See* **12550**.

20547. BEHLAU, ULRIKE; REITZ, BERNHARD (eds). Jewish women's writing of the 1990s and beyond in Great Britain and the United States. *See* **12556**.

20548. BELL, ELEANOR. Questioning Scotland: literature, nationalism, postmodernism. *See* **12557**.

20549. BERTACCO, SIMONA. Beyond 'ethnicity' and 'race': new perspectives in English Canadian literature. *In* (pp. 66–77) **3690**.

20550. BOTTALICO, MICHELE; CHIALANT, MARIA TERESA (eds). L'impulso autobiografico: Inghilterra, Stati Uniti, Canada … e altrove. *See* **12577**.

20551. CHEN, TINA MAI. Introduction: thinking through embeddedness: globalization, culture, and the popular. *See* **12601**.

20552. CHEVIGNY, BELL GALE. 'All I have, a lament and a boast': why prisoners write. *In* (pp. 246–71) **12821**.

20553. CHLEBEK, DIANA (comp.). Annual bibliography of Commonwealth literature 2004: Canada 2003–04. JCL (40:4) 2005, 25–88.

20554. CHUH, KANDICE. Imagine otherwise: on Asian Americanist critique. *See* **12605**.

20555. CONNOR, STEVEN (ed.). The Cambridge companion to postmodernism. *See* **12617**.

20556. CORNELL, M. DORETTA. Mother of all the living: reinterpretations of Eve in contemporary literature. *See* **12620**.

20557. CROWTHER, HAL. Gather at the river: notes from the post-millennial South. Foreword by Louis D. Rubin. Baton Rouge: Louisiana State UP, 2005. pp. 165. (Southern literary studies.)

20558. DELROSSO, JEANA. Writing Catholic women: contemporary international Catholic girlhood narratives. *See* **12633**.

20559. EK, AULI. Race and masculinity in contemporary American prison narratives. *See* **12654**.

20560. EZENWA-OHAETO. Winging words: interviews with Nigerian writers. *See* **12668**.

20561. FISCHER, HEINZ-D.; FISCHER, ERIKA J. Complete bibliographical manual of books about the Pulitzer Prizes, 1935–2003: monographs and anthologies on the coveted awards. *See* **12675**.

20562. GILROY, PAUL. After empire: melancholia or convivial culture? *See* **12695.**

20563. GREGSON, IAN. Postmodern literature. *See* **12708.**

20564. GUNDY, JEFF. New maps of the territories: on Mennonite writing. *See* **12710.**

20565. GUNEW, SNEJA. 'Mouthwork': food and language as the corporeal home for the unhoused diasporic body in South Asian women's writing. *See* **12711.**

20566. HAMILTON, STEPHEN (comp.). Annual bibliography of Commonwealth literature 2004: New Zealand. JCL (40:4) 2005, 157–71.

20567. HARGREAVES, TRACY. Androgyny in modern literature. *See* **12718.**

20568. HOPKINS, RICHARD. Book signing: the view from both sides of the table. *See* **404.**

20569. IKIN, VAN; JORGENSEN, DARREN (comps). Annual bibliography of Commonwealth literature 2004: Australia. JCL (40:4) 2005, 7–23.

20570. KAPLAN, E. ANN. Trauma culture: the politics of terror and loss in media and literature. *See* **12752.**

20571. KEOWN, MICHELLE. Postcolonial Pacific writing: representations of the body. *See* **12755.**

20572. KING, BRUCE. Kiwi nationalism and identity. *See* **12760.**

20573. LAMBERT, GREGG. The return of baroque in modern culture. *See* **12771.**

20574. LEMBERT, ALEXANDRA. The heritage of Hermes: alchemy in contemporary British literature. *See* **12778.**

20575. LEONARD, FRANCES; CEARLEY, RAMONA (eds). Conversations with Texas writers. Introd. by Joe Holley. *See* **12779.**

20576. LI, GUICANG. Review of the national perspective on Chinese American identity. *See* **12783.**

20577. LIU, YABIN. Culture representation in postcolonial literatures. *See* **12785.**

20578. McCANN, ANDREW. The obstinacy of the sacred. *See* **11544.**

20579. McLAUGHLIN, ROBERT L. Anthologizing contemporary literature. *In* (pp. 141–54) **3749.**

20580. MAZZA, CRIS. Finding the chic in lit. *In* (pp. 155–69) **3749.**

20581. MILLER, DANNY L.; HATFIELD, SHARON; NORMAN, GURNEY (eds). An American vein: critical readings in Appalachian literature. *See* **12822.**

20582. MODJESKA, DRUSILLA. PNG writing, writing PNG. *See* **12824.**

20583. NIELSEN, ALDON LYNN. The future of an allusion: the color of modernity. *In* (pp. 17–30) **12640.**

20584. PERERA, S. W. (comp.). Annual bibliography of Commonwealth literature 2004: Sri Lanka. JCL (40:4) 2005, 235–51.

20585. RIEMENSCHNEIDER, DIETER. Global fantasy – glocal imagination: the new literatures in English and their fantastic imagiNations. *See* **12884.**

20586. RUBIN, DEREK (ed.). Who we are: on being (and not being) a Jewish American writer. *See* **12893.**

20587. Ryan, Judylyn S. Spirituality as ideology in Black women's film and literature. See 12899.

20588. Scafe, Suzanne (comp.). Annual bibliography of Commonwealth literature 2004: the Caribbean. JCL (40:4) 2005, 89–108.

20589. Shamsie, Muneeza. Annual bibliography of Commonwealth literature 2004: Pakistan 2001–04. JCL (40:4) 2005, 173–94.

20590. Spahr, Juliana. Connected disconnection and localized globalism in Pacific multilingual literature. See 19731.

20591. Stella, Regis. Untying the cultural knot. See 12933.

20592. Talib, Ismail S. (comp.). Annual bibliography of Commonwealth literature 2004: Malaysia and Singapore. JCL (40:4) 2005, 139–56.

20593. Wanjala, Chris L.; Wanjala, Alex Nelungo. Annual bibliography of Commonwealth literature 2004: Central and East Africa – a personal overview. JCL (40:4) 2005, 253–65.

THEATRE

20594. Bennett, Susan. Theatre/tourism. See 12989.

20595. Bourgault, Louise M. Playing for life: performance in Africa in the age of AIDS. See 12997.

20596. Chávez, Karma R. Beyond complicity: coherence, queer theory, and the rhetoric of the 'Gay Christian Movement'. TPQ (24:3/4) 2004, 255–75.

20597. Clarke, Denise. Memory from the deep rodeo barrel. See 13006.

20598. Frayling, Christopher. Mad, bad and dangerous? The scientist and the cinema. See 13024.

20599. Freeman, John. Fading away: remembering to forget what theatre was. JDTC (19:2) 2005, 31–41.

20600. Gale, Maggie B.; Gardner, Viv (eds). Auto/biography and identity: women, theatre, and performance. See 13027.

20601. Grace, Sherrill. Performing the auto/biographical pact: towards a theory of identity in performance. In (pp. 65–79) 12750.

20602. Kaplan, Ellen W. Going the distance: trauma, social rupture, and the work of repair. TT (15:2) 2005, 171–83.

20603. Kershaw, Baz (ed.). The Cambridge history of British theatre: vol. 3, Since 1895. See 9486.

20604. Kuppers, Petra. Disability and contemporary performance: bodies on edge. See 13064.

20605. Lim, Eng-Beng. The Mardi Gras boys of Singapore's English-language theatre. ATJ (22:2) 2005, 293–309.

20606. Mendelsohn, Judith. One Yellow Rabbit's High Performance Rodeo, 1987–2005: a chronology. See 13075.

20607. Milne, Geoffrey. Theatre Australia (un)limited: Australian theatre since the 1950s. See 13077.

20608. Moe, Christian H.; Parker, Scott J.; McCalmon, George. Creating historical drama: a guide for communities, theatre groups, and playwrights.

Foreword by Romulus Linney. (Bibl. 1967, 2087.) Carbondale: Southern Illinois UP, 2005. pp. xvi, 318. (Second ed.: first ed. 1965.)

20609. MÜNDEL, INGRID. Radical storytelling: performance process in popular Canadian theatre. *See* **13081.**

20610. O'REILLY, ANNE F. Sacred play: soul-journeys in contemporary Irish theatre. *See* **13088.**

20611. RIVELLINO, STEVEN. Bright lights, big changes: transatlantic theatre at the turn of the century. *See* **13097.**

20612. SHTEIR, RACHEL. Notes on New York theater criticism. *See* **13109.**

20613. SIMON, JOHN IVAN. John Simon on theater: criticism, 1974–2003. Introd. by Jack O'Brien. *See* **13110.**

20614. SMITH, ANNA DEVEARE, *et al.* A forum on Black theatre. The questions: what is a Black play? And/or what is playing Black? *See* **13111.**

20615. SOMERSET-WARD, RICHARD. An American theatre: the story of Westport Country Playhouse, 1931–2005. Foreword by Joanne Woodward and Paul Newman. *See* **13113.**

20616. TAYLOR, DIANA. The archive and the repertoire: performing cultural memory in the Americas. *See* **13119.**

20617. WARRINGTON, LISA. Brave 'New World': Asian voices in the theatre of Aotearoa. *See* **13128.**

20618. WEHLE, PHILIPPA. A wild man of the theatre: Josh Fox and his International WOW Company. *See* **13129.**

20619. WELTON, MARTIN. Once more with feeling. *See* **11715.**

CINEMA
General

20620. ANON. Note on the comedy romantic rights of women. Iris (51) 2005, 30–1.

20621. ARONSTEIN, SUSAN. Hollywood knights: Arthurian cinema and the politics of nostalgia. *See* **13139.**

20622. AZZARO, GABRIELE. Four-letter films: taboo language in movies. *See* **1722.**

20623. BAETENS, JAN. Novelization, a contaminated genre? Trans. by Pieter Verrmeulen. *See* **4008.**

20624. BAINBRIDGE, CAROLINE; YATES, CANDIDA. Cinematic symptoms of masculinity in transition: memory, history and mythology in contemporary film. PsCS (10:3) 2005, 299–318.

20625. BARON, LAWRENCE. Projecting the Holocaust into the present: the changing focus of contemporary Holocaust cinema. *See* **13146.**

20626. BLESSING, KIMBERLY A.; TUDICO, PAUL J. (eds). Movies and the meaning of life: philosophers take on Hollywood. *See* **13158.**

20627. BONILA, PAUL C. Is there more to Hollywood lowbrow than meets the eye? *See* **13164.**

20628. BORDWELL, DAVID; THOMPSON, KRISTIN.   Film art: an introduction. *See* **13165.**

20629. BUSCOMBE, EDWARD.   Cinema today. *See* **13175.**

20630. CHIN, DARYL; QUALLS, LARRY.   Ain't nothin' like the real thing: Hollywood comes to New York. PAJ (73) 2003, 39–47.

20631. CONNOR, STEVEN (ed.).   The Cambridge companion to postmodernism. *See* **12617.**

20632. CONRICH, IAN.   Global pressure and the political state: New Zealand's cinema of crisis. *See* **13190.**

20633. DALZIELL, TANYA; HUGHES-D'AETH, TONY.   Thematising the global: recent Australian film. *See* **13200.**

20634. DEACY, CHRISTOPHER.   Faith in film: religious themes in contemporary cinema. *See* **13204.**

20635. DELTCHEVA, ROUMIANA.   Eastern women in Western chronotopes: the representation of East European women in Western films after 1989. *In* (pp. 161–85) **12697.**

20636. DE VALCK, MARIJKE; HAGENER, MALTE (eds).   Cinephilia: movies, love and memory. *See* **13210.**

20637. DIKA, VERA.   Recycled culture in contemporary art and film: the uses of nostalgia. *See* **13213.**

20638. DIXON, WHEELER WINSTON.   Visions of the apocalypse: spectacles of destruction in American cinema. *See* **13217.**

20639. EBERWEIN, ROBERT (ed.).   The war film. *See* **13226.**

20640. FITZPATRICK, KATHLEEN.   From the crisis to the commons. *See* **1037.**

20641. GATES, PHILIPPA.   'Fighting the good fight': the real and the moral in the contemporary Hollywood combat film. QRFV (22:4) 2005, 297–310.

20642. —— Manhunting: the female detective in the serial-killer film. PS (24:1) 2004, 42–61.

20643. GIBBS, JOHN; PYE, DOUGLAS (eds).   Style and meaning: studies in the detailed analysis of film. *See* **13241.**

20644. GLAJAR, VALENTINA; RADULESCU, DOMNICA (eds).   Vampirettes, wretches, and Amazons: Western representations of East European women. *See* **12697.**

20645. GRANT, BARRY KEITH; SHARRETT, CHRISTOPHER (eds).   Planks of reason: essays on the horror film. *See* **13245.**

20646. HOLMLUND, CHRIS; WYATT, JUSTIN (eds).   Contemporary American independent film: from the margins to the mainstream. London; New York: Routledge, 2005. pp. xvi, 299.

20647. JACKSON, LAUREN.   The film connection: twenty years of contacts between the film cultures of New Zealand and Germany. *See* **13265.**

20648. JENKINS, TRICIA.   'Potential lesbians at two o'clock': the hetero-sexualization of lesbianism in the recent teen film. *See* **13268.**

20649. KAPLAN, E. ANN.   Trauma culture: the politics of terror and loss in media and literature. *See* **12752.**

20650. KEATING, NICOLE MARIE.   Mamma's boy: counting on ghosts, sending smoke signals, and finding surrogate fathers in contemporary film. *In* (pp. 246–63) **13342.**

20651. KING, GEOFF.   American independent cinema. *See* **13277.**

20652. KIRBY, DAVID A.; GAITHER, LAURA A.   Genetic coming of age: genomics, enhancement, and identity in film. *See* **13278.**

20653. KOWALSKI, DEAN A.   Classic questions & contemporary film: an introduction to philosophy. *See* **13282.**

20654. LACEY, NICK.   Introduction to film. *See* **13284.**

20655. LAWN, JENNIFER; BEATTY, BRONWYN.   Getting to Wellywood: national branding and the globalisation of the New Zealand film industry. *See* **13285.**

20656. LEVI, ROSS D.   The celluloid courtroom: a history of legal cinema. *See* **13289.**

20657. LOUGHLIN, GERARD.   Alien sex: the body and desire in cinema and theology. *See* **13295.**

20658. LUCIA, CYNTHIA.   Framing female lawyers: women on trial in film. *See* **13297.**

20659. McCRISKEN, TREVOR B.; PEPPER, ANDREW.   American history and contemporary Hollywood film. *See* **13303.**

20660. McFARLANE, BRIAN.   Change is not a choice. *See* **13304.**

20661. McGINN, COLIN.   The power of movies: how screen and mind interact. *See* **13306.**

20662. MITCHNER, LESLIE.   'Oy vey! Is it a crisis or is it just me?' *See* **13315.**

20663. NERONI, HILARY.   The violent woman: femininity, narrative, and violence in contemporary American cinema. *See* **13323.**

20664. ONEGA, SUSANA; GUTLEBEN, CHRISTIAN (eds).   Refracting the canon in contemporary British literature and film. *See* **3879.**

20665. PETRO, PATRICE.   Whose crisis is it? *See* **13333.**

20666. PLUNKETT, FELICITY.   B[l]acktracking towards Australia: *Australian Film after Mabo*. *See* **13340.**

20667. POSTER, JAMIE.   Code orange: career fear and publishing. *See* **13343.**

20668. RADER, DEAN.   Composition, visual culture, and the problems of class. CE (67:6) 2005, 636–50 (review-article).

20669. REID, MARK A.   Black lenses, Black voices: African American film now. Lanham, MD; Oxford: Rowman & Littlefield, 2005. pp. viii, 136. (Genre and beyond.)

20670. RENZI, THOMAS C. (ed.).   H. G. Wells: six scientific romances adapted for film. *See* **20061.**

20671. RICH, NATHANIEL.   San Francisco *noir*: the city in *film noir* from 1940 to the present. *See* **13352.**

20672. RICHTER, DAVID H.   Your cheatin' art: double dealing in cinematic narrative. *See* **13353.**

20673. ROBB, DAVID L.   Operation Hollywood: how the Pentagon shapes and censors the movies. *See* **13354.**

20674. ROMBES, NICHOLAS.   Avant-garde realism. *See* **13360.**

20675. RYAN, JUDYLYN S.   Spirituality as ideology in Black women's film and literature. *See* **12899.**

20676. SCHNEIDER, STEVEN JAY (ed.).   New Hollywood violence. Manchester; New York: Manchester UP, 2004. pp. xvi, 331. (Inside popular film.)

20677. SCHWARTZ, RONALD.   Neo-*noir*: the new *film noir* style from *Psycho* to *Collateral*. *See* **13376.**

20678. SHAPIRO, HARRY.   Shooting stars: drugs, Hollywood, and the movies. *See* **13379.**

20679. SHORT, SUE.   Cyborg cinema and contemporary subjectivity. *See* **13384.**

20680. SIMPSON, PAUL.   The Rough Guide to kids' movies. *See* **13387.**

20681. STAM, ROBERT; RAENGO, ALESSANDRA (eds).   Literature and film: a guide to the theory and practice of film adaptation. Oxford; Malden, MA: Blackwell, 2005. pp. xiv, 359. Rev. by Thomas Leitch in LitFQ (33:3) 2005, 233–45; by James Naremore in Cineaste (31:1) 2005, 75–6.

20682. SUID, LAWRENCE H.; HAVERSTICK, DOLORES A.   Stars and stripes on screen: a comprehensive guide to portrayals of American military on film. *See* **13404.**

20683. TELOTTE, J. P.   Annual bibliography of Film Studies – 2003. *See* **13409.**

20684. —— Annual bibliography of Film Studies – 2004. *See* **13410.**

20685. VOIGTS-VIRCHOW, ECKART (ed.).   Janespotting and beyond: British heritage retrovisions since the mid-1990s. *See* **13415.**

20686. WELSCH, JANICE R.; ADAMS, J. Q.   Multicultural films: a reference guide. *See* **13423.**

20687. WORLEY, ALEC.   Empires of the imagination: a critical survey of fantasy cinema from Georges Méliès to *The Lord of the Rings*. Foreword by Brian Sibley. *See* **13428.**

20688. ZATLIN, PHYLLIS.   Theatrical translation and film adaptation: a practitioner's view. *See* **4006.**

20689. ZIMMERMAN, STEVE; WEISS, KEN.   Food in the movies. *See* **13433.**

Individual Films

Alexander (2004)

20690. CROWDUS, GARY.   Dramatizing issues that historians don't address: an interview with Oliver Stone. *See* **13942.**

Artificial Intelligence: AI (2001)

20691. NAREMORE, JAMES.   Love and death in *AI: Artificial Intelligence*. MichQR (44:2) 2005, 257–84.

Australian Rules (2002)

20692. MCFARLANE, BRIAN.   Back tracking. *See* **20781.**

The Believer (2001)

20693. CARR, STEVEN ALAN.   *L.I.E.*, *The Believer*, and the sexuality of the Jewish boy. *In* (pp. 316–32) **13342.**

Bend It Like Beckham (2002)

20694. ASHBY, JUSTINE.   Postfeminism in the British frame. CinJ (44:2) 2005, 127–32.

Birthday Girl (2001)

20695. TUSZYNSKA, AGNIESZKA.   Eastern girls, Western boys: the image of the Eastern European woman in *Birthday Girl*. In (pp. 203–14) **12697**.

Black and White (2002)

20696. MCFARLANE, BRIAN.   Back tracking. See **20781**.

Black Hawk Down (2001)

20697. BOUGHN, MICHAEL.   Representations of postmodern spaces in Ridley Scott's *Black Hawk Down*. WCL (39:1) 2005, 5–16.

Bride & Prejudice (2004)

20698. RESNICK, LAURA.   *Bride and Prejudice*. In (pp. 87–96) **9971**.

Bridget Jones's Diary (2001)

20699. MURPHY, OLIVIA.   Books, bras and Bridget Jones: reading adaptions of *Pride and Prejudice*. See **10026**.

Bully (2001)

20700. MAHADEVAN, SADHIR.   'Perfect childhoods': Larry Clark puts boys on screen. In (pp. 98–113) **13342**.

Captain Corelli's Mandolin (2001)

20701. WATSON, WILLIAM VAN.   Escape from patria(rchy), return to the (m)other: the Italian invasion of Greece in *Mediterraneo* and *Captain Corelli's Mandolin*. LitFQ (33:4) 2005, 313–21.

The Chronicles of Narnia (2005–)

20702. BAJETTA, CARLO M.   Più magico di Harry Potter: Lewis al cinema. See **17717**.

Corpse Bride (2005)

20703. SALISBURY, MARK.   Tim Burton's *Corpse Bride*: an invitation to the wedding. New York: Newmarket Press, 2005. pp. 156.

Dogville (2003)

20704. SHILOH, ILANA.   Lars von Trier: *Breaking the Waves*; *Dancer in the Dark*; *Dogville*. See **13492**.

Donnie Darko (2001)

20705. MATHEWS, PETER.   Spinoza's stone: the logic of *Donnie Darko*. PS (25:1) 2005, 38–48.

Elephant (2003)

20706. GARRY, JOHN P., III.   Gus Van Sant's *Elephant*: an ordinary high school movie, except that it's not. JuC (47) 2005.

Far from Heaven (2002)

20707. PAUL, WILLIAM.   Off the deep end far from heaven: social topography in *The Reckless Moment*. See **13730**.

The Fast and the Furious (2001)

20708. BELTRÁN, MARY C.   The new Hollywood racelessness: only the fast, furious, (and multiracial) will survive. *See* **13742**.

The Guru (2002)

20709. FORDHAM, FINN.   Hoaxer visions of the global. WLWE (40:2) 2004, 11–22.

Harry Potter Films (2001–)

20710. ANDERSEN, KARA LYNN.   Harry Potter and the susceptible child audience. *See* **19192**.

20711. HOPKINS, LISA.   Screening the gothic. *See* **13263**.

Hotel Rwanda (2004)

20712. HARROW, KENNETH W.   '*Un train peut en cacher un* "autre"': narrating the Rwandan genocide and *Hotel Rwanda*. RAL (36:4) 2005, 223–32.

Human Error (2004)

20713. BOHR, DENNIS.   From script to screen: adaptation of Richard Dresser's *Below the Belt*. *In* (pp. 219–38) **13950**.

The Human Stain (2003)

20714. GELDER, RACHEL.   Passing and failing: reflections on the limitations of showing the passer in *The Human Stain*. WP (15:1) 2005, 293–312.

In My Father's Den (2004)

20715. PETRIE, DUNCAN.   From the cinema of poetry to the cinema of unease: Brad McGann's *In My Father's Den*. Illusions (37) 2005, 2–8.

Intimacy (2001)

20716. EMIG, RAINER.   Alien sex fiends: the metaphoricity of sexuality in postmodernity. *See* **12656**.

Kill Bill (2003–)

20717. ANDERSON, AARON.   Mindful violence: the visibility of power and inner life in *Kill Bill*. JuC (47) 2005.

20718. BIDERMAN, SHAI.   The roar and the rampage: a tale of revenge in *Kill Bill, Volumes 1 and 2*. *In* (pp. 199–209) **13158**.

King Arthur (2004)

20719. BLANTON, VIRGINIA.   'Don't worry, I won't let them rape you': Guinevere's agency in Jerry Bruckheimer's *King Arthur*. Arthuriana (15:3) 2005, 91–111.

Kinsey (2004)

20720. GRUNDMANN, ROY.   Sex, science, and the biopic: an interview with Bill Condon. *See* **13864**.

A Knight's Tale (2001)

20721. TRIGG, STEPHANIE.   Walking through cathedrals: scholars, pilgrims, and medieval tourists. *See* **5039**.

The Laramie Project (2002)

20722. BAGLIA, JAY; FOSTER, ELISSA. Performing the 'really' real: cultural criticism, representation, and commodification in *The Laramie Project*. *See* **17367**.

Legally Blonde (2001)

20723. MARSH, KELLY A. Dear husbands and other 'girls' stuff': the *Trifles* in *Legally Blonde*. LitFQ (33:3) 2005, 201–6.

L.I.E. (2001)

20724. CARR, STEVEN ALAN. *L.I.E.*, *The Believer*, and the sexuality of the Jewish boy. *In* (pp. 316–32) **13342**.

The Lord of the Rings (2001–2003)

20725. CROFT, JANET BRENNAN (ed.). Tolkien on film: essays on Peter Jackson's *The Lord of the Rings*. Altadena, CA: Mythopoeic Press, 2004. pp. ix, 323.

20726. HOPKINS, LISA. Screening the gothic. *See* **13263**.

20727. PHILLIPSON, ALLAN. Dollarman *vs The Lord of the Rings*: the battle of nature and progress. WLWE (39:2) 2002/03, 18–37.

20728. PORTER, LYNNETTE R. Unsung heroes of *The Lord of the Rings*: from the page to the screen. *See* **19840**.

20729. SELLING, KIM. J. R. R. Tolkien's *The Lord of the Rings*: the book, the film, and genre criticism. *See* **19845**.

20730. VELDHOEN, BART. J. R. R. Tolkien, philologist and holist. *See* **19853**.

20731. WILDE, DANA. This moral core: J. R. R. Tolkien's books and Peter Jackson's films. *See* **19858**.

Lost in Translation (2003)

20732. ANTEPARA, ROBIN. Culture matters: Americans through Japanese eyes. Cweal (132:7) 2005, 10–11.

Minority Report (2002)

20733. EISIKOVITS, NIR; BIDERMAN, SHAI. So tired of the future: free will and determinism in Spielberg's *Minority Report*. *In* (pp. 242–56) **13158**.

20734. SHARPE, MATTHEW. Is there a *Minority Report*? Or, What is subjectivity? OV (2:3) 2005.

20735. SUTTON, BRIAN. Sophocles's *Oedipus the King* and Spielberg's *Minority Report*. Exp (63:4) 2005, 194–7.

Moulin Rouge! (2001)

20736. KEHLER, GRACE. Still for sale: love songs and prostitutes from *La traviata* to *Moulin Rouge!* Mosaic (38:2) 2005, 145–62.

20737. O'CONNOR, ROBERT. Baz Luhrmann's *Moulin Rouge!* Orpheus again descending. LJH (30:2) 2005, 21–32.

Mulholland Drive (2001)

20738. EKEBERG, BJORN. *No hay banda*: prosthetic memory and identity in David Lynch's *Mulholland Drive*. ImN (10) 2005.

20739. LENTZNER, JAY R.; ROSS, DONALD R. The dreams that blister sleep: latent content and cinematic form in *Mulholland Drive*. AI (62:1) 2005, 101–23.

20740. McDowell, Kelly.   Unleashing the feminine unconscious: female oedipal desires and lesbian sadomasochism in *Mulholland Dr.* JPC (38:6) 2005, 1037–49.

20741. Perlmutter, Ruth.   Memories, dreams, screens. QRFV (22:2) 2005, 125–34.

20742. Roche, David.   The death of the subject in David Lynch's *Lost Highway* and *Mulholland Drive*. See **13643**.

20743. Sherwin, Richard K.   Anti-Oedipus, Lynch: initiatory rites and the ordeal of justice. *In* (pp. 106–50) **13368**.

20744. Toles, George.   Auditioning Betty in *Mulholland Drive*. FilmQ (58:1) 2004, 2–13.

Mystic River (2003)

20745. Morrey, Douglas.   'The acorn don't fall far from the tree': genealogy and eternal return in *Mystic River*. Storytelling (5:1) 2005, 41–52.

Not Another Teen Movie (2001)

20746. Schneider, Steven Jay.   Jerkus interruptus: the terrible trials of masturbating boys in recent Hollywood cinema. *In* (pp. 377–93) **13342**.

O (2001)

20747. Brown, Eric C.   Cinema in the round: self-reflexivity in Tim Blake Nelson's *O*. *In* (pp. 73–85) **13273**.

20748. Colón Semenza, Gregory M.   Shakespeare after Columbine: teen violence in Tim Blake Nelson's *O*. ColLit (32:4) 2005, 99–124.

The Passion of the Christ (2004)

20749. Apostolos-Cappadona, Diane.   On seeing *The Passion*. Is there a painting in this film? Or is this film a painting? *In* (pp. 97–108) **20763**.

20750. Ariel, Yaakov.   *The Passion of the Christ* and the passion of the Jews: Mel Gibson's film in the light of Jewish–Christian relations. *In* (pp. 21–41) **20763**.

20751. Chattaway, Peter T.   Come and see: how movies encourage us to look at (and with) Jesus. *In* (pp. 121–33) **20763**.

20752. Corley, Kathleen E.; Webb, Robert L. (eds).   Jesus and Mel Gibson's *The Passion of the Christ*: the film, the Gospels, and the claims of history. London; New York: Continuum, 2004. pp. x, 198. Rev. by Anthony Burke Smith in Cweal (132:10) 2005, 26–7.

20753. Gracia, Jorge J. E. (ed.).   Mel Gibson's *Passion* and philosophy: the Cross, the questions, the controversy. (Bibl. 2004, 20709.) Rev. by Anthony Burke Smith in Cweal (132:10) 2005, 26–7.

20754. Jacobs, Steven Leonard.   Can there be Jewish–Christian dialogue after *The Passion*? *In* (pp. 43–52) **20763**.

20755. Johnston, Robert K.   *The Passion* as dynamic icon: a theological reflection. *In* (pp. 55–70) **20763**.

20756. King, Neal.   Truth at last: evangelical communities embrace *The Passion of the Christ*. *In* (pp. 151–62) **20763**.

20757. Levine, Amy-Jill.   Mel Gibson, the scribes, and the Pharisees. *In* (pp. 137–49) **20763**.

20758. Middleton, Darren J. N.   Celluloid synoptics: viewing the gospels of Marty and Mel together. *In* (pp. 71–81) **20763**.

20759. Miller, Monica Migliorino.   The theology of *The Passion of the Christ*. New York: St Pauls/Alba House, 2005. pp. xxix, 170.

20760. Morgan, David.   Catholic visual piety and *The Passion of the Christ*. *In* (pp. 85–96) **20763**.

20761. Ortiz, Gaye W.   'Passion'-ate women: the female presence in *The Passion of the Christ*. *In* (pp. 109–20) **20763**.

20762. Perry, Marvin; Schweitzer, Frederick M.   The medieval Passion play revisited. *In* (pp. 3–19) **20763**.

20763. Plate, S. Brent (ed.).   Re-viewing *The Passion*: Mel Gibson's film and its critics. Basingstoke; New York: Palgrave Macmillan, 2004. pp. xxiii, 198.

20764. Sandmel, David Fox.   Jews, Christians, and Gibson's *The Passion of the Christ*. JudQ (53:1/2) 2004, 12–20.

20765. Smart, Robert.   *The Passion of the Christ*: reflections on Mel's monstrous Messiah movie and the culture wars. JuC (47) 2005.

20766. Smith, Anthony Burke.   He's an *auteur*. Cweal (132:10) 2005, 26–7 (review-article).

20767. Woods, Robert H.; Jindra, Michael C.; Baker, Jason D.   The audience responds to *The Passion of the Christ*. *In* (pp. 163–80) **20763**.

The Pianist (2002)

20768. Mazierska, Ewa.   The autobiographical effect in the cinema of Roman Polanski. FilCr (29:3) 2005, 28–45.

Proteus (2003)

20769. Ben-Asher, Noa, *et al.*   Screening historical sexualities: a roundtable on sodomy, South Africa and *Proteus*. GLQ (11:3) 2005, 437–55.

Rabbit-Proof Fence (2002)

20770. McFarlane, Brian.   Back tracking. *See* **20781**.

Real Women Have Curves (2002)

20771. Holmlund, Chris.   Postfeminism from A to G. CinJ (44:2) 2005, 116–21.

Resident Evil (2002–)

20772. Hand, Richard J.   Proliferating horrors: survival horror and the *Resident Evil* franchise. *In* (pp. 117–34) **13250**.

Scotland, PA (2001)

20773. Shohet, Lauren.   The banquet of Scotland (PA). ShS (57) 2004, 186–95.

Serenity (2005)

20774. Espenson, Jane; Yeffeth, Glenn (eds).   Finding serenity: anti-heroes, lost shepherds and space hookers in Joss Whedon's *Firefly*. *See* **20809**.

20775. LACKEY, MERCEDES. *Serenity* and Bobby McGee: freedom and the illusion of freedom in Joss Whedon's *Firefly*. In (pp. 63–73) **20809.**

20776. TAYLOR, ROBERT B. The captain may wear the tight pants, but it's the gals who make *Serenity* soar. In (pp. 131–7) **20809.**

Shattered Glass (2003)

20777. EHRLICH, MATTHEW C. *Shattered Glass*, movies, and the free-press myth. JCI (29:2) 2005, 103–18.

Spider-Man (2002–)

20778. SANFORD, JONATHAN J. Of *Spider-Man*, *Spider-Man 2*, and living like a hero. In (pp. 228–41) **13158.**

20779. SCHNEIDER, STEVEN JAY. Jerkus interruptus: the terrible trials of masturbating boys in recent Hollywood cinema. In (pp. 377–93) **13342.**

Taking Lives (2004)

20780. MIZEJEWSKI, LINDA. Dressed to kill: postfeminist *noir*. See **20783.**

The Tracker (2002)

20781. MCFARLANE, BRIAN. Back tracking. Meanjin (62:1) 2003, 59–68. (Racism in Australian cinema.)

Troy (2004)

20782. MANION, LEE. The trouble with Troy: misrepresenting myth. Iris (49) 2004, 29–34.

Twisted (2004)

20783. MIZEJEWSKI, LINDA. Dressed to kill: postfeminist *noir*. CinJ (44:2) 2005, 121–7.

Vanilla Sky (2001)

20784. SIMERKA, BARBARA; WEIMER, CHRISTOPHER. Tom Cruise and the seven dwarves: cinematic postmodernisms in *Abre los ojos* and *Vanilla Sky*. AmDr (14:2) 2005, 1–15.

Vanity Fair (2004)

20785. SUTHERLAND, JOHN. Some nabob: the sometimes useful errors of Edward Said. See **15032.**

Waking Life (2001)

20786. STOEHR, KEVIN. The on-going wow: *Waking Life* and the waltz between detachment and immersion. In (pp. 32–44) **13158.**

Yes (2004)

20787. LUCIA, CYNTHIA. Saying *Yes* to taking risks: an interview with Sally Potter. See **13927.**

Directors

Noah Baumbach

20788. QUART, LEONARD. Divorce Brooklyn style: an interview with Noah Baumbach. Cineaste (31:1) 2005, 27–39.

Kathryn Bigelow

20789. JERMYN, DEBORAH; REDMOND, SEAN (eds). The cinema of Kathryn Bigelow: Hollywood transgressor. London: Wallflower, 2003. pp. viii, 232. (Directors' cuts.) Rev. by Jim Hemphill in FilmQ (58:1) 2004, 61–3.

Pawel Pawlikowski

20790. PORTON, RICHARD. Going against the grain: an interview with Pawel Pawlikowski. Cineaste (30:3) 2005, 37–41.

Takashi Shimizu

20791. DIXON, WHEELER WINSTON. An interview with Takashi Shimizu. QRFV (22:1) 2005, 1–16.

Joss Whedon

20792. ESPENSON, JANE; YEFFETH, GLENN (eds). Finding serenity: anti-heroes, lost shepherds and space hookers in Joss Whedon's *Firefly*. See **20809.**

20793. SCHIFF, LEN. Joss Whedon: absolute admiration for Sondheim. SondR (11:4) 2005, 34–5.

RADIO, TELEVISION, INTERACTIVE MEDIA

20794. AKASS, KIM; MCCABE, JANET (eds). Reading *Sex and the City*. See **13954.**

20795. ATKINS, BARRY. More than a game: the computer game as fictional form. See **13956.**

20796. BATTIS, JES. Blood relations: chosen families in *Buffy, the Vampire Slayer* and *Angel*. See **13958.**

20797. BROGLIO, RON. Criticism from inside the poem: MOOs and Blake's *Milton. See* **8361.**

20798. BUCHANAN, GINJER. Who killed *Firefly? In* (pp. 47–53) **20809.**

20799. CASTIGLIA, CHRISTOPHER; REED, CHRISTOPHER. 'Ah, yes, I remember it well': memory and queer culture in *Will and Grace*. CultC (56) 2004, 158–88.

20800. CAZEAUX, CLIVE. Phenomenology and radio drama. BJA (45:2) 2005, 157–74.

20801. CHAOULI, MICHEL. How interactive can fiction be? See **13968.**

20802. CONRAD, ROXANNE LONGSTREET. Mirror/mirror: a parody. *In* (pp. 169–82) **20809.**

20803. CREEBER, GLEN (ed.). Fifty key television programmes. See **13973.**

20804. DAVIDSON, JOY. Whores and goddesses: the archetypal domain of Inara Serra. *In* (pp. 113–29) **20809.**

20805. DEBRANDT, DON. *Firefly* vs *The Tick. In* (pp. 75–84) **20809.**

20806. DECANDIDO, KEITH R. A. 'The train job' didn't do the job: poor opening contributed to *Firefly*'s doom. *In* (pp. 55–61) **20809.**

20807. DIXON, LARRY. The reward, the details, the devils, the due. *In* (pp. 5–15) **20809.**

20808. EARLY, FRANCES; KENNEDY, KATHLEEN (eds). Athena's daughters: television's new women warriors. Foreword by Rhonda V. Wilcox. See **13979.**

20809. ESPENSON, JANE; YEFFETH, GLENN (eds).   Finding serenity: anti-heroes, lost shepherds and space hookers in Joss Whedon's *Firefly*. Dallas, TX: BenBella, 2005. pp. x, 238.

20810. GANS-BORISKIN, RACHEL TISINGER.   The Bushlet administration: terrorism and war on *The West Wing*. See **13984**.

20811. GERROLD, DAVID.   Star truck. *In* (pp. 183–95) **20809**.

20812. GOLTZ, JENNIFER.   Listening to *Firefly*. *In* (pp. 209–15) **20809**.

20813. GREELEY, ANDREW M.   Is God one of us? The many voices of God in *Joan of Arcadia*. ANCW (192:12) 2005, 12–15.

20814. HAND, RICHARD J.   Proliferating horrors: survival horror and the *Resident Evil* franchise. *In* (pp. 117–34) **13250**.

20815. HEINECKEN, DAWN.   The warrior women of television: a feminist cultural analysis of the female body in popular media. See **13994**.

20816. HELLER, DANA.   Sex and the series: Paris, New York, and the post-national romance. See **13995**.

20817. HOLBERT, R. LANCE, *et al*.   The *West Wing* and depictions of the American Presidency: expanding the domains of framing in political communication. ComQ (53:4) 2005, 505–22.

20818. HOLDER, NANCY.   I want your sex: gender and power in Joss Whedon's dystopian future world. *In* (pp. 139–53) **20809**.

20819. HUFF, TANYA.   'Thanks for the reenactment, sir.' Zoe: updating the woman warrior. *In* (pp. 105–12) **20809**.

20820. HUNT, DARRELL M.   Channeling Blackness: studies on television and race in America. See **14000**.

20821. JIWANI, YASMIN.   The Eurasian female hero(ine): Sydney Fox as relic hunter. See **14004**.

20822. JOHNSON, MERRI LISA.   From relationship autopsy to romantic utopia: the missing discourse of egalitarian marriage on HBO's *Six Feet Under*. Discourse (26:3) 2004, 18–40.

20823. JOHNSON-SMITH, JAN.   American science fiction TV: *Star Trek*, *Stargate* and beyond. See **14006**.

20824. JOWETT, LORNA.   Sex and the slayer: a Gender Studies primer for the *Buffy* fan. See **14007**.

20825. LACKEY, MERCEDES.   *Serenity* and Bobby McGee: freedom and the illusion of freedom in Joss Whedon's *Firefly*. *In* (pp. 63–73) **20809**.

20826. MITCHELL, DANIELLE.   Producing containment: the rhetorical construction of difference in *Will & Grace*. JPC (38:6) 2005, 1050–68.

20827. NADEL, ALAN.   Television in Black-and-White America: race and national identity. See **14025**.

20828. NELSON, ROBIN.   Live or wired? Technologizing the event. *In* (pp. 303–16) **3974**.

20829. NEWCOMB, HORACE.   Studying television: same questions, different contexts. See **14030**.

20830. QUIMBY, KARIN.   *Will & Grace*: negotiating (gay) marriage on prime-time television. JPC (38:4) 2004, 713–31.

20831. RADER, DEAN.   Composition, visual culture, and the problems of class. *See* **20668.**

20832. SAUNDERS, IAN.   Virtual cultures. YWCCT (12) 2004, 130–42 (review-article).

20833. SCHIFF, LEN.   Vision and voice: Marc Cherry shows no desperation in his devotion to Sondheim. SondR (12:2) 2005, 30–1. (Interview.)

20834. STAITE, JEWEL.   Kaylee speaks: Jewel Staite on *Firefly*.   *In* (pp. 217–27) **20809.**

20835. SULLIVAN, KEVIN M.   Chinese words in the 'verse. *In* (pp. 197–207) **20809.**

20836. TAGLIAMONTE, SALI; ROBERTS, CHRIS.   So weird; so cool; so innovative: the use of intensifiers in the television series *Friends*. *See* **1647.**

20837. TAVINOR, GRANT.   Videogames and interactive fiction. PhilL (29:1) 2005, 24–40.

20838. TAYLOR, ROBERT B.   The captain may wear the tight pants, but it's the gals who make *Serenity* soar. *In* (pp. 131–7) **20809.**

20839. TEA, ALAN J. H.; LEE, BENNY P. H.   Reference and blending in a computer role-playing game. *See* **1699.**

20840. THORBURN, DAVID; JENKINS, HENRY (eds); SEAWELL, BRAD (assoc. ed.). Rethinking media change: the aesthetics of transition. *See* **24.**

20841. THORNHAM, SUE; PURVIS, TONY.   Television drama: theories and identities. *See* **14053.**

20842. TURNER, CHRIS.   Planet Simpson: how a cartoon masterpiece defined a generation. *See* **14056.**

20843. VOIGTS-VIRCHOW, ECKART (ed.).   Janespotting and beyond: British heritage retrovisions since the mid-1990s. *See* **13415.**

20844. WASKO, JANET (ed.).   A companion to television. *See* **14058.**

20845. WATT-EVANS, LAWRENCE.   The heirs of Sawney Beane. *In* (pp. 17–28) **20809.**

20846. WEST, MICHELLE SAGARA.   More than a marriage of convenience. *In* (pp. 97–104) **20809.**

20847. WILKERSON, MARGARET B.   The *Theatre Journal* auto/archive: Margaret B. Wilkerson. *See* **16880.**

20848. WOLF, MARK J. P.; PERRON, BERNARD (eds).   The video game theory reader. *See* **14064.**

20849. WRIGHT, JOHN C.   Just shove him in the engine; or, The role of chivalry in *Firefly*. *In* (pp. 155–67) **20809.**

20850. WRIGHT, LEIGH ADAMS.   Asian objects in space. *In* (pp. 29–35) **20809.**

20851. WRIGHT, ZACHARY C.; RABKIN, ERIC S.; SIMON, CARL P.   The exaggerated reports of the death of science fiction. *See* **20895.**

20852. YEFFETH, GLENN.   The rise and fall (and rise) of *Firefly* (the behind-the-scenes story). *In* (pp. 37–46) **20809.**

20853. ZYNDA, LYLE.   We're all just floating in space. *In* (pp. 85–95) **20809.**

FICTION

20854. ARMITT, LUCIE.   Fantasy fiction: an introduction. *See* **14078**.

20855. BEAN, ETHELLE S.   Technology and detective fiction. Clues (24:1) 2005, 27–34.

20856. BONE, MARTYN.   The postsouthern sense of place in contemporary fiction. *See* **14087**.

20857. BRENNAN, ZOE.   The older woman in recent fiction. *See* **14089**.

20858. BRODERICK, DAMIEN.   Transreal nostalgia in a time of singularity. *See* **14091**.

20859. BURGESS, MICHAEL; VASSILAKOS, JILL H.   Murder in retrospect: a selective guide to historical mystery fiction. *See* **14097**.

20860. BYERMAN, KEITH.   Remembering the past in contemporary African American fiction. *See* **14100**.

20861. COALE, SAMUEL CHASE.   Paradigms of paranoia: the culture of conspiracy in contemporary American fiction. *See* **14109**.

20862. CUNNINGHAM, SOPHIE.   Alien star. *See* **14116**.

20863. DICKSON-CARR, DARRYL.   The Columbia guide to contemporary African American fiction. *See* **14124**.

20864. DISCH, THOMAS M.   On SF. *See* **14125**.

20865. DURHAM, CAROLYN A.   Literary globalism: Anglo-American fiction set in France. *See* **14129**.

20866. FREIER, MARY P.   Information ethics in the detective novel. Clues (24:1) 2005, 18–26.

20867. GANNON, CHARLES E.   Rumors of war and infernal machines: technomilitary agenda-setting in American and British speculative fiction. *See* **14142**.

20868. GREEN, JEREMY.   Late postmodernism: American fiction at the millennium. *See* **14150**.

20869. GRIBBEN, CRAWFORD.   Rapture fictions and the changing evangelical condition. *See* **14152**.

20870. HAHN, TORSTEN.   Risk communication and paranoid hermeneutics: towards a distinction between 'medical thrillers' and 'mind-control thrillers' in narrations on biocontrol. *See* **14155**.

20871. HARRIS-FAIN, DARREN.   Understanding contemporary American science fiction: the age of maturity, 1970–2000. *See* **14158**.

20872. HAWLITSCHKA, KATJA.   Detection, deconstruction, and academic death sentences: female scholars reading the mysteries of high and low culture. *See* **14160**.

20873. HEGERFELDT, ANNE C.   Lies that tell the truth: magic realism seen through contemporary fiction from Britain. *See* **14162**.

20874. HOPKINSON, NALO; MEHAN, UPPINDER (eds).   So long been dreaming: postcolonial science fiction & fantasy. Vancouver: Arsenal Pulp Press, 2004. pp. 270. Rev. by Michelle Reid in Foundation (94) 2005, 124–7.

20875. HOWELLS, CORAL ANN.   Contemporary Canadian women's fiction: refiguring identities. *See* **14175**.

20876. JAFFE, HAROLD.   The writer in wartime. AmBR (26:4) 2005, 3, 6.

20877. KELMAN, SUANNE.   The glittering prizes: the struggle between merit and Mammon continues, ten years after the birth of the Giller. *See* **14188.**

20878. KENYON, KAY.   Reading by flashlight: what fantasy writers can learn from Pullman. *In* (pp. 97–107) **18973.**

20879. KIDMAN, FIONA (ed.).   The best New Zealand fiction: vol. 2. Auckland: Vintage, 2005. pp. 239.

20880. LAY, GRAEME; STRATFORD, STEPHEN (eds).   Home: new short short stories by New Zealand writers. Auckland: Random House, 2005. pp. 254.

20881. LEAVIS, L. R.   Current literature 2001: 1, New writing: novels and short stories. EngS (84:5) 2003, 464–72.

20882. McNEER, REBECCA.   'What might be true': the diverse relationships of Australian novels to fact. *See* **14215.**

20883. MARCUS, DAVID (ed.).   The Faber book of best new Irish short stories 2004–5. London; Boston, MA: Faber & Faber, 2005. pp. viii, 325. Rev. by Paddy Bullard in TLS, 13 May 2005, 21–2.

20884. MONTEITH, SHARON; NEWMAN, JENNY; WHEELER, PAT (eds). Contemporary British & Irish fiction: an introduction through interviews. *See* **14231.**

20885. MONTFORT, NICK.   Twisty little passages: an approach to interactive fiction. (Bibl. 2004, 20792.) Rev. by Steven Malliet in ImN (9) 2004.

20886. MOSELEY, MERRITT.   Henry James and novelistic impersonation. *See* **11437.**

20887. PARKER, EMMA.   Introduction: 'the proper stuff of fiction': defending the domestic, reappraising the parochial. *See* **14245.**

20888. SCHNEIDER, RALF.   Hypertext narrative and the reader: a view from cognitive theory. EJES (9:2) 2005, 197–208.

20889. SHOWALTER, ELAINE.   Faculty towers: the academic novel and its discontents. *See* **14275.**

20890. SNODGRASS, KATHLEEN.   The ties that bind. GaR (59:1) 2005, 200–13 (review-article).

20891. TURCHI, PETER; BARRETT, ANDREA (eds).   The story behind the story: 26 writers and how they work. Introd. by Richard Russo. *See* **14294.**

20892. WEINBAUM, BATYA.   Early US sci fi: post-nationalist exploration for Jews in outer space? *See* **14303.**

20893. WELLS, LYNN.   Allegories of telling: self-referential narrative in contemporary British fiction. *See* **14306.**

20894. WOLEDGE, ELIZABETH.   From slash to the mainstream: female writers and gender-blending men. *See* **14313.**

20895. WRIGHT, ZACHARY C.; RABKIN, ERIC S.; SIMON, CARL P.   The exaggerated reports of the death of science fiction. NYRSF (18:4) 2005, 1, 4–8.

20896. WYTENBROEK, LYNN (J. R.).   Harry Potter and the Canadian fantasy. *See* **19243.**

LITERATURE FOR CHILDREN

20897. ARONSON, MARC. Beyond the pale: new essays for a new era. (Bibl. 2004, 20801.) Rev. by Giselle Liza Anatol in LU (29:1) 2005, 124–8.

20898. FLYNN, RICHARD; HAGER, KELLY; THOMAS, JOSEPH T., JR. It could be verse: the 2005 *Lion and the Unicorn* Award for Excellence in North American Poetry. *See* **18499**.

20899. GANGI, JANE M. Inclusive aesthetics and social justice: the vanguard of small, multicultural presses. *See* **1038**.

20900. HOGAN, WALTER. Humor in young adult literature: a time to laugh. *See* **14335**.

20901. HUNT, PETER. Alternative worlds in fantasy fiction – revisited. *See* **14337**.

20902. REYNOLDS, KIMBERLEY. Frightening fiction: beyond horror. *See* **14351**.

20903. —— (ed.). Modern children's literature: an introduction. *See* **14352**.

20904. SCHALL, LUCY. Teen genre connections: from booktalking to booklearning. *See* **14353**.

20905. WATSON, GREER. Tertiary reality in children's fantasy. *See* **21205**.

20906. WATSON, VICTOR. Has children's literature come of age? *See* **14358**.

20907. YAMPBELL, CAT. Judging a book by its cover: publishing trends in young adult literature. *See* **1028**.

POETRY

20908. BAKER, ROBERT. The extravagant: crossings of modern poetry and modern philosophy. *See* **14364**.

20909. BRAUNE, BEV. Who is the reader? And how many of us are there? *See* **14371**.

20910. BROWER, BRYAN. Articles of chap. AmBR (26:3) 2005, 3.

20911. BUTLING, PAULINE; RUDY, SUSAN. Writing in our time: Canada's radical poetries in English (1957–2003). *See* **14374**.

20912. CAMBONI, MARINA. 'Disarmonia perfetta': polilinguismo e transnazionalismo nella poesia sperimentale contemporanea. *In* (pp. 9–33) **14377**.

20913. CAPLAN, DAVID. Questions of possibility: contemporary poetry and poetic form. *See* **14379**.

20914. CLARK, J. ELIZABETH. *Versus* verse: poets against war. RT (74) 2005, 6–11.

20915. CLARK, KEVIN. Poetic modernism and the Oceanic divide. *See* **14380**.

20916. CONSTANTINE, DAVID. A living language. Newcastle upon Tyne: Dept of English Literary & Linguistic Studies, Univ. of Newcastle, in assn with Bloodaxe, 2004. pp. 64. (Newcastle/Bloodaxe poetry series, 2.) (Newcastle/Bloodaxe poetry lectures.) Rev. by Stephen Burt in TLS, 25 Nov. 2005, 3–4.

20917. COOLEY, DENNIS. Documents in the postmodern long prairie poem. *In* (pp. 175–211) **12587**.

20918. DAVIDSON, IAN. Visual poetry as performance. *See* **15814**.

20919. DELVILLE, MICHEL; PAGNOULLE, CHRISTINE (eds). Sound as sense: contemporary US poetry &/in music. (Bibl. 2004, 20813.) Rev. by Jelle Dierickx in ImN (9) 2004.

20920. FLAJŠAR, JIŘÍ. Issues of form in contemporary American poetry. *In* (pp. 51–6) **3734**.

20921. GIOIA, DANA. Disappearing ink: poetry at the end of print culture. HR (56:1) 2003, 21–49.

20922. —— Disappearing ink: poetry at the end of print culture. Saint Paul, MN: Graywolf Press, 2004. pp. xiv, 271. Rev. by Brenda Wineapple in Poetry (186:2) 2005, 175–9; by Lynnell Edwards in AmBR (26:5) 2005, 10–12.

20923. HENNESSY, CHRISTOPHER. Outside the lines: talking with contemporary gay poets. *See* **14417**.

20924. HENRY, BRIAN; ZAWACKI, ANDREW (eds). The Verse book of interviews: 27 poets on language, craft & culture. *See* **14419**.

20925. INCKLE, KAY. Who's hurting who? The ethics of engaging the marked body. Auto/Biography (13:3) 2005, 227–48.

20926. KINDSETH, TIM. The wide, wide world of chapbooks. *See* **14430**.

20927. KITCHEN, JUDITH. The properties of rain. GaR (59:1) 2005, 181–99 (review-article). (Nature poetry.)

20928. LONGENBACH, JAMES. The resistance to poetry. (Bibl. 2004, 20820.) Rev. by Edward Butscher in GaR (59:1) 2005, 167–80.

20929. MANHIRE, BILL (sel. and introd.). 121 New Zealand poems. *See* **14451**.

20930. MIDDLETON, PETER. Distant reading: performance, readership, and consumption in contemporary poetry. Tuscaloosa; London: Alabama UP, 2005. pp. xviii, 241. (Modern and contemporary poetics.) Rev. by Hannah Lavery in RMER (59:2) 2005.

20931. MILLER, WAYNE. Chapbooks: democratic ephemera. *See* **14457**.

20932. MILOVANOVIČ, ČELICA. A Classicist reads some modern poetry. *See* **14458**.

20933. PATERSON, DON. The dark art of poetry. Brick (75) 2005, 19–33.

20934. PFEFFERLE, W. T. (comp.). Poets on place: tales and interviews from the road. Foreword by David St John. *See* **14473**.

20935. PIRIE, MARK. The new American poetry. PNZ (31) 2005, 90–8.

20936. REES-JONES, DERYN (ed.). Consorting with angels: essays on modern women poets. *See* **14478**.

20937. ROBINSON, JEFFREY CANE. Wordsworth, day by day: reading his work into poetry now. *See* **12516**.

20938. SAJÉ, NATASHA. Dynamic design: the structure of books of poems. IowaR (35:2) 2005, 149–62.

20939. SCHNEIDERMAN, JASON; SIKEN, RICHARD; SMITH, AARON. Young poets on the state of the craft. GLRW (12:5) 2005, 28–30.

20940. SCHULTZ, SUSAN M. A poetics of impasse in modern and contemporary American poetry. *See* **14487**.

20941. SOLE, KELWYN. 'The deep thoughts the one in need falls into': quotidian experience and the perspectives of poetry in postliberation South Africa. *In* (pp. 182–205) **12789**.

20942. SOMERS-WILLETT, SUSAN B. A. Slam poetry and the cultural politics of performing identity. *See* **14494**.

20943. SPERBER, HANNAH. Poetry in from the cold. NorS, July 2005, 64–71.

20944. SPIEGELMAN, WILLARD. How poets see the world: the art of description in contemporary poetry. *See* **14495**.

20945. SZIRTES, GEORGE. An update on British poetry. ChattR (25:1/2) 2005, 107–13.

20946. WALDROP, ROSMARIE. Dissonance (if you are interested). *See* **14508**.

20947. WALKER, JEANNE MURRAY. A comment on the state of the art: poetry in 2004. ChrisL (54:1) 2004, 93–110 (review-article).

20948. ZIMMER, PAUL. Hello, sky. GaR (59:2) 2005, 400–21 (review-article).

PROSE

20949. ADAMS, MARY E. Mending the schism: an optimistic approach to academic writing. Lit (16:4) 2005, 405–15.

20950. BAUERLEIN, MARK. Interpretation against the essay. Lit (16:4) 2005, 371–9.

20951. BLOOM, LYNN Z. Academic essays and the vertical pronoun. Lit (16:4) 2005, 417–30.

20952. BOYNTON, ROBERT S. The new New Journalism: conversations with America's best nonfiction writers on their craft. *See* **14520**.

20953. GERMANO, WILLIAM. Final thoughts. *See* **1078**.

20954. GUNN, JOSHUA. Mourning speech: haunting and the spectral voices of nine-eleven. *See* **2326**.

20955. LOW, GRAHAM. Explaining evolution: the use of animacy in an example of semi-formal science writing. *See* **2861**.

20956. MÉMET, MONIQUE. Letters to the editor: a multi-faceted genre. *See* **2868**.

20957. POSNER, DAVID M. Rhetoric, redemption, and fraud: what we do when we end books. *See* **1088**.

20958. RICHARDT, SUSANNE. Metaphor in languages for special purposes: the function of conceptual metaphor in written expert language and expert–lay communication in the domains of economics, medicine, and computing. *See* **2449**.

20959. SCHOENFELDT, MICHAEL. First impressions and last thoughts: the importance of scholarly introductions. *See* **1091**.

20960. SCHULTE, RAINER. The dynamics of scholarly and essayistic writing. Lit (16:4) 2005, 389–95.

20961. TONELLO, FABRIZIO. Il giornalismo americano. *See* **14552**.

20962. WOOD, JAMES HUNTER. Interventional narratology: form and function of the narrative medical write-up. *See* **10764**.

20963. ZIOLKOWSKI, THEODORE. The quest for cultural community. Lit (16:4) 2005, 397–403.

BIOGRAPHY AND AUTOBIOGRAPHY

20964. AMIGONI, DAVID. Distinctively queer little morsels: imagining distinction, groups, and difference in the *DNB* and the *ODNB*. *See* **9798.**

20965. BARRETT, MARVIN. Touched by Aldous Huxley. *See* **17145.**

20966. BOOTH, ALISON. Fighting for lives in the *ODNB*; or, Taking prosopography personally. JVC (10:2) 2005, 267–79.

20967. —— How to make it as a woman: collective biographical history from Victoria to the present. *See* **9803.**

20968. BROSMAN, CATHARINE SAVAGE. Autobiography and the complications of postmodernism and feminism. *See* **14576.**

20969. GALE, MAGGIE B.; GARDNER, VIV (eds). Auto/biography and identity: women, theatre, and performance. *See* **13027.**

20970. GOELLER, ALISON D. The politics of food in Italian American women's autobiography. *See* **14595.**

20971. GOLDMAN, LAWRENCE. No smoking dons: the *ODNB* and the new structures of knowledge. *See* **14596.**

20972. HARRISON-KAHAN, LORI. Passing for White, passing for Jewish: mixed-race identity in Danzy Senna and Rebecca Walker. *See* **19359.**

20973. JOHNSON, GREG. Modern writers, modern lives. GaR (57:1) 2003, 176–85 (review-article).

20974. McHANEY, PEARL AMELIA. Interview with Suzanne Marrs, author of *Eudora Welty: a Biography*. *See* **20079.**

20975. NADEL, IRA B. Writing the life of *Tom Stoppard*. *See* **19698.**

20976. PERKINS, MAUREEN. The role of colour and 'ethnic' autobiography: Fanon, Capécia and difference. *See* **14621.**

20977. POLETTI, ANNA. Self-publishing in the global and local: situating life writing in zines. *See* **14625.**

20978. POTTER, LOIS. Having our Will: imagination in recent Shakespeare biographies. *See* **6056.**

20979. RAK, JULIE. The digital queer: weblogs and Internet identity. Biography (28:1) 2005, 166–82.

20980. SHAPIRO, JAMES. Toward a new biography of Shakespeare. *See* **6077.**

RELATED STUDIES

20981. CROSS, GARY. The cute and the cool: wondrous innocence and modern American children's culture. Oxford; New York: OUP, 2004. pp. 259. Rev. by Susan J. Matt in JAH (92:1) 2005, 282–4.

20982. FREEMAN, SUZANNE. End of discussion: why I'm leaving my book group. *See* **14659.**

20983. FYNSK, CHRISTOPHER. The claim of language: a case for the humanities. *See* **14660.**

20984. KEARNEY, RICHARD. Strangers, gods, and monsters: interpreting otherness. *See* **14668.**

20985. NKANDAWIRE, THANDIKA (ed.). African intellectuals: rethinking politics, language, gender and development. London; Atlantic Highlands, NJ: Zed, 2005. pp. 248. (Africa in the new millennium.)

20986. WOOD, RALPH C. Contending for the faith: the Church's engagement with culture. See **14681.**

20987. ZHANG, XUDONG. Multiplicity or homogeneity? The cultural-political paradox of the age of globalization. CultC (58) 2004, 30–55.

LITERARY THEORY

20988. ADAMS, JAMES ELI. The function of journals at the present time. JVC (10:2) 2005, 257–66. (Perspectives.)

20989. ADÉÈKÓ, ADÉLÉKÈ. Symptoms of the present in Ato Quayson's *Calibrations*. RAL (36:2) 2005, 104–11.

20990. ALLMENDINGER, BLAKE. Through the looking-glass: what Western historians and literary critics can learn from each other. PacHR (72:3) 2003, 415–20.

20991. ALTIERI, CHARLES. Some problems with being contemporary: aging critics, younger poets and the new century. See **18389.**

20992. ANDERSON, AMANDA. Victorian Studies and the two modernities. See **14687.**

20993. APTER, EMILY. Afterlife of a discipline. CL (57:3) 2005, 201–6 (review-article).

20994. BADMINGTON, NEIL. From *Critical Practice* to cultural criticism: an interview with Catherine Belsey. See **14693.**

20995. BAETENS, JAN. Novelization, a contaminated genre? Trans. by Pieter Verrmeulen. See **4008.**

20996. BENEDETTI, CARLA. The empty cage: inquiry into the mysterious disappearance of the author. Trans. by William J. Hartley. See **14701.**

20997. BENNETT, LYN. Boundaries and frontiers: metaphor and the rhetoric of interdisciplinarity in literary studies. See **14702.**

20998. BENNETT, SUSAN. Theatre/tourism. See **12989.**

20999. BERRY, AMANDA. Some of my best friends are Romanticists: Shelley and the queer project in Romanticism. See **11996.**

21000. BEYERS, CHRIS. Critical studies in a post-theoretical age: three books sort of about Wallace Stevens. See **19646.**

21001. BOWMAN, PAUL. Marxism(s) and postmarxism(s). YWCCT (12) 2004, 29–57 (review-article).

21002. BOYD, BRIAN. Literature and evolution: a bio-cultural approach. PhilL (29:1) 2005, 1–23.

21003. BREWSTER, SCOTT. Psychoanalysis. YWCCT (12) 2004, 89–97 (review-article).

21004. BROWN, KIMBERLY NICHELE. Sniffing the 'calypso magnolia': unearthing the Caribbean presence in the South (response to John Lowe). See **10600.**

21005. BUELL, LAWRENCE. The future of environmental criticism: environmental crisis and literary imagination. Oxford; Malden, MA: Blackwell, 2005. pp. ix, 195. (Blackwell manifestos.)

21006. BUSH, CHRISTOPHER. Deaths of a discipline. CL (57:3) 2005, 207–13 (review-article).

21007. BUTLER, JUDITH. Undoing gender. See 14727.

21008. CAESAR, TERRY. Anthologies, literature, and theory in Japan. In (pp. 298–325) 3749.

21009. CAPLAN, BEN. Creatures of fiction, myth, and imagination. See 3726.

21010. CARRILLO ROWE, AIMEE. Be longing: toward a feminist politics of relation. See 19065.

21011. CASTRONOVO, RUSS. Death to the American renaissance: history, Heidegger, Poe. See 11800.

21012. CHAMBERS, ROSS. The queer and the creepy: Western fictions of artificial life. See 11964.

21013. CHANG, FANG. The current situation and disciplinary construction of comparative literature in China: an interview with Professor Cao Shunqing. FLS (114) 2005, 1–7. (In Chinese.)

21014. CHAPLEAU, SEBASTIEN. New voices in children's literature criticism. See 4080.

21015. CHÁVEZ, KARMA R. Beyond complicity: coherence, queer theory, and the rhetoric of the 'Gay Christian Movement'. See 20596.

21016. COOK, MALCOLM. The Modern Language Review: the first hundred years. See 1181.

21017. CSICSILA, JOSEPH. Canons by consensus: critical trends and American literature anthologies. Foreword by Tom Quirk. See 3739.

21018. DEAN, PAUL. Current literature 2002: literary theory, history and criticism. EngS (84:6) 2003, 558–72.

21019. DI LEO, JEFFREY R. (ed.). On anthologies: politics and pedagogy. See 3749.

21020. DILLARD, R. H. W. Notes from after the deluge. See 14758.

21021. DOWNING, DAVID B. Theorizing the discipline and the disciplining of theory. In (pp. 342–70) 3749.

21022. EDELMAN, LEE. No future: queer theory and the death drive. Durham, NC; London: Duke UP, 2004. pp. x, 191. (Series Q.) Rev. by Carolyn Dever in VS (47:4) 2005, 601–2.

21023. ENTERLINE, LYNN; HILLMAN, DAVID. Other selves, other bodies. SStud (33) 2005, 62–72.

21024. ERKKILÄ, BETSY. Revolution in the renaissance. See 9246.

21025. ESONWANNE, UZOMA. Calibrations: literary reference and the ethics of reading. RAL (36:2) 2005, 112–21.

21026. ESTOK, SIMON C. Shakespeare and ecocriticism: an analysis of 'home' and 'power' in King Lear. See 6463.

21027. FARBER, JERRY. What is literature? What is art? Integrating essence and history. JAE (39:3) 2005, 1–21.

21028. FELSKI, RITA. Redescriptions of female masochism. MinnR (63/64) 2005, 127–39.

21029. FERNIE, EWAN. Introduction: Shakespeare, spirituality and contemporary criticism. *In* (pp. 1–27) **5928.**

21030. —— (ed.). Spiritual Shakespeares. *See* **5928.**

21031. FERRETTER, LUKE. Towards a Christian literary theory. (Bibl. 2004, 20873.) Rev. by Beulah P. Baker in CSR (34:2) 2005, 259–62; by Gillen D. Wood in ReLit (37:1) 2005, 119–21.

21032. FINKE, LAURIE. The hidden curriculum. *In* (pp. 395–404) **3749.**

21033. FISHKIN, SHELLEY FISHER. Crossroads of cultures: the transnational turn in American Studies – Presidential Address to the American Studies Association, November 12, 2004. *See* **14782.**

21034. FLINT, KATE. Why 'Victorian'? Response. VS (47:2) 2005, 230–9.

21035. FORD, SARAH. Listening to the ghosts: the 'New Southern Studies': a response to Michael Kreyling. *See* **14788.**

21036. FREEMAN, MARGARET H. Poetry as power: the dynamics of cognitive poetics as a scientific and literary paradigm. *In* (pp. 31–57) **3888.**

21037. FROMM, HAROLD. The new Darwinism in the humanities: part II, Back to nature, again. *See* **14792.**

21038. GALLAGHER, CATHERINE. Theoretical answers to interdisciplinary questions or interdisciplinary answers to theoretical questions? VS (47:2) 2005, 253–9.

21039. GALLOP, JANE. Acknowledgments. CL (57:3) 2005, 214–18 (review-article).

21040. GAVINS, JOANNA. Text world theory in literary practice. *In* (pp. 89–104) **3888.**

21041. GILES, PAUL; ELLIS, R. J. *E pluribus multitudinum*: the new world of journal publishing in American Studies. *See* **1039.**

21042. GRABBE, HANS-JÜRGEN. 50 Jahre Deutsche Gesellschaft für Amerikastudien. *See* **14809.**

21043. GRAFF, GERALD; DI LEO, JEFFREY R. Anthologies, literary theory, and the teaching of literature. *In* (pp. 279–97) **3749.**

21044. GRAHAM, COLIN. Irish studies. YWCCT (12) 2004, 279–83.

21045. GREEN, DIANE (comp.). Welsh writing in English: a bibliography of criticism 2004. *See* **3789.**

21046. GREENBERG, GERALD S. Poststructuralism and communication: an annotated bibliography. *See* **14811.**

21047. GUPTA, SUMAN. Sociological speculations on the professions of children's literature. *See* **4087.**

21048. HAGEMANN, SUSANNE. Postcolonial translation studies and James Kelman's *Translated Accounts*. *See* **17383.**

21049. HAWES, CLEMENT. The British eighteenth century and global critique. *See* **7997.**

21050. HAYNES, CHRISTINE. Reassessing 'genius' in studies of authorship: the state of the discipline. *See* **875.**

21051. HAYOT, ERIC.   I/O: a comparative literature in a digital age. CL (57:3) 2005, 219–26 (review-article).

21052. —— 'The slightness of my endeavor': an interview with Gayatri Chakravorty Spivak. CL (57:3) 2005, 256–72.

21053. HERMAN, DAVID; JAHN, MANFRED; RYAN, MARIE-LAURE (eds). Routledge encyclopedia of narrative theory. See **14834**.

21054. HERMAN, LUC; VERVAECK, BART.   Handbook of narrative analysis. Lincoln; London: Nebraska UP, 2005. pp. 231. (Frontiers of narrative.)

21055. HETHERINGTON, CAROL; PETERSSON, IRMTRAUD (comps).   Annual bibliography of studies in Australian literature: 2004. ALS (22:1) 2005, 94–112.

21056. HOFFMAN, MICHAEL J.; MURPHY, PATRICK D. (eds).   Essentials of the theory of fiction. See **4031**.

21057. HONES, SHEILA; LEYDA, JULIA.   Geographies of American Studies. AmQ (57:4) 2005, 1019–32.

21058. HORNUNG, ALFRED.   Transnational American Studies: response to the Presidential Address. See **14838**.

21059. HUME, ROBERT D.   Construction and legitimation in literary history. RES (56:226) 2005, 632–61. (Opinion.)

21060. HUNTER, LATHAM.   'What's natural about it?': a baseball movie as introduction to key concepts in Cultural Studies. See **13686**.

21061. JOHANSEN, JÜRGEN DINES.   Theory and/vs interpretation in literary studies. In (pp. 241–66) **3888**.

21062. JOHNSON, BARBARA.   Headnotes. In (pp. 384–94) **3749**.

21063. JOUGHIN, JOHN J.; MALPAS, SIMON (eds).   The New Aestheticism. See **14850**.

21064. KAPLAN, AMY.   A call for a truce. See **14856**.

21065. KINDT, TOM; MÜLLER, HANS-HARALD (eds).   What is narratology? Questions and answers regarding the status of a theory. See **14864**.

21066. KREYLING, MICHAEL.   Toward 'a New Southern Studies'. See **14870**.

21067. KUBIAK, ANTHONY.   Soul death and the death of the soul in critical theory: a polemic. JDTC (20:1) 2005, 85–92.

21068. LACAPRA, DOMINICK.   History in transit: experience, identity, critical theory. See **14872**.

21069. LARSEN, SVEND ERIK.   Self-reference: theory and didactics between language and literature. JAE (39:1) 2005, 13–30.

21070. LEES, CLARE A.   Analytical survey 7: actually existing Anglo-Saxon studies. See **4214**.

21071. LEITCH, VINCENT B.   Ideology of headnotes. In (pp. 373–83) **3749**.

21072. LI, GUICANG.   Review of the national perspective on Chinese American identity. See **12783**.

21073. LI, KEHE; ZHANG, WEIJIA.   A comparative study of the 'blankness' in Chinese and Western aesthetics. See **14880**.

21074. LICONA, ADELA C.   (B)orderlands' rhetorics and representations: the transformative potential of feminist third-space scholarship and zines. See **14881**.

21075. —— CARRILLO ROWE, AIMEE. After words: feminist praxis as a bridge between theory and practice. See 15179.

21076. LIGGINS, EMMA. Feminisms. YWCCT (12) 2004, 16–28 (review-article).

21077. LIU, JIANJUN. The current nature of literary ethical criticism. See 14886.

21078. LJUNGBERG, CHRISTINA. Models of reading: diagrammatic aspects of literary texts. In (pp. 105–25) 3888.

21079. LOCATELLI, CARLA. Is s/he my gaze? (Feminist) possibilities for autobiographical co(n)texts. In (pp. 3–18) 12577.

21080. LONG, MARK C. Ecocriticism as a practice of reading. See 14890.

21081. LOWE, JOHN. 'Calypso magnolia': the Caribbean side of the South. See 10601.

21082. MCQUILLAN, MARTIN. Deconstruction. YWCCT (12) 2004, 255–78 (review-article).

21083. MALPAS, SIMON; WAKE, PAUL. Postmodernism. YWCCT (12) 2004, 75–88 (review-article).

21084. MARX, LEO. On recovering the 'Ur' theory of American Studies. See 14906.

21085. MAX, D. T. The literary Darwinists. See 10019.

21086. MEDOVARSKI, ANDREA. Unstable post(-)colonialities: speculations through punctuation. See 14910.

21087. MEISTER, JAN CHRISTOPH (ed.); KINDT, TOM; SCHERNUS, WILHELM (asst eds). Narratology beyond literary criticism: mediality, disciplinarity. Berlin; New York: Mouton de Gruyter, 2005. pp. xvi, 296. (Narratologia, 6.)

21088. MIALL, DAVID S. Beyond interpretation: the cognitive significance of reading. In (pp. 129–56) 3888.

21089. MISHRA, VIJAY. Multiculturalism. YWCCT (12) 2004, 180–98 (review-article).

21090. MITCHELL, SALLY. Reading class. See 9353.

21091. —— Victorian 'companions': forward to the past? JVC (10:1) 2005, 87–95. (Perspectives, 2.)

21092. MOHANTY, CHANDRA TALPADE. Feminism without borders: decolonizing theory, practicing solidarity. See 14925.

21093. MORETTI, FRANCO. Graphs, maps, trees: abstract models for a literary history. See 14926.

21094. MUFTI, AAMIR R. Global comparativism. See 14930.

21095. NGAI, MAE M. Transnationalism and the transformation of the 'Other': response to the Presidential Address. See 14935.

21096. NIE, ZHENZHAO. On literary ethical criticism. See 14937.

21097. NIXON, ROB. Environmentalism and postcolonialism. In (pp. 233–51) 12789.

21098. PATAI, DAPHNE; CORRAL, WILL (eds). Theory's empire: an anthology of dissent. See 14957.

21099. PAYNE, MICHAEL. What difference has theory made? From Freud to Adam Phillips. See 14959.

21100. POLVINEN, MERJA (ed.). Cognition and literary interpretation in practice. Introd. by Harri Veivo. Afterword by Bo Pettersson. *See* **3888**.

21101. PRABHU, ANJALI. Reading *Calibrations*: re-reading for the social. RAL (36:2) 2005, 97–103.

21102. PRESSMAN, RICHARD S. Is there a future for the *Heath Anthology* in the neoliberal State? *In* (pp. 264–76) **3749**.

21103. PROCTER, JAMES; MOREY, PETER. Colonial discourse, postcolonial theory. YWCCT (12) 2004, 58–74 (review-article).

21104. QIAO, GUOQIANG. A peep into literary ethical criticism. *See* **14974**.

21105. QUAYSON, ATO. Incessant particularities: *Calibrations* as close reading. RAL (36:2) 2005, 122–31.

21106. RAJAN, RAJESWARI SUNDER. Critical responses, recent. *In* (pp. 101–10) **10060**.

21107. RAMNARAYAN, AKHILA. Veiled wor(l)ds: the postcolonial feminist and the question of where. *In* (pp. 159–70) **2457**.

21108. RINTOUL, SUZANNE. Gothic anxieties: struggling with a definition. ECF (17:4) 2005, 701–9 (review-article).

21109. ROBERTS, ANDREW MICHAEL. Conrad and the territory of ethics. *See* **15916**.

21110. ROCHE, MARK WILLIAM. Why literature matters in the 21st century. *See* **3903**.

21111. ROHR, SUSANNE. Pragmaticism – a new approach to literary and cultural analysis. *See* **14992**.

21112. ROMBES, NICHOLAS. The rebirth of the author. CTHEORY, 6 Oct. 2005.

21113. ROORDA, RANDALL. Wonderful world: comic frames, dissolution of scene, the temper of ecocriticism. *See* **15552**.

21114. ROUND, PHILLIP H. The return of the native: recent scholarship in the literature of Christianization and contact. *See* **6932**.

21115. ROWLINSON, MATTHEW. Theory of Victorian Studies: anachronism and self-reflexivity. VS (47:2) 2005, 241–52.

21116. RUBIK, MARGARETE. Navigating through fantasy worlds: cognition and the intricacies of reading Jasper Fforde's *The Eyre Affair*. *In* (pp. 183–200) **3888**.

21117. RUSH, FRED (ed.). The Cambridge companion to critical theory. *See* **14998**.

21118. SAUNDERS, IAN. Virtual cultures. *See* **20832**.

21119. SAUSSY, HAUN. Chiasmus. CL (57:3) 2005, 234–8.

21120. SCHEINER, CORINNE. *Teleiopoiesis, telepoesis*, and the practice of comparative literature. CL (57:3) 2005, 239–45 (review-article).

21121. SCHLOBIN, ROGER C. Character, the fantastic, and the failure of contemporary literary theory. *See* **15007**.

21122. SCHOLES, ROBERT. What is happening in literary studies? LPub (18:4) 2005, 311–15.

21123. SCHRIFT, ALAN D. Confessions of an anthology editor. *In* (pp. 186–204) **3749**.

21124. SHAWCROSS, JOHN T.   Works of love or enmity: do not let our minor poets disappear. *See* **4134**.

21125. SHEN, DAN.   Narratology in China and in the West. *See* **15013**.

21126. SNEDEKER, GEORGE.   The politics of critical theory: language/discourse/society. *See* **15021**.

21127. SNYDER, ANN VIRTU.   Location, location, location: reflections of an itinerant practitioner. NWSAJ (17:2) 2005, 142–9.

21128. STANITZEK, GEORG.   Texts and paratexts in media. *See* **15025**.

21129. SULLIVAN, NIKKI.   A critical introduction to queer theory. *See* **15029**.

21130. SUSSMAN, HENRY.   The task of the critic: poetics, philosophy, and religion. *See* **15031**.

21131. SWIBODA, MARCEL.   Immanence. YWCCT (12) 2004, 105–15 (review-article).

21132. TANSELLE, G. THOMAS.   The prospect for textual criticism. *See* **722**.

21133. TREVOR, DOUGLAS.   Love, humoralism, and 'soft' psychoanalysis. *See* **6702**.

21134. TRIFONAS, PETER PERICLES; PETERS, MICHAEL A. (eds).   Deconstructing Derrida: tasks for the new humanities. *See* **15036**.

21135. VEIVO, HARRI; KNUUTTILA, TARJA.   Modelling, theorising and interpretation in cognitive literary studies. *In* (pp. 283–305) **3888**.

21136. VERNON, JAMES.   Historians and the Victorian Studies question: response. VS (47:2) 2005, 272–9.

21137. VINE, STEVE (ed.).   Literature in psychoanalysis: a reader. *See* **15041**.

21138. WANG, NING.   Environmental ethics of literature: the significance of ecocriticism. *See* **15046**.

21139. WARNES, CHRISTOPHER.   The hermeneutics of vagueness: magical realism in current literary critical discourse. *See* **15047**.

21140. WEAVER, ANDY.   Synchronous foreignicity: Fred Wah's poetry and the recuperation of experimental texts. *See* **19926**.

21141. WEBER, JEAN JACQUES.   A new paradigm for literary studies; or, The teething troubles of cognitive poetics. Style (38:4) 2004, 515–23 (review-article).

21142. WILLIAMS, JEFFREY.   The ubiquity of culture. PMC (16:1) 2005, (review-article).

21143. WILLIAMS, JEFFREY J.   Articulating feminism: an interview with Rita Felski. MinnR (63/64) 2005, 113–25.

21144. WINTER, SARAH.   Cultural politics and the sociology of the university. YJC (18:2) 2005, 473–8.

21145. WOLFREYS, JULIAN (ed.); THOMAS, HARUN KARIM (asst ed.).   Glossalalia: an alphabet of critical keywords. *See* **1979**.

21146. WOOD, PHILIP R.   Beyond the simulacrum of religion *versus* secularism: modernist aesthetic 'mysticism'; or, Why we will not stop revering 'great books'. ReLit (37:1) 2005, 93–117.

21147. YAO, STEVEN G.   The *unheimlich* maneuver; or, The gap, the gradient, and the spaces of comparison. CL (57:3) 2005, 246–55 (review-article).

21148. ZIMMERMAN, SUSAN.   Psychoanalysis and the corpse. SStud (33) 2005, 101–8.

AUTHORS

Christopher Abani

21149. ELLIS, SHERRY.   Coming to Elvis: an interview with Chris Abani. BRev (25:1) 2005, 22–3.

Pearl Abraham (b.1960)

21150. ABRAHAM, PEARL.   Divinity school; or, Trusting the act of writing. *In* (pp. 227–37) **12893.**

Daniel Alarcón (b.1977)

21151. WENDORFF, LILIANA.   Interview with Daniel Alarcón, New York City on October 6, 2004. PemM (37) 2005, 98–107.

Quiara Alegría Hudes

21152. SVICH, CARIDAD.   In conversation with Quiara Alegría Hudes. Dramatist (8:1) 2005, 26–9.

Alfian Sa'at (b.1977)

21153. POON, ANGELIA.   Performing national service in Singapore: (re)imagining nation in the poetry and short stories of Alfian Sa'at. JCL (40:3) 2005, 118–38.

Monica Ali (b.1967)

21154. HIDDLESTON, JANE.   Shapes and shadows: (un)veiling the immigrant in Monica Ali's *Brick Lane*. JCL (40:1) 2005, 57–72.

Robert Joseph Barclay (b.1962)

21155. OETTLI-VAN DELDEN, SIMONE.   Problematizing the postcolonial: deterritorialization and cultural identity in Robert Barclay's *Melal*. WLWE (39:2) 2002/03, 38–51.

Joan Bauer (b.1951)

21156. BLASINGAME, JAMES.   Interview with Joan Bauer. JAAL (49:3) 2005, 244–5.

Thomas Beller

21157. BELLER, THOMAS.   How to be a man: scenes from a protracted boyhood. New York; London: Norton, 2005. pp. 231.

John Bemrose (b.1947)

21158. JIRGENS, KARL.   Walking the island: interview with John Bemrose. Rampike (14:1) 2005, 26–8.

John Biguenet

21159. TRUSSLER, MICHAEL.   Rips in the fabric of the mundane: an interview with John Biguenet. WasRCPSF (38:1) 2003, 234–40.

Jessica Blank (b.1975)

21160. BLANK, JESSICA; JENSEN, ERIK. The uses of empathy: theater and the real world. THS (25) 2005, 15–22. (Creation of *The Exonerated* from interviews with Death Row prisoners.)

A. D. (Anne D.) Blonstein (b.1958)

21161. COLLECOTT, DIANA. The experimental writings of Anne Blonstein. *In* (pp. 117–26) **14377.**

Merlinda C. (Merlinda Carullo) Bobis

21162. HERRERO GRANADO, M. DOLORES. Merlinda Bobis's use of magic realism as reflected in *White Turtle*: moving across cultures, redefining the multicultural and dialogic self. RAEI (16) 2003, 147–63.

Patrick Bone

21163. RUBIN, RACHEL. 'What ain't called Melungeons is called hillbillies': Southern Appalachia's in-between people. *See* **17936.**

Karen Brennan (b.1941)

21164. BRENNAN, KAREN. Behind the story. *In* (pp. 134–6) **14294.**

Christopher Brookmyre (b.1968)

21165. CLANDFIELD, PETER. Putting the 'black' into 'tartan *noir*'. *In* (pp. 211–38) **14191.**

Amanda Brown

21166. MARSH, KELLY A. Dear husbands and other 'girls' stuff': the *Trifles* in *Legally Blonde*. *See* **20723.**

Dan Brown (b.1964)

21167. BOCK, DARRELL L. Breaking *The Da Vinci Code*: answers to the questions everyone's asking. (Bibl. 2004, 20943.) Rev. by James Bibza in CSR (34:2) 2005, 262–3.

21168. EHRMAN, BART D. Truth and fiction in *The Da Vinci Code*: a historian reveals what we really know about Jesus, Mary Magdalene, and Constantine. Oxford; New York: OUP, 2004. pp. xxiv, 207.

21169. GARLOW, JAMES L.; JONES, PETER. Cracking Da Vinci's code. Colorado Springs, CO: Victor, 2004. pp. 252.

21170. HAMILTON, BERNARD. Puzzling success: specious history, religious bigotry and the power of symbols in *The Da Vinci Code*. TLS, 10 June 2005, 20–1.

21171. LUNN, MARTIN. *Da Vinci Code* decoded. New York: Disinformation, 2004. pp. x, 181.

21172. MCDERMOTT, JIM. Krispy Kremes and *The Da Vinci Code*. ANCW (193:7) 2005, 8–11.

21173. PRICE, ROBERT M. The Da Vinci fraud: why the truth is stranger than fiction. Amherst, NY: Prometheus, 2005. pp. 296.

21174. ROGAK, LISA. The man behind *The Da Vinci Code*: an unauthorized biography of Dan Brown. Kansas City, MO: Andrews McMeel, 2005. pp. xvi, 140, (plates) 8.

Scott Cairns

21175. DUNNE, GREGORY. A conversation with Scott Cairns. PrS (79:1) 2005, 44–52.

Linda Cargill

21176. RAVAL, SHILPA. The three faces of Helen: 1970s and 1980s feminist revisions of the myth of Helen of Troy. See **19371.**

Kirsten Childs

21177. COHEN, PATRICIA. Guild seminar: race & politics in theater. See **15101.**

Rita Ciresi

21178. ANTONUCCI, CLARA. Scrittura e memoria: i luoghi del sé nella creatività italoamericana. In (pp. 105–18) **12577.**

Basil B. Clark

21179. HUGLEN, MARK E. (commentary); BROCK, BERNARD L. (afterword). Poetic healing: a Vietnam veteran's journey from a communication perspective. West Lafayette, IN: Parlor Press, 2005. pp. xxi, 297.

Marie Humber Clements (b.1962)

21180. GILBERG, REID. Marie Clements's *The Unnatural and Accidental Women*: 'denaturalizing' genre. TRC (24:1/2) 2003, 125–46.

John Clute (b.1940)

21181. BARBOUR, DOUGLAS. Archive fever in the technological far future histories *Appleseed*, *Permanence* and *Psychohistorical Crisis*. Foundation (94) 2005, 39–49.

Robert Cohen (b.1957)

21182. COHEN, ROBERT. Behind the story. In (pp. 96–9) **14294.**

21183. —— Living, loving, temple-going. In (pp. 202–16) **12893.**

Imraan Coovadia

21184. RASTOGI, PALLAVI. From South Asia to South Africa: locating other postcolonial diasporas. See **16380.**

Doreen Cronin

21185. JACK, KIMBERLY. Trouble in the farm yard: labor relations and politics in Doreen Cronin's Duck books. CLAQ (30:4) 2005, 407–25.

Tracy Daugherty (b.1955)

21186. DAUGHERTY, TRACY. Behind the story. In (pp. 122–4) **14294.**

Linh Dinh (b.1963)

21187. PELAUD, ISABELLE THUY. Entering Linh Dinh's *Fake House*: literature of displacement. AmerJ (31:2) 2005, 37–49.

Stella Pope Duarte

21188. FOSTER, DAVID WILLIAM. Out of the *barrio*: Stella Pope Duarte's *Let Their Spirits Dance*. BR (27:2) 2003, 171–9.

Tananarive Due (b.1966)

21189. GLAVE, DIANNE. 'My characters are teaching me to be strong': an interview with Tananarive Due. AAR (38:4) 2004, 695–705.

Martin Edmond (b.1952)

21190. EDMOND, MARTIN. Chronicle of the unsung. Auckland: Auckland UP, 2004. pp. 207.

Anne Enright (b.1962)

21191. SHUMAKER, JEANETT. Uncanny doubles: the fiction of Anne Enright. NewHR (9:3) 2005, 107–22.

Percival L. Everett

21192. BELL, MADISON SMARTT. A note on *God's Country*. Callaloo (28:2) 2005, 343–4.

21193. HANDLEY, WILLIAM R. Detecting the real fictions of history in *Watershed*. Callaloo (28:2) 2005, 305–12.

21194. KINCAID, JIM. An interview with Percival Everett. Callaloo (28:2) 2005, 377–81.

21195. KRAUTH, LELAND. Undoing and redoing the western. Callaloo (28:2) 2005, 313–27.

21196. RAMSEY, WILLIAM M. Knowing their place: three Black writers and the postmodern South. See **17532**.

21197. RUSSETT, MARGARET. Race under *Erasure*: for Percival Everett, 'a piece of fiction'. Callaloo (28:2) 2005, 358–68.

21198. WOLFREYS, JULIAN. 'A self-referential density': *Glyph* and the 'theory' thing. Callaloo (28:2) 2005, 345–57.

Michel Faber

21199. HARGER-GRINLING, VIRGINIA; JORDAAN, CHANTAL. Fifty years on: *Animal Farm* gets under the skin. See **18682**.

Jim Ferris

21200. HOLMES, MARTHA STODDARD; CHAMBERS, TOD. Thinking through pain. See **3807**.

Jasper Fforde (b.1961)

21201. HATELEY, ERICA. The end of *The Eyre Affair*: *Jane Eyre*, parody, and popular culture. JPC (38:6) 2005, 1022–36.

21202. HORSTKOTTE, MARTIN. The worlds of the fantastic Other in postmodern English fiction. See **19215**.

21203. LUSTY, HEATHER. Struggling to remember: war, trauma, and the adventures of Thursday Next. PCR (16:2) 2005, 117–30.

21204. RUBIK, MARGARETE. Navigating through fantasy worlds: cognition and the intricacies of reading Jasper Fforde's *The Eyre Affair*. *In* (pp. 183–200) **3888**.

21205. WATSON, GREER. Tertiary reality in children's fantasy. JFA (14:3) 2004, 350–66.

Ann W. Fisher-Wirth (b.1947)

21206. HOLMSTEN, ELIN.   Shifting boundaries: an interview with Ann Fisher-Wirth. ISLE (12:1) 2005, 131–7.

Jeffrey Ford (b.1955)

21207. DONATO, CLORINDA.   Jeffrey Ford's *The Physiognomy*: postmodern Lavater at the cusp of the twenty-first century. *In* (pp. 230–41) **3884**.

Graham W. Foust (b.1970)

21208. HENRY, BRIAN.   The art of leaving out: on Graham Foust. DQ (40:1) 2005, 56–73.

Karen Joy Fowler

21209. NEILL, EDWARD.   'Little women?': Karen Joy Fowler's adventure in Austenland. Persuasions (26) 2004, 249–54.

Yael Goldstein (b.1978)

21210. GOLDSTEIN, YAEL.   When God's your favorite writer. *In* (pp. 319–31) **12893**.

Philip Kan Gotanda (b.1951)

21211. DUNBAR, ANN-MARIE.   From ethnic to mainstream theater: negotiating 'Asian American' in the plays of Philip Kan Gotanda. AmDr (14:1) 2005, 15–31.

Michael Griffith (b.1965)

21212. GRIFFITH, MICHAEL.   Jostling with the actual: my summer with Saul Bellow. *See* **15444**.

Stephen Adly Guirgis

21213. HORNBY, RICHARD.   New York hot *versus* L.A. cool. HR (56:2) 2003, 338–44.

Camille Suzanne Guthrie (b.1971)

21214. ELSHTAIN, ERIC P.   It takes a thief: an interview with Camille Guthrie. ChiR (51:1/2) 2005, 187–99.

Sands Hall

21215. KARELL, LINDA.   The postmodern author on stage: *Fair Use* and Wallace Stegner. *See* **19576**.

Barbara Hamby (b.1952)

21216. CRUTCHFIELD, JOHN.   Speaking in forked tongues. CaroQ (57:3) 2005, 74–7 (review-article).

Pete Hautman (b.1952)

21217. BLASINGAME, JAMES.   Interview with Pete Hautman. JAAL (48:5) 2005, 438–9.

Tom Holland (b.1947)

21218. STEIN, ATARA.   Fictionalized Romantics: Byron, Shelley, and Keats as characters in contemporary genre fiction. JFA (13:4) 2003, 379–88.

Chloe Hooper (b.1973)

21219. WEBBY, ELIZABETH.   Books and covers: reflections on some recent Australian novels. *See* **131**.

Dara Horn (b.1977)

21220. HORN, DARA. On the interpretation of dreams. *In* (pp. 310–18) **12893**.

Kate Horsley (b.1952)

21221. RAWLINGS, DONN. Kate Horsley's New Mexico trilogy: masks of ambivalence in the Southwest. WAL (39:1) 2004, 105–20.

Colette Inez

21222. DALTON, MARY. Journey of an exiled daughter: an interview with poet Colette Inez. BRev (25:3) 2005, 31–2.

21223. INEZ, COLETTE. The secret of M. Dulong: a memoir. Madison; London: Wisconsin UP, 2005. pp. xi, 256. (Wisconsin studies in autobiography.)

Ian Irvine (b.1950)

21224. SIMONS, KATE. Thresholds crossed and boundaries broken? A Kristevan insight into Ian Irvine's quartet *The View from the Mirror*. JFA (13:4) 2003, 368–78.

Frances Itani (b.1942)

21225. FISHER, SUSAN. Hear, overhear, observe, remember: a dialogue with Frances Itani. CanL (183) 2004, 40–56.

Heidi L. Janz

21226. JANZ, HEIDI L. My continuing adventures as a 'challenged' playwright. CanTR (122) 2005, 21–2.

Nada A. Jarrar

21227. HOUT, SYRINE C. Memory, home, and exile in contemporary anglophone Lebanese fiction. *See* **15099**.

Erik Jensen (b.1970)

21228. BLANK, JESSICA; JENSEN, ERIK. The uses of empathy: theater and the real world. *See* **21160**.

Liz Jensen (b.1959)

21229. ESTRIN, BARBARA L. Mutating literary form and literalizing scientific theory in Liz Jensen's *Ark Baby*. CritW (47:1) 2005, 41–56.

Sarah Jones (b.1973)

21230. HAIRSTON, ANDREA. Driving Mr Lenny: notes on race and gender as a transport to another reality, another dimension. *See* **13808**.

Tayari Jones (b.1970)

21231. GRANDT, JÜRGEN E. (Un-)telling truth: an interview with Tayari Jones. LHR (19:2) 2005, 71–81.

Sue Monk Kidd (b.1948)

21232. HARKEN, AMY LIGNITZ. Unveiling *The Secret Life of Bees*. St Louis, MO: Chalice Press, 2005. pp. 100. (Popular insights.)

Binnie Kirshenbaum

21233. KIRSHENBAUM, BINNIE. Princess. *In* (pp. 217–26) **12893**.

Matthew Kneale (b.1960)

21234. KRAL, FRANÇOISE. Récits d'un voyage: *English Passengers* de Matthew Neale et l'art de l'entre genres. EREA (3:1) 2005, 94–101.

21235. WALLHEAD, CELIA. To voice or not to voice the Tasmanian Aborigines: novels by Matthew Kneale and Richard Flanagan. *See* **16509.**

India Knight (b.1965)

21236. COCKIN, KATHARINE. Inventing the suffragettes: anachronism, gnosticism and corporeality in contemporary fiction. *See* **16469.**

Gretchen Moran Laskas

21237. BIGGERS, JEFF. Out of Appalachia: new writing from an old region, including an interview with Gretchen Laskas and Ron Rash. *See* **19028.**

21238. BROSI, GEORGE. A rising star in Appalachian literature. AppH (33:1) 2005, 8–12.

21239. WILLIS, MEREDITH SUE. Examining the truth about women's lives in Appalachia: the fiction of Gretchen Moran Laskas. AppH (33:1) 2005, 19–27.

Julia Lawrinson (b.1969)

21240. MALLAN, KERRY. (M)other love: constructing queer families in *Girl Walking Backwards* and *Obsession*. CLAQ (29:4) 2004, 345–57.

Shawna Lemay (b.1966)

21241. LEMAY, SHAWNA. Women writing horses. *See* **16890.**

Toby Litt (b.1968)

21242. FLANNERY, DENIS. The powers of apostrophe and the boundaries of mourning: Henry James, Alan Hollinghurst, and Toby Litt. *See* **11401.**

Tim Lott (b.1956)

21243. PARK, CHRISTINE COHEN. Close comfort? Sons as their mothers' memoirists. *See* **17235.**

Lisa M. Lubasch

21244. ELSHTAIN, ERIC. Mind as an opening book: an e-mail interview with Lisa Lubasch. DQ (40:1) 2005, 41–9.

Alexander McCall Smith (b.1948)

21245. GAVINS, JOANNA. Text world theory in literary practice. *In* (pp. 89–104) **3888.**

S. Siobhan McCarthy

21246. MCCARTHY, S. SIOBHAN. Using the arts as a tool for healing, self-discovery, empowerment and catharsis. CanTR (122) 2005, 59–61.

Nick McDonell (b.1984)

21247. BRITAIN, IAN. Striking twelve. Meanjin (62:1) 2003, 144–54.

21248. ZIEGLER, ROBERT. Countdown to *Twelve*: Nick McDonell's midnight special. NCL (35:1) 2005, 10–13.

Alice Major (b.1949)

21249. QUERENGESSER, NEIL. Domestic science in the poetry of Alice Major. CanP (56) 2005, 53–64.

Melina Marchetta (b.1965)

21250. ANTONUCCI, CLARA.   Scrittura e memoria: i luoghi del sé nella creatività italoamericana. *In* (pp. 105–18) **12577.**

Stefanie Marlis (b.1951)

21251. ELSHTAIN, ERIC P.   On the quiet: an interview with Stefanie Marlis. ChiR (51:3) 2005, 94–102.

Victoria Maxwell

21252. MAXWELL, VICTORIA.   Making the invisible visible. CanTR (122) 2005, 26–8. (Drama about disability and mental illness.)

Cris Mazza

21253. MAZZA, CRIS.   Indigenous: growing up Californian. San Francisco, CA: City Lights, 2003. pp. xix, 293.

Ana Menéndez (b.1970)

21254. JOHANNESSEN, LENE.   The lonely figure: memory of exile in Ana Menéndez's *In Cuba I Was a German Shepherd.* JPW (41:1) 2005, 54–68.

21255. PERERA, JENNIFER BALLANTINE.   'Only in Miami is Cuba so far away': the politics of exile in Ana Menéndez's *In Cuba I Was a German Shepherd.* WLWE (39:2) 2002/03, 8–17.

21256. SOCOLOVSKY, MAYA.   Cuba interrupted: the loss of center and story in Ana Menéndez's collection *In Cuba I Was a German Shepherd.* CritW (46:3) 2005, 235–51.

Denise Mina (b.1966)

21257. CLANDFIELD, PETER.   Putting the 'black' into 'tartan *noir*'. *In* (pp. 211–38) **14191.**

Tova Mirvis (b.1972)

21258. MIRVIS, TOVA.   Writing between worlds. *In* (pp. 300–9) **12893.**

Phaswane Mpe (1970–2004)

21259. ATTREE, LIZZY.   Healing with words: Phaswane Mpe interviewed. JCL (40:3) 2005, 139–48.

Kate Muir (b.1964)

21260. COCKIN, KATHARINE.   Inventing the suffragettes: anachronism, gnosticism and corporeality in contemporary fiction. *See* **16469.**

Stephen Murabito (b.1956)

21261. TURCO, LEWIS.   Oswego poems and poets: Murabito and Davis. HC (42:3) 2005, 1–15.

Allison Muri (b.1965)

21262. WAESE, REBECCA.   'Mystory' in Allison Muri's *the hystery of the broken fether.* CanL (185) 2005, 111–30.

Sabina Murray

21263. HONG, TERRY.   Writing from a different place: a profile of 2003 PEN/Faulkner Award winner Sabina Murray. BRev (24:1) 2004, 7.

Anita Nair

21264. ROMEO, MARCELLA. 'Akhila felt within her a queer itinerant sensation': *Ladies Coupé*: 'new' literatures and new feminisms. *In* (pp. 244–54) **3690.**

Melissa Nathan

21265. WHELEHAN, IMELDA. Sex and the single girl: Helen Fielding, Erica Jong and Helen Gurley Brown. *See* **16473.**

D. Nurkse (b.1949)

21266. JANSEN, REAMY. Poetry and endless war: an interview with poet Dennis Nurkse. BRev (23:5) 2003, 14.

Margaret A. Ogola

21267. MUKUNDI, PAUL M. Looking beyond the horizon at all times at all places: the triumphant African woman in Zora Neale Hurston's *Their Eyes Were Watching God*, Mariama Bâ's *So Long a Letter* and Margaret Ogola's *The River and the Source*. *See* **17136.**

Jamie O'Neill (b.1962)

21268. VALENTE, JOSEPH. Race/sex/shame: the queer nationalism of *At Swim Two Boys*. EI (40:3/4) 2005, 58–84.

Yu Ouyang (b.1955)

21269. OUYANG, YU. Motherland, otherland: small issues. Antipodes (18:1) 2004, 50–5.

Michael Parker (b.1959)

21270. LLOYD, JEREMY; WALKER, KATHRYN. Time, place, and a lament for the loss of the chicken house: an interview with Michael Parker. NCLR (14) 2005, 169–79.

Brian Payton (b.1966)

21271. LEFEBVRE, BENJAMIN. From *Bad Boy* to dead boy: homophobia, adolescent problem fiction, and male bodies that matter. *See* **20166.**

Tyler Perry (b.1969)

21272. SAINE, K. B. The Black American's chitlin/gospel/urban show: Tyler Perry and the Madea plays. ThSym (13) 2005, 105–15.

Donald Pfarrer

21273. PFARRER, DONALD. American fighter. BosR (29:6) 2004/05, 50.

Jodi Picoult (b.1966)

21274. PICOULT, JODI. The writing life. BkW, 6 Mar. 2005, 10.

Manuel A. Ramos

21275. SOTELO, SUSAN BAKER. Chicano detective fiction: a critical study of five novelists. *See* **15153.**

Adam Rapp (b.1968)

21276. MILLER, BRUCE. Profile: Adam Rapp. AmDr (14:1) 2005, 110–14.

Hannie Rayson (b.1957)

21277. GLOW, HILARY. Class action. Meanjin (64:1/2) 2005, 326–35.

Elizabeth Robinson (b.1961)

21278. MORRISON, RUSTY. An echoing after the object. *See* 16835.

Kathleen Rooney (b.1980)

21279. ARMILLAS-TISEYRA, MAGALI. Interview: Kathleen Rooney. GWR (26:1) 2004, 21–5.

Graham Salisbury (b.1944)

21280. GILL, DAVID MACINNIS. Graham Salisbury: island boy. Lanham, MD; London: Scarecrow Press, 2005. pp. xvii, 109. (Scarecrow studies in young adult literature, 20.)

Alex Sanchez (b.1957)

21281. BLASINGAME, JAMES. Interview with Alex Sanchez. JAAL (48:7) 2005, 619–21.

Marjorie Sandor

21282. SANTASIERO, ELLEN. An interview with Marjorie Sandor. NwR (43:2) 2005, 81–95.

Karl Schroeder (b.1962)

21283. BARBOUR, DOUGLAS. Archive fever in the technological far future histories *Appleseed, Permanence* and *Psychohistorical Crisis*. *See* 21181.

Leslie Schwartz (b.1962)

21284. KOEPPEL, MARY SUE. Developing and creating character: an interview with Leslie Schwartz. Kalliope (27:2) 2005, 39–46.

Kamila Shamsie (b.1973)

21285. AHMED, REHANA. Unsettling cosmopolitanisms: representations of London in Kamila Shamsie's *Salt and Saffron*. WLWE (40:1) 2002/03, 12–28.

Jim Shepard (b.1956)

21286. SHEPARD, JIM. Behind the story. *In* (pp. 424–6) 14294.

Jenny Siler (b.1971)

21287. SCHAFFER, RACHEL. The mean streets of Montana: Jenny Siler's hard-boiled protagonists. Storytelling (4:1) 2004, 44–59.

Anne Simpson (b.1956)

21288. COMPTON, ANNE. Writing paintings and thinking physics: Anne Simpson's poetry. CanL (185) 2005, 30–42.

21289. MCNEILLY, KEVIN. What remains: Anne Simpson's *Loop*. CanL (185) 2005, 197–200.

Joseph Skibell

21290. STADDEN, PAMELA. Narrative techniques and Holocaust literature: Joseph Skibell's *A Blessing on the Moon*. StudAJL (24) 2005, 153–7.

Ali Smith (b.1962)

21291. ESHELMAN, RAOUL. Checking out of the epoch: performatism in Olga Tokarczuk's *The Hotel Capital* vs late postmodernism in Ali Smith's *Hotel World* (with remarks on Arundhati Roy's *The God of Small Things* and Miloš Urban's *Sevenchurch*). Anthropoetics (10:2) 2004/05.

Tracy K. Smith

21292. BROWN, JERICHO. The body's boundaries, the body's questions. GC (17:1) 2005, 123–37. (Interview.)

Cole Swensen (b.1955)

21293. ANON. Interview with Cole Swensen. Jubilat (10) 2005, 81–94.

21294. KELLER, LYNN. Poems living with paintings: Cole Swensen's ekphrastic *Try.* ConLit (46:2) 2005, 176–212.

Janet Tashjian (b.1956)

21295. BLASINGAME, JAMES. Interview with Janet Tashjian. JAAL (48:4) 2004/05, 350–1.

Polly Teale

21296. CROUCH, KRISTIN. 'Inside out': the creative process of Shared Experience theatre. TheatreForum (26) 2005, 76–83.

Harry Turtledove
('Eric G. Iverson', 'H. N. Turteltaub') (b.1949)

21297. BILSON, FRED. The colonialists' fear of colonisation and the alternate worlds of Ward Moore, Philip K. Dick and Keith Roberts. See **18333**.

21298. ROCHELLE, WARREN. The patriotic rhetoric of Harry Turtledove's alternate America. Foundation (94) 2005, 75–86.

Lara Vapnyar (b.1971)

21299. VAPNYAR, LARA. On becoming a Russian Jewish American. *In* (pp. 293–9) **12893**.

Karen Volkman (b.1967)

21300. ALTIERI, CHARLES. Some problems with being contemporary: aging critics, younger poets and the new century. See **18389**.

Susan Vreeland (b.1946)

21301. KOEPPEL, MARY SUE. The writer who loves artists: an interview with Susan Vreeland. Kalliope (26:2) 2004, 37–44.

Frank X. Walker (b.1961)

21302. BURRISS, THERESA L. Claiming a space: the Affrilachian Poets. *In* (pp. 315–36) **12822**.

Jess Walter (b.1969)

21303. FISTER, BARBARA. Copycat crimes: crime fiction and the marketplace of anxieties. See **18931**.

Sarah Waters (b.1966)

21304. PALMER, PAULINA. Lesbian gothic: genre, transformation, transgression. GothS (6:1) 2004, 118–30.

Crystal E. Wilkinson (b.1962)

21305. BURRISS, THERESA L. Claiming a space: the Affrilachian Poets. *In* (pp. 315–36) **12822**.

21306. WILKINSON, CRYSTAL E. Harvesting *Blackberries, Blackberries*: a Black woman's publishing tale. *In* (pp. 189–93) **14204**.

Bett Williams

21307. MALLAN, KERRY. (M)other love: constructing queer families in *Girl Walking Backwards* and *Obsession*. See **21240**.

Jonathan Wilson (b.1950)

21308. WILSON, JONATHAN. How I became a Jewish writer in America. *In* (pp. 151–8) **12893**.

Robert Charles Wilson (b.1953)

21309. MURPHY, GRAHAM J. Ideas and inhabitations. Foundation (94) 2005, 5–12. (Profession of science fiction, 61.)

Michael Winter (b.1965)

21310. SALEM-WISEMAN, LISA. Divided cities, divided selves: portraits of the artist as ambivalent urban hipster. *In* (pp. 142–65) **9243**.

C. Dale Young (b.1969)

21311. WEST, SASHA. There is light and there is dark. GC (17:1) 2005, 138–53. (Interview.)

Mary Zimmerman

21312. GARWOOD, DEBORAH. Myth as public dream: the metamorphosis of Mary Zimmerman's *Metamorphoses*. PAJ (73) 2003, 69–78.

INDEXES

INDEX OF AUTHORS AND FILM DIRECTORS

INDEX OF SCHOLARS

including compilers, editors, translators and reviewers

—— R. Philip, 13296
Lucas, Angela M., 5012
—— Ann Lawson, 9647
—— John, 11136, 11142
—— Peter J., 4772
—— Rebecca Garcia, 14194
—— Scott, 5320, 5378, 5428
Lucia, Cynthia, 13297, 13927, 20658, 20787
Luciano, Dana, 9907, 11952
Luckhurst, Mary, 3985, 17362
—— Roger, 1263, 4042, 9223, 9768, 12060
Lucy, Robin, 18778
Ludington, Charles C., 6905, 8020
Luey, Beth, 14132
Luhr, William G., 13565
Lukens, Margo, 9521
Lukes, H. N., 14727
Lukinbeal, Chris, 13298
Lull, Janis, 5845, 6390, 6439, 6512
Lumsden, Alison, 11909, 11987
Luna, Alina M., 10498, 13719
Lund, Roger, 7208, 8021
Lunde, Arne, 13231
Lundeen, Kathleen, 8384
Lundin, Anne, 4089, 8526, 9648–50, 14342
—— Roger, 10985, 11472
Lundquist, Robert, 4123
Lunn, Martin, 21171
Lunney, Ruth, 5542
Luo, Lianggong, 17094, 19303
—— Shiping, 14208
—— Yihua, 11523
Lupack, Alan, 3845
—— Barbara Tepa, 4090
Lupo, Scott, 3643
Lupoff, Richard A., 15626
Lupton, Christina, 620, 8636, 9037
—— Julia Reinhard, 2862, 6008, 7130
—— Mary Jane, 15811, 20030
Lurcock, A. F. T., 7995, 8760
Lurie, Alison, 4091
—— Peter, 14892, 15957, 16426
Lustig, T. J., 3962, 10935, 11209, 11344, 11428
Lusty, Heather, 21203
Luther, Carol, 3699
Lutz, Hartmut, 15187
Lux, Elaine, 17083
Luxon, Thomas H., 7712
Luyster, Amanda, 5075
Lv, Hongling, 20384

Lyall, Roderick J., 3846, 4791, 8408
Lyday, Margaret M., 2318
Lyden, John C., 13299
Lye, Colleen, 9332, 12794
—— Hui Min, 1577, 3038, 3219
Lynall, Gregory, 9075
Lynch, Beth, 7284
—— Deidre, 4076
—— Deidre Shauna, 8140, 9870, 10014–15, 14209, 14893
—— Jack, 1934, 3847, 6194, 6476, 7188, 8297, 8769–70, 9871
—— Kathryn L., 4788, 4955, 5013, 6816, 7448
—— Lisa, 17559
—— William F., 3848
Lynn, Michael R., 7786
—— Thomas J., 18530
Lyon, John, 17634, 18407
—— John M., 17028
—— Philippa, 14443
Lyons, Bonnie, 19157–8
—— Bridget Gellert, 5879
—— James, 14003
—— William, 5910
Lysack, Krista, 11012, 11862
Lysandrou, Yvonne, 16594
Lystra, Karen, 12256
Lyytinen, Maria, 18274

Ma, Jianjun, 19546
Maar, Michael, 18461
Maas, Christel-Maria, 11613
Mabey, Richard, 10441
McAlindon, Tom, 6009
Macalister, John, 1963, 3063, 3326
McAllister, Marvin, 9491
MacArthur, Fiona, 2386, 3327
McArthur, Lewis A., 2003
MacArthur, Marit J., 16607
Macaulay, Ronald, 2928
McAuliffe, Jody, 17307, 17337
McAvoy, Liz Herbert, 4830–1
McBratney, John, 10860, 17473
McBride, Charlotte, 6408, 6586, 7449
—— Sam, 17758
—— Tom, 19653
MacCabe, Colin, 17308
McCabe, Douglas, 18605
—— Janet, 13954, 20794
—— Richard, 4547

—— Richard A., 5707, 5717, 8894
—— Susan, 9170, 9907, 13300, 14444, 15598, 17866
McCaffrey, Lawrence J., 3772, 18593
McCall, John C., 13301–2
McCallum, Pamela, 14894
McCalmon, George, 13078, 20608
McCann, Andrew, 11544, 11832, 12795, 20578
—— Paul, 16481, 17095
—— Sean, 14210, 14250, 18056
MacCannell, Juliet, 14895
McCarthy, Conor, 4450, 15700, 16018
—— Michael, 2387, 2570
—— Patrick J., 10713, 10717, 11484
—— Penny, 5461, 5592, 6010
—— S. Siobhan, 21246
—— Tom, 6596
McCarty, Steve, 11137
McCauley, Elizabeth Anne, 9333, 11429
McCaw, Neil, 9334, 9426–7, 14016, 16768
McClanahan, Ed, 18516
McClatchy, J. D., 3849
McCleery, Alistair, 9, 913
McClellan, William, 5014
McClendon, Aaron, 11693
McClennen, Sophia A., 16117
McClish, Glen, 2388
McClure, J. Derrick, 2943, 3328, 6557
McCluskey, Peter M., 914, 5414, 5580, 5763, 6709
McClymond, Michael J., 8560, 8589
MacColl, Alan, 5382, 5440, 5475, 5491, 5708
McCollum, Sarah C., 6906
McCombe, John P., 6757, 10499, 13473–4, 13745, 14445
McConachie, Bruce, 4003, 8108, 9476, 13069
McConkey, James, 3850, 4124, 17933–4
McConnell-Ginet, Sally, 3164
McCooey, David, 4178, 15082, 16914
McCoole, Sinéad, 16743
McCorkle, Ben, 169, 2389, 9769
McCormack, Jerusha, 9703
—— Kathleen, 4039, 10936

Roemer, Kenneth M., 2454,
10832, 12863, 18666
Roff, Sandra Shoiock, 1134
Rogak, Lisa, 21174
Roger, Catherine, 15255
— Vincent, 6497
Rogers, G. A. J., 7514
— Helen, 2836
— James Silas, 18552
— John, 7744
— Jonathan, 17783
— Linda, 19116
— Margaret, 3213
— Nicholas, 3651, 4278,
4474
— Pat, 3652, 8494, 8540,
8654, 8851, 8900–5, 10041
— Philip, 10180
— Rebecca, 1090, 3199,
6216, 6221, 6568, 8111
— Scott, 11863
— Shannon, 11160, 13816
— William Elford, 4858
— William W., 12415
Rogiers, Hella, 1606
Rognoni, Francesco, 15497
Rohdenburg, Günter, 1671
Rohman, Carrie, 20063
Rohr, Susanne, 14992, 21111
Rohrbach, Emily, 8318,
10042, 11530
Roldán Vera, Eugenia, 981
Rollin, Lucy, 4096
Rollings, Andrew G., 1536
Rollins, Peter C., 13357–8,
14040
Rollyson, Carl, 4177
Romack, Katherine, 5347
Romaine, Suzanne, 1537,
2007, 3134–5
Roman, Christopher, 4825,
4838
Romance, Joseph, 11676,
12238, 14121, 16441
Romanik, Barbara, 16670
Romano, Frederick V., 13359
Romanska, Magda, 119,
6217, 6361–2
Romberg, Osvaldo, 17303
Rombes, Nicholas, 13360,
20674, 21112
Romeo, Marcella, 21264
Römer, Ute, 1635, 3368
Romero, Chanette, 18369
Romero Allué, Milena, 5188
Romesburg, Rod, 15067
Romine, Scott, 9400
Romines, Ann, 15744
Romotsky, Sally Robertson,
5291, 6428
Ronald, Ann, 3904
Ronk, Martha, 6658

Rood, Tim, 3905
Roof, Judith, 13361, 16527
Rooks, John, 5226
— Noliwe M., 1323
Rooksby, Rikky, 12123
Rooney, Brigid, 16647
— Charles J., Jr, 3949
— Elizabeth, 10885
— Monique, 18735
Roorda, Randall, 14993,
15552, 21113
Roos, Anna Marie, 1155
Root, Robert, 12211, 20144
— William Pitt, 16891
Roper, Alan, 2017, 2019,
7076–7, 7424–5, 7515
— John Herbert, 16810
— Michael, 17007, 19430
Roppolo, Kimberly, 14476,
18711
Roraback, Erik S., 13676,
17334, 18993
Roscher, Jennifer, 18058
Rosdeitcher, Liz, 9545
Rose, D. C., 12416
— Margaret, 16139
— Marilyn, 456, 14633,
18109
— Natalie, 10734
— Norman, 18510
— Spencer, 1126, 16803,
19080
Rosebury, Brian, 19814,
19843
Rosen, Alan, 2759, 12887
— Carol, 19427
— David, 7745, 11531,
16301, 18830
— Susan C., 3904
Rosenbaum, S. P., 12888
— Susan, 15498
— Thane, 19121
Rosenberg, John D., 9715
— Tracey S., 10352, 15204
Rosenblum, Andrew E.,
11222
— Joseph, 4994
Rosendale, Steven, 9401,
12889
Rosenfeld, Aaron S., 17691
— Jason, 9805
— Nancy, 5317, 7286, 7439,
7746, 7832, 16804
Rosenhan, Claudia, 17152,
17628, 17895
Rosenman, Ellen Bayuk,
10213
Rosenthal, Caroline, 16370
— Jane E., 318
— Joel T., 4426–7, 4909
— Laura J., 7254
— Sarah, 18728

Rosier, Pat, 14428
Rosner, Victoria, 12890,
20409
Ross, Catherine Sheldrick,
4060
— Charles, 5189
— Cheri Louise, 9911
— David, 20360
— Donald R., 20739
— Jack, 16010, 18412
— Margaret Clunies, 4241
— Melanie H., 2455, 6659,
11450
— Michael L., 16388,
16564
— Stephen, 2760, 2956,
15917, 16821, 18696
— Steven, 2558
— William T., 20064
Rosser, Susan, 4231
Rossholm, Göran, 4054
Rossi, John P., 18697, 20015
— Matti, 6627
— William, 10967, 10996
Rossignol, Benoît, 17008
Rossington, Michael, 457,
12028
Rossini, Manuela, 7649
— Manuela S., 6442, 6517
Rosslyn, Felicity, 17220
Roston, Murray, 7078, 7390
Rotella, Guy, 15499, 19681
Roth, Elaine, 13362
— Marty, 3906
— Wolff-Michael, 2195
Rothman, Irving N., 8541
— William, 13363, 13779
Rothmayer, Michael A.,
13005
Rothstein, Eric, 3691, 3927
Rothwell, Kenneth Sprague,
6218
Rotunno, Laura, 10735
Roud, Steve, 3584, 3653
Roudeau, Cécile, 14266,
18831
Rounce, Adam, 8337, 8472,
9121
Round, Phillip H., 3716,
6851, 6932, 6947, 7435,
8063, 21114
Rountree, Kathryn, 3424
Rouse, Andrew C., 3585
— Robert, 4569, 4571,
4589
— Robert Allen, 4279,
4554, 4646
Roush, Jan, 3907
Rousseau, G. S., 10520
— George S., 12891
Roussel, Emmanuelle, 1636